BUTTERWORTHS CHARITY LAW HANDBOOK

Second edition

CONSULTANT EDITORS

MICHAEL SCOTT, MA (Hons) (Oxon)

SIMON WETHERED, MA (Hons) (Oxon)

Partners, Charles Russell

LexisNexis® Butterworths

Members of the LexisNexis Group Worldwide

United Kingdom	LexisNexis Butterworths, a Division of Reed Elsevier (UK) Ltd, Halsbury House, 35 Chancery Lane, London, WC2A 1EL, and London House, 20–22 East London Street, Edinburgh EH7 4BQ
Argentina	LexisNexis Argentina, Buenos Aires
Australia	LexisNexis Butterworths, Chatswood, New South Wales
Austria	LexisNexis Verlag ARD Orac GmbH & Co KG, Vienna
Benelux	LexisNexis Benelux, Amsterdam
Canada	LexisNexis Canada, Markham, Ontario
Chile	LexisNexis Chile Ltda, Santiago
China	LexisNexis China, Beijing and Shanghai
France	LexisNexis SA, Paris
Germany	LexisNexis Deutschland GmbH, Munster
Hong Kong	LexisNexis Hong Kong, Hong Kong
India	LexisNexis India, New Delhi
Italy	Giuffrè Editore, Milan
Japan	LexisNexis Japan, Tokyo
Malaysia	Malayan Law Journal Sdn Bhd, Kuala Lumpur
Mexico	LexisNexis Mexico, Mexico
New Zealand	LexisNexis NZ Ltd, Wellington
Poland	Wydawnictwo Prawnicze LexisNexis Sp, Warsaw
Singapore	LexisNexis Singapore, Singapore
South Africa	LexisNexis Butterworths, Durban
USA	LexisNexis, Dayton, Ohio

Published by LexisNexis Butterworths

A CIP Catalogue record for this book is available from the British Library.

ISBN 978 1 4057 0895 1

Typeset by Columns Design Ltd, Reading, UK
Printed and bound in Great Britain by CPI Bath Press, Bath

Visit LexisNexis Butterworths at www.lexisnexis.co.uk

PREFACE

The enactment, on 8 November 2006, of the Charities Act 2006 has in any event rendered necessary a second edition of this handbook, though there have been several other relevant changes in the statute law affecting charities since the first edition was published in November 2000.

However, the fact that the Charities Act 2006 is to be brought into force in a piecemeal fashion over the next 18 months or so does present difficulties in ensuring that practitioners can discern from this volume what parts of the Act are indeed in force, and what are due to come into force. We have sought to deal with this by including a table of commencement at the beginning of the Act and by indicating throughout the text where appropriate those parts that have already been brought into force at the date of publication and in respect of the remainder of the Act, by alluding to the fact that the provisions are to be brought into force. The Office of the Third Sector have published a provisional implementation timetable which is available at www.cabinetoffice.gov.uk/third_sector.

The contemporaneous passing of the Companies Act 2006 has also presented us with something of a conundrum: charity law practitioners will often need to advise incorporated charities, and our first edition included substantial extracts from the Companies Act 1985 which were likely to be of assistance for that purpose. Again, at the time of going to press, much of the Companies Act 2006 has yet to be brought into force, and accordingly the most sensible solution appeared to be to leave in the provisions of the 1985 Act which are still in force and of relevance while confining those parts of the Companies Act 2006 which are here set out to those which are likely to be relevant to charities incorporated as companies limited by guarantee.

There is a distinct prospect of the Charities Acts being consolidated within the next couple of years or so, and at that stage the opportunity will be taken to review the extent to which the Companies Act 2006 has been brought into force and can be more fully set out in what will then be the third edition of this handbook.

As with the first edition, we would be the first to acknowledge that there are large tracts of law relating to charities – for example that relating to education, housing, health and ecclesiastical law – which receive no treatment in this handbook, if only for reasons of ensuring that it remains of a manageable size and weight.

However, we would welcome any comments from practitioners as to materials that they would find useful for inclusion in the third edition, which will be put in hand shortly after the passing of the consolidating Charities Act.

Again, we would like to thank the editorial team at Butterworth's for their painstaking assistance in the preparation of this handbook, and in particular for the preparation of the comprehensive Index.

The law here collated is that in force as at 1 March 2007, although later amendments have been noted wherever possible.

Michael Scott, Simon Wethered

March 2007

CONTENTS

PART II STATUTORY INSTRUMENTS

PART I
STATUTES

CHARITABLE USES ACT 1601

(43 Eliz 1, c 4)

NOTES

This Act was repealed by the Mortmain and Charitable Uses Act 1888, s 13(1), Schedule; however, s 13(2) of the 1888 Act preserved the preamble to the 1601 Act for the limited purpose of making references in other documents to charities within the meaning, purview and interpretation of that Act intelligible. The 1888 Act was repealed by the Charities Act 1960, ss 38(1), 48(2), Sch 7, Pt II. However, the 1960 Act, s 38(4) provided that any reference in any enactment or document to a charity within the meaning, purview and interpretation of the 1601 Act or the preamble to it shall be construed as a reference to a charity within the meaning that the word bears as a legal term according to the law of England and Wales, and the preamble is therefore reproduced below. The 1960 Act is repealed as from a day to be appointed (subject to transitional provisions and savings) by the Charities Act 2006, s 75(2), (3), Sch 9, Sch 10, paras 21–27, 29.

Whereas Landes Tenementes Rentes Annuities Profittes Hereditamentes, Goodes Chattels Money and Stockes of Money, have bene heretofore given limitted appointed and assigned, as well by the Queenes most excellent Majestie and her moste noble Progenitors, as by sondrie other well disposed persons, some for Releife of aged impotent and poore people, some for Maintenance of sicke and maymed Souldiers and Marriners, Schooles of Learninge, Free Schooles and Schollers in Universities, some for Repaire of Bridges Portes Havens Causwaies Churches Seabankes and Highwaies, some for Educacion and prefermente of Orphans, some for or towardes Reliefe Stocke or Maintenance of Howses of Correccion, some for Mariages of poore Maides, some for Supportacion Ayde and Helpe of younge tradesmen Handicraftesmen and persons decayed, and others for reliefe or redemption of Prisoners or Captives, and for aide or ease of any poore Inhabitantes concerninge paymente of Fifteenes, setting out of Souldiers and other Taxes; Whiche Landes Tenementes Rents Annuities Profitts Hereditaments Goodes Chattells Money and Stockes of Money nevertheles have not byn imployed accordinge to the charitable intente of the givers and founders thereof, by reason of Fraudes breaches of Truste and Negligence in those that shoulde pay delyver and imploy the same:

[1]

POLICE, FACTORIES, &C (MISCELLANEOUS PROVISIONS) ACT 1916

(6 & 7 Geo 5 c 31)

An Act to amend the Enactments relating to the Police and certain other Enactments with the administration of which the Secretary of State for the Home Department is concerned

[3 August 1916]

PART I
POLICE

1–4 *(S 1 repealed by the Police (Pensions) Act 1918, s 3; s 2 repealed by the Statute Law Revision Act 1927; s 3 repealed by the Statute Law (Repeals) Act 1973; s 4 repealed by the Local Government Act 1929, s 137, Sch 12, Pt VI.)*

5 Regulation of street collections

(1) [Each of the authorities specified in subsection (1A) below] may make regulations with respect to the places where and the conditions under which persons may be permitted in any street or public place, within [their] area, to collect money or sell articles for the benefit of charitable or other purposes, and any person who acts in contravention of any such regulation shall be liable on summary conviction to a fine not exceeding [level 1 on the standard scale]:

Provided that—

(a) regulations made under this section shall not come into operation until they have been confirmed by the Secretary of State [or the Minister for the Cabinet Office],

and published for such time and in such manner as the Secretary of State [or the Minister for the Cabinet Office] may direct; and

(*b*) *regulations made under this section shall not apply to the selling of articles in any street or public place when the articles are sold in the ordinary course of trade, and for the purpose of earning a livelihood, and no representation is made by or on behalf of the seller that any part of the proceeds of sale will be devoted to any charitable purpose.*

[(1A) The authorities referred to in subsection (1) above are—

(*a*) *the Common Council of the City of London,*

(*b*) *the police authority for the Metropolitan Police District, and*

(*c*) *the council of each district;*

but any regulations made by a district council under that subsection shall not have effect with respect to any street or public place which is within the Metropolitan Police District as well as within the district.]

(2) *This section, except subsection (3) thereof, shall apply to Ireland with the following modifications:—*

(*a*) *references to the Secretary of State [or the Minister for the Cabinet Office] shall be construed as references to the Lord Lieutenant; and*

(*b*) *references to a police authority shall ... be construed as references to the Inspector General of the [Police Service of Northern Ireland].*

(3) ...

(4) *In this section—*

["charitable appeal" has the same meaning as in Chapter 1 of Part 3 of the Charities Act 2006;]

the expression "street" includes any highway and any public bridge, road, lane, footway, square, court, alley, or passage, whether a thoroughfare or not.

[2]

NOTES

In so far as unrepealed, this Act is repealed, except in relation to Northern Ireland, by the Charities Act 1992, ss 78(2), 79(7), Sch 7, as from a day to be appointed under s 79(2) of that Act; that repeal is itself repealed by the Charities Act 2006, s 75(1), (2), Sch 8, paras 89, 95, Sch 9 as from a day to be appointed.

Sub-s (1): words in first and second pairs of square brackets substituted by the Local Government Act 1972, s 251, Sch 29, Pt II, para 22; reference to level 1 on the standard scale substituted by virtue of the Criminal Justice Act 1982, ss 38, 46; words in first and second pairs of square brackets of para (a) of the proviso substituted by the Transfer of Functions (Third Sector, Communities and Equality) Order 2006, SI 2006/2951, art 6, Schedule, para 1; for the words "the benefit of charitable or other purposes," there are substituted the words "any purposes in circumstances not involving the making of a charitable appeal," and in para (b) of the proviso, words from ", and no representation" onwards repealed by the Charities Act 2006, s 75(1), (2), Sch 8, para 15(1)–(3), Sch 9, as from a day to be appointed under s 79(2) of that Act.

Sub-s (1A): inserted by the Local Government Act 1972, s 251, Sch 29, Pt II, para 22.

Sub-s (2): words in square brackets in para (a) substituted by SI 2006/2951, art 6, Schedule, para 1; words omitted from para (b) repealed by virtue of the Statute Law Revision Act 1927, s 3; words in square brackets in para (b) substituted by the Police (Northern Ireland) Act 2000, s 78(2)(f).

Sub-s (3): repealed by the Civic Government (Scotland) Act 1982, ss 119(15), 137, Sch 4.

Sub-s (4): definition "charitable appeal" inserted by the Charities Act 2006, s 75(1), Sch 8, para 15(1), (4), as from a day to be appointed under s 79(2) of that Act.

Regulations: the Street Collections (Metropolitan Police District) Regulations 1979, SI 1979/1230.

6 Extent of Part I

This Part of this Act shall not apply, except where otherwise expressly provided, to Scotland or Ireland.

[3]

NOTES

Repealed as noted to s 5 at **[2]**.

7–9 *((Pt II) repealed by the Factories Act 1937, ss 159, 160(3), Sch 4, and the Factories Act (Northern Ireland) 1938, s 161(1), Sch 3.)*

PART III
MISCELLANEOUS AND GENERAL

10–12 (*S 10 repealed by the Mines and Quarries Act 1954, s 189, Sch 5, and the Mines Act (Northern Ireland) 1969, s 163, Sch 5; s 11 repealed by the Mental Health Act 1959, s 149(2), Sch 8, Pt I; s 12 repealed by the Criminal Justice Act 1948, s 83(3), Sch 10, Pt I, and the Magistrates' Courts Act (Northern Ireland) 1964, s 172, Sch 7.*)

13 Short title

This Act may be cited as the Police, Factories, etc (Miscellaneous Provisions) Act 1916.
[4]–[14]

NOTES
Repealed as noted to s 5 at **[2]**.

(*Schedule repealed by the Statute Law Revision Act 1927.*)

TRUSTEE ACT 1925

(15 & 16 Geo 5 c 19)

ARRANGEMENT OF SECTIONS

PART II
GENERAL POWERS OF TRUSTEES AND PERSONAL REPRESENTATIVES

General Powers

Indemnities

Maintenance, Advancement and Protective Trusts

PART III
APPOINTMENT AND DISCHARGE OF TRUSTEES

PART IV
POWERS OF THE COURT

Appointment of new Trustees

An Act to consolidate certain enactments relating to trustees in England and Wales

[9 April 1925]

NOTES

Modification: this Act has been modified by the Solicitors' Incorporated Practices Order 1991, SI 1991/2684, arts 2–5, Sch 1, so that any reference to a solicitor is to be construed as including a reference to a recognised body within the meaning of the Administration of Justice Act 1985, s 9.

1–11 *((Pt 1) s 1 repealed by the Trustee Investments Act 1961, s 16(2), Sch 5; ss 2–11 repealed by the Trustee Act 2000, s 40(1), (3), Sch 2, Pt II, para 18, Sch 4, Pt II.)*

PART II
GENERAL POWERS OF TRUSTEES AND PERSONAL REPRESENTATIVES

General Powers

12 Power of trustees for sale to sell by auction, etc

(1) Where [a trustee has a duty or power to sell property], he may sell or concur with any other person in selling all or any part of the property, either subject to prior charges or not, and

either together or in lots, by public auction or by private contract, subject to any such conditions respecting title or evidence of title or other matter as the trustee thinks fit, with power to vary any contract for sale, and to buy in at any auction, or to rescind any contract for sale and to re-sell, without being answerable for any loss.

(2) A trust or power to sell or dispose of land includes a trust or power to sell or dispose of part thereof, whether the division is horizontal, vertical, or made in any other way.

(3) This section does not enable an express power to sell settled land to be exercised where the power is not vested in the tenant for life or statutory owner.

[15]

NOTES

Sub-s (1): words in square brackets substituted for original words "a trust for sale or a power of sale of property is vested in a trustee" by the Trusts of Land and Appointment of Trustees Act 1996, s 25(1), Sch 3, para 3(1), (2); for savings see ss 3, 18(3), 25(5) of the 1996 Act, at **[1009]**, **[1025]** and **[1032]**.

13 Power to sell subject to depreciatory conditions

(1) No sale made by a trustee shall be impeached by any beneficiary upon the ground that any of the conditions subject to which the sale was made may have been unnecessarily depreciatory, unless it also appears that the consideration for the sale was thereby rendered inadequate.

(2) No sale made by a trustee shall, after the execution of the conveyance, be impeached as against the purchaser upon the ground that any of the conditions subject to which the sale was made may have been unnecessarily depreciatory, unless it appears that the purchaser was acting in collusion with the trustee at the time when the contract for sale was made.

(3) No purchaser, upon any sale made by a trustee, shall be at liberty to make any objection against the title upon any of the grounds aforesaid.

(4) This section applies to sales made before or after the commencement of this Act.

[16]

14 Power of trustees to give receipts

(1) The receipt in writing of a trustee for any money, securities, [investments] or other personal property or effects payable, transferable, or deliverable to him under any trust or power shall be a sufficient discharge to the person paying, transferring, or delivering the same and shall effectually exonerate him from seeing to the application or being answerable for any loss or misapplication thereof.

(2) This section does not, except where the trustee is a trust corporation, enable a sole trustee to give a valid receipt for—

[(a) proceeds of sale or other capital money arising under a trust for land;]
(b) capital money arising under the Settled Land Act 1925.

(3) This section applies notwithstanding anything to the contrary in the instrument, if any, creating the trust.

[17]

NOTES

Sub-s (1): word in square brackets inserted by the Trustee Act 2000, s 40(1), Sch 2, Pt II, para 19.

Sub-s (2): para (a) substituted by the Trusts of Land and Appointment of Trustees Act 1996, s 25(1), Sch 3, para 3(1), (3); for savings see ss 3, 18(3), 25(5) of the 1996 Act at **[1009]**, **[1025]** and **[1032]**.

15 Power to compound liabilities

A personal representative, or two or more trustees acting together, or, subject to the restrictions imposed in regard to receipts by a sole trustee not being a trust corporation, a sole acting trustee where by the instrument, if any, creating the trust, or by statute, a sole trustee is authorised to execute the trusts and powers reposed in him, may, if and as he or they think fit—

(a) accept any property, real or personal, before the time at which it is made transferable or payable; or
(b) sever and apportion any blended trust funds or property; or
(c) pay or allow any debt or claim on any evidence that he or they think sufficient; or

(d) accept any composition or any security, real or personal, for any debt or for any property, real or personal, claimed; or
(e) allow any time of payment of any debt; or
(f) compromise, compound, abandon, submit to arbitration, or otherwise settle any debt, account, claim, or thing whatever relating to the testator's or intestate's estate or to the trust;

and for any of these purposes may enter into, give, execute, and do such agreements, instruments of composition or arrangement, releases, and other things as to him or them seem expedient, without being responsible for any loss occasioned by any act or thing so done by him or them [if he has or they have discharged the duty of care set out in section 1(1) of the Trustee Act 2000].

[18]

NOTES

Words in square brackets substituted by the Trustee Act 2000, s 40(1), Sch 2, Pt II, para 20.

16 Power to raise money by sale, mortgage, etc

(1) Where trustees are authorised by the instrument, if any, creating the trust or by law to pay or apply capital money subject to the trust for any purpose or in any manner, they shall have and shall be deemed always to have had power to raise the money required by sale, conversion, calling in, or mortgage of all or any part of the trust property for the time being in possession.

(2) This section applies notwithstanding anything to the contrary contained in the instrument, if any, creating the trust, but does not apply to trustees of property held for charitable purposes, or to trustees of a settlement for the purposes of the Settled Land Act 1925, not being also the statutory owners.

[19]

17 Protection to purchasers and mortgagees dealing with trustees

No purchaser or mortgagee, paying or advancing money on a sale or mortgage purporting to be made under any trust or power vested in trustees, shall be concerned to see that such money is wanted, or that no more than is wanted is raised, or otherwise as to the application thereof.

[20]

18 Devolution of powers or trusts

(1) Where a power or trust is given to or imposed on two or more trustees jointly, the same may be exercised or performed by the survivors or survivor of them for the time being.

(2) Until the appointment of new trustees, the personal representatives or representative for the time being of a sole trustee, or, where there were two or more trustees of the last surviving or continuing trustee, shall be capable of exercising or performing any power or trust which was given to, or capable of being exercised by, the sole or last surviving or continuing trustee, or the other trustees or trustee for the time being of the trust.

(3) This section takes effect subject to the restrictions imposed in regard to receipts by a sole trustee, not being a trust corporation.

(4) In this section "personal representative" does not include an executor who has renounced or has not proved.

[21]

[19 Power to insure

(1) A trustee may—
(a) insure any property which is subject to the trust against risks of loss or damage due to any event, and
(b) pay the premiums out of the trust funds.

(2) In the case of property held on a bare trust, the power to insure is subject to any direction given by the beneficiary or each of the beneficiaries—
(a) that any property specified in the direction is not to be insured;
(b) that any property specified in the direction is not to be insured except on such conditions as may be so specified.

(3) Property is held on a bare trust if it is held on trust for—

(a) a beneficiary who is of full age and capacity and absolutely entitled to the property subject to the trust, or

(b) beneficiaries each of whom is of full age and capacity and who (taken together) are absolutely entitled to the property subject to the trust.

(4) If a direction under subsection (2) of this section is given, the power to insure, so far as it is subject to the direction, ceases to be a delegable function for the purposes of section 11 of the Trustee Act 2000 (power to employ agents).

(5) In this section "trust funds" means any income or capital funds of the trust.]

[22]

NOTES

Substituted by the Trustee Act 2000, s 34(1), (3) in relation to trusts created before or after 1 February 2001.

20 Application of insurance money where policy kept up under any trust, power or obligation

(1) Money receivable by trustees or any beneficiary under a policy of insurance against the loss or damage of any property subject to a trust or to a settlement within the meaning of the Settled Land Act 1925, … , shall, where the policy has been kept up under any trust in that behalf or under any power statutory or otherwise, or in performance of any covenant or of any obligation statutory or otherwise, or by a tenant for life impeachable for waste, be capital money for the purposes of the trust or settlement, as the case may be.

(2) If any such money is receivable by any person, other than the trustees of the trust or settlement, that person shall use his best endeavours to recover and receive the money, and shall pay the net residue thereof, after discharging any costs of recovering and receiving it, to the trustees of the trust or settlement, or, if there are no trustees capable of giving a discharge therefor, into court.

(3) Any such money—

(a) if it was receivable in respect of settled land within the meaning of the Settled Land Act 1925, or any building or works thereon, shall be deemed to be capital money arising under that Act from the settled land, and shall be invested or applied by the trustees, or, if in court, under the direction of the court, accordingly;

(b) if it was receivable in respect of personal chattels settled as heirlooms within the meaning of the Settled Land Act 1925, shall be deemed to be capital money arising under that Act, and shall be applicable by the trustees, or, if in court, under the direction of the court, in like manner as provided by that Act with respect to money arising by sale of chattels as heirlooms as aforesaid;

(c) if it was receivable in respect of [land subject to a trust for land or personal property held on a trust for sale], shall be held upon the trusts and subject to the powers and provisions applicable to money arising by a sale under such trust;

(d) in any other case, shall be held upon trusts corresponding as nearly as may be with the trusts affecting the property in respect of which it was payable.

(4) Such money, or any part thereof, may also be applied by the trustees, or, if in court, under the direction of the court, in rebuilding, reinstating, replacing, or repairing the property lost or damaged, but any such application by the trustees shall be subject to the consent of any person whose consent is required by the instrument, if any, creating the trust to the investment of money subject to the trust, and, in the case of money which is deemed to be capital money arising under the Settled Land Act 1925, be subject to the provisions of that Act with respect to the application of capital money by the trustees of the settlement.

(5) Nothing contained in this section prejudices or affects the right of any person to require any such money or any part thereof to be applied in rebuilding, reinstating, or repairing the property lost or damaged, or the rights of any mortgagee, lessor, or lessee, whether under any statute or otherwise.

(6) This section applies to policies effected either before or after the commencement of this Act, but only to money received after such commencement.

[23]–[24]

NOTES

Sub-s (1): words omitted repealed by the Trustee Act 2000, ss 34(2), (3), 40(3), Sch 4, Pt II in relation to a trust created before the commencement of s 34 (1 February 2001) as it applies to one created after that date.

Sub-s (3): words in square brackets substituted for original words "property held upon trust for sale" by the Trusts of Land and Appointment of Trustees Act 1996, s 25(1), Sch 3, para 3(1), (5); for savings see ss 3, 18(3), 25(5) of the 1996 Act at **[1009]**, **[1025]** and **[1032]**.

21 *(Repealed by the Trustee Act 2000, s 40(1), (3), Sch 2, Pt II, para 21, Sch 4, Pt II.)*

22 Reversionary interests, valuations, and audit

(1) Where the trust property includes any share or interest in property not vested in the trustees, or the proceeds of the sale of any such property, or any other thing in action, the trustees on the same falling into possession, or becoming payable or transferable may—

(a) agree or ascertain the amount or value thereof or any part thereof in such manner as they may think fit;

(b) accept in or towards satisfaction thereof, at the market or current value, or upon any valuation or estimate of value which they may think fit, any authorised investments;

(c) allow any deductions for duties, costs, charges and expenses which they may think proper or reasonable;

(d) execute any release in respect of the premises so as effectually to discharge all accountable parties from all liability in respect of any matters coming within the scope of such release;

without being responsible in any such case for any loss occasioned by any act or thing so done by them [if they have discharged the duty of care set out in section 1(1) of the Trustee Act 2000].

(2) The trustees shall not be under any obligation and shall not be chargeable with any breach of trust by reason of any omission—

(a) to place any distringas notice or apply for any stop or other like order upon any securities or other property out of or on which such share or interest or other thing in action as aforesaid is derived, payable or charged; or

(b) to take any proceedings on account of any act, default, or neglect on the part of the persons in whom such securities or other property or any of them or any part thereof are for the time being, or had at any time been, vested;

unless and until required in writing so to do by some person, or the guardian of some person, beneficially interested under the trust, and unless also due provision is made to their satisfaction for payment of the costs of any proceedings required to be taken:

Provided that nothing in this subsection shall relieve the trustees of the obligation to get in and obtain payment or transfer of such share or interest or other thing in action on the same falling into possession.

(3) Trustees may, for the purpose of giving effect to the trust, or any of the provisions of the instrument, if any, creating the trust or of any statute, from time to time (by duly qualified agents) ascertain and fix the value of any trust property in such manner as they think proper, and any valuation so made ... shall be binding upon all persons interested under the trust [if the trustees have discharged the duty of care set out in section 1(1) of the Trustee Act 2000].

(4) Trustees may, in their absolute discretion, from time to time, but not more than once in every three years unless the nature of the trust or any special dealings with the trust property make a more frequent exercise of the right reasonable, cause the accounts of the trust property to be examined or audited by an independent accountant, and shall, for that purpose, produce such vouchers and give such information to him as he may require; and the costs of such examination or audit, including the fee of the auditor, shall be paid out of the capital or income of the trust property, or partly in one way and partly in the other as the trustees, in their absolute discretion, think fit, but, in default of any direction by the trustees to the contrary in any special case, costs attributable to capital shall be borne by capital and those attributable to income by income.

[25]–[26]

NOTES

Sub-s (1): words in square brackets substituted by the Trustee Act 2000, s 40(1), Sch 2, Pt II, para 22(a).

Sub-s (3): words omitted repealed and words in square brackets added by the Trustee Act 2000, s 40(1), Sch 2, Pt II, para 22(b).

23 *(Repealed by the Trustee Act 2000, s 40(1), (3), Sch 2, Pt II, para 23, Sch 4, Pt II, subject to transitional provisions and savings contained in Sch 3, para 6 to that Act at* **[1317]***.)*

24 Power to concur with others

Where an undivided share in [any] property, is subject to a trust, or forms part of the estate of a testator or intestate, the trustees or personal representatives may (without prejudice to the [trust] affecting the entirety of the land and the powers of the [trustees] in reference thereto) execute or exercise any [duty or] power vested in them in relation to such share in conjunction with the persons entitled to or having power in that behalf over the other share or shares, and notwithstanding that any one or more of the trustees or personal representatives may be entitled to or interested in any such other share, either in his or their own right or in a fiduciary capacity.

[27]

NOTES

Word in first pair of square brackets substituted for original words "the proceeds of sale of land directed to be sold, or in any other", word in second pair of square brackets substituted for original words "trust for sale", word in third pair of square brackets substituted for original words "trustees for sale" and words in final pair of square brackets substituted for original words "trust or" by the Trusts of Land and Appointment of Trustees Act 1996, s 25(1), Sch 3, para 3(1), (6); for savings see ss 3, 18(3), 25(5) of the 1996 Act at **[1009]**, **[1025]** and **[1032]**.

[25 Delegation of trustee's functions by power of attorney

(1) Notwithstanding any rule of law or equity to the contrary, a trustee may, by power of attorney, delegate the execution or exercise of all or any of the trusts, powers and discretions vested in him as trustee either alone or jointly with any other person or persons.

(2) A delegation under this section—

(a) commences as provided by the instrument creating the power or, if the instrument makes no provision as to the commencement of the delegation, with the date of the execution of the instrument by the donor; and

(b) continues for a period of twelve months or any shorter period provided by the instrument creating the power.

(3) The persons who may be donees of a power of attorney under this section include a trust corporation.

(4) Before or within seven days after giving a power of attorney under this section the donor shall give written notice of it (specifying the date on which the power comes into operation and its duration, the donee of the power, the reason why the power is given and, where some only are delegated, the trusts, powers and discretions delegated) to—

(a) each person (other than himself), if any, who under any instrument creating the trust has power (whether alone or jointly) to appoint a new trustee; and

(b) each of the other trustees, if any;

but failure to comply with this subsection shall not, in favour of a person dealing with the donee of the power, invalidate any act done or instrument executed by the donee.

(5) A power of attorney given under this section by a single donor—

(a) in the form set out in subsection (6) of this section; or

(b) in a form to the like effect but expressed to be made under this subsection,

shall operate to delegate to the person identified in the form as the single donee of the power the execution and exercise of all the trusts, powers and discretions vested in the donor as trustee (either alone or jointly with any other person or persons) under the single trust so identified.

(6) The form referred to in subsection (5) of this section is as follows—

"THIS GENERAL TRUSTEE POWER OF ATTORNEY is made on [date] by [name of one donor] of [address of donor] as trustee of [name or details of one trust].

I appoint [name of one donee] of [address of donee] to be my attorney [if desired, the date on which the delegation commences or the period for which it continues (or both)] in accordance with section 25(5) of the Trustee Act 1925.

[To be executed as a deed]".

(7) The donor of a power of attorney given under this section shall be liable for the acts or defaults of the donee in the same manner as if they were the acts or defaults of the donor.

(8) For the purpose of executing or exercising the trusts or powers delegated to him, the donee may exercise any of the powers conferred on the donor as trustee by statute or by the instrument creating the trust, including power, for the purpose of the transfer of any inscribed stock, himself to delegate to an attorney power to transfer, but not including the power of delegation conferred by this section.

(9) The fact that it appears from any power of attorney given under this section, or from any evidence required for the purposes of any such power of attorney or otherwise, that in dealing with any stock the donee of the power is acting in the execution of a trust shall not be deemed for any purpose to affect any person in whose books the stock is inscribed or registered with any notice of the trust.

(10) This section applies to a personal representative, tenant for life and statutory owner as it applies to a trustee except that subsection (4) shall apply as if it required the notice there mentioned to be given—

(a) in the case of a personal representative, to each of the other personal representatives, if any, except any executor who has renounced probate;

(b) in the case of a tenant for life, to the trustees of the settlement and to each person, if any, who together with the person giving the notice constitutes the tenant for life; and

(c) in the case of a statutory owner, to each of the persons, if any, who together with the person giving the notice constitute the statutory owner and, in the case of a statutory owner by virtue of section 23(1)(a) of the Settled Land Act 1925, to the trustees of the settlement.]

[28]

NOTES

Commencement: 1 March 2000.

Substituted by the Trustee Delegation Act 1999, s 5(1), (2), in relation to enduring powers of attorney created after 1 March 2000.

Indemnities

26 Protection against liability in respect of rents and covenants

(1) Where a personal representative or trustee liable as such for—

(a) any rent, covenant, or agreement reserved by or contained in any lease; or

(b) any rent, covenant or agreement payable under or contained in any grant made in consideration of a rentcharge; or

(c) any indemnity given in respect of any rent, covenant or agreement referred to in either of the foregoing paragraphs;

satisfies all liabilities under the lease or grant [which may have accrued and been claimed] up to the date of the conveyance hereinafter mentioned, and, where necessary, sets apart a sufficient fund to answer any future claim that may be made in respect of any fixed and ascertained sum which the lessee or grantee agreed to lay out on the property demised or granted, although the period for laying out the same may not have arrived, then and in any such case the personal representative or trustee may convey the property demised or granted to a purchaser, legatee, devisee, or other person entitled to call for a conveyance thereof and thereafter—

(i) he may distribute the residuary real and personal estate of the deceased testator or intestate, or, as the case may be, the trust estate (other than the fund, if any, set apart as aforesaid) to or amongst the persons entitled thereto, without appropriating any part, or any further part, as the case may be, of the estate of the deceased or of the trust estate to meet any future liability under the said lease or grant;

(ii) notwithstanding such distribution, he shall not be personally liable in respect of *any subsequent claim* under the said lease or grant.

[(1A) Where a personal representative or trustee has as such entered into, or may as such be required to enter into, an authorised guarantee agreement with respect to any lease comprised in the estate of a deceased testator or intestate or a trust estate (and, in a case where he has entered into such an agreement, he has satisfied all liabilities under it which may have accrued and been claimed up to the date of distribution)—

(a) he may distribute the residuary real and personal estate of the deceased testator or intestate, or the trust estate, to or amongst the persons entitled thereto—

(i) without appropriating any part of the estate of the deceased, or the trust estate, to meet any future liability (or, as the case may be, any liability) under any such agreement, and

(ii) notwithstanding any potential liability of his to enter into any such agreement; and

(b) notwithstanding such distribution, he shall not be personally liable in respect of any subsequent claim (or, as the case may be, any claim) under any such agreement.

In this subsection "authorised guarantee agreement" has the same meaning as in the Landlord and Tenant (Covenants) Act 1995.]

(2) This section operates without prejudice to the right of the lessor or grantor, or the persons deriving title under the lessor or grantor, to follow the assets of the deceased or the trust property into the hands of the persons amongst whom the same may have been respectively distributed, and applies notwithstanding anything to the contrary in the will or other instrument, if any, creating the trust.

(3) In this section "lease" includes an underlease and an agreement for a lease or underlease and any instrument giving any such indemnity as aforesaid or varying the liabilities under the lease; "grant" applies to a grant whether the rent is created by limitation, grant, reservation, or otherwise, and includes an agreement for a grant and any instrument giving any such indemnity as aforesaid or varying the liabilities under the grant; "lessee" and "grantee" include persons respectively deriving title under them.

[29]

NOTES

Sub-s (1): words in square brackets substituted with retrospective effect by the Law of Property (Amendment) Act 1926, ss 7, 8(2), Schedule.

Sub-s (1A): inserted by the Landlord and Tenant (Covenants) Act 1995, s 30(1), Sch 1, para 1.

27 Protection by means of advertisements

(1) With a view to the conveyance to or distribution among the persons entitled to any real or personal property, the trustees of a settlement[, trustees of land, trustees for sale of personal property] or personal representatives, may give notice by advertisement in the Gazette, and [in a newspaper circulating in the district in which the land is situated] and such other like notices, including notices elsewhere than in England and Wales, as would, in any special case, have been directed by a court of competent jurisdiction in an action for administration, of their intention to make such conveyance or distribution as aforesaid, and requiring any person interested to send to the trustees or personal representatives within the time, not being less than two months, fixed in the notice or, where more than one notice is given, in the last of the notices, particulars of his claim in respect of the property or any part thereof to which the notice relates.

(2) At the expiration of the time fixed by the notice the trustees or personal representatives may convey or distribute the property or any part thereof to which the notice relates, to or among the persons entitled thereto, having regard only to the claims, whether formal or not, of which the trustees or personal representatives then had notice and shall not, as respects the property so conveyed or distributed, be liable to any person of whose claim the trustees or personal representatives have not had notice at the time of conveyance or distribution; but nothing in this section—

(a) prejudices the right of any person to follow the property, or any property representing the same, into the hands of any person, other than a purchaser, who may have received it; or

(b) frees the trustees or personal representatives from any obligation to make searches or obtain official certificates of search similar to those which an intending purchaser would be advised to make or obtain.

(3) This section applies notwithstanding anything to the contrary in the will or other instrument, if any, creating the trust.

[30]

NOTES

Sub-s (1): words in first pair of square brackets substituted for original words "or of a disposition on trust for sale" by the Trusts of Land and Appointment of Trustees Act 1996, s 25(1), Sch 3, para 3(1),(7); for savings see ss 3, 18(3), 25(5) of the 1996 Act at **[1009]**, **[1025]** and **[1032]**; words in second pair of square brackets substituted with retrospective effect by the Law of Property (Amendment) Act 1926, ss 7, 8(2),Schedule.

28 Protection in regard to notice

A trustee or personal representative acting for the purposes of more than one trust or estate shall not, in the absence of fraud, be affected by notice of any instrument, matter, fact or thing in relation to any particular trust or estate if he has obtained notice thereof merely by reason of his acting or having acted for the purposes of another trust or estate.

[31]–[32]

29, 30 *(S 29 repealed by the Powers of Attorney Act 1971, s 11(2), (4), Sch 2; s 30 repealed by the Trustee Act 2000, s 40(1), (3), Sch 2, Pt II, para 24, Sch 4, Pt II.)*

Maintenance, Advancement and Protective Trusts

31 Power to apply income for maintenance and to accumulate surplus income during a minority

(1) Where any property is held by trustees in trust for any person for any interest whatsoever, whether vested or contingent, then, subject to any prior interests or charges affecting that property—

(i) during the infancy of any such person, if his interest so long continues, the trustees may, at their sole discretion, pay to his parent or guardian, if any, or otherwise apply for or towards his maintenance, education, or benefit, the whole or such part, if any, of the income of that property as may, in all the circumstances, be reasonable, whether or not there is—

(a) any other fund applicable to the same purpose; or

(b) any person bound by law to provide for his maintenance or education; and

(ii) if such person on attaining the age of [eighteen years] has not a vested interest in such income, the trustees shall thenceforth pay the income of that property and of any accretion thereto under subsection (2) of this section to him, until he either attains a vested interest therein or dies, or until failure of his interest:

Provided that, in deciding whether the whole or any part of the income of the property is during a minority to be paid or applied for the purposes aforesaid, the trustees shall have regard to the age of the infant and his requirements and generally to the circumstances of the case, and in particular to what other income, if any, is applicable for the same purposes; and where trustees have notice that the income of more than one fund is applicable for those purposes, then, so far as practicable, unless the entire income of the funds is paid or applied as aforesaid or the court otherwise directs, a proportionate part only of the income of each fund shall be so paid or applied.

(2) During the infancy of any such person, if his interest so long continues, the trustees shall accumulate all the residue of that income [by investing it, and any profits from so investing it] from time to time in authorised investments, and shall hold those accumulations as follows:—

(i) If any such person—

(a) attains the age of [eighteen years], or marries under that age [or forms a civil partnership under that age], and his interest in such income during his infancy[, or until his marriage or his formation of a civil partnership,] is a vested interest; or

(b) on attaining the age of [eighteen years] or on marriage[, or formation of a civil partnership,] under that age becomes entitled to the property from which such income arose in fee simple, absolute or determinable, or absolutely, or for an entailed interest;

the trustees shall hold the accumulations in trust for such person absolutely, but without prejudice to any provision with respect thereto contained in any settlement by him made under any statutory powers during his infancy, and so that the receipt of such person after marriage [or formation of a civil partnership], and though still an infant, shall be a good discharge; and

(ii) In any other case the trustees shall, notwithstanding that such person had a vested interest in such income, hold the accumulations as an accretion to the capital of the property from which such accumulations arose, and as one fund with such capital for all purposes, and so that, if such property is settled land, such accumulations shall be held upon the same trusts as if the same were capital money arising therefrom;

but the trustees may, at any time during the infancy of such person if his interest so long continues, apply those accumulations, or any part thereof, as if they were income arising in the then current year.

(3) This section applies in the case of a contingent interest only if the limitation or trust carries the intermediate income of the property, but it applies to a future or contingent legacy by the parent of, or a person standing in loco parentis to, the legatee, if and for such period as, under the general law, the legacy carries interest for the maintenance of the legatee, and in any such case as last aforesaid the rate of interest shall (if the income available is sufficient, and subject to any rules of court to the contrary) be five pounds per centum per annum.

(4) This section applies to a vested annuity in like manner as if the annuity were the income of property held by trustees in trust to pay the income thereof to the annuitant for the same period for which the annuity is payable, save that in any case accumulations made during the infancy of the annuitant shall be held in trust for the annuitant or his personal representatives absolutely.

(5) This section does not apply where the instrument, if any, under which the interest arises came into operation before the commencement of this Act.

[33]

NOTES

Sub-s (1): words in square brackets substituted by the Family Law Reform Act 1969, s 1(3), (4), Sch 1, Pt I, Sch 3, paras 5(1), 9.

Sub-s (2): words in first pair of square brackets substituted by the Trustee Act 2000, s 40(1), Sch 2, Pt II, para 25; words in first pair of square brackets in para (i)(a) and words in first pair of square brackets in para (i)(b) substituted by the Family Law Reform Act 1969, s 1(3), (4), Sch 1, Pt I, Sch 3, paras 5(1), 9; words in second and third pairs of square brackets in para (i)(a) substituted, words in second pair of square brackets in para (i)(b) inserted and words in square brackets in the closing paragraph of para (i) inserted by the Civil Partnership Act 2004, s 261(1), Sch 27, para 5.

32 Power of advancement

(1) Trustees may at any time or times pay or apply any capital money subject to a trust, for the advancement or benefit, in such manner as they may, in their absolute discretion, think fit, of any person entitled to the capital of the trust property or of any share thereof, whether absolutely or contingently on his attaining any specified age or on the occurrence of any other event, or subject to a gift over on his death under any specified age or on the occurrence of any other event, and whether in possession or in remainder or reversion, and such payment or application may be made notwithstanding that the interest of such person is liable to be defeated by the exercise of a power of appointment or revocation, or to be diminished by the increase of the class to which he belongs:

Provided that—

(a) the money so paid or applied for the advancement or benefit of any person shall not exceed altogether in amount one-half of the presumptive or vested share or interest of that person in the trust property; and

(b) if that person is or becomes absolutely and indefeasibly entitled to a share in the trust property the money so paid or applied shall be brought into account as part of such share; and

(c) no such payment or application shall be made so as to prejudice any person entitled to any prior life or other interest, whether vested or contingent, in the money paid or applied unless such person is in existence and of full age and consents in writing to such payment or application.

[(2) This section does not apply to capital money arising under the Settled Land Act 1925.]

(3) This section does not apply to trusts constituted or created before the commencement of this Act.

[34]

NOTES

Sub-s (2): substituted by the Trusts of Land and Appointment of Trustees Act 1996, s 25(1), Sch 3, para 3(1), (8); for savings see ss 3, 18(3), 25(5) of the 1996 Act at **[1009]**, **[1025]** and **[1032]**.

33 Protective trusts

(1) Where any income, including an annuity or other periodical income payment, is directed to be held on protective trusts for the benefit of any person (in this section called "the principal beneficiary") for the period of his life or for any less period, then, during that period (in this section called the "trust period") the said income shall, without prejudice to any prior interest, be held on the following trusts, namely:—

(i) Upon trust for the principal beneficiary during the trust period or until he, whether before or after the termination of any prior interest, does or attempts to do or suffers any act or thing, or until any event happens, other than an advance under any statutory or express power, whereby, if the said income were payable during the trust period to the principal beneficiary absolutely during that period, he would be deprived of the right to receive the same or any part thereof, in any of which cases, as well as on the termination of the trust period, whichever first happens, this trust of the said income shall fail or determine;

(ii) If the trust aforesaid fails or determines during the subsistence of the trust period, then, during the residue of that period, the said income shall be held upon trust for the application thereof for the maintenance or support, or otherwise for the benefit, of all or any one or more exclusively of the other or others of the following persons (that is to say)—

(a) the principal beneficiary and his or her [spouse or civil partner], if any, and his or her children or more remote issue, if any; or

(b) if there is no [spouse or civil partner] or issue of the principal beneficiary in existence, the principal beneficiary and the persons who would, if he were actually dead, be entitled to the trust property or the income thereof or to the annuity fund, if any, or arrears of the annuity, as the case may be;

as the trustees in their absolute discretion, without being liable to account for the exercise of such discretion, think fit.

(2) This section does not apply to trusts coming into operation before the commencement of this Act, and has effect subject to any variation of the implied trusts aforesaid contained in the instrument creating the trust.

(3) Nothing in this section operates to validate any trust which would, if contained in the instrument creating the trust, be liable to be set aside.

[(4) In relation to the dispositions mentioned in section 19(1) of the Family Law Reform Act 1987, this section shall have effect as if any reference (however expressed) to any relationship between two persons were construed in accordance with section 1 of that Act.]

[35]

NOTES

Sub-s (1): words in square brackets substituted by the Civil Partnership Act 2004, s 261(1), Sch 27, para 6.

Sub-s (4): added by the Family Law Reform Act 1987, s 33(1), Sch 2, para 2.

PART III
APPOINTMENT AND DISCHARGE OF TRUSTEES

34 Limitation of the number of trustees

(1) Where, at the commencement of this Act, there are more than four trustees of a settlement of land, or more than four trustees holding land on trust for sale, no new trustees shall (except where as a result of the appointment the number is reduced to four or less) be capable of being appointed until the number is reduced to less than four, and thereafter the number shall not be increased beyond four.

(2) In the case of settlements and dispositions [creating trusts of land] made or coming into operation after the commencement of this Act—

(a) the number of trustees thereof shall not in any case exceed four, and where more than four persons are named as such trustees, the four first named (who are able and willing to act) shall alone be the trustees, and the other persons named shall not be trustees unless appointed on the occurrence of a vacancy;

(b) the number of the trustees shall not be increased beyond four.

(3) This section only applies to settlements and dispositions of land, and the restrictions imposed on the number of trustees do not apply—

(a) in the case of land vested in trustees for charitable, ecclesiastical, or public purposes; or

(b) where the net proceeds of the sale of the land are held for like purposes; or

(c) to the trustees of a term of years absolute limited by a settlement on trusts for raising money, or of a like term created under the statutory remedies relating to annual sums charged on land.

[36]

NOTES

Sub-s (2): words in square brackets substituted for original words "on trust for sale of land" by the Trusts of Land and Appointment of Trustees Act 1996, s 25(1), Sch 3, para 3(1), (9); for savings see ss 3, 18(3), 25(5) of the 1996 Act, at **[1009]**, **[1025]** and **[1032]**.

35 Appointments of trustees of settlements and [and trustees of land]

[(1) Appointments of new trustees of land and of new trustees of any trust of the proceeds of sale of the land shall, subject to any order of the court, be effected by separate instruments, but in such manner as to secure that the same persons become trustees of land and trustees of the trust of the proceeds of sale.]

(2) Where new trustees of a settlement are appointed, a memorandum of the names and addresses of the persons who are for the time being the trustees thereof for the purposes of the Settled Land Act 1925, shall be endorsed on or annexed to the last or only principal vesting instrument by or on behalf of the trustees of the settlement, and such vesting instrument shall, for that purpose, be produced by the person having the possession thereof to the trustees of the settlement when so required.

[(3) Where new trustees of land are appointed, a memorandum of the persons who are for the time being the trustees of the land shall be endorsed on or annexed to the conveyance by which the land was vested in trustees of land; and that conveyance shall be produced to the persons who are for the time being the trustees of the land by the person in possession of it in order for that to be done when the trustees require its production.]

(4) This section applies only to settlements and dispositions of land.

[37]

NOTES

Section heading: words in square brackets substituted for original words "dispositions on trust for sale of land" by the Trusts of Land and Appointment of Trustees Act 1996, s 25(1), Sch 3, para 3(1), (10)(c); for savings see ss 3, 18(3), 25(5) of the 1996 Act at **[1009]**, **[1025]** and **[1032]**.

Sub-s (1), (3): substituted by the Trusts of Land and Appointment of Trustees Act 1996, s 25(1), Sch 3, para 3(1), (10)(a); for savings see ss 3, 18(3), 25(5) of the 1996 Act at **[1009]**, **[1025]** and **[1032]**.

36 Power of appointing new or additional trustees

(1) Where a trustee, either original or substituted, and whether appointed by a court or otherwise, is dead, or remains out of the United Kingdom for more than twelve months, or desires to be discharged from all or any of the trusts or powers reposed in or conferred on him, or refuses or is unfit to act therein, or is incapable of acting therein, or is an infant, then, subject to the restrictions imposed by this Act on the number of trustees,—

(a) the person or persons nominated for the purpose of appointing new trustees by the instrument, if any, creating the trust; or

(b) if there is no such person, or no such person able and willing to act, then the surviving or continuing trustees or trustee for the time being, or the personal representatives of the last surviving or continuing trustee;

may, by writing, appoint one or more other persons (whether or not being the persons exercising the power) to be a trustee or trustees in the place of the trustee so deceased remaining out of the United Kingdom, desiring to be discharged, refusing, or being unfit or being incapable, or being an infant, as aforesaid.

(2) Where a trustee has been removed under a power contained in the instrument creating the trust, a new trustee or new trustees may be appointed in the place of the trustee who is removed, as if he were dead, or, in the case of a corporation, as if the corporation desired to be discharged from the trust, and the provisions of this section shall apply accordingly, but subject to the restrictions imposed by this Act on the number of trustees.

(3) Where a corporation being a trustee is or has been dissolved, either before or after the commencement of this Act, then, for the purposes of this section and of any enactment replaced thereby, the corporation shall be deemed to be and to have been from the date of the dissolution incapable of acting in the trusts or powers reposed in or conferred on the corporation.

(4) The power of appointment given by subsection (1) of this section or any similar previous enactment to the personal representatives of a last surviving or continuing trustee shall be and shall be deemed always to have been exercisable by the executors for the time being (whether original or by representation) of such surviving or continuing trustee who have proved the will of their testator or by the administrators for the time being of such trustee without the concurrence of any executor who has renounced or has not proved.

(5) But a sole or last surviving executor intending to renounce, or all the executors where they all intend to renounce, shall have and shall be deemed always to have had power, at any time before renouncing probate, to exercise the power of appointment given by this section, or by any similar previous enactment, if willing to act for that purpose and without thereby accepting the office of executor.

[(6) Where, in the case of any trust, there are not more that three trustees—]

(a) the person or persons nominated for the purpose of appointing new trustees by the instrument, if any, creating the trust; or

(b) if there is no such person, or no such person able and willing to act, then the trustee or trustees for the time being;

may, by writing appoint another person or other persons to be an additional trustee or additional trustees, but it shall not be obligatory to appoint any additional trustee, unless the instrument, if any, creating the trust, or any statutory enactment provides to the contrary, nor shall the number of trustees be increased beyond four by virtue of any such appointment.

[(6A) A person who is either—

(a) both a trustee and attorney for the other trustee (if one other), or for both of the other trustees (if two others), under a registered power; or

(b) attorney under a registered power for the trustee (if one) or for both or each of the trustees (if two or three),

may, if subsection (6B) of this section is satisfied in relation to him, make an appointment under subsection (6)(b) of this section on behalf of the trustee or trustees.

(6B) This subsection is satisfied in relation to an attorney under a registered power for one or more trustees if (as attorney under the power)—

(a) he intends to exercise any function of the trustee or trustees by virtue of section 1(1) of the Trustee Delegation Act 1999; or

(b) he intends to exercise any function of the trustee or trustees in relation to any land, capital proceeds of a conveyance of land or income from land by virtue of its delegation to him under section 25 of this Act or the instrument (if any) creating the trust.

(6C) In subsections (6A) and (6B) of this section "registered power" means *a power of attorney created by an instrument which is for the time being registered under section 6 of the Enduring Powers of Attorney Act 1985*.

(6D) Subsection (6A) of this section—

(a) applies only if and so far as a contrary intention is not expressed in the instrument creating the power of attorney (or, where more than one, any of them) or the instrument (if any) creating the trust; and

(b) has effect subject to the terms of those instruments.]

(7) Every new trustee appointed under this section as well before as after all the trust property becomes by law, or by assurance, or otherwise, vested in him, shall have the same powers, authorities, and discretions, and may in all respects act as if he had been originally appointed a trustee by the instrument, if any, creating the trust.

(8) The provisions of this section relating to a trustee who is dead include the case of a person nominated trustee in a will but dying before the testator, and those relative to a continuing trustee include a refusing or retiring trustee, if willing to act in the execution of the provisions of this section.

[(9) Where a trustee *is incapable, by reason of mental disorder within the meaning of [the Mental Health Act 1983], of exercising* his functions as trustee and is also entitled in possession to some beneficial interest in the trust property, no appointment of a new trustee in his place shall be made by virtue of paragraph (b) of subsection (1) of this section unless leave to make the appointment has been given by *the authority having jurisdiction under [Part VII of the Mental Health Act 1983]*.]

[38]

NOTES

Sub-s (6): words in square brackets substituted by the Trusts of Land and Appointment of Trustees Act 1996, s 25(1), Sch 3, para 3(1), (11); for savings see ss 3, 18(3), 25(5) of the 1996 Act at **[1009]**, **[1025]** and **[1032]**.

Sub-ss (6A), (6B), (6D): inserted, together with sub-s (6C), by the Trustee Delegation Act 1999, s 8, in relation to any power (or where there is more than one, each of them) created before 1 March 2000.

Sub-s (6C): inserted, together with sub-ss (6A), (6B), (6D), by the Trustee Delegation Act 1999, s 8, in relation to any power (or where there is more than one, each of them) created before 1 March 2000; for the words in italics there are substituted the words "an enduring power of attorney or lasting power of attorney registered under the Mental Capacity Act 2005" by the Mental Capacity Act 2005, s 67(1), Sch 6, para 3(1), (2)(a), as from a day to be appointed under s 68(1) of that Act.

Sub-s (9): substituted by the Mental Health Act 1959, s 149(1), Sch 7, Pt I; words in square brackets substituted by the Mental Health Act 1983, s 148, Sch 4, para 4(a); words in italics in the first place substituted by the words "lacks capacity to exercise" and words in italics in the second place substituted by the words "the Court of Protection" by the Mental Capacity Act 2005, s 67(1), Sch 6, para 3(1), (2)(b), as from a day to be appointed under s 68(1) of that Act.

37 Supplemental provisions as to appointment of trustees

(1) On the appointment of a trustee for the whole or any part of trust property—

(a) the number of trustees may, subject to the restrictions imposed by this Act on the number of trustees, be increased; and

(b) a separate set of trustees, not exceeding four, may be appointed for any part of the trust property held on trusts distinct from those relating to any other part or parts of the trust property, notwithstanding that no new trustees or trustee are or is to be appointed for other parts of the trust property, and any existing trustee may be appointed or remain one of such separate set of trustees, or, if only one trustee was originally appointed, then, save as hereinafter provided, one separate trustee may be so appointed; and

(c) it shall not be obligatory, save as hereinafter provided, to appoint more than one new trustee where only one trustee was originally appointed, or to fill up the original number of trustees where more than two trustees were originally appointed, but, except where only one trustee was originally appointed, and a sole trustee when appointed will be able to give valid receipts for all capital money, a trustee shall not be discharged from his trust unless there will be either a trust corporation or at least two [persons] to act as trustees to perform the trust; and

(d) any assurance or thing requisite for vesting the trust property, or any part thereof, in a sole trustee, or jointly in the persons who are the trustees, shall be executed or done.

(2) Nothing in this Act shall authorise the appointment of a sole trustee, not being a trust corporation, where the trustee, when appointed, would not be able to give valid receipts for all capital money arising under the trust.

[39]

NOTES

Sub-s (1): word in square brackets substituted for original word "individuals" by the Trusts of Land and Appointment of Trustees Act 1996, s 25(1), Sch 3, para 3(1), (12); for savings see ss 3, 18(3), 25(5) of the 1996 Act at **[1009]**, **[1025]** and **[1032]**.

38 Evidence as to a vacancy in a trust

(1) A statement, contained in any instrument coming into operation after the commencement of this Act by which a new trustee is appointed for any purpose connected

with land, to the effect that a trustee has remained out of the United Kingdom for more than twelve months or refuses or is unfit to act, or is incapable of acting, or that he is not entitled to a beneficial interest in the trust property in possession, shall, in favour of a purchaser of a legal estate, be conclusive evidence of the matter stated.

(2) In favour of such purchaser any appointment of a new trustee depending on that statement, and any vesting declaration, express or implied, consequent on the appointment, shall be valid.

[40]

39 Retirement of trustee without a new appointment

(1) Where a trustee is desirous of being discharged from the trust, and after his discharge there will be either a trust corporation or at least two [persons] to act as trustees to perform the trust, then, if such trustee as aforesaid by deed declares that he is desirous of being discharged from the trust, and if his co-trustees and such other person, if any, as is empowered to appoint trustees, by deed consent to the discharge of the trustee, and to the vesting in the co-trustees alone of the trust property, the trustee desirous of being discharged shall be deemed to have retired from the trust, and shall, by the deed, be discharged therefrom under this Act, without any new trustee being appointed in his place.

(2) Any assurance or thing requisite for vesting the trust property in the continuing trustees alone shall be executed or done.

[41]

NOTES

Sub-s (1): word in square brackets substituted for original word "individuals" by the Trusts of Land and Appointment of Trustees Act 1996, s 25(1), Sch 3, para 3(1), (13); for savings see ss 3, 18(3), 25(5) of the 1996 Act at **[1009]**, **[1025]** and **[1032]**.

40 Vesting of trust property in new or continuing trustees

(1) Where by a deed a new trustee is appointed to perform any trust, then—

(a) if the deed contains a declaration by the appointor to the effect that any estate or interest in any land subject to the trust, or in any chattel so subject, or the right to recover or receive any debt or other thing in action so subject, shall vest in the persons who by virtue of the deed become or are the trustees for performing the trust, the deed shall operate, without any conveyance or assignment, to vest in those persons as joint tenants and for the purposes of the trust the estate interest or right to which the declaration relates; and

(b) if the deed is made after the commencement of this Act and does not contain such a declaration, the deed shall, subject to any express provision to the contrary therein contained, operate as if it had contained such a declaration by the appointor extending to all the estates interests and rights with respect to which a declaration could have been made.

(2) Where by a deed a retiring trustee is discharged under [section 39 of this Act or section 19 of the Trusts of Land and Appointment of Trustees Act 1996] without a new trustee being appointed, then—

(a) if the deed contains such a declaration as aforesaid by the retiring and continuing trustees, and by the other person, if any, empowered to appoint trustees, the deed shall, without any conveyance or assignment, operate to vest in the continuing trustees alone, as joint tenants, and for the purposes of the trust, the estate, interest, or right to which the declaration relates; and

(b) if the deed is made after the commencement of this Act and does not contain such a declaration, the deed shall, subject to any express provision to the contrary therein contained, operate as if it had contained such a declaration by such persons as aforesaid extending to all the estates, interests and rights with respect to which a declaration could have been made.

(3) An express vesting declaration, whether made before or after the commencement of this Act, shall, notwithstanding that the estate, interest or right to be vested is not expressly referred to, and provided that the other statutory requirements were or are complied with, operate and be deemed always to have operated (but without prejudice to any express provision to the contrary contained in the deed of appointment or discharge) to vest in the persons respectively referred to in subsections (1) and (2) of this section, as the case may require, such estates, interests and rights as are capable of being and ought to be vested in those persons.

(4) This section does not extend—

(a) to land conveyed by way of mortgage for securing money subject to the trust, except land conveyed on trust for securing debentures or debenture stock;

(b) to land held under a lease which contains any covenant, condition or agreement against assignment or disposing of the land without licence or consent, unless, prior to the execution of the deed containing expressly or impliedly the vesting declaration, the requisite licence or consent has been obtained, or unless, by virtue of any statute or rule of law, the vesting declaration, express or implied, would not operate as a breach of covenant or give rise to a forfeiture;

(c) to any share, stock, annuity or property which is only transferable in books kept by a company or other body, or in manner directed by or under an Act of Parliament.

In this subsection "lease" includes an underlease and an agreement for a lease or underlease.

(5) For purposes of registration of the deed in any registry, the person or persons making the declaration expressly or impliedly, shall be deemed the conveying party or parties, and the conveyance shall be deemed to be made by him or them under a power conferred by this Act.

(6) This section applies to deeds of appointment or discharge executed on or after the first day of January, eighteen hundred and eighty-two.

[42]

NOTES

Sub-s (2): words in square brackets substituted for original words "the statutory power" by the Trusts of Land and Appointment of Trustees Act 1996, s 25(1), Sch 3, para 3(1), (14); for savings see ss 3, 18(3), 25(5) of the 1996 Act at **[1009]**, **[1025]** and **[1032]**.

PART IV
POWERS OF THE COURT

Appointment of new Trustees

41 Power of court to appoint new trustees

(1) The court may, whenever it is expedient to appoint a new trustee or new trustees, and it is found inexpedient difficult or impracticable so to do without the assistance of the court, make an order appointing a new trustee or new trustees either in substitution for or in addition to any existing trustee or trustees, or although there is no existing trustee.

In particular and without prejudice to the generality of the foregoing provision, the court may make an order appointing a new trustee in substitution for a trustee who … *is [incapable, by reason of mental disorder within the meaning of [the Mental Health Act 1983], of exercising* his functions as trustee], or is a bankrupt, or is a corporation which is in liquidation or has been dissolved.

(2) The power conferred by this section may, in the case of a deed of arrangement within the meaning of the Deeds of Arrangement Act 1914, be exercised either by the High Court or by the court having jurisdiction in bankruptcy in the district in which the debtor resided or carried on business at the date of the execution of the deed.

(3) An order under this section, and any consequential vesting order or conveyance, shall not operate further or otherwise as a discharge to any former or continuing trustee than an appointment of new trustees under any power for that purpose contained in any instrument would have operated.

(4) Nothing in this section gives power to appoint an executor or administrator.

[43]

NOTES

Sub-s (1): words omitted repealed by the Criminal Law Act 1967, s 10, Sch 3, Pt III; for the words in italics there are substituted the words "lacks capacity to exercise" by the Mental Capacity Act 2005, s 67(1), Sch 6, para 3(1), (3), as from a day to be appointed under s 68(1) of that Act; words in first (outer) pair of square brackets substituted by the Mental Health Act 1959, s 149(1), Sch 7, Pt I, words in second (inner) pair of square brackets substituted by the Mental Health Act 1983, s 148, Sch 4, para 4(b).

42 Power to authorise remuneration

Where the court appoints a corporation, other than the Public Trustee, to be a trustee either solely or jointly with another person, the court may authorise the corporation to charge such remuneration for its services as trustee as the court may think fit.

[44]

43 Powers of new trustee appointed by the court

Every trustee appointed by a court of competent jurisdiction shall, as well before as after the trust property becomes by law, or by assurance, or otherwise, vested in him, have the same powers, authorities, and discretions, and may in all respects act as if he had been originally appointed a trustee by the instrument, if any, creating the trust.

[45]

Vesting Orders

44 Vesting orders of land

In any of the following cases, namely:—

(i) Where the court appoints or has appointed a trustee, or where a trustee has been appointed out of court under any statutory or express power;

(ii) Where a trustee entitled to or possessed of any land or interest therein, whether by way of mortgage or otherwise, or entitled to a contingent right therein, either solely or jointly with any other person—

(a) is under disability; or

(b) is out of the jurisdiction of the High Court; or

(c) cannot be found, or, being a corporation, has been dissolved;

(iii) Where it is uncertain who was the survivor of two or more trustees jointly entitled to or possessed of any interest in land;

(iv) Where it is uncertain whether the last trustee known to have been entitled to or possessed of any interest in land is living or dead;

(v) Where there is no personal representative of a deceased trustee who was entitled to or possessed of any interest in land, or where it is uncertain who is the personal representative of a deceased trustee who was entitled to or possessed of any interest in land;

(vi) Where a trustee jointly or solely entitled to or possessed of any interest in land, or entitled to a contingent right therein, has been required, by or on behalf of a person entitled to require a conveyance of the land or interest or a release of the right, to convey the land or interest or to release the right, and has wilfully refused or neglected to convey the land or interest or release the right for twenty-eight days after the date of the requirement;

(vii) Where land or any interest therein is vested in a trustee whether by way of mortgage or otherwise, and it appears to the court to be expedient;

the court may make an order (in this Act called a vesting order) vesting the land or interest therein in any such person in any such manner and for any such estate or interest as the court may direct, or releasing or disposing of the contingent right to such person as the court may direct:

Provided that—

(a) Where the order is consequential on the appointment of a trustee the land or interest therein shall be vested for such estate as the court may direct in the persons who on the appointment are the trustees; and

(b) Where the order relates to a trustee entitled or formerly entitled jointly with another person, and such trustee is under disability or out of the jurisdiction of the High Court or cannot be found, or being a corporation has been dissolved, the land interest or right shall be vested in such other person who remains entitled, either alone or with any other person the court may appoint.

[46]

45 Orders as to contingent rights of unborn persons

Where any interest in land is subject to a contingent right in an unborn person or class of unborn persons who, on coming into existence would, in respect thereof, become entitled to or possessed of that interest on any trust, the court may make an order releasing the land or interest therein from the contingent right, or may make an order vesting in any person the estate or interest to or of which the unborn person or class of unborn persons would, on coming into existence, be entitled or possessed in the land.

[47]

46 Vesting order in place of conveyance by infant mortgagee

Where any person entitled to or possessed of any interest in land, or entitled to a contingent right in land, by way of security for money, is an infant, the court may make an order vesting or releasing or disposing of the interest in the land or the right in like manner as in the case of a trustee under disability.

[48]

47 Vesting order consequential on order for sale or mortgage of land

Where any court gives a judgment or makes an order directing the sale or mortgage of any land, every person who is entitled to or possessed of any interest in the land, or entitled to a contingent right therein, and is a party to the action or proceeding in which the judgment or order is given or made or is otherwise bound by the judgment or order, shall be deemed to be so entitled or possessed, as the case may be, as a trustee for the purposes of this Act, and the court may, if it thinks expedient, make an order vesting the land or any part thereof for such estate or interest as that court thinks fit in the purchaser or mortgagee or in any other person:

Provided that, in the case of a legal mortgage, the estate to be vested in the mortgagee shall be a term of years absolute.

[49]

48 Vesting order consequential on judgment for specific performance, etc

Where a judgment is given for the specific performance of a contract concerning any interest in land, or for sale or exchange of any interest in land, or generally where any judgment is given for the conveyance of any interest in land either in cases arising out of the doctrine of election or otherwise, the court may declare—

(a) that any of the parties to the action are trustees of any interest in the land or any part thereof within the meaning of this Act; or

(b) that the interests of unborn persons who might claim under any party to the action, or under the will or voluntary settlement of any deceased person who was during his lifetime a party to the contract or transaction concerning which the judgment is given, are the interests of persons who, on coming into existence, would be trustees within the meaning of this Act;

and thereupon the court may make a vesting order relating to the rights of those persons, born and unborn, as if they had been trustees.

[50]

49 Effect of vesting order

A vesting order under any of the foregoing provisions shall in the case of a vesting order consequential on the appointment of a trustee, have the same effect—

(a) as if the persons who before the appointment were the trustees, if any, had duly executed all proper conveyances of the land for such estate or interest as the court directs; or

(b) if there is no such person, or no such person of full capacity, as if such person had existed and been of full capacity and had duly executed all proper conveyances of the land for such estate or interest as the court directs;

and shall in every other case have the same effect as if the trustee or other person or description or class of persons to whose rights or supposed rights the said provisions respectively relate had been an ascertained and existing person of full capacity, and had executed a conveyance or release to the effect intended by the order.

[51]

50 Power to appoint person to convey

In all cases where a vesting order can be made under any of the foregoing provisions, the court may, if it is more convenient, appoint a person to convey the land or any interest therein or release the contingent right, and a conveyance or release by that person in conformity with the order shall have the same effect as an order under the appropriate provision.

[52]

51 Vesting orders as to stock and things in action

(1) In any of the following cases, namely:—

(i) Where the court appoints or has appointed a trustee, or where a trustee has been appointed out of court under any statutory or express power;

(ii) Where a trustee entitled, whether by way of mortgage or otherwise, alone or jointly with another person to stock or to a thing in action—

(a) is under disability; or

(b) is out of the jurisdiction of the High Court; or

(c) cannot be found, or, being a corporation, has been dissolved; or

(d) neglects or refuses to transfer stock or receive the dividends or income thereof, or to sue for or recover a thing in action, according to the direction of the person absolutely entitled thereto for twenty-eight days next after a request in writing has been made to him by the person so entitled; or

(e) neglects or refuses to transfer stock or receive the dividends or income thereof, or to sue for or recover a thing in action for twenty-eight days next after an order of the court for that purpose has been served on him;

(iii) Where it is uncertain whether a trustee entitled alone or jointly with another person to stock or to a thing in action is alive or dead;

(iv) Where stock is standing in the name of a deceased person whose personal representative is under disability;

(v) Where stock or a thing in action is vested in a trustee whether by way of mortgage or otherwise and it appears to the court to be expedient;

the court may make an order vesting the right to transfer or call for a transfer of stock, or to receive the dividends or income thereof, or to sue for or recover the thing in action, in any such person as the court may appoint:

Provided that—

(a) Where the order is consequential on the appointment of a trustee, the right shall be vested in the persons who, on the appointment, are the trustees; and

(b) Where the person whose right is dealt with by the order was entitled jointly with another person, the right shall be vested in that last-mentioned person either alone or jointly with any other person whom the court may appoint.

(2) In all cases where a vesting order can be made under this section, the court may, if it is more convenient, appoint some proper person to make or join in making the transfer:

Provided that the person appointed to make or join in making a transfer of stock shall be some proper officer of the bank, or the company or society whose stock is to be transferred.

(3) The person in whom the right to transfer or call for the transfer of any stock is vested by an order of the court under this Act, may transfer the stock to himself or any other person, according to the order, and the [Registrar of Government Stock and any company] shall obey every order under this section according to its tenor.

(4) After notice in writing of an order under this section it shall not be lawful for the [Registrar of Government Stock or any company] to transfer any stock to which the order relates or to pay any dividends thereon except in accordance with the order.

(5) The court may make declarations and give directions concerning the manner in which the right to transfer any stock or thing in action vested under the provisions of this Act is to be exercised.

(6) The provisions of this Act as to vesting orders shall apply to shares in ships registered under the [Merchant Shipping Act 1995] as if they were stock.

[53]

NOTES

Sub-ss (3), (4): words in square brackets substituted by the Government Stock (Consequential and Transitional Provision) (No 2) Order 2004, SI 2004/1662, art 2, Schedule, para 10, subject to a transitional provision in art 3 of that Order.

Sub-s (6): words in square brackets substituted by the Merchant Shipping Act 1995, s 314(2), Sch 13, para 13.

52 Vesting orders of charity property

The powers conferred by this Act as to vesting orders may be exercised for vesting any interest in land, stock, or thing in action in any trustee of a charity or society over which the court would have jurisdiction upon action duly instituted, whether the appointment of the trustee was made by instrument under a power or by the court under its general or statutory jurisdiction.

[54]

53 Vesting orders in relation to infant's beneficial interests

Where an infant is beneficially entitled to any property the court may, with a view to the application of the capital or income thereof for the maintenance, education, or benefit of the infant, make an order—

(a) appointing a person to convey such property; or

(b) in the case of stock, or a thing in action, vesting in any person the right to transfer or call for a transfer of such stock, or to receive the dividends or income thereof, or to sue for and recover such thing in action, upon such terms as the court may think fit.

[55]

[54 Jurisdiction in regard to mental patients

(1) Subject to the provisions of this section, the authority having jurisdiction under [Part VII of the Mental Health Act 1983] shall not have power to make any order, or give any direction or authority, in relation to a patient who is a trustee if the High Court has power under this Act to make an order to the like effect.

(2) *Where a patient is a trustee and a receiver appointed by the said authority is acting for him or an application for the appointment of a receiver* has been made but not determined, then, except as respects a trust which is subject to an order for administration made by the High Court, *the said authority* shall have concurrent jurisdiction with the High Court in relation to—

(a) mortgaged property of which *the patient* has become a trustee merely by reason of the mortgage having been paid off;

(b) matters consequent on the making of provision by *the said authority* for the exercise of a power of appointing trustees or retiring from a trust;

(c) matters consequent on the making of provision by *the said authority* for the carrying out of any contract entered into by *the patient*;

(d) property to some interest in which *the patient* is beneficially entitled but which, or some interest in which, is held by *the patient* under an express, implied or constructive trust.

[(2A) Rules may be made in accordance with Part 1 of Schedule 1 to the Constitutional Reform Act 2005 with respect to the exercise of the jurisdiction referred to in subsection (2).]

(3) In this section "patient" means a patient as defined by [section 94 of the Mental Health Act 1983], or a person as to whom powers are [exercisable under section 98 of that Act and have been exercised under that section or section 104 of the Mental Health Act 1959].]

[56]

NOTES

Substituted by the Mental Health Act 1959, s 149(1), Sch 7, Pt I.

Sub-s (1): words in square brackets substituted by the Mental Health Act 1983, s 148, Sch 4, para 4(c); substituted by the Mental Capacity Act 2005, s 67(1), Sch 6, para 3(1), (4)(a), as from a day to be appointed under s 68(1) of that Act, as follows—

"(1) Subject to subsection (2), the Court of Protection may not make an order, or give a direction or authority, in relation to a person who lacks capacity to exercise his functions as trustee, if the High Court may make an order to that effect under this Act.".

Sub-s (2): for the words in italics in the first place there are substituted the words "Where a person lacks capacity to exercise his functions as a trustee and a deputy is appointed for him by the Court of Protection or an application for the appointment of a deputy", for the words "the said authority" in italics there are substituted the words "the Court of Protection" and for the words "the patient" in italics there are substituted the words "the person concerned" by the Mental Capacity Act 2005, s 67(1), Sch 6, para 3(1), (4)(b), as from a day to be appointed under s 68(1) of that Act.

Sub-s (2A): substituted for the closing words of sub-s (2) by the Constitutional Reform Act 2005, s 12(2), Sch 1, Pt 2, para 6.

Sub-s (3): repealed by the Mental Capacity Act 2005, s 67(1), (2), Sch 6, para 3(1), (4)(c), Sch 7, as from a day to be appointed under s 68(1) of that Act; words in square brackets substituted by the Mental Health Act 1983, s 148, Sch 4, para 4(c).

Mental Health Act 1959, s 104: repealed by the Mental Health Act 1983, s 148, Sch 6 and replaced by s 98 of that Act.

Rules: the Court of Protection Rules 2001, SI 2001/824.

55 Orders made upon certain allegations to be conclusive evidence

Where a vesting order is made as to any land under this Act or under *[Part VII of the Mental Health Act 1983], as amended by any subsequent enactment, or under any Act relating to lunacy in Northern Ireland*, founded on an allegation of any of the following matters namely—

(*a*) *the personal incapacity of a trustee or mortgagee;* or

(b) that a trustee or mortgagee or the personal representative of or other person deriving title under a trustee or mortgagee is out of the jurisdiction of the High Court or cannot be found, or being a corporation has been dissolved; or

(c) that it is uncertain which of two or more trustees, or which of two or more persons interested in a mortgage, was the survivor; or

(d) that it is uncertain whether the last trustee or the personal representative of or other person deriving title under a trustee or mortgagee, or the last surviving person interested in a mortgage is living or dead; or

(e) that any trustee or mortgagee has died intestate without leaving a person beneficially interested under the intestacy or has died and it is not known who is his personal representative or the person interested;

the fact that the order has been so made shall be conclusive evidence of the matter so alleged in any court upon any question as to the validity of the order; but this section does not prevent the court from directing a reconveyance or surrender or the payment of costs occasioned by any such order if improperly obtained.

[57]

NOTES

Words in square brackets substituted by the Mental Health Act 1983, s 148, Sch 4, para 4(d).

Words in italics in the first place substituted by the words "sections 15 to 20 of the Mental Capacity Act 2005 or any corresponding provisions having effect in Northern Ireland" by the Mental Capacity Act 2005, s 67(1), Sch 6, para 3(1), (5)(a), as from a day to be appointed under s 68(1) of that Act.

Para (a): substituted by the Mental Capacity Act 2005, s 67(1), Sch 6, para 3(1), (5)(b), as from a day to be appointed under s 68(1) of that Act, as follows—

"(a) that a trustee or mortgagee lacks capacity in relation to the matter in question;".

56 Application of vesting order to property out of England

The powers of the court to make vesting orders under this Act shall extend to all property in any part of His Majesty's dominions except Scotland.

[58]

Jurisdiction to make other Orders

57 Power of court to authorise dealings with trust property

(1) Where in the management or administration of any property vested in trustees, any sale, lease, mortgage, surrender, release, or other disposition, or any purchase, investment, acquisition, expenditure, or other transaction, is in the opinion of the court expedient, but the same cannot be effected by reason of the absence of any power for that purpose vested in the trustees by the trust instrument, if any, or by law, the court may by order confer upon the trustees, either generally or in any particular instance, the necessary power for the purpose, on such terms, and subject to such provisions and conditions, if any, as the court may think fit and may direct in what manner any money authorised to be expended, and the costs of any transaction, are to be paid or borne as between capital and income.

(2) The court may, from time to time, rescind or vary any order made under this section, or may make any new or further order.

(3) An application to the court under this section may be made by the trustees, or by any of them, or by any person beneficially interested under the trust.

(4) This section does not apply to trustees of a settlement for the purposes of the Settled Land Act 1925.

[59]

58 Persons entitled to apply for orders

(1) An order under this Act for the appointment of a new trustee or concerning any interest in land, stock, or thing in action subject to a trust, may be made on the application of any person beneficially interested in the land, stock, or thing in action, whether under disability or not, or on the application of any person duly appointed trustee thereof.

(2) An order under this Act concerning any interest in land, stock, or thing in action subject to a mortgage may be made on the application of any person beneficially interested in the equity of redemption, whether under disability or not, or of any person interested in the money secured by the mortgage.

[60]

59 Power to give judgment in absence of a trustee

Where in any action the court is satisfied that diligent search has been made for any person who, in the character of trustee, is made a defendant in any action, to serve him with a process of the court, and that he cannot be found, the court may hear and determine the action and give judgment therein against that person in his character of a trustee as if he had been duly served, or had entered an appearance in the action, and had also appeared by his counsel and solicitor at the hearing, but without prejudice to any interest he may have in the matters in question in the action in any other character.

[61]

NOTES

Solicitors' Incorporated Practices: this section is applied, with modifications, in relation to a recognised body under the Administration of Justice Act 1985, s 9; see the Solicitors' Incorporated Practices Order 1991, SI 1991/2684, arts 2–5, Sch 1.

60 Power to charge costs on trust estate

The court may order the costs and expenses of and incident to any application for an order appointing a new trustee, or for a vesting order, or of and incident to any such order, or any conveyance or transfer in pursuance thereof, to be raised and paid out of the property in respect whereof the same is made, or out of the income thereof, or to be borne and paid in such manner and by such persons as to the court may seem just.

[62]

61 Power to relieve trustee from personal liability

If it appears to the court that a trustee, whether appointed by the court or otherwise, is or may be personally liable for any breach of trust, whether the transaction alleged to be a breach of trust occurred before or after the commencement of this Act, but has acted honestly and reasonably, and ought fairly to be excused for the breach of trust and for omitting to obtain the directions of the court in the matter in which he committed such breach, then the court may relieve him either wholly or partly from personal liability for the same.

[63]

62 Power to make beneficiary indemnify for breach of trust

(1) Where a trustee commits a breach of trust at the instigation or request or with the consent in writing of a beneficiary, the court may, if it thinks fit, … make such order as to the court seems just, for impounding all or any part of the interest of the beneficiary in the trust estate by way of indemnity to the trustee or persons claiming through him.

(2) This section applies to breaches of trust committed as well before as after the commencement of this Act.

[64]

NOTES

Sub-s (1): words omitted repealed by the Married Women (Restraint upon Anticipation) Act 1949, s 1(4), Sch 2.

PART I STATUTES

Payment into Court

63 Payment into court by trustees

(1) Trustees, or the majority of trustees, having in their hands or under their control money or securities belonging to a trust, may pay the same into court; …

(2) The receipt or certificate of the proper officer shall be a sufficient discharge to trustees for the money or securities so paid into court.

(3) Where money or securities are vested in any persons as trustees, and the majority are desirous of paying the same into court, but the concurrence of the other or others cannot be obtained, the court may order the payment into court to be made by the majority without the concurrence of the other or others.

(4) Where any such money or securities are deposited with any banker, broker, or other depositary, the court may order payment or delivery of the money or securities to the majority of the trustees for the purpose of payment into court.

(5) Every transfer payment and delivery made in pursuance of any such order shall be valid and take effect as if the same had been made on the authority or by the act of all the persons entitled to the money and securities so transferred, paid, or delivered.

[65]

NOTES

Sub-s (1): words omitted repealed by the Administration of Justice Act 1965, s 36(4), Sch 3.

[63A Jurisdiction of County Court

(1) The county court has jurisdiction under the following provisions where the amount or value of the trust estate or fund to be dealt with in the court does not exceed the county court limit—

section 41;
section 42;
section 51;
section 57;
section 60;
section 61;
section 62.

(2) The county court has jurisdiction under the following provisions where the land or the interest or contingent right in land which is to be dealt with in the court forms part of a trust estate which does not exceed in amount or value the county court limit—section 44; section 45; section 46.

(3) The county court has jurisdiction—

(a) under sections 47 and 48 of this Act, where the judgment is given or order is made by the court;
(b) under sections 50 and 56, where a vesting order can be made by the court;
(c) under section 53, where the amount or value of the property to be dealt with in the court does not exceed the county court limit; and
(d) under section 63 (including power to receive payment of money or securities into court) where the money or securities to be paid into court do not exceed in amount or value the county court limit.

(4) Any reference to the court in section 59 of this Act includes a reference to the county court.

(5) In this section, in its application to any enactment, "the county court limit" means the amount for the time being specified by an Order in Council under section 145 of the County Courts Act 1984 as the county court limit for the purposes of that enactment (or, where no such Order in Council has been made, the corresponding limit specified by Order in Council under section 192 of the County Courts Act 1959).]

[66]

NOTES

Inserted by the County Courts Act 1984, s 148(1), Sch 2, Pt I, para 1.
County Courts Act 1959, s 192: repealed by the County Courts Act 1984, s 148(3), Sch 4.

PART V
GENERAL PROVISIONS

64 Application of Act to Settled Land Act Trustees

(1) All the powers and provisions contained in this Act with reference to the appointment of new trustees, and the discharge and retirement of trustees, apply to and include trustees for the purposes of the Settled Land Act 1925, and trustees for the purpose of the management of land during a minority, whether such trustees are appointed by the court or by the settlement, or under provisions contained in any instrument.

(2) Where, either before or after the commencement of this Act, trustees of a settlement have been appointed by the court for the purposes of the Settled Land Acts 1882 to 1890, or of the Settled Land Act 1925, then, after the commencement of this Act—

(a) the person or persons nominated for the purpose of appointing new trustees by the instrument, if any, creating the settlement, though no trustees for the purposes of the said Acts were thereby appointed; or

(b) if there is no such person, or no such person able and willing to act, the surviving or continuing trustees or trustee for the time being for the purposes of the said Acts or the personal representatives of the last surviving or continuing trustee for those purposes,

shall have the powers conferred by this Act to appoint new or additional trustees of the settlement for the purposes of the said Acts.

(3) Appointments of new trustees for the purposes of the said Acts made or expressed to be made before the commencement of this Act by the trustees or trustee or personal representatives referred to in paragraph (b) of the last preceding subsection or by the persons referred to in paragraph (a) of that subsection are, without prejudice to any order of the court made before such commencement, hereby confirmed.

[67]

NOTES

Settled Land Acts 1882 to 1890: the Settled Land Act 1882 (repealed except for s 30), the Settled Land Act 1884 (repealed), the Settled Land Acts (Amendment) Act 1887 (repealed), the Settled Land Act 1889 (repealed) and the Settled Land Act 1890 (repealed). All such repeals are without prejudice to transactions completed, and instruments made, before 1926.

65 (*Repealed by the Criminal Law Act 1967, s 10, Sch 3, Pt I.*)

66 Indemnity to banks, etc

This Act, and every order purporting to be made under this Act, shall be a complete indemnity to the Bank of England[, the Registrar of Government Stock, any previous Registrar of Government Stock], and to all persons for any acts done pursuant thereto, and it shall not be necessary for the Bank [, the Registrar of Government Stock, any previous Registrar of Government Stock] or for any person to inquire concerning the propriety of the order, or whether the court by which the order was made had jurisdiction to make it.

[68]

NOTES

Words in square brackets inserted by the Government Stock (Consequential and Transitional Provision) (No 2) Order 2004, SI 2004/1662, art 2, Schedule, para 10, subject to transitional provisions in art 3 of that Order.

67 Jurisdiction of the "court"

(1) In this Act "the court" means the High Court … or the county court, where those courts respectively have jurisdiction.

(2) The procedure under this Act in … county courts shall be in accordance with the Acts and rules regulating the procedure of those courts.

[69]

NOTES

Words omitted repealed by the Courts Act 1971, s 56, Sch 11, Pt II.

68 Definitions

[(1)] In this Act, unless the context otherwise requires, the following expressions have the meanings hereby assigned to them respectively, that is to say:—

(1) "Authorised investments" mean investments authorised by the instrument, if any, creating the trust for the investment of money subject to the trust, or by law;

(2) "Contingent right" as applied to land includes a contingent or executory interest, a possibility coupled with an interest, whether the object of the gift or limitation of the interest, or possibility is or is not ascertained, also a right of entry, whether immediate or future, and whether vested or contingent;

(3) "Convey" and "conveyance" as applied to any person include the execution by that person of every necessary or suitable assurance (including an assent) for conveying, assigning, appointing, surrendering, or otherwise transferring or disposing of land whereof he is seised or possessed, or wherein he is entitled to a contingent right, either for his whole estate or for any less estate, together with the performance of all formalities required by law for the validity of the conveyance; "sale" includes an exchange;

(4) "Gazette" means the London Gazette;

(5) "Instrument" includes Act of Parliament;

(6) "Land" includes land of any tenure, and mines and minerals, whether or not severed from the surface, buildings or parts of buildings, whether the division is horizontal, vertical or made in any other way, and other corporeal hereditaments; also a manor, an advowson, and a rent and other incorporeal hereditaments, and an easement, right, privilege, or benefit in, over, or derived from land, ...; and in this definition "mines and minerals" include any strata or seam of minerals or substances in or under any land, and powers of working and getting the same, ...; and "hereditaments" mean real property which under an intestacy occurring before the commencement of this Act might have devolved on an heir;

(7) "Mortgage" and "mortgagee" include a charge or chargee by way of legal mortgage, and relate to every estate and interest regarded in equity as merely a security for money, and every person deriving title under the original mortgagee;

(8) ...

(9) "Personal representative" means the executor, original or by representation, or administrator for the time being of a deceased person;

(10) "Possession" includes receipt of rents and profits or the right to receive the same, if any; "income" includes rents and profits; and "possessed" applies to receipt of income of and to any vested estate less than a life interest in possession or in expectancy in any land;

(11) "Property" includes real and personal property, and any estate share and interest in any property, real or personal, and any debt, and any thing in action, and any other right or interest, whether in possession or not;

(12) "Rights" include estates and interests;

(13) "Securities" include stocks, funds, and shares; ... and "securities payable to bearer" include securities transferable by delivery or by delivery and endorsement;

(14) "Stock" includes fully paid up shares, and so far as relates to vesting orders made by the court under this Act, includes any fund, annuity, or security transferable in books kept by any company or society, or by instrument of transfer either alone or accompanied by other formalities, and any share or interest therein;

(15) "Tenant for life," "statutory owner," "settled land," "settlement," "trust instrument," "trustees of the settlement" ... "term of years absolute" and "vesting instrument" have the same meanings as in the Settled Land Act 1925, and "entailed interest" has the same meaning as in the Law of Property Act 1925;

(16) "Transfer" in relation to stock or securities, includes the performance and execution of every deed, power of attorney, act, and thing on the part of the transferor to effect and complete the title in the transferee;

(17) "Trust" does not include the duties incident to an estate conveyed by way of mortgage, but with this exception the expressions "trust" and "trustee" extend to implied and constructive trusts, and to cases where the trustee has a beneficial interest in the trust property, and to the duties incident to the office of a personal representative, and "trustee" where the context admits, includes a personal representative, and "new trustee" includes an additional trustee;

(18) "Trust corporation" means the Public Trustee or a corporation either appointed by the court in any particular case to be a trustee, or entitled by rules made under subsection (3) of section four of the Public Trustee Act 1906, to act as custodian trustee;

(19) "Trust for sale" in relation to land means an immediate … trust for sale, whether or not exercisable at the request or with the consent of any person, …;

(20) "United Kingdom" means Great Britain and Northern Ireland.

[(2) Any reference in this Act to paying money or securities into court shall be construed as referring to paying the money or transferring or depositing the securities into or in the *Supreme Court* or into or in any other court that has jurisdiction, and any reference in this Act to payment of money or securities into court shall be construed—

(a) with reference to an order of the High Court, as referring to payment of the money or transfer or deposit of the securities into or in the *Supreme Court*; and

(b) with reference to an order of any other court, as referring to payment of the money or transfer or deposit of the securities into or in that court.]

[(3) Any reference in this Act to a person who lacks capacity in relation to a matter is to a person—

(a) who lacks capacity within the meaning of the Mental Capacity Act 2005 in relation to that matter, or

(b) in respect of whom the powers conferred by section 48 of that Act are exercisable and have been exercised in relation to that matter.]

[70]

NOTES

Sub-s (1): numbered as such by virtue of the Administration of Justice Act 1965, s 17(1), Sch 1.

Sub-s (1), para (8): repealed by the Administration of Justice Act 1965, s 17(1), Sch 1.

Sub-s (1), para (13): words omitted repealed by the Administration of Justice Act 1965, s 17(1), Sch 1.

Sub-s (1), paras (6), (19): words omitted repealed by the Trusts of Land and Appointment of Trustees Act 1996, s 25(2), Sch 4; for savings see ss 3, 18(3), 25(5) of the 1996 Act at **[1009]**, **[1025]** and **[1032]**.

Sub-s (1), para (15): words omitted repealed by the Mental Health Act 1959 s 149(2), Sch 8, Pt I.

Sub-s (2): added by the Administration of Justice Act 1965, s 17(1), Sch 1; for the words in italics there are substituted the words "Senior Courts" in both places by the Constitutional Reform Act 2005, s 59(5), Sch 11, Pt 2, para 4(1), (3), as from a day to be appointed under s 148(1) of that Act.

Sub-s (3): added by the Mental Capacity Act 2005, s 67(1), Sch 6, para 3(1), (6), as from a day to be appointed under s 68(1) of that Act.

Trust corporation: the definition of "trust corporation" is modified by the Charities Act 1993, s 35 at **[799]**.

69 Application of Act

(1) This Act, except where otherwise expressly provided, applies to trusts including, so far as this Act applies thereto, executorships and administratorships constituted or created either before or after the commencement of this Act.

(2) The powers conferred by this Act on trustees are in addition to the powers conferred by the instrument, if any, creating the trust, but those powers, unless otherwise stated, apply if and so far only as a contrary intention is not expressed in the instrument, if any, creating the trust, and have effect subject to the terms of that instrument.

(3) …

[71]

NOTES

Sub-s (3): repealed by the Statute Law (Repeals) Act 1978.

70 Enactments repealed

… without prejudice to the provisions of section thirty-eight of the Interpretation Act 1889:

(a) Nothing in this repeal shall affect any vesting order or appointment made or other thing done under any enactment so repealed, and any order or appointment so made may be revoked or varied in like manner as if it has been made under this Act;

(b) References in any document to any enactment repealed by this Act shall be construed as references to this Act or to the corresponding enactment in this Act.

[72]

NOTES

Words omitted repealed by the Statute Law Revision Act 1950.

Interpretation Act 1889, s 38: repealed, see now the Interpretation Act 1978, ss 16(1), 17(2)(a), Sch 2, para 3.

71 Short title, commencement, extent

(1) This Act may be cited as the Trustee Act 1925.

(2) …

(3) This Act, except where otherwise expressly provided, extends to England and Wales only.

(4) The provisions of this Act bind the Crown.

[73]

NOTES

Sub-s (2): repealed by the Statute Law Revision Act 1950.

(Sch 1 repealed by the Statute Law (Repeals) Act 1978; Sch 2 repealed by the Statute Law Revision Act 1950.)

HOUSE TO HOUSE COLLECTIONS ACT 1939

(2 & 3 Geo 6 c 44)

ARRANGEMENT OF SECTIONS

An Act to provide for the regulation of house to house collections for charitable purposes; and for matters connected therewith

[28 July 1939]

1 Charitable collections from house to house to be licensed

(1) Subject to the provisions of this Act, no collection for a charitable purpose shall be made unless the requirements of this Act as to a licence for the promotion thereof are satisfied.

(2) If a person promotes a collection for a charitable purpose, and a collection for that purpose is made in any locality pursuant to his promotion, then, unless there is in force, throughout the period during which the collection is made in that locality, a licence authorising him, or authorising another under whose authority he acts, to promote a collection therein for that purpose, he shall be guilty of an offence.

(3) If a person acts as a collector in any locality for the purposes of a collection for a charitable purpose, then, unless there is in force, at all times when he so acts, a licence authorising a promoter under whose authority he acts, or authorising the collector himself, to promote a collection therein for that purpose, he shall be guilty of an offence.

(4) If the chief officer of police for the police area comprising a locality in which a collection for a charitable purpose is being, or is proposed to be, made is satisfied that that purpose is local in character and that the collection is likely to be completed within a short period of time, he may grant to the person who appears to him to be principally concerned in

the promotion of the collection a certificate in the prescribed form, and, where a certificate is so granted, the provisions of this Act, except the provisions of sections five and six thereof and the provisions of section eight thereof in so far as they relate to those sections, shall not apply, in relation to a collection made for that purpose within such locality and within such period as may be specified in the certificate, to the person to whom the certificate is granted or to any person authorised by him to promote the collection or to act as a collector for the purposes thereof.

[74]

NOTES

This Act is repealed by the Charities Act 1992, s 78(2), Sch 7, as from a day to be appointed under s 79(2) of that Act; for provisions of the Charities Act 2006 relating to house to house collections, see ss 45–66 of that Act at **[2142]** et seq. The Act is also repealed, in relation to Scotland, by the Civic Government (Scotland) Act 1982, ss 119(15), 137(8), Sch 4.

2 Licences

(1) Where a person who is promoting, or proposes to promote, a collection in any locality for a charitable purpose makes to the [licensing] authority for the … area comprising that locality an application in the prescribed manner specifying the purpose of the collection and the locality (whether being the whole of the area of the authority or a part thereof) within which the collection is to be made, and furnishes them with the prescribed information, the authority shall, subject to the following provisions of this section, grant to him a licence authorising him to promote a collection within that locality for that purpose.

[(1A) In this section "licensing authority" means—
- *(a) in relation to the City of London, the Common Council;*
- *(b) in relation to the Metropolitan Police District, the Commissioner of Police for the Metropolis; and*
- *(c) in relation to a district exclusive of any part thereof within the Metropolitan Police District, the district council.]*

(2) A licence shall be granted for such period, not being longer than twelve months, as may be specified in the application, and shall, unless it is previously revoked, remain in force for the period so specified:

Provided that, if it appears to a [licensing] authority to be expedient to provide for the simultaneous expiration of licences to be granted by them in respect of collections which in their opinion are likely to be proposed to be made annually or continuously over a long period, they may, on the grant of such a licence, grant it for a period shorter or longer than that specified in the application therefor, or for a period longer than twelve months (but not exceeding eighteen months), as may be requisite for that purpose.

(3) A [licensing] authority may refuse to grant a licence, or, where a licence has been granted, may revoke it, if it appears to the authority—
- *(a) that the total amount likely to be applied for charitable purposes as the result of the collection (including any amount already so applied) is inadequate in proportion to the value of the proceeds likely to be received (including any proceeds already received);*
- *(b) that remuneration which is excessive in relation to the total amount aforesaid is likely to be, or has been, retained or received out of the proceeds of the collection by any person;*
- *(c) that the grant of a licence would be likely to facilitate the commission of an offence under section three of the Vagrancy Act 1824, or that an offence under that section has been committed in connection with the collection;*
- *(d) that the applicant or the holder of the licence is not a fit and proper person to hold a licence by reason of the fact that he has been convicted in the United Kingdom of any of the offences specified in the Schedule to this Act, or has been convicted in any part of His Majesty's dominions of any offence conviction for which necessarily involved a finding that he acted fraudulently or dishonestly, or of an offence of a kind the commission of which would be likely to be facilitated by the grant of a licence;*
- *(e) that the applicant or the holder of the licence, in promoting a collection in respect of which a licence has been granted to him, has failed to exercise due diligence to secure that persons authorised by him to act as collectors for the purposes of the collection were fit and proper persons, to secure compliance on the part of*

persons so authorised with the provisions of regulations made under this Act, or to prevent prescribed badges or prescribed certificates of authority being obtained by persons other than persons so authorised; or

(*f*) *that the applicant or holder of the licence has refused or neglected to furnish to the authority such information as they may have reasonably required for the purpose of informing themselves as to any of the matters specified in the foregoing paragraphs.*

(*4*) *When a [licensing] authority refuse to grant a licence or revoke a licence which has been granted, they shall forthwith give written notice to the applicant or holder of the licence stating upon which one or more of the grounds set out in subsection* (*3*) *of this section the licence has been refused or revoked and informing him of the right of appeal given by this section, and the applicant or holder of the licence may thereupon appeal to the [Minister for the Cabinet Office] against the refusal or revocation of the licence as the case may be and the decision of the [Minister for the Cabinet Office] shall be final.*

(*5*) *The time within which any such appeal may be brought shall be fourteen days from the date on which notice is given under subsection* (*4*) *of this section.*

(*6*) *If the [Minister for the Cabinet Office] decides that the appeal shall be allowed, the [licensing] authority shall forthwith issue a licence or cancel the revocation as the case may be in accordance with the decision of the [Minister for the Cabinet Office].*

[75]

NOTES

Repealed as noted to s 1 at **[74]**.

Sub-s (1): word in square brackets substituted and words omitted repealed by the Local Government Act 1972, ss 251(2), 252(2), 272(1), Sch 29, para 23(1), (3), Sch 30.

Sub-s (1A): inserted by the Local Government Act 1972, s 251(2), Sch 29, para 23(2).

Sub-ss (2), (3): words in square brackets substituted by the Local Government Act 1972, s 251(2), Sch 29, para 23(1), (3).

Sub-s (4): word in first pair of square brackets substituted by the Local Government Act 1972, s 251(2), Sch 29, para 23(1), (3); words in second and third pairs of square brackets substituted by the Transfer of Functions (Third Sector, Communities and Equality) Order 2006, SI 2006/2951, art 6, Schedule, para 2(a).

Sub-s (6): words in first and third pairs of square brackets substituted by SI 2006/2951, art 6, Schedule, para 2(a); words in second pair of square brackets substituted by the Local Government Act 1972, s 251(2), Sch 29, para 23(1), (3).

3 Exemptions in the case of collections over wide areas

(*1*) *Where the [Minister for the Cabinet Office] is satisfied that a person pursues a charitable purpose throughout the whole of England or a substantial part thereof and is desirous of promoting collections for that purpose, the [Minister for the Cabinet Office] may by order direct that he shall be exempt from the provisions of subsection* (2) *of section one of this Act as respects all collections for that purpose in such localities as may be prescribed in the order, and whilst an order so made in the case of any person is in force as respects collections in any locality, the provisions of this Act shall have effect in relation to the person exempted, to a promoter of a collection in that locality for that purpose who acts under the authority of the person exempted, and to a person who so acts as a collector for the purposes of any such collection, as if a licence authorising the person exempted to promote a collection in that locality for that purpose had been in force.*

(*2*) *Any order made under this section may be revoked or varied by a subsequent order made by the [Minister for the Cabinet Office].*

[76]

NOTES

Repealed as noted to s 1 at **[74]**.

Words in square brackets substituted by the Transfer of Functions (Third Sector, Communities and Equality) Order 2006, SI 2006/2951, art 6, Schedule, para 2(b).

4 Regulations

(*1*) *The [Minister for the Cabinet Office] may make regulations for prescribing anything which by this Act is required to be prescribed, and for regulating the manner in which collections, in respect of which licences have been granted or orders have been made under the last foregoing section, may be carried out and the conduct of promoters and collectors in relation to such collections.*

(2) *Without prejudice to the generality of the powers conferred by the foregoing subsection, regulations made thereunder may make provision for all or any of the following matters, that is to say:—*

(*a*) *for requiring and regulating the use by collectors, of prescribed badges and prescribed certificates of authority, and the issue, custody, production and return thereof, and, in particular, for requiring collectors on demand by a police constable or by any occupant of a house visited to produce their certificates of authority;*

(*b*) *in the case of collections in respect of which licences have been granted, for requiring that the prescribed certificates of authority of the collectors shall be authenticated in a manner approved by the chief officer of police for the area in respect of which the licence was granted, and that their prescribed badges shall have inserted therein or annexed thereto in a manner and form so approved a general indication of the purpose of the collection;*

(*c*) *for prohibiting persons below a prescribed age from acting, and others from causing them to act, as collectors;*

(*d*) *for preventing annoyance to the occupants of houses visited by collectors;*

(*e*) *for requiring the prescribed information with respect to the expenses, proceeds and application of the proceeds of collections to be furnished, in the case of collections in respect of which licences have been granted, by the person to whom the licence was granted to the … authority by whom it was granted, and, in the case of collections in respect of which an order has been made, by the person thereby exempted from the provisions of subsection (2) of section one of this Act to the [Minister for the Cabinet Office], and for requiring the information furnished to be vouched and authenticated in such manner as may be prescribed.*

(3) *Any person who contravenes or fails to comply with the provisions of a regulation made under this Act shall be guilty of an offence.*

(4) *Any regulations made under this Act shall be laid before Parliament as soon as may be after they are made, and if either House of Parliament, within the period of forty days beginning with the date on which the regulations are laid before it, resolves that the regulations be annulled, the regulations shall thereupon become void, without prejudice, however, to anything previously done thereunder or to the making of new regulations.*

In reckoning any such period of forty days as aforesaid, no account shall be taken of any time during which Parliament is dissolved or prorogued or during which both Houses are adjourned for more than four days.

[77]

NOTES

Repealed as noted to s 1 at **[74]**.

Sub-s (1): words in square brackets substituted by the Transfer of Functions (Third Sector, Communities and Equality) Order 2006, SI 2006/2951, art 6, Schedule, para 2(c).

Sub-s (2)(e): word omitted repealed by the Local Government Act 1972, ss 251(2), 271(1), Sch 29, para 23(4), Sch 30; words in square brackets substituted by SI 2006/2951, art 6, Schedule, para 2(c).

Regulations: the House to House Collections Regulations 1947, SR & O 1947/2662 at **[3013]** et seq; the House to House Collections Regulations 1963, SI 1963/684.

5 Unauthorised use of badges, etc

If any person, in connection with any appeal made by him to the public in association with a representation that the appeal is for a charitable purpose, displays or uses—

(*a*) *a prescribed badge, or a prescribed certificate of authority, not being a badge or certificate for the time being held by him for the purposes of the appeal pursuant to regulations made under this Act, or*

(*b*) *any badge or device, or any certificate or other document, so nearly resembling a prescribed badge or, as the case may be, a prescribed certificate of authority as to be calculated to deceive,*

he shall be guilty of an offence.

[78]

NOTES

Repealed as noted to s 1 at **[74]**.

6 Collector to give name, etc, to police on demand

A police constable may require any person whom he believes to be acting as a collector for the purposes of a collection for a charitable purpose to declare to him immediately his name and address and to sign his name, and if any person fails to comply with a requirement duly made to him under this section, he shall be guilty of an offence.

[79]

NOTES

Repealed as noted to s 1 at **[74]**.

7 Delegation of functions

(1) ...

(2) The functions conferred on a chief officer of police by this Act or regulations made thereunder may be delegated by him to any police officer not below the rank of inspector.

[80]

NOTES

Repealed as noted to s 1 at **[74]**.

Sub-s (1): repealed by the Local Government Act 1972, s 272(1), Sch 30.

8 Penalties

(1) Any promoter guilty of an offence under subsection (2) of section one of this Act shall be liable, on summary conviction, to imprisonment for a term not exceeding six months or to a fine not exceeding [level 3 on the standard scale] or to both such imprisonment and such fine.

(2) Any collector guilty of an offence under subsection (3) of section one of this Act shall be liable, on summary conviction, [to a fine not exceeding level 2 on the standard scale or imprisonment for a term not exceeding three months, or to both such imprisonment and such fine].

(3) Any person guilty of an offence under subsection (3) of section four of this Act shall be liable, on summary conviction, to a fine not exceeding [level 1 on the standard scale].

(4) Any person guilty of an offence under section five of this Act shall be liable, on summary conviction, to imprisonment for a term not exceeding six months or to a fine not exceeding [level 3 on the standard scale], or to both such imprisonment and such fine.

(5) Any person guilty of an offence under section six of this Act shall be liable, on summary conviction, to a fine not exceeding [level 1 on the standard scale].

(6) If any person in furnishing any information for the purposes of this Act knowingly or recklessly makes a statement false in a material particular, he shall be guilty of an offence, and shall be liable, on summary conviction, to imprisonment for a term not exceeding six months or to a fine not exceeding [level 3 on the standard scale], or to both such imprisonment and such fine.

(7) Where an offence under this Act committed by a corporation is proved to have been committed with the consent or connivance of, or to be attributable to any culpable neglect of duty on the part of, any director, manager, secretary, or other officer of the corporation, he, as well as the corporation, shall be deemed to be guilty of that offence and shall be liable to be proceeded against and punished accordingly.

[81]

NOTES

Repealed as noted to s 1 at **[74]**.

Sub-ss (1), (4), (6): references to level 3 on the standard scale substituted by virtue of the Criminal Justice Act 1982, ss 38, 46.

Sub-s (2): words in square brackets substituted by virtue of the Criminal Justice Act 1982, s 46; for the words "three months" there are substituted the words "51 weeks" by the Criminal Justice Act 2003, s 280(2), Sch 26, para 10, as from a day to be appointed under s 336 of that Act.

Sub-ss (3), (5): references to level 1 on the standard scale substituted by virtue of the Criminal Justice Act 1982, ss 38, 46.

9 Application to metropolitan police district

(1) ...

(2) The functions which may be delegated by a chief officer of police by virtue of subsection (2) of section seven of this Act shall not include any functions conferred on the [Commissioner of Police for the Metropolis by virtue of his being a licensing authority within the meaning of section 2 of this Act].

[82]

NOTES

Repealed as noted to s 1 at **[74]**.

Sub-s (1): repealed by the Local Government Act 1972, s 272(1), Sch 30.

Sub-s (2): words in square brackets substituted by the Local Government Act 1972, s 251(2), Sch 29, para 23(5).

10 *(Repealed by the Civic Government (Scotland) Act 1982, ss 119(15), 137, Sch 4.)*

11 Interpretation

(1) In this Act the following expressions have the meanings hereby respectively assigned to them, that is to say:—

"charitable purpose" means any charitable, benevolent or philanthropic purpose, whether or not the purpose is charitable within the meaning of any rule of law;

"collection" means an appeal to the public, made by means of visits from house to house, to give, whether for consideration or not, money or other property; and "collector" means, in relation to a collection, a person who makes the appeal in the course of such visits as aforesaid;

"house" includes a place of business;

"licence" means a licence under this Act;

. . .

"prescribed" means prescribed by regulations made under this Act;

"proceeds" means, in relation to a collection, all money and all other property given, whether for consideration or not, in response to the appeal made;

"promoter" means, in relation to a collection, a person who causes others to act, whether for remuneration or otherwise, as collectors for the purposes of the collection; and "promote" and "promotion" have corresponding meanings.

(2) For the purposes of this Act, a collection shall be deemed to be made for a particular purpose where the appeal is made in association with a representation that the money or other property appealed for, or part thereof, will be applied for that purpose.

[83]

NOTES

Repealed as noted to s 1 at **[74]**.

Sub-s (1): words omitted repealed by the Police Act 1964, s 64(3), Sch 10, Pt I.

12 Short title, commencement, interpretation and extent

(1) This Act may be cited as the House to House Collections Act 1939.

(2) ...

(3) References in this Act to any enactment shall be construed as references to that enactment as amended by any subsequent enactment.

(4) This Act shall not extend to Northern Ireland.

[84]

NOTES

Repealed as noted to s 1 at **[74]**.

Sub-s (2): repealed by the Statute Law Revision Act 1950.

SCHEDULE
OFFENCES TO WHICH PARAGRAPH (D) OF SUBSECTION (3) OF SECTION TWO APPLIES

Section 2

Offences under sections forty-seven to fifty-six of the Offences against the Person Act 1861.

[Robbery, burglary and blackmail]

Offences in Scotland involving personal violence or lewd, indecent, or libidinous conduct, or dishonest appropriation of property.

Offences under the Street Collections Regulation (Scotland) Act 1915.

Offences under section five of the Police, Factories, etc (Miscellaneous Provisions) Act 1916.
[85]

NOTES

Repealed as noted to s 1 at **[74]**.

Words in square brackets substituted by the Theft Act 1968, s 33(2), Sch 2, Pt III.

Offences against the Person Act 1861, ss 47–56: ss 48–56 repealed by various enactments, s 47 (assault occasioning actual bodily harm—common assault) is still in force.

Police, Factories, etc (Miscellaneous Provisions) Act 1916, s 5: repealed by the Charities Act 1992, ss 78(2), 79(7), Sch 7, as from a day to be appointed under s 79(2) of that Act.

CHARITABLE TRUSTS (VALIDATION) ACT 1954

(2 & 3 Eliz 2 c 58)

ARRANGEMENT OF SECTIONS

An Act to validate under the law of England and Wales, and restrict to charitable objects, certain instruments taking effect before the sixteenth day of December, nineteen hundred and fifty-two, and providing for property to be held or applied for objects partly but not exclusively charitable, and to enable corresponding provision to be made by the Parliament of Northern Ireland

[30 July 1954]

1 Validation and modification of imperfect trust instruments

(1) In this Act, "imperfect trust provision" means any provision declaring the objects for which property is to be held or applied, and so describing those objects that, consistently with the terms of the provision, the property could be used exclusively for charitable purposes, but could nevertheless be used for purposes which are not charitable.

(2) Subject to the following provisions of this Act, any imperfect trust provision contained in an instrument taking effect before the sixteenth day of December, nineteen hundred and fifty-two, shall have, and be deemed to have had, effect in relation to any disposition or covenant to which this Act applies—

(a) as respects the period before the commencement of this Act, as if the whole of the declared objects were charitable; and

(b) as respects the period after that commencement as if the provision had required the property to be held or applied for the declared objects in so far only as they authorise use for charitable purposes.

(3) A document inviting gifts of property to be held or applied for objects declared by the document shall be treated for the purposes of this section as an instrument taking effect when it is first issued.

(4) In this Act, "covenant" includes any agreement, whether under seal or not, and "covenantor" is to be construed accordingly.

[86]

2 Dispositions and covenants to which the Act applies

(1) Subject to the next following subsection, this Act applies to any disposition of property to be held or applied for objects declared by an imperfect trust provision, and to any covenant to make such a disposition, where apart from this Act the disposition or covenant is invalid under the law of England and Wales, but would be valid if the objects were exclusively charitable.

(2) This Act does not apply to a disposition if before the sixteenth day of December, nineteen hundred and fifty-two, property comprised in, or representing that comprised in, the disposition in question or another disposition made for the objects declared by the same imperfect trust provision, or income arising from any such property, had been paid or conveyed to, or applied for the benefit of, the persons entitled by reason of the invalidity of the disposition in question or of such other disposition as aforesaid, as the case may be.

(3) A disposition in settlement or other disposition creating more than one interest in the same property shall be treated for the purposes of this Act as a separate disposition in relation to each of the interests created.

[87]

3 Savings for adverse claims, etc

(1) Subject to the next following subsection, where a disposition to which this Act applies was made before, and is not confirmed after, the commencement of this Act, the foregoing sections shall not prejudice a person's right, by reason of the invalidity of the disposition, to property comprised in, or representing that comprised in, the disposition as against the persons administering the imperfect trust provision or the persons on whose behalf they do so, unless the right accrued to him or some person through whom he claims more than six years before the sixteenth day of December, nineteen hundred and fifty-two; but the persons administering the imperfect trust provision, and any trustee for them or for the persons on whose behalf they do so, shall be entitled, as against a person whose right to the property is saved by this subsection, to deal with the property as if this subsection had not been passed, unless they have express notice of a claim by him to enforce his right to the property.

(2) No proceedings shall be begun by any person to enforce his right to any property by virtue of the foregoing subsection after the expiration of one year beginning with the date of the passing of this Act or the date when the right first accrues to him or to some person through whom he claims, whichever is the later, unless the right (before or after its accrual) either—

- (a) has been concealed by the fraud of some person administering the imperfect trust provision or his agent; or
- (b) has been acknowledged by some such person or his agent by means of a written acknowledgment given to the person having the right or his agent and signed by the person making it, or by means of a payment or transfer of property in respect of the right;

and if the period prescribed by this subsection for any person to bring proceedings to recover any property expires without his having recovered the property or begun proceedings to do so, his title to the property shall be extinguished.

This subsection shall not be taken as extending the time for bringing any proceedings beyond the period of limitation prescribed by any other enactment.

(3) For the purposes of the foregoing subsections, a right by reason of the invalidity of a disposition to property comprised in, or representing that comprised in, the disposition shall not be deemed to accrue to anyone so long as he is under a disability or has a future interest only, or so long as the disposition is subject to another disposition made by the same person, and the whole of the property or the income arising from it is held or applied for the purposes of that other disposition.

(4) [Subsections (2) to (6) of section thirty-eight of the Limitation Act 1980] (which define the circumstances in which, for the purposes of that Act, a person is to be deemed to be under a disability or to claim through another person), shall apply for the purposes of the foregoing subsections as they apply for the purposes of that Act.

(5) Where subsection (1) of this section applies to save a person's right to property comprised in, or representing that comprised in, a disposition, or would have so applied but for some dealing with the property by persons administering the imperfect trust provision, or by any trustee for them or for the persons on whose behalf they do so, the foregoing sections shall not prejudice the first-mentioned person's right by virtue of his interest in the property to damages or other relief in respect of any dealing with the property by any person administering the imperfect trust provision or by any such trustee as aforesaid, if the person dealing with the property had at the time express notice of a claim by him to enforce his right to the property.

(6) A covenant entered into before the commencement of this Act shall not be enforceable by virtue of this Act unless confirmed by the covenantor after that commencement, but a disposition made in accordance with such a covenant shall be treated for the purposes of this Act as confirming the covenant and any previous disposition made in accordance with it.

[88]

NOTES

Sub-s (4): words in square brackets substituted by the Limitation Act 1980, s 40(2), Sch 3, para 4.

4 Provisions as to pending proceedings and past decisions and tax payments

(1)–(3) ...

(4) This Act shall not, by its operation on any instrument as respects the period before the commencement of the Act, impose or increase any liability to tax nor entitle any person to reclaim any tax paid or borne before that commencement, nor (save as respects taxation) require the objects declared by the instrument to be treated for the purposes of any enactment as having been charitable so as to invalidate anything done or any determination given before that commencement.

[89]

NOTES

Sub-ss (1)–(3): repealed by the Statute Law (Repeals) Act 2004.

5 (*Repealed by the Northern Ireland Constitution Act 1973, s 41(1), Sch 6, Pt I.*)

6 Application to Crown

This Act, and (except in so far as the contrary intention appears) any enactment of the Parliament of Northern Ireland passed for purposes similar to the purposes of this Act, shall bind the Crown.

[90]

7 Short title

This Act may be cited as the Charitable Trusts (Validation) Act 1954.

[91]

RECREATIONAL CHARITIES ACT 1958

(6 & 7 Eliz 2 c 17)

An Act to declare charitable under the law of England and Wales the provision in the interests of social welfare of facilities for recreation or other leisure-time occupation, to make similar provision as to certain trusts heretofore established for carrying out social welfare activities within the meaning of the Miners' Welfare Act 1952, to enable laws for corresponding purposes to be passed by the Parliament of Northern Ireland, and for purposes connected therewith

[13 March 1958]

1 General provision as to recreational and similar trusts, etc

(1) Subject to the provisions of this Act, it shall be and be deemed always to have been charitable to provide, or assist in the provision of, facilities for recreation or other leisure-time occupation, if the facilities are provided in the interests of social welfare:

Provided that nothing in this section shall be taken to derogate from the principle that a trust or institution to be charitable must be for the public benefit.

(2) *The requirement of the foregoing subsection that the facilities are provided in the interests of social welfare shall not be treated as satisfied unless—*

(*a*) *the facilities are provided with the object of improving the conditions of life for the persons for whom the facilities are primarily intended; and*

(*b*) *either—*

(*i*) *those persons have need of such facilities as aforesaid by reason of their youth, age, infirmity or disablement, poverty or social and economic circumstances; or*

(*ii*) *the facilities are to be available to the members or female members of the public at large.*

(3) Subject to the said requirement, subsection (1) of this section applies in particular to the provision of facilities at village halls, community centres and women's institutes, and to the provision and maintenance of grounds and buildings to be used for purposes of recreation or leisure-time occupation, and extends to the provision of facilities for those purposes by the organising of any activity.

[92]

NOTES

Sub-s (2): substituted by sub-ss (2), (2A) by the Charities Act 2006, s 5(1), (2), as from a day to be appointed under s 79(2) of that Act, as follows—

"(2) The requirement in subsection (1) that the facilities are provided in the interests of social welfare cannot be satisfied if the basic conditions are not met.

(2A) The basic conditions are—

(a) that the facilities are provided with the object of improving the conditions of life for the persons for whom the facilities are primarily intended; and

(b) that either—

(i) those persons have need of the facilities by reason of their youth, age, infirmity or disability, poverty, or social and economic circumstances, or

(ii) the facilities are to be available to members of the public at large or to male, or to female, members of the public at large.".

2 Miners' welfare trusts

(*1*) *Where trusts declared before the seventeenth day of December, nineteen hundred and fifty-seven, required or purported to require property to be held for the purpose of activities which are social welfare activities within the meaning of the Miners' Welfare Act 1952, and at that date the whole or part of the property held on those trusts or of any property held with that property represented an application of moneys standing to the credit of the miners' welfare fund or moneys provided by the Coal Industry Social Welfare Organisation, those trusts shall be treated as if they were and always had been charitable.*

(2) *For the purposes of this section property held on the same trusts as other property shall be deemed to be held with it, though vested in different trustees.*

NOTES

Repealed by the Charities Act 2006, ss 5(1), (3), 75(2), Sch 9, as from a day to be appointed under s 79(2) of that Act, subject to transitional provisions and savings in Sch 10, para 2 to that Act at **[2176]**.

[93]

3 Savings and other provisions as to past transactions

(1) Nothing in this Act shall be taken to restrict the purposes which are to be regarded as charitable independently of this Act.

(2) Nothing in this Act—

(a) shall apply to make charitable any trust, or validate any disposition, of property if before the seventeenth day of December, nineteen hundred and fifty-seven, that property or any property representing or forming part of it, or any income arising from any such property, has been paid or conveyed to, or applied for the benefit of, the persons entitled by reason of the invalidity of the trust or disposition; or

(b) shall affect any order or judgment made or given (whether before or after the passing of this Act) in legal proceedings begun before that day; or

(c) shall require anything properly done before that day, or anything done or to be done in pursuance of a contract entered into before that day, to be treated for any purpose as wrongful or ineffectual.

(3) … nothing in this Act shall require anything to be treated for the purposes of any enactment as having been charitable at a time before the date of the passing of this Act, so as to invalidate anything done or any determination given before that date.

(4), (5) …

[94]

NOTES

Sub-s (3): words omitted repealed by the Statute Law (Repeals) Act 2004.
Sub-ss (4), (5): repealed by the Statute Law (Repeals) Act 2004.

4 *(Repealed by the Northern Ireland Constitution Act 1973, s 41(1), Sch 6, Pt I.)*

5 Application to Crown

This Act, and (except in so far as the contrary intention appears) any enactment of the Parliament of Northern Ireland passed for purposes similar to section one of this Act, shall bind the Crown.

[95]

6 Short title and extent

(1) This Act may be cited as the Recreational Charities Act 1958.

(2) *Sections one and two of this Act shall affect the law of Scotland and Northern Ireland only in so far as they affect the operation of the Income Tax Acts or of other enactments in which references to charity are to be construed in accordance with the law of England and Wales […].*

[96]

NOTES

Sub-s (2): words omitted from square brackets added by the Local Government (Financial Provisions, etc) (Scotland) Act 1962, s 12(1), Sch 2, repealed by the Charities and Trustee Investment (Scotland) Act 2005, s 104, Sch 4, para 1; substituted by sub-ss (2), (3) by the Charities Act 2006, s 75(1), Sch 8, para 39, as from a day to be appointed under s 79(2) of that Act, as follows—

"(2) Section 1 of this Act, as amended by section 5 of the Charities Act 2006, has the same effect in relation to the law of Scotland or Northern Ireland as section 5 of that Act has by virtue of section 80(3) to (6) of that Act.

(3) Sections 1 and 2 of this Act, as in force before the commencement of section 5 of that Act, continue to have effect in relation to the law of Scotland or Northern Ireland so far as they affect the construction of any references to charities or charitable purposes which—

(a) are to be construed in accordance with the law of England and Wales, but

(b) are not contained in enactments relating to matters of the kind mentioned in section 80(4) or (6) of that Act.".

CHARITIES ACT 1960

(8 & 9 Eliz 2 c 58)

ARRANGEMENT OF SECTIONS

PART III

APPLICATION OF PROPERTY CY-PRES, AND ASSISTANCE AND SUPERVISION OF CHARITIES BY COURT AND CENTRAL AUTHORITIES

Miscellaneous

An Act to replace with new provisions the Charitable Trusts Acts 1853 to 1939, and other enactments relating to charities, to repeal the mortmain Acts, to make further provision as to the powers exercisable by or with respect to charities or with respect to gifts to charity, and for purposes connected therewith

[29 July 1960]

NOTES

Charities Act 1960 and 1985: this Act and the Charities Act 1985 may be cited together by this collective title; see s 7(1) of the 1985 Act.

1–12 *((Pts I, II) Ss 1, 3–12 repealed by the Charities Act 1993, s 98(2), Sch 7, subject to transitional provisions concerning s 8; s 2 repealed, with savings, by the Education Act 1973, s 1(1)(a), (3)–(5), Sch 1, para 1(2)–(7), Sch 2, Pts II, III.)*

PART III
APPLICATION OF PROPERTY CY-PRES, AND ASSISTANCE AND SUPERVISION OF CHARITIES BY COURT AND CENTRAL AUTHORITIES

13–27 *(Ss 13–26, 26A repealed by the Charities Act 1993, s 98(2), Sch 7; s 27 repealed by the Charities Act 1992, ss 37(5), 78(2), Sch 7.)*

Miscellaneous

28 Taking of legal proceedings

(1)–(8) …

(9) … *so much of any local or private Act establishing or regulating a charity as relates to the persons by whom or the manner or form in which any charity proceedings may be brought shall cease to have effect.*

[97]

NOTES

This Act, in so far as unrepealed, is repealed by the Charities Act 2006, s 75(2), Sch 9, as from a day to be appointed under s 79(2) of that Act, subject to savings in Sch 10, paras 21–27, 29(1), (2)(a) to that Act at **[2176]**.

Sub-ss (1)–(8): repealed by the Charities Act 1993, s 98(2), Sch 7.

Sub-s (9): words omitted repealed by the Statute Law (Repeals) Act 2004.

29–31 *(Ss 29, 30, 30A–30C repealed by the Charities Act 1993, s 98(2), Sch 7; s 31 repealed by the Charities Act 1992, ss 47, 78(2), Sch 3, para 12, Sch 7.)*

PART IV
MISCELLANEOUS PROVISIONS AS TO CHARITIES AND THEIR AFFAIRS

32–34 *(Repealed by the Charities Act 1993, s 98(2), Sch 7, subject to transitional provisions concerning s 32.)*

35 Transfer and evidence of title to property vested in trustees

(1)–(5) …

(*6*) *The Trustee Appointment Act 1850, the Trustee Appointment Act 1869, the Trustees Appointment Act 1890, and in so far as it applies any of those Acts the School Sites Act 1852, shall cease to have effect; but where, at the commencement of this Act, the provisions of those Acts providing for the appointment of trustees apply in relation to any land, those provisions shall have effect as if contained in the conveyance or other instrument declaring the trusts on which the land is then held.*

[98]

NOTES

Repealed as noted to s 28 at **[97]**.
Sub-ss (1)–(5): repealed by the Charities Act 1993, s 98(2), Sch 7.

36, 37 (*Repealed by the Charities Act 1993, s 98(2), Sch 7.*)

38 Repeal of law of mortmain

(*1*), (*2*) ...

(*3*) *The repeal by this Act of the Mortmain and Charitable Uses Act 1891 shall have effect in relation to the wills of persons dying before the passing of this Act so as to abrogate any requirement to sell land then unsold, but not so as to enable effect to be given to a direction to lay out personal estate in land without an order under section eight of that Act or so as to affect the power to make such an order.*

(*4*) *Any reference in any enactment or document to a charity within the meaning, purview and interpretation of the Charitable Uses Act 1601 or of the preamble to it, shall be construed as a reference to a charity within the meaning which the word bears as a legal term according to the law of England and Wales.*

(*5*) *No repeal made by this Act shall affect any power to hold land in Northern Ireland without licence in mortmain;* ...

[99]

NOTES

Repealed as noted to s 28 at **[97]**.
Sub-ss (1), (2): repealed by the Education Act 1973, s 1(4), Sch 2, Pt I.
Sub-s (5): words omitted repealed by the Northern Ireland Constitution Act 1973, s 41(1), Sch 6, Pt I.
Charitable Uses Act 1601: repealed by the Mortmain and Charitable Uses Act 1888, s 13(1).

39 Repeal of obsolete enactments

(*1*) ...

(*2*) *Where the trusts of a charity are at the commencement of this Act wholly or partly comprised in an enactment specified in the Fifth Schedule to this Act, or in an instrument having effect under such an enactment, the operation of those trusts shall not be affected by the repeal of that enactment by this Act.*

[100]

NOTES

Repealed as noted to s 28 at **[97]**.
Sub-s (1): repealed by the Education Act 1973, s 1(4), Sch 2, Pt I.
Fifth Schedule: repealed by the Education Act 1973, s 1(4), Sch 2, Pt I.

PART V
SUPPLEMENTARY

40–47 (*Ss 40, 40A, 41–43, 45, 46 repealed by the Charities Act 1993, s 98(2), Sch 7, subject to transitional provisions; s 44 repealed by the Charities Act 1992, s 78(2), Sch 7; s 47 repealed by the Northern Ireland Constitution Act 1973, s 41(1), Sch 6, Pt I.*)

***48 Consequential amendments*, general repeal and transitional provisions**

(*1*) *The enactments mentioned in the first column of the Sixth Schedule to this Act shall be amended as provided in the second column of that Schedule.*

(2) …

(3) *The Commissioners may take the like action under this Act in consequence of any application or enquiry under the Charitable Trusts Acts 1853 to 1939, as if the application or enquiry had been made for the corresponding purpose under this Act; and subsections (3) to (5) of section twenty-five of this Act shall extend (with any necessary adaptations) to documents enrolled by the Commissioners or deposited with them under those Acts.*

(4) *The repeal by this Act of the Charitable Trusts Acts 1853 to 1939 shall not invalidate any scheme, order, certificate or other document issued under or for the purposes of those Acts, so far as the document is capable after the commencement of this Act of having effect either for its original purpose or for any corresponding purpose of this Act; but any such documents shall continue to have effect for any such purpose (except in so far as they are modified or superseded under the powers of this Act), and shall in the case of an order be appealable, enforceable and liable to be discharged as if this Act had not been passed; and any such document, and any document under the seal of the official trustees of charitable funds, may be proved as if this Act had not been passed.*

(5) …

(6) *The official custodian for charities shall be treated as the successor for all purposes both of the official trustee of charity lands and of the official trustees of charitable funds, as if the functions of the said trustee or trustees had been functions of the official custodian, and as if any such trustee or trustees had been, and had discharged his or their functions as, holder of the office of the official custodian; and accordingly (but without prejudice to the generality of the foregoing provision, and subject to any express amendment or repeal made by this Act) as from the commencement of this Act—*

(*a*) *all property vested in the said trustee or trustees shall vest in the official custodian, and shall be held by him as if vested in him under section sixteen of this Act for the purposes for which it was held by the said trustee or trustees; and*

(*b*) *any Act, scheme, deed or other document referring or relating to the said trustee or trustees shall, in so far as the context permits, have effect as if the official custodian had been mentioned instead.*

(7) *The specific provisions of this Act as to the effect of any repeal shall not be taken to exclude the general provisions contained in section thirty-eight of the Interpretation Act 1889 except in so far as those general provisions are inconsistent with specific provisions in this Act.*

[101]

NOTES

Repealed as noted to s 28 at **[97]**.
Sub-s (2): repealed by the Education Act 1973, s 1(4), Sch 2, Pt I.
Sub-s (5): repealed by the Statute Law (Repeals) Act 2004.
Charitable Trusts Acts 1853 to 1939: all these Acts were repealed by sub-s (2) of this section and Sch 7 to this Act.
Interpretation Act 1889, s 38: repealed by the Interpretation Act 1978, s 25(1), Sch 3, and replaced by s 17(2)(a) of that Act.

49 Short title, extent and commencement

(1) *This Act may be cited as the Charities Act 1960.*

(2) *This Act shall extend—*

(*a*), (*b*) …

(*c*) *to Northern Ireland in so far as it relates to the amendment of Royal Charters; but, subject to that, this Act shall not extend to Scotland or Northern Ireland.*

(3) …

[102]

NOTES

Repealed as noted to s 28 at **[97]**.
Sub-s (2): paras (a), (b) repealed by the Statute Law (Repeals) Act 1978.
Sub-s (3): repealed by the Education Act 1973, s 1(4), Sch 2, Pt I.

(Schs 1–4 repealed by the Charities Act 1993, s 98(2), Sch 7; Schs 5, 7 repealed by the Education Act 1973, s 1(4), Sch 2, Pt I; Sch 6 in so far as unrepealed, contains amendments which are outside the scope of this work.)

TRUSTEE INVESTMENTS ACT 1961

(1961 c 62)

ARRANGEMENT OF SECTIONS

An Act to make fresh provision with respect to investment by trustees and persons having the investment powers of trustees, and by local authorities, and for purposes connected therewith

[3 August 1961]

1 New powers of investment of trustees

(1) A trustee may invest any property in his hands, whether at the time in a state of investment or not, in any manner specified in Part I or II of the First Schedule to this Act or, subject to the next following section, in any manner specified in Part III of that Schedule, and may also from time to time vary any such investments.

(2) The supplemental provisions contained in Part IV of that Schedule shall have effect for the interpretation and for restricting the operation of the said Parts I to III.

(3) No provision relating to the powers of the trustee contained in any instrument (not being an enactment or an instrument made under an enactment) made before the passing of this Act shall limit the powers conferred by this section, but those powers are exerciseable only in so far as a contrary intention is not expressed in any Act or instrument made under an enactment, whenever passed or made, and so relating or in any other instrument so relating which is made after the passing of this Act.

For the purposes of this subsection any rule of the law of Scotland whereby a testamentary writing may be deemed to be made on a date other than that on which it was actually executed shall be disregarded.

(4) In this Act "narrower-range investment" means an investment falling within Part I or II of the First Schedule to this Act and "wider-range investment" means an investment falling within Part III of that Schedule.

[103]

NOTES

Ss 1, 2, 5, 6, 12, 13 and 15 repealed, except in so far as applied by or under any other enactment, by the *Trustee Act 2000, s 40(1), (3), Sch 2, Pt I,* para 1(1), Sch 4, Pt I, and, in relation to Scotland, by the Charities and Trustee Investment (Scotland) Act 2005, s 95, Sch 3, para 4(1), (2).

This Act is applied by the Industrial and Provident Societies Act 1965, s 31(c) at **[170]**.

2 Restrictions on wider-range investment

(1) A trustee shall not have power by virtue of the foregoing section to make or retain any wider-range investment unless the trust fund has been divided into two parts (hereinafter referred to as the narrower-range part and the wider-range part), the parts being, subject to the provisions of this Act, equal in value at the time of the division; and where such a division has been made no subsequent division of the same fund shall be made for the purposes of this section, and no property shall be transferred from one part of the fund to the other unless either—

(a) the transfer is authorised or required by the following provisions of this Act, or

(b) a compensating transfer is made at the same time.

In this section "compensating transfer", in relation to any transferred property, means a transfer in the opposite direction of property of equal value.

(2) Property belonging to the narrower-range part of a trust fund shall not by virtue of the foregoing section be invested except in narrower-range investments, and any property invested in any other manner which is or becomes comprised in that part of the trust fund shall either be transferred to the wider-range part of the fund, with a compensating transfer, or be reinvested in narrower-range investments as soon as may be.

(3) Where any property accrues to a trust fund after the fund has been divided in pursuance of subsection (1) of this section, then—

(a) if the property accrues to the trustee as owner or former owner of property comprised in either part of the fund, it shall be treated as belonging to that part of the fund;

(b) in any other case, the trustee shall secure, by apportionment of the accruing property or the transfer of property from one part of the fund to the other, or both, that the value of each part of the fund is increased by the same amount.

Where a trustee acquires property in consideration of a money payment the acquisition of the property shall be treated for the purposes of this section as investment and not as the accrual of property to the trust fund, notwithstanding that the amount of the consideration is less than the value of the property acquired; and paragraph (a) of this subsection shall not include the case of a dividend or interest becoming part of a trust fund.

(4) Where in the exercise of any power or duty of a trustee property falls to be taken out of the trust fund, nothing in this section shall restrict his discretion as to the choice of property to be taken out.

[104]–[105]

NOTES

Repealed as noted to s 1 at **[103]**.

See further, the Trustee Investments (Division of Trust Fund) Order 1996, SI 1996/845, art 2, which provides that, subject to s 4(3) of this Act, any division of a trust fund made in pursuance of sub-s (1) above must be made so that the value of the wider-range part at the time of the division bears to the then value of the narrower-range part the proportion of three to one.

3 *(Repealed, except in so far as this section relates to a trustee having a power of investment conferred on him under any enactment which was passed before 3 August 1961 and which is not amended by the Trustee Act 2000, Sch 2 or by the Charities and Trustee Investment (Scotland) Act 2005, Sch 3, by the Trustee Act 2000, s 40(1), (3), Sch 2, Pt I, para 1(2), Sch 4, Pt I and by the Charities and Trustee Investment (Scotland) Act 2005, s 95, Sch 3, para 4(1), (3).)*

4 Interpretation of references to trust property and trust funds

(1) In this Act "property" includes real or personal property of any description, including money and things in action:

Provided that it does not include an interest in expectancy, but the falling into possession of such an interest, or the receipt of proceeds of the sale thereof, shall be treated for the purposes of this Act as an accrual of property to the trust fund.

(2) So much of the property in the hands of a trustee shall for the purposes of this Act constitute one trust fund as is held on trusts which (as respects the beneficiaries or their respective interests or the purposes of the trust or as respects the powers of the trustee) are not identical with those on which any other property in his hands is held.

(3) Where property is taken out of a trust fund by way of appropriation so as to form a separate fund, and at the time of the appropriation the trust fund had (as to the whole or a part thereof) been divided in pursuance of subsection (1) of section two of this Act, or that subsection as modified by the Second Schedule to this Act, then if the separate fund is so divided the narrower-range and wider-range parts of the separate fund may be constituted so as either to be equal, or to bear to each other the same proportion as the two corresponding parts of the fund out of which it was so appropriated (the values of those parts of those funds being ascertained as at the time of appropriation), or some intermediate proportion.

(4) *(Applies to Scotland only.)*

[106]

5 Certain valuations to be conclusive for purposes of division of trust fund

(1) If for the purposes of section two or four of this Act or the Second Schedule thereto a trustee obtains, from a person reasonably believed by the trustee to be qualified to make it, a valuation in writing of any property, the valuation shall be conclusive in determining whether the division of the trust fund in pursuance of subsection (1) of the said section two, or any transfer or apportionment of property under that section or the said Second Schedule, has been duly made.

(2) The foregoing subsection applies to any such valuation notwithstanding that it is made by a person in the course of his employment as an officer or servant.

[107]

NOTES

Repealed as noted to s 1 at **[103]**.

6 Duty of trustees in choosing investments

(1) In the exercise of his powers of investment a trustee shall have regard—

(a) to the need for diversification of investments of the trust, in so far as is appropriate to the circumstances of the trust;

(b) to the suitability to the trust of investments of the description of investment proposed and of the investment proposed as an investment of that description.

(2) Before exercising any power conferred by section one of this Act to invest in a manner specified in Part II or III of the First Schedule to this Act, or before investing in any such manner in the exercise of a power falling within subsection (2) of section three of this Act, a trustee shall obtain and consider proper advice on the question whether the investment is satisfactory having regard to the matters mentioned in paragraphs (a) and (b) of the foregoing subsection.

(3) A trustee retaining any investment made in the exercise of such a power and in such a manner as aforesaid shall determine at what intervals the circumstances, and in particular the nature of the investment, make it desirable to obtain such advice as aforesaid, and shall obtain and consider such advice accordingly.

(4) For the purposes of the two foregoing subsections, proper advice is the advice of a person who is reasonably believed by the trustee to be qualified by his ability in and practical experience of financial matters; and such advice may be given by a person notwithstanding that he gives it in the course of his employment as an officer or servant.

(5) A trustee shall not be treated as having complied with subsection (2) or (3) of this section unless the advice was given or has been subsequently confirmed in writing.

(6) Subsections (2) and (3) of this section shall not apply to one of two or more trustees where he is the person giving the advice required by this section to his co-trustee or co-trustees, and shall not apply where powers of a trustee are lawfully exercised by an officer or servant competent under subsection (4) of this section to give proper advice.

(7) Without prejudice to section eight of the Trustee Act 1925, or section thirty of the Trusts (Scotland) Act 1921 (which relate to valuation, and the proportion of the value to be lent, where a trustee lends on the security of property) the advice required by this section shall not include, in the case of a loan on the security of freehold or leasehold property in England and Wales or Northern Ireland or on heritable security in Scotland, advice on the suitability of the particular loan.

[108]

NOTES

Repealed as noted to s 1 at **[103]**.

Trustee Act 1925, s 8: repealed by Trustee Act 2000, s 40(1), (3), Sch 2, Pt II, para 18, Sch 4, Pt II, subject to transitional provisions and savings contained in Sch 3, paras 1–3 to that Act.

7 Application of ss 1–6 to persons, other than trustees, having trustee investment powers

(1) Where any persons, not being trustees, have a statutory power of making investments which is or includes power—

(a) to make the like investments as are authorised by section one of the Trustee Act 1925, or section ten of the Trusts (Scotland) Act 1921, or

(b) to make the like investments as trustees are for the time being by law authorised to make,

however the power is expressed, the foregoing provisions of this Act shall with the necessary modifications apply in relation to them as if they were trustees:

Provided that property belonging to a Consolidated Loans Fund or any other fund applicable wholly or partly for the redemption of debt shall not by virtue of the foregoing provisions of this Act be invested or held invested in any manner specified in paragraph 6 of Part II of the First Schedule to this Act or in wider-range investments.

(2) Where, in the exercise of powers conferred by any enactment, an authority to which paragraph 9 of Part II of the First Schedule to this Act applies uses money belonging to any fund for a purpose for which the authority has power to borrow, the foregoing provisions of this Act, as applied by the foregoing subsection, shall apply as if there were comprised in the fund (in addition to the actual content thereof) property, being narrower-range investments, having a value equal to so much of the said money as for the time being has not been repaid to the fund, and accordingly any repayment of such money to the fund shall not be treated for the said purposes as the accrual of property to the fund:

Provided that nothing in this subsection shall be taken to require compliance with any of the provisions of section six of this Act in relation to the exercise of such powers as aforesaid.

(3) In this section "Consolidated Loans Fund" means a fund established under section fifty-five of the Local Government Act 1958, and includes a loans fund established under [Schedule 3 to the Local Government (Scotland) Act 1975] and "statutory power" means a power conferred by an enactment passed before the passing of this Act or by any instrument made under any such enactment.

[109]–[111]

NOTES

Sub-s (3): words in square brackets substituted by the Local Government and Planning (Scotland) Act 1982, s 66(1), Sch 3, para 4.

Trustee Act 1925, s 1: repealed by s 16(2) of, and Sch 5 to, this Act.

Trusts (Scotland) Act 1921, s 10: repealed by s 16(2) of, and Sch 5 to, this Act.

Local Government Act 1958, s 55: repealed by the Local Government Act 1972, s 272(1), Sch 30.

8–10 *(S 8 repealed by the Trustee Act 2000, s 40(1), (3), Sch 2, Pt I, para 1(3)(a), Sch 4, Pt I and by the Charities and Trustee Investment (Scotland) Act 2005, s 95, Sch 3, para 4(1), (4); s 9 repealed by the Trustee Act 2000, s 40(1), (3), Sch 2, Pt I, para 1(3)(a), Sch 4, Pt I; s 10 applies to Scotland only.)*

11 Local Authority investment schemes

(1) Without prejudice to powers conferred by or under any other enactment, any authority to which this section applies may invest property held by the authority in accordance with a scheme submitted to the Treasury by any association of local authorities ... and approved by the Treasury as enabling investments to be made collectively without in substance extending the scope of powers of investment.

(2) A scheme under this section may apply to a specified authority or to a specified class of authorities, may make different provisions as respects different authorities or different classes of authorities or as respects different descriptions of property or property held for different purposes, and may impose restrictions on the extent to which the power controlled by the foregoing subsection shall be exerciseable.

(3) In approving a scheme under this section, the Treasury may direct that [the [Financial Services and Markets Act 2000]] shall not apply to dealings undertaken or documents issued for the purposes of the scheme, or to such dealings or documents of such descriptions as may be specified in the direction.

(4) The authorities to which this section applies are—

(a) in England and Wales [, the Greater London Authority,] the council of a county [a county borough], a … borough … a … district or a [parish, the Common] Council of the City of London [, a functional body (within the meaning of the Greater London Authority Act 1999),] [the Broads Authority] [a National Park authority][, a police authority established under [section 3 of the Police Act 1996]][…][, … , a joint authority established by Part IV of the Local Government Act 1985] … and the Council of the Isles of Scilly;

(b) in Scotland, a local authority within the meaning of the Local Government (Scotland) Act 1947;

(c) in any part of Great Britain, a joint board or joint committee constituted to discharge or advise on the discharge of the functions of any two or more of the authorities mentioned in the foregoing paragraphs (including a joint committee established by [those authorities acting in combination in accordance with regulations made under section 7 of the Superannuation Act 1972];

(d) in Northern Ireland [a district council established under the Local Government Act (Northern Ireland) 1972] and the Northern Ireland Local Government Officers' Superannuation Committee established under the Local Government (Superannuation) Act (Northern Ireland) 1950;

[(e) …]

[112]

NOTES

Sub-s (1): words omitted repealed by the Local Government Act 1985, s 102(2), Sch 17 and by the London Government Act 1963, s 93(1), Sch 18, Pt II.

Sub-s (3): words in first (outer) pair of square brackets substituted by the Financial Services Act 1986, s 212(2), Sch 16, para 2(a); words in second (inner) pair of square brackets substituted by the Financial Services and Markets Act 2000 (Consequential Amendments and Repeals) Order 2001, SI 2001/3649, art 268.

Sub-s (4)(a): words in first pair of square brackets inserted by the Greater London Authority Act 1999, s 387(1), (2)(a); words in second pair of square brackets inserted by the Local Government (Wales) Act 1994, s 66(6), Sch 16, para 19(1); words omitted in the first place repealed by the London Government Act 1963, s 93(1), Sch 18, Pt II; words omitted in the second and third places repealed by the Local Government Act 1972, s 272(1), Sch 30; words omitted in the fourth place (as inserted by the Local Government Act 1985, s 84, Sch 14, Pt II, para 38) repealed by the Education Reform Act 1988, s 237(2), Sch 13, Pt 1; words in third pair of square brackets substituted by the Water Act 1989, s 190(1), Sch 25, para 29(1); words in fourth pair of square brackets inserted by the Greater London Authority Act 1999, s 387(1), (2)(b); words in fifth pair of square brackets inserted by the Norfolk and Suffolk Broads Act 1988, s 21, Sch 6, para 3; words in sixth pair of square brackets inserted by the Environment Act 1995, s 78, Sch 10, para 5; words in seventh (outer) pair of square brackets inserted by the Police and Magistrates' Courts Act 1994, s 43, Sch 4, Pt II, para 46; words in eighth (inner) pair of square brackets substituted by the Police Act 1996, s 103, Sch 7, para 1(2)(a); words omitted from ninth pair of square brackets inserted by the Police Act 1997, s 134(1), Sch 9, para 4(a) and repealed by the Serious Organised Crime and Police Act 2005, ss 59, 174(2), Sch 4, paras 7, 8(a), Sch 17, Pt 2; words in final pair of square brackets inserted by the Local Government Act 1985, s 84, Sch 14, Pt II, para 38 and words omitted in the final place repealed by s 102(2) of, and Sch 17 to, the 1985 Act.

Sub-s (4)(c): words in square brackets substituted by the Superannuation Act 1972, s 29(1), Sch 6, para 40.

Sub-s (4)(d): words in square brackets substituted by the Transfer of Functions (Local Government, etc) (Northern Ireland) Order 1973, SR & O (NI) 1973/256, art 3, Sch 2.

Sub-s (4)(e): added by the Police Act 1997, s 134(1), Sch 9, para 4(b) and repealed by the Serious Organised Crime and Police Act 2005, ss 59, 174(2), Sch 4, paras 7, 8(b), Sch 17, Pt 2.

12 Power to confer additional powers of investment

(1) Her Majesty may by Order in Council extend the powers of investment conferred by section one of this Act by adding to Part I, Part II or Part III of the First Schedule to this Act any manner of investment specified in the Order.

(2) Any Order under this section shall be subject to annulment in pursuance of a resolution of either House of Parliament.

[113]

NOTES

Repealed as noted to s 1 at **[103]**.

Orders: the Trustee Investments (Additional Powers) Order 1962, SI 1962/658; the Trustee Investments (Additional Powers) (No 2) Order 1962, SI 1962/2611; the Trustee Investments (Additional Powers) Order 1964, SI 1964/703; the Trustee Investments (Additional Powers) (No 2) Order 1964, SI 1964/1404; the Trustee Investments (Additional Powers) Order 1966, SI 1966/401; the Trustee Investments (Additional Powers) Order 1968, SI 1968/470; the Trustee Investments (Additional Powers) Order 1972, SI 1972/1818; the Trustee Investments (Additional Powers) Order 1973, SI 1973/1332; the Trustee Investments (Additional Powers) Order 1975, SI 1975/1710; the Trustee Investments (Additional Powers) Order 1977, SI 1977/831; the Trustee Investments (Additional Powers) (No 2) Order 1977, SI 1977/1878; the Trustee Investments (Additional Powers) Order 1982, SI 1982/1086; the Trustee Investments (Additional Powers) Order 1983, SI 1983/772; the Trustee Investments (Additional Powers) (No 2) Order 1983, SI 1983/1525; the Trustee Investments (Additional Powers) Order 1985, SI 1985/1780; the Trustee Investments (Additional Powers) Order 1986, SI 1986/601; the Trustee Investments (Additional Powers) Order 1988, SI 1988/2254; the Trustee Investments (Additional Powers) Order 1991, SI 1991/999; the Trustee Investments (Additional Powers) Order 1992, SI 1992/1738; the Trustee Investments (Additional Powers) Order 1994, SI 1994/265; the Trustee Investments (Additional Powers) (No 2) Order 1994, SI 1994/1908 and the Trustee Investments (Additional Powers) Order 1995, SI 1995/768.

13 Power to modify provisions as to division of trust fund

(1) The Treasury may by order made by statutory instrument direct that, subject to subsection (3) of section four of this Act, any division of a trust fund made in pursuance of subsection (1) of section two of this Act during the continuance in force of the order shall be made so that the value of the wider-range part at the time of the division bears to the then value of the narrower-range part such proportion, greater than one but not greater than three to one, as may be prescribed by the order; and in this Act "the prescribed proportion" means the proportion for the time being prescribed under this subsection.

(2) A fund which has been divided in pursuance of subsection (1) of section two of this Act before the coming into operation of an order under the foregoing subsection may notwithstanding anything in that subsection be again divided (once only) in pursuance of the said subsection (1) during the continuance in force of the order.

(3) If an order is made under subsection (1) of this section, then as from the coming into operation of the order—

- *(a) paragraph (b) of subsection (3) of section two of this Act and sub-paragraph (b) of paragraph 3 of the Second Schedule thereto shall have effect with the substitution, for the words from "each" to the end, of the words "the wider-range part of the fund is increased by an amount which bears the prescribed proportion to the amount by which the value of the narrower-range part of the fund is increased";*
- *(b) subsection (3) of section four of this Act shall have effect as if for the words "so as either" to "each other" there were substituted the words "so as to bear to each other either the prescribed proportion or".*

(4) An order under this section may be revoked by a subsequent order thereunder prescribing a greater proportion.

(5) An order under this section shall not have effect unless approved by a resolution of each House of Parliament.

[114]

NOTES

Repealed as noted to s 1 at **[103]**.

Orders: the Trustee Investments (Division of Trust Fund) Order 1996, SI 1996/845.

14 (*Applies to Scotland only.*)

15 Saving for powers of court

The enlargement of the investment powers of trustees by this Act shall not lessen any power of a court to confer wider powers of investment on trustees, or affect the extent to which any such power is to be exercised.

[115]

NOTES

Repealed as noted to s 1 at **[103]**.

16 Minor and consequential amendments and repeals

(*1*) *The provisions of the Fourth Schedule to this Act (which contain minor amendments and amendments consequential on the foregoing provisions of this Act) shall have effect.*

(2) …

[116]

NOTES

Sub-s (1): repealed, in so far as it relates to Sch 4, para 1(1), by the Trustee Act 2000, s 40(1), (3), Sch 2, Pt I, para 1(3)(c), Sch 4, Pt I.

Sub-s (2): repealed by the Statute Law (Repeals) Act 1974.

17 Short title, extent and construction

(1) This Act may be cited as the Trustee Investments Act 1961.

[(2) Section 11 of this Act extends to Northern Ireland, but, except as aforesaid and except so far as any other provisions of this Act apply by virtue of Northern Ireland legislation to trusts the execution of which is governed by the law of Northern Ireland, this Act does not apply to such trusts.]

(3) So much of section sixteen of this Act as relates to [the National Savings Bank] … shall extend to the Isle of Man and the Channel Islands.

(4) Except where the context otherwise requires, in this Act, in its application to trusts the execution of which is governed by the law in force in England and Wales, expressions have the same meaning as in the Trustee Act 1925.

(5) (*Applies to Scotland only.*)

[117]

NOTES

Sub-s (2): substituted by the Trustee Act (Northern Ireland) 2001, s 44(1), Sch 2, para 20.

Sub-s (3): words in square brackets substituted by the Post Office Act 1969, ss 94, 114, Sch 6, Pt III; words omitted repealed by the Trustee Savings Banks Act 1985, ss 4(3), 7(3), Sch 4.

SCHEDULES

FIRST SCHEDULE
MANNER OF INVESTMENT

Section 1

PART I
NARROWER-RANGE INVESTMENTS NOT REQUIRING ADVICE

1. In Defence Bonds, National Savings Certificates Ulster Savings Certificates, [Ulster Development Bonds] [National Development Bonds], [British Savings Bonds], [National Savings Income Bonds] [National Savings Deposit Bonds] [National Savings Indexed-Income Bonds] [National Savings Capital Bonds] [National Savings FIRST Option Bonds] [National Savings Pensioners Guaranteed Income Bonds].

2. In deposits in [the National Savings Bank], … and deposits in a bank or department thereof certified under subsection (3) of section nine of the Finance Act 1956.

[118]

NOTES

Repealed, except in so far as this Schedule is applied by or under any other enactment, by virtue of the Trustee Act 2000, s 40(1), (3), Sch 2, Pt I, para 1(1), Sch 4, Pt I. As to the application of this Act, see the note to s 1 at **[103]**.

Para 1: words in first pair of square brackets added by the Trustee Investments (Additional Powers) (No 2) Order 1962, SI 1962/2611, art 1; words in second pair of square brackets added by the Trustee Investments (Additional Powers) Order 1964, SI 1964/703, art 1; words in third pair of square brackets added by the Trustee Investments (Additional Powers) Order 1968, SI 1968/470, art 1; words in fourth pair of square brackets added by the Trustee Investments (Additional Powers) Order 1982, SI 1982/1086, art 2; words in fifth pair of square brackets added by the Trustee Investments (Additional Powers) (No 2) Order 1983, SI 1983/1525, art 2; words in sixth pair of square brackets added by the Trustee Investments (Additional Powers) Order 1985, SI 1985/1780, art 2; words in seventh pair of square brackets added by the Trustee Investments (Additional Powers) Order 1988, SI 1988/2254, art 2; words in eighth pair of square brackets added by the Trustee Investments (Additional Powers) Order 1992, SI 1992/1738, art 2; words in final pair of square brackets added by the Trustee Investments (Additional Powers) Order 1994, SI 1994/265, art 2.

Para 2: words in square brackets substituted by the Post Office Act 1969, ss 94, 114, Sch 6, Pt III; words omitted repealed by the Trustee Savings Bank Act 1986, s 36(2), Sch 6.

Finance Act 1956, s 9(3): repealed by the Income and Corporation Taxes Act 1988, s 538(1), Sch 16.

PART II
NARROWER-RANGE OF INVESTMENTS REQUIRING ADVICE

1. In securities issued by Her Majesty's Government in the United Kingdom, the Government of Northern Ireland or the Government of the Isle of Man, not being securities falling within Part I of this Schedule and being fixed-interest securities registered in the United Kingdom or the Isle of Man, Treasury Bills or Tax Reserve Certificates [or any variable interest securities issued by Her Majesty's Government in the United Kingdom and registered in the United Kingdom].

2. In any securities the payment of interest on which is guaranteed by Her Majesty's Government in the United Kingdom or the Government of Northern Ireland.

3. In fixed-interest securities issued in the United Kingdom by any public authority or nationalised industry or undertaking in the United Kingdom.

4. In fixed-interest securities issued in the United Kingdom by the government of any overseas territory within the Commonwealth or by any public or local authority within such a territory, being securities registered in the United Kingdom.

References in this paragraph to an overseas territory or to the government of such a territory shall be construed as if they occurred in the Overseas Service Act 1958.

[4A. In securities issued in the United Kingdom by the government of an overseas territory within the Commonwealth or by any public or local authority within such a territory, being securities registered in the United Kingdom and in respect of which the rate of interest is variable by reference to one or more of the following:—

(*a*) *the Bank of England's minimum lending rate;*
(*b*) *the average rate of discount on allotment on 91-day Treasury bills;*
(*c*) *a yield on 91-day Treasury bills;*
(*d*) *a London sterling inter-bank offered rate;*
(*e*) *a London sterling certificate of deposit rate.*

References in this paragraph to an overseas territory or to the government of such a territory shall be construed as if they occurred in the Overseas Service Act 1958.]

5. In fixed-interest securities issued in the United Kingdom by [the African Development Bank, the Asian Development Bank, the Caribbean Development Bank, [the European Bank for Reconstruction and Development,] the International Finance Corporation, the International Monetary Fund or by] the International Bank for Reconstruction and Development, being securities registered in the United Kingdom.

[In fixed-interest securities issued in the United Kingdom by the Inter-American Development Bank],

[In fixed interest securities issued in the United Kingdom by [the European Atomic Energy Community, the European Economic Community,] the European Investment Bank or by the European Coal and Steel Community, being securities registered in the United Kingdom.]

[5A. In securities issued in the United Kingdom by

(i) the International Bank for Reconstruction and Development or by the European Investment Bank or by the European Coal and Steel Community, being securities registered in the United Kingdom or
(ii) the Inter-American Development Bank

being securities in respect of which the rate of interest is variable by reference to one or more of the following:—
(a) the Bank of England's minimum lending rate;
(b) the average rate of discount on allotment on 91-day Treasury bills;
(c) a yield on 91-day Treasury bills;
(d) a London sterling inter-bank offered rate;
(e) a London sterling certificate of deposit rate.]

[5B. In securities issued in the United Kingdom by the African Development Bank, the Asian Development Bank, the Caribbean Development Bank, the European Atomic Energy Community, [the European Bank for Reconstruction and Development,] the European Economic Community, the International Finance Corporation or by the International Monetary Fund, being securities registered in the United Kingdom and in respect of which the rate of interest is variable by reference to one or more of the following:—
(a) the average rate of discount on allotment on 91-day Treasury Bills;
(b) a yield on 91-day Treasury Bills;
(c) a London sterling inter-bank offered rate;
(d) a London sterling certificate of deposit rate.]

6. In debentures issued in the United Kingdom by a company incorporated in the United Kingdom, being debentures registered in the United Kingdom.

7. In stock of the Bank of Ireland.

[In Bank of Ireland 7 per cent Loan Stock 1968/91].

8. …

9. In loans to any authority to which this paragraph applies charged on all or any of the revenues of the authority or on a fund into which all or any of those revenues are payable, in any fixed-interest securities issued in the United Kingdom by any such authority for the purpose of borrowing money so charged, and in deposits with any such authority by way of temporary loan made on the giving of a receipt for the loan by the treasurer or other similar officer of the authority and on the giving of an undertaking by the authority that, if requested to charge the loan as aforesaid, it will either comply with the request or repay the loan.

This paragraph applies to the following authorities, that is to say—
(a) any local authority in the United Kingdom;
[(aa) the Greater London Authority;
(ab) any functional body, within the meaning of the Greater London Authority Act 1999;]
(b) any authority all the members of which are appointed or elected by one or more local authorities in the United Kingdom;
(c) any authority the majority of the members of which are appointed or elected by one or more local authorities in the United Kingdom, being an authority which by virtue of any enactment has power to issue a precept to a local authority in England and Wales, or a requisition to a local authority in Scotland, or to the expenses of which, by virtue of any enactment, a local authority in the United Kingdom is or can be required to contribute;
(d) … [a police authority established under [section 3 of the Police Act 1996];]
[(da) …]
(e) the Belfast City and District Water Commissioners
[(f) the Great Ouse Water Authority]
(g) any district council in Northern Ireland]
[(h) …;
(i) any residuary body established by section 57 of the Local Government Act 1985.]

[9A. In any securities issued in the United Kingdom by any authority to which paragraph 9 applies for the purpose of borrowing money charged on all or any of the revenues of the authority or on a fund into which all or any of those revenues are payable and being securities in respect of which the rate of interest is variable by reference to one or more of the following:—

(a) the Bank of England's minimum lending rate;
(b) the average rate of discount on allotment on 91-day Treasury bills;
(c) a yield on 91-day Treasury bills;
(d) a London sterling inter-bank offered rate;
(e) a London sterling certificate of deposit rate.]

10. In debentures or in the guaranteed or preference stock of any incorporated company, being statutory water undertakers within the meaning of the Water Act 1945, or any corresponding enactment in force in Northern Ireland, and having during each of the ten years immediately preceding the calendar year in which the investment was made paid a dividend of not less than five per cent. on its ordinary shares.

[10A. In any units of a gilt unit trust scheme.

A gilt unit trust scheme is an authorised unit trust scheme, or a recognised scheme, the objective of which is—

(a) to invest at least 90% of the property of the scheme in loan stock, bonds or other instruments creating indebtedness which—
  (i) are transferable; and
  (ii) are issued or guaranteed by the government of the United Kingdom or of any other country or territory, by a local authority in the United Kingdom or in a relevant state, or by an international organisation the members of which include the United Kingdom or a relevant state;

(b) to invest the remainder of the property of the scheme in shares, debentures or other instruments creating or acknowledging indebtedness, certificates representing securities or units in a collective investment scheme.

Sub-paragraphs (a) and (b) must be read with—
(i) section 22 of the Financial Services and Markets Act 2000;
(ii) any relevant order under that section; and
(iii) Schedule 2 to that Act.]

11. …

12. In deposits with a building society within the meaning of the Building Societies Act 1986.]

13. In mortgages of freehold property in England and Wales or Northern Ireland and of leasehold property in those countries of which the unexpired term at the time of investment is not less than sixty years, and in loans on heritable security in Scotland.

14. In perpetual rent-charges charged on land in England and Wales or Northern Ireland and fee-farm rents (not being rent-charges) issuing out of such land …

[15. In Certificates of Tax Deposit.]

[16. In fixed-interest or variable interest securities issued by the government of a relevant state.

17. In any securities the payment of interest on which is guaranteed by the government of a relevant state.

18. In fixed-interest securities issued in any relevant state by any public authority or nationalised industry or undertaking in that state.

19. In fixed-interest or variable interest securities issued in a relevant state by the government of any overseas territory within the Commonwealth or by any public or local authority within such a territory.

[For this purpose—
(a) "overseas territory" means any territory or country outside the United Kingdom, and
(b) the reference to the government of any overseas territory includes a reference to a government constituted for two or more overseas territories, and to any authority

established for the purpose of providing or administering services which are common to, or relate to matters of common interest to, two or more such territories.]

20. In the fixed-interest or variable interest securities issued in a relevant state by—
(a) the African Development Bank;
(b) the Asian Development Bank;
(c) the Caribbean Development Bank;
(d) the International Finance Corporation;
(e) the International Monetary Fund;
(f) the International Bank for Reconstruction and Development;
(g) the Inter-American Development Bank;
(h) the European Atomic Energy Community;
(i) the European Bank for Reconstruction and Development;
(j) the European Economic Community;
(k) the European Investment Bank; or
(l) the European Coal and Steel Community.

21. In debentures issued in any relevant state by a company incorporated in that state.

22. In loans to any authority to which this paragraph applies secured on all or any of the revenues of the authority or on a fund into which all or any of those revenues are payable, in fixed-interest or variable interest securities issued in a relevant state by any such authority in that state for the purpose of borrowing money so secured, and in deposits with any authority to which this paragraph applies by way of temporary loan made on the giving of a receipt for the loan by the treasurer or other similar officer of the authority and on the giving of an undertaking by the authority that, if requested to charge the loan as aforesaid, it will either comply with the request or repay the loan.

This paragraph applies to the following authorities, that is to say—
(a) any local authority in a relevant state; or
(b) any local authority all the members of which are appointed or elected by one or more local authorities in any such state.

23. In deposits with a mutual investment society whose head office is located in a relevant state.

24. In loans secured on any interest in property in a relevant state which corresponds to an interest in property falling within paragraph 13 of this Part of this Schedule.]

[119]

NOTES

Repealed as noted to Pt I at **[118]**.

Para 1: words in square brackets added by the Trustee Investments (Additional Powers) Order 1977, SI 1977/831, art 3.

Paras 4A, 5A, 9A: inserted by the Trustee Investments (Additional Powers) (No 2) Order 1977, SI 1977/1878, art 3.

Para 5: words in first (outer) and final (inner) pairs of square brackets inserted by the Trustee Investments (Additional Powers) Order 1983, SI 1983/772, art 2, words in second (inner) pair of square brackets inserted by the Trustee Investments (Additional Powers) Order 1991, SI 1991/999, art 2; words in third pair of square brackets inserted by the Trustee Investments (Additional Powers) (No 2) Order 1964, SI 1964/1404, art 1; words in fourth (outer) pair of square brackets added by the Trustee Investments (Additional Powers) Order 1972, SI 1972/1818, art 3.

Para 5B: inserted by SI 1983/772, art 2; words in square brackets inserted by SI 1991/999, art 2.

Para 7: words in square brackets inserted by the Trustee Investments (Additional Powers) Order 1966, SI 1966/401, art 1.

Para 8: repealed by the Agriculture and Forestry (Financial Provisions) Act 1991, s 1(1), (5), Schedule, Pt IV.

Para 9: sub-paras (aa), (ab) inserted and words omitted from sub-para (d) repealed by the Greater London Authority Act 1999, ss 387(1), (3)(a), (b), 423, Sch 34, Pt I; words in first (outer) pair of square brackets in sub-para (d) substituted by the Police and Magistrates' Courts Act 1994, s 43, Sch 4, Pt II, para 47; words in second (inner) pair of square brackets substituted by the Police Act 1996, s 103(1), Sch 7, Pt I, para 1(1), (2)(a); sub-para (da) inserted by the Police Act 1997, s 134(1), Sch 9, para 5 and repealed by the Serious Organised Crime and Police Act 2005, ss 59, 174(2), Sch 4, paras 7, 9, Sch 17, Pt 2; sub-para (f) added by the Trustee Investments (Additional Powers) Order 1962, SI 1962/658, art 1; sub-para (g) added by the Trustee Investments (Additional Powers) Order 1973, SI 1973/1332, art 3; sub-para (h) added by the Trustee Investments (Additional Powers) Order 1986, SI 1986/601, art 2, repealed by the Education Reform Act 1988, s 237(2), Sch 13, Pt I; sub-para (i) added by SI 1986/601, art 2.

Para 10: repealed, except in so far as it relates to the debentures or guaranteed or preference stock of a company which is a statutory water undertaker within the meaning of an enactment in Northern Ireland, by the Water Act 1989, s 190(1), Sch 25, para 29(2), (3).
Para 10A: inserted by the Finance Act 1982, s 150; substituted by the Financial Services and Markets Act 2000 (Consequential Amendments and Repeals) Order 2001, SI 2001/3649, art 269(1), (2).
Para 11: repealed by the Trustee Savings Bank Act 1976, s 36(2), Sch 6.
Para 12: substituted by the Building Societies Act 1986, s 120(1), Sch 18, Pt I, para 4(2).
Para 14: words omitted repealed by the Abolition of Feudal Tenure etc (Scotland) Act 2000, s 76(2), Sch 13, Pt 1.
Para 15: added by the Trustee Investments (Additional Powers) Order 1975, SI 1975/1710, art 3.
Paras 16–18: added by the Trustee Investments (Additional Powers) (No 2) Order 1994, SI 1994/1908, art 2(2).
Para 19: added by the Trustee Investments (Additional Powers) (No 2) Order 1994, SI 1994/1908, art 2(2); words in square brackets substituted by the International Development Act 2002, s 19(1), Sch 3, para 1.
Paras 20–24: added by the Trustee Investments (Additional Powers) (No 2) Order 1994, SI 1994/1908, art 2(2).
Overseas Service Act 1958: repealed by the Overseas Development and Co-operation Act 1980, s 18(1), Sch 2, Pt I.
Water Act 1945: the definition of "statutory water undertakers" was found in s 59(1) of the 1945 Act and was repealed by the Water Act 1973, s 40(3), Sch 9; see now the Water Industry Act 1991, s 6.
Local Government Act 1985, s 57: repealed by the Statute Law (Repeals) Act 2004, s 1(1), Sch 1, Pt 10, Group 3.

PART III
WIDER-RANGE INVESTMENTS

1. In any securities issued in the United Kingdom by a company incorporated in the United Kingdom, being securities registered in the United Kingdom and not being securities falling within Part II of this Schedule.

[2. In shares in a building society within the meaning of the Building Societies Act 1986.]

[2A. In any shares in an open-ended investment company within the meaning of the Open-Ended Investment Companies Regulations 2001.]

[3. In any units of an authorised unit trust scheme ...]

[4. In any securities issued in any relevant state by a company incorporated in that state or by any unincorporated body constituted under the law of that state, not being (in either case) securities falling within Part II of this Schedule or paragraph 6 of this Part of this Schedule.

5. In shares in a mutual investment society whose head office is located in a relevant state.

[6. In any units of a recognised scheme which does not fall within Part 2 of this Schedule.]]
[120]

NOTES

Repealed as noted to Pt I at **[118]**.
Para 2: substituted by the Building Societies Act 1986, s 120(1), Sch 18, Pt I, para 4(3).
Para 2A: inserted by the Open-Ended Investment Companies (Investment Companies with Variable Capital) Regulations 1996, SI 1996/2827, reg 75, Sch 8, Pt I, para 1; substituted by the Open-Ended Investment Companies Regulations 2001, SI 2001/1228, reg 84, Sch 7, para 1.
Para 3: substituted by the Financial Services Act 1986, s 212(2), Sch 16, para 2(6); words omitted repealed by the Financial Services and Markets Act 2000 (Consequential Amendments and Repeals) Order 2001, SI 2001/3649, art 269(1), (3).
Paras 4, 5: added, together with para 6, by the Trustee Investments (Additional Powers) (No 2) Order 1994, SI 1994/1908, art 2(3).
Para 6: added, together with paras 4, 5, by SI 1994/1908, art 2(3); substituted by SI 2001/3649, art 269(1), (4).

PART IV
SUPPLEMENTAL

1. The securities mentioned in Parts I to III of this Schedule do not include any securities where the holder can be required to accept repayment of the principal, or the payment of any interest, otherwise than in sterling[, in the currency of a relevant state or in the European currency unit (as defined in article 1 of Council Regulation No 3180/78/EEC)].

2. The securities mentioned in paragraphs 1 to 8 of Part II, other than Treasury Bills or Tax Reserve Certificates, securities issued before the passing of this Act by the Government of the Isle of Man, securities falling within paragraph 4 of the said Part II issued before the passing of this Act or securities falling within paragraph 9 of that Part, and the securities mentioned in paragraph 1 of Part III of this Schedule, do not include—

- *(a) securities the price of which is not quoted on [a recognised investment exchange ...] [or on an investment exchange which constitutes the principal or only market established in a relevant state on which securities admitted to official listing are dealt in or traded];*
- *(b) shares or debenture stock not fully paid up (except shares or debenture stock which by the terms of issue are required to be fully paid up within nine months of the date of issue).*

[2A. The securities mentioned in paragraphs 16 to 21 of Part II of this Schedule, other than securities traded on a relevant money market or securities falling within paragraph 22 of Part II of this Schedule, and the securities mentioned in paragraph 4 of Part III of this Schedule do not include—

- *(a) securities the price for which is not quoted on a recognised investment exchange ... or on an investment exchange which constitutes the principal or only market established in a relevant state on which securities admitted to official listing are dealt in or traded;*
- *(b) shares or debenture stock not fully paid up (except shares or debenture stock which by the terms of issue are required to be fully paid up within nine months of the date of issue or shares issued with no nominal value).]*

3. The securities mentioned in paragraphs 6 [and 21] of Part II and paragraph 1 [or 4] of Part III of this Schedule do not include—

- *(a) shares or debentures of an incorporated company of which the total issued and paid up share capital is less than one million pounds;*
- *[(ab) shares or debentures of an incorporated company of which the total issued and paid up share capital at any time on the business day before the investment is made is less than the equivalent of one million pounds in the currency of a relevant state (at the exchange rate prevailing in the United Kingdom at the close of business on the day before the investment is made);]*
- *(b) shares or debentures of an incorporated company which has not in each of the five years immediately preceding the calendar year in which the investment is made paid a dividend on all the shares issued by the company, excluding any shares issued after the dividend was declared and any shares which by their terms of issue did not rank for the dividend for that year.*

For the purposes of sub-paragraph (b) of this paragraph a company formed—

- *(i) to take over the business of another company or other companies, or*
- *(ii) to acquire the securities of, or control of, another company or other companies, or for either of those purposes and for other purposes shall be deemed to have paid a dividend as mentioned in that sub-paragraph in any year in which such a dividend has been paid by the other company or all the other companies, as the case may be.*

[For the purposes of sub-paragraph (b) of this paragraph in relation to investment in shares or debentures of a successor company within the meaning of the Electricity (Northern Ireland) Order 1992 the company shall be deemed to have paid a dividend as mentioned in that sub-paragraph—

- *(iii) in every year preceding the calendar year in which the transfer date within the meaning of Part III of that Order of 1992 falls ("the first investment year") which is included in the relevant five years; and*
- *(iv) in the first investment year, if that year is included in the relevant five years and that company does not in fact pay such a dividend in that year; and*

"the relevant five years" means the five years immediately preceding the year in which the investment in question is made or proposed to be made.]

[3A. …]

4. In this Schedule, unless the context otherwise requires, the following expressions have the meanings hereby respectively assigned to them, that is to say—

"debenture" includes debenture stock and bonds, whether constituting a charge on assets or not, and loan stock or notes;

"enactment" includes an enactment of the Parliament of Northern Ireland;

"fixed-interest securities" means securities which under their terms of issue bear a fixed rate of interest;

"local authority" in relation to the United Kingdom, means any of the following authorities—

(*a*) *in England and Wales, the council of a county[, a county borough], a … borough … an urban or rural district or a parish, the Common Council of the City of London [the Greater London Council] and the Council of the Isles of Scilly;*

(*b*) *in Scotland, a local authority within the meaning of the Local Government (Scotland) Act 1947;*

(*c*) …

.....

["mutual investment society" means a credit institution which operates on mutual principles and which is authorised by the appropriate supervisory authority of a relevant state;

"relevant money market" means a money market which is supervised by the central bank, or a government agency, of a relevant state;

"relevant state" means Austria, Finland, Iceland, [Liechtenstein,] Norway, Sweden or a member state other than the United Kingdom;]

"securities" includes shares, debentures, [units within paragraph 3 [or 6] of Part III of this Schedule], Treasury Bills and Tax Reserve Certificates;

"shares" includes stock;

"Treasury Bills" includes … bills issued by Her Majesty's Government in the United Kingdom and Northern Ireland Treasury Bills.

[4A. In this Schedule—

"authorised unit trust scheme" and "recognised scheme" have the meaning given by section 237(3) of the Financial Services and Markets Act 2000;

"collective investment scheme" has the meaning given by section 235 of that Act; and

"recognised investment exchange" has the meaning given by section 285 of that Act.]

5. It is hereby declared that in this Schedule "mortgage", in relation to freehold or leasehold property in Northern Ireland, includes a registered charge which, by virtue of subsection (4) of section forty of the Local Registration of Title (Ireland) Act 1891, or any other enactment, operates as a mortgage by deed.

6. [In relation to the United Kingdom,] references in this Schedule to an incorporated company are references to a company incorporated by or under any enactment and include references to a body of persons established for the purpose of trading for profit and incorporated by Royal Charter.

[6A. …]

7. …

[121]–[124]

NOTES

Repealed as noted to Pt I at **[118]**.

Para 1: words in square brackets added by the Trustee Investments (Additional Powers) (No 2) Order 1994, SI 1994/1908, art 3(1), (2).

Para 2: words in first pair of square brackets in sub-para (a) substituted by the Financial Services Act 1986, s 212(2), Sch 16, para 2; words omitted repealed by the Financial Services and Markets Act 2000 (Consequential Amendments and Repeals) Order 2001, SI 2001/3649, art 269(1), (5); words in second pair of square brackets in sub-para (a) inserted by SI 1994/1908, art 3(1),(3).

Para 2A: inserted by SI 1994/1908, art 3(1), (4), (8); words omitted repealed by SI 2001/3649, art 269(1), (5).

PART I STATUTES

Para 3: words in first, second and third pairs of square brackets inserted by SI 1994/1908, art 3(1), (5); words in fourth pair of square brackets added by the Electricity (Northern Ireland Consequential Amendments) Order 1992, SI 1992/232, art 4.

Para 3A: inserted by the Housing (Consequential Provisions) Act 1985, s 4, Sch 2, para 5(3); repealed by the Building Societies Act 1986, s 120(2), Sch 19, Pt I.

Para 4: in definition "local authority", words in first pair of square brackets inserted by the Local Government (Wales) Act 1994, s 66(6), Sch 16, para 19(2), words omitted in the first place repealed by the London Government Act 1963, ss 83(1), 93(1), Sch 17, para 25, Sch 18, Pt II, words omitted in the second place repealed by the Local Government Act 1972, s 272(1), Sch 30, sub-para (c) repealed by the Statute Law (Repeals) Act 1981, words in square brackets inserted by the London Government Act 1963, s 83(1), Sch 17; definitions omitted repealed by the Trustee Savings Banks Act 1976, s 36(2), Sch 6; definitions "mutual investment society", "relevant money market" and "relevant state" inserted by SI 1994/1908, arts 3(1), (6)(a); words in square brackets in definition "relevant state" inserted by the Trustee Investments (Additional Powers) Order 1995, SI 1995/768, art 2; in definition "securities" words in first (outer) pair of square brackets inserted by the Financial Services Act 1986, s 212(2), Sch 16, para 2, words in second (inner) pair of square brackets inserted by SI 1994/1908, art 3(1), (6)(b); in definition "Treasury Bills", words omitted repealed by the National Loans Act 1968, s 24(2), Sch 6, Pt I.

Para 4A: inserted by SI 2001/3649, art 269(1), (6).

Para 6: words in square brackets inserted by SI 1994/1908, art 3(1), (7).

Para 6A: inserted by SI 1994/1908, art 3(1), (4), (8); repealed by SI 2001/3649, art 269(1), (7).

Para 7: repealed by the Building Societies Act 1986, s 120, Sch 19, Pt I.

Local Registration of Title (Ireland) Act 1891: repealed with a saving by the Land Registration Act (Northern Ireland) 1970, ss 96, 97, Sch 13, Pt I, Sch 14.

(Second and Third Schedules repealed by the Trustee Act 2000, s 40(1), (3), Sch 2, Pt I, para 1(2), Sch 4, Pt I, as from 1 February 2001, except in so far as relating to a trustee having a power of investment conferred on him under an enactment passed before the passing of this Act and which is not amended by the Trustee Act 2000, Sch 2. Fourth Schedule: para 1(1) repealed by the Trustee Act 2000, s 40(1), (3), Sch 2, Pt I, para 1(3)(b), Sch 4, Pt I; para 1(2) repealed by the Charities and Trustee Investment (Scotland) Act 2005, s 95, Sch 3, para 4(1), (4); para 2 repealed by the Building Societies Act 1962, s 131, Sch 10, Pt I; para 3: repealed by the Water Act 1989, s 190(3), Sch 27, Pt II; paras 4, 5: repealed by the National Savings Bank Act 1971, s 28, Sch 2; para 6: repealed by the Housing (Consequential Provisions) Act 1985, s 3, Sch 1, Pt I. Fifth Schedule repealed by the Statute Law (Repeals) Act 1974.)

PERPETUITIES AND ACCUMULATIONS ACT 1964

(1964 c 55)

ARRANGEMENT OF SECTIONS

Perpetuities

Accumulations

Supplemental

An Act to modify the law of England and Wales relating to the avoidance of future interests in property on grounds of remoteness and governing accumulations of income from property

[16 July 1964]

Perpetuities

1 Power to specify perpetuity period

(1) Subject to section 9(2) of this Act and subsection (2) below, where the instrument by which any disposition is made so provides, the perpetuity period applicable to the disposition under the rule against perpetuities, instead of being of any other duration, shall be of a duration equal to such number of years not exceeding eighty as is specified in that behalf in the instrument.

(2) Subsection (1) above shall not have effect where the disposition is made in exercise of a special power of appointment, but where a period is specified under that subsection in the instrument creating such a power the period shall apply in relation to any disposition under the power as it applies in relation to the power itself.

[125]

2 Presumptions and evidence as to future parenthood

(1) Where in any proceedings there arises on the rule against perpetuities a question which turns on the ability of a person to have a child at some future time, then—

(a) subject to paragraph (b) below, it shall be presumed that a male can have a child at the age of fourteen years or over, but not under that age, and that a female can have a child at the age of twelve years or over, but not under that age or over the age of fifty-five years; but

(b) in the case of a living person evidence may be given to show that he or she will or will not be able to have a child at the time in question.

(2) Where any such question is decided by treating a person as unable to have a child at a particular time, and he or she does so, the High Court may make such order as it thinks fit for placing the persons interested in the property comprised in the disposition, so far as may be just, in the position they would have held if the question had not been so decided.

(3) Subject to subsection (2) above, where any such question is decided in relation to a disposition by treating a person as able or unable to have a child at a particular time, then he or she shall be so treated for the purpose of any question which may arise on the rule against perpetuities in relation to the same disposition in any subsequent proceedings.

(4) In the foregoing provisions of this section references to having a child are references to begetting or giving birth to a child, but those provisions (except subsection (1)(b)) shall apply in relation to the possibility that a person will at any time have a child by adoption, legitimation or other means as they apply to his or her ability at that time to beget or give birth to a child.

[126]

3 Uncertainty as to remoteness

(1) Where, apart from the provisions of this section and sections 4 and 5 of this Act, a disposition would be void on the ground that the interest disposed of might not become vested until too remote a time, the disposition shall be treated, until such time (if any) as it becomes established that the vesting must occur, if at all, after the end of the perpetuity period, as if the disposition were not subject to the rule against perpetuities; and its becoming so established shall not affect the validity of anything previously done in relation to the interest disposed of by way of advancement, application of intermediate income or otherwise.

(2) Where, apart from the said provisions, a disposition consisting of the conferring of a general power of appointment would be void on the ground that the power might not become exercisable until too remote a time, the disposition shall be treated, until such time (if any) as it becomes established that the power will not be exercisable within the perpetuity period, as if the disposition were not subject to the rule against perpetuities.

(3) Where, apart from the said provisions, a disposition consisting of the conferring of any power, option or other right would be void on the ground that the right might be exercised at too remote a time, the disposition shall be treated as regards any exercise of the right within the perpetuity period as if it were not subject to the rule against perpetuities and, subject to the said provisions, shall be treated as void for remoteness only if, and so far as, the right is not fully exercised within that period.

(4) Where this section applies to a disposition and the duration of the perpetuity period is not determined by virtue of section 1 or 9(2) of this Act, it shall be determined as follows:—

(a) where any persons falling within subsection (5) below are individuals in being and ascertainable at the commencement of the perpetuity period the duration of the period shall be determined by reference to their lives and no others, but so that the lives of any description of persons falling within paragraph (b) or (c) of that subsection shall be disregarded if the number of persons of that description is such as to render it impracticable to ascertain the date of death of the survivor;

(b) where there are no lives under paragraph (a) above the period shall be twenty-one years.

(5) The said persons are as follows:—

(a) the person by whom the disposition was made;

(b) a person to whom or in whose favour the disposition was made, that is to say—

(i) in the case of a disposition to a class of persons, any member or potential member of the class;

(ii) in the case of an individual disposition to a person taking only on certain conditions being satisfied, any person as to whom some of the conditions are satisfied and the remainder may in time be satisfied;

(iii) in the case of a special power of appointment exercisable in favour of members of a class, any member or potential member of the class;

(iv) in the case of a special power of appointment exercisable in favour of one person only, that person or, where the object of the power is ascertainable only on certain conditions being satisfied, any person as to whom some of the conditions are satisfied and the remainder may in time be satisfied;

(v) in the case of any power, option or other right, the person on whom the right is conferred;

(c) a person having a child or grandchild within sub-paragraphs (i) to (iv) of paragraph (b) above, or any of whose children or grandchildren, if subsequently born, would by virtue of his or her descent fall within those sub-paragraphs;

(d) any person on the failure or determination of whose prior interest the disposition is limited to take effect.

[127]

4 Reduction of age and exclusion of class members to avoid remoteness

(1) Where a disposition is limited by reference to the attainment by any person or persons of a specified age exceeding twenty-one years, and it is apparent at the time the disposition is made or becomes apparent at a subsequent time—

(a) that the disposition would, apart from this section, be void for remoteness, but

(b) that it would not be so void if the specified age had been twenty-one years,

the disposition shall be treated for all purposes as if, instead of being limited by reference to the age in fact specified, it had been limited by reference to the age nearest to that age which would, if specified instead, have prevented the disposition from being so void.

(2) Where in the case of any disposition different ages exceeding twenty-one years are specified in relation to different persons—

(a) the reference in paragraph (b) of subsection (1) above to the specified age shall be construed as a reference to all the specified ages, and

(b) that subsection shall operate to reduce each such age so far as is necessary to save the disposition from being void for remoteness.

(3) Where the inclusion of any persons, being potential members of a class or unborn persons who at birth would become members or potential members of the class, prevents the foregoing provisions of this section from operating to save a disposition from being void for remoteness, those persons shall thenceforth be deemed for all the purposes of the disposition to be excluded from the class, and the said provisions shall thereupon have effect accordingly.

(4) Where, in the case of a disposition to which subsection (3) above does not apply, it is apparent at the time the disposition is made or becomes apparent at a subsequent time that, apart from this subsection, the inclusion of any persons, being potential members of a class or unborn persons who at birth would become members or potential members of the class, would cause the disposition to be treated as void for remoteness, those persons shall, unless their exclusion would exhaust the class, thenceforth be deemed for all the purposes of the disposition to be excluded from the class.

(5) Where this section has effect in relation to a disposition to which section 3 above applies, the operation of this section shall not affect the validity of anything previously done in relation to the interest disposed of by way of advancement, application of intermediate income or otherwise.

(6) …

[(7) For the avoidance of doubt it is hereby declared that a question arising under section 3 of this Act or subsection (1)(a) above of whether a disposition would be void apart from this section is to be determined as if subsection (6) above had been a separate section of this Act.]

[128]

PART I STATUTES

NOTES

Sub-s (6): repeals the Law of Property Act 1925, s 163.
Sub-s (7): added by the Children Act 1975, s 108(1)(a), Sch 3, para 43.

5 Condition relating to death of surviving spouse

Where a disposition is limited by reference to the time of death of the survivor of a person in being at the commencement of the perpetuity period and any spouse of that person, and that time has not arrived at the end of the perpetuity period, the disposition shall be treated for all purposes, where to do so would save it from being void for remoteness, as if it had instead been limited by reference to the time immediately before the end of that period.

[129]

6 Saving and acceleration of expectant interests

A disposition shall not be treated as void for remoteness by reason only that the interest disposed of is ulterior to and dependent upon an interest under a disposition which is so void, and the vesting of an interest shall not be prevented from being accelerated on the failure of a prior interest by reason only that the failure arises because of remoteness.

[130]

7 Powers of appointment

For the purposes of the rule against perpetuities, a power of appointment shall be treated as a special power unless—

(a) in the instrument creating the power it is expressed to be exercisable by one person only, and

(b) it could, at all times during its currency when that person is of full age and capacity, be exercised by him so as immediately to transfer to himself the whole of the interest governed by the power without the consent of any other person or compliance with any other condition, not being a formal condition relating only to the mode of exercise of the power:

Provided that for the purpose of determining whether a disposition made under a power of appointment exercisable by will only is void for remoteness, the power shall be treated as a general power where it would have fallen to be so treated if exercisable by deed.

[131]

8 Administrative powers of trustees

(1) The rule against perpetuities shall not operate to invalidate a power conferred on trustees or other persons to sell, lease, exchange or otherwise dispose of any property for full consideration, or to do any other act in the administration (as opposed to the distribution) of any property, and shall not prevent the payment to trustees or other persons of reasonable remuneration for their services.

(2) Subsection (1) above shall apply for the purpose of enabling a power to be exercised at any time after the commencement of this Act notwithstanding that the power is conferred by an instrument which took effect before that commencement.

[132]

9 Options relating to land

(1) The rule against perpetuities shall not apply to a disposition consisting of the conferring of an option to acquire for valuable consideration an interest reversionary (whether directly or indirectly) on the term of a lease if—

(a) the option is exercisable only by the lessee or his successors in title, and
(b) it ceases to be exercisable at or before the expiration of one year following the determination of the lease.

This subsection shall apply in relation to an agreement for a lease as it applies in relation to a lease, and "lessee" shall be construed accordingly.

(2) In the case of a disposition consisting of the conferring of an option to acquire for valuable consideration any interest in land, the perpetuity period under the rule against perpetuities shall be twenty-one years, and section 1 of this Act shall not apply:

Provided that this subsection shall not apply to a right of pre-emption conferred on a public or local authority in respect of land used or to be used for religious purposes where the right becomes exercisable only if the land ceases to be used for such purposes.

[133]

10 Avoidance of contractual and other rights in cases of remoteness

Where a disposition inter vivos would fall to be treated as void for remoteness if the rights and duties thereunder were capable of transmission to persons other than the original parties and had been so transmitted, it shall be treated as void as between the person by whom it was made and the person to whom or in whose favour it was made or any successor of his, and no remedy shall lie in contract or otherwise for giving effect to it or making restitution for its lack of effect.

[134]

11 Rights for enforcement of rentcharges

(1) The rule against perpetuities shall not apply to any powers or remedies for recovering or compelling the payment of an annual sum to which section 121 or 122 of the Law of Property Act 1925 applies, or otherwise becoming exercisable or enforceable on the breach of any condition or other requirement relating to that sum.

(2) …

[135]

NOTES

Sub-s (2): amends the Law of Property Act 1925, s 121(6).

12 Possibilities of reverter, conditions subsequent, exceptions and reservations

(1) In the case of—

(a) a possibility of reverter on the determination of a determinable fee simple, or
(b) a possibility of a resulting trust on the determination of any other determinable interest in property,

the rule against perpetuities shall apply in relation to the provision causing the interest to be determinable as it would apply if that provision were expressed in the form of a condition subsequent giving rise, on breach thereof, to a right of re-entry or an equivalent right in the case of property other than land, and where the provision falls to be treated as void for remoteness the determinable interest shall become an absolute interest.

(2) Where a disposition is subject to any such provision, or to any such condition subsequent, or to any exception or reservation, the disposition shall be treated for the purposes of this Act as including a separate disposition of any rights arising by virtue of the provision, condition subsequent, exception or reservation.

[136]

Accumulations

13 Amendment of s 164 of Law of Property Act 1925

(1) The periods for which accumulations of income under a settlement or other disposition are permitted by section 164 of the Law of Property Act 1925 shall include—

(a) a term of twenty-one years from the date of the making of the disposition, and
(b) the duration of the minority or respective minorities of any person or persons in being at that date.

(2) It is hereby declared that the restrictions imposed by the said section 164 apply in relation to a power to accumulate income whether or not there is a duty to exercise that power, and that they apply whether or not the power to accumulate extends to income produced by the investment of income previously accumulated.

[137]

14 Right to stop accumulations

Section 2 above shall apply to any question as to the right of beneficiaries to put an end to accumulations of income under any disposition as it applies to questions arising on the rule against perpetuities.

[138]

Supplemental

15 Short title, interpretation and extent

(1) This Act may be cited as the Perpetuities and Accumulations Act 1964.

(2) In this Act—

"disposition" includes the conferring of a power of appointment and any other disposition of an interest in or right over property, and references to the interest disposed of shall be construed accordingly;

"in being" means living or en ventre sa mere;

"power of appointment" includes any discretionary power to transfer a beneficial interest in property without the furnishing of valuable consideration;

"will" includes a codicil; and for the purposes of this Act a disposition contained in a will shall be deemed to be made at the death of the testator.

(3) For the purposes of this Act a person shall be treated as a member of a class if in his case all the conditions identifying a member of the class are satisfied, and shall be treated as a potential member if in his case some only of those conditions are satisfied but there is a possibility that the remainder will in time be satisfied.

(4) Nothing in this Act shall affect the operation of the rule of law rendering void for remoteness certain dispositions under which property is limited to be applied for purposes other than the benefit of any person or class of persons in cases where the property may be so applied after the end of the perpetuity period.

(5) The foregoing sections of this Act shall apply (except as provided in section 8(2) above) only in relation to instruments taking effect after the commencement of this Act, and in the case of an instrument made in the exercise of a special power of appointment shall apply only where the instrument creating the power takes effect after that commencement;

Provided that section 7 above shall apply in all cases for construing the foregoing reference to a special power of appointment.

(6) This Act shall apply in relation to a disposition made otherwise than by an instrument as if the disposition had been contained in an instrument taking effect when the disposition was made.

[139]

INDUSTRIAL AND PROVIDENT SOCIETIES ACT 1965

(1965 c 12)

ARRANGEMENT OF SECTIONS

Registered societies

Name and maximum shareholding

Operations of registered society

Capacity of society and power of committee to bind it

Provisions as to rules

Cancellations, suspension or refusal of registration of society or rules

Membership and special provisions affecting members

Contracts, property etc, of society

Accounts, etc

Officers, receivers, etc

An Act to consolidate certain enactments relating to industrial and provident societies, being those enactments as they apply in Great Britain and the Channel Islands with corrections and improvements made under the Consolidation of Enactments (Procedure) Act 1949

[2 June 1965]

NOTES

Industrial and Provident Societies Acts 1965 to 2003: by the Co-operatives and Community Benefit Societies Act 2003, s 9(1), this Act, the Industrial and Provident Societies Act 1967, the Friendly and Industrial and Provident Societies Act 1968, the Industrial and Provident Societies Act 1975, the Industrial and Provident Societies Act 1978, the Industrial and Provident Societies Act 2002, and the Co-operatives and Community Benefit Societies Act 2003 may be cited by this collective title.

Application with modifications: see the Credit Unions Act 1979 as to the registration of such unions under this Act and its application to them.

Registered societies

1 Societies which may be registered

(1) Subject to sections 2(1) and 7(1) of this Act, a society for carrying on any industry, business or trade (including dealings of any description with land), whether wholesale or retail, may be registered under this Act if—

(a) it is shown to the satisfaction of [the Authority] that one of the conditions specified in subsection (2) of this section is fulfilled; and

(b) the society's rules contain provision in respect of the matters mentioned in Schedule 1 to this Act; and

(c) the place which under those rules is to be the society's registered office is situated in Great Britain or the Channel Islands.

(2) The conditions referred to in subsection (1) (a) of this section are—

(a) that the society is a bona fide co-operative society; or

(b) that, in view of the fact that the business of the society is being, or is intended to be, conducted for the benefit of the community, there are special reasons why the society should be registered under this Act rather than as a company under the [Companies Act 1985].

(3) In this section, the expression "co-operative society" does not include a society which carries on, or intends to carry on, business with the object of making profits mainly for the payment of interest, dividends or bonuses on money invested or deposited with, or lent to, the society or any other person.

[140]

NOTES

Sub-s (1): words in square brackets substituted by the Financial Services and Markets Act 2000 (Mutual Societies) Order 2001, SI 2001/2617, art 13(1), Sch 3, Pt III, paras 214, 215(i).

Sub-s (2): words in square brackets substituted by the Companies Consolidation (Consequential Provisions) Act 1985, s 30, Sch 2.

2 Registration of society

(1) Subject to subsection (2) of this section—

(a) no society shall be registered under this Act if the number of the members thereof is less than [three]; and

(b) an application for the registration of a society under this Act shall be signed by [three] members and the secretary of the society and shall be sent with two printed copies of the society's rules to [the Authority].

(2) A society whose members consist solely of two or more registered societies may be registered under this Act if the application for registration is signed by ... the secretary of each [(or, if more than two, of each of any two)] of the constituent societies and is accompanied by two printed copies ... of the rules of the society sought to be registered.

(3) On being satisfied that a society has complied with the provisions of this Act as to registration thereunder, [the Authority] shall issue to the society an acknowledgment of registration [bearing the Authority's seal].

[141]

NOTES

Sub-s (1): words in first and second pairs of square brackets substituted by he Deregulation (Industrial and Provident Societies) Order 1996, SI 1996/1738, art 3(1); words in third pair of square brackets substituted by the Financial Services and Markets Act 2000 (Mutual Societies) Order 2001, SI 2001/2617, art 13(1), Sch 3, Pt III, paras 214, 215(i).

Sub-s (2): words omitted repealed and words in square brackets substituted by SI 1996/1738, art 4(1).

Sub-s (3): words in first pair of square brackets substituted by SI 2001/2617, art 13(1), Sch 3, Pt III, paras 214, 215(i); words in second pair of square brackets substituted by the Financial Services and Markets Act 2000 (Consequential Amendments and Repeals) Order 2001, SI 2001/3649, art 181(2).

3 Registration to effect incorporation of society with limited liability

A registered society shall by virtue of its registration be a body corporate by its registered name, by which it may sue and be sued, with perpetual succession and … with limited liability; and that registration shall vest in the society all property for the time being vested in any person in trust for the society, and all legal proceedings pending by or against the trustees of the society may be brought or continued by or against the society in its registered name. **[142]**

NOTES

Words omitted repealed by the Co-operatives and Community Benefit Societies Act 2003, s 5(2), (9), Schedule.

4 Existing societies deemed to be registered

Any society which at the date immediately before the commencement of this Act was registered or deemed to be registered under the Industrial and Provident Societies Act 1893 (hereafter in this Act referred to as "the Act of 1893"), being a society whose registered office was at that date in Great Britain or the Channel Islands, shall be deemed to be registered under this Act; and—

(a) any acknowledgment of registry of that society issued by virtue of section 5(4), 6 or 7(2) of the Act of 1893 shall be deemed to be an acknowledgment of the registration under this Act of that society and, by virtue of section 9 of this Act, of the rules of the society in force at the date of the acknowledgment;

(b) any acknowledgment of registry of an amendment of the society's rules issued by virtue of section 7(2) or 10(3) of the Act of 1893 shall be deemed to be an acknowledgment of the registration of that amendment under this Act;

(c) any change of the society's name duly made before the date of commencement of this Act in accordance with section 52 of the Act of 1893 as in force at the time of the change, and any change in the situation of the society's registered office of which notice was duly given before that date under section 11 of that Act, shall be deemed for the purposes of this Act to be a duly registered amendment of the society's rules;

(d) any rules of that society which, having been made before 1st January 1894, continued in force immediately before the commencement of this Act by virtue of section 3 of the Act of 1893 shall be deemed to be registered under this Act. **[143]**

NOTES

Industrial and Provident Societies Act 1893: repealed by s 77(1) of, and Sch 5 to, this Act.

Name and maximum shareholding

5 Name of society

(1) No society shall be registered under this Act under a name which in the opinion of [the Authority] is undesirable.

(2) Subject to subsection (5) of this section, [the last word in the name of every society registered under this Act shall be "limited" or, if the rules of the society state that its registered office is to be in Wales, either that word or the word "cyfyngedig"].

(3) A registered society may change its name in the following manner and in that manner only, that is to say—

(a) by a resolution for the purpose passed at a general meeting of the society after the giving of such notice as is required by the rules of the society of such a resolution or, if the rules do not make special provision as to notice of such a resolution, after the giving of such notice as is required by the rules of a resolution to amend the rules; and

(b) with the approval in writing [of the Authority].

(4) No change in the name of a registered society shall affect any right or obligation of the society, or of any member thereof, and any pending legal proceedings may be continued by or against the society notwithstanding its new name.

(5) If [the Authority] is satisfied that the objects of a society applying for registration under this Act or of a registered society are wholly charitable or benevolent, [the Authority] may register the society by a name which does not contain the word "limited" [or the word "cyfyngedig"] or, as the case may be, permit the society to change its name to one which does not contain [either of those words]; but if it subsequently appears to [the Authority] that the society, whether in consequence of a change in its rules or otherwise, is not being conducted wholly for charitable or benevolent objects, [the Authority] may direct that the word "limited"[, or in an appropriate case the word "cyfyngedig",] be added as the last word in the name of the society and shall notify the society accordingly.

(6) Every registered society shall cause its registered name to be painted or affixed, and to be kept painted or affixed, in a conspicuous position and in letters easily legible, on the outside of its registered office and every other office or place in which the business of the society is carried on, and shall have that name … mentioned in legible characters—

(a) in all notices, advertisements and other official publications of the society;
(b) in all business letters of the society;
(c) in all bills of exchange, promissory notes, endorsements, cheques, and orders for money or goods, purporting to be signed by or on behalf of the society;
(d) in all bills, invoices, receipts, and letters of credit of the society.

(7) Any officer of a registered society, or any other person acting on such a society's behalf, who—

(a) …
(b) issues or authorises the issue of any document such as is mentioned in subsection (6)(a) or (d) of this section in which [the society's registered name] is not mentioned in legible characters; or
(c) signs or authorises to be signed on behalf of the society any document such as is mentioned in subsection (6)(c) of this section in which that name is not so mentioned,

shall be liable on summary conviction to a fine not exceeding [level 3 on the standard scale] and, in the case of a conviction by virtue of paragraph (c) of this subsection, shall further be personally liable to the holder of any such document as is referred to in that paragraph for the amount specified in the document unless that amount is duly paid by the society.

[144]

NOTES

Sub-ss (1), (3): words in square brackets substituted by the Financial Services and Markets Act 2000 (Mutual Societies) Order 2001, SI 2001/2617, art 13(1), Sch 3, Pt III, paras 214, 215(i), 216(a).

Sub-s (2): words in square brackets substituted by the Welsh Language Act 1993, s 28(1), (2).

Sub-s (5): words in first, second, fifth and sixth pairs of square brackets substituted by SI 2001/2617, art 13(1), Sch 3, Pt III, paras 214, 215(i), (ii), 216(b); words in third and seventh pairs of square brackets inserted and words in fourth pair of square brackets substituted by the Welsh Language Act 1993, s 28(1), (3).

Sub-s (6): words omitted repealed by the Co-operatives and Community Benefit Societies Act 2003, s 5(3), (9), Schedule.

Sub-s (7): para (a) repealed and words in square brackets in para (b) substituted by the Co-operatives and Community Benefit Societies Act 2003, s 5(4), (9), Schedule; maximum fine increased and converted to a level on the standard scale by the Criminal Justice Act 1982, ss 37, 38, 46.

[5A Status of charitable societies to appear on correspondence etc

(1) Where a registered society is a charity and its registered name does not include the word "charity" or the word "charitable", the society must state the fact that it is a charity in legible characters—

(a) in all notices, advertisements and other official publications of the society;
(b) in all business letters of the society;
(c) in all bills of exchange, promissory notes, endorsements, cheques and orders for money or goods, purporting to be signed by or on behalf of the society;
(d) in all bills, invoices, receipts and letters of credit of the society; and
(e) in all conveyances purporting to be executed by or on behalf of the society.

(2) Where a society's registered name includes the words "elusen" or the word "elusennol", subsection (1) of this section shall not apply in relation to any document which is wholly in Welsh.

(3) The statement required by subsection (1) of this section shall be in English, except that, in the case of a document which is otherwise wholly in Welsh, the statement may be in Welsh if it consists of or includes the word "elusen" or the word "elusennol".

(4) Section 62 of this Act does not apply in respect of an offence committed by a registered society under section 61 of this Act where the offence consists of a failure to comply with this section.

(5) Any officer of a registered society, or any other person acting on such a society's behalf, who—
- (a) issues or authorises the issue of any document such as is mentioned in subsection (1)(a), (b) or (d) of this section;
- (b) signs or authorises to be signed on behalf of the society any document such as is mentioned in subsection (1)(c) of this section; or
- (c) executes or authorises to be executed on behalf of the society any document such as is mentioned in subsection (1)(e) of this section,

in which a statement required by subsection (1) is not made in accordance with this section shall be liable on summary conviction to a fine not exceeding level 3 on the standard scale.

(6) In the case of a conviction by virtue of paragraph (b) of subsection (5) of this section, the officer or other person shall further be personally liable to the holder of any such document as is referred to in that paragraph for the amount specified in the document unless that amount is duly paid by the society.

(7) In this section "charity"—
- (a) in relation to a society whose registered office is situated in England or Wales, has the same meaning as in the Charities Act 1993;
- (b) in relation to a society whose registered office is situated in Scotland, means a body established for charitable purposes only (that expression having the same meaning as in the Income Tax Acts);
- (c) in relation to a society whose registered office is situated in one of the Channel Islands, means a society established for charitable purposes only ("charitable purposes" having the meaning given by the law of the Island in question).

(8) In this section "conveyance" means any document for the creation, transfer, variation or extinction of an interest in land.

(9) In subsection (5)(c) of this section the references to execution include—
- (a) purported execution; and
- (b) the doing of any act which (though not by itself execution) combined with other acts constitutes execution or purported execution.]

[144A]

NOTES

Commencement: 1 April 2004.
Inserted by the Co-operatives and Community Benefit Societies Act 2003, s 2.

6 Maximum shareholding in society

(1) Where a society is, or is to be, registered under this Act, no member thereof other than—
- (a) a registered society; or
- (b) an authority who acquired the holding by virtue of [section [58] or 59(2) of the Housing Associations Act 1985] [or section 22 of the Housing Act 1996]; or
- (c) a member who acquired the holding by virtue of paragraph 2 of Part I of the Schedule to the Agricultural Credits Act 1923 at a time when section 2 of that Act applied to the society,

shall have or claim any interest in the shares of the society exceeding [twenty thousand pounds].

(2) Where in the case of a society to which section 4 of this Act applies—
- (a) immediately before 27th April 1952 the rules of the society provided for the maximum amount of the interest in the shares of the society permitted to be held by a member (other than a registered society) to be two hundred pounds; and
- (b) no amendment of the rules of the society has been registered since that date; and
- (c) on or after that date and before 22nd July 1961 the society's committee has by a resolution recorded in writing resolved that the said maximum amount shall be a specified amount greater than two hundred pounds but not greater than five hundred pounds,

then, subject to subsection (4) of this section, the registered rules of the society shall have effect subject to that resolution.

(3) Where in the case of a society to which section 4 of this Act applies—
(a) immediately before 22nd July 1961 the rules of the society provided for the maximum amount aforesaid to be five hundred pounds; and
(b) no amendment of the society's rules has been registered since that date; and
(c) on or after that date and before 22nd January 1963 the society's committee has by a resolution recorded in writing resolved that the said maximum amount shall be a specified amount greater than five hundred pounds but not greater than one thousand pounds,

then, subject to subsection (4) of this section, the registered rules of the society shall have effect subject to that resolution.

(4) Where subsections (2) or (3) of this section applies to any society, the society's committee shall not have power to vary or revoke the resolution referred to in that subsection; but upon the registration after the commencement of this Act under section 10 thereof of any amendment of the society's rules the registered rules of the society shall have effect as if the resolution had not been passed, so, however, that this subsection shall not affect any interest in the shares of the society held by a member immediately before the date of that registration.
[145]

NOTES

Sub-s (1): words in first (outer) pair of square brackets substituted by the Housing (Consequential Provisions) Act 1985, s 4, Sch 2, para 8; figure in second (inner) pair of square brackets substituted and words in third pair of square brackets inserted by the Housing Act 1996 (Consequential Amendments) (No 2) Order 1997, SI 1997/627, art 2, Schedule, para 1; words in the final pair of square brackets substituted the Industrial and Provident Societies (Increase in Shareholding Limit) Order 1994, SI 1994/341, art 3.

Agricultural Credits Act 1923, Schedule, Pt I, para 2: repealed by the Statute Law Revision Act 1950.

Operations of registered society

7 Carrying on of banking by societies

(1) A society which has any withdrawable share capital—
(a) shall not be registered with the object of carrying on, and
(b) if a registered society shall not carry on,

the business of banking.

(2) Every registered society which carries on the business of banking shall on the first Monday in February and August in each year make out, and until the next such Monday keep hung up in a conspicuous position in its registered office and in every other office or place of business belonging to the society where the business of banking is carried on, a statement in the form set out in Schedule 2 to this Act or as near thereto as the circumstances admit.

(3) The taking of deposits of not more than [four hundred pounds] in any one payment and not more than [four hundred pounds] for any one depositor, payable on not less than two clear days' notice, shall not be treated for the purposes of subsections (1) and (2) of this section as carrying on the business of banking; but no society which takes such deposits shall make any payment of withdrawable capital while any payment due on account of any such deposit is unsatisfied.

(4) Where, in the case of a society to which section 4 of this Act applies, being a society registered under the Act of 1893 before 27th April 1952—
(a) no amendment of the society's registered rules has been registered since that date; and
(b) those rules permit the taking of deposits up to, but not in excess of, ten shillings in any one payment and twenty pounds for any one depositor; and
(c) the society's committee has since that date by a resolution recorded in writing, whether passed before or after the commencement of this Act, resolved that there shall be substituted for the said limits of ten shillings and twenty pounds specified higher limits not exceeding two pounds and fifty pounds respectively,

then, subject to subsection (5) of this section, the society's registered rules shall have effect subject to that resolution.

(5) Where subsection (4) of this section applies to any society, the society's committee shall not have power to vary or revoke any resolution such as is mentioned in paragraph (c) of

that subsection; but upon the registration after the commencement of this Act under section 10 thereof of any amendment of the rules of the society—

(a) the registered rules of the society shall have effect as if any such resolution had not been passed; and

(b) if not already exercised, the power of the society's committee to pass such a resolution shall determine,

so, however, that paragraph (a) of this subsection shall not affect any sums standing deposited with the society immediately before the date of registration of the amendment.

(6) Any registered society which—

(a) carries on the business of banking in contravention of subsection (1) of this section; or

(b) fails to comply with subsection (2) of this section; or

(c) makes any payment of withdrawable capital in contravention of subsection (3) of this section,

shall be liable on summary conviction to a fine not exceeding [level 1 on the standard scale].

[146]

NOTES

Sub-s (3): words in square brackets substituted by the Industrial and Provident Societies (Increase in Deposit-taking Limits) Order 1981, SI 1981/394, art 3.

Sub-s (6): maximum fine increased by the Criminal Law Act 1977, s 31(6), (9), and converted to a level on the standard scale by the Criminal Justice Act 1982, ss 37, 46.

Act of 1893: the Industrial and Provident Societies Act 1893: repealed by s 77(1) of, and Sch 5 to, this Act.

[Capacity of society and power of committee to bind it

7A Capacity of society not limited by its rules

(1) The validity of an act done by a registered society shall not be called into question on the ground of lack of capacity by reason of anything in the society's registered rules.

(2) A member of a registered society may bring proceedings to restrain the doing of an act which but for subsection (1) of this section would be beyond the society's capacity; but no such proceedings shall lie in respect of an act to be done in fulfilment of a legal obligation arising from a previous act of the society.

(3) It remains the duty of the members of the committee of a registered society to observe any limitations on their powers flowing from the society's registered rules; and action by the members of the committee which but for subsection (1) of this section would be beyond the society's capacity may only be ratified by the society by special resolution.

(4) A resolution ratifying such action shall not affect any liability incurred by a member of the committee or any other person; relief from any such liability must be agreed to separately by special resolution.

(5) The operation of this section is restricted by section 7D of this Act (application to charitable societies); and section 7E of this Act (transactions with members of the committee and connected persons in excess of powers) has effect notwithstanding this section.

(6) In this section "special resolution" means a resolution passed by not less than 75% of such members of the society as (being entitled to do so) vote in person, or by proxy where the society's rules allow proxies, at a general meeting of which not less than 21 days' notice, specifying the intention to propose the resolution, has been duly given according to those rules.

(7) A copy of every special resolution for the purposes of this section signed by the chairman of the meeting at which the resolution was passed and countersigned by the secretary of the society shall be sent to the Authority and registered by it; and until that copy is so registered the special resolution shall not take effect.]

[146A]

NOTES

Commencement: 1 April 2004.

Inserted, together with preceding cross-heading and ss 7B–7F, by the Co-operatives and Community Benefit Societies Act 2003, s 3.

[7B Power of committee to bind society

(1) In favour of a person dealing with a registered society in good faith, the power of the committee to bind the society, or authorise others to do so, shall be deemed to be free of any limitation under the society's registered rules.

(2) For this purpose—

(a) a person "deals with" a society if he is a party to any transaction or other act to which the society is a party;

(b) a person shall not be regarded as acting in bad faith by reason only of his knowing that an act is beyond the powers of the committee under the society's registered rules; and

(c) a person shall be presumed to have acted in good faith unless the contrary is proved.

(3) The references above to limitations on the powers of the committee under the society's registered rules include limitations deriving—

(a) from a resolution of the society in general meeting or a meeting of any class of members; or

(b) from any agreement between the members of the society or of any class of members.

(4) Subsection (1) of this section does not affect any right of a member of the society to bring proceedings to restrain the doing of an act which is beyond the powers of the committee; but no such proceedings shall lie in respect of an act to be done in fulfilment of a legal obligation arising from a previous act of the society.

(5) Nor does subsection (1) affect any liability incurred by a member of the committee, or any other person, by reason of the committee's exceeding its powers.

(6) The operation of this section is restricted by section 7D of this Act (application to charitable societies); and section 7E of this Act (transactions with members of the committee and connected persons in excess of powers) has effect notwithstanding this section.

[146B]

NOTES

Commencement: 1 April 2004.
Inserted as noted to s 7A at **[146A]**.

[7C No duty to enquire as to capacity of society or authority of committee

A party to a transaction with a registered society is not bound to enquire as to whether it is permitted by the society's registered rules or as to any limitation on the powers of the committee to bind the society or authorise others to do so.]

[146C]

NOTES

Commencement: 1 April 2004.
Inserted as noted to s 7A at **[146A]**.

[7D Application of sections 7A and 7B to charitable societies

(1) Sections 7A and 7B of this Act (capacity of society not limited by its rules and power of committee to bind society) do not apply to the acts of a registered society which is a charity except in favour of a person who—

(a) gives full consideration in money or money's worth in relation to the act in question; and

(b) does not know that the act is not permitted by the society's registered rules or, as the case may be, is beyond the powers of the committee,

or who does not know at the time the act is done that the society is a charity.

(2) However, where such a society purports to transfer or grant an interest in property, the fact that the act was not permitted by the society's registered rules or, as the case may be, that the committee in connection with the act exceeded any limitation on its powers under those rules, does not affect the title of a person who subsequently acquires the property or any interest in it for full consideration without actual notice of any such circumstances affecting the validity of the society's act.

(3) In any proceedings arising out of subsection (1) of this section the burden of proving—

(a) that a person knew that an act was not permitted by the society's registered rules or was beyond the powers of the committee, or

(b) that a person knew that the society was a charity,

lies on the person making that allegation.

(4) Where a registered society is a charity with its registered office situated in England or Wales, the ratification of an act under section 7A(3) of this Act, or the ratification of a transaction to which section 7E of this Act applies, is ineffective without the prior written consent of the [Charity Commission] for England and Wales.

(5) In this section "charity"—

(a) in relation to a society whose registered office is situated in England or Wales, has the same meaning as in the Charities Act 1993;

(b) in relation to a society whose registered office is situated in Scotland, means a body established for charitable purposes only (that expression having the same meaning as in the Income Tax Acts);

(c) in relation to a society whose registered office is situated in one of the Channel Islands, means a society established for charitable purposes only ("charitable purposes" having the meaning given by the law of the Island in question).]

[146D]

NOTES

Commencement: 1 April 2004.
Inserted as noted to s 7A at **[146A]**.
Sub-s (4): words in square brackets substituted by the Charities Act 2006, s 75(1), Sch 8, para 47.

[7E Transactions with committee members and other persons in excess of powers

(1) This section applies where a registered society enters into a transaction to which the parties include—

(a) a member of the committee of the society, or

(b) a person connected with such a member or a company with whom such a member is associated,

and the committee of the society, in connection with the transaction, exceeds any limitation on its powers under the society's registered rules.

(2) The transaction is voidable at the instance of the society.

(3) Whether or not it is avoided, any such party to the transaction as is mentioned in subsection (1)(a) or (b) of this section, and any member of the committee who authorised the transaction, is liable—

(a) to account to the society for any gain which he has made directly or indirectly by the transaction; and

(b) to indemnify the society for any loss or damage resulting from the transaction.

(4) Nothing in the above provisions shall be construed as excluding the operation of any other enactment or rule of law by virtue of which the transaction may be called in question or any liability to the society may arise.

(5) The transaction ceases to be voidable if—

(a) restitution of any money or other asset which was the subject-matter of the transaction is no longer possible; or

(b) the society is indemnified for any loss or damage resulting from the transaction; or

(c) rights acquired bona fide for value and without actual notice of the committee's exceeding its powers by a person who is not party to the transaction would be affected by the avoidance; or

(d) the transaction is ratified by the society in general meeting in such a way as the case may require.

(6) A person other than a member of the committee is not liable under subsection (3) of this section if he shows that at the time the transaction was entered into he did not know that the committee was exceeding its powers.

(7) This section does not affect the operation of section 7B of this Act in relation to any party to the transaction not within subsection (1)(a) or (b) of this section.

(8) But where a transaction is voidable by virtue of this section and valid by virtue of that section in favour of such a person, the court may, on the application of that person or of the society, make such order affirming, severing or setting aside the transaction, on such terms, as appear to the court to be just.]

[146E]

NOTES

Commencement: 1 April 2004.
Inserted as noted to s 7A at **[146A]**.

[7F Definitions relating to section 7E

(1) In section 7E of this Act "transaction" includes any act; and the reference in subsection (1) of that section to limitations under the society's registered rules includes limitations deriving—

(a) from a resolution of the society in general meeting or a meeting of any class of members; or
(b) from any agreement between the members of the society or of any class of members.

(2) In section 7E(1) of this Act "company" has the same meaning as in the Companies Act 1985.

(3) Section 346(2) to (8) of the Companies Act 1985 shall apply for the purposes of references in section 7E(1) of this Act to a person's being "connected" with a committee member or to a committee member's being "associated with" a company, but shall so apply—

(a) as if any reference to a director of a company were a reference to a member of a committee of a registered society; and
(b) subject to such other adaptations and modifications as may be specified by regulations made by the Treasury under this section.

(4) Any regulations made under this section shall be made by statutory instrument which shall be subject to annulment in pursuance of a resolution of either House of Parliament.

(5) In section 7E(4) of this Act "enactment" includes an enactment comprised in—

(a) an Act of the Scottish Parliament;
(b) subordinate legislation, whether made under an Act or an Act of the Scottish Parliament.

(6) In section 7E(8) of this Act "the court", in relation to a registered society, means the court having jurisdiction to wind up the society under the provisions of the Insolvency Act 1986 as applied by section 55 of this Act.]

[146F]–[147]

NOTES

Commencement: 1 April 2004.
Inserted as noted to s 7A at **[146A]**.

8 *(Repealed by the Financial Services and Markets Act 2000, ss 338(3), 432(3), Sch 18, Pt IV, para 19, Sch 22.)*

Provisions as to rules

9 Acknowledgment of registration of rules

Without prejudice to section 53(3) of this Act, an acknowledgment of the registration of a society issued under section 2(3) of this Act shall also constitute an acknowledgment, and be conclusive evidence, of the registration under this Act of the rules of that society in force at the date of the society's registration.

[148]

10 Amendment of registered rules

(1) Subject to subsection (2) of this section, any amendment of a society's rules as for the time being registered under this Act shall not be valid until the amendment has been so registered, for which purpose there shall be sent to [the Authority] two copies of the amendment signed—

(a) in the case of a society for the time being consisting solely of registered societies, by the secretary of the society and by … the secretary of each [(or, if more than two, of each of any two)] of the constituent societies;

(b) in any other case, by three members and the secretary of the society.

(2) The foregoing subsection shall not apply to a change in the situation of a society's registered office or in the name of a society; but—

(a) notice of any change in the situation of a society's registered office shall be sent to [the Authority]; and

(b) where such a notice is duly sent, or where a change in the name of a registered society is made in accordance with section 5(3) of this Act, the change in the situation of the society's registered office or, as the case may be, the change in the society's name shall be registered by [the Authority] as an amendment of the society's rules.

(3) [The Authority], on being satisfied that any amendment of a society's rules is not contrary to the provisions of this Act, shall issue to the society in respect of that amendment an acknowledgment of registration [bearing the Authority's seal].

[149]

NOTES

Sub-s (1): words in first pair of square brackets substituted by the Financial Services and Markets Act 2000 (Mutual Societies) Order 2001, SI 2001/2617, art 13(1), Sch 3, Pt III, paras 214, 215(i); words omitted repealed and words in second pair of square brackets substituted by the Deregulation (Industrial and Provident Societies) Order 1996, SI 1996/1738, art 4(2).

Sub-s (2): words in square brackets substituted by SI 2001/2617, art 13(1), Sch 3, Pt III, paras 214, 215(i).

Sub-s (3): words in first pair of square brackets substituted by SI 2001/2617, art 13(1), Sch 3, Pt III, paras 214, 215(i); words in second pair of square brackets substituted by the Financial Services and Markets Act 2000 (Consequential Amendments and Repeals) Order 2001, SI 2001/3649, art 181(2).

11 Rules as to fund for purchase of government securities

(1) The rules of a society registered or to be registered under this Act may make provision for the setting up and administration by the society of a fund for the purchase on behalf of the members contributing to the fund of defence bonds or national saving certificates or such other securities of Her Majesty's Government in the United Kingdom as may for the time being be prescribed under [section 47(1) of the Friendly Societies Act 1974] by the [Treasurer]; and any such rules may make provision for enabling persons to become members of the society for the purpose only of contributing to that fund and without being entitled to any rights as members other than rights as contributors to that fund.

(2) Any rule which, immediately before the commencement of this Act, was included among the registered rules of a registered society by virtue of section 8(3) of the [Societies (Miscellaneous Provisions) Act 1940] shall have effect as if it had been duly passed by the society.

[150]

NOTES

Sub-s (1): words in first pair of square brackets substituted by the Friendly Societies Act 1974, s 116(1), Sch 9, para 8; word in second pair of square brackets substituted by the Financial Services and Markets Act 2000 (Mutual Societies) Order 2001, SI 2001/2617, art 13(1), Sch 3, Pt III, paras 214, 217.

Sub-s (2): words in first pair of square brackets substituted by the Friendly Societies Act 1974, s 116(1), Sch 9, para 8.

Societies (Miscellaneous Provisions) Act 1940, s 8(3): repealed by the Friendly Societies Act 1974, s 116(4), Sch 11 and replaced by s 47(1)–(3) of that Act.

12 Rules of agricultural, horticultural or forestry society

Where a society registered or to be registered under this Act consists mainly of members who are producers of agricultural or horticultural produce or persons engaged in forestry, or organisations of such producers or persons so engaged, and the object or principal object of the society is the making to its members of advances of money for agricultural, horticultural or forestry purposes, registration under this Act of the rules of the society or any amendment thereof shall not be refused on the ground that the rules provide, or would as amended provide, for the making of such advances without security.

[151]

13 Supplementary provisions as to rules

(1) The rules of a registered society or any schedule thereto may specify the form of any instrument necessary for carrying the purposes of the society into effect.

(2) The rules of a registered society may impose reasonable fines on persons who contravene or fail to comply with any of those rules.

(3) Any fine imposed by the rules of a registered society shall be recoverable on the summary conviction of the offender.

(4) Any provision of, or of any instrument made under, this or any other Act requiring or authorising the rules of a registered society to deal with particular matters shall be without prejudice to the power of such a society to make rules with respect to any other matter which are not inconsistent with any such provision or with any other provision of this or any other Act and which are not otherwise unlawful.

[152]

14 Rules to bind members

(1) Subject to subsections (2) and (3) of this section, the registered rules of a registered society shall bind the society and all members thereof and all persons claiming through them respectively to the same extent as if each member had subscribed his name and affixed his seal thereto and there were contained in those rules a covenant on the part of each member and any person claiming through him to conform thereto subject to the provisions of this Act.

(2) A member of a registered society shall not, without his consent in writing having been first obtained, be bound by any amendment of the society's rules registered after he became a member, being an amendment registered after 27th March 1928, if and so far as that amendment requires him to take or subscribe for more shares than the number held by him at the date of registration of the amendment, or to pay upon the shares so held any sum exceeding the amount unpaid upon them at that date, or in any other way increases the liability of that member to contribute to the share or loan capital of the society.

(3) In the case of a society to which section 4 of this Act applies which was a registered society under the Act of 1893 on 1st January 1894, the society or the members thereof may respectively exercise any power given by this Act and not made to depend on the provisions of the society's rules notwithstanding anything in any of those rules registered before 12th September 1893.

(4) (*Applies to Scotland only.*)

[153]

NOTES

Act of 1893: the Industrial and Provident Societies Act 1893: repealed by s 77(1) of, and Sch 5 to, this Act.

15 Provision of copies of rules

(1) A copy of the registered rules of any registered society shall be delivered by the society to any person who demands it, subject to payment by that person of such sum not exceeding [10 pence] as the society may see fit to charge.

(2) If any person, with intent to mislead or defraud, gives to any other person—

(a) a copy of any rules other than rules for the time being registered under this Act on the pretence that they are the existing rules, or that there are no other rules, of a registered society; or

(b) a copy of the rules of a society which is not registered under this Act on the pretence that they are the rules of a registered society,

he shall be liable on summary conviction to a fine not exceeding [level 1 on the standard scale].

[154]

NOTES

Sub-s (1): words in square brackets substituted by virtue of the Decimal Currency Act 1969, s 10(1).

Sub-s (2): maximum fine increased by the Criminal Law Act 1977, s 31(6), (9), and converted to a level on the standard scale by the Criminal Justice Act 1982, ss 37, 46.

manner as [the Authority] shall from time to time direct;

(c) ...

(i) on proof to [the Authority's] satisfaction that the society exists for an illegal purpose, or has wilfully and after notice from [the Authority] violated any of the provisions of this Act or any enactment repealed thereby; or

(ii) if at any time it appears to [the Authority] that neither of the conditions specified in section 1(2) of this Act is fulfilled in the case of that society; or

(iii) in the case of a society whose registered rules contain such a provision as is authorised by section 12 of this Act, if it appears to [the Authority] that the society no longer consists mainly of such members as are mentioned in that section or that the activities carried on by it do not mainly consist in making advances to its members for such purposes as are so mentioned.

(2) Subsection (1)(c)(ii) of this section shall not authorise the cancellation of the registration of any society to which section 4 of this Act applies which was registered or deemed to be registered under the Act of 1893 before 26th July 1938 if no invitation to subscribe for or to acquire or offer to acquire securities, or to lend or deposit money, has been made on or after that date by or on behalf of the society.

(3) Not less than two months previous notice in writing specifying briefly the ground of the proposed cancellation shall be given by the appropriate registrar to a society before its registration is cancelled otherwise than—

(a) at its own request; or

(b) by virtue of section 52(4) of this Act; or

(c) after the lodging with the appropriate registrar of such a certificate as is referred to in section 59 of this Act;

and if before the expiration of the period of that notice the society duly lodges an appeal under section 18(1)(c) of this Act, then, without prejudice to section 17(2) of this Act, the society's registration shall not be cancelled before the date of the determination or abandonment of the appeal.

(4) Where the ground specified in any notice under subsection (3) of this section is that referred to in subsection (1)(c)(ii) thereof—

(a) [the Authority] shall consider any representations with respect to the proposed cancellation made to [the Authority] by the society within the period of duration of the notice and, if the society so requests, afford it an opportunity of being heard by [the Authority] before its registration is cancelled;

(b) if it appears to [the Authority] at any time after the expiration of one month from the date of the giving of the notice that there have not been taken the steps which by that time could reasonably have been taken for the purpose—

(i) of converting the society into, or amalgamating it with, or transferring its engagements to, a company in accordance with section 52 of this Act; or

(ii) of dissolving the society under section 55 of this Act, [the Authority] may give such directions as [it] thinks fit for securing that the affairs of the society are wound up before cancellation of the registration takes effect.

(5) Any person who contravenes or fails to comply with any directions given by [the Authority] under subsection (4)(b) of this section shall be liable on summary conviction to a fine not exceeding [level 3 on the standard scale] *or to imprisonment for a term not exceeding three months or to both.*

[notice in writing] suspend the society's registration from the expiration of that period until the date of the determination or abandonment of the appeal.

(3) Not less than two months previous notice in writing specifying briefly the ground of the proposed suspension shall be given by [the Authority] to a society before its registration is suspended under subsection (1)(a) of this section.

(4) Notice of every suspension of a society's registration under subsection (1)(a) or (2) of this section and of any renewal of a suspension under subsection (1)(b) thereof shall, as soon as practicable after it takes place, be published in the Gazette and in some local newspaper circulating in or about the locality in which the society's registered office is situated.

(5) From the date of publication in the Gazette of a notice under subsection (4) of this section of the suspension of any society's registration under subsection (1)(a) or (2) of this section until the period of that suspension and any renewal thereof under subsection (1)(b) of this section ends (whether on the expiration of that period or on a successful appeal under section 18(1)(d) of this Act from such a renewal) the society shall not be entitled to any of the privileges of this Act as a registered society, but without prejudice to any liability actually incurred by the society which may be enforced against it as if the suspension had not taken place.

(6) …

[156]

NOTES

Sub-s (1): words in square brackets substituted, and words omitted repealed, by the Financial Services and Markets Act 2000 (Mutual Societies) Order 2001, SI 2001/2617, art 13(1), (2), Sch 3, Pt III, paras 214, 215(i), (ii), 220(a), Sch 4.

Sub-ss (2), (3): words in square brackets substituted by SI 2001/2617, art 13(1), Sch 3, Pt III, paras 214, 215(i), 220(b).

Sub-s (6): repealed by SI 2001/2617, art 13(1), Sch 3, Pt III, paras 214, 220(c), Sch 4.

18 Appeal from refusal, cancellation or suspension of registration of society or rules

(1) A society may appeal from any decision of [the Authority]—

(a) to refuse registration of the society (including a refusal by reason only of anything contained in or omitted from the society's rules) on any ground other than that [the Authority] is not satisfied that either of the conditions specified in section 1(2) of this Act is fulfilled; or

(b) to refuse registration of any amendment of the society's rules; or

(c) to cancel the society's registration (being a cancellation of which notice is required under section 16(3), and not being a cancellation by virtue of section 16(1)(c)(ii), of this Act) if the appeal is lodged before the expiration of the period of notice of the proposed cancellation given under the said section 16(3); or

(d) to renew under section 17(1)(b) of this Act a suspension of the society's registration so far as that renewal provides for the suspension to continue more than three months from the original date of suspension.

(2) An appeal under the foregoing subsection shall lie [to the High Court or, in the case of a society whose registered office is situated in Scotland, to the Court of Session.]

(3) If any decision such as is mentioned in subsection (1)(a) or (b) of this section is overruled on appeal, [the Authority] shall thereupon issue to the society an acknowledgment of registration of the society under section 2(3), or, as the case may be, of the amendment under section 10(3), of this Act.

[157]

NOTES

Sub-s (1): words in square brackets substituted, and words omitted repealed, by the Financial Services and Markets Act 2000 (Mutual Societies) Order 2001, SI 2001/2617, art 13(1), Sch 3, Pt III, paras 214, 215(i), (ii), 221(a).

Sub-s (2): words in square brackets substituted for paras (a), (b) by SI 2001/2617, art 13(1), Sch 3, Pt III, paras 214, 215(i), 221(b).

Sub-s (3): words in square brackets substituted by SI 2001/2617, art 13(1), Sch 3, Pt III, paras 214, 215(i).

Membership and special provisions affecting members

19 Bodies corporate as members of society

(1) Shares in a registered society may be held by any other body corporate (if that body's regulations so permit) by its corporate name.

(2) Where a registered society is a member of another registered society, then, for the purposes of any enactment with respect to the making or signing of any application, instrument or document by members of a registered society, any reference therein to such a member shall, in relation to the first-mentioned society as a member of the second-mentioned society, be construed as a reference to two members of the committee and the secretary of the society.

[158]

20 Members under [18]

A person under the age of [eighteen] but above the age of sixteen may be a member of a registered society unless provision to the contrary is made by the society's registered rules and may, subject to those rules and to the provisions of this Act, enjoy all the rights of a member and execute all instruments and give all receipts necessary to be executed or given under those rules, but shall not be a member of the committee, trustee, manager or treasurer of the society.

[159]

NOTES

Words in square brackets substituted by the Family Law Reform Act 1969, ss 1(3), 28(3), Sch 1, Pt I; the section heading has been adjusted accordingly.

21 Advance to members

Without prejudice to any provision included by virtue of section 12 of this Act, the rules of a registered society may provide for advances of money to members—

(a) on the security of real or personal property or, in Scotland, of heritable or moveable estate; or

(b) if the society is registered to carry on banking business, in any manner customary in the conduct of such business.

[160]

22 Remedy for debts from members

(1) All moneys payable to a registered society by a member thereof shall be a debt due from that member to the society and shall be recoverable as such in the county court, or, in Scotland, before the sheriff, within whose jurisdiction the society's registered office is situate or within whose jurisdiction the member resides, at the option of the society.

(2) A registered society shall have a lien on the shares of any member for any debt due to the society by that member, and may set off any sum credited to the member on those shares in or towards the payment of that debt.

[161]

23 Nomination to property in society

(1) Subject to subsections (2) and (3) of this section, a member of a registered society may, by a written statement signed by him and delivered at or sent to the society's registered office during his lifetime or made in any book kept at that office, nominate a person or persons to become entitled at his death to the whole, or to such part or respective parts as may be specified in the nomination, of any property in the society (whether in shares, loans or deposits or otherwise) which he may have—

(a) in the case of a nomination made before 1st January 1914, at the date of the nomination; or

(b) in any other case, at the time of his death.

(2) The nomination by a member of a society under the foregoing subsection of a person who is at the date of the nomination an officer or servant of the society shall not be valid unless that person is the [spouse, civil partner,] father, mother, child, brother, sister, nephew or niece of the nominator.

(3) For the purposes of the disposal of any property which is the subject of a nomination under subsection (1) of this section—

(a) if the nomination was made before 1st January 1914 and at the date of the nomination the amount credited to the nominator in the society's books exceeded one hundred pounds, the nomination shall not be valid;

(b) if the nomination was made after 31st December 1913 and before 5th August 1954 and at the date of the nominator's death the amount of his property in the society comprised in the nomination exceeds one hundred pounds, the nomination shall be valid to the extent of one hundred pounds but not further or otherwise;

(c) if the nomination was made after 4th August 1954 and at the date of the nominator's death the amount of his property in the society comprised in the nomination exceeds [£5,000], the nomination shall be valid to the extent of [£5,000], but not further or otherwise.

(4) A nomination by a member of a society under subsection (1) of this section may be varied or revoked by a subsequent nomination by him thereunder or by any similar document in the nature of a revocation or variation signed by the nominator and delivered at or sent to the society's registered office during his lifetime, but shall not be revocable or variable by the will of the nominator or by any codicil thereto.

(5) Every registered society shall keep a book in which the names of all persons nominated under subsection (1) of this section and any revocation or variation of any nomination under that subsection shall be recorded.

(6) The marriage of a member of a society shall operate as a revocation of any nomination made by him before the marriage and after 31st December 1913; but if any property of that member has been transferred by an officer of the society in pursuance of that nomination in ignorance of a marriage contracted by the nominator subsequent to the date of the nomination, the receipt of the nominee shall be a valid discharge to the society and the society shall be under no liability to any other person claiming the property.

[(7) The formation of a civil partnership by a member of a society revokes any nomination made by him before the formation of the civil partnership; but if any property of that member has been transferred by an officer of the society in pursuance of the nomination in ignorance of a civil partnership formed by the nominator after the date of the nomination—

(a) the receipt of the nominee shall be a valid discharge to the society, and

(b) the society shall be under no liability to any other person claiming the property.]

[162]

NOTES

Sub-s (2): words in square brackets substituted by the Civil Partnership Act 2004, s 261(1), Sch 27, para 24(1), (2).

Sub-s (3): sums in square brackets substituted by virtue of the Administration of Estates (Small Payments) (Increase of Limit) Order 1984, SI 1984/539, in relation to deaths occurring after 11 May 1984.

Sub-s (7): added by the Civil Partnership Act 2004, s 261(1), Sch 27, para 24(1), (3).

24 Proceedings on death of nominator

(1) Subject to subsections (2) and (4) of this section, where any member of a registered society has made a nomination under section 23 of this Act, the committee of the society, on receiving satisfactory proof of the death of that member, and if and to the extent that the nomination is valid under subsections (2) and (3) of that section, shall in the case of each person entitled under the nomination either transfer to him, or pay him the full value of, any property to which he is so entitled.

(2) Where any of the property comprised in such a nomination as aforesaid consists of shares in the society, the foregoing subsection shall have effect notwithstanding that the rules of the society declare the shares therein not to be transferable; but if the transfer of any shares comprised in the nomination in the manner directed by the nominator would raise the share capital of any nominee beyond the maximum for the time being permitted in the case of that society, the committee of the society shall not transfer to that nominee more of those shares than will raise his share capital to that maximum and shall pay him the value of any of those shares not transferred.

(3) Where any sum falls to be paid under the foregoing provisions of this section to a nominee who is under sixteen years of age, the society may pay that sum to either parent, or to a guardian, of the nominee or to any other person of full age who will undertake to hold it in trust for the nominee or to apply it for his benefit and whom the society may think a fit and proper person for the purpose, and the receipt of that parent, guardian or other person shall be a sufficient discharge to the society for all moneys so paid.

(4) …

[163]

NOTES

Sub-s (4): repealed by the Administration of Estates (Small Payments) Act 1965, ss 4(1), (3), 7(6), Sch 4.

25 Provision for intestacy

(1) If any member of a registered society dies … and at his death his property in the society in respect of shares, loans or deposits does not exceed in the whole [£5,000] and is not the subject of any nomination under section 23 of this Act, then, *subject to subsection (2) of this section,* the committee of the society may, without letters of administration [or probate of any will] or, in Scotland, without confirmation having been obtained, distribute that property among such persons as appear to the committee on such evidence as they deem satisfactory to be entitled by law to receive it.

(2) If the member aforesaid was illegitimate [and leaves no widow, widower[, surviving civil partner] or issue (including any illegitimate child of the member) and neither of his parents survives him] the committee shall deal with his property in the society as the Treasury shall direct.

[164]

NOTES

Sub-s (1): words omitted repealed and words in second pair of square brackets substituted by the Administration of Estates (Small Payments) Act 1965, ss 3, 7(5), Schs 3, 4; sum in square brackets substituted by virtue of the Administration of Estates (Small Payments) (Increase of Limit) Order 1984, SI 1984/539, in relation to deaths occurring after 11 May 1984; words in italics repealed, in relation to Scotland, by the Family Law (Scotland) Act 2006, s 45(2), Sch 3.

Sub-s (2): repealed, in relation to Scotland, by the Family Law (Scotland) Act 2006, s 45(2), Sch 3; words in first (outer) pair of square brackets substituted by the Family Law Reform Act 1969, s 19(2), (3); words in second (inner) pair of square brackets substituted by the Civil Partnership Act 2004, s 261(1), Sch 27, para 25.

26 Payments in respect of mentally incapable persons

(1) Subject to subsection (2) of this section, where in the case of a member of a registered society or a person claiming through such a member the society's committee are satisfied after considering medical evidence that the member or person is incapable through disorder or disability of mind of managing his own affairs and are also satisfied that no person has been duly appointed to administer his property on his behalf, and it is proved to the satisfaction of the committee that it is just and expedient so to do, the society may pay the amount of any shares, loans, and deposits belonging to that member or person to any person whom they judge proper to receive it on his behalf, whose receipt shall be a good discharge to the society for any sum so paid.

(2) The foregoing subsection shall not apply when the member or person in question is—

(a) a patient within the meaning of Part VIII of the Mental Health Act 1959; or

(b) a person as to whom powers are exercisable and have been exercised under section 104 of that Act.

[165]

NOTES

Sub-s (2): substituted as follows by the Mental Capacity Act 2005, s 67(1), Sch 6, para 11, as from a day to be appointed under s 68(1) of that Act—

"(2) Subsection (1) does not apply where the member or person concerned lacks capacity (within the meaning of the Mental Capacity Act 2005) for the purposes of this Act and—

(a) there is a donee of an enduring power of attorney or lasting power of attorney (within the meaning of the 2005 Act), or a deputy appointed for the member or person by the Court of Protection, and

(b) the donee or deputy has power in relation to the member or person for the purposes of this Act.".

Mental Health Act 1959, Pt VIII, s 104: repealed by the Mental Health Act 1983, s 148(3), Sch 6 and replaced by Pt VII and s 98 of that Act respectively.

27 Validity of payment to persons apparently entitled

All payments or transfers made by the committee of a registered society under section 25 or 26(1) of this Act or any corresponding provision of any Act repealed by this Act to any person appearing to the committee at the time of the payment or transfer to be entitled thereunder shall be valid and effectual against any demand made upon the committee or society by any other person.

[166]

Contracts, property etc, of society

28 Promissory notes and bills of exchange

A promissory note or bill of exchange shall be deemed to have been made, accepted or endorsed on behalf of any registered society if made, accepted or endorsed in the name of the society or by or on behalf or account of the society, by any person acting under the authority of the society.

[167]

29 Contracts

(1) Any contract which, if made between private persons, would be by law required to be in writing and, if made according to English law, to be under seal may be made, varied or discharged on behalf of a registered society in writing under the common seal of the society; and any contract which may be or have been made, varied or discharged in accordance with

this subsection shall, so far as concerns its form, be effectual in law and binding on all parties thereto, their heirs, executors or administrators, as the case may be.

(2) A signature purporting to be made by a person holding any office in a registered society attached to a writing whereby any contract purports to be made, varied or discharged by or on behalf of the society shall, until the contrary is proved, be taken to be the signature of a person holding that office at the time when the signature was made.

(3) Subsection (1) of this section shall not apply to Scotland; and nothing in that subsection shall prejudice the operation in England and Wales of the Corporate Bodies' Contracts Act 1960.

[168]

[29A Purported contracts, deeds and obligations

(1) A contract which purports to be made by or on behalf of a registered society at a time when the society has not been registered under this Act has effect, subject to any agreement to the contrary, as one made with the person purporting to act for the society or as agent for it.

(2) Accordingly, the contract is to be treated—

(a) as imposing on that person all the obligations it purports to impose on the society; and

(b) as conferring on him all the rights it purports to confer on the society.

(3) Subsections (1) and (2) of this section apply—

(a) to the making of a deed under the law of England and Wales, and

(b) to the undertaking of an obligation under the law of Scotland,

as they apply to the making of a contract.]

[168A]

NOTES

Commencement: 20 October 2003 (in relation to contracts or deeds made, and obligations undertaken, on or after that date).

Inserted by the Co-operatives and Community Benefit Societies Act 2003, s 4(1).

[29B Common seal

(1) Notwithstanding any enactment or rule of law, a registered society need not have a common seal.

(2) If a registered society has a common seal, the society shall have its registered name engraved on the seal in legible characters.

(3) If, after the coming into force of subsection (1) of this section, a registered society decides to have a common seal, it shall not cause such a seal to be made unless the registered rules of the society contain provision for the custody and use of that seal.

(4) Section 62 of this Act does not apply in respect of an offence committed by a registered society under section 61 of this Act where the offence consists of a failure to comply with subsection (2) or (3) of this section.

(5) Any officer of a registered society, or any other person acting on such a society's behalf, who uses or authorises the use of any seal purporting to be the common seal of the society which does not have the society's registered name engraved on it in legible characters shall be liable on summary conviction to a fine not exceeding level 3 on the standard scale.

(6) In this section "enactment" includes an enactment comprised in—

(a) an Act of the Scottish Parliament;

(b) subordinate legislation, whether made under an Act or an Act of the Scottish Parliament.]

[168B]

NOTES

Commencement: 20 October 2003.

Inserted, together with ss 29C–29G, by the Co-operatives and Community Benefit Societies Act 2003, s 5(1).

[29C Methods for execution of documents: England and Wales

(1) The following provisions have effect with respect to the execution of documents by a registered society under the law of England and Wales.

(2) A registered society may, if it has a common seal, execute a document by affixing that seal to it.

(3) A document—

(a) signed by a member of the committee of a registered society and the secretary of the society, or by two members of that committee, and

(b) expressed (in whatever form of words) to be executed by the society,

has the same effect as if it were executed under the common seal of the society.

(4) A document executed by a registered society which makes it clear on its face that it is intended by the person or persons making it to be a deed has effect, upon delivery, as a deed; and it shall be presumed, unless a contrary intention is proved, to be delivered upon its being so executed.

(5) In favour of a purchaser a document shall be deemed to have been duly executed by a registered society if it purports to be signed by a member of the committee of the society and the secretary of the society, or by two members of the committee, and, where it makes it clear on its face that it is intended by the person or persons making it to be a deed, to have been delivered upon its being executed.

(6) Subsections (3) to (5) of this section apply whether or not the society has a common seal; and, in subsection (5) of this section, "purchaser" means a purchaser in good faith for valuable consideration and includes a lessee, mortgagee or other person who for valuable consideration acquires an interest in property.]

[168C]

NOTES

Commencement: 20 October 2003.
Inserted as noted to s 29B at **[168B]**.

[29D Execution of documents: Scotland

(1) Under the law of Scotland, for the purposes of any enactment—

(a) providing for a document to be executed by a registered society by affixing its common seal, or

(b) referring (in whatever terms) to a document so executed,

a document signed or subscribed by or on behalf of the society in accordance with the provisions of the Requirements of Writing (Scotland) Act 1995 shall have effect as if so executed.

(2) In this section "enactment" includes an enactment comprised in—

(a) an Act of the Scottish Parliament;

(b) subordinate legislation, whether made under an Act or an Act of the Scottish Parliament.]

[168D]

NOTES

Commencement: 20 October 2003.
Inserted as noted to s 29B at **[168B]**.

[29E Power of society to have official seal for use abroad

(1) This section applies to a registered society if—

(a) it has a common seal; and

(b) its objects require or comprise the transaction of business in foreign countries.

(2) The society may, if authorised by its registered rules, have an official seal for use in any territory, district, or place elsewhere than in the United Kingdom.

(3) An "official seal" is a facsimile of the society's common seal with the addition on its face of the name of every territory, district or place where it is to be used.]

[168E]

NOTES

Commencement: 20 October 2003.
Inserted as noted to s 29B at **[168B]**.

[29F Effect of use of official seal

The official seal of a registered society when duly affixed to a document has the same effect as the society's common seal.]

[168F]

NOTES

Commencement: 20 October 2003.
Inserted as noted to s 29B at **[168B]**.

[29G Authorisation of use of official seal

(1) If a registered society has an official seal, it may authorise any person appointed for the purpose as respects any territory, district or place appearing on the face of that seal to affix it to any deed or other document to which the society is party there.

(2) An authorisation for the purposes of subsection (1) of this section must be given—

(a) in the case of a society with its registered office in Scotland, by writing subscribed in accordance with the Requirements of Writing (Scotland) Act 1995; and

(b) in any other case, by writing under the society's common seal.

(3) As between the society and a person dealing with such an agent, the agent's authority continues—

(a) if a period is mentioned in the authorisation, during that period; or

(b) if no period is there mentioned, until notice of the revocation or determination of the agent's authority has been given to the person dealing with him.

(4) The person affixing the official seal shall certify in writing on the deed or other instrument to which the seal is affixed the date on which and the place at which it is affixed.]

[168G]

NOTES

Commencement: 20 October 2003.
Inserted as noted to s 29B at **[168B]**.

30 Holding of land

(1) A registered society may, unless its registered rules direct otherwise, hold, purchase or take on lease in its own name any land and may sell, exchange, mortgage or lease any such land and erect, alter or pull down buildings on it; and—

(a) no purchaser, assignee, mortgagee or tenant shall be bound to inquire as to the authority for any such dealing with the land by the society; and

(b) the receipt of the society shall be a discharge for all moneys arising from or in connection with any such dealing.

(2) (*Applies to Scotland only.*)

[169]

31 Investments

A registered society may invest any part of its funds in or upon any security authorised by its registered rules, and also, unless those rules direct otherwise—

(a) in or upon any mortgage, bond, debenture, debenture stock, corporation stock, annuity, rentcharge, rent or other security (not being securities payable to bearer) authorised by or under any Act of

[[(i) a billing authority or a precepting authority, as defined in section 69 of the Local Government Finance Act 1992;

[(ia) a fire and rescue authority in Wales constituted by a scheme under section 2 of the Fire and Rescue Services Act 2004 or a scheme to which section 4 of that Act applies;]]

(ii) a levying body within the meaning of section 74 of [the Local Government Finance Act 1988]; and

(iii) a body as regards which section 75 of that Act applies];

(b) in the shares or on the security of any other registered society, of any [building society within the meaning of the Building Societies Act 1986], or of any company registered under the Companies Acts or incorporated by Act of Parliament or by charter, being a society or company with limited liability;

(c) in or upon any other security, being a security in which trustees are for the time being authorised by law to invest, for which purpose sections 1 to 6 of the Trustee Investments Act 1961 shall apply as if the society were a trustee and its funds were trust property.

[170]

NOTES

In para (a) sub-paras (i)–(iii) substituted by the Local Government Finance (Repeals, Savings and Consequential Amendments) Order 1990, SI 1990/776, art 8, Sch 3, para 9, sub-paras (i), (ia) further substituted for the previously substituted sub-para (i) by the Local Government Finance Act 1992, s 117(1), Sch 13, para 13; sub-para (ia) further substituted and words in square brackets in sub-para (a)(ii) substituted by the Fire and Rescue Services Act 2004, s 53(1), Sch 1, para 19; in para (b) words in square brackets substituted by the Building Societies Act 1986, s 120(1), Sch 18, Pt I, para 6.

32 Proxy voting by societies

(1) A registered society which has invested any part of its funds in the shares or on the security of any other body corporate may appoint as proxy any one of its members notwithstanding that he is not personally a shareholder of that other body corporate.

(2) Any member of the society so appointed shall during the continuance of his appointment be taken by virtue thereof as holding the number of shares held by the society for all purposes other than the transfer of any such share or the giving of a receipt for any dividend thereon.

[171]

33 Discharge of mortgages in England and Wales

(1) Where, in the case of any mortgage or other assurance to a registered society of any property in England or Wales, a receipt in full for all moneys secured thereby on that property is endorsed on or annexed to the mortgage or other assurance, being a receipt—

(a) signed by two members of the committee and countersigned by the secretary of the society or, if the society is in liquidation, signed by the liquidator or liquidators for the time being, described as such; and

(b) in one of the forms set out in Part I of Schedule 3 to this Act, or in any other form specified in the rules of the society or any schedule thereto,

then, for the purposes of the provisions of section 115 of the Law of Property Act 1925 specified in subsection (2) of this section, that receipt shall be deemed to be a receipt which fulfils the requirements of subsection (1) of that section.

(2) The provisions of the said section 115 referred to in the foregoing subsection are—

(a) subsection (1) so far as it relates to the operation of such a receipt as is mentioned in that subsection;

(b) if, but only if, the receipt under this section states the name of the person who pays the money, subsection (2);

(c) subsections (3), (6), (8), (10) and (11);

(d) where consistent with the terms of the form authorised by subsection (1)(b) of this section which is used for the receipt, subsection (7).

[172]

34 *(Applies to Scotland only.)*

35 Receipt on payment of moneys secured to a society

On payment of all moneys intended to be secured to a registered society on the security of any property, the debtor or his successor or representatives shall be entitled to a receipt in the appropriate form specified in Schedule 3 to this Act.

[173]

36 (*Repealed by the Requirements of Writing (Scotland) Act 1995, s 14(2), Sch 5 and the Co-operatives and Community Benefit Societies Act 2003, s 5(5), (9), Schedule.*)

Accounts, etc

37, 38 (*Repealed with savings by the Friendly and Industrial and Provident Societies Act 1968, s 20(1)(b), (2), Schs 2, 3.*)

39 Annual returns

(1) Every registered society shall [within the period of 7 months beginning immediately after the end of the period required by this section to be included in the return] send to [the Authority] a return [relating to its affairs for that period] together with—

[(a) where the period required to be included in the return is one at the end of which there is in force in relation to the period a disapplication under section 4A(1) of the Friendly and Industrial and Provident Societies Act 1968 (power to disapply the obligation under section 4 of that Act to have accounts audited), the documents mentioned in subsection (1A) of this section, and

(b) where it is not, the documents mentioned in subsection (1B) of this section.

(1A) The documents referred to in subsection (1)(a) of this section are—

(a) copies of the reports, if any, which the society is required, because of the disapplication, to obtain under section 9A of the Friendly and Industrial and Provident Societies Act 1968 (duty to obtain accountant's reports where section 4 of that Act disapplied); and

(b) a copy of each balance sheet made during the period included in the return.

(1B) The documents referred to in subsection (1)(b) of this section are—]

(a) a copy of the report of the auditor or auditors on the society's accounts for the period included in the return; and

(b) a copy of each balance sheet made during that period and of any report of the auditor or auditors on that balance sheet.

(2) The said return shall—

(a), (b) ...

(c) subject to subsections (3) and (4) of this section, be made up for the period beginning with the date of the society's registration under this Act or [with the date to which the society's last annual return was made up, whichever is the later, and ending—

(i) with the date of the last balance sheet published by the society before the appropriate date; or

(ii) if the date of that balance sheet is earlier than 31st August immediately preceding the appropriate date or later than 31st January of the year in which the appropriate date falls, with 31st December immediately preceding the appropriate date].

[(2A) For the purposes of paragraph (c) of subsection (2) of this section "the appropriate date", in relation to an annual return of a society, is 31st March of the year in which that return is required by subsection (1) of this section to be sent to [the Authority] or the date on which that return is so sent, whichever is the earlier.]

(3) If [the Authority] is of opinion that special circumstances exist [it] may allow a society to make a return under this section up to a date other than that specified in subsection (2)(c)(i) or (ii) of this section, ...

(4) The last return under this section by a registered society which is being terminated by an instrument of dissolution under section 55(b) of this Act shall be made up to the date of the instrument of dissolution.

(5) Every registered society shall supply free of charge to every member or person interested in the funds of the society who applies for it a copy of the latest return of the society under this section.

[174]

NOTES

Sub-s (1): words in first and third pairs of square brackets substituted and words in third pair of square brackets inserted by the Deregulation (Industrial and Provident Societies) Order 1996, SI 1996/1738, art 5(1), (2), 9(1); words in second pair of square brackets substituted by the Financial Services and Markets Act 2000 (Mutual Societies) Order 2001, SI 2001/2617, art 13(1), Sch 3, Pt III, paras 214, 215(i).

Sub-ss (1A), (1B): inserted by SI 1996/1738, art 9(1).

Sub-s (2): paras (a), (b) repealed and in para (c) words in square brackets substituted by the Friendly and Industrial and Provident Societies Act 1968, ss 11(1), (8), 20, Sch 1, para 10, Sch 2.

Sub-s (2A): inserted by the Friendly and Industrial and Provident Societies Act 1968, ss 11, 20, Sch 1, para 10; words in second pair of square brackets substituted by SI 2001/2617, art 13(1), Sch 3, Pt III, paras 214, 215(i).

Sub-s (3): words in second pair of square brackets substituted by SI 2001/2617, art 13(1), Sch 3, Pt III, paras 214, 215(i); words omitted repealed by SI 1996/1738, art 5(1), (3).

40 Display of latest balance sheet

Every registered society shall keep a copy of the latest balance sheet of the society … hung up at all times in a conspicuous position at the registered office of the society.

[175]

NOTES

Words omitted repealed by the Deregulation (Industrial and Provident Societies) Order 1996, SI 1996/1738, art 9(2).

Officers, receivers, etc

41 Security by officers

(1) Every officer of a registered society having receipt or charge of money shall, if the rules of the society so require, before entering upon the execution of his office give security in such sum as the society's committee may direct conditioned for his rendering a just and true account of all moneys received and paid by him on account of the society at such times as its rules appoint or as the society or its committee require him so to do and for the payment by him of all sums due from him to the society.

(2) An officer of a registered society shall give security in accordance with the foregoing subsection either—

(a) by becoming bound, either with or without a surety as the society's committee may require, in a bond in one of the forms set out in Schedule 4 to this Act or such other form as the society's committee may approve; or

(b) by giving the security of a guarantee society.

(3) (*Applies to Scotland only.*)

[176]

42 Duty of officers

(1) Every officer of a registered society having receipt or charge of money, and every servant of such a society in receipt or charge of money who is not engaged under a special agreement to account, shall—

(a) at such time as he is required so to do by the rules of the society; or

(b) on demand; or

(c) on notice in writing requiring him so to do given or left at his last or usual place of residence,

render an account as may be required by the society or its committee to be examined and allowed or disallowed by them, and shall, on demand or on such notice as aforesaid, pay over all moneys and deliver all property for the time being in his hands or custody to such person as the society or committee may appoint.

(2) Any duty imposed by the foregoing subsection on an officer or servant of a society shall, after his death, be taken to be imposed on his personal representatives.

(3) In case of any neglect or refusal to comply with the foregoing provisions of this section, the society—

(a) may sue on any bond or security given under section 41 of this Act; or

(b) *may apply to the county court* (which may proceed in a summary way) or to a magistrates' court and, notwithstanding anything in [section 77 of the County Courts Act 1984], the order of that county court or magistrates' court shall be final and conclusive.

(4) (*Applies to Scotland only.*)

[177]

NOTES

Sub-s (3): words in square brackets substituted by the County Courts Act 1984, s 148(1), Sch 2, Pt V, para 29.

43 Duties of receiver or manager of society's property

Every receiver or manager of the property of a registered society who has been appointed under the powers contained in any instrument shall—

(a) within one month from the date of his appointment notify [the Authority] of his appointment; and

(b) within one month (or such longer period as [the Authority] may allow) after the expiration of the period of six months from that date, and of every subsequent period of six months, deliver to [the Authority] a return showing his receipts and his payments during that period of six months; and

(c) within one month after he ceases to act as receiver or manager deliver to [the Authority] a return showing his receipts and his payments during the final period and the aggregate amount of his receipts and of his payments during all preceding periods since his appointment.

[178]

NOTES

Words in square brackets substituted by the Financial Services and Markets Act 2000 (Mutual Societies) Order 2001, SI 2001/2617, art 13(1), Sch 3, Pt III, paras 214, 215(i).

Registers, books, etc

44 Register of members and officers

(1) Every registered society shall keep at its registered office a register and enter therein the following particulars:—

(a) the names and addresses of the members;

(b) a statement of the number of shares held by each member and of the amount paid or agreed to be considered as paid on the shares of each member;

(c) a statement of other property in the society, whether in loans, deposits or otherwise, held by each member;

(d) the date at which each person was entered in the register as a member, and the date at which any person ceased to be a member;

(e) the names and addresses of the officers of the society, with the offices held by them respectively, and the dates on which they assumed office.

(2) The said register may be kept either by making entries in bound books or by recording the matters in question in any other manner; but, where it is not kept by making entries in a bound book but by some other means, adequate precautions shall be taken for guarding against falsification and facilitating its discovery.

(3) Every registered society shall either—

(a) keep at its registered office a duplicate register containing the particulars in the register kept under subsection (1) of this section other than those entered under paragraph (b) or (c) of that subsection; or

(b) so construct the register kept under the said subsection (1) that it is possible to open to inspection the particulars therein other than the particulars entered under the said paragraph (b) or (c) without exposing those last-mentioned particulars.

(4) [Any person authorised for the purpose by the Authority may, on producing evidence of his authority,] at all reasonable hours inspect any particulars in any register or duplicate register kept under this section.

(5) A registered society's register or duplicate register kept under this section, or any other register or list of members or shares kept by the society, shall be prima facie evidence of any of the following particulars entered therein, that is to say—

(a) the names, addresses and occupations of the members;

(b) the number of shares respectively held by the members, the distinguishing numbers of those shares, if they are distinguished by numbers, and the amount paid or agreed to be considered as paid on any of those shares;

(c) the date at which the name of any person, company or society was entered in that register or list as a member;

(d) the date at which any such person, company or society ceased to be a member.

[179]

NOTES

Sub-s (4): words in square brackets substituted by the Financial Services and Markets Act 2000 (Mutual Societies) Order 2001, SI 2001/2617, art 13(1), Sch 3, Pt III, paras 214, 223.

45 Restriction on inspection of books

(1) Save as provided by this Act, no member or other person shall have any right to inspect the books of a registered society.

(2) In the case of a society to which section 4 of this Act applies, the foregoing subsection shall have effect notwithstanding anything relating to such inspection in any rules of the society made before 12th September 1893.

[180]

46 Inspection of books by members, etc

(1) Subject to any regulations as to the time and manner of inspection which may be made from time to time by the general meetings of a registered society, any member, and any person having an interest in the funds, of the society shall be allowed to inspect at all reasonable hours—

(a) his own account; and

(b) all the particulars contained in the duplicate register kept under section 44(3)(a) of this Act or, if no duplicate register is so kept, all the particulars in the register kept under section 44(1) of this Act other than those entered under paragraph (b) or (c) thereof.

(2) A registered society may by its rules (not being rules made earlier than 12th September 1893) authorise, in addition to any inspection in pursuance of the foregoing subsection, the inspection of such of the society's books upon such conditions as may be specified in the rules, but no person who is not an officer of the society or specially authorised by a resolution of the society shall be authorised by the rules to inspect the loan or deposit account of any other person without that other person's written consent.

[181]

47 Inspection of books by order of [the Authority]

(1) Subject to subsection (2) of this section, [the Authority] may, if [it] thinks fit, on the application of ten members of a registered society each of whom has been a member of the society for not less than twelve months immediately preceding the date of the application, appoint an accountant or actuary to inspect the books of the society and to report thereon.

(2) The members making an application under the foregoing subsection shall deposit with [the Authority] as security for the costs of the proposed inspection such sum as [it] may require; and all expenses of and incidental to the inspection shall be defrayed by the applicants, or out of the funds of the society, or by the members or officers, or former members or officers, of the society, in such proportions as [the Authority] may direct.

(3) A person appointed under this section shall have power to make copies of any books of the society, and to take extracts therefrom, at all reasonable hours at the society's registered office or at any other place where those books are kept.

(4) [The Authority] shall communicate the results of any inspection under this section to the applicants and to the society.

[182]

NOTES

Section heading: words in square brackets substituted by virtue of the Financial Services and Markets Act 2000 (Mutual Societies) Order 2001, SI 2001/2617, art 13(1), Sch 3, Pt III, paras 214, 215.

Sub-ss (1), (2), (4): words in square brackets substituted by SI 2001/2617, art 13(1), Sch 3, Pt III, paras 214, 215(i), 224.

48 Production of documents and provision of information for certain purposes

(1) [The Authority] may at any time, by notice in writing served on a registered society or on any person who is or has been an officer of such a society, require that society or person to produce to [the Authority] such books, accounts and other documents relating to the business of the society, and to furnish to [it] such other information relating to that business, as [the Authority] considers necessary for the exercise of any of the powers which [it] has by virtue of section 16(1)(c)(ii), 16(4) or 56 of this Act; and any such notice may contain a requirement that any information to be furnished in accordance with the notice shall be verified by a statutory declaration.

(2) Any society or other person failing to comply with the requirements of a notice under the foregoing subsection shall be liable on summary conviction to a fine not exceeding [level 3 on the standard scale] *or to imprisonment for a term not exceeding three months or to both*.

(3) [The Authority] may, if [it] considers it just, direct that all or any of the expenses incurred by [it] in exercising [its] powers under subsection (1) of this section in relation to any society shall, either wholly or to such extent as [it] may determine, be defrayed out of the funds of the society or by the officers or former officers thereof or any of them; and any sum which any society or other person is required by such a direction to pay shall be a debt due to [the Authority] from that society or person.

[183]

NOTES

Sub-ss (1), (3): words in square brackets substituted by the Financial Services and Markets Act 2000 (Mutual Societies) Order 2001, SI 2001/2617, art 13(1), Sch 3, Pt III, paras 214, 215(i), (ii), 225.

Sub-s (2): maximum fine increased and converted to a level on the standard scale by the Criminal Justice Act 1982, ss 37, 38, 46; words in italics repealed by the Criminal Justice Act 2003, s 332, Sch 37, Pt 9, as from a day to be appointed under s 336(3) of that Act.

49 Appointment of inspectors and calling of special meetings

(1) Upon the application of one-tenth of the whole number of members of a registered society or, in the case of a society with more than one thousand members, of one hundred of those members, [the Authority] may ...—

(a) appoint an inspector or inspectors to examine into and report on the affairs of the society; or

(b) call a special meeting of the society.

(2) An application under this section shall be supported by such evidence for the purpose of showing that the applicants have good reason for requiring the examination or meeting and are not actuated by malicious motives, and such notice of the application shall be given to the society, as [the Authority] shall direct.

(3) [The Authority] may, if [it] thinks fit, require the applicants to give security for the costs of the proposed examination or meeting before appointing any inspector or calling the meeting.

(4) All expenses of and incidental or preliminary to any such examination or meeting shall be defrayed by the members applying for it, or out of the funds of the society, or by the members or officers, or former members or officers, of the society, in such proportions as [the Authority] shall direct.

(5) An inspector appointed under this section may require the production of all or any of the books, accounts, securities, and documents of the society, and may examine on oath its officers, members, agents and servants in relation to its business, and may for that purpose administer oaths.

(6) [The Authority] may direct at what time and place a special meeting under this section is to be held, and what matters are to be discussed and determined at the meeting; and the meeting shall have all the powers of a meeting called according to the rules of the society, and shall have power to appoint its own chairman notwithstanding any rule of the society to the contrary.

(7) ...

[184]

NOTES

Sub-s (1): words in square brackets substituted and words omitted repealed by the Financial Services and Markets Act 2000 (Mutual Societies) Order 2001, SI 2001/2617, art 13(1), (2), Sch 3, Pt III, paras 214, 226(a), Sch 4.

Sub-ss (2), (3), (4), (6): words in square brackets substituted by SI 2001/2617, art 13(1), Sch 3, Pt III, paras 214, 215(iii), 226(b).

Sub-s (7): repealed by SI 2001/2617, art 13(1), (2), Sch 3, Pt III, paras 214, 226(c), Sch 4.

Amalgamations, transfers of engagements and conversions

50 Amalgamation of societies

(1) Any two or more registered societies may by special resolution of each of those societies become amalgamated together as one society, with or without any dissolution or division of the funds of those societies or any of them; and the property of each of those societies shall become vested in the amalgamated society without the necessity of any form of conveyance other than that contained in the special resolution.

(2) In this section the expression "special resolution" means a resolution which is—

(a) passed by not less than two-thirds of such members of the society for the time being entitled under the society's rules to vote as may have voted in person, or by proxy where the rules allow proxies, at any general meeting of which notice, specifying the intention to propose the resolution, has been duly given according to those rules; and

(b) confirmed by a majority of such members of the society for the time being entitled as aforesaid as may have voted as aforesaid at a subsequent general meeting of which notice has been duly given held not less than fourteen days nor more than one month from the day of the meeting at which the resolution was passed in accordance with paragraph (a) of this subsection.

(3) At any such meeting as aforesaid, a declaration by the chairman that the resolution has been carried shall be deemed conclusive evidence of that fact.

(4) A copy of every special resolution for the purposes of this section signed by the chairman of the meeting at which the resolution was confirmed and countersigned by the secretary of the society shall be sent to [the Authority] and registered by [it]; and until that copy is so registered the special resolution shall not take effect.

(5) It shall be the duty of a registered society to send any special resolution for registration in accordance with the last foregoing subsection within fourteen days from the day on which the resolution is confirmed under subsection (2)(b) of this section, but this subsection shall not invalidate registration of the resolution after that time.

[185]

NOTES

Sub-s (4): words in square brackets substituted and words omitted repealed by the Financial Services and Markets Act 2000 (Mutual Societies) Order 2001, SI 2001/2617, art 13(1), Sch 3, Pt III, paras 214, 215(i), 226(a).

Sub-ss (2), (3), (4), (6): words in square brackets substituted by SI 2001/2617, art 13(1), Sch 3, Pt III, paras 214, 215(iii), 226(b).

Sub-s (7): repealed by SI 2001/2617, art 13(1), (2), Sch 3, Pt III, paras 214, 226(c), Sch 4.

51 Transfer of engagements between societies

(1) Any registered society may by special resolution transfer its engagements to any other registered society which may undertake to fulfil those engagements; and if that resolution approves the transfer of the whole or any part of the society's property to that other society, the whole or, as the case may be, that part of the society's property shall vest in that other society without any conveyance or assignment.

(2) Subsections (2) to (5) of section 50 of this Act shall have effect for the purposes of this section as they have effect for the purposes of that section.

(3) (*Applies to Scotland only.*)

[186]

52 Conversion into, amalgamation with, or transfer of engagements to company

(1) A registered society may by special resolution determine to convert itself into, or to amalgamate with or transfer its engagements to, a company under the Companies Acts.

(2) If a special resolution for converting a registered society into a company contains the particulars required by the [Companies Act 1985] to be contained in the memorandum of association of a company and a copy thereof has been registered by [the Authority], a copy of that resolution under the seal and stamp of [the Authority] … shall have the same effect as a memorandum of association duly signed and attested under the said [Act of 1985].

[(3) In this section the expression "special resolution" means a resolution—

(a) which is passed at a general meeting of which notice, specifying the intention to propose the resolution, has been duly given according to the rules of the society ("the rules");

(b) which is passed by not less than three-fourths of such of the qualifying members of the society as may have voted in person or, where the rules allow proxies, by proxy;

(c) on which not less than half of the qualifying members of the society voted either in person or, where the rules allow proxies, by proxy; and

(d) which is confirmed by a majority of such of the qualifying members of the society as may have voted in person or, where the rules allow proxies, by proxy at a subsequent general meeting of which notice has been duly given held not less than fourteen days nor more than one month from the day of the meeting at which the resolution was passed in accordance with paragraphs (a) to (c) of this subsection,

and references to the qualifying members of a society are references to the members of the society who are for the time being entitled under the society's rules to vote.

(3A) At any such meeting as aforesaid, a declaration by the chairman that—

(a) all reasonably practicable steps have been taken to ascertain the number of qualifying members of the society; and

(b) the resolution has been carried,

shall be deemed conclusive evidence of those facts.

(3B) Subsections (4) and (5) of section 50 of this Act shall have effect for the purposes of this section as they have effect for the purposes of that section but as if in subsection (5) of that section for the reference to subsection (2)(b) of that section there were substituted a reference to subsection (3)(d) of this section.]

(4) Subject to subsection (5) of this section, if a registered society is registered as, or amalgamates with, or transfers all its engagements to, a company under the Companies Acts, the registration of that society under this Act shall thereupon become void and, subject to section 59 of this Act, shall be cancelled by [the Authority] …

(5) Registration of a registered society as a company shall not affect any right or claim for the time being subsisting against the society or any penalty for the time being incurred by the society; and—

(a) for the purpose of enforcing any such right, claim or penalty, the society may be sued and proceeded against in the same manner as if it had not become registered as a company; and

(b) every such right or claim, or the liability to any such penalty, shall have priority as against the property of the company over all other rights or claims against or liabilities of the company.

[187]

NOTES

Sub-s (2): words in first and fourth pairs of square brackets substituted by the Companies Consolidation (Consequential Provisions) Act 1985, s 30, Sch 2; words omitted repealed and words in second and third pairs of square brackets substituted by the Financial Services and Markets Act 2000 (Mutual Societies) Order 2001, SI 2001/2617, art 13(1), (2), Sch 3, Pt III, paras 214, 215(i), (iv), 228(a), Sch 4.

Sub-ss (3)–(3A): substituted for sub-s (3) as originally enacted by the Industrial and Provident Societies Act 2002, s 1.

Sub-s (4): words in square brackets substituted and words omitted repealed by SI 2001/2617, art 13(1), (2), Sch 3, Pt III, paras 214, 215(iii), 228(b), Sch 4.

53 Conversion of company into registered society

(1) A company registered under the Companies Acts may, by a special resolution as defined by [section 378 of the Companies Act 1985], determine to convert itself into a registered society; and for this purpose, in any case where the nominal value of the company's shares held by any member other than a registered society exceeds [the maximum for the time being permitted by section 6(1) of this Act in the case of a member of a registered society] the resolution may provide for the conversion of the shares representing that excess into a transferable loan stock bearing such rate of interest as may be fixed, and repayable on such conditions only as are determined by the resolution.

(2) Any such resolution as aforesaid shall be accompanied by a copy of the rules of the society therein referred to and shall appoint [three] persons, being members of the company, who, together with the secretary, shall sign the rules and who may either—

(a) be authorised to accept any alterations made by [the Authority] therein without further consulting the company; or

(b) be required to lay any such alterations before the company in general meeting for acceptance as the resolution may direct.

(3) A copy of the resolution aforesaid shall be sent with a copy of the rules aforesaid to [the Authority] who, upon the registration of the society under this Act, shall give to it, in addition to an acknowledgement of registration under section 2(3) of this Act, a certificate similarly sealed or signed that the rules of the society referred to in the resolution have been registered.

(4) A copy of any such resolution as aforesaid under the seal of the company together with the certificate issued as aforesaid by the appropriate registrar shall be sent for registration to the office of the registrar of companies within the meaning of the [Companies Act 1985] and, upon his registering that resolution and certificate, the conversion shall take effect.

(5) The name under which any company is registered under this section as a registered society shall not include the word "company".

(6) Subject to the next following subsection, upon the conversion of a company into a registered society under this section, the registration of the company under the Companies Acts shall become void and shall be cancelled by the registrar of companies aforesaid.

(7) The registration of a company as a registered society shall not affect any right or claim for the time being subsisting against the company or any penalty for the time being incurred by the company; and—

(a) for the purpose of enforcing any such right, penalty or claim the company may be sued and proceeded against in the same manner as if it had not been registered as a society;

(b) any such right or claim and the liability to any such penalty shall have priority as against the property of the registered society over all other rights or claims against or liabilities of the society.

[188]

NOTES

Sub-s (1): words in first pair of square brackets substituted by the Companies Consolidation (Consequential Provisions) Act 1985, s 30, Sch 2; words in second pair of square brackets substituted by the Industrial and Provident Societies Act 1975, s 3(3).

Sub-s (2): words in first pair of square brackets substituted by the Deregulation (Industrial and Provident Societies) Order 1996, SI 1996/1738, art 3(3); words in second pair of square brackets substituted by the Financial Services and Markets Act 2000 (Mutual Societies) Order 2001, SI 2001/2617, art 13(1), Sch 3, Pt III, paras 214, 215(i).

Sub-s (3): words in square brackets substituted by SI 2001/2617, art 13(1), Sch 3, Pt III, paras 214, 215(i).

Sub-s (4): words in first pair of square brackets substituted by SI 2001/2617, art 13(1), Sch 3, Pt III, paras 214, 215(i); words in second pair of square brackets substituted by the Companies Consolidation (Consequential Provisions) Act 1985, s 30, Sch 2.

---

54 Saving for rights of creditors

An amalgamation or transfer of engagements in pursuance of section 50, 51 or 52 of this Act shall not prejudice any right of a creditor of any registered society which is a party thereto.

[189]

Dissolution of society

55 Dissolution of registered society

Subject to section 59 of this Act, a registered society may be dissolved—

(a) on its being wound up in pursuance of an order or resolution made as is directed in regard to companies by the [Insolvency Act 1986], the provisions whereof shall apply to that order or resolution as if the society were a company, but subject to the following modifications, that is to say—

(i) any reference in those provisions to the registrar within the meaning of that Act shall for the purposes of the society's winding up be construed as a reference to [the Authority] . . .; and

[(ia) any reference in those provisions to a company registered in Scotland shall have effect as a reference to a society registered under this Act whose registered office is situated in Scotland;]

(ii) if the society is wound up in Scotland, the court having jurisdiction shall be the sheriff court within whose jurisdiction the society's registered office is situated; or

(b) in accordance with section 58 of this Act, by an instrument of dissolution to which not less than three-fourths of the members of the society have given their consent testified by their signatures to the instrument.

[190]

NOTES

Words in first pair of square brackets substituted by the Insolvency Act 1986, s 439(2), Sch 14; in sub-para (a)(i) words in square brackets substituted and words omitted repealed and sub-para (a)(ii) inserted by the Financial Services and Markets Act 2000 (Mutual Societies) Order 2001, SI 2001/2617, art 13(1), (2), Sch 3, Pt III, paras 214, 215(i), 229, Sch 4.

56 Power of [the Authority] to petition for winding up

In the case of a society to which section 4 of this Act applies which was registered or deemed to be registered under the Act of 1893 before 26th July 1938, a petition for the winding up of the society may be presented to the court by [the Authority] if it appears to [the Authority]—

(a) that neither of the conditions specified in section 1(2) of this Act is fulfilled in the case of that society;

(b) that it would be in the interests of persons who have invested or deposited money with the society or of any other person that the society should be wound up.

[191]

NOTES

Section heading: words in square brackets substituted by virtue of the Financial Services and Markets Act 2000 (Mutual Societies) Order 2001, SI 2001/2617, art 13(1), Sch 3, Pt III, paras 214, 215(i).

Words in square brackets substituted by SI 2001/2617, art 13(1), Sch 3, Pt III, paras 214, 215(i).

Act of 1893: the Industrial and Provident Societies Act 1893: repealed by s 77(1) of, and Sch 5 to, this Act.

57 Liability of members in winding up

Where a registered society is wound up by virtue of section 55(a) of this Act, the liability of a present or past member of the society to contribute for payment of the debts and liabilities of the society, the expenses of winding up, and the adjustment of the rights of contributories amongst themselves, shall be qualified as follows, that is to say—

(a) no person who ceased to be a member not less than one year before the beginning of the winding up shall be liable to contribute;

(b) no person shall be liable to contribute in respect of any debt or liability contracted after he ceased to be a member;

(c) no person who is not a member shall be liable to contribute unless it appears to the court that the contributions of the existing members are insufficient to satisfy the just demands on the society;

(d) no contribution shall be required from any person exceeding the amount, if any, unpaid on the shares in respect of which he is liable as a past or present member;

(e) in the case of a withdrawable share which has been withdrawn, a person shall be taken to have ceased to be a member in respect of that share as from the date of the notice or application for withdrawal.

[192]

58 Instrument of dissolution

(1) The following provisions of this section shall have effect where a society is to be dissolved by an instrument of dissolution under section 55(b) of this Act,

(2) The instrument of dissolution shall set forth—

(a) the liabilities and assets of the society in detail;

(b) the number of the members and the nature of their respective interests in the society;

(c) the claims of creditors, if any, and the provision to be made for their payment; and

(d) unless stated in the instrument of dissolution to be left to the award of [the Authority], the intended appropriation or division of the funds and property of the society.

(3) Alterations in the instrument of dissolution may be made by the consent of not less than three-fourths of the members of the society testified by their signatures to the alteration.

(4) The instrument of dissolution shall be sent to [the Authority] accompanied by a statutory declaration made by three members and the secretary of the society that all relevant provisions of this Act have been complied with; and any person knowingly making a false or fraudulent declaration in the matter shall be guilty of a misdemeanour or, in Scotland, an offence.

(5) The instrument of dissolution and any alterations thereto shall be registered in like manner as an amendment of the rules of the society and shall be binding upon all the members of the society, but shall not be so registered until [the Authority] has received such a final return from the society as is referred to in section 39(4) of this Act.

(6) [The Authority] shall cause notice of the dissolution to be advertised ... in the Gazette and in some newspaper circulating in or about the locality in which the society's registered office is situated; and unless—

(a) within three months from the date of the Gazette in which that advertisement appears a member or other person interested in or having any claim on the funds of the society commences in the county court, or in Scotland before the sheriff, having jurisdiction in that locality proceedings to set aside the dissolution of the society; and

(b) that dissolution is set aside accordingly,

then, subject to subsection (7) of this section, the society shall be legally dissolved from the date of the advertisement and the requisite consents to the instrument of dissolution shall be deemed to have been duly obtained without proof of the signatures thereto.

(7) If the certificate referred to in section 59 of this Act has not been lodged with [the Authority] by the date of the advertisement referred to in subsection (6) of this section, the society shall be legally dissolved only from the date when that certificate is so lodged.

(8) Notice of any proceedings to set aside the dissolution of a society shall be sent to [the Authority] by the person taking those proceedings not later than seven days after they are commenced or not later than the expiration of the period of three months referred to in subsection (6) of this section, whichever is the earlier; and notice of any order setting the dissolution aside shall be sent by the society to [the Authority] within seven days after the making of the order.

(9) In the application of this section to a society which for the time being consists solely of two registered societies, the reference in subsection (4) thereof to three members shall be construed as a reference to both members.

[193]

NOTES

Sub-ss (2), (4), (5), (7), (8): words in square brackets substituted by the Financial Services and Markets Act 2000 (Mutual Societies) Order 2001, SI 2001/2617, art 13(1), Sch 3, Pt III, paras 214, 215(i), (iii).

Sub-s (6): words in square brackets substituted by SI 2001/2617, art 13(1), Sch 3, Pt III, paras 214, 215(i); words omitted repealed by the Financial Services and Markets Act 2000 (Consequential Amendments and Repeals) Order 2001, SI 2001/3649, art 180.

60 Decision of disputes

(1) Subject to subsections (2), [(2A),] (4) and (5) of this section, every dispute between a registered society or an officer thereof and—

(a) a member of the society; or

(b) any person aggrieved who has ceased to be a member of the society not more than six months previously; or

(c) any person claiming through a member of the society or any such person aggrieved; or

(d) any person claiming under the rules of the society,

shall, if the society's rules give directions as to the manner in which such disputes are to be decided, be decided in that manner.

[(1A) Nothing in subsection (1) above or in rules of a kind mentioned in that subsection prevents any person, in accordance with the scheme for which Part XVI of the Financial Services and Markets Act 2000 provides (the ombudsman scheme), from having a complaint dealt with under such a scheme before, or instead of, determination in the manner directed in the rules.]

[(2) The county court or, in Scotland, the sheriff may determine a dispute in a registered society if—

(a) both parties to the dispute consent; or

(b) the rules of the society concerned contain no directions as to disputes.]

[(2A) If the rules contain directions by virtue of which a dispute would fall to be determined by the Authority, the dispute shall instead be referred to the county court or, in Scotland, to the sheriff for determination.]

(3) A decision made under subsection (1) *or* (2) of this section on any dispute shall be binding and conclusive on all parties without appeal; and—

(a) the decision shall not be removable into any court of law or restrainable by injunction; and

(b) application for the enforcement of the decision may be made to the county court.

(4) Subject to subsection (5) of this section, any dispute directed by the rules of a registered society to be referred to justices shall be determined by a magistrates' court.

(5) Where, whether by virtue of subsection (4) of this section or otherwise, a dispute is cognisable under the rules of a registered society by a magistrates' court, the parties to the dispute may by agreement refer the dispute to the county court, who may hear and determine it.

(6) Where the rules of a registered society contain no direction as to disputes, or where no decision is made on a dispute within forty days after application to the society for a reference under its rules, any person such as is mentioned in subsection (1)(a) to (d) of this section who is a party to the dispute may apply either to the county court or to a magistrates' court, who may hear and determine the matter in dispute.

[196]

NOTES

In para (b) words in square brackets substituted and words omitted repealed by the Financial Services and Markets Act 2000 (Mutual Societies) Order 2001, SI 2001/2617, art 13(1), (2), Sch 3, Pt III, paras 214, 215(iii), 231, Sch 4; maximum fine increased and converted to a level on the standard scale by the Criminal Justice Act 1982, ss 37, 39(2), 46, Sch 3.

62 Offences by societies to be also offences by officers, etc

Every offence committed by a registered society under this Act shall be deemed to have been also committed by every officer of that society bound by the society's rules to fulfil the duty of which that offence is a breach or, if there is no such officer, by every member of the society's committee who is not proved to have been ignorant of, or to have attempted to prevent, the commission of that offence.

[197]

63 Continuing offences

Every act or default under this Act constituting an offence shall constitute a new offence in every week during which it continues.

[198]

64 Punishment of fraud or misappropriation

(1) Subject to subsection (2) of this section, any person who obtains possession by false representation or imposition of any property of a registered society, or having any such

property in his possession withholds or misapplies it or wilfully applies any part of it to purposes which are not authorised by the rules of the society or which are not in accordance with this Act, shall be liable on summary conviction to a fine not exceeding [level 2 on the standard scale] with costs or expenses and to be ordered to deliver up that property or to repay all moneys improperly applied and, in default of such delivery or repayment or of the payment of any such fine, to be imprisoned for a term not exceeding three months; but nothing in this subsection shall prevent any such person from being proceeded against by way of indictment for any offence if he has not previously been convicted in respect of the same matters under this subsection.

(2) If on proceedings under the foregoing subsection it is not proved that the person charged acted with any fraudulent intent, he may be ordered to deliver up any property belonging to the society or to repay any money improperly applied, with costs or expenses, but shall not be liable to conviction under that subsection.

[199]

NOTES

Sub-s (1): maximum fine increased by the Criminal Law Act 1977, s 31(6), (9), and converted to a level on the standard scale by the Criminal Justice Act 1982, ss 37, 46.

65 Penalty for falsification

If any person, with intent to falsify it or to evade any of the provisions of this Act, wilfully makes, or orders or allows to be made, any entry or erasure in, or omission from, any balance-sheet of a registered society, or any contribution or collecting book, or any return or document required to be sent, produced or delivered for the purposes of this Act, he shall be liable on summary conviction to a fine not exceeding [level 3 on the standard scale].

[200]

NOTES

Maximum fine increased and converted to a level on the standard scale by the Criminal Justice Act 1982, ss 37, 38, 46.

66 Institution of proceedings

(1) Proceedings for the recovery of a fine which under this Act is recoverable on the summary conviction of the offender may be instituted by ... the following persons, that is to say—

- (a) in the case of proceedings by virtue of section 64(1) of this Act—
  - (i) the registered society concerned; or
  - (ii) any member of that society authorised by the society or its committee or by the central office; or
  - [(iii) other than in Scotland, the Authority;]
- (b) in the case of proceedings by virtue of section 13(3) of this Act, the registered society concerned;
- [(c) in any other case—
  - (i) any person aggrieved; or
  - (ii) other than in Scotland, the Authority

and (except in Scotland) no other person may institute such proceedings.]

(2) Notwithstanding any limitation on the time for the taking of proceedings contained in any Act, any proceedings such as are mentioned in subsection (1) of this section which are instituted by [the Authority or by the Lord Advocate] may be brought at any time within one year of the first discovery of the offence by the [Authority (or the Lord Advocate, as the case may be)], but not in any case more than three years after the commission of the offence.

[201]

NOTES

Sub-s (1): words omitted repealed, sub-para (a)(iii) substituted, para (c) substituted by the Financial Services and Markets Act 2000 (Mutual Societies) Order 2001, SI 2001/2617, art 13(1), (2), Sch 3, Pt III, paras 214, 232(a), Sch 4.

Sub-s (2): words in square brackets substituted by SI 2001/2617, art 13(1), Sch 3, Pt III, paras 214, 232(b).

67 Recovery of costs, etc

(1) Any costs or expenses ordered or directed by [the Authority] … to be paid by any person under this Act shall be recoverable summarily as a civil debt.

(2) (*Applies to Scotland only.*)

[202]

NOTES

Sub-s (1): words in square brackets substituted and words omitted repealed by the Financial Services and Markets Act 2000 (Mutual Societies) Order 2001, SI 2001/2617, art 13(1), (2), Sch 3, Pt III, paras 214, 215(iii), 233, Sch 4.

Sub-s (2): words in square brackets substituted by SI 2001/2617, art 13(1), Sch 3, Pt III, paras 214, 232(b).

68 Service of process

Where proceedings are taken against a registered society for the recovery of any fine under this Act, the summons or other process shall be sufficiently served by leaving a true copy thereof at the registered office of the society or, if that office is closed, by posting that copy on the outer door of that office.

[203]

Miscellaneous and general

69 Remuneration of county court registrars

Registrars of county courts shall be remunerated for any duties to be performed by them under this Act in such manner as the Treasury may with the consent of the Lord Chancellor from time to time direct.

[204]–[205]

70 (*Repealed by the Financial Services and Markets Act 2000, ss 338(3), 432(3), Sch 18, Pt IV, para 20, Sch 22.*)

[70A Fees for inspection or copying of documents

Before the Authority allows any person to inspect any document held by it in connection with this Act, or provides any person with a copy of any such document (or part of such document), it may charge that person a reasonable fee.]

[206]

NOTES

Commencement: 1 December 2001.

Inserted by the Financial Services and Markets Act 2000 (Mutual Societies) Order 2001, SI 2001/2617, art 13(1), Sch 3, Pt III, paras 214, 234.

71 (*Repealed by the Financial Services and Markets Act 2000 (Consequential Amendments and Repeals) Order 2001, SI 2001/3649, art 181(1).*)

72 Form, deposit and evidence of documents

[(1) Every return and other document required for the purposes of this Act shall be made in such form, shall contain such particulars and shall be deposited in such manner as the Authority may direct and the Authority shall register and record those documents with such observations thereon (if any) as it considers appropriate.]

[(2) Any document bearing the seal or stamp of the Authority shall be received in evidence without further proof.

(3) Any document purporting to have been signed by a person authorised to do so on behalf of the Authority, and every document purporting to be signed by any inspector under this Act, shall, in the absence of any evidence to the contrary, be received in evidence without proof of the signature.

(4) In subsections (2) and (3), "document" means any document issued, received or created by the Authority (or, as the case may be, by any inspector under this Act) for the

purposes of or in connection with this Act, the Industrial and Provident Societies Act 1967 or the Friendly and Industrial and Provident Societies Act 1968.]

[207]–[208]

NOTES

Sub-s (1): substituted by the Financial Services and Markets Act 2000 (Consequential Amendments and Repeals) Order 2001, SI 2001/3649, art 235.

Sub-ss (2)–(4): substituted for sub-s (2) as originally enacted by the Financial Services and Markets Act 2000 (Mutual Societies) Order 2001, SI 2001/2617, art 13(1), Sch 3, Pt III, paras 214, 235, subject to transitional provisions in Sch 5, paras 1, 2(d) to that Act.

73 *(Repealed by the Financial Services and Markets Act 2000 (Mutual Societies) Order 2001, SI 2001/2617, art 13(1), (2), Sch 3, Pt III, paras 214, 236, Sch 4.)*

74 Interpretation—general

[(1)] In this Act, except where the context otherwise requires, the following expressions have the following meanings respectively, that is to say—

"Act of 1893", means the Industrial and Provident Societies Act 1893;

"amendment", in relation to the rules of a registered society, includes a new rule, and a resolution rescinding a rule, of the society;

["the Authority" means the Financial Services Authority;]

"committee", in relation to a society, means the committee of management or other directing body of the society;

"Companies Acts" includes the [Companies Act 1985], any earlier enactment for the like purposes which has been repealed, and any law for the like purposes which is or has been in force in Northern Ireland or any of the Channel Islands;

"Gazette", in relation to a registered society, means such one or more of the following as may be appropriate in the circumstances of the case, that is to say—

(a) the London Gazette if the society's registered office is situated, [or the society carries on business], in England, Wales or the Channel Islands;

(b) the Edinburgh Gazette if the society's registered office is situated, [or the society carries on business], in Scotland;

(c) the Belfast Gazette if the society's rules are recorded in Northern Ireland;

"heritable security" has the same meaning as in the Conveyancing (Scotland) Act 1924 except that it includes a security constituted by *ex facie* absolute disposition or assignation;

"land" includes hereditaments and chattels real, and in Scotland, heritable subjects of whatever description;

"meeting", in relation to a society, includes, where the rules of that society so allow, a meeting of delegates appointed by members;

"officer", in relation to a registered society, includes any treasurer, secretary, member of the committee, manager or servant of the society other than a servant appointed by the society's committee, but does not include an [auditor appointed by the society in accordance with the requirements of the Friendly and Industrial and Provident Societies Act 1968];

"persons claiming through a member", in relation to a registered society, includes the heirs, executors or administrators and assignees of a member and, where nomination is allowed, his nominee;

"prescribed" means prescribed by regulations under section 71 of this Act;

"property" includes all real, personal or heritable and moveable estate, including books and papers;

"registered" in relation to the name or an office of a society means for the time being registered under this Act;

"registered rules", in relation to a registered society, means the rules of the society registered or deemed to be registered under this Act as for the time being in force after any amendment thereof so registered;

"registered society" means, subject to section 76 of this Act, a society registered or deemed to be registered under this Act.

[(2) Any reference in this Act to the seal of the Authority is a reference to the seal provided for in regulations made under section 109(1)(b) of the Friendly Societies Act 1974 (and not to the Authority's common seal), and any reference to a document sealed by the Authority is a reference to a document sealed with that seal.]

[209]

NOTES

Sub-s (1): numbered as such, definition "the Authority" inserted and in definition "Gazette" words in square brackets substituted by the Financial Services and Markets Act 2000 (Mutual Societies) Order 2001, SI 2001/2617, art 13(1), Sch 3, Pt III, paras 214, 237; in definition "Companies Acts" words in square brackets substituted by the Companies Consolidation (Consequential Provisions) Act 1985, s 30, Sch 2; in definition "officer" words in square brackets substituted by the Friendly and Industrial and Provident Societies Act 1968, s 20(1)(a), Sch 1, para 11.

Sub-s (2): added by SI 2001/2617, art 13(1), Sch 3, Pt III, paras 214, 237(c).

Industrial and Provident Societies Act 1893: repealed by s 77(1) of, and Sch 5 to, this Act.

75 Channel Islands

(1) Subject to any express provision of this Act with respect to the Channel Islands, this Act in its application to those Islands shall have effect subject to such adaptations and modifications as Her Majesty may by Order in Council specify.

(2) Any Order in Council under the foregoing subsection may be varied or revoked by a subsequent Order in Council so made.

[210]

NOTES

Orders in Council: the Industrial and Provident Societies (Channel Islands) Order 1965, SI 1965/2165.

76 Northern Ireland Societies

(1) Where, in the case of any society for the time being registered under the law for the time being in force in Northern Ireland for purposes corresponding to those of this Act, copies of that society's rules so registered have been sent to the [Authority to be recorded by it and have been so recorded, then, for the purposes of the operation of this Act in Great Britain and the Channel Islands], references to a registered society in such, but such only, of the provisions of this Act as are specified in subsection (2) of this section shall, subject to subsection (3) of this section include a reference to that society, and for the purposes of those provisions that society, those rules and any amendment of those rules registered and recorded as aforesaid shall in that area be deemed to be a society, rules or an amendment duly registered under this Act by the [Authority].

(2) The provisions of this Act referred to in the foregoing subsection are sections 2(2), 3, 5(4), (6) and (7), 6(1)(a), 7(1)(b), (2), (3) and (6), 10(1)(a), 13(3), 14, 15, 16(1)(a)(i), 19(2), 22, [26 to 29, 29B to 29D,] 30, 31(b), 32 to 36, 41, 42, 44(5), 45(1), 50, 51, 52(5), 54, 60 to 62, 64 to 66 and 72.

[(2A) In section 29A(1) of this Act—

(a) the reference to a registered society includes a reference to a society registered under the law for the time being in force in Northern Ireland for purposes corresponding to those of this Act; and

(b) the reference to this Act includes a reference to that law.]

(3) Nothing in this section shall confer any power or impose any obligation or liability with respect to the taking or refraining from taking of, or a failure to take, any action outside Great Britain and the Channel Islands; and in the application of section 45(1) of this Act by virtue of this section the reference therein to this Act shall be construed as a reference to the law for the time being in force in Northern Ireland for purposes corresponding to those of this Act.

(4) In relation to any society for the time being registered as mentioned in subsection (1) of this section, Article 22 of the Government of Ireland (Companies, Societies, &c) Order 1922 shall have effect as if the words from "a society registered in Northern Ireland" to "United Kingdom, and" and the words "both in their application to the United Kingdom exclusive of Northern Ireland and" were omitted.

[211]

NOTES

Sub-s (1): words in square brackets substituted by the Financial Services and Markets Act 2000 (Mutual Societies) Order 2001, SI 2001/2617, art 13(1), Sch 3, Pt III, paras 214, 238.

Sub-s (2): words in square brackets substituted by the Co-operatives and Community Benefit Societies Act 2003, s 5(6).

Sub-s (2A): inserted by the Co-operatives and Community Benefit Societies Act 2003, s 4(2).

77 Repeals and savings

(1) …

(2) Without prejudice to section 4 of this Act, any regulations, application or notice made or given and any other thing whatsoever done under or in pursuance of any of the enactments repealed by this Act shall be deemed for the purposes of this Act to have been made, given or done, as the case may be, under or in pursuance of the corresponding provision of this Act; and anything begun under any of the said enactments may be continued under this Act as if begun under this Act.

(3) So much of any document as refers expressly or by implication to any enactment repealed by this Act shall, if and so far as the context permits, be construed as referring to this Act or the corresponding enactment therein.

(4) Nothing in section 4 of this Act or in this section shall be taken as affecting the general application of section 38 of the Interpretation Act 1889 with regard to the effect of repeals.

[212]

NOTES

Sub-s (1): repealed by the Statute Law (Repeals) Act 1974.

Interpretation Act 1889, s 38: repealed by the Interpretation Act 1978, s 25, Sch 3 and replaced by ss 16(1), 17(2)(a) of, and Sch 2, para 3 to, that Act.

78 Short title, extent and commencement

(1) This Act may be cited as the Industrial and Provident Societies Act 1965.

(2) This Act extends to the Channel Islands but does not extend to Northern Ireland.

(3) This Act shall come into operation on such day as Her Majesty may by Order in Council appoint.

[213]

NOTES

Orders in Council: the Industrial and Provident Societies Act 1965 (Commencement) Order 1965, SI 1965/2051.

SCHEDULES

SCHEDULE 1
MATTERS TO BE PROVIDED FOR IN SOCIETY'S RULES

Section 1

1. The name of the society, which shall comply with the requirements of section 5 of this Act.

2. The objects of the society.

3. The place which is to be the registered office of the society to which all communications and notices to the society may be addressed.

4. The terms of admission of the members, including any society or company investing funds in the society under the provisions of this Act.

5. The mode of holding meetings, the scale and right of voting, and the mode of making, altering or rescinding rules.

6. The appointment and removal of a committee, by whatever name, and of managers or other officers and their respective powers and remuneration.

7. Determination in accordance with section 6 of this Act of the maximum amount of the interest in the shares of the society which may be held by any member otherwise than by virtue of section 6(1)(a), (b) or (c) of this Act.

8. Determination whether the society may contract loans or receive moneys on deposit subject to the provisions of this Act from members or others; and, if so, under what conditions, under what security, and to what limits of amount.

9. Determination whether the shares or any of them shall be transferable, and provision for the form of transfer and registration of the shares, and for the consent of the committee thereto; determination whether the shares or any of them shall be withdrawable, and provision for the mode of withdrawal and for payment of the balance due thereon on withdrawing from the society.

10. Provision for the audit of accounts by one or more [auditors appointed by the society in accordance with the requirements of the Friendly and Industrial and Provident Societies Act 1968].

11. Determination whether and, if so, how members may withdraw from the society, and provision for the claims of the representatives of deceased members, or the trustees of the property of bankrupt members or, in Scotland, members whose estate has been sequestrated, and for the payment of nominees.

12. The mode of application of profits of the society. 13. Provision for the custody and use of the society's seal.

[13 If the society is to have a common seal, provision for its custody and use.]

14. Determination whether and, if so, by what authority, and in what manner, any part of the society's funds may be invested.

[214]

NOTES

Para 10: words in square brackets substituted by the Friendly and Industrial and Provident Societies Act 1968, s 20(1)(a), Sch 1, para 12.

Para 13: substituted by the Co-operatives and Community Benefit Societies Act 2003, s 5(7).

SCHEDULE 2
FORM OF STATEMENT BY SOCIETY CARRYING ON BANKING

Section 7

1. Capital of the society:—
   - (a) nominal amount of each share;
   - (b) number of shares issued;
   - (c) amount paid up on shares.
2. Liabilities of the society on 1st January or 1st July last previous:—
   - (a) on judgments;
   - (b) on specialty;
   - (c) on notes or bills;
   - (d) on simple contract;
   - (e) on estimated liabilities.
3. Assets of the society on the same date:—
   - (a) government securities (stating them);
   - (b) bills of exchange and promissory notes;
   - (c) cash at the bankers;
   - (d) other securities.

[215]

SCHEDULE 3
FORM OF RECEIPT ON MORTGAGE, HERITABLE SECURITY, ETC

Sections 33, 34, 35

PART I
FORMS APPLICABLE IN ENGLAND AND WALES

Form A

The   Limited hereby acknowledges to have received all moneys intended to be secured by the (within (or above) written) (annexed) deed (and by a further charge dated, etc, *or otherwise as required*).

Dated this   day of

Members of the Committee.

Secretary.

Form B

The   Limited hereby acknowledges that it has this   day of   received the sum of   pounds representing all moneys intended to be secured by the (within (or above) written) (annexed) deed (and by a further charge dated, etc *or otherwise as required*), the payment having been made by C.D. of   and E. F. of

Members of the Committee.

Secretary.

NOTE. If the persons paying are not entitled to the equity of redemption but are paying the money out of a fund applicable to the discharge of the mortgage or other assurance, insert a statement to that effect.

A statement may also be inserted as to whether the receipt is or is not to operate as a transfer of the benefit of the mortgage or other assurance.

[216]

(*Sch 3, Pt II applies to Scotland only.*)

SCHEDULE 4
FORMS OF BOND FOR OFFICERS OF SOCIETY

Section 41

PART I
FORMS APPLICABLE IN ENGLAND, WALES AND THE CHANNEL ISLANDS

Form A

Know all men by these presents, that we, *A, B,* of   , one of the officers of the   Limited, hereinafter referred to as "the Society," whose registered office is at   in the county of   , and *C.D.*, of   (as surety on behalf of the said *A.B.*), are jointly and severally held and firmly bound to the said society in the sum of   , to be paid to the said society, or its certain attorney, for which payment well and truly to be made we jointly and severally bind ourselves, and each of us by himself, our and each of our heirs, executors, and administrators, firmly by these presents. Sealed with out seals. Dated the   day of   .

Whereas the above-bounden *A.B.* has been duly appointed to the office of   of the   Society, and he, together with the above-bounden *C.D.* as his surety, have entered into the above-written bond, subject to the condition herein-after contained: Now therefore the condition of the above-written bond is such, that if the said *A.B.* do render a just and true account of all moneys received and paid by him on account of the society, at such times as the rules thereof appoint, and do pay over all the moneys remaining in his hands, and assign and transfer or deliver all property (including books and papers) belonging to the society in his hands or custody to such person or persons as the society or the committee thereof appoint, according to the rules of the society, together with the proper and legal receipts or vouchers for such payments, then the above-written bond shall be void, but otherwise shall remain in full force.

Sealed and delivered in the presence of

Form B

Know all men by these presents that I   , of   , in the county of   , am firmly bound to

Limited, herein-after referred to as "the Society," whose registered office is at , in the county of , in the sum of pounds sterling to be paid to the said society or its assigns, for which payment to be truly made to the said society or its certain attorney or assigns I bind myself, my heirs, executors, and administrators, by these presents sealed with my seal.
(And know further that I (we) as surety (sureties) for the above-named principal obligor and such obligor are jointly and severally bound to the society in the sum aforesaid to be paid to the society or its assigns, for which payment to be truly made to the society or its certain attorney or assigns we firmly bind ourselves and each of us and each of our heirs, executors, and administrators by these presents sealed with our seals.
Dated the day of .
The condition of the above-contained bond is that if the said faithfully execute the office of to the society during such time as he continues to hold the same in virtue either of his present appointment, or of any renewal thereof if such office is of a renewable character (without wasting, embezzling, losing, misspending, misapplying, or unlawfully making away with any of the moneys, goods, chattels, wares, merchandise or effects whatsoever of the said society at any time committed to his charge, custody, or keeping by reason or means of his said office), and render a true and full account of all moneys received or paid by him on its behalf as and when he is required by the committee of the society for the time being, and pay over all the moneys remaining in his hands from time to time, and assign, transfer, and deliver up all securities, books, papers, property, and effects whatsoever of or belonging to the society in his charge, custody, or keeping, to such person or persons as the said committee may appoint, according to the rules or regulations of the society for the time being, together with the proper or legal receipts or vouchers for such payments; and in all other respects well and faithfully perform and fulfil the said office of to the society according to the rules thereof, then the above-mentioned bond shall be void and of no effect; but otherwise shall remain in full force.
Sealed and delivered by the above named .
(The words between brackets against which we have set out initials being first struck out*) in the presence of us and
*If no words are struck out in the bond or condition, strike out these words and let the witnesses set their initials in the margin.

[217]

(Sch 4, Pt II applies to Scotland only; Sch 5 repealed by the Statute Law (Repeals) Act 1974.)

LOCAL GOVERNMENT ACT 1972

(1972 c 70)

An Act to make provision with respect to local government and the functions of local authorities in England and Wales; to amend Part II of the Transport Act 1968; to confer rights of appeal in respect of decisions relating to licences under the Home Counties (Music and Dancing) Licensing Act 1926; to make further provision with respect to magistrates' courts committees; to abolish certain inferior courts of record; and for connected purposes

[26 October 1972]

1–110 ((*Pts I–VI) outside the scope of this work.*)

PART VII
MISCELLANEOUS POWERS OF LOCAL AUTHORITIES

Miscellaneous

111–138 (*Outside the scope of this work.*)

139 Acceptance of gifts of property

(1) Subject to the provisions of this section a local authority may accept, hold and administer—

(a) for the purpose of discharging any of their functions, gifts of property, whether real or personal, made for that purpose; or

(b) for the benefit of the inhabitants of their area or of some part of it, gifts made for that purpose;

and may execute any work (including works of maintenance or improvement) incidental to or consequential on the exercise of the powers conferred by this section.

(2) Where any such work is executed in connection with a gift made for the benefit of the inhabitants of the area of a local authority or of some part of that area, the cost of executing the work shall be added to any expenditure under section 137 above in computing the limit imposed on that expenditure by subsection (4) of that section.

(3) This section shall not authorise the acceptance by a local authority of property which, when accepted, would be held in trust for an ecclesiastical charity or for a charity for the relief of poverty.

(4) Nothing in this section shall affect any powers exercisable by a local authority under or by virtue of [the Education Act 1996].

[218]

NOTES

Sub-s (4): words in square brackets substituted by the Education Act 1996, s 582(1), Sch 37, Pt I, para 24.

Modification: this section has effect as if a National Park authority were a principal council for the purposes of this Act and as if the relevant Park were the authority's area, by virtue of the Environment Act 1995, s 65, Sch 8, para 3(1).

140–178 *(Ss 140–146A, ss 147–178 (Pt VIII) outside the scope of this work.)*

PART IX
FUNCTIONS

179–195 *(Outside the scope of this work.)*

Miscellaneous functions

196–209 *(Ss 196, 197, 202, 204, 206, 208 outside the scope of this work; ss 198, 199 repealed by the Food Act 1984, s 134, Sch 11; ss 200, 207 repealed by the Local Government (Wales) Act 1994, s 66(5), (8), Sch 15, paras 1, 42, Sch 18; s 201 repealed by the Weights and Measures Act 1985, s 98(1), Sch 13, Pt I; s 203 repealed by the Transport Act 1978, s 24(4), Sch 4; s 205 repealed by the Rent Act 1977, s 155, Sch 25; s 209 repealed by the Employment and Training Act 1973, s 14(2), Sch 4.)*

210 Charities

(1) Where, immediately before 1st April 1974, any property is held, as sole trustee, exclusively for charitable purposes by an existing local authority for an area outside Greater London, other than the parish council, parish meeting or representative body of an existing rural parish in England (but including the corporation of a borough included in a rural district), that property shall vest (on the same trusts) in a new local authority in accordance with subsections (2) to (5) below.

(2) Subject to subsection (3) below, where the property is held by one of the existing authorities specified below, and is so held for the benefit of, or of the inhabitants of, or of any particular class or body of persons in, a specified area, the property shall vest in the new authority specified below, the area of which comprises the whole or the greater part of that specified area, and where the property is so held but is not held for such a benefit, it shall vest in the new authority specified below, the area of which comprises the whole or the greater part of the area of the existing authority, that is to say—

(a) where the existing authority is a county council, the new authority is the council of the new county;

(b) where the existing authority is the council of a borough or urban district in England, the new authority is the council of the parish constituted under Part V of Schedule 1 to this Act or, where there is no such parish, the council of the district;

(c) where the existing authority is the council of a borough or urban district in Wales, the new authority is the council of the community or, where there is no such council, the council of the district; and

(d) where the existing authority is a rural district council, then, if the rural district is co-extensive with a parish, the new authority is the parish council, and in any other case the new authority is the council of the district.

(3) Where the property is held by an existing county council or county borough council for the purposes of a charity registered in the register established under section 4 of the Charities Act 1960 in any part of that register which is maintained by the Secretary of State by virtue of section 2 of that Act (educational charities) then—

(a) if the property is so held for the benefit of, or of the inhabitants of, or of any particular class or body of persons in, a specified area, the property shall vest in the new authority which is the local education authority for the whole or the greater part of that specified area, and

(b) in any other case, the property shall vest in the new authority which is the local education authority for the whole or the greater part of the area of the existing county council or county borough council by which the property is held.

(4) Where the property is held by the corporation of a borough included in a rural district, it shall vest in the parish council for the parish consisting of the area of the existing borough.

(5) Where the property is held by the parish council, parish meeting or representative body of an existing rural parish in Wales, then—

(a) in the case of property held by an existing parish council, the property shall vest in the community council for the community or group of communities, the area or areas of which are co-extensive with the area of the parish or parishes for which the existing parish council act;

(b) in the case of property held by the parish meeting or representative body of an existing parish the area of which is comprised in a community for which there is a community council, the property shall vest in that community council; and

(c) in any other case, the property shall vest in the council of the district which comprises the area of the existing rural parish.

(6) Where, immediately before 1st April 1974, any power with respect to a charity, not being a charity incorporated under the Companies Acts or by charter, is under the trusts of the charity or by virtue of any enactment vested in, or in the holder of an office connected with, any existing local authority to which subsection (1) above applies, that power shall vest in, or in the holder of the corresponding office connected with, or (if there is no such office) the proper officer of, the corresponding new authority, that is to say, the new authority in which, had the property of the charity been vested in the existing local authority, that property would have been vested under subsections (1) to (5) above.

(7) References in subsection (6) above to a power with respect to a charity do not include references to a power of any person by virtue of being a charity trustee thereof; but where under the trusts of any charity, not being a charity incorporated under the Companies Acts or by charter, the charity trustees immediately before 1st April 1974 include either an existing local authority to which subsection (1) above applies or the holder of an office connected with such an existing local authority, those trustees shall instead include the corresponding new authority as defined in subsection (6) above or, as the case may require, the holder of the corresponding office connected with, or (if there is no such office) the proper officer of, that authority.

(8), (9) …

(10) Nothing in the foregoing provisions of this section shall affect any power of Her Majesty, the court or any other person to alter the trusts of any charity and nothing in those provisions shall apply in a case to which section 211 below applies.

(11) In this section the expression "local authority", in relation to a parish, includes a parish meeting and the representative body of a parish, and the expressions "charitable purposes", "charity", "charity trustees", "court" and "trusts" have the same meanings as in the Charities Act 1960.

[219]

NOTES

Sub-s (8): repealed by the Charities Act 1992, s 78(2), Sch 7.
Sub-s (9): repealed by the Charities Act 1993, s 98(2), Sch 7.

211–244A *(Ss 211, 213–215, ss 216–244A (Pts X, XI) outside the scope of this work; s 212 repealed by the Local Land Charges Act 1975, s 19(1), Sch 2.)*

PART XII
MISCELLANEOUS AND GENERAL

245–250 *(Outside the scope of this work.)*

General

251–272 *(Ss 251–263, 265–267, 269–272 outside the scope of this work; s 264 repealed by the Local Government Act 1985, s 101(2), Sch 17; s 268 repealed by the House of Commons Disqualification Act 1975, s 10(2), Sch 3 and the Northern Ireland Assembly Disqualification Act 1975, s 5(2), Sch 3, Pt I.)*

273 Commencement

(1) The provisions of this Act to which this subsection applies shall, except so far as brought into force earlier by an order under subsection (2) below, come into force on 1st April 1974.

(2)–(10) *(Outside the scope of this work.)*

[220]

NOTES

This Act largely came into force on Royal Assent, and the whole Act was effective from 1 April 1974; for more details of its commencement (for administrative reasons earlier dates were prescribed for the coming into force of certain provisions) see: the Local Government Act 1972 (Commencement No 1) (England) Order 1973, SI 1973/373, and the Local Government Act 1972 (Commencement No 2) (Wales) Order 1973, SI 1973/375.

274 Short title and extent

(1) This Act may be cited as the Local Government Act 1972.

(2) … this Act shall not extend to Scotland.

(3) … this Act shall not extend to Northern Ireland.

[221]

NOTES

Sub-s (2): words omitted repealed by the Statute Law (Repeals) Act 2004.
Sub-s (3): words omitted repealed by the House of Commons Disqualification Act 1875, s 10(2), Sch 3, and the Northern Ireland Assembly Disqualification Act 1975, s 5(2), Sch 3, Part I.

(Schs 1–30 in so far as unrepealed, outside the scope of this work.)

EDUCATION ACT 1973

(1973 c 16)

An Act to make provision for terminating and in part replacing the powers possessed by the Secretary of State for Education and Science and the Secretary of State for Wales under the Charities Act 1960 concurrently with the Charity Commissioners or under the Endowed Schools Acts 1869 to 1948, and enlarging certain other powers of modifying educational trusts, and for supplementing awards under section 1 and restricting awards under section 2 of the Education Act 1962, and for purposes connected therewith

[18 April 1973]

Educational trusts

1 General provisions as to educational trusts

(1), (2) …

(3) In connection with the operation of this section there shall have effect the transitional and other consequential or supplementary provisions contained in Schedule 1 to this Act.

(4) The enactments mentioned in Schedule 2 to this Act (which includes in Part I certain enactments already spent or otherwise no longer required apart from the foregoing provisions of this section) are hereby repealed to the extent specified in column 3 of the Schedule.

(5) Subsection (1)(a) above and Part III of Schedule 2 to this Act shall not come into force until such date as may be appointed by order made by statutory instrument by the Secretary of State.

[222]

NOTES

Sub-s (1): repeals the Charities Act 1960, s 2, and the Endowed Schools Acts 1869 to 1948 (ie the Endowed Schools Act 1869, the Endowed Schools Act 1873, the Education (Miscellaneous Provisions) Act 1948, s 2, Sch 1, Pt II).

Sub-s (2): repealed by the Education Act 1996, s 582(2), Sch 38, Pt I.

Orders: the Education Act 1973 (Commencement) Order 1973, SI 1973/1661.

2–4 *(S 2 repealed by the Education Act 1996, s 582(2), Sch 38, Pt I; s 3 repealed by the Teaching and Higher Education Act 1998, s 44(2), Sch 4; s 4 outside the scope of this work.)*

Supplementary

5 Citation and extent

(1) This Act may be cited as the Education Act 1973 …

(2) Nothing in this Act extends to Scotland or to Northern Ireland.

[223]

NOTES

Sub-s (1): words omitted repealed by the Education Act 1996, s 582(2), Sch 38, Pt I.

SCHEDULE 1
TRANSITIONAL AND SUPPLEMENTARY PROVISIONS AS TO CHARITIES ETC

1.—(1) …

(2) Section 210(3) of the Local Government Act 1972 (which makes special provision for certain charitable property to vest in local education authorities, if it is held for purposes of a charity registered in a part of the charities register maintained by the Secretary of State by virtue of section 2 of the Charities Act 1960) shall have effect, unless the appointed day is later than the end of March 1974, as if the reference to a charity registered in a part of the register which is maintained by the Secretary of State were a reference to a charity so registered immediately before the appointed day.

(3) …

(4) The repeal by this Act of section 2(1) of the Charities Act 1960 shall not affect the operation of section 2(1)—

(a) in conferring on the Charity Commissioners functions belonging at the passing of that Act to the Minister of Education; or

(b) in extending to the Charity Commissioners references to the Secretary of State for Education and Science or the Secretary of State for Wales (or references having effect as if either of them were mentioned) so as to enable the Commissioners to discharge any such functions as aforesaid or to act under or for the purposes of the trusts of a charity;

but on the appointed day any functions so conferred and any reference so extended shall, subject to sub-paragraph (5) below, cease to be functions of or to extend to either Secretary of State.

[(5) Where it appears to the Secretary of State that any reference, which in accordance with sub-paragraph (4) above ceased on the appointed day to extend to the Secretary of State for Education and Science or the Secretary of State for Wales, was not related (or not wholly related) to the functions ceasing to belong to that Minister by the repeal of section 2(1) of the Charities Act 1960, he may by order exclude the operation of that sub-paragraph in relation to the reference and make such modifications of the relevant instrument as appear to him appropriate in the circumstances.]

(6) The repeal of section 2(1) of the Charities Act 1960 shall not affect the validity of anything done (or having effect as if done) before the appointed day by or in relation to the Secretary of State for Education and Science or the Secretary of State for Wales, and anything so done (or having effect as if so done) in so far as it could by virtue of section 2(1) have been done by or in relation to the Charity Commissioners shall thereafter have effect as if done by or in relation to them.

(7) In this paragraph "appointed day" means the day appointed under section 1(5) of this Act.

2.—(1) Where before the passing of this Act a scheme under the Endowed Schools Acts 1869 to 1948 has been published as required by section 13 of the Endowed Schools Act 1873, the scheme may be proceeded with as if section 1 of this Act had not been passed.

(2) Where before the passing of this Act a draft scheme under the Endowed Schools Acts 1869 to 1948 has been prepared in a case in which effect might be given to the scheme by order under section 2 of this Act, and the draft scheme has been published as required by section 33 of the Endowed Schools Act 1869, the scheme may be proceeded with in pursuance of section 2 of this Act as if section 2(2)(a) and (b) had been complied with on the date this Act is passed.

3. …

[224]

NOTES

Para 1: sub-paras (1), (3) repealed by the Charities Act 1993, s 98(2); sub-para (5) substituted by the Transfer of Functions (Education and Employment) Order 1995, SI 1995/2986, art 11(1), Schedule, para 7.

Para 3: repealed by the Education Act 1996, s 582(2), Sch 38, Pt I.

(*Sch 2 contains repeals.*)

CONSUMER CREDIT ACT 1974

(1974 c 39)

An Act to establish for the protection of consumers a new system, administered by the Director General of Fair Trading, of licensing and other control of traders concerned with the provision of credit, or the supply of goods on hire or hire-purchase, and their transactions, in place of the present enactments regulating moneylenders, pawnbrokers and hire-purchase traders and their transactions, and for related matters

[31 July 1974]

1–7 ((*Pt I*) *outside the scope of this work.*)

PART II
CREDIT AGREEMENTS, HIRE AGREEMENTS AND LINKED TRANSACTIONS

8–15 (*Outside the scope of this work.*)

16 Exempt agreements

(1) This Act does not regulate a consumer credit agreement where the creditor is a local authority … , or a body specified, or of a description specified, in an order made by the Secretary of State, being—

[(a) an insurer,]
(b) a friendly society,
(c) an organisation of employers or organisation of workers,
(d) a charity,
(e) a land improvement company, …
(f) a body corporate named or specifically referred to in any public general Act
[(ff) a body corporate named or specifically referred to in an order made under—
section 156(4), *444(1)* or 447(2)(a) of the Housing Act 1985,
[section 156(4) of that Act as it has effect by virtue of section 17 of the Housing Act 1996 (the right to acquire),],
…
Article 154(1)(a) or 156AA of the Housing (Northern Ireland) Order 1981 or Article 10(6A) of the Housing (Northern Ireland) Order 1983; or]
[(g) a building society][, or
[(h) a deposit-taker]].

(2) Subsection (1) applies only where the agreement is—

(a) a debtor-creditor-supplier agreement financing—
(i) the purchase of land, or
(ii) the provision of dwellings on any land, and secured by a land mortgage on that land, or
(b) a debtor-creditor agreement secured by any land mortgage; or
(c) a debtor-creditor-supplier agreement financing a transaction which is a linked transaction in relation to—
(i) an agreement falling within paragraph (a), or
(ii) an agreement falling within paragraph (b) financing—
(aa) the purchase of any land, or
(bb) the provision of dwellings on any land,

and secured by a land mortgage on the land referred to in paragraph (a) or, as the case may be, the land referred to in sub-paragraph (ii).

[(3) Before he makes, varies or revokes an order under subsection (1), the Secretary of State must undertake the necessary consultation.

(3A) The necessary consultation means consultation with the bodies mentioned in the following table in relation to the provision under which the order is to be made, varied or revoked:

TABLE

Provision of subsection (1)	*Consultee*
Paragraph (a) or (b)	The Financial Services Authority
Paragraph (d)	The [Charity Commission]
Paragraph (e), (f) or (ff)	Any Minister of the Crown with responsibilities in relation to the body in question
Paragraph (g) or (h)	The Treasury and the Financial Services Authority]

(4) An order under subsection (1) relating to a body may be limited so as to apply only to agreements by that body of a description specified in the order.

(5) The Secretary of State may by order provide that this Act shall not regulate other consumer credit agreements where—

(a) the number of payments to be made by the debtor does not exceed the number specified for that purpose in the order, or
(b) the rate of the total charge for credit does not exceed the rate so specified, or
(c) an agreement has a connection with a country outside the United Kingdom.

(6) The Secretary of State may by order provide that this Act shall not regulate consumer hire agreements of a description specified in the order where—

(a) the owner is a body corporate authorised by or under any enactment to supply electricity, gas or water, and

(b) the subject of the agreement is a meter or metering equipment, [or where the owner is a [provider of a public electronic communications service who is specified in the order]].

[(6A) This Act does not regulate a consumer credit agreement where the creditor is a housing authority and the agreement is secured by a land mortgage of a dwelling.

(6B) In subsection (6A) "housing authority" means—

(a) as regards England and Wales, [the Housing Corporation, … and] an authority or body within section 80(1) of the Housing Act 1985 (the landlord condition for secure tenancies), other than a housing association or a housing trust which is a charity;

(b) as regards Scotland, a development corporation established under an order made, or having effect as if made under the New Towns (Scotland) Act 1968, the Scottish Special Housing Association or the Housing Corporation;

(c) as regards Northern Ireland, the Northern Ireland Housing Executive.]

[*(6C) This Act does not regulate a consumer credit agreement if—*

(a) it is secured by a land mortgage; and

(b) entering into that agreement as lender is a regulated activity for the purposes of the Financial Services and Markets Act 2000.

(6D) But section 126, and any other provision so far as it relates to section 126, applies to an agreement which would (but for *subsection (6C)*) be a regulated agreement.

(6E) Subsection (6C) must be read with—

(a) section 22 of the Financial Services and Markets Act 2000 (regulated activities: power to specify classes of activity and categories of investment);

(b) any order for the time being in force under that section; and

(c) Schedule 2 to that Act.]

(7) Nothing in this section affects the application of sections 137 to 140 (extortionate credit bargains).

[(7A) Nothing in this section affects the application of sections 140A to 140C.]

[(8) In the application of this section to Scotland, subsection (3A) shall have effect as if the reference to the [Charity Commission] were a reference to the Lord Advocate.]

(9) In the application of this section to Northern Ireland [subsection (3A)] shall have effect as if any reference to a Minister of the Crown were a reference to a Northern Ireland department, … and any reference to the [Charity Commission] were a reference to the Department of Finance for Northern Ireland.

[(10) In this section—

(a) "deposit-taker" means—

(i) a person who has permission under Part 4 of the Financial Services and Markets Act 2000 to accept deposits,

(ii) an EEA firm of the kind mentioned in paragraph 5(b) of Schedule 3 to that Act which has permission under paragraph 15 of that Schedule (as a result of qualifying for authorisation under paragraph 12 of that Schedule) to accept deposits,

(iii) any wholly owned subsidiary (within the meaning of the Companies Act 1985) of a person mentioned in sub-paragraph (i), or

(iv) any undertaking which, in relation to a person mentioned in sub-paragraph (ii), is a subsidiary undertaking within the meaning of any rule of law in force in the EEA State in question for purposes connected with the implementation of the European Council Seventh Company Law Directive of 13 June 1983 on consolidated accounts (No 83/349/EEC), and which has no members other than that person;

(b) "insurer" means—

(i) a person who has permission under Part 4 of the Financial Services and Markets Act 2000 to effect or carry out contracts of insurance, or

(ii) an EEA firm of the kind mentioned in paragraph 5(d) of Schedule 3 to that Act, which has permission under paragraph 15 of that Schedule (as a result of qualifying for authorisation under paragraph 12 of that Schedule) to effect or carry out contracts of insurance,

but does not include a friendly society or an organisation of workers or of employers.

(11) Subsection (10) must be read with—
(a) section 22 of the Financial Services and Markets Act 2000;
(b) any relevant order under that section; and
(c) Schedule 2 to that Act.]

[225]

NOTES

Sub-s (1): words omitted in the first place repealed and para (g) inserted by the Building Societies Act 1986, s 120(1), (2), Sch 18, Pt I, para 10(2), Sch 19, Pt I; para (a) substituted by the Financial Services and Markets Act 2000 (Consequential Amendments and Repeals) Order 2001, SI 2001/3649, art 165(1), (2)(a); para (ff) inserted by the Housing and Planning Act 1986, s 22(2), (4), with respect to agreements made after 7 January 1987, number "444(1)" in italics repealed by the Housing Act 1996, s 227, Sch 19, Pt XIV, as from a day to be appointed, and words in square brackets inserted by the Housing Act 1996 (Consequential Amendments) (No 2) Order 1997, SI 1997/627, art 2, Schedule, para 2; para (h) and the word immediately preceding it inserted by the Banking Act 1987, s 88(2), substituted by SI 2001/3649, art 165(1), (2)(b).

Sub-s (3): substituted, together with sub-s (3A), for sub-s (3) as originally enacted, by SI 2001/3649, art 165(1), (3).

Sub-s (3A): substituted, together with sub-s (3), for sub-s (3) as originally enacted, by SI 2001/3649, art 165(1), (3); words in square brackets in the Table substituted by the Charities Act 2006, s 75(1), Sch 8, para 56.

Sub-s (6): words in first (outer) pair of square brackets substituted by the Telecommunications Act 1984, s 109, Sch 4, para 60(1); words in second (inner) pair of square brackets substituted by the Communications Act 2003, s 406(1), Sch 17, para 47.

Sub-s (6A): inserted, together with sub-s (6B), by the Housing and Planning Act 1986, s 22(3), with respect to agreements made after 7 January 1987.

Sub-s (6B): inserted, together with sub-s (6A), by the Housing and Planning Act 1986, s 22(3), with respect to agreements made after 7 January 1987; words in square brackets inserted by the Housing Act 1988, s 140(1), Sch 17, Pt I, para 20; words omitted repealed by the Government of Wales Act 1998, ss 141, 152, Sch 18, Pt VI, subject to transitional provisions.

Sub-s (6C): inserted, together with sub-ss (6D), (6E), by the Financial Services and Markets Act 2000 (Regulated Activities) Order 2001, SI 2001/544, art 90(1), (2); substituted as follows partly as from 6 November 2006 and fully as from 6 April 2007 by the Financial Services and Markets Act 2000 (Regulated Activities) (Amendment) (No 2) Order 2006, SI 2006/2383, art 25(1), (2)(a), subject to transitional provisions in arts 37–39 of that Order—

"(6C) This Act does not regulate a consumer credit agreement if—
(a) it is secured by a land mortgage and entering into the agreement as lender is a regulated activity for the purposes of the Financial Services and Markets Act 2000; or
(b) it is or forms part of a regulated home purchase plan and entering into the agreement as home purchase provider is a regulated activity for the purposes of that Act.".

Sub-s (6D): inserted, together with sub-s (6E), by SI 2001/544, art 90(1), (2); for the words in italics there are substituted the words "subsection (6C)(a)" partly as from 6 November 2006 and fully as from 6 April 2007 by SI 2006/2383, art 25(1), (2)(b), subject to transitional provisions in arts 37–39 of that Order.

Sub-s (6E): inserted, together with sub-s (6D), by SI 2001/544, art 90(1), (2).

Sub-s (7): repealed by the Consumer Credit Act 2006, s 70, Sch 4, as from 6 April 2007, subject to transitional provisions and savings in Sch 3, paras 1, 15(5)(a), (7) to that Act.

Sub-s (7A): inserted by the Consumer Credit Act 2006, s 22(2), as from 6 April 2007.

Sub-s (8): substituted by SI 2001/3649, art 165(1), (4); words in square brackets substituted by the Charities Act 2006, s 75(1), Sch 8, para 56.

Sub-s (9): words in first pair of square brackets substituted and words omitted repealed by SI 2001/3649, art 165(1), (5); words in second pair of square brackets substituted by the Charities Act 2006, s 75(1), Sch 8, para 56.

Sub-ss (10), (11): added by SI 2001/3649, art 165(1), (6).

Orders: the Consumer Credit (Exempt Agreements) Order 1989, SI 1989/869.

17–173 (*Ss 17–20, ss 21–173 (Pts III–XI) outside the scope of this work.*)

PART XII
SUPPLEMENTAL

174–189 (*Outside the scope of this work.*)

Miscellaneous

190–192 (*Outside the scope of this work.*)

193 Short title and extent

(1) This Act may be cited as the Consumer Credit Act 1974.

(2) This Act extends to Northern Ireland.

[226]

(*Schs 1–5 outside the scope of this work.*)

SEX DISCRIMINATION ACT 1975

(1975 c 65)

An Act to render unlawful certain kinds of sex discrimination and discrimination on the ground of marriage, and establish a Commission with the function of working towards the elimination of such discrimination and promoting equality of opportunity between men and women generally; and for related purposes

[12 November 1975]

1–42 ((*Pts I–IV*) *outside the scope of this work.*)

PART V
GENERAL EXCEPTIONS FROM PARTS II TO IV

43 Charities

(1) Nothing in Parts II to IV shall—
- (a) be construed as affecting a provision to which this subsection applies, or
- (b) render unlawful an act which is done in order to give effect to such a provision.

(2) Subsection (1) applies to a provision for conferring benefits on persons of one sex only (disregarding any benefits to persons of the opposite sex which are exceptional or are relatively insignificant), being a provision which is contained in a charitable instrument.

[(3) In this section "charitable instrument" means an enactment or other instrument so far as it relates to charitable purposes, and in Scotland includes the governing instrument of an endowment or of an educational endowment as those expressions are defined in section 135(1) of the Education (Scotland) Act 1962.

In the application of this section to England and Wales, "charitable purposes" means purposes which are exclusively charitable according to the law of England and Wales.]

[227]

NOTES

Sub-s (3): substituted for original sub-ss (3), (4) by the Sex Discrimination Act 1975 (Amendment of section 43) Order 1977, SI 1977/528, art 2.

44–76 (*Ss 44–52A, ss 53–76* (*Pts VI, VII*) *outside the scope of this work.*)

PART VIII
SUPPLEMENTAL

77–86 (*Ss 77, 78, 80–86 outside the scope of this work; s 79 applies to Scotland only.*)

87 Short title and extent

(1) This Act may be cited as the Sex Discrimination Act 1975.

(2) This Act (except paragraph 16 of Schedule 3) does not extend to Northern Ireland.

[228]

(*Schs 1–6 outside the scope of this work.*)

LOTTERIES AND AMUSEMENTS ACT 1976

(1976 c 32)

ARRANGEMENT OF SECTIONS

PART I
LEGAL AND ILLEGAL LOTTERIES

General illegality of lotteries

An Act to consolidate certain enactments relating to lotteries, prize competitions and amusements with prizes

[22 July 1976]

PART I
LEGAL AND ILLEGAL LOTTERIES

General illegality of lotteries

1 Illegality of lotteries

All lotteries which do not constitute gaming are unlawful, except as provided by this Act [and section 2(1) of the National Lottery etc Act 1993].

[229]

NOTES

This Act is repealed by the Gambling Act 2005, s 356(3)(i), (4), Sch 17, as from 1 September 2007, subject to savings and transitional provisions in Sch 18, Pt 2, paras 8–11 to that Act and in the Gambling Act 2005 (Commencement No 6 and Transitional Provisions) Order 2006, SI 2006/3272, arts 5, 6, Sch 4, paras 13–16, 67–77, 101–107.

Words in square brackets inserted by the National Lottery etc Act 1993, s 2(2), Sch 1, para 2(1).

2 General lottery offences

(1) Subject to the provisions of this section, every person who in connection with any lottery promoted or proposed to be promoted either in Great Britain or elsewhere—

(a) prints any tickets for use in the lottery; or

(b) sells or distributes, or offers or advertises for sale or distribution, or has in his possession for the purpose of sale or distribution, any tickets or chances in the lottery; or

(c) prints, publishes or distributes, or has in his possession for the purpose of publication or distribution—

(i) any advertisement of the lottery; or

(ii) any list, whether complete or not, of prize winners or winning tickets in the lottery; or

(iii) any such matter descriptive of the drawing or intended drawing of the lottery, or otherwise relating to the lottery, as is calculated to act as an inducement to persons to participate in that lottery or in other lotteries; or

(d) brings, or invites any person to send, into Great Britain [from a place outside the British Islands and the member States] for the purpose of sale or distribution any ticket in, or advertisement of, the lottery; or

(e) sends or attempts to send out of Great Britain [to a place outside the British Islands and the member States] any money or valuable thing received in respect of the sale or distribution, or any document recording the sale or distribution, or the identity of the holder, of any ticket or chance in the lottery; or

(f) uses any premises, or causes or knowingly permits any premises to be used, for purposes connected with the promotion or conduct of the lottery; or

(g) causes, procures or attempts to procure any person to do any of the above-mentioned acts, shall be guilty of an offence.

(2) In any proceedings instituted under subsection (1) above, it shall be a defence to prove either—

(a) that the lottery to which the proceedings relate was a lottery declared not to be unlawful by section 3, 4 or 25(6) below, and that at the date of the alleged offence the person charged believed, and had reasonable ground for believing, that none of the conditions required by the relevant enactment to be observed in connection with the promotion and conduct of the lottery had been broken; or

(b) that the lottery to which the proceedings relate was a society's lottery or a local

lottery, and that at the date of the alleged offence the person charged believed, and had reasonable ground for believing, that it was being conducted in accordance with the requirements of this Act; or

(*c*) *that the lottery to which the proceedings relate was not promoted wholly or partly outside Great Britain and constituted gaming as well as a lottery[; or* (*d*) *that the lottery to which the proceedings relate was a lottery forming part of the National Lottery for the purposes of Part I of the National Lottery etc Act 1993 or that at the date of the alleged offence the person charged believed, and had reasonable ground for believing, it to be such a lottery.]*

[(2A) In any proceedings instituted under subsection (*1*) *above in respect of the printing, sale or possession of any tickets, advertisements or other documents or in respect of anything done with a view to or in connection with the printing, sale or export from Great Britain of any tickets, advertisements or other documents, it shall be a defence to prove that at the date of the alleged offence the person charged believed, and had reasonable ground for believing—*

(*a*) *that the lottery to which the proceedings relate was not being, and would not be, promoted or conducted wholly or partly in Great Britain; and*

(*b*) *that the tickets, advertisements or other documents were not being, and would not be, used in Great Britain in or in connection with that or any other lottery.]*

(3) In England and Wales, proceedings under subsection (*1*)(*c*)(*iii*) *above in respect of any matter published in a newspaper shall not be instituted except by, or by direction of, the Director of Public Prosecutions.*

[230]

NOTES

Repealed as noted to s 1 at **[229]**.

Sub-s (1): in paras (d), (e) words in square brackets inserted by the National Lottery etc Act 1993, s 46(3).

Sub-s (2): para (d), and the word immediately preceding it added by the National Lottery etc Act 1993, s 2(2), Sch 1, para 2(2).

Sub-s (2A): inserted by the Lotteries (Amendment) Act 1984, s 1.

Exceptions

3 Small lotteries incidental to exempt entertainments

(1) In this Act "exempt entertainment" means a bazaar, sale of work, fete, dinner, dance, sporting or athletic event or other entertainment of a similar character, whether limited to one day or extending over two or more days.

(2) Where a lottery is promoted as an incident of an exempt entertainment, that lottery is not unlawful, but the conditions set out in subsection (*3*) *below shall be observed in connection with its promotion and conduct and, if any of those conditions is contravened, every person concerned in the promotion or conduct of the lottery shall be guilty of an offence unless he proves that the contravention occurred without his consent or connivance and that he exercised all due diligence to prevent it.*

(3) The conditions referred to in subsection (2) *above are that—*

(*a*) *the whole proceeds of the entertainment* (*including the proceeds of the lottery*) *after deducting—*

(*i*) *the expenses of the entertainment, excluding expenses incurred in connection with the lottery; and*

(*ii*) *the expenses incurred in printing tickets in the lottery; and*

(*iii*) *such sum, if any, not exceeding £50 or such other sum as may be specified in an order made by the Secretary of State, as the promoters of the lottery think fit to appropriate on account of any expenses incurred by them in purchasing prizes in the lottery, shall be devoted to purposes other than private gain;*

(*b*) *none of the prizes in the lottery shall be money prizes;*

(*c*) *tickets or chances in the lottery shall not be sold or issued, nor shall the result of the lottery be declared, except on the premises on which the entertainment takes place and during the progress of the entertainment; and*

(*d*) *the facilities for participating in lotteries under this section, or those facilities together with any other facilities for participating in lotteries or gaming, shall not be the only, or the only substantial, inducement to persons to attend the entertainment.*

[231]

NOTES

Repealed as noted to s 1 at **[229]**.
Orders: the Exempt Entertainments (Variation of Monetary Limit) Order 1993, SI 1992/3222.

4 Private lotteries

[(1) In this Act "private lottery" means a lottery in Great Britain which is promoted—

(*a*) *for members of one society established and conducted for purposes not connected with gaming, betting or lotteries;*

(*b*) *for persons all of whom work on the same premises; or*

(*c*) *for persons all of whom reside on the same premises,*

and which satisfies the conditions in subsections (1A) and (1B) below.

(*1A*) *The lottery must be promoted by persons each of whom—*

(*a*) *is one of the persons for whom the lottery is promoted; and*

(*b*) *in the case of a lottery promoted for the members of a society, is authorised in writing by the governing body of the society to promote the lottery.*

(*1B*) *The sale of tickets or chances in the lottery must be confined—*

(*a*) *to the persons for whom the lottery is promoted; and*

(*b*) *in the case of a lottery promoted for the members of a society, to any other persons on the society's premises.]*

(*2*) *For the purposes of this section, each local or affiliated branch or section of a society shall be regarded as a separate and distinct society.*

(*3*) *A private lottery is not unlawful, but the following conditions shall be observed in connection with its promotion and conduct, that is to say—*

(*a*) *the whole proceeds, after deducting only expenses incurred for printing and stationery, shall be devoted to the provision of prizes for purchasers of tickets or chances, or, in the case of a lottery promoted for the members of a society, shall be devoted either—*

(*i*) *to the provision of prizes as aforesaid; or*

(*ii*) *to purposes which are purposes of the society; or*

(*iii*) *as to part to the provision of prizes as aforesaid and as to the remainder to such purposes as aforesaid;*

(*b*) *there shall not be exhibited, published or distributed any written notice or advertisement of the lottery other than—*

(*i*) *a notice of it exhibited on the premises of the society for whose members it is promoted or, as the case may be, on the premises on which the persons for whom it is promoted work or reside; and*

(*ii*) *such announcement or advertisement of it as is contained in the tickets, if any;*

(*c*) *the price of every ticket or chance shall be the same, and the price of any ticket shall be stated on the ticket;*

(*d*) *every ticket shall bear upon the face of it the name and address of each of the promoters and a statement of the persons to whom the sale of tickets or chances by the promoters is restricted, and a statement that no prize won in the lottery shall be paid or delivered by the promoters to any person other than the person to whom the winning ticket or chance was sold by them, and no prize shall be paid or delivered except in accordance with that statement;*

(*e*) *no ticket or chance shall be issued or allotted by the promoters except by way of sale and upon receipt of its full price, and no money or valuable thing so received by a promoter shall in any circumstances be returned; and*

(*f*) *no tickets in the lottery shall be sent through the post.*

(*4*) *Subject to subsection (5) below, if any of the conditions set out in subsection (3) above is contravened, each of the promoters of the lottery, and, where the person by whom the condition is broken is not one of the promoters, that person also, shall be guilty of an offence.*

(5) It shall be a defence for a person charged with an offence under subsection (4) above only by reason of his being a promoter of the lottery to prove that the contravention occurred without his consent or connivance and that he exercised all due diligence to prevent it.

[232]

NOTES

Repealed as noted to s 1 at **[229]**.

Sub-ss (1)–(1B): substituted for original sub-s (1) by the National Lottery etc Act 1993, s 47.

5 Societies' lotteries

(1) In this Act "society's lottery" means a lottery promoted on behalf of a society which is established and conducted wholly or mainly for one or more of the following purposes, that is to say—

- *(a) charitable purposes;*
- *(b) participation in or support of athletic sports or games or cultural activities;*
- *(c) purposes which are not described in paragraph (a) or (b) above but are neither purposes of private gain nor purposes of any commercial undertaking.*

(2) Any purpose for which a society is established and conducted and which is calculated to benefit the society as a whole shall not be held to be a purpose of private gain by reason only that action in its fulfilment would result in benefit to any person as an individual.

(3) Subject to the provisions of this Act, a society's lottery is not unlawful if—

- *(a) it is promoted in Great Britain; and*
- *(b) the society is for the time being registered under [the appropriate Schedule]; and*
- *(c) it is promoted in accordance with a scheme approved by the society; …*
- *(d) …*

[(3A) The appropriate Schedule for the purposes of subsection (3)(b) above—

- *(a) is Schedule 1 to this Act if none of subsections (3B) to (3D) below applies to the lottery;*
- *(b) is Schedule 1A to this Act if any of those subsections applies to the lottery.*

(3B) This subsection applies to a lottery if the total value of the tickets or chances sold or to be sold in the lottery is more than £20,000.

(3C) This subsection applies to a lottery if the total value of—

- *(a) the tickets or chances sold or to be sold in the lottery, and*
- *(b) the tickets or chances sold or to be sold in all earlier lotteries held by the same society in the same year,*

is more than £250,000.

(3D) This subsection applies to a lottery if subsection (3B) or (3C) above applied to any earlier lottery held by the same society in the same year or any of the three preceding years.

(3E) For the purposes of this section—

- *(a) a lottery is earlier than another lottery if any tickets or chances in it are sold, distributed or offered for sale before any tickets or chances in the other lottery are sold, distributed or offered for sale, and*
- *(b) a lottery is held in the year in which the date of the lottery falls.*

(3F) In this section "year" means a period of twelve months beginning with 1st January.]

(4) The whole proceeds of a society's lottery, after deducting sums lawfully appropriated on account of expenses or for the provision of prizes, shall be applied to purposes of the society such as are described in subsection (1) above.

(5) [Schedules 1 and 1A] to this Act shall have effect.

[233]

NOTES

Repealed as noted to s 1 at **[229]**.

Sub-s (3): words in square brackets substituted and words omitted repealed by the National Lottery etc Act 1993, ss 48(1), (2), 49(1), 64, Sch 10.

Sub-ss (3A)–(3F): inserted by the National Lottery etc Act 1993, s 48(1), (3).

Sub-s (5): words in square brackets substituted by the National Lottery etc Act 1993, s 48(1), (4).

6 Local lotteries

(*1*) *In this Act "local lottery" means a lottery promoted by a local authority.*

(*2*) *Subject to the provisions of this Act, a local lottery is not unlawful if—*

(*a*) *it is promoted in Great Britain; and*

(*b*) *it is promoted in accordance with a scheme approved by the local authority; and*

(*c*) *the scheme is registered with the Board before any tickets or chances are sold.*

(*3*) *The functions of local authorities for the discharge of which arrangements may be made under section 101 of the Local Government Act 1972 or section 56 of the Local Government (Scotland) Act 1973 (arrangements for the discharge of a local authority's functions by a committee, a sub-committee or an officer of the authority, or by another local authority) do not include the approval of schemes for local lotteries.*

[(4) Schedule 2 to this Act shall have effect.]

[234]

NOTES

Repealed as noted to s 1 at **[229]**.
Sub-s (4): added by the National Lottery etc Act 1993, s 49(2).

PART II
PROVISIONS RELATING TO SOCIETIES' LOTTERIES AND LOCAL LOTTERIES

Provisions relating to local lotteries

7 Purposes of a local lottery

(*1*) *A local authority may promote a local lottery for any purpose for which they have power to incur expenditure under any enactment, including, without prejudice to the generality of this subsection, section 137 of the Local Government Act 1972 and section 83 of the Local Government (Scotland) Act 1973 (power of local authorities to incur expenditure for certain purposes not otherwise authorised).*

(*2*) *It shall be the duty of a local authority—*

(*a*) *to give such publicity to the object of a local lottery as will be likely to bring it to the attention of persons purchasing tickets or chances; and*

(*b*) *subject to the following provisions of this section, to apply money accruing from a local lottery only to the object of the lottery.*

(*3*) *In this section "object" means the particular purpose or purposes for which a local authority promote a local lottery.*

(*4*) *The Secretary of State, upon receipt of an application from a local authority for his consent to the use of money accruing from a local lottery for a purpose suggested by the local authority other than the object of the lottery, may give that consent if and only if he is satisfied—*

(*a*) *that the object of the lottery, in whole or in part—*

(*i*) *has been as far as may be fulfilled; or*

(*ii*) *cannot be carried out; or*

(*b*) *that the object provides a use for part only of the money accruing from the lottery; or*

(*c*) *that the money accruing from the lottery and other money applicable for similar purposes can be more effectively used in conjunction, and to that end can suitably be made applicable to common purposes; or*

(*d*) *that the object was specified by reference to an area which was, when the object was specified, but has since ceased to be, a unit for some other purpose, or by reference to a class of persons or to an area which has for any reason since ceased to be suitable; or*

(*e*) *that the object, in whole or in part, has since it was specified—*

(*i*) *been adequately provided for by other means; or*

(*ii*) *ceased in any other way to provide a suitable and effective method of using money accruing from the lottery.*

(5) *If the Secretary of State consents to the use of money accruing from a local lottery for a purpose other than its object, it shall be the duty of the local authority to use it only for the purpose for which the consent is given.*

[235]

NOTES

Repealed as noted to s 1 at **[229]**.

8 Proceeds of local lotteries

(1) *A local authority shall pay the whole proceeds of a local lottery, after deducting the expenses of promoting it and the sums required for prizes, into a fund (in this section referred to as a "lottery fund"), and any money in such a fund shall be invested by the local authority and any income arising from such investment shall be credited to the fund.*

(2) *It shall be the duty of a local authority to maintain a separate lottery fund for each local lottery which they promote.*

(3) ...

[236]

NOTES

Repealed as noted to s 1 at **[229]**.
Sub-s (3): repealed by the Local Government Finance Act 1987, s 11(2), Sch 5.

Provisions relating to societies' lotteries and local lotteries

9 (*Repealed by the National Lottery etc Act 1993, ss 49(3), 64, Sch 10.*)

[9A Lottery managers

(1) *No person shall manage a society's lottery or a local lottery unless that person is—*
 (a) *a member of the society on whose behalf or of the local authority by whom the lottery is promoted, acting in his capacity as such,*
 (b) *an employee of that society or authority acting in the course of his employment,*
 (c) *in the case of a society's lottery, a company that is wholly owned by the society,*
 (d) *a person certified as a lottery manager under Schedule 2A to this Act, or*
 (e) *an employee of a person so certified acting in the course of his employment.*

(2) *In subsection (1) above "employee", in relation to an unincorporated body, includes an employee of a member of the body employed by him in his capacity as a member.*

(3) *For the purposes of subsection (1)(c) above—*
 (a) *"company" means a company formed and registered under the Companies Act 1985 or a company to which the provisions of that Act apply as they apply to a company so formed and registered, and*
 (b) *a company is wholly owned by a society if the society is entitled (whether directly or through one or more nominees) to exercise, or control the exercise of, the whole of the voting power at any general meeting of the company.*

(4) *In subsection (1) above and Schedule 2A to this Act references to managing a lottery are to managing the promotion, or any part of the promotion, of a lottery.*

(5) *Schedule 2A to this Act shall have effect.]*

[237]

NOTES

Repealed as noted to s 1 at **[229]**.
Inserted by the National Lottery etc Act 1993, s 50(1).

[10 Frequency of lotteries

(1) *The Secretary of State may by order prescribe—*
 (a) *the maximum number of lotteries that may be promoted under section 5 or 6 above in any period of twelve months on behalf of the same society or by the same local authority; and*

(*b*) *the minimum number of days that must elapse between the dates of any two lotteries promoted under section 5 or 6 above on behalf of the same society or by the same local authority.*

(*2*) *An order under subsection* (*1*) *above may make different provision for different cases or circumstances.]*

[238]

NOTES

Repealed as noted to s 1 at **[229]**.
Substituted by the National Lottery etc Act 1993, s 51.

11 Rules for authorised lotteries

(*1*) *In the case of a society's lottery—*

(*a*) *the promoter of the lottery shall be a member of the society authorised in writing by the governing body of the society to act as the promoter; and*

(*b*) *every ticket [distributed or sold] shall specify the name of the society, the name and address of the promoter and the date of the lottery.*

(*2*) *No ticket or chance in a society's lottery or a local lottery shall be sold at a price exceeding [£2].*

(*3*) *The price of every ticket or chance shall be the same, and the price of any ticket [distributed or sold] shall be stated on the ticket.*

(*4*) *No person shall be admitted to participate in a society's lottery or a local lottery in respect of a ticket or chance except after payment to the society or authority of the whole price of the ticket or chance; and no money received for or on account of a ticket or chance shall in any circumstances be returned.*

[(*4A*) *No payment other than the price of a ticket or chance shall be required of a person as a condition of his admission to participate in a society's lottery or a local lottery.]*

[(*5*) *No prize in a society's lottery or a local lottery shall exceed in amount or value £25,000 or 10 per cent of the total value of the tickets or chances sold in the lottery* (*whichever is greater*).

(*6*) *The total value of the tickets or chances sold in any one such lottery shall not exceed [£2,000,000].*

(*7*) *The total value of the tickets or chances sold in all such lotteries held in any one year and promoted on behalf of the same society or by the same local authority shall not exceed [£10,000,000].*

(*8*) *For the purposes of subsection* (*7*) *above, a lottery is held in the year in which the date of the lottery falls.*

(*9*) *In this section "year" means a period of twelve months beginning with 1st January; but if subsection* (*7*) *above* (*as substituted by section 52 of the National Lottery etc Act 1993*) *comes into force on a date other than 1st January—*

(*a*) *the period beginning with that date and ending with the next 31st December shall be taken to be the first year for the purposes of that subsection, and*

(*b*) *in relation to that period, the reference to £5,000,000 in that subsection shall be read as a reference to a proportionately smaller amount.]*

(*11*) *The amount of the proceeds of a society's lottery or a local lottery appropriated for the provision of prizes shall not exceed [55 per cent] of the whole proceeds of the lottery.*

(*12*) *The amount of the proceeds of a society's lottery or a local lottery appropriated on account of expenses* (*exclusive of prizes*) *shall not exceed whichever is the less of—*

(*a*) *the expenses actually incurred; and*

(*b*) *whichever of the amounts specified in subsection* (*13*) *below applies.*

(*13*) *The amounts referred to in subsection* (*12*)(*b*) *above are—*

(*a*) *where the whole proceeds of the lottery do not exceed [£20,000], [35 per cent] of those proceeds; or*

(*b*) *where the whole proceeds of the lottery exceed [£20,000], 15 per cent of those proceeds or such larger percentage, not exceeding [35 per cent], as the Board may authorise in the case of a particular lottery.*

[(14) For the purposes of subsection (12) above, the amount of any expenses that are met—

(a) by the society on whose behalf, or the local authority by whom, the lottery is promoted, or

(b) by any beneficiary of the lottery,

shall be treated as having been appropriated on account of expenses from the proceeds of the lottery.

(15) In subsection (14) above "beneficiary of the lottery" means a person (other than the society on whose behalf, or the local authority by whom, the lottery is promoted) to whom or for whose benefit any of the proceeds of the lottery, other than amounts appropriated in respect of expenses or prizes, are lawfully paid or applied.

(16) The amount of the proceeds of a society's lottery or a local lottery appropriated for the provision of prizes and the amount of those proceeds appropriated on account of expenses (exclusive of prizes) shall not exceed in aggregate a prescribed percentage of the whole proceeds of the lottery.]

[239]

NOTES

Repealed as noted to s 1 at **[229]**.

Sub-s (1): words in square brackets substituted by the National Lottery etc Act 1993, s 52(1), (2).

Sub-s (2): sum in square brackets substituted by the Lotteries (Variation of Monetary Limits) Order 2002, SI 2002/1410, art 2.

Sub-s (3): words in square brackets inserted by the National Lottery etc Act 1993, s 52(1), (3).

Sub-s (4A): inserted by the National Lottery etc Act 1993, s 52(1), (4).

Sub-ss (5), (8), (9): substituted, together with sub-ss (6), (7), for original sub-ss (5)–(10), by the National Lottery etc Act 1993, s 52(1), (5).

Sub-ss (6), (7): substituted, together with sub-ss (5), (8), (9), for original sub-ss (5)–(10) by the National Lottery etc Act 1993, s 52(1), (5); sums in square brackets substituted by SI 2002/1410, arts 3, 4.

Sub-s (11): words in square brackets substituted by the Lotteries (Prizes and Expenses: Variation and Prescription of Percentage Limits) Order 1997, SI 1997/43, art 2.

Sub-s (13): sums in square brackets substituted by the National Lottery etc Act 1993, s 52(1), (7); words in square brackets substituted by SI 1997/43, arts 3, 4.

Sub-ss (14)–(16): added by the National Lottery etc Act 1993, s 52(1), (8).

Orders: the Lotteries (Prizes and Expenses: Variation and Prescription of Percentage Limits) Order 1997, SI 1997/43.

12 Regulations

(1) The Secretary of State may by regulations prescribe provisions to be included in—

(a) any scheme approved by a society for the promotion of a society's lottery; and

(b) any scheme approved by a local authority for the promotion of a local lottery.

(2) The Secretary of State may by regulations make such provision with respect to the promotion of society's lotteries or local lotteries as he may consider necessary or expedient.

(3) Without prejudice to the generality of subsection (2) above, the Secretary of State may by regulations impose requirements or restrictions with respect to all or any of the following matters—

(a) the persons to whom and by whom tickets or chances in a lottery may or may not be sold;

(b) the circumstances in which tickets or chances may be sold and in which persons may be invited to purchase tickets or chances;

(c) the minimum age at which any person may buy a ticket or chance;

(d) any information which must, or must not, appear on a ticket;

(e) the manner in which a lottery may be advertised;

(f) the use of postal services in connection with lotteries;

(g) the matters in respect of which expenses in a lottery may be incurred.

(4) Any power to make regulations under this section may be exercised so as to make different provision in relation to different cases or different circumstances.

(5) It shall be the duty of the Secretary of State before making any regulations under this section to consult—

(a) the Board, and,

(b) such associations of local authorities as appear to him to be concerned.

[240]

NOTES

Repealed as noted to s 1 at **[229]**.
Regulations: the Lotteries Regulations 1993, SI 1993/3223 at **[3120]**.

13 Offences relating to societies' lotteries and local lotteries

(1) If any requirement of this Act[, of any regulations made under it or of any order made under section 10 above] in respect of a society's lottery or a local lottery is contravened, the promoter of that lottery and any other person who is party to the contravention shall be guilty of an offence.

(2) It shall be a defence for a person charged with any such offence only by reason of his being the promoter to prove that the contravention occurred without his consent or connivance and that he exercised all due diligence to prevent it.

[(2A) It shall be a defence for a person charged with an offence in respect of a contravention of section 11(5) above to prove—

(a) that the total value of the tickets or chances sold in the lottery fell short of the sum reasonably estimated; and

(b) that the amount or value of the prize in question would not have contravened section 11(5) above if the total value of the tickets or chances sold had amounted to the sum reasonably estimated; and

(c) that, if the amount or value of the prize had been any less, an unconditional undertaking as to prizes given in connection with the sale of tickets or chances would have been broken.]

(3) It shall be a defence for any person charged with an offence in respect of an appropriation made in contravention of section 11(11) or (12) above to prove—

(a) that the proceeds of the lottery fell short of the sum reasonably estimated; and

(b) that the appropriation was made in order to fulfil an unconditional undertaking as to prizes given in connection with the sale of the relevant tickets or chances, or in respect of expenses actually incurred; and

(c) that the total amounts appropriated in respect of prizes or expenses did not exceed the amounts which could lawfully have been appropriated out of the proceeds of the lottery under the said subsections if the proceeds had amounted to the sum reasonably estimated.

(4) It shall be a defence for any person charged with an offence in respect of a contravention of [an order made under] section 10 above … to prove that the date of a lottery was later than he had expected for reasons which he could not foresee.

[241]

NOTES

Repealed as noted to s 1 at **[229]**.
Sub-s (1): words in square brackets substituted by the National Lotteries etc Act 1993, s 53(1), (2).
Sub-s (2A): inserted by the National Lottery etc Act 1993, s 53(1), (3).
Sub-s (4): words in square brackets inserted and words omitted repealed by the National Lottery etc Act 1993, ss 53(1), (4), 64, Sch 10.

PART III
COMPETITIONS AND AMUSEMENTS

Newspaper and other competitions

14 Prize competitions

(1) Subject to subsection (2) below, it shall be unlawful to conduct in or through any newspaper, or in connection with any trade or business or the sale of any article to the public—

(a) any competition in which prizes are offered for forecasts of the result either—

(i) of a future event; or

(ii) of a past event the result of which is not yet ascertained, or not yet generally known;

(*b*) *any other competition in which success does not depend to a substantial degree on the exercise of skill.*

(*2*) *Nothing in subsection* (*1*) *above with respect to the conducting of competitions in connection with a trade or business shall apply in relation to sponsored pool betting or in relation to pool betting operations carried on by a person whose only trade or business is that of a bookmaker.*

(*3*) *Any person who contravenes this section shall, without prejudice to any liability to be proceeded against under section 2 above, be guilty of an offence.*

(*4*) *In this section "bookmaker", "pool betting" and "sponsored pool betting" have the meanings assigned to them by section 55 of the Betting, Gaming and Lotteries Act 1963.*

[242]

NOTES

Repealed as noted to s 1 at **[229]**.

Amusements with prizes

15 Provision of amusements with prizes at exempt entertainments

(*1*) *This section applies to the provision at any exempt entertainment of any amusement with prizes which constitutes a lottery or gaming or both but does not constitute—*

(*a*) *gaming to which Part II of the Gaming Act 1968 applies, or*

(*b*) *gaming by means of a machine to which Part III of that Act applies.*

(*2*) *Where any such amusement constitutes a lottery, nothing in section 1 or 2 above shall apply to it.*

(*3*) *In relation to any such amusement* (*whether it constitutes a lottery or not*) *the conditions set out in subsection* (*4*) *below shall be observed, and if either of those conditions is contravened every person concerned in the provision or conduct of that amusement shall be guilty of an offence unless he proves that the contravention occurred without his consent or connivance and that he exercised all due diligence to prevent it.*

(*4*) *The conditions referred to in subsection* (*3*) *above are—*

(*a*) *that the whole proceeds of the entertainment, after deducting the expenses of the entertainment, shall be devoted to purposes other than private gain;*

(*b*) *that the facilities for winning prizes at amusements to which this section applies, or those facilities together with any other facilities for participating in lotteries or gaming, shall not be the only, or the only substantial, inducement to persons to attend the entertainment.*

(*5*) *Where any payment falls to be made—*

(*a*) *by way of a hiring, maintenance or other charge in respect of a machine to which Part III of the Gaming Act 1968 applies, or*

(*b*) *in respect of any equipment for holding a lottery or gaming at any entertainment,*

then if, but only if, the amount of that charge falls to be determined wholly or partly by reference to the extent to which that or some other such machine or equipment is used for the purposes of lotteries or gaming, that payment shall be held to be an application of the proceeds of the entertainment for the purposes of private gain.

(*6*) *The reference to expenses in subsection* (*4*)(*a*) *above shall accordingly not include a reference to any charge mentioned in subsection* (*5*) *above and falling to be determined as there mentioned.*

[243]

NOTES

Repealed as noted to s 1 at **[229]**.

16 Provision of amusements with prizes at certain commercial entertainments

(*1*) *This section shall have effect for the purpose of permitting the provision of amusements with prizes where those amusements constitute a lottery or gaming or both but do not constitute gaming to which Part II of the Gaming Act 1968 applies or gaming by means of a machine to which Part III applies, and they are provided—*

(*a*) *on any premises in respect of which a permit under this section has been granted in accordance with Schedule 3 to this Act and is for the time being in force, or*

(*b*) *on any premises used mainly for the purposes of amusements by means of machines to which Part III of the Gaming Act 1968 applies, being premises in respect of which a permit granted under section 34 of that Act is for the time being in force, or*

(*c*) *at a pleasure fair consisting wholly or mainly of amusements provided by travelling showmen which is held on any day of the year on premises not previously used in that year on more than 27 days for the holding of such a pleasure fair.*

(*2*) *Nothing in section 1 or 2 above shall apply in relation to amusements falling within subsection* (*1*) *above, but in relation to any such amusement the conditions set out in subsection* (*3*) *below shall be observed, and if any of those conditions is contravened every person concerned in the provision or conduct of that amusement shall be guilty of an offence unless he proves that the contravention occurred without his consent or connivance and that he exercised all due diligence to prevent it.*

(*3*) *The conditions referred to in subsection* (*2*) *above are—*

(*a*) *that the amount paid by any person for any one chance to win a prize does not exceed [50p], and*

(*b*) *that the aggregate amount taken by way of the sale of chances in any one determination of winners, if any, of prizes does not exceed [£90], and that the sale of those chances and the declaration of the result take place on the same day and on the premises on which, and during the time when, the amusement is provided, and*

(*c*) *that no money prize is distributed or offered which exceeds [£25], and*

(*d*) *that the winning of, or the purchase of a chance to win, a prize does not entitle any person, whether or not subject to a further payment by him, to any further opportunity to win money or money's worth by taking part in any amusement with prizes or in any gaming or lottery, and*

(*e*) *in the case of such a pleasure fair as is mentioned in subsection* (*1*)(*c*) *above, that the opportunity to win prizes at amusements to which this subsection applies is not the only, or the only substantial, inducement to persons to attend the fair.*

(*4*) *Schedule 3 to this Act shall have effect.*

[244]

NOTES

Repealed as noted to s 1 at **[229]**; for transitional provisions in relation to any permit which is due to expire in accordance with Sch 3, para 15 to this Act in the period beginning on 1 September 2006 and ending on 30 August 2007 see the Gambling Act 2005 (Transitional Provisions) (No 2) Order 2006, SI 2006/1758, art 7.

Sub-s (3): sum in square brackets in para (a) substituted by the Amusements with Prizes (Variation of Monetary Limits) Order 1999, SI 1999/1259, art 2(a); sums in square brackets in paras (b), (c) substituted by the Amusements with Prizes (Variation of Monetary Limits) Order 2001, SI 2001/4034, art 2.

17 Restriction on grant and provisions as to duration and forfeiture of permits

(*1*) *No permit under section 16 above shall be granted in respect of any premises where a licence under the Gaming Act 1968 is for the time being in force in respect of them or where a club or a miners' welfare institute is for the time being registered in respect of them under Part II of that Act; and, where such a licence is granted or a club or a miners' welfare institute is so registered in respect of any premises, and a permit under section 16 above is then in force in respect of those premises, the permit shall thereupon cease to have effect.*

(*2*) *The court by or before which the holder of a permit under section 16 above is convicted of an offence under that section in connection with the premises to which the permit relates may, if the court thinks fit, order that the permit shall be forfeited and cancelled.*

(*3*) *An order under subsection* (*2*) *above shall be deemed for the purposes of any appeal to be part of the sentence for the offence; and the permit shall not be forfeited or cancelled under that order—*

(*a*) *until the date of expiry of the period within which notice of appeal against the conviction or sentence may be given, nor* (*b*) *if notice of appeal against the conviction or sentence is duly given within that period, until the date of the determination or abandonment of the appeal.*

(4) (*Applies to Scotland only.*)

[245]

NOTES

Repealed as noted to s 1 at **[229]**.

PART IV
SUPPLEMENTARY

18 Powers of Secretary of State as to monetary limits, fees etc

(*1*) *The Secretary of State may by order—*

[(a) vary the sum specified in section 5(3B) or (3C) above;]

[(b) vary any sum or percentage specified in section 11 above or prescribe the percentage referred to in subsection (16) of that section;]

(*c*) *direct that any provision of section 16 above which is specified in the order and which specifies a sum shall have effect as if for that sum there were substituted such other sum as may be specified in the order;*

(*d*) *vary the fee payable under paragraph 3 or 9 of Schedule 1 below;*

(*e*) *prescribe the fees to be payable[, or provide that no fees are to be payable, under paragraph 2, 6 or 10 of Schedule 1A below or paragraph 6A or 7 of Schedule 2 below]; …*

[(ee) vary the sum specified in paragraph 13(1) of Schedule 1A below or paragraph 6D(1) of Schedule 2 below;

(*eee*) *vary the fee payable under paragraph 1 of Schedule 2A below; and]*

(*f*) *vary the fee payable under paragraph 18 of Schedule 3 below, or provide that it shall cease to be payable.*

(2) *An order made by virtue of [subsection (1) above may make different provision for different cases or circumstances and an order made by virtue of paragraph (e) of that subsection] may, instead of specifying the amount of any fee, authorise the Board to determine the amount subject to such limit, or in accordance with such provisions, as may be prescribed by the order.*

[246]

NOTES

Repealed as noted to s 1 at **[229]**.

Sub-s (1): paras (a), (b) substituted, words in square brackets in para (e) substituted, word omitted repealed, and paras (ee), (eee) inserted, by the National Lottery etc Act 1993, ss 54(1)–(5), 64, Sch 10.

Sub-s (2): words in square brackets substituted by the National Lottery etc Act 1993, s 54(1), (6).

Orders: the Amusements with Prizes (Variation of Fees) Order 1991, SI 1991/2174; the Lotteries (Registration Authority Fees) Order 1991, SI 1991/2178; the Lotteries (Prizes and Expenses: Variation and Prescription of Percentage Limits) Order 1997, SI 1997/43; the Amusements with Prizes (Variation of Monetary Limits) Order 1999, SI 1999/1259; the Amusements with Prizes (Variation of Monetary Limits) Order 2001, SI 2001/4034; the Lotteries (Variation of Monetary Limits) Order 2002, SI 2002/1410; the Lotteries (Gaming Board Fees) Order 2006, SI 2006/542.

19 Search warrants

If—

(*a*) *in England or Wales, a justice of the peace, or*

(*b*) (*applies to Scotland only*),

is satisfied on information on oath that there is reasonable ground for suspecting that an offence under this Act is being, has been or is about to be committed on any premises, he may issue a warrant in writing authorising any constable to enter those premises, if necessary by force, … and search them; and any constable who enters the premises under the authority of the warrant may—

(*a*) *seize and remove any document, money or valuable thing, instrument or other thing whatsoever found on the premises which he has reasonable cause to believe may be required as evidence for the purposes of proceedings in respect of any such offence, and* (*b*) *arrest and search any person found on the premises whom he has reasonable cause to believe to be committing or to have committed any such offence.*

[247]

NOTES

Repealed as noted to s 1 at **[229]**.

Words omitted repealed by the Police and Criminal Evidence Act 1984, s 119(2), Sch 7, Pt I; second para (b) repealed, in so far as it confers a power of arrest without warrant upon a constable or persons in general by the Serious Organised Crime and Police Act 2005, s 111, Sch 7, Pt 2, para 38.

20 Penalties and forfeitures

(*1*) *A person guilty of an offence under this Act shall be liable—*

(*a*) *on summary conviction, to a fine not exceeding [the prescribed sum]; or*

(*b*) *on conviction on indictment, to imprisonment for a term not exceeding two years or a fine, or both.*

(*2*) *The court by or before which a person is convicted of any offence under this Act may order anything produced to the court and shown to the satisfaction of the court to relate to the offence to be forfeited and either destroyed or dealt with in such other manner as the court may order.*

[248]

NOTES

Repealed as noted to s 1 at **[229]**.

Sub-s (1): words in square brackets substituted by virtue of the Magistrates' Courts Act 1980, s 32(2).

21 Offences by bodies corporate

(*1*) *Where an offence under this Act committed by a body corporate is proved to have been committed with the consent or connivance of, or to have been attributable to any neglect on the part of, any director, manager, secretary or other similar officer of the body corporate or any person who was purporting to act in any such capacity, he, as well as the body corporate, shall be guilty of that offence and be liable to be proceeded against and punished accordingly.*

(*2*) *In subsection (1) above, except as it applies for the purposes of section 13 above, "director", in relation to a body corporate established by or under any enactment for the purpose of carrying on under national ownership any industry or part of an industry or undertaking, being a body corporate whose affairs are managed by its members, means a member of that body corporate.*

[249]

NOTES

Repealed as noted to s 1 at **[229]**.

22 Meaning of "private gain" in relation to proceeds of entertainments, lotteries and gaming promoted on behalf of certain societies

(*1*) *For the purposes of this Act proceeds of any entertainment, lottery or gaming promoted on behalf of a society to which this subsection extends which are applied for any purpose calculated to benefit the society as a whole shall not be held to be applied for purposes of private gain by reason only that their application for that purpose results in benefit to any person as an individual.*

(*2*) *Subsection (1) above extends to any society which is established and conducted either—*

(*a*) *wholly for purposes other than purposes of any commercial undertaking; or*

(*b*) *wholly or mainly for the purpose of participation in or support of athletic sports or athletic games.*

[250]

NOTES

Repealed as noted to s 1 at **[229]**.

23 Interpretation

(1) In this Act, except where the context otherwise requires—

"the Board" means the Gaming Board for Great Britain;

"contravention", in relation to any requirement, includes a failure to comply with that requirement, and cognate expressions shall be construed accordingly;

"date", in relation to a lottery, means the date on which the winners in that lottery are ascertained;

"distribute", in relation to documents or other matters, includes distribution to persons or places within or outside Great Britain, and "distribution" shall be construed accordingly;

["employee" and "employment" have the [same meanings as in the Employment Rights Act 1996]];

"exempt entertainment" has the meaning assigned to it by section 3(1) above;

"gaming" has the same meaning as in the Gaming Act 1968;

"local authority" means—

- *(a) in England, a county council, ..., a district council, a London borough council, the Common Council of the City of London, the Council of the Isles of Scilly and a parish council;*
- *(b) in Wales, a county council, a [county borough] council and a community council; and*
- *(c) (applies to Scotland only);*

"local lottery" has the meaning assigned to it by section 6(1) above;

"money" includes a cheque, banknote, postal order or money order;

"newspaper" includes any journal, magazine or other periodical publication;

"premises" includes any place;

"printing" includes writing and other modes of reproducing words in a visible form;

"private lottery" has the meaning assigned to it by section 4(1) above;

["registration authority" has the meaning given by paragraph 1 of Schedule 1 below;]

"society" includes any club, institution, organisation or association of persons, by whatever name called, and any separate branch or section of such a club, institution, organisation or association;

"society's lottery" has the meaning assigned to it by section 5(1) above;

"ticket", in relation to any lottery, includes any document evidencing the claim of a person to participate in the chances of the lottery.

(2) In this Act, unless the context otherwise requires, a reference to the promotion of a society's lottery or a local lottery includes a reference to the conduct of that lottery, and "promote" shall be construed accordingly.

[251]

NOTES

Repealed as noted to s 1 at **[229]**.

Sub-s (1): definitions "employee" and "employment" inserted by the National Lottery etc Act 1993, s 55, words in square brackets therein substituted by the Employment Rights Act 1996, s 240, Sch 1, para 9; definition "registration authority" inserted by the National Lottery etc Act 1993, s 55; in definition "local authority" words omitted repealed by the Local Government Act 1985, s 102(2), Sch 17, words in square brackets substituted by the Local Government (Wales) Act 1994, s 66(6), Sch 16, para 50(1).

24 Orders and regulations

(1) Any power to make an order or regulations under this Act shall be exercisable by statutory instrument subject, except in the case of an order under section 25(7) below, to annulment in pursuance of a resolution of either House of Parliament.

(2) Any power conferred by this Act to make an order includes power to vary or revoke the order by a subsequent order.

[252]

NOTES

Repealed as noted to s 1 at **[229]**.

25 Citation, etc

(1) This Act may be cited as the Lotteries and Amusements Act 1976.

(2) The amendments specified in Schedule 4 to this Act shall have effect.

(3) The enactments specified in Schedule 5 to this Act are repealed to the extent specified in column 3 of that Schedule.

(4) In so far as any instrument made or any other thing whatsoever done under any enactment repealed by this Act could have been made or done under a corresponding enactment in this Act, it shall not be invalidated by the repeal of that enactment but shall have effect as if made or done under that corresponding enactment; and for the purposes of this provision anything which under section 57(3) of the Betting, Gaming and Lotteries Act 1963 had effect as if done under any enactment in that Act shall, so far as may be necessary for the continuity of the law, be treated as done under the corresponding enactment in this Act.

(5) Any enactment or other document referring to an enactment repealed by this Act or by the Betting, Gaming and Lotteries Act 1963 shall, so far as may be necessary for preserving its effect, be construed as referring, or as including a reference, to the corresponding enactment in this Act.

(6) …

(7) Where any provision contained in any local Act passed before the Betting and Gaming Act 1960 appears to the Secretary of State to have been superseded by, or to be inconsistent with, section 15 or 16 above, the Secretary of State may by order, a draft of which shall be laid before Parliament, specify that provision for the purposes of this subsection; and, without prejudice to the operation of any rule of law relating to the effect on any such provision of the relevant enactment in the said Act of 1960, any provision so specified is hereby repealed as from the date of the making of the order.

(8) Section 254(2)(c) of the Local Government Act 1972 (power of Secretary of State to amend, etc, enactments by order) shall apply to this Act as if it had been passed before 1st April 1974.

(9) This Act shall come into force immediately after the coming into force of the Lotteries Act 1975, or, if the provisions of that Act come into force on different dates, immediately after the coming into force of the last of them; but

- *(a) nothing in this subsection shall be taken as prejudicing the exercise, by virtue of section 37 of the Interpretation Act 1889 (exercise of statutory powers between passing and commencing of Act) of any powers under the Lotteries Act 1975 or this Act in respect of the registration of schemes for societies' lotteries or local lotteries; and*
- *(b) nothing in this Act shall be taken as prejudicing the operation of section 38 of that Act (which relates to the effect of repeals).*

(10) This Act does not extend to Northern Ireland.

[253]

NOTES

Repealed as noted to s 1 at **[229]**.
Sub-s (6): repealed by the Statute Law (Repeals) Act 2004.

SCHEDULES

SCHEDULE 1
[REGISTRATION OF SOCIETIES BY LOCAL AUTHORITIES]

Section 5

PART I
REGISTRATION

1.—(1) …

(2) [In this Act] "registration authority", in relation to any society, means—

- *(a) in England, a London borough council, a district council, the Common Council of the City of London, or the Council of the Isles of Scilly;*
- *(b) in Wales, a [county council or county borough] council;*
- *(c) (applies to Scotland only),*

being the authority within whose area the office or head office of the society is situated.

2. [An application to the registration authority for the registration of a society] shall specify the purposes for which the society is established and conducted.

3. Subject to the provisions of this Schedule, upon application being duly made on behalf of a society and upon payment of a fee of [£35], the registration authority shall register the society in a register to be kept for the purposes of section 5 above and notify the society in writing that they have done so.

[3A.—(1) The registration authority shall refuse or revoke the registration of the society under this Part of this Schedule if the Board have refused or revoked the registration of the society under Schedule 1A below within the last five years.

(2) Sub-paragraph (1) above does not apply where the ground for the Board's refusal or revocation was that specified in paragraph 3(2)(e) of Schedule 1A below.

(3) Where the registration authority refuse or revoke the registration of a society under sub-paragraph (1) above, they shall notify the society in writing that they have done so.]

4.—(1) The registration authority may, after giving the society an opportunity of being heard, refuse or revoke the registration of the society under this Part of this Schedule if it appears to the authority—
- *[(a) that any person who is or will be a person connected with a lottery promoted or proposed to be promoted on behalf of the society has been convicted of an offence to which this paragraph applies; or]*
- *(b) that the society does not satisfy or has ceased to satisfy the conditions specified in section 5(1) above[; or*
- *(c) that any information given by the society to the authority in or in connection with the society's application for registration was false in a material particular.]*

(2) This paragraph applies to any of the following offences, namely—
- *(a) an offence under section 2 or 13 above;*
- *(b) an offence under paragraph 14 below[, paragraph 14 of Schedule 1A below, paragraph 8 or 9 of Schedule 2 below, paragraph 12 of Schedule 2A below] or paragraph 12 of Schedule 7 to the Betting, Gaming and Lotteries Act 1963;*
- *(c) an offence under section 42 or 45 of that Act; and*
- *(d) an offence involving fraud or dishonesty.*

[(3) For the purposes of sub-paragraph (1)(a) above, a person connected with a lottery is a person who is or has been—
- *(a) involved in the promotion of the lottery; or*
- *(b) employed for reward in connection with the promotion of any other lottery on behalf of the same society.]*

[4A. The registration authority may, after giving the society an opportunity of being heard, revoke the registration of the society under this Part of this Schedule if it appears to the authority that the society has failed to comply with a requirement imposed on it under paragraph 16 below.]

5. Where the registration of any society has been refused or revoked under [paragraph 4 or 4A] above by a registration authority in England or Wales, that authority shall forthwith notify the society of the refusal or revocation and the society may appeal to the Crown Court, and any such appeal shall be commenced by giving notice to the appropriate officer of the Crown Court and to the registration authority within 21 days of the day on which notice of the refusal or revocation is given to the society.

6. (Applies to Scotland only.)

7. Where the registration authority revoke a registration under [paragraph 4 or 4A] above, then, until the time within which notice of appeal under paragraph 5 or 6 above may be given has expired and, if such notice is duly given, until the determination or abandonment of the appeal, the registration shall be deemed to continue in force, and if the Crown Court or, as the case may be, the sheriff confirms the decision of the registration authority, the Court or the sheriff may, if it or he thinks fit, order that the registration shall continue in force for a further period not exceeding two months from the date of the order.

8. A society which is for the time being registered under this part of this Schedule may at any time apply to the registration authority for the cancellation of the registration; and in any such case the authority shall cancel the registration accordingly.

9. Every society which is registered under this part of the Schedule shall pay to the registration authority on 1st January in each year while it is registered a fee of [£17.50], and any such fee which remains unpaid after the date on which it becomes payable may be recovered by the authority as a debt.

10. Subject to the provisions of this Schedule, the registration of any society under Schedule 7 to the Betting, Gaming and Lotteries Act 1963 shall have effect as registration under this Schedule.

[254]

NOTES

Repealed as noted to s 1 at **[229]**.

Schedule heading: substituted by the National Lottery etc Act 1993, s 48, Sch 7, para 1.

Para 1: sub-para (1) repealed and words in first pair of square brackets in sub-para (2) substituted by the National Lottery etc Act 1993, ss 48(5), 64, Sch 7, Pt I, paras 1, 2, Sch 10; in sub-para (2)(b) words in square brackets substituted by the Local Government (Wales) Act 1994, s 66(6), Sch 16, para 50(2).

Paras 2, 5, 7: words in square brackets substituted by the National Lottery etc Act 1993, s 48, Sch 7, paras 1, 3, 6.

Paras 3, 9: sums in square brackets substituted by the Lotteries (Registration Authority Fees) Order 1991, SI 1991/2178, arts 2, 3.

Paras 3A, 4A: inserted by the National Lottery etc Act 1993, s 48, Sch 7, paras 1, 4, 5(2).

Para 4: sub-para (1)(a) substituted and other words in square brackets inserted by the National Lottery etc Act 1993, s 48, Sch 7, paras 1, 5(1).

Betting, Gaming and Lotteries Act 1963, ss 42, 45, Sch 7: s 45 and Sch 7 repealed by the Lotteries Act 1975, s 20(4), Sch 5; s 42 repealed by s 25(3) of, and Sch 5 to, this Act.

PART II
RETURNS

11. Subject to paragraph 12 below, the promoter of a society's lottery shall, not later than the end of the third month after the date of the lottery, send to the registration authority a return certified by two other members of the society, being persons of full age appointed in writing by the governing body of the society, showing—

- *(a) a copy of the scheme under which the lottery was promoted;*
- *(b) the whole proceeds of the lottery;*
- *(c) the sums appropriated out of those proceeds on account of expenses and on account of prizes respectively;*
- *[(cc) whether any expenses were met otherwise than out of proceeds of the lottery and, if so, the amount and source of any sums used to meet them;]*
- *(d) the particular purpose or purposes to which proceeds of the lottery were applied in pursuance of section 5(4) above, and the amount applied for that purpose, or for each of those purposes, as the case may be; and*
- *(e) the date of the lottery.*

12. Paragraph 11 above shall not apply to a society's lottery [if on the date of the lottery the society was registered with the Board under Schedule 1A below].

13. The registration authority shall preserve any return sent to them under paragraph 11 above for a period of at least 18 months, and during that period shall keep it deposited at their office and permit any member of the public to inspect it during office hours free of charge.

14. Any person who fails to send a return in accordance with the provisions of this Part of this Schedule, or who knowingly gives in any such return sent by him any information which is false in a material particular, or who certifies any such return knowing it to contain such information, shall be guilty of an offence.

[15.—(1) Where it appears to the registration authority that section 5(3C) above applies to a lottery in respect of which a return has been sent to them under paragraph 11 above, they shall notify the Board in writing of that fact.

(2) The notification shall have attached to it a copy of the return and of all other returns sent to the registration authority in respect of the earlier lotteries mentioned in section 5(3C)(b) above. 16. The registration authority may require a society that is registered under this Part of this Schedule—

- *(a) to allow the authority to inspect and take copies of any documents of the society, including any information kept by the society otherwise than in writing, relating to any lottery promoted on behalf of the society; and*
- *(b) where such information is kept by means of a computer, to give the authority such assistance as they may require to enable them to inspect and take copies of the information in a visible and legible form and to inspect and check the operation of any computer, and any associated apparatus or material, that is or has been in use in connection with the keeping of the information.]*

[255]

NOTES

Repealed as noted to s 1 at **[229]**.

Para 11: sub-para (cc) inserted by the National Lottery etc Act 1993, s 48(5), Sch 7, para 7.

Para 12: words in square brackets substituted by the National Lottery etc Act 1993, s 48(5), Sch 7, para 8.

Paras 15, 16: added by the National Lottery etc Act 1993, s 48(5), Sch 7, Pt I, para 9.

[SCHEDULE 1A
REGISTRATION OF SOCIETIES BY THE GAMING BOARD

Section 5

PART I
REGISTRATION

1. An application to the Board for the registration of a society shall—

- *(a) specify the address of the office or head office of the society,*
- *(b) specify the purposes for which the society is established and conducted, and*
- *(c) have attached to it a copy of any scheme approved by the society under section 5(3)(c) above.*

2.—(1) Subject to the provisions of this Schedule, upon application being duly made on behalf of a society and upon payment of a prescribed fee, the Board shall register the society in a register to be kept for the purposes of section 5 above and notify the society in writing that they have done so.

(2) Any fees received by the Board by virtue of this paragraph shall be paid into the Consolidated Fund.

3.—(1) The Board shall refuse or revoke the registration of a society under this Schedule if any scheme attached to its application for registration, or any other scheme subsequently approved by the society under section 5(3)(c) above, is contrary to law.

(2) The Board may refuse or revoke the registration of a society under this Schedule if it appears to the Board—

- *(a) that the ground specified in paragraph 4(1)(a) or (b) of Schedule 1 above applies;*
- *(b) that any information given by the society to the Board in or in connection with the society's application for registration was false in a material particular;*
- *(c) that the address of the office or head office of the society is the same as that of the office or head office of another society that is established for the same or a connected purpose and is registered under this Schedule;*
- *(d) that any lottery promoted on behalf of the society within the last five years has not been properly conducted;*
- *(e) that any fees payable by the society under this Act have not been paid;*
- *(f) that the society has failed to comply with a requirement imposed on it under paragraph 12 below; or*
- *(g) that an act or omission of a person who is or will be a person connected with a lottery promoted or proposed to be promoted on behalf of the society was a cause—*
  - *(i) of the registration of another society being refused or revoked on the ground specified in paragraph (b) or (f) above or under sub-paragraph (5) below;*

(ii) of the registration of a scheme being refused or revoked on a ground specified in paragraph 3(1)(e) or 4(2)(c) of Schedule 2 below; or

(iii) of a relevant lottery, in the promotion of which the person was involved, not being properly conducted.

(3) In considering whether sub-paragraph (2)(g) above applies, the Board shall disregard any act or omission that occurred more than five years previously.

(4) For the purposes of sub-paragraph (2)(g) above—

(a) a person connected with a lottery is a person who is or has been—

(i) involved in the promotion of the lottery; or

(ii) employed for reward in connection with the promotion of any other lottery on behalf of the same society; and

(b) "relevant lottery", in relation to a society and a person, means a lottery promoted—

(i) on behalf of another society that at the time of the person's involvement with the promotion of the lottery was registered with the Board; or

(ii) under a scheme that at the time of the person's involvement with the promotion of the lottery was registered with the Board.

(5) The Board may revoke the registration of a society under this Schedule if it appears to the Board that the society has failed to comply with a requirement imposed on it by or under paragraph 7, 8, 9, 11 or 13 below.

(6) The Board shall not refuse or revoke the registration of a society without giving the society an opportunity of being heard.

(7) Where the Board refuse or revoke the registration of a society, they shall notify the society and, except in the case of a refusal or revocation on the ground specified in subparagraph (2)(e) above, the registration authority in writing of the refusal or revocation and the ground for it.

(8) The revocation of the registration of a society under this Schedule shall not have effect in relation to any lottery in respect of which any tickets or chances have already been sold at the date of revocation.

4.—(1) The Secretary of State may direct the Board—

(a) to register under this Schedule any society that they have refused to register on any ground mentioned in paragraph 3(2) above; or

(b) to restore any registration that the Board have revoked on any ground mentioned in paragraph 3(2) or (5) above;

and the Board shall give effect to any such direction.

(2) The Board shall notify the society and the registration authority in writing of any direction that has been given to the Board under sub-paragraph (1) above.

(3) The restoration of any registration under sub-paragraph (1) above shall have effect from the date of revocation or such later date as may be specified in the direction.

5. The Board shall cancel the registration of a society under this Schedule if the society requests them to do so.

6.—(1) A society that is registered under this Schedule shall pay to the Board—

(a) a prescribed fee at such intervals whilst the society is so registered as the Secretary of State may by order direct; and

(b) a prescribed fee for each society's lottery promoted on behalf of the society whilst it is so registered.

(2) Any fees received by the Board by virtue of this paragraph shall be paid into the Consolidated Fund.]

[256]

NOTES

Repealed as noted to s 1 at **[229]**.
Inserted by the National Lottery etc Act 1993, s 48(6), Sch 7, Pt II.
Orders: the Lotteries (Gambling Commission Fees) Order 2006, SI 2006/542.

[PART II
INFORMATION

7. A society registered under this Schedule shall notify the Board in writing of any change in the address of the society's office or head office within the period of twenty-one days beginning with the day on which the change takes effect.

8.—(1) A society registered under this Schedule shall notify the Board in writing of any modification of a scheme approved by the society under section 5(3)(c) above.

(2) A copy of the scheme as modified shall be attached to the notification.

(3) The notification shall be given to the Board at least four weeks before any tickets or chances in a lottery promoted in accordance with the scheme as modified are sold, distributed or offered for sale.

(4) In this paragraph references to the modification of a scheme include the substitution for that scheme of another scheme (and references to the scheme as modified are to be read accordingly).

9.—(1) Where a society is registered under this Schedule on the date of a society's lottery promoted on its behalf, it shall, before the end of the period of three months beginning with that date, send a return in respect of the lottery to the Board.

(2) The return shall be in such form and contain such information as the Board may direct.

(3) A direction under sub-paragraph (2) above shall be given in writing and may be varied or revoked by a subsequent direction.

10.—(1) The Board shall preserve any return sent to them under paragraph 9 above for a period of at least eighteen months, and during that period shall keep it deposited at their office and permit any member of the public to inspect it during office hours on payment of a prescribed fee.

(2) Any fees received by the Board by virtue of this paragraph shall be paid into the Consolidated Fund.

11.—(1) A society registered under this Schedule shall preserve all documents of the society, including all information kept by the society otherwise than in writing, relating to a lottery promoted on the society's behalf until the end of the period of two years beginning with the date of the lottery.

(2) The Board may direct that, subject to such conditions as may be specified in the direction, sub-paragraph (1) above shall not apply to documents or information specified, or of a description specified, in the direction.

(3) A direction under sub-paragraph (2) above shall be given in writing and may be varied or revoked by a subsequent direction.

12. The Board may require a society that is registered or has applied to be registered under this Schedule—

- *(a) to provide the Board with such information relating to any lottery promoted or to be promoted on behalf of the society as they may require;*
- *(b) to allow the Board to inspect and take copies of any documents of the society, including any information kept by the society otherwise than in writing, relating to such a lottery;*
- *(c) where such information is kept by means of a computer, to give the Board such assistance as they may require to enable them to inspect and take copies of the information in a visible and legible form and to inspect and check the operation of any computer, and any associated apparatus or material, that is or has been in use in connection with the keeping of the information;*
- *(d) to allow the Board to inspect any aspect of the management of such a lottery.*

13.—(1) Subject to sub-paragraph (10) below, where the total value of the tickets or chances sold in all lotteries held in any one year and promoted on behalf of the same society is more than £100,000 and any of those lotteries is a lottery to which section 5(3B), (3C) or

(3D) above applies, the society shall send to the Board accounts in respect of those lotteries together with a report on the accounts prepared by a qualifying auditor.

(2) The accounts shall be sent to the Board within ten months of the end of the year in which the lotteries to which they relate were held.

(3) Accounts under this paragraph shall comply with any directions given by the Board as to the information to be contained in such accounts, the manner in which such information is to be presented or the methods and principles according to which such accounts are to be prepared.

(4) Any directions under sub-paragraph (3) above shall be given in writing and may be varied or revoked by subsequent directions.

(5) In sub-paragraph (1) above "qualifying auditor" means a person who—
- *(a) is eligible for appointment as a company auditor under section 25 of the Companies Act 1989; and*
- *(b) is not disqualified by sub-paragraph (6) below.*

(6) The following persons are disqualified—
- *(a) a member of the society;*
- *(b) a partner, officer or employee of such a member;*
- *(c) a partnership of which a person disqualified by paragraph (a) or (b) above is a member.*

(7) The auditor's report on any accounts under this paragraph shall state whether in the auditor's opinion the accounts have been properly prepared in accordance with any directions given under sub-paragraph (3) above.

(8) The auditor shall, in preparing his report, carry out such investigations as will enable him to form an opinion as to—
- *(a) whether proper accounting records have been kept by the society; and*
- *(b) whether the society's accounts are in agreement with the accounting records.*

(9) If the auditor fails to obtain all the information and explanations that, to the best of his knowledge and belief, are necessary for the purposes of his audit, his report shall state that fact.

(10) Sub-paragraph (1) above does not apply to a society in relation to any year if the promotion of every lottery promoted on behalf of the society held in that year is managed by a person certified under Schedule 2A below as a lottery manager.

(11) For the purposes of this paragraph a lottery is held in the year in which the date of the lottery falls.

(12) In this paragraph "year" means a period of twelve months beginning with 1st January.

14.—(1) Any person who, in pursuance of a requirement imposed by or under paragraph 7, 9, 12 or 13 above, knowingly or recklessly gives to the Board any information which is false in a material particular shall be guilty of an offence.

(2) Any person who knowingly or recklessly includes in a report under paragraph 13 above any information which is false in a material particular shall be guilty of an offence.]
[257]

NOTES

Repealed as noted to s 1 at **[229]**.
Inserted by the National Lottery etc Act 1993, s 48(6), Sch 7, Pt II.

SCHEDULE 2
REGISTRATION OF SCHEMES

Section 9

1. A local authority shall submit to the Board any scheme approved by the authority under section 6(2)(b) above.

2. …

3.—(1) The Board shall register a scheme submitted to them under this Schedule[, and notify the local authority in writing that they have done so,] unless—

- (a) ...
- (b) *the scheme is contrary to law; or*
- (c) *except where the Secretary of State otherwise directs, the Board is not satisfied either—*
  - (i) *that all lotteries promoted by or on behalf of the [local authority] within the last five years have been properly conducted; or*
  - (ii) *that all fees payable [by the local authority] under this Act have been paid; or*
  - (iii) ...
- (d) *except where the Secretary of State otherwise directs, it appears to the Board that an unsuitable person will be [a person connected with] a lottery under the scheme[; or*
- (e) *except where the Secretary of State otherwise directs, it appears to the Board that the local authority—*
  - (i) *have given to the Board in or in connection with the authority's application for registration of the scheme any information which was false in a material particular; or*
  - (ii) *have failed to comply with a requirement imposed on them under paragraph 6C below; or*
- (f) *except where the Secretary of State otherwise directs, it appears to the Board that an act or omission of a person who will be a person connected with a lottery under the scheme was a cause—*
  - (i) *of the registration of another scheme being refused or revoked on a ground specified in paragraph (e) above or paragraph 4(2)(c) below;*
  - (ii) *of the registration of a society being refused or revoked on the ground specified in paragraph 3(2)(b) or (f) of Schedule 1A above or under paragraph 3(5) of that Schedule; or*
  - (iii) *of a relevant lottery, in the promotion of which that person was involved, not being properly conducted.]*

[(1A) In considering whether sub-paragraph (1)(f) above applies, the Board shall disregard any act or omission that occurred more than five years previously.

(1B) Where a scheme submitted to the Board under this Schedule is not registered by them, the Board shall notify the local authority concerned in writing of that fact and the reason for it.]

(2) In this paragraph and in paragraph 4 below "unsuitable person" means a person who has been convicted of—

- (a) *an offence under section 2 or 13 above;*
- (b) *an offence under paragraph 14 of Schedule 1 above[, paragraph 14 of Schedule 1A above, paragraph 8 or 9 below, paragraph 12 of Schedule 2A below] or paragraph 12 of Schedule 7 to the Betting, Gaming and Lotteries Act 1963;*
- (c) *an offence under section 42 or 45 of that Act; or*
- (d) *an offence involving fraud or dishonesty.*

[(3) For the purposes of this paragraph and paragraph 4 below—

- (a) *a person connected with a lottery is a person who is or has been—*
  - (i) *involved in the promotion of the lottery; or*
  - (ii) *employed for reward in connection with the promotion of any other lottery under the same scheme; and*
- (b) *"relevant lottery", in relation to a scheme and a person, means a lottery promoted—*
  - (i) *under another scheme that at the time of the person's involvement with the promotion of the lottery was registered with the Board; or*
  - (ii) *on behalf of a society that at the time of the person's involvement with the promotion of the lottery was registered with the Board.]*

4.—[(1) The Board shall revoke the registration of a scheme if it comes to their attention that the scheme has become, or has always been, contrary to law.

(2) The Board may revoke the registration of a scheme—

- (a) *on any of the grounds (c), (d) or (e) specified in paragraph 3(1) above;*
- (b) *if it appears to them that an unsuitable person is a person connected with any lottery under the scheme;*

(*c*) *if it appears to them that the local authority have failed to comply with a requirement imposed on them by or under paragraph 5A, 6, 6B, 6C or 6D below; or*

(*d*) *if it appears to them that an act or omission of a person who is or will be a person connected with a lottery under the scheme was a cause—*

(*i*) *of the registration of another scheme being refused or revoked on a ground specified in paragraph 3(1)(e) or paragraph (c) above;*

(*ii*) *of the registration of a society being refused or revoked on the ground specified in paragraph 3(2)(b) or (f) of Schedule 1A above or under paragraph 3(5) of that Schedule; or*

(*iii*) *of a relevant lottery, in the promotion of which that person was involved, not being properly conducted.*

(2A) In considering whether sub-paragraph (2)(d) above applies, the Board shall disregard any act or omission that occurred more than five years previously.]

(3) The revocation of the registration of any scheme under this paragraph shall not have effect in relation to any lottery in respect of which any tickets or chances have already been sold at the date of revocation.

[4A. Where the Board revoke the registration of a scheme, they shall notify the local authority in writing of the revocation and of the ground for it.

4B. The Board shall cancel the registration of a scheme if the local authority request them to do so.]

5.—[(1) The Secretary of State may direct the Board to restore any registration that has been revoked under paragraph 4(2) above, and the Board shall give effect to any such direction.

(1A) The Board shall notify a local authority in writing of any direction that has been given to the Board under sub-paragraph (1) above in relation to a scheme approved by the authority under section 6(2)(b) above.]

(2) The restoration of any registration under sub-paragraph (1) above shall have effect from the date of revocation or such later date as may be specified in the direction.

[5A.—(1) A local authority shall notify the Board in writing of any modification of a scheme approved by the authority under section 6(2)(b) above and registered under this Schedule.

(2) A copy of the scheme as modified shall be attached to the notification.

(3) The notification shall be given to the Board at least four weeks before any tickets or chances in a lottery promoted in accordance with the scheme as modified are sold, distributed or offered for sale.]

[6.—(1) A local authority shall, before the end of the period of three months beginning with the date of any local lottery promoted by them, send a return in respect of the lottery to the Board.

(2) The return shall be in such form and contain such information as the Board may direct.

(3) A direction under sub-paragraph (2) above shall be given in writing and may be varied or revoked by a subsequent direction.

6A.—(1) The Board shall preserve any return sent to them under paragraph 6 above for a period of at least eighteen months, and during that period shall keep it deposited at their office and permit any member of the public to inspect it during office hours on payment of a prescribed fee.

(2) Any fees received by the Board by virtue of this paragraph shall be paid into the Consolidated Fund.

6B.—(1) A local authority shall preserve all documents of theirs, including all information kept by them otherwise than in writing, relating to a local lottery promoted by them until the end of the period of two years beginning with the date of the lottery.

(2) The Board may direct that, subject to such conditions as may be specified in the direction, sub-paragraph (1) above shall not apply to documents or information specified, or of a description specified, in the direction.

(3) A direction under sub-paragraph (2) above shall be given in writing and may be varied or revoked by a subsequent direction.

6C. The Board may require a local authority—

(a) to provide the Board with such information as they may require relating to a local lottery promoted or to be promoted by the authority;

(b) to allow the Board to inspect and take copies of any documents of the authority, including any information kept by the authority otherwise than in writing, relating to such a lottery;

(c) where such information is kept by means of a computer, to give the Board such assistance as they may require to enable them to inspect and take copies of the information in a visible and legible form and to inspect and check the operation of any computer, and any associated apparatus or material, that is or has been in use in connection with the keeping of the information;

(d) to allow the Board to inspect any aspect of the management of such a lottery.

6D.—(1) Subject to sub-paragraph (10) below, where the total value of the tickets or chances sold in all local lotteries held in any one financial year and promoted by the same local authority is more than £100,000, the authority shall send to the Board accounts for those lotteries together with a report on the accounts prepared by a qualifying auditor.

(2) The accounts shall be sent to the Board within ten months of the end of the financial year in which the lotteries to which they relate were held.

(3) Accounts under this paragraph shall comply with any directions given by the Board as to the information to be contained in such accounts, the manner in which such information is to be presented or the methods and principles according to which such accounts are to be prepared.

(4) Any directions under sub-paragraph (3) above shall be given in writing and may be varied or revoked by subsequent directions.

(5) In sub-paragraph (1) above "qualifying auditor" means a person who is—

(a) eligible for appointment as a company auditor under section 25 of the Companies Act 1989;

(b) a member of the Chartered Institute of Public Finance and Accountancy; or

(c) a firm each of the members of which is a member of that institute;

and who is not disqualified by sub-paragraph (6) below.

(6) The following persons are disqualified—

(a) a member, officer or employee of the local authority;

(b) a partner or employee of such a person;

(c) a partnership of which a person disqualified by paragraph (a) or (b) above is a member.

(7) The auditor's report on any accounts under this paragraph shall state whether in the auditor's opinion the accounts have been properly prepared in accordance with any directions given under sub-paragraph (3) above.

(8) The auditor shall, in preparing his report, carry out such investigations as will enable him to form an opinion as to—

(a) whether proper accounting records have been kept by the local authority; and

(b) whether the authority's accounts are in agreement with the accounting records.

(9) If the auditor fails to obtain all the information and explanations that, to the best of his knowledge and belief, are necessary for the purposes of his audit, his report shall state that fact.

(10) Sub-paragraph (1) above does not apply to a local authority in relation to any financial year if the promotion of every local lottery promoted by them held in that year is managed by a person certified under Schedule 2A below as a lottery manager.

(11) For the purposes of this paragraph a lottery is held in the financial year in which the date of the lottery falls.

(12) In this paragraph "financial year" means a period of twelve months beginning with 1st April.]

7.—[(1) The following fees shall be payable by a local authority to the Board—
(a) a prescribed fee on an application for a scheme approved by the authority to be registered under this Schedule;
(b) a prescribed fee at such intervals whilst such a scheme is so registered as the Secretary of State may by order direct; and
(c) a prescribed fee for each lottery promoted under such a scheme.]

(2) Any such fees received by the Board shall be paid into the Consolidated Fund.

8. Any person who, in pursuance of a requirement under [paragraph 6, 6C or 6D] above knowingly or recklessly gives to the Board any information which is false in a material particular shall be guilty of an offence.

[9. A person who knowingly or recklessly includes in a report under paragraph 6D above any information which is false in a material particular shall be guilty of an offence.]

[258]

NOTES

Repealed as noted to s 1 at **[229]**.
Para 2: repealed by the National Lottery etc Act 1993, ss 49(4), 64, Sch 8, para 1, Sch 10.
Para 3: sub-paras (1)(a), (c)(iii) repealed, words in square brackets in sub-paras (1)(c)(i), (d) substituted, and other words in square brackets inserted by the National Lottery etc Act 1993, ss 49(4), 64, Sch 8, para 2, Sch 10.
Para 4: sub-paras (1)–(2A) substituted for original sub-paras (1), (2) by the National Lottery etc Act 1993, s 49(4), Sch 8, para 3.
Paras 4A, 4B, 5A: inserted by the National Lottery etc Act 1993, s 49(4), Sch 8, paras 4, 6.
Para 5: sub-paras (1), (1A) substituted for original sub-para (1) by the National Lottery etc Act 1993, s 49(4), Sch 8, para 5.
Paras 6–6D: substituted for original para 6 by the National Lottery etc Act 1993, s 49(4), Sch 8, para 7.
Para 7: sub-para (1) substituted by the National Lottery etc Act 1993, s 49(4), Sch 8, para 8.
Para 8: words in square brackets substituted by the National Lottery etc Act 1993, s 49(4), Sch 8, para 9.
Para 9: added by the National Lottery etc Act 1993, s 49(4), Sch 8, para 10.
Orders: the Lotteries (Gambling Commission Fees) Order 2006, SI 2006/542.

[SCHEDULE 2A
LOTTERY MANAGERS

Section 9A

PART I
CERTIFICATION

Application and fee

1.—(1) An application for a person to be certified as a lottery manager shall be made to the Board.

(2) The application shall be in such form and contain such information as the Board may require.

(3) A fee of [£2,735] shall be payable to the Board when the application is made.

(4) Any fees received by the Board by virtue of this paragraph shall be paid into the Consolidated Fund.

Grant or refusal of certificate

2.—(1) Subject to sub-paragraphs (2) and (3) below, on the making of an application and the payment of a fee in accordance with paragraph 1 above, the Board shall grant a certificate to the applicant certifying him as a lottery manager.

(2) The Board shall refuse to grant the certificate if, after giving the applicant an opportunity of being heard, they are not satisfied that he is a fit and proper person to manage a lottery.

(3) The Board may refuse to grant the certificate if, after giving the applicant an opportunity of being heard, it appears to them that—

(a) any person who would be likely to manage the business or any part of the business of managing lotteries under the certificate is not a fit and proper person to do so,

(b) any person for whose benefit that business would be likely to be carried on is not a fit and proper person to benefit from it, or

(c) any information given by the applicant to the Board in or in connection with the application is false in a material particular.

(4) Where the Board refuse to grant a certificate, they shall notify the applicant in writing of the refusal and the ground for it.

Conditions

3. A certificate may include such conditions as the Board consider appropriate for protecting the interests—

(a) of any societies or local authorities whose lotteries the certificate holder may manage, or

(b) of the persons who participate in any lottery that the certificate holder may manage.

4.—(1) The Board may, after giving the certificate holder an opportunity of being heard, vary any condition in a certificate.

(2) The Board's power to vary a condition in a certificate under this paragraph includes power to add a condition to the certificate or omit a condition from it (and references in this paragraph to the variation of a condition are to be read accordingly).

(3) Where the Board vary a condition under this paragraph they shall serve a notice on the certificate holder, by post, informing him—

(a) of the variation, and

(b) of the effect of sub-paragraph (4) below.

(4) The variation shall take effect at the end of the period of twenty-one days beginning with the date of service of the notice.

Duration of certificate

5. A certificate shall have effect until it is revoked by the Board.

Revocation of certificate

6. The Board may revoke a certificate if the certificate holder consents.

7.—(1) The Board shall revoke a certificate if, after giving the certificate holder an opportunity of being heard, they are satisfied that he is no longer, or never was, a fit and proper person to manage a lottery.

(2) The Board may revoke a certificate if, after giving the certificate holder an opportunity of being heard, it appears to them that—

(a) any person who is managing the business or any part of the business of managing lotteries under the certificate is not a fit and proper person to do so,

(b) any person for whose benefit the business of managing lotteries under the certificate is carried on is not a fit and proper person to benefit from it,

(c) any information given by the certificate holder to the Board in or in connection with the application for the certificate was false in a material particular, or

(d) the certificate holder has failed to comply with a condition in the certificate or with a requirement imposed on him by or under this Act.

(3) Where the Board revoke a certificate under this paragraph they shall serve a notice on the certificate holder, by post, informing him—

(*a*) *of the revocation,*
(*b*) *of the ground for the revocation, and*
(*c*) *of the effect of sub-paragraph (4) below.*

(4) The revocation shall take effect at the end of the period of twenty-one days beginning with the date of service of the notice.]

[259]

NOTES

Repealed as noted to s 1 at **[229]**, subject to savings and transitional provisions in the Gambling Act 2005 (Commencement No 6 and Transitional Provisions) Order 2006, SI 2006/3272, arts 5, 6, Sch 4, paras 13–16.

Inserted by the National Lottery etc Act 1993, s 50(2), Sch 9.

Para 1: in sub-para (3) sum in square brackets substituted by virtue of the Lotteries (Gaming Board Fees) Order 2000, SI 2000/1210, art 8.

[PART II
INFORMATION

8.—(1) A certificate holder shall preserve all documents of his, including all information kept by him otherwise than in writing, relating to the management of a society's lottery or a local lottery until the end of the period of two years beginning with the date of the lottery.

(2) The Board may direct that, subject to such conditions as may be specified in the direction, sub-paragraph (1) above shall not apply to documents or information specified, or of a description specified, in the direction: (3) A direction under sub-paragraph (2) above shall be given in writing and may be varied or revoked by a subsequent direction.

9. The Board may require a certificate holder—
(*a*) *to provide the Board with such information relating to the management of a society's lottery or a local lottery as they may require;*
(*b*) *to allow the Board to inspect and take copies of any documents of the certificate holder, including any information kept by him otherwise than in writing, relating to the management of such a lottery;*
(*c*) *where such information is kept by means of a computer, to give the Board such assistance as they may require to enable them to inspect and take copies of the information in a visible and legible form and to inspect and check the operation of any computer, and any associated apparatus or material, that is or has been in use in connection with the keeping of the information;*
(*d*) *to allow the Board to inspect any aspect of the management of such a lottery.*

10. Where a certificate holder is a company to which section 241 of the Companies Act 1985 (directors' duty to lay and deliver accounts) applies, the company shall, immediately after copies of its accounts for a financial year have been laid before it under that section, send a copy of its profit and loss account for that year and the related auditors' report to the Board.

11.—(1) A certificate holder to whom paragraph 10 above does not apply shall, in respect of each year in which he holds a certificate, send to the Board a profit and loss account of his business of managing lotteries under the certificate together with a report on the account prepared by a qualifying auditor.

(2) The account shall be sent to the Board within ten months of the end of the year to which it relates.

(3) An account under this paragraph shall comply with any directions given by the Board as to the information to be contained in such an account, the manner in which such information is to be presented or the methods and principles according to which such an account is to be prepared.

(4) Any directions under sub-paragraph (3) above shall be given in writing and may be varied or revoked by subsequent directions.

(5) In sub-paragraph (1) above "qualifying auditor" means a person who—
(*a*) *is eligible for appointment as a company auditor under section 25 of the Companies Act 1989, and*

(*b*) *is not disqualified by sub-paragraph* (*6*) *below.*

(*6*) *The following persons are disqualified—*
(*a*) *the certificate holder;*
(*b*) *where the certificate holder is an unincorporated body of persons, any of those persons;*
(*c*) *a partner, officer or employee of the certificate holder or a person disqualified by paragraph* (*b*) *above;*
(*d*) *a partner or employee of a person disqualified by paragraph* (*c*) *above;*
(*e*) *a partnership of which any person disqualified by paragraph* (*a*), (*b*) *or* (*c*) *above is a member.*

(*7*) *The auditor's report on an account under this paragraph shall state whether in the auditor's opinion the account has been properly prepared in accordance with any directions given under sub-paragraph* (*3*) *above.*

(*8*) *The auditor shall, in preparing his report, carry out such investigations as will enable him to form an opinion as to—*
(*a*) *whether proper accounting records have been kept by the certificate holder, and*
(*b*) *whether the certificate holder's account is in agreement with the accounting records.*

(*9*) *If the auditor fails to obtain all the information and explanations that, to the best of his knowledge and belief, are necessary for the purposes of his audit, his report shall state that fact.*

(*10*) *In this paragraph "year" means a period of twelve months beginning with 1st January.*

12.—(*1*) *A person who, in pursuance of a requirement imposed on him by or under paragraph 9, 10 or 11 above, knowingly or recklessly gives to the Board any information which is false in a material particular shall be guilty of an offence.*

(*2*) *A person who knowingly or recklessly includes in a report under paragraph 11 above any information which is false in a material particular shall be guilty of an offence.]*

[260]

NOTES

Repealed as noted to s 1 at **[229]**, subject to savings and transitional provisions in the Gambling Act 2005 (Commencement No 6 and Transitional Provisions) Order 2006, SI 2006/3272, arts 5, 6, Sch 4, paras 13–16.

Inserted by the National Lottery etc Act 1993, s 50(2), Sch 9.

SCHEDULE 3
PERMITS FOR COMMERCIAL PROVISION OF AMUSEMENTS WITH PRIZES

Section 16

Interpretation

1.—(*1*) *In this Schedule "the appropriate authority" means—*
[(*a*) *in relation to any premises in England and Wales in respect of which there is in force a premises licence authorising the supply of alcohol for consumption on the premises, the relevant licensing authority in relation to those premises;]*
(*b*) *in relation to any other premises in England or Wales, the local authority within whose area the premises are situated;*
(*c*), (*d*) (*Apply to Scotland only*).

(*2*) *In this Schedule—*
["alcohol", "licensing authority" and "premises licence" have the same meaning as in the Licensing Act 2003,]

… ..

"local authority" means—
(*a*) *in England, a district council, a London borough council and the Common Council of the City of London;*
(*b*) *in Wales a [county council or county borough] council; and*
(*c*) (*applies to Scotland only*); *and*
"permit" means a permit under section 16 above; [and

..... *]*

["relevant licensing authority", in relation to premises in respect of which a premises licence is in force, means the licensing authority in relation to those premises determined in accordance with section 12 of the Licensing Act 2003;]
["supply of alcohol" has the same meaning as in section 14 of the Licensing Act 2003].

[(3) A function conferred by this Schedule on a licensing authority is, for the purposes of section 7 of the Licensing Act 2003 (exercise and delegation by licensing authority of licensing functions), to be treated as a licensing function within the meaning of that Act.]

Resolution by local authority as to grant or renewal of permits

2. Any local authority may pass either of the following resolutions, that is to say—
- *(a) that (subject to paragraph 3 below) the authority will not grant any permits in respect of premises of a class specified in the resolution; or*
- *(b) that (subject to paragraph 3 below) the authority will neither grant nor renew any permit in respect of premises of a class specified in the resolution.*

3.—(1) No resolution under paragraph 2 above shall have effect in relation to the grant or renewal of permits in respect of premises to which this paragraph applies.

(2) This paragraph applies to any premises used or to be used wholly or mainly for the purposes of a pleasure fair consisting wholly or mainly of amusements.

Application for grant or renewal of permit

4.—(1) An application to the appropriate authority for the grant of a permit in respect of any premises may be made—
- *(a) by the holder of the licence or certificate, in the case of premises such as are mentioned in paragraph 1(1)(a) or (c) above, and*
- *(b) in any other case, by the person who is, or by any person who proposes if the permit is granted to become, the occupier of the premises.*

(2) The holder of a permit may apply from time to time for the renewal of the permit.

5. The appropriate authority shall not refuse to grant or renew a permit without affording to the applicant or a person acting for him an opportunity of appearing before, and being heard by, the appropriate authority or (where that authority is a local authority) a committee of the local authority.

Grounds for refusal to grant or renew permit

6.—(1) Where an application for the grant or renewal of a permit is made to a local authority, then if—
- *(a) there is for the time being in force a resolution passed by that authority in accordance with paragraph 2 above which is applicable to the premises to which the application relates, and*
- *(b) the permit could not be granted or renewed without contravening that resolution,*

it shall be the duty of the authority to refuse to grant or renew the permit.

(2) The grant or renewal of a permit shall not be invalidated by any failure to comply with this paragraph, and no duty of a local authority to comply with this paragraph shall be enforced by legal proceedings.

7.—(1) In the case of premises to which paragraph 3 above applies—
- *(a) the grant of a permit shall be at the discretion of the appropriate authority; but*
- *(b) the appropriate authority shall not refuse to renew a permit except either on the grounds that they or their authorised representatives have been refused reasonable facilities to inspect the premises or by reason of the conditions in which amusements with prizes have been provided on the premises, or the manner in which any such amusements have been conducted, while the permit has been in force.*

(2) In the case of premises other than premises to which paragraph 3 above applies, the grant or renewal of a permit shall (subject to paragraph 6 above) be at the discretion of the

appropriate authority; and in particular, and without prejudice to the generality of that discretion, the appropriate authority may refuse to grant or renew any such permit on the grounds that, by reason of the purposes for which, or the persons by whom, or any circumstances in which, the premises are or are to be used, it is undesirable that amusements with prizes should be provided on those premises.

(3) *The preceding provisions of this paragraph shall have effect subject to section 17(1) above.*

(4) *In this paragraph any reference to amusements with prizes includes any amusements provided by means of a machine to which Part III of the Gaming Act 1968 applies.*

Appeal in England or Wales against decision of appropriate authority

8.—(1) *Where on an application under this Schedule in England or Wales the appropriate authority refuse to grant or renew a permit, or grant or renew it subject to a condition, the authority shall forthwith give to the applicant notice of their decision and of the grounds on which it is made.*

(2) *Where such a notice has been given the applicant may, by notice to the [clerk to] the appropriate authority, appeal against the decision to the Crown Court.*

(3) *As soon as practicable after receiving notice of appeal against a decision of the appropriate authority, the [clerk to] the authority shall send the notice to the appropriate officer of the Crown Court together with a statement of the decision against which the appeal is brought and of the name and last-known residence or place of business of the appellant, and on receipt of the notice, that officer shall enter the appeal and give to the appellant and to the appropriate authority not less than seven days' notice in writing of the date, time and place appointed for the hearing of the appeal.*

(4) …

9. *The Court shall not allow an appeal under this Schedule if satisfied that, by virtue of paragraph 6 above, it was the duty of the appropriate authority to refuse to grant or renew the permit.*

10. *Subject to paragraph 9 above, on any such appeal the Court may by its order allow or dismiss the appeal, or reverse or vary any part of the decision of the appropriate authority, and may deal with the application as if it had been made to the Court in the first instance; and the judgment of the Court on the appeal shall be final.*

11. …

12, 13. (*Apply to Scotland only.*)

14. …

Duration of permit

15. *Subject to the following provisions of this Schedule, and without prejudice to the cancellation of any permit under section 17(2) above, a permit—*

- (*a*) *if not renewed, shall cease to have effect on such date, not being less than three years beginning with the date on which it was granted, as may be specified in the permit, or*
- (*b*) *if renewed, shall, unless further renewed, cease to have effect on such date, not being less than three years beginning with the date on which it was renewed or last renewed, as the case may be, as may be specified in the decision to renew it.*

16.—(1) *Where an application for the renewal of a permit is made not less than one month before the date on which it is due to expire, the permit shall not cease to have effect by virtue of paragraph 15 above before the appropriate authority have determined the application or the application has been withdrawn.*

(2) *Where, on such an application, the appropriate authority refuse to renew the permit, it shall not cease to have effect by virtue of paragraph 15 above before the time within which*

beginning with the date of his death, and

(*b*) *except for the purposes of a renewal of the permit, his personal representatives shall be deemed to be the holder of the permit;*

and the appropriate authority may from time to time on the application of those personal representatives, extend or further extend the period for which the permit continues to have effect by virtue of this sub-paragraph if satisfied that the extension is necessary for the purpose of winding up the estate of the deceased and that no other circumstances make it undesirable.

[*17A.—(1) This paragraph applies where—*

(*a*) *a premises licence authorising the supply of alcohol for consumption on particular premises has been granted under paragraph 4 of Schedule 8 to the Licensing Act 2003 (conversion of existing justices' licences to premises licences),*

(*b*) *the application for the licence was made by virtue of paragraph 2(3)(b) of that Schedule (application made by a person with the consent of the existing licence holder), and*

(*c*) *a permit granted by the licensing justices has effect in respect of the premises immediately before the premises licence takes effect.*

(2) *This paragraph also applies where—*

(*a*) *a premises licence authorising the supply of alcohol for consumption on particular premises has been granted under section 18 of the Licensing Act 2003 (determination of application for premises licence) before 24th November 2005,*

(*b*) *a justices' licence granted under the Licensing Act 1964 has effect in respect of the premises immediately before that day ("the existing licence"),*

(*c*) *the application for the premises licence was made by a person other than the holder of the existing licence, and*

(*d*) *a permit granted by the licensing justices has effect in respect of the premises immediately before the premises licence takes effect.*

(3) *The permit is transferred, at the time the premises licence takes effect, to the holder of that licence (and, accordingly, does not cease to have effect at that time under paragraph 17(1)(a)).*

(4) *Subject to that, the permit continues to have effect in accordance with this Schedule.*]

Payment of fees

18. Notwithstanding anything in the preceding provisions of this Schedule, no permit shall be granted or renewed except on payment by the applicant to the appropriate authority or their [clerk] of a fee of [£32].

[261]

NOTES

Repealed as noted to s 1 at **[229]**.

Para 1: sub-para (1)(a) substituted, in sub-para (2) definitions "alcohol", "licensing authority" and "premises licence" substituted, for definitions "justices' on-licence", "licensing district" and "Part IV licence" as originally enacted, definitions "relevant licensing authority", "supply of alcohol" inserted and sub-para (3) added by the Licensing Act 2003, s 198(1), Sch 6, paras 62, 63(1), (2), (3)(a), (4), subject to transitional provisions in respect of a permit made in relation to premises licensed under the Licensing Act 2003 and savings: see the Licensing Act 2003 (Commencement No 7 and Transitional Provisions) Order 2005, SI 2005/3056, arts 3, 4, Schedule, Pt 4; definitions omitted apply to Scotland only; words in square brackets in definition "local authority" substituted by the Local Government (Wales) Act 1994, *amendments for bringing provisions in that Act relating to its administration and enforcement into conformity with the corresponding provisions in this Act*

[22 November 1976]

1–33 ((*Pts I–IV*) *outside the scope of this work.*)

PART V
CHARITIES

34 Charities

(1) A provision which is contained in a charitable instrument (whenever that instrument took or takes effect) and which provides for conferring benefits on persons of a class defined by reference to colour shall have effect for all purposes as if it provided for conferring the like benefits—

- (a) on persons of the class which results if the restriction by reference to colour is disregarded; or
- (b) where the original class is defined by reference to colour only, on persons generally; but nothing in this subsection shall be taken to alter the effect of any provision as regards any time before the coming into operation of this subsection.

(2) Nothing in Parts II to IV shall—

- (a) be construed as affecting a provision to which this subsection applies; or
- (b) render unlawful an act which is done in order to give effect to such a provision.

(3) Subsection (2) applies to any provision which is contained in a charitable instrument (whenever that instrument took or takes effect) and which provides for conferring benefits on persons of a class defined otherwise than by reference to colour (including a class resulting from the operation of subsection (1)).

[(3A) Subsection (2) (b) does not apply to an act which is unlawful, on grounds of race or ethnic or national origins, by virtue of section 4 or 7.]

(4) In this section "charitable instrument" means an enactment or other instrument passed or made for charitable purposes, or an enactment or other instrument so far as it relates to charitable purposes …

In the application of this section to England and Wales, "charitable purposes" means purposes which are exclusively charitable according to the law of England and Wales.

[262]

NOTES

Sub-s (3A): inserted by the Race Relations Act 1976 (Amendment) Regulations 2003, SI 2003/1626, reg 33.

Sub-s (4): words omitted apply to Scotland only.

35–70 (*Ss 35–69* (*Pts VI–VIII*) *outside the scope of this work; s 70* (*Pt IX*) *repealed by the Public Order Act 1986, s 40(3), Sch 3.*)

PART X
SUPPLEMENTAL

71–78 (*Outside the scope of this work.*)

79 Transitional and commencement provisions, amendments and repeals

(1) The provisions of Schedule 2 shall have effect for making transitional provision for the purposes of this Act.

(2) This Act shall come into operation on such day as the Secretary of State may by order appoint, and different days may be so appointed for different provisions and for different purposes.

(3) The enactments specified in Schedule 3 shall have effect subject to the amendments specified in that Schedule (being minor amendments or amendments consequential on the preceding provisions of this Act).

(4) The Sex Discrimination Act 1975 shall have effect subject to the amendments specified in Schedule 4, being amendments for bringing provisions in that Act relating to its administration and enforcement into conformity with the corresponding provisions in this Act.

(5) Subject to the provisions of Schedule 2, the enactments specified in Schedule 5 are hereby repealed to the extent shown in column 3 of that Schedule.

(6) …

(7) An order under this section may make such transitional provision as appears to the Secretary of State to be necessary or expedient in connection with the provisions thereby brought into operation, including such adaptations of those provisions, or of any provisions of this Act then in operation, as appear to the Secretary of State necessary or expedient in consequence of the partial operation of this Act.

[263]

NOTES

Sub-s (6): repealed by the Public Order Act 1986, s 40(3), Sch 3.

Orders: the Race Relations Act 1976 (Commencement No 1) Order 1977, SI 1977/680; the Race Relations Act 1976 (Commencement No 2) Order 1977, SI 1977/840.

80 Short title and extent

(1) This Act may be cited as the Race Relations Act 1976.

(2) This Act, except so far as it amends or repeals any provision of the House of Commons Disqualification Act 1975 or the Northern Ireland Assembly Disqualification Act 1975, does not extend to Northern Ireland.

[264]

(*Schs 1,1A, 2, 4, 5 outside the scope of this work; Sch 3 repealed by the Trade Union and Labour Relations* (*Consolidation*) *Act 1992, s 300(1), Sch 1.*)

INDUSTRIAL AND PROVIDENT SOCIETIES ACT 1978

(1978 c 34)

An Act to raise the amounts of deposits which an industrial and provident society may take without thereby carrying on the business of banking; and to authorise the further alteration of those amounts from time to time

[20 July 1978]

1 Raising of maximum deposit

(1) …

(2) Where immediately before the coming into force of this Act the registered rules of a society registered under the Act of 1965 permitted depositors under the said section 7(3) to deposit a maximum of £50 then laid down thereby, the committee may, by a resolution recorded in writing, resolve that depositors may be permitted to hold such greater amount not exceeding £250 as may be specified in the resolution, and the registered rules shall have effect accordingly.

(3) Where immediately before the coming into force of this Act the registered rules of a society registered under the Act of 1965 permitted depositors under the said section 7(3) to deposit a maximum of not more than £2 in any one payment, the committee may, by resolution recorded in writing, resolve that depositors may be permitted to deposit a maximum of not more than £10 in any one payment as may be specified in the resolution, and the registered rules shall have effect accordingly.

(4) The powers conferred on the committees of registered societies by subsections (2) and (3) above shall not be exercisable after the expiration of the period of eighteen months beginning with the date on which this Act comes into force or after the coming into force of an order under section 2 below; and if any amendment of the rules of a society is made after the coming into force of this Act and before the expiration of the time allowed by this subsection for exercising that power the power shall cease to be exercisable by the committee of that society on the date on which the amendment is registered under section 10 of the Act of 1965.

(5) The committee of a registered society shall not have power to vary or revoke a resolution under subsections (2) or (3) above except in so far as they may be authorised to do so by an order under section 2 below.

(6) Where the committee of a registered society have exercised the power to pass a resolution under subsection (2) or (3) above and an amendment of the society's rules is subsequently registered under section 10 of the Act of 1965 the registered rules of the society shall thereupon have effect as if the resolution had not been passed, so however, that this subsection shall not affect any interest in the funds of the society held by a depositor immediately before the date on which the amendment is registered.

[265]

NOTES

Sub-s (1): amended the Industrial and Provident Societies Act 1965, s 7(3): now superseded by the amendment to that section by the Industrial and Provident Societies (Increase in Deposit-taking Limits) Order 1981, SI 1981/394, art 3.

Act of 1965: Industrial and Provident Societies Act 1965.

2 Further alterations of limits

(1) The [Treasury] may from time to time … by order substitute for the sums for the time being specified in section 7(3) of the Act of 1965 as the limits applicable thereunder such other sums, not being less than £10 (denoting the limit of deposits which can be taken at any one time) and £250 (denoting the maximum amount which can be taken from any one depositor), as may be specified in the order.

(2) An order under this section may make any such provision in connection with altering the limits for the time being applicable under the said section 7(3) as is made by section 1 above, and may contain such other transitional, consequential, incidental or supplementary provisions as appear to the [Treasury] to be necessary or appropriate in that connection.

(3) An order made under this section may vary or revoke any previous order so made.

(4) The power to make an order under this section shall be exercisable by statutory instrument which shall be subject to annulment in pursuance of a resolution of either House of Parliament; …

[266]

NOTES

Sub-s (1): word in square brackets substituted and words omitted repealed by the Financial Services and Markets Act 2000 (Mutual Societies) Order 2001, SI 2001/2617, art 13(1), (2), Sch 3, Pt III, paras 246, 263(a), Sch 4.

Sub-s (2): word in square brackets substituted by SI 2001/2617, art 13(1), Sch 3, Pt III, para 263(b).

Sub-s (4): words omitted repealed by SI 2001/2617, art 13(1), (2), Sch 3, Pt III, paras 246, 263(c), Sch 4.

Orders: the Industrial and Provident Societies (Increase in Deposit-taking Limits) Order 1981, SI 1981/394.

3 Construction, citation, commencement and extent

(1) The Act of 1965 and this Act shall be construed as one.

(2) This Act may be cited as the Industrial and Provident Societies Act 1978, and this Act and the Industrial Provident Societies Acts 1965 to 1975 may be cited together as the Industrial and Provident Societies Acts 1965 to 1978.

(3) This Act shall come into force on the expiration of the period of one month beginning with the date on which it is passed.

(4) This Act extends to the Channel Islands but does not extend to Northern Ireland.

[267]

FINANCE ACT 1982

(1982 c 39)

An Act to grant certain duties, to alter other duties, and to amend the law relating to the National Debt and the Public Revenue, and to make further provision in connection with Finance

[30 July 1982]

1–127 *((Pts I–IV) in so far as unrepealed, outside the scope of this work.)*

PART V
STAMP DUTY

128 *(Repealed by the Finance Act 1999, s 139, Sch 20, Pt V(2), in relation to instruments executed, or bearer instruments issued, on or after 1 October 1999.)*

129 Exemption from duty on grants, transfers to charities, etc

(1) Where any conveyance, transfer or lease is made or agreed to be made to a body of persons established for charitable purposes only or to the trustees of a trust so established or to the Trustees of the National Heritage Memorial Fund [or to the National Endowment for Science, Technology and the Arts], no stamp duty shall be chargeable [under Part I or II, or paragraph 16, of Schedule 13 to the Finance Act 1999] …

(2) An instrument in respect of which stamp duty is not chargeable by virtue only of subsection (1) above shall not be treated as duly stamped unless it is stamped in accordance with section 12 of the Stamp Act 1891 with a stamp denoting that it is not chargeable with any duty.

(3) This section applies to instruments executed on or after 22nd March 1982 and shall be deemed to have come into force on that date.

[268]

PART I STATUTES

NOTES

Sub-s (1): words in first pair of square brackets inserted by the National Lottery Act 1998, s 24(4); words in second pair of square brackets substituted by the Finance Act 1999, s 112(4), Sch 14, para 7, in relation to instruments executed on or after 1 October 1999 but does not apply to transfers or other instruments relating to units under a unit trust scheme: see the Finance Act 1999, ss 112(4), 122(1) (for further provision in relation to the exception see s 122(2) thereof). The Finance Act 1999, s 122(4), Sch 19, para 1, abolishes stamp duty on transfers or other instruments relating to a unit under a unit trust scheme, in relation to instruments executed on or after 6 February 2000, and, accordingly, the original wording ceased to have effect, in relation to such transfers or instruments, from that date; words omitted repealed by the Finance Act 1985, s 98, Sch 27, Pt IX(1).

130–142 *(S 130 repealed by the Inheritance Act 1984, s 277, Sch 9; s 131 repealed by the Finance Act 1989, s 187(1), Sch 17, Pt IX, in relation to instruments made on or after 1 January 1990; ss 132–142 (Pt VI) outside the scope of this work.)*

PART VII
MISCELLANEOUS AND SUPPLEMENTARY

143–156 *(In so far as unrepealed, outside the scope of this work.)*

157 Short title, interpretation, construction and repeals

(1) This Act may be cited as the Finance Act 1982.

[(2) In this Act—
(a) "the Taxes Act 1970" means the Income and Corporation Taxes Act 1970; and
(b) "the Taxes Act 1988" means the Income and Corporation Taxes Act 1988.]

(3) Part III of this Act, so far as it relates to income tax, shall be construed as one with the Income Tax Acts, so far as it relates to corporation tax, shall be construed as one with the Corporation Tax Acts and, so far as it relates to capital gains tax shall be construed as one with the Capital Gains Tax Act 1979.

(4) …

(5) Part VI of this Act shall be construed as one with Part I of the Oil Taxation Act 1975 … and references in Part VI to the principal Act are references to that Act.

(6) The enactments and Orders mentioned in Schedule 22 to this Act (which include spent enactments) are hereby repealed to the extent specified in the third column of that Schedule, but subject to any provision at the end of any part of that Schedule.

(7) The provisions of Part XI of Schedule 22 to this Act, except in so far as they relate to the Wellington Museum Act 1947 and the Finance (No 2) Act 1975, shall have effect in substitution for the provisions of Section B of Part VI of Schedule 20 to the Finance Act 1980 and, accordingly, that Section shall be deemed not to have taken effect at the beginning of the year 1982–83.

[269]

NOTES

Sub-s (2): substituted by the Income and Corporation Taxes Act 1988, s 844(1), Sch 29, para 32.
Sub-s (4): repealed by the Inheritance Tax Act 1984, s 277, Sch 9.
Sub-s (5): words omitted repealed by the Income and Corporation Taxes Act 1988, s 844(4), Sch 31.

INHERITANCE TAX ACT 1984

(1984 c 51)

ARRANGEMENT OF SECTIONS

PART II
EXEMPT TRANSFERS

CHAPTER I
GENERAL

PART I
STATUTES

PART VIII
ADMINISTRATION AND COLLECTION

Payment

PART IX
MISCELLANEOUS AND SUPPLEMENTARY

Supplementary

An Act to consolidate provisions of Part III of the Finance Act 1975 and other enactments relating to inheritance tax

[31 July 1984]

NOTES

Inheritance Tax: except in relation to a liability to tax arising before 25 July 1986 capital transfer tax shall be known as inheritance tax and the Capital Transfer Tax Act 1984 may be cited as the Inheritance Tax Act 1984, by virtue of the Finance Act 1986, s 100. Accordingly references to capital transfer tax have been changed to references to inheritance tax throughout this Act.

1–17 ((*Pt I*) *outside the scope of this work.*)

PART II
EXEMPT TRANSFERS

CHAPTER I
GENERAL

18–22 (*Outside the scope of this work.*)

23 Gifts to charities

(1) Transfers of value are exempt to the extent that the values transferred by them are attributable to property which is given to charities.

(2) Subsection (1) above shall not apply in relation to property if the testamentary or other disposition by which it is given—

(a) takes effect on the termination after the transfer of value of any interest or period, or

(b) depends on a condition which is not satisfied within twelve months after the transfer, or

(c) is defeasible;

and for this purpose any disposition which has not been defeated at a time twelve months after the transfer of value and is not defeasible after that time shall be treated as not being defeasible (whether or not it was capable of being defeated before that time).

(3) Subsection (1) above shall not apply in relation to property which is an interest in other property if—

(a) that interest is less than the donor's, or

(b) the property is given for a limited period;

and for this purpose any question whether an interest is less than the donor's shall be decided as at a time twelve months after the transfer of value.

(4) Subsection (1) above shall not apply in relation to any property if—

(a) the property is land or a building and is given subject to an interest reserved or created by the donor which entitles him, his spouse [or civil partner] or a person connected with him to possession of, or to occupy, the whole or any part of the land or building rent-free or at a rent less than might be expected to be obtained in a transaction at arm's length between persons not connected with each other, or

(b) the property is not land or a building and is given subject to an interest reserved or created by the donor other than—

(i) an interest created by him for full consideration in money or money's worth, or

(ii) an interest which does not substantially affect the enjoyment of the property by the person or body to whom it is given;

and for this purpose any question whether property is given subject to an interest shall be decided as at a time twelve months after the transfer of value.

(5) Subsection (1) above shall not apply in relation to property if it or any part of it may become applicable for purposes other than charitable purposes or those of a body mentioned in section 24 [or 25] below [or, where it is land, of a body mentioned in section 24A below].

(6) For the purposes of this section property is given to charities if it becomes the property of charities or is held on trust for charitable purposes only, and "donor" shall be construed accordingly.

[270]

NOTES

Sub-s (4): words in square brackets in para (a) inserted by the Tax and Civil Partnership Regulations 2005, SI 2005/3229, regs 3, 9.

Sub-s (5): words in first pair of square brackets substituted by the Finance Act 1998, s 143(1), (2), in relation to any transfer of value made on or after 17 March 1998; words in second pair of square brackets inserted by the Finance Act 1989, s 171(2), (6), in relation to transfers of value made on or after 14 March 1989.

For the modification of this section in relation to amateur sports clubs, see the Finance Act 2002, s 58, Sch 18, Pt 3, para 9(2).

24 (*Outside the scope of this work.*)

[24A Gifts to housing associations

(1) A transfer of value is exempt to the extent that the value transferred by it is attributable to land in the United Kingdom given to a [body falling within subsection (2) below].

[(2) A body falls within this subsection if it is—

(a) a registered social landlord within the meaning of Part I of the Housing Act 1996;

(b) a registered housing association within the meaning of the Housing Associations Act 1985; or

(c) a registered housing association within the meaning of Part II of the Housing (Northern Ireland) Order 1992.]

(3) Subsections (2) to (5) of section 23 and subsection (4) of section 24 above shall apply in relation to subsection (1) above as they apply in relation to section 24(1).]

[271]

NOTES

Inserted by the Finance Act 1989, s 171(1), (6), in relation to transfers of value made on or after 14 March 1989.

Sub-s (1): words in square brackets substituted by the Housing Act 1996 (Consequential Provisions) Order 1996, SI 1996/2325, art 5(1), Sch 2, para 12(1), (2).

Sub-s (2): substituted by SI 1996/2325, art 5(1), Sch 2, para 12(1), (3).

25 Gifts for national purposes, etc

(1) A transfer of value is an exempt transfer to the extent that the value transferred by it is attributable to property which becomes the property of a body within Schedule 3 to this Act.

(2) Subsections (2) to (5) of section 23 and subsection (4) of section 24 above shall apply in relation to subsection (1) above as they apply in relation to section 24(1), except that

section 23(3) shall not prevent subsection (1) above from applying in relation to property consisting of the benefit of an agreement restricting the use of land.

[272]

26 (*Repealed by the Finance Act 1998, ss 143(1), 165, Sch 27, Pt IV, in relation to any transfer of value made on or after 17 March 1998.*)

[26A Potentially exempt transfer of property subsequently held for national purposes etc

A potentially exempt transfer which would (apart from this section) have proved to be a chargeable transfer shall be an exempt transfer to the extent that the value transferred by it is attributable to property which has been or could be designated under section 31(1) below and which, during the period beginning with the date of the transfer and ending with the death of the transferor,—

(a) has been disposed of by sale by private treaty to a body mentioned in Schedule 3 to this Act or has been disposed of to such a body otherwise than by sale, or

(b) has been disposed of in pursuance of section 230 below.]

[273]

NOTES

Inserted by the Finance Act 1986, s 101(1), (3), Sch 19, Pt I, para 6, with respect to transfers of value made, and other events occurring, on or after 18 March 1986.

27 Maintenance funds for historic buildings, etc

(1) [Subject to subsection (1A) below,] A transfer of value is an exempt transfer to the extent that the value transferred by it is attributable to property which by virtue of the transfer becomes comprised in a settlement and in respect of which—

(a) a direction under paragraph 1 of Schedule 4 to this Act has effect at the time of the transfer, or

(b) such a direction is given after the time of the transfer.

[(1A) Subsection (1) above does not apply in the case of a direction given after the time of the transfer unless the claim for the direction (if it is not made before that time) is made no more than two years after the date of that transfer, or within such longer period as the Board may allow.]

(2) Subsections (2) and (3) of section 23 and subsection (4) of section 24 above shall apply in relation to subsection (1) above as they apply in relation to section 24(1).

[274]

NOTES

Sub-s (1): words in square brackets inserted by the Finance Act 1998, s 144, in relation to transfers of value made on or after 17 March 1998.

Sub-s (1A): inserted by the Finance Act 1998, s 144, in relation to transfers of value made on or after 17 March 1998.

28–29A (*Outside the scope of this work.*)

CHAPTER II
CONDITIONAL EXEMPTION

30, 31 (*Outside the scope of this work.*)

32 Chargeable events

(1) Where there has been a conditionally exempt transfer of any property, tax shall be charged under this section on the first occurrence after the transfer [(or, if the transfer was a potentially exempt transfer, after the death of the transferor)] of an event which under this section is a chargeable event with respect to the property.

(2) If the Treasury are satisfied that at any time an undertaking given with respect to the property under section 30 above or [subsection (5AA)] below has not been observed in a material respect, the failure to observe the undertaking is a chargeable event with respect to the property.

(3) If—
(a) the person beneficially entitled to the property dies, or
(b) the property is disposed of, whether by sale or gift or otherwise,

the death or disposal is, subject to subsections (4) and (5) below, a chargeable event with respect to the property.

(4) A death or disposal is not a chargeable event with respect to any property if the personal representatives of the deceased (or, in the case of settled property, the trustees or the person next entitled) within three years of the death make or, as the case may be, the disposal is—
(a) a disposal of the property by sale by private treaty to a body mentioned in Schedule 3 to this Act, or a disposal of it to such a body otherwise than by sale, or
(b) a disposal in pursuance of section 230 below,

and a death or disposal of the property after such a disposal as is mentioned in paragraph (a) or (b) above is not a chargeable event with respect to the property unless there has again been a conditionally exempt transfer of it after that disposal.

(5) A death or disposal otherwise than by sale is not a chargeable event with respect to any property if—
(a) the transfer of value made on the death or the disposal is itself a conditionally exempt transfer of the property, or
[(b) the condition specified in subsection (5AA) below is satisfied with respect to the property.]

[(5A) This section does not apply where section 32A below applies.]

[(5AA) The condition referred to in subsection (5)(b) above is satisfied if—
(a) the requisite undertaking described in section 31 above is given with respect to the property by such person as the Board think appropriate in the circumstances of the case, or
(b) (where the property is an area of land within section 31(1)(d) above) the requisite undertakings described in that section are given with respect to the property by such person or persons as the Board think appropriate in the circumstances of the case.]

(6), (7) ...

[275]

NOTES

Sub-s (1): words in square brackets inserted by the Finance Act 1986, s 101(1), (3), Sch 19, Pt I, para 9, with respect to transfers of value made, and other events occurring, on or after 18 March 1986.

Sub-ss (2), (5): words in square brackets substituted by the Finance Act 1998, s 142, Sch 25, para 7(1), (2), (9), in relation to the giving of any undertaking on or after 31 July 1998.

Sub-s (5A): inserted by the Finance Act 1985, s 94, Sch 26, para 3(1), (2), in relation to events on or after 19 March 1985.

Sub-s (5AA): inserted by the Finance Act 1998, s 142, Sch 25, para 7(3), (9), in relation to the giving of any undertaking on or after 31 July 1998.

Sub-ss (6), (7): repealed by the Finance Act 1985, ss 94, 98(6), Sch 26, para 3(1), (3), Sch 27, Pt XI, in relation to events on or after 19 March 1985.

Functions of the Treasury under this section transferred to the Commissioners of Inland Revenue by the Finance Act 1985, s 95(1).

[32A Associated properties

(1) For the purposes of this section the following properties are associated with each other, namely, a building falling within section 31(1)(c) above and (to the extent that any of the following exists) an area or areas of land falling within section 31(1)(d) above in relation to the building and an object or objects falling within section 31(1)(e) above in relation to the building; and this section applies where there are such properties, which are referred to as *associated properties*.

(2) Where there has been a conditionally exempt transfer of any property (or part), tax shall be charged under this section in respect of that property (or part) on the first occurrence after the transfer [(or, if the transfer was a potentially exempt transfer, after the death of the transferor)] of an event which under this section is a chargeable event with respect to that property (or part).

(3) If the Treasury are satisfied that at any time an undertaking given under section 30 above or this section for the maintenance, repair, preservation, access or keeping of any of the

associated properties has not been observed in a material respect, then (subject to subsection (10) below) the failure to observe the undertaking is a chargeable event with respect to the whole of each of the associated properties of which there has been a conditionally exempt transfer.

(4) If—

(a) the person beneficially entitled to property dies, or

(b) property (or part of it) is disposed of, whether by sale or gift or otherwise,

then, if the property is one of the associated properties and an undertaking for its maintenance, repair, preservation, access or keeping has been given under section 30 above or this section, the death or disposal is (subject to subsections (5) to (10) below) a chargeable event with respect to the whole of each of the associated properties of which there has been a conditionally exempt transfer.

(5) Subject to subsection (6) below, the death of a person beneficially entitled to property, or the disposal of property (or part), is not a chargeable event if the personal representatives of the deceased (or, in the case of settled property, the trustees or the person next entitled) within three years of the death make or, as the case may be, the disposal is—

(a) a disposal of the property (or part) concerned by sale by private treaty to a body mentioned in Schedule 3 to this Act, or to such a body otherwise than by sale, or

(b) a disposal of the property (or part) concerned in pursuance of section 230 below.

(6) Where a disposal mentioned in subsection (5)(a) or (b) above is a part disposal, that subsection does not make the event non-chargeable with respect to property other than that disposed of [unless—

(a) the requisite undertaking described in section 31 above is given with respect to the property (or part) not disposed of by such person as the Board think appropriate in the circumstances of the case, or

(b) (where any of the property or part not disposed of is an area of land within section 31(1)(d) above) the requisite undertakings described in that section are given with respect to that property (or that part) by such person or persons as the Board think appropriate in the circumstances of the case;

and] in this subsection "part disposal" means a disposal of property which does not consist of or include the whole of each property which is one of the associated properties and of which there has been a conditionally exempt transfer.

(7) Where, after a relevant disposal (that is, a disposal mentioned in subsection (5)(a) or (b) above made in circumstances where that subsection applies), a person beneficially entitled to the property (or part) concerned dies or the property (or part) concerned is disposed of, the death or disposal is not a chargeable event with respect to the property (or part) concerned unless there has again been a conditionally exempt transfer of the property (or part) concerned after the relevant disposal.

(8) The death of a person beneficially entitled to property, or the disposal of property (or part) otherwise than by sale, is not a chargeable event if—

(a) the transfer of value made on the death or the disposal is itself a conditionally exempt transfer of the property (or part) concerned, or

[(b) the condition specified in subsection (8A) below is satisfied with respect to the property (or part) concerned.]

[(8A) The condition referred to in subsection (8)(b) above is satisfied if—

(a) the requisite undertaking described in section 31 above is given with respect to the property (or part) by such person as the Board think appropriate in the circumstances of the case, or

(b) (where any of the property or part is an area of land within section 31(1)(d) above) the requisite undertakings described in that section are given with respect to the property (or part) by such person or persons as the Board think appropriate in the circumstances of the case.]

[(9) If the whole or part of any property is disposed of by sale and—

(a) the requisite undertaking described in section 31 above is given with respect to the property (or part) by such person as the Board think appropriate in the circumstances of the case, or

(b) (where any of the property or part is an area of land within section 31(1)(d) above) the requisite undertakings described in that section are given with respect to the property (or part) by such person or persons as the Board think appropriate in the circumstances of the case, the disposal is a chargeable event only with respect to the whole or part actually disposed of (if it is a chargeable event with respect to such whole or part apart from this subsection).]

(10) If—

(a) the Treasury are satisfied that there has been a failure to observe, as to one of the associated properties or part of it, an undertaking for the property's maintenance, repair, preservation, access or keeping, or

(b) there is a disposal of one of the associated properties or part of it,

and it appears to the Treasury that the entity consisting of the associated properties has not been materially affected by the failure or disposal, they may direct that it shall be a chargeable event only with respect to the property or part as to which there has been a failure or disposal (if it is a chargeable event with respect to that property or part apart from this subsection).]

[276]

NOTES

Inserted by the Finance Act 1985, s 94, Sch 26, para 4, in relation to events on or after 19 March 1985.

Sub-s (2): words in square brackets inserted by the Finance Act 1986, s 101(1), (3), Sch 19, Pt I, para 10, with respect to transfers of value made, and other events occurring, on or after 18 March 1986.

Sub-ss (6), (8): words in square brackets substituted by the Finance Act 1998, s 142, Sch 25, para 7(4), (5), (9), in relation to the giving of any undertaking on or after 31 July 1998.

Sub-s (8A): inserted by the Finance Act 1998, s 142, Sch 25, para 7(6), (9), in relation to the giving of any undertaking on or after 31 July 1998.

Sub-s (9): substituted by the Finance Act 1998, s 142, Sch 25, para 7(7), (9), in relation to the giving of any undertaking on or after 31 July 1998.

Functions of the Treasury under this section transferred to the Commissioners of Inland Revenue by the Finance Act 1985, s 95(1).

33–42 (*Ss 33–35A, ss 36–42 (Ch III) outside the scope of this work.*)

PART III
SETTLED PROPERTY

43–57A (*(Chs I, II) outside the scope of this work.*)

CHAPTER III
SETTLEMENTS WITHOUT INTERESTS IN POSSESSION

Interpretation

58 Relevant property

(1) In this Chapter "relevant property" means settled property in which no qualifying interest in possession subsists, other than—

(a) property held for charitable purposes only, whether for a limited time or otherwise;

(b)–(f) (*outside the scope of this work.*)

(1A)–(3) (*outside the scope of this work.*)

[277]

59 Qualifying interest in possession

[(1) In this Chapter "qualifying interest in possession" means-

(a) an interest in possession—

(i) to which an individual is beneficially entitled, and

(ii) which, if the individual became beneficially entitled to the interest in possession on or after 22nd March 2006, is an immediate post-death interest, a disabled person's interest or a transitional serial interest, or

(b) an interest in possession to which, where subsection (2) below applies, a company is beneficially entitled.]

(2) This subsection applies where—

(a) the business of the company consists wholly or mainly in the acquisition of interests in settled property, and

(b) the company has acquired the interest for full consideration in money or money's worth from an individual who was beneficially entitled to it, [and

(c) if the individual became beneficially entitled to the interest in possession on or after 22nd March 2006, the interest is an immediate post-death interest, or a disabled person's interest within section 89B(1)(c) or (d) below or a transitional serial interest, immediately before the company acquires it.]

(3) Where the acquisition mentioned in paragraph (b) of subsection (2) above was before 14th March 1975—

(a) the condition set out in paragraph (a) of that subsection shall be treated as satisfied if the business of the company was at the time of the acquisition such as is described in that paragraph, and

(b) that condition need not be satisfied [if the company is an insurance company (within the meaning of Chapter I of Part XII of the Taxes Act 1988) and [has permission—

(i) under Part 4 of the Financial Services and Markets Act 2000, or

(ii) under paragraph 15 of Schedule 3 to that Act (as a result of qualifying for authorisation under paragraph 12(1) of that Schedule)

to effect or carry out contracts of long-term insurance.]]

[(4) In subsection (3)(b) above "contracts of long-term insurance" means contracts which fall within Part II of Schedule 1 to the Financial Services and Markets Act 2000 (Regulated Activities) Order 2001.]

[278]

NOTES

Sub-s (1): substituted by the Finance Act 2006, s 156, Sch 20, Pt 3, paras 7, 20(1), (2).

Sub-s (2): sub-para (c) added by the Finance Act 2006, s 156, Sch 20, Pt 3, paras 7, 20(1), (3).

Sub-s (3): words in first (outer) pair of square brackets substituted by the Finance Act 1995, s 52(4), (5), with effect for the purposes of the making, on an anniversary or other occasion after 30 June 1994, of any charge to tax under s 64 or 65 of this Act; words in second (inner) pair of square brackets substituted by the Financial Services and Markets Act 2000 (Consequential Amendments) (Taxes) Order 2001, SI 2001/3629, art 5(1), (2), (4), with effect in relation to the making, on an anniversary or other occasion on or after 1 December 2001, of any charge to tax under s 64 or 65 of this Act.

Sub-s (4): added by SI 2001/3629, art 5(1), (3), (4), with effect in relation to the making, on an anniversary or other occasion on or after 1 December 2001, of any charge to tax under s 64 or 65 of this Act.

60 Commencement of settlement

In this Chapter references to the commencement of a settlement are references to the time when property first becomes comprised in it.

[279]

61 Ten-year anniversary

(1) In this Chapter "ten-year anniversary" in relation to a settlement means the tenth anniversary of the date on which the settlement commenced and subsequent anniversaries at ten-yearly intervals, but subject to subsections (2) to (4) below.

(2) The ten-year anniversaries of a settlement treated as made under section 80 below shall be the dates that are (or would but for that section be) the ten-year anniversaries of the settlement first mentioned in that section.

(3) No date falling before 1st April 1983 shall be a ten-year anniversary.

(4) Where—

(a) the first ten-year anniversary of a settlement would apart from this subsection fall during the year ending with 31st March 1984, and

(b) during that year an event occurs in respect of the settlement which could not have occurred except as the result of some proceedings before a court, and

(c) the event is one on which tax was chargeable under Chapter II of Part IV of the Finance Act 1982 (or, apart from Part II of Schedule 15 to that Act, would have been so chargeable),

the first ten-year anniversary shall be taken to be 1st April 1984 (but without affecting the dates of later anniversaries).

[280]

NOTES

Finance Act 1982, Pt IV, Chapter II, Sch 15, Pt II: repealed by s 277 of, and Sch 9 to, this Act, and replaced, in the case of Pt IV, Chapter II, by this Chapter, and in the case of Sch 15, Pt II, by ss 66(6), 68(6)(b)(ii), 70(9)(b).

62 Related settlements

(1) For the purposes of this Chapter two settlements are related if and only if—

(a) the settlor is the same in each case, and

(b) they commenced on the same day, but subject to subsection (2) below.

(2) Two settlements are not related for the purposes of this Chapter if all the property comprised in one or both of them was immediately after the settlement commenced held for charitable purposes only without limit of time (defined by a date or otherwise).

[281]

63 Minor interpretative provisions

In this Chapter, unless the context otherwise requires—

"payment" includes a transfer of assets other than money;

"quarter" means period of three months.

[282]

Principal charge to tax

64 Charge at ten-year anniversary

Where immediately before a ten-year anniversary all or any part of the property comprised in a settlement is relevant property, tax shall be charged at the rate applicable under sections 66 and 67 below on the value of the property or part at that time.

[283]

65 Charge at other times

(1) There shall be a charge to tax under this section—

(a) where the property comprised in a settlement or any part of that property ceases to be relevant property (whether because it ceases to be comprised in the settlement or otherwise); and

(b) in a case in which paragraph (a) above does not apply, where the trustees of the settlement make a disposition as a result of which the value of relevant property comprised in the settlement is less than it would be but for the disposition.

(2) The amount on which tax is charged under this section shall be—

(a) the amount by which the value of relevant property comprised in the settlement is less immediately after the event in question than it would be but for the event, or

(b) where the tax payable is paid out of relevant property comprised in the settlement immediately after the event, the amount which, after deducting the tax, is equal to the amount on which tax would be charged by virtue of paragraph (a) above.

(3) The rate at which tax is charged under this section shall be the rate applicable under section 68 or 69 below.

(4) Subsection (1) above does not apply if the event in question occurs in a quarter beginning with the day on which the settlement commenced or with a ten-year anniversary.

(5) Tax shall not be charged under this section in respect of—

(a) a payment of costs or expenses (so far as they are fairly attributable to relevant property), or

(b) a payment which is (or will be) income of any person for any of the purposes of income tax or would for any of those purposes be income of a person not resident in the United Kingdom if he were so resident,

or in respect of a liability to make such a payment.

(6) Tax shall not be charged under this section by virtue of subsection (1)(b) above if the disposition is such that, were the trustees beneficially entitled to the settled property, section 10 or section 16 above would prevent the disposition from being a transfer of value.

(7) Tax shall not be charged under this section by reason only that property comprised in a settlement ceases to be situated in the United Kingdom and thereby becomes excluded property by virtue of section 48(3)(a) above.

(8) If the settlor of a settlement was not domiciled in the United Kingdom when the settlement was made, tax shall not be charged under this section by reason only that property comprised in the settlement is invested in securities issued by the Treasury subject to a condition of the kind mentioned in section 6(2) above and thereby becomes excluded property by virtue of section 48(4)(b) above.

(9) For the purposes of this section trustees shall be treated as making a disposition if they omit to exercise a right (unless it is shown that the omission was not deliberate) and the disposition shall be treated as made at the time or latest time when they could have exercised the right.

[284]

Rates of principal charge

66 Rate of ten-yearly charge

(1) Subject to subsection (2) below, the rate at which tax is charged under section 64 above at any time shall be three tenths of the effective rate (that is to say the rate found by expressing the tax chargeable as a percentage of the amount on which it is charged) at which tax would be charged on the value transferred by a chargeable transfer of the description specified in subsection (3) below.

(2) Where the whole or part of the value mentioned in section 64 above is attributable to property which was not relevant property, or was not comprised in the settlement, throughout the period of ten years ending immediately before the ten-year anniversary concerned, the rate at which tax is charged on that value or part shall be reduced by one-fortieth for each of the successive quarters in that period which expired before the property became, or last became, relevant property comprised in the settlement.

(3) The chargeable transfer postulated in subsection (1) above is one—

(a) the value transferred by which is equal to an amount determined in accordance with subsection (4) below;

(b) which is made immediately before the ten-year anniversary concerned by a transferor who has in the [preceding seven years] made chargeable transfers having an aggregate value determined in accordance with subsection (5) below; and

[(c) on which tax is charged in accordance with section 7(2) of this Act].

(4) The amount referred to in subsection (3)(a) above is equal to the aggregate of—

(a) the value on which tax is charged under section 64 above;

(b) the value immediately after it became comprised in the settlement of any property which was not then relevant property and has not subsequently become relevant property while remaining comprised in the settlement; and

(c) the value, immediately after a related settlement commenced, of the property then comprised in it; but subject to subsection (6) below.

(5) The aggregate value referred to in subsection (3)(b) above is equal to the aggregate of—

(a) the values transferred by any chargeable transfers made by the settlor in the period of [seven] years ending with the day on which the settlement commenced, disregarding transfers made on that day or before 27th March 1974, and

(b) the amounts on which any charges to tax were imposed under section 65 above in respect of the settlement in the ten years before the anniversary concerned;

but subject to subsection (6) and section 67 below.

(6) In relation to a settlement which commenced before 27th March 1974—

(a) subsection (4) above shall have effect with the omission of paragraphs (b) and (c); and

(b) subsection (5) above shall have effect with the omission of paragraph (a);

and where tax is chargeable under section 64 above by reference to the first ten-year anniversary of a settlement which commenced before 9th March 1982, the aggregate mentioned in subsection (5) above shall be increased by the amounts of any distribution payments (determined in accordance with the rules applicable under paragraph 11 of

Schedule 5 to the Finance Act 1975) made out of the settled property before 9th March 1982 (or, where paragraph 6, 7 or 8 of Schedule 15 to the Finance Act 1982 applied, 1st April 1983, or as the case may be, 1st April 1984) and within the period of ten years before the anniversary concerned.

[285]

NOTES

Sub-ss (3), (5): words in square brackets substituted by the Finance Act 1986, s 101(1), (3), Sch 19, Pt I, para 16, with respect to transfers of value made, and other events occurring, on or after 18 March 1986.

Finance Act 1975, Sch 5, para 11: repealed by the Finance Act 1982, s 157(6), Sch 22, Pt VII, in relation to events after 8 March 1982.

Finance Act 1982, Sch 15, paras 6–8: repealed by s 277 of, and Sch 9 to, this Act, and replaced by sub-s (6) above and ss 68(6)(b)(ii), 70(9)(b).

67 Added property, etc

(1) This subsection applies where, after the settlement commenced and after 8th March 1982, but before the anniversary concerned, the settlor made a chargeable transfer as a result of which the value of the property comprised in the settlement was increased.

(2) For the purposes of subsection (1) above, it is immaterial whether the amount of the property so comprised was increased as a result of the transfer, but a transfer as a result of which the value increased but the amount did not shall be disregarded if it is shown that the transfer—

(a) was not primarily intended to increase the value, and

(b) did not result in the value being greater immediately after the transfer by an amount exceeding five per cent. of the value immediately before the transfer.

(3) Where subsection (1) above applies in relation to a settlement which commenced after 26th March 1974, section 66(5)(a) above shall have effect as if it referred to the greater of—

(a) the aggregate of the values there specified, and

(b) the aggregate of the values transferred by any chargeable transfers made by the settlor in the period of [seven] years ending with the day on which the chargeable transfer falling within subsection (1) above was made—

(i) disregarding transfers made on that day or before 27th March 1974, and

(ii) excluding the values mentioned in subsection (5) below;

and where the settlor made two or more chargeable transfers falling within subsection (1) above, paragraph (b) above shall be taken to refer to the transfer in relation to which the aggregate there mentioned is the greatest.

(4) Where subsection (1) above applies in relation to a settlement which commenced before 27th March 1974, the aggregate mentioned in section 66(5) above shall be increased (or further increased) by the aggregate of the values transferred by any chargeable transfers made by the settlor in the period of [seven] years ending with the day on which the chargeable transfer falling within subsection (1) above was made—

(a) disregarding transfers made on that day or before 27th March 1974, and

(b) excluding the values mentioned in subsection (5) below; and where the settlor made two or more chargeable transfers falling within subsection (1) above, this subsection shall be taken to refer to the transfer in relation to which the aggregate to be added is the greatest.

(5) The values excluded by subsections (3)(b)(ii) and (4)(b) above are—

(a) any value attributable to property whose value is taken into account in determining the amount mentioned in section 66(4) above; and

(b) any value attributable to property in respect of which a charge to tax has been made under section 65 above and by reference to which an amount mentioned in section 66(5)(b) above is determined.

(6) Where the property comprised in a settlement immediately before the ten-year anniversary concerned, or any part of that property, had on any occasion within the preceding ten years ceased to be relevant property then, if on that occasion tax was charged in respect of the settlement under section 65 above, the aggregate mentioned in section 66(5) above shall be reduced by an amount equal to the lesser of—

(a) the amount on which tax was charged under section 65 (or so much of that amount as is attributable to the part in question), and

(b) the value on which tax is charged under section 64 above (or so much of that value as is attributable to the part in question);

and if there were two or more such occasions relating to the property or the same part of it, this subsection shall have effect in relation to each of them.

(7) References in subsection (6) above to the property comprised in a settlement immediately before an anniversary shall, if part only of the settled property was then relevant property, be construed as references to that part.

[286]

NOTES

Sub-ss (3), (4): words in square brackets substituted by the Finance Act 1986, s 101(1), (3), Sch 19, Pt I, para 17, with respect to transfers of value made, and other events occurring, on or after 18 March 1986.

68 Rate before first ten-year anniversary

(1) The rate at which tax is charged under section 65 above on an occasion preceding the first ten-year anniversary after the settlement's commencement shall be the appropriate fraction of the effective rate at which tax would be charged on the value transferred by a chargeable transfer of the description specified in subsection (4) below (but subject to subsection (6) below).

(2) For the purposes of this section the appropriate fraction is three tenths multiplied by so many fortieths as there are complete successive quarters in the period beginning with the day on which the settlement commenced and ending with the day before the occasion of the charge, but subject to subsection (3) below.

(3) Where the whole or part of the amount on which tax is charged is attributable to property which was not relevant property, or was not comprised in the settlement, throughout the period referred to in subsection (2) above, then in determining the appropriate fraction in relation to that amount or part—

(a) no quarter which expired before the day on which the property became, or last became, relevant property comprised in the settlement shall be counted, but

(b) if that day fell in the same quarter as that in which the period ends, that quarter shall be counted whether complete or not.

(4) The chargeable transfer postulated in subsection (1) above is one—

(a) the value transferred by which is equal to an amount determined in accordance with subsection (5) below;

(b) which is made at the time of the charge to tax under section 65 by a transferor who has in the period of [seven] years ending with the day of the occasion of the charge made chargeable transfers having an aggregate value equal to that of any chargeable transfers made by the settlor in the period of [seven] years ending with the day on which the settlement commenced, disregarding transfers made on that day or before 27th March 1974; and

[(c) on which tax is charged in accordance with section 7(2) of this Act].

(5) The amount referred to in subsection (4)(a) above is equal to the aggregate of—

(a) the value, immediately after the settlement commenced, of the property then comprised in it;

(b) the value, immediately after a related settlement commenced, of the property then comprised in it; and

(c) the value, immediately after it became comprised in the settlement, of any property which became so comprised after the settlement commenced and before the occasion of the charge under section 65 (whether or not it has remained so comprised).

(6) Where the settlement commenced before 27th March 1974, subsection (1) above shall have effect with the substitution of a reference to three tenths for the reference to the appropriate fraction; and in relation to such a settlement the chargeable transfer postulated in that subsection is one—

(a) the value transferred by which is equal to the amount on which tax is charged under section 65 above;

(b) which is made at the time of that charge to tax by a transferor who has in the period of [seven] years ending with the day of the occasion of the charge made chargeable transfers having an aggregate value equal to the aggregate of—

(i) any amounts on which any charges to tax have been imposed under section 65 above in respect of the settlement in [the period of ten years ending with that day]; and

(ii) the amounts of any distribution payments (determined in accordance with the rules applicable under paragraph 11 of Schedule 5 to the Finance Act 1975) made out of the settled property before 9th March 1982 (or, where paragraph 6, 7 or 8 of Schedule 15 to the Finance Act 1982 applied, 1st April 1983, or, as the case may be, 1st April 1984) and within the said period of ten years; and

[(c) on which tax is charged in accordance with section 7(2) of this Act].

[287]

NOTES

Sub-ss (4), (6): words in square brackets substituted by the Finance Act 1986, s 101(1), (3), Sch 19, Pt I, para 18, with respect to transfers of value made, and other events occurring, on or after 18 March 1986.

Finance Act 1975, Sch 5, para 11: repealed by the Finance Act 1982, s 157(6), Sch 22, Pt VII, in relation to events after 8 March 1982.

Finance Act 1982, Sch 15, paras 6–8: repealed by s 277 of, and Sch 9 to, this Act, and replaced by sub-s (6)(b)(ii) above and ss 66(6), 70(9)(b).

69 Rate between ten-year anniversaries

(1) Subject to subsection (2) below, the rate at which tax is charged under section 65 above on an occasion following one or more ten-year anniversaries after the settlement's commencement shall be the appropriate fraction of the rate at which it was last charged under section 64 (or would have been charged apart from section 66(2)).

(2) If at any time before the occasion of the charge under section 65 and on or after the most recent ten-year anniversary—

(a) property has become comprised in the settlement, or

(b) property which was comprised in the settlement immediately before the anniversary, but was not then relevant property, has become relevant property,

then, whether or not the property has remained comprised in the settlement or has remained relevant property, the rate at which tax is charged under section 65 shall be the appropriate fraction of the rate at which it would last have been charged under section 64 (apart from section 66(2)) if immediately before that anniversary the property had been relevant property comprised in the settlement with a value determined in accordance with subsection (3) below.

(3) In the case of property within subsection (2)(a) above which either—

(a) was relevant property immediately after it became comprised in the settlement, or

(b) was not then relevant property and has not subsequently become relevant property while remaining comprised in the settlement,

the value to be attributed to it for the purposes of subsection (2) above is its value immediately after it became comprised in the settlement; and in any other case the value to be so attributed is the value of the property when it became (or last became) relevant property.

(4) For the purposes of this section the appropriate fraction is so many fortieths as there are complete successive quarters in the period beginning with the most recent ten-year anniversary and ending with the day before the occasion of the charge; but subsection (3) of section 68 above shall have effect for the purposes of this subsection as it has effect for the purposes of subsection (2) of that section.

[288]

Special cases—charges to tax

70 Property leaving temporary charitable trusts

(1) This section applies to settled property held for charitable purposes only until the end of a period (whether defined by a date or in some other way).

(2) Subject to subsections (3) and (4) below, there shall be a charge to tax under this section—

(a) where settled property ceases to be property to which this section applies, otherwise than by virtue of an application for charitable purposes, and

(b) in a case in which paragraph (a) above does not apply, where the trustees make a disposition (otherwise than by an application of property for charitable purposes) as a result of which the value of settled property to which this section applies is less than it would be but for the disposition.

(3) Tax shall not be charged under this section in respect of—

(a) a payment of costs or expenses (so far as they are fairly attributable to property to which this section applies), or

(b) a payment which is (or will be) income of any person for any of the purposes of income tax or would for any of those purposes be income of a person not resident in the United Kingdom if he were so resident,

or in respect of a liability to make such a payment.

(4) Tax shall not be charged under this section by virtue of subsection (2)(b) above if the disposition is such that, were the trustees beneficially entitled to the settled property, section 10 or section 16 above would prevent the disposition from being a transfer of value.

(5) The amount on which tax is charged under this section shall be—

(a) the amount by which the value of property which is comprised in the settlement and to which this section applies is less immediately after the event giving rise to the charge than it would be but for the event, or

(b) where the tax payable is paid out of settled property to which this section applies immediately after the event, the amount which, after deducting the tax, is equal to the amount on which tax would be charged by virtue of paragraph (a) above.

(6) The rate at which tax is charged under this section shall be the aggregate of the following percentages—

(a) 0.25 per cent for each of the first forty complete successive quarters in the relevant period,

(b) 0.20 per cent for each of the next forty,

(c) 0.15 per cent for each of the next forty,

(d) 0.10 per cent for each of the next forty, and

(e) 0.05 per cent for each of the next forty.

(7) Where the whole or part of the amount on which tax is charged under this section is attributable to property which was excluded property at any time during the relevant period then, in determining the rate at which tax is charged under this section in respect of that amount or part, no quarter throughout which that property was excluded property shall be counted.

(8) In subsections (6) and (7) above "the relevant period" means the period beginning with the later of—

(a) the day on which the property in respect of which tax is chargeable became (or last became) property to which this section applies, and

(b) 13th March 1975, and ending with the day before the event giving rise to the charge.

(9) Where the property in respect of which tax is chargeable—

(a) was relevant property immediately before 10th December 1981, and

(b) became (or last became) property to which this section applies on or after that day and before 9th March 1982 (or, where paragraph 6, 7 or 8 of Schedule 15 to the Finance Act 1982 applied, 1st April 1983 or, as the case may be, 1st April 1984),

subsection (8) above shall have effect as if the day referred to in paragraph (a) of that subsection were the day on which the property became (or last became) relevant property before 10th December 1981.

(10) For the purposes of this section trustees shall be treated as making a disposition if they omit to exercise a right (unless it is shown that the omission was not deliberate) and the disposition shall be treated as made at the time or latest time when they could have exercised the right.

[289]

NOTES

Finance Act 1982, Sch 15, paras 6–8: repealed by s 277 of, and Sch 9 to, this Act, and replaced by sub-s (9)(b) above and ss 66(6), 68(6)(b)(ii).

71 Accumulation and maintenance trusts

(1) Subject to [subsections (1A)] to (2) below, this section applies to settled property if—

(a) one or more persons (in this section referred to as beneficiaries) will, on or before attaining a specified age not exceeding *twenty-five*, become beneficially entitled to it *or to an interest in possession in it*, and
(b) no interest in possession subsists in it and the income from it is to be accumulated so far as not applied for the maintenance, education or benefit of a beneficiary.

[(1A) This section does not apply to settled property at any particular time on or after 22nd March 2006 unless this section—
(a) applied to the settled property immediately before 22nd March 2006, and
(b) has applied to the settled property at all subsequent times up to the particular time.

(1B) This section does not apply to settled property at any particular time on or after 22nd March 2006 if, at that time, section 71A below applies to the settled property.]

(2) This section does not apply to settled property unless either—
(a) not more than twenty-five years have elapsed since the commencement of the settlement or, if it was later, since the time (or latest time) when the conditions stated in paragraphs (a) and (b) of subsection (1) above became satisfied with respect to the property, or
(b) all the persons who are or have been beneficiaries are or were either—
(i) grandchildren of a common grandparent, or
(ii) children, widows or widowers [or surviving civil partners] of such grandchildren who were themselves beneficiaries but died before the time when, had they survived, they would have become entitled as mentioned in subsection (1)(a) above.

(3) Subject to subsections (4) and (5) below, there shall be a charge to tax under this section—
(a) where settled property ceases to be property to which this section applies, and
(b) in a case in which paragraph (a) above does not apply, where the trustees make a disposition as a result of which the value of settled property to which this section applies is less than it would be but for the disposition.

(4) Tax shall not be charged under this section—
(a) on a beneficiary's becoming beneficially entitled to, or to an interest in possession in, settled property on or before attaining the specified age, or
(b) on the death of a beneficiary before attaining the specified age.

(5) Subsections (3) to (8) and (10) of section 70 above shall apply for the purposes of this section as they apply for the purposes of that section (with the substitution of a reference to subsection (3)(b) above for the reference in section 70(4) to section 70(2)(b)).

(6) Where the conditions stated in paragraphs (a) and (b) of subsection (1) above were satisfied on 15th April 1976 with respect to property comprised in a settlement which commenced before that day, subsection (2)(a) above shall have effect with the substitution of a reference to that day for the reference to the commencement of the settlement, and the condition stated in subsection (2)(b) above shall be treated as satisfied if—
(a) it is satisfied in respect of the period beginning with 15th April 1976, or
(b) it is satisfied in respect of the period beginning with 1st April 1977 and either there was no beneficiary living on 15th April 1976 or the beneficiaries on 1st April 1977 included a living beneficiary, or
(c) there is no power under the terms of the settlement whereby it could have become satisfied in respect of the period beginning with 1st April 1977, and the trusts of the settlement have not been varied at any time after 15th April 1976.

(7) In subsection (1) above "persons" includes unborn persons; but the conditions stated in that subsection shall be treated as not satisfied unless there is or has been a living beneficiary.

(8) For the purposes of this section a person's children shall be taken to include his illegitimate children, his adopted children and his stepchildren.

[290]

NOTES

Sub-s (1): words in square brackets substituted substituted by the Finance Act 2006, s 156, Sch 20, Pt 1, para 2(1), (2), (4)–(6); for the first word in italics in para (a) there is substituted the word "eighteen" and other words in italics repealed as from 6 April 2008, by the Finance Act 2006, s 156, 178, Sch 20, Pt 1, para 3, Sch 26, Pt 6.

Sub-ss (1A)–(1B): inserted by the Finance Act 2006, s 156, Sch 20, Pt 1, para 2(1), (3), (4)–(6).

Sub-s (2): words in square brackets in para (b)(ii) inserted by the Tax and Civil Partnership Regulations 2005, SI 2005/3229, regs 3, 16.

[71A Trusts for bereaved minors

(1) This section applies to settled property (including property settled before 22nd March 2006) if—

(a) it is held on statutory trusts for the benefit of a bereaved minor under sections 46 and 47(1) of the Administration of Estates Act 1925 (succession on intestacy and statutory trusts in favour of issue of intestate), or

(b) it is held on trusts for the benefit of a bereaved minor and subsection (2) below applies to the trusts,

but this section does not apply to property in which a disabled person's interest subsists.

(2) This subsection applies to trusts—

(a) established under the will of a deceased parent of the bereaved minor, or

(b) established under the Criminal Injuries Compensation Scheme,

which secure that the conditions in subsection (3) below are met.

(3) Those conditions are—

(a) that the bereaved minor, if he has not done so before attaining the age of 18, will on attaining that age become absolutely entitled to—

(i) the settled property,

(ii) any income arising from it, and

(iii) any income that has arisen from the property held on the trusts for his benefit and been accumulated before that time,

(b) that, for so long as the bereaved minor is living and under the age of 18, if any of the settled property is applied for the benefit of a beneficiary, it is applied for the benefit of the bereaved minor, and

(c) that, for so long as the bereaved minor is living and under the age of 18, either—

(i) the bereaved minor is entitled to all of the income (if there is any) arising from any of the settled property, or

(ii) no such income may be applied for the benefit of any other person.

(4) Trusts such as are mentioned in paragraph (a) or (b) of subsection (2) above are not to be treated as failing to secure that the conditions in subsection (3) above are met by reason only of—

(a) the trustees' having the powers conferred by section 32 of the Trustee Act 1925 (powers of advancement),

(b) the trustees' having those powers but free from, or subject to a less restrictive limitation than, the limitation imposed by proviso (a) of subsection (1) of that section,

(c) the trustees' having the powers conferred by section 33 of the Trustee Act (Northern Ireland) 1958 (corresponding provision for Northern Ireland),

(d) the trustees' having those powers but free from, or subject to a less restrictive limitation than, the limitation imposed by subsection (1)(a) of that section, or

(e) the trustees' having powers to the like effect as the powers mentioned in any of paragraphs (a) to (d) above.

(5) In this section "the Criminal Injuries Compensation Scheme" means—

(a) the schemes established by arrangements made under the Criminal Injuries Compensation Act 1995,

(b) arrangements made by the Secretary of State for compensation for criminal injuries in operation before the commencement of those schemes, and

(c) the scheme established under the Criminal Injuries Compensation (Northern Ireland) Order 2002.

(6) The preceding provisions of this section apply in relation to Scotland as if, in subsection (2) above, before "which" there were inserted "the purposes of".]

[290A]

NOTES

Commencement: 22 March 2006.

Inserted, together with ss 71B–71H, by the Finance Act 2006, s 156, Sch 20, Pt 1, para 1(1).

[71B Charge to tax on property to which section 71A applies

(1) Subject to subsections (2) and (3) below, there shall be a charge to tax under this section—

(a) where settled property ceases to be property to which section 71A above applies, and

(b) in a case where paragraph (a) above does not apply, where the trustees make a disposition as a result of which the value of settled property to which section 71A above applies is less than it would be but for the disposition.

(2) Tax is not charged under this section where settled property ceases to be property to which section 71A applies as a result of—

(a) the bereaved minor attaining the age of 18 or becoming, under that age, absolutely entitled as mentioned in section 71A(3)(a) above, or

(b) the death under that age of the bereaved minor, or

(c) being paid or applied for the advancement or benefit of the bereaved minor.

(3) Subsections (3) to (8) and (10) of section 70 above apply for the purposes of this section as they apply for the purposes of that section, but—

(a) with the substitution of a reference to subsection (1)(b) above for the reference in subsection (4) of section 70 above to subsection (2)(b) of that section,

(b) with the substitution of a reference to property to which section 71A above applies for each of the references in subsections (3), (5) and (8) of section 70 above to property to which that section applies,

(c) as if, for the purposes of section 70(8) above as applied by this subsection, property—

(i) which is property to which section 71A above applies,

(ii) which, immediately before it became property to which section 71A above applies, was property to which section 71 above applied, and

(iii) which, by the operation of section 71(1B) above, ceased on that occasion to be property to which section 71 above applied,

had become property to which section 71A above applies not on that occasion but on the occasion (or last occasion) before then when it became property to which section 71 above applied, and

(d) as if, for the purposes of section 70(8) above as applied by this subsection, property—

(i) which is property to which section 71A above applies,

(ii) which, immediately before it became property to which section 71A above applies, was property to which section 71D below applied, and

(iii) which, by the operation of section 71D(5)(a) below, ceased on that occasion ("the 71D-to-71A occasion") to be property to which section 71D below applied,

had become property to which section 71A above applies not on the 71D-to-71A occasion but on the relevant earlier occasion.

(4) In subsection (3)(d) above—

(a) "the relevant earlier occasion" means the occasion (or last occasion) before the 71D-to-71A occasion when the property became property to which section 71D below applied, but

(b) if the property, when it became property to which section 71D below applied, ceased at the same time to be property to which section 71 above applied without ceasing to be settled property, "the relevant earlier occasion" means the occasion (or last occasion) when the property became property to which section 71 above applied.]

[290B]

NOTES

Commencement: 22 March 2006.
Inserted as noted to s 71A at **[290A]**.

[71C Sections 71A and 71B: meaning of "bereaved minor"

In sections 71A and 71B above "bereaved minor" means a person—

(a) who has not yet attained the age of 18, and

(b) at least one of whose parents has died.]

[290C]

NOTES
Commencement: 22 March 2006.
Inserted as noted to s 71A at **[290A]**.

[71D Age 18-to-25 trusts

(1) This section applies to settled property (including property settled before 22nd March 2006), but subject to subsection (5) below, if—
- (a) the property is held on trusts for the benefit of a person who has not yet attained the age of 25,
- (b) at least one of the person's parents has died, and
- (c) subsection (2) below applies to the trusts.

(2) This subsection applies to trusts—
- (a) established under the will of a deceased parent of the person mentioned in subsection (1)(a) above, or
- (b) established under the Criminal Injuries Compensation Scheme,

which secure that the conditions in subsection (6) below are met.

(3) Subsection (4) has effect where—
- (a) at any time on or after 22nd March 2006 but before 6th April 2008, or on the coming into force of paragraph 3(1) of Schedule 20 to the Finance Act 2006, any property ceases to be property to which section 71 above applies without ceasing to be settled property, and
- (b) immediately after the property ceases to be property to which section 71 above applies—
  - (i) it is held on trusts for the benefit of a person who has not yet attained the age of 25, and
  - (ii) the trusts secure that the conditions in subsection (6) below are met.

(4) From the time when the property ceases to be property to which section 71 above applies, but subject to subsection (5) below, this section applies to the property (if it would not apply to the property by virtue of subsection (1) above) for so long as—
- (a) the property continues to be settled property held on trusts such as are mentioned in subsection (3)(b)(i) above, and
- (b) the trusts continue to secure that the conditions in subsection (6) below are met.

(5) This section does not apply—
- (a) to property to which section 71A above applies,
- (b) to property to which section 71 above, or section 89 below, applies, or
- (c) to settled property if a person is beneficially entitled to an interest in possession in the settled property and—
  - (i) the person became beneficially entitled to the interest in possession before 22nd March 2006, or
  - (ii) the interest in possession is an immediate post-death interest, or a transitional serial interest, and the person became beneficially entitled to it on or after 22nd March 2006.

(6) Those conditions are—
- (a) that the person mentioned in subsection (1)(a) or (3)(b)(i) above ("B"), if he has not done so before attaining the age of 25, will on attaining that age become absolutely entitled to—
  - (i) the settled property,
  - (ii) any income arising from it, and
  - (iii) any income that has arisen from the property held on the trusts for his benefit and been accumulated before that time,
- (b) that, for so long as B is living and under the age of 25, if any of the settled property is applied for the benefit of a beneficiary, it is applied for the benefit of B, and
- (c) that, for so long as B is living and under the age of 25, either—
  - (i) B is entitled to all of the income (if there is any) arising from any of the settled property, or
  - (ii) no such income may be applied for the benefit of any other person.

(7) For the purposes of this section, trusts are not to be treated as failing to secure that the conditions in subsection (6) above are met by reason only of—

(a) the trustees' having the powers conferred by section 32 of the Trustee Act 1925 (powers of advancement),

(b) the trustees' having those powers but free from, or subject to a less restrictive limitation than, the limitation imposed by proviso (a) of subsection (1) of that section,

(c) the trustees' having the powers conferred by section 33 of the Trustee Act (Northern Ireland) 1958 (corresponding provision for Northern Ireland),

(d) the trustees' having those powers but free from, or subject to a less restrictive limitation than, the limitation imposed by subsection (1)(a) of that section, or

(e) the trustees' having powers to the like effect as the powers mentioned in any of paragraphs (a) to (d) above.

(8) In this section "the Criminal Injuries Compensation Scheme" means—

(a) the schemes established by arrangements made under the Criminal Injuries Compensation Act 1995,

(b) arrangements made by the Secretary of State for compensation for criminal injuries in operation before the commencement of those schemes, and

(c) the scheme established under the Criminal Injuries Compensation (Northern Ireland) Order 2002.

(9) The preceding provisions of this section apply in relation to Scotland—

(a) as if, in subsection (2) above, before "which" there were inserted "the purposes of", and

(b) as if, in subsections (3)(b)(ii) and (4)(b) above, before "trusts" there were inserted "purposes of the".]

[290D]

NOTES

Commencement: 22 March 2006.
Inserted as noted to s 71A at **[290A]**.

[71E Charge to tax on property to which section 71D applies

(1) Subject to subsections (2) to (4) below, there shall be a charge to tax under this section—

(a) where settled property ceases to be property to which section 71D above applies, or

(b) in a case where paragraph (a) above does not apply, where the trustees make a disposition as a result of which the value of the settled property to which section 71D above applies is less than it would be but for the disposition.

(2) Tax is not charged under this section where settled property ceases to be property to which section 71D above applies as a result of—

(a) B becoming, at or under the age of 18, absolutely entitled as mentioned in section 71D(6)(a) above,

(b) the death, under the age of 18, of B,

(c) becoming, at a time when B is living and under the age of 18, property to which section 71A above applies, or

(d) being paid or applied for the advancement or benefit of B—
  (i) at a time when B is living and under the age of 18, or
  (ii) on B's attaining the age of 18.

(3) Tax is not charged under this section in respect of—

(a) a payment of costs or expenses (so far as they are fairly attributable to property to which section 71D above applies), or

(b) a payment which is (or will be) income of any person for any of the purposes of income tax or would for any of those purposes be income of a person not resident in the United Kingdom if he were so resident,

or in respect of a liability to make such a payment.

(4) Tax is not charged under this section by virtue of subsection (1)(b) above if the disposition is such that, were the trustees beneficially entitled to the settled property, section 10 or section 16 above would prevent the disposition from being a transfer of value.

(5) For the purposes of this section the trustees shall be treated as making a disposition if they omit to exercise a right (unless it is shown that the omission was not deliberate) and the disposition shall be treated as made at the time or latest time when they could have exercised the right.]

[290E]

NOTES

Commencement: 22 March 2006.
Inserted as noted to s 71A at **[290A]**.

[71F Calculation of tax charged under section 71E in certain cases

(1) Where—

(a) tax is charged under section 71E above by reason of the happening of an event within subsection (2) below, and

(b) that event happens after B has attained the age of 18,

the tax is calculated in accordance with this section.

(2) Those events are—

(a) B becoming absolutely entitled as mentioned in section 71D(6)(a) above,

(b) the death of B, and

(c) property being paid or applied for the advancement or benefit of B.

(3) The amount of the tax is given by—

Chargeable amount x Relevant fraction x Settlement rate

(4) For the purposes of subsection (3) above, the "Chargeable amount" is—

(a) the amount by which the value of property which is comprised in the settlement and to which section 71D above applies is less immediately after the event giving rise to the charge than it would be but for the event, or

(b) where the tax is payable out of settled property to which section 71D above applies immediately after the event, the amount which, after deducting the tax, is equal to the amount on which tax would be charged by virtue of paragraph (a) above.

(5) For the purposes of subsection (3) above, the "Relevant fraction" is three tenths multiplied by so many fortieths as there are complete successive quarters in the period—

(a) beginning with the day on which B attained the age of 18 or, if later, the day on which the property became property to which section 71D above applies, and

(b) ending with the day before the occasion of the charge.

(6) Where the whole or part of the Chargeable amount is attributable to property that was excluded property at any time during the period mentioned in subsection (5) above then, in determining the "Relevant fraction" in relation to that amount or part, no quarter throughout which that property was excluded property shall be counted.

(7) For the purposes of subsection (3) above, the "Settlement rate" is the effective rate (that is to say, the rate found by expressing the tax chargeable as a percentage of the amount on which it is charged) at which tax would be charged on the value transferred by a chargeable transfer of the description specified in subsection (8) below.

(8) The chargeable transfer postulated in subsection (7) above is one—

(a) the value transferred by which is equal to an amount determined in accordance with subsection (9) below,

(b) which is made at the time of the charge to tax under section 71E above by a transferor who has in the period of seven years ending with the day of the occasion of the charge made chargeable transfers having an aggregate value equal to that of any chargeable transfers made by the settlor in the period of seven years ending with the day on which the settlement commenced, disregarding transfers made on that day, and

(c) on which tax is charged in accordance with section 7(2) above.

(9) The amount referred to in subsection (8)(a) above is equal to the aggregate of—

(a) the value, immediately after the settlement commenced, of the property then comprised in it,

(b) the value, immediately after a related settlement commenced, of the property then comprised in it, and

(c) the value, immediately after it became comprised in the settlement, of any property which became so comprised after the settlement commenced and before the occasion of the charge under section 71E above (whether or not it has remained so comprised).]

[290F]

NOTES

Commencement: 22 March 2006.
Inserted as noted to s 71A at **[290A]**.

[71G Calculation of tax charged under section 71E in all other cases

(1) Where—

(a) tax is charged under section 71E above, and
(b) the tax does not fall to be calculated in accordance with section 71F above,

the tax is calculated in accordance with this section.

(2) The amount on which the tax is charged is—

(a) the amount by which the value of property which is comprised in the settlement and to which section 71D above applies is less immediately after the event giving rise to the charge than it would be but for the event, or
(b) where the tax is payable out of settled property to which section 71D above applies immediately after the event, the amount which, after deducting the tax, is equal to the amount on which tax would be charged by virtue of paragraph (a) above.

(3) The rate at which the tax is charged is the rate that would be given by subsections (6) to (8) of section 70 above—

(a) if the reference to section 70 above in subsection (8)(a) of that section were a reference to section 71D above,
(b) if the other references in those subsections to section 70 above were references to section 71E above, and
(c) if, for the purposes of section 70(8) above, property—
  (i) which is property to which section 71D above applies,
  (ii) which, immediately before it became property to which section 71D above applies, was property to which section 71 applied, and
  (iii) which ceased on that occasion to be property to which section 71 above applied without ceasing to be settled property,

had become property to which section 71D above applies not on that occasion but on the occasion (or last occasion) before then when it became property to which section 71 above applied.]

[290G]

NOTES

Commencement: 22 March 2006.
Inserted as noted to s 71A at **[290A]**.

[71H Sections 71A to 71G: meaning of "parent"

(1) In sections 71A to 71G above "parent" includes step-parent.

(2) For the purposes of sections 71A to 71G above, a deceased individual ("D") shall be taken to have been a parent of another individual ("Y") if, immediately before D died, D had—

(a) parental responsibility for Y under the law of England and Wales,
(b) parental responsibilities in relation to Y under the law of Scotland, or
(c) parental responsibility for Y under the law of Northern Ireland.

(3) In subsection (2)(a) above "parental responsibility" has the same meaning as in the Children Act 1989.

(4) In subsection (2)(b) above "parental responsibilities" has the meaning given by section 1(3) of the Children (Scotland) Act 1995.

(5) In subsection (2)(c) above "parental responsibility" has the same meaning as in the Children (Northern Ireland) Order 1995.]

[290H]

NOTES
Commencement: 22 March 2006.
Inserted as noted to s 71A at **[290A]**.

72 Property leaving employee trusts and newspaper trusts

(1) This section applies to settled property to which section 86 below applies [if—
(a) no interest in possession subsists in it to which an individual is beneficially entitled, and
(b) no company-purchased interest in possession subsists in it.]

[(1A) For the purposes of subsection (1)(b) above, an interest in possession is "company-purchased" if—
(a) a company is beneficially entitled to the interest in possession,
(b) the business of the company consists wholly or mainly in the acquisition of interests in settled property, and
(c) the company has acquired the interest in possession for full consideration in money or money's worth from an individual who was beneficially entitled to it.

(1B) Section 59(3) and (4) above apply for the purposes of subsection (1A)(c) above as for those of section 59(2)(b) above, but as if the references to the condition set out in section 59(2)(a) above were to the condition set out in subsection (1A)(b) above.]

(2) Subject to subsections (4)[, (4A)] and (5) below, there shall be a charge to tax under this section—
(a) where settled property ceases to be property to which this section applies, otherwise than by virtue of a payment out of the settled property, and
(b) where a payment is made out of settled property to which this section applies for the benefit of a person within subsection (3) below, or a person connected with such a person, and
(c) in a case in which paragraphs (a) and (b) above do not apply, where the trustees make a disposition (otherwise than by way of a payment out of the settled property) as a result of which the value of settled property to which this section applies is less than it would be but for the disposition.

(3) A person is within this subsection if—
(a) he has directly or indirectly provided any of the settled property otherwise than by additions not exceeding in value £1,000 in any one year; or
(b) in a case where the employment in question is employment by a close company, he is a participator in relation to that company and either—
(i) is beneficially entitled to, or to rights entitling him to acquire, not less than 5 per cent. of, or of any class of the shares comprised in, its issued share capital, or
(ii) would, on a winding-up of the company, be entitled to not less than 5 per cent. of its assets; or
(c) he has acquired an interest in the settled property for a consideration in money or money's worth.

(4) If the trusts are those of a profit sharing scheme approved in accordance with Schedule 9 to the [Taxes Act 1988], tax shall not be chargeable under this section by virtue of subsection (3)(b) above on an appropriation of shares in pursuance of the scheme.

[(4A) If the trusts are those of [a share incentive plan approved under Schedule 2 to the Income Tax (Earnings and Pensions) Act 2003], tax shall not be chargeable under this section by virtue of subsection (3)(b) above on an appropriation of shares to, or acquisition of shares on behalf of, an individual under the plan.]

(5) Subsections (3) to (10) of section 70 above shall apply for the purposes of this section as they apply for the purposes of that section (with the substitution of a reference to subsection (2)(c) above for the reference in section 70(4) to section 70(2)(b)).

(6) In this section—
(a) "close company" and "participator" have the same meanings as in Part IV of this Act; and
(b) "year" means the period beginning with 26th March 1974 and ending with 5th April 1974, and any subsequent period of twelve months ending with 5th April;

and a person shall be treated for the purposes of this section as acquiring an interest for a consideration in money or money's worth if he becomes entitled to it as a result of transactions which include a disposition for such consideration (whether to him or another) of that interest or of other property.

[291]

NOTES

Sub-s (1): words in square brackets substituted by the Finance Act 2006, s 156, Sch 20, Pt 3, paras 7, 21(1), (2).

Sub-ss (1A), (1B): inserted by the Finance Act 2006, s 156, Sch 20, Pt 3, paras 7, 21(1), (3).

Sub-s (2): number in square brackets inserted by the Finance Act 2000, s 138(1), (3)(a).

Sub-s (4): words in square brackets substituted by the Income and Corporation Taxes Act 1988, s 844(1), Sch 29, para 32.

Sub-s (4A): inserted by the Finance Act 2000, s 138(1), (3)(b); words in square brackets substituted by the Income Tax (Earnings and Pensions) Act 2003, ss 722, 723, Sch 6, Pt 2, paras 150, 151(1)(b), (2), with effect for the purposes of income tax, for the tax year 2003–04 and subsequent tax years, and for the purposes of corporation tax, for accounting periods ending after 5 April 2003.

73 Pre-1978 protective trusts

(1) This section applies to settled property which is held on trusts to the like effect as those specified in section 33(1)(ii) of the Trustee Act 1925 and which became held on those trusts on the failure or determination before 12th April 1978 of trusts to the like effect as those specified in section 33(1)(i).

(2) Subject to subsection (3) below, there shall be a charge to tax under this section—

(a) where settled property ceases to be property to which this section applies, otherwise than by virtue of a payment out of the settled property for the benefit of the principal beneficiary within the meaning of section 33 of the Trustee Act 1925, and

(b) in a case in which paragraph (a) above does not apply, where the trustees make a disposition (otherwise than by way of such a payment) as a result of which the value of settled property to which this section applies is less than it would be but for the disposition.

(3) Subsections (3) to (10) of section 70 above shall apply for the purposes of this section as they apply for the purposes of that section.

[292]

74 Pre-1981 trusts for disabled persons

(1) This section applies to settled property transferred into settlement before 10th March 1981 and held on trusts under which, during the life of a disabled person, no interest in possession in the settled property subsists, and which secure that any of the settled property which is applied during his life is applied only or mainly for his benefit.

(2) Subject to subsection (3) below, there shall be a charge to tax under this section—

(a) where settled property ceases to be property to which this section applies, otherwise than by virtue of a payment out of the settled property for the benefit of the person mentioned in subsection (1) above, and

(b) in a case in which paragraph (a) above does not apply, where the trustees make a disposition (otherwise than by way of such a payment) as a result of which the value of settled property to which this section applies is less than it would be but for the disposition.

(3) Subsections (3) to (10) of section 70 above shall apply for the purposes of this section as they apply for the purposes of that section.

(4) In this section "disabled person" means a person who—

(a) is by reason of mental disorder (within the meaning of the Mental Health Act 1983) incapable of administering his property or managing his affairs, or

(b) is in receipt of an attendance allowance under section [64 of the Social Security Contributions and Benefits Act 1992 or section 64 of the Social Security Contributions and Benefits (Northern Ireland) Act 1992][, or

(c) is in receipt of a disability living allowance under section [71 of the Social Security Contributions and Benefits Act 1992 or section 71 of the Social Security Contributions and Benefits (Northern Ireland) Act 1992] by virtue of entitlement to the care component at the highest or middle rate].

[293]

NOTES

Sub-s (4): words in square brackets in para (b) substituted by the combined effect of the Social Security (Consequential Provisions) Act 1992, s 4, Sch 2, para 66(1) and the Social Security (Consequential Provisions) (Northern Ireland) Act 1992, s 4, Sch 2, para 29(1); para (c) and the preceding word inserted by the Disability Living Allowance and Disability Working Allowance Act 1991, s 4, Sch 2, para 14, and the words in square brackets substituted by the combined effect of the Social Security (Consequential Provisions) Act 1992, s 4, Sch 2, para 66(2), the Disability Living Allowance and Disability Working Allowance (Northern Ireland Consequential Amendments) Order 1991, SI 1991/2874, art 4(1), (2) and the Social Security (Consequential Provisions) (Northern Ireland) Act 1992, s 4, Sch 2, para 29(2).

Special cases—reliefs

75 Property becoming subject to employee trusts

(1) Tax shall not be charged under section 65 above in respect of shares in or securities of a company which cease to be relevant property on becoming held on trusts of the description specified in section 86(1) below if the conditions in subsection (2) below are satisfied.

(2) The conditions referred to in subsection (1) above are—

(a) that the persons for whose benefit the trusts permit the settled property to be applied include all or most of the persons employed by or holding office with the company;

(b) that, at the date when the shares or securities cease to be relevant property or at a subsequent date not more than one year thereafter, both the conditions mentioned in subsection (2) of section 28 above (read with subsections (3) and (7)) are satisfied, without taking account of shares or securities held on other trusts; and

(c) that the trusts do not permit any of the property to be applied at any time (whether during any such period as is referred to in section 86(1) below or later) for the benefit of any of the persons mentioned in subsection (4) of section 28 above (read with subsections (5) to (7)) or for the benefit of the settlor or of any person connected with him.

(3) In its application for the purposes of subsection (2)(c) above, section 28(4) shall be construed as if—

(a) references to section 28(1) were references to subsection (2) above, and

(b) references to the time of the transfer of value were references to the time when the property ceases to be relevant property.

[294]

76 Property becoming held for charitable purposes, etc

(1) Tax shall not be charged under this Chapter (apart from section 79 below) in respect of property which ceases to be relevant property, or ceases to be property to which section 70, 71, [71A, 71D,] 72, 73 or 74 above or paragraph 8 of Schedule 4 to this Act applies, on becoming—

(a) property held for charitable purposes only without limit of time (defined by a date or otherwise);

(b) the property of a political party qualifying for exemption under section 24 above; [or]

(c) the property of a body within Schedule 3 to this Act; …

(d) …

(2) …

(3) If the amount on which tax would be charged apart from this section in respect of any property exceeds the value of the property immediately after it becomes property of a description specified in paragraphs (a) [to (c)] of subsection (1) above (less the amount of any consideration for its transfer received by the trustees), that subsection shall not apply but the amount on which tax is charged shall be equal to the excess.

(4) The reference in subsection (3) above to the amount on which tax would be charged is a reference to the amount on which it would be charged—

(a) assuming (if it is not in fact so) that the tax is not paid out of settled property, and

(b) apart from Chapters I and II of Part V of this Act;

and the reference in that subsection to the amount on which tax is charged is a reference to the amount on which it would be charged on that assumption and apart from those Chapters.

(5) Subsection (1) above shall not apply in relation to any property if the disposition by which it becomes property of the relevant description is defeasible; but for this purpose a disposition which has not been defeated at a time twelve months after the property concerned becomes property of the relevant description and is not defeasible after that time shall be treated as not being defeasible, whether or not it was capable of being defeated before that time.

(6) Subsection (1) above shall not apply in relation to any property if it or any part of it may become applicable for purposes other than charitable purposes or purposes of a body mentioned in subsection (1)(b) [or (c)] above.

(7) Subsection (1) shall not apply in relation to any property if, at or before the time when it becomes property of the relevant description, an interest under the settlement is or has been acquired for a consideration in money or money's worth by an exempt body otherwise than from a charity or a body mentioned in subsection (1)(b) or (c) above.

(8) In subsection (7) above "exempt body" means a charity or a body mentioned in subsection (1)(b) [or (c)] above; and for the purposes of subsection (7) above a body shall be treated as acquiring an interest for a consideration in money or money's worth if it becomes entitled to the interest as a result of transactions which include a disposition for such consideration (whether to that body or to another person) of that interest or of other property.

[295]

NOTES

Sub-s (1): numbers in first pair of square brackets inserted by the Finance Act 2006, s 156, Sch 20, Pt 3, paras 7, 22; word in square brackets after para (b) inserted and words omitted repealed by the Finance Act 1998, ss 143(1), (4)(a), (5), 165, Sch 27, Pt IV, in relation to property which ceases to be relevant property, or to be property to which any of sections 70 to 74 of this Act or paragraph 8 of Schedule 4 to this Act applies, on or after 17 March 1998.

Sub-s (2): repealed by the Finance Act 1998, ss 143(1), (4)(a), (5), 165, Sch 27, Pt IV, in relation to property which ceases to be relevant property, or to be property to which any of sections 70 to 74 of this Act or paragraph 8 of Schedule 4 to this Act applies, on or after 17 March 1998.

Sub-ss (3), (6), (8): words in square brackets substituted by the Finance Act 1998, s 143(1), (4)(b), (c), (5), in relation to property which ceases to be relevant property, or to be property to which any of sections 70 to 74 of this Act or paragraph 8 of Schedule 4 to this Act applies, on or after 17 March 1998.

Functions of the Treasury under this section transferred to the Commissioners of Inland Revenue by the Finance Act 1985, s 95(1).

Works of art, historic buildings, etc

77 Maintenance funds for historic buildings, etc

Schedule 4 to this Act shall have effect.

[295A]

78 Conditionally exempt occasions

(1) A transfer of property or other event shall not constitute an occasion on which tax is chargeable under any provision of this Chapter other than section 64 if the property in respect of which the charge would have been made has been comprised in the settlement throughout the six years ending with the transfer or event, and—

(a) the property is, on a claim made for the purpose, designated by the Treasury under section 31 above, and

(b) the requisite undertaking described in that section is given with respect to the property by such person as the Treasury think appropriate in the circumstances of the case [or (where the property is an area of land within subsection (1)(d) of that section) the requisite undertakings described in that section are given with respect to the property by such person or persons as the Treasury think appropriate in the circumstances of the case].

[(1A) A claim under subsection (1) above must be made no more than two years after the date of the transfer or other event in question or within such longer period as the Board may allow.]

(2) References in this Chapter to a conditionally exempt occasion are to—

(a) a transfer or event which by virtue of subsection (1) above does not constitute an occasion on which tax is chargeable under this Chapter;

(b) a transfer or event which, by virtue of section 81(1) of the Finance Act 1976, did not constitute an occasion on which tax was chargeable under Chapter II of Part IV of the Finance Act 1982;

(c) a conditionally exempt distribution within the meaning given by section 81(2) of the Finance Act 1976 as it had effect in relation to events before 9th March 1982.

(3) Where there has been a conditionally exempt occasion in respect of any property, sections 32, [32A,] 33(1), 33(3) to (7) and 35(2) above shall have effect (and tax shall accordingly be chargeable under section 32 [or 32A]) as if—

(a) references to a conditionally exempt transfer and to such a transfer of property included references respectively to a conditionally exempt occasion and to such an occasion in respect of property;

(b) references to a disposal otherwise than by sale included references to any occasion on which tax is chargeable under any provision of this Chapter other than section 64;

(c) references to an undertaking given under section 30 above included references to an undertaking given under this section;

and the references in section 33(5) above to the person who made a conditionally exempt transfer shall have effect in relation to a conditionally exempt occasion as references to the person who is the settlor of the settlement in respect of which the occasion occurred (or if there is more than one such person, whichever of them the Board may select).

(4) Where by virtue of subsection (3) above the relevant person for the purposes of section 33 above is the settlor of a settlement, the rate (or each of the rates) mentioned in section 33(1)(b)(i) or (ii)—

(a) shall, if the occasion occurred before the first ten-year anniversary to fall after the property became comprised in the settlement concerned, be 30 per cent of what it would be apart from this subsection, and

(b) shall, if the occasion occurred after the first and before the second ten-year anniversary to fall after the property became so comprised, be 60 per cent of what it would be apart from this subsection;

[and the appropriate provision of section 7 for the purposes of section 33(1)(b)(ii) is, if the settlement was created on his death, subsection (1) and, if not, subsection (2)].

(5) Where by virtue of subsection (3) above the relevant person for the purposes of section 33 above is the settlor of a settlement and that settlor died before 13th March 1975, section 33(1)(b) above shall have effect (subject to subsection (4) above) with the substitution for sub-paragraph (ii) of the following sub-paragraph—

"(ii) the rate or rates that would have applied to that amount ("the chargeable amount") [in accordance with the appropriate provision of section 7 above] if the relevant person had died when the chargeable event occurred, the value transferred on his death had been equal to the amount on which estate duty was chargeable when he in fact died, and the chargeable amount had been added to that value and had formed the highest part of it."

(6) Section 34 above shall not apply to a chargeable event in respect of property if the last conditionally exempt transfer of the property has been followed by a conditionally exempt occasion in respect of it.

[296]

NOTES

Sub-ss (1), (3): words in square brackets inserted by the Finance Act 1985, s 94, Sch 26, para 8, in relation to events occurring on or after 19 March 1985.

Sub-s (1A): inserted by the Finance Act 1998, s 142, Sch 25, para 3(1), in relation to transfers of property made, and other events occurring, on or after 17 March 1998.

Sub-ss (4), (5): words in square brackets substituted by the Finance Act 1986, s 101(1), (3), Sch 19, Pt I, para 19, as respects transfers of value made, and other events occurring, on or after 18 March 1986.

---

79 Exemption from ten-yearly charge

(1) Where property is comprised in a settlement and there has been a conditionally exempt transfer of the property on or before the occasion on which it became comprised in the settlement, section 64 above shall not have effect in relation to the property on any ten-year anniversary falling before the first occurrence after the transfer of a chargeable event with respect to the property.

(2) Where property is comprised in a settlement and there has been, on or before the occasion on which it became comprised in the settlement, a disposal of the property in relation to which subsection (4) of section [258 of the 1992 Act] (capital gains tax relief for works of art etc) had effect, section 64 above shall not have effect in relation to the property on any ten-year anniversary falling before the first occurrence after the disposal of an event on the happening of which the property is treated as sold under subsection (5) of the said section [258].

(3) Where property is comprised in a settlement and there has been no such transfer or disposal of the property as is mentioned in subsection (1) or (2) above on or before the occasion on which it became comprised in the settlement, then, if—

(a) the property has, on a claim made for the purpose, been designated by the Treasury under section 31 above,
(b) the requisite undertaking described in that section has been given [with respect to the property] by such person as the Treasury think appropriate in the circumstances of the case [or (where the property is an area of land within subsection (1)(d) of that section) the requisite undertakings described in that section have been given with respect to the property by such person or persons as the Treasury think appropriate in the circumstances of the case], and
(c) the property is relevant property,

section 64 above shall not have effect in relation to the property; but there shall be a charge to tax under this subsection on the first occurrence of an event which, if there had been a conditionally exempt transfer of the property when the claim was made and the undertaking had been given under section 30 above, would be a chargeable event with respect to the property.

(4) Tax shall not be charged under subsection (3) above in respect of property if, after the occasion and before the occurrence there mentioned, there has been a conditionally exempt occasion in respect of the property.

(5) The amount on which tax is charged under subsection (3) above shall be an amount equal to the value of the property at the time of the event.

[(5A) Where the event giving rise to a charge to tax under subsection (3) above is a disposal on sale, and the sale—

(a) was not intended to confer any gratuitous benefit on any person, and
(b) was either a transaction at arm's length between persons not connected with each other or a transaction such as might be expected to be made at arm's length between persons not connected with each other,

the value of the property at the time of that event shall be taken for the purposes of subsection (5) above to be equal to the proceeds of the sale.]

(6) The rate at which tax is charged under subsection (3) above shall be the aggregate of the following percentages—

(a) 0.25 per cent for each of the first forty complete successive quarters in the relevant period,
(b) 0.20 per cent for each of the next forty,
(c) 0.15 per cent for each of the next forty,
(d) 0.10 per cent for each of the next forty, and
(e) 0.05 per cent for each of the next forty.

[(7) In subsection (6) above "the relevant period" means the period given by subsection (7A) below or, if shorter, the period given by subsection (7B) below.

(7A) The period given by this subsection is the period beginning with the latest of—

(a) the day on which the settlement commenced,
(b) the date of the last ten-year anniversary of the settlement to fall before the day on which the property became comprised in the settlement,
(c) the date of the last ten-year anniversary of the settlement to fall before the day on which the property was designated under section 31 above on a claim under this section, and
(d) 13th March 1975,

and ending with the day before the event giving rise to the charge.

(7B) The period given by this subsection is the period equal in length to the number of relevant-property days in the period—

(a) beginning with the day that is the latest of those referred to in paragraphs (a) to (d) of subsection (7A) above, and

(b) ending with the day before the event giving rise to the charge.

(7C) For the purposes of subsection (7B) above, a day is a "relevant-property day" if at any time on that day the property was relevant property.]

(8) Subsection (9) below shall have effect where—

(a) by virtue of subsection (3) above, section 64 does not have effect in relation to property on the first ten-year anniversary of the settlement to fall after the making of the claim and the giving of the undertaking,

(b) on that anniversary a charge to tax falls to be made in respect of the settlement under section 64, and

(c) the property became comprised in the settlement, and the claim was made and the undertaking was given, within the period of ten years ending with that anniversary.

(9) In calculating the rate at which tax is charged under section 64 above, the value of the consideration given for the property on its becoming comprised in the settlement shall be treated for the purposes of section 66(5)(b) above as if it were an amount on which a charge to tax was imposed in respect of the settlement under section 65 above at the time of the property becoming so comprised.

[(9A) Subsection (9B) below applies where the same event gives rise—

(a) to a charge under subsection (3) above in relation to any property, and

(b) to a charge under section 32 or 32A above in relation to that property.

(9B) If the amount of each of the charges is the same, each charge shall have effect as a charge for one half of the amount that would be charged apart from this subsection; otherwise, whichever of the charges is lower in amount shall have effect as if it were a charge the amount of which is nil.]

(10) In subsection (1) above, the reference to a conditionally exempt transfer of any property includes a reference to a transfer of value in relation to which the value of any property has been left out of account under the provisions of sections 31 to 34 of the Finance Act 1975 and, in relation to such property, the reference to a chargeable event includes a reference to an event on the occurrence of which tax becomes chargeable under Schedule 5 to this Act.

[297]

NOTES

Sub-s (2): words in square brackets substituted by the Taxation of Chargeable Gains Act 1992, s 290(1), Sch 10, para 8(1), (3).

Sub-s (3): words in square brackets substituted by the Finance Act 1985, s 94, Sch 26, para 9, in relation to events occurring on or after 19 March 1985.

Sub-s (5A): inserted by the Finance Act 2006, s 156, Sch 20, Pt 6, para 34(1), (2).

Sub-ss (7), (7A)–(7C): substituted, for sub-s (7) as originally enacted, by the Finance Act 2006, s 156, Sch 20, Pt 6, para 34(1), (3).

Sub-ss (9A), (9B): inserted by the Finance Act 2006, s 156, Sch 20, Pt 6, para 34(1), (4).

1992 Act: the Taxation of Chargeable Gains Act 1992.

Finance Act 1975, ss 31–34: by virtue of the Finance Act 1976, s 83(1), those sections applied only to deaths occurring before 6 April 1976; they are repealed by s 277 of, and Sch 9 to, this Act.

[79A Variation of undertakings

(1) An undertaking given under section 78 or 79 above may be varied from time to time by agreement between the Board and the person bound by the undertaking.

(2) Where a Special Commissioner is satisfied that—

(a) the Board have made a proposal for the variation of such an undertaking to the person bound by the undertaking,

(b) that person has failed to agree to the proposed variation within six months after the date on which the proposal was made, and

(c) it is just and reasonable, in all the circumstances, to require the proposed variation to be made,

the Commissioner may direct that the undertaking is to have effect from a date specified by him as if the proposed variation had been agreed to by the person bound by the undertaking.

(3) The date specified by the Special Commissioner must not be less than sixty days after the date of his direction.

(4) A direction under this section shall not take effect if, before the date specified by the Special Commissioner, a variation different from that to which the direction relates is agreed between the Board and the person bound by the undertaking.]

[298]

NOTES

Inserted by the Finance Act 1998, s 142, Sch 25, paras 1, 8, (2), (4), in relation to undertakings given on or after 31 July 1998.

Miscellaneous

80 Initial interest of settlor or spouse [or civil partner]

(1) Where a settlor or his spouse [or civil partner] is beneficially entitled to an interest in possession in property immediately after it becomes comprised in the settlement, the property shall for the purposes of this Chapter be treated as not having become comprised in the settlement on that occasion; but when the property or any part of it becomes held on trusts under which neither of those persons is beneficially entitled to an interest in possession, the property or part shall for those purposes be treated as becoming comprised in a separate settlement made by that one of them who ceased (or last ceased) to be beneficially entitled to an interest in possession in it.

(2) References in subsection (1) above to the spouse [or civil partner] of a settlor include references to the widow or widower [or surviving civil partner] of a settlor.

(3) This section shall not apply if the occasion first referred to in subsection (1) above occurred before 27th March 1974.

[(4) Where the occasion first referred to in subsection (1) above occurs on or after 22nd March 2006, this section applies—

(a) as though for "an interest in possession" in each place where that appears in subsection (1) above there were substituted "a postponing interest", and

(b) as though, for the purposes of that subsection, each of the following were a "postponing interest"—

(i) an immediate post-death interest;

(ii) a disabled person's interest.]

[299]

NOTES

Section heading: words in square brackets inserted by the Tax and Civil Partnership Regulations 2005, SI 2005/3229, regs 3, 17(1), (4).

Sub-ss (1), (2): words in square brackets inserted by SI 2005/3229, regs 3, 17(1)–(3).

Sub-s (4): added by the Finance Act 2006, s 156, Sch 20, Pt 3, para 7.

81 Property moving between settlements

(1) Where property which ceases to be comprised in one settlement becomes comprised in another then, unless in the meantime any person becomes beneficially entitled to the property (and not merely to an interest in possession in the property), it shall for the purposes of this Chapter be treated as remaining comprised in the first settlement.

(2) Subsection (1) above shall not apply where the property ceased to be comprised in the first settlement before 10th December 1981; but where property ceased to be comprised in one settlement before 10th December 1981 and after 26th March 1974 and, by the same disposition, became comprised in another settlement, it shall for the purposes of this Chapter be treated as remaining comprised in the first settlement.

(3) Subsection (1) above shall not apply where a reversionary interest in the property expectant on the termination of a qualifying interest in possession subsisting under the first settlement was settled on the trusts of the other settlement before 10th December 1981.

[300]

82 Excluded property

(1) For the purposes of this Chapter (except sections 78 and 79) property to which section 80 or 81 above applies shall not be taken to be excluded property by virtue of

section 48(3)(a) above unless the condition in subsection (3) below is satisfied (in addition to the conditions in section 48(3) that the property is situated outside the United Kingdom and that the settlor was not domiciled there when the settlement was made).

(2) Section 65(8) above shall not have effect in relation to property to which section 80 or 81 above applies unless the condition in subsection (3) below is satisfied (in addition to the condition in section 65(8) that the settlor was not domiciled in the United Kingdom when the settlement was made).

(3) The condition referred to in subsections (1) and (2) above is—

(a) in the case of property to which section 80 above applies, that the person who is the settlor in relation to the settlement first mentioned in that section, and

(b) in the case of property to which subsection (1) or (2) of section 81 above applies, that the person who is the settlor in relation to the second of the settlements mentioned in the subsection concerned,

was not domiciled in the United Kingdom when that settlement was made.

[301]

83 Property becoming settled on a death

Property which becomes comprised in a settlement in pursuance of a will or intestacy shall for the purposes of this Chapter be taken to have become comprised in it on the death of the testator or intestate (whether it occurred before or after the passing of this Act).

[302]

84 Income applied for charitable purposes

For the purposes of this Chapter (except sections 78 and 79) where the trusts on which settled property is held require part of the income of the property to be applied for charitable purposes, a corresponding part of the settled property shall be regarded as held for charitable purposes.

[303]

85–214 (*S 85, ss 86–93 (Ch IV), ss 94–214 (Pts IV–VII) outside the scope of this work.*)

PART VIII
ADMINISTRATION AND COLLECTION

215–225A (*Outside the scope of this work.*)

Payment

226–229 (*Outside the scope of this work.*)

230 Acceptance of property in satisfaction of tax

(1) The Board may, if they think fit and the [Secretary of State agrees], on the application of any person liable to pay tax or interest payable under section 233 below, accept in satisfaction of the whole or any part of it any property to which this section applies.

(2) This section applies to any such land as may be agreed upon between the Board and the person liable to pay tax.

(3) This section also applies to any objects which are or have been kept in any building—

(a) if the Board have determined to accept or have accepted that building in satisfaction or part satisfaction of tax or of estate duty, or

(b) if the building or any interest in it belongs to Her Majesty in right of the Crown or of the Duchy of Lancaster, or belongs to the Duchy of Cornwall or belongs to a Government department or is held for the purposes of a Government department, or

(c) if the building is one of which the Secretary of State is guardian under the Ancient Monuments and Archaeological Areas Act 1979 or of which the Department of the Environment for Northern Ireland is guardian under [the Historic Monuments and Archaeological Objects (Northern Ireland) Order 1995], or

(d) if the building belongs to any body within Schedule 3 to this Act, in any case where it appears to the [Secretary of State] desirable for the objects to remain associated with the building.

(4) This section also applies to—

(a) any picture, print, book, manuscript, work of art, scientific object or other thing which the [Secretary of State is] satisfied is pre-eminent for its national, scientific, historic or artistic interest, and

(b) any collection or group of pictures, prints, books, manuscripts, works of art, scientific objects or other things if the [Secretary of State is] satisfied that the collection or group, taken as a whole, is pre-eminent for its national, scientific, historic or artistic interest.

(5) In this section—

. . . .

"national interest" includes interest within any part of the United Kingdom;

and in determining under subsection (4) above whether an object or collection or group of objects is pre-eminent, regard shall be had to any significant association of the object, collection or group with a particular place.

[(6) The functions of the Ministers under this section in relation to the acceptance, in satisfaction of tax, of property in which there is a Scottish interest may be exercised separately.

(7) For the purposes of subsection (6) a Scottish interest in the property exists—

(a) where the property is located in Scotland; or

(b) the person liable to pay the tax has expressed a wish or imposed a condition on his offer of the property in satisfaction of tax that it be displayed in Scotland or disposed of or transferred to a body or institution in Scotland.]

[304]

NOTES

Sub-ss (1), (4): words in square brackets substituted by the Transfer of Functions (National Heritage) Order 1992, SI 1992/1311, art 12(2), para 6(1), (2), (4).

Sub-s (3): words in first pair of square brackets substituted by the Historic Monuments and Archaeological Objects (Northern Ireland) Order 1995, SI 1995/1625, art 45(1), Sch 3, para 1(2)(e); words in second pair of square brackets substituted by SI 1992/1311, art 12(2), Sch 2, para 6(1), (3).

Sub-s (5): definition omitted repealed by SI 1992/1311, art 12(2), Sch 2, para 6(1), (5).

Sub-ss (6), (7): inserted by the Scotland Act 1998 (Modification of Functions) Order 1999, SI 1999/1756, art 2, Schedule, para 8.

231–261 (*Outside the scope of this work.*)

PART IX
MISCELLANEOUS AND SUPPLEMENTARY

262–272 (*Outside the scope of this work.*)

Supplementary

273 (*Outside the scope of this work.*)

274 Commencement

(1) This Act shall come into force on 1st January 1985, but shall not apply to transfers of value made before that date or to other events before that date on which inheritance tax is chargeable or would be chargeable but for an exemption, exception or relief.

(2) Subsection (1) above shall have effect subject to section 275 below, to Schedule 7 to this Act and to any other provision to the contrary.

[305]

275 Continuity, and construction of references to old and new law

(1) The continuity of the operation of the law relating to inheritance tax shall not be affected by the substitution of this Act for the repealed enactments.

(2) Any reference, whether express or implied, in any enactment, instrument or document (including this Act and any enactment amended by Schedule 8 to this Act) to, or to things done or falling to be done under or for the purposes of, any provision of this Act shall, if and so far as the nature of the reference permits, be construed as including, in relation to the times, circumstances or purposes in relation to which the corresponding provision in the repealed enactments has or had effect, a reference to, or as the case may be, to things done or falling to be done under or for the purposes of, that corresponding provision.

(3) Any reference, whether express or implied, in any enactment, instrument or document (including the repealed enactments and enactments, instruments and documents passed or made after the passing of this Act) to, or to things done or falling to be done under or for the purposes of, any of the repealed enactments shall, if and so far as the nature of the reference permits, be construed as including, in relation to the times, circumstances or purposes in relation to which the corresponding provision of this Act has effect, a reference to, or as the case may be, to things done or falling to be done under or for the purposes of, that corresponding provision.

(4) Subsection (2) above shall have effect without prejudice to section 17(2) of the Interpretation Act 1978.

(5) In this section "the repealed enactments" means the enactments repealed by this Act. **[306]**

276, 277 (*Outside the scope of this work.*)

278 Short title

This Act may be cited as the Inheritance Tax Act 1984.

[307]

SCHEDULES

(*Schs 1, 2 outside the scope of this work.*)

SCHEDULE 3
GIFTS FOR NATIONAL PURPOSES, ETC

Sections 25, 32, 230 etc

The National Gallery.

The British Museum.

[The National Museums of Scotland.]

The National Museum of Wales.

The Ulster Museum.

Any other similar national institution which exists wholly or mainly for the purpose of preserving for the public benefit a collection of scientific, historic or artistic interest and which is approved for the purposes of this Schedule by the Treasury.

Any museum or art gallery in the United Kingdom which exists wholly or mainly for that purpose and is maintained by a local authority or university in the United Kingdom.

Any library the main function of which is to serve the needs of teaching and research at a university in the United Kingdom.

The Historic Buildings and Monuments Commission for England.

The National Trust for Places of Historic Interest or Natural Beauty.

The National Trust for Scotland for Places of Historic Interest or Natural Beauty.

The National Art Collections Fund.

The Trustees of the National Heritage Memorial Fund.

[The National Endowment for Science, Technology and the Arts.]

The Friends of the National Libraries.

The Historic Churches Preservation Trust.

[[Commission for Rural Communities.

Natural England.].

[Scottish Natural Heritage.]

Countryside Council for Wales.]

Any local authority.

Any Government department (including the National Debt Commissioners).

Any university or university college in the United Kingdom.

[A health service body, within the meaning of section 519A of the Income and Corporation Taxes Act 1988.]

[308]

NOTES

Entry "The National Museums of Scotland" substituted by the National Heritage (Scotland) Act 1985, s 24(1), Sch 2, Pt I, para 4; entry "The National Endowment for Science, Technology and the Arts" inserted by the National Lottery Act 1998, s 24(3); entries "Nature Conservancy Council for England" and "Countryside Council for Wales" substituted by the Environmental Protection Act 1990, s 128, Sch 6, para 25; entries "Commission for Rural Communities", "Natural England" substituted by the Natural Environment and Rural Communities Act 2006, s 105(1), Sch 11, Pt 1, para 105; entry "Scottish Natural Heritage" substituted by the Natural Heritage (Scotland) Act 1991, s 4(10), Sch 2, para 9; final entry in square brackets added by the National Health Service and Community Care Act 1990, s 61(5).

Functions of the Treasury under this Schedule transferred to the Commissioners of Inland Revenue by the Finance Act 1985, s 95(1).

SCHEDULE 4
MAINTENANCE FUNDS FOR HISTORIC BUILDINGS, ETC

Sections 27, 58, 77 etc

PART I
TREASURY DIRECTIONS

Giving of directions

1.—(1) If the conditions mentioned in paragraph 2(1) below are fulfilled in respect of settled property, the Treasury shall, on a claim made for the purpose, give a direction under this paragraph in respect of the property.

(2) The Treasury may give a direction under this paragraph in respect of property proposed to be comprised in a settlement or to be held on particular trusts in any case where, if the property were already so comprised or held, they would be obliged to give the direction.

(3) Property comprised in a settlement by virtue of a transfer of value made before the coming into force of section 94 of the Finance Act 1982 and exempt under section 84 of the Finance Act 1976 shall be treated as property in respect of which a direction has been given under this paragraph.

Conditions

2.—(1) The conditions referred to in paragraph 1 above are—

(a) that the Treasury are satisfied—

(i) that the trusts on which the property is held comply with the requirements mentioned in paragraph 3 below, and

(ii) that the property is of a character and amount appropriate for the purposes of those trusts; and (b) that the trustees—

(i) are approved by the Treasury,

(ii) include a trust corporation, a solicitor, an accountant or a member of such other professional body as the Treasury may allow in the case of the property concerned, and

(iii) are, at the time the direction is given, resident in the United Kingdom.

(2) For the purposes of this paragraph trustees shall be regarded as resident in the United Kingdom if—

(a) the general administration of the trusts is ordinarily carried on in the United Kingdom, and

(b) the trustees or a majority of them (and, where there is more than one class of trustees, a majority of each class) are resident in the United Kingdom;

and where a trustee is a trust corporation, the question whether the trustee is resident in the United Kingdom shall, for the purposes of paragraph (b) above, be determined as for the purposes of corporation tax.

(3) In this paragraph—

"accountant" means a member of an incorporated society of accountants;

"trust corporation" means a person that is a trust corporation for the purposes of the Law of Property Act 1925 or for the purposes of Article 9 of the Administration of Estates (Northern Ireland) Order 1979.

3.—(1) The requirements referred to in paragraph 2(1)(a)(i) above are (subject to paragraph 4 below)—

(a) that none of the property held on the trusts can at any time in the period of six years beginning with the date on which it became so held be applied otherwise than—

(i) for the maintenance, repair or preservation of, or making provision for public access to, property which is for the time being qualifying property, for the maintenance, repair or preservation of property held on the trusts or for such improvement of property so held as is reasonable having regard to the purposes of the trusts, or for defraying the expenses of the trustees in relation to the property so held;

(ii) as respects income not so applied and not accumulated, for the benefit of a body within Schedule 3 to this Act or of a qualifying charity; and

(b) that none of the property can, on ceasing to be held on the trusts at any time in that period or, if the settlor dies in that period, at any time before his death, devolve otherwise than on any such body or charity; and

(c) that income arising from property held on the trusts cannot at any time after the end of that period be applied except as mentioned in paragraph (a)(i) or (ii) above.

(2) Property is qualifying property for the purposes of sub-paragraph (1) above if—

(a) it has been designated under section 34(1) of the Finance Act 1975 or section 77(1)(b), (c), (d) or (e) of the Finance Act 1976 or section 31(1)(b), (c), (d) or (e) of this Act; and

(b) the requisite undertaking has been given with respect to it under section 34 of the Finance Act 1975 or under section 76, 78(5)(b) or 82(3) of the Finance Act 1976 or under section 30, 32(5)(b) [, 32A(6), (8)(b) or (9)(b)] or 79(3) of this Act or paragraph 5 of Schedule 5 to this Act; and

(c) tax has not (since the last occasion on which such an undertaking was given) become chargeable with respect to it under the said section 34 or under section 78 or 82(3) of the Finance Act 1976 or under section 32 [, 32A] or 79(3) of this Act or paragraph 3 of Schedule 5 to this Act.

(3) If it appears to the Treasury that provision is, or is to be, made by a settlement for the maintenance, repair or preservation of any such property as is mentioned in subsection (1)(b), (c), (d) or (e) of section 31 of this Act they may, on a claim made for the purpose—

(a) designate that property under this sub-paragraph, and

(b) accept with respect to it an undertaking such as is described in subsection (4) [, or (as the case may be) undertakings such as are described in subsections (4) and (4A),] of that section;

and, if they do so, sub-paragraph (2) above shall have effect as if the designation were under that section and the undertaking [or undertakings] under section 30 of this Act and as if the reference to tax becoming chargeable were a reference to the occurrence of an event on which tax would become chargeable under section 32 [or 32A] of this Act if there had been a conditionally exempt transfer of the property when the claim was made and the undertaking [or undertakings] had been given under section 30.

[(3A) Section 35A of this Act shall apply in relation to an undertaking given under sub-paragraph (3) above as it applies in relation to an undertaking given under section 30 of *this Act.]*

(4) A charity is a qualifying charity for the purposes of sub-paragraph (1) above if it exists wholly or mainly for maintaining, repairing or preserving for the public benefit

buildings of historic or architectural interest, land of scenic, historic or scientific interest or objects of national, scientific, historic or artistic interest; and in this sub-paragraph "national interest" includes interest within any part of the United Kingdom.

(5) Designations, undertakings and acceptances made under section 84(6) of the Finance Act 1976 or section 94(3) of the Finance Act 1982 shall be treated as made under subparagraph (3) above.

[(5A) In the case of property which, if a direction is given under paragraph 1 above, will be property to which paragraph 15A below applies, sub-paragraph (1)(b) above shall have effect as if for the reference to the settlor there were substituted a reference to either the settlor or the person referred to in paragraph 15A(2).]

4.—(1) Paragraphs (a) and (b) of paragraph 3(1) above do not apply to property which—

(a) was previously comprised in another settlement, and

(b) ceased to be comprised in that settlement and became comprised in the current settlement in circumstances such that by virtue of paragraph 9(1) below there was no charge (or, but for paragraph 9(4), there would have been no charge) to tax in respect of it;

and in relation to any such property paragraph 3(1)(c) above shall apply with the omission of the words "at any time after the end of that period".

(2) Sub-paragraph (1) above shall not have effect if the time when the property comprised in the previous settlement devolved otherwise than on any such body or charity as is mentioned in paragraph 3(1)(a) above fell before the expiration of the period of six years there mentioned; but in such a case paragraph 3(1) above shall apply to the current settlement as if for the references to that period of six years there were substituted references to the period beginning with the date on which the property became comprised in the current settlement and ending six years after the date on which it became held on the relevant trusts of the previous settlement (or, where this sub-paragraph has already had effect in relation to the property, the date on which it became held on the relevant trusts of the first settlement in the series).

Withdrawal

5. If in the Treasury's opinion the facts concerning any property or its administration cease to warrant the continuance of the effect of a direction given under paragraph 1 above in respect of the property, they may at any time by notice in writing to the trustees withdraw the direction on such grounds, and from such date, as may be specified in the notice; and the direction shall cease to have effect accordingly.

Information

6. Where a direction under paragraph 1 above has effect in respect of property, the trustees shall from time to time furnish the Treasury with such accounts and other information relating to the property as the Treasury may reasonably require.

Enforcement of trusts

7. Where a direction under paragraph 1 above has effect in respect of property, the trusts on which the property is held shall be enforceable at the suit of the Treasury and the Treasury shall, as respects the appointment, removal and retirement of trustees, have the rights and powers of a beneficiary.

[308A]

NOTES

Para 3: words in square brackets in sub-paras (2), (3) inserted by the Finance Act 1985, s 94, Sch 26, para 12, in relation to events occurring on or after 19 March 1985.

Para 3: sub-para (3A) inserted by the Finance Act 1998, s 142, Sch 25, para 8(3), in relation to undertakings given on or after 31 July 1998: see the Finance Act 1998, Sch 25, para 8(4) (for further provision as to the application of this amendment see para 10 thereof).

Para 3: sub-para (5A) inserted by the Finance Act 1987, s 59, Sch 9, paras 2, 5, in relation to directions given on or after 17 March 1987.

Transfer of Functions: functions of the Treasury under this Schedule transferred to the Commissioners of Inland Revenue by the Finance Act 1985, s 95(1).

PART II
PROPERTY LEAVING MAINTENANCE FUNDS

Charge to tax

8.—(1) This paragraph applies to settled property which is held on trusts which comply with the requirements mentioned in paragraph 3(1) above, and in respect of which a direction given under paragraph 1 above has effect.

(2) Subject to paragraphs 9 and 10 below, there shall be a charge to tax under this paragraph—

(a) where settled property ceases to be property to which this paragraph applies, otherwise than by virtue of an application of the kind mentioned in paragraph 3(1)(a)(i) or (ii) above or by devolving on any such body or charity as is mentioned in paragraph 3(1)(a)(ii);

(b) in a case in which paragraph (a) above does not apply, where the trustees make a disposition (otherwise than by such an application) as a result of which the value of settled property to which this paragraph applies is less than it would be but for the disposition.

(3) Subsections (4), (5) and (10) of section 70 of this Act shall apply for the purposes of this paragraph as they apply for the purposes of that section (with the substitution of a reference to sub-paragraph (2)(b) above for the reference in section 70(4) to section 70(2)(b)).

(4) The rate at which tax is charged under this paragraph shall be determined in accordance with paragraphs 11 to 15 below.

(5) The devolution of property on a body or charity shall not be free from charge by virtue of sub-paragraph (2)(a) above if, at or before the time of devolution, an interest under the settlement in which the property was comprised immediately before the devolution is or has been acquired for a consideration in money or money's worth by that or another such body or charity; but for the purposes of this sub-paragraph any acquisition from another such body or charity shall be disregarded.

(6) For the purposes of sub-paragraph (5) above a body or charity shall be treated as acquiring an interest for a consideration in money or money's worth if it becomes entitled to the interest as a result of transactions which include a disposition for such consideration (whether to that body or charity or to another person) of that interest or of other property.

Exceptions from charge

9.—(1) Tax shall not be charged under paragraph 8 above in respect of property which, within the permitted period after the occasion on which tax would be chargeable under that paragraph, becomes comprised in another settlement as a result of a transfer of value which is exempt under section 27 of this Act.

(2) In sub-paragraph (1) above "the permitted period" means the period of thirty days except in a case where the occasion referred to is the death of the settlor, and in such a case means the period of two years.

(3) Sub-paragraph (1) above shall not apply to any property if the person who makes the transfer of value has acquired it for a consideration in money or money's worth; and for the purposes of this sub-paragraph a person shall be treated as acquiring any property for such consideration if he becomes entitled to it as a result of transactions which include a disposition for such consideration (whether to him or another) of that or other property.

(4) If the amount on which tax would be charged apart from sub-paragraph (1) above in respect of any property exceeds the value of the property immediately after it becomes comprised in the other settlement (less the amount of any consideration for its transfer received by the person who makes the transfer of value), that sub-paragraph shall not apply but the amount on which tax is charged shall be equal to the excess.

(5) The reference in sub-paragraph (4) above to the amount on which tax would be charged is a reference to the amount on which it would be charged apart from—

(a) section 70(5)(b) of this Act (as applied by paragraph 8(3) above), and

(b) Chapters I and II of Part V of this Act; and the reference in that sub-paragraph to the amount on which tax is charged is a reference to the amount on which it would be charged apart from section 70(5)(b) and those Chapters.

10.—(1) Tax shall not be charged under paragraph 8 above in respect of property which ceases to be property to which that paragraph applies on becoming—

(a) property to which the settlor or his spouse [or civil partner] is beneficially entitled, or

(b) property to which the settlor's widow or widower [or surviving civil partner] is beneficially entitled if the settlor has died in the two years preceding the time when it becomes such property.

(2) If the amount on which tax would be charged apart from sub-paragraph (1) above in respect of any property exceeds the value of the property immediately after it becomes property of a description specified in paragraph (a) or (b) of that sub-paragraph (less the amount of any consideration for its transfer received by the trustees), that sub-paragraph shall not apply but the amount on which tax is charged shall be equal to the excess.

(3) The reference in sub-paragraph (2) above to the amount on which tax would be charged is a reference to the amount on which it would be charged apart from—

(a) section 70(5)(b) of this Act (as applied by paragraph 8(3) above), and

(b) Chapters I and II of Part V of this Act;

and the reference in sub-paragraph (2) above to the amount on which tax is charged is a reference to the amount on which it would be charged apart from section 70(5)(b) and those Chapters.

(4) Sub-paragraph (1) above shall not apply in relation to any property if, at or before the time when it becomes property of a description specified in paragraph (a) or (b) of that sub-paragraph, an interest under the settlement in which the property was comprised immediately before it ceased to be property to which paragraph 8 above applies is or has been acquired for a consideration in money or money's worth by the person who becomes beneficially entitled.

(5) For the purposes of sub-paragraph (4) above a person shall be treated as acquiring an interest for a consideration in money or money's worth if he becomes entitled to the interest as a result of transactions which include a disposition for such consideration (whether to him or to another person) of that interest or of other property.

(6) Sub-paragraph (1) above shall not apply in respect of property if it was relevant property before it became (or last became) property to which paragraph 8 above applies and, by virtue of paragraph 16(1) or 17(1) below, tax was not chargeable (or, but for paragraph 16(2) or 17(4), would not have been chargeable) under section 65 of this Act in respect of its ceasing to be relevant property before becoming (or last becoming) property to which paragraph 8 above applies.

(7) Sub-paragraph (1) above shall not apply in respect of property if—

(a) before it last became property to which paragraph 8 above applies it was comprised in another settlement in which it was property to which that paragraph applies, and

(b) it ceased to be comprised in the other settlement and last became property to which that paragraph applies in circumstances such that by virtue of paragraph 9(1) above there was no charge (or, but for paragraph 9(4), there would have been no charge) to tax in respect of it.

(8) Sub-paragraph (1) above shall not apply unless the person who becomes beneficially entitled to the property is domiciled in the United Kingdom at the time when he becomes so entitled.

Rates of charge

11.—(1) This paragraph applies where tax is chargeable under paragraph 8 above and—

(a) the property in respect of which the tax is chargeable was relevant property before it became (or last became) property to which that paragraph applies, and

(b) by virtue of paragraph 16(1) or 17(1) below tax was not chargeable (or, but for paragraph 16(2) or 17(4), would not have been chargeable) under section 65 of this Act in respect of its ceasing to be relevant property on or before becoming (or last becoming) property to which paragraph 8 above applies.

(2) Where this paragraph applies, the rate at which the tax is charged shall be the aggregate of the following percentages—

(a) 0.25 per cent for each of the first forty complete successive quarters in the relevant period,
(b) 0.20 per cent for each of the next forty,
(c) 0.15 per cent for each of the next forty,
(d) 0.10 per cent for each of the next forty, and
(e) 0.05 per cent for each of the next forty.

(3) In sub-paragraph (2) above "the relevant period" means the period beginning with the latest of—

(a) the date of the last ten-year anniversary of the settlement in which the property was comprised before it ceased (or last ceased) to be relevant property,
(b) the day on which the property became (or last became) relevant property before it ceased (or last ceased) to be such property, and
(c) 13th March 1975,

and ending with the day before the event giving rise to the charge.

(4) Where the property in respect of which the tax is chargeable has at any time ceased to be and again become property to which paragraph 8 above applies in circumstances such that by virtue of paragraph 9(1) above there was no charge to tax in respect of it (or, but for paragraph 9(4), there would have been no charge), it shall for the purposes of this paragraph be treated as having been property to which paragraph 8 above applies throughout the period mentioned in paragraph 9(1).

12.—(1) This paragraph applies where tax is chargeable under paragraph 8 above and paragraph 11 above does not apply.

(2) Where this paragraph applies, the rate at which the tax is charged shall be the higher of—

(a) the first rate (as determined in accordance with paragraph 13 below), and
(b) the second rate (as determined in accordance with paragraph 14 below).

13.—(1) The first rate is the aggregate of the following percentages—

(a) 0.25 per cent for each of the first forty complete successive quarters in the relevant period,
(b) 0.20 per cent for each of the next forty,
(c) 0.15 per cent for each of the next forty,
(d) 0.10 per cent for each of the next forty, and
(e) 0.05 per cent for each of the next forty.

(2) In sub-paragraph (1) above "the relevant period" means the period beginning with the day on which the property in respect of which the tax is chargeable became (or first became) property to which paragraph 8 above applies, and ending with the day before the event giving rise to the charge.

(3) For the purposes of sub-paragraph (2) above, any occasion on which property became property to which paragraph 8 above applies, and which occurred before an occasion of charge to tax under that paragraph in respect of the property, shall be disregarded.

(4) The reference in sub-paragraph (3) above to an occasion of charge to tax under paragraph 8 does not include a reference to—

(a) the occasion by reference to which the rate is being determined in accordance with this Schedule, or
(b) an occasion which would not be an occasion of charge but for paragraph 9(4) above.

14.—(1) If the settlor is alive, the second rate is the effective rate at which tax would be charged, on the amount on which it is chargeable, [in accordance with the appropriate provision of section 7 of this Act] if the amount were the value transferred by a chargeable transfer made by him on the occasion on which the tax becomes chargeable.

[(1A) The rate or rates of tax determined under sub-paragraph (1) above in respect of any occasion shall not be affected by the death of the settlor after that occasion.]

(2) If the settlor is dead, the second rate is (subject to sub-paragraph (3) below) the effective rate at which tax would have been charged, on the amount on which it is chargeable, [in accordance with the appropriate provision of section 7 of this Act] if the amount had been added to the value transferred on his death and had formed the highest part of it.

(3) If the settlor died before 13th March 1975, the second rate is the effective rate at which tax would have been charged, on the amount on which it is chargeable ("the chargeable amount"), [in accordance with the appropriate provision of section 7 of this Act] if the settlor had died when the event occasioning the charge under paragraph 8 above occurred, the value transferred on his death had been equal to the amount on which estate duty was chargeable when he in fact died, and the chargeable amount had been added to that value and had formed the highest part of it.

(4) Where, in the case of a settlement ("the current settlement"), tax is chargeable under paragraph 8 above in respect of property which—

(a) was previously comprised in another settlement, and

(b) ceased to be comprised in that settlement and became comprised in the current settlement in circumstances such that by virtue of paragraph 9(1) above there was no charge (or, but for paragraph 9(4), there would have been no charge) to tax in respect of it,

then, subject to sub-paragraph (5) below, references in sub-paragraphs (1) to (3) above to the settlor shall be construed as references to the person who was the settlor in relation to the settlement mentioned in paragraph (a) above (or, if the Board so determine, the person who was the settlor in relation to the current settlement).

(5) Where, in the case of a settlement ("the current settlement"), tax is chargeable under paragraph 8 above in respect of property which—

(a) was previously comprised at different times in other settlements ("the previous settlements"), and

(b) ceased to be comprised in each of them, and became comprised in another of them or in the current settlement, in circumstances such that by virtue of paragraph 9(1) above there was no charge (or, but for paragraph 9(4), there would have been no charge) to tax in respect of it,

references in sub-paragraphs (1) to (3) above to the settlor shall be construed as references to the person who was the settlor in relation to the previous settlement in which the property was first comprised (or, if the Board so determine, any person selected by them who was the settlor in relation to any of the other previous settlements or the current settlement).

(6) Sub-paragraph (7) below shall apply if—

(a) in the period of [seven years] preceding a charge under paragraph 8 above (the "current charge"), there has been another charge under that paragraph where tax was charged at the second rate, and

(b) the person who is the settlor for the purposes of the current charge is the settlor for the purposes of the other charge (whether or not the settlements are the same and, if the settlor is dead, whether or not he has died since the other charge);

and in sub-paragraph (7) below the other charge is referred to as the "previous charge".

(7) Where this sub-paragraph applies, the amount on which tax was charged on the previous charge (or, if there have been more than one, the aggregate of the amounts on which tax was charged on each)—

(a) shall, for the purposes of calculating the rate of the current charge under sub-paragraph (1) above, be taken to be the value transferred by a chargeable transfer made by the settlor immediately before the occasion of the current charge, and

(b) shall, for the purposes of calculating the rate of the current charge under sub-paragraph (2) or (3) above, be taken to increase the value there mentioned by an amount equal to that amount (or aggregate).

(8) References in sub-paragraphs (1) to (3) above to the effective rate are to the rate found by expressing the tax chargeable as a percentage of the amount on which it is charged.

[(9) For the purposes of sub-paragraph (1) above the appropriate provision of section 7 of this Act is subsection (2), and for the purposes of sub-paragraphs (2) and (3) above it is (if the settlement was made on death) subsection (1) and (if not) subsection (2).]

15. Where property is, by virtue of paragraph 1(3) above, treated as property in respect of which a direction has been given under paragraph 1, it shall for the purposes of paragraphs 11

to 14 above be treated as having become property to which paragraph 8 above applies when the transfer of value mentioned in paragraph 1(3) was made.

[Maintenance fund following interest in possession

15A.—(1) In relation to settled property to which this paragraph applies, the provisions of this Part of this Schedule shall have effect with the modifications set out in the following subparagraphs.

(2) This paragraph applies to property which became property to which paragraph 8 above applies on the occasion of a transfer of value which was made by a person beneficially entitled to an interest in possession in the property, and which (so far as the value transferred by it was attributable to the property)—

(a) was an exempt transfer by virtue of the combined effect of either—

(i) sections 27 and 57(5) of this Act, or

(ii) sections 27 and 57A of this Act, and

(b) would but for those sections have been a chargeable transfer;

and in the following sub-paragraphs "the person entitled to the interest in possession" means the person above referred to.

(3) Paragraph 9(2) shall have effect as if for the reference to the settlor there were substituted a reference to either the settlor or the person entitled to the interest in possession.

(4) Paragraph 10 shall not apply if the person entitled to the interest in possession had died at or before the time when the property became property to which paragraph 8 above applies; and in any other case shall have effect with the substitution in sub-paragraph (1) of the following words for the words from "on becoming" onwards—

"(a) on becoming property to which the person entitled to the interest in possession is beneficially entitled, or

(b) on becoming—

(i) property to which that person's spouse [or civil partner] is beneficially entitled, or

(ii) property to which that person's widow or widower [or surviving civil partner] is beneficially entitled if that person has died in the two years preceding the time when it becomes such property;

but paragraph (b) above applies only where the [spouse or civil partner, or widow or widower or surviving civil partner,] would have become beneficially entitled to the property on the termination of the interest in possession had the property not then become property to which paragraph 8 above applies.".

(5) Paragraph 11 shall not apply.

(6) Sub-paragraphs (1) to (3) of paragraph 14 shall have effect as if for the references to the settlor there were substituted references to the person entitled to the interest in possession.

(7) Sub-paragraph (4) of paragraph 14 shall have effect with the insertion after paragraph (b) of the words

"and

(c) was, in relation to either of those settlements, property to which paragraph 15A below applied,",

and with the substitution for the words from "settlor shall" onwards of the words "person entitled to the interest in possession shall, if the Board so determine, be construed as references to the person who was the settlor in relation to the current settlement.".

(8) Sub-paragraph (5) of paragraph 14 shall have effect with the insertion after paragraph (b) of the words

"and

(c) was, in relation to any of those settlements, property to which paragraph 15A below applied,",

and with the substitution for the words from "settlor shall" onwards of the words "person entitled to the interest in possession shall, if the Board so determine, be construed as references to any person selected by them who was the settlor in relation to any of the previous settlements or the current settlement."

(9) Except in a case where the Board have made a determination under sub-paragraph (4) or (5) of paragraph 14, sub-paragraphs (6) and (7) of that paragraph shall have effect as if for the references to the settlor there were substituted references to the person entitled to the interest in possession.

(10) Sub-paragraph (9) of paragraph 14 shall have effect with the substitution for the words "(if the settlement was made on death)" of the words "(if the person entitled to the interest in possession had died at or before the time when the property became property to which paragraph 8 above applies)".]

[308B]

NOTES

Para 10: words in square brackets in sub-para (1) inserted by the Tax and Civil Partnership Regulations 2005, SI 2005/3229, regs 3, 39(1), (2).

Para 14: words in square brackets substituted or inserted by the Finance Act 1986, s 101, Sch 19, Pt I, in relation to transfers of value made, and other events occurring, on or after 18 March 1986.

Para 15A: inserted by the Finance Act 1987, s 59, Sch 9, paras 3, 6, with effect where the occasion of the charge or potential charge to tax under para 8 of this Schedule falls on or after 17 March 1987; words in first and second pairs of square brackets in sub-para (4) inserted and words in third pair of square brackets substituted by SI 2005/3229, regs 3, 39(1), (3).

See further, in relation to transitional provisions: the Finance Act 1986, s 101, Sch 19, Pt II.

PART III
PROPERTY BECOMING COMPRISED IN MAINTENANCE FUNDS

16.—(1) Tax shall not be charged under section 65 of this Act in respect of property which ceases to be relevant property on becoming property in respect of which a direction under paragraph 1 above then has effect.

(2) If the amount on which tax would be charged apart from sub-paragraph (1) above in respect of any property exceeds the value of the property immediately after it becomes property in respect of which the direction has effect (less the amount of any consideration for its transfer received by the trustees of the settlement in which it was comprised immediately before it ceased to be relevant property), that sub-paragraph shall not apply but the amount on which tax is charged shall be equal to the excess.

(3) Sub-paragraph (1) above shall not apply in relation to any property if, at or before the time when it becomes property in respect of which the direction has effect, an interest under the settlement in which it was comprised immediately before it ceased to be relevant property is or has been acquired for a consideration in money or money's worth by the trustees of the settlement in which it becomes comprised on ceasing to be relevant property.

(4) For the purposes of sub-paragraph (3) above trustees shall be treated as acquiring an interest for a consideration in money or money's worth if they become entitled to the interest as a result of transactions which include a disposition for such consideration (whether to them or to another person) of that interest or of other property.

17.—(1) Tax shall not be charged under section 65 of this Act in respect of property which ceases to be relevant property if within the permitted period an individual makes a transfer of value—

(a) which is exempt under section 27 of this Act, and
(b) the value transferred by which is attributable to that property.

(2) In sub-paragraph (1) above "the permitted period" means the period of thirty days beginning with the day on which the property ceases to be relevant property except in a case where it does so on the death of any person, and in such a case means the period of two years beginning with that day.

(3) Sub-paragraph (1) above shall not apply if the individual has acquired the property concerned for a consideration in money or money's worth; and for the purposes of this sub-paragraph an individual shall be treated as acquiring any property for such consideration if he becomes entitled to it as a result of transactions which include a disposition for such consideration (whether to him or another) of that or other property.

(4) If the amount on which tax would be charged apart from sub-paragraph (1) above in respect of any property exceeds the value of the property immediately after the transfer there

PART I STATUTES

referred to (less the amount of any consideration for its transfer received by the individual), that sub-paragraph shall not apply but the amount on which tax is charged shall be equal to the excess.

18. In paragraphs 16(2) and 17(4) above the references to the amount on which tax would be charged are references to the amount on which it would be charged apart from—
(a) paragraph (b) of section 65(2) of this Act, and
(b) Chapters I and II of Part V of this Act;

and the references to the amount on which tax is charged are references to the amount on which it would be charged apart from that paragraph and those Chapters.

[308C]

(*Schs 5–9 outside the scope of this work.*)

COMPANIES ACT 1985

(1985 c 6)

ARRANGEMENT OF SECTIONS

PART I
FORMATION AND REGISTRATION OF COMPANIES; JURIDICAL STATUS AND MEMBERSHIP

CHAPTER I
COMPANY FORMATION

Memorandum of association

Articles of association

Registration and its consequences

A company's membership

CHAPTER II
COMPANY NAMES

CHAPTER III
A COMPANY'S CAPACITY; FORMALITIES OF CARRYING ON BUSINESS

PART VII
ACCOUNTS AND AUDIT

CHAPTER I
PROVISIONS APPLYING TO COMPANIES GENERALLY

Accounting records

A company's financial year and accounting reference periods

Annual accounts

Approval and signing of accounts

Directors' report

Quoted companies: directors' remuneration report

Auditors' report

Publication of accounts and reports

Laying and delivering of accounts and reports

Revision of defective accounts and reports

CHAPTER II
EXEMPTIONS, EXCEPTIONS AND SPECIAL PROVISIONS

Small and medium-sized companies and groups

Exemptions from audit for certain categories of small company

Summary financial statement

Private companies

Unlimited companies

Banking and insurance companies and groups

CHAPTER III
SUPPLEMENTARY PROVISIONS

Accounting standards

Power to alter accounting requirements

Parents and subsidiary undertakings

Other interpretation provisions

PART IX
A COMPANY'S MANAGEMENT;
DIRECTORS AND SECRETARIES;
THEIR QUALIFICATIONS, DUTIES AND RESPONSIBILITIES

Officers and registered office

Provisions governing appointment of directors

Removal of directors

Other provisions about directors and officers

PART X
ENFORCEMENT OF FAIR DEALING BY DIRECTORS

Restrictions on directors taking financial advantage

CHAPTER III
ANNUAL RETURN

CHAPTER IV
MEETINGS AND RESOLUTIONS

Meetings

Resolutions

Written resolutions of private companies

Records of proceedings

CHAPTER V
AUDITORS

Appointment of auditors

PART I
STATUTES

An Act to consolidate the greater part of the Companies Acts

[11 March 1985]

NOTES

Repeal and amendment of this Act by the Companies Act 2006:

The vast majority of this Act is repealed by the Companies Act 2006, as from a day to be appointed (see s 1295 of, and Sch 16 to, the 2006 Act which repeal ss 1–430F, 438, 446, 458–461, 651–746 of, and Schs 1–15B, 20–25 to, this Act). For provision relating to the continuity of law, see s 1297 of the 2006 Act. The 2006 Act also makes a number of amendments to this Act (including amendments to provisions which it also repeals). Details of all repeals and amendments are noted to the provisions affected.

Application of this Act to other companies, etc:

This Act is applied to various other types of companies and bodies, as follows:

Community interest companies: as to the application of this Act (subject to certain modifications) to community interest companies, see the Companies (Audit, Investigations and Community Enterprise) Act 2004. See, in particular, Part 2 of that Act.

Societas Europaea: as to the application of certain provisions of this Act to SEs, see the European Public Limited-Liability Company Regulations 2004, SI 2004/2326. See in particular, Sch 2 (provisions of the 1985 Act applying to the registration of SEs), and Sch 4 (modifications of the 1985 Act and the Insolvency Act 1986).

PART I
FORMATION AND REGISTRATION OF COMPANIES; JURIDICAL STATUS AND MEMBERSHIP

CHAPTER I
COMPANY FORMATION

Memorandum of association

1 Mode of forming incorporated company

(*1*) *Any two or more persons associated for a lawful purpose may, by subscribing their names to a memorandum of association and otherwise complying with the requirements of this Act in respect of registration, form an incorporated company, with or without limited liability.*

(2) *A company so formed may be either—*

(*a*) *a company having the liability of its members limited by the memorandum to the amount, if any, unpaid on the shares respectively held by them ("a company limited by shares");*

(*b*) *a company having the liability of its members limited by the memorandum to such amount as the members may respectively thereby undertake to contribute to the assets of the company in the event of its being wound up ("a company limited by guarantee"); or*

(*c*) *a company not having any limit on the liability of its members ("an unlimited company").*

(3) A "public company" is a company limited by shares or limited by guarantee and having a share capital, being a company—

(*a*) *the memorandum of which states that it is to be a public company, and*

(*b*) *in relation to which the provisions of this Act or the former Companies Acts as to the registration or re-registration of a company as a public company have been complied with on or after 22nd December 1980;*

and a "private company" is a company that is not a public company.

[(3A) Notwithstanding subsection (1), one person may, for a lawful purpose, by subscribing his name to a memorandum of association and otherwise complying with the requirements of this Act in respect of registration, form an incorporated company being a private company limited by shares or by guarantee.]

(4) With effect from 22nd December 1980, a company cannot be formed as, or become, a company limited by guarantee with a share capital.

[309]

NOTES

Repealed by the Companies Act 2006, s 1295, Sch 16, as from a day to be appointed under s 1300(2) of that Act; see further the introductory note to this Act.

Sub-s (3A): inserted by the Companies (Single Member Private Limited Companies) Regulations 1992, SI 1992/1699, reg 2, Schedule, para 1.

2 Requirements with respect to memorandum

(1) The memorandum of every company must state—

(*a*) *the name of the company;*

(*b*) *whether the registered office of the company is to be situated in England and Wales, or in Scotland;*

(*c*) *the objects of the company.*

(2) Alternatively to subsection (1)(b), the memorandum may contain a statement that the company's registered office is to be situated in Wales; and a company whose registered office is situated in Wales may by special resolution alter its memorandum so as to provide that its registered office is to be so situated.

(3) The memorandum of a company limited by shares or by guarantee must also state that the liability of its members is limited.

(4) The memorandum of a company limited by guarantee must also state that each member undertakes to contribute to the assets of the company if it should be wound up while he is a member, or within one year after he ceases to be a member, for payment of the debts and liabilities of the company contracted before he ceases to be a member, and of the costs, charges and expenses of winding up, and for adjustment of the rights of the contributories among themselves, such amount as may be required, not exceeding a specified amount.

(5) In the case of a company having a share capital—

(*a*) *the memorandum must also (unless it is an unlimited company) state the amount of the share capital with which the company proposes to be registered and the division of the share capital into shares of a fixed amount;*

(*b*) *no subscriber of the memorandum may take less than one share; and*

(*c*) *there must be shown in the memorandum against the name of each subscriber the number of shares he takes.*

(6) [Subject to subsection (6A), the memorandum] must be signed by each subscriber in the presence of at least one witness, who must attest the signature; and that attestation is sufficient in Scotland as well as in England and Wales.

[(6A) Where the memorandum is delivered to the registrar otherwise than in legible form and is authenticated by each subscriber in such manner as is directed by the registrar, the requirements in subsection (6) for signature in the presence of at least one witness and for attestation of the signature do not apply.]

(7) A company may not alter the conditions contained in its memorandum except in the cases, in the mode and to the extent, for which express provision is made by this Act.

[310]

NOTES

Repealed as noted to s 1 at **[309]**.

Sub-s (6): words in square brackets substituted by the Companies Act 1985 (Electronic Communications) Order 2000, SI 2000/3373, art 2(1), (2); words "; and that attestation is sufficient in Scotland as well as in England and Wales" repealed in relation to Scotland by the Requirements of Writing (Scotland) Act 1995, s 14(2), Sch 5.

Sub-s (6A): inserted by SI 2000/3373, art 2(1), (3).

3 Forms of memorandum

(1) Subject to the provisions of sections 1 and 2, the form of the memorandum of association of—

- *(a) a public company, being a company limited by shares,*
- *(b) a public company, being a company limited by guarantee and having a share capital,*
- *(c) a private company limited by shares,*
- *(d) a private company limited by guarantee and not having a share capital,*
- *(e) a private company limited by guarantee and having a share capital, and*
- *(f) an unlimited company having a share capital,*

shall be as specified respectively for such companies by regulations made by the Secretary of State, or as near to that form as circumstances admit.

(2) Regulations under this section shall be made by statutory instrument subject to annulment in pursuance of a resolution of either House of Parliament.

[311]

NOTES

Repealed as noted to s 1 at **[309]**.

Regulations: the Companies (Tables A to F) Regulations 1985, SI 1985/805.

[3A Statement of company's objects: general commercial company

Where the company's memorandum states that the object of the company is to carry on business as a general commercial company—

- *(a) the object of the company is to carry on any trade or business whatsoever, and*
- *(b) the company has power to do all such things as are incidental or conducive to the carrying on of any trade or business by it.]*

[312]

NOTES

Repealed as noted to s 1 at **[309]**.

Inserted by the Companies Act 1989, s 110(1).

[4 Resolution to alter objects

(1) A company may by special resolution alter its memorandum with respect to the statement of the company's objects.

(2) If an application is made under the following section, an alteration does not have effect except in so far as it is confirmed by the court.]

[313]

NOTES

Repealed as noted to s 1 at **[309]**.

Substituted by the Companies Act 1989, s 110(2).

5 Procedure for objecting to alteration

(1) Where a company's memorandum has been altered by special resolution under section 4, application may be made to the court for the alteration to be cancelled.

(2) Such an application may be made—

(a) by the holders of not less in the aggregate than 15 per cent in nominal value of the company's issued share capital or any class of it or, if the company is not limited by shares, not less than 15 per cent of the company's members; or

(b) by the holders of not less than 15 per cent of the company's debentures entitling the holders to object to an alteration of its objects;

but an application shall not be made by any person who has consented to or voted in favour of the alteration.

(3) The application must be made within 21 days after the date on which the resolution altering the company's objects was passed, and may be made on behalf of the persons entitled to make the application by such one or more of their number as they may appoint in writing for the purpose.

(4) The court may on such an application make an order confirming the alteration either wholly or in part and on such terms and conditions as it thinks fit, and may—

(a) if it thinks fit, adjourn the proceedings in order that an arrangement may be made to its satisfaction for the purchase of the interests of dissentient members, and

(b) give such directions and make such orders as it thinks expedient for facilitating or carrying into effect any such arrangement.

(5) The court's order may (if the court thinks fit) provide for the purchase by the company of the shares of any members of the company, and for the reduction accordingly of its capital, and may make such alterations in the company's memorandum and articles as may be required in consequence of that provision.

(6) If the court's order requires the company not to make any, or any specified, alteration in its memorandum or articles, the company does not then have power without the leave of the court to make any such alteration in breach of that requirement.

(7) An alteration in the memorandum or articles of a company made by virtue of an order under this section, other than one made by resolution of the company, is of the same effect as if duly made by resolution; and this Act applies accordingly to the memorandum or articles as so altered.

[(7A) For the purposes of subsection (2)(a), any of the company's issued share capital held as treasury shares must be disregarded.]

(8) The debentures entitling the holders to object to an alteration of a company's objects are any debentures secured by a floating charge which were issued or first issued before 1st December 1947 or form part of the same series as any debentures so issued; and a special resolution altering a company's objects requires the same notice to the holders of any such debentures as to members of the company.

In the absence of provisions regulating the giving of notice to any such debenture holders, the provisions of the company's articles regulating the giving of notice to members apply.

[314]

NOTES

Repealed as noted to s 1 at **[309]**.

Sub-s (7A): inserted by the Companies (Acquisition of Own Shares) (Treasury Shares) Regulations 2003, SI 2003/1116, reg 4, Schedule, para 1.

6 Provisions supplementing ss 4, 5

(1) Where a company passes a resolution altering its objects, then—

(a) if with respect to the resolution no application is made under section 5, the company shall within 15 days from the end of the period for making such an application deliver to the registrar of companies a printed copy of its memorandum as altered; and

(b) if such an application is made, the company shall—

(i) forthwith give notice (in the prescribed form) of that fact to the registrar, and

(ii) within 15 days from the date of any order cancelling or confirming the alteration, deliver to the registrar an office copy of the order and, in the case of an order confirming the alteration, a printed copy of the memorandum as altered.

(2) The court may by order at any time extend the time for the delivery of documents to the registrar under subsection (1)(b) for such period as the court may think proper.

(3) If a company makes default in giving notice or delivering any document to the registrar of companies as required by subsection (1), the company and every officer of it who is in default is liable to a fine and, for continued contravention, to a daily default fine.

(4) The validity of an alteration of a company's memorandum with respect to the objects of the company shall not be questioned on the ground that it was not authorised by section 4, except in proceedings taken for the purpose (whether under section 5 or otherwise) before the expiration of 21 days after the date of the resolution in that behalf.

(5) Where such proceedings are taken otherwise than under section 5, subsections (1) to (3) above apply in relation to the proceedings as if they had been taken under that section, and as if an order declaring the alteration invalid were an order cancelling it, and as if an order dismissing the proceedings were an order confirming the alteration.

[315]

NOTES

Repealed as noted to s 1 at **[309]**.

Prescribed form: see the Companies (Forms) Regulations 1985, SI 1985/854, Form 6, as prescribed by the Companies (Forms) (Amendment) Regulations 1995, SI 1995/736.

Articles of association

7 Articles prescribing regulations for companies

(1) There may in the case of a company limited by shares, and there shall in the case of a company limited by guarantee or unlimited, be registered with the memorandum articles of association signed by the subscribers to the memorandum and prescribing regulations for the company.

(2) In the case of an unlimited company having a share capital, the articles must state the amount of share capital with which the company proposes to be registered.

(3) Articles must—
- *(a) be printed,*
- *(b) be divided into paragraphs numbered consecutively, and*
- *(c) [subject to subsection (3A),] be signed by each subscriber of the memorandum in the presence of at least one witness who must attest the signature (which attestation is sufficient in Scotland as well as in England and Wales).*

[(3A) Where the articles are delivered to the registrar otherwise than in legible form and are authenticated by each subscriber to the memorandum in such manner as is directed by the registrar, the requirements in subsection (3)(c) for signature in the presence of at least one witness and for attestation of the signature do not apply.]

[316]

NOTES

Repealed as noted to s 1 at **[309]**.

Sub-s (3): words in square brackets in para (c) inserted by the Companies Act 1985 (Electronic Communications) Order 2000, SI 2000/3373, art 3(1), (2); words "(which attestation is sufficient in Scotland as well as in England and Wales)" in para (c) repealed in relation to Scotland by the Requirements of Writing (Scotland) Act 1995, s 14(2), Sch 5.

Sub-s (3A): added by SI 2000/3373, art 3(1), (3).

8 Tables A, C, D and E

(1) Table A is as prescribed by regulations made by the Secretary of State; and a company may for its articles adopt the whole or any part of that Table.

(2) In the case of a company limited by shares, if articles are not registered or, if articles are registered, in so far as they do not exclude or modify Table A, that Table (so far as

applicable, and as in force at the date of the company's registration) constitutes the company's articles, in the same manner and to the same extent as if articles in the form of that Table had been duly registered.

(*3*) *If in consequence of regulations under this section Table A is altered, the alteration does not affect a company registered before the alteration takes effect, or repeal as respects that company any portion of the Table.*

(*4*) *The form of the articles of association of—*

(*a*) *a company limited by guarantee and not having a share capital,*

(*b*) *a company limited by guarantee and having a share capital, and*

(*c*) *an unlimited company having a share capital,*

shall be respectively in accordance with Table C, D or E prescribed by regulations made by the Secretary of State, or as near to that form as circumstances admit.

(*5*) *Regulations under this section shall be made by statutory instrument subject to annulment in pursuance of a resolution of either House of Parliament.*

[317]

NOTES

Repealed as noted to s 1 at **[309]**.
Regulations: the Companies (Tables A to F) Regulations 1985, SI 1985/805.

[8A Table G

(*1*) *The Secretary of State may by regulations prescribe a Table G containing articles of association appropriate for a partnership company, that is, a company limited by shares whose shares are intended to be held to a substantial extent by or on behalf of its employees.*

(*2*) *A company limited by shares may for its articles adopt the whole or any part of that Table.*

(*3*) *If in consequence of regulations under this section Table G is altered, the alteration does not affect a company registered before the alteration takes effect, or repeal as respects that company any portion of the Table.*

(*4*) *Regulations under this section shall be made by statutory instrument which shall be subject to annulment in pursuance of a resolution of either House of Parliament.]*

[318]

NOTES

Commencement: to be appointed.
Repealed as noted to s 1 at **[309]**.
Inserted by the Companies Act 1989, s 128, as from a day to be appointed.

9 Alteration of articles by special resolution

(*1*) *Subject to the provisions of this Act and to the conditions contained in its memorandum, a company may by special resolution alter its articles.*

(*2*) *Alterations so made in the articles are (subject to this Act) as valid as if originally contained in them, and are subject in like manner to alteration by special resolution.*

[319]

NOTES

Repealed as noted to s 1 at **[309]**.

Registration and its consequences

10 Documents to be sent to registrar

(*1*) *The company's memorandum and articles (if any) shall be delivered—*

(*a*) *to the registrar of companies for England and Wales, if the memorandum states that the registered office of the company is to be situated in England and Wales, or that it is to be situated in Wales; and* (*b*) *to the registrar of companies for Scotland, if the memorandum states that the registered office of the company is to be situated in Scotland.*

(*2*) *With the memorandum there shall be delivered a statement in the prescribed form containing the names and requisite particulars of—*

(*a*) *the person who is, or the persons who are, to be the first director or directors of the company; and*

(*b*) *the person who is, or the persons who are, to be the first secretary or joint secretaries of the company;*

and the requisite particulars in each case are those set out in Schedule 1.

[(2A) Where any statement delivered under subsection (2) includes an address specified in reliance on paragraph 5 of Schedule 1 there shall be delivered with the statement, a statement in the prescribed form containing particulars of the usual residential address of the director or secretary whose address is so specified.]

(*3*) *The statement [under subsection (2)] shall be signed by or on behalf of the subscribers of the memorandum and shall contain a consent signed by each of the persons named in it as a director, as secretary or as one of joint secretaries, to act in the relevant capacity.*

(*4*) *Where a memorandum is delivered by a person as agent for the subscribers, the statement shall specify that fact and the person's name and address.*

(*5*) *An appointment by any articles delivered with the memorandum of a person as director or secretary of the company is void unless he is named as a director or secretary in the statement.*

(*6*) *There shall in the statement be specified the intended situation of the company's registered office on incorporation.*

[320]

NOTES

Repealed as noted to s 1 at [**309**].

Sub-s (2A): inserted by the Companies (Particulars of Usual Residential Address) (Confidentiality Orders) Regulations 2002, SI 2002/912, reg 16, Sch 2, para 1(1), (2).

Sub-s (3): words in square brackets inserted by SI 2002/912, reg 16, Sch 2, para 1(1), (3).

Prescribed forms: see the Companies (Forms) Regulations 1985, SI 1985/854, Forms 10, 10CYM, as prescribed by the Companies (Forms) (Amendment) Regulations 1995, SI 1995/736 and the Companies (Welsh Language Forms and Documents) (Amendment) Regulations 1995, SI 1995/734 respectively.

11 Minimum authorised capital (public companies)

When a memorandum delivered to the registrar of companies under section 10 states that the association to be registered is to be a public company, the amount of the share capital stated in the memorandum to be that with which the company proposes to be registered must not be less than the authorised minimum (defined in section 118).

[321]

NOTES

Repealed as noted to s 1 at [**309**].

12 Duty of registrar

(*1*) *The registrar of companies shall not register a company's memorandum delivered under section 10 unless he is satisfied that all the requirements of this Act in respect of registration and of matters precedent and incidental to it have been complied with.*

(*2*) *Subject to this, the registrar shall retain and register the memorandum and articles (if any) delivered to him under that section.*

(*3*) *[Subject to subsection (3A), a statutory declaration] in the prescribed form by—*

(*a*) *a solicitor engaged in the formation of a company, or*

(*b*) *a person named as a director or secretary of the company in the statement delivered under section 10(2),*

that those requirements have been complied with shall be delivered to the registrar of companies, and the registrar may accept such a declaration as sufficient evidence of compliance.

[(3A) In place of the statutory declaration referred to in subsection (3), there may be delivered to the registrar of companies using electronic communications a statement made by a person mentioned in paragraph (a) or (b) of subsection (3) that the requirements mentioned in subsection (1) have been complied with; and the registrar may accept such a statement as sufficient evidence of compliance.

(3B) Any person who makes a false statement under subsection (3A) which he knows to be false or does not believe to be true is liable to imprisonment or a fine, or both.]

[322]

NOTES

Repealed as noted to s 1 at **[309]**.

Sub-s (3): words in square brackets substituted by the Companies Act 1985 (Electronic Communications) Order 2000, SI 2000/3373, art 4(1), (2).

Sub-ss (3A), (3B): added by SI 2000/3373, art 4(1), (3).

Prescribed forms: see the Companies (Forms) Regulations 1985, SI 1985/854, Forms 12, 12CYM, as prescribed by the Companies (Forms) (Amendment) Regulations 1995, SI 1995/736 and the Companies (Welsh Language Forms and Documents) (No 3) Regulations 1995, SI 1995/1508 respectively.

13 Effect of registration

(1) On the registration of a company's memorandum, the registrar of companies shall give a certificate that the company is incorporated and, in the case of a limited company, that it is limited.

(2) The certificate may be signed by the registrar, or authenticated by his official seal.

(3) From the date of incorporation mentioned in the certificate, the subscribers of the memorandum, together with such other persons as may from time to time become members of the company, shall be a body corporate by the name contained in the memorandum.

(4) That body corporate is then capable forthwith of exercising all the functions of an incorporated company, but with such liability on the part of its members to contribute to its assets in the event of its being wound up as is provided by this Act [and the Insolvency Act].

This is subject, in the case of a public company, to section 117 (additional certificate as to amount of allotted share capital).

(5) The persons named in the statement under section 10 as directors, secretary or joint secretaries are, on the company's incorporation, deemed to have been respectively appointed as its first directors, secretary or joint secretaries.

(6) Where the registrar registers an association's memorandum which states that the association is to be a public company, the certificate of incorporation shall contain a statement that the company is a public company.

(7) A certificate of incorporation given in respect of an association is conclusive evidence—

- *(a) that the requirements of this Act in respect of registration and of matters precedent and incidental to it have been complied with, and that the association is a company authorised to be registered, and is duly registered, under this Act, and*
- *(b) if the certificate contains a statement that the company is a public company, that the company is such a company.*

[323]

NOTES

Repealed as noted to s 1 at **[309]**.

Sub-s (4): words in square brackets inserted by the Insolvency Act 1986, s 439(1), Sch 13, Pt I.

Insolvency Act: ie, the Insolvency Act 1986.

14 Effect of memorandum and articles

(1) Subject to the provisions of this Act, the memorandum and articles, when registered, bind the company and its members to the same extent as if they respectively had been signed and sealed by each member, and contained covenants on the part of each member to observe all the provisions of the memorandum and of the articles.

(2) *Money payable by a member to the company under the memorandum or articles is a debt due from him to the company, and in England and Wales is of the nature of a specialty debt.*

[324]

NOTES

Repealed as noted to s 1 at **[309]**.

15 Memorandum and articles of company limited by guarantee

(*1*) *In the case of a company limited by guarantee and not having a share capital, every provision in the memorandum or articles, or in any resolution of the company purporting to give any person a right to participate in the divisible profits of the company otherwise than as a member, is void.*

(2) *For purposes of provisions of this Act relating to the memorandum of a company limited by guarantee, and for those of section 1(4) and this section, every provision in the memorandum or articles, or in any resolution, of a company so limited purporting to divide the company's undertaking into shares or interests is to be treated as a provision for a share capital, notwithstanding that the nominal amount or number of the shares or interests is not specified by the provision.*

[325]

NOTES

Repealed as noted to s 1 at **[309]**.

16 Effect of alteration on company's members

(*1*) *A member of a company is not bound by an alteration made in the memorandum or articles after the date on which he became a member, if and so far as the alteration—*

- (*a*) *requires him to take or subscribe for more shares than the number held by him at the date on which the alteration is made; or*
- (*b*) *in any way increases his liability as at that date to contribute to the company's share capital or otherwise to pay money to the company.*

(2) *Subsection* (*1*) *operates notwithstanding anything in the memorandum or articles; but it does not apply in a case where the member agrees in writing, either before or after the alteration is made, to be bound by the alteration.*

[326]

NOTES

Repealed as noted to s 1 at **[309]**.

17 Conditions in memorandum which could have been in articles

(*1*) *A condition contained in a company's memorandum which could lawfully have been contained in articles of association instead of in the memorandum may be altered by the company by special resolution; but if an application is made to the court for the alteration to be cancelled, the alteration does not have effect except in so far as it is confirmed by the court.*

(2) *This section—*

- (*a*) *is subject to section 16, and also to Part XVII* (*court order protecting minority*), *and*
- (*b*) *does not apply where the memorandum itself provides for or prohibits the alteration of all or any of the conditions above referred to, and does not authorise any variation or abrogation of the special rights of any class of members.*

(*3*) *Section 5* (*except subsections* (2)(*b*) *and* (8)) *and section 6*(*1*) *to* (*3*) *apply in relation to any alteration and to any application made under this section as they apply in relation to alterations and applications under sections 4 to 6.*

[327]

NOTES

Repealed as noted to s 1 at **[309]**.

18 Amendments of memorandum or articles to be registered

(1) Where an alteration is made in a company's memorandum or articles by any statutory provision, whether contained in an Act of Parliament or in an instrument made under an Act, a printed copy of the Act or instrument shall, not later than 15 days after that provision comes into force, be forwarded to the registrar of companies and recorded by him.

(2) Where a company is required (by this section or otherwise) to send to the registrar any document making or evidencing an alteration in the company's memorandum or articles (other than a special resolution under section 4), the company shall send with it a printed copy of the memorandum or articles as altered.

(3) If a company fails to comply with this section, the company and any officer of it who is in default is liable to a fine and, for continued contravention, to a daily default fine.

[328]

NOTES

Repealed as noted to s 1 at **[309]**.

19 Copies of memorandum and articles to be given to members

(1) A company shall, on being so required by any member, send to him a copy of the memorandum and of the articles (if any), and a copy of any Act of Parliament which alters the memorandum, subject to payment—

(a) in the case of a copy of the memorandum and of the articles, of 5 pence or such less sum as the company may prescribe, and

(b) in the case of a copy of an Act, of such sum not exceeding its published price as the company may require.

(2) If a company makes default in complying with this section, the company and every officer of it who is in default is liable for each offence to a fine.

[329]

NOTES

Repealed as noted to s 1 at **[309]**.

20 Issued copy of memorandum to embody alterations

(1) Where an alteration is made in a company's memorandum, every copy of the memorandum issued after the date of the alteration shall be in accordance with the alteration.

(2) If, where any such alteration has been made, the company at any time after the date of the alteration issues any copies of the memorandum which are not in accordance with the alteration, it is liable to a fine, and so too is every officer of the company who is in default.

[330]

NOTES

Repealed as noted to s 1 at **[309]**.

21 *(Repealed by the Welsh Language Act 1993, ss 30(1), (2), 35(1), Sch 2.)*

A company's membership

22 Definition of "member"

(1) The subscribers of a company's memorandum are deemed to have agreed to become members of the company, and on its registration shall be entered as such in its register of members.

(2) Every other person who agrees to become a member of a company, and whose name is entered in its register of members, is a member of the company.

[331]

NOTES

Repealed as noted to s 1 at **[309]**.

[23 Membership of holding company

(1) Except as mentioned in this section, a body corporate cannot be a member of a company which is its holding company and any allotment or transfer of shares in a company to its subsidiary is void.

(2) The prohibition does not apply where the subsidiary is concerned only as personal representative or trustee unless, in the latter case, the holding company or a subsidiary of it is beneficially interested under the trust.

For the purpose of ascertaining whether the holding company or a subsidiary is so interested, there shall be disregarded—

(a) any interest held only by way of security for the purposes of a transaction entered into by the holding company or subsidiary in the ordinary course of a business which includes the lending of money;

(b) any such interest as is mentioned in Part I of Schedule 2.

[(3) The prohibition does not apply where shares in the holding company are held by the subsidiary in the ordinary course of its business as an intermediary.

For this purpose a person is an intermediary if that person—

(a) carries on a bona fide business of dealing in securities;

(b) is a member of an EEA exchange (and satisfies any requirements for recognition as a dealer in securities laid down by that exchange) or is otherwise approved or supervised as a dealer in securities under the laws of an EEA State; and

(c) does not carry on an excluded business.

(3A) The excluded businesses are the following—

(a) any business which consists wholly or mainly in the making or managing of investments;

(b) any business which consists wholly or mainly in, or is carried on wholly or mainly for the purpose of, providing services to persons who are connected with the person carrying on the business;

(c) any business which consists in insurance business;

(d) any business which consists in managing or acting as trustee in relation to a pension scheme or which is carried on by the manager or trustee of such a scheme in connection with or for the purposes of the scheme;

(e) any business which consists in operating or acting as trustee in relation to a collective investment scheme or is carried on by the operator or trustee of such a scheme in connection with or for the purposes of the scheme.

(3B) For the purposes of subsections (3) and (3A)—

(a) the question whether a person is connected with another shall be determined in accordance with the provisions of section 839 of the Income and Corporation Taxes Act 1988;

(b) "collective investment scheme" has the meaning given in [section 236 of the Financial Services and Markets Act 2000];

(c) "EEA exchange" means a market which appears on the list drawn up by an EEA State pursuant to Article 16 of Council Directive 93/22/EEC on investment services in the securities field;

[(d) "insurance business" means business which consists of the effecting or carrying out of contracts of insurance;

(e) "securities" includes—

(i) options,

(ii) futures, and

(iii) contracts for differences,

and rights or interests in those investments;]

(f) "trustee" and "the operator" shall, in relation to a collective investment scheme, be construed in accordance with [section 237(2) of the Financial Services and Markets Act 2000].

[(3BA) Subsection (3B) must be read with—

(a) section 22 of the Financial Services and Markets Act 2000;

(b) any relevant order under that section; and

(c) Schedule 2 to that Act.]

(3C) Where—

(a) a subsidiary which is a dealer in securities has purportedly acquired shares in its holding company in contravention of the prohibition in subsection (1); and

PART I STATUTES

(*b*) *a person acting in good faith has agreed, for value and without notice of that contravention, to acquire shares in the holding company from the subsidiary or from someone who has purportedly acquired the shares after their disposal by the subsidiary,*

any transfer to that person of the shares mentioned in paragraph (a) shall have the same effect as it would have had if their original acquisition by the subsidiary had not been in contravention of the prohibition.]

(4) *Where a body corporate became a holder of shares in a company—*

(*a*) *before 1st July 1948, or*

(*b*) *on or after that date and before [20th October 1997], in circumstances in which this section as it then had effect did not apply,*

but at any time [on or after [20th October 1997]] falls within the prohibition in subsection (1) above in respect of those shares, it may continue to be a member of that company; but for so long as that prohibition would apply, apart from this subsection, it has no right to vote in respect of those shares at meetings of the company or of any class of its members.

(5) *Where a body corporate becomes a holder of shares in a company [on or after [20th October 1997]] in circumstances in which the prohibition in subsection (1) does not apply, but subsequently falls within that prohibition in respect of those shares, it may continue to be a member of that company; but for so long as that prohibition would apply, apart from this subsection, it has no right to vote in respect of those shares at meetings of the company or of any class of its members.*

(6) *Where a body corporate is permitted to continue as a member of a company by virtue of subsection (4) or (5), an allotment to it of fully paid shares in the company may be validly made by way of capitalisation of reserves of the company; but for so long as the prohibition in subsection (1) would apply, apart from subsection (4) or (5), it has no right to vote in respect of those shares at meetings of the company or of any class of its members.*

(7) *The provisions of this section apply to a nominee acting on behalf of a subsidiary as to the subsidiary itself.*

(8) *In relation to a company other than a company limited by shares, the references in this section to shares shall be construed as references to the interest of its members as such, whatever the form of that interest.]*

[332]

NOTES

Repealed as noted to s 1 at **[309]**.

Substituted by the Companies Act 1989, s 129(1).

Sub-ss (3), (3A), (3C): substituted, together with sub-s (3B) for original sub-s (3), by the Companies (Membership of Holding Company) (Dealers in Securities) Regulations 1997, SI 1997/2306, reg 2.

Sub-s (3B): substituted as noted above; words in square brackets in paras (b), (f), and whole of paras (d), (e), substituted by the Financial Services and Markets Act 2000 (Consequential Amendments and Repeals) Order 2001, SI 2001/3649, art 4(1)–(4); for the words "Article 16 of Council Directive 93/22/EEC on investment services in the securities field" in para (c) there are substituted the words "Article 47 of Directive 2004/39/EC of the European Parliament and of the Council of 21 April 2004 on markets in financial instruments" by the Financial Services and Markets Act 2000 (Markets in Financial Instruments) Regulations 2007, SI 2007/126, art 3(6), Sch 6, Pt 1, para 7(1), (2), as from 1 April 2007 for certain purposes and as from 1 November 2007 otherwise (for purposes see reg 1 of those Regulations).

Sub-s (3BA): inserted by SI 2001/3649, art 4(1), (5).

Sub-s (4): words in first and third (inner) pairs of square brackets substituted by SI 1997/2306, reg 3; words in second (outer) pair of square brackets substituted by the Companies Act 1989 (Commencement No 6 and Transitional and Saving Provisions) Order 1990, SI 1990/1392, art 8.

Sub-s (5): words in first (outer) pair of square brackets substituted by SI 1990/1392, art 8; words in second (inner) pair of square brackets substituted by SI 1997/2306, reg 3.

24 Minimum membership for carrying on business

[(1)] If a company[, other than a private company limited by shares or by guarantee,] carries on business without having at least two members and does so for more than 6 months, a person who, for the whole or any part of the period that it so carries on business after those 6 months—

(*a*) *is a member of the company, and*

(*b*) *knows that it is carrying on business with only one member,*

is liable (jointly and severally with the company) for the payment of the company's debts contracted during the period or, as the case may be, that part of it.

[(2) For the purposes of this section references to a member of a company do not include the company itself where it is such a member only by virtue of its holding shares as treasury shares.]

[333]

NOTES

Repealed as noted to s 1 at **[309]**.

Sub-s (1): numbered as such by the Companies (Acquisition of Own Shares) (Treasury Shares) Regulations 2003, SI 2003/1116, reg 4, Schedule, para 2; words in square brackets inserted by the Companies (Single Member Private Limited Companies) Regulations 1992, SI 1992/1699, reg 2(1)(b), Schedule, para 2.

Sub-s (2): added by SI 2003/1116, reg 4, Schedule, para 2.

CHAPTER II
COMPANY NAMES

25 Name as stated in memorandum

(1) The name of a public company must end with the words "public limited company" or, if the memorandum states that the company's registered office is to be situated in Wales, those words or their equivalent in Welsh ("cwmni cyfyngedig cyhoeddus"); and those words or that equivalent may not be preceded by the word "limited" or its equivalent in Welsh ("cyfyngedig").

(2) In the case of a company limited by shares or by guarantee (not being a public company), the name must have "limited" as its last word, except that—

(a) this is subject to section 30 (exempting, in certain circumstances, a company from the requirement to have "limited" as part of the name), and

(b) if the company is to be registered with a memorandum stating that its registered office is to be situated in Wales, the name may have "cyfyngedig" as its last word.

[334]

NOTES

Repealed as noted to s 1 at **[309]**.

26 Prohibition on registration of certain names

(1) A company shall not be registered under this Act by a name—

(a) which includes, otherwise than at the end of the name, any of the following words or expressions, that is to say, "limited", "unlimited"[, "public limited company", "community interest company" or "community interest public limited company"] or their Welsh equivalents ("cyfyngedig", "anghyfyngedig"[, "cwmni cyfyngedig cyhoeddus", "cwmni buddiant cymunedol" and "cwmni buddiant cymunedol cyhoeddus cyfyngedig"] respectively);

(b) which includes, otherwise than at the end of the name, an abbreviation of any of those words or expressions;

[(bb) which includes, at any place in the name, the expressions "investment company with variable capital" or "open-ended investment company" or their Welsh equivalents ("cwmni buddsoddi â chyfalaf newidiol" and "cwmni buddsoddiant penagored" respectively);]

[(bbb) which includes, at any place in the name, the expression "limited liability partnership" or its Welsh equivalent ("partneriaeth atebolrwydd cyfyngedig");]

(c) which is the same as a name appearing in the registrar's index of company names;

(d) the use of which by the company would in the opinion of the Secretary of State constitute a criminal offence; or

(e) which in the opinion of the Secretary of State is offensive.

(2) Except with the approval of the Secretary of State, a company shall not be registered under this Act by a name which—

(a) in the opinion of the Secretary of State would be likely to give the impression that the company is connected in any way with Her Majesty's Government or with any local authority; or

(b) includes any word or expression for the time being specified in regulations under section 29.

"Local authority" means any local authority within the meaning of the Local Government Act 1972 or the Local Government (Scotland) Act 1973, the Common Council of the City of London or the Council of the Isles of Scilly.

(3) In determining for purposes of subsection (1)(c) whether one name is the same as another, there are to be disregarded—

(a) the definite article, where it is the first word of the name;

(b) the following words and expressions where they appear at the end of the name, that is to say—

"company" or its Welsh equivalent ("cwmni"),

"and company" or its Welsh equivalent ("a'r cwmni"),

"company limited" or its Welsh equivalent ("cwmni cyfyngedig"),

"and company limited" or its Welsh equivalent ("a'r cwmni cyfyngedig"),

"limited" or its Welsh equivalent ("cyfyngedig"),

"unlimited" or its Welsh equivalent ("anghyfyngedig"), …

"public limited company" or its Welsh equivalent ("cwmni cyfyngedig cyhoeddus"); […

["community interest company" or its Welsh equivalent ("cwmni buddiant cymunedol");

"community interest public limited company" or its Welsh equivalent ("cwmni buddiant cymunedol cyhoeddus cyfyngedig");]

"investment company with variable capital" or its Welsh equivalent ("cwmni buddsoddi â chyfalaf newidiol");] [and

"open-ended investment company" or its Welsh equivalent ("cwmni buddsoddiant penagored");]

(c) abbreviations of any of those words or expressions where they appear at the end of the name; and

(d) type and case of letters, accents, spaces between letters and punctuation marks;

and "and" and "&" are to be taken as the same.

[335]

NOTES

Repealed as noted to s 1 at **[309]**.

Sub-s (1): words in square brackets in para (a) substituted by the Companies (Audit, Investigations and Community Enterprise) Act 2004, s 33, Sch 6, paras 1, 2(1), (2); para (bb) inserted by the Open-Ended Investment Companies (Investment Companies with Variable Capital) Regulations 1996, SI 1996/2827, reg 75, Sch 8, Pt I, para 4(a), substituted by the Open-Ended Investment Companies Regulations 2001, SI 2001/1228, reg 84, Sch 7, para 3(1), (2); para (bbb) inserted by the Limited Liability Partnerships Regulations 2001, SI 2001/1090, reg 9, Sch 5, para 9.

Sub-s (3): word omitted at the end of the entry beginning "unlimited" repealed, and entry beginning "investment company with variable capital" (and the word "and" which originally preceded it) inserted by SI 1996/2827, reg 75, Sch 8, Pt I, para 4(b); entries beginning "community interest company" and "community interest public limited company" inserted by the Companies (Audit, Investigations and Community Enterprise) Act 2004, s 33, Sch 6, paras 1, 2(1), (3); word omitted at the end of the entry beginning "public limited company" repealed, and entry beginning "open-ended investment company" inserted, by SI 2001/1228, reg 84, Sch 7, para 3(1), (3).

Secretary of State: by the Contracting Out (Functions in relation to the Registration of Companies) Order 1995, SI 1995/1013, art 5, Sch 3, para 1, the functions of the Secretary of State conferred by or under sub-s (2) above and s 244(5), may be exercised by, or by employees of, such person (if any) as may be authorised in that behalf by the Secretary of State.

27 Alternatives of statutory designations

(1) A company which by any provision of this Act is either required or entitled to include in its name, as its last part, any of the words specified in subsection (4) below may, instead of those words, include as the last part of the name the abbreviations there specified as alternatives in relation to those words.

(2) A reference in this Act to the name of a company or to the inclusion of any of those words in a company's name includes a reference to the name including (in place of any of the words so specified) the appropriate alternative, or to the inclusion of the appropriate alternative, as the case may be.

(3) A provision of this Act requiring a company not to include any of those words in its name also requires it not to include the abbreviated alternative specified in subsection (4).

(4) For the purposes of this section—

(a) the alternative of "limited" is "ltd.";

(*b*) *the alternative of "public limited company" is "p.l.c.";*
(*c*) *the alternative of "cyfyngedig" is "cyf."; …*
(*d*) *the alternative of "cwmni cyfyngedig cyhoeddus" is "c.c.c."*
[(*e*) *the alternative of "community interest company" is "cic";*
(*f*) *the alternative of "cwmni buddiant cymunedol" is "cbc";*
(*g*) *the alternative of "community interest public limited company" is "community interest plc"; and*
(*h*) *the alternative of "cwmni buddiant cymunedol cyhoeddus cyfyngedig" is "cwmni buddiant cymunedol ccc."*].

[336]

NOTES

Repealed as noted to s 1 at **[309]**.

Sub-s (4): word omitted from para (c) repealed, and paras (e)–(h) added, by the Companies (Audit, Investigations and Community Enterprise) Act 2004, ss 33, 64, Sch 6, paras 1, 3, Sch 8.

28 Change of name

(1) A company may by special resolution change its name (but subject to section 31 in the case of a company which has received a direction under subsection (2) of that section from the Secretary of State).

(2) Where a company has been registered by a name which—

(*a*) *is the same as or, in the opinion of the Secretary of State, too like a name appearing at the time of the registration in the registrar's index of company names, or*

(*b*) *is the same as or, in the opinion of the Secretary of State, too like a name which should have appeared in that index at that time,*

the Secretary of State may within 12 months of that time, in writing, direct the company to change its name within such period as he may specify.

Section 26(3) applies in determining under this subsection whether a name is the same as or too like another.

(3) If it appears to the Secretary of State that misleading information has been given for the purpose of a company's registration with a particular name, or that undertakings or assurances have been given for that purpose and have not been fulfilled, he may within 5 years of the date of its registration with that name in writing direct the company to change its name within such period as he may specify.

(4) Where a direction has been given under subsection (2) or (3), the Secretary of State may by a further direction in writing extend the period within which the company is to change its name, at any time before the end of that period.

(5) A company which fails to comply with a direction under this section, and any officer of it who is in default, is liable to a fine and, for continued contravention, to a daily default fine.

(6) Where a company changes its name under this section, the registrar of companies shall (subject to section 26) enter the new name on the register in place of the former name, and shall issue a certificate of incorporation altered to meet the circumstances of the case; and the change of name has effect from the date on which the altered certificate is issued.

(7) A change of name by a company under this section does not affect any rights or obligations of the company or render defective any legal proceedings by or against it; and any legal proceedings that might have been continued or commenced against it by its former name may be continued or commenced against it by its new name.

[337]

NOTES

Repealed as noted to s 1 at **[309]**.

29 Regulations about names

(1) The Secretary of State may by regulations—

(*a*) *specify words or expressions for the registration of which as or as part of a company's corporate name his approval is required under section 26(2)(b), and* (*b*) *in relation to any such word or expression, specify a Government department or other body as the relevant body for purposes of the following subsection.*

(*2*) *Where a company proposes to have as, or as part of, its corporate name any such word or expression and a Government department or other body is specified under subsection (1)(b) in relation to that word or expression, a request shall be made (in writing) to the relevant body to indicate whether (and if so why) it has any objections to the proposal; and the person to make the request is—*

(*a*) *in the case of a company seeking to be registered under this Part, the person making the statutory declaration [under section 12(3) or statement under section 12(3A) (as the case may be)],*

(*b*) *in the case of a company seeking to be registered under section 680, the persons making the statutory declaration [under section 686(2) or statement under section 686(2A) (as the case may be)], and*

(*c*) *in any other case, a director or secretary of the company concerned.*

(*3*) *The person who has made that request to the relevant body shall submit to the registrar of companies a statement that it has been made and a copy of any response received from that body, together with—*

(*a*) *the requisite statutory declaration [or statement], or*

(*b*) *a copy of the special resolution changing the company's name,*

according as the case is one or other of those mentioned in subsection (2).

(*4*) ...

(*5*) *Regulations under this section may contain such transitional provisions and savings as the Secretary of State thinks appropriate and may make different provision for different cases or classes of case.*

(*6*) *The regulations shall be made by statutory instrument, to be laid before Parliament after it is made; and the regulations shall cease to have effect at the end of 28 days beginning with the day on which the regulations were made (but without prejudice to anything previously done by virtue of them or to the making of new regulations), unless during that period they are approved by resolution of each House. In reckoning that period, no account is to be taken of any time during which Parliament is dissolved or prorogued or during which both Houses are adjourned for more than 4 days.*

[338]

NOTES

Repealed as noted to s 1 at **[309]**.

Sub-s (2): words in square brackets substituted by the Companies Act 1985 (Electronic Communications) Order 2000, SI 2000/3373, art 31(1)(a), (b).

Sub-s (3): words in square brackets inserted by SI 2000/3373, art 31(1)(c).

Sub-s (4): repealed by the Companies Act 2006, s 1295, Sch 16.

Regulations: by virtue of the Companies Consolidation (Consequential Provisions) Act 1985, s 31(2) and the Interpretation Act 1978, the Company and Business Names Regulations 1981, SI 1981/1685 have effect as if made under this section.

30 Exemption from requirement of "limited" as part of the name

(*1*) *Certain companies are exempt from requirements of this Act relating to the use of "limited" as part of the company name.*

(*2*) *A private company limited by guarantee is exempt from those requirements, and so too is a company which on 25th February 1982 was a private company limited by shares with a name which, by virtue of a licence under section 19 of the Companies Act 1948, did not include "limited"; but in either case the company must, to have the exemption, comply with the requirements of the following subsection.*

(*3*) *Those requirements are that—*

(*a*) *the objects of the company are (or, in the case of a company about to be registered, are to be) the promotion of commerce, art, science, education, religion, charity or any profession, and anything incidental or conducive to any of those objects; and*

(*b*) *the company's memorandum or articles—*

(*i*) *require its profits (if any) or other income to be applied in promoting its objects,*

(*ii*) *prohibit the payment of dividends to its members, and*

(iii) *require all the assets which would otherwise be available to its members generally to be transferred on its winding up either to another body with objects similar to its own or to another body the objects of which are the promotion of charity and anything incidental or conducive thereto (whether or not the body is a member of the company).*

(4) *[Subject to subsection (5A), a statutory declaration] that a company complies with the requirements of subsection (3) may be delivered to the registrar of companies, who may accept the declaration as sufficient evidence of the matters stated in it …*

(5) *The statutory declaration must be in the prescribed form and be made—*

(a) *in the case of a company to be formed, by a solicitor engaged in its formation or by a person named as director or secretary in the statement delivered under section 10(2);*

(b) *in the case of a company to be registered in pursuance of section 680, by two or more directors or other principal officers of the company; and*

(c) *in the case of a company proposing to change its name so that it ceases to have the word "limited" as part of its name, by a director or secretary of the company.*

[(5A) In place of the statutory declaration referred to in subsection (4), there may be delivered to the registrar of companies using electronic communications a statement made by a person falling within the applicable paragraph of subsection (5) stating that the company complies with the requirements of subsection (3); and the registrar may accept such a statement as sufficient evidence of the matters stated in it.

(5B) The registrar may refuse to register a company by a name which does not include the word "limited" unless a statutory declaration under subsection (4) or statement under subsection (5A) has been delivered to him.

(5C) Any person who makes a false statement under subsection (5A) which he knows to be false or does not believe to be true is liable to imprisonment or a fine, or both.]

(6) *References in this section to the word "limited" include (in an appropriate case) its Welsh equivalent ("cyfyngedig"), and the appropriate alternative ("ltd." or "cyf.", as the case may be).*

(7) *A company which [under this section] is exempt from requirements relating to the use of "limited" and does not include that word as part of its name, is also exempt from the requirements of this Act relating to the publication of its name and the sending of lists of members to the registrar of companies.*

[339]

NOTES

Repealed as noted to s 1 at **[309]**.

Sub-s (4): words in square brackets substituted, and words omitted repealed, by the Companies Act 1985 (Electronic Communications) Order 2000, SI 2000/3373, art 5(1), (2).

Sub-ss (5A)–(5C): inserted by SI 2000/3373, art 5(1), (3).

Sub-s (7): words in square brackets inserted by the Companies (Audit, Investigations and Community Enterprise) Act 2004, s 33, Sch 6, paras 1, 4.

Prescribed forms: see the Companies (Forms) Regulations 1985, SI 1985/854, Forms 30(5)(a), 30(5)(b), 30(5)(c) and 30(5)(a)CYM, 30(5)(b)CYM, 30(5)(c)CYM, as prescribed by the Companies (Forms) (Amendment) Regulations 1995, SI 1995/736 and the Companies (Welsh Language Forms and Documents) (No 3) Regulations 1995, SI 1995/1508 respectively.

Companies Act 1948, s 19: repealed by the Companies Act 1981, s 119, Sch 4.

31 Provisions applying to company exempt under s 30

(1) *A company which is exempt under section 30 and whose name does not include "limited" shall not alter its memorandum or articles of association so that it ceases to comply with the requirements of subsection (3) of that section.*

(2) *If it appears to the Secretary of State that such a company—*

(a) *has carried on any business other than the promotion of any of the objects mentioned in that subsection, or*

(b) *has applied any of its profits or other income otherwise than in promoting such objects, or*

(c) *has paid a dividend to any of its members, he may, in writing, direct the company to change its name by resolution of the directors within such period as may be specified in the direction, so that its name ends with "limited".*

A resolution passed by the directors in compliance with a direction under this subsection is subject to section 380 of this Act (copy to be forwarded to the registrar of companies within 15 days).

(3) A company which has received a direction under subsection (2) shall not thereafter be registered by a name which does not include "limited", without the approval of the Secretary of State.

(4) References in this section to the word "limited" include (in an appropriate case) its Welsh equivalent ("cyfyngedig"), and the appropriate alternative ("ltd." or "cyf.", as the case may be).

(5) A company which contravenes subsection (1), and any officer of it who is in default, is liable to a fine and, for continued contravention, to a daily default fine.

(6) A company which fails to comply with a direction by the Secretary of State under subsection (2), and any officer of the company who is in default, is liable to a fine and, for continued contravention, to a daily default fine.

[340]

NOTES

Repealed as noted to s 1 at **[309]**.

32 Power to require company to abandon misleading name

(1) If in the Secretary of State's opinion the name by which a company is registered gives so misleading an indication of the nature of its activities as to be likely to cause harm to the public, he may direct it to change its name.

(2) The direction must, if not duly made the subject of an application to the court under the following subsection, be complied with within a period of 6 weeks from the date of the direction or such longer period as the Secretary of State may think fit to allow.

(3) The company may, within a period of 3 weeks from the date of the direction, apply to the court to set it aside; and the court may set the direction aside or confirm it and, if it confirms the direction, shall specify a period within which it must be complied with.

(4) If a company makes default in complying with a direction under this section, it is liable to a fine and, for continued contravention, to a daily default fine.

(5) Where a company changes its name under this section, the registrar shall (subject to section 26) enter the new name on the register in place of the former name, and shall issue a certificate of incorporation altered to meet the circumstances of the case; and the change of name has effect from the date on which the altered certificate is issued.

(6) A change of name by a company under this section does not affect any of the rights or obligations of the company, or render defective any legal proceedings by or against it; and any legal proceedings that might have been continued or commenced against it by its former name may be continued or commenced against it by its new name.

[341]

NOTES

Repealed as noted to s 1 at **[309]**.

33 Prohibition on trading under misleading name

(1) A person who is not a public company is guilty of an offence if he carries on any trade, profession or business under a name which includes, as its last part, the words "public limited company" or their equivalent in Welsh ("cwmni cyfyngedig cyhoeddus").

(2) A public company is guilty of an offence if, in circumstances in which the fact that it is a public company is likely to be material to any person, it uses a name which may reasonably be expected to give the impression that it is a private company.

(3) A person guilty of an offence under subsection (1) or (2) and, if that person is a company, any officer of the company who is in default, is liable to a fine and, for continued contravention, to a daily default fine.

[342]

NOTES

Repealed as noted to s 1 at **[309]**.

Sub-s (1): words in square brackets inserted by the Companies (Audit, Investigations and Community Enterprise) Act 2004, s 33, Sch 6, paras 1, 5.

34 Penalty for improper use of "limited" or "cyfyngedig"

If any person trades or carries on business under a name or title of which "limited" or "cyfyngedig", or any contraction or imitation of either of those words, is the last word, that person, unless duly incorporated with limited liability, is liable to a fine and, for continued contravention, to a daily default fine.

[343]

NOTES

Repealed as noted to s 1 at **[309]**.

[34A Penalty for improper use of "community interest company" etc

(1) A company which is not a community interest company is guilty of an offence if it carries on any trade, profession or business under a name which includes any of the expressions specified in subsection (3).

(2) A person other than a company is guilty of an offence if it carries on any trade, profession or business under a name which includes any of those expressions (or any contraction of them) as its last part.

(3) The expressions are—

(a) "community interest company" or its Welsh equivalent ("cwmni buddiant cymunedol"), and

(b) "community interest public limited company" or its Welsh equivalent ("cwmni buddiant cymunedol cyhoeddus cyfyngedig").

(4) Subsections (1) and (2) do not apply—

(a) to a person who was carrying on a trade, profession or business under the name in question at any time during the period beginning with 1st September 2003 and ending with 4th December 2003, or

(b) if the name in question was on 4th December 2003 a registered trade mark or Community trade mark (within the meaning of the Trade Marks Act 1994 (c 26)), to a person who was on that date a proprietor or licensee of that trade mark.

(5) A person guilty of an offence under subsection (1) or (2) and, if that person is a company, any officer of the company who is in default, is liable to a fine and, for continued contravention, to a daily default fine.]

[343A]

NOTES

Commencement: 1 July 2005.

Repealed as noted to s 1 at **[309]**.

Inserted by the Companies (Audit, Investigations and Community Enterprise) Act 2004, s 33, Sch 6, paras 1, 6.

CHAPTER III
A COMPANY'S CAPACITY; FORMALITIES OF CARRYING ON BUSINESS

[35 A company's capacity not limited by its memorandum

(1) The validity of an act done by a company shall not be called into question on the ground of lack of capacity by reason of anything in the company's memorandum.

(2) A member of a company may bring proceedings to restrain the doing of an act which but for subsection (1) would be beyond the company's capacity; but no such proceedings shall lie in respect of an act to be done in fulfilment of a legal obligation arising from a previous act of the company.

(3) It remains the duty of the directors to observe any limitations on their powers flowing from the company's memorandum; and action by the directors which but for subsection (1) would be beyond the company's capacity may only be ratified by the company by special resolution.

A resolution ratifying such action shall not affect any liability incurred by the directors or any other person; relief from any such liability must be agreed to separately by special resolution.

(4) The operation of this section is restricted by [section 65(1) of the Charities Act 1993] and section 112(3) of the Companies Act 1989 in relation to companies which are charities; and section 322A below (invalidity of certain transactions to which directors or their associates are parties) has effect notwithstanding this section.]

[344]

NOTES

Repealed as noted to s 1 at **[309]**.

Substituted, together with ss 35A, 35B for original s 35, by the Companies Act 1989, s 108(1), subject to transitional provisions contained in the Companies Act 1989 (Commencement No 8 and Transitional and Saving Provisions) Order 1990, SI 1990/2569.

Sub-s (4): words in square brackets substituted by the Charities Act 1993, s 98(1), Sch 6, para 20(1), (2).

[35A Power of directors to bind the company

(1) In favour of a person dealing with a company in good faith, the power of the board of directors to bind the company, or authorise others to do so, shall be deemed to be free of any limitation under the company's constitution.

(2) For this purpose—

(a) a person "deals with" a company if he is a party to any transaction or other act to which the company is a party;

(b) a person shall not be regarded as acting in bad faith by reason only of his knowing that an act is beyond the powers of the directors under the company's constitution; and

(c) a person shall be presumed to have acted in good faith unless the contrary is proved.

(3) The references above to limitations on the directors' power under the company's constitution include limitations deriving—

(a) from a resolution of the company in general meeting or a meeting of any class of shareholders, or

(b) from any agreement between the members of the company or of any class of shareholders.

(4) Subsection (1) does not affect any right of a member of the company to bring proceedings to restrain the doing of an act which is beyond the powers of the directors; but no such proceedings shall lie in respect of an act to be done in fulfilment of a legal obligation arising from a previous act of the company.

(5) Nor does that subsection affect any liability incurred by the directors, or any other person, by reason of the directors' exceeding their powers.

(6) The operation of this section is restricted by [section 65(1) of the Charities Act 1993] and section 112(3) of the Companies Act 1989 in relation to companies which are charities; and section 322A below (invalidity of certain transactions to which directors or their associates are parties) has effect notwithstanding this section.]

[345]

NOTES

Repealed as noted to s 1 at **[309]**.

Substituted as noted to s 35 at **[344]**.

Sub-s (6): words in square brackets substituted by the Charities Act 1993, s 98(1), Sch 6, para 20(1), (2).

[35B No duty to enquire as to capacity of company or authority of directors

A party to a transaction with a company is not bound to enquire as to whether it is permitted by the company's memorandum or as to any limitation on the powers of the board of directors to bind the company or authorise others to do so.]

[346]

NOTES

Repealed as noted to s 1 at **[309]**.
Substituted as noted to s 35 at **[344]**.

[36 Company contracts: England and Wales

Under the law of England and Wales a contract may be made—

(*a*) *by a company, by writing under its common seal, or*
(*b*) *on behalf of a company, by any person acting under its authority, express or implied;*

and any formalities required by law in the case of a contract made by an individual also apply, unless a contrary intention appears, to a contract made by or on behalf of a company.]

[347]

NOTES

Repealed as noted to s 1 at **[309]**.
Substituted by the Companies Act 1989, s 130(1).
Modification: this section, and s 36A, are modified, in relation to companies incorporated outside Great Britain, by the Foreign Companies (Execution of Documents) Regulations 1994, SI 1994/950.

[36A Execution of documents: England and Wales

(*1*) *Under the law of England and Wales the following provisions have effect with respect to the execution of documents by a company.*

(*2*) *A document is executed by a company by the affixing of its common seal.*

(*3*) *A company need not have a common seal, however, and the following subsections apply whether it does or not.*

(*4*) *A document signed by a director and the secretary of a company, or by two directors of a company, and expressed (in whatever form of words) to be executed by the company has the same effect as if executed under the common seal of the company.*

[(4A) Where a document is to be signed by a person as a director or the secretary of more than one company, it shall not be taken to be duly signed by that person for the purposes of subsection (4) unless the person signs it separately in each capacity.]

(*5*) …

(*6*) *In favour of a purchaser a document shall be deemed to have been duly executed by a company if it purports to be signed by a director and the secretary of the company, or by two directors of the company, …*

A "purchaser" means a purchaser in good faith for valuable consideration and includes a lessee, mortgagee or other person who for valuable consideration acquires an interest in property.]

[(7) This section applies in the case of a document which is (or purports to be) executed by a company in the name or on behalf of another person whether or not that person is also a company.]

[(8) For the purposes of this section, a document is (or purports to be) signed, in the case of a director or the secretary of a company which is not an individual, if it is (or purports to be) signed by an individual authorised by the director or secretary to sign on its behalf.]

[348]

NOTES

Repealed as noted to s 1 at **[309]**.
Inserted by the Companies Act 1989, s 130(2).
Sub-ss (4A), (7), (8): inserted and added by the Regulatory Reform (Execution of Deeds and Documents) Order 2005, SI 2005/1906, arts 7(2), 10(1), Sch 1, paras 9–11, except in relation to any instrument executed before 15 September 2005.

Sub-s (5): repealed by SI 2005/1906, art 10(2), Sch 2, except in relation to any instrument executed before 15 September 2005; before that date the subsection read as follows—

"(5) A document executed by a company which makes it clear on its face that it is intended by the person or persons making it to be a deed has effect, upon delivery, as a deed; and it shall be presumed, unless a contrary intention is proved, to be delivered upon its being so executed.".

Sub-s (6): words "and, where it makes it clear on its face that it is intended by the person or persons making it to be a deed, to have been delivered upon its being executed" repealed by SI 2005/1906, arts 5, 10(2), Sch 2, except in relation to any instrument executed before 15 September 2005.
Modified as noted to s 36 at **[347]**.

[36AA Execution of deeds: England and Wales

(1) A document is validly executed by a company as a deed for the purposes of section 1(2)(b) of the Law of Property (Miscellaneous Provisions) Act 1989, if and only if—
(a) it is duly executed by the company, and
(b) it is delivered as a deed.

(2) A document shall be presumed to be delivered for the purposes of subsection (1)(b) upon its being executed, unless a contrary intention is proved.]

[348A]

NOTES
Commencement: 15 September 2005.
Repealed as noted to s 1 at **[309]**.
Inserted by the Regulatory Reform (Execution of Deeds and Documents) Order 2005, SI 2005/1906, art 6, except in relation to any instrument executed before 15 September 2005.

36B *(Applies to Scotland only.)*

[36C Pre-incorporation contracts, deeds and obligations

(1) A contract which purports to be made by or on behalf of a company at a time when the company has not been formed has effect, subject to any agreement to the contrary, as one made with the person purporting to act for the company or as agent for it, and he is personally liable on the contract accordingly.

(2) Subsection (1) applies—
(a) to the making of a deed under the law of England and Wales, and
(b) to the undertaking of an obligation under the law of Scotland,
as it applies to the making of a contract.]

[349]

NOTES
Repealed as noted to s 1 at **[309]**.
Inserted by the Companies Act 1989, s 130(4).

37 Bills of exchange and promissory notes

A bill of exchange or promissory note is deemed to have been made, accepted or endorsed on behalf of a company if made, accepted or endorsed in the name of, or by or on behalf or on account of, the company by a person acting under its authority.

[350]

NOTES
Repealed as noted to s 1 at **[309]**.

38 Execution of deeds abroad

(1) A company may [...], by writing under its common seal, empower any person, either generally or in respect of any specified matters, as its attorney, to execute deeds on its behalf in any place elsewhere than in the United Kingdom.

[(2) A deed executed by such an attorney on behalf of the company has the same effect as if it were executed under the company's common seal.]

[(3) This section does not extend to Scotland.]

[351]

NOTES

Repealed as noted to s 1 at **[309]**.

Sub-s (1): words omitted (which were inserted by the Companies Act 1989, s 130(7), Sch 17, para 1) repealed by the Law Reform (Miscellaneous Provisions) (Scotland) Act 1990, s 74(1), (2), Sch 8, para 33(2), Sch 9.

Sub-s (2): substituted by the Companies Act 1989, s 130(7), Sch 17, para 1.

Sub-s (3): added by the Requirements of Writing (Scotland) Act 1995, s 14(1), Sch 4, para 52.

39 Power of company to have official seal for use abroad

(1) A company [which has a common seal] whose objects require or comprise the transaction of business in foreign countries may, if authorised by its articles, have for use in any territory, district, or place elsewhere than in the United Kingdom, an official seal, which shall be a facsimile of [its common seal], with the addition on its face of the name of every territory, district or place where it is to be used.

[(2) The official seal when duly affixed to a document has the same effect as the company's common seal.]

[(2A) Subsection (2) does not extend to Scotland.]

(3) A company having an official seal for use in any such territory, district or place may, by writing under its common seal [or as respects Scotland by writing subscribed in accordance with the Requirements of Writing (Scotland) Act 1995] [...] authorise any person appointed for the purpose in that territory, district or place to affix the official seal to any deed or other document to which the company is party in that territory, district or place.

(4) As between the company and a person dealing with such an agent, the agent's authority continues during the period (if any) mentioned in the instrument conferring the authority, or if no period is there mentioned, then until notice of the revocation or determination of the agent's authority has been given to the person dealing with him.

(5) The person affixing the official seal shall certify in writing on the deed or other instrument to which the seal is affixed the date on which and the place at which it is affixed.

[352]

NOTES

Repealed as noted to s 1 at **[309]**.

Sub-s (1): words in first pair of square brackets inserted and words in second pair of square brackets substituted by the Companies Act 1989, s 130(7), Sch 17, para 2.

Sub-s (2): substituted by the Companies Act 1989, s 130(7), Sch 17, para 2.

Sub-s (2A): inserted by the Requirements of Writing (Scotland) Act 1995, s 14(1), Sch 4, para 53(a).

Sub-s (3): words in square brackets inserted by the Requirements of Writing (Scotland) Act 1995, s 14(1), Sch 4, para 53(b); words omitted (which were inserted by the Companies Act 1989, s 130(7), Sch 17, para 2) repealed by the Law Reform (Miscellaneous Provisions) (Scotland) Act 1990, s 74(1), (2), Sch 8, para 33(3), Sch 9.

40 Official seal for share certificates, etc

[(1)] A company [which has a common seal] may have, for use for sealing securities issued by the company and for sealing documents creating or evidencing securities so issued, an official seal which is a facsimile of [its common seal] with the addition on its face of the word "Securities".

[The official seal when duly affixed to a document has the same effect as the company's common seal.]

[(2) Nothing in this section shall affect the right of a company registered in Scotland to subscribe such securities and documents in accordance with the Requirements of Writing (Scotland) Act 1995.]

[353]

NOTES

Repealed as noted to s 1 at **[309]**.

Sub-s (1): original section numbered as sub-s (1) by the Requirements of Writing (Scotland) Act 1995, s 14(1), Sch 4, para 54; words in first pair of square brackets inserted, words in second pair of square brackets substituted, and words in third pair of square brackets added by the Companies Act 1989, s 130(7), Sch 17, para 3.

Sub-s (2): added by the Requirements of Writing (Scotland) Act 1995, s 14(1), Sch 4, para 54.

41 Authentication of documents

A document or proceeding requiring authentication by a company [is sufficiently authenticated for the purposes of the law of England and Wales by the signature of a director, secretary or other authorised officer of the company].

[354]–[355]

NOTES

Repealed by the Companies Act 2006, s 1295, Sch 16, as from 6 April 2007.

Words in square brackets substituted by the Companies Act 1989, s 130(7), Sch 17, para 4.

42–220 *(S 42 repealed by the Companies Act 2006, s 1295, Sch 16, as from 1 January 2007, subject to a saving in relation to limited liability partnerships (see the Companies Act 2006 (Commencement No 1, Transitional Provisions and Savings) Order 2006, SI 2006/3428, art 8(2)); ss 43–220 (Pts II–VI) outside the scope of this work.)*

PART VII
ACCOUNTS AND AUDIT

NOTES

Original Part VII (ss 221–262) replaced by the insertion of new ss 221–262A, by the Companies Act 1989, ss 2–22. Extensive transitional provisions and savings relating to this insertion are made by the Companies Act 1989 (Commencement No 4 and Transitional and Saving Provisions) Order 1990, SI 1990/335. Principally, these provide that the rules relating to accounts and reports of companies under this Part prior to its amendment by the 1989 Act can have effect for financial years of a company commencing before 23 December 1989. Savings are also made to ensure the continuity of the law between the old and new Part VII.

Application: as to the application of this Part of this Act, subject to modifications, to overseas companies, and the requirements from which overseas companies are exempted, see the Oversea Companies (Accounts) (Modifications and Exemptions) Order 1990, SI 1990/440; as to the application of this Part of this Act, subject to modifications, to accounts prepared under the Partnerships and Unlimited Companies (Accounts) Regulations 1993, SI 1993/1820, see reg 4 of, and the Schedule to, those Regulations; as to the application of this Part to accounts prepared under the Insurance Accounts Directive (Miscellaneous Insurance Undertakings) Regulations 1993, SI 1993/3245, see reg 3 of those Regulations.

CHAPTER I
PROVISIONS APPLYING TO COMPANIES GENERALLY

[Accounting records

221 Duty to keep accounting records

(1) Every company shall keep accounting records which are sufficient to show and explain the company's transactions and are such as to—

(a) disclose with reasonable accuracy, at any time, the financial position of the company at that time, and

(b) enable the directors to ensure that [any accounts required to be prepared under this Part comply] with the requirements of this Act [(and, where applicable, of Article 4 of the IAS Regulation)].

(2) The accounting records shall in particular contain—

(a) entries from day to day of all sums of money received and expended by the company, and the matters in respect of which the receipt and expenditure takes place, and

(b) a record of the assets and liabilities of the company.

(3) If the company's business involves dealing in goods, the accounting records shall contain—

(*a*) *statements of stock held by the company at the end of each financial year of the company,*

(*b*) *all statements of stocktakings from which any such statement of stock as is mentioned in paragraph (a) has been or is to be prepared, and*

(*c*) *except in the case of goods sold by way of ordinary retail trade, statements of all goods sold and purchased, showing the goods and the buyers and sellers in sufficient detail to enable all these to be identified.*

(4) A parent company which has a subsidiary undertaking in relation to which the above requirements do not apply shall take reasonable steps to secure that the undertaking keeps such accounting records as to enable the directors of the parent company to ensure that [any accounts required to be prepared under this Part comply] with the requirements of this Act [(and, where applicable, of Article 4 of the IAS Regulation)].

(5) If a company fails to comply with any provision of this section, every officer of the company who is in default is guilty of an offence unless he shows that he acted honestly and that in the circumstances in which the company's business was carried on the default was excusable.

(6) A person guilty of an offence under this section is liable to imprisonment or a fine, or both.]

[356]

NOTES

Repealed as noted to s 1 at **[309]**.

Inserted, together with the preceding heading and s 222, by the Companies Act 1989, s 2.

Sub-ss (1), (4): words in first pair of square brackets substituted, and words in second pair of square brackets inserted, by the Companies Act 1985 (International Accounting Standards and Other Accounting Amendments) Regulations 2004, SI 2004/2947, reg 3, Sch 1, paras 1, 4, in relation to companies' financial years which begin on or after 1 January 2005.

[222 Where and for how long records to be kept

(1) A company's accounting records shall be kept at its registered office or such other place as the directors think fit, and shall at all times be open to inspection by the company's officers.

(2) If accounting records are kept at a place outside Great Britain, accounts and returns with respect to the business dealt with in the accounting records so kept shall be sent to, and kept at, a place in Great Britain, and shall at all times be open to such inspection.

(3) The accounts and returns to be sent to Great Britain shall be such as to—

(*a*) *disclose with reasonable accuracy the financial position of the business in question at intervals of not more than six months, and*

(*b*) *enable the directors to ensure that [the accounts required to be prepared under this Part] comply with the requirements of this Act [(and, where applicable, Article 4 of the IAS Regulation)].*

(4) If a company fails to comply with any provision of subsections (1) to (3), every officer of the company who is in default is guilty of an offence, and liable to imprisonment or a fine or both, unless he shows that he acted honestly and that in the circumstances in which the company's business was carried on the default was excusable.

(5) Accounting records which a company is required by section 221 to keep shall be preserved by it—

(*a*) *in the case of a private company, for three years from the date on which they are made, and*

(*b*) *in the case of a public company, for six years from the date on which they are made.*

This is subject to any provision contained in rules made under section 411 of the Insolvency Act 1986 (company insolvency rules).

(6) An officer of a company is guilty of an offence, and liable to imprisonment or a fine or both, if he fails to take all reasonable steps for securing compliance by the company with subsection (5) or intentionally causes any default by the company under that subsection.]

[357]

NOTES

Repealed as noted to s 1 at **[309]**.

Inserted as noted to s 221 at **[356]**.

Sub-s (3): words in first pair of square brackets in para (b) substituted, and words in second pair of square brackets inserted, by the Companies Act 1985 (International Accounting Standards and Other Accounting Amendments) Regulations 2004, SI 2004/2947, reg 3, Sch 1, paras 1, 5, in relation to companies' financial years which begin on or after 1 January 2005.

[A company's financial year and accounting reference periods

223 A company's financial year

(1) A company's "financial year" is determined as follows.

(2) Its first financial year begins with the first day of its first accounting reference period and ends with the last day of that period or such other date, not more than seven days before or after the end of that period, as the directors may determine.

(3) Subsequent financial years begin with the day immediately following the end of the company's previous financial year and end with the last day of its next accounting reference period or such other date, not more than seven days before or after the end of that period, as the directors may determine.

(4) In relation to an undertaking which is not a company, references in this Act to its financial year are to any period in respect of which a profit and loss account of the undertaking is required to be made up (by its constitution or by the law under which it is established), whether that period is a year or not.

(5) The directors of a parent company shall secure that, except where in their opinion there are good reasons against it, the financial year of each of its subsidiary undertakings coincides with the company's own financial year.]

[358]

NOTES

Repealed as noted to s 1 at **[309]**.

Inserted, together with the preceding heading and ss 224, 225, by the Companies Act 1989, s 3.

[224 Accounting reference periods and accounting reference date

(1) A company's accounting reference periods are determined according to its accounting reference date.

(2) A company [incorporated before 1st April 1996] may, at any time before the end of the period of nine months beginning with the date of its incorporation, by notice in the prescribed form given to the registrar specify its accounting reference date, that is, the date on which its accounting reference period ends in each calendar year.

(3) Failing such notice, [the accounting reference date of such a company] is—

(a) in the case of a company incorporated before [1st April 1990], 31st March;

(b) in the case of a company incorporated after [1st April 1990], the last day of the month in which the anniversary of its incorporation falls.

[(3A) The accounting reference date of a company incorporated on or after 1st April 1996 is the last day of the month in which the anniversary of its incorporation falls.]

(4) A company's first accounting reference period is the period of more than six months, but not more than 18 months, beginning with the date of its incorporation and ending with its accounting reference date.

(5) Its subsequent accounting reference periods are successive periods of twelve months beginning immediately after the end of the previous accounting reference period and ending with its accounting reference date.

(6) This section has effect subject to the provisions of section 225 relating to the alteration of accounting reference dates and the consequences of such alteration.]

[359]

NOTES

Repealed as noted to s 1 at **[309]**.
Inserted as noted to s 223 at **[358]**.
Sub-s (2): words in square brackets inserted by the Companies Act 1985 (Miscellaneous Accounting Amendments) Regulations 1996, SI 1996/189, reg 2(1), (2).
Sub-s (3): words in first pair of square brackets substituted by SI 1996/189, reg 2(1), (3); words in second and third pairs of square brackets substituted by the Companies Act 1989 (Commencement No 4 and Transitional and Saving Provisions) Order 1990, SI 1990/355, art 15.
Sub-s (3A): inserted by SI 1996/189, reg 2(1), (4).
Prescribed form: see the Companies (Forms) Regulations 1985, SI 1985/854, Form 224, as prescribed by the Companies (Forms) (Amendment) Regulations 1990, SI 1990/572.

[225 Alteration of accounting reference date

(1) A company may by notice in the prescribed form given to the registrar specify a new accounting reference date [having effect in relation to—
- *(a) the company's current accounting reference period and subsequent periods; or*
- *(b) the company's previous accounting reference period and subsequent periods.*

A company's "previous accounting reference period" means that immediately preceding its current accounting reference period.]

(2) …

(3) The notice shall state whether the current or previous accounting reference period—
- *(a) is to be shortened, so as to come to an end on the first occasion on which the new accounting reference date falls or fell after the beginning of the period, or*
- *(b) is to be extended, so as to come to an end on the second occasion on which that date falls or fell after the beginning of the period.*

(4) A notice under subsection (1) stating that the current [or previous] accounting reference period is to be extended is ineffective, except as mentioned below, if given less than five years after the end of an earlier accounting reference period of the company which was extended by virtue of this section.

This subsection does not apply—
- *[(a) to a notice given by a company which is a subsidiary undertaking or parent undertaking of another EEA undertaking if the new accounting reference date coincides with that of the other EEA undertaking or, where that undertaking is not a company, with the last day of its financial year, or]*
- *(b) where [the company is in administration] under Part II of the Insolvency Act 1986,*

or where the Secretary of State directs that it should not apply, which he may do with respect to a notice which has been given or which may be given.

(5) A notice under [subsection (1)] may not be given [in respect of a previous accounting reference period] if the period allowed for laying and delivering accounts and reports in relation to [that period] has already expired.

(6) [A company's accounting reference period may not in any case, unless the company is in administration] under Part II of the Insolvency Act 1986, be extended so as to exceed 18 months and a notice under this section is ineffective if the current or previous accounting reference period as extended in accordance with the notice would exceed that limit.]

[(7) In this section "EEA undertaking" means an undertaking established under the law of any part of the United Kingdom or the law of any other EEA State.]

[360]

NOTES

Repealed as noted to s 1 at **[309]**.
Inserted as noted to s 223 at **[358]**.
Sub-s (1): words in square brackets substituted by the Companies Act 1985 (Miscellaneous Accounting Amendments) Regulations 1996, SI 1996/189, reg 3(1), (2).
Sub-s (2): repealed by SI 1996/189, reg 3(1), (3).
Sub-s (4): words in first pair of square brackets inserted and para (a) substituted by SI 1996/189, reg 3(1), (4); words in square brackets in para (b) substituted by the Enterprise Act 2002, s 248(3), Sch 17, paras 3, 4(a).
Sub-s (5): words in first and third pairs of square brackets substituted and words in second pair of square brackets inserted by SI 1996/189, reg 3(1), (5).

Sub-s (6): words in square brackets substituted by the Enterprise Act 2002, s 248(3), Sch 17, paras 3, 4(b).
Sub-s (7): added by SI 1996/189, reg 3(1), (6).
Prescribed forms: see the Companies (Forms) Regulations 1985, SI 1985/854, Forms 225, 225CYM, as prescribed by the Companies (Forms) (Amendment) Regulations 1996, SI 1996/594 and the Companies (Welsh Language Forms and Documents) Regulations 1996, SI 1996/595 respectively.

[Annual accounts

[226 Duty to prepare individual accounts

(1) The directors of every company shall prepare accounts for the company for each of its financial years.

Those accounts are referred to in this Part as the company's "individual accounts".

(2) A company's individual accounts may be prepared—
(a) in accordance with section 226A ("Companies Act individual accounts"), or
(b) in accordance with international accounting standards ("IAS individual accounts").

This subsection is subject to the following provisions of this section and section 227C (consistency of accounts).

(3) The individual accounts of a company that is a charity must be Companies Act individual accounts.

(4) After the first financial year in which the directors of a company prepare IAS individual accounts ("the first IAS year"), all subsequent individual accounts of the company must be prepared in accordance with international accounting standards unless there is a relevant change of circumstance.

(5) There is a relevant change of circumstance if, at any time during or after the first IAS year—
(a) the company becomes a subsidiary undertaking of another undertaking that does not prepare IAS individual accounts,
(b) the company ceases to be a company with securities admitted to trading on a regulated market, or
(c) a parent undertaking of the company ceases to be an undertaking with securities admitted to trading on a regulated market.

In this subsection "regulated market" has the same meaning as it has in Council Directive 93/22/EEC on investment services in the securities field.

(6) If, having changed to preparing Companies Act individual accounts following a relevant change of circumstance, the directors again prepare IAS individual accounts for the company, subsections (4) and (5) apply again as if the first financial year for which such accounts are again prepared were the first IAS year.]]

[361]

NOTES

Repealed as noted to s 1 at **[309]**.
Originally inserted, together with the preceding heading, by the Companies Act 1989, s 4(1).
Ss 226, 227 subsequently substituted by new ss 226, 226A, 226B, 227, 227A–227C by the Companies Act 1985 (International Accounting Standards and Other Accounting Amendments) Regulations 2004, SI 2004/2947, reg 2, in relation to companies' financial years which begin on or after 1 January 2005.
Sub-s (5): for the words "Council Directive 93/22/EEC on investment services in the securities field" there are substituted the words "Directive 2004/39/EC of the European Parliament and of the Council of 21 April 2004 on markets in financial instruments" by the Financial Services and Markets Act 2000 (Markets in Financial Instruments) Regulations 2007, SI 2007/126, art 3(6), Sch 6, Pt 1, para 7(1), (5), as from 1 April 2007 for certain purposes and as from 1 November 2007 otherwise (for purposes see reg 1 of those Regulations).

[226A Companies Act individual accounts

(1) Companies Act individual accounts must comprise—
(a) a balance sheet as at the last day of the financial year, and
(b) a profit and loss account.

(2) The balance sheet must give a true and fair view of the state of affairs of the company as at the end of the financial year; and the profit and loss account must give a true and fair view of the profit or loss of the company for the financial year.

(3) Companies Act individual accounts must comply with the provisions of Schedule 4 as to the form and content of the balance sheet and profit and loss account and additional information to be provided by way of notes to the accounts.

(4) Where compliance with the provisions of that Schedule, and the other provisions of this Act as to the matters to be included in a company's individual accounts or in notes to those accounts, would not be sufficient to give a true and fair view, the necessary additional information must be given in the accounts or in a note to them.

(5) If in special circumstances compliance with any of those provisions is inconsistent with the requirement to give a true and fair view, the directors must depart from that provision to the extent necessary to give a true and fair view.

(6) Particulars of any such departure, the reasons for it and its effect must be given in a note to the accounts.]

[361A]

NOTES

Commencement: 12 November 2004 (in relation to companies' financial years which begin on or after 1 January 2005).

Repealed as noted to s 1 at **[309]**.

Substituted as noted to s 226 at **[361]**.

[226B IAS individual accounts

Where the directors of a company prepare IAS individual accounts, they must state in the notes to those accounts that the accounts have been prepared in accordance with international accounting standards.]

[361B]

NOTES

Commencement: 12 November 2004 (in relation to companies' financial years which begin on or after 1 January 2005).

Repealed as noted to s 1 at **[309]**.

Substituted as noted to s 226 at **[361]**.

[227 Duty to prepare group accounts

(1) If at the end of a financial year a company is a parent company the directors, as well as preparing individual accounts for the year, shall prepare consolidated accounts for the group for the year.

Those accounts are referred to in this Part as the company's "group accounts".

(2) The group accounts of certain parent companies are required by Article 4 of the IAS Regulation to be prepared in accordance with international accounting standards ("IAS group accounts").

(3) The group accounts of other companies may be prepared—

(a) in accordance with section 227A ("Companies Act group accounts"), or

(b) in accordance with international accounting standards ("IAS group accounts").

This subsection is subject to the following provisions of this section.

(4) The group accounts of a parent company that is a charity must be Companies Act group accounts.

(5) After the first financial year in which the directors of a parent company prepare IAS group accounts ("the first IAS year"), all subsequent group accounts of the company must be prepared in accordance with international accounting standards unless there is a relevant change of circumstance.

(6) There is a relevant change of circumstance if, at any time during or after the first IAS year—

(a) the company becomes a subsidiary undertaking of another undertaking that does not prepare IAS group accounts,

(*b*) *the company ceases to be a company with securities admitted to trading on a regulated market, or*

(*c*) *a parent undertaking of the company ceases to be an undertaking with securities admitted to trading on a regulated market.*

In this subsection "regulated market" has the same meaning as it has in Council Directive 93/22/EEC on investment services in the securities field.

(7) If, having changed to preparing Companies Act group accounts following a relevant change of circumstance, the directors again prepare IAS group accounts for the company, subsections (5) and (6) apply again as if the first financial year for which such accounts are again prepared were the first IAS year.

(8) This section is subject to the exemptions provided by sections 228 (parent companies included in accounts of larger EEA group), 228A (parent companies included in non-EEA group accounts), 229(5) (all subsidiary undertakings excluded from consolidation) and 248 (small and medium-sized groups).]

[362]

NOTES

Commencement: 12 November 2004 (in relation to companies' financial years which begin on or after 1 January 2005).

Repealed as noted to s 1 at **[309]**.

Originally inserted by the Companies Act 1989, s 5(1), subject to transitional provisions.

Substituted as noted to s 226 at **[361]**.

Sub-s (6): for the words "Council Directive 93/22/EEC on investment services in the securities field" there are substituted the words "Directive 2004/39/EC of the European Parliament and of the Council of 21 April 2004 on markets in financial instruments" by the Financial Services and Markets Act 2000 (Markets in Financial Instruments) Regulations 2007, SI 2007/126, art 3(6), Sch 6, Pt 1, para 7(1), (6), as from 1 April 2007 for certain purposes and as from 1 November 2007 otherwise (for purposes see reg 1 of those Regulations).

[227A Companies Act group accounts

(1) Companies Act group accounts must comprise—

(*a*) *a consolidated balance sheet dealing with the state of affairs of the parent company and its subsidiary undertakings, and*

(*b*) *a consolidated profit and loss account dealing with the profit or loss of the parent company and its subsidiary undertakings.*

(2) The accounts must give a true and fair view of the state of affairs as at the end of the financial year, and the profit or loss for the financial year, of the undertakings included in the consolidation as a whole, so far as concerns members of the company.

(3) Companies Act group accounts must comply with the provisions of Schedule 4A as to the form and content of the consolidated balance sheet and consolidated profit and loss account and additional information to be provided by way of notes to the accounts.

(4) Where compliance with the provisions of that Schedule, and the other provisions of this Act as to the matters to be included in a company's group accounts or in notes to those accounts, would not be sufficient to give a true and fair view, the necessary additional information must be given in the accounts or in a note to them.

(5) If in special circumstances compliance with any of those provisions is inconsistent with the requirement to give a true and fair view, the directors must depart from that provision to the extent necessary to give a true and fair view.

(6) Particulars of any such departure, the reasons for it and its effect must be given in a note to the accounts.]

[362A]

NOTES

Commencement: 12 November 2004 (in relation to companies' financial years which begin on or after 1 January 2005).

Repealed as noted to s 1 at **[309]**.

Substituted as noted to s 226 at **[361]**.

[227B IAS group accounts

Where the directors of a parent company prepare IAS group accounts, they must state in the notes to those accounts that the accounts have been prepared in accordance with international accounting standards.]

[362B]

NOTES

Commencement: 12 November 2004 (in relation to companies' financial years which begin on or after 1 January 2005).

Repealed as noted to s 1 at **[309]**.

Substituted as noted to s 226 at **[361]**.

[227C Consistency of accounts

(1) The directors of a parent company must secure that the individual accounts of—

(a) the parent company, and

(b) each of its subsidiary undertakings,

are all prepared using the same financial reporting framework, except to the extent that in their opinion there are good reasons for not doing so.

(2) Subsection (1) does not apply if the directors do not prepare group accounts for the parent company.

(3) Subsection (1) only applies to accounts of subsidiary undertakings that are required to be prepared under this Part.

(4) Subsection (1) does not require accounts of undertakings that are charities to be prepared using the same financial reporting framework as accounts of undertakings which are not charities.

(5) Subsection (1)(a) does not apply where the directors of a parent company prepare IAS group accounts and IAS individual accounts.]

[362C]

NOTES

Commencement: 12 November 2004 (in relation to companies' financial years which begin on or after 1 January 2005).

Repealed as noted to s 1 at **[309]**.

Substituted as noted to s 226 at **[361]**.

[228 Exemption for parent companies included in accounts of larger group

(1) A company is exempt from the requirement to prepare group accounts if it is itself a subsidiary undertaking and its immediate parent undertaking is established under the law of [an EEA State], in the following cases—

(a) where the company is a wholly-owned subsidiary of that parent undertaking;

(b) where that parent undertaking holds more than 50 per cent of the shares in the company and notice requesting the preparation of group accounts has not been served on the company by shareholders holding in aggregate—

(i) more than half of the remaining shares in the company, or

(ii) 5 per cent of the total shares in the company.

Such notice must be served not later than six months after the end of the financial year before that to which it relates.

(2) Exemption is conditional upon compliance with all of the following conditions—

(a) that the company is included in consolidated accounts for a larger group drawn up to the same date, or to an earlier date in the same financial year, by a parent undertaking established under the law of [an EEA State];

(b) that those accounts are drawn up and audited, and that parent undertaking's annual report is drawn up, according to that law, in accordance with the provisions of the Seventh Directive (83/349/EEC) [(where applicable as modified by the provisions of the Bank Accounts Directive (86/635/EEC) [or the Insurance Accounts Directive (91/674/EEC)]) [or in accordance with international accounting standards]];

(c) that the company discloses in its individual accounts that it is exempt from the obligation to prepare and deliver group accounts;

(*d*) *that the company states in its individual accounts the name of the parent undertaking which draws up the group accounts referred to above and—*
(*i*) *if it is incorporated outside Great Britain, the country in which it is incorporated,*
(*ii*) *… , and*
(*iii*) *if it is unincorporated, the address of its principal place of business;*
(*e*) *that the company delivers to the registrar, within the period allowed for delivering its individual accounts, copies of those group accounts and of the parent undertaking's annual report, together with the auditors' report on them; and*
(*f*) *[…] that if any document comprised in accounts and reports delivered in accordance with paragraph (e) is in a language other than English, there is annexed to the copy of that document delivered a translation of it into English, certified in the prescribed manner to be a correct translation.*

(3) The exemption does not apply to a company any of whose securities are [admitted to trading on a regulated market of any EEA State within the meaning of Council Directive 93/22/EEC on investment services in the securities field].

(4) Shares held by directors of a company for the purpose of complying with any share qualification requirement shall be disregarded in determining for the purposes of subsection (1)(a) whether the company is a wholly-owned subsidiary.

(5) For the purposes of subsection (1)(b) shares held by a wholly-owned subsidiary of the parent undertaking, or held on behalf of the parent undertaking or a wholly-owned subsidiary, shall be attributed to the parent undertaking.

(6) In subsection (3) "securities" includes—
(*a*) *shares and stock,*
(*b*) *debentures, including debenture stock, loan stock, bonds, certificates of deposit and other instruments creating or acknowledging indebtedness,*
(*c*) *warrants or other instruments entitling the holder to subscribe for securities falling within paragraph (a) or (b), and*
(*d*) *certificates or other instruments which confer—*
(*i*) *property rights in respect of a security falling within paragraph (a), (b) or (c),*
(*ii*) *any right to acquire, dispose of, underwrite or convert a security, being a right to which the holder would be entitled if he held any such security to which the certificate or other instrument relates, or*
(*iii*) *a contractual right (other than an option) to acquire any such security otherwise than by subscription.]*

[363]

NOTES

Repealed as noted to s 1 at **[309]**.

Inserted, together with s 229, by the Companies Act 1989, s 5(3).

Sub-s (1): words in square brackets substituted by the Companies Act 1985 (International Accounting Standards and Other Accounting Amendments) Regulations 2004, SI 2004/2947, reg 15, Sch 7, Pt 1, para 4(1), (2), in relation to companies' financial years which begin on or after 1 January 2005.

Sub-s (2): words in square brackets in para (a) substituted by SI 2004/2947, reg 15, Sch 7, Pt 1, para 4(1), (2), in relation to companies' financial years which begin on or after 1 January 2005; words in first (outer) pair of square brackets in para (b) added by the Companies Act 1985 (Disclosure of Branches and Bank Accounts) Regulations 1992, SI 1992/3178, reg 4, and words in second (inner) pair of square brackets in para (b) added by the Companies Act 1985 (Insurance Companies Accounts) Regulations 1993, SI 1993/3246, reg 5(1), Sch 2, para 1, subject to transitional provisions contained in regs 6, 7 thereof; words in third (inner) pair of square brackets in para (b) inserted by the Companies Act 1985 (International Accounting Standards and Other Accounting Amendments) Regulations 2004, SI 2004/2947, reg 3, Sch 1, paras 1, 6, in relation to companies' financial years which begin on or after 1 January 2005; para (d)(ii) repealed, in relation to any financial year ending on or after 2 February 1996, by the Companies Act 1985 (Miscellaneous Accounting Amendments) Regulations 1996, SI 1996/189, regs 4, 16(1), subject to a transitional provision in reg 16(2) of the 1996 Regulations; words omitted in square brackets in para (f) inserted by the Welsh Language Act 1993, s 30(1), (3), repealed by the Companies Act 2006, s 1295, Sch 16.

Sub-s (3): words in square brackets substituted by SI 2004/2947, reg 15, Sch 7, Pt 1, para 4(1), (3), in relation to companies' financial years which begin on or after 1 January 2005; for the words "Council Directive 93/22/EEC on investment services in the securities field" there are substituted the words "Directive 2004/39/EC of the European Parliament and of the Council of 21 April 2004 on markets in financial instruments" by the Financial Services and Markets Act 2000 (Markets in Financial Instruments) Regulations 2007, SI 2007/126, art 3(6), Sch 6, Pt 1, para 7(1), (7), as from 1 April 2007 for certain purposes and as from 1 November 2007 otherwise (for purposes see reg 1 of those Regulations).

[228A Exemption for parent companies included in non-EEA group accounts

(1) A company is exempt from the requirement to prepare group accounts if it is itself a subsidiary undertaking and its parent undertaking is not established under the law of an EEA State, in the following cases—

(*a*) *where the company is a wholly-owned subsidiary of that parent undertaking;*

(*b*) *where that parent undertaking holds more than 50 per cent of the shares in the company and notice requesting the preparation of group accounts has not been served on the company by shareholders holding in aggregate—*

 (*i*) *more than half of the remaining shares in the company, or*

 (*ii*) *5 per cent of the total shares in the company.*

Such notice must be served not later than six months after the end of the financial year before that to which it relates.

(2) *Exemption is conditional upon compliance with all of the following conditions—*

(*a*) *that the company and all of its subsidiary undertakings are included in consolidated accounts for a larger group drawn up to the same date, or to an earlier date in the same financial year, by a parent undertaking;*

(*b*) *that those accounts and, where appropriate, the group's annual report, are drawn up in accordance with the provisions of the Seventh Directive (83/349/EEC) (where applicable as modified by the provisions of the Bank Accounts Directive (86/635/EEC) or the Insurance Accounts Directive (91/674/EEC)), or in a manner equivalent to consolidated accounts and consolidated annual reports so drawn up;*

(*c*) *that the consolidated accounts are audited by one or more persons authorised to audit accounts under the law under which the parent undertaking which draws them up is established;*

(*d*) *that the company discloses in its individual accounts that it is exempt from the obligation to prepare and deliver group accounts;*

(*e*) *that the company states in its individual accounts the name of the parent undertaking which draws up the group accounts referred to above and—*

 (*i*) *if it is incorporated outside Great Britain, the country in which it is incorporated, and*

 (*ii*) *if it is unincorporated, the address of its principal place of business;*

(*f*) *that the company delivers to the registrar, within the period allowed for delivering its individual accounts, copies of the group accounts and, where appropriate, of the consolidated annual report, together with the auditors' report on them; and*

(*g*) *... that if any document comprised in accounts and reports delivered in accordance with paragraph (f) is in a language other than English, there is annexed to the copy of that document delivered a translation of it into English, certified in the prescribed manner to be a correct translation.*

(3) The exemption does not apply to a company any of whose securities are admitted to trading on a regulated market of any EEA State within the meaning of Council Directive 93/22/EEC on investment services in the securities field.

(4) Shares held by directors of a company for the purpose of complying with any share qualification requirement are disregarded in determining for the purposes of subsection (1)(a) whether the company is a wholly-owned subsidiary.

(5) For the purposes of subsection (1)(b), shares held by a wholly-owned subsidiary of the parent undertaking, or held on behalf of the parent undertaking or a wholly-owned subsidiary, are attributed to the parent undertaking.

(6) *In subsection (3) "securities" includes—*

(*a*) *shares and stock,*

(*b*) *debentures, including debenture stock, loan stock, bonds, certificates of deposit and other instruments creating or acknowledging indebtedness,*

(*c*) *warrants or other instruments entitling the holder to subscribe for securities falling within paragraph (a) or (b), and*

(*d*) *certificates or other instruments which confer—*

 (*i*) *property rights in respect of a security falling within paragraph (a), (b) or (c),*

 (*ii*) *any right to acquire, dispose of, underwrite or convert a security, being a right to which the holder would be entitled if he held any such security to which the certificate or other instrument relates, or*

(iii) a contractual right (other than an option) to acquire any such security otherwise than by subscription.]

[363A]

NOTES

Commencement: 12 November 2004 (in relation to companies' financial years which begin on or after 1 January 2005).

Repealed as noted to s 1 at **[309]**.

Inserted by the Companies Act 1985 (International Accounting Standards and Other Accounting Amendments) Regulations 2004, SI 2004/2947, reg 4, in relation to companies' financial years which begin on or after 1 January 2005.

Sub-s (2): words omitted from para (g) repealed by the Companies Act 2006, s 1295, Sch 16, subject to a saving in relation to limited liability partnerships; see the Companies Act 2006 (Commencement No 1, Transitional Provisions and Savings) Order 2006, SI 2006/3428, art 8(2).

Sub-s (3): for the words "Council Directive 93/22/EEC on investment services in the securities field" there are substituted the words "Directive 2004/39/EC of the European Parliament and of the Council of 21 April 2004 on markets in financial instruments" by the Financial Services and Markets Act 2000 (Markets in Financial Instruments) Regulations 2007, SI 2007/126, art 3(6), Sch 6, Pt 1, para 7(1), (8), as from 1 April 2007 for certain purposes and as from 1 November 2007 otherwise (for purposes see reg 1 of those Regulations).

[229 Subsidiary undertakings included in the consolidation

(1) [In the case of Companies Act group accounts,] subject to the exceptions authorised ... by this section, all the subsidiary undertakings of the parent company shall be included in the consolidation.

(2) A subsidiary undertaking may be excluded from consolidation [in Companies Act group accounts] if its inclusion is not material for the purpose of giving a true and fair view; but two or more undertakings may be excluded only if they are not material taken together.

(3) In addition, a subsidiary undertaking may be excluded from consolidation [in Companies Act group accounts] where—

(a) severe long-term restrictions substantially hinder the exercise of the rights of the parent company over the assets or management of that undertaking, or

(b) the information necessary for the preparation of group accounts cannot be obtained without disproportionate expense or undue delay, or

(c) the interest of the parent company is held exclusively with a view to subsequent resale ...

The reference in paragraph (a) to the rights of the parent company and the reference in paragraph (c) to the interest of the parent company are, respectively, to rights and interests held by or attributed to the company for the purposes of section 258 (definition of "parent undertaking") in the absence of which it would not be the parent company.

(4) ...

[(5) A parent company is exempt from the requirement to prepare group accounts if under subsection (2) or (3) all of its subsidiary undertakings could be excluded from consolidation in Companies Act group accounts.]]

[364]

NOTES

Repealed as noted to s 1 at **[309]**.

Inserted as noted to s 228 at **[363]**.

Sub-ss (1), (3): words in square brackets inserted, and words omitted repealed, by the Companies Act 1985 (International Accounting Standards and Other Accounting Amendments) Regulations 2004, SI 2004/2947, regs 3, 5(a), Sch 1, paras 1, 7(a), (b), in relation to companies' financial years which begin on or after 1 January 2005.

Sub-s (2): words in square brackets inserted by SI 2004/2947, reg 3, Sch 1, paras 1, 7(b), in relation to companies' financial years which begin on or after 1 January 2005.

Sub-s (4): repealed by SI 2004/2947, reg 5(b), in relation to companies' financial years which begin on or after 1 January 2005.

Sub-s (5): substituted by SI 2004/2947, reg 3, Sch 1, paras 1, 7(c), in relation to companies' financial years which begin on or after 1 January 2005.

[230 Treatment of individual profit and loss account where group accounts prepared

(1) The following provisions apply with respect to the individual profit and loss account of a parent company where—

(*a*) *the company is required to prepare and does prepare group accounts in accordance with this Act, and*

(*b*) *the notes to the company's individual balance sheet show the company's profit or loss for the financial year determined in accordance with this Act.*

(2) *[Where the company prepares Companies Act individual accounts,] the profit and loss account need not contain the information specified in paragraphs 52 to 57 of Schedule 4 (information supplementing the profit and loss account).*

(3) *The profit and loss account must be approved in accordance with section 233(1) (approval by board of directors) but may be omitted from the company's annual accounts for the purposes of the other provisions below in this Chapter.*

(4) *The exemption conferred by this section is conditional upon its being disclosed in the company's annual accounts that the exemption applies.]*

[365]

NOTES

Repealed as noted to s 1 at **[309]**.
Inserted by the Companies Act 1989, s 5(4).
Sub-s (2): words in square brackets inserted by the Companies Act 1985 (International Accounting Standards and Other Accounting Amendments) Regulations 2004, SI 2004/2947, reg 3, Sch 1, paras 1, 8, in relation to companies' financial years which begin on or after 1 January 2005.

[231 Disclosure required in notes to accounts: related undertakings

(1) *The information specified in Schedule 5 shall be given in notes to a company's annual accounts.*

(2) *Where the company is not required to prepare group accounts, the information specified in Part I of that Schedule shall be given; and where the company is required to prepare group accounts, the information specified in Part II of that Schedule shall be given.*

(3) *The information required by Schedule 5 need not be disclosed with respect to an undertaking which—*

(*a*) *is established under the law of a country outside the United Kingdom, or*

(*b*) *carries on business outside the United Kingdom,*

if in the opinion of the directors of the company the disclosure would be seriously prejudicial to the business of that undertaking, or to the business of the company or any of its subsidiary undertakings, and the Secretary of State agrees that the information need not be disclosed.

This subsection does not apply in relation to the information required under [paragraph … 6, 9A, 20 or 28A] of that Schedule.

(4) *Where advantage is taken of subsection (3), that fact shall be stated in a note to the company's annual accounts.*

(5) *If the directors of the company are of the opinion that the number of undertakings in respect of which the company is required to disclose information under any provision of Schedule 5 to this Act is such that compliance with that provision would result in information of excessive length being given, the information need only be given in respect of—*

(*a*) *the undertakings whose results or financial position, in the opinion of the directors, principally affected the figures shown in the company's annual accounts, and*

(*b*) *undertakings excluded from consolidation under section 229(3) …*

…

(6) *If advantage is taken of subsection (5)—*

(*a*) *there shall be included in the notes to the company's annual accounts a statement that the information is given only with respect to such undertakings as are mentioned in that subsection, and*

(*b*) *the full information (both that which is disclosed in the notes to the accounts and that which is not) shall be annexed to the company's next annual return.*

For this purpose the "next annual return" means that next delivered to the registrar after the accounts in question have been approved under section 233.

(7) *If a company fails to comply with subsection (6)(b), the company and every officer of it who is in default is liable to a fine and, for continued contravention, to a daily default fine.]*

[366]

NOTES

Repealed as noted to s 1 at **[309]**.

Inserted by the Companies Act 1989, s 6(1).

Sub-s (3): words in square brackets substituted by the Partnerships and Unlimited Companies (Accounts) Regulations 1993, SI 1993/1820, reg 11(1), subject to transitional provisions in reg 12 thereof; number omitted repealed in relation to any financial year ending on or after 2 February 1996, by the Companies Act 1985 (Miscellaneous Accounting Amendments) Regulations 1996, SI 1996/189, regs 15(1), 16(1), for a transitional provision see reg 16(2) of the 1996 Regulations.

Sub-s (5): words omitted in the first place repealed by the Companies Act 1985 (International Accounting Standards and Other Accounting Amendments) Regulations 2004, SI 2004/2947, reg 15, Sch 7, Pt 1, paras 1, 5, in relation to companies' financial years which begin on or after 1 January 2005; words omitted in the second place repealed in relation to any financial year ending on or after 2 February 1996, by SI 1996/189, regs 15(1), 16(1); for a transitional provision see reg 16(2) of the 1996 Regulations.

[231A Disclosure required in notes to annual accounts: particulars of staff

(1) The following information with respect to the employees of the company must be given in notes to the company's annual accounts—

(a) the average number of persons employed by the company in the financial year, and

(b) the average number of persons so employed within each category of persons employed by the company.

(2) The average number required by subsection (1)(a) or (b) is determined by dividing the relevant annual number by the number of months in the financial year.

(3) The relevant annual number is determined by ascertaining for each month in the financial year—

(a) for the purposes of subsection (1)(a), the number of persons employed under contracts of service by the company in that month (whether throughout the month or not);

(b) for the purposes of subsection (1)(b), the number of persons in the category in question of persons so employed;

and, in either case, adding together all the monthly numbers.

(4) In respect of all persons employed by the company during the financial year who are taken into account in determining the relevant annual number for the purposes of subsection (1)(a) there must also be stated the aggregate amounts respectively of—

(a) wages and salaries paid or payable in respect of that year to those persons;

(b) social security costs incurred by the company on their behalf; and

(c) other pension costs so incurred.

This does not apply in so far as those amounts, or any of them, are stated elsewhere in the company's accounts.

(5) For the purposes of subsection (1)(b), the categories of person employed by the company are such as the directors may select, having regard to the manner in which the company's activities are organised.

(6) This section applies in relation to group accounts as if the undertakings included in the consolidation were a single company.

(7) In this section "social security costs" and "pension costs" have the same meaning as in Schedule 4 (see paragraph 94(1) and (2) of that Schedule).]

[366A]

NOTES

Commencement: 12 November 2004 (in relation to companies' financial years which begin on or after 1 January 2005).

Repealed as noted to s 1 at **[309]**.

Inserted by the Companies Act 1985 (International Accounting Standards and Other Accounting Amendments) Regulations 2004, SI 2004/2947, reg 3, Sch 1, paras 1, 9, in relation to companies' financial years which begin on or after 1 January 2005.

[232 Disclosure required in notes to accounts: emoluments and other benefits of directors and others

[(1) The information specified in Schedule 6 shall be given in notes to a company's annual accounts, save that the information specified in paragraphs 2–14 in Part I of Schedule 6 shall be given only in the case of a company which is not a quoted company.]

(2) In that Schedule—

Part I relates to the emoluments of directors (including emoluments waived), pensions of directors and past directors, compensation for loss of office to directors and past directors and sums paid to third parties in respect of directors' services,

Part II relates to loans, quasi-loans and other dealings in favour of directors and connected persons, and

Part III relates to transactions, arrangements and agreements made by the company or a subsidiary undertaking for officers of the company other than directors.

(3) It is the duty of any director of a company, and any person who is or has at any time in the preceding five years been an officer of the company, to give notice to the company of such matters relating to himself as may be necessary for the purposes of Part I of Schedule 6.

(4) A person who makes default in complying with subsection (3) commits an offence and is liable to a fine.]

[367]

NOTES

Repealed as noted to s 1 at **[309]**.

Inserted by the Companies Act 1989, s 6(3).

Sub-s (1): substituted by the Directors' Remuneration Report Regulations 2002, SI 2002/1986, reg 2, with effect as respects companies' financial years ending on or after 31 December 2002.

[Approval and signing of accounts

233 Approval and signing of accounts

(1) A company's annual accounts shall be approved by the board of directors and signed on behalf of the board by a director of the company.

(2) The signature shall be on the company's balance sheet.

(3) Every copy of the balance sheet which is laid before the company in general meeting, or which is otherwise circulated, published or issued, shall state the name of the person who signed the balance sheet on behalf of the board.

(4) The copy of the company's balance sheet which is delivered to the registrar shall be signed on behalf of the board by a director of the company.

(5) If annual accounts are approved which do not comply with the requirements of this Act [(or, where applicable, of Article 4 of the IAS Regulation)], every director of the company who is party to their approval and who knows that they do not comply or is reckless as to whether they comply is guilty of an offence and liable to a fine.

For this purpose every director of the company at the time the accounts are approved shall be taken to be a party to their approval unless he shows that he took all reasonable steps to prevent their being approved.

(6) If a copy of the balance sheet—

(a) is laid before the company, or otherwise circulated, published or issued, without the balance sheet having been signed as required by this section or without the required statement of the signatory's name being included, or

(b) is delivered to the registrar without being signed as required by this section,

the company and every officer of it who is in default is guilty of an offence and liable to a fine.]

[368]

NOTES

Repealed as noted to s 1 at **[309]**.

Inserted, together with the preceding heading, by the Companies Act 1989, s 7.

Sub-s (5): words in square brackets inserted by the Companies Act 1985 (International Accounting Standards and Other Accounting Amendments) Regulations 2004, SI 2004/2947, reg 3, Sch 1, paras 1, 10, in relation to companies' financial years which begin on or after 1 January 2005.

[Directors' report

234 Duty to prepare directors' report

(1) The directors of a company shall for each financial year prepare a report (a "directors' report") complying with the general requirements of section 234ZZA and containing—

(a) the business review specified in section 234ZZB, and

(b) if section 234ZA applies to the report, the statement as to disclosure of information to auditors required by that section.

(2) For a financial year in which—

(a) the company is a parent company, and

(b) the directors of the company prepare group accounts,

the directors' report must be a consolidated report (a "group directors' report") relating, to the extent specified in the following provisions of this Part, to the company and its subsidiary undertakings included in the consolidation.

(3) A group directors' report may, where appropriate, give greater emphasis to the matters that are significant to the company and its subsidiary undertakings included in the consolidation, taken as a whole.

(4) …

(5) If a directors' report does not comply with the provisions of this Part relating to the preparation and contents of the report, every director of the company who—

(a) knew that it did not comply or was reckless as to whether it complied, and

(b) failed to take all reasonable steps to secure compliance with the provision in question,

is guilty of an offence and liable to a fine.]

[369]

NOTES

Repealed as noted to s 1 at **[309]**.

Inserted, together with the preceding heading and s 234A, by the Companies Act 1989, s 8(1).

Substituted by new ss 234, 234ZZA, 234ZZB, by the Companies Act 1985 (Operating and Financial Review and Directors' Report etc) Regulations 2005, SI 2005/1011, reg 2, in relation to companies' financial years which begin on or after 1 April 2005.

Sub-s (4): repealed by the Companies Act 1985 (Operating and Financial Review) (Repeal) Regulations 2005, SI 2005/3442, reg 2(2)(a), Sch 1, para 1.

[234ZZA Directors' report: general requirements

(1) The directors' report for a financial year must state—

(a) the names of the persons who, at any time during the financial year, were directors of the company,

(b) the principal activities of the company in the course of the year, and

(c) the amount (if any) that the directors recommend should be paid by way of dividend.

(2) In relation to a group directors' report subsection (1)(b) has effect as if the reference to the company was a reference to the company and its subsidiary undertakings included in the consolidation.

(3) The report must also comply with Schedule 7 as regards the disclosure of the matters mentioned there.

(4) In Schedule 7—

Part 1 relates to matters of a general nature, including changes in asset values, directors' shareholdings and other interests and contributions for political and charitable purposes;

Part 2 relates to the acquisition by a company of its own shares or a charge on them;

Part 3 relates to the employment, training and advancement of disabled persons;

Part 5 relates to the involvement of employees in the affairs, policy and performance of the company;
Part 6 relates to the company's policy and practice on the payment of creditors;
[Part 7 specifies information to be disclosed by certain publicly- traded companies].

[(5) A directors' report shall also contain any necessary explanatory material with regard to information that is required to be included in the report by Part 7 of Schedule 7.]

[369ZA]

NOTES

Commencement: 22 March 2005 (in relation to companies' financial years which begin on or after 1 April 2005).

Repealed as noted to s 1 at **[309]**. Note that this section is also amended by the 2006 Act (see below).

Substituted as noted to s 234 at **[369]**.

Sub-s (4): words in square brackets inserted by the Companies Act 2006, s 992(1), (3), (6), as from a day to be appointed, in relation to directors' reports for financial years beginning on or after 20 May 2006.

Sub-s (5): added by the Companies Act 2006, s 992(1), (4), (6), as from a day to be appointed, in relation to directors' reports for financial years beginning on or after 20 May 2006.

[234ZZB Directors' report: business review

(1) The directors' report for a financial year must contain—
- *(a) a fair review of the business of the company, and*
- *(b) a description of the principal risks and uncertainties facing the company.*

(2) The review required is a balanced and comprehensive analysis of—
- *(a) the development and performance of the business of the company during the financial year, and*
- *(b) the position of the company at the end of that year,*

consistent with the size and complexity of the business.

(3) The review must, to the extent necessary for an understanding of the development, performance or position of the business of the company, include—
- *(a) analysis using financial key performance indicators, and*
- *(b) where appropriate, analysis using other key performance indicators, including information relating to environmental matters and employee matters.*

(4) The review must, where appropriate, include references to, and additional explanations of, amounts included in the annual accounts of the company.

(5) In this section, "key performance indicators" means factors by reference to which the development, performance or position of the business of the company can be measured effectively.

(6) In relation to a group directors' report this section has effect as if the references to the company were references to the company and its subsidiary undertakings included in the consolidation.]

[369ZB]

NOTES

Commencement: 22 March 2005 (in relation to companies' financial years which begin on or after 1 April 2005).

Repealed as noted to s 1 at **[309]**.

Substituted as noted to s 234 at **[369]**.

[234ZA Statement as to disclosure of information to auditors

(1) This section applies to a directors' report unless the directors have taken advantage of the exemption conferred by section 249A(1) or 249AA(1).

(2) The report must contain a statement to the effect that, in the case of each of the persons who are directors at the time when the report is approved under section 234A, the following applies—
- *(a) so far as the director is aware, there is no relevant audit information of which the company's auditors are unaware, and*
- *(b) he has taken all the steps that he ought to have taken as a director in order to*

make himself aware of any relevant audit information and to establish that the company's auditors are aware of that information.

(3) In subsection (2) "relevant audit information" means information needed by the company's auditors in connection with preparing their report.

(4) For the purposes of subsection (2) a director has taken all the steps that he ought to have taken as a director in order to do the things mentioned in paragraph (b) of that subsection if he has—

(a) made such enquiries of his fellow directors and of the company's auditors for that purpose, and

(b) taken such other steps (if any) for that purpose,

as were required by his duty as a director of the company to exercise due care, skill and diligence.

(5) In determining for the purposes of subsection (2) the extent of that duty in the case of a particular director, the following considerations (in particular) are relevant—

(a) the knowledge, skill and experience that may reasonably be expected of a person carrying out the same functions as are carried out by the director in relation to the company, and

(b) (so far as they exceed what may reasonably be so expected) the knowledge, skill and experience that the director in fact has.

(6) Where a directors' report containing the statement required by subsection (2) is approved under section 234A but the statement is false, every director of the company who—

(a) knew that the statement was false, or was reckless as to whether it was false, and

(b) failed to take reasonable steps to prevent the report from being approved,

is guilty of an offence and liable to imprisonment or a fine, or both.]

[369A]

NOTES

Commencement: 6 April 2005.

Repealed as noted to s 1 at **[309]**.

Inserted by the Companies (Audit, Investigations and Community Enterprise) Act 2004, s 9(1), (3) (except in relation to any report of the directors of a company prepared under s 234 concerning a financial year beginning before 1 April 2005 or ending before 6 April 2005; see the Companies (Audit, Investigations and Community Enterprise) Act 2004 (Commencement) and Companies Act 1989 (Commencement No 18) Order 2004, SI 2004/3322, art 4).

[234A Approval and signing of directors' report

(1) The directors' report shall be approved by the board of directors and signed on behalf of the board by a director or the secretary of the company.

(2) Every copy of the directors' report which is laid before the company in general meeting, or which is otherwise circulated, published or issued, shall state the name of the person who signed it on behalf of the board.

(3) The copy of the directors' report which is delivered to the registrar shall be signed on behalf of the board by a director or the secretary of the company.

(4) If a copy of the directors' report—

(a) is laid before the company, or otherwise circulated, published or issued, without the report having been signed as required by this section or without the required statement of the signatory's name being included, or

(b) is delivered to the registrar without being signed as required by this section,

the company and every officer of it who is in default is guilty of an offence and liable to a fine.]

[370]

NOTES

Repealed as noted to s 1 at **[309]**.

Inserted as noted to s 234 at **[369]**.

234AA, 234AB *(Inserted by the Companies Act 1985 (Operating and Financial Review and Directors' Report etc) Regulations 2005, SI 2005/1011, reg 8, in relation to companies'* *financial years which begin on or after 1 April 2005; repealed by the Companies Act 1985 (Operating and Financial Review) (Repeal) Regulations 2005, SI 2005/3442, reg 2(1), (2)(a), Sch 1, paras 2, 3.)*

[Quoted companies: directors' remuneration report

234B Duty to prepare directors' remuneration report

(1) The directors of a quoted company shall for each financial year prepare a directors' remuneration report which shall contain the information specified in Schedule 7A and comply with any requirement of that Schedule as to how information is to be set out in the report.

(2) In Schedule 7A—
Part 1 is introductory,
Part 2 relates to information about remuneration committees, performance related remuneration and liabilities in respect of directors' contracts,
Part 3 relates to detailed information about directors' remuneration (information included under Part 3 is required to be reported on by the auditors, see section 235), and
Part 4 contains interpretative and supplementary provisions.

(3) In the case of any failure to comply with the provisions of this Part as to the preparation of a directors' remuneration report and the contents of the report, every person who was a director of the quoted company immediately before the end of the period for laying and delivering accounts and reports for the financial year in question is guilty of an offence and liable to a fine.

(4) In proceedings against a person for an offence under subsection (3) it is a defence for him to prove that he took all reasonable steps for securing compliance with the requirements in question.

(5) It is the duty of any director of a company, and any person who has at any time in the preceding five years been a director of the company, to give notice to the company of such matters relating to himself as may be necessary for the purposes of Parts 2 and 3 of Schedule 7A.

(6) A person who makes default in complying with subsection (5) commits an offence and is liable to a fine.]

[370A]

NOTES

Commencement: 1 August 2002 (with effect as respects companies' financial years ending on or after 31 December 2002).

Repealed as noted to s 1 at **[309]**.

Inserted, together with the preceding heading and s 234C, by the Directors' Remuneration Report Regulations 2002, SI 2002/1986, reg 3, with effect as respects companies' financial years ending on or after 31 December 2002.

[234C Approval and signing of directors' remuneration report

(1) The directors' remuneration report shall be approved by the board of directors and signed on behalf of the board by a director or the secretary of the company.

(2) Every copy of the directors' remuneration report which is laid before the company in general meeting, or which is otherwise circulated, published or issued, shall state the name of the person who signed it on behalf of the board.

(3) The copy of the directors' remuneration report which is delivered to the registrar shall be signed on behalf of the board by a director or the secretary of the company.

(4) If a copy of the directors' remuneration report—
(a) is laid before the company, or otherwise circulated, published or issued, without the report having been signed as required by this section or without the required statement of the signatory's name being included, or
(b) is delivered to the registrar without being signed as required by this section,
the company and every officer of it who is in default is guilty of an offence and liable to a fine.]

[370B]

NOTES

Commencement: 1 August 2002 (with effect as respects companies' financial years ending on or after 31 December 2002).

Repealed as noted to s 1 at **[309]**.

Inserted as noted to s 234B at **[370A]**.

[Auditors' report

235 Auditors' report

(1) A company's auditors shall make a report to the company's members on all annual accounts of the company of which copies are to be laid before the company in general meeting during their tenure of office.

[(1A) The auditors' report must include—
- *(a) an introduction identifying the annual accounts that are the subject of the audit and the financial reporting framework that has been applied in their preparation;*
- *(b) a description of the scope of the audit identifying the auditing standards in accordance with which the audit was conducted.*

(1B) The report must state clearly whether in the auditors' opinion the annual accounts have been properly prepared in accordance with the requirements of this Act (and, where applicable, Article 4 of the IAS Regulation).

(2) The report must state in particular whether the annual accounts give a true and fair view, in accordance with the relevant financial reporting framework—
- *(a) in the case of an individual balance sheet, of the state of affairs of the company as at the end of the financial year,*
- *(b) in the case of an individual profit and loss account, of the profit or loss of the company for the financial year,*
- *(c) in the case of group accounts, of the state of affairs as at the end of the financial year and of the profit or loss for the financial year, of the undertakings included in the consolidation as a whole, so far as concerns members of the company.*

(2A) The auditors' report—
- *(a) must be either unqualified or qualified, and*
- *(b) must include a reference to any matters to which the auditors wish to draw attention by way of emphasis without qualifying the report.]*

[(3) The auditors must state in their report whether in their opinion the information given in the directors' report for the financial year for which the annual accounts are prepared is consistent with those accounts.]

[(3A) ...]

[(4) If a directors' remuneration report is prepared for the financial year for which the annual accounts are prepared the auditors shall in their report
- *(a) report to the company's members on the auditable part of the directors' remuneration report, and*
- *(b) state whether in their opinion that part of the directors' remuneration report has been properly prepared in accordance with this Act.*

(5) For the purposes of this Part, "the auditable part" of a directors' remuneration report is the part containing the information required by Part 3 of Schedule 7A.]]

[371]

NOTES

Repealed as noted to s 1 at **[309]**.

Inserted, together with the preceding heading and ss 236, 237, by the Companies Act 1989, s 9.

Sub-ss (1A), (1B), (2), (2A): substituted, for original sub-s (2), by the Companies Act 1985 (International Accounting Standards and Other Accounting Amendments) Regulations 2004, SI 2004/2947, reg 6, in relation to companies' financial years which begin on or after 1 January 2005.

Sub-s (3): substituted by the Companies Act 1985 (Operating and Financial Review and Directors' Report etc) Regulations 2005, SI 2005/1011, reg 3, in relation to companies' financial years which begin on or after 1 April 2005.

Sub-s (3A): inserted by SI 2005/1011, reg 10, in relation to companies' financial years which begin on or after 1 April 2005; repealed by the Companies Act 1985 (Operating and Financial Review) (Repeal) Regulations 2005, SI 2005/3442, reg 2(2)(a), Sch 1, para 4.

Sub-ss (4), (5): added by the Directors' Remuneration Report Regulations 2002, SI 2002/1986, reg 4, with effect as respects companies' financial years ending on or after 31 December 2002.

[236 Signature of auditors' report

(1) The auditors' report shall state the names of the auditors and be signed [and dated] by them.

(2) Every copy of the auditors' report which is laid before the company in general meeting, or which is otherwise circulated, published or issued, shall state the names of the auditors.

(3) The copy of the auditors' report which is delivered to the registrar shall state the names of the auditors and be signed by them.

(4) If a copy of the auditors' report—

- *(a) is laid before the company, or otherwise circulated, published or issued, without the required statement of the auditors' names, or*
- *(b) is delivered to the registrar without the required statement of the auditors' names or without being signed as required by this section,*

the company and every officer of it who is in default is guilty of an offence and liable to a fine.

(5) References in this section to signature by the auditors are, where the office of auditor is held by a body corporate or partnership, to signature in the name of the body corporate or partnership by a person authorised to sign on its behalf.]

[372]

NOTES

Repealed as noted to s 1 at **[309]**.
Inserted as noted to s 235 at **[371]**.
Sub-s (1): words in square brackets inserted by the Companies Act 1985 (International Accounting Standards and Other Accounting Amendments) Regulations 2004, SI 2004/2947, reg 7, in relation to companies' financial years which begin on or after 1 January 2005.

[237 Duties of auditors

(1) A company's auditors shall, in preparing their report, carry out such investigations as will enable them to form an opinion as to—

- *(a) whether proper accounting records have been kept by the company and proper returns adequate for their audit have been received from branches not visited by them, and*
- *(b) whether the company's individual accounts are in agreement with the accounting records and returns, [and*
- *(c) (in the case of a quoted company) whether the auditable part of the company's directors' remuneration report is in agreement with the accounting records and returns.]*

(2) If the auditors are of opinion that proper accounting records have not been kept, or that proper returns adequate for their audit have not been received from branches not visited by them, or if the company's individual accounts are not in agreement with the accounting records and returns, [or if in the case of a quoted company the auditable part of its directors' remuneration report is not in agreement with the accounting records and returns,] the auditors shall state that fact in their report.

(3) If the auditors fail to obtain all the information and explanations which, to the best of their knowledge and belief, are necessary for the purposes of their audit, they shall state that fact in their report.

[(4) If—

- *(a) the requirements of Schedule 6 (disclosure of information: emoluments and other benefits of directors and others) are not complied with in the annual accounts, or*
- *(b) where a directors' remuneration report is required to be prepared, the requirements of Part 3 of Schedule 7A (directors' remuneration report) are not complied with in that report,*

the auditors shall include in their report, so far as they are reasonably able to do so, a statement giving the required particulars.]

[(4A) *If the directors of the company have taken advantage of the exemption conferred by section 248 (exemption for small and medium-sized groups from the need to prepare group accounts) and in the auditors' opinion they were not entitled so to do, the auditors shall state that fact in their report.*]]

[373]

NOTES

Repealed as noted to s 1 at **[309]**.

Inserted as noted to s 235 at **[371]**.

Sub-s (1): para (c) and the word immediately preceding it added by the Directors' Remuneration Report Regulations 2002, SI 2002/1986, reg 5, with effect as respects companies' financial years ending on or after 31 December 2002.

Sub-s (2): words in square brackets inserted by SI 2002/1986, reg 10(1), (2), with effect as respects companies' financial years ending on or after 31 December 2002.

Sub-s (4): substituted by SI 2002/1986, reg 6, with effect as respects companies' financial years ending on or after 31 December 2002.

Sub-s (4A): added by the Companies Act 1985 (Miscellaneous Accounting Amendments) Regulations 1996, SI 1996/189, regs 6, 16(5), in relation to any annual accounts of a company which are approved by the board of directors on or after 2 February 1996.

[Publication of accounts and reports

238 Persons entitled to receive copies of accounts and reports

(1) [*A copy of each of the documents mentioned in subsection (1A)*] *shall be sent to—*

(*a*) *every member of the company,*

(*b*) *every holder of the company's debentures, and*

(*c*) *every person who is entitled to receive notice of general meetings,*

not less than 21 days before the date of the meeting at which copies of those documents are to be laid in accordance with section 241.

[(1A) *Those documents are—*

(*a*) *the company's annual accounts for the financial year,*

(*b*) *the directors' report for that financial year,*

[(*ba*) ...]

(*c*) *(in the case of a quoted company) the directors' remuneration report for that financial year, and*

[(*d*) *the auditors' report on those accounts and that directors' report and (in the case of a quoted company) on ... the auditable part of that directors' remuneration report.*]]

(2) *Copies need not be sent—*

(*a*) *to a person who is not entitled to receive notices of general meetings and of whose address the company is unaware, or*

(*b*) *to more than one of the joint holders of shares or debentures none of whom is entitled to receive such notices, or*

(*c*) *in the case of joint holders of shares or debentures some of whom are, and some not, entitled to receive such notices, to those who are not so entitled.*

(3) *In the case of a company not having a share capital, copies need not be sent to anyone who is not entitled to receive notices of general meetings of the company.*

(4) *If copies are sent less than 21 days before the date of the meeting, they shall, notwithstanding that fact, be deemed to have been duly sent if it is so agreed by all the members entitled to attend and vote at the meeting.*

[(4A)–(4E) ...]

(5) *If default is made in complying with this section, the company and every officer of it who is in default is guilty of an offence and liable to a fine.*

(6) *Where copies are sent out under this section over a period of days, references elsewhere in this Act to the day on which copies are sent out shall be construed as references to the last day of that period.*]

[374]

NOTES

Repealed as noted to s 1 at **[309]**.

Inserted, together with the preceding heading and ss 239, 240, by the Companies Act 1989, s 10.

Sub-s (1): words in square brackets substituted by the Directors' Remuneration Report Regulations 2002, SI 2002/1986, reg 10(1), (3), with effect as respects companies' financial years ending on or after 31 December 2002.

Sub-s (1A): inserted by SI 2002/1986, reg 10(1), (4), with effect as respects companies' financial years ending on or after 31 December 2002; para (ba) inserted, and para (d) substituted, by the Companies Act 1985 (Operating and Financial Review and Directors' Report etc) Regulations 2005, SI 2005/1011, reg 19, Schedule, paras 1, 2, in relation to companies' financial years which begin on or after 1 April 2005; para (ba) repealed and the words omitted from para (d) repealed by the Companies Act 1985 (Operating and Financial Review) (Repeal) Regulations 2005, SI 2005/3442, reg 2(2)(a), Sch 1, para 5.

Sub-ss (4A)–(4E): inserted by the Companies Act 1985 (Electronic Communications) Order 2000, SI 2000/3373, SI 2000/3373, art 12; repealed, subject to transitional provisions as noted below, by the Companies Act 2006, s 1295, Sch 16.

Transitional provisions: the Companies Act 2006 (Commencement No 1, Transitional Provisions and Savings) Order 2006, SI 2006/3428, Sch 5, paras 3–5 provide as follows—

3 False or misleading statements in reports

Section 463 of the Companies Act 2006 (liability for false or misleading statements in reports) does not apply to a directors' report, directors' remuneration report or summary financial statement first sent to members and others under section 238 or 251 of the 1985 Act, or Article 246 or 259 of the 1986 Order, before 20th January 2007.

4 Existing agreements to communication by electronic means

(1) This paragraph applies where an address has been notified by a person to a company for the purposes of—

(a) section 238(4A) or 239(2A) of the 1985 Act or Article 246(4A) or 247(2A) of the 1986 Order (sending or supply of accounts and reports by means of electronic communications);

(b) section 251(2A) of the 1985 Act or Article 259(2A) of the 1986 Order (sending of summary financial statement by means of electronic communications); or

(c) section 369(4A) or 379A(2B) of the 1985 Act or Article 377(5) or 387A(2B) of the 1986 Order (notice of meeting given by means of electronic communications).

(2) Any such notification that is in force immediately before 20th January 2007 shall have effect on and after that date, in relation to the matters to which it relates, as an agreement under paragraph 6(a) of Schedule 5 to the Companies Act 2006 (agreement to accept documents or information in electronic form) and as an address specified under paragraph 7(1) of Schedule 5 to that Act (address for communications in electronic form).

5.—(1) This paragraph applies where an agreement between a person and a company has been entered into for the purposes of—

(a) section 238(4B) of the 1985 Act or Article 246(4B) of the 1986 Order (sending or supply of copies of accounts and reports by means of website);

(b) section 251(2B) of the 1985 Act or Article 259(2B) of the 1986 Order (sending of summary financial statement by means of website); or

(c) section 369(4B) or 379A(2C) of the 1985 Act or Article 377(6) or 387A(2C) of the 1986 Order (notice of meeting given by means of website).

(2) Any such agreement that is in force immediately before 20th January 2007 shall have effect on and after that date, in relation to the matters to which it relates, as an agreement under paragraph 9(a) of Schedule 5 to the Companies Act 2006 (agreement to accept documents or information by means of a website).

[239 Right to demand copies of accounts and reports

(1) Any member of a company and any holder of a company's debentures is entitled to be furnished, on demand and without charge, [with a copy of—

(a) the company's last annual accounts,

(b) the last directors' report,

[(ba) …]

(c) (in the case of a quoted company) the last directors' remuneration report, and

[(d) the auditors' report on those accounts and that directors' report and (in the case of a quoted company) on … the auditable part of that directors' remuneration report.]]

(2) The entitlement under this section is to a single copy of those documents, but that is in addition to any copy to which a person may be entitled under section 238.

[(2A) Any obligation by virtue of subsection (1) to furnish a person with a document may be complied with by using electronic communications for sending that document to such address as may for the time being be notified to the company by that person for that purpose.

(2B) A company may, notwithstanding any provision to the contrary in its articles, take advantage of subsection (2A).]

(3) If a demand under this section is not complied with within seven days, the company and every officer of it who is in default is guilty of an offence and liable to a fine and, for continued contravention, to a daily default fine.

(4) If in proceedings for such an offence the issue arises whether a person had already been furnished with a copy of the relevant document under this section, it is for the defendant to prove that he had.]

[375]

NOTES

Repealed as noted to s 1 at **[309]**.

Inserted as noted to s 238 at **[374]**.

Sub-s (1): words in first (outer) pair of square brackets substituted by the Directors' Remuneration Report Regulations 2002, SI 2002/1986, reg 10(1), (6), with effect as respects companies' financial years ending on or after 31 December 2002; para (ba) inserted, and para (d) substituted, by the Companies Act 1985 (Operating and Financial Review and Directors' Report etc) Regulations 2005, SI 2005/1011, reg 19, Schedule, paras 1, 3, in relation to companies' financial years which begin on or after 1 April 2005; para (ba) and the words omitted from para (d) repealed by the Companies Act 1985 (Operating and Financial Review) (Repeal) Regulations 2005, SI 2005/3442, reg 2(2)(a), Sch 1, para 6.

Sub-ss (2A), (2B): inserted by the Companies Act 1985 (Electronic Communications) Order 2000, SI 2000/3373, art 13; repealed by the Companies Act 2006, s 1295, Sch 16, subject to a saving for limited liability partnerships (for transitional provisions see the note to s 238 at **[374]**).

[240 Requirements in connection with publication of accounts

(1) If a company publishes any of its statutory accounts, they must be accompanied by the relevant auditors' report under section 235 [or, as the case may be, the relevant report made for the purposes of section 249A(2)].

(2) A company which is required to prepare group accounts for a financial year shall not publish its statutory individual accounts for that year without also publishing with them its statutory group accounts.

(3) If a company publishes non-statutory accounts, it shall publish with them a statement indicating—

(a) that they are not the company's statutory accounts,

(b) whether statutory accounts dealing with any financial year with which the non-statutory accounts purport to deal have been delivered to the registrar,

(c) whether the company's auditors have made a report under section 235 on the statutory accounts for any such financial year [and, if no such report has been made, whether the company's reporting accountant has made a report for the purposes of section 249A(2) on the statutory accounts for any financial year], … [and]

[(d) whether any such auditors' report—

(i) was qualified or unqualified, or included a reference to any matters to which the auditors drew attention by way of emphasis without qualifying the report, or

(ii) contained a statement under section 237(2) or (3) (accounting records or returns inadequate, accounts not agreeing with records and returns or failure to obtain necessary information and explanations); and

(e) whether any report made for the purposes of section 249A(2) was qualified;]

and it shall not publish with the non-statutory accounts any auditors' report under section 235 [or any report made for the purposes of section 249A(2)].

(4) For the purposes of this section a company shall be regarded as publishing a document if it publishes, issues or circulates it or otherwise makes it available for public inspection in a manner calculated to invite members of the public generally, or any class of members of the public, to read it.

(5) *References in this section to a company's statutory accounts are to its individual or group accounts for a financial year as required to be delivered to the registrar under section 242; and references to the publication by a company of "non-statutory accounts" are to the publication of—*

(*a*) *any balance sheet or profit and loss account relating to, or purporting to deal with, a financial year of the company, or*

(*b*) *an account in any form purporting to be a balance sheet or profit and loss account for the group consisting of the company and its subsidiary undertakings relating to, or purporting to deal with, a financial year of the company,*

otherwise than as part of the company's statutory accounts.

(6) *A company which contravenes any provision of this section, and any officer of it who is in default, is guilty of an offence and liable to a fine.]*

[376]

NOTES

Repealed as noted to s 1 at **[309]**.

Inserted as noted to s 238 at **[374]**.

Sub-s (1): words in square brackets added by the Companies Act 1985 (Audit Exemption) Regulations 1994, SI 1994/1935, reg 4, Sch 1, para 1(1), subject to transitional provisions contained in reg 6 thereof; repealed by the Companies Act 2006, s 1175, Sch 9, Pt 1, para 1(a), as from a day to be appointed under s 1300(2) of that Act.

Sub-s (3): words in first and final pairs of square brackets inserted by SI 1994/1935, reg 4, Sch 1, para 1(1), (3)(a), (c), subject to transitional provisions contained in reg 6 thereof, repealed by the Companies Act 2006, s 1175, Sch 9, Pt 1, para 1(b), (e), as from a day to be appointed under s 1300(2) of that Act; word omitted from para (c) repealed by the Companies Act 1985 (International Accounting Standards and Other Accounting Amendments) Regulations 2004, SI 2004/2947, reg 8(a), in relation to companies' financial years which begin on or after 1 January 2005; word "and" at the end of para (c) added by the Companies Act 2006, s 1175, Sch 9, Pt 1, para 1(c), as from a day to be appointed under s 1300(2) of that Act; paras (d), (e) substituted for original para (d) by SI 2004/2947, reg 8(b), in relation to companies' financial years which begin on or after 1 January 2005; para (e) and the word immediately preceding it repealed by the Companies Act 2006, s 1175, Sch 9, Pt 1, para 1(d), as from a day to be appointed under s 1300(2) of that Act.

[Laying and delivering of accounts and reports

241 Accounts and reports to be laid before company in general meeting

(*1*) *The directors of a company shall in respect of each financial year lay before the company in general meeting [copies of—*

(*a*) *the company's annual accounts,*

(*b*) *the directors' report,*

[(ba) …]

(*c*) *(in the case of a quoted company) the directors' remuneration report, and*

[(d) the auditors' report on those accounts and that directors' report and (in the case of a quoted company) on … the auditable part of that directors' remuneration report.]]

(*2*) *If the requirements of subsection (1) are not complied with before the end of the period allowed for laying and delivering accounts and reports, every person who immediately before the end of that period was a director of the company is guilty of an offence and liable to a fine and, for continued contravention, to a daily default fine.*

(*3*) *It is a defence for a person charged with such an offence to prove that he took all reasonable steps for securing that those requirements would be complied with before the end of that period.*

(*4*) *It is not a defence to prove that the documents in question were not in fact prepared as required by this Part.]*

[377]

NOTES

Repealed as noted to s 1 at **[309]**.

Inserted, together with the preceding heading and ss 242, 243, 244, by the Companies Act 1989, s 11.

Sub-s (1): words in first (outer) pair of square brackets substituted by the Directors' Remuneration Report Regulations 2002, SI 2002/1986, reg 10(1), (7), with effect as respects companies' financial years ending on or after 31 December 2002; para (ba) inserted, and para (d) substituted, by the Companies Act 1985 (Operating and Financial Review and Directors' Report etc) Regulations 2005, SI 2005/1011, reg 19, Schedule, paras 1, 4, in relation to companies' financial years which begin on or after 1 April 2005; para (ba) and the words omitted from para (d) repealed by the Companies Act 1985 (Operating and Financial Review) (Repeal) Regulations 2005, SI 2005/3442, reg 2(2)(a), Sch 1, para 7.

[241A Members' approval of directors' remuneration report

(1) This section applies to every company that is a quoted company immediately before the end of a financial year.

(2) In this section "the meeting" means the general meeting of the company before which the company's annual accounts for the financial year are to be laid.

(3) The company must, prior to the meeting, give to the members of the company entitled to be sent notice of the meeting notice of the intention to move at the meeting, as an ordinary resolution, a resolution approving the directors' remuneration report for the financial year.

(4) Notice under subsection (3) shall be given to each such member in any manner permitted for the service on him of notice of the meeting.

(5) The business that may be dealt with at the meeting includes the resolution.

(6) The existing directors must ensure that the resolution is put to the vote of the meeting.

(7) Subsection (5) has effect notwithstanding—

(a) any default in complying with subsections (3) and (4);
(b) anything in the company's articles.

(8) No entitlement of a person to remuneration is made conditional on the resolution being passed by reason only of the provision made by this section.

(9) In the event of default in complying with the requirements of subsections (3) and (4), every officer of the company who is in default is liable to a fine.

(10) If the resolution is not put to the vote of the meeting, each existing director is guilty of an offence and liable to a fine.

(11) If an existing director is charged with an offence under subsection (10), it is a defence for him to prove that he took all reasonable steps for securing that the resolution was put to the vote of the meeting.

(12) In this section "existing director" means a person who, immediately before the meeting, is a director of the company.]

[377A]

NOTES

Commencement: 1 August 2002 (with effect as respects companies' financial years ending on or after 31 December 2002).

Repealed as noted to s 1 at **[309]**.

Inserted by the Directors' Remuneration Report Regulations 2002, SI 2002/1986, reg 7, with effect as respects companies' financial years ending on or after 31 December 2002.

[242 Accounts and reports to be delivered to the registrar

(1) The directors of a company shall in respect of each financial year deliver to the registrar [a copy of—

(a) the company's annual accounts,
(b) the directors' report,
[(ba) ...]
(c) (in the case of a quoted company) the directors' remuneration report, and
[(d) the auditors' report on those accounts and that directors' report and (in the case of a quoted company) on ... the auditable part of that directors' remuneration report.]]

[If any document comprised in those accounts or reports is in a language other than English ... , the directors must annex to the copy of that document delivered a translation of it into English, certified in the prescribed manner to be a correct translation.]

(2) If the requirements of subsection (1) are not complied with before the end of the period allowed for laying and delivering accounts and reports, every person who immediately before the end of that period was a director of the company is guilty of an offence and liable to a fine and, for continued contravention, to a daily default fine.

(3) Further, if the directors of the company fail to make good the default within 14 days after the service of a notice on them requiring compliance, the court may on the application of any member or creditor of the company or of the registrar, make an order directing the directors (or any of them) to make good the default within such time as may be specified in the order.

The court's order may provide that all costs of and incidental to the application shall be borne by the directors.

(4) It is a defence for a person charged with an offence under this section to prove that he took all reasonable steps for securing that the requirements of subsection (1) would be complied with before the end of the period allowed for laying and delivering accounts and reports.

(5) It is not a defence in any proceedings under this section to prove that the documents in question were not in fact prepared as required by this Part].

[378]

NOTES

Repealed as noted to s 1 at **[309]**.

Inserted as noted to s 241 at **[377]**.

Sub-s (1): words in first (outer) pair of square brackets substituted by the Directors' Remuneration Report Regulations 2002, SI 2002/1986, reg 10(1), (8), with effect as respects companies' financial years ending on or after 31 December 2002; para (ba) and the final words in square brackets inserted, and para (d) substituted, by the Companies Act 1985 (Operating and Financial Review and Directors' Report etc) Regulations 2005, SI 2005/1011, reg 19, Schedule, paras 1, 5, in relation to companies' financial years which begin on or after 1 April 2005; para (ba) and the words omitted from para (d) repealed by the Companies Act 1985 (Operating and Financial Review) (Repeal) Regulations 2005, SI 2005/3442, reg 2(2)(a), Sch 1, para 8; final words omitted repealed by the Companies Act 2006, s 1295, Sch 16, subject to a saving for limited liability partnerships.

Community interest companies: sub-s (1) of this section is to be treated as requiring the directors of a community interest company to deliver to the registrar of companies a copy of the community interest company report; see the Companies (Audit, Investigations and Community Enterprise) Act 2004, ss 26, 34(1), (2).

[242A Civil penalty for failure to deliver accounts

(1) Where the requirements of section 242(1) are not complied with before the end of the period allowed for laying and delivering accounts and reports, the company is liable to a civil penalty.

This is in addition to any liability of the directors under section 242.

(2) The amount of the penalty is determined by reference to the length of the period between the end of the period allowed for laying and delivering accounts and reports and the day on which the requirements are complied with, and whether the company is a public or private company, as follows—

Length of period	*Public company*	*Private company*
Not more than 3 months	*£500*	*£100*
More than 3 months but not more than 6 months	*£1,000*	*£250*
More than 6 months but not more than 12 months	*£2,000*	*£500*
More than 12 months	*£5,000*	*£1,000*

(3) The penalty may be recovered by the registrar and shall be paid by him into the Consolidated Fund.

(4) It is not a defence in proceedings under this section to prove that the documents in question were not in fact prepared as required by this Part.]

[379]

NOTES

Repealed as noted to s 1 at **[309]**.

Inserted by the Companies Act 1989, s 11.

[242B Delivery and publication of accounts in ECUs

(1) The amounts set out in the annual accounts of a company may also be shown in the same accounts translated into ECUs.

(2) When complying with section 242, the directors of a company may deliver to the registrar an additional copy of the company's annual accounts in which the amounts have been translated into ECUs.

(3) In both cases—

(a) the amounts must have been translated at the relevant exchange rate prevailing on the balance sheet date, and

(b) that rate must be disclosed in the notes to the accounts.

(4) For the purposes of section 240 any additional copy of the company's annual accounts delivered to the registrar under subsection (2) shall be treated as statutory accounts of the company and, in the case of such a copy, references in section 240 to the auditors' report under section 235 shall be read as references to the auditors' report on the annual accounts of which it is a copy.

(5) In this section—

"ECU" means a unit with a value equal to the value of the unit known as the ecu used in the European Monetary System, and

"relevant exchange rate" means the rate of exchange used for translating the value of the ecu for the purposes of that System.]

[380]–[381]

NOTES

Repealed as noted to s 1 at **[309]**.

Inserted by the Companies Act 1985 (Accounts of Small and Medium-Sized Enterprises and Publication of Accounts in ECUs) Regulations 1992, SI 1992/2452, reg 3.

243 *(Repealed by the Companies Act 1985 (International Accounting Standards and Other Accounting Amendments) Regulations 2004, SI 2004/2947, reg 15, Sch 7, Pt 1, paras 1, 6, in relation to companies' financial years which begin on or after 1 January 2005.)*

[244 Period allowed for laying and delivering accounts and reports

(1) The period allowed for laying and delivering accounts and reports is—

(a) for a private company, 10 months after the end of the relevant accounting reference period, and

(b) for a public company, 7 months after the end of that period.

This is subject to the following provisions of this section.

(2) If the relevant accounting reference period is the company's first and is a period of more than 12 months, the period allowed is—

(a) 10 months or 7 months, as the case may be, from the first anniversary of the incorporation of the company, or

(b) 3 months from the end of the accounting reference period,

whichever last expires.

(3) …

(4) If the relevant accounting period is treated as shortened by virtue of a notice given by the company under section 225 (alteration of accounting reference date), the period allowed for laying and delivering accounts is that applicable in accordance with the above provisions or 3 months from the date of the notice under that section, whichever last expires.

(5) If for any special reason the Secretary of State thinks fit he may, on an application made before the expiry of the period otherwise allowed, by notice in writing to a company extend that period by such further period as may be specified in the notice.

(6) In this section "the relevant accounting reference period" means the accounting reference period by reference to which the financial year for the accounts in question was determined.]

[382]

NOTES

Repealed as noted to s 1 at **[309]**.

Inserted as noted to s 241 at **[377]**.

Sub-s (3): repealed by the Companies Act 1985 (International Accounting Standards and Other Accounting Amendments) Regulations 2004, SI 2004/2947, reg 9, in relation to companies' financial years which begin on or after 1 January 2005.

Secretary of State: as to the contracting out of the function of the Secretary of State under sub-s (5) above, see the note to s 26 at **[335]**.

Prescribed form: see the Companies (Forms) Regulations 1985, SI 1985/854, Form 244, as prescribed by the Companies (Forms) (Amendment) Regulations 1990, SI 1990/572.

[Revision of defective accounts and reports

245 Voluntary revision of annual accounts or directors' report

(1) If it appears to the directors of a company that any annual accounts [or summary financial statement] of the company, or any directors' report […] [or directors' remuneration report], did not comply with the requirements of this Act [(or, where applicable, of Article 4 of the IAS Regulation)], they may prepare revised accounts or a [revised statement or report].

(2) Where copies of the previous accounts [or report] have been laid before the company in general meeting or delivered to the registrar, the revisions shall be confined to—

(a) the correction of those respects in which the previous accounts [or report] did not comply with the requirements of this Act [(or, where applicable, of Article 4 of the IAS Regulation)], and

(b) the making of any necessary consequential alterations.

(3) The Secretary of State may make provision by regulations as to the application of the provisions of this Act in relation to revised annual accounts [or a revised summary financial statement] or a revised directors' report […] [or a revised directors' remuneration report].

(4) The regulations may, in particular—

(a) make different provision according to whether the previous accounts [statement or report] are replaced or are supplemented by a document indicating the corrections to be made;

(b) make provision with respect to the functions of the company's auditors [or reporting accountant] in relation to the revised accounts [statement or report];

(c) require the directors to take such steps as may be specified in the regulations where the previous accounts [or report] have been—

(i) sent out to members and others under section 238(1),

(ii) laid before the company in general meeting, or

(iii) delivered to the registrar,

or where a summary financial statement [containing information [derived from the previous accounts or report]] has been sent to members under section 251;

(d) apply the provisions of this Act (including those creating criminal offences) subject to such additions, exceptions and modifications as are specified in the regulations.

(5) Regulations under this section shall be made by statutory instrument which shall be subject to annulment in pursuance of a resolution of either House of Parliament.]

[383]

NOTES

Repealed as noted to s 1 at **[309]**.

Inserted, together with the preceding heading and ss 245A–245C, by the Companies Act 1989, s 12.

Sub-s (1): words in first and fourth pairs of square brackets inserted by the Companies Act 1985 (International Accounting Standards and Other Accounting Amendments) Regulations 2004, SI 2004/2947, regs 3, 10(1), (2)(a), Sch 1, paras 1, 11, in relation to companies' financial years which begin on or after 1 January 2005; words in second pair of square brackets originally inserted by the Companies Act 1985 (Operating and Financial Review and Directors' Report etc) Regulations 2005, SI 2005/1011, reg 14(1), (2), with effect from 1 April 2005; repealed by the Companies Act 1985 (Operating and Financial Review) (Repeal) Regulations 2005, SI 2005/3442, reg 2(2)(a), Sch 1, para 9(1), (2)(a); words in third pair of square brackets inserted by the Directors' Remuneration Report Regulations 2002, SI 2002/1986, reg 10(1), (9)(a), with effect as respects companies' financial years ending on or after 31 December 2002; words in final pair of square brackets substituted by SI 2005/3442, reg 2(2)(a), Sch 1, para 9(1), (2)(b).

Sub-s (2): words in first and second pairs of square brackets substituted by SI 2005/3442, reg 2(2)(a), Sch 1, para 9(1), (3); words in third pair of square brackets inserted by SI 2004/2947, reg 3, Sch 1, paras 1, 11, in relation to companies' financial years which begin on or after 1 January 2005.

Sub-s (3): words in first pair of square brackets inserted by SI 2004/2947, reg 10(1), (3), in relation to companies' financial years which begin on or after 1 January 2005; words in second pair of square brackets originally inserted by SI 2005/1011, reg 14(1), (4), with effect from 1 April 2005, and repealed by SI 2005/3442, reg 2(2)(a), Sch 1, para 9(1), (4); words in third pair of square brackets added by SI 2002/1986, reg 10(1), (9)(b), with effect as respects companies' financial years ending on or after 31 December 2002.

Sub-s (4): words in square brackets in para (a) and words in second pair of square brackets in para (b) substituted by SI 2005/3442, reg 2(2)(a), Sch 1, para 9(1), (5); words in first pair of square brackets in para (b) inserted by the Companies Act 1985 (Audit Exemption) Regulations 1994, SI 1994/1935, reg 4, Sch 1, Pt I, para 2, subject to transitional provisions contained in reg 6 thereof, repealed by the Companies Act 2006, s 1175, Sch 9, Pt 1, para 2, as from a day to be appointed under s 1300(2) of that Act; words in first pair and third (inner) pair of square brackets in para (c) substituted by SI 2005/3442, reg 2(2)(a), Sch 1, para 9(1), (6); words in second (outer) pair of square brackets in para (c) substituted by SI 2005/1011, reg 14(1), (6), with effect from 1 April 2005.

Regulations: the Companies (Revision of Defective Accounts and Report) Regulations 1990, SI 1990/2570; the Companies Act 1985 (Audit Exemption) Regulations 1994, SI 1994/1935; the Companies (Summary Financial Statement) Regulations 1995, SI 1995/2092.

[245A Secretary of State's notice in respect of annual accounts

[(1) Where—

(a) copies of a company's annual accounts, [or directors' report] have been sent out under section 238, or

(b) a copy of a company's annual accounts, [or directors' report] has been laid before the company in general meeting or delivered to the registrar,

and it appears to the Secretary of State that there is, or may be, a question whether the accounts [or report] comply with the requirements of this Act, he may give notice to the directors of the company indicating the respects in which it appears to him that such a question arises or may arise.]

(2) The notice shall specify a period of not less than one month for the directors to give him an explanation of the accounts [[or report] or prepare revised accounts or [a revised report]].

(3) If at the end of the specified period, or such longer period as he may allow, it appears to the Secretary of State that [the directors have not—

(a) given a satisfactory explanation of the accounts [or report], or

(b) revised the accounts [or report] so as to comply with the requirements of this Act,

he may if he thinks fit apply to the court].

[(4) The provisions of this section apply equally to revised annual accounts [and revised directors' reports], in which case they have effect as if the references to revised accounts [or reports] were references to further revised accounts [or reports].]]

[384]

NOTES

Repealed as noted to s 1 at **[309]**.

Inserted as noted to s 245 at **[383]**.

Sub-s (1): substituted by the Companies Act 1985 (Operating and Financial Review and Directors' Report etc) Regulations 2005, SI 2005/1011, reg 15(1), (2), in relation to annual accounts, directors' reports and operating and financial reviews prepared for companies' financial years which begin on or after 1 April 2006; words in square brackets substituted by the Companies Act 1985 (Operating and Financial Review) (Repeal) Regulations 2005, SI 2005/3442, reg 2(2)(a), Sch 1, para 10(1), (2). The original subsection (as amended by the Companies Act 1985 (International Accounting Standards and Other Accounting Amendments) Regulations 2004, SI 2004/2947, reg 3, Sch 1, paras 1, 11, in relation to companies' financial years which begin on or after 1 January 2005) read as follows—

"(1) Where copies of a company's annual accounts have been sent out under section 238, or a copy of a company's annual accounts has been laid before the company in general meeting or delivered to the registrar, and it appears to the Secretary of State that there is, or may be, a question whether the accounts comply with the requirements of this Act [(or, where applicable, of Article 4 of the IAS Regulation)], he may give notice to the directors of the company indicating the respects in which it appears to him that such a question arises, or may arise.".

Sub-s (2): words in first (outer) pair of square brackets substituted (for the original words "or prepare revised accounts") by SI 2005/1011, reg 15(1), (3), in relation to annual accounts, directors' reports and operating and financial reviews prepared for companies' financial years which begin on or after 1 April 2006; words in second and third (inner) pairs of square brackets substituted by SI 2005/3442, reg 2(2)(a), Sch 1, para 10(1), (3).

Sub-s (3): words in first (outer) pair of square brackets substituted (for the original words "no satisfactory explanation of the accounts has been given and that the accounts have not been revised so as to comply with the requirements of this Act, he may if he thinks fit apply to the court") by SI 2005/1011, reg 15(1), (4), in relation to annual accounts, directors' reports and operating and financial reviews prepared for companies' financial years which begin on or after 1 April 2006; words in second and third (inner) pairs of square brackets substituted by SI 2005/3442, reg 2(2)(a), Sch 1, para 10(1), (4).

Sub-s (4): substituted by SI 2005/1011, reg 15(1), (5), in relation to annual accounts, directors' reports and operating and financial reviews prepared for companies' financial years which begin on or after 1 April 2006; words in square brackets substituted by SI 2005/3442, reg 2(2)(a), Sch 1, para 10(1), (5). The original subsection read as follows—

"(4) The provisions of this section apply equally to revised annual accounts, in which case the references to revised accounts shall be read as references to further revised accounts.".

[245B Application to court in respect of defective accounts

(1) An application may be made to the court—

(a) by the Secretary of State, after having complied with section 245A, or

(b) by a person authorised by the Secretary of State for the purposes of this section,

for a declaration or declarator that the annual accounts of a company do not comply[, or a directors' report … does not comply,] with the requirements of this Act [(or, where applicable, of Article 4 of the IAS Regulation)] and for an order requiring the directors of the company to prepare revised accounts [or a revised report …].

(2) Notice of the application, together with a general statement of the matters at issue in the proceedings, shall be given by the applicant to the registrar for registration.

(3) If the court orders the preparation of revised accounts, it may give directions with respect to—

(a) the auditing of the accounts,

(b) the revision of any directors' report[, directors' remuneration report] or summary financial statement, and

(c) the taking of steps by the directors to bring the making of the order to the notice of persons likely to rely on the previous accounts,

and such other matters as the court thinks fit.

[(3A) If the court orders the preparation of a revised directors' report … it may give directions with respect to—

(a) the review of the directors' report … by the auditors,

(b) the revision of any directors' report, directors' remuneration report … or summary financial statement,

(c) the taking of steps by the directors to bring the making of the order to the notice of persons likely to rely on the previous report …, and

(d) such other matters as the court thinks fit.]

(4) If the court finds that the accounts [or report] did not comply with the requirements of this Act [(or, where applicable, of Article 4 of the IAS Regulation)] it may order that all or part of—

(a) the costs (or in Scotland expenses) of and incidental to the application, and

(b) any reasonable expenses incurred by the company in connection with or in consequence of the preparation of revised accounts [or a revised report …],

shall be borne by such of the directors as were party to the approval of the [defective accounts or report].

For this purpose every director of the company at the time [of the [approval of the accounts or report]] shall be taken to have been a party to [the approval] unless he shows that he took all reasonable steps to prevent [that approval].

(5) Where the court makes an order under subsection (4) it shall have regard to whether the directors party to the approval of the defective accounts [or report] knew or ought to have known that the accounts [or report] did not comply with the requirements of this Act [(or, where applicable, of Article 4 of the IAS Regulation)], and it may exclude one or more directors from the order or order the payment of different amounts by different directors.

(6) On the conclusion of proceedings on an application under this section, the applicant shall give to the registrar for registration an office copy of the court order or, as the case may be, notice that the application has failed or been withdrawn.

[(7) The provisions of this section apply equally to revised annual accounts [and revised directors' reports], in which case they have effect as if the references to revised accounts [or reports] were references to further revised accounts [or reports].]]

[385]

NOTES

Repealed as noted to s 1 at **[309]**.

Inserted as noted to s 245 at **[383]**.

Sub-s (1): words in first and third pairs of square brackets inserted by the Companies Act 1985 (Operating and Financial Review and Directors' Report etc) Regulations 2005, SI 2005/1011, reg 16(1), (2), in relation to annual accounts, directors' reports and operating and financial reviews prepared for companies' financial years which begin on or after 1 April 2006; words omitted repealed by the Companies Act 1985 (Operating and Financial Review) (Repeal) Regulations 2005, SI 2005/3442, reg 2(2)(a), Sch 1, para 11(1), (2); words in second pair of square brackets inserted by the Companies Act 1985 (International Accounting Standards and Other Accounting Amendments) Regulations 2004, SI 2004/2947, reg 3, Sch 1, paras 1, 11, in relation to companies' financial years which begin on or after 1 January 2005.

Sub-s (3): words in square brackets inserted by the Directors' Remuneration Report Regulations 2002, SI 2002/1986, reg 10(1), (10), with effect as respects companies' financial years ending on or after 31 December 2002.

Sub-s (3A): inserted by SI 2005/1011, reg 16(1), (3), in relation to annual accounts, directors' reports and operating and financial reviews prepared for companies' financial years which begin on or after 1 April 2006; words omitted repealed by SI 2005/3442, reg 2(2)(a), Sch 1, para 11(1), (3).

Sub-s (4): words in first and fourth pairs of square brackets substituted by SI 2005/3442, reg 2(2)(a), Sch 1, para 11(1), (4)(a), (c); words in second pair of square brackets inserted by SI 2004/2947, reg 3, Sch 1, paras 1, 11, in relation to companies' financial years which begin on or after 1 January 2005; words in third pair of square brackets inserted by SI 2005/1011, reg 16(1), (4)(b), in relation to annual accounts, directors' reports and operating and financial reviews prepared for companies' financial years which begin on or after 1 April 2006; words omitted therefrom repealed by SI 2005/3442, reg 2(2)(a), Sch 1, para 11(1), (4)(b); words in fifth (outer) pair of square brackets substituted (for the original words "the accounts were approved") by SI 2005/1011, reg 16(1), (4)(d), in relation to annual accounts, directors' reports and operating and financial reviews prepared for companies' financial years which begin on or after 1 April 2006; words in sixth (inner) pair of square brackets substituted by SI 2005/3442, reg 2(2)(a), Sch 1, para 11(1), (4)(d); words in seventh and final pairs of square brackets substituted (for the original words "their approval" and "their being approved" respectively) by SI 2005/1011, reg 16(1), (4)(e), (f), in relation to annual accounts, directors' reports and operating and financial reviews prepared for companies' financial years which begin on or after 1 April 2006.

Sub-s (5): words in first and second pairs of square brackets originally inserted by SI 2005/1011, reg 16(1), (5), in relation to annual accounts, directors' reports and operating and financial reviews prepared for companies' financial years which begin on or after 1 April 2006, and substituted by SI 2005/3442, reg 2(2)(a), Sch 1, para 11(1), (4)(d); words in third pair of square brackets inserted by SI 2004/2947, reg 3, Sch 1, paras 1, 11, in relation to companies' financial years which begin on or after 1 January 2005.

Sub-s (7): substituted by SI 2005/1011, reg 16(1), (6), in relation to annual accounts, directors' reports and operating and financial reviews prepared for companies' financial years which begin on or after 1 April 2006; words in square brackets substituted by SI 2005/3442, reg 2(2)(a), Sch 1, para 11(1), (6). The original subsection read as follows—

"(7) The provisions of this section apply equally to revised annual accounts, in which case the references to revised accounts shall be read as references to further revised accounts.".

[245C Other persons authorised to apply to court

(1) The Secretary of State may authorise for the purposes of section 245B any person appearing to him—

- *(a) to have an interest in, and to have satisfactory procedures directed to securing, compliance by companies with [the requirements of this Act relating to accounts [and directors' reports]] [(or, where applicable, of Article 4 of the IAS Regulation)],*
- *(b) to have satisfactory procedures for receiving and investigating complaints about the [companies' annual accounts [and directors' reports]], and*
- *(c) otherwise to be a fit and proper person to be authorised.*

[(1A) But where the order giving authorisation (see subsection (4)) is to contain any requirements or other provisions specified under subsection (4A), the Secretary of State may not authorise a person unless, in addition, it appears to him that the person would, if authorised, exercise his functions as an authorised person in accordance with any such requirements or provisions.]

(2) A person may be authorised generally or in respect of particular classes of case, and different persons may be authorised in respect of different classes of case.

(3) The Secretary of State may refuse to authorise a person if he considers that his authorisation is unnecessary having regard to the fact that there are one or more other persons who have been or are likely to be authorised.

(4) Authorisation shall be by order made by statutory instrument which shall be subject to annulment in pursuance of a resolution of either House of Parliament.

[(4A) An order under subsection (4) may contain such requirements or other provisions relating to the exercise of functions by the authorised person as appear to the Secretary of State to be appropriate.

(4B) If the authorised person is an unincorporated association, any relevant proceedings may be brought by or against that association in the name of any body corporate whose constitution provides for the establishment of the association.

For this purpose "relevant proceedings" means proceedings brought in, or in connection with, the exercise of any function by the association as an authorised person.]

(5) Where authorisation is revoked, the revoking order may make such provision as the Secretary of State thinks fit with respect to pending proceedings.

(6) ...]

[386]

NOTES

Repealed as noted to s 1 at **[309]**.
Inserted as noted to s 245 at **[383]**.
Sub-s (1): words in first (outer) pair of square brackets in para (a) substituted (for the original words "the accounting requirements of this Act") by the Companies Act 1985 (Operating and Financial Review and Directors' Report etc) Regulations 2005, SI 2005/1011, reg 17(a), in relation to annual accounts, directors' reports and operating and financial reviews prepared for companies' financial years which begin on or after 1 April 2006; words in second (inner) pair of square brackets in para (a) substituted by the Companies Act 1985 (Operating and Financial Review) (Repeal) Regulations 2005, SI 2005/3442, reg 2(2)(a), Sch 1, para 12; words in third pair of square brackets in para (a) inserted by the Companies Act 1985 (International Accounting Standards and Other Accounting Amendments) Regulations 2004, SI 2004/2947, reg 3, Sch 1, paras 1, 11, in relation to companies' financial years which begin on or after 1 January 2005; words in first (outer) pair of square brackets in para (b) substituted (for the original words "annual accounts of companies") by SI 2005/1011, reg 17(b), in relation to annual accounts, directors' reports and operating and financial reviews prepared for companies' financial years which begin on or after 1 April 2006; words in second (inner) pair of square brackets in para (b) substituted by SI 2005/3442, reg 2(2)(a), Sch 1, para 12.
Sub-ss (1A), (4A), (4B): inserted by the Companies (Audit, Investigations and Community Enterprise) Act 2004, s 10.
Sub-s (6): repealed by the Companies (Audit, Investigations and Community Enterprise) Act 2004, s 64, Sch 8.
Orders: the Companies (Defective Accounts) (Authorised Person) Order 1991, SI 1991/13.

[245D Disclosure of information held by Inland Revenue to persons authorised to apply to court

(1) Information which is held by or on behalf of the Commissioners of Inland Revenue may be disclosed to a person who is authorised under section 245C of this Act, or under Article 253C of the Companies (Northern Ireland) Order 1986 (SI 1986/1032 (NI 6)), if the disclosure—

(a) is made for a permitted purpose, and

(b) is made by the Commissioners or is authorised by them.

(2) Such information—

(a) may be so disclosed despite any other restriction on the disclosure of information whether imposed by any statutory provision or otherwise, but

(b) in the case of personal data (within the meaning of the Data Protection Act 1998), may not be disclosed in contravention of that Act.

(3) For the purposes of subsection (1), a disclosure is made for a permitted purpose if it is made for the purpose of facilitating—

(a) the taking of steps by the authorised person to discover whether there are grounds for an application to the court under section 245B of this Act or Article 253B of the Companies (Northern Ireland) Order 1986; or

(b) a determination by the authorised person as to whether or not to make such an application.

(4) The power of the Commissioners to authorise a disclosure under subsection (1)(b) may be delegated (either generally or for a specified purpose) to an officer of the Board of Inland Revenue.]

[386A]

NOTES

Commencement: 6 April 2005.
Repealed as noted to s 1 at **[309]**.
Inserted, together with s 245E, by the Companies (Audit, Investigations and Community Enterprise) Act 2004, s 11(1).
Commissioners of Inland Revenue: a reference to the Commissioners of Inland Revenue is now to be taken as a reference to the Commissioners for Her Majesty's Revenue and Customs; see the Commissioners for Revenue and Customs Act 2005, s 50(1), (7).

[245E Restrictions on use and further disclosure of information disclosed under section 245D

(1) Information that is disclosed to an authorised person under section 245D may not be used except in or in connection with—
- *(a) taking steps to discover whether there are grounds for an application to the court as mentioned in section 245D(3)(a);*
- *(b) determining whether or not to make such an application; or*
- *(c) proceedings on any such application.*

(2) Information that is disclosed to an authorised person under section 245D may not be further disclosed except—
- *(a) to the person to whom the information relates; or*
- *(b) in or in connection with proceedings on any such application to the court.*

(3) A person who contravenes subsection (1) or (2) is guilty of an offence and liable to imprisonment or a fine, or both.

(4) It is a defence for a person charged with an offence under subsection (3) to prove—
- *(a) that he did not know, and had no reason to suspect, that the information had been disclosed under section 245D; or*
- *(b) that he took all reasonable steps and exercised all due diligence to avoid the commission of the offence.*

(5) Sections 732 (restriction on prosecutions), 733(2) and (3) (liability of individuals for corporate default) and 734 (criminal proceedings against unincorporated bodies) apply to offences under this section.]

[386B]

NOTES

Commencement: 6 April 2005.
Repealed as noted to s 1 at **[309]**.
Inserted as noted to s 245D at **[386A]**.

[245F Power of authorised persons to require documents, information and explanations

(1) This section applies where it appears to a person who is authorised under section 245C of this Act that there is, or may be, a question whether the [a company's annual accounts [or directors' report]] comply with the requirements of this Act [(or, where applicable, of Article 4 of the IAS Regulation)].

(2) The authorised person may require any of the persons mentioned in subsection (3) to produce any document, or to provide him with any information or explanations, that he may reasonably require for the purpose of—
- *(a) discovering whether there are grounds for an application to the court under section 245B; or*
- *(b) determining whether or not to make such an application.*

(3) Those persons are—
- *(a) the company;*
- *(b) any officer, employee, or auditor of the company;*
- *(c) any persons who fell within paragraph (b) at a time to which the document or information required by the authorised person relates.*

(4) If a person fails to comply with a requirement under subsection (2), the authorised person may apply to the court for an order under subsection (5).

(5) If on such an application the court decides that the person has failed to comply with the requirement under subsection (2), it may order the person to take such steps as it directs for securing that the documents are produced or the information or explanations are provided.

(6) A statement made by a person in response to a requirement under subsection (2) or an order under subsection (5) may not be used in evidence against him in any criminal proceedings.

(7) Nothing in this section compels any person to disclose documents or information in respect of which in an action in the High Court a claim to legal professional privilege, or in an action in the Court of Session a claim to confidentiality of communications, could be maintained.

(8) In this section "document" includes information recorded in any form.]

[386C]

NOTES

Commencement: 6 April 2005.

Repealed as noted to s 1 at **[309]**.

Inserted, together with s 245G, by the Companies (Audit, Investigations and Community Enterprise) Act 2004, s 12(1).

Sub-s (1): words in first (outer) pair of square brackets substituted (for the original words "annual accounts of a company") by the Companies Act 1985 (Operating and Financial Review and Directors' Report etc) Regulations 2005, SI 2005/1011, reg 18, in relation to annual accounts, directors' reports and operating and financial reviews prepared for companies' financial years which begin on or after 1 April 2006; words in second (inner) pair of square brackets substituted by the Companies Act 1985 (Operating and Financial Review) (Repeal) Regulations 2005, SI 2005/3442, reg 2(2)(a), Sch 1, para 13; words in third pair of square brackets inserted by SI 2005/1011, reg 19, Schedule, paras 1, 6, in relation to companies' financial years which begin on or after 1 April 2005.

[245G Restrictions on further disclosure of information obtained under section 245F

(1) This section applies to information (in whatever form) which—

(a) has been obtained in pursuance of a requirement or order under section 245F, and

(b) relates to the private affairs of an individual or to any particular business.

(2) No such information may, during the lifetime of that individual or so long as that business continues to be carried on, be disclosed without the consent of that individual or the person for the time being carrying on that business.

(3) Subsection (2) does not apply to any disclosure of information which—

(a) is made for the purpose of facilitating the carrying out by a person authorised under section 245C of his functions under section 245B;

(b) is made to a person specified in Part 1 of Schedule 7B;

(c) is of a description specified in Part 2 of that Schedule; or

(d) is made in accordance with Part 3 of that Schedule.

(4) The Secretary of State may by order amend Schedule 7B.

(5) An order under subsection (4) must not—

(a) amend Part 1 of Schedule 7B by specifying a person unless the person exercises functions of a public nature (whether or not he exercises any other function);

(b) amend Part 2 of Schedule 7B by adding or modifying a description of disclosure unless the purpose for which the disclosure is permitted is likely to facilitate the exercise of a function of a public nature;

(c) amend Part 3 of Schedule 7B so as to have the effect of permitting disclosures to be made to a body other than one that exercises functions of a public nature in a country or territory outside the United Kingdom.

(6) An order under subsection (4) shall be made by statutory instrument which shall be subject to annulment in pursuance of a resolution of either House of Parliament.

(7) A person who discloses any information in contravention of this section—

(a) is guilty of an offence, and

(b) is liable on conviction to imprisonment or a fine, or both.

(8) However, it is a defence for a person charged with an offence under subsection (7) to prove—

(a) that he did not know, and had no reason to suspect, that the information had been disclosed under section 245F; or

(b) that he took all reasonable steps and exercised all due diligence to avoid the commission of the offence.

(9) Sections 732 (restriction on prosecutions), 733 (liability of individuals for corporate default) and 734 (criminal proceedings against unincorporated bodies) apply to offences under this section.

(10) This section does not prohibit the disclosure of information if the information is or has been available to the public from any other source.

(11) Nothing in this section authorises the making of a disclosure in contravention of the Data Protection Act 1998.]

[386D]

NOTES

Commencement: 6 April 2005.
Repealed as noted to s 1 at **[309]**.
Inserted as noted to s 245F at **[386C]**.

[CHAPTER II
EXEMPTIONS, EXCEPTIONS AND SPECIAL PROVISIONS

Small and medium-sized companies and groups

[246 Special provisions for small companies

(1) Subject to section 247A, this section applies where a company qualifies as a small company in relation to a financial year.

(2) If the company's individual accounts for the year [are Companies Act individual accounts and]—

(a) comply with the provisions of Schedule 8, or

(b) fail to comply with those provisions only in so far as they comply instead with one or more corresponding provisions of Schedule 4,

they need not comply with the provisions or, as the case may be, the remaining provisions of Schedule 4; and where advantage is taken of this subsection, references in [section 226A] to compliance with the provisions of Schedule 4 shall be construed accordingly.

[(3) The company's individual accounts for the year—

(a) may give the total of the aggregates required by paragraphs (a), (c) and (d) of paragraph 1(1) of Schedule 6 (emoluments and other benefits etc of directors) instead of giving those aggregates individually; and

(b) need not give the information required by—

[(ai) section 231A (disclosure required in notes to annual accounts: particulars of staff);]

(i) paragraph 4 of Schedule 5 (financial years of subsidiary undertakings);

(ii) paragraph 1(2)(b) of Schedule 6 (numbers of directors exercising share options and receiving shares under long term incentive schemes);

(iii) paragraph 2 of Schedule 6 (details of highest paid director's emoluments etc); or

(iv) paragraph 7 of Schedule 6 (excess retirement benefits of directors and past directors).]

(4) The directors' report for the year need not give the information required by—

[(a) sections 234ZZA(1)(c) (directors' report: amount to be paid as dividend) and 234ZZB (directors' report: business review);]

(b) paragraph 1(2) of Schedule 7 (statement of market value of fixed assets where substantially different from balance sheet amount);

[(ba) paragraph 5A of Schedule 7 (disclosures relating to the use of financial instruments);]

(c) paragraph 6 of Schedule 7 (miscellaneous disclosures); or

(d) paragraph 11 of Schedule 7 (employee involvement).

(5) Notwithstanding anything in section 242(1), the directors of the company need not deliver to the registrar any of the following, namely—

- *(a) a copy of the company's profit and loss account for the year;*
- *(b) a copy of the directors' report for the year; and*
- *(c) if [they prepare Companies Act individual accounts and] they deliver a copy of a balance sheet drawn up as at the last day of the year which complies with the requirements of Schedule 8A, a copy of the company's balance sheet drawn up as at that day.*

(6) Neither a copy of the company's accounts for the year delivered to the registrar under section 242(1), nor a copy of a balance sheet delivered to the registrar under subsection (5)(c), need give the information required by—

- *(a) paragraph 4 of Schedule 5 (financial years of subsidiary undertakings);*
- *(b) paragraph 6 of Schedule 5 (shares of company held by subsidiary undertakings);*
- *(c) Part I of Schedule 6 (directors' and chairman's emoluments, pensions and compensation for loss of office); or*
- *(d) section 390A(3) (amount of auditors' remuneration).*

(7) The provisions of section 233 as to the signing of the copy of the balance sheet delivered to the registrar apply to a copy of a balance sheet delivered under subsection (5)(c).

(8) Subject to subsection (9), each of the following, namely—

- *(a) accounts prepared in accordance with subsection (2) or (3),*
- *(b) a report prepared in accordance with subsection (4), and*
- *(c) a copy of accounts delivered to the registrar in accordance with subsection (5) or (6),*

shall contain a statement in a prominent position on the balance sheet, in the report or, as the case may be, on the copy of the balance sheet, above the signature required by section 233, 234A or subsection (7), that they are prepared in accordance with the special provisions of this Part relating to small companies.

(9) Subsection (8) does not apply where [the directors of the company have taken advantage of the exemption from audit conferred by section 249AA (dormant companies].]

[387]

NOTES

Repealed as noted to s 1 at **[309]**.

Inserted, together with the preceding heading and s 247, by the Companies Act 1989, s 13(1). Substituted by the Companies Act 1985 (Accounts of Small and Medium-sized Companies and Minor Accounting Amendments) Regulations 1997, SI 1997/220, reg 2(1), in relation to annual accounts approved by the board of directors on or after 1 March 1997, and to directors' and auditors' reports on such accounts; for a transitional provision, see reg 1(4) of the 1997 Regulations.

Sub-s (2): words in first pair of square brackets inserted, and words in second pair of square brackets substituted, by the Companies Act 1985 (International Accounting Standards and Other Accounting Amendments) Regulations 2004, SI 2004/2947, reg 3, Sch 1, paras 1, 12(1), (2), in relation to companies' financial years which begin on or after 1 January 2005.

Sub-s (3): substituted by the Company Accounts (Disclosure of Directors' Emoluments) Regulations 1997, SI 1997/570, reg 6(1), with effect in relation to companies' financial years ending on or after that date; sub-para (b)(ai) inserted by the Companies Act 1985 (Investment Companies and Accounting and Audit Amendments) Regulations 2005, SI 2005/2280, reg 12, in relation to companies' financial years which begin on or after 1 January 2005 and which end on or after 1 October 2005.

Sub-s (4): para (ba) inserted by SI 2004/2947, reg 13(2), in relation to companies' financial years which begin on or after 1 January 2005; para (a) substituted by the Companies Act 1985 (Operating and Financial Review and Directors' Report etc) Regulations 2005, SI 2005/1011, reg 4, in relation to companies' financial years which begin on or after 1 April 2005.

Sub-s (5): words in square brackets inserted by SI 2004/2947, reg 3, Sch 1, paras 1, 12(1), (3), in relation to companies' financial years which begin on or after 1 January 2005.

Sub-s (9): words in square brackets substituted by the Companies Act 1985 (Audit Exemption) (Amendment) Regulations 2000, SI 2000/1430, reg 8(1), in relation to annual reports and reports in respect of financial years ending two months or more after 26 May 2000.

[246A Special provisions for medium-sized companies

(1) Subject to section 247A, this section applies where a company qualifies as a medium-sized company in relation to a financial year [and its directors prepare Companies Act individual accounts for that year].

(2) The company's individual accounts for the year need not comply with the requirements of paragraph 36A of Schedule 4 (disclosure with respect to compliance with accounting standards).

[(2A) The directors' report for the year need not comply with the requirements of section 234ZZB(3) (business review to include analysis using key performance indicators) so far as they relate to non-financial information.]

(3) The company may deliver to the registrar a copy of the company's accounts for the year—

(a) which includes a profit and loss account in which the following items listed in the profit and loss account formats set out in Part I of Schedule 4 are combined as one item under the heading "gross profit or loss"—
Items 1, 2, 3 and 6 in Format 1;
Items 1 to 5 in Format 2;
Items A.1, B.1 and B.2 in Format 3;
Items A.1, A.2 and B.1 to B.4 in Format 4;

(b) which does not contain the information required by paragraph 55 of Schedule 4 (particulars of turnover).

(4) A copy of accounts delivered to the registrar in accordance with subsection (3) shall contain a statement in a prominent position on the copy of the balance sheet, above the signature required by section 233, that the accounts are prepared in accordance with the special provisions of this Part relating to medium-sized companies.]

[388]

NOTES

Repealed as noted to s 1 at **[309]**.

Inserted by the Companies Act 1985 (Accounts of Small and Medium-sized Companies and Minor Accounting Amendments) Regulations 1997, SI 1997/220, reg 3, in relation to annual accounts approved by the board of directors on or after 1 March 1997, and to directors' and auditors' reports on such accounts; for a transitional provision see reg 1(4) of the 1997 Regulations.

Sub-s (1): words in square brackets added by the Companies Act 1985 (International Accounting Standards and Other Accounting Amendments) Regulations 2004, SI 2004/2947, reg 3, Sch 1, paras 1, 13, in relation to companies' financial years which begin on or after 1 January 2005.

Sub-s (2A): inserted by the Companies Act 1985 (Operating and Financial Review and Directors' Report etc) Regulations 2005, SI 2005/1011, reg 5, in relation to companies' financial years which begin on or after 1 April 2005.

[247 Qualification of company as small or medium-sized

(1) A company qualifies as small or medium-sized in relation to a financial year if the qualifying conditions are met—

(a) in the case of the company's first financial year, in that year, and

(b) in the case of any subsequent financial year, in that year and the preceding year.

(2) A company shall be treated as qualifying as small or medium-sized in relation to a financial year—

(a) if it so qualified in relation to the previous financial year under [subsection (1) above or was treated as so qualifying under paragraph

(b) below]; or (b) if it was treated as so qualifying in relation to the previous year by virtue of paragraph (a) and the qualifying conditions are met in the year in question.

(3) The qualifying conditions are met by a company in a year in which it satisfies two or more of the following requirements—

		Small company
1.	*Turnover*	*[Not more than £2.8 million]*
2.	*Balance sheet total*	*[Not more than £1.4 million]*
3.	*Number of employees*	*Not more than 50*
		Medium-sized company
1.	*Turnover*	*[Not more than £11.2 million]*
2.	*Balance sheet total*	*[Not more than £5.6 million]*
3.	*Number of employees*	*Not more than 250.*

(4) For a period which is a company's financial year but not in fact a year the maximum figures for turnover shall be proportionately adjusted.

(5) The balance sheet total means—

(a) where in the company's accounts Format 1 of the balance sheet formats set out in Part I of Schedule 4 [or Part I of Schedule 8] is adopted, the aggregate of the amounts shown in the balance sheet under the headings corresponding to items A to D in that Format, and

(b) where Format 2 is adopted, the aggregate of the amounts shown under the general heading "Assets".

(6) The number of employees means the average number of persons employed by the company in the year (determined on a [monthly] basis).

That number shall be determined by applying the method of calculation prescribed by paragraph 56(2) and (3) of Schedule 4 for determining the corresponding number required to be stated in a note to the company's accounts.]

[389]

NOTES

Repealed as noted to s 1 at **[309]**.

Inserted as noted to s 246 at **[387]**.

Sub-s (2): words in square brackets substituted by the Companies Act 1985 (Accounts of Small and Medium-Sized Enterprises and Publication of Accounts in ECUs) Regulations 1992, SI 1992/2452, reg 5(1), (2), in relation to annual accounts in respect of financial years ending on or after 16 November 1992, and to directors' and auditors' reports on such accounts; subject to transitional provisions contained in reg 7 thereof.

Sub-s (3): words in square brackets substituted by the Companies Act 1985 (Accounts of Small and Medium-Sized Enterprises and Audit Exemption) (Amendment) Regulations 2004, SI 2004/16, reg 2, in relation to financial years ending on or after that date.

Sub-s (5): substituted by the Companies Act 1985 (International Accounting Standards and Other Accounting Amendments) Regulations 2004, SI 2004/2947, reg 3, Sch 1, paras 1, 14, in relation to companies' financial years which begin on or after 1 January 2005.

Sub-s (6): word in square brackets substituted by the Companies Act 1985 (Miscellaneous Accounting Amendments) Regulations 1996, SI 1996/189, regs 8, 16(5), in relation to any annual accounts of a company which are approved by the board of directors on or after 2 February 1996.

[247A Cases in which special provisions do not apply

[(1) If a company is, or was at any time within the financial year to which the accounts relate, an ineligible company, sections 246 and 246A do not apply.

(1A) If a company does not fall within subsection (1) but is, or was at any time within the financial year to which the accounts relate, a member of an ineligible group—

(a) section 246(4) and (5)(b) and section 246A(2A) (provisions relating to directors' report) apply;

(b) the other provisions of sections 246 and 246A do not apply.

[(1B) A company that qualifies as small in relation to the financial year to which the accounts relate is ineligible if—

(a) it is a public company,

(b) it is an authorised insurance company, a banking company, an e-money issuer, an ISD investment firm or a UCITS management company, or

(c) it carries on an insurance market activity.

(1C) A company that qualifies as medium-sized in relation to the financial year to which the accounts relate is ineligible if—

(a) it is a public company,

(b) it has permission under Part 4 of the Financial Services and Markets Act 2000 to carry on a regulated activity, or

(c) it carries on an insurance market activity.]]

(2) A group is ineligible if any of its members is—

(a) a public company or a body corporate which (not being a company) has power under its constitution to offer its shares or debentures to the public and may lawfully exercise that power,

[(b) a person [(other than a small company)] who has permission under Part 4 of the Financial Services and Markets Act 2000 to carry on a regulated activity,

[(ba) a small company that is an authorised insurance company, a banking company, an e-money issuer, an ISD investment firm or a UCITS management company, or]
(c) a person who carries on an insurance market activity.]

[(2A) A company is a small company for the purposes of subsection (2) if it qualified as small in relation to its last financial year ending on or before the end of the financial year to which the accounts relate.]

(3) A parent company shall not be treated as qualifying as a small company in relation to a financial year unless the group headed by it qualifies as a small group, and shall not be treated as qualifying as a medium-sized company in relation to a financial year unless that group qualifies as a medium-sized group (see section 249).]

[390]

NOTES

Repealed as noted to s 1 at **[309]**.

Inserted by the Companies Act 1985 (Accounts of Small and Medium-sized Companies and Minor Accounting Amendments) Regulations 1997, SI 1997/220, reg 4, in relation to annual accounts approved by the board of directors on or after 1 March 1997, and to directors' and auditors' reports on such accounts; for a transitional provision see reg 1(4) of the 1997 Regulations.

Sub-ss (1), (1A): substituted, together with sub-s (1B) for original sub-s (1), by the Companies Act 1985 (Operating and Financial Review and Directors' Report etc) Regulations 2005, SI 2005/1011, reg 6.

Sub-s (1B): originally substituted as noted above; further substituted, together with sub-s (1C), by the Companies Act 1985 (Small Companies' Accounts and Audit) Regulations 2006, SI 2006/2782, reg 2(1), (2), in relation to annual accounts and reports in respect of financial years ending on or after 31 December 2006. The original sub-s (1B) (as amended by the Companies Act 1985 (Investment Companies and Accounting and Audit Amendments) Regulations 2005, SI 2005/2280, reg 13, in relation to accounts copies of which are delivered to the registrar of companies on or after that date) read as follows—

"(1B) A company is ineligible if—
(a) it is a public company,
(b) it has permission under Part 4 of the Financial Services and Markets Act 2000 to carry on [a regulated activity], or
(c) it carries on an insurance market activity.".

Sub-s (1C): substituted as noted above.

Sub-s (2): paras (b), (c) substituted, for original paras (b)–(d), by SI 2001/3649, art 11(1), (3); words in square brackets in para (b) inserted, and para (ba) substituted for the original word "or" at the end of para (b), by SI 2006/2782, reg 2(1), (3), in relation to annual accounts and reports in respect of financial years ending on or after 31 December 2006.

Sub-s (2A): inserted by SI 2006/2782, reg 2(1), (4), in relation to annual accounts and reports in respect of financial years ending on or after 31 December 2006.

Note: the Companies Act 1985 (Operating and Financial Review and Directors' Report etc) Regulations 2005, SI 2005/1011, reg 1(3) originally provided that the amendment made by reg 6 of those Regulations to this section would have effect as respects companies' financial years which begin on or after 1 April 2005. See now, the Companies Act 1985 (Investment Companies and Accounting and Audit Amendments) Regulations 2005, SI 2005/2280, reg 14, which provides as follows—

"14 Application of SI 2005/1011, regulation 6

Regulation 6 of the Companies Act 1985 (Operating and Financial Review and Directors. Report etc) Regulations 2005 (which amends section 247A of the 1985 Act so as to enable a small company to take advantage of certain exemptions despite being a member of an ineligible group) has effect in relation to a financial year—
(a) beginning before 1st April 2005 but on or after 1st January 2005, and
(b) ending on or after 1st October 2005,
as it has effect in relation to a financial year beginning on or after 1st April 2005.".

[247B Special auditors' report

(1) This section applies where—
(a) the directors of a company propose to deliver to the registrar copies of accounts ("abbreviated accounts") prepared in accordance with section 246(5) or (6) or 246A(3) ("the relevant provision"),
(b) the directors have not taken advantage of the exemption from audit conferred by section 249A(1) or (2) [or section 249AA], ...
(c) ...

(2) If abbreviated accounts prepared in accordance with the relevant provision are delivered to the registrar, they shall be accompanied by a copy of a special report of the auditors stating that in their opinion—

(*a*) *the company is entitled to deliver abbreviated accounts prepared in accordance with that provision, and*

(*b*) *the abbreviated accounts to be delivered are properly prepared in accordance with that provision.*

(*3*) *In such a case a copy of the auditors' report under section 235 need not be delivered, but—*

(*a*) *if that report was qualified, the special report shall set out that report in full together with any further material necessary to understand the qualification; and*

(*b*) *if that report contained a statement under—*

(*i*) *section 237(2) (accounts, records or returns inadequate or accounts not agreeing with records and returns), or*

(*ii*) *section 237(3) (failure to obtain necessary information and explanations),*

the special report shall set out that statement in full.

(*4*) *Section 236 (signature of auditors' report) applies to a special report under this section as it applies to a report under section 235.*

(*5*) *If abbreviated accounts prepared in accordance with the relevant provision are delivered to the registrar, references in section 240 (requirements in connection with publication of accounts) to the auditors' report under section 235 shall be read as references to the special auditors' report under this section.]*

[391]

NOTES

Repealed as noted to s 1 at **[309]**.

Inserted by the Companies Act 1985 (Accounts of Small and Medium-sized Companies and Minor Accounting Amendments) Regulations 1997, SI 1997/220, reg 5, in relation to annual accounts approved by the board of directors on or after 1 March 1997, and to directors' and auditors' reports on such accounts; for a transitional provision see reg 1(4) of the 1997 Regulations.

Sub-s (1): words in square brackets inserted and words omitted repealed by the Companies Act 1985 (Audit Exemption) (Amendment) Regulations 2000, SI 2000/1430, reg 8(2), in relation to annual reports and reports in respect of financial years ending two months or more after 26 May 2000.

[248 Exemption for small and medium-sized groups

(*1*) *A parent company need not prepare group accounts for a financial year in relation to which the group headed by that company qualifies as a small or medium-sized group and is not an ineligible group.*

(*2*) *A group is ineligible if any of its members is—*

(*a*) *a public company or body corporate which (not being a company) has power under its constitution to offer its shares or debentures to the public and may lawfully exercise that power,*

[(b) a person [(other than a small company)] who has permission under Part 4 of the Financial Services and Markets Act 2000 to carry on a regulated activity,

[(ba) a small company that is an authorised insurance company, a banking company, an e-money issuer, an ISD investment firm or a UCITS management company, or]

(*c*) *a person who carries on an insurance market activity.]*

[(2A) A company is a small company for the purposes of subsection (2) if it qualified as small in relation to its last financial year ending on or before the end of the financial year to which the group accounts relate.]

(3), (4) …]

[392]

NOTES

Repealed as noted to s 1 at **[309]**.

Inserted, together with s 249, by the Companies Act 1989, s 13(3).

Sub-s (2): paras (b), (c) substituted, for original paras (b)–(d), by the Financial Services and Markets Act 2000 (Consequential Amendments and Repeals) Order 2001, SI 2001/3649, art 12; words in square brackets in para (b) inserted, and para (ba) substituted for the original word "or" at the end of para (b), by the Companies Act 1985 (Small Companies' Accounts and Audit) Regulations 2006, SI 2006/2782, reg 3(1), (2), in relation to annual accounts and reports in respect of financial years ending on or after 31 December 2006.

Sub-s (2A): inserted by SI 2006/2782, reg 3(1), (3), in relation to annual accounts and reports in respect of financial years ending on or after 31 December 2006.

PART I STATUTES

Sub-ss (3), (4): repealed by the Companies Act 1985 (Miscellaneous Accounting Amendments) Regulations 1996, SI 1996/189, regs 9, 16(1), in relation to any financial year ending on or after 2 February 1996; for a transitional provision see reg 16(2) of the 1996 Regulations.

Modification: by the Insurance Companies (Third Insurance Directive) Regulations 1994, SI 1994/1696, reg 68(1), Sch 8, Pt I, para 9(1), sub-s (2) above has effect as if the reference to an insurance company to which the Insurance Companies Act 1982, Pt II, applies includes a reference to an EC company lawfully carrying on insurance business in the United Kingdom.

[248A Group accounts prepared by small company

(1) This section applies where a small company—

(a) has prepared individual accounts for a financial year in accordance with section 246(2) or (3), and

(b) is preparing [Companies Act group accounts] in respect of the same year.

(2) If the group accounts—

(a) comply with the provisions of Schedule 8, or

(b) fail to comply with those provisions only in so far as they comply instead with one or more corresponding provisions of Schedule 4,

they need not comply with the provisions or, as the case may be, the remaining provisions of Schedule 4; and where advantage is taken of this subsection, references in Schedule 4A to compliance with the provisions of Schedule 4 shall be construed accordingly.

(3) For the purposes of this section, Schedule 8 shall have effect as if, in each balance sheet format set out in that Schedule, for item B.III there were substituted the following item—

"B.III Investments

1 Shares in group undertakings
2 Interests in associated undertakings
3 Other participating interests
4 Loans to group undertakings and undertakings in which a participating interest is held
5 Other investments other than loans
6 Others."

(4) The group accounts need not give the information required by the provisions specified in section 246(3).

(5) Group accounts prepared in accordance with this section shall contain a statement in a prominent position on the balance sheet, above the signature required by section 233, that they are prepared in accordance with the special provisions of this Part relating to small companies.]

[393]

NOTES

Repealed as noted to s 1 at **[309]**.

Inserted by the Companies Act 1985 (Accounts of Small and Medium-sized Companies and Minor Accounting Amendments) Regulations 1997, SI 1997/220, reg 6, in relation to annual accounts approved by the board of directors on or after 1 March 1997, and to directors' and auditors' reports on such accounts; for a transitional provision see reg 1(4) of the 1997 Regulations.

Sub-s (1): words in square brackets substituted by the Companies Act 1985 (International Accounting Standards and Other Accounting Amendments) Regulations 2004, SI 2004/2947, reg 3, Sch 1, paras 1, 15, in relation to companies' financial years which begin on or after 1 January 2005.

[249 Qualification of group as small or medium-sized

(1) A group qualifies as small or medium-sized in relation to a financial year if the qualifying conditions are met—

(a) in the case of the parent company's first financial year, in that year, and

(b) in the case of any subsequent financial year, in that year and the preceding year.

(2) A group shall be treated as qualifying as small or medium-sized in relation to a financial year—

(a) if it so qualified in relation to the previous financial year under [subsection (1) above or was treated as so qualifying under paragraph (b) below]; or

(b) if it was treated as so qualifying in relation to the previous year by virtue of paragraph (a) and the qualifying conditions are met in the year in question.

(3) The qualifying conditions are met by a group in a year in which it satisfies two or more of the following requirements—

Small group

1. Aggregate turnover	*[Not more than £5.6 million net (or £6.72 million gross)]*
2. Aggregate balance sheet total	*[Not more than £2.8 million net (or £3.36 million gross)]*
3. Aggregate number of employees	*Not more than 50*

Medium-sized group

1. Aggregate turnover	*[Not more than £22.8 million net (or £27.36 million gross)]*
2. Aggregate balance sheet total	*[Not more than £11.4 million net (or £13.68 million gross)]*
3. Aggregate number of employees	*Not more than 250.*

(4) The aggregate figures shall be ascertained by aggregating the relevant figures determined in accordance with section 247 for each member of the group.

In relation to the aggregate figures for turnover and balance sheet total, "net" means with the set-offs and other adjustments required by Schedule 4A in the case of group accounts and "gross" means without those set-offs and other adjustments; and a company may satisfy the relevant requirements on the basis of either the net or the gross figure.

(5) The figures for each subsidiary undertaking shall be those included in its accounts for the relevant financial year, that is—

(a) if its financial year ends with that of the parent company, that financial year, and

(b) if not, its financial year ending last before the end of the financial year of the parent company.

(6) If those figures cannot be obtained without disproportionate expense or undue delay, the latest available figures shall be taken.]

[394]

NOTES

Repealed as noted to s 1 at **[309]**.

Inserted as noted to s 248 at **[392]**.

Sub-s (2): words in square brackets substituted by the Companies Act 1985 (Accounts of Small and Medium-Sized Enterprises and Publication of Accounts in ECUs) Regulations 1992, SI 1992/2452, reg 6(1), (2), in relation to annual accounts in respect of financial years ending on or after 16 November 1992, and to directors' and auditors' reports on such accounts; subject to transitional provisions contained in reg 7 thereof.

Sub-s (3): words in square brackets substituted by the Companies Act 1985 (Accounts of Small and Medium-Sized Enterprises and Audit Exemption) (Amendment) Regulations 2004, SI 2004/16, reg 3, in relation to financial years ending on or after that date.

[Exemptions from audit for certain categories of small company

249A Exemptions from audit

(1) Subject to section 249B, a company which meets the total exemption conditions set out below in respect of a financial year is exempt from the provisions of this Part relating to the audit of accounts in respect of that year.

(2) Subject to section 249B, [a company which is a charity and] which meets the report conditions set out below in respect of a financial year is exempt from the provisions of this

Part relating to the audit of accounts in respect of that year if the directors cause a report in respect of the company's individual accounts for that year to be prepared in accordance with section 249C and made to the company's members.

(3) The total exemption conditions are met by a company in respect of a financial year if—

(a) it qualifies as a small company in relation to that year for the purposes of section 246,

(b) its turnover in that year is not more than [£5.6 million], and

(c) its balance sheet total for that year is not more than [£2.8 million].

[(3A) In relation to any company which is a charity, subsection (3)(b) shall have effect with the substitution—

(a) for the reference to turnover of a reference to gross income, and

(b) for the reference to [£5.6 million] of a reference to £90,000.]

(4) The report conditions are met by [a company which is a charity] in respect of a financial year if—

(a) it qualifies as a small company in relation to that year for the purposes of section 246,

(b) its [gross income] in that year is more than £90,000 but not more than [£500,000], and

(c) its balance sheet total for that year is not more than [£2.8 million].

(5) …

(6) For a period which is a company's financial year but not in fact a year the maximum figures for turnover or gross income shall be proportionately adjusted.

[(6A) A company is entitled to the exemption conferred by subsection (1) or (2) notwithstanding that it falls within paragraph (a) or (b) of [section 249AA(1)].]

(7) In this section—

"balance sheet total" has the meaning given by section 247(5), and

"gross income" means the company's income from all sources, as shown in the company's income and expenditure account.]

[395]

NOTES

Repealed as noted to s 1 at **[309]**.

Inserted, together with the preceding heading and ss 249B–249E, by the Companies Act 1985 (Audit Exemption) Regulations 1994, SI 1994/1935, reg 2, subject to transitional provisions contained in reg 6 thereof.

Sub-s (2): repealed by the Companies Act 2006, s 1175, Sch 9, Pt 1, para 3(a), as from a day to be appointed under s 1300(2) of that Act; words in square brackets substituted by the Companies Act 1985 (Audit Exemption) (Amendment) Regulations 1997, SI 1997/936, reg 2(1), (2), in relation to the annual accounts of any company for any financial year ending two months or more after 15 April 1997.

Sub-s (3): words in square brackets substituted by the Companies Act 1985 (Accounts of Small and Medium-Sized Enterprises and Audit Exemption) (Amendment) Regulations 2004, SI 2004/16, regs 4, 7(4), in relation to financial years ending two months or more after that date.

Sub-s (3A): inserted by SI 1997/936, reg 2(1), (4), in relation to the annual accounts of any company for any financial year ending two months or more after that date, and repealed by the Companies Act 2006, s 1175, Sch 9, Pt 1, para 3(a), as from a day to be appointed under s 1300(2) of that Act; words in square brackets substituted by SI 2004/16, regs 4, 7(4), in relation to financial years ending two months or more after that date.

Sub-s (4): repealed by the Companies Act 2006, s 1175, Sch 9, Pt 1, para 3(a), as from a day to be appointed under s 1300(2) of that Act; words in first pair of square brackets, and words in first pair of square brackets in para (b), substituted by SI 1997/936, reg 2(1), (5), in relation to the annual accounts of any company for any financial year ending two months or more after that date; sums in square brackets in paras (b), (c) substituted in relation to any financial year of a charity which begins on or after 27 February 2007 by the Charities Act 2006, ss 32(1), 75(3), Sch 10, para 9.

Sub-s (5): repealed by SI 1997/936, reg 2(1), (6), in relation to the annual accounts of any company for any financial year ending two months or more after 15 April 1997.

Sub-s (6): for the words "figures for turnover or gross income" there are substituted the words "figure for turnover" by the Companies Act 2006, s 1175, Sch 9, Pt 1, para 3(b), as from a day to be appointed under s 1300(2) of that Act.

Sub-s (6A): inserted by SI 1997/936, reg 2(1), (7), (8), which amendment is deemed always to have had effect; words in square brackets substituted by SI 2000/1430, reg 2(1), (3), in relation to annual reports and reports in respect of financial years ending two months or more after 26 May 2000.

Sub-s (7): definition "gross income" and the word immediately preceding it repealed by the Companies Act 2006, s 1175, Sch 9, Pt 1, para 3(b), as from a day to be appointed under s 1300(2) of that Act.

[249AA Dormant companies

(1) Subject to section 249B(2) to (5), a company is exempt from the provisions of this Part relating to the audit of accounts in respect of a financial year if—

(a) it has been dormant since its formation, or

(b) it has been dormant since the end of the previous financial year and subsection (2) applies.

(2) This subsection applies if the company—

(a) is entitled in respect of its individual accounts for the financial year in question to prepare accounts in accordance with section 246, or would be so entitled but for the application [to it of subsection (1A), (1B)(a) or (1C)(a) of section 247A], and

(b) is not required to prepare group accounts for that year.

(3) Subsection (1) does not apply if at any time in the financial year in question the company was—

[[(a) an authorised insurance company, a banking company, an e-money issuer, an ISD investment firm or a UCITS management company;]

(b) a person who carries on insurance market activity].

(4) A company is "dormant" during any period in which it has no significant accounting transaction.

(5) "Significant accounting transaction" means a transaction which—

(a) is required by section 221 to be entered in the company's accounting records; but

(b) is not a transaction to which subsection (6) or (7) applies.

(6) This subsection applies to a transaction arising from the taking of shares in the company by a subscriber to the memorandum as a result of an undertaking of his in the memorandum.

(7) This subsection applies to a transaction consisting of the payment of—

(a) a fee to the registrar on a change of name under section 28 (change of name),

(b) a fee to the registrar on the re-registration of a company under Part II (re-registration as a means of altering a company's status),

(c) a penalty under section 242A (penalty for failure to deliver accounts), or

(d) a fee to the registrar for the registration of an annual return under Chapter III of Part XI.]

[396]

NOTES

Repealed as noted to s 1 at **[309]**.

Inserted by the Companies Act 1985 (Audit Exemption) (Amendment) Regulations 2000, SI 2000/1430, reg 3, in relation to annual reports and reports in respect of financial years ending two months or more after 26 May 2000.

Sub-s (2): words in square brackets in para (a) substituted (for the original words "of section 247A(1)(a)(i) or (b)") by the Companies Act 1985 (Small Companies' Accounts and Audit) Regulations 2006, SI 2006/2782, reg 4(1), (2), in relation to annual accounts and reports in respect of financial years ending on or after 31 December 2006.

Sub-s (3): paras (a), (b) originally substituted by the Financial Services and Markets Act 2000 (Consequential Amendments and Repeals) Order 2001, SI 2001/3649, art 13; para (a) further substituted by SI 2006/2782, reg 4(1), (3), in relation to annual accounts and reports in respect of financial years ending on or after 31 December 2006. The original para (a) (as amended by the Companies Act 1985 (Investment Companies and Accounting and Audit Amendments) Regulations 2005, SI 2005/2280, reg 15, in relation to accounts copies of which are delivered to the registrar of companies on or after that date) read as follows—

"(a) a person who has permission under Part 4 of the Financial Services and Markets Act 2000 to carry on [a regulated activity]; or".

[249B Cases where exemptions not available

(1) [Subject to [subsections (1A) to (1C)],] a company is not entitled to the exemption conferred by subsection (1) or (2) of section 249A in respect of a financial year if at any time within that year—

(a) it was a public company,

[(b) it was an authorised insurance company, a banking company, an e-money issuer, an ISD investment firm or a UCITS management company,]

[(bb) it carried on an insurance market activity,]

(c), (d) …

PART I STATUTES

(*e*) *it was a special register body as defined in section 117(1) of the Trade Union and Labour Relations (Consolidation) Act 1992 or an employers' association as defined in section 122 of that Act, or*

(*f*) *it was a parent company or a subsidiary undertaking.*

[(1A) A company which, apart from this subsection, would fall within subsection (1)(f) by virtue of its being a subsidiary undertaking for any period within a financial year shall not be treated as so falling if it is dormant (within the meaning of [section 249AA]) throughout that period.]

[(1B) A company which, apart from this subsection, would fall within subsection (1)(f) by virtue of its being a parent company or a subsidiary undertaking for any period within a financial year, shall not be treated as so falling if throughout that period it was a member of a group meeting the conditions set out in subsection (1C).

(1C) The conditions referred to in subsection (1B) are—

(*a*) *that the group qualifies as a small group, in relation to the financial year within which the period falls, for the purposes of section 249 [(or if all bodies corporate in such group were companies, would so qualify)] and is not, and was not at any time within that year, an ineligible group within the meaning of section 248(2),*

(*b*) *that the group's aggregate turnover in that year (calculated in accordance with section 249) is[, where the company referred to in subsection (1B) is a charity,] not more than [£700,000 net (or £840,000 gross)] [or, where the company so referred to is not a charity, [not more than £5.6 million net (or £6.72 million gross)]], and*

(*c*) *that the group's aggregate balance sheet total for that year (calculated in accordance with section 249) is [not more than £2.8 million net (or £3.36 million gross)].]*

(2) Any member or members holding not less in the aggregate than 10 per cent in nominal value of the company's issued share capital or any class of it or, if the company does not have a share capital, not less than 10 per cent in number of the members of the company, may, by notice in writing deposited at the registered office of the company during a financial year but not later than one month before the end of that year, require the company to obtain an audit of its accounts for that year.

(3) Where a notice has been deposited under subsection (2), the company is not entitled to the exemption conferred by subsection (1) or (2) of section 249A [or by subsection (1) of section 249AA] in respect of the financial year to which the notice relates.

(4) A company is not entitled to the exemption conferred by subsection (1) or (2) of section 249A [or by subsection (1) of section 249AA] unless its balance sheet contains a statement by the directors—

(*a*) *[to the effect] that for the year in question the company was entitled to exemption under subsection (1) or (2) ... of section 249A [or subsection (1) of section 249AA],*

[(*b*) *to the effect that members have not required the company to obtain an audit of its accounts for the year in question in accordance with subsection (2) of this section], and*

(*c*) *[to the effect] that the directors acknowledge their responsibilities for—*

(*i*) *ensuring that the company keeps accounting records which comply with section 221, and*

(*ii*) *preparing accounts which give a true and fair view of the state of affairs of the company as at the end of the financial year and of its profit or loss for the financial year in accordance with the requirements of section 226, and which otherwise comply with the requirements of this Act relating to accounts, so far as applicable to the company.*

(5) The statement required by subsection (4) shall appear in the balance sheet [above the signature required by section 233].]

[397]

NOTES

Repealed as noted to s 1 at **[309]**.

Inserted as noted to s 249A at **[395]**.

Sub-s (1): words in first (outer) pair of square brackets inserted by the Companies Act 1985 (Miscellaneous Accounting Amendments) Regulations 1996, SI 1996/189, regs 10(1), (2), 16(5), in relation to any annual accounts of a company which are approved by the board of directors on or after

2 February 1996; words in second (inner) pair of square brackets substituted by the Companies Act 1985 (Audit Exemption) (Amendment) Regulations 1997, SI 1997/936, reg 3(1), (2), in relation to the annual accounts of any company for any financial year ending two months or more after 15 April 1997.

Sub-s (1A): inserted by SI 1996/189, regs 10(1), (3), 16(5), in relation to any annual accounts of a company which are approved by the board of directors on or after 2 February 1996; words in square brackets substituted by the Companies Act 1985 (Audit Exemption) (Amendment) Regulations 2000, SI 2000/1430, reg 4(1), (2), in relation to annual reports and reports in respect of financial years ending two months or more after 26 May 2000.

Sub-s (1B): inserted by SI 1997/936, reg 3(1), (3), in relation to the annual accounts of any company for any financial year ending two months or more after 15 April 1997.

Sub-s (1C): inserted by SI 1997/936, reg 3(1), (3), in relation to the annual accounts of any company for any financial year ending two months or more after 15 April 1997; words in first, second and fourth (outer) pairs of square brackets inserted by SI 2000/1430, reg 4(1), (3), in relation to annual reports and reports in respect of financial years ending two months or more after 26 May 2000; words in fifth (inner) and sixth pairs of square brackets substituted by the Companies Act 1985 (Accounts of Small and Medium-Sized Enterprises and Audit Exemption) (Amendment) Regulations 2004, SI 2004/16, regs 5, 7(4), in relation to financial years ending two months or more after that date; words in third pair of square brackets substituted for the words "£350,000 net (or £420,000 gross)" in relation to any financial year of a charity which begins on or after 27 February 2007 by the Charities Act 2006, ss 32(2), 75(3), Sch 10, except in relation to Scotland; words from "where the company referred to in subsection (1B)" to "is not a charity" repealed by the Companies Act 2006, s 1175, Sch 9, Pt 1, para 4(b), as from a day to be appointed under s 1300(2) of that Act.

Sub-s (3): words in square brackets inserted by SI 2000/1430, reg 4(1), (4), in relation to annual reports and reports in respect of financial years ending two months or more after 26 May 2000.

Sub-s (4): words in first and third pairs of square brackets inserted, words omitted repealed and para (b) substituted by SI 2000/1430, reg 4(1), (5), in relation to annual reports and reports in respect of financial years ending two months or more after 26 May 2000; words in second and fourth pairs of square brackets inserted by SI 1996/189, regs 10(1), (4), 16(1), in relation to any financial year ending on or after 2 February 1996, for a transitional provision see reg 16(2) of the 1996 Regulations.

Sub-s (5): words in square brackets substituted by SI 1996/189, regs 10(1), (5), 16(1), in relation to any financial year ending on or after 2 February 1996; for a transitional provision see reg 16(2) of the 1996 Regulations.

[249C The report required for the purposes of section 249A(2)

(1) The report required for the purposes of section 249A(2) shall be prepared by a person (referred to in this Part as "the reporting accountant") who is eligible under section 249D.

(2) The report shall state whether in the opinion of the reporting accountant making it—
- *(a) the accounts of the company for the financial year in question are in agreement with the accounting records kept by the company under section 221, and*
- *(b) having regard only to, and on the basis of, the information contained in those accounting records, those accounts have been drawn up in a manner consistent with the provisions of this Act specified in subsection (6), so far as applicable to the company.*

(3) The report shall also state that in the opinion of the reporting accountant, having regard only to, and on the basis of, the information contained in the accounting records kept by the company under section 221, the company satisfied the requirements of subsection (4) of section 249A … for the financial year in question, and did not fall within section 249B(1)(a) to (f) at any time within that financial year.

(4) The report shall state the name of the reporting accountant and be signed by him.

(5) Where the reporting accountant is a body corporate or partnership, any reference to signature of the report, or any copy of the report, by the reporting accountant is a reference to signature in the name of the body corporate or partnership by a person authorised to sign on its behalf.

(6) The provisions referred to in subsection (2)(b) are—
- *(a) [section 226A(3)] and Schedule 4,*
- *(b) section 231 and paragraphs 7 to 9A and 13(1), (3) and (4) of Schedule 5, and*
- *(c) section 232 and Schedule 6,*

where appropriate as modified by [section 246(2) and (3)].]

[398]

NOTES

Repealed as noted to s 1 at **[309]**.

Inserted as noted to s 249A at **[395]**.

Sub-s (3): words omitted repealed by the Companies Act 1985 (Audit Exemption) (Amendment) Regulations 2000, SI 2000/1430, reg 8(3), in relation to annual reports and reports in respect of financial years ending two months or more after 26 May 2000.

Sub-s (6): words in first pair of square brackets substituted by the Companies Act 1985 (International Accounting Standards and Other Accounting Amendments) Regulations 2004, SI 2004/2947, reg 3, Sch 1, para 16, in relation to companies' financial years which begin on or after 1 January 2005; words in second pair of square brackets substituted by the Companies Act 1985 (Accounts of Small and Medium-sized Companies and Minor Accounting Amendments) Regulations 1997, SI 1997/220, reg 7(3), in relation to annual accounts approved by the board of directors on or after 1 March 1997, and to directors' and auditors' reports on such accounts (for a transitional provision, see reg 1(4) of the 1997 Regulations).

[249D The reporting accountant

[(1) The reporting accountant shall be either—

(a) any member of a body listed in subsection (3) who, under the rules of the body—

(i) is entitled to engage in public practice, and

(ii) is not ineligible for appointment as a reporting accountant, or

(b) any person (whether or not a member of any such body) who—

(i) is subject to the rules of any such body in seeking appointment or acting as auditor under Chapter V of Part XI, and

(ii) under those rules, is eligible for appointment as auditor under that Chapter.

(1A) In subsection (1), references to the rules of a body listed in subsection (3) are to the rules (whether or not laid down by the body itself) which the body has power to enforce and which are relevant for the purposes of Part II of the Companies Act 1989 or this section.

This includes rules relating to the admission and expulsion of members of the body, so far as relevant for the purposes of that Part or this section.]

(2) An individual, a body corporate or a partnership may be appointed as a reporting accountant, and section 26 of the Companies Act 1989 (effect of appointment of partnership) shall apply to the appointment as reporting accountant of a partnership constituted under the law of England and Wales or Northern Ireland, or under the law of any other country or territory in which a partnership is not a legal person.

(3) The bodies referred to in [subsections (1) and (1A)] are—

(a) the Institute of Chartered Accountants in England and Wales,

(b) the Institute of Chartered Accountants of Scotland,

(c) the Institute of Chartered Accountants in Ireland,

(d) [the Association of Chartered Certified Accountants], ...

(e) the Association of Authorised Public Accountants.

(f) the Association of Accounting Technicians,

(g) the Association of International Accountants, ...

(h) the Chartered Institute of Management Accountants[, and

(i) the Institute of Chartered Secretaries and Administrators].]

(4) A person is ineligible for appointment by a company as reporting accountant if he would be ineligible for appointment as an auditor of that company under section 27 of the Companies Act 1989 (ineligibility on ground of lack of independence).]

[399]

NOTES

Repealed as noted to s 1 at **[309]**.

Inserted as noted to s 249A at **[395]**.

Sub-ss (1), (1A): substituted for original sub-s (1) by the Companies Act 1985 (Audit Exemption) (Amendment) Regulations 1995, SI 1995/589, reg 2(1), (2), subject to a transitional provision in reg 3 thereof.

Sub-s (3): words in first pair of square brackets substituted by SI 1995/589, reg 2(1), (3), subject to a transitional provision in reg 3 thereof; words in second pair of square brackets substituted by the Companies Act 1985 (Audit Exemption) (Amendment) Regulations 1997, SI 1997/936, reg 4, in relation to the annual accounts of any company for any financial year ending two months or more after 15 April 1997; word omitted repealed and paras (f)–(h) added by the Companies Act 1985 (Audit Exemption) (Amendment) Regulations 1996, SI 1996/3080, reg 2; word omitted from para (g) repealed, and para (i) added, by the Companies Act 1985 (Accounts of Small and Medium-Sized Enterprises and Audit Exemption) (Amendment) Regulations 2004, SI 2004/16, regs 6, 7(5), in relation to financial years ending on or after that date.

[249E Effect of exemptions

(1) Where the directors of a company have taken advantage of the exemption conferred by section 249A(1) [or 249AA(1)]—

(*a*) *sections 238 and 239* (*right to receive or demand copies of accounts and reports*) *shall have effect with the omission of references to the auditors' report;*

(*b*) *no copy of an auditors' report need be delivered to the registrar or laid before the company in general meeting;*

(*c*) *subsections* (*3*) *to* (*5*) *of section 271* (*accounts by reference to which distribution to be justified*) *shall not apply.*

[(1A) Where the directors of a company have taken advantage of the exemption conferred by section 249AA, then for the purposes of that section the company shall be treated as a company entitled to prepare accounts in accordance with section 246 even though it is a member of an ineligible group.]

(2) *Where the directors of a company have taken advantage of the exemption conferred by section 249A*(2)*—*

(*a*) *subsections* (2) *to* (4) *of section 236* (*which require copies of the auditors' report to state the names of the auditors*) *shall have effect with the substitution for references to the auditors and the auditors' report of references to the reporting accountant and the report made for the purposes of section 249A*(2) *respectively;*

(*b*) *sections 238 and 239* (*right to receive or demand copies of accounts and reports*), *section 241* (*accounts and reports to be laid before company in general meeting*) *and section 242* (*accounts and reports to be delivered to the registrar*) *shall have effect with the substitution for references to the auditors' report of references to the report made for the purposes of section 249A*(2)*;*

(*c*) *subsections* (3) *to* (5) *of section 271* (*accounts by reference to which distribution to be justified*) *shall not apply;*

(*d*) *[sections 389A*(*1*) *and 389B*(*1*) *and* (*5*)*]* (*rights to information*) *shall have effect with the substitution for references to [an auditor] of references to the reporting accountant.]*

[400]

NOTES

Repealed as noted to s 1 at **[309]**.

Inserted as noted to s 249A at **[395]**.

Sub-s (1): words in square brackets inserted by the Companies Act 1985 (Audit Exemption) (Amendment) Regulations 2000, SI 2000/1430, reg 8(4), in relation to annual reports and reports in respect of financial years ending two months or more after 26 May 2000.

Sub-s (1A): inserted by SI 2000/1430, reg 8(5), in relation to annual reports and reports in respect of financial years ending two months or more after 26 May 2000.

Sub-s (2): repealed by the Companies Act 2006, s 1175, Sch 9, Pt 1, para 7, as from a day to be appointed under s 1300(2) of that Act; words in square brackets in para (d) substituted by the Companies (Audit, Investigations and Community Enterprise) Act 2004, s 25, Sch 2, Pt 2, paras 5, 6.

250 (*Repealed by the Companies Act 1985* (*Audit Exemption*) (*Amendment*) *Regulations 2000, SI 2000/1430, reg 8*(*6*)*, in relation to annual reports and reports in respect of financial years ending two months or more after 26 May 2000.*)

[[Summary financial statement]

251 Provision of summary financial statement to shareholders

(*1*) *[A company] need not, in such cases as may be specified by regulations made by the Secretary of State, and provided any conditions so specified are complied with, send copies of the documents referred to in [section 238*(*1A*)*] to [entitled persons], but may instead send them a summary financial statement.*

[In this section—

"entitled persons", in relation to a company, means such of the persons specified in paragraphs (*a*) *to* (*c*) *of subsection* (*1*) *of section 238 as are or would apart from this section be entitled to be sent copies of those documents relating to the company which are referred to in that subsection;*

["summary financial statement" means a statement that is derived from the company's annual accounts and (*in the case of a quoted company*) *the directors' remuneration report and prepared in accordance with this section and regulations made under it;]*

[.....

.....]]

(2) Copies of the documents referred to in [section 238(1A)] shall, however, be sent to [any entitled person] who wishes to receive them; and the Secretary of State may by regulations make provision as to the manner in which it is to be ascertained [(whether before or after he becomes an entitled person)] whether [an entitled person] wishes to receive them.

[(2ZA) …]

[(2ZB) A company that sends to an entitled person a summary financial statement instead of a copy of its directors' report shall—
- *(a) include in the statement the explanatory material required to be included in the directors' report by section 234ZZA(5), or*
- *(b) send that material to the entitled person at the same time as it sends the statement.*

For the purposes of paragraph (b), subsections (2A) to (2E) apply in relation to the material referred to in that paragraph as they apply in relation to a summary financial statement.]

[(2A)–(2E) …]

[(3) The summary financial statement must—
- *(a) be in such form, and*
- *(b) contain such information,*

as the Secretary of State may by regulations specify, including information derived from the company's directors' report …

(3A) Nothing in this section or regulations made under it prevents a company from including in its summary financial statement additional information derived from the company's annual accounts, directors' remuneration report [or directors' report].]

[(4) Every summary financial statement shall—
- *(a) state that it is only a summary of information in the company's annual accounts, … and (in the case of a quoted company) the directors' remuneration report;*
- *[(aa) state whether it contains additional information derived from the directors' report … and, if so, state that it does not contain the full text of that report … ;*
- *(ab) state how an entitled person can obtain a full copy of the documents referred to in section 238(1A);*
- *(ac) …]*
- *(b) contain a statement by the company's auditors of their opinion as to whether the summary financial statement—*
  - *[(i) is consistent with the company's annual accounts and directors' remuneration report and (where information derived from the directors' report … is included in the statement) with that report … , and*
  - *(ii)] complies with the requirements of this section and regulations made under it;*
- *(c) state whether the auditors' report on the annual accounts, or on the annual accounts and the auditable part of the directors' remuneration report, was unqualified or qualified, and if it was qualified set out the report in full together with any further material needed to understand the qualification;*
- *[(ca) state whether, in that report, the auditor's statement under section 235(3) (whether directors' report is consistent with accounts) was qualified or unqualified and, if qualified, set out the qualified statement in full together with any further material needed to understand the qualification;]*
- *(d) state whether that auditors' report contained a statement under—*
  - *(i) section 237(2) (accounting records or returns inadequate or accounts or directors' remuneration report not agreeing with records and returns); or*
  - *(ii) section 237(3) (failure to obtain necessary information and explanations),*

and if so, set out the statement in full.]

(5) Regulations under this section shall be made by statutory instrument which shall be subject to annulment in pursuance of a resolution of either House of Parliament.

(6) If default is made in complying with this section or regulations made under it, the company and every officer of it who is in default is guilty of an offence and liable to a fine.

(7) Section 240 (requirements in connection with publication of accounts) does not apply in relation to the provision to [entitled persons] of a summary financial statement in accordance with this section.]

[401]

NOTES

Repealed as noted to s 1 at **[309]**.

Inserted, together with the preceding heading, by the Companies Act 1989, s 15.

Cross-heading preceding this section substituted by the Companies Act 1985 (International Accounting Standards and Other Accounting Amendments) Regulations 2004, SI 2004/2947, reg 11(1), in relation to companies' financial years which begin on or after 1 January 2005.

Sub-s (1): words in first and second pairs of square brackets inserted, and words in third and fourth pairs of square brackets substituted by the Companies Act 1985 (Amendment of Sections 250 and 251) Regulations 1992, SI 1992/3003, reg 3(1)–(3).

Sub-s (2): words in first pair of square brackets substituted by SI 2005/1011, reg 12(1), (3), in relation to companies' financial years which begin on or after 1 April 2005; words in second and fourth pairs of square brackets substituted, and words in third pair of square brackets inserted, by SI 1992/3003, reg 3(1), (4).

Sub-s (2ZA): inserted by SI 2005/1011, reg 12(1), (4), in relation to companies' financial years which begin on or after 1 April 2005; repealed by the Companies Act 1985 (Operating and Financial Review) (Repeal) Regulations 2005, SI 2005/3442, reg 2(2)(a), Sch 1, para 14(1), (2).

Sub-s (2ZB): inserted by the Companies Act 2006, s 992(1), (5), (6), as from a day to be appointed under s 1300(2) of that Act, in relation to directors' reports for financial years beginning on or after 20 May 2006.

Sub-ss (2A)–(2E): inserted by the Companies Act 1985 (Electronic Communications) Order 2000, SI 2000/3373, art 14; repealed by the Companies Act 2006, s 1295, Sch 16, for transitional provisions see the note to s 238 at **[374]**.

Sub-s (3): substituted by the Directors' Remuneration Report Regulations 2002, SI 2002/1986, reg 8(1), (2), with effect as respects companies' financial years ending on or after 31 December 2002; further substituted by new sub-s (3), (3A) by SI 2005/1011, reg 12(1), (7), in relation to companies' financial years which begin on or after 1 April 2005; words omitted repealed by SI 2005/3442, reg 2(2)(a), Sch 1, para 14(1), (4).

Sub-s (3A): substituted by SI 2002/1986, reg 8(1), (2), with effect as respects companies' financial years ending on or after 31 December 2002; words in square brackets substituted by SI 2005/3442, reg 2(2)(a), Sch 1, para 14(1), (5).

Sub-s (4): substituted by SI 2002/1986, reg 8(1), (3), with effect as respects companies' financial years ending on or after 31 December 2002; words omitted from para (a) repealed, paras (aa)–(a), (ca) inserted, and words in square brackets in para (b) substituted, by SI 2005/1011, reg 12(1), (8), in relation to companies' financial years which begin on or after 1 April 2005; words omitted from paras (aa), (b)(i), and the whole of para (ac), repealed, and para (ca) substituted, by SI 2005/3442, reg 2(2)(a), Sch 1, para 14(1), (6).

Transitional provisions: the Companies Act 1985 (Operating and Financial Review and Directors' Report etc) Regulations 2005, SI 2005/1011, reg 13 provides as follows (note that by virtue of reg 1(2) of the 2005 Regulations, they came into force on 22 March 2005)—

"13 Transitional provision

As respects companies' financial years beginning on or after 1st April 2005, regulations made by the Secretary of State under section 251 of the 1985 Act before the date on which these Regulations come into force have effect as if—

(a) any requirement in the regulations that a summary financial statement contain information derived from the company's directors' report was omitted, and

(b) the regulations had been made (with those omissions) under section 251 as amended by these Regulations.".

Modification: reference to the Official List as maintained by The London Stock Exchange Limited (formerly known as The International Stock Exchange of the United Kingdom and the Republic of Ireland Limited) shall have effect, in certain circumstances, as a reference to the Official List as maintained by the Financial Services Authority, by virtue of the Official Listing of Securities (Change of Competent Authority) Regulations 2000, SI 2000/968, reg 4.

Regulations: the Companies (Summary Financial Statement) Regulations 1995, SI 1995/2092.

[Private companies

252 Election to dispense with laying of accounts and reports before general meeting

(1) A private company may elect (by elective resolution in accordance with section 379A) to dispense with the laying of accounts and reports before the company in general meeting.

(2) An election has effect in relation to the accounts and reports in respect of the financial year in which the election is made and subsequent financial years.

(3) Whilst an election is in force, the references in the following provisions of this Act to the laying of accounts before the company in general meeting shall be read as references to the sending of copies of the accounts to members and others under section 238(1)—

(*a*) *section 235(1) (accounts on which auditors are to report),*

(*b*) *section 270(3) and (4) (accounts by reference to which distributions are justified), and*

(*c*) *section 320(2) (accounts relevant for determining company's net assets for purposes of ascertaining whether approval required for certain transactions);*

and the requirement in section 271(4) that the auditors' statement under that provision be laid before the company in general meeting shall be read as a requirement that it be sent to members and others along with the copies of the accounts sent to them under section 238(1).

(4) If an election under this section ceases to have effect, section 241 applies in relation to the accounts and reports in respect of the financial year in which the election ceases to have effect and subsequent financial years.]

[402]

NOTES

Repealed as noted to s 1 at **[309]**.
Inserted, together with the preceding heading and s 253, by the Companies Act 1989, s 16.

[253 Right of shareholder to require laying of accounts

(1) Where an election under section 252 is in force, the copies of the accounts and reports sent out in accordance with section 238(1)—

(*a*) *shall be sent not less than 28 days before the end of the period allowed for laying and delivering accounts and reports, and*

(*b*) *shall be accompanied, in the case of a member of the company, by a notice informing him of his right to require the laying of the accounts and reports before a general meeting;*

and section 238(5) (penalty for default) applies in relation to the above requirements as to the requirements contained in that section.

(2) Before the end of the period of 28 days beginning with the day on which the accounts and reports are sent out in accordance with section 238(1), any member or auditor of the company may by notice in writing deposited at the registered office of the company require that a general meeting be held for the purpose of laying the accounts and reports before the company.

[(2A) …]

(3) If the directors do not within 21 days from the date of[—

(*a*) *the deposit of a notice containing a requirement under subsection (2), or*

(*b*) *the receipt of such a requirement contained in an electronic communication,*

proceed] duly to convene a meeting, the person who [required the holding of the meeting] may do so himself.

(4) A meeting so convened shall not be held more than three months from that date and shall be convened in the same manner, as nearly as possible, as that in which meetings are to be convened by directors.

(5) Where the directors do not duly convene a meeting, any reasonable expenses incurred by reason of that failure by the person who [required the holding of the meeting] shall be made good to him by the company, and shall be recouped by the company out of any fees, or other remuneration in respect of their services, due or to become due to such of the directors as were in default.

(6) The directors shall be deemed not to have duly convened a meeting if they convene a meeting for a date more than 28 days after the date of the notice convening it.]

[403]

NOTES

Repealed as noted to s 1 at **[309]**.
Inserted as noted to s 252 at **[402]**.
Sub-s (2A): inserted by the Companies Act 1985 (Electronic Communications) Order 2000, SI 2000/3373, art 15(1), (2); repealed by the Companies Act 2006, s 1295, Sch 16.
Sub-ss (3), (5): words in square brackets substituted by SI 2000/3373, art 15(1), (3), (4).

[Unlimited companies

254 Exemption from requirement to deliver accounts and reports

(1) The directors of an unlimited company are not required to deliver accounts and reports to the registrar in respect of a financial year if the following conditions are met.

(2) The conditions are that at no time during the relevant accounting reference period—

(a) has the company been, to its knowledge, a subsidiary undertaking of an undertaking which was then limited, or

(b) have there been, to its knowledge, exercisable by or on behalf of two or more undertakings which were then limited, rights which if exercisable by one of them would have made the company a subsidiary undertaking of it, or

(c) has the company been a parent company of an undertaking which was then limited.

The references above to an undertaking being limited at a particular time are to an undertaking (under whatever law established) the liability of whose members is at that time limited.

(3) The exemption conferred by this section does not apply [if—

(a) the company is a banking [or insurance] company or the parent company of a banking [or insurance] group, or

(b) the company is a qualifying company within the meaning of the Partnerships and Unlimited Companies (Accounts) Regulations 1993, ...

(c)] ...

(4) Where a company is exempt by virtue of this section from the obligation to deliver accounts, section 240 (requirements in connection with publication of accounts) has effect with the following modifications—

(a) in subsection (3)(b) for the words from "whether statutory accounts" to "have been delivered to the registrar" substitute "that the company is exempt from the requirement to deliver statutory accounts", and

(b) in subsection (5) for "as required to be delivered to the registrar under section 242" substitute "as prepared in accordance with this Part and approved by the board of directors".]

[404]

NOTES

Repealed as noted to s 1 at **[309]**.

Inserted, together with the preceding heading, by the Companies Act 1989, s 17.

Sub-s (3): words in first (outer) pair of square brackets substituted (for the words inserted by the Companies Act 1985 (Bank Accounts) Regulations 1991, SI 1991/2705, reg 6, Sch 2, para 1), by the Partnerships and Unlimited Companies (Accounts) Regulations 1993, SI 1993/1820, reg 10; words in second and third (inner) pairs of square brackets inserted by the Companies Act 1985 (Insurance Companies Accounts) Regulations 1993, SI 1993/3246, reg 5(1), Sch 2, para 2, subject to transitional provisions contained in regs 6, 7 thereof; para (c) and the word immediately preceding it repealed by the Regulatory Reform (Trading Stamps) Order 2005, SI 2005/781, art 6, Schedule.

[Banking and insurance companies and groups

255 Special provisions for banking and insurance companies

(1) A banking company shall prepare its individual accounts in accordance with Part I of Schedule 9 rather than Schedule 4.

(2) An insurance company [shall] prepare its individual accounts in accordance with Part I of Schedule 9A rather than Schedule 4.

(3) Accounts so prepared shall contain a statement that they are prepared in accordance with the special provisions of this Part relating to banking companies or insurance companies, as the case may be.

(4) In relation to the preparation of individual accounts in accordance with the special provisions of this Part, the references to Schedule 4 in section 226(4) and (5) (relationship between specific requirements and duty to give true and fair view) shall be read as references to the provisions of Part I of Schedule 9, in the case of the accounts of banking companies, or to the provisions of Part I of Schedule 9A, in the case of the accounts of insurance companies.

[(4A) References to Companies Act individual accounts include accounts prepared in accordance with this section.

(4B) This section does not apply to banking companies and insurance companies that prepare IAS individual accounts.]

(5) ...]

[405]

NOTES

Repealed as noted to s 1 at **[309]**.

Substituted, together with ss 255A, 255B for ss 255, 255A, 255B (as inserted by the Companies Act 1989, s 18(1)), by the Companies Act 1985 (Bank Accounts) Regulations 1991, SI 1991/2705, regs 3, 9, subject to transitional provisions.

Sub-s (2): word in square brackets substituted by the Companies Act 1985 (Insurance Companies Accounts) Regulations 1993, SI 1993/3246, reg 2(1), subject to transitional provisions contained in regs 6, 7 thereof.

Sub-ss (4A), (4B): inserted by the Companies Act 1985 (International Accounting Standards and Other Accounting Amendments) Regulations 2004, SI 2004/2947, reg 3, Sch 1, paras 1, 17, in relation to companies' financial years which begin on or after 1 January 2005.

Sub-s (5): repealed by SI 1993/3246, reg 2(2), subject to transitional provisions contained in regs 6, 7 thereof.

[255A Special provisions for banking and insurance groups

(1) The parent company of a banking group shall prepare group accounts in accordance with the provisions of this Part as modified by Part II of Schedule 9.

(2) The parent company of an insurance group [shall] prepare group accounts in accordance with the provisions of this Part as modified by Part II of Schedule 9A.

(3) Accounts so prepared shall contain a statement that they are prepared in accordance with the special provisions of this Part relating to banking groups or to insurance groups, as the case may be.

[(4) References in this Part to a banking group are to a group where the parent company is a banking company or where—

(a) the parent company's principal subsidiary undertakings are wholly or mainly credit institutions, and

(b) the parent company does not itself carry on any material business apart from the acquisition, management and disposal of interests in subsidiary undertakings.

(5) References in this Part to an insurance group are to a group where the parent company is an insurance company or where—

(a) the parent company's principal subsidiary undertakings are wholly or mainly insurance companies, and

(b) the parent company does not itself carry on any material business apart from the acquisition, management and disposal of interests in subsidiary undertakings.

(5A) For the purposes of subsections (4) and (5) above—

(a) a parent company's principal subsidiary undertakings are the subsidiary undertakings of the company whose results or financial position would principally affect the figures shown in the group accounts, and

(b) the management of interests in subsidiary undertakings includes the provision of services to such undertakings.]

(6) In relation to the preparation of group accounts in accordance with the special provisions of this Part:

(a) the references to the provisions of Schedule 4A in [section 227A(4) and (5)] (relationship between specific requirements and duty to give true and fair view) shall be read as references to those provisions as modified by Part II of Schedule 9, in the case of the group accounts of a banking group, or Part II of Schedule 9A, in the case of the group accounts of an insurance group; and

(b) the reference to paragraphs 52 to 57 of Schedule 4 in section 230(2) (relief from obligation to comply with those paragraphs where group accounts prepared) shall be read as a reference to paragraphs [75 to 77], 80 and 81 of Part I of Schedule 9, in the case of the group accounts of a banking group[, and as a reference to paragraphs 73, 74, 79 and 80 of Part I of Schedule 9A, in the case of the group accounts of an insurance group].

[(6A) References to Companies Act group accounts include accounts prepared in accordance with subsections (1) to (3).

(6B) Subsections (1) to (3) and (6) do not apply to parent companies of banking groups or insurance groups that prepare IAS group accounts.]

(7) ...

[406]

NOTES

Repealed as noted to s 1 at **[309]**.
Substituted as noted to s 255 at **[405]**.
Sub-s (2): word in square brackets substituted by the Companies Act 1985 (Insurance Companies Accounts) Regulations 1993, SI 1993/3246, regs 3(1), subject to transitional provisions in regs 6, 7 thereof.
Sub-ss (4), (5), (5A): substituted for original sub-ss (4), (5) by SI 1993/3246, reg 3(2), subject to transitional provisions in regs 6, 7.
Sub-s (6): words in first pair of square brackets substituted by the Companies Act 1985 (International Accounting Standards and Other Accounting Amendments) Regulations 2004, SI 2004/2947, reg 3, Sch 1, paras 1, 18(1), (2), in relation to companies' financial years which begin on or after 1 January 2005; words in second pair of square brackets substituted by the Companies Act 1985 (Miscellaneous Accounting Amendments) Regulations 1996, SI 1996/189, regs 15(2), 16(1), in relation to any financial year ending on or after 2 February 1996, for a transitional provision, see reg 16(2) of the 1996 Regulations (note, in relation to this amendment, the word "paragraphs" has not been substituted as specified, in order to preserve the sense of the text); words in third pair of square brackets added by SI 1993/3246, reg 3(3), subject to exemptions in relation to certain companies contained in reg 6 and general transitional provisions in reg 7.
Sub-ss (6A), (6B): inserted by SI 2004/2947, reg 3, Sch 1, paras 1, 18(1), (3), in relation to companies' financial years which begin on or after 1 January 2005.
Sub-s (7): repealed by SI 1993/3246, reg 3(4), subject to transitional provisions contained in regs 6, 7 thereof.

[255B Modification of disclosure requirements in relation to banking company or group

(1) In relation to a banking company, or the [parent company of a banking group], the provisions of Schedule 5 (Disclosure of information: related undertakings) have effect subject to Part III of Schedule 9.

(2) In relation to a banking company, or the [holding company of a credit institution], the provisions of Schedule 6 (Disclosure of information: emoluments and other benefits of directors and others) have effect subject to Part IV of Schedule 9.]

[407]

NOTES

Repealed as noted to s 1 at **[309]**.
Substituted as noted to s 255 at **[405]**.
Sub-s (1): words in square brackets substituted by the Companies Act 1985 (Disclosure of Branches and Bank Accounts) Regulations 1992, SI 1992/3178, regs 6, 8(b), subject to a transitional provision.
Sub-s (2): words in square brackets substituted by the Companies Act 1985 (Bank Accounts) Regulations 1994, SI 1994/233, reg 3.

255C *(Inserted by the Companies Act 1989, s 18(1), and repealed by the Companies Act 1985 (Insurance Companies Accounts) Regulations 1993, SI 1993/3246, reg 5(1), Sch 2, para 3, subject to transitional provisions contained in regs 6, 7 thereof.)*

[255D Power to apply provisions to banking partnerships

(1) The Secretary of State may by regulations apply to banking partnerships, subject to such exceptions, adaptations and modifications as he considers appropriate, the provisions of this Part applying to banking companies.

[(2) A "banking partnership" means a partnership which has permission under Part 4 of the Financial Services and Markets Act 2000.

(2A) But a partnership is not a banking partnership if it has permission to accept deposits only for the purpose of carrying on another regulated activity in accordance with that permission.]

(3) Regulations under this section shall be made by statutory instrument.

(4) No regulations under this section shall be made unless a draft of the instrument containing the regulations has been laid before Parliament and approved by a resolution of each House.

[(5) Subsections (2) *and* (2A) *must be read with—*

(a) section 22 of the Financial Services and Markets Act 2000;

(b) any relevant order under that section; and

(c) Schedule 2 to that Act.]]

[408]

NOTES

Repealed as noted to s 1 at **[309]**.

Inserted by the Companies Act 1989, s 18(2).

Sub-ss (2), (2A): substituted, for original sub-s (2), by the Financial Services and Markets Act 2000 (Consequential Amendments and Repeals) Order 2001, SI 2001/3649, art 16(1).

Sub-s (5): added by SI 2001/3649, art 16(2).

255E *(Inserted by the Companies Act 1985 (Welsh Language Accounts) Regulations 1992, SI 1992/1083, reg 2(1), (4), and repealed by the Welsh Language Act 1993, ss 30(1), (5), 35(1), Sch 2.)*

[CHAPTER III
SUPPLEMENTARY PROVISIONS

Accounting standards

256 Accounting standards

(1) In this Part "accounting standards" means statements of standard accounting practice issued by such body or bodies as may be prescribed by regulations.

(2) References in this Part to accounting standards applicable to a company's annual accounts are to such standards as are, in accordance with their terms, relevant to the company's circumstances and to the accounts.

(3) ...

(4) Regulations under this section may contain such transitional and other supplementary and incidental provisions as appear to the Secretary of State to be appropriate.]

[409]

NOTES

Repealed as noted to s 1 at **[309]**.

Inserted, together with the preceding headings, by the Companies Act 1989, s 19.

Sub-s (3): repealed by the Companies (Audit, Investigations and Community Enterprise) Act 2004, ss 16(7), 64, Sch 8.

Regulations: the Accounting Standards (Prescribed Body) Regulations 2005, SI 2005/697.

[Power to alter accounting requirements

257 Power of Secretary of State to alter accounting requirements

(1) The Secretary of State may by regulations made by statutory instrument modify the provisions of this Part.

(2) Regulations which—

(a) add to the classes of documents required to be prepared, laid before the company in general meeting or delivered to the registrar,

(b) restrict the classes of company which have the benefit of any exemption, exception or special provision,

(c) require additional matter to be included in a document of any class, or

(d) otherwise render the requirements of this Part more onerous,

shall not be made unless a draft of the instrument containing the regulations has been laid before Parliament and approved by a resolution of each House.

(3) Otherwise, a statutory instrument containing regulations under this section shall be subject to annulment in pursuance of a resolution of either House of Parliament.

(4) Regulations under this section may—

(a) make different provision for different cases or classes of case,

(b) repeal and re-enact provisions with modifications of form or arrangement, whether or not they are modified in substance,

(c) make consequential amendments or repeals in other provisions of this Act, or in other enactments, and

(d) contain such transitional and other incidental and supplementary provisions as the Secretary of State thinks fit.

[(4A) Regulations under this section may also make provision—

(a) for the issuing, by such body or bodies as may be specified, of standards in relation to matters to be contained in reports which are required by this Part to be prepared by the directors of a company;

(b) for directors of a company who have complied with any such standard, or any of its provisions, in relation to any such report, to be presumed (unless the contrary is proved) to have complied with any requirements of this Part relating to the contents of the report to which the standard or provision relates.

(4B) In subsection (4A) "specified" means specified in an order made by the Secretary of State; and such an order—

(a) shall be made by statutory instrument which shall be subject to annulment in pursuance of a resolution of either House of Parliament;

(b) may contain such transitional provisions as the Secretary of State thinks fit.]

(5) Any modification by regulations under this section of section 258 or Schedule 10A (parent and subsidiary undertakings) does not apply for the purposes of enactments outside the Companies Acts unless the regulations so provide.]

[410]

NOTES

Repealed as noted to s 1 at **[309]**.

Inserted, together with the preceding heading, by the Companies Act 1989, s 20.

Sub-ss (4A), (4B): inserted by the Companies (Audit, Investigations and Community Enterprise) Act 2004, s 13.

Regulations: the Companies Act 1985 (Bank Accounts) Regulations 1991, SI 1991/2705; the Companies Act 1985 (Accounts of Small and Medium-sized Enterprises and Publication of Accounts in ECUs) Regulations 1992, SI 1992/2452; the Companies Act 1985 (Amendment of Sections 250 and 251) Regulations 1992, SI 1992/3003; the Companies Act 1985 (Disclosure of Branches and Bank Accounts) Regulations 1992, SI 1992/3178; the Partnerships and Unlimited (Accounts) Regulations 1993, SI 1993/1820; the Companies Act 1985 (Insurance Companies Accounts) Regulations 1993, SI 1993/3246; the Companies Act 1985 (Bank Accounts) Regulations 1994, SI 1994/233; the Companies Act 1985 (Audit Exemption) Regulations 1994, SI 1994/1935; the Companies Act 1985 (Audit Exemption) (Amendment) Regulations 1995, SI 1995/589; the Companies Act 1985 (Miscellaneous Accounting Amendments) Regulations 1996, SI 1996/189; the Companies Act 1985 (Audit Exemption) (Amendment) Regulations 1996, SI 1996/3080; the Companies Act 1985 (Accounts of Small and Medium-sized Companies and Minor Accounting Amendments) Regulations 1997, SI 1997/220; the Company Accounts (Disclosure of Directors' Emoluments) Regulations 1997, SI 1997/570; the Companies Act 1985 (Directors' Report) (Statement of Payment Practice) Regulations 1997, SI 1997/571; the Companies Act 1985 (Audit Exemption) (Amendment) Regulations 1997, SI 1997/936; the Companies Act 1985 (Insurance Companies Accounts) (Minor Amendments) Regulations 1997, SI 1997/2704; the Companies Act 1985 (Audit Exemption) (Amendment) Regulations 2000, SI 2000/1430; the Directors' Remuneration Report Regulations 2002, SI 2002/1986; the Companies Act 1985 (Accounts of Small and Medium-Sized Enterprises and Audit Exemption) (Amendment) Regulations 2004, SI 2004/16; the Companies Act 1985 (International Accounting Standards and Other Accounting Amendments) Regulations 2004, SI 2004/2947; the Companies Act 1985 (Operating and Financial Review and Directors' Report etc) Regulations 2005, SI 2005/1011; the Companies Act 1985 (Investment Companies and Accounting and Audit Amendments) Regulations 2005, SI 2005/2280; the Companies Act 1985 (Operating and Financial Review) (Repeal) Regulations 2005, SI 2005/3442; the Companies Act 1985 (Small Companies' Accounts and Audit) Regulations 2006, SI 2006/2782.

Orders: the Reporting Standards (Specified Body) Order 2005, SI 2005/692.

[Parent and subsidiary undertakings

258 Parent and subsidiary undertakings

(1) The expressions "parent undertaking" and "subsidiary undertaking" in this Part shall be construed as follows; and a "parent company" means a parent undertaking which is a company.

(2) An undertaking is a parent undertaking in relation to another undertaking, a subsidiary undertaking, if—

- *(a) it holds a majority of the voting rights in the undertaking, or*
- *(b) it is a member of the undertaking and has the right to appoint or remove a majority of its board of directors, or*
- *(c) it has the right to exercise a dominant influence over the undertaking—*
  - *(i) by virtue of provisions contained in the undertaking's memorandum or articles, or*
  - *(ii) by virtue of a control contract, or*
- *(d) it is a member of the undertaking and controls alone, pursuant to an agreement with other shareholders or members, a majority of the voting rights in the undertaking.*

(3) For the purposes of subsection (2) an undertaking shall be treated as a member of another undertaking—

- *(a) if any of its subsidiary undertakings is a member of that undertaking, or*
- *(b) if any shares in that other undertaking are held by a person acting on behalf of the undertaking or any of its subsidiary undertakings.*

(4) An undertaking is also a parent undertaking in relation to another undertaking, a subsidiary undertaking, if ...—

- *[(a) it has the power to exercise, or actually exercises, dominant influence or control over it, or]*
- *(b) it and the subsidiary undertaking are managed on a unified basis.*

(5) A parent undertaking shall be treated as the parent undertaking of undertakings in relation to which any of its subsidiary undertakings are, or are to be treated as, parent undertakings; and references to its subsidiary undertakings shall be construed accordingly.

(6) Schedule 10A contains provisions explaining expressions used in this section and otherwise supplementing this section.]

[411]

NOTES

Repealed as noted to s 1 at **[309]**.

Inserted, together with the preceding heading, by the Companies Act 1989, s 21(1).

Sub-s (4): words omitted repealed, and para (a) substituted, by the Companies Act 1985 (International Accounting Standards and Other Accounting Amendments) Regulations 2004, SI 2004/2947, reg 12(1), in relation to companies' financial years which begin on or after 1 January 2005.

Note that SI 2004/2947, reg 12(2) also provides that the amendments noted above also apply for the purposes of he Building Societies Act 1986, and the Financial Services and Markets Act 2000.

[Other interpretation provisions

259 Meaning of "undertaking" and related expressions

(1) In this Part "undertaking" means—

- *(a) a body corporate or partnership, or*
- *(b) an unincorporated association carrying on a trade or business, with or without a view to profit.*

(2) In this Part references to shares—

- *(a) in relation to an undertaking with a share capital, are to allotted shares;*
- *(b) in relation to an undertaking with capital but no share capital, are to rights to share in the capital of the undertaking; and*
- *(c) in relation to an undertaking without capital, are to interests—*
  - *(i) conferring any right to share in the profits or liability to contribute to the losses of the undertaking, or*

(ii) giving rise to an obligation to contribute to the debts or expenses of the undertaking in the event of a winding up.

(3) Other expressions appropriate to companies shall be construed, in relation to an undertaking which is not a company, as references to the corresponding persons, officers, documents or organs, as the case may be, appropriate to undertakings of that description.

This is subject to provision in any specific context providing for the translation of such expressions.

(4) References in this Part to "fellow subsidiary undertakings" are to undertakings which are subsidiary undertakings of the same parent undertaking but are not parent undertakings or subsidiary undertakings of each other.

(5) In this Part "group undertaking", in relation to an undertaking, means an undertaking which is—

(a) a parent undertaking or subsidiary undertaking of that undertaking, or

(b) a subsidiary undertaking of any parent undertaking of that undertaking.]

[412]

NOTES

Repealed as noted to s 1 at **[309]**.

Inserted, together with the preceding heading and ss 260, 261, 262, 262A, by the Companies Act 1989, s 22.

[260 Participating interests

(1) In this Part a "participating interest" means an interest held by an undertaking in the shares of another undertaking which it holds on a long-term basis for the purpose of securing a contribution to its activities by the exercise of control or influence arising from or related to that interest.

(2) A holding of 20 per cent or more of the shares of an undertaking shall be presumed to be a participating interest unless the contrary is shown.

(3) The reference in subsection (1) to an interest in shares includes—

(a) an interest which is convertible into an interest in shares, and

(b) an option to acquire shares or any such interest;

and an interest or option falls within paragraph (a) or (b) notwithstanding that the shares to which it relates are, until the conversion or the exercise of the option, unissued.

(4) For the purposes of this section an interest held on behalf of an undertaking shall be treated as held by it.

(5) …

(6) In the balance sheet and profit and loss formats set out in Part I of Schedule 4[, [Part I of Schedule 8, Schedule 8A,] Chapter I of Part I of Schedule 9 and Chapter I of Part I of Schedule 9A], "participating interest" does not include an interest in a group undertaking.

(7) For the purposes of this section as it applies in relation to the expression "participating interest"—

(a) in those formats as they apply in relation to group accounts, and

(b) in paragraph 20 of Schedule 4A (group accounts: undertakings to be accounted for as associated undertakings),

the references in subsections (1) to (4) to the interest held by, and the purposes and activities of, the undertaking concerned shall be construed as references to the interest held by, and the purposes and activities of, the group (within the meaning of paragraph 1 of that Schedule).]

[413]

NOTES

Repealed as noted to s 1 at **[309]**.

Inserted as noted to s 259 at **[412]**.

Sub-s (5): repealed by the Companies Act 1985 (International Accounting Standards and Other Accounting Amendments) Regulations 2004, SI 2004/2947, reg 15, Sch 7, Pt 1, paras 1, 7, in relation to companies' financial years which begin on or after 1 January 2005.

Sub-s (6): words in first (outer) pair of square brackets (originally inserted by the Companies Act 1985 (Bank Accounts) Regulations 1991, SI 1991/2705, reg 6, Sch 2, para 2) substituted by the Companies Act 1985 (Insurance Companies Accounts) Regulations 1993, SI 1993/3246, reg 5(1), Sch 2, para 4, subject to transitional provisions in regs 6, 7 thereof; words in second (inner) pair of square brackets inserted by the Companies Act 1985 (Accounts of Small and Medium-sized Companies and Minor Accounting Amendments) Regulations 1997, SI 1997/220, reg 7(5), in relation to annual accounts approved by the board of directors on or after 1 March 1997, and to directors' and auditors' reports on such accounts, for a transitional provision see reg 1(4) of the 1997 Regulations.

[261 Notes to the accounts

(1) Information required by this Part to be given in notes to a company's annual accounts may be contained in the accounts or in a separate document annexed to the accounts.

(2) References in this Part to a company's annual accounts, or to a balance sheet or profit and loss account, include notes to the accounts giving information which is required by any provision of this Act [or international accounting standards], and required or allowed by any such provision to be given in a note to company accounts.]

[414]

NOTES

Repealed as noted to s 1 at **[309]**.

Inserted as noted to s 259 at **[412]**.

Sub-s (2): words in square brackets inserted by the Companies Act 1985 (International Accounting Standards and Other Accounting Amendments) Regulations 2004, SI 2004/2947, reg 3, Sch 1, paras 1, 19, in relation to companies' financial years which begin on or after 1 January 2005.

[262 Minor definitions

(1) In this Part—

[.....]

"annual accounts" means—

(a) the individual accounts required by section 226, and

(b) any group accounts required by section 227,

(but see also section 230 (treatment of individual profit and loss account where group accounts prepared));

"annual report", in relation to a company, means the directors' report required by section 234;

"balance sheet date" means the date as at which the balance sheet was made up;

"capitalisation", in relation to work or costs, means treating that work or those costs as a fixed asset;

["Companies Act accounts" means Companies Act individual accounts or Companies Act group accounts;]

["credit institution" means a credit institution as defined in [Article 4(1)(a) of Directive 2006/48/EC of the European Parliament and of the Council of 14 June 2006] relating to the taking up and pursuit of the business of credit institutions, that is to say an undertaking whose business is to receive deposits or other repayable funds from the public and to grant credits for its own account;]

[.....]

["e-money issuer" means a person who has permission under Part 4 of the Financial Services and Markets Act 2000 to carry on the activity of issuing electronic money within the meaning of article 9B of the Financial Services and Markets Act 2000 (Regulated Activities) Order 2001;]

"fixed assets" means assets of a company which are intended for use on a continuing basis in the company's activities, and "current assets" means assets not intended for such use;

"group" means a parent undertaking and its subsidiary undertakings;

["IAS accounts" means IAS individual accounts or IAS group accounts;]

["IAS Regulation" means EC Regulation No 1606/2002 of the European Parliament and of the Council of 19th July 2002 on the application of international accounting standards;]

"included in the consolidation", in relation to group accounts, or "included in consolidated group accounts", means that the undertaking is included in the accounts by the method of full (and not proportional) consolidation, and references to an undertaking excluded from consolidation shall be construed accordingly;

["international accounting standards" means the international accounting standards, within the meaning of the IAS Regulation, adopted from time to time by the European Commission in accordance with that Regulation;]

["ISD investment firm" has the same meaning as in the General Provisions and Glossary Instrument 2001 made by the Financial Services Authority under the Financial Services and Markets Act 2000;]

["profit and loss account", in relation to a company that prepares IAS accounts, includes an income statement or other equivalent financial statement required to be prepared by international accounting standards;]

"purchase price", in relation to an asset of a company or any raw materials or consumables used in the production of such an asset, includes any consideration (whether in cash or otherwise) given by the company in respect of that asset or those materials or consumables, as the case may be;

"qualified", in relation to an auditors' report, means that the report does not state the auditors' unqualified opinion that the accounts have been properly prepared in accordance with this Act or, in the case of an undertaking not required to prepare accounts in accordance with this Act, under any corresponding legislation under which it is required to prepare accounts;

["quoted company" means a company whose equity share capital—

- *(a) has been included in the official list in accordance with the provisions of Part VI of the Financial Services and Markets Act 2000; or*
- *(b) is officially listed in an EEA State; or*
- *(c) is admitted to dealing on either the New York Stock Exchange or the exchange known as Nasdaq;*

and in paragraph (a) "the official list" shall have the meaning given it by section 103(1) of the Financial Services and Markets Act 2000;]

["regulated activity" has the meaning given by section 744, except that it does not include activities of the kind specified in any of the following provisions of the Financial Services and Markets Act 2000 (Regulated Activities) Order 2001—

- *(a) article 25A (arranging regulated mortgage contracts),*
- *[(aa) article 25B (arranging regulated home reversion plans),*
- *(ab) article 25C (arranging regulated home purchase plans),]*
- *(b) article 39A (assisting administration and performance of a contract of insurance),*
- *(c) article 53A (advising on regulated mortgage contracts), or*
- *[(ca) article 53B (advising on regulated home reversion plans),*
- *(cb) article 53C (advising on regulated home purchase plans), ...]*
- *(d) article 21 (dealing as agent), article 25 (arranging deals in investments) or article 53 (advising on investments) where the activity concerns relevant investments that are not contractually based investments (within the meaning of article 3 of that Order)[, or*
- *(e) article 64 (agreeing to carry on a regulated activity of the kind mentioned in paragraphs (a) to (d) above);]]*

.....

"turnover", in relation to a company, means the amounts derived from the provision of goods and services falling within the company's ordinary activities, after deduction of—

- *(i) trade discounts,*
- *(ii) value added tax, and*
- *(iii) any other taxes based on the amounts so derived;*

["UCITS management company" has the same meaning as in the Collective Investment Schemes (UCITS Amending Directive) Instrument 2003 made by the Financial Services Authority under the Financial Services and Markets Act 2000].

(2) In the case of an undertaking not trading for profit, any reference in this Part to a profit and loss account is to an income and expenditure account; and references to profit and loss and, in relation to group accounts, to a consolidated profit and loss account shall be construed accordingly.

[(2A) References in this Part to accounts giving a "true and fair view" are references—

- *(a) in the case of Companies Act individual accounts, to the requirement under section 226A that such accounts give a true and fair view;*
- *(b) in the case of Companies Act group accounts, to the requirement under section 227A that such accounts give a true and fair view; and*
- *(c) in the case of IAS accounts, to the requirement under international accounting standards that such accounts achieve a fair presentation.]*

(3) References in this Part to "realised profits" and "realised losses", in relation to a company's accounts, are to such profits or losses of the company as fall to be treated as

realised in accordance with principles generally accepted, at the time when the accounts are prepared, with respect to the determination for accounting purposes of realised profits or losses.

This is without prejudice to—

(*a*) *the construction of any other expression (where appropriate) by reference to accepted accounting principles or practice, or*

(*b*) *any specific provision for the treatment of profits or losses of any description as realised.]*

[415]

NOTES

Repealed as noted to s 1 at **[309]**.

Inserted as noted to s 259 at **[412]**.

Sub-s (1): definition "address" inserted by the Companies Act 1985 (Electronic Communications) Order 2000, SI 2000/3373, art 16(1), and repealed by the Companies Act 2006, s 1295, Sch 16; definitions "Companies Act accounts", "IAS accounts", "IAS Regulation", "international accounting standards", and "profit and loss account" inserted, and definition "true and fair view" repealed, by the Companies Act 1985 (International Accounting Standards and Other Accounting Amendments) Regulations 2004, SI 2004/2947, reg 3, Sch 1, paras 1, 20(1), (2), in relation to companies' financial years which begin on or after 1 January 2005; definition "credit institution" substituted by the Banking Consolidation Directive (Consequential Amendments) Regulations 2000, SI 2000/2952, reg 2(1), (3); words in square brackets substituted by the Capital Requirements Regulations 2006, SI 2006/3221, reg 29(2), Sch 4, para 2(1), (3); definition "EEA State" originally inserted by the Companies Act 1985 (Miscellaneous Accounting Amendments) Regulations 1996, SI 1996/189, regs 12(1), 16(1), in relation to any financial year ending on or after 2 February 1996; repealed by the Companies (Membership of Holding Company) (Dealers in Securities) Regulations 1997, SI 1997/2306, reg 4(2); definitions "e-money issuer", "ISD investment firm", and "UCITS management company" inserted by the Companies Act 1985 (Small Companies' Accounts and Audit) Regulations 2006, SI 2006/2782, reg 6(1), (2), in relation to annual accounts and reports in respect of financial years ending on or after 31 December 2006; definition "quoted company" inserted by the Directors' Remuneration Report Regulations 2002, SI 2002/1986, reg 10(1), (11), with effect as respects companies' financial years ending on or after 31 December 2002; definition "regulated activity" inserted by the Companies Act 1985 (Investment Companies and Accounting and Audit Amendments) Regulations 2005, SI 2005/2280, reg 17(1), in relation to accounts copies of which are delivered to the registrar of companies on or after that date; paras (aa), (ab), (ca), (cb) inserted, and the word "or" in para (c) is repealed, by the Financial Services and Markets Act 2000 (Regulated Activities) (Amendment) (No 2) Order 2006, SI 2006/2383, art 26, as from 6 April 2007; word "or" at the end of para (cb) repealed, and para (e) inserted, by SI 2006/2782, reg 6(1), (3), in relation to annual accounts and reports in respect of financial years ending on or after 31 December 2006.

Sub-s (2A): inserted by SI 2004/2947, reg 3, Sch 1, paras 1, 20(1), (3), in relation to companies' financial years which begin on or after 1 January 2005.

[262A Index of defined expressions

The following Table shows the provisions of this Part defining or otherwise explaining expressions used in this Part (other than expressions used only in the same section or paragraph)—

[the 1982 Act (in Schedule 9A)	*paragraph 81 of Part I of that Schedule]*
accounting reference date and accounting reference period	*section 224*
accounting standards and applicable accounting standards	*section 256*
[.....]	
annual accounts	
(generally)	*section 262(1)*
(includes notes to the accounts)	*section 261(2)*
annual report	*section 262(1)*
associated undertaking (in Schedule 4A)	*paragraph 20 of that Schedule*
[auditable part (of a directors' remuneration report)	*section 235(5)]*

balance sheet (includes notes)	*section 261(2)*
balance sheet date	*section 262(1)*
[.....]	
banking group	*[section 255A(4)]*
[.....]	
capitalisation (in relation to work or costs)	*section 262(1)*
[Companies Act accounts	*Section 262(1)]*
[Companies Act group accounts	*Sections 227(2) and 255A(6A)]*
[Companies Act individual accounts	*Sections 226(2) and 255(4A)]*
credit institution	*section 262(1)*
current assets	*section 262(1)*
[directors' report	*section 23]*
[.....]	
[e-money issuer	*section 262]*
fellow subsidiary undertaking	*section 259(4)*
[financial fixed assets (in Schedule 9)	*paragraph 82 of Part I of that Schedule]*
financial year	*section 223*
fixed assets	*section 262(1)*
[general business (in Schedule 9A)	*paragraph 81 of Part I of that Schedule]*
group	*section 262(1)*
[group accounts	*Section 227(1)]*
[group directors' report	*section 234]*
[.....]	
group undertaking	*section 259(5)*
[historical cost accounting rules	
—in Schedule 4	*paragraph 29 of that Schedule*
[—in Schedule 8	*paragraph 29 of that Schedule]*
—in Schedule 9	*paragraph 39 of Part I of that Schedule*
[—in Schedule 9A	*paragraph 20(1) of Part I of that Schedule]]*
[IAS accounts	*Section 262(1)]*
[IAS group accounts	*Section 227(2) and (3)]*
[IAS individual accounts	*Section 226(2)]*
[IAS Regulation	*Section 262(1)]*
included in the consolidation and related expressions	*section 262(1)*
individual accounts	*section 226(1)*
insurance group	*[section 255A(5)]*
[international accounting standards	*Section 262(1)]*
[ISD investment firm	*section 262]*
land of freehold tenure and land of leasehold tenure (in relation to Scotland)	
—in Schedule 4	*paragraph 93 of that Schedule*
[—in Schedule 9	*paragraph 86 of Part I of that Schedule]*
[—in Schedule 9A	*paragraph 85 of Part I of that Schedule]*

PART I STATUTES

lease, long lease and short lease	
—in Schedule 4	*paragraph 83 of that Schedule*
[—in Schedule 9	*paragraph 82 of Part I of that Schedule]*
[—in Schedule 9A	*paragraph 81 of Part I of that Schedule]*
listed investment	
—in Schedule 4	*paragraph 84 of that Schedule*
[—in Schedule 8	*paragraph 54 of that Schedule]*
[—in Schedule 9A	*paragraph 81 of Part I of that Schedule]*
[listed security (in Schedule 9)	*paragraph 82 of Part I of that Schedule]*
[long term business (in Schedule 9A)	*paragraph 81 of Part I of that Schedule*
long term fund (in Schedule 9A)	*paragraph 81 of Part I of that Schedule]*
notes to the accounts	*section 261(1)*
[.....]	
parent undertaking (and parent company)	*section 258 and Schedule 10A*
participating interest	*section 260*
[pension costs	
—in Schedule 4	*paragraph 94(2) of that Schedule*
—in Schedule 8	*paragraph 59(2) of that Schedule*
—in Schedule 9	*paragraph 87(b) of Part I of that Schedule*
—in Schedule 9A	*paragraph 86(b) of Part I of that Schedule]*
period allowed for laying and delivering accounts and reports	*section 244*
[policy holder (in Schedule 9A)	*paragraph 81 of Part I of that Schedule]*
profit and loss account	
(includes notes)	*section 261(2)*
[(in relation to IAS accounts)	*Section 262(1)]*
(in relation to a company not trading for profit)	*section 262(2)*
provision	
—in Schedule 4	*paragraphs 88 and 89 of that Schedule*
[—in Schedule 8	*paragraphs 57 and 58 of that Schedule]*
[—in Schedule 9	*paragraph 85 of Part I of that Schedule]*
[—in Schedule 9A	*paragraph 84 of Part I of that Schedule]*
[provision for unexpired risks (in Schedule 9A)	*paragraph 81 of Part I of that Schedule]*
purchase price	*section 262(1)*
qualified	*section 262(1)*
[quoted company	*section 262(1)]*
realised losses and realised profits	*section 262(3)*
[regulated activity	*sections 262 and 744]*
[repayable on demand (in Schedule 9)	*paragraph 82 of Part I of that Schedule]*
[reporting accountant	*section 249C(1)]*
[.....]	
reserve (in [Schedule 9A])	*paragraph 32 of that Schedule*

[sale and repurchase transaction (in Schedule 9)	*paragraph 82 of Part I of that Schedule*
sale and option to resell transaction (in Schedule 9)	*paragraph 82 of Part I of that Schedule]*
shares	*section 259(2)*
[social security costs	
—in Schedule 4	*paragraph 94(1) and (3) of that Schedule*
[—in Schedule 8	*paragraph 59(1) and (3) of that Schedule]*
—in Schedule 9	*paragraph 87(a) and (c) of Part I of that Schedule*
[—in Schedule 9A	*paragraph 86(a) and (c) of Part I of that Schedule]]*
special provisions for banking and insurance companies and groups	*sections 255 and 255A*
subsidiary undertaking	*section 258 and Schedule 10A*
[true and fair view	*section 262(2A)]*
turnover	*section 262(1)*
[UCITS management company	*section 262]*
undertaking and related expressions	*section 259(1) to (3).]*

[416]

NOTES

Repealed as noted to s 1 at **[309]**. Note that this section is also amended by the 2006 Act (see below).

Inserted as noted to s 259 at **[412]**.

Entries relating to "the 1982 Act (in Schedule 9A)", "general business (in Schedule 9A)", "long term business (in Schedule 9A)", "long term fund (in Schedule 9A)", "policy holder (in Schedule 9A)", "provision for unexpired risks (in Schedule 9A)" inserted by the Companies Act 1985 (Insurance Companies Accounts) Regulations 1993, SI 1993/3246, regs 5(1), Sch 2, para 5(a), subject to exemptions in relation to certain companies contained in reg 6 and general transitional provisions in reg 7.

Entry relating to "address" inserted by the Companies Act 1985 (Electronic Communications) Order 2000, SI 2000/3373, art 16(2), and repealed by the Companies Act 2006, s 1295, Sch 16, subject to a saving for limited liability partnerships.

Entries relating to "auditable part (of a directors' remuneration report)" and "quoted company" inserted by the Directors' Remuneration Report Regulations 2002, SI 2002/1986, reg 10(1), (12), with effect as respects companies' financial years ending on or after 31 December 2002.

Entries relating to "banking activities" and "banking transactions" (originally inserted by the Companies Act 1985 (Bank Accounts) Regulations 1991, SI 1991/2705, reg 6, Sch 2, para 3) repealed by the Companies Act 1985 (Bank Accounts) Regulations 1994, SI 1994/233, reg 4(2), subject to transitional provisions in reg 7 thereof.

Entries "Companies Act accounts", "Companies Act group accounts", "Companies Act individual accounts", "group accounts", "IAS accounts", "IAS group accounts", "IAS individual accounts", "IAS Regulation", "international accounting standards", and "(in relation to IAS accounts)" inserted, and entry "true and fair view" substituted, by the Companies Act 1985 (International Accounting Standards and Other Accounting Amendments) Regulations 2004, SI 2004/2947, reg 3, Sch 1, paras 1, 21, in relation to companies' financial years which begin on or after 1 January 2005.

Entries "directors' report", "group directors' report", "group operating and financial review", "operating and financial review", and "reporting standards and relevant reporting standards" inserted by the Companies Act 1985 (Operating and Financial Review and Directors' Report etc) Regulations 2005, SI 2005/1011, reg 19, Schedule, paras 1, 7, in relation to companies' financial years which begin on or after 1 April 2005.

Entry relating to "EEA State" (originally inserted by the Companies Act 1985 (Miscellaneous Accounting Amendments) Regulations 1996, SI 1996/189, regs 12(2), 16(1), in relation to any financial year ending on or after 2 February 1996); repealed by the Companies (Membership of Holding Company) (Dealers in Securities) Regulations 1997, SI 1997/2306, reg 4(4).

Entries "e-money issuer", "ISD investment firm", and "UCITS management company" inserted by the Companies Act 1985 (Small Companies' Accounts and Audit) Regulations 2006, SI 2006/2782, reg 6(1), (4), in relation to annual accounts and reports in respect of financial years ending on or after 31 December 2006.

Entries relating to "financial fixed assets", "listed security", "repayable on demand", "sale and repurchase transaction", "sale and option to resell transaction" inserted, and words in square brackets in entries relating to "banking group" and "insurance group" substituted, by SI 1991/2705, reg 6, Sch 2, para 3.

Entries "group operating and financial review", "operating and financial review", and "reporting standards and relevant reporting standards" repealed by the Companies Act 1985 (Operating and Financial Review) (Repeal) Regulations 2005, SI 2005/3442, reg 2(2)(a), Sch 1, para 16.

Entry relating to "historical cost accounting rules" substituted by SI 1991/2705, reg 6, Sch 2, para 3; words in first pair of square brackets in that entry inserted by the Companies Act 1985 (Accounts of Small and Medium-sized Companies and Minor Accounting Amendments) Regulations 1997, SI 1997/220, reg 7(6)(a), in relation to annual accounts approved by the board of directors on or after 1 March 1997, and to directors' and auditors' reports on such accounts (for a transitional provision, see reg 1(4) of the 1997 Regulations); words in second pair of square brackets in that entry inserted by SI 1993/3246, reg 5(1), Sch 2, para 5(b), subject to exemptions in relation to certain companies contained in reg 6 and general transitional provisions in reg 7.

In entries relating to "land of freehold tenure and land of leasehold tenure (in relation to Scotland)" and "lease, long lease and short lease" words in first pair of square brackets inserted by SI 1991/2705, reg 6, Sch 2, para 3; words in second pair of square brackets in those entries substituted by SI 1993/3246, reg 5(1), Sch 2, para 5(c), (d), (g), subject to exemptions in relation to certain companies contained in reg 6 and general transitional provisions in reg 7.

In entry relating to "listed investment" words in first pair of square brackets inserted by SI 1997/220, reg 7(6)(b), in relation to annual accounts approved by the board of directors on or after 1 March 1997, and to directors' and auditors' reports on such accounts (for a transitional provision, see reg 1(4) of the 1997 Regulations); words in second pair of square brackets in that entry substituted by SI 1993/3246, reg 5(1), Sch 2, para 5(e), subject to exemptions in relation to certain companies contained in reg 6 and general transitional provisions in reg 7.

Entry relating to "pension costs" substituted by SI 1997/220, reg 7(6)(c), in relation to annual accounts approved by the board of directors on or after 1 March 1997, and to directors' and auditors' reports on such accounts; for a transitional provision, see reg 1(4) of the 1997 Regulations.

In entry relating to "provision" words in first pair of square brackets inserted by SI 1997/220, reg 7(6)(d), in relation to annual accounts approved by the board of directors on or after 1 March 1997, and to directors' and auditors' reports on such accounts (for a transitional provision, see reg 1(4) of the 1997 Regulations); words in second pair of square brackets in that entry inserted by SI 1991/2705, reg 6, Sch 2, para 3; words in third pair of square brackets substituted by SI 1993/3246, reg 5(1), Sch 2, para 5(c), (d), (g), subject to exemptions in relation to certain companies contained in reg 6 and general transitional provisions in reg 7.

Entry relating to "regulated activity" inserted by the Companies Act 1985 (Investment Companies and Accounting and Audit Amendments) Regulations 2005, SI 2005/2280, reg 17(2), in relation to accounts copies of which are delivered to the registrar of companies on or after that date.

Entry relating to "reporting accountant" inserted by the Companies Act 1985 (Audit Exemption) Regulations 1994, SI 1994/1935, reg 4, Sch 1, para 3 (subject to transitional provisions in reg 6 thereof); repealed by the Companies Act 2006, s 1175, Sch 9, Pt 1, para 8, as from a day to be appointed under s 1300(2) of that Act.

Entry relating to "social security costs" substituted by SI 1991/2705, reg 6, Sch 2, para 3; words in first pair of square brackets in that entry inserted by SI 1997/220, reg 7(6)(e), in relation to annual accounts approved by the board of directors on or after 1 March 1997, and to directors' and auditors' reports on such accounts (for a transitional provision, see reg 1(4) of the 1997 Regulations); words in second pair of square brackets inserted by SI 1993/3246, reg 5(1), Sch 2, para 5(h), subject to exemptions in relation to certain companies contained in reg 6 and general transitional provisions in reg 7.

263–281 *((Pt VII) outside the scope of this work.)*

PART IX
A COMPANY'S MANAGEMENT; DIRECTORS AND SECRETARIES; THEIR QUALIFICATIONS, DUTIES AND RESPONSIBILITIES

Officers and registered office

282 Directors

(1) Every company registered on or after 1st November 1929 (other than a private company) shall have at least two directors.

(2) Every company registered before that date (other than a private company) shall have at least one director.

(3) Every private company shall have at least one director.

[417]

NOTES

Repealed as noted to s 1 at **[309]**.

283 Secretary

(*1*) *Every company shall have a secretary.*

(*2*) *A sole director shall not also be secretary.*

(*3*) *Anything required or authorised to be done by or to the secretary may, if the office is vacant or there is for any other reason no secretary capable of acting, be done by or to any assistant or deputy secretary or, if there is no assistant or deputy secretary capable of acting, by or to any officer of the company authorised generally or specially in that behalf by the directors.*

(*4*) *No company shall—*

(*a*) *have as secretary to the company a corporation the sole director of which is a sole director of the company;*

(*b*) *have as sole director of the company a corporation the sole director of which is secretary to the company.*

[418]

NOTES

Repealed as noted to s 1 at **[309]**.

284 Acts done by person in dual capacity

A provision requiring or authorising a thing to be done by or to a director and the secretary is not satisfied by its being done by or to the same person acting both as director and as, or in place of, the secretary.

[419]

NOTES

Repealed as noted to s 1 at **[309]**.

285 Validity of acts of directors

The acts of a director or manager are valid notwithstanding any defect that may afterwards be discovered in his appointment or qualification; and this provision is not excluded by section 292(2) (void resolution to appoint).

[420]

NOTES

Repealed as noted to s 1 at **[309]**.

286 Qualifications of company secretaries

(*1*) *It is the duty of the directors of a public company to take all reasonable steps to secure that the secretary (or each joint secretary) of the company is a person who appears to them to have the requisite knowledge and experience to discharge the functions of secretary of the company and who—*

(*a*) *on 22nd December 1980 held the office of secretary or assistant or deputy secretary of the company; or*

(*b*) *for at least 3 of the 5 years immediately preceding his appointment as secretary held the office of secretary of a company other than a private company; or*

(*c*) *is a member of any of the bodies specified in the following subsection; or*

(*d*) *is a barrister, advocate or solicitor called or admitted in any part of the United Kingdom; or*

(*e*) *is a person who, by virtue of his holding or having held any other position or his being a member of any other body, appears to the directors to be capable of discharging those functions.*

(*2*) *The bodies referred to in subsection (1)(c) are—*

(*a*) *the Institute of Chartered Accountants in England and Wales;*

(*b*) *the Institute of Chartered Accountants of Scotland;*

(*c*) *the Chartered Association of Certified Accountants;*

(*d*) *the Institute of Chartered Accountants in Ireland;*

(*e*) *the Institute of Chartered Secretaries and Administrators;*

(*f*) *the Institute of Cost and Management Accountants;*

(*g*) *the Chartered Institute of Public Finance and Accountancy.*

[421]

NOTES

Repealed as noted to s 1 at **[309]**.

[287 Registered office

(*1*) *A company shall at all times have a registered office to which all communications and notices may be addressed.*

(*2*) *On incorporation the situation of the company's registered office is that specified in the statement sent to the registrar under section 10.*

(*3*) *The company may change the situation of its registered office from time to time by giving notice in the prescribed form to the registrar.*

(*4*) *The change takes effect upon the notice being registered by the registrar, but until the end of the period of 14 days beginning with the date on which it is registered a person may validly serve any document on the company at its previous registered office.*

(*5*) *For the purposes of any duty of a company—*

(*a*) *to keep at its registered office, or make available for public inspection there, any register, index or other document, or*

(*b*) *to mention the address of its registered office in any document,*

a company which has given notice to the registrar of a change in the situation of its registered office may act on the change as from such date, not more than 14 days after the notice is given, as it may determine.

(*6*) *Where a company unavoidably ceases to perform at its registered office any such duty as is mentioned in subsection (5)(a) in circumstances in which it was not practicable to give prior notice to the registrar of a change in the situation of its registered office, but—*

(*a*) *resumes performance of that duty at other premises as soon as practicable, and*

(*b*) *gives notice accordingly to the registrar of a change in the situation of its registered office within 14 days of doing so,*

it shall not be treated as having failed to comply with that duty.

(*7*) *In proceedings for an offence of failing to comply with any such duty as is mentioned in subsection (5), it is for the person charged to show that by reason of the matters referred to in that subsection or subsection (6) no offence was committed.]*

[422]

NOTES

Repealed as noted to s 1 at **[309]**.

Substituted by the Companies Act 1989, s 136, subject to transitional provisions contained in the Companies Act 1989 (Commencement No 4 and Transitional and Saving Provisions) Order 1990, SI 1990/355.

Prescribed forms: see the Companies (Forms) Regulations 1985, SI 1985/854, Forms 287, 287(I) and 287CYM, as prescribed by the Companies (Forms) (Amendment) Regulations 1995, SI 1995/736, the Companies (Forms) (Amendment) Regulations 1998, SI 1998/1702 and the Companies (Welsh Language Forms and Documents) (Amendment) Regulations 1995, SI 1995/734 respectively.

288 Register of directors and secretaries

(*1*) *Every company shall keep at its registered office a register of its directors and secretaries; and the register shall, with respect to the particulars to be contained in it of those persons, comply with sections 289 and 290 below.*

(*2*) *The company shall, within the period of 14 days from the occurrence of—*

(*a*) *any change among its directors or in its secretary, or*

(*b*) *any change in the particulars contained in the register,*

send to the registrar of companies a notification in the prescribed form of the change and of the date on which it occurred; and a notification of a person having become a director or secretary, or one of joint secretaries, of the company shall contain a consent, signed by that person, to act in the relevant capacity.

(3) The register shall … be open to the inspection of any member of the company without charge and of any other person on payment of [such fee as may be prescribed].

(4) If an inspection required under this section is refused, or if default is made in complying with subsection (1) or (2), the company and every officer of it who is in default is liable to a fine and, for continued contravention, to a daily default fine.

(5) In the case of a refusal of inspection of the register, the court may by order compel an immediate inspection of it.

[(5A) Where a confidentiality order made under section 723B is in force in respect of a director or secretary of a company, subsections (3) and (5) shall not apply in relation to that part of the register of the company as contains particulars of the usual residential address of that individual.]

(6) For purposes of this and the next section, a shadow director of a company is deemed a director and officer of it.

[(7) …]

[423]

PART I STATUTES

NOTES

Repealed as noted to s 1 at **[309]**.

Sub-s (3): words omitted repealed and words in square brackets substituted by the Companies Act 1989, ss 143(6), 212, Sch 24.

Sub-s (5A): inserted by the Companies (Particulars of Usual Residential Address) (Confidentiality Orders) Regulations 2002, SI 2002/912, reg 16, Sch 2, para 2(1), (2).

Sub-s (7): added by the Criminal Justice and Police Act 2001, s 45(1), (3); repealed by SI 2002/912, reg 16, Sch 2, para 2(1), (3).

Regulations: the Companies (Inspection and Copying of Registers, Indices and Documents) Regulations 1991, SI 1991/1998.

Prescribed forms: see the Companies (Forms) Regulations 1985, SI 1985/854, Forms 288a, 288b, 288c, as prescribed by the Companies (Forms) (Amendment) Regulations 1995, SI 1995/736, Forms 288a(I), 288b(I), 288c(I), as prescribed by the Companies (Forms) (Amendment) Regulations 1998, SI 1998/1702, and Forms 288aCYM, 288bCYM, 288cCYM, as prescribed by the Companies (Welsh Language Forms and Documents) (Amendment) Regulations 1995, SI 1995/734.

288A (*Outside the scope of this work.*)

289 Particulars of directors to be registered under s 288

(1) Subject to the provisions of this section, the register kept by a company under section 288 shall contain the following particulars with respect to each director—

- *(a) in the case of an individual—*
  - *(i) his present [name],*
  - *(ii) any former [name],*
  - *(iii) his usual residential address,*
  - *(iv) his nationality,*
  - *(v) his business occupation (if any),*
  - *(vi) particulars of any other directorships held by him or which have been held by him, and*
  - *[(vii) the date of his birth;]*
- *(b) in the case of a corporation [or Scottish firm], its corporate [or firm] name and registered or principal office.*

[(1A) Where a confidentiality order made under section 723B is in force in respect of a director, the register shall contain, in addition to the particulars specified in subsection (1)(a), such address as is for the time being notified by the director to the company under regulations made under sections 723B to 723F.]

[(2) In subsection (1)(a)—

- *(a) "name" means a person's Christian name (or other forename) and surname, except that in the case of a peer, or an individual usually known by a title, the title may be stated instead of his Christian name (or other forename) and surname, or in addition to either or both of them; and*
- *(b) the reference to a former name does not include—*
  - *(i) in the case of a peer, or an individual normally known by a British title, the name by which he was known previous to the adoption of or succession to the title, or*

(ii) *in the case of any person, a former name which was changed or disused before he attained the age of 18 years or which has been changed or disused for 20 years or more, or*

(iii) *in the case of a married woman, the name by which she was known previous to the marriage.]*

(3) It is not necessary for the register to contain on any day particulars of a directorship—

(a) *which has not been held by a director at any time during the 5 years preceding that day,*

(b) *which is held by a director in a company which—*

(i) *is dormant or grouped with the company keeping the register, and*

(ii) *if he also held that directorship for any period during those 5 years, was for the whole of that period either dormant or so grouped,*

(c) *which was held by a director for any period during those 5 years in a company which for the whole of that period was either dormant or grouped with the company keeping the register.*

(4) For purposes of subsection (3), "company" includes any body corporate incorporated in Great Britain; and—

(a) *[section 249AA(3)] applies as regards whether and when a company is or has been dormant, and*

(b) *a company is to be regarded as being, or having been, grouped with another at any time if at that time it is or was a company of which the other is or was a wholly-owned subsidiary, or if it is or was a wholly-owned subsidiary of the other or of another company of which that other is or was a wholly-owned subsidiary.*

[424]

NOTES

Repealed as noted to s 1 at **[309]**.

Sub-s (1): words in square brackets in para (a) substituted and words in square brackets in para (b) inserted by the Companies Act 1989, s 145, Sch 19, para 2, subject to transitional provisions contained in the Companies Act 1989 (Commencement No 7 and Transitional and Saving Provisions) Order 1990, SI 1990/1707.

Sub-s (1A): inserted by the Companies (Particulars of Usual Residential Address) (Confidentiality Orders) Regulations 2002, SI 2002/912, reg 16, Sch 2, para 3.

Sub-s (2): substituted by the Companies Act 1989, s 145, Sch 19, para 2, subject to transitional provisions as noted above.

Sub-s (4): words in square brackets substituted by the Companies Act 1985 (Audit Exemption) (Amendment) Regulations 2000, SI 2000/1430, reg 8(7), in relation to annual reports and reports in respect of financial years ending two months or more after 26 May 2000.

290 Particulars of secretaries to be registered under s 288

(1) The register to be kept by a company under section 288 shall contain the following particulars with respect to the secretary or, where there are joint secretaries, with respect to each of them—

(a) *in the case of an individual, his present [name], any former [name] and his usual residential address, and*

(b) *in the case of a corporation or a Scottish firm, its corporate or firm name and registered or principal office.*

[(1A) Where a confidentiality order made under section 723B is in force in respect of a secretary the register shall contain, in addition to the particulars specified in subsection (1)(a), such address as is for the time being notified by the secretary to the company under regulations made under sections 723B to 723F.]

(2) Where all the partners in a firm are joint secretaries, the name and principal office of the firm may be stated instead of the particulars specified above.

[(3) Section 289(2)(a) and (b) apply for the purposes of the obligation under subsection (1)(a) of this section to state the name or former name of an individual.]

[425]

NOTES

Repealed as noted to s 1 at **[309]**.

Sub-s (1): words in square brackets in para (a) substituted by the Companies Act 1989, s 145, Sch 19, para 3.

Sub-s (1A): inserted by the Companies (Particulars of Usual Residential Address) (Confidentiality Orders) Regulations 2002, SI 2002/912, reg 16, Sch 2, para 4.
Sub-s (3): substituted by the Companies Act 1989, s 145, Sch 19, para 3.

Provisions governing appointment of directors

291 Share qualification of directors

(1) It is the duty of every director who is by the company's articles required to hold a specified share qualification, and who is not already qualified, to obtain his qualification within 2 months after his appointment, or such shorter time as may be fixed by the articles.

(2) For the purpose of any provision of the articles requiring a director or manager to hold any specified share qualification, the bearer of a share warrant is not deemed the holder of the shares specified in the warrant.

(3) The office of director of a company is vacated if the director does not within 2 months from the date of his appointment (or within such shorter time as may be fixed by the articles) obtain his qualification, or if after the expiration of that period or shorter time he ceases at any time to hold his qualification.

(4) A person vacating office under this section is incapable of being reappointed to be a director of the company until he has obtained his qualification.

(5) If after the expiration of that period or shorter time any unqualified person acts as a director of the company, he is liable to a fine and, for continued contravention, to a daily default fine.

[426]

NOTES

Repealed as noted to s 1 at **[309]**.

292 Appointment of directors to be voted on individually

(1) At a general meeting of a public company, a motion for the appointment of two or more persons as directors of the company by a single resolution shall not be made, unless a resolution that it shall be so made has first been agreed to by the meeting without any vote being given against it.

(2) A resolution moved in contravention of this section is void, whether or not its being so moved was objected to at the time; but where a resolution so moved is passed, no provision for the automatic reappointment of retiring directors in default of another appointment applies.

(3) For purposes of this section, a motion for approving a person's appointment, or for nominating a person for appointment, is to be treated as a motion for his appointment.

(4) Nothing in this section applies to a resolution altering the company's articles.

[427]–[429]

NOTES

Repealed as noted to s 1 at **[309]**.

293–302 *(Ss 293, 294 repealed by the Companies Act 2006, s 1295, Sch 16, as from 6 April 2007 (subject to the transitional provision that the repeal of s 293(3) does not affect the validity of acts done by a person acting as director to whom that section applied; ss 295–299, 301, 302 repealed by the Company Directors Disqualification Act 1986, s 23(2), Sch 4; s 300 repealed by the Insolvency Act 1985, s 235(3), Sch 10, Pt II.)*

Removal of directors

303 Resolution to remove director

(1) A company may by ordinary resolution remove a director before the expiration of his period of office, notwithstanding anything in its articles or in any agreement between it and him.

(2) Special notice is required of a resolution to remove a director under this section or to appoint somebody instead of a director so removed at the meeting at which he is removed.

(3) A vacancy created by the removal of a director under this section, if not filled at the meeting at which he is removed, may be filled as a casual vacancy.

(4) A person appointed director in place of a person removed under this section is treated, for the purpose of determining the time at which he or any other director is to retire, as if he had become director on the day on which the person in whose place he is appointed was last appointed a director.

(5) This section is not to be taken as depriving a person removed under it of compensation or damages payable to him in respect of the termination of his appointment as director or of any appointment terminating with that as director, or as derogating from any power to remove a director which may exist apart from this section.

[430]

NOTES

Repealed as noted to s 1 at **[309]**.

304 Director's right to protest removal

(1) On receipt of notice of an intended resolution to remove a director under section 303, the company shall forthwith send a copy of the notice to the director concerned; and he (whether or not a member of the company) is entitled to be heard on the resolution at the meeting.

(2) Where notice is given of an intended resolution to remove a director under that section, and the director concerned makes with respect to it representations in writing to the company (not exceeding a reasonable length) and requests their notification to members of the company, the company shall, unless the representations are received by it too late for it to do so—

(a) in any notice of the resolution given to members of the company state the fact of the representations having been made; and

(b) send a copy of the representations to every member of the company to whom notice of the meeting is sent (whether before or after receipt of the representations by the company).

(3) If a copy of the representations is not sent as required by subsection (2) because received too late or because of the company's default, the director may (without prejudice to his right to be heard orally) require that the representations shall be read out at the meeting.

(4) But copies of the representations need not be sent out and the representations need not be read out at the meeting if, on the application either of the company or of any other person who claims to be aggrieved, the court is satisfied that the rights conferred by this section are being abused to secure needless publicity for defamatory matter.

(5) The court may order the company's costs on an application under this section to be paid in whole or in part by the director, notwithstanding that he is not a party to the application.

[431]

NOTES

Repealed as noted to s 1 at **[309]**.

Other provisions about directors and officers

305 Directors' names on company correspondence, etc

(1) A company to which this section applies shall not state, in any form, the name of any of its directors (otherwise than in the text or as a signatory) on any business letter on which the company's name appears unless it states on the letter in legible characters [the name of every director of the company].

(2) This section applies to—

(a) every company registered under this Act or under the former Companies Acts (except a company registered before 23rd November 1916); and

(*b*) *every company incorporated outside Great Britain which has an established place of business within Great Britain, unless it had established such a place of business before that date.*

(*3*) *If a company makes default in complying with this section, every officer of the company who is in default is liable for each offence to a fine; and for this purpose, where a corporation is an officer of the company, any officer of the corporation is deemed an officer of the company.*

[(4) For the purposes of the obligation under subsection (1) to state the name of every director of the company, a person's "name" means—

(*a*) *in the case of an individual, his Christian name (or other forename) and surname; and*

(*b*) *in the case of a corporation or Scottish firm, its corporate or firm name.*

(*5*) *The initial or a recognised abbreviation of a person's Christian name or other forename may be stated instead of the full Christian name or other forename.*

(*6*) *In the case of a peer, or an individual usually known by a title, the title may be stated instead of his Christian name (or other forename) and surname or in addition to either or both of them.*

(*7*) *In this section "director" includes a shadow director and the reference in subsection (3) to an "officer" shall be construed accordingly.]*

[432]

NOTES

Repealed as noted to s 1 at **[309]**.

Sub-s (1): words in square brackets substituted by the Companies Act 1989, s 145, Sch 19, para 4.

Sub-ss (4)–(7): substituted for original sub-s (4) by the Companies Act 1989, s 145, Sch 19, para 4.

306 Limited company may have directors with unlimited liability

(*1*) *In the case of a limited company the liability of the directors or managers, or of the managing director, may, if so provided by the memorandum, be unlimited.*

(*2*) *In the case of a limited company in which the liability of a director or manager is unlimited, the directors and any managers of the company and the member who proposes any person for election or appointment to the office of director or manager, shall add to that proposal a statement that the liability of the person holding that office will be unlimited.*

(*3*) *Before the person accepts the office or acts in it, notice in writing that his liability will be unlimited shall be given to him by the following or one of the following persons, namely—*

(*a*) *the promoters of the company,*

(*b*) *the directors of the company,*

(*c*) *any managers of the company,*

(*d*) *the company secretary.*

(*4*) *If a director, manager or proposer makes default in adding such a statement, or if a promoter, director, manager or secretary makes default in giving the notice required by subsection (3), then—*

(*a*) *he is liable to a fine, and*

(*b*) *he is also liable for any damage which the person so elected or appointed may sustain from the default;*

but the liability of the person elected or appointed is not affected by the default.

[433]

NOTES

Repealed as noted to s 1 at **[309]**.

307 Special resolution making liability of directors unlimited

(*1*) *A limited company, if so authorised by its articles, may by special resolution alter its memorandum so as to render unlimited the liability of its directors or managers, or of any managing director.*

PART I STATUTES

(2) When such a special resolution is passed, its provisions are as valid as if they had been originally contained in the memorandum.

[434]

NOTES

Repealed as noted to s 1 at **[309]**.

308 Assignment of office by directors

If provision is made by a company's articles, or by any agreement entered into between any person and the company, for empowering a director or manager of the company to assign his office as such to another person, any assignment of office made in pursuance of that provision is (notwithstanding anything to the contrary contained in the provision) of no effect unless and until it is approved by a special resolution of the company.

[435]

NOTES

Repealed as noted to s 1 at **[309]**.

309 Directors to have regard to interests of employees

(1) The matters to which the directors of a company are to have regard in the performance of their functions include the interests of the company's employees in general, as well as the interests of its members.

(2) Accordingly, the duty imposed by this section on the directors is owed by them to the company (and the company alone) and is enforceable in the same way as any other fiduciary duty owed to a company by its directors.

(3) This section applies to shadow directors as it does to directors.

[436]

NOTES

Repealed as noted to s 1 at **[309]**.

[309A Provisions protecting directors from liability

(1) This section applies in relation to any liability attaching to a director of a company in connection with any negligence, default, breach of duty or breach of trust by him in relation to the company.

(2) Any provision which purports to exempt (to any extent) a director of a company from any liability within subsection (1) is void.

(3) Any provision by which a company directly or indirectly provides (to any extent) an indemnity for a director of—

(a) the company, or
(b) an associated company,

against any liability within subsection (1) is void

This is subject to subsections (4) and (5).

(4) Subsection (3) does not apply to a qualifying third party indemnity provision (see section 309B(1)).

(5) Subsection (3) does not prevent a company from purchasing and maintaining for a director of—

(a) the company, or
(b) an associated company,

insurance against any liability within subsection (1).

(6) In this section—

"associated company", in relation to a company ("C"), means a company which is C's subsidiary, or C's holding company or a subsidiary of C's holding company;

"provision" means a provision of any nature, whether or not it is contained in a company's articles or in any contract with a company.]

[436A]

NOTES

Commencement: 6 April 2005.
Repealed as noted to s 1 at [**309**].
Inserted, together with ss 309B, 309C, by the Companies (Audit, Investigations and Community Enterprise) Act 2004, s 19(1), except in relation to provisions made before 29 October 2004 which are not void under old s 310; see the Companies (Audit, Investigations and Community Enterprise) Act 2004 (Commencement) and Companies Act 1989 (Commencement No 18) Order 2004, SI 2004/3322, art 5.

[309B Qualifying third party indemnity provisions

(1) For the purposes of section 309A(4) a provision is a qualifying third party indemnity provision if it is a provision such as is mentioned in section 309A(3) in relation to which conditions A to C below are satisfied.

(2) Condition A is that the provision does not provide any indemnity against any liability incurred by the director—
- *(a) to the company, or*
- *(b) to any associated company.*

(3) Condition B is that the provision does not provide any indemnity against any liability incurred by the director to pay—
- *(a) a fine imposed in criminal proceedings, or*
- *(b) a sum payable to a regulatory authority by way of a penalty in respect of non-compliance with any requirement of a regulatory nature (however arising).*

(4) Condition C is that the provision does not provide any indemnity against any liability incurred by the director—
- *(a) in defending any criminal proceedings in which he is convicted, or*
- *(b) in defending any civil proceedings brought by the company, or an associated company, in which judgment is given against him, or*
- *(c) in connection with any application under any of the following provisions in which the court refuses to grant him relief, namely—*
  - *(i) section 144(3) or (4) (acquisition of shares by innocent nominee), or*
  - *(ii) section 727 (general power to grant relief in case of honest and reasonable conduct).*

(5) In paragraph (a), (b) or (c) of subsection (4) the reference to any such conviction, judgment or refusal of relief is a reference to one that has become final.

(6) For the purposes of subsection (5) a conviction, judgment or refusal of relief becomes final—
- *(a) if not appealed against, at the end of the period for bringing an appeal, or*
- *(b) if appealed against, at the time when the appeal (or any further appeal) is disposed of.*

(7) An appeal is disposed of—
- *(a) if it is determined and the period for bringing any further appeal has ended, or*
- *(b) if it is abandoned or otherwise ceases to have effect.*

(8) In this section "associated company" and "provision" have the same meaning as in section 309A.]

[436B]

NOTES

Commencement: 6 April 2005.
Repealed as noted to s 1 at [**309**].
Inserted as noted to s 309A at [**436A**].

[309C Disclosure of qualifying third party indemnity provisions

(1) Subsections (2) and (3) impose disclosure requirements in relation to a directors' report under section 234 in respect of a financial year.

(2) If—
- *(a) at the time when the report is approved under section 234A, any qualifying third party indemnity provision (whether made by the company or otherwise) is in force for the benefit of one or more directors of the company, or*

(*b*) *at any time during the financial year, any such provision was in force for the benefit of one or more persons who were then directors of the company,*

the report must state that any such provision is or (as the case may be) was so in force.

(*3*) *If the company has made a qualifying third party indemnity provision and—*

(*a*) *at the time when the report is approved under section 234A, any qualifying third party indemnity provision made by the company is in force for the benefit of one or more directors of an associated company, or*

(*b*) *at any time during the financial year, any such provision was in force for the benefit of one or more persons who were then directors of an associated company,*

the report must state that any such provision is or (as the case may be) was so in force.

(*4*) *Subsection (5) applies where a company has made a qualifying third party indemnity provision for the benefit of a director of the company or of an associated company.*

(*5*) *Section 318 shall apply to—*

(*a*) *the company, and*

(*b*) *if the director is a director of an associated company, the associated company,*

as if a copy of the provision, or (if it is not in writing) a memorandum setting out its terms, were included in the list of documents in section 318(1).

(*6*) *In this section—*

"associated company" and "provision" have the same meaning as in section 309A; and

"qualifying third party indemnity provision" has the meaning given by section 309B(1).]

[436C]

NOTES

Commencement: 6 April 2005.
Repealed as noted to s 1 at **[309]**.
Inserted as noted to s 309A at **[436A]**.

310 Provisions [protecting] auditors from liability

(*1*) *This section applies to any provision, whether contained in a company's articles or in any contract with the company or otherwise, for exempting ... any person (whether an officer or not) employed by the company as auditor from, or indemnifying him against, any liability which by virtue of any rule of law would otherwise attach to him in respect of any negligence, default, breach of duty or breach of trust of which he may be guilty in relation to the company.*

(2) *Except as provided by the following subsection, any such provision is void.*

[(3) This section does not prevent a company—

(*a*) *from purchasing and maintaining for any such ... auditor insurance against any such liability, or*

(*b*) *from indemnifying any such ... auditor against any liability incurred by him—*

(*i*) *in defending any proceedings (whether civil or criminal) in which judgment is given in his favour or he is acquitted, or*

(*ii*) *in connection with any application under ... section 727 (general power to grant relief in case of honest and reasonable conduct) in which relief is granted to him by the court.]*

[437]–[438]

NOTES

Repealed as noted to s 1 at **[309]**.
Section heading: word in square brackets substituted by the Companies (Audit, Investigations and Community Enterprise) Act 2004, s 19(2)(b) (for transitional provisions see the note to s 309A at **[436A]**).
Sub-s (1): words omitted repealed by the Companies (Audit, Investigations and Community Enterprise) Act 2004, ss 19(2)(a), 64, Sch 8 (for transitional provisions see the note to s 309A at **[436A]**).
Sub-s (3): substituted by the Companies Act 1989, s 137(1); words omitted repealed by the Companies (Audit, Investigations and Community Enterprise) Act 2004, ss 19(2)(b), 64, Sch 8 (for transitional provisions see the note to s 309A at **[436A]**).

PART X
ENFORCEMENT OF FAIR DEALING BY DIRECTORS

Restrictions on directors taking financial advantage

311 (*Repealed by the Companies Act 2006, ss 1177, 1295, Sch 16, as from 6 April 2007.*)

312 Payment to director for loss of office, etc

It is not lawful for a company to make to a director of the company any payment by way of compensation for loss of office, or as consideration for or in connection with his retirement from office, without particulars of the proposed payment (including its amount) being disclosed to members of the company and the proposal being approved by the company.

[439]

NOTES

Repealed as noted to s 1 at **[309]**.

313 Company approval for property transfer

(1) It is not lawful, in connection with the transfer of the whole or any part of the undertaking or property of a company, for any payment to be made to a director of the company by way of compensation for loss of office, or as consideration for or in connection with his retirement from office, unless particulars of the proposed payment (including its amount) have been disclosed to members of the company and the proposal approved by the company.

(2) Where a payment unlawful under this section is made to a director, the amount received is deemed to be received by him in trust for the company.

[440]

NOTES

Repealed as noted to s 1 at **[309]**.

314 Director's duty of disclosure on takeover, etc

(1) This section applies where, in connection with the transfer to any persons of all or any of the shares in a company, being a transfer resulting from—

- *(a) an offer made to the general body of shareholders; or*
- *(b) an offer made by or on behalf of some other body corporate with a view to the company becoming its subsidiary or a subsidiary of its holding company; or*
- *(c) an offer made by or on behalf of an individual with a view to his obtaining the right to exercise or control the exercise of not less than one-third of the voting power at any general meeting of the company; or*
- *(d) any other offer which is conditional on acceptance to a given extent,*

a payment is to be made to a director of the company by way of compensation for loss of office, or as consideration for or in connection with his retirement from office.

(2) It is in those circumstances the director's duty to take all reasonable steps to secure that particulars of the proposed payment (including its amount) are included in or sent with any notice of the offer made for their shares which is given to any shareholders.

(3) If—

- *(a) the director fails to take those steps, or*
- *(b) any person who has been properly required by the director to include those particulars in or send them with the notice required by subsection (2) fails to do so,*

he is liable to a fine.

[441]

NOTES

Repealed as noted to s 1 at **[309]**.

315 Consequences of non-compliance with s 314

(1) If in the case of any such payment to a director as is mentioned in section 314(1)—

(*a*) *his duty under that section is not complied with, or*

(*b*) *the making of the proposed payment is not, before the transfer of any shares in pursuance of the offer, approved by a meeting (summoned for the purpose) of the holders of the shares to which the offer relates and of other holders of shares of the same class as any of those shares,*

any sum received by the director on account of the payment is deemed to have been received by him in trust for persons who have sold their shares as a result of the offer made; and the expenses incurred by him in distributing that sum amongst those persons shall be borne by him and not retained out of that sum.

(2) *Where—*

(*a*) *the shareholders referred to in subsection (1)(b) are not all the members of the company, and*

(*b*) *no provision is made by the articles for summoning or regulating the meeting referred to in that paragraph,*

the provisions of this Act and of the company's articles relating to general meetings of the company apply (for that purpose) to the meeting either without modification or with such modifications as the Secretary of State on the application of any person concerned may direct for the purpose of adapting them to the circumstances of the meeting.

(3) *If at a meeting summoned for the purpose of approving any payment as required by subsection (1)(b) a quorum is not present and, after the meeting has been adjourned to a later date, a quorum is again not present, the payment is deemed for the purposes of that subsection to have been approved.*

[442]

NOTES

Repealed as noted to s 1 at **[309]**.

316 Provisions supplementing ss 312 to 315

(*1*) *Where in proceedings for the recovery of any payment as having, by virtue of section 313(2) or 315(1) been received by any person in trust, it is shown that—*

(*a*) *the payment was made in pursuance of any arrangement entered into as part of the agreement for the transfer in question, or within one year before or two years after that agreement or the offer leading to it; and*

(*b*) *the company or any person to whom the transfer was made was privy to that arrangement,*

the payment is deemed, except in so far as the contrary is shown, to be one to which the provisions mentioned above in this subsection apply.

(2) *If in connection with any such transfer as is mentioned in any of sections 313 to 315—*

(*a*) *the price to be paid to a director of the company whose office is to be abolished or who is to retire from office for any shares in the company held by him is in excess of the price which could at the time have been obtained by other holders of the like shares; or*

(*b*) *any valuable consideration is given to any such director,*

the excess or the money value of the consideration (as the case may be) is deemed for the purposes of that section to have been a payment made to him by way of compensation for loss of office or as consideration for or in connection with his retirement from office.

(3) *References in sections 312 to 315 to payments made to a director by way of compensation for loss of office or as consideration for or in connection with his retirement from office, do not include any bona fide payment by way of damages for breach of contract or by way of pension in respect of past services.*

"Pension" here includes any superannuation allowance, superannuation gratuity or similar payment.

(4) *Nothing in sections 313 to 315 prejudices the operation of any rule of law requiring disclosure to be made with respect to such payments as are there mentioned, or with respect to any other like payments made or to be made to a company's directors.*

[443]

NOTES

Repealed as noted to s 1 at **[309]**.

317 Directors to disclose interest in contracts

(*1*) *It is the duty of a director of a company who is in any way, whether directly or indirectly, interested in a contract or proposed contract with the company to declare the nature of his interest at a meeting of the directors of the company.*

(*2*) *In the case of a proposed contract, the declaration shall be made—*

(*a*) *at the meeting of the directors at which the question of entering into the contract is first taken into consideration; or*

(*b*) *if the director was not at the date of that meeting interested in the proposed contract, at the next meeting of the directors held after he became so interested;*

and, in a case where the director becomes interested in a contract after it is made, the declaration shall be made at the first meeting of the directors held after he becomes so interested.

(*3*) *For purposes of this section, a general notice given to the directors of a company by a director to the effect that—*

(*a*) *he is a member of a specified company or firm and is to be regarded as interested in any contract which may, after the date of the notice, be made with that company or firm; or*

(*b*) *he is to be regarded as interested in any contract which may after the date of the notice be made with a specified person who is connected with him (within the meaning of section 346 below),*

is deemed a sufficient declaration of interest in relation to any such contract.

(*4*) *However, no such notice is of effect unless either it is given at a meeting of the directors or the director takes reasonable steps to secure that it is brought up and read at the next meeting of the directors after it is given.*

(*5*) *A reference in this section to a contract includes any transaction or arrangement (whether or not constituting a contract) made or entered into on or after 22nd December 1980.*

(*6*) *For purposes of this section, a transaction or arrangement of a kind described in section 330 (prohibition of loans, quasi-loans etc to directors) made by a company for a director of the company or a person connected with such a director is treated (if it would not otherwise be so treated, and whether or not it is prohibited by that section) as a transaction or arrangement in which that director is interested.*

(*7*) *A director who fails to comply with this section is liable to a fine.*

(*8*) *This section applies to a shadow director as it applies to a director, except that a shadow director shall declare his interest, not at a meeting of the directors, but by a notice in writing to the directors which is either—*

(*a*) *a specific notice given before the date of the meeting at which, if he had been a director, the declaration would be required by subsection (2) to be made; or*

(*b*) *a notice which under subsection (3) falls to be treated as a sufficient declaration of that interest (or would fall to be so treated apart from subsection (4)).*

(*9*) *Nothing in this section prejudices the operation of any rule of law restricting directors of a company from having an interest in contracts with the company.*

[444]

NOTES

Repealed as noted to s 1 at **[309]**.

318 Directors' service contracts to be open to inspection

(*1*) *Subject to the following provisions, every company shall keep at an appropriate place—*

(*a*) *in the case of each director whose contract of service with the company is in writing, a copy of that contract;*

(*b*) *in the case of each director whose contract of service with the company is not in writing, a written memorandum setting out its terms; and*

(*c*) *in the case of each director who is employed under a contract of service with a subsidiary of the company, a copy of that contract or, if it is not in writing, a written memorandum setting out its terms.*

(2) *All copies and memoranda kept by a company in pursuance of subsection (1) shall be kept at the same place.*

(3) *The following are appropriate places for the purposes of subsection (1)—*

(*a*) *the company's registered office;*

(*b*) *the place where its register of members is kept (if other than its registered office);*

(*c*) *its principal place of business, provided that is situated in that part of Great Britain in which the company is registered.*

(4) *Every company shall send notice in the prescribed form to the registrar of companies of the place where copies and memoranda are kept in compliance with subsection (1), and of any change in that place, save in a case in which they have at all times been kept at the company's registered office.*

(5) *Subsection (1) does not apply to a director's contract of service with the company or with a subsidiary of it if that contract required him to work wholly or mainly outside the United Kingdom; but the company shall keep a memorandum—*

(*a*) *in the case of a contract of service with the company, giving the director's name and setting out the provisions of the contract relating to its duration;*

(*b*) *in the case of a contract of service with a subsidiary, giving the director's name and the name and place of incorporation of the subsidiary, and setting out the provisions of the contract relating to its duration,*

at the same place as copies and memoranda are kept by the company in pursuance of subsection (1).

(6) *A shadow director is treated for purposes of this section as a director.*

(7) *Every copy and memorandum required by subsection (1) or (5) to be kept shall, ... , be open to inspection of any member of the company without charge.*

(8) *If—*

(*a*) *default is made in complying with subsection (1) or (5), or*

(*b*) *an inspection required under subsection (7) is refused, or*

(*c*) *default is made for 14 days in complying with subsection (4),*

the company and every officer of it who is in default is liable to a fine and, for continued contravention, to a daily default fine.

(9) *In the case of a refusal of an inspection required under subsection (7) of a copy or memorandum, the court may by order compel an immediate inspection of it.*

(10) *Subsections (1) and (5) apply to a variation of a director's contract of service as they apply to the contract.*

(11) *This section does not require that there be kept a copy of, or memorandum setting out the terms of, a contract (or its variation) at a time when the unexpired portion of the term for which the contract is to be in force is less than 12 months, or at a time at which the contract can, within the next ensuing 12 months, be terminated by the company without payment of compensation.*

[445]

NOTES

Repealed as noted to s 1 at **[309]**.

Sub-s (7): words omitted repealed by the Companies Act 1989, ss 143(7), 212, Sch 24,.

Prescribed form: see the Companies (Forms) Regulations 1985, SI 1985/854, Form 318, as prescribed by the Companies (Forms) (Amendment) Regulations 1995, SI 1995/736.

319 Director's contract of employment for more than 5 years

(1) *This section applies in respect of any term of an agreement whereby a director's employment with the company of which he is a director or, where he is the director of a holding company, his employment within the group is to continue, or may be continued,*

otherwise than at the instance of the company (whether under the original agreement or under a new agreement entered into in pursuance of it), for a period of more than 5 years during which the employment—

(*a*) *cannot be terminated by the company by notice; or*

(*b*) *can be so terminated only in specified circumstances.*

(*2*) *In any case where—*

(*a*) *a person is or is to be employed with a company under an agreement which cannot be terminated by the company by notice or can be so terminated only in specified circumstances; and*

(*b*) *more than 6 months before the expiration of the period for which he is or is to be so employed, the company enters into a further agreement (otherwise than in pursuance of a right conferred by or under the original agreement on the other party to it) under which he is to be employed with the company or, where he is a director of a holding company, within the group,*

this section applies as if to the period for which he is to be employed under that further agreement there were added a further period equal to the unexpired period of the original agreement.

(*3*) *A company shall not incorporate in an agreement such a term as is mentioned in subsection (1), unless the term is first approved by a resolution of the company in general meeting and, in the case of a director of a holding company, by a resolution of that company in general meeting.*

(*4*) *No approval is required to be given under this section by any body corporate unless it is a company within the meaning of this Act, or is registered under section 680, or if it is a wholly-owned subsidiary of any body corporate, wherever incorporated.*

(*5*) *A resolution of a company approving such a term as is mentioned in subsection (1) shall not be passed at a general meeting of the company unless a written memorandum setting out the proposed agreement incorporating the term is available for inspection by members of the company both—*

(*a*) *at the company's registered office for not less than 15 days ending with the date of the meeting; and*

(*b*) *at the meeting itself.*

(*6*) *A term incorporated in an agreement in contravention of this section is, to the extent that it contravenes the section, void; and that agreement and, in a case where subsection (2) applies, the original agreement are deemed to contain a term entitling the company to terminate it at any time by the giving of reasonable notice.*

(*7*) *In this section—*

(*a*) *"employment" includes employment under a contract for services; and*

(*b*) *"group", in relation to a director of a holding company, means the group which consists of that company and its subsidiaries;*

and for purposes of this section a shadow director is treated as a director.

[446]

NOTES

Repealed as noted to s 1 at **[309]**.

320 Substantial property transactions involving directors, etc

(*1*) *With the exceptions provided by the section next following, a company shall not enter into an arrangement—*

(*a*) *whereby a director of the company or its holding company, or a person connected with such a director, acquires or is to acquire one or more non-cash assets of the requisite value from the company; or*

(*b*) *whereby the company acquires or is to acquire one or more non-cash assets of the requisite value from such a director or a person so connected,*

unless the arrangement is first approved by a resolution of the company in general meeting and, if the director or connected person is a director of its holding company or a person connected with such a director, by a resolution in general meeting of the holding company.

(*2*) *For this purpose a non-cash asset is of the requisite value if at the time the arrangement in question is entered into its value is not less than [£2,000] but (subject to that) exceeds [£100,000] or 10 per cent of the company's asset value, that is—*

(*a*) *except in a case falling within paragraph (b) below, the value of the company's net assets determined by reference to the accounts prepared and laid under Part VII in respect of the last preceding financial year in respect of which such accounts were so laid; and*

(*b*) *where no accounts have been so prepared and laid before that time, the amount of the company's called-up share capital.*

(*3*) *For purposes of this section and sections 321 and 322, a shadow director is treated as a director.*

[447]

NOTES

Repealed as noted to s 1 at **[309]**.

Sub-s (2): sums in square brackets substituted by the Companies (Fair Dealing by Directors) (Increase in Financial Limits) Order 1990, SI 1990/1393, art 2.

321 Exceptions from s 320

(*1*) *No approval is required to be given under section 320 by any body corporate unless it is a company within the meaning of this Act or registered under section 680 or, if it is a wholly-owned subsidiary of any body corporate, wherever incorporated.*

(*2*) *Section 320(1) does not apply to an arrangement for the acquisition of a non-cash asset—*

(*a*) *if the asset is to be acquired by a holding company from any of its wholly-owned subsidiaries or from a holding company by any of its wholly-owned subsidiaries, or by one wholly-owned subsidiary of a holding company from another wholly-owned subsidiary of that same holding company, or*

(*b*) *if the arrangement is entered into by a company which is being wound up, unless the winding up is a members' voluntary winding up.*

(*3*) *Section 320(1)(a) does not apply to an arrangement whereby a person is to acquire an asset from a company of which he is a member, if the arrangement is made with that person in his character as a member.*

[(4) Section 320(1) does not apply to a transaction on a recognised investment exchange which is effected by a director, or a person connected with him, through the agency of a person who in relation to the transaction acts as an independent broker.

For this purpose an "independent broker" means—

(*a*) *in relation to a transaction on behalf of a director, a person who independently of the director selects the person with whom the transaction is to be effected, and*

(*b*) *in relation to a transaction on behalf of a person connected with a director, a person who independently of that person or the director selects the person with whom the transaction is to be effected;*

and "recognised", in relation to an investment exchange, means recognised under the [Financial Services and Markets Act 2000].]

[448]

NOTES

Repealed as noted to s 1 at **[309]**.

Sub-s (4): added by the Companies Act 1989, s 145, Sch 19, para 8; words in square brackets substituted by the Financial Services and Markets Act 2000 (Consequential Amendments and Repeals) Order 2001, SI 2001/3649, art 19.

322 Liabilities arising from contravention of s 320

(*1*) *An arrangement entered into by a company in contravention of section 320, and any transaction entered into in pursuance of the arrangement (whether by the company or any other person) is voidable at the instance of the company unless one or more of the conditions specified in the next subsection is satisfied.*

(*2*) *Those conditions are that—*

(*a*) *restitution of any money or other asset which is the subject-matter of the arrangement or transaction is no longer possible or the company has been indemnified in pursuance of this section by any other person for the loss or damage suffered by it; or* (*b*) *any rights acquired bona fide for value and without actual notice of the contravention by any person who is not a party to the arrangement or transaction would be affected by its avoidance; or*

(*c*) *the arrangement is, within a reasonable period, affirmed by the company in general meeting and, if it is an arrangement for the transfer of an asset to or by a director of its holding company or a person who is connected with such a director, is so affirmed with the approval of the holding company given by a resolution in general meeting.*

(*3*) *If an arrangement is entered into with a company by a director of the company or its holding company or a person connected with him in contravention of section 320, that director and the person so connected, and any other director of the company who authorised the arrangement or any transaction entered into in pursuance of such an arrangement, is liable—*

(*a*) *to account to the company for any gain which he has made directly or indirectly by the arrangement or transaction, and*

(*b*) *(jointly and severally with any other person liable under this subsection) to indemnify the company for any loss or damage resulting from the arrangement or transaction.*

(*4*) *Subsection (3) is without prejudice to any liability imposed otherwise than by that subsection, and is subject to the following two subsections; and the liability under subsection (3) arises whether or not the arrangement or transaction entered into has been avoided in pursuance of subsection (1).*

(*5*) *If an arrangement is entered into by a company and a person connected with a director of the company or its holding company in contravention of section 320, that director is not liable under subsection (3) if he shows that he took all reasonable steps to secure the company's compliance with that section.*

(*6*) *In any case, a person so connected and any such other director as is mentioned in subsection (3) is not so liable if he shows that, at the time the arrangement was entered into, he did not know the relevant circumstances constituting the contravention.*

[449]

NOTES

Repealed as noted to s 1 at **[309]**.

[322A Invalidity of certain transactions involving directors, etc

(*1*) *This section applies where a company enters into a transaction to which the parties include—*

(*a*) *a director of the company or of its holding company, or*

(*b*) *a person connected with such a director or a company with whom such a director is associated,*

and the board of directors, in connection with the transaction, exceed any limitation on their powers under the company's constitution.

(*2*) *The transaction is voidable at the instance of the company.*

(*3*) *Whether or not it is avoided, any such party to the transaction as is mentioned in subsection (1)(a) or (b), and any director of the company who authorised the transaction, is liable—*

(*a*) *to account to the company for any gain which he has made directly or indirectly by the transaction, and*

(*b*) *to indemnify the company for any loss or damage resulting from the transaction.*

(*4*) *Nothing in the above provisions shall be construed as excluding the operation of any other enactment or rule of law by virtue of which the transaction may be called in question or any liability to the company may arise.*

(*5*) *The transaction ceases to be voidable if—*

(*a*) *restitution of any money or other asset which was the subject-matter of the transaction is no longer possible, or*

(*b*) *the company is indemnified for any loss or damage resulting from the transaction, or* (*c*) *rights acquired bona fide for value and without actual notice of the directors' exceeding their powers by a person who is not party to the transaction would be affected by the avoidance, or*

(*d*) *the transaction is ratified by the company in general meeting, by ordinary or special resolution or otherwise as the case may require.*

(6) A person other than a director of the company is not liable under subsection (3) if he shows that at the time the transaction was entered into he did not know that the directors were exceeding their powers.

(7) This section does not affect the operation of section 35A in relation to any party to the transaction not within subsection (1)(a) or (b).

But where a transaction is voidable by virtue of this section and valid by virtue of that section in favour of such a person, the court may, on the application of that person or of the company, make such order affirming, severing or setting aside the transaction, on such terms, as appear to the court to be just.

(8) In this section "transaction" includes any act; and the reference in subsection (1) to limitations under the company's constitution includes limitations deriving—

(*a*) *from a resolution of the company in general meeting or a meeting of any class of shareholders, or*

(*b*) *from any agreement between the members of the company or of any class of shareholders.]*

[450]

NOTES

Repealed as noted to s 1 at **[309]**.

Inserted by the Companies Act 1989, s 109(1), subject to transitional provisions contained in the Companies Act 1989 (Commencement No 8 and Transitional and Saving Provisions) Order 1990, SI 1990/2569.

[322B Contracts with sole members who are directors

(1) Subject to subsection (2), where a private company limited by shares or by guarantee having only one member enters into a contract with the sole member of the company and the sole member is also a director of the company, the company shall, unless the contract is in writing, ensure that the terms of the contract are either set out in a written memorandum or are recorded in the minutes of the first meeting of the directors of the company following the making of the contract.

(2) Subsection (1) shall not apply to contracts entered into in the ordinary course of the company's business.

(3) For the purposes of this section a sole member who is a shadow director is treated as a director.

(4) If a company fails to comply with subsection (1), the company and every officer of it who is in default is liable to a fine.

(5) Subject to subsection (6), nothing in this section shall be construed as excluding the operation of any other enactment or rule of law applying to contracts between a company and a director of that company.

(6) Failure to comply with subsection (1) with respect to a contract shall not affect the validity of that contract.]

[451]

NOTES

Repealed as noted to s 1 at **[309]**.

Inserted by the Companies (Single Member Private Limited Companies) Regulations 1992, SI 1992/1699, reg 2, Schedule, para 3.

323–329 (*Outside the scope of this work.*)

Restrictions on a company's power to make loans, etc, to directors and persons connected with them

330 General restriction on loans etc to directors and persons connected with them

(1) The prohibitions listed below in this section are subject to the exceptions in sections 332 to 338.

(2) A company shall not—

(a) make a loan to a director of the company or of its holding company;

(b) enter into any guarantee or provide any security in connection with a loan made by any person to such a director.

(3) A relevant company shall not—

(a) make a quasi-loan to a director of the company or of its holding company;

(b) make a loan or a quasi-loan to a person connected with such a director;

(c) enter into a guarantee or provide any security in connection with a loan or quasi-loan made by any other person for such a director or a person so connected.

(4) A relevant company shall not—

(a) enter into a credit transaction as creditor for such a director or a person so connected;

(b) enter into any guarantee or provide any security in connection with a credit transaction made by any other person for such a director or a person so connected.

(5) For purposes of sections 330 to 346, a shadow director is treated as a director.

(6) A company shall not arrange for the assignment to it, or the assumption by it, of any rights, obligations or liabilities under a transaction which, if it had been entered into by the company, would have contravened subsection (2), (3) or (4); but for the purposes of sections 330 to 347 the transaction is to be treated as having been entered into on the date of the arrangement.

(7) A company shall not take part in any arrangement whereby—

(a) another person enters into a transaction which, if it had been entered into by the company, would have contravened any of subsections (2), (3), (4) or (6); and

(b) that other person, in pursuance of the arrangement, has obtained or is to obtain any benefit from the company or its holding company or a subsidiary of the company or its holding company.

[452]

NOTES

Repealed as noted to s 1 at **[309]**.

331 Definitions for ss 330 ff

(1) The following subsections apply for the interpretation of sections 330 to 346.

(2) "Guarantee" includes indemnity, and cognate expressions are to be construed accordingly.

(3) A quasi-loan is a transaction under which one party ("the creditor") agrees to pay, or pays otherwise than in pursuance of an agreement, a sum for another ("the borrower") or agrees to reimburse, or reimburses otherwise than in pursuance of an agreement, expenditure incurred by another party for another ("the borrower")—

(a) on terms that the borrower (or a person on his behalf) will reimburse the creditor; or

(b) in circumstances giving rise to a liability on the borrower to reimburse the creditor.

(4) Any reference to the person to whom a quasi-loan is made is a reference to the borrower; and the liabilities of a borrower under a quasi-loan include the liabilities of any person who has agreed to reimburse the creditor on behalf of the borrower.

(5) …

(6) "Relevant company" means a company which—

(a) *is a public company, or*
(b) *is a subsidiary of a public company, or*
(c) *is a subsidiary of a company which has as another subsidiary a public company, or*
(d) *has a subsidiary which is a public company.*

(7) *A credit transaction is a transaction under which one party ("the creditor")—*
(a) *supplies any goods or sells any land under a hire-purchase agreement or a conditional sale agreement;*
(b) *leases or hires any land or goods in return for periodical payments;*
(c) *otherwise disposes of land or supplies goods or services on the understanding that payment (whether in a lump sum or instalments or by way of periodical payments or otherwise) is to be deferred.*

(8) *"Services" means anything other than goods or land.*

(9) *A transaction or arrangement is made "for" a person if—*
(a) *in the case of a loan or quasi-loan, it is made to him;*
(b) *in the case of a credit transaction, he is the person to whom goods or services are supplied, or land is sold or otherwise disposed of, under the transaction;*
(c) *in the case of a guarantee or security, it is entered into or provided in connection with a loan or quasi-loan made to him or a credit transaction made for him;*
(d) *in the case of an arrangement within subsection (6) or (7) of section 330, the transaction to which the arrangement relates was made for him; and*
(e) *in the case of any other transaction or arrangement for the supply or transfer of, or of any interest in, goods, land or services, he is the person to whom the goods, land or services (or the interest) are supplied or transferred.*

(10) *"Conditional sale agreement" means the same as in the Consumer Credit Act 1974.*
[453]

NOTES

Repealed as noted to s 1 at **[309]**.
Sub-s (5): repealed by the Banking Act 1987, s 108(2), Sch 7, Pt I.

332 Short-term quasi-loans

(1) *Subsection (3) of section 330 does not prohibit a company ("the creditor") from making a quasi-loan to one of its directors or to a director of its holding company if—*
(a) *the quasi-loan contains a term requiring the director or a person on his behalf to reimburse the creditor his expenditure within 2 months of its being incurred; and*
(b) *the aggregate of the amount of that quasi-loan and of the amount outstanding under each relevant quasi-loan does not exceed [£5,000].*

(2) *A quasi-loan is relevant for this purpose if it was made to the director by virtue of this section by the creditor or its subsidiary or, where the director is a director of the creditor's holding company, any other subsidiary of that company; and "the amount outstanding" is the amount of the outstanding liabilities of the person to whom the quasi-loan was made.*
[454]

NOTES

Repealed as noted to s 1 at **[309]**.
Sub-s (1): sum in square brackets substituted by the Companies Act 1989, s 138(a), subject to transitional provisions.

333 Inter-company loans in same group

In the case of a relevant company which is a member of a group of companies (meaning a holding company and its subsidiaries), paragraphs (b) and (c) of section 330(3) do not prohibit the company from—
(a) *making a loan or quasi-loan to another member of that group; or*
(b) *entering into a guarantee or providing any security in connection with a loan or quasi-loan made by any person to another member of the group,*

by reason only that a director of one member of the group is associated with another.
[455]

NOTES

Repealed as noted to s 1 at **[309]**.

334 Loans of small amounts

Without prejudice to any other provision of sections 332 to 338, paragraph (a) of section 330(2) does not prohibit a company from making a loan to a director of the company or of its holding company if the aggregate of the relevant amounts does not exceed [£5,000].

[456]

NOTES

Repealed as noted to s 1 at **[309]**.

Sum in square brackets substituted by the Companies Act 1989, s 138(b), subject to transitional provisions.

335 Minor and business transactions

(1) Section 330(4) does not prohibit a company from entering into a transaction for a person if the aggregate of the relevant amounts does not exceed [£10,000].

(2) Section 330(4) does not prohibit a company from entering into a transaction for a person if—

(a) the transaction is entered into by the company in the ordinary course of its business; and

(b) the value of the transaction is not greater, and the terms on which it is entered into are no more favourable, in respect of the person for whom the transaction is made, than that or those which it is reasonable to expect the company to have offered to or in respect of a person of the same financial standing but unconnected with the company.

[457]

NOTES

Repealed as noted to s 1 at **[309]**.

Sub-s (1): sum in square brackets substituted by the Companies (Fair Dealing by Directors) (Increase in Financial Limits) Order 1990, SI 1990/1393, art 2.

336 Transactions at behest of holding company

The following transactions are excepted from the prohibitions of section 330—

(a) a loan or quasi-loan by a company to its holding company, or a company entering into a guarantee or providing any security in connection with a loan or quasi-loan made by any person to its holding company;

(b) a company entering into a credit transaction as creditor for its holding company, or entering into a guarantee or providing any security in connection with a credit transaction made by any other person for its holding company.

[458]

NOTES

Repealed as noted to s 1 at **[309]**.

337 Funding of director's expenditure on duty to company

(1) A company is not prohibited by section 330 from doing anything to provide a director with funds to meet expenditure incurred or to be incurred by him for the purposes of the company or for the purpose of enabling him properly to perform his duties as an officer of the company.

(2) Nor does the section prohibit a company from doing any thing to enable a director to avoid incurring such expenditure.

(3) Subsections (1) and (2) apply only if one of the following conditions is satisfied—

(a) the thing in question is done with prior approval of the company given at a general meeting at which there are disclosed all the matters mentioned in the next subsection;

(*b*) *that thing is done on condition that, if the approval of the company is not so given at or before the next annual general meeting, the loan is to be repaid, or any other liability arising under any such transaction discharged, within 6 months from the conclusion of that meeting;*

but those subsections do not authorise a relevant company to enter into any transaction if the aggregate of the relevant amounts exceeds [£20,000].

(*4*) *The matters to be disclosed under subsection* (*3*)(*a*) *are—*

(*a*) *the purpose of the expenditure incurred or to be incurred, or which would otherwise be incurred, by the director,*

(*b*) *the amount of the funds to be provided by the company, and*

(*c*) *the extent of the company's liability under any transaction which is or is connected with the thing in question.*

[459]

NOTES

Repealed as noted to s 1 at **[309]**.

Sub-s (3): sum in square brackets substituted by the Companies (Fair Dealing by Directors) (Increase in Financial Limits) Order 1990, SI 1990/1393, art 2.

[337A Funding of director's expenditure on defending proceedings

(*1*) *A company is not prohibited by section 330 from doing anything to provide a director with funds to meet expenditure incurred or to be incurred by him—*

(*a*) *in defending any criminal or civil proceedings, or*

(*b*) *in connection with any application under any of the provisions mentioned in subsection* (*2*).

(*2*) *The provisions are—*

section 144(*3*) *and* (*4*) (*acquisition of shares by innocent nominee*), *and*

section 727 (*general power to grant relief in case of honest and reasonable conduct*).

(*3*) *Nor does section 330 prohibit a company from doing anything to enable a director to avoid incurring such expenditure.*

(*4*) *Subsections* (*1*) *and* (*3*) *only apply to a loan or other thing done as mentioned in those subsections if the terms on which it is made or done will result in the loan falling to be repaid, or any liability of the company under any transaction connected with the thing in question falling to be discharged, not later than—*

(*a*) *in the event of the director being convicted in the proceedings, the date when the conviction becomes final,*

(*b*) *in the event of judgment being given against him in the proceedings, the date when the judgment becomes final, or*

(*c*) *in the event of the court refusing to grant him relief on the application, the date when the refusal of relief becomes final.*

(*5*) *For the purposes of subsection* (*4*) *a conviction, judgment or refusal of relief becomes final—*

(*a*) *if not appealed against, at the end of the period for bringing an appeal, or*

(*b*) *if appealed against, at the time when the appeal* (*or any further appeal*) *is disposed of.*

(*6*) *An appeal is disposed of—*

(*a*) *if it is determined and the period for bringing any further appeal has ended, or*

(*b*) *if it is abandoned or otherwise ceases to have effect.]*

[459A]

NOTES

Commencement: 6 April 2005.

Repealed as noted to s 1 at **[309]**.

Inserted by the Companies (Audit, Investigations and Community Enterprise) Act 2004, s 20.

338 Loan or quasi-loan by money-lending company

(*1*) *There is excepted from the prohibitions in section 330—*

(*a*) *a loan or quasi-loan made by a money-lending company to any person; or* (*b*) *a money-lending company entering into a guarantee in connection with any other loan or quasi-loan.*

(2) *"Money-lending company" means a company whose ordinary business includes the making of loans or quasi-loans, or the giving of guarantees in connection with loans or quasi-loans.*

(3) *Subsection (1) applies only if both the following conditions are satisfied—*

(*a*) *the loan or quasi-loan in question is made by the company, or it enters into the guarantee, in the ordinary course of the company's business; and*

(*b*) *the amount of the loan or quasi-loan, or the amount guaranteed, is not greater, and the terms of the loan, quasi-loan or guarantee are not more favourable, in the case of the person to whom the loan or quasi-loan is made or in respect of whom the guarantee is entered into, than that or those which it is reasonable to expect that company to have offered to or in respect of a person of the same financial standing but unconnected with the company.*

(4) *But subsection (1) does not authorise a relevant company (unless it is [a banking company]) to enter into any transaction if the aggregate of the relevant amounts exceeds [£100,000].*

(5) *In determining that aggregate, a company which a director does not control is deemed not to be connected with him.*

(6) *The condition specified in subsection (3)(b) does not of itself prevent a company from making a loan to one of its directors or a director of its holding company—*

(*a*) *for the purpose of facilitating the purchase, for use as that director's only or main residence, of the whole or part of any dwelling-house together with any land to be occupied and enjoyed with it;*

(*b*) *for the purpose of improving a dwelling-house or part of a dwelling-house so used or any land occupied and enjoyed with it;*

(*c*) *in substitution for any loan made by any person and falling within paragraph (a) or (b) of this subsection,*

if loans of that description are ordinarily made by the company to its employees and on terms no less favourable than those on which the transaction in question is made, and the aggregate of the relevant amounts does not exceed [£100,000].

[460]

NOTES

Repealed as noted to s 1 at **[309]**.

Sub-s (4): words in first pair of square brackets further substituted (having been previously substituted by the Banking Act 1987, s 108(1), Sch 6, para 18(6)), by the Companies Act 1989, s 23, Sch 10, para 10, subject to transitional provisions; sum in second pair of square brackets substituted by the Companies Act 1989, s 138(c), subject to transitional provisions.

Sub-s (6): sum in square brackets substituted by the Companies Act 1989, s 138(c), subject to transitional provisions.

339 "Relevant amounts" for purposes of ss 334 ff

(1) *This section has effect for defining the "relevant amounts" to be aggregated under sections 334, 335(1), 337(3) and 338(4); and in relation to any proposed transaction or arrangement and the question whether it falls within one or other of the exceptions provided by those sections, "the relevant exception" is that exception; but where the relevant exception is the one provided by section 334 (loan of small amount), references in this section to a person connected with a director are to be disregarded.*

(2) *Subject as follows, the relevant amounts in relation to a proposed transaction or arrangement are—*

(*a*) *the value of the proposed transaction or arrangement,*

(*b*) *the value of any existing arrangement which—*

(*i*) *falls within subsection (6) or (7) of section 330, and*

(*ii*) *also falls within subsection (3) of this section, and*

(*iii*) *was entered into by virtue of the relevant exception by the company or by a subsidiary of the company or, where the proposed transaction or arrangement is to be made for a director of its holding company or a person connected with such a director, by that holding company or any of its subsidiaries;*

(*c*) *the amount outstanding under any other transaction—*
(*i*) *falling within subsection* (*3*) *below, and*
(*ii*) *made by virtue of the relevant exception, and*
(*iii*) *made by the company or by a subsidiary of the company or, where the proposed transaction or arrangement is to be made for a director of its holding company or a person connected with such a director, by that holding company or any of its subsidiaries.*

(*3*) *A transaction falls within this subsection if it was made—*

(*a*) *for the director for whom the proposed transaction or arrangement is to be made, or for any person connected with that director; or*

(*b*) *where the proposed transaction or arrangement is to be made for a person connected with a director of a company, for that director or any person connected with him;*

and an arrangement also falls within this subsection if it relates to a transaction which does so.

(*4*) *But where the proposed transaction falls within section 338 and is one which [a banking company] proposes to enter into under subsection* (*6*) *of that section* (*housing loans, etc*), *any other transaction or arrangement which apart from this subsection would fall within subsection* (*3*) *of this section does not do so unless it was entered into in pursuance of section 338*(*6*).

(*5*) *A transaction entered into by a company which is* (*at the time of that transaction being entered into*) *a subsidiary of the company which is to make the proposed transaction, or is a subsidiary of that company's holding company, does not fall within subsection* (*3*) *if at the time when the question arises* (*that is to say, the question whether the proposed transaction or arrangement falls within any relevant exception*), *it no longer is such a subsidiary.*

(*6*) *Values for purposes of subsection* (*2*) *of this section are to be determined in accordance with the section next following; and "the amount outstanding" for purposes of subsection* (*2*)(*c*) *above is the value of the transaction less any amount by which that value has been reduced.*

[461]

NOTES

Repealed as noted to s 1 at **[309]**.

Sub-s (4): words in square brackets further substituted (having been previously substituted by the Banking Act 1987, s 108(1), Sch 6, para 18(6)), by the Companies Act 1989, s 23, Sch 10, para 10, subject to transitional provisions.

340 "Value" of transactions and arrangements

(*1*) *This section has effect for determining the value of a transaction or arrangement for purposes of sections 330 to 339.*

(*2*) *The value of a loan is the amount of its principal.*

(*3*) *The value of a quasi-loan is the amount, or maximum amount, which the person to whom the quasi-loan is made is liable to reimburse the creditor.*

(*4*) *The value of a guarantee or security is the amount guaranteed or secured.*

(*5*) *The value of an arrangement to which section 330*(*6*) *or* (*7*) *applies is the value of the transaction to which the arrangement relates less any amount by which the liabilities under the arrangement or transaction of the person for whom the transaction was made have been reduced.*

(*6*) *The value of a transaction or arrangement not falling within subsections* (*2*) *to* (*5*) *above is the price which it is reasonable to expect could be obtained for the goods, land or services to which the transaction or arrangement relates if they had been supplied* (*at the time the transaction or arrangement is entered into*) *in the ordinary course of business and on the same terms* (*apart from price*) *as they have been supplied, or are to be supplied, under the transaction or arrangement in question.*

(*7*) *For purposes of this section, the value of a transaction or arrangement which is not capable of being expressed as a specific sum of money* (*because the amount of any liability arising under the transaction or arrangement is unascertainable, or for any other reason), whether or not any liability under the transaction or arrangement has been reduced, is deemed to exceed [£100,000].*

[462]

NOTES

Repealed as noted to s 1 at **[309]**.

Sub-s (7): sum in square brackets substituted by the Companies (Fair Dealing by Directors) (Increase in Financial Limits) Order 1990, SI 1990/1393, art 2.

341 Civil remedies for breach of s 330

(1) If a company enters into a transaction or arrangement in contravention of section 330, the transaction or arrangement is voidable at the instance of the company unless—

- *(a) restitution of any money or any other asset which is the subject matter of the arrangement or transaction is no longer possible, or the company has been indemnified in pursuance of subsection (2)(b) below for the loss or damage suffered by it, or*
- *(b) any rights acquired bona fide for value and without actual notice of the contravention by a person other than the person for whom the transaction or arrangement was made would be affected by its avoidance.*

(2) Where an arrangement or transaction is made by a company for a director of the company or its holding company or a person connected with such a director in contravention of section 330, that director and the person so connected and any other director of the company who authorised the transaction or arrangement (whether or not it has been avoided in pursuance of subsection (1)) is liable—

- *(a) to account to the company for any gain which he has made directly or indirectly by the arrangement or transaction; and*
- *(b) (jointly and severally with any other person liable under this subsection) to indemnify the company for any loss or damage resulting from the arrangement or transaction.*

(3) Subsection (2) is without prejudice to any liability imposed otherwise than by that subsection, but is subject to the next two subsections.

(4) Where an arrangement or transaction is entered into by a company and a person connected with a director of the company or its holding company in contravention of section 330, that director is not liable under subsection (2) of this section if he shows that he took all reasonable steps to secure the company's compliance with that section.

(5) In any case, a person so connected and any such other director as is mentioned in subsection (2) is not so liable if he shows that, at the time the arrangement or transaction was entered into, he did not know the relevant circumstances constituting the contravention.

[463]

NOTES

Repealed as noted to s 1 at **[309]**.

342 Criminal penalties for breach of s 330

(1) A director of a relevant company who authorises or permits the company to enter into a transaction or arrangement knowing or having reasonable cause to believe that the company was thereby contravening section 330 is guilty of an offence.

(2) A relevant company which enters into a transaction or arrangement for one of its directors or for a director of its holding company in contravention of section 330 is guilty of an offence.

(3) A person who procures a relevant company to enter into a transaction or arrangement knowing or having reasonable cause to believe that the company was thereby contravening section 330 is guilty of an offence.

(4) A person guilty of an offence under this section is liable to imprisonment or a fine, or both.

(*5*) *A relevant company is not guilty of an offence under subsection* (2) *if it shows that, at the time the transaction or arrangement was entered into, it did not know the relevant circumstances.*

[464]–[466]

NOTES

Repealed as noted to s 1 at **[309]**.

343, 344 (*Repealed by the Companies Act 2006, ss 1177, 1295, Sch 16, as from 6 April 2007.*)

Supplementary

345 Power to increase financial limits

(*1*) *The Secretary of State may by order in a statutory instrument substitute for any sum of money specified in this Part a larger sum specified in the order.*

(*2*) *An order under this section is subject to annulment in pursuance of a resolution of either House of Parliament.*

(*3*) *Such an order does not have effect in relation to anything done or not done before its coming into force; and accordingly, proceedings in respect of any liability* (*whether civil or criminal*) *incurred before that time may be continued or instituted as if the order had not been made.*

[467]

NOTES

Repealed as noted to s 1 at **[309]**.

Orders: the Companies (Fair Dealing by Directors) (Increase in Financial Limits) Order 1990, SI 1990/1393.

346 "Connected persons", etc

(*1*) *This section has effect with respect to references in this Part to a person being "connected" with a director of a company, and to a director being "associated with" or "controlling" a body corporate.*

(*2*) *A person is connected with a director of a company if, but only if, he* (*not being himself a director of it*) *is—*

(*a*) *that director's spouse, [civil partner,] child or step-child; or*

(*b*) *except where the context otherwise requires, a body corporate with which the director is associated; or*

(*c*) *a person acting in his capacity as trustee of any trust the beneficiaries of which include—*

(*i*) *the director, his spouse [or civil partner] or any children or step-children of his, or*

(*ii*) *a body corporate with which he is associated,*

or of a trust whose terms confer a power on the trustees that may be exercised for the benefit of the director, his spouse [or civil partner], or any children or step-children of his, or any such body corporate; or

(*d*) *a person acting in his capacity as partner of that director or of any person who, by virtue of paragraph* (*a*), (*b*) *or* (*c*) *of this subsection, is connected with that director; or*

(*e*) *a Scottish firm in which—*

(*i*) *that director is a partner,*

(*ii*) *a partner is a person who, by virtue of paragraph* (*a*), (*b*) *or* (*c*) *above, is connected with that director, or*

(*iii*) *a partner is a Scottish firm in which that director is a partner or in which there is a partner who, by virtue of paragraph* (*a*), (*b*) *or* (*c*) *above, is connected with that director.*

(*3*) *In subsection* (2)*—*

(*a*) *a reference to the child or step-child of any person includes an illegitimate child of his, but does not include any person who has attained the age of 18; and* (*b*) *paragraph (c) does not apply to a person acting in his capacity as trustee under an employees' share scheme or a pension scheme.*

(*4*) *A director of a company is associated with a body corporate if, but only if, he and the persons connected with him, together—*

(*a*) *are interested in shares comprised in the equity share capital of that body corporate of a nominal value equal to at least one-fifth of that share capital [(excluding any shares in the company held as treasury shares)]; or*

(*b*) *are entitled to exercise or control the exercise of more than one-fifth of the voting power at any general meeting of that body [(excluding any voting rights attached to any shares in the company held as treasury shares)].*

(*5*) *A director of a company is deemed to control a body corporate if, but only if—*

(*a*) *he or any person connected with him is interested in any part of the equity share capital of that body or is entitled to exercise or control the exercise of any part of the voting power at any general meeting of that body; and*

(*b*) *that director, the persons connected with him and the other directors of that company, together, are interested in more than one-half of that share capital [(excluding any shares in the company held as treasury shares)] or are entitled to exercise or control the exercise of more than one-half of that voting power [(excluding any voting rights attached to any shares in the company held as treasury shares)].*

(*6*) *For purposes of subsections (4) and (5)—*

(*a*) *a body corporate with which a director is associated is not to be treated as connected with that director unless it is also connected with him by virtue of subsection (2)(c) or (d); and*

(*b*) *a trustee of a trust the beneficiaries of which include (or may include) a body corporate with which a director is associated is not to be treated as connected with a director by reason only of that fact.*

(*7*) *The rules set out in Part I of Schedule 13 apply for the purposes of subsections (4) and (5).*

(*8*) *References in those subsections to voting power the exercise of which is controlled by a director include voting power whose exercise is controlled by a body corporate controlled by him; but this is without prejudice to other provisions of subsections (4) and (5).*

[468]

NOTES

Repealed as noted to s 1 at **[309]**.

Sub-s (2): words in square brackets inserted by the Civil Partnership Act 2004, s 261(1), Sch 27, para 102.

Sub-ss (4), (5): words in square brackets inserted by the Companies (Acquisition of Own Shares) (Treasury Shares) Regulations 2003, SI 2003/1116, reg 4, Schedule, para 17.

Step-child: this includes relationships arising through civil partnership; see the Civil Partnership Act 2004, ss 246, 247, Sch 21.

347 Transactions under foreign law

For purposes of sections 319 to 322 and 330 to 343, it is immaterial whether the law which (apart from this Act) governs any arrangement or transaction is the law of the United Kingdom, or of a part of it, or not.

[469]

NOTES

Repealed as noted to s 1 at **[309]**.

[PART XA
CONTROL OF POLITICAL DONATIONS

347A Introductory provisions

(*1*) *This Part has effect for controlling—*

(*a*) *contributions and other donations made by companies to registered parties and other EU political organisations; and* (*b*) *EU political expenditure incurred by companies.*

(*2*) *The following provisions have effect for the purposes of this Part, but subsections (4) and (7) have effect subject to section 347B.*

(*3*) *"Director" includes shadow director.*

(*4*) *"Donation", in relation to an organisation, means anything that would constitute a donation for the purposes of Part IV of the Political Parties, Elections and Referendums Act 2000 in accordance with sections 50 to 52 of that Act (references in those sections to a registered party being read as applying equally to an organisation which is not such a party); and—*

(*a*) *subsections (3) to (8) of section 50 of that Act shall apply, with any necessary modifications, for the purpose of determining whether something is a donation to an organisation for the purposes of this Part as they apply for the purpose of determining whether something is a donation to a registered party for the purposes of Part IV of that Act; and*

(*b*) *section 53 of that Act shall similarly apply for the purpose of determining, for the purposes of this Part, the value of any donation.*

(*5*) *"EU political expenditure", in relation to a company, means any expenditure incurred by the company—*

(*a*) *in respect of the preparation, publication or dissemination of any advertising or any other promotional or publicity material—*

(*i*) *of whatever nature, and*

(*ii*) *however published or otherwise disseminated,*

which, at the time of publication or dissemination, is capable of being reasonably regarded as intended to affect public support for any EU political organisation, or

(*b*) *in respect of any activities on the part of the company such as are mentioned in subsection (7)(b) or (c).*

(*6*) *"EU political organisation" means—*

(*a*) *a registered party; or*

(*b*) *any other organisation to which subsection (7) applies.*

(*7*) *This subsection applies to an organisation if—*

(*a*) *it is a political party which carries on, or proposes to carry on, activities for the purpose of or in connection with the participation of the party in any election or elections to public office held in a member State other than the United Kingdom;*

(*b*) *it carries on, or proposes to carry on, activities which are capable of being reasonably regarded as intended to affect public support for—*

(*i*) *any registered party,*

(*ii*) *any other political party within paragraph (a), or*

(*iii*) *independent candidates at any election or elections of the kind mentioned in that paragraph; or*

(*c*) *it carries on, or proposes to carry on, activities which are capable of being reasonably regarded as intended to influence voters in relation to any national or regional referendum held under the law of any member State.*

(*8*) *"Organisation" includes any body corporate and any combination of persons or other unincorporated association.*

(*9*) *"Registered party" means a party registered under Part II of the Political Parties, Elections and Referendums Act 2000.*

(*10*) *"The relevant time", in relation to any donation or expenditure made or incurred by a company or subsidiary undertaking, means—*

(*a*) *the time when the donation or expenditure is made or incurred; or*

(*b*) *if earlier, the time when any contract is entered into by the company or undertaking in pursuance of which the donation or expenditure is made or incurred.*

(*11*) *"Subsidiary undertaking" has the same meaning as in Part VII.]*

[469A]

NOTES

Commencement: 30 November 2000 (in so far as confers power to make an order or regulation), 16 February 2001 (otherwise).

Repealed as noted to s 1 at **[309]**.

Inserted, together with preceding heading and ss 347B–347K (Pt XA) by the Political Parties, Elections and Referendums Act 2000, s 139(1), Sch 19. By virtue of s 163(7) of, and Sch 23, Pt II, para 12 to, the 2000 Act, Pt XA shall not apply to a company in relation to any time falling before the relevant date for the company; namely the date (if held within the first year after s 139(1) comes into force) of the annual general meeting of the company, or otherwise the date immediately following the end of that year.

[347B Exemptions

(1) Section 347A(4) does not extend to a subscription paid to an EU trade association for membership of the association, and accordingly such a payment is not a donation to the association for the purposes of this Part.

(2) In subsection (1)—

"EU trade association" means any organisation formed for the purpose of furthering the trade interests—

(a) of its members, or

(b) of persons represented by its members,

which carries on its activities wholly or mainly in one or more of the member States;

"subscription", in relation to a trade association, does not include any payment to the association to the extent that it is made for the purpose of financing any particular activity of the association.

(3) Section 347A(7) does not apply to any all-party parliamentary group composed of members of one or both of the Houses of Parliament (or of such members and other persons), and accordingly any such group is not an EU political organisation for the purposes of this Part.

(4) For the purposes of this Part—

(a) a company does not need to be authorised as mentioned in section 347C(1) or section 347D(2) or (3), and

(b) a subsidiary undertaking does not need to be authorised as mentioned in section 347E(2),

in connection with any donation or donations to any EU political organisation or organisations made in a particular qualifying period, except to the extent (if any) that the amount or aggregate amount of any such donation or donations made in that period exceeds £5,000.

(5) The restrictions imposed by sections 347C(1), 347D(2) and (3) and 347E(2) accordingly have effect subject to subsection (4); and, where a resolution is passed for the purposes of any of those provisions, any amount of donations in relation to which, by virtue of subsection (4), no authorisation is needed shall accordingly not count towards the sum specified in the resolution.

(6) In subsection (4) "qualifying period" means—

(a) the period of 12 months beginning with the relevant date for the company or (in the case of a subsidiary undertaking) the parent company; and

(b) each succeeding period of twelve months.

(7) For the purposes of subsection (6) the relevant date for a company is—

(a) if an annual general meeting of the company is held within the period of 12 months beginning with the date of the coming into force of this section, the date of that meeting; and

(b) otherwise, the date immediately following the end of that period.

(8) For the purposes of this Part—

(a) a company does not need to be authorised as mentioned in section 347C(1) or section 347D(2) or (3), and

(b) a subsidiary undertaking does not need to be authorised as mentioned in section 347E(2),

in connection with any EU political expenditure in relation to which an exemption is conferred on the company or (as the case may be) subsidiary undertaking by virtue of an order made by the Secretary of State by statutory instrument.

(9) The restrictions imposed by sections 347C(1), 347D(2) and (3) and 347E(2) accordingly have effect subject to subsection (8); and, where a resolution is passed for the purposes of any of those provisions, any amount of EU political expenditure in relation to which, by virtue of subsection (8), no authorisation is needed shall accordingly not count towards the sum specified in the resolution.

PART I STATUTES

(10) An order under subsection (8) may confer an exemption for the purposes of that subsection in relation to—

- *(a) companies or subsidiary undertakings of any description or category specified in the order, or*
- *(b) expenditure of any description or category so specified (whether framed by reference to goods, services or other matters in respect of which such expenditure is incurred or otherwise),*

or both.

(11) An order shall not be made under subsection (8) unless a draft of the statutory instrument containing the order has been laid before and approved by each House of Parliament.]

[469B]

NOTES

Commencement: 30 November 2000 (in so far as confers power to make an order or regulation), 16 February 2001 (otherwise).

Repealed as noted to s 1 at **[309]**.

Inserted as noted to s 347A at **[469A]**.

Orders: the Companies (EU Political Expenditure) Exemption Order 2001, SI 2001/445.

[347C Prohibition on donations and political expenditure by companies

(1) A company must not—

- *(a) make any donation to any registered party or to any other EU political organisation, or*
- *(b) incur any EU political expenditure,*

unless the donation or expenditure is authorised by virtue of an approval resolution passed by the company in general meeting before the relevant time.

This subsection has effect subject to section 347D(3).

(2) For the purposes of this section an approval resolution is a qualifying resolution which authorises the company to do either (or both) of the following, namely—

- *(a) make donations to EU political organisations not exceeding in total a sum specified in the resolution, or*
- *(b) incur EU political expenditure not exceeding in total a sum so specified,*

during the requisite period beginning with the date of the resolution.

(3) In subsection (2)—

- *(a) "qualifying resolution" means an ordinary resolution or, if the directors so determine or the articles so require—*
  - *(i) a special resolution, or*
  - *(ii) a resolution passed by any percentage of the members greater than that required for an ordinary resolution;*
- *(b) "the requisite period" means four years or such shorter period as the directors may determine or the articles may require;*

and the directors may make a determination for the purposes of paragraph (a) or (b) above except where any provision of the articles operates to prevent them from doing so.

(4) The resolution must be expressed in general terms conforming with subsection (2), and accordingly may not purport to authorise particular donations or expenditure.

(5) Where a company makes any donation or incurs any expenditure in contravention of subsection (1), no ratification or other approval made or given by the company or its members after the relevant time is capable of operating to nullify that contravention.

(6) Nothing in this section enables a company to be authorised to do anything that it could not lawfully do apart from this section.]

[469C]

NOTES

Commencement: 30 November 2000 (in so far as confers power to make an order or regulation), 16 February 2001 (otherwise).

Repealed as noted to s 1 at **[309]**.

Inserted as noted to s 347A at **[469A]**.

[347D Special rules for subsidiaries

(1) This section applies where a company is a subsidiary of another company ("the holding company").

(2) Where the subsidiary is not a wholly-owned subsidiary of the holding company—

(a) it must not make any donation or incur any expenditure to which subsection (1) of section 347C applies unless the donation or expenditure is authorised by virtue of a subsidiary approval resolution passed by the holding company in general meeting before the relevant time; and

(b) this requirement applies in addition to that imposed by that subsection.

(3) Where the subsidiary is a wholly-owned subsidiary of the holding company—

(a) it must not make any donation or incur any expenditure to which subsection (1) of section 347C applies unless the donation or expenditure is authorised by virtue of a subsidiary approval resolution passed by the holding company in general meeting before the relevant time; and

(b) this requirement applies in place of that imposed by that subsection.

(4) For the purposes of this section a subsidiary approval resolution is a qualifying resolution of the holding company which authorises the subsidiary to do either (or both) of the following, namely—

(a) make donations to EU political organisations not exceeding in total a sum specified in the resolution, or

(b) incur EU political expenditure not exceeding in total a sum so specified,

during the requisite period beginning with the date of the resolution.

(5) Subsection (3) of section 347C shall apply for the purposes of subsection (4) above as it applies for the purposes of subsection (2) of that section.

(6) The resolution must be expressed in general terms conforming with subsection (4), and accordingly may not purport to authorise particular donations or expenditure.

(7) The resolution may not relate to donations or expenditure by more than one subsidiary.

(8) Where a subsidiary makes any donation or incurs any expenditure in contravention of subsection (2) or (3), no ratification or other approval made or given by the holding company or its members after the relevant time is capable of operating to nullify that contravention.

(9) Nothing in this section enables a company to be authorised to do anything that it could not lawfully do apart from this section.]

[469D]

NOTES

Commencement: 30 November 2000 (in so far as confers power to make an order or regulation), 16 February 2001 (otherwise).

Repealed as noted to s 1 at **[309]**.

Inserted as noted to s 347A at **[469A]**.

[347E Special rule for parent company of non-GB subsidiary undertaking

(1) This section applies where a company ("the parent company") has a subsidiary undertaking which is incorporated or otherwise established outside Great Britain.

(2) The parent company shall take all such steps as are reasonably open to it to secure that the subsidiary undertaking does not make any donation or incur any expenditure to which subsection (1) of section 347C applies except to the extent that the donation or expenditure is authorised by virtue of a subsidiary approval resolution passed by the parent company in general meeting before the relevant time.

(3) For the purposes of this section a subsidiary approval resolution is a qualifying resolution of the parent company which authorises the subsidiary undertaking to do either (or both) of the following, namely—

(a) make donations to EU political organisations not exceeding in total a sum specified in the resolution, or

(b) incur EU political expenditure not exceeding in total a sum so specified,

during the requisite period beginning with the date of the resolution.

(4) Subsection (3) of section 347C shall apply for the purposes of subsection (3) above as it applies for the purposes of subsection (2) of that section.

(5) The resolution must be expressed in general terms conforming with subsection (3), and accordingly may not purport to authorise particular donations or expenditure.

(6) The resolution may not relate to donations or expenditure by more than one subsidiary undertaking.

(7) Where a subsidiary undertaking makes any donation or incurs any expenditure which (to any extent) is not authorised as mentioned in subsection (2), no ratification or other approval made or given by the parent company or its members after the relevant time is capable of operating to authorise that donation or expenditure.]

[469E]

NOTES

Commencement: 30 November 2000 (in so far as confers power to make an order or regulation), 16 February 2001 (otherwise).

Repealed as noted to s 1 at **[309]**.

Inserted as noted to s 347A at **[469A]**.

[347F Remedies for breach of prohibitions on company donations etc

(1) This section applies where a company has made any donation or incurred any expenditure in contravention of any of the provisions of sections 347C and 347D.

(2) Every person who was a director of the company at the relevant time is liable to pay the company—

(a) the amount of the donation or expenditure made or incurred in contravention of the provisions in question; and

(b) damages in respect of any loss or damage sustained by the company as a result of the donation or expenditure having been made or incurred in contravention of those provisions.

(3) Every such person is also liable to pay the company interest on the amount mentioned in subsection (2)(a) in respect of the period—

(a) beginning with the date when the donation or expenditure was made or incurred, and

(b) ending with the date when that amount is paid to the company by any such person;

and such interest shall be payable at such rate as the Secretary of State may prescribe by regulations.

(4) Where two or more persons are subject to a particular liability arising by virtue of any provision of this section, each of those persons is jointly and severally liable.

(5) Where only part of any donation or expenditure was made or incurred in contravention of any of the provisions of sections 347C and 347D, this section applies only to so much of it as was so made or incurred.

(6) Where—

(a) this section applies as mentioned in subsection (1), and

(b) the company in question is a subsidiary of another company ("the holding company"),

then (subject to subsection (7)) subsections (2) to (5) shall, in connection with the donation or expenditure made or incurred by the subsidiary, apply in relation to the holding company as they apply in relation to the subsidiary.

(7) Those subsections do not apply in relation to the holding company if—

(a) the subsidiary is not a wholly-owned subsidiary of the holding company; and

(b) the donation or expenditure was authorised by such a resolution of the holding company as is mentioned in section 347D(2)(a).

(8) Nothing in section 727 shall apply in relation to any liability of any person arising under this section.]

[469F]

PART I STATUTES

NOTES

Commencement: 30 November 2000 (in so far as confers power to make an order or regulation), 16 February 2001 (otherwise).

Repealed as noted to s 1 at **[309]**.

Inserted as noted to s 347A at **[469A]**.

[347G Remedy for unauthorised donation or expenditure by non-GB subsidiary

(*1*) *This section applies where—*

(*a*) *a company ("the parent company") has a subsidiary undertaking falling within subsection (1) of section 347E;*

(*b*) *the subsidiary undertaking has made any donation or incurred any expenditure to which subsection (1) of section 347C applies; and*

(*c*) *the parent company has, in relation to that donation or expenditure, failed to discharge its duty under subsection (2) of section 347E to take all such steps as are mentioned in that subsection.*

(2) *Subsections (2) to (4) of section 347F shall, in connection with the donation or expenditure made or incurred by the subsidiary undertaking, apply in relation to the holding company as if—*

(*a*) *it were a company falling within subsection (1) of that section, and*

(*b*) *the donation or expenditure had been made or incurred by it in contravention of section 347C or 347D.*

(*3*) *Where only part of the donation or expenditure was not authorised as mentioned in section 347E(2), those subsections shall so apply only to that part of it.*

(*4*) *Section 347F(8) applies to any liability of any person arising under section 347F by virtue of this section.]*

[469G]

NOTES

Commencement: 30 November 2000 (in so far as confers power to make an order or regulation), 16 February 2001 (otherwise).

Repealed as noted to s 1 at **[309]**.

Inserted as noted to s 347A at **[469A]**.

[347H Exemption of directors from liability in respect of unauthorised donation or expenditure

(*1*) *Where proceedings are brought against a director or former director of a company in respect of any liability arising under section 347F(2)(a) in connection with a donation or expenditure made or incurred by the company, it shall be a defence for that person to show that—*

(*a*) *the unauthorised amount has been repaid to the company, together with any interest on that amount due under section 347F(3);*

(*b*) *that repayment has been approved by the company in general meeting; and*

(*c*) *in the notice of the relevant resolution submitted to that meeting full disclosure was made—*

(*i*) *of the circumstances in which the donation or expenditure was made or incurred in contravention of section 347C or 347D, and*

(*ii*) *of the circumstances in which, and the person or persons by whom, the repayment was made.*

(2) *Where proceedings are brought against a director or former director of a holding company in respect of any liability arising under section 347F(2)(a) in connection with a donation or expenditure made or incurred by a subsidiary of the company, it shall be a defence for that person to show that—*

(*a*) *the unauthorised amount has been repaid either to the subsidiary or to the holding company, together with any interest on that amount due under section 347F(3);*

(*b*) *that repayment has been approved—*

(*i*) *(if made to the subsidiary) by both the subsidiary and the holding company in general meeting, or*

(*ii*) *(if made to the holding company) by the holding company in general meeting; and*

(*c*) *in the notice of the relevant resolution submitted to each of those meetings or (as the case may be) to that meeting, full disclosure was made—*
  (*i*) *of the circumstances in which the donation or expenditure was made in contravention of section 347D, and*
  (*ii*) *of the circumstances in which, and the person or persons by whom, the repayment was made.*

(3) If the subsidiary is a wholly-owned subsidiary of the holding company, it is not necessary for the purposes of subsection (2) to show (where the repayment was made to the subsidiary) that the repayment has been approved by the subsidiary, and paragraphs (b) and (c) of that subsection shall apply accordingly.

(4) Where proceedings are brought against a director or former director of a holding company in respect of any liability arising under section 347F(2)(a) in connection with a donation or expenditure made or incurred by a subsidiary of the company which is not a wholly-owned subsidiary, then (subject to subsection (5)) it shall be a defence for that person to show that—
(*a*) *proceedings have been instituted by the subsidiary against all or any of its directors in respect of the unauthorised amount; and*
(*b*) *those proceedings are being pursued with due diligence by the subsidiary.*

(5) A person may not avail himself of the defence provided by subsection (4) except with the leave of the court; and on an application for leave under this subsection the court may make such order as it thinks fit, including an order adjourning, or sanctioning the continuation of, the proceedings against the applicant on such terms and conditions as it thinks fit.

(6) Where proceedings are brought against a director or former director of a company in respect of any liability arising under section 347F(2)(a) (as applied by virtue of section 347G) in connection with a donation or expenditure made or incurred by a subsidiary undertaking of the company, it shall be a defence for that person to show that—
(*a*) *the unauthorised amount has been repaid to the subsidiary undertaking, together with any interest on that amount due under section 347F(3) (as so applied);*
(*b*) *that repayment has been approved by the company in general meeting; and*
(*c*) *in the notice of the relevant resolution submitted to that meeting full disclosure was made—*
  (*i*) *of the circumstances in which the donation or expenditure was made without having been authorised as mentioned in section 347E(2), and*
  (*ii*) *of the circumstances in which, and the person or persons by whom, the repayment was made.*

(7) In this section "the unauthorised amount", in relation to any donation or expenditure, means the amount of the donation or expenditure—
(*a*) *which was made or incurred in contravention of section 347C or 347D, or*
(*b*) *which was not authorised as mentioned in section 347E(2),*
as the case may be.]

[469H]

NOTES

Commencement: 30 November 2000 (in so far as confers power to make an order or regulation), 16 February 2001 (otherwise).

Repealed as noted to s 1 at **[309]**.

Inserted as noted to s 347A at **[469A]**.

[347I Enforcement of directors' liabilities by shareholder action

(1) Any liability of any person under section 347F or 347G as a director or former director of a company is (in addition to being enforceable by proceedings brought by the company) enforceable by proceedings brought under this section in the name of the company by an authorised group of members of the company.

(2) For the purposes of this section "authorised group", in relation to the members of a company, means any such combination of members as is specified in section 54(2)(a), (b) or (c).

(3) An authorised group of members of a company may not bring proceedings under this section unless—
(*a*) *the group has given written notice to the company stating—*

(i) *the cause of action and a summary of the facts on which the proceedings are to be based,*

(ii) *the names and addresses of the members of the company comprising the group, and*

(iii) *the grounds on which it is alleged that those members constitute an authorised group; and*

(b) *not less than 28 days have elapsed between the date of the giving of the notice to the company and the institution of the proceedings.*

(4) *Where such a notice is given to a company, any director may apply to the court within the period of 28 days beginning with the date of the giving of the notice for an order directing that the proposed proceedings are not to be instituted.*

(5) *An application under subsection (4) may be made on one or more of the following grounds—*

(a) *that the unauthorised amount within the meaning of section 347H has been repaid to the company or subsidiary undertaking as mentioned in subsection (1), (2), (4) or (6) of that section (as the case may be) and the other conditions mentioned in that subsection were satisfied with respect to that repayment;*

(b) *that proceedings to enforce the liability have been instituted by the company and are being pursued with due diligence by the company;*

(c) *that the members proposing to institute proceedings under this section do not constitute an authorised group.*

(6) *Where such an application is made on the ground mentioned in subsection (5)(b), the court may make such order as it thinks fit; and such an order may, as an alternative to directing that the proposed proceedings under this section are not to be instituted, direct—*

(a) *that those proceedings may be instituted on such terms and conditions as the court thinks fit;*

(b) *that the proceedings instituted by the company are to be discontinued;*

(c) *that the proceedings instituted by the company may be continued on such terms and conditions as the court thinks fit.*

(7) *If proceedings are brought under this section by an authorised group of members of a company, the group shall owe the same duties to the company in relation to the bringing of those proceedings on behalf of the company as would be owed by the directors of the company if the proceedings were being brought by the company itself; but no proceedings to enforce any duty owed by virtue of this subsection shall be brought by the company except with the leave of the court.*

(8) *Proceedings brought under this section may not be discontinued or settled by the group except with the leave of the court; and the court may grant leave under this subsection on such terms as it thinks fit.]*

[469I]

NOTES

Commencement: 30 November 2000 (in so far as confers power to make an order or regulation), 16 February 2001 (otherwise).

Repealed as noted to s 1 at **[309]**.

Inserted as noted to s 347A at **[469A]**.

[347J Costs of shareholder action

(1) *This section applies in relation to proceedings brought under section 347I by an authorised group of members of a company ("the group").*

(2) *The group may apply to the court for an order directing the company to indemnify the group in respect of costs incurred or to be incurred by the group in connection with the proceedings; and on such an application the court may make such an order on such terms as it thinks fit.*

(3) *The group shall not be entitled to be paid any such costs out of the assets of the company except by virtue of such an order.*

(4) *If—*

(a) *the company is awarded costs in connection with the proceedings or it is agreed that costs incurred by the company in connection with the proceedings should be paid by any defendant, and* (*b*) *no order has been made with respect to the proceedings under subsection* (*2*),

the costs shall be paid to the group.

(*5*) *If—*

(*a*) *any defendant is awarded costs in connection with the proceedings or it is agreed that any defendant should be paid costs incurred by him in connection with the proceedings, and*

(*b*) *no order has been made with respect to the proceedings under subsection* (*2*),

the costs shall be paid by the group.

(*6*) *In the application of this section to Scotland references to costs are to expenses and references to any defendant are to any defender.]*

[469J]

NOTES

Commencement: 30 November 2000 (in so far as confers power to make an order or regulation), 16 February 2001 (otherwise).

Repealed as noted to s 1 at **[309]**.

Inserted as noted to s 347A at **[469A]**.

[347K Information for purposes of shareholder action

(*1*) *Where any proceedings have been instituted under section 347I by an authorised group within the meaning of that section, the group is entitled to require the company to provide the group with all information relating to the subject matter of the proceedings which is in the company's possession or under its control or which is reasonably obtainable by it.*

(*2*) *If the company, having been required by the group to provide the information referred to in subsection* (*1*), *refuses to provide the group with all or any of the information, the court may, on an application made by the group, make an order directing—*

(*a*) *the company, and*

(*b*) *any of its officers or employees specified in the application,*

to provide the group with the information in question in such form and by such means as the court may direct.]

[469K]

NOTES

Commencement: 30 November 2000 (in so far as confers power to make an order or regulation), 16 February 2001 (otherwise).

Repealed as noted to s 1 at **[309]**.

Inserted as noted to s 347A at **[469A]**.

PART XI
COMPANY ADMINISTRATION AND PROCEDURE

CHAPTER I
COMPANY IDENTIFICATION

348 Company name to appear outside place of business

(*1*) *Every company shall paint or affix, and keep painted or affixed, its name on the outside of every office or place in which its business is carried on, in a conspicuous position and in letters easily legible.*

(*2*) *If a company does not paint or affix its name as required above, the company and every officer of it who is in default is liable to a fine; and if a company does not keep its name painted or affixed as so required, the company and every officer of it who is in default is liable to a fine and, for continued contravention, to a daily default fine.*

[470]

NOTES

Repealed as noted to s 1 at **[309]**.

349 Company's name to appear in its correspondence, etc

(*1*) *Every company shall have its name mentioned in legible characters—*

(*a*) *in all business letters [and order forms] of the company,*
(*b*) *in all its notices and other official publications,*
[(*ba*) *on all its websites,]*
(*c*) *in all bills of exchange, promissory notes, endorsements, cheques and orders for money or goods purporting to be signed by or on behalf of the company, and*
(*d*) *in all its bills of parcels, invoices, receipts and letters of credit.*

(*2*) *If a company fails to comply with subsection (1) it is liable to a fine.*

(*3*) *If an officer of a company or a person on its behalf—*
(*a*) *issues or authorises the issue of any business letter [or order form] of the company, or any notice or other official publication of the company, in which the company's name is not mentioned as required by subsection (1), ...*
[(*aa*) *causes or authorises the appearance of a website of the company on which the company's name is not so mentioned, or]*
(*b*) *issues or authorises the issue of any bill of parcels, invoice, receipt or letter of credit of the company in which its name is not so mentioned,*
he is liable to a fine.

(*4*) *If an officer of a company or a person on its behalf signs or authorises to be signed on behalf of the company any bill of exchange, promissory note, endorsement, cheque or order for money or goods in which the company's name is not mentioned as required by subsection (1), he is liable to a fine; and he is further personally liable to the holder of the bill of exchange, promissory note, cheque or order for money or goods for the amount of it (unless it is duly paid by the company).*

[(*5*) *References in this section to a document of any type are to a document of that type in hard copy, electronic or any other form.]*

[471]

NOTES

Repealed as noted to s 1 at **[309]**.

Sub-s (1): words in square brackets in para (a) and the whole of para (ba) inserted by the Companies (Registrar, Languages and Trading Disclosures) Regulations 2006, SI 2006/3429, reg 6, Sch 1, para 1(1), (2).

Sub-s (3): words in square brackets in para (a) and the whole of para (aa) inserted, and word omitted from para (a) repealed, by SI 2006/3429, reg 6, Sch 1, para 1(1), (3).

Sub-s (5): added by the Companies (Registrar, Languages and Trading Disclosures) Regulations 2006, SI 2006/3429, reg 6, Sch 1, para 1(1), (4).

350 Company seal

[(*1*) *A company which has a common seal shall have its name engraved in legible characters on the seal; and if it fails to comply with this subsection it is liable to a fine.]*

(*2*) *If an officer of a company or a person on its behalf uses or authorises the use of any seal purporting to be a seal of the company on which its name is not engraved as required by subsection (1), he is liable to a fine.*

[472]

NOTES

Repealed as noted to s 1 at **[309]**.

Sub-s (1): substituted by the Companies Act 1989, s 130(7), Sch 17, para 7.

351 Particulars in correspondence etc

(*1*) *Every company shall have the following particulars mentioned in legible characters in all business letters and order forms of the company[, and on all the company's websites], that is to say—*
(*a*) *the company's place of registration and the number with which it is registered,*
(*b*) *the address of its registered office,*
(*c*) *in the case of an investment company (as defined in section 266), the fact that it is such a company, and*
(*d*) *in the case of a limited company exempt from the obligation to use the word "limited" as part of its name [under section 30 or a community interest company which is not a public company], the fact that it is a limited company.*

[(2) If in the case of a company having a share capital there is a reference to the amount of share capital—

(a) on the stationery used for any such letters,

(b) on the company's order forms, or

(c) on any of the company's websites,

the reference must be to paid-up share capital.]

(3), (4) …

(5) As to contraventions of this section, the following applies—

(a) if a company fails to comply with subsection (1) or (2), it is liable to a fine,

(b) if an officer of a company or a person on its behalf issues or authorises the issue of any business letter or order form not complying with those subsections, he is liable to a fine, …

[(ba) if an officer of a company or a person on its behalf causes or authorises the appearance of a website not complying with those subsections, he is liable to a fine].

(c) …

[(6) References in this section to a document of any type are to a document of that type in hard copy, electronic or any other form.]

[473]

NOTES

Repealed as noted to s 1 at **[309]**.

Sub-s (1): words in first pair of square brackets inserted by the Companies (Registrar, Languages and Trading Disclosures) Regulations 2006, SI 2006/3429, reg 6, Sch 1, para 2(1), (2); words in square brackets in para (d) inserted by the Companies (Audit, Investigations and Community Enterprise) Act 2004, s 33, Sch 6, paras 1, 8.

Sub-s (2): substituted by SI 2006/3429, reg 6, Sch 1, para 2(1), (3).

Sub-ss (3), (4): repealed by the Welsh Language Act 1993, ss 31, 35(1), Sch 2.

Sub-s (5): para (ba) inserted by SI 2006/3429, reg 6, Sch 1, para 2(1), (4); para (c) and the word immediately preceding it repealed by the Welsh Language Act 1993, s 35(1), Sch 2.

Sub-s (6): added by SI 2006/3429, reg 6, Sch 1, para 2(1), (5).

CHAPTER II
REGISTER OF MEMBERS

352 Obligation to keep and enter up register

(1) Every company shall keep a register of its members and enter in it the particulars required by this section.

(2) There shall be entered in the register—

(a) the names and addresses of the members;

(b) the date on which each person was registered as a member; and

(c) the date at which any person ceased to be a member.

(3) The following applies in the case of a company having a share capital—

(a) with the names and addresses of the members there shall be entered a statement—

(i) of the shares held by each member, distinguishing each share by its number (so long as the share has a number) and, where the company has more than one class of issued shares, by its class, and

(ii) of the amount paid or agreed to be considered as paid on the shares of each member;

(b) where the company has converted any of its shares into stock and given notice of the conversion to the registrar of companies, the register shall show the amount and class of stock held by each member, instead of the amount of shares and the particulars relating to shares specified in paragraph (a).

(4) In the case of a company which does not have a share capital but has more than one class of members, there shall be entered in the register, with the names and addresses of the members, the class to which each member belongs.

(5) If a company makes default in complying with this section, the company and every officer of it who is in default is liable to a fine and, for continued contravention, to a daily default fine.

(6) An entry relating to a former member of the company may be removed from the register after the expiration of 20 years from the date on which he ceased to be a member.

(7) Liability incurred by a company from the making or deletion of an entry in its register of members, or from a failure to make or delete any such entry, is not enforceable more than 20 years after the date on which the entry was made or deleted or, in the case of any such failure, the failure first occurred.

This is without prejudice to any lesser period of limitation.

[474]

NOTES

Repealed as noted to s 1 at **[309]**.

Sub-s (3A): inserted by the Companies (Acquisition of Own Shares) (Treasury Shares) Regulations 2003, SI 2003/1116, reg 4, Schedule, para 18.

[352A Statement that company has only one member

(1) If the number of members of a private company limited by shares or by guarantee falls to one there shall upon the occurrence of that event be entered in the company's register of members with the name and address of the sole member—

- *(i) a statement that the company has only one member, and*
- *(ii) the date on which the company became a company having only one member.*

(2) If the membership of a private company limited by shares or by guarantee increases from one to two or more members there shall upon the occurrence of that event be entered in the company's register of members, with the name and address of the person who was formerly the sole member, a statement that the company has ceased to have only one member together with the date on which that event occurred.

(3) If a company makes default in complying with this section, the company and every officer of it who is in default is liable to a fine and, for continued contravention, to a daily default fine.]

[475]

NOTES

Repealed as noted to s 1 at **[309]**.

Inserted by the Companies (Single Member Private Limited Companies) Regulations 1992, SI 1992/1699, reg 2, Schedule, para 4.

353 Location of register

(1) A company's register of members shall be kept at its registered office, except that—

- *(a) if the work of making it up is done at another office of the company, it may be kept there; and*
- *(b) if the company arranges with some other person for the making up of the register to be undertaken on its behalf by that other, it may be kept at the office of the other at which the work is done;*

but it must not be kept, in the case of a company registered in England and Wales, at any place elsewhere than in England and Wales or, in the case of a company registered in Scotland, at any place elsewhere than in Scotland.

(2) Subject as follows, every company shall send notice in the prescribed form to the registrar of companies of the place where its register of members is kept, and of any change in that place.

(3) The notice need not be sent if the register has, at all times since it came into existence (or, in the case of a register in existence on 1st July 1948, at all times since then) been kept at the company's registered office.

(4) If a company makes default for 14 days in complying with subsection (2), the company and every officer of it who is in default is liable to a fine and, for continued contravention, to a daily default fine.

[476]

NOTES

Repealed as noted to s 1 at **[309]**.

Prescribed form: see the Companies (Forms) Regulations 1985, SI 1985/854, Form 353, as prescribed by the Companies (Forms) (Amendment) Regulations 1995, SI 1995/736.

354 Index of members

(1) Every company having more than 50 members shall, unless the register of members is in such a form as to constitute in itself an index, keep an index of the names of the members of the company and shall, within 14 days after the date on which any alteration is made in the register of members, make any necessary alteration in the index.

(2) The index shall in respect of each member contain a sufficient indication to enable the account of that member in the register to be readily found.

(3) The index shall be at all times kept at the same place as the register of members.

(4) If default is made in complying with this section, the company and every officer of it who is in default is liable to a fine and, for continued contravention, to a daily default fine.

[477]

NOTES

Repealed as noted to s 1 at **[309]**.

355 Entries in register in relation to share warrants

(1) On the issue of a share warrant the company shall strike out of its register of members the name of the member then entered in it as holding the shares specified in the warrant as if he had ceased to be a member, and shall enter in the register the following particulars, namely—

(a) the fact of the issue of the warrant;

(b) a statement of the shares included in the warrant, distinguishing each share by its number so long as the share has a number; and

(c) the date of the issue of the warrant.

(2) Subject to the company's articles, the bearer of a share warrant is entitled, on surrendering it for cancellation, to have his name entered as a member in the register of members.

(3) The company is responsible for any loss incurred by any person by reason of the company entering in the register the name of a bearer of a share warrant in respect of the shares specified in it without the warrant being surrendered and cancelled.

(4) Until the warrant is surrendered, the particulars specified in subsection (1) are deemed to be those required by this Act to be entered in the register of members; and, on the surrender, the date of the surrender must be entered.

(5) Except as provided by section 291(2) (director's share qualification), the bearer of a share warrant may, if the articles of the company so provide, be deemed a member of the company within the meaning of this Act, either to the full extent or for any purposes defined in the articles.

[478]

NOTES

Repealed as noted to s 1 at **[309]**.

356 Inspection of register and index

(1) Except when the register of members is closed under the provisions of this Act, the register and the index of members' names shall … be open to the inspection of any member of the company without charge, and of any other person on payment of [such fee as may be prescribed].

(2) …

(3) Any member of the company or other person may require a copy of the register, or of any part of it, on payment of [such fee as may be prescribed]; and the company shall cause any copy so required by a person to be sent to him within 10 days beginning with the day next following that on which the requirement is received by the company.

(4) ...

(5) If an inspection required under this section is refused, or if a copy so required is not sent within the proper period, the company and every officer of it who is in default is liable in respect of each offence to a fine.

(6) In the case of such refusal or default, the court may by order compel an immediate inspection of the register and index, or direct that the copies required be sent to the persons requiring them.

[479]

NOTES

Repealed as noted to s 1 at **[309]**.

Sub-s (1): words omitted repealed and words in square brackets substituted by the Companies Act 1989, ss 143(8), 212, Sch 24.

Sub-ss (2), (4): repealed by the Companies Act 1989, ss 143(8), 212, Sch 24.

Sub-s (3): words in square brackets substituted by the Companies Act 1989, s 143(8).

Regulations: the Companies (Inspection and Copying of Registers, Indices and Documents) Regulations 1991, SI 1991/1998.

357 Non-compliance with ss 353, 354, 356; agent's default

Where under section 353(1)(b), the register of members is kept at the office of some person other than the company, and by reason of any default of his the company fails to comply with—

section 353(2) (notice to registrar),
section 354(3) (index to be kept with register), or
section 356 (inspection),

or with any requirement of this Act as to the production of the register, that other person is liable to the same penalties as if he were an officer of the company who was in default, and the power of the court under section 356(6) extends to the making of orders against that other and his officers and servants.

[480]

NOTES

Repealed as noted to s 1 at **[309]**.

358 Power to close register

A company may, on giving notice by advertisement in a newspaper circulating in the district in which the company's registered office is situated, close the register of members for any time or times not exceeding in the whole 30 days in each year.

[481]

NOTES

Repealed as noted to s 1 at **[309]**.

359 Power of court to rectify register

(1) If—

(a) the name of any person is, without sufficient cause, entered in or omitted from a company's register of members, or

(b) default is made or unnecessary delay takes place in entering on the register the fact of any person having ceased to be a member,

the person aggrieved, or any member of the company, or the company, may apply to the court for rectification of the register.

(2) The court may either refuse the application or may order rectification of the register and payment by the company of any damages sustained by any party aggrieved.

(3) On such an application the court may decide any question relating to the title of a person who is a party to the application to have his name entered in or omitted from the register, whether the question arises between members or alleged members, or between members or alleged members on the one hand and the company on the other hand, and generally may decide any question necessary or expedient to be decided for rectification of the register.

(4) In the case of a company required by this Act to send a list of its members to the registrar of companies, the court, when making an order for rectification of the register, shall by its order direct notice of the rectification to be given to the registrar.

[482]

NOTES

Repealed as noted to s 1 at **[309]**.

360 Trusts not to be entered on register in England and Wales

No notice of any trust, expressed, implied or constructive, shall be entered on the register, or be receivable by the registrar, in the case of companies registered in England and Wales.

[483]

NOTES

Repealed as noted to s 1 at **[309]**.

361 Register to be evidence

The register of members is prima facie evidence of any matters which are by this Act directed or authorised to be inserted in it.

[484]

NOTES

Repealed as noted to s 1 at **[309]**.

362 Overseas branch registers

(1) A company having a share capital whose objects comprise the transaction of business in any of the countries or territories specified in Part I of Schedule 14 to this Act may cause to be kept in any such country or territory in which it transacts business a branch register of members resident in that country or territory.

(2) Such a branch register is to be known as an "overseas branch register"; and—

(a) any dominion register kept by a company under section 119 of the Companies Act 1948 is to become known as an overseas branch register of the company;

(b) where any Act or instrument (including in particular a company's articles) refers to a company's dominion register, that reference is to be read (unless the context otherwise requires) as being to an overseas branch register kept under this section; and

(c) references to a colonial register occurring in articles registered before 1st November 1929 are to be read as referring to an overseas branch register.

(3) Part II of Schedule 14 has effect with respect to overseas branch registers kept under this section; and Part III of the Schedule enables corresponding facilities in Great Britain to be accorded to companies incorporated in other parts of the world.

(4) The Foreign Jurisdiction Act 1890 has effect as if subsection (1) of this section, and Part II of Schedule 14, were included among the enactments which by virtue of section 5 of that Act may be applied by Order in Council to foreign countries in which for the time being Her Majesty has jurisdiction.

(5) Her Majesty may by Order in Council direct that subsection (1) above and Part II of Schedule 14 shall extend, with such exceptions, modifications or adaptations (if any) as may be specified in the Order, to any territories under Her Majesty's protection to which those provisions cannot be extended under the Foreign Jurisdiction Act 1890.

[485]

NOTES

Repealed as noted to s 1 at **[309]**.
Prescribed form: see the Companies (Forms) Regulations 1985, SI 1985/854, Form 362.
Companies Act 1948, s 119: repealed by the Companies Consolidation (Consequential Provisions) Act 1985, s 29, Sch 1, and replaced by this section and Sch 14.

[CHAPTER III
ANNUAL RETURN

363 Duty to deliver annual returns

(1) Every company shall deliver to the registrar successive annual returns each of which is made up to a date not later than the date which is from time to time the company's "return date", that is—

(*a*) *the anniversary of the company's incorporation, or*

(*b*) *if the company's last return delivered in accordance with this Chapter was made up to a different date, the anniversary of that date.*

(2) *Each return shall—*

(*a*) *be in the prescribed form,*

(*b*) *contain the information required by or under the following provisions of this Chapter, and*

(*c*) *be signed by a director or the secretary of the company;*

and it shall be delivered to the registrar within 28 days after the date to which it is made up.

(3) If a company fails to deliver an annual return in accordance with this Chapter before the end of the period of 28 days after a return date, the company is guilty of an offence and liable to a fine and, in the case of continued contravention, to a daily default fine.

The contravention continues until such time as an annual return made up to that return date and complying with the requirements of subsection (2) *(except as to date of delivery) is delivered by the company to the registrar.*

(4) Where a company is guilty of an offence under subsection (3), every director or secretary of the company is similarly liable unless he shows that he took all reasonable steps to avoid the commission or continuation of the offence.

(5) The references in this section to a return being delivered "in accordance with this Chapter" are—

(*a*) *in relation to a return made [on or after 1st October 1990], to a return with respect to which all the requirements of subsection* (2) *are complied with;*

(*b*) *in relation to a return made before [1st October 1990], to a return with respect to which the formal and substantive requirements of this Chapter as it then had effect were complied with, whether or not the return was delivered in time.]*

[486]

NOTES

Repealed as noted to s 1 at **[309]**.

This Chapter (ie Chapter III (ss 363, 364, 364A, 365)) substituted for original Chapter III by the Companies Act 1989, s 139(1), subject to transitional provisions contained in the Companies Act 1989 (Commencement No 7 and Transitional and Saving Provisions) Order 1990, SI 1990/1707.

Sub-s (5): words in square brackets substituted by SI 1990/1707, art 7.

Prescribed forms: see the Companies (Forms) Regulations 1985, SI 1985/854, Form 363a as prescribed by the Companies (Forms) (Amendment) Regulations 1995, SI 1995/736; Forms 363b, 363s as prescribed by the Companies (Forms) (Amendment) Regulations 1991, SI 1991/1259; Form 363CYM as prescribed by the Companies (Welsh Language Forms and Documents) (Amendment) Regulations 1995, SI 1995/734. In addition, the Companies (Forms) (Amendment) Regulations 1995, SI 1995/736, reg 5 provides that Form 288a (prescribed by those Regulations) if annexed to a return in Form 363a is a prescribed form for the purposes of sub-s (2) above to the extent that it gives the information required by s 364(1)(d)–(f).

[364 Contents of annual return: general

(1) Every annual return shall state the date to which it is made up and shall contain the following information—

(*a*) *the address of the company's registered office;*

(*b*) *the type of company it is and its principal business activities;*

(*c*) *the name and address of the company secretary;*

(*d*) *the name and address of every director of the company;*

(*e*) *in the case of each individual director—*

(*i*) *his nationality, date of birth and business occupation, …*

(*ii*) *… ;*

(*f*) *… ;*

(*g*) *if the register of members is not kept at the company's registered office, the address of the place where it is kept;*

(*h*) *if any register of debenture holders (or a duplicate of any such register or a part of it) is not kept at the company's registered office, the address of the place where it is kept;*

(*i*) ...

(2) *The information as to the company's type shall be given by reference to the classification scheme prescribed for the purposes of this section.*

(3) *The information as to the company's principal business activities may be given by reference to one or more categories of any prescribed system of classifying business activities.*

(4) *A person's "name" and "address" mean, respectively—*

(*a*) *in the case of an individual, his Christian name (or other forename) and surname and his usual residential address;*

(*b*) *in the case of a corporation or Scottish firm, its corporate or firm name and its registered or principal office.*

(5) *In the case of a peer, or an individual usually known by a title, the title may be stated instead of his Christian name (or other forename) and surname or in addition to either or both of them.*

(6) *Where all the partners in a firm are joint secretaries, the name and principal office of the firm may be stated instead of the names and addresses of the partners.]*

[487]

NOTES

Repealed as noted to s 1 at **[309]**.

Substituted as noted to s 363 at **[486]**.

Sub-s (1): para (e)(ii) and the word immediately preceding it, and paras (f), (i) repealed by the Companies (Contents of Annual Return) Regulations 1999, SI 1999/2322, reg 2.

Prescribed scheme; prescribed system: see the Companies (Forms Amendment No 2 and Company's Type and Principal Business Activities) Regulations 1990, SI 1990/1766.

[364A Contents of annual return: particulars of share capital and shareholders

(1) *The annual return of a company having a share capital shall contain the following information with respect to its share capital and members.*

(2) *The return shall state the total number of issued shares of the company at the date to which the return is made up and the aggregate nominal value of those shares.*

(3) *The return shall state with respect to each class of shares in the company—*

(*a*) *the nature of the class, and*

(*b*) *the total number and aggregate nominal value of issued shares of that class at the date to which the return is made up.*

(4) *The return shall contain a list of the names and addresses of every person who—*

(*a*) *is a member of the company on the date to which the return is made up, or*

(*b*) *has ceased to be a member of the company since the date to which the last return was made up (or, in the case of the first return, since the incorporation of the company);*

and if the names are not arranged in alphabetical order the return shall have annexed to it an index sufficient to enable the name of any person in the list to be easily found.

(5) *The return shall also state—*

(*a*) *the number of shares of each class held by each member of the company at the date to which the return is made up, and*

(*b*) *the number of shares of each class transferred since the date to which the last return was made up (or, in the case of the first return, since the incorporation of the company) by each member or person who has ceased to be a member, and the dates of registration of the transfers.*

(6) *The return may, if either of the two immediately preceding returns has given the full particulars required by subsections (4) and (5), give only such particulars as relate to persons ceasing to be or becoming members since the date of the last return and to shares transferred since that date.*

(7) Subsections (4) and (5) do not require the inclusion of particulars entered in an overseas branch register if copies of those entries have not been received at the company's registered office by the date to which the return is made up.

Those particulars shall be included in the company's next annual return after they are received.

(8) Where the company has converted any of its shares into stock, the return shall give the corresponding information in relation to that stock, stating the amount of stock instead of the number or nominal value of shares.]

[488]

NOTES

Repealed as noted to s 1 at **[309]**.
Substituted as noted to s 363 at **[486]**.

[365 Supplementary provisions: regulations and interpretation

(1) The Secretary of State may by regulations make further provision as to the information to be given in a company's annual return, which may amend or repeal the provisions of sections 364 and 364A.

(2) Regulations under this section shall be made by statutory instrument which shall be subject to annulment in pursuance of a resolution of either House of Parliament.

(3) For the purposes of this Chapter, except section 363(2)(c) (signature of annual return), a shadow director shall be deemed to be a director.]

[489]

NOTES

Repealed as noted to s 1 at **[309]**.
Substituted as noted to s 363 at **[486]**.
Regulations: the Companies (Contents of Annual Return) Regulations 1999, SI 1999/2322.

CHAPTER IV
MEETINGS AND RESOLUTIONS

Meetings

366 Annual general meeting

(1) Every company shall in each year hold a general meeting as its annual general meeting in addition to any other meetings in that year, and shall specify the meeting as such in the notices calling it.

(2) However, so long as a company holds its first annual general meeting within 18 months of its incorporation, it need not hold it in the year of its incorporation or in the following year.

(3) Not more than 15 months shall elapse between the date of one annual general meeting of a company and that of the next.

(4) If default is made in holding a meeting in accordance with this section, the company and every officer of it who is in default is liable to a fine.

[490]

NOTES

Repealed as noted to s 1 at **[309]**.

[366A Election by private company to dispense with annual general meetings

(1) A private company may elect (by elective resolution in accordance with section 379A) to dispense with the holding of annual general meetings.

(2) An election has effect for the year in which it is made and subsequent years, but does not affect any liability already incurred by reason of default in holding an annual general meeting.

(3) In any year in which an annual general meeting would be required to be held but for the election, and in which no such meeting has been held, any member of the company may, by notice to the company not later than three months before the end of the year, require the holding of an annual general meeting in that year.

[(3A) ...]

(4) If such a notice is given [or electronic communication is transmitted], the provisions of section 366(1) and (4) apply with respect to the calling of the meeting and the consequences of default.

(5) If the election ceases to have effect, the company is not obliged under section 366 to hold an annual general meeting in that year if, when the election ceases to have effect, less than three months of the year remains.

This does not affect any obligation of the company to hold an annual general meeting in that year in pursuance of a notice given [or electronic communication transmitted] under subsection (3).

[(5A) ...]]

[491]

NOTES

Repealed as noted to s 1 at **[309]**.

Inserted by the Companies Act 1989, s 115(2), subject to transitional provisions contained in the Companies Act 1989 (Commencement No 4 and Transitional and Saving Provisions) Order 1990, SI 1990/355 and the Companies Act 1989 (Commencement No 7 and Transitional and Saving Provisions) Order 1990, SI 1990/1707.

Sub-s (3A): inserted by the Companies Act 1985 (Electronic Communications) Order 2000, SI 2000/3373, art 17(1), (2); repealed by the Companies Act 2006, s 1295, Sch 16.

Sub-ss (4), (5): words in square brackets inserted by SI 2000/3373, art 17(1), (3), (4).

Sub-s (5A): added by SI 2000/3373, art 17(1), (5); repealed by the Companies Act 2006, s 1295, Sch 16.

367 Secretary of State's power to call meeting in default

(1) If default is made in holding a meeting in accordance with section 366, the Secretary of State may, on the application of any member of the company, call, or direct the calling of, a general meeting of the company and give such ancillary or consequential directions as he thinks expedient, including directions modifying or supplementing, in relation to the calling, holding and conduct of the meeting, the operation of the company's articles.

(2) The directions that may be given under subsection (1) include a direction that one member of the company present in person or by proxy shall be deemed to constitute a meeting.

(3) If default is made in complying with directions of the Secretary of State under subsection (1), the company and every officer of it who is in default is liable to a fine.

(4) A general meeting held under this section shall, subject to any directions of the Secretary of State, be deemed to be an annual general meeting of the company; but, where a meeting so held is not held in the year in which the default in holding the company's annual general meeting occurred, the meeting so held shall not be treated as the annual general meeting for the year in which it is held unless at that meeting the company resolves that it be so treated.

(5) Where a company so resolves, a copy of the resolution shall, within 15 days after its passing, be forwarded to the registrar of companies and recorded by him; and if default is made in complying with this subsection, the company and every officer of it who is in default is liable to a fine and, for continued contravention, to a daily default fine.

[492]

NOTES

Repealed as noted to s 1 at **[309]**.

368 Extraordinary general meeting on members' requisition

(1) The directors of a company shall, on a members' requisition, forthwith proceed duly to convene an extraordinary general meeting of the company.

This applies notwithstanding anything in the company's articles.

(2) A members' requisition is a requisition of—

(a) members of the company holding at the date of the deposit of the requisition not less than one-tenth of such of the paid-up capital of the company as at that date carries the right of voting at general meetings of the company; or

(b) in the case of a company not having a share capital, members of it representing not less than one-tenth of the total voting rights of all the members having at the date of deposit of the requisition a right to vote at general meetings.

[(2A) For the purposes of subsection (2)(a) any of the company's paid up capital held as treasury shares must be disregarded.]

(3) The requisition must state the objects of the meeting, and must be signed by the requisitionists and deposited at the registered office of the company, and may consist of several documents in like form each signed by one or more requisitionists.

(4) If the directors do not within 21 days from the date of the deposit of the requisition proceed duly to convene a meeting, the requisitionists, or any of them representing more than one half of the total voting rights of all of them, may themselves convene a meeting, but any meeting so convened shall not be held after the expiration of 3 months from that date.

(5) A meeting convened under this section by requisitionists shall be convened in the same manner, as nearly as possible, as that in which meetings are to be convened by directors.

(6) Any reasonable expenses incurred by the requisitionists by reason of the failure of the directors duly to convene a meeting shall be repaid to the requisitionists by the company, and any sum so repaid shall be retained by the company out of any sums due or to become due from the company by way of fees or other remuneration in respect of their services to such of the directors as were in default.

(7) In the case of a meeting at which a resolution is to be proposed as a special resolution, the directors are deemed not to have duly convened the meeting if they do not give the notice required for special resolutions by section 378(2).

[(8) The directors are deemed not to have duly convened a meeting if they convene a meeting for a date more than 28 days after the date of the notice convening the meeting.]
[493]

NOTES

Repealed as noted to s 1 at **[309]**.

Sub-s (2A): inserted by the Companies (Acquisition of Own Shares) (Treasury Shares) Regulations 2003, SI 2003/1116, reg 4, Schedule, para 19.

Sub-s (8): added by the Companies Act 1989, s 145, Sch 19, para 9.

369 Length of notice for calling meetings

(1) A provision of a company's articles is void in so far as it provides for the calling of a meeting of the company (other than an adjourned meeting) by a shorter notice than—

(a) in the case of the annual general meeting, 21 days' notice in writing; and

(b) in the case of a meeting other than an annual general meeting or a meeting for the passing of a special resolution—

(i) 7 days' notice in writing in the case of an unlimited company, and

(ii) otherwise, 14 days' notice in writing.

(2) Save in so far as the articles of a company make other provision in that behalf (not being a provision avoided by subsection (1)), a meeting of the company (other than an adjourned meeting) may be called—

(a) in the case of the annual general meeting, by 21 days' notice in writing; and

(b) in the case of a meeting other than an annual general meeting or a meeting for the passing of a special resolution—

(i) by 7 days' notice in writing in the case of an unlimited company, and

(ii) otherwise, 14 days' notice in writing.

(3) Notwithstanding that a meeting is called by shorter notice than that specified in subsection (2) or in the company's articles (as the case may be), it is deemed to have been duly called if it is so agreed—

(a) in the case of a meeting called as the annual general meeting, by all the members entitled to attend and vote at it; and

(*b*) *otherwise, by the requisite majority.*

(*4*) *The requisite majority for this purpose is a majority in number of the members having a right to attend and vote at the meeting, being a majority—*

(*a*) *together holding not less than 95 per cent in nominal value of the shares giving a right to attend and vote at the meeting [(excluding any shares in the company held as treasury shares)]; or*

(*b*) *in the case of a company not having a share capital, together representing not less than 95 per cent of the total voting rights at that meeting of all the members.*

[A private company may elect (by elective resolution in accordance with section 379A) that the above provisions shall have effect in relation to the company as if for the references to 95 per cent there were substituted references to such lesser percentage, but not less than 90 per cent, as may be specified in the resolution or subsequently determined by the company in general meeting.]

[(4A)–(4G) ...]

[494]

NOTES

Repealed as noted to s 1 at **[309]**.

Sub-s (4): words in square brackets in para (a) inserted by the Companies (Acquisition of Own Shares) (Treasury Shares) Regulations 2003, SI 2003/1116, reg 4, Schedule, para 20; words in second pair of square brackets added by the Companies Act 1989, s 115(3).

Sub-ss (4A)–(4G): added by the Companies Act 1985 (Electronic Communications) Order 2000, SI 2000/3373, art 18; repealed by the Companies Act 2006, s 1295, Sch 16.

370 General provisions as to meetings and votes

(*1*) *The following provisions have effect in so far as the articles of the company do not make other provision in that behalf.*

(*2*) *Notice of the meeting of a company shall be served on every member of it in the manner in which notices are required to be served by Table A (as for the time being in force).*

(*3*) *Two or more members holding not less than one-tenth of the issued share capital [(excluding any shares in the company held as treasury shares)] or, if the company does not have a share capital, not less than 5 per cent in number of the members of the company may call a meeting.*

(*4*) *Two members personally present are a quorum.*

(*5*) *Any member elected by the members present at a meeting may be chairman of it.*

(*6*) *In the case of a company originally having a share capital, every member has one vote in respect of each share or each £10 of stock held by him; and in any other case every member has one vote.*

[495]

NOTES

Repealed as noted to s 1 at **[309]**.

Sub-s (3): words in square brackets inserted by the Companies (Acquisition of Own Shares) (Treasury Shares) Regulations 2003, SI 2003/1116, reg 4, Schedule, para 21.

[370A Quorum at meetings of the sole member

Notwithstanding any provision to the contrary in the articles of a private company limited by shares or by guarantee having only one member, one member present in person or by proxy shall be a quorum.]

[496]

NOTES

Repealed as noted to s 1 at **[309]**.

Inserted by the Companies (Single Member Private Limited Companies) Regulations 1992, SI 1992/1699, reg 2, Schedule, para 5.

371 Power of court to order meeting

(1) If for any reason it is impracticable to call a meeting of a company in any manner in which meetings of that company may be called, or to conduct the meeting in manner prescribed by the articles or this Act, the court may, either of its own motion or on the application—

(a) of any director of the company, or

(b) of any member of the company who would be entitled to vote at the meeting,

order a meeting to be called, held and conducted in any manner the court thinks fit.

(2) Where such an order is made, the court may give such ancillary or consequential directions as it thinks expedient; and these may include a direction that one member of the company present in person or by proxy be deemed to constitute a meeting.

(3) A meeting called, held and conducted in accordance with an order under subsection (1) is deemed for all purposes a meeting of the company duly called, held and conducted.

[497]

NOTES

Repealed as noted to s 1 at **[309]**.

372 Proxies

(1) Any member of a company entitled to attend and vote at a meeting of it is entitled to appoint another person (whether a member or not) as his proxy to attend and vote instead of him; and in the case of a private company a proxy appointed to attend and vote instead of a member has also the same right as the member to speak at the meeting.

(2) But, unless the articles otherwise provide—

(a) subsection (1) does not apply in the case of a company not having a share capital; and

(b) a member of a private company is not entitled to appoint more than one proxy to attend on the same occasion; and

(c) a proxy is not entitled to vote except on a poll.

[(2A), (2B) …]

(3) In the case of a company having a share capital, in every notice calling a meeting of the company there shall appear with reasonable prominence a statement that a member entitled to attend and vote is entitled to appoint a proxy or, where that is allowed, one or more proxies to attend and vote instead of him, and that a proxy need not also be a member.

(4) If default is made in complying with subsection (3) as respects any meeting, every officer of the company who is in default is liable to a fine.

(5) A provision contained in a company's articles is void in so far as it would have the effect of requiring [the appointment of a proxy or any] document necessary to show the validity of, or otherwise relating to, the appointment of a proxy, to be received by the company or any other person more than 48 hours before a meeting or adjourned meeting in order that the appointment may be effective.

(6) If for the purpose of any meeting of a company invitations to appoint as proxy a person or one of a number of persons specified in the invitations are issued at the company's expense to some only of the members entitled to be sent a notice of the meeting and to vote at it by proxy, then every officer of the company who knowingly and wilfully authorises or permits their issue in that manner is liable to a fine.

However, an officer is not so liable by reason only of the issue to a member at his request … of a form of appointment naming the proxy, or of a list of persons willing to act as proxy, if the form or list is available on request … to every member entitled to vote at the meeting by proxy.

[(6A) …]

(7) This section applies to meetings of any class of members of a company as it applies to general meetings of the company.

[498]

NOTES

Repealed as noted to s 1 at **[309]**.

Sub-ss (2A), (2B), (6A): inserted by the Companies Act 1985 (Electronic Communications) Order 2000, SI 2000/3373, art 19(1), (2), (5); repealed by the Companies Act 2006, s 1295, Sch 16.

Sub-s (5): words in square brackets substituted by SI 2000/3373, art 19(1), (3).

Sub-s (6): words omitted repealed by SI 2000/3373, art 19(1), (4).

373 Right to demand a poll

(1) A provision contained in a company's articles is void in so far as it would have the effect either—

- *(a) of excluding the right to demand a poll at a general meeting on any question other than the election of the chairman of the meeting or the adjournment of the meeting; or*
- *(b) of making ineffective a demand for a poll on any such question which is made either—*
  - *(i) by not less than 5 members having the right to vote at the meeting; or*
  - *(ii) by a member or members representing not less than one-tenth of the total voting rights of all the members having the right to vote at the meeting [(excluding any voting rights attached to any shares in the company held as treasury shares)]; or*
  - *(iii) by a member or members holding shares in the company conferring a right to vote at the meeting, being shares on which an aggregate sum has been paid up equal to not less than one-tenth of the total sum paid up on all the shares conferring that right [(excluding any shares in the company conferring a right to vote at the meeting which are held as treasury shares)].*

(2) [The appointment of] a proxy to vote at a meeting of a company is deemed also to confer authority to demand or join in demanding a poll; and for the purposes of subsection (1) a demand by a person as proxy for a member is the same as a demand by the member.

[499]

NOTES

Repealed as noted to s 1 at **[309]**.

Sub-s (1): words in square brackets inserted by the Companies (Acquisition of Own Shares) (Treasury Shares) Regulations 2003, SI 2003/1116, reg 4, Schedule, para 22.

Sub-s (2): words in square brackets substituted by the Companies Act 1985 (Electronic Communications) Order 2000, SI 2000/3373, art 20.

374 Voting on a poll

On a poll taken at a meeting of a company or a meeting of any class of members of a company, a member entitled to more than one vote need not, if he votes, use all his votes or cast all the votes he uses in the same way.

[500]

NOTES

Repealed as noted to s 1 at **[309]**.

375 Representation of corporations at meetings

(1) A corporation, whether or not a company within the meaning of this Act, may—

- *(a) if it is a member of another corporation, being such a company, by resolution of its directors or other governing body authorise such person as it thinks fit to act as its representative at any meeting of the company or at any meeting of any class of members of the company;*
- *(b) if it is a creditor (including a holder of debentures) of another corporation, being such a company, by resolution of its directors or other governing body authorise such person as it thinks fit to act as its representative at any meeting of creditors of the company held in pursuance of this Act or of rules made under it, or in pursuance of the provisions contained in any debenture or trust deed, as the case may be.*

(2) A person so authorised is entitled to exercise the same powers on behalf of the corporation which he represents as that corporation could exercise if it were an individual shareholder, creditor or debenture-holder of the other company.

[501]

NOTES

Repealed as noted to s 1 at **[309]**.

Resolutions

376 Circulation of members' resolutions

(1) Subject to the section next following, it is the duty of a company, on the requisition in writing of such number of members as is specified below and (unless the company otherwise resolves) at the expense of the requisitionists—

- *(a) any number representing not less than one-twentieth of the total voting rights of all the members having at the date of the requisition a right to vote at the meeting to which the requisition relates [(excluding any voting rights attached to any shares in the company held as treasury shares)]; or*
- *(b) to circulate to members entitled to have notice of any general meeting sent to them any statement of not more than 1,000 words with respect to the matter referred to in any proposed resolution or the business to be dealt with at that meeting.*

(2) The number of members necessary for a requisition under subsection (1) is—

- *(a) any number representing not less than one-twentieth of the total voting rights of all the members having at the date of the requisition a right to vote at the meeting to which the requisition relates; or*
- *(b) not less than 100 members holding shares in the company on which there has been paid up an average sum, per member, of not less than £100.*

(3) Notice of any such resolution shall be given, and any such statement shall be circulated, to members of the company entitled to have notice of the meeting sent to them, by serving a copy of the resolution or statement on each such member in any manner permitted for service of notice of the meeting.

(4) Notice of any such resolution shall be given to any other member of the company by giving notice of the general effect of the resolution in any manner permitted for giving him notice of meetings of the company.

(5) For compliance with subsections (3) and (4), the copy must be served, or notice of the effect of the resolution be given (as the case may be) in the same manner and (so far as practicable) at the same time as notice of the meeting; and, where it is not practicable for it to be served or given at the same time, it must be served or given as soon as practicable thereafter.

(6) The business which may be dealt with at an annual general meeting includes any resolution of which notice is given in accordance with this section; and for purposes of this subsection notice is deemed to have been so given notwithstanding the accidental omission, in giving it, of one or more members. This has effect notwithstanding anything in the company's articles.

(7) In the event of default in complying with this section, every officer of the company who is in default is liable to a fine.

[502]

NOTES

Repealed as noted to s 1 at **[309]**.
Sub-s (2): words in square brackets in para (a) inserted by the Companies (Acquisition of Own Shares) (Treasury Shares) Regulations 2003, SI 2003/1116, reg 4, Schedule, para 23.

377 In certain cases, compliance with s 376 not required

(1) A company is not bound under section 376 to give notice of a resolution or to circulate a statement unless—

- *(a) a copy of the requisition signed by the requisitionists (or two or more copies which between them contain the signatures of all the requisitionists) is deposited at the registered office of the company—*

(i) *in the case of a requisition requiring notice of a resolution, not less than 6 weeks before the meeting, and*

(ii) *otherwise, not less than one week before the meeting; and*

(b) *there is deposited or tendered with the requisition a sum reasonably sufficient to meet the company's expenses in giving effect to it.*

(2) *But if, after a copy of a requisition requiring notice of a resolution has been deposited at the company's registered office, an annual general meeting is called for a date 6 weeks or less after the copy has been deposited, the copy (though not deposited within the time required by subsection (1)) is deemed properly deposited for the purposes of that subsection.*

(3) *The company is also not bound under section 376 to circulate a statement if, on the application either of the company or of any other person who claims to be aggrieved, the court is satisfied that the rights conferred by that section are being abused to secure needless publicity for defamatory matter; and the court may order the company's costs on such an application to be paid in whole or in part by the requisitionists, notwithstanding that they are not parties to the application.*

[503]

NOTES

Repealed as noted to s 1 at **[309]**.

378 Extraordinary and special resolutions

(1) *A resolution is an extraordinary resolution when it has been passed by a majority of not less than three-fourths of such members as (being entitled to do so) vote in person or, where proxies are allowed, by proxy, at a general meeting of which notice specifying the intention to propose the resolution as an extraordinary resolution has been duly given.*

(2) *A resolution is a special resolution when it has been passed by such a majority as is required for the passing of an extraordinary resolution and at a general meeting of which not less than 21 days' notice, specifying the intention to propose the resolution as a special resolution, has been duly given.*

(3) *If it is so agreed by a majority in number of the members having the right to attend and vote at such a meeting, being a majority—*

(a) *together holding not less than 95 per cent in nominal value of the shares giving that right; or*

(b) *in the case of a company not having a share capital, together representing not less than 95 per cent of the total voting rights at that meeting of all the members,*

a resolution may be proposed and passed as a special resolution at a meeting of which less than 21 days' notice has been given.

[A private company may elect (by elective resolution in accordance with section 379A) that the above provisions shall have effect in relation to the company as if for the references to 95 per cent there were substituted references to such lesser percentage, but not less than 90 per cent, as may be specified in the resolution or subsequently determined by the company in general meeting.]

(4) *At any meeting at which an extraordinary resolution or a special resolution is submitted to be passed, a declaration by the chairman that the resolution is carried is, unless a poll is demanded, conclusive evidence of the fact without proof of the number or proportion of the votes recorded in favour of or against the resolution.*

(5) *In computing the majority on a poll demanded on the question that an extraordinary resolution or a special resolution be passed, reference is to be had to the number of votes cast for and against the resolution.*

(6) *For purposes of this section, notice of a meeting is deemed duly given, and the meeting duly held, when the notice is given and the meeting held in the manner provided by this Act or the company's articles.*

[504]

NOTES

Repealed as noted to s 1 at **[309]**.

Sub-s (3): words in square brackets in para (a) inserted by the Companies (Acquisition of Own Shares) (Treasury Shares) Regulations 2003, SI 2003/1116, reg 4, Schedule, para 24; words in square brackets added by the Companies Act 1989, s 115(3), subject to transitional provisions.

379 Resolution requiring special notice

(1) Where by any provision of this Act special notice is required of a resolution, the resolution is not effective unless notice of the intention to move it has been given to the company at least 28 days before the meeting at which it is moved.

(2) The company shall give its members notice of any such resolution at the same time and in the same manner as it gives notice of the meeting or, if that is not practicable, shall give them notice either by advertisement in a newspaper having an appropriate circulation or in any other mode allowed by the company's articles, at least 21 days before the meeting.

(3) If, after notice of the intention to move such a resolution has been given to the company, a meeting is called for a date 28 days or less after the notice has been given, the notice is deemed properly given, though not given within the time required.

[505]

NOTES

Repealed as noted to s 1 at **[309]**.

[379A Elective resolution of private company

(1) An election by a private company for the purposes of—

(a) section 80A (election as to duration of authority to allot shares),

(b) section 252 (election to dispense with laying of accounts and reports before general meeting),

(c) section 366A (election to dispense with holding of annual general meeting),

(d) section 369(4) or 378(3) (election as to majority required to authorise short notice of meeting), or

(e) section 386 (election to dispense with appointment of auditors annually),

shall be made by resolution of the company in general meeting in accordance with this section.

Such a resolution is referred to in this Act as an "elective resolution".

(2) An elective resolution is not effective unless—

(a) at least 21 days' notice in writing is given of the meeting, stating that an elective resolution is to be proposed and stating the terms of the resolution, and

(b) the resolution is agreed to at the meeting, in person or by proxy, by all the members entitled to attend and vote at the meeting.

[(2A) An elective resolution is effective notwithstanding the fact that less than 21 days' notice in writing of the meeting is given if all the members entitled to attend and vote at the meeting so agree.]

[(2B)–(2F) ...]

(3) The company may revoke an elective resolution by passing an ordinary resolution to that effect.

(4) An elective resolution shall cease to have effect if the company is re-registered as a public company.

(5) An elective resolution may be passed or revoked in accordance with this section, and the provisions referred to in [subsections (1) and (2B) to (2E)] have effect, notwithstanding any contrary provision in the company's articles of association.

[(5A) ...]

[506]

NOTES

Repealed as noted to s 1 at **[309]**.
Inserted by the Companies Act 1989, s 116(1), (2).
Sub-s (2A): inserted by the Deregulation (Resolutions of Private Companies) Order 1996, SI 1996/1471, art 2; repealed by the Companies Act 2006, s 1295, Sch 16.

Sub-ss (2B)–(2F): inserted by the Companies Act 1985 (Electronic Communications) Order 2000, SI 2000/3373, art 21(1), (2); repealed by the Companies Act 2006, s 1295, Sch 16.

Sub-s (5): words in square brackets substituted by SI 2000/3373, art 21(1), (3).

Sub-s (5A): added by SI 2000/3373, art 21(1), (4); repealed by the Companies Act 2006, s 1295, Sch 16.

380 Registration, etc of resolutions and agreements

(1) A copy of every resolution or agreement to which this section applies shall, within 15 days after it is passed or made, be forwarded to the registrar of companies and recorded by him; and it must be either a printed copy or else a copy in some other form approved by the registrar.

(2) Where articles have been registered, a copy of every such resolution or agreement for the time being in force shall be embodied in or annexed to every copy of the articles issued after the passing of the resolution or the making of the agreement.

(3) Where articles have not been registered, a printed copy of every such resolution or agreement shall be forwarded to any member at his request on payment of 5 pence or such less sum as the company may direct.

(4) [Except as mentioned in subsection (4ZB),] this section applies to—

(a) special resolutions;

(b) extraordinary resolutions;

[(bb) an elective resolution or a resolution revoking such a resolution;]

(c) resolutions or agreements which have been agreed to by all the members of a company but which, if not so agreed to, would not have been effective for their purpose unless (as the case may be) they had been passed as special resolutions or as extraordinary resolutions;

(d) resolutions or agreements which have been agreed to by all the members of some class of shareholders but which, if not so agreed to, would not have been effective for their purpose unless they had been passed by some particular majority or otherwise in some particular manner, and all resolutions or agreements which effectively bind all the members of any class of shareholders though not agreed to by all those members;

(e) a resolution passed by the directors of a company in compliance with a direction under section 31(2) (change of name on Secretary of State's direction);

(f) a resolution of a company to give, vary, revoke or renew an authority to the directors for the purposes of section 80 (allotment of relevant securities);

(g) a resolution of the directors passed under section 147(2) (alteration of memorandum on company ceasing to be a public company, following acquisition of its own shares);

(h) a resolution conferring, varying, revoking or renewing authority under section 166 (market purchase of company's own shares);

(j) a resolution for voluntary winding up, passed under [section 84(1)(a) of the Insolvency Act];

(k) a resolution passed by the directors of an old public company, under section 2(1) of the Consequential Provisions Act, that the company should be re-registered as a public company;

[(l) a resolution of the directors passed by virtue of regulation 16(2) of the Uncertificated Securities Regulations 2001 (which allows title to a company's shares to be evidenced and transferred without written instrument); and

(m) a resolution of a company passed by virtue of regulation 16(6) of the Uncertificated Securities Regulations 2001 (which prevents or reverses a resolution of the directors under regulation 16(2) of those Regulations)].

[(4ZA) This section does not, despite paragraphs (a) to (c) of subsection (4), apply to any resolution of a company which is—

(a) registered as a company in Scotland, and

(b) entered in the Scottish Charity Register,

where that resolution is of either of the types mentioned in section 56(5) of the Charities and Trustee Investment (Scotland) Act 2005 (asp 10).]

[(4ZB) Paragraphs (a) and (c) of subsection (4) do not apply to the resolutions of a charitable company mentioned in paragraphs (a) and (b) respectively of section 69G(6) of the Charities Act 1993.]

[(4A) For the purposes of this section, references to a member of a company do not include the company itself where it is such a member by virtue only of its holding shares as treasury shares, and accordingly, in such circumstances, the company is not, for those purposes, to be treated as a member of any class of the company's shareholders.]

(5) If a company fails to comply with subsection (1), the company and every officer of it who is in default is liable to a fine and, for continued contravention, to a daily default fine.

(6) If a company fails to comply with subsection (2) or (3), the company and every officer of it who is in default is liable to a fine.

(7) For purposes of subsections (5) and (6), a liquidator of a company is deemed an officer of it.

[507]

NOTES

Repealed as noted to s 1 at **[309]**.

Sub-s (4): words in first pair of square brackets inserted by the Charities Act 2006, s 75, Sch 8, paras 74, 75(1), (2), as from a day to be appointed under s 79(2) of that Act; para (bb) inserted by the Companies Act 1989, s 116(3); words in square brackets in para (j) substituted by the Insolvency Act 1986, s 439(1), Sch 13, Pt I; paras (l), (m) originally added by the Uncertificated Securities Regulations 1995, SI 1995/3272, reg 40(3); the 1995 Regulations were revoked by the Uncertificated Securities Regulations 2001, SI 2001/3755, reg 52, and reg 51 of, and Sch 7, Pt 1, para 10 to, the 2001 Regulations added new paras (l), (m).

Sub-s (4ZA): inserted by the Charities and Trustee Investment (Scotland) Act 2005, s 104, Sch 4, Pt 1, para 6.

Sub-s (4ZB): inserted by the Charities Act 2006, s 75, Sch 8, paras 74, 75(1), (3), as from a day to be appointed under s 79(2) of that Act.

Sub-s (4A): inserted by the Companies (Acquisition of Own Shares) (Treasury Shares) Regulations 2003, SI 2003/1116, reg 4, Schedule, para 25.

Insolvency Act: ie, the Insolvency Act 1986.

Consequential Provisions Act: ie, the Companies Consolidation (Consequential Provisions) Act 1985.

381 Resolution passed at adjourned meeting

Where a resolution is passed at an adjourned meeting of—

(a) a company;

(b) the holders of any class of shares in a company;

(c) the directors of a company;

the resolution is for all purposes to be treated as having been passed on the date on which it was in fact passed, and is not to be deemed passed on any earlier date.

[508]

NOTES

Repealed as noted to s 1 at **[309]**.

[Written resolutions of private companies

381A Written resolutions of private companies

(1) Anything which in the case of a private company may be done—

(a) by resolution of the company in general meeting, or

(b) by resolution of a meeting of any class of members of the company,

may be done, without a meeting and without any previous notice being required, by resolution in writing signed by or on behalf of all the members of the company who at the date of the resolution would be entitled to attend and vote at such meeting.

(2) The signatures need not be on a single document provided each is on a document which accurately states the terms of the resolution.

(3) The date of the resolution means when the resolution is signed by or on behalf of the last member to sign.

(4) A resolution agreed to in accordance with this section has effect as if passed—

(a) by the company in general meeting, or

(b) by a meeting of the relevant class of members of the company,

as the case may be; and any reference in any enactment to a meeting at which a resolution is passed or to members voting in favour of a resolution shall be construed accordingly.

(5) Any reference in any enactment to the date of passing of a resolution is, in relation to a resolution agreed to in accordance with this section, a reference to the date of the resolution, ...

(6) A resolution may be agreed to in accordance with this section which would otherwise be required to be passed as a special, extraordinary or elective resolution; and any reference in any enactment to a special, extraordinary or elective resolution includes such a resolution.

(7) This section has effect subject to the exceptions specified in Part I of Schedule 15A; and in relation to certain descriptions of resolution under this section the procedural requirements of this Act have effect with the adaptations specified in Part II of that Schedule.]

[509]

NOTES

Repealed as noted to s 1 at **[309]**.

Inserted, together with preceding heading and ss 381B, 381C, by the Companies Act 1989, s 113(1), (2).

Sub-s (5): words omitted repealed by the Deregulation (Resolutions of Private Companies) Order 1996, SI 1996/1471, art 3(2)(a), (3), with effect in relation to written resolutions first proposed on or after 19 June 1996.

[381B Duty to notify auditors of proposed written resolution

(1) If a director or secretary of a company—

(a) knows that it is proposed to seek agreement to a resolution in accordance with section 381A, and

(b) knows the terms of the resolution,

he shall, if the company has auditors, secure that a copy of the resolution is sent to them, or that they are otherwise notified of its contents, at or before the time the resolution is supplied to a member for signature.

(2) A person who fails to comply with subsection (1) is liable to a fine.

(3) In any proceedings for an offence under this section it is a defence for the accused to prove—

(a) that the circumstances were such that it was not practicable for him to comply with subsection (1), or

(b) that he believed on reasonable grounds that a copy of the resolution had been sent to the company's auditors or that they had otherwise been informed of its contents.

(4) Nothing in this section affects the validity of any resolution.]

[510]

NOTES

Repealed as noted to s 1 at **[309]**.

Inserted as noted to s 381A at **[509]** and substituted by the Deregulation (Resolutions of Private Companies) Order 1996, SI 1996/1471, art 3(1), (3), with effect in relation to written resolutions first proposed on or after 19 June 1996.

[381C Written resolutions: supplementary provisions

(1) Sections 381A and 381B have effect notwithstanding any provision of the company's memorandum or article[, but do not prejudice any power conferred by any such provision].

(2) Nothing in those sections affects any enactment or rule of law as to—

(a) things done otherwise than by passing a resolution, or

(b) cases in which a resolution is treated as having been passed, or a person is precluded from alleging that a resolution has not been duly passed.]

[511]

NOTES

Repealed as noted to s 1 at **[309]**.

Inserted as noted to s 381A at **[509]**.

Sub-s (1): words in square brackets added by the Deregulation (Resolutions of Private Companies) Order 1996, SI 1996/1471, art 4.

Records of proceedings

382 Minutes of meetings

(1) Every company shall cause minutes of all proceedings of general meetings, all proceedings at meetings of its directors and, where there are managers, all proceedings at meetings of its managers to be entered in books kept for that purpose.

(2) Any such minute, if purporting to be signed by the chairman of the meeting at which the proceedings were had, or by the chairman of the next succeeding meeting, is evidence of the proceedings.

(3) Where a shadow director by means of a notice required by section 317(8) declares an interest in a contract or proposed contract, this section applies—

(a) if it is a specific notice under paragraph (a) of that subsection, as if the declaration had been made at the meeting there referred to, and

(b) otherwise, as if it had been made at the meeting of the directors next following the giving of the notice;

and the making of the declaration is in either case deemed to form part of the proceedings at the meeting.

(4) Where minutes have been made in accordance with this section of the proceedings at any general meeting of the company or meeting of directors or managers, then, until the contrary is proved, the meeting is deemed duly held and convened, and all proceedings had at the meeting to have been duly had; and all appointments of directors, managers or liquidators are deemed valid.

(5) If a company fails to comply with subsection (1), the company and every officer of it who is in default is liable to a fine and, for continued contravention, to a daily default fine.
[512]

NOTES

Repealed as noted to s 1 at **[309]**.

[382A Recording of written resolutions

(1) Where a written resolution is agreed to in accordance with section 381A which has effect as if agreed by the company in general meeting, the company shall cause a record of the resolution (and of the signatures) to be entered in a book in the same way as minutes of proceedings of a general meeting of the company.

(2) Any such record, if purporting to be signed by a director of the company or by the company secretary, is evidence of the proceedings in agreeing to the resolution; and where a record is made in accordance with this section, then, until the contrary is proved, the requirements of this Act with respect to those proceedings shall be deemed to be complied with.

(3) Section 382(5) (penalties) applies in relation to a failure to comply with subsection (1) above as it applies in relation to a failure to comply with subsection (1) of that section; and section 383 (inspection of minute books) applies in relation to a record made in accordance with this section as it applies in relation to the minutes of a general meeting.]
[513]

NOTES

Repealed as noted to s 1 at **[309]**.
Inserted by the Companies Act 1989, s 113(1), (3).

[382B Recording of decisions by the sole member

(1) Where a private company limited by shares or by guarantee has only one member and he takes any decision which may be taken by the company in general meeting and which has effect as if agreed by the company in general meeting, he shall (unless that decision is taken by way of a written resolution) provide the company with a written record of that decision.

(2) *If the sole member fails to comply with subsection (1) he shall be liable to a fine.*

(3) *Failure by the sole member to comply with section (1) shall not affect the validity of any decision referred to in that subsection.]*

[514]

NOTES

Repealed as noted to s 1 at **[309]**.
Inserted by the Companies (Single Member Private Limited Companies) Regulations 1992, SI 1992/1699, reg 2, Schedule, para 6.

383 Inspection of minute books

(1) *The books containing the minutes of proceedings of any general meeting of a company held on or after 1st November 1929 shall be kept at the company's registered office, and shall ... be open to the inspection of any member without charge.*

(2) ...

(3) *Any member shall be entitled [on payment of such fee as may be prescribed] to be furnished, within 7 days after he has made a request in that behalf to the company, with a copy of any such minutes as are referred to above, ...*

(4) *If an inspection required under this section is refused or if a copy required under this section is not sent within the proper time, the company and every officer of it who is in default is liable in respect of each offence to a fine.*

(5) *In the case of any such refusal or default, the court may by order compel an immediate inspection of the books in respect of all proceedings of general meetings, or direct that the copies required be sent to the persons requiring them.*

[515]

NOTES

Repealed as noted to s 1 at **[309]**.
Sub-s (1): words omitted repealed by the Companies Act 1989, ss 143(9), 212, Sch 24.
Sub-s (2): repealed by the Companies Act 1989, ss 143(9), 212, Sch 24.
Sub-s (3): words in square brackets inserted and words omitted repealed by the Companies Act 1989, ss 143(9), 212, Sch 24.
Regulations: the Companies (Inspection and Copying of Registers, Indices and Documents) Regulations 1991, SI 1991/1998.

CHAPTER V
AUDITORS

[Appointment of auditors

384 Duty to appoint auditors

(1) *Every company shall appoint an auditor or auditors in accordance with this Chapter.*

This is subject to section 388A ([certain companies] exempt from obligation to appoint auditors).

(2) *Auditors shall be appointed in accordance with section 385 (appointment at general meeting at which accounts are laid), except in the case of a private company which has elected to dispense with the laying of accounts in which case the appointment shall be made in accordance with section 385A.*

(3) *References in this Chapter to the end of the time for appointing auditors are to the end of the time within which an appointment must be made under section 385(2) or 385A(2), according to whichever of those sections applies.*

(4) *Sections 385 and 385A have effect subject to section 386 under which a private company may elect to dispense with the obligation to appoint auditors annually.]*

[516]

NOTES

Repealed as noted to s 1 at **[309]**.

Substituted, together with the preceding heading and ss 385, 385A, 386–388, 388A, by the Companies Act 1989, ss 118, 119(1), subject to transitional provisions contained in the Companies Act 1989 (Commencement No 4 and Transitional and Saving Provisions) Order 1990, SI 1990/355.

Sub-s (1): words in square brackets substituted by the Companies Act 1985 (Audit Exemption) Regulations 1994, SI 1994/1935, reg 4, Sch 1, Pt I, para 4, subject to transitional provisions in reg 6 thereof.

[385 Appointment at general meeting at which accounts laid

(1) This section applies to every public company and to a private company which has not elected to dispense with the laying of accounts.

(2) The company shall, at each general meeting at which accounts are laid, appoint an auditor or auditors to hold office from the conclusion of that meeting until the conclusion of the next general meeting at which accounts are laid.

(3) The first auditors of the company may be appointed by the directors at any time before the first general meeting of the company at which accounts are laid; and auditors so appointed shall hold office until the conclusion of that meeting.

(4) If the directors fail to exercise their powers under subsection (3), the powers may be exercised by the company in general meeting.]

[517]

NOTES

Repealed as noted to s 1 at **[309]**.
Substituted as noted to s 384 at **[516]**.

[385A Appointment by private company which is not obliged to lay accounts

(1) This section applies to a private company which has elected in accordance with section 252 to dispense with the laying of accounts before the company in general meeting.

(2) Auditors shall be appointed by the company in general meeting before the end of the period of 28 days beginning with the day on which copies of the company's annual accounts for the previous financial year are sent to members under section 238 or, if notice is given under section 253(2) requiring the laying of the accounts before the company in general meeting, the conclusion of that meeting.

Auditors so appointed shall hold office from the end of that period or, as the case may be, the conclusion of that meeting until the end of the time for appointing auditors for the next financial year.

(3) The first auditors of the company may be appointed by the directors at any time before—

- *(a) the end of the period of 28 days beginning with the day on which copies of the company's first annual accounts are sent to members under section 238, or*
- *(b) if notice is given under section 253(2) requiring the laying of the accounts before the company in general meeting, the beginning of that meeting;*

and auditors so appointed shall hold office until the end of that period or, as the case may be, the conclusion of that meeting.

(4) If the directors fail to exercise their powers under subsection (3), the powers may be exercised by the company in general meeting.

(5) Auditors holding office when the election is made shall, unless the company in general meeting determines otherwise, continue to hold office until the end of the time for appointing auditors for the next financial year; and auditors holding office when an election ceases to have effect shall continue to hold office until the conclusion of the next general meeting of the company at which accounts are laid.]

[518]

NOTES

Repealed as noted to s 1 at **[309]**.
Substituted as noted to s 384 at **[516]**.

[386 Election by private company to dispense with annual appointment

(1) A private company may elect (by elective resolution in accordance with section 379A) to dispense with the obligation to appoint auditors annually.

(2) When such an election is in force the company's auditors shall be deemed to be re-appointed for each succeeding financial year on the expiry of the time for appointing auditors for that year, unless—

[(a) the directors of the company have taken advantage of the exemption conferred by section 249A or 249AA, or]

(b) a resolution has been passed under section 393 to the effect that their appointment should be brought to an end.

(3) If the election ceases to be in force, the auditors then holding office shall continue to hold office—

(a) where section 385 then applies, until the conclusion of the next general meeting of the company at which accounts are laid;

(b) where section 385A then applies, until the end of the time for appointing auditors for the next financial year under that section.

(4) No account shall be taken of any loss of the opportunity of further deemed re-appointment under this section in ascertaining the amount of any compensation or damages payable to an auditor on his ceasing to hold office for any reason.]

[519]

NOTES

Repealed as noted to s 1 at **[309]**.

Substituted as noted to s 384 at **[516]**.

Sub-s (2): para (a) substituted by the Companies Act 1985 (Audit Exemption) (Amendment) Regulations 2000, SI 2000/1430, reg 8(8), in relation to annual reports and reports in respect of financial years ending two months or more after 26 May 2000.

[387 Appointment by Secretary of State in default of appointment by company

(1) If in any case no auditors are appointed, re-appointed or deemed to be re-appointed before the end of the time for appointing auditors, the Secretary of State may appoint a person to fill the vacancy.

(2) In such a case the company shall within one week of the end of the time for appointing auditors give notice to the Secretary of State of his power having become exercisable.

If a company fails to give the notice required by this subsection, the company and every officer of it who is in default is guilty of an offence and liable to a fine and, for continued contravention, to a daily default fine.]

[520]

NOTES

Repealed as noted to s 1 at **[309]**.

Substituted as noted to s 384 at **[516]**.

[388 Filling of casual vacancies

(1) The directors, or the company in general meeting, may fill a casual vacancy in the office of auditor.

(2) While such a vacancy continues, any surviving or continuing auditor or auditors may continue to act.

(3) Special notice is required for a resolution at a general meeting of a company—

(a) filling a casual vacancy in the office of auditor, or

(b) re-appointing as auditor a retiring auditor who was appointed by the directors to fill a casual vacancy.

(4) On receipt of notice of such an intended resolution the company shall forthwith send a copy of it—

(a) to the person proposed to be appointed, and

(b) if the casual vacancy was caused by the resignation of an auditor, to the auditor who resigned.]

[521]

PART I STATUTES

NOTES

Repealed as noted to s 1 at **[309]**.
Substituted as noted to s 384 at **[516]**.

[388A Certain companies exempt from obligation to appoint auditors

(1) A company which by virtue of section 249A (certain categories of small company) or [section 249AA] (dormant companies) is exempt from the provisions of Part VII relating to the audit of accounts is also exempt from the obligation to appoint auditors.

(2) The following provisions apply if a company which has been exempt from those provisions ceases to be so exempt.

(3) Where section 385 applies (appointment at general meeting at which accounts are laid), the directors may appoint auditors at any time before the next meeting of the company at which accounts are to be laid; and auditors so appointed shall hold office until the conclusion of that meeting.

(4) Where section 385A applies (appointment by private company not obliged to lay accounts), the directors may appoint auditors at any time before—

(a) the end of the period of 28 days beginning with the day on which copies of the company's annual accounts are next sent to members under section 238, or

(b) if notice is given under section 253(2) requiring the laying of the accounts before the company in general meeting, the beginning of that meeting;

and auditors so appointed shall hold office until the end of that period or, as the case may be, the conclusion of that meeting.

(5) If the directors fail to exercise their powers under subsection (3) or (4), the powers may be exercised by the company in general meeting.]

[522]

NOTES

Repealed as noted to s 1 at **[309]**.
Substituted as noted to s 384 at **[516]**, and further substituted by the Companies Act 1985 (Audit Exemption) Regulations 1994, SI 1994/1935, reg 3, subject to transitional provisions contained in reg 6 thereof.
Sub-s (1): words in square brackets substituted by the Companies Act 1985 (Audit Exemption) (Amendment) Regulations 2000, SI 2000/1430, reg 8(9), in relation to annual reports and reports in respect of financial years ending two months or more after 26 May 2000.

389 *(Repealed by the Companies Act 1989, s 212, Sch 24.)*

[Rights of auditors

389A Rights to information

(1) The auditors of a company have a right of access at all times to the company's books, accounts and vouchers, and are entitled to require from the company's officers such information and explanations as they think necessary for the performance of their duties as auditors.

(2) An officer of a company commits an offence if he knowingly or recklessly makes to the company's auditors a statement (whether written or oral) which—

(a) conveys or purports to convey any information or explanations which the auditors require, or are entitled to require, as auditors of the company, and

(b) is misleading, false or deceptive in a material particular.

A person guilty of an offence under this subsection is liable to imprisonment or a fine, or both.

(3) A subsidiary undertaking which is a body corporate incorporated in Great Britain, and the auditors of such an undertaking, shall give to the auditors of any parent company of the undertaking such information and explanations as they may reasonably require for the purposes of their duties as auditors of that company.

If a subsidiary undertaking fails to comply with this subsection, the undertaking and every officer of it who is in default is guilty of an offence and liable to a fine; and if an auditor fails without reasonable excuse to comply with this subsection he is guilty of an offence and liable to a fine.

(4) A parent company having a subsidiary undertaking which is not a body corporate incorporated in Great Britain shall, if required by its auditors to do so, take all such steps as are reasonably open to it to obtain from the subsidiary undertaking such information and explanations as they may reasonably require for the purposes of their duties as auditors of that company.

If a parent company fails to comply with this subsection, the company and every officer of it who is in default is guilty of an offence and liable to a fine.

(5) Section 734 (criminal proceedings against unincorporated bodies) applies to an offence under subsection (3).]

[523]

NOTES

Repealed as noted to s 1 at **[309]**.

Inserted, together with the preceding heading and s 390, by the Companies Act 1989, ss 118, 120(1), subject to transitional provisions contained in the Companies Act 1989 (Commencement No 4 and Transitional and Saving Provisions) Order 1990, SI 1990/355.

Substituted, together with s 389B, by the Companies (Audit, Investigations and Community Enterprise) Act 2004.

[389B Offences relating to the provision of information to auditors

(1) If a person knowingly or recklessly makes to an auditor of a company a statement (oral or written) that—

- *(a) conveys or purports to convey any information or explanations which the auditor requires, or is entitled to require, under section 389A(1)(b), and*
- *(b) is misleading, false or deceptive in a material particular,*

the person is guilty of an offence and liable to imprisonment or a fine, or both.

(2) A person who fails to comply with a requirement under section 389A(1)(b) without delay is guilty of an offence and is liable to a fine.

(3) However, it is a defence for a person charged with an offence under subsection (2) to prove that it was not reasonably practicable for him to provide the required information or explanations.

(4) If a company fails to comply with section 389A(5), the company and every officer of it who is in default is guilty of an offence and liable to a fine.

(5) Nothing in this section affects any right of an auditor to apply for an injunction to enforce any of his rights under section 389A.]

[523A]

NOTES

Commencement: 6 April 2005.

Repealed as noted to s 1 at **[309]**.

Substituted as noted to s 389A at **[523]**.

[390 Right to attend company meetings, &c

(1) A company's auditors are entitled—

- *(a) to receive all notices of, and other communications relating to, any general meeting which a member of the company is entitled to receive;*
- *(b) to attend any general meeting of the company; and*
- *(c) to be heard at any general meeting which they attend on any part of the business of the meeting which concerns them as auditors.*

[(1A) Subsections (4A) to (4G) of section 369 (electronic communication of notices of meetings) apply for the purpose of determining whether notice of a meeting is received by the company's auditors as they apply in determining whether such a notice is given to any person.]

(2) In relation to a written resolution proposed to be agreed to by a private company in accordance with section 381A, the company's auditors are entitled—

(a) to receive all such communications relating to the resolution as, by virtue of any provision of Schedule 15A, are required to be supplied to a member of the company,

(b)–(d) …

(3) The right to attend or be heard at a meeting is exercisable in the case of a body corporate or partnership by an individual authorised by it in writing to act as its representative at the meeting.]

[524]

NOTES

Repealed as noted to s 1 at **[309]**.

Inserted as noted to s 389A at **[523]**.

Sub-s (1A): inserted by the Companies Act 1985 (Electronic Communications) Order 2000, SI 2000/3373, art 31(3).

Sub-s (2): paras (b)–(d) repealed by the Deregulation (Resolutions of Private Companies) Order 1996, SI 1996/1471, art 3(2)(b), (3), with effect in relation to written resolutions first proposed on or after 19 June 1996.

[Remuneration of auditors

390A Remuneration of auditors

(1) The remuneration of auditors appointed by the company in general meeting shall be fixed by the company in general meeting or in such manner as the company in general meeting may determine.

(2) The remuneration of auditors appointed by the directors or the Secretary of State shall be fixed by the directors or the Secretary of State, as the case may be.

(3) …

(4) For the purposes of this section "remuneration" includes sums paid in respect of expenses.

(5) This section applies in relation to benefits in kind as to [payments of money].]

[525]

NOTES

Repealed as noted to s 1 at **[309]**.

Inserted, together with the preceding heading and s 390B, by the Companies Act 1989, ss 118, 121, subject to transitional provisions contained in the Companies Act 1989 (Commencement No 4 and Transitional and Saving Provisions) Order 1990, SI 1990/355.

Sub-s (3): repealed by the Companies (Audit, Investigations and Community Enterprise) Act 2004, ss 7(2)(a), 64, Sch 8, except in relation to the accounts of a company for a financial year beginning before 1 October 2005; see the Companies (Audit, Investigations and Community Enterprise) Act 2004 (Commencement) and Companies Act 1989 (Commencement No 18) Order 2004, SI 2004/3322, art 3.

Sub-s (5): words in square brackets substituted by the Companies (Audit, Investigations and Community Enterprise) Act 2004, s 7(2)(b).

[390B Disclosure of services provided by auditors or associates and related remuneration

(1) The Secretary of State may make provision by regulations for securing the disclosure of—

(a) the nature of any services provided for a company by the company's auditors (whether in their capacity as such or otherwise) or by their associates;

(b) the amount of any remuneration received or receivable by a company's auditors, or their associates, in respect of any services within paragraph (a).

(2) The regulations may provide—

(a) for disclosure of the nature of any services provided to be made by reference to any class or description of services specified in the regulations (or any combination of services, however described);

(b) for the disclosure of amounts of remuneration received or receivable in respect of

services of any class or description specified in the regulations (or any combination of services, however described);

(*c*) *for the disclosure of separate amounts so received or receivable by the company's auditors or any of their associates, or of aggregate amounts so received or receivable by all or any of those persons.*

(*3*) *The regulations may—*

(*a*) *provide that "remuneration" includes sums paid in respect of expenses;*

(*b*) *apply to benefits in kind as well as to payments of money, and require the disclosure of the nature of any such benefits and their estimated money value;*

(*c*) *apply to services provided for associates of a company as well as to those provided for a company;*

(*d*) *define "associate" in relation to an auditor and a company respectively.*

(*4*) *The regulations may provide that any disclosure required by the regulations is to be made—*

(*a*) *in a note to the company's annual accounts (in the case of its individual accounts) or in such manner as is specified in the regulations (in the case of group accounts),*

(*b*) *in the directors' report required by section 234, or*

(*c*) *in the auditors' report under section 235.*

(*5*) *If the regulations provide that any such disclosure is to be made as mentioned in subsection (4)(a) or (b), the regulations may—*

(*a*) *require the auditors to supply the directors of the company with any information necessary to enable the disclosure to be made;*

(*b*) *provide for any provision within subsection (6) to apply in relation to a failure to make the disclosure as it applies in relation to a failure to comply with a requirement of this Act or (as the case may be) a provision of Part 7.*

(*6*) *The provisions are—*

(*a*) *sections 233(5) and 234(5); and*

(*b*) *any provision of sections 245 to 245C*

(*7*) *The regulations may make different provision for different cases.*

(*8*) *Nothing in subsections (2) to (7) affects the generality of subsection (1).*

(*9*) *Regulations under this section shall be made by statutory instrument which shall be subject to annulment in pursuance of a resolution of either House of Parliament.]*

[526]

NOTES

Repealed as noted to s 1 at **[309]**.

Inserted as noted to s 390A at **[525]**.

Substituted by the Companies (Audit, Investigations and Community Enterprise) Act 2004, s 7(1), except in relation to the accounts of a company for a financial year beginning before 1 October 2005 (see the Companies (Audit, Investigations and Community Enterprise) Act 2004 (Commencement) and Companies Act 1989 (Commencement No 18) Order 2004, SI 2004/3322, art 3).

Regulations: the Companies Act 1985 (Disclosure of Remuneration for Non-Audit Work) Regulations 1991, SI 1991/2128 (which are disapplied in relation to the accounts of a company for any financial year beginning on or after 1 October 2005); the Companies (Disclosure of Auditor Remuneration) Regulations 2005, SI 2005/2417.

[Removal, resignation, &c of auditors

391 Removal of auditors

(*1*) *A company may by ordinary resolution at any time remove an auditor from office, notwithstanding anything in any agreement between it and him.*

(*2*) *Where a resolution removing an auditor is passed at a general meeting of a company, the company shall within 14 days give notice of that fact in the prescribed form to the registrar.*

If a company fails to give the notice required by this subsection, the company and every officer of it who is in default is guilty of an offence and liable to a fine and, for continued contravention, to a daily default fine.

(3) Nothing in this section shall be taken as depriving a person removed under it of compensation or damages payable to him in respect of the termination of his appointment as auditor or of any appointment terminating with that as auditor.

(4) An auditor of a company who has been removed has, notwithstanding his removal, the rights conferred by section 390 in relation to any general meeting of the company—

(a) at which his term of office would otherwise have expired, or

(b) at which it is proposed to fill the vacancy caused by his removal.

In such a case the references in that section to matters concerning the auditors as auditors shall be construed as references to matters concerning him as a former auditor.]

[527]

NOTES

Repealed as noted to s 1 at **[309]**.

Inserted, together with the preceding heading and ss 391A, 392, 392A, 393, by the Companies Act 1989, ss 118, 122(1), subject to transitional provisions contained in the Companies Act 1989 (Commencement No 4 and Transitional and Saving Provisions) Order 1990, SI 1990/355.

Prescribed form: see the Companies (Forms) Regulations 1985, SI 1985/854, Form 391, as prescribed by the Companies (Forms) (Amendment) Regulations 1995, SI 1995/736.

[391A Rights of auditors who are removed or not re-appointed

(1) Special notice is required for a resolution at a general meeting of a company—

(a) removing an auditor before the expiration of his term of office, or

(b) appointing as auditor a person other than a retiring auditor.

(2) On receipt of notice of such an intended resolution the company shall forthwith send a copy of it to the person proposed to be removed or, as the case may be, to the person proposed to be appointed and to the retiring auditor.

(3) The auditor proposed to be removed or (as the case may be) the retiring auditor may make with respect to the intended resolution representations in writing to the company (not exceeding a reasonable length) and request their notification to members of the company.

(4) The company shall (unless the representations are received by it too late for it to do so)—

(a) in any notice of the resolution given to members of the company, state the fact of the representations having been made, and

(b) send a copy of the representations to every member of the company to whom notice of the meeting is or has been sent.

(5) If a copy of any such representations is not sent out as required because received too late or because of the company's default, the auditor may (without prejudice to his right to be heard orally) require that the representations be read out at the meeting.

(6) Copies of the representations need not be sent out and the representations need not be read at the meeting if, on the application either of the company or of any other person claiming to be aggrieved, the court is satisfied that the rights conferred by this section are being abused to secure needless publicity for defamatory matter; and the court may order the company's costs on the application to be paid in whole or in part by the auditor, notwithstanding that he is not a party to the application.]

[528]

NOTES

Repealed as noted to s 1 at **[309]**.

Inserted as noted to s 391 at **[527]**.

[392 Resignation of auditors

(1) An auditor of a company may resign his office by depositing a notice in writing to that effect at the company's registered office.

The notice is not effective unless it is accompanied by the statement required by section 394.

(2) An effective notice of resignation operates to bring the auditor's term of office to an end as of the date on which the notice is deposited or on such later date as may be specified in it.

(3) The company shall within 14 days of the deposit of a notice of resignation send a copy of the notice to the registrar of companies.

If default is made in complying with this subsection, the company and every officer of it who is in default is guilty of an offence and liable to a fine and, for continued contravention, a daily default fine.]

[529]

NOTES

Repealed as noted to s 1 at **[309]**.
Inserted as noted to s 391 at **[527]**.

[392A Rights of resigning auditors

(1) This section applies where an auditor's notice of resignation is accompanied by a statement of circumstances which he considers should be brought to the attention of members or creditors of the company.

(2) He may deposit with the notice a signed requisition calling on the directors of the company forthwith duly to convene an extraordinary general meeting of the company for the purpose of receiving and considering such explanation of the circumstances connected with his resignation as he may wish to place before the meeting.

(3) He may request the company to circulate to its members—

(a) before the meeting convened on his requisition, or

(b) before any general meeting at which his term of office would otherwise have expired or at which it is proposed to fill the vacancy caused by his resignation,

a statement in writing (not exceeding a reasonable length) of the circumstances connected with his resignation.

(4) The company shall (unless the statement is received too late for it to comply)—

(a) in any notice of the meeting given to members of the company, state the fact of the statement having been made, and

(b) send a copy of the statement to every member of the company to whom notice of the meeting is or has been sent.

(5) If the directors do not within 21 days from the date of the deposit of a requisition under this section proceed duly to convene a meeting for a day not more than 28 days after the date on which the notice convening the meeting is given, every director who failed to take all reasonable steps to secure that a meeting was convened as mentioned above is guilty of an offence and liable to a fine.

(6) If a copy of the statement mentioned above is not sent out as required because received too late or because of the company's default, the auditor may (without prejudice to his right to be heard orally) require that the statement be read out at the meeting.

(7) Copies of a statement need not be sent out and the statement need not be read out at the meeting if, on the application either of the company or of any other person who claims to be aggrieved, the court is satisfied that the rights conferred by this section are being abused to secure needless publicity for defamatory matter; and the court may order the company's costs on such an application to be paid in whole or in part by the auditor, notwithstanding that he is not a party to the application.

(8) An auditor who has resigned has, notwithstanding his resignation, the rights conferred by section 390 in relation to any such general meeting of the company as is mentioned in subsection (3)(a) or (b).

In such a case the references in that section to matters concerning the auditors as auditors shall be construed as references to matters concerning him as a former auditor.]

[530]

NOTES

Repealed as noted to s 1 at **[309]**.
Inserted as noted to s 391 at **[527]**.

[393 Termination of appointment of auditors not appointed annually

(1) When an election is in force under section 386 (election by private company to dispense with annual appointment), any member of the company may deposit notice in writing at the company's registered office proposing that the appointment of the company's auditors be brought to an end.

No member may deposit more than one such notice in any financial year of the company.

(2) If such a notice is deposited it is the duty of the directors—

(a) to convene a general meeting of the company for a date not more than 28 days after the date on which the notice was given, and

(b) to propose at the meeting a resolution in a form enabling the company to decide whether the appointment of the company's auditors should be brought to an end.

(3) If the decision of the company at the meeting is that the appointment of the auditors should be brought to an end, the auditors shall not be deemed to be reappointed when next they would be and, if the notice was deposited within the period immediately following the distribution of accounts, any deemed reappointment for the financial year following that to which those accounts relate which has already occurred shall cease to have effect.

The period immediately following the distribution of accounts means the period beginning with the day on which copies of the company's annual accounts are sent to members of the company under section 238 and ending 14 days after that day.

(4) If the directors do not within 14 days from the date of the deposit of the notice proceed duly to convene a meeting, the member who deposited the notice (or, if there was more than one, any of them) may himself convene the meeting; but any meeting so convened shall not be held after the expiration of three months from that date.

(5) A meeting convened under this section by a member shall be convened in the same manner, as nearly as possible, as that in which meetings are to be convened by directors.

(6) Any reasonable expenses incurred by a member by reason of the failure of the directors duly to convene a meeting shall be made good to him by the company; and any such sums shall be recouped by the company from such of the directors as were in default out of any sums payable, or to become payable, by the company by way of fees or other remuneration in respect of their services.

(7) This section has effect notwithstanding anything in any agreement between the company and its auditors; and no compensation or damages shall be payable by reason of the auditors' appointment being terminated under this section.]

[531]

NOTES

Repealed as noted to s 1 at **[309]**.
Inserted as noted to s 391 at **[527]**.

[394 Statement by person ceasing to hold office as auditor

(1) Where an auditor ceases for any reason to hold office, he shall deposit at the company's registered office a statement of any circumstances connected with his ceasing to hold office which he considers should be brought to the attention of the members or creditors of the company or, if he considers that there are no such circumstances, a statement that there are none.

(2) In the case of resignation, the statement shall be deposited along with the notice of resignation; in the case of failure to seek re-appointment, the statement shall be deposited not less than 14 days before the end of the time allowed for next appointing auditors; in any other case, the statement shall be deposited not later than the end of the period of 14 days beginning with the date on which he ceases to hold office.

(3) If the statement is of circumstances which the auditor considers should be brought to the attention of the members or creditors of the company, the company shall within 14 days of the deposit of the statement either—

(a) send a copy of it to every person who under section 238 is entitled to be sent copies of the accounts, or

(b) apply to the court.

(4) The company shall if it applies to the court notify the auditor of the application.

(5) Unless the auditor receives notice of such an application before the end of the period of 21 days beginning with the day on which he deposited the statement, he shall within a further seven days send a copy of the statement to the registrar.

(6) If the court is satisfied that the auditor is using the statement to secure needless publicity for defamatory matter—

(a) it shall direct that copies of the statement need not be sent out, and

(b) it may further order the company's costs on the application to be paid in whole or in part by the auditor, notwithstanding that he is not a party to the application;

and the company shall within 14 days of the court's decision send to the persons mentioned in subsection (3)(a) a statement setting out the effect of the order.

(7) If the court is not so satisfied, the company shall within 14 days of the court's decision—

(a) send copies of the statement to the persons mentioned in subsection (3)(a), and

(b) notify the auditor of the court's decision;

and the auditor shall within seven days of receiving such notice send a copy of the statement to the registrar.]

[532]

NOTES

Repealed as noted to s 1 at **[309]**.

Inserted, together with s 394A, by the Companies Act 1989, ss 118, 123(1), subject to transitional provisions contained in the Companies Act 1989 (Commencement No 4 and Transitional and Saving Provisions) Order 1990, SI 1990/355.

[394A Offences of failing to comply with s 394

(1) If a person ceasing to hold office as auditor fails to comply with section 394 he is guilty of an offence and liable to a fine.

(2) In proceedings for an offence under subsection (1) it is a defence for the person charged to show that he took all reasonable steps and exercised all due diligence to avoid the commission of the offence.

(3) Sections 733 (liability of individuals for corporate default) and 734 (criminal proceedings against unincorporated bodies) apply to an offence under subsection (1).

(4) If a company makes default in complying with section 394, the company and every officer of it who is in default is guilty of an offence and liable to a fine and, for continued contravention, to a daily default fine.]

[533]

NOTES

Repealed as noted to s 1 at **[309]**.

Inserted as noted to s 394 at **[532]**.

PART XII
REGISTRATION OF CHARGES

NOTES

Prospective amendment.

(a) New ss 395–420 (provisions relating to the registration of charges with respect to companies registered in Great Britain) which apply throughout Great Britain are inserted in this Part of this Act by the Companies Act 1989, ss 92–104, in place of the original ss 395–408 applying to England and Wales, and ss 410–423 applying to Scotland, as from a day to be appointed as follows (it is understood that these substitutions are now unlikely to be brought into force in their present form and the Companies Act 1989, ss 92–104 are repealed by the Companies Act 2006, ss 1180, 1295, Sch 16, as from a day to be appointed)—

"Registration in the company charges register

395 Introductory provisions

(1) The purpose of this Part is to secure the registration of charges on a company's property.

(2) In this Part—

"charge" means any form of security interest (fixed or floating) over property, other than an interest arising by operation of law; and
"property", in the context of what is the subject of a charge, includes future property.

(3) *It is immaterial for the purposes of this Part where the property subject to a charge is situated.*

(4) *References in this Part to "the registrar" are—*
(*a*) *in relation to a company registered in England and Wales, to the registrar of companies for England and Wales, and*
(*b*) *in relation to a company registered in Scotland, to the registrar of companies for Scotland;*
and references to registration, in relation to a charge, are to registration in the register kept by him under this Part.

396 Charges requiring registration

(*1*) *The charges requiring registration under this Part are—*
(*a*) *a charge on land or any interest in land, other than—*
(*i*) *in England and Wales, a charge for rent or any other periodical sum issuing out of the land,*
(*ii*) *in Scotland, a charge for any rent, ground annual or other periodical sum payable in respect of the land;*
(*b*) *a charge on goods or any interest in goods, other than a charge under which the chargee is entitled to possession either of the goods or of a document of title to them;*
(*c*) *a charge on intangible movable property (in Scotland, incorporeal moveable property) of any of the following descriptions—*
(*i*) *goodwill,*
(*ii*) *intellectual property,*
(*iii*) *book debts (whether book debts of the company or assigned to the company),*
(*iv*) *uncalled share capital of the company or calls made but not paid;*
(*d*) *a charge for securing an issue of debentures; or*
(*e*) *a floating charge on the whole or part of the company's property.*

(2) *The descriptions of charge mentioned in subsection (1) shall be construed as follows—*
(*a*) *a charge on a debenture forming part of an issue or series shall not be treated as falling within paragraph (a) or (b) by reason of the fact that the debenture is secured by a charge on land or goods (or on an interest in land or goods);*
(*b*) *in paragraph (b) "goods" means any tangible movable property (in Scotland, corporeal moveable property) other than money;*
(*c*) *a charge is not excluded from paragraph (b) because the chargee is entitled to take possession in case of default or on the occurrence of some other event;*
(*d*) *in paragraph (c)(ii) "intellectual property" means—*
(*i*) *any patent, trade mark, ... registered design, copyright or design right, or*
(*ii*) *any licence under or in respect of any such right;*
(*e*) *a debenture which is part of an issue or series shall not be treated as a book debt for the purposes of paragraph (c)(iii);*
(*f*) *the deposit by way of security of a negotiable instrument given to secure the payment of book debts shall not be treated for the purposes of paragraph (c)(iii) as a charge on book debts;*
(*g*) *a shipowner's lien on subfreights shall not be treated as a charge on book debts for the purposes of paragraph (c)(iii) or as a floating charge for the purposes of paragraph (e).*

(3) *Whether a charge is one requiring registration under this Part shall be determined—*
(*a*) *in the case of a charge created by a company, as at the date the charge is created, and*
(*b*) *in the case of a charge over property acquired by a company, as at the date of the acquisition.*

(*4*) *The Secretary of State may by regulations amend subsections (1) and (2) so as to add any description of charge to, or remove any description of charge from, the charges requiring registration under this Part.*

(*5*) *Regulations under this section shall be made by statutory instrument which shall be subject to annulment in pursuance of a resolution of either House of Parliament.*

(*6*) *In the following provisions of this Part references to a charge are, unless the context otherwise requires, to a charge requiring registration under this Part.*

Where a charge not otherwise requiring registration relates to property, by virtue of which it requires to be registered and to other property, the references are to the charge so far as it relates to property of the former description.

397 The companies charges register

(*1*) *The registrar shall keep for each company a register, in such form as he thinks fit, of charges on property of the company.*

(2) *The register shall consist of a file containing with respect to each charge the particulars and other information delivered to the registrar under the provisions of this Part.*

(*3*) *Any person may require the registrar to provide a certificate stating the date on which any specified particulars of, or other information relating to, a charge were delivered to him.*

(4) The certificate shall be signed by the registrar or authenticated by his official seal.

(5) The certificate shall be conclusive evidence that the specified particulars or other information were delivered to the registrar no later than the date stated in the certificate; and it shall be presumed unless the contrary is proved that they were not delivered earlier than that date.

398 Company's duty to deliver particulars of charge for registration

(1) It is the duty of a company which creates a charge, or acquires property subject to a charge—
- *(a) to deliver the prescribed particulars of the charge, in the prescribed form, to the registrar for registration, and*
- *(b) to do so within 21 days after the date of the charge's creation or, as the case may be, the date of the acquisition;*

but particulars of a charge may be delivered for registration by any person interested in the charge.

(2) Where the particulars are delivered for registration by a person other than the company concerned, that person is entitled to recover from the company the amount of any fees paid by him to the registrar in connection with the registration.

(3) If a company fails to comply with subsection (1), then, unless particulars of the charge have been delivered for registration by another person, the company and every officer of it who is in default is liable to a fine.

(4) Where prescribed particulars in the prescribed form are delivered to the registrar for registration, he shall file the particulars in the register and shall note, in such form as he thinks fit, the date on which they were delivered to him.

(5) The registrar shall send to the company and any person appearing from the particulars to be the chargee, and if the particulars were delivered by another person interested in the charge to that person, a copy of the particulars filed by him and of the note made by him as to the date on which they were delivered.

399 Effect of failure to deliver particulars for registration

(1) Where a charge is created by a company and no prescribed particulars in the prescribed form are delivered for registration within the period of 21 days after the date of the charge's creation, the charge is void against—
- *(a) an administrator or liquidator of the company, and*
- *(b) any person who for value acquires an interest in or right over property subject to the charge,*

where the relevant event occurs after the creation of the charge, whether before or after the end of the 21 day period.

This is subject to section 400 (late delivery of particulars).

(2) In this Part "the relevant event" means—
- *(a) in relation to the voidness of a charge as against an administrator or liquidator, the beginning of the insolvency proceedings, and*
- *(b) in relation to the voidness of a charge as against a person acquiring an interest in or right over property subject to a charge, the acquisition of that interest or right;*

and references to "a relevant event" shall be construed accordingly.

(3) Where a relevant event occurs on the same day as the charge is created, it shall be presumed to have occurred after the charge is created unless the contrary is proved.

400 Late delivery of particulars

(1) Where prescribed particulars of a charge created by a company, in the prescribed form, are delivered for registration more than 21 days after the date of the charge's creation, section 399(1) does not apply in relation to relevant events occurring after the particulars are delivered.

(2) However, where in such a case—
- *(a) the company is at the date of delivery of the particulars unable to pay its debts, or subsequently becomes unable to pay its debts in consequence of the transaction under which the charge is created, and*
- *(b) insolvency proceedings begin before the end of the relevant period beginning with the date of delivery of the particulars,*

the charge is void as against the administrator or liquidator.

(3) For this purpose—
- *(a) the company is "unable to pay its debts" in the circumstances specified in section 123 of the Insolvency Act 1986; and*
- *(b) the "relevant period" is—*
  - *(i) two years in the case of a floating charge created in favour of a person connected with the company (within the meaning of section 249 of that Act),*
  - *(ii) one year in the case of a floating charge created in favour of a person not so connected, and*
  - *(iii) six months in any other case.*

(4) *Where a relevant event occurs on the same day as the particulars are delivered, it shall be presumed to have occurred before the particulars are delivered unless the contrary is proved.*

401 Delivery of further particulars

(1) *Further particulars of a charge, supplementing or varying the registered particulars, may be delivered to the registrar for registration at any time.*

(2) *Further particulars must be in the prescribed form signed by or on behalf of both the company and the chargee.*

(3) *Where further particulars are delivered to the registrar for registration and appear to him to be duly signed, he shall file the particulars in the register and shall note, in such form as he thinks fit, the date on which they were delivered to him.*

(4) *The registrar shall send to the company and any person appearing from the particulars to be the chargee, and if the particulars were delivered by another person interested in the charge to that other person, a copy of the further particulars filed by him and of the note made by him as to the date on which they were delivered.*

402 Effect of omissions and errors in registered particulars

(1) *Where the registered particulars of a charge created by a company are not complete and accurate, the charge is void, as mentioned below, to the extent that rights are not disclosed by the registered particulars which would be disclosed if they were complete and accurate.*

(2) *The charge is void to that extent, unless the court on the application of the chargee orders otherwise, as against—*

(a) *an administrator or liquidator of the company, and*

(b) *any person who for value acquires an interest in or right over property subject to the charge,*

where the relevant event occurs at a time when the particulars are incomplete or inaccurate in a relevant respect.

(3) *Where a relevant event occurs on the same day as particulars or further particulars are delivered, it shall be presumed to have occurred before those particulars are delivered unless the contrary is proved.*

(4) *The court may order that the charge is effective as against an administrator or liquidator of the company if it is satisfied—*

(a) *that the omission or error is not likely to have misled materially to his prejudice any unsecured creditor of the company, or*

(b) *that no person became an unsecured creditor of the company at a time when the registered particulars of the charge were incomplete or inaccurate in a relevant respect.*

(5) *The court may order that the charge is effective as against a person acquiring an interest in or right over property subject to the charge if it is satisfied that he did not rely, in connection with the acquisition, on registered particulars which were incomplete or inaccurate in a relevant respect.*

(6) *For the purposes of this section an omission or inaccuracy with respect to the name of the chargee shall not be regarded as a failure to disclose the rights of the chargee.*

403 Memorandum of charge ceasing to affect company's property

(1) *Where a charge of which particulars have been delivered ceases to affect the company's property, a memorandum to that effect may be delivered to the registrar for registration.*

(2) *The memorandum must be in the prescribed form signed by or on behalf of both the company and the chargee.*

(3) *Where a memorandum is delivered to the registrar for registration and appears to him to be duly signed, he shall file it in the register, and shall note, in such form as he thinks fit, the date on which it was delivered to him.*

(4) *The registrar shall send to the company and any person appearing from the memorandum to be the chargee, and if the memorandum was delivered by another person interested in the charge to that person, a copy of the memorandum filed by him and of the note made by him as to the date on which it was delivered.*

(5) *if a duly signed memorandum is delivered in a case where the charge in fact continues to affect the company's property, the charge is void as against—*

(a) *an administrator or liquidator of the company, and*

(b) *any person who for value acquires an interest in or right over property subject to the charge,*

where the relevant event occurs after the delivery of the memorandum.

(6) *Where a relevant event occurs on the same day as the memorandum is delivered, it shall be presumed to have occurred before the memorandum is delivered unless the contrary is proved.*

Further provisions with respect to voidness of charges

404 Exclusion of voidness as against unregistered charges

(1) A charge is not void by virtue of this Part as against a subsequent charge unless some or all of the relevant particulars of that charge are duly delivered for registration—

(a) within 21 days after the date of its creation, or

(b) before complete and accurate relevant particulars of the earlier charge are duly delivered for registration.

(2) Where relevant particulars of the subsequent charge so delivered are incomplete or inaccurate, the earlier charge is void as against that charge only to the extent that rights are disclosed by registered particulars of the subsequent charge duly delivered for registration before the corresponding relevant particulars of the earlier charge.

(3) The relevant particulars of a charge for the purposes of this section are those prescribed particulars relating to rights inconsistent with those conferred by or in relation to the other charge.

405 Restrictions on voidness by virtue of this Part

(1) A charge is not void by virtue of this Part as against a person acquiring an interest in or right over property where the acquisition is expressly subject to the charge.

(2) Nor is a charge void by virtue of this Part in relation to any property by reason of a relevant event occurring after the company which created the charge has disposed of the whole of its interest in that property.

406 Effect of exercise of power of sale

(1) A chargee exercising a power of sale may dispose of property to a purchaser freed from any interest or right arising from the charge having become void to any extent by virtue of this Part—

(a) against an administrator or liquidator of the company, or

(b) against a person acquiring a security interest over property subject to the charge;

and a purchaser is not concerned to see or inquire whether the charge has become so void.

(2) The proceeds of the sale shall be held by the chargee in trust to be applied—

First, in discharge of any sum effectively secured by prior incumbrances to which the sale is not made subject;

Second, in payment of all costs, charges and expenses properly incurred by him in connection with the sale, or any previous attempted sale, of the property;

Third, in discharge of any sum effectively secured by the charge and incumbrances ranking pari passu with the charge;

Fourth, in discharge of any sum effectively secured by incumbrances ranking after the charge;

and any residue is payable to the company or to a person authorised to give a receipt for the proceeds of the sale of the property.

(3) For the purposes of subsection (2)—

(a) prior incumbrances include any incumbrance to the extent that the charge is void as against it by virtue of this Part; and

(b) no sum is effectively secured by a charge to the extent that it is void as against an administrator or liquidator of the company.

(4) In this section—

(a) references to things done by a chargee include things done by a receiver appointed by him, whether or not the receiver acts as his agent;

(b) "power of sale" includes any power to dispose of, or grant an interest out of, property for the purpose of enforcing a charge (but in relation to Scotland does not include the power to grant a lease), and references to "sale" shall be construed accordingly; and

(c) "purchaser" means a person who in good faith and for valuable consideration acquires an interest in property.

(5) The provisions of this section as to the order of application of the proceeds of sale have effect subject to any other statutory provision (in Scotland, any other statutory provision or rule of law) applicable in any case.

(6) Where a chargee exercising a power of sale purports to dispose of property freed from any such interest or right as is mentioned in subsection (1) to a person other than a purchaser, the above provisions apply, with any necessary modifications, in relation to a disposition to a purchaser by that person or any successor in title of his.

(7) In Scotland, subsections (2) and (7) of section 27 of the Conveyancing and Feudal Reform (Scotland) Act 1970 apply to a chargee unable to obtain a discharge for any payment which he is required to make under subsection (2) above as they apply to a creditor in the circumstances mentioned in those subsections.

407 Effect of voidness on obligation secured

(1) Where a charge becomes void to any extent by virtue of this Part, the whole of the sum secured by the charge is payable forthwith on demand; and this applies notwithstanding that the sum secured by the charge is also the subject of other security.

(2) Where the charge is to secure the repayment of money, the references in subsection (1) to the sum secured include any interest payable.

Additional information to be registered

408 Particulars of taking up of issue of debentures

(1) Where particulars of a charge for securing an issue of debentures have been delivered for registration, it is the duty of the company—

- *(a) to deliver to the registrar for registration particulars in the prescribed form of the date on which any debentures of the issue are taken up, and of the amount taken up, and*
- *(b) to do so before the end of the period of 21 days after the date on which they are taken up.*

(2) Where particulars in the prescribed form are delivered to the registrar for registration under this section, he shall file them in the register.

(3) If a company fails to comply with subsection (1), the company and every officer of it who is in default is liable to a fine.

409 Notice of appointment of receiver or manager, &c

(1) If a person obtains an order for the appointment of a receiver or manager of a company's property, or appoints such a receiver or manager under powers contained in an instrument, he shall within seven days of the order or of the appointment under those powers, give notice of that fact in the prescribed form to the registrar for registration.

(2) Where a person appointed receiver or manager of a company's property under powers contained in an instrument ceases to act as such receiver or manager, he shall, on so ceasing, give notice of that fact in the prescribed form to the registrar for registration.

(3) Where a notice under this section in the prescribed form is delivered to the registrar for registration, he shall file it in the register.

(4) If a person makes default in complying with the requirements of subsection (1) or (2), he is liable to a fine.

(5) This section does not apply in relation to companies registered in Scotland (for which corresponding provision is made by sections 53, 54 and 62 of the Insolvency Act 1986).

410 Notice of crystallisation of floating charge, &c

(1) The Secretary of State may by regulations require notice in the prescribed form to be given to the registrar of—

- *(a) the occurrence of such events as may be prescribed affecting the nature of the security under a floating charge of which particulars have been delivered for registration, and*
- *(b) the taking of such action in exercise of powers conferred by a fixed or floating charge of which particulars have been delivered for registration, or conferred in relation to such a charge by an order of the court, as may be prescribed.*

(2) The regulations may make provision as to—

- *(a) the persons by whom notice is required to be, or may be, given, and the period within which notice is required to be given;*
- *(b) the filing in the register of the particulars contained in the notice and the noting of the date on which the notice was given; and*
- *(c) the consequences of failure to give notice.*

(3) As regards the consequences of failure to give notice of an event causing a floating charge to crystallise, the regulations may include provision to the effect that the crystallisation—

- *(a) shall be treated as ineffective until the prescribed particulars are delivered, and*
- *(b) if the prescribed particulars are delivered after the expiry of the prescribed period, shall continue to be ineffective against such persons as may be prescribed,*

subject to the exercise of such powers as may be conferred by the regulations on the court.

(4) The regulations may provide that if there is a failure to comply with such of the requirements of the regulations as may be prescribed, such persons as may be prescribed are liable to a fine.

(5) Regulations under this section shall be made by statutory instrument which shall be subject to annulment in pursuance of a resolution of either House of Parliament.

(6) Regulations under this section shall not apply in relation to a floating charge created under the law of Scotland by a company registered in Scotland.

Copies of instruments and register to be kept by company

411 Duty to keep copies of instruments and register

(1) Every company shall keep at its registered office a copy of every instrument creating or evidencing a charge over the company's property.

In the case of a series of uniform debentures, a copy of one debenture of the series is sufficient.

(2) Every company shall also keep at its registered office a register of all such charges, containing entries for each charge giving a short description of the property charged, the amount of the charge and (except in the case of securities to bearer) the names of the persons entitled to it.

(3) This section applies to any charge, whether or not particulars are required to be delivered to the registrar for registration.

(4) If a company fails to comply with any requirement of this section, the company and every officer of it who is in default is liable to a fine.

412 Inspection of copies and register

(1) The copies and the register referred to in section 411 shall be open to the inspection of any creditor or member of the company without fee; and to the inspection of any other person on payment of such fee as may be prescribed.

(2) Any person may request the company to provide him with a copy of—

(a) any instrument creating or evidencing a charge over the company's property, or

(b) any entry in the register of charges kept by the company, on payment of such fee as may be prescribed.

This subsection applies to any charge, whether or not particulars are required to be delivered to the registrar for registration.

(3) The company shall send the copy to him not later than ten days after the day on which the request is received or, if later, on which payment is received.

(4) If inspection of the copies or register is refused, or a copy requested is not sent within the time specified above—

(a) the company and every officer of it who is in default is liable to a fine, and

(b) the court may by order compel an immediate inspection of the copies or register or, as the case may be, direct that the copy be sent immediately.

Supplementary provisions

413 Power to make further provision by regulations

(1) The Secretary of State may by regulations make further provision as to the application of the provisions of this Part in relation to charges of any description specified in the regulations.

Nothing in the following provisions shall be construed as restricting the generality of that power.

(2) The regulations may require that where the charge is contained in or evidenced or varied by a written instrument, there shall be delivered to the registrar for registration, instead of particulars or further particulars of the charge, the instrument itself or a certified copy of it together with such particulars as may be prescribed.

(3) The regulations may provide that a memorandum of a charge ceasing to affect property of the company shall not be accepted by the registrar unless supported by such evidence as may be prescribed, and that a memorandum not so supported shall be treated as not having been delivered.

(4) The regulations may also provide that where the instrument creating the charge is delivered to the registrar in support of such a memorandum, the registrar may mark the instrument as cancelled before returning it and shall send copies of the instrument cancelled to such persons as may be prescribed.

(5) The regulations may exclude or modify, in such circumstances and to such extent as may be prescribed, the operation of the provisions of this Part relating to the voidness of a charge.

(6) The regulations may require, in connection with the delivery of particulars, further particulars or a memorandum of the charge's ceasing to affect property of the company, the delivery of such supplementary information as may be prescribed, and may—

(a) apply in relation to such supplementary information any provisions of this Part relating to particulars, further particulars or such a memorandum, and

(b) provide that the particulars, further particulars or memorandum shall be treated as not having been delivered until the required supplementary information is delivered.

(7) Regulations under this section shall be made by statutory instrument which shall be subject to annulment in pursuance of a resolution of either House of Parliament.

414 Date of creation of charge

(1) References in this Part to the date of creation of a charge by a company shall be construed as follows.

(2) A charge created under the law of England and Wales shall be taken to be created—

(a) in the case of a charge created by an instrument in writing, when the instrument is executed by the company or, if its execution by the company is conditional, upon the conditions being fulfilled, and

(b) in any other case, when an enforceable agreement is entered into by the company conferring a security interest intended to take effect forthwith or upon the company acquiring an interest in property subject to the charge.

(3) A charge created under the law of Scotland shall be taken to be created—

(a) in the case of a floating charge, when the instrument creating the floating charge is executed by the company, and

(b) in any other case, when the right of the person entitled to the benefit of the charge is constituted as a real right.

(4) Where a charge is created in the United Kingdom but comprises property outside the United Kingdom, any further proceedings necessary to make the charge valid or effectual under the law of the country where the property is situated shall be disregarded in ascertaining the date on which the charge is to be taken to be created.

415 Prescribed particulars and related expressions

(1) References in this Part to the prescribed particulars of a charge are to such particulars of, or relating to, the charge as may be prescribed.

(2) The prescribed particulars may, without prejudice to the generality of subsection (1), include—

(a) whether the company has undertaken not to create other charges ranking in priority to or pari passu with the charge, and

(b) whether the charge is a market charge within the meaning of Part VII of the Companies Act 1989 or a charge to which the provisions of that Part apply as they apply to a market charge.

(3) References in this Part to the registered particulars of a charge at any time are to such particulars and further particulars of the charge as have at that time been duly delivered for registration.

(4) References in this Part to the registered particulars of a charge being complete and accurate at any time are to their including all the prescribed particulars which would be required to be delivered if the charge were then newly created.

416 Notice of matters disclosed on register

(1) A person taking a charge over a company's property shall be taken to have notice of any matter requiring registration and disclosed on the register at the time the charge is created.

(2) Otherwise, a person shall not be taken to have notice of any matter by reason of its being disclosed on the register or by reason of his having failed to search the register in the course of making such inquiries as ought reasonably to be made.

(3) The above provisions have effect subject to any other statutory provision as to whether a person is to be taken to have notice of any matter disclosed on the register.

417 Power of court to dispense with signature

(1) Where it is proposed to deliver further particulars of a charge, or to deliver a memorandum of a charge ceasing to affect the company's property, and—

(a) the chargee refuses to sign or authorise a person to sign on his behalf, or cannot be found, or

(b) the company refuses to authorise a person to sign on its behalf,

the court may on the application of the company or the chargee, or of any other person having a sufficient interest in the matter, authorise the delivery of the particulars or memorandum without that signature.

(2) The order may be made on such terms as appear to the court to be appropriate.

(3) Where particulars or a memorandum are delivered to the registrar for registration in reliance on an order under this section, they must be accompanied by an office copy of the order.

In such a case the references in sections 401 and 403 to the particulars or memorandum being duly signed are to their being otherwise duly signed.

(4) The registrar shall file the office copy of the court order along with the particulars or memorandum.

418 Regulations

Regulations under any provision of this Part, or prescribing anything for the purposes of any such provision—

(a) may make different provision for different cases, and

(b) may contain such supplementary, incidental and transitional provisions as appear to the Secretary of State to be appropriate.

419 Minor definitions

(1) In this Part—

"chargee" means the person for the time being entitled to exercise the security rights conferred by the charge;

"issue of debentures" means a group of debentures, or an amount of debenture stock, secured by the same charge; and

"series of debentures" means a group of debentures each containing or giving by reference to another instrument a charge to the benefit of which the holders of debentures of the series are entitled pari passu.

(2) References in this Part to the creation of a charge include the variation of a charge which is not registrable so as to include property by virtue of which it becomes registrable.

The provisions of section 414 (construction of references to date of creation of charge) apply in such a case with any necessary modifications.

(3) References in this Part to the date of acquisition of property by a company are—

(a) in England and Wales, to the date on which the acquisition is completed, and

(b) in Scotland, to the date on which the transaction is settled.

(4) In the application of this Part to a floating charge created under the law of Scotland, references to crystallisation shall be construed as references to the attachment of the charge.

(5) References in this Part to the beginning of insolvency proceedings are to—

(a) the presentation of a petition on which an administration order or winding-up order is made, or

(b) the passing of a resolution for voluntary winding up.

420 Index of defined expressions

The following Table shows the provisions of this Part defining or otherwise explaining expressions used in this Part (other than expressions used only in the same section)—

charge	*sections 395(2) and 396(6)*
charge requiring registration	*section 396*
chargee	*section 419(1)*
complete and accurate (in relation to registered particulars)	*section 415(4)*
creation of charge	*section 419(2)*
crystallisation (in relation to Scottish floating charge)	*section 419(4)*
date of acquisition (of property by a company)	*section 419(3)*
date of creation of charge	*section 414*
further particulars	*section 401*
insolvency proceedings, beginning of	*section 419(5)*
issue of debentures	*section 419(1)*
memorandum of charge ceasing to affect company's property	*section 403*
prescribed particulars	*section 415(1) and (2)*
property	*section 395(2)*
registered particulars	*section 415(3)*
registrar and registration in relation to a charge	*section 395(4)*
relevant event	*section 399(2)*
series of debentures	*section 419(1).".*

Notes relating to the substituted sections above: the words "ground annual" in s 396(1) repealed by the Abolition of Feudal Tenure etc (Scotland) Act 2000, s 76(1), (2), Sch 12, Pt I, para 46(1)–(4), Sch 13, Pt I, as from the date of the coming into force of the Companies Act 1989, s 92. The words omitted from s 396(2)(d)(i) repealed by the Trade Marks Act 1994, s 106(2), Sch 5, and the reference in that subsection to a trade mark is to be construed as a reference to a trade mark within the meaning of the 1994 Act, by virtue of s 106(1) of, and Sch 4, para 1, to that Act.

(b) Ss 409, 424 (relating to registration of charges with respect to oversea companies) replaced by insertion of new Chapter III (ss 703A–703N) of Part XXIII by the Companies Act 1989, ss 92(b), 105, Sch 15, as from a day to be appointed; those sections are outside the scope of this work.

CHAPTER I
REGISTRATION OF CHARGES (ENGLAND AND WALES)

395 Certain charges void if not registered

(1) Subject to the provisions of this Chapter, a charge created by a company registered in England and Wales and being a charge to which this section applies is, so far as any security on the company's property or undertaking is conferred by the charge, void against the liquidator [or administrator] and any creditor of the company, unless the prescribed particulars of the charge together with the instrument (if any) by which the charge is created or evidenced, are delivered to or received by the registrar of companies for registration in the manner required by this Chapter within 21 days after the date of the charge's creation.

(2) Subsection (1) is without prejudice to any contract or obligation for repayment of the money secured by the charge; and when a charge becomes void under this section, the money secured by it immediately becomes payable.

[534]

NOTES

Repealed as noted to s 1 at **[309]**.

Sub-s (1): words in square brackets inserted by the Insolvency Act 1985, s 109(1), Sch 6, para 10.

Prospective replacement: see note (a) preceding this section.

Prescribed form: see the Companies (Forms) Regulations 1985, SI 1985/854, Form 395.

396 Charges which have to be registered

(1) Section 395 applies to the following charges—

(a) a charge for the purpose of securing any issue of debentures,

(b) a charge on uncalled share capital of the company,

(c) a charge created or evidenced by an instrument which, if executed by an individual, would require registration as a bill of sale,

(d) a charge on land (wherever situated) or any interest in it, but not including a charge for any rent or other periodical sum issuing out of the land,

(e) a charge on book debts of the company,

(f) a floating charge on the company's undertaking or property,

(g) a charge on calls made but not paid,

(h) a charge on a ship or aircraft, or any share in a ship,

(j) a charge on goodwill, [or on any intellectual property].

(2) Where a negotiable instrument has been given to secure the payment of any book debts of a company, the deposit of the instrument for the purpose of securing an advance to the company is not, for purposes of section 395, to be treated as a charge on those book debts.

(3) The holding of debentures entitling the holder to a charge on land is not for purposes of this section deemed to be an interest in land.

[(3A) The following are "intellectual property" for the purposes of this section—

(a) any patent, trade mark, ... registered design, copyright or design right;

(b) any licence under or in respect of any such right.]

(4) In this Chapter, "charge" includes mortgage.

[535]

NOTES

Repealed as noted to s 1 at **[309]**.

Sub-s (1): words in square brackets substituted by the Copyright, Designs and Patents Act 1988, s 303(1), Sch 7, para 31(1), (2).

Sub-s (3A): inserted by the Copyright, Designs and Patents Act 1988, s 303(1), Sch 7, para 31(1), (2); words omitted repealed by the Trade Marks Act 1994, s 106(2), Sch 5.

Prospective replacement: see note (a) preceding s 395 at **[534]**.

Trade mark: by the Trade Marks Act 1994, s 106(1), Sch 4, para 1, the reference in sub-s (3A)(a) above to a trade mark is to be construed as a reference to a trade mark within the meaning of the 1994 Act.

397 Formalities of registration (debentures)

(1) Where a series of debentures containing, or giving by reference to another instrument, any charge to the benefit of which the debenture holders of that series are entitled pari passu is created by a company, it is for purposes of section 395 sufficient if there are

delivered to or received by the registrar, within 21 days after the execution of the deed containing the charge (or, if there is no such deed, after the execution of any debentures of the series), the following particulars in the prescribed form—

(*a*) *the total amount secured by the whole series, and*

(*b*) *the dates of the resolutions authorising the issue of the series and the date of the covering deed (if any) by which the security is created or defined, and*

(*c*) *a general description of the property charged, and*

(*d*) *the names of the trustees (if any) for the debenture holders,*

together with the deed containing the charge or, if there is no such deed, one of the debentures of the series:

Provided that there shall be sent to the registrar of companies, for entry in the register, particulars in the prescribed form of the date and amount of each issue of debentures of the series, but any omission to do this does not affect the validity of any of those debentures.

(*2*) *Where any commission, allowance or discount has been paid or made either directly or indirectly by a company to a person in consideration of his—*

(*a*) *subscribing or agreeing to subscribe, whether absolutely or conditionally, for debentures of the company, or*

(*b*) *procuring or agreeing to procure subscriptions, whether absolute or conditional, for such debentures,*

the particulars required to be sent for registration under section 395 shall include particulars as to the amount or rate per cent of the commission, discount or allowance so paid or made, but omission to do this does not affect the validity of the debentures issued.

(*3*) *The deposit of debentures as security for a debt of the company is not, for the purposes of subsection (2), treated as the issue of the debentures at a discount.*

[536]

NOTES

Repealed as noted to s 1 at **[309]**.
Prospective replacement: see note (a) preceding s 395 at **[534]**.
Prescribed form: see the Companies (Forms) Regulations 1985, SI 1985/854, Forms 397, 397a.

398 Verification of charge on property outside United Kingdom

(*1*) *In the case of a charge created out of the United Kingdom comprising property situated outside the United Kingdom, the delivery to and the receipt by the registrar of companies of a copy (verified in the prescribed manner) of the instrument by which the charge is created or evidenced has the same effect for purposes of sections 395 to 398 as the delivery and receipt of the instrument itself.*

(*2*) *In that case, 21 days after the date on which the instrument or copy could, in due course of post (and if despatched with due diligence), have been received in the United Kingdom are substituted for the 21 days mentioned in section 395(1) (or as the case may be, section 397(1)) as the time within which the particulars and instrument or copy are to be delivered to the registrar.*

(*3*) *Where a charge is created in the United Kingdom but comprises property outside the United Kingdom, the instrument creating or purporting to create the charge may be sent for registration under section 395 notwithstanding that further proceedings may be necessary to make the charge valid or effectual according to the law of the country in which the property is situated.*

(*4*) *Where a charge comprises property situated in Scotland or Northern Ireland and registration in the country where the property is situated is necessary to make the charge valid or effectual according to the law of that country, the delivery to and receipt by the registrar of a copy (verified in the prescribed manner) of the instrument by which the charge is created or evidenced, together with a certificate in the prescribed form stating that the charge was presented for registration in Scotland or Northern Ireland (as the case may be) on the date on which it was so presented has, for purposes of sections 395 to 398, the same effect as the delivery and receipt of the instrument itself.*

[537]

NOTES

Repealed as noted to s 1 at **[309]**.
Prospective replacement: see note (a) preceding s 395 at **[534]**.

Prescribed form: see the Companies (Forms) Regulations 1985, SI 1985/854, Form 398.
Prescribed manner: see reg 7 of the 1985 Regulations.

399 Company's duty to register charges it creates

(1) It is a company's duty to send to the registrar of companies for registration the particulars of every charge created by the company and of the issues of debentures of a series requiring registration under sections 395 to 398; but registration of any such charge may be effected on the application of any person interested in it.

(2) Where registration is effected on the application of some person other than the company, that person is entitled to recover from the company the amount of any fees properly paid by him to the registrar on the registration.

(3) If a company fails to comply with subsection (1), then, unless the registration has been effected on the application of some other person, the company and every officer of it who is in default is liable to a fine and, for continued contravention, to a daily default fine.

[538]

NOTES

Repealed as noted to s 1 at **[309]**.
Prospective replacement: see note (a) preceding s 395 at **[534]**.

400 Charges existing on property acquired

(1) This section applies where a company registered in England and Wales acquires property which is subject to a charge of any such kind as would, if it had been created by the company after the acquisition of the property, have been required to be registered under this Chapter.

(2) The company shall cause the prescribed particulars of the charge, together with a copy (certified in the prescribed manner to be a correct copy) of the instrument (if any) by which the charge was created or is evidenced, to be delivered to the registrar of companies for registration in manner required by this Chapter within 21 days after the date on which the acquisition is completed.

(3) However, if the property is situated and the charge was created outside Great Britain, 21 days after the date on which the copy of the instrument could in due course of post, and if despatched with due diligence, have been received in the United Kingdom is substituted for the 21 days above-mentioned as the time within which the particulars and copy of the instrument are to be delivered to the registrar.

(4) If default is made in complying with this section, the company and every officer of it who is in default is liable to a fine and, for continued contravention, to a daily default fine.

[539]

NOTES

Repealed as noted to s 1 at **[309]**.
Prospective replacement: see note (a) preceding s 395 at **[534]**.
Prescribed form: see the Companies (Forms) Regulations 1985, SI 1985/854, Form 400.
Prescribed manner: see reg 7 of the 1985 Regulations.

401 Register of charges to be kept by registrar of companies

(1) The registrar of companies shall keep, with respect to each company, a register in the prescribed form of all the charges requiring registration under this Chapter; and he shall enter in the register with respect to such charges the following particulars—

- *(a) in the case of a charge to the benefit of which the holders of a series of debentures are entitled, the particulars specified in section 397(1),*
- *(b) in the case of any other charge—*
  - *(i) if it is a charge created by the company, the date of its creation, and if it is a charge which was existing on property acquired by the company, the date of the acquisition of the property, and*
  - *(ii) the amount secured by the charge, and*
  - *(iii) short particulars of the property charged, and*
  - *(iv) the persons entitled to the charge.*

(2) The registrar shall give a certificate of the registration of any charge registered in pursuance of this Chapter, stating the amount secured by the charge.

The certificate—

(a) shall be either signed by the registrar, or authenticated by his official seal, and
(b) is conclusive evidence that the requirements of this Chapter as to registration have been satisfied.

(3) The register kept in pursuance of this section shall be open to inspection by any person.

[540]

NOTES

Repealed as noted to s 1 at **[309]**.
Prospective replacement: see note (a) preceding s 395 at **[534]**.
Prescribed form: see the Companies (Forms) Regulations 1985, SI 1985/854, Form 401.

402 Endorsement of certificate on debentures

(1) The company shall cause a copy of every certificate of registration given under section 401 to be endorsed on every debenture or certificate of debenture stock which is issued by the company, and the payment of which is secured by the charge so registered.

(2) But this does not require a company to cause a certificate of registration of any charge so given to be endorsed on any debenture or certificate of debenture stock issued by the company before the charge was created.

(3) If a person knowingly and wilfully authorises or permits the delivery of a debenture or certificate of debenture stock which under this section is required to have endorsed on it a copy of a certificate of registration, without the copy being so endorsed upon it, he is liable (without prejudice to any other liability) to a fine.

[541]

NOTES

Repealed as noted to s 1 at **[309]**.
Prospective replacement: see note (a) preceding s 395 at **[534]**.

403 Entries of satisfaction and release

(1) [Subject to subsection (1A), the registrar] of companies, on receipt of a statutory declaration in the prescribed form verifying, with respect to a registered charge,—

(a) that the debt for which the charge was given has been paid or satisfied in whole or in part, or
(b) that part of the property or undertaking charged has been released from the charge or has ceased to form part of the company's property or undertaking,

may enter on the register a memorandum of satisfaction in whole or in part, or of the fact that part of the property or undertaking has been released from the charge or has ceased to form part of the company's property or undertaking (as the case may be).

[(1A) The registrar of companies may make any such entry as is mentioned in subsection (1) where, instead of receiving such a statutory declaration as is mentioned in that subsection, he receives a statement by a director, secretary, administrator or administrative receiver of the company which is contained in an electronic communication and that statement—

(a) verifies the matters set out in paragraph (a) or (b) of that subsection,
(b) contains a description of the charge,
(c) states the date of creation of the charge and the date of its registration under this Chapter,
(d) states the name and address of the chargee or, in the case of a debenture, trustee, and
(e) where paragraph (b) of subsection (1) applies, contains short particulars of the property or undertaking which has been released from the charge, or which has ceased to form part of the company's property or undertaking (as the case may be).]

(2) Where the registrar enters a memorandum of satisfaction in whole, he shall if required furnish the company with a copy of it.

[(2A) Any person who makes a false statement under subsection (1A) which he knows to be false or does not believe to be true is liable to imprisonment or a fine, or both.]

[542]

NOTES

Repealed as noted to s 1 at **[309]**.

Prospective replacement: see note (a) preceding s 395 at **[534]**.

Sub-s (1): words in square brackets substituted by the Companies Act 1985 (Electronic Communications) Order 2000, SI 2000/3373, art 22(1), (2).

Sub-ss (1A), (2A): inserted by SI 2000/3373, art 22(1), (3), (4).

Prescribed form: see the Companies (Forms) Regulations 1985, SI 1985/854, Forms 403a, 403b.

404 Rectification of register of charges

(1) The following applies if the court is satisfied that the omission to register a charge within the time required by this Chapter or that the omission or mis-statement of any particular with respect to any such charge or in a memorandum of satisfaction was accidental, or due to inadvertence or to some other sufficient cause, or is not of a nature to prejudice the position of creditors or shareholders of the company, or that on other grounds it is just and equitable to grant relief.

(2) The court may, on the application of the company or a person interested, and on such terms and conditions as seem to the court just and expedient, order that the time for registration shall be extended or, as the case may be, that the omission or mis-statement shall be rectified.

[543]

NOTES

Repealed as noted to s 1 at **[309]**.

Prospective replacement: see note (a) preceding s 395 at **[534]**.

405 Registration of enforcement of security

(1) If a person obtains an order for the appointment of a receiver or manager of a company's property, or appoints such a receiver or manager under powers contained in an instrument, he shall within 7 days of the order or of the appointment under those powers, give notice of the fact to the registrar of companies; and the registrar shall enter the fact in the register of charges.

(2) Where a person appointed receiver or manager of a company's property under powers contained in an instrument ceases to act as such receiver or manager, he shall, on so ceasing, give the registrar notice to that effect, and the registrar shall enter the fact in the register of charges.

(3) A notice under this section shall be in the prescribed form.

(4) If a person makes default in complying with the requirements of this section, he is liable to a fine and, for continued contravention, to a daily default fine.

[544]

NOTES

Repealed as noted to s 1 at **[309]**.

Prospective replacement: see note (a) preceding s 395 at **[534]**.

Prescribed form: see the Companies (Forms) Regulations 1985, SI 1985/854, Forms 405(1), 405(2).

406 Companies to keep copies of instruments creating charges

(1) Every company shall cause a copy of every instrument creating a charge requiring registration under this Chapter to be kept at its registered office.

(2) In the case of a series of uniform debentures, a copy of one debenture of the series is sufficient.

[545]

NOTES

Repealed as noted to s 1 at **[309]**.

Prospective replacement: see note (a) preceding s 395 at **[534]**.

407 Company's register of charges

(1) Every limited company shall keep at its registered office a register of charges and enter in it all charges specifically affecting property of the company and all floating charges on the company's undertaking or any of its property.

(2) The entry shall in each case give a short description of the property charged, the amount of the charge and, except in the case of securities to bearer, the names of the persons entitled to it.

(3) If an officer of the company knowingly and wilfully authorises or permits the omission of an entry required to be made in pursuance of this section, he is liable to a fine.
[546]

NOTES

Repealed as noted to s 1 at **[309]**.
Prospective replacement: see note (a) preceding s 395 at **[534]**.

408 Right to inspect instruments which create charges, etc

(1) The copies of instruments creating any charge requiring registration under this Chapter with the registrar of companies, and the register of charges kept in pursuance of section 407, shall be open during business hours (but subject to such reasonable restrictions as the company in general meeting may impose, so that not less than 2 hours in each day be allowed for inspection) to the inspection of any creditor or member of the company without fee.

(2) The register of charges shall also be open to the inspection of any other person on payment of such fee, not exceeding 5 pence, for each inspection, as the company may prescribe.

(3) If inspection of the copies referred to, or of the register, is refused, every officer of the company who is in default is liable to a fine and, for continued contravention, to a daily default fine.

(4) If such a refusal occurs in relation to a company registered in England and Wales, the court may by order compel an immediate inspection of the copies or register.
[547]

NOTES

Repealed as noted to s 1 at **[309]**.
Prospective replacement: see note (a) preceding s 395 at **[534]**.

409 Charges on property in England and Wales created by overseas company

(1) This Chapter extends to charges on property in England and Wales which are created, and to charges on property in England and Wales which is acquired, by a company (whether a company within the meaning of this Act or not) incorporated outside Great Britain which has an established place of business in England and Wales.

(2) In relation to such a company, sections 406 and 407 apply with the substitution, for the reference to the company's registered office, of a reference to its principal place of business in England and Wales.
[548]

NOTES

Repealed as noted to s 1 at **[309]**.
Prospective replacement: see note (b) preceding s 395 at **[534]**.

410–715A *(Ss 410–424 (Pt XII, Chapter II) apply to Scotland only (see further the introductory note preceding s 395 at* **[534]***); ss 425–715A (Pts XIII–XXIV) outside the scope of this work.)*

PART XXV
MISCELLANEOUS AND SUPPLEMENTARY PROVISIONS

716–726 (*Ss 716–723A, 725, 726 outside the scope of this work; s 724 repealed by the Insolvency Act 1986, s 438, Sch 12.*)

727 Power of court to grant relief in certain cases

(1) If in any proceedings for negligence, default, breach of duty or breach of trust against an officer of a company or a person employed by a company as auditor (whether he is or is not an officer of the company) it appears to the court hearing the case that that officer or person is or may be liable in respect of the negligence, default, breach of duty or breach of trust, but that he has acted honestly and reasonably, and that having regard to all the circumstances of the case (including those connected with his appointment) he ought fairly to be excused for the negligence, default, breach of duty or breach of trust, that court may relieve him, either wholly or partly, from his liability on such terms as it thinks fit.

(2) If any such officer or person as above-mentioned has reason to apprehend that any claim will or might be made against him in respect of any negligence, default, breach of duty or breach of trust, he may apply to the court for relief; and the court on the application has the same power to relieve him as under this section it would have had if it had been a court before which proceedings against that person for negligence, default, breach of duty or breach of trust had been brought.

(3) Where a case to which subsection (1) applies is being tried by a judge with a jury, the judge, after hearing the evidence, may, if he is satisfied that the defendant or defender ought in pursuance of that subsection to be relieved either in whole or in part from the liability sought to be enforced against him, withdraw the case in whole or in part from the jury and forthwith direct judgment to be entered for the defendant or defender on such terms as to costs or otherwise as the judge may think proper.

[549]

NOTES
Repealed as noted to s 1 at **[309]**.

728–734 (*Outside the scope of this work.*)

PART XXVI
INTERPRETATION

735 "Company", etc

(1) In this Act—

(a) "company" means a company formed and registered under this Act, or an existing company;

(b) "existing company" means a company formed and registered under the former Companies Acts, but does not include a company registered under the Joint Stock Companies Acts, the Companies Act 1862 or the Companies (Consolidation) Act 1908 in what was then Ireland;

(c) "the former Companies Acts" means the Joint Stock Companies Acts, the Companies Act 1862, the Companies (Consolidation) Act 1908, the Companies Act 1929 and the Companies Acts 1948 to 1983.

(2) "Public company" and "private company" have the meanings given by section 1(3).

(3) "The Joint Stock Companies Acts" means the Joint Stock Companies Act 1856, the Joint Stock Companies Acts 1856, 1857, the Joint Stock Banking Companies Act 1857 and the Act to enable Joint Stock Banking Companies to be formed on the principle of limited liability, or any one or more of those Acts (as the case may require), but does not include the Joint Stock Companies Act 1844.

(4) The definitions in this section apply unless the contrary intention appears.

[550]

NOTES
Repealed as noted to s 1 at **[309]**.
Companies Act 1862: repealed by the Companies (Consolidation) Act 1908, s 286, Sch 6.

Companies (Consolidation) Act 1908: repealed by the Companies Act 1929, s 381, Sch 12.
Companies Act 1929: repealed by the Companies Act 1948, s 459, Sch 17.
Companies Acts 1948 to 1983: by virtue of the Companies Act 1981, s 119(2) as read with the Companies Act 1983 s 7(2), the following Acts could be cited by this collective title: the Companies Act 1948, the Companies Act 1967 (Pts I, III), the Companies (Floating Charges and Receivers) (Scotland) Act 1972, the European Communities Act 1972, s 9, the Stock Exchange (Completion of Bargains) Act 1976, ss 1–4, the Insolvency Act 1976, s 9, the Companies Act 1976, the Companies Act 1980, the Companies Act 1981 (except ss 28, 29), and the Companies (Beneficial Interests) Act 1983. All of these provisions were repealed by the Companies Consolidation (Consequential Provisions) Act 1985, s 29, Sch 1.
Joint Stock Companies Acts: the Joint Stock Companies Act 1856, the Joint Stock Companies Act 1857, the Joint Stock Banking Companies Act 1857 and the Act to enable Joint Stock Banking Companies to be formed on the principle of limited liability (21 & 22 Vict c 91) (1858): repealed by the Companies Act 1862, s 205, Sch 3 (repealed).
Joint Stock Companies Act 1844: repealed by the Companies Act 1862, s 205, Sch 3 (repealed).

735A, 735B *(Outside the scope of this work.)*

[736 "Subsidiary", "holding company" and "wholly-owned subsidiary"

(1) A company is a "subsidiary" of another company, its "holding company", if that other company—

(a) holds a majority of the voting rights in it, or

(b) is a member of it and has the right to appoint or remove a majority of its board of directors, or

(c) is a member of it and controls alone, pursuant to an agreement with other shareholders or members, a majority of the voting rights in it,

or if it is a subsidiary of a company which is itself a subsidiary of that other company.

(2) A company is a "wholly-owned subsidiary" of another company if it has no members except that other and that other's wholly-owned subsidiaries or persons acting on behalf of that other or its wholly-owned subsidiaries.

(3) In this section "company" includes any body corporate.]

[551]

NOTES

Repealed as noted to s 1 at **[309]**.
Substituted, together with s 736A for original s 736, by the Companies Act 1989, s 144(1).
The original s 736 is reproduced here because of its continuing application for certain purposes (see in particular the Companies Act 1989 (Commencement No 6 and Transitional and Saving Provisions) Order 1990, SI 1990/1392, art 6)—

"736 "Holding company", "subsidiary" and "wholly-owned subsidiary"

(1) For the purposes of this Act, a company is deemed to be a subsidiary of another if (but only if)—

(a) that other either—

(i) is a member of it and controls the composition of its board of directors, or

(ii) holds more than half in nominal value of its equity share capital, or

(b) the first-mentioned company is a subsidiary of any company which is that other's subsidiary.

The above is subject to subsection (4) below in this section.

(2) For purposes of subsection (1), the composition of a company's board of directors is deemed to be controlled by another company if (but only if) that other company by the exercise of some power exercisable by it without the consent or concurrence of any other person can appoint or remove the holders of all or a majority of the directorships.

(3) For purposes of this last provision, the other company is deemed to have power to appoint to a directorship with respect to which any of the following conditions is satisfied—

(a) that a person cannot be appointed to it without the exercise in his favour by the other company of such a power as is mentioned above, or

(b) that a person's appointment to the directorship follows necessarily from his appointment as director of the other company, or

(c) that the directorship is held by the other company itself or by a subsidiary of it.

(4) In determining whether one company is a subsidiary of another—

(a) any shares held or power exercisable by the other in a fiduciary capacity are to be treated as not held or exercisable by it,

(b) subject to the two following paragraphs, any shares held or power exercisable—

(i) by any person as nominee for the other (except where the other is concerned only in a fiduciary capacity), or

(ii) by, or by a nominee for, a subsidiary of the other (not being a subsidiary which is concerned only in a fiduciary capacity),

are to be treated as held or exercisable by the other,

(c) any shares held or power exercisable by any person by virtue of the provisions of any debentures of the first-mentioned company or of a trust deed for securing any issue of such debentures are to be disregarded,

(d) any shares held or power exercisable by, or by a nominee for, the other or its subsidiary (not being held or exercisable as mentioned in paragraph (c)) are to be treated as not held or exercisable by the other if the ordinary business of the other or its subsidiary (as the case may be) includes the lending of money and the shares are held or the power is exercisable as above mentioned by way of security only for the purposes of a transaction entered into in the ordinary course of that business.

(5) For purposes of this Act—

(a) a company is deemed to be another's holding company if (but only if) the other is its subsidiary, and

(b) a body corporate is deemed the wholly-owned subsidiary of another if it has no members except that other and that other's wholly-owned subsidiaries and its or their nominees.

(6) In this section "company" includes any body corporate.".

736A–736B, 737, 738 (*Outside the scope of this work.*)

739 "Non-cash asset"

(1) In this Act "non-cash asset" means any property or interest in property other than cash; and for this purpose "cash" includes foreign currency.

(2) A reference to the transfer or acquisition of a non-cash asset includes the creation or extinction of an estate or interest in, or a right over, any property and also the discharge of any person's liability, other than a liability for a liquidated sum.

[552]

NOTES

Repealed as noted to s 1 at **[309]**.

740 "Body corporate" and "corporation"

References in this Act to a body corporate or to a corporation do not include a corporation sole, but include a company incorporated elsewhere than in Great Britain.

Such references to a body corporate do not include a Scottish firm.

[553]

NOTES

Repealed as noted to s 1 at **[309]**.

741 "Director" and "shadow director"

(1) In this Act, "director" includes any person occupying the position of director, by whatever name called.

(2) In relation to a company, "shadow director" means a person in accordance with whose directions or instructions the directors of the company are accustomed to act.

However, a person is not deemed a shadow director by reason only that the directors act on advice given by him in a professional capacity.

(3) For the purposes of the following provisions of this Act, namely—

section 309 (directors' duty to have regard to interests of employees),

section 319 (directors' long-term contracts of employment),

sections 320 to 322 (substantial property transactions involving directors), …

[section 322B (contracts with sole members who are directors), and]

sections 330 to 346 (general restrictions on power of companies to make loans, etc, to directors and others connected with them),

(being provisions under which shadow directors are treated as directors), a body corporate is not to be treated as a shadow director of any of its subsidiary companies by reason only that the directors of the subsidiary are accustomed to act in accordance with its directions or instructions.

[554]

NOTES

Repealed as noted to s 1 at **[309]**.

Sub-s (3): word omitted repealed and words in square brackets inserted by the Companies (Single Member Private Limited Companies) Regulations 1992, SI 1992/1699, reg 2, Schedule, para 3(2).

[742 Expressions used in connection with accounts

(1) In this Act, unless a contrary intention appears, the following expressions have the same meaning as in Part VII (accounts)—

"annual accounts",
"accounting reference date" and "accounting reference period",
"balance sheet" and "balance sheet date",
["Companies Act accounts"]
["Companies Act individual accounts"]
"current assets",
"financial year", in relation to a company,
"fixed assets",
["IAS accounts"]
["IAS individual accounts"]
"parent company" and "parent undertaking",
"profit and loss account", and
"subsidiary undertaking".

(2) References in this Act to "realised profits" and "realised losses", in relation to a company's accounts, shall be construed in accordance with section 262(3).]

[(2A) References in this Act to sending or sending out copies of any of the documents referred to in section 238(1) include sending or sending out such copies in accordance with section 238(4A) or (4B).]

[555]

NOTES

Repealed as noted to s 1 at **[309]**.

Substituted by the Companies Act 1989, s 23, Sch 10, para 15, subject to transitional provisions.

Sub-s (1): entries in square brackets inserted the Companies Act 1985 (International Accounting Standards and Other Accounting Amendments) Regulations 2004, SI 2004/2947, reg 3, Sch 1, paras 1, 29, in relation to companies' financial years which begin on or after 1 January 2005.

Sub-s (2A): added by the Companies Act 1985 (Electronic Communications) Order 2000, SI 2000/3373, art 28.

743, 743A (*Outside the scope of this work.*)

744 Expressions used generally in this Act

In this Act, unless the contrary intention appears, the following definitions apply—

"agent" does not include a person's counsel acting as such;

.....

"articles" means, in relation to a company, its articles of association, as originally framed or as altered by resolution, including (so far as applicable to the company) regulations contained in or annexed to any enactment relating to companies passed before this Act, as altered by or under any such enactment;

[.....]

"authorised minimum" has the meaning given by section 118;

"bank holiday" means a holiday under the Banking and Financial Dealings Act 1971;

[.....]

"books and papers" and "books or papers" include accounts, deeds, writings and documents;

["communication" means the same as in the Electronic Communications Act 2000;]

"the Companies Acts" means this Act, the [insider dealing legislation] and the Consequential Provisions Act;

"the Consequential Provisions Act" means the Companies Consolidation (Consequential Provisions) Act 1985;

"the court", in relation to a company, means the court having jurisdiction to wind up the company;

"debenture" includes debenture stock, bonds and any other securities of a company, whether constituting a charge on the assets of the company or not;
"document" includes summons, notice, order, and other legal process, and registers;
["EEA State" means a State which is a Contracting Party to the Agreement on the European Economic Area signed at Oporto on 2nd May 1992 as adjusted by the Protocol signed at Brussels on 17th March 1993.]
["electronic communication" means the same as in the Electronic Communications Act 2000;]
"equity share capital" means, in relation to a company, its issued share capital excluding any part of that capital which, neither as respects dividends nor as respects capital, carries any right to participate beyond a specified amount in a distribution;
"expert" has the meaning given by section 62;
"floating charge" includes a floating charge within the meaning given by section 462;
"the Gazette" means, as respects companies registered in England and Wales, the London Gazette and, as respects companies registered in Scotland, the Edinburgh Gazette;

.....

"hire-purchase agreement" has the same meaning as in the Consumer Credit Act 1974;
["the insider dealing legislation" means Part V of the Criminal Justice Act 1993 (insider dealing).]

.....

["insurance market activity" has the meaning given in section 316(3) of the Financial Services and Markets Act 2000;]
"joint stock company" has the meaning given by section 683;
"memorandum", in relation to a company, means its memorandum of association, as originally framed or as altered in pursuance of any enactment;
"number", in relation to shares, includes amount, where the context admits of the reference to shares being construed to include stock;
"officer", in relation to a body corporate, includes a director, manager or secretary;
"official seal", in relation to the registrar of companies, means a seal prepared under section 704(4) for the authentication of documents required for or in connection with the registration of companies;
"oversea company" means—

(*a*) *a company incorporated elsewhere than in Great Britain which, after the commencement of this Act, establishes a place of business in Great Britain, and*

(*b*) *a company so incorporated which has, before that commencement, established a place of business and continues to have an established place of business in Great Britain at that commencement;*

"place of business" includes a share transfer or share registration office;
"prescribed" means—

(*a*) *as respects provisions of this Act relating to winding up, prescribed by general rules ... , and*

(*b*) *otherwise, prescribed by statutory instrument made by the Secretary of State;*

"prospectus" means any prospectus, notice, circular, advertisement, or other invitation, offering to the public for subscription or purchase any shares in or debentures of a company;
"prospectus issued generally" means a prospectus issued to persons who are not existing members of the company or holders of its debentures;

.....

["regulated activity" has the meaning given in section 22 of the Financial Services and Markets Act 2000;]
"the registrar of companies" and "the registrar" mean the registrar or other officer performing under this Act the duty of registration of companies in England and Wales or in Scotland, as the case may require;
"share" means share in the share capital of a company, and includes stock (except where a distinction between shares and stock is express or implied); and
"undistributable reserves" has the meaning given by section 264(3).

[556]

NOTES

Repealed as noted to s 1 at **[309]**.
Definition "annual return" repealed by the Companies Act 1989, s 212, Sch 24.

Definitions "authorised minimum", "expert", "floating charge", "joint stock company" and "undistributable reserves" repealed by the Companies Act 1989, s 212, Sch 24, as from a day to be appointed.

Definition "authorised institution" (inserted by the Banking Act 1987, s 108(1), Sch 6, para 18(8)) repealed by the Companies Act 1989, ss 23, 212, Sch 10, Pt I, para 16, Sch 24, subject to transitional provisions contained in the Companies Act 1989 (Commencement No 4 and Transitional and Saving Provisions) Order 1990, SI 1990/355.

Definition "banking company" inserted by the Companies Act 1989, s 23, Sch 10, Pt I, para 16, subject to transitional provisions; repealed by the Financial Services and Markets Act 2000 (Consequential Amendments and Repeals) Order 2001, SI 2001/3649, art 30(a).

Definitions "communication" and "electronic communication" inserted by the Companies Act 1985 (Electronic Communications) Order 2000, SI 2000/3373, art 29.

Words in square brackets in definition "the Companies Acts" and whole of definition "the insider dealing legislation" substituted by the Criminal Justice Act 1993, s 79(13), Sch 5, Pt I, para 4.

Definition "EEA State" inserted by the Companies (Membership of Holding Company) (Dealers in Securities) Regulations 1997, SI 1997/2306, reg 4(1).

Definition "general rules", and words omitted from definition "prescribed" repealed by the Insolvency Act 1985, s 235(3), Sch 10, Pt II.

Definition "insurance company" repealed by SI 2001/3649, art 30(a).

Definition "insurance market activity" inserted by SI 2001/3649, art 30(b).

Definition "prospectus issued generally" and "recognised stock exchange" repealed by Financial Services Act 1986, s 212(3), Sch 17, subject to savings.

Definition "recognised bank" repealed by the Banking Act 1987, s 108, Sch 6, para 18(8), Sch 7, Pt I.

Definition "regulated activity" inserted by SI 2001/3649, art 30(c).

Prescribed: by virtue of the Transfer of Functions (Financial Services) Order 1992, SI 1992/1315, art 10(1), Sch 4, para 2, this section has effect, in relation to any provision of this Act conferring a function transferred to the Treasury by that Order as if "prescribed" means prescribed by statutory instrument made by the Treasury.

Regulations: the Partnerships (Unrestricted Size) No 13 Regulations 1999, SI 1999/2464; the Partnerships (Unrestricted Size) No 14 Regulations 2000, SI 2000/486.

744A (*Outside the scope of this work.*)

PART XXVII
FINAL PROVISIONS

745 (*Outside the scope of this work.*)

746 Commencement

... this Act comes into force on 1st July 1985.

[557]

NOTES

Repealed as noted to s 1 at **[309]**.

Words omitted repealed by the Companies Act 1989, s 212, Sch 24.

747 Citation

This Act may be cited as the Companies Act 1985.

[558]

SCHEDULES

(*Schs 1, 2 outside the scope of this work; Sch 3 repealed, with savings, by Financial Services Act 1986, s 212(3), Sch 17, Pt I.*)

SCHEDULE 4
FORM AND CONTENT OF COMPANY ACCOUNTS

Sections 228, 230

PART I
GENERAL RULES AND FORMATS

SECTION A
GENERAL RULES

1.—(1) Subject to the following provisions of this Schedule—

(*a*) *every balance sheet of a company shall show the items listed in either of the balance sheet formats set out below in section B of this Part; and*

(*b*) *every profit and loss account of a company shall show the items listed in any one of the profit and loss account formats so set out;*

in either case in the order and under the headings and sub-headings given in the format adopted.

(2) *Sub-paragraph (1) above is not to be read as requiring the heading or sub-heading for any item to be distinguished by any letter or number assigned to that item in the format adopted.*

2.—(1) Where in accordance with paragraph 1 a company's balance sheet or profit and loss account for any financial year has been prepared by reference to one of the formats set out in section B below, the directors of the company shall adopt the same format in preparing the accounts for subsequent financial years of the company unless in their opinion there are special reasons for a change.

(2) *Particulars of any change in the format adopted in preparing a company's balance sheet or profit and loss account in accordance with paragraph 1 shall be disclosed, and the reasons for the change shall be explained, in a note to the accounts in which the new format is first adopted.*

3.—(1) Any item required in accordance with paragraph 1 to be shown in a company's balance sheet or profit and loss account may be shown in greater detail than required by the format adopted.

(2) *A company's balance sheet or profit and loss account may include an item representing or covering the amount of any asset or liability, income or expenditure not otherwise covered by any of the items listed in the format adopted, but the following shall not be treated as assets in any company's balance sheet—*

(*a*) *preliminary expenses;*

(*b*) *expenses of and commission on any issue of shares or debentures; and*

(*c*) *costs of research.*

(3) *In preparing a company's balance sheet or profit and loss account the directors of the company shall adapt the arrangement and headings and sub-headings otherwise required by paragraph 1 in respect of items to which an Arabic number is assigned in the format adopted, in any case where the special nature of the company's business requires such adaptation.*

(4) *Items to which Arabic numbers are assigned in any of the formats set out in section B below may be combined in a company's accounts for any financial year if either—*

(*a*) *their individual amounts are not material to assessing the state of affairs or profit or loss of the company for that year; or*

(*b*) *the combination facilitates that assessment;*

but in a case within paragraph (*b*) *the individual amounts of any items so combined shall be disclosed in a note to the accounts.*

(5) *Subject to paragraph 4(3) below, a heading or sub-heading corresponding to an item listed in the format adopted in preparing a company's balance sheet or profit and loss account shall not be included if there is no amount to be shown for that item in respect of the financial year to which the balance sheet or profit and loss account relates.*

(6) *Every profit and loss account of a company shall show the amount of the company's profit or loss on ordinary activities before taxation.*

(7) *Every profit and loss account of a company shall show separately as additional items—*

(*a*) *any amount set aside or proposed to be set aside to, or withdrawn or proposed to be withdrawn from, reserves; …*

(*b*) *the aggregate amount of any dividends paid and proposed.*

[(*c*) *if it is not shown in the notes to the accounts, the aggregate amount of any dividends proposed.*]

4.—(1) In respect of every item shown in a company's balance sheet or profit and loss account the corresponding amount for the financial year immediately preceding that to which the balance sheet or profit and loss account relates shall also be shown.

(2) Where that corresponding amount is not comparable with the amount to be shown for the item in question in respect of the financial year to which the balance sheet or profit and loss account relates, the former amount [may be adjusted] and [particulars of the non-comparability and of any adjustment] shall be disclosed in a note to the accounts.

(3) Paragraph 3(5) does not apply in any case where an amount can be shown for the item in question in respect of the financial year immediately preceding that to which the balance sheet or profit and loss account relates, and that amount shall be shown under the heading or sub-heading required by paragraph 1 for that item.

5. Amounts in respect of items representing assets or income may not be set off against amounts in respect of items representing liabilities or expenditure (as the case may be), or vice versa.

[5A. The directors of a company must, in determining how amounts are presented within items in the profit and loss account and balance sheet, have regard to the substance of the reported transaction or arrangement, in accordance with generally accepted accounting principles or practice.]

SECTION B
THE REQUIRED FORMATS FOR ACCOUNTS

PRELIMINARY

6. References in this Part of this Schedule to the items listed in any of the formats set out below are to those items read together with any of the notes following the formats which apply to any of those items, and the requirement imposed by paragraph 1 to show the items listed in any such format in the order adopted in the format is subject to any provision in those notes for alternative positions for any particular items.

7. A number in brackets following any item in any of the formats set out below is a reference to the note of that number in the notes following the formats.

8. In the notes following the formats—
- *(a) the heading of each note gives the required heading or sub-heading for the item to which it applies and a reference to any letters and numbers assigned to that item in the formats set out below (taking a reference in the case of Format 2 of the balance sheet formats to the item listed under "Assets" or under "Liabilities" as the case may require); and*
- *(b) references to a numbered format are to the balance sheet format or (as the case may require) to the profit and loss account format of that number set out below.*

Balance Sheet Formats

Format 1

A. Called up share capital not paid (1)

B. Fixed assets
- *I Intangible assets*
  - *1. Development costs*
  - *2. Concessions, patents, licences, trade marks and similar rights and assets (2)*
  - *3. Goodwill (3)*
  - *4. Payments on account*
- *II Tangible assets*
  - *1. Land and buildings*
  - *2. Plant and machinery*
  - *3. Fixtures, fittings, tools and equipment*
  - *4. Payments on account and assets in course of construction*
- *III Investments*
  - *1. Shares in [group undertakings]*
  - *2. Loans to [group undertakings]*
  - *3. [Participating interests]*
  - *4. Loans to [undertakings in which the company has a participating interest]*
  - *5. Other investments other than loans*

6. *Other loans*
7. *Own shares (4)*

C. *Current assets*

I *Stocks*
1. *Raw materials and consumables*
2. *Work in progress*
3. *Finished goods and goods for resale*
4. *Payments on account*

II *Debtors (5)*
1. *Trade debtors*
2. *Amounts owed by [group undertakings]*
3. *Amounts owed by [undertakings in which the company has a participating interest]*
4. *Other debtors*
5. *Called up share capital not paid (1)*
6. *Prepayments and accrued income (6)*

III *Investments*
1. *Shares in [group undertakings]*
2. *Own shares (4)*
3. *Other investments*

IV *Cash at bank and in hand*

D. *Prepayments and accrued income (6)*

E. *Creditors: amounts falling due within one year*
1. *Debenture loans (7)*
2. *Bank loans and overdrafts*
3. *Payments received on account (8)*
4. *Trade creditors*
5. *Bills of exchange payable*
6. *Amounts owed to [group undertakings]*
7. *Amounts owed to [undertakings in which the company has a participating interest]*
8. *Other creditors including taxation and social security (9)*
9. *Accruals and deferred income (10)*

F. *Net current assets (liabilities) (11)*

G. *Total assets less current liabilities*

H. *Creditors: amounts falling due after more than one year*
1. *Debenture loans (7)*
2. *Bank loans and overdrafts*
3. *Payments received on account (8)*
4. *Trade creditors*
5. *Bills of exchange payable*
6. *Amounts owed to [group undertakings]*
7. *Amounts owed to [undertakings in which the company has a participating interest]*
8. *Other creditors including taxation and social security (9)*
9. *Accruals and deferred income (10)*

I. *[Provisions for liabilities]*
1. *Pensions and similar obligations*
2. *Taxation, including deferred taxation*
3. *Other provisions*

J. *Accruals and deferred income (10)*

K. *Capital and reserves*

I *Called up share capital (12)*

II *Share premium account*

III *Revaluation reserve*

IV *Other reserves*
1. *Capital redemption reserve*
2. *Reserve for own shares*
3. *Reserves provided for by the articles of association*
4. *Other reserves*

V *Profit and loss account*

Balance Sheet Formats

Format 2

ASSETS

A. *Called up share capital not paid* (*1*)

B. *Fixed assets*
- I *Intangible assets*
  - 1. *Development costs*
  - 2. *Concessions, patents, licences, trade marks and similar rights and assets* (2)
  - 3. *Goodwill* (*3*)
  - 4. *Payments on account*
- II *Tangible assets*
  - 1. *Land and buildings*
  - 2. *Plant and machinery*
  - 3. *Fixtures, fittings, tools and equipment*
  - 4. *Payments on account and assets in course of construction*
- III *Investments*
  - 1. *Shares in [group undertakings]*
  - 2. *Loans to [group undertakings]*
  - 3. *[Participating interests]*
  - 4. *Loans to [undertakings in which the company has a participating interest]*
  - 5. *Other investments other than loans*
  - 6. *Other loans*
  - 7. *Own shares* (*4*)

C. *Current assets*
- I *Stocks*
  - 1. *Raw materials and consumables*
  - 2. *Work in progress*
  - 3. *Finished goods and goods for resale*
  - 4. *Payments on account*
- II *Debtors* (*5*)
  - 1. *Trade debtors*
  - 2. *Amounts owed by [group undertakings]*
  - 3. *Amounts owed by [undertakings in which the company has a participating interest]*
  - 4. *Other debtors*
  - 5. *Called up share capital not paid* (*1*)
  - 6. *Prepayments and accrued income* (*6*)
- III *Investments*
  - 1. *Shares in [group undertakings]*
  - 2. *Own shares* (*4*)
  - 3. *Other investments*
- IV *Cash at bank and in hand*

D. *Prepayments and accrued income* (*6*)

LIABILITIES

A. *Capital and reserves*
- I *Called up share capital* (*12*)
- II *Share premium account*
- III *Revaluation reserve*
- IV *Other reserves*
  - 1. *Capital redemption reserve*
  - 2. *Reserve for own shares*
  - 3. *Reserves provided for by the articles of association*
  - 4. *Other reserves*
- V *Profit and loss account*

B. *[Provisions for liabilities]*
  - 1. *Pensions and similar obligations*
  - 2. *Taxation including deferred taxation*
  - 3. *Other provisions*

C. *Creditors* (*13*)
  - 1. *Debenture loans* (*7*)

2. *Bank loans and overdrafts*
3. *Payments received on account (8)*
4. *Trade creditors*
5. *Bills of exchange payable*
6. *Amounts owed to [group undertakings]*
7. *Amounts owed to [undertakings in which the company has a participating interest]*
8. *Other creditors including taxation and social security (9)*
9. *Accruals and deferred income (10)*

D. *Accruals and deferred income (10)*

Notes on the balance sheet formats

(1) Called up share capital not paid

(Formats 1 and 2, items A and C.II.5.)

This item may be shown in either of the two positions given in Formats 1 and 2.

(2) Concessions, patents, licences, trade marks and similar rights and assets

(Formats 1 and 2, item B.I.2.)

Amounts in respect of assets shall only be included in a company's balance sheet under this item if either—

(a) the assets were acquired for valuable consideration and are not required to be shown under goodwill; or

(b) the assets in question were created by the company itself.

(3) Goodwill

(Formats 1 and 2, item B.I.3.)

Amounts representing goodwill shall only be included to the extent that the goodwill was acquired for valuable consideration.

(4) Own shares

(Formats 1 and 2, items B.III.7 and C.III.2.)

The nominal value of the shares held shall be shown separately.

(5) Debtors

(Formats 1 and 2, items C.II.1 to 6.)

The amount falling due after more than one year shall be shown separately for each item included under debtors.

(6) Prepayments and accrued income

(Formats 1 and 2, items C.II.6 and D.)

This item may be shown in either of the two positions given in Formats 1 and 2.

(7) Debenture loans

(Format 1, items E.1 and H.1 and Format 2, item C.1.)

The amount of any convertible loans shall be shown separately.

(8) Payments received on account

(Format 1, items E.3 and H.3 and Format 2, item C.3.)

Payments received on account of orders shall be shown for each of these items in so far as they are not shown as deductions from stocks.

(9) Other creditors including taxation and social security

(Format 1, items E.8 and H.8 and Format 2, item C.8.)

The amount for creditors in respect of taxation and social security shall be shown separately from the amount for other creditors.

(10) Accruals and deferred income

(Format 1, items E.9, H.9 and J and Format 2, items C.9 and D.)

The two positions given for this item in Format 1 at E.9 and H.9 are an alternative to the position at J, but if the item is not shown in a position corresponding to that at J it may be shown in either or both of the other two positions (as the case may require).

The two positions given for this item in Format 2 are alternatives.

(11) Net current assets (liabilities)

(Format 1, item F.)

In determining the amount to be shown for this item any amounts shown under "prepayments and accrued income" shall be taken into account wherever shown.

(12) Called up share capital

(Format 1, item K.I and Format 2, item A.I.)

The amount of allotted share capital and the amount of called up share capital which has been paid up shall be shown separately.

(13) Creditors

(Format 2, items C.1 to 9.)

Amounts falling due within one year and after one year shall be shown separately for each of these items [and for the aggregate of all of these items].

Profit and loss account formats

Format 1
(see note (17) below)

1. *Turnover*
2. *Cost of sales (14)*
3. *Gross profit or loss*
4. *Distribution costs (14)*
5. *Administrative expenses (14)*
6. *Other operating income*
7. *Income from shares in [group undertakings]*
8. *Income from [participating interests]*
9. *Income from other fixed asset investments (15)*
10. *Other interest receivable and similar income (15)*
11. *Amounts written off investments*
12. *Interest payable and similar charges (16)*
13. *Tax on profit or loss on ordinary activities*
14. *Profit or loss on ordinary activities after taxation*
15. *Extraordinary income*
16. *Extraordinary charges*
17. *Extraordinary profit or loss*
18. *Tax on extraordinary profit or loss*
19. *Other taxes not shown under the above items*
20. *Profit or loss for the financial year*

Profit and loss account formats

Format 2

1. *Turnover*
2. *Change in stocks of finished goods and in work in progress*
3. *Own work capitalised*

4. *Other operating income*

5.
   (*a*) *Raw materials and consumables*
   (*b*) *Other external charges*

6. *Staff costs—*
   (*a*) *wages and salaries*
   (*b*) *social security costs*
   (*c*) *other pension costs*

7.
   (*a*) *Depreciation and other amounts written off tangible and intangible fixed assets*
   (*b*) *Exceptional amounts written off current assets*

8. *Other operating charges*

9. *Income from shares in [group undertakings]*

10. *Income from [participating interests]*

11. *Income from other fixed asset investments (15)*

12. *Other interest receivable and similar income (15)*

13. *Amounts written off investments*

14. *Interest payable and similar charges (16)*

15. *Tax on profit or loss on ordinary activities*

16. *Profit or loss on ordinary activities after taxation*

17. *Extraordinary income*

18. *Extraordinary charges*

19. *Extraordinary profit or loss*

20. *Tax on extraordinary profit or loss*

21. *Other taxes not shown under the above items*

22. *Profit or loss for the financial year*

Profit and loss account formats

Format 3
(*see note (17) below*)

A. *Charges*
   1. *Cost of sales (14)*
   2. *Distribution costs (14)*
   3. *Administrative expenses (14)*
   4. *Amounts written off investments*
   5. *Interest payable and similar charges (16)*
   6. *Tax on profit or loss on ordinary activities*
   7. *Profit or loss on ordinary activities after taxation*
   8. *Extraordinary charges*
   9. *Tax on extraordinary profit or loss*
   10. *Other taxes not shown under the above items*
   11. *Profit or loss for the financial year*

B. *Income*
   1. *Turnover*
   2. *Other operating income*
   3. *Income from shares in [group undertakings]*
   4. *Income from [participating interests]*
   5. *Income from other fixed asset investments (15)*
   6. *Other interest receivable and similar income (15)*
   7. *Profit or loss on ordinary activities after taxation*
   8. *Extraordinary income*
   9. *Profit or loss for the financial year*

Profit and loss account formats

Format 4

A. *Charges*

1. *Reduction in stocks of finished goods and in work in progress*
2.
   (*a*) *Raw materials and consumables*
   (*b*) *Other external charges*
3. *Staff costs—*
   (*a*) *wages and salaries*
   (*b*) *social security costs*
   (*c*) *other pension costs*
4.
   (*a*) *Depreciation and other amounts written off tangible and intangible fixed assets*
   (*b*) *Exceptional amounts written off current assets*
5. *Other operating charges*
6. *Amounts written off investments*
7. *Interest payable and similar charges* (*16*)
8. *Tax on profit or loss on ordinary activities*
9. *Profit or loss on ordinary activities after taxation*
10. *Extraordinary charges*
11. *Tax on extraordinary profit or loss*
12. *Other taxes not shown under the above items*
13. *Profit or loss for the financial year*

B. *Income*

1. *Turnover*
2. *Increase in stocks of finished goods and in work in progress*
3. *Own work capitalised*
4. *Other operating income*
5. *Income from shares in [group undertakings]*
6. *Income from [participating interests]*
7. *Income from other fixed asset investments* (*15*)
8. *Other interest receivable and similar income* (*15*)
9. *Profit or loss on ordinary activities after taxation*
10. *Extraordinary income*
11. *Profit or loss for the financial year*

Notes on the profit and loss account formats

(*14*) *Cost of sales: distribution costs: administrative expenses*

(*Format 1, items 2, 4 and 5 and Format 3, items A.1, 2 and 3.*)

These items shall be stated after taking into account any necessary provisions for depreciation or diminution in value of assets.

(*15*) *Income from other fixed asset investments: other interest receivable and similar income*

(*Format 1, items 9 and 10: Format 2, items 11 and 12: Format 3, items B.5 and 6: Format 4, items B.7 and 8.*)

Income and interest derived from [group undertakings] shall be shown separately from income and interest derived from other sources.

(*16*) *Interest payable and similar charges*

(*Format 1, item 12: Format 2, item 14: Format 3, item A.5: Format 4, item A.7.*)

The amount payable to [group undertakings] shall be shown separately.

(*17*) *Formats 1 and 3*

The amount of any provisions for depreciation and diminution in value of tangible and intangible fixed assets falling to be shown under items 7(a) and A.4(a) respectively in Formats 2 and 4 shall be disclosed in a note to the accounts in any case where the profit and loss account is prepared by reference to Format 1 or Format 3.

[559]

NOTES

Repealed as noted to s 1 at **[309]**.

Para 3: word omitted from sub-para (7)(a) repealed and sub-para (7)(c) added by the Companies Act 1985 (Miscellaneous Accounting Amendments) Regulations 1996, SI 1996/189, regs 14(1), 16(1), Sch 1, paras 1, 2, in relation to any financial year ending on or after 2 February 1996; for a transitional provision see reg 16(2) of the 1996 Regulations.

Para 4: words in square brackets substituted by the Companies Act 1985 (Investment Companies and Accounting and Audit Amendments) Regulations 2005, SI 2005/2280, reg 3, in relation to companies' financial years which begin on or after 1 January 2005 and which end on or after 1 October 2005.

Para 5A: inserted by SI 2004/2947, reg 14(1), Sch 2, paras 1, 3, in relation to companies' financial years which begin on or after 1 January 2005.

Words "provisions for liabilities" in square brackets in balance sheet format 1 and balance sheet format 2 substituted by SI 2004/2947, reg 14(1), Sch 2, paras 1, 4, in relation to companies' financial years which begin on or after 1 January 2005.

Words in square brackets in note (13) substituted by SI 1996/189, regs 14(1), 16(1), Sch 1, paras 1, 3, in relation to any financial year ending on or after 2 February 1996; for a transitional provision see reg 16(2) of the 1996 Regulations.

Other words in square brackets substituted by the Companies Act 1989, s 4(2), Sch 1, paras 1–4, subject to transitional provisions contained in the Companies Act 1989 (Commencement No 4 and Transitional and Saving Provisions) Order 1990, SI 1990/355. See the transitional provisions note preceding s 221 at **[356]**.

Trade marks: by the Trade Marks Act 1994, s 106(1), Sch 4, para 1, references in Balance Sheet Formats 1 and 2 and Note (2) to trade marks are to be construed as references to trade marks within the meaning of the 1994 Act.

PART II
ACCOUNTING PRINCIPLES AND RULES

SECTION A
ACCOUNTING PRINCIPLES

Preliminary

9. Subject to paragraph 15 below, the amounts to be included in respect of all items shown in a company's accounts shall be determined in accordance with the principles set out in paragraphs 10 to 14.

Accounting principles

10. The company shall be presumed to be carrying on business as a going concern.

[11. Accounting policies shall be applied consistently within the same accounts as from one financial year to the next.]

12. The amount of any item shall be determined on a prudent basis, and in particular—

(a) only profits realised at the balance sheet date shall be included in the profit and loss account; and

(b) all liabilities … which have arisen … in respect of the financial year to which the accounts relate or a previous financial year shall be taken into account, including those which only become apparent between the balance sheet date and the date on which it is signed on behalf of the board of directors in pursuance of [section 233] of this Act.

13. All income and charges relating to the financial year to which the accounts relate shall be taken into account, without regard to the date of receipt or payment.

14. In determining the aggregate amount of any item the amount of each individual asset or liability that falls to be taken into account shall be determined separately.

Departure from the accounting principles

15. If it appears to the directors of a company that there are special reasons for departing from any of the principles stated above in preparing the company's accounts in respect of any financial year they may do so, but particulars of the departure, the reasons for it and its effect shall be given in a note to the accounts.

SECTION B
HISTORICAL COST ACCOUNTING RULES

Preliminary

16. [Subject to sections C and D] of this Part of this Schedule, the amounts to be included in respect of all items shown in a company's accounts shall be determined in accordance with the rules set out in paragraphs 17 to 28.

Fixed assets

General rules

17. Subject to any provision for depreciation or diminution in value made in accordance with paragraph 18 or 19 the amount to be included in respect of any fixed asset shall be its purchase price or production cost.

18. In the case of any fixed asset which has a limited useful economic life, the amount of—
- *(a) its purchase price or production cost; or*
- *(b) where it is estimated that any such asset will have a residual value at the end of the period of its useful economic life, its purchase price or production cost less that estimated residual value;*

shall be reduced by provisions for depreciation calculated to write off that amount systematically over the period of the asset's useful economic life.

19.—(1) Where a fixed asset investment of a description falling to be included under item B.III of either of the balance sheet formats set out in Part I of this Schedule has diminished in value provisions for diminution in value may be made in respect of it and the amount to be included in respect of it may be reduced accordingly; and any such provisions which are not shown in the profit and loss account shall be disclosed (either separately or in aggregate) in a note to the accounts.

(2) Provisions for diminution in value shall be made in respect of any fixed asset which has diminished in value if the reduction in its value is expected to be permanent (whether its useful economic life is limited or not), and the amount to be included in respect of it shall be reduced accordingly; and any such provisions which are not shown in the profit and loss account shall be disclosed (either separately or in aggregate) in a note to the accounts.

(3) Where the reasons for which any provision was made in accordance with sub-paragraph (1) or (2) have ceased to apply to any extent, that provision shall be written back to the extent that it is no longer necessary; and any amounts written back in accordance with this sub-paragraph which are not shown in the profit and loss account shall be disclosed (either separately or in aggregate) in a note to the accounts.

Rules for determining particular fixed asset items

20.—(1) Notwithstanding that an item in respect of "development costs" is included under "fixed assets" in the balance sheet formats set out in Part I of this Schedule, an amount may only be included in a company's balance sheet in respect of development costs in special circumstances.

(2) If any amount is included in a company's balance sheet in respect of development costs the following information shall be given in a note to the accounts—
- *(a) the period over which the amount of those costs originally capitalised is being or is to be written off; and*
- *(b) the reasons for capitalising the development costs in question.*

21.—(1) The application of paragraphs 17 to 19 in relation to goodwill (in any case where goodwill is treated as an asset) is subject to the following provisions of this paragraph.

(2) Subject to sub-paragraph (3) below, the amount of the consideration for any goodwill acquired by a company shall be reduced by provisions for depreciation calculated to write off that amount systematically over a period chosen by the directors of the company.

(3) The period chosen shall not exceed the useful economic life of the goodwill in question.

(4) In any case where any goodwill acquired by a company is shown or included as an asset in the company's balance sheet the period chosen for writing off the consideration for that goodwill and the reasons for choosing that period shall be disclosed in a note to the accounts.

Current assets

22. Subject to paragraph 23, the amount to be included in respect of any current asset shall be its purchase price or production cost.

23.—(1) If the net realisable value of any current asset is lower than its purchase price or production cost the amount to be included in respect of that asset shall be the net realisable value.

(2) Where the reasons for which any provision for diminution in value was made in accordance with sub-paragraph (1) have ceased to apply to any extent, that provision shall be written back to the extent that it is no longer necessary.

Miscellaneous and supplementary provisions

Excess of money owed over value received as an asset item

24.—(1) Where the amount repayable on any debt owed by a company is greater than the value of the consideration received in the transaction giving rise to the debt, the amount of the difference may be treated as an asset.

(2) Where any such amount is so treated—
(a) it shall be written off by reasonable amounts each year and must be completely written off before repayment of the debt; and
(b) if the current amount is not shown as a separate item in the company's balance sheet it must be disclosed in a note to the accounts.

Assets included at a fixed amount

25.—(1) Subject to the following sub-paragraph, assets which fall to be included—
(a) amongst the fixed assets of a company under the item "tangible assets"; or
(b) amongst the current assets of a company under the item "raw materials and consumables";
may be included at a fixed quantity and value.

(2) Sub-paragraph (1) applies to assets of a kind which are constantly being replaced, where—
(a) their overall value is not material to assessing the company's state of affairs; and
(b) their quantity, value and composition are not subject to material variation.

Determination of purchase price or production cost

26.—(1) The purchase price of an asset shall be determined by adding to the actual price paid any expenses incidental to its acquisition.

(2) The production cost of an asset shall be determined by adding to the purchase price of the raw materials and consumables used the amount of the costs incurred by the company which are directly attributable to the production of that asset.

(3) In addition, there may be included in the production cost of an asset—
(a) a reasonable proportion of the costs incurred by the company which are only indirectly attributable to the production of that asset, but only to the extent that they relate to the period of production; and
(b) interest on capital borrowed to finance the production of that asset, to the extent that it accrues in respect of the period of production;
provided, however, in a case within paragraph (b) above, that the inclusion of the interest in determining the cost of that asset and the amount of the interest so included is disclosed in a note to the accounts.

(4) In the case of current assets distribution costs may not be included in production costs.

27.—(1) Subject to the qualification mentioned below, the purchase price or production cost of—

(a) any assets which fall to be included under any item shown in a company's balance sheet under the general item "stocks"; and

(b) any assets which are fungible assets (including investments);

may be determined by the application of any of the methods mentioned in sub-paragraph (2) below in relation to any such assets of the same class.

The method chosen must be one which appears to the directors to be appropriate in the circumstances of the company.

(2) Those methods are—

(a) the method known as "first in, first out" (FIFO);

(b) the method known as "last in, first out" (LIFO);

(c) a weighted average price; and

(d) any other method similar to any of the methods mentioned above.

(3) Where in the case of any company—

(a) the purchase price or production cost of assets falling to be included under any item shown in the company's balance sheet has been determined by the application of any method permitted by this paragraph; and

(b) the amount shown in respect of that item differs materially from the relevant alternative amount given below in this paragraph;

the amount of that difference shall be disclosed in a note to the accounts.

(4) Subject to sub-paragraph (5) below, for the purposes of sub-paragraph (3)(b) above, the relevant alternative amount, in relation to any item shown in a company's balance sheet, is the amount which would have been shown in respect of that item if assets of any class included under that item at an amount determined by any method permitted by this paragraph had instead been included at their replacement cost as at the balance sheet date.

(5) The relevant alternative amount may be determined by reference to the most recent actual purchase price or production cost before the balance sheet date of assets of any class included under the item in question instead of by reference to their replacement cost as at that date, but only if the former appears to the directors of the company to constitute the more appropriate standard of comparison in the case of assets of that class.

(6) For the purposes of this paragraph, assets of any description shall be regarded as fungible if assets of that description are substantially indistinguishable one from another.

Substitution of original stated amount where price or cost unknown

28. Where there is no record of the purchase price or production cost of any asset of a company or of any price, expenses or costs relevant for determining its purchase price or production cost in accordance with paragraph 26, or any such record cannot be obtained without unreasonable expense or delay, its purchase price or production cost shall be taken for the purposes of paragraphs 17 to 23 to be the value ascribed to it in the earliest available record of its value made on or after its acquisition or production by the company.

SECTION C
ALTERNATIVE ACCOUNTING RULES

Preliminary

29.—(1) The rules set out in section B are referred to below in this Schedule as the historical cost accounting rules.

(2) Those rules, with the omission of paragraphs 16, 21 and 25 to 28, are referred to below in this Part of this Schedule as the depreciation rules; and references below in this Schedule to the historical cost accounting rules do not include the depreciation rules as they apply by virtue of paragraph 32.

30. Subject to paragraphs 32 to 34, the amounts to be included in respect of assets of any description mentioned in paragraph 31 may be determined on any basis so mentioned.

Alternative accounting rules

31.—(1) Intangible fixed assets, other than goodwill, may be included at their current cost.

(2) Tangible fixed assets may be included at a market value determined as at the date of their last valuation or at their current cost.

(3) Investments of any description falling to be included under item B.III of either of the balance sheet formats set out in Part I of this Schedule may be included either—

(a) at a market value determined as at the date of their last valuation; or

(b) at a value determined on any basis which appears to the directors to be appropriate in the circumstances of the company;

but in the latter case particulars of the method of valuation adopted and of the reasons for adopting it shall be disclosed in a note to the accounts.

(4) Investments of any description falling to be included under item C.III of either of the balance sheet formats set out in Part I of this Schedule may be included at their current cost.

(5) Stocks may be included at their current cost.

Application of the depreciation rules

32.—(1) Where the value of any asset of a company is determined on any basis mentioned in paragraph 31, that value shall be, or (as the case may require) be the starting point for determining, the amount to be included in respect of that asset in the company's accounts, instead of its purchase price or production cost or any value previously so determined for that asset; and the depreciation rules shall apply accordingly in relation to any such asset with the substitution for any reference to its purchase price or production cost of a reference to the value most recently determined for that asset on any basis mentioned in paragraph 31.

(2) The amount of any provision for depreciation required in the case of any fixed asset by paragraph 18 or 19 as it applies by virtue of sub-paragraph (1) is referred to below in this paragraph as the adjusted amount, and the amount of any provision which would be required by that paragraph in the case of that asset according to the historical cost accounting rules is referred to as the historical cost amount.

(3) Where sub-paragraph (1) applies in the case of any fixed asset the amount of any provision for depreciation in respect of that asset—

(a) included in any item shown in the profit and loss account in respect of amounts written off assets of the description in question; or

(b) taken into account in stating any item so shown which is required by note (14) of the notes on the profit and loss account formats set out in Part I of this Schedule to be stated after taking into account any necessary provisions for depreciation or diminution in value of assets included under it;

may be the historical cost amount instead of the adjusted amount, provided that the amount of any difference between the two is shown separately in the profit and loss account or in a note to the accounts.

Additional information to be provided in case of departure from historical cost accounting rules

33.—(1) This paragraph applies where the amounts to be included in respect of assets covered by any items shown in a company's accounts have been determined on any basis mentioned in paragraph 31.

(2) The items affected and the basis of valuation adopted in determining the amounts of the assets in question in the case of each such item shall be disclosed in a note to the accounts.

(3) In the case of each balance sheet item affected (except stocks) either—

(a) the comparable amounts determined according to the historical cost accounting rules; or

(b) the differences between those amounts and the corresponding amounts actually shown in the balance sheet in respect of that item;

shall be shown separately in the balance sheet or in a note to the accounts.

(4) In sub-paragraph (3) above, references in relation to any item to the comparable amounts determined as there mentioned are references to—

(*a*) *the aggregate amount which would be required to be shown in respect of that item if the amounts to be included in respect of all the assets covered by that item were determined according to the historical cost accounting rules; and*

(*b*) *the aggregate amount of the cumulative provisions for depreciation or diminution in value which would be permitted or required in determining those amounts according to those rules.*

Revaluation reserve

34.—(1) With respect to any determination of the value of an asset of a company on any basis mentioned in paragraph 31, the amount of any profit or loss arising from that determination (after allowing, where appropriate, for any provisions for depreciation or diminution in value made otherwise than by reference to the value so determined and any adjustments of any such provisions made in the light of that determination) shall be credited or (as the case may be) debited to a separate reserve ("the revaluation reserve").

(2) The amount of the revaluation reserve shall be shown in the company's balance sheet under a separate sub-heading in the position given for the item "revaluation reserve" in Format 1 or 2 of the balance sheet formats set out in Part I of this Schedule, but need not be shown under that name.

[(3) An amount may be transferred—

[(a) from the revaluation reserve—

(i) to the profit and loss account, if the amount was previously charged to that account or represents realised profit, or

(ii) on capitalisation,

(b) to or from the revaluation reserve in respect of the taxation relating to any profit or loss credited or debited to the reserve;]

and the revaluation reserve shall be reduced to the extent that the amounts transferred to it are no longer necessary for the purposes of the valuation method used.

(3A) In [sub-paragraph (3)(a)(ii)] "capitalisation", in relation to an amount standing to the credit of the revaluation reserve, means applying it in wholly or partly paying up unissued shares in the company to be allotted to members of the company as fully or partly paid shares.

(3B) The revaluation reserve shall not be reduced except as mentioned in this paragraph.]

(4) The treatment for taxation purposes of amounts credited or debited to the revaluation reserve shall be disclosed in a note to the accounts.

[SECTION D
FAIR VALUE ACCOUNTING

Inclusion of financial instruments at fair value

34A.—(1) Subject to sub-paragraphs (2) to (4), financial instruments (including derivatives) may be included at fair value.

(2) Sub-paragraph (1) does not apply to financial instruments which constitute liabilities unless—

(*a*) *they are held as part of a trading portfolio, or*

(*b*) *they are derivatives.*

(3) Sub-paragraph (1) does not apply to—

(*a*) *financial instruments (other than derivatives) held to maturity;*

(*b*) *loans and receivables originated by the company and not held for trading purposes;*

(*c*) *interests in subsidiary undertakings, associated undertakings and joint ventures;*

(*d*) *equity instruments issued by the company;*

(*e*) *contracts for contingent consideration in a business combination;*

(*f*) *other financial instruments with such special characteristics that the instruments, according to generally accepted accounting principles or practice, should be accounted for differently from other financial instruments.*

(4) If the fair value of a financial instrument cannot be determined reliably in accordance with paragraph 34B, sub-paragraph (1) does not apply to that financial instrument.

(5) *In this paragraph—*

"associated undertaking" has the meaning given by paragraph 20 of Schedule 4A; and
"joint venture" has the meaning given by paragraph 19 of that Schedule.

Determination of fair value

34B.—(1) The fair value of a financial instrument is determined in accordance with this paragraph.

(2) If a reliable market can readily be identified for the financial instrument, its fair value is determined by reference to its market value.

(3) If a reliable market cannot readily be identified for the financial instrument but can be identified for its components or for a similar instrument, its fair value is determined by reference to the market value of its components or of the similar instrument.

(4) If neither sub-paragraph (2) nor (3) applies, the fair value of the financial instrument is a value resulting from generally accepted valuation models and techniques.

(5) Any valuation models and techniques used for the purposes of sub-paragraph (4) must ensure a reasonable approximation of the market value.

Inclusion of hedged items at fair value

34C. A company may include any assets and liabilities that qualify as hedged items under a fair value hedge accounting system, or identified portions of such assets or liabilities, at the amount required under that system.

Other assets that may be included at fair value

34D.—(1) This paragraph applies to—

(a) investment property, and

(b) living animals and plants,

that, under international accounting standards, may be included in accounts at fair value.

(2) Such investment property and such living animals and plants may be included at fair value, provided that all such investment property or, as the case may be, all such living animals and plants are so included where their fair value can reliably be determined.

(3) In this paragraph, "fair value" means fair value determined in accordance with relevant international accounting standards.

Accounting for changes in value

34E.—(1) This paragraph applies where a financial instrument is valued in accordance with paragraph 34A or 34C or an asset is valued in accordance with paragraph 34D.

(2) Notwithstanding paragraph 12 of this Schedule, and subject to sub-paragraphs (3) and (4) below, a change in the value of the financial instrument or of the investment property or living animal or plant must be included in the profit and loss account.

(3) Where—

(a) the financial instrument accounted for is a hedging instrument under a hedge accounting system that allows some or all of the change in value not to be shown in the profit and loss account, or

(b) the change in value relates to an exchange difference arising on a monetary item that forms part of a company's net investment in a foreign entity,

the amount of the change in value must be credited to or (as the case may be) debited from a separate reserve ("the fair value reserve").

(4) Where the instrument accounted for—

(a) is an available for sale financial asset, and

(b) is not a derivative,

the change in value may be credited to or (as the case may be) debited from the fair value reserve.

The fair value reserve

34F.—(1) The fair value reserve must be adjusted to the extent that the amounts shown in it are no longer necessary for the purposes of paragraph 34E(3) or (4).

(2) The treatment for taxation purposes of amounts credited or debited to the fair value reserve must be disclosed in a note to the accounts.]

[560]

NOTES

Para 11: substituted by the Companies Act 1989, s 4(2), Sch 1, para 5, subject to transitional provisions contained in the Companies Act 1989 (Commencement No 4 and Transitional and Saving Provisions) Order 1990, SI 1990/355. See the transitional provisions note preceding s 221 at **[356]**.

Para 12: words omitted repealed by the Companies Act 1985 (International Accounting Standards and Other Accounting Amendments) Regulations 2004, SI 2004/2947, reg 14(1), Sch 2, paras 1, 5, in relation to companies' financial years which begin on or after 1 January 2005; words in square brackets in sub-para (b) substituted by the Companies Act 1989, s 23, Sch 10, para 20, subject to transitional provisions contained in SI 1990/355 as noted above.

Para 16: words in square brackets substituted by SI 2004/2947, reg 14(1), Sch 2, paras 1, 6(1), (2), in relation to companies' financial years which begin on or after 1 January 2005.

Para 34: sub-paras (3), (3A), (3B) substituted for original sub-para (3) by the Companies Act 1989, s 4(2), Sch 1, para 6, subject to transitional provisions contained in SI 1990/355 as noted above; words in square brackets in sub-paras (3), (3A) substituted by the Companies Act 1985 (Miscellaneous Accounting Amendments) Regulations 1996, SI 1996/189, regs 14(1), 16(1), Sch 1, paras 1, 4, in relation to any financial year ending on or after 2 February 1996, for a transitional provision see reg 16(2) of the 1996 Regulations.

Paras 34A–34F: added by SI 2004/2947, reg 14(1), Sch 2, paras 1, 6(1), (3), in relation to companies' financial years which begin on or after 1 January 2005.

PART III
NOTES TO THE ACCOUNTS

Preliminary

35. Any information required in the case of any company by the following provisions of this Part of this Schedule shall (if not given in the company's accounts) be given by way of a note to those accounts.

[Reserves and dividends

35A. There must be stated—

(a) any amount set aside or proposed to be set aside to, or withdrawn or proposed to be withdrawn from, reserves,

(b) the aggregate amount of dividends paid in the financial year (other than those for which a liability existed at the immediately preceding balance sheet date),

(c) the aggregate amount of dividends that the company is liable to pay at the balance sheet date, and

(d) the aggregate amount of dividends that are proposed before the date of approval of the accounts, and not otherwise disclosed under paragraph (b) or (c).]

Disclosure of accounting policies

36. The accounting policies adopted by the company in determining the amounts to be included in respect of items shown in the balance sheet and in determining the profit or loss of the company shall be stated (including such policies with respect to the depreciation and diminution in value of assets).

[36A. It shall be stated whether the accounts have been prepared in accordance with applicable accounting standards and particulars of any material departure from those standards and the reasons for it shall be given.]

Information supplementing the balance sheet

37. Paragraphs 38 to 51 require information which either supplements the information given with respect to any particular items shown in the balance sheet or is otherwise relevant to assessing the company's state of affairs in the light of the information so given.

Share capital and debentures

38.—(1) The following information shall be given with respect to the company's share capital—

- (*a*) *the authorised share capital; …*
- (*b*) *where shares of more than one class have been allotted, the number and aggregate nominal value of shares of each class allotted[; and*
- (*c*) *where shares are held as treasury shares, the number and aggregate nominal value of the treasury shares and, where shares of more than one class have been allotted, the number and aggregate nominal value of the shares of each class held as treasury shares.]*

(2) In the case of any part of the allotted share capital that consists of redeemable shares, the following information shall be given—

- (*a*) *the earliest and latest dates on which the company has power to redeem those shares;*
- (*b*) *whether those shares must be redeemed in any event or are liable to be redeemed at the option of the company or of the shareholder; and*
- (*c*) *whether any (and, if so, what) premium is payable on redemption.*

39. If the company has allotted any shares during the financial year, the following information shall be given—

- (*a*) …
- (*b*) *the classes of shares allotted; and*
- (*c*) *as respects each class of shares, the number allotted, their aggregate nominal value, and the consideration received by the company for the allotment.*

40.—(1) With respect to any contingent right to the allotment of shares in the company the following particulars shall be given—

- (*a*) *the number, description and amount of the shares in relation to which the right is exercisable;*
- (*b*) *the period during which it is exercisable; and*
- (*c*) *the price to be paid for the shares allotted.*

(2) In sub-paragraph (1) above "contingent right to the allotment of shares" means any option to subscribe for shares and any other right to require the allotment of shares to any person whether arising on the conversion into shares of securities of any other description or otherwise.

41.—(1) If the company has issued any debentures during the financial year to which the accounts relate, the following information shall be given—

- (*a*) …
- (*b*) *the classes of debentures issued; and*
- (*c*) *as respects each class of debentures, the amount issued and the consideration received by the company for the issue.*

(2) …

(3) Where any of the company's debentures are held by a nominee of or trustee for the company, the nominal amount of the debentures and the amount at which they are stated in the accounting records kept by the company in accordance with section 221 of this Act shall be stated.

Fixed assets

42.—(1) In respect of each item which is or would but for paragraph 3(4)(b) be shown under the general item "fixed assets" in the company's balance sheet the following information shall be given—

- (*a*) *the appropriate amounts in respect of that item as at the date of the beginning of the financial year and as at the balance sheet date respectively;*
- (*b*) *the effect on any amount shown in the balance sheet in respect of that item of—*
  - (*i*) *any revision of the amount in respect of any assets included under that item made during that year on any basis mentioned in paragraph 31;*
  - (*ii*) *acquisitions during that year of any assets;*
  - (*iii*) *disposals during that year of any assets; and*

(iv) any transfers of assets of the company to and from that item during that year.

(2) The reference in sub-paragraph (1)(a) to the appropriate amounts in respect of any item as at any date there mentioned is a reference to amounts representing the aggregate amounts determined, as at that date, in respect of assets falling to be included under that item on either of the following bases, that is to say—

(a) on the basis of purchase price or production cost (determined in accordance with paragraphs 26 and 27); or

(b) on any basis mentioned in paragraph 31,

(leaving out of account in either case any provisions for depreciation or diminution in value).

(3) In respect of each item within sub-paragraph (1)—

(a) the cumulative amount of provisions for depreciation or diminution in value of assets included under that item as at each date mentioned in sub-paragraph (1)(a);

(b) the amount of any such provisions made in respect of the financial year;

(c) the amount of any adjustments made in respect of any such provisions during that year in consequence of the disposal of any assets; and

(d) the amount of any other adjustments made in respect of any such provisions during that year;

shall also be stated.

43. Where any fixed assets of the company (other than listed investments) are included under any item shown in the company's balance sheet at an amount determined on any basis mentioned in paragraph 31, the following information shall be given—

(a) the years (so far as they are known to the directors) in which the assets were severally valued and the several values; and

(b) in the case of assets that have been valued during the financial year, the names of the persons who valued them or particulars of their qualifications for doing so and (whichever is stated) the bases of valuation used by them.

44. In relation to any amount which is or would but for paragraph 3(4)(b) be shown in respect of the item "land and buildings" in the company's balance sheet there shall be stated—

(a) how much of that amount is ascribable to land of freehold tenure and how much to land of leasehold tenure; and

(b) how much of the amount ascribable to land of leasehold tenure is ascribable to land held on long lease and how much to land held on short lease.

Investments

45.—(1) In respect of the amount of each item which is or would but for paragraph 3(4)(b) be shown in the company's balance sheet under the general item "investments" (whether as fixed assets or as current assets) there shall be stated—

(a) how much of that amount is ascribable to listed investments; …

(b) …

(2) Where the amount of any listed investments is stated for any item in accordance with sub-paragraph (1)(a), the following amounts shall also be stated—

(a) the aggregate market value of those investments where it differs from the amount so stated; and

(b) both the market value and the stock exchange value of any investments of which the former value is, for the purposes of the accounts, taken as being higher than the latter.

[Information about fair value of assets and liabilities

45A.—(1) This paragraph applies where financial instruments have been valued in accordance with paragraph 34A or 34C

(2) There must be stated—

(a) where the fair value of the instruments has been determined in accordance with paragraph 34B(4), the significant assumptions underlying the valuation models and techniques used,

(*b*) *for each category of financial instrument, the fair value of the instruments in that category and the changes in value—*

(*i*) *included in the profit and loss account, or*

(*ii*) *credited to or (as the case may be) debited from the fair value reserve,*

in respect of those instruments, and

(*c*) *for each class of derivatives, the extent and nature of the instruments, including significant terms and conditions that may affect the amount, timing and certainty of future cash flows.*

(*3*) *Where any amount is transferred to or from the fair value reserve during the financial year, there must be stated in tabular form—*

(*a*) *the amount of the reserve as at the date of the beginning of the financial year and as at the balance sheet date respectively;*

(*b*) *the amount transferred to or from the reserve during that year; and*

(*c*) *the source and application respectively of the amounts so transferred.*

45B. Where the company has derivatives that it has not included at fair value, there must be stated for each class of such derivatives—

(*a*) *the fair value of the derivatives in that class, if such a value can be determined in accordance with paragraph 34B, and*

(*b*) *the extent and nature of the derivatives.*

45C.—(1) Sub-paragraph (2) applies if—

(*a*) *the company has financial fixed assets that could be included at fair value by virtue of paragraph 34A,*

(*b*) *the amount at which those assets are included under any item in the company's accounts is in excess of their fair value, and*

(*c*) *the company has not made provision for diminution in value of those assets in accordance with paragraph 19(1) of this Schedule.*

(2) *There must be stated—*

(*a*) *the amount at which either the individual assets or appropriate groupings of those individual assets are included in the company's accounts,*

(*b*) *the fair value of those assets or groupings, and*

(*c*) *the reasons for not making a provision for diminution in value of those assets, including the nature of the evidence that provides the basis for the belief that the amount at which they are stated in the accounts will be recovered.*

Information where investment property and living animals and plants included at fair value

45D.—(1) This paragraph applies where the amounts to be included in a company's accounts in respect of investment property or living animals and plants have been determined in accordance with paragraph 34D.

(*2*) *The balance sheet items affected and the basis of valuation adopted in determining the amounts of the assets in question in the case of each such item must be disclosed in a note to the accounts.*

(*3*) *In the case of investment property, for each balance sheet item affected there must be shown, either separately in the balance sheet or in a note to the accounts—*

(*a*) *the comparable amounts determined according to the historical cost accounting rules; or*

(*b*) *the differences between those amounts and the corresponding amounts actually shown in the balance sheet in respect of that item.*

(*4*) *In sub-paragraph (3) above, references in relation to any item to the comparable amounts determined in accordance with that sub-paragraph are references to—*

(*a*) *the aggregate amount which would be required to be shown in respect of that item if the amounts to be included in respect of all the assets covered by that item were determined according to the historical cost accounting rules; and*

(*b*) *the aggregate amount of the cumulative provisions for depreciation or diminution in value which would be permitted or required in determining those amounts according to those rules.]*

Reserves and provisions

46.—(1) Where any amount is transferred—

(a) to or from any reserves; or

(b) to any [provisions for liabilities]; or

(c) from any [provision for liabilities] otherwise than for the purpose for which the provision was established;

and the reserves or provisions are or would but for paragraph 3(4)(b) be shown as separate items in the company's balance sheet, the information mentioned in the following sub-paragraph shall be given in respect of the aggregate of reserves or provisions included in the same item.

(2) That information is—

(a) the amount of the reserves or provisions as at the date of the beginning of the financial year and as at the balance sheet date respectively;

(b) any amounts transferred to or from the reserves or provisions during that year; and

(c) the source and application respectively of any amounts so transferred.

(3) Particulars shall be given of each provision included in the item "other provisions" in the company's balance sheet in any case where the amount of that provision is material.

Provision for taxation

[47. The amount of any provision for deferred taxation shall be stated separately from the amount of any provision for other taxation.]

Details of indebtedness

48.—[(1) In respect of each item shown under "creditors" in the company's balance sheet there shall be stated the aggregate of the following amounts, that is to say—

(a) the amount of any debts included under that item which are payable or repayable otherwise than by instalments and fall due for payment or repayment after the end of the period of five years beginning with the day next following the end of the financial year; and

[(b) in the case of any debts so included which are payable or repayable by instalments, the amount of any instalments which fall due for payment after the end of that period.]]

(2) Subject to sub-paragraph (3), in relation to each debt falling to be taken into account under sub-paragraph (1), the terms of payment or repayment and the rate of any interest payable on the debt shall be stated.

(3) If the number of debts is such that, in the opinion of the directors, compliance with sub-paragraph (2) would result in a statement of excessive length, it shall be sufficient to give a general indication of the terms of payment or repayment and the rates of any interest payable on the debts.

(4) In respect of each item shown under "creditors" in the company's balance sheet there shall be stated—

(a) the aggregate amount of any debts included under that item in respect of which any security has been given by the company; and

(b) an indication of the nature of the securities so given.

(5) References above in this paragraph to an item shown under "creditors" in the company's balance sheet include references, where amounts falling due to creditors within one year and after more than one year are distinguished in the balance sheet—

(a) in a case within sub-paragraph (1), to an item shown under the latter of those categories; and

(b) in a case within sub-paragraph (4), to an item shown under either of those categories;

and references to items shown under "creditors" include references to items which would but for paragraph 3(4)(b) be shown under that heading.

49. If any fixed cumulative dividends on the company's shares are in arrear, there shall be stated—

(a) *the amount of the arrears; and*
(b) *the period for which the dividends or, if there is more than one class, each class of them are in arrear.*

Guarantees and other financial commitments

50.—(1) Particulars shall be given of any charge on the assets of the company to secure the liabilities of any other person, including, where practicable, the amount secured.

(2) The following information shall be given with respect to any other contingent liability not provided for—
(a) *the amount or estimated amount of that liability;*
(b) *its legal nature; and*
(c) *whether any valuable security has been provided by the company in connection with that liability and if so, what.*

(3) There shall be stated, where practicable—
(a) *the aggregate amount or estimated amount of contracts for capital expenditure, so far as not provided for; ...*
(b) *...*

(4) Particulars shall be given of—
(a) *any pension commitments included under any provision shown in the company's balance sheet; and*
(b) *any such commitments for which no provision has been made;*
and where any such commitment relates wholly or partly to pensions payable to past directors of the company separate particulars shall be given of that commitment so far as it relates to such pensions.

(5) Particulars shall also be given of any other financial commitments which—
(a) *have not been provided for; and*
(b) *are relevant to assessing the company's state of affairs.*

(6) ...

Miscellaneous matters

51.—(1) Particulars shall be given of any case where the purchase price or production cost of any asset is for the first time determined under paragraph 28.

(2) Where any outstanding loans made under the authority of section 153(4)(b)[, (bb)] or (c) or section 155 of this Act (various cases of financial assistance by a company for purchase of its own shares) are included under any item shown in the company's balance sheet, the aggregate amount of those loans shall be disclosed for each item in question.

(3) ...

Information supplementing the profit and loss account

52. Paragraphs 53 to 57 require information which either supplements the information given with respect to any particular items shown in the profit and loss account or otherwise provides particulars of income or expenditure of the company or of circumstances affecting the items shown in the profit and loss account.

Separate statement of certain items of income and expenditure

53.—(1) Subject to the following provisions of this paragraph, each of the amounts mentioned below shall be stated.

(2) The amount of the interest on or any similar charges in respect of—
(a) *bank loans and overdrafts, ... ; and*
(b) *loans of any other kind made to the company.*

This sub-paragraph does not apply to interest or charges on loans to the company from [group undertakings], but, with that exception, it applies to interest or charges on all loans, whether made on the security of debentures or not.

(3)–(7) ...

Particulars of tax

54.—(1) ...

(2) Particulars shall be given of any special circumstances which affect liability in respect of taxation of profits, income or capital gains for the financial year or liability in respect of taxation of profits, income or capital gains for succeeding financial years.

(3) The following amounts shall be stated—

(a) the amount of the charge for United Kingdom corporation tax;

(b) if that amount would have been greater but for relief from double taxation, the amount which it would have been but for such relief;

(c) the amount of the charge for United Kingdom income tax; and

(d) the amount of the charge for taxation imposed outside the United Kingdom of profits, income and (so far as charged to revenue) capital gains.

These amounts shall be stated separately in respect of each of the amounts which is or would but for paragraph 3(4)(b) be shown under the following items in the profit and loss account, that is to say "tax on profit or loss on ordinary activities" and "tax on extraordinary profit or loss".

Particulars of turnover

55.—(1) If in the course of the financial year the company has carried on business of two or more classes that, in the opinion of the directors, differ substantially from each other, there shall be stated in respect of each class (describing it)—

(a) the amount of the turnover attributable to that class; ...

(b) ...

(2) If in the course of the financial year the company has supplied markets that, in the opinion of the directors, differ substantially from each other, the amount of the turnover attributable to each such market shall also be stated.

In this paragraph "market" means a market delimited by geographical bounds.

(3) In analysing for the purposes of this paragraph the source (in terms of business or in terms of market) of turnover ... , the directors of the company shall have regard to the manner in which the company's activities are organised.

(4) For the purposes of this paragraph—

(a) classes of business which, in the opinion of the directors, do not differ substantially from each other shall be treated as one class; and

(b) markets which, in the opinion of the directors, do not differ substantially from each other shall be treated as one market;

and any amounts properly attributable to one class of business or (as the case may be) to one market which are not material may be included in the amount stated in respect of another.

(5) Where in the opinion of the directors the disclosure of any information required by this paragraph would be seriously prejudicial to the interests of the company, that information need not be disclosed, but the fact that any such information has not been disclosed must be stated.

56. ...

Miscellaneous matters

57.—(1) Where any amount relating to any preceding financial year is included in any item in the profit and loss account, the effect shall be stated.

(2) Particulars shall be given of any extraordinary income or charges arising in the financial year.

(3) The effect shall be stated of any transactions that are exceptional by virtue of size or incidence though they fall within the ordinary activities of the company.

General

58.—(1) Where sums originally denominated in foreign currencies have been brought into account under any items shown in the balance sheet or profit and loss account, the basis on which those sums have been translated into sterling shall be stated.

(2), (3) ...

[Dormant Companies Acting as Agents

58A. Where the directors of a company take advantage of the exemption conferred by section 249AA, and the company has during the financial year in question acted as an agent for any person, the fact that it has so acted must be stated.]

[561]

NOTES

Repealed as noted to s 1 at **[309]**.

Para 35A: inserted by the Companies Act 1985 (International Accounting Standards and Other Accounting Amendments) Regulations 2004, SI 2004/2947, reg 14(1), Sch 2, paras 1, 7(1), (2), in relation to companies' financial years which begin on or after 1 January 2005.

Para 36A: inserted by the Companies Act 1989, s 4(2), Sch 1, para 7, subject to transitional provisions contained in the Companies Act 1989 (Commencement No 4 and Transitional and Saving Provisions) Order 1990, SI 1990/355. See the transitional provisions note preceding s 221 at **[356]**.

Para 38: word omitted repealed, and sub-para (1)(c) and the word immediately preceding it added, by the Companies (Acquisition of Own Shares) (Treasury Shares) Regulations 2003, SI 2003/1116, reg 4, Schedule, para 30, as from 1 December 2003.

Para 39: sub-para (a) repealed by the Companies Act 1985 (Miscellaneous Accounting Amendments) Regulations 1996, SI 1996/189, regs 14(1), 16(1), Sch 1, paras 1, 5, in relation to any financial year ending on or after 2 February 1996; for a transitional provision see reg 16(2) of the 1996 Regulations.

Para 41: sub-paras (1)(a), (2) repealed by SI 1996/189, regs 14(1), 16(1), Sch 1, paras 1, 6, in relation to any financial year ending on or after 2 February 1996; for a transitional provision see reg 16(2) of the 1996 Regulations.

Para 45: sub-para (1)(b) and the word omitted immediately preceding it repealed by SI 1996/189, regs 14(1), 16(1), Sch 1, paras 1, 7, in relation to any financial year ending on or after 2 February 1996; for a transitional provision see reg 16(2) of the 1996.

Paras 45A–45D: inserted by SI 2004/2947, reg 14(1), Sch 2, paras 1, 7(1), (3), in relation to companies' financial years which begin on or after 1 January 2005.

Para 46: words in square brackets in sub-para (1)(b), (c) substituted by SI 2004/2947, reg 14(1), Sch 2, paras 1, 8, in relation to companies' financial years which begin on or after 1 January 2005.

Para 47: substituted by the Companies Act 1989, s 4(2), Sch 1, para 8, subject to transitional provisions contained in SI 1990/355 as noted above.

Para 48: sub-para (1) substituted by SI 1996/189, regs 14(1), 16(1), Sch 1, paras 1, 8, in relation to any financial year ending on or after 2 February 1996, for a transitional provision see reg 16(2) of the 1996 Regulations; sub-para (1)(b) further substituted, in relation to annual accounts approved by the board of directors on or after 1 March 1997, and to directors' and auditors' reports on such accounts, by the Companies Act 1985 (Accounts of Small and Medium-sized Companies and Minor Accounting Amendments) Regulations 1997, SI 1997/220, reg 7(9), for a transitional provision see reg 1(4) of the 1997 Regulations.

Para 50: sub-para (3)(b) and the word omitted immediately preceding it repealed by SI 1996/189, regs 14(1), 16(1), Sch 1, paras 1, 9, in relation to any financial year ending on or after 2 February 1996, for a transitional provision see reg 16(2) of the 1996 Regulations; sub-para (6) repealed by the Companies Act 1989, s 212, Sch 24.

Para 51: words in square brackets in sub-para (2) inserted by the Companies Act 1989, s 4(2), Sch 1, para 9, subject to transitional provisions contained in SI 1990/355 as noted above; sub-para (3) repealed by SI 1996/189, regs 14(1), 16(1), Sch 1, paras 1, 10, in relation to any financial year ending on or after 2 February 1996, for a transitional provision see reg 16(2) of the 1996 Regulations.

Para 53: words omitted from sub-para (2), and sub-paras (3)–(6), repealed by SI 1996/189, regs 14(1), 16(1), Sch 1, paras 1, 11, in relation to any financial year ending on or after 2 February 1996, for a transitional provision see reg 16(2) of the 1996 Regulations; words in square brackets in sub-para (2) substituted and sub-para (7) repealed by the Companies Act 1989, ss 4(2), 212, Sch 1, para 2, Sch 24, subject to transitional provisions contained in SI 1990/355 as noted above.

Para 54: sub-para (1) repealed by SI 1996/189, regs 14(1), 16(1), Sch 1, paras 1, 12, in relation to any financial year ending on or after 2 February 1996; for a transitional provision see reg 16(2) of the 1996 Regulations.

Para 55: sub-para (1)(b), the word omitted immediately preceding it, and words omitted from sub-para (3) repealed by SI 1996/189, regs 14(1), 16(1), Sch 1, paras 1, 13, in relation to any financial year ending on or after 2 February 1996; for a transitional provision see reg 16(2) of the 1996 Regulations.

Para 56: repealed by SI 2004/2947, reg 3, Sch 1, paras 1, 31(1), (2), in relation to companies' financial years which begin on or after 1 January 2005.

Para 56: words in square brackets in sub-paras (2) and (3) substituted by SI 1996/189, regs 14(1), 16(1), Sch 1, paras 1, 14, in relation to any financial year ending on or after 2 February 1996; for a transitional provision see reg 16(2) of the 1996 Regulations.

Para 58: sub-paras (2), (3) repealed by the Companies Act 1985 (Investment Companies and Accounting and Audit Amendments) Regulations 2005, SI 2005/2280, reg 4, in relation to companies' financial years which begin on or after 1 January 2005 and which end on or after 1 October 2005.

Para 58A: added by the Companies Act 1985 (Audit Exemption) (Amendment) Regulations 2000, SI 2000/1430, reg 5, in relation to annual reports and reports in respect of financial years ending two months or more after 26 May 2000.

Disapplication: para 58(2) does not apply to any amount which, in relation to a financial year of a company ending before 31 March 1998, is shown by virtue of Sch 6, para 2(2) of this Act; see the Company Accounts (Disclosure of Directors' Emoluments) Regulations 1997, SI 1997/570, reg 3(2).

[PART IV
SPECIAL PROVISIONS WHERE COMPANY IS A PARENT COMPANY OR SUBSIDIARY UNDERTAKING]

COMPANY'S OWN ACCOUNTS

59. …

[Guarantees and other financial commitments in favour of group undertakings

59A. Commitments within any of sub-paragraphs (1) to (5) of paragraph 50 (guarantees and other financial commitments) which are undertaken on behalf of or for the benefit of—

(a) any parent undertaking or fellow subsidiary undertaking, or

(b) any subsidiary undertaking of the company,

shall be stated separately from the other commitments within that sub-paragraph, and commitments within paragraph (a) shall also be stated separately from those within paragraph (b).]

60–70. …

[562]

NOTES

Repealed as noted to s 1 at **[309]**.

Para 59: repealed by the Companies Act 1985 (Miscellaneous Accounting Amendments) Regulations 1996, SI 1996/189, regs 14(1), 16(1), Sch 1, paras 1, 15, in relation to any financial year ending on or after 2 February 1996; for a transitional provision see reg 16(2) of the 1996 Regulations.

Para 59A: substituted (together with para 59, the preceding heading and the heading to this Part of the Schedule) by the Companies Act 1989, s 4(2), Sch 1, para 11, subject to transitional provisions contained in the Companies Act 1989 (Commencement No 4 and Transitional and Saving Provisions) Order 1990, SI 1990/355. See the transitional provisions note preceding s 221 at **[356]**.

Paras 60–70: repealed by the Companies Act 1989, s 212, Sch 24.

(*Pt V outside the scope of this work; Pt VI repealed by the Companies 1989, s 212, Sch 24.*)

PART VII
INTERPRETATION OF SCHEDULE

76. The following paragraphs apply for the purposes of this Schedule and its interpretation.

[Financial instruments

76A. References to "derivatives" include commodity-based contracts that give either contracting party the right to settle in cash or in some other financial instrument, except when such contracts—

(a) were entered into for the purpose of, and continue to meet, the company's expected purchase, sale or usage requirements,

(b) were designated for such purpose at their inception, and

(c) are expected to be settled by delivery of the commodity.

76B.—(1) The expressions listed in sub-paragraph (2) have the same meaning as they have in Council Directive 78/660/EEC on the annual accounts of certain types of companies, as amended.

(2) Those expressions are "available for sale financial asset", "business combination", "commodity-based contracts", "derivative", "equity instrument", "exchange difference", "fair value hedge accounting system", "financial fixed asset", "financial instrument", "foreign entity", "hedge accounting", "hedge accounting system", "hedged items",

"hedging instrument", "held for trading purposes", "held to maturity", "monetary item", "receivables", "reliable market" and "trading portfolio".]

Historical cost accounting rules

77.–81. …

82. References to the historical cost accounting rules shall be read in accordance with paragraph 29.

[Investment property

82A "Investment property" means land held to earn rent or for capital appreciation.]

Leases

83.—(1) "Long lease" means a lease in the case of which the portion of the term for which it was granted remaining unexpired at the end of the financial year is not less than 50 years.

(2) "Short lease" means a lease which is not a long lease.

(3) "Lease" includes an agreement for a lease.

Listed investments

[84. "Listed investment" means an investment as respects which there has been granted a listing [on a recognised investment exchange other than an overseas investment exchange within the meaning of the Financial Services Act 1986 or on any stock exchange of repute outside Great Britain].

Loans

85. A loan is treated as falling due for repayment, and an instalment of a loan is treated as falling due for payment, on the earliest date on which the lender could require repayment or (as the case may be) payment, if he exercised all options and rights available to him.

Materiality

86. Amounts which in the particular context of any provision of this Schedule are not material may be disregarded for the purposes of that provision.

87. …

Provisions

88.—(1) References to provisions for depreciation or diminution in value of assets are to any amount written off by way of providing for depreciation or diminution in value of assets.

(2) Any reference in the profit and loss account formats set out in Part I of this Schedule to the depreciation of, or amounts written off, assets of any description is to any provision for depreciation or diminution in value of assets of that description.

89. References to [provisions for liabilities] are to any amount retained as reasonably necessary for the purpose of providing for any liability [the nature of which is clearly defined and] which is either likely to be incurred, or certain to be incurred but uncertain as to amount or as to the date on which it will arise.

90.–92. …

Scots land tenure

93. In the application of this Schedule to Scotland, "land of freehold tenure" means land in respect of which the company … is the owner; "land of leasehold tenure" means land of which the company is the tenant under a lease …

Staff costs

94.—(1) "Social security costs" means any contributions by the company to any state social security or pension scheme, fund or arrangement.

[(2) "Pension costs" includes any costs incurred by the company in respect of any pension scheme established for the purpose of providing pensions for persons currently or formerly employed by the company, any sums set aside for the future payment of pensions directly by the company to current or former employees and any pensions paid directly to such persons without having first been set aside.]

(3) Any amount stated in respect of [the item "social security costs"] or in respect of the item "wages and salaries" in the company's profit and loss account shall be determined by reference to payments made or costs incurred in respect of all persons employed by the company during the financial year who are taken into account in determining the relevant annual number for the purposes of [section 231A(1)(a)].

95. …

[563]

NOTES

Repealed as noted to s 1 at **[309]**.

Paras 76A, 76B, 82A: inserted by the Companies Act 1985 (International Accounting Standards and Other Accounting Amendments) Regulations 2004, SI 2004/2947, reg 14(1), Sch 2, paras 1, 10, 11, in relation to companies' financial years which begin on or after 1 January 2005.

Paras 77–81, 87, 90–92, 95: repealed by the Companies Act 1989, s 212, Sch 24.

Para 84: substituted by the Financial Services and Markets Act 2000 (Consequential Amendments and Repeals) Order 2001, SI 2001/3649, art 32.

Para 93: words omitted repealed by the Abolition of Feudal Tenure etc (Scotland) Act 2000, s 76(1), (2), Sch 12, Pt I, para 46(1), (5), Sch 13, Pt I.

Para 94: sub-para (2) and words in first pair of square brackets in sub-para (3) substituted by the Companies Act 1985 (Miscellaneous Accounting Amendments) Regulations 1996, SI 1996/189, regs 14(1), 16(1), Sch 1, paras 1, 16, in relation to any financial year ending on or after 2 February 1996; for a transitional provision see reg 16(2) of the 1996 Regulations; words in second pair of square brackets in sub-para (3) substituted by SI 2004/2947, reg 3, Sch 1, paras 1, 31(1), (4), in relation to companies' financial years which begin on or after 1 January 2005.

[SCHEDULE 4A
FORM AND CONTENT OF GROUP ACCOUNTS

Section 227

General rules

1.—(1) Group accounts shall comply so far as practicable with the [provisions of … Schedule 4 (form and content of company accounts)] as if the undertakings included in the consolidation ("the group") were a single company.

(2) …

(3) Where the parent company is treated as an investment company for the purposes of Part V of that Schedule (special provisions for investment companies) the group shall be similarly treated.

2.—(1) The consolidated balance sheet and profit and loss account shall incorporate in full the information contained in the individual accounts of the undertakings included in the consolidation, subject to the adjustments authorised or required by the following provisions of this Schedule and to such other adjustments (if any) as may be appropriate in accordance with generally accepted accounting principles or practice.

(2) If the financial year of a subsidiary undertaking included in the consolidation [does not end with that of the parent company], the group accounts shall be made up—

(a) from the accounts of the subsidiary undertaking for its financial year last ending before the end of the parent company's financial year, provided that year ended no more than three months before that of the parent company, or

(b) from interim accounts prepared by the subsidiary undertaking as at the end of the parent company's financial year.

3.—(1) Where assets and liabilities to be included in the group accounts have been valued or otherwise determined by undertakings according to accounting rules differing from those used for the group accounts, the values or amounts shall be adjusted so as to accord with the rules used for the group accounts.

(2) If it appears to the directors of the parent company that there are special reasons for departing from sub-paragraph (1) they may do so, but particulars of any such departure, the reasons for it and its effect shall be given in a note to the accounts.

(3) The adjustments referred to in this paragraph need not be made if they are not material for the purpose of giving a true and fair view.

4. Any differences of accounting rules as between a parent company's individual accounts for a financial year and its group accounts shall be disclosed in a note to the latter accounts and the reasons for the difference given.

5. Amounts which in the particular context of any provision of this Schedule are not material may be disregarded for the purposes of that provision.

Elimination of group transactions

6.—(1) Debts and claims between undertakings included in the consolidation, and income and expenditure relating to transactions between such undertakings, shall be eliminated in preparing the group accounts.

(2) Where profits and losses resulting from transactions between undertakings included in the consolidation are included in the book value of assets, they shall be eliminated in preparing the group accounts.

(3) The elimination required by sub-paragraph (2) may be effected in proportion to the group's interest in the shares of the undertakings.

(4) Sub-paragraphs (1) and (2) need not be complied with if the amounts concerned are not material for the purpose of giving a true and fair view.

Acquisition and merger accounting

7.—(1) The following provisions apply where an undertaking becomes a subsidiary undertaking of the parent company.

(2) That event is referred to in those provisions as an "acquisition", and references to the "undertaking acquired" shall be construed accordingly.

8. An acquisition shall be accounted for by the acquisition method of accounting unless the conditions for accounting for it as a merger are met and the merger method of accounting is adopted.

9.—(1) The acquisition method of accounting is as follows.

(2) The identifiable assets and liabilities of the undertaking acquired shall be included in the consolidated balance sheet at their fair values as at the date of acquisition.

In this paragraph the "identifiable" assets or liabilities of the undertaking acquired means the assets or liabilities which are capable of being disposed of or discharged separately, without disposing of a business of the undertaking.

(3) The income and expenditure of the undertaking acquired shall be brought into the group accounts only as from the date of the acquisition.

(4) There shall be set off against the acquisition cost of the interest in the shares of the undertaking held by the parent company and its subsidiary undertakings the interest of the parent company and its subsidiary undertakings in the adjusted capital and reserves of the undertaking acquired.

For this purpose—

"the acquisition cost" means the amount of any cash consideration and the fair value of any other consideration, together with such amount (if any) in respect of fees and other expenses of the acquisition as the company may determine, and

"the adjusted capital and reserves" of the undertaking acquired means its capital and reserves at the date of the acquisition after adjusting the identifiable assets and liabilities of the undertaking to fair values as at that date.

(5) The resulting amount if positive shall be treated as goodwill, and if negative as a negative consolidation difference.

10.—(1) The conditions for accounting for an acquisition as a merger are—

(a) that at least 90 per cent of the nominal value of the relevant shares in the undertaking acquired [(excluding any shares in the undertaking held as treasury shares)] is held by or on behalf of the parent company and its subsidiary undertakings,

(b) that the proportion referred to in paragraph (a) was attained pursuant to an arrangement providing for the issue of equity shares by the parent company or one or more of its subsidiary undertakings,

(c) that the fair value of any consideration other than the issue of equity shares given pursuant to the arrangement by the parent company and its subsidiary undertakings did not exceed 10 per cent of the nominal value of the equity shares issued, and

(d) that adoption of the merger method of accounting accords with generally accepted accounting principles or practice.

(2) The reference in sub-paragraph (1)(a) to the "relevant shares" in an undertaking acquired is to those carrying unrestricted rights to participate both in distributions and in the assets of the undertaking upon liquidation.

11.—(1) The merger method of accounting is as follows.

(2) The assets and liabilities of the undertaking acquired shall be brought into the group accounts at the figures at which they stand in the undertaking's accounts, subject to any adjustment authorised or required by this Schedule.

(3) The income and expenditure of the undertaking acquired shall be included in the group accounts for the entire financial year, including the period before the acquisition.

(4) The group accounts shall show corresponding amounts relating to the previous financial year as if the undertaking acquired had been included in the consolidation throughout that year.

(5) There shall be set off against the aggregate of—

(a) the appropriate amount in respect of qualifying shares issued by the parent company or its subsidiary undertakings in consideration for the acquisition of shares in the undertaking acquired, and

(b) the fair value of any other consideration for the acquisition of shares in the undertaking acquired, determined as at the date when those shares were acquired,

the nominal value of the issued share capital of the undertaking acquired held by the parent company and its subsidiary undertakings.

(6) The resulting amount shall be shown as an adjustment to the consolidated reserves.

(7) In sub-paragraph (5)(a) "qualifying shares" means—

(a) shares in relation to which section 131 (merger relief) applies, in respect of which the appropriate amount is the nominal value; or

(b) shares in relation to which section 132 (relief in respect of group reconstructions) applies, in respect of which the appropriate amount is the nominal value together with any minimum premium value within the meaning of that section.

12.—(1) Where a group is acquired, paragraphs 9 to 11 apply with the following adaptations.

(2) References to shares of the undertaking acquired shall be construed as references to shares of the parent undertaking of the group.

(3) Other references to the undertaking acquired shall be construed as references to the group; and references to the assets and liabilities, income and expenditure and capital and reserves of the undertaking acquired shall be construed as references to the assets and liabilities, income and expenditure and capital and reserves of the group after making the set-offs and other adjustments required by this Schedule in the case of group accounts.

13.—(1) The following information with respect to acquisitions taking place in the financial year shall be given in a note to the accounts.

(2) There shall be stated—

- *(a) the name of the undertaking acquired or, where a group was acquired, the name of the parent undertaking of that group, and*
- *(b) whether the acquisition has been accounted for by the acquisition or the merger method of accounting;*

and in relation to an acquisition which significantly affects the figures shown in the group accounts, the following further information shall be given.

(3) The composition and fair value of the consideration for the acquisition given by the parent company and its subsidiary undertakings shall be stated.

(4) …

(5) Where the acquisition method of accounting has been adopted, the book values immediately prior to the acquisition, and the fair values at the date of acquisition, of each class of assets and liabilities of the undertaking or group acquired shall be stated in tabular form, including a statement of the amount of any goodwill or negative consolidation difference arising on the acquisition, together with an explanation of any significant adjustments made.

(6) Where the merger method of accounting has been adopted, an explanation shall be given of any significant adjustments made in relation to the amounts of the assets and liabilities of the undertaking or group acquired, together with a statement of any resulting adjustment to the consolidated reserves (including the re-statement of opening consolidated reserves).

(7) In ascertaining for the purposes of sub-paragraph … , (5) or (6) the profit or loss of a group, the book values and fair values of assets and liabilities of a group or the amount of the assets and liabilities of a group, the set-offs and other adjustments required by this Schedule in the case of group accounts shall be made.

14.—(1) There shall also be stated in a note to the accounts the cumulative amount of goodwill resulting from acquisitions in that and earlier financial years which has been written off [otherwise than in the consolidated profit and loss account for that or any earlier financial year].

(2) That figure shall be shown net of any goodwill attributable to subsidiary undertakings or businesses disposed of prior to the balance sheet date.

15. Where during the financial year there has been a disposal of an undertaking or group which significantly affects the figures shown in the group accounts, there shall be stated in a note to the accounts—

- *(a) the name of that undertaking or, as the case may be, of the parent undertaking of that group, and*
- *(b) the extent to which the profit or loss shown in the group accounts is attributable to profit or loss of that undertaking or group.*

16. The information required by paragraph 13, 14 or 15 above need not be disclosed with respect to an undertaking which—

- *(a) is established under the law of a country outside the United Kingdom, or*
- *(b) carries on business outside the United Kingdom,*

if in the opinion of the directors of the parent company the disclosure would be seriously prejudicial to the business of that undertaking or to the business of the parent company or any of its subsidiary undertakings and the Secretary of State agrees that the information should not be disclosed.

Minority interests

17.—(1) The formats set out in Schedule 4 have effect in relation to group accounts with the following additions.

(2) In the Balance Sheet Formats a further item headed "Minority interests" shall be added—

(a) in Format 1, either after item J or at the end (after item K), and

(b) in Format 2, under the general heading "LIABILITIES", between items A and B;

and under that item shall be shown the amount of capital and reserves attributable to shares in subsidiary undertakings included in the consolidation held by or on behalf of persons other than the parent company and its subsidiary undertakings.

(3) In the Profit and Loss Account Formats a further item headed "Minority interests" shall be added—

(a) in Format 1, between items 14 and 15,

(b) in Format 2, between items 16 and 17,

(c) in Format 3, between items 7 and 8 in both sections A and B, and

(d) in Format 4, between items 9 and 10 in both sections A and B;

and under that item shall be shown the amount of any profit or loss on ordinary activities attributable to shares in subsidiary undertakings included in the consolidation held by or on behalf of persons other than the parent company and its subsidiary undertakings.

(4) In the Profit and Loss Account Formats a further item headed "Minority interests" shall be added—

(a) in Format 1, between items 18 and 19,

(b) in Format 2, between items 20 and 21,

(c) in Format 3, between items 9 and 10 in section A and between items 8 and 9 in section B, and

(d) in Format 4, between items 11 and 12 in section A and between items 10 and 11 in section B;

and under that item shall be shown the amount of any profit or loss on extraordinary activities attributable to shares in subsidiary undertakings included in the consolidation held by or on behalf of persons other than the parent company and its subsidiary undertakings.

(5) For the purposes of paragraph 3(3) and (4) of Schedule 4 (power to adapt or combine items)—

(a) the additional item required by sub-paragraph (2) above shall be treated as one to which a letter is assigned, and

(b) the additional items required by sub-paragraphs (3) and (4) above shall be treated as ones to which an Arabic number is assigned.

Interests in subsidiary undertakings excluded from consolidation

18. …

Joint ventures

19.—(1) Where an undertaking included in the consolidation manages another undertaking jointly with one or more undertakings not included in the consolidation, that other undertaking ("the joint venture") may, if it is not—

(a) a body corporate, or

(b) a subsidiary undertaking of the parent company,

be dealt with in the group accounts by the method of proportional consolidation.

(2) The provisions of [this Schedule] relating to the preparation of consolidated accounts apply, with any necessary modifications, to proportional consolidation under this paragraph.

Associated undertakings

20.—(1) An "associated undertaking" means an undertaking in which an undertaking included in the consolidation has a participating interest and over whose operating and financial policy it exercises a significant influence, and which is not—

(a) a subsidiary undertaking of the parent company, or

(*b*) *a joint venture dealt with in accordance with paragraph 19.*

(2) *Where an undertaking holds 20 per cent or more of the voting rights in another undertaking, it shall be presumed to exercise such an influence over it unless the contrary is shown.*

(3) *The voting rights in an undertaking means the rights conferred on shareholders in respect of their shares or, in the case of an undertaking not having a share capital, on members, to vote at general meetings of the undertaking on all, or substantially all, matters.*

(4) *The provisions of paragraphs 5 to 11 of Schedule 10A (rights to be taken into account and attribution of rights) apply in determining for the purposes of this paragraph whether an undertaking holds 20 per cent or more of the voting rights in another undertaking.*

21.—(1) The formats set out in Schedule 4 have effect in relation to group accounts with the following modifications.

(2) *In the Balance Sheet Formats the items headed "Participating interests", that is—*

(*a*) *in Format 1, item B.III.3, and*

(*b*) *in Format 2, item B.III.3 under the heading "ASSETS",*

shall be replaced by two items, "Interests in associated undertakings" and "Other participating interests".

(3) *In the Profit and Loss Account Formats, the items headed "Income from participating interests", that is—*

(*a*) *in Format 1, item 8,*

(*b*) *in Format 2, item 10,*

(*c*) *in Format 3, item B.4, and*

(*d*) *in Format 4, item B.6,*

shall be replaced by two items, "Income from interests in associated undertakings" and "Income from other participating interests".

22.—(1) The interest of an undertaking in an associated undertaking, and the amount of profit or loss attributable to such an interest, shall be shown by the equity method of accounting (including dealing with any goodwill arising in accordance with paragraphs 17 to 19 and 21 of Schedule 4).

(2) *Where the associated undertaking is itself a parent undertaking, the net assets and profits or losses to be taken into account are those of the parent and its subsidiary undertakings (after making any consolidation adjustments).*

(3) *The equity method of accounting need not be applied if the amounts in question are not material for the purpose of giving a true and fair view.]*

[564]

NOTES

Repealed as noted to s 1 at **[309]**.

Inserted by the Companies Act 1989, s 5(2), Sch 2, subject to transitional provisions contained in the Companies Act 1989 (Commencement No 4 and Transitional and Saving Provisions) Order 1990, SI 1990/355. See the transitional provisions note preceding s 221 at **[356]**.

Para 1: words in square brackets in sub-para (1) substituted by the Companies Act 1985 (Miscellaneous Accounting Amendments) Regulations 1996, SI 1996/189, regs 14(2), 16(1), Sch 2, paras 1, 2, in relation to any financial year ending on or after 2 February 1996, for a transitional provision, see reg 16(2) of the 1996 Regulations; words omitted from sub-para (1) repealed by the Companies (Audit, Investigations and Community Enterprise) Act 2004, ss 7(3), 64, Sch 8, as from 1 October 2005 (except in relation to the accounts of a company for a financial year beginning before that date, see the Companies (Audit, Investigations and Community Enterprise) Act 2004 (Commencement) and Companies Act 1989 (Commencement No 18) Order 2004, SI 2004/3322, art 3; sub-para (2) repealed, in relation to annual accounts approved by the board of directors on or after 1 March 1997, and to directors' and auditors' reports on such accounts, by the Companies Act 1985 (Accounts of Small and Medium-sized Companies and Minor Accounting Amendments) Regulations 1997, SI 1997/220, reg 7(10)(a), for a transitional provision see reg 1(4) of the 1997 Regulations.

Para 2: words in square brackets in sub-para (2) substituted by SI 1996/189, regs 14(2), 16(1), Sch 2, paras 1, 3, in relation to any financial year ending on or after 2 February 1996; for a transitional provision see reg 16(2) of the 1996 Regulations.

Para 10: words in square brackets inserted by the Companies (Acquisition of Own Shares) (Treasury Shares) Regulations 2003, SI 2003/1116, reg 4, Schedule, para 31, as from 31 December 2003.

Para 13: sub-para (4) and figure omitted from sub-para (7) repealed by SI 1996/189, regs 14(2), 16(1), Sch 2, paras 1, 4, in relation to any financial year ending on or after 2 February 1996; for a transitional provision see reg 16(2) of the 1996 Regulations.

Para 14: words in square brackets in sub-para (1) added by SI 1996/189, regs 14(2), 16(1), Sch 2, paras 1, 5, in relation to any financial year ending on or after 2 February 1996; for a transitional provision see reg 16(2) of the 1996.

Para 18: repealed by the Companies Act 1985 (International Accounting Standards and Other Accounting Amendments) Regulations 2004, SI 2004/2947, reg 15, Sch 7, Pt 1, paras 1, 10, in relation to companies' financial years which begin on or after 1 January 2005.

Para 19: words in square brackets in sub-para (2) substituted by SI 1997/220, reg 7(10)(b), in relation to annual accounts approved by the board of directors on or after 1 March 1997, and to directors' and auditors' reports on such accounts; for a transitional provision see reg 1(4) of the 1997 Regulations.

[SCHEDULE 5
DISCLOSURE OF INFORMATION: RELATED UNDERTAKINGS

Section 231

PART I
COMPANIES NOT REQUIRED TO PREPARE GROUP ACCOUNTS

Subsidiary undertakings

1.—(1) The following information shall be given where at the end of the financial year the company has subsidiary undertakings.

(2) The name of each subsidiary undertaking shall be stated.

(3) There shall be stated with respect to each subsidiary undertaking—
(a) if it is incorporated outside Great Britain, the country in which it is incorporated;
(b) …
(c) if it is unincorporated, the address of its principal place of business.

(4) The reason why the company is not required to prepare group accounts shall be stated.

(5) If the reason is that all the subsidiary undertakings of the company fall within the exclusions provided for in section 229, it shall be stated with respect to each subsidiary undertaking which of those exclusions applies.

Holdings in subsidiary undertakings

2.—(1) There shall be stated in relation to shares of each class held by the company in a subsidiary undertaking—
(a) the identity of the class, and
(b) the proportion of the nominal value of the shares of that class represented by those shares.

(2) The shares held by or on behalf of the company itself shall be distinguished from those attributed to the company which are held by or on behalf of a subsidiary undertaking.

Financial information about subsidiary undertakings

3.—(1) There shall be disclosed with respect to each subsidiary undertaking—
(a) the aggregate amount of its capital and reserves as at the end of its relevant financial year, and
(b) its profit or loss for that year.

(2) That information need not be given if the company is exempt by virtue of section 228 from the requirement to prepare group accounts (parent company included in accounts of larger group).

[(2A) That information need not be given if the company's investment in the subsidiary undertaking is included in the company's accounts by way of the equity method of valuation.]

(3) That information need not be given if—
(a) the subsidiary undertaking is not required by any provision of this Act to deliver a copy of its balance sheet for its relevant financial year and does not otherwise publish that balance sheet in Great Britain or elsewhere, and

(b) *the company's holding is less than 50 per cent of the nominal value of the shares in the undertaking.*

(4) *Information otherwise required by this paragraph need not be given if it is not material.*

(5) *For the purposes of this paragraph the "relevant financial year" of a subsidiary undertaking is—*

(a) *if its financial year ends with that of the company, that year, and*
(b) *if not, its financial year ending last before the end of the company's financial year.*

Financial years of subsidiary undertakings

[4. Where—

(a) *disclosure is made under paragraph 3(1) with respect to a subsidiary undertaking, and*
(b) *that undertaking's financial year does not end with that of the company,*

there shall be stated in relation to that undertaking the date on which its last financial year ended (last before the end of the company's financial year).]

Further information about subsidiary undertakings

5. …

Shares and debentures of company held by subsidiary undertakings

6.—(1) The number, description and amount of the shares in … the company held by or on behalf of its subsidiary undertakings shall be disclosed.

(2) Sub-paragraph (1) does not apply in relation to shares … in the case of which the subsidiary undertaking is concerned as personal representative or, subject as follows, as trustee.

(3) The exception for shares … in relation to which the subsidiary undertaking is concerned as trustee does not apply if the company, or any subsidiary undertaking of the company, is beneficially interested under the trust, otherwise than by way of security only for the purposes of a transaction entered into by it in the ordinary course of a business which includes the lending of money.

(4) Schedule 2 to this Act has effect for the interpretation of the reference in sub-paragraph (3) to a beneficial interest under a trust.

Significant holdings in undertakings other than subsidiary undertakings

7.—(1) The information required by paragraphs 8 and 9 shall be given where at the end of the financial year the company has a significant holding in an undertaking which is not a subsidiary undertaking of the company.

(2) A holding is significant for this purpose if—

(a) *it amounts to [20 per cent] or more of the nominal value of any class of shares in the undertaking, or*
(b) *the amount of the holding (as stated or included in the company's accounts) exceeds [one-fifth] of the amount (as so stated) of the company's assets.*

8.—(1) The name of the undertaking shall be stated.

(2) There shall be stated—

(a) *if the undertaking is incorporated outside Great Britain, the country in which it is incorporated;*
(b) …
(c) *if it is unincorporated, the address of its principal place of business.*

(3) There shall also be stated—

(a) *the identity of each class of shares in the undertaking held by the company, and (b)* *the proportion of the nominal value of the shares of that class represented by those shares.*

9.—(1) … there shall also be stated—

(a) the aggregate amount of the capital and reserves of the undertaking as at the end of its relevant financial year, and

(b) its profit or loss for that year.

(2) That information need not be given if—

(a) the company is exempt by virtue of section 228 from the requirement to prepare group accounts (parent company included in accounts of larger group), and

(b) the investment of the company in all undertakings in which it has such a holding as is mentioned in sub-paragraph (1) is shown, in aggregate, in the notes to the accounts by way of the equity method of valuation.

(3) That information need not be given in respect of an undertaking if—

(a) the undertaking is not required by any provision of this Act to deliver a copy of its balance sheet for its relevant financial year and does not otherwise publish that balance sheet in Great Britain or elsewhere, and

(b) the company's holding is less than 50 per cent of the nominal value of the shares in the undertaking.

(4) Information otherwise required by this paragraph need not be given if it is not material.

(5) For the purposes of this paragraph the "relevant financial year" of an undertaking is—

(a) if its financial year ends with that of the company, that year, and

(b) if not, its financial year ending last before the end of the company's financial year.

[Membership of certain undertakings

9A.—(1) The information required by this paragraph shall be given where at the end of the financial year the company is a member of a qualifying undertaking.

(2) There shall be stated—

(a) the name and legal form of the undertaking, and

(b) the address of the undertaking's registered office (whether in or outside Great Britain) or, if it does not have such an office, its head office (whether in or outside Great Britain).

(3) Where the undertaking is a qualifying partnership there shall also be stated either—

(a) that a copy of the latest accounts of the undertaking has been or is to be appended to the copy of the company's accounts sent to the registrar under section 242 of this Act, or

(b) the name of at least one body corporate (which may be the company) in whose group accounts the undertaking has been or is to be dealt with on a consolidated basis.

(4) Information otherwise required by sub-paragraph (2) above need not be given if it is not material.

(5) Information otherwise required by sub-paragraph (3)(b) above need not be given if the notes to the company's accounts disclose that advantage has been taken of the exemption conferred by regulation 7 of the Partnerships and Unlimited Companies (Accounts) Regulations 1993.

(6) In this paragraph—

"dealt with on a consolidated basis", "member", "qualifying company" and "qualifying partnership" have the same meanings as in the Partnerships and Unlimited Companies (Accounts) Regulations 1993;

"qualifying undertaking" means a qualifying partnership or a qualifying company.]

10. …

Parent undertaking drawing up accounts for larger group

11.—(1) Where the company is a subsidiary undertaking, the following information shall be given with respect to the parent undertaking of—

- (*a*) *the largest group of undertakings for which group accounts are drawn up and of which the company is a member, and*
- (*b*) *the smallest such group of undertakings.*

(2) The name of the parent undertaking shall be stated.

(3) There shall be stated—

- (*a*) *if the undertaking is incorporated outside Great Britain, the country in which it is incorporated;*
- (*b*) …
- (*c*) *if it is unincorporated, the address of its principal place of business.*

(4) If copies of the group accounts referred to in sub-paragraph (1) are available to the public, there shall also be stated the addresses from which copies of the accounts can be obtained.

Identification of ultimate parent company

12.—(1) Where the company is a subsidiary undertaking, the following information shall be given with respect to the company (if any) regarded by the directors as being the company's ultimate parent company.

(2) The name of that company shall be stated.

(3) If known to the directors, there shall be stated—

- (*a*) *if that company is incorporated outside Great Britain, the country in which it is incorporated;*
- (*b*) …

(4) In this paragraph "company" includes any body corporate.

Constructions of references to shares held by company

13.—(1) References in this Part of this Schedule to shares held by a company shall be construed as follows.

(2) For the purposes of [paragraphs 2 to 4] (information about subsidiary undertakings)—

- (*a*) *there shall be attributed to the company any shares held by a subsidiary undertaking, or by a person acting on behalf of the company or a subsidiary undertaking; but*
- (*b*) *there shall be treated as not held by the company any shares held on behalf of a person other than the company or a subsidiary undertaking.*

(3) For the purposes of paragraphs 7 to 9 (information about undertakings other than subsidiary undertakings)—

- (*a*) *there shall be attributed to the company shares held on its behalf by any person; but*
- (*b*) *there shall be treated as not held by a company shares held on behalf of a person other than the company.*

(4) For the purposes of any of those provisions, shares held by way of security shall be treated as held by the person providing the security—

- (*a*) *where apart from the right to exercise them for the purpose of preserving the value of the security, or of realising it, the rights attached to the shares are exercisable only in accordance with his instructions, and*
- (*b*) *where the shares are held in connection with the granting of loans as part of normal business activities and apart from the right to exercise them for the purpose of preserving the value of the security, or of realising it, the rights attached to the shares are exercisable only in his interests.]*

[565]

NOTES

Repealed as noted to s 1 at **[309]**.

Whole Schedule substituted by the Companies Act 1989, s 6(2), Sch 3, subject to transitional provisions contained in the Companies Act 1989 (Commencement No 4 and Transitional and Saving Provisions) Order 1990, SI 1990/355. See the transitional provisions note preceding s 221 at **[356]**.

Para 1: sub-para (3)(b) repealed by the Companies Act 1985 (Miscellaneous Accounting Amendments) Regulations 1996, SI 1996/189, regs 14(3), 16(1), Sch 3, paras 1, 2, in relation to any financial year ending on or after 2 February 1996; for a transitional provision see reg 16(2) of the 1996 Regulations.

Para 3: sub-para (2A) inserted by SI 1996/189, regs 14(3), 16(1), Sch 3, paras 1, 3, in relation to any financial year ending on or after 2 February 1996; for a transitional provision see reg 16(2) thereof.

Para 4: substituted by SI 1996/189, regs 14(3), 16(1), Sch 3, paras 1, 4, in relation to any financial year ending on or after 2 February 1996; for a transitional provision see reg 16(2) of the 1996 Regulations.

Para 5: repealed by SI 1996/189, regs 14(3), 16(1), Sch 3, paras 1, 5, in relation to any financial year ending on or after 2 February 1996; for a transitional provision see reg 16(2) of the 1996 Regulations.

Para 6: words omitted from sub-paras (1), (2), (3) repealed by SI 1996/189, regs 14(3), 16(1), Sch 3, paras 1, 6, in relation to any financial year ending on or after 2 February 1996; for a transitional provision see reg 16(2) of the 1996 Regulations.

Para 7: words in square brackets in sub-para (2) substituted by SI 1996/189, regs 14(3), 16(1), Sch 3, paras 1, 7, in relation to any financial year ending on or after 2 February 1996; for a transitional provision see reg 16(2) of the 1996 Regulations.

Para 8: sub-para (2)(b) repealed by SI 1996/189, regs 14(3), 16(1), Sch 3, paras 1, 8, in relation to any financial year ending on or after 2 February 1996; for a transitional provision see reg 16(2) of the 1996 Regulations.

Para 9: words omitted repealed by SI 1996/189, regs 14(3), 16(1), Sch 3, paras 1, 9, in relation to any financial year ending on or after 2 February 1996; for a transitional provision see reg 16(2) thereof.

Para 9A: inserted by the Partnerships and Unlimited Companies (Accounts) Regulations 1993, SI 1993/1820, reg 11(2), subject to transitional provisions in reg 12 thereof.

Para 10: repealed by SI 1996/189, regs 14(3), 16(1), Sch 3, paras 1, 10, in relation to any financial year ending on or after 2 February 1996; for a transitional provision see reg 16(2) of the 1996 Regulations.

Para 11: sub-para (3)(b) repealed by SI 1996/189, regs 14(3), 16(1), Sch 3, paras 1, 11, in relation to any financial year ending on or after 2 February 1996; for a transitional provision see reg 16(2) of the 1996 Regulations.

Para 12: sub-para (3)(b) repealed by SI 1996/189, regs 14(3), 16(1), Sch 3, paras 1, 12, in relation to any financial year ending on or after 2 February 1996; for a transitional provision see reg 16(2) of the 1996 Regulations.

Para 13: words in square brackets in sub-para (2) substituted by SI 1996/189, regs 14(3), 16(1), Sch 3, paras 1, 13, in relation to any financial year ending on or after 2 February 1996; for a transitional provision see reg 16(2) of the 1996 Regulations.

[PART II
COMPANIES REQUIRED TO PREPARE GROUP ACCOUNTS

Introductory

14. In this Part of this Schedule "the group" means the group consisting of the parent company and its subsidiary undertakings.

Subsidiary undertakings

15.—(1) The following information shall be given with respect to the undertakings which are subsidiary undertakings of the parent company at the end of the financial year.

(2) The name of each undertaking shall be stated.

(3) There shall be stated—

(a) if the undertaking is incorporated outside Great Britain, the country in which it is incorporated;

(b) …

(c) if it is unincorporated, the address of its principal place of business.

(4) It shall also be stated whether the subsidiary undertaking is included in the consolidation and, if it is not, the reasons for excluding it from consolidation shall be given.

(5) It shall be stated with respect to each subsidiary undertaking by virtue of which of the conditions specified in section 258(2) or (4) it is a subsidiary undertaking of its immediate parent undertaking.

That information need not be given if the relevant condition is that specified in subsection (2)(a) of that section (holding of a majority of the voting rights) and the immediate parent undertaking holds the same proportion of the shares in the undertaking as it holds voting rights.

Holdings in subsidiary undertakings

16.—(1) The following information shall be given with respect to the shares of a subsidiary undertaking held—

(a) by the parent company, and
(b) by the group;

and the information under paragraphs (a) and (b) shall (if different) be shown separately.

(2) There shall be stated—

(a) the identity of each class of shares held, and
(b) the proportion of the nominal value of the shares of that class represented by those shares.

Financial information about subsidiary undertakings not included in the consolidation

17.—(1) There shall be shown with respect to each subsidiary undertaking not included in the consolidation—

(a) the aggregate amount of its capital and reserves as at the end of its relevant financial year, and
(b) its profit or loss for that year.

(2) That information need not be given if the group's investment in the undertaking is included in the accounts by way of the equity method of valuation or if—

(a) the undertaking is not required by any provision of this Act to deliver a copy of its balance sheet for its relevant financial year and does not otherwise publish that balance sheet in Great Britain or elsewhere, and
(b) the holding of the group is less than 50 per cent of the nominal value of the shares in the undertaking.

(3) Information otherwise required by this paragraph need not be given if it is not material.

(4) For the purposes of this paragraph the "relevant financial year" of a subsidiary undertaking is—

(a) if its financial year ends with that of the company, that year, and
(b) if not, its financial year ending last before the end of the company's financial year.

18, 19. …

Shares and debentures of company held by subsidiary undertakings

20.—(1) The number, description and amount of the shares in … the company held by or on behalf of its subsidiary undertakings shall be disclosed.

(2) Sub-paragraph (1) does not apply in relation to shares … in the case of which the subsidiary undertaking is concerned as personal representative or, subject as follows, as trustee.

(3) The exception for shares … in relation to which the subsidiary undertaking is concerned as trustee does not apply if the company or any of its subsidiary undertakings is beneficially interested under the trust, otherwise than by way of security only for the purposes of a transaction entered into by it in the ordinary course of a business which includes the lending of money.

(4) Schedule 2 to this Act has effect for the interpretation of the reference in sub-paragraph (3) to a beneficial interest under a trust.

Joint ventures

21.—(1) The following information shall be given where an undertaking is dealt with in the consolidated accounts by the method of proportional consolidation in accordance with paragraph 19 of Schedule 4A (joint ventures)—
- *(a) the name of the undertaking;*
- *(b) the address of the principal place of business of the undertaking;*
- *(c) the factors on which joint management of the undertaking is based; and*
- *(d) the proportion of the capital of the undertaking held by undertakings included in the consolidation.*

(2) Where the financial year of the undertaking did not end with that of the company, there shall be stated the date on which a financial year of the undertaking last ended before that date.

Associated undertakings

22.—(1) The following information shall be given where an undertaking included in the consolidation has an interest in an associated undertaking.

(2) The name of the associated undertaking shall be stated.

(3) There shall be stated—
- *(a) if the undertaking is incorporated outside Great Britain, the country in which it is incorporated;*
- *(b) …*
- *(c) if it is unincorporated, the address of its principal place of business.*

(4) The following information shall be given with respect to the shares of the undertaking held—
- *(a) by the parent company, and*
- *(b) by the group;*

and the information under paragraphs (a) and (b) shall be shown separately.

(5) There shall be stated—
- *(a) the identity of each class of shares held, and*
- *(b) the proportion of the nominal value of the shares of that class represented by those shares.*

(6) In this paragraph "associated undertaking" has the meaning given by paragraph 20 of Schedule 4A; and the information required by this paragraph shall be given notwithstanding that paragraph 22(3) of that Schedule (materiality) applies in relation to the accounts themselves.

Other significant holdings of parent company or group

23.—(1) The information required by paragraphs 24 and 25 shall be given where at the end of the financial year the parent company has a significant holding in an undertaking which is not one of its subsidiary undertakings and does not fall within paragraph 21 (joint ventures) or paragraph 22 (associated undertakings).

(2) A holding is significant for this purpose if—
- *(a) it amounts to [20 per cent] or more of the nominal value of any class of shares in the undertaking, or*
- *(b) the amount of the holding (as stated or included in the company's individual accounts) exceeds [one-fifth] of the amount of its assets (as so stated).*

24.—(1) The name of the undertaking shall be stated.

(2) There shall be stated—
- *(a) if the undertaking is incorporated outside Great Britain, the country in which it is incorporated;*
- *(b) …*
- *(c) if it is unincorporated, the address of its principal place of business.*

(3) The following information shall be given with respect to the shares of the undertaking held by the parent company.

(4) There shall be stated—
(a) the identity of each class of shares held, and
(b) the proportion of the nominal value of the shares of that class represented by those shares.

25.—(1) ... there shall also be stated—
(a) the aggregate amount of the capital and reserves of the undertaking as at the end of its relevant financial year, and
(b) its profit or loss for that year.

(2) That information need not be given in respect of an undertaking if—
(a) the undertaking is not required by any provision of this Act to deliver a copy of its balance sheet for its relevant financial year and does not otherwise publish that balance sheet in Great Britain or elsewhere, and
(b) the company's holding is less than 50 per cent of the nominal value of the shares in the undertaking.

(3) Information otherwise required by this paragraph need not be given if it is not material.

(4) For the purposes of this paragraph the "relevant financial year" of an undertaking is—
(a) if its financial year ends with that of the company, that year, and
(b) if not, its financial year ending last before the end of the company's financial year.

26.—(1) The information required by paragraphs 27 and 28 shall be given where at the end of the financial year the group has a significant holding in an undertaking which is not a subsidiary undertaking of the parent company and does not fall within paragraph 21 (joint ventures) or paragraph 22 (associated undertakings).

(2) A holding is significant for this purpose if—
(a) it amounts to [20 per cent] or more of the nominal value of any class of shares in the undertaking, or
(b) the amount of the holding (as stated or included in the group accounts) exceeds [one-fifth] of the amount of the group's assets (as so stated).

27.—(1) The name of the undertaking shall be stated.

(2) There shall be stated—
(a) if the undertaking is incorporated outside Great Britain, the country in which it is incorporated;
(b) ...
(c) if it is unincorporated, the address of its principal place of business.

(3) The following information shall be given with respect to the shares of the undertaking held by the group.

(4) There shall be stated—
(a) the identity of each class of shares held, and
(b) the proportion of the nominal value of the shares of that class represented by those shares.

28.—(1) ... there shall also be stated—
(a) the aggregate amount of the capital and reserves of the undertaking as at the end of its relevant financial year, and
(b) its profit or loss for that year.

(2) That information need not be given if—
(a) the undertaking is not required by any provision of this Act to deliver a copy of its balance sheet for its relevant financial year and does not otherwise publish that balance sheet in Great Britain or elsewhere, and
(b) the holding of the group is less than 50 per cent of the nominal value of the shares in the undertaking.

(3) Information otherwise required by this paragraph need not be given if it is not material.

(4) For the purposes of this paragraph the "relevant financial year" of an outside undertaking is—
(a) if its financial year ends with that of the parent company, that year, and

(*b*) *if not, its financial year ending last before the end of the parent company's financial year.*

[Parent company's or group's membership of certain undertakings

28A.—(1) The information required by this paragraph shall be given where at the end of the financial year the parent company or group is a member of a qualifying undertaking.

(2) There shall be stated—

(*a*) *the name and legal form of the undertaking, and*

(*b*) *the address of the undertaking's registered office (whether in or outside Great Britain) or, if it does not have such an office, its head office (whether in or outside Great Britain).*

(3) Where the undertaking is a qualifying partnership there shall also be stated either—

(*a*) *that a copy of the latest accounts of the undertaking has been or is to be appended to the copy of the company's accounts sent to the registrar under section 242 of this Act, or*

(*b*) *the name of at least one body corporate (which may be the company) in whose group accounts the undertaking has been or is to be dealt with on a consolidated basis.*

(4) Information otherwise required by sub-paragraph (2) above need not be given if it is not material.

(5) Information otherwise required by sub-paragraph (3)(b) above need not be given if the notes to the company's accounts disclose that advantage has been taken of the exemption conferred by regulation 7 of the Partnerships and Unlimited Companies (Accounts) Regulations 1993.

(6) In this paragraph—

"dealt with on a consolidated basis", "member", "qualifying company" and "qualifying partnership" have the same meanings as in the Partnerships and Unlimited Companies (Accounts) Regulations 1993;

"qualifying undertaking" means a qualifying partnership or a qualifying company.]

29. …

Parent undertaking drawing up accounts for larger group

30.—(1) Where the parent company is itself a subsidiary undertaking, the following information shall be given with respect to that parent undertaking of the company which heads—

(*a*) *the largest group of undertakings for which group accounts are drawn up and of which that company is a member, and*

(*b*) *the smallest such group of undertakings.*

(2) The name of the parent undertaking shall be stated.

(3) There shall be stated—

(*a*) *if the undertaking is incorporated outside Great Britain, the country in which it is incorporated;*

(*b*) …

(*c*) *if it is unincorporated, the address of its principal place of business.*

(4) If copies of the group accounts referred to in sub-paragraph (1) are available to the public, there shall also be stated the addresses from which copies of the accounts can be obtained.

Identification of ultimate parent company

31.—(1) Where the parent company is itself a subsidiary undertaking, the following information shall be given with respect to the company (if any) regarded by the directors as being that company's ultimate parent company.

(2) The name of that company shall be stated.

(3) If known to the directors, there shall be stated—

(a) if that company is incorporated outside Great Britain, the country in which it is incorporated;

(b) …

(4) In this paragraph "company" includes any body corporate.

Construction of references to shares held by parent company or group

32.—(1) References in this Part of this Schedule to shares held by the parent company or the group shall be construed as follows.

(2) For the purposes of paragraphs 16, 22(4) and (5) and 23 to 25 (information about holdings in subsidiary and other undertakings)—

(a) there shall be attributed to the parent company shares held on its behalf by any person; but

(b) there shall be treated as not held by the parent company shares held on behalf of a person other than the company.

(3) References to shares held by the group are to any shares held by or on behalf of the parent company or any of its subsidiary undertakings; but there shall be treated as not held by the group any shares held on behalf of a person other than the parent company or any of its subsidiary undertakings.

(4) Shares held by way of security shall be treated as held by the person providing the security—

(a) where apart from the right to exercise them for the purpose of preserving the value of the security, or of realising it, the rights attached to the shares are exercisable only in accordance with his instructions, and

(b) where the shares are held in connection with the granting of loans as part of normal business activities and apart from the right to exercise them for the purpose of preserving the value of the security, or of realising it, the rights attached to the shares are exercisable only in his interests.]

[566]

NOTES

Repealed as noted to s 1 at **[309]**.

Substituted as noted to Pt I of this Schedule at **[565]**.

Para 15: sub-para (3)(b) repealed by the Companies Act 1985 (Miscellaneous Accounting Amendments) Regulations 1996, SI 1996/189, regs 14(3), 16(1), Sch 3, paras 1, 14, in relation to any financial year ending on or after 2 February 1996; for a transitional provision see reg 16(2) of the 1996 Regulations.

Paras 18, 19: repealed by SI 1996/189, regs 14(3), 16(1), Sch 3, paras 1, 15, 16, in relation to any financial year ending on or after 2 February 1996; for a transitional provision see reg 16(2) of the 1996 Regulations.

Para 20: words omitted in sub-paras (1), (2), (3) repealed by SI 1996/189, regs 14(3), 16(1), Sch 3, paras 1, 17, in relation to any financial year ending on or after 2 February 1996; for a transitional provision see reg 16(2) of the 1996 Regulations.

Para 22: sub-para (3)(b) repealed by SI 1996/189, regs 14(3), 16(1), Sch 3, paras 1, 18, in relation to any financial year ending on or after 2 February 1996; for a transitional provision see reg 16(2) of the 1996 Regulations.

Para 23: words in square brackets in sub-para (2) substituted by SI 1996/189, regs 14(3), 16(1), Sch 3, paras 1, 19, in relation to any financial year ending on or after 2 February 1996; for a transitional provision see reg 16(2) of the 1996 Regulations.

Para 24: sub-para (2)(b) repealed by SI 1996/189, regs 14(3), 16(1), Sch 3, paras 1, 20, in relation to any financial year ending on or after 2 February 1996; for a transitional provision see reg 16(2) of the 1996 Regulations.

Para 25: words omitted in sub-para (1) repealed by SI 1996/189, regs 14(3), 16(1), Sch 3, paras 1, 21, in relation to any financial year ending on or after 2 February 1996; for a transitional provision see reg 16(2) of the 1996 Regulations.

Para 26: words in square brackets in sub-para (2) substituted by SI 1996/189, regs 14(3), 16(1), Sch 3, paras 1, 19, in relation to any financial year ending on or after 2 February 1996; for a transitional provision see reg 16(2) of the 1996 Regulations.

Para 27: sub-para (2)(b) repealed by SI 1996/189, regs 14(3), 16(1), Sch 3, paras 1, 22, in relation to any financial year ending on or after 2 February 1996; for a transitional provision see reg 16(2) of the 1996 Regulations.

Para 28: words omitted from sub-para (1) repealed by SI 1996/189, regs 14(3), 16(1), Sch 3, paras 1, 21, in relation to any financial year ending on or after 2 February 1996; for a transitional provision see reg 16(2) of the 1996 Regulations.

Para 28A: inserted by the Partnerships and Unlimited Companies (Accounts) Regulations 1993, SI 1993/1820, reg 11(3), subject to transitional provisions in reg 12 thereof.

Para 29: repealed by SI 1996/189, regs 14(3), 16(1), Sch 3, paras 1, 23, in relation to any financial year ending on or after 2 February 1996; for a transitional provision see reg 16(2) of the 1996 Regulations.

Para 30: sub-para (3)(b) repealed by SI 1996/189, regs 14(3), 16(1), Sch 3, paras 1, 24, in relation to any financial year ending on or after 2 February 1996; for a transitional provision see reg 16(2) of the 1996 Regulations.

Para 31: sub-para (3)(b) repealed by SI 1996/189, regs 14(3), 16(1), Sch 3, paras 1, 25, in relation to any financial year ending on or after 2 February 1996; for a transitional provision see reg 16(2) of the 1996 Regulations.

SCHEDULE 6
[DISCLOSURE OF INFORMATION: EMOLUMENTS AND OTHER BENEFITS OF DIRECTORS AND OTHERS]

Section 232

(Pt I outside the scope of this work.)

[PART II
LOANS, QUASI-LOANS AND OTHER DEALINGS IN FAVOUR OF DIRECTORS]

[15]. [The group accounts of a holding company, or if it is not required to prepare group accounts its individual accounts,] shall contain the particulars required by this Schedule of—

(*a*) *any transaction or arrangement of a kind described in section 330 entered into by the company or by a subsidiary of the company for a person who at any time during the financial year was a director of the company or its holding company, or was connected with such a director;*

(*b*) *an agreement by the company or by a subsidiary of the company to enter into any such transaction or arrangement for a person who was at any time during the financial year a director of the company or its holding company, or was connected with such a director; and*

(*c*) *any other transaction or arrangement with the company or a subsidiary of it in which a person who at any time during the financial year was a director of the company or its holding company had, directly or indirectly, a material interest.*

[16]. The accounts prepared by a company other than a holding company shall contain the particulars required by this Schedule of—

(*a*) *any transaction or arrangement of a kind described in section 330 entered into by the company for a person who at any time during the financial year was a director of it or of its holding company or was connected with such a director;*

(*b*) *an agreement by the company to enter into any such transaction or arrangement for a person who at any time during the financial year was a director of the company or its holding company or was connected with such a director; and*

(*c*) *any other transaction or arrangement with the company in which a person who at any time during the financial year was a director of the company or of its holding company had, directly or indirectly, a material interest.*

[17].—(1) For purposes of paragraphs [15](c) and [16](c), a transaction or arrangement between a company and a director of it or of its holding company, or a person connected with such a director, is to be treated (if it would not otherwise be so) as a transaction, arrangement or agreement in which that director is interested.

(2) An interest in such a transaction or arrangement is not "material" for purposes of those sub-paragraphs if in the board's opinion it is not so; but this is without prejudice to the question whether or not such an interest is material in a case where the board have not considered the matter.

"The board" here means the directors of the company preparing the accounts, or a majority of those directors, but excluding in either case the director whose interest it is.

.....

[18]. Paragraphs [15] and [16] do not apply in relation to the following transactions, arrangements and agreements—

(*a*) *a transaction, arrangement or agreement between one company and another in which a director of the former or of its subsidiary or holding company is interested only by virtue of his being a director of the latter;*

(*b*) *a contract of service between a company and one of its directors or a director of its holding company, or between a director of a company and any of that company's subsidiaries;*

(*c*) *a transaction, arrangement or agreement which was not entered into during the financial year and which did not subsist at any time during that year.*

[19]. Paragraphs [15] and [16] apply whether or not—

(*a*) *the transaction or arrangement was prohibited by section 330;*

(*b*) *the person for whom it was made was a director of the company or was connected with a director of it at the time it was made;*

(*c*) *in the case of a transaction or arrangement made by a company which at any time during a financial year is a subsidiary of another company, it was a subsidiary of that other company at the time the transaction or arrangement was made.*

[20]. Neither paragraph [15](c) nor paragraph [16](c) applies in relation to any transaction or arrangement if—

(*a*) *each party to the transaction or arrangement which is a member of the same group of companies (meaning a holding company and its subsidiaries) as the company entered into the transaction or arrangement in the ordinary course of business, and*

(*b*) *the terms of the transaction or arrangement are not less favourable to any such party than it would be reasonable to expect if the interest mentioned in that sub-paragraph had not been an interest of a person who was a director of the company or of its holding company.*

[21]. Neither paragraph [15](c) nor paragraph [16](c) applies in relation to any transaction or arrangement if—

(*a*) *the company is a member of a group of companies (meaning a holding company and its subsidiaries), and*

(*b*) *either the company is a wholly-owned subsidiary or no body corporate (other than the company or a subsidiary of the company) which is a member of the group of companies which includes the company's ultimate holding company was a party to the transaction or arrangement, and*

(*c*) *the director in question was at some time during the relevant period associated with the company, and*

(*d*) *the material interest of the director in question in the transaction or arrangement would not have arisen if he had not been associated with the company at any time during the relevant period.*

The particulars required by this Part

[22].—(1) Subject to the next paragraph, the particulars required by this Part are those of the principal terms of the transaction, arrangement or agreement.

(2) *Without prejudice to the generality of sub-paragraph (1), the following particulars are required—*

(*a*) *a statement of the fact either that the transaction, arrangement or agreement was made or subsisted (as the case may be) during the financial year;*

(*b*) *the name of the person for whom it was made and, where that person is or was connected with a director of the company or of its holding company, the name of that director;*

(*c*) *in a case where paragraph [15](c) or [16](c) applies, the name of the director with the material interest and the nature of that interest;*

(*d*) *in the case of a loan or an agreement for a loan or an arrangement within section 330(6) or (7) of this Act relating to a loan—*

(*i*) *the amount of the liability of the person to whom the loan was or was agreed to be made, in respect of principal and interest, at the beginning and at the end of the financial year;*

(*ii*) *the maximum amount of that liability during that year;*

(*iii*) *the amount of any interest which, having fallen due, has not been paid; and*

(*iv*) *the amount of any provision (within the meaning of Schedule 4 to this Act) made in respect of any failure or anticipated failure by the borrower to repay the whole or part of the loan or to pay the whole or part of any interest on it;*

(*e*) *in the case of a guarantee or security or an arrangement within section 330(6) relating to a guarantee or security—*

(i) the amount for which the company (or its subsidiary) was liable under the guarantee or in respect of the security both at the beginning and at the end of the financial year;

(ii) the maximum amount for which the company (or its subsidiary) may become so liable; and

(iii) any amount paid and any liability incurred by the company (or its subsidiary) for the purpose of fulfilling the guarantee or discharging the security (including any loss incurred by reason of the enforcement of the guarantee or security); and

(f) in the case of any transaction, arrangement or agreement other than those mentioned in sub-paragraphs (d) and (e), the value of the transaction or arrangement or (as the case may be) the value of the transaction or arrangement to which the agreement relates.

[23]. In paragraph [22](2) above, sub-paragraphs (c) to (f) do not apply in the case of a loan or quasi-loan made or agreed to be made by a company to or for a body corporate which is either—

(a) a body corporate of which that company is a wholly-owned subsidiary, or

(b) a wholly-owned subsidiary of a body corporate of which that company is a wholly-owned subsidiary, or

(c) a wholly-owned subsidiary of that company,

if particulars of that loan, quasi-loan or agreement for it would not have been required to be included in that company's annual accounts if the first-mentioned body corporate had not been associated with a director of that company at any time during the relevant period.

[Excluded transactions]

[24].—(1) In relation to a company's accounts for a financial year, compliance with this Part is not required in the case of transactions of a kind mentioned in the following sub-paragraph which are made by the company or a subsidiary of it for a person who at any time during that financial year was a director of the company or of its holding company, or was connected with such a director, if the aggregate of the values of each transaction, arrangement or agreement so made for that director or any person connected with him, less the amount (if any) by which the liabilities of the person for whom the transaction or arrangement was made has been reduced, did not at any time during the financial year exceed £5,000.

(2) The transactions in question are—

(a) credit transactions,

(b) guarantees provided or securities entered into in connection with credit transactions,

(c) arrangements within subsection (6) or (7) of section 330 relating to credit transactions,

(d) agreements to enter into credit transactions.

[25]. In relation to a company's accounts for a financial year, compliance with this Part is not required by virtue of paragraph [15](c) or [16](c) in the case of any transaction or arrangement with a company or any of its subsidiaries in which a director of the company or its holding company had, directly or indirectly, a material interest if—

(a) the value of each transaction or arrangement within paragraph [15](c) or [16](c) (as the case may be) in which that director had (directly or indirectly) a material interest and which was made after the commencement of the financial year with the company or any of its subsidiaries, and

(b) the value of each such transaction or arrangement which was made before the commencement of the financial year less the amount (if any) by which the liabilities of the person for whom the transaction or arrangement was made have been reduced,

did not at any time during the financial year exceed in the aggregate £1,000 or, if more, did not exceed £5,000 or 1 per cent of the value of the net assets of the company preparing the accounts in question as at the end of the financial year, whichever is the less.

For this purpose a company's net assets are the aggregate of its assets, less the aggregate of its liabilities ("liabilities" to include any [provisions for liabilities] within paragraph 89 of Schedule 4 [that is made in Companies Act accounts and any provision that is made in IAS accounts]).

[26]. Section 345 of this Act (power of Secretary of State to alter sums by statutory instrument subject to negative resolution in Parliament) applies as if the money sums specified in paragraph [24] or [25] above were specified in Part X.

Interpretation

[27].—[(1)] The following provisions of this Act apply for purposes of this Part of this Schedule—

(*a*) *section 331(2), ... and (7), as regards the meaning of "guarantee", ... and "credit transaction";*

(*b*) *section 331(9), as to the interpretation of references to a transaction or arrangement being made "for" a person;*

(*c*) *section 340, in assigning values to transactions and arrangements, and*

(*d*) *section 346, as to the interpretation of references to a person being "connected with" a director of a company.*

[(2) In this Part of this Schedule "director" includes a shadow director.]

[567]

NOTES

Repealed as noted to s 1 at **[309]**.

Heading to this Part of this Schedule (renumbered Pt II) substituted, paragraphs of this Part renumbered 15–27 and internal cross-references accordingly renumbered, para 4 (as originally numbered) repealed, words in square brackets in para 15 (as renumbered) and heading preceding para 24 (as renumbered) substituted, and the original para 27 (as renumbered) renumbered para 27(1), and para 27(2) inserted, by the Companies Act 1989, s 6(4), Sch 4, paras 1, 4, 5, subject to transitional provisions contained in the Companies Act 1989 (Commencement No 4 and Transitional and Saving Provisions) Order 1990, SI 1990/355. See the transitional provisions note preceding s 221 at **[356]**.

Para 25: words in first pair of square brackets substituted, and words in second pair of square brackets inserted, by the Companies Act 1985 (International Accounting Standards and Other Accounting Amendments) Regulations 2004, SI 2004/2947, regs 3, 15, Sch 1, paras 1, 32, Sch 7, Pt 1, paras 1, 11, in relation to companies' financial years which begin on or after 1 January 2005.

Para 27: words omitted from sub-para (1) (as renumbered) repealed by the Banking Act 1987, s 108(2), Sch 7, Pt I.

[PART III
OTHER TRANSACTIONS, ARRANGEMENTS AND AGREEMENTS]

[28]. This Part of this Schedule applies in relation to the following classes of transactions, arrangements and agreements—

(*a*) *loans, guarantees and securities relating to loans, arrangements of a kind described in subsection (6) or (7) of section 330 of this Act relating to loans and agreements to enter into any of the foregoing transactions and arrangements;*

(*b*) *quasi-loans, guarantees and securities relating to quasi-loans, arrangements of a kind described in either of those subsections relating to quasi-loans and agreements to enter into any of the foregoing transactions and arrangements;*

(*c*) *credit transactions, guarantees and securities relating to credit transactions, arrangements of a kind described in either of those subsections relating to credit transactions and agreements to enter into any of the foregoing transactions and arrangements.*

[29].—(1) To comply with this Part of this Schedule, the accounts must contain a statement, in relation to transactions, arrangements and agreements [made by the company or a subsidiary of it for persons who at any time during the financial year were officers of the company (but not directors or shadow directors)], of—

(*a*) *the aggregate amounts outstanding at the end of the financial year under transactions, arrangements and agreements within sub-paragraphs (a), (b) and (c) respectively of paragraph [28] above, and*

(*b*) *the numbers of officers for whom the transactions, arrangements and agreements falling within each of those sub-paragraphs were made.*

(2) This paragraph does not apply to transactions, arrangements and agreements made by the company or any of its subsidiaries for an officer of the company if the aggregate amount outstanding at the end of the financial year under the transactions, arrangements and agreements so made for that officer does not exceed £2,500.

(3) Section 345 of this Act (power of Secretary of State to alter money sums by statutory instrument subject to negative resolution in Parliament) applies as if the money sum specified above in this paragraph were specified in Part X.

[30]. The following provisions of this Act apply for purposes of this Part—

- *(a) section 331(2), (3), ... and (7), as regards the meaning of "guarantee", "quasi-loan", ... and "credit transaction", and*
- *(b) section 331(9), as to the interpretation of references to a transaction or arrangement being made "for" a person;*

and "amount outstanding" means the amount of the outstanding liabilities of the person for whom the transaction, arrangement or agreement was made or, in the case of a guarantee or security, the amount guaranteed or secured.

[568]

NOTES

Repealed as noted to s 1 at **[309]**.

Heading to this Part of this Schedule (renumbered Pt III) substituted, paragraphs of this Part renumbered 28–30 and internal cross-references accordingly renumbered, words in square brackets in para 29 (as renumbered) substituted, and original Pt III of this Schedule repealed, by the Companies Act 1989, s 6(4), Sch 4, paras 1, 6, 7, subject to transitional provisions contained in the Companies Act 1989 (Commencement No 4 and Transitional and Saving Provisions) Order 1990, SI 1990/355. See the transitional provisions note preceding s 221 at **[356]**.

Para 30: words omitted from sub-para (a) (as renumbered) repealed by the Banking Act 1987, s 108(2), Sch 7, Pt I.

SCHEDULE 7
MATTERS TO BE DEALT WITH IN DIRECTORS' REPORT

Section 234

PART I
MATTERS OF A GENERAL NATURE

Asset values

1.—(1) ...

(2) If, in the case of [such of the fixed assets of the company ...] as consist in interests in land, their market value (as at the end of the financial year) differs substantially from the amount at which they are included in the balance sheet, and the difference is, in the directors' opinion, of such significance as to require that the attention of members of the company or of holders of its debentures should be drawn to it, the report shall indicate the difference with such degree of precision as is practicable.

[(3) In relation to a group directors' report sub-paragraph (2) has effect as if the reference to the fixed assets of the company was a reference to the fixed assets of the company and of its subsidiary undertakings included in the consolidation.]

Directors' interests

[2.—(1) The information required by paragraphs 2A and 2B shall be given in the directors' report, or by way of notes to the company's annual accounts, with respect to each person who at the end of the financial year was a director of the company.

(2) In those paragraphs—

- *(a) "the register" means the register of directors' interests kept by the company under section 325; and*
- *(b) references to a body corporate being in the same group as the company are to its being a subsidiary or holding company, or another subsidiary of a holding company, of the company.*

2A.—(1) It shall be stated with respect to each director whether, according to the register, he was at the end of the financial year interested in shares in or debentures of the company or any other body corporate in the same group.

(2) If he was so interested, there shall be stated the number of shares in and amount of debentures of each body (specifying it) in which, according to the register, he was then interested.

(3) If a director was interested at the end of the financial year in shares in or debentures of the company or any other body corporate in the same group—

(a) it shall also be stated whether, according to the register, he was at the beginning of the financial year (or, if he was not then a director, when he became one) interested in shares in or debentures of the company or any other body corporate in the same group, and

(b) if he was so interested, there shall be stated the number of shares in and amount of debentures of each body (specifying it) in which, according to the register, he was then interested.

(4) In this paragraph references to an interest in shares or debentures have the same meaning as in section 324; and references to the interest of a director include any interest falling to be treated as his for the purposes of that section.

(5) The reference above to the time when a person became a director is, in the case of a person who became a director on more than one occasion, to the time when he first became a director.

2B.—(1) It shall be stated with respect to each director whether, according to the register, any right to subscribe for shares in or debentures of the company or another body corporate in the same group was during the financial year granted to, or exercised by, the director or a member of his immediate family.

(2) If any such right was granted to, or exercised by, any such person during the financial year, there shall be stated the number of shares in and amount of debentures of each body (specifying it) in respect of which, according to the register, the right was granted or exercised.

(3) A director's "immediate family" means his or her spouse [or civil partner] and infant children; and for this purpose "children" includes step-children, and "infant", in relation to Scotland, means pupil or minor.

(4) The reference above to a member of the director's immediate family does not include a person who is himself or herself a director of the company.]

[Political donations and expenditure

3.—(1) If—

(a) the company (not being the wholly-owned subsidiary of a company incorporated in Great Britain) has in the financial year—

(i) made any donation to any registered party or to any other EU political organisation, or

(ii) incurred any EU political expenditure, and

(b) the amount of the donation or expenditure, or (as the case may be) the aggregate amount of all donations and expenditure falling within paragraph (a), exceeded £200,

the directors' report for the year shall contain the particulars specified in sub-paragraph (2).

(2) Those particulars are—

(a) as respects donations falling within sub-paragraph (1)(a)(i)—

(i) the name of each registered party or other organisation to whom any such donation has been made, and

(ii) the total amount given to that party or organisation by way of such donations in the financial year; and

(b) as respects expenditure falling within sub-paragraph (1)(a)(ii), the total amount incurred by way of such expenditure in the financial year.

(3) If—

(a) at the end of the financial year the company has subsidiaries which have, in that year, made any donations or incurred any such expenditure as is mentioned in sub-paragraph (1)(a), and

(b) it is not itself the wholly-owned subsidiary of a company incorporated in Great Britain,

the directors' report for the year is not, by virtue of sub-paragraph (1), required to contain the particulars specified in sub-paragraph (2); but, if the total amount of any such donations or expenditure (or both) made or incurred in that year by the company and the subsidiaries between them exceeds £200, the directors' report for the year shall contain those particulars in relation to each body by whom any such donation or expenditure has been made or incurred.

(4) Any expression used in this paragraph which is also used in Part XA of this Act has the same meaning as in that Part.

4.—(1) If the company (not being the wholly-owned subsidiary of a company incorporated in Great Britain) has in the financial year made any contribution to a non-EU political party, the directors' report for the year shall contain—

(a) a statement of the amount of the contribution, or

(b) (if it has made two or more such contributions in the year) a statement of the total amount of the contributions.

(2) If—

(a) at the end of the financial year the company has subsidiaries which have, in that year, made any such contributions as are mentioned in sub-paragraph (1), and

(b) it is not itself the wholly-owned subsidiary of a company incorporated in Great Britain,

the directors' report for the year is not, by virtue of sub-paragraph (1), required to contain any such statement as is there mentioned, but it shall instead contain a statement of the total amount of the contributions made in the year by the company and the subsidiaries between them.

(3) In this paragraph "contribution", in relation to an organisation, means—

(a) any gift of money to the organisation (whether made directly or indirectly);

(b) any subscription or other fee paid for affiliation to, or membership of, the organisation; or

(c) any money spent (otherwise than by the organisation or a person acting on its behalf) in paying any expenses incurred directly or indirectly by the organisation.

(4) In this paragraph "non-EU political party" means any political party which carries on, or proposes to carry on, its activities wholly outside the member States.

Charitable donations

5.—(1) If—

(a) the company (not being the wholly-owned subsidiary of a company incorporated in Great Britain) has in the financial year given money for charitable purposes, and

(b) the money given exceeded £200 in amount,

the directors' report for the year shall contain, in the case of each of the purposes for which money has been given, a statement of the amount of money given for that purpose.

(2) If—

(a) at the end of the financial year the company has subsidiaries which have, in that year, given money for charitable purposes, and

(b) it is not itself the wholly-owned subsidiary of a company incorporated in Great Britain,

sub-paragraph (1) does not apply to the company; but, if the amount given in that year for charitable purposes by the company and the subsidiaries between them exceeds £200, the directors' report for the year shall contain, in the case of each of the purposes for which money has been given by the company and the subsidiaries between them, a statement of the amount of money given for that purpose.

(3) Money given for charitable purposes to a person who, when it was given, was ordinarily resident outside the United Kingdom is to be left out of account for the purposes of this paragraph.

(4) For the purposes of this paragraph "charitable purposes" means purposes which are exclusively charitable, and as respects Scotland [a purpose is charitable if it is listed in section 7(2) of the Charities and Trustee Investment (Scotland) Act 2005].]

[Financial instruments

5A.—(1) In relation to the use of financial instruments by a company ... the directors' report must contain an indication of—

(*a*) *the financial risk management objectives and policies of the company ... , including the policy for hedging each major type of forecasted transaction for which hedge accounting is used, and*

(*b*) *the exposure of the company ... to price risk, credit risk, liquidity risk and cash flow risk,*

unless such information is not material for the assessment of the assets, liabilities, financial position and profit or loss of the company ...

[(1A) In relation to a group directors' report sub-paragraph (1) has effect as if the references to the company were references to the company and its subsidiary undertakings included in the consolidation.]

(2) In sub-paragraph (1) the expressions "hedge accounting", "price risk", "credit risk", "liquidity risk" and "cash flow risk" have the same meaning as they have in Council Directive 78/660/EEC on the annual accounts of certain types of companies, and in Council Directive 83/349/EEC on consolidated accounts, as amended.]

Miscellaneous

6.—[(1)] The directors' report shall contain—

(*a*) *particulars of any important events affecting the company ... which have occurred since the end of the financial year,*

(*b*) *an indication of likely future developments in the business of the company ...*

(*c*) *an indication of the activities (if any) of the company ... in the field of research and development[, and*

(*d*) *(unless the company is an unlimited company) an indication of the existence of branches (as defined in section 698(2)) of the company outside the United Kingdom].*

[(2) In relation to a group directors' report paragraphs (a), (b) and (c) of sub-paragraph (1) have effect as if the references to the company were references to the company and its subsidiary undertakings included in the consolidation.]

[569]

NOTES

Repealed as noted to s 1 at **[309]**.

Para 1: sub-para (1) repealed and words in square brackets in sub-para (2) substituted by the Companies Act 1985 (Miscellaneous Accounting Amendments) Regulations 1996, SI 1996/189, regs 14(4)(a), 15(3), 16(1), in relation to any financial year ending on or after 2 February 1996; for a transitional provision see reg 16(2) of the 1996 Regulations; words omitted from sub-para (2) repealed, and sub-para (3) added, by the Companies Act 1985 (Operating and Financial Review and Directors' Report etc) Regulations 2005, SI 2005/1011, reg 7(1), (2), in relation to companies' financial years which begin on or after 1 April 2005.

Paras 2, 2A: substituted, together with para 2B for original para 2, by the Companies Act 1989, s 8(2), Sch 5, subject to transitional provisions contained in the Companies Act 1989 (Commencement No 4 and Transitional and Saving Provisions) Order 1990, SI 1990/355. See the transitional provisions note preceding s 221 at **[356]**.

Para 2B: substituted, together with paras 2, 2A, for original para 2, by the Companies Act 1989, s 8(2), Sch 5, subject to transitional provisions contained in the Companies Act 1989 (Commencement No 4 and Transitional and Saving Provisions) Order 1990, SI 1990/355; words in square brackets in sub-para (3) inserted by the Civil Partnership Act 2004, s 261(1), Sch 27, para 105.

Paras 3, 4: substituted, together with para 5, by the Political Parties, Elections and Referendums Act 2000, s 140. By virtue of s 163(7), Sch 23, Pt II, para 13 to the 2000 Act, this substitution applies only in relation to directors' reports for financial years beginning on or after the first anniversary of the date which is the relevant date for the purposes of Sch 23, Pt II, para 12 to that Act; namely the date (if held within the first year after s 139(1) comes into force) of the annual general meeting of the company, or otherwise the date immediately following the end of that year.

Para 5: substituted, together with paras 3, 4, by the Political Parties, Elections and Referendums Act 2000, s 140; words in square brackets in sub-para (4) substituted by the Charities and Trustee Investment (Scotland) Act 2005 (Consequential Provisions and Modifications) Order 2006, SI 2006/242, art 5, Schedule, Pt 1, para 3.

Para 5A: inserted by the Companies Act 1985 (International Accounting Standards and Other Accounting Amendments) Regulations 2004, SI 2004/2947, reg 13(1), as from 12 November 2004, in relation to companies' financial years which begin on or after 1 January 2005 (note that previously a para 5A had been inserted by the Companies Act 1989, s 137(2), partly as from 1 April 1990 (certain purposes), partly as from a day to be appointed (otherwise) and repealed by SI 1996/189, regs 14(4)(b), 16(1), in relation to any financial year ending on or after 2 February 1996, for a transitional provision see reg 16(2) of the 1996 Regulations); words omitted from sub-para (1) repealed, and sub-para (1A) inserted, by the Companies Act 1985 (Operating and Financial Review and Directors' Report etc) Regulations 2005, SI 2005/1011, reg 7(1), (3), in relation to companies' financial years which begin on or after 1 April 2005.

Para 6: sub-para (1) numbered as such, words omitted from that sub-paragraph repealed, and sub-para (2) added, by the Companies Act 1985 (Operating and Financial Review and Directors' Report etc) Regulations 2005, SI 2005/1011, reg 7(1), (4), in relation to companies' financial years which begin on or after 1 April 2005; sub-para (1)(d) and the word immediately preceding it added, by the Companies Act 1985 (Disclosure of Branches and Bank Accounts) Regulations 1992, SI 1992/3178, regs 3, 8(a), subject to a transitional provision.

(Pt II outside the scope of this work.)

PART III
DISCLOSURE CONCERNING EMPLOYMENT, ETC, OF DISABLED PERSONS

9.—(1) This Part of this Schedule applies to the directors' report where the average number of persons employed by the company in each week during the financial year exceeded 250.

(2) That average number is the quotient derived by dividing, by the number of weeks in the financial year, the number derived by ascertaining, in relation to each of those weeks, the number of persons who, under contracts of service, were employed in the week (whether throughout it or not) by the company, and adding up the numbers ascertained.

(3) The directors' report shall in that case contain a statement describing such policy as the company has applied during the financial year—

(a) for giving full and fair consideration to applications for employment by the company made by disabled persons, having regard to their particular aptitudes and abilities,

(b) for continuing the employment of, and for arranging appropriate training for, employees of the company who have become disabled persons during the period when they were employed by the company, and

(c) otherwise for the training, career development and promotion of disabled persons employed by the company.

(4) In this Part—

(a) "employment" means employment other than employment to work wholly or mainly outside the United Kingdom, and "employed" and "employee" shall be construed accordingly; and

(b) "disabled person" means the same as in the [Disability Discrimination Act 1995].

[570]

NOTES

Repealed as noted to s 1 at **[309]**.

Para 9: words in square brackets substituted by the Disability Discrimination Act 1995, s 70(4), Sch 6, para 4.

(Pt IV repealed, in relation to any financial year ending on or after 2 February 1996, by the Companies Act 1985 (Miscellaneous Accounting Amendments) Regulations 1996, SI 1996/189, regs 14(4)(c), 16(1); for a transitional provision see reg 16(2) of the 1996 Regulations.)

PART V
EMPLOYEE INVOLVEMENT

11.—(1) This Part of this Schedule applies to the directors' report where the average number of persons employed by the company in each week during the financial year exceeded 250.

(2) That average number is the quotient derived by dividing by the number of weeks in the financial year the number derived by ascertaining, in relation to each of those weeks, the number of persons who, under contracts of service, were employed in the week (whether throughout it or not) by the company, and adding up the numbers ascertained.

(3) The directors' report shall in that case contain a statement describing the action that has been taken during the financial year to introduce, maintain or develop arrangements aimed at—

(*a*) *providing employees systematically with information on matters of concern to them as employees,*

(*b*) *consulting employees or their representatives on a regular basis so that the views of employees can be taken into account in making decisions which are likely to affect their interests,*

(*c*) *encouraging the involvement of employees in the company's performance through an employees' share scheme or by some other means,*

(*d*) *achieving a common awareness on the part of all employees of the financial and economic factors affecting the performance of the company.*

(4) In sub-paragraph (3) "employee" does not include a person employed to work wholly or mainly outside the United Kingdom; and for the purposes of sub-paragraph (2) no regard is to be had to such a person.

[571]

NOTES

Repealed as noted to s 1 at **[309]**.

[PART VI
POLICY AND PRACTICE ON PAYMENT OF CREDITORS

12.—(1) This Part of this Schedule applies to the directors' report for a financial year if—

(*a*) *the company was at any time within the year a public company, or*

(*b*) *the company did not qualify as small or medium-sized in relation to the year by virtue of section 247 and was at any time within the year a member of a group of which the parent company was a public company.*

(2) The report shall state, with respect to the next following financial year—

(*a*) *whether in respect of some or all of its suppliers it is the company's policy to follow any code or standard on payment practice and, if so, the name of the code or standard and the place where information about, and copies of, the code or standard can be obtained,*

(*b*) *whether in respect of some or all of its suppliers it is the company's policy—*

(i) to settle the terms of payment with those suppliers when agreeing the terms of each transaction,

(ii) to ensure that those suppliers are made aware of the terms of payment, and

(iii) to abide by the terms of payment,

(*c*) *where the company's policy is not as mentioned in paragraph* (*a*) *or* (*b*) *in respect of some or all of its suppliers, what its policy is with respect to the payment of those suppliers;*

and if the company's policy is different for different suppliers or classes of suppliers, the report shall identify the suppliers to which the different policies apply.

In this sub-paragraph references to the company's suppliers are references to persons who are or may become its suppliers.

(3) The report shall also state the number of days which bears to the number of days in the financial year the same proportion as X bears to Y where—

X = the aggregate of the amounts which were owed to trade creditors at the end of the year; and

Y = the aggregate of the amounts in which the company was invoiced by suppliers during the year.

(4) For the purposes of sub-paragraphs (2) *and* (3) *a person is a supplier of the company at any time if—*

(*a*) *at that time, he is owed an amount in respect of goods or services supplied, and*

(*b*) *that amount would be included under the heading corresponding to itemE.4* (*trade creditors*) *in Format 1 if—*

(i) the company's accounts fell to be prepared as at that time,

(ii) those accounts were prepared in accordance with Schedule 4, and

(iii) that Format were adopted.

(5) *For the purpose of sub-paragraph (3), the aggregate of the amounts which at the end of the financial year were owed to trade creditors shall be taken to be—*

(*a*) *where in the company's accounts Format 1 of the balance sheet formats set out in Part I of Schedule 4 is adopted, the amount shown under the heading corresponding to item E.4 (trade creditors) in that Format,*

(*b*) *where Format 2 is adopted, the amount which, under the heading corresponding to item C.4 (trade creditors) in that Format, is shown as falling due within one year, and*

(*c*) *where the company's accounts are prepared in accordance with Schedule 9 or 9A [or the company's accounts are IAS accounts], the amount which would be shown under the heading corresponding to item E.4 (trade creditors) in Format 1 if the company's accounts were prepared in accordance with Schedule 4 and that Format were adopted.]*

[572]

NOTES

Repealed as noted to s 1 at **[309]**.

Inserted by the Companies Act 1985 (Miscellaneous Accounting Amendments) Regulations 1996, SI 1996/189, regs 14(5), 16(1), in relation to any financial year ending on or after 2 February 1996, for a transitional provision see reg 16(2) of the 1996 Regulations; substituted by the Companies Act 1985 (Directors' Report) (Statement of Payment Practice) Regulations 1997, SI 1997/571, reg 2(2), for a transitional provision see reg 3 of the 1997 Regulations.

Para 12: words in square brackets in sub-para (5)(c) inserted by the Companies Act 1985 (International Accounting Standards and Other Accounting Amendments) Regulations 2004, SI 2004/2947, reg 3, Sch 1, paras 1, 33, in relation to companies' financial years which begin on or after 1 January 2005.

(Sch 7, Pt VII outside the scope of this work; Sch 7ZA inserted by the Companies Act 1985 (Operating and Financial Review and Directors' Report etc) Regulations 2005, SI 2005/1011, reg 9, in relation to companies' financial years which begin on or after 1 April 2005; repealed by the Companies Act 1985 (Operating and Financial Review) (Repeal) Regulations 2005, SI 2005/3442, reg 2(2)(a), Sch 1, para 17; Schs 7A, 7B outside the scope of this work.)

[SCHEDULE 8
FORM AND CONTENT OF ACCOUNTS PREPARED BY SMALL COMPANIES

Sections 246, 248A

PART I
GENERAL RULES AND FORMATS

SECTION A
GENERAL RULES

1.—(1) Subject to the following provisions of this Schedule—

(*a*) *every balance sheet of a small company shall show the items listed in either of the balance sheet formats set out below in section B of this Part; and*

(*b*) *every profit and loss account of a small company shall show the items listed in any one of the profit and loss account formats so set out;*

in either case in the order and under the headings and sub-headings given in the format adopted.

(2) *Sub-paragraph (1) above is not to be read as requiring the heading or sub-heading for any item to be distinguished by any letter or number assigned to that item in the format adopted.*

2.—(1) Where in accordance with paragraph 1 a small company's balance sheet or profit and loss account for any financial year has been prepared by reference to one of the formats set out in section B below, the directors of the company shall adopt the same format in preparing the accounts for subsequent financial years of the company unless in their opinion there are special reasons for a change.

(2) *Particulars of any change in the format adopted in preparing a small company's balance sheet or profit and loss account in accordance with paragraph 1 shall be disclosed, and the reasons for the change shall be explained, in a note to the accounts in which the new format is first adopted.*

3.—(1) Any item required in accordance with paragraph 1 to be shown in a small company's balance sheet or profit and loss account may be shown in greater detail than required by the format adopted.

(2) A small company's balance sheet or profit and loss account may include an item representing or covering the amount of any asset or liability, income or expenditure not otherwise covered by any of the items listed in the format adopted, but the following shall not be treated as assets in any small company's balance sheet—
- *(a) preliminary expenses;*
- *(b) expenses of and commission on any issue of shares or debentures; and*
- *(c) costs of research.*

(3) In preparing a small company's balance sheet or profit and loss account the directors of the company shall adapt the arrangement and headings and sub-headings otherwise required by paragraph 1 in respect of items to which an Arabic number is assigned in the format adopted, in any case where the special nature of the company's business requires such adaptation.

(4) Items to which Arabic numbers are assigned in any of the formats set out in section B below may be combined in a small company's accounts for any financial year if either—
- *(a) their individual amounts are not material to assessing the state of affairs or profit or loss of the company for that year; or*
- *(b) the combination facilitates that assessment;*

but in a case within paragraph (b) the individual amounts of any items so combined shall be disclosed in a note to the accounts.

(5) Subject to paragraph 4(3) below, a heading or sub-heading corresponding to an item listed in the format adopted in preparing a small company's balance sheet or profit and loss account shall not be included if there is no amount to be shown for that item in respect of the financial year to which the balance sheet or profit and loss account relates.

(6) Every profit and loss account of a small company shall show the amount of the company's profit or loss on ordinary activities before taxation.

(7) …

4.—(1) In respect of every item shown in a small company's balance sheet or profit and loss account the corresponding amount for the financial year immediately preceding that to which the balance sheet or profit and loss account relates shall also be shown.

(2) Where that corresponding amount is not comparable with the amount to be shown for the item in question in respect of the financial year to which the balance sheet or profit and loss account relates, the former amount [may be adjusted] and [particulars of the non-comparability and of any adjustment] shall be disclosed in a note to the accounts.

(3) Paragraph 3(5) does not apply in any case where an amount can be shown for the item in question in respect of the financial year immediately preceding that to which the balance sheet or profit and loss account relates, and that amount shall be shown under the heading or sub-heading required by paragraph 1 for that item.

5. Amounts in respect of items representing assets or income may not be set off against amounts in respect of items representing liabilities or expenditure (as the case may be), or vice versa.

[5A. The directors of a company must, in determining how amounts are presented within items in the profit and loss account and balance sheet, have regard to the substance of the reported transaction or arrangement, in accordance with generally accepted accounting principles or practice.]

SECTION B
THE REQUIRED FORMATS FOR ACCOUNTS

Preliminary

6. References in this Part of this Schedule to the items listed in any of the formats set out below are to those items read together with any of the notes following the formats which apply to any of those items, and the requirement imposed by paragraph 1 to show the items listed in any such format in the order adopted in the format is subject to any provision in those notes for alternative positions for any particular items.

7. A number in brackets following any item in any of the formats set out below is a reference to the note of that number in the notes following the formats.

8. In the notes following the formats—

(a) the heading of each note gives the required heading or sub-heading for the item to which it applies and a reference to any letters and numbers assigned to that item in the formats set out below (taking a reference in the case of Format 2 of the balance sheet formats to the item listed under "Assets" or under "Liabilities" as the case may require); and

(b) references to a numbered format are to the balance sheet format or (as the case may require) to the profit and loss account format of that number set out below.

Balance Sheet Formats

Format 1

A. Called up share capital not paid (1)

B. Fixed assets
- *I Intangible assets*
  - *1. Goodwill (2)*
  - *2. Other intangible assets (3)*
- *II Tangible assets*
  - *1. Land and buildings*
  - *2. Plant and machinery etc*
- *III Investments*
  - *1. Shares in group undertakings and participating interests*
  - *2. Loans to group undertakings and undertakings in which the company has a participating interest*
  - *3. Other investments other than loans*
  - *4. Other investments (4)*

C. Current assets
- *I Stocks*
  - *1. Stocks*
  - *2. Payments on account*
- *II Debtors (5)*
  - *1. Trade debtors*
  - *2. Amounts owed by group undertakings and undertakings in which the company has a participating interest*
  - *3. Other debtors*
- *III Investments*
  - *1. Shares in group undertakings*
  - *2. Other investments*
- *IV Cash at bank and in hand*

D. Prepayments and accrued income (6)

E. Creditors: amounts falling due within one year
- *1. Bank loans and overdrafts*
- *2. Trade creditors*
- *3. Amounts owed to group undertakings and undertakings in which the company has a participating interest*
- *4. Other creditors (7)*

F. Net current assets (liabilities) (8)

G. Total assets less current liabilities

H. Creditors: amounts falling due after more than one year
- *1. Bank loans and overdrafts*
- *2. Trade creditors*
- *3. Amounts owed to group undertakings and undertakings in which the company has a participating interest*
- *4. Other creditors (7)*

I. [Provisions for liabilities]

J. Accruals and deferred income (7)

K. Capital and reserves
I Called up share capital (9)
II Share premium account
III Revaluation reserve
IV Other reserves
V Profit and loss account

Balance Sheet Formats

Format 2

ASSETS

A. Called up share capital not paid (1)

B. Fixed assets
I Intangible assets
1. Goodwill (2)
2. Other intangible assets (3)
II Tangible assets
1. Land and buildings
2. Plant and machinery etc
III Investments
1. Shares in group undertakings and participating interests
2. Loans to group undertakings and undertakings in which the company has a participating interest
3. Other investments other than loans
4. Other investments (4)

C. Current assets
I Stocks
1. Stocks
2. Payments on account
II Debtors (5)
1. Trade debtors
2. Amounts owed by group undertakings and undertakings in which the company has a participating interest
3. Other debtors
III Investments
1. Shares in group undertakings
2. Other investments
IV Cash at bank and in hand

D. Prepayments and accrued income (6)

LIABILITIES

A. Capital and reserves
I Called up share capital (9)
II Share premium account
III Revaluation reserve
IV Other reserves
V Profit and loss account

B. [Provisions for liabilities]

C. Creditors (10)
1. Bank loans and overdrafts
2. Trade creditors
3. Amounts owed to group undertakings and undertakings in which the company has a participating interest
4. Other creditors (7)

D. Accruals and deferred income (7)

Notes on the balance sheet formats

(1) Called up share capital not paid

(Formats 1 and 2, items A and C.II.3.)

This item may either be shown at item A or included under item C.II.3 in Format 1 or 2.

(2) Goodwill

(Formats 1 and 2, item B.I.1.)

Amounts representing goodwill shall only be included to the extent that the goodwill was acquired for valuable consideration.

(3) Other intangible assets

(Formats 1 and 2, item B.I.2.)

Amounts in respect of concessions, patents, licences, trade marks and similar rights and assets shall only be included in a company's balance sheet under this item if either—

(a) the assets were acquired for valuable consideration and are not required to be shown under goodwill; or

(b) the assets in question were created by the company itself.

(4) Others: Other investments

(Formats 1 and 2, items B.III.4 and C.III.2.)

Where amounts in respect of own shares held are included under either of these items, the nominal value of such shares shall be shown separately.

(5) Debtors

(Formats 1 and 2, items C.II.1 to 3.)

The amount falling due after more than one year shall be shown separately for each item included under debtors unless the aggregate amount of debtors falling due after more than one year is disclosed in the notes to the accounts.

(6) Prepayments and accrued income

(Formats 1 and 2, item D.)

This item may alternatively be included under item C.II.3 in Format 1 or 2.

(7) Other creditors

(Format 1, items E.4, H.4 and J and Format 2, items C.4 and D.)

There shall be shown separately—

(a) the amount of any convertible loans, and

(b) the amount for creditors in respect of taxation and social security.

Payments received on account of orders shall be included in so far as they are not shown as deductions from stocks.

In Format 1, accruals and deferred income may be shown under item J or included under item E.4 or H.4, or both (as the case may require). In Format 2, accruals and deferred income may be shown under item D or within item C.4 under Liabilities.

(8) Net current assets (liabilities)

(Format 1, item F.)

In determining the amount to be shown under this item any prepayments and accrued income shall be taken into account wherever shown.

(9) Called up share capital

(Format 1, item K.I and Format 2, item A.I.)

The amount of allotted share capital and the amount of called up share capital which has been paid up shall be shown separately.

(10) Creditors

(Format 2, items C.I to 4.)

Amounts falling due within one year and after one year shall be shown separately for each of these items and for the aggregate of all of these items unless the aggregate amount of creditors falling due within one year and the aggregate amount of creditors falling due after more than one year is disclosed in the notes to the accounts.

Profit and loss account formats

Format 1
(see note (14) below)

1. *Turnover*
2. *Cost of sales (11)*
3. *Gross profit or loss*
4. *Distribution costs (11)*
5. *Administrative expenses (11)*
6. *Other operating income*
7. *Income from shares in group undertakings*
8. *Income from participating interests*
8. *Income from other fixed asset investments (12)*
10. *Other interest receivable and similar income (12)*
11. *Amounts written off investments*
12. *Interest payable and similar charges (13)*
13. *Tax on profit or loss on ordinary activities*
14. *Profit or loss on ordinary activities after taxation*
15. *Extraordinary income*
16. *Extraordinary charges*
17. *Extraordinary profit or loss*
18. *Tax on extraordinary profit or loss*
19. *Other taxes not shown under the above items*
20. *Profit or loss for the financial year*

Profit and loss account formats

Format 2

1. *Turnover*
2. *Change in stocks of finished goods and in work in progress*
3. *Own work capitalised*
4. *Other operating income*
5.
   (*a*) *Raw materials and consumables*
   (*b*) *Other external charges*
6. *Staff costs:*
   (*a*) *wages and salaries*
   (*b*) *social security costs*
   (*c*) *other pension costs*
7.
   (*a*) *Depreciation and other amounts written off tangible and intangible fixed assets*
   (*b*) *Exceptional amounts written off current assets*
8. *Other operating charges*
9. *Income from shares in group undertakings*

10. *Income from participating interests*

11. *Income from other fixed asset investments (12)*

12. *Other interest receivable and similar income (12)*

13. *Amounts written off investments*

14. *Interest payable and similar charges (13)*

15. *Tax on profit or loss on ordinary activities*

16. *Profit or loss on ordinary activities after taxation*

17. *Extraordinary income*

18. *Extraordinary charges*

19. *Extraordinary profit or loss*

20. *Tax on extraordinary profit or loss*

21. *Other taxes not shown under the above items*

22. *Profit or loss for the financial year*

Profit and loss account formats

Format 3

(see note (14) below)

A. *Charges*
1. *Cost of sales (11)*
2. *Distribution costs (11)*
3. *Administrative expenses (11)*
4. *Amounts written off investments*
5. *Interest payable and similar charges (13)*
6. *Tax on profit or loss on ordinary activities*
7. *Profit or loss on ordinary activities after taxation*
8. *Extraordinary charges*
9. *Tax on extraordinary profit or loss*
10. *Other taxes not shown under the above items*
11. *Profit or loss for the financial year*

B. *Income*
1. *Turnover*
2. *Other operating income*
3. *Income from shares in group undertakings*
4. *Income from participating interests*
5. *Income from other fixed asset investments (12)*
6. *Other interest receivable and similar income (12)*
7. *Profit or loss on ordinary activities after taxation*
8. *Extraordinary income*
9. *Profit or loss for the financial year*

Profit and loss account formats

Format 4

A. *Charges*
1. *Reduction in stocks of finished goods and in work in progress*
2.
   (a) *Raw materials and consumables*
   (b) *Other external charges*
3. *Staff costs:*
   (a) *wages and salaries*
   (b) *social security costs*
   (c) *other pension costs*
4.
   (a) *Depreciation and other amounts written off tangible and intangible fixed assets*
   (b) *Exceptional amounts written off current assets*
5. *Other operating charges*

8. *Other interest receivable and similar income (12)*
9. *Profit or loss on ordinary activities after taxation*
10. *Extraordinary income*
11. *Profit or loss for the financial year*

Notes on the profit and loss account formats

(11) Cost of sales: distribution costs: administrative expenses

(Format 1, items 2, 4 and 5 and Format 3, items A.1, 2 and 3.)

These items shall be stated after taking into account any necessary provisions for depreciation or diminution in value of assets.

(12) Income from other fixed asset investments: other interest receivable and similar income

(Format 1, items 9 and 10: Format 2, items 11 and 12: Format 3, items B.5 and 6: Format 4, items B.7 and 8.)

Income and interest derived from group undertakings shall be shown separately from income and interest derived from other sources.

(13) Interest payable and similar charges

(Format 1, item 12: Format 2, item 14: Format 3, item A.5: Format 4, item A.7.)

The amount payable to group undertakings shall be shown separately.

(14) Formats 1 and 3

The amount of any provisions for depreciation and diminution in value of tangible and intangible fixed assets falling to be shown under items 7(a) and A.4(a) respectively in Formats 2 and 4 shall be disclosed in a note to the accounts in any case where the profit and loss account is prepared by reference to Format 1 or Format 3.]

[573]

NOTES

Repealed as noted to s 1 at **[309]**.

Whole Schedule substituted by the Companies Act 1985 (Accounts of Small and Medium-sized Companies and Minor Accounting Amendments) Regulations 1997, SI 1997/220, reg 2(2), Sch 1, in relation to annual accounts approved by the board of directors on or after 1 March 1997, and to directors' and auditors' reports on such accounts; for a transitional provision see reg 1(4) of the 1997 Regulations.

Para 3: sub-para (7) repealed by the Companies Act 1985 (International Accounting Standards and Other Accounting Amendments) Regulations 2004, SI 2004/2947, reg 14(2), Sch 3, paras 1, 2, in relation to companies' financial years which begin on or after 1 January 2005.

Para 4: words in square brackets in sub-para (2) substituted by the Companies Act 1985 (Investment Companies and Accounting and Audit Amendments) Regulations 2005, SI 2005/2280, reg 5, in relation to companies' financial years which begin on or after 1 January 2005 and which end on or after 1 October 2005.

Para 5A: inserted by SI 2004/2947, reg 14(2), Sch 3, paras 1, 3, in relation to companies' financial years which begin on or after 1 January 2005.

Words in square brackets in balance sheet format 1 and balance sheet format 2 substituted by SI 2004/2947, reg 14(2), Sch 3, paras 1, 4, in relation to companies' financial years which begin on or after 1 January 2005.

6. *Amounts written off investments*
7. *Interest payable and similar charges (13)*
8. *Tax on profit or loss on ordinary activities*
9. *Profit or loss on ordinary activities after taxation*
10. *Extraordinary charges*
11. *Tax on extraordinary profit or loss*
12. *Other taxes not shown under the above items*
13. *Profit or loss for the financial year*

B. *Income*

1. *Turnover*
2. *Increase in stocks of finished goods and in work in progress*
3. *Own work capitalised*
4. *Other operating income*
5. *Income from shares in group undertakings*
6. *Income from participating interests*
7. *Income from other fixed asset investments (12)*

... stated above in preparing the company's accounts in respect of any financial year they may do so, but particulars of the departure, the reasons for it and its effect shall be given in a note to the accounts.

SECTION B
HISTORICAL COST ACCOUNTING RULES

Preliminary

16. [Subject to sections C and D] of this Part of this Schedule, the amounts to be included in respect of all items shown in a small company's accounts shall be determined in accordance with the rules set out in paragraphs 17 to 28.

Fixed assets

General rules

17. Subject to any provision for depreciation or diminution in value made in accordance with paragraph 18 or 19 the amount to be included in respect of any fixed asset shall be its purchase price or production cost.

18. In the case of any fixed asset which has a limited useful economic life, the amount of—

(a) its purchase price or production cost; or

(b) where it is estimated that any such asset will have a residual value at the end of the period of its useful economic life, its purchase price or production cost less that estimated residual value;

shall be reduced by provisions for depreciation calculated to write off that amount systematically over the period of the asset's useful economic life.

19.—(1) Where a fixed asset investment of a description falling to be included under item B.III of either of the balance sheet formats set out in Part I of this Schedule has diminished in value provisions for diminution in value may be made in respect of it and the amount to be included in respect of it may be reduced accordingly; and any such provisions which are not shown in the profit and loss account shall be disclosed (either separately or in aggregate) in a note to the accounts.

(2) Provisions for diminution in value shall be made in respect of any fixed asset which has diminished in value if the reduction in its value is expected to be permanent (whether its useful economic life is limited or not), and the amount to be included in respect of it shall be reduced accordingly; and any such provisions which are not shown in the profit and loss account shall be disclosed (either separately or in aggregate) in a note to the accounts.

(3) Where the reasons for which any provision was made in accordance with sub-paragraph (1) or (2) have ceased to apply to any extent, that provision shall be written back to the extent that it is no longer necessary; and any amounts written back in accordance with this sub-paragraph which are not shown in the profit and loss account shall be disclosed (either separately or in aggregate) in a note to the accounts.

Rules for determining particular fixed asset items

20.—(1) Notwithstanding that an item in respect of "development costs" is included under "fixed assets" in the balance sheet formats set out in Part I of this Schedule, an amount may only be included in a small company's balance sheet in respect of development costs in special circumstances.

(2) If any amount is included in a small company's balance sheet in respect of development costs the following information shall be given in a note to the accounts—
- *(a) the period over which the amount of those costs originally capitalised is being or is to be written off; and*
- *(b) the reasons for capitalising the development costs in question.*

21.—(1) The application of paragraphs 17 to 19 in relation to goodwill (in any case where goodwill is treated as an asset) is subject to the following provisions of this paragraph.

(2) Subject to sub-paragraph (3) below, the amount of the consideration for any goodwill acquired by a small company shall be reduced by provisions for depreciation calculated to write off that amount systematically over a period chosen by the directors of the company.

(3) The period chosen shall not exceed the useful economic life of the goodwill in question.

(4) In any case where any goodwill acquired by a small company is shown or included as an asset in the company's balance sheet the period chosen for writing off the consideration for that goodwill and the reasons for choosing that period shall be disclosed in a note to the accounts.

Current assets

22. Subject to paragraph 23, the amount to be included in respect of any current asset shall be its purchase price or production cost.

23.—(1) If the net realisable value of any current asset is lower than its purchase price or production cost the amount to be included in respect of that asset shall be the net realisable value.

(2) Where the reasons for which any provision for diminution in value was made in accordance with sub-paragraph (1) have ceased to apply to any extent, that provision shall be written back to the extent that it is no longer necessary.

Miscellaneous and supplementary provisions

Excess of money owed over value received as an asset item

24.—(1) Where the amount repayable on any debt owed by a small company is greater than the value of the consideration received in the transaction giving rise to the debt, the amount of the difference may be treated as an asset.

(2) Where any such amount is so treated—

(a) it shall be written off by reasonable amounts each year and must be completely written off before repayment of the debt; and

(b) if the current amount is not shown as a separate item in the company's balance sheet it must be disclosed in a note to the accounts.

Assets included at a fixed amount

25.—(1) Subject to the following sub-paragraph, assets which fall to be included—

(a) amongst the fixed assets of a small company under the item "tangible assets"; or

(b) amongst the current assets of a small company under the item "raw materials and consumables";

may be included at a fixed quantity and value.

(2) Sub-paragraph (1) applies to assets of a kind which are constantly being replaced, where—

(a) their overall value is not material to assessing the company's state of affairs; and

(b) their quantity, value and composition are not subject to material variation.

Determination of purchase price or production cost

26.—(1) The purchase price of an asset shall be determined by adding to the actual price paid any expenses incidental to its acquisition.

(2) The production cost of an asset shall be determined by adding to the purchase price of the raw materials and consumables used the amount of the costs incurred by the company which are directly attributable to the production of that asset.

(3) In addition, there may be included in the production cost of an asset—

(a) a reasonable proportion of the costs incurred by the company which are only indirectly attributable to the production of that asset, but only to the extent that they relate to the period of production; and

(b) interest on capital borrowed to finance the production of that asset, to the extent that it accrues in respect of the period of production;

provided, however, in a case within paragraph (b) above, that the inclusion of the interest in determining the cost of that asset and the amount of the interest so included is disclosed in a note to the accounts.

(4) In the case of current assets distribution costs may not be included in production costs.

27.—(1) Subject to the qualification mentioned below, the purchase price or production cost of—

(a) any assets which fall to be included under any item shown in a small company's balance sheet under the general item "stocks"; and

(b) any assets which are fungible assets (including investments);

may be determined by the application of any of the methods mentioned in sub-paragraph (2) below in relation to any such assets of the same class.

The method chosen must be one which appears to the directors to be appropriate in the circumstances of the company.

(2) Those methods are—

(a) the method known as "first in, first out" (FIFO);

(b) the method known as "last in, first out" (LIFO);

(c) a weighted average price; and

(d) any other method similar to any of the methods mentioned above.

(3) For the purposes of this paragraph, assets of any description shall be regarded as fungible if assets of that description are substantially indistinguishable one from another.

Substitution of original stated amount where price or cost unknown

28. Where there is no record of the purchase price or production cost of any asset of a small company or of any price, expenses or costs relevant for determining its purchase price or production cost in accordance with paragraph 26, or any such record cannot be obtained without unreasonable expense or delay, its purchase price or production cost shall be taken for the purposes of paragraphs 17 to 23 to be the value ascribed to it in the earliest available record of its value made on or after its acquisition or production by the company.

SECTION C
ALTERNATIVE ACCOUNTING RULES

Preliminary

29.—(1) The rules set out in section B are referred to below in this Schedule as the historical cost accounting rules.

(2) Those rules, with the omission of paragraphs 16, 21 and 25 to 28, are referred to below in this Part of this Schedule as the depreciation rules; and references below in this Schedule to the historical cost accounting rules do not include the depreciation rules as they apply by virtue of paragraph 32.

30. Subject to paragraphs 32 to 34, the amounts to be included in respect of assets of any description mentioned in paragraph 31 may be determined on any basis so mentioned.

Alternative accounting rules

31.—(1) Intangible fixed assets, other than goodwill, may be included at their current cost.

(2) Tangible fixed assets may be included at a market value determined as at the date of their last valuation or at their current cost.

(3) Investments of any description falling to be included under item B III of either of the balance sheet formats set out in Part I of this Schedule may be included either—

(a) at a market value determined as at the date of their last valuation; or

(b) at a value determined on any basis which appears to the directors to be appropriate in the circumstances of the company;

but in the latter case particulars of the method of valuation adopted and of the reasons for adopting it shall be disclosed in a note to the accounts.

(4) Investments of any description falling to be included under item C III of either of the balance sheet formats set out in Part I of this Schedule may be included at their current cost.

(5) Stocks may be included at their current cost.

Application of the depreciation rules

32.—(1) Where the value of any asset of a small company is determined on any basis mentioned in paragraph 31, that value shall be, or (as the case may require) be the starting point for determining, the amount to be included in respect of that asset in the company's accounts, instead of its purchase price or production cost or any value previously so determined for that asset; and the depreciation rules shall apply accordingly in relation to any such asset with the substitution for any reference to its purchase price or production cost of a reference to the value most recently determined for that asset on any basis mentioned in paragraph 31.

(2) The amount of any provision for depreciation required in the case of any fixed asset by paragraph 18 or 19 as it applies by virtue of sub-paragraph (1) is referred to below in this paragraph as the adjusted amount, and the amount of any provision which would be required by that paragraph in the case of that asset according to the historical cost accounting rules is referred to as the historical cost amount.

(3) Where sub-paragraph (1) applies in the case of any fixed asset the amount of any provision for depreciation in respect of that asset—

(a) included in any item shown in the profit and loss account in respect of amounts written off assets of the description in question; or

(b) taken into account in stating any item so shown which is required by note (11) of the notes on the profit and loss account formats set out in Part I of this Schedule to be stated after taking into account any necessary provision for depreciation or diminution in value of assets included under it;

may be the historical cost amount instead of the adjusted amount, provided that the amount of any difference between the two is shown separately in the profit and loss account or in a note to the accounts.

Additional information to be provided in case of departure from historical cost accounting rules

33.—(1) This paragraph applies where the amounts to be included in respect of assets covered by any items shown in a small company's accounts have been determined on any basis mentioned in paragraph 31.

(2) The items affected and the basis of valuation adopted in determining the amounts of the assets in question in the case of each such item shall be disclosed in a note to the accounts.

(3) In the case of each balance sheet item affected (except stocks) either—

(a) the comparable amounts determined according to the historical cost accounting rules; or

(b) the differences between those amounts and the corresponding amounts actually shown in the balance sheet in respect of that item;

shall be shown separately in the balance sheet or in a note to the accounts.

(4) In sub-paragraph (3) above, references in relation to any item to the comparable amounts determined as there mentioned are references to—

(a) the aggregate amount which would be required to be shown in respect of that item if the amounts to be included in respect of all the assets covered by that item were determined according to the historical cost accounting rules; and

(b) the aggregate amount of the cumulative provisions for depreciation or diminution in value which would be permitted or required in determining those amounts according to those rules.

Revaluation reserve

34.—(1) With respect to any determination of the value of an asset of a small company on any basis mentioned in paragraph 31, the amount of any profit or loss arising from that determination (after allowing, where appropriate, for any provisions for depreciation or diminution in value made otherwise than by reference to the value so determined and any adjustments of any such provisions made in the light of that determination) shall be credited or (as the case may be) debited to a separate reserve ("the revaluation reserve").

(2) The amount of the revaluation reserve shall be shown in the company's balance sheet under a separate sub-heading in the position given for the item "revaluation reserve" in Format 1 or 2 of the balance sheet formats set out in Part I of this Schedule, but need not be shown under that name.

(3) An amount may be transferred—

(a) from the revaluation reserve—

(i) to the profit and loss account, if the amount was previously charged to that account or represents realised profit, or

(ii) on capitalisation,

(b) to or from the revaluation reserve in respect of the taxation relating to any profit or loss credited or debited to the reserve;

and the revaluation reserve shall be reduced to the extent that the amounts transferred to it are no longer necessary for the purposes of the valuation method used.

(4) In sub-paragraph (3)(a)(ii) "capitalisation", in relation to an amount standing to the credit of the revaluation reserve, means applying it in wholly or partly paying up unissued shares in the company to be allotted to members of the company as fully or partly paid shares.

(5) The revaluation reserve shall not be reduced except as mentioned in this paragraph.

(6) The treatment for taxation purposes of amounts credited or debited to the revaluation reserve shall be disclosed in a note to the accounts.]

[SECTION D
FAIR VALUE ACCOUNTING

Inclusion of financial instruments at fair value

34A.—(1) Subject to sub-paragraphs (2) to (4), financial instruments (including derivatives) may be included at fair value.

(2) Sub-paragraph (1) does not apply to financial instruments which constitute liabilities unless—
(a) they are held as part of a trading portfolio, or
(b) they are derivatives.

(3) Sub-paragraph (1) does not apply to—
(a) financial instruments (other than derivatives) held to maturity;
(b) loans and receivables originated by the company and not held for trading purposes;
(c) interests in subsidiary undertakings, associated undertakings and joint ventures;
(d) equity instruments issued by the company;
(e) contracts for contingent consideration in a business combination;
(f) other financial instruments with such special characteristics that the instruments, according to generally accepted accounting principles or practice, should be accounted for differently from other financial instruments.

(4) If the fair value of a financial instrument cannot be determined reliably in accordance with paragraph 34B, sub-paragraph (1) does not apply to that financial instrument.

(5) In this paragraph—
"associated undertaking" has the meaning given by paragraph 20 of Schedule 4A; and
"joint venture" has the meaning given by paragraph 19 of that Schedule.

Determination of fair value

34B.—(1) The fair value of a financial instrument is determined in accordance with this paragraph.

(2) If a reliable market can readily be identified for the financial instrument, its fair value is determined by reference to its market value.

(3) If a reliable market cannot readily be identified for the financial instrument but can be identified for its components or for a similar instrument, its fair value is determined by reference to the market value of its components or of the similar instrument.

(4) If neither sub-paragraph (2) nor (3) applies, the fair value of the financial instrument is a value resulting from generally accepted valuation models and techniques.

(5) Any valuation models and techniques used for the purposes of sub-paragraph (4) must ensure a reasonable approximation of the market value.

Inclusion of hedged items at fair value

34C. A company may include any assets and liabilities that qualify as hedged items under a fair value hedge accounting system, or identified portions of such assets or liabilities, at the amount required under that system.

Other assets that may be included at fair value

34D.—(1) This paragraph applies to—
(a) investment property, and
(b) living animals and plants,

that, under international accounting standards, may be included in accounts at fair value.

(2) Such investment property and such living animals and plants may be included at fair value, provided that all such investment property or, as the case may be, all such living animals and plants are so included where their fair value can reliably be determined.

(3) In this paragraph, "fair value" means fair value determined in accordance with relevant international accounting standards.

Accounting for changes in value

34E.—(1) This paragraph applies where a financial instrument is valued in accordance with paragraph 34A or 34C or an asset is valued in accordance with paragraph 34D.

(2) Notwithstanding paragraph 12 of this Schedule, and subject to sub-paragraphs (3) and (4) below, a change in the value of the financial instrument or of the investment property or living animal or plant must be included in the profit and loss account.

(3) Where—
- *(a) the financial instrument accounted for is a hedging instrument under a hedge accounting system that allows some or all of the change in value not to be shown in the profit and loss account, or*
- *(b) the change in value relates to an exchange difference arising on a monetary item that forms part of a company's net investment in a foreign entity,*

the amount of the change in value must be credited to or (as the case may be) debited from a separate reserve ("the fair value reserve").

(4) Where the instrument accounted for—
- *(a) is an available for sale financial asset, and*
- *(b) is not a derivative,*

the change in value may be credited to or (as the case may be) debited from the fair value reserve.

The fair value reserve

34F.—(1) The fair value reserve must be adjusted to the extent that the amounts shown in it are no longer necessary for the purposes of paragraph 34E(3) or (4).

(2) The treatment for taxation purposes of amounts credited or debited to the fair value reserve must be disclosed in a note to the accounts.]

[574]

NOTES

Repealed as noted to s 1 at **[309]**.
Substituted as noted to Pt I at **[573]**.
Para 12: words omitted repealed by the Companies Act 1985 (International Accounting Standards and Other Accounting Amendments) Regulations 2004, SI 2004/2947, reg 14(2), Sch 3, paras 1, 5, in relation to companies' financial years which begin on or after 1 January 2005.
Para 16: words in square brackets substituted by SI 2004/2947, reg 14(2), Sch 3, paras 1, 6(1), (2), in relation to companies' financial years which begin on or after 1 January 2005.
Paras 34A–34F: added by SI 2004/2947, reg 14(2), Sch 3, paras 1, 6(1), (3), in relation to companies' financial years which begin on or after 1 January 2005.

[PART III
NOTES TO THE ACCOUNTS

Preliminary

35. Any information required in the case of any small company by the following provisions of this Part of this Schedule shall (if not given in the company's accounts) be given by way of a note to those accounts.

[Reserves and dividends

35A. There must be stated—
- *(a) any amount set aside or proposed to be set aside to, or withdrawn or proposed to be withdrawn from, reserves,*

(*b*) *the aggregate amount of dividends paid in the financial year (other than those for which a liability existed at the immediately preceding balance sheet date),*
(*c*) *the aggregate amount of dividends that the company is liable to pay at the balance sheet date, and*
(*d*) *the aggregate amount of dividends that are proposed before the date of approval of the accounts, and not otherwise disclosed under paragraph (b) or (c).]*

Disclosure of accounting policies

36. The accounting policies adopted by the company in determining the amounts to be included in respect of items shown in the balance sheet and in determining the profit or loss of the company shall be stated (including such policies with respect to the depreciation and diminution in value of assets).

Information supplementing the balance sheet

37. Paragraphs 38 to 47 require information which either supplements the information given with respect to any particular items shown in the balance sheet or is otherwise relevant to assessing the company's state of affairs in the light of the information so given.

Share capital and debentures

38.—(1) The following information shall be given with respect to the company's share capital—
(*a*) *the authorised share capital; and*
(*b*) *where shares of more than one class have been allotted, the number and aggregate nominal value of shares of each class allotted.*

(2) In the case of any part of the allotted share capital that consists of redeemable shares, the following information shall be given—
(*a*) *the earliest and latest dates on which the company has power to redeem those shares;*
(*b*) *whether those shares must be redeemed in any event or are liable to be redeemed at the option of the company or of the shareholder; and*
(*c*) *whether any (and, if so, what) premium is payable on redemption.*

39. If the company has allotted any shares during the financial year, the following information shall be given—
(*a*) *the classes of shares allotted; and*
(*b*) *as respects each class of shares, the number allotted, their aggregate nominal value, and the consideration received by the company for the allotment.*

Fixed assets

40.—(1) In respect of each item which is or would but for paragraph 3(4)(b) be shown under the general item "fixed assets" in the company's balance sheet the following information shall be given—
(*a*) *the appropriate amounts in respect of that item as at the date of the beginning of the financial year and as at the balance sheet date respectively;*
(*b*) *the effect on any amount shown in the balance sheet in respect of that item of—*
  (*i*) *any revision of the amount in respect of any assets included under that item made during that year on any basis mentioned in paragraph 31;*
  (*ii*) *acquisitions during that year of any assets;*
  (*iii*) *disposals during that year of any assets; and*
  (*iv*) *any transfers of assets of the company to and from that item during that year.*

(2) The reference in sub-paragraph (1)(a) to the appropriate amounts in respect of any item as at any date there mentioned is a reference to amounts representing the aggregate amounts determined, as at that date, in respect of assets falling to be included under that item on either of the following bases, that is to say—
(*a*) *on the basis of purchase price or production cost (determined in accordance with paragraphs 26 and 27); or*
(*b*) *on any basis mentioned in paragraph 31,*

PART I STATUTES

(leaving out of account in either case any provisions for depreciation or diminution in value).

(3) In respect of each item within sub-paragraph (1)—

(a) the cumulative amount of provisions for depreciation or diminution in value of assets included under that item as at each date mentioned in sub-paragraph (1)(a);

(b) the amount of any such provisions made in respect of the financial year;

(c) the amount of any adjustments made in respect of any such provisions during that year in consequence of the disposal of any assets; and

(d) the amount of any other adjustments made in respect of any such provisions during that year;

shall also be stated.

41. Where any fixed assets of the company (other than listed investments) are included under any item shown in the company's balance sheet at an amount determined on any basis mentioned in paragraph 31, the following information shall be given—

(a) the years (so far as they are known to the directors) in which the assets were severally valued and the several values; and

(b) in the case of assets that have been valued during the financial year, the names of the persons who valued them or particulars of their qualifications for doing so and (whichever is stated) the bases of valuation used by them.

Investments

42.—(1) In respect of the amount of each item which is or would but for paragraph 3(4)(b) be shown in the company's balance sheet under the general item "investments" (whether as fixed assets or as current assets) there shall be stated how much of that amount is ascribable to listed investments.

(2) Where the amount of any listed investments is stated for any item in accordance with sub-paragraph (1), the following amounts shall also be stated—

(a) the aggregate market value of those investments where it differs from the amount so stated; and

(b) both the market value and the stock exchange value of any investments of which the former value is, for the purposes of the accounts, taken as being higher than the latter.

[Information about fair value of assets and liabilities

42A.—(1) This paragraph applies where financial instruments have been valued in accordance with paragraph 34A or 34C

(2) There must be stated—

(a) where the fair value of the instruments has been determined in accordance with paragraph 34B(4), the significant assumptions underlying the valuation models and techniques used,

(b) for each category of financial instrument, the fair value of the instruments in that category and the changes in value—

(i) included in the profit and loss account, and

(ii) credited to or (as the case may be) debited from the fair value reserve,

in respect of those instruments, and

(c) for each class of derivatives, the extent and nature of the instruments, including significant terms and conditions that may affect the amount, timing and certainty of future cash flows.

(3) Where any amount is transferred to or from the fair value reserve during the financial year, there must be stated in tabular form—

(a) the amount of the reserve as at the date of the beginning of the financial year and as at the balance sheet date respectively;

(b) the amount transferred to or from the reserve during that year; and

(c) the source and application respectively of the amounts so transferred.

42B.—(1) Sub-paragraph (2) applies if—

(a) the company has financial fixed assets that could be included at fair value by virtue of paragraph 34A,

(b) *the amount at which those assets are included under any item in the company's accounts is in excess of their fair value, and*
(c) *the company has not made provision for diminution in value of those assets in accordance with paragraph 19(1) of this Schedule.*

(2) *There must be stated—*
(a) *the amount at which either the individual assets or appropriate groupings of those individual assets are included in the company's accounts,*
(b) *the fair value of those assets or groupings, and*
(c) *the reasons for not making a provision for diminution in value of those assets, including the nature of the evidence that provides the basis for the belief that the amount at which they are stated in the accounts will be recovered.*

Information where investment property and living animals and plants included at fair value

42C.—(1) This paragraph applies where the amounts to be included in a company's accounts in respect of investment property or living animals and plants have been determined in accordance with paragraph 34D.

(2) *The balance sheet items affected and the basis of valuation adopted in determining the amounts of the assets in question in the case of each such item must be disclosed in a note to the accounts.*

(3) *In the case of investment property, for each balance sheet item affected there must be shown, either separately in the balance sheet or in a note to the accounts—*
(a) *the comparable amounts determined according to the historical cost accounting rules; or*
(b) *the differences between those amounts and the corresponding amounts actually shown in the balance sheet in respect of that item.*

(4) *In sub-paragraph (3) above, references in relation to any item to the comparable amounts determined in accordance with that sub-paragraph are references to—*
(a) *the aggregate amount which would be required to be shown in respect of that item if the amounts to be included in respect of all the assets covered by that item were determined according to the historical cost accounting rules; and*
(b) *the aggregate amount of the cumulative provisions for depreciation or diminution in value which would be permitted or required in determining those amounts according to those rules.]*

Reserves and provisions

43.—(1) Where any amount is transferred—
(a) *to or from any reserves; or*
(b) *to any [provisions for liabilities]; or*
(c) *from any [provision for liabilities] otherwise than for the purpose for which the provision was established;*

and the reserves or provisions are or would but for paragraph 3(4)(b) be shown as separate items in the company's balance sheet, the information mentioned in the following sub-paragraph shall be given in respect of the aggregate of reserves or provisions included in the same item.

(2) *That information is—*
(a) *the amount of the reserves or provisions as at the date of the beginning of the financial year and as at the balance sheet date respectively;*
(b) *any amounts transferred to or from the reserves or provisions during that year; and*
(c) *the source and application respectively of any amounts so transferred.*

(3) *Particulars shall be given of each provision included in the item "other provisions" in the company's balance sheet in any case where the amount of that provision is material.*

Details of indebtedness

44.—(1) For the aggregate of all items shown under "creditors" in the company's balance sheet there shall be stated the aggregate of the following amounts, that is to say—

(a) the amount of any debts included under "creditors" which are payable or repayable otherwise than by instalments and fall due for payment or repayment after the end of the period of five years beginning with the day next following the end of the financial year; and

(b) in the case of any debts so included which are payable or repayable by instalments, the amount of any instalments which fall due for payment after the end of that period.

(2) In respect of each item shown under "creditors" in the company's balance sheet there shall be stated the aggregate amount of any debts included under that item in respect of which any security has been given by the company.

(3) References above in this paragraph to an item shown under "creditors" in the company's balance sheet include references, where amounts falling due to creditors within one year and after more than one year are distinguished in the balance sheet—

(a) in a case within sub-paragraph (1), to an item shown under the latter of those categories; and

(b) in a case within sub-paragraph (2), to an item shown under either of those categories;

and references to items shown under "creditors" include references to items which would but for paragraph 3(4)(b) be shown under that heading.

45. If any fixed cumulative dividends on the company's shares are in arrear, there shall be stated—

(a) the amount of the arrears; and

(b) the period for which the dividends or, if there is more than one class, each class of them are in arrear.

Guarantees and other financial commitments

46.—(1) Particulars shall be given of any charge on the assets of the company to secure the liabilities of any other person, including, where practicable, the amount secured.

(2) The following information shall be given with respect to any other contingent liability not provided for—

(a) the amount or estimated amount of that liability;

(b) its legal nature; and

(c) whether any valuable security has been provided by the company in connection with that liability and if so, what.

(3) There shall be stated, where practicable, the aggregate amount or estimated amount of contracts for capital expenditure, so far as not provided for.

(4) Particulars shall be given of—

(a) any pension commitments included under any provision shown in the company's balance sheet; and

(b) any such commitments for which no provision has been made;

and where any such commitment relates wholly or partly to pensions payable to past directors of the company separate particulars shall be given of that commitment so far as it relates to such pensions.

(5) Particulars shall also be given of any other financial commitments which—

(a) have not been provided for; and

(b) are relevant to assessing the company's state of affairs.

(6) Commitments within any of sub-paragraphs (1) to (5) which are undertaken on behalf of or for the benefit of—

(a) any parent undertaking or fellow subsidiary undertaking, or

(b) any subsidiary undertaking of the company,

shall be stated separately from the other commitments within that sub-paragraph, and commitments within paragraph (a) shall also be stated separately from those within paragraph (b).

Miscellaneous matters

47. Particulars shall be given of any case where the purchase price or production cost of any asset is for the first time determined under paragraph 28.

Information supplementing the profit and loss account

48. Paragraphs 49 and 50 require information which either supplements the information given with respect to any particular items shown in the profit and loss account or otherwise provides particulars of income or expenditure of the company or of circumstances affecting the items shown in the profit and loss account.

Particulars of turnover

49.—(1) If the company has supplied geographical markets outside the United Kingdom during the financial year in question, there shall be stated the percentage of its turnover that, in the opinion of the directors, is attributable to those markets.

(2) In analysing for the purposes of this paragraph the source of turnover, the directors of the company shall have regard to the manner in which the company's activities are organised.

Miscellaneous matters

50.—(1) Where any amount relating to any preceding financial year is included in any item in the profit and loss account, the effect shall be stated.

(2) Particulars shall be given of any extraordinary income or charges arising in the financial year.

(3) The effect shall be stated of any transactions that are exceptional by virtue of size or incidence though they fall within the ordinary activities of the company.

General

51.—(1) Where sums originally denominated in foreign currencies have been brought into account under any items shown in the balance sheet or profit and loss account, the basis on which those sums have been translated into sterling shall be stated.

(2), (3) …

[Dormant Companies Acting as Agents

51A. Where the directors of a company take advantage of the exemption conferred by section 249AA, and the company has during the financial year in question acted as an agent for any person, the fact that it has so acted must be stated.]

[575]

NOTES

Repealed as noted to s 1 at **[309]**.

Substituted as noted to Pt I at **[573]**.

Paras 35A, 42A–42C: inserted by the Companies Act 1985 (International Accounting Standards and Other Accounting Amendments) Regulations 2004, SI 2004/2947, reg 14(2), Sch 3, paras 1, 7, in relation to companies' financial years which begin on or after 1 January 2005.

Para 43: words in square brackets in sub-para (1) substituted by SI 2004/2947, reg 14(2), Sch 3, paras 1, 8, in relation to companies' financial years which begin on or after 1 January 2005.

Para 51: sub-paras (2), (3) repealed by the Companies Act 1985 (Investment Companies and Accounting and Audit Amendments) Regulations 2005, SI 2005/2280, reg 6, in relation to companies' financial years which begin on or after 1 January 2005 and which end on or after 1 October 2005.

Para 51A: added by the Companies Act 1985 (Audit Exemption) (Amendment) Regulations 2000, SI 2000/1430, reg 6, in relation to annual reports and reports in respect of financial years ending two months or more after 26 May 2000.

[PART IV
INTERPRETATION OF SCHEDULE

52. The following paragraphs apply for the purposes of this Schedule and its interpretation.

[Financial instruments

52A. References to "derivatives" include commodity-based contracts that give either contracting party the right to settle in cash or in some other financial instrument, except when such contracts—

- (*a*) *were entered into for the purpose of, and continue to meet, the company's expected purchase, sale or usage requirements,*
- (*b*) *were designated for such purpose at their inception, and*
- (*c*) *are expected to be settled by delivery of the commodity.*

52B.—(1) The expressions listed in sub-paragraph (2) have the same meaning as they have in Council Directive 78/660/EEC on the annual accounts of certain types of companies, as amended.

(2) Those expressions are "available for sale financial asset", "business combination", "commodity-based contracts", "derivative", "equity instrument", "exchange difference", "fair value hedge accounting system", "financial fixed asset", "financial instrument", "foreign entity", "hedge accounting", "hedge accounting system", "hedged items", "hedging instrument", "held for trading purposes", "held to maturity", "monetary item", "receivables", "reliable market" and "trading portfolio".]

Historical cost accounting rules

53. References to the historical cost accounting rules shall be read in accordance with paragraph 29.

[Investment property

53A. "Investment property" means land held to earn rent or for capital appreciation.]

Listed investments

[54.—(1) "Listed investment" means an investment as respects which there has been granted a listing on—

- (*a*) *a recognised investment exchange other than an overseas investment exchange; or*
- (*b*) *a stock exchange of repute outside Great Britain.*

(2) "Recognised investment exchange" and "overseas investment exchange" have the meaning given in Part 18 of the Financial Services and Markets Act 2000.]

Loans

55. A loan is treated as falling due for repayment, and an instalment of a loan is treated as falling due for payment, on the earliest date on which the lender could require repayment or (as the case may be) payment, if he exercised all options and rights available to him.

Materiality

56. Amounts which in the particular context of any provision of this Schedule are not material may be disregarded for the purposes of that provision.

Provisions

57.—(1) References to provisions for depreciation or diminution in value of assets are to any amount written off by way of providing for depreciation or diminution in value of assets.

(2) Any reference in the profit and loss account formats set out in Part I of this Schedule to the depreciation of, or amounts written off, assets of any description is to any provision for depreciation or diminution in value of assets of that description.

58. References to [provisions for liabilities] are to any amount retained as reasonably necessary for the purpose of providing for any liability [the nature of which is clearly defined and] which is either likely to be incurred, or certain to be incurred but uncertain as to amount or as to the date on which it will arise.

Staff costs

59.—(1) "Social security costs" means any contributions by the company to any state social security or pension scheme, fund or arrangement.

(2) "Pension costs" includes any costs incurred by the company in respect of any pension scheme established for the purpose of providing pensions for persons currently or formerly employed by the company, any sums set aside for the future payment of pensions directly by the company to current or former employees and any pensions paid directly to such persons without having first been set aside.

(3) Any amount stated in respect of the item "social security costs" or in respect of the item "wages and salaries" in the company's profit and loss account shall be determined by reference to payments made or costs incurred in respect of all persons employed by the company during the financial year under contracts of service.]

[576]

NOTES

Repealed as noted to s 1 at **[309]**.

Substituted as noted to Pt I at **[573]**.

Paras 52A, 52B, 53A: inserted by the Companies Act 1985 (International Accounting Standards and Other Accounting Amendments) Regulations 2004, SI 2004/2947, reg 14(2), Sch 3, paras 1, 9, 10, in relation to companies' financial years which begin on or after 1 January 2005.

Para 54: substituted by the Financial Services and Markets Act 2000 (Consequential Amendments and Repeals) Order 2001, SI 2001/3649, art 34.

Para 58: words in square brackets substituted by SI 2004/2947, reg 14(2), Sch 3, paras 1, 11, in relation to companies' financial years which begin on or after 1 January 2005.

[SCHEDULE 8A
FORM AND CONTENT OF ABBREVIATED ACCOUNTS OF SMALL COMPANIES DELIVERED TO REGISTRAR

Section 246

PART I
BALANCE SHEET FORMATS

1. A small company may deliver to the registrar a copy of the balance sheet showing the items listed in either of the balance sheet formats set out in paragraph 2 below in the order and under the headings and sub-headings given in the format adopted, but in other respects corresponding to the full balance sheet.

2. The formats referred to in paragraph 1 are as follows—

Balance Sheet Formats

Format 1

A. Called up share capital not paid

B. Fixed assets

I Intangible assets

II Tangible assets
III Investments

C. Current assets
I Stocks
II Debtors (1)
III Investments
IV Cash at bank and in hand

D. Prepayments and accrued income

E. Creditors: amounts falling due within one year

F. Net current assets (liabilities)

G. Total assets less current liabilities

H. Creditors: amounts falling due after more than one year

I. [Provisions for liabilities]

J. Accruals and deferred income

K. Capital and reserves
I Called up share capital
II Share premium account
III Revaluation reserve
IV Other reserves
V Profit and loss account

Balance Sheet Formats

Format 2

ASSETS

A. Called up share capital not paid

B. Fixed assets
I Intangible assets
II Tangible assets
III Investments

C. Current assets
I Stocks
II Debtors (1)
III Investments
IV Cash at bank and in hand

D. Prepayments and accrued income

LIABILITIES

A. Capital and reserves
I Called up share capital
II Share premium account
III Revaluation reserve
IV Other reserves
V Profit and loss account

B. [Provisions for liabilities]

C. Creditors (2)

D. Accruals and deferred income

Notes on the balance sheet formats

(1) Debtors

(Formats 1 and 2, item C.II.)

The aggregate amount of debtors falling due after more than one year shall be shown separately, unless it is disclosed in the notes to the accounts.

(2) Creditors

(Format 2, Liabilities item C.)

The aggregate amount of creditors falling due within one year and of creditors falling due after more than one year shall be shown separately, unless it is disclosed in the notes to the accounts.

[577]

NOTES

Repealed as noted to s 1 at **[309]**.

Inserted by the Companies Act 1985 (Accounts of Small and Medium-sized Companies and Minor Accounting Amendments) Regulations 1997, SI 1997/220, reg 2(3), Sch 2, in relation to annual accounts approved by the board of directors on or after 1 March 1997, and to directors' and auditors' reports on such accounts; for a transitional provision see reg 1(4) of the 1997 Regulations.

Words in square brackets in balance sheet format 1 and balance sheet format 2 substituted by the Companies Act 1985 (International Accounting Standards and Other Accounting Amendments) Regulations 2004, SI 2004/2947, reg 14(3), Sch 4, paras 1, 2, in relation to companies' financial years which begin on or after 1 January 2005.

PART II
NOTES TO THE ACCOUNTS

Preliminary

3. Any information required in the case of any small company by the following provisions of this Part of this Schedule shall (if not given in the company's accounts) be given by way of a note to those accounts.

Disclosure of accounting policies

4. The accounting policies adopted by the company in determining the amounts to be included in respect of items shown in the balance sheet and in determining the profit or loss of the company shall be stated (including such policies with respect to the depreciation and diminution in value of assets).

Information supplementing the balance sheet

Share capital and debentures

5.—(1) The following information shall be given with respect to the company's share capital—

- *(a) the authorised share capital; and*
- *(b) where shares of more than one class have been allotted, the number and aggregate nominal value of shares of each class allotted.*

(2) In the case of any part of the allotted share capital that consists of redeemable shares, the following information shall be given—

- *(a) the earliest and latest dates on which the company has power to redeem those shares;*
- *(b) whether those shares must be redeemed in any event or are liable to be redeemed at the option of the company or of the shareholder; and*
- *(c) whether any (and, if so, what) premium is payable on redemption.*

6. If the company has allotted any shares during the financial year, the following information shall be given—

- *(a) the classes of shares allotted; and*
- *(b) as respects each class of shares, the number allotted, their aggregate nominal value, and the consideration received by the company for the allotment.*

Fixed assets

7.—(1) In respect of each item to which a letter or Roman number is assigned under the general item "fixed assets" in the company's balance sheet the following information shall be given—

(a) the appropriate amounts in respect of that item as at the date of the beginning of the financial year and as at the balance sheet date respectively;
(b) the effect on any amount shown in the balance sheet in respect of that item of—
(i) any revision of the amount in respect of any assets included under that item made during that year on any basis mentioned in paragraph 31 of Schedule 8;
(ii) acquisitions during that year of any assets;
(iii) disposals during that year of any assets; and
(iv) any transfers of assets of the company to and from that item during that year.

(2) The reference in sub-paragraph (1)(a) to the appropriate amounts in respect of any item as at any date there mentioned is a reference to amounts representing the aggregate amounts determined, as at that date, in respect of assets falling to be included under that item on either of the following bases, that is to say—
(a) on the basis of purchase price or production cost (determined in accordance with paragraphs 26 and 27 of Schedule 8); or
(b) on any basis mentioned in paragraph 31 of that Schedule,
(leaving out of account in either case any provisions for depreciation or diminution in value).

(3) In respect of each item within sub-paragraph (1)—
(a) the cumulative amount of provisions for depreciation or diminution in value of assets included under that item as at each date mentioned in sub-paragraph (1)(a);
(b) the amount of any such provisions made in respect of the financial year;
(c) the amount of any adjustments made in respect of any such provisions during that year in consequence of the disposal of any assets; and
(d) the amount of any other adjustments made in respect of any such provisions during that year;
shall also be stated.

[Financial fixed assets

7A.—(1) Sub-paragraph (2) applies if—
(a) the company has financial fixed assets that could be included at fair value by virtue of paragraph 34A of Schedule 8,
(b) the amount at which those assets are included under any item in the company's accounts is in excess of their fair value, and
(c) the company has not made provision for diminution in value of those assets in accordance with paragraph 19(1) of that Schedule.

(2) There must be stated—
(a) the amount at which either the individual assets or appropriate groupings of those individual assets are included in the company's accounts,
(b) the fair value of those assets or groupings, and
(c) the reasons for not making a provision for diminution in value of those assets, including the nature of the evidence that provides the basis for the belief that the amount at which they are stated in the accounts will be recovered.]

Details of indebtedness

8.—(1) For the aggregate of all items shown under "creditors" in the company's balance sheet there shall be stated the aggregate of the following amounts, that is to say—
(a) the amount of any debts included under "creditors" which are payable or repayable otherwise than by instalments and fall due for payment or repayment after the end of the period of five years beginning with the day next following the end of the financial year; and
(b) in the case of any debts so included which are payable or repayable by instalments, the amount of any instalments which fall due for payment after the end of that period.

(2) In respect of each item shown under "creditors" in the company's balance sheet there shall be stated the aggregate amount of any debts included under that item, in respect of which any security has been given by the company.

General

9.—(1) Where sums originally denominated in foreign currencies have been brought into account under any items shown in the balance sheet or profit and loss account, the basis on which those sums have been translated into sterling shall be stated.

(2), (3) …

[Dormant Companies Acting as Agents

9A. Where the directors of a company take advantage of the exemption conferred by section 249AA, and the company has during the financial year in question acted as an agent for any person, the fact that it has so acted must be stated.]]

[578]

NOTES

Repealed as noted to s 1 at **[309]**.

Inserted as noted to Pt I at **[577]**.

Para 7A: inserted by the Companies Act 1985 (International Accounting Standards and Other Accounting Amendments) Regulations 2004, SI 2004/2947, reg 14(3), Sch 4, paras 1, 3, in relation to companies' financial years which begin on or after 1 January 2005.

Para 9: sub-paras (2), (3) repealed by the Companies Act 1985 (Investment Companies and Accounting and Audit Amendments) Regulations 2005, SI 2005/2280, reg 7, in relation to companies' financial years which begin on or after 1 January 2005 and which end on or after 1 October 2005.

Para 9A: added by the Companies Act 1985 (Audit Exemption) (Amendment) Regulations 2000, SI 2000/1430, reg 7, in relation to annual reports and reports in respect of financial years ending two months or more after 26 May 2000.

(Schs 9, 9A outside the scope of this work; Sch 10 repealed by the Companies Act 1985 (Insurance Companies Accounts) Regulations 1993, SI 1993/3246, reg 5(1), Sch 2, para 7, for transitional provisions see regs 6, 7 thereof.)

SCHEDULE 10A
PARENT AND SUBSIDIARY UNDERTAKINGS: SUPPLEMENTARY PROVISIONS

Section 258

Introduction

1. The provisions of this Schedule explain expressions used in section 258 (parent and subsidiary undertakings) and otherwise supplement that section.

Voting rights in an undertaking

2.—(1) In section 258(2)(a) and (d) the references to the voting rights in an undertaking are to the rights conferred on shareholders in respect of their shares or, in the case of an undertaking not having a share capital, on members, to vote at general meetings of the undertaking on all, or substantially all, matters.

(2) In relation to an undertaking which does not have general meetings at which matters are decided by the exercise of voting rights, the references to holding a majority of the voting rights in the undertaking shall be construed as references to having the right under the constitution of the undertaking to direct the overall policy of the undertaking or to alter the terms of its constitution.

Right to appoint or remove a majority of the directors

3.—(1) In section 258(2)(b) the reference to the right to appoint or remove a majority of the board of directors is to the right to appoint or remove directors holding a majority of the voting rights at meetings of the board on all, or substantially all, matters.

(2) An undertaking shall be treated as having the right to appoint to a directorship if—

(a) a person's appointment to it follows necessarily from his appointment as director of the undertaking, or

(b) the directorship is held by the undertaking itself.

(3) A right to appoint or remove which is exercisable only with the consent or concurrence of another person shall be left out of account unless no other person has a right to appoint or, as the case may be, remove in relation to that directorship.

Right to exercise dominant influence

4.—(1) For the purposes of section 258(2)(c) an undertaking shall not be regarded as having the right to exercise a dominant influence over another undertaking unless it has a right to give directions with respect to the operating and financial policies of that other undertaking which its directors are obliged to comply with whether or not they are for the benefit of that other undertaking.

(2) A "control contract" means a contract in writing conferring such a right which—

(a) is of a kind authorised by the memorandum or articles of the undertaking in relation to which the right is exercisable, and

(b) is permitted by the law under which that undertaking is established.

(3) This paragraph shall not be read as affecting the construction of the expression "actually exercises a dominant influence" in section 258(4)(a).

Rights exercisable only in certain circumstances or temporarily incapable of exercise

5.—(1) Rights which are exercisable only in certain circumstances shall be taken into account only—

(a) when the circumstances have arisen, and for so long as they continue to obtain, or

(b) when the circumstances are within the control of the person having the rights.

(2) Rights which are normally exercisable but are temporarily incapable of exercise shall continue to be taken into account.

Rights held by one person on behalf of another

6. Rights held by a person in a fiduciary capacity shall be treated as not held by him.

7.—(1) Rights held by a person as nominee for another shall be treated as held by the other.

(2) Rights shall be regarded as held as nominee for another if they are exercisable only on his instructions or with his consent or concurrence.

Rights attached to shares held by way of security

8. Rights attached to shares held by way of security shall be treated as held by the person providing the security—

(a) where apart from the right to exercise them for the purpose of preserving the value of the security, or of realising it, the rights are exercisable only in accordance with his instructions, and

(b) where the shares are held in connection with the granting of loans as part of normal business activities and apart from the right to exercise them for the purpose of preserving the value of the security, or of realising it, the rights are exercisable only in his interests.

Rights attributed to parent undertaking

9.—(1) Rights shall be treated as held by a parent undertaking if they are held by any of its subsidiary undertakings.

(2) Nothing in paragraph 7 or 8 shall be construed as requiring rights held by a parent undertaking to be treated as held by any of its subsidiary undertakings.

(3) For the purposes of paragraph 8 rights shall be treated as being exercisable in accordance with the instructions or in the interests of an undertaking if they are exercisable in accordance with the instructions of or, as the case may be, in the interests of any group undertaking.

Disregard of certain rights

10. The voting rights in an undertaking shall be reduced by any rights held by the undertaking itself.

Supplementary

11. References in any provision of paragraphs 6 to 10 to rights held by a person include rights falling to be treated as held by him by virtue of any other provision of those paragraphs but not rights which by virtue of any such provision are to be treated as not held by him.]

[579]

NOTES

Repealed as noted to s 1 at **[309]**.

Inserted by the Companies Act 1989, s 21(2), Sch 9, subject to transitional provisions contained in the Companies Act 1989 (Commencement No 4 and Transitional and Saving Provisions) Order 1990, SI 1990/355. See the transitional provisions note preceding s 221 at **[356]**.

(Schs 11, 13, 14 outside the scope of this work; Sch 12 repealed, subject to transitional provisions and savings, by the Company Directors Disqualification Act 1986, s 23(1), (2), Schs 3, 4: Sch 15 repealed by the Companies Act 1989, s 212, Sch 24, though the Schedule is still of limited effect by virtue of the Companies Act 1989 (Commencement No 7 and Transitional and Saving Provisions) Order 1990, SI 1990/1707.)

[SCHEDULE 15A
WRITTEN RESOLUTIONS OF PRIVATE COMPANIES

Section 381A(7)

PART I
EXCEPTIONS

1. Section 381A does not apply to—

- *(a) a resolution under section 303 removing a director before the expiration of his period of office, or*
- *(b) a resolution under section 391 removing an auditor before the expiration of his term of office.*

[580]

NOTES

Repealed as noted to s 1 at **[309]**.

Inserted by the Companies Act 1989, s 114(1).

PART II
ADAPTATION OF PROCEDURAL REQUIREMENTS

Introductory

2.—(1) In this Part of this Schedule (which adapts certain requirements of this Act in relation to proceedings under section 381A)—

- *(a) a "written resolution" means a resolution agreed to, or proposed to be agreed to, in accordance with that section, and*
- *(b) a "relevant member" means a member by whom, or on whose behalf, the resolution is required to be signed in accordance with that section.*

(2) A written resolution is not effective if any of the requirements of this Part of this Schedule is not complied with.

Section 95 (disapplication of pre-emption rights)

3.—(1) The following adaptations have effect in relation to a written resolution under section 95(2) (disapplication of pre-emption rights), or renewing a resolution under that provision.

(2) So much of section 95(5) as requires the circulation of a written statement by the directors with a notice of meeting does not apply, but such a statement must be supplied to each relevant member at or before the time at which the resolution is supplied to him for signature.

(3) Section 95(6) (offences) applies in relation to the inclusion in any such statement of matter which is misleading, false or deceptive in a material particular.

Section 155 (financial assistance for purchase of company's own shares or those of holding company)

4. In relation to a written resolution giving approval under section 155(4) or (5) (financial assistance for purchase of company's own shares or those of holding company), section 157(4)(a) (documents to be available at meeting) does not apply, but the documents referred to in that provision must be supplied to each relevant member at or before the time at which the resolution is supplied to him for signature.

Sections 164, 165 and 167 (authority for off-market purchase or contingent purchase contract of company's own shares)

5.—(1) The following adaptations have effect in relation to a written resolution—
- *(a) conferring authority to make an off-market purchase of the company's own shares under section 164(2),*
- *(b) conferring authority to vary a contract for an off-market purchase of the company's own shares under section 164(7), or*
- *(c) varying, revoking or renewing any such authority under section 164(3).*

(2) Section 164(5) (resolution ineffective if passed by exercise of voting rights by member holding shares to which the resolution relates) does not apply; but for the purposes of section 381A(1) a member holding shares to which the resolution relates shall not be regarded as a member who would be entitled to attend and vote.

(3) Section 164(6) (documents to be available at company's registered office and at meeting) does not apply, but the documents referred to in that provision and, where that provision applies by virtue of section 164(7), the further documents referred to in that provision must be supplied to each relevant member at or before the time at which the resolution is supplied to him for signature.

(4) The above adaptations also have effect in relation to a written resolution in relation to which the provisions of section 164(3) to (7) apply by virtue of—
- *(a) section 165(2) (authority for contingent purchase contract), or*
- *(b) section 167(2) (approval of release of rights under contract approved under section 164 or 165).*

Section 173 (approval for payment out of capital)

6.—(1) The following adaptations have effect in relation to a written resolution giving approval under section 173(2) (redemption or purchase of company's own shares out of capital).

(2) Section 174(2) (resolution ineffective if passed by exercise of voting rights by member holding shares to which the resolution relates) does not apply; but for the purposes of section 381A(1) a member holding shares to which the resolution relates shall not be regarded as a member who would be entitled to attend and vote.

(3) Section 174(4) (documents to be available at meeting) does not apply, but the documents referred to in that provision must be supplied to each relevant member at or before the time at which the resolution is supplied to him for signature.

Section 319 (approval of director's service contract)

7. In relation to a written resolution approving any such term as is mentioned in section 319(1) (director's contract of employment for more than five years), section 319(5) (documents to be available at company's registered office and at meeting) does not apply, but the documents referred to in that provision must be supplied to each relevant member at or before the time at which the resolution is supplied to him for signature.

Section 337 (funding of director's expenditure in performing his duties)

8. In relation to a written resolution giving approval under section 337(3)(a) (funding a director's expenditure in performing his duties), the requirement of that provision that certain matters be disclosed at the meeting at which the resolution is passed does not apply, but those matters must be disclosed to each relevant member at or before the time at which the resolution is supplied to him for signature.]

[581]

NOTES

Repealed as noted to s 1 at **[309]**.
Inserted as noted to Pt I at **[580]**.

(Schs 15B, 21, 21A, 21B, 21C, 21D, 22–25 outside the scope of this work; Sch 16 repealed by the Insolvency Act 1986, s 438, Sch 12; Schs 17–19, 20, Pt I repealed by the Insolvency Act 1985, s 235(3), Sch 10, Pt II; Sch 20, Pt II applies to Scotland only.)

BUSINESS NAMES ACT 1985

(1985 c 7)

ARRANGEMENT OF SECTIONS

An Act to consolidate certain enactments relating to the names under which persons may carry on business in Great Britain

[11 March 1985]

1 Persons subject to this Act

(1) This Act applies to any person who has a place of business in Great Britain and who carries on business in Great Britain under a name which—

(a) *in the case of a partnership, does not consist of the surnames of all partners who are individuals and the corporate names of all partners who are bodies corporate without any addition other than an addition permitted by this Act;*

(b) *in the case of an individual, does not consist of his surname without any addition other than one so permitted;*

(c) *in the case of a company, being a company which is capable of being wound up under the Companies Act 1985, does not consist of its corporate name without any addition other than one so permitted;*

[(d) *in the case of a limited liability partnership, does not consist of its corporate name without any addition other than one so permitted].*

(2) *The following are permitted additions for the purposes of subsection (1)—*

(*a*) *in the case of a partnership, the forenames of individual partners or the initials of those forenames or, where two or more individual partners have the same surname, the addition of "s" at the end of that surname; or*

(*b*) *in the case of an individual, his forename or its initial;*

(*c*) *in any case, any addition merely indicating that the business is carried on in succession to a former owner of the business.*

[582]

NOTES

This Act is repealed by the Companies Act 2006, s 1295, Sch 16, as from a day to be appointed under s 1300(2) of that Act. For provision relating to the continuity of law, see s 1297 of the 2006 Act.

Sub-s (1): para (d) added by the Limited Liability Partnerships Regulations 2001, SI 2001/1090, reg 9(1), Sch 5, para 10.

2 Prohibition of use of certain business names

(*1*) *Subject to the following subsections, a person to whom this Act applies shall not, without the written approval of the Secretary of State, carry on business in Great Britain under a name which—*

(*a*) *would be likely to give the impression that the business is connected with Her Majesty's Government[, with any part of the Scottish Administration,] or with any local authority; or*

(*b*) *includes any word or expression for the time being specified in regulations made under this Act.*

(*2*) *Subsection (1) does not apply to the carrying on of a business by a person—*

(*a*) *to whom the business has been transferred on or after 26th February 1982; and*

(*b*) *who carries on the business under the name which was its lawful business name immediately before that transfer,*

during the period of 12 months beginning with the date of that transfer.

(*3*) *Subsection (1) does not apply to the carrying on of a business by a person who—*

(*a*) *carried on that business immediately before 26th February 1982; and*

(*b*) *continues to carry it on under the name which immediately before that date was its lawful business name.*

(*4*) *A person who contravenes subsection (1) is guilty of an offence.*

[583]

NOTES

Repealed as noted to s 1 at **[582]**.

Sub-s (1): words in square brackets in para (a) inserted by the Scotland Act 1998 (Consequential Modifications) (No 2) Order 1999, SI 1999/1820, art 4, Sch 2, Pt I, para 79.

Secretary of State: by the Contracting Out (Functions in relation to the Registration of Companies) Order 1995, SI 1995/1013, art 5, Sch 3, paras 2, 3, the functions of the Secretary of State conferred by or under this section may be exercised by, or by employees of, such person (if any) as may be authorised in that behalf by the Secretary of State.

3 Words and expressions requiring Secretary of State's approval

(*1*) *The Secretary of State may by regulations—*

(*a*) *specify words or expressions for the use of which as or as part of a business name his approval is required by section 2(1)(b); and*

(*b*) *in relation to any such word or expression, specify a Government department or other body as the relevant body for purposes of the following subsection.*

(*2*) *Where a person to whom this Act applies proposes to carry on a business under a name which is or includes any such word or expression, and a Government department or other body is specified under subsection (1)(b) in relation to that word or expression, that person shall—*

(*a*) *request (in writing) the relevant body to indicate whether (and if so why) it has any objections to the proposal; and*

(*b*) *submit to the Secretary of State a statement that such a request has been made and a copy of any response received from the relevant body.*

[584]

NOTES

Repealed as noted to s 1 at **[582]**.
Regulations: the Company and Business Names Regulations 1981, SI 1981/1685.

4 Disclosure required of persons using business names

(1) A person to whom this Act applies shall—

(a) [subject to subsections (3) and (3A)], state in legible characters on all business letters, written orders for goods or services to be supplied to the business, invoices and receipts issued in the course of the business and written demands for payment of debts arising in the course of the business—

(i) in the case of a partnership, the name of each partner,

(ii) in the case of an individual, his name,

(iii) in the case of a company, its corporate name, …

[(iiia) in the case of a limited liability partnership, its corporate name and the name of each member, and]

(iv) in relation to each person so named, an address in Great Britain at which service of any document relating in any way to the business will be effective; and

(b) in any premises where the business is carried on and to which the customers of the business or suppliers of any goods or services to the business have access, display in a prominent position so that it may easily be read by such customers or suppliers a notice containing such names and addresses.

(2) A person to whom this Act applies shall secure that the names and addresses required by subsection (1)(a) to be stated on his business letters, or which would have been so required but for [subsection (3) or (3A], are immediately given, by written notice to any person with whom anything is done or discussed in the course of the business and who asks for such names and addresses.

(3) Subsection (1)(a) does not apply in relation to any document issued by a partnership of more than 20 persons which maintains at its principal place of business a list of the names of all the partners if—

(a) none of the names of the partners appears in the document otherwise than in the text or as a signatory; and

(b) the document states in legible characters the address of the partnership's principal place of business and that the list of the partners' names is open to inspection at that place.

[(3A) Subsection (1)(a) does not apply in relation to any document issued by a limited liability partnership with more than 20 members which maintains at its principal place of business a list of the names of all the members—

(a) none of the names of the members appears in the document otherwise than in the text or as a signatory; and

(b) the document states in legible characters the address of the principal place of business of the limited liability partnership and that the list of the members' names is open to inspection at that place.]

(4) Where a partnership maintains a list of the partners' names for purposes of subsection (3), any person may inspect the list during office hours.

[(4A) Where a limited liability partnership maintains a list of the members' names for the purposes of subsection (3A), any person may inspect the list during office hours.]

(5) The Secretary of State may by regulations require notices under subsection (1)(b) or (2) to be displayed or given in a specified form.

(6) A person who without reasonable excuse contravenes subsection (1) or (2), or any regulations made under subsection (5), is guilty of an offence.

(7) Where an inspection required by a person in accordance with subsection (4) [or (4A)] is refused, any partner of the partnership concerned[, or any member of the limited liability partnership concerned,] who without reasonable excuse refused that inspection, or permitted it to be refused, is guilty of an offence.

[585]

NOTES

Repealed as noted to s 1 at **[582]**.

Sub-s (1): words in first pair of square brackets substituted, word omitted repealed, and sub-para (iiia) inserted by the Limited Liability Partnerships Regulations 2001, SI 2001/1090, reg 9(1), Sch 5, para 11(1), (2).

Sub-s (2): words in square brackets substituted by SI 2001/1090, reg 9(1), Sch 5, para 11(1), (3).

Sub-s (3A): inserted by SI 2001/1090, reg 9(1), Sch 5, para 11(1), (4).

Sub-s (4A): inserted by SI 2001/1090, reg 9(1), Sch 5, para 11(1), (5).

Sub-s (7): words in square brackets inserted by SI 2001/1090, reg 9(1), Sch 5, para 11(1), (6).

5 Civil remedies for breach of s 4

(1) Any legal proceedings brought by a person to whom this Act applies to enforce a right arising out of a contract made in the course of a business in respect of which he was, at the time the contract was made, in breach of subsection (1) or (2) of section 4 shall be dismissed if the defendant (or, in Scotland, the defender) to the proceedings shows—

(a) that he has a claim against the plaintiff (pursuer) arising out of that contract which he has been unable to pursue by reason of the latter's breach of section 4(1) or (2), or

(b) that he has suffered some financial loss in connection with the contract by reason of the plaintiff's (pursuer's) breach of section 4(1) or (2),

unless the court before which the proceedings are brought is satisfied that it is just and equitable to permit the proceedings to continue.

(2) This section is without prejudice to the right of any person to enforce such rights as he may have against another person in any proceedings brought by that person.

[586]

NOTES

Repealed as noted to s 1 at **[582]**.

6 Regulations

(1) Regulations under this Act shall be made by statutory instrument and may contain such transitional provisions and savings as the Secretary of State thinks appropriate, and may make different provision for different cases or classes of case.

(2) In the case of regulations made under section 3, the statutory instrument containing them shall be laid before Parliament after the regulations are made and shall cease to have effect at the end of the period of 28 days beginning with the day on which they were made (but without prejudice to anything previously done by virtue of them or to the making of new regulations) unless during that period they are approved by a resolution of each House of Parliament.

In reckoning this period of 28 days, no account is to be taken of any time during which Parliament is dissolved or prorogued, or during which both Houses are adjourned for more than 4 days.

(3) In the case of regulations made under section 4, the statutory instrument containing them is subject to annulment in pursuance of a resolution of either House of Parliament.

[587]

NOTES

Repealed as noted to s 1 at **[582]**.

7 Offences

(1) Offences under this Act are punishable on summary conviction.

(2) A person guilty of an offence under this Act is liable to a fine not exceeding one-fifth of the statutory maximum.

(3) If after a person has been convicted summarily of an offence under section 2 or 4(6) the original contravention is continued, he is liable on a second or subsequent summary conviction of the offence to a fine not exceeding one-fiftieth of the statutory maximum for each day on which the contravention is continued (instead of to the penalty which may be imposed on the first conviction of the offence).

(4) Where an offence under section 2 or 4(6) or (7) committed by a body corporate is proved to have been committed with the consent or connivance of, or to be attributable to any neglect on the part of, any director, manager, secretary or other similar officer of the body corporate, or any person who was purporting to act in any such capacity, he as well as the body corporate is guilty of the offence and liable to be proceeded against and punished accordingly.

(5) Where the affairs of a body corporate are managed by its members, subsection (4) applies in relation to the acts and defaults of a member in connection with his functions of managements as if he were a director of the body corporate.

(6) For purposes of the following provisions of the Companies Act 1985—
(a) section 731 (summary proceedings under the Companies Acts), and
(b) section 732(3) (legal professional privilege),
this Act is to be treated as included in those Acts.

[588]

NOTES

Repealed as noted to s 1 at **[582]**.

8 Interpretation

(1) The following definitions apply for purposes of this Act—
"business" includes a profession;
"initial" includes any recognised abbreviation of a name;
"lawful business name", in relation to a business, means a name under which the business was carried on without contravening section 2(1) of this Act or section 2 of the Registration of Business Names Act 1916;
"local authority" means any local authority within the meaning of the Local Government Act 1972 or the Local Government (Scotland) Act 1973, the Common Council of the City of London or the Council of the Isles of Scilly;
"partnership" includes a foreign partnership;

.....

and "surname", in relation to a peer or person usually known by a British title different from his surname, means the title by which he is known.

(2) Any expression used in this Act and also in the Companies Act 1985 has the same meaning in this Act as in that.

[589]

NOTES

Repealed as noted to s 1 at **[582]**.
Sub-s (1): definition "statutory maximum" repealed by the Statute Law (Repeals) Act 1993.

9 Northern Ireland

This Act does not extend to Northern Ireland.

[590]

NOTES

Repealed as noted to s 1 at **[582]**.

10 Commencement

This Act comes into force on 1st July 1985.

[591]

NOTES

Repealed as noted to s 1 at **[582]**.

11 Citation

This Act may be cited as the Business Names Act 1985.

[592]

NOTES
Repealed as noted to s 1 at **[582]**.

HOUSING ACT 1985

(1985 c 68)

An Act to consolidate the Housing Acts (except those provisions consolidated in the Housing Associations Act 1985 and the Landlord and Tenant Act 1985), and certain related provisions, with amendments to give effect to recommendations of the Law Commission
[30 October 1985]

1–117 ((*Pts I–IV*) *outside the scope of this work.*)

PART V
THE RIGHT TO BUY

118–171H (*Outside the scope of this work.*)

Modifications of Leasehold Reform Act 1967 in relation to leases granted under this Part

172 Exclusion of leases where landlord is housing association and freeholder is a charity

(1) Part I of the Leasehold Reform Act 1967 (enfranchisement and extension of long leaseholds) does not apply where, in the case of a tenancy or sub-tenancy to which this section applies, the landlord is a housing association and the freehold is owned by a body of persons or trust established for charitable purposes only.

(2) This section applies to a tenancy created by the grant of a lease in pursuance of this Part of a dwelling-house which is a house.

(3) Where Part I of the 1967 Act applies as if there had been a single tenancy granted for a term beginning at the same time as the term under a tenancy falling within subsection (2) and expiring at the same time as the term under a later tenancy, this section also applies to that later tenancy.

(4) This section applies to any sub-tenancy directly or indirectly derived out of a tenancy falling within subsection (2) or (3).

[593]

NOTES
Charitable purposes: see the Charities Act 2006, s 2 at **[2132]**.

173–603 (*Ss 173–188, ss 189–603* (*Pts VI–XVII*) *outside the scope of this work.*)

PART XVIII
MISCELLANEOUS AND GENERAL PROVISIONS

604–624 (*Outside the scope of this work.*)

Final provisions

625 Short title, commencement and extent

(1) This Act may be cited as the Housing Act 1985.

(2) This Act comes into force on 1st April 1986.

(3) This Act extends to England and Wales only.

[594]

SCHEDULES
SCHEDULE 1

Section 79

TENANCIES WHICH ARE NOT SECURE TENANCIES

1, 1A, 2–4, 4A, 5–11. (*Outside the scope of this work.*)

Almshouses

[12. A licence to occupy a dwelling-house is not a secure tenancy if—
(a) the dwelling-house is an almshouse, and
(b) the licence was granted by or on behalf of a charity which—
(i) is authorised under its trusts to maintain the dwelling-house as an almshouse, and
(ii) has no power under its trusts to grant a tenancy of the dwelling-house;

and in this paragraph "almshouse" means any premises maintained as an almshouse, whether they are called an almshouse or not; and "trusts", in relation to a charity, means the provisions establishing it as a charity and regulating its purposes and administration, whether those provisions take effect by way of trust or not.]

[595]

NOTES

Para 12: substituted by the Charities Act 1992, s 78(1), Sch 6, para 12.

(*Schs 2–24 outside the scope of this work.*)

HOUSING ASSOCIATIONS ACT 1985

(1985 c 69)

ARRANGEMENT OF SECTIONS

PART I
REGULATION OF HOUSING ASSOCIATIONS

Introductory

PART I STATUTES

PART II
HOUSING ASSOCIATION FINANCE

Arrangements with local authorities

Miscellaneous

Supplementary provisions

PART III
THE HOUSING CORPORATION

Constitution and other general matters

Relevant Authority's powers with respect to grants and loans

Relevant Authority's powers with respect to land and works

The Relevant Authority's finances

Acquisition of securities and control of subsidiaries

Supplementary provisions

PART IV
GENERAL PROVISIONS

General provisions

An Act to consolidate certain provisions of the Housing Acts relating to housing associations, with amendments to give effect to recommendations of the Law Commission and of the Scottish Law Commission

[30 October 1985]

NOTES

Transfer of functions in relation to Wales: as to the transfer of functions under this Act from Ministers of the Crown to the National Assembly for Wales, see the National Assembly for Wales (Transfer of Functions) Order 1999, SI 1999/672.

PART I
REGULATION OF HOUSING ASSOCIATIONS

INTRODUCTORY

1 Meaning of "housing association" and related expressions

(1) In this Act "housing association" means a society, body of trustees or company—

(a) which is established for the purpose of, or amongst whose objects or powers are included those of, providing, constructing, improving or managing, or facilitating or encouraging the construction or improvement of, housing accommodation, and

(b) which does not trade for profit or whose constitution or rules prohibit the issue of capital with interest or dividend exceeding such rate as may be prescribed by the Treasury, whether with or without differentiation as between share and loan capital[...]

(2) In this Act "fully mutual", in relation to a housing association, means that the rules of the association—

(a) restrict membership to persons who are tenants or prospective tenants of the association, and

(b) preclude the granting or assignment of tenancies to persons other than members;

and "co-operative housing association" means a fully mutual housing association which is a society registered under the Industrial and Provident Societies Act 1965...

(3) In this Act "self-build society" means a housing association whose object is to provide, for sale to, or occupation by, its members, dwellings built or improved principally with the use of its members' own labour.

[596]

NOTES

Sub-s (1): words omitted from square brackets added by the Housing (Scotland) Act 1988, ss 1, 3, Sch 2, para 6, repealed by the Housing (Scotland) Act 2001 (asp 10), s 112, Sch 10, para 11(1), (2).

Sub-s (2): words omitted repealed, in relation to England and Wales, by the Housing Act 1996 (Consequential Provisions) Order 1996, SI 1996/2325, art 4(1), Sch 1, Pt I.

2 Meaning of "housing trust"

In this Act "housing trust" means a corporation or body of persons which—

(a) is required by the terms of its constituent instrument to use the whole of its funds, including any surplus which may arise from its operations, for the purpose of providing housing accommodation, or

(b) is required by the terms of its constituent instrument to devote the whole, or substantially the whole, of its funds to charitable purposes and in fact uses the whole, or substantially the whole, of its funds for the purpose of providing housing accommodation.

[597]

NOTES

Charitable purposes: see the Charities Act 2006, s 2 at **[2132]**.

2A (*Inserted by the Housing Act 1988, s 59, Sch 6, para 1; repealed by the Housing Act 1996 (Consequential Provisions) Order 1996, SI 1996/2325, art 4(1), Sch 1, Pts I, II.*)

[2B Meaning of "registered housing association", "registered social landlord" etc

In this Act, unless the context otherwise requires—

"registered housing association" means a housing association registered in the register [of social landlords maintained under section 57 of the Housing (Scotland) Act 2001 (asp 10)],

"registered social landlord" has the same meaning as in Part I of the Housing Act 1996, and

"unregistered", in relation to a housing association, means neither registered in the register [of social landlords maintained under section 57 of the Housing (Scotland) Act 2001 (asp 10)] nor registered as a social landlord under Part I of the Housing Act 1996.]

[598]

NOTES

Commencement: 1 October 1996.

Inserted by the Housing Act 1996 (Consequential Provisions) Order 1996, SI 1996/2325, art 5(1), Sch 2, para 15(1), (1), (2).

In definitions "registered housing association", "unregistered" words in square brackets substituted (and definition "registered social landlord" repealed in relation to Scotland) by the Housing (Scotland) Act 2001 (asp 10), s 112, Sch 10, para 11(1), (3)(a), (c).

3–7 (*Repealed, in relation to England and Wales, by the Housing Act 1996, s 227, Sch 19, Pt I; but note that the repeal of s 4(6) does not affect the priority of mortgages entered into before 1 October 1996, see the Housing Act 1996 (Commencement No 3 and Transitional Provisions) Order 1996, SI 1996/2402, art 3, Schedule, para 2.*)

Disposal of land

8 (*Repealed, in relation to England and Wales, by the Housing Act 1996, s 227, Sch 19, Pt I.*)

9 Control by [Corporation] of dispositions of land by housing associations

[(1) …

(1A) Subject to section 10, the consent of the relevant Corporation is required for any disposition of grant-aided land (as defined in Schedule 1) by an unregistered housing association; and for this purpose "the relevant Corporation" means,—

(a) if the land is in England, the Housing Corporation;
(b) (*applies to Scotland only*); and
(c) if the land is in Wales, [the Secretary of State].]

(2) [Consent under this section] may be so given—
(a) generally to all housing associations or to a particular housing association or description of association;
(b) in relation to particular land or in relation to a particular description of land;
and may be given subject to conditions.

(3) A disposition by a housing association which requires [consent] under this section is valid in favour of a person claiming under the association notwithstanding that [that consent] has not been given; and a person dealing with the association, or with a person claiming under the association, shall not be concerned to see or inquire whether any such consent has been given.

This subsection has effect subject to section 12 (avoidance of certain dispositions of houses without consent).

(4) …

(5) For the purposes of this section "disposition" means sale, lease, mortgage, charge or any other disposal.

[(6 References in this section to consent are references,—
(a) in the case of the Housing Corporation …; to consent given by order under the seal of the Corporation; and
(b) (*applies to Scotland only.*)]

[599]

NOTES

Repealed, in relation to Scotland, by the Housing (Scotland) Act 2001, s 112, Sch 10, para 11(1), (4).
Section heading: word in square brackets substituted by the Housing Act 1988, s 59, Sch 6, Pt I, para 2.
Sub-s (1): substituted, together with sub-s (1A) for original sub-s (1), by the Housing Act 1988, s 59, Sch 6, Pt I, para 7; repealed, in relation to England and Wales, by the Housing Act 1996, s 227, Sch 19, Pt I.
Sub-s (1A): substituted, together with sub-s (1) for original sub-s (1), by the Housing Act 1988, s 59, Sch 6, Pt I, para 7; words in square brackets substituted by the Government of Wales Act 1998, s 140, Sch 16, paras 23, 24(1), (2).
Sub-s (2): words in square brackets substituted by the Housing Act 1996 (Consequential Provisions) Order 1996, SI 1996/2325, art 5(1), Sch 2, para 15(1), (1), (10).
Sub-s (3): words in square brackets substituted by the Housing Act 1988, s 59, Sch 6, Pt I, para 7.
Sub-s (4): repealed, in relation to England and Wales, by the Housing Act 1996, s 227, Sch 19, Pt I.
Sub-s (6): added by the Housing Act 1988, s 59, Sch 6, Pt I, para 7; words omitted from para (a) repealed by the Government of Wales Act 1998, ss 140, 152, Sch 16, paras 23, 24(1), (3)(a), Sch 18, Pt VI.

10 Dispositions excepted from s 9

(1) A disposition by an unregistered housing association which is a charity is not within section 9 if by virtue of [sections 36 and 38 of the Charities Act 1993] it cannot be made without an order of the court or the [Charity Commission]; but [before making an order in such a case the [Charity Commission] shall consult,—
(a) in the case of dispositions of land in England, the Housing Corporation;
(b) (*applies to Scotland only*); and
(c) in the case of dispositions of land in Wales, [the Secretary of State]].

(2) A letting … by an unregistered housing association which is a housing trust, is not within section 9 if it is—
(a) a letting of land under a secure tenancy, or
(b) a letting of land under what would be a secure tenancy but for any of paragraphs 2 to 12 of [Schedule 1 to the Housing Act 1985] or [paragraphs 1 to 8 of Schedule 2 to the Housing (Scotland) Act 1987] (tenancies excepted from being secure tenancies for reasons other than that they are long leases) [or
(c) a letting of land under an assured tenancy or an assured agricultural occupancy, or
(d) a letting of land in England or Wales under what would be an assured tenancy or an assured agricultural occupancy but for any of paragraphs 4 to 8 of Schedule 1 to the Housing Act 1988, or
(e) (*applies to Scotland only.*)

(3) The grant by an unregistered housing association which does not satisfy the landlord condition in section 80 of the Housing Act 1985 (bodies which are capable of granting secure tenancies) of a lease for a term ending within the period of seven years and three months beginning on the date of the grant is not within section 9 unless—

(a) there is conferred on the lessee (by the lease or otherwise) an option for renewal for a term which, together with the original term, would expire outside that period, or

(b) the lease is granted wholly or partly in consideration of a fine.

(4) In subsection (3) the expression "lease" includes an agreement for a lease and a licence to occupy, and the expressions "grant" and "term" shall be construed accordingly.
[600]

NOTES

Repealed, in relation to Scotland, by the Housing (Scotland) Act 2001, s 112, Sch 10, para 11(1), (4).

Sub-s (1): words in first pair of square brackets substituted by the Charities Act 1993, s 98(1), Sch 6, para 21(1), (2); words in second and fourth (inner) pairs of square brackets substituted by the Charities Act 2006, s 75(1), Sch 8, para 78; words in third (outer) pair of square brackets substituted by the Housing Act 1988, s 59, Sch 6, Pt I, para 8(1); words in fifth (inner) pair of square brackets substituted by the Government of Wales Act 1998, s 140, Sch 16, paras 23, 25.

Sub-s (2): words omitted repealed, in relation to England and Wales, by the Housing Act 1996 (Consequential Provisions) Order 1996, SI 1996/2325, art 4(1), Sch 1, Pt I; in para (b) words in first pair of square brackets substituted by the Housing and Planning Act 1986, s 24(1)(j), Sch 5, Pt I, para 10(6), (9), words in second pair of square brackets substituted by the Housing (Scotland) Act 1987, s 339(2), Sch 23, para 31(2), and by the Housing (Scotland) Act 1988, s 72, Sch 9, para 6(a); paras (c)–(e) added by the Housing Act 1988, s 59, Sch 6, Pt I, para 8(2).

11 *(Repealed by the Housing Act 1996, s 227, Sch 19, Pt I.)*

12 Avoidance of certain disposals of houses without consent

A disposal of a house by a housing association made without the consent required by section 9 is void unless—

(a) the disposal is to an individual (or to two or more individuals), and

(b) the disposal does not extend to any other house.
[601]

13–32 *(Repealed, in relation to England and Wales, by the Housing Act 1996, s 227, Sch 19, Pt I; but note that the repeal of s 24 does not affect the application of an order made under that section in relation to periods ending on or before 30 September 1996, see the Housing Act 1996 (Commencement No 3 and Transitional Provisions) Order 1996, SI 1996/2402, art 3, Schedule, para 4, and repealed in relation to Scotland by the Housing (Scotland) Act 2001 (asp 10), s 112, Sch 10, para 11(1), (4).)*

Miscellaneous

33 *(Repealed, in relation to England and Wales, by the Housing Act 1996, s 227, Sch 19, Pt I and, in relation to Scotland, by the Housing (Scotland) Act 2001 (asp 10), s 112, Sch 10, para 11(1), (4).)*

[33A Provision of services between the Corporations

Any of the [following[, that is to say, the Housing Corporation, the Secretary of State] or Scottish Homes,] may enter into an agreement with the others or either of them for the provision of services of any description by the one to the other or others on such terms, as to payment or otherwise, as the parties to the agreement consider appropriate.]
[602]

NOTES

Inserted by the Housing Act 1988, s 59, Sch 6, Pt I, para 24.

Words in first (outer) pair of square brackets substituted by the Housing Act 1996 (Consequential Provisions) Order 1996, SI 1996/2325, art 5(1), Sch 2, para 15(1), (1), (19); words in second (inner) pair of square brackets substituted by the Government of Wales Act 1998, s 140, Sch 16, paras 23, 26.

34 Provision of land by county councils

(1) Where a housing association wishes to erect houses [in England] which in the opinion of the Secretary of State are required and the local housing authority in whose district the houses are proposed to be built are unwilling to acquire land with a view to selling or leasing it to the association, the county council, on the application of the association, may acquire land for that purpose.

(2) For that purpose the county council may exercise all the powers of a local housing authority under Part II of the Housing Act 1985 (provision of housing) in regard to the acquisition and disposal of land; and the provisions of that Act as to the acquisition of land by local housing authorities for the purposes of that Part apply accordingly.

[603]

NOTES

Sub-s (1): words in square brackets inserted by the Local Government (Wales) Act 1994, s 22(2), Sch 8, para 6(1).

35 Housing trusts: power to transfer housing to local housing authority

(1) A housing trust may—
- (a) sell or lease to the local housing authority the houses provided by the trust, or
- (b) make over to the authority the management of the houses.

(2) So far as subsection (1) confers power to dispose of land—
- [(a) it does not apply to registered social landlords (on whom power to dispose of land is conferred by section 8 of the Housing Act 1996);]
- (b) it has effect subject to section 9 (dispositions requiring consent ...) where the housing trust is an unregistered housing association and the land is grant-aided land (as defined in Schedule 1); and
- (c) it has effect subject to [[section 36 of the Charities Act 1993] (restrictions on dispositions of charity land)] where the housing trust is a charity.

[604]

NOTES

Sub-s (2): para (a) substituted by the Housing Act 1996 (Consequential Provisions) Order 1996, SI 1996/2325, art 5(1), Sch 2, para 15(1), (1), (20); words omitted from para (b) repealed by the Government of Wales Act 1998, s 152, Sch 18, Pt VI; words in first (outer) pair of square brackets in para (c) substituted by the Charities Act 1992, s 78(1), Sch 6, para 13(3), words in second (inner) pair of square brackets substituted by the Charities Act 1993, s 98(1), Sch 6, para 21(1), (4).

36 Housing trusts: functions of Secretary of State with respect to legal proceedings

(1) If it appears to the Secretary of State—
- (a) that the institution of legal proceedings is requisite or desirable with respect to any property belonging to a housing trust, or
- (b) that the expediting of any such legal proceedings is requisite or desirable,

he may certify the case to the Attorney-General who may institute legal proceedings or intervene in legal proceedings already instituted in such manner as he thinks proper in the circumstances.

(2) Before preparing a scheme with reference to property belonging to a housing trust, the court or body which is responsible for making the scheme shall communicate with the Secretary of State and consider any recommendations made by him with reference to the proposed scheme.

[605]

36A (*Inserted by the Housing Act 1988, s 49; repealed, in relation to England and Wales, by the Housing Act 1996, s 227, Sch 19, Pt I, and, in relation to Scotland, by the Housing (Scotland) Act 2001 (asp 10), s 112, Sch 10, para 11(1), (4).*)

Supplementary

37 (*Repealed, in relation to England and Wales, by the Housing Act 1996 (Consequential Provisions) Order 1996, SI 1996/2325, art 4(1), Sch 1, Pt and, in relation to Scotland, by the Housing (Scotland) Act 2001 (asp 10), s 112, Sch 10, para 11(1), (4).*)

38 Definitions relating to charities

In this Part—

(a) "charity" has the same meaning as in [the Charities Act 1993]; and

(b) …

[606]

NOTES

Repealed in relation to Scotland by the Housing (Scotland) Act 2001 (asp 10), s 112, Sch 10, para 11(1), (4).

Words in square brackets substituted by the Charities Act 1993, s 98(1), Sch 6, para 21(1), (5)(a); para (b) repealed by the Housing Act 1996 (Consequential Provisions) Order 1996, SI 1996/2325, art 4(1), Sch 1, Pt I.

39 Minor definitions

In this Part—

["assured tenancy" has, in England and Wales, the same meaning as in Part I of the Housing Act 1988 and, in Scotland, the same meaning as in Part II of the Housing (Scotland) Act 1988;

"assured agricultural occupancy" has the same meaning as in Part I of the Housing Act 1988,]

.....

"secure tenancy" has the same meaning as in section 79 of the Housing Act 1985 or section [44 of the Housing (Scotland) Act 1987];

.....

[607]

NOTES

Repealed in relation to Scotland by the Housing (Scotland) Act 2001 (asp 10), s 112, Sch 10, para 11(1), (4).

Definitions "assured tenancy" and "assured agricultural occupancy" inserted by the Housing Act 1988, s 59, Sch 6, Pt I, para 25; definition "mental disorder" repealed, in relation to England and Wales, by the Housing Act 1996 (Consequential Provisions) Order 1996, SI 1996/2325, art 4(1), Sch 1, Pt I; in definition "secure tenancy" words in square brackets substituted by the Housing (Scotland) Act 1987, s 339(2), Sch 23, para 31(3), and also by the Housing (Scotland) Act 1988, s 72(2), Sch 9, para 8; definition "standard scale" repealed by the Statute Law (Repeals) Act 1993.

40 Index of defined expressions: Part I

The following Table shows provisions defining or explaining expressions used in this Part (other than provisions defining or explaining an expression used only in the same section or paragraph)—

… ..	
[assured agricultural occupancy	section 39
assured tenancy	section 39]
… ..	
charity	section 38(a)
… ..	
co-operative housing association	section 1(2)
… ..	
district (of a local housing authority)	section 104(2)
… ..	
fully mutual (in relation to a housing association)	section 1(2)
… ..	
house	section 106
… ..	

housing association	section 1(1)
... ..	
housing trust	section 2
... ..	
local housing authority	section 104
... ..	
[registered social landlord	section 2B]
... ..	
secure tenancy	section 39
... ..	
[unregistered (in relation to a housing association)	section 2B]

[608]

NOTES

Repealed in relation to Scotland by the Housing (Scotland) Act 2001 (asp 10), s 112, Sch 10, para 11(1), (4).

Entries "appropriate registrar", "bank", "committee", "compulsory disposal", "co-opted member", "the Companies Act", "the Corporation", "dissolved under the 1965 Act", "dwelling", "eligible for registration", "exempted disposal", "friendly society", "hostel", "housing activities", "insurance company", "member of family", "mental disorder", "the 1965 Act", "register, registered, registration and unregistered (in relation to a housing association)", "registered charity", "relevant disposal", "shared ownership lease", "standard scale" and "trustee savings bank" repealed, in relation to England and Wales, by the Housing Act 1996 (Consequential Provisions) Order 1996, SI 1996/2325, art 4(1), Sch 1, Pt I.

Entries "assured agricultural occupancy" and "assured tenancy" inserted and entries "housing association grant" and "revenue deficit grant" repealed by the Housing Act 1988, ss 59, 140(2), Sch 6, Pt I, para 26, Sch 18.

Entries "registered social landlord" and "unregistered (in relation to a housing association)" inserted by SI 1996/2325, art 5(1), Sch 2, para 15(1), (21).

Other entries omitted (as inserted in part by the Housing (Scotland) Act 1986, s 25(1), Sch 2, para 4) apply to Scotland only.

PART II
HOUSING ASSOCIATION FINANCE

41–57 *(Ss 41–53 repealed by the Housing Act 1988, s 140(2), Sch 18; s 54 repealed by the Housing Act 1988, s 140(2), Sch 18, except in relation to a revenue deficit grant payable to an association for a period that expires before 1 April 1989 (see the Housing Act 1988 (Commencement No 4) Order 1989, SI 1989/404, art 3(c)); s 55 repealed by the Housing Act 1988, s 140(2), Sch 18, except in relation to a hostel deficit grant payable to an association for a period that expires before 1 April 1991 (see the Housing Act 1988 (Commencement No 5 and Transitional Provisions) Order 1991, SI 1991/954, art 3); ss 56, 57 repealed by the Housing Act 1988, s 140(2), Sch 18, except in relation to a revenue deficit grant payable to an association for a period that expires before 1 April 1989 and except in relation to a hostel deficit grant payable to an association for a period that expires before 1 April 1991 (see SI 1989/404, art 3(c) and SI 1991/954, art 3.)*

Arrangements with local authorities

[58 Powers of local authorities to promote and assist housing associations: England and Wales

(1) A local authority may promote the formation or extension of a housing association.

(2) A local authority may for the assistance of a housing association subscribe for share or loan capital of the association.

(3) A local authority may make a loan to an unregistered self-build society for the purpose of enabling it to meet the whole or part of the expenditure incurred, or to be incurred by it, in carrying out its objects.

(4) This section does not apply where the housing association is a registered social landlord (for which corresponding provision is made by section 22 of the Housing Act 1996).] **[609]**

NOTES

Commencement: 1 October 1996.

Substituted by the Housing Act 1996 (Consequential Provisions) Order 1996, SI 1996/2325, art 5(1), Sch 2, para 15(1), (22).

59, 60 *(S 59 repealed by the Housing (Scotland) Act 2001 (asp 10), s 112, Sch 10, para 11(1), (4); s 60 repealed, in relation to England and Wales, by the Housing Act 1996 (Consequential Provisions) Order 1996, SI 1996/2325, art 4(1), Sch 1, Pt I and, in relation to Scotland, by the Housing (Scotland) Act 2001 (asp 10), s 112, Sch 10, para 11(1), (4).)*

61 Power of local housing authority to supply furniture to housing association tenants

(1) A local housing authority may sell, or supply under a hire-purchase agreement, furniture to the occupants of houses provided by a housing association under arrangements made with the authority, and may buy furniture for the purpose.

(2) In this section "hire-purchase agreement" means a hire-purchase agreement or conditional sale agreement within the meaning of the Consumer Credit Act 1974.

[(3) This section does not apply where the housing association is a registered social landlord (for which corresponding provision is made by section 22 of the Housing Act 1996).] **[610]**

NOTES

Repealed in relation to Scotland by the Housing (Scotland) Act 2001 (asp 10), s 112, Sch 10, para 11(1), (4).

Sub-s (3): added, in relation to England and Wales, by the Housing Act 1996 (Consequential Provisions) Order 1996, SI 1996/2325, art 5(1), Sch 2, para 15(1), (23).

62–68 *(S 62 repealed by the Housing Act 1988, s 140(2), Sch 18, except in relation to a grant payable to an association in respect of a period that commences before 1 April 1989 (see the Housing Act 1988 (Commencement No 4) Order 1989, SI 1989/404, art 3(d)); ss 63–66 repealed by the Building Societies Act 1986, s 120(1), (2), Sch 18, Pt I, para 19(2), Sch 19, Pt I (s 64(4) was again repealed by the Statute Law (Repeals) Act 1993); s 67 repealed by the Housing Act 1996, s 227, Sch 19, Pt I; s 68 applies to Scotland only.)*

Miscellaneous

69 Power to vary or terminate certain agreements with housing associations

(1) This section applies to agreements of the following descriptions—

(a) an agreement for a loan to a housing association by the Housing Corporation under section 2 of the Housing Act 1964 [(including such an agreement under which rights and obligations have been transferred to Housing for Wales [and then to the Secretary of State])];

(b) an agreement which continues in force under Part I of Schedule 4 (arrangements with local authority for the provision or improvement of housing);

(c) an agreement to which Part II of Schedule 4 applies (subsidy agreements with local authorities);

(d) *(applies to Scotland only)*;

(e) …

(f) a scheme which continues in force under Part V of Schedule 5 (schemes for unification of grant conditions)

[(g) …]

(2) [If any person (other than the Secretary of State) who is a party to an agreement to which this section applies makes an application to the Secretary of State, he] may, if he thinks fit, direct—

(a) that the agreement shall have effect with such variations, determined by him or agreed by the parties, as may be specified in the direction, or

(b) that the agreement shall be terminated,

[and where the Secretary of State is a party to such an agreement, he may agree that it shall have effect with any variations or that it shall be terminated.]

[(2A) In the case of an agreement under which rights and obligations have been transferred to Housing for Wales [and then to the Secretary of State], the reference to a party to the agreement includes a reference to [the Secretary of State].]

(3) No variation shall be directed under subsection (2) which would have the effect of including in an agreement a term—

(a) limiting the aggregate amount of rents payable in respect of dwellings to which the agreement relates or contributions towards the cost of maintaining such dwellings, or

(b) specifying a limit which the rent of a dwelling is not to exceed.

This subsection does not extend to Scotland.

(4) (*Applies to Scotland only.*)

[611]

NOTES

Sub-s (1): in para (a) words in first (outer) pair of square brackets inserted by the Housing Act 1988, s 59, Sch 6, Pt II, para 28, words in second (inner) pair of square brackets inserted by the Government of Wales Act 1998, s 140, Sch 16, paras 23, 27(1), (2); paras (e), (g) (as added in the case of para (g) by the Local Government Act 1988, s 24(5)(c)) repealed, in relation to England and Wales, by the Housing Act 1996, ss 55(1), 227, Sch 3, para 3, Sch 19, Pt I.

Sub-s (2): words in first pair of square brackets substituted and words in second pair of square brackets added by the Government of Wales Act 1998, s 140, Sch 16, paras 23, 27(1), (3).

Sub-s (2A): inserted by the Housing Act 1988, s 59, Sch 6, Pt II, para 28; words in square brackets inserted and added respectively by the Government of Wales Act 1998, s 140, Sch 16, paras 23, 27(1), (4).

Housing Act 1964, s 2: repealed by the Housing (Consequential Provisions) Act 1985, s 3, Sch 1, Pt I (but for powers that are exercisable where a loan is outstanding under s 2 of the 1964 Act, see s 82 of, and Sch 7 to, this Act).

[69A Land subject to housing management agreement

A housing association is not entitled to a [grant under section 50 (housing association grant) or section 51 (revenue deficit grant) of the Housing Act 1988] in respect of land comprised in—

(a) a management agreement within the meaning of the Housing Act 1985 (see sections 27(2) and 27B(4) of that Act: delegation of housing management functions by certain authorities), or

(b) (*applies to Scotland only.*)]

[612]

NOTES

Inserted by the Housing and Planning Act 1986, s 24(2), Sch 5, Pt II, para 42.

Words in square brackets substituted by the Housing Act 1988, s 59, Sch 6, Pt II, para 29, except in relation to a revenue deficit grant payable to an association for a period that expires before 1 April 1989, or in relation to a hostel deficit grant payable under s 55; see the Housing Act 1988 (Commencement No 4) Order 1989, SI 1989/404, arts 3(c), 4.

70 Continuation of arrangements under repealed enactments

The provisions of Schedule 4 have effect in relation to certain arrangements affecting housing associations which continue in force despite the repeal of the enactments under or by reference to which they were made, as follows—

Part I—Arrangements with local authorities for the provision or improvement of housing.

Part II—Subsidy agreements with local authorities.

…

[613]

NOTES

Words omitted apply to Scotland only.

71 Superseded contributions, subsidies and grants

The provisions of Schedule 5 have effect with respect to superseded subsidies, contributions and grants, as follows—

Part I—Residual subsidies: England and Wales.

…

Part III—Contributions and grants under arrangements with local authorities.

…

Part V—Schemes for the unification of grant conditions.

Part VI—New building subsidy and improvement subsidy.

…

[614]

NOTES

Words omitted apply to Scotland only.

Supplementary provisions

72 (*Repealed, in relation to England and Wales, by the Housing Act 1996* (*Consequential Provisions*) *Order 1996, SI 1996/2325, art 4*(*1*), *Sch 1, Pt I.*)

73 Index of defined expressions: Part II

The following Table shows provisions defining or explaining expressions used in this Part (other than provisions defining or explaining an expression in the same section):—

… ..	
co-operative housing association	section 1(2)
Dwelling	section 106
… ..	
Hostel	section 106
… ..	
House	section 106
… ..	
housing association	section 1(1)
… ..	
local authority	section 106
local housing authority	section 104
… ..	
[registered social landlord	section 2B]
self-build society	section 1(3)
… ..	
[unregistered (in relation to a housing association)	section 2B]

[615]

NOTES

Entries "Building Society", "Chief Registrar" and "officer" repealed by the Building Societies Act 1986, s 120(1), (2), Sch 18, Pt I, para 19(2), Sch 19, Pt I.

Entries "approved development programme", "hostel deficit grant", "housing association grant", "housing project", "revenue deficit grant" and "shared ownership lease" repealed by the Housing *Act 1988, s 140(2), Sch 18.*

Entries "fully mutual", housing activities" and "registered charity" repealed, in relation to England and Wales, entry "registered and related expressions (in relation to a housing association)" repealed, in relation to England and Wales and Scotland, and entries "registered social landlord" and "unregistered (in

relation to a housing association)" inserted by the Housing Act 1996 (Consequential Provisions) Order 1996, SI 1996/2325, arts 4(1), 5(1), Sch 1, Pt I, Sch 2, para 15(1), (24).
Other entries omitted (inserted in part by SI 1996/2325) apply to Scotland only.

PART III
THE HOUSING CORPORATION

Constitution and other general matters

74 The Housing Corporation

(1) This Part has effect with respect to the Housing Corporation [and the Secretary of State.

(1A) Each of them] is referred to in this Part as "the [Relevant Authority]".

(2) The provisions of Schedule 6 have effect with respect to the constitution and proceedings of, and other matters relating to, [the Housing Corporation].

[(3) The functions conferred by this Part in relation to registered social landlords are exercisable by the [Relevant Authority] in whose register they are registered.

As to which [Relevant Authority] that is, see section 56 of the Housing Act 1996.]

(4) In this Part,—
- (a) in relation to land in Wales held by an unregistered housing association, "the [Relevant Authority]" means [the Secretary of State]; and
- (b) in relation to land outside Wales held by such an association, "the [Relevant Authority]" means the Housing Corporation.]

[616]

NOTES

Sub-ss (1), (1A): words from "and the Secretary of State" in sub-s (1) to "Each of them" in sub-s (1A) were substituted and words in square brackets in sub-s (1A) substituted by the Government of Wales Act 1998, s 140, Sch 16, paras 23, 28(a), 29(1), (2).
Sub-s (2): words in square brackets substituted by the Housing Act 1988, s 59, Sch 6, para 31(2).
Sub-s (3): inserted together with sub-s (4) by the Housing Act 1988, s 59, Sch 6, Pt III, para 31(1), (3); substituted, in relation to England and Wales, by the Housing Act 1996 (Consequential Provisions) Order 1996, SI 1996/2325, art 5(1), Sch 2, para 15(1), (25); words in square brackets substituted by the Government of Wales Act 1998, s 140, Sch 16, paras 23, 28(a).
Sub-s (4): inserted as noted to sub-s (3); words in square brackets substituted by the Government of Wales Act 1998, s 140, Sch 16, paras 23, 28(a), 29(1), (3).

75 General functions of the [Relevant Authority]

(1) The [Relevant Authority] has the following general functions—
- [(a) to facilitate the proper performance of the functions of registered social landlords;
- (b) to maintain a register of social landlords and to exercise supervision and control over such persons;
- (c) to promote and assist the development of self-build societies (other than registered social landlords) and to facilitate the proper performance of the functions, and to publicise the aims and principles, of such societies;]
- (d) …
- (e) to undertake, to such extent as the [Relevant Authority] considers necessary, the provision (by construction, acquisition, conversion, improvement or otherwise) of dwellings for letting or for sale and of hostels, and the management of dwellings or hostels so provided;
- [(f) …].

[(1A) The Housing Corporation also has the general function of providing, on request, to such extent as the Housing Corporation considers appropriate, advice and assistance to the Audit Commission for Local Authorities and the National Health Service in England and Wales in relation to the functions of the Commission mentioned in subsection (1B).

(1B) The functions referred to in subsection (1A) are the functions of the Commission under Part 1 of the Local Government Act 1999 (best value), except to the extent that those functions are exercisable in relation to best value authorities in Wales (within the meaning given in that Act).]

(2) The [Relevant Authority] shall exercise its general functions subject to and in accordance with the provisions of this Act [and Part I of the Housing Act 1996].

(3) Subsection (1) is without prejudice to specific functions conferred on the [Relevant Authority] by or under this Act [or Part I of the Housing Act 1996].

(4) The [Relevant Authority] may do such things and enter into such transactions as are incidental to or conducive to the exercise of any of its functions, general or specific, under this Act [or Part I of the Housing Act 1996].

[(5) ...]

[617]

NOTES

Section heading: words in square brackets substituted by the Government of Wales Act 1998, s 140, Sch 16, paras 23, 28(a).

Sub-s (1): words in first pair of square brackets and words in square brackets in para (e) substituted by the Government of Wales Act 1998, s 140, Sch 16, paras 23, 28(a); paras (a)–(c) substituted, in relation to England and Wales, by the Housing Act 1996, s 55(1), Sch 3, para 5; para (d) repealed by the Housing Act 1988, s 140, Sch 18; para (f) added by the Local Government Act 1999, s 22(7), repealed by the Public Audit (Wales) Act 2004, ss 66, 72, Sch 2, para 5(1), (2), Sch 4.

Sub-ss (1A), (1B): inserted by Public Audit (Wales) Act 2004, s 66, Sch 2, para 5(1), (3).

Sub-ss (2)–(4): words in first pair of square brackets substituted by the Government of Wales Act 1998, s 140, Sch 16, paras 23, 28(a); words in second pair of square brackets added, in relation to England and Wales, by the Housing Act 1996 (Consequential Provisions) Order 1996, SI 1996/2325, art 5(1), Sch 2, para 15(1), (26).

Sub-s (5): added by the Housing Act 1988, s 56; repealed by the Race Relations (Amendment) Act 2000, s 9(2), Sch 3.

76 Directions by the Secretary of State

(1) The Secretary of State may give directions to the [Housing Corporation] as to the exercise of its functions.

(2) A direction as to the terms of loans made under section 79 (lending powers of [Housing Corporation]) requires the consent of the Treasury.

(3) Directions may be of a general or particular character and may be varied or revoked by subsequent directions.

(4) Non-compliance with a direction does not invalidate a transaction between a person and the [Housing Corporation] unless the person had actual notice of the direction.

[618]

NOTES

Sub-ss (1), (2), (4): words in square brackets substituted by the Government of Wales Act 1998, s 140, Sch 16, paras 23, 31.

[76A Realisation of value of [Housing Corporation's] loans portfolio

(1) The [Housing Corporation] may, and if so directed by the Secretary of State (under section 76) shall, enter into arrangements of a description approved by the Secretary of State for the purpose of realising the value of the whole or part of its loans portfolio.

(2) The arrangements may provide for—

(a) the transfer of any estate or interest of the [Housing Corporation], or

(b) the creation or disposal of economic interests not involving a transfer of an estate or interest,

and may extend to such incidental or ancillary matters as the [Housing Corporation] or the Secretary of State considers appropriate.

(3) In this section the [Housing Corporation's] "loans portfolio" means the [Housing Corporation's] rights and obligations in relation to any loans or related securities.

(4) Nothing in the terms of any loan or related transaction entered into by the [Housing Corporation] shall be construed as impliedly prohibiting or restricting the [Housing Corporation] from dealing with its loans portfolio in accordance with arrangements under this section.]

[619]

NOTES

Commencement: 1 August 1996.

Inserted, in relation to England and Wales, by the Housing Act 1996, s 55(1), Sch 3, para 6.

Words in square brackets in each place they occur (including the section heading) substituted by the Government of Wales Act 1998, s 140, Sch 16, paras 23, 32.

77 Advisory service

(1) The [Relevant Authority] may provide an advisory service for the purpose of giving advice on legal, architectural and other technical matters to [registered social landlords or unregistered housing associations] and to persons who are forming a housing association or are interested in the possibility of doing so.

(2) The [Relevant Authority] may make charges for the service.

[(3) The powers conferred on the [Relevant Authority] by subsections (1) and (2) may be exercised by the Housing Corporation and [the Secretary of State] acting jointly.]

[620]

NOTES

Sub-s (1): words in first pair of square brackets substituted by the Government of Wales Act 1998, s 140, Sch 16, paras 23, 28(a); words in second pair of square brackets substituted for the words "housing associations (whether registered or unregistered)", in relation to England and Wales, by the Housing Act 1996 (Consequential Provisions) Order 1996, SI 1996/2325, art 5(1), Sch 2, para 15(1), (27).

Sub-s (2): words in square brackets substituted by the Government of Wales Act 1998, s 140, Sch 16, paras 23, 28(a).

Sub-s (3): added by the Housing Act 1988, s 59, Sch 6, Pt III, para 33; words in square brackets substituted by the Government of Wales Act 1998, s 140, Sch 16, paras 23, 28(a), 33.

78 Annual report

(1) The [Housing Corporation] shall, as soon as possible after the end of each financial year, make a report to the Secretary of State on the exercise of its functions during the year.

(2) It shall include in the report a copy of its audited accounts and shall set out in the report any directions given to it by the Secretary of State during the year.

(3) The Secretary of State shall lay a copy of the report before each House of Parliament.

[621]

NOTES

Sub-s (1): words in square brackets substituted by the Government of Wales Act 1998, s 140, Sch 16, paras 23, 34.

[Relevant Authority's] powers with respect to grants and loans

79 Lending powers

[(1) The Relevant Authority may lend to a registered social landlord or an unregistered self-build society, and the Housing Corporation may lend to any of its subsidiaries or to any other body in which it holds an interest, for the purpose of enabling the body to meet the whole or part of expenditure incurred or to be incurred by it in carrying out its objects.

(2) The Relevant Authority may lend to an individual for the purpose of enabling him to acquire from—

(a) the Relevant Authority, or

(b) any body to which the Relevant Authority may lend under subsection (1),

a legal estate or interest in a dwelling which he intends to occupy.]

(3) A loan under this section may be by way of temporary loan or otherwise, and the terms of a loan made under subsection (1) may include (though the terms of a loan made under subsection (2) may not) terms for preventing repayment of the loan or part of it before a specified date without the consent of the [Relevant Authority].

(4) The terms of a loan under this section shall, subject to subsection (3) and [(in the case of a loan by the Housing Corporation)] to any direction under section 76 (general power of Secretary of State to give directions), be such as the [Relevant Authority] may determine, either generally or in a particular case.

[622]

NOTES

Words in square brackets in the heading preceding this section substituted by the Government of Wales Act 1998, s 140, Sch 16, paras 23, 28(b).

Sub-ss (1), (2): substituted by the Government of Wales Act 1998, s 140, Sch 16, paras 23, 35(1), (2).

Sub-s (3): words in square brackets substituted by the Government of Wales Act 1998, s 140, Sch 16, paras 23, 28(a).

Sub-s (4): words in first pair of square brackets inserted and words in second pair of square brackets substituted by the Government of Wales Act 1998, s 140, Sch 16, paras 23, 28(a), 35(1), (3).

80 Security for loans to unregistered self-build societies

(1) Where the [Relevant Authority]—

(a) makes a loan to an unregistered self-build society under section 79(1); and

(b) under a mortgage or heritable security entered into by the society to secure the loan has an interest as mortgagee or creditor in land belonging to the society,

it may … give the society directions with respect to the disposal of the land.

(2) The society shall comply with directions so given so long as the [Relevant Authority] continues to have such an interest in the land.

(3) Directions so given may be varied or revoked by subsequent directions …

[(3A) The written consent of the Secretary of State is required for the giving, varying or revoking of directions by the Housing Corporation.]

(4) The Secretary of State shall not [give directions under this section requiring a society to transfer its interest in land to him or any other person, and shall not consent to the Housing Corporation's giving such directions requiring a society to transfer its interest in land to the Housing Corporation or] any other person, unless he is satisfied that arrangements have been made which will secure that the members of the society receive fair treatment in connection with the transfer.

[623]

NOTES

Sub-s (1): word in square brackets substituted and words omitted repealed by the Government of Wales Act 1998, ss 140, 152, Sch 16, paras 23, 28(a), 36(1), (2), Sch 18, Pt VI.

Sub-ss (2), (4): words in square brackets substituted by the Government of Wales Act 1998, s 140, Sch 16, paras 23, 28(a), 36(1), (5).

Sub-s (3): words omitted repealed by the Government of Wales Act 1998, ss 140, 152, Sch 16, paras 23, 36(1), (3), Sch 18, Pt VI.

Sub-s (3A): inserted by the Government of Wales Act 1998, s 140, Sch 16, paras 23, 36(1), (4).

81 Further advances in case of disposal on shared ownership lease

Where—

(a) a lease of a dwelling, granted otherwise than in pursuance of the provisions of Part V of the Housing Act 1985 (the right to buy) relating to shared ownership leases, contains a provision to the like effect as that required by paragraph 1 of Schedule 8 to that Act (terms of shared ownership lease: right of tenant to acquire additional shares), and

(b) the [Relevant Authority] has, in exercise of any of its powers, left outstanding or advanced any amount on the security of the dwelling,

that power includes power to advance further amounts for the purpose of assisting the tenant to make payments in pursuance of that provision.

[624]

NOTES

Words in square brackets substituted by the Government of Wales Act 1998, s 140, Sch 16, paras 23, 28(a).

82 Loans made under s 2 of the Housing Act 1964

Schedule 7 (further powers of [Relevant Authority] with respect to land of certain housing associations) applies where a loan has been made to a housing association under section 2 of the Housing Act 1964 and the loan has not been repaid.

[625]

NOTES

Words in square brackets substituted by the Government of Wales Act 1998, s 140, Sch 16, paras 23, 28(a).

Housing Act 1964, s 2: repealed by the Housing (Consequential Provisions) Act 1985, s 3, Sch 1, Pt I (but for powers that are exercisable where a loan is outstanding under s 2 of the 1964 Act, see this section and Sch 7 to this Act).

83 Power to guarantee loans

[(1) The Relevant Authority may guarantee the repayment of the principal of, and the payment of interest on, sums borrowed by registered social landlords or unregistered self-build societies; and the Housing Corporation may guarantee the repayment of the principal of, and the payment of interest on, sums borrowed by other bodies in which it holds an interest.]

[(1A) The consent of the Secretary of State given with the approval of the Treasury is required for the giving of a guarantee by the Housing Corporation and the approval of the Treasury is required for the giving of a guarantee by the Secretary of State.]

(2) Where the [Relevant Authority] gives such a guarantee, it may impose such terms and conditions as it thinks fit.

(3) The aggregate amount outstanding in respect of—

(a) loans for which [the Housing Corporation] has given a guarantee under this section, and

(b) payments made by [the Housing Corporation] in meeting an obligation arising by virtue of such a guarantee and not repaid to [the Housing Corporation],

shall not exceed £300 million or such greater sum not exceeding £500 million as the Secretary of State may specify by order made with the approval of the Treasury.

[(3A) The aggregate amount outstanding in respect of—

(a) loans for which [the Secretary of State (or Housing for Wales)] has given a guarantee under this section, and

(b) payments made by [the Secretary of State (or Housing for Wales)] in meeting an obligation arising by virtue of such a guarantee and not repaid to [the Secretary of State (or Housing for Wales)],

shall not exceed £30 million or such greater sum not exceeding £50 million as the Secretary of State may specify by order made with the approval of the Treasury.]

(4) An order under subsection (3) [or subsection (3A)] shall be made by statutory instrument and no such order shall be made unless a draft of it has been laid before and approved by the House of Commons.

[626]

NOTES

Sub-s (1): substituted by the Government of Wales Act 1998, s 140, Sch 16, paras 23, 37(1), (2).

Sub-s (1A): inserted by the Government of Wales Act 1998, s 140, Sch 16, paras 23, 37(1), (3).

Sub-s (2): words in square brackets substituted by the Government of Wales Act 1998, s 140, Sch 16, paras 23, 28(a).

Sub-s (3): words in square brackets substituted by the Housing Act 1988, s 59, Sch 6, Pt III, para 34.

Sub-s (3A): inserted by the Housing Act 1988, s 59, Sch 6, Pt III, para 34; words in square brackets substituted by the Government of Wales Act 1998, s 140, Sch 16, paras 23, 37(1), (4).

Sub-s (4): words in square brackets inserted by the Housing Act 1988, s 59, Sch 6, Pt III, para 34.

84 Agreements to indemnify certain lenders: England and Wales

(1) The [Relevant Authority] may … enter into an agreement with—

(a) a building society lending on the security of a house, or

(b) a recognised body making a relevant advance on the security of a house,

whereby, in the event of default by the mortgagor, and in circumstances and subject to conditions specified in the agreement, the [Relevant Authority] binds itself to indemnify the society or body in respect of the whole or part of the mortgagor's outstanding indebtedness and any loss or expense falling on the society or body in consequence of the mortgagor's default.

(2) The agreement may also, if the mortgagor is made party to it, enable or require the [Relevant Authority] in specified circumstances to take a transfer of the mortgage and assume rights and liabilities under it, the building society or recognised body being then discharged in respect of them.

(3) The transfer may be made to take effect—

(a) on terms provided for by the agreement (including terms involving substitution of a new mortgage agreement or modification of the existing one), and

(b) so that the [Relevant Authority] is treated as acquiring (for and in relation to the purposes of the mortgage) the benefit and burden of all preceding acts, omissions and events.

(4) The [Housing Corporation may not enter into an agreement without the approval of the Secretary of State who] may approve particular agreements or give notice that particular forms of agreement have his approval, and in either case may make his approval subject to conditions.

(5) The Secretary of State shall, before giving notice that a particular form of agreement has his approval [and before himself entering into an agreement in a form about which he has not previously consulted under this subsection], consult—

(a) in the case of a form of agreement with a building society, the [Financial Services Authority] and such organisations representative of building societies and local authorities as he thinks expedient, and

(b) in the case of a form of agreement with a recognised body, such organisations representative of such bodies and local authorities as he thinks expedient.

(6) …

[627]

NOTES

Sub-s (1): words in square brackets substituted and words omitted repealed by the Government of Wales Act 1998, ss 140, 152, Sch 16, paras 23, 28(a), 38(1), (2), Sch 18, Pt VI.

Sub-ss (2)–(4): words in square brackets substituted by the Government of Wales Act 1998, s 140, Sch 16, paras 23, 28(a), 38(1), (3).

Sub-s (5): words in first pair of square brackets inserted by the Government of Wales Act 1998, s 140, Sch 16, paras 23, 38(1), (4); words in second pair of square brackets substituted by the Financial Services and Markets Act 2000 (Consequential Amendments and Repeals) Order 2001, SI 2001/3649, art 301.

Sub-s (6): repealed by the Competition Act 1998 (Transitional, Consequential and Supplemental Provisions) Order 2000, SI 2000/311, art 16.

Local authorities: the Residuary Body for Wales and the Local Government Residuary Body (England) are to be treated as a local authorities for the purposes of subsection (5)(b) above, see the Local Government (Wales) Act 1994, Sch 13, para 20(l) and the Local Government Residuary Body (England) Order 1995, SI 1995/401, Schedule, para 9.

85 Meaning of "recognised body" and "relevant advance"

(1) The expressions "recognised body" and "relevant advance" in section 84 (agreements to indemnify certain lenders) shall be construed in accordance with the following provisions.

(2) A "recognised body" means a body specified, or of a class or description specified, in an order made by statutory instrument by the Secretary of State …

(3) Before making such an order varying or revoking an order previously made, the Secretary of State shall give an opportunity for representations to be made on behalf of a recognised body which, if the order were made, would cease to be such a body.

(4) A "relevant advance" means an advance made to a person whose interest in the dwelling is or was acquired by virtue of a conveyance of the freehold or an assignment of a long lease, or a grant of a long lease by—

a local authority,
a new town corporation,
an urban development corporation,
…
the [Housing Corporation], or
a [registered social landlord],

[or an advance made to such a person by the Secretary of State if the conveyance, assignment or grant was made under section 90.]

(5) In subsection (4) "long lease" has the same meaning as in Part V of the Housing Act 1985 (the right to buy).

[628]

NOTES

Sub-s (2): words omitted repealed by the Housing Act 1996, ss 222, 227, Sch 18, Pt IV, para 22(1)(d), Sch 19, Pt XIII.

Sub-s (4): words omitted repealed, words in first pair of square brackets substituted and words in third pair of square brackets added by the Government of Wales Act 1998, ss 140, 152, Sch 16, paras 23, 39, Sch 18, Pt IV; words in second pair of square brackets substituted by the Housing Act 1996 (Consequential Provisions) Order 1996, SI 1996/2325, art 5(1), Sch 2, para 15(1), (30).

Local authorities: the Residuary Body for Wales and the Local Government Residuary Body (England) are to be treated as a local authorities for the purposes of subsection (4) above, see the Local Government (Wales) Act 1994, Sch 13, para 20(l) and the Local Government Residuary Body (England) Order 1995, SI 1995/401, Schedule, para 9.

Orders: no orders have been made under sub-s (2) above but, by virtue of the Housing (Consequential Provisions) Act 1985, s 2(2), the Mortgage Indemnities (Recognised Bodies) Order 1984, SI 1984/1555 as modified by SI 1994/1696, and the Mortgage Indemnities (Recognised Bodies) Order 1985, SI 1985/1978, have effect thereunder.

86 (*Applies to Scotland only.*)

[87 Financial assistance with respect to formation, management, etc of certain housing associations

(1) The [Relevant Authority] may give financial assistance to any person to facilitate the proper performance of the functions of registered social landlords or co-operative housing associations.]

(2) Assistance under this section may be in the form of grants, loans, guarantees or incurring expenditure for the benefit of the person assisted or in such other way as the [Relevant Authority] considers appropriate, except that the [Relevant Authority] may not, in giving any form of financial assistance [under this section] purchase loan or share capital in a company.

(3) With respect to financial assistance under this section, the following—

(a) the procedure to be followed in relation to applications for assistance,

(b) the circumstances in which assistance is or is not to be given,

(c) the method for calculating, and any limitations on, the amount of assistance, and

(d) the manner in which, and the time or times at which, assistance is to be given,

shall be such as may be specified by the [Relevant Authority] …

(4) In giving assistance under this section, the [Relevant Authority] may provide that the assistance is conditional upon compliance by the person to whom the assistance is given with such conditions as it may specify.

(5) Where assistance under this section is given in the form of a grant, subsections (1), (2) and (7) to (9) of section 52 of the Housing Act 1988 (recovery, etc of grants) shall apply as they apply in relation to a grant to which that section applies, but with the substitution, for any reference in those subsections to the … housing association to which the grant has been given, of a reference to the person to whom assistance is given under this section.

(6) …]

[629]

NOTES

Substituted, in relation to England and Wales, by the Local Government and Housing Act 1989, s 183.

Sub-s (1): substituted, in relation to England and Wales, by the Housing Act 1996, s 55(1), Sch 3, para 7; words in square brackets substituted by the Government of Wales Act 1998, s 140, Sch 16, paras 23, 28(a).

Sub-s (2): words in first and second pairs of square brackets substituted and words in third pair of square brackets inserted by the Government of Wales Act 1998, s 140, Sch 16, paras 23, 28(a), 40.

Sub-s (3): words in square brackets substituted by the Government of Wales Act 1998, s 140, Sch 16, paras 23, 28(a); words omitted repealed by the Housing Act 2004, ss 218, 266, Sch 11, para 1(a), Sch 16.

Sub-s (4): words in square brackets substituted by the Government of Wales Act 1998, s 140, Sch 16, paras 23, 28(a).

Sub-s (5): word omitted repealed by the Housing Act 1996 (Consequential Provisions) Order 1996, SI 1996/2325, art 4(1), Sch 1, Pt I.

Sub-s (6): repealed by the Housing Act 2004, ss 218, 266, Sch 11, para 1(b), Sch 16.

Note: the Housing Act 1996 (Consequential Provisions) Order 1996, SI 1996/2325, art 4(1), Sch 1, Pt I provides for the repeal of the word "registered" in this section. According to the Department of the Environment, Transport and the Regions that repeal is limited to the word as it appears in sub-s (5) above and not sub-s (1) above. The Housing Act 1996, s 55 confers a power on the Secretary of State to make such repeals as appear to him to be necessary or expedient in consequence of Part I of that Act. The repeal of the word "registered" in sub-s (1) above could not be said to be consequent on the said Part I and must therefore be viewed as ultra vires.

[Relevant Authority's] powers with respect to land and works

88 Acquisition of land

(1) The [Relevant Authority] may acquire land by agreement for the purpose of—

(a) selling or leasing it to a [registered social landlord] or an unregistered self-build society, or

(b) providing dwellings (for letting or for sale) or hostels,

and [the Housing Corporation may be authorised by the Secretary of State to, and the Secretary of State may,] acquire land compulsorily for any such purpose.

(2) Land may be so acquired by the [Relevant Authority] notwithstanding that it is not immediately required for any such purpose.

(3) In relation to a compulsory purchase of land by the [Relevant Authority] under this section—

(a) in England and Wales, the Acquisition of Land Act 1981 applies;

(b) *(applies to Scotland only.)*

(4), (5) *(Apply to Scotland only.)*

[630]

NOTES

Words in square brackets in the heading preceding this section substituted by the Government of Wales Act 1998, s 140, Sch 16, paras 23, 28(b).

Sub-s (1): words in first and third pairs of square brackets substituted by the Government of Wales Act 1998, s 140, Sch 16, paras 23, 28(a), 41; words in second pair of square brackets substituted, in relation to England and Wales, by the Housing Act 1996 (Consequential Provisions) Order 1996, SI 1996/2325, art 5(1), Sch 2, para 15(1), (31).

Sub-ss (2), (3): words in square brackets substituted by the Government of Wales Act 1998, s 140, Sch 16, paras 23, 28(a).

89 Provision of dwellings or hostels and clearance, management and development of land

(1) The [Relevant Authority] may provide or improve dwellings or hostels on land belonging to it.

(2) The [Relevant Authority] may clear land belonging to it and carry out other work on the land to prepare it as a building site or estate, including—

(a) the laying out and construction of streets or roads and open spaces, and

(b) the provision of sewerage facilities and supplies of gas, electricity and water.

(3) The [Relevant Authority] may repair, maintain and insure buildings or works on land belonging to it, may generally deal in the proper course of management with such land and buildings or works on it, and may charge for the tenancy or occupation of such land, buildings or works.

(4) The [Relevant Authority] may carry out such operations on, and do such other things in relation to, land belonging to it as appear to it to be conducive to facilitating the provision or improvement of dwellings or hostels on the land—

(a) by the [Relevant Authority] itself, or

(b) by a [registered social landlord] or unregistered self-build society.

(5) In the exercise of its powers under subsection (4) the [Relevant Authority] may carry out any development ancillary to or in connection with the provision of dwellings or hostels,

including development which makes provision for buildings or land to be used for commercial, recreational or other non-domestic purposes.

[631]

NOTES

Sub-ss (1)–(3), (5): words in square brackets substituted by the Government of Wales Act 1998, s 140, Sch 16, paras 23, 28(a).

Sub-s (4): words in first and second pairs of square brackets substituted by the Government of Wales Act 1998, s 140, Sch 16, paras 23, 28(a); words in second pair of square brackets substituted, in relation to England and Wales, by the Housing Act 1996 (Consequential Provisions) Order 1996, SI 1996/2325, art 5(1), Sch 2, para 15(1), (32).

90 Disposal of land

(1) The [Relevant Authority] may dispose of land in respect of which it has not exercised its powers under section 89(1) (provision or improvement of dwellings or hostels) and on which it has not carried out any such development as is mentioned in section 89(5) [(ancillary development) to a registered social landlord or an unregistered self-build society; and the Housing Corporation may dispose of such land to any of its subsidiaries or to any other body in which it holds an interest.]

(2) The [Relevant Authority] may dispose of land on which dwellings or hostels have been provided or improved in exercise of its powers under section 89 to—

a [registered social landlord],
a local authority,
a new town corporation[, or
Scottish Homes;

and the Housing Corporation may dispose of any such land to any of its subsidiaries.]

(3) The [Relevant Authority] may sell or lease individual dwellings to persons for their own occupation; but where the dwelling concerned was acquired [by the Housing Corporation] by compulsory purchase under section 88(1), it shall not be disposed of under this subsection without the written consent of the Secretary of State.

(4) The [Relevant Authority] may dispose of a building or land intended for use for commercial, recreational or other non-domestic purposes in respect of which development has been carried out by virtue of section 89; but no such building or land shall be disposed of [by the Housing Corporation] for less than the best consideration it commands except with the written consent of the Secretary of State.

(5) The [Relevant Authority] may dispose of land which is not required for the purposes for which it was acquired; but where the land—

(a) was acquired compulsorily by, or on behalf of, the [Housing Corporation] or by a local housing authority who transferred it to the [Housing Corporation], or

(b) is disposed of [by the Housing Corporation] (otherwise than for use as, or in connection with, a highway or street) for less than the best consideration it commands,

the [Housing Corporation] shall not dispose of the land except with the written consent of the Secretary of State.

(6) The [Housing Corporation] may not dispose of land except in accordance with the provisions of this section.

[632]

NOTES

Sub-ss (1), (6): words in square brackets substituted by the Government of Wales Act 1998, s 140, Sch 16, paras 23, 28(a), 42(1), (2), (7).

Sub-s (2): words in first and third pairs of square brackets substituted by the Government of Wales Act 1998, s 140, Sch 16, paras 23, 28(a), 42(1), (3); words in second pair of square brackets substituted, in relation to England and Wales, by the Housing Act 1996 (Consequential Provisions) Order 1996, SI 1996/2325, art 5(1), Sch 2, para 15(1), (33).

Sub-ss (3), (4): words in first pair of square brackets substituted and words in second pair of square brackets inserted by the Government of Wales Act 1998, s 140, Sch 16, paras 23, 28(a), 42(1), (4), (5).

Sub-s (5): words in first, second, third and final pairs of square brackets substituted and words in fourth pair of square brackets inserted by the Government of Wales Act 1998, s 140, Sch 16, paras 23, 28(a), 42(1), (6).

91 Protection of persons deriving title under transactions requiring consent

Where the [Housing Corporation] purport to acquire or dispose of land—

(a) in favour of a person claiming under the [Housing Corporation] the transaction is not invalid by reason that any consent of the Secretary of State which is required has not been given, and

(b) a person dealing with the [Housing Corporation], or with a person claiming under the [Housing Corporation], shall not be concerned to see or inquire whether any such consent has been given.

[633]

NOTES

Words in square brackets substituted by the Government of Wales Act 1998, s 140, Sch 16, paras 23, 43.

The [Relevant Authority's] finances

92 Borrowing powers

(1) The [Housing Corporation] may borrow from the Secretary of State, and the Secretary of State may lend to the [Housing Corporation], by way of temporary loan or otherwise, such sums in sterling as the [Housing Corporation] may require.

(2) The [Housing Corporation] may, with the consent of the Secretary of State or in accordance with a general authorisation given by him, borrow temporarily by overdraft or otherwise such sums in sterling as the [Housing Corporation] may require.

(3) The [Housing Corporation] may, with the consent of the Secretary of State, borrow—

(a) from the European Investment Bank or the Commission of the European Communities, sums in any currency, and

(b) from any other person, sums in a currency other than sterling.

(4) A loan made to the [Housing Corporation] by the Secretary of State shall be repaid to him at such times and by such methods, and interest on the loan shall be paid to him at such rates and at such times, as he may from time to time determine.

(5) The Treasury may issue to the Secretary of State out of the National Loans Fund such sums as are necessary to enable him to make loans to the [Housing Corporation] in pursuance of this section; and sums received by the Secretary of State in pursuance of subsection (4) shall be paid into that Fund.

(6) The Secretary of State may act under this section only with the approval of the Treasury.

[634]

NOTES

Words in square brackets in the heading preceding this section substituted by the Government of Wales Act 1998, s 140, Sch 16, paras 23, 28(b).

Sub-ss (1)–(5): words in square brackets substituted by the Government of Wales Act 1998, s 140, Sch 16, paras 23, 44.

93 Limit on borrowing

(1) The [Housing Corporation] has only the borrowing powers conferred by section 92 and those powers are exercisable subject to the following limit.

(2) The aggregate amount outstanding by way of principal of—

(a) advances made to the [Housing Corporation] under section 9 of the Housing Act 1964 before 18th September 1974 (when that section was repealed),

(b) advances made to housing associations before 1st April 1975 in respect of which the rights and obligations of the Secretary of State were then transferred to the [Housing Corporation] by section 34 of the Housing Act 1974,

(c) money borrowed by the [Housing Corporation] under section 92, and

(d) money borrowed by a subsidiary of the [Housing Corporation] otherwise than from the [Housing Corporation],

[shall not exceed the limit [specified] under subsection (2A)].

[(2A) The limit referred to in subsection (2) is,—

(a) … [£2,300 million] or such greater sum not exceeding £3,000 million as the Secretary of State may specify by order made with the consent of the Treasury; …

(b) …]

(3) An order under subsection [(2A)] shall be made by statutory instrument and no such order shall be made unless a draft of it has been laid before and approved by the House of Commons.

(4) In ascertaining the limit imposed by subsection [(2A)], interest payable on a loan made by the Secretary of State to the [Housing Corporation] which, with the approval of the Treasury, is deferred and treated as part of the loan, shall, so far as outstanding, be treated as outstanding by way of principal.

(5) The power of the [Housing Corporation] to borrow from a subsidiary of the [Housing Corporation] is not affected by subsection (1) and borrowing from such a subsidiary shall be left out of account for the purposes of subsection [(2A)].

[635]

PART I
STATUTES

NOTES

Sub-s (1): words in square brackets substituted by the Government of Wales Act 1998, s 140, Sch 16, paras 23, 45(1), (2).

Sub-s (2): words "Housing Corporation" and "specified" in square brackets substituted by the Government of Wales Act 1998, s 140, Sch 16, paras 23, 45(3); other words in square brackets substituted by the Housing Act 1988, s 59, Sch 6, Pt III, para 35(1).

Sub-s (2A): inserted by the Housing Act 1988, s 59, Sch 6, Pt III, para 35(2); words omitted repealed by the Government of Wales Act 1998, ss 140, 152, Sch 16, para 45(4), Sch 18, Pt VI; sum in square brackets substituted by virtue of the Housing Corporation Advances (Increase of Limit) Order 1990, SI 1990/779, art 2.

Sub-s (3): reference to "(2A)" in square brackets substituted by the Housing Act 1988, s 59, Sch 6, Pt III, para 35(3).

Sub-ss (4), (5): reference to "(2A)" in square brackets substituted by the Housing Act 1988, s 59, Sch 6, Pt III, para 35(3); words in square brackets substituted by the Government of Wales Act 1998, s 140, Sch 16, paras 23, 45(1), (2).

Housing Act 1964, s 9: repealed by the Housing Act 1974, s 130(4), Sch 15.

Housing Act 1974, s 34: repealed, subject to savings, by the Housing (Consequential Provisions) Act 1985, ss 3, 5(2), Sch 1, Sch 4, para 15(2).

Orders: the Housing Corporation Advances (Increase of Limit) Order 1990, SI 1990/779.

94 Treasury guarantees of borrowing

(1) The Treasury may guarantee, in such manner and on such conditions as they think fit, the repayment of the principal of and the payment of interest on and the discharge of any other financial obligation in connection with sums which the [Housing Corporation] borrows from a person other than the Secretary of State.

(2) Immediately after a guarantee is given the Treasury shall lay a statement of the guarantee before each House of Parliament.

(3) Any sums required by the Treasury for fulfilling the guarantee shall be charged on and issued out of the Consolidated Fund.

(4) If any sums are so issued, the [Housing Corporation] shall make to the Treasury, at such times and in such manner as the Treasury may from time to time direct—

(a) payments of such amounts as the Treasury so direct in or towards repayment of the sums so issued, and

(b) payments of interest, at such rate as the Treasury so direct, on what is outstanding for the time being in respect of sums so issued.

(5) Sums received by the Treasury in pursuance of subsection (4) shall be paid into the Consolidated Fund.

(6) Where a sum is issued for fulfilling a guarantee given under this section, the Treasury shall, as soon as possible after the end of each financial year, beginning with that in which the sum is issued and ending with that in which all liability in respect of the principal of the sum and in respect of interest on it is finally discharged, lay before each House of Parliament a statement relating to the sum.

[636]

NOTES

Sub-ss (1), (4): words in square brackets substituted by the Government of Wales Act 1998, s 140, Sch 16, paras 23, 46.

95 Grants to the [Housing Corporation]

(1) The Secretary of State may make such grants to the [Housing Corporation] as appear to him to be required to enable the [Housing Corporation] to meet the expenses incurred by it in the exercise of its functions.

(2) A grant may be made subject to such conditions as the Secretary of State may determine.

(3) The Secretary of State may act under this section only with the consent of the Treasury.

[637]

NOTES

Section heading: words in square brackets substituted by the Government of Wales Act 1998, s 140, Sch 16, paras 23, 47.

Sub-s (1): words in square brackets substituted by the Government of Wales Act 1998, s 140, Sch 16, paras 23, 47.

96 General financial provisions

(1) The [Housing Corporation] may turn its resources to account so far as they are not required for the exercise of its functions.

(2) If for an accounting year the revenues of the [Housing Corporation] exceed the total sums properly chargeable to revenue account, the [Housing Corporation] shall apply the excess in such manner as the Secretary of State may, after consultation with the [Housing Corporation], direct; and the Secretary of State may direct that the whole or part of the excess be paid to him.

(3) The Secretary of State may give directions to the [Housing Corporation] as to matters relating to—

(a) the establishment or management of reserves,
(b) the carrying of sums to the credit of reserves, or
(c) the application of reserves for the purposes of the [Housing Corporation's] functions.

(4) The Secretary of State may, after consultation with the [Housing Corporation], direct the [Housing Corporation] to pay to him the whole or part of any sums for the time being standing to the credit of reserves of the [Housing Corporation] or being of a capital nature and not required for the exercise of the [Housing Corporation's] functions.

(5) The Secretary of State may act under this section only with the approval of the Treasury.

[638]

NOTES

Sub-ss (1)–(4): words in square brackets substituted by the Government of Wales Act 1998, s 140, Sch 16, paras 23, 48.

97 Accounts and audit

(1) The [Housing Corporation] shall keep proper accounts and proper records in relation to the accounts and shall prepare in respect of each financial year annual accounts in such form as the Secretary of State may, with the approval of the Treasury, direct.

(2) The accounts of the [Housing Corporation] for each financial year [ending on or before 31st March 2003] shall be audited by a qualified accountant appointed for the purpose by the Secretary of State.

[(2A) The Housing Corporation shall send a copy of the accounts prepared under subsection (1) in respect of each financial year ending on or after 31st March 2004 to the Comptroller and Auditor General as soon as reasonably practicable after the end of the financial year to which the accounts relate.

(2B) The Comptroller and Auditor General shall examine and certify the accounts sent to him by the Housing Corporation under subsection (2A) and shall lay before each House of Parliament a copy of the accounts and his report on them.]

(3) As soon as the annual accounts of the [Housing Corporation] for a financial year have been audited [under subsection (2) or (2A)], the [Housing Corporation] shall send to the Secretary of State a copy of the accounts prepared by it for the year in accordance with this section, together with a copy of any report made on them by the auditor.

(4) The Secretary of State shall prepare in respect of each financial year, in such form and manner as the Treasury may direct, an account of—
- (a) the sums issued to him and lent to the [Housing Corporation], and
- (b) sums received by him from the [Housing Corporation] and paid into the National Loans Fund in respect of the principal and interest on sums so lent, or on sums advanced to the [Housing Corporation] under section 9 of the Housing Act 1964, and shall transmit the accounts so prepared by him to the Comptroller and Auditor General on or before 30th November in the following financial year.

(5) The Comptroller and Auditor General shall examine and certify the accounts prepared by the Secretary of State and lay before each House of Parliament copies of the accounts together with his report on them.

[(6) In this section "qualified accountant" means a person who is eligible for appointment as a company auditor under section 25 of the Companies Act 1989.]

[639]

NOTES

Sub-ss (1), (4): words in square brackets substituted by the Government of Wales Act 1998, s 140, Sch 16, paras 23, 49.

Sub-s (2): words in first pair of square brackets substituted by the Government of Wales Act 1998, s 140, Sch 16, paras 23, 49; words in second pair of square brackets inserted by the Government Resources and Accounts Act 2000 (Audit of Public Bodies) Order 2003, SI 2003/1326, art 16(1), (2).

Sub-ss (2A), (2B): inserted by SI 2003/1326, art 16(1), (3).

Sub-s (3): words in first and third pairs of square brackets substituted by the Government of Wales Act 1998, s 140, Sch 16, paras 23, 49; words in second pair of square brackets inserted by SI 2003/1326, art 16(1), (4).

Sub-s (6): substituted by the Companies Act 1989 (Eligibility for Appointment as Company Auditor) (Consequential Amendments) Regulations 1991, SI 1991/1997, reg 2, Schedule, para 59(2), subject to transitional provisions relating to the termination and resignation of appointments, contained in reg 4 thereof.

Housing Act 1964, s 9: repealed by the Housing Act 1974, s 130(4), Sch 15.

Acquisition of securities and control of subsidiaries

98 Acquisition of securities and promotion of body corporate

(1) The [Housing Corporation] may with the consent of the Secretary of State—
- (a) subscribe for or acquire securities of a body corporate, and
- (b) promote or participate in the promotion of a body corporate.

(2) In this section "securities" means shares, stock, debenture stock and other securities of a like nature.

[640]

NOTES

Sub-s (1): words in square brackets substituted by the Government of Wales Act 1998, s 140, Sch 16, paras 23, 50.

99 Control of subsidiaries

(1) The [Housing Corporation] shall exercise its control over its subsidiaries so as to secure that no subsidiary—
- (a) engages in an activity which the [Housing Corporation] is not empowered to carry on, or
- (b) engages in an activity in a manner in which the [Housing Corporation] itself could not engage by reason of a direction given to it under section 76 (directions by Secretary of State).

(2) The [Housing Corporation] shall also exercise its control over its subsidiaries so as to secure that no subsidiary of its—

(a) borrows money from a person other than the [Housing Corporation], or

(b) raises money by the issue of shares or stock to a person other than the [Housing Corporation],

without the consent of the Secretary of State.

[641]

NOTES

Words in square brackets substituted by the Government of Wales Act 1998, s 140, Sch 16, paras 23, 51.

Supplementary provisions

100 (*Repealed by the Housing* (*Scotland*) *Act 1986, s 25*(*2*), *Sch 3.*)

101 Minor definitions

In this Part—

["building society" means a building society within the meaning of the Building Societies Act 1986;]

"financial year" means the period of 12 months ending with the 31st March;

... ..

"subsidiary" has [the meaning given by section 736 of] the Companies Act.

[642]

NOTES

Definition "building society" substituted by the Building Societies Act 1986, s 120, Sch 18, Pt I, para 19(4); in definition "subsidiary" words in square brackets substituted by the Companies Act 1989, s 144(4), Sch 18, para 41.

Definition omitted applies to Scotland only.

102 Index of defined expressions: Part III

The following Table shows provisions defining or explaining expressions used in this Part (other than provisions defining or explaining an expression in the same section or paragraph)—

building society	section 101
the Companies Act	section 106
[co-operative housing association	section 1]
dwelling	section 106
financial year	section 101
... ..	
hostel	section 106
housing association	section 1(1)
local authority	section 106
local housing authority	section 104
new town corporation	section 106
recognised body	section 85(2)
[registered social landlord	section 2B]
relevant advance	section 85(4)
self-build society	section 1(3)
subsidiary	section 101

[unregistered (in relation to a housing association)	section 2B]
urban development corporation	section 106

[643]

NOTES

First entry in square brackets inserted and second and third entries in square brackets substituted, in relation to England and Wales, by the Housing Act 1996 (Consequential Provisions) Order 1996, SI 1996/2325, art 5(1), Sch 2, para 15(1), (34).

Entries omitted apply to Scotland only.

PART IV
GENERAL PROVISIONS

General provisions

103 Application to Isles of Scilly

(1) This Act applies to the Isles of Scilly subject to such exceptions, adaptations and modifications as the Secretary of State may by order direct.

(2) An order shall be made by statutory instrument which shall be subject to annulment in pursuance of a resolution of either House of Parliament.

[644]

104 Local housing authorities

(1) In this Act "local housing authority"—

(a) in relation to England and Wales, has the meaning given by section 1 of the Housing Act 1985, and

(b) *(applies to Scotland only.)*

(2) References in this Act to the district of a local housing authority—

(a) in England and Wales shall be construed in accordance with section 2 of the Housing Act 1985, and

(b) *(applies to Scotland only.)*

[645]

105 *(Repealed in relation to England and Wales by the Housing Act 1996 (Consequential Provisions) Order 1996, SI 1996/2325, art 4(1), Sch 1, Pt I.)*

106 Minor definitions—general

(1) In the application of this Act in England and Wales—

. . . . .

"dwelling" means a building or part of a building occupied or intended to be occupied as a separate dwelling, together with any yard, garden, outhouses and appurtenances belonging to it or usually enjoyed with it;

. . . . .

"hostel" means a building in which is provided for persons generally or for a class or classes of persons—

(a) residential accommodation otherwise than in separate and self-contained sets of premises, and

(b) either board or facilities for the preparation of food adequate to the needs of those persons, or both;

"house" includes—

(a) any part of a building which is occupied or intended to be occupied as a separate dwelling;

(b) any yard, garden, outhouses and appurtenances belonging to the house or usually enjoyed with it;

. . . . .

"local authority" means a county, [county borough,] district, or London borough council, the Common Council of the City of London or the Council of the Isles of

Scilly and in [section 84(5)] includes … a joint authority established by Part IV of the Local Government Act 1985 [and the London Fire and Emergency Planning Authority] [and in section 85(4) includes such a joint authority[, the London Fire and Emergency Planning Authority] and a police authority established under [section 3 of the Police Act 1996] [and the Metropolitan Police Authority];

"new town corporation" means the Commission for the New Towns or a development corporation within the meaning of the New Towns Act 1981;

"shared ownership lease" means a lease—

(a) granted on payment of a premium calculated by reference to a percentage of the value of the house or dwelling or of the cost of providing it, or

(b) under which the tenant (or his personal representatives) will or may be entitled to a sum calculated by reference directly or indirectly to the value of the house or dwelling;

… ..

"urban development corporation" means an urban development corporation established under Part XVI of the Local Government, Planning and Land Act 1980.

(2), [(3)] (*Apply to Scotland only.*)

[646]

NOTES

Definitions "bank", "the Companies Act", "friendly society", "insurance company" and "trustee savings bank" repealed, in relation to England and Wales, by the Housing Act 1996 (Consequential Provisions) Order 1996, SI 1996/2325, art 4(1), Sch 1, Pt I; definition "housing activities" (as substituted by the Housing Act 1988, s 59, Sch 6, Pt III, para 36, except in relation to revenue deficit grants payable to an association for a period which expires before 1 April 1989; see the Housing Act 1988 (Commencement No 4) Order 1989, SI 1989/404, art 3(c)) repealed by SI 1996/2325, art 4(1), Sch 1, Pt I, subject to savings in relation to its continued application to the Housing Act 1988, ss 50–55 (see art 4(4) of the 1996 Order)

In definition "local authority" words "county borough" in square brackets inserted by the Local Government (Wales) Act 1994, s 22(2), Sch 8, para 6(2); words and "section 84(5)" in square brackets substituted and words in square brackets beginning with the words "and in section 85(4)" inserted by the Police and Magistrates' Courts Act 1994, s 43, Sch 4, Pt II, para 59; words omitted repealed by the Education Reform Act 1988, s 237(2), Sch 13, Pt I; words "and the London Fire and Emergency Planning Authority", ", the London Fire and Emergency Planning Authority" in square brackets inserted by the Greater London Authority Act 1999, ss 325, 328, Sch 27, para 52, Sch 29, Pt I, para 43; words "section 3 of the Police Act 1996" in square brackets substituted by the Police Act 1996, s 103, Sch 7, Pt I, para 1(1), (2)(w); words "and the Metropolitan Police Authority" substituted by the Criminal Justice and Police Act 2001, s 128(1), Sch 6, Pt 3, para 68.

Final provisions

107 Short title, commencement and extent

(1) This Act may be cited as the Housing Associations Act 1985.

(2) This Act comes into force on 1st April 1986.

(3) The following provisions of this Act apply to England and Wales only—

section 2,
…
section 8(2) and (3),
sections 11 and 12,
…
section 18,
section 20,
section 31,
sections 34 to 36,
section 38,
…
…
section 58,
section 67,
section 69(3),
section 81,
sections 84 and 85,
section 103,

...
Schedules 2 and 3,
In Schedule 4, Part I,
In Schedule 5, Part I, paragraphs 1 and 2 of Part III and paragraph 1 of Part V.

(4) The following provisions of this Act apply to Scotland only—

...
[section 15A,]
section 59,
section 66,
section 68,
section 69(4),
section 86,
In Schedule 4, Part III,
In Schedule 5, Part II, paragraphs 3 and 4 of Part III, Part IV and Part VII.

(5) This Act does not extend to Northern Ireland.

[647]

NOTES

Sub-s (3): words omitted repealed by the Housing Act 1988, s 140, Sch 18.
Sub-s (4): words omitted repealed by the Housing Act 1988, s 140, Sch 18; words in square brackets inserted by the Housing (Scotland) Act 1986, s 25(1), Sch 2, para 4(8).

SCHEDULES

SCHEDULE 1
GRANT-AIDED LAND

Sections 6, 9

Definition of "grant-aided land"

1. For the purposes of [section 9(1A)] (control ... of dispositions of land by unregistered housing associations) "grant-aided land" means land—
   - (a) in respect of which a payment of a description specified in paragraph 2 falls or fell to be made in respect of a period ending after 24th January 1974, or
   - (b) on which is, or has been, secured a loan of a description specified in paragraph 3 in respect of which a repayment (by way of principal or interest or both) falls or fell to be made after 24th January 1974.

Payments

2. The payments referred to in paragraph 1(a) are—
   - (a) payments by way of annual grants or exchequer contributions under—
     section 31(3) of the Housing Act 1949,
     ... ..
     (arrangements by local authorities for improvement of housing accommodation);
   - (b) payments by way of annual grants or exchequer contributions under—
     section 12(1) or 15 of the Housing (Financial Provisions) Act 1958,
     ... ..
     (contributions for dwellings improved under arrangements with local authorities or grants for hostels);
   - (c) payments by way of annual grant or exchequer contributions under—
     section 12(6) of the Housing Subsidies Act 1967,
     ... ..
     section 62 of the Housing Act 1964, or
     ... ..
     (subsidies for conversions or improvements by housing associations);
   - (d) payments by way of annual grant under—
     section 21(8) of the Housing Act 1969 (contributions for dwellings provided or improved by housing associations under arrangements with local authorities);
   - (e) payments by way of subsidy under—
     section 72, 73, 75 or 92 of the Housing Finance Act 1972,

... ..

Parts I, II, VI and VII of Schedule 5 to this Act (basic or special residual subsidy, new building or improvement subsidy, hostel subsidy).

Loans

3. The loans referred to in paragraph 1(b) are—

(a) loans under—
section 119 of the Housing Act 1957,

... ..

section 58 of this Act, or

... ..

(powers of certain local authorities to promote and assist housing associations);

(b) loans to housing associations under—
section 47 of the Housing (Financial Provisions) Act 1958,

... ..

section 67 of this Act, or

... ..

(loans by Public Works Loan Commissioners to certain bodies);

(c) advances made under—
section 7 of the Housing Act 1961,

... ..

(advances to housing associations providing housing accommodation for letting);

(d) loans under—
section 2 of the Housing Act 1964

(loan by Housing Corporation to housing associations).

[648]

NOTES

Para 1: words in square brackets substituted by the Housing Act 1996 (Consequential Provisions) Order 1996, SI 1996/2325, art 5(1), Sch 2, para 15(1), (36); words omitted repealed by the Government of Wales Act 1998, s 152, Sch 18, Pt VI.

Paras 2, 3: words omitted apply to Scotland only.

Housing Act 1949, s 31(3): repealed by the Housing (Financial Provisions) Act 1958, s 59, Sch 6.

Housing (Financial Provisions) Act 1958, ss 12(1), 15, 47: s 12 was repealed, subject to savings, by the Housing Act 1969, s 89, Sch 10; s 15 was repealed, subject to savings, by the Housing Finance Act 1972, s 108(4), Sch 11, Pt V and by the Housing Act 1980, s 152, Sch 26; s 47 was repealed, subject to savings, by the Housing (Consequential Provisions) Act 1985, ss 3, 5(2), Sch 1, Pt I, Sch 4, para 4.

Housing Subsidies Act 1967, s 12(6): repealed, subject to savings, by the Housing Act 1969, s 89(3), Sch 10.

Housing Act 1964, ss 2, 62: s 2 was repealed by the Housing (Consequential Provisions) Act 1985, s 3, Sch 1, Pt I (but for powers that are exercisable where a loan is outstanding under s 2 of the 1964 Act, see s 82 of, and Sch 7 to, this Act); s 62 repealed, subject to savings, by the Housing Act 1969, s 89(3), Sch 10.

Housing Act 1969, s 21(8): s 21 was repealed, subject to savings, by the Housing Act 1974, s 130(3), (4), Sch 14, para 6, Sch 15.

Housing Finance Act 1972, ss 72, 73, 75, 92: repealed by the Housing (Consequential Provisions) Act 1985, s 3, Sch 1, Pt I.

Housing Act 1961, s 7: repealed, subject to savings, by the Housing (Consequential Provisions) Act 1985, ss 3, 5(2), Sch 1, Pt I, Sch 4, para 15(1).

(Schs 2, 3, repealed by the Housing Act 1996, s 227, Sch 19, Pt I.)

SCHEDULE 4
HOUSING ASSOCIATIONS: CONTINUATION OF ARRANGEMENTS UNDER REPEALED ENACTMENTS

Sections 69, 70

PART I
ARRANGEMENTS WITH LOCAL AUTHORITIES FOR PROVISION OR IMPROVEMENT OF HOUSING

(*ss 120 and 121 of the Housing Act 1957*)

1. Arrangements between a local authority and a housing association under section 120 of the Housing Act 1957 (arrangements for provision of housing) which were made before 10th August 1972 and are in force immediately before the commencement of this Act remain in force under this paragraph.

2. Arrangements between a local authority and a housing association under section 121 of the Housing Act 1957 (arrangements for improvement or conversion of housing) which were made before 1st April 1975 and are in force immediately before the commencement of this Act remain in force under this paragraph.

[649]

NOTES

Housing Act 1957, ss 120, 121: s 120 was repealed by the Housing Finance Act 1972, ss 78, 108(4), Sch 11, Pt VI; s 121 was repealed by the Housing Act 1974, s 130(1), (4), Sch 13, para 5, Sch 15.

PART II
SUBSIDY AGREEMENTS WITH LOCAL AUTHORITIES

(s 79 of the Housing Finance Act 1972 and s 59 of the Housing (Financial Provisions) (Scotland) Act 1972)

1. In this Part "subsidy agreement" means an agreement made between a local authority and a housing association which provides for payments to be made under or by reference to any of the following enactments—

section 2 of the Housing (Financial Provisions) Act 1924,
section 29(1) of the Housing Act 1930,
section 27(3) of the Housing Act 1935,
. . .
section 94(3) of the Housing Act 1936,
. . .
section 1(2)(b) of the Housing Subsidies Act 1956,
. . .
section 1(2)(b) of the Housing (Financial Provisions) Act 1958,
section 1(2) of the Housing Act 1961,
. . .
section 1(5) or 9(4) of the Housing Subsidies Act 1967,
. . .

(being enactments with respect to which it was provided by the Housing Finance Act 1972 or the Housing (Financial Provisions) (Scotland) Act 1972 that no further payments were to be made for 1972–73 or any subsequent year).

2. Where a subsidy agreement provides for the payment of greater amounts than those which the authority would have been obliged to pay under the relevant enactment, the authority shall continue to pay to the housing association sums equal to the difference between the amounts for the payment of which the agreement provides and the amounts which they would have been obliged to pay by that enactment.

[650]

NOTES

Words omitted apply to Scotland only.

Housing (Financial Provisions) Act 1924, s 2: repealed by the Housing (Financial Provisions) Act 1958, s 59(1), Sch 6.

Housing Act 1930, s 29(1): that section was repealed by the Housing Act s 99, Sch 7, Pt I.

Housing Act 1935, s 27(3): that section was repealed by the Housing Finance Act 1972, s 108(4), Sch 11, Pt III.

Housing Act 1936, s 94(3): repealed by the Housing (Financial Provisions) 1958, s 59, Sch 6.

Housing Subsidies Act 1956, s 1(2)(b): that section was repealed, with savings, by the Housing (Financial Provisions) Act 1958, s 59. Sch 6, and the whole Act was repealed by the Housing Finance Act 1972, s 108(4), Sch 11, Pt III.

Housing (Financial Provisions) Act 1958, s 1(2)(b): repealed, as respects certain dwellings, by the Housing Subsidies Act 1961, s 36(5), Sch 4 and the whole section was repealed by the Housing Finance Act 1972, s 108(4), Sch 11, Pt III.

Housing Act 1961, s 1(2): repealed, as respects certain dwellings, by the Housing Subsidies Act 1967, s 23(1), Sch 4, Pt II and the whole section was repealed by the Housing Finance Act 1972, s 108(4), Sch 11, Pt III.

Housing Subsidies Act 1967, ss 1(5), 9(4): those sections were repealed by the Housing Finance Act 1972, s 108(4), Sch 11, Pt III.
Housing Finance Act 1972: repealed by the Housing (Consequential Provisions) Act 1985, s 3, Sch 1, Pt I.

(Pt III applies to Scotland only.)

SCHEDULE 5
HOUSING ASSOCIATION FINANCE: SUPERSEDED SUBSIDIES, CONTRIBUTIONS AND GRANTS

Sections 69, 71

PART I
RESIDUAL SUBSIDIES: ENGLAND AND WALES

(ss 72 and 73 of the Housing Finance Act 1972)

Entitlement to residual subsidies

1.—(1) Basic residual subsidy is payable to a housing association in accordance with the following provisions where the association received payments from the Secretary of State for the financial year 1971–72 under certain enactments under which, in accordance with the Housing Finance Act 1972, no payments were to be made for 1972–73 or any subsequent year.

(2) A housing association is entitled to basic residual subsidy for a financial year if—
(a) it was entitled to basic residual subsidy under section 72 of the Housing Finance Act 1972 for the financial year 1972–73, and
(b) it has continued to be entitled to basic residual subsidy, under that section or this Schedule, for each succeeding financial year up to and including that immediately before the year in question.

(3) The amount of basic residual subsidy payable to an association for any year is the amount (if any) by which the basic residual subsidy payable for the previous year exceeds the withdrawal factor.

(4) Subject to any direction of the Secretary of State under paragraph 4(2), the withdrawal factor is the sum produced by multiplying £20 by the number of dwellings as at 31st March 1972 in respect of which the association's subsidies for 1971–72 (as defined in section 72(4) of the Housing Finance Act 1972) were payable.

2.—(1) Special residual subsidy is payable to a housing association in accordance with the following provisions in respect of dwellings which—
(a) were approved by the Secretary of State for the purposes of Part I of the Housing Subsidies Act 1967 before 10th August 1972, and
(b) were completed during the year 1972–73, 1973–74 or 1974–75.

(2) A housing association is entitled to special residual subsidy for a financial year if—
(a) it was entitled by virtue of section 73 of the Housing Finance Act 1972 to special residual subsidy for any of the years 1972–73, 1973–74 or 1974–75, and
(b) it has continued to be entitled to special residual subsidy, under that section or this Schedule, for each succeeding financial year up to and including that immediately before the year in question.

(3) The amount of special residual subsidy payable to an association for any year is the amount (if any) by which the special residual subsidy payable for the previous year exceeds the reduction factor.

(4) Subject to any direction of the Secretary of State under paragraph 4(2), the reduction factor is the sum produced by multiplying £20 by the number of dwellings satisfying the description in sub-paragraph (1).

3. No basic or special residual subsidy is payable to a co-operative housing association.

Power to vary withdrawal factor or reduction factor

4.—(1) This paragraph applies where a housing association, by furnishing to the Secretary of State such information as to its financial position as he may require, satisfies him as regards any financial year that its income from its dwellings will be, or was, inadequate having regard to its normal sources of income to meet such expenditure (including loan charges) as in his opinion it would be, or was, reasonable for the association to incur for that financial year in the exercise of its housing functions.

(2) Where this paragraph applies, the Secretary of State may direct that the amount of basic residual subsidy or special residual subsidy payable to the association for the financial year in question shall be determined—

(a) by reference to a withdrawal factor or reduction factor calculated by reference to a smaller sum of money per dwelling than that mentioned in paragraph 1(4) or 2(4), or

(b) by reference to a withdrawal factor or reduction factor of zero.

(3) A direction under this paragraph may be varied or revoked by the Secretary of State by a further direction.

(4) In sub-paragraph (1) "housing functions" means—

(a) constructing or improving, or facilitating or encouraging the construction or improvement, of dwellings,

(b) managing dwellings,

(c) the provision of dwellings by conversion, and

(d) the acquisition of dwellings;

and includes functions which are supplementary or incidental to any of those functions.

(5) For the purposes of this paragraph "loan charges", in relation to money borrowed by an association, means—

(a) the sums required for the payment of interest on the money and for its repayment, either by instalments or by means of a sinking fund, and

(b) the expenses of managing the debt,

and includes any such charges made by the association itself, whether in respect of borrowing from a capital fund kept by the association or in respect of borrowing between accounts kept by the association for different functions, or otherwise.

Administrative provisions

5.—(1) Payment of basic or special residual subsidy is subject to the making of a claim for the payment in such form, and containing such particulars, as the Secretary of State may from time to time determine.

(2) The amount of basic or special residual subsidy payable to a housing association for a financial year shall be calculated to the nearest pound by rounding up any odd amount of 50p or more and rounding down any lesser amount.

(3) Basic or special residual subsidy is payable ... subject to such conditions as to records, certificates, audit or otherwise as the Secretary of State may, ... , impose.

Powers exercisable in case of disposal of dwellings by association

6.—(1) The Secretary of State may reduce, suspend or discontinue the payment of basic or special residual subsidy to an association if the association leases for a term exceeding seven years or otherwise disposes of any of the dwellings in respect of which the association is entitled to the payment.

(2) If any dwellings of an association are leased for a term exceeding seven years to, or become vested in—

(a) another housing association, or trustees for another housing association, or

(b) the Housing Corporation [...],

the Secretary of State may pay to them any basic or special residual subsidy which he would otherwise have paid to the former association for any financial year, beginning with that in which the dwellings are so leased or become so vested.

(3) For the purposes of this paragraph a lease shall be treated as being for a term exceeding seven years where the original term is for a lesser period but the lease confers on the lessee an option for renewal for a term which, together with the original term, exceeds seven years.

Saving for financial years beginning before the commencement of this Act

7.—(1) The preceding provisions apply in relation to the financial year 1986–87 and subsequent financial years.

(2) The repeal by the Housing (Consequential Provisions) Act 1985 of the provisions of the Housing Finance Act 1972 relating to basic and special residual subsidies does not affect the operation of those provisions in relation to previous financial years.

[651]

NOTES

Para 5: words omitted repealed by the Housing Act 1988, ss 59, 140(2), Sch 6, Pt II, para 30(1), Sch 18.

Para 6: in sub-para (2)(b) words omitted originally inserted by the Housing Act 1988, s 59, Sch 6, para 30(1), and repealed by the Government of Wales Act 1998, ss 140, 152, Sch 16, para 52, Sch 18, Pt VI.

Housing Finance Act 1972, ss 72, 73: repealed by the Housing (Consequential Provisions) Act 1985, s 3, Sch 1, Pt I, subject to savings contained in para 7(2).

Housing Subsidies Act 1967, Pt I: largely repealed by the Housing Finance Act 1972, s 108(4), Sch 11, Pt III, and the whole Act was repealed by the Housing (Consequential Provisions) Act 1985, s 3, Sch 1, Pt I.

(*Pt II applies to Scotland only.*)

PART III
CONTRIBUTIONS AND GRANTS UNDER ARRANGEMENTS WITH LOCAL AUTHORITIES

(*s 12 of the Housing* (*Financial Provisions*) *Act 1958; s 12 of the Housing Subsidies Act 1967; s 21 of the Housing Act 1969*)

1.—(1) Contributions by the Secretary of State in connection with arrangements made under section 121 of the Housing Act 1957 (arrangements between housing associations and local authorities for improvement of housing) remain payable—

(a) under section 12 of the Housing (Financial Provisions) Act 1958 and section 12 of the Housing Subsidies Act 1967 as regards arrangements made before 25th August 1969, and

(b) under section 21 of the Housing Act 1969 as regards arrangements made on or after that date and approved under subsection (2) of that section before 1st April 1975.

(2) The contributions are payable at such times and in such manner as the Treasury may direct, and subject to such conditions, as to records, certificates, audit or otherwise as the Secretary of State may, with the approval of the Treasury, impose.

(3) Where such a contribution is paid to a local authority, the authority shall pay to the housing association by way of annual grant an amount not less than the contribution.

2. If the Secretary of State is satisfied, in the case of contributions payable under section 12 of the Housing (Financial Provisions) Act 1958, that the housing association have made default in giving effect to the terms of the arrangements, he may, as he thinks just—

(a) reduce the amount of the contribution payable to the local authority, or

(b) suspend or discontinue the payment;

and the local authority may reduce to a proportionate or any less extent the annual grant payable by them to the association or, as the case may be, suspend the payment for a corresponding period or discontinue the payment.

3, 4. (*Apply to Scotland only.*)

[652]

NOTES

Housing Act 1957, s 121: repealed by the Housing Act 1974, s 130(4), Sch 15; for a saving see Sch 4, Pt I to this Act at **[649]**.

Housing (Financial Provisions) Act 1958, s 12: repealed, subject to savings, by the Housing Act 1969, s 89, Sch 9, para 1, Sch 10.

Housing (Subsidies) Act 1967, s 12: repealed, subject to savings, by the Housing Act 1969, s 89, Sch 9, para 1, Sch 10.

Housing Act 1969, s 21: repealed, subject to savings, by the Housing Act 1974, s 130(3), (4), Sch 14, para 6, Sch 15.

(*Pt IV applies to Scotland only.*)

PART V
SCHEMES FOR THE UNIFICATION OF GRANT CONDITIONS

(*s 123 of the Housing Act 1957; s 157 of the Housing (Scotland) Act 1966*)

1. A scheme under section 123 of the Housing Act 1957 (schemes for the unification of divergent grant conditions affecting the management of a housing association's houses) which was made before 10th August 1972 and is in force immediately before the commencement of this Act remains in force under this paragraph.

2. (*Applies to Scotland only.*)

[653]

NOTES

Housing Act 1957, s 123: repealed by the Housing Finance Act 1972, ss 78, 108(4), Sch 11, Pt VI.

PART VI
NEW BUILDING SUBSIDY AND IMPROVEMENT SUBSIDY

(*s 75 of the Housing Finance Act 1972; ss 55 and 57 of the Housing (Financial Provisions) (Scotland) Act 1972*)

1.—(1) The following subsidies remain payable in respect of building schemes or improvement schemes approved by the Secretary of State before 1st April 1975—

- (a) new building subsidy under section 75 of the Housing Finance Act 1972 or section 55 of the Housing (Financial Provisions) (Scotland) Act 1972, and
- (b) (*applies to Scotland only.*)

(2) Payment of the subsidy is subject to the making of a claim for the payment in such form, and containing such particulars as the Secretary of State may from time to time determine.

(3) The amount of the subsidy payable for a financial year shall be calculated to the nearest pound by rounding up any odd amount of 50p or more and rounding down any lesser amount.

(4) The subsidy is payable at such times and in such manner as the Treasury may direct, and subject to such conditions as to records, certificates, audit or otherwise as the Secretary of State may, with the approval of the Treasury, impose.

2.—(1) The Secretary of State may make reduced payments of subsidy, or suspend or discontinue such payments, if—

- (a) he made his approval of the scheme subject to conditions and is satisfied that any of the conditions has not been complied with, or
- (b) he is satisfied that a dwelling comprised in the scheme has been converted, demolished or destroyed, is not fit to be used or is not being used for the purpose for which it was intended, has been sold or leased for a term exceeding seven years or has ceased for any reason whatsoever to be vested in the association or trustees for the association.

(2) If any of the dwellings comprised in the scheme become vested in, or are leased for a term exceeding seven years to—

(a) a housing association, or trustees for a housing association other than the association which received approval for the scheme, or

(b) the Housing Corporation,

the Secretary of State may, for any year beginning with that in which they come to be so vested or are so leased, pay them the whole or any part of the subsidy which he would otherwise have paid to the association which received approval for the scheme.

(3) For the purposes of this paragraph a dwelling shall be treated as leased for a term exceeding seven years if it is leased for a lesser term by a lease which confers on the lessee an option for renewal for a term which, together with the original term, exceeds seven years.

3.—(1) Where a housing association satisfies the Secretary of State, by furnishing him with such information as to its financial position as he may require, that the amount of new building subsidy for a year will be, or was, inadequate having regard to its normal sources of income to enable it to meet such expenditure (including loan charges) as in his opinion it would be, or was, reasonable for it to incur for that year in the exercise of its housing functions, he may direct that for that year the percentage of the initial deficit to be met by subsidy shall be greater than that otherwise applicable.

(2) The percentage shall not, however, be greater than 90 per cent or the percentage met by subsidy for the immediately preceding year, whichever is less.

(3) This paragraph does not apply in relation to the year of completion or the second or third year for which new building subsidy is payable.

(4) In this paragraph—

"housing functions" means constructing, improving or managing, or facilitating or encouraging the construction or improvement of dwellings, the provision of dwellings by conversion and the acquisition of dwellings, and includes functions which are supplementary or incidental to any of those functions;

"loan charges" includes any loan charges made by a housing association (including charges for debt management whether in respect of borrowing from a capital fund kept by the association or in respect of borrowing between accounts kept by the association for different functions or otherwise.

4.—(1) Where before 1st April 1976 a registered housing association made an application for housing association grant in respect of a housing project which was or included a building scheme or improvement scheme which had been previously approved for the purposes of any of the provisions mentioned in paragraph 1 and the Secretary of State gave his approval to that project for the purposes of housing association grant, no further payments of new building subsidy or improvement subsidy shall be made in respect of that approved scheme.

(2) A condition imposed by the Secretary of State in such a case by virtue of section 35(2)(b) of the Housing Act 1974, requiring the repayment of all or any of the payments of new building subsidy or improvement subsidy already paid, if in force immediately before the commencement of this Act, remains in force under this sub-paragraph.

(3) No account shall be taken under section 47(2)(b) (estimation of net cost of project for purposes of housing association grant; income to include subsidies) of payments of subsidy received which are required to be repaid in pursuance of such a condition.

[654]

NOTES

Housing Finance Act 1972, s 75: repealed by the Housing (Consequential Provisions) Act 1985, s 3, Sch 1, Pt I.

Housing Act 1974, s 35(2)(b): that section was repealed by the Housing (Consequential Provisions) Act 1985, s 3, Sch 1, Pt I.

(*Pt VII applies to Scotland only.*)

SCHEDULE 6
CONSTITUTION OF HOUSING CORPORATION

Section 74

Status of Corporation

1.—(1) The Housing Corporation is a body corporate.

(2) It is a public body for the purposes of the Prevention of Corruption Acts 1889 to 1916.

(3) It shall not be regarded—
- (a) as the servant or agent of the Crown, or
- (b) as enjoying any status, immunity or privilege of the Crown, or
- (c) as exempt from any tax, duty, rate, levy or other charge whatsoever, whether general or local;

and its property shall not be regarded as property of, or held on behalf of, the Crown.

Membership of Corporation

2.—(1) The members of the Housing Corporation, of whom there shall be not more than fifteen, shall be appointed by the Secretary of State.

(2) Before appointing a person to be a member of the Corporation the Secretary of State shall satisfy himself that he will have no financial or other interest likely to affect prejudicially the exercise of his functions as member; and the Secretary of State may require a person whom he proposes to appoint to give him such information as he considers necessary for that purpose.

3.—(1) The members of the Housing Corporation shall hold and vacate office in accordance with the terms of their appointment, subject to the following provisions.

(2) A member may resign his membership by notice in writing addressed to the Secretary of State.

(3) The Secretary of State may remove a member from office if he is satisfied that—
- (a) he has been adjudged bankrupt or made an arrangement with his creditors or (in Scotland) has had his estate sequestrated or has made a trust deed for behoof of his creditors or a composition contract,
- (b) … ,
- (c) he has been absent from meetings of the Corporation for a period longer than three consecutive months without the permission of the Corporation, or
- (d) he is otherwise unable or unfit to discharge the functions of a member, or is unsuitable to continue as a member.

(4) The Secretary of State shall satisfy himself from time to time with respect to every member that he has no financial or other interest likely to affect prejudicially the exercise of his functions as a member; and he may require a member to give him such information as he considers necessary for that purpose.

Chairman and Deputy Chairman

4.—(1) The Secretary of State shall appoint one of the members to be Chairman and one to be Deputy Chairman; and the members so appointed shall hold and vacate those offices in accordance with the terms of their appointment, subject to the following provisions.

(2) The Chairman or Deputy Chairman may resign his office by notice in writing addressed to the Secretary of State.

(3) If the Chairman or Deputy Chairman ceases to be a member of the Corporation, he also ceases to be Chairman or Deputy Chairman.

Remuneration and allowances

5.—(1) The Secretary of State may pay the Chairman, Deputy Chairman and members such remuneration as he may, … determine.

(2) The Housing Corporation may pay them such reasonable allowances as may be so determined in respect of expenses properly incurred by them in the performance of their duties.

Pensions

6.—(1) The Secretary of State may, … determine to pay in respect of a person's office as Chairman, Deputy Chairman or member—

(a) such pension, allowance or gratuity to or in respect of that person on his retirement or death as may be so determined, or

(b) such contributions or other payments towards provision for such pension, allowance or gratuity as may be so determined.

(2) As soon as may be after the making of such a determination the Secretary of State shall lay before each House of Parliament a statement of the amount payable in pursuance of the determination.

(3) Sub-paragraph (1) does not apply in the case of a member who has been admitted in pursuance of regulations under section 7 of the Superannuation Act 1972 to participate in the benefits of a superannuation fund maintained by a local authority.

(4) In such a case the Secretary of State shall make any payments required to be made to the fund in respect of the member by the employing authority and may make such deductions from his remuneration as the employing authority might make in respect of his contributions to the fund.

[Delegation of functions

6A. The Housing Corporation may delegate the exercise of any of its functions to any of its members, committees, sub-committees or employees.]

Proceedings of the Corporation

7.—(1) The quorum of the Housing Corporation and the arrangements relating to its meetings shall, subject to any directions given by the Secretary of State, be such as the Corporation may determine.

(2) The validity of proceedings of the Corporation is not affected by any defect in the appointment of any of its members.

8.—(1) Where a member of the Housing Corporation is in any way directly or indirectly interested in a contract made or proposed to be made by the Corporation—

(a) he shall disclose the nature of his interest at a meeting of the Corporation, and the disclosure shall be recorded in the minutes of the Corporation, and

(b) he shall not take any part in any decision of the Corporation with respect to the contract.

(2) A general notice given by a member at a meeting of the Corporation to the effect that he is a member of a specified company or firm and is to be regarded as interested in any contract which may be made with the company or firm is a sufficient disclosure of his interest for the purposes of this paragraph in relation to a contract made after the date of the notice.

(3) A member need not attend in person at a meeting of the Corporation in order to make any disclosure which he is required to make under this paragraph provided he takes reasonable steps to secure that the disclosure is brought up and read at the meeting.

9.—(1) The fixing of the Housing Corporation's seal may be authenticated by the signature of the Chairman or of any other person authorised for the purpose.

(2) A document purporting to be duly executed under the seal of the Corporation shall be received in evidence and be deemed to be so executed unless the contrary is proved.

[655]

NOTES

Para 3: sub-para (3)(b) repealed by the Housing Act 1988, ss 59, 140(2), Sch 6, Pt III, para 37, Sch 18.

Paras 5, 6: words omitted repealed, in relation to England and Wales, by the Housing Act 1996, ss 222, 227, Sch 18, Pt IV, para 22(1)(d), Sch 19, Pt XIII.

Para 6A: inserted, together with preceding cross-heading, by the Housing Corporation (Delegation) etc Act 2006, s 1(1).

SCHEDULE 7
POWERS EXERCISABLE WHERE LOAN OUTSTANDING UNDER SECTION 2 OF THE HOUSING ACT 1964

Section 82

Introductory

1. This Schedule applies where the Housing Corporation has made a loan to a housing association under section 2 of the Housing Act 1964 before the repeal of that section by the Housing (Consequential Provisions) Act 1985 and the loan has not been repaid.

Directions as to disposal of land securing loan

2.—(1) The Corporation may … give the association directions with respect to the disposal of land belonging to the association in which the Corporation has an interest as mortgagee under a mortgage, or as creditor in a heritable security, entered into by the association to secure the loan.

(2) Directions so given may be varied or revoked by subsequent directions …

[(3) The written consent of the Secretary of State is required for the giving, varying or revoking of directions by the Housing Corporation.]

3. Where the [Housing Corporation] proposes to give a housing association directions under paragraph 2 requiring the association to transfer to the [Housing Corporation] the association's interest in any land, the Secretary of State shall not consent to the giving of the directions unless he at the same time approves, or has previously approved, a scheme under paragraph 5 with respect to that land[; and the Secretary of State shall not give a housing association directions under paragraph 2 unless he at the same time makes, or has previously made, such a scheme].

4.—[(1)] Where the [Housing Corporation] proposes to give directions under paragraph 2 to an association whose rules restrict membership to persons entitled or prospectively entitled (whether as tenants or otherwise) to occupy a dwelling provided or managed by the association requiring the association to transfer its interest in any such land to the [Housing Corporation], or to any other person, the Secretary of State shall not consent to the giving of the directions unless he is satisfied that arrangements have been made which, if the directions are given, will secure that the members of the association receive fair treatment in connection with the transfer.

[(2) The Secretary of State shall not give to such an association directions under paragraph 2 requiring the association to transfer any land to the Secretary of State, or to any other person, unless he is so satisfied.]

Schemes for [Housing Corporation] to provide housing accommodation in place of association

5.—(1) If it appears to the [Housing Corporation]—

(a) that the association is experiencing difficulty in providing housing accommodation on any land which it has acquired or in managing housing accommodation provided by it on any land, or is in any way failing to perform its functions as a housing association in relation to any land, and that accordingly it is undesirable for the land in question to remain in the hands of the association,

(b) that there is no other housing association, whether in existence or about to be formed, to which the association's interest in the land in question can suitably be transferred, and

(c) that the land is capable of being, or continuing to be, used to provide housing accommodation for letting,

the [Housing Corporation] may prepare and submit to the Secretary of State a scheme.

[(1A) If it so appears to the Secretary of State, he may make a scheme.]

(2) The scheme shall be for the Corporation—

(a) to acquire the association's interest in the land,

(b) to undertake all such operations as may be required for the provision or continued provision on the land of housing accommodation for letting (including any operation which might have been carried out by a housing association in connection with the provision of housing accommodation), and

(c) to retain the accommodation and keep it available for letting so long as the scheme has not been terminated in any manner provided for in the scheme.

(3) Where such a scheme is submitted to the Secretary of State by the [Housing Corporation], the Secretary of State, on being satisfied of—

(a) the undesirability of the land remaining in the hands of the association, and

(b) the lack of any housing association to which it can suitably be transferred,

may, if he thinks fit, approve the scheme.

(4) If he does so the [Housing Corporation] shall have power to acquire for the purposes of the scheme the association's interest in the land and to carry through the provisions of the scheme.

(5) A scheme approved by the Secretary of State under this paragraph may be varied from time to time in accordance with proposals in that behalf made by the [Housing Corporation] and approved by the Secretary of State.

[(6) Where the Secretary of State makes the scheme, he shall have power to acquire for the purposes of the scheme the association's interest in the land and to carry through the provisions of the scheme.]

[656]

NOTES

Para 2: words omitted repealed and sub-para (3) added by the Government of Wales Act 1998, ss 140, 152, Sch 16, para 53(1), (2), Sch 18, Pt VI.

Para 3: words in first and second pairs of square brackets substituted and words in third pair of square brackets added by the Government of Wales Act 1998, s 140, Sch 16, paras 23, 53(1), (3).

Para 4: sub-para (1) numbered as such, words in square brackets therein substituted and sub-para (2) added by the Government of Wales Act 1998, s 140, Sch 16, paras 23, 53(1), (4).

Para 5: words in square brackets in the heading preceding this paragraph and in sub-paras (1), (3), (4), (5) substituted, sub-para (1A) inserted, and sub-para (6) added by the Government of Wales Act 1998, s 140, Sch 16, paras 23, 53(1), (5).

Housing Act 1964, s 2: repealed by the Housing (Consequential Provisions) Act 1985, s 3, Sch 1, Pt I (but for powers that are exercisable where a loan is outstanding under s 2 of the 1964 Act, see s 82 of this Act and this Schedule.

INSOLVENCY ACT 1986

(1986 c 45)

ARRANGEMENT OF SECTIONS

THE FIRST GROUP OF PARTS
COMPANY INSOLVENCY; COMPANIES WINDING UP

PART IV
WINDING UP OF COMPANIES REGISTERED UNDER THE COMPANIES ACTS

CHAPTER X
MALPRACTICE BEFORE AND DURING LIQUIDATION; PENALISATION OF COMPANIES AND COMPANY OFFICERS; INVESTIGATIONS AND PROSECUTIONS

Offences of fraud, deception, etc

Penalisation of directors and officers

Investigation and prosecution of malpractice

PART VII
INTERPRETATION FOR FIRST GROUP OF PARTS

THE THIRD GROUP OF PARTS
MISCELLANEOUS MATTERS BEARING ON BOTH COMPANY AND INDIVIDUAL INSOLVENCY; GENERAL INTERPRETATION; FINAL PROVISIONS

PART XIX
FINAL PROVISIONS

An Act to consolidate the enactments relating to company insolvency and winding up (including the winding up of companies that are not insolvent, and of unregistered companies); enactments relating to the insolvency and bankruptcy of individuals; and other enactments bearing on those two subject matters, including the functions and qualification of insolvency practitioners, the public administration of insolvency, the penalisation and redress of malpractice and wrongdoing, and the avoidance of certain transactions at an undervalue

[25 July 1986]

NOTES

Modification: the provisions of this Act, except s 413 and Sch 7, are applied, with modifications, in relation to a "recognised body" under the Administration of Justice Act 1985, s 9, by the Solicitors' Incorporated Practices Order 1991, SI 1991/2684, arts 2–5, Sch 1.

Insolvent partnerships: this Act is extensively applied and modified in relation to insolvent partnerships by the Insolvent Partnerships Order 1994, SI 1994/2421.

Official Receiver: as to the contracting out of functions of the Official Receiver conferred by or under this Act, see the Contracting Out (Functions of the Official Receiver) Order 1995, SI 1995/1386.

THE FIRST GROUP OF PARTS
COMPANY INSOLVENCY; COMPANIES WINDING UP

1–72 ((*Pts I–III*) *outside the scope of this work.*)

PART IV
WINDING UP OF COMPANIES REGISTERED UNDER THE COMPANIES ACTS

NOTES

Application: as to the application, with modifications, of this Part of this Act to the winding up of incorporated friendly societies by virtue of the Friendly Societies Act 1992, s 21(1) or 22(2), see s 23 of, and Sch 10 to, that Act; as to the application, with modifications, of this Part of this Act to the winding up of Industrial and Provident Societies, see the Industrial and Provident Societies Act 1965, s 55 at **[190]**.

73–205 ((*Chs I–IX*) *outside the scope of this work.*)

CHAPTER X
MALPRACTICE BEFORE AND DURING LIQUIDATION; PENALISATION OF COMPANIES AND COMPANY OFFICERS; INVESTIGATIONS AND PROSECUTIONS

Offences of fraud, deception, etc

206 Fraud, etc in anticipation of winding up

(1) When a company is ordered to be wound up by the court, or passes a resolution for voluntary winding up, any person, being a past or present officer of the company, is deemed to have committed an offence if, within the 12 months immediately preceding the commencement of the winding up, he has—

(a) concealed any part of the company's property to the value of [£500] or more, or concealed any debt due to or from the company, or

(b) fraudulently removed any part of the company's property to the value of [£500] or more, or

(c) concealed, destroyed, mutilated or falsified any book or paper affecting or relating to the company's property or affairs, or

(d) made any false entry in any book or paper affecting or relating to the company's property or affairs, or

(e) fraudulently parted with, altered or made any omission in any document affecting or relating to the company's property or affairs, or

(f) pawned, pledged or disposed of any property of the company which has been obtained on credit and has not been paid for (unless the pawning, pledging or disposal was in the ordinary way of the company's business).

(2) Such a person is deemed to have committed an offence if within the period above mentioned he has been privy to the doing by others of any of the things mentioned in paragraphs (c), (d) and (e) of subsection (1); and he commits an offence if, at any time after the commencement of the winding up, he does any of the things mentioned in paragraphs (a) to (f) of that subsection, or is privy to the doing by others of any of the things mentioned in paragraphs (c) to (e) of it.

(3) For purposes of this section, "officer" includes a shadow director.

(4) It is a defence—

(a) for a person charged under paragraph (a) or (f) of subsection (1) (or under subsection (2) in respect of the things mentioned in either of those two paragraphs) to prove that he had no intent to defraud, and

(b) for a person charged under paragraph (c) or (d) of subsection (1) (or under subsection (2) in respect of the things mentioned in either of those two paragraphs) to prove that he had no intent to conceal the state of affairs of the company or to defeat the law.

(5) Where a person pawns, pledges or disposes of any property in circumstances which amount to an offence under subsection (1)(f), every person who takes in pawn or pledge, or otherwise receives, the property knowing it to be pawned, pledged or disposed of in such circumstances, is guilty of an offence.

(6) A person guilty of an offence under this section is liable to imprisonment or a fine, or both.

(7) The money sums specified in paragraphs (a) and (b) of subsection (1) are subject to increase or reduction by order under section 416 in Part XV.

[657]

NOTES

Sub-s (1): amounts in square brackets in sub-paras (a), (b) increased from £120 by the Insolvency Proceedings (Monetary Limits) Order 1986, SI 1986/1996, art 2(1), Schedule, Pt I.

207 Transactions in fraud of creditors

(1) When a company is ordered to be wound up by the court or passes a resolution for voluntary winding up, a person is deemed to have committed an offence if he, being at the time an officer of the company—

(a) has made or caused to be made any gift or transfer of, or charge on, or has caused or connived at the levying of any execution against, the company's property, or

(b) has concealed or removed any part of the company's property since, or within 2 months before, the date of any unsatisfied judgment or order for the payment of money obtained against the company.

(2) A person is not guilty of an offence under this section—

(a) by reason of conduct constituting an offence under subsection (1)(a) which occurred more than 5 years before the commencement of the winding up, or

(b) if he proves that, at the time of the conduct constituting the offence, he had no intent to defraud the company's creditors.

(3) A person guilty of an offence under this section is liable to imprisonment or a fine, or both.

[658]

208 Misconduct in course of winding up

(1) When a company is being wound up, whether by the court or voluntarily, any person, being a past or present officer of the company, commits an offence if he—

(a) does not to the best of his knowledge and belief fully and truly discover to the liquidator all the company's property, and how and to whom and for what consideration and when the company disposed of any part of that property (except such part as has been disposed of in the ordinary way of the company's business), or

(b) does not deliver up to the liquidator (or as he directs) all such part of the company's property as is in his custody or under his control, and which he is required by law to deliver up, or

(c) does not deliver up to the liquidator (or as he directs) all books and papers in his custody or under his control belonging to the company and which he is required by law to deliver up, or

(d) knowing or believing that a false debt has been proved by any person in the winding up, fails to inform the liquidator as soon as practicable, or

(e) after the commencement of the winding up, prevents the production of any book or paper affecting or relating to the company's property or affairs.

(2) Such a person commits an offence if after the commencement of the winding up he attempts to account for any part of the company's property by fictitious losses or expenses;

and he is deemed to have committed that offence if he has so attempted at any meeting of the company's creditors within the 12 months immediately preceding the commencement of the winding up.

(3) For purposes of this section, "officer" includes a shadow director.

(4) It is a defence—
  (a) for a person charged under paragraph (a), (b) or (c) of subsection (1) to prove that he had no intent to defraud, and
  (b) for a person charged under paragraph (e) of that subsection to prove that he had no intent to conceal the state of affairs of the company or to defeat the law.

(5) A person guilty of an offence under this section is liable to imprisonment or a fine, or both.

[659]

209 Falsification of company's books

(1) When a company is being wound up, an officer or contributory of the company commits an offence if he destroys, mutilates, alters or falsifies any books, papers or securities, or makes or is privy to the making of any false or fraudulent entry in any register, book of account or document belonging to the company with intent to defraud or deceive any person.

(2) A person guilty of an offence under this section is liable to imprisonment or a fine, or both.

[660]

210 Material omissions from statement relating to company's affairs

(1) When a company is being wound up, whether by the court or voluntarily, any person, being a past or present officer of the company, commits an offence if he makes any material omission in any statement relating to the company's affairs.

(2) When a company has been ordered to be wound up by the court, or has passed a resolution for voluntary winding up, any such person is deemed to have committed that offence if, prior to the winding up, he has made any material omission in any such statement.

(3) For purposes of this section, "officer" includes a shadow director.

(4) It is a defence for a person charged under this section to prove that he had no intent to defraud.

(5) A person guilty of an offence under this section is liable to imprisonment or a fine, or both.

[661]

211 False representations to creditors

(1) When a company is being wound up, whether by the court or voluntarily, any person, being a past or present officer of the company—
  (a) commits an offence if he makes any false representation or commits any other fraud for the purpose of obtaining the consent of the company's creditors or any of them to an agreement with reference to the company's affairs or to the winding up, and
  (b) is deemed to have committed that offence if, prior to the winding up, he has made any false representation, or committed any other fraud, for that purpose.

(2) For purposes of this section, "officer" includes a shadow director.

(3) A person guilty of an offence under this section is liable to imprisonment or a fine, or both.

[662]

Penalisation of directors and officers

212 Summary remedy against delinquent directors, liquidators, etc

(1) This section applies if in the course of the winding up of a company it appears that a person who—
  (a) is or has been an officer of the company,

(b) has acted as liquidator … or administrative receiver of the company, or
(c) not being a person falling within paragraph (a) or (b), is or has been concerned, or has taken part, in the promotion, formation or management of the company,

has misapplied or retained, or become accountable for, any money or other property of the company, or been guilty of any misfeasance or breach of any fiduciary or other duty in relation to the company.

(2) The reference in subsection (1) to any misfeasance or breach of any fiduciary or other duty in relation to the company includes, in the case of a person who has acted as liquidator … of the company, any misfeasance or breach of any fiduciary or other duty in connection with the carrying out of his functions as liquidator … of the company.

(3) The court may, on the application of the official receiver or the liquidator, or of any creditor or contributory, examine into the conduct of the person falling within subsection (1) and compel him—

(a) to repay, restore or account for the money or property or any part of it, with interest at such rate as the court thinks just, or
(b) to contribute such sum to the company's assets by way of compensation in respect of the misfeasance or breach of fiduciary or other duty as the court thinks just.

(4) The power to make an application under subsection (3) in relation to a person who has acted as liquidator … of the company is not exercisable, except with the leave of the court, after [he] has had his release.

(5) The power of a contributory to make an application under subsection (3) is not exercisable except with the leave of the court, but is exercisable notwithstanding that he will not benefit from any order the court may make on the application.

[663]

NOTES

Sub-ss (1), (2): words omitted repealed by the Enterprise Act 2002, ss 248(3), 278(2), Sch 17, paras 9, 18(a), (b), Sch 26.

Sub-s (4): words omitted repealed and word in square brackets substituted by the Enterprise Act 2002, ss 248(3), 278(2), Sch 17, paras 9, 18(c), Sch 26.

213 Fraudulent trading

(1) If in the course of the winding up of a company it appears that any business of the company has been carried on with intent to defraud creditors of the company or creditors of any other person, or for any fraudulent purpose, the following has effect.

(2) The court, on the application of the liquidator may declare that any persons who were knowingly parties to the carrying on of the business in the manner above-mentioned are to be liable to make such contributions (if any) to the company's assets as the court thinks proper.

[664]

214 Wrongful trading

(1) Subject to subsection (3) below, if in the course of the winding up of a company it appears that subsection (2) of this section applies in relation to a person who is or has been a director of the company, the court, on the application of the liquidator, may declare that that person is to be liable to make such contribution (if any) to the company's assets as the court thinks proper.

(2) This subsection applies in relation to a person if—

(a) the company has gone into insolvent liquidation,
(b) at some time before the commencement of the winding up of the company, that person knew or ought to have concluded that there was no reasonable prospect that the company would avoid going into insolvent liquidation, and
(c) that person was a director of the company at that time; but the court shall not make a declaration under this section in any case where the time mentioned in paragraph (b) above was before 28th April 1986.

(3) The court shall not make a declaration under this section with respect to any person if it is satisfied that after the condition specified in subsection (2)(b) was first satisfied in relation to him that person took every step with a view to minimising the potential loss to the company's creditors as (assuming him to have known that there was no reasonable prospect that the company would avoid going into insolvent liquidation) he ought to have taken.

(4) For the purposes of subsections (2) and (3), the facts which a director of a company ought to know or ascertain, the conclusions which he ought to reach and the steps which he ought to take are those which would be known or ascertained, or reached or taken, by a reasonably diligent person having both—

- (a) the general knowledge, skill and experience that may reasonably be expected of a person carrying out the same functions as are carried out by that director in relation to the company, and
- (b) the general knowledge, skill and experience that that director has.

(5) The reference in subsection (4) to the functions carried out in relation to a company by a director of the company includes any functions which he does not carry out but which have been entrusted to him.

(6) For the purposes of this section a company goes into insolvent liquidation if it goes into liquidation at a time when its assets are insufficient for the payment of its debts and other liabilities and the expenses of the winding up.

(7) In this section "director" includes a shadow director.

(8) This section is without prejudice to section 213.

[665]

215 Proceedings under ss 213, 214

(1) On the hearing of an application under section 213 or 214, the liquidator may himself give evidence or call witnesses.

(2) Where under either section the court makes a declaration, it may give such further directions as it thinks proper for giving effect to the declaration; and in particular, the court may—

- (a) provide for the liability of any person under the declaration to be a charge on any debt or obligation due from the company to him, or on any mortgage or charge or any interest in a mortgage or charge on assets of the company held by or vested in him, or any person on his behalf, or any person claiming as assignee from or through the person liable or any person acting on his behalf, and
- (b) from time to time make such further order as may be necessary for enforcing any charge imposed under this subsection.

(3) For the purposes of subsection (2), "assignee"—

- (a) includes a person to whom or in whose favour, by the directions of the person made liable, the debt, obligation, mortgage or charge was created, issued or transferred or the interest created, but
- (b) does not include an assignee for valuable consideration (not including consideration by way of marriage [or the formation of a civil partnership]) given in good faith and without notice of any of the matters on the ground of which the declaration is made.

(4) Where the court makes a declaration under either section in relation to a person who is a creditor of the company, it may direct that the whole or any part of any debt owed by the company to that person and any interest thereon shall rank in priority after all other debts owed by the company and after any interest on those debts.

(5) Sections 213 and 214 have effect notwithstanding that the person concerned may be criminally liable in respect of matters on the ground of which the declaration under the section is to be made.

[666]

NOTES

Sub-s (3): words in square brackets inserted by the Civil Partnership Act 2004, s 261(1), Sch 27, para 112.

216 Restriction on re-use of company names

(1) This section applies to a person where a company ("the liquidating company") has gone into insolvent liquidation on or after the appointed day and he was a director or shadow director of the company at any time in the period of 12 months ending with the day before it went into liquidation.

(2) For the purposes of this section, a name is a prohibited name in relation to such a person if—

(a) it is a name by which the liquidating company was known at any time in that period of 12 months, or

(b) it is a name which is so similar to a name falling within paragraph (a) as to suggest an association with that company.

(3) Except with leave of the court or in such circumstances as may be prescribed, a person to whom this section applies shall not at any time in the period of 5 years beginning with the day on which the liquidating company went into liquidation—

(a) be a director of any other company that is known by a prohibited name, or

(b) in any way, whether directly or indirectly, be concerned or take part in the promotion, formation or management of any such company, or

(c) in any way, whether directly or indirectly, be concerned or take part in the carrying on of a business carried on (otherwise than by a company) under a prohibited name.

(4) If a person acts in contravention of this section, he is liable to imprisonment or a fine, or both.

(5) In subsection (3) "the court" means any court having jurisdiction to wind up companies; and on an application for leave under that subsection, the Secretary of State or the official receiver may appear and call the attention of the court to any matters which seem to him to be relevant.

(6) References in this section, in relation to any time, to a name by which a company is known are to the name of the company at that time or to any name under which the company carries on business at that time.

(7) For the purposes of this section a company goes into insolvent liquidation if it goes into liquidation at a time when its assets are insufficient for the payment of its debts and other liabilities and the expenses of the winding up.

(8) In this section "company" includes a company which may be wound up under Part V of this Act.

[667]

217 Personal liability for debts, following contravention of s 216

(1) A person is personally responsible for all the relevant debts of a company if at any time—

(a) in contravention of section 216, he is involved in the management of the company, or

(b) as a person who is involved in the management of the company, he acts or is willing to act on instructions given (without the leave of the court) by a person whom he knows at that time to be in contravention in relation to the company of section 216.

(2) Where a person is personally responsible under this section for the relevant debts of a company, he is jointly and severally liable in respect of those debts with the company and any other person who, whether under this section or otherwise, is so liable.

(3) For the purposes of this section the relevant debts of a company are—

(a) in relation to a person who is personally responsible under paragraph (a) of subsection (1), such debts and other liabilities of the company as are incurred at a time when that person was involved in the management of the company, and

(b) in relation to a person who is personally responsible under paragraph (b) of that subsection, such debts and other liabilities of the company as are incurred at a time when that person was acting or was willing to act on instructions given as mentioned in that paragraph.

(4) For the purposes of this section, a person is involved in the management of a company if he is a director of the company or if he is concerned, whether directly or indirectly, or takes part, in the management of the company.

(5) For the purposes of this section a person who, as a person involved in the management of a company, has at any time acted on instructions given (without the leave of the court) by a person whom he knew at that time to be in contravention in relation to the company of section 216 is presumed, unless the contrary is shown, to have been willing at any time thereafter to act on any instructions given by that person.

(6) In this section "company" includes a company which may be wound up under Part V.

[668]

Investigation and prosecution of malpractice

218 Prosecution of delinquent officers and members of company

(1) If it appears to the court in the course of a winding up by the court that any past or present officer, or any member, of the company has been guilty of any offence in relation to the company for which he is criminally liable, the court may (either on the application of a person interested in the winding up or of its own motion) direct the liquidator to refer the matter

[(a) in the case of a winding up in England and Wales, to the Secretary of State, and

(b) in the case of a winding up in Scotland, to the Lord Advocate].

(2) …

(3) If in the case of a winding up by the court in England and Wales it appears to the liquidator, not being the official receiver, that any past or present officer of the company, or any member of it, has been guilty of an offence in relation to the company for which he is criminally liable, the liquidator shall report the matter to the official receiver.

(4) If it appears to the liquidator in the course of a voluntary winding up that any past or present officer of the company, or any member of it, has been guilty of an offence in relation to the company for which he is criminally liable, he shall [forthwith report the matter—

(a) in the case of a winding up in England and Wales, to the Secretary of State, and

(b) in the case of a winding up in Scotland, to the Lord Advocate,

and shall furnish to the Secretary of State or (as the case may be) the Lord Advocate] such information and give to him such access to and facilities for inspecting and taking copies of documents (being information or documents in the possession or under the control of the liquidator and relating to the matter in question) as [the Secretary of State or (as the case may be) the Lord Advocate] requires.

[(5) Where a report is made to the Secretary of State under subsection (4) he may, for the purpose of investigating the matter reported to him and such other matters relating to the affairs of the company as appear to him to require investigation, exercise any of the powers which are exercisable by inspectors appointed under section 431 or 432 of the Companies Act to investigate a company's affairs.]

(6) If it appears to the court in the course of a voluntary winding up that—

(a) any past or present officer of the company, or any member of it, has been guilty as above-mentioned, and

(b) no report with respect to the matter has been made by the liquidator … under subsection (4),

the court may (on the application of any person interested in the winding up or of its own motion) direct the liquidator to make such a report.

On a report being made accordingly, this section has effect as though the report had been made in pursuance of subsection (4).

[669]

NOTES

Sub-s (1): paras (a), (b) substituted by the Insolvency Act 2000, s 10(1), (2).
Sub-s (2): repealed by the Insolvency Act 2000, ss 10(1), (3), 15(1), Sch 5.
Sub-s (4): words in square brackets substituted by the Insolvency Act 2000, s 10(1), (4).
Sub-s (5): substituted by the Insolvency Act 2000, s 10(1), (5).
Sub-s (6): words omitted from para (b) repealed by the Insolvency Act 2000, ss 10(1), (6), 15(1), Sch 5.

219 Obligations arising under s 218

(1) For the purpose of an investigation by the Secretary of State [in consequence of a report made to him under section 218(4)], any obligation imposed on a person by any provision of the Companies Act to produce documents or give information to, or otherwise to assist, inspectors appointed as mentioned in [section 218(5)] is to be regarded as an obligation similarly to assist the Secretary of State in his investigation.

(2) An answer given by a person to a question put to him in exercise of the powers conferred by section 218(5) may be used in evidence against him.

[(2A) However, in criminal proceedings in which that person is charged with an offence to which this subsection applies—

(a) no evidence relating to the answer may be adduced, and
(b) no question relating to it may be asked,

by or on behalf of the prosecution, unless evidence relating to it is adduced, or a question relating to it is asked, in the proceedings by or on behalf of that person.

(2B) Subsection (2A) applies to any offence other than—

(a) an offence under section 2 or 5 of the Perjury Act 1911 (false statements made on oath otherwise than in judicial proceedings or made otherwise than on oath), or
(b) an offence under section 44(1) or (2) of the Criminal Law (Consolidation) (Scotland) Act 1995 (false statements made on oath or otherwise than on oath).]

(3) Where criminal proceedings are instituted by the [the Director of Public Prosecutions, the Lord Advocate] or the Secretary of State following any report or reference under section 218, it is the duty of the liquidator and every officer and agent of the company past and present (other than the defendant or defender) to give to [the Director of Public Prosecutions, the Lord Advocate] or the Secretary of State (as the case may be) all assistance in connection with the prosecution which he is reasonably able to give.

For this purpose "agent" includes any banker or solicitor of the company and any person employed by the company as auditor, whether that person is or is not an officer of the company.

(4) If a person fails or neglects to give assistance in the manner required by subsection (3), the court may, on the application of the [Director of Public Prosecutions, the Lord Advocate] or the Secretary of State (as the case may be) direct the person to comply with that subsection; and if the application is made with respect to a liquidator, the court may (unless it appears that the failure or neglect to comply was due to the liquidator not having in his hands sufficient assets of the company to enable him to do so) direct that the costs shall be borne by the liquidator personally.

[670]

NOTES

Sub-ss (1), (3), (4): words in square brackets substituted by the Insolvency Act 2000, s 10(7).
Sub-ss (2A), (2B): inserted by the Insolvency Act 2000, s 11.

220–246 *((Pts V, VI) outside the scope of this work.)*

PART VII
INTERPRETATION FOR FIRST GROUP OF PARTS

NOTES

Application: as to the application of this Part of this Act, with modifications, to the winding up of incorporated friendly societies by virtue of the Friendly Societies Act 1992, s 21(1) or 22(2), see s 23 of, and Sch 10 to, the 1992 Act.

247 "Insolvency" and "go into liquidation"

(1) In this Group of Parts, except in so far as the context otherwise requires, "insolvency", in relation to a company, includes the approval of a voluntary arrangement under Part I, [or the appointment of an administrator or administrative receiver].

(2) For the purposes of any provision in this Group of Parts, a company goes into liquidation if it passes a resolution for voluntary winding up or an order for its winding up is made by the court at a time when it has not already gone into liquidation by passing such a resolution.

[(3) The reference to a resolution for voluntary winding up in subsection (2) includes a reference to a resolution which is deemed to occur by virtue of—

(a) paragraph 83(6)(b) of Schedule B1, or
(b) an order made following conversion of administration or a voluntary arrangement into winding up by virtue of Article 37 of the EC Regulation.]

[671]

NOTES

Sub-s (1): words in square brackets substituted by the Enterprise Act 2002, s 248(3), Sch 17, paras 9, 33(1), (2).

Sub-s (3): added by the Insolvency Act 1986 (Amendment) (No 2) Regulations 2002, SI 2002/1240, regs 3, 12; substituted by the Enterprise Act 2002, s 248(3), Sch 17, paras 9, 33(1), (3).

248 "Secured creditor", etc

In this Group of Parts, except in so far as the context otherwise requires—

(a) "secured creditor", in relation to a company, means a creditor of the company who holds in respect of his debt a security over property of the company, and "unsecured creditor" is to be read accordingly; and

(b) "security" means—

(i) in relation to England and Wales, any mortgage, charge, lien or other security, and

(ii) (*applies to Scotland only.*)

[672]

249 "Connected" with a company

For the purposes of any provision in this Group of Parts, a person is connected with a company if—

(a) he is a director or shadow director of the company or an associate of such a director or shadow director, or

(b) he is an associate of the company;

and "associate" has the meaning given by section 435 in Part XVIII of this Act.

[673]

250 "Member" of a company

For the purposes of any provision in this Group of Parts, a person who is not a member of a company but to whom shares in the company have been transferred, or transmitted by operation of law, is to be regarded as a member of the company, and references to a member or members are to be read accordingly.

[674]

251 Expressions used generally

In this Group of Parts, except in so far as the context otherwise requires—

"administrative receiver" means—

(a) an administrative receiver as defined by section 29(2) in Chapter I of Part III, or

(b) (*applies to Scotland only*);

"business day" means any day other than a Saturday, a Sunday, Christmas Day, Good Friday or a day which is a bank holiday in any part of Great Britain;

"chattel leasing agreement" means an agreement for the bailment or, in Scotland, the hiring of goods which is capable of subsisting for more than 3 months;

"contributory" has the meaning given by section 79;

"director" includes any person occupying the position of director, by whatever name called;

"floating charge" means a charge which, as created, was a floating charge and includes a floating charge within section 462 of the Companies Act (Scottish floating charges);

. . . . .

"the official rate", in relation to interest, means the rate payable under section 189(4);

"prescribed" means prescribed by the rules;

. . . . .

"retention of title agreement" means an agreement for the sale of goods to a company, being an agreement—

(a) which does not constitute a charge on the goods, but

(b) under which, if the seller is not paid and the company is wound up, the seller will have priority over all other creditors of the company as respects the goods or any property representing the goods;

"the rules" means rules under section 411 in Part XV; and

"shadow director", in relation to a company, means a person in accordance with whose directions or instructions the directors of the company are accustomed to act (but so that a person is not deemed a shadow director by reason only that the directors act on advice given by him in a professional capacity);

and any expression for whose interpretation provision is made by Part XXVI of the Companies Act, other than an expression defined above in this section, is to be construed in accordance with that provision.

[675]

NOTES

Definitions omitted apply to Scotland only.
Companies Act: ie, the Companies Act 1985.

252–385 ((*Pts VIII–XI*) *outside the scope of this work.*)

THE THIRD GROUP OF PARTS
MISCELLANEOUS MATTERS BEARING ON BOTH COMPANY AND INDIVIDUAL INSOLVENCY; GENERAL INTERPRETATION; FINAL PROVISIONS

386–436A ((*Pts XII–XVIII*) *outside the scope of this work.*)

PART XIX
FINAL PROVISIONS

437–442 (*Outside the scope of this work.*)

443 Commencement

This Act comes into force on the day appointed under section 236(2) of the Insolvency Act 1985 for the coming into force of Part III of that Act (individual insolvency and bankruptcy), immediately after that Part of that Act comes into force for England and Wales.

[676]

NOTES

Commencement: this Act came into force on 29 December 1986 by virtue of this section and the Insolvency Act 1985 (Commencement No 5) Order 1986, SI 1986/1924, art 3.

444 Citation

This Act may be cited as the Insolvency Act 1986.

[677]–[681]

(*Schs A1–14 outside the scope of this work.*)

REVERTER OF SITES ACT 1987

(1987 c 15)

ARRANGEMENT OF SECTIONS

An Act to amend the law with respect to the reverter of sites that have ceased to be used for particular purposes; and for connected purposes

[9 April 1987]

1 Right of reverter replaced by [trust]

(1) Where any relevant enactment provides for land to revert to the ownership of any person at any time, being a time when the land ceases, or has ceased for a specified period, to be used for particular purposes, that enactment shall have effect, and (subject to subsection (4) below) shall be deemed always to have had effect, as if it provided (instead of for the reverter) for the land to be vested after that time, on the trust arising under this section, in the persons in whom it was vested immediately before that time.

(2) Subject to the following provisions of this Act, the trust arising under this section in relation to any land is a trust [for the persons who (but for this Act) would from time to time be entitled to the ownership of the land by virtue of its reverter with a power, without consulting them,] to sell the land and to stand possessed of the net proceeds of sale (after payment of costs and expenses) and of the net rents and profits until sale (after payment of rates, taxes, costs of insurance, repairs and other outgoings) [in trust for those persons; but they shall not be entitled by reason of their interest to occupy the land].

(3) Where—

(a) a trust in relation to any land has arisen or is treated as having arisen under this section at such a time as is mentioned in subsection (1) above; and

(b) immediately before that time the land was vested in any persons in their capacity as the minister and churchwardens of any parish,

those persons shall be treated as having become [trustees] under this section in that capacity and, accordingly, their interest in the land shall pass and, if the case so requires, be treated as having passed to their successors from time to time.

(4) This section shall not confer any right on any person as a beneficiary—

(a) in relation to any property in respect of which that person's claim was statute-barred before the commencement of this Act, or in relation to any property derived from any such property; or

(b) in relation to any rents or profits received, or breach of trust committed, before the commencement of this Act;

and anything validly done before the commencement of this Act in relation to any land which by virtue of this section is deemed to have been held at the time [in trust] shall, if done by the beneficiaries, be deemed, so far as necessary for preserving its validity, to have been done by the trustees.

(5) Where any property is held by any persons as trustees of a trust which has arisen under this section and, in consequence of subsection (4) above, there are no beneficiaries of that trust, the trustees shall have no power to act in relation to that property except—

(a) for the purposes for which they could have acted in relation to that property if this Act had not been passed; or

(b) for the purpose of securing the establishment of a scheme under section 2 below or the making of an order under [section 554 of the Education Act 1996] (special powers as to trusts for religious education).

(6) In this section—

"churchwardens" includes chapel wardens;

"minister" includes a rector, vicar or perpetual curate; and

"parish" includes a parish of the Church in Wales;

and the reference to a person's claim being statute-barred is a reference to the Limitation Act 1980 providing that no proceedings shall be brought by that person to recover the property in respect of which the claim subsists.

[682]

NOTES

Section heading: word in square brackets substituted for the words "trust for sale" by the Trusts of Land and Appointment of Trustees Act 1996, s 5(1), Sch 2, para 6(1), (5), (6), whether the trust arises before or after 1 January 1997; for savings in connection with the abolition of the doctrine of conversion, see ss 3, 18(3), 25(5) of the 1996 Act, at **[1009]**, **[1025]** and **[1032]**.

Sub-s (2): words in first pair of square brackets inserted and words in second pair of square brackets substituted for the words "upon trust for the persons who but for this Act would from time to time be entitled to the ownership of the land by virtue of its reverter" by the Trusts of Land and Appointment of Trustees Act 1996, s 5(1), Sch 2, para 6(1), (2), (6), whether the trust arises before or after 1 January 1997; for savings in connection with the abolition of the doctrine of conversion, see ss 3, 18(3), 25(5) of the 1996 Act, at **[1009]**, **[1025]** and **[1032]**.

Sub-s (3): word in square brackets substituted for the words "trustees for sale" by the Trusts of Land and Appointment of Trustees Act 1996, s 5(1), Sch 2, para 6(1), (3), (6), whether the trust arises before or after 1 January 1997; for savings in connection with the abolition of the doctrine of conversion, see ss 3, 18(3), 25(5) of the 1996 Act, at **[1009]**, **[1025]** and **[1032]**.

Sub-s (4): words in square brackets substituted for the words "on trust for sale" by the Trusts of Land and Appointment of Trustees Act 1996, s 5(1), Sch 2, para 6(1), (4), (6), whether the trust arises before or after 1 January 1997; for savings in connection with the abolition of the doctrine of conversion, see ss 3, 18(3), 25(5) of the 1996 Act, at **[1009]**, **[1025]** and **[1032]**.

Sub-s (5): words in square brackets substituted by the Education Act 1996, s 582(1), Sch 37, Pt I, para 67.

2 [Charity Commission's] schemes

(1) Subject to the following provisions of this section and to sections 3 and 4 below, where any persons hold any property as trustees of a trust which has arisen under section 1 above, the [Charity Commission] may, on the application of the trustees, by order establish a scheme which—

(a) extinguishes the rights of beneficiaries under the trust; and

(b) requires the trustees to hold the property on trust for such charitable purposes as may be specified in the order.

(2) Subject to subsections (3) and (4) below, an order made under this section—

(a) may contain any such provision as may be contained in an order made by the High Court for establishing a scheme for the administration of a charity; and

(b) shall have the same effect as an order so made.

(3) The charitable purposes specified in an order made under this section on an application with respect to any trust shall be as similar in character as the Charity Commissioners think is practicable in all the circumstances to the purposes (whether charitable or not) for which the trustees held the relevant land before the cesser of use in consequence of which the trust arose; but in determining the character of the last-mentioned purposes the Commissioners, if they think it appropriate to do so, may give greater weight to the persons or locality benefited by the purposes than to the nature of the benefit.

(4) An order made under this section on an application with respect to any trust shall be so framed as to secure that if a person who—

(a) but for the making of the order would have been a beneficiary under the trust; and

(b) has not consented to the establishment of a scheme under this section, notifies a claim to the trustees within the period of five years after the date of the making of the order, that person shall be paid an amount equal to the value of his rights at the time of their extinguishment.

(5) The [Charity Commission] shall not make any order under this section establishing a scheme unless—

(a) the requirements of section 3 below with respect to the making of the application for the order are satisfied or, by virtue of subsection (4) of that section, do not apply;

(b) one of the conditions specified in subsection (6) below is fulfilled;

(c) public notice of the [Commission's] proposals has been given inviting representations to be made to [it] within a period specified in the notice, being a period ending not less than one month after the date of the giving of the notice; and

(d) that period has ended and the [Commission has] taken into consideration any representations which have been made within that period and not withdrawn.

(6) The conditions mentioned in subsection (5)(b) above are—

(a) that there is no claim by any person to be a beneficiary in respect of rights proposed to be extinguished—

  (i) which is outstanding; or

  (ii) which has at any time been accepted as valid by the trustees or by persons whose acceptance binds the trustees; or

  (iii) which has been upheld in proceedings that have been concluded;

(b) that consent to the establishment of a scheme under this section has been given by every person whose claim to be a beneficiary in respect of those rights is outstanding or has been so accepted or upheld.

(7) The [Charity Commission] shall refuse to consider an application under this section unless it is accompanied by a statutory declaration by the applicants—

(a) that the requirements of section 3 below are satisfied with respect to the making of the application or, if the declaration so declares, do not apply; and

(b) that a condition specified in subsection (6) above and identified in the declaration is fulfilled;

and the declaration shall be conclusive for the purposes of this section of the matters declared therein.

(8) A notice given for the purposes of subsection (5)(c) above shall contain such particulars of the [Commission's] proposals, or such directions for obtaining information about them, and shall be given in such manner, as [it thinks] sufficient and appropriate; and a further such notice shall not be required where the [Commission decides], before proceeding with any proposals of which notice has been so given, to modify them.

[683]

NOTES

Section heading: words in square brackets substituted by the Charities Act 2006, s 75(1), Sch 8, paras 81, 82(1), (7).

Sub-ss (1), (5), (7), (8): words in square brackets substituted the words "Charity Commission" by the Charities Act 2006, s 75(1), Sch 8, paras 81, 82(1), (2), (4)–(6).

Sub-s (3): substituted by sub-ss (3), (3A), (3B) by the Charities Act 2006, s 75(1), Sch 8, paras 81, 82(1), (3), as from a day to be appointed under s 79(2) of that Act, as follows—

"(3) The charitable purposes specified in an order made under this section on an application with respect to any trust shall be such as the Charity Commission consider appropriate, having regard to the matters set out in subsection (3A).

(3A) The matters are—

(a) the desirability of securing that the property is held for charitable purposes ("the new purposes") which are close to the purposes, whether charitable or not, for which the trustees held the relevant land before the cesser of use in consequence of which the trust arose ("the former purposes); and

(b) the need for the new purposes to be capable of having a significant social or economic effect.

(3B) In determining the character of the former purposes, the Commission may, if they think it appropriate to do so, give greater weight to the persons or locality benefited by those purposes than to the nature of the benefit.".

3 Applications for schemes

(1) Where an application is made under section 2 above by the trustees of any trust that has arisen under section 1 above, the requirements of this section are satisfied with respect to the making of that application if, before the application is made—

(a) notices under subsection (2) below have been published in two national newspapers and in a local newspaper circulating in the locality where the relevant land is situated;

(b) each of those notices specified a period for the notification to the trustees of claims by beneficiaries, being a period ending not less than three months after the date of publication of the last of those notices to be published;

(c) that period has ended;

(d) for a period of not less than twenty-one days during the first month of that period, a copy of one of those notices was affixed to some object on the relevant land in such a position and manner as, so far as practicable, to make the notice easy for members of the public to see and read without going on to the land; and

(e) the trustees have considered what other steps could be taken to trace the persons who are or may be beneficiaries and to inform those persons of the application to be made under section 2 above and have taken such of the steps considered by them as it was reasonably practicable for them to take.

(2) A notice under this subsection shall—

(a) set out the circumstances that have resulted in a trust having arisen under section 1 above;

(b) state that an application is to be made for the establishment of a scheme with respect to the property subject to the trust; and

(c) contain a warning to every beneficiary that, if he wishes to oppose the extinguishment of his rights, he should notify his claim to the trustees in the manner, and within the period, specified in the notice.

(3) Where at the time when the trustees publish a notice for the purposes of subsection (2) above—

(a) the relevant land is not under their control; and

(b) it is not reasonably practicable for them to arrange for a copy of the notice to be affixed as required by paragraph (d) of subsection (1) above to some object on the land,

that paragraph shall be disregarded for the purposes of this section.

(4) The requirements of this section shall not apply in the case of an application made in respect of any trust if—

(a) the time when that trust is treated as having arisen was before the commencement of this Act; and

(b) more than twelve years have elapsed since that time.

[684]

4 Provisions supplemental to ss 2 and 3

(1) Where an order is made under section 2 above—

(a) public notice of the order shall be given in such manner as the [Charity Commission thinks] sufficient and appropriate; and

(b) a copy of the order shall, for not less than one month after the date of the giving of the notice, be available for public inspection at all reasonable times at the [Commission's] office and at some convenient place in the locality where the relevant land is situated;

and a notice given for the purposes of paragraph (a) above shall contain such particulars of the order, or such directions for obtaining information about it, as [the Commission thinks] sufficient and appropriate.

(2) *Subject to subsection (3) below, an appeal against an order made under section 2 above may be brought in the High Court by any of the following, that is to say—*

(a) the Attorney General;

(b) the trustees of the trust established under the order;

(c) a beneficiary of, or the trustees of, the trust in respect of which the application for the order had been made;

(d) any person interested in the purposes for which the last-mentioned trustees or any of their predecessors held the relevant land before the cesser of use in consequence of which the trust arose under section 1 above;

(e) any two or more inhabitants of the locality where that land is situated.

(3) An appeal shall not be brought under subsection (2) above against any order—

(a) after the end of the period of three months beginning with the day following the date on which public notice of the order is given; or

(b) without either a certificate by the Charity Commissioners that it is a proper case for an appeal or the leave of the High Court,

unless it is brought by the Attorney General.

(4) [*Sections 89, 91 and 92* of the Charities Act 1993] (supplemental provisions with respect to orders *and appeals*) shall apply in relation to, *and to appeals against,* orders under section 2 above as they apply in relation to, *and to appeals against,* orders under that Act.

(5) Trustees of a trust which has arisen under section 1 above may pay or apply capital money for any of the purposes of section 2 or 3 above or of this section.

[685]

NOTES

Sub-s (1): words in square brackets substituted by the Charities Act 2006, s 75(1), Sch 8, paras 81, 83(1), (2).

Sub-ss (2), (3): substituted by sub-s (2) by the Charities Act 2006, s 75(1), Sch 8, paras 81, 83(1), (3), as from a day to be appointed under s 79(2) of that Act, subject to savings in Sch 10, para 18 to that Act at **[2176]**, as follows—

"(2) Schedule 1C to the Charities Act 1993 shall apply in relation to an order made under section 2 above as it applies in relation to an order made under section 16(1) of that Act, except that the persons who may bring an appeal against an order made under section 2 above are—

(a) the Attorney General;

(b) the trustees of the trust established under the order;

(c) a beneficiary of, or the trustees of, the trust in respect of which the application for the order had been made;

(d) any person interested in the purposes for which the lastmentioned trustees or any of their predecessors held the relevant land before the cesser of use in consequence of which the trust arose under section 1 above;

(e) any two or more inhabitants of the locality where that land is situated;

(f) any other person who is or may be affected by the order.".

Sub-s (4): words in square brackets substituted by the Charities Act 1993, s 98(1), Sch 6, para 24; for the words in italics in the first place there are substituted the words "Sections 89 and 91" and other words in italics repealed by the Charities Act 2006, s 75(1), (2), Sch 8, paras 81, 83(1), (4), Sch 9, as from a day to be appointed under s 79(2) of that Act, subject to savings in Sch 10, para 18 to that Act at **[2176]**.

5 Orders under the Education Act 1973

(1) An order made under [section 554 of the Education Act 1996] (special powers as to certain trusts for religious education) with respect to so much of any endowment as consists of—

(a) land in relation to which a trust under section 1 above has arisen or will arise after the land ceased or ceases to be used for particular purposes; or

(b) any other property subject to a trust under that section,

may extinguish any rights to which a person is or may become entitled as a beneficiary under the trust.

(2) The Secretary of State shall not by an order under [section 554 of the 1996 Act] extinguish any such rights unless he is satisfied that all reasonably practicable steps to trace the persons who are or may become entitled to any of those rights have been taken and either—

(a) that there is no claim by any person to be a person who is or may become so entitled—

(i) which is outstanding; or

(ii) which has at any time been accepted as valid by the trustees or by persons whose acceptance binds or will bind the trustees; or

(iii) which has been upheld in proceedings that have been concluded; or

(b) that consent to the making of an order under [section 554 of the 1996 Act] has been given by every person whose claim to be such a person is outstanding or has been so accepted or upheld.

(3) Where applications for the extinguishment of the rights of any beneficiaries are made with respect to the same trust property both to the Secretary of State under [section 554 of the 1996 Act] and to the [Charity Commission] under section 2 above, [the Commission] shall not consider, or further consider, the application made to [it], unless the Secretary of State either—

(a) consents to the application made to the [Charity Commission] being considered before the application made to him; or

(b) disposes of the application made to him without extinguishing the rights of one or more of the beneficiaries.

(4) Trustees of a trust which has arisen under section 1 above may pay or apply capital money for the purposes of any provision of this section or [section 554 of the 1996 Act].

[686]

NOTES

Sub-ss (1), (2), (4): words in square brackets substituted by the Education Act 1996, s 582(1), Sch 37, Pt I, para 67.

Sub-s (3): words in first pair of square brackets substituted by the Education Act 1996, s 582(1), Sch 37, Pt I, para 67; words in second, third, fourth and fifth pairs of square brackets substituted by the Charities Act 2006, s 75(1), Sch 8, paras 81, 84.

The reference to the Education Act 1973 in the heading of this section should be read in light of the amendments made to this section by the Education Act 1996 as noted above.

6 Classification of status etc of land before reverter

(1) Nothing in this Act shall require any land which is or has been the subject of any grant, conveyance or other assurance under any relevant enactment to be treated as or as having been settled land.

(2) It is hereby declared—

(a) that the power conferred by section 14 of the School Sites Act 1841 (power of sale etc) is exercisable at any time in relation to land in relation to which (but for the exercise of the power) a trust might subsequently arise under section 1 above; and

(b) that the exercise of that power in respect of any land prevents any trust from arising under section 1 above in relation to that land or any land representing the proceeds of sale of that land.

[687]

7 Construction

(1) In this Act—

"relevant enactment" means any enactment contained in—

(a) the School Sites Acts;

(b) the Literary and Scientific Institutions Act 1854; or

(c) the Places of Worship Sites Act 1873;

"relevant land", in relation to a trust which has arisen under section 1 above, means the land which but for this Act would have reverted to the persons who are the first beneficiaries under the trust.

(2) In this Act references to land include references to—

(a) any part of any land which has been the subject of a grant, conveyance or other assurance under any relevant enactment; and

(b) any land an interest in which (including any future or contingent interest arising under any such enactment) belongs to the Crown, the Duchy of Lancaster or the Duchy of Cornwall.

(3) For the purposes of this Act a claim by any person to be a beneficiary under a trust is outstanding if—

(a) it has been notified to the trustees;

(b) it has not been withdrawn; and

(c) proceedings for determining whether it should be upheld have not been commenced or (if commenced) have not been concluded.

(4) For the purposes of this Act proceedings shall not, in relation to any person's claim, be treated as concluded where the time for appealing is unexpired or an appeal is pending unless that person has indicated his intention not to appeal or, as the case may be, not to continue with the appeal.

[688]

8 Consequential amendments, repeals and saving

(1), (2) …

(3) The enactments mentioned in the Schedule to this Act are hereby repealed to the extent specified in the third column of that Schedule.

(4) The repeals contained in the Schedule to this Act shall not affect the operation at any time after the commencement of this Act of so much of any order made before the commencement of this Act under section 2 of the Education Act 1973 as has excluded the operation of the third proviso to section 2 of the School Sites Act 1841.

[689]

NOTES

Sub-s (1): repealed by the Education Act 1996, s 582(2), Sch 38, Pt I.
Sub-s (2): amends the Law of Property Act 1925, s 3(3).

9 Short title, commencement and extent

(1) This Act may be cited as the Reverter of Sites Act 1987.

(2) This Act shall come into force on such day as the Lord Chancellor may by order made by statutory instrument appoint.

(3) This Act shall extend to England and Wales only.

[690]

NOTES

Orders: the Reverter of Sites Act 1987 (Commencement) Order 1987, SI 1987/1260.

(*Schedule contains repeals only.*)

INCOME AND CORPORATION TAXES ACT 1988

(1988 c 1)

ARRANGEMENT OF SECTIONS

PART I
THE CHARGE TO TAX

The six Schedules

PART IV
PROVISIONS RELATING TO THE SCHEDULE D CHARGE

CHAPTER V
COMPUTATIONAL PROVISIONS

Deductions

PART VIII
TAXATION OF INCOME AND CHARGEABLE GAINS OF COMPANIES

Taxation of income

PART IX
ANNUAL PAYMENTS AND INTEREST

Annual payments

PART XII
SPECIAL CLASSES OF COMPANIES AND BUSINESSES

CHAPTER VI
MISCELLANEOUS BUSINESSES AND BODIES

PART XVII
TAX AVOIDANCE

CHAPTER VI
MISCELLANEOUS

Other provisions

PART XIX
SUPPLEMENTAL

Commencement, savings, repeals etc

An Act to consolidate certain of the enactments relating to income tax and corporation tax, including certain enactments relating also to capital gains tax; and to repeal as obsolete section 339(1) of the Income and Corporation Taxes Act 1970 and paragraphs 3 and 4 of Schedule 11 to the Finance Act 1980

[9 February 1988]

PART I
THE CHARGE TO TAX

1–14 (*Outside the scope of this work.*)

The six Schedules

15 Schedule A

(1) The Schedule referred to as Schedule A is as follows:—

[SCHEDULE A

1.—(1) Tax is charged under this Schedule on the annual profits arising from a business carried on for the exploitation, as a source of rents or other receipts, of any estate, interest or rights in or over land in the United Kingdom.

(2) To the extent that any transaction is entered into for the exploitation, as a source of rents or other receipts, of any estate, interest or rights in or over land in the United Kingdom, it is taken to be entered into in the course of such a business.

(3) All businesses and transactions carried on or entered into by a particular person or partnership, so far as they are businesses or transactions the profits of which are chargeable to tax under this Schedule, are treated for the purposes of this Schedule as, or as entered into in the course of carrying on, a single business.

There are qualifications to this rule in the case of—

(a) companies not resident in the United Kingdom (see subsection (1A) below); and
(b) insurance companies (see sections 432AA and 441B(2A)).

(4) The receipts referred to in the expression "as a source of rents or other receipts" include—

(a) payments in respect of a licence to occupy or otherwise to use land or the exercise of any other right over land, and
(b) rentcharges, … and other annual payments reserved in respect of, or charged on or issuing out of, the land.

2.—(1) This Schedule does not apply to profits arising from the occupation of land.

(2) This Schedule does not apply to—

(a) profits charged to tax under Case I of Schedule D under—
section 53(1) (farming and market gardening), or
section 55 (mines, quarries and other concerns);
(b) receipts or expenses taken into account as trading receipts or expenses under section 98 (tied premises);

(c) rent charged to tax under Schedule D under—
section 119 (rent, etc payable in connection with mines, quarries and other concerns), or
section 120(1) (certain rent, etc payable in respect of electric line wayleaves).

(3) The profits of a Schedule A business carried on by a company shall be computed without regard to items giving rise to—
credits or debits within Chapter II of Part IV of the Finance Act 1996 (loan relationships), or
. . .
[credits or debits within Schedule 26 to the Finance Act 2002 (derivative contracts)].

This Schedule does not affect the operation of those provisions.

3.—(1) For the purposes of this Schedule a right to use a caravan or houseboat, where the use to which the caravan or houseboat may be put in pursuance of the right is confined to use at a single location in the United Kingdom, is treated as a right deriving from an estate or interest in land in the United Kingdom.

(2) In sub-paragraph (1)—
"caravan" has the meaning given by section 29(1) of the Caravan Sites and Control of Development Act 1960; and
"houseboat" means a boat or similar structure designed or adapted for use as a place of human habitation.

4.—(1) In the case of a furnished letting, any sum payable for the use of furniture shall be taken into account in computing the profits chargeable to tax under this Schedule in the same way as rent.

Expenses in connection with the provision of furniture shall similarly be taken into account in the same way as expenses in connection with the premises.

(2) A furnished letting means where—
(a) a sum is payable in respect of the use of premises, and
(b) the tenant or other person entitled to the use of the premises is also entitled, in connection with that use, to the use of furniture.

(3) This paragraph does not apply if the receipts and expenses are taken into account in computing the profits of a trade consisting in, or involving, making furniture available for use in premises.

(4) In this paragraph—
(a) any reference to a sum includes the value of consideration other than money, and references to a sum being payable shall be construed accordingly; and
(b) "premises" includes a caravan or houseboat within the meaning of paragraph 3.]

[(1A) In the case of a company which is not resident in the United Kingdom—
(a) businesses carried on and transactions entered into by it the profits of which are within the charge to corporation tax under Schedule A, and
(b) businesses carried on and transactions entered into by it the profits of which are [the profits of a UK property business within the charge to income tax under Chapter 3 of Part 3 of ITTOIA 2005],

are treated [for the purposes of those charges as separate businesses].]

(2), (3) . . .

[(3A) Subsection (1) applies for corporation tax purposes (and does not apply for income tax purposes except so far as necessary to ensure its application for corporation tax purposes by virtue of section 9).]

(4) Part II contains further provisions relating to the charge to tax under Schedule A [and under Chapter 3 of Part 3 of ITTOIA 2005 (profits of a property business)].

[691]

NOTES

Sub-s (1): Schedule A substituted, subject to transitional provisions, by the Finance Act 1998, s 38, *Sch 5, Pt I, para 1, Pt IV, as from 1 April 1998* in so far as relating to corporation tax, and, in so far as relating to income tax, for the year 1998–99 and subsequent years of assessment; in para 1(4)(b) of Schedule A words omitted repealed by the Abolition of Feudal Tenure etc (Scotland) Act 2000, s 76(1), (2), Sch 12, para 50(1), (2), Sch 13; in para 2(3) of Schedule A words omitted repealed and words in square brackets substituted by the Finance Act 2002, ss 83(1)(b), 141, Sch 27, paras 1, 2, Sch 40, Pt 3(10) in relation to accounting periods beginning on or after 1 October 2002.

Sub-s (1A): inserted, subject to transitional provisions, by the Finance Act 1998, s 38, Sch 5, Pt I, para 2, Pt IV, as from 1 April 1998 in so far as relating to corporation tax, and, in so far as relating to income tax, for the year 1998–99 and subsequent years of assessment; words in square brackets substituted by the Income Tax (Trading and Other Income) Act 2005, s 882(1), Sch 1, Pt 1, paras 1, 8(1), (2), with effect, for the purposes of income tax for the year 2005–06 and subsequent tax years, and for the purposes of corporation tax for accounting periods ending after 5 April 2005.

Sub-s (2): repealed (except as applied by virtue of s 9 of this Act for the purposes of corporation tax), by the Finance Act 1995, s 39(1), (3), (4)(a), Sch 6, para 1, in relation to the year 1995–96 and subsequent years of assessment; for provision as to circumstances in which this repeal does not apply in the year 1995–96 see s 39(5) thereof. Further repealed, in relation to corporation tax, by the Finance Act 1998, s 165, Sch 27, Pt III(4), with effect from 1 April 1998.

Sub-s (3): repealed by the Finance Act 1988, s 148, Sch 14, Pt V.

Sub-s (3A): inserted by the Income Tax (Trading and Other Income) Act 2005, s 882(1), Sch 1, Pt 1, paras 1, 8(1), (3), with effect, for the purposes of income tax for the year 2005–06 and subsequent tax years, and for the purposes of corporation tax for accounting periods ending after 5 April 2005.

Sub-s (4): words in square brackets inserted by the Income Tax (Trading and Other Income) Act 2005, s 882(1), Sch 1, Pt 1, paras 1, 8(1), (4), with effect, for the purposes of income tax for the year 2005–06 and subsequent tax years, and for the purposes of corporation tax for accounting periods ending after 5 April 2005.

16, 17 *(S 16 repealed by the Finance Act 1988, s 148, Sch 14, Pt V, consequent on the abolition of Schedule B tax by s 65 of, and Sch 6, para 2 to, that Act; s 17 repealed by the Finance Act 1996, ss 79(2), 205, Sch 7, paras 1, 3, 32, Sch 41, Pt V(2), for the purposes of income tax in relation to the year 1996–97 and subsequent years of assessment, and for the purposes of corporation tax for accounting periods ending after 31 March 1996, consequent on the abolition of Schedule C tax by s 79(2) of that Act.)*

18 Schedule D

(1) The Schedule referred to as Schedule D is as follows:—

SCHEDULE D

Tax under this Schedule shall be charged in respect of—

(a) the annual profits or gains arising or accruing—

(i) to any person residing in the United Kingdom from any kind of property whatever, whether situated in the United Kingdom or elsewhere, and

(ii) to any person residing in the United Kingdom from any trade, profession or vocation, whether carried on in the United Kingdom or elsewhere, and

(iii) to any person, whether a Commonwealth citizen or not, although not resident in the United Kingdom from any property whatever in the United Kingdom or from any trade, profession or vocation exercised within the United Kingdom, and

(b) all interest of money, annuities and other annual profits or gains [not charged under Schedule A [or under ITEPA 2003 as employment income, pension income or social security income]], and not specially exempted from tax.

(2) Tax under Schedule D shall be charged under the Cases set out in subsection (3) below, and subject to and in accordance with the provisions of the Tax Acts applicable to those Cases respectively.

(3) The Cases are—

Case I: tax in respect of any trade carried on in the United Kingdom or elsewhere [but not contained in Schedule A];

Case II: tax in respect of any profession or vocation not contained in any other Schedule;

Case III: tax in respect of—

(a) any interest of money, whether yearly or otherwise, or any annuity or other annual payment, whether such payment is payable within or out of the United Kingdom, either as a charge on any property of the person paying the same by virtue of any deed or will or otherwise, or as a reservation out of it, or as a personal debt or obligation by virtue of any contract, or whether the same is received and payable half-yearly or at any shorter or more distant periods, but not including any payment chargeable under Schedule A, and

(b) all discounts, and

(c) income, [from securities which is payable out of the public revenue of the United Kingdom or Northern Ireland];

Case IV: tax in respect of income arising from securities out of the United Kingdom …;

Case V: tax in respect of income arising from possessions out of the United Kingdom not being [employment income, pension income or social security income on which tax is charged under ITEPA 2003];

Case VI: tax in respect of any annual profits or gains not falling under any other Case of Schedule D and not charged by virtue of [Schedule A [or by virtue of ITEPA 2003 as employment income, pension income or social security income]].

[(3A) For the purposes of corporation tax subsection (3) above shall have effect as if the following Case were substituted for Cases III and IV, that is to say—

"Case III: tax in respect of—

(a) profits and gains which, as profits and gains arising from loan relationships, are to be treated as chargeable under this Case by virtue of Chapter II of Part IV of the Finance Act 1996;

(b) any annuity or other annual payment which—

(i) is payable (whether inside or outside the United Kingdom and whether annually or at shorter or longer intervals) in respect of anything other than a loan relationship; and

(ii) is not a payment chargeable under Schedule A;

(c) …"

and as if Case V did not include tax in respect of any income falling within paragraph (a) of the substituted Case III.]

[(3B) The references in Case IV of Schedule D to income arising from securities out of the United Kingdom, and in Case V of Schedule D to income arising from possessions out of the United Kingdom, shall be taken, in the case of relevant foreign holdings, to include references to the following—

(a) any proceeds of such a sale or other realisation of coupons for foreign dividends as is effected by a bank in the United Kingdom which pays the proceeds over or carries them into an account;

(b) any proceeds of a sale of such coupons to a dealer in coupons in the United Kingdom by a person who is not a bank or another dealer in coupons.

(3C) In this section "relevant foreign holdings" means—

(a) any securities issued by or on behalf of a government or a public or local authority in a country outside the United Kingdom; or

(b) any shares or securities issued by or on behalf of a body of persons not resident in the United Kingdom;

and "securities" here includes loan stock and similar securities.

(3D) In this section "foreign dividends" means—

(a) in relation to relevant foreign holdings falling within subsection (3C)(a) above, interest or annual payments payable out of the revenue of the government or authority in question; and

(b) in relation to relevant foreign holdings falling within subsection (3C)(b) above, any dividends, interest or annual payments payable in respect of the holdings in question.

(3E) In this section—

(a) "bank" has the meaning given by section 840A; and

(b) references to coupons include, in relation to any foreign dividends, warrants for and bills of exchange purporting to be drawn or made in payment of those dividends.]

(4) The provisions of Schedule D and of subsection (2) above are without prejudice to any other provision of the Tax Acts directing tax to be charged under Schedule D or under one or other of the Cases set out in subsection (3) above, and tax directed to be so charged shall be charged accordingly.

[(4A) Subsections (1) to (4) apply for corporation tax purposes (and do not apply for income tax purposes except so far as necessary to ensure their application for corporation tax purposes by virtue of section 9).]

(5) [Parts III and IV contain] further provisions relating to the charge to tax under Schedule D [and under ITTOIA 2005 (see, in particular, the charge under Chapter 2 of Part 2 of that Act (trade profits))].

[(6) …]

[692]–[693]

NOTES

Sub-s (1): words in first (outer) pair of square brackets substituted, for the purposes of income tax in relation to the year 1996–97 and subsequent years of assessment and, for the purposes of corporation tax, in relation to accounting periods ending after 31 March 1996, by the Finance Act 1996, s 79, Sch 7, paras 4(1), 32, for transitional provision relating to the period before 29 April 1996 see paras 33–35 thereof; words in second (inner) pair of square brackets substituted by the Income Tax (Earnings and Pensions) Act 2003, s 722, Sch 6, Pt 1, paras 1, 5(1), (2), with effect, for the purposes of income tax for the year 2003–04 and subsequent years of assessment, and for the purposes of corporation tax for accounting periods ending after 5 April 2003.

Sub-s (3): words in square brackets in Case I inserted, for the purposes of income tax, in relation to the year 1995–96 and subsequent years of assessment and, for the purposes of corporation tax, in relation to accounting periods ending on or after 31 March 1995, by the Finance Act 1995, s 39(3), (4), Sch 6, para 2, for provision as to circumstances in which this amendment does not apply in the year 1995–96 see s 39(5) thereof; words in square brackets in Case III(c) substituted, for the purposes of income tax, in relation to the year 1996–97 and subsequent years of assessment and, for the purposes of corporation tax, in relation to accounting periods ending after 31 March 1996, by the Finance Act 1996, s 79, Sch 7, paras 4(2), 32, for transitional provision relating to the period before 29 April 1996 see Sch 7, paras 33–35 thereof; words omitted repealed, for the purposes of income tax, in relation to the year 1996–97 and subsequent years of assessment and, for the purposes of corporation tax, in relation to accounting periods ending after 31 March 1996, by the Finance Act 1996, s 205, Sch 41, Part V(2); for transitional provision relating to the period before 29 April 1996 see Sch 7, paras 33–35 thereof; words in square brackets in Case V substituted by the Income Tax (Earnings and Pensions) Act 2003, s 722, Sch 6, Pt 1, paras 1, 5(1), (3)(a), with effect, for the purposes of income tax for the year 2003–04 and subsequent years of assessment, and for the purposes of corporation tax for accounting periods ending after 5 April 2003; words in first (outer) pair of square brackets in Case VI substituted, for the purposes of income tax, in relation to the year 1996–97 and subsequent years of assessment and, for the purposes of corporation tax, in relation to accounting periods ending after 31 March 1996, by the Finance Act 1996, ss 79, 205, Sch 7, paras 4(2), 32, Sch 41, Pt V(2), for transitional provision relating to the period before 29 April 1996 see Sch 7, paras 33–35 thereof; words in second (inner) pair of square brackets in Case VI substituted by the Income Tax (Earnings and Pensions) Act 2003, s 722, Sch 6, Pt 1, paras 1, 5(1), (3)(b), with effect, for the purposes of income tax for the year 2003–04 and subsequent years of assessment, and for the purposes of corporation tax for accounting periods ending after 5 April 2003.

Sub-s (3A): inserted for the purposes of income tax, in relation to the year 1996–97 and subsequent years of assessment and, for the purposes of corporation tax, in relation to accounting periods ending after 31 March 1996, by the Finance Act 1996, ss 104, 105(1), Sch 14, para 5; for transitional provisions see Sch 7, paras 33–35 and Sch 15, Pt I; Case III para (c) repealed by the Finance (No 2) Act 2005, ss 39, 70(1), Sch 7, para 12(9), Sch 11, Pt 2(8), with effect in relation to any discount arising in an accounting period beginning on or after 16 March 2005.

Sub-ss (3B)–(3E): inserted for the purposes of income tax, in relation to the year 1996–97 and subsequent years of assessment and, for the purposes of corporation tax, in relation to accounting periods ending after 31 March 1996, by the Finance Act 1996, s 79(2), Sch 7, paras 4(3), 32; for transitional provisions see Sch 7, paras 33–35 and Sch 15, Pt I.

Sub-s (4A): inserted by the Income Tax (Trading and Other Income) Act 2005, s 882(1), Sch 1, Pt 1, paras 1, 9(1), (2), with effect, for the purposes of income tax for the year 2005–06 and subsequent tax years, and for the purposes of corporation tax for accounting periods ending after 5 April 2005.

Sub-s (5): words in first pair of square brackets substituted, for the purposes of income tax, in relation to the year 1996–97 and subsequent years of assessment and, for the purposes of corporation tax, in relation to accounting periods ending after 31 March 1996, by the Finance Act 1996, s 79, Sch 7, paras 4(4), 32, for transitional provision relating to the period before 29 April 1996 see paras 33–35 thereof; words in second pair of square brackets inserted by the Income Tax (Trading and Other Income) Act 2005, s 882(1), Sch 1, Pt 1, paras 1, 9(1), (3), with effect, for the purposes of income tax for the year 2005–06 and subsequent tax years, and for the purposes of corporation tax for accounting periods ending after 5 April 2005.

Sub-s (6): inserted by the Finance Act 2004, s 105(4); repealed by the Income Tax (Trading and Other Income) Act 2005, ss 882(1), 884, Sch 1, Pt 1, paras 1, 9(1), (4), Sch 3, with effect, for the purposes of income tax for the year 2005–06 and subsequent tax years, and for the purposes of corporation tax for accounting periods ending after 5 April 2005.

19, 20 *(S 19 outside the scope of this work; s 20 repealed by the Income Tax (Trading and Other Income) Act 2005, ss 882(1), 884, Sch 1, Pt 1, paras 1, 10, Sch 3, with effect, for the purposes of income tax for the year 2005–06 and subsequent tax years, and for the purposes of corporation tax for accounting periods ending after 5 April 2005.)*

21–52 *((Pts II, III) outside the scope of this work.)*

PART IV
PROVISIONS RELATING TO THE SCHEDULE D CHARGE

53–73 ((*Chs I–IV*) *outside the scope of this work.*)

CHAPTER V
COMPUTATIONAL PROVISIONS

Deductions

74–83 (*Ss 74–77, 79–83 outside the scope of this work; s 78 repealed by the Finance Act 1996, ss 104, 105(1), 205, Sch 14, para 10(1), Sch 41, Pt V(3), except in relation to bills drawn before 1 April 1996.*)

[83A Gifts in kind to charities etc

(1) This section applies where [a company carrying on a trade or profession] gives an article falling within subsection (2) below to—

(a) a charity within the meaning of section 506, or

(b) a body listed in section 507(1).

(2) An article falls within this subsection if—

(a) it is an article manufactured, or of a class or description sold, by [the company in the course of its trade]; …

(b) …

(3) Subject to subsection (4) below, where this section applies in the case of the gift of an article—

(a) no amount shall be required, in consequence of [the company's] disposal of that article from trading stock, to be brought into account for [corporation tax purposes] as a trading receipt of [the company]; …

(b) …

(4) In any case where—

(a) relief is given under subsection (3) above [or section 63(2) of the Capital Allowances Act] in respect of the gift of an article [made by a company], and

(b) any benefit received in any [accounting period] by [the company or any person connected with the company] is in any way attributable to the making of that gift,

[the company shall] in respect of that [accounting period] be charged to [corporation] tax under Case I or Case II of Schedule D or, if [the company] is not chargeable to [corporation] tax under either of those Cases for that period, under Case VI of Schedule D on an amount equal to the value of that benefit.

(5) Section 839 applies for the purposes of this section.]

[694]

NOTES

Commencement: 27 July 1999.

Inserted by the Finance Act 1999, s 55(1), (3), in relation to gifts made on or after 27 July 1999.

Sub-s (1): words in square brackets substituted by the Income Tax (Trading and Other Income) Act 2005, s 882(1), Sch 1, Pt 1, paras 1, 57(1), (2), with effect, for the purposes of income tax for the year 2005–06 and subsequent tax years, and for the purposes of corporation tax for accounting periods ending after 5 April 2005.

Sub-s (2): words in square brackets in para (a) substituted by the Income Tax (Trading and Other Income) Act 2005, s 882(1), Sch 1, Pt 1, paras 1, 57(1), (3), with effect, for the purposes of income tax for the year 2005–06 and subsequent tax years, and for the purposes of corporation tax for accounting periods ending after 5 April 2005; para (b) and the word omitted immediately preceding it repealed by the Capital Allowances Act 2001, ss 578, 580, Sch 2, para 16(1), Sch 4, with effect, in relation to corporation tax, as respects allowances and charges falling to be made for chargeable periods ending on or after 1 April 2001 and, in relation to income tax, as respects allowances and charges falling to be made for chargeable periods ending on or after 6 April 2001.

Sub-s (3): words in square brackets in para (a) substituted by the Income Tax (Trading and Other Income) Act 2005, s 882(1), Sch 1, Pt 1, paras 1, 57(1), (4), with effect, for the purposes of income tax for the year 2005–06 and subsequent tax years, and for the purposes of corporation tax for accounting periods ending after 5 April 2005; para (b) and the word omitted immediately preceding it repealed by the Capital Allowances Act 2001, ss 578, 580, Sch 2, para 16(2), Sch 4, with effect, in relation to corporation tax, as respects allowances and charges falling to be made for chargeable periods ending on or after 1 April 2001 and, in relation to income tax, as respects allowances and charges falling to be made for chargeable periods ending on or after 6 April 2001.

Sub-s (4): words in first pair of square brackets in para (a) inserted by the Capital Allowances Act 2001, s 578, Sch 2, para 16(3), with effect, in relation to corporation tax, as respects allowances and charges falling to be made for chargeable periods ending on or after 1 April 2001 and, in relation to income tax, as respects allowances and charges falling to be made for chargeable periods ending on or after 6 April 2001; words in second pair of square brackets in para (a) and word "corporation" in square brackets in both places it occurs inserted and other words in square brackets substituted by the Income Tax (Trading and Other Income) Act 2005, s 882(1), Sch 1, Pt 1, paras 1, 57(1), (5), with effect, for the purposes of income tax for the year 2005–06 and subsequent tax years, and for the purposes of corporation tax for accounting periods ending after 5 April 2005.

For the application of this section in relation to amateur sports clubs, see the Finance Act 2002, s 58, Sch 18, Pt 3, para 9(3).

84, 84A, 85, 85A, 85B (*Outside the scope of this work.*)

86 Employees seconded to charities and educational establishments

(1) [If a company ("the employer") carrying on a trade, profession or business for the purposes of which it] employs a person ("the employee") makes available to a charity, on a basis which is expressed and intended to be of a temporary nature, the services of the employee then, [notwithstanding anything in section 74, 75 or 76, any expenditure incurred] by the employer which is attributable to the employment of that employee shall continue to be deductible in the manner and to the like extent as if, during the time that his services are so made available to the charity, they continued to be available for the purposes of the employer's trade, business [or profession].

(2) In subsection (1) above—
"charity" has the same meaning as in section 506;
["deductible" means—
(a) deductible as an expense in computing the profits of the employer to be charged [to corporation tax] under Case I or II of Schedule D,
(b) deductible as expenses of management for the purposes of section 75, or
(c) falling to be brought into account in accordance with section 76 as expenses payable which fall to be brought into account at Step 1 in subsection (7) of that section,
as the case may be].

(3) With respect to expenditure attributable to the employment of a person on or after 26th November 1986 … , this section shall have effect as if the references to a charity included references to any of the following bodies, that is to say—
[(a) in England and Wales, any body falling within subsection (4) below;
(b) in Scotland, any body falling within subsection (5) below;
(c) in Northern Ireland, any body falling within subsection (6) below; and]
(d) any other educational body which is for the time being approved for the purposes of this section by the Secretary of State or, in Northern Ireland, the Department of Education for Northern Ireland.

[(4) A body falls within this subsection if it is—
(a) a local education authority;
(b) an educational institution maintained or otherwise supported by such an authority (including a grant-maintained school or a grant-maintained special school within the meaning of the Education Act 1996);
(c) an independent school, within the meaning of the Education Act 1996, whose registration under section 465 of that Act is final; or
(d) an institution within the further education sector, or the higher education sector, within the meaning of the Further and Higher Education Act 1992.

(5) A body falls within this subsection if it is—
(a) an education authority;
(b) an educational establishment managed by such an authority within the meaning of the Education (Scotland) Act 1980 ("the 1980 Act");
(c) a public or grant-aided school within the meaning of the 1980 Act;
(d) a self-governing school within the meaning of the Self-Governing Schools etc (Scotland) Act 1989;
(e) an independent school within the meaning of the 1980 Act;
(f) a central institution within the meaning of the 1980 Act;
(g) an institution within the higher education sector within the meaning of section 56(2) of the Further and Higher Education (Scotland) Act 1992; or

(h) a college of further education within the meaning of section 36(1) of that Act.

(6) A body falls within this subsection if it is—

(a) an education or library board within the meaning of the Education and Libraries (Northern Ireland) Order 1986;

(b) a college of education or a controlled, maintained, grant-maintained integrated, controlled integrated, voluntary or independent school within the meaning of that Order; or

(c) an institution of further education within the meaning of the Further Education (Northern Ireland) Order 1997.]

[695]

NOTES

Sub-s (1): words in first and third pairs of square brackets substituted by the Income Tax (Trading and Other Income) Act 2005, s 882(1), Sch 1, Pt 1, paras 1, 60(1), (2), with effect, for the purposes of income tax for the year 2005–06 and subsequent tax years, and for the purposes of corporation tax for accounting periods ending after 5 April 2005; words in second pair of square brackets substituted by the Finance Act 2004, Sections 38 to 40 and 45 and Schedule 6 (Consequential Amendment of Enactments) Order 2004, SI 2004/2310, reg 2, Schedule, paras 2, 7(1), (2), with effect in relation to accounting periods beginning on or after 1 April 2004.

Sub-s (2): definition "deductible" substituted by SI 2004/2310, reg 2, Schedule, paras 2, 7(1), (3), with effect in relation to accounting periods beginning on or after 1 April 2004; in definition "deductible" words in square brackets inserted by the Income Tax (Trading and Other Income) Act 2005, s 882(1), Sch 1, Pt 1, paras 1, 60(1), (3), with effect, for the purposes of income tax for the year 2005–06 and subsequent tax years, and for the purposes of corporation tax for accounting periods ending after 5 April 2005.

Sub-s (3): words omitted repealed, with retrospective effect, by the Finance Act 1999, ss 58(1), (2), 139, Sch 20, Pt III(14); paras (a)–(c) substituted by the Finance Act 1999, s 58(1), (3), (6), with effect for the year 1999–2000 and subsequent years of assessment.

Sub-ss (4)–(6): added by the Finance Act 1999, s 58(1), (4), (6), with effect for the year 1999–2000 and subsequent years of assessment.

[86A Charitable donations: contributions to agent's expenses

(1) This section applies where—

(a) [a company] (the employer) is liable to make to any individual payments from which income tax falls to be deducted [under PAYE regulations], and

(b) the employer withholds sums from those payments in accordance with [an approved scheme and pays the sums to an approved agent].

[(1A) In subsection (1)(b) "approved scheme" and "approved agent" have the same meaning as in section 714 of ITEPA 2003.]

(2) Any relevant expenditure incurred by the employer on or after 16th March 1993—

(a) shall be deducted in computing for the purposes of Schedule D the [profits] of a trade [or profession] carried on by the employer, or

[(b) if the employer is a company with investment business, shall be treated as expenses of management deductible under section 75].

(3) Relevant expenditure is expenditure incurred in making to the agent any payment in respect of expenses which have been or are to be incurred by the agent in connection with his functions under the scheme.]

[696]–[697]

NOTES

Inserted by the Finance Act 1993, s 69, with effect for expenditure incurred after 15 March 1993.

Sub-s (1): words in first pair of square brackets substituted by the Income Tax (Trading and Other Income) Act 2005, s 882(1), Sch 1, Pt 1, paras 1, 61, with effect, for the purposes of income tax for the year 2005–06 and subsequent tax years, and for the purposes of corporation tax for accounting periods ending after 5 April 2005; words in second and third pairs of square brackets substituted by the Income Tax (Earnings and Pensions) Act 2003, s 722, Sch 6, Pt 1, paras 1, 13(1)–(3), with effect, for the purposes of income tax for the year 2003–04 and subsequent years of assessment, and for the purposes of corporation tax for accounting periods ending after 5 April 2003.

Sub-s (1A): inserted by the Income Tax (Earnings and Pensions) Act 2003, s 722, Sch 6, Pt 1, paras 1, 13(1), (4), with effect, for the purposes of income tax for the year 2003–04 and subsequent years of assessment, and for the purposes of corporation tax for accounting periods ending after 5 April 2003.

Sub-s (2): in para (a) word in first pair of square brackets substituted by the Finance Act 1998, s 46(3)(a), Sch 7, para 1, words in second pair of square brackets substituted by the Income Tax (Trading and Other Income) Act 2005, s 882(1), Sch 1, Pt 1, paras 1, 61(b), with effect, for the purposes of income tax for the year 2005–06 and subsequent tax years, and for the purposes of corporation tax for accounting periods ending after 5 April 2005; para (b) substituted by the Finance Act 2004, Sections 38 to 40 and 45 and Schedule 6 (Consequential Amendment of Enactments) Order 2004, SI 2004/2310, reg 2, Schedule, paras 2, 8, in relation to accounting periods beginning on or after 1 April 2004.

87–130 (*Ss 87–99, ss 100–130 (Chs VI–VIII) outside the scope of this work.*)

PART V
PROVISIONS RELATING TO THE SCHEDULE E CHARGE

131–184 (*(Chs I–III) outside the scope of this work.*)

CHAPTER IV
OTHER EXEMPTIONS AND RELIEFS

185–197G (*Outside the scope of this work.*)

Other expenses, subscriptions etc

198–202 (*Ss 198, 199–202 repealed by the Income Tax (Earnings and Pensions) Act 2003, ss 722, 724(1), Sch 6, Pt 1, paras 1, 28, Sch 8, Pt 1, with effect, for the purposes of income tax for the year 2003–04 and subsequent years of assessment, and for the purposes of corporation tax for accounting periods ending after 5 April 2003; s 198A (as inserted, in relation to the year 1998–99 and subsequent years of assessment, by the Finance Act 1997, s 62(2), (5)) repealed by the Finance Act 1998, s 165, Sch 27, Pt III(10), with effect for the year 1998–99 and subsequent years of assessment.*)

202A–336 (*Ss 202A–207 (Ch V), ss 208–336 (Pts VI, VII) outside the scope of this work.*)

PART VIII
TAXATION OF INCOME AND CHARGEABLE GAINS OF COMPANIES

Taxation of income

337, 337A (*Outside the scope of this work.*)

[338 Charges on income deducted from total profits

(1) Charges on income are allowed as deductions from a company's total profits in computing the corporation tax chargeable for an accounting period.

(2) They are deducted from the company's total profits for the period as reduced by any other relief from tax other than group relief.

(3) The amount of the deduction is limited to the amount that reduces the company's total profits for the period to nil.

(4) Except as otherwise provided, a deduction is allowed only in respect of payments made by the company in the accounting period concerned.

(5) The above provisions are subject to any express exceptions in the Corporation Tax Acts.]

[698]

NOTES

Commencement: 24 July 2002.

Substituted, together with new ss 338A, 338B, for s 338 as originally enacted, by the Finance Act 2002, s 84(2), Sch 30, para 1(2).

[338A Meaning of "charges on income"

(1) This section defines what payments or other amounts are "charges on income" for the purposes of corporation tax.

This section has effect subject to any express exceptions in the Corporation Tax Acts.

(2) Subject to the following provisions of this section, the following (and only the following) are charges on income—

(a) …

(b) qualifying donations within the meaning of section 339 (qualifying donations to charity);

(c) amounts allowed as charges on income under section 587B(2)(a)(ii) (gifts of shares etc to charity).

(3) No payment that is deductible in computing profits or any description of profits for the purposes of corporation tax shall be treated as a charge on income.

(4) …]

[698A]

NOTES

Commencement: 24 July 2002.

Substituted as noted to s 338 at **[698]**. An original s 338A was inserted by the Finance Act 1995, s 42(6), Sch 7, para 2 and repealed by the Finance Act 1996, ss 104, 105, 205, Sch 14, para 17, Sch 41, Pt V(3), with effect for accounting periods ending after 31 March 1996.

Sub-s (2): para (a) repealed by the Finance (No 2) Act 2005, ss 38(1), (2), 70(1), Sch 11, Pt 2(7), with effect in relation to payments made on or after 16 March 2005 in respect of annuities or other annual payments.

Sub-s (4): repealed by the Finance (No 2) Act 2005, s 70(1), Sch 11, Pt 2(7), with effect in relation to payments made on or after 16 March 2005 in respect of annuities or other annual payments.

338B *(Substituted as noted to s 338 at* **[698]***; repealed by the Finance (No 2) Act 2005, s 70(1), Sch 11, Pt 2(7), with effect in relation to payments made on or after 16 March 2005 in respect of annuities or other annual payments.)*

339 Charges on income: donations to charity

(1) A qualifying donation is a payment [of a sum of money] made by a company to a charity, other than—

[(a) a payment which, by reason of any provision of the Taxes Acts (within the meaning of the Management Act) except section 209(4), is to be regarded as a distribution [(but see subsections (1A) and (1B) below)]; and]

(b) a payment which is deductible in computing profits or any description of profits for purposes of corporation tax.

[(1A) In determining whether a payment is to be regarded as a distribution for the purposes of subsection (1)(a) above, the words in section 209(5) from "; and any amount" to the end are to be disregarded.

(1B) A payment (other than a dividend) made by a company which is wholly owned by a charity is not to be regarded as a distribution for the purposes of subsection (1)(a) above.]

(2), (3), [(3A) …

(3B) A payment made by a [company] is not a qualifying donation if—

(a) it is made subject to a condition as to repayment, or

(b) the company or a connected person receives a benefit in consequence of making it and either the relevant value in relation to the payment exceeds [the limit imposed by subsection (3DA) below] or the amount to be taken into account for the purposes of this paragraph in relation to the payment exceeds £250.

(3C) For the purposes of subsections (3B) above and (3D) below, the relevant value in relation to a payment to a charity is—

(a) where there is one benefit received in consequence of making it which is received by the company or a connected person, the value of that benefit;

(b) where there is more than one benefit received in consequence of making it which is received by the company or a connected person, the aggregate value of all the benefits received in consequence of making it which are received by the company or a connected person.

(3D) The amount to be taken into account for the purposes of subsection (3B)(b) above in relation to a payment to a charity is an amount equal to the aggregate of—

(a) the relevant value in relation to the payment, and

(b) the relevant value in relation to each payment already made to the charity by the company in the accounting period in which the payment is made which is a qualifying donation within the meaning of this section.

[(3DA) The limit imposed by this subsection is—

(a) where the amount of the payment does not exceed £100, 25 per cent of the amount of the payment;

(b) where the amount of the payment exceeds £100 but does not exceed £1,000, £25;

(c) where the amount of the payment exceeds £1,000, 2.5 per cent of the amount of the payment.

(3DB) Where a benefit received in consequence of making a payment—

(a) consists of the right to receive benefits at intervals over a period of less than twelve months;

(b) relates to a period of less than twelve months; or

(c) is one of a series of benefits received at intervals in consequence of making a series of payments at intervals of less than twelve months,

the value of the benefit shall be adjusted for the purposes of subsection (3C) above and the amount of the payment shall be adjusted for the purposes of subsection (3DA) above.

(3DC) Where a benefit, other than a benefit which is one of a series of benefits received at intervals, is received in consequence of making a payment which is one of a series of payments made at intervals of less than twelve months, the amount of the payment shall be adjusted for the purposes of subsection (3DA) above.

(3DD) Where the value of a benefit, or the amount of a payment, falls to be adjusted under subsection (3DB) or (3DC) above, the value or amount shall be multiplied by 365 and the result shall be divided by—

(a) in a case falling within subsection (3DB)(a) or (b) above, the number of days in the period of less than twelve months;

(b) in a case falling within subsection (3DB)(c) or (3DC) above, the average number of days in the intervals of less than twelve months;

and the reference in subsection (3DB) to subsection (3C) above is a reference to that subsection as it applies for the purposes of subsection (3B) above.]

(3E) A payment made by a [company] is not a qualifying donation if it is conditional on, or associated with, or part of an arrangement involving, the acquisition of property by the charity, otherwise than by way of gift, from the company or a connected person.

(3F) ...

(3G) A payment made by a company is not a qualifying donation if the company is itself a charity.]

[(4) Where a company gives a sum of money to a charity, the gift shall in the hands of the charity be treated for the purposes of this Act as if it were an annual payment.]

(5)–(7) ...

[[(7AA) Where—

(a) a qualifying donation to a charity is made by a company which is wholly owned by a charity, and

(b) the company makes a claim for the donation, or any part of it, to be deemed for the purposes of section 338 to be a charge on income paid in an accounting period falling wholly or partly within the period of nine months ending with the date of the making of the donation,

the donation or part shall be deemed for those purposes to be a charge on income paid in that accounting period, and not in any later period.

A claim under this subsection must be made within the period of two years immediately following the accounting period in which the donation is made, or such longer period as the Board may allow.]

(7AB) For the purposes of this section a company is wholly owned by a charity if it is either—

(a) a company with an ordinary share capital every part of which is owned by a charity (whether or not the same charity); or

(b) a company limited by guarantee in whose case every person who—

(i) is beneficially entitled to participate in the divisible profits of the company, or

(ii) will be beneficially entitled to share in any net assets of the company available for distribution on its winding up,

is or must be a charity or a company wholly owned by a charity.

(7AC) For the purposes of subsection (7AB) above ordinary share capital of a company shall be taken to be owned by a charity if there is a charity which—

(a) within the meaning of section 838 directly or indirectly owns that share capital; or

(b) would be taken so to own that share capital if references in that section to a body corporate included references to a charity which is not a body corporate.]

[(7A) In subsections (3B) to (3E) above references to a connected person are to a person connected with—

(a) the company, or

(b) a person connected with the company;

and section 839 applies for the purposes of this subsection.]

(8) ...

(9) For the purposes of this section "charity" includes [each of the bodies mentioned in section 507, and ...] any Association of a description specified in section 508, but, subject to that, in this section "charity" has the same meaning as in section 506.

[699]

NOTES

Sub-s (1): words in first pair of square brackets inserted by the Finance Act 1990, s 26(1), (2), (6), in relation to payments made on or after 1 October 1990; para (a) substituted by the Finance Act 2000, s 40(1), (2), (11), in relation to payments made on or after 1 April 2000; words in square brackets in para (a) inserted by the Finance Act 2006, s 57(1), (2), with effect in relation to payments made on or after 1 April 2006.

Sub-ss (1A), (1B): inserted by the Finance Act 2006, s 57(1), (3), with effect in relation to payments made on or after 1 April 2006.

Sub-ss (2), (3), (6), (7), (8): repealed by the Finance Act 2000, ss 40(1), (3), (11), 156, Sch 40, Pt II(1), in relation to payments made on or after 1 April 2000.

Sub-ss (3A), (3F): inserted, together with sub-ss (3B)–(3E), (3G), by the Finance Act 1990, s 26(1), (4)–(6), in relation to payments made on or after 1 October 1990; repealed by the Finance Act 2000, ss 40(1), (3), (11), 156, Sch 40, Pt II(1), in relation to payments made on or after 1 April 2000.

Sub-s (3B): inserted, together with sub-ss (3A), (3C)–(3G) by the Finance Act 1990, s 26(1), (4)–(6), in relation to payments made on or after 1 October 1990; word in first pair of square brackets substituted by the Finance Act 2006, s 58(1), (2), in relation to payments made on or after 1 April 2006; words in square brackets in para (b) substituted by the Finance Act 2000, s 40(1), (4), (11), in relation to payments made on or after 1 April 2000.

Sub-ss (3C), (3D), (3G): inserted, together with sub-ss (3A), (3B), (3F), by the Finance Act 1990, s 26(1), (4)–(6), in relation to payments made on or after 1 October 1990.

Sub-s (3E): inserted, together with sub-ss (3A)–(3D), (3F), (3G), by the Finance Act 1990, s 26(1), (4)–(6), in relation to payments made on or after 1 October 1990; word in square brackets substituted by the Finance Act 2006, s 58(1), (3), in relation to payments made on or after 1 April 2006.

Sub-ss (3DA)–(3DD): inserted by the Finance Act 2000, s 40(1), (5), (11), in relation to payments made on or after 1 April 2000, and so much of an accounting period as falls before that date and so much of it that falls after 31 March 2000 shall be treated as separate accounting periods for the purposes of this amendment.

Sub-s (4): substituted by the Finance Act 2000, s 40(1), (6), (11), in relation to payments made on or after 1 April 2000.

Sub-s (5): repealed by the Finance Act 1990, ss 27(2), (4), 132, Sch 19, Pt V, in relation to accounting periods ending on or after 1 October 1990.

Sub-ss (7AA)–(7AC): inserted by the Finance Act 1997, s 64, in relation to donations made in accounting periods beginning on or after 1 April 1997; sub-s (7AA) was substituted by the Finance Act 2000, s 40(1), (7), (11), in relation to payments made on or after 1 April 2000.

Sub-s (7A): inserted by the Finance Act 1990, s 26(1), (4)–(6), in relation to payments made on or after 1 October 1990.

Sub-s (9): words in square brackets substituted by the Finance Act 1989, s 60(2), (4), in relation to payments due on or after 14 March 1989; words omitted repealed by the Finance Act 2000, s 40(1), (8), (11), in relation to payments made on or after 1 April 2000.

339A–347 *(S 339A (as inserted by the Finance Act 1990, s 27(3), (4)) repealed by the Finance Act 1991, ss 71(1), (3), 123, Sch 19, Pt V; ss 340, 341 repealed by the Finance Act 1996, ss 104, 105(1), 205, Sch 14, para 17, Sch 41, Pt V(3), with effect for accounting periods ending after 31 March 1996 and subject to transitional provisions; ss 342–344 outside the scope of this work; ss 345–347 repealed by the Taxation of Chargeable Gains Act 1992, s 209(3), Sch 12.)*

PART IX
ANNUAL PAYMENTS AND INTEREST

Annual payments

[347A General rule

(1) A payment to which this section applies shall not be a charge on the income of the person liable to make it, and accordingly—

(a) his income shall be computed without any deduction being made on account of the payment, and

(b) the payment shall not[, for the purposes of corporation tax,] form part of the income of [any company] to whom it is made or of any [other company].

(2) This section applies to any annual payment made by an individual which would otherwise be within the charge to tax under Case III of Schedule D except—

(a) a payment of interest;

(b) …;

(c) a payment made for bona fide commercial reasons in connection with the individual's trade, profession or vocation; and

(d) a payment to which section 125(1) applies.

[(2A) This section applies to any annual payment made by an individual which—

(a) arises in the United Kingdom, and

(b) is exempt from any charge under Part 5 of ITTOIA 2005 (miscellaneous income) as a result of section 727 of that Act.]

(3)–(6) (*Outside the scope of this work.*)

[(7), (8)] …

[700]

NOTES

Inserted by the Finance Act 1988, s 36, in relation to any payment falling due on or after 15 March 1988, unless made in pursuance of an existing obligation. By virtue of the Finance Act 1999, s 36(7), this section now has effect in relation to payments made in pursuance of an existing obligation as it has effect in relation to a payment made otherwise than in pursuance of such an obligation.

Sub-s (1): words in first pair of square brackets inserted and words in second and third pairs of square brackets substituted by the Income Tax (Trading and Other Income) Act 2005, s 882(1), Sch 1, Pt 1, paras 1, 146(1), (2), with effect, for the purposes of income tax for the year 2005–06 and subsequent tax years, and for the purposes of corporation tax for accounting periods ending after 5 April 2005.

Sub-s (2): para (b) repealed by the Finance Act 2000, ss 41(2), (9), 156, Sch 40, Pt II(1), in relation to covenanted payments made by companies on or after 1 April 2000 and in relation to covenanted payments falling to be made by individuals on or after 6 April 2000.

Sub-s (2A): inserted by the Income Tax (Trading and Other Income) Act 2005, s 882(1), Sch 1, Pt 1, paras 1, 146(1), (3), with effect, for the purposes of income tax for the year 2005–06 and subsequent tax years, and for the purposes of corporation tax for accounting periods ending after 5 April 2005.

Sub-ss (7), (8): inserted, in relation to the year 1995–96 and subsequent years of assessment, by the Finance Act 1995, s 74, Sch 17, Pt II, para 4(2); repealed by the Finance Act 2000, ss 41(2), (9), 156, Sch 40, Pt II(1), in relation to covenanted payments made by companies on or after 1 April 2000 and in relation to covenanted payments falling to be made by individuals on or after 6 April 2000.

Modified, in relation to payments becoming due after 6 April 1994, and after 6 April 1996, by the Finance Act 1994, s 79(2) and the Finance Act 1996, s 149, respectively.

347B (*Outside the scope of this work.*)

348 Payments out of profits or gains brought into charge to income tax: deduction of tax

(1) Subject to any provision to the contrary in the Income Tax Acts, where any annuity or other annual payment [to which this subsection applies] is payable wholly out of profits or gains brought into charge to income tax—

(a) the whole of the profits or gains shall be assessed and charged with income tax on the person liable to the annuity or other annual payment, without distinguishing the annuity or other annual payment; and

(b) the person liable to make the payment, whether out of the profits or gains charged with income tax or out of any annual payment liable to deduction, or from which a deduction has been made, shall be entitled on making the payment to deduct and retain out of it a sum representing the amount of income tax thereon; and

(c) the person to whom the payment is made shall allow the deduction on receipt of the residue of the payment, and the person making the deduction shall be acquitted and discharged of so much money as is represented by the deduction, as if that sum had been actually paid; and

(d) the deduction shall be treated as income tax paid by the person to whom the payment is made.

[(1A) Subsection (1) applies to any annuity or other annual payment, not being interest—

(a) which is charged with tax under Case III of Schedule D,

[(aa) which—

(i) is charged with tax under Chapter 7 of Part 4 of ITTOIA 2005 (purchased life annuity payments), Chapter 10 of that Part (distributions from unauthorised unit trusts), section 579 of that Act (royalties etc from intellectual property), Chapter 4 of Part 5 of that Act (certain telecommunication rights: non-trading income) or Chapter 7 of Part 5 of that Act (annual payments not otherwise charged), and

(ii) is not relevant foreign income,]

(b) *which is charged with tax under Part 9 of ITEPA 2003 (pension income) because section [579A of that Act applies to it because it is an annuity under an annuity contract that is a registered pension scheme,*] or

(c) which arises from a source in the United Kingdom and is charged with tax under Part 9 of ITEPA 2003 because section 609, *610* or 611 of that Act applies to it (certain employment-related annuities).]

(2) Subject to any provision to the contrary in the Income Tax Acts, where—

(a) any royalty or other sum paid in respect of the user of a patent; …

(b) …

is paid wholly out of profits or gains brought into charge to income tax, the person making the payment shall be entitled on making the payment to deduct and retain out of it a sum representing the amount of the income tax thereon.

(3) This section does not apply to … any payment to which section 687 applies […] [or to any payment which is a qualifying donation for the purposes of section 25 of the Finance Act 1990].

[(4) For the purposes of this section and section 349(1), the following income shall be treated as not brought into charge to income tax—

(a) income on which income tax is treated as paid under section 399(2) or 400(2) of ITTOIA 2005 (distributions from UK resident companies etc on which there is no tax credit),

(b) income on which an individual is liable to income tax as a result of section 413(2) of that Act or trustees are so liable as a result of section 413(3) of that Act (stock dividend income),

(c) income on which any person is liable to income tax under Chapter 6 of Part 4 of that Act (release of loan to participator in close company),

(d) income on which an individual is liable to income tax as a result of section 465 of that Act or trustees are so liable as a result of section 467 of that Act (gains from contracts for life insurance etc), being income to which section 530 of that Act applies (income tax treated as paid etc), and

(e) income which is included in the aggregate income of an estate as a result of section 664(2)(c), (d) or (e) of that Act (income arising to personal representatives and corresponding to income within paragraph (b), (c) or (d)).]

[701]

NOTES

Sub-s (1): words in square brackets substituted by the Income Tax (Earnings and Pensions) Act 2003, s 722, Sch 6, Pt 1, paras 1, 50(1), (2), with effect, for the purposes of income tax for the year 2003–04 and subsequent years of assessment, and for the purposes of corporation tax for accounting periods ending after 5 April 2003.

Sub-s (1A): inserted by the Income Tax (Earnings and Pensions) Act 2003, s 722, Sch 6, Pt 1, paras 1, 50(1), (3), with effect, for the purposes of income tax for the year 2003–04 and subsequent years of assessment, and for the purposes of corporation tax for accounting periods ending after 5 April 2003; para (aa) inserted by the Income Tax (Trading and Other Income) Act 2005, s 882(1), Sch 1, Pt 1, paras 1, 147(1), (2), with effect, for the purposes of income tax for the year 2005–06 and subsequent tax years, and for the purposes of corporation tax for accounting periods ending after 5 April 2005; para (b) and reference in italics in para (c) repealed by the Finance Act 2005, ss 101, 104, Sch 10, para 62, Sch 11, Pt 4, as from 6 April 2007; words in square brackets in para (b) substituted by the Finance Act 2004, s 281(1), Sch 35, paras 2, 14.

Sub-s (2): words omitted repealed by the Finance Act 1997, s 113, Sch 18, Pt VI(2), in relation to payments made on or after 6 April 1997.

Sub-s (3): words omitted in the first place repealed by the Finance Act 1988, s 148, Sch 14, Pt IV, in relation to payments made on or after 6 April 1989; words omitted in the second place originally inserted by the Finance Act 1996, s 156, Sch 29, para 5(1), repealed by the Finance Act 2000, ss 111(6)(a), 156, Sch 40, Pt II(17), in relation to relevant payments or receipts in relation to which the chargeable date for the purposes of Chapter VIIA of Pt IV is on or after 1 April 2001; words in second pair of square brackets inserted by the Finance Act 2000, s 41(3), (9), in relation to covenanted payments made by companies on or after 1 April 2000 and in relation to covenanted payments falling to be made by individuals on or after 6 April 2000.

Sub-s (4): added by the Income Tax (Trading and Other Income) Act 2005, s 882(1), Sch 1, Pt 1, paras 1, 147(1), (3), with effect, for the purposes of income tax for the year 2005–06 and subsequent tax years, and for the purposes of corporation tax for accounting periods ending after 5 April 2005.

349 Payments not out of profits or gains brought into charge to income tax, and annual interest

(1) Where—

(a) any annuity or other annual payment [to which this paragraph applies]; or

(b) any royalty or other sum paid in respect of the user of a patent; …

(c) …

is not payable or not wholly payable out of profits or gains brought into charge to income tax, the person by or through whom any payment thereof is made shall, on making the payment, deduct out of it a sum representing the amount of income tax thereon.

[(1A) Paragraph (a) of subsection (1) applies to any annuity or other annual payment, not being interest—

(a) which is charged with tax under Case III of Schedule D,

[(aa) which—

(i) is charged with tax under Chapter 7 of Part 4 of ITTOIA 2005 (purchased life annuity payments), Chapter 10 of that Part (distributions from unauthorised unit trusts), section 579 of that Act (royalties etc from intellectual property), Chapter 4 of Part 5 of that Act (certain telecommunication rights: non-trading income) or Chapter 7 of Part 5 of that Act (annual payments not otherwise charged), and

(ii) is not relevant foreign income,]

(b) *which is charged with tax under Part 9 of ITEPA 2003 (pension income) because section [579A of that Act applies to it because it is an annuity under an annuity contract that is a registered pension scheme,]* or

(c) which arises from a source in the United Kingdom and is charged with tax under Part 9 of ITEPA 2003 because section 609, *610* or 611 of that Act applies to it.]

[(1B)] [Subsection (1)] does not apply to any payment to which section 687 applies […] [or to any payment which is a qualifying donation (within the meaning of section 339) or a qualifying donation for the purposes of section 25 of the Finance Act 1990].

(2) Subject to subsection (3) below and to any other provision to the contrary in the Income Tax Acts, where any yearly interest of money [which falls within Chapter 2 of Part 4 of ITTOIA 2005 (interest) (excluding anything specially exempted from income tax and discounts treated as interest by section 381 of that Act) or which is chargeable to corporation] tax under Case III of Schedule D [(as that Schedule has effect apart from the modification made for the purposes of corporation tax by section 18(3A))] is paid—

(a) otherwise than in a fiduciary or representative capacity, by a company [(other than a building society)] or local authority; or

(b) by or on behalf of a partnership of which a company is a member; or

(c) by any person to another person whose usual place of abode is outside the United Kingdom;

the person by or through whom the payment is made shall, on making the payment, deduct out of it a sum representing the amount of income tax thereon for the year in which the payment is made.

(3) Subsection (2) above does not apply—

[(za) to interest chargeable to income tax as relevant foreign income; or]

(a) to interest payable [on an advance from a bank, if at the time when the interest is paid the person beneficially entitled to the interest is within the charge to corporation tax as respects the interest]

(b) to interest paid by [a bank in the ordinary course of its] business; or

[(ba) to interest paid on deposits with the National Savings Bank; or]

(c) to any [payment of interest on a quoted Eurobond]; or

(d) to any payment to which section 369 … applies [or

[(e) …]

(f) to any payment in respect of which a liability to deduct income tax is imposed by section 480A(1); or

(g) to any payment in respect of which a liability to deduct income tax would be imposed by section 480A(1) if conditions prescribed by regulations under section 480B were not fulfilled.] [or]

[(h) to any payment in respect of which a liability to deduct income tax would, but for section 481(5)(k), be imposed by section 480A(1)]; [or

(i) in the case of a person who is authorised for the purposes of the Financial Services and Markets Act 2000 and whose business consists wholly or mainly of dealing in financial instruments as principal, to interest paid by that person in the ordinary course of his business]; [or—

(j) to interest paid by a recognised clearing house or recognised investment exchange carrying on business as provider of a central counterparty clearing service, in the ordinary course of that business, on margin or other collateral deposited with it by users of the service; or

(k) to interest treated by virtue of section 730A(2)(a) or (b) (repos) as paid by a recognised clearing house or recognised investment exchange in respect of contracts made by it as provider of a central counterparty clearing service].

…

[(3AA) In this section "bank" has the meaning given by section 840A.]

[(3AB) An order under section 840A(1)(d) designating an organisation as a bank for the purposes of paragraph (a) of subsection (3) above may provide that that paragraph shall apply to the organisation as if the words from "if" to the end were omitted.]

[(3A) Subject to subsection (3B) below and to any other provision to the contrary in the Income Tax Acts, where—

(a) any dividend or interest is paid in respect of a security issued by a building society other than a qualifying certificate of deposit [and other than a qualifying deposit right], and

(b) the security was [listed], or capable of being [listed], on a recognised stock exchange at the time the dividend or interest became payable,

the person by or through whom the payment is made shall, on making the payment, deduct out of it a sum representing the amount of income tax thereon for the year in which the payment is made.

(3B) Subsection (3A) above does not apply to any [payment of interest on a quoted Eurobond].]

[(3C) Subject to any provision to the contrary in the Income Tax Acts, where any UK public revenue dividend is paid, the person by or through whom the payment is made shall, on making the payment, deduct out of it a sum representing the amount of income tax on it for the year in which the payment is made.]

[(4) In [this section]—

["central counterparty clearing service" means the service provided by a clearing house or investment exchange to the parties to a transaction where there are contracts between each of the parties and the clearing house or investment exchange (in place of, or as an alternative to, a contract directly between the parties);]

["certificate of deposit" means a document falling within the definition of that expression in section 56(5) above or section 552(2) of ITTOIA 2005;]

"dividend" has the same meaning as in section 477A,

["qualifying certificate of deposit" means a certificate of deposit … under which[, or uncertificated eligible debt security units under which]—

(a) the amount payable by the issuing society, exclusive of interest, is not less than £50,000 (or, for a deposit denominated in foreign currency, not less than the equivalent of £50,000 at the time when the deposit is made), and

(b) the obligation of the society to pay that amount arises after a period of not more than five years beginning with the date on which the deposit is made; and

["qualifying deposit right" means a right to receive an amount (with or without interest) in pursuance of a deposit of money, where—

(a) the right subsists under an arrangement falling within section 56A [above or is an uncertificated right, as defined in section 552(2) of ITTOIA 2005],

(b) no certificate of deposit … has been issued[, and no uncertificated eligible debt security units have been issued,] in respect of the right at the time the dividend or interest concerned is paid, and

(c) the conditions set out in paragraphs (a) and (b) in the definition of "qualifying certificate of deposit" apply; and]

["quoted Eurobond" means any security that—

(i) is issued by a company,

(ii) is listed on a recognised stock exchange, and

(iii) carries a right to interest;]

["recognised clearing house" and "recognised investment exchange" have the same meaning as in the Financial Services and Markets Act 2000 (see section 285 of that Act);]

"security" includes share].

["UK public revenue dividend" means any income from securities which is paid out of the public revenue of the United Kingdom or Northern Ireland, but does not include interest on local authority stock.]

["uncertificated eligible debt security units" has the same meaning as in section 552(2) of ITTOIA 2005].]

[(5) For the purposes of subsection (3)(i) above, a financial instrument includes—

(a) any money,

(b) any shares or securities,

(c) an option, future or contract for differences if, but only if, its underlying subject-matter is (or is primarily) a financial instrument, or financial instruments, and

(d) an instrument the underlying subject-matter of which is (or is primarily) creditworthiness.

(6) For the purposes of subsection (5) above, the "underlying" subject-matter of an instrument the effect of which depends on an index or factor is the matter by reference to which the index or factor is determined.]

[(7) This section is subject to section 101 of the Finance Act 2004 (payment of royalties without deduction at source).]

[702]

NOTES

Sub-s (1): words in square brackets in para (a) substituted by the Income Tax (Earnings and Pensions) Act 2003, s 722, Sch 6, Pt 1, paras 1, 51(1), (2), with effect, for the purposes of income tax for the year 2003–04 and subsequent years of assessment, and for the purposes of corporation tax for accounting periods ending after 5 April 2003; words omitted repealed by the Finance Act 1997, s 113, Sch 18, Pt VI(2), in relation to payments made on or after 6 April 1997.

Sub-s (1A): inserted by the Income Tax (Earnings and Pensions) Act 2003, s 722, Sch 6, Pt 1, paras 1, 51(1), (3), with effect, for the purposes of income tax for the year 2003–04 and subsequent years of assessment, and for the purposes of corporation tax for accounting periods ending after 5 April 2003; para (aa) inserted by the Income Tax (Trading and Other Income) Act 2005, s 882(1), Sch 1, Pt 1, paras 1, 148(1), (2), with effect, for the purposes of income tax for the year 2005–06 and subsequent tax years, and for the purposes of corporation tax for accounting periods ending after 5 April 2005; para (b) and reference in italics in para (c) repealed by the Finance Act 2005, ss 101, 104, Sch 10, para 62, Sch 11, Pt 4, as from 6 April 2007; words in square brackets in para (b) substituted by the Finance Act 2004, s 281(1), Sch 35, paras 2, 15;

Sub-s (1B): numbered as such and words in first pair of square brackets substituted by the Income Tax (Earnings and Pensions) Act 2003, s 722, Sch 6, Pt 1, paras 1, 51(1), (4), (5), with effect, for the purposes of income tax for the year 2003–04 and subsequent years of assessment, and for the purposes of corporation tax for accounting periods ending after 5 April 2003; words omitted originally inserted by the Finance Act 1996, s 156, Sch 29, para 5(1), repealed by the Finance Act 2000, ss 111(6)(a), 156, Sch 40, Pt II(17), in relation to relevant payments or receipts in relation to which the chargeable date for the purposes of Chapter VIIA of Pt IV is on or after 1 April 2001; words in third pair of square brackets inserted by the Finance Act 2000, s 41(4), (9), in relation to covenanted payments made by companies on or after 1 April 2000 and in relation to covenanted payments falling to be made by individuals on or after 6 April 2000.

Sub-s (2): words in first pair of square brackets substituted by the Income Tax (Trading and Other Income) Act 2005, s 882(1), Sch 1, Pt 1, paras 1, 148(1), (3), with effect, for the purposes of income tax for the year 2005–06 and subsequent tax years, and for the purposes of corporation tax for accounting periods ending after 5 April 2005; words in second pair of square brackets inserted by the Finance Act 1996, ss 104, 105, Sch 14, para 18, in relation to the year 1996–97 and subsequent years of assessment; words in third pair of square brackets inserted by the Finance Act 1991, s 52, Sch 11, para 1(2).

Sub-s (3): para (za) inserted by the Income Tax (Trading and Other Income) Act 2005, s 882(1), Sch 1, Pt 1, paras 1, 148(1), (4), with effect, for the purposes of income tax for the year 2005–06 and subsequent tax years, and for the purposes of corporation tax for accounting periods ending after 5 April 2005; words in square brackets in para (a) substituted by the Finance Act 1996, s 198, Sch 37, para 3(a), 6, 8(1), (2), with effect in relation to interest payable after 29 April 1996, and subject to para 8(3)–(6) thereof; words in square brackets in para (b) substituted by s 198 of, and Sch 37, paras 3(b), 6, 8(7) to, the 1996 Act, in relation to interest paid on or after 29 April 1996 on an advance made on or after that date and subject to para 8(8) thereof; para (ba) inserted by the Finance Act 1997, s 78, in relation to interest whenever paid (including interest paid before 19 March 1997); words in square brackets in para (c) substituted by the Finance Act 2000, s 111(2)(a), (6)(b), in relation to payments of interest made on or after 1 April 2001; para (d) repealed by the Finance Act 1990. S 132, Sch 19, Pt IV and paras (e)–(g), and the word immediately preceding them, added by s 30 of and, Sch 5, para 10 to, that Act in relation to payment made on or after 6 April 1991; para (e) repealed by the Finance Act 1991, ss 52, 123, Sch 11, para 1(3), Sch 19, Pt V, new para (e) subsequently inserted by the Finance Act 1996, s 156, Sch 29, para 5(2) and repealed by the Finance Act 2000, ss 111(6)(a), 156, Sch 40, Pt II(17), in relation to relevant payments or receipts in relation to which the chargeable date for the purposes of Chapter VIIA of Part IV is on or after 1 April 2001; para (h) and the word immediately preceding it added by the Finance Act 1993, s 59; para (i) and word "or" immediately preceding it inserted by the Finance Act 2002, s 95(1), (2), in relation to the payment of interest on or after 1 October 2002; paras (j), (k) and word "or" immediately preceding them inserted by the Finance Act 2003, s 202(1), (2), in relation to payments of interest on or after 14 April 2003; final words omitted repealed by the Finance Act 1988, s 148, Sch 14, Pt IV, in relation to payments made on or after 6 April 1989.

Sub-s (3AA): inserted by the Finance Act 1996, s 196, Sch 37, paras 2(1), (2)(b), with effect as provided for by paras 6 and 8 of that Schedule.

Sub-s (3AB): inserted by the Finance Act 1996, s 196, Sch 37, para 4.

Sub-s (3A): inserted by the Finance Act 1991, s 52, Sch 11, para 1(4); words in square brackets in para (a) inserted by the Finance (No 2) Act 1992, s 34, Sch 8, para 2(2), in relation to arrangements made after 16 July 1992; words in square brackets in para (b) substituted by the Finance Act 1996, s 199, Sch 38, para 6(1), (2)(e), (7), in relation to dividends or interest which become payable on or after 1 April 1996.

Sub-s (3B): inserted by the Finance Act 1991, s 52, Sch 11, para 1(4); words in square brackets substituted by the Finance Act 2000, s 111(2)(a), (6)(b), in relation to payments of interest made on or after 1 April 2001.

Sub-s (3C): inserted by the Finance Act 2000, s 112(2), (5), in relation to payments made on or after 1 April 2001.

Sub-s (4): added by the Finance Act 1990, s 30, Sch 5, para 10(1), (3), in relation to a payment made on or after 6 April 1991; words in first pair of square brackets and definitions "qualifying certificate of deposit" and "security" substituted by the Finance Act 1991, s 52, Sch 11, para 1(5); definitions "central counterparty clearing service", "recognised clearing house" and "recognised investment exchange" inserted by the Finance Act 2003, s 202(1), (3), in relation to payments of interest on or after 14 April 2003; definitions "certificate of deposit", "uncertificated eligible debt security units" inserted, and in definitions "qualifying certificate of deposit" and "qualifying deposit right" (as inserted by the Finance (No 2) Act 1992, s 34, Sch 8, para 2(3), in relation to arrangements made after 16 July 1992), words omitted repealed and words in square brackets inserted by the Income Tax (Trading and Other Income) Act 2005, s 882(1), 884, Sch 1, Pt 1, paras 1, 148(1), (5), Sch 3, with effect, for the purposes of income tax for the year 2005–06 and subsequent tax years, and for the purposes of corporation tax for accounting periods ending after 5 April 2005; definition "quoted Eurobond" inserted by the Finance Act 2000, s 111(2)(b), (6)(b), in relation to payments of interest made on or after 1 April 2001 and definition "UK public revenue dividend" inserted by s 112(3), (5) of the 2000 Act, in relation to payments made on or after 1 April 2001.

Sub-ss (5), (6): inserted by the Finance Act 2002, s 95(1), (3), in relation to the payment of interest on or after 1 October 2002.

Sub-s (7): inserted by the Finance Act 2004, s 105(5); substituted by the Income Tax (Trading and Other Income) Act 2005, s 882(1), Sch 1, Pt 1, paras 1, 148(1), (6), with effect, for the purposes of income tax for the year 2005–06 and subsequent tax years, and for the purposes of corporation tax for accounting periods ending after 5 April 2005.

Orders: the European Investment Bank (Designated International Organisation) Order 1996, SI 1996/1179.

349ZA (*Outside the scope of this work.*)

[349A Exceptions to section 349 for payments between companies etc

(1) The provisions specified in subsection (3) below (which require tax to be deducted on making certain payments) do not apply to a payment made by a company [or a local

authority] if, at the time the payment is made, the company [or authority] reasonably believes that one of the conditions specified in section 349B is satisfied.

(2) Subsection (1) above has effect subject to any directions under section 349C.

(3) The provisions are—

section 349(1) (certain annuities and other annual payments, and royalties and other sums paid for use of UK patents),

section 349(2)(a) and (b) (UK interest),

section 349(3A) (dividend or interest on securities issued by building societies), and

section [349ZA(2)] (which provides for section 349(1) to apply to proceeds of sale of UK patent rights).

(4) References in subsection (3) above to any provision of section 349 do not include that provision as applied—

(a) under section 777(9) (directions applying section 349(1) to certain payments to non-residents), or

(b) by paragraph 4(2) of Schedule 23A (manufactured overseas dividends to be treated as annual payments within section 349).

(5) References in this section to the company by which a payment is made do not include a company acting as trustee or agent for another person.

(6) For the purposes of this section,

[(a)] a payment by a partnership is treated as made by a company if any member of the partnership is a company[, and

(b) a payment by a partnership is treated as made by a local authority if any member of the partnership is a local authority].]

[702B]

NOTES

Inserted, together with ss 349B–349D, by the Finance Act 2001, s 85(1), in relation to payments made on or after 1 April 2001.

Sub-s (1): words in square brackets inserted by the Finance Act 2002, s 94(1)(a), in relation to payments made on or after 1 October 2002.

Sub-s (3): reference in square brackets substituted by the Income Tax (Trading and Other Income) Act 2005, s 882(1), Sch 1, Pt 1, paras 1, 150, with effect, for the purposes of income tax for the year 2005–06 and subsequent tax years, and for the purposes of corporation tax for accounting periods ending after 5 April 2005.

Sub-s (6): para (a) numbered as such and para (b) and word immediately preceding it inserted by the Finance Act 2002, s 94(1)(b), in relation to payments made on or after 1 October 2002.

[349B The conditions mentioned in section 349A(1)

(1) The first of the conditions mentioned in section 349A(1) is that the person beneficially entitled to the income in respect of which the payment is made is—

(a) a company resident in the United Kingdom, …

(b) …

(2) The second of those conditions is that—

(a) the person beneficially entitled to the income in respect of which the payment is made is a company not resident in the United Kingdom ("the non-resident company"),

(b) the non-resident company carries on a trade in the United Kingdom through a [permanent establishment], and

(c) the payment falls to be brought into account in computing the chargeable profits (within the meaning given by section 11(2)) of the non-resident company.

[(3) The third of those conditions is that the payment is made to[, or to the nominee of]—

(a) a local authority;

(b) a health service body within the meaning of section 519A(2);

(c) a public office or department of the Crown to which section 829(1) applies;

(d) a charity (within the meaning of section 506(1));

(e) a body for the time being mentioned in section 507(1) (bodies that are allowed the same exemption from tax as charities the whole income of which is applied to charitable purposes);

(f) an Association of a description specified in section 508 (scientific research organisations);

(g), (h) …
[(i) the scheme administrator of a registered pension scheme;
(ia) the sub-scheme administrator of a sub-scheme which forms part of a split scheme pursuant to the Registered Pensions (Splitting of Schemes) Regulations 2006;]
(j) the trustees of a scheme entitled to exemption under section 613(4) (Parliamentary pension funds); [or]
(k) the persons entitled to receive the income of a fund entitled to exemption under section 614(3) (certain colonial, etc pension funds);
(l), (m) …

(4) The fourth of those conditions is that—
(a) the person to whom the payment is made is, or is the nominee of, the plan manager of a plan [of a kind to which regulations under Chapter 3 of Part 6 of ITTOIA 2005 (income from individual investment plans) apply],
(b) …
(c) the plan manager receives the payment in respect of investments under the plan.

(5) …

(6) The sixth of those conditions is that the person beneficially entitled to the income in respect of which the payment is made is a partnership each member of which is—
(a) a person or body mentioned in subsection (3) above, or
(b) a person or body mentioned in subsection (7) below.

(7) The persons and bodies referred to in subsection (6)(b) above are—
(a) a company resident in the United Kingdom;
(b) a company that—
(i) is not resident in the United Kingdom,
(ii) carries on a trade there through a [permanent establishment], and
(iii) is required to bring into account, in computing its chargeable profits (within the meaning of section 11(2)), the whole of any share of that payment that falls to it by reason of sections 114 and 115;
(c) the European Investment Fund.

(8) The Treasury may by order amend—
(a) subsection (3) above;
(b) subsection (7) above;

so as to add to, restrict or otherwise alter the persons and bodies falling within that subsection.]]

[702C]

NOTES

Inserted as noted to s 349A at **[702B]**.

Sub-s (1): para (b) and word omitted immediately preceding it repealed by the Finance Act 2002, s 141, Sch 40, Pt 3(14), in relation to payments made on or after 1 October 2002.

Sub-s (2): words in square brackets in para (b) substituted by the Finance Act 2003, s 153(1)(a), in relation to accounting periods beginning on or after 1 January 2003.

Sub-s (3): added, together with sub-ss (4)–(8), by the Finance Act 2002, s 94(2), in relation to payments made on or after 1 October 2002; words in first pair of square brackets inserted by the Income and Corporation Taxes Act 1988, Section 349B(3) Order 2002, SI 2002/2931, art 2; paras (g), (h) repealed by the Finance (No 2) Act 2005, ss 46(2)(a), 70(1), Sch 11, Pt 2(12), in relation to payments made on or after 1 April 2005; paras (i), (ia) substituted, for para (i), by the Finance Act 2004, s 281(1), Sch 35, paras 2, 16(1), (2); in para (j) word "or" in square brackets inserted, and paras (l), (m) repealed by the Finance Act 2004, s 281(1), 326, Sch 35, paras 2, 16(1), (3), (4), Sch 42, Pt 3.

Sub-s (4): added, together with sub-ss (3), (5)–(8), by the Finance Act 2002, s 94(2), in relation to payments made on or after 1 October 2002; words in square brackets in para (a) inserted and para (b) repealed by the Finance (No 2) Act 2005, ss 22, 70(1), Sch 11, Pt 2(3), with effect in relation to payments made on or after 6 April 2005.

Sub-s (5): added, together with sub-ss (3), (4), (6)–(8), by the Finance Act 2002, s 94(2), in relation to payments made on or after 1 October 2002; repealed by the Income Tax (Trading and Other Income) Act 2005, ss 882(1), 884, Sch 1, Pt 1, paras 1, 151(1), (3), Sch 3, with effect, for the purposes of income tax for the year 2005–06 and subsequent tax years, and for the purposes of corporation tax for accounting periods ending after 5 April 2005.

Sub-ss (6), (8): added, together with sub-ss (3), (4), (5), (7), by the Finance Act 2002, s 94(2), in relation to payments made on or after 1 October 2002

Sub-s (7): added, together with sub-ss (3)–(6), (8), by the Finance Act 2002, s 94(2), in relation to payments made on or after 1 October 2002; words in square brackets in para (b)(ii) substituted by the Finance Act 2003, s 153(1)(a), in relation to accounting periods beginning on or after 1 January 2003.

Orders: the Income and Corporation Taxes Act 1988, Section 349B(3) Order 2002, SI 2002/2931.

349C–349E (*Outside the scope of this work.*)

350 Charge to tax where payments made under section 349

(1) Where any payment within section 349 is made by or through any person, that person shall forthwith deliver to the inspector an account of the payment, and shall be assessable and chargeable with income tax at the [applicable rate] on the payment, or on so much thereof as is not made out of profits or gains brought into charge to income tax.

[(1A) In subsection (1) above "the applicable rate" means the rate which is applicable to the payment under section 4 [(or, where the payment is one to which subsection (1) of section 349E applies, the rate referred to in that subsection)].]

(2) In section 349(1) any reference to a payment or sum as being not payable, or not wholly payable, out of profits or gains brought into charge to income tax shall be construed as a reference to it as being payable wholly or in part out of a source other than profits or gains brought into charge; and any such reference elsewhere in the Tax Acts shall be construed accordingly.

(3) All the provisions of the Income Tax Acts relating to persons who are to be chargeable with income tax, to income tax assessments, and to the collection and recovery of income tax, shall, so far as they are applicable, apply to the charge, assessment, collection and recovery of income tax under this section.

(4) Section 349 and this section have effect subject to the provisions of Schedule 16 which has effect for the purpose of regulating the time and manner in which companies resident in the United Kingdom—

(a) are to account for and pay income tax in respect of payments from which tax is deductible under section 349, and

(b) are to be repaid income tax in respect of payments received by them;

and for that purpose the Board may by regulations modify, supplement or replace any of the provisions of Schedule 16; and references in this Act and in any other enactment to any of those provisions shall be construed as including references to any such regulations.

(5) Without prejudice to the generality of subsection (4) above, regulations under that subsection may, in relation to income tax for which a company is liable to account, modify any provision of Parts II to VI of the Management Act or apply any such provision with or without modifications.

(6) Regulations under this section may—

(a) make different provision for different descriptions of companies and for different circumstances and may authorise the Board, where in their opinion there are special circumstances justifying it, to make special arrangements as respects income tax for which a company is liable to account or the repayment of income tax borne by a company;

(b) include such transitional and other supplemental provisions as appear to the Board to be expedient or necessary.

(7) The Board shall not make any regulations under this section unless a draft of them has been laid before and approved by a resolution of the House of Commons.

[703]

NOTES

Sub-s (1): words in square brackets substituted by the Finance Act 1996, s 73, Sch 6, paras 8, 28, in relation to the year 1996–97 and subsequent years of assessment.

Sub-s (1A): inserted by the Finance Act 1996, s 73, Sch 6, paras 8, 28, in relation to the year 1996–97 and subsequent years of assessment; words in square brackets added by the Finance Act 2002, s 96(2), in relation to payments made on or after 1 October 2002.

Management Act: ie, the Taxes Management Act 1970.

Regulations: the Income Tax (Building Societies) (Annual Payments) Regulations 1991, SI 1991/512.

350A, 351 (*S 350A outside the scope of this work; s 351 repealed by the Finance Act 1988, s 148, Sch 14, Pt IV.*)

352 Certificates of deduction of tax

(1) A person making any payment which is subject to deduction of income tax by virtue of section 339, 348, 349[, 480A or 687 or by virtue of regulations under section 477A(1)]

shall, if the recipient so requests in writing, furnish him with a statement in writing showing the gross amount of the payment, the amount of tax deducted, and the actual amount paid.

(2) The duty imposed by subsection (1) above shall be enforceable at the suit or instance of the person requesting the statement.

[704]

NOTES

Sub-s (1): words in square brackets substituted, in relation to payments made on or after 6 April 1991, by the Finance Act 1990, s 30, Sch 5, paras 1, 11.

353–430 (*Ss 353–379, ss 379A–430* (*Pts X, XI*) *outside the scope of this work.*)

PART XII
SPECIAL CLASSES OF COMPANIES AND BUSINESSES

431–502L ((*Chs I–5A*) *outside the scope of this work.*)

CHAPTER VI
MISCELLANEOUS BUSINESSES AND BODIES

503, 504, 504A (*Outside the scope of this work.*)

505 Charities: general

(1) Subject to subsections (2) and (3) below, the following exemptions shall be granted on a claim in that behalf to the Board—

[(a) exemption from tax under Schedules A and D[, or under Parts 2 and 3 of ITTOIA 2005,] in respect of any profits or gains arising in respect of rents or other receipts from an estate, interest or right in or over any land (whether situated in the United Kingdom or elsewhere) to the extent that the profits or gains—
(i) arise in respect of rents or receipts from an estate, interest or right vested in any person for charitable purposes; and
(ii) are applied to charitable purposes only;]

(b) …;

(c) exemption—
(i) …
[(ii) from tax under Case III of Schedule D [or under Chapter 2, 7, 8 or 10 of Part 4 of ITTOIA 2005 (interest, purchased life annuity payments, profits from deeply discounted securities and distributions from unauthorised unit trusts), section 579 of that Act so far as it relates to annual payments (royalties etc from intellectual property), Chapter 4 of Part 5 of that Act so far as it relates to annual payments (certain telecommunication rights: non-trading income) or Chapter 7 of Part 5 of that Act (annual payments not otherwise charged)],
(iia) from tax under Case … V of Schedule D in respect of income equivalent to income chargeable under Case III of that Schedule but arising from securities or other possessions outside the United Kingdom,
[(iiaa) from tax under Chapter 4 of Part 4 of ITTOIA 2005 (dividends from non-UK resident companies) or from tax under Chapter 8 of Part 5 of that Act (income not otherwise charged) so far as it applies to relevant foreign distributions,]
(iib) from tax under Case V of Schedule D in respect of [such dividends as would, in the case of income tax, be chargeable to tax under Chapter 4 of Part 4 of ITTOIA 2005 or such distributions (other than dividends) as would, in the case of income tax, be chargeable to tax under Chapter 8 of Part 5 of that Act so far as it would apply to what would be a relevant foreign distribution,]]
[(iic) from tax under Case VI of Schedule D in respect of non-trading gains on intangible fixed assets under Schedule 29 to the Finance Act 2002, and]
(iii) from tax under [Chapter 3 of Part 4 of ITTOIA 2005 (dividends etc from UK resident companies etc)] in respect of any distribution,

where the income in question forms part of the income of a charity, or is, according to rules or regulations established by Act of Parliament, charter, decree, deed of trust or will, applicable to charitable purposes only, and so far as it is applied to charitable purposes only;

[(d) exemption from tax under Schedule D [or Chapter 2 of Part 4 of ITTOIA 2005 (interest)] in respect of public revenue dividends on securities which are in the name of trustees, to the extent that the dividends are applicable and applied only for the repair of—
  (i) any cathedral, college, church or chapel, or
  (ii) any building used only for the purposes of divine worship;]

(e) exemption from tax under Schedule D [or Part 2 of ITTOIA 2005 (trading income)] in respect of the profits of any trade carried on by a charity [(whether in the United Kingdom or elsewhere)], if the profits are applied solely to the purposes of the charity and either—
  (i) the trade is exercised in the course of the actual carrying out of a primary purpose of the charity; or
  (ii) the work in connection with the trade is mainly carried out by beneficiaries of the charity;

[(f) exemption from tax under Schedule D [or Part 2 or 5 of ITTOIA 2005 (trading and miscellaneous income)] in respect of profits accruing to a charity from a lottery if—
  (i) the lottery is promoted and conducted in accordance with section 3 or 5 of the Lotteries and Amusements Act 1976 or Article 133 or 135 of the Betting, Gaming, Lotteries and Amusements (Northern Ireland) Order 1985; and
  (ii) the profits are applied solely to the charity's purposes.]

[(1AA) In subsection (1)(c)(iiaa) and (iib) "relevant foreign distribution" means any distribution of a company not resident in the United Kingdom which—
  (a) is not chargeable under Chapter 4 of Part 4 of ITTOIA 2005, but
  (b) would be chargeable under Chapter 3 of that Part of that Act if the company were resident in the United Kingdom.]

[(1A) In subsection (1)(d) above "public revenue dividends" means—
  (a) income from securities which is payable out of the public revenue of the United Kingdom or Northern Ireland;
  (b) income from securities issued by or on behalf of a government or a public or local authority in a country outside the United Kingdom.]

[(1B) For the purpose of subsection (1)(e)—
  (a) where a trade is exercised partly in the course of the actual carrying out of a primary purpose of the charity and partly otherwise, each part shall be treated as a separate trade (for which purpose reasonable apportionment of expenses and receipts shall be made), and
  (b) where the work in connection with the trade is carried out partly but not mainly by beneficiaries, the part in connection with which work is carried on by beneficiaries and the other part shall be treated as separate trades (for which purpose reasonable apportionment of expenses and receipts shall be made).]

(2) Any payment which—
  (a) is received by a charity from another charity; and
  (b) is not made for full consideration in money or money's worth; and
  (c) is not chargeable to tax apart from this subsection; and
  (d) is not, apart from this subsection, of a description which (on a claim) would be eligible for relief from tax by virtue of any provision of subsection (1) above;

shall be chargeable to [income tax under Chapter 7 of Part 5 of ITTOIA 2005 (annual payments not otherwise charged) so far as it does not apply to relevant foreign income and shall be chargeable to corporation] tax under Case III of Schedule D but shall be eligible for relief from tax under subsection (1)(c) above as if it were an annual payment.

[(3) In subsections (4) to (7)—
  (a) "charitable expenditure" has the meaning given by section 506,
  (b) "relief" means relief or exemption under—
    (i) subsection (1) above,
    (ii) section 56(3)(c) above,
    (iii) section 761(6) below,
    (iv) section 256 of the 1992 Act (charities), or

(v) section 46 of the Finance Act 2000 (small trades),

(c) "relievable income and gains" means income and gains which would be eligible for relief or exemption under any of those provisions (disregarding subsections (4) to (6)), and

(d) "total income and gains" means the aggregate of—

(i) relievable income and gains,

(ii) income and gains, other than relievable income and gains, chargeable to tax, and

(iii) donations, legacies and other similar receipts that are not chargeable to tax.

(4) If a charity incurs (or is treated as incurring) non-charitable expenditure in a chargeable period, relief shall be disallowed in respect of such amount of relievable income and gains as equals the amount of the non-charitable expenditure.

(5) If in a chargeable period a charity's non-charitable expenditure exceeds its total income and gains the excess shall be treated as non-charitable expenditure of the previous period for the purposes of subsection (4); and any necessary adjustments shall be made, whether by making assessments or otherwise.

(6) Subsection (5) may apply to a chargeable period wholly or partly as a result of the application of that subsection in respect of a later period; but no excess of non-charitable expenditure shall be treated as non-charitable expenditure of a chargeable period which ended more than six years before the end of the period in which the expenditure was actually incurred.

(7) Where an amount of a charity's relievable income and gains is disallowed for relief by subsection (4) (whether or not as a result of the application of subsection (5))—

(a) the charity may by notice to the Board specify which items of income or gains are to be disallowed, but

(b) if the Board requires the charity to give a notice under paragraph (a) and the charity fails to comply within the period of 30 days beginning with the date on which the requirement is imposed, the Board shall determine which items to disallow.]

[705]

NOTES

Sub-s (1): paras (a), (d) substituted, para (c)(i) repealed, sub-paras (c)(ii), (iia), (iib) substituted for original sub-para (c)(ii) and words in second pair of square brackets in para (e) inserted, for the purposes of income tax in relation to the year 1996–97 and subsequent years of assessment, and for the purposes of corporation tax in relation to accounting periods ending after 31 March 1996, by the Finance Act 1996, ss 79, 146, 205, Sch 7, paras 19, 32, Sch 41, Pt V(2); words in square brackets in paras (a), (c)(ii), (d), (e), (f), inserted, words omitted from sub-para (c)(iia) repealed, para (c)(iiaa) inserted, and words in square brackets in sub-paras (c)(iib), (iii) substituted by the Income Tax (Trading and Other Income) Act 2005, s 882(1), 884, Sch 1, Pt 1, paras 1, 198(1), (2), Sch 3, with effect, for the purposes of income tax for the year 2005–06 and subsequent tax years, and for the purposes of corporation tax for accounting periods ending after 5 April 2005; para (b) repealed by the Finance Act 1988, s 148, Sch 14, Pt V; para (c)(iic) inserted by the Finance Act 2002, s 84(2), Sch 30, para 3; para (f) added, in relation to chargeable periods beginning after 31 March 1995 in the case of a company, and after 5 April 1995 in any other case, by the Finance Act 1995, s 138.

Sub-s (1AA): inserted by the Income Tax (Trading and Other Income) Act 2005, s 882(1), Sch 1, Pt 1, paras 1, 198(1), (3), with effect, for the purposes of income tax for the year 2005–06 and subsequent tax years, and for the purposes of corporation tax for accounting periods ending after 5 April 2005.

Sub-s (1A): inserted, for the purposes of income tax in relation to the year 1996–97 and subsequent years of assessment, and for the purposes of corporation tax in relation to accounting periods ending after 31 March 1996, by the Finance Act 1996, s 79, Sch 7, paras 19(3), 32.

Sub-s (1B): inserted by the Finance Act 2006, s 56(1), with effect in respect of chargeable periods beginning on or after 22 March 2006.

Sub-s (2): words in square brackets inserted by the Income Tax (Trading and Other Income) Act 2005, s 882(1), Sch 1, Pt 1, paras 1, 198(1), (4), with effect, for the purposes of income tax for the year 2005–06 and subsequent tax years, and for the purposes of corporation tax for accounting periods ending after 5 April 2005.

Sub-ss (3)–(7): substituted, for sub-ss (3)–(8) as originally enacted, by the Finance Act 2006, s 55(1), with effect in relation to chargeable periods beginning on or after 22 March 2006.

1992 Act: Taxation of Chargeable Gains Act 1992.

[506 Charitable and non-charitable expenditure]

(1) In this section, section 505 and Schedule 20—

"charity" means any body of persons or trust established for charitable purposes only;

["charitable expenditure" means (subject to subsections (3) to (5) below) expenditure which is exclusively for charitable purposes].

(2) For the purposes of section 505 … where expenditure which is not actually incurred in a particular chargeable period properly falls to be charged against the income of that chargeable period as being referable to commitments (whether or not of a contractual nature) which the charity has entered into before or during that period, it shall be treated as incurred in that period.

(3) A payment made (or to be made) to a body situated outside the United Kingdom shall not be [charitable expenditure] by virtue of this section unless the charity concerned has taken such steps as may be reasonable in the circumstances to ensure that the payment will be applied for charitable purposes.

(4) If in any chargeable period a charity—

(a) invests any of its funds in an investment which is not a qualifying investment, as defined in Part I of Schedule 20; or

(b) makes a loan (not being an investment) which is not a qualifying loan, as defined in Part II of that Schedule;

then, subject to subsection (5) below, the amount so invested or lent in that period shall be treated for the purposes of this section as being an amount of expenditure incurred by the charity, and, accordingly, as being [non-charitable expenditure].

(5) If, in any chargeable period, a charity which has in that period made an investment or loan falling within subsection (4) above—

(a) realises the whole or part of that investment; or

(b) is repaid the whole or part of that loan;

any further investment or lending in that period of the sum realised or repaid shall, to the extent that it does not exceed the sum originally invested or lent, be left out of account in determining the amount which, by virtue of subsection (4) above, is treated as [non-charitable expenditure] incurred in that period.

(6) …

[706]

NOTES

Section heading: substituted by the Finance Act 2006, s 55(2)(g), with effect in relation to chargeable periods beginning on or after 22 March 2006.

Sub-s (1): definition "charitable expenditure" substituted, for definitions "qualifying expenditure" and "non-qualifying expenditure" as originally enacted, by the Finance Act 2006, s 55(2)(a), with effect in relation to chargeable periods beginning on or after 22 March 2006.

Sub-s (2): words omitted repealed by the Finance Act 2006, ss 55(2)(b), 178, Sch 26, Pt 3(5), with effect in relation to chargeable periods beginning on or after 22 March 2006.

Sub-ss (3)–(5): words in square brackets substituted by the Finance Act 2006, s 55(2)(c)–(e), with effect in relation to chargeable periods beginning on or after 22 March 2006.

Sub-s (6): repealed by the Finance Act 2006, ss 55(2)(f), 178, Sch 26, Pt 3(5), with effect in relation to chargeable periods beginning on or after 22 March 2006.

[506A Transactions with substantial donors

(1) This section applies to the following transactions—

(a) the sale or letting of property by a charity to a substantial donor,

(b) the sale or letting of property to a charity by a substantial donor,

(c) the provision of services by a charity to a substantial donor,

(d) the provision of services to a charity by a substantial donor,

(e) an exchange of property between a charity and a substantial donor,

(f) the provision of financial assistance by a charity to a substantial donor,

(g) the provision of financial assistance to a charity by a substantial donor, and

(h) investment by a charity in the business of a substantial donor.

(2) For the purposes of this section a person is a substantial donor to a charity in respect of a chargeable period if—

(a) the charity receives relievable gifts of at least £25,000 from him in a period of 12 months in which the chargeable period wholly or partly falls, or

(b) the charity receives relievable gifts of at least £100,000 from him in a period of six years in which the chargeable period wholly or partly falls;

and if a person is a substantial donor to a charity in respect of a chargeable period by virtue of paragraph (a) or (b), he is a substantial donor to the charity in respect of the following five chargeable periods.

(3) A payment made by a charity to a substantial donor in the course of or for the purposes of a transaction to which this section applies shall be treated for the purposes of section 505 as non-charitable expenditure.

(4) If the terms of a transaction to which this section applies are less beneficial to the charity than terms which might be expected in a transaction at arm's length, the charity shall be treated for the purposes of section 505 as incurring non-charitable expenditure equal to that amount which the Commissioners for Her Majesty's Revenue and Customs determine as the cost to the charity of the difference in terms.

(5) A payment by a charity of remuneration to a substantial donor shall be treated for the purposes of section 505 as non-charitable expenditure unless it is remuneration, for services as a trustee, which is approved by—

(a) the Charity Commission,

(b) another body with responsibility for regulating charities by virtue of legislation having effect in respect of any Part of the United Kingdom, or

(c) a court.]

[706A]

NOTES

Inserted, together with ss 506B, 506C, by the Finance Act 2006, s 54(1), with effect in relation to transactions occurring on or after 22 March 2006.

[506B Section 506A: exceptions

(1) Section 506A shall not apply to a transaction within section 506A(1)(b) or (d) if the Commissioners for Her Majesty's Revenue and Customs determine that the transaction—

(a) takes place in the course of a business carried on by the substantial donor,

(b) is on terms which are no less beneficial to the charity than those which might be expected in a transaction at arm's length, and

(c) is not part of an arrangement for the avoidance of any tax.

(2) Section 506A shall not apply to the provision of services to a substantial donor if the Commissioners determine that the services are provided—

(a) in the course of the actual carrying out of a primary purpose of the charity, and

(b) on terms which are no more beneficial to the substantial donor than those on which services are provided to others.

(3) Section 506A shall not apply to the provision of financial assistance to a charity by a substantial donor if the Commissioners determine that the assistance—

(a) is on terms which are no less beneficial to the charity than those which might be expected in a transaction at arm's length, and

(b) is not part of an arrangement for the avoidance of any tax.

(4) Section 506A shall not apply to investment by a charity in the business of a substantial donor where the investment takes the form of the purchase of shares or securities listed on a recognised stock exchange.

(5) A disposal at an undervalue to which section 587B applies shall not be a transaction to which section 506A applies (but may be taken into account in the application of section 506A(2)).

(6) A disposal at an undervalue to which section 257(2) of the 1992 Act (gifts of chargeable assets) applies shall not be a transaction to which section 506A applies (but may be taken into account in the application of section 506A(2)).

(7) In the application of section 506A payments by a charity, or benefits arising to a substantial donor from a transaction, shall be disregarded in so far as they—

(a) relate to a donation by the donor, and

(b) do not exceed the relevant limit in relation to the donation for the purposes of section 339 or section 25 of the Finance Act 1990.

(8) A company which is wholly owned by a charity within the meaning of section 339(7AB) shall not be treated as a substantial donor in relation to the charity which owns it (or any of the charities which own it).

(9) A registered social landlord or housing association shall not be treated as a substantial donor in relation to a charity with which it is connected; and for that purpose—

(a) "registered social landlord or housing association" means a body entered on a register maintained under—

(i) section 1 of the Housing Act 1996,

(ii) section 57 of the Housing (Scotland) Act 2001, or

(iii) Article 14 of the Housing (Northern Ireland) Order 1992, and

(b) a body and a charity are connected if (and only if)—

(i) the one is wholly owned, or subject to control, by the other, or

(ii) both are wholly owned, or subject to control, by the same person.]

[706B]

NOTES

Inserted as noted to 506A at **[706A]**.

[506C Sections 506A and 506B: supplemental

(1) A gift is "relievable" for the purposes of section 506A(2) if relief is available in respect of it under—

(a) section 83A,

(b) section 339,

(c) sections 587B and 587C,

(d) section 25 of the Finance Act 1990 (individual gift aid),

(e) section 257 of the 1992 Act (gifts of chargeable assets),

(f) section 63 of the Capital Allowances Act (gifts of plant and machinery),

(g) sections 713 to 715 of ITEPA 2003 (payroll giving),

(h) section 108 of ITTOIA 2005 (gifts of trading stock), or

(i) sections 628 and 630 of ITTOIA 2005 (gifts from settlor-interested trusts).

(2) A charity is treated as incurring expenditure in accordance with section 506A(4) at such time (or times) as the Commissioners determine.

(3) Section 506A applies to a transaction entered into in a chargeable period with a person who is a substantial donor in respect of that period, even if it was not until after the transaction was entered into that he first satisfied the definition of "substantial donor" in respect of that period.

(4) Either or both of subsections (3) and (4) of section 506A may be applied to a single transaction; but any amount of non-charitable expenditure which a charity is treated as incurring under section 506A(3) in respect of a transaction shall be deducted from any amount which it would otherwise be treated as incurring under section 506A(4) in respect of the transaction.

(5) Two or more connected charities shall be treated as a single charity for the purposes of section 506A and 506B and this section; and for this purpose "connected" means connected in a matter relating to the structure, administration or control of a charity.

(6) Where remuneration is paid otherwise than in money, section 506A(5) shall apply as to a payment in money of the amount that would, under Part 3 of ITEPA 2003, be the cash equivalent of the remuneration as a benefit.

(7) In sections 506A and 506B and this section—

(a) a reference to a substantial donor or other person includes a reference to a person connected with him within the meaning of section 839,

(b) "financial assistance" includes, in particular—

(i) the provision of a loan, guarantee or indemnity, and

(ii) entering into alternative finance arrangements within the meaning of *section* 46 of the Finance Act 2005, and

(c) a reference to a gift of a specified amount includes a reference to a non-monetary gift of that value.

(8) On an appeal against an assessment the Special Commissioners may review a decision of the Commissioners in connection with section 506A.

(9) The Treasury may by regulations vary a sum, or a period of time, specified in section 506A(2).]

[706C]

NOTES

Inserted as noted to 506A at **[706A]**.

507 The National Heritage Memorial Fund, the Historic Buildings and Monuments Commission for England and the British Museum

(1) There shall on a claim in that behalf to the Board be allowed in the case of—

(a) the Trustees of the National Heritage Memorial Fund;

(b) the Historic Buildings and Monuments Commission for England;

[(c) the Trustees of the British Museum;

(d) the Trustees of the [Natural History Museum];]

[(e) …]

[(f) the National Endowment for Science, Technology and the Arts;]

such exemption from tax as falls to be allowed under section 505 in the case of a charity the whole income of which is applied to charitable purposes.

(2) …

[707]

NOTES

Sub-s (1): paras (c), (d) added, in relation to accounting periods ending on or after 14 March 1989, by the Finance Act 1989, s 60(1); words in square brackets in para (d) substituted by the Museums and Galleries Act 1992, s 11(2), Sch 8, para 1(8); para (e) added by the United Kingdom Ecolabelling Board Regulations 1992, SI 1992/2383, reg 2(2), Schedule, para 11, repealed by the United Kingdom Ecolabelling Board (Abolition) Regulations 1999, SI 1999/931, reg 9; para (f) added by the National Lottery Act 1998, s 24(1).

Sub-s (2): repealed by the Finance Act 1989, ss 60, 187, Sch 17, Pt IV, in relation to accounting periods ending on or after 14 March 1989.

508 Scientific research organisations

(1) Where—

(*a*) *an Association which has as its object the undertaking of scientific research which may lead to or facilitate an extension of any class or classes of trade is approved for the purposes of this section by the Secretary of State; and*

(b) the memorandum of association or other similar instrument regulating the functions of the Association precludes the direct or indirect payment or transfer to any of its members of any of its income or property by way of dividend, gift, division, bonus or otherwise howsoever by way of profit;

there shall, on a claim in that behalf to the Board, *be allowed in the case of the Association* such exemption from tax as falls to be allowed under section 505 in the case of a charity the whole income of which is applied to charitable purposes.

(2) The condition specified in paragraph (b) of subsection (1) above shall not be deemed not to be complied with in the case of any Association by reason only that the memorandum or other similar instrument regulating its functions does not prevent the payment to its members of reasonable remuneration for goods, labour or power supplied, or for services rendered, of reasonable interest for money lent, or of reasonable rent for any premises.

(3) In this section "scientific research" means any activities in the fields of natural or applied science for the extension of knowledge.

[708]

NOTES

Sub-s (1): para (a) substituted as follows—

"(a) an Association has as its object the undertaking of research and development which may lead to or facilitate an extension of any class or classes of trade; and"

and for the words in italics there are substituted the words "in relation to any accounting period, be allowed in the case of the Association for that accounting period" by the Finance (No 2) Act 2005, s 13(1)–(3), with effect in relation to accounting periods beginning on or after such day as the Treasury may by order made by statutory instrument appoint.

Sub-ss (1A), (1B): inserted by the Finance (No 2) Act 2005, s 13(1), (4), with effect in relation to accounting periods beginning on or after such day as the Treasury may by order made by statutory instrument appoint—

"(1A) The Treasury may by regulations prescribe circumstances in which the conditions in subsection (1) above shall be deemed not to be complied with.

(1B) The Treasury may by regulations make provision specifying for the purposes of paragraph (a) of that subsection—

(a) what shall be deemed to be, or not to be, an Association,
(b) circumstances in which an Association shall be deemed to have, or not to have, the undertaking of research and development as its object,
(c) circumstances in which the undertaking of research and development shall be deemed to be, or not to be, capable of leading to or facilitating an extension of a class of trade, or
(d) what shall be deemed to be, or not to be, a class of trade."

Sub-s (3): substituted as follows, by sub-ss (3), (4), by the Finance (No 2) Act 2005, s 13(1), (5), with effect in relation to accounting periods beginning on or after such day as the Treasury may by order made by statutory instrument appoint—

"(3) Section 837A (meaning of "research and development") applies for the purposes of subsection (1)(a) above.

(4) Regulations under subsection (3) of that section (power to prescribe activities which are, or are not, research and development) may make provision for the purposes of that section as it applies by virtue of subsection (3) of this section which is additional to, or different from, the provision made otherwise for the purposes of that section.".

508A–702 (*Ss 508A–519A, ss 520–702 (Pts XIII–XVI) outside the scope of this work.*)

PART XVII
TAX AVOIDANCE

703–764 ((*Chs I–V) outside the scope of this work.*)

CHAPTER VI
MISCELLANEOUS

765–774G (*Outside the scope of this work.*)

Other provisions

775–786 (*Outside the scope of this work.*)

787 Restriction of relief for payments of interest

(1) Relief shall not be given to any person under any provision of the Tax Acts in respect of any payment of interest if a scheme has been effected or arrangements have been made (whether before or after the time when the payment is made) such that the sole or main benefit that might be expected to accrue to that person from the transaction under which the interest is paid was the obtaining of a reduction in tax liability by means of any such relief.

[(1A) This section has effect in relation to Chapter 2 of Part 4 of the Finance Act 1996 (loan relationships) but taking the reference in subsection (1) above to giving relief to any person in respect of any payment of interest as including a reference to the bringing into account by any person in accordance with that Chapter of any debit in respect of interest (whether a payment or not); and other references in this section to relief shall be construed accordingly.]

(2) In this section "relief" means relief by way of deduction in computing profits or gains or deduction or set off against income or total profits.

[(3) Where the relief is claimed by virtue of section 403—

(a) in respect of a deficit to which section 83 of the Finance Act 1996 applies (non-trading deficit on loan relationships), or
(b) in respect of trading losses, in a case where in computing those losses debits in respect of loan relationships are treated under section 82(2)(b) of that Act as expenses of the trade which are deductible in computing the profits of the trade,

any question under this section as to what benefit might be expected to accrue from the transaction in question shall be determined by reference to the claimant company and the surrendering company taken together.]

[709]

PART I STATUTES

NOTES

Sub-s (1A): inserted by the Finance Act 2002, s 82(1), Sch 25, Pt 2, paras 43, 53(1), (2), with effect in relation to accounting periods beginning on or after 1 October 2002.

Sub-s (3): substituted by the Finance Act 2002, s 82(1), Sch 25, Pt 2, paras 43, 53(1), (3), with effect in relation to accounting periods beginning on or after 1 October 2002.

See further, in relation to alternative finance arrangements: the Finance Act 2005, s 55, Sch 2, para 8.

788–816 *((Pt XVIII) outside the scope of this work.)*

PART XIX
SUPPLEMENTAL

817–842B *(Outside the scope of this work.)*

Commencement, savings, repeals etc

843 Commencement

(1) Except as otherwise provided by the following provisions of this section, this Act shall come into force in relation to tax for the year 1988–89 and subsequent years of assessment, and for companies' accounting periods ending after 5th April 1988.

(2) Except as otherwise provided by the following provisions of this section, such of the provisions of this Act as relate to capital gains tax (including the provisions of Part XVIII as applied to capital gains tax by section [277 of [the 1992 Act]]) shall come into force in relation to that tax for the year 1988–89 and subsequent years of assessment.

(3) The following provisions of this Act, that is to say—

(a) so much of any provision as authorises the making of any Order in Council or regulations or other instrument;

(b) so much of any provision as relates to the making of a return, the furnishing of a certificate or the giving of any other information, including any such provision which imposes a duty on the Board or an officer of the Board as well as any such provision which imposes a duty on any other person;

(c) so much of any provision as imposes any penalty;

(d) except where the tax concerned is all tax for years of assessment before the year 1988–89 or accounting periods ending before 6th April 1988, so much of any other provision as confers any power or imposes any duty the exercise or performance of which operates or may operate in relation to tax for more than one chargeable period,

shall come into force for all purposes on 6th April 1988 to the exclusion of the corresponding enactments repealed by this Act.

(4) This section has effect except as otherwise provided by any other provision of this Act, and in particular except as provided by sections 96, 380 to 384, 393 … 400, 703 and 812.

[710]

NOTES

Sub-s (2): words in first (outer) pair of square brackets substituted by the Taxation of Chargeable Gains Act 1992, s 290(1), Sch 10, para 14(1), (56); words in second (inner) pair of square brackets substituted with retrospective effect by the Finance Act 1994, s 146, Sch 17, para 8.

Sub-s (4): figure omitted repealed, with retrospective effect, in relation to losses incurred in accounting periods ending on after 1 April 1991, by the Finance Act 1991, ss 73(3), (4), 123, Sch 15, para 24, Sch 19, Pt V.

1992 Act: Taxation of Chargeable Gains Act 1992.

844 *(Outside the scope of this work.)*

845 Short title

This Act may be cited as the Income and Corporation Taxes Act 1988.

[711]

SCHEDULES

(*Schs A1–19C outside the scope of this work.*)

SCHEDULE 20
CHARITIES: QUALIFYING INVESTMENTS AND LOANS

Section 506

PART I
QUALIFYING INVESTMENTS

1. Investments specified in any of the following paragraphs of this Part of this Schedule are qualifying investments for the purposes of section 506.

2. Any investment falling within Part I, Part II, apart from paragraph 13 (mortgages etc) or Part III of Schedule 1 to the Trustee Investments Act 1961.

3. Any investment in a common investment fund established under section 22 of the Charities Act 1960[, section 24 of the Charities Act 1993] or section 25 of the Charities Act (Northern Ireland) 1964 or in any similar fund established for the exclusive benefit of charities by or under any enactment relating to any particular charities or class of charities.

[3A. Any investment in a common deposit fund established under section 22A of the Charities Act 1960 [or section 25 of the Charities Act 1993] or in any similar fund established for the exclusive benefit of charities by or under any enactment relating to any particular charities or class of charities.]

4. Any interest in land, other than an interest held as security for a debt of any description.

5. Shares in, or securities of, a company which are [listed] on a recognised stock exchange, or which are dealt in on the Unlisted Securities Market.

6. Units, or other shares of the investments subject to the trusts, of a unit trust scheme within the meaning [given by section 237(1) of the Financial Services and Markets Act 2000].

7.—(1) Deposits with [a bank] in respect of which interest is payable at a commercial rate.

(2) A deposit mentioned in sub-paragraph (1) above is not a qualifying investment if it is made as part of an arrangement under which a loan is made by the authorised institution to some other person.

[(3) In this paragraph "bank" has the meaning given by section 840A.]

[7A. Uncertificated eligible debt security units as defined in section 552(2) of ITTOIA 2005.]

8. Certificates of deposit as defined in [for corporation tax purposes in section 56(5) above and for income tax purposes in section 552(2) of ITTOIA 2005].

9.—(1) Any loan or other investment as to which the Board are satisfied, on a claim made to them in that behalf, that the loan or other investment is made for the benefit of the charity and not for the avoidance of tax (whether by the charity or any other person).

(2) The reference in sub-paragraph (1) above to a loan includes a loan which is secured by a mortgage or charge of any kind over land.

[712]

NOTES

Para 3: words in square brackets inserted by the Charities Act 1993, s 98(1), Sch 6, para 25(a).

Para 3A: inserted by the Charities Act 1992, s 78(1), Sch 6, para 17; words in square brackets inserted by the Charities Act 1993, s 98(1), Sch 6, para 25(b).

Para 5: word in square brackets substituted, in relation to chargeable periods ending on or after 1 April 1996, by the Finance Act 1996, s 199, Sch 38, para 6(1), (2)(l), (11).

Para 6: words in square brackets substituted by the Financial Services and Markets Act 2000 (Consequential Amendments) (Taxes) Order 2001, SI 2001/3629, arts 13, 50.

Para 7: in sub-para (1) words in square brackets substituted, in relation to deposits made or, as the case may be, money placed on or after 29 April 1996, by the Finance Act 1996, s 198, Sch 37, paras 5, 10; sub-para (3) added, in relation to deposits made or, as the case may be, money placed on or after 29 April 1996, by the Finance Act 1996, s 198, Sch 37, paras 2(3), 10.

Para 7A: inserted by the Income Tax (Trading and Other Income) Act 2005, s 882(1), Sch 1, Pt 1, paras 1, 347(1), (2), with effect, for the purposes of income tax for the year 2005–06 and subsequent tax years, and for the purposes of corporation tax for accounting periods ending after 5 April 2005.

Para 8: words in square brackets substituted by the Income Tax (Trading and Other Income) Act 2005, s 882(1), Sch 1, Pt 1, paras 1, 347(1), (3), with effect, for the purposes of income tax for the year 2005–06 and subsequent tax years, and for the purposes of corporation tax for accounting periods ending after 5 April 2005.

See further, in relation to the application of this Part of this Schedule, with modifications: in relation to eligible debt securities, the Uncertificated Securities (Amendment) (Eligible Debt Securities) Regulations 2003, SI 2003/1633, reg 15, Sch 2, para 6(1), (2)(a); in relation to authorised investment funds, shareholders or unit holders in authorised investment funds and transactions involving authorised investment funds, the Authorised Investment Funds (Tax) Regulations 2006, SI 2006/964, regs 93, 94(1), (7).

PART II
QUALIFYING LOANS

10.—[(1)] For the purposes of section 506, a loan which is not made by way of investment is a qualifying loan if it consists of—

(a) a loan made to another charity for charitable purposes only; or

(b) a loan to a beneficiary of the charity which is made in the course of carrying out the purposes of the charity; or

(c) money placed on current account with [a bank] otherwise than as part of such an arrangement as is mentioned in paragraph 7(2) above; or

(d) any other loan as to which the Board are satisfied, on a claim made to them in that behalf, that the loan is made for the benefit of the charity and not for the avoidance of tax (whether by the charity or by some other person).

[(2) In this paragraph "bank" has the meaning given by section 840A.]

[713]–[714]

NOTES

Sub-para (1) numbered as such, words in square brackets therein substituted and sub-para (2) added, in relation to deposits made or, as the case may be, money placed on or after 29 April 1996, by the Finance Act 1996, s 198, Sch 37, paras 2(3), (4), 5, 10.

(Sch 20, Pt III repealed by the Finance Act 2006, ss 55(3), 178, Sch 26, Pt 3(5), with effect in relation to chargeable periods beginning on or after 22 March 2006; Schs 21–31 outside the scope of this work.)

LOCAL GOVERNMENT FINANCE ACT 1988

(1988 c 41)

ARRANGEMENT OF SECTIONS

PART III
NON-DOMESTIC RATING

Local rating

PART XI
MISCELLANEOUS AND GENERAL

General

An Act to create community charges in favour of certain authorities, to create new rating systems, to provide for precepting by certain authorities and levying by certain bodies, to make provision about the payment of grants to certain authorities, to require certain authorities to maintain certain funds, to make provision about the capital expenditure and the administration of the financial affairs of certain authorities, to abolish existing rates, precepts and similar rights, to abolish rate support grants and supplementary grants for transport purposes, to make amendments as to rates and certain grants, to make certain amendments to the law of Scotland as regards community charges, rating and valuation, to provide for the establishment of valuation and community charge tribunals, and for connected purposes

[29 July 1988]

NOTES

Transfer of functions in relation to Wales: as to the transfer of functions under this Act from Ministers of the Crown to the National Assembly for Wales, see the National Assembly for Wales (Transfer of Functions) Order 1999, SI 1999/672.

1–40 ((*Pts I, II*) *repealed by the Local Government Finance Act 1992, ss 117(2), 118(1), Sch 14, except in relation to community charges for days, or financial years, beginning before 1 April 1993.*)

PART III
NON-DOMESTIC RATING

Local rating

41, 41A, 42, 42A, 42B (*Outside the scope of this work.*)

43 Occupied hereditaments: liability

(1) A person (the ratepayer) shall as regards a hereditament be subject to a non-domestic rate in respect of a chargeable financial year if the following conditions are fulfilled in respect of any day in the year—

(a) on the day the ratepayer is in occupation of all or part of the hereditament, and
(b) the hereditament is shown for the day in a local non-domestic rating list in force for the year.

(2) In such a case the ratepayer shall be liable to pay an amount calculated by—

(a) finding the chargeable amount for each chargeable day, and
(b) aggregating the amounts found under paragraph (a) above.

(3) A chargeable day is one which falls within the financial year and in respect of which the conditions mentioned in subsection (1) above are fulfilled.

(4) Subject to [subsections [(4A),] (5) and (6A)] below, the chargeable amount for a chargeable day shall be calculated in accordance with the formula—

$$\frac{A \times B}{C}$$

[(4A) Where subsection (4B) below applies, the chargeable amount for a chargeable day shall be calculated—

(a) in relation to England, in accordance with the formula—

$$\frac{A \times D}{C \times E}$$

(b) in relation to Wales, in accordance with the formula—

$$\frac{A \times B}{C \times E}$$

(4B) This subsection applies—

(a) in relation to England, where—
(i) the rateable value of the hereditament shown in the local non-domestic rating list for the first day of the chargeable financial year is not more than any amount prescribed by the Secretary of State by order,
(ii) on the day concerned any conditions prescribed by the Secretary of State by order are satisfied, and
(iii) the ratepayer has made an application for the purposes of this subsection to the billing authority concerned by such date as may be prescribed by the Secretary of State by order,

(b) in relation to Wales, where—
(i) the rateable value of the hereditament shown in the local non-domestic rating list for the first day of the chargeable financial year is not more than any amount prescribed by the National Assembly for Wales by order, and
(ii) on the day concerned any conditions prescribed by the National Assembly for Wales by order are satisfied.

(4C) An application under subsection (4B)(a)(iii) above shall be made in such form, and contain such information, as may be prescribed by the Secretary of State by order.

(4D) If the ratepayer—

(a) makes a statement in an application under subsection (4B)(a)(iii) above which he knows to be false in a material particular, or

(b) recklessly makes a statement in such an application which is false in a material particular,

he shall be liable on summary conviction to imprisonment for a term not exceeding 3 months or to a fine not exceeding level 3 on the standard scale or to both.]

(5) Where subsection (6) below applies the chargeable amount for a chargeable day shall be calculated in accordance with the formula—

$$\frac{A \times B}{C \times 5}$$

(6) This subsection applies where on the day concerned—

[(a)] the ratepayer is a charity or trustees for a charity and the hereditament is wholly or mainly used for charitable purposes (whether of that charity or of that and other charities)[, or

(b) the ratepayer is a registered club for the purposes of Schedule 18 to the Finance Act 2002 (community amateur sports clubs) and the hereditament is wholly or mainly used—
(i) for the purposes of that club, or
(ii) for the purposes of that club and of other such registered clubs].

(6A)–(8) (*Outside the scope of this work.*)

[715]

NOTES

Sub-s (4): words in first (outer) pair of square brackets substituted by the Local Government and Rating Act 1997, s 1, Sch 1, para 2(a); number in second (inner) pair of square brackets inserted by the Local Government Act 2003, s 61(1), (2).

Sub-ss (4A)–(4D): inserted by the Local Government Act 2003, s 61(1), (3).

Sub-s (6): para (a) numbered as such and para (b) and word ", or" immediately preceding it inserted by the Local Government Act 2003, s 64(1).

Orders: the Non-Domestic Rating (Small Business Rate Relief) (England) Order 2004, SI 2004/3315; the Non-Domestic Rating (Small Business Relief) (Wales) Order 2006, SI 2006/3345.

44 Occupied hereditaments: supplementary

(1) This section applies for the purposes of section 43 above.

(2) A is the rateable value shown for the day under section 42(4) above as regards the hereditament …

(3) …

(4) Subject to subsection (5) below, B is the non-domestic rating multiplier for the financial year.

(5) Where the [billing authority] is a special authority, B is the authority's non-domestic rating multiplier for the financial year.

(6) C is the number of days in the financial year.

[(7) Subject to subsection (8) below, D is the small business non-domestic rating multiplier for the financial year.

(8) Where the billing authority is a special authority, D is the authority's small business non-domestic rating multiplier for the financial year.

(9) E is such amount as may be prescribed—

- (a) in relation to England, by the Secretary of State by order,
- (b) in relation to Wales, by the National Assembly for Wales by order.]

[716]

NOTES

Sub-s (2): words omitted repealed with retrospective effect by the Local Government and Housing Act 1989, ss 139, 194(4), Sch 5, paras 1, 21(2), 79(3), Sch 12, Pt II.

Sub-s (3): repealed with retrospective effect by the Local Government and Housing Act 1989, ss 139, 194(4), Sch 5, paras 1, 21(2), 79(3), Sch 12, Pt II.

Sub-s (5): words in square brackets substituted by the Local Government Finance Act 1992, s 117(1), 118(1), Sch 13, para 61, with effect in relation to financial years beginning on or after 1 April 1993.

Sub-ss (7)–(9): added by the Local Government Act 2003, s 61(5).

Orders: the Non-Domestic Rating (Small Business Rate Relief) (England) Order 2004, SI 2004/3315; the Non-Domestic Rating (Small Business Relief) (Wales) Order 2006, SI 2006/3345

44A (*Outside the scope of this work.*)

45 Unoccupied hereditaments: liability

(1) A person (the ratepayer) shall as regards a hereditament be subject to a non-domestic rate in respect of a chargeable financial year if the following conditions are fulfilled in respect of any day in the year—

- (a) on the day none of the hereditament is occupied,
- (b) on the day the ratepayer is the owner of the whole of the hereditament,
- (c) the hereditament is shown for the day in a local non-domestic rating list in force for the year, and
- (d) on the day the hereditament falls within a [class] prescribed by the Secretary of State by regulations.

(2) In such a case the ratepayer shall be liable to pay an amount calculated by—

- (a) finding the chargeable amount for each chargeable day, and
- (b) aggregating the amounts found under paragraph (a) above.

(3) A chargeable day is one which falls within the financial year and in respect of which the conditions mentioned in subsection (1) above are fulfilled.

(4) Subject to subsection (5) below, the chargeable amount for a chargeable day shall be calculated in accordance with the formula—

$$\frac{A \times B}{C \times 2}$$

(5) Where subsection (6) below applies the chargeable amount for a chargeable day shall be calculated in accordance with the formula—

(6) This subsection applies where on the day concerned—

[(a)] the ratepayer is a charity or trustees for a charity and it appears that when next in use the hereditament will be wholly or mainly used for charitable purposes (whether of that charity or of that and other charities)[, or

(b) the ratepayer is a registered club for the purposes of Schedule 18 to the Finance Act 2002 (community amateur sports clubs) and it appears that when the hereditament is next in use—
 (i) it will be wholly or mainly used for the purposes of that club, and that club will be such a registered club, or
 (ii) it will be wholly or mainly used for the purposes of two or more clubs including that club, and each of those clubs will be such a registered club].

(7) The amount the ratepayer is liable to pay under this section shall be paid to the [billing authority] in whose local non-domestic rating list the hereditament is shown.

(8) The liability to pay any such amount shall be discharged by making a payment or payments in accordance with regulations under Schedule 9 below.

[(9) For the purposes of subsection (1)(d) above a class may be prescribed by reference to such factors as the Secretary of State sees fit.

(10) Without prejudice to the generality of subsection (9) above, a class may be prescribed by reference to one or more of the following factors—
(a) the physical characteristics of the hereditaments;
(b) the fact that hereditaments have been unoccupied at any time preceding the day mentioned in subsection (1) above;
(c) the fact that the owners of hereditaments fall within prescribed descriptions.]

[717]

NOTES

Sub-s (1): word in square brackets substituted with retrospective effect by the Local Government and Housing Act 1989, s 139, Sch 5, paras 1, 23(2), 79(3).

Sub-s (7): words in square brackets substituted by the Local Government Finance Act 1992, s 117(1), 118(1), Sch 13, para 63, with effect in relation to financial years beginning on or after 1 April 1993.

Sub-s (6): para (a) numbered as such and para (b) and word ", or" immediately preceding it inserted by the Local Government Act 2003, s 64(2).

Sub-ss (9), (10): added with retrospective effect by the Local Government and Housing Act 1989, s 139, Sch 5, paras 1, 23(3), 79(3).

Regulations: the Non-Domestic Rating (Unoccupied Property) Regulations 1989, SI 1989/2261.

46, 46A (*Outside the scope of this work.*)

47 Discretionary relief

(1) Where the first and second conditions mentioned in subsections (2) and (3) below [or the rural settlement condition and the second condition mentioned in subsection (3) below][, or the condition relating to relief for former agricultural premises mentioned in subsection (3C) below and the second condition mentioned in subsection (3) below,] [or the small business condition and the second condition mentioned in subsection (3) below,] are fulfilled for a day which is a chargeable day within the meaning of section 43 or 45 above (as the case may be)—
(a) the chargeable amount for the day shall be such as is determined by, or found in accordance with rules determined by, the [billing authority] concerned, and
(b) sections [43(4) to (6B)] and 44 above, sections 45(4) to (6) and 46 above, [regulations under [section 57A or 58] below or any provision of or made under Schedule 7A below] (as the case may be) shall not apply as regards the day.

(2) The first condition is that one or more of the following applies on the chargeable day—
(a) the ratepayer is a charity or trustees for a charity, and the hereditament is wholly or mainly used for charitable purposes (whether of that charity or of that and other charities);
(b) the hereditament is not an excepted hereditament, and all or part of it is occupied for the purposes of one or more institutions or other organisations none of which is established or conducted for profit and each of whose main objects are charitable or are otherwise philanthropic or religious or concerned with education, social welfare, science, literature or the fine arts;
[(ba) the ratepayer is a registered club for the purposes of Schedule 18 to the Finance Act 2002 (community amateur sports clubs), and the hereditament is not an excepted hereditament and is wholly or mainly used—
 (i) for the purposes of that club, or

(ii) for the purposes of that club and of other such registered clubs;]

(c) the hereditament is not an excepted hereditament, it is wholly or mainly used for purposes of recreation, and all or part of it is occupied for the purposes of a club, society or other organisation not established or conducted for profit.

(3) The second condition is that, during a period which consists of or includes the chargeable day, a decision of the [billing authority] concerned operates to the effect that this section applies as regards the hereditament concerned.

(3A)–(9) (*Outside the scope of this work.*)

[718]

NOTES

Sub-s (1): words in first pair of square brackets inserted and words in first pair of square brackets in para (b) substituted by the Local Government and Rating Act 1997, s 1, Sch 1, para 3(a); words in second pair of square brackets inserted in relation to England and inserted as from a day to be appointed in relation to Wales by the Rating (Former Agricultural Premises and Rural Shops) Act 2001, s 2(1), (2); words in third pair of square brackets inserted by the Local Government Act 2003, s 61(6); words in square brackets in para (a) substituted by the Local Government Finance Act 1992, ss 117(1), 118(1), Sch 13, para 65(1), with effect in relation to financial years beginning on or after 1 April 1993; words in second (outer) pair of square brackets in para (b) substituted with retrospective effect by the Local Government and Housing Act 1989, s 139, Sch 5, paras 1, 26, 79(3); words in third (inner) pair of square brackets in para (b) substituted by the Local Government Act 2003, s 127(1), Sch 7, paras 9(1), 10.

Sub-s (2): para (ba) inserted by the Local Government Act 2003, s 64(3).

Sub-s (3): words in square brackets substituted by the Local Government Finance Act 1992, ss 117(1), 118(1), Sch 13, para 65, with effect in relation to financial years beginning on or after 1 April 1993.

48 Discretionary relief: supplementary

(1) This section applies for the purposes of section 47 above [(but subsection (5) below does not apply for the purposes of subsection (3B)(a) of that section)].

(2) A hereditament not in use shall be treated as wholly or mainly used for charitable purposes if it appears that when next in use it will be wholly or mainly used for charitable purposes.

[(2A) A hereditament not in use shall be treated as wholly or mainly used for the purposes of a club that is a registered club for the purposes of Schedule 18 to the Finance Act 2002 (community amateur sports clubs) if it appears that when next in use it will be wholly or mainly used for the purposes of a club that is then, or two or more clubs each of which is then, such a registered club.]

(3) A hereditament not in use shall be treated as wholly or mainly used for purposes of recreation if it appears that when next in use it will be wholly or mainly used for purposes of recreation.

(4) A hereditament which is wholly unoccupied shall be treated as an excepted hereditament if it appears that when any of it is next occupied the hereditament will be an excepted hereditament.

(5) If a hereditament is wholly unoccupied but it appears that it or any part of it when next occupied will be occupied for particular purposes, the hereditament or part concerned (as the case may be) shall be treated as occupied for those purposes.

[719]–[721]

NOTES

Sub-s (1): words in square brackets added by the Local Government and Rating Act 1997, s 1, Sch 1, para 4.

Sub-s (2A): inserted by the Local Government Act 2003, s 64(4).

49, 50 (*Outside the scope of this work.*)

51 Exemption

Schedule 5 below shall have effect to determine the extent (if any) to which a hereditament is for the purposes of this Part exempt from local non-domestic rating.

[722]

52–63 (*Outside the scope of this work.*)

Interpretation

64 Hereditaments

(1)–(9) (*Outside the scope of this work.*)

(10) A hereditament shall be treated as wholly or mainly used for charitable purposes at any time if at the time it is wholly or mainly used for the sale of goods donated to a charity and the proceeds of sale of the goods (after any deduction of expenses) are applied for the purposes of a charity.

(11)–(12) (*Outside the scope of this work.*)

[722A]

65, 66 (*Outside the scope of this work.*)

67 Interpretation: other provisions

(1), (2) (*Outside the scope of this work.*)

(3) A right or other property is a hereditament on a particular day if (and only if) it is a hereditament immediately before the day ends.

(4)–(9) (*Outside the scope of this work.*)

(10) A charity is an institution or other organisation established for charitable purposes only or any persons administering a trust established for charitable purposes only.

(10A)–(13) (*Outside the scope of this work.*)

[722B]

68–129 ((*Pts IV–X*) *in so far as unrepealed outside the scope of this work.*)

PART XI
MISCELLANEOUS AND GENERAL

130–137 (*In so far as unrepealed outside the scope of this work.*)

General

138–144 (*Ss 138, 139, 139A, 140, 141, 142–144 outside the scope of this work; ss 141A, 141B, 145A inserted, with retrospective effect, by the Local Government and Housing Act 1989, s 139, Sch 5, paras 1, 71, 73 and repealed by the Local Government Finance Act 1992, ss 117(2), 118(1), Sch 14.*)

145 Interpretation: financial years etc

(1) Chargeable financial years are financial years beginning in 1990 and subsequent years.

(2) (*Outside the scope of this work.*)

(3) A financial year is a period of 12 months beginning with 1 April.

[722C]

145A–151 (*Outside the scope of this work.*)

152 Citation

This Act may be cited as the Local Government Finance Act 1988.

[723]

SCHEDULES

(*Schs 1–4 ceased to have effect on the repeal of Pt I of this Act by the Local Government Finance Act 1992, ss 117(2), 118(1), Sch 14; Sch 4A outside the scope of this work.*)

SCHEDULE 5
NON-DOMESTIC RATING: EXEMPTION

Section 51

1–10. (*Outside the scope of this work.*)

Places of religious worship etc

11.—(1) A hereditament is exempt to the extent that it consists of any of the following—

(*a*) *a place of public religious worship which belongs to the Church of England or the Church in Wales (within the meaning of the Welsh Church Act 1914) or is for the time being certified as required by law as a place of religious worship;*

(b) a church hall, chapel hall or similar building used in connection with a place falling within paragraph (a) above for the purposes of the organisation responsible for the conduct of public religious worship in that place.

[(2) A hereditament is exempt to the extent that it is occupied by an organisation responsible for the conduct of public religious worship in a place falling within sub-paragraph (1)(a) above and—

(a) is used for carrying out administrative or other activities relating to the organisation of the conduct of public religious worship in such a place; or

(b) is used as an office or for office purposes, or for purposes ancillary to its use as an office or for office purposes.

(3) In this paragraph "office purposes" include administration, clerical work and handling money; and "clerical work" includes writing, book-keeping, sorting papers or information, filing, typing, duplicating, calculating (by whatever means), drawing and the editorial preparation of matter for publication.]

12–15. (*Outside the scope of this work.*)

Property used for the disabled

16.—(1) A hereditament is exempt to the extent that it consists of property used wholly for any of the following purposes—

(a) the provision of facilities for training, or keeping suitably occupied, persons who are disabled or who are or have been suffering from illness;

(b) the provision of welfare services for disabled persons;

(c) the provision of facilities under section 15 of the Disabled Persons (Employment) Act 1944;

(d) the provision of a workshop or of other facilities under section 3(1) of the Disabled Persons (Employment) Act 1958.

(2) A person is disabled if he is blind, deaf or dumb or suffers from mental disorder of any description or is substantially and permanently handicapped by illness, injury, congenital deformity or any other disability for the time being prescribed for the purposes of section 29(1) of the National Assistance Act 1948.

(3) "Illness" has the meaning given by [section 275 of the National Health Service Act 2006].

(4) "Welfare services for disabled persons" means services or facilities (by whomsoever provided) of a kind which a local authority has power to provide under section 29 of the National Assistance Act 1948.

17–21. (*Outside the scope of this work.*)

[724]

NOTES

Para 11: sub-para (1)(a) substituted as follows by the Local Government Act 2003, s 68, as from a day to be appointed under s 128(6) of that Act—

"(a) a place of public religious worship;".

Para 11: sub-paras (2), (3) substituted for original sub-para (2) by the Local Government Finance Act 1992, s 104, Sch 10, para 3.

Para 16: words in square brackets in sub-para (3) substituted by the National Health Service (Consequential Provisions) Act 2006, s 2, Sch 1, paras 109, 110.

(Schs 6–13 outside the scope of this work.)

LOCAL GOVERNMENT AND HOUSING ACT 1989

(1989 c 42)

ARRANGEMENT OF SECTIONS

PART V
COMPANIES IN WHICH LOCAL AUTHORITIES HAVE INTERESTS

PART IX
MISCELLANEOUS AND GENERAL

Supplementary

An Act to make provision with respect to the members, officers and other staff and the procedure of local authorities; to amend Part III of the Local Government Act 1974 and Part II of the Local Government (Scotland) Act 1975 and to provide for a national code of local government conduct; to make further provision about the finances and expenditure of local authorities (including provision with respect to housing subsidies) and about companies in which local authorities have interests; to make provision for and in connection with renewal areas, grants towards the cost of improvement and repair of housing accommodation and the carrying out of works of maintenance, repair and improvement; to amend the Housing Act 1985 and Part III of the Local Government Finance Act 1982; to make amendments of and consequential upon Parts I, II and IV of the Housing Act 1988; to amend the Local Government Finance Act 1988 and the Abolition of Domestic Rates Etc (Scotland) Act 1987 and certain enactments relating, as respects Scotland, to rating and valuation, and to provide for the making of grants; to make provision with respect to the imposition of charges by local authorities; to make further provision about certain existing grants and about financial assistance to and planning by local authorities in respect of emergencies; to amend sections 102 and 211 of the Local Government (Scotland) Act 1973; to amend the Local Land Charges Act 1975; to enable local authorities in Wales to be known solely by Welsh language names; to provide for the transfer of new town housing stock; to amend certain of the provisions of the Housing (Scotland) Act 1987 relating to a secure tenant's right to purchase his house; to amend section 47 of the Race Relations Act 1976; to confer certain powers on the Housing Corporation, Housing for Wales and Scottish Homes; to make provision about security of tenure for certain tenants under long tenancies; to provide for the making of grants and giving of guarantees in respect of certain activities carried on in relation to the construction industry; to provide for the repeal of certain enactments relating to improvement notices, town development and education support grants; to make, as respects Scotland, further provision in relation to the phasing of progression to registered rent for houses let by housing associations or Scottish Homes and in relation to the circumstances in which rent increases under assured tenancies may be secured; and for connected purposes

[16 November 1989]

NOTES

Transfer of functions in relation to Wales: as to the transfer of functions under this Act from Ministers of the Crown to the National Assembly for Wales, see the National Assembly for Wales (Transfer of Functions) Order 1999, SI 1999/672.

1–66 (*(Pts I–IV) outside the scope of this work.*)

PART V
COMPANIES IN WHICH LOCAL AUTHORITIES HAVE INTERESTS

67 Application of, and orders under, Part V

(1) Any reference in this Part to a company is a reference to a body corporate of one of the following descriptions—

(a) a company limited by shares;
(b) a company limited by guarantee and not having a share capital;
(c) a company limited by guarantee and having a share capital;
(d) an unlimited company; and
(e) a society registered or deemed to be registered under the Industrial and Provident Societies Act 1965 or under the Industrial and Provident Societies Act (Northern Ireland) 1969.

(2) Expressions used in paragraphs (a) to (d) of subsection (1) above have the same meaning as in Chapter I of Part I of the Companies Act 1985 or the corresponding enactment for the time being in force in Northern Ireland.

(3) Any reference in this Part to a local authority is a reference to a body of one of the following descriptions—

(a) a county council;
[(aa) a county borough council;]
(b) a district council;
[(bb) the Greater London Authority;
(bc) a functional body, within the meaning of the Greater London Authority Act 1999;]
(c) a London borough council;
(d) the Common Council of the City of London in its capacity as a local authority, police authority or port health authority;
(e) the Council of the Isles of Scilly;
(f) a parish council;
(g) a community council;
[(ga) …]
[(h) a fire and rescue authority constituted by a scheme under section 2 of the Fire and Rescue Services Act 2004 or a scheme to which section 4 of that Act applies;]
[(i) a police authority established under [section 3 of the Police Act 1996] […];]
(j) an authority established under section 10 of the Local Government Act 1985 (waste disposal authorities);
(k) a joint authority established by Part IV of that Act [(fire and rescue services and transport)];
(l) any body established pursuant to an order under section 67 of that Act (successors to residuary bodies);
(m) the Broads Authority;
[(ma) a National Park authority;]
(n) any joint board the constituent members of which consist of any of the bodies specified above;
(o) …
[(oo) a joint planning board constituted for an area in Wales outside a National Park by an order under section 2(1B) of the Town and Country Planning Act 1990; and]
(p) a Passenger Transport Executive.

(4) Any power to make an order under this Part shall be exercisable by statutory instrument subject to annulment in pursuance of a resolution of either House of Parliament; and under any such power different provision may be made for different cases and different descriptions of cases (including different provision for different areas).

[(5) The power under subsection (4) above to make differential provision includes, in particular, power to make different provision for different local authorities or descriptions of local authority.]

[725]

NOTES

Sub-s (3): para (aa) inserted by the Local Government Reorganisation (Wales) (Consequential Amendments No 3) Order 1996, SI 1996/3071, art 2, Schedule, para 3(6); paras (bb), (bc) inserted by the Greater London Authority Act 1999, s 393; para (ga) inserted by the Access to Justice Act 1999, s 83(3), Sch 12, paras 4, 6, repealed by the Courts Act 2003, s 109(1), (3), Sch 8, para 342, Sch 10; para (h) substituted by the Fire and Rescue Services Act 2004, s 53(1), Sch 1, para 71(1), (3); para (i) substituted by the Police and Magistrates' Courts Act 1994, s 43, Sch 4, Pt I, para 39; words in first pair of square brackets in para (i) substituted by the Police Act 1996, s 103, Sch 7, para 1(2)(zd), words in second pair of square brackets in para (i) added by the Police Act 1997, s 88, Sch 6, para 30 and repealed by the Criminal Justice and Police Act 2001, ss 128(1), 137, Sch 6, Pt 2, paras 49, 52, Sch 7, Pt 5(1); words in square brackets in para (k) substituted by the Civil Contingencies Act 2004, s 32(1), Sch 2, Pt 1, para 10(3)(b); paras (ma), (oo) inserted and para (o) repealed by the Environment Act 1995, ss 65, 78, 120, Sch 8, para 10, Sch 10, para 31(3), Sch 24.

Sub-s (5): added by the Local Government Act 2003, s 100(3), Sch 3, paras 1, 2.

68 Companies controlled by local authorities and arm's length companies

(1) For the purposes of this Part, unless the Secretary of State otherwise directs, a company is for the time being under the control of a local authority if—

(a) by virtue of section 736 of the Companies Act 1985 the company is at that time a subsidiary of the local authority for the purposes of that Act; or

(b) paragraph (a) above does not apply but the local authority have at that time power to control a majority of the votes at a general meeting of the company as mentioned in subsection (3) below; or

(c) paragraph (a) above does not apply but the local authority have at that time power to appoint or remove a majority of the board of directors of the company; or

(d) the company is under the control of another company which, by virtue of this subsection, is itself under the control of the local authority;

and, for the purposes of paragraph (d) above, any question whether one company is under the control of another shall be determined by applying the preceding provisions of this subsection, substituting a reference to the other company for any reference to the local authority.

(2) A direction under subsection (1) above—

(a) may be limited in time and may be made conditional upon such matters as appear to the Secretary of State to be appropriate; and

(b) may be made with respect to a particular company or a description of companies specified in the direction.

(3) The reference in subsection (1)(b) above to a power to control a majority of votes at a general meeting of the company is a reference to a power which is exercisable—

(a) in the case of a company limited by shares, through the holding of equity share capital in any one or more of the following ways, namely, by the local authority, by nominees of the local authority and by persons whose shareholding is under the control of the local authority; or

(b) in the case of any company, through the holding of votes at a general meeting of the company in any one or more of the following ways, namely, by the local authority, by a group of members of the company the composition of which is controlled by the local authority and by persons who have contractually bound themselves to vote in accordance with the instructions of the local authority; or

(c) partly in one of those ways and partly in the other.

(4) Subsection (3) of section 736A of the Companies Act 1985 (right to appoint or remove a majority of a company's board of directors) and the following provisions of that section as they have effect in relation to subsection (3) apply for the purposes of subsection (1)(c) above with the substitution for the word "right", wherever it occurs, of the word "power".

(5) For the purposes of subsection (3)(a) above, a person's shareholding is under the control of a local authority if—

(a) his right to hold the shares arose because of some action which the authority took, or refrained from taking, in order to enable him to have the right; and

(b) the local authority, alone or jointly with one or more other persons can require him to transfer his shareholding (or any part of it) to another person.

(6) Notwithstanding that, by virtue of the preceding provisions of this section, a company is for the time being under the control of a local authority, the company is for the purposes of this Part an "arm's length company", in relation to any financial year if, at a time before the beginning of that year, the authority resolved that the company should be an arm's length company and, at all times from the passing of that resolution up to the end of the financial year in question, the following conditions have applied while the company has been under the control of the local authority,—

(a) that each of the directors of the company was appointed for a fixed term of at least two years;

(b) that, subject to subsection (7) below, no director of the company has been removed by resolution under section 303 of the Companies Act 1985;

(c) that not more than one-fifth of the directors of the company have been members or officers of the authority;

(d) that the company has not occupied (as tenant or otherwise) any land in which the authority have an interest, otherwise than for the best consideration reasonably obtainable;

(e) that the company has entered into an agreement with the authority that the company will use its best endeavours to produce a specified positive return on its assets;

(f) that, except for the purpose of enabling the company to acquire fixed assets or to provide it with working capital, the authority have not lent money to the company or guaranteed any sum borrowed by it or subscribed for any securities in the company;

(g) that the authority have not made any grant to the company except in pursuance of an agreement or undertaking entered into before the financial year (within the meaning of the Companies Act 1985) of the company in which the grant was made; and

(h) that the authority have not made any grant to the company the amount of which is in any way related to the financial results of the company in any period.

(7) If the Secretary of State so directs, the removal of a director shall be disregarded for the purposes of subsection (6)(b) above; but the Secretary of State shall not give such a direction if it appears to him that the director was removed with a view to influencing the management of the company for other than commercial reasons.

[726]

69 Companies subject to local authority influence

(1) For the purposes of this Part, unless the Secretary of State otherwise directs, a company which is not at the time under the control of a local authority is for the time being subject to the influence of a local authority if it is not a banking or insurance company or a member of a banking or insurance group and at that time there is such a business relationship between the company and the authority as is referred to in subsection (3) below and either—

(a) at least 20 per cent of the total voting rights of all the members having the right to vote at a general meeting of the company are held by persons who are associated with the authority as mentioned in subsection (5) below; or

(b) at least 20 per cent of the directors of the company are persons who are so associated; or

(c) at least 20 per cent of the total voting rights at a meeting of the directors of the company are held by persons who are so associated.

(2) A direction under subsection (1) above—

(a) may be limited in time and may be made conditional upon such matters as appear to the Secretary of State to be appropriate; and

(b) may be made with respect to a particular company or a description of companies specified in the direction.

(3) For the purposes of this section there is a business relationship between a company and a local authority at any time if the condition in any one or more of the following paragraphs is fulfilled—

(a) within a period of twelve months which includes that time the aggregate of the payments to the company by the authority or by another company which is under the control of the authority represents more than one-half of the company's turnover, as shown in its profit and loss account for the most recent financial year for which the company's auditors have made a report on the accounts or, if there is no such account, as estimated by the authority for the period of twelve months preceding the date of the estimate or for such part of that period as follows the formation of the company;

(b) more than one-half of the company's turnover referred to in paragraph (a) above is derived from the exploitation of assets of any description in which the local authority or a company under the control of the authority has an interest (disregarding an interest in land which is in reversion on a lease granted for more than 7 years);

(c) the aggregate of—

(i) grants made either by the authority and being expenditure for capital purposes or by a company under the control of the authority, and

(ii) the nominal value of shares or stock in the company which is owned by the authority or by a company under the control of the authority,

exceeds one-half of the net assets of the company;

(d) the aggregate of—

(i) grants falling within paragraph (c)(i) above,

(ii) loans or other advances made or guaranteed by the authority or by a company under the control of the authority, and

(iii) the nominal value referred to in paragraph (c)(ii) above,

exceeds one-half of the fixed and current assets of the company;

(e) the company at that time occupies land by virtue of an interest which it obtained from the local authority or a company under the control of the authority and which it so obtained at less than the best consideration reasonably obtainable; and

(f) the company intends at that time to enter into (or complete) a transaction and, when that is done, there will then be a business relationship between the company and the authority by virtue of any of paragraphs (a) to (e) above.

(4) In subsection (3) above—

(a) the reference in paragraph (c) to the net assets of the company shall be construed in accordance with section 152(2) of the Companies Act 1985; and

(b) the reference in paragraph (d) to the fixed and current assets of the company shall be construed in accordance with paragraph 77 of Schedule 4 to that Act;

and in either case, the reference is a reference to those assets as shown in the most recent balance sheet of the company on which, at the time in question, the auditors have made a report or, if there is no such balance sheet, as estimated by the local authority for the time in question.

(5) For the purposes of this section, a person is at any time associated with a local authority if—

(a) he is at that time a member of the authority;

(b) he is at that time an officer of the authority;

(c) he is at that time both an employee and either a director, manager, secretary or other similar officer of a company which is under the control of the authority; or

(d) at any time within the preceding four years he has been associated with the authority by virtue of paragraph (a) above.

(6) If and to the extent that the Secretary of State by order so provides, a person is at any time associated with a local authority if—

(a) at that time he is, or is employed by or by a subsidiary of, a person who for the time being has a contractual relationship with the authority to provide—

(i) advice with regard to the authority's interest in any company (whether existing or proposed to be formed), or

(ii) advice with regard to the management of an undertaking or the development of land by a company (whether existing or proposed to be formed) with which it is proposed that the authority should enter into any lease, licence or other contract or to which it is proposed that the authority should make any grant or loan, or

(iii) services which facilitate the exercise of the authority's rights in any company (whether by acting as the authority's representative at a meeting of the company or as a director appointed by the authority or otherwise);

(b) at any time within the preceding four years, he has been associated with the authority by virtue of paragraph (b) or paragraph (c) of subsection (5) above;

(c) he is at that time the spouse [or civil partner] of, or carries on business in partnership with, a person who is associated with the authority by virtue of subsection (5)(a) above; or

(d) he holds a relevant office in a political association or other body which, in the nomination paper of a person who is an elected member of the authority, formed part of that person's description.

(7) For the purposes of subsection (6)(d) above, an office in a political association or body is relevant to a local authority in the following circumstances—

(a) if the association or body is active only in the area of the local authority, any office in it is relevant; and

(b) in any other case, an office is relevant only if it is in a branch or other part of the association or body which is active in the area of the local authority.

(8) In relation to a company which is an industrial and provident society, any reference in this section to the directors of the company is a reference to the members of the committee of management.

(9) Subject to subsections (4) and (8) and section 67 above, expressions used in this section have the same meaning as in the Companies Act 1985.

[727]

NOTES

Sub-s (6): words in square brackets in para (c) inserted by the Civil Partnership Act 2004, s 261(1), Sch 27, para 134.

70 Requirements for companies under control or subject to influence of local authorities

(1) In relation to companies under the control of local authorities and companies subject to the influence of local authorities, the Secretary of State may by order make provision regulating, forbidding or requiring the taking of certain actions or courses of action; and an order under this subsection may—

(a) make provision in relation to those companies which are arm's length companies different from that applicable to companies which are not; and

(b) make provision in relation to companies under the control of local authorities different from that applicable in relation to companies under the influence of local authorities.

(2) It shall be the duty of every local authority to ensure, so far as practicable, that any company under its control complies with [any provisions made by order under subsection (1) above which are for the time being applicable to it]; and if a local authority fails to perform that duty in relation to any company, any payment made by the authority to that company and any other expenditure incurred by the authority in contravention of any such provisions shall be deemed for the purposes of [the Audit Commission Act 1998] [and Part 2 of the Public Audit (Wales) Act 2004] to be expenditure which is unlawful.

(3) In order to secure compliance, in relation to companies subject to the influence of [a local authority], with provisions made by virtue of subsection (1) above, an order under that subsection may prescribe requirements to be complied with by [the] local authority in relation to conditions to be included in such leases, licences, contracts, gifts, grants or loans as may be so prescribed which are made with or to a company subject to the influence of the local authority.

(4) It shall be the duty of [local authority to comply with any requirements for the time being applicable to it] under subsection (3) above; and if a local authority fails to perform that duty, any expenditure which is incurred by the local authority under the lease, licence, contract, gift, grant or loan in question shall be deemed for the purposes of [the Audit Commission Act 1998] [and Part 2 of the Public Audit (Wales) Act 2004] to be expenditure which is unlawful.

(5) Without prejudice to the generality of the power conferred by subsection (1) above, an order under that subsection may make provision requiring a company or local authority to obtain the consent of the Secretary of State, or of the Audit Commission for Local Authorities in England and Wales, [or of the Auditor General for Wales,] before taking any particular action or course of action.

[(6) An order under subsection (1) may be made in relation to—

(a) all local authorities,

(b) particular local authorities, or
(c) particular descriptions of local authority.]

[728]

NOTES

Sub-s (2): words in first pair of square brackets substituted by the Local Government Act 2003, s 127(1), Sch 7, paras 28, 30(1), (2); words in second pair of square brackets substituted by the Audit Commission Act 1998, s 54(1), Sch 3, para 18(3)(a); words in third pair of square brackets inserted by the Public Audit (Wales) Act 2004, s 66, Sch 2, paras 10, 12(1), (2).

Sub-s (3): words in square brackets substituted by the Local Government Act 2003, s 127(1), Sch 7, paras 28, 30(1), (3).

Sub-s (4): words in first pair of square brackets substituted by the Local Government Act 2003, s 127(1), Sch 7, paras 28, 30(1), (4); words in second pair of square brackets substituted by the Audit Commission Act 1998, s 54(1), Sch 3, para 18(3)(b); words in third pair of square brackets inserted by the Public Audit (Wales) Act 2004, s 66, Sch 2, paras 10, 12(1), (3).

Sub-s (5): words in square brackets inserted by the Public Audit (Wales) Act 2004, s 66, Sch 2, paras 10, 12(1), (4).

Sub-s (6): added by the Local Government Act 2003, s 100(3), Sch 3, paras 1, 3.

Audit Commission for Local Authorities in England and Wales: this body was established by the Local Government Finance Act 1982, s 11, Sch 3 and was renamed the Audit Commission for Local Authorities and the National Health Service in England and Wales by virtue of the National Health Service and Community Care Act 1990, s 20(8).

Orders: the Local Authorities (Companies) Order 1995, SI 1995/849; the Public Audit (Wales) Act 2004 (Consequential Amendments) (Wales) Order 2005, SI 2005/757.

71 Controls of minority interests etc in certain companies

(1) In relation to a local authority, subsection (2) below applies to any company other than—

(a) a company which is or, if the action referred to in that subsection is taken, will be under the control of the local authority; and
(b) a company of a description specified for the purposes of this section by an order made by the Secretary of State;

and in this section an "authorised company" means a company falling within paragraph (b) above.

(2) Except with the approval of the Secretary of State, in relation to a company to which this subsection applies, a local authority may not—

(a) subscribe for, or acquire, whether in their own name or in the name of a nominee, any shares or share warrants in the company;
(b) become or remain a member of the company if it is limited by guarantee;
(c) exercise any power, however arising, to nominate any person to become a member of the company;
(d) exercise any power to appoint directors of the company;
(e) permit any officer of the authority, in the course of his employment, to make any such nomination or appointment as is referred to in paragraph (c) or paragraph (d) above; or
(f) permit an officer of the authority, in the course of his employment, to become or remain a member or director of the company.

(3) Any approval of the Secretary of State under subsection (2) above may be general or relate to any specific matter or company.

(4) A local authority may not take any action, or refrain from exercising any right, which would have the result that a person who is disqualified from membership of the authority (otherwise than by being employed by that or any other local authority or by a company which is under the control of a local authority) becomes a member or director of an authorised company or is authorised, in accordance with section 375 of the Companies Act 1985, to act as the authority's representative at a general meeting of an authorised company (or at meetings of an authorised company which include a general meeting).

(5) In any case where,—

(a) in accordance with section 375 of the Companies Act 1985, a local authority have authorised a member or officer of the authority to act as mentioned in subsection (4) above, or
(b) a member or officer of a local authority has become a member or director of an authorised company as mentioned in subsection (7) below,

the authority shall make arrangements (whether by standing orders or otherwise) for enabling members of the authority, in the course of proceedings of the authority (or of any committee or sub-committee thereof), [or, where a local authority is operating executive arrangements under Part II of the Local Government Act 2000, for enabling members of the executive, in the course of proceedings of the executive (or of any committee of the executive),] to put to the member or officer concerned questions about the activities of the company.

(6) Nothing in subsection (5) above shall require the member or officer referred to in that subsection to disclose any information about the company which has been communicated to him in confidence.

(7) Any member or officer of a local authority who has become a member or director of an authorised company by virtue of—

(a) a nomination made by the authority, or

(b) election at a meeting of the company at which voting rights were exercisable (whether or not exercised) by the authority or by a person bound to vote in accordance with the instructions of the authority, or

(c) an appointment made by the directors of another company, the majority of whom became directors of that company by virtue of a nomination made by the authority or election at a meeting of the company at which voting rights were exercisable as mentioned in paragraph (b) above,

shall make a declaration to the authority, in such form as they may require, of any remuneration or re-imbursement of expenses which he receives from the company as a member or director or in respect of anything done on behalf of the company.

(8) Subject to section 67 above, expressions used in this section have the same meaning as in the Companies Act 1985.

[729]

NOTES

Sub-s (5): words in square brackets inserted in relation to England by the Local Authorities (Executive and Alternative Arrangements) (Modification of Enactments and Other Provisions) (England) Order 2001, SI 2001/2237, arts 2(l), 26(1), and in relation to Wales by the Local Authorities (Executive and Alternative Arrangements) (Modification of Enactments and Other Provisions) (Wales) Order 2002, SI 2002/808, arts 2(k), 25(1).

Orders: the Local Authorities (Companies) Order 1995, SI 1995/849.

72 Trusts influenced by local authorities

(1) The Secretary of State may by order made by statutory instrument adapt the provisions of section 69 above so as to make them applicable to trusts which are not charitable; and, subject to subsection (2) below, this Part shall apply in relation to trusts which are subject to local authority influence by virtue of that section as so adapted as it applies in relation to companies which are subject to local authority influence.

(2) In the exercise of the power conferred by section 70 above, as applied in relation to trusts by subsection (1) above, the Secretary of State may make different provision for trusts as compared with companies.

[730]

73 Authorities acting jointly and by committees

(1) In any case where—

(a) apart from this section a company would not be under the control of any one local authority, but

(b) if the actions, powers and interests of two or more local authorities were treated as those of one authority alone, the company would be under the control of that one authority,

the company shall be treated for the purposes of this Part as under the control of each of the two or more local authorities mentioned in paragraph (b) above.

(2) In any case where, apart from this section, a company would not be treated as being subject to the influence of any one local authority, it shall be treated as being subject to the influence of each of a number of local authorities (in this section referred to as a "group") if the conditions in subsection (3) below are fulfilled with respect to the company and the group of authorities.

(3) The conditions referred to in subsection (2) above are—

(a) that at least one of the conditions in paragraphs (a) to (e) of subsection (3) of section 69 above would be fulfilled—
  (i) if any reference therein to the company being under the control of a local authority were a reference to its being under the control of any one of the authorities in the group or of any two or more of them taken together; and
  (ii) if any other reference therein to the local authority were a reference to any two or more of the authorities in the group taken together; and

(b) that at least one of the conditions in paragraphs (a) to (c) of subsection (1) of section 69 above would be fulfilled if any reference therein to the local authority were a reference to those local authorities who are taken into account under sub-paragraph (i) or sub-paragraph (ii) of paragraph (a) above taken together; and

(c) that if the condition (or one of the conditions) which would be fulfilled as mentioned in paragraph (b) above is that in subsection (1)(a) of section 69 above, then, so far as concerns each local authority in the group, at least one person who, in terms of subsection (5) of that section, is associated with that authority has the right to vote at a general meeting of the company; and

(d) that, if paragraph (c) above does not apply, then, so far as concerns each local authority in the group, a person who, in terms of section 69(5) above, is associated with the authority is a director of the company.

(4) For the purposes of this Part, anything done, and any power exercisable, by a committee or sub-committee of a local authority, or by any of the authority's officers [or, where a local authority is operating executive arrangements under Part II of the Local Government Act 2000, by the authority's executive, any committee of the executive, or any member of the executive], shall be treated as done or, as the case may be, exercisable by the authority.

(5) For the purposes of this Part, anything done, and any power exercisable, by a joint committee of two or more local authorities or by a sub-committee of such a joint committee shall be treated as done or, as the case may be, exercisable by each of the local authorities concerned.

[731]

NOTES

Sub-s (4): words in square brackets inserted in relation to England by the Local Authorities (Executive and Alternative Arrangements) (Modification of Enactments and Other Provisions) (England) Order 2001, SI 2001/2237, arts 2(1), 26(2), and in relation to Wales by the Local Authorities (Executive and Alternative Arrangements) (Modification of Enactments and Other Provisions) (Wales) Order 2002, SI 2002/808, arts 2(k), 25(2).

74–138 ((*Pts VI–VIII*) *outside the scope of this work.*)

PART IX
MISCELLANEOUS AND GENERAL

139–189 (*Outside the scope of this work.*)

Supplementary

190–194 (*Outside the scope of this work.*)

195 Short title, commencement and extent

(1) This Act may be cited as the Local Government and Housing Act 1989.

(2)–(6) (*Outside the scope of this work.*)

[732]

(*Schs 1–12 outside the scope of this work.*)

FINANCE ACT 1990

(1990 c 29)

An Act to grant certain duties, to alter other duties, and to amend the law relating to the National Debt and the Public Revenue, and to make further provision in connection with Finance

[26 July 1990]

1–16 ((*Pt I*) *outside the scope of this work.*)

PART II
INCOME TAX, CORPORATION TAX AND CAPITAL GAINS TAX

CHAPTER I
GENERAL

17–23 (*Outside the scope of this work.*)

Charities

24 (*Repealed by the Finance Act 1993, s 213, Sch 23, Pt III(10), with effect for the year 1994–95 and subsequent years of assessment.*)

25 Donations to charity by individuals

(1) For the purposes of this section, a gift to a charity by an individual ("the donor") is a qualifying donation if—

(a) it is made on or after 1st October 1990,

(b) it satisfies the requirements of subsection (2) below, and

(c) the donor gives [an appropriate declaration] in relation to it to the charity.

(2) A gift satisfies the requirements of this subsection if—

(a) it takes the form of a payment of a sum of money;

(b) it is not subject to a condition as to repayment;

(c) . . .

(d) it does not constitute a sum falling within [section 713(3) of the Income Tax (Earnings and Pensions) Act 2003] (payroll deduction scheme);

(e) neither the donor nor any person connected with him receives a benefit in consequence of making it or, where the donor or a person connected with him does receive a benefit in consequence of making it, the relevant value in relation to the gift does not exceed [the limit imposed by subsection (5A) below] and the amount to be taken into account for the purposes of this paragraph in relation to the gift does not exceed £250;

(f) it is not conditional on or associated with, or part of an arrangement involving, the acquisition of property by the charity, otherwise than by way of gift, from the donor or a person connected with him;

(g), (h) . . .; and

[(i) either—

(i) at the time the gift is made, the donor is resident in the United Kingdom [or is in Crown employment as defined in section 28(2) of the Income Tax (Earnings and Pensions) Act 2003]; or

(ii) the grossed up amount of the gift would, if in fact made, be payable out of profits or gains brought into charge to income tax or capital gains tax.]

[(3) The reference in subsection (1)(c) above to an appropriate declaration is a reference to a declaration which—

(a) is given in such manner as may be prescribed by regulations made by the Board; and

(b) contains such information and such statements as may be so prescribed.

(3A) Regulations made for the purposes of subsection (3) above may—

(a) provide for declarations to have effect, to cease to have effect or to be deemed never to have had effect in such circumstances and for such purposes as may be prescribed by the regulations;
(b) require charities to keep records with respect to declarations given to them by donors; and
(c) make different provision for declarations made in a different manner.]

(4) For the purposes of subsections (2)(e) above and (5) below, the relevant value in relation to a gift is—
(a) where there is one benefit received in consequence of making it which is received by the donor or a person connected with him, the value of that benefit;
(b) where there is more than one benefit received in consequence of making it which is received by the donor or a person connected with him, the aggregate value of all the benefits received in consequence of making it which are received by the donor or a person connected with him.

(5) The amount to be taken into account for the purposes of subsection (2)(e) above in relation to a gift to a charity is an amount equal to the aggregate of—
(a) the relevant value in relation to the gift, and
(b) the relevant value in relation to each gift, already made to the charity by the donor in the relevant year of assessment which is a qualifying donation for the purposes of this section.

[(5A) The limit imposed by this subsection is—
(a) where the amount of the gift does not exceed £100, 25 per cent of the amount of the gift;
(b) where the amount of the gift exceeds £100 but does not exceed £1,000, £25;
(c) where the amount of the gift exceeds £1,000, 2.5 per cent of the amount of the gift.

(5B) Where a benefit received in consequence of making a gift—
(a) consists of the right to receive benefits at intervals over a period of less than twelve months;
(b) relates to a period of less than twelve months; or
(c) is one of a series of benefits received at intervals in consequence of making a series of gifts at intervals of less than twelve months,

the value of the benefit shall be adjusted for the purposes of subsection (4) above and the amount of the gift shall be adjusted for the purposes of subsection (5A) above.

(5C) Where a benefit, other than a benefit which is one of a series of benefits received at intervals, is received in consequence of making a gift which is one of a series of gifts made at intervals of less than twelve months, the amount of the gift shall be adjusted for the purposes of subsection (5A) above.

(5D) Where the value of a benefit, or the amount of a gift, falls to be adjusted under subsection (5B) or (5C) above, the value or amount shall be multiplied by 365 and the result shall be divided by—
(a) in a case falling within subsection (5B)(a) or (b) above, the number of days in the period of less than twelve months;
(b) in a case falling within subsection (5B)(c) or (5C) above, the average number of days in the intervals of less than twelve months;

and the reference in subsection (5B) above to subsection (4) above is a reference to that subsection as it applies for the purposes of subsection (2)(e) above.

[(5E) In determining whether a gift to a charity is a qualifying donation the benefit of any right of admission received in consequence of the gift shall be disregarded if subsections (5F) to (5H) are satisfied in relation to the right.

(5F) This subsection is satisfied if the opportunity to make a gift and to receive the right of admission in consequence is available to the public.

(5G) This subsection is satisfied if the right of admission is a right granted by the charity for the purpose of viewing property preserved, maintained, kept or created by a charity in pursuance of its charitable purposes, including, in particular—
(a) buildings,
(b) grounds or other land,
(c) plants,
(d) animals,

(e) works of art (but not performances),
(f) artefacts, and
(g) property of a scientific nature.

(5H) This subsection is satisfied if—
(a) the right of admission applies, during a period of at least one year, at all times at which the public can obtain admission, or
(b) a member of the public could purchase the same right of admission and the amount of the gift is greater by at least 10% than the amount which he would have to pay.

(5I) In subsection (5E) "right of admission" means a right of admission—
(a) of the person who makes the gift or of that person and one or more members of his family (whether or not the right must be exercised by all those persons at the same time),
(b) to premises or property to which the public are admitted on payment of an admission fee, and
(c) without payment of the admission fee or on payment of a reduced fee;

and in the application of subsection (5H)(b) "the same right of admission" means a right relating to the same property, classes of person and periods of time as the right received in consequence of the gift.

(5J) For the purposes of subsection (5H)(a) a right of admission shall be treated as applying at all times at which the public can obtain admission despite the fact that the right does not apply on days specified by the charity, being days on each of which an event is to take place on the premises to which the right relates; provided that no more than 5 days are specified for that purpose in relation to—
(a) the period during which the right applies, in the case of a period of one year, or
(b) each calendar year during all or part of which the right applies, in the case of a right applying for a period of more than one year.]]

[(6) Where any gift made by the donor in a year of assessment is a qualifying donation, then, for that year—
(a) the Income Tax Acts and the Taxation of Chargeable Gains Act 1992 shall have effect, in their application to him, as if—
(i) the gift had been made after deduction of income tax at the basic rate; and
(ii) the basic rate limit were increased by an amount equal to the grossed up amount of the gift;
(b) the provisions mentioned in subsection (7) below shall have effect, in their application to him, as if any reference to income tax which he is entitled to charge against any person included a reference to the tax treated as deducted from the gift; and
(c) to the extent, if any, necessary to ensure that he is charged to an amount of income tax and capital gains tax equal to the tax treated as deducted from the gift, he shall not be entitled to relief under Chapter I of Part VII of the Taxes Act 1988;

but paragraph (a)(ii) above shall not apply for the purposes of any computation under [sections 535 to 537 of the Income Tax (Trading and Other Income) Act 2005 (top slicing relief)].

(7) The provisions referred to in subsection (6)(b) above are—
(a) section 289A(5)(e) of the Taxes Act 1988 (relief under enterprise investment scheme);
(b) section 796(3) of that Act (credit for foreign tax); …
(c) paragraph 1(6)(f) of Schedule 15B to that Act (venture capital trusts) [and
(d) paragraph 19(6)(d) of Schedule 16 to the Finance Act 2002.]

(8) Where the tax treated as deducted from a gift by virtue of subsection (6) above exceeds the amount of income tax and capital gains tax with which the donor is charged for the year of assessment, the donor shall be assessable and chargeable with income tax at the basic rate on so much of the gift as is necessary to recover an amount of tax equal to the excess.

(9) In determining for the purposes of subsection (8) above the total amount of income tax and capital gains tax with which the donor is charged for the year of assessment, there shall be disregarded—
(a) any tax charged at the basic rate by virtue of—
(i) section 348 of the Taxes Act 1988 (read with section 3 of that Act); or

(ii) section 349 of that Act (read with section 350 of that Act);

[(b) any tax treated as having been paid under—

(i) section 399(2) or 400(2) of the Income Tax (Trading and Other Income) Act 2005 (distributions from UK resident companies etc on which there is no tax credit);

(ii) section 414(1) of that Act (stock dividend income);

(iii) section 421(1) of that Act (release of loan to participator in close company); …

(iv) section 530(1) of that Act (gains from contracts for life insurance etc); [or

(v) section 685A(2) of that Act (payments from settlor-interested settlements);]]

[(ba) any tax paid to meet the lifetime allowance charge or the annual allowance charge (under Part 4 of the Finance Act 2004);]

(c) any relief to which section 256(2) [of the Taxes Act 1988] applies (relief by way of income tax reduction);

(d) any relief under—

(i) section 347B of that Act (relief for maintenance payments);

(ii) section 788 of that Act (relief by agreement with other countries); or

(iii) section 790(1) of that Act (unilateral relief);

(e) any set off of tax deducted, or treated as deducted, from income other than—

(i) …

(ii) tax treated as deducted from [estate income under section 656(3) or 657(4) of the Income Tax (Trading and Other Income) Act 2005, so far as that income is treated under section 679 of that Act as paid from sums within section 680(3)(b) or (4) of that Act]; and

(f) any set off of tax credits.

(9A) For the purposes of sections 257(5)[, 257A(5) and 257AB(4)] of the Taxes Act 1988 (age related allowances), the donor's total income shall be treated as reduced by the aggregate amount of gifts from which tax is treated as deducted by virtue of subsection (6) above.]

(10) The receipt by a charity of a gift which is a qualifying donation shall be treated for the purposes of the Tax Acts, in their application to the charity, as the receipt, under deduction of income tax at the basic rate for the relevant year of assessment, of an annual payment of an amount equal to the grossed up amount of the gift.

(11) Section 839 of the Taxes Act 1988 applies for the purposes of subsections (2) and (4) above.

(12) For the purposes of this section—

(a) "charity" has the same meaning as in section 506 of the Taxes Act 1988 and includes each of the bodies mentioned in section 507 of that Act;

(b) …

(c) "relevant year of assessment", in relation to a gift, means the year of assessment in which the gift is made;

(d) references, in relation to a gift, to the grossed up amount are to the amount which after deducting income tax at the basic rate for the relevant year of assessment leaves the amount of the gift; …

(e) …

[(13) This section is to be read with—

(a) section 98 of the Finance Act 2002 (gift aid: election to be treated as if gift made in previous tax year);

(b) section 83 of the Finance Act 2004 (gift aid: giving through the self-assessment return).]

[733]

NOTES

Sub-s (1): in para (c) words in square brackets substituted by the Finance Act 2000, s 39(1), (2), (10), in relation to gifts made on or after 6 April 2000 which are not covenanted payments and covenanted payments falling to be made on or after that date.

Sub-s (2): paras (c), (g) repealed and words in square brackets in para (e) substituted by the Finance Act 2000, ss 39(1), (3)(a), (b), (10), 156, Sch 40, Pt II(1), in relation to gifts made on or after 6 April 2000 which are not covenanted payments and covenanted payments falling to be made on or after that date; words in square brackets in para (d) substituted by the Income Tax (Earnings and Pensions) Act 2003, ss 722, 723, Sch 6, Pt 2, paras 165, 166(1), (2), with effect for income tax purposes, for the tax year 2003–04 and subsequent tax years, and for corporation tax purposes, for accounting periods ending after

5 April 2003; para (h) repealed by the Finance Act 1991, ss 71(5), (6), 123, Sch 19, Pt V, in relation to gifts made on or after 19 March 1991; para (i) substituted by the Finance Act 2000, s 39(1), (3)(c) (10), in relation to gifts made on or after 6 April 2000 which are not covenanted payments and covenanted payments falling to be made on or after that date; words in square brackets in para (i) substituted by the Finance Act 2004, s 92, Sch 7, para 5, with effect for the year 2003–2004 and subsequent years of assessment.

Sub-ss (3), (3A): substituted for original sub-s (3) by the Finance Act 2000, s 39(1), (4), (10), in relation to gifts made on or after 6 April 2000 which are not covenanted payments and covenanted payments falling to be made on or after that date.

Sub-ss (5A)–(5D): inserted, together with sub-ss (5E)–(5G), by the Finance Act 2000, s 39(1), (5), (10), in relation to gifts made on or after 6 April 2000 which are not covenanted payments and covenanted payments falling to be made on or after that date.

Sub-ss (5E)–(5G): inserted, together with sub-ss (5A)–(5D), by the Finance Act 2000, s 39(1), (5), (10), in relation to gifts made on or after 6 April 2000 which are not covenanted payments and covenanted payments falling to be made on or after that date; substituted, together with sub-ss (5H)–(5J), for original sub-ss (5E)–(5G), by the Finance (No 2) Act 2005, s 11, with effect in relation to gifts made on or after 6 April 2006.

Sub-ss (5H)–(5J): substituted, together with sub-ss (5E)–(5G), for original sub-ss (5E)–(5G), by the Finance (No 2) Act 2005, s 11, with effect in relation to gifts made on or after 6 April 2006

Sub-s (6): substituted, together with sub-ss (7)–(9), (9A), for original sub-ss (6)–(9) by the Finance Act 2000, s 39(1), (6), (10), in relation to gifts made on or after 6 April 2000 which are not covenanted payments and covenanted payments falling to be made on or after that date; words in square brackets substituted by the Income Tax (Trading and Other Income) Act 2005, ss 882(1), 883, Sch 1, Pt 2, paras 414, 415(1), (2), with effect for income tax purposes, for the tax year 2005–06 and subsequent tax years, and for corporation tax purposes, for accounting periods ending after 5 April 2005.

Sub-s (7): substituted, together with sub-ss (6), (8), (9), (9A), for original sub-ss (6)–(9) by the Finance Act 2000, s 39(1), (6), (10), in relation to gifts made on or after 6 April 2000 which are not covenanted payments and covenanted payments falling to be made on or after that date; words omitted repealed, and para (d) and word 'and' immediately preceding it added, by the Finance Act 2002, ss 57(2)–(4), 141, Sch 17, para 4, Sch 40, Pt 3(6), with effect in relation to years of assessment ending on or after 17 April 2002.

Sub-s (8): substituted, together with sub-ss (6), (7), (9), (9A), for original sub-ss (6)–(9) by the Finance Act 2000, s 39(1), (6), (10), in relation to gifts made on or after 6 April 2000 which are not covenanted payments and covenanted payments falling to be made on or after that date.

Sub-s (9): substituted, together with sub-ss (6)–(8), (9A), for original sub-ss (6)–(9) by the Finance Act 2000, s 39(1), (6), (10), in relation to gifts made on or after 6 April 2000 which are not covenanted payments and covenanted payments falling to be made on or after that date; para (b) substituted by the Income Tax (Trading and Other Income) Act 2005, ss 882(1), 883, Sch 1, Pt 2, paras 414, 415(1), (3)(a), with effect for income tax purposes, for the tax year 2005–06 and subsequent tax years, and for corporation tax purposes, for accounting periods ending after 5 April 2005, word omitted from para (b)(iii) repealed, and para (b)(v) and word 'or' immediately preceding it added by the Finance Act 2006, ss 89, 178, Sch 13, Pt 2, para 30, Pt 3(15); para (ba) inserted by the Finance Act 2004, s 281(1), Sch 35, para 37, for transitional provisions and savings see s 283(1) of, and Sch 36 to, that Act; words in square brackets in paras (c), (e) substituted and words omitted from para (e) repealed by the Income Tax (Trading and Other Income) Act 2005, ss 882(1), 883, 884, Sch 1, Pt 2, paras 414, 415(1), (3)(b), (c), Sch 4, with effect for income tax purposes, for the tax year 2005–06 and subsequent tax years, and for corporation tax purposes, for accounting periods ending after 5 April 2005.

Sub-s (9A): substituted, together with sub-ss (6)–(9), for original sub-ss (6)–(9) by the Finance Act 2000, s 39(1), (6), (10), in relation to gifts made on or after 6 April 2000 which are not covenanted payments and covenanted payments falling to be made on or after that date; words in square brackets substituted by the Tax and Civil Partnership Regulations 2005, SI 2005/3229, reg 104 with effect for the year 2005–06 and subsequent years.

Sub-s (12): para (b), and para (e) and the word omitted preceding it, repealed by the Finance Act 2000, ss 39(1), (7), (10), 156, Sch 40, Pt II(1), in relation to gifts made on or after 6 April 2000 which are not covenanted payments and covenanted payments falling to be made on or after that date.

Sub-s (13): added by the Finance Act 2004, s 83(6), (7), with effect in relation to personal returns for the year 2003–04 and subsequent years of assessment

Taxes Act 1988: ie, the Income and Corporation Taxes Act 1988.

For the application of this section in relation to amateur sports clubs, see the Finance Act 2002, s 58, Sch 18, Pt 3, para 9(1).

Regulations: the Donations to Charity by Individuals (Appropriate Declarations) Regulations 2000, SI 2000/2074, at **[3351]**.

26–114 *(Ss 26, 27(2) amend the Income and Corporation Tax Act 1988,s 339 at* **[699]**; *s 27(1), (3) repealed by the Finance Act 1991, s 123, Sch 19, Part V, in relation to accounting periods beginning on or after 19 March 1991; ss 28–106, ss 107–114 (Pt III) outside the scope of this work.)*

PART IV
MISCELLANEOUS AND GENERAL

115–130 (*In so far as unrepealed outside the scope of this work.*)

General

131, 132 (*Outside the scope of this work.*)

133 Short title

This Act may be cited as the Finance Act 1990.

[734]

(*Schs 1–19 outside the scope of this work.*)

TAXATION OF CHARGEABLE GAINS ACT 1992

(1992 c 12)

An Act to consolidate certain enactments relating to the taxation of chargeable gains

[6 March 1992]

1–221 ((*Pts I–VI*) *outside the scope of this work.*)

PART VII
OTHER PROPERTY, BUSINESSES, INVESTMENTS ETC

222–255 (*Outside the scope of this work.*)

Charities and gifts of non-business assets etc

256 Charities

(1) Subject to [section 505(4)] of the Taxes Act and subsection (2) below, a gain shall not be a chargeable gain if it accrues to a charity and is applicable and applied for charitable purposes.

(2) If property held on charitable trusts ceases to be subject to charitable trusts—

(a) the trustees shall be treated as if they had disposed of, and immediately reacquired, the property for a consideration equal to its market value, any gain on the disposal being treated as not accruing to a charity, and

(b) if and so far as any of that property represents, directly or indirectly, the consideration for the disposal of assets by the trustees, any gain accruing on that disposal shall be treated as not having accrued to a charity,

and an assessment to capital gains tax chargeable by virtue of paragraph (b) above may be made at any time not more than 3 years after the end of the year of assessment in which the property ceases to be subject to charitable trusts.

[735]

NOTES

Sub-s (1): words in square brackets substituted by the Finance Act 2006, s 55(4), with effect in relation to chargeable periods beginning on or after 22 March 2006.

Taxes Act: ie, the Income and Corporation Taxes Act 1988.

For the application of this section in relation to amateur sports clubs, see the Finance Act 2002, s 58, Sch 18, Pt 3, para 9(3).

257 Gifts to charities etc

(1) Subsection (2) below shall apply where a disposal of an asset is made otherwise than under a bargain at arm's length—

(a) to a charity, or

(b) to any bodies mentioned in Schedule 3 to the Inheritance Tax Act 1984 (gifts for national purposes, etc)

[and the disposal is not one in relation to which section 151A(1) has effect.]

(2) Sections 17(1) and 258(3) shall not apply; but if the disposal is by way of gift (including a gift in settlement) or for a consideration not exceeding the sums allowable as a deduction under section 38, then—

(a) the disposal and acquisition shall be treated for the purposes of this Act as being made for such consideration as to secure that neither a gain nor a loss accrues on the disposal, and

(b) where, after the disposal, the asset is disposed of by the person who acquired it under the disposal, its acquisition by the person making the earlier disposal shall be treated for the purposes of this Act as the acquisition of the person making the later disposal.

(3) Where—

(a) otherwise than on the termination of a life interest (within the meaning of section 72) by the death of the person entitled thereto, any assets or parts of any assets forming part of settled property are, under section 71, deemed to be disposed of and reacquired by the trustee, and

(b) the person becoming entitled as mentioned in section 71(1) is a charity, or a body mentioned in Schedule 3 to the Inheritance Tax Act 1984 (gifts for national purposes, etc),

then, if no consideration is received by any person for or in connection with any transaction by virtue of which the charity or other body becomes so entitled, the disposal and reacquisition of the assets to which the charity or other body becomes so entitled shall, notwithstanding section 71, be treated for the purposes of this Act as made for such consideration as to secure that neither a gain nor a loss accrues on the disposal.

(4) In subsection (2)(b) above the first reference to a disposal includes a disposal to which section 146(2) of the 1979 Act applied where the person who acquired the asset on that disposal disposes of the asset after the coming into force of this section.

[736]

NOTES

Sub-s (1): words in square brackets added by the Finance Act 1995, s 72(1), (5), (8), in relation to the year 1995–96 and subsequent years of assessment.

1972 Act: Capital Gains Act 1972: repealed by s 290(3) of, and Sch 12 to, this Act.

258–271 (*Outside the scope of this work.*)

PART VIII
SUPPLEMENTAL

272–288 (*Outside the scope of this work.*)

289 Commencement

(1) Except where the context otherwise requires, this Act has effect in relation to tax for the year 1992–93 and subsequent years of assessment, and tax for other chargeable periods beginning on or after 6th April 1992, and references to the coming into force of this Act or any provision in this Act shall be construed accordingly.

(2) The following provisions of this Act, that is—

(a) so much of any provision of this Act as authorises the making of any order or other instrument, and

(b) except where the tax concerned is all tax for chargeable periods to which this Act does not apply, so much of any provision of this Act as confers any power or imposes any duty the exercise or performance of which operates or may operate in relation to tax for more than one chargeable period,

shall come into force for all purposes on 6th April 1992 to the exclusion of the corresponding enactments repealed by this Act.

[737]

290 (*Outside the scope of this work.*)

291 Short title

This Act may be cited as the Taxation of Chargeable Gains Act 1992.

[738]

(*Schs A1–12 outside the scope of this work.*)

CHARITIES ACT 1992

(1992 c 41)

ARRANGEMENT OF SECTIONS

PART I
CHARITIES

Preliminary

Charity property

Miscellaneous and supplementary

PART II
CONTROL OF FUND-RAISING FOR CHARITABLE INSTITUTIONS

Preliminary

Control of fund-raising

Supplementary

PART IV
GENERAL

An Act to amend the Charities Act 1960 and make other provision with respect to charities; to regulate fund-raising activities carried on in connection with charities and other institutions; to make fresh provision with respect to public charitable collections; and for connected purposes

[16 March 1992]

PART I
CHARITIES

Preliminary

1 Interpretation of Part I, etc

(1) In this Part—

"the 1960 Act" means the Charities Act 1960;

"financial year"—

(*a*) *in relation to a charity which is a company, shall be construed in accordance with section 223 of the Companies Act 1985; and*

(*b*) *in relation to any other charity, shall be construed in accordance with regulations made by virtue of section 20(2);*

"gross income", in relation to a charity, means its gross recorded income from all sources, including special trusts;

"independent examiner", in relation to a charity, means such a person as is mentioned in section 21(3)(a);

"the official custodian" means the official custodian for charities;

"the register" (unless the context otherwise requires) means the register of charities kept under section 4 of the 1960 Act, and "registered" shall be construed accordingly;

"special trust" means property which is held and administered by or on behalf of a charity for any special purposes of the charity, and is so held and administered on separate trusts relating only to that property.

(2), (3) ...

(4) No vesting or transfer of any property in pursuance of any provision of this Part, or of any provision of the 1960 Act as amended by this Part, shall operate as a breach of a covenant or condition against alienation or give rise to a forfeiture.

[739]

NOTES

Commencement: 1 September 1992 (sub-s (1) (except definitions "financial year", "independent examiner" and "special trust"), sub-s (4)); to be appointed (definitions noted above).

Pt I (in so far as unrepealed) and Pt III of this Act are repealed by the Charities Act 2006, s 75(2), Sch 9, as from a day to be appointed under s 79(2) of that Act.

Sub-ss (2), (3): repealed by the Charities Act 1993, s 98(2), Sch 7.

2–28 (*Repealed by the Charities Act 1993, s 98(2), Sch 7.*)

Charity property

29 Divestment of charity property held by official custodian for charities

(1) The official custodian shall, in accordance with this section, divest himself of all property to which this subsection applies.

(2) Subsection (1) applies to any property held by the official custodian in his capacity as such, with the exception of—

(*a*) *any land; and*

(*b*) *any property (other than land) which is vested in him by virtue of an order of the Commissioners under section 20 of the 1960 Act [or section 18 of the Charities Act 1993] (power to act for protection of charities).*

(3) Where property to which subsection (1) applies is held by the official custodian in trust for particular charities, he shall (subject to subsection (7)) divest himself of that property in such manner as the Commissioners may direct.

(4) *Without prejudice to the generality of subsection (3), directions given by the Commissioners under that subsection may make different provision in relation to different property held by the official custodian or in relation to different classes or descriptions of property held by him, including (in particular)—*

(*a*) *provision designed to secure that the divestment required by subsection (1) is effected in stages or by means of transfers or other disposals taking place at different times;*

(*b*) *provision requiring the official custodian to transfer any specified investments, or any specified class or description of investments, held by him in trust for a charity—*

(*i*) *to the charity trustees or any trustee for the charity, or*

(*ii*) *to a person nominated by the charity trustees to hold any such investments in trust for the charity;*

(*c*) *provision requiring the official custodian to sell or call in any specified investments, or any specified class or description of investments, so held by him and to pay any proceeds of sale or other money accruing therefrom—*

(*i*) *to the charity trustees or any trustee for the charity, or*

(*ii*) *into any bank account kept in its name.*

(5) *The charity trustees of a charity may, in the case of any property falling to be transferred by the official custodian in accordance with a direction under subsection (3), nominate a person to hold any such property in trust for the charity; but a person shall not be so nominated unless—*

(*a*) *if an individual, he resides in England and Wales; or*

(*b*) *if a body corporate, it has a place of business there.*

(6) *Directions under subsection (3) shall, in the case of any property vested in the official custodian by virtue of section 22(6) of the 1960 Act (common investment funds), provide for any such property to be transferred—*

(*a*) *to the trustees appointed to manage the common investment fund concerned; or*

(*b*) *to any person nominated by those trustees who is authorised by or under the common investment scheme concerned to hold that fund or any part of it.*

(7) *Where the official custodian—*

(*a*) *holds any relevant property in trust for a charity, but*

(*b*) *after making reasonable inquiries is unable to locate the charity or any of its trustees,*

he shall—

(*i*) *unless the relevant property is money, sell the property and hold the proceeds of sale pending the giving by the Commissioners of a direction under subsection (8);*

(*ii*) *if the relevant property is money, hold it pending the giving of any such direction;*

and for this purpose "relevant property" means any property to which subsection (1) applies or any proceeds of sale or other money accruing to the official custodian in consequence of a direction under subsection (3).

(8) *Where subsection (7) applies in relation to a charity ("the dormant charity"), the Commissioners may direct the official custodian—*

(*a*) *to pay such amount as is held by him in accordance with that subsection to such other charity as is specified in the direction in accordance with subsection (9), or*

(*b*) *to pay to each of two or more other charities so specified in the direction such part of that amount as is there specified in relation to that charity.*

(9) *The Commissioners may specify in a direction under subsection (8) such charity or charities as they consider appropriate, being in each case a charity whose purposes are, in the opinion of the Commissioners, as similar in character to those of the dormant charity as is reasonably practicable; but the Commissioners shall not so specify any charity unless they have received from the charity trustees written confirmation that they are willing to accept the amount proposed to be paid to the charity.*

(10) *Any amount received by a charity by virtue of subsection (8) shall be received by the charity on terms that—*

(*a*) *it shall be held and applied by the charity for the purposes of the charity, but*

(*b*) *it shall, as property of the charity, nevertheless be subject to any restrictions on expenditure to which it, or (as the case may be) the property which it represents, was subject as property of the dormant charity.*

(11) At such time as the Commissioners are satisfied that the official custodian has divested himself of all property held by him in trust for particular charities, all remaining funds held by him as official custodian shall be paid by him into the Consolidated Fund.

(12) Nothing in subsection (11) applies in relation to any property held by the official custodian which falls within subsection (2)(a) or (b).

(13) In this section "land" does not include any interest in land by way of mortgage or other security.

[740]

NOTES

Repealed as noted to s 1 at **[739]**.

Sub-s (2): words in square brackets inserted by the Charities Act 1993, s 98(1), Sch 6, para 29(1), (2).

1960 Act: i e Charities Act 1960: s 20 was repealed by the Charities Act 1993, s 98(2), Sch 7 and replaced by s 18 of that Act. S 22(6) was repealed by ss 47, 78(2) of, and Sch 3, para 9, Sch 7 to, this Act.

30 Provisions supplementary to s 29

(1) Any directions of the Commissioners under section 29 above shall have effect notwithstanding anything—

- *(a) in the trusts of a charity, or*
- *(b) in section 17(1) of the 1960 Act [or section 22(1) of the Charities Act 1993] (supplementary provisions as to property vested in official custodian).*

(2) Subject to subsection (3), any provision—

- *(a) of the trusts of a charity, or*
- *(b) of any directions given by an order of the Commissioners made in connection with a transaction requiring the sanction of an order under section 29(1) of the 1960 Act (restrictions on dealing with charity property),*

shall cease to have effect if and to the extent that it requires or authorises personal property of the charity to be transferred to or held by the official custodian; and for this purpose "personal property" extends to any mortgage or other real security, but does not include any interest in land other than such an interest by way of mortgage or other security.

(3) Subsection (2) does not apply to—

- *(a) any provision of an order made under section 20 of the 1960 Act [or section 18 of the Charities Act 1993] (power to act for protection of charities); or*
- *(b) any provision of any other order, or of any scheme, of the Commissioners if the provision requires trustees of a charity to make payments into an account maintained by the official custodian with a view to the accumulation of a sum as capital of the charity (whether or not by way of recoupment of a sum expended out of the charity's permanent endowment);*

but any such provision as is mentioned in paragraph (b) shall have effect as if, instead of requiring the trustees to make such payments into an account maintained by the official custodian, it required the trustees to make such payments into an account maintained by them or by any other person (apart from the official custodian) who is either a trustee for the charity or a person nominated by them to hold such payments in trust for the charity.

(4) The disposal of any property by the official custodian in accordance with section 29 above shall operate to discharge him from his trusteeship of that property.

(5) Where any instrument issued by the official custodian in connection with any such disposal contains a printed reproduction of his official seal, that instrument shall have the same effect as if it were duly sealed with his official seal.

[741]

NOTES

Repealed as noted to s 1 at **[739]**.

Sub-ss (1), (3): words in square brackets inserted by the Charities Act 1993, s 98(1), Sch 6, para 29(1), (3), (4).

1960 Act: i e Charities Act 1960: ss 17(1), 20 was repealed by the Charities Act 1993, s 98(2), Sch 7. S 29 was repealed by s 78(2) of, and Sch 7 to, this Act.

31–35 (*Repealed by the Charities Act 1993, s 98(2), Sch 7.*)

36 Removal of requirements under statutory provisions for consent to dealings with charity land

(1) Any provision—

(a) establishing or regulating a particular charity and contained in, or having effect under, any Act of Parliament, or

(b) contained in the trusts of a charity,

shall cease to have effect if and to the extent that it provides for dispositions of, or other dealings with, land held by or in trust for the charity to require the consent of the Commissioners (whether signified by order or otherwise).

(2) Any provision of an order or scheme under the Education Act 1944 or the Education Act 1973 relating to a charity shall cease to have effect if and to the extent that it requires, in relation to any sale, lease or other disposition of land held by or in trust for the charity, approval by the Commissioners or the Secretary of State of the amount for which the land is to be sold, leased or otherwise disposed of.

(3) In this section "land" means land in England or Wales.

[742]

NOTES

Repealed as noted to s 1 at **[739]**, subject to savings in Sch 10, para 29(1), (2)(b) to that Act at **[2176]**.
Education Act 1944: repealed by the Education Act 1996, s 582(2), Sch 38, Pt I.

37–46 *(Repealed by the Charities Act 1993, s 98(2), Sch 7.)*

Miscellaneous and supplementary

47–49 *(Ss 47, 48 repealed by the Charities Act 1993, s 98(2), Sch 7; s 49 introduces Sch 5 to this Act (outside the scope of this work).)*

50 Contributions towards maintenance etc of almshouses

(1) Any provision in the trusts of an almshouse charity which relates to the payment by persons resident in the charity's almshouses of contributions towards the cost of maintaining those almshouses and essential services in them shall cease to have effect if and to the extent that it provides for the amount, or the maximum amount, of such contributions to be a sum specified, approved or authorised by the Commissioners.

(2) In subsection (1)—

"almshouse" means any premises maintained as an almshouse, whether they are called an almshouse or not; and

"almshouse charity" means a charity which is authorised under its trusts to maintain almshouses.

[743]

NOTES

Repealed as noted to s 1 at **[739]**, subject to savings in Sch 10, para 29(1), (2)(c) to that Act at **[2176]**.

51–57 *(Repealed by the Charities Act 1993, s 98(2), Sch 7.)*

PART II
CONTROL OF FUND-RAISING FOR CHARITABLE INSTITUTIONS

Preliminary

58 Interpretation of Part II

(1) In this Part—

"charitable contributions", in relation to any representation made by any commercial participator or other person, means—

(a) the whole or part of—

(i) the consideration given for goods or services sold or supplied by him, or
(ii) any proceeds (other than such consideration) of a promotional venture undertaken by him, or

(b) sums given by him by way of donation in connection with the sale or supply of any such goods or services (whether the amount of such sums is determined by reference to the value of any such goods or services or otherwise);

"charitable institution" means a charity or an institution (other than a charity) which is established for charitable, benevolent or philanthropic purposes;

"charity" means a charity within the meaning of [the Charities Act 1993];

"commercial participator", in relation to any charitable institution, means any person [(apart from a company connected with the institution)] who—

(a) carries on for gain a business other than a fund-raising business, but
(b) in the course of that business, engages in any promotional venture in the course of which it is represented that charitable contributions are to be given to or applied for the benefit of the institution;

"company" has the meaning given by section [97 of the Charities Act 1993];

"the court" means the High Court or a county court;

"credit card" means a card which is a credit-token within the meaning of the Consumer Credit Act 1974;

"debit card" means a card the use of which by its holder to make a payment results in a current account of his at a bank, or at any other institution providing banking services, being debited with the payment;

"fund-raising business" means any business carried on for gain and wholly or primarily engaged in soliciting or otherwise procuring money or other property for charitable, benevolent or philanthropic purposes;

"institution" includes any trust or undertaking;

["the Minister" means the Minister for the Cabinet Office;]

"professional fund-raiser" means—

(a) any person (apart from a charitable institution [or a company connected with such an institution]) who carries on a fund-raising business, or
(b) any other person (apart from a person excluded by virtue of subsection (2) or (3)) who for reward solicits money or other property for the benefit of a charitable institution, if he does so otherwise than in the course of any fund-raising venture undertaken by a person falling within paragraph (a) above;

"promotional venture" means any advertising or sales campaign or any other venture undertaken for promotional purposes;

"radio or television programme" includes any item included in a programme service within the meaning of the Broadcasting Act 1990.

(2) In subsection (1), paragraph (b) of the definition of "professional fund-raiser" does not apply to any of the following, namely—

(a) any charitable institution or any company connected with any such institution;
(b) any officer or employee of any such institution or company, or any trustee of any such institution, acting (in each case) in his capacity as such;
(c) any person acting as a collector in respect of a public charitable collection (apart from a person who is *to be treated as a promoter of such a collection by virtue of section 65(3)*);
(d) any person who in the course of a relevant programme, that is to say a radio or television programme in the course of which a fund-raising venture is undertaken by—
 (i) a charitable institution, or
 (ii) a company connected with such an institution,

makes any solicitation at the instance of that institution or company; or

(e) any commercial participator;

and for this purpose "collector" and "public charitable collection" have the same meaning as in *Part III of this Act*.

(3) In addition, paragraph (b) of the definition of "professional fund-raiser" does not apply to a person if he does not receive—

(a) more than—
 (i) £5 per day, or
 (ii) £500 per year,

by way of remuneration in connection with soliciting money or other property for the benefit of the charitable institution referred to in that paragraph; or

(b) more than £500 by way of remuneration in connection with any fund-raising venture in the course of which he solicits money or other property for the benefit of that institution.

(4) In this Part any reference to charitable purposes, where occurring in the context of a reference to charitable, benevolent or philanthropic purposes, is a reference to charitable purposes *whether or not the purposes are charitable within the meaning of any rule of law*.

(5) For the purposes of this Part a company is connected with a charitable institution if—

(a) the institution, or

(b) the institution and one or more other charitable institutions, taken together,

is or are entitled (whether directly or through one or more nominees) to exercise, or control the exercise of, the whole of the voting power at any general meeting of the company.

(6) In this Part—

(a) "represent" and "solicit" mean respectively represent and solicit in any manner whatever, whether expressly or impliedly and whether done—

(i) by speaking directly to the person or persons to whom the representation or solicitation is addressed (whether when in his or their presence or not), or

(ii) by means of a statement published in any newspaper, film or radio or television programme,

or otherwise, and references to a representation or solicitation shall be construed accordingly; and

(b) any reference to soliciting or otherwise procuring money or other property is a reference to soliciting or otherwise procuring money or other property whether any consideration is, or is to be, given in return for the money or other property or not.

(7) Where—

(a) any solicitation of money or other property for the benefit of a charitable institution is made in accordance with arrangements between any person and that institution, and

(b) under those arrangements that person will be responsible for receiving on behalf of the institution money or other property given in response to the solicitation,

then (if he would not be so regarded apart from this subsection) that person shall be regarded for the purposes of this Part as soliciting money or other property for the benefit of the institution.

(8) Where any fund-raising venture is undertaken by a professional fund-raiser in the course of a radio or television programme, any solicitation which is made by a person in the course of the programme at the instance of the fund-raiser shall be regarded for the purposes of this Part as made by the fund-raiser and not by that person (and shall be so regarded whether or not the solicitation is made by that person for any reward).

(9) In this Part "services" includes facilities, and in particular—

(a) access to any premises or event;

(b) membership of any organisation;

(c) the provision of advertising space; and

(d) the provision of any financial facilities;

and references to the supply of services shall be construed accordingly.

(10) The [Minister] may by order amend subsection (3) by substituting a different sum for any sum for the time being specified there.

[744]

NOTES

Sub-s (1): in definitions "charity" and "company" words in square brackets substituted by the Charities Act 1993, s 98(1), Sch 6, para 29(1), (5); in definitions "commercial participator" and "professional fund-raiser" words in square brackets inserted by the Deregulation and Contracting Out Act 1994, s 25; definition "the Minister" inserted by the Charities Act 2006, s 75(1), Sch 8, paras 89, 90(1), (2).

Sub-s (2): for the words in italics in para (c) there are substituted the words "a promoter of such a collection as defined in section 47(1) of the Charities Act 2006" and for the words in italics in the second place there are substituted the words "Chapter 1 of Part 3 of the Charities Act 2006" by the Charities Act 2006, s 75(1), Sch 8, paras 89, 90(1), (3), as from a day to be appointed under s 79(2) of that Act.

Sub-s (4): for the words in italics there are substituted the words "as defined by section 2(1) of the Charities Act 2006" by the Charities Act 2006, s 75(1), Sch 8, paras 89, 90(1), (4), as from a day to be appointed under s 79(2) of that Act.

Sub-s (10): word in square brackets substituted by the Transfer of Functions (Third Sector, Communities and Equality) Order 2006, SI 2006/2951, art 6, Schedule, para 3(a).

Control of fund-raising

59 Prohibition on professional fund-raiser etc raising funds for charitable institution without an agreement in prescribed form

(1) It shall be unlawful for a professional fund-raiser to solicit money or other property for the benefit of a charitable institution unless he does so in accordance with an agreement with the institution satisfying the prescribed requirements.

(2) It shall be unlawful for a commercial participator to represent that charitable contributions are to be given to or applied for the benefit of a charitable institution unless he does so in accordance with an agreement with the institution satisfying the prescribed requirements.

(3) Where on the application of a charitable institution the court is satisfied—

(a) that any person has contravened or is contravening subsection (1) or (2) in relation to the institution, and

(b) that, unless restrained, any such contravention is likely to continue or be repeated,

the court may grant an injunction restraining the contravention; and compliance with subsection (1) or (2) shall not be enforceable otherwise than in accordance with this subsection.

(4) Where—

(a) a charitable institution makes any agreement with a professional fund-raiser or a commercial participator by virtue of which—

(i) the professional fund-raiser is authorised to solicit money or other property for the benefit of the institution, or

(ii) the commercial participator is authorised to represent that charitable contributions are to be given to or applied for the benefit of the institution,

as the case may be, but

(b) the agreement does not satisfy the prescribed requirements in any respect,

the agreement shall not be enforceable against the institution except to such extent (if any) as may be provided by an order of the court.

(5) A professional fund-raiser or commercial participator who is a party to such an agreement as is mentioned in subsection (4)(a) shall not be entitled to receive any amount by way of remuneration or expenses in respect of anything done by him in pursuance of the agreement unless—

(a) he is so entitled under any provision of the agreement, and

(b) either—

(i) the agreement satisfies the prescribed requirements, or

(ii) any such provision has effect by virtue of an order of the court under subsection (4).

(6) In this section "the prescribed requirements" means such requirements as are prescribed by regulations made by virtue of section 64(2)(a).

[745]

NOTES

Regulations: the Charitable Institutions (Fund-Raising) Regulations 1994, SI 1994/3024 at **[3134]**.

60 Professional fund-raisers etc required to indicate institutions benefiting and arrangements for remuneration

(1) Where a professional fund-raiser solicits money or other property for the benefit of one or more particular charitable institutions, the solicitation shall be accompanied by a statement clearly indicating—

(a) the name or names of the institution or institutions concerned;

(b) if there is more than one institution concerned, the proportions in which the institutions are respectively to benefit; and

(c) *(in general terms) the method by which the fund-raiser's remuneration in connection with the appeal is to be determined.*

(2) Where a professional fund-raiser solicits money or other property for charitable, benevolent or philanthropic purposes of any description (rather than for the benefit of one or more particular charitable institutions), the solicitation shall be accompanied by a statement clearly indicating—

(a) the fact that he is soliciting money or other property for those purposes and not for the benefit of any particular charitable institution or institutions;

(b) the method by which it is to be determined how the proceeds of the appeal are to be distributed between different charitable institutions; and

(c) *(in general terms) the method by which his remuneration in connection with the appeal is to be determined.*

(3) Where any representation is made by a commercial participator to the effect that charitable contributions are to be given to or applied for the benefit of one or more particular charitable institutions, the representation shall be accompanied by a statement clearly indicating—

(a) the name or names of the institution or institutions concerned;

(b) if there is more than one institution concerned, the proportions in which the institutions are respectively to benefit; and

(c) *(in general terms) the method by which it is to be determined—*

(i) what proportion of the consideration given for goods or services sold or supplied by him, or of any other proceeds of a promotional venture undertaken by him, is to be given to or applied for the benefit of the institution or institutions concerned, or

(ii) what sums by way of donations by him in connection with the sale or supply of any such goods or services are to be so given or applied,

as the case may require.

(4) If any such solicitation or representation as is mentioned in any of subsections (1) to (3) is made—

(a) in the course of a radio or television programme, and

(b) in association with an announcement to the effect that payment may be made, in response to the solicitation or representation, by means of a credit or debit card,

the statement required by virtue of subsection (1), (2) or (3) (as the case may be) shall include full details of the right to have refunded under section 61(1) any payment of £50 or more which is so made.

(5) If any such solicitation or representation as is mentioned in any of subsections (1) to (3) is made orally but is not made—

(a) by speaking directly to the particular person or persons to whom it is addressed and in his or their presence, or

(b) in the course of any radio or television programme,

the professional fund-raiser or commercial participator concerned shall, within seven days of any payment of £50 or more being made to him in response to the solicitation or representation, give to the person making the payment a written statement—

(i) of the matters specified in paragraphs (a) to (c) of that subsection; and

(ii) including full details of the right to cancel under section 61(2) an agreement made in response to the solicitation or representation, and the right to have refunded under section 61(2) or (3) any payment of £50 or more made in response thereto.

(6) In subsection (5) above the reference to the making of a payment is a reference to the making of a payment of whatever nature and by whatever means, including a payment made by means of a credit card or a debit card; and for the purposes of that subsection—

(a) where the person making any such payment makes it in person, it shall be regarded as made at the time when it is so made;

(b) where the person making any such payment sends it by post, it shall be regarded as made at the time when it is posted; and

(c) where the person making any such payment makes it by giving, by telephone or by means of any other [electronic communications apparatus], authority for an account to be debited with the payment, it shall be regarded as made at the time when any such authority is given.

(7) Where any requirement of subsections (1) to (5) is not complied with in relation to any solicitation or representation, the professional fund-raiser or commercial participator concerned shall be guilty of an offence and liable on summary conviction to a fine not exceeding the fifth level on the standard scale.

(8) It shall be a defence for a person charged with any such offence to prove that he took all reasonable precautions and exercised all due diligence to avoid the commission of the offence.

(9) Where the commission by any person of an offence under subsection (7) is due to the act or default of some other person, that other person shall be guilty of the offence; and a person may be charged with and convicted of the offence by virtue of this subsection whether or not proceedings are taken against the first-mentioned person.

(10) In this section—

"the appeal", in relation to any solicitation by a professional fund-raiser, means the campaign or other fund-raising venture in the course of which the solicitation is made;

.....

[746]

NOTES

Sub-s (1): para (c) substituted as follows by the Charities Act 2006, s 67(1), (2), as from a day to be appointed under s 79(2) of that Act, subject to transitional provisions in Sch 10, para 15 to that Act at **[2176]**—

"(c) the method by which the fund-raiser's remuneration in connection with the appeal is to be determined and the notifiable amount of that remuneration.".

Sub-s (2): para (c) substituted as follows by the Charities Act 2006, s 67(1), (3), as from a day to be appointed under s 79(2) of that Act, subject to transitional provisions in Sch 10, para 15 to that Act at **[2176]**—

"(c) the method by which his remuneration in connection with the appeal is to be determined and the notifiable amount of that remuneration.".

Sub-s (3): para (c) substituted as follows by the Charities Act 2006, s 67(1), (4), as from a day to be appointed under s 79(2) of that Act, subject to transitional provisions in Sch 10, para 15 to that Act at **[2176]**—

"(c) the notifiable amount of whichever of the following sums is applicable in the circumstances—
(i) the sum representing so much of the consideration given for goods or services sold or supplied by him as is to be given to or applied for the benefit of the institution or institutions concerned,
(ii) the sum representing so much of any other proceeds of a promotional venture undertaken by him as is to be so given or applied, or
(iii) the sum of the donations by him in connection with the sale or supply of any such goods or services which are to be so given or supplied.".

Sub-s (3A): inserted as follows by the Charities Act 2006, s 67(1), (5), as from a day to be appointed under s 79(2) of that Act, subject to transitional provisions in Sch 10, para 15 to that Act at **[2176]**—

"(3A) In subsections (1) to (3) a reference to the "notifiable amount" of any remuneration or other sum is a reference—
(a) to the actual amount of the remuneration or sum, if that is known at the time when the statement is made; and
(b) otherwise to the estimated amount of the remuneration or sum, calculated as accurately as is reasonably possible in the circumstances."

Sub-s (6): words in square brackets in para (c) substituted by the Communications Act 2003, s 406(1), Sch 17, para 118, subject to transitional provisions in Sch 18 to that Act.

Sub-s (10): definition omitted repealed by the Communications Act 2003, s 406(7), Sch 19(1), subject to transitional provisions in Sch 18 to that Act.

[60A Other persons making appeals required to indicate institutions benefiting and arrangements for remuneration

(1) Subsections (1) and (2) of section 60 apply to a person acting for reward as a collector in respect of a public charitable collection as they apply to a professional fund-raiser.

(2) But those subsections do not so apply to a person excluded by virtue of—
(a) subsection (3) below, or
(b) section 60B(1) (exclusion of lower-paid collectors).

(3) Those subsections do not so apply to a person if—

(a) section 60(1) or (2) applies apart from subsection (1) (by virtue of the exception in section 58(2)(c) for persons treated as promoters), or

(b) subsection (4) or (5) applies,

in relation to his acting for reward as a collector in respect of the collection mentioned in subsection (1) above.

(4) Where a person within subsection (6) solicits money or other property for the benefit of one or more particular charitable institutions, the solicitation shall be accompanied by a statement clearly indicating—

(a) the name or names of the institution or institutions for whose benefit the solicitation is being made;

(b) if there is more than one such institution, the proportions in which the institutions are respectively to benefit;

(c) the fact that he is an officer, employee or trustee of the institution or company mentioned in subsection (6); and

(d) the fact that he is receiving remuneration as an officer, employee or trustee or (as the case may be) for acting as a collector.

(5) Where a person within subsection (6) solicits money or other property for charitable, benevolent or philanthropic purposes of any description (rather than for the benefit of one or more particular charitable institutions), the solicitation shall be accompanied by a statement clearly indicating—

(a) the fact that he is soliciting money or other property for those purposes and not for the benefit of any particular charitable institution or institutions;

(b) the method by which it is to be determined how the proceeds of the appeal are to be distributed between different charitable institutions;

(c) the fact that he is an officer, employee or trustee of the institution or company mentioned in subsection (6); and

(d) the fact that he is receiving remuneration as an officer, employee or trustee or (as the case may be) for acting as a collector.

(6) A person is within this subsection if—

(a) he is an officer or employee of a charitable institution or a company connected with any such institution, or a trustee of any such institution,

(b) he is acting as a collector in that capacity, and

(c) he receives remuneration either in his capacity as officer, employee or trustee or for acting as a collector.

(7) But a person is not within subsection (6) if he is excluded by virtue of section 60B(4).

(8) Where any requirement of—

(a) subsection (1) or (2) of section 60, as it applies by virtue of subsection (1) above, or

(b) subsection (4) or (5) above,

is not complied with in relation to any solicitation, the collector concerned shall be guilty of an offence and liable on summary conviction to a fine not exceeding level 5 on the standard scale.

(9) Section 60(8) and (9) apply in relation to an offence under subsection (8) above as they apply in relation to an offence under section 60(7).

(10) In this section—

"the appeal", in relation to any solicitation by a collector, means the campaign or other fund-raising venture in the course of which the solicitation is made;

"collector" has the meaning given by section 47(1) of the Charities Act 2006;

"public charitable collection" has the meaning given by section 45 of that Act.]

[746A]

NOTES

Commencement: to be appointed.

Inserted, together with s 60B, by the Charities Act 2006, s 68, as from a day to be appointed under s 79(2) of that Act.

[60B Exclusion of lower-paid collectors from provisions of section 60A

(1) Section 60(1) and (2) do not apply (by virtue of section 60A(1)) to a person who is under the earnings limit in subsection (2) below.

(2) A person is under the earnings limit in this subsection if he does not receive—
(a) more than—
(i) £5 per day, or
(ii) £500 per year,
by way of remuneration for acting as a collector in relation to relevant collections, or
(b) more than £500 by way of remuneration for acting as a collector in relation to the collection mentioned in section 60A(1).

(3) In subsection (2) "relevant collections" means public charitable collections conducted for the benefit of—
(a) the charitable institution or institutions, or
(b) the charitable, benevolent or philanthropic purposes,
for whose benefit the collection mentioned in section 60A(1) is conducted.

(4) A person is not within section 60A(6) if he is under the earnings limit in subsection (5) below.

(5) A person is under the earnings limit in this subsection if the remuneration received by him as mentioned in section 60A(6)(c)—
(a) is not more than—
(i) £5 per day, or
(ii) £500 per year, or
(b) if a lump sum, is not more than £500.

(6) The Minister may by order amend subsections (2) and (5) by substituting a different sum for any sum for the time being specified there.]

[746B]

NOTES

Commencement: 27 February 2007 (sub-s (6) for the purposes of enabling the Minister to exercise the power to make subordinate legislation); to be appointed (otherwise).
Inserted as noted to s 60A at **[746A]**.

61 Cancellation of payments and agreements made in response to appeals

(1) Where—
(a) a person ("the donor"), in response to any such solicitation or representation as is mentioned in any of subsections (1) to (3) of section 60 which is made in the course of a radio or television programme, makes any payment of £50 or more to the relevant fund-raiser by means of a credit card or a debit card, but
(b) before the end of the period of seven days beginning with the date of the solicitation or representation, the donor serves on the relevant fund-raiser a notice in writing which, however expressed, indicates the donor's intention to cancel the payment,
the donor shall (subject to subsection (4) below) be entitled to have the payment refunded to him forthwith by the relevant fund-raiser.

(2) Where—
(a) a person ("the donor"), in response to any solicitation or representation falling within subsection (5) of section 60, enters into an agreement with the relevant fund-raiser under which the donor is, or may be, liable to make any payment or payments to the relevant fund-raiser, and the amount or aggregate amount which the donor is, or may be, liable to pay to him under the agreement is £50 or more, but
(b) before the end of the period of seven days beginning with the date when he is given any such written statement as is referred to in that subsection, the donor serves on the relevant fund-raiser a notice in writing which, however expressed, indicates the donor's intention to cancel the agreement,
the notice shall operate, as from the time when it is so served, to cancel the agreement and any liability of any person other than the donor in connection with the making of any such payment or payments, and the donor shall (subject to subsection (4) below) be entitled to have any payment of £50 or more made by him under the agreement refunded to him forthwith by the relevant fund-raiser.

(3) Where, in response to any solicitation or representation falling within subsection (5) of section 60, a person ("the donor")—
(a) makes any payment of £50 or more to the relevant fund-raiser, but

(b) does not enter into any such agreement as is mentioned in subsection (2) above,

then, if before the end of the period of seven days beginning with the date when the donor is given any such written statement as is referred to in subsection (5) of that section, the donor serves on the relevant fund-raiser a notice in writing which, however expressed, indicates the donor's intention to cancel the payment, the donor shall (subject to subsection (4) below) be entitled to have the payment refunded to him forthwith by the relevant fund-raiser.

(4) The right of any person to have a payment refunded to him under any of subsections (1) to (3) above—

(a) is a right to have refunded to him the amount of the payment less any administrative expenses reasonably incurred by the relevant fund-raiser in connection with—

(i) the making of the refund, or

(ii) (in the case of a refund under subsection (2)) dealing with the notice of cancellation served by that person; and

(b) shall, in the case of a payment for goods already received, be conditional upon restitution being made by him of the goods in question.

(5) Nothing in subsections (1) to (3) above has effect in relation to any payment made or to be made in respect of services which have been supplied at the time when the relevant notice is served.

(6) In this section any reference to the making of a payment is a reference to the making of a payment of whatever nature and (in the case of subsection (2) or (3)) a payment made by whatever means, including a payment made by means of a credit card or a debit card; and subsection (6) of section 60 shall have effect for determining when a payment is made for the purposes of this section as it has effect for determining when a payment is made for the purposes of subsection (5) of that section.

(7) In this section "the relevant fund-raiser", in relation to any solicitation or representation, means the professional fund-raiser or commercial participator by whom it is made.

(8) The [Minister] may by order—

(a) amend any provision of this section by substituting a different sum for the sum for the time being specified there; and

(b) make such consequential amendments in section 60 as he considers appropriate.

[747]

NOTES

Sub-s (8): word in square brackets substituted by the Transfer of Functions (Third Sector, Communities and Equality) Order 2006, SI 2006/2951, art 6, Schedule, para 3(b).

62 Right of charitable institution to prevent unauthorised fund-raising

(1) Where on the application of any charitable institution—

(a) the court is satisfied that any person has done or is doing either of the following, namely—

(i) soliciting money or other property for the benefit of the institution, or

(ii) representing that charitable contributions are to be given to or applied for the benefit of the institution,

and that, unless restrained, he is likely to do further acts of that nature, and

(b) the court is also satisfied as to one or more of the matters specified in subsection (2),

then (subject to subsection (3)) the court may grant an injunction restraining the doing of any such acts.

(2) The matters referred to in subsection (1)(b) are—

(a) that the person in question is using methods of fund-raising to which the institution objects;

(b) that that person is not a fit and proper person to raise funds for the institution; and

(c) where the conduct complained of is the making of such representations as are mentioned in subsection (1)(a)(ii), that the institution does not wish to be associated with the particular promotional or other fund-raising venture in which that person is engaged.

(3) The power to grant an injunction under subsecction (1) shall not be exercisable on the application of a charitable institution unless the institution has, not less than 28 days before making the application, served on the person in question a notice in writing—

(a) requesting him to cease forthwith—

(i) soliciting money or other property for the benefit of the institution, or

(ii) representing that charitable contributions are to be given to or applied for the benefit of the institution,

as the case may be; and

(b) stating that, if he does not comply with the notice, the institution will make an application under this section for an injunction.

(4) Where—

(a) a charitable institution has served on any person a notice under subsection (3) ("the relevant notice") and that person has complied with the notice, but

(b) that person has subsequently begun to carry on activities which are the same, or substantially the same, as those in respect of which the relevant notice was served,

the institution shall not, in connection with an application made by it under this section in respect of the activities carried on by that person, be required by virtue of that subsection to serve a further notice on him, if the application is made not more than 12 months after the date of service of the relevant notice.

(5) This section shall not have the effect of authorising a charitable institution to make an application under this section in respect of anything done by a professional fund-raiser or commercial participator in relation to the institution.

[748]

63 False statements relating to institutions which are not registered charities

(1) Where—

(a) a person solicits money or other property for the benefit of an institution in association with a representation that the institution is a registered charity, and

(b) the institution is not such a charity,

he shall be guilty of an offence and liable on summary conviction to a fine not exceeding the fifth level on the standard scale.

[(1A) In any proceedings for an offence under subsection (1), it shall be a defence for the accused to prove that he believed on reasonable grounds that the institution was a registered charity.]

(2) In [this section] "registered charity" means a charity which is for the time being registered in the register of charities kept under [section 3 of the Charities Act 1993].

[749]

NOTES

Sub-s (1A): inserted by the Deregulation and Contracting Out Act 1994, s 26(1), (2).

Sub-s (2): words in first pair of square brackets substituted by the Deregulation and Contracting Out Act 1994, s 26(1), (3); words in second pair of square brackets substituted by the Charities Act 1993, s 98(1), Sch 6, para 29(1), (6).

Supplementary

64 Regulations about fund-raising

(1) The [Minister] may make such regulations as appear to him to be necessary or desirable for any purposes connected with any of the preceding provisions of this Part.

(2) Without prejudice to the generality of subsection (1), any such regulations may—

(a) prescribe the form and content of—

(i) agreements made for the purposes of section 59, and

(ii) notices served under section 62(3);

(b) require professional fund-raisers or commercial participators who are parties to such agreements with charitable institutions to make available to the institutions books, documents or other records (however kept) which relate to the institutions;

(c) specify the manner in which money or other property acquired by professional fund-raisers or commercial participators for the benefit of, or otherwise falling to be given to or applied by such persons for the benefit of, charitable institutions is to be transmitted to such institutions;

(d) provide for any provisions of section 60 or 61 having effect in relation to solicitations or representations made in the course of radio or television programmes to have effect, subject to any modifications specified in the regulations, in relation to solicitations or representations made in the course of such programmes—
  (i) by charitable institutions, or
  (ii) by companies connected with such institutions,

and, in that connection, provide for any other provisions of this Part to have effect for the purposes of the regulations subject to any modifications so specified;

(e) make other provision regulating the raising of funds for charitable, benevolent or philanthropic purposes (whether by professional fund-raisers or commercial participators or otherwise).

(3) In subsection (2)(c) the reference to such money or other property as is there mentioned includes a reference to money or other property which, in the case of a professional fund-raiser or commercial participator—

(a) has been acquired by him otherwise than in accordance with an agreement with a charitable institution, but

(b) by reason of any solicitation or representation in consequence of which it has been acquired, is held by him on trust for such an institution.

(4) Regulations under this section may provide that any failure to comply with a specified provision of the regulations shall be an offence punishable on summary conviction by a fine not exceeding the second level on the standard scale.

[750]

NOTES

Sub-s (1): word in square brackets substituted by the Transfer of Functions (Third Sector, Communities and Equality) Order 2006, SI 2006/2951, art 6, Schedule, para 3(c).

Regulations: the Charitable Institutions (Fund-Raising) Regulations 1994, SI 1994/3024 at **[3134]**.

[64A Reserve power to control fund-raising by charitable institutions

(1) The Minister may make such regulations as appear to him to be necessary or desirable for or in connection with regulating charity fund-raising.

(2) In this section "charity fund-raising" means activities which are carried on by—

(a) charitable institutions,

(b) persons managing charitable institutions, or

(c) persons or companies connected with such institutions,

and involve soliciting or otherwise procuring funds for the benefit of such institutions or companies connected with them, or for general charitable, benevolent or philanthropic purposes.

But "activities" does not include primary purpose trading.

(3) Regulations under this section may, in particular, impose a good practice requirement on the persons managing charitable institutions in circumstances where—

(a) those institutions,

(b) the persons managing them, or

(c) persons or companies connected with such institutions,

are engaged in charity fund-raising.

(4) A "good practice requirement" is a requirement to take all reasonable steps to ensure that the fund-raising is carried out in such a way that—

(a) it does not unreasonably intrude on the privacy of those from whom funds are being solicited or procured;

(b) it does not involve the making of unreasonably persistent approaches to persons to donate funds;

(c) it does not result in undue pressure being placed on persons to donate funds;

(d) it does not involve the making of any false or misleading representation about any of the matters mentioned in subsection (5).

(5) The matters are—

(a) the extent or urgency of any need for funds on the part of any charitable institution or company connected with such an institution;

(b) any use to which funds donated in response to the fund-raising are to be put by such an institution or company;

(c) the activities, achievements or finances of such an institution or company.

(6) Regulations under this section may provide that a person who persistently fails, without reasonable excuse, to comply with any specified requirement of the regulations is to be guilty of an offence and liable on summary conviction to a fine not exceeding level 2 on the standard scale.

(7) For the purposes of this section—

(a) "funds" means money or other property;

(b) "general charitable, benevolent or philanthropic purposes" means charitable, benevolent or philanthropic purposes other than those associated with one or more particular institutions;

(c) the persons "managing" a charitable institution are the charity trustees or other persons having the general control and management of the administration of the institution; and

(d) a person is "connected" with a charitable institution if he is an employee or agent of—

(i) the institution,

(ii) the persons managing it, or

(iii) a company connected with it,

or he is a volunteer acting on behalf of the institution or such a company.

(8) In this section "primary purpose trading", in relation to a charitable institution, means any trade carried on by the institution or a company connected with it where—

(a) the trade is carried on in the course of the actual carrying out of a primary purpose of the institution; or

(b) the work in connection with the trade is mainly carried out by beneficiaries of the institution.]

[751]–[760]

NOTES

Commencement: 27 February 2007.
Inserted by the Charities Act 2006, s 69.

65–74 *(Pt III (ss 65–74) repealed by the Charities Act 2006, s 75(1), (2), Sch 8, paras 89, 91, Sch 9.)*

PART IV
GENERAL

75 Offences by bodies corporate

Where any offence—

(a) under this Act or any regulations made under it, or

(b) … is committed by a body corporate and is proved to have been committed with the consent or connivance of, or to be attributable to any neglect on the part of, any director, manager, secretary or other similar officer of the body corporate, or any person who was purporting to act in any such capacity, he as well as the body corporate shall be guilty of that offence and shall be liable to be proceeded against and punished accordingly.

In relation to a body corporate whose affairs are managed by its members, "director" means a member of the body corporate.

[761]

NOTES

Words omitted repealed by the Charities Act 1993, s 98(2), Sch 7.

76 Service of documents

(1) This section applies to—

(a) …

(b) any notice or other document required or authorised to be given or served under Part II of this Act; ...
(c) ...

(2) A document to which this section applies may be served on or given to a person (other than a body corporate)—
(a) by delivering it to that person;
(b) by leaving it at his last known address in the United Kingdom; or
(c) by sending it by post to him at that address.

(3) A document to which this section applies may be served on or given to a body corporate by delivering it or sending it by post—
(a) to the registered or principal office of the body in the United Kingdom, or
(b) if it has no such office in the United Kingdom, to any place in the United Kingdom where it carries on business or conducts its activities (as the case may be).

(4) Any such document may also be served on or given to a person (including a body corporate) by sending it by post to that person at an address notified by that person for the purposes of this subsection to the person or persons by whom it is required or authorised to be served or given.

[762]

NOTES

Sub-s (1): para (a) repealed by the Charities Act 1993, s 98(2), Sch 7; para (c) and word omitted from para (b) repealed by the Charities Act 2006, s 75(1), (2), Sch 8, paras 89, 92, Sch 9.

77 Regulations and orders

(1) Any regulations or order of the [Minister] under this Act—
(a) shall be made by statutory instrument; and
(b) (subject to [subsections (2) and (2A)]) shall be subject to annulment in pursuance of a resolution of either House of Parliament.

(2) Subsection (1)(b) does not apply—
(a)–(c) ...; or
(d) to an order under section 79(2).

[(2A) Subsection (1)(b) does not apply to regulations under section 64A, and no such regulations may be made unless a draft of the statutory instrument containing the regulations has been laid before, and approved by a resolution of, each House of Parliament.]

(3) Any regulations or order of the [Minister] under this Act may make—
(a) different provision for different cases; and
(b) such supplemental, incidental, consequential or transitional provision or savings as the [Minister] considers appropriate.

(4) Before making any regulations under section ... 64 [or 64A] ... the [Minister] shall consult such persons or bodies of persons as he considers appropriate.

[763]

NOTES

Sub-s (1): word in first pair of square brackets substituted by the Transfer of Functions (Third Sector, Communities and Equality) Order 2006, SI 2006/2951, art 6, Schedule, para 3(e); words in square brackets in para (b) substituted by the Charities Act 2006, s 75(1), Sch 8, paras 89, 93(1), (2).

Sub-s (2): words omitted repealed by the Charities Act 1993, s 98(2), Sch 7.

Sub-s (2A): inserted by the Charities Act 2006, s 75(1), Sch 8, paras 89, 93(1), (3).

Sub-s (3): words in square brackets substituted by SI 2006/2951, art 6, Schedule, para 3(e).

Sub-s (4): words omitted in the first place repealed by the Charities Act 1993, s 98(2), Sch 7; words in first pair of square brackets inserted and words omitted in the second place repealed by the Charities Act 2006, s 75(1), (2), Sch 8, paras 89, 93(1), (4), Sch 9; word in second pair of square brackets substituted by SI 2006/2951, art 6, Schedule, para 3(e).

78 Minor and consequential amendments and repeals

(1) The enactments mentioned in Schedule 6 to this Act shall have effect subject to the amendments there specified (which are either minor amendments or amendments consequential on the provisions of this Act).

(2) The enactments mentioned in Schedule 7 to this Act (which include some that are already spent or are no longer of practical utility) are hereby repealed to the extent specified in the third column of that Schedule.

[764]

79 Short title, commencement and extent

(1) This Act may be cited as the Charities Act 1992.

(2) This Act shall come into force on such day as the [Minister] may by order appoint; and different days may be so appointed for different provisions or for different purposes.

(3) Subject to subsections (4) to (6) below, this Act extends only to England and Wales.

(4), (5) …

(6) The amendments in Schedule 6, and (*subject to subsection (7)*) the repeals in Schedule 7, have the same extent as the enactments to which they refer, and section 78 extends accordingly.

(7) *The repeal in Schedule 7 of the Police, Factories, &c (Miscellaneous Provisions) Act 1916 does not extend to Northern Ireland.*

[765]–[766]

NOTES

Sub-s (2): word in square brackets substituted by the Transfer of Functions (Third Sector, Communities and Equality) Order 2006, SI 2006/2951, art 6, Schedule, para 3(e).

Sub-ss (4), (5): repealed by the Charities Act 1993, s 98(2), Sch 7.

Sub-s (6): words in italics repealed by the Charities Act 2006, s 75(1), (2), Sch 8, paras 89, 94(a), Sch 9, as from a day to be appointed under s 79(2) of that Act.

Sub-s (7): repealed by the Charities Act 2006, s 75(1), (2), Sch 8, paras 89, 94(b), Sch 9, as from a day to be appointed under s 79(2) of that Act.

Orders: the Charities Act 1992 (Commencement No 1 and Transitional Provisions) Order 1992, SI 1992/1900; the Charities Act 1992 (Commencement No 2) Order 1994, SI 1994/3023.

(Schs 1–4 repealed by the Charities Act 1993, s 98(2), Sch 7; Sch 5 substitutes the Redundant Churches and Other Religious Buildings Act 1969, ss 4, 5, repealed by the Charities Act 2006, s 75(2), Sch 9, as from a day to be appointed under s 79(2) of that Act; Sch 6 in so far as unrepealed contains minor and consequential amendments; Sch 7 contains repeals only, repealed in part by the Charities Act 2006, s 75(1), (2), Sch 8, paras 89, 95, Sch 9, as from a day to be appointed under s 79(2) of that Act.)

CHARITIES ACT 1993

(1993 c 10)

ARRANGEMENT OF SECTIONS

PART I
THE CHARITY COMMISSION AND THE OFFICIAL CUSTODIAN FOR CHARITIES

PART 1A
THE CHARITY TRIBUNAL

PART II
REGISTRATION AND NAMES OF CHARITIES

Registration of charities

Legal proceedings relating to charities

Meaning of "trust corporation"

PART V
CHARITY LAND

PART VI
CHARITY ACCOUNTS, REPORTS AND RETURNS

PART VII
INCORPORATION OF CHARITY TRUSTEES

PART VIII
CHARITABLE COMPANIES

PART 8A
CHARITABLE INCORPORATED ORGANISATIONS

Nature and constitution

An Act to consolidate the Charitable Trustees Incorporation Act 1872 and, except for certain spent or transitional provisions, the Charities Act 1960 and Part I of the Charities Act 1992

[27 May 1993]

PART I
THE [CHARITY COMMISSION] AND THE OFFICIAL CUSTODIAN FOR CHARITIES

NOTES

Part heading: words in square brackets substituted by the Charities Act 2006, s 75(1), Sch 8, paras 96, 97, as from 27 February 2007.

1 *(Repealed by the Charities Act 2006, ss 6(6), 75(2), Sch 9, as from 27 February 2007.)*

[1A The Charity Commission

(1) There shall be a body corporate to be known as the Charity Commission for England and Wales (in this Act referred to as "the Commission").

(2) In Welsh the Commission shall be known as "Comisiwn Elusennau Cymru a Lloegr".

(3) The functions of the Commission shall be performed on behalf of the Crown.

(4) In the exercise of its functions the Commission shall not be subject to the direction or control of any Minister of the Crown or other government department.

(5) But subsection (4) above does not affect—

(a) any provision made by or under any enactment;

(b) any administrative controls exercised over the Commission's expenditure by the Treasury.

(6) The provisions of Schedule 1A to this Act shall have effect with respect to the Commission.]

[766A]

NOTES

Commencement: 27 February 2007.
Inserted by the Charities Act 2006, s 6(1).

[1B The Commission's objectives

(1) The Commission has the objectives set out in subsection (2).

(2) The objectives are—

1. The public confidence objective.
2. The public benefit objective.
3. The compliance objective.
4. The charitable resources objective.
5. The accountability objective.

(3) Those objectives are defined as follows—

1. The public confidence objective is to increase public trust and confidence in charities.
2. The public benefit objective is to promote awareness and understanding of the operation of the public benefit requirement.
3. The compliance objective is to promote compliance by charity trustees with their legal obligations in exercising control and management of the administration of their charities.
4. The charitable resources objective is to promote the effective use of charitable resources.
5. The accountability objective is to enhance the accountability of charities to donors, beneficiaries and the general public.

(4) In this section "the public benefit requirement" means the requirement in section 2(1)(b) of the Charities Act 2006 that a purpose falling within section 2(2) of that Act must be for the public benefit if it is to be a charitable purpose.]

[766B]

NOTES

Commencement: 27 February 2007.
Inserted, together with ss 1C–1E, by the Charities Act 2006, s 7.

[1C The Commission's general functions

(1) The Commission has the general functions set out in subsection (2).

(2) The general functions are—

1. Determining whether institutions are or are not charities.
2. Encouraging and facilitating the better administration of charities.
3. Identifying and investigating apparent misconduct or mismanagement in the administration of charities and taking remedial or protective action in connection with misconduct or mismanagement therein.
4. Determining whether public collections certificates should be issued, and remain in force, in respect of public charitable collections.
5. Obtaining, evaluating and disseminating information in connection with the performance of any of the Commission's functions or meeting any of its objectives.
6. Giving information or advice, or making proposals, to any Minister of the Crown on matters relating to any of the Commission's functions or meeting any of its objectives.

(3) The Commission's fifth general function includes (among other things) the maintenance of an accurate and up-to-date register of charities under section 3 below.

(4) The Commission's sixth general function includes (among other things) complying, so far as is reasonably practicable, with any request made by a Minister of the Crown for information or advice on any matter relating to any of its functions.

(5) In this section "public charitable collection" and "public collections certificate" have the same meanings as in Chapter 1 of Part 3 of the Charities Act 2006.]

[766C]

NOTES

Commencement: 27 February 2007 (sub-ss (1), (3), (4), sub-s (2) paras 1–3, 5, 6); to be appointed (otherwise).

Inserted as noted to s 1B at **[766B]**.

[1D The Commission's general duties

(1) The Commission has the general duties set out in subsection (2).

(2) The general duties are—

1. So far as is reasonably practicable the Commission must, in performing its functions, act in a way—
   (a) which is compatible with its objectives, and
   (b) which it considers most appropriate for the purpose of meeting those objectives.
2. So far as is reasonably practicable the Commission must, in performing its functions, act in a way which is compatible with the encouragement of—
   (a) all forms of charitable giving, and
   (b) voluntary participation in charity work.
3. In performing its functions the Commission must have regard to the need to use its resources in the most efficient, effective and economic way.
4. In performing its functions the Commission must, so far as relevant, have regard to the principles of best regulatory practice (including the principles under which regulatory activities should be proportionate, accountable, consistent, transparent and targeted only at cases in which action is needed).
5. In performing its functions the Commission must, in appropriate cases, have regard to the desirability of facilitating innovation by or on behalf of charities.
6. In managing its affairs the Commission must have regard to such generally accepted principles of good corporate governance as it is reasonable to regard as applicable to it.]

[766D]

NOTES

Commencement: 27 February 2007.

Inserted as noted to s 1B at **[766B]**.

[1E The Commission's incidental powers

(1) The Commission has power to do anything which is calculated to facilitate, or is conducive or incidental to, the performance of any of its functions or general duties.

(2) However, nothing in this Act authorises the Commission—

(a) to exercise functions corresponding to those of a charity trustee in relation to a charity, or

(b) otherwise to be directly involved in the administration of a charity.

(3) Subsection (2) does not affect the operation of section 19A or 19B below (power of Commission to give directions as to action to be taken or as to application of charity property).]

[766E]

NOTES

Commencement: 27 February 2007 (sub-ss (1), (2)); to be appointed (otherwise).

Inserted as noted to s 1B at **[766B]**.

2 The official custodian for charities

(1) There shall continue to be an officer known as the official custodian for charities (in this Act referred to as "the official custodian") whose function it shall be to act as trustee for

charities in the cases provided for by this Act; and the official custodian shall be by that name a corporation sole having perpetual succession and using an official seal which shall be officially and judicially noticed.

[(2) Such individual as the Commission may from time to time designate shall be the official custodian.]

(3) The official custodian shall perform his duties in accordance with such general or special directions as may be given him by the [Commission], and his expenses (except those re-imbursed to him or recovered by him as trustee for any charity) shall be defrayed by the [Commission].

(4) Anything which is required to or may be done by, to or before the official custodian may be done by, to or before any [member of the staff of the Commission] generally or specially authorised [by it] to act for him during a vacancy in his office or otherwise.

(5) The official custodian shall not be liable as trustee for any charity in respect of any loss or of the mis-application of any property unless it is occasioned by or through the wilful neglect or default of the custodian or of any person acting for him; but the Consolidated Fund shall be liable to make good to a charity any sums for which the custodian may be liable by reason of any such neglect or default.

(6) The official custodian shall keep such books of account and such records in relation thereto as may be directed by the Treasury and shall prepare accounts in such form, in such manner and at such times as may be so directed.

(7) The accounts so prepared shall be examined and certified by the Comptroller and Auditor General, *and the report to be made by the Commissioners to the [Minister] for any year shall include a copy of the accounts so prepared for any period ending in or with the year and of the certificate and report of the Comptroller and Auditor General with respect to those accounts.*

[(8) The Comptroller and Auditor General shall send to the Commission a copy of the accounts as certified by him together with his report on them.

(9) The Commission shall publish and lay before Parliament a copy of the documents sent to it under subsection (8) above.]

[767]

NOTES

Sub-s (2): substituted by the Charities Act 2006, s 75(1), Sch 8, paras 96, 98(1), (2), as from 27 February 2007, subject to savings in Sch 10, para 19 to that Act at **[2176]**.

Sub-ss (3), (4): words in square brackets substituted by the Charities Act 2006, s 75(1), Sch 8, paras 96, 98(1), (3), (4), as from 27 February 2007.

Sub-s (7): words in italics repealed by the Charities Act 2006, s 75(1), (2), Sch 8, paras 96, 98(1), (5), Sch 9, in relation to any financial year of a charity which begins on or after 27 February 2007: see the Charities Act 2006 (Commencement No 1, Transitional Provisions and Savings) Order 2007, SI 2007/309, art 4; word in square brackets substituted by the Transfer of Functions (Third Sector, Communities and Equality) Order 2006, SI 2006/2951, art 6, Schedule, para 4(b).

Sub-ss (8), (9): added by the Charities Act 2006, s 75(1), Sch 8, paras 96, 98(1), (6), in relation to any financial year of a charity which begins on or after 27 February 2007: see the Charities Act 2006 (Commencement No 1, Transitional Provisions and Savings) Order 2007, SI 2007/309, art 4.

[PART 1A
THE CHARITY TRIBUNAL

2A The Charity Tribunal

(1) There shall be a tribunal to be known as the Charity Tribunal (in this Act referred to as "the Tribunal").

(2) In Welsh the Tribunal shall be known as "Tribiwnlys Elusennau".

(3) The provisions of Schedule 1B to this Act shall have effect with respect to the constitution of the Tribunal and other matters relating to it.

(4) The Tribunal shall have jurisdiction to hear and determine—

(a) such appeals and applications as may be made to the Tribunal in accordance with Schedule 1C to this Act, or any other enactment, in respect of decisions, orders or directions of the Commission, and

(b) such matters as may be referred to the Tribunal in accordance with Schedule 1D to this Act by the Commission or the Attorney General.

(5) Such appeals, applications and matters shall be heard and determined by the Tribunal in accordance with those Schedules, or any such enactment, taken with section 2B below and rules made under that section.]

[767A]

NOTES

Commencement: to be appointed.

Pt 1A (ss 2A–2D) inserted by the Charities Act 2006, s 8(1), as from a day to be appointed under s 79(2) of that Act.

[2B Practice and procedure

(1) The Lord Chancellor may make rules—

(a) regulating the exercise of rights to appeal or to apply to the Tribunal and matters relating to the making of references to it;

(b) about the practice and procedure to be followed in relation to proceedings before the Tribunal.

(2) Rules under subsection (1)(a) above may, in particular, make provision—

(a) specifying steps which must be taken before appeals, applications or references are made to the Tribunal (and the period within which any such steps must be taken);

(b) specifying the period following the Commission's final decision, direction or order within which such appeals or applications may be made;

(c) requiring the Commission to inform persons of their right to appeal or apply to the Tribunal following a final decision, direction or order of the Commission;

(d) specifying the manner in which appeals, applications or references to the Tribunal are to be made.

(3) Rules under subsection (1)(b) above may, in particular, make provision—

(a) for the President or a legal member of the Tribunal (see paragraph 1(2)(b) of Schedule 1B to this Act) to determine preliminary, interlocutory or ancillary matters;

(b) for matters to be determined without an oral hearing in specified circumstances;

(c) for the Tribunal to deal with urgent cases expeditiously;

(d) about the disclosure of documents;

(e) about evidence;

(f) about the admission of members of the public to proceedings;

(g) about the representation of parties to proceedings;

(h) about the withdrawal of appeals, applications or references;

(i) about the recording and promulgation of decisions;

(j) about the award of costs.

(4) Rules under subsection (1)(a) or (b) above may confer a discretion on—

(a) the Tribunal,

(b) a member of the Tribunal, or

(c) any other person.

(5) The Tribunal may award costs only in accordance with subsections (6) and (7) below.

(6) If the Tribunal considers that any party to proceedings before it has acted vexatiously, frivolously or unreasonably, the Tribunal may order that party to pay to any other party to the proceedings the whole or part of the costs incurred by that other party in connection with the proceedings.

(7) If the Tribunal considers that a decision, direction or order of the Commission which is the subject of proceedings before it was unreasonable, the Tribunal may order the Commission to pay to any other party to the proceedings the whole or part of the costs incurred by that other party in connection with the proceedings.

(8) Rules of the Lord Chancellor under this section—

(a) shall be made by statutory instrument, and

(b) shall be subject to annulment in pursuance of a resolution of either House of Parliament.

(9) Section 86(3) below applies in relation to rules of the Lord Chancellor under this section as it applies in relation to regulations and orders of the Minister under this Act.]

[767B]

NOTES

Commencement: 27 February 2007 (sub-ss (1), (4), (8), (9) for the purposes of enabling the Lord Chancellor to exercise the power to make subordinate legislation); to be appointed (otherwise).

Inserted as noted to s 2A at **[767A]**.

[2C Appeal from Tribunal

(1) A party to proceedings before the Tribunal may appeal to the High Court against a decision of the Tribunal.

(2) Subject to subsection (3) below, an appeal may be brought under this section against a decision of the Tribunal only on a point of law.

(3) In the case of an appeal under this section against a decision of the Tribunal which determines a question referred to it by the Commission or the Attorney General, the High Court—

(a) shall consider afresh the question referred to the Tribunal, and
(b) may take into account evidence which was not available to the Tribunal.

(4) An appeal under this section may be brought only with the permission of—

(a) the Tribunal, or
(b) if the Tribunal refuses permission, the High Court.

(5) For the purposes of subsection (1) above—

(a) the Commission and the Attorney General are to be treated as parties to all proceedings before the Tribunal, and
(b) rules under section 2B(1) above may include provision as to who else is to be treated as being (or not being) a party to proceedings before the Tribunal.]

[767C]

NOTES

Commencement: 27 February 2007 (sub-s (5)(c) for the purposes of enabling the Lord Chancellor to exercise the power to make subordinate legislation); to be appointed (otherwise).

Inserted as noted to s 2A at **[767A]**.

[2D Intervention by Attorney General

(1) This section applies to any proceedings—

(a) before the Tribunal, or
(b) on an appeal from the Tribunal,

to which the Attorney General is not a party.

(2) The Tribunal or, in the case of an appeal from the Tribunal, the court may at any stage of the proceedings direct that all the necessary papers in the proceedings be sent to the Attorney General.

(3) A direction under subsection (2) may be made by the Tribunal or court—

(a) of its own motion, or
(b) on the application of any party to the proceedings.

(4) The Attorney General may—

(a) intervene in the proceedings in such manner as he thinks necessary or expedient, and
(b) argue before the Tribunal or court any question in relation to the proceedings which the Tribunal or court considers it necessary to have fully argued.

(5) Subsection (4) applies whether or not the Tribunal or court has given a direction under subsection (2).]

[767D]

NOTES

Commencement: to be appointed.

Inserted as noted to s 2A at **[767A]**.

PART II
REGISTRATION AND NAMES OF CHARITIES

Registration of charities

3 The register of charities

(1) The Commissioners shall continue to keep a register of charities, which shall be kept by them in such manner as they think fit.

(2) There shall be entered in the register every charity not excepted by subsection (5) below; and a charity so excepted (other than one excepted by paragraph (a) of that subsection) may be entered in the register at the request of the charity, but (whether or not it was excepted at the time of registration) may at any time, and shall at the request of the charity, be removed from the register.

(3) The register shall contain—
- (a) the name of every registered charity; and
- (b) such other particulars of, and such other information relating to, every such charity as the Commissioners think fit.

(4) Any institution which no longer appears to the Commissioners to be a charity shall be removed from the register, with effect, where the removal is due to any change in its purposes or trusts, from the date of that change; and there shall also be removed from the register any charity which ceases to exist or does not operate.

(5) The following charities are not required to be registered—
- (a) any charity comprised in Schedule 2 to this Act (in this Act referred to as an "exempt charity");
- (b) any charity which is excepted by order or regulations;
- (c) any charity which has neither—
  - (i) any permanent endowment, nor
  - (ii) the use or occupation of any land,

  and whose income from all sources does not in aggregate amount to more than £1,000 a year;

and no charity is required to be registered in respect of any registered place of worship.

[(5A) In subsection (5) above, paragraph (a) shall be read as referring also to—
- (a) any higher education corporation within the meaning of the Education Reform Act 1988, and
- (b) any further education corporation within the meaning of the Further and Higher Education Act 1992.]

[(5B) In addition, in subsection (5) above—
- (a) paragraph (a) shall be read as referring also to—
  - (i) any body to which section 23(1)(a) or (b) of the School Standards and Framework Act 1998 applies, and
  - (ii) any Education Action Forum established by virtue of section 10(1) of that Act; and
- (b) paragraph (b) shall be read as referring also to any foundation to which section 23(3) of that Act applies;

but an order of the Commissioners, or regulations made by the [Minister], may provide that section 23(3) of that Act shall cease to apply to any such foundation as is mentioned in that provision or to any such foundation of a description specified in the order or regulations.]

(6) With any application for a charity to be registered there shall be supplied to the Commissioners copies of its trusts (or, if they are not set out in any extant document, particulars of them), and such other documents or information as may be prescribed by regulations made by the [Minister] or as the Commissioners may require for the purpose of the application.

(7) It shall be the duty—
- (a) of the charity trustees of any charity which is not registered nor excepted from registration to apply for it to be registered, and to supply the documents and information required by subsection (6) above; and
- (b) of the charity trustees (or last charity trustees) of any institution which is for the time being registered to notify the Commissioners if it ceases to exist, or if there is

any change in its trusts or in the particulars of it entered in the register, and to supply to the Commissioners particulars of any such change and copies of any new trusts or alterations of the trusts.

(8) The register (including the entries cancelled when institutions are removed from the register) shall be open to public inspection at all reasonable times; and copies (or particulars) of the trusts of any registered charity as supplied to the Commissioners under this section shall, so long as it remains on the register, be kept by them and be open to public inspection at all reasonable times, except in so far as regulations made by the [Minister] otherwise provide.

(9) Where any information contained in the register is not in documentary form, subsection (8) above shall be construed as requiring the information to be available for public inspection in legible form at all reasonable times.

(10) If the Commissioners so determine, subsection (8) above shall not apply to any particular information contained in the register and specified in their determination.

(11) Nothing in the foregoing subsections shall require any person to supply the Commissioners with copies of schemes for the administration of a charity made otherwise than by the court, or to notify the Commissioners of any change made with respect to a registered charity by such a scheme, or require a person, if he refers the Commissioners to a document or copy already in the possession of the Commissioners, to supply a further copy of the document; but where by virtue of this subsection a copy of any document need not be supplied to the Commissioners, a copy of it, if it relates to a registered charity, shall be open to inspection under subsection (8) above as if supplied to the Commissioners under this section.

(12) If the [Minister] thinks it expedient to do so—

(a) in consequence of changes in the value of money, or

(b) with a view to extending the scope of the exception provided for by subsection (5)(c) above,

he may by order amend subsection (5)(c) by substituting a different sum for the sum for the time being specified there.

(13) The reference in subsection (5)(b) above to a charity which is excepted by order or regulations is to a charity which—

(a) is for the time being permanently or temporarily excepted by order of the Commissioners; or

(b) is of a description permanently or temporarily excepted by regulations made by the [Minister],

and which complies with any conditions of the exception.

(14) In this section "registered place of worship" means any land or building falling within section 9 of the Places of Worship Registration Act 1855 (that is to say, the land and buildings which if the Charities Act 1960 had not been passed, would by virtue of that section as amended by subsequent enactments be partially exempted from the operation of the Charitable Trusts Act 1853), and for the purposes of this subsection "building" includes part of a building.

[768]

NOTES

Sub-s (5A): inserted by the Teaching and Higher Education Act 1998, s 44(1), Sch 3, para 9.

Sub-s (5B): inserted by the School Standards and Framework Act 1998, s 140(1), Sch 30, para 48; word in square brackets substituted by the Transfer of Functions (Third Sector, Communities and Equality) Order 2006, SI 2006/2951, art 6, Schedule, para 4(c).

Sub-ss (6), (8), (12), (13): words in square brackets substituted by SI 2006/2951, art 6, Schedule, para 4(c).

Substituted, together with ss 3A, 3B, for s 3 as originally enacted, by the Charities Act 2006, s 9, as from a day to be appointed under s 79(2) of that Act, as follows—

"3 Register of charities

(1) There shall continue to be a register of charities, which shall be kept by the Commission.

(2) The register shall be kept by the Commission in such manner as it thinks fit.

(3) The register shall contain—

(a) the name of every charity registered in accordance with section 3A below (registration), and

(b) such other particulars of, and such other information relating

to, every such charity as the Commission thinks fit.

(4) The Commission shall remove from the register—
(a) any institution which it no longer considers is a charity, and
(b) any charity which has ceased to exist or does not operate.

(5) If the removal of an institution under subsection (4)(a) above is due to any change in its trusts, the removal shall take effect from the date of that change.

(6) A charity which is for the time being registered under section 3A(6) below (voluntary registration) shall be removed from the register if it so requests.

(7) The register (including the entries cancelled when institutions are removed from the register) shall be open to public inspection at all reasonable times.

(8) Where any information contained in the register is not in documentary form, subsection (7) above shall be construed as requiring the information to be available for public inspection in legible form at all reasonable times.

(9) If the Commission so determines, subsection (7) shall not apply to any particular information contained in the register that is specified in the determination.

(10) Copies (or particulars) of the trusts of any registered charity as supplied to the Commission under section 3B below (applications for registration etc) shall, so long as the charity remains on the register—
(a) be kept by the Commission, and
(b) be open to public inspection at all reasonable times.".

Regulations: the Charities (Exception from Registration) Regulations 1996, SI 1996/180 at **[3206]**.
In addition, by virtue of the Interpretation Act 1978, s 17(2)(b), the following regulations have effect as if made under sub-s (13) above: the Charities (Exception of Voluntary Schools from Registration) Regulations 1960, SI 1960/2366; the Charities (Exception of Certain Charities for Boy Scouts and Girl Guides from Registration) Regulations 1961, SI 1961/1044; the Charities (Baptist, Congregational and Unitarian Churches and Presbyterian Church of England) Regulations 1961, SI 1961/1282; the Charities (Religious Premises) Regulations 1962, SI 1962/1421; the Charities (Society of Friends, Fellowship of Independent Evangelical Churches and Presbyterian Church of Wales) Regulations 1962, SI 1962/1815; the Charities (Church of England) Regulations 1963, SI 1963/1062; the Charities (Exception from Registration and Accounts) Regulations 1965, SI 1965/1056; the Charities (Exception of Universities from Registration) Regulations 1966, SI 1966/965; the Charities (Methodist Church) Regulations 1978, SI 1978/1836.

[3A Registration of charities

(1) Every charity must be registered in the register of charities unless subsection (2) below applies to it.

(2) The following are not required to be registered—
(a) any exempt charity (see Schedule 2 to this Act);
(b) any charity which for the time being—
 (i) is permanently or temporarily excepted by order of the Commission, and
 (ii) complies with any conditions of the exception, and whose gross income does not exceed £100,000;
(c) any charity which for the time being—
 (i) is, or is of a description, permanently or temporarily excepted by regulations made by the [Minister], and
 (ii) complies with any conditions of the exception, and whose gross income does not exceed £100,000; and
(d) any charity whose gross income does not exceed £5,000.

(3) For the purposes of subsection (2)(b) above—
(a) any order made or having effect as if made under section 3(5)(b) of this Act (as originally enacted) and in force immediately before the appointed day has effect as from that day as if made under subsection (2)(b) (and may be varied or revoked accordingly); and
(b) no order may be made under subsection (2)(b) so as to except on or after the appointed day any charity that was not excepted immediately before that day.

(4) For the purposes of subsection (2)(c) above—
(a) any regulations made or having effect as if made under section 3(5)(b) of this Act (as originally enacted) and in force immediately before the appointed day have effect as from that day as if made under subsection (2)(c) (and may be varied or revoked accordingly);
(b) such regulations shall be made under subsection (2)(c) as are necessary to secure

that all of the formerly specified institutions are excepted under that provision (subject to compliance with any conditions of the exception and the financial limit mentioned in that provision); but

(c) otherwise no regulations may be made under subsection (2)(c) so as to except on or after the appointed day any description of charities that was not excepted immediately before that day.

(5) In subsection (4)(b) above "formerly specified institutions" means—

(a) any institution falling within section 3(5B)(a) or (b) of this Act as in force immediately before the appointed day (certain educational institutions); or

(b) any institution ceasing to be an exempt charity by virtue of section 11 of the Charities Act 2006 or any order made under that section.

(6) A charity within—

(a) subsection (2)(b) or (c) above, or

(b) subsection (2)(d) above,

must, if it so requests, be registered in the register of charities.

(7) The Minister may by order amend—

(a) subsection (2)(b) and (c) above, or

(b) subsection (2)(d) above,

by substituting a different sum for the sum for the time being specified there.

(8) The Minister may only make an order under subsection (7) above—

(a) so far as it amends subsection (2)(b) and (c), if he considers it expedient to so with a view to reducing the scope of the exception provided by those provisions;

(b) so far as it amends subsection (2)(d), if he considers it expedient to do so in consequence of changes in the value of money or with a view to extending the scope of the exception provided by that provision, and no order may be made by him under subsection (7)(a) unless a copy of a report under section 73 of the Charities Act 2006 (report on operation of that Act) has been laid before Parliament in accordance

with that section.

(9) In this section "the appointed day" means the day on which subsections (1) to (5) above come into force by virtue of an order under section 79 of the Charities Act 2006 relating to section 9 of that Act (registration of charities).

(10) In this section any reference to a charity's "gross income" shall be construed, in relation to a particular time—

(a) as a reference to the charity's gross income in its financial year immediately preceding that time, or

(b) if the Commission so determines, as a reference to the amount which the Commission estimates to be the likely amount of the charity's gross income in such financial year of the charity as is specified in the determination.

(11) The following provisions of this section—

(a) subsection (2)(b) and (c),

(b) subsections (3) to (5), and

(c) subsections (6)(a), (7)(a), (8)(a) and (9),

shall cease to have effect on such day as the Minister may by order appoint for the purposes of this subsection.]

[768A]

NOTES

Commencement: 27 February 2007 (sub-ss (2)(c), (4)(b), (5) for the purposes of enabling the Minister to exercise the power to make subordinate legislation); to be appointed (otherwise).

Substituted as noted to s 3 at **[768]**.

Sub-s (2): word in square brackets in para (c) substituted by the Transfer of Functions (Third Sector, Communities and Equality) Order 2006, SI 2006/2951, art 6, Schedule, para 4(d).

[3B Duties of trustees in connection with registration

(1) Where a charity required to be registered by virtue of section 3A(1) above is not registered, it is the duty of the charity trustees—

(a) to apply to the Commission for the charity to be registered, and

(b) to supply the Commission with the required documents and information.

(2) The "required documents and information" are—
 (a) copies of the charity's trusts or (if they are not set out in any extant document) particulars of them,
 (b) such other documents or information as may be prescribed by regulations made by the Minister, and
 (c) such other documents or information as the Commission may require for the purposes of the application.

(3) Where an institution is for the time being registered, it is the duty of the charity trustees (or the last charity trustees)—
 (a) to notify the Commission if the institution ceases to exist, or if there is any change in its trusts or in the particulars of it entered in the register, and
 (b) (so far as appropriate), to supply the Commission with particulars of any such change and copies of any new trusts or alterations of the trusts.

(4) Nothing in subsection (3) above requires a person—
 (a) to supply the Commission with copies of schemes for the administration of a charity made otherwise than by the court,
 (b) to notify the Commission of any change made with respect to a registered charity by such a scheme, or
 (c) if he refers the Commission to a document or copy already in the possession of the Commission, to supply a further copy of the document.

(5) Where a copy of a document relating to a registered charity—
 (a) is not required to be supplied to the Commission as the result of subsection (4) above, but
 (b) is in the possession of the Commission, a copy of the document shall be open to inspection under section 3(10) above as if supplied to the Commission under this section.".

[768B]

NOTES

Commencement: 27 February 2007 (sub-s (2)(b) for the purposes of enabling the Minister to exercise the power to make subordinate legislation); to be appointed (otherwise).

Substituted as noted to s 3 at **[768]**.

4 Effect of, and claims and objections to, registration

(1) An institution shall for all purposes other than rectification of the register be conclusively presumed to be or to have been a charity at any time when it is or was on the register of charities.

(2) Any person who is or may be affected by the registration of an institution as a charity may, on the ground that it is not a charity, object to its being entered by [the Commission] in the register, or apply [to the Commission] for it to be removed from the register; and provision may be made by regulations made by the [Minister] as to the manner in which any such objection or application is to be made, prosecuted or dealt with.

(3) An appeal against any decision of the Commissioners to enter or not to enter an institution in the register of charities, or to remove or not to remove an institution from the register, may be brought in the High Court by the Attorney General, or by the persons who are or claim to be the charity trustees of the institution, or by any person whose objection or application under subsection (2) above is disallowed by the decision.

(4) If there is an appeal to the *High Court* against any decision of [the Commission] to enter an institution in the register, or not to remove an institution from the register, then until [the Commissioners is] satisfied whether the decision of [the Commission] is or is not to stand, the entry in the register shall be maintained, but shall be in suspense and marked to indicate that it is in suspense; and for the purposes of subsection (1) above an institution shall be deemed not to be on the register during any period when the entry relating to it is in suspense under this subsection.

(5) Any question affecting the registration or removal from the register of an institution may, notwithstanding that it has been determined by a decision on appeal under *subsection (3) above*, be considered afresh by [the Commission] and shall not be concluded by that decision, if it appears to [the Commission] that there has been a change of circumstances or that the decision is inconsistent with a later judicial decision, *whether given on such an appeal or not*.

[769]

PART I STATUTES

NOTES

Sub-s (2): words in first and second pairs of square brackets substituted by the Charities Act 2006, s 75(1), Sch 8, paras 96, 99(1), (2), as from 27 February 2007; word in third pair of square brackets substituted by the Transfer of Functions (Third Sector, Communities and Equality) Order 2006, SI 2006/2951, art 6, Schedule, para 4(e).

Sub-s (3): repealed by the Charities Act 2006, s 75(1), (2), Sch 8, paras 96, 99(1), (3), Sch 9, as from a day to be appointed under s 79(2) of that Act, subject to savings in Sch 10, para 18 to that Act at **[2176]**.

Sub-s (4): for the words in italics there is substituted the word "Tribunal" by the Charities Act 2006, s 75(1), Sch 8, paras 96, 99(1), (4)(a), as from a day to be appointed under s 79(2) of that Act, subject to savings in Sch 10, para 18 to that Act at **[2176]**, and words in square brackets substituted, by s 75(1) of, and Sch 8, paras 96, 99(1), (4)(b), (c) to, that Act, as from 27 February 2007.

Sub-s (5): for the words in italics in the first place there are substituted the words "Schedule 1C to this Act" and words in italics in the second place repealed by the Charities Act 2006, s 75(1), Sch 8, paras 96, 99(1), (5)(a), (c), as from a day to be appointed under s 79(2) of that Act, subject to savings in Sch 10, para 18 to that Act at **[2176]**, and words in square brackets substituted by s 75(1), (2) of, and Sch 8, paras 96, 99(1), (5)(b) to, that Act, as from 27 February 2007.

5 Status of registered charity (other than small charity) to appear on official publications etc

(1) This section applies to a registered charity if its gross income in its last financial year exceeded [£10,000].

(2) Where this section applies to a registered charity, the fact that it is a registered charity shall be stated … in legible characters—

(a) in all notices, advertisements and other documents issued by or on behalf of the charity and soliciting money or other property for the benefit of the charity;

(b) in all bills of exchange, promissory notes, endorsements, cheques and orders for money or goods purporting to be signed on behalf of the charity; and

(c) in all bills rendered by it and in all its invoices, receipts and letters of credit.

[(2A) The statement required by subsection (2) above shall be in English, except that, in the case of a document which is otherwise wholly in Welsh, the statement may be in Welsh if it consists of or includes the words "elusen cofrestredig" (the Welsh equivalent of "registered charity").]

(3) Subsection (2)(a) above has effect whether the solicitation is express or implied, and whether the money or other property is to be given for any consideration or not.

(4) If, in the case of a registered charity to which this section applies, any person issues or authorises the issue of any document falling within paragraph (a) or (c) of subsection (2) above [which does not contain the statement] required by that subsection, he shall be guilty of an offence and liable on summary conviction to a fine not exceeding level 3 on the standard scale.

(5) If, in the case of any such registered charity, any person signs any document falling within paragraph (b) of subsection (2) above [which does not contain the statement] required by that subsection, he shall be guilty of an offence and liable on summary conviction to a fine not exceeding level 3 on the standard scale.

(6) The [Minister] may by order amend subsection (1) above by substituting a different sum for the sum for the time being specified there.

[770]

NOTES

Sub-s (1): sum in square brackets substituted by the Charities Act 1993 (Substitution of Sums) Order 1995, SI 1995/2696, art 2(1), (2).

Sub-s (2): words omitted repealed by the Welsh Language Act 1993, ss 32(1), (2), 35(1), Sch 2.

Sub-s (2A): inserted by the Welsh Language Act 1993, s 32(1), (3).

Sub-ss (4), (5): words in square brackets substituted by the Welsh Language Act 1993, s 32(1), (4), (5).

Sub-s (6): word in square brackets substituted by the Transfer of Functions (Third Sector, Communities and Equality) Order 2006, SI 2006/2951, art 6, Schedule, para 4(f).

Orders: the Charities Act 1993 (Substitution of Sums) Order 1995, SI 1995/2696.

Charity names

6 Power of [Commission] to require charity's name to be changed

(1) Where this subsection applies to a charity, the [Commission] may give a direction requiring the name of the charity to be changed, within such period as is specified in the direction, to such other name as the charity trustees may determine with the approval of the [Commission].

(2) Subsection (1) above applies to a charity if—

(a) it is a registered charity and its name ("the registered name")—

(i) is the same as, or

(ii) is in the opinion of the [Commission] too like,

the name, at the time when the registered name was entered in the register in respect of the charity, of any other charity (whether registered or not);

(b) the name of the charity is in the opinion of the [Commission] likely to mislead the public as to the true nature—

(i) of the purposes of the charity as set out in its trusts, or

(ii) of the activities which the charity carries on under its trusts in pursuit of those purposes;

(c) the name of the charity includes any word or expression for the time being specified in regulations made by the [Minister] and the inclusion in its name of that word or expression is in the opinion of the [Commission] likely to mislead the public in any respect as to the status of the charity;

(d) the name of the charity is in the opinion of the [Commission] likely to give the impression that the charity is connected in some way with Her Majesty's Government or any local authority, or with any other body of persons or any individual, when it is not so connected; or

(e) the name of the charity is in the opinion of the [Commission] offensive;

and in this subsection any reference to the name of a charity is, in relation to a registered charity, a reference to the name by which it is registered.

(3) Any direction given by virtue of subsection (2)(a) above must be given within twelve months of the time when the registered name was entered in the register in respect of the charity.

(4) Any direction given under this section with respect to a charity shall be given to the charity trustees; and on receiving any such direction the charity trustees shall give effect to it notwithstanding anything in the trusts of the charity.

(5) Where the name of any charity is changed under this section, then (without prejudice to *section 3(7)(b) above*) it shall be the duty of the charity trustees forthwith to notify the [Commission] of the charity's new name and of the date on which the change occurred.

(6) A change of name by a charity under this section does not affect any rights or obligations of the charity; and any legal proceedings that might have been continued or commenced by or against it in its former name may be continued or commenced by or against it in its new name.

(7) Section 26(3) of the Companies Act 1985 (minor variations in names to be disregarded) shall apply for the purposes of this section as if the reference to section 26(1)(c) of that Act were a reference to subsection (2)(a) above.

(8) Any reference in this section to the charity trustees of a charity shall, in relation to a charity which is a company, be read as a reference to the directors of the company.

(9) Nothing in this section applies to an exempt charity.

[771]

NOTES

Section heading: word in square brackets substituted by the Charities Act 2006, s 75(1), Sch 8, paras 96, 100(1), (2), as from 27 February 2007.

Sub-s (1): words in square brackets substituted by the Charities Act 2006, s 75(1), Sch 8, paras 96, 100(1), (2), as from 27 February 2007.

Sub-s (2): word in first pair of square brackets in para (c) substituted by the Transfer of Functions (Third Sector, Communities and Equality) Order 2006, SI 2006/2951, art 6, Schedule, para 4(g); other words in square brackets substituted by the Charities Act 2006, s 75(1), Sch 8, paras 96, 100(1), (2), as from 27 February 2007.

Sub-s (5): for the words in italics in the first place there are substituted the words "section 3B(3)" by the Charities Act 2006, s 75(1), Sch 8, paras 96, 100(1), (3), as from a day to be appointed under the Charities Act 2006, s 79(2); word in square brackets substituted by s 75(1) of, and Sch 8, paras 96, 100(1), (2) to, that Act, as from 27 February 2007.

Sub-s (9): repealed by the Charities Act 2006, ss 12, 75(2), Sch 5, para 1, Sch 9, as from a day to be appointed under s 79(2) of that Act.

Regulations: by virtue of the Interpretation Act 1978, s 17(2)(b), the Charities (Misleading Names) Regulations 1992, SI 1992/1901 at **[3094]**, have effect as if made under this section.

---

7 Effect of direction under s 6 where charity is a company

(1) Where any direction is given under section 6 above with respect to a charity which is a company, the direction shall be taken to require the name of the charity to be changed by resolution of the directors of the company.

(2) Section 380 of the Companies Act 1985 (registration etc of resolutions and agreements) shall apply to any resolution passed by the directors in compliance with any such direction.

(3) Where the name of such a charity is changed in compliance with any such direction, the registrar of companies—

(a) shall, subject to section 26 of the Companies Act 1985 (prohibition on registration of certain names), enter the new name on the register of companies in place of the former name, and

(b) shall issue a certificate of incorporation altered to meet the circumstances of the case;

and the change of name has effect from the date on which the altered certificate is issued.

[772]

PART III
[INFORMATION POWERS]

8 General power to institute inquiries

(1) [The Commission] may from time to time institute inquiries with regard to charities or a particular charity or class of charities, either generally or for particular purposes, but no such inquiry shall extend to any exempt charity [except where this has been requested by its principal regulator].

(2) [The Commission] may either conduct such an inquiry [itself] or appoint a person to conduct it and make a report [to the Commission].

(3) For the purposes of any such inquiry [the Commission, or a person appointed by the Commission] to conduct it, may direct any person (subject to the provisions of this section)—

(a) to furnish accounts and statements in writing with respect to any matter in question at the inquiry, being a matter on which he has or can reasonably obtain information, or to return answers in writing to any questions or inquiries addressed to him on any such matter, and to verify any such accounts, statements or answers by statutory declaration;

(b) to furnish copies of documents in his custody or under his control which relate to any matter in question at the inquiry, and to verify any such copies by statutory declaration;

(c) to attend at a specified time and place and give evidence or produce any such documents.

(4) For the purposes of any such inquiry evidence may be taken on oath, and the person conducting the inquiry may for that purpose administer oaths, or may instead of administering an oath require the person examined to make and subscribe a declaration of the truth of the matters about which he is examined.

(5) [The Commission] may pay to any person the necessary expenses of his attendance to give evidence or produce documents for the purpose of an inquiry under this section, and a person shall not be required in obedience to a direction under paragraph (c) of subsection (3) above to go more than ten miles from his place of residence unless those expenses are paid or tendered to him.

(6) Where an inquiry has been held under this section, [the Commission] may either—

(a) cause the report of the person conducting the inquiry, or such other statement of the results of the inquiry as [the Commission thinks] fit, to be printed and published, or

(b) publish any such report or statement in some other way which is calculated in [the Commission's opinion] to bring it to the attention of persons who may wish to make representations [to the Commission] about the action to be taken.

(7) The council of a county or district, the Common Council of the City of London and the council of a London borough may contribute to the expenses of [the Commission] in connection with inquiries under this section into local charities in the council's area.

[773]

NOTES

Words in square brackets in the Part Heading preceding this section substituted by the Charities Act 2006, s 75(1), Sch 8, paras 96, 101, as from 27 February 2007.

Sub-s (1): words in first pair of square brackets substituted by the Charities Act 2006, s 75(1), Sch 8, paras 96, 102(1), (2), as from 27 February 2007, and words in second pair of square brackets inserted, as from a day to be appointed under s 79(2) of that Act, by s 12 of, and Sch 5, para 2 to, that Act.

Sub-ss (2), (3), (5)–(7): words in square brackets substituted by the Charities Act 2006, s 75(1), Sch 8, paras 96, 102(1), (3)–(7), as from 27 February 2007.

9 Power to call for documents and search records

(1) [The Commission] may by order—

(a) require any person to [furnish the Commission] with any information in his possession which relates to any charity and is relevant to the discharge of [the Commission's functions] or of the functions of the official custodian;

(b) require any person who has in his custody or under his control any document which relates to any charity and is relevant to the discharge of [the Commission's functions] or of the functions of the official custodian—

(i) to [furnish the Commission] with a copy of or extract from the document, or

(ii) (unless the document forms part of the records or other documents of a court or of a public or local authority) to transmit the document itself to [the Commission for its] inspection.

(2) Any [member of the staff of the Commission, if so authorised by it], shall be entitled without payment to inspect and take copies of or extracts from the records or other documents of any court, or of any public registry or office of records, for any purpose connected with the discharge of the functions of [the Commission] or of the official custodian.

(3) [The Commission] shall be entitled without payment to keep any copy or extract furnished [to it] under subsection (1) above; and where a document transmitted [to the Commission] under that subsection for [it to inspect] relates only to one or more charities and is not held by any person entitled as trustee or otherwise to the custody of it, [the Commission] may keep it or may deliver it to the charity trustees or to any other person who may be so entitled.

(4) No person properly having the custody of documents relating only to an exempt charity shall be required under subsection (1) above to transmit to the Commissioners any of those documents, or to furnish any copy of or extract from any of them.

(5) The rights conferred by subsection (2) above shall, in relation to information recorded otherwise than in legible form, include the right to require the information to be made available in legible form for inspection or for a copy or extract to be made of or from it.

[(6) In subsection (2) the reference to a member of the staff of the Commission includes the official custodian even if he is not a member of the staff of the Commission.]

[774]

NOTES

Sub-ss (1)–(3): words in square brackets substituted by the Charities Act 2006, s 75(1), Sch 8, paras 96, 103(1)–(4), as from 27 February 2007.

Sub-s (4): repealed by the Charities Act 2006, ss 12, 75(2), Sch 5, para 3, Sch 9, as from a day to be appointed under s 79(2) of that Act.

Sub-s (6): added by the Charities Act 2006, s 75(1), Sch 8, paras 96, 103(1), (5), as from 27 February 2007.

[10 Disclosure of information to Commission

(1) Any relevant public authority may disclose information to the Commission if the disclosure is made for the purpose of enabling or assisting the Commission to discharge any of its functions.

(2) But Revenue and Customs information may be disclosed under subsection (1) only if it relates to an institution, undertaking or body falling within one (or more) of the following paragraphs—

(a) a charity;

(b) an institution which is established for charitable, benevolent or philanthropic purposes;

(c) an institution by or in respect of which a claim for exemption has at any time been made under section 505(1) of the Income and Corporation Taxes Act 1988;

(d) a subsidiary undertaking of a charity;

(e) a body entered in the Scottish Charity Register which is managed or controlled wholly or mainly in or from England or Wales.

(3) In subsection (2)(d) above "subsidiary undertaking of a charity" means an undertaking (as defined by section 259(1) of the Companies Act 1985) in relation to which—

(a) a charity is (or is to be treated as) a parent undertaking in accordance with the provisions of section 258 of, and Schedule 10A to, the Companies Act 1985, or

(b) two or more charities would, if they were a single charity, be (or be treated as) a parent undertaking in accordance with those provisions.

(4) For the purposes of the references to a parent undertaking—

(a) in subsection (3) above, and

(b) in section 258 of, and Schedule 10A to, the Companies Act 1985 as they apply for the purposes of that subsection,

"undertaking" includes a charity which is not an undertaking as defined by section 259(1) of that Act.]

[775]

NOTES

Commencement: 8 November 2006 (so far as it confers power to make regulations); 27 February 2007 (otherwise).

Substituted, together with ss 10A–10C, by the Charities Act 2006, s 75(1), Sch 8, paras 96, 104.

[10A Disclosure of information by Commission

(1) Subject to subsections (2) and (3) below, the Commission may disclose to any relevant public authority any information received by the Commission in connection with any of the Commission's functions—

(a) if the disclosure is made for the purpose of enabling or assisting the relevant public authority to discharge any of its functions, or

(b) if the information so disclosed is otherwise relevant to the discharge of any of the functions of the relevant public authority.

(2) In the case of information disclosed to the Commission under section 10(1) above, the Commission's power to disclose the information under subsection (1) above is exercisable subject to any express restriction subject to which the information was disclosed to the Commission.

(3) Subsection (2) above does not apply in relation to Revenue and Customs information disclosed to the Commission under section 10(1) above; but any such information may not be further disclosed (whether under subsection (1) above or otherwise) except with the consent of the Commissioners for Her Majesty's Revenue and Customs.

(4) Any responsible person who discloses information in contravention of subsection (3) above is guilty of an offence and liable—

(a) on summary conviction, to imprisonment for a term not exceeding 12 months or to a fine not exceeding the statutory maximum, or both;

(b) on conviction on indictment, to imprisonment for a term not exceeding two years or to a fine, or both.

(5) It is a defence for a responsible person charged with an offence under subsection (4) above of disclosing information to prove that he reasonably believed—

(a) that the disclosure was lawful, or

(b) that the information had already and lawfully been made available to the public.

(6) In the application of this section to Scotland or Northern Ireland, the reference to 12 months in subsection (4) is to be read as a reference to 6 months.

(7) In this section "responsible person" means a person who is or was—

(a) a member of the Commission,

(b) a member of the staff of the Commission,

(c) a person acting on behalf of the Commission or a member of the staff of the Commission, or

(d) a member of a committee established by the Commission.]

[775A]

NOTES

Commencement: 8 November 2006 (so far as it confers power to make regulations); 27 February 2007 (otherwise).

Substituted as noted to s 10 at **[775]**, subject to transitional provisions in the Charities Act 2006, s 75(3), Sch 10, para 20 at **[2176]**.

By the Charities Act 2006 (Commencement No 1, Transitional Provisions and Savings) Order 2007, SI 2007/309, art 5, the restriction on the Charity Commission's power of disclosure under sub-s (2) applies whether the information was disclosed to the Charity Commission before, on or after 27 February 2007. In relation to information disclosed to the Charity Commission before 27 February 2007, the reference in sub-s (2) to s 10(1) is to be taken as a reference to s 10(1) as originally enacted, which read as follows—

"(1) Subject to subsection (2) below and to any express restriction imposed by or under any other enactment, a body or person to whom this section applies may disclose to the Charity Commissioners any information received by that body or person under or for the purposes of any enactment, where the disclosure is made by the body or person for the purpose of enabling or assisting the Commissioners to discharge any of their functions.".

[10B Disclosure to and by principal regulators of exempt charities

(1) Sections 10 and 10A above apply with the modifications in subsections (2) to (4) below in relation to the disclosure of information to or by the principal regulator of an exempt charity.

(2) References in those sections to the Commission or to any of its functions are to be read as references to the principal regulator of an exempt charity or to any of the functions of that body or person as principal regulator in relation to the charity.

(3) Section 10 above has effect as if for subsections (2) and (3) there were substituted—

"(2) But Revenue and Customs information may be disclosed under subsection (1) only if it relates to—

(a) the exempt charity in relation to which the principal regulator has functions as such, or

(b) a subsidiary undertaking of the exempt charity.

(3) In subsection (2)(b) above "subsidiary undertaking of the exempt charity" means an undertaking (as defined by section 259(1) of the Companies Act 1985) in relation to which—

(a) the exempt charity is (or is to be treated as) a parent undertaking in accordance with the provisions of section 258 of, and Schedule 10A to, the Companies Act 1985, or

(b) the exempt charity and one or more other charities would, if they were a single charity, be (or be treated as) a parent undertaking in accordance with those provisions."

(4) Section 10A above has effect as if for the definition of "responsible person" in subsection (7) there were substituted a definition specified by regulations under section 13(4)(b) of the Charities Act 2006 (regulations prescribing principal regulators).

(5) Regulations under section 13(4)(b) of that Act may also make such amendments or other modifications of any enactment as the [Minister] considers appropriate for securing that any disclosure provisions that would otherwise apply in relation to the principal regulator of an exempt charity do not apply in relation to that body or person in its or his capacity as principal regulator.

(6) In subsection (5) above "disclosure provisions" means provisions having effect for authorising, or otherwise in connection with, the disclosure of information by or to the principal regulator concerned.]

[775B]

NOTES

Commencement: 8 November 2006 (so far as it confers power to make regulations); to be appointed (otherwise).

Substituted as noted to s 10 at **[775]**.

Sub-s (5): word in square brackets substituted by the Transfer of Functions (Third Sector, Communities and Equality) Order 2006, SI 2006/2951, art 6, Schedule, para 4(h).

[10C Disclosure of information: supplementary

(1) In sections 10 and 10A above "relevant public authority" means—

(a) any government department (including a Northern Ireland department),

(b) any local authority,

(c) any constable, and

(d) any other body or person discharging functions of a public nature (including a body or person discharging regulatory functions in relation to any description of activities).

(2) In section 10A above "relevant public authority" also includes any body or person within subsection (1)(d) above in a country or territory outside the United Kingdom.

(3) In sections 10 to 10B above and this section—

"enactment" has the same meaning as in the Charities Act 2006;

"Revenue and Customs information" means information held as mentioned in section 18(1) of the Commissioners for Revenue and Customs Act 2005.

(4) Nothing in sections 10 and 10A above (or in those sections as applied by section 10B(1) to (4) above) authorises the making of a disclosure which—

(a) contravenes the Data Protection Act 1998, or

(b) is prohibited by Part 1 of the Regulation of Investigatory Powers Act 2000.]

[775C]

NOTES

Commencement: 8 November 2006 (so far as it confers power to make regulations); 27 February 2007 (otherwise, except in so far as this section refers to s 10B).

Substituted as noted to s 10 at **[775]**.

11 Supply of false or misleading information to [Commission], etc

(1) Any person who knowingly or recklessly provides the [Commission] with information which is false or misleading in a material particular shall be guilty of an offence if the information—

(a) is provided in purported compliance with a requirement imposed by or under this Act; or

(b) is provided otherwise than as mentioned in paragraph (a) above but in circumstances in which the person providing the information intends, or could reasonably be expected to know, that it would be used by the [Commission] for the purpose of discharging [its functions] under this Act.

(2) Any person who wilfully alters, suppresses, conceals or destroys any document which he is or is liable to be required, by or under this Act, to produce to the [Commission]shall be guilty of an offence.

(3) Any person guilty of an offence under this section shall be liable—

(a) on summary conviction, to a fine not exceeding the statutory maximum;

(b) on conviction on indictment, to imprisonment for a term not exceeding two years or to a fine, or both.

(4) In this section references to the [Commission] include references to any person conducting an inquiry under section 8 above.

[776]

NOTES

Section heading: words in square brackets substituted by the Charities Act 2006, s 75(1), Sch 8, paras 96, 105(1), (2), as from 27 February 2007.

Sub-ss (1), (2), (4): words in square brackets substituted by the Charities Act 2006, s 75(1), Sch 8, paras 96, 105, as from 27 February 2007.

12 (*Repealed by the Data Protection Act 1998, s 74(2), Sch 16, Pt I.*)

PART IV
APPLICATION OF PROPERTY CY-PRÈS AND ASSISTANCE AND SUPERVISION OF CHARITIES BY COURT [AND COMMISSION]

Extended powers of court and variation of charters

13 Occasions for applying property cy-près

(1) Subject to subsection (2) below, the circumstances in which the original purposes of a charitable gift can be altered to allow the property given or part of it to be applied cy-près shall be as follows—

(a) where the original purposes, in whole or in part—
  (i) have been as far as may be fulfilled; or
  (ii) cannot be carried out, or not according to the directions given and to the spirit of the gift; or

(b) where the original purposes provide a use for part only of the property available by virtue of the gift; or

(c) where the property available by virtue of the gift and other property applicable for similar purposes can be more effectively used in conjunction, and to that end can suitably, regard being had to *the spirit of the gift*, be made applicable to common purposes; or

(d) where the original purposes were laid down by reference to an area which then was but has since ceased to be a unit for some other purpose, or by reference to a class of persons or to an area which has for any reason since ceased to be suitable, regard being had to *the spirit of the gift*, or to be practical in administering the gift; or

(e) where the original purposes, in whole or in part, have, since they were laid down,—
  (i) been adequately provided for by other means; or
  (ii) ceased, as being useless or harmful to the community or for other reasons, to be in law charitable; or
  (iii) ceased in any other way to provide a suitable and effective method of using the property available by virtue of the gift, regard being had to *the spirit of the gift*.

[(1A) In subsection (1) above "the appropriate considerations" means—

(a) (on the one hand) the spirit of the gift concerned, and

(b) (on the other) the social and economic circumstances prevailing at the time of the proposed alteration of the original purposes.]

(2) Subsection (1) above shall not affect the conditions which must be satisfied in order that property given for charitable purposes may be applied cy-près except in so far as those conditions require a failure of the original purposes.

(3) References in the foregoing subsections to the original purposes of a gift shall be construed, where the application of the property given has been altered or regulated by a scheme or otherwise, as referring to the purposes for which the property is for the time being applicable.

(4) Without prejudice to the power to make schemes in circumstances falling within subsection (1) above, the court may by scheme made under the court's jurisdiction with respect to charities, in any case where the purposes for which the property is held are laid down by reference to any such area as is mentioned in the first column in Schedule 3 to this Act, provide for enlarging the area to any such area as is mentioned in the second column in the same entry in that Schedule.

(5) It is hereby declared that a trust for charitable purposes places a trustee under a duty, where the case permits and requires the property or some part of it to be applied cy-près, to secure its effective use for charity by taking steps to enable it to be so applied.

[777]

NOTES

Words in square brackets in the Part Heading preceding this section substituted by the Charities Act 2006, s 75(1), Sch 8, paras 96, 106, as from 27 February 2007.

Sub-s (1): for the words in italics in paras (c), (d), (e)(iii) there are substituted the words "the appropriate considerations" by the Charities Act 2006, s 15(1), (2), as from a day to be appointed under s 79(2)of that Act.

Sub-s (1A): inserted by the Charities Act 2006, s 15(1), (3), as from a day to be appointed under s 79(2) of that Act.

14 Application cy-près of gifts of donors unknown or disclaiming

(1) Property given for specific charitable purposes which fail shall be applicable cy-près as if given for charitable purposes generally, where it belongs—

- (a) to a donor who after—
  - (i) the prescribed advertisements and inquiries have been published and made, and
  - (ii) the prescribed period beginning with the publication of those advertisements has expired,

  cannot be identified or cannot be found; or
- (b) to a donor who has executed a disclaimer in the prescribed form of his right to have the property returned.

(2) Where the prescribed advertisements and inquiries have been published and made by or on behalf of trustees with respect to any such property, the trustees shall not be liable to any person in respect of the property if no claim by him to be interested in it is received by them before the expiry of the period mentioned in subsection (1)(a)(ii) above.

(3) For the purposes of this section property shall be conclusively presumed (without any advertisement or inquiry) to belong to donors who cannot be identified, in so far as it consists—

- (a) of the proceeds of cash collections made by means of collecting boxes or by other means not adapted for distinguishing one gift from another; or
- (b) of the proceeds of any lottery, competition, entertainment, sale or similar money-raising activity, after allowing for property given to provide prizes or articles for sale or otherwise to enable the activity to be undertaken.

(4) The court [or the Commission] may by order direct that property not falling within subsection (3) above shall for the purposes of this section be treated (without any advertisement or inquiry) as belonging to donors who cannot be identified where it appears to the court [or the Commission] either—

- (a) that it would be unreasonable, having regard to the amounts likely to be returned to the donors, to incur expense with a view to returning the property; or
- (b) that it would be unreasonable, having regard to the nature, circumstances and amounts of the gifts, and to the lapse of time since the gifts were made, for the donors to expect the property to be returned.

(5) Where property is applied cy-près by virtue of this section, the donor shall be deemed to have parted with all his interest at the time when the gift was made; but where property is so applied as belonging to donors who cannot be identified or cannot be found, and is not so applied by virtue of subsection (3) or (4) above—

- (a) the scheme shall specify the total amount of that property; and
- (b) the donor of any part of that amount shall be entitled, if he makes a claim not later than six months after the date on which the scheme is made, to recover from the charity for which the property is applied a sum equal to that part, less any expenses properly incurred by the charity trustees after that date in connection with claims relating to his gift; and
- (c) the scheme may include directions as to the provision to be made for meeting any such claim.

(6) Where—

- (a) any sum is, in accordance with any such directions, set aside for meeting any such claims, but

(b) the aggregate amount of any such claims actually made exceeds the relevant amount,

then, if [the Commission so directs], each of the donors in question shall be entitled only to such proportion of the relevant amount as the amount of his claim bears to the aggregate amount referred to in paragraph (b) above; and for this purpose "the relevant amount" means the amount of the sum so set aside after deduction of any expenses properly incurred by the charity trustees in connection with claims relating to the donors' gifts.

(7) For the purposes of this section, charitable purposes shall be deemed to "fail" where any difficulty in applying property to those purposes makes that property or the part not applicable cy-près available to be returned to the donors.

(8) In this section "prescribed" means prescribed by regulations made by [the Commission]; and such regulations may, as respects the advertisements which are to be published for the purposes of subsection (1)(a) above, make provision as to the form and content of such advertisements as well as the manner in which they are to be published.

(9) Any regulations made by [the Commission] under this section shall be published by [the Commission] in such manner as [it thinks fit].

(10) In this section, except in so far as the context otherwise requires, references to a donor include persons claiming through or under the original donor, and references to property given include the property for the time being representing the property originally given or property derived from it.

(11) This section shall apply to property given for charitable purposes, notwithstanding that it was so given before the commencement of this Act.

[778]

NOTES

Sub-s (4): words in square brackets inserted by the Charities Act 2006, s 16, as from a day to be appointed under s 79(2) of that Act.

Sub-ss (6), (8), (9): words in square brackets substituted by the Charities Act 2006, s 75(1), Sch 8, paras 96, 107, as from 27 February 2007.

[14A Application cy-près of gifts made in response to certain solicitations

(1) This section applies to property given—
- (a) for specific charitable purposes, and
- (b) in response to a solicitation within subsection (2) below.

(2) A solicitation is within this subsection if—
- (a) it is made for specific charitable purposes, and
- (b) it is accompanied by a statement to the effect that property given in response to it will, in the event of those purposes failing, be applicable cy-près as if given for charitable purposes generally, unless the donor makes a relevant declaration at the time of making the gift.

(3) A "relevant declaration" is a declaration in writing by the donor to the effect that, in the event of the specific charitable purposes failing, he wishes the trustees holding the property to give him the opportunity to request the return of the property in question (or a sum equal to its value at the time of the making of the gift).

(4) Subsections (5) and (6) below apply if—
- (a) a person has given property as mentioned in subsection (1) above,
- (b) the specific charitable purposes fail, and
- (c) the donor has made a relevant declaration.

(5) The trustees holding the property must take the prescribed steps for the purpose of—
- (a) informing the donor of the failure of the purposes,
- (b) enquiring whether he wishes to request the return of the property (or a sum equal to its value), and
- (c) if within the prescribed period he makes such a request, returning the property (or such a sum) to him.

(6) If those trustees have taken all appropriate prescribed steps but—
- (a) they have failed to find the donor, or
- (b) the donor does not within the prescribed period request the return of the property (or a sum equal to its value),

section 14(1) above shall apply to the property as if it belonged to a donor within paragraph (b) of that subsection (application of property where donor has disclaimed right to return of property).

(7) If—

(a) a person has given property as mentioned in subsection (1) above,
(b) the specific charitable purposes fail, and
(c) the donor has not made a relevant declaration,

section 14(1) above shall similarly apply to the property as if it belonged to a donor within paragraph (b) of that subsection.

(8) For the purposes of this section—

(a) "solicitation" means a solicitation made in any manner and however communicated to the persons to whom it is addressed,
(b) it is irrelevant whether any consideration is or is to be given in return for the property in question, and
(c) where any appeal consists of both solicitations that are accompanied by statements within subsection (2)(b) and solicitations that are not so accompanied, a person giving property as a result of the appeal is to be taken to have responded to the former solicitations and not the latter, unless he proves otherwise.

(9) In this section "prescribed" means prescribed by regulations made by the Commission, and any such regulations shall be published by the Commission in such manner as it thinks fit.

(10) Subsections (7) and (10) of section 14 shall apply for the purposes of this section as they apply for the purposes of section 14.]

[778A]

NOTES

Commencement: 27 February 2007 (sub-s (9), enabling the Charity Commission to make regulations); to be appointed (otherwise).

Inserted by the Charities Act 2006, s 17, partly as from 27 February 2007, and fully as from a day to be appointed under s 79(2) of that Act.

[14B Cy-près schemes

(1) The power of the court or the Commission to make schemes for the application of property cy-près shall be exercised in accordance with this section.

(2) Where any property given for charitable purposes is applicable cy-près, the court or the Commission may make a scheme providing for the property to be applied—

(a) for such charitable purposes, and
(b) (if the scheme provides for the property to be transferred to another charity) by or on trust for such other charity,

as it considers appropriate, having regard to the matters set out in subsection (3).

(3) The matters are—

(a) the spirit of the original gift,
(b) the desirability of securing that the property is applied for charitable purposes which are close to the original purposes, and
(c) the need for the relevant charity to have purposes which are suitable and effective in the light of current social and economic circumstances.

The "relevant charity" means the charity by or on behalf of which the property is to be applied under the scheme.

(4) If a scheme provides for the property to be transferred to another charity, the scheme may impose on the charity trustees of that charity a duty to secure that the property is applied for purposes which are, so far as is reasonably practicable, similar in character to the original purposes.

(5) In this section references to property given include the property for the time being representing the property originally given or property derived from it.

(6) In this section references to the transfer of property to a charity are references to its transfer—

(a) to the charity, or
(b) to the charity trustees, or

(c) to any trustee for the charity, or

(d) to a person nominated by the charity trustees to hold it in trust for the charity,

as the scheme may provide."

[778B]

NOTES

Commencement: to be appointed.

Inserted by the Charities Act 2006, s 18, as from a day to be appointed under s 79(2) of that Act, subject to transitional provisions in Sch 10, para 3 to that Act at **[2176]**.

15 Charities governed by charter, or by or under statute

(1) Where a Royal charter establishing or regulating a body corporate is amendable by the grant and acceptance of a further charter, a scheme relating to the body corporate or to the administration of property held by the body (including a scheme for the cy-près application of any such property) may be made by the court under the court's jurisdiction with respect to charities notwithstanding that the scheme cannot take effect without the alteration of the charter, but shall be so framed that the scheme, or such part of it as cannot take effect without the alteration of the charter, does not purport to come into operation unless or until Her Majesty thinks fit to amend the charter in such manner as will permit the scheme or that part of it to have effect.

(2) Where under the court's jurisdiction with respect to charities or the corresponding jurisdiction of a court in Northern Ireland, or under powers conferred by this Act or by any Northern Ireland legislation relating to charities, a scheme is made with respect to a body corporate, and it appears to Her Majesty expedient, having regard to the scheme, to amend any Royal charter relating to that body, Her Majesty may, on the application of that body, amend the charter accordingly by Order in Council in any way in which the charter could be amended by the grant and acceptance of a further charter; and any such Order in Council may be revoked or varied in like manner as the charter it amends.

(3) The jurisdiction of the court with respect to charities shall not be excluded or restricted in the case of a charity of any description mentioned in Schedule 4 to this Act by the operation of the enactments or instruments there mentioned in relation to that description, and a scheme established for any such charity may modify or supersede in relation to it the provision made by any such enactment or instrument as if made by a scheme of the court, and may also make any such provision as is authorised by that Schedule.

[779]

NOTES

Orders in Council: by virtue of the Interpretation Act 1978, s 17(2)(b), the King George Fund for Sailors (Amendment of Charter) Order 1989, SI 1989/2414, has effect as if made under this section. In addition, the Royal College of Ophthalmologists (Charter Amendment) Order 1998, SI 1998/2252; the Corporation of the Cranleigh and Bramley Schools (Charter Amendments) Order 1999, SI 1999/656, the Royal College of Physicians of London (Charter Amendment) Order 1999, SI 1999/667; Licensed Victualler's National Homes (Charter Amendment) Order 2000, SI 2000/1348; the Institution of Chemical Engineers (Charter Amendment) Order 2004, SI 2004/1986.

[Powers of Commission] to make schemes and act for protection of charities etc

16 Concurrent jurisdiction with High Court for certain purposes

(1) Subject to the provisions of this Act, [the Commission] may by order exercise the same jurisdiction and powers as are exercisable by the High Court in charity proceedings for the following purposes—

(a) establishing a scheme for the administration of a charity;

(b) appointing, discharging or removing a charity trustee or trustee for a charity, or removing an officer or employee;

(c) vesting or transferring property, or requiring or entitling any person to call for or make any transfer of property or any payment.

(2) Where the court directs a scheme for the administration of a charity to be established, the court may by order refer the matter to [the Commission for it] to prepare or settle a scheme in accordance with such directions (if any) as the court sees fit to give, and any such

order may provide for the scheme to be put into effect by order of [the Commission] as if prepared under subsection (1) above and without any further order of the court.

(3) [The Commission] shall not have jurisdiction under this section to try or determine the title at law or in equity to any property as between a charity or trustee for a charity and a person holding or claiming the property or an interest in it adversely to the charity, or to try or determine any question as to the existence or extent of any charge or trust.

(4) Subject to the following subsections, [the Commission shall not exercise its] jurisdiction under this section as respects any charity, except—

(a) on the application of the charity; or

(b) on an order of the court under subsection (2) above; or

(c) *in the case of a charity other than an exempt charity,* on the application of the Attorney General.

(5) In the case of a charity *which is not an exempt charity and* whose [gross income does not] exceed £500 a year, [the Commission may exercise its] jurisdiction under this section on the application—

(a) of any one or more of the charity trustees; or

(b) of any person interested in the charity; or

(c) of any two or more inhabitants of the area of the charity if it is a local charity.

(6) Where in the case of a charity, other than an exempt charity, [the Commission is] satisfied that the charity trustees ought in the interests of the charity to apply for a scheme, but have unreasonably refused or neglected to do so and [the Commission has] given the charity trustees an opportunity to make representations to them, [the Commission] may proceed as if an application for a scheme had been made by the charity but [the Commission] shall not have power in a case where [it acts] by virtue of this subsection to alter the purposes of a charity, unless forty years have elapsed from the date of its foundation.

(7) Where—

(a) a charity cannot apply to [the Commission] for a scheme by reason of any vacancy among the charity trustees or the absence or incapacity of any of them, but

(b) such an application is made by such number of the charity trustees as [the Commission considers] appropriate in the circumstances of the case,

[the Commission] may nevertheless proceed as if the application were an application made by the charity.

(8) [The Commission] may on the application of any charity trustee or trustee for a charity exercise [its jurisdiction] under this section for the purpose of discharging him from his trusteeship.

(9) Before exercising any jurisdiction under this section otherwise than on an order of the court, [the Commission shall give notice of its] intention to do so to each of the charity trustees, except any that cannot be found or has no known address in the United Kingdom or who is party or privy to an application for the exercise of the jurisdiction; and any such notice may be given by post, and, if given by post, may be addressed to the recipient's last known address in the United Kingdom.

(10) [The Commission shall not exercise its] jurisdiction under this section in any case (not referred to them by order of the court) which, by reason of its contentious character, or of any special question of law or of fact which it may involve, or for other reasons, [the Commission] may consider more fit to be adjudicated on by the court.

(11) An appeal against any order of the Commissioners under this section may be brought in the High Court by the Attorney General.

(12) An appeal against any order of the Commissioners under this section may also, at any time within the three months beginning with the day following that on which the order is published, be brought in the High Court by the charity or any of the charity trustees, or by any person removed from any office or employment by the order (unless he is removed with the concurrence of the charity trustees or with the approval of the special visitor, if any, of the charity).

(13) No appeal shall be brought under subsection (12) above except with a certificate of the Commissioners that it is a proper case for an appeal or with the leave of one of the judges of the High Court attached to the Chancery Division.

(14) Where an order of the Commissioners under this section establishes a scheme for the administration of a charity, any person interested in the charity shall have the like right of

appeal under subsection (12) above as a charity trustee, and so also, in the case of a charity which is a local charity in any area, shall any two or more inhabitants of the area and the council of any parish or (in Wales) any community comprising the area or any part of it.

(15) If the [Minister] thinks it expedient to do so—

(a) in consequence of changes in the value of money, or

(b) with a view to increasing the number of charities in respect of which [the Commission may exercise its] jurisdiction under this section in accordance with subsection (5) above,

he may by order amend that subsection by substituting a different sum for the sum for the time being specified there.

[780]

NOTES

Words in square brackets in the cross-heading preceding this section substituted by the Charities Act 2006, s 75(1), Sch 8, paras 96, 108, as from 27 February 2007.

Sub-ss (1)–(3), (6)–(10): words in square brackets substituted by the Charities Act 2006, s 75(1), Sch 8, paras 96, 109(1)–(4), (7)–(11), as from 27 February 2007.

Sub-ss (4), (5): words in italics repealed by the Charities Act 2006, ss 12, 75(2), Sch 5, para 4, Sch 9, as from a day to be appointed under s 79(2) of that Act, and words in square brackets substituted by s 75(1) of, and Sch 8, paras 96, 109(1), (5), (6) to, that Act, as from 27 February 2007.

Sub-ss (11)–(14): repealed by the Charities Act 2006, s 75(1), (2), Sch 8, paras 96, 109(1), (12), Sch 9, as from a day to be appointed under s 79(2) of that Act, subject to savings in Sch 10, para 18 to that Act at **[2176]**.

Sub-s (15): word in first pair of square brackets substituted by the Transfer of Functions (Third Sector, Communities and Equality) Order 2006, SI 2006/2951, art 6, Schedule, para 4(i); words in second pair of square brackets substituted by the Charities Act 2006, s 75(1), Sch 8, paras 96, 109(1), (13), as from 27 February 2007.

By the Charities Act 2006 (Commencement No 1, Transitional Provisions and Savings) Order 2007, SI 2007/309, art 13, until sub-s (12) is repealed, it has effect as if the reference to a period of three months beginning with the day following that on which the order is published were a reference to a period of three months beginning with the day following that on which the order is made.

17 Further powers to make schemes or alter application of charitable property

(1) Where it appears to [the Commission] that a scheme should be established for the administration of a charity, but also that it is necessary or desirable for the scheme to alter the provision made by an Act of Parliament establishing or regulating the charity or to make any other provision which goes or might go beyond the powers exercisable [by the Commission] apart from this section, or that it is for any reason proper for the scheme to be subject to parliamentary review, then (subject to subsection (6) below) [the Commission] may settle a scheme accordingly with a view to its being given effect under this section.

(2) A scheme settled by [the Commission] under this section may be given effect by order of the [Minister], and a draft of the order shall be laid before Parliament.

(3) Without prejudice to the operation of section 6 of the Statutory Instruments Act 1946 in other cases, in the case of a scheme which goes beyond the powers exercisable apart from this section in altering a statutory provision contained in or having effect under any public general Act of Parliament, the order shall not be made unless the draft has been approved by resolution of each House of Parliament.

(4) Subject to subsection (5) below, any provision of a scheme brought into effect under this section may be modified or superseded by the court or [the Commission] as if it were a scheme brought into effect by order of [the Commission] under section 16 above.

(5) Where subsection (3) above applies to a scheme, the order giving effect to it may direct that the scheme shall not be modified or superseded by a scheme brought into effect otherwise than under this section, and may also direct that that subsection shall apply to any scheme modifying or superseding the scheme to which the order gives effect.

(6) The [Commission] shall not proceed under this section without the like application and the like notice to the charity trustees, as would be required [if the Commission was] proceeding (without an order of the court) under section 16 above; but on any application for a scheme, or in a case where [it acts] by virtue of subsection (6) or (7) of that section, the [Commission] may proceed under this section or that section as appears [to it] appropriate.

(7) Notwithstanding anything in the trusts of a charity, no expenditure incurred in preparing or promoting a Bill in Parliament shall without the consent of the court or [the

Commission] be defrayed out of any moneys applicable for the purposes of a charity *but this subsection shall not apply in the case of an exempt charity*.

(8) Where [the Commission is] satisfied—

(a) that the whole of the income of a charity cannot in existing circumstances be effectively applied for the purposes of the charity; and

(b) that, if those circumstances continue, a scheme might be made for applying the surplus cy-près; and

(c) that it is for any reason not yet desirable to make such a scheme;

then [the Commission] may by order authorise the charity trustees at their discretion (but subject to any conditions imposed by the order) to apply any accrued or accruing income for any purposes for which it might be made applicable by such a scheme, and any application authorised by the order shall be deemed to be within the purposes of the charity.

(9) An order under subsection (8) above shall not extend to more than £300 out of income accrued before the date of the order, nor to income accruing more than three years after that date, nor to more than £100 out of the income accruing in any of those three years. **[781]**

NOTES

Sub-ss (1), (4), (6), (8): words in square brackets substituted by the Charities Act 2006, s 75(1), Sch 8, paras 96, 110(1), (2), (4), (5), (7), as from 27 February 2007.

Sub-s (2): words in first pair of square brackets substituted by the Charities Act 2006, s 75(1), Sch 8, paras 96, 110(1), (3), as from 27 February 2007; word in second pair of square brackets substituted by the Transfer of Functions (Third Sector, Communities and Equality) Order 2006, SI 2006/2951, art 6, Schedule, para 4(j).

Sub-s (7): words in square brackets substituted by the Charities Act 2006, s 75(1), Sch 8, paras 96, 110(1), (6), as from 27 February 2007, and words in italics repealed by ss 12, 75(2) of, and Sch 5, para 5, Sch 9 to, that Act, as from a day to be appointed under s 79(2) of that Act.

Orders under this section: orders made under sub-s (2) above are not recorded in this work as they apply only to particular charities.

18 Power to act for protection of charities

(1) Where, at any time [after it has] instituted an inquiry under section 8 above with respect to any charity, [the Commission is] satisfied—

(a) that there is or has been any misconduct or mismanagement in the administration of the charity; or

(b) that it is necessary or desirable to act for the purpose of protecting the property of the charity or securing a proper application for the purposes of the charity of that property or of property coming to the charity,

[the Commission may of its] own motion do one or more of the following things—

(i) by order suspend any trustee, charity trustee, officer, agent or employee of the charity from the exercise of his office or employment pending consideration being given to his removal (whether under this section or otherwise);

(ii) by order appoint such number of additional charity trustees [as it considers] necessary for the proper administration of the charity;

(iii) by order vest any property held by or in trust for the charity in the official custodian, or require the persons in whom any such property is vested to transfer it to him, or appoint any person to transfer any such property to him;

(iv) order any person who holds any property on behalf of the charity, or of any trustee for it, not to part with the property without the approval of [the Commission];

(v) order any debtor of the charity not to make any payment in or towards the discharge of his liability to the charity without the approval of [the Commission];

(vi) by order restrict (notwithstanding anything in the trusts of the charity) the transactions which may be entered into, or the nature or amount of the payments which may be made, in the administration of the charity without the approval of [the Commission];

(vii) by order appoint (in accordance with section 19 below) *a receiver* and manager in respect of the property and affairs of the charity.

(2) Where, at any time after [it has] instituted an inquiry under section 8 above with respect to any charity, [the Commission is] satisfied—

(a) that there is or has been any misconduct or mismanagement in the administration of the charity; and

(b) that it is necessary or desirable to act for the purpose of protecting the property of the charity or securing a proper application for the purposes of the charity of that property or of property coming to the charity,

[the Commission may of its] own motion do either or both of the following things—

(i) by order remove any trustee, charity trustee, officer, agent or employee of the charity who has been responsible for or privy to the misconduct or mismanagement or has by his conduct contributed to it or facilitated it;

(ii) by order establish a scheme for the administration of the charity.

(3) The references in subsection (1) or (2) above to misconduct or mismanagement shall (notwithstanding anything in the trusts of the charity) extend to the employment for the remuneration or reward of persons acting in the affairs of the charity, or for other administrative purposes, of sums which are excessive in relation to the property which is or is likely to be applied or applicable for the purposes of the charity.

(4) [The Commission] may also remove a charity trustee by order made of [its own motion]—

(a) where, within the last five years, the trustee—

(i) having previously been adjudged bankrupt or had his estate sequestrated, has been discharged, or

(ii) having previously made a composition or arrangement with, or granted a trust deed for, his creditors, has been discharged in respect of it;

(b) where the trustee is a corporation in liquidation;

(c) where the trustee is incapable of acting by reason of mental disorder within the meaning of the Mental Health Act 1983;

(d) where the trustee has not acted, and will not declare his willingness or unwillingness to act;

(e) where the trustee is outside England and Wales or cannot be found or does not act, and his absence or failure to act impedes the proper administration of the charity.

(5) [The Commission may by order made of its] own motion appoint a person to be a charity trustee—

(a) in place of a charity trustee [removed by the Commission] under this section or otherwise;

(b) where there are no charity trustees, or where by reason of vacancies in their number or the absence or incapacity of any of their number the charity cannot apply for the appointment;

(c) where there is a single charity trustee, not being a corporation aggregate, and [the Commission is of] opinion that it is necessary to increase the number for the proper administration of the charity;

(d) where [the Commission is of] opinion that it is necessary for the proper administration of the charity to have an additional charity trustee because one of the existing charity trustees who ought nevertheless to remain a charity trustee either cannot be found or does not act or is outside England and Wales.

(6) The powers of [the Commission] under this section to remove or appoint charity trustees of [its own motion] shall include power to make any such order with respect to the vesting in or transfer to the charity trustees of any property as [the Commission] could make on the removal or appointment of a charity trustee [by it] under section 16 above.

(7) Any order under this section for the removal or appointment of a charity trustee or trustee for a charity, or for the vesting or transfer of any property, shall be of the like effect as an order made under section 16 above.

(8) Subject to subsection (9) below, subsections (11) to (13) of section 16 above shall apply to orders under this section as they apply to orders under that section.

(9) The requirement to obtain any such certificate or leave as is mentioned in section 16(13) above shall not apply to—

(a) an appeal by a charity or any of the charity trustees of a charity against an order under subsection (1)(vii) above appointing a receiver and manager in respect of the charity's property and affairs, or

(b) an appeal by a person against an order under subsection (2)(i) or (4)(a) above removing him from his office or employment.

(10) Subsection (14) of section 16 above shall apply to an order under this section which establishes a scheme for the administration of a charity as it applies to such an order under that section.

(11) The power of [the Commission] to make an order under subsection (1)(i) above shall not be exercisable so as to suspend any person from the exercise of his office or employment for a period of more than twelve months; but (without prejudice to the generality of section 89(1) below), any such order made in the case of any person may make provision as respects the period of his suspension for matters arising out of it, and in particular for enabling any person to execute any instrument in his name or otherwise act for him and, in the case of a charity trustee, for adjusting any rules governing the proceedings of the charity trustees to take account of the reduction in the number capable of acting.

(12) Before exercising any jurisdiction under this section otherwise than by virtue of subsection (1) above, [the Commission] shall give notice of [its intention] to do so to each of the charity trustees, except any that cannot be found or has no known address in the United Kingdom; and any such notice may be given by post and, if given by post, may be addressed to the recipient's last known address in the United Kingdom.

(13) [The Commission] shall, at such intervals as [it thinks fit], review any order made [by it] under paragraph (i), or any of paragraphs (iii) to (vii), of subsection (1) above; and, if on any such review it appears [to the Commission] that it would be appropriate to discharge the order in whole or in part, [the Commission shall] so discharge it (whether subject to any savings or other transitional provisions or not).

(14) If any person contravenes an order under subsection (1)(iv), (v) or (vi) above, he shall be guilty of an offence and liable on summary conviction to a fine not exceeding level 5 on the standard scale.

(15) Subsection (14) above shall not be taken to preclude the bringing of proceedings for breach of trust against any charity trustee or trustee for a charity in respect of a contravention of an order under subsection (1)(iv) or (vi) above (whether proceedings in respect of the contravention are brought against him under subsection (14) above or not).

(16) This section shall not apply to an exempt charity.

[782]

NOTES

Sub-ss (1), (2), (4)–(6), (11)–(13): words in square brackets substituted by the Charities Act 2006, s 75(1), Sch 8, paras 96, 111(1)–(6), (8)–(10), as from 27 February 2007.

Sub-ss (8)–(10): repealed by the Charities Act 2006, s 75(1), (2), Sch 8, paras 96, 111(1), (7), Sch 9, as from a day to be appointed under s 79(2) of that Act, subject to savings in Sch 10, para 18 to that Act at **[2176]**.

Sub-s (16): substituted as follows by the Charities Act 2006, s 12, Sch 5, para 6, as from a day to be appointed under s 79(2) of that Act—

"(16) In this section—

(a) subsections (1) to (3) apply in relation to an exempt charity, and

(b) subsections (4) to (6) apply in relation to such a charity at any time after the Commission have instituted an inquiry under section 8 with respect to it,

and the other provisions of this section apply accordingly.".

[18A Power to suspend or remove trustees etc from membership of charity

(1) This section applies where the Commission makes—

(a) an order under section 18(1) above suspending from his office or employment any trustee, charity trustee, officer, agent or employee of a charity, or

(b) an order under section 18(2) above removing from his office or employment any officer, agent or employee of a charity,

and the trustee, charity trustee, officer, agent or employee (as the case may be) is a member of the charity.

(2) If the order suspends the person in question from his office or employment, the Commission may also make an order suspending his membership of the charity for the period for which he is suspended from his office or employment.

(3) If the order removes the person in question from his office or employment, the Commission may also make an order—

(a) terminating his membership of the charity, and

(b) prohibiting him from resuming his membership of the charity without the Commission's consent.

(4) If an application for the Commission's consent under subsection (3)(b) above is made five years or more after the order was made, the Commission must grant the application unless satisfied that, by reason of any special circumstances, it should be refused.]

[782A]

NOTES

Commencement: to be appointed.

Inserted by the Charities Act 2006, s 19, as from a day to be appointed under s 79(2) of that Act, subject to transitional provisions in Sch 10, para 4 to that Act at **[2176]**.

19 Supplementary provisions relating to [interim manager] appointed for a charity

[(1) The Commission may under section 18(1)(vii) above appoint to be interim manager in respect of a charity such person (other than a member of its staff) as it thinks fit.]

(2) Without prejudice to the generality of section 89(1) below, any order made by [the Commission] under section 18(1)(vii) above may make provision with respect to the functions to be discharged by the [interim manager] appointed by the order; and those functions shall be discharged by him under the supervision of [the Commission].

(3) In connection with the discharge of those functions any such order may provide—

(a) for the [interim manager] appointed by the order to have such powers and duties of the charity trustees of the charity concerned (whether arising under this Act or otherwise) as are specified in the order;

(b) for any powers or duties exercisable or falling to be performed by the [interim manager] by virtue of paragraph (a) above to be exercisable or performed by him to the exclusion of those trustees.

(4) Where a person has been appointed [interim manager] by any such order—

(a) section 29 below shall apply to him and to his functions as a person so appointed as it applies to a charity trustee of the charity concerned and to his duties as such; and

(b) [the Commission] may apply to the High Court for directions in relation to any particular matter arising in connection with the discharge of those functions.

(5) The High Court may on an application under subsection (4)(b) above—

(a) give such directions, or

(b) make such orders declaring the rights of any persons (whether before the court or not),

as it thinks just; and the costs of any such application shall be paid by the charity concerned.

(6) Regulations made by the [Minister] may make provision with respect to—

(a) the appointment and removal of persons appointed in accordance with this section;

(b) the remuneration of such persons out of the income of the charities concerned;

(c) the making of reports to [the Commission] by such persons.

(7) Regulations under subsection (6) above may, in particular, authorise [the Commission]—

(a) to require security for the due discharge of his functions to be given by a person so appointed;

(b) to determine the amount of such a person's remuneration;

(c) to disallow any amount of remuneration in such circumstances as are prescribed by the regulations.

[783]

NOTES

Section heading: words in square brackets substituted by the Charities Act 2006, s 75(1), Sch 8, paras 96, 112(1), (7), as from 27 February 2007.

Sub-s (1): substituted by the Charities Act 2006, s 75(1), Sch 8, paras 96, 112(1), (2), as from 27 February 2007.

Sub-ss (2)–(4), (7): words in square brackets substituted by the Charities Act 2006, s 75(1), Sch 8, paras 96, 112(1), (3)–(6), as from 27 February 2007.

Sub-s (6): word in first pair of square brackets substituted by the Transfer of Functions (Third Sector, Communities and Equality) Order 2006, SI 2006/2951, art 6, Schedule, para 4(k); words in square brackets in para (c) substituted by the Charities Act 2006, s 75(1), Sch 8, paras 96, 112(1), (6), as from 27 February 2007.

Regulations: by virtue of the Interpretation Act 1978, s 17(2)(b), the Charities (Receiver and Manager) Regulations 1992, SI 1992/2355, have effect as if made under this section.

[19A Power to give specific directions for protection of charity

(1) This section applies where, at any time after the Commission has instituted an inquiry under section 8 above with respect to any charity, it is satisfied as mentioned in section 18(1)(a) or (b) above.

(2) The Commission may by order direct—
(a) the charity trustees,
(b) any trustee for the charity,
(c) any officer or employee of the charity, or
(d) (if a body corporate) the charity itself,

to take any action specified in the order which the Commission considers to be expedient in the interests of the charity.

(3) An order under this section—
(a) may require action to be taken whether or not it would otherwise be within the powers exercisable by the person or persons concerned, or by the charity, in relation to the administration of the charity or to its property, but
(b) may not require any action to be taken which is prohibited by any Act of Parliament or expressly prohibited by the trusts of the charity or is inconsistent with its purposes.

(4) Anything done by a person or body under the authority of an order under this section shall be deemed to be properly done in the exercise of the powers mentioned in subsection (3)(a) above.

(5) Subsection (4) does not affect any contractual or other rights arising in connection with anything which has been done under the authority of such an order.]

[783A]

NOTES

Commencement: to be appointed.
Inserted by the Charities Act 2006, s 20, as from a day to be appointed under s 79(2) of that Act, subject to transitional provisions in Sch 10, para 5 to that Act at **[2176]**.

[19B Power to direct application of charity property

(1) This section applies where the Commission is satisfied—
(a) that a person or persons in possession or control of any property held by or on trust for a charity is or are unwilling to apply it properly for the purposes of the charity, and
(b) that it is necessary or desirable to make an order under this section for the purpose of securing a proper application of that property for the purposes of the charity.

(2) The Commission may by order direct the person or persons concerned to apply the property in such manner as is specified in the order.

(3) An order under this section—
(a) may require action to be taken whether or not it would otherwise be within the powers exercisable by the person or persons concerned in relation to the property, but
(b) may not require any action to be taken which is prohibited by any Act of Parliament or expressly prohibited by the trusts of the charity.

(4) Anything done by a person under the authority of an order under this section shall be deemed to be properly done in the exercise of the powers mentioned in subsection (3)(a) above.

(5) Subsection (4) does not affect any contractual or other rights arising in connection with anything which has been done under the authority of such an order.]

[783B]

NOTES

Commencement: to be appointed.
Inserted by the Charities Act 2006, s 21, as from a day to be appointed under s 79(2) of that Act.

[19C Copy of order under section 18, 18A, 19A or 19B, and Commission's reasons, to be sent to charity

(1) Where the Commission makes an order under section 18, 18A, 19A or 19B, it must send the documents mentioned in subsection (2) below—
- (a) to the charity concerned (if a body corporate), or
- (b) (if not) to each of the charity trustees.

(2) The documents are—
- (a) a copy of the order, and
- (b) a statement of the Commission's reasons for making it.

(3) The documents must be sent to the charity or charity trustees as soon as practicable after the making of the order.

(4) The Commission need not, however, comply with subsection (3) above in relation to the documents, or (as the case may be) the statement of its reasons, if it considers that to do so—
- (a) would prejudice any inquiry or investigation, or
- (b) would not be in the interests of the charity;

but, once the Commission considers that this is no longer the case, it must send the documents, or (as the case may be) the statement, to the charity or charity trustees as soon as practicable.

(5) Nothing in this section requires any document to be sent to a person who cannot be found or who has no known address in the United Kingdom.

(6) Any documents required to be sent to a person under this section may be sent to, or otherwise served on, that person in the same way as an order made by the Commission under this Act could be served on him in accordance with section 91 below.]

[783C]

NOTES

Commencement: 27 February 2007 (except in so far as it refers to ss 18A, 19A and 19B of this Act); to be appointed (otherwise).

Inserted by the Charities Act 2006, s 75(1), Sch 8, paras 96, 113.

[20 Publicity relating to schemes

(1) The Commission may not—
- (a) make any order under this Act to establish a scheme for the administration of a charity, or
- (b) submit such a scheme to the court or the Minister for an order giving it effect,

unless, before doing so, the Commission has complied with the publicity requirements in subsection (2) below.

This is subject to any disapplication of those requirements under subsection (4) below.

(2) The publicity requirements are—
- (a) that the Commission must give public notice of its proposals, inviting representations to be made to it within a period specified in the notice; and
- (b) that, in the case of a scheme relating to a local charity (other than an ecclesiastical charity) in a parish or in a community in Wales, the Commission must communicate a draft of the scheme to the parish or community council (or, where a parish has no council, to the chairman of the parish meeting).

(3) The time when any such notice is given or any such communication takes place is to be decided by the Commission.

(4) The Commission may determine that either or both of the publicity requirements is or are not to apply in relation to a particular scheme if it is satisfied that—
- (a) by reason of the nature of the scheme, or
- (b) for any other reason,

compliance with the requirement or requirements is unnecessary.

(5) Where the Commission gives public notice of any proposals under this section, the Commission—
- (a) must take into account any representations made to it within the period specified in the notice, and

(b) may (without further notice) proceed with the proposals either without modifications or with such modifications as it thinks desirable.

(6) Where the Commission makes an order under this Act to establish a scheme for the administration of a charity, a copy of the order must be available, for at least a month after the order is published, for public inspection at all reasonable times—

(a) at the Commission's office, and

(b) if the charity is a local charity, at some convenient place in the area of the charity.

Paragraph (b) does not apply if the Commission is satisfied that for any reason it is unnecessary for a copy of the scheme to be available locally.

(7) Any public notice of any proposals which is to be given under this section—

(a) is to contain such particulars of the proposals, or such directions for obtaining information about them, as the Commission thinks sufficient and appropriate, and

(b) is to be given in such manner as the Commission thinks sufficient and appropriate.]

[784]

NOTES

Commencement: 27 February 2007.

Substituted, together with s 20A, for s 20 as originally enacted, by the Charities Act 2006, s 22.

[20A Publicity for orders relating to trustees or other individuals

(1) The Commission may not make any order under this Act to appoint, discharge or remove a charity trustee or trustee for a charity, other than—

(a) an order relating to the official custodian, or

(b) an order under section 18(1)(ii) above,

unless, before doing so, the Commission has complied with the publicity requirement in subsection (2) below.

This is subject to any disapplication of that requirement under subsection (4) below.

(2) The publicity requirement is that the Commission must give public notice of its proposals, inviting representations to be made to it within a period specified in the notice.

(3) The time when any such notice is given is to be decided by the Commission.

(4) The Commission may determine that the publicity requirement is not to apply in relation to a particular order if it is satisfied that for any reason compliance with the requirement is unnecessary.

(5) Before the Commission makes an order under this Act to remove without his consent—

(a) a charity trustee or trustee for a charity, or

(b) an officer, agent or employee of a charity,

the Commission must give him not less than one month's notice of its proposals, inviting representations to be made to it within a period specified in the notice.

This does not apply if the person cannot be found or has no known address in the United Kingdom.

(6) Where the Commission gives notice of any proposals under this section, the Commission—

(a) must take into account any representations made to it within the period specified in the notice, and

(b) may (without further notice) proceed with the proposals either without modifications or with such modifications as it thinks desirable.

(7) Any notice of any proposals which is to be given under this section—

(a) is to contain such particulars of the proposals, or such directions for obtaining information about them, as the Commission thinks sufficient and appropriate, and

(b) (in the case of a public notice) is to be given in such manner as the Commission thinks sufficient and appropriate.

(8) Any notice to be given under subsection (5)—

(a) may be given by post, and

(b) if given by post, may be addressed to the recipient's last known address in the United Kingdom.]

[784A]

NOTES

Commencement: 27 February 2007.
Substituted as noted to s 20 at **[784]**.

Property vested in official custodian

21 Entrusting charity property to official custodian, and termination of trust

(1) The court may by order—

(a) vest in the official custodian any land held by or in trust for a charity;

(b) authorise or require the persons in whom any such land is vested to transfer it to him; or

(c) appoint any person to transfer any such land to him;

but this subsection does not apply to any interest in land by way of mortgage or other security.

(2) Where property is vested in the official custodian in trust for a charity, the court may make an order discharging him from the trusteeship as respects all or any of that property.

(3) Where the official custodian is discharged from his trusteeship of any property, or the trusts on which he holds any property come to an end, the court may make such vesting orders and give such directions as may seem to the court to be necessary or expedient in consequence.

(4) No person shall be liable for any loss occasioned by his acting in conformity with an order under this section or by his giving effect to anything done in pursuance of such an order, or be excused from so doing by reason of the order having been in any respect improperly obtained.

[785]

22 Supplementary provisions as to property vested in official custodian

(1) Subject to the provisions of this Act, where property is vested in the official custodian in trust for a charity, he shall not exercise any powers of management, but he shall as trustee of any property have all the same powers, duties and liabilities, and be entitled to the same rights and immunities, and be subject to the control and orders of the court, as a corporation appointed custodian trustee under section 4 of the Public Trustee Act 1906 except that he shall have no power to charge fees.

(2) Subject to subsection (3) below, where any land is vested in the official custodian in trust for a charity, the charity trustees shall have power in his name and on his behalf to execute and do all assurances and things which they could properly execute or do in their own name and on their own behalf if the land were vested in them.

(3) If any land is so vested in the official custodian by virtue of an order under section 18 above, the power conferred on the charity trustees by subsection (2) above shall not be exercisable by them in relation to any transaction affecting the land, unless the transaction is authorised by order of the court or of [the Commission].

(4) Where any land is vested in the official custodian in trust for a charity, the charity trustees shall have the like power to make obligations entered into by them binding on the land as if it were vested in them; and any covenant, agreement or condition which is enforceable by or against the custodian by reason of the land being vested in him shall be enforceable by or against the charity trustees as if the land were vested in them.

(5) In relation to a corporate charity, subsections (2), (3) and (4) above shall apply with the substitution of references to the charity for references to the charity trustees.

(6) Subsections (2), (3) and (4) above shall not authorise any charity trustees or charity to impose any personal liability on the official custodian.

(7) Where the official custodian is entitled as trustee for a charity to the custody of securities or documents of title relating to the trust property, he may permit them to be in the possession or under the control of the charity trustees without thereby incurring any liability.

[786]

NOTES

Sub-s (3): words in square brackets substituted by the Charities Act 2006, s 75(1), Sch 8, paras 96, 114, as from 27 February 2007.

23 Divestment in the case of land subject to Reverter of Sites Act 1987

(1) Where—

(a) any land is vested in the official custodian in trust for a charity, and

(b) it appears to [the Commission] that section 1 of the Reverter of Sites Act 1987 (right of reverter replaced by [trust]) will, or is likely to, operate in relation to the land at a particular time or in particular circumstances,

the jurisdiction which, under section 16 above, is exercisable by [the Commission] for the purpose of discharging a trustee for a charity may, at any time before section 1 of that Act ("the 1987 Act") operates in relation to the land, be exercised [by the Commission of its own] motion for the purpose of—

(i) making an order discharging the official custodian from his trusteeship of the land, and

(ii) making such vesting orders and giving such directions as [appear to the Commission] to be necessary or expedient in consequence.

(2) Where—

(a) section 1 of the 1987 Act has operated in relation to any land which, immediately before the time when that section so operated, was vested in the official custodian in trust for a charity, and

(b) the land remains vested in him but on the trust arising under that section,

the court or [the Commission (of its own motion)] may—

(i) make an order discharging the official custodian from his trusteeship of the land, and

(ii) (subject to the following provisions of this section) make such vesting orders and give such directions as appear to it ... to be necessary or expedient in consequence.

(3) Where any order discharging the official custodian from his trusteeship of any land—

(a) is made by the court under section 21(2) above, or by [the Commission] under section 16 above, on the grounds that section 1 of the 1987 Act will, or is likely to, operate in relation to the land, or

(b) is made by the court or [the Commission] under subsection (2) above,

the persons in whom the land is to be vested on the discharge of the official custodian shall be the relevant charity trustees (as defined in subsection (4) below), unless the court or (as the case may be) [the Commission is] satisfied that it would be appropriate for it to be vested in some other persons.

(4) In subsection (3) above "the relevant charity trustees" means—

(a) in relation to an order made as mentioned in paragraph (a) of that subsection, the charity trustees of the charity in trust for which the land is vested in the official custodian immediately before the time when the order takes effect, or

(b) in relation to an order made under subsection (2) above, the charity trustees of the charity in trust for which the land was vested in the official custodian immediately before the time when section 1 of the 1987 Act operated in relation to the land.

(5) Where—

(a) section 1 of the 1987 Act has operated in relation to any such land as is mentioned in subsection (2)(a) above, and

(b) the land remains vested in the official custodian as mentioned in subsection (2)(b) above,

then (subject to subsection (6) below), all the powers, duties and liabilities that would, apart from this section, be those of the official custodian as [trustee] of the land shall instead be those of the charity trustees of the charity concerned; and those trustees shall have power in his name and on his behalf to execute and do all assurances and things which they could properly execute or do in their own name and on their own behalf if the land were vested in them.

(6) Subsection (5) above shall not be taken to require or authorise those trustees to sell the land at a time when it remains vested in the official custodian.

(7) Where—

(a) the official custodian has been discharged from his trusteeship of any land by an order under subsection (2) above, and

(b) the land has, in accordance with subsection (3) above, been vested in the charity trustees concerned or (as the case may be) in any persons other than those trustees,

the land shall be held by those trustees, or (as the case may be) by those persons, as [trustees] on the terms of the trust arising under section 1 of the 1987 Act.

(8) The official custodian shall not be liable to any person in respect of any loss or misapplication of any land vested in him in accordance with that section unless it is occasioned by or through any wilful neglect or default of his or of any person acting for him; but the Consolidated Fund shall be liable to make good to any person any sums for which the official custodian may be liable by reason of any such neglect or default.

(9) In this section any reference to section 1 of the 1987 Act operating in relation to any land is a reference to a [trust] arising in relation to the land under that section.

[787]

NOTES

Sub-s (1): word in second pair of square brackets substituted by the Trusts of Land and Appointment of Trustees Act 1996, s 25(1), Sch 3, para 26(a); other words in square brackets substituted by the Charities Act 2006, s 75(1), Sch 8, paras 96, 115(1), (2), as from 27 February 2007.

Sub-s (2): words in square brackets substituted and words omitted repealed by the Charities Act 2006, s 75(1), (2), Sch 8, paras 96, 115(1), (3), Sch 9, as from 27 February 2007.

Sub-s (3): words in square brackets substituted by the Charities Act 2006, s 75(1), Sch 8, paras 96, 115(1), (4), as from 27 February 2007.

Sub-ss (5), (7), (9): words in square brackets substituted by the Trusts of Land and Appointment of Trustees Act 1996, s 25(1), Sch 3, para 26(b)–(d).

Establishment of common investment or deposit funds

24 Schemes to establish common investment funds

(1) The court or [the Commission] may by order make and bring into effect schemes (in this section referred to as "common investment schemes") for the establishment of common investment funds under trusts which provide—

(a) for property transferred to the fund by or on behalf of a charity participating in the scheme to be invested under the control of trustees appointed to manage the fund; and

(b) for the participating charities to be entitled (subject to the provisions of the scheme) to the capital and income of the fund in shares determined by reference to the amount or value of the property transferred to it by or on behalf of each of them and to the value of the fund at the time of the transfers.

(2) The court or [the Commission] may make a common investment scheme on the application of any two or more charities.

(3) A common investment scheme may be made in terms admitting any charity to participate, or the scheme may restrict the right to participate in any manner.

[(3A) A common investment scheme may provide for appropriate bodies to be admitted to participate in the scheme (in addition to the participating charities) to such extent as the trustees appointed to manage the fund may determine.

(3B) In this section "appropriate body" means—

(a) a Scottish recognised body, or

(b) a Northern Ireland charity,

and, in the application of the relevant provisions in relation to a scheme which contains provisions authorised by subsection (3A) above, "charity" includes an appropriate body.

"The relevant provisions" are subsections (1) and (4) to (6) and (in relation only to a charity within paragraph (b)) subsection (7).]

(4) A common investment scheme may make provision for, and for all matters connected with, the establishment, investment, management and winding up of the common investment fund, and may in particular include provision—

(a) for remunerating persons appointed trustees to hold or manage the fund or any part of it, with or without provision authorising a person to receive the remuneration notwithstanding that he is also a charity trustee of or trustee for a participating charity;

(b) for restricting the size of the fund, and for regulating as to time, amount or otherwise the right to transfer property to or withdraw it from the fund, and for enabling sums to be advanced out of the fund by way of loan to a participating charity pending the withdrawal of property from the fund by the charity;

(c) for enabling income to be withheld from distribution with a view to avoiding fluctuations in the amounts distributed, and generally for regulating distributions of income;

(d) for enabling money to be borrowed temporarily for the purpose of meeting payments to be made out of the funds;

(e) for enabling questions arising under the scheme as to the right of a charity to participate, or as to the rights of participating charities, or as to any other matter, to be conclusively determined by the decision of the trustees managing the fund or in any other manner;

(f) for regulating the accounts and information to be supplied to participating charities.

(5) A common investment scheme, in addition to the provision for property to be transferred to the fund on the basis that the charity shall be entitled to a share in the capital and income of the fund, may include provision for enabling sums to be deposited by or on behalf of a charity on the basis that (subject to the provisions of the scheme) the charity shall be entitled to repayment of the sums deposited and to interest thereon at a rate determined by or under the scheme; and where a scheme makes any such provision it shall also provide for excluding from the amount of capital and income to be shared between charities participating otherwise than by way of deposit such amounts (not exceeding the amounts properly attributable to the making of deposits) as are from time to time reasonably required in respect of the liabilities of the fund for the repayment of deposits and for the interest on deposits, including amounts required by way of reserve.

(6) Except in so far as a common investment scheme provides to the contrary, the rights under it of a participating charity shall not be capable of being assigned or charged, nor shall any trustee or other person concerned in the management of the common investment fund be required or entitled to take account of any trust or other equity affecting a participating charity or its property or rights.

(7) The powers of investment of every charity shall include power to participate in common investment schemes unless the power is excluded by a provision specifically referring to common investment schemes in the trusts of the charity.

(8) A common investment fund shall be deemed for all purposes to be a charity*; and if the scheme admits only exempt charities, the fund shall be an exempt charity for the purposes of this Act*.

(9) Subsection (8) above shall apply not only to common investment funds established under the powers of this section, but also to any similar fund established for the exclusive benefit of charities by or under any enactment relating to any particular charities or class of charity.

[788]

Sub-ss (1), (2): words in square brackets substituted by the Charities Act 2006, s 75(1), Sch 8, paras 96, 116, as from 27 February 2007.

Sub-ss (3A), (3B): inserted by the Charities Act 2006, s 23(1), as from 27 February 2007.

Sub-s (8): words in italics repealed by the Charities Act 2006, ss 11(1), (10), 75(2), Sch 9, as from a day to be appointed under s 79(2) of that Act.

25 Schemes to establish common deposit funds

(1) The court or [the Commission] may by order make and bring into effect schemes (in this section referred to as "common deposit schemes") for the establishment of common deposit funds under trusts which provide—

(a) for sums to be deposited by or on behalf of a charity participating in the scheme and invested under the control of trustees appointed to manage the fund; and

(b) for any such charity to be entitled (subject to the provisions of the scheme) to repayment of any sums so deposited and to interest thereon at a rate determined under the scheme.

(2) Subject to subsection (3) below, the following provisions of section 24 above, namely—

(a) [subsections (2), (3) and (4)], and

(b) subsections (6) to (9),

shall have effect in relation to common deposit schemes and common deposit funds as they have effect in relation to common investment schemes and common investment funds.

(3) In its application in accordance with subsection (2) above, subsection (4) of that section shall have effect with the substitution for paragraphs (b) and (c) of the following paragraphs—

"(b) for regulating as to time, amount or otherwise the right to repayment of sums deposited in the fund;

(c) for authorising a part of the income for any year to be credited to a reserve account maintained for the purpose of counteracting any losses accruing to the fund, and generally for regulating the manner in which the rate of interest on deposits is to be determined from time to time;".

[(4) A common deposit scheme may provide for appropriate bodies to be admitted to participate in the scheme (in addition to the participating charities) to such extent as the trustees appointed to manage the fund may determine.

(5) In this section "appropriate body" means—

(a) a Scottish recognised body, or

(b) a Northern Ireland charity,

and, in the application of the relevant provisions in relation to a scheme which contains provisions authorised by subsection (4) above, "charity" includes an appropriate body.

(6) "The relevant provisions" are—

(a) subsection (1) above, and

(b) subsections (4) and (6) of section 24 above, as they apply in accordance with subsections (2) and (3) above, and

(c) (in relation only to a charity within subsection (5)(b) above) subsection (7) of that section, as it so applies.]

[789]

NOTES

Sub-s (1): words in square brackets substituted by the Charities Act 2006, s 75(1), Sch 8, paras 96, 117, as from 27 February 2007.

Sub-s (2): words in square brackets substituted by the Charities Act 2006, s 23(2), as from 27 February 2007.

Sub-ss (4)–(6): added by the Charities Act 2006, s 23(3), as from 27 February 2007.

[25A Meaning of "Scottish recognised body" and "Northern Ireland charity" in sections 24 and 25

(1) In sections 24 and 25 above "Scottish recognised body" means a body—

(a) established under the law of Scotland, or

(b) managed or controlled wholly or mainly in or from Scotland,

to which the Commissioners for Her Majesty's Revenue and Customs have given intimation, which has not subsequently been withdrawn, that relief is due under section 505 of the Income and Corporation Taxes Act 1988 in respect of income of the body which is applicable and applied to charitable purposes only.

(2) In those sections "Northern Ireland charity" means an institution—

(a) which is a charity under the law of Northern Ireland, and

(b) to which the Commissioners for Her Majesty's Revenue and Customs have given intimation, which has not subsequently been withdrawn, that relief is due under section 505 of the Income and Corporation Taxes Act 1988 in respect of income of the institution which is applicable and applied to charitable purposes only.]

[789A]

NOTES

Commencement: 27 February 2007.

Inserted by the Charities Act 2006, s 23(4).

[Additional powers of Commission]

26 Power to authorise dealings with charity property etc

(1) Subject to the provisions of this section, where it appears to [the Commission] that any action proposed or contemplated in the administration of a charity is expedient in the interests of the charity, [the Commission may] by order sanction that action, whether or not it would otherwise be within the powers exercisable by the charity trustees in the administration of the charity; and anything done under the authority of such an order shall be deemed to be properly done in the exercise of those powers.

(2) An order under this section may be made so as to authorise a particular transaction, compromise or the like, or a particular application of property, or so as to give a more general authority, and (without prejudice to the generality of subsection (1) above) may authorise a charity to use common premises, or employ a common staff, or otherwise combine for any purpose of administration, with any other charity.

(3) An order under this section may give directions as to the manner in which any expenditure is to be borne and as to other matters connected with or arising out of the action thereby authorised; and where anything is done in pursuance of an authority given by any such order, any directions given in connection therewith shall be binding on the charity trustees for the time being as if contained in the trusts of the charity; but any such directions may on the application of the charity be modified or superseded by a further order.

(4) Without prejudice to the generality of subsection (3) above, the directions which may be given by an order under this section shall in particular include directions for meeting any expenditure out of a specified fund, for charging any expenditure to capital or to income, for requiring expenditure charged to capital to be recouped out of income within a specified period, for restricting the costs to be incurred at the expense of the charity, or for the investment of moneys arising from any transaction.

(5) An order under this section may authorise any act notwithstanding that it is prohibited by any of the disabling Acts mentioned in subsection (6) below or that the trusts of the charity provide for the act to be done by or under the authority of the court; but no such order shall authorise the doing of any act expressly prohibited by Act of Parliament other than the disabling Acts or by the trusts of the charity or shall extend or alter the purposes of the charity.

[(5A) In the case of a charity that is a company, an order under this section may authorise an act notwithstanding that it involves the breach of a duty imposed on a director of the company under Chapter 2 of Part 10 of the Companies Act 2006 (general duties of directors).]

(6) The Acts referred to in subsection (5) above as the disabling Acts are the Ecclesiastical Leases Act 1571, the Ecclesiastical Leases Act 1572, the Ecclesiastical Leases Act 1575 and the Ecclesiastical Leases Act 1836.

(7) An order under this section shall not confer any authority in relation to a building which has been consecrated and of which the use or disposal is regulated, and can be further regulated, by a scheme having effect under the Union of Benefices Measures 1923 to 1952, the Reorganisation Areas Measures 1944 and 1954, the Pastoral Measure 1968 or the Pastoral Measure 1983, the reference to a building being taken to include part of a building and any land which under such a scheme is to be used or disposed of with a building to which the scheme applies.

[790]

NOTES

Cross-heading preceding this section substituted by the Charities Act 2006, s 75(1), Sch 8, paras 96, 118, as from 27 February 2007.

Sub-s (1): words in square brackets substituted by the Charities Act 2006, s 75(1), Sch 8, paras 96, 119, as from 27 February 2007.

Sub-s (5A): inserted by the Companies Act 2006, s 181(4), as from a day to be appointed under s 1300(2) of that Act.

Union of Benefices Measures 1923 to 1952; Reorganisation Areas Measures 1944 and 1954; Pastoral Measure 1968; Pastoral Measure 1983: the Union of Benefices Measures 1923 to 1952 and the Reorganisation Areas Measures 1944 and 1954 were repealed and replaced by the Pastoral Measure 1968, which is itself repealed and replaced by the Pastoral Measure 1983.

27 Power to authorise ex gratia payments etc

(1) Subject to subsection (3) below, [the Commission] may by order exercise the same power as is exercisable by the Attorney General to authorise the charity trustees of a charity—

(a) to make any application of property of the charity, or

(b) to waive to any extent, on behalf of the charity, its entitlement to receive any property,

in a case where the charity trustees—

(i) (apart from this section) have no power to do so, but

(ii) in all the circumstances regard themselves as being under a moral obligation to do so.

(2) The power conferred on [the Commission] by subsection (1) above shall be exercisable [by the Commission] under the supervision of, and in accordance with such directions as may be given by, the Attorney General; and any such directions may in particular require [the Commission], in such circumstances as are specified in the directions—

(a) to refrain from exercising that power; or

(b) to consult the Attorney General before exercising it.

(3) Where—

(a) an application is made to [the Commission for it] to exercise that power in a case where [it is not] precluded from doing so by any such directions, but

(b) [the Commission considers] that it would nevertheless be desirable for the application to be entertained by the Attorney General rather than [by the Commission],

[the Commission shall] refer the application to the Attorney General.

(4) It is hereby declared that where, in the case of any application made [to the Commission] as mentioned in subsection (3)(a) above, [the Commission determines] the application by refusing to authorise charity trustees to take any action falling within subsection (1)(a) or (b) above, that refusal shall not preclude the Attorney General, on an application subsequently made to him by the trustees, from authorising the trustees to take that action.

[791]

NOTES

Words in square brackets substituted by the Charities Act 2006, s 75(1), Sch 8, paras 96, 120, as from 27 February 2007.

28 Power to give directions about dormant bank accounts of charities

(1) Where [the Commission]—

(a) [is informed] by a relevant institution—

(i) that it holds one or more accounts in the name of or on behalf of a particular charity ("the relevant charity"), and

(ii) that the account, or (if it so holds two or more accounts) each of the accounts, is dormant, and

(b) [is unable], after making reasonable inquiries, to locate that charity or any of its trustees,

[it may give] a direction under subsection (2) below.

(2) A direction under this subsection is a direction which—

(a) requires the institution concerned to transfer the amount, or (as the case may be) the aggregate amount, standing to the credit of the relevant charity in the account or accounts in question to such other charity as is specified in the direction in accordance with subsection (3) below; or

(b) requires the institution concerned to transfer to each of two or more other charities so specified in the direction such part of that amount or aggregate amount as is there specified in relation to that charity.

(3) The [Commission] may specify in a direction under subsection (2) above such other charity or charities as [it considers] appropriate, having regard, in a case where the purposes of the relevant charity are known [to the Commission], to those purposes and to the purposes of the other charity or charities; but the [Commission] shall not so specify any charity unless [it has received] from the charity trustees written confirmation that those trustees are willing to accept the amount proposed to be transferred to the charity.

(4) Any amount received by a charity by virtue of this section shall be received by the charity on terms that—

(a) it shall be held and applied by the charity for the purposes of the charity, but

(b) it shall, as property of the charity, nevertheless be subject to any restrictions on expenditure to which it was subject as property of the relevant charity.

(5) Where—

(a) [the Commission has been] informed as mentioned in subsection (1)(a) above by any relevant institution, and

(b) before any transfer is made by the institution in pursuance of a direction under subsection (2) above, the institution has, by reason of any circumstances, cause to believe that the account, or (as the case may be) any of the accounts, held by it in the name of or on behalf of the relevant charity is no longer dormant,

the institution shall forthwith notify those circumstances in writing to [the Commission]; and, if it appears to [the Commission] that the account or accounts in question is or are no longer dormant, [it shall revoke] any direction under subsection (2) above which has previously been given [by it] to the institution with respect to the relevant charity.

(6) The receipt of any charity trustees or trustee for a charity in respect of any amount received from a relevant institution by virtue of this section shall be a complete discharge of the institution in respect of that amount.

(7) No obligation as to secrecy or other restriction on disclosure (however imposed) shall preclude a relevant institution from disclosing any information to [the Commission] for the purpose of enabling [the Commission to discharge its functions] under this section.

(8) For the purposes of this section—

(a) an account is dormant if no transaction, other than—

(i) a transaction consisting in a payment into the account, or

(ii) a transaction which the institution holding the account has itself caused to be effected,

has been effected in relation to the account within the period of five years immediately preceding the date when [the Commission is informed] as mentioned in paragraph (a) of subsection (1) above;

(b) a "relevant institution" means—

(i) the Bank of England;

[(ii) a person who has permission under Part 4 of the Financial Services and Markets Act 2000 to accept deposits;

(iii) an EEA firm of the kind mentioned in paragraph 5(b) of Schedule 3 to that Act which has permission under paragraph 15 of that Schedule (as a result of qualifying for authorisation under paragraph 12(1) of that Schedule) to accept deposits; or

(iv) such other person who may lawfully accept deposits in the United Kingdom as may be prescribed by the [Minister].]

(c) references to the transfer of any amount to a charity are references to its transfer—

(i) to the charity trustees, or

(ii) to any trustee for the charity,

as the charity trustees may determine (and any reference to any amount received by a charity shall be construed accordingly).

[(8A) Sub-paragraphs (ii) to (iv) of the definition of "relevant institution" in subsection (8)(b) must be read with—

(a) section 22 of the Financial Services and Markets Act 2000;

(b) any relevant order under that section; and

(c) Schedule 2 to that Act.]

(9) For the purpose of determining the matters in respect of which any of the powers conferred by section 8 or 9 above may be exercised it shall be assumed that [the Commission has] no functions under this section in relation to accounts to which this subsection applies (with the result that, for example, a relevant institution shall not, in connection with the functions of [the Commission] under this section, be required under section 8(3)(a) above to furnish any statements, or answer any questions or inquiries, with respect to any such accounts held by the institution).

This subsection applies to accounts which are dormant accounts by virtue of subsection (8)(a) above but would not be such accounts if sub-paragraph (i) of that provision were omitted.

(10) Subsection (1) above shall not apply to any account held in the name of or on behalf of an exempt charity.

[792]

NOTES

Sub-ss (1), (3), (5), (7), (9): words in square brackets substituted by by the Charities Act 2006, s 75(1), Sch 8, paras 96, 121(1)–(5), (7), as from 27 February 2007.

Sub-s (8): words in square brackets in para (a) substituted by the Charities Act 2006, s 75(1), Sch 8, paras 96, 121(1), (6), as from 27 February 2007; sub-paras (b)(ii)–(iv) substituted for sub-paras (b)(ii)–(v) as originally enacted by the Financial Services and Markets Act 2000 (Consequential Amendments and Repeals) Order 2001, SI 2001/3649, art 339(1), (2); word in square brackets in para (b)(iv) substituted by the Transfer of Functions (Third Sector, Communities and Equality) Order 2006, SI 2006/2951, art 6, Schedule, para 4(m).

Sub-s (8A): inserted by SI 2001/3649, art 339(1), (3).

Sub-s (10): repealed by the Charities Act 2006, ss 12, 75(2), Sch 5, para 7, Sch 9, as from a day to be appointed under s 79(2) of that Act.

[29 Power to give advice and guidance

(1) The Commission may, on the written application of any charity trustee or trustee for a charity, give that person its opinion or advice in relation to any matter—

(a) relating to the performance of any duties of his, as such a trustee, in relation to the charity concerned, or

(b) otherwise relating to the proper administration of the charity.

(2) A charity trustee or trustee for a charity who acts in accordance with any opinion or advice given by the Commission under subsection (1) above (whether to him or to another trustee) is to be taken, as regards his responsibility for so acting, to have acted in accordance with his trust.

(3) But subsection (2) above does not apply to a person if, when so acting, either—

(a) he knows or has reasonable cause to suspect that the opinion or advice was given in ignorance of material facts, or

(b) a decision of the court or the Tribunal has been obtained on the matter or proceedings are pending to obtain one.

(4) The Commission may, in connection with its second general function mentioned in section 1C(2) above, give such advice or guidance with respect to the administration of charities as it considers appropriate.

(5) Any advice or guidance so given may relate to—

(a) charities generally,

(b) any class of charities, or

(c) any particular charity,

and may take such form, and be given in such manner, as the Commission considers appropriate.]

[793]

NOTES

Commencement: 27 February 2007.

Substituted by the Charities Act 2006, s 24.

[29A Power to determine membership of charity

(1) The Commission may—

(a) on the application of a charity, or

(b) at any time after the institution of an inquiry under section 8 above with respect to a charity,

determine who are the members of the charity.

(2) The Commission's power under subsection (1) may also be exercised by a person appointed by the Commission for the purpose.

(3) In a case within subsection (1)(b) the Commission may, if it thinks fit, so appoint the person appointed to conduct the inquiry.]

[793A]

NOTES

Commencement: 27 February 2007.
Inserted by the Charities Act 2006, s 25.

30 Powers for preservation of charity documents

(1) [The Commission] may provide books in which any deed, will or other document relating to a charity may be enrolled.

(2) The [Commission] may accept for safe keeping any document of or relating to a charity, and the charity trustees or other persons having the custody of documents of or relating to a charity (including a charity which has ceased to exist) may with the consent of the [Commission] deposit them with the [Commission] for safe keeping, except in the case of documents required by some other enactment to be kept elsewhere.

(3) Where a document is enrolled by [the Commission] or is for the time being deposited [with the Commission] under this section, evidence of its contents may be given by means of a copy certified by any [member of the staff of the Commission generally or specially authorised by the Commission] to act for this purpose; and a document purporting to be such a copy shall be received in evidence without proof of the official position, authority or handwriting of the person certifying it or of the original document being enrolled or deposited as aforesaid.

(4) Regulations made by the [Minister] may make provision for such documents deposited with [the Commission] under this section as may be prescribed by the regulations to be destroyed or otherwise disposed of after such period or in such circumstances as may be so prescribed.

(5) Subsections (3) and (4) above shall apply to any document transmitted to [the Commission] under section 9 above and kept [by the Commission] under subsection (3) of that section, as if the document had been deposited [with the Commission] for safe keeping under this section.

[794]

NOTES

Sub-ss (1)–(3), (5): words in square brackets substituted by the Charities Act 2006, s 75(1), Sch 8, paras 96, 122(1)–(4), (6), as from 27 February 2007.

Sub-s (4): word in first pair of square brackets substituted by the Transfer of Functions (Third Sector, Communities and Equality) Order 2006, SI 2006/2951, art 6, Schedule, para 4(n); words in square brackets in para (c) substituted by the Charities Act 2006, s 75(1), Sch 8, paras 96, 122(1), (5), as from 27 February 2007.

31 Power to order taxation of solicitor's bill

(1) [The Commission] may order that a solicitor's bill of costs for business done for a charity, or for charity trustees or trustees for a charity, shall be taxed, together with the costs of the taxation, by a taxing officer in such division of the High Court as may be specified in the order, or by the taxing officer of any other court having jurisdiction to order the taxation of the bill.

(2) On any order under this section for the taxation of a solicitor's bill the taxation shall proceed, and the taxing officer shall have the same powers and duties, and the costs of the taxation shall be borne, as if the order had been made, on the application of the person chargeable with the bill, by the court in which the costs are taxed.

(3) No order under this section for the taxation of a solicitor's bill shall be made after payment of the bill unless [the Commission is] of opinion that it contains exorbitant charges; and no such order shall in any case be made where the solicitor's costs are not subject to taxation on an order of the High Court by reason either of an agreement as to his remuneration or the lapse of time since payment of the bill.

[795]

NOTES

Sub-ss (1), (3): words in square brackets substituted by the Charities Act 2006, s 75(1), Sch 8, paras 96, 123, as from 27 February 2007.

[31A Power to enter premises

(1) A justice of the peace may issue a warrant under this section if satisfied, on information given on oath by a member of the Commission's staff, that there are reasonable grounds for believing that each of the conditions in subsection (2) below is satisfied.

(2) The conditions are—

(a) that an inquiry has been instituted under section 8 above;

(b) that there is on the premises to be specified in the warrant any document or information relevant to that inquiry which the Commission could require to be produced or furnished under section 9(1) above; and

(c) that, if the Commission were to make an order requiring the document or information to be so produced or furnished—

(i) the order would not be complied with, or

(ii) the document or information would be removed, tampered with, concealed or destroyed.

(3) A warrant under this section is a warrant authorising the member of the Commission's staff who is named in it—

(a) to enter and search the premises specified in it;

(b) to take such other persons with him as the Commission considers are needed to assist him in doing anything that he is authorised to do under the warrant;

(c) to take possession of any documents which appear to fall within subsection (2)(b) above, or to take any other steps which appear to be necessary for preserving, or preventing interference with, any such documents;

(d) to take possession of any computer disk or other electronic storage device which appears to contain information falling within subsection (2)(b), or information contained in a document so falling, or to take any other steps which appear to be necessary for preserving, or preventing interference with, any such information;

(e) to take copies of, or extracts from, any documents or information falling within paragraph (c) or (d);

(f) to require any person on the premises to provide an explanation of any such document or information or to state where any such documents or information may be found;

(g) to require any such person to give him such assistance as he may reasonably require for the taking of copies or extracts as mentioned in paragraph (e) above.

(4) Entry and search under such a warrant must be at a reasonable hour and within one month of the date of its issue.

(5) The member of the Commission's staff who is authorised under such a warrant ("the authorised person") must, if required to do so, produce—

(a) the warrant, and

(b) documentary evidence that he is a member of the Commission's staff,

for inspection by the occupier of the premises or anyone acting on his behalf.

(6) The authorised person must make a written record of—

(a) the date and time of his entry on the premises;

(b) the number of persons (if any) who accompanied him onto the premises, and the names of any such persons;

(c) the period for which he (and any such persons) remained on the premises;

(d) what he (and any such persons) did while on the premises; and

(e) any document or device of which he took possession while there.

(7) If required to do so, the authorised person must give a copy of the record to the occupier of the premises or someone acting on his behalf.

(8) Unless it is not reasonably practicable to do so, the authorised person must comply with the following requirements before leaving the premises, namely—

(a) the requirements of subsection (6), and

(b) any requirement made under subsection (7) before he leaves the premises.

(9) Where possession of any document or device is taken under this section—

(a) the document may be retained for so long as the Commission considers that it is necessary to retain it (rather than a copy of it) for the purposes of the relevant inquiry under section 8 above, or

(b) the device may be retained for so long as the Commission considers that it is necessary to retain it for the purposes of that inquiry, as the case may be.

(10) Once it appears to the Commission that the retention of any document or device has ceased to be so necessary, it shall arrange for the document or device to be returned as soon as is reasonably practicable—

(a) to the person from whose possession it was taken, or
(b) to any of the charity trustees of the charity to which it belonged or related.

(11) A person who intentionally obstructs the exercise of any rights conferred by a warrant under this section is guilty of an offence and liable on summary conviction—

(a) to imprisonment for a term not exceeding 51 weeks, or
(b) to a fine not exceeding level 5 on the standard scale,

or to both.]

[795A]

NOTES

Commencement: 27 February 2007, subject to transitional provisions in Sch 10, para 6 at **[2176]**.
Inserted by the Charities Act 2006, s 26(1).

Legal proceedings relating to charities

32 Proceedings by [Commission]

(1) Subject to subsection (2) below, [the Commission] may exercise the same powers with respect to—

(a) the taking of legal proceedings with reference to charities or the property or affairs of charities, or
(b) the compromise of claims with a view to avoiding or ending such proceedings,

as are exercisable by the Attorney General acting ex officio.

(2) Subsection (1) above does not apply to the power of the Attorney General under section 63(1) below to present a petition for the winding up of a charity.

(3) The practice and procedure to be followed in relation to any proceedings taken by [the Commission] under subsection (1) above shall be the same in all respects (and in particular as regards costs) as if they were proceedings taken by the Attorney General acting ex officio.

(4) No rule of law or practice shall be taken to require the Attorney General to be a party to any such proceedings.

(5) The powers exercisable by [the Commission] by virtue of this section shall be exercisable [by the Commission of its own] motion, but shall be exercisable only with the agreement of the Attorney General on each occasion.

[796]

NOTES

Section heading: word in square brackets substituted by the Charities Act 2006, s 75(1), Sch 8, paras 96, 124(1), (4), as from 27 February 2007.
Sub-ss (1), (3), (5): words in square brackets substituted by the Charities Act 2006, s 75(1), Sch 8, paras 96, 124(1)–(3), as from 27 February 2007.

33 Proceedings by other persons

(1) Charity proceedings may be taken with reference to a charity either by the charity, or by any of the charity trustees, or by any person interested in the charity, or by any two or more inhabitants of the area of the charity if it is a local charity, but not by any other person.

(2) Subject to the following provisions of this section, no charity proceedings relating to a charity (*other than an exempt charity*) shall be entertained or proceeded with in any court unless the taking of the proceedings is authorised by order of [the Commission].

(3) [The Commission] shall not, without special reasons, authorise the taking of charity proceedings where in [its opinion] the case can be dealt with [by the Commission] under the powers of this Act other than those conferred by section 32 above.

(4) This section shall not require any order for the taking of proceedings in a pending cause or matter or for the bringing of any appeal.

(5) Where the foregoing provisions of this section require the taking of charity proceedings to be authorised by an order of [the Commission], the proceedings may nevertheless be entertained or proceeded with if, after the order had been applied for and refused, leave to take the proceedings was obtained from one of the judges of the High Court attached to the Chancery Division.

(6) Nothing in the foregoing subsections shall apply to the taking of proceedings by the Attorney General, with or without a relator, or to the taking of proceedings by [the Commission] in accordance with section 32 above.

(7) Where it appears to [the Commission], on an application for an order under this section or otherwise, that it is desirable for legal proceedings to be taken with reference to any charity (*other than an exempt charity*) or its property or affairs, and for the proceedings to be taken by the Attorney General, [the Commission] shall so inform the Attorney General, and send him such statements and particulars as [the Commission thinks] necessary to explain the matter.

(8) In this section "charity proceedings" means proceedings in any court in England or Wales brought under the court's jurisdiction with respect to charities, or brought under the court's jurisdiction with respect to trusts in relation to the administration of a trust for charitable purposes.

[797]

NOTES

Sub-s (2): words in italics repealed by the Charities Act 2006, ss 12, 75 (2), Sch 5, para 8(1), (2), Sch 9, as from a day to be appointed under s 79(2) of that Act, and words in square brackets substituted by s 75(1) of, and Sch 8, paras 96, 125(1), (2) to, that Act, as from 27 February 2007.

Sub-ss (3), (5), (6): words in square brackets substituted by the Charities Act 2006, s 75(1), Sch 8, paras 125(1), (3), (4), as from 27 February 2007.

Sub-s (7): words in square brackets substituted by the Charities Act 2006, s 75(1), Sch 8, paras 96, 125(1), (5), as from 27 February 2007, and words in italics repealed by ss 12, 75(2) of, and Sch 5, para 8(1), (3), Sch 9 to, that Act, as from a day to be appointed under s 79(2) of that Act.

34 Report of s 8 inquiry to be evidence in certain proceedings

(1) A copy of the report of the person conducting an inquiry under section 8 above shall, if certified by [the Commission] to be a true copy, be admissible in any proceedings to which this section applies—

(a) as evidence of any fact stated in the report; and
(b) as evidence of the opinion of that person as to any matter referred to in it.

(2) This section applies to—

(a) any legal proceedings instituted by [the Commission] under this Part of this Act; and
(b) any legal proceedings instituted by the Attorney General in respect of a charity.

(3) A document purporting to be a certificate issued for the purposes of subsection (1) above shall be received in evidence and be deemed to be such a certificate, unless the contrary is proved.

[798]

NOTES

Sub-ss (1), (2): words in square brackets substituted by the Charities Act 2006, s 75(1), Sch 8, paras 96, 126, as from 27 February 2007.

Meaning of "trust corporation"

35 Application of provisions to trust corporations appointed under s 16 or 18

(1) In the definition of "trust corporation" contained in the following provisions—

(a) section 117(xxx) of the Settled Land Act 1925,
(b) section 68(18) of the Trustee Act 1925,
(c) section 205(xxviii) of the Law of Property Act 1925,
(d) section 55(xxvi) of the Administration of Estates Act 1925, and
(e) section 128 of the *Supreme Court Act 1981*,

the reference to a corporation appointed by the court in any particular case to be a trustee includes a reference to a corporation appointed by [the Commission] under this Act to be a trustee.

(2) This section shall be deemed always to have had effect; but the reference to section 128 of the *Supreme Court Act 1981* shall, in relation to any time before 1st January 1982, be construed as a reference to section 175(1) of the Supreme Court of Judicature (Consolidation) Act 1925.

[799]

NOTES

Sub-s (1): for the words in italics in para (e) there are substituted the words "Senior Courts Act 1981" by the Constitutional Reform Act 2005, s 59(5), Sch 11, Pt 1, para 1(2), as from a day to be appointed under s 148(1) of that Act; words in square brackets substituted by the Charities Act 2006, s 75(1), Sch 8, paras 96, 127, as from 27 February 2007.

Sub-s (2): for the words in italics there are substituted the words "Senior Courts Act 1981" by the Constitutional Reform Act 2005, s 59(5), Sch 11, Pt 1, para 1(2), as from a day to be appointed under s 148(1) of that Act.

Supreme Court of Judicature (Consolidation) Act 1925, s 175(1): repealed by the Supreme Court Act 1981, s 152(4), Sch 7, and replaced by s 128 of that Act.

PART V
CHARITY LAND

36 Restrictions on dispositions

(1) Subject to the following provisions of this section and section 40 below, no land held by or in trust for a charity shall be [conveyed, transferred], leased or otherwise disposed of without an order of the court or of [the Commission].

(2) Subsection (1) above shall not apply to a disposition of such land if—

(a) the disposition is made to a person who is not—

(i) a connected person (as defined in Schedule 5 to this Act), or

(ii) a trustee for, or nominee of, a connected person; and

(b) the requirements of subsection (3) or (5) below have been complied with in relation to it.

(3) Except where the proposed disposition is the granting of such a lease as is mentioned in subsection (5) below [the requirements mentioned in subsection (2)(b) above are that], the charity trustees must, before entering into an agreement for the sale, or (as the case may be) for a lease or other disposition, of the land—

(a) obtain and consider a written report on the proposed disposition from a qualified surveyor instructed by the trustees and acting exclusively for the charity;

(b) advertise the proposed disposition for such period and in such manner as the surveyor has advised in his report (unless he has there advised that it would not be in the best interests of the charity to advertise the proposed disposition); and

(c) decide that they are satisfied, having considered the surveyor's report, that the terms on which the disposition is proposed to be made are the best that can reasonably be obtained for the charity.

(4) For the purposes of subsection (3) above a person is a qualified surveyor if—

(a) he is a fellow or professional associate of the Royal Institution of Chartered Surveyors or of the Incorporated Society of Valuers and Auctioneers or satisfies such other requirement or requirements as may be prescribed by regulations made by the [Minister]; and

(b) he is reasonably believed by the charity trustees to have ability in, and experience of, the valuation of land of the particular kind, and in the particular area, in question;

and any report prepared for the purposes of that subsection shall contain such information, and deal with such matters, as may be prescribed by regulations so made.

(5) Where the proposed disposition is the granting of a lease for a term ending not more than seven years after it is granted (other than one granted wholly or partly in consideration of a fine), [the requirements mentioned in subsection (2)(b) above are that] the charity trustees must, before entering into an agreement for the lease—

(a) obtain and consider the advice on the proposed disposition of a person who is reasonably believed by the trustees to have the requisite ability and practical experience to provide them with competent advice on the proposed disposition; and

(b) decide that they are satisfied, having considered that person's advice, that the terms on which the disposition is proposed to be made are the best that can reasonably be obtained for the charity.

(6) Where—

(a) any land is held by or in trust for a charity, and

(b) the trusts on which it is so held stipulate that it is to be used for the purposes, or any particular purposes, of the charity,

then (subject to subsections (7) and (8) below and without prejudice to the operation of the preceding provisions of this section) the land shall not be *sold*, leased or otherwise disposed of unless the charity trustees have *previously*—

(i) given public notice of the proposed disposition, inviting representations to be made to them within a time specified in the notice, being not less than one month from the date of the notice; and

(ii) taken into consideration any representations made to them within that time about the proposed disposition.

[(6A) In subsection (6) above "the relevant time" means—

(a) where the charity trustees enter into an agreement for the sale, or (as the case may be) for the lease or other disposition, the time when they enter into that agreement, and

(b) in any other case, the time of the disposition.]

(7) Subsection (6) above shall not apply to any such disposition of land as is there mentioned if—

(a) the disposition is to be effected with a view to acquiring by way of replacement other property which is to be held on the trusts referred to in paragraph (b) of that subsection; or

(b) the disposition is the granting of a lease for a term ending not more than two years after it is granted (other than one granted wholly or partly in consideration of a fine).

(8) [The Commission] may direct—

(a) that subsection (6) above shall not apply to dispositions of land held by or in trust for a charity or class of charities (whether generally or only in the case of a specified class of dispositions or land, or otherwise as may be provided in the direction), or

(b) that that subsection shall not apply to a particular disposition of land held by or in trust for a charity,

if, on an application made to them in writing by or on behalf of the charity or charities in question, [the Commission is satisfied] that it would be in the interests of the charity or charities [for the Commission] to give the direction.

(9) The restrictions on disposition imposed by this section apply notwithstanding anything in the trusts of a charity; but nothing in this section applies—

(a) to any disposition for which general or special authority is expressly given (without the authority being made subject to the sanction of an order of the court) by any statutory provision contained in or having effect under an Act of Parliament or by any scheme legally established; or

(b) to any disposition of land held by or in trust for a charity which—

(i) is made to another charity otherwise than for the best price that can reasonably be obtained, and

(ii) is authorised to be so made by the trusts of the first-mentioned charity; or

(c) to the granting, by or on behalf of a charity and in accordance with its trusts, of a lease to any beneficiary under those trusts where the lease—

(i) is granted otherwise than for the best rent that can reasonably be obtained; and

(ii) is intended to enable the demised premises to be occupied for the purposes, or any particular purposes, of the charity.

(10) Nothing in this section applies—

(a) to any disposition of land held by or in trust for an exempt charity;

(b) to any disposition of land by way of mortgage or other security; or

(c) to any disposition of an advowson.

(11) In this section "land" means land in England or Wales.

[800]

NOTES

Sub-ss (1), (8): words in square brackets substituted by the Charities Act 2006, s 75(1), Sch 8, paras 96, 128(1), (2), (7), as from 27 February 2007.

Sub-ss (3), (5): words in square brackets inserted by the Charities Act 2006, s 75(1), Sch 8, paras 96, 128(1), (3), (4), as from 27 February 2007.

Sub-s (4): word in square brackets in para (a) substituted by the Transfer of Functions (Third Sector, Communities and Equality) Order 2006, SI 2006/2951, art 6, Schedule, para 4(o).

Sub-s (6): words in square brackets substituted for the word "sold" by the Charities Act 2006, s 75(1), Sch 8, paras 96, 128(1), (5), except in relation to any sale, lease or other disposition where before 27 February 2007 the charity trustees have entered into an agreement for the disposition; see the Charities Act 2006 (Commencement No 1, Transitional Provisions and Savings) Order 2007, SI 2007/309, art 6(1).

Sub-s (6A): inserted by the Charities Act 2006, s 75(1), Sch 8, paras 96, 128(1), (6), except in relation to any sale, lease or other disposition where before 27 February 2007 the charity trustees have entered into an agreement for the disposition; see the Charities Act 2006 (Commencement No 1, Transitional Provisions and Savings) Order 2007, SI 2007/309, art 6(1).

Regulations: by virtue of the Interpretation Act 1978, s 17(2)(b), the Charities (Qualified Surveyors' Reports) Regulations 1992, SI 1992/2980 at **[3102]**, have effect as if made under this section.

37 Supplementary provisions relating to dispositions

(1) Any of the following instruments, namely—

(a) any contract for the sale, or for a lease or other disposition, of land which is held by or in trust for a charity, and

(b) any conveyance, transfer, lease or other instrument effecting a disposition of such land,

shall state—

(i) that the land is held by or in trust for a charity,

(ii) whether the charity is an exempt charity and whether the disposition is one falling within paragraph (a), (b) or (c) of subsection (9) of section 36 above, and

(iii) if it is not an exempt charity and the disposition is not one falling within any of those paragraphs, that the land is land to which the restrictions on disposition imposed by that section apply.

(2) Where any land held by or in trust for a charity is [conveyed, transferred], leased or otherwise disposed of by a disposition to which subsection (1) or (2) of section 36 above applies, the charity trustees shall certify in the instrument by which the disposition is effected—

(a) (where subsection (1) of that section applies) that the disposition has been sanctioned by an order of the court or of [the Commission] (as the case may be), or

(b) (where subsection (2) of that section applies) that the charity trustees have power under the trusts of the charity to effect the disposition, and that they have complied with the provisions of that section so far as applicable to it.

(3) Where subsection (2) above has been complied with in relation to any disposition of land, then in favour of a person who (whether under the disposition or afterwards) acquires an interest in the land for money or money's worth, it shall be conclusively presumed that the facts were as stated in the certificate.

(4) Where—

(a) any land held by or in trust for a charity is [conveyed, transferred], leased or otherwise disposed of by a disposition to which subsection (1) or (2) of section 36 above applies, but

(b) subsection (2) above has not been complied with in relation to the disposition,

then in favour of a person who (whether under the disposition or afterwards) in good faith acquires an interest in the land for money or money's worth, the disposition shall be valid whether or not—

(i) the disposition has been sanctioned by an order of the court or of [the Commission], or

(ii) the charity trustees have power under the trusts of the charity to effect the disposition and have complied with the provisions of that section so far as applicable to it.

(5) Any of the following instruments, namely—

(a) any contract for the sale, or for a lease or other disposition, of land which will, as a result of the disposition, be held by or in trust for a charity, and

(b) any conveyance, transfer, lease or other instrument effecting a disposition of such land,

shall state—

(i) that the land will, as a result of the disposition, be held by or in trust for a charity,

(ii) whether the charity is an exempt charity, and

(iii) if it is not an exempt charity, that the restrictions on disposition imposed by section 36 above will apply to the land (subject to subsection (9) of that section).

(6) …

[(7)Where the disposition to be effected by any such instrument as is mentioned in subsection (1)(b) or (5)(b) above will be—

(a) a registrable disposition, or

(b) a disposition which triggers the requirement of registration,

the statement which, by virtue of subsection (1) or (5) above, is to be contained in the instrument shall be in such form as may be prescribed by land registration rules.

(8)Where the registrar approves an application for registration of—

(a) a disposition of registered land, or

(b) a person's title under a disposition of unregistered land,

and the instrument effecting the disposition contains a statement complying with subsections (5) and (7) above, he shall enter in the register a restriction reflecting the limitation under section 36 above on subsequent disposal.]

(9) Where—

(a) any such restriction is entered in the register in respect of any land, and

(b) the charity by or in trust for which the land is held becomes an exempt charity,

the charity trustees shall apply to the registrar for [the removal of the entry]; and on receiving any application duly made under this subsection the registrar shall [remove the entry].

(10) Where—

(a) any registered land is held by or in trust for an exempt charity and the charity ceases to be an exempt charity, or

(b) any registered land becomes, as a result of a declaration of trust by the registered proprietor, land held in trust for a charity (other than an exempt charity),

the charity trustees shall apply to the registrar for such a restriction as is mentioned in subsection (8) above to be entered in the register in respect of the land; and on receiving any application duly made under this subsection the registrar shall enter such a restriction in the register in respect of the land.

(11) In this section—

(a) references to a disposition of land do not include references to—

(i) a disposition of land by way of mortgage or other security,

(ii) any disposition of an advowson, or

(iii) any release of a rentcharge falling within section 40(1) below; and

(b) "land" means land in England or Wales;

and subsections (7) to (10) above shall be construed as one with the [Land Registration Act 2002].

[801]

NOTES

Sub-ss (2), (4): words in square brackets substituted by the Charities Act 2006, s 75(1), Sch 8, paras 96, 129, as from 27 February 2007.

Sub-s (6): repealed by the Trusts of Land and Appointment of Trustees Act 1996, s 25(2), Sch 4.

Sub-ss (7), (8): substituted by the Land Registration Act 2002, s 133, Sch 11, para 29(1), (2).

Sub-ss (9), (11): words in square brackets substituted by the Land Registration Act 2002, s 133, Sch 11, para 29(1), (3), (4).

Rules: the Land Registration Rules 2003, SI 2003/1417.

38 Restrictions on mortgaging

(1) Subject to subsection (2) below, no mortgage of land held by or in trust for a charity shall be granted without an order of the court or of [the Commission].

[(2) Subsection (1) above shall not apply to a mortgage of any such land if the charity trustees have, before executing the mortgage, obtained and considered proper advice, given to them in writing, on the relevant matters or matter mentioned in subsection (3) or (3A) below (as the case may be).

(3) In the case of a mortgage to secure the repayment of a proposed loan or grant, the relevant matters are—

(a) whether the loan or grant is necessary in order for the charity trustees to be able to pursue the particular course of action in connection with which they are seeking the loan or grant;

(b) whether the terms of the loan or grant are reasonable having regard to the status of the charity as the prospective recipient of the loan or grant; and

(c) the ability of the charity to repay on those terms the sum proposed to be paid by way of loan or grant.

(3A) In the case of a mortgage to secure the discharge of any other proposed obligation, the relevant matter is whether it is reasonable for the charity trustees to undertake to discharge the obligation, having regard to the charity's purposes.

(3B) Subsection (3) or (as the case may be) subsection (3A) above applies in relation to such a mortgage as is mentioned in that subsection whether the mortgage—

(a) would only have effect to secure the repayment of the proposed loan or grant or the discharge of the proposed obligation, or

(b) would also have effect to secure the repayment of sums paid by way of loan or grant, or the discharge of other obligations undertaken, after the date of its execution.

(3C) Subsection (3D) below applies where—

(a) the charity trustees of a charity have executed a mortgage of land held by or in trust for a charity in accordance with subsection (2) above, and

(b) the mortgage has effect to secure the repayment of sums paid by way of loan or grant, or the discharge of other obligations undertaken, after the date of its execution.

(3D) In such a case, the charity trustees must not after that date enter into any transaction involving—

(a) the payment of any such sums, or

(b) the undertaking of any such obligations,

unless they have, before entering into the transaction, obtained and considered proper advice, given to them in writing, on the matters or matter mentioned in subsection (3)(a) to (c) or (3A) above (as the case may be).]

(4) For the purposes of [this section] proper advice is the advice of a person—

(a) who is reasonably believed by the charity trustees to be qualified by his ability in and practical experience of financial matters; and

(b) who has no financial interest in [relation to the loan, grant or other transaction in connection with which his advice is given];

and such advice may constitute proper advice for those purposes notwithstanding that the person giving it does so in the course of his employment as an officer or employee of the charity or of the charity trustees.

(5) This section applies notwithstanding anything in the trusts of a charity; but nothing in this section applies to any mortgage for which general or special authority is given as mentioned in section 36(9)(a) above.

(6) In this section—

"land" means land in England or Wales;

"mortgage" includes a charge.

(7) Nothing in this section applies to an exempt charity.

[802]

NOTES

Sub-s (1): words in square brackets substituted by the Charities Act 2006, s 75(1), Sch 8, paras 96, 130, as from 27 February 2007.

Sub-ss (2), (3)–(3D): substituted, for sub-ss (2), (3) as originally enacted, by the Charities Act 2006, s 27(1), (2), as from 27 February 2007.

Sub-s (4): words in square brackets substituted by the Charities Act 2006, s 27(1), (3), as from 27 February 2007.

39 Supplementary provisions relating to mortgaging

(1) Any mortgage of land held by or in trust for a charity shall state—

(a) that the land is held by or in trust for a charity,

(b) whether the charity is an exempt charity and whether the mortgage is one falling within subsection (5) of section 38 above, and

(c) if it is not an exempt charity and the mortgage is not one falling within that subsection, that the mortgage is one to which the restrictions imposed by that section apply;

and where the mortgage will be a registered disposition any such statement shall be in such form as may be prescribed [by land registration rules].

[(1A) Where any such mortgage will be one to which section 4(1)(g) of the Land Registration Act 2002 applies—

(a) the statement required by subsection (1) above shall be in such form as may be prescribed by land registration rules; and

(b) if the charity is not an exempt charity, the mortgage shall also contain a statement, in such form as may be prescribed by land registration rules, that the restrictions on disposition imposed by section 36 above apply to the land (subject to subsection (9) of that section).

(1B) Where—

(a) the registrar approves an application for registration of a person's title to land in connection with such a mortgage as is mentioned in subsection (1A) above,

(b) the mortgage contains statements complying with subsections (1) and (1A) above, and

(c) the charity is not an exempt charity,

the registrar shall enter in the register a restriction reflecting the limitation under section 36 above on subsequent disposal.

(1C) Section 37(9) above shall apply in relation to any restriction entered under subsection (1B) as it applies in relation to any restriction entered under section 37(8).]

(2) Where subsection (1) or (2) of section 38 above applies to any mortgage of land held by or in trust for a charity, the charity trustees shall certify in the mortgage—

(a) (where subsection (1) of that section applies) that the mortgage has been sanctioned by an order of the court or of [the Commission] (as the case may be), or

(b) (where subsection (2) of that section applies) that the charity trustees have power under the trusts of the charity to grant the mortgage, and that they have obtained and considered such advice as is mentioned in that subsection.

(3) Where subsection (2) above has been complied with in relation to any mortgage, then in favour of a person who (whether under the mortgage or afterwards) acquires an interest in the land in question for money or money's worth, it shall be conclusively presumed that the facts were as stated in the certificate.

(4) Where—

(a) subsection (1) or (2) of section 38 above applies to any mortgage of land held by or in trust for a charity, but

(b) subsection (2) above has not been complied with in relation to the mortgage,

then in favour of a person who (whether under the mortgage or afterwards) in good faith acquires an interest in the land for money or money's worth, the mortgage shall be valid whether or not—

(i) the mortgage has been sanctioned by an order of the court or of [the Commission], or

(ii) the charity trustees have power under the trusts of the charity to grant the mortgage and have obtained and considered such advice as is mentioned in subsection (2) of that section.

[(4A) Where subsection (3D) of section 38 above applies to any mortgage of land held by or in trust for a charity, the charity trustees shall certify in relation to any transaction falling within that subsection that they have obtained and considered such advice as is mentioned in that subsection.

(4B) Where subsection (4A) above has been complied with in relation to any transaction, then, in favour of a person who (whether under the mortgage or afterwards) has acquired or acquires an interest in the land for money or money's worth, it shall be conclusively presumed that the facts were as stated in the certificate.]

(5) …

(6) In this section—

"mortgage" includes a charge, and "mortgagee" shall be construed accordingly;

"land" means land in England or Wales;

[and subsections (1) to (1B) above shall be construed as one with the Land Registration Act 2002.]

[803]

NOTES

Sub-s (1): words in square brackets added by the Land Registration Act 2002, s 133, Sch 11, para 29(1), (5).

Sub-ss (1A)–(1C): substituted for sub-ss (1A), (1B) (as inserted by the Land Registration Act 1997, s 4(1), Sch 1, para 6(2), in relation to dispositions made on or after 1 April 1998) by the Land Registration Act 2002, s 133, Sch 11, para 29(1), (6).

Sub-ss (2), (4): words in square brackets substituted by the Charities Act 2006, s 75(1), Sch 8, paras 96, 131(1), (2), as from 27 February 2007.

Sub-ss (4A), (4B): inserted by the Charities Act 2006, s 75(1), Sch 8, paras 96, 131(1), (3), as from 27 February 2007.

Sub-s (5): repealed by the Trusts of Land and Appointment of Trustees Act 1996, s 25(2), Sch 4.

Sub-s (6): words in square brackets substituted by the Land Registration Act 2002, s 133, Sch 11, para 29(1), (7).

Rules: the Land Registration Rules 2003, SI 2003/1417.

40 Release of charity rentcharges

(1) Section 36(1) above shall not apply to the release by a charity of a rentcharge which it is entitled to receive if the release is given in consideration of the payment of an amount which is not less than ten times the annual amount of the rentcharge.

(2) Where a charity which is entitled to receive a rentcharge releases it in consideration of the payment of an amount not exceeding £500, any costs incurred by the charity in connection with proving its title to the rentcharge shall be recoverable by the charity from the person or persons in whose favour the rentcharge is being released.

(3) Neither section 36(1) nor subsection (2) above applies where a rentcharge which a charity is entitled to receive is redeemed under sections 8 to 10 of the Rentcharges Act 1977.

(4) The [Minister] may by order amend subsection (2) above by substituting a different sum for the sum for the time being specified there.

[804]

NOTES

Sub-s (4): word in square brackets substituted by the Transfer of Functions (Third Sector, Communities and Equality) Order 2006, SI 2006/2951, art 6, Schedule, para 4(p).

PART VI
CHARITY ACCOUNTS, REPORTS AND RETURNS

41 Duty to keep accounting records

(1) The charity trustees of a charity shall ensure that accounting records are kept in respect of the charity which are sufficient to show and explain all the charity's transactions, and which are such as to—

(a) disclose at any time, with reasonable accuracy, the financial position of the charity at that time, and

(b) enable the trustees to ensure that, where any statements of accounts are prepared by them under section 42(1) below, those statements of accounts comply with the requirements of regulations under that provision.

(2) The accounting records shall in particular contain—

(a) entries showing from day to day all sums of money received and expended by the charity, and the matters in respect of which the receipt and expenditure takes place; and

(b) a record of the assets and liabilities of the charity.

(3) The charity trustees of a charity shall preserve any accounting records made for the purposes of this section in respect of the charity for at least six years from the end of the financial year of the charity in which they are made.

(4) Where a charity ceases to exist within the period of six years mentioned in subsection (3) above as it applies to any accounting records, the obligation to preserve those records in accordance with that subsection shall continue to be discharged by the last charity trustees of the charity, unless [the Commission consents] in writing to the records being destroyed or otherwise disposed of.

(5) Nothing in this section applies to a charity which is a company.

[805]

NOTES

Commencement: this Part (ss 41–49) was brought into force on 15 October 1995 for the purpose of making Orders and Regulations, and on 1 March 1996 for all other purposes: see the Charities Act 1993 (Commencement and Transitional Provisions) Order 1995, SI 1995/2695, which also provides that no requirement imposed by ss 42, 43, 45, 46(5) or 48 in respect of a financial year of a charity shall apply in relation to any financial year which begins before 1 March 1996.

Sub-s (4): words in square brackets substituted by the Charities Act 2006, s 75(1), Sch 8, paras 96, 132, as from 27 February 2007.

42 Annual statements of accounts

(1) The charity trustees of a charity shall (subject to subsection (3) below) prepare in respect of each financial year of the charity a statement of accounts complying with such requirements as to its form and contents as may be prescribed by regulations made by the [Minister].

(2) Without prejudice to the generality of subsection (1) above, regulations under that subsection may make provision—

(a) for any such statement to be prepared in accordance with such methods and principles as are specified or referred to in the regulations;

(b) as to any information to be provided by way of notes to the accounts;

and regulations under that subsection may also make provision for determining the financial years of a charity for the purposes of this Act and any regulations made under it.

[(2A) Such regulations may, however, not impose on the charity trustees of a charity that is a charitable trust created by any person ("the settlor") any requirement to disclose, in any statement of accounts prepared by them under subsection (1)—

(a) the identities of recipients of grants made out of the funds of the charity, or

(b) the amounts of any individual grants so made,

if the disclosure would fall to be made at a time when the settlor or any spouse or civil partner of his was still alive.]

(3) Where a charity's gross income in any financial year does not exceed [£100,000], the charity trustees may, in respect of that year, elect to prepare the following, namely—

(a) a receipts and payments account, and

(b) a statement of assets and liabilities,

instead of a statement of accounts under subsection (1) above.

(4) The charity trustees of a charity shall preserve—

(a) any statement of accounts prepared by them under subsection (1) above, or

(b) any account and statement prepared by them under subsection (3) above,

for at least six years from the end of the financial year to which any such statement relates or (as the case may be) to which any such account and statement relate.

(5) Subsection (4) of section 41 above shall apply in relation to the preservation of any such statement or account and statement as it applies in relation to the preservation of any accounting records (the references to subsection (3) of that section being read as references to subsection (4) above).

(6) The [Minister] may by order amend subsection (3) above by substituting a different sum for the sum for the time being specified there.

(7) Nothing in this section applies to a charity which is a company.

[(8) Provisions about the preparation of accounts in respect of groups consisting of certain charities and their subsidiary undertakings, and about other matters relating to such groups, are contained in Schedule 5A to this Act (see section 49A below).]

[806]

NOTES

Commencement: see the note to s 41 at **[805]**.

Sub-ss (1), (6): words in square brackets substituted by the Transfer of Functions (Third Sector, Communities and Equality) Order 2006, SI 2006/2951, art 6, Schedule, para 4(q).

Sub-s (2A): inserted by the Charities Act 2006, s 75(1), Sch 8, paras 96, 133(1), (2), as from a day to be appointed under s 79(2) of that Act.

Sub-s (3): sum in square brackets substituted by the Charities Act 1993 (Substitution of Sums) Order 1995, SI 1995/2696, art 2(1), (3).

Sub-s (8): added by the Charities Act 2006, s 75(1), Sch 8, paras 96, 133(1), (3), as from a day to be appointed under s 79(2) of that Act.

Regulations: the Charities (Accounts and Reports) Regulations 2005, SI 2005/572 at **[3398]**.

Orders: the Charities Act 1993 (Substitution of Sums) Order 1995, SI 1995/2696.

43 Annual audit or examination of charity accounts

[(1) Subsection (2) below applies to a financial year of a charity if—

(a) the charity's gross income in that year exceeds £500,000; or

(b) the charity's gross income in that year exceeds the accounts threshold and at the end of the year the aggregate value of its assets (before deduction of liabilities) exceeds £2.8 million.

"The accounts threshold" means £100,000 or such other sum as is for the time being specified in section 42(3) above.]

(2) If this subsection applies to a financial year of a charity, the accounts of the charity for that year shall be audited by a person who—

[(a) would be eligible for appointment as auditor of the charity under Part 2 of the Companies Act 1989 if the charity were a company, or]

(b) is a member of a body for the time being specified in regulations under section 44 below and is under the rules of that body eligible for appointment as auditor of the charity.

(3) If subsection (2) above does not apply to a financial year of a charity [but its gross income in that year exceeds £10,000,] the accounts of the charity for that year shall, at the election of the charity trustees, either—

(a) be examined by an independent examiner, that is to say an independent person who is reasonably believed by the trustees to have the requisite ability and practical experience to carry out a competent examination of the accounts, or

(b) be audited by such a person as is mentioned in subsection (2) above.

[This is subject to the requirements of subsection (3A) below where the gross income exceeds £250,000, and to any order under subsection (4) below.]

[(3A) If subsection (3) above applies to the accounts of a charity for a year and the charity's gross income in that year exceeds £250,000, a person qualifies as an independent examiner for the purposes of paragraph (a) of that subsection if (and only if) he is an independent person who is—

(a) a member of a body for the time being specified in section 249D(3) of the Companies Act 1985 (reporting accountants);

(b) a member of the Chartered Institute of Public Finance and Accountancy; or

(c) a Fellow of the Association of Charity Independent Examiners.]

(4) Where it appears to [the Commission]—

(a) that subsection (2), or (as the case may be) subsection (3) above, has not been complied with in relation to a financial year of a charity within ten months from the end of that year, or

(b) that, although subsection (2) above does not apply to a financial year of a charity, it would nevertheless be desirable for the accounts of the charity for that year to be audited by such a person as is mentioned in that subsection, [the Commission] may by order require the accounts of the charity for that year to be audited by such a person as is mentioned in that subsection.

(5) If [the Commission makes] an order under subsection (4) above with respect to a charity, then unless—

(a) the order is made by virtue of paragraph (b) of that subsection, and

(b) the charity trustees themselves appoint an auditor in accordance with the order,

the auditor shall be a person appointed by [the Commission].

(6) The expenses of any audit carried out by an auditor appointed by [the Commission] under subsection (5) above, including the auditor's remuneration, shall be recoverable by [the Commission]—

(a) from the charity trustees of the charity concerned, who shall be personally liable, jointly and severally, for those expenses; or

(b) to the extent that it appears to [the Commission] not to be practical to seek recovery of those expenses in accordance with paragraph (a) above, from the funds of the charity.

(7) [The Commission] may—

(a) give guidance to charity trustees in connection with the selection of a person for appointment as an independent examiner;

(b) give such directions as [it thinks] appropriate with respect to the carrying out of an examination in pursuance of subsection (3)(a) above;

and any such guidance or directions may either be of general application or apply to a particular charity only.

[(8) The Minister may by order—

(a) amend subsection (1)(a) or (b), (3) or (3A) above by substituting a different sum for any sum for the time being specified there;

(b) amend subsection (3A) by adding or removing a description of person to or from the list in that subsection or by varying any entry for the time being included in that list.]

(9) Nothing in this section applies to a charity which is a company.

[(10) Nothing in this section applies in relation to a financial year of a charity where, at any time in the year, a charity is an English National Health Service charity or Welsh National Health Service charity (as defined in sections 43A and 43B respectively).]

[807]

NOTES

Commencement: see the note to s 41 at **[805]**.

Sub-s (1): substituted by the Charities Act 2006, s 28(1), (2), as from 27 February 2007, subject to transitional provisions in Sch 10, para 7 at **[2176]**.

Sub-s (2): para (a) substituted by the Charities Act 2006, s 28(1), (3), as from 27 February 2007, subject to transitional provisions in Sch 10, para 7 at **[2176]**.

Sub-s (3): words in first pair of square brackets substituted and words in second pair of square brackets inserted by the Charities Act 2006, s 28(1), (4), as from 27 February 2007, subject to transitional provisions in Sch 10, para 7 at **[2176]**.

Sub-s (3A): inserted by the Charities Act 2006, s 28(1), (5), as from 27 February 2007, subject to transitional provisions in Sch 10, para 7 at **[2176]**.

Sub-ss (4)–(7): words in square brackets substituted by the Charities Act 2006, s 75(1), Sch 8, paras 96, 134, as from 27 February 2007.

Sub-s (8): substituted by the Charities Act 2006, s 28(1), (6), as from 27 February 2007, subject to transitional provisions and savings in Sch 10, para 7 at **[2176]**.

Sub-s (10): added by the Regulatory Reform (National Health Service Charitable and Non-Charitable Trust Accounts and Audit) Order 2005, SI 2005/1074, art 3(1), (2), in relation to the financial year of a trust starting on or after 1 April 2004.

Orders: the Charities Act 1993 (Substitution of Sums) Order 1995, SI 1995/2696.

[43A Annual audit or examination of English National Health Service charity accounts

(1) This section applies in relation to a financial year of a charity where, at any time in the year, the charity is an English National Health Service charity.

(2) In any case where [paragraph (a) or (b) of section 43(1) is satisfied in relation to] a financial year of an English National Health Service charity, the accounts of the charity for that financial year shall be audited by a person appointed by the Audit Commission.

(3) In any other case, the accounts of the charity for that financial year shall, at the election of the Audit Commission, be—

(a) audited by a person appointed by the Audit Commission; or
(b) examined by a person so appointed.

(4) Section 3 of the Audit Commission Act 1998 (c.18) applies in relation to any appointment under subsection (2) or (3)(a).

(5) [The Commission] may give such directions as [it thinks] appropriate with respect to the carrying out of an examination in pursuance of subsection (3)(b); and any such directions may either be of general application or apply to a particular charity only.

(6) The Comptroller and Auditor General may at any time examine and inspect—

(a) the accounts of the charity for the financial year;
(b) any records relating to those accounts; and
(c) any report of a person appointed under subsection (2) or (3) to audit or examine those accounts.

(7) In this section—

"Audit Commission" means the Audit Commission for Local Authorities and the National Health Service in England and Wales; and

"English National Health Service charity" means a charitable trust, the trustees of which are—

(a) a Strategic Health Authority;
(b) a Primary Care Trust;
(c) a National Health Service trust all or most of whose hospitals, establishments and facilities are situated in England;
[(d) trustees appointed in pursuance of paragraph 10 of Schedule 4 to the National Health Service Act 2006 for a National Health Service trust falling within paragraph (c);
(da) special trustees appointed in pursuance of section 29(1) of the National Health Service Reorganisation Act 1973, section 95(1) of the National Health Service Act 1977 and section 212(1) of the National Health Service Act 2006 for such a National Health Service trust, or]
(e) trustees for a Primary Care Trust appointed in pursuance of [paragraph 12 of Schedule 3 to the National Health Service Act 2006].]

[807A]

NOTES

Commencement: 31 March 2005.

Inserted, together with s 43B, by the Regulatory Reform (National Health Service Charitable and Non-Charitable Trust Accounts and Audit) Order 2005, SI 2005/1074, art 3(1), (3), with effect in relation to the financial year of a trust starting on or after 1 April 2004.

Sub-s (2): words in square brackets substituted for the words "the criterion set out in subsection (1) of section 43 is met in respect of" by the Charities Act 2006, s 75(1), Sch 8, paras 96, 135(1), (2), in relation to any financial year of an English NHS charity which begins on or after 27 February 2007; see the Charities Act 2006 (Commencement No 1, Transitional Provisions and Savings) Order 2007, SI 2007/309, art 7.

Sub-s (5): words in square brackets substituted by the Charities Act 2006, s 75(1), Sch 8, paras 96, 135(1), (3), as from 27 February 2007.

Sub-s (7): in definition "English National Health Service charity" paras (d), (da) substituted, for para (d) as originally enacted, and words in square brackets in para (e) substituted, by the National Health Service (Consequential Provisions) Act 2006, s 2, Sch 1, paras 160, 161.

[43B Annual audit or examination of Welsh National Health Service charity accounts

(1) This section applies in relation to a financial year of a charity where, at any time in the year, the charity is a Welsh National Health Service charity.

(2) In any case where [paragraph (a) or (b) of section 43(1) is satisfied in relation to] a financial year of a Welsh National Health Service charity, the accounts of the charity for that financial year shall be audited by the Auditor General for Wales.

(3) In any other case, the accounts of the charity for that financial year shall, at the election of the Auditor General for Wales, be audited or examined by the Auditor General for Wales.

(4) In this section—

"Welsh National Health Service charity" means a charitable trust, the trustees of which are—

(a) a Local Health Board;
(b) a National Health Service trust all or most of whose hospitals, establishments and facilities are situated in Wales;
[(c) trustees appointed in pursuance of paragraph 10 of Schedule 3 to the National Health Service (Wales) Act 2006 for a National Health Service trust falling within paragraph (b); or
(d) special trustees appointed in pursuance of section 29(1) of the National Health Service Reorganisation Act 1973, section 95(1) of the National Health Service Act 1977 and section 160(1) of the National Health Service (Wales) Act 2006 for such a National Health Service trust.]]

[(5) References in this Act to an auditor or an examiner have effect in relation to this section as references to the Auditor General for Wales acting under this section as an auditor or examiner.]

[807B]

NOTES

Commencement: 31 March 2005.

Inserted as noted to s 43A at **[807A]**.

Sub-s (2): words in square brackets substituted for the words "the criterion set out in subsection (1) of section 43 is met in respect of" by the Charities Act 2006, s 75(1), Sch 8, paras 96, 136(1), (2), in relation to any financial year of a Welsh NHS charity which begins on or after 27 February 2007; see the Charities Act 2006 (Commencement No 1, Transitional Provisions and Savings) Order 2007, SI 2007/309, art 8.

Sub-s (4): in definition "Welsh National Health Service charity" paras (c), (d) substituted for para (c) and word "or" immediately preceding it, by the National Health Service (Consequential Provisions) Act 2006, s 2, Sch 1, paras 160, 162

Sub-s (5): added by the Charities Act 2006, s 75(1), Sch 8, paras 96, 136(1), (3), as from 27 February 2007.

44 Supplementary provisions relating to audits etc

(1) The [Minister] may by regulations make provision—
(a) specifying one or more bodies for the purposes of section 43(2)(b) above;
(b) with respect to the duties of an auditor carrying out an audit under section 43[, 43A or 43B] above, including provision with respect to the making by him of a report on—
(i) the statement of accounts prepared for the financial year in question under section 42(1) above, or
(ii) the account and statement so prepared under section 42(3) above, as the case may be;
[(c) with respect to the making of a report—
(i) by an independent examiner in respect of an examination carried out by him under section 43 above; or
(ii) by an examiner in respect of an examination carried out by him under section 43A or 43B above;]
(d) conferring on such an auditor or on an independent examiner [or examiner] a right of access with respect to books, documents and other records (however kept) which relate to the charity concerned;
(e) entitling such an auditor or an independent examiner [or examiner] to require, in the case of a charity, information and explanations from past or present charity trustees or trustees for the charity, or from past or present officers or employees of the charity;
(f) enabling [the Commission], in circumstances specified in the regulations, to dispense with the requirements of section 43(2) or (3) above in the case of a particular charity or in the case of any particular financial year of a charity.

(2) If any person fails to afford an auditor or an independent examiner [or examiner] any facility to which he is entitled by virtue of subsection (1)(d) or (e) above, [the Commission] may by order give—
(a) to that person, or
(b) to the charity trustees for the time being of the charity concerned,

such directions as [the Commission thinks] appropriate for securing that the default is made good.

(3) ...

[808]

NOTES

Commencement: see the note to s 41 at **[805]**.

Sub-ss (1)–(3) contain provisions formerly in the Charities Act 1992, s 22(1)–(3), respectively.

Sub-s (1): word in first pair of square brackets substituted by the Transfer of Functions (Third Sector, Communities and Equality) Order 2006, SI 2006/2951, art 6, Schedule, para 4(s); words in square brackets in paras (b), (d), (e) inserted, para (c) substituted, and words in square brackets in para (f) substituted, by the Charities Act 2006, s 75(1), Sch 8, paras 96, 137(1), (2), as from 27 February 2007.

Sub-s (2): words in first pair of square brackets inserted, and words in second and third pairs of square brackets substituted by the Charities Act 2006, s 75(1), Sch 8, paras 96, 137(1), (3), as from 27 February 2007.

Sub-s (3): repealed by the Charities Act 2006, s 75(1), (2), Sch 8, paras 96, 137(1), (4), Sch 9, as from 27 February 2007.

Regulations: the Charities (Accounts and Reports) Regulations 2005, SI 2005/572 at **[3398]**.

[44A Duty of auditors etc to report matters to Commission

(1) This section applies to—

(a) a person acting as an auditor or independent examiner appointed by or in relation to a charity under section 43 above,

(b) a person acting as an auditor or examiner appointed under section 43A(2) or (3) above, and

(c) the Auditor General for Wales acting under section 43B(2) or (3) above.

(2) If, in the course of acting in the capacity mentioned in subsection (1) above, a person to whom this section applies becomes aware of a matter—

(a) which relates to the activities or affairs of the charity or of any connected institution or body, and

(b) which he has reasonable cause to believe is likely to be of material significance for the purposes of the exercise by the Commission of its functions under section 8 or 18 above,

he must immediately make a written report on the matter to the Commission.

(3) If, in the course of acting in the capacity mentioned in subsection (1) above, a person to whom this section applies becomes aware of any matter—

(a) which does not appear to him to be one that he is required to report under subsection (2) above, but

(b) which he has reasonable cause to believe is likely to be relevant for the purposes of the exercise by the Commission of any of its functions,

he may make a report on the matter to the Commission.

(4) Where the duty or power under subsection (2) or (3) above has arisen in relation to a person acting in the capacity mentioned in subsection (1), the duty or power is not affected by his subsequently ceasing to act in that capacity.

(5) Where a person makes a report as required or authorised by subsection (2) or (3), no duty to which he is subject is to be regarded as contravened merely because of any information or opinion contained in the report.

(6) In this section "connected institution or body", in relation to a charity, means—

(a) an institution which is controlled by, or

(b) a body corporate in which a substantial interest is held by,

the charity or any one or more of the charity trustees acting in his or their capacity as such.

(7) Paragraphs 3 and 4 of Schedule 5 to this Act apply for the purposes of subsection (6) above as they apply for the purposes of provisions of that Schedule.]

[808A]

NOTES

Commencement: to be appointed.

Inserted by the Charities Act 2006, s 29(1), subject to transitional provisions in Sch 10, para 8 to that Act at **[2176]**, as from a day to be appointed under s 79(2) of that Act.

45 Annual reports

(1) The charity trustees of a charity shall prepare in respect of each financial year of the charity an annual report containing—

(a) such a report by the trustees on the activities of the charity during that year, and

(b) such other information relating to the charity or to its trustees or officers, as may be prescribed by regulations made by the [Minister].

(2) Without prejudice to the generality of subsection (1) above, regulations under that subsection may make provision—

(a) for any such report as is mentioned in paragraph (a) of that subsection to be prepared in accordance with such principles as are specified or referred to in the regulations;

(b) enabling [the Commission] to dispense with any requirement prescribed by virtue of subsection (1)(b) above in the case of a particular charity or a particular class of charities, or in the case of a particular financial year of a charity or of any class of charities.

(3) [Where [a charity's gross income in any financial year] exceeds £10,000, [a copy of] the annual report required to be prepared under this section in respect of that year] shall be transmitted to [the Commission] by the charity trustees—

(a) within ten months from the end of that year, or

(b) within such longer period as [the Commission] may for any special reason allow in the case of that report.

[(3A) Where [a charity's gross income in any financial year does not exceed] £10,000, [a copy of] the annual report required to be prepared under this section in respect of that year shall, if [the Commission so requests, be transmitted to it] by the charity trustees—

(a) in the case of a request made before the end of seven months from the end of the financial year to which the report relates, within ten months from the end of that year, and

(b) in the case of a request not so made, within three months from the date of the request,

or, in either case, within such longer period as [the Commission] may for any special reason allow in the case of that report.]

[(3B) But in the case of a charity which is constituted as a CIO—

(a) the requirement imposed by subsection (3) applies whatever the charity's gross income is, and

(b) subsection (3A) does not apply.]

(4) Subject to subsection (5) below, [any [copy of an annual report transmitted to the Commission] under this section] shall have attached to it [a copy of] the statement of accounts prepared for the financial year in question under section 42(1) above or (as the case may be) [a copy of] the account and statement so prepared under section 42(3) above, together with—

(a) where the accounts of the charity for that year have been audited under section 43[, 43A or 43B] above, a copy of the report made by the auditor on that statement of accounts or (as the case may be) on that account and statement;

(b) where the accounts of the charity for that year have been examined under section 43[, 43A or 43B] above, a copy of the report made by the [person carrying out the examination].

(5) Subsection (4) above does not apply to a charity which is a company, and any [copy of an] annual report transmitted by the charity trustees of such a charity under [this section] shall instead have attached to it a copy of the charity's annual accounts prepared for the financial year in question under Part VII of the Companies Act 1985, together with a copy of [any auditors' report or report made for the purposes of section 249A(2) of that Act] on those accounts.

(6) Any [copy of an] annual report transmitted to [the Commission] under [this section], together with the documents attached to it, shall be kept by [the Commission] for such period as [it thinks fit].

[(7) The charity trustees of a charity shall preserve, for at least six years from the end of the financial year to which it relates, any annual report prepared by them under subsection (1) above [of which they have not been required to transmit a copy to the Commission].

(8) Subsection (4) of section 41 above shall apply in relation to the preservation of any such annual report as it applies in relation to the preservation of any accounting records (the references [to subsection (3)] of that section being read as references to subsection (7) above).

(9) The [Minister] may by order amend subsection (3) or (3A) above by substituting a different sum for the sum for the time being specified there.]

[809]

NOTES

Commencement: see the note to s 41 at **[805]**.

Sub-s (1): word in square brackets substituted by the Transfer of Functions (Third Sector, Communities and Equality) Order 2006, SI 2006/2951, art 6, Schedule, para 4(t).

Sub-s (2): words in square brackets substituted by the Charities Act 2006, s 75(1), Sch 8, paras 96, 138(1), (2), as from 27 February 2007.

Sub-s (3): words in first (outer) pair of square brackets substituted by the Deregulation and Contracting Out Act 1994, s 29(1), (3), (5); words in second (inner) pair of square brackets substituted for the words "in any financial year of a charity its gross income or total expenditure" and words in third (inner) pair of square brackets inserted in relation to any financial year of a charity which begins on or after 27 February 2007 and words in fourth pair of square brackets substituted by the Charities Act 2006, s 75(1), Sch 8, paras 96, 138(1), (3), as from 27 February 2007.

Sub-s (3A): inserted by the Deregulation and Contracting Out Act 1994, s 29(2); words in first pair of square brackets substituted for the words "a charity's gross income in any financial year does not exceed", words in second pair of square brackets inserted and words in third pair of square brackets substituted for the words "the Commissioners so request, be transmitted to them" in relation to any financial year of a charity which begins on or after 27 February 2007 by the Charities Act 2006, s 75(1), Sch 8, paras 96, 138(1), (4) (see the Charities Act 2006 (Commencement No 1, Transitional Provisions and Savings) Order 2007, SI 2007/309, art 9); and words in fourth pair of square brackets substituted by the Charities Act 2006, s 75(1), Sch 8, paras 96, 138(1), (4), as from 27 February 2007.

Sub-s (3B): inserted by the Charities Act 2006, s 34, Sch 7, Pt 2, paras 3, 4, as from a day to be appointed under s 79(2) of that Act.

Sub-s (4): words in first (outer) pair of square brackets substituted by the Deregulation and Contracting Out Act 1994, s 29(1), (3), (5); words in second (inner) pair of square brackets substituted for the words "annual report transmitted to the Commissioners", and words in third and fourth pairs of square brackets inserted, in relation to any financial year of a charity which begins on or after 27 February 2007, by the Charities Act 2006, s 75(1), Sch 8, paras 96, 138(1), (5) (see the Charities Act 2006 (Commencement No 1, Transitional Provisions and Savings) Order 2007, SI 2007/309, art 9); words in square brackets in para (a) inserted, and in para (b) words in first pair of square brackets inserted and words in second pair of square brackets substituted in relation to the financial year of a trust starting on or after 1 April 2004 by the Regulatory Reform (National Health Service Charitable and Non-Charitable Trust Accounts and Audit) Order 2005, SI 2005/1074, art 3(1), (4).

Sub-s (5): words in first pair of square brackets inserted in relation to any financial year of a charity which begins on or after 27 February 2007 by the Charities Act 2006, s 75(1), Sch 8, paras 96, 138(1), (6) (see the Charities Act 2006 (Commencement No 1, Transitional Provisions and Savings) Order 2007, SI 2007/309, art 9); words in second pair of square brackets substituted by the Deregulation and Contracting Out Act 1994, s 29(4); words in third pair of square brackets substituted by the Companies Act 1985 (Audit Exemption) Regulations 1994, SI 1994/1935, reg 4, Sch 1, Pt II, para 6.

Sub-s (6): words in first pair of square brackets inserted in relation to any financial year of a charity which begins on or after 27 February 2007, and words in second, fourth and fifth pairs of square brackets substituted by the Charities Act 2006, s 75(1), Sch 8, paras 96, 138(1), (7), as from 27 February 2007; words in third pair of square brackets substituted by the Deregulation and Contracting Out Act 1994, s 29(1), (3), (5).

Sub-s (7): added, together with sub-ss (8), (9), by the Deregulation and Contracting Out Act 1994, s 29(6); words in square brackets substituted for the words "which they have not "in relation to any financial year of a charity which begins on or after 27 February 2007 by the Charities Act 2006, s 75(1), Sch 8, paras 96, 138(1), (8) (see the Charities Act 2006 (Commencement No 1, Transitional Provisions and Savings) Order 2007, SI 2007/309, art 9).

Sub-s (8): added, together with sub-ss (7), (9), by the Deregulation and Contracting Out Act 1994, s 29(6); words in square brackets substituted for the words "in subsection (3)" in relation to any financial year of a charity which begins on or after 27 February 2007 by the Charities Act 2006, s 75(1), Sch 8, paras 96, 138(1), (9) (see the Charities Act 2006 (Commencement No 1, Transitional Provisions and Savings) Order 2007, SI 2007/309, art 9).

Sub-s (9): added, together with sub-ss (7), (8), by the Deregulation and Contracting Out Act 1994, s 29(6); word in square brackets substituted by SI 2006/2951, art 6, Schedule, para 4(t).

Regulations: the Charities (Accounts and Reports) Regulations 2005, SI 2005/572 at **[3398]**.

46 Special provision as respects accounts and annual reports of exempt and other excepted charities

(1) Nothing in *sections 41 to 45* above applies to any exempt charity; but the charity trustees of an exempt charity shall keep proper books of account with respect to the affairs of the charity, and if not required by or under the authority of any other Act to prepare periodical statements of account shall prepare consecutive statements of account consisting on each occasion of an income and expenditure account relating to a period of not more than fifteen months and a balance sheet relating to the end of that period.

(2) The books of accounts and statements of account relating to an exempt charity shall be preserved for a period of six years at least unless the charity ceases to exist and [the Commission consents] in writing to their being destroyed or otherwise disposed of.

[(2A) Section 44A(2) to (7) above shall apply in relation to a person appointed to audit, or report on, the accounts of an exempt charity which is not a company as they apply in relation to a person such as is mentioned in section 44A(1).

(2B) But section 44A(2) to (7) so apply with the following modifications—

(a) any reference to a person acting in the capacity mentioned in section 44A(1) is to be read as a reference to his acting as a person appointed as mentioned in subsection (2A) above; and

(b) any reference to the Commission or to any of its functions is to be read as a reference to the charity's principal regulator or to any of that person's functions in relation to the charity as such.]

(3) Nothing in [section 43 44 or 45] above applies to any charity which—

(a) falls within section 3(5)(c) above, and

(b) is not registered.

(4) Except in accordance with subsection (7) below, nothing in section 45 above applies to any charity (*other than an exempt charity or a charity which falls within section 3(5)(c) above) which—*

(a) is excepted by section 3(5) above, and

(b) is not registered.

(5) If requested to do so by [the Commission], the charity trustees of any such charity as is mentioned in subsection (4) above shall prepare an annual report in respect of such financial year of the charity as is specified in [the Commission's request].

(6) Any report prepared under subsection (5) above shall contain—

(a) such a report by the charity trustees on the activities of the charity during the year in question, and

(b) such other information relating to the charity or to its trustees or officers,

as may be prescribed by regulations made under section 45(1) above in relation to annual reports prepared under that provision.

(7) Subsections (3) to (6) of section 45 [(as originally enacted)] above shall apply to any report required to be prepared under subsection (5) above as if it were an annual report required to be prepared under subsection (1) of that section.

(8) Any reference in this section to a charity which falls within section 3(5)(c) above includes a reference to a charity which falls within that provision but is also excepted from registration by section 3(5)(b) above.

[810]

NOTES

Commencement: see the note to s 41 at **[805]**.

Sub-s (1): for the words in italics there are substituted the words "sections 41 to 44 or section 45" by the Charities Act 2006, s 29(2)(a), as from a day to be appointed under s 79(2) of that Act, subject to transitional provisions in Sch 10, para 8 to that Act at **[2176]**.

Sub-ss (2), (5): words in square brackets substituted by the Charities Act 2006, s 75(1), Sch 8, paras 96, 139(1), (2), (5), as from 27 February 2007.

Sub-ss (2A), (2B): inserted by the Charities Act 2006, s 29(2)(b), as from a day to be appointed under s 79(2) of that Act, subject to transitional provisions in Sch 10, para 8 to that Act **[2176]**.

Sub-s (3): words in square brackets substituted in relation to the financial year of a trust starting on or after 1 April 2004 by the Regulatory Reform (National Health Service Charitable and Non-Charitable Trust Accounts and Audit) Order 2005, SI 2005/1074, art 3(1), (5); substituted as follows by the Charities Act 2006, s 75(1), Sch 8, paras 96, 139(1), (3), as from a day to be appointed under s 79(2) of that Act—

"(3) Except in accordance with subsections (3A) and (3B) below, nothing in section 43, 44, 44A or 45 applies to any charity which—

(a) falls within section 3A(2)(d) above (whether or not it also falls within section 3A(2)(b) or (c)), and

(b) is not registered.

(3A) Section 44A above applies in accordance with subsections (2A) and (2B) above to a charity mentioned in subsection (3) above which is also an exempt charity.

(3B) Sections 44 and 44A above apply to a charity mentioned in subsection (3) above which is also an English National Health Service charity or a Welsh National Health Service charity (as defined in sections 43A and 43B above).".

Sub-s (4): for the words in italics there is substituted the following by the Charities Act 2006, s 75(1), Sch 8, paras 96, 139(1), (4), as from a day to be appointed under s 79(2) of that Act—

"which—

(a) falls within section 3A(2)(b) or (c) above but does not fall within section 3A(2)(d), and
(b) is not registered.".

Sub-s (7): words in square brackets inserted by the Deregulation and Contracting Out Act 1994, s 29(7); substituted by the Charities Act 2006, s 75(1), Sch 8, paras 96, 139(1), (6), as from a day to be appointed under s 79(2) of that Act—

"(7) The following provisions of section 45 above shall apply in relation to any report required to be prepared under subsection (5) above as if it were an annual report required to be prepared under subsection (1) of that section—

(a) subsection (3), with the omission of the words preceding "a copy of the annual report", and
(b) subsections (4) to (6).".

Sub-s (8): repealed by the Charities Act 2006, s 75(1), (2), Sch 8, paras 96, 139(1), (7), Sch 9, as from a day to be appointed under s 79(2) of that Act.

47 Public inspection of annual reports etc

(1) [Any document kept by the Commission] in pursuance of section 45(6) above shall be open to public inspection at all reasonable times—

(a) during the period for which it is so kept; or
(b) if [the Commission so determines], during such lesser period as [it may] specify.

(2) Where any person—

(a) requests the charity trustees of a charity in writing to provide him with a copy of the charity's most recent accounts [or (if subsection (4) below applies) of its most recent annual report], and
(b) pays them such reasonable fee (if any) as they may require in respect of the costs of complying with the request,

those trustees shall comply with the request within the period of two months beginning with the date on which it is made.

(3) In subsection (2) above the reference to a charity's most recent accounts is—

(a) …
(b) in the case of [a charity other than one falling within paragraph (c) or (d) below], a reference to the statement of accounts or account and statement prepared in pursuance of section 42(1) or (3) above in respect of the last financial year of the charity in respect of which a statement of accounts or account and statement has or have been so prepared;
[(c) in the case of a charity which is a company, a reference to the most recent annual accounts of the company prepared under Part VII of the Companies Act 1985 in relation to which any of the following conditions is satisfied—
   (i) they have been audited;
   (ii) a report required for the purposes of section 249A(2) of that Act has been made in respect of them; or
   (iii) they relate to a year in respect of which the company is exempt from audit by virtue of section 249A(1) of that Act; and]
(d) in the case of an exempt charity, a reference to the accounts of the charity most recently audited in pursuance of any statutory or other requirement or, if its accounts are not required to be audited, the accounts most recently prepared in respect of the charity.

[(4) This subsection applies if an annual report has been prepared in respect of any financial year of a charity in pursuance of section 45(1) or 46(5) above.

(5) In subsection (2) above the reference to a charity's most recent annual report is a reference to the annual report prepared in pursuance of section 45(1) or 46(5) in respect of the last financial year of the charity in respect of which an annual report has been so prepared.]

[811]

NOTES

Commencement: see the note to s 41 at **[805]**.

Sub-s (1): words in square brackets substituted by the Charities Act 2006, s 75(1), Sch 8, paras 96, 140(1), (2), as from 27 February 2007.

Sub-s (2): words in square brackets in para (a) inserted by the Charities Act 2006, s 75(1), Sch 8, paras 96, 140(1), (3), as from 27 February 2007.

Sub-s (3): para (a) repealed and words in square brackets in para (b) substituted by the Deregulation and Contracting Out Act 1994, ss 39, 81(1), Sch 11, para 12, Sch 17; para (c) substituted by the Companies Act 1985 (Audit Exemption) Regulations 1994, SI 1994/1935, reg 4, Sch 1, Pt II, para 7.

Sub-ss (4), (5): added by the Charities Act 2006, s 75(1), Sch 8, paras 96, 140(1), (4), as from 27 February 2007.

48 Annual returns by registered charities

(1) [Subject to subsection (1A) below,] every registered charity shall prepare in respect of each of its financial years an annual return in such form, and containing such information, as may be prescribed by regulations made by [the Commission].

[(1A) Subsection (1) above shall not apply in relation to any financial year of a charity in which [the charity's gross income does not exceed] £10,000 [(but this subsection does not apply if the charity is constituted as a CIO)].]

(2) Any such return shall be transmitted to [the Commission] by the date by which the charity trustees are, by virtue of section 45(3) above, required to transmit [to the Commission] the annual report required to be prepared in respect of the financial year in question.

(3) [The Commission] may dispense with the requirements of subsection (1) above in the case of a particular charity or a particular class of charities, or in the case of a particular financial year of a charity or of any class of charities.

[(4) The [Minister] may by order amend subsection (1A) above by substituting a different sum for the sum for the time being specified there.]

[812]

NOTES

Commencement: see the note to s 41 at **[805]**.

Sub-s (1): words in first pair of square brackets inserted by the Deregulation and Contracting Out Act 1994, s 30(1), (2); word in second pair of square brackets substituted by the Charities Act 2006, s 75(1), Sch 8, paras 96, 141(1), (2), as from 27 February 2007.

Sub-s (1A): inserted by the Deregulation and Contracting Out Act 1994, s 30(1), (3); words in first pair of square brackets substituted for the words "neither the gross income nor the total expenditure of the charity exceeds" in relation to any financial year of a charity which begins on or after 27 February 2007 by the Charities Act 2006, s 75(1), Sch 8, paras 96, 141(1), (3) (see the Charities Act 2006 (Commencement No 1, Transitional Provisions and Savings) Order 2007, SI 2007/309, art 10) and words in second pair of square brackets added by s 34 of, and Sch 7, Pt 2, paras 3, 5 to, that Act, as from a day to be appointed under s 79(2) of that Act.

Sub-ss (2), (3): words in square brackets substituted by the Charities Act 2006, s 75(1), Sch 8, paras 96, 141(1), (4), (5), as from 27 February 2007.

Sub-s (4): added by the Deregulation and Contracting Out Act 1994, s 30(1), (4); word in square brackets substituted by the Transfer of Functions (Third Sector, Communities and Equality) Order 2006, SI 2006/2951, art 6, Schedule, para 4(u).

[49 Offences

(1) If any requirement imposed—

(a) by section 45(3) or (3A) above (taken with section 45(3B), (4) and (5), as applicable), or

(b) by section 47(2) or 48(2) above,

is not complied with, each person who immediately before the date for compliance specified in the section in question was a charity trustee of the charity shall be guilty of an offence and liable on summary conviction to the penalty mentioned in subsection (2).

(2) The penalty is—

(a) a fine not exceeding level 4 on the standard scale, and

(b) for continued contravention, a daily default fine not exceeding 10% of level 4 on the standard scale for so long as the person in question remains a charity trustee of the charity.

(3) It is a defence for a person charged with an offence under subsection (1) to prove that he took all reasonable steps for securing that the requirement in question would be complied with in time.]

[813]

NOTES

Commencement: 27 February 2007.

Substituted by the Charities Act 2006, s 75(1), Sch 8, paras 96, 142, in relation to non-compliance with any requirement where the specified date for compliance is 1 April 2008 or later. Original s 49 continues to apply to non-compliance with any requirement where the specified date for compliance is before 1 April 2008: see the Charities Act 2006 (Commencement No 1, Transitional Provisions and Savings) Order 2007, SI 2007/309, art 11. Original s 49 as amended reads as follows—

"49 Offences

Any person who, without reasonable excuse, is persistently in default in relation to any requirement imposed—

(a) by section 45(3) [or (3A)] above (taken with section 45(4) or (5), as the case may require), or

(b) by section 47(2) or 48(2) above,

shall be guilty of an offence and liable on summary conviction to a fine not exceeding level 4 on the standard scale.".

Words in square brackets in para (a) of original s 49 inserted by the Deregulation and Contracting Out Act 1994, s 29(8).

[49A Group accounts

The provisions of Schedule 5A to this Act shall have effect with respect to—

(a) the preparation and auditing of accounts in respect of groups consisting of parent charities and their subsidiary undertakings (within the meaning of that Schedule), and

(b) other matters relating to such groups.]

[813A]

NOTES

Commencement: to be appointed.

Inserted by the Charities Act 2006, s 30(1), as from a day to be appointed under s 79(2) of that Act.

PART VII
INCORPORATION OF CHARITY TRUSTEES

50 Incorporation of trustees of a charity

(1) Where—

(a) the trustees of a charity, in accordance with section 52 below, apply to [the Commission] for a certificate of incorporation of the trustees as a body corporate, and

(b) [the Commission considers] that the incorporation of the trustees would be in the interests of the charity,

[the Commission] may grant such a certificate, subject to such conditions or directions as [the Commission thinks fit] to insert in it.

(2) [The Commission] shall not, however, grant such a certificate in a case where the charity appears [to the Commission] to be required to be registered *under section 3* above but is not so registered.

(3) On the grant of such a certificate—

(a) the trustees of the charity shall become a body corporate by such name as is specified in the certificate; and

(b) (without prejudice to the operation of section 54 below) any relevant rights or liabilities of those trustees shall become rights or liabilities of that body.

(4) After their incorporation the trustees—

(a) may sue and be sued in their corporate name; and

(b) shall have the same powers, and be subject to the same restrictions and limitations, as respects the holding, acquisition and disposal of property for or in connection with the purposes of the charity as they had or were subject to while unincorporated;

and any relevant legal proceedings that might have been continued or commenced by or against the trustees may be continued or commenced by or against them in their corporate name.

(5) A body incorporated under this section need not have a common seal.

(6) In this section—

"relevant rights or liabilities" means rights or liabilities in connection with any property vesting in the body in question under section 51 below; and

"relevant legal proceedings" means legal proceedings in connection with any such property.

[814]

NOTES

Sub-s (1): words in square brackets substituted by the Charities Act 2006, s 75(1), Sch 8, paras 96, 143(1), (2), as from 27 February 2007.

Sub-s (2): words in square brackets substituted by the Charities Act 2006, s 75(1), Sch 8, paras 96, 143(1), (3)(a), (b), as from 27 February 2007, and for the words in italics there are substituted the words "in accordance with section 3A" by s 75(1) of, and Sch 8, paras 96, 143(1), (3)(c) to, that Act, as from a day to be appointed under s 79(2) of that Act.

51 Estate to vest in body corporate

The certificate of incorporation shall vest in the body corporate all real and personal estate, of whatever nature or tenure, belonging to or held by any person or persons in trust for the charity, and thereupon any person or persons in whose name or names any stocks, funds or securities are standing in trust for the charity, shall transfer them into the name of the body corporate, except that the foregoing provisions shall not apply to property vested in the official custodian.

[815]

52 Applications for incorporation

(1) Every application to [the Commission] for a certificate of incorporation under this Part of this Act shall—

(a) be in writing and signed by the trustees of the charity concerned; and

(b) be accompanied by such documents or information as [the Commission] may require for the purpose of the application.

(2) [The Commission] may require—

(a) any statement contained in any such application, or

(b) any document or information supplied under subsection (1)(b) above,

to be verified in such manner as [it may specify].

[816]

NOTES

Words in square brackets substituted by the Charities Act 2006, s 75(1), Sch 8, paras 96, 144, as from 27 February 2007.

53 Nomination of trustees, and filling up vacancies

(1) Before a certificate of incorporation is granted under this Part of this Act, trustees of the charity must have been effectually appointed to the satisfaction of [the Commission].

(2) Where a certificate of incorporation is granted vacancies in the number of the trustees of the charity shall from time to time be filled up so far as required by the constitution or settlement of the charity, or by any conditions or directions in the certificate, by such legal means as would have been available for the appointment of new trustees of the charity if no certificate of incorporation had been granted, or otherwise as required by such conditions or directions.

[817]

NOTES

Sub-s (1): words in square brackets substituted by the Charities Act 2006, s 75(1), Sch 8, paras 96, 145, as from 27 February 2007.

54 Liability of trustees and others, notwithstanding incorporation

After a certificate of incorporation has been granted under this Part of this Act all trustees of the charity, notwithstanding their incorporation, shall be chargeable for such property as shall come into their hands, and shall be answerable and accountable for their own acts, receipts, neglects, and defaults, and for the due administration of the charity and its property, in the same manner and to the same extent as if no such incorporation had been effected.

[818]

55 Certificate to be evidence of compliance with requirements for incorporation

A certificate of incorporation granted under this Part of this Act shall be conclusive evidence that all the preliminary requirements for incorporation under this Part of this Act have been complied with, and the date of incorporation mentioned in the certificate shall be deemed to be the date at which incorporation has taken place.

[819]

56 Power of [Commission] to amend certificate of incorporation

(1) [The Commission] may amend a certificate of incorporation either on the application of the incorporated body to which it relates or [of the Commission's own motion].

(2) Before making any such amendment [of its own motion, the Commission] shall by notice in writing—

(a) inform the trustees of the relevant charity of [its proposals], and

(b) invite those trustees to make representations [to it] within a time specified in the notice, being not less than one month from the date of the notice.

(3) [The Commission] shall take into consideration any representations made by those trustees within the time so specified, and may then (without further notice) proceed with [its proposals] either without modification or with such modifications as appear [to it] to be desirable.

(4) [The Commission] may amend a certificate of incorporation either—

(a) by making an order specifying the amendment; or

(b) by issuing a new certificate of incorporation taking account of the amendment.

[820]

NOTES

Section heading: word in square brackets substituted by the Charities Act 2006, s 75(1), Sch 8, paras 96, 146(1), (6), as from 27 February 2007.

Words in square brackets substituted by the Charities Act 2006, s 75(1), Sch 8, paras 96, 146(1)–(5), as from 27 February 2007.

57 Records of applications and certificates

(1) [The Commission] shall keep a record of all applications for, and certificates of, incorporation under this Part of this Act and shall preserve all documents sent [to it] under this Part of this Act.

(2) Any person may inspect such documents, under the direction of [the Commission], and any person may require a copy or extract of any such document to be certified by a certificate signed by [a member of the staff of the Commission].

[821]

NOTES

Words in square brackets substituted by the Charities Act 2006, s 75(1), Sch 8, paras 96, 147, as from 27 February 2007.

58 Enforcement of orders and directions

All conditions and directions inserted in any certificate of incorporation shall be binding upon and performed or observed by the trustees as trusts of the charity, and section 88 below shall apply to any trustee who fails to perform or observe any such condition or direction as it applies to a person guilty of disobedience to any such order of [the Commission] as is mentioned in that section.

[822]

NOTES

Words in square brackets substituted by the Charities Act 2006, s 75(1), Sch 8, paras 96, 148, as from 27 February 2007.

59 Gifts to charity before incorporation to have same effect afterwards

After the incorporation of the trustees of any charity under this Part of this Act every donation, gift and disposition of property, real or personal, lawfully made before the incorporation but not having actually taken effect, or thereafter lawfully made, by deed, will or otherwise to or in favour of the charity, or the trustees of the charity, or otherwise for the purposes of the charity, shall take effect as if made to or in favour of the incorporated body or otherwise for the like purposes.

[823]

60 Execution of documents by incorporated body

(1) This section has effect as respects the execution of documents by an incorporated body.

(2) If an incorporated body has a common seal, a document may be executed by the body by the affixing of its common seal.

(3) Whether or not it has a common seal, a document may be executed by an incorporated body either—

(a) by being signed by a majority of the trustees of the relevant charity and expressed (in whatever form of words) to be executed by the body; or

(b) by being executed in pursuance of an authority given under subsection (4) below.

(4) For the purposes of subsection (3)(b) above the trustees of the relevant charity in the case of an incorporated body may, subject to the trusts of the charity, confer on any two or more of their number—

(a) a general authority, or

(b) an authority limited in such manner as the trustees think fit,

to execute in the name and on behalf of the body documents for giving effect to transactions to which the body is a party.

(5) An authority under subsection (4) above—

(a) shall suffice for any document if it is given in writing or by resolution of a meeting of the trustees of the relevant charity, notwithstanding the want of any formality that would be required in giving an authority apart from that subsection;

(b) may be given so as to make the powers conferred exercisable by any of the trustees, or may be restricted to named persons or in any other way;

(c) subject to any such restriction, and until it is revoked, shall, notwithstanding any change in the trustees of the relevant charity, have effect as a continuing authority given by the trustees from time to time of the charity and exercisable by such trustees.

(6) In any authority under subsection (4) above to execute a document in the name and on behalf of an incorporated body there shall, unless the contrary intention appears, be implied authority also to execute it for the body in the name and on behalf of the official custodian or of any other person, in any case in which the trustees could do so.

(7) A document duly executed by an incorporated body which makes it clear on its face that it is intended by the person or persons making it to be a deed has effect, upon delivery, as a deed; and it shall be presumed, unless a contrary intention is proved, to be delivered upon its being so executed.

(8) In favour of a purchaser a document shall be deemed to have been duly executed by such a body if it purports to be signed—

(a) by a majority of the trustees of the relevant charity, or

(b) by such of the trustees of the relevant charity as are authorised by the trustees of that charity to execute it in the name and on behalf of the body,

and, where the document makes it clear on its face that it is intended by the person or persons making it to be a deed, it shall be deemed to have been delivered upon its being executed.

For this purpose "purchaser" means a purchaser in good faith for valuable consideration and includes a lessee, mortgagee or other person who for valuable consideration acquires an interest in property.

[824]

61 Power of [Commission] to dissolve incorporated body

(1) Where [the Commission is] satisfied—

(a) that an incorporated body has no assets or does not operate, or
(b) that the relevant charity in the case of an incorporated body has ceased to exist, or
(c) that the institution previously constituting, or [treated by the Commission] as constituting, any such charity has ceased to be, or (as the case may be) was not at the time of the body's incorporation, a charity, or
(d) that the purposes of the relevant charity in the case of an incorporated body have been achieved so far as is possible or are in practice incapable of being achieved,

[the Commission may of its own motion] make an order dissolving the body as from such date as is specified in the order.

(2) Where [the Commission is] satisfied, on the application of the trustees of the relevant charity in the case of an incorporated body, that it would be in the interests of the charity for that body to be dissolved, [the Commission] may make an order dissolving the body as from such date as is specified in the order.

(3) Subject to subsection (4) below, an order made under this section with respect to an incorporated body shall have the effect of vesting in the trustees of the relevant charity, in trust for that charity, all property for the time being vested—
(a) in the body, or
(b) in any other person (apart from the official custodian),

in trust for that charity.

(4) If [the Commission so directs] in the order—
(a) all or any specified part of that property shall, instead of vesting in the trustees of the relevant charity, vest—
(i) in a specified person as trustee for, or nominee of, that charity, or
(ii) in such persons (other than the trustees of the relevant charity) as may be specified;
(b) any specified investments, or any specified class or description of investments, held by any person in trust for the relevant charity shall be transferred—
(i) to the trustees of that charity, or
(ii) to any such person or persons as is or are mentioned in paragraph (a)(i) or (ii) above;

and for this purpose "specified" means specified by [the Commission] in the order.

(5) Where an order to which this subsection applies is made with respect to an incorporated body—
(a) any rights or liabilities of the body shall become rights or liabilities of the trustees of the relevant charity; and
(b) any legal proceedings that might have been continued or commenced by or against the body may be continued or commenced by or against those trustees.

(6) Subsection (5) above applies to any order under this section by virtue of which—
(a) any property vested as mentioned in subsection (3) above is vested—
(i) in the trustees of the relevant charity, or
(ii) in any person as trustee for, or nominee of, that charity; or
(b) any investments held by any person in trust for the relevant charity are required to be transferred—
(i) to the trustees of that charity, or
(ii) to any person as trustee for, or nominee of, that charity.

(7) ...

NOTES

Section heading: words in square brackets substituted by the Charities Act 2006, s 75(1), Sch 8, paras 96, 149(1), (6), as from 27 February 2007.

Sub-ss (1), (2), (4): words in square brackets substituted by the Charities Act 2006, s 75(1), Sch 8, paras 96, 149(1)–(4), as from 27 February 2007.

Sub-s (7): repealed by the Charities Act 2006, s 75(1), (2), Sch 8, paras 96, 149(1), (5), Sch 9, as from 27 February 2007.

[825]

62 Interpretation of Part VII

In this Part of this Act—

"incorporated body" means a body incorporated under section 50 above;

"the relevant charity", in relation to an incorporated body, means the charity the trustees of which have been incorporated as that body;

"the trustees", in relation to a charity, means the charity trustees.

[826]

PART VIII
CHARITABLE COMPANIES

63 Winding up

(1) Where a charity may be wound up by the High Court under the Insolvency Act 1986, a petition for it to be wound up under that Act by any court in England or Wales having jurisdiction may be presented by the Attorney General, as well as by any person authorised by that Act.

(2) Where a charity may be so wound up by the High Court, such a petition may also be presented by [the Commission] if, at any time after [it has instituted] an inquiry under section 8 above with respect to the charity, [it is satisfied] as mentioned in section 18(1)(a) or (b) above.

(3) Where a charitable company is dissolved, [the Commission] may make an application under section 651 of the Companies Act 1985 (power of court to declare dissolution of company void) for an order to be made under that section with respect to the company; and for this purpose subsection (1) of that section shall have effect in relation to a charitable company as if the reference to the liquidator of the company included a reference to [the Commission].

(4) Where a charitable company's name has been struck off the register of companies under section 652 of the Companies Act 1985 (power of registrar to strike defunct company off register), [the Commission] may make an application under section 653(2) of that Act (objection to striking off by person aggrieved) for an order restoring the company's name to that register; and for this purpose section 653(2) shall have effect in relation to a charitable company as if the reference to any such person aggrieved as is there mentioned included a reference to [the Commission].

(5) The powers exercisable by [the Commission] by virtue of this section shall be exercisable [by the Commission of its own motion], but shall be exercisable only with the agreement of the Attorney General on each occasion.

(6) In this section "charitable company" means a company which is a charity.

[827]

NOTES

Sub-ss (2)–(5): words in square brackets substituted by the Charities Act 2006, s 75(1), Sch 8, paras 96, 150, as from 27 February 2007.

64 Alteration of objects clause

(1) Where a charity is a company or other body corporate having power to alter the instruments establishing or regulating it as a body corporate, no exercise of that power which has the effect of the body ceasing to be a charity shall be valid so as to affect the application of—

(a) any property acquired under any disposition or agreement previously made otherwise than for full consideration in money or money's worth, or any property representing property so acquired,

(b) any property representing income which has accrued before the alteration is made, or

(c) the income from any such property as aforesaid.

(2) Where a charity is a company, any alteration by it—

(a) of the objects clause in its memorandum of association, or

(b) of any other provision in its memorandum of association, or any provision in its articles of association, which is a provision directing or restricting the manner in which property of the company may be used or applied,

is ineffective without the prior written consent of the Commissioners.

(3) Where a company has made *any such alteration* in accordance with subsection (2) above and—

(a) in connection with the alteration is required by virtue of—

(i) section 6(1) of the Companies Act 1985 (delivery of documents following alteration of objects), or

(ii) that provision as applied by section 17(3) of that Act (alteration of condition in memorandum which could have been contained in articles),

to deliver to the registrar of companies a printed copy of its memorandum, as altered, or

(b) is required by virtue of section 380(1) of that Act (registration etc of resolutions and agreements) to forward to the registrar a printed or other copy of the special resolution effecting the alteration,

the copy so delivered or forwarded by the company shall be accompanied by a copy of [the Commission's consent].

(4) Section 6(3) of that Act (offences) shall apply to any default by a company in complying with subsection (3) above as it applies to any such default as is mentioned in that provision.

[828]

NOTES

Sub-s (2): substituted as follows by the Charities Act 2006, s 31(1), (2), as from a day to be appointed under s 79(2) of that Act—

"(2) Where a charity is a company, any regulated alteration by the company—

(a) requires the prior written consent of the Commission, and

(b) is ineffective if such consent has not been obtained.

(2A) The following are "regulated alterations"—

(a) any alteration of the objects clause in the company's memorandum of association,

(b) any alteration of any provision of its memorandum or articles of association directing the application of property of the company on its dissolution, and

(c) any alteration of any provision of its memorandum or articles of association where the alteration would provide authorisation for any benefit to be obtained by directors or members of the company or persons connected with them.

(2B) For the purposes of subsection (2A) above—

(a) "benefit" means a direct or indirect benefit of any nature, except that it does not include any remuneration (within the meaning of section 73A below) whose receipt may be authorised under that section; and

(b) the same rules apply for determining whether a person is connected with a director or member of the company as apply, in accordance with section 73B(5) and (6) below, for determining whether a person is connected with a charity trustee for the purposes of section 73A.".

Sub-s (3): for the words in italics there are substituted the words "a regulated alteration" by the Charities Act 2006, s 31(1), (3), as from a day to be appointed under s 79(2) of that Act, and words in square brackets substituted by s 75(1) of, and Sch 8, paras 96, 151 to, that Act, as from 27 February 2007.

---

65 Invalidity of certain transactions

(1) Sections 35 and 35A of the Companies Act 1985 (capacity of company not limited by its memorandum; power of directors to bind company) do not apply to the acts of a company which is a charity except in favour of a person who—

(a) gives full consideration in money or money's worth in relation to the act in question, and

(b) does not know that the act is not permitted by the company's memorandum or, as the case may be, is beyond the powers of the directors,

or who does not know at the time the act is done that the company is a charity.

(2) However, where such a company purports to transfer or grant an interest in property, the fact that the act was not permitted by the company's memorandum or, as the case may be, that the directors in connection with the act exceeded any limitation on their powers under the company's constitution, does not affect the title of a person who subsequently acquires the property or any interest in it for full consideration without actual notice of any such circumstances affecting the validity of the company's act.

(3) In any proceedings arising out of subsection (1) above the burden of proving—

(a) that a person knew that an act was not permitted by the company's memorandum or was beyond the powers of the directors, or

(b) that a person knew that the company was a charity,

lies on the person making that allegation.

(4) Where a company is a charity, the ratification of an act under section 35(3) of the Companies Act 1985, or the ratification of a transaction to which section 322A of that Act applies (invalidity of certain transactions to which directors or their associates are parties), is ineffective without the prior written consent of [the Commission].

[829]

NOTES

Sub-s (4): words in square brackets substituted by the Charities Act 2006, s 75(1), Sch 8, paras 96, 152, as from 27 February 2007.

66 Requirement of consent of [Commission] to certain acts

(1) Where a company is a charity—

(a) any approval given by the company for the purposes of any of the provisions of the Companies Act 1985 specified in subsection (2) below, and

(b) any affirmation by it for the purposes of section 322(2)(c) of that Act (affirmation of voidable arrangements under which assets are acquired by or from a director or person connected with him),

is ineffective without the prior written consent of the [Commission].

(2) The provisions of the Companies Act 1985 referred to in subsection (1)(a) above are—

(a) section 312 (payment to director in respect of loss of office or retirement);

(b) section 313(1) (payment to director in respect of loss of office or retirement made in connection with transfer of undertaking or property of company);

(c) section 319(3) (incorporation in director's service contract of term whereby his employment will or may continue for a period of more than five years);

(d) section 320(1) (arrangement whereby assets are acquired by or from director or person connected with him);

(e) section 337(3)(a) (provision of funds to meet certain expenses incurred by director).

[830]

NOTES

Section heading, and sub-s (1): word in square brackets substituted by the Charities Act 2006, s 75(1), Sch 8, paras 96, 153, as from 27 February 2007.

Substituted, together with s 66A, for s 66 as originally enacted, as follows, by the Companies Act 2006, s 226, as from a day to be appointed under s 1300(2) of that Act—

"66 Consent of Commission required for approval etc by members of charitable companies

(1) Where a company is a charity—

(a) any approval given by the members of the company under any provision of Chapter 4 of Part 10 of the Companies Act 2006 (transactions with directors requiring approval by members) listed in subsection (2) below, and

(b) any affirmation given by members of the company under section 196 or 214 of that Act (affirmation of unapproved property transactions and loans),

is ineffective without the prior written consent of the Commission.

(2) The provisions are—

(a) section 188 (directors' long-term service contracts);

(b) section 190 (substantial property transactions with directors etc);

(c) section 197, 198 or 200 (loans and quasi-loans to directors etc);

(d) section 201 (credit transactions for benefit of directors etc);

(e) section 203 (related arrangements);

(f) section 217 (payments to directors for loss of office);

(g) section 218 (payments to directors for loss of office: transfer of undertaking etc).

66A Consent of Commission required for certain acts of charitable company

(1) A company that is a charity may not do an act to which this section applies without the prior written consent of the Commission.

(2) This section applies to an act that—

(a) does not require approval under a listed provision of Chapter 4 of Part 10 of the Companies Act 2006 (transactions with directors) by the members of the company, but

(b) would require such approval but for an exemption in the provision in question that disapplies the need for approval on the part of the members of a body corporate which is a wholly-owned subsidiary of another body corporate.

(3) The reference to a listed provision is a reference to a provision listed in section 66(2) above.

(4) If a company acts in contravention of this section, the exemption referred to in subsection (2)(b) shall be treated as of no effect in relation to the act.".

67 Name to appear on correspondence etc

Section 30(7) of the Companies Act 1985 (exemption from requirements relating to publication of name etc) shall not, in its application to any company which is a charity, have the effect of exempting the company from the requirements of section 349(1) of that Act (company's name to appear in its correspondence etc).

[831]

68 Status to appear on correspondence etc

(1) Where a company is a charity and its name does not include the word "charity" or the word "charitable" [then, subject to subsection (1A)], the fact that the company is a charity shall be stated … in legible characters—

[(1A) Where a company's name includes the words "elusen" or the word "elusennol" (the Welsh equivalents of the words "charity" and "charitable"), subsection (1) above shall not apply in relation to any document which is wholly in Welsh.

(1B) The statement required by subsection (1) above shall be in English, except that, in the case of a document which is otherwise wholly in Welsh, the statement may be in Welsh if it consists of or includes the word "elusen" or the word "elusennol".]

(a) in all business letters of the company,

(b) in all its notices and other official publications,

(c) in all bills of exchange, promissory notes, endorsements, cheques and orders for money or goods purporting to be signed on behalf of the company,

(d) in all conveyances purporting to be executed by the company, and

(e) in all bills rendered by it and in all its invoices, receipts, and letters of credit.

(2) In subsection (1)(d) above "conveyance" means any instrument creating, transferring, varying or extinguishing an interest in land.

(3) Subsections (2) to (4) of section 349 of the Companies Act 1985 (offences in connection with failure to include required particulars in business letters etc) shall apply in relation to a contravention of subsection (1) above, taking the reference in subsection (3)(b) of that section to a bill of parcels as a reference to any such bill as is mentioned in subsection (1)(e) above.

[832]

NOTES

Sub-s (1): words in square brackets inserted and words omitted repealed by the Welsh Language Act 1993, ss 33(1), (2), 35(1), Sch 2.

Sub-ss (1A), (1B): inserted by the Welsh Language Act 1993, s 33(1), (3).

[68A Duty of charity's auditors etc to report matters to Commission

(1) Section 44A(2) to (7) above shall apply in relation to a person acting as—

(a) an auditor of a charitable company appointed under Chapter 5 of Part 11 of the Companies Act 1985 (auditors), or

(b) a reporting accountant appointed by a charitable company for the purposes of section 249C of that Act (report required instead of audit),

as they apply in relation to a person such as is mentioned in section 44A(1).

(2) For this purpose any reference in section 44A to a person acting in the capacity mentioned in section 44A(1) is to be read as a reference to his acting in the capacity mentioned in subsection (1) of this section.

(3) In this section "charitable company" means a charity which is a company.]

[832A]

NOTES

Commencement: to be appointed.

Inserted by the Charities Act 2006, s 33, as from a day to be appointed under s 79(2) of that Act, subject to transitional provisions in Sch 10, para 10 to that Act at **[2176]**.

69 Investigation of accounts

(1) In the case of a charity which is a company [the Commission] may by order require that the condition and accounts of the charity for such period as [the Commission thinks fit] shall be investigated and audited by an auditor appointed [by the Commission], being a person eligible for appointment as a company auditor under section 25 of the Companies Act 1989.

(2) An auditor acting under subsection (1) above—

(a) shall have a right of access to all books, accounts and documents relating to the charity which are in the possession or control of the charity trustees or to which the charity trustees have access;

(b) shall be entitled to require from any charity trustee, past or present, and from any past or present officer or employee of the charity such information and explanation as he thinks necessary for the performance of his duties;

(c) shall at the conclusion or during the progress of the audit make such reports to [the Commission] about the audit or about the accounts or affairs of the charity as he thinks the case requires, and shall send a copy of any such report to the charity trustees.

(3) The expenses of any audit under subsection (1) above, including the remuneration of the auditor, shall be paid by [the Commission].

(4) If any person fails to afford an auditor any facility to which he is entitled under subsection (2) above [the Commission] may by order give to that person or to the charity trustees for the time being such directions as [the Commission thinks] appropriate for securing that the default is made good.

[833]

NOTES

Commencement: 1 March 1996.

Words in square brackets substituted by the Charities Act 2006, s 75(1), Sch 8, paras 96, 154.

[PART 8A
CHARITABLE INCORPORATED ORGANISATIONS

Nature and constitution

69A Charitable incorporated organisations

(1) In this Act, a charitable incorporated organisation is referred to as a "CIO".

(2) A CIO shall be a body corporate.

(3) A CIO shall have a constitution.

(4) A CIO shall have a principal office, which shall be in England or in Wales.

(5) A CIO shall have one or more members.

(6) The members may be either—

(a) not liable to contribute to the assets of the CIO if it is wound up, or

(b) liable to do so up to a maximum amount each.]

[833A]

NOTES

Commencement: to be appointed.

Pt 8A (ss 69A–69Q) inserted by the Charities Act 2006, s 34, Sch 7, Pt 1, para 1, partly as from 27 February 2007 and partly as from a day to be appointed under s 79(2) of that Act.

[69B Constitution

(1) A CIO's constitution shall state—

(a) its name,
(b) its purposes,
(c) whether its principal office is in England or in Wales, and
(d) whether or not its members are liable to contribute to its assets if it is wound up, and (if they are) up to what amount.

(2) A CIO's constitution shall make provision—
(a) about who is eligible for membership, and how a person becomes a member,
(b) about the appointment of one or more persons who are to be charity trustees of the CIO, and about any conditions of eligibility for appointment, and
(c) containing directions about the application of property of the CIO on its dissolution.

(3) A CIO's constitution shall also provide for such other matters, and comply with such requirements, as are specified in regulations made by the Minister.

(4) A CIO's constitution—
(a) shall be in English if its principal office is in England,
(b) may be in English or in Welsh if its principal office is in Wales.

(5) A CIO's constitution shall be in the form specified in regulations made by the Commission, or as near to that form as the circumstances admit.

(6) Subject to anything in a CIO's constitution: a charity trustee of the CIO may, but need not, be a member of it; a member of the CIO may, but need not, be one of its charity trustees; and those who are members of the CIO and those who are its charity trustees may, but need not, be identical.]

[833B]

NOTES

Commencement: 27 February 2007 (sub-ss (3), (5) for the purposes of enabling the Minister (and the Charity Commission in relation to section 69B(5)) to exercise the power to make subordinate legislation); to be appointed (otherwise).

Inserted as noted to s 69A at **[833A]**.

[69C Name and status

(1) The name of a CIO shall appear in legible characters—
(a) in all business letters of the CIO,
(b) in all its notices and other official publications,
(c) in all bills of exchange, promissory notes, endorsements, cheques and orders for money or goods purporting to be signed on behalf of the CIO,
(d) in all conveyances purporting to be executed by the CIO, and
(e) in all bills rendered by it and in all its invoices, receipts, and letters of credit.

(2) In subsection (1)(d), "conveyance" means any instrument creating, transferring, varying or extinguishing an interest in land.

(3) Subsection (5) applies if the name of a CIO does not include—
(a) "charitable incorporated organisation", or
(b) "CIO", with or without full stops after each letter, or
(c) a Welsh equivalent mentioned in subsection (4) (but this option applies only if the CIO's constitution is in Welsh),

and it is irrelevant, in any such case, whether or not capital letters are used.

(4) The Welsh equivalents referred to in subsection (3)(c) are—
(a) "sefydliad elusennol corfforedig", or
(b) "SEC", with or without full stops after each letter.

(5) If this subsection applies, the fact that a CIO is a CIO shall be stated in legible characters in all the documents mentioned in subsection (1).

(6) The statement required by subsection (5) shall be in English, except that in the case of a document which is otherwise wholly in Welsh, the statement may be in Welsh.]

[833C]

NOTES

Commencement: to be appointed.

Inserted as noted to s 69A at **[833A]**.

[69D Offences connected with name and status

(1) A charity trustee of a CIO or a person on the CIO's behalf who issues or authorises the issue of any document referred to in paragraph (a), (b), (d) or (e) of section 69C(1) above which fails to comply with the requirements of section 69C(1), (5) or (6) is liable on summary conviction to a fine not exceeding level 3 on the standard scale.

(2) A charity trustee of a CIO or a person on the CIO's behalf who signs or authorises to be signed on behalf of the CIO any document referred to in paragraph (c) of section 69C(1) above which fails to comply with the requirements of section 69C(1), (5) or (6)—

(a) is liable on summary conviction to a fine not exceeding level 3 on the standard scale, and

(b) is personally liable to the holder of the bill of exchange (etc) for the amount of it, unless it is duly paid by the CIO.

(3) A person who holds any body out as being a CIO when it is not (however he does this) is guilty of an offence and is liable on summary conviction to a fine not exceeding level 3 on the standard scale.

(4) It is a defence for a person charged with an offence under subsection (3) to prove that he believed on reasonable grounds that the body was a CIO.]

[833D]

NOTES

Commencement: to be appointed.
Inserted as noted to s 69A at **[833A]**.

[Registration

69E Application for registration

(1) Any one or more persons ("the applicants") may apply to the Commission for a CIO to be constituted and for its registration as a charity.

(2) The applicants shall supply the Commission with—

(a) a copy of the proposed constitution of the CIO,

(b) such other documents or information as may be prescribed by regulations made by the Minister, and

(c) such other documents or information as the Commission may require for the purposes of the application.

(3) The Commission shall refuse such an application if—

(a) it is not satisfied that the CIO would be a charity at the time it would be registered, or

(b) the CIO's proposed constitution does not comply with one or more of the requirements of section 69B above and any regulations made under that section.

(4) The Commission may refuse such an application if—

(a) the proposed name of the CIO is the same as, or is in the opinion of the Commission too like, the name of any other charity (whether registered or not), or

(b) the Commission is of the opinion referred to in any of paragraphs (b) to (e) of section 6(2) above (power of Commission to require change in charity's name) in relation to the proposed name of the CIO (reading paragraph (b) as referring to the proposed purposes of the CIO and to the activities which it is proposed it should carry on).]

[833E]

NOTES

Commencement: 27 February 2007 (sub-s (2)(b) for the purposes of enabling the Minister to exercise the power to make subordinate legislation); to be appointed (otherwise).
Inserted as noted to s 69A at **[833A]**.

[69F Effect of registration

(1) If the Commission grants an application under section 69E above it shall register the CIO to which the application relates as a charity in the register of charities.

(2) Upon the registration of the CIO in the register of charities, it becomes by virtue of the registration a body corporate—

(a) whose constitution is that proposed in the application,

(b) whose name is that specified in the constitution, and

(c) whose first member is, or first members are, the applicants referred to in section 69E above.

(3) All property for the time being vested in the applicants (or, if more than one, any of them) on trust for the charitable purposes of the CIO (when incorporated) shall by virtue of this subsection become vested in the CIO upon its registration.

(4) The entry relating to the charity's registration in the register of charities shall include—

(a) the date of the charity's registration, and

(b) a note saying that it is constituted as a CIO.

(5) A copy of the entry in the register shall be sent to the charity at the principal office of the CIO.]

[833F]

NOTES

Commencement: to be appointed.
Inserted as noted to s 69A at **[833A]**.

[Conversion, amalgamation and transfer

69G Conversion of charitable company or registered industrial and provident society

(1) The following may apply to the Commission to be converted into a CIO, and for the CIO's registration as a charity, in accordance with this section—

(a) a charitable company,

(b) a charity which is a registered society within the meaning of the Industrial and Provident Societies Act 1965.

(2) But such an application may not be made by—

(a) a company or registered society having a share capital if any of the shares are not fully paid up, or

(b) an exempt charity.

(3) Such an application is referred to in this section and sections 69H and 69I below as an "application for conversion".

(4) The Commission shall notify the following of any application for conversion—

(a) the appropriate registrar, and

(b) such other persons (if any) as the Commission thinks appropriate in the particular case.

(5) The company or registered society shall supply the Commission with—

(a) a copy of a resolution of the company or registered society that it be converted into a CIO,

(b) a copy of the proposed constitution of the CIO,

(c) a copy of a resolution of the company or registered society adopting the proposed constitution of the CIO,

(d) such other documents or information as may be prescribed by regulations made by the Minister, and

(e) such other documents or information as the Commission may require for the purposes of the application.

(6) The resolution referred to in subsection (5)(a) shall be—

(a) a special resolution of the company or registered society, or

(b) a unanimous written resolution signed by or on behalf of all the members of the company or registered society who would be entitled to vote on a special resolution.

(7) In the case of a registered society, "special resolution" has the meaning given in section 52(3) of the Industrial and Provident Societies Act 1965.

(8) In the case of a company limited by guarantee which makes an application for conversion (whether or not it also has a share capital), the proposed constitution of the CIO shall (unless subsection (10) applies) provide for the CIO's members to be liable to contribute to its assets if it is wound up, and for the amount up to which they are so liable.

(9) That amount shall not be less than the amount up to which they were liable to contribute to the assets of the company if it was wound up.

(10) If the amount each member of the company is liable to contribute to its assets on its winding up is £10 or less, the guarantee shall be extinguished on the conversion of the company into a CIO, and the requirements of subsections (8) and (9) do not apply.

(11) In subsection (4), and in sections 69H and 69I below, "the appropriate registrar" means—

(a) in the case of an application for conversion by a charitable company, the registrar of companies,

(b) in the case of an application for conversion by a registered society, the Financial Services Authority.

(12) In this section, "charitable company" means a company which is a charity.]

[833G]

NOTES

Commencement: 27 February 2007 (sub-s (5)(d) for the purposes of enabling the Minister to exercise the power to make subordinate legislation); to be appointed (otherwise).

Inserted as noted to s 69A at **[833A]**.

[69H Conversion: consideration of application

(1) The Commission shall consult those to whom it has given notice of an application for conversion under section 69G(4) above about whether the application should be granted.

(2) The Commission shall refuse an application for conversion if—

(a) it is not satisfied that the CIO would be a charity at the time it would be registered,

(b) the CIO's proposed constitution does not comply with one or more of the requirements of section 69B above and any regulations made under that section, or

(c) in the case of an application for conversion made by a company limited by guarantee, the CIO's proposed constitution does not comply with the requirements of subsections (8) and (9) of section 69G above.

(3) The Commission may refuse an application for conversion if—

(a) the proposed name of the CIO is the same as, or is in the opinion of the Commission too like, the name of any other charity (whether registered or not),

(b) the Commission is of the opinion referred to in any of paragraphs (b) to (e) of section 6(2) above (power of Commission to require change in charity's name) in relation to the proposed name of the CIO (reading paragraph (b) as referring to the proposed purposes of the CIO and to the activities which it is proposed it should carry on), or

(c) having considered any representations received from those whom it has consulted under subsection (1), the Commission considers (having regard to any regulations made under subsection (4)) that it would not be appropriate to grant the application.

(4) The Minister may make provision in regulations about circumstances in which it would not be appropriate to grant an application for conversion.

(5) If the Commission refuses an application for conversion, it shall so notify the appropriate registrar (see section 69G(11) above).]

[833H]

NOTES

Commencement: 27 February 2007 (sub-s (4) for the purposes of enabling the Minister to exercise the power to make subordinate legislation); to be appointed (otherwise).

Inserted as noted to s 69A at **[833A]**.

[69I Conversion: supplementary

(1) If the Commission grants an application for conversion, it shall—

(a) register the CIO to which the application related in the register of charities, and

(b) send to the appropriate registrar (see section 69G(11) above) a copy of each of the resolutions of the converting company or registered society referred to in section 69G(5)(a) and (c) above, and a copy of the entry in the register relating to the CIO.

(2) The registration of the CIO in the register shall be provisional only until the appropriate registrar cancels the registration of the company or registered society as required by subsection (3)(b).

(3) The appropriate registrar shall—

(a) register the documents sent to him under subsection (1)(b), and

(b) cancel the registration of the company in the register of companies, or of the society in the register of friendly societies,

and shall notify the Commission that he has done so.

(4) When the appropriate registrar cancels the registration of the company or of the registered society, the company or registered society is thereupon converted into a CIO, being a body corporate—

(a) whose constitution is that proposed in the application for conversion,

(b) whose name is that specified in the constitution, and

(c) whose first members are the members of the converting company or society immediately before the moment of conversion.

(5) If the converting company or registered society had a share capital, upon the conversion of the company or registered society all the shares shall by virtue of this subsection be cancelled, and no former holder of any cancelled share shall have any right in respect of it after its cancellation.

(6) Subsection (5) does not affect any right which accrued in respect of a share before its cancellation.

(7) The entry relating to the charity's registration in the register shall include—

(a) a note that it is constituted as a CIO,

(b) the date on which it became so constituted, and

(c) a note of the name of the company or society which was converted into the CIO,

but the matters mentioned in paragraphs (a) and (b) are to be included only when the appropriate registrar has notified the Commission as required by subsection (3).

(8) A copy of the entry in the register shall be sent to the charity at the principal office of the CIO.

(9) The conversion of a charitable company or of a registered society into a CIO does not affect, in particular, any liability to which the company or registered society was subject by virtue of its being a charitable company or registered society.]

[833I]

NOTES

Commencement: to be appointed.
Inserted as noted to s 69A at **[833A]**.

[69J Conversion of community interest company

(1) The Minister may by regulations make provision for the conversion of a community interest company into a CIO, and for the CIO's registration as a charity.

(2) The regulations may, in particular, apply, or apply with modifications specified in the regulations, or disapply, anything in sections 53 to 55 of the Companies (Audit, Investigations and Community Enterprise) Act 2004 or in sections 69G to 69I above.]

[833J]

NOTES

Commencement: 27 February 2007 (for the purposes of enabling the Minister to exercise the power to make subordinate legislation); to be appointed (otherwise).
Inserted as noted to s 69A at **[833A]**.

[69K Amalgamation of CIOs

(1) Any two or more CIOs ("the old CIOs") may, in accordance with this section, apply to the Commission to be amalgamated, and for the incorporation and registration as a charity of a new CIO ("the new CIO") as their successor.

(2) Such an application is referred to in this section and section 69L below as an "application for amalgamation".

(3) Subsections (2) to (4) of section 69E above apply in relation to an application for amalgamation as they apply to an application for a CIO to be constituted, but in those subsections—

(a) "the applicants" shall be construed as meaning the old CIOs, and
(b) references to the CIO are to the new CIO.

(4) In addition to the documents and information referred to in section 69E(2) above, the old CIOs shall supply the Commission with—

(a) a copy of a resolution of each of the old CIOs approving the proposed amalgamation, and
(b) a copy of a resolution of each of the old CIOs adopting the proposed constitution of the new CIO.

(5) The resolutions referred to in subsection (4) must have been passed—

(a) by a 75% majority of those voting at a general meeting of the CIO (including those voting by proxy or by post, if voting that way is permitted), or
(b) unanimously by the CIO's members, otherwise than at a general meeting.

(6) The date of passing of such a resolution is—

(a) the date of the general meeting at which it was passed, or
(b) if it was passed otherwise than at a general meeting, the date on which provision in the CIO's constitution or in regulations made under paragraph 13 of Schedule 5B to this Act deems it to have been passed (but that date may not be earlier than that on which the last member agreed to it).

(7) Each old CIO shall—

(a) give notice of the proposed amalgamation in the way (or ways) that in the opinion of its charity trustees will make it most likely to come to the attention of those who would be affected by the amalgamation, and
(b) send a copy of the notice to the Commission.

(8) The notice shall invite any person who considers that he would be affected by the proposed amalgamation to make written representations to the Commission not later than a date determined by the Commission and specified in the notice.

(9) In addition to being required to refuse it on one of the grounds mentioned in section 69E(3) above as applied by subsection (3) of this section, the Commission shall refuse an application for amalgamation if it considers that there is a serious risk that the new CIO would be unable properly to pursue its purposes.

(10) The Commission may refuse an application for amalgamation if it is not satisfied that the provision in the constitution of the new CIO about the matters mentioned in subsection (11) is the same, or substantially the same, as the provision about those matters in the constitutions of each of the old CIOs.

(11) The matters are—

(a) the purposes of the CIO,
(b) the application of property of the CIO on its dissolution, and
(c) authorisation for any benefit to be obtained by charity trustees or members of the CIO or persons connected with them.

(12) For the purposes of subsection (11)(c)—

(a) "benefit" means a direct or indirect benefit of any nature, except that it does not include any remuneration (within the meaning of section 73A below) whose receipt may be authorised under that section, and
(b) the same rules apply for determining whether a person is connected with a charity trustee or member of the CIO as apply, in accordance with section 73B(5) and (6) below, for determining whether a person is connected with a charity trustee for the purposes of section 73A.]

[833K]

NOTES

Commencement: to be appointed.
Inserted as noted to s 69A at **[833A]**.

[69L Amalgamation: supplementary

(1) If the Commission grants an application for amalgamation, it shall register the new CIO in the register of charities.

(2) Upon the registration of the new CIO it thereupon becomes by virtue of the registration a body corporate—

(a) whose constitution is that proposed in the application for amalgamation,

(b) whose name is that specified in the constitution, and

(c) whose first members are the members of the old CIOs immediately before the new CIO was registered.

(3) Upon the registration of the new CIO—

(a) all the property, rights and liabilities of each of the old CIOs shall become by virtue of this subsection the property, rights and liabilities of the new CIO, and

(b) each of the old CIOs shall be dissolved.

(4) Any gift which—

(a) is expressed as a gift to one of the old CIOs, and

(b) takes effect on or after the date of registration of the new CIO,

takes effect as a gift to the new CIO.

(5) The entry relating to the registration in the register of the charity constituted as the new CIO shall include—

(a) a note that it is constituted as a CIO,

(b) the date of the charity's registration, and

(c) a note that the CIO was formed following amalgamation, and of the name of each of the old CIOs.

(6) A copy of the entry in the register shall be sent to the charity at the principal office of the new CIO.]

[833L]

NOTES

Commencement: to be appointed.
Inserted as noted to s 69A at **[833A]**.

[69M Transfer of CIO's undertaking

(1) A CIO may resolve that all its property, rights and liabilities should be transferred to another CIO specified in the resolution.

(2) Where a CIO has passed such a resolution, it shall send to the Commission—

(a) a copy of the resolution, and

(b) a copy of a resolution of the transferee CIO agreeing to the transfer to it.

(3) Subsections (5) and (6) of section 69K above apply to the resolutions referred to in subsections (1) and (2)(b) as they apply to the resolutions referred to in section 69K(4).

(4) Having received the copy resolutions referred to in subsection (2), the Commission—

(a) may direct the transferor CIO to give public notice of its resolution in such manner as is specified in the direction, and

(b) if it gives such a direction, must take into account any representations made to it by persons appearing to it to be interested in the transferor CIO, where those representations are made to it within the period of 28 days beginning with the date when public notice of the resolution is given by the transferor CIO.

(5) The resolution shall not take effect until confirmed by the Commission.

(6) The Commission shall refuse to confirm the resolution if it considers that there is a serious risk that the transferee CIO would be unable properly to pursue the purposes of the transferor CIO.

(7) The Commission may refuse to confirm the resolution if it is not satisfied that the provision in the constitution of the transferee CIO about the matters mentioned in section 69K(11) above is the same, or substantially the same, as the provision about those matters in the constitution of the transferor CIO.

(8) If the Commission does not notify the transferor CIO within the relevant period that it is either confirming or refusing to confirm the resolution, the resolution is to be treated as confirmed by the Commission on the day after the end of that period.

(9) Subject to subsection (10), "the relevant period" means—

(a) in a case where the Commission directs the transferor CIO under subsection (4) to give public notice of its resolution, the period of six months beginning with the date when that notice is given, or

(b) in any other case, the period of six months beginning with the date when both of the copy resolutions referred to in subsection (2) have been received by the Commission.

(10) The Commission may at any time within the period of six months mentioned in subsection (9)(a) or (b) give the transferor CIO a notice extending the relevant period by such period (not exceeding six months) as is specified in the notice.

(11) A notice under subsection (10) must set out the Commission's reasons for the extension.

(12) If the resolution is confirmed (or treated as confirmed) by the Commission—

(a) all the property, rights and liabilities of the transferor CIO shall become by virtue of this subsection the property, rights and liabilities of the transferee CIO in accordance with the resolution, and

(b) the transferor CIO shall be dissolved.

(13) Any gift which—

(a) is expressed as a gift to the transferor CIO, and

(b) takes effect on or after the date on which the resolution is confirmed (or treated as confirmed),

takes effect as a gift to the transferee CIO.]

[833M]

NOTES

Commencement: to be appointed.
Inserted as noted to s 69A at **[833A]**.

[Winding up, insolvency and dissolution

69N Regulations about winding up, insolvency and dissolution

(1) The Minister may by regulations make provision about—

(a) the winding up of CIOs,

(b) their insolvency,

(c) their dissolution, and

(d) their revival and restoration to the register following dissolution.

(2) The regulations may, in particular, make provision—

(a) about the transfer on the dissolution of a CIO of its property and rights (including property and rights held on trust for the CIO) to the official custodian or another person or body,

(b) requiring any person in whose name any stocks, funds or securities are standing in trust for a CIO to transfer them into the name of the official custodian or another person or body,

(c) about the disclaiming, by the official custodian or other transferee of a CIO's property, of title to any of that property,

(d) about the application of a CIO's property cy-près,

(e) about circumstances in which charity trustees may be personally liable for contributions to the assets of a CIO or for its debts,

(f) about the reversal on a CIO's revival of anything done on its dissolution.

(3) The regulations may—

(a) apply any enactment which would not otherwise apply, either without modification or with modifications specified in the regulations,

(b) disapply, or modify (in ways specified in the regulations) the application of, any enactment which would otherwise apply.

(4) In subsection (3), "enactment" includes a provision of subordinate legislation within the meaning of the Interpretation Act 1978.]

[833N]

NOTES

Commencement: 27 February 2007 (for the purposes of enabling the Minister to exercise the power to make subordinate legislation); to be appointed (otherwise).

Inserted as noted to s 69A at **[833A]**.

[Miscellaneous

69O Power to transfer all property of unincorporated charity to one or more CIOs

Section 74 below (power to transfer all property of unincorporated charity) applies with the omission of paragraph (a) of subsection (1) in relation to a resolution by the charity trustees of a charity to transfer all its property to a CIO or to divide its property between two or more CIOs.]

[833O]

NOTES

Commencement: to be appointed.

Inserted as noted to s 69A at **[833A]**.

[69P Further provision about CIOs

The provisions of Schedule 5B to this Act shall have effect with respect to CIOs.]

[833P]

NOTES

Commencement: to be appointed.

Inserted as noted to s 69A at **[833A]**.

[69Q Regulations

(1) The Minister may by regulations make further provision about applications for registration of CIOs, the administration of CIOs, the conversion of charitable companies, registered societies and community interest companies into CIOs, the amalgamation of CIOs, and in relation to CIOs generally.

(2) The regulations may, in particular, make provision about—

(a) the execution of deeds and documents,

(b) the electronic communication of messages or documents relevant to a CIO or to any dealing with the Commission in relation to one,

(c) the maintenance of registers of members and of charity trustees,

(d) the maintenance of other registers (for example, a register of charges over the CIO's assets).

(3) The regulations may, in relation to charities constituted as CIOs—

(a) disapply any of sections 3 to 4 above,

(b) modify the application of any of those sections in ways specified in the regulations.

(4) Subsections (3) and (4) of section 69N above apply for the purposes of this section as they apply for the purposes of that.]

[833Q]–[835]

NOTES

Commencement: 27 February 2007 (for the purposes of enabling the Minister to exercise the power to make subordinate legislation); to be appointed (otherwise).

Inserted as noted to s 69A at **[833A]**.

PART IX
MISCELLANEOUS

70, 71 (*Repealed in relation to England and Wales by the Trustee Act 2000, s 40(1), (3), Sch 2, Pt I, para 2(1), Sch 4, Pt I and in relation to Scotland by the Charities and Trustee Investment (Scotland) Act 2005, s 95, Sch 3, para 9.*)

[Charity trustees]

72 Persons disqualified for being trustees of a charity

(1) Subject to the following provisions of this section, a person shall be disqualified for being a charity trustee or trustee for a charity if—

(a) he has been convicted of any offence involving dishonesty or deception;

(b) he has been adjudged bankrupt or sequestration of his estate has been awarded and (in either case) he has not been discharged [or he is the subject of a bankruptcy restrictions order or an interim order];

(c) he has made a composition or arrangement with, or granted a trust deed for, his creditors and has not been discharged in respect of it;

(d) he has been removed from the office of charity trustee or trustee for a charity by an order made—

(i) by the [Commission or] Commissioners under section 18(2)(i) above, or

(ii) by the Commissioners under section 20(1A)(i) of the Charities Act 1960 (power to act for protection of charities) or under section 20(1)(i) of that Act (as in force before the commencement of section 8 of the Charities Act 1992), or

(iii) by the High Court,

on the grounds of any misconduct or mismanagement in the administration of the charity for which he was responsible or to which he was privy, or which he by his conduct contributed to or facilitated;

(e) he has been removed, under section 7 of the Law Reform (Miscellaneous Provisions) (Scotland) Act 1990 (powers of Court of Session to deal with management of charities) [or section 34(5)(e) of the Charities and Trustee Investment (Scotland) Act 2005 (powers of the Court of Session)], from being concerned in the management or control of any body;

(f) he is subject to a disqualification order [or disqualification undertaking] under the Company Directors Disqualification Act 1986 [to a disqualification order under Part II of the Companies (Northern Ireland) Order 1989] [or disqualification undertaking under the Company Directors Disqualification (Northern Ireland) Order 2002] or to an order made under section 429(2)(b) of the Insolvency Act 1986 (failure to pay under county court administration order).

(2) In subsection (1) above—

(a) paragraph (a) applies whether the conviction occurred before or after the commencement of that subsection, but does not apply in relation to any conviction which is a spent conviction for the purposes of the Rehabilitation of Offenders Act 1974;

(b) paragraph (b) applies whether the adjudication of bankruptcy or the sequestration [or the making of a bankruptcy restrictions order or an interim order] occurred before or after the commencement of that subsection;

(c) paragraph (c) applies whether the composition or arrangement was made, or the trust deed was granted, before or after the commencement of that subsection; and

(d) paragraphs (d) to (f) apply in relation to orders made and removals effected before or after the commencement of that subsection.

(3) Where (apart from this subsection) a person is disqualified under subsection (1)(b) above for being a charity trustee or trustee for any charity which is a company, he shall not be so disqualified if leave has been granted under section 11 of the Company Directors

Disqualification Act 1986 (undischarged bankrupts) for him to act as director of the charity; and similarly a person shall not be disqualified under subsection (1)(f) above for being a charity trustee or trustee for such a charity if—

[(a) in the case of a person subject to a disqualification order or disqualification undertaking under the Company Directors Disqualification Act 1986, leave for the purposes of section 1(1)(a) or 1A(1)(a) of that Act has been granted for him to act as director of the charity,

(aa) in the case of a person subject to a disqualification order under Part II of the Companies (Northern Ireland) Order 1989 [or disqualification undertaking under the Company Directors Disqualification (Northern Ireland) Order 2002], leave has been granted by the High Court in Northern Ireland for him to act as director of the charity,]

(b) in the case of a person subject to an order under section 429(2)(b) of the Insolvency Act 1986, leave has been granted by the court which made the order for him to so act.

(4) [The Commission] may, on the application of any person disqualified under subsection (1) above, waive his disqualification either generally or in relation to a particular charity or a particular class of charities; but no such waiver may be granted in relation to any charity which is a company if—

(a) the person concerned is for the time being prohibited, by virtue of—

(i) a disqualification order [or disqualification undertaking] under the Company Directors Disqualification Act 1986, or

(ii) section 11(1) [12(2)[,12A or 12B]] of that Act (undischarged bankrupts; failure to pay under county court administration order [Northern Irish disqualification orders][; Northern Irish disqualification undertakings]),

from acting as director of the charity; and

(b) leave has not been granted for him to act as director of any other company.

[(4A) If—

(a) a person disqualified under subsection (1)(d) or (e) makes an application under subsection (4) above five years or more after the date on which his disqualification took effect, and

(b) the Commission is not prevented from granting the application by virtue of paragraphs (a) and (b) of subsection (4),

the Commission must grant the application unless satisfied that, by reason of any special circumstances, it should be refused.]

(5) Any waiver under subsection (4) above shall be notified in writing to the person concerned.

(6) For the purposes of this section [the Commission] shall keep, in such manner as [it thinks fit], a register of all persons who have been removed from office as mentioned in subsection (1)(d) above either—

(a) by an order of [the Commission or] the Commissioners made before or after the commencement of subsection (1) above, or

(b) by an order of the High Court made after the commencement of section 45(1) of the Charities Act 1992;

and, where any person is so removed from office by an order of the High Court, the court shall notify [the Commission] of his removal.

(7) The entries in the register kept under subsection (6) above shall be available for public inspection in legible form at all reasonable times.

[(8) In this section "the Commissioners" means the Charity Commissioners for England and Wales.]

[836]

NOTES

Cross-heading preceding this section substituted by the Charities Act 2006, s 75(1), Sch 8, paras 96, 155, as from 27 February 2007.

Sub-s (1): words in square brackets in para (b) inserted by the Enterprise Act 2002 (Disqualification from Office: General) Order 2006, SI 2006/1722, art 2(2), Sch 2, Pt 1, para 4(a); words in square brackets in para (d)(i) inserted by the Charities Act 2006, s 75(1), Sch 8, paras 96, 156(1), (2), as from 27 February 2007; words in square brackets in para (e) inserted by the Charities and Trustee Investment (Scotland) Act 2005 (Consequential Provisions and Modifications) Order 2006, SI 2006/242, art 5, Schedule, Pt 1, para 6(1), (2); in para (f) words in first and second pairs of square brackets inserted by the Insolvency

Act 2000, s 8, Sch 4, Pt II, para 18(a), words in third pair of square brackets inserted by the Insolvency Act 2000 (Company Directors Disqualification Undertakings) Order 2004, SI 2004/1941, art 3, Schedule, para 5(a).

Sub-s (2): words in square brackets in para (b) inserted by SI 2006/1722, art 2(2), Sch 2, Pt 1, para 4(b).

Sub-s (3): paras (a), (aa) substituted, for para (a) as originally enacted, by the Insolvency Act 2000, s 8, Sch 4, Pt II, para 18(b); words in square brackets in para (aa) inserted by SI 2004/1941, art 3, Schedule, para 5(b).

Sub-s (4): words in first pair of square brackets substituted by the Charities Act 2006, s 75(1), Sch 8, paras 96, 156(1), (3), as from 27 February 2007; words in square brackets in para (a)(i) inserted and in para (a)(ii) words in first (outer) pair of square brackets inserted and words in third pair of square brackets substituted by the Insolvency Act 2000, s 8, Sch 4, Pt II, para 18(c); in para (a)(ii) words in second (inner) pair of square brackets substituted and words in fourth pair of square brackets inserted by SI 2004/1941, art 3, Schedule, para 5(c).

Sub-s (4A): inserted by the Charities Act 2006, s 35, as from 27 February 2007, subject to transitional provisions in Sch 10, para 11 to that Act at **[2176]**.

Sub-s (6): words in first, second and fourth pairs of square brackets substituted and words in square brackets in para (a) inserted by the Charities Act 2006, s 75(1), Sch 8, paras 96, 156(1), (4), as from 27 February 2007.

Sub-s (8): added by the Charities Act 2006, s 75(1), Sch 8, paras 96, 156(1), (5), as from 27 February 2007.

Charities Act 1960, s 20(1)(i), (1A)(i): repealed by s 98(2) of and, Sch 7 to, this Act.

Charities Act 1992, ss 8, 45(1): repealed by s 98(2) of and, Sch 7 to, this Act.

73 Persons acting as charity trustee while disqualified

(1) Subject to subsection (2) below, any person who acts as a charity trustee or trustee for a charity while he is disqualified for being such a trustee by virtue of section 72 above shall be guilty of an offence and liable—

(a) on summary conviction, to imprisonment for a term not exceeding six months or to a fine not exceeding the statutory maximum, or both;

(b) on conviction on indictment, to imprisonment for a term not exceeding two years or to a fine, or both.

(2) Subsection (1) above shall not apply where—

(a) the charity concerned is a company; and

(b) the disqualified person is disqualified by virtue only of paragraph (b) or (f) of section 72(1) above.

(3) Any acts done as charity trustee or trustee for a charity by a person disqualified for being such a trustee by virtue of section 72 above shall not be invalid by reason only of that disqualification.

(4) Where [the Commission is] satisfied—

(a) that any person has acted as charity trustee or trustee for a charity (*other than an exempt charity*) while disqualified for being such a trustee by virtue of section 72 above, and

(b) that, while so acting, he has received from the charity any sums by way of remuneration or expenses, or any benefit in kind, in connection with his acting as charity trustee or trustee for the charity,

[the Commission may by order] direct him to repay to the charity the whole or part of any such sums, or (as the case may be) to pay to the charity the whole or part of the monetary value [(as determined by the Commission)] of any such benefit.

(5) Subsection (4) above does not apply to any sums received by way of remuneration or expenses in respect of any time when the person concerned was not disqualified for being a charity trustee or trustee for the charity.

[837]

NOTES

Sub-s (4): words in square brackets substituted by the Charities Act 2006, s 75(1), Sch 8, paras 96, 157, as from 27 February 2007, and words in italics repealed as from a day to be appointed under s 79(2) of that Act, by ss 12, 75 (2) of, and Sch 5, para 9, Sch 9 to, that Act.

[73A Remuneration of trustees etc providing services to charity

(1) This section applies to remuneration for services provided by a person to or on behalf of a charity where—

(a) he is a charity trustee or trustee for the charity, or

(b) he is connected with a charity trustee or trustee for the charity and the remuneration might result in that trustee obtaining any benefit.

This is subject to subsection (7) below.

(2) If conditions A to D are met in relation to remuneration within subsection (1), the person providing the services ("the relevant person") is entitled to receive the remuneration out of the funds of the charity.

(3) Condition A is that the amount or maximum amount of the remuneration—

(a) is set out in an agreement in writing between—

(i) the charity or its charity trustees (as the case may be), and

(ii) the relevant person,

under which the relevant person is to provide the services in question to or on behalf of the charity, and

(b) does not exceed what is reasonable in the circumstances for the provision by that person of the services in question.

(4) Condition B is that, before entering into that agreement, the charity trustees decided that they were satisfied that it would be in the best interests of the charity for the services to be provided by the relevant person to or on behalf of the charity for the amount or maximum amount of remuneration set out in the agreement.

(5) Condition C is that if immediately after the agreement is entered into there is, in the case of the charity, more than one person who is a charity trustee and is—

(a) a person in respect of whom an agreement within subsection (3) above is in force, or

(b) a person who is entitled to receive remuneration out of the funds of the charity otherwise than by virtue of such an agreement, or

(c) a person connected with a person falling within paragraph (a) or (b) above,

the total number of them constitute a minority of the persons for the time being holding office as charity trustees of the charity.

(6) Condition D is that the trusts of the charity do not contain any express provision that prohibits the relevant person from receiving the remuneration.

(7) Nothing in this section applies to—

(a) any remuneration for services provided by a person in his capacity as a charity trustee or trustee for a charity or under a contract of employment, or

(b) any remuneration not within paragraph (a) which a person is entitled to receive out of the funds of a charity by virtue of any provision or order within subsection (8).

(8) The provisions or orders within this subsection are—

(a) any provision contained in the trusts of the charity,

(b) any order of the court or the Commission,

(c) any statutory provision contained in or having effect under an Act of Parliament other than this section.

(9) Section 73B below applies for the purposes of this section.]

[837A]

NOTES

Commencement: to be appointed.

Inserted, together with s 73B, by the Charities Act 2006, s 36, as from a day to be appointed under s 79(2) of that Act, subject to savings in Sch 10, para 12 to that Act at **[2176]**.

[73B Supplementary provisions for purposes of section 73A

(1) Before entering into an agreement within section 73A(3) the charity trustees must have regard to any guidance given by the Commission concerning the making of such agreements.

(2) The duty of care in section 1(1) of the Trustee Act 2000 applies to a charity trustee when making such a decision as is mentioned in section 73A(4).

(3) For the purposes of section 73A(5) an agreement within section 73A(3) is in force so long as any obligations under the agreement have not been fully discharged by a party to it.

(4) In section 73A—

"benefit" means a direct or indirect benefit of any nature;

"maximum amount", in relation to remuneration, means the maximum amount of the remuneration whether specified in or ascertainable under the terms of the agreement in question;

"remuneration" includes any benefit in kind (and "amount" accordingly includes monetary value);

"services", in the context of remuneration for services, includes goods that are supplied in connection with the provision of services.

(5) For the purposes of section 73A the following persons are "connected" with a charity trustee or trustee for a charity—

(a) a child, parent, grandchild, grandparent, brother or sister of the trustee;

(b) the spouse or civil partner of the trustee or of any person falling within paragraph (a);

(c) a person carrying on business in partnership with the trustee or with any person falling within paragraph (a) or (b);

(d) an institution which is controlled—

(i) by the trustee or by any person falling within paragraph (a), (b) or (c), or

(ii) by two or more persons falling within sub-paragraph (i), when taken together;

(e) a body corporate in which—

(i) the trustee or any connected person falling within any of paragraphs (a) to (c) has a substantial interest, or

(ii) two or more persons falling within sub-paragraph (i), when taken together, have a substantial interest.

(6) Paragraphs 2 to 4 of Schedule 5 to this Act apply for the purposes of subsection (5) above as they apply for the purposes of provisions of that Schedule.]

[837B]

NOTES

Commencement: to be appointed.

Inserted as noted to s 73A at **[837A]**.

[73C Disqualification of trustee receiving remuneration under section 73A

(1) This section applies to any charity trustee or trustee for a charity—

(a) who is or would be entitled to remuneration under an agreement or proposed agreement within section 73A(3) above, or

(b) who is connected with a person who is or would be so entitled.

(2) The charity trustee or trustee for a charity is disqualified from acting as such in relation to any decision or other matter connected with the agreement.

(3) But any act done by such a person which he is disqualified from doing by virtue of subsection (2) above shall not be invalid by reason only of that disqualification.

(4) Where the Commission is satisfied—

(a) that a person ("the disqualified trustee") has done any act which he was disqualified from doing by virtue of subsection (2) above, and

(b) that the disqualified trustee or a person connected with him has received or is to receive from the charity any remuneration under the agreement in question,

it may make an order under subsection (5) or (6) below (as appropriate).

(5) An order under this subsection is one requiring the disqualified trustee—

(a) to reimburse to the charity the whole or part of the remuneration received as mentioned in subsection (4)(b) above;

(b) to the extent that the remuneration consists of a benefit in kind, to reimburse to the charity the whole or part of the monetary value (as determined by the Commission) of the benefit in kind.

(6) An order under this subsection is one directing that the disqualified trustee or (as the case may be) connected person is not to be paid the whole or part of the remuneration mentioned in subsection (4)(b) above.

(7) If the Commission makes an order under subsection (5) or (6) above, the disqualified trustee or (as the case may be) connected person accordingly ceases to have any entitlement

under the agreement to so much of the remuneration (or its monetary value) as the order requires him to reimburse to the charity or (as the case may be) as it directs is not to be paid to him.

(8) Subsections (4) to (6) of section 73B above apply for the purposes of this section as they apply for the purposes of section 73A above.]

[837C]

NOTES

Commencement: to be appointed.

Inserted by the Charities Act 2006, s 37, as from a day to be appointed under s 79(2) of that Act.

[73D Power to relieve trustees, auditors etc from liability for breach of trust or duty

(1) This section applies to a person who is or has been—

(a) a charity trustee or trustee for a charity,

(b) a person appointed to audit a charity's accounts (whether appointed under an enactment or otherwise), or

(c) an independent examiner, reporting accountant or other person appointed to examine or report on a charity's accounts (whether appointed under an enactment or otherwise).

(2) If the Commission considers—

(a) that a person to whom this section applies is or may be personally liable for a breach of trust or breach of duty committed in his capacity as a person within paragraph (a), (b) or (c) of subsection (1) above, but

(b) that he has acted honestly and reasonably and ought fairly to be excused for the breach of trust or duty,

the Commission may make an order relieving him wholly or partly from any such liability.

(3) An order under subsection (2) above may grant the relief on such terms as the Commission thinks fit.

(4) Subsection (2) does not apply in relation to any personal contractual liability of a charity trustee or trustee for a charity.

(5) For the purposes of this section and section 73E below—

(a) subsection (1)(b) above is to be read as including a reference to the Auditor General for Wales acting as auditor under section 43B above, and

(b) subsection (1)(c) above is to be read as including a reference to the Auditor General for Wales acting as examiner under that section;

and in subsection (1)(b) and (c) any reference to a charity's accounts is to be read as including any group accounts prepared by the charity trustees of a charity.

(6) This section does not affect the operation of—

(a) section 61 of the Trustee Act 1925 (power of court to grant relief to trustees),

(b) section 727 of the Companies Act 1985 (power of court to grant relief to officers or auditors of companies), or

(c) section 73E below (which extends section 727 to auditors etc of charities which are not companies).]

[837D]

NOTES

Commencement: 27 February 2007 (except in so far as this section refers to group accounts as required to be prepared under the new Sch 5A to this Act).

Inserted, together with s 73E, by the Charities Act 2006, s 38, subject to transitional provisions in Sch 10, para 13 to that Act at **[2176]**.

[73E Court's power to grant relief to apply to all auditors etc of charities which are not companies

(1) Section 727 of the Companies Act 1985 (power of court to grant relief to officers or auditors of companies) shall have effect in relation to a person to whom this section applies as it has effect in relation to a person employed as an auditor by a company.

(2) This section applies to—

(a) a person acting in a capacity within section 73D(1)(b) or (c) above in a case where, apart from this section, section 727 would not apply in relation to him as a person so acting, and

(b) a charity trustee of a CIO.]

[837E]

NOTES

Commencement: 27 February 2007 (sub-ss (1), (2)(a)); to be appointed (otherwise).
Inserted as noted to s 73D at **[837D]**.

[73F Trustees' indemnity insurance

(1) The charity trustees of a charity may arrange for the purchase, out of the funds of the charity, of insurance designed to indemnify the charity trustees or any trustees for the charity against any personal liability in respect of—

(a) any breach of trust or breach of duty committed by them in their capacity as charity trustees or trustees for the charity, or

(b) any negligence, default, breach of duty or breach of trust committed by them in their capacity as directors or officers of the charity (if it is a body corporate) or of any body corporate carrying on any activities on behalf of the charity.

(2) The terms of such insurance must, however, be so framed as to exclude the provision of any indemnity for a person in respect of—

(a) any liability incurred by him to pay—

(i) a fine imposed in criminal proceedings, or

(ii) a sum payable to a regulatory authority by way of a penalty in respect of non-compliance with any requirement of a regulatory nature (however arising);

(b) any liability incurred by him in defending any criminal proceedings in which he is convicted of an offence arising out of any fraud or dishonesty, or wilful or reckless misconduct, by him; or

(c) any liability incurred by him to the charity that arises out of any conduct which he knew (or must reasonably be assumed to have known) was not in the interests of the charity or in the case of which he did not care whether it was in the best interests of the charity or not.

(3) For the purposes of subsection (2)(b) above—

(a) the reference to any such conviction is a reference to one that has become final;

(b) a conviction becomes final—

(i) if not appealed against, at the end of the period for bringing an appeal, or

(ii) if appealed against, at the time when the appeal (or any further appeal) is disposed of; and

(c) an appeal is disposed of—

(i) if it is determined and the period for bringing any further appeal has ended, or

(ii) if it is abandoned or otherwise ceases to have effect.

(4) The charity trustees of a charity may not purchase insurance under this section unless they decide that they are satisfied that it is in the best interests of the charity for them to do so.

(5) The duty of care in section 1(1) of the Trustee Act 2000 applies to a charity trustee when making such a decision.

(6) The Minister may by order make such amendments of subsections (2) and (3) above as he considers appropriate.

(7) No order may be made under subsection (6) above unless a draft of the order has been laid before and approved by a resolution of each House of Parliament.

(8) This section—

(a) does not authorise the purchase of any insurance whose purchase is expressly prohibited by the trusts of the charity, but

(b) has effect despite any provision prohibiting the charity trustees or trustees for the charity receiving any personal benefit out of the funds of the charity.]

[837F]

NOTES

Commencement: 27 February 2007.
Inserted by the Charities Act 2006, s 39.

[Miscellaneous powers of charities]

74 Power to transfer all property, modify objects etc

(*1*) *This section applies to a charity if—*

(*a*) *its gross income in its last financial year did not exceed £5,000, and*

(*b*) *it does not hold any land on trusts which stipulate that the land is to be used for the purposes, or any particular purposes, of the charity,*

and it is neither an exempt charity nor a charitable company.

(2) *Subject to the following provisions of this section, the charity trustees of a charity to which this section applies may resolve for the purposes of this section—*

(*a*) *that all the property of the charity should be transferred to such other charity as is specified in the resolution, being either a registered charity or a charity which is not required to be registered;*

(*b*) *that all the property of the charity should be divided, in such manner as is specified in the resolution, between such two or more other charities as are so specified, being in each case either a registered charity or a charity which is not required to be registered;*

(*c*) *that the trusts of the charity should be modified by replacing all or any of the purposes of the charity with such other purposes, being in law charitable, as are specified in the resolution;*

(*d*) *that any provision of the trusts of the charity—*

(*i*) *relating to any of the powers exercisable by the charity trustees in the administration of the charity, or*

(*ii*) *regulating the procedure to be followed in any respect in connection with its administration,*

should be modified in such manner as is specified in the resolution.

(3) *Any resolution passed under subsection* (2) *above must be passed by a majority of not less than two-thirds of such charity trustees as vote on the resolution.*

(4) *The charity trustees of a charity to which this section applies ("the transferor charity") shall not have power to pass a resolution under subsection* (2)(*a*) *or* (*b*) *above unless they are satisfied—*

(*a*) *that the existing purposes of the transferor charity have ceased to be conducive to a suitable and effective application of the charity's resources; and*

(*b*) *that the purposes of the charity or charities specified in the resolution are as similar in character to the purposes of the transferor charity as is reasonably practicable;*

and before passing the resolution they must have received from the charity trustees of the charity, or (as the case may be) of each of the charities, specified in the resolution written confirmation that those trustees are willing to accept a transfer of property under this section.

(5) *The charity trustees of any such charity shall not have power to pass a resolution under subsection* (2)(*c*) *above unless they are satisfied—*

(*a*) *that the existing purposes of the charity (or, as the case may be, such of them as it is proposed to replace) have ceased to be conducive to a suitable and effective application of the charity's resources; and*

(*b*) *that the purposes specified in the resolution are as similar in character to those existing purposes as is practical in the circumstances.*

(6) *Where charity trustees have passed a resolution under subsection* (2) *above, they shall—*

(*a*) *give public notice of the resolution in such manner as they think reasonable in the circumstances; and*

(*b*) *send a copy of the resolution to the Commissioners, together with a statement of their reasons for passing it.*

(7) *The Commissioners may, when considering the resolution, require the charity trustees to provide additional information or explanation—*

(*a*) *as to the circumstances in and by reference to which they have determined to act under this section, or*

(*b*) *relating to their compliance with this section in connection with the resolution;*

and the Commissioners shall take into account any representations made to them by persons appearing to them to be interested in the charity where those representations are made within the period of six weeks beginning with the date when the Commissioners receive a copy of the resolution by virtue of subsection (6)(b) above.

(*8*) *Where the Commissioners have so received a copy of a resolution from any charity trustees and it appears to them that the trustees have complied with this section in connection with the resolution, the Commissioners shall, within the period of three months beginning with the date when they receive the copy of the resolution, notify the trustees in writing either—*

(*a*) *that the Commissioners concur with the resolution; or*

(*b*) *that they do not concur with it.*

(*9*) *Where the Commissioners so notify their concurrence with the resolution, then—*

(*a*) *if the resolution was passed under subsection (2)(a) or (b) above, the charity trustees shall arrange for all the property of the transferor charity to be transferred in accordance with the resolution and on terms that any property so transferred—*

(*i*) *shall be held and applied by the charity to which it is transferred ("the transferee charity") for the purposes of that charity, but*

(*ii*) *shall, as property of the transferee charity, nevertheless be subject to any restrictions on expenditure to which it is subject as property of the transferor charity,*

and those trustees shall arrange for it to be so transferred by such date as may be specified in the notification; and

(*b*) *if the resolution was passed under subsection (2)(c) or (d) above, the trusts of the charity shall be deemed, as from such date as may be specified in the notification, to have been modified in accordance with the terms of the resolution.*

(*10*) *For the purpose of enabling any property to be transferred to a charity under this section, the Commissioners shall have power, at the request of the charity trustees of that charity, to make orders vesting any property of the transferor charity—*

(*a*) *in the charity trustees of the first-mentioned charity or in any trustee for that charity, or*

(*b*) *in any other person nominated by those charity trustees to hold the property in trust for that charity.*

(*11*) *The [Minister] may by order amend subsection (1) above by substituting a different sum for the sum for the time being specified there.*

(*12*) *In this section—*

(*a*) *"charitable company" means a charity which is a company or other body corporate; and*

(*b*) *references to the transfer of property to a charity are references to its transfer—*

(*i*) *to the charity trustees, or*

(*ii*) *to any trustee for the charity, or*

(*iii*) *to a person nominated by the charity trustees to hold it in trust for the charity, as the charity trustees may determine.*

[838]

NOTES

Cross-heading preceding this section substituted by the Charities Act 2006, s 75(1), Sch 8, paras 96, 158, as from 27 February 2007.

Sub-s (11): word in square brackets substituted by the Transfer of Functions (Third Sector, Communities and Equality) Order 2006, SI 2006/2951, art 6, Schedule, para 4(v).

Substituted as follows, together with ss 74A, 74B, for s 74 as originally enacted, by the Charities Act 2006, s 40, as from a day to be appointed under s 79(2) of that Act—

"74 Power to transfer all property of unincorporated charity

(1) This section applies to a charity if—

(a) its gross income in its last financial year did not exceed £10,000,

(b) it does not hold any designated land, and

(c) it is not a company or other body corporate.

"Designated land" means land held on trusts which stipulate that it is to be used for the purposes, or any particular purposes, of the charity.

(2) The charity trustees of such a charity may resolve for the purposes of this section—
(a) that all the property of the charity should be transferred to another charity specified in the resolution, or
(b) that all the property of the charity should be transferred to two or more charities specified in the resolution in accordance with such division of the property between them as is so specified.

(3) Any charity so specified may be either a registered charity or a charity which is not required to be registered.

(4) But the charity trustees of a charity ("the transferor charity") do not have power to pass a resolution under subsection (2) above unless they are satisfied—
(a) that it is expedient in the interests of furthering the purposes for which the property is held by the transferor charity for the property to be transferred in accordance with the resolution, and
(b) that the purposes (or any of the purposes) of any charity to which property is to be transferred under the resolution are substantially similar to the purposes (or any of the purposes) of the transferor charity.

(5) Any resolution under subsection (2) above must be passed by a majority of not less than two-thirds of the charity trustees who vote on the resolution.

(6) Where charity trustees have passed a resolution under subsection (2), they must send a copy of it to the Commission, together with a statement of their reasons for passing it.

(7) Having received the copy of the resolution, the Commission—
(a) may direct the charity trustees to give public notice of the resolution in such manner as is specified in the direction, and
(b) if it gives such a direction, must take into account any representations made to it by persons appearing to it to be interested in the charity, where those representations are made to it within the period of 28 days beginning with the date when public notice of the resolution is given by the charity trustees.

(8) The Commission may also direct the charity trustees to provide the Commission with additional information or explanations relating to—
(a) the circumstances in and by reference to which they have decided to act under this section, or
(b) their compliance with any obligation imposed on them by or under this section in connection with the resolution.

(9) Subject to the provisions of section 74A below, a resolution under subsection (2) above takes effect at the end of the period of 60 days beginning with the date on which the copy of it was received by the Commission.

(10) Where such a resolution has taken effect, the charity trustees must arrange for all the property of the transferor charity to be transferred in accordance with the resolution, and on terms that any property so transferred—
(a) is to be held by the charity to which it is transferred ("the transferee charity") in accordance with subsection (11) below, but
(b) when so held is nevertheless to be subject to any restrictions on expenditure to which it was subject as property of the transferor charity;

and the charity trustees must arrange for the property to be so transferred by such date after the resolution takes effect as they agree with the charity trustees of the transferee charity or charities concerned.

(11) The charity trustees of any charity to which property is transferred under this section must secure, so far as is reasonably practicable, that the property is applied for such of its purposes as are substantially similar to those of the transferor charity.

But this requirement does not apply if those charity trustees consider that complying with it would not result in a suitable and effective method of applying the property.

(12) For the purpose of enabling any property to be transferred to a charity under this section, the Commission may, at the request of the charity trustees of that charity, make orders vesting any property of the transferor charity—
(a) in the transferee charity, in its charity trustees or in any trustee for that charity, or
(b) in any other person nominated by those charity trustees to hold property in trust for that charity.

(13) The Minister may by order amend subsection (1) above by substituting a different sum for the sum for the time being specified there.

(14) In this section references to the transfer of property to a charity are references to its transfer—
(a) to the charity, or
(b) to the charity trustees, or
(c) to any trustee for the charity, or
(d) to a person nominated by the charity trustees to hold it in trust for the charity,

as the charity trustees may determine.

(15) Where a charity has a permanent endowment, this section has effect in accordance with section 74B.

74A Resolution not to take effect or to take effect at later date

(1) This section deals with circumstances in which a resolution under section 74(2) above either—

(a) does not take effect under section 74(9) above, or

(b) takes effect at a time later than that mentioned in section 74(9).

(2) A resolution does not take effect under section 74(9) above if before the end of—

(a) the period of 60 days mentioned in section 74(9) ("the 60-day period"), or

(b) that period as modified by subsection (3) or (4) below,

the Commission notifies the charity trustees in writing that it objects to the resolution, either on procedural grounds or on the merits of the proposals contained in the resolution.

"On procedural grounds" means on the grounds that any obligation imposed on the charity trustees by or under section 74 above has not been complied with in connection with the resolution.

(3) If under section 74(7) above the Commission directs the charity trustees to give public notice of a resolution, the running of the 60-day period is suspended by virtue of this subsection—

(a) as from the date on which the direction is given to the charity trustees, and

(b) until the end of the period of 42 days beginning with the date on which public notice of the resolution is given by the charity trustees.

(4) If under section 74(8) above the Commission directs the charity trustees to provide any information or explanations, the running of the 60-day period is suspended by virtue of this subsection—

(a) as from the date on which the direction is given to the charity trustees, and

(b) until the date on which the information or explanations is or are provided to the Commission.

(5) Subsection (6) below applies once the period of time, or the total period of time, during which the 60-day period is suspended by virtue of either or both of subsections (3) and (4) above exceeds 120 days.

(6) At that point the resolution (if not previously objected to by the Commission) is to be treated as if it had never been passed.

74B Transfer where charity has permanent endowment

(1) This section provides for the operation of section 74 above where a charity within section 74(1) has a permanent endowment (whether or not the charity's trusts contain provision for the termination of the charity).

(2) In such a case section 74 applies as follows—

(a) if the charity has both a permanent endowment and other property ("unrestricted property")—

(i) a resolution under section 74(2) must relate to both its permanent endowment and its unrestricted property, and

(ii) that section applies in relation to its unrestricted property in accordance with subsection (3) below and in relation to its permanent endowment in accordance with subsections (4) to (11) below;

(b) if all of the property of the charity is comprised in its permanent endowment, that section applies in relation to its permanent endowment in accordance with subsections (4) to (11) below.

(3) Section 74 applies in relation to unrestricted property of the charity as if references in that section to all or any of the property of the charity were references to all or any of its unrestricted property.

(4) Section 74 applies in relation to the permanent endowment of the charity with the following modifications.

(5) References in that section to all or any of the property of the charity are references to all or any of the property comprised in its permanent endowment.

(6) If the property comprised in its permanent endowment is to be transferred to a single charity, the charity trustees must (instead of being satisfied as mentioned in section 74(4)(b)) be satisfied that the proposed transferee charity has purposes which are substantially similar to all of the purposes of the transferor charity.

(7) If the property comprised in its permanent endowment is to be transferred to two or more charities, the charity trustees must (instead of being satisfied as mentioned in section 74(4)(b)) be satisfied—

(a) that the proposed transferee charities, taken together, have purposes which are substantially similar to all of the purposes of the transferor charity, and

(b) that each of the proposed transferee charities has purposes which are substantially similar to one or more of the purposes of the transferor charity.

(8) In the case of a transfer to which subsection (7) above applies, the resolution under section 74(2) must provide for the property comprised in the permanent endowment of the charity to be divided between the transferee charities in such a way as to take account of such guidance as may be given by the Commission for the purposes of this section.

(9) The requirement in section 74(11) shall apply in the case of every such transfer, and in complying with that requirement the charity trustees of a transferee charity must secure that the application of property transferred to the charity takes account of any such guidance.

(10) Any guidance given by the Commission for the purposes of this section may take such form and be given in such manner as the Commission considers appropriate.

(11) For the purposes of sections 74 and 74A above, any reference to any obligation imposed on the charity trustees by or under section 74 includes a reference to any obligation imposed on them by virtue of any of subsections (6) to (8) above.

(12) Section 74(14) applies for the purposes of this section as it applies for the purposes of section 74.".

[74C Power to replace purposes of unincorporated charity

(1) This section applies to a charity if—

(a) its gross income in its last financial year did not exceed £10,000,

(b) it does not hold any designated land, and

(c) it is not a company or other body corporate.

"Designated land" means land held on trusts which stipulate that it is to be used for the purposes, or any particular purposes, of the charity.

(2) The charity trustees of such a charity may resolve for the purposes of this section that the trusts of the charity should be modified by replacing all or any of the purposes of the charity with other purposes specified in the resolution.

(3) The other purposes so specified must be charitable purposes.

(4) But the charity trustees of a charity do not have power to pass a resolution under subsection (2) above unless they are satisfied—

(a) that it is expedient in the interests of the charity for the purposes in question to be replaced, and

(b) that, so far as is reasonably practicable, the new purposes consist of or include purposes that are similar in character to those that are to be replaced.

(5) Any resolution under subsection (2) above must be passed by a majority of not less than two-thirds of the charity trustees who vote on the resolution.

(6) Where charity trustees have passed a resolution under subsection (2), they must send a copy of it to the Commission, together with a statement of their reasons for passing it.

(7) Having received the copy of the resolution, the Commission—

(a) may direct the charity trustees to give public notice of the resolution in such manner as is specified in the direction, and

(b) if it gives such a direction, must take into account any representations made to it by persons appearing to it to be interested in the charity, where those representations are made to it within the period of 28 days beginning with the date when public notice of the resolution is given by the charity trustees.

(8) The Commission may also direct the charity trustees to provide the Commission with additional information or explanations relating to—

(a) the circumstances in and by reference to which they have decided to act under this section, or

(b) their compliance with any obligation imposed on them by or under this section in connection with the resolution.

(9) Subject to the provisions of section 74A above (as they apply in accordance with subsection (10) below), a resolution under subsection (2) above takes effect at the end of the period of 60 days beginning with the date on which the copy of it was received by the Commission.

(10) Section 74A above applies to a resolution under subsection (2) of this section as it applies to a resolution under subsection (2) of section 74 above, except that any reference to section 74(7), (8) or (9) is to be read as a reference to subsection (7), (8) or (9) above.

(11) As from the time when a resolution takes effect under subsection (9) above, the trusts of the charity concerned are to be taken to have been modified in accordance with the terms of the resolution.

(12) The Minister may by order amend subsection (1) above by substituting a different sum for the sum for the time being specified there.]

[838A]

NOTES

Commencement: to be appointed.
Inserted by the Charities Act 2006, s 41, as from a day to be appointed under s 79(2) of that Act.

[74D Power to modify powers or procedures of unincorporated charity

(1) This section applies to any charity which is not a company or other body corporate.

(2) The charity trustees of such a charity may resolve for the purposes of this section that any provision of the trusts of the charity—

(a) relating to any of the powers exercisable by the charity trustees in the administration of the charity, or

(b) regulating the procedure to be followed in any respect in connection with its administration,

should be modified in such manner as is specified in the resolution.

(3) Subsection (4) applies if the charity is an unincorporated association with a body of members distinct from the charity trustees.

(4) Any resolution of the charity trustees under subsection (2) must be approved by a further resolution which is passed at a general meeting of the body either—

(a) by a majority of not less than two-thirds of the members entitled to attend and vote at the meeting who vote on the resolution, or

(b) by a decision taken without a vote and without any expression of dissent in response to the question put to the meeting.

(5) Where—

(a) the charity trustees have passed a resolution under subsection (2), and

(b) (if subsection (4) applies) a further resolution has been passed under that subsection,

the trusts of the charity are to be taken to have been modified in accordance with the terms of the resolution.

(6) The trusts are to be taken to have been so modified as from such date as is specified for this purpose in the resolution under subsection (2), or (if later) the date when any such further resolution was passed under subsection (4).]

[838B]

NOTES

Commencement: 27 February 2007.
Inserted by the Charities Act 2006, s 42.

75 Power to spend capital

(1) This section applies to a charity if—

(a) it has a permanent endowment which does not consist of or comprise any land, and

(b) its gross income in its last financial year did not exceed £1,000,

and it is neither an exempt charity nor a charitable company.

(2) Where the charity trustees of a charity to which this section applies are of the opinion that the property of the charity is too small, in relation to its purposes, for any useful purpose to be achieved by the expenditure of income alone, they may resolve for the purposes of this section that the charity ought to be freed from the restrictions with respect to expenditure of capital to which its permanent endowment is subject.

(3) Any resolution passed under subsection (2) above must be passed by a majority of not less than two-thirds of such charity trustees as vote on the resolution.

(4) Before passing such a resolution the charity trustees must consider whether any reasonable possibility exists of effecting a transfer or division of all the charity's property under section 74 above (disregarding any such transfer or division as would, in their opinion, impose on the charity an unacceptable burden of costs).

(5) Where charity trustees have passed a resolution under subsection (2) above, they shall—

(a) give public notice of the resolution in such manner as they think reasonable in the circumstances; and

(b) send a copy of the resolution to the Commissioners, together with a statement of their reasons for passing it.

(6) The Commissioners may, when considering the resolution, require the charity trustees to provide additional information or explanation—

(a) as to the circumstances in and by reference to which they have determined to act under this section, or

(b) relating to their compliance with this section in connection with the resolution;

and the Commissioners shall take into account any representations made to them by persons appearing to them to be interested in the charity where those representations are made within the period of six weeks beginning with the date when the Commissioners receive a copy of the resolution by virtue of subsection (5)(b) above.

(7) Where the Commissioners have so received a copy of a resolution from any charity trustees and it appears to them that the trustees have complied with this section in connection with the resolution, the Commissioners shall, within the period of three months beginning with the date when they receive the copy of the resolution, notify the trustees in writing either—

(a) that the Commissioners concur with the resolution; or

(b) that they do not concur with it.

(8) Where the Commissioners so notify their concurrence with the resolution, the charity trustees shall have, as from such date as may be specified in the notification, power by virtue of this section to expend any property of the charity without regard to any such restrictions as are mentioned in subsection (2) above.

(9) The [Minister] may by order amend subsection (1) above by substituting a different sum for the sum for the time being specified there.

(10) In this section "charitable company" means a charity which is a company or other body corporate.

[839]

NOTES

Sub-s (9): word in square brackets substituted by the Transfer of Functions (Third Sector, Communities and Equality) Order 2006, SI 2006/2951, art 6, Schedule, para 4(w).

Substituted as follows, together with ss 75A, 75B, for s 75 as originally enacted, by the Charities Act 2006, s 43, as from a day to be appointed under s 79(2) of that Act—

"75 Power of unincorporated charities to spend capital: general

(1) This section applies to any available endowment fund of a charity which is not a company or other body corporate.

(2) But this section does not apply to a fund if section 75A below (power of larger charities to spend capital given for particular purpose) applies to it.

(3) Where the condition in subsection (4) below is met in relation to the charity, the charity trustees may resolve for the purposes of this section that the fund, or a portion of it, ought to be freed from the restrictions with respect to expenditure of capital that apply to it.

(4) The condition in this subsection is that the charity trustees are satisfied that the purposes set out in the trusts to which the fund is subject could be carried out more effectively if the capital of the fund, or the relevant portion of the capital, could be expended as well as income accruing to it, rather than just such income.

(5) Once the charity trustees have passed a resolution under subsection (3) above, the fund or portion may by virtue of this section be expended in carrying out the purposes set out in the trusts to which the fund is subject without regard to the restrictions mentioned in that subsection.

(6) The fund or portion may be so expended as from such date as is specified for this purpose in the resolution.

(7) In this section "available endowment fund", in relation to a charity, means—

(a) the whole of the charity's permanent endowment if it is all subject to the same trusts, or

(b) any part of its permanent endowment which is subject to any particular trusts that are different from those to which any other part is subject.

75A Power of larger unincorporated charities to spend capital given for particular purpose

(1) This section applies to any available endowment fund of a charity which is not a company or other body corporate if—

(a) the capital of the fund consists entirely of property given—

(i) by a particular individual,

(ii) by a particular institution (by way of grant or otherwise), or

(iii) by two or more individuals or institutions in pursuit of a common purpose, and

(b) the financial condition in subsection (2) below is met.

(2) The financial condition in this subsection is met if—

(a) the relevant charity's gross income in its last financial year exceeded £1,000, and

(b) the market value of the endowment fund exceeds £10,000.

(3) Where the condition in subsection (4) below is met in relation to the charity, the charity trustees may resolve for the purposes of this section that the fund, or a portion of it, ought to be freed from the restrictions with respect to expenditure of capital that apply to it.

(4) The condition in this subsection is that the charity trustees are satisfied that the purposes set out in the trusts to which the fund is subject could be carried out more effectively if the capital of the fund, or the relevant portion of the capital, could be expended as well as income accruing to it, rather than just such income.

(5) The charity trustees—

(a) must send a copy of any resolution under subsection (3) above to the Commission, together with a statement of their reasons for passing it, and

(b) may not implement the resolution except in accordance with the following provisions of this section.

(6) Having received the copy of the resolution the Commission may—

(a) direct the charity trustees to give public notice of the resolution in such manner as is specified in the direction, and

(b) if it gives such a direction, must take into account any representations made to it by persons appearing to it to be interested in the charity, where those representations are made to it within the period of 28 days beginning with the date when public notice of the resolution is given by the charity trustees.

(7) The Commission may also direct the charity trustees to provide the Commission with additional information or explanations relating to—

(a) the circumstances in and by reference to which they have decided to act under this section, or

(b) their compliance with any obligation imposed on them by or under this section in connection with the resolution.

(8) When considering whether to concur with the resolution the Commission must take into account—

(a) any evidence available to it as to the wishes of the donor or donors mentioned in subsection (1)(a) above, and

(b) any changes in the circumstances relating to the charity since the making of the gift or gifts (including, in particular, its financial position, the needs of its beneficiaries, and the social, economic and legal environment in which it operates).

(9) The Commission must not concur with the resolution unless it is satisfied—

(a) that its implementation would accord with the spirit of the gift or gifts mentioned in subsection (1)(a) above (even though it would be inconsistent with the restrictions mentioned in subsection (3) above), and

(b) that the charity trustees have complied with the obligations imposed on them by or under this section in connection with the resolution.

(10) Before the end of the period of three months beginning with the relevant date, the Commission must notify the charity trustees in writing either—

(a) that the Commission concurs with the resolution, or

(b) that it does not concur with it.

(11) In subsection (10) "the relevant date" means—

(a) in a case where the Commission directs the charity trustees under subsection (6) above to give public notice of the resolution, the date when that notice is given, and

(b) in any other case, the date on which the Commission receives the copy of the resolution in accordance with subsection (5) above.

(12) Where—

(a) the charity trustees are notified by the Commission that it concurs with the resolution, or

(b) the period of three months mentioned in subsection (10) above has elapsed without the Commission notifying them that it does not concur with the resolution,

the fund or portion may, by virtue of this section, be expended in carrying out the purposes set out in the trusts to which the fund is subject without regard to the restrictions mentioned in subsection (3).

(13) The Minister may by order amend subsection (2) above by substituting a different sum for any sum specified there.

(14) In this section—

(a) "available endowment fund" has the same meaning as in section 75 above,

(b) "market value", in relation to an endowment fund, means—

(i) the market value of the fund as recorded in the accounts for the last financial year of the relevant charity, or

(ii) if no such value was so recorded, the current market value of the fund as determined on a valuation carried out for the purpose, and

(c) the reference in subsection (1) to the giving of property by an individual includes his giving it under his will.

75B Power to spend capital subject to special trusts

(1) This section applies to any available endowment fund of a special trust which, as the result of a direction under section 96(5) below, is to be treated as a separate charity ("the relevant charity") for the purposes of this section.

(2) Where the condition in subsection (3) below is met in relation to the relevant charity, the charity trustees may resolve for the purposes of this section that the fund, or a portion of it, ought to be freed from the restrictions with respect to expenditure of capital that apply to it.

(3) The condition in this subsection is that the charity trustees are satisfied that the purposes set out in the trusts to which the fund is subject could be carried out more effectively if the capital of the fund, or the relevant portion of the capital, could be expended as well as income accruing to it, rather than just such income.

(4) Where the market value of the fund exceeds £10,000 and the capital of the fund consists entirely of property given—

(a) by a particular individual,

(b) by a particular institution (by way of grant or otherwise), or

(c) by two or more individuals or institutions in pursuit of a common purpose,

subsections (5) to (11) of section 75A above apply in relation to the resolution and that gift or gifts as they apply in relation to a resolution under section 75A(3) and the gift or gifts mentioned in section 75A(1)(a).

(5) Where—

(a) the charity trustees have passed a resolution under subsection (2) above, and

(b) (in a case where section 75A(5) to (11) above apply in accordance with subsection (4) above) either—

(i) the charity trustees are notified by the Commission that it concurs with the resolution, or

(ii) the period of three months mentioned in section 75A(10) has elapsed without the Commission notifying them that it does not concur with the resolution,

the fund or portion may, by virtue of this section, be expended in carrying out the purposes set out in the trusts to which the fund is subject without regard to the restrictions mentioned in subsection (2).

(6) The fund or portion may be so expended as from such date as is specified for this purpose in the resolution.

(7) The Minister may by order amend subsection (4) above by substituting a different sum for the sum specified there.

(8) In this section—

(a) "available endowment fund" has the same meaning as in section 75 above,

(b) "market value" has the same meaning as in section 75A above, and

(c) the reference in subsection (4) to the giving of property by an individual includes his giving it under his will.".

[Mergers

75C Register of charity mergers

(1) The Commission shall establish and maintain a register of charity mergers.

(2) The register shall be kept by the Commission in such manner as it thinks fit.

(3) The register shall contain an entry in respect of every relevant charity merger which is notified to the Commission in accordance with subsections (6) to (9) and such procedures as it may determine.

(4) In this section "relevant charity merger" means—

(a) a merger of two or more charities in connection with which one of them ("the transferee") has transferred to it all the property of the other or others, each of which (a "transferor") ceases to exist, or is to cease to exist, on or after the transfer of its property to the transferee, or

(b) a merger of two or more charities ("transferors") in connection with which both or all of them cease to exist, or are to cease to exist, on or after the transfer of all of their property to a new charity ("the transferee").

(5) In the case of a merger involving the transfer of property of any charity which has both a permanent endowment and other property ("unrestricted property") and whose trusts do not contain provision for the termination of the charity, subsection (4)(a) or (b) applies in relation to any such charity as if—

(a) the reference to all of its property were a reference to all of its unrestricted property, and

(b) any reference to its ceasing to exist were omitted.

(6) A notification under subsection (3) above may be given in respect of a relevant charity merger at any time after—

(a) the transfer of property involved in the merger has taken place, or

(b) (if more than one transfer of property is so involved) the last of those transfers has taken place.

(7) If a vesting declaration is made in connection with a relevant charity merger, a notification under subsection (3) above must be given in respect of the merger once the transfer, or the last of the transfers, mentioned in subsection (6) above has taken place.

(8) A notification under subsection (3) is to be given by the charity trustees of the transferee and must—

(a) specify the transfer or transfers of property involved in the merger and the date or dates on which it or they took place;

(b) include a statement that appropriate arrangements have been made with respect to the discharge of any liabilities of the transferor charity or charities; and

(c) in the case of a notification required by subsection (7), set out the matters mentioned in subsection (9).

(9) The matters are—

(a) the fact that the vesting declaration in question has been made;

(b) the date when the declaration was made; and

(c) the date on which the vesting of title under the declaration took place by virtue of section 75E(2) below.

(10) In this section and section 75D—

(a) any reference to a transfer of property includes a transfer effected by a vesting declaration; and

(b) "vesting declaration" means a declaration to which section 75E(2) below applies.

(11) Nothing in this section or section 75E or 75F applies in a case where section 69K (amalgamation of CIOs) or 69M (transfer of CIO's undertaking) applies.]

[839A]

NOTES

Commencement: to be appointed.

Inserted, together with preceding cross-heading and ss 75D–75F, by the Charities Act 2006, s 44, as from a day to be appointed under s 79(2) of that Act, subject to transitional provisions in Sch 10, para 14 to that Act at **[2176]**.

[75D Register of charity mergers: supplementary

(1) Subsection (2) applies to the entry to be made in the register in respect of a relevant charity merger, as required by section 75C(3) above.

(2) The entry must—

(a) specify the date when the transfer or transfers of property involved in the merger took place,

(b) if a vesting declaration was made in connection with the merger, set out the matters mentioned in section 75C(9) above, and

(c) contain such other particulars of the merger as the Commission thinks fit.

(3) The register shall be open to public inspection at all reasonable times.

(4) Where any information contained in the register is not in documentary form, subsection (3) above shall be construed as requiring the information to be available for public inspection in legible form at all reasonable times.

(5) In this section—

"the register" means the register of charity mergers;

"relevant charity merger" has the same meaning as in section 75C.]

[839B]

NOTES

Commencement: to be appointed.

Inserted as noted to s 75C at **[839A]**.

[75E Pre-merger vesting declarations

(1) Subsection (2) below applies to a declaration which—

(a) is made by deed for the purposes of this section by the charity trustees of the transferor,

(b) is made in connection with a relevant charity merger, and

(c) is to the effect that (subject to subsections (3) and (4)) all of the transferor's property is to vest in the transferee on such date as is specified in the declaration ("the specified date").

(2) The declaration operates on the specified date to vest the legal title to all of the transferor's property in the transferee, without the need for any further document transferring it.

This is subject to subsections (3) and (4).

(3) Subsection (2) does not apply to—

(a) any land held by the transferor as security for money subject to the trusts of the transferor (other than land held on trust for securing debentures or debenture stock);

(b) any land held by the transferor under a lease or agreement which contains any covenant (however described) against assignment of the transferor's interest without the consent of some other person, unless that consent has been obtained before the specified date; or

(c) any shares, stock, annuity or other property which is only transferable in books kept by a company or other body or in a manner directed by or under any enactment.

(4) In its application to registered land within the meaning of the Land Registration Act 2002, subsection (2) has effect subject to section 27 of that Act (dispositions required to be registered).

(5) In this section "relevant charity merger" has the same meaning as in section 75C.

(6) In this section—

(a) any reference to the transferor, in relation to a relevant charity merger, is a reference to the transferor (or one of the transferors) within the meaning of section 75C above, and

(b) any reference to all of the transferor's property, where the transferor is a charity within section 75C(5), is a reference to all of the transferor's unrestricted property (within the meaning of that provision).

(7) In this section any reference to the transferee, in relation to a relevant charity merger, is a reference to—

(a) the transferee (within the meaning of section 75C above), if it is a company or other body corporate, and

(b) otherwise, to the charity trustees of the transferee (within the meaning of that section).]

[839C]

NOTES

Commencement: to be appointed.

Inserted as noted to s 75C at **[839A]**.

[75F Effect of registering charity merger on gifts to transferor

(1) This section applies where a relevant charity merger is registered in the register of charity mergers.

(2) Any gift which—

(a) is expressed as a gift to the transferor, and

(b) takes effect on or after the date of registration of the merger,

takes effect as a gift to the transferee, unless it is an excluded gift.

(3) A gift is an "excluded gift" if—

(a) the transferor is a charity within section 75C(5), and

(b) the gift is intended to be held subject to the trusts on which the whole or part of the charity's permanent endowment is held.

(4) In this section—

"relevant charity merger" has the same meaning as in section 75C; and

"transferor" and "transferee" have the same meanings as in section 75E.]

[839D]

NOTES

Commencement: to be appointed.

Inserted as noted to s 75C at **[839A]**.

Local charities

76 Local authority's index of local charities

(1) The council of a county [or county borough] or of a district or London borough and the Common Council of the City of London may maintain an index of local charities or of any class of local charities in the council's area, and may publish information contained in the index, or summaries or extracts taken from it.

(2) A council proposing to establish or maintaining under this section an index of local charities or of any class of local charities shall, on request, be supplied by [the Commission] free of charge with copies of such entries in the register of charities as are relevant to the index or with particulars of any changes in the entries of which copies have been supplied before; and [the Commission] may arrange that [it will] without further request supply a council with particulars of any such changes.

(3) An index maintained under this section shall be open to public inspection at all reasonable times.

(4) A council may employ any voluntary organisation as their agent for the purposes of this section, on such terms and within such limits (if any) or in such cases as they may agree; and for this purpose "voluntary organisation" means any body of which the activities are carried on otherwise than for profit, not being a public or local authority.

(5) A joint board discharging any of a council's functions shall have the same powers under this section as the council as respects local charities in the council's area which are established for purposes similar or complementary to any services provided by the board.

[840]

NOTES

Sub-s (1): words in square brackets inserted by the Local Government (Wales) Act 1994, s 66(6), Sch 16, para 101(1).

Sub-s (2): words in square brackets substituted by the Charities Act 2006, s 75(1), Sch 8, paras 96, 159, as from 27 February 2007.

Modification: this section and ss 77, 78 have effect as if the references to a council for any area included references to a National Park authority and as if the relevant Parks were in the authority's area; see the Environment Act 1995, s 70, Sch 9, para 15. As to the establishment of National Park authorities, see ss 63, 64 of that Act.

77 Reviews of local charities by local authority

(1) The council of a county [or county borough] or of a district or London borough and the Common Council of the City of London may, subject to the following provisions of this

section, initiate, and carry out in co-operation with the charity trustees, a review of the working of any group of local charities with the same or similar purposes in the council's area, and may make to [the Commission] such report on the review and such recommendations arising from it as the council after consultation with the trustees think fit.

(2) A council having power to initiate reviews under this section may co-operate with other persons in any review by them of the working of local charities in the council's area (with or without other charities), or may join with other persons in initiating and carrying out such a review.

(3) No review initiated by a council under this section shall extend to any charity without the consent of the charity trustees, nor to any ecclesiastical charity.

(4) No review initiated under this section by the council of a district shall extend to the working in any county of a local charity established for purposes similar or complementary to any services provided by county councils unless the review so extends with the consent of the council of that county.

[(4A) Subsection (4) above does not apply in relation to Wales.]

(5) Subsections (4) and (5) of section 76 above shall apply for the purposes of this section as they apply for the purposes of that section.

[841]

NOTES

Sub-s (1): words in first pair of square brackets inserted by the Local Government (Wales) Act 1994, s 66(6), Sch 16, para 101(2); words in second pair of square brackets substituted by the Charities Act 2006, s 75(1), Sch 8, paras 96, 160, as from 27 February 2007.

Sub-s (4A): inserted by the Local Government (Wales) Act 1994, s 66(6), Sch 16, para 101(2). Modified as noted to s 76 at **[840]**.

78 Co-operation between charities, and between charities and local authorities

(1) Any local council and any joint board discharging any functions of such a council—

(a) may make, with any charity established for purposes similar or complementary to services provided by the council or board, arrangements for co-ordinating the activities of the council or board and those of the charity in the interests of persons who may benefit from those services or from the charity; and

(b) shall be at liberty to disclose to any such charity in the interests of those persons any information obtained in connection with the services provided by the council or board, whether or not arrangements have been made with the charity under this subsection.

In this subsection "local council" means[, in relation to England,] the council of a county, or of a district, London borough, [or parish], and includes also the Common Council of the City of London and the Council of the Isles of Scilly [and, in relation to Wales, the council of a county, county borough or community].

(2) Charity trustees shall, notwithstanding anything in the trusts of the charity, have power by virtue of this subsection to do all or any of the following things, where it appears to them likely to promote or make more effective the work of the charity, and may defray the expense of so doing out of any income or money applicable as income of the charity, that is to say—

(a) they may co-operate in any review undertaken under section 77 above or otherwise of the working of charities or any class of charities;

(b) they may make arrangements with an authority acting under subsection (1) above or with another charity for co-ordinating their activities and those of the authority or of the other charity;

(c) they may publish information of other charities with a view to bringing them to the notice of those for whose benefit they are intended.

[842]

NOTES

Sub-s (1): words in first pair of square brackets inserted, words in second pair of square brackets substituted, and words in final pairs of square brackets added by the Local Government (Wales) Act 1994, s 66(6), Sch 16, para 101(3).

Modified as noted to s 76 at **[840]**.

79 Parochial charities

(1) Where trustees hold any property for the purposes of a public recreation ground, or of allotments (whether under inclosure Acts or otherwise), for the benefit of inhabitants of a parish having a parish council, or for other charitable purposes connected with such a parish, except for an ecclesiastical charity, they may with the approval of [the Commission] and with the consent of the parish council transfer the property to the parish council or to persons appointed by the parish council; and the council or their appointees shall hold the property on the same trusts and subject to the same conditions as the trustees did.

This subsection shall apply to property held for any public purposes as it applies to property held for charitable purposes.

(2) Where the charity trustees of a parochial charity in a parish, not being an ecclesiastical charity nor a charity founded within the preceding forty years, do not include persons elected by the local government electors, ratepayers or inhabitants of the parish or appointed by the parish council or parish meeting, the parish council or parish meeting may appoint additional charity trustees, to such number as [the Commission] may allow; and if there is a sole charity trustee not elected or appointed as aforesaid of any such charity, the number of the charity trustees may, with the approval of [the Commission], be increased to three of whom one may be nominated by the person holding the office of the sole trustee and one by the parish council or parish meeting.

(3) Where, under the trusts of a charity other than an ecclesiastical charity, the inhabitants of a rural parish (whether in vestry or not) or a select vestry were formerly (in 1894) entitled to appoint charity trustees for, or trustees or beneficiaries of, the charity, then—

(a) in a parish having a parish council, the appointment shall be made by the parish council or, in the case of beneficiaries, by persons appointed by the parish council; and

(b) in a parish not having a parish council, the appointment shall be made by the parish meeting.

(4) Where overseers as such or, except in the case of an ecclesiastical charity, churchwardens as such were formerly (in 1894) charity trustees of or trustees for a parochial charity in a rural parish, either alone or jointly with other persons, then instead of the former overseer or church warden trustees there shall be trustees (to a number not greater than that of the former overseer or churchwarden trustees) appointed by the parish council or, if there is no parish council, by the parish meeting.

(5) Where, outside Greater London (other than the outer London boroughs), overseers of a parish as such were formerly (in 1927) charity trustees of or trustees for any charity, either alone or jointly with other persons, then instead of the former overseer trustees there shall be trustees (to a number not greater than that of the former overseer trustees) appointed by the parish council or, if there is no parish council, by the parish meeting.

(6) In the case of an urban parish existing immediately before the passing of the Local Government Act 1972 which after 1st April 1974 is not comprised in a parish, the power of appointment under subsection (5) above shall be exercisable by the district council.

(7) In the application of the foregoing provisions of this section to Wales—

(a) for references in subsections (1) and (2) to a parish or a parish council there shall be substituted respectively references to a community or a community council;

(b) for references in subsections (3)(a) and (b) to a parish, a parish council or a parish meeting there shall be substituted respectively references to a community, a community council or the [council of the county or (as the case may be) county borough];

(c) for references in subsections (4) and (5) to a parish council or a parish meeting there shall be substituted respectively references to a community council or the [council of the county or (as the case may be) county borough].

(8) Any appointment of a charity trustee or trustee for a charity which is made by virtue of this section shall be for a term of four years, and a retiring trustee shall be eligible for re-appointment but—

(a) on an appointment under subsection (2) above, where no previous appointments have been made by virtue of that subsection or of the corresponding provision of the Local Government Act 1894 or the Charities Act 1960, and more than one trustee is appointed, half of those appointed (or as nearly as may be) shall be appointed for a term of two years; and

(b) an appointment made to fill a casual vacancy shall be for the remainder of the term of the previous appointment.

[(9) This section shall not affect the trusteeship, control or management of any [foundation or voluntary school within the meaning of the School Standards and Framework Act 1998.]]

(10) The provisions of this section shall not extend to the Isles of Scilly, and shall have effect subject to any order (including any future order) made under any enactment relating to local government with respect to local government areas or the powers of local authorities.

(11) In this section the expression "formerly (in 1894)" relates to the period immediately before the passing of the Local Government Act 1894, and the expression "formerly (in 1927)" to the period immediately before 1st April 1927; and the word "former" shall be construed accordingly.

[843]

NOTES

Sub-ss (1), (2): words in square brackets substituted by the Charities Act 2006, s 75(1), Sch 8, paras 96, 161, as from 27 February 2007.

Sub-s (7): words in square brackets in paras (b), (c) substituted by the Local Government (Wales) Act 1994, s 66(6), Sch 16, para 101(4).

Sub-s (9): substituted by the Education Act 1996, s 582(1), Sch 37, Pt I, para 119; words in square brackets substituted by the School Standards and Framework Act 1998, s 140(1), Sch 30, para 49.

Scottish charities

80 Supervision by [Commission] of certain Scottish charities

(1) The following provisions of this Act, namely—

(a) sections 8 and 9,

(b) section 18 (except subsection (2)(ii)),

(c) section 19,

[(d) section 31A,]

shall have effect in relation to any recognised body which is managed or controlled wholly or mainly in or from England or Wales as they have effect in relation to a charity.

(2) Where—

(a) a recognised body is managed or controlled wholly or mainly in or from Scotland, but

(b) any person in England and Wales holds any property on behalf of the body or of any person concerned in its management or control,

then, if [the Commission is satisfied] as to the matters mentioned in subsection (3) below, [it may make] an order requiring the person holding the property not to part with it without [the Commission's approval].

(3) The matters referred to in subsection (2) above are—

(a) that there has been any misconduct or mismanagement in the administration of the body; and

(b) that it is necessary or desirable to make an order under that subsection for the purpose of protecting the property of the body or securing a proper application of such property for the purposes of the body;

and the reference in that subsection to [the Commission] being satisfied as to those matters is a reference to [the Commission being] so satisfied on the basis of such information as may be [supplied to it] by the [Scottish Charity Regulator].

(4) Where—

(a) any person in England and Wales holds any property on behalf of a recognised body or of any person concerned in the management or control of such a body, and

(b) [the Commission is satisfied] (whether on the basis of such information as may be [supplied to it] by the [Scottish Charity Regulator] or otherwise)—

(i) that there has been any misconduct or mismanagement in the administration of the body, and

(ii) that it is necessary or desirable to make an order under this subsection for the purpose of protecting the property of the body or securing a proper application of such property for the purposes of the body,

[the Commission] may by order vest the property in such recognised body or charity as is specified in the order in accordance with subsection (5) below, or require any persons in whom the property is vested to transfer it to any such body or charity, or appoint any person to transfer the property to any such body or charity.

(5) The [Commission] may specify in an order under subsection (4) above such other recognised body or such charity as [it considers] appropriate, being a body or charity whose purposes are, in the opinion of the [Commission], as similar in character to those of the body referred to in paragraph (a) of that subsection as is reasonably practicable; but the [Commission] shall not so specify any body or charity unless [it has received]—

(a) from the persons concerned in the management or control of the body, or

(b) from the charity trustees of the charity,

as the case may be, written confirmation that they are willing to accept the property.

(6) In this section "recognised body" [means a body entered in the Scottish Charity Register].

[844]

NOTES

Section heading: word in square brackets substituted by the Charities Act 2006, s 75(1), Sch 8, paras 96, 162(1), (7), as from 27 February 2007.

Sub-s (1): paras (c), (d) substituted for existing para (c) (in italics) by the Charities Act 2006, s 75(1), Sch 8, paras 96, 162(1), (2), as from 27 February 2007, except in so far as new para (c) is inserted. New para (c) reads as follows—

"(c) sections 19 to 19C, and"

Sub-ss (2), (5): words in square brackets substituted by the Charities Act 2006, s 75(1), Sch 8, paras 96, 162(1), (3), (6), as from 27 February 2007.

Sub-s (3): words in first, second and third pairs of square brackets substituted by the Charities Act 2006, s 75(1), Sch 8, paras 96, 162(1), (4), as from 27 February 2007; words in fourth pair of square brackets substituted by the Charities and Trustee Investment (Scotland) Act 2005 (Consequential Provisions and Modifications) Order 2006, SI 2006/242, art 5, Schedule, Pt 1, para 6(1), (3)(a).

Sub-s (4): words in first, second and fourth pairs of square brackets substituted by the Charities Act 2006, s 75(1), Sch 8, paras 96, 162(1), (5), as from 27 February 2007; words in third pair of square brackets substituted by SI 2006/242, art 5, Schedule, Pt 1, para 6(1), (3)(a).

Sub-s (6): words in square brackets substituted by SI 2006/242, art 5, Schedule, Pt 1, para 6(1), (3)(b).

Administrative provisions about charities

81 Manner of giving notice of charity meetings, etc

(1) All notices which are required or authorised by the trusts of a charity to be given to a charity trustee, member or subscriber may be sent by post, and, if sent by post, may be addressed to any address given as his in the list of charity trustees, members or subscribers for the time being in use at the office or principal office of the charity.

(2) Where any such notice required to be given as aforesaid is given by post, it shall be deemed to have been given by the time at which the letter containing it would be delivered in the ordinary course of post.

(3) No notice required to be given as aforesaid of any meeting or election need be given to any charity trustee, member or subscriber, if in the list above mentioned he has no address in the United Kingdom.

[845]

82 Manner of executing instruments

(1) Charity trustees may, subject to the trusts of the charity, confer on any of their body (not being less than two in number) a general authority, or an authority limited in such manner as the trustees think fit, to execute in the names and on behalf of the trustees assurances or other deeds or instruments for giving effect to transactions to which the trustees are a party; and any deed or instrument executed in pursuance of an authority so given shall be of the same effect as if executed by the whole body.

(2) An authority under subsection (1) above—

(a) shall suffice for any deed or instrument if it is given in writing or by resolution of a meeting of the trustees, notwithstanding the want of any formality that would be required in giving an authority apart from that subsection;

(b) may be given so as to make the powers conferred exercisable by any of the trustees, or may be restricted to named persons or in any other way;

(c) subject to any such restriction, and until it is revoked, shall, notwithstanding any change in the charity trustees, have effect as a continuing authority given by the charity trustees from time to time of the charity and exercisable by such trustees.

(3) In any authority under this section to execute a deed or instrument in the names and on behalf of charity trustees there shall, unless the contrary intention appears, be implied authority also to execute it for them in the name and on behalf of the official custodian or of any other person, in any case in which the charity trustees could do so.

(4) Where a deed or instrument purports to be executed in pursuance of this section, then in favour of a person who (then or afterwards) in good faith acquires for money or money's worth an interest in or charge on property or the benefit of any covenant or agreement expressed to be entered into by the charity trustees, it shall be conclusively presumed to have been duly executed by virtue of this section.

(5) The powers conferred by this section shall be in addition to and not in derogation of any other powers.

[846]

83 Transfer and evidence of title to property vested in trustees

(1) Where, under the trusts of a charity, trustees of property held for the purposes of the charity may be appointed or discharged by resolution of a meeting of the charity trustees, members or other persons, a memorandum declaring a trustee to have been so appointed or discharged shall be sufficient evidence of that fact if the memorandum is signed either at the meeting by the person presiding or in some other manner directed by the meeting and is attested by two persons present at the meeting.

(2) A memorandum evidencing the appointment or discharge of a trustee under subsection (1) above, if executed as a deed, shall have the like operation under section 40 of the Trustee Act 1925 (which relates to vesting declarations as respects trust property in deeds appointing or discharging trustees) as if the appointment or discharge were effected by the deed.

(3) For the purposes of this section, where a document purports to have been signed and attested as mentioned in subsection (1) above, then on proof (whether by evidence or as a matter of presumption) of the signature the document shall be presumed to have been so signed and attested, unless the contrary is shown.

(4) This section shall apply to a memorandum made at any time, except that subsection (2) shall apply only to those made after the commencement of the Charities Act 1960.

(5) This section shall apply in relation to any institution to which the Literary and Scientific Institutions Act 1854 applies as it applies in relation to a charity.

[847]

PART X
SUPPLEMENTARY

84 Supply by [Commission] of copies of documents open to public inspection

[The Commission] shall, at the request of any person, furnish him with copies of, or extracts from, any document in [the Commission's possession] which is for the time being open to inspection under Parts II to VI of this Act [or section 75D].

[848]

NOTES

Section heading: word in square brackets substituted by the Charities Act 2006, s 75(1), Sch 8, paras 96, 163(1), (5), as from 27 February 2007.

Words in first and second pairs of square brackets substituted by the Charities Act 2006, s 75(1), Sch 8, paras 96, 163(1)–(3), as from 27 February 2007, and words in third pair of square brackets added as from a day to be appointed under s 79(2) of that Act, by s 75(1) of, and Sch 8, paras 96, 163(1), (4) to, that Act.

85 Fees and other amounts payable to [Commission]

(1) The [Minister] may by regulations require the payment to [the Commission] of such fees as may be prescribed by the regulations in respect of—

(a) the discharge by [the Commission] of such functions under the enactments relating to charities as may be so prescribed;

(b) the inspection of the register of charities or of other material [kept by the Commission] under those enactments, or the furnishing of copies of or extracts from documents so kept.

(2) Regulations under this section may—

(a) confer, or provide for the conferring of, exemptions from liability to pay a prescribed fee;

(b) provide for the remission or refunding of a prescribed fee (in whole or in part) in circumstances prescribed by the regulations.

(3) Any regulations under this section which require the payment of a fee in respect of any matter for which no fee was previously payable shall not be made unless a draft of the regulations has been laid before and approved by a resolution of each House of Parliament.

(4) [The Commission] may impose charges of such amounts as [it considers] reasonable in respect of the supply of any publications produced [by it].

(5) Any fees and other payments received by [the Commission] by virtue of this section shall be paid into the Consolidated Fund.

[849]

NOTES

Section heading: word in square brackets substituted by the Charities Act 2006, s 75(1), Sch 8, paras 96, 164(1), (5), as from 27 February 2007.

Sub-s (1): word in first pair of square brackets substituted by the Transfer of Functions (Third Sector, Communities and Equality) Order 2006, SI 2006/2951, art 6, Schedule, para 4(x); words in second, third and fourth pairs of square brackets substituted by the Charities Act 2006, s 75(1), Sch 8, paras 96, 164(1), (2), as from 27 February 2007.

Sub-ss (4), (5): words in square brackets substituted by the Charities Act 2006, s 75(1), Sch 8, paras 96, 164(1), (3), (4), as from 27 February 2007.

Regulations: by virtue of the Interpretation Act 1978, s 17(2)(b), the Charity Commissioners' Fees (Copies and Extracts) Regulations 1992, SI 1992/2986, have effect as if made under this section.

86 Regulations and orders

(1) Any regulations or order of the [Minister] under this Act—

(a) shall be made by statutory instrument; and

(b) (subject to subsection (2) below) shall be subject to annulment in pursuance of a resolution of either House of Parliament.

(2) Subsection (1)(b) above does not apply—

(a) to an order under section 17(2), [73F(6)]... or 99(2) [or paragraph 6 of Schedule 1C]; [or]

[(aa) to regulations under section 69N above; and no regulations shall be made under that section unless a draft of the regulations has been laid before and approved by a resolution of each House of Parliament; or]

(b) ...

(c) to any regulations to which section 85(3) applies.

(3) Any regulations of the [Minister] or [the Commission] and any order of the [Minister] under this Act may make—

(a) different provision for different cases; and

(b) such supplemental, incidental, consequential or transitional provision or savings as the [Minister] or, as the case may be, [the Commission considers] appropriate.

(4) Before making any regulations under section 42, 44[, 45, 69N or 69Q] above [or Schedule 5A] the [Minister] shall consult such persons or bodies of persons as he considers appropriate.

[850]

NOTES

Sub-s (1): word in square brackets substituted by the Transfer of Functions (Third Sector, Communities and Equality) Order 2006, SI 2006/2951, art 6, Schedule, para 4(y).

Sub-s (2): number in first pair of square brackets in para (a) and the whole of para (aa) inserted by the Charities Act 2006, ss 34, 75(1), Sch 7, Pt 2, paras 3, 6(a), Sch 8, paras 96, 165(1), (2)(a), as from 27 February 2007, and words in second pair of square brackets in para (a) inserted as from a day to be appointed under s 79(2) of that Act, by s 75(1) of, and Sch 8, paras 96, 165(1), (2)(b) to, that Act; words omitted repealed in relation to England and Wales by the Trustee Act 2000, s 40(1), (3), Sch 2, Pt I, para 2(2)(a), (3), Sch 4, Pt I and in relation to Scotland by the Charities and Trustee Investment (Scotland) Act 2005, s 95, Sch 3, para 9; word in third pair of square brackets in para (a) inserted by the Trustee Act 2000, s 40(1), (3), Sch 2, Pt I, para 2(2), (3), Sch 4, Pt I.

Sub-s (3): words in first, third and fourth pairs of square brackets substituted by SI 2006/2951, art 6, Schedule, para 4(y); words in second and fifth pairs of square brackets substituted by the Charities Act 2006, s 75(1), Sch 8, paras 96, 165(1), (3), as from 27 February 2007.

Sub-s (4): words in first pair of square brackets substituted and words in second pair of square brackets inserted by the Charities Act 2006, ss 34, 75(1), Sch 7, Pt 2, paras 3, 6(b), Sch 8, paras 96, 165(1), (4), as from 27 February 2007; word in third pair of square brackets substituted by SI 2006/2951, art 6, Schedule, para 4(y).

Orders: the Charities Act 1993 (Commencement and Transitional Provisions) Order 1995, SI 1995/2695.

[86A Consultation by Commission before exercising powers in relation to exempt charity

Before exercising in relation to an exempt charity any specific power exercisable by it in relation to the charity, the Commission must consult the charity's principal regulator.]

[850A]

NOTES

Commencement: to be appointed.

Inserted by the Charities Act 2006, s 14, as from a day to be appointed under s 79(2) of that Act.

87 Enforcement of requirements by order of [Commission]

(1) If a person fails to comply with any requirement imposed by or under this Act then (subject to subsection (2) below) [the Commission] may by order give him such directions as [it considers] appropriate for securing that the default is made good.

(2) Subsection (1) above does not apply to any such requirement if—

(a) a person who fails to comply with, or is persistently in default in relation to, the requirement is liable to any criminal penalty; or

(b) the requirement is imposed—

(i) by an order of [the Commission] to which section 88 below applies, or

(ii) by a direction of [the Commission] to which that section applies by virtue of section 90(2) below.

[851]

NOTES

Section heading: word in square brackets substituted by the Charities Act 2006, s 75(1), Sch 8, paras 96, 166(1), (4), as from 27 February 2007.

Words in square brackets substituted by the Charities Act 2006, s 75(1), Sch 8, paras 96, 166(1)–(3), as from 27 February 2007.

88 Enforcement of orders of [Commission]

A person guilty of disobedience—

(*a*) *to an order of the Commissioners under section 9(1), 44(2), 61, 73 or 80 above; or*

(b) to an order of [the Commission] under section 16 or 18 above requiring a transfer of property or payment to be called for or made; or

(c) to an order of [the Commission] requiring a default under this Act to be made good;

may on the application of [the Commission to] the High Court be dealt with as for disobedience to an order of the High Court.

[852]

NOTES

Section heading: word in square brackets substituted by the Charities Act 2006, s 75(1), Sch 8, paras 96, 167(1), (5), as from 27 February 2007.

Words in square brackets substituted by the Charities Act 2006, s 75(1), Sch 8, paras 96, 167(1), (3), (4), as from 27 February 2007; para (a) substituted as follows by s 75(1) of, and Sch 8, paras 96, 167(1), (2) to, that Act, as from a day to be appointed under s 79(2) of that Act—

"(a) to an order of the Commission under section 9(1), 19A, 19B, 44(2), 61, 73, 73C or 80 above; or".

89 Other provisions as to orders of [Commission]

(1) Any order made by [the Commission] under this Act may include such incidental or supplementary provisions as [the Commission thinks] expedient for carrying into effect the objects of the orders, and where [the Commission exercises] any jurisdiction to make such an order on an application or reference [to it, it may] insert any such provisions in the order notwithstanding that the application or reference does not propose their insertion.

(2) Where [the Commission makes] an order under this Act, then (without prejudice to the requirements of this Act where the order is subject to appeal) [the Commission may itself] give such public notice as [it thinks fit] of the making or contents of the order, or may require it to be given by any person on whose application the order is made or by any charity affected by the order.

(3) [The Commission] at any time within twelve months after [it has] made an order under any provision of this Act other than section 61 if [it is] satisfied that the order was made by mistake or on misrepresentation or otherwise than in conformity with this Act, may with or without any application or reference [to it] discharge the order in whole or in part, and subject or not to any savings or other transitional provisions.

(4) Except for the purposes of subsection (3) above or of an appeal under this Act, an order made by [the Commission] under this Act shall be deemed to have been duly and formally made and not be called in question on the ground only of irregularity or informality, but (subject to any further order) have effect according to its tenor.

[(5) Any order made by the Commission under any provision of this Act may be varied or revoked by a subsequent order so made.]

[853]

NOTES

Section heading: word in square brackets substituted by the Charities Act 2006, s 75(1), Sch 8, paras 96, 168(1), (7), as from 27 February 2007.

Sub-ss (1)–(4): words in square brackets substituted by the Charities Act 2006, s 75(1), Sch 8, paras 96, 168(1)–(5), as from 27 February 2007.

Sub-s (5): added by the Charities Act 2006, s 75(1), Sch 8, paras 96, 168(1), (6), as from 27 February 2007.

90 Directions of [the Commission]

(1) Any direction given by [the Commission] under any provision contained in this Act—

(a) may be varied or revoked by a further direction given under that provision; and

(b) shall be given in writing.

(2) Sections 88 and 89(1), (2) and (4) above shall apply to any such directions as they apply to an order of [the Commission].

(3) In subsection (1) above the reference to [the Commission] includes, in relation to a direction under subsection (3) of section 8 above, a reference to any person conducting an inquiry under that section.

(4) Nothing in this section shall be read as applying to any directions contained in an order made by [the Commission] under section 87(1) above.

[854]

NOTES

Section heading: words in square brackets substituted by the Charities Act 2006, s 75(1), Sch 8, paras 96, 169, as from 27 February 2007.

Words in square brackets substituted by the Charities Act 2006, s 75(1), Sch 8, paras 96, 169, as from 27 February 2007.

91 Service of orders and directions

(1) This section applies to any order or direction made or given by [the Commission] under this Act.

(2) An order or direction to which this section applies may be served on a person (other than a body corporate)—

(a) by delivering it to that person;
(b) by leaving it at his last known address in the United Kingdom; or
(c) by sending it by post to him at that address.

(3) An order or direction to which this section applies may be served on a body corporate by delivering it or sending it by post—

(a) to the registered or principal office of the body in the United Kingdom, or
(b) if it has no such office in the United Kingdom, to any place in the United Kingdom where it carries on business or conducts its activities (as the case may be).

(4) Any such order or direction may also be served on a person (including a body corporate) by sending it by post to that person at an address notified by that person to [the Commission] for the purposes of this subsection.

(5) In this section any reference to [the Commission] includes, in relation to a direction given under subsection (3) of section 8 above, a reference to any person conducting an inquiry under that section.

[855]

NOTES

Sub-ss (1), (4), (5): words in square brackets substituted by the Charities Act 2006, s 75(1), Sch 8, paras 96, 170, as from 27 February 2007.

92 Appeals from Commissioners

(1) *Provision shall be made by rules of court for regulating appeals to the High Court under this Act against orders or decisions of the Commissioners.*

(2) *On such an appeal the Attorney General shall be entitled to appear and be heard, and such other persons as the rules allow or as the court may direct.*

[856]

NOTES

Repealed by the Charities Act 2006, s 75(1), (2), Sch 8, paras 96, 171, Sch 9, as from a day to be appointed under s 79(2) of that Act, subject to savings in Sch 10, para 18 to that Act at **[2176]**.

93 Miscellaneous provisions as to evidence

(1) Where, in any proceedings to recover or compel payment of any rentcharge or other periodical payment claimed by or on behalf of a charity out of land or of the rents, profits or other income of land, otherwise than as rent incident to a reversion, it is shown that the rentcharge or other periodical payment has at any time been paid for twelve consecutive years to or for the benefit of the charity, that shall be prima facie evidence of the perpetual liability to it of the land or income, and no proof of its origin shall be necessary.

(2) In any proceedings, the following documents, that is to say,—

(a) the printed copies of the reports of the Commissioners for enquiring concerning charities, 1818 to 1837, who were appointed under the Act 58 Geo 3 c 91 and subsequent Acts; and
(b) the printed copies of the reports which were made for various counties and county boroughs to the Charity Commissioners by their assistant commissioners and presented to the House of Commons as returns to orders of various dates beginning with 8th December 1890, and ending with 9th September 1909,

shall be admissible as evidence of the documents and facts stated in them.

[(3) Evidence of any order, certificate or other document issued by the Commission may be given by means of a copy which it retained, or which is taken from a copy so retained, and evidence of an entry in any register kept by it may be given by means of a copy of the entry, if (in each case) the copy is certified in accordance with subsection (4).

(4) The copy shall be certified to be a true copy by any member of the staff of the Commission generally or specially authorised by the Commission to act for that purpose.

(5) A document purporting to be such a copy shall be received in evidence without proof of the official position, authority or handwriting of the person certifying it.

(6) In subsection (3) above "the Commission" includes the Charity Commissioners for England and Wales.]

[857]

NOTES

Sub-ss (3)–(6): substituted, for sub-s (3) as originally enacted, by the Charities Act 2006, s 75(1), Sch 8, paras 96, 172, as from 27 February 2007.

Act 58 Geo 3 c 91: i e the Inquiry Concerning Charities Act 1818: repealed by the Statute Law Revision Act 1873.

94 Restriction on institution of proceedings for certain offences

(1) No proceedings for an offence under this Act to which this section applies shall be instituted except by or with the consent of the Director of Public Prosecutions.

(2) This section applies to any offence under—

(a) section 5;
(b) section 11;
(c) section 18(14);
(d) section 49; or
(e) section 73(1).

[858]

95 Offences by bodies corporate

Where any offence under this Act is committed by a body corporate and is proved to have been committed with the consent or connivance of, or to be attributable to any neglect on the part of, any director, manager, secretary or other similar officer of the body corporate, or any person who was purporting to act in any such capacity, he as well as the body corporate shall be guilty of that offence and shall be liable to be proceeded against and punished accordingly.

In relation to a body corporate whose affairs are managed by its members, "director" means a member of the body corporate.

[859]

96 Construction of references to a "charity" or to particular classes of charity

(1) In this Act, except in so far as the context otherwise requires—

"charity" means any institution, corporate or not, which is established for charitable purposes and is subject to the control of the High Court in the exercise of the court's jurisdiction with respect to charities;

"ecclesiastical charity" has the same meaning as in the Local Government Act 1894;

"exempt charity" means (*subject to section 24(8) above*) a charity comprised in Schedule 2 to this Act;

"local charity" means, in relation to any area, a charity established for purposes which are by their nature or by the trusts of the charity directed wholly or mainly to the benefit of that area or of part of it;

"parochial charity" means, in relation to any parish or (in Wales) community, a charity the benefits of which are, or the separate distribution of the benefits of which is, confined to inhabitants of the parish or community, or of a single ancient ecclesiastical parish which included that parish or community or part of it, or of an area consisting of that parish or community with not more than four neighbouring parishes or communities.

(2) The expression "charity" is not in this Act applicable—

(a) to any ecclesiastical corporation (that is to say, any corporation in the Church of England, whether sole or aggregate, which is established for spiritual purposes) in respect of the corporate property of the corporation, except to a corporation aggregate having some purposes which are not ecclesiastical in respect of its corporate property held for those purposes; or

(b) to any Diocesan Board of Finance [(or any subsidiary thereof)] within the meaning of the Endowments and Glebe Measure 1976 for any diocese in respect of the diocesan glebe land of that diocese within the meaning of that Measure; or

(c) to any trust of property for purposes for which the property has been consecrated.

(3) A charity shall be deemed for the purposes of this Act to have a permanent endowment unless all property held for the purposes of the charity may be expended for those purposes without distinction between capital and income, and in this Act "permanent endowment" means, in relation to any charity, property held subject to a restriction on its being expended for the purposes of the charity.

(4) References in this Act to a charity whose income from all sources does not in aggregate amount to more than a specified amount shall be construed—

(a) by reference to the gross revenues of the charity, or

(b) if the Commissioners so determine, by reference to the amount which they estimate to be the likely amount of those revenues,

but without (in either case) bringing into account anything for the yearly value of land occupied by the charity apart from the pecuniary income (if any) received from that land; and any question as to the application of any such reference to a charity shall be determined by the Commissioners, whose decision shall be final.

(5) [The Commission] may direct that for all or any of the purposes of this Act an institution established for any special purposes of or in connection with a charity (being charitable purposes) shall be treated as forming part of that charity or as forming a distinct charity.

[(6) [The Commission] may direct that for all or any of the purposes of this Act two or more charities having the same charity trustees shall be treated as a single charity.]

[860]

NOTES

Sub-s (1): definition "charity" substituted as follows—

""charity" has the meaning given by section 1(1) of the Charities Act 2006;", and

in definition "exempt charity" words in italics repealed by the Charities Act 2006, s 75(1), (2), Sch 8, paras 96, 173(1), (2), (3)(a), Sch 9, as from a day to be appointed under s 79(2) of that Act.

Sub-s (2): in para (b) words in square brackets inserted by the Church of England (Miscellaneous Provisions) Measure 2000, s 11, subject to transitional provisions in s 19 of, and Sch 7 to, that Measure.

Sub-s (4): repealed by the Charities Act 2006, s 75(1), (2), Sch 8, paras 96, 173(1), (3)(b), Sch 9, as from a day to be appointed under s 79(2) of that Act.

Sub-s (5): words in square brackets substituted by the Charities Act 2006, s 75(1), Sch 8, paras 96, 173(1), (4), as from 27 February 2007.

Sub-s (6): added by the Charities (Amendment) Act 1995, s 1; words in square brackets substituted by the Charities Act 2006, s 75(1), Sch 8, paras 96, 173(1), (4), as from 27 February 2007.

97 General interpretation

(1) In this Act, except in so far as the context otherwise requires—

"charitable purposes" means purposes which are exclusively *charitable according to the law of England and Wales;*

"charity trustees" means the persons having the general control and management of the administration of a charity;

["CIO" means charitable incorporated organisation;]

["the Commission" means the Charity Commission;]

"company" means a company formed and registered under the Companies Act 1985 or to which the provisions of that Act apply as they apply to such a company;

"the court" means the High Court and, within the limits of its jurisdiction, any other court in England and Wales having a jurisdiction in respect of charities concurrent (within any limit of area or amount) with that of the High Court, and includes any judge or officer of the court exercising the jurisdiction of the court;

"financial year"—

(a) in relation to a charity which is a company, shall be construed in accordance with section 223 of the Companies Act 1985; and

(b) in relation to any other charity, shall be construed in accordance with regulations made by virtue of section 42(2) above;

but this definition is subject to the transitional provisions in section 99(4) below and Part II of Schedule 8 to this Act;

"gross income", in relation to charity, means its gross recorded income from all sources including special trusts;

"independent examiner", in relation to a charity, means such a person as is mentioned in section 43(3)(a) above;

"institution" [means an institution whether incorporated or not, and] includes any trust or undertaking;

["members", in relation to a charity with a body of members distinct from the charity trustees, means any of those members;]

["the Minister" means the Minister for the Cabinet Office;]

"the official custodian" means the official custodian for charities;

"permanent endowment" shall be construed in accordance with section 96(3) above;

["principal regulator", in relation to an exempt charity, means the charity's principal regulator within the meaning of section 13 of the Charities Act 2006;]

"the register" means the register of charities kept under section 3 above and "registered" shall be construed accordingly;

"special trust" means property which is held and administered by or on behalf of a charity for any special purposes of the charity, and is so held and administered on separate trusts relating only to that property but a special trust shall not, by itself, constitute a charity for the purposes of Part VI of this Act;

["the Tribunal" means the Charity Tribunal;]

"trusts" in relation to a charity, means the provisions establishing it as a charity and regulating its purposes and administration, whether those provisions take effect by way of trust or not, and in relation to other institutions has a corresponding meaning.

(2) In this Act, except in so far as the context otherwise requires, "document" includes information recorded in any form, and, in relation to information recorded otherwise than in legible form—

(a) any reference to its production shall be construed as a reference to the furnishing of a copy of it in legible form; and

(b) any reference to the furnishing of a copy of, or extract from, it shall accordingly be construed as a reference to the furnishing of a copy of, or extract from, it in legible form.

(3) No vesting or transfer of any property in pursuance of any provision of [Part 4, 7, 8A or 9] of this Act shall operate as a breach of a covenant or condition against alienation or give rise to a forfeiture.

[861]

NOTES

Sub-s (1): in definition "charitable purpose" for the words in italics there are substituted the words "charitable purposes as defined by section 2(1) of the Charities Act 2006;" and definition "CIO" inserted by the Charities Act 2006, ss 34, 75(1), Sch 7, Pt 2, paras 3, 7, Sch 8, paras 96, 174(a), as from a day to be appointed under s 79(2) of that Act, and definitions "members", "the Minister", "principal regulator" and "the Tribunal" inserted as from 8 November 2006, definition "the Commissioners" substituted, as from 27 February 2007, and in definition "institution" words in square brackets inserted, as from 27 February 2007, by s 75(1) of, and Sch 8, paras 96, 174(b)–(d) to, that Act.

Sub-s (3): words in square brackets substituted, as from 27 February 2007 except in so far as they refer to Part 8A, for the words "Part IV or IX" by the Charities Act 2006, s 75(1), Sch 8, paras 96, 175.

98 Consequential amendments and repeals

(1) The enactments mentioned in Schedule 6 to this Act shall be amended as provided in that Schedule.

(2) The enactments mentioned in Schedule 7 to this Act are hereby repealed to the extent specified in the third column of the Schedule.

[862]–[863]

99 (*Repealed by the Statute Law (Repeals) Act 2004.*)

100 Short title and extent

(1) This Act may be cited as the Charities Act 1993.

(2) Subject to subsection (3) to (6) below, this Act extends only to England and Wales.

(3) [Sections 10 to 10C] above and this section extend to the whole of the United Kingdom.

(4) Section 15(2) [and sections 24 to 25A extend] also to Northern Ireland.

(5) ....

(6) The amendments in Schedule 6 and the repeals in Schedule 7 have the same extent as the enactments to which they refer and section 98 above extends accordingly.

[864]–[865]

NOTES

Sub-s (3): words in square brackets substituted, as from 27 February 2007 except in so far as they refer to s 10B, for the words "Section 10" by the Charities Act 2006, s 75(1), Sch 8, paras 96, 176.

Sub-s (4): words in square brackets substituted by the Charities Act 2006, s 23(5), as from 27 February 2007.

Sub-s (5): repealed by the Charities and Investment (Scotland) Act 2005, s 95, Sch 3, para 9.

SCHEDULES

(Sch 1 repealed by the Charities Act 2006, ss 6(6), 75(2), Sch 9, as from 27 February 2007.)

[SCHEDULE 1A
THE CHARITY COMMISSION

Section 1A

Membership

1.—(1) The Commission shall consist of a chairman and at least four, but not more than eight, other members.

(2) The members shall be appointed by the Minister.

(3) The Minister shall exercise the power in sub-paragraph (2) so as to secure that—
- (a) the knowledge and experience of the members of the Commission (taken together) includes knowledge and experience of the matters mentioned in sub-paragraph (4),
- (b) at least two members have a seven year general qualification within the meaning of section 71 of the Courts and Legal Services Act 1990, and
- (c) at least one member knows about conditions in Wales and has been appointed following consultation with the National Assembly for Wales.

(4) The matters mentioned in this sub-paragraph are—
- (a) the law relating to charities,
- (b) charity accounts and the financing of charities, and
- (c) the operation and regulation of charities of different sizes and descriptions.

(5) In sub-paragraph (3)(c) "member" does not include the chairman of the Commission.

Terms of appointment and remuneration

2. The members of the Commission shall hold and vacate office as such in accordance with the terms of their respective appointments.

3.—(1) An appointment of a person to hold office as a member of the Commission shall be for a term not exceeding three years.

(2) A person holding office as a member of the Commission—
- (a) may resign that office by giving notice in writing to the Minister, and
- (b) may be removed from office by the Minister on the ground of incapacity or misbehaviour.

(3) Before removing a member of the Commission the Minister shall consult—
- (a) the Commission, and
- (b) if the member was appointed following consultation with the National Assembly for Wales, the Assembly.

(4) No person may hold office as a member of the Commission for more than ten years in total.

(5) For the purposes of sub-paragraph (4), time spent holding office as a Charity Commissioner for England and Wales shall be counted as time spent holding office as a member of the Commission.

4.—(1) The Commission shall pay to its members such remuneration, and such other allowances, as may be determined by the Minister.

(2) The Commission shall, if required to do so by the Minister—

(a) pay such pension, allowances or gratuities as may be determined by the Minister to or in respect of a person who is or has been a member of the Commission, or

(b) make such payments as may be so determined towards provision for the payment of a pension, allowances or gratuities to or in respect of such a person.

(3) If the Minister determines that there are special circumstances which make it right for a person ceasing to hold office as a member of the Commission to receive compensation, the Commission shall pay to him a sum by way of compensation of such amount as may be determined by the Minister.

Staff

5.—(1) The Commission—

(a) shall appoint a chief executive, and

(b) may appoint such other staff as it may determine.

(2) The terms and conditions of service of persons appointed under sub-paragraph (1) are to be such as the Commission may determine with the approval of the Minister for the Civil Service.

Committees

6.—(1) The Commission may establish committees and any committee of the Commission may establish sub-committees.

(2) The members of a committee of the Commission may include persons who are not members of the Commission (and the members of a sub-committee may include persons who are not members of the committee or of the Commission).

Procedure etc

7.—(1) The Commission may regulate its own procedure (including quorum).

(2) The validity of anything done by the Commission is not affected by a vacancy among its members or by a defect in the appointment of a member.

Performance of functions

8. Anything authorised or required to be done by the Commission may be done by—

(a) any member or member of staff of the Commission who is authorised for that purpose by the Commission, whether generally or specially;

(b) any committee of the Commission which has been so authorised.

Evidence

9. The Documentary Evidence Act 1868 shall have effect as if—

(a) the Commission were mentioned in the first column of the Schedule to that Act,

(b) any member or member of staff of the Commission authorised to act on behalf of the Commission were specified in the second column of that Schedule in connection with the Commission, and

(c) the regulations referred to in that Act included any document issued by or under the authority of the Commission.

Execution of documents

10.—(1) A document is executed by the Commission by the fixing of its common seal to the document.

(2) But the fixing of that seal to a document must be authenticated by the signature of—
(a) any member of the Commission, or
(b) any member of its staff,
who is authorised for the purpose by the Commission.

(3) A document which is expressed (in whatever form of words) to be executed by the Commission and is signed by—
(a) any member of the Commission, or
(b) any member of its staff,
who is authorised for the purpose by the Commission has the same effect as if executed in accordance with sub-paragraphs (1) and (2).

(4) A document executed by the Commission which makes it clear on its face that it is intended to be a deed has effect, upon delivery, as a deed; and it is to be presumed (unless a contrary intention is proved) to be delivered upon its being executed.

(5) In favour of a purchaser a document is to be deemed to have been duly executed by the Commission if it purports to be signed on its behalf by—
(a) any member of the Commission, or
(b) any member of its staff;
and, where it makes it clear on its face that it is intended to be a deed, it is to be deemed to have been delivered upon its being executed.

(6) For the purposes of this paragraph—
"authorised" means authorised whether generally or specially; and
"purchaser" means a purchaser in good faith for valuable consideration and includes a lessee, mortgagee or other person who for valuable consideration acquired an interest in property.

Annual report

11.—(1) As soon as practicable after the end of each financial year the Commission shall publish a report on—
(a) the discharge of its functions,
(b) the extent to which, in its opinion, its objectives (see section 1B of this Act) have been met,
(c) the performance of its general duties (see section 1D of this Act), and
(d) the management of its affairs,
during that year.

(2) The Commission shall lay a copy of each such report before Parliament.

(3) In sub-paragraph (1) above, "financial year" means—
(a) the period beginning with the date on which the Commission is established and ending with the next 31st March following that date, and
(b) each successive period of 12 months ending with 31st March.

Annual public meeting

12.—(1) The Commission shall hold a public meeting ("the annual meeting") for the purpose of enabling a report under paragraph 11 above to be considered.

(2) The annual meeting shall be held within the period of three months beginning with the day on which the report is published.

(3) The Commission shall organise the annual meeting so as to allow—
(a) a general discussion of the contents of the report which is being considered, and
(b) a reasonable opportunity for those attending the meeting to put questions to the Commission about matters to which the report relates.

(4) But subject to sub-paragraph (3) above the annual meeting is to be organised and conducted in such a way as the Commission considers appropriate.

(5) The Commission shall—
(a) take such steps as are reasonable in the circumstances to ensure that notice of the annual meeting is given to every registered charity, and
(b) publish notice of the annual meeting in the way appearing to it to be best calculated to bring it to the attention of members of the public.

(6) Each such notice shall—
(a) give details of the time and place at which the meeting is to be held,
(b) set out the proposed agenda for the meeting,
(c) indicate the proposed duration of the meeting, and
(d) give details of the Commission's arrangements for enabling persons to attend.

(7) If the Commission proposes to alter any of the arrangements which have been included in notices given or published under sub-paragraph (5) above it shall—
(a) give reasonable notice of the alteration, and
(b) publish the notice in the way appearing to it to be best calculated to bring it to the attention of registered charities and members of the public.]

[865A]

NOTES
Commencement: 27 February 2007.
Inserted by the Charities Act 2006, s 6(2), Sch 1, para 1; for effect see s 6(7), Sch 2, para 2(6) to that Act at **[2175]**.

[SCHEDULE 1B
THE CHARITY TRIBUNAL

Section 2A(3)

Membership

1.—(1) The Tribunal shall consist of the President and its other members.

(2) The Lord Chancellor shall appoint—
(a) a President of the Tribunal,
(b) legal members of the Tribunal, and
(c) ordinary members of the Tribunal.

(3) A person may be appointed as the President or a legal member of the Tribunal only if he has a seven year general qualification within the meaning of section 71 of the Courts and Legal Services Act 1990.

(4) A person may be appointed as an ordinary member of the Tribunal only if he appears to the Lord Chancellor to have appropriate knowledge or experience relating to charities.

Deputy President

2.—(1) The Lord Chancellor may appoint a legal member as deputy President of the Tribunal.

(2) The deputy President—
(a) may act for the President when he is unable to act or unavailable, and
(b) shall perform such other functions as the President may delegate or assign to him.

Terms of appointment

3.—(1) The members of the Tribunal shall hold and vacate office as such in accordance with the terms of their respective appointments.

(2) A person holding office as a member of the Tribunal—
(a) may resign that office by giving notice in writing to the Lord Chancellor, and
(b) may be removed from office by the Lord Chancellor on the ground of incapacity or misbehaviour.

(3) A previous appointment of a person as a member of the Tribunal does not affect his eligibility for re-appointment as a member of the Tribunal.

Retirement etc

4.—(1) A person shall not hold office as a member of the Tribunal after reaching the age of 70.

(2) Section 26(5) and (6) of the Judicial Pensions and Retirement Act 1993 (extension to age 75) apply in relation to a member of the Tribunal as they apply in relation to a holder of a relevant office.

Remuneration etc

5.—(1) The Lord Chancellor may pay to the members of the Tribunal such remuneration, and such other allowances, as he may determine.

(2) The Lord Chancellor may—
- (a) pay such pension, allowances or gratuities as he may determine to or in respect of a person who is or has been a member of the Tribunal, or
- (b) make such payments as he may determine towards provision for the payment of a pension, allowances or gratuities to or in respect of such a person.

(3) If the Lord Chancellor determines that there are special circumstances which make it right for a person ceasing to hold office as a member of the Tribunal to receive compensation, the Lord Chancellor may pay to him a sum by way of compensation of such amount as may be determined by the Lord Chancellor.

Staff and facilities

6. The Lord Chancellor may make staff and facilities available to the Tribunal.

Panels

7.—(1) The functions of the Tribunal shall be exercised by panels of the Tribunal.

(2) Panels of the Tribunal shall sit at such times and in such places as the President may direct.

(3) Before giving a direction under sub-paragraph (2) above the President shall consult the Lord Chancellor.

(4) More than one panel may sit at a time.

8.—(1) The President shall make arrangements for determining which of the members of the Tribunal are to constitute a panel of the Tribunal in relation to the exercise of any function.

(2) Those arrangements shall, in particular, ensure that each panel is constituted in one of the following ways—
- (a) as the President sitting alone,
- (b) as a legal member sitting alone,
- (c) as the President sitting with two other members,
- (d) as a legal member sitting with two other members,
- (e) as the President sitting with one other member,
- (f) as a legal member sitting with one other member,

(and references in paragraphs (d) and (f) to other members do not include the President).

(3) The President shall publish arrangements made under this paragraph.

Practice and procedure

9.—(1) Decisions of the Tribunal may be taken by majority vote.

(2) In the case of a panel constituted in accordance with paragraph 8(2)(e), the President shall have a casting vote.

(3) In the case of a panel constituted in accordance with paragraph 8(2)(f) which consists of a legal member and an ordinary member, the legal member shall have a casting vote.

(4) The President shall make and publish arrangements as to who is to have a casting vote in the case of a panel constituted in accordance with paragraph 8(2)(f) which consists of two legal members.

10. The President may, subject to rules under section 2B of this Act, give directions about the practice and procedure of the Tribunal.]

[865B]

NOTES

Commencement: to be appointed.

Inserted by the Charities Act 2006, s 8(2), Sch 3, as from a day to be appointed under s 79(2) of that Act.

[SCHEDULE 1C
APPEALS AND APPLICATIONS TO CHARITY TRIBUNAL

Section 2A(4)

Appeals: general

1.—(1) Except in the case of a reviewable matter (see paragraph 3) an appeal may be brought to the Tribunal against any decision, direction or order mentioned in column 1 of the Table.

(2) Such an appeal may be brought by—

(a) the Attorney General, or

(b) any person specified in the corresponding entry in column 2 of the Table.

(3) The Commission shall be the respondent to such an appeal.

(4) In determining such an appeal the Tribunal—

(a) shall consider afresh the decision, direction or order appealed against, and

(b) may take into account evidence which was not available to the Commission.

(5) The Tribunal may—

(a) dismiss the appeal, or

(b) if it allows the appeal, exercise any power specified in the corresponding entry in column 3 of the Table.

Appeals: orders under section 9

2.—(1) Paragraph 1(4)(a) above does not apply in relation to an appeal against an order made under section 9 of this Act.

(2) On such an appeal the Tribunal shall consider whether the information or document in question—

(a) relates to a charity;

(b) is relevant to the discharge of the functions of the Commission or the official custodian.

(3) The Tribunal may allow such an appeal only if it is satisfied that the information or document in question does not fall within either paragraph (a) or paragraph (b) of sub-paragraph (2) above.

Reviewable matters

3.—(1) In this Schedule references to "reviewable matters" are to—

(a) decisions to which sub-paragraph (2) applies, and

(b) orders to which sub-paragraph (3) applies.

(2) This sub-paragraph applies to decisions of the Commission—

(a) to institute an inquiry under section 8 of this Act with regard to a particular institution,

(b) to institute an inquiry under section 8 of this Act with regard to a class of institutions,

(c) not to make a common investment scheme under section 24 of this Act,

(d) not to make a common deposit scheme under section 25 of this Act,
(e) not to make an order under section 26 of this Act in relation to a charity,
(f) not to make an order under section 36 of this Act in relation to land held by or in trust for a charity,
(g) not to make an order under section 38 of this Act in relation to a mortgage of land held by or in trust for a charity.

(3) This sub-paragraph applies to an order made by the Commission under section 69(1) of this Act in relation to a company which is a charity.

Reviews

4.—(1) An application may be made to the Tribunal for the review of a reviewable matter.

(2) Such an application may be made by—
(a) the Attorney General, or
(b) any person mentioned in the entry in column 2 of the Table which corresponds to the entry in column 1 which relates to the reviewable matter.

(3) The Commission shall be the respondent to such an application.

(4) In determining such an application the Tribunal shall apply the principles which would be applied by the High Court on an application for judicial review.

(5) The Tribunal may—
(a) dismiss the application, or
(b) if it allows the application, exercise any power mentioned in the entry in column 3 of the Table which corresponds to the entry in column 1 which relates to the reviewable matter.

Interpretation: remission of matters to Commission

5. References in column 3 of the Table to the power to remit a matter to the Commission are to the power to remit the matter either—
(a) generally, or
(b) for determination in accordance with a finding made or direction given by the Tribunal.

TABLE

1	2	3
Decision of the Commission under section 3 or 3A of this Act— (a) to enter or not to enter an institution in the register of charities, or (b) to remove or not to remove an institution from the register.	The persons are— (a) the persons who are or claim to be the charity trustees of the institution, (b) (if a body corporate) the institution itself, and (c) any other person who is or may be affected by the decision.	Power to quash the decision and (if appropriate)— (a) remit the matter to the Commission, (b) direct the Commission to rectify the register.
Decision of the Commission not to make a determination under section 3(9) of this Act in relation to particular information contained in the register.	The persons are— (a)the charity trustees of the charity to which the information relates, (b) (if a body corporate) the charity itself, and (c) any other person who is or may be affected by the decision.	Power to quash the decision and (if appropriate) remit the matter to the Commission.

1	2	3
Direction given by the Commission under section 6 of this Act requiring the name of a charity to be changed.	The persons are— (a) the charity trustees of the charity to which the direction relates, (b) (if a body corporate) the charity itself, and (c) any other person who is or may be affected by the direction.	Power to— (a) quash the direction and (if appropriate) remit the matter to the Commission, (b) substitute for the direction any other direction which could have been given by the Commission.
Decision of the Commission to institute an inquiry under section 8 of this Act with regard to a particular institution.	The persons are— (a) the persons who have control or management of the institution, and (b) (if a body corporate) the institution itself.	Power to direct the Commission to end the inquiry.
Decision of the Commission to institute an inquiry under section 8 of this Act with regard to a class of institutions.	The persons are— (a) the persons who have control or management of any institution which is a member of the class of institutions, and (b) (if a body corporate) any such institution.	Power to— (a) direct the Commission that the inquiry should not consider a particular institution, (b) direct the Commission to end the inquiry.
Order made by the Commission under section 9 of this Act requiring a person to supply information or a document.	The persons are any person who is required to supply the information or document.	Power to— (a) quash the order, (b) substitute for all or part of the order any other order which could have been made by the Commission.
Order made by the Commission under section 16(1) of this Act (including such an order made by virtue of section 23(1)).	The persons are— (a) in a section 16(1)(a) case, the charity trustees of the charity to which the order relates or (if a body corporate) the charity itself, (b) in a section 16(1)(b) case, any person discharged or removed by the order, and (c) any other person who is or may be affected by the order.	Power to— (a) quash the order in whole or in part and (if appropriate) remit the matter to the Commission, (b) substitute for all or part of the order any other order which could have been made by the Commission, (c) add to the order anything which could have been contained in an order made by the Commission.
Order made by the Commission under section 18(1) of this Act in relation to a charity.	The persons are— (a) the charity trustees of the charity, (b) (if a body corporate) the charity itself, (c) in a section 18(1)(i) case, any person suspended by the order, and (d) any other person who is or may be affected by the order.	Power to— (a) quash the order in whole or in part and (if appropriate) remit the matter to the Commission, (b) substitute for all or part of the order any other order which could have been made by the Commission, (c) add to the order anything which could have been contained in an order made by the Commission.

1	2	3
Order made by the Commission under section 18(2) of this Act in relation to a charity.	The persons are— (a) the charity trustees of the charity, (b) (if a body corporate) the charity itself, (c) in a section 18(2)(i) case, any person removed by the order, and (d) any other person who is or may be affected by the order.	Power to— (a) quash the order in whole or in part and (if appropriate) remit the matter to the Commission, (b) substitute for all or part of the order any other order which could have been made by the Commission, (c) add to the order anything which could have been contained in an order made by the Commission.
Order made by the Commission under section 18(4) of this Act removing a charity trustee.	The persons are— (a) the charity trustee, (b) the remaining charity trustees of the charity of which he was a charity trustee, (c) (if a body corporate) the charity itself, and (d) any other person who is or may be affected by the order.	Power to— (a) quash the order in whole or in part and (if appropriate) remit the matter to the Commission, (b) substitute for all or part of the order any other order which could have been made by the Commission, (c) add to the order anything which could have been contained in an order made by the Commission.
Order made by the Commission under section 18(5) of this Act appointing a charity trustee.	The persons are— (a) the other charity trustees of the charity, (b) (if a body corporate) the charity itself, and (c) any other person who is or may be affected by the order.	Power to— (a) quash the order in whole or in part and (if appropriate) remit the matter to the Commission, (b) substitute for all or part of the order any other order which could have been made by the Commission, (c) add to the order anything which could have been contained in an order made by the Commission.
Decision of the Commission— (a) to discharge an order following a review under section 18(13) of this Act, or (b) not to discharge an order following such a review.	The persons are— (a) the charity trustees of the charity to which the order relates, (b) (if a body corporate) the charity itself, (c) if the order in question was made under section 18(1)(i), any person suspended by it, and (d) any other person who is or may be affected by the order.	Power to— (a) quash the decision and (if appropriate) remit the matter to the Commission, (b) make the discharge of the order subject to savings or other transitional provisions, (c) remove any savings or other transitional provisions to which the discharge of the order was subject, (d) discharge the order in whole or in part (whether subject to any savings or other transitional provisions or not).

1	2	3
Order made by the Commission under section 18A(2) of this Act which suspends a person's membership of a charity	The persons are— (a) the person whose membership is suspended by the order, and (b) any other person who is or may be affected by the order.	Power to quash the order and (if appropriate) remit the matter to the Commission.
Order made by the Commission under section 19A(2) of this Act which directs a person to take action specified in the order.	The persons are any person who is directed by the order to take the specified action.	Power to quash the order and (if appropriate) remit the matter to the Commission.
Order made by the Commission under section 19B(2) of this Act which directs a person to apply property in a specified manner.	The persons are any person who is directed by the order to apply the property in the specified manner.	Power to quash the order and (if appropriate) remit the matter to the Commission.
Order made by the Commission under section 23(2) of this Act in relation to any land vested in the official custodian in trust for a charity.	The persons are— (a) the charity trustees of the charity, (b) (if a body corporate) the charity itself, and (c) any other person who is or may be affected by the order.	Power to— (a) quash the order and (if appropriate) remit the matter to the Commission, (b) substitute for the order any other order which could have been made by the Commission, (c) add to the order anything which could have been contained in an order made by the Commission.
Decision of the Commission not to make a common investment scheme under section 24 of this Act.	The persons are— (a) the charity trustees of a charity which applied to the Commission for the scheme, (b) (if a body corporate) the charity itself, and (c) any other person who is or may be affected by the decision.	Power to quash the decision and (if appropriate) remit the matter to the Commission.
Decision of the Commission not to make a common deposit scheme under section 25 of this Act.	The persons are— (a) the charity trustees of a charity which applied to the Commission for the scheme, (b) (if a body corporate) the charity itself, and (c) any other person who is or may be affected by the decision.	Power to quash the decision and (if appropriate) remit the matter to the Commission.
Decision by the Commission not to make an order under section 26 of this Act in relation to a charity.	The persons are— (a) the charity trustees of the charity, and (b) (if a body corporate) the charity itself.	Power to quash the decision and (if appropriate) remit the matter to the Commission.

1	2	3
Direction given by the Commission under section 28 of this Act in relation to an account held in the name of or on behalf of a charity.	The persons are— (a) the charity trustees of the charity, (b) (if a body corporate) the charity itself, and (c) any other person who is or may be affected by the order.	Power to— (a) quash the direction and (if appropriate) remit the matter to the Commission, (b) substitute for the direction any other direction which could have been given by the Commission, (c) add to the direction anything which could have been contained in a direction given by the Commission.
Order made by the Commission under section 31 of this Act for the taxation of a solicitor's bill.	The persons are— (a) the solicitor, (b) any person for whom the work was done by the solicitor, and (c) any other person who is or may be affected by the order.	Power to— (a) quash the order, (b) substitute for the order any other order which could have been made by the Commission, (c) add to the order anything which could have been contained in an order made by the Commission.
Decision of the Commission not to make an order under section 36 of this Act in relation to land held by or in trust for a charity.	The persons are— (a) the charity trustees of the charity, (b) (if a body corporate) the charity itself, and (c) any other person who is or may be affected by the decision.	Power to quash the decision and (if appropriate) remit the matter to the Commission.
Decision of the Commission not to make an order under section 38 of this Act in relation to a mortgage of land held by or in trust for a charity.	The persons are— (a) the charity trustees of the charity, (b) (if a body corporate) the charity itself, and (c) any other person who is or may be affected by the decision.	Power to quash the decision and (if appropriate) remit the matter to the Commission.
Order made by the Commission under section 43(4) of this Act requiring the accounts of a charity to be audited.	The persons are— (a) the charity trustees of the charity, (b) (if a body corporate) the charity itself, and (c) any other person who is or may be affected by the order.	Power to— (a) quash the order, (b) substitute for the order any other order which could have been made by the Commission, (c) add to the order anything which could have been contained in an order made by the Commission.

1	2	3
Order made by the Commission under section 44(2) of this Act in relation to a charity, or a decision of the Commission not to make such an order in relation to a charity.	The persons are— (a) the charity trustees of the charity, (b) (if a body corporate) the charity itself, (c) in the case of a decision not to make an order, the auditor, independent examiner or examiner, and (d) any other person who is or may be affected by the order or the decision.	Power to— (a) quash the order or decision and (if appropriate) remit the matter to the Commission, (b) substitute for the order any other order of a kind the Commission could have made, (c) make any order which the Commission could have made.
Decision of the Commission under section 46(5) of this Act to request charity trustees to prepare an annual report for a charity.	The persons are— (a) the charity trustees, and (b) (if a body corporate) the charity itself.	Power to quash the decision and (if appropriate) remit the matter to the Commission.
Decision of the Commission not to dispense with the requirements of section 48(1) in relation to a charity or class of charities.	The persons are the charity trustees of any charity affected by the decision.	Power to quash the decision and (if appropriate) remit the matter to the Commission.
Decision of the Commission— (a)to grant a certificate of incorporation under section 50(1) of this Act to the trustees of a charity, or (b)not to grant such a certificate.	The persons are— (a) the trustees of the charity, and (b) any other person who is or may be affected by the decision.	Power to quash— (a) the decision, (b) any conditions or directions inserted in the certificate, and (if appropriate) remit the matter to the Commission.
Decision of the Commission to amend a certificate of incorporation of a charity under section 56(4) of this Act.	The persons are— (a) the trustees of the charity, and (b) any other person who is or may be affected by the amended certificate of incorporation.	Power to quash the decision and (if appropriate) remit the matter to the Commission.
Decision of the Commission not to amend a certificate of incorporation under section 56(4) of this Act.	The persons are— (a) the trustees of the charity, and (b) any other person who is or may be affected by the decision not to amend the certificate of incorporation.	Power to— (a) quash the decision and (if appropriate) remit the matter to the Commission, (b) make any order the Commission could have made under section 56(4).
Order of the Commission under section 61(1) or (2) of this Act which dissolves a charity which is an incorporated body.	The persons are— (a) the trustees of the charity, (b) the charity itself, and (c) any other person who is or may be affected by the order.	Power to— (a) quash the order and (if appropriate) remit the matter to the Commission, (b) substitute for the order any other order which could have been made by the Commission, (c) add to the order anything which could have been contained in an order made by the Commission.

1	2	3
Decision of the Commission to give, or withhold, consent under section 64(2), 65(4) or 66(1) of this Act in relation to a body corporate which is a charity.	The persons are— (a) the charity trustees of the charity, (b) the body corporate itself, and (c) any other person who is or may be affected by the decision.	Power to quash the decision and (if appropriate) remit the matter to the Commission.
Order made by the Commission under section 69(1) of this Act in relation to a company which is a charity.	The persons are— (a) the directors of the company, (b) the company itself, and (c) any other person who is or may be affected by the order.	Power to— (a) quash the order and (if appropriate) remit the matter to the Commission, (b) substitute for the order any other order which could have been made by the Commission, (c) add to the order anything which could have been contained in an order made by the Commission.
Order made by the Commission under section 69(4) of this Act which gives directions to a person or to charity trustees.	The persons are— (a) in the case of directions given to a person, that person, (b) in the case of directions given to charity trustees, those charity trustees and (if a body corporate) the charity of which they are charity trustees, and (c) any other person who is or may be affected by the directions.	Power to— (a) quash the order, (b) substitute for the order any other order which could have been made by the Commission, (c) add to the order anything which could have been contained in an order made by the Commission.
Decision of the Commission under section 69E of this Act to grant an application for the constitution of a CIO and its registration as a charity.	The persons are any person (other than the persons who made the application) who is or may be affected by the decision.	Power to quash the decision and (if appropriate)— (a) remit the matter to the Commission, (b) direct the Commission to rectify the register of charities.
Decision of the Commission under section 69E of this Act not to grant an application for the constitution of a CIO and its registration as a charity.	The persons are— (a) the persons who made the application, and (b) any other person who is or may be affected by the decision.	Power to— (a) quash the decision and (if appropriate) remit the matter to the Commission, (b) direct the Commission to grant the application.
Decision of the Commission under section 69H of this Act not to grant an application for the conversion of a charitable company or a registered society into a CIO and the CIO's registration as a charity.	The persons are— (a) the charity which made the application, (b) the charity trustees of the charity, and (c) any other person who is or may be affected by the decision.	Power to— (a) quash the decision and (if appropriate) remit the matter to the Commission, (b) direct the Commission to grant the application.

1	2	3
Decision of the Commission under section 69K of this Act to grant an application for the amalgamation of two or more CIOs and the incorporation and registration as a charity of a new CIO as their successor.	The persons are any creditor of any of the CIOs being amalgamated.	Power to quash the decision and (if appropriate) remit the matter to the Commission.
Decision of the Commission under section 69K of this Act not to grant an application for the amalgamation of two or more CIOs and the incorporation and registration as a charity of a new CIO as their successor.	The persons are— (a) the CIOs which applied for the amalgamation, (b) the charity trustees of the CIOs, and (c) any other person who is or may be affected by the decision.	Power to— (a) quash the decision and (if appropriate) remit the matter to the Commission, (b) direct the Commission to grant the application.
Decision of the Commission to confirm a resolution passed by a CIO under section 69M(1) of this Act.	The persons are any creditor of the CIO.	Power to quash the decision and (if appropriate) remit the matter to the Commission.
Decision of the Commission not to confirm a resolution passed by a CIO under section 69M(1) of this Act.	The persons are— (a) the CIO, (b) the charity trustees of the CIO, and (c) any other person who is or may be affected by the decision.	Power to— (a) quash the decision and (if appropriate) remit the matter to the Commission, (b) direct the Commission to confirm the resolution.
Decision of the Commission under section 72(4) of this Act to waive, or not to waive, a person's disqualification.	The persons are— (a) the person who applied for the waiver, and (b) any other person who is or may be affected by the decision.	Power to— (a) quash the decision and (if appropriate) remit the matter to the Commission, (b) substitute for the decision any other decision of a kind which could have been made by the Commission.
Order made by the Commission under section 73(4) of this Act in relation to a person who has acted as charity trustee or trustee for a charity.	The persons are— (a) the person subject to the order, and (b) any other person who is or may be affected by the order.	Power to— (a) quash the order and (if appropriate) remit the matter to the Commission, (b) substitute for the order any other order which could have been made by the Commission.
Order made by the Commission under section 73C(5) or (6) of this Act requiring a trustee or connected person to repay, or not to receive, remuneration.	The persons are— (a) the trustee or connected person, (b) the other charity trustees of the charity concerned, and (c) any other person who is or may be affected by the order.	Power to— (a) quash the order and (if appropriate) remit the matter to the Commission, (b) substitute for the order any other order which could have been made by the Commission.

PART I STATUTES

1	2	3
Decision of the Commission to notify charity trustees under section 74A(2) of this Act that it objects to a resolution of the charity trustees under section 74(2) or 74C(2).	The persons are— (a) the charity trustees, and (b) any other person who is or may be affected by the decision.	Power to quash the decision.
Decision of the Commission not to concur under section 75A of this Act with a resolution of charity trustees under section 75A(3) or 75B(2).	The persons are— (a) the charity trustees, (b) (if a body corporate) the charity itself, and (c) any other person who is or may be affected by the decision.	Power to quash the decision and (if appropriate) remit the matter to the Commission.
Decision of the Commission to withhold approval for the transfer of property from trustees to a parish council under section 79(1) of this Act.	The persons are— (a) the trustees, (b) the parish council, and (c) any other person who is or may be affected by the decision.	Power to quash the decision and (if appropriate) remit the matter to the Commission.
Order made by the Commission under section 80(2) of this Act in relation to a person holding property on behalf of a recognised body or of any person concerned in its management or control.	The persons are— (a) the person holding the property in question, and (b) any other person who is or may be affected by the order.	Power to quash the order and (if appropriate) remit the matter to the Commission.
Decision of the Commission not to give a direction under section 96(5) or (6) of this Act in relation to an institution or a charity.	The persons are the trustees of the institution or charity concerned.	Power to quash the decision and (if appropriate) remit the matter to the Commission.
Decision of the Commission under paragraph 15 of Schedule 5B to this Act to refuse to register an amendment to the constitution of a CIO.	The persons are— (a) the CIO, (b) the charity trustees of the CIO, and (c) any other person who is or may be affected by the decision.	Power to quash the decision and (if appropriate)— (a) remit the matter to the Commission, (b) direct the Commission to register the amendment.

Power to amend Table etc

6.—(1) The Minister may by order—

(a) amend or otherwise modify an entry in the Table,

(b) add an entry to the Table, or

(c) remove an entry from the Table.

(2) An order under sub-paragraph (1) may make such amendments, repeals or other modifications of paragraphs 1 to 5 of this Schedule, or of an enactment which applies this Schedule, as the Minister considers appropriate in consequence of any change in the Table made by the order.

(3) No order shall be made under this paragraph unless a draft of the order has been laid before and approved by a resolution of each House of Parliament.

7. Paragraph 6 above applies (with the necessary modifications) in relation to section 57 of the Charities Act 2006 as if—

(a) the provisions of that section were contained in this Schedule, and
(b) the reference in that paragraph to paragraphs 1 to 5 of this Schedule included a reference to any other provision relating to appeals to the Tribunal which is contained in Chapter 1 of Part 3 of the Charities Act 2006.]

[865C]

NOTES

Commencement: 27 February 2007 (para 6 for the purposes of enabling the Lord Chancellor to exercise the power to make subordinate legislation); to be appointed (otherwise).

Inserted, together with Sch 1D, by the Charities Act 2006, s 8(3), Sch 4, partly as from 27 February 2007, and fully as from a day to be appointed under s 79(2) of that Act.

[SCHEDULE 1D
REFERENCES TO CHARITY TRIBUNAL

Section 2A(4)

References by Commission

1.—(1) A question which—
(a) has arisen in connection with the exercise by the Commission of any of its functions, and
(b) involves either the operation of charity law in any respect or its application to a particular state of affairs,

may be referred to the Tribunal by the Commission if the Commission considers it desirable to refer the question to the Tribunal.

(2) The Commission may make such a reference only with the consent of the Attorney General.

(3) The Commission shall be a party to proceedings before the Tribunal on the reference.

(4) The following shall be entitled to be parties to proceedings before the Tribunal on the reference—
(a) the Attorney General, and
(b) with the Tribunal's permission—
(i) the charity trustees of any charity which is likely to be affected by the Tribunal's decision on the reference,
(ii) any such charity which is a body corporate, and
(iii) any other person who is likely to be so affected.

References by Attorney General

2.—(1) A question which involves either—
(a) the operation of charity law in any respect, or
(b) the application of charity law to a particular state of affairs,

may be referred to the Tribunal by the Attorney General if the Attorney General considers it desirable to refer the question to the Tribunal.

(2) The Attorney General shall be a party to proceedings before the Tribunal on the reference.

(3) The following shall be entitled to be parties to proceedings before the Tribunal on the reference—
(a) the Commission, and
(b) with the Tribunal's permission—
(i) the charity trustees of any charity which is likely to be affected by the Tribunal's decision on the reference,
(ii) any such charity which is a body corporate, and
(iii) any other person who is likely to be so affected.

Powers of Commission in relation to matters referred to Tribunal

3.—(1) This paragraph applies where a question which involves the application of charity law to a particular state of affairs has been referred to the Tribunal under paragraph 1 or 2 above.

(2) The Commission shall not take any steps in reliance on any view as to the application of charity law to that state of affairs until—
(a) proceedings on the reference (including any proceedings on appeal) have been concluded, and
(b) any period during which an appeal (or further appeal) may ordinarily be made has ended.

(3) Where—
(a) paragraphs (a) and (b) of sub-paragraph (2) above are satisfied, and
(b) the question has been decided in proceedings on the reference,
the Commission shall give effect to that decision when dealing with the particular state of affairs to which the reference related.

Suspension of time limits while reference in progress

4.—(1) Sub-paragraph (2) below applies if—
(a) paragraph 3(2) above prevents the Commission from taking any steps which it would otherwise be permitted or required to take, and
(b) the steps in question may be taken only during a period specified in an enactment ("the specified period").

(2) The running of the specified period is suspended for the period which—
(a) begins with the date on which the question is referred to the Tribunal, and
(b) ends with the date on which paragraphs (a) and (b) of paragraph 3(2) above are satisfied.

(3) Nothing in this paragraph or section 74A of this Act prevents the specified period being suspended concurrently by virtue of sub-paragraph (2) above and that section.

Agreement for Commission to act while reference in progress

5.—(1) Paragraph 3(2) above does not apply in relation to any steps taken by the Commission with the agreement of—
(a) the persons who are parties to the proceedings on the reference at the time when those steps are taken, and
(b) (if not within paragraph (a) above) the charity trustees of any charity which—
(i) is likely to be directly affected by the taking of those steps, and
(ii) is not a party to the proceedings at that time.

(2) The Commission may take those steps despite the suspension in accordance with paragraph 4(2) above of any period during which it would otherwise be permitted or required to take them.

(3) Paragraph 3(3) above does not require the Commission to give effect to a decision as to the application of charity law to a particular state of affairs to the extent that the decision is inconsistent with any steps already taken by the Commission in relation to that state of affairs in accordance with this paragraph.

Appeals and applications in respect of matters determined on references

6.—(1) No appeal or application may be made to the Tribunal by a person to whom sub-paragraph (2) below applies in respect of an order or decision made, or direction given, by the Commission in accordance with paragraph 3(3) above.

(2) This sub-paragraph applies to a person who was at any stage a party to the proceedings in which the question referred to the Tribunal was decided.

(3) Rules under section 2B(1) of this Act may include provision as to who is to be treated for the purposes of sub-paragraph (2) above as being (or not being) a party to the proceedings.

(4) Any enactment (including one contained in this Act) which provides for an appeal or application to be made to the Tribunal has effect subject to sub-paragraph (1) above.

Interpretation

7.—(1) In this Schedule—
"charity law" means—

(a) any enactment contained in, or made under, this Act or the Charities Act 2006,
(b) any other enactment specified in regulations made by the Minister, and
(c) any rule of law which relates to charities, and

"enactment" includes an enactment comprised in subordinate legislation (within the meaning of the Interpretation Act 1978), and includes an enactment whenever passed or made.

(2) The exclusions contained in section 96(2) of this Act (ecclesiastical corporations etc) do not have effect for the purposes of this Schedule.]

[865D]

NOTES

Commencement: to be appointed.
Inserted as noted to Sch 1C at **[865C]**.

SCHEDULE 2
EXEMPT CHARITIES

Sections 3 and 96

The following institutions, so far as they are charities, are exempt charities within the meaning of this Act, that is to say—

(a) any institution which, if the Charities Act 1960 had not been passed, would be exempted from the powers and jurisdiction, under the Charitable Trusts Acts 1853 to 1939, of [the Commission] or Minister of Education (apart from any power of the Commissioners or Minister to apply those Acts in whole or in part to charities otherwise exempt) by the terms of any enactment not contained in those Acts other than section 9 of the Places of Worship Registration Act 1855 [(*but see Note 1*)];
(b) the universities of Oxford, Cambridge, London, Durham and Newcastle, the colleges and halls in the universities of Oxford, Cambridge, Durham and Newcastle, [and] Queen Mary and Westfield College in the University of London *and the colleges of Winchester and Eton*;
(c) any university, university college, or institution connected with a university or university college, which Her Majesty declares by Order in Council to be an exempt charity for the purposes of this Act;
(d) …
[(da) the Qualifications and Curriculum Authority;]
(e) …
[(f) …]
(g), (h) …
[(h) a higher education corporation;]
(i) a successor company to a higher education corporation (within the meaning of section 129(5) of the Education Reform Act 1988) at a time when an institution conducted by the company is for the time being designated under that section;
[(j) a further education corporation;]
(j) …
(k) the Board of Trustees of the Victoria and Albert Museum;
(l) the Board of Trustees of the Science Museum;
(m) the Board of Trustees of the Armouries;
(n) the Board of Trustees of the Royal Botanic Gardens, Kew;
(o) the Board of Trustees of the National Museums and Galleries on Merseyside;
(p) the trustees of the British Museum and the trustees of the Natural History Museum;
(q) the Board of Trustees of the National Gallery;
(r) the Board of Trustees of the Tate Gallery;
(s) the Board of Trustees of the National Portrait Gallery;
(t) the Board of Trustees of the Wallace Collection;
(u) the Trustees of the Imperial War Museum;
(v) the Trustees of the National Maritime Museum;
(w) any institution which is administered by or on behalf of an institution included above and is established for the general purposes of, or for any special purpose of or in connection with, the last-mentioned institution [(*but see Note 2*)];
(*x*) *the Church Commissioners and any institution which is administered by them;*

(y) any registered society within the meaning of the Industrial and Provident Societies Act 1965 *and any registered society or branch within the meaning of the Friendly Societies Act 1974*;

(z) the Board of Governors of the Museum of London;

(za) the British Library Board.

[(zb) …]

[*Notes*

1. Paragraph (a) above does not include—

(a) any Investment Fund or Deposit Fund within the meaning of the Church Funds Investment Measure 1958,

(b) any investment fund or deposit fund within the meaning of the Methodist Church Funds Act 1960, or

(c) the representative body of the Welsh Church or property administered by it.

2. Paragraph (w) above does not include any students' union.]

[866]

NOTES

Para (a): words in first pair of square brackets substituted by the Charities Act 2006, s 75(1), Sch 8, paras 96, 177, as from 27 February 2007, and words in second pair of square brackets inserted, as from a day to be appointed under s 79(2) of that Act, by s 11(1), (2) of that Act.

Para (b): word in square brackets inserted and words in italics repealed by the Charities Act 2006, ss 11(1), (3), 75(2), Sch 9, as from a day to be appointed under s 79(2) of that Act.

Para (d): repealed by the School Standards and Framework Act 1998, s 140(3), Sch 31.

Para (da): substituted (originally inserted by the Education Act 1993, s 307(1), Sch 19, para 175 and continued in force by the Education Act 1996, s 582(1), Sch 37, para 120(2)) by the Education Act 1997, s 57(1), Sch 7, para 7, subject to savings contained in the Education Act 1997 (Commencement No 2 and Transitional Provisions) Order 1997, SI 1997/1468, Pt II.

Paras (e), (g): repealed by the Education Act 1996, s 582(2), Sch 38, Pt I.

Para (f): substituted by the Education Act 1997, s 57(1), Sch 7, para 7, subject to savings contained in SI 1997/1468, Pt II; repealed by the Qualifications, Curriculum and Assessment Authority for Wales (Transfer of Functions to the National Assembly for Wales and Abolition) Order 2005, SI 2005/3239, art 9(1), Sch 1, para 4.

Paras (h), (j): repealed by the Teaching and Higher Education Act 1998, s 44(2), Sch 4; new paras (h), (j) inserted by the Charities Act 2006, s 11(1), (4), (5), as from a day to be appointed under s 79(2) of that Act.

Para (w): words in square brackets inserted by the Charities Act 2006, s 11(1), (6), as from a day to be appointed under s 79(2) of that Act.

Para (x): repealed by the Charities Act 2006, ss 11(1), (7), 75(2), Sch 9, as from a day to be appointed under s 79(2) of that Act.

Para (y): for the words in italics there are substituted the words "and which is also registered in the register of social landlords under Part 1 of the Housing Act 1996;" by the Charities Act 2006, s 11(1), (8), as from a day to be appointed under s 79(2) of that Act.

Para (zb): added by the National Lottery etc Act 1993, s 37(2), Sch 5, para 12; repealed by the National Lottery Act 2006, s 21, Sch 3.

Notes inserted by the Charities Act 2006, s 11(1), (9), as from a day to be appointed under s 79(2) of that Act.

Charitable Trusts Acts 1853 to 1939: repealed by the Charities Act 1960, s 48(2), Sch 7.

Orders in Council: the Exempt Charities Order 1993, SI 1993/2359; the Exempt Charities Order 1994, SI 1994/1905; the Exempt Charities (No 2) Order 1994, SI 1994/2956; the Exempt Charities Order 1995, SI 1995/2998; the Exempt Charities Order 1996, SI 1996/1637; the Exempt Charities (No 2) Order 1996, SI 1996/1932; the Exempt Charities (No 3) Order 1996, SI 1996/1933; the Exempt Charities Order 1999, SI 1999/3139; the Exempt Charities Order 2000, SI 2000/1826; the Exempt Charities Order 2002, SI 2002/1626; the Exempt Charities Order 2003, SI 2003/1881; the Exempt Charities Order 2004, SI 2004/1995; the Exempt Charities Order 2006, SI 2006/1452.

In addition, by virtue of the Interpretation Act 1978, s 17(2)(b), the Exempt Charities Order 1962, SI 1962/1343; the Exempt Charities Order 1965, SI 1965/1715; the Exempt Charities Order 1966, SI 1966/1460; the Exempt Charities Order 1967, SI 1967/821; the Exempt Charities Order 1969, SI 1969/1496; the Exempt Charities Order 1978, SI 1978/453; the Exempt Charities Order 1982, SI 1982/1661; the Exempt Charities Order 1983, SI 1983/1516; the Exempt Charities Order 1984, SI 1984/1976; the Exempt Charities Order 1987, SI 1987/1823; the Exempt Charities Order 1989, SI 1989/2394, now have effect as if made under this Schedule.

PART I STATUTES

SCHEDULE 3
ENLARGEMENT OF AREAS OF LOCAL CHARITIES

Section 13

Existing area	*Permissible enlargement*
1. Greater London	Any area comprising Greater London.
2. Any area in Greater London and not in, or partly in, the City of London.	(i) Any area in Greater London and not in, or partly in, the City of London; (ii) the area of Greater London exclusive of the City of London; (iii) any area comprising the area of Greater London, exclusive of the City of London; (iv) any area partly in Greater London and partly in any adjacent parish or parishes (civil or ecclesiastical), and not partly in the City of London.
3. A district	Any area comprising the district
[3A. Welsh county or county borough ...	Any area comprising that county or county borough.]
4. Any area in a district	(i) Any area in the district; (ii) the district; (iii) any area comprising the district; (iv) any area partly in the district and partly in any adjacent district [or in any adjacent Welsh county or county borough].
[4A. Any area in a Welsh county or county borough	(i) Any area in the county or county borough; (ii) the county or county borough; (iii) any area comprising the county or county borough; (iv) any area partly in the county or county borough and partly in any adjacent Welsh county or county borough or in any adjacent district.]
5. A parish (civil or ecclesiastical), or two or more parishes, or an area in a parish, or partly in each of two or more parishes.	Any area not extending beyond the parish or parishes comprising or adjacent to the area in column 1.
6. In Wales, a community, or two or more communities, or an area in a community, or partly in each of two or more communities.	Any area not extending beyond the community or communities comprising or adjacent to the area in column 1.

[867]

NOTES

Paras 3A, 4A: inserted by the Local Government (Wales) Act 1994, s 66(6), Sch 16, para 101(5), (6).

Para 4: in para (iv) words in square brackets added by the Local Government (Wales) Act 1994, s 66(6), Sch 16, para 101(6).

SCHEDULE 4
COURT'S JURISDICTION OVER CERTAIN CHARITIES GOVERNED BY OR UNDER STATUTE

Section 15

1. The court may by virtue of section 15(3) of this Act exercise its jurisdiction with respect to charities—
   (a) in relation to charities established or regulated by any provision of the Seamen's Fund Winding-up Act 1851 which is repealed by the Charities Act 1960;
   (b) in relation to charities established or regulated by schemes under the Endowed Schools Act 1869 to 1948, or section 75 of the Elementary Education Act 1870 or by schemes given effect under section 2 of the Education Act 1973 [or section 554 of the Education Act 1996];
   (c) . . .
   (d) in relation to fuel allotments, that is to say, land which, by any enactment relating to inclosure or any instrument having effect under such an enactment, is vested in trustees upon trust that the land or the rents and profits of the land shall be used for the purpose of providing poor persons with fuel;
   (e) in relation to charities established or regulated by any provision of the Municipal Corporations Act 1883 which is repealed by the Charities Act 1960 or by any scheme having effect under any such provision;
   (f) in relation to charities regulated by schemes under the London Government Act 1899;
   (g) in relation to charities established or regulated by orders or regulations under section 2 of the Regimental Charitable Funds Act 1935;
   (h) in relation to charities regulated by section 79 of this Act, or by any such order as is mentioned in that section.

2. Notwithstanding anything in section 19 of the Commons Act 1876 a scheme for the administration of a fuel allotment (within the meaning of the foregoing paragraph) may provide—
   (a) for the sale or letting of the allotment or any part thereof, for the discharge of the land sold or let from any restrictions as to the use thereof imposed by or under any enactment relating to inclosure and for the application of the sums payable to the trustees of the allotment in respect of the sale or lease; or
   (b) for the exchange of the allotment or any part thereof for other land, for the discharge as aforesaid of the land given in exchange by the said trustees, and for the application of any money payable to the said trustees for equality of exchange; or
   (c) for the use of the allotment or any part thereof for any purposes specified in the scheme.

[868]

NOTES

Para 1: words in square brackets in sub-para (b) added by the Education Act 1996, s 582(1), Sch 37, Pt I, para 121; sub-para (c) repealed by the Statute Law (Repeals) Act 1993, s 1(1), Sch 1, Pt III.

Endowed Schools Act 1869–1948: the Acts which were cited by this collective title have all been repealed.

Elementary Education Act 1870, s 75: repealed by the Charities Act 1960, s 39(1), Sch 5.

Education Act 1973, s 2: repealed by the Education Act 1996, s 582(2), Sch 38, Pt I.

London Government Act 1899: now wholly repealed.

SCHEDULE 5
MEANING OF "CONNECTED PERSON" FOR PURPOSES OF SECTION 36(2)

Section 36(2)

1.—[(1) In section 36(2) of this Act "connected person", in relation to a charity, means any person who falls within sub-paragraph (2)—
   (a) at the time of the disposition in question, or
   (b) at the time of any contract for the disposition in question.

(2) The persons falling within this sub-paragraph are—]
   (a) a charity trustee or trustee for the charity;
   (b) a person who is the donor of any land to the charity (whether the gift was made on or after the establishment of the charity);

(c) a child, parent, grandchild, grandparent, brother or sister of any such trustee or donor;
(d) an officer, agent or employee of the charity;
(e) the spouse [or civil partner] of any person falling within any of sub-paragraphs (a) to (d) above;
[(ea) a person carrying on business in partnership with any person falling within any of sub-paragraphs (a) to (e) above;]
(f) an institution which is controlled—
  (i) by any person falling within any of sub-paragraphs (a) to [(ea)] above, or
  (ii) by two or more such persons taken together; or
(g) a body corporate in which—
  (i) any connected person falling within any of sub-paragraphs (a) to (f) above has a substantial interest, or
  (ii) two or more such persons, taken together, have a substantial interest.

2.—(1) In paragraph [1(2)(c)] above "child" includes a stepchild and an illegitimate child.

(2) For the purposes of paragraph [1(2)(e)] above a person living with another as that person's husband or wife shall be treated as that person's spouse.

[(3) Where two persons of the same sex are not civil partners but live together as if they were, each of them shall be treated for those purposes as the civil partner of the other.]

3. For the purposes of paragraph [1(2)(f)] above a person controls an institution if he is able to secure that the affairs of the institution are conducted in accordance with his wishes.

4.—(1) For the purposes of paragraph [1(2)(g)] above any such connected person as is there mentioned has a substantial interest in a body corporate if the person or institution in question—
(a) is interested in shares comprised in the equity share capital of that body of a nominal value of more than one-fifth of that share capital, or
(b) is entitled to exercise, or control the exercise of, more than one-fifth of the voting power at any general meeting of that body.

(2) The rules set out in Part I of Schedule 13 to the Companies Act 1985 (rules for interpretation of certain provisions of that Act) shall apply for the purposes of sub-paragraph (1) above as they apply for the purposes of section 346(4) of that Act ("connected persons" etc).

(3) In this paragraph "equity share capital" and "share" have the same meaning as in that Act.

[869]

NOTES

Para 1: words in first pair of square brackets substituted for the words "In section 36(2) of this Act "connected person", in relation to a charity, means—", sub-para (2)(ea) inserted and number in square brackets in sub-para (f)(i) substituted for "(e)" by the Charities Act 2006, s 75(1), Sch 8, paras 96, 178(1)–(4), as from 27 February 2007, except that the insertion of para (1)(b) and (2)(ea) shall not apply in relation to any disposition for which the contract was entered into before 27 February 2007 (see the Charities Act 2006 (Commencement No 1, Transitional Provisions and Savings) Order 2007, SI 2007/309, art 6(2)); words in square brackets in para (2)(e) inserted by the Civil Partnership Act 2004, s 261(1), Sch 27, para 147.

Para 2: numbers in square brackets in sub-paras (1), (2) substituted and sub-para (3) added by the Charities Act 2006, s 75(1), Sch 8, paras 96, 178(1), (5), as from 27 February 2007.

Paras 3, 4: numbers in square brackets substituted by the Charities Act 2006, s 75(1), Sch 8, paras 96, 178(1), (6), (7), as from 27 February 2007.

[SCHEDULE 5A
GROUP ACCOUNTS

Section 49A

Interpretation

1.—(1) This paragraph applies for the purposes of this Schedule.

(2) A charity is a "parent charity" if—
(a) it is (or is to be treated as) a parent undertaking in relation to one or more other

undertakings in accordance with the provisions of section 258 of, and Schedule 10A to, the Companies Act 1985, and

(b) it is not a company.

(3) Each undertaking in relation to which a parent charity is (or is to be treated as) a parent undertaking in accordance with those provisions is a "subsidiary undertaking" in relation to the parent charity.

(4) But sub-paragraph (3) does not have the result that any of the following is a "subsidiary undertaking"—

(a) any special trusts of a charity,

(b) any institution which, by virtue of a direction under section 96(5) of this Act, is to be treated as forming part of a charity for the purposes of this Part of this Act, or

(c) any charity to which a direction under section 96(6) of this Act applies for those purposes.

(5) "The group", in relation to a parent charity, means that charity and its subsidiary undertaking or undertakings, and any reference to the members of the group is to be construed accordingly.

(6) For the purposes of—

(a) this paragraph, and

(b) the operation of the provisions mentioned in sub-paragraph (2) above for the purposes of this paragraph,

"undertaking" has the meaning given by sub-paragraph (7) below.

(7) For those purposes "undertaking" means—

(a) an undertaking as defined by section 259(1) of the Companies Act 1985, or

(b) a charity which is not an undertaking as so defined.

Accounting records

2.—(1) The charity trustees—

(a) of a parent charity, or

(b) of any charity which is a subsidiary undertaking,

must ensure that the accounting records kept in respect of the charity under section 41(1) of this Act not only comply with the requirements of that provision but also are such as to enable the charity trustees of the parent charity to ensure that, where any group accounts are prepared by them under paragraph 3(2), those accounts comply with the relevant requirements.

(2) If a parent charity has a subsidiary undertaking in relation to which the requirements of section 41(1) of this Act do not apply, the charity trustees of the parent charity must take reasonable steps to secure that the undertaking keeps such accounting records as to enable the trustees to ensure that, where any group accounts are prepared by them under paragraph 3(2), those accounts comply with the relevant requirements.

(3) In this paragraph "the relevant requirements" means the requirements of regulations under paragraph 3.

Preparation of group accounts

3.—(1) This paragraph applies in relation to a financial year of a charity if it is a parent charity at the end of that year.

(2) The charity trustees of the parent charity must prepare group accounts in respect of that year.

(3) "Group accounts" means consolidated accounts—

(a) relating to the group, and

(b) complying with such requirements as to their form and contents as may be prescribed by regulations made by the Minister.

(4) Without prejudice to the generality of sub-paragraph (3), regulations under that sub-paragraph may make provision—

(a) for any such accounts to be prepared in accordance with such methods and principles as are specified or referred to in the regulations;

(b) for dealing with cases where the financial years of the members of the group do not all coincide;

(c) as to any information to be provided by way of notes to the accounts.

(5) Regulations under that sub-paragraph may also make provision—

(a) for determining the financial years of subsidiary undertakings for the purposes of this Schedule;

(b) for imposing on the charity trustees of a parent charity requirements with respect to securing that such financial years coincide with that of the charity.

(6) If the requirement in sub-paragraph (2) applies to the charity trustees of a parent charity in relation to a financial year—

(a) that requirement so applies in addition to the requirement in section 42(1) of this Act, and

(b) the option of preparing the documents mentioned in section 42(3) of this Act is not available in relation to that year (whatever the amount of the charity's gross income for that year).

(7) Sub-paragraph (2) has effect subject to paragraph 4.

Exceptions relating to requirement to prepare group accounts

4.—(1) The requirement in paragraph 3(2) does not apply to the charity trustees of a parent charity in relation to a financial year if at the end of that year it is itself a subsidiary undertaking in relation to another charity.

(2) The requirement in paragraph 3(2) does not apply to the charity trustees of a parent charity in relation to a financial year if the aggregate gross income of the group for that year does not exceed such sum as is specified in regulations made by the Minister.

(3) Regulations made by the Minister may prescribe circumstances in which a subsidiary undertaking may or (as the case may be) must be excluded from group accounts required to be prepared under paragraph 3(2) for a financial year.

(4) Where, by virtue of such regulations, each of the subsidiary undertakings which are members of a group is either permitted or required to be excluded from any such group accounts for a financial year, the requirement in paragraph 3(2) does not apply to the charity trustees of the parent charity in relation to that year.

Preservation of group accounts

5.—(1) The charity trustees of a charity shall preserve any group accounts prepared by them under paragraph 3(2) for at least six years from the end of the financial year to which the accounts relate.

(2) Subsection (4) of section 41 of this Act shall apply in relation to the preservation of any such accounts as it applies in relation to the preservation of any accounting records (the references to subsection (3) of that section being construed as references to sub-paragraph (1) above).

Audit of accounts of larger groups

6.—(1) This paragraph applies where group accounts are prepared for a financial year of a parent charity under paragraph 3(2) and—

(a) the aggregate gross income of the group in that year exceeds the relevant income threshold, or

(b) the aggregate gross income of the group in that year exceeds the relevant income threshold and at the end of the year the aggregate value of the assets of the group (before deduction of liabilities) exceeds the relevant assets threshold.

(2) In sub-paragraph (1)—

(a) the reference in paragraph (a) or (b) to the relevant income threshold is a reference to the sum prescribed as the relevant income threshold for the purposes of that paragraph, and

(b) the reference in paragraph (b) to the relevant assets threshold is a reference to the sum prescribed as the relevant assets threshold for the purposes of that paragraph.

"Prescribed" means prescribed by regulations made by the Minister.

(3) This paragraph also applies where group accounts are prepared for a financial year of a parent charity under paragraph 3(2) and the appropriate audit provision applies in relation to the parent charity's own accounts for that year.

(4) If this paragraph applies in relation to a financial year of a parent charity by virtue of sub-paragraph (1) or (3), the group accounts for that year shall be audited—
- (a) (subject to paragraph (b) or (c) below) by a person within section 43(2)(a) or (b) of this Act;
- (b) if section 43A of this Act applies in relation to that year, by a person appointed by the Audit Commission (see section 43A(7));
- (c) if section 43B of this Act applies in relation to that year, by the Auditor General for Wales.

(5) Where it appears to the Commission that sub-paragraph (4)(a) above has not been complied with in relation to that year within ten months from the end of that year—
- (a) the Commission may by order require the group accounts for that year to be audited by a person within section 43(2)(a) or (b) of this Act, and
- (b) if it so orders, the auditor shall be a person appointed by the Commission.

(6) Section 43(6) of this Act shall apply in relation to any such audit as it applies in relation to an audit carried out by an auditor appointed under section 43(5) (reading the reference to the funds of the charity as a reference to the funds of the parent charity).

(7) Section 43A(4) and (6) of this Act apply in relation to any appointment under sub-paragraph (4)(b) above as they apply in relation to an appointment under section 43A(2).

(8) If this paragraph applies in relation to a financial year of a parent charity by virtue of sub-paragraph (1), the appropriate audit provision shall apply in relation to the parent charity's own accounts for that year (whether or not it would otherwise so apply).

(9) In this paragraph "the appropriate audit provision", in relation to a financial year of a parent charity, means—
- (a) (subject to paragraph (b) or (c) below) section 43(2) of this Act;
- (b) if section 43A of this Act applies in relation to that year, section 43A(2);
- (c) if section 43B of this Act applies in relation to that year, section 43B(2).

Examination of accounts of smaller groups

7.—(1) This paragraph applies where—
- (a) group accounts are prepared for a financial year of a parent charity under paragraph 3(2), and
- (b) paragraph 6 does not apply in relation to that year.

(2) If—
- (a) this paragraph applies in relation to a financial year of a parent charity, and
- (b) sub-paragraph (4) or (5) below does not apply in relation to it,

subsections (3) to (7) of section 43 of this Act shall apply in relation to the group accounts for that year as they apply in relation to the accounts of a charity for a financial year in relation to which subsection (2) of that section does not apply, but subject to the modifications in sub-paragraph (3) below.

(3) The modifications are—
- (a) any reference to the charity trustees of the charity is to be construed as a reference to the charity trustees of the parent charity;
- (b) any reference to the charity's gross income in the financial year in question is to be construed as a reference to the aggregate gross income of the group in that year; and
- (c) any reference to the funds of the charity is to be construed as a reference to the funds of the parent charity.

(4) If—
- (a) this paragraph applies in relation to a financial year of a parent charity, and
- (b) section 43A of this Act also applies in relation to that year,

subsections (3) to (6) of that section shall apply in relation to the group accounts for that year as they apply in relation to the accounts of a charity for a financial year in relation to which subsection (2) of that section does not apply.

(5) If—

(a) this paragraph applies in relation to a financial year of a parent charity, and

(b) section 43B of this Act also applies in relation to that year,

subsection (3) of that section shall apply in relation to the group accounts for that year as they apply in relation to the accounts of a charity for a financial year in relation to which subsection (2) of that section does not apply.

(6) If the group accounts for a financial year of a parent charity are to be examined or audited in accordance with section 43(3) of this Act (as applied by sub-paragraph (2) above), section 43(3) shall apply in relation to the parent charity's own accounts for that year (whether or not it would otherwise so apply).

(7) Nothing in sub-paragraph (4) or (5) above affects the operation of section 43A(3) to (6) or (as the case may be) section 43B(3) in relation to the parent charity's own accounts for the financial year in question.

Supplementary provisions relating to audits etc

8.—(1) Section 44(1) of this Act shall apply in relation to audits and examinations carried out under or by virtue of paragraph 6 or 7, but subject to the modifications in sub-paragraph (2) below.

(2) The modifications are—

(a) in paragraph (b), the reference to section 43, 43A or 43B of this Act is to be construed as a reference to paragraph 6 above or to any of those sections as applied by paragraph 7 above;

(b) also in paragraph (b), the reference to any such statement of accounts as is mentioned in sub-paragraph (i) of that paragraph is to be construed as a reference to group accounts prepared for a financial year under paragraph 3(2) above;

(c) in paragraph (c), any reference to section 43, 43A or 43B of this Act is to be construed as a reference to that section as applied by paragraph 7 above;

(d) in paragraphs (d) and (e), any reference to the charity concerned or a charity is to be construed as a reference to any member of the group; and

(e) in paragraph (f), the reference to the requirements of section 43(2) or (3) of this Act is to be construed as a reference to the requirements of paragraph 6(4)(a) or those applied by paragraph 7(2) above.

(3) Without prejudice to the generality of section 44(1)(e), as modified by sub-paragraph (2)(d) above, regulations made under that provision may make provision corresponding or similar to any provision made by section 389A of the Companies Act 1985 (c 6) in connection with the rights exercisable by an auditor of a company in relation to a subsidiary undertaking of the company.

(4) In section 44(2) of this Act the reference to section 44(1)(d) or (e) includes a reference to that provision as it applies in accordance with this paragraph.

Duty of auditors etc to report matters to Commission

9.—(1) Section 44A(2) to (5) and (7) of this Act shall apply in relation to a person appointed to audit, or report on, any group accounts under or by virtue of paragraph 6 or 7 above as they apply in relation to a person such as is mentioned in section 44A(1).

(2) In section 44A(2)(a), as it applies in accordance with sub-paragraph (1) above, the reference to the charity or any connected institution or body is to be construed as a reference to the parent charity or any of its subsidiary undertakings.

Annual reports

10.—(1) This paragraph applies where group accounts are prepared for a financial year of a parent charity under paragraph 3(2).

(2) The annual report prepared by the charity trustees of the parent charity in respect of that year under section 45 of this Act shall include—

(a) such a report by the trustees on the activities of the charity's subsidiary undertakings during that year, and

(b) such other information relating to any of those undertakings,

as may be prescribed by regulations made by the Minister.

(3) Without prejudice to the generality of sub-paragraph (2), regulations under that sub-paragraph may make provision—

(a) for any such report as is mentioned in paragraph (a) of that sub-paragraph to be prepared in accordance with such principles as are specified or referred to in the regulations;

(b) enabling the Commission to dispense with any requirement prescribed by virtue of sub-paragraph (2)(b) in the case of a particular subsidiary undertaking or a particular class of subsidiary undertaking.

(4) Section 45(3) to (3B) shall apply in relation to the annual report referred to in sub-paragraph (2) above as if any reference to the charity's gross income in the financial year in question were a reference to the aggregate gross income of the group in that year.

(5) When transmitted to the Commission in accordance with sub-paragraph (4) above, the copy of the annual report shall have attached to it both a copy of the group accounts prepared for that year under paragraph 3(2) and—

(a) a copy of the report made by the auditor on those accounts; or

(b) where those accounts have been examined under section 43, 43A or 43B of this Act (as applied by paragraph 7 above), a copy of the report made by the person carrying out the examination.

(6) The requirements in this paragraph are in addition to those in section 45 of this Act.

Excepted charities

11.—(1) This paragraph applies where—

(a) a charity is required to prepare an annual report in respect of a financial year by virtue of section 46(5) of this Act,

(b) the charity is a parent charity at the end of the year, and

(c) group accounts are prepared for that year under paragraph 3(2) by the charity trustees of the charity.

(2) When transmitted to the Commission in accordance with section 46(7) of this Act, the copy of the annual report shall have attached to it both a copy of the group accounts and—

(a) a copy of the report made by the auditor on those accounts; or

(b) where those accounts have been examined under section 43, 43A or 43B of this Act (as applied by paragraph 7 above), a copy of the report made by the person carrying out the examination.

(3) The requirement in sub-paragraph (2) is in addition to that in section 46(6) of this Act.

Exempt charities

12. Nothing in the preceding provisions of this Schedule applies to an exempt charity.

Public inspection of annual reports etc

13. In section 47(2) of this Act, the reference to a charity's most recent accounts includes, in relation to a charity whose charity trustees have prepared any group accounts under paragraph 3(2), the group accounts most recently prepared by them.

Offences

14.—(1) Section 49(1) of this Act applies in relation to a requirement within sub-paragraph (2) as it applies in relation to a requirement within section 49(1)(a).

(2) A requirement is within this sub-paragraph where it is imposed by section 45(3) or (3A) of this Act, taken with—

(a) section 45(3B), (4) and (5), and

(b) paragraph 10(5) or 11(2) above,

as applicable.

(3) In sub-paragraph (2) any reference to section 45(3), (3A) or (3B) of this Act is a reference to that provision as applied by paragraph 10(4) above.

(4) In section 49(1)(b) the reference to section 47(2) of this Act includes a reference to that provision as extended by paragraph 13 above.

Aggregate gross income

15. The Minister may by regulations make provision for determining for the purposes of this Schedule the amount of the aggregate gross income for a financial year of a group consisting of a parent charity and its subsidiary undertaking or undertakings.]

[869A]

NOTES

Commencement: 27 February 2007 (paras 3(3)(b), (4), (5), 4(2), (3), 6(2), 8, 10(2), (3), 15 for the purposes of enabling the Minister to exercise the power to make subordinate legislation); to be appointed (otherwise).

Inserted by the Charities Act 2006, s 30(2), Sch 6, partly as from 27 February 2007, and fully as from a day to be appointed under s 79(2) of that Act, subject to transitional provisions in Sch 10, para 17 to that Act at **[2176]**.

[SCHEDULE 5B

FURTHER PROVISION ABOUT CHARITABLE INCORPORATED ORGANISATIONS

Section 69P

Powers

1.—(1) Subject to anything in its constitution, a CIO has power to do anything which is calculated to further its purposes or is conducive or incidental to doing so.

(2) The CIO's charity trustees shall manage the affairs of the CIO and may for that purpose exercise all the powers of the CIO.

Constitutional requirements

2. A CIO shall use and apply its property in furtherance of its purposes and in accordance with its constitution.

3. If the CIO is one whose members are liable to contribute to its assets if it is wound up, its constitution binds the CIO and its members for the time being to the same extent as if its provisions were contained in a contract—

(a) to which the CIO and each of its members was a party, and

(b) which contained obligations on the part of the CIO and each member to observe all the provisions of the constitution.

4. Money payable by a member to the CIO under the constitution is a debt due from him to the CIO, and is of the nature of a specialty debt.

Third parties

5.—(1) Sub-paragraphs (2) and (3) are subject to sub-paragraph (4).

(2) The validity of an act done (or purportedly done) by a CIO shall not be called into question on the ground that it lacked constitutional capacity.

(3) The power of the charity trustees of a CIO to act so as to bind the CIO (or authorise others to do so) shall not be called into question on the ground of any constitutional limitations on their powers.

(4) But sub-paragraphs (2) and (3) apply only in favour of a person who gives full consideration in money or money's worth in relation to the act in question, and does not know—

(a) in a sub-paragraph (2) case, that the act is beyond the CIO's constitutional capacity, or
(b) in a sub-paragraph (3) case, that the act is beyond the constitutional powers of its charity trustees,

and (in addition) sub-paragraph (3) applies only if the person dealt with the CIO in good faith (which he shall be presumed to have done unless the contrary is proved).

(5) A party to an arrangement or transaction with a CIO is not bound to inquire—
(a) whether it is within the CIO's constitutional capacity, or
(b) as to any constitutional limitations on the powers of its charity trustees to bind the CIO or authorise others to do so.

(6) If a CIO purports to transfer or grant an interest in property, the fact that the act was beyond its constitutional capacity, or that its charity trustees in connection with the act exceeded their constitutional powers, does not affect the title of a person who subsequently acquires the property or any interest in it for full consideration without actual notice of any such circumstances affecting the validity of the CIO's act.

(7) In any proceedings arising out of sub-paragraphs (2) to (4), the burden of proving that a person knew that an act—
(a) was beyond the CIO's constitutional capacity, or
(b) was beyond the constitutional powers of its charity trustees,

lies on the person making that allegation.

(8) In this paragraph and paragraphs 6 to 8—
(a) references to a CIO's lack of "constitutional capacity" are to lack of capacity because of anything in its constitution, and
(b) references to "constitutional limitations" on the powers of a CIO's charity trustees are to limitations on their powers under its constitution, including limitations deriving from a resolution of the CIO in general meeting, or from an agreement between the CIO's members, and "constitutional powers" is to be construed accordingly.

6.—(1) Nothing in paragraph 5 prevents a person from bringing proceedings to restrain the doing of an act which would be—
(a) beyond the CIO's constitutional capacity, or
(b) beyond the constitutional powers of the CIO's charity trustees.

(2) But no such proceedings may be brought in respect of an act to be done in fulfilment of a legal obligation arising from a previous act of the CIO.

(3) Sub-paragraph (2) does not prevent the Commission from exercising any of its powers.

7. Nothing in paragraph 5(3) affects any liability incurred by the CIO's charity trustees (or any one of them) for acting beyond his or their constitutional powers.

8. Nothing in paragraph 5 absolves the CIO's charity trustees from their duty to act within the CIO's constitution and in accordance with any constitutional limitations on their powers.

Duties

9. It is the duty of—
(a) each member of a CIO, and
(b) each charity trustee of a CIO,

to exercise his powers, and (in the case of a charity trustee) to perform his functions, in his capacity as such, in the way he decides, in good faith, would be most likely to further the purposes of the CIO.

10.—(1) Subject to any provision of a CIO's constitution permitted by virtue of regulations made under sub-paragraph (2), each charity trustee of a CIO shall in the performance of his functions in that capacity exercise such care and skill as is reasonable in the circumstances, having regard in particular—
(a) to any special knowledge or experience that he has or holds himself out as having, and
(b) if he acts as a charity trustee in the course of a business or profession, to any

special knowledge or experience that it is reasonable to expect of a person acting in the course of that kind of business or profession.

(2) The Minister may make regulations permitting a CIO's constitution to provide that the duty in sub-paragraph (1) does not apply, or does not apply in so far as is specified in the constitution.

(3) Regulations under sub-paragraph (2) may provide for limits on the extent to which, or the cases in which, a CIO's constitution may disapply the duty in sub-paragraph (1).

Personal benefit and payments

11.—(1) A charity trustee of a CIO may not benefit personally from any arrangement or transaction entered into by the CIO if, before the arrangement or transaction was entered into, he did not disclose to all the charity trustees of the CIO any material interest of his in it or in any other person or body party to it (whether that interest is direct or indirect).

(2) Nothing in sub-paragraph (1) confers authority for a charity trustee of a CIO to benefit personally from any arrangement or transaction entered into by the CIO.

12. A charity trustee of a CIO—
(a) is entitled to be reimbursed by the CIO, or
(b) may pay out of the CIO's funds,

expenses properly incurred by him in the performance of his functions as such.

Procedure

13.—(1) The Minister may by regulations make provision about the procedure of CIOs.

(2) Subject to—
(a) any such regulations,
(b) any other requirement imposed by or by virtue of this Act or any other enactment, and
(c) anything in the CIO's constitution,

a CIO may regulate its own procedure.

(3) But a CIO's procedure shall include provision for the holding of a general meeting of its members, and the regulations referred to in sub-paragraph (1) may in particular make provision about such meetings.

Amendment of constitution

14.—(1) A CIO may by resolution of its members amend its constitution (and a single resolution may provide for more than one amendment).

(2) Such a resolution must be passed—
(a) by a 75% majority of those voting at a general meeting of the CIO (including those voting by proxy or by post, if voting that way is permitted), or
(b) unanimously by the CIO's members, otherwise than at a general meeting.

(3) The date of passing of such a resolution is—
(a) the date of the general meeting at which it was passed, or
(b) if it was passed otherwise than at a general meeting, the date on which provision in the CIO's constitution or in regulations made under paragraph 13 deems it to have been passed (but that date may not be earlier than that on which the last member agreed to it).

(4) The power of a CIO to amend its constitution is not exercisable in any way which would result in the CIO's ceasing to be a charity.

(5) Subject to paragraph 15(5) below, a resolution containing an amendment which would make any regulated alteration is to that extent ineffective unless the prior written consent of the Commission has been obtained to the making of the amendment.

(6) The following are regulated alterations—
(a) any alteration of the CIO's purposes,

(b) any alteration of any provision of the CIO's constitution directing the application of property of the CIO on its dissolution,

(c) any alteration of any provision of the CIO's constitution where the alteration would provide authorisation for any benefit to be obtained by charity trustees or members of the CIO or persons connected with them.

(7) For the purposes of sub-paragraph (6)(c)—

(a) "benefit" means a direct or indirect benefit of any nature, except that it does not include any remuneration (within the meaning of section 73A of this Act) whose receipt may be authorised under that section, and

(b) the same rules apply for determining whether a person is connected with a charity trustee or member of the CIO as apply, in accordance with section 73B(5) and (6) of this Act, for determining whether a person is connected with a charity trustee for the purposes of section 73A.

Registration and coming into effect of amendments

15.—(1) A CIO shall send to the Commission a copy of a resolution containing an amendment to its constitution, together with—

(a) a copy of the constitution as amended, and

(b) such other documents and information as the Commission may require,

by the end of the period of 15 days beginning with the date of passing of the resolution (see paragraph 14(3)).

(2) An amendment to a CIO's constitution does not take effect until it has been registered.

(3) The Commission shall refuse to register an amendment if—

(a) in the opinion of the Commission the CIO had no power to make it (for example, because the effect of making it would be that the CIO ceased to be a charity, or that the CIO or its constitution did not comply with any requirement imposed by or by virtue of this Act or any other enactment), or

(b) the amendment would change the name of the CIO, and the Commission could have refused an application under section 69E of this Act for the constitution and registration of a CIO with the name specified in the amendment on a ground set out in subsection (4) of that section.

(4) The Commission may refuse to register an amendment if the amendment would make a regulated alteration and the consent referred to in paragraph 14(5) had not been obtained.

(5) But if the Commission does register such an amendment, paragraph 14(5) does not apply."

[869B]–[871]

NOTES

Commencement: 27 February 2007 (paras 10(2), (3), 13 for the purposes of enabling the Minister to exercise the power to make subordinate legislation); to be appointed (otherwise).

Inserted by the Charities Act 2006, s 34, Sch 7, Pt 1, para 2, partly as from 27 February 2007, and fully as from a day to be appointed under s 79(2) of that Act.

(Sch 6 contains consequential amendments, Sch 7 contains repeals; Sch 8 repealed by the Statute Law (Repeals) Act 2004.)

NATIONAL LOTTERY ETC ACT 1993

(1993 c 39)

ARRANGEMENT OF SECTIONS

PART I
AUTHORISATION AND REGULATION OF THE NATIONAL LOTTERY

Preliminary

An Act to authorise lotteries to be promoted as part of a National Lottery; to make provision with respect to the running and regulation of that National Lottery and with respect to the distribution of its net proceeds; to increase the membership and extend the powers of the Trustees of the National Heritage Memorial Fund; to amend section 1 of the Revenue Act 1898 and the Lotteries and Amusements Act 1976; to amend the law relating to pool betting; and for connected purposes

[21 October 1993]

NOTES

Transfer of functions in relation to Wales: as to the transfer of functions under this Act from Ministers of the Crown to the National Assembly for Wales and modifications consequential thereon, see the National Assembly for Wales (Transfer of Functions) Order 1999, SI 1999/672.

PART I
AUTHORISATION AND REGULATION OF THE NATIONAL LOTTERY

Preliminary

1 The National Lottery

(1) In this Act "the National Lottery" means all the lotteries that form part of the National Lottery, taken as a whole.

(2) A lottery forms part of the National Lottery if the following conditions are satisfied.

(3) The lottery must be promoted or proposed to be promoted—

(a) by the [person] licensed to run the National Lottery under section 5, or

(b) in pursuance of an agreement that has been made between that [person] and the lottery's promoter or proposed promoter.

(4) The promotion of the lottery must be authorised by a licence that has been granted to its promoter or proposed promoter under section 6.

[872]

NOTES

Substituted as follows by National Lottery Act 2006, s 6, Sch 1, paras 1, 2, as from a day to be appointed under s 6(1) of that Act—

"1 The National Lottery

(1) A lottery forms part of the National Lottery if it is promoted in accordance with a licence under section 5.

(2) A reference to the National Lottery is a reference to the lotteries forming part of the National Lottery in accordance with subsection (1).".

Sub-s (3): in paras (a), (b) word in square brackets substituted by the National Lottery Act 2006, s 3(a).

2 Legality of lotteries forming part of the National Lottery

(1) A lottery that forms part of the National Lottery shall not be unlawful.

(2) Schedule 1 contains amendments consequential on subsection (1).

[873]

NOTES

Repealed, in relation to England, Wales and Scotland, by the Gambling Act 2005, s 356(4), Sch 17, as from 1 September 2007, subject to savings and transitional provisions in Sch 18, Pt 2, paras 8–11 to that Act and in the Gambling Act 2005 (Commencement No 6 and Transitional Provisions) Order 2006, SI 2006/3272, arts 5, 6, Sch 4, paras 13–16.

3 (*Repealed by the National Lottery Act 1998, ss 1(2), 26, Sch 5, Pt I.*)

[3A The National Lottery Commission

(1) There shall be a body corporate known as the National Lottery Commission.

(2) Schedule 2A makes provision in relation to the Commission.]

[874]

NOTES

Commencement: 1 April 1999.
Inserted by the National Lottery Act 1998, s 1(3).

4 Overriding duties of the Secretary of State and [Commission]

(1) The Secretary of State and (subject to any directions [they] may be given by the Secretary of State under section 11) the [Commission] shall each exercise [their] functions under this Part in the manner [they consider] the most likely to secure—

(a) that the National Lottery is run, and every lottery that forms part of it is promoted, with all due propriety, and

(b) that the interests of every participant in a lottery that forms part of the National Lottery are protected.

(2) Subject to subsection (1), the Secretary of State and the [Commission] shall each in exercising those functions do [their] best to secure that the net proceeds of the National Lottery are as great as possible.

(3) In subsection (2) "the net proceeds of the National Lottery" means *the sums that are paid to the Secretary of State by virtue of section 5(6).*

[875]

NOTES

Section heading: words in square brackets substituted by virtue of the National Lottery Act 1998, s 1(5), Sch 1, para 4.

Sub-ss (1), (2): words in square brackets substituted by virtue of the National Lottery Act 1998, s 1(5), Sch 1, para 4.

Sub-s (3): for the words in italics there are substituted the words "the sums paid into the National Lottery Distribution Fund under section 5(2)(c)" by the National Lottery Act 2006, s 6, Sch 1, paras 1, 3, as from a day to be appointed under s 6(1) of that Act.

Reference to functions under Part I of this Act shall be treated as including a reference to functions under the Horserace Betting and Olympic Lottery Act 2004, Part 3 and the definition in sub-s (3) above of "net proceeds of the National Lottery" shall be treated as including a reference to sums paid into the Olympic Lottery Distribution Fund by virtue of s 24 thereof: see the Horserace Betting and Olympic Lottery Act 2004, s 34(2).

[4A Consultation with Gambling Commission

(1) If in the course of the exercise of its functions the National Lottery Commission becomes aware of a matter about which the Gambling Commission is likely to have an opinion, the National Lottery Commission shall consult the Gambling Commission.

(2) The National Lottery Commission shall comply with any direction of the Secretary of State (which may be general or specific) to consult the Gambling Commission.]

[875A]

NOTES

Commencement: 1 October 2005.
Inserted by the Gambling Act 2005, s 15(5), Sch 3, para 2.

[4B Disclosure of information

(1) The Commissioners for Her Majesty's Revenue and Customs may disclose information to the National Lottery Commission.

(2) The National Lottery Commission may disclose information to the Commissioners for Her Majesty's Revenue and Customs.

(3) Information disclosed under this section shall not be further disclosed except in accordance with subsection (4).

(4) Information may be further disclosed—

(a) for the purpose of complying with an enactment,
(b) in pursuance of an order of a court,
(c) for the purpose of legal proceedings connected with the operation of an enactment relating to lotteries,
(d) with the consent of the Commissioners for Her Majesty's Revenue and Customs,
(e) with the consent of each person to whom the information relates, or
(f) to the National Audit Office for the purposes of the exercise of functions under Part II of the National Audit Act 1983 (c 44).

(5) This section has effect despite any prohibition or restriction that would otherwise prevent disclosure of information.]

[875B]

NOTES

Commencement: 1 October 2006.
Inserted, together with s 4C, by the National Lottery Act 2006, s 2.

[4C Wrongful disclosure

(1) This section applies to a person—

(a) who is or was an officer or employee of the National Lottery Commission, or
(b) who acts or acted on behalf of the National Lottery Commission.

(2) A person to whom this section applies commits an offence if he discloses information received from the Commissioners for Her Majesty's Revenue and Customs in contravention of section 4B(3) and the information relates to a person whose identity—

(a) is specified in the disclosure, or
(b) can be deduced from it.

(3) It is a defence for a person charged with an offence under this section of disclosing information to prove that he reasonably believed—

(a) that the disclosure was lawful, or
(b) that the information had already and lawfully been made available to the public.

(4) A person guilty of an offence under this section shall be liable—

(a) on conviction on indictment, to imprisonment for a term not exceeding two years, to a fine or to both, or
(b) on summary conviction, to imprisonment for a term not exceeding 12 months, to a fine not exceeding the statutory maximum or to both.

(5) In relation to a conviction occurring before the commencement of section 282 of the Criminal Justice Act 2003 (c 44) (short sentences) the reference in subsection (4)(b) to 12 months shall have effect as if it were a reference to six months.

(6) In the application of this section to Scotland or Northern Ireland the reference in subsection (4)(b) to 12 months shall be taken as a reference to six months.]

[875C]

NOTES

Commencement: 1 October 2006.
Inserted as noted to s 4B at **[875B]**.

The licensing system

5 Licensing of a [person] to run the National Lottery

(1) The [Commission] may by licence authorise a [person] to run the National Lottery.

(2) Only one [person] may be licensed under this section at any one time.

(3) The [Commission] shall not grant a licence under this section unless an application in writing, containing such information as [it] has specified as necessary for enabling [it] to determine whether to grant it, has been made to [it] by such date as [it] has specified.

(4) The [Commission] shall not grant such a licence unless [it] is satisfied that the applicant is a fit and proper [person] to run the National Lottery.

(5) In determining whether to grant such a licence, the [Commission] may consider—

(a) whether any person who appears to [it] to be likely to manage the business or any part of the business of running the National Lottery under the licence is a fit and proper person to do so, and

(b) whether any person who appears to [it] to be likely to be a person for whose benefit that business would be carried on is a fit and proper person to benefit from it.

(6) A licence under this section shall include a condition requiring the licensee to pay to the Secretary of State at such times as may be determined by or under the licence such sums out of the proceeds of lotteries forming part of the National Lottery as may be so determined.

(7) A licence under this section may include a condition requiring the licensee to make such arrangements as may be determined by or under the licence for securing that, in circumstances specified in the licence, such sums as may be so determined are paid to the [Commission] for distribution to participants in lotteries forming part of the National Lottery.

[876]

NOTES

Substituted as follows, together with ss 6, 6A, for ss 5, 6 as originally enacted, by the National Lottery Act 2006, s 6, Sch 1, paras 1, 4, as from a day to be appointed under s 6(1) of that Act—

"5 Licence to promote lottery

(1) The Commission may by licence authorise a person to promote a lottery.

(2) A licence—

(a) may make provision about any matter connected with the promotion of a lottery (including, in particular, arrangements for advertising, for the sale of tickets, for the distribution of prizes or for compliance with a provision of this Act),

(b) may, in particular, require the licensee to—

(i) obtain in advance the Commission's approval of the rules of a lottery, and

(ii) pay a fee of such amount as may be prescribed by regulations made by the Secretary of State in respect of an application for approval of the rules of a lottery,

(c) shall include a condition requiring the licensee to pay into the National Lottery Distribution Fund sums out of the proceeds of any lottery promoted in reliance on the licence,

(d) shall include provision for determining—

(i) the amount of payments under paragraph (c), and

(ii) the timing of payments under paragraph (c), and

(e) may include provision requiring the licensee to make arrangements (which may include payments to the Commission) for securing the payment of prizes in certain circumstances.

(3) No more than one licence may be issued in relation to any one lottery; but—

(a) a licence may relate to one or more specified lotteries or to lotteries of a specified description,

(b) a person may hold more than one licence at a time, and

(c) a licence may require or permit the holder to make arrangements with another person for the performance of specified functions.

6 Section 5 licence: procedure

(1) The Commission may issue a licence under section 5 to a person only if—
(a) he has applied in writing for the licence,
(b) he has supplied such information or documents in or with the application as the Commission directs,
(c) having considered the application the Commission is satisfied that the applicant is a suitable person to promote the lottery or lotteries to which the licence relates, and
(d) the Commission has complied with any relevant regulations under section 6A (but this paragraph is subject to section 6A(3)).

(2) For the purposes of subsection (1)(c) the Commission may, in particular, have regard to—
(a) the integrity of the applicant or of a person relevant to the application;
(b) the competence of the applicant or of any person relevant to the application;
(c) the financial and other circumstances of the applicant or of a person relevant to the application.

(3) A person is relevant to an application under section 5 for the purposes of this section if, in particular—
(a) he is likely to exercise a function in connection with the promotion of a lottery in reliance on the licence applied for, or
(b) he is likely to have an interest in a lottery promoted in reliance on the licence applied for.

6A Competition for licences

(1) The Commission may not issue a licence under section 5 unless it has complied, in relation to the licence, with regulations of the Secretary of State about inviting competing applications for licences.

(2) The regulations shall, in particular, make provision—
(a) about the publication of invitations (including provision as to the manner and timing of publication and the matters to be published), and
(b) about the timing of responses.

(3) Where an application for a licence under section 5 relates to a lottery already licensed the Commission may issue the licence without complying with the regulations (whether or not compliance has begun) if the Commission thinks it—
(a) is likely to be in the interests of compliance with the duty under section 4(2), or
(b) is necessary in order to prevent the lapse of the lottery.

(4) Where a licence is issued in reliance on subsection (3)(b), the period specified for the duration of the licence under section 7(1A) shall be no longer than the Commission thinks necessary to enable a further licence to be issued having complied with the regulations.

(5) This section applies to a variation of a licence which expands the class of authorised activities as it applies to the issue of a licence.

(6) Before making regulations under subsection (1) the Secretary of State shall consult the Commission."

Section heading: word in square brackets substituted by the National Lottery Act 2006, s 3(b).
Sub-s (1): word in first pair of square brackets substituted by virtue of the National Lottery Act 1998, s 1(5), Sch 1, para 4; word in second pair of square brackets substituted by the National Lottery Act 2006, s 3(b).
Sub-s (2): word in square brackets substituted by the National Lottery Act 2006, s 3(b).
Sub-ss (3), (5), (7): words in square brackets substituted by virtue of the National Lottery Act 1998, s 1(5), Sch 1, para 4.
Sub-s (4): words in first and second pairs of square brackets substituted by virtue of the National Lottery Act 1998, s 1(5), Sch 1, para 4; word in third pair of square brackets substituted by the National Lottery Act 2006, s 3(b).

---

6 Licensing of [persons] to promote lotteries

(1) The [Commission] may by licence authorise a [person] to promote lotteries as part of the National Lottery.

(2) A licence under this section shall specify the lotteries, or descriptions of lottery, the promotion of which it authorises.

(3) The [Commission] shall not grant such a licence unless an application in writing, containing such information as [it] has specified as necessary for enabling [it] to determine whether to grant it, has been made to [it].

(4) The [Commission] shall not grant such a licence unless [it] is satisfied that the applicant is a fit and proper [person] to promote lotteries under the licence.

(5) In determining whether to grant such a licence, the [Commission] may consider—

(a) whether any person who appears to [it] to be likely to manage the business or any part of the business of promoting lotteries under the licence is a fit and proper person to do so, and

(b) whether any person who appears to [it] to be likely to be a person for whose benefit that business would be carried on is a fit and proper person to benefit from it.

(6) A licence under this section may include a condition requiring the licensee to obtain the [Commission's] approval of the rules of any lottery before the lottery is promoted under the licence.

[877]

NOTES

Substituted as noted to s 5. at **[876]**.

Section heading: word in first pair of square brackets substituted by virtue of the National Lottery Act 1998, s 1(5), Sch 1, para 4; word in second pair of square brackets substituted by the National Lottery Act 2006, s 3(c).

Sub-s (1): word in square brackets substituted by the National Lottery Act 2006, s 3(c).

Sub-ss (3), (5), (6): words in square brackets substituted by virtue of the National Lottery Act 1998, s 1(5), Sch 1, para 4.

Sub-s (4): words in first and second pairs of square brackets substituted by virtue of the National Lottery Act 1998, s 1(5), Sch 1, para 4; word in third pair of square brackets substituted by the National Lottery Act 2006, s 3(c).

7 Licences under *sections 5 and 6*: further provisions

(1) A licence granted under section 5 or 6 shall be in writing and shall specify the period for which (subject to being revoked or suspended) it is to have effect.

[*(1A) The period specified under subsection (1) must—*

(a) begin with the date of grant of the licence, and

(b) not exceed 15 years.

(1B) A licence granted under *section 5 or 6* may (subject to the restriction in subsection (1A)(b)) include—

(a) provision enabling the period specified under subsection (1) to be extended by the Commission;

(b) provision enabling the period specified under subsection (1) to be extended by agreement between the Commission and the licensee.]

(2) [*A licence granted under section 5 or 6*] may include such conditions (in addition to those required or authorised *by section 5 or 6*) as the [Commission] considers appropriate and in particular may include conditions requiring the licensee—

(a) to obtain the consent of the [Commission] before doing anything specified, or of a description specified, in the licence;

(b) to refer matters to the [Commission] for approval;

(c) to ensure that such requirements as the [Commission] may from time to time determine or approve are complied with;

(d) to provide the [Commission] at times specified by [it] with such information as [it] may require (including, if the information is of a description specified in the licence, information for publication by [it]);

(e) to allow the [Commission] to inspect and take copies of any documents of the licensee, including any information kept by the licensee otherwise than in writing, relating to the National Lottery or a lottery forming part of it;

(f) where such information is kept by means of a computer, to give the [Commission] such assistance as [it] may require to enable [it] to inspect and take copies of the information in a visible and legible form or to inspect and check the operation of any computer, and any associated apparatus or material, that is or has been in use in connection with the keeping of the information;

(g) to do such things (and, in particular, to effect such transfers of property or rights) as the [Commission] may require in connection with the licence ceasing to have effect and the grant of a licence to another [person].

(3) In subsection (2)(e) and (f) "the [Commission]" includes any representative of the [Commission], as well as any member of [its] staff, who has been authorised by [it] (whether generally or specially) to make such an inspection.

[(3A) Conditions under subsection (2), or requirements under subsection (2)(c), may, in particular, require the holder of a licence under section 5—

(a) to provide information in connection with the licensed activities to—

(i) the holder of another licence under section 5,

(ii) a person who is applying, or considering whether to apply, for a licence under section 5, or

(iii) such other person as the condition or requirement may specify or may enable the Commission to specify;

(b) to make facilities in connection with the licensed activities available to—

(i) the holder of another licence under section 5,

(ii) a person who is applying, or considering whether to apply, for a licence under section 5, or

(iii) such other person as the condition or requirement may specify or may enable the Commission to specify;

(c) to co-operate with the holder of another licence under section 5 in a specified matter;

(d) to participate in or co-operate with arrangements designed for the purposes of—

(i) holders of section 5 licences generally, or

(ii) a class of holders of section 5 licences generally;

(e) not to enter into an arrangement of a specified kind that would or might be harmful to the interests of the holder of another licence under section 5.]

(4) Conditions in a licence granted under *section 5 or 6* may impose requirements to be complied with by the licensee after the licence has ceased to have effect.

(5), (6) ...

[878]

NOTES

Section heading: for the words in italics there are substituted the words "section 5" by the National Lottery Act 2006, s 6, Sch 1, paras 1, 5(1), (7), as from a day to be appointed under s 6(1) of that Act.

Sub-s (1): substituted, together with sub-s (1A), as follows by the National Lottery Act 2006, s 6, Sch 1, paras 1, 5(1), (2), as from a day to be appointed under s 6(1) of that Act—

"(1) A licence under section 5 must be in writing.

(1A) A licence under section 5 must specify a period during which it has effect (unless revoked or suspended)—

(a) beginning with the date of issue, and

(b) not exceeding 15 years.".

Sub-s (1A): inserted, together with sub-s (1B), by the National Lottery Act 2006, s 4(1); substituted, together with sub-s (1), as set out under sub-s (1), by the National Lottery Act 2006, s 6, Sch 1, paras 1, 5(1), (2), as from a day to be appointed under s 6(1) of that Act.

Sub-s (1B): inserted, together with sub-s (1A), by the National Lottery Act 2006, s 4(1); for the words in italics there are substituted the words "section 5" by the National Lottery Act 2006, s 6, Sch 1, paras 1, 5(1), (3), as from a day to be appointed under s 6(1) of that Act.

Sub-s (2): words in first pair of square brackets substituted by the National Lottery Act 2006, s 4(2), further substituted by the words "section 5" and for the words in italics in the second place there are substituted the words "section 5" by the National Lottery Act 2006, s 6, Sch 1, paras 1, 5(1), (4), as from a day to be appointed under s 6(1) of that Act; word "Commission" in square brackets in each place it occurs, words in square brackets in paras (d), (f) and words in first pair of square bracket in para (g) substituted by virtue of the National Lottery Act 1998, s 1(5), Sch 1, para 4; words in second pair of square brackets in para (g) substituted by the National Lottery Act 2006, s 3(g).

Sub-s (3): words in square brackets substituted by virtue of the National Lottery Act 1998, s 1(5), Sch 1, para 4.

Sub-s (3A): inserted by the National Lottery Act 2006, s 6, Sch 1, paras 1, 5(1), (5), as from a day to be appointed under s 6(1) of that Act.

Sub-s (4): for the words in italics there are substituted the words "section 5" by the National Lottery Act 2006, s 6, Sch 1, paras 1, 5(1), (6), as from a day to be appointed under s 6(1) of that Act.

Sub-ss (5), (6): repealed by the National Lottery Act 2006, ss 5(2), 21, Sch 3.

Orders: the National Lottery (Licence Fees) Order 2001, SI 2001/2506.

[7A Annual fee

(1) The holder of a licence *under section 5 or 6*—

(a) shall pay a first annual fee to the Commission within such period after the issue of the licence as may be prescribed, and

(b) shall pay an annual fee to the Commission before each anniversary of the issue of the licence.

(2) In this section—
"annual fee" means a fee of such amount as may be prescribed, and
"prescribed" means prescribed by regulations made by the Secretary of State.

(3) Subsection (1)(b) does not apply in relation to an anniversary of the issue of a licence on or immediately before which the licence ceases, by virtue of its terms, to have effect.

(4) The Commission shall pay fees received by virtue of this section into the Consolidated Fund.]

[878A]

NOTES

Commencement: to be appointed.

Inserted by the National Lottery Act 2006, s 5(1), as from a day to be appointed under s 22(1) of that Act.

Sub-s (1): for the words in italics there are substituted the words "section 5" by the National Lottery Act 2006, s 6, Sch 1, paras 1, 6, as from a day to be appointed under s 6(1) of that Act.

8 Variation of conditions in licences

(1) The [Commission] may vary any condition in a licence granted under *section 5 or 6* if the licensee consents.

(2) Subject to subsection (3), the [Commission] may vary any condition in such a licence without the licensee's consent if the licensee has been given a reasonable opportunity of making representations to the [Commission] about the variation.

(3) Subsection (2) does not apply—
- (a) where the variation would result in a condition requiring the licensee to transfer any property or rights, or
- (b) *in the case of a licence granted under section 5*, in relation to a condition that the licence provides may only be varied with the consent of the licensee.

(4) Where the [Commission] varies a condition in a licence under subsection (2)—
- (a) [it] shall serve a notice on the licensee informing the licensee of the variation, and
- (b) the variation shall take effect at the end of such period as may be specified in the notice.

(5) The period specified in the notice shall be a period of at least twenty-one days beginning with the date of the notice.

(6) The [Commission's] power to vary a condition in a licence under subsection (1) or (2) includes power to add a condition to the licence or omit a condition from it (and references in this section to the variation of a condition are to be read accordingly).

[879]

NOTES

Sub-s (1): word in square brackets substituted by virtue of the National Lottery Act 1998, s 1(5), Sch 1, para 4; for the words in italics there are substituted the words "section 5" by the National Lottery Act 2006, s 6, Sch 1, paras 1, 7(a), as from a day to be appointed under s 6(1) of that Act.

Sub-ss (2), (4), (6): words in square brackets substituted by virtue of the National Lottery Act 1998, s 1(5), Sch 1, para 4.

Sub-s (3): words in italics repealed by the National Lottery Act 2006, s 6, Sch 1, paras 1, 7(b), as from a day to be appointed under s 6(1) of that Act.

9 Enforcement of conditions in licences

(1) If, on an application made by the [Commission], the court is satisfied—
- (a) that there is a reasonable likelihood that a person will contravene a condition in a licence granted under *section 5 or 6*,
- (b) that a person has contravened such a condition and there is a reasonable likelihood that the contravention will continue or be repeated, or
- (c) that a person has contravened such a condition and there are steps that could be taken for remedying the contravention,

the court may grant an injunction restraining the contravention or, in Scotland, an interdict prohibiting the contravention or (as the case may be) make an order requiring the licensee, and any other person who appears to the court to have been party to the contravention, to take such steps as the court may direct to remedy it.

(2) In subsection (1) "the court" means the High Court or, in Scotland, the Court of Session.

[(3) Where a sum is due to be paid to the National Lottery Distribution Fund by virtue of *section 5(6)*—

(a) the sum shall be recoverable by the Secretary of State as a debt due to the Fund, and

(b) the licensee's liability to pay shall not be affected by his licence ceasing to have effect.]

[880]

NOTES

Sub-s (1): word in square brackets substituted by virtue of the National Lottery Act 1998, s 1(5), Sch 1, para 4; for the words in italics there are substituted the words "section 5" by the National Lottery Act 2006, s 6, Sch 1, paras 1, 8(a), as from a day to be appointed under s 6(1) of that Act.

Sub-s (3): substituted by the Horserace Betting and Olympic Lottery Act 2004, s 34(1), (5); for further effect see s 24(2) of that Act; for the words in italics there are substituted the words "section 5(2)(c)" by the National Lottery Act 2006, s 6, Sch 1, paras 1, 8(b), as from a day to be appointed under s 6(1) of that Act.

10 Revocation of licences

(1) The [Commission] shall revoke a licence granted under section 5 if [it] is satisfied that the licensee no longer is, or never was, *a fit and proper [person] to run the National Lottery*.

(2) *The [Commission] shall revoke a licence granted under section 6 if [it] is satisfied that the licensee no longer is, or never was, a fit and proper [person] to promote lotteries under the licence.*

(3) The [Commission] may revoke a licence granted under *section 5 or 6*—

(a) if it appears to [it] that any of the grounds for revocation set out in Part I of Schedule 3 applies, or

(b) if the licensee consents.

[(3A) The Commission shall revoke a licence granted under *section 5 or 6* if the licensee fails to pay the annual fee in accordance with section 7A; but the Commission may disapply this subsection if it thinks that a failure to pay is attributable to administrative error.]

(4) Part II of Schedule 3 shall have effect in relation to the revocation of a licence under this section, other than a revocation with the licensee's consent [or under subsection (3A)].

[881]

NOTES

Sub-s (1): words in first and second pairs of square brackets substituted by virtue of the National Lottery Act 1998, s 1(5), Sch 1, para 4; for the words in italics there are substituted the words "a suitable person to promote the lottery or lotteries to which the licence relates" by the National Lottery Act 2006, s 6, Sch 1, paras 1, 9(a), as from a day to be appointed under s 6(1) of that Act; words in third pair of square brackets substituted by the National Lottery Act 2006, s 3(e).

Sub-s (2): repealed by the National Lottery Act 2006, s 6, Sch 1, paras 1, 9(b), as from a day to be appointed under s 6(1) of that Act; words in first and second pairs of square brackets substituted by virtue of the National Lottery Act 1998, s 1(5), Sch 1, para 4; words in third pair of square brackets substituted by the National Lottery Act 2006, s 3(e).

Sub-s (3): words in square brackets substituted by virtue of the National Lottery Act 1998, s 1(5), Sch 1, para 4; for the words in italics there are substituted the words "section 5" by the National Lottery Act 2006, s 6, Sch 1, paras 1, 9(c), as from a day to be appointed under s 6(1) of that Act.

Sub-s (3A): inserted by the National Lottery Act 2006, s 5(3)(a), as from a day to be appointed under s 22(1) of that Act; for the words in italics there are substituted the words "section 5" by the National Lottery Act 2006, s 6, Sch 1, paras 1, 9(d), as from a day to be appointed under s 6(1) of that Act.

Sub-s (4): words in square brackets added by the National Lottery Act 2006, s 5(3)(b), as from a day to be appointed under s 22(1) of that Act.

[10A Financial penalties for breach of conditions in licences

(1) If the Director General is satisfied that a person has contravened a condition in a licence under *section 5 or 6*, he may impose a financial penalty on that person in respect of the contravention.

(2) The matters to which the Director General may have regard in imposing a financial penalty include the desirability of both—

(a) deterring persons from contravening conditions in licences under *section 5 or 6*, and
(b) recovering any diminution in the sums *paid to the Secretary of State under section 5(6)* which is attributable to the contravention.

(3) If the Director General proposes to impose a financial penalty on a person, he shall serve on that person a notice—
(a) stating that the person has contravened conditions in the licence,
(b) identifying the contraventions in question,
(c) stating that the Director General proposes to impose a financial penalty,
(d) specifying the amount of the financial penalty,
(e) stating the Director General's reasons—
 (i) for the imposition of a financial penalty, and
 (ii) for the amount of the financial penalty,
(f) stating the person to whom the financial penalty is to be paid and the manner in which, and place at which, payment may be made, and
(g) stating the effect of subsections (5) and (12).

(4) A notice under subsection (3) must state that the person may, within the period of 21 days beginning with the date of the notice, either—
(a) make written representations about the matter to the Director General, or
(b) notify the Director General in writing of the person's intention to make oral representations,

and that the right of appeal conferred by section 10B is dependent on the person having made such written or oral representations.

(5) If, within the period mentioned in subsection (4), the Director General receives neither—
(a) written representations, nor
(b) written notification of the person's intention to make oral representations,

the financial penalty shall become payable at the end of that period.

(6) The Secretary of State may make regulations as to the procedure to be followed where a person's intention to make oral representations is notified to the Director General as mentioned in subsection (4).

(7) The regulations may in particular make provision—
(a) for the financial penalty to become payable if the person fails to comply with any requirements imposed by or under the regulations, and
(b) as to the hearing by the Director General of oral representations.

(8) If—
(a) any written representations against the imposition of the financial penalty are made as mentioned in subsection (4), or
(b) any oral representations against the imposition of the financial penalty are made in accordance with regulations under subsection (6),

subsection (9) shall apply.

(9) Where this subsection applies, the Director General shall after taking the representations into account—
(a) decide whether or not to impose a financial penalty, and
(b) serve a further notice on the person informing the person of the decision.

(10) Where the decision is to impose a financial penalty, the further notice must—
(a) identify the contraventions in question,
(b) specify the amount of the financial penalty imposed,
(c) state the Director General's reasons—
 (i) for the imposition of a financial penalty, and
 (ii) for the amount of the financial penalty,
(d) state the person to whom the financial penalty is to be paid and the manner in which, and place at which, payment may be made, and
(e) state the effect of subsections (11) and (12).

(11) A financial penalty imposed by virtue of a decision under subsection (9) becomes payable on the date of the further notice.

(12) A person on whom a financial penalty is imposed is required to pay the penalty within the period of fourteen days beginning with the date on which the financial penalty becomes payable.

(13) If the whole or any part of a financial penalty is not paid within the period mentioned in subsection (12), then as from the end of that period the unpaid balance from time to time shall carry interest at the rate for the time being specified in section 17 of the Judgments Act 1838.

[(14) Where under this section one person ("the debtor") becomes liable to pay a penalty to another person ("the creditor")—

(a) the penalty and any interest accrued under subsection (13) shall be recoverable by the Secretary of State from the debtor as a debt due to the creditor, and

(b) the debtor's liability to pay shall not be affected by his licence ceasing to have effect.

(15) A penalty under this section may be payable partly to the National Lottery Distribution Fund and partly to the Olympic Lottery Distribution Fund.]]

[882]

NOTES

Commencement: 2 September 1998.

Inserted, in relation to any contravention, after 2 September 1998, of a condition in a licence under s 5 or 6, whenever granted, by the National Lottery Act 1998, s 2(1), (5).

Sub-s (1): for the words in italics there are substituted the words "section 5" by the National Lottery Act 2006, s 6, Sch 1, paras 1, 10(a), as from a day to be appointed under s 6(1) of that Act.

Sub-s (2): for the words in italics in para (a) there are substituted the words "section 5" and for the words in italics in para (b) there are substituted the words "payable under section 5(2)(c)" by the National Lottery Act 2006, s 6, Sch 1, paras 1, 10, as from a day to be appointed under s 6(1) of that Act.

Sub-ss (14), (15): substituted, for existing sub-s (14), by the Horserace Betting and Olympic Lottery Act 2004, s 34(1), (6).

Regulations: the National Lottery (Imposition of Penalties and Revocation of Licences) Procedure Regulations 1999, SI 1999/137.

[10B Appeals against financial penalties

(1) Where the Director General decides under subsection (9) of section 10A to impose a financial penalty on a person, the person may appeal against the decision on the grounds specified in subsection (2) or, as the case may be, subsection (3).

(2) To the extent that an appeal under this section is against a finding by the Director General that a person contravened a condition of a licence, the grounds for the appeal are—

(a) that the Director General made an error as to the facts,

(b) that there was a material procedural error, or

(c) that the Director General made some other error of law.

(3) To the extent that an appeal under this section is against the amount of a financial penalty, the grounds for the appeal are—

(a) that the amount of the penalty is unreasonable,

(b) that there was a material procedural error, or

(c) that the decision was based on a manifest material misapprehension as to the facts.

(4) Where on an appeal under this section a court reduces the amount of a financial penalty, the powers of the court shall include power to make such orders as to interest on the penalty as the court considers just and equitable in all the circumstances of the case.

(5) The power conferred by subsection (4) includes power to make orders as to—

(a) the rates of interest which are to apply, and

(b) the date from which interest is to run.

(6) An appeal under this section lies to the High Court or, in Scotland, to the Court of Session.

(7) Any appeal under this section to the Court of Session shall be heard in the Outer House.]

[883]

NOTES

Commencement: 2 September 1998.

Inserted by the National Lottery Act 1998, s 3.

[10C Annual levy

(1) The Secretary of State may make regulations requiring holders of licences under *section 5 or 6* to pay an annual levy to the Gambling Commission.

(2) The regulations shall, in particular, make provision for—
- (a) timing of payment of the levy, and
- (b) the amount of the levy.

(3) The regulations may, in particular, make provision—
- (a) determining the amount of the levy by reference to a percentage of specified receipts of the holder of a licence under *section 5 or 6*,
- (b) determining the amount of the levy by reference to a percentage of specified profits of the holder of a licence under *section 5 or 6*,
- (c) providing for the determination of the amount of the levy according to a specified formula, or
- (d) providing for the determination of the amount of the levy in some other way.

(4) Any sum due by way of levy by virtue of this section shall be treated for the purposes of this Act as if its payment were a condition of the licence under *section 5 or 6*.

(5) The Gambling Commission shall, with the consent of the Treasury and of the Secretary of State, expend money received by way of levy for purposes related to, or by providing financial assistance for projects related to—
- (a) addiction to gambling,
- (b) other forms of harm or exploitation associated with gambling, or
- (c) any of the licensing objectives for the purposes of the Gambling Act 2005.

(6) In subsection (5) the reference to financial assistance is a reference to grants, loans and any other form of financial assistance, which may be made or given on terms or conditions (which may include terms and conditions as to repayment with or without interest).

(7) The Secretary of State may make regulations under this section only if—
- (a) he has made regulations under the Gambling Act 2005 requiring holders of operating licences to pay an annual levy to the Gambling Commission, and
- (b) he has consulted the National Lottery Commission.

(8) The Gambling Commission shall consult the National Lottery Commission before incurring expenditure under subsection (5).]

[883A]

NOTES

Commencement: 1 September 2007.

Inserted by the Gambling Act 2005, s 15(5), Sch 3, para 1, as from 1 September 2007.

Sub-ss (1), (3), (4): for the words in italics in each place they occur there are substituted the words "section 5" by the National Lottery Act 2006, s 6, Sch 1, paras 1, 11, as from a day to be appointed under s 6(1) of that Act.

Control by the Secretary of State

11 Directions to the [Commission]

(1) The [Commission] shall in exercising [its] functions under [sections 5 to 10A] comply with any directions that [it] may be given by the Secretary of State.

(2) Such directions may deal in particular—
- (a) with the matters that the [Commission] should take into account in deciding whether or not to grant licences;
- (b) with the conditions that licences should contain.

[884]

NOTES

Words in third pair of square brackets in sub-s (1) substituted by the National Lottery Act 1998, s 2(2); other words in square brackets substituted by virtue of s 1(5) of, and Sch 1, para 4 to, the 1998 Act.

12 Regulations as to the promotion of lotteries

(1) The Secretary of State may by regulations make such provision in relation to the promotion of lotteries that form part of the National Lottery as he considers necessary or expedient.

(2) Such regulations may in particular impose requirements or restrictions as to—
- (a) the minimum age of persons to whom or by whom tickets or chances may be sold;
- (b) the places, circumstances or manner in which tickets or chances may be sold or persons may be invited to buy them;
- (c) the information that must appear in an advertisement for a lottery;
- (d) the places, circumstances or manner in which signs relating to a lottery may be displayed.

(3) In subsection (2) "tickets" includes any document providing evidence of a person's claim to participate in the chances of a lottery.

(4) Regulations under this section may make different provision for different areas.

[885]

NOTES

Regulations: the National Lottery Regulations 1994, SI 1994/189.

13 Contravention of regulations an offence

(1) If any requirement or restriction imposed by regulations made under section 12 is contravened in relation to the promotion of a lottery that forms part of the National Lottery—
- (a) the promoter of the lottery shall be guilty of an offence, except if the contravention occurred without the consent or connivance of the promoter and the promoter exercised all due diligence to prevent such a contravention,
- (b) any director, manager, secretary or other similar officer of the promoter, or any person purporting to act in such a capacity, shall be guilty of an offence if he consented to or connived at the contravention or if the contravention was attributable to any neglect on his part, and
- (c) any other person who was party to the contravention shall be guilty of an offence.

(2) A person guilty of an offence under this section shall be liable—
- (a) on summary conviction, to a fine not exceeding the statutory maximum;
- (b) on conviction on indictment, to imprisonment for a term not exceeding two years, to a fine or to both.

(3), (4) (*Apply to Scotland only.*)

[886]

Provision of information by the [Commission]

14 Annual report

(1) As soon as possible after the end of every financial year, the [Commission] shall make a report on the exercise of [their] functions during that year to the Secretary of State.

(2) In subsection (1) "financial year" means—
- (a) …
- [(aa) the period beginning with the date on which section 3A comes into force and ending with the next 31st March, and]
- (b) each successive period of twelve months ending with 31st March.

(3) The Secretary of State shall lay a copy of every report received by him under this section before Parliament.

[887]

NOTES

Words in square brackets in the heading preceding this section substituted by virtue of the National Lottery Act 1998, s 1(5), Sch 1, para 4.

Sub-s (1): words in square brackets substituted by virtue of the National Lottery Act 1998, s 1(5), Sch 1, para 4.

Sub-s (2): para (a) repealed and para (aa) inserted by the National Lottery Act 1998, ss 1(5), 26, Sch 1, para 13(a), (b), Sch 5, Pt I.

15 Power of the Secretary of State to require information

The [Commission] shall provide the Secretary of State with such information relating to the National Lottery or a lottery forming part of it as the Secretary of State may direct.

[888]

NOTES

Words in square brackets substituted by virtue of the National Lottery Act 1998, s 1(5), Sch 1, para 4.

Miscellaneous and supplementary

16 False representations as to the National Lottery

(1) If a person advertising, or offering the opportunity to participate in, a lottery, competition or game of another description gives, by whatever means, a false indication that it is a lottery forming part of, or is otherwise connected with, the National Lottery, he shall be guilty of an offence.

(2) A person guilty of an offence under this section shall be liable—

(a) on summary conviction, to a fine not exceeding the statutory maximum;

(b) on conviction on indictment, to imprisonment for a term not exceeding two years, to a fine or to both.

[889]

17 Extension of powers of Horserace Totalisator Board

(1) The Horserace Totalisator Board may hold a licence under section 5 or 6.

(2) The Horserace Totalisator Board may hold an interest in a body corporate the only or principal object of which is the holding of a licence under section 5 or 6.

(3) In subsection (2) the reference to holding an interest in a body corporate is to holding, or being beneficially entitled to, shares in that body or to possessing voting power in that body.

[890]

NOTES

Repealed by the Horserace Betting and Olympic Lottery Act 2004, ss 13, 38, Sch 2, para 21, Sch 6, as from a day to be appointed under s 40(1) of that Act.

18 *(Amends the Betting, Gaming and Lotteries Act 1963, Sch 1, and the Betting, Gaming, Lotteries and Amusements (Northern Ireland) Order 1985, SI 1985/1204, arts 8, 17, 27; repealed in part by the Gambling Act 2005, s 356(4), Sch 17, as from 1 September 2007.)*

19 Restriction of enactments relating to the rehabilitation of offenders

(1) Neither section 4(1) of the Rehabilitation of Offenders Act 1974 nor Article 5(1) of the Rehabilitation of Offenders (Northern Ireland) Order 1978 (exclusion of evidence and questions relating to an individual's previous convictions) shall apply in relation to any proceedings—

(a) before the [Commission] in respect of the grant or revocation of a licence, or

(b) by way of appeal to the Secretary of State against the revocation of a licence by the [Commission].

(2) A conviction shall not be regarded as spent for the purposes of section 4(2) of that Act or Article 5(2) of that Order (restrictions in respect of such questions put otherwise than in proceedings) if the question is put by the [Commission] and the following conditions are satisfied.

(3) The question must be put for the purpose of determining whether to grant or revoke a licence.

(4) The question must relate to an individual—

(a) *who manages the business or any part of the business carried on under the licence (or who is likely to do so if the licence is granted), or*
(b) *for whose benefit that business is carried on (or is likely to be carried on if the licence is granted).*

(5) When the question is asked, the person questioned must be informed that by virtue of this section all the individual's previous convictions are to be disclosed.

[891]

NOTES

Repealed by the Police Act 1997, ss 133(d), 134(2), Sch 10, as from a day to be appointed.
Sub-ss (1), (2): words in square brackets substituted by virtue of the National Lottery Act 1998, s 1(5), Sch 1, para 4.

20 Interpretation of Part I

In this Part—

["the Commission" means the National Lottery Commission;]

"contravention", in relation to a condition or requirement, includes a failure to comply with that condition or requirement (and "contravened" is to be read accordingly);

.....

["lottery" has the same meaning as in the Gambling Act 2005;]

"participant", in relation to a lottery, means a person who has bought a ticket or chance in the lottery;

"promote" includes conduct (and "promotion" is to be read accordingly);

and any reference to a lottery forming part of the National Lottery is to be read in accordance with section 1.

[892]

NOTES

Definition "the Commission" inserted and definition "the Director General" (omitted) repealed by the National Lottery Act 1998, ss 1(5), 26, Sch 1, para 14(a), (b), Sch 5, Pt I; definition "lottery" inserted by the Gambling Act 2005, s 15(5), Sch 3, para 3, as from 1 September 2007.

PART II
DISTRIBUTION OF THE NET PROCEEDS OF THE NATIONAL LOTTERY

The distribution system

21 The National Lottery Distribution Fund

(1) There shall be a fund maintained under the control and management of the Secretary of State and known as the National Lottery Distribution Fund.

(2) …

[893]

NOTES

Sub-s (2): repealed by the Horserace Betting and Olympic Lottery Act 2004, ss 34(1), (8), 38, Sch 6.

22 Apportionment of money in Distribution Fund

(1) Every sum that is paid into the Distribution Fund [by virtue of *section 5(6)* or 10A] shall be apportioned as follows.

(2) So much of the sum as the Secretary of State considers appropriate shall be allocated for making payments under section 31 and held in the Distribution Fund for that purpose.

(3) Of the balance—
(a) [16⅔per cent] shall be allocated for expenditure on or connected with the arts,
(b) [16⅔per cent] shall be allocated for expenditure on or connected with sport,
(c) [16⅔ per cent] shall be allocated for expenditure on or connected with the national heritage, [and]
[(d) 50 per cent shall be allocated for prescribed expenditure that is—

(i) charitable, or
(ii) connected with health, or
(iii) connected with education, or
(iv) connected with the environment]

[(including, in each case, for establishing or contributing to endowments in connection with such expenditure)].

[(3A) In subsection (3)(d) "prescribed expenditure" means expenditure of a description prescribed by order of the Secretary of State.

(3B) A description of expenditure under subsection (3A) may, in particular, refer to expenditure in relation to—

(a) England,
(b) Wales,
(c) Scotland,
(d) Northern Ireland,
(e) any of the Channel Islands, or
(f) the Isle of Man;

and expenditure described by virtue of this subsection is referred to in this Act as "devolved expenditure".

(3C) Before making an order under subsection (3A) the Secretary of State shall consult—

(a) the Big Lottery Fund,
(b) the National Assembly for Wales,
(c) the Scottish Ministers,
(d) the Northern Ireland Department of Culture, Arts and Leisure, and
(e) such other persons (if any) as he thinks appropriate.]

[(4) This section has effect subject to section 19 of the National Lottery Act 1998 [and to section 25 of the Horserace Betting and Olympic Lottery Act 2004].]

[894]

NOTES

Sub-s (1): words in square brackets substituted by the Horserace Betting and Olympic Lottery Act 2004, s 34(1), (9)(a); for the words in italics there are substituted the words "section 5(2)(c)" by the National Lottery Act 2006, s 6, Sch 1, paras 1, 12, as from a day to be appointed under s 6(1) of that Act.

Sub-s (3): in paras (a)–(c) words in square brackets substituted, in relation to sums paid into the National Lottery Distribution Fund, by the Apportionment of Money in the National Lottery Distribution Fund Order 1999, SI 1999/344, arts 2, 3(1)–(4), with effect from 17 May 1999; in para (c) word "and" in square brackets inserted and para (d) substituted, for paras (d), (f) as originally enacted, by the National Lottery Act 2006, s 7(1), (2); words in final pair of square brackets added with retrospective effect by the National Lottery (Funding of Endowments) Act 2003, s 1(1), (2).

Sub-ss (3A)–(3C): inserted by the National Lottery Act 2006, s 7(1), (3), as from 1 December 2006 except in so far as it relates to sub-s (3B)(e).

Sub-s (4): added by the National Lottery Act 1998, s 19(7); words in square brackets added by the Horserace Betting and Olympic Lottery Act 2004, s 34(1), (9)(c).

Orders: the Big Lottery Fund (Prescribed Expenditure) Order 2006, SI 2006/3202 at **[3418]**.

23 The distributing bodies

(1) So much of any sum paid into the Distribution Fund as is allocated for expenditure on or connected with the arts shall be held in the Distribution Fund—

[(a) as to [71.1 per cent], for distribution by the Arts Council of England,
(b) (*applies to Scotland only*),
(c) as to 5 per cent, for distribution by the Arts Council of Wales, …
(d) as to 2.8 per cent, for distribution by [the Arts Council of Northern Ireland]][, *and*
(e) as to 12.2 per cent, for distribution by the Film Council]

(2) So much of any sum paid into the Distribution Fund as is allocated for expenditure on or connected with sport shall be held in the Distribution Fund—

(a) as to [62 per cent], for distribution by [the English Sports Council],
(b) as to [8.1 per cent], for distribution by the Scottish Sports Council,
(c) as to [4.5 per cent], for distribution by the Sports Council for Wales, and
(d) as to [2.6 per cent], for distribution by the Sports Council for Northern Ireland [and
(e) as to [22.8 per cent], for distribution by the United Kingdom Sports Council].

(3) So much of any sum paid into the Distribution Fund as is allocated for expenditure on or connected with the national heritage shall be held in the Distribution Fund for distribution by the Trustees of the National Heritage Memorial Fund.

[(4) So much of any sum paid into the Distribution Fund as is allocated under section 22(3)(d) shall be held by the Distribution Fund for distribution by the Big Lottery Fund (established under section 36A).]

[895]

NOTES

Sub-s (1): paras (a)–(d) substituted for original paras (a), (b) by the National Lottery etc Act 1993 (Amendment of Section 23) Order 1994, SI 1994/1342, art 2; words in square brackets in para (a) substituted, word omitted from para (c) repealed and para (e) and the word immediately preceding it added, by the National Lottery etc Act 1993 (Amendment of Section 23) (No 2) Order 1999, SI 1999/2090, art 2; words in square brackets in para (d) substituted by the National Lottery etc Act 1993 (Amendment of Section 23) Order 1995. SI 1995/2088, art 2.

Sub-s (2): words in first pair of square brackets in para (a) substituted by the National Lottery etc Act 1993 (Amendment of Section 23) Order 2006, SI 2006/654, art 2(1), (2); words in square brackets in paras (b)–(d) substituted, and para (e) and the word immediately preceding it added, by the National Lottery etc Act 1993 (Amendment of Section 23) Order 1999, SI 1999/1563, art 2; words in second pair of square brackets in para (a) substituted by the National Lottery etc Act 1993 (Amendment of Section 23) Order 1996, SI 1996/3095, art 2; words in square brackets in para (e) substituted by SI 2006/654, art 2(1), (3).

Sub-s (4): substituted, for sub-ss (4)–(6) as originally enacted, by the National Lottery Act 2006, s 15(1).

24 Payments from Distribution Fund to distributing bodies

At such times as the Secretary of State thinks appropriate, payments of such amounts as he thinks appropriate may be made to a body specified in section 23 [or in an order under section 29A] out of so much of any money in the Distribution Fund as is held for distribution by that body.

[896]

NOTES

Words in square brackets inserted by the National Lottery Act 2006, s 8(2).

25 Application of money by distributing bodies

(1) Subject to the provisions of this Part, a body shall distribute any money paid to it under section 24 for meeting expenditure of the relevant description mentioned in section 22(3).

[(1A) The manner in which a body may distribute any money paid to it under section 24 includes making or entering into arrangements for or in connection with meeting expenditure (including arrangements with respect to vouchers); and this subsection shall apply notwithstanding anything to the contrary in any enactment or instrument relating to the functions of the body.]

(2) A body shall not under subsection (1) distribute money for any purpose or in any manner if it does not have power to distribute money for that purpose or in that manner apart from subsection (1).

[(2A) A body which distributes money under subsection (1) shall have power to solicit applications from other bodies or persons for any of the money which the body so distributes, notwithstanding anything to the contrary in any enactment or instrument relating to the functions of the body.

(2B) In determining whether a decision of a body concerning its distribution of money under subsection (1) was unlawful, it shall be immaterial whether or not the body, or any person acting on behalf of the body, solicited an application from a body or person for such money.]

[(2C) In determining how to distribute money in accordance with subsection (1) a body may—

(a) consult any person;
(b) take account of opinions expressed to it or information submitted to it.]

(3) A body may defray out of any money paid to it under section 24 any expenses incurred by the body in consequence of this Act.

(4) The Trustees of the National Heritage Memorial Fund may apply any money paid to them under section 24 for any purpose for which they have power to apply money under section 4 of the National Heritage Act 1980 [(other expenditure out of the fund)].

[(5) References in this section (however expressed) to the distribution of money for meeting expenditure are to be construed as including distribution of money for the purpose of establishing, or contributing to, endowments in connection with expenditure of the description concerned.]

[(6) A reference in this section to meeting expenditure includes a reference to meeting expenditure which relates to—

(a) the Isle of Man, or

(b) any of the Channel Islands.]

[897]

NOTES

Sub-ss (1A), (2A), (2B): inserted by the National Lottery Act 1998, ss 9(1), 10.

Sub-s (2C): inserted by the National Lottery Act 2006, s 10.

Sub-s (4): words in square brackets substituted by the National Heritage Act 1997, s 3, Schedule, Pt I, para 4.

Sub-s (5): inserted with retrospective effect by the National Lottery (Funding of Endowments) Act 2003, s 1(1), (3).

Sub-s (6): added by the National Lottery Act 2006, s 13(1), as from 1 December 2006 except in so far as it relates to para (b).

[25A Delegation by distributing bodies of their powers of distribution

(1) A body which distributes money under subsection (1) of section 25 may appoint any other body or person to exercise on its behalf any of its functions relating to, or connected with, the distribution of money under that subsection (including its function of making decisions as to the persons to whom such distributions are to be made)—

(a) in any particular case, or

(b) in cases of any particular description.

(2) The persons who may be appointed by a body under subsection (1) include a member, employee or committee of the body itself.

(3) A body which makes an appointment under subsection (1) may defray out of any money paid to it under section 24 any expenses incurred by the appointee in consequence of the appointment.

(4) Power to accept any such appointment as is mentioned in subsection (1) is conferred by this subsection on the following bodies—

(a) any body which distributes money under section 25(1),

(b) any charity or any charitable, benevolent or philanthropic institution,

(c) any body established by or under an enactment, and

(d) any body established by Royal Charter.

(5) A body appointed by virtue of subsection (1) to exercise a function on behalf of another may itself appoint any of its members or employees, or a committee, to exercise the function in its stead, but only if—

(a) the terms of the body's appointment by virtue of subsection (1) so permit, and

(b) the body has power apart from this section to appoint a member or, as the case may be, an employee or committee of the body to exercise some or all of its functions.

(6) Subject to the following provisions of this section—

(a) a body which distributes money under section 25(1) may establish a committee for the purpose of exercising on behalf of the body any such function as is mentioned in subsection (1), and

(b) a body falling within any paragraph of subsection (4) may establish a committee for the purpose of exercising on behalf of any body which distributes money under section 25(1) any such function as is mentioned in subsection (1).

(7) A committee established under subsection (6)—

(a) must consist of or include one or more members, or one or more employees, of the body establishing the committee, but

(b) may include persons who are neither members nor employees of that body.

(8) Any power conferred on a body by subsections (1) to (7) is so conferred—

(a) to the extent that the body would not have the power apart from this section, and

(b) notwithstanding anything to the contrary in any enactment or instrument relating to the functions of the body.

(9) In this section—

"charity" means a body, or the trustees of a trust, established for charitable purposes only;

"charitable, benevolent or philanthropic institution" means a body, or the trustees of a trust, which is established for charitable purposes (whether or not those purposes are charitable within the meaning of any rule of law), benevolent purposes or philanthropic purposes, and which is not a charity.

(10) For the purposes of this section—

(a) the trustees of a trust shall be regarded as a body, and

(b) any reference to a member of a body shall, in the case of a body of trustees, be taken as a reference to any of the trustees,

and references to a committee shall be construed accordingly.

(11) Any reference in this section to a member of a body includes a reference to the chairman or deputy chairman of (or the holder of any corresponding office in relation to) the body.]

[(12) A body established under the law of the Isle of Man may be the subject of an appointment under this section in connection with expenditure which relates to the Isle of Man.

(13) A body established under the law of any of the Channel Islands may be the subject of an appointment under this section in connection with expenditure which relates to that Island.]

[898]

NOTES

Commencement: 2 July 1998.
Inserted by the National Lottery Act 1998, s 11(1).
Sub-s (12): added by the National Lottery Act 2006, s 13(2).
Sub-s (13): added by the National Lottery Act 2006, s 13(2) as from a day to be appointed.

[25B Joint schemes for distribution of money by distributing bodies

(1) A body which distributes money under subsection (1) of section 25 may, in accordance with the following provisions of this section, participate with one or more other such bodies in a joint scheme for the distribution of money under that subsection.

(2) A body may participate in a joint scheme if the principal purposes of the joint scheme include purposes for which the body has power to distribute money under subsection (1) of section 25, notwithstanding that the body would not, apart from this section, have power to distribute money under that subsection for meeting expenditure on some of the particular projects for which money may be distributed under the scheme.

(3) Money shall not, under a joint scheme, be distributed for meeting expenditure on any particular project unless the expenditure is such that—

(a) at least one of the bodies participating in the joint scheme has power, acting alone, to distribute money under section 25(1) for meeting the expenditure, or

(b) two or more of the bodies participating in the joint scheme, taken together, have power between them to distribute money under section 25(1) for meeting the expenditure.

(4) Nothing in subsection (3) affects the liability of each body participating in a scheme in relation to the distribution of any money under section 25(1) under the scheme.

(5) Schedule 3A contains supplementary provision in relation to joint schemes.]

[(6) References in this section (however expressed) to distribution under section 25(1) of money for meeting expenditure are to be construed in accordance with section 25(5).]

[899]

NOTES

Commencement: 2 July 1998.

Inserted by the National Lottery Act 1998, s 12(1).

Sub-s (6): inserted with retrospective effect by the National Lottery (Funding of Endowments) Act 2003, s 1(1), (4).

[25C Strategic plans for distributing bodies

(1) If the Secretary of State instructs it do so, a body which distributes money under section 25(1) shall, in accordance with the following provisions of this section,—

(a) prepare and adopt a strategic plan, or

(b) review and modify any strategic plan which it has adopted, or

(c) replace any strategic plan which it has adopted by preparing and adopting another.

(2) In this section "strategic plan", in the case of any body, means a statement containing the body's policies for the distribution of the money likely to be available to it for distribution under section 25(1).

(3) A strategic plan must also contain—

(a) a statement of any directions given to the body by the Secretary of State under section 26(1) [or 36E],

(b) a statement of the estimate given to the body by the Secretary of State of the money likely to be available for distribution by the body under section 25(1),

(c) a statement of the body's assessment of the needs which the body has power to deal with, in whole or in part, by distributing money under section 25(1), and

(d) a statement of the body's priorities in dealing with those needs by the distribution of money under section 25(1).

(4) A strategic plan must be such as to demonstrate how the body is taking into account or, as the case may be, complying with the directions mentioned in subsection (3)(a).

(5) Before adopting a strategic plan, a body shall—

(a) consult such other bodies as it thinks fit for the purpose of identifying the needs mentioned in subsection (3)(c) and formulating the policies to be adopted for dealing with those needs,

(b) prepare a draft of the proposed plan,

(c) send a copy of the draft to the Secretary of State, and

(d) after consultation with the Secretary of State, make such modifications to the draft as it considers necessary or expedient.

(6) Where a body adopts a strategic plan—

(a) the body shall send copies of the document containing the plan to the Secretary of State, and

(b) the Secretary of State shall lay a copy of the document before each House of Parliament.

(7) Nothing in this section applies in relation to any body which distributes under section 25(1) money allocated under section 22(3)(e).]

[900]

NOTES

Commencement: 2 July 1998.

Inserted by the National Lottery Act 1998, s 13.

Sub-s (3): words in square brackets in para (a) substituted by the National Lottery Act 2006, s 19(1), (2).

[25D] *(Inserted by the Scotland Act 1998 (Modification of Functions) Order 1999, SI 1999/1756, art 2, Schedule, para 15(2); outside the scope of this work.)*

[25E Distribution of funds: publicity

A body which distributes money under section 25(1) may make or participate in arrangements for—

(a) publishing information relating to the effect of a provision of this Act,

(b) publishing information relating to the distribution of money under this Act or the expenditure of money distributed under this Act, or

(c) encouraging participation in activities relating to the distribution of money under this Act.]

[901]

NOTES

Commencement: 1 October 2006.
Inserted by the National Lottery Act 2006, s 11.

Control by the Secretary of State

26 Directions to distributing bodies

(1) A body shall comply with any directions given to it by the Secretary of State as to the matters to be taken into account in determining the persons to whom, the purposes for which and the conditions subject to which the body distributes any money under section 25(1).

(2) The Trustees of the National Heritage Memorial Fund shall comply with any directions given to them by the Secretary of State as to the matters to be taken into account in determining the purposes for which and the conditions subject to which the Trustees apply any money under section 25(4).

(3) A body shall comply with any directions that the Secretary of State considers it appropriate to give the body for securing the proper management and control of money paid to the body under section 24.

[(3A) In exercising any power under section 25A, a body which distributes money under section 25(1) shall comply with any directions given to it by the Secretary of State.]

(4) Directions under subsection (3) [or (3A)] may in particular require a body—

(a) to obtain the consent of the Secretary of State before doing anything specified, or of a description specified, in the directions;

(b) to provide the Secretary of State at times specified by him with such information as he may require.

[(4A) Directions under subsection (3A) may in particular—

(a) impose limits on the amount of money which may be distributed by a body under section 25(1) by virtue of decisions made on its behalf by bodies or persons not falling within section 25A(2), and

(b) require a body, before appointing any body or person not falling within section 25A(2) to exercise on its behalf any function of making decisions concerning the distribution of money under section 25(1), to obtain the approval of the Secretary of State to its plans for making such appointments.]

(5) The Secretary of State shall consult a body before giving any directions to it under this section.

[(6) This section does not apply to the Big Lottery Fund.]

[902]–[903]

NOTES

Sub-ss (3A), (4A): inserted by the National Lottery Act 1998, s 11(2), (4).
Sub-s (4): words in square brackets inserted by the National Lottery Act 1998, s 11(3).
Sub-s (6): added by the National Lottery Act 2006, s 19(1), (3).

[26A] (*Inserted by the Scotland Act 1998 (Modification of Functions) Order 1999, SI 1999/1756, art 2, Schedule, para 15(3); outside the scope of this work.*)

27 Power to prohibit distribution in certain cases

(1) Where subsection (2) applies, the Secretary of State may by order prohibit a body from distributing money under section 25(1) to a person specified in the order.

(2) This subsection applies if at the time the order is made—

(a) the person specified is a company of which the body, or a wholly-owned subsidiary of the body, is a member, or

(b) the Secretary of State considers that the body is able (whether directly or indirectly) to control or materially to influence the policy of the person specified in carrying on any undertaking or performing any functions.

(3) In subsection (2)—

(a) "company" means a company formed and registered under the Companies Act 1985 or the Companies (Northern Ireland) Order 1986 or a company to which the provisions of that Act or Order apply as they apply to a company so formed and registered, and

(b) "wholly-owned subsidiary" has the meaning given by section 736 of that Act or Article 4 of that Order.

(4) Where subsection (5) applies, the Secretary of State may give directions to a body—

(a) prohibiting it from distributing money under section 25(1) to a person in Northern Ireland specified in the directions, or

(b) requiring it to secure that any money distributed by it under section 25(1) to such a person is not applied for a purpose specified in the directions.

(5) This subsection applies if at the time the directions are given the Secretary of State considers that—

(a) a proscribed organisation for the purposes of the Northern Ireland (Emergency Provisions) Act 1991, or

(b) any other organisation that appears to him to be concerned in terrorism in Northern Ireland or in promoting or encouraging it,

might directly or indirectly derive benefit from the distribution of money to the person specified.

(6) In subsection (5) "benefit" includes benefit of a non-financial nature and, in particular, an enhancement of reputation.

(7) A body may not disclose to any other person either the identity of any person specified in directions given to it under subsection (4) or any information that might lead to the identification of such a person.

(8) A body shall provide the Secretary of State with such information as he may require for the purpose of exercising his powers under this section in relation to the body.

[(9) The function of the Secretary of State—

(a) under subsection (1) to prohibit a body from distributing money; or

(b) under subsection (8) to require information,

may, in relation to—

(i) any body specified in section 23(1) whose functions exclusively or mainly relate to the arts in Scotland; or

(ii) any body specified in section 23(2) whose functions exclusively or mainly relate to sport in Scotland,.

be exercised separately.]

[904]

NOTES

Sub-s (9): added by the Scotland Act 1998 (Modification of Functions) Order 1999, SI 1999/1756, art 2, Schedule, para 15(4).

28 Power to amend section 22

(1) The Secretary of State may by order amend section 22(3) so as to substitute different percentages for any of the percentages for the time being specified there.

(2) Any amendment made under this section shall be such that—

(a) no percentage lower than 5 per cent is specified in section 22(3), and

(b) the percentages specified in section 22(3) amount in total to 100 per cent.

(3) Without prejudice to the generality of section 60(5), an order under this section may provide for sums that apart from the order would be held in the Distribution Fund for distribution by a particular body to be held in the Distribution Fund for distribution by another body specified in section 23.

[905]

NOTES

Orders: the Apportionment of Money in the National Lottery Distribution Fund Order 1999, SI 1999/344; the Apportionment of Money in the National Lottery Distribution Fund Order 2000, SI 2000/3356.

29 Power to amend section 23

(1) The Secretary of State may by order amend subsection (1), (2), (3) or (4) of section 23 so as—

- (a) to substitute a different body for any body for the time being specified in that subsection;
- (b) to add another body to the bodies or body for the time being specified in it;
- (c) to omit any body for the time being specified in it;
- (d) to substitute different percentages for any percentages for the time being specified in it.

(2) Any amendment made under subsection (1) shall be such that the amended subsection—

- (a) provides for the whole of the sum mentioned in that subsection to be held for distribution by the one body specified in that subsection, or
- (b) provides for the whole of that sum to be held for distribution by the two or more bodies specified in that subsection and specifies, in relation to each of those bodies, what percentage of that sum is to be held for distribution by that body.

(3) The Secretary of State may by order provide that subsection (1), (2), (3) or (4) of section 23 shall, pending the making of an order amending that subsection under subsection (1),—

- (a) cease to have effect, or
- (b) have effect as if any of the bodies for the time being specified in it were omitted.

(4) Without prejudice to the generality of section 60(5)—

- (a) an order made under subsection (1) may provide for sums that apart from the order would be held in the Distribution Fund for distribution by a particular body to be held in the Distribution Fund for distribution by another body (being a body that on the coming into force of the order is specified in the subsection amended by the order);
- (b) an order made under subsection (3) may provide for sums that apart from the order would be held in the Distribution Fund for distribution by a particular body to be held in the Distribution Fund in the name of the Secretary of State, pending being held for distribution by another body in accordance with the order to be made under subsection (1).

(5) Without prejudice to the generality of subsection (1), the Secretary of State may exercise his powers under that subsection so as to remove from section 23 any body that has contravened or failed to comply with a requirement or prohibition imposed on it by or under section 26 or 27.

[(6) The functions of the Secretary of State under this section shall, in so far as they relate to—

- (a) substitution of a different body for, or addition of another body to, the body specified in section 23(3) or (4) or omission of a body specified in either of those subsections; or
- (b) substitution of a different percentage for the total aggregate percentage specified as held in the Distribution Fund for—
  - (i) any body or bodies specified in section 23(1) whose functions exclusively or mainly relate to the arts in Scotland, or
  - (ii) any body or bodies specified in section 23(2) whose functions exclusively or mainly relate to sport in Scotland;
- (c) substitution of a different body for, or addition of another body to, any such body specified in section 23(1) or (2) as is mentioned in paragraph (b) above or omission of any such body specified in section 23(1) or (2); or
- (d) where more than one such body is specified in section 23(1) or (2), specification of the particular percentage held in the Distribution Fund for distribution by any one of those bodies,

be treated as exercisable in or as regards Scotland and may be exercised separately.]

[906]

NOTES

Sub-s (6): added by the Scotland Act 1998 (Modification of Functions) Order 1999, SI 1999/1756, art 2, Schedule, para 15(5).

Orders: the National Lottery etc Act 1993 (Amendment of Section 23) Order 1994, SI 1994/1342; the National Lottery etc Act 1993 (Amendment of Section 23) Order 1995, SI 1995/2088; the National Lottery etc Act 1993 (Amendment of Section 23) Order 1996, SI 1996/3095; the National Lottery etc Act 1993 (Amendment of Section 23) Order 1999, SI 1999/1563; the National Lottery etc Act 1993 (Amendment of Section 23) (No 2) Order 1999, SI 1999/2090; the National Lottery etc Act 1993 (Amendment of Section 23) Order 2006, SI 2006/654; the National Lottery etc Act 1993 (Amendment of Section 23) (Scotland) Order 2000, SSI 2000/78.

[29A Reallocation of funds

(1) This section applies where money is—
(a) allocated for a purpose under section 22(3), and
(b) held for distribution by a body under section 23.

(2) The Secretary of State may by order provide for the money to be held for distribution by a different body specified in the order (without altering the purpose for which the money is allocated).

(3) Before making an order under this section the Secretary of State shall consult—
(a) each body mentioned in the order,
(b) the National Assembly for Wales,
(c) the Scottish Ministers,
(d) the Northern Ireland Department of Culture, Arts and Leisure, and
(e) such other persons (if any) as he thinks appropriate.]

[907]

NOTES

Commencement: 1 October 2006.

Inserted by the National Lottery Act 2006, s 8(1).

30 *(Repealed by the Horserace Betting and Olympic Lottery Act 2004, ss 34(1), (10), 38, Sch 6.)*

Distribution Fund: further provisions

31 Payments from Distribution Fund in respect of expenses

(1) At such times as the Secretary of State with the approval of the Treasury determines to be appropriate, payments shall be made into the Consolidated Fund out of so much of any money in the Distribution Fund as is held under section 22(2).

(2) The payments shall be of such amounts as the Secretary of State with the approval of the Treasury determines to be appropriate for—
(a) …
[(aa) meeting payments made or to be made under paragraph 10 of Schedule 2A,]
(b) defraying expenses incurred or to be incurred by the Secretary of State in exercising his functions under this Act, and
(c) defraying expenses incurred or to be incurred by the National Debt Commissioners in making investments under section 32.

(3) …

[(4) In determining what amounts are appropriate for meeting the payments referred to in subsection (2)(aa), the Secretary of State shall take into account sums paid or to be paid into the Consolidated Fund under section 7(6).]

[908]

NOTES

Sub-s (2): para (a) repealed and para (aa) inserted by the National Lottery Act 1998, ss 1(5), 26, Sch 1, para 15(2)(a), (b), Sch 5, Pt I.

Sub-s (3): repealed by the National Lottery Act 1998, ss 1(5), 26, Sch 1, para 15(3), Sch 5, Pt I.

Sub-s (4): added by the National Lottery Act 1998, s 1(5), Sch 1, para 15(4).

32 Investment of Distribution Fund

(1) So much of any money in the Distribution Fund as is neither held under section 22(2) nor immediately required for making payments under section 24 may be paid over to the National Debt Commissioners and invested by them in accordance with such directions as may be given by the Treasury.

(2) The proceeds of any investment made under subsection (1) or this subsection may be re-invested by the National Debt Commissioners in accordance with such directions as may be given by the Treasury.

(3) The proceeds of any investment made under subsection (1) or (2) shall, if they are not re-invested under subsection (2), be paid into the Distribution Fund and [treated as if paid into the Fund by virtue of *section 5(6)*].

(4) In this section "proceeds", in relation to an investment, means any interest or dividends received in respect of the investment and any sums received on the realisation of the investment.

(5) …

[909]

NOTES

Sub-s (3): words in square brackets substituted by the National Lottery Act 2006, s 9(a), and for words in italics there are substituted the words "section 5(2)(c)" by the National Lottery Act 2006, s 6, Sch 1, paras 1, 13, as from a day to be appointed under s 6(1) thereof.

Sub-s (5): repealed by the National Lottery Act 2006, ss 9(b), 21, Sch 3.

33 Accounts of the Secretary of State and National Debt Commissioners

(1) The Secretary of State shall prepare accounts in respect of the Distribution Fund in such form, and in such manner and at such times, as the Treasury may direct.

(2) The National Debt Commissioners shall prepare accounts in respect of any investments under section 32 in such form, and in such manner and at such times, as the Treasury may direct.

(3) Each account prepared under subsection (1) or (2) shall be sent to the Comptroller and Auditor General who shall examine, certify and report on it and shall lay copies of it and of his report before Parliament.

[(4) For the purpose of exercising his examination function in relation to any accounts prepared under subsection (1), the Comptroller and Auditor General—

(a) shall have a right of access at all reasonable times to any documents which he reasonably requires which are in the custody or under the control of any section 5 licensee; and

(b) shall have a right to require from any officer or employee of any section 5 licensee, or from the auditors of any section 5 licensee, an explanation of, or information relating to, any such documents;

but a section 5 licensee shall not, by virtue only of this subsection, be a body to which section 6 of the National Audit Act 1983 applies.

(5) For the purpose of—

(a) exercising his examination function in relation to any accounts prepared under subsection (1), or

(b) deciding whether, or to what extent, to exercise any right conferred by subsection (4),

the Comptroller and Auditor General shall have regard to any information which the Director General has obtained from any section 5 licensee and which is relevant to the exercise of that function.

(6) Where, in exercising his examination function in relation to any accounts prepared under subsection (1), the Comptroller and Auditor General obtains any information which gives him grounds to believe that a section 5 licensee has, or may have, contravened any of the conditions of its licence under section 5, the Comptroller and Auditor General shall as soon as practicable disclose that information to the Director General.

(7) A section 5 licensee shall be under a duty—

(a) to permit the Comptroller and Auditor General to exercise the right conferred by subsection (4)(a); and

(b) to do all that may be reasonably practicable to secure that any person who under subsection (4)(b) is required to provide an explanation of, or information relating to, any document complies with that requirement;

and any breach of that duty shall be actionable at the suit of the Comptroller and Auditor General.

(8) The right of access to documents conferred by subsection (4)(a) includes a right to take copies of or make extracts from documents.

(9) In this section any reference to documents includes a reference to information held by means of a computer or in any other electronic form; and in the case of information so held the right of access conferred by subsection (4)(a) includes a right of access to, and to take copies of, that information in a visible and legible form.

(10) In this section—

"examination function", in relation to the Comptroller and Auditor General, means his function under subsection (3);

"section 5 licensee" means a body which holds or has held a licence under section 5.]

[910]

NOTES

Sub-ss (4)–(10): added, in relation to accounts prepared under sub-s (1) of this section, so far as they relate to periods beginning on or after 1 April 1999, by the National Lottery Act 1998, s 5.

Reports and accounts of distributing bodies

34 Annual reports by distributing bodies …

(1) As soon as possible after the end of every financial year, each body that in that year was paid any money under section 24 or distributed or applied any money under section 25 shall make a report to the Secretary of State on the exercise during that year of its functions under this Act.

(2) The report shall set out any directions given to the body under section 26 that had effect during the financial year to which the report relates.

[(2A) The report shall set out the body's policy and practice in relation to the principle that proceeds of the National Lottery should be used to fund projects, or aspects of projects, for which funds would be unlikely to be made available by—

(a) a Government department,

(b) the Scottish Ministers,

(c) a Northern Ireland department, or

(d) the National Assembly for Wales.]

(3) The Secretary of State shall lay a copy of every report received by him under this section before Parliament.

(4) …

[(5) The functions of the Secretary of State under this section shall, in so far as they relate to any body other than—

(a) any body specified in section 23(1) whose functions relate exclusively or mainly to the arts in any one of England, Wales or Northern Ireland; or

(b) any body specified in section 23(2) whose functions relate exclusively or mainly to sport in any one of England, Wales or Northern Ireland,

be treated as exercisable in or as regards Scotland and may be exercised separately.]

[(6) Where a report is made under subsection (1) to the Scottish Ministers (by virtue of provision made under section 63 of the Scotland Act 1998), the Scottish Ministers shall lay a copy of the report before the Scottish Parliament.]

[911]

NOTES

Section heading: words omitted repealed by the National Lottery Act 2006, s 19(1), (4)(b).
Sub-s (2A): inserted by the National Lottery Act 2006, s 12.
Sub-s (4): repealed by the National Lottery Act 2006, ss 19(1), (4)(a), 21, Sch 3.

Sub-s (5): inserted by the Scotland Act 1998 (Modification of Functions) Order 1999, SI 1999/1756, art 2, Schedule, para 15(6).

Sub-s (6): inserted by the Scotland Act 1998 (Transfer of Functions to the Scottish Ministers etc) Order 1999, SI 1999/1750, art 6(1), Sch 5, para 12(1), (3).

35 Accounts of distributing bodies other than [the Big Lottery Fund]

(1) A body shall keep proper accounts in respect of any money paid to it under section 24 and proper records in relation to the accounts.

(2) A body shall prepare a statement of accounts in respect of each financial year in which it was paid any money under section 24 or distributed or applied any money under section 25.

(3) The statement shall comply with any directions that may be given by the Secretary of State as to the information to be contained in such a statement, the manner in which such information is to be presented or the methods and principles according to which such a statement is to be prepared.

(4) Copies of the statement shall be sent to the Secretary of State and the Comptroller and Auditor General within such period after the end of the financial year to which the statement relates as the Secretary of State may direct.

(5) The Comptroller and Auditor General shall examine, certify and report on the statement and shall lay copies of the statement and of his report before Parliament.

(6) The Secretary of State shall not give a direction under this section without the Treasury's approval.

(7) This section does not apply to [the Big Lottery Fund].

[(8) The functions of the Secretary of State—

(a) under subsection (3) to give directions shall, in so far as they relate to—

(i) any body specified in section 23(1) whose functions exclusively or mainly relate to the arts in Scotland; or

(ii) any body specified in section 23(2) whose functions exclusively or mainly relate to sport in Scotland; and

(b) under subsection (4) to receive copies of the statement shall, in so far as they relate to any body other than—

(i) any body specified in section 23(1) whose functions relate exclusively or mainly to the arts in any one of England, Wales or Northern Ireland; or

(ii) any body specified in section 23(2) whose functions relate exclusively or mainly to sport in any one of England, Wales or Northern Ireland,

be treated as exercisable in or as regards Scotland and may be exercised separately.]

[912]

NOTES

Section heading: words in square brackets substituted by the National Lottery Act 2006, s 19(1), (5)(b).

Sub-s (7): words in square brackets substituted by the National Lottery Act 2006, s 19(1), (5)(a).

Sub-s (8): inserted by the Scotland Act 1998 (Modification of Functions) Order 1999, SI 1999/1756, art 2, Schedule, para 15(7).

The Trustees of the National Heritage Memorial Fund

36 Amendment of the National Heritage Act 1980

The National Heritage Act 1980 shall have effect with the amendments set out in Schedule 4.

[913]

[The Big Lottery Fund

36A The Fund

(1) There shall be a body corporate known as the Big Lottery Fund.

(2) Schedule 4A (which makes provision in relation to the Fund) shall have effect.]

[914]

NOTES

Commencement: 14 August 2006.
Inserted, together with preceding cross-heading, by the National Lottery Act 2006, s 14(1).

[36B Power to distribute funds

(1) The Big Lottery Fund may make grants or loans, or make or enter into other arrangements, for the purpose of complying with section 25(1).

(2) A grant or loan may be subject to conditions (which may, in particular, include conditions as to repayment with interest).

(3) The Secretary of State may by order make provision limiting the amounts distributed under subsection (1).

(4) An order under subsection (3) may in particular—
- (a) specify a maximum amount that may be distributed during a specified period for expenditure of a description prescribed under section 22(3A);
- (b) specify a minimum amount that must be distributed during a specified period for expenditure of a description prescribed under section 22(3A);
- (c) make provision by reference to the aggregate of amounts distributed, to a percentage of amounts available for distribution or otherwise;
- (d) make provision (which may, in particular, confer a power on the Fund) for the treatment of expenditure which satisfies more than one prescribed description.

(5) Before making an order under subsection (3) the Secretary of State shall consult—
- (a) the Fund,
- (b) the National Assembly for Wales,
- (c) the Scottish Ministers,
- (d) the Northern Ireland Department of Culture, Arts and Leisure, and
- (e) such other persons (if any) as he thinks appropriate.]

[915]

NOTES

Commencement: 1 December 2006.
Inserted, together with ss 36C–36E, by the National Lottery Act 2006, s 15(2).
Orders: the Big Lottery Fund (Prescribed Expenditure) Order 2006, SI 2006/3202 at **[3418]**.

[36C Non-lottery funds

(1) The Fund may enter into an arrangement with a person under which—
- (a) the person pays money to the Fund, and
- (b) the Fund distributes the money to a third party.

(2) An arrangement under subsection (1) may, in particular—
- (a) identify the third party, or
- (b) otherwise limit the Fund's freedom of action in relation to the distribution of the money paid under the arrangement.

(3) The Fund shall distribute money received under subsection (1) for meeting expenditure that is—
- (a) charitable,
- (b) connected with health,
- (c) connected with education, or
- (d) connected with the environment.

(4) The reference in subsection (3) to the distribution of money received under subsection (1) is a reference to doing anything of a kind that the Fund can do under section 36B.

(5) A reference in this Act to payment under section 25(1) shall include a reference to payment under subsection (3) above.]

[916]

NOTES

Commencement: 1 December 2006.
Inserted as noted to s 36B at **[915]**.

[36D Power to give advice

The Big Lottery Fund may give advice about—

(a) the distribution of money under any provision of this Act;
(b) inviting, making or considering applications for grants and loans under any provision of this Act;
(c) the use of money paid under any provision of this Act.]

[917]

NOTES

Commencement: 1 December 2006.
Inserted as noted to s 36B at **[915]**.

[36E Directions

(1) In exercising any of its functions the Big Lottery Fund shall comply with any direction given to it by the Secretary of State (subject to subsection (4)).

(2) A direction under this section may, in particular, specify matters to be taken into account in determining the persons to whom, the purposes for which and the conditions subject to which the Fund distributes money.

(3) A direction under this section may, in particular—

(a) relate to the management and control of money received by the Fund;
(b) relate to the employment of staff;
(c) with the consent of the Treasury, relate to—
  (i) the form of accounts, or
  (ii) methods and principles for the preparation of accounts;
(d) in so far as it relates to a matter specified in paragraphs (a) to (c)—
  (i) relate to the persons to whom or the terms on which the Fund delegates functions;
  (ii) require the Fund to obtain the Secretary of State's consent before taking action of a specified kind;
  (iii) require the Fund to provide information to the Secretary of State.

(4) A direction under this section, other than a direction given by virtue only of subsection (3), may not be given by the Secretary of State in relation to Welsh, Scottish or Northern Ireland devolved expenditure, but—

(a) may be given by the National Assembly for Wales in relation to Welsh devolved expenditure,
(b) may be given by the Scottish Ministers in relation to Scottish devolved expenditure, and
(c) may be given by the Northern Ireland Department of Culture, Arts and Leisure in relation to Northern Ireland devolved expenditure.

(5) Before giving a direction under this section, other than by virtue only of subsection (3), the Secretary of State shall consult—

(a) the Fund,
(b) the National Assembly for Wales,
(c) the Scottish Ministers, and
(d) the Northern Ireland Department of Culture, Arts and Leisure.

(6) But subsection (5)(b) to (d) shall not apply to a direction which relates only to English devolved expenditure.

(7) Before giving a direction to the Fund by virtue only of subsection (3) the Secretary of State shall consult the Fund.

(8) Before giving a direction to the Fund by virtue of subsection (4)(a) to (c) the person giving the direction shall—

(a) consult the Fund, and
(b) obtain the consent of the Secretary of State.

(9) A report of the Fund under section 34 shall set out any directions given to the Fund under subsection (1) that had effect during the financial year to which the report relates.]

[918]–[925]

NOTES

Commencement: 1 December 2006.
Inserted as noted to s 36B at **[915]**.

37–43D (*Repealed by the National Lottery Act 2006, ss 19(1), (6)(a), 21, Sch 3.*)

Supplementary

44 Interpretation of Part II

(1) In this Part—

["charitable", in relation to expenditure, means expenditure for a charitable, benevolent or philanthropic purpose];

.....

"the Distribution Fund" means the National Lottery Distribution Fund;

["education" includes training and the provision of activities for children;

["endowment" includes permanent endowment;]

"the environment" includes the living and social environment;]

"expenditure on or connected with the national heritage" [means expenditure for any purpose for which expenditure may be incurred under section 3, 3A or 4 of the National Heritage Act 1980];

"financial year", in relation to a body, means—

(a) the period beginning with the date on which the body is established and ending with the next 31st March, and

(b) each successive period of twelve months ending with 31st March

["joint scheme" means a joint scheme under section 25B].

(2) For the purposes of the definition of "expenditure on or connected with the national heritage" in subsection (1), any reference in section 3 [3A or 4] of the National Heritage Act 1980 to the opinion of the Trustees shall be read, in relation to any body other than the Trustees of the National Heritage Memorial Fund that is for the time being specified in section 23(3), as a reference to the opinion of that body.

[(3) A project or arrangement shall be regarded for the purposes of this Part as concerned or connected with health, education or the environment notwithstanding that it contains incidental provision—

(a) which is not concerned or connected with any of those matters; but

(b) which is necessary or expedient for the purposes of the project or arrangement.]

[(4) Any reference in this Part to the distribution of money shall be construed as including the making or entering into of arrangements in accordance with section 25(1A) …; and related expressions used in this Part shall be construed accordingly.]

[926]

NOTES

Sub-s (1): definition "charitable" substituted, for definition "charitable expenditure" as originally enacted, and definition "the Charities Board" (omitted) repealed by the National Lottery Act 2006, ss 19(1), (7), 20; definitions "education" and "the environment" inserted, in relation to sums paid into the National Lottery Distribution Fund, on or after 14 October 1997, and the definition "joint scheme" inserted, by the National Lottery Act 1998, ss 6(8), (9), 12(2); definition "endowment" inserted with retrospective effect by the National Lottery (Funding of Endowments) Act 2003, s 1(1), (8); in definition "expenditure on or connected with the national heritage" words in square brackets substituted by the National Heritage Act 1997, s 3, Schedule, Pt I, para 5(a).

Sub-s (2): words in square brackets inserted by the National Heritage Act 1997, s 3, Schedule, Pt I, para 5(b).

Sub-s (3): added, together with sub-s (4), by the National Lottery Act 1998, ss 8(2), 9(2).

Sub-s (4): added, together with sub-s (3), by the National Lottery Act 1998, ss 8(2), 9(2); words omitted repealed by the National Lottery Act 2006, s 21, Sch 3.

45–59 ((*Pts III, IV*) *outside the scope of this work.*)

PART V
SUPPLEMENTARY

60 Orders and regulations

(1) Any power to make an order or regulations under this Act shall be exercisable by statutory instrument.

(2) An order shall not be made under—

[[(a) section 22(3A), 28 or 36B(3),]
[(aa) section 29A,] or
(b) paragraph 2(5) of Schedule 3A,]

unless a draft of the statutory instrument containing it has been laid before, and approved by a resolution of, each House of Parliament.

[(2A) Subsection (2) does not apply to an order which contains only provision revoking an order under [section 22(3A) or 36B(3)].]

(3) A statutory instrument containing any order or regulations under this Act, other than—

[(a) an order to which subsection (2) applies, or
(b) an order under section 65],

shall be subject to annulment in pursuance of a resolution of either House of Parliament.

[(3A) Subsection (3) does not apply to a statutory instrument which contains only provision revoking an order under paragraph 2(1) of Schedule 3A.

(3B) A statutory instrument which contains only provision revoking an order under paragraph 2(1) of Schedule 3A shall be laid before each House of Parliament.]

(4) Any order or regulations under this Act may make different provision for different cases or circumstances.

(5) Any order or regulations under this Act may make such incidental, supplemental and transitional provision as the person making the order or regulations thinks appropriate.

[(6) Any reference in this section to an order is a reference to an order of the Secretary of State.]

[927]

NOTES

Sub-s (2): paras (a), (b) in square brackets substituted by the National Lottery Act 1998, s 15(1), (2); para (a) further substituted and para (aa) inserted by the National Lottery Act 2006, ss 8(3), 19(1), (8)(a).

Sub-s (2A): inserted by the National Lottery Act 1998, s 15(1), (3); words in square brackets substituted by the National Lottery Act 2006, s 19(1), (8)(b).

Sub-s (3): words in square brackets substituted by the National Lottery Act 1998, s 15(1), (4).

Sub-ss (3A), (3B): inserted by the National Lottery Act 1998, s 15(1), (5).

Sub-s (6): added by the National Lottery Act 1998, s 15(1), (6).

Modification: sub-s (6) is modified, in relation to the National Assembly for Wales, by the National Assembly for Wales (Transfer of Functions) Order 1999, SI 1999/672, art 2, Sch 1.

61 Directions

Any directions under this Act shall be given in writing and may be varied or revoked by subsequent directions.

[928]

62 Expenses

There shall be paid out of money provided by Parliament—

(a) any expenses of the Secretary of State or the National Debt Commissioners attributable to this Act, and
(b) any increase attributable to this Act in the sums payable out of money so provided under any other enactment.

[929]

63 Northern Ireland

(1) This Act extends to Northern Ireland (except so far as it amends enactments that do not extend there).

(2) …

[930]

NOTES

Sub-s (2): repealed by the Northern Ireland Act 1998, s 100(2), Sch 15.

64 (*Outside the scope of this work.*)

65 Commencement

This Act shall come into force on such date as the Secretary of State may by order appoint; and different dates may be so appointed for different provisions or for different purposes.

[931]

NOTES

Orders: the National Lottery etc Act 1993 (Commencement No 1 and Transitional Provisions) Order 1993, SI 1993/2632; the National Lottery etc Act 1993 (Commencement No 2 and Transitional Provisions) Order 1994, SI 1994/1055; the National Lottery etc Act 1993 (Commencement No 3) Order 1994, SI 1994/2659.

66 Short title

This Act may be cited as the National Lottery etc Act 1993.

[932]

SCHEDULES

(*Schs 1, 2A, 3, 3A, 4, outside the scope of this work; Sch 2 repealed by the National Lottery Act 1998, ss 1(2), 26, Sch 5, Pt I.*)

[SCHEDULE 4A
THE BIG LOTTERY FUND

Section 36A

PART 1
CONSTITUTION

Membership

1.—(1) The Big Lottery Fund shall consist of 12 members appointed by the Secretary of State.

(2) The Secretary of State shall appoint one of the members as Chairman.

(3) The Secretary of State shall ensure that at any time—

(a) one of the members is appointed to represent the interests of England,

(b) one of the members is appointed to represent the interests of Wales,

(c) one of the members is appointed to represent the interests of Scotland, and

(d) one of the members is appointed to represent the interests of Northern Ireland.

(4) In complying with paragraphs (a) to (d) of sub-paragraph (3) the Secretary of State—

(a) may not appoint a member for the purpose of satisfying more than one of those paragraphs,

(b) may appoint the Chairman for the purpose of satisfying one of those paragraphs,

(c) shall obtain the agreement of the National Assembly for Wales before appointing a person to satisfy paragraph (b),

(d) shall obtain the agreement of the Scottish Ministers before appointing a person to satisfy paragraph (c), and

(e) shall obtain the agreement of the Northern Ireland Department of Culture, Arts and Leisure before appointing a person to satisfy paragraph (d).

(5) The Secretary of State may by order vary the number specified in sub-paragraph (1).

(6) Before making an order under sub-paragraph (5) the Secretary of State shall consult—

(a) the National Assembly for Wales,
(b) the Scottish Ministers, and
(c) the Northern Ireland Department of Culture, Arts and Leisure.

Tenure

2. A person shall hold and vacate office as Chairman or other member of the Fund in accordance with the terms of his appointment (subject to this Schedule).

3. The Chairman or another member may resign his office by notice in writing to the Secretary of State.

4.—(1) The Chairman or another member may be removed from office by the Secretary of State on the grounds that—
(a) a bankruptcy order has been made against him, his estate has been sequestrated or he has made a composition or arrangement with, or granted a trust deed for, his creditors, or
(b) he is, in the opinion of the Secretary of State, unable, unfit or unwilling to discharge the functions of his office.

(2) Before exercising the power under sub-paragraph (1) in respect of a person appointed for the purpose of satisfying paragraph 1(3)(b), (c) or (d) the Secretary of State shall consult—
(a) the National Assembly for Wales, in the case of a person appointed for the purpose of satisfying paragraph 1(3)(b),
(b) the Scottish Ministers, in the case of a person appointed for the purpose of satisfying paragraph 1(3)(c), and
(c) the Northern Ireland Department of Culture, Arts and Leisure, in the case of a person appointed for the purpose of satisfying paragraph 1(3)(d).

5. A person who ceases, otherwise than by virtue of paragraph 4, to be Chairman or another member may be re-appointed.

Staff

6. The Fund may appoint staff (subject to any directions under section 36E(3)(b)).

Committees

7.—(1) The Fund shall establish—
(a) a committee, chaired by the member appointed under paragraph 1(3)(a), for the purpose of exercising the Fund's functions in relation to English devolved expenditure,
(b) a committee, chaired by the member appointed under paragraph 1(3)(b), for the purpose of exercising the Fund's functions in relation to Welsh devolved expenditure,
(c) a committee, chaired by the member appointed under paragraph 1(3)(c), for the purpose of exercising the Fund's functions in relation to Scottish devolved expenditure, and
(d) a committee, chaired by the member appointed under paragraph 1(3)(d), for the purpose of exercising the Fund's functions in relation to Northern Ireland devolved expenditure.

(2) Before appointing the members of a committee established under sub-paragraph (1) the Fund shall obtain the consent of—
(a) in the case of the committee concerned with England, the Secretary of State;
(b) in the case of the committee concerned with Wales, the National Assembly for Wales;
(c) in the case of the committee concerned with Scotland, the Scottish Ministers;
(d) in the case of the committee concerned with Northern Ireland, the Northern Ireland Department of Culture, Arts and Leisure.

(3) A committee established under sub-paragraph (1) shall carry on its activities under such name as the committee may determine with the consent of the Secretary of State and—

(a) in the case of the committee concerned with Wales, with the consent of the National Assembly for Wales;

(b) in the case of the committee concerned with Scotland, with the consent of the Scottish Ministers;

(c) in the case of the committee concerned with Northern Ireland, with the consent of the Northern Ireland Department of Culture, Arts and Leisure.

8. Nothing in paragraph 7 or section 25A(6) shall prevent the Fund from—

(a) establishing a committee otherwise than in accordance with that paragraph or section, or

(b) authorising a committee (whether or not established in accordance with that paragraph or section) to exercise a function of the Fund.

9. Section 25A(7) shall apply in relation to any committee of the Fund as it applies in relation to a committee established under section 25A(6).

Status

10. The Fund shall not be regarded as the servant or agent of the Crown or as enjoying any status, immunity or privilege of the Crown.

Supervision

11. In Schedule 2 to the Parliamentary Commissioner Act 1967 (c 13) (departments, &c. subject to investigation) insert at the appropriate place—

"The Big Lottery Fund."

Disqualification

12. In Part III of Schedule 1 to the House of Commons Disqualification Act 1975 (c 24) (other disqualifying offices) insert at the appropriate place—

"Chairman, or member in receipt of remuneration, of the Big Lottery Fund. "

13. In Part III of Schedule 1 to the Northern Ireland Assembly Disqualification Act 1975 (c 25) (other disqualifying offices) insert at the appropriate place—

"Chairman, or member in receipt of remuneration, of the Big Lottery Fund. "]

[933]

NOTES

Commencement: 14 August 2006.
Sch 4A inserted by the National Lottery Act 2006, s 14(2), Sch 2.

[PART 2
PROCEEDINGS

Self-regulation

14. The Fund may, subject to this Schedule, regulate its procedure and the procedure of its committees (and may, in particular, make provision for a quorum).

Records

15. In Schedule 1 to the Public Records Act 1958 (definition of public records) the following entry shall be inserted at the appropriate place in Part II of the Table at the end of paragraph 3—

"The Big Lottery Fund."

Saving

16. The validity of proceedings of the Fund or a committee shall not be affected by—
(a) a vacancy among its members, or
(b) a defect in the appointment of a person as Chairman or member.]

[934]

NOTES
Commencement: 14 August 2006.
Inserted as noted to Pt 1 at **[933]**.

[PART 3
MONEY

Remuneration, &c

17.—(1) The Fund may pay to the Chairman, another member or a member of a committee—
(a) such remuneration as the Secretary of State may determine, and
(b) such travelling and other allowances as the Secretary of State may determine.

(2) The Fund may pay to or in respect of the Chairman or another member such sums as the Secretary of State may determine by way of, or in respect of, pensions, allowances or gratuities.

(3) If the Secretary of State thinks that there are special circumstances that make it right for a person ceasing to hold office as Chairman or member to receive compensation, the Fund may pay him such compensation as the Secretary of State may determine.

18.—(1) The Fund may (subject to any directions under section 36E(3)(b)) pay sums to or in respect of a member or former member of staff by way of or in respect of—
(a) remuneration,
(b) allowances,
(c) pensions,
(d) gratuities, or
(e) compensation for loss of employment.

(2) In Schedule 1 to the Superannuation Act 1972 (c 11) (employment to which superannuation schemes may extend) in the list of other bodies insert at the appropriate place—

"The Big Lottery Fund."

Payments

19. The Fund may make payments in respect of expenditure (which may include expenditure of a capital nature) of—
(a) the Fund, or
(b) a person to whom it delegates a function under section 25A(1).

Investment

20.—(1) The Fund may deposit money in an interest-bearing account (but may not otherwise invest).

(2) The proceeds of money received by the Fund and invested under sub-paragraph (1) shall be treated for the purposes of Part II of this Act as part of that money.

Accounts

21.—(1) The Fund shall—
(a) keep proper accounting records, and
(b) prepare a statement of accounts in respect of each financial year.

(2) The Fund shall send a copy of a statement under sub-paragraph (1)(b)—
- (a) to the Secretary of State,
- (b) to the National Assembly for Wales,
- (c) to the Scottish Ministers,
- (d) to the Northern Ireland Department of Culture, Arts and Leisure, and
- (e) to the Comptroller and Auditor General.

(3) A copy of a statement must be sent under sub-paragraph (2) within such period, beginning with the end of the financial year to which the statement relates, as the Secretary of State may, with the consent of the Treasury, direct.

(4) The Comptroller and Auditor General shall—
- (a) examine, certify and report on a statement received under this paragraph, and
- (b) lay a copy of the statement and his report before Parliament.]

[934A]

NOTES

Commencement: 14 August 2006.
Inserted as noted to Pt 1 at **[933]**.

(Schs 5, 6, 6A repealed by the National Lottery Act 2006, ss 19(1), (6)(a), 21, Sch 3; Schs 7–10 outside the scope of this work.)

LOCAL GOVERNMENT (WALES) ACT 1994

(1994 c 19)

An Act to make provision with respect to local government in Wales

[5 July 1994]

NOTES

Transfer of functions in relation to Wales: as to the transfer of functions under this Act from Ministers of the Crown to the National Assembly for Wales, see the National Assembly for Wales (Transfer of Functions) Order 1999, SI 1999/672.

1–45 ((*Pts I–V*) *outside the scope of this work.*)

PART VI
TRANSITIONAL PROVISIONS

46–48 (*Outside the scope of this work.*)

49 Charities

(1) Where, immediately before the commencement of this section, any property is held exclusively for charitable purposes by any of the old authorities, as sole trustee, that property shall vest on the same trusts in the appropriate council.

(2) Where, immediately before the commencement of this section, any power with respect to a charity was vested in the proper officer of an old authority or in the holder of any other office of an old authority that power shall vest in the corresponding officer of the appropriate council.

(3) Where, immediately before the commencement of this section, an old authority or any officer of an old authority is included among the charity trustees of a charity, those trustees shall include instead the appropriate council or (as the case may be) the corresponding officer of that council.

(4) Where subsection (1) applies and the property in question is held for the benefit of—
- (a) a specified area,
- (b) the inhabitants of a specified area, or
- (c) any particular class or body of persons in a specified area,

the appropriate council is the new principal council whose area comprises the whole, or the greater part, of the specified area.

(5) In any other case falling within this section, the appropriate council is the new principal council whose area comprises the whole, or the greater part, of the area of the old authority in question.

(6) The Secretary of State may by order make provision with respect to any of the matters dealt with by this section, either in substitution for the provision made by this section or by way of supplementing or modifying that provision, and either generally or in relation to prescribed cases or classes of case.

(7) Nothing in this section—

(a) affects any power of Her Majesty, the court or any other person to alter the trusts of any charity; or

(b) applies in a case to which section 50 applies.

(8) In this section "charity", "charitable purposes", "charity trustees", "court" and "trusts" have the same meaning as in the Charities Act 1993.

[935]

NOTES

Commencement: 1 April 1996.

Orders: the Local Government Reorganisation (Wales) (Charities) Order 1996, SI 1996/1983.

50–59 (*Outside the scope of this work.*)

PART VII

MISCELLANEOUS AND SUPPLEMENTAL

60–63 (*Outside the scope of this work.*)

64 Interpretation

(1) In this Act—

"the 1972 Act" means the Local Government Act 1972;

"the Commission" means the Staff Commission for Wales or Comisiwn Staff Cymru;

"decentralisation scheme" has the meaning given in section 27;

"financial year" means the period of twelve months beginning with 1st April;

"new", in relation to any area or authority, means an area or authority established by or under this Act;

"old authority" means an authority which ceases to exist as a result of this Act;

"the planning Act" means the Town and Country Planning Act 1990;

"prescribed" means prescribed by an order or by regulations made by the Secretary of State;

"preserved county" means any county created by the 1972 Act as a county in Wales, as that county stood immediately before the passing of this Act but subject to any provision of this Act, or made under the 1972 Act, redrawing its boundaries;

"the Residuary Body" means the Residuary Body for Wales or Corff Gweddilliol Cymru.

(2) A county borough established by this Act shall not be treated as a borough for the purposes of any Act passed before 1st April 1974.

(3) Subject to the provisions of this section, this Act and the 1972 Act shall be construed as one.

(4) Subject to any provision to the contrary, in any amendment of an enactment made by or under this Act "Wales" has the same meaning as in section 269 of the 1972 Act.

[936]

65 (*Outside the scope of this work.*)

66 Short title, commencement, extent etc

(1) This Act may be cited as the Local Government (Wales) Act 1994.

(2) The following provisions of this Act—

(a) sections 1(1), (2) and (7), 3, 6, 7, 39, 40, 43, 46, 47, 48, 54, 55, 63 and 64,
(b) Schedules 1, 3, 13 and 14 and paragraphs 1, 4, 6 and 9 of Schedule 17, and
(c) subsections (1) to (4) and (9) of this section,

shall come into force on the passing of this Act.

(3) The other provisions of this Act shall come into force on such day as the Secretary of State may by order appoint.

(4) Different days may be appointed by an order under subsection (3) for different purposes and different provisions.

(5) Schedule 15 makes minor and consequential amendments of the 1972 Act.

(6) Schedule 16 makes certain miscellaneous consequential amendments. (7) Schedule 17 contains transitional provisions and savings.

(8) The repeals set out in Schedule 18, which include repeals of certain enactments which are spent, shall have effect.

(9) This Act does not extend to Scotland or Northern Ireland except that any amendment or repeal of another enactment by this Act has the same extent as the enactment amended or repealed.

[937]

NOTES

Orders: the Local Government (Wales) Act 1994 (Commencement No 1) Order 1994, SI 1994/2109; the Local Government (Wales) Act 1994 (Commencement No 2) Order 1994, SI 1994/2790; the Local Government (Wales) Act 1994 (Commencement No 3) Order 1995, SI 1995/546; the Local Government (Wales) Act 1994 (Commencement No 4) Order 1995, SI 1995/852; the Local Government (Wales) Act 1994 (Commencement No 5) Order 1995, SI 1995/2490; the Local Government (Wales) Act 1994 (Commencement No 6) Order 1995, SI 1995/3198; the Local Government (Wales) Act 1994 (Commencement No 7) Order 1996 SI 1996/396;

(Schs 1–18 outside the scope of this work.)

VALUE ADDED TAX ACT 1994

(1994 c 23)

ARRANGEMENT OF SECTIONS

PART II
RELIEFS, EXCEPTIONS AND REPAYMENTS

Reliefs etc generally available

Acquisitions

Imports, overseas businesses etc

PART III
APPLICATION OF ACT IN PARTICULAR CASES

PART VI
SUPPLEMENTARY PROVISIONS

Supplementary provisions

An Act to consolidate the enactments relating to value added tax, including certain enactments relating to VAT tribunals

[5 July 1994]

1–29 ((*Pt I*) *outside the scope of this work.*)

PART II
RELIEFS, EXCEPTIONS AND REPAYMENTS

Reliefs etc generally available

29A (*Outside the scope of this work.*)

30 Zero-rating

(1) Where a taxable person supplies goods or services and the supply is zero-rated, then, whether or not VAT would be chargeable on the supply apart from this section—

(a) no VAT shall be charged on the supply; but

(b) it shall in all other respects be treated as a taxable supply;

and accordingly the rate at which VAT is treated as charged on the supply shall be nil.

(2) A supply of goods or services is zero-rated by virtue of this subsection if the goods or services are of a description for the time being specified in Schedule 8 or the supply is of a description for the time being so specified.

[(2A) A supply by a person of services which consist of applying a treatment or process to another person's goods is zero-rated by virtue of this subsection if by doing so he produces goods, and either—

(a) those goods are of a description for the time being specified in Schedule 8; or

(b) a supply by him of those goods to the person to whom he supplies the services would be of a description so specified.]

(3) Where goods of a description for the time being specified in that Schedule, or of a description forming part of a description of supply for the time being so specified, are

acquired in the United Kingdom from another member State or imported from a place outside the member States, no VAT shall be chargeable on their acquisition or importation, except as otherwise provided in that Schedule.

(4) The Treasury may by order vary Schedule 8 by adding to or deleting from it any description or by varying any description for the time being specified in it.

[(5) The export of any goods by a charity to a place outside the member States shall for the purposes of this Act be treated as a supply made by the charity—

(a) in the United Kingdom, and

(b) in the course or furtherance of a business carried on by the charity.]

(6) A supply of goods is zero-rated by virtue of this subsection if the Commissioners are satisfied that the person supplying the goods—

(a) has exported them to a place outside the member States; or

(b) has shipped them for use as stores on a voyage or flight to an eventual destination outside the United Kingdom, or as merchandise for sale by retail to persons carried on such a voyage or flight in a ship or aircraft,

and in either case if such other conditions, if any, as may be specified in regulations or the Commissioners may impose are fulfilled.

(7) Subsection (6)(b) above shall not apply in the case of goods shipped for use as stores on a voyage or flight to be made by the person to whom the goods were supplied and to be made for a purpose which is private.

(8) Regulations may provide for the zero-rating of supplies of goods, or of such goods as may be specified in the regulations, in cases where—

(a) the Commissioners are satisfied that the goods have been or are to be exported to a place outside the member States or that the supply in question involves both—

(i) the removal of the goods from the United Kingdom; and

(ii) their acquisition in another member State by a person who is liable for VAT on the acquisition in accordance with provisions of the law of that member State corresponding, in relation to that member State, to the provisions of section 10; and

(b) such other conditions, if any, as may be specified in the regulations or the Commissioners may impose are fulfilled.

[(8A) Regulations may provide for the zero-rating of supplies of goods, or of such goods as may be specified in regulations, in cases where—

(a) the Commissioners are satisfied that the supply in question involves both—

(i) the removal of the goods from a fiscal warehousing regime within the meaning of section 18F(2); and

(ii) their being placed in a warehousing regime in another member State, or in such member State or States as may be prescribed, where that regime is established by provisions of the law of that member State corresponding, in relation to that member State, to the provisions of sections 18A and 18B; and

(b) such other conditions, if any, as may be specified in the regulations or the Commissioners may impose are fulfilled.]

(9) Regulations may provide for the zero-rating of a supply of services which is made where goods are let on hire and the Commissioners are satisfied that the goods have been or are to be removed from the United Kingdom during the period of the letting, and such other conditions, if any, as may be specified in the regulations or the Commissioners may impose are fulfilled.

(10) Where the supply of any goods has been zero-rated by virtue of subsection (6) above or in pursuance of regulations made under [subsection (8), (8A) or (9)] above and—

(a) the goods are found in the United Kingdom after the date on which they were alleged to have been or were to be exported or shipped or otherwise removed from the United Kingdom; or

(b) any condition specified in the relevant regulations under [subsection (6), (8), (8A) or (9)] above or imposed by the Commissioners is not complied with,

and the presence of the goods in the United Kingdom after that date or the non-observance of the condition has not been authorised for the purposes of this subsection by the Commissioners, the goods shall be liable to forfeiture under the Management Act and the VAT that would have been chargeable on the supply but for the zero-rating shall become payable forthwith by the person to whom the goods were supplied or by any person in whose possession the goods are found in the United Kingdom; but the Commissioners may, if they think fit, waive payment of the whole or part of that VAT.

[938]

NOTES

Sub-s (2A): inserted, in relation to supplies made on or after 1 January 1996, by the Finance Act 1996, s 29(1), (2), (5).

Sub-s (5): substituted, in relation to transactions occurring on or after 1 May 1995, by the Finance Act 1995, s 28.

Sub-s (8A): inserted, in relation to any acquisition of goods from another member State and any supply taking place on or after 1 June 1996, by the Finance Act 1996, s 26, Sch 3, para 7.

Sub-s (10): words in square brackets substituted, in relation to any acquisition of goods from another member State and any supply taking place on or after 1 June 1996, by the Finance Act 1996, s 26, Sch 3, para 7.

Management Act: Customs and Excise Management Act 1979.

Orders: the Value Added Tax (Transport) Order 1994, SI 1994/3014; the Value Added Tax (Construction of Buildings) Order 1995, SI 1995/280; the Value Added Tax (Protected Buildings) Order 1995, SI 1995/283; the Value Added Tax (Supply of Pharmaceutical Goods) Order 1995, SI 1995/652; the Value Added Tax (Transport) Order 1995, SI 1995/653; the Value Added Tax (Ships and Aircraft) Order 1995, SI 1995/3039; the Value Added Tax (Tax Free Shops) Order 1995, SI 1995/3041 (revoked); the Value Added Tax (Anti-avoidance (Heating)) Order 1996, SI 1996/1661; the Value Added Tax (Registered Social Landlords) (No 1) Order 1997, SI 1997/50; the Value Added Tax (Drugs, Medicines and Aids for the Handicapped) Order 1997, SI 1997/2744; the Value Added Tax (Abolition of Zero-Rating for Tax-Free Shops) Order 1999, SI 1999/1642; the Value Added Tax (Drugs, Medicines, Aids for the Handicapped and Charities Etc) Order 2000, SI 2000/503; Value Added Tax (Charities and Aids for the Handicapped) Order 2000, SI 2000/805; Value Added Tax (Protective Helmets) Order 2000, SI 2000/1517; the Value Added Tax (Protective Helmets) Order 2001, SI 2001/732; the Value Added Tax (Passenger Vehicles) Order 2001, SI 2001/753; the Value Added Tax (Vehicles Designed or Adapted for Handicapped Persons) Order 2001, SI 2001/754; the Value Added Tax (Conversion of Buildings) Order 2001, SI 2001/2305; the Value Added Tax (Construction of Buildings) Order 2002, SI 2002/1101; the Value Added Tax (Equipment in Lifeboats) Order 2002, SI 2002/456; the Value Added Tax (Transport) Order 2002, SI 2002/1173; the Value Added Tax (Drugs, Medicines, Aids for the Handicapped and Charities Etc) Order 2002, SI 2002/2813; the Value Added Tax (Food) Order 2004, SI 2004/3343; the Value Added Tax (Lifeboats) Order 2006, SI 2006/1750.

Regulations: the Value Added Tax Regulations 1995, SI 1995/2518.

31 Exempt supplies and acquisitions

(1) A supply of goods or services is an exempt supply if it is of a description for the time being specified in Schedule 9 and an acquisition of goods from another member State is an exempt acquisition if the goods are acquired in pursuance of an exempt supply.

(2) The Treasury may by order vary that Schedule by adding to or deleting from it any description of supply or by varying any description of supply for the time being specified in it, and the Schedule may be varied so as to describe a supply of goods by reference to the use which has been made of them or to other matters unrelated to the characteristics of the goods themselves.

[939]

NOTES

See further, in relation to the making of orders under sub-s (2): the Finance Act 1999, s 13(2), (4).

Orders: the Value Added Tax (Education) (No 2) Order 1994, SI 1994/2969; the Value Added Tax (Land) Order 1995, SI 1995/282; the Value Added Tax (Cultural Services) Order 1996, SI 1996/1256; the Value Added Tax (Pharmaceutical Chemists) Order 1996, SI 1996/2949; the Value Added Tax (Finance) Order 1997, SI 1997/510; the Value Added Tax (Osteopaths) Order 1998, SI 1998/1294; the Value Added Tax (Finance) Order 1999, SI 1999/594; the Value Added Tax (Chiropractors) Order 1999, SI 1999/1575; the Value Added Tax (Sport, Sports Competitions and Physical Education) Order 1999, SI 1999/1994; the Value Added Tax (Supplies of Goods where Input Tax cannot be recovered) Order 1999, SI 1999/2833; the Value Added Tax (Investment Gold) Order 1999, SI 1999/3116; the Value Added Tax (Fund-Raising Events by Charities and Other Qualifying Bodies) Order 2000, SI 2000/802; the Value Added Tax (Health and Welfare) Order 2002, SI 2002/762; the Value Added Tax (Health and Welfare) Order 2003, SI 2003/24; the Value Added Tax (Finance) Order 2003, SI 2003/1568; the Value Added Tax (Finance) (No 2) Order 2003, SI 2003/1569; the Value Added Tax (Insurance) Order 2004, SI 2004/3083; the Value Added Tax (Betting, Gaming and Lotteries) Order 2006, SI 2006/2685; the Value Added Tax (Health and Welfare) Order 2007, SI 2007/206.

32 (*Repealed by the Finance Act 1995, ss 24(2), 162, Sch 29, Pt VI(3).*)

33 Refunds of VAT in certain cases

(1) Subject to the following provisions of this section, where—

(a) VAT is chargeable on the supply of goods or services to a body to which this section applies, on the acquisition of any goods by such a body from another member State or on the importation of any goods by such a body from a place outside the member States, and

(b) the supply, acquisition or importation is not for the purpose of any business carried on by the body,

the Commissioners shall, on a claim made by the body at such time and in such form and manner as the Commissioners may determine, refund to it the amount of the VAT so chargeable.

(2) Where goods or services so supplied to or acquired or imported by the body cannot be conveniently distinguished from goods or services supplied to or acquired or imported by it for the purpose of a business carried on by it, the amount to be refunded under this section shall be such amount as remains after deducting from the whole of the VAT chargeable on any supply to or acquisition or importation by the body such proportion thereof as appears to the Commissioners to be attributable to the carrying on of the business; but where—

(a) the VAT so attributable is or includes VAT attributable, in accordance with regulations under section 26, to exempt supplies by the body, and

(b) the VAT attributable to the exempt supplies is in the opinion of the Commissioners an insignificant proportion of the VAT so chargeable,

they may include it in the VAT refunded under this section.

(3) The bodies to which this section applies are—

(a) a local authority;

(b) a river purification board established under section 135 of the Local Government (Scotland) Act 1973, and a water development board within the meaning of section 109 of the Water (Scotland) Act 1980;

(c) an internal drainage board;

(d) a passenger transport authority or executive within the meaning of Part II of the Transport Act 1968;

(e) a port health authority within the meaning of the Public Health (Control of Disease) Act 1984, and a port local authority and joint port local authority constituted under Part X of the Public Health (Scotland) Act 1897;

(f) a police authority *and the Receiver for the Metropolitan Police District*;

(g) a development corporation within the meaning of the New Towns Act 1981 or the New Towns (Scotland) Act 1968, a new town commission within the meaning of the New Towns Act (Northern Ireland) 1965 and the Commission for the New Towns;

(h) a general lighthouse authority within the meaning of [Part VIII of the Merchant Shipping Act 1995];

(i) the British Broadcasting Corporation;

[(j) the appointed news provider referred to in section 280 of the Communications Act 2003; and]

(k) any body specified for the purposes of this section by an order made by the Treasury.

(4) No VAT shall be refunded under this section to a general lighthouse authority which in the opinion of the Commissioners is attributable to activities other than those concerned with the provision, maintenance or management of lights or other navigational aids.

(5) No VAT shall be refunded under this section to [an appointed] news provider which in the opinion of the Commissioners is attributable to activities other than the provision of news programmes for broadcasting by holders of regional Channel 3 licences (within the meaning of Part I of the Broadcasting Act 1990).

(6) References in this section to VAT chargeable do not include any VAT which, by virtue of any order under section 25(7), is excluded from credit under that section.

[940]

NOTES

Sub-s (3): in para (f) words in italics repealed by the Greater London Authority Act 1999, ss 325, 423, Sch 27, para 68, Sch 34, Pt VII, as from a day to be appointed; in para (h) words in square brackets substituted by the Merchant Shipping Act 1995, s 314(2), Sch 13, para 95; para (j) substituted by the Communications Act 2003, s 406(1), Sch 17, para 129(1), (2)(a).

Sub-s (5): words in square brackets substituted by the Communications Act 2003, s 406(1), Sch 17, para 129(1), (2)(b).

Orders: the Value Added Tax (Refund of Tax) Order 1995, SI 1995/1978; the Value Added Tax (Refund of Tax) (No 2) Order 1995, SI 1995/2999; the Value Added Tax (Refund of Tax) Order 1997, SI 1997/2558; the Value Added Tax (Refund of Tax) Order 1999, SI 1999/2076; the Value Added Tax (Refund of Tax) Order 2000, SI 2000/1046; the Value Added Tax (Refund of Tax) (No 2) Order 2000, SI 2000/1515; the Value Added Tax (Refund of Tax) (No 3) Order 2000, SI 2000/1672; the Value Added Tax (Refund of Tax) Order 2001, SI 2001/3453; the Value Added Tax (Refund of Tax) Order 2006, SI 2006/1793. In addition, by virtue of the Interpretation Act 1978, s 17(2)(b), the following orders have effect as if made under this section: the Value Added Tax (Refund of Tax) Order 1976, SI 1976/2028; the Value Added Tax (Refund of Tax) Order 1985, SI 1985/1101; the Value Added Tax (Refund of Tax) Order 1986, SI 1986/336; the Value Added Tax (Refund of Tax) (No 2) Order 1986, SI 1986/532; the Value Added Tax (Refund of Tax) Order 1989, SI 1989/1217.

[33A Refunds of VAT to museums and galleries

(1) Subsections (2) to (5) below apply where—

(a) VAT is chargeable on—

(i) the supply of goods or services to a body to which this section applies,

(ii) the acquisition of any goods by such a body from another member State, or

(iii) the importation of any goods by such a body from a place outside the member States,

(b) the supply, acquisition or importation is attributable to the provision by the body of free rights of admission to a relevant museum or gallery, and

(c) the supply is made, or the acquisition or importation takes place, on or after 1st April 2001.

(2) The Commissioners shall, on a claim made by the body in such form and manner as the Commissioners may determine, refund to the body the amount of VAT so chargeable.

(3) The claim must be made before the end of the claim period.

(4) Subject to subsection (5) below, "the claim period" is the period of 3 years beginning with the day on which the supply is made or the acquisition or importation takes place.

(5) If the Commissioners so determine, the claim period is such shorter period beginning with that day as the Commissioners may determine.

(6) Subsection (7) below applies where goods or services supplied to, or acquired or imported by, a body to which this section applies that are attributable to free admissions cannot conveniently be distinguished from goods or services supplied to, or acquired or imported by, the body that are not attributable to free admissions.

(7) The amount to be refunded on a claim by the body under this section shall be such amount as remains after deducting from the VAT related to the claim such proportion of that VAT as appears to the Commissioners to be attributable otherwise than to free admissions.

(8) For the purposes of subsections (6) and (7) above—

(a) goods or services are, and VAT is, attributable to free admissions if they are, or it is, attributable to the provision by the body of free rights of admission to a relevant museum or gallery;

(b) the VAT related to a claim is the whole of the VAT chargeable on—

(i) the supplies to the body, and

(ii) the acquisitions and importations by the body,

to which the claim relates.

(9) The Treasury may by order—

(a) specify a body as being a body to which this section applies;

(b) when specifying a body under paragraph (a), specify any museum or gallery that, for the purposes of this section, is a "relevant" museum or gallery in relation to the body;

(c) specify an additional museum or gallery as being, for the purposes of this section, a "relevant" museum or gallery in relation to a body to which this section applies;

(d) when specifying a museum or gallery under paragraph (b) or (c), provide that this section shall have effect in the case of the museum or gallery as if in subsection (1)(c) there were substituted for 1st April 2001 a later date specified in the order.

(10) References in this section to VAT do not include any VAT which, by virtue of any order under section 25(7), is excluded from credit under that section.]

[940A]

NOTES

Commencement: 11 May 2001 (for the purpose of exercising the power to make orders); 1 September 2001 (otherwise).

Inserted by the Finance Act 2001, s 98(1), (2).

Orders: the Value Added Tax (Refund of Tax to Museums and Galleries) Order 2001, SI 2001/2879.

34 Capital goods

(1) The Treasury may by order make provision for the giving of relief, in such cases, to such extent and subject to such exceptions as may be specified in the order, from VAT paid on the supply, acquisition or importation for the purpose of a business carried on by any person of machinery or plant or any specified description of machinery or plant in cases where that VAT or part of that VAT cannot be credited under section 25 and such other conditions are satisfied as may be specified in the order.

(2) Without prejudice to the generality of subsection (1) above, an order under this section may provide for relief to be given by deduction or refunding of VAT and for aggregating or excluding the aggregation of value where goods of the same description are supplied, acquired or imported together.

[941]

35 Refund of VAT to persons constructing certain buildings

[(1) Where—

(a) a person carries out works to which this section applies,

(b) his carrying out of the works is lawful and otherwise than in the course or furtherance of any business, and

(c) VAT is chargeable on the supply, acquisition or importation of any goods used by him for the purposes of the works,

the Commissioners shall, on a claim made in that behalf, refund to that person the amount of VAT so chargeable.

(1A) The works to which this section applies are—

(a) the construction of a building designed as a dwelling or number of dwellings;

(b) the construction of a building for use solely for a relevant residential purpose or relevant charitable purpose; and

(c) a residential conversion.

(1B) For the purposes of this section goods shall be treated as used for the purposes of works to which this section applies by the person carrying out the works in so far only as they are building materials which, in the course of the works, are incorporated in the building in question or its site.

(1C) Where—

(a) a person ("the relevant person") carries out a residential conversion by arranging for any of the work of the conversion to be done by another ("a contractor"),

(b) the relevant person's carrying out of the conversion is lawful and otherwise than in the course or furtherance of any business,

(c) the contractor is not acting as an architect, surveyor or consultant or in a supervisory capacity, and

(d) VAT is chargeable on services consisting in the work done by the contractor,

the Commissioners shall, on a claim made in that behalf, refund to the relevant person the amount of VAT so chargeable.

(1D) For the purposes of this section works constitute a residential conversion to the extent that they consist in the conversion of a non-residential building, or a non-residential part of a building, into—

(a) a building designed as a dwelling or a number of dwellings;

(b) a building intended for use solely for a relevant residential purpose; or

(c) anything which would fall within paragraph (a) or (b) above if different parts of a building were treated as separate buildings.]

(2) The Commissioners shall not be required to entertain a claim for a refund of VAT under this section unless the claim—

(a) is made within such time and in such form and manner, and

(b) contains such information, and

(c) is accompanied by such documents, whether by way of evidence or otherwise,

as the Commissioners may by regulations prescribe [or, in the case of documents, as the Commissioners may determine in accordance with the regulations].

(3) This section shall have effect—

(a) as if the reference in subsection (1) above to the VAT chargeable on the supply of any goods included a reference to VAT chargeable on the supply in accordance with the law of another member State; and

(b) in relation to VAT chargeable in accordance with the law of another member State, as if references to refunding VAT to any person were references to paying that person an amount equal to the VAT chargeable in accordance with the law of that member State;

and the provisions of this Act and of any other enactment or subordinate legislation (whenever passed or made) so far as they relate to a refund under this section shall be construed accordingly.

[(4) The notes to Group 5 of Schedule 8 shall apply for construing this section as they apply for construing that Group [but this is subject to subsection (4A) below].

[(4A) The meaning of "non-residential" given by Note (7A) of Group 5 of Schedule 8 (and not that given by Note (7) of that Group) applies for the purposes of this section but as if—

(a) references in that Note to item 3 of that Group were references to this section, and

(b) paragraph (b)(iii) of that Note were omitted.]

(5) The power of the Treasury by order under section 30 to vary Schedule 8 shall include—

(a) power to apply any variation made by the order for the purposes of this section; and

(b) power to make such consequential modifications of this section as they may think fit.]

[942]

NOTES

Sub-ss (1), (1A)–(1D): substituted for original sub-s (1), in relation to any case in which a claim for repayment is made under this section at any time on or after 29 April 1996, by the Finance Act 1996, s 30(1), (4).

Sub-s (2): words in square brackets inserted, in relation to any case in which a claim for repayment is made under this section at any time on or after 29 April 1996, by the Finance Act 1996, s 30(2), (4).

Sub-s (4): added, together with sub-s (5), in relation to any case in which a claim for repayment is made under this section at any time on or after 29 April 1996, by the Finance Act 1996, s 30(3), (4); words in square brackets inserted by the Value Added Tax (Conversion of Buildings) Order 2001, SI 2001/2305, arts 2, 4(a), in relation to supplies made on or after 1 August 2001.

Sub-s (4A): inserted by SI 2001/2305, arts 2, 4(b), in relation to supplies made on or after 1 August 2001.

Sub-s (5): added, together with sub-s (4), in relation to any case in which a claim for repayment is made under this section at any time on or after 29 April 1996, by the Finance Act 1996, s 30(3), (4).

Regulations: the Value Added Tax Regulations 1995, SI 1995/2518.

Orders: the Value Added Tax (Conversion of Buildings) Order 2001, SI 2001/2305.

---

36 Bad debts

(1) Subsection (2) below applies where—

(a) a person has supplied goods or services … and has accounted for and paid VAT on the supply,

(b) the whole or any part of the consideration for the supply has been written off in his accounts as a bad debt, and

(c) a period of 6 months (beginning with the date of the supply) has elapsed.

(2) Subject to the following provisions of this section and to regulations under it the person shall be entitled, on making a claim to the Commissioners, to a refund of the amount of VAT chargeable by reference to the outstanding amount.

[(3) In subsection (2) above "the outstanding amount" means—

(a) if at the time of the claim no part of the consideration written off in the claimant's accounts as a bad debt has been received, an amount equal to the amount of the consideration so written off;

(b) if at that time any part of the consideration so written off has been received, an amount by which that part is exceeded by the amount of the consideration written off;

and in this subsection "received" means received either by the claimant or by a person to whom has been assigned a right to receive the whole or any part of the consideration written off.]

[(3A) For the purposes of this section, where the whole or any part of the consideration for the supply does not consist of money, the amount in money that shall be taken to represent any non-monetary part of the consideration shall be so much of the amount made up of—

(a) the value of the supply, and
(b) the VAT charged on the supply,

as is attributable to the non-monetary consideration in question.]

(4) A person shall not be entitled to a refund under subsection (2) above unless—

(a) the value of the supply is equal to or less than its open market value, …
(b) …

[(4A) …]

(5) Regulations under this section may—

(a) require a claim to be made at such time and in such form and manner as may be specified by or under the regulations;
(b) require a claim to be evidenced and quantified by reference to such records and other documents as may be so specified;
(c) require the claimant to keep, for such period and in such form and manner as may be so specified, those records and documents and a record of such information relating to the claim and to [anything subsequently received] by way of consideration as may be so specified;
(d) require the repayment of a refund allowed under this section where any requirement of the regulations is not complied with;
(e) require the repayment of the whole or, as the case may be, an appropriate part of a refund allowed under this section [where any part (or further part) of the consideration written off in the claimant's accounts as a bad debt is subsequently received either by the claimant or, except in such circumstances as may be prescribed, by a person to whom has been assigned a right to receive the whole or any part of that consideration;]
[(ea) …]
(e) above, for restoring the whole or any part of an entitlement to credit for input tax;]
(f) include such supplementary, incidental, consequential or transitional provisions as appear to the Commissioners to be necessary or expedient for the purposes of this section;
(g) make different provision for different circumstances.

(6) The provisions which may be included in regulations by virtue of subsection (5)(f) above may include rules for ascertaining—

(a) whether, when and to what extent consideration is to be taken to have been written off in accounts as a bad debt;
(b) whether [anything received] is to be taken as received by way of consideration for a particular supply;
(c) whether, and to what extent, [anything received] is to be taken as received by way of consideration written off in accounts as a bad debt.

(7) The provisions which may be included in regulations by virtue of subsection (5)(f) above may include rules dealing with particular cases, such as those involving [receipt of part of the consideration] or mutual debts; and in particular such rules may vary the way in which the following amounts are to be calculated—

(a) the outstanding amount mentioned in subsection (2) above, and
(b) the amount of any repayment where a refund has been allowed under this section.

(8) Section 6 shall apply for determining the time when a supply is to be treated as taking place for the purposes of construing this section.

[943]

NOTES

Sub-s (1): in para (a) words omitted repealed, in relation to claims made on or after 31 July 1998, by the Finance Act 1998, ss 23(1), (7), 165, Sch 27, Pt II.

Sub-s (3): substituted by the Finance Act 1999, s 15(1), (5); this amendment has effect for the purposes of the making of any refund or repayment after 9 March 1999, but does not have effect in relation to anything received on or before that day.
Sub-s (3A): inserted, in relation to claims made on or after 31 July 1998, by the Finance Act 1998, s 23(3), (7).
Sub-s (4): para (b) repealed, in relation to a supply of goods made after 19 March 1997, by the Finance Act 1997, ss 39(1), 113, Sch 18, Part IV(3).
Sub-s (4A): inserted, in relation to any entitlement to a refund of VAT charged on a supply made after 26 November 1996, by the Finance Act 1997, s 39(2), (3); repealed by the Finance Act 2002, ss 22(2), 141, Sch 40, Pt 2(1), with effect in relation to supplies made on or after 1 January 2003.
Sub-s (5): in para (c) words in square brackets substituted by the Finance Act 1998, s 23(4)(a); in para (e) words in square brackets substituted by the Finance Act 1999, s 15(2); para (ea) inserted by the Finance Act 1997, s 39(4), repealed by the Finance Act 2002, ss 22(2), 141, Sch 40, Pt 2(1), with effect in relation to supplies made on or after 1 January 2003.
Sub-ss (6), (7): words in square brackets substituted by the Finance Act 1998, s 23(5), (6).
Regulations: the Value Added Tax Regulations 1995, SI 1995/2518; the Value Added Tax Regulations 1999, SI 1999/3029.

[Acquisitions

36A Relief from VAT on acquisition if importation would attract relief

(1) The Treasury may by order make provision for relieving from VAT the acquisition from another member State of any goods if, or to the extent that, relief from VAT would be given by an order under section 37 if the acquisition were an importation from a place outside the member States.

(2) An order under this section may provide for relief to be subject to such conditions as appear to the Treasury to be necessary or expedient.

These may—

(a) include conditions prohibiting or restricting the disposal of or dealing with the goods concerned;

(b) be framed by reference to the conditions to which, by virtue of any order under section 37 in force at the time of the acquisition, relief under such an order would be subject in the case of an importation of the goods concerned.

(3) Where relief from VAT given by an order under this section was subject to a condition that has been breached or not complied with, the VAT shall become payable at the time of the breach or, as the case may be, at the latest time allowed for compliance.]

[943A]

NOTES

Commencement: 24 July 2002.
Inserted, together with preceding cross-heading, by the Finance Act 2002, s 25.
Orders: the Value Added Tax (Acquisitions) Relief Order 2002, SI 2002/1935.

Imports, overseas businesses etc

37 Relief from VAT on importation of goods

(1) The Treasury may by order make provision for giving relief from the whole or part of the VAT chargeable on the importation of goods from places outside the member States, subject to such conditions (including conditions prohibiting or restricting the disposal of or dealing with the goods) as may be imposed by or under the order, if and so far as the relief appears to the Treasury to be necessary or expedient, having regard to any international agreement or arrangements.

(2) In any case where—

(a) it is proposed that goods which have been imported from a place outside the member States by any person ("the original importer") with the benefit of relief under subsection (1) above shall be transferred to another person ("the transferee"), and

(b) on an application made by the transferee, the Commissioners direct that this subsection shall apply,

this Act shall have effect as if, on the date of the transfer of the goods (and in place of the transfer), the goods were exported by the original importer and imported by the transferee and, accordingly, where appropriate, provision made under subsection (1) above shall have effect in relation to the VAT chargeable on the importation of the goods by the transferee.

(3) The Commissioners may by regulations make provision for remitting or repaying, if they think fit, the whole or part of the VAT chargeable on the importation of any goods from places outside the member States which are shown to their satisfaction to have been previously exported from the United Kingdom or removed from any member State.

(4) The Commissioners may by regulations make provision for remitting or repaying the whole or part of the VAT chargeable on the importation of any goods from places outside the member States if they are satisfied that the goods have been or are to be re-exported or otherwise removed from the United Kingdom and they think fit to do so in all the circumstances and having regard—

- (a) to the VAT chargeable on the supply of like goods in the United Kingdom;
- (b) to any VAT which may have become chargeable in another member State in respect of the goods.

[944]

NOTES

See further, in relation to the making of orders under sub-s (1): the Finance Act 1999, s 13(3), (4).
Orders: the Value Added Tax (Importation of Investment Gold) Relief Order 1999, SI 1999/3115; the Value Added Tax (Imported Gas and Electricity) Relief Order 2004, SI 2004/3147. In addition, by virtue of the Interpretation Act 1978, s 17(2)(b), the following orders have effect as if made under this section: the Value Added Tax (Imported Goods) Relief Order 1986, SI 1986746; the Value Added Tax (Small Non-Commercial Consignments) Relief 1986, SI 1986/939; the Value Added Tax (Imported Gold) Relief Order 1992, SI 1992/3124.

Regulations: the Value Added Tax Regulations 1995, SI 1995/2518.

38 Importation of goods by taxable persons

The Commissioners may by regulations make provision for enabling goods imported from a place outside the member States by a taxable person in the course or furtherance of any business carried on by him to be delivered or removed, subject to such conditions or restrictions as the Commissioners may impose for the protection of the revenue, without payment of the VAT chargeable on the importation, and for that VAT to be accounted for together with the VAT chargeable on the supply of goods or services by him or on the acquisition of goods by him from other member States.

[945]

NOTES

Regulations: the Value Added Tax Regulations 1995, SI 1995/2518.

39 Repayment of VAT to those in business overseas

(1) The Commissioners may, by means of a scheme embodied in regulations, provide for the repayment, to persons to whom this section applies, of VAT on supplies to them in the United Kingdom or on the importation of goods by them from places outside the member States which would be input tax of theirs if they were taxable persons in the United Kingdom.

(2) This section—

- (a) applies to persons carrying on business in another member State, and
- (b) shall apply also to persons carrying on business in other countries, if, pursuant to any Community Directive, rules are adopted by the Council of the Communities about refunds of VAT to persons established elsewhere than in the member States,

but does not apply to persons carrying on business in the United Kingdom.

(3) Repayment shall be made in such cases only, and subject to such conditions, as the scheme may prescribe (being conditions specified in the regulations or imposed by the Commissioners either generally or in particular cases); and the scheme may provide—

- (a) for claims and repayments to be made only through agents in the United Kingdom;
- (b) either generally or for specified purposes—
  - (i) for the agents to be treated under this Act as if they were taxable persons; and
  - (ii) for treating claims as if they were returns under this Act and repayments as if they were repayments of input tax; and

(c) for generally regulating the methods by which the amount of any repayment is to be determined and the repayment is to be made.

[946]

NOTES

Regulations: the Value Added Tax Regulations 1995, SI 1995/2518.

40 Refunds in relation to new means of transport supplied to other member States

(1) Subject to subsection (2) below, where a person who is not a taxable person makes such a supply of goods consisting in a new means of transport as involves the removal of the goods to another member State, the Commissioners shall, on a claim made in that behalf, refund to that person, as the case may be—

(a) the amount of any VAT on the supply of that means of transport to that person, or

(b) the amount of any VAT paid by that person on the acquisition of that means of transport from another member State or on its importation from a place outside the member States.

(2) The amount of VAT refunded under this section shall not exceed the amount that would have been payable on the supply involving the removal if it had been a taxable supply by a taxable person and had not been zero-rated.

(3) The Commissioners shall not be entitled to entertain a claim for refund of VAT under this section unless the claim—

(a) is made within such time and in such form and manner;

(b) contains such information; and

(c) is accompanied by such documents, whether by way of evidence or otherwise,

as the Commissioners may by regulations prescribe.

[947]

NOTES

Regulations: the Value Added Tax Regulations 1995, SI 1995/2518.

PART III
APPLICATION OF ACT IN PARTICULAR CASES

41–50A (*Outside the scope of this work.*)

51 Buildings and land

(1) Schedule 10 shall have effect with respect to buildings and land.

(2) The Treasury may by order amend Schedule 10.

[948]

NOTES

Orders: the Value Added Tax (Buildings and Land) Order 1994, SI 1994/3013; the Value Added Tax (Buildings and Land) Order 1995, SI 1995/279; the Value Added Tax (Registered Social Landlords) (No 2) Order 1997, SI 1997/51; the Value Added Tax (Buildings and Land) Order 1999, SI 1999/593; the Value Added Tax (Buildings and Land) Order 2002, SI 2002/1102; the Value Added Tax (Buildings and Land) Order 2004, SI 2004/778.

51A–87 (*Ss 51A–57, ss 58–87 (Pts IV, V) outside the scope of this work.*)

PART VI
SUPPLEMENTARY PROVISIONS

88–96 (*Outside the scope of this work.*)

Supplementary provisions

97, 97A, 98–100 (*Outside the scope of this work.*)

101 Commencement and extent

(1) This Act shall come into force on 1st September 1994 and Part I shall have effect in relation to the charge to VAT on supplies, acquisitions and importations in prescribed accounting periods ending on or after that date.

(2) Without prejudice to section 16 of the Interpretation Act 1978 (continuation of proceedings under repealed enactments) except in so far as it enables proceedings to be continued under repealed enactments, section 72 shall have effect on the commencement of this Act to the exclusion of section 39 of the 1983 Act.

(3) This Act extends to Northern Ireland.

(4) Paragraph 23 of Schedule 13 and paragraph 7 of Schedule 14 shall extend to the Isle of Man but no other provision of this Act shall extend there.

[949]

NOTES

1983 Act: Value Added Tax Act 1983.

102 Short title

This Act may be cited as the Value Added Tax Act 1994.

[950]

SCHEDULES

(*Schs A1–7A outside the scope of this work.*)

SCHEDULE 8
ZERO-RATING

Section 30

(*Sch 8, Pt I outside the scope of this work.*)

PART II
THE GROUPS

GROUP 1—FOOD

The supply of anything comprised in the general items set out below, except—

(a) a supply in the course of catering; and

(b) a supply of anything comprised in any of the excepted items set out below, unless it is also comprised in any of the items overriding the exceptions set out below which relates to that excepted item.

General items

Item No.

1. Food of a kind used for human consumption.

2. Animal feeding stuffs.

3. Seeds or other means of propagation of plants comprised in item 1 or 2.

4. Live animals of a kind generally used as, or yielding or producing, food for human consumption.

Excepted items

Item No.

1. Ice cream, ice lollies, frozen yogurt, water ices and similar frozen products, and prepared mixes and powders for making such products.

2. Confectionery, not including cakes or biscuits other than biscuits wholly or partly covered with chocolate or some product similar in taste and appearance.

3. Beverages chargeable with any duty of excise specifically charged on spirits, beer, wine or made-wine and preparations thereof.

4. Other beverages (including fruit juices and bottled waters) and syrups, concentrates, essences, powders, crystals or other products for the preparation of beverages.

5. Any of the following when packaged for human consumption without further preparation, namely, potato crisps, potato sticks, potato puffs, and similar products made from the potato, or from potato flour, or from potato starch, and savoury food products obtained by the swelling of cereals or cereal products; and salted or roasted nuts other than nuts in shell.

6. Pet foods, canned, packaged or prepared; packaged foods (not being pet foods) for birds other than poultry or game; and biscuits and meal for cats and dogs.

7. Goods described in items 1, 2 and 3 of the general items which are canned, bottled, packaged or prepared for use—

(a) in the domestic brewing of any beer;
(b) in the domestic making of any cider or perry;
(c) in the domestic production of any wine or made-wine.

Items overriding the exceptions

Item No.

1. Yoghurt unsuitable for immediate consumption when frozen.

2. Drained cherries.

3. Candied peels.

4. Tea, maté, herbal teas and similar products, and preparations and extracts thereof.

5. Cocoa, coffee and chicory and other roasted coffee substitutes, and preparations and extracts thereof.

6. Milk and preparations and extracts thereof.

7. Preparations and extracts of meat, yeast or egg.

Notes:

(1) "Food" includes drink.

(2) "Animal" includes bird, fish, crustacean and mollusc.

(3) A supply of anything in the course of catering includes—

(a) any supply of it for consumption on the premises on which it is supplied; and
(b) any supply of hot food for consumption off those premises;

and for the purposes of paragraph (b) above "hot food" means food which, or any part of which—

(i) has been heated for the purposes of enabling it to be consumed at a temperature above the ambient air temperature; and
[(ii) is above that temperature at the time it is provided to the customer].

(4) Item 1 of the items overriding the exceptions relates to item 1 of the excepted items.

(5) Items 2 and 3 of the items overriding the exceptions relate to item 2 of the excepted items; and for the purposes of item 2 of the excepted items "confectionery" includes chocolates, sweets and biscuits; drained, glacé or crystallised fruits; and any item of sweetened prepared food which is normally eaten with the fingers.

(6) [Items 4 to 7] of the items overriding the exceptions relate to item 4 of the excepted items.

(7) Any supply described in this Group shall include a supply of services described in paragraph 1(1) of Schedule 4.

[951]

NOTES

Note (3): sub-para (ii) substituted by the Value Added Tax (Food) Order 2004, SI 2004/3343, art 2.
Note (6): words in square brackets substituted, with retrospective effect, by the Finance Act 1999, s 14.

(*Sch 8, Pt II, Group 2 outside the scope of this work.*)

GROUP 3—BOOKS, ETC

Item No.

1. Books, booklets, brochures, pamphlets and leaflets.
2. Newspapers, journals and periodicals.
3. Children's picture books and painting books.
4. Music (printed, duplicated or manuscript).
5. Maps, charts and topographical plans.
6. Covers, cases and other articles supplied with items 1 to 5 and not separately accounted for.

Note: Items 1 to 6—
(a) do not include plans or drawings for industrial, architectural, engineering, commercial or similar purposes; but
(b) include the supply of the services described in paragraph 1(1) of Schedule 4 in respect of goods comprised in the items.

[952]

GROUP 4—TALKING BOOKS FOR THE BLIND AND HANDICAPPED AND WIRELESS SETS FOR THE BLIND

Item No.

1. The supply to the Royal National Institute for the Blind, the National Listening Library or other similar charities of—
(a) magnetic tape specially adapted for the recording and reproduction of speech for the blind or severely handicapped;
(b) apparatus designed or specially adapted for the making on a magnetic tape, by way of the transfer of recorded speech from another magnetic tape, of a recording described in paragraph (f) below;
(c) apparatus designed or specially adapted for transfer to magnetic tapes of a recording made by apparatus described in paragraph (b) above;
(d) apparatus for re-winding magnetic tape described in paragraph (f) below;
(e) apparatus designed or specially adapted for the reproduction from recorded magnetic tape of speech for the blind or severely handicapped which is not available for use otherwise than by the blind or severely handicapped;
(f) magnetic tape upon which has been recorded speech for the blind or severely handicapped, such recording being suitable for reproduction only in the apparatus mentioned in paragraph (e) above;
(g) apparatus solely for the making on a magnetic tape of a sound recording which is for use by the blind or severely handicapped;
(h) parts and accessories (other than a magnetic tape for use with apparatus described in paragraph (g) above) for goods comprised in paragraphs (a) to (g) above;
(i) the supply of a service of repair or maintenance of any goods comprised in paragraphs (a) to (h) above.

2. The supply to a charity of—
(a) wireless receiving sets; or
(b) apparatus solely for the making and reproduction of a sound recording on a magnetic tape permanently contained in a cassette,

being goods solely for gratuitous loan to the blind.

Note: The supply mentioned in items 1 and 2 includes the letting on hire of goods comprised in the items.

[953]

[GROUP 5—CONSTRUCTION OF BUILDINGS, ETC

Item No.

1. The first grant by a person—
(a) constructing a building—
(i) designed as a dwelling or number of dwellings; or
(ii) intended for use solely for a relevant residential or a relevant charitable purpose; or
(b) converting a non-residential building or a non-residential part of a building into a

building designed as a dwelling or number of dwellings or a building intended for use solely for a relevant residential purpose,

of a major interest in, or in any part of, the building, dwelling or its site.

2. The supply in the course of the construction of—

(a) a building designed as a dwelling or number of dwellings or intended for use solely for a relevant residential purpose or a relevant charitable purpose; or

(b) any civil engineering work necessary for the development of a permanent park for residential caravans,

of any services related to the construction other than the services of an architect, surveyor or any person acting as a consultant or in a supervisory capacity.

3. The supply to a [relevant housing association] in the course of conversion of a non-residential building or a non-residential part of a building into—

(a) a building or part of a building designed as a dwelling or number of dwellings; or

(b) a building or part of a building intended for use solely for a relevant residential purpose,

of any services related to the conversion other than the services of an architect, surveyor or any person acting as a consultant or in a supervisory capacity.

4. The supply of building materials to a person to whom the supplier is supplying services within item 2 or 3 of this Group which include the incorporation of the materials into the building (or its site) in question.

Notes:

(1) "Grant" includes an assignment or surrender.

(2) A building is designed as a dwelling or a number of dwellings where in relation to each dwelling the following conditions are satisfied—

(a) the dwelling consists of self-contained living accommodation;

(b) there is no provision for direct internal access from the dwelling to any other dwelling or part of a dwelling;

(c) the separate use, or disposal of the dwelling is not prohibited by the term of any covenant, statutory planning consent or similar provision; and

(d) statutory planning consent has been granted in respect of that dwelling and its construction or conversion has been carried out in accordance with that consent.

(3) The construction of, or conversion of a non-residential building to, a building designed as a dwelling or a number of dwellings includes the construction of, or conversion of a non-residential building to, a garage provided that—

(a) the dwelling and the garage are constructed or converted at the same time; and

(b) the garage is intended to be occupied with the dwelling or one of the dwellings.

(4) Use for a relevant residential purpose means use as—

(a) a home or other institution providing residential accommodation for children;

(b) a home or other institution providing residential accommodation with personal care for persons in need of personal care by reason of old age, disablement, past or present dependence on alcohol or drugs or past or present mental disorder;

(c) a hospice;

(d) residential accommodation for students or school pupils;

(e) residential accommodation for members of any of the armed forces;

(f) a monastery, nunnery or similar establishment; or

(g) an institution which is the sole or main residence of at least 90 per cent of its residents,

except use as a hospital, prison or similar institution or an hotel, inn or similar establishment.

(5) Where a number of buildings are—

(a) constructed at the same time and on the same site; and

(b) are intended to be used together as a unit solely for a relevant residential purpose;

then each of those buildings, to the extent that they would not be so regarded but for this Note, are to be treated as intended for use solely for a relevant residential purpose.

(6) Use for a relevant charitable purpose means use by a charity in either or both the following ways, namely—

(a) otherwise than in the course or furtherance of a business;

(b) as a village hall or similarly in providing social or recreational facilities for a local community.

[(7) For the purposes of item 1(b), and for the purposes of these Notes so far as having effect for the purposes of item 1(b), a building or part of a building is "non-residential" if—

(a) it is neither designed nor adapted for use—

(i) as a dwelling or number of dwellings, or

(ii) for a relevant residential purpose, or

(b) it is designed, or adapted, for such use but—

(i) it was constructed more than 10 years before the grant of the major interest; and

(ii) no part of it has, in the period of 10 years immediately preceding the grant, been used as a dwelling or for a relevant residential purpose.

(7A) For the purposes of item 3, and for the purposes of these Notes so far as having effect for the purposes of item 3, a building or part of a building is "non-residential" if—

(a) it is neither designed nor adapted for use—

(i) as a dwelling or number of dwellings, or

(ii) for a relevant residential purpose, or

(b) it is designed, or adapted, for such use but—

(i) it was constructed more than 10 years before the commencement of the works of conversion, and

(ii) no part of it has, in the period of 10 years immediately preceding the commencement of those works, been used as a dwelling or for a relevant residential purpose, and

(iii) no part of it is being so used.]

(8) References to a non-residential building or a non-residential part of a building do not include a reference to a garage occupied together with a dwelling.

(9) The conversion, other than to a building designed for a relevant residential purpose, of a non-residential part of a building which already contains a residential part is not included within items 1(b) or 3 unless the result of that conversion is to create an additional dwelling or dwellings.

(10) Where—

(a) part of a building that is constructed is designed as a dwelling or number of dwellings or is intended for use solely for a relevant residential purpose or relevant charitable purpose (and part is not); or

(b) part of a building that is converted is designed as a dwelling or number of dwellings or is used solely for a relevant residential purpose (and part is not)—

then in the case of—

(i) a grant or other supply relating only to the part so designed or intended for that use (or its site) shall be treated as relating to a building so designed or intended for such use;

(ii) a grant or other supply relating only to the part neither so designed nor intended for such use (or its site) shall not be so treated; and

(iii) any other grant or other supply relating to, or to any part of, the building (or its site), an apportionment shall be made to determine the extent to which it is to be so treated.

(11) Where, a service falling within the description in items 2 or 3 is supplied in part in relation to the construction or conversion of a building and in part for other purposes, an apportionment may be made to determine the extent to which the supply is to be treated as falling within items 2 or 3.

(12) Where all or part of a building is intended for use solely for a relevant residential purpose or a relevant charitable purpose—

(a) a supply relating to the building (or any part of it) shall not be taken for the purposes of items 2 and 4 as relating to a building intended for such use unless it is made to a person who intends to use the building (or part) for such a purpose; and

(b) a grant or other supply relating to the building (or any part of it) shall not be taken as relating to a building intended for such use unless before it is made the person to whom it is made has given to the person making it a certificate in such form as may be specified in a notice published by the Commissioners stating that the grant or other supply (or a specified part of it) so relates.

(13) The grant of an interest in, or in any part of—

(a) a building designed as a dwelling or number of dwellings; or

(b) the site of such a building,

is not within item 1 if—

(i) the interest granted is such that the grantee is not entitled to reside in the building or part, throughout the year; or
(ii) residence there throughout the year, or the use of the building or part as the grantee's principal private residence, is prevented by the terms of a covenant, statutory planning consent or similar permission.

(14) Where the major interest referred to in item 1 is a tenancy or lease—
(a) if a premium is payable, the grant falls within that item only to the extent that it is made for consideration in the form of the premium; and
(b) if a premium is not payable, the grant falls within that item only to the extent that it is made for consideration in the form of the first payment of rent due under the tenancy or lease.

(15) The reference in item 2(b) of this Group to the construction of a civil engineering work does not include a reference to the conversion, reconstruction, alteration or enlargement of a work.

(16) For the purpose of this Group, the construction of a building does not include—
(a) the conversion, reconstruction or alteration of an existing building; or
(b) any enlargement of, or extension to, an existing building except to the extent the enlargement or extension creates an additional dwelling or dwellings; or
(c) subject to Note (17) below, the construction of an annexe to an existing building.

(17) Note 16(c) above shall not apply [where the whole or a part of an annexe is intended for use solely for a relevant charitable purpose and]—
(a) [the annexe] is capable of functioning independently from the existing building; and
(b) the only access or where there is more than one means of access, the main access to:
(i) the annexe is not via the existing building; and
(ii) the existing building is not via the annexe.

(18) A building only ceases to be an existing building when:
(a) demolished completely to ground level; or
(b) the part remaining above ground level consists of no more than a single facade or where a corner site, a double facade, the retention of which is a condition or requirement of statutory planning consent or similar permission.

(19) A caravan is not a residential caravan if residence in it throughout the year is prevented by the terms of a covenant, statutory planning consent or similar permission.

(20) Item 2 and Item 3 do not include the supply of services described in paragraph 1(1) or 5(4) of Schedule 4.

[(21) In item 3 "relevant housing association" means—
(a) a registered social landlord within the meaning of Part I of the Housing Act 1996,
(b) a registered housing association within the meaning of the Housing Associations Act 1985 (Scottish registered housing associations), or
(c) a registered housing association within the meaning of Part II of the Housing (Northern Ireland) Order 1992 (Northern Irish registered housing associations).]

(22) "Building materials", in relation to any description of building, means goods of a description ordinarily incorporated by builders in a building of that description, (or its site), but does not include—
(a) finished or prefabricated furniture, other than furniture designed to be fitted in kitchens;
(b) materials for the construction of fitted furniture, other than kitchen furniture;
(c) electrical or gas appliances, unless the appliance is an appliance which is—
(i) designed to heat space or water (or both) or to provide ventilation, air cooling, air purification, or dust extraction; or
(ii) intended for use in a building designed as a number of dwellings and is a door-entry system, a waste disposal unit or a machine for compacting waste; or
(iii) a burglar alarm, a fire alarm, or fire safety equipment or designed solely for the purpose of enabling aid to be summoned in an emergency; or
(iv) a lift or hoist;
(d) carpets or carpeting material.

(23) For the purposes of Note (22) above the incorporation of goods in a building includes their installation as fittings.

(24) Section 30(3) does not apply to goods forming part of a description of supply in this Group.]

[954]

NOTES

Substituted by the Value Added Tax (Construction of Buildings) Order 1995, SI 1995/280, art 2.

Item No 1: words in square brackets substituted by the Value Added Tax (Registered Social Landlords) (No 1) Order 1997, SI 1997/50, art 2(a).

Notes (7), (7A): substituted for Note (7) as originally enacted by the Value Added Tax (Conversion of Buildings) Order 2001, SI 2001/2305, arts 2, 3, with effect in relation to supplies made on or after 1 August 2001.

Note (17): words in first pair of square brackets substituted and words in second pair of square brackets inserted by the Value Added Tax (Construction of Buildings) Order 2002, SI 2002/1101, art 2.

Note (21): substituted by SI 1997/50, art 2(b).

[GROUP 6—PROTECTED BUILDINGS

Item No.

1. The first grant by a person substantially reconstructing a protected building, of a major interest in, or in any part of, the building or its site.

2. The supply, in the course of an approved alteration of a protected building, of any services other than the services of an architect, surveyor or any person acting as consultant or in a supervisory capacity.

3. The supply of building materials to a person to whom the supplier is supplying services within item 2 of this Group which include the incorporation of the materials into the building (or its site) in question.

Notes:

(1) "Protected building" means a building which is designed to remain as or become a dwelling or number of dwellings (as defined in Note (2) below) or is intended for use solely for a relevant residential purpose or a relevant charitable purpose after the reconstruction or alteration and which, in either case, is—

(a) a listed building, within the meaning of—
  (i) the Planning (Listed Buildings and Conservation Areas) Act 1990; or
  (ii) [the Planning (Listed Buildings and Conservation Areas) (Scotland) Act 1997]; or
  (iii) the Planning (Northern Ireland) Order 1991; or
(b) a scheduled monument, within the meaning of—
  (i) the Ancient Monuments and Archaeological Areas Act 1979; or
  (ii) [the Historic Monuments and Archaeological Objects (Northern Ireland) Order 1995].

(2) A building is designed to remain as or become a dwelling or number of dwellings where in relation to each dwelling the following conditions are satisfied—

(a) the dwelling consists of self-contained living accommodation;
(b) there is no provision for direct internal access from the dwelling to any other dwelling or part of a dwelling;
(c) the separate use, or disposal of the dwelling is not prohibited by the terms of any covenant, statutory planning consent or similar provision,

and includes a garage (occupied together with a dwelling) either constructed at the same time as the building or where the building has been substantially reconstructed at the same time as that reconstruction.

(3) Notes (1), (4), (6), (12) to (14) and (22) to (24) of Group 5 apply in relation to this Group as they apply in relation to that Group but subject to any appropriate modifications.

(4) For the purposes of item 1, a protected building shall not be regarded as substantially reconstructed unless the reconstruction is such that at least one of the following conditions is fulfilled when the reconstruction is completed—

(a) that, of the works carried out to effect the reconstruction, at least three-fifths, measured by reference to cost, are of such a nature that the supply of services (other than excluded services), materials and other items to carry out the works, would, if supplied by a taxable person, be within either item 2 or item 3 of this Group; and
(b) that the reconstructed building incorporates no more of the original building (that

is to say, the building as it was before the reconstruction began) than the external walls, together with other external features of architectural or historic interest;

and in paragraph (a) above "excluded services" means the services of an architect, surveyor or other person acting as consultant or in a supervisory capacity.

(5) Where part of a protected building that is substantially reconstructed is designed to remain as or become a dwelling or a number of dwellings or is intended for use solely for a relevant residential or relevant charitable purpose (and part is not)—

(a) a grant or other supply relating only to the part so designed or intended for such use (or its site) shall be treated as relating to a building so designed or intended for such use;

(b) a grant or other supply relating only to the part neither so designed nor intended for such use (or its site) shall not be so treated; and

(c) in the case of any other grant or other supply relating to, or to any part of, the building (or its site), an apportionment shall be made to determine the extent to which it is to be so treated.

(6) "Approved alteration" means—

(a) in the case of a protected building which is an ecclesiastical building to which section 60 of the Planning (Listed Buildings and Conservation Areas) Act 1990 applies, any works of alteration; and

(b) …

(c) in any other case, works of alteration which may not, or but for the existence of a Crown interest or Duchy interest could not, be carried out unless authorised under, or under any provision of—

(i) Part I of the Planning (Listed Buildings and Conservation Areas) Act 1990,

(ii) [Part I of the Planning (Listed Buildings and Conservation Areas) (Scotland) Act 1997],

(iii) Part V of the Planning (Northern Ireland) Order 1991,

(iv) Part I of the Ancient Monuments and Archaeological Areas Act 1979, [or

(v) Part II of the Historic Monuments and Archaeological Objects (Northern Ireland) Order 1995,]

and for which, except in the case of a Crown interest or Duchy interest, consent has been obtained under any provision of that Part,

but does not include any works of repair or maintenance, or any incidental alteration to the fabric of a building which results from the carrying out of repairs, or maintenance work.

(7) For the purposes of paragraph (a) of Note (6), a building used or available for use by a minister of religion wholly or mainly as a residence from which to perform the duties of his office shall be treated as not being an ecclesiastical building.

(8) For the purposes of paragraph (c) of Note (6) "Crown interest" and "Duchy interest" have the same meaning as in section 50 of the Ancient Monuments and Archaeological Areas Act 1979.

(9) Where a service is supplied in part in relation to an approved alteration of a building, and in part for other purposes, an apportionment may be made to determine the extent to which the supply is to be treated as falling within item 2.

(10) For the purposes of item 2 the construction of a building separate from, but in the curtilage of, a protected building does not constitute an alteration of the protected building.

(11) Item 2 does not include the supply of services described in paragraph 1(1) or 5(4) of Schedule 4.]

[955]

NOTES

Substituted by the Value Added Tax (Protected Buildings) Order 1995, SI 1995/283, art 2.

Note (1): words in first pair of square brackets substituted by the Planning (Consequential Provisions) (Scotland) Act 1997, s 4, Sch 2, para 57(a); words in second pair of square brackets substituted by the Historic Monuments and Archaeological Objects (Northern Ireland) Order 1995, SI 1995/1625, art 45(1), Sch 3, para 4(1).

Note (6): para (b) repealed and words in second pair of square brackets inserted by SI 1995/1625, art 45, Sch 3, para 4, Sch 4; words in first pair of square brackets substituted by the Planning (Consequential Provisions) (Scotland) Act 1997, s 4, Sch 2, para 57(b).

(Sch 8, Pt II, Groups 7–11 outside the scope of this work.)

GROUP 12—DRUGS, MEDICINES, AIDS FOR THE HANDICAPPED

Item No.

1. The [supply of any qualifying goods dispensed to an individual for his personal use where the dispensing is] by a person registered in *the register of pharmaceutical chemists kept under the Pharmacy Act 1954 or* the Pharmacy (Northern Ireland) Order 1976, on the prescription of a person registered in the register of medical practitioners, *the register of medical practitioners with limited registration* or the dentists' register.

[1A. The supply of any [qualifying] goods in accordance with a requirement or authorisation under—

(a) regulation 20 of the National Health Service (Pharmaceutical Services) Regulations 1992;

(b) regulation 34 of the National Health Service (General Medical Services) (Scotland) Regulations 1995; or

(c) [regulation 12 of the Pharmaceutical Services Regulations (Northern Ireland) 1997],

by a person registered in the register of medical practitioners *or the register of medical practitioners with limited registration.*]

2. The supply to a handicapped person for domestic or his personal use, or to a charity for making available to handicapped persons by sale or otherwise, for domestic or their personal use, of—

(a) medical or surgical appliances designed solely for the relief of a severe abnormality or severe injury;

(b) electrically or mechanically adjustable beds designed for invalids;

(c) commode chairs, commode stools, devices incorporating a bidet jet and warm air drier and frames or other devices for sitting over or rising from a sanitary appliance;

(d) chair lifts or stair lifts designed for use in connection with invalid wheelchairs;

(e) hoists and lifters designed for use by invalids;

(f) motor vehicles designed or substantially and permanently adapted for the carriage of a person in a wheelchair or on a stretcher and of no more than [11] other persons;

(g) equipment and appliances not included in paragraphs (a) to (f) above designed solely for use by a handicapped person;

(h) parts and accessories designed solely for use in or with goods described in paragraphs (a) to (g) above;

(i) boats designed or substantially and permanently adapted for use by handicapped persons.

[2A. The supply of a qualifying motor vehicle—

(a) to a handicapped person—

(i) who usually uses a wheelchair, or

(ii) who is usually carried on a stretcher, for domestic or his personal use; or

(b) to a charity for making available to such a handicapped person by sale or otherwise, for domestic or his personal use.]

3. The supply to a handicapped person of services of adapting goods to suit his condition.

4. The supply to a charity of services of adapting goods to suit the condition of a handicapped person to whom the goods are to be made available, by sale or otherwise, by the charity.

5. The supply to a handicapped person or to a charity of a service of repair or maintenance of any goods specified in item 2, [2A,] 6, 18 or 19 and supplied as described in that item.

6. The supply of goods in connection with a supply described in item 3, 4 or 5.

7. The supply to a handicapped person or to a charity of services necessarily performed in the installation of equipment or appliances (including parts and accessories therefor) specified in item 2 and supplied as described in that item.

8. The supply to a handicapped person of a service of constructing ramps or widening doorways or passages for the purpose of facilitating his entry to or movement within his private residence.

9. The supply to a charity of a service described in item 8 for the purpose of facilitating a handicapped person's entry to or movement within any building.

10. The supply to a handicapped person of a service of providing, extending or adapting a bathroom, washroom or lavatory in his private residence where such provision, extension or adaptation is necessary by reason of his condition.

[11. The supply to a charity of a service of providing, extending or adapting a bathroom, washroom or lavatory for use by handicapped persons—

(a) in residential accommodation, or

(b) in a day-centre where at least 20 per cent of the individuals using the centre are handicapped persons,

where such provision, extension or adaptation is necessary by reason of the condition of the handicapped persons.]

12. The supply to a charity of a service of providing, extending or adapting a washroom or lavatory for use by handicapped persons in a building, or any part of a building, used principally by a charity for charitable purposes where such provision, extension or adaptation is necessary to facilitate the use of the washroom or lavatory by handicapped persons.

13. The supply of goods in connection with a supply described in items 8, 9, 10 or 11.

14. The letting on hire of a motor vehicle for a period of not less than 3 years to a handicapped person in receipt of a disability living allowance by virtue of entitlement to the mobility component or of mobility supplement where the lessor's business consists predominantly of the provision of motor vehicles to such persons.

15. The sale of a motor vehicle which had been let on hire in the circumstances described in item 14, where such sale constitutes the first supply of the vehicle after the end of the period of such letting.

16. The supply to a handicapped person of services necessarily performed in the installation of a lift for the purpose of facilitating his movement between floors within his private residence.

17. The supply to a charity providing a permanent or temporary residence or day-centre for handicapped persons of services necessarily performed in the installation of a lift for the purpose of facilitating the movement of handicapped persons between floors within that building.

18. The supply of goods in connection with a supply described in item 16 or 17.

19. The supply to a handicapped person for domestic or his personal use, or to a charity for making available to handicapped persons by sale or otherwise for domestic or their personal use, of an alarm system designed to be capable of operation by a handicapped person, and to enable him to alert directly a specified person or a control centre.

20. The supply of services necessarily performed by a control centre in receiving and responding to calls from an alarm system specified in item 19.

Notes:

(1) Section 30(3) does not apply to goods forming part of a description of supply in item 1 [or item 1A], nor to other goods forming part of a description of supply in this Group, except where those other goods are acquired from another member State or imported from a place outside the member States by a handicapped person for domestic or his personal use, or by a charity for making available to handicapped persons, by sale or otherwise, for domestic or their personal use.

(2) For the purposes of item 1 a person who is not registered in the visiting EEC practitioners list in the register of medical practitioners at the time he performs services in an urgent case as mentioned in subsection (3) of section 18 of the Medical Act 1983 is to be treated as being registered in that list where he is entitled to be registered in accordance with that section.

[(2A) In items 1 and 1A, "qualifying goods" means any goods designed or adapted for use in connection with any medical or surgical treatment except—

(a) hearing aids;

(b) dentures; and

(c) spectacles and contact lenses.]

(3) "Handicapped" means chronically sick or disabled.

(4) Item 2 shall not include hearing aids (except hearing aids designed for the auditory training of deaf children), dentures, spectacles and contact lenses but shall be deemed to include—

(a) clothing, footwear and wigs;
(b) invalid wheelchairs, and invalid carriages … ; and
(c) renal haemodialysis units, oxygen concentrators, artificial respirators and other similar apparatus.

(5) The supplies described in items 1[, 1A][, 2 and 2A] include supplies of services of letting on hire of the goods respectively comprised in those items.

[(5A) In item 1 the reference to personal use does not include any use which is, or involves, a use by or in relation to an individual while that individual, for the purposes of being provided (whether or not by the person making the supply) with medical or surgical treatment, or with any form of care—

(a) is an in-patient or resident in a relevant institution which is a hospital or nursing home; or
(b) is attending at the premises of a relevant institution which is a hospital or nursing home.

(5B) Subject to Notes (5C) and (5D), in item 2 the reference to domestic or personal use does not include any use which is, or involves, a use by or in relation to a handicapped person while that person, for the purposes of being provided (whether or not by the person making the supply) with medical or surgical treatment, or with any form of care—

(a) is an in-patient or resident in a relevant institution; or
(b) is attending at the premises of a relevant institution.

(5C) Note (5B) does not apply for the purpose of determining whether any of the following supplies falls within item 2, that is to say—

(a) a supply to a charity;
(b) a supply by a person mentioned in any of paragraphs (a) to (g) of Note (5H) of an invalid wheelchair or invalid carriage;
(c) a supply by a person so mentioned of any parts or accessories designed solely for use in or with an invalid wheelchair or invalid carriage.

(5D) Note (5B) applies for the purpose of determining whether a supply of goods by a person not mentioned in any of paragraphs (a) to (g) of Note (5H) falls within item 2 only if those goods are—

(a) goods falling within paragraph (a) of that item;
(b) incontinence products and wound dressings; or
(c) parts and accessories designed solely for use in or with goods falling within paragraph (a) of this Note.

(5E) Subject to Note (5F), item 2 does not include—

(a) a supply made in accordance with any agreement, arrangement or understanding (whether or not legally enforceable) to which any of the persons mentioned in paragraphs (a) to (g) of Note (5H) is or has been a party otherwise than as the supplier; or
(b) any supply the whole or any part of the consideration for which is provided (whether directly or indirectly) by a person so mentioned.

(5F) A supply to a handicapped person of an invalid wheelchair or invalid carriage is excluded from item 2 by Note (5E) only if—

(a) that Note applies in relation to that supply by reference to a person falling within paragraph (g) of Note (5H); or
(b) the whole of the consideration for the supply is provided (whether directly or indirectly) by a person falling within any of paragraphs (a) to (f) of Note (5H).

(5G) In Notes (4), (5C) and (5F), the references to an invalid wheelchair and to an invalid carriage do not include references to any mechanically propelled vehicle which is intended or adapted for use on roads.

(5H) The persons referred to in Notes (5C) to (5F) are—

[(a) a Strategic Health Authority or Special Health Authority in England;
(aa) a Health Authority, Special Health Authority or Local Health Board in Wales;]
(b) a Health Board or Special Health Board in Scotland;
(c) a Health and Social Services Board in Northern Ireland;
(d) the Common Services Agency for the Scottish Health Service, the Northern Ireland Central Services Agency for Health and Social Services and the Isle of Man Health Services Board;

(e) a National Health Service trust established under [the National Health Service Act 2006 or the National Health Service (Wales) Act 2006] or the National Health Service (Scotland) Act 1978;

[(eaa) an NHS foundation trust;]

[(ea) a Primary Care Trust established under [section 18 of the National Health Service Act 2006];]

(f) a Health and Social Services trust established under Article 10 of the Health and Personal Social Services (Northern Ireland) Order 1991; or

(g) any person not falling within any of paragraphs (a) to (f) above who is engaged in the carrying on of any activity in respect of which a relevant institution is required to be approved, licensed or registered or as the case may be, would be so required if not exempt.

(5I) In Notes (5A), (5B) and (5H), "relevant institution" means any institution (whether a hospital, nursing home or other institution) which provides care or medical or surgical treatment and is either—

(a) approved, licensed or registered in accordance with the provisions of any enactment or Northern Ireland legislation; or

(b) exempted by or under the provisions of any enactment or Northern Ireland legislation from any requirement to be approved, licensed or registered,

and in this Note the references to the provisions of any enactment or Northern Ireland legislation include references only to provisions which, so far as relating to England, Wales, Scotland or Northern Ireland, have the same effect in every locality within that part of the United Kingdom.]

[(5J) For the purposes of item 11 "residential accommodation" means—

(a) a residential home, or

(b) self-contained living accommodation,

provided as a residence (whether on a permanent or temporary basis or both) for handicapped persons, but does not include an inn, hotel, boarding house or similar establishment or accommodation in any such type of establishment.

(5K) In this Group "washroom" means a room that contains a lavatory or washbasin (or both) but does not contain a bath or a shower or cooking, sleeping or laundry facilities.]

[(5L) A "qualifying motor vehicle" for the purposes of item 2A is a motor vehicle (other than a motor vehicle capable of carrying more than 12 persons including the driver)—

(a) that is designed or substantially and permanently adapted to enable a handicapped person—

(i) who usually uses a wheelchair, or

(ii) who is usually carried on a stretcher,

to enter, and drive or be otherwise carried in, the motor vehicle; or

(b) that by reason of its design, or being substantially and permanently adapted, includes features whose design is such that their sole purpose is to allow a wheelchair used by a handicapped person to be carried in or on the motor vehicle.]

(6) Item 14 applies only—

(a) where the vehicle is unused at the commencement of the period of letting; and

(b) where the consideration for the letting consists wholly or partly of sums paid to the lessor by [the Department for Work and Pensions] or the Ministry of Defence on behalf of the lessee in respect of the mobility component of the disability living allowance or mobility supplement to which he is entitled.

(7) In item 14—

(a) "disability living allowance" is a disability living allowance within the meaning of section 71 of the Social Security Contributions and Benefits Act 1992, or section 71 of the Social Security Contributions and Benefits (Northern Ireland) Act 1992; and

(b) "mobility supplement" is a mobility supplement within the meaning of Article 26A of the Naval, Military and Air Forces etc (Disablement and Death) Service Pensions Order 1983, Article 25A of the Personal Injuries (Civilians) Scheme 1983, Article 3 of the Motor Vehicles (Exemption from Vehicles Excise Duty) Order 1985 or Article 3 of the Motor Vehicles (Exemption from Vehicles Excise Duty) (Northern Ireland) Order 1985.

(8) Where in item 3 or 4 the goods are adapted in accordance with that item prior to their supply to the handicapped person or the charity, an apportionment shall be made to determine the supply of services which falls within item 3 or 4.

(9) In item 19 or 20, a specified person or control centre is a person or centre who or which—

(a) is appointed to receive directly calls activated by an alarm system described in that item, and

(b) retains information about the handicapped person to assist him in the event of illness, injury or similar emergency.

[956]

NOTES

Item 1: words in square brackets substituted by the Value Added Tax (Drugs, Medicines and Aids for the Handicapped) Order 1997, SI 1997/2744, art 3; first words in italics substituted for words "the Register of Pharmacists maintained under the Pharmacists and Pharmacy Technicians Order 2007 or in the register of pharmaceutical chemists kept under" by the Pharmacists and Pharmacy Technicians Order 2007, SI 2007/289, art 67, Sch 1, para 5(1), (2), as from a day to be notified in the London, Edinburgh and Belfast Gazettes; second words in italics repealed by the Medical Act 1983 (Amendment) and Miscellaneous Amendments Order 2006, SI 2006/1914, art 75(1)(a), as from a day to be notified in the London, Edinburgh and Belfast Gazettes.

Item 1A: inserted by the Value Added Tax (Supply of Pharmaceutical Goods) Order 1995, SI 1995/652, arts 2, 3; words in first pair of square brackets inserted and words in second pair of square brackets substituted by SI 1997/2744, art 4; words in italics repealed by SI 2006/1914, art 75(1)(b), as from a day to be notified in the London, Edinburgh and Belfast Gazettes.

Item 2: in para (f) number in square brackets substituted, in relation to supplies made on or after 1 April 2000, by the Value Added Tax (Vehicles Designed or Adapted for Handicapped Persons) Order 2001, SI 2001/754, art 2.

Item 2A: inserted, in relation to supplies made on or after 1 April 2000, by SI 2001/754, art 3.

Item 5: number in square brackets inserted, in relation to supplies made on or after 1 April 2000, by SI 2001/754, art 4.

Item 11: substituted, in relation to supplies made on or after 1 April 2000, by the Value Added Tax (Charities and Aids for the Handicapped) Order 2000, SI 2000/805, arts 2, 3.

Note (1): words in square brackets inserted by SI 1995/652, arts 2, 4.

Notes (2A), (5A)–(5I): inserted by SI 1997/2744, arts 5, 7.

Note (4): words omitted repealed by SI 1997/2744, art 6.

Note (5): reference in first pair of square brackets inserted by SI 1995/652, arts 2, 5; reference in second pair of square brackets substituted, in relation to supplies made on or after 1 April 2000, by SI 2001/754, art 5.

Note (5H): paras (a), (aa) substituted, for para (a), by the Value Added Tax (Drugs, Medicines, Aids for the Handicapped and Charities Etc) Order 2002, SI 2002/2813, arts 2, 3; words in square brackets in para (e) substituted for the words "Part I of the National Health Service and Community Care Act 1990" by the National Health Service (Consequential Provisions) Act 2006, s 2, Sch 1, paras 173, 174(a), as from 1 March 2007; para (eaa) inserted by the Health and Social Care (Community Health and Standards) Act 2003, s 34, Sch 4, paras 97, 98; para (ea) inserted, in relation to supplies made on or after 1 April 2000, by the Value Added Tax (Drugs, Medicines, Aids for the Handicapped and Charities Etc) Order 2000, SI 2000/503, arts 2, 3, words in square brackets substituted for the words "section 16A of the National Health Service Act 1977" by the National Health Service (Consequential Provisions) Act 2006, s 2, Sch 1, paras 173, 174(b), as from 1 March 2007.

Notes (5J), (5K): inserted, in relation to supplies made on or after 1 April 2000, by SI 2000/805, arts 2, 4.

Note (5L): added by SI 2001/754, art 6, in relation to supplies, acquisitions or importations made on or after 1 April 2001.

Note (6): in para (b) words in square brackets substituted by the Secretaries of State for Education and Skills and for Work and Pensions Order 2002, SI 2002/1397, art 12, Schedule, Pt I, para 11.

(Sch 8, Pt II, Group 13 outside the scope of this work; Sch 8, Pt II, Group 14 repealed, in relation to supplies made on or after 1 July 1999 by the Value Added Tax (Abolition of Zero-Rating for Tax-Free Shops) Order 1999, SI 1999/1642, art 2(b).)

GROUP 15—CHARITIES ETC

Item No.

[1. The sale, or letting on hire, by a charity of any goods donated to it for—

(a) sale,
(b) letting,
(c) sale or letting,
(d) sale or export,
(e) letting or export, or
(f) sale, letting or export.

1A. The sale, or letting on hire, by a taxable person of any goods donated to him for—

(a) sale,
(b) letting,

(c) sale or letting,
(d) sale or export,
(e) letting or export, or
(f) sale, letting or export,

if he is a profits-to-charity person in respect of the goods.

2. The donation of any goods for any one or more of the following purposes—
(a) sale by a charity or a taxable person who is a profits-to-charity person in respect of the goods;
(b) export by a charity or such a taxable person;
(c) letting by a charity or such a taxable person.]

3. The export of any goods by a charity to a place outside the member States.

4. The supply of any relevant goods for donation to a nominated eligible body where the goods are purchased with funds provided by a charity or from voluntary contributions.

5. The supply of any relevant goods to an eligible body which pays for them with funds provided by a charity or from voluntary contributions or to an eligible body which is a charitable institution providing care or medical or surgical treatment for handicapped persons.

6. Repair and maintenance of relevant goods owned by an eligible body.

7. The supply of goods in connection with the supply described in item 6.

[8. The supply to a charity of a right to promulgate an advertisement by means of a medium of communication with the public.

8A. A supply to a charity that consists in the promulgation of an advertisement by means of such a medium.

8B. The supply to a charity of services of design or production of an advertisement that is, or was intended to be, promulgated by means of such a medium.

8C. The supply to a charity of goods closely related to a supply within item 8B.]

9. The supply to a charity, providing care or medical or surgical treatment for human beings or animals, or engaging in medical or veterinary research, of a medicinal product [or veterinary medicinal product] where the supply is solely for use by the charity in such care, treatment or research.

10. The supply to a charity of a substance directly used for synthesis or testing in the course of medical or veterinary research.

Notes:

[(1) Item 1 or 1A does not apply unless the sale or letting—
(a) takes place as a result of the goods having been made available—
(i) to two or more specified persons, or
(ii) to the general public, for purchase or hire (whether so made available in a shop or elsewhere) and
(b) does not take place as a result of any arrangements (whether legally binding or not) relating to the goods and entered into, before the goods were made so available, by—
(i) each of the parties to the sale or letting, or
(ii) the donor of the goods and either or both of those parties.

(1A) For the purposes of items 1, 1A and 2, goods are donated for letting only if they are donated for—
(a) letting, and
(b) re-letting after the end of any first or subsequent letting, and
(c) all or any of—
(i) sale,
(ii) export, or
(iii) disposal as waste,

if not, or when no longer, used for letting.

(1B) Items 1 and 1A do not include (and shall be treated as having not included) any sale, or letting on hire, of particular donated goods if the goods, at any time after they are donated but before they are sold, exported or disposed of as waste, are whilst unlet used for any purpose other than, or in addition to, that of being available for purchase, hire or export.

(1C) In Note (1) "specified person" means a person who—

(a) is handicapped, or
(b) is entitled to any one or more of the specified benefits, or
(c) is both handicapped and so entitled.

(1D) For the purposes of Note (1C) the specified benefits are—
(a) income support under Part VII of the Social Security Contributions and Benefits Act 1992 or Part VII of the Social Security Contributions and Benefits (Northern Ireland) Act 1992;
(b) housing benefit under Part VII of the Social Security Contributions and Benefits Act 1992 or Part VII of the Social Security Contributions and Benefits (Northern Ireland) Act 1992;
(c) council tax benefit under Part VII of the Social Security Contributions and Benefits Act 1992;
(d) an income-based jobseeker's allowance within the meaning of section 1(4) of the Jobseekers Act 1995 or article 3(4) of the Jobseekers (Northern Ireland) Order 1995;
[(e) any element of child tax credit other than the family element; and
(f) working tax credit].

(1E) For the purposes of items 1A and 2 a taxable person is a "profits-to-charity" person in respect of any goods if—
(a) he has agreed in writing (whether or not contained in a deed) to transfer to a charity his profits from supplies and lettings of the goods, or
(b) his profits from supplies and lettings of the goods are otherwise payable to a charity.

(1F) In items 1, 1A and 2, and any Notes relating to any of those items, "goods" means goods (and, in particular, does not include anything that is not goods even though provision made by or under an enactment provides for a supply of that thing to be, or be treated as, a supply of goods).]

(2) "Animals" includes any species of the animal kingdom.

(3) "Relevant goods" means—
(a) medical, scientific, computer, video, sterilising, laboratory or refrigeration equipment for use in medical or veterinary research, training, diagnosis or treatment;
(b) ambulances;
(c) parts or accessories for use in or with goods described in paragraph (a) or (b) above;
(d) goods of a kind described in item 2 of Group 12 of this Schedule;
(e) motor vehicles (other than vehicles with more than 50 seats) designed or substantially and permanently adapted for the safe carriage of a handicapped person in a wheelchair provided that—
(i) in the case of vehicles with more than 16 but fewer than 27 seats, the number of persons for which such provision shall exist shall be at least 2;
(ii) in the case of vehicles with more than 26 but fewer than 37 seats, the number of persons for which such provision shall exist shall be at least 3;
(iii) in the case of vehicles with more than 36 but fewer than 47 seats, the number of persons for which such provision shall exist shall be at least 4;
(iv) in the case of vehicles with more than 46 seats, the number of persons for which such provision shall exist shall be at least 5;
(v) there is either a fitted electrically or hydraulically operated lift or, in the case of vehicles with fewer than 17 seats, a fitted ramp to provide access for a passenger in a wheelchair;
(f) motor vehicles (with more than 6 but fewer than 51 seats) for use by an eligible body providing care for blind, deaf, mentally handicapped or terminally sick persons mainly to transport such persons;
(g) telecommunication, aural, visual, light enhancing or heat detecting equipment (not being equipment ordinarily supplied for private or recreational use) solely for use for the purpose of rescue or first aid services undertaken by a charitable institution providing such services.

(4) "Eligible body" means—
[(a) a Strategic Health Authority or Special Health Authority in England;
(aa) a Health Authority, Special Health Authority or Local Health Board in Wales;]
(b) a Health Board in Scotland;
(c) a Health and Social Services Board in Northern Ireland;
(d) a hospital whose activities are not carried on for profit;

(e) a research institution whose activities are not carried on for profit;
(f) a charitable institution providing care or medical or surgical treatment for handicapped persons;
(g) the Common Services Agency for the Scottish Health Service, the Northern Ireland Central Services Agency for Health and Social Services or the Isle of Man Health Services Board;
(h) a charitable institution providing rescue or first aid services;
(i) a National Health Service trust established under Part I of the National Health Service and Community Care Act 1990 or the National Health Service (Scotland) Act 1978;
[(j) a Primary Care Trust established under section 16A of the National Health Service Act 1977].

[(4A) Subject to Note (5B), a charitable institution shall not be regarded as providing care or medical or surgical treatment for handicapped persons unless—
(a) it provides care or medical or surgical treatment in a relevant establishment; and
(b) the majority of the persons who receive care or medical or surgical treatment in that establishment are handicapped persons.

(4B) "Relevant establishment" means—
(a) a day-centre, other than a day-centre which exists primarily as a place for activities that are social or recreational or both; or
(b) an institution which is—
(i) approved, licensed or registered in accordance with the provisions of any enactment or Northern Ireland legislation; or
(ii) exempted by or under the provisions of any enactment or Northern Ireland legislation from any requirement to be approved, licensed or registered;

and in paragraph (b) above the references to the provisions of any enactment or Northern Ireland legislation are references only to provisions which, so far as relating to England, Wales, Scotland or Northern Ireland, have the same effect in every locality within that part of the United Kingdom.]

(5) "Handicapped" means chronically sick or disabled.

[(5A) Subject to Note (5B), items 4 to 7 do not apply where the eligible body falls within Note (4)(f) unless the relevant goods are or are to be used in a relevant establishment in which that body provides care or medical or surgical treatment to persons the majority of whom are handicapped.

(5B) Nothing in Note (4A) or (5A) shall prevent a supply from falling within items 4 to 7 where—
(a) the eligible body provides medical care to handicapped persons in their own homes;
(b) the relevant goods fall within Note (3)(a) or are parts or accessories for use in or with goods described in Note (3)(a); and
(c) those goods are or are to be used in or in connection with the provision of that care.]

(6) Item 4 does not apply where the donee of the goods is not a charity and has contributed in whole or in part to the funds for the purchase of the goods.

(7) Item 5 does not apply where the body to whom the goods are supplied is not a charity and has contributed in whole or in part to the funds for the purchase of the goods.

(8) Items 6 and 7 do not apply unless—
(a) the supply is paid for with funds which have been provided by a charity or from voluntary contributions, and
(b) in a case where the owner of the goods repaired or maintained is not a charity, it has not contributed in whole or in part to those funds.

(9) Items 4 and 5 include the letting on hire of relevant goods; accordingly in items 4, 5 and 6 and the notes relating thereto, references to the purchase or ownership of goods shall be deemed to include references respectively to their hiring and possession.

(10) Item 5 includes computer services by way of the provision of computer software solely for use in medical research, diagnosis or treatment.

[(10A) Neither of items 8 and 8A includes a supply where any of the members of the public (whether individuals or other persons) who are reached through the medium are selected by or on behalf of the charity.

For this purpose "selected" includes selected by address (whether postal address or telephone number, e-mail address or other address for electronic communications purposes) or at random.

(10B) None of items 8 to 8C includes a supply used to create, or contribute to, a website that is the charity's own.

For this purpose a website is a charity's own even though hosted by another person.

(10C) Neither of items 8B and 8C includes a supply to a charity that is used directly by the charity to design or produce an advertisement.]

(11) In item 9—

(a) a "medicinal product" means any substance or article (not being an instrument, apparatus or appliance) which is for use wholly or mainly in either or both of the following ways—

(i) by being administered to one or more human beings ... for a medicinal purpose;

(ii) as an ingredient in the preparation of a substance or article which is to be administered to one or more human beings ... for a medicinal purpose;

(b) a "medicinal purpose" has the meaning assigned to it by section 130(2) of the Medicines Act 1968;

(c) "administer" has the meaning assigned to it by section 130(9) of the Medicines Act 1968;

[(d) "veterinary medicinal product" has the meaning assigned to it by regulation 2 of the Veterinary Medicines Regulations 2006.]

(12) In items 9 and 10 "substance" and "ingredient" have the meanings assigned to them by section 132 of the Medicines Act 1968.

[957]

NOTES

Items 1, 1A, 2: substituted for original item 1, in relation to supplies made on or after 1 April 2000, by the Value Added Tax (Charities and Aids for the Handicapped) Order 2000, SI 2000/805, arts 5, 6.

Items 8–8C: substituted for original item 8, in relation to supplies made on or after 1 April 2000, by SI 2000/805, arts 5, 7.

Item 9: words in square brackets inserted by the Veterinary Medicines Regulations 2006, SI 2006/2407, reg 44(3), Sch 9, Pt 1, para 10(a).

Notes (1)–(1C), (1E), (1F): substituted, together with Note (1D), for original note (1), in relation to supplies made on or after 1 April 2000, by SI 2000/805, arts 5, 8.

Note (1D): substituted, together with Notes (1)–(1C), (1E), (1F), for original note (1), in relation to supplies made on or after 1 April 2000, by SI 2000/805, arts 5, 8; paras (e), (f) substituted by the Tax Credits Act 2002, s 47, Sch 3, paras 47, 49.

Note (4): paras (a), (aa) substituted, for para (a) as originally enacted, by the Value Added Tax (Drugs, Medicines, Aids for the Handicapped and Charities Etc) Order 2002, SI 2002/2813, arts 2, 4; para (j) added, in relation to supplies made on or after 1 April 2000, by the Value Added Tax (Drugs, Medicines, Aids for the Handicapped and Charities Etc) Order 2000, SI 2000/503, arts 2, 4.

Notes (4A), (4B), (5A), (5B): inserted, in relation to supplies made on or after 26 November 1996, by the Finance Act 1997, s 34.

Notes (10A)–(10C): inserted, in relation to supplies made on or after 1 April 2000, by SI 2000/805, arts 5, 9.

Note (11): words omitted repealed and para (d) added by SI 2006/2407, reg 44(3), Sch 9, Pt 1, para 10(b).

(*Sch 8, Pt II, Group 16 outside the scope of this work.*)

SCHEDULE 9
EXEMPTIONS

Sections 8, 31

(*Sch 9, Pt I outside the scope of this work.*)

PART II
THE GROUPS

GROUP 1—LAND

Item No

1. The grant of any interest in or right over land or of any licence to occupy land, or, in relation to land in Scotland, any personal right to call for or be granted any such interest or right, other than—

(a) the grant of the fee simple in—

(i) a building which has not been completed and which is neither designed as a dwelling or number of dwellings nor intended for use solely for a relevant residential purpose or a relevant charitable purpose;

(ii) a new building which is neither designed as a dwelling or number of dwellings nor intended for use solely for a relevant residential purpose or a relevant charitable purpose after the grant;

(iii) a civil engineering work which has not been completed;

(iv) a new civil engineering work;

(b) a supply made pursuant to a developmental tenancy, developmental lease or developmental licence;

(c) the grant of any interest, right or licence consisting of a right to take game or fish unless at the time of the grant the grantor grants to the grantee the fee simple of the land over which the right to take game or fish is exercisable;

(d) the provision in an hotel, inn, boarding house or similar establishment of sleeping accommodation or of accommodation in rooms which are provided in conjunction with sleeping accommodation or for the purpose of a supply of catering;

(e) the grant of any interest in, right over or licence to occupy holiday accommodation;

(f) the provision of seasonal pitches for caravans, and the grant of facilities at caravan parks to persons for whom such pitches are provided;

(g) the provision of pitches for tents or of camping facilities;

(h) the grant of facilities for parking a vehicle;

(j) the grant of any right to fell and remove standing timber;

(k) the grant of facilities for housing, or storage of, an aircraft or for mooring, or storage of, a ship, boat or other vessel;

(l) the grant of any right to occupy a box, seat or other accommodation at a sports ground, theatre, concert hall or other place of entertainment;

(m) the grant of facilities for playing any sport or participating in any physical recreation; and

(n) the grant of any right, including—

(i) an equitable right,

(ii) a right under an option or right of pre-emption, or

(iii) in relation to land in Scotland, a personal right,

to call for or be granted an interest or right which would fall within any of paragraphs (a) or (c) to (m) above.

Notes:

[(1) "Grant" includes an assignment or surrender and the supply made by the person to whom an interest is surrendered when there is a reverse surrender.]

[(1A) A "reverse surrender" is one in which the person to whom the interest is surrendered is paid by the person by whom the interest is being surrendered to accept the surrender.]

(2) A building shall be taken to be completed when an architect issues a certificate of practical completion in relation to it or it is first fully occupied, whichever happens first; and a civil engineering work shall be taken to be completed when an engineer issues a certificate of completion in relation to it or it is first fully used, whichever happens first.

(3) [Notes (2) to (10) and (12)] to Group 5 of Schedule 8 apply in relation to this Group as they apply in relation to that Group.

(4) A building or civil engineering work is new if it was completed less than three years before the grant.

(5) Subject to Note (6), the grant of the fee simple in a building or work completed before 1st April 1989 is not excluded from this Group by paragraph (a)(ii) or (iv).

(6) Note (5) does not apply where the grant is the first grant of the fee simple made on or after 1st April 1989 and the building was not fully occupied, or the work not fully used, before that date.

(7) A tenancy of, lease of or licence to occupy a building or work is treated as becoming a developmental tenancy, developmental lease or developmental licence (as the case may be) when a tenancy of, lease of or licence to occupy a building or work, whose construction, reconstruction, enlargement or extension commenced on or after 1st January 1992, is treated as being supplied to and by the developer under paragraph 6(1) of Schedule 10 [(except where that paragraph applies by virtue of paragraph 5(1)(b) of that Schedule)].

(8) Where a grant of an interest in, right over or licence to occupy land includes a valuable right to take game or fish, an apportionment shall be made to determine the supply falling outside this Group by virtue of paragraph (c).

(9) "Similar establishment" includes premises in which there is provided furnished sleeping accommodation, whether with or without the provision of board or facilities for the preparation of food, which are used by or held out as being suitable for use by visitors or travellers.

(10) "Houseboat" includes a houseboat within the meaning of Group 9 of Schedule 8.

(11) Paragraph (e) includes—
(a) any grant excluded from item 1 of Group 5 of Schedule 8 by [Note (13)] in that Group;
(b) any supply made pursuant to a tenancy, lease or licence under which the grantee is or has been permitted to erect and occupy holiday accommodation.

(12) Paragraph (e) does not include a grant in respect of a building or part which is not a new building of—
(a) the fee simple, or
(b) a tenancy, lease or licence to the extent that the grant is made for a consideration in the form of a premium.

(13) "Holiday accommodation" includes any accommodation in a building, hut (including a beach hut or chalet), caravan, houseboat or tent which is advertised or held out as holiday accommodation or as suitable for holiday or leisure use, but excludes any accommodation within paragraph (d).

(14) A seasonal pitch is a pitch—
(a) which is provided for a period of less than a year, or
(b) which is provided for a year or a period longer than a year but which the person to whom it is provided is prevented by the terms of any covenant, statutory planning consent or similar permission from occupying by living in a caravan at all times throughout the period for which the pitch is provided.

(15) "Mooring" includes anchoring or berthing.

(16) Paragraph (m) shall not apply where the grant of the facilities is for—
(a) a continuous period of use exceeding 24 hours; or
(b) a series of 10 or more periods, whether or not exceeding 24 hours in total, where the following conditions are satisfied—
(i) each period is in respect of the same activity carried on at the same place;
(ii) the interval between each period is not less than one day and not more than 14 days;
(iii) consideration is payable by reference to the whole series and is evidenced by written agreement;
(iv) the grantee has exclusive use of the facilities; and
(v) the grantee is a school, a club, an association or an organisation representing affiliated clubs or constituent associations.

[957A]

NOTES

Note (1): substituted by the Value Added Tax (Land) Order 1995, SI 1995/282, arts 2, 3.
Note (1A): inserted by SI 1995/282, arts 2, 4.
Notes (3), (11): words in square brackets substituted by SI 1995/282, arts 2, 5, 7.
Note (7): words in square brackets inserted by SI 1995/282, arts 2, 6.

(*Sch 9, Pt II, Groups 2–5 outside the scope of this work.*)

GROUP 6—EDUCATION

Item No.

1. The provision by an eligible body of—
   (a) education;
   (b) research, where supplied to an eligible body; or
   (c) vocational training.

2. The supply of private tuition, in a subject ordinarily taught in a school or university, by an individual teacher acting independently of an employer.

3. The provision of examination services—
   (a) by or to an eligible body; or
   (b) to a person receiving education or vocational training which is—
      (i) exempt by virtue of items 1, 2[, 5 or 5A]; or
      (ii) provided otherwise than in the course or furtherance of a business.

4. The supply of any goods or services (other than examination services) which are closely related to a supply of a description falling within item 1 (the principal supply) by or to the eligible body making the principal supply provided—
   (a) the goods or services are for the direct use of the pupil, student or trainee (as the case may be) receiving the principal supply; and
   (b) where the supply is to the eligible body making the principal supply, it is made by another eligible body.

5. The provision of vocational training, and the supply of any goods or services essential thereto by the person providing the vocational training, to the extent that the consideration payable is ultimately a charge to funds provided pursuant to arrangements made under section 2 of the Employment and Training Act 1973, section 1A of the Employment and Training Act (Northern Ireland) 1950 or section 2 of the Enterprise and New Towns (Scotland) Act 1990.

[5A. The provision of education or vocational training and the supply, by the person providing that education or training, of any goods or services essential to that provision, to the extent that the consideration payable is ultimately a charge to funds provided by the Learning and Skills Council for England or the [National Assembly for Wales] under Part I or Part II of the Learning and Skills Act 2000.]

6. The provision of facilities by—
   (a) a youth club or an association of youth clubs to its members; or
   (b) an association of youth clubs to members of a youth club which is a member of that association.

Notes:

(1) For the purposes of this Group an "eligible body" is—
   (a) a school within the meaning of [the Education Act 1996], the Education (Scotland) Act 1980, the Education and Libraries (Northern Ireland) Order 1986 or the Education Reform (Northern Ireland) Order 1989, which is—
      (i) provisionally or finally registered or deemed to be registered as a school within the meaning of the aforesaid legislation in a register of independent schools; or
      (ii) a school in respect of which of which grants are made by the Secretary of State to the proprietor or managers; or
      (iii) [[a community, foundation or voluntary school within the meaning of the School Standards and Framework Act 1998, a special school within the meaning of section 337 of the Education Act 1996] or a maintained school within the meaning of] the Education and Libraries (Northern Ireland) Order 1986; or
      (iv) a public school within the meaning of section 135(1) of the Education (Scotland) Act 1980; or
      (v)–(vii) ...
      (viii) a grant-maintained integrated school within the meaning of Article 65 of the Education Reform (Northern Ireland) Order 1989;
   (b) a United Kingdom university, and any college, institution, school or hall of such a university;
   (c) an institution—
      (i) falling within section 91(3)(a) or (b) or section 91(5)(b) or (c) of the Further and Higher Education Act 1992; or

(ii) which is a designated institution as defined in section 44(2) of the Further and Higher Education (Scotland) Act 1992; or

(iii) managed by a board of management as defined in section 36(1) of the Further and Higher Education (Scotland) Act 1992; or

(iv) to which grants are paid by the Department of Education for Northern Ireland under Article 66(2) of the Education and Libraries (Northern Ireland) Order 1986; [or]

[(v) managed by a governing body established under the Further Education (Northern Ireland) Order 1997;]

(d) a public body of a description in Note (5) to Group 7 below;

[(e) a body which—

(i) is precluded from distributing and does not distribute any profit it makes; and

(ii) applies any profits made from supplies of a description within this Group to the continuance or improvement of such supplies;]

[(f) a body not falling within paragraphs (a) to (e) above which provides the teaching of English as a foreign language].

(2) A supply by a body, which is an eligible body only by virtue of falling within Note[(1)(f)], shall not fall within this Group insofar as it consists of the provision of anything other than the teaching of English as a foreign language.

[(3) "Vocational training" means—training, re-training or the provision of work experience for—

(a) any trade, profession or employment; or

(b) any voluntary work connected with—

(i) education, health, safety, or welfare; or

(ii) the carrying out of activities of a charitable nature.]

(4) "Examination services" include the setting and marking of examinations, the setting of educational or training standards, the making of assessments and other services provided with a view to ensuring educational and training standards are maintained.

(5) For the purposes of item 5 a supply of any goods or services shall not be taken to be essential to the provision of vocational training unless the goods or services in question are provided directly to the trainee.

[(5A) For the purposes of item 5A a supply of any goods or services shall not be taken to be essential to the provision of education or vocational training unless—

(a) in the case of the provision of education, the goods or services are provided directly to the person receiving the education;

(b) in the case of the provision of vocational training, the goods or services are provided directly to the person receiving the training.]

(6) For the purposes of item 6 a club is a "youth club" if—

(a) it is established to promote the social, physical, educational or spiritual development of its members;

(b) its members are mainly under 21 years of age; and

(c) it satisfies the requirements of Note (1)(f)(i) and (ii).

[958]

NOTES

Item 3: words in square brackets substituted by the Learning and Skills Act 2000, s 149, Sch 9, paras 1, 47(1), (2).

Item 5A: inserted by the Learning and Skills Act 2000, s 149, Sch 9, paras 1, 47(1), (3); words in square brackets substituted by the National Council for Education and Training for Wales (Transfer of Functions to the National Assembly for Wales and Abolition) Order 2005, SI 2005/3238, art 9(1), Sch 1, para 30, subject to transitional provisions in art 7 of that Order.

Note (1): words in first pair of square brackets in para (a) and words in first (outer) pair of square brackets in para (a)(iii) substituted by the Education Act 1996, s 582(1), Sch 37, para 125; words in second (inner) pair of square brackets in para (a)(iii) substituted and paras (a)(v), (vii) repealed by the School Standards and Framework Act 1998, s 140(1), (3), Sch 30, para 51(a), (b), Sch 31; para (a)(vi) repealed by the Standards in Scotland's Schools etc Act 2000, s 60(2), Sch 3; para (c)(v) inserted by the Further Education (Northern Ireland) Order 1997, SI 1997/1772, art 25, Sch 4; paras (e), (f) substituted by the Value Added Tax (Education) (No 2) Order 1994, SI 1994/2969, arts 2–4.

Note (2): words in square brackets substituted by SI 1994/2969, arts 2, 5.

Note (3): substituted by SI 1994/2969, arts 2, 6.

Note (5A): inserted by the Learning and Skills Act 2000, s 149, Sch 9, paras 1, 47(1), (4).

GROUP 7—HEALTH AND WELFARE

Item No.

1. The supply of services [consisting in the provision of medical care] by a person registered or enrolled in any of the following—
   - (a) the register of medical practitioners *or the register of medical practitioners with limited registration*;
   - (b) either of the registers of ophthalmic opticians or the register of dispensing opticians kept under the Opticians Act 1989 or either of the lists kept under section 9 of that Act of bodies corporate carrying on business as ophthalmic opticians or as dispensing opticians;
   - [(c) the register kept under the Health Professions Order 2001;]
   - [(ca) the register of osteopaths maintained in accordance with the provisions of the Osteopaths Act 1993;]
   - [(cb) the register of chiropractors maintained in accordance with the provisions of the Chiropractors Act 1994;]
   - [(d) the register of qualified nurses and midwives maintained under article 5 of the Nursing and Midwifery Order 2001;]
   - (e) the register of dispensers of hearing aids or the register of persons employing such dispensers maintained under section 2 of the Hearing Aid Council Act 1968.

2. *The supply of any services or dental prostheses by—*
   - (a) a person registered in the dentists' register;
   - [(b) a person registered in the dental care professionals register established under section 36B of the Dentists Act 1984; *or*]
   - *(c) a dental technician.*

[2A. The supply of any services or dental prostheses by a dental technician.]

3. The supply of any services [consisting in the provision of medical care] by a person registered in *the register of pharmaceutical chemists kept under the Pharmacy Act 1954 or* the Pharmacy (Northern Ireland) Order 1976.

4. The provision of care or medical or surgical treatment and, in connection with it, the supply of any goods, in any hospital [or state-regulated institution].

5. The provision of a deputy for a person registered in the register of medical practitioners *or the register of medical practitioners with limited registration.*

6. Human blood.

7. Products for therapeutic purposes, derived from human blood.

8. Human (including foetal) organs or tissue for diagnostic or therapeutic purposes or medical research.

[9. The supply by—
   - (a) a charity,
   - (b) a state-regulated private welfare institution [or agency], or
   - (c) a public body,

of welfare services and of goods supplied in connection with those welfare services.]

10. The supply, otherwise than for profit, of goods and services incidental to the provision of spiritual welfare by a religious community to a resident member of that community in return for a subscription or other consideration paid as a condition of membership.

11. The supply of transport services for sick or injured persons in vehicles specially designed for that purpose.

Notes:

(1) Item 1 does not include the letting on hire of goods except where the letting is in connection with a supply of other services comprised in the item.

(2) Paragraphs (a) to (d) of item 1 and paragraphs (a) and (b) of item 2 include supplies of services made by a person who is not registered or enrolled in any of the registers or rolls specified in those paragraphs where the services are wholly performed or directly supervised by a person who is so registered or enrolled.

[(2A) Item 3 includes supplies of services made by a person who is not registered in either of the registers specified in that item where the services are wholly performed by a person who is so registered.]

(3) Item 3 does not include the letting on hire of goods.

(4) For the purposes of this Group a person who is not registered in the visiting EEC practitioners list in the register of medical practitioners at the time he performs services in an urgent case as mentioned in subsection (3) of section 18 of the Medical Act 1983 is to be treated as being registered in that list where he is entitled to be registered in accordance with that section.

(5) In item 9 "public body" means—
- (a) a Government department within the meaning of section 41(6);
- (b) a local authority;
- (c) a body which acts under any enactment or instrument for public purposes and not for its own profit and which performs functions similar to those of a Government department or local authority.

[(6) In item 9 "welfare services" means services which are directly connected with—
- (a) the provision of care, treatment or instruction designed to promote the physical or mental welfare of elderly, sick, distressed or disabled persons,
- (b) the care or protection of children and young persons, or
- (c) the provision of spiritual welfare by a religious institution as part of a course of instruction or a retreat, not being a course or a retreat designed primarily to provide recreation or a holiday,

and, in the case of services supplied by a state-regulated private welfare institution, includes only those services in respect of which the institution is so regulated.]

(7) Item 9 does not include the supply of accommodation or catering except where it is ancillary to the provision of care, treatment or instruction.

[(8) In this Group "state-regulated" means approved, licensed, registered or exempted from registration by any Minister or other authority pursuant to a provision of a public general Act, other than a provision that is capable of being brought into effect at different times in relation to different local authority areas.

Here "Act" means—
- (a) an Act of Parliament;
- (b) an Act of the Scottish Parliament;
- (c) an Act of the Northern Ireland Assembly;
- (d) an Order in Council under Schedule 1 to the Northern Ireland Act 1974;
- (e) a Measure of the Northern Ireland Assembly established under section 1 of the Northern Ireland Assembly Act 1973;
- (f) an Order in Council under section 1(3) of the Northern Ireland (Temporary Provisions) Act 1972;
- (g) an Act of the Parliament of Northern Ireland.]

[959]

NOTES

Item 1: words in first pair of square brackets inserted by the Value Added Tax (Health and Welfare) Order 2007, SI 2007/206, arts 2, 3, as from 1 May 2007; words in italics in para (a) repealed by the Medical Act 1983 (Amendment) and Miscellaneous Amendments Order 2006, SI 2006/1914, art 75(2)(a), as from a day to be notified in the London, Edinburgh and Belfast Gazettes; para (c) substituted by the Health Professions Order 2001, SI 2002/254, art 48(3), Sch 4, para 6; para (ca) inserted, in relation to supplies made on or after 12 June 1998, by the Value Added Tax (Osteopaths) Order 1998, SI 1998/1294, art 2; para (cb) inserted, in relation to supplies made on or after 29 June 1999, by the Value Added Tax (Chiropractors) Order 1999, SI 1999/1575, art 2, subject to transitional provisions in Sch 2 of that Order; para (d) substituted by the Nursing and Midwifery Order 2001, SI 2002/253, art 54(3), Sch 5, para 12, subject to transitional provisions in Sch 2 to that Order.

Item 2: for the words in italics in the first place there are substituted the words "The supply of any services consisting in the provision of medical care, or the supply of dental prostheses, by", and para (c) and word "or" immediately preceding it repealed, by SI 2007/206, arts 2, 4, as from 1 May 2007; para (b) substituted by the Dentists Act 1984 (Amendment) Order 2005, SI 2005/2011, arts 2(1), 49, Sch 6, Pt 1, para 3.

Item 2A: inserted by SI 2007/206, arts 2, 5, as from 1 May 2007.

Item 3: words in square brackets inserted by SI 2007/206, arts 2, 6, as from 1 May 2007; words in italics substituted for words "the Register of Pharmacists maintained under the Pharmacists and Pharmacy Technicians Order 2007 or in the register of pharmaceutical chemists kept under" by the Pharmacists and Pharmacy Technicians Order 2007, SI 2007/289, art 67, Sch 1, Pt 1, para 5(1), (3), as from a day to be notified in the London, Edinburgh and Belfast Gazettes.

Item 4: words in square brackets substituted by the Value Added Tax (Health and Welfare) Order 2002, SI 2002/762, arts 2, 3.

Item 5: words in italics repealed by SI 2006/1914, art 75(2)(b), as from a day to be notified in the London, Edinburgh and Belfast Gazettes.

Item 9: substituted by SI 2002/762, arts 2, 4; words in square brackets in para (b) inserted by the Value Added Tax (Health and Welfare) Order 2003, SI 2003/24, arts 2, 3.

Note (2A): inserted, in relation to supplies made on or after 1 January 1997, by the Value Added Tax (Pharmaceutical Chemists) Order 1996, SI 1996/2949, art 2.

Note (6): substituted by SI 2002/762, arts 2, 5.

Note (8): added by SI 2002/762, arts 2, 6.

GROUP 8—BURIAL AND CREMATION

Item No.

1. The disposal of the remains of the dead.

2. The making of arrangements for or in connection with the disposal of the remains of the dead.

[960]

[GROUP 9—SUBSCRIPTIONS TO TRADE UNIONS, PROFESSIONAL AND OTHER PUBLIC INTEREST BODIES]

Item No.

1. The supply to its members of such services and, in connection with those services, of such goods as are both referable only to its aims and available without payment other than a membership subscription by any of the following non-profit-making organisations—
   - (a) a trade union or other organisation of persons having as its main object the negotiation on behalf of its members of the terms and conditions of their employment;
   - (b) a professional association, membership of which is wholly or mainly restricted to individuals who have or are seeking a qualification appropriate to the practice of the profession concerned;
   - (c) an association, the primary purpose of which is the advancement of a particular branch of knowledge, or the fostering of professional expertise, connected with the past or present professions or employments of its members;
   - (d) an association, the primary purpose of which is to make representations to the Government on legislation and other public matters which affect the business or professional interests of its members.
   - [(e) a body which has objects which are in the public domain and are of a political, religious, patriotic, philosophical, philanthropic or civic nature.]

Notes:

(1) Item 1 does not include any right of admission to any premises, event or performance, to which non-members are admitted for a consideration.

(2) "Trade union" has the meaning assigned to it by section 1 of the Trade Union and Labour Relations (Consolidation) Act 1992.

(3) Item 1 shall include organisations and associations the membership of which consists wholly or mainly of constituent or affiliated associations which as individual associations would be comprised in the item; and "member" shall be construed as including such an association and "membership subscription" shall include an affiliation fee or similar levy.

(4) Paragraph (c) does not apply unless the association restricts its membership wholly or mainly to individuals whose present or previous professions or employments are directly connected with the purposes of the association.

(5) Paragraph (d) does not apply unless the association restricts its membership wholly or mainly to individuals or corporate bodies whose business or professional interests are directly connected with the purposes of the association.

[961]

NOTES

Heading substituted in relation to supplies made on or after 1 December 1999, by the Value Added Tax (Subscriptions to Trade Unions, Professional and Other Public Interest Bodies) Order 1999, SI 1999/2834, arts 2, 4(a).

Item 1: para (e) inserted, in relation to supplies made on or after 1 December 1999, by SI 1999/2834, arts 2, 4(b).

GROUP 10—SPORT, SPORTS COMPETITIONS AND PHYSICAL EDUCATION

Item No.

1. The grant of a right to enter a competition in sport or physical recreation where the consideration for the grant consists in money which is to be allocated wholly towards the provision of a prize or prizes awarded in that competition.

2. The grant, by [an eligible body] established for the purposes of sport or physical recreation, of a right to enter a competition in such an activity.

3. The supply by [an eligible body] to an individual, except, where the body operates a membership scheme, an individual who is not a member, of services closely linked with and essential to sport or physical education in which the individual is taking part.

Notes

(1) Item 3 does not include the supply of any services by [an eligible body] of residential accommodation, catering or transport.

(2) An individual shall only be considered to be a member of [an eligible body] for the purpose of Item 3 where he is granted membership for a period of three months or more.

[(2A) Subject to Notes (2C) and (3), in this Group "eligible body" means a non-profit making body which—

(a) is precluded from distributing any profit it makes, or is allowed to distribute any such profit by means only of distributions to a non-profit making body;

(b) applies in accordance with Note (2B) any profits it makes from supplies of a description within Item 2 or 3; and

(c) is not subject to commercial influence.

(2B) For the purposes of Note (2A)(b) the application of profits made by any body from supplies of a description within Item 2 or 3 is in accordance with this Note only if those profits are applied for one or more of the following purposes, namely—

(a) the continuance or improvement of any facilities made available in or in connection with the making of the supplies of those descriptions made by that body;

(b) the purposes of a non-profit making body.

(2C) In determining whether the requirements of Note (2A) for being an eligible body are satisfied in the case of any body, there shall be disregarded any distribution of amounts representing unapplied or undistributed profits that falls to be made to the body's members on its winding-up or dissolution.]

(3) In Item 3 [an "eligible body"] does not include—

(a) a local authority;

(b) a Government department within the meaning of section 41(6); or

(c) a non-departmental public body which is listed in the 1993 edition of the publication prepared by the Office of Public Service and Science and known as Public Bodies.

[(4) For the purposes of this Group a body shall be taken, in relation to a sports supply, to be subject to commercial influence if, and only if, there is a time in the relevant period when—

(a) a relevant supply was made to that body by a person associated with it at that time;

(b) an emolument was paid by that body to such a person;

(c) an agreement existed for either or both of the following to take place after the end of that period, namely—

 (i) the making of a relevant supply to that body by such a person; or

 (ii) the payment by that body to such a person of any emoluments.

(5) In this Group "the relevant period", in relation to a sports supply, means—

(a) where that supply is one made before 1st January 2003, the period beginning with 14th January 1999 and ending with the making of that sports supply; and

(b) where that supply is one made on or after 1st January 2003, the period of three years ending with the making of that sports supply.

(6) Subject to Note (7), in this Group "relevant supply", in relation to any body, means a supply falling within any of the following paragraphs—

(a) the grant of any interest in or right over land which at any time in the relevant period was or was expected to become sports land;
(b) the grant of any licence to occupy any land which at any such time was or was expected to become sports land;
(c) the grant, in the case of land in Scotland, of any personal right to call for or be granted any such interest or right as is mentioned in paragraph (a) above;
(d) a supply arising from a grant falling within paragraph (a), (b) or (c) above, other than a grant made before 1st April 1996;
(e) the supply of any services consisting in the management or administration of any facilities provided by that body;
(f) the supply of any goods or services for a consideration in excess of what would have been agreed between parties entering into a commercial transaction at arm's length.

(7) A supply which has been, or is to be or may be, made by any person shall not be taken, in relation to a sports supply made by any body, to be a relevant supply for the purposes of this Group if—

(a) the principal purpose of that body is confined, at the time when the sports supply is made, to the provision for employees of that person of facilities for use for or in connection with sport or physical recreation, or both;
(b) the supply in question is one made by a charity or local authority or one which (if it is made) will be made by a person who is a charity or local authority at the time when the sports supply is made;
(c) the supply in question is a grant falling within Note (6)(a) to (c) which has been made, or (if it is made) will be made, for a nominal consideration;
(d) the supply in question is one arising from such a grant as is mentioned in paragraph (c) above and is not itself a supply the consideration for which was, or will or may be, more than a nominal consideration; or
(e) the supply in question—
    (i) is a grant falling within Note (6)(a) to (c) which is made for no consideration; but
    (ii) falls to be treated as a supply of goods or services, or (if it is made) will fall to be so treated, by reason only of the application, in accordance with paragraph 9 of Schedule 4, of paragraph 5 of that Schedule.

(8) Subject to Note (10), a person shall be taken, for the purposes of this Group, to have been associated with a body at any of the following times, that is to say—

(a) the time when a supply was made to that body by that person;
(b) the time when an emolument was paid by that body to that person; or
(c) the time when an agreement was in existence for the making of a relevant supply or the payment of emoluments, if, at that time, or at another time (whether before or after that time) in the relevant period, that person was an officer or shadow officer of that body or an intermediary for supplies to that body.

(9) Subject to Note (10), a person shall also be taken, for the purposes of this Group, to have been associated with a body at a time mentioned in paragraph (a), (b) or (c) of Note (8) if, at that time, he was connected with another person who in accordance with that Note—

(a) is to be taken to have been so associated at that time; or
(b) would be taken to have been so associated were that time the time of a supply by the other person to that body.

(10) Subject to Note (11), a person shall not be taken for the purposes of this Group to have been associated with a body at a time mentioned in paragraph (a), (b) or (c) of Note (8) if the only times in the relevant period when that person or the person connected with him was an officer or shadow officer of the body are times before 1st January 2000.

(11) Note (10) does not apply where (but for that Note) the body would be treated as subject to commercial influence at any time in the relevant period by virtue of—

(a) the existence of any agreement entered into on or after 14th January 1999 and before 1st January 2000; or
(b) anything done in pursuance of any such agreement.

(12) For the purposes of this Group a person shall be taken, in relation to a sports supply, to have been at all times in the relevant period an intermediary for supplies to the body making that supply if—

(a) at any time in that period either a supply was made to him by another person or an agreement for the making of a supply to him by another was in existence; and

(b) the circumstances were such that, if—
  (i) that body had been the person to whom the supply was made or (in the case of an agreement) the person to whom it was to be or might be made; and
  (ii) Note (7) above were to be disregarded to the extent (if at all) that it would prevent the supply from being a relevant supply, the body would have fallen to be regarded in relation to the sports supply as subject to commercial influence.

(13) In determining for the purposes of Note (12) or this Note whether there are such circumstances as are mentioned in paragraph (b) of that Note in the case of any supply, that Note and this Note shall be applied first for determining whether the person by whom the supply was made, or was to be or might be made, was himself an intermediary for supplies to the body in question, and so on through any number of other supplies or agreements.

(14) In determining for the purposes of this Group whether a supply made by any person was made by an intermediary for supplies to a body, it shall be immaterial that the supply by that person was made before the making of the supply or agreement by reference to which that person falls to be regarded as such an intermediary.

(15) Without prejudice to the generality of subsection (1AA) of section 43, for the purpose of determining—
(a) whether a relevant supply has at any time been made to any person;
(b) whether there has at any time been an agreement for the making of a relevant supply to any person; and
(c) whether a person falls to be treated as an intermediary for the supplies to any body by reference to supplies that have been, were to be or might have been made to him,

references in the preceding Notes to a supply shall be deemed to include references to a supply falling for other purposes to be disregarded in accordance with section 43(1)(a).

(16) In this Group—
"agreement" includes any arrangement or understanding (whether or not legally enforceable); "emolument" means any emolument (within the meaning of the Income Tax Acts) the amount of which falls or may fall, in accordance with the agreement under which it is payable, to be determined or varied wholly or partly by reference—
  (i) to the profits from some or all of the activities of the body paying the emolument; or
  (ii) to the level of that body's gross income from some or all of its activities; "employees", in relation to a person, includes retired employees of that person; "grant" includes an assignment or surrender; "officer", in relation to a body, includes—
  (i) a director of a body corporate; and
  (ii) any committee member or trustee concerned in the general control and management of the administration of the body;
"shadow officer", in relation to a body, means a person in accordance with whose directions or instructions the members or officers of the body are accustomed to act;
"sports land", in relation to any body, means any land used or held for use for or in connection with the provision by that body of facilities for use for or in connection with sport or physical recreation, or both;
"sports supply" means a supply which, if made by an eligible body, would fall within Item 2 or 3.

(17) For the purposes of this Group any question whether a person is connected with another shall be determined in accordance with section 839 of the Taxes Act (connected persons).]

[962]

NOTES

Items 2, 3: words in square brackets substituted by the Value Added Tax (Sport, Sports Competitions and Physical Education) Order 1999, SI 1999/1994, arts 2, 3.

Notes (1), (2), (3): words in square brackets substituted by SI 1999/1994, arts 2, 3.

Notes (2A)–(2C): inserted by SI 1999/1994, arts 2, 4.

Notes (4)–(17): added by SI 1999/1994, arts 2, 5.

GROUP 11—WORKS OF ART ETC

Item No.

1. The disposal of an object with respect to which estate duty is not chargeable by virtue of section 30(3) of the Finance Act 1953, section 34(1) of the Finance Act 1956 or the proviso to section 40(2) of the Finance Act 1930.

2. The disposal of an object with respect to which inheritance tax is not chargeable by virtue of paragraph 1(3)(a) or (4), paragraph 3(4)(a), or the words following paragraph 3(4), of Schedule 5 to the Inheritance Tax Act 1984.

3. The disposal of property with respect to which inheritance tax is not chargeable by virtue of section 32(4) or 32A(5) or (7) of the Inheritance Tax Act 1984.

4. The disposal of an asset in a case in which any gain accruing on that disposal is not a chargeable gain by virtue of section 258(2) of the Taxation of Chargeable Gains Act 1992.

[963]

NOTES

Finance Act 1953, s 30(3); Finance Act 1956, s 34(1); Finance Act 1930, s 40(2): repealed by the Finance Act 1975, ss 52(2), 59(5), Sch 13, Pt I, in relation to deaths occurring after 13 March 1975, and so far as they relate to any duty mentioned in s 50 of the 1975 Act in relation to any death.

[GROUP 12—FUND-RAISING EVENTS BY CHARITIES AND OTHER QUALIFYING BODIES

Item No.

1. The supply of goods and services by a charity in connection with an event—
   (a) that is organised for charitable purposes by a charity or jointly by more than one charity,
   (b) whose primary purpose is the raising of money, and
   (c) that is promoted as being primarily for the raising of money.
2. The supply of goods and services by a qualifying body in connection with an event—
   (a) that is organised exclusively for the body's own benefit,
   (b) whose primary purpose is the raising of money, and
   (c) that is promoted as being primarily for the raising of money.
3. The supply of goods and services by a charity or a qualifying body in connection with an event—
   (a) that is organised jointly by a charity, or two or more charities, and the qualifying body,
   (b) that is so organised exclusively for charitable purposes or exclusively for the body's own benefit or exclusively for a combination of those purposes and that benefit,
   (c) whose primary purpose is the raising of money, and
   (d) that is promoted as being primarily for the raising of money.

Notes:

(1) For the purposes of this Group "event" includes an event accessed (wholly or partly) by means of electronic communications.

For this purpose "electronic communications" includes any communications by means of [an electronic communications network].

(2) For the purposes of this Group "charity" includes a body corporate that is wholly owned by a charity if—
   (a) the body has agreed in writing (whether or not contained in a deed) to transfer its profits (from whatever source) to a charity, or
   (b) the body's profits (from whatever source) are otherwise payable to a charity.

(3) For the purposes of this Group "qualifying body" means—
   (a) any non-profit making organisation mentioned in item 1 of Group 9;
   (b) any body that is an eligible body for the purposes of Group 10 and whose principal purpose is the provision of facilities for persons to take part in sport or physical education; or
   (c) any body that is an eligible body for the purposes of item 2 of Group 13.

(4) Where in a financial year of a charity or qualifying body there are held at the same location more than 15 events involving the charity or body that are of the same kind, items 1 to 3 do not apply (or shall be treated as having not applied) to a supply in connection with any event involving the charity or body that is of that kind and is held in that financial year at that location.

(5) In determining whether the limit of 15 events mentioned in Note (4) has been exceeded in the case of events of any one kind held at the same location, disregard any event of that kind held at that location in a week during which the aggregate gross takings from events involving the charity or body that are of that kind and are held in that location do not exceed £1,000.

(6) In the case of a financial year that is longer or shorter than a year, Notes (4) and (5) have effect as if for "15" there were substituted the whole number nearest to the number obtained by—

(a) first multiplying the number of days in the financial year by 15, and
(b) then dividing the result by 365.

(7) For the purposes of Notes (4) and (5)—

(a) an event involves a charity if the event is organised by the charity or a connected charity;
(b) an event involves a qualifying body if the event is organised by the body.

In this Note "organised" means organised alone or jointly in any combination, and "organising" in Note (8) shall be construed accordingly.

(8) Items 1 to 3 do not include any supply in connection with an event if—

(a) accommodation in connection with the event is provided to a person by means of a supply, or in pursuance of arrangements, made by—
 (i) the charity or any of the charities, or the qualifying body, organising the event, or
 (ii) a charity connected with any charity organising the event,

and

(b) the provision of the accommodation is not incidental to the event.

(9) For the purposes of Note (8) the provision of accommodation is incidental to the event only if accommodation provided to the person by such means, or in pursuance of such arrangements, as are mentioned in paragraph (a) of that Note—

(a) does not exceed two nights in total (whether or not consecutive), and
(b) is not to any extent provided by means of a supply to which an order under section 53 applies.

(10) For the purposes of Notes (7)(a) and (8), two charities are connected if—

(a) one is a charity for the purposes of this Group only by virtue of Note (2) and the other is the charity that owns it, or
(b) each is a charity for the purposes of this Group only by virtue of Note (2) and the two of them are owned by the same charity.

(11) Items 1 to 3 do not include any supply the exemption of which would be likely to create distortions of competition such as to place a commercial enterprise carried on by a taxable person at a disadvantage.]

[964]

NOTES

Substituted, in relation to supplies made on or after 1 April 2000, by the Value Added Tax (Fund-Raising Events by Charities and Other Qualifying Bodies) Order 2000, SI 2000/802, arts 2, 3.

Note (1): words in square brackets substituted by the Communications Act 2003, s 406(1), Sch 17, para 129(1), (3).

[GROUP 13—CULTURAL SERVICES ETC

Item No.

1. The supply by a public body of a right of admission to—
 (a) a museum, gallery, art exhibition or zoo; or
 (b) a theatrical, musical or choreographic performance of a cultural nature.

2. The supply by an eligible body of a right of admission to—
 (a) a museum, gallery, art exhibition or zoo; or
 (b) a theatrical, musical or choreographic performance of a cultural nature.

Notes

(1) For the purposes of this Group "public body" means—
- (a) a local authority;
- (b) a government department within the meaning of section 41(6); or
- (c) a non-departmental public body which is listed in the 1995 edition of the publication prepared by the Office of Public Service and known as "Public Bodies".

(2) For the purposes of item 2 "eligible body" means any body (other than a public body) which—
- (a) is precluded from distributing, and does not distribute, any profit it makes;
- (b) applies any profits made from supplies of a description falling within item 2 to the continuance or improvement of the facilities made available by means of the supplies; and
- (c) is managed and administered on a voluntary basis by persons who have no direct or indirect financial interest in its activities.

(3) Item 1 does not include any supply the exemption of which would be likely to create distortions of competition such as to place a commercial enterprise carried on by a taxable person at a disadvantage.

(4) Item 1(b) includes the supply of a right of admission to a performance only if the performance is provided exclusively by one or more public bodies, one or more eligible bodies or any combination of public bodies and eligible bodies.]

[965]

NOTES

Commencement: 1 June 1996.
Added by the Value Added Tax (Cultural Services) Order 1996, SI 1996/1256, art 2(b).

(Sch 9, Pt II, Groups 14, 15, Sch 9A outside the scope of this work.)

SCHEDULE 10
BUILDINGS AND LAND

Section 51

Residential and charitable buildings: change of use etc

1.—(1) In this paragraph "relevant zero-rated supply" means a grant or other supply taking place on or after 1st April 1989 which—
- (a) relates to a building intended for use solely for a relevant residential purpose or a relevant charitable purpose or part of such a building; and
- (b) is zero-rated, in whole or in part, by virtue of Group 5 of Schedule 8.

(2) Sub-paragraph (3) below applies where—
- (a) one or more relevant zero-rated supplies relating to a building (or part of a building) have been made to any person,
- (b) within the period of 10 years beginning with the day on which the building is completed, the person grants an interest in, right over or licence to occupy the building or any part of it (or the building or any part of it including, consisting of or forming part of the part to which the relevant zero-rated supply or supplies related), and
- (c) after the grant the whole or any part of the building, or of the part to which the grant relates, (or the whole of the building or of the part to which the grant relates, or any part of it including, consisting of or forming part of the part to which the relevant zero-rated supply or supplies related) is not intended for use solely for a relevant residential purpose or a relevant charitable purpose.

(3) Where this sub-paragraph applies, to the extent that the grant relates to so much of the building as—
- (a) by reason of its intended use gave rise to the relevant zero-rated supply or supplies; and
- (b) is not intended for use solely for a relevant residential purpose or a relevant charitable purpose after the grant,

it shall be taken to be a taxable supply in the course or furtherance of a business which is not zero-rated by virtue of Group 5 of Schedule 8 (if it would not otherwise be such a supply).

(4) Sub-paragraph (5) below applies where—

(a) one or more relevant zero-rated supplies relating to a building (or part of a building) have been made to any person; and

(b) within the period of 10 years beginning with the day on which the building is completed, the person uses the building or any part of it (or the building or any part of it including, consisting of or forming part of the part to which the relevant zero-rated supply or supplies related) for a purpose which is neither a relevant residential purpose nor a relevant charitable purpose.

(5) Where this sub-paragraph applies, his interest in, right over or licence to occupy so much of the building as—

(a) by reason of its intended use gave rise to the relevant zero-rated supply or supplies, and

(b) is used otherwise than for a relevant residential purpose or a relevant charitable purpose,

shall be treated for the purposes of this Act as supplied to him for the purpose of a business carried on by him and supplied by him in the course or furtherance of the business when he first uses it for a purpose which is neither a relevant residential purpose nor a relevant charitable purpose.

(6) Where sub-paragraph (5) applies—

(a) the supply shall be taken to be a taxable supply which is not zero-rated by virtue of Group 5 of Schedule 8 (if it would not otherwise be such a supply); and

[(b) the value of the supply shall be taken to be such amount as is obtained by using the formula—

$$A \times \frac{(10-B)}{10}$$

where—

A is the amount that yields an amount of VAT chargeable on it equal to the VAT which would have been chargeable on the relevant zero-rated supply (or, where there was more than one supply, the aggregate amount which would have been chargeable on them) had so much of the building as is mentioned in sub-paragraph (5) above not been intended for use solely for a relevant residential purpose or a relevant charitable purpose; and

B is the number of whole years since the day the building was completed for which the building or part concerned has been used for a relevant residential purpose or a relevant charitable purpose].

Election to waive exemption

2.—(1) Subject to sub-paragraphs [(2), (3) and (3A)] and paragraph 3 below, where an election under this paragraph has effect in relation to any land, if and to the extent that any grant made in relation to it at a time when the election has effect by the person who made the election, or where that person is a body corporate by that person or a relevant associate, would (apart from this sub-paragraph) fall within Group 1 of Schedule 9, the grant shall not fall within that Group.

(2) Sub-paragraph (1) above shall not apply in relation to a grant if the grant is made in relation to—

(a) a building or part of a building intended for use as a dwelling or number of dwellings or solely for a relevant residential purpose; or

(b) a building or part of a building intended for use solely for a relevant charitable purpose, other than as an office;

[(c) a pitch for a residential caravan;

(d) facilities for the mooring of a residential houseboat.]

[(2A) Subject to the following provisions of this paragraph, where—

(a) an election has been made for the purposes of this paragraph in relation to any land, and

(b) a supply is made that would fall, but for sub-paragraph (2)(a) above, to be treated as excluded by virtue of that election from Group 1 of Schedule 9,

then, notwithstanding sub-paragraph (2)(a) above, that supply shall be treated as so excluded if the conditions in sub-paragraph (2B) below are satisfied.

(2B) The conditions mentioned in sub-paragraph (2A) above are—

(a) that an agreement in writing made, at or before the time of the grant, between—

(i) the person making the grant, and

(ii) the person to whom it is made,

declares that the election is to apply in relation to the grant; and

(b) that the person to whom the supply is made intends, at the time when it is made, to use the land for the purpose only of making a supply which is zero-rated by virtue of paragraph (b) of item 1 of Group 5 of Schedule 8.]

(3) Sub-paragraph (1) above shall not apply in relation to a grant if—

(a) the grant is made to a [relevant housing association] and the association has given to the grantor a certificate stating that the land is to be used (after any necessary demolition work) for the construction of a building or buildings intended for use as a dwelling or number of dwellings or solely for a relevant residential purpose; or

(b) the grant is made to an individual and the land is to be used for the construction, otherwise than in the course or furtherance of a business carried on by him, of a building intended for use by him as a dwelling.

[(3AA) Where an election has been made under this paragraph in relation to any land, a supply shall not be taken by virtue of that election to be a taxable supply if—

(a) the grant giving rise to the supply was made by a person ("the grantor") who was a developer of the land; and

(b) at the time of the grant, [or at the time it was treated as made by virtue of [sub-paragraphs (3AAA) or (3B)] below,] it was the intention or expectation of—

(i) the grantor, or

(ii) a person responsible for financing the grantor's development of the land for exempt use,

that the land would become exempt land (whether immediately or eventually and whether or not by virtue of the grant) or, as the case may be, would continue, for a period at least, to be such land.]

[(3AAA) For the purposes of sub-paragraph (3AA) above a grant (the original grant) in relation to land made on or after 19th March 1997 and before 10th March 1999 shall be treated as being made on 10th March 1999 if at the time of the original grant—

(a) the grantor or a person responsible for financing the grantor's development of the land for exempt use, intended or expected that the land or a building or part of a building on, or to be constructed on, that land would become an asset falling in relation to—

(i) the grantor, or

(ii) any person to whom that land, building or part of a building was to be transferred either in the course of a supply or in the course of a transfer of a business or part of a business as a going concern,

to be treated as a capital item for the purposes of any regulations made under section 26(3) and (4) providing for adjustments relating to the deduction of input tax to be made as respects that item, and

(b) the land or a building or part of a building on, or to be constructed on, that land had not become such an asset.]

[(3A) ...]

[(3B) Where a supply is made by a person other than the person who made the grant giving rise to it, then for the purposes of sub-paragraph (3AA) above—

(a) the person making the supply shall be treated as the person who made the grant that gave rise to that supply; and

(b) the grant shall be treated as made at the time when that person made his first supply arising from the grant.]

(4) Subject to the following provisions of this paragraph, no input tax on any supply or importation which, apart from this sub-paragraph, would be allowable by virtue of the operation of this paragraph shall be allowed if the supply or importation took place before the first day for which the election in question has effect.

(5) Subject to sub-paragraph (6) below, sub-paragraph (4) above shall not apply where the person by whom the election was made—

(a) has not, before the first day for which the election has effect, made in relation to the land in relation to which the election has effect any grant falling within Group 1 of Schedule 9; or

(b) has before that day made in relation to that land a grant or grants so falling but the grant, or all the grants—

(i) were made in the period beginning with 1st April 1989 and ending with 31st July 1989; and
(ii) would have been taxable supplies but for the amendments made by Schedule 3 to the Finance Act 1989.

(6) Sub-paragraph (5) above does not make allowable any input tax on supplies or importations taking place before 1st August 1989 unless—
(a) it is attributable by or under regulations to grants made by the person on or after 1st April 1989 which would have been taxable supplies but for the amendments made by Schedule 3 to the Finance Act 1989, and
(b) the election has effect from 1st August 1989.

(7) Sub-paragraph (4) above shall not apply in relation to input tax on grants or other supplies which are made in the period beginning with 1st April 1989 and ending with 31st July 1989 [if]—
(a) they would have been zero-rated by virtue of item 1 or 2 of Group 5 of Schedule 8 or exempt by virtue of item 1 of Group 1 of Schedule 9 but for the amendments made by Schedule 3 to the Finance Act 1989; and
(b) the election has effect from 1st August 1989.

(8) Sub-paragraph (4) above shall not apply in relation to any election having effect from any day on or after 1st January 1992, except in respect of the input tax on a supply or importation which took place before 1st August 1989.

(9) Where a person has made an exempt grant in relation to any land and has made an election in relation to that land which has effect from any day before 1st January 1992, he may apply to the Commissioners for sub-paragraph (4) above to be disapplied in respect of any input tax on a supply or importation which took place on or after 1st August 1989, but the Commissioners shall only permit the disapplication of that sub-paragraph if they are satisfied, having regard to all the circumstances of the case, and in particular to—
(a) the total value of—
(i) exempt grants made;
(ii) taxable grants made or expected to be made, in relation to the land; and
(b) the total amount of input tax in relation to the land which had been incurred before the day from which the election had effect,

that a fair and reasonable attribution of the input tax mentioned in paragraph (b) above will be secured.

3.—(1) An election under paragraph 2 above shall have effect—
(a) subject to the following provisions of this paragraph, from the beginning of the day on which the election is made or of any later day specified in the election; or
(b) where the election was made before 1st November 1989, from the beginning of 1st August 1989 or of any later day so specified.

(2) An election under paragraph 2 above shall have effect in relation to any land specified, or of a description specified, in the election.

(3) Where such an election is made in relation to, or to part of, a building (or planned building), it shall have effect in relation to the whole of the building and all the land within its curtilage and for the purposes of this sub-paragraph buildings linked internally or by a covered walkway, and [complexes consisting of a number of units grouped around a fully enclosed concourse], shall be taken to be a single building (if they otherwise would not be).

[(4) Subject to sub-paragraph (5) below, an election under paragraph 2 above shall be irrevocable.

(5) Where—
(a) the time that has elapsed since the day on which an election had effect is—
(i) less than 3 months; or
(ii) more than 20 years;
(b) in a case to which paragraph (a)(i) above applies—
(i) no tax has become chargeable and no credit for input tax has been claimed by virtue of the election; and
(ii) no grant in relation to the land which is the subject of the election has been made which, by virtue of being a supply of the assets of a business to a person to whom the business (or part of it) is being transferred as a going concern, has been treated as neither a supply of goods nor a supply of services; and
(c) the person making the election obtains the written consent of the Commissioners;

the election shall be revoked, in a case to which paragraph (a)(i) above applies, from the date on which it was made, and in a case to which paragraph (a)(ii) above applies, from the date on which the written consent of the Commissioners is given or such later date as they may specify in their written consent.

[(5A) Where—
(a) an election under paragraph 2 above is made in relation to any land, and
(b) apart from this sub-paragraph, a grant in relation to that land would be taken to have been made (whether in whole or in part) before the time when the election takes effect,

that paragraph shall have effect, in relation to any supplies to which the grant gives rise which are treated for the purposes of this Act as taking place after that time, as if the grant had been made after that time.

(5B) Accordingly, the references in paragraph 2(9) above and sub-paragraph (9) below to grants being exempt or taxable shall be construed as references to supplies to which a grant gives rise being exempt or, as the case may be, taxable.]

(6) An election under paragraph 2 above shall have effect after 1st March 1995 only if—
(a) in the case of an election made before that date—
(i) it also had effect before that date; or
(ii) written notification of the election is given to the Commissioners not later than the end of the period of 30 days beginning with the day on which the election was made, or not later than the end of such longer period beginning with that day as the Commissioners may in any particular case allow, together with such information as the Commissioners may require;
(b) in the case of an election made on or after that date—
(i) written notification of the election is given to the Commissioners not later than the end of the period of 30 days beginning with the day on which the election is made, or not later than the end of such longer period beginning with that day as the Commissioners may in any particular case allow, together with such information as the Commissioners may require; and
(ii) in a case in which sub-paragraph (9) below requires the prior written permission of the Commissioners to be obtained, that permission has been given.]

(7) In paragraph 2 above and this paragraph "relevant associate", in relation to a body corporate by which an election under paragraph 2 above has been made in relation to any building or land, means a body corporate which under section 43—
(a) was treated as a member of the same group as the body corporate by which the election was made at the time when the election first had effect;
(b) has been so treated at any later time when the body corporate by which the election was made had an interest in, right over or licence to occupy the building or land (or any part of it); or
(c) has been treated as a member of the same group as a body corporate within paragraph (a) or (b) above or this paragraph at a time when that body corporate had an interest in, right over or licence to occupy the building or land (or any part of it).

[(7A) In paragraph 2 above—
(a) "houseboat" means a houseboat within the meaning of Group 9 of Schedule 8; and
(b) a houseboat is not a residential houseboat if residence in it throughout the year is prevented by the terms of a covenant, statutory planning consent or similar permission.]

[(8) In paragraph 2 above "relevant housing association" means—
(a) a registered social landlord within the meaning of Part I of the Housing Act 1996,
(b) a registered housing association within the meaning of the Housing Associations Act 1985 (Scottish registered housing associations), or
(c) a registered housing association within the meaning of Part II of the Housing (Northern Ireland) Order 1992 (Northern Irish registered housing associations).]

[(8A) …]

(9) Where a person who wishes to make an election in relation to any land (the relevant land) to have effect on or after 1st January 1992, has made, makes or intends to make, an exempt grant in relation to the relevant land at any time between 1st August 1989 and before the beginning of the day from which he wishes an election in relation to the relevant land to

have effect, he shall not make an election in relation to the relevant land unless [the conditions for automatic permission specified in a notice published by the Commissioners are met or] he obtains the prior written permission of the Commissioners, who shall only give such permission if they are satisfied having regard to all the circumstances of the case and in particular to—

(a) the total value of exempt grants in relation to the relevant land made or to be made before the day from which the person wishes his election to have effect;

(b) the expected total value of grants relating to the relevant land that would be taxable if the election were to have effect; and

(c) the total amount of input tax which has been incurred on or after 1st August 1989 or is likely to be incurred in relation to the relevant land,

that there would be secured a fair and reasonable attribution of the input tax mentioned in paragraph (c) above to grants in relation to the relevant land which, if the election were to have effect, would be taxable.

[3A.—(1) This paragraph shall have effect for the construction of paragraph 2(3AA)[, (3AAA) and (3B)] above.

[(2) For the purposes of paragraph 2(3AA)[, (3AAA) and (3B)] above, a grant made by any person in relation to any land is a grant made by a developer of that land if—

(a) the land or building or part of a building on that land is an asset falling in relation to that person to be treated as a capital item for the purposes of any regulations under section 26(3) and (4) providing for adjustments relating to the deduction of input tax; or

(b) that person or a person financing his development of the land for exempt use intended or expected that the land or a building or part of a building on, or to be constructed on, that land would become an asset falling in relation to—

(i) the grantor, or

(ii) any person to whom it was to be transferred either in the course of a supply or in the course of a transfer of a business or part of a business as a going concern,

to be treated as a capital item for the purposes of the regulations referred to in sub-paragraph (a) above,

unless the grant was made at a time falling after the expiry of the period over which such regulations require or allow adjustments relating to the deduction of input tax to be made as respects that item.]

[(2A) For the purposes of paragraph 2(3AA) where—

(a) by virtue of paragraph 2(3B), a person is treated as making the grant of the land giving rise to a supply made by him; and

(b) the grant is not a grant made by a developer of that land within sub-paragraph (2) above only because it is treated as made at a time falling after the expiry of the period for adjustments of input tax by virtue of regulations made under section 26(3) and (4),

the grant shall be treated as having been made by a developer of the land to which the grant relates.]

(3) In paragraph 2(3AA)[, (3AAA) and (3B)] above and this paragraph the references to a person's being responsible for financing the grantor's development of the land for exempt use are references to his being a person who, with the intention or in the expectation that the land will become, or continue (for a period at least) to be, exempt land—

(a) has provided finance for the grantor's development of the land; or

(b) has entered into any agreement, arrangement or understanding (whether or not legally enforceable) to provide finance for the grantor's development of the land.

(4) In sub-paragraph (3)(a) and (b) above the references to providing finance for the grantor's development of the land are references to doing any one or more of the following, that is to say—

(a) directly or indirectly providing funds for meeting the whole or any part of the cost of the grantor's development of the land;

(b) directly or indirectly procuring the provision of such funds by another;

(c) directly or indirectly providing funds for discharging, in whole or in part, any liability that has been or may be incurred by any person for or in connection with the raising of funds to meet the cost of the grantor's development of the land;

(d) directly or indirectly procuring that any such liability is or will be discharged, in whole or in part, by another.

(5) The references in sub-paragraph (4) above to the provision of funds for a purpose referred to in that sub-paragraph include references to—

(a) the making of a loan of funds that are or are to be used for that purpose;

(b) the provision of any guarantee or other security in relation to such a loan;

(c) the provision of any of the consideration for the issue of any shares or other securities issued wholly or partly for raising those funds; …

[(cc) the provision of any consideration for the acquisition by any person of any shares or other securities described in paragraph (c) above; or]

(d) any other transfer of assets or value as a consequence of which any of those funds are made available for that purpose.

[(6) In sub-paragraph (4) above the references to the grantor's development of the land are references to the acquisition by the grantor of the asset which—

(a) consists in the land or a building or part of a building on the land, and

(b) in relation to the grantor falls or, as the case may be, is intended or expected to fall to be treated for the purposes mentioned in sub-paragraph (2)(a) or (b) above as a capital item;

and for the purposes of this sub-paragraph the acquisition of an asset shall be taken to include its construction or reconstruction and the carrying out in relation to that asset of any other works by reference to which it falls or, as the case may be, is intended or expected to fall, to be treated for the purposes mentioned in sub-paragraph (2)(a) or (b) above as a capital item.]

(7) For the purposes of paragraph 2(3AA)[, (3AAA) and (3B)] above and this paragraph land is exempt land if, [at a time falling before the expiry of the period provided in regulations made under section 26(3) and (4) for the making of adjustments relating to the deduction of input tax as respects that land]—

(a) the grantor,

(b) a person responsible for financing the grantor's development of the land for exempt use, or

(c) a person connected with the grantor or with a person responsible for financing the grantor's development of the land for exempt use,

is in occupation of the land without being in occupation of it wholly or mainly for eligible purposes.

(8) For the purposes of this paragraph, but subject to sub-paragraphs (10) and (12) below, a person's occupation at any time of any land is not capable of being occupation for eligible purposes unless he is a taxable person at that time.

(9) Subject to sub-paragraphs (10) to (12) below, a taxable person in occupation of any land shall be taken for the purposes of this paragraph to be in occupation of that land for eligible purposes to the extent only that his occupation of that land is for the purpose of making supplies which—

(a) are or are to be made in the course or furtherance of a business carried on by him; and

(b) are supplies of such a description that any input tax of his which was wholly attributable to those supplies would be input tax for which he would be entitled to a credit.

(10) For the purposes of this paragraph—

(a) occupation of land by a body to which section 33 applies is occupation of the land for eligible purposes to the extent that the body occupies the land for purposes other than those of a business carried on by that body; and

(b) any occupation of land by a Government department (within the meaning of section 41) is occupation of the land for eligible purposes.

(11) For the purposes of this paragraph, where land of which any person is in occupation—

(a) is being held by that person in order to be put to use by him for particular purposes, and

(b) is not land of which he is in occupation for any other purpose,

that person shall be deemed, for so long as the conditions in paragraphs (a) and (b) above are satisfied, to be in occupation of that land for the purposes for which he proposes to use it.

(12) Sub-paragraphs (8) to (11) above shall have effect where land is in the occupation of a person who—

(a) is not a taxable person, but

(b) is a person whose supplies are treated for the purposes of this Act as supplies made by another person who is a taxable person, as if the person in occupation of the land and that other person were a single taxable person.

(13) For the purposes of this paragraph a person shall be taken to be in occupation of any land whether he occupies it alone or together with one or more other persons and whether he occupies all of that land or only part of it.

(14) Any question for the purposes of this paragraph whether one person is connected with another shall be determined in accordance with section 839 of the Taxes Act.]

4. …

5–9. (*Outside the scope of this work.*)

[966]

NOTES

Para 1: sub-para (6)(b) substituted by the Value Added Tax (Buildings and Land) Order 2002, SI 2002/1102, art 2

Para 2: words in square brackets in sub-para (1) substituted by the Value Added Tax (Buildings and Land) Order 1994, SI 1994/3013, art 2(a); sub-paras (2)(c), (d) and word in square brackets in sub-para (7) inserted by the Value Added Tax (Buildings and Land) Order 1995, SI 1995/279, arts 2, 3; sub-paras (2A), (2B) inserted, in relation to supplies made on or after 19 March 1997, by the Finance Act 1997, s 36; words in square brackets in sub-para (3)(a) substituted by the Value Added Tax (Registered Social Landlords) (No 2) Order 1997, SI 1997/51, art 2(a); sub-para (3AA) inserted, in relation to any supply made on or after 19 March 1997, other than a supply arising from a relevant pre-commencement grant, by the Finance Act 1997, s 37(2), (4)–(6); sub-para (3AAA), inserted, and words in first (outer) pair of square brackets in sub-para (3AA)(b) inserted, in relation to supplies, other than a supply arising from a relevant pre-commencement grant within the meaning of the Finance Act 1997, s 37, made on or after 10 March 1999, by the Value Added Tax (Buildings and Land) Order 1999, SI 1999/593, arts 2, 3; words in second (inner) pair of square brackets in sub-para (3AA)(b) substituted, and sub-para (3B) inserted, in relation to supplies made on or after 18 March 2004, by the Value Added Tax (Buildings and Land) Order 2004, SI 2004/778, arts 2–4; sub-para (3A) (as inserted by SI 1994/3013, art 2(a)), repealed, in relation to any supply made on or after 26 November 1996, by the Finance Act 1997, ss 37(1), 113, Sch 18, Pt IV(2).

Para 3: words in square brackets in sub-paras (3), (9) and sub-para (7A), inserted, and sub-paras (4)–(6) substituted, by SI 1995/279, arts 2, 4; sub-paras (5A), (5B) inserted, with retrospective, effect by the Finance Act 1997, s 35(2); sub-para (8) substituted by SI 1997/51, art 2(b); sub-para (8A) (as inserted by SI 1994/3013, art 2(b)), repealed, in relation to any supply made on or after 26 November 1996, by the Finance Act 1997, ss 37(1), 113, Sch 18, Part IV(2).

Para 3A: inserted, in relation to any supply made on or after 19 March 1997, other than a supply arising from a relevant pre-commencement grant, by the Finance Act 1997, s 37(3), (4)–(6); in sub-paras (1), (2), (3), (7) words ", (3AAA) and (3B)" in square brackets substituted, sub-para (2A) inserted, in sub-para (5)(c) word omitted repealed and sub-para (5)(cc) inserted, in relation to supplies made on or after 18 March 2004, by SI 2004/778, arts 2, 5(1), (2); words in second pair of square brackets in sub-para (7) inserted, and sub-paras (2), (6) substituted, in relation to supplies, other than a supply arising from a relevant pre-commencement grant within the meaning of the Finance Act 1997, s 37, made on or after 10 March 1999, by SI 1999/593, arts 2, 5.

Para 4: repealed by SI 1995/279, arts 2, 5.

(*Schs 10A–15 outside the scope of this work.*)

DISABILITY DISCRIMINATION ACT 1995

(1995 c 50)

ARRANGEMENT OF SECTIONS

PART I
DISABILITY

An Act to make it unlawful to discriminate against disabled persons in connection with employment, the provision of goods, facilities and services or the disposal or management of premises; to make provision about the employment of disabled persons; and to establish a National Disability Council

[8 November 1995]

NOTES

The Disability Rights Commission Act 1999, s 1, provides for the abolition of the National Disability Council and its replacement by a body known as the Disability Rights Commission.

Modification: this Act is modified, in its application to employment by the governing body of a school having a right to a delegated budget, by the Education (Modification of Enactments Relating to Employment) Order 1999, SI 1999/2256, art 3, Schedule.

PART I
DISABILITY

1 Meaning of "disability" and "disabled person"

(1) Subject to the provisions of Schedule 1, a person has a disability for the purposes of this Act if he has a physical or mental impairment which has a substantial and long-term adverse effect on his ability to carry out normal day-today activities.

PART I STATUTES

(2) In this Act "disabled person" means a person who has a disability.

[967]

NOTES

Commencement: 17 May 1996.

2 Past disabilities

(1) The provisions of this Part and Parts II [to 4] [and 5A] apply in relation to a person who has had a disability as they apply in relation to a person who has that disability.

(2) Those provisions are subject to the modifications made by Schedule 2.

(3) Any regulations or order made under this Act [by the Secretary of State, the Scottish Ministers or the National Assembly for Wales] may include provision with respect to persons who have had a disability.

(4) In any proceedings under Part [2, 3, 4 or 5A] of this Act, the question whether a person had a disability at a particular time ("the relevant time") shall be determined, for the purposes of this section, as if the provisions of, or made under, this Act in force when the act complained of was done had been in force at the relevant time.

(5) The relevant time may be a time before the passing of this Act.

[968]

NOTES

Commencement: 17 May 1996.

Sub-s (1): words in first pair of square brackets substituted by the Special Educational Needs and Disability Act 2001, s 38(1), (2); words in second pair of square brackets inserted by the Disability Discrimination Act 2005, s 19(1), Sch 1, Pt 1, paras 1, 2(1), (2).

Sub-s (3): words in square brackets inserted by the Disability Discrimination Act 2005, s 19(1), Sch 1, Pt 1, paras 1, 2(1), (3).

Sub-s (4): words in square brackets substituted by the Disability Discrimination Act 2005, s 19(1), Sch 1, Pt 1, paras 1, 2(1), (4).

3 Guidance

[(A1) The Secretary of State may issue guidance about matters to be taken into account in determining whether a person is a disabled person.]

(1) [Without prejudice to the generality of subsection (A1),] the Secretary of State may[, in particular,] issue guidance about the matters to be taken into account in determining—

- (a) whether an impairment has a substantial adverse effect on a person's ability to carry out normal day-to-day activities; or
- (b) whether such an impairment has a long-term effect.

(2) [Without prejudice to the generality of subsection (A1), guidance about the matters mentioned in subsection (1)] may, among other things, give examples of—

- (a) effects which it would be reasonable, in relation to particular activities, to regard for purposes of this Act as substantial adverse effects;
- (b) effects which it would not be reasonable, in relation to particular activities, to regard for such purposes as substantial adverse effects;
- (c) substantial adverse effects which it would be reasonable to regard, for such purposes, as long-term;
- (d) substantial adverse effects which it would not be reasonable to regard, for such purposes, as long-term.

(3) [An adjudicating body] determining, for any purpose of this Act, whether [a person is a disabled person], shall take into account any guidance which appears to it to be relevant.

[(3A) "Adjudicating body" means—

- (a) a court;
- (b) a tribunal; and
- (c) any other person who, or body which, may decide a claim under Part 4.]

(4) In preparing a draft of any guidance, the Secretary of State shall consult such persons as he considers appropriate.

(5) Where the Secretary of State proposes to issue any guidance, he shall publish a draft of it, consider any representations that are made to him about the draft and, if he thinks it appropriate, modify his proposals in the light of any of those representations.

(6) If the Secretary of State decides to proceed with any proposed guidance, he shall lay a draft of it before each House of Parliament.

(7) If, within the 40-day period, either House resolves not to approve the draft, the Secretary of State shall take no further steps in relation to the proposed guidance.

(8) If no such resolution is made within the 40-day period, the Secretary of State shall issue the guidance in the form of his draft.

(9) The guidance shall come into force on such date as the Secretary of State may appoint by order.

(10) Subsection (7) does not prevent a new draft of the proposed guidance from being laid before Parliament.

(11) The Secretary of State may—

(a) from time to time revise the whole or part of any guidance and re-issue it;

(b) by order revoke any guidance.

(12) In this section—

"40-day period", in relation to the draft of any proposed guidance, means—

(a) if the draft is laid before one House on a day later than the day on which it is laid before the other House, the period of 40 days beginning with the later of the two days, and

(b) in any other case, the period of 40 days beginning with the day on which the draft is laid before each House,

no account being taken of any period during which Parliament is dissolved or prorogued or during which both Houses are adjourned for more than 4 days; and

"guidance" means guidance issued by the Secretary of State under this section and includes guidance which has been revised and re-issued.

[969]

NOTES

Commencement: 17 May 1996.

Sub-s (A1): inserted by the Disability Discrimination Act 2005, s 19(1), Sch 1, Pt 1, paras 1, 3(1), (2).

Sub-s (1): words in square brackets inserted by the Disability Discrimination Act 2005, s 19(1), Sch 1, Pt 1, paras 1, 3(1), (3).

Sub-s (2): words in square brackets substituted by the Disability Discrimination Act 2005, s 19(1), Sch 1, Pt 1, paras 1, 3(1), (4).

Sub-s (3): words in first pair of square brackets substituted by the Special Educational Needs and Disability Act 2001, s 38(1), (3); words in second pair of square brackets substituted by the Disability Discrimination Act 2005, s 19(1), Sch 1, Pt 1, paras 1, 3(1), (5).

Sub-s (3A): inserted by the Special Educational Needs and Disability Act 2001, s 38(1), (4).

Orders: the Disability Discrimination (Guidance and Code of Practice) (Appointed Day) Order 1996, SI 1996/1996 (appointing 31 July 1996 for the purposes of sub-s (9) above for England and Wales); the Disability Discrimination (Guidance on the Definition of Disability) Appointed Day Order 2006, SI 2006/1005; the Disability Discrimination (Guidance on the Definition of Disability) Revocation Order 2006, SI 2006/1007.

PART II
[THE EMPLOYMENT FIELD [AND MEMBERS OF LOCALLY-ELECTABLE AUTHORITIES]

NOTES

Part heading: substituted by the Disability Discrimination Act 1995 (Amendment) Regulations 2003, SI 2003/1673, regs 3(1), 4(1); words in square brackets added by the Disability Discrimination Act 2005, s 19(1), Sch 1, Pt 1, paras 1, 4.

[Meaning of "discrimination" and "harassment"

3A Meaning of "discrimination"

(1) For the purposes of this Part, a person discriminates against a disabled person if—

(a) for a reason which relates to the disabled person's disability, he treats him less favourably than he treats or would treat others to whom that reason does not or would not apply, and
(b) he cannot show that the treatment in question is justified.

(2) For the purposes of this Part, a person also discriminates against a disabled person if he fails to comply with a duty to make reasonable adjustments imposed on him in relation to the disabled person.

(3) Treatment is justified for the purposes of subsection (1)(b) if, but only if, the reason for it is both material to the circumstances of the particular case and substantial.

(4) But treatment of a disabled person cannot be justified under subsection (3) if it amounts to direct discrimination falling within subsection (5).

(5) A person directly discriminates against a disabled person if, on the ground of the disabled person's disability, he treats the disabled person less favourably than he treats or would treat a person not having that particular disability whose relevant circumstances, including his abilities, are the same as, or not materially different from, those of the disabled person.

(6) If, in a case falling within subsection (1), a person is under a duty to make reasonable adjustments in relation to a disabled person but fails to comply with that duty, his treatment of that person cannot be justified under subsection (3) unless it would have been justified even if he had complied with that duty.]

[969A]

NOTES

Commencement: 3 July 2003 (so far as enabling anything to be done for the purposes of preparing and bringing into force on or after 1 October 2004 a code of practice under section 53A of this Act); 1 October 2004 (otherwise).

Inserted, together with preceding cross-heading and s 3B, by the Disability Discrimination Act 1995 (Amendment) Regulations 2003, SI 2003/1673, regs 3(1), 4(2).

[3B Meaning of "harassment"

(1) For the purposes of this Part, a person subjects a disabled person to harassment where, for a reason which relates to the disabled person's disability, he engages in unwanted conduct which has the purpose or effect of—
(a) violating the disabled person's dignity, or
(b) creating an intimidating, hostile, degrading, humiliating or offensive environment for him.

(2) Conduct shall be regarded as having the effect referred to in paragraph (a) or (b) of subsection (1) only if, having regard to all the circumstances, including in particular the perception of the disabled person, it should reasonably be considered as having that effect.]

[969B]

NOTES

Commencement: 3 July 2003 (so far as enabling anything to be done for the purposes of preparing and bringing into force on or after 1 October 2004 a code of practice under section 53A of this Act); 1 October 2004 (otherwise).

Inserted as noted to s 3A at **[969A]**.

[Employment

4 Employers: discrimination and harassment

(1) It is unlawful for an employer to discriminate against a disabled person—
(a) in the arrangements which he makes for the purpose of determining to whom he should offer employment;
(b) in the terms on which he offers that person employment; or
(c) by refusing to offer, or deliberately not offering, him employment.

(2) It is unlawful for an employer to discriminate against a disabled person whom he employs—
(a) in the terms of employment which he affords him;

(b) in the opportunities which he affords him for promotion, a transfer, training or receiving any other benefit;
(c) by refusing to afford him, or deliberately not affording him, any such opportunity; or
(d) by dismissing him, or subjecting him to any other detriment.

(3) It is also unlawful for an employer, in relation to employment by him, to subject to harassment—
(a) a disabled person whom he employs; or
(b) a disabled person who has applied to him for employment.

(4) Subsection (2) does not apply to benefits of any description if the employer is concerned with the provision (whether or not for payment) of benefits of that description to the public, or to a section of the public which includes the employee in question, unless—
(a) that provision differs in a material respect from the provision of the benefits by the employer to his employees;
(b) the provision of the benefits to the employee in question is regulated by his contract of employment; or
(c) the benefits relate to training.

(5) The reference in subsection (2)(d) to the dismissal of a person includes a reference—
(a) to the termination of that person's employment by the expiration of any period (including a period expiring by reference to an event or circumstance), not being a termination immediately after which the employment is renewed on the same terms; and
(b) to the termination of that person's employment by any act of his (including the giving of notice) in circumstances such that he is entitled to terminate it without notice by reason of the conduct of the employer.

(6) This section applies only in relation to employment at an establishment in Great Britain.]

[970]

NOTES

Commencement: 3 July 2003 (so far as enabling anything to be done for the purposes of preparing and bringing into force on or after 1 October 2004 a code of practice under section 53A of this Act); 1 October 2004 (otherwise).

Substituted, together with preceding cross-heading and ss 4A–4F and associated cross-headings, for ss 4–6 as originally enacted, in relation to England, Wales and Scotland, by the Disability Discrimination Act 1995 (Amendment) Regulations 2003, SI 2003/1673, regs 3(1), 5.

[4A Employers: duty to make adjustments

(1) Where—
(a) a provision, criterion or practice applied by or on behalf of an employer, or
(b) any physical feature of premises occupied by the employer,

places the disabled person concerned at a substantial disadvantage in comparison with persons who are not disabled, it is the duty of the employer to take such steps as it is reasonable, in all the circumstances of the case, for him to have to take in order to prevent the provision, criterion or practice, or feature, having that effect.

(2) In subsection (1), "the disabled person concerned" means—
(a) in the case of a provision, criterion or practice for determining to whom employment should be offered, any disabled person who is, or has notified the employer that he may be, an applicant for that employment;
(b) in any other case, a disabled person who is—
(i) an applicant for the employment concerned, or
(ii) an employee of the employer concerned.

(3) Nothing in this section imposes any duty on an employer in relation to a disabled person if the employer does not know, and could not reasonably be expected to know—
(a) in the case of an applicant or potential applicant, that the disabled person concerned is, or may be, an applicant for the employment; or
(b) in any case, that that person has a disability and is likely to be affected in the way mentioned in subsection (1).]

[971]

NOTES

Commencement: 3 July 2003 (so far as enabling anything to be done for the purposes of preparing and bringing into force on or after 1 October 2004 a code of practice under section 53A of this Act); 1 October 2004 (otherwise).

Substituted as noted to s 4 at **[970]**.

[Contract workers

4B Contract workers

(1) It is unlawful for a principal, in relation to contract work, to discriminate against a disabled person who is a contract worker (a "disabled contract worker")—

(a) in the terms on which he allows him to do that work;

(b) by not allowing him to do it or continue to do it;

(c) in the way he affords him access to any benefits or by refusing or deliberately omitting to afford him access to them; or

(d) by subjecting him to any other detriment.

(2) It is also unlawful for a principal, in relation to contract work, to subject a disabled contract worker to harassment.

(3) Subsection (1) does not apply to benefits of any description if the principal is concerned with the provision (whether or not for payment) of benefits of that description to the public, or to a section of the public which includes the contract worker in question, unless that provision differs in a material respect from the provision of the benefits by the principal to contract workers.

(4) This subsection applies to a disabled contract worker where, by virtue of—

(a) a provision, criterion or practice applied by or on behalf of all or most of the principals to whom he is or might be supplied, or

(b) a physical feature of premises occupied by such persons,

he is likely, on each occasion when he is supplied to a principal to do contract work, to be placed at a substantial disadvantage in comparison with persons who are not disabled which is the same or similar in each case.

(5) Where subsection (4) applies to a disabled contract worker, his employer must take such steps as he would have to take under section 4A if the provision, criterion or practice were applied by him or on his behalf or (as the case may be) if the premises were occupied by him.

(6) Section 4A applies to any principal, in relation to contract work, as if he were, or would be, the employer of the disabled contract worker and as if any contract worker supplied to do work for him were an employee of his.

(7) However, for the purposes of section 4A as applied by subsection (6), a principal is not required to take a step in relation to a disabled contract worker if under that section the disabled contract worker's employer is required to take the step in relation to him.

(8) This section applies only in relation to contract work done at an establishment in Great Britain (the provisions of section 68 about the meaning of "employment at an establishment in Great Britain" applying for the purposes of this subsection with the appropriate modifications).

(9) In this section—

"principal" means a person ("A") who makes work available for doing by individuals who are employed by another person who supplies them under a contract made with A;

"contract work" means work so made available; and

"contract worker" means any individual who is supplied to the principal under such a contract.]

[972]

NOTES

Commencement: 3 July 2003 (so far as enabling anything to be done for the purposes of preparing and bringing into force on or after 1 October 2004 a code of practice under section 53A of this Act); 1 October 2004 (otherwise).

Substituted as noted to s 4 at **[970]**.

[Office-holders

4C Office-holders: introductory

(1) Subject to subsection (5), sections 4D and 4E apply to an office or post if—

(a) no relevant provision of this Part applies in relation to an appointment to the office or post; and

(b) one or more of the conditions specified in subsection (3) is satisfied.

(2) The following are relevant provisions of this Part for the purposes of subsection (1)(a): section 4, section 4B, section 6A, section 7A, section 7C[, section 14C and section 15B(3)(b)].

(3) The conditions specified in this subsection are that—

(a) the office or post is one to which persons are appointed to discharge functions personally under the direction of another person, and in respect of which they are entitled to remuneration;

(b) the office or post is one to which appointments are made by a Minister of the Crown, a government department, the National Assembly for Wales or any part of the Scottish Administration;

(c) the office or post is one to which appointments are made on the recommendation of, or subject to the approval of, a person referred to in paragraph (b).

(4) For the purposes of subsection (3)(a) the holder of an office or post—

(a) is to be regarded as discharging his functions under the direction of another person if that other person is entitled to direct him as to when and where he discharges those functions;

(b) is not to be regarded as entitled to remuneration merely because he is entitled to payments—

(i) in respect of expenses incurred by him in carrying out the functions of the office or post, or

(ii) by way of compensation for the loss of income or benefits he would or might have received from any person had he not been carrying out the functions of the office or post.

(5) Sections 4D and 4E do not apply to—

(a) any office of the House of Commons held by a member of it,

(b) a life peerage within the meaning of the Life Peerages Act 1958, or any office of the House of Lords held by a member of it,

(c) any office mentioned in Schedule 2 (Ministerial offices) to the House of Commons Disqualification Act 1975,

(d) the offices of Leader of the Opposition, Chief Opposition Whip or Assistant Opposition Whip within the meaning of the Ministerial and other Salaries Act 1975,

(e) any office of the Scottish Parliament held by a member of it,

(f) a member of the Scottish Executive within the meaning of section 44 of the Scotland Act 1998, or a junior Scottish Minister within the meaning of section 49 of that Act,

(g) any office of the National Assembly for Wales held by a member of it,

(h) in England, any office of a county council, a London borough council, a district council or a parish council held by a member of it,

(i) in Wales, any office of a county council, a county borough council or a community council held by a member of it,

(j) in relation to a council constituted under section 2 of the Local Government etc (Scotland) Act 1994 or a community council established under section 51 of the Local Government (Scotland) Act 1973, any office of such a council held by a member of it,

(k) any office of the Greater London Authority held by a member of it,

(l) any office of the Common Council of the City of London held by a member of it,

(m) any office of the Council of the Isles of Scilly held by a member of it, or

(n) any office of a political party.

NOTES

Commencement: 3 July 2003 (so far as enabling anything to be done for the purposes of preparing and bringing into force on or after 1 October 2004 a code of practice under section 53A of this Act); 1 October 2004 (otherwise).

Substituted as noted to s 4 at **[970]**.

Sub-s (2): words in square brackets substituted by the Disability Discrimination Act 2005, s 19(1), Sch 1, Pt 1, paras 1, 5.

Sub-s (3): substituted by the Disability Discrimination Act 2005, s 19(1), Sch 1, Pt 1, paras 1, 6.

[4D Office-holders: discrimination and harassment

(1) It is unlawful for a relevant person, in relation to an appointment to an office or post to which this section applies, to discriminate against a disabled person—

(a) in the arrangements which he makes for the purpose of determining who should be offered the appointment;

(b) in the terms on which he offers him the appointment; or

(c) by refusing to offer him the appointment.

(2) It is unlawful for a relevant person, in relation to an appointment to an office or post to which this section applies and which satisfies the condition set out in section 4C(3)(c), to discriminate against a disabled person—

(a) in the arrangements which he makes for the purpose of determining who should be recommended or approved in relation to the appointment; or

(b) in making or refusing to make a recommendation, or giving or refusing to give an approval, in relation to the appointment.

(3) It is unlawful for a relevant person, in relation to a disabled person who has been appointed to an office or post to which this section applies, to discriminate against him—

(a) in the terms of the appointment;

(b) in the opportunities which he affords him for promotion, a transfer, training or receiving any other benefit, or by refusing to afford him any such opportunity;

(c) by terminating the appointment; or

(d) by subjecting him to any other detriment in relation to the appointment.

(4) It is also unlawful for a relevant person, in relation to an office or post to which this section applies, to subject to harassment a disabled person—

(a) who has been appointed to the office or post;

(b) who is seeking or being considered for appointment to the office or post; or

(c) who is seeking or being considered for a recommendation or approval in relation to an appointment to an office or post satisfying the condition set out in section 4C(3)(c).

(5) Subsection (3) does not apply to benefits of any description if the relevant person is concerned with the provision (for payment or not) of benefits of that description to the public, or a section of the public to which the disabled person belongs, unless—

(a) that provision differs in a material respect from the provision of the benefits to persons appointed to offices or posts which are the same as, or not materially different from, that to which the disabled person has been appointed;

(b) the provision of the benefits to the person appointed is regulated by the terms and conditions of his appointment; or

(c) the benefits relate to training.

(6) In subsection (3)(c) the reference to the termination of the appointment includes a reference—

(a) to the termination of the appointment by the expiration of any period (including a period expiring by reference to an event or circumstance), not being a termination immediately after which the appointment is renewed on the same terms and conditions; and

(b) to the termination of the appointment by any act of the person appointed (including the giving of notice) in circumstances such that he is entitled to terminate the appointment by reason of the conduct of the relevant person.

(7) In this section—

(a) references to making a recommendation include references to making a negative recommendation; and

(b) references to refusal include references to deliberate omission.]

[972B]

NOTES

Commencement: 3 July 2003 (so far as enabling anything to be done for the purposes of preparing and bringing into force on or after 1 October 2004 a code of practice under section 53A of this Act); 1 October 2004 (otherwise).

Substituted as noted to s 4 at **[970]**.

[4E Office-holders: duty to make adjustments

(1) Where—

(a) a provision, criterion or practice applied by or on behalf of a relevant person, or

(b) any physical feature of premises—

(i) under the control of a relevant person, and

(ii) at or from which the functions of an office or post to which this section applies are performed,

places the disabled person concerned at a substantial disadvantage in comparison with persons who are not disabled, it is the duty of the relevant person to take such steps as it is reasonable, in all the circumstances of the case, for him to have to take in order to prevent the provision, criterion or practice, or feature, having that effect.

(2) In this section, "the disabled person concerned" means—

(a) in the case of a provision, criterion or practice for determining who should be appointed to, or recommended or approved in relation to, an office or post to which this section applies, any disabled person who—

(i) is, or has notified the relevant person that he may be, seeking appointment to, or (as the case may be) seeking a recommendation or approval in relation to, that office or post, or

(ii) is being considered for appointment to, or (as the case may be) for a recommendation or approval in relation to, that office or post;

(b) in any other case, a disabled person—

(i) who is seeking or being considered for appointment to, or a recommendation or approval in relation to, the office or post concerned, or

(ii) who has been appointed to the office or post concerned.

(3) Nothing in this section imposes any duty on the relevant person in relation to a disabled person if the relevant person does not know, and could not reasonably be expected to know—

(a) in the case of a person who is being considered for, or is or may be seeking, appointment to, or a recommendation or approval in relation to, an office or post, that the disabled person concerned—

(i) is, or may be, seeking appointment to, or (as the case may be) seeking a recommendation or approval in relation to, that office or post, or

(ii) is being considered for appointment to, or (as the case may be) for a recommendation or approval in relation to, that office or post; or

(b) in any case, that that person has a disability and is likely to be affected in the way mentioned in subsection (1).]

[972C]

NOTES

Commencement: 3 July 2003 (so far as enabling anything to be done for the purposes of preparing and bringing into force on or after 1 October 2004 a code of practice under section 53A of this Act); 1 October 2004 (otherwise).

Substituted as noted to s 4 at **[970]**.

[4F Office-holders: supplementary

(1) In sections 4C to 4E, appointment to an office or post does not include election to an office or post.

(2) In sections 4D and 4E, "relevant person" means—

(a) in a case relating to an appointment to an office or post, the person with power to make that appointment;

(b) in a case relating to the making of a recommendation or the giving of an approval in relation to an appointment, a person or body referred to in section 4C(3)(b) with power to make that recommendation or (as the case may be) to give that approval;

(c) in a case relating to a term of an appointment, the person with power to determine that term;

(d) in a case relating to a working condition afforded in relation to an appointment—

(i) the person with power to determine that working condition; or

(ii) where there is no such person, the person with power to make the appointment;

(e) in a case relating to the termination of an appointment, the person with power to terminate the appointment;

(f) in a case relating to the subjection of a disabled person to any other detriment or to harassment, any person or body falling within one or more of paragraphs (a) to (e) in relation to such cases as are there mentioned.

(3) In subsection (2)(d), "working condition" includes—

(a) any opportunity for promotion, a transfer, training or receiving any other benefit; and

(b) any physical feature of premises at or from which the functions of an office or post are performed.]

[972D]–[978]

NOTES

Commencement: 3 July 2003 (so far as enabling anything to be done for the purposes of preparing and bringing into force on or after 1 October 2004 a code of practice under section 53A of this Act); 1 October 2004 (otherwise).

Substituted as noted to s 4 at **[970]**.

4G–12 *(Ss 4G–6C, 7A–7D, outside the scope of this work; s 7 repealed in relation to England, Wales and Scotland, by the Disability Discrimination Act 1995 (Amendment) Regulations 2003, SI 2003/1673, regs 3(1), 7; s 8 renumbered as s 17A and moved together with preceding cross-heading to appear after s 17 in relation to England, Wales and Scotland, by the Disability Discrimination Act 1995 (Amendment) Regulations 2003, SI 2003/1673, regs 3(1), 9(1); s 9 repealed in relation to England, Wales and Scotland by SI 2003/1673, regs 3(1), 10; s 10 renumbered as s 18C and moved together with preceding cross-heading to appear after s 18B in relation to England, Wales and Scotland, by SI 2003/1673, regs 3(1), 9(1); ss 11, 12 repealed in relation to England, Wales and Scotland by SI 2003/1673, regs 3(1), 12.)*

[Trade and professional bodies

13, 14 *(Outside the scope of this work.)*

[14A Qualifications bodies: discrimination and harassment

(1) It is unlawful for a qualifications body to discriminate against a disabled person—

(a) in the arrangements which it makes for the purpose of determining upon whom to confer a professional or trade qualification;

(b) in the terms on which it is prepared to confer a professional or trade qualification on him;

(c) by refusing or deliberately omitting to grant any application by him for such a qualification; or

(d) by withdrawing such a qualification from him or varying the terms on which he holds it.

(2) It is also unlawful for a qualifications body, in relation to a professional or trade qualification conferred by it, to subject to harassment a disabled person who holds or applies for such a qualification.

(3) In determining for the purposes of subsection (1) whether the application by a qualifications body of a competence standard to a disabled person constitutes discrimination within the meaning of section 3A, the application of the standard is justified for the purposes of section 3A(1)(b) if, but only if, the qualifications body can show that—

(a) the standard is, or would be, applied equally to persons who do not have his particular disability; and

(b) its application is a proportionate means of achieving a legitimate aim.

(4) For the purposes of subsection (3)—

(a) section 3A(2) (and (6)) does not apply; and

(b) section 3A(4) has effect as if the reference to section 3A(3) were a reference to subsection (3) of this section.

(5) In this section and section 14B—

"qualifications body" means any authority or body which can confer a professional or trade qualification, but it does not include—

(a) a responsible body (within the meaning of Chapter 1 or 2 of Part 4),

(b) a local education authority in England or Wales, or

(c) an education authority (within the meaning of section 135(1) of the Education (Scotland) Act 1980);

"confer" includes renew or extend;

"professional or trade qualification" means an authorisation, qualification, recognition, registration, enrolment, approval or certification which is needed for, or facilitates engagement in, a particular profession or trade;

"competence standard" means an academic, medical or other standard applied by or on behalf of a qualifications body for the purpose of determining whether or not a person has a particular level of competence or ability.]

[979]

NOTES

Commencement: 3 July 2003 (so far as enabling anything to be done for the purposes of preparing and bringing into force on or after 1 October 2004 a code of practice under section 53A of this Act); 1 October 2004 (otherwise).

Substituted, together with preceding cross-heading and ss 13, 14, 14B–14D and associated cross-headings, for ss 13–15 as originally enacted, in relation to England, Wales and Scotland, by the Disability Discrimination Act 1995 (Amendment) Regulations 2003, SI 2003/1673, regs 3(1), 13.

[14B Qualifications bodies: duty to make adjustments

(1) Where—

(a) a provision, criterion or practice, other than a competence standard, applied by or on behalf of a qualifications body; or

(b) any physical feature of premises occupied by a qualifications body,

places the disabled person concerned at a substantial disadvantage in comparison with persons who are not disabled, it is the duty of the qualifications body to take such steps as it is reasonable, in all the circumstances of the case, for it to have to take in order to prevent the provision, criterion or practice, or feature, having that effect.

(2) In this section "the disabled person concerned" means—

(a) in the case of a provision, criterion or practice for determining on whom a professional or trade qualification is to be conferred, any disabled person who is, or has notified the qualifications body that he may be, an applicant for the conferment of that qualification;

(b) in any other case, a disabled person who—

(i) holds a professional or trade qualification conferred by the qualifications body, or

(ii) applies for a professional or trade qualification which it confers.

(3) Nothing in this section imposes a duty on a qualifications body in relation to a disabled person if the body does not know, and could not reasonably be expected to know—

(a) in the case of an applicant or potential applicant, that the disabled person concerned is, or may be, an applicant for the conferment of a professional or trade qualification; or

(b) in any case, that that person has a disability and is likely to be affected in the way mentioned in subsection (1).]

[980]

NOTES

Commencement: 3 July 2003 (so far as enabling anything to be done for the purposes of preparing and bringing into force on or after 1 October 2004 a code of practice under section 53A of this Act); 1 October 2004 (otherwise).

Substituted as noted to s 14A at **[979]**.

[Practical work experience

14C Practical work experience: discrimination and harassment

(1) It is unlawful, in the case of a disabled person seeking or undertaking a work placement, for a placement provider to discriminate against him—

(a) in the arrangements which he makes for the purpose of determining who should be offered a work placement;

(b) in the terms on which he affords him access to any work placement or any facilities concerned with such a placement;

(c) by refusing or deliberately omitting to afford him such access;

(d) by terminating the placement; or

(e) by subjecting him to any other detriment in relation to the placement.

(2) It is also unlawful for a placement provider, in relation to a work placement, to subject to harassment—

(a) a disabled person to whom he is providing a placement; or

(b) a disabled person who has applied to him for a placement.

[(3) This section and section 14D do not apply—

(a) to anything which is unlawful under any provision of section 4, sections 19 to 21A, sections 21F to 21J or Part 4; or

(b) to anything which would be unlawful under any such provision but for the operation of any provision in or made under this Act.]

(4) In this section and section 14D—

"work placement" means practical work experience undertaken for a limited period for the purposes of a person's vocational training;

"placement provider" means any person who provides a work placement to a person whom he does not employ.

(5) This section and section 14D do not apply to a work placement undertaken in any of the naval, military and air forces of the Crown.]

[980A]

NOTES

Commencement: 3 July 2003 (so far as enabling anything to be done for the purposes of preparing and bringing into force on or after 1 October 2004 a code of practice under section 53A of this Act); 1 October 2004 (otherwise).

Substituted as noted to s 14A at **[979]**.

Sub-s (3): substituted by the Disability Discrimination Act 2005, s 19(1), Sch 1, Pt 1, paras 1, 6.

[14D Practical work experience: duty to make adjustments

(1) Where—

(a) a provision, criterion or practice applied by or on behalf of a placement provider, or

(b) any physical feature of premises occupied by the placement provider,

places the disabled person concerned at a substantial disadvantage in comparison with persons who are not disabled, it is the duty of the placement provider to take such steps as it is reasonable, in all the circumstances of the case, for him to have to take in order to prevent the provision, criterion or practice, or feature, having that effect.

(2) In this section, "the disabled person concerned" means—

(a) in the case of a provision, criterion or practice for determining to whom a work placement should be offered, any disabled person who is, or has notified the placement provider that he may be, an applicant for that work placement;

(b) in any other case, a disabled person who is—

(i) an applicant for the work placement concerned, or

(ii) undertaking a work placement with the placement provider.

(3) Nothing in this section imposes any duty on a placement provider in relation to the disabled person concerned if he does not know, and could not reasonably be expected to know—

(a) in the case of an applicant or potential applicant, that the disabled person concerned is, or may be, an applicant for the work placement; or

(b) in any case, that that person has a disability and is likely to be affected in the way mentioned in subsection (1).]

[980B]–[981]

NOTES

Commencement: 3 July 2003 (so far as enabling anything to be done for the purposes of preparing and bringing into force on or after 1 October 2004 a code of practice under section 53A of this Act); 1 October 2004 (otherwise).

Substituted as noted to s 14A at **[979]**.

15, 16 (*S 15 substituted as noted to s 14A at* **[979]**; *s 16 renumbered as s 18A and moved to appear after s 18 in relation to England, Wales and Scotland, by the Disability Discrimination Act 1995 (Amendment) Regulations 2003, SI 2003/1673, regs 3(1), 14(2).*)

[Other unlawful acts

16A Relationships which have come to an end

(1) This section applies where—

(a) there has been a relevant relationship between a disabled person and another person ("the relevant person"), and

(b) the relationship has come to an end.

(2) In this section a "relevant relationship" is—

(a) a relationship during the course of which an act of discrimination against, or harassment of, one party to the relationship by the other party to it is unlawful under any preceding provision of this Part[, other than sections 15B and 15C]; or

(b) a relationship between a person providing employment services … and a person receiving such services.

(3) It is unlawful for the relevant person—

(a) to discriminate against the disabled person by subjecting him to a detriment, or

(b) to subject the disabled person to harassment,

where the discrimination or harassment arises out of and is closely connected to the relevant relationship.

(4) This subsection applies where—

(a) a provision, criterion or practice applied by the relevant person to the disabled person in relation to any matter arising out of the relevant relationship, or

(b) a physical feature of premises which are occupied by the relevant person,

places the disabled person at a substantial disadvantage in comparison with persons who are not disabled, but are in the same position as the disabled person in relation to the relevant person.

(5) Where subsection (4) applies, it is the duty of the relevant person to take such steps as it is reasonable, in all the circumstances of the case, for him to have to take in order to prevent the provision, practice or criterion, or feature, having that effect.

(6) Nothing in subsection (5) imposes any duty on the relevant person if he does not know, and could not reasonably be expected to know, that the disabled person has a disability and is likely to be affected in the way mentioned in that subsection.

(7) In subsection (2), reference to an act of discrimination or harassment which is unlawful includes, in the case of a relationship which has come to an end before the commencement of this section, reference to such an act which would, after the commencement of this section, be unlawful.]

[982]

NOTES

Commencement: 3 July 2003 (so far as enabling anything to be done for the purposes of preparing and bringing into force on or after 1 October 2004 a code of practice under section 53A of this Act); 1 October 2004 (otherwise).

Inserted, together with preceding cross-heading and ss 16B, 16C, by the Disability Discrimination Act 1995 (Amendment) Regulations 2003, SI 2003/1673, regs 3(1), 15(1).

Sub-s (2): words in square brackets in para (a) inserted and words omitted from para (b) repealed by the Disability Discrimination Act 2005, s 19, Sch 1, Pt 1, paras 1, 7, Sch 2.

[16B Discriminatory advertisements

[(1) It is unlawful for a person to publish or cause to be published an advertisement which—

(a) invites applications for a relevant appointment or benefit; and

(b) indicates, or might reasonably be understood to indicate, that an application will or may be determined to any extent by reference to—

(i) the applicant not having any disability, or any particular disability,

(ii) the applicant not having had any disability, or any particular disability, or

(iii) any reluctance of the person determining the application to comply with a duty to make reasonable adjustments or (in relation to employment services) with the duty imposed by section 21(1) as modified by section 21A(6).]

(2) Subsection (1) does not apply where it would not in fact be unlawful under this Part or, to the extent that it relates to the provision of employment services, Part 3 for an application to be determined in the manner indicated (or understood to be indicated) in the advertisement.

[(2A) A person who publishes an advertisement of the kind described in subsection (1) shall not be subject to any liability under subsection (1) in respect of the publication of the advertisement if he proves—

(a) that the advertisement was published in reliance on a statement made to him by the person who caused it to be published to the effect that, by reason of the operation of subsection (2), the publication would not be unlawful; and

(b) that it was reasonable for him to rely on the statement.

(2B) A person who knowingly or recklessly makes a statement such as is mentioned in subsection (2A)(a) which in a material respect is false or misleading commits an offence, and shall be liable on summary conviction to a fine not exceeding level 5 on the standard scale.]

[(2C) Subsection (1) does not apply in relation to an advertisement so far as it invites persons to apply, in their capacity as members of an authority to which sections 15B and 15C apply, for a relevant appointment or benefit which the authority is intending to make or confer.]

(3) In [this section], "relevant appointment or benefit" means—

(a) any employment, promotion or transfer of employment;

(b) membership of, or a benefit under, an occupational pension scheme;

(c) an appointment to any office or post to which section 4D applies;

(d) any partnership in a firm (within the meaning of section 6A);

(e) any tenancy or pupillage (within the meaning of section 7A or 7C);

(f) any membership of a trade organisation (within the meaning of section 13);

(g) any professional or trade qualification (within the meaning of section 14A);

(h) any work placement (within the meaning of section 14C);

(i) any employment services …

(4) In this section, "advertisement" includes every form of advertisement or notice, whether to the public or not.

[(5) Proceedings in respect of a contravention of subsection (1) may be brought only—

(a) by the Commission for Equality and Human Rights, and

(b) in accordance with section 25 of the Equality Act 2006.]]

[982A]

NOTES

Commencement: 3 July 2003 (so far as enabling anything to be done for the purposes of preparing and bringing into force on or after 1 October 2004 a code of practice under section 53A of this Act); 1 October 2004 (otherwise).

Inserted as noted to s 16A at **[982]**.

Sub-s (1): substituted by the Disability Discrimination Act 2005, s 10(1), (2).

Sub-ss (2A)–(2C): inserted by the Disability Discrimination Act 2005, ss 10(1), (3), 19(1), Sch 1, Pt 1, paras 1, 8(1), (2).

Sub-s (3): words in square brackets substituted and words omitted repealed by the Disability Discrimination Act 2005, ss 10(1), (4), 19, Sch 1, Pt 1, paras 1, 8(1), (3), Sch 2.

Sub-s (5): added by the Equality Act 2006, s 40, Sch 3, paras 41, 42, as from a day to be appointed under s 93 of that Act.

[16C Instructions and pressure to discriminate

(1) It is unlawful for a person—

(a) who has authority over another person, or

(b) in accordance with whose wishes that other person is accustomed to act,

to instruct him to do any act which is unlawful under this Part or, to the extent that it relates to the provision of employment services, Part 3, or to procure or attempt to procure the doing by him of any such act.

(2) It is also unlawful to induce, or attempt to induce, a person to do any act which contravenes this Part or, to the extent that it relates to the provision of employment services, Part 3 by—

(a) providing or offering to provide him with any benefit, or

(b) subjecting or threatening to subject him to any detriment.

(3) An attempted inducement is not prevented from falling within subsection (2) because it is not made directly to the person in question, if it is made in such a way that he is likely to hear of it.

[(4) Proceedings in respect of a contravention of this section may be brought only—

(a) by the Commission for Equality and Human Rights, and

(b) in accordance with section 25 of the Equality Act 2006.]]

[982B]

NOTES

Commencement: 3 July 2003 (so far as enabling anything to be done for the purposes of preparing and bringing into force on or after 1 October 2004 a code of practice under section 53A of this Act); 1 October 2004 (otherwise).

Inserted as noted to s 16A at **[982]**.

Sub-s (4): added by the Equality Act 2006, s 40, Sch 3, paras 41, 43, as from a day to be appointed under s 93 of that Act.

17 (*Repealed, together with preceding cross-heading, in relation to England, Wales and Scotland, by the Disability Discrimination Act 1995 (Amendment) Regulations 2003, SI 2003/2770, reg 4 (1).*)

[Enforcement etc

[17A] Enforcement, remedies and procedure

(1) A complaint by any person that another person—

(a) has discriminated against him[, or subjected him to harassment,] in a way which is unlawful under this Part, or

(b) is, by virtue of section 57 or 58, to be treated as having [done so],

may be presented to an [employment tribunal].

[(1A) Subsection (1) does not apply to a complaint under section 14A(1) or (2) of an act in respect of which an appeal, or proceedings in the nature of an appeal, may be brought under any enactment.

(1B) …

(1C) Where, on the hearing of a complaint under subsection (1), the complainant proves facts from which the tribunal could, apart from this subsection, conclude in the absence of an adequate explanation that the respondent has acted in a way which is unlawful under this Part, the tribunal shall uphold the complaint unless the respondent proves that he did not so act.]

(2) Where an [employment tribunal] finds that a complaint presented to it under this section is well-founded, it shall take such of the following steps as it considers just and equitable—

(a) making a declaration as to the rights of the complainant and the respondent in relation to the matters to which the complaint relates;

(b) ordering the respondent to pay compensation to the complainant;

(c) recommending that the respondent take, within a specified period, action appearing to the tribunal to be reasonable, in all the circumstances of the case, for the purpose of obviating or reducing the adverse effect on the complainant of any matter to which the complaint relates.

(3) Where a tribunal orders compensation under subsection (2)(b), the amount of the compensation shall be calculated by applying the principles applicable to the calculation of damages in claims in tort or (in Scotland) in reparation for breach of statutory duty.

(4) For the avoidance of doubt it is hereby declared that compensation in respect of discrimination in a way which is unlawful under this Part may include compensation for injury to feelings whether or not it includes compensation under any other head.

(5) If the respondent to a complaint fails, without reasonable justification, to comply with a recommendation made by an [employment tribunal] under subsection (2)(c) the tribunal may, if it thinks it just and equitable to do so—

(a) increase the amount of compensation required to be paid to the complainant in respect of the complaint, where an order was made under subsection (2)(b); or

(b) make an order under subsection (2)(b).

(6) Regulations may make provision—

(a) for enabling a tribunal, where an amount of compensation falls to be awarded under subsection (2)(b), to include in the award interest on that amount; and

(b) specifying, for cases where a tribunal decides that an award is to include an amount in respect of interest, the manner in which and the periods and rate by reference to which the interest is to be determined.

(7) Regulations may modify the operation of any order made under [section 14 of [the Employment Tribunals Act 1996]] (power to make provision as to interest on sums payable in pursuance of [employment tribunal] decisions) to the extent that it relates to an award of compensation under subsection (2)(b).

(8) Part I of Schedule 3 makes further provision about the enforcement of this Part and about procedure.

[983]

NOTES

Commencement: 2 December 1996 (sub-ss (1)–(5), (8)); 6 June 1996 (sub-ss (6), (7)).

Originally enacted as s 8, but renumbered as s 17A, in relation to England, Wales and Scotland, by the Disability Discrimination Act 1995 (Amendment) Regulations 2003, SI 2003/1673, regs 3(1), 9(1).

Sub-s (1): words in square brackets in para (a) inserted and words in square brackets in para (b) substituted, in relation to England, Wales and Scotland, by SI 2003/1673, regs 3(1), 9(2); words in third pair of square brackets substituted by the Employment Rights (Dispute Resolution) Act 1998, s 1(2)(a).

Sub-ss (1A), (1C): inserted, together with sub-s (1B), in relation to England, Wales and Scotland, by SI 2003/1673, regs 3(1), 9(3).

Sub-s (1B): inserted, together with sub-ss (1A), (1B), in relation to England, Wales and Scotland, by SI 2003/1673, regs 3(1), 9(3); repealed by the Disability Discrimination Act 2005, s 19, Sch 1, Pt 1, paras 1, 9, Sch 2.

Sub-ss (2), (5): words in square brackets substituted by the Employment Rights (Dispute Resolution) Act 1998, s 1(2)(a).

Sub-s (7): words in first (outer) pair of square brackets substituted by the Employment Tribunals Act 1996, s 43, Sch 1, para 12(1), (2); words in second (inner) pair and third pair of square brackets substituted by the Employment Rights (Dispute Resolution) Act 1998, s 1(2)(a), (c).

By virtue of the Employment Rights (Dispute Resolution) Act 1998, s 1(2), the Industrial Tribunals Act 1996 shall be cited as the Employment Tribunals Act 1996; the reference in the above note to the Industrial Tribunals Act 1996 has been changed accordingly.

[17B Enforcement of sections [16B(1)] and 16C

(1) Only the Disability Rights Commission may bring proceedings in respect of a contravention of section [16B(1)] (discriminatory advertisements) or section 16C (instructions and pressure to discriminate).

(2) The Commission shall bring any such proceedings in accordance with subsection (3) or (4).

(3) The Commission may present to an employment tribunal a complaint that a person has done an act which is unlawful under section [16B(1)] or 16C; and if the tribunal finds that the complaint is well-founded it shall make a declaration to that effect.

(4) Where—

(a) a tribunal has made a finding pursuant to subsection (3) that a person has done an act which is unlawful under section [16B(1)] or 16C,

(b) that finding has become final, and

(c) it appears to the Commission that, unless restrained, he is likely to do a further act which is unlawful under [section 16B(1) or (as the case may be) section 16C],

the Commission may apply to a county court for an injunction, or (in Scotland) to a sheriff court for an interdict, restraining him from doing such an act; and the court, if satisfied that the application is well-founded, may grant the injunction or interdict in the terms applied for or in more limited terms.

(5) A finding of a tribunal under subsection (3) in respect of any act shall, if it has become final, be treated as conclusive by a county court or sheriff court upon an application under subsection (4).

(6) A finding of a tribunal becomes final for the purposes of this section when an appeal against it is dismissed, withdrawn or abandoned or when the time for appealing expires without an appeal having been brought.

(7) An employment tribunal shall not consider a complaint under subsection (3) unless it is presented before the end of the period of six months beginning when the act to which it relates was done; and a county court or sheriff court shall not consider an application under subsection (4) unless it is made before the end of the period of five years so beginning.

(8) A court or tribunal may consider any such complaint or application which is out of time if, in all the circumstances of the case, it considers that it is just and equitable to do so.

(9) The provisions of paragraph 3(3) and (4) of Schedule 3 apply for the purposes of subsection (7) as they apply for the purposes of paragraph 3(1) of that Schedule.]

[983A]

NOTES

Commencement: 3 July 2003 (so far as enabling anything to be done for the purposes of preparing and bringing into force on or after 1 October 2004 a code of practice under section 53A of this Act); 1 October 2004 (otherwise).

Repealed by the Equality Act 2006, ss 40, 91, Sch 3, paras 41, 44, Sch 4, as from a day to be appointed under s 93 of that Act.

Inserted, together with s 17C, in relation to England, Wales and Scotland, by the Disability Discrimination Act 1995 (Amendment) Regulations 2003, SI 2003/1673, regs 3(1), 16(1).

Section heading: number in square brackets substituted by the Disability Discrimination Act 2005, s 19(1), Sch 1, Pt 1, paras 1, 10(1), (2).

Sub-ss (1), (3): number in square brackets substituted by the Disability Discrimination Act 2005, s 19(1), Sch 1, Pt 1, paras 1, 10(1), (2).

Sub-s (4): number and words in square brackets substituted by the Disability Discrimination Act 2005, s 19(1), Sch 1, Pt 1, paras 1, 10.

[17C Validity of contracts, collective agreements and rules of undertakings

Schedule 3A shall have effect.]

[983B]–[984]

NOTES

Commencement: 3 July 2003 (so far as enabling anything to be done for the purposes of preparing and bringing into force on or after 1 October 2004 a code of practice under section 53A of this Act); 1 October 2004 (otherwise).

Inserted as noted to s 17B at **[980A]**.

[Supplementary and general]

NOTES

Cross-heading inserted, in relation to England, Wales and Scotland, by the Disability Discrimination Act 1995 (Amendment) Regulations 2003, SI 2003/1673, regs 3(1), 17(1).

18 *(Repealed by the Disability Discrimination Act 2005, ss 11(1), 19(2), Sch 2.)*

[18A] Alterations to premises occupied under leases

(1) This section applies where—

(a) [a person to whom a duty to make reasonable adjustments applies] ("the occupier") occupies premises under a lease;

(b) but for this section, the occupier would not be entitled to make a particular alteration to the premises; and

(c) the alteration is one which the occupier proposes to make in order to comply with [that duty].

(2) Except to the extent to which it expressly so provides, the lease shall have effect by virtue of this subsection as if it provided—

(a) for the occupier to be entitled to make the alteration with the written consent of the lessor;

(b) for the occupier to have to make a written application to the lessor for consent if he wishes to make the alteration;

(c) if such an application is made, for the lessor not to withhold his consent unreasonably; and

(d) for the lessor to be entitled to make his consent subject to reasonable conditions.

(3) In this section—

"lease" includes a tenancy, sub-lease or sub-tenancy and an agreement for a lease, tenancy, sub-lease or sub-tenancy; and

"sub-lease" and "sub-tenancy" have such meaning as may be prescribed.

(4) If the terms and conditions of a lease—

(a) impose conditions which are to apply if the occupier alters the premises, or

(b) entitle the lessor to impose conditions when consenting to the occupier's altering the premises,

the occupier is to be treated for the purposes of subsection (1) as not being entitled to make the alteration.

(5) Part I of Schedule 4 supplements the provisions of this section.

[984A]

NOTES

Commencement: sub-ss (1)–(4) (except for the definitions of "sub-lease" and "sub-tenancy" in sub-s (3)) were brought into force on 2 December 1996; the definitions noted above in sub-s (3) were brought into force on 17 May 1996; sub-s (5) was brought into force on 17 May 1996 for certain purposes, 6 June 1996 for certain purposes, and 2 December 1996 for remaining purposes.

Originally enacted as s 16, but renumbered as s 18A, in relation to England, Wales and Scotland, by the Disability Discrimination Act 1995 (Amendment) Regulations 2003, SI 2003/1673, regs 3(1), 14(2).

Sub-s (1): words in square brackets substituted, in relation to England, Wales and Scotland, by SI 2003.1673, regs 3(1), 14(3).

Regulations: the Disability Discrimination (Employment Field) (Leasehold Premises) Regulations 2004, SI 2004/153.

[18B Reasonable adjustments: supplementary

(1) In determining whether it is reasonable for a person to have to take a particular step in order to comply with a duty to make reasonable adjustments, regard shall be had, in particular, to—

(a) the extent to which taking the step would prevent the effect in relation to which the duty is imposed;

(b) the extent to which it is practicable for him to take the step;

(c) the financial and other costs which would be incurred by him in taking the step and the extent to which taking it would disrupt any of his activities;

(d) the extent of his financial and other resources;

(e) the availability to him of financial or other assistance with respect to taking the step;

(f) the nature of his activities and the size of his undertaking;

(g) where the step would be taken in relation to a private household, the extent to which taking it would—

(i) disrupt that household, or

(ii) disturb any person residing there.

(2) The following are examples of steps which a person may need to take in relation to a disabled person in order to comply with a duty to make reasonable adjustments—

(a) making adjustments to premises;

(b) allocating some of the disabled person's duties to another person;

(c) transferring him to fill an existing vacancy;

(d) altering his hours of working or training;

(e) assigning him to a different place of work or training;

(f) allowing him to be absent during working or training hours for rehabilitation, assessment or treatment;
(g) giving, or arranging for, training or mentoring (whether for the disabled person or any other person);
(h) acquiring or modifying equipment;
(i) modifying instructions or reference manuals;
(j) modifying procedures for testing or assessment;
(k) providing a reader or interpreter;
(l) providing supervision or other support.

(3) For the purposes of a duty to make reasonable adjustments, where under any binding obligation a person is required to obtain the consent of another person to any alteration of the premises occupied by him—
(a) it is always reasonable for him to have to take steps to obtain that consent; and
(b) it is never reasonable for him to have to make that alteration before that consent is obtained.

(4) The steps referred to in subsection (3)(a) shall not be taken to include an application to a court or tribunal.

(5) In subsection (3), "binding obligation" means a legally binding obligation (not contained in a lease (within the meaning of section 18A(3)) in relation to the premises, whether arising from an agreement or otherwise.

(6) A provision of this Part imposing a duty to make reasonable adjustments applies only for the purpose of determining whether a person has discriminated against a disabled person; and accordingly a breach of any such duty is not actionable as such.]

[984B]

NOTES

Commencement: 3 July 2003 (so far as enabling anything to be done for the purposes of preparing and bringing into force on or after 1 October 2004 a code of practice under section 53A of this Act); 1 October 2004 (otherwise).

Inserted, in relation to England, Wales and Scotland, by the Disability Discrimination Act 1995 (Amendment) Regulations 2003, SI 2003/1673, regs 3(1), 17(2).

[18C Charities and support for particular groups of persons

(1) Nothing in this Part—
(a) affects any charitable instrument which provides for conferring benefits on one or more categories of person determined by reference to any physical or mental capacity; or
(b) makes unlawful any act done by a charity or recognised body in pursuance of any of its charitable purposes, so far as those purposes are connected with persons so determined.

(2) Nothing in this Part prevents—
(a) a person who provides supported employment from treating members of a particular group of disabled persons more favourably than other persons in providing such employment; or
(b) the Secretary of State from agreeing to arrangements for the provision of supported employment which will, or may, have that effect.

(3) In this section—

"charitable instrument" means an enactment or other instrument (whenever taking effect) so far as it relates to charitable purposes;

"charity" has the same meaning as in the Charities Act 1993;

"recognised body" means a body which is a recognised body for the purposes of Part I of the Law Reform (Miscellaneous Provisions) (Scotland) Act 1990; and

"supported employment" means facilities provided, or in respect of which payments are made, under section 15 of the Disabled Persons (Employment) Act 1944.

(4) In the application of this section to England and Wales, "charitable purposes" means purposes which are exclusively charitable according to the law of England and Wales.

(5) (*Applies to Scotland only.*)

[984C]

NOTES

Commencement: 2 December 1996.

Originally enacted as s 10, but renumbered as s 18C, in relation to England, Wales and Scotland, by the Disability Discrimination Act 1995 (Amendment) Regulations 2003, SI 2003/1673, regs 3(1), 11.

[18D Interpretation of Part 2

(1) Subject to any duty to make reasonable adjustments, nothing in this Part is to be taken to require a person to treat a disabled person more favourably than he treats or would treat others.

(2) In this Part—

"benefits"[, except in sections 4G to 4K,] includes facilities and services;

"detriment", except in section 16C(2)(b), does not include conduct of the nature referred to in section 3B (harassment);

"discriminate", "discrimination" and other related expressions are to be construed in accordance with section 3A;

"duty to make reasonable adjustments" means a duty imposed by or under section 4A, 4B(5) or (6), 4E, [4H,] 6B, 7B, 7D, 14, 14B, 14D[, 15C] or 16A(5);

"employer" includes a person who has no employees but is seeking to employ another person;

"harassment" is to be construed in accordance with section 3B;

"physical feature", in relation to any premises, includes [(subject to any provision under section 15C(4)(e))] any of the following (whether permanent or temporary)—

(a) any feature arising from the design or construction of a building on the premises,

(b) any feature on the premises of any approach to, exit from or access to such a building,

(c) any fixtures, fittings, furnishings, furniture, equipment or material in or on the premises,

(d) any other physical element or quality of any land comprised in the premises;

"provision, criterion or practice" includes any arrangements.]

[984D]

NOTES

Commencement: 3 July 2003 (so far as enabling anything to be done for the purposes of preparing and bringing into force on or after 1 October 2004 a code of practice under section 53A of this Act); 1 October 2004 (otherwise).

Inserted in relation to England, Wales and Scotland by the Disability Discrimination Act 1995 (Amendment) Regulations 2003, SI 2003/1673, regs 3(1), 18.

Sub-s (2): in definition "benefits", words in square brackets inserted by the Disability Discrimination Act 1995 (Pensions) Regulations 2003, SI 2003/2770, regs 2, 4(2)(a); in definition "duty to make reasonable adjustments", number in first pair of square brackets inserted by SI 2003/2770, regs 2, 4(2)(b), number in second pair of square brackets inserted by the Disability Discrimination Act 2005, s 19(1), Sch 1, Pt 1, paras 1, 11(a); in definition "physical feature", words in square brackets inserted by the Disability Discrimination Act 2005, s 19(1), Sch 1, Pt 1, paras 1, 11(b).

[18E Premises provided otherwise than in course of a Part 2 relationship

(1) This Part does not apply in relation to the provision, otherwise than in the course of a Part 2 relationship, of premises by the regulated party to the other party.

(2) For the purposes of subsection (1)—

(a) "Part 2 relationship" means a relationship during the course of which an act of discrimination against, or harassment of, one party to the relationship by the other party to it is unlawful under sections 4 to 15C; and

(b) in relation to a Part 2 relationship, "regulated party" means the party whose acts of discrimination, or harassment, are made unlawful by sections 4 to 15C.]

[984E]

NOTES

Commencement: 4 December 2006.

Inserted by the Disability Discrimination Act 2005, s 19(1), Sch 1, Pt 1, paras 1, 12.

PART III
DISCRIMINATION IN OTHER AREAS

Goods, facilities and services

19 Discrimination in relation to goods, facilities and services

(1) It is unlawful for a provider of services to discriminate against a disabled person—

(a) in refusing to provide, or deliberately not providing, to the disabled person any service which he provides, or is prepared to provide, to members of the public;

(b) in failing to comply with any duty imposed on him by section 21 in circumstances in which the effect of that failure is to make it impossible or unreasonably difficult for the disabled person to make use of any such service;

(c) in the standard of service which he provides to the disabled person or the manner in which he provides it to him; or

(d) in the terms on which he provides a service to the disabled person.

(2) For the purposes of this section and sections 20 [to 21ZA]—

(a) the provision of services includes the provision of any goods or facilities;

(b) a person is "a provider of services" if he is concerned with the provision, in the United Kingdom, of services to the public or to a section of the public; and

(c) it is irrelevant whether a service is provided on payment or without payment.

(3) The following are examples of services to which this section and sections 20 and 21 apply—

(a) access to and use of any place which members of the public are permitted to enter;

(b) access to and use of means of communication;

(c) access to and use of information services;

(d) accommodation in a hotel, boarding house or other similar establishment;

(e) facilities by way of banking or insurance or for grants, loans, credit or finance;

(f) facilities for entertainment, recreation or refreshment;

(g) facilities provided by employment agencies or under section 2 of the Employment and Training Act 1973;

(h) the services of any profession or trade, or any local or other public authority.

(4) In the case of an act which constitutes discrimination by virtue of section 55, this section also applies to discrimination against a person who is not disabled.

[(5) Regulations may provide for subsection (1) and section 21(1), (2) and (4) not to apply, or to apply only to a prescribed extent, in relation to a service of a prescribed description.]

[(5A) Nothing in this section or sections 20 to 21A applies to the provision of a service in relation to which discrimination is unlawful under Part 4.]

(6) …

[985]

NOTES

Commencement: 6 June 1996 (sub-s (5)(c)); 2 December 1996 (sub-ss (1)(a), (c), (d), (2)–(4), (5)(a), (b), (6)); 1 October 1999 (sub-s (1)(b)).

Sub-s (2): words in square brackets substituted by the Disability Discrimination Act 2005, s 19(1), Sch 1, Pt 1, paras 1, 13(1), (2).

Sub-s (5): substituted by the Disability Discrimination Act 2005, s 19(1), Sch 1, Pt 1, paras 1, 13(1), (3).

Sub-s (5A): inserted by the Special Educational Needs and Disability Act 2001, s 38(1), (6); substituted by the Disability Discrimination Act 2005, s 19(1), Sch 1, Pt 1, paras 1, 13(1), (4).

Sub-s (6): repealed by the Special Educational Needs and Disability Act 2001, s 38(1), (5)(b).

20 Meaning of "discrimination"

(1) For the purposes of section 19, a provider of services discriminates against a disabled person if—

(a) for a reason which relates to the disabled person's disability, he treats him less favourably than he treats or would treat others to whom that reason does not or would not apply; and

(b) he cannot show that the treatment in question is justified.

(2) For the purposes of section 19, a providers of services also discriminates against a disabled person if—

(a) he fails to comply with a section 21 duty imposed on him in relation to the disabled person; and

(b) he cannot show that his failure to comply with that duty is justified.

(3) For the purposes of this section, treatment is justified only if—

(a) in the opinion of the provider of services, one or more of the conditions mentioned in subsection (4) are satisfied; and

(b) it is reasonable, in all the circumstances of the case, for him to hold that opinion.

(4) The conditions are that—

(a) in any case, the treatment is necessary in order not to endanger the health or safety of any person (which may include that of the disabled person);

(b) in any case, the disabled person is incapable of entering into an enforceable agreement, or of giving an informed consent, and for that reason the treatment is reasonable in that case;

(c) in a case falling within section 19(1)(a), the treatment is necessary because the provider of services would otherwise be unable to provide the service to members of the public;

(d) in a case falling within section 19(1)(c) or (d), the treatment is necessary in order for the provider of services to be able to provide the service to the disabled person or to other members of the public;

(e) in a case falling within section 19(1)(d), the difference in the terms on which the service is provided to the disabled person and those on which it is provided to other members of the public reflects the greater cost to the provider of services in providing the service to the disabled person.

(5) Any increase in the cost of providing a service to a disabled person which results from compliance by a provider of services with a section 21 duty shall be disregarded for the purposes of subsection (4)(e).

(6) Regulations may make provision, for purposes of this section, as to circumstances in which—

(a) it is reasonable for a provider of services to hold the opinion mentioned in subsection (3)(a);

(b) it is not reasonable for a provider of services to hold that opinion.

(7) Regulations may make provision for subsection (4)(b) not to apply in prescribed circumstances where—

(a) a person is acting for a disabled person under a power of attorney;

(b) functions conferred by or under *Part VII of the Mental Health Act 1983* are exercisable in relation to a disabled person's property or affairs; or

[(c) powers are exercisable in relation to a disabled person's property or affairs in consequence of the appointment, under the law of Scotland, of a guardian, tutor or judicial factor.]

(8) Regulations may make provision, for purposes of this section, as to circumstances (other than those mentioned in subsection (4)) in which treatment is to be taken to be justified.

(9) In subsections (3), (4) and (8) "treatment" includes failure to comply with a section 21 duty.

[986]

NOTES

Commencement: 1 October 1999 (sub-ss (2), (5), (9)); 2 December 1996 (sub-ss (1), (3), (4)); 6 June 1996 (sub-ss (6)–(8)).

Sub-s (7): for the words in italics in para (b) there are substituted the words "the Mental Capacity Act 2005" by the Mental Capacity Act 2005, s 67(1), Sch 6, para 41, as from a day to be appointed under s 68(1) of that Act; para (c) substituted by the Disability Discrimination Act 2005, s 19(1), Sch 1, Pt 1, paras 1, 14.

Regulations: the Disability Discrimination (Services and Premises) Regulations 1996, SI 1996/1836; the Disability Discrimination (Service Providers and Public Authorities Carrying Out Functions) Regulations 2005, SI 2005/2901.

21 Duty of providers of services to make adjustments

(1) Where a provider of services has a practice, policy or procedure which makes it impossible or unreasonably difficult for disabled persons to make use of a service which he

provides, or is prepared to provide, to other members of the public, it is his duty to take such steps as it is reasonable, in all the circumstances of the case, for him to have to take in order to change that practice, policy or procedure so that it no longer has that effect.

(2) Where a physical feature (for example, one arising from the design or construction of a building or the approach or access to premises) makes it impossible or unreasonably difficult for disabled persons to make use of such a service, it is the duty of the provider of that service to take such steps as it is reasonable, in all the circumstances of the case, for him to have to take in order to—

(a) remove the feature;
(b) alter it so that it no longer has that effect;
(c) provide a reasonable means of avoiding the feature; or
(d) provide a reasonable alternative method of making the service in question available to disabled persons.

(3) Regulations may prescribe—

(a) matters which are to be taken into account in determining whether any provision of a kind mentioned in subsection (2)(c) or (d) is reasonable; and
(b) categories of providers of services to whom subsection (2) does not apply.

(4) Where an auxiliary aid or service (for example, the provision of information on audio tape or of a sign language interpreter) would—

(a) enable disabled persons to make use of a service which a provider of services provides, or is prepared to provide, to members of the public, or
(b) facilitate the use by disabled persons of such a service,

it is the duty of the provider of that service to take such steps as it is reasonable, in all the circumstances of the case, for him to have to take in order to provide that auxiliary aid or service.

(5) Regulations may make provision, for the purposes of this section—

(a) as to circumstances in which it is reasonable for a provider of services to have to take steps of a prescribed description;
(b) as to circumstances in which it is not reasonable for a provider of services to have to take steps of a prescribed description;
(c) as to what is to be included within the meaning of "practice, policy or procedure";
(d) as to what is not to be included within the meaning of that expression;
(e) as to things which are to be treated as physical features;
(f) as to things which are not to be treated as such features;
(g) as to things which are to be treated as auxiliary aids or services;
(h) as to things which are not to be treated as auxiliary aids or services.

(6) Nothing in this section requires a provider of services to take any steps which would fundamentally alter the nature of the service in question or the nature of his trade, profession or business.

(7) Nothing in this section requires a provider of services to take any steps which would cause him to incur expenditure exceeding the prescribed maximum.

(8) Regulations under subsection (7) may provide for the prescribed maximum to be calculated by reference to—

(a) aggregate amounts of expenditure incurred in relation to different cases;
(b) prescribed periods;
(c) services of a prescribed description;
(d) premises of a prescribed description; or
(e) such other criteria as may be prescribed.

(9) Regulations may provide, for the purposes of subsection (7), for expenditure incurred by one provider of services to be treated as incurred by another.

(10) This section imposes duties only for the purpose of determining whether a provider of services has discriminated against a disabled person; and accordingly a breach of any such duty is not actionable as such.

[987]

NOTES

Commencement: 1 October 1999 (sub-ss (1), (2)(d), (4), (6), (10)); 26 April 1999 (sub-ss (3), (5)); 1 October 2004 (sub-ss (2)(a)–(c)); to be appointed (sub-ss (7)–(9)).

Orders: the Disability Discrimination (Providers of Services) (Adjustment of Premises) Regulations 2001, SI 2001/3253; the Disability Discrimination (Service Providers and Public Authorities Carrying Out Functions) Regulations 2005, SI 2005/2901; the Disability Discrimination (Transport Vehicles) Regulations 2005, SI 2005/3190.

[21ZA Application of sections 19 to 21 to transport vehicles

(1) Section 19(1) (a), (c) and (d) do not apply in relation to a case where the service is a transport service and, as provider of that service, the provider of services discriminates against a disabled person—

(a) in not providing, or in providing, him with a vehicle; or

(b) in not providing, or in providing, him with services when he is travelling in a vehicle provided in the course of the transport service.

(2) For the purposes of section 21(1), (2) and (4), it is never reasonable for a provider of services, as a provider of a transport service—

(a) to have to take steps which would involve the alteration or removal of a physical feature of a vehicle used in providing the service;

(b) to have to take steps which would—

(i) affect whether vehicles are provided in the course of the service or what vehicles are so provided, or

(ii) where a vehicle is provided in the course of the service, affect what happens in the vehicle while someone is travelling in it.

(3) Regulations may provide for subsection (1) or (2) not to apply, or to apply only to a prescribed extent, in relation to vehicles of a prescribed description.

(4) In this section—

"transport service" means a service which (to any extent) involves transport of people by vehicle;

"vehicle" means a vehicle for transporting people by land, air or water, and includes (in particular)—

(a) a vehicle not having wheels, and

(b) a vehicle constructed or adapted to carry passengers on a system using a mode of guided transport;

"guided transport" has the same meaning as in the Transport and Works Act 1992.]

[987ZA]

NOTES

Commencement: 30 June 2005.
Inserted by the Disability Discrimination Act 2005, s 5.

[21A Employment services

(1) In [this Act], "employment services" means—

(a) vocational guidance;

(b) vocational training; or

(c) services to assist a person to obtain or retain employment, or to establish himself as self-employed.

(2) It is unlawful for a provider of employment services, in relation to such services, to subject to harassment a disabled person—

(a) to whom he is providing such services, or

(b) who has requested him to provide such services;

and section 3B (meaning of "harassment") applies for the purposes of this subsection as it applies for the purposes of Part 2.

(3) In their application to employment services, the preceding provisions of this Part have effect as follows.

(4) Section 19 has effect as if—

(a) after subsection (1)(a), there were inserted the following paragraph—

"(aa) in failing to comply with a duty imposed on him by subsection (1) of section 21 in circumstances in which the effect of that failure is to place the disabled person at a substantial disadvantage in comparison with persons who are not disabled in relation to the provision of the service;";

(b) in subsection (1)(b), for "section 21" there were substituted "subsection (2) or (4) of section 21";

[(c) in subsection (2), for "sections 20 to 21ZA" there is substituted "sections 20 to 21A".]

(5) Section 20 has effect as if—

(a) after subsection (1), there were inserted the following subsection—

"(1A) For the purposes of section 19, a provider of services also discriminates against a disabled person if he fails to comply with a duty imposed on him by subsection (1) of section 21 in relation to the disabled person.";

(b) in subsection (2)(a), for "a section 21 duty imposed" there were substituted "a duty imposed by subsection (2) or (4) of section 21";

(c) after subsection (3), there were inserted the following subsection—

"(3A) But treatment of a disabled person cannot be justified under subsection (3) if it amounts to direct discrimination falling within section 3A(5).".

(6) Section 21 has effect as if—

(a) in subsection (1), for "makes it impossible or unreasonably difficult for disabled persons to make use of" there were substituted "places disabled persons at a substantial disadvantage in comparison with persons who are not disabled in relation to the provision of";

(b) after subsection (1), there were inserted the following subsection—

"(1A) In subsection (1), "practice, policy or procedure" includes a provision or criterion.".]

[987A]

NOTES

Commencement: 3 July 2003 (so far as enabling anything to be done for the purposes of preparing and bringing into force on or after 1 October 2004 a code of practice under section 53A of this Act); 1 October 2004 (otherwise).

Inserted, in relation to England, Wales and Scotland, by the Disability Discrimination Act 1995 (Amendment) Regulations 2003, SI 2003/1673, regs 3(1), 19(1).

Sub-s (1): words in square brackets substituted by the Disability Discrimination Act 2005, s 19(1), Sch 1, Pt 1, paras 1, 15(1), (2).

Sub-s (4): para (c) substituted by the Disability Discrimination Act 2005, s 19(1), Sch 1, Pt 1, paras 1, 15(1), (3).

[Public authorities

21B Discrimination by public authorities

(1) It is unlawful for a public authority to discriminate against a disabled person in carrying out its functions.

(2) In this section, and sections 21D and 21E, "public authority"—

(a) includes any person certain of whose functions are functions of a public nature; but

(b) does not include any person mentioned in subsection (3).

(3) The persons are—

(a) either House of Parliament;

(b) a person exercising functions in connection with proceedings in Parliament;

(c) the Security Service;

(d) the Secret Intelligence Service;

(e) the Government Communications Headquarters; and

(f) a unit, or part of a unit, of any of the naval, military or air forces of the Crown which is for the time being required by the Secretary of State to assist the Government Communications Headquarters in carrying out its functions.

(4) In relation to a particular act, a person is not a public authority by virtue only of subsection (2)(a) if the nature of the act is private.

(5) Regulations may provide for a person of a prescribed description to be treated as not being a public authority for purposes of this section and sections 21D and 21E.

(6) In the case of an act which constitutes discrimination by virtue of section 55, subsection (1) of this section also applies to discrimination against a person who is not disabled.

(7) Subsection (1)—
- (a) does not apply to anything which is unlawful under any provision of this Act other than subsection (1); and
- (b) does not, subject to subsections (8) and (9), apply to anything which would be unlawful under any such provision but for the operation of any provision in or made under this Act.

(8) Subsection (1) does apply in relation to a public authority's function of appointing a person to, and in relation to a public authority's functions with respect to a person as holder of, an office or post if—
- (a) none of the conditions specified in section 4C(3) is satisfied in relation to the office or post; and
- (b) sections 4D and 4E would apply in relation to an appointment to the office or post if any of those conditions was satisfied.

(9) Subsection (1) does apply in relation to a public authority's functions with respect to a person as candidate or prospective candidate for election to, and in relation to a public authority's functions with respect to a person as elected holder of, an office or post if—
- (a) the office or post is not membership of a House of Parliament, the Scottish Parliament, the National Assembly for Wales or an authority mentioned in section 15A(1);
- (b) none of the conditions specified in section 4C(3) is satisfied in relation to the office or post; and
- (c) sections 4D and 4E would apply in relation to an appointment to the office or post if—
  - (i) any of those conditions was satisfied, and
  - (ii) section 4F(1) (but not section 4C(5)) was omitted.

(10) Subsections (8) and (9)—
- (a) shall not be taken to prejudice the generality of subsection (1); but
- (b) are subject to section 21C(5).]

[987B]

NOTES

Commencement: 4 December 2006.
Inserted, together with preceding cross-heading and ss 21C–21E, by the Disability Discrimination Act 2005, s 2.

[21C Exceptions from section 21B(1)

(1) Section 21B(1) does not apply to—
- (a) a judicial act (whether done by a court, tribunal or other person); or
- (b) an act done on the instructions, or on behalf, of a person acting in a judicial capacity.

(2) Section 21B(1) does not apply to any act of, or relating to, making, confirming or approving—
- (a) an Act, an Act of the Scottish Parliament or an Order in Council; or
- (b) an instrument made under an Act, or under an Act of the Scottish Parliament, by—
  - (i) a Minister of the Crown;
  - (ii) a member of the Scottish Executive; or
  - (iii) the National Assembly for Wales.

(3) Section 21B(1) does not apply to any act of, or relating to, imposing conditions or requirements of a kind falling within section 59(1)(c).

(4) Section 21B(1) does not apply to—
- (a) a decision not to institute criminal proceedings;
- (b) where such a decision is made, an act done for the purpose of enabling the decision to be made;
- (c) a decision not to continue criminal proceedings; or
- (d) where such a decision is made—
  - (i) an act done for the purpose of enabling the decision to be made; or

(ii) an act done for the purpose of securing that the proceedings are not continued.

(5) Section 21B(1) does not apply to an act of a prescribed description.]

[987C]

NOTES

Commencement: 4 December 2006.
Inserted as noted to s 21B at **[987B]**.

[21D Meaning of "discrimination" in section 21B

(1) For the purposes of section 21B(1), a public authority discriminates against a disabled person if—

(a) for a reason which relates to the disabled person's disability, it treats him less favourably than it treats or would treat others to whom that reason does not or would not apply; and

(b) it cannot show that the treatment in question is justified under subsection (3), (5) or (7)(c).

(2) For the purposes of section 21B(1), a public authority also discriminates against a disabled person if—

(a) it fails to comply with a duty imposed on it by section 21E in circumstances in which the effect of that failure is to make it—

(i) impossible or unreasonably difficult for the disabled person to receive any benefit that is or may be conferred, or

(ii) unreasonably adverse for the disabled person to experience being subjected to any detriment to which a person is or may be subjected,

by the carrying-out of a function by the authority; and

(b) it cannot show that its failure to comply with that duty is justified under subsection (3), (5) or (7)(c).

(3) Treatment, or a failure to comply with a duty, is justified under this subsection if—

(a) in the opinion of the public authority, one or more of the conditions specified in subsection (4) are satisfied; and

(b) it is reasonable, in all the circumstances of the case, for it to hold that opinion.

(4) The conditions are—

(a) that the treatment, or non-compliance with the duty, is necessary in order not to endanger the health or safety of any person (which may include that of the disabled person);

(b) that the disabled person is incapable of entering into an enforceable agreement, or of giving an informed consent, and for that reason the treatment, or non-compliance with the duty, is reasonable in the particular case;

(c) that, in the case of treatment mentioned in subsection (1), treating the disabled person equally favourably would in the particular case involve substantial extra costs and, having regard to resources, the extra costs in that particular case would be too great;

(d) that the treatment, or non-compliance with the duty, is necessary for the protection of rights and freedoms of other persons.

(5) Treatment, or a failure to comply with a duty, is justified under this subsection if the acts of the public authority which give rise to the treatment or failure are a proportionate means of achieving a legitimate aim.

(6) Regulations may make provision, for purposes of this section, as to circumstances in which it is, or as to circumstances in which it is not, reasonable for a public authority to hold the opinion mentioned in subsection (3)(a).

(7) Regulations may—

(a) amend or omit a condition specified in subsection (4) or make provision for it not to apply in prescribed circumstances;

(b) amend or omit subsection (5) or make provision for it not to apply in prescribed circumstances;

(c) make provision for purposes of this section (in addition to any provision for the time being made by subsections (3) to (5)) as to circumstances in which treatment, or a failure to comply with a duty, is to be taken to be justified.]

[987D]

NOTES

Commencement: 30 June 2005 (for the purpose of exercising any power to make regulations, orders or rules of court); 4 December 2006 (otherwise).

Inserted as noted to s 21B at **[987B]**.

Regulations: the Disability Discrimination (Service Providers and Public Authorities Carrying Out Functions) Regulations 2005, SI 2005/2901.

[21E Duties for purposes of section 21D(2) to make adjustments

(1) Subsection (2) applies where a public authority has a practice, policy or procedure which makes it—

(a) impossible or unreasonably difficult for disabled persons to receive any benefit that is or may be conferred, or

(b) unreasonably adverse for disabled persons to experience being subjected to any detriment to which a person is or may be subjected,

by the carrying-out of a function by the authority.

(2) It is the duty of the authority to take such steps as it is reasonable, in all the circumstances of the case, for the authority to have to take in order to change that practice, policy or procedure so that it no longer has that effect.

(3) Subsection (4) applies where a physical feature makes it—

(a) impossible or unreasonably difficult for disabled persons to receive any benefit that is or may be conferred, or

(b) unreasonably adverse for disabled persons to experience being subjected to any detriment to which a person is or may be subjected,

by the carrying-out of a function by a public authority.

(4) It is the duty of the authority to take such steps as it is reasonable, in all the circumstances of the case, for the authority to have to take in order to—

(a) remove the feature;

(b) alter it so that it no longer has that effect;

(c) provide a reasonable means of avoiding the feature; or

(d) adopt a reasonable alternative method of carrying out the function.

(5) Regulations may prescribe—

(a) matters which are to be taken into account in determining whether any provision of a kind mentioned in subsection (4)(c) or (d) is reasonable;

(b) categories of public authorities to whom subsection (4) does not apply.

(6) Subsection (7) applies where an auxiliary aid or service would—

(a) enable disabled persons to receive, or facilitate the receiving by disabled persons of, any benefit that is or may be conferred, or

(b) reduce the extent to which it is adverse for disabled persons to experience being subjected to any detriment to which a person is or may be subjected,

by the carrying-out of a function by a public authority.

(7) It is the duty of the authority to take such steps as it is reasonable, in all the circumstances of the case, for the authority to have to take in order to provide that auxiliary aid or service.

(8) Regulations may make provision, for purposes of this section—

(a) as to circumstances in which it is, or as to circumstances in which it is not, reasonable for a public authority to have to take steps of a prescribed description;

(b) as to steps which it is always, or as to steps which it is never, reasonable for a public authority to have to take;

(c) as to what is, or as to what is not, to be included within the meaning of "practice, policy or procedure";

(d) as to things which are, or as to things which are not, to be treated as physical features;

(e) as to things which are, or as to things which are not, to be treated as auxiliary aids or services.

(9) Nothing in this section requires a public authority to take any steps which, apart from this section, it has no power to take.

(10) This section imposes duties only for the purposes of determining whether a public authority has, for the purposes of section 21B(1), discriminated against a disabled person; and accordingly a breach of any such duty is not actionable as such.]

[987E]

NOTES

Commencement: 30 June 2005 (for the purpose of exercising any power to make regulations, orders or rules of court); 4 December 2006 (otherwise).

Inserted as noted to s 21B at **[987B]**.

Regulations: the Disability Discrimination (Service Providers and Public Authorities Carrying Out Functions) Regulations 2005, SI 2005/2901.

[Private clubs etc

21F Discrimination by private clubs etc

(1) This section applies to any association of persons (however described, whether corporate or unincorporate, and whether or not its activities are carried on for profit) if—

(a) it has twenty-five or more members;
(b) admission to membership is regulated by its constitution and is so conducted that the members do not constitute a section of the public within the meaning of section 19(2); and
(c) it is not an organisation to which section 13 applies.

(2) It is unlawful for an association to which this section applies, in the case of a disabled person who is not a member of the association, to discriminate against him—

(a) in the terms on which it is prepared to admit him to membership; or
(b) by refusing or deliberately omitting to accept his application for membership.

(3) It is unlawful for an association to which this section applies, in the case of a disabled person who is a member, or associate, of the association, to discriminate against him—

(a) in the way it affords him access to a benefit, facility or service;
(b) by refusing or deliberately omitting to afford him access to a benefit, facility or service;
(c) in the case of a member—
  (i) by depriving him of membership, or
  (ii) by varying the terms on which he is a member;
(d) in the case of an associate—
  (i) by depriving him of his rights as an associate, or
  (ii) by varying those rights; or
(e) in either case, by subjecting him to any other detriment.

(4) It is unlawful for an association to which this section applies to discriminate against a disabled person—

(a) in the way it affords him access to a benefit, facility or service,
(b) by refusing or deliberately omitting to afford him access to a benefit, facility or service, or
(c) by subjecting him to any other detriment,

in his capacity as a guest of the association.

(5) It is unlawful for an association to which this section applies to discriminate against a disabled person—

(a) in the terms on which it is prepared to invite him, or permit a member or associate to invite him, to be a guest of the association;
(b) by refusing or deliberately omitting to invite him to be a guest of the association; or
(c) by not permitting a member or associate to invite him to be a guest of the association.

(6) It is unlawful for an association to which this section applies to discriminate against a disabled person in failing in prescribed circumstances to comply with a duty imposed on it under section 21H.

(7) In the case of an act which constitutes discrimination by virtue of section 55, this section also applies to discrimination against a person who is not disabled.]

[987F]

PART I STATUTES

NOTES

Commencement: 10 October 2005 (for the purpose of exercising any power to make regulations); 5 December 2005 (otherwise).

Inserted, together with preceding cross-heading and ss 21G, 21H, 21J, by the Disability Discrimination Act 2005, s 12.

Regulations: the Disability Discrimination (Private Clubs etc) Regulations 2005, SI 2005/3258.

[21G Meaning of "discrimination"

(1) For the purposes of section 21F, an association discriminates against a disabled person if—

(a) for a reason which relates to the disabled person's disability, the association treats him less favourably than it treats or would treat others to whom that reason does not or would not apply; and

(b) it cannot show that the treatment in question is justified.

(2) For the purposes of subsection (1), treatment is justified only if—

(a) in the opinion of the association, one or more of the conditions mentioned in subsection (3) are satisfied; and

(b) it is reasonable, in all the circumstances, for it to hold that opinion.

(3) The conditions are that—

(a) the treatment is necessary in order not to endanger the health or safety of any person (which may include that of the disabled person);

(b) the disabled person is incapable of entering into an enforceable agreement, or giving an informed consent, and for that reason the treatment is reasonable in that case;

(c) in a case falling within section 21F(2)(a), (3)(a), (c)(ii), (d)(ii) or (e), (4)(a) or (c) or (5)(a), the treatment is necessary in order for the association to be able to afford members, associates or guests of the association, or the disabled person, access to a benefit, facility or service;

(d) in a case falling within section 21F(2)(b), (3)(b), (c)(i) or (d)(i), (4)(b) or (5)(b) or (c), the treatment is necessary because the association would otherwise be unable to afford members, associates or guests of the association access to a benefit, facility or service;

(e) in a case falling within section 21F(2)(a), the difference between—

(i) the terms on which membership is offered to the disabled person, and

(ii) those on which it is offered to other persons,

reflects the greater cost to the association of affording the disabled person access to a benefit, facility or service;

(f) in a case falling within section 21F(3)(a), (c)(ii) or (d)(ii) or (4)(a), the difference between—

(i) the association's treatment of the disabled person, and

(ii) its treatment of other members or (as the case may be) other associates or other guests of the association,

reflects the greater cost to the association of affording the disabled person access to a benefit, facility or service;

(g) in a case falling within section 21F(5)(a), the difference between—

(i) the terms on which the disabled person is invited, or permitted to be invited, to be a guest of the association, and

(ii) those on which other persons are invited, or permitted to be invited, to be guests of the association,

reflects the greater cost to the association of affording the disabled person access to a benefit, facility or service.

(4) Any increase in the cost of affording a disabled person access to a benefit, facility or service which results from compliance with a duty under section 21H shall be disregarded for the purposes of subsection (3)(e), (f) and (g).

(5) Regulations may—

(a) make provision, for purposes of this section, as to circumstances in which it is, or as to circumstances in which it is not, reasonable for an association to hold the opinion mentioned in subsection (2)(a);

(b) amend or omit a condition specified in subsection (3) or make provision for it not to apply in prescribed circumstances;

(c) make provision as to circumstances (other than any for the time being mentioned in subsection (3)) in which treatment is to be taken to be justified for the purposes of subsection (1).

(6) For the purposes of section 21F, an association also discriminates against a disabled person if—

(a) it fails to comply with a duty under section 21H imposed on it in relation to the disabled person; and

(b) it cannot show that its failure to comply with that duty is justified.

(7) Regulations may make provision as to circumstances in which failure to comply with a duty under section 21H is to be taken to be justified for the purposes of subsection (6).]

[987G]

NOTES

Commencement: 30 June 2005 (for the purpose of exercising any power to make regulations, orders or rules of court); 5 December 2005 (otherwise).

Inserted as noted to s 21F at **[987F]**.

Regulations: the Disability Discrimination (Private Clubs etc) Regulations 2005, SI 2005/3258.

[21H Duty to make adjustments

(1) Regulations may make provision imposing on an association to which section 21F applies—

(a) a duty to take steps for a purpose relating to a policy, practice or procedure of the association, or a physical feature, which adversely affects disabled persons who—

(i) are, or might wish to become, members or associates of the association, or

(ii) are, or are likely to become, guests of the association;

(b) a duty to take steps for the purpose of making an auxiliary aid or service available to any such disabled persons.

(2) Regulations under subsection (1) may (in particular)—

(a) make provision as to the cases in which a duty is imposed;

(b) make provision as to the steps which a duty requires to be taken;

(c) make provision as to the purpose for which a duty requires steps to be taken.

(3) Any duty imposed under this section is imposed only for the purpose of determining whether an association has, for the purposes of section 21F, discriminated against a disabled person; and accordingly a breach of any such duty is not actionable as such.]

[987H]

NOTES

Commencement: 30 June 2005 (for the purpose of exercising any power to make regulations, orders or rules of court); 5 December 2005 (otherwise).

Inserted as noted to s 21F at **[987F]**.

Regulations: the Disability Discrimination (Private Clubs etc) Regulations 2005, SI 2005/3258.

[21J "Member", "associate" and "guest"

(1) For the purposes of sections 21F to 21H and this section—

(a) a person is a member of an association to which section 21F applies if he belongs to it by virtue of his admission to any sort of membership provided for by its constitution (and is not merely a person with certain rights under its constitution by virtue of his membership of some other association), and references to membership of an association shall be construed accordingly;

(b) a person is an associate of an association to which section 21F applies if, not being a member of it, he has under its constitution some or all of the rights enjoyed by members (or would have apart from any provision in its constitution authorising the refusal of those rights in particular cases).

(2) References in sections 21F to 21H to a guest of an association include a person who is a guest of the association by virtue of an invitation issued by a member or associate of the association and permitted by the association.

(3) Regulations may make provision, for purposes of sections 21F to 21H, as to circumstances in which a person is to be treated as being, or as to circumstances in which a person is to be treated as not being, a guest of an association.]

[987J]

NOTES

Commencement: 5 December 2005.
Inserted as noted to s 21F at **[987F]**.

Premises

22 Discrimination in relation to premises

(1) It is unlawful for a person with power to dispose of any premises to discriminate against a disabled person—

(a) in the terms on which he offers to dispose of those premises to the disabled person;
(b) by refusing to dispose of those premises to the disabled person; or
(c) in his treatment of the disabled person in relation to any list of persons in need of premises of that description.

(2) Subsection (1) does not apply to a person who owns an estate or interest in the premises and wholly occupies them unless, for the purpose of disposing of the premises, he—

(a) uses the services of an estate agent, or
(b) publishes an advertisement or causes an advertisement to be published.

(3) It is unlawful for a person managing any premises to discriminate against a disabled person occupying those premises—

(a) in the way he permits the disabled person to make use of any benefits or facilities;
(b) by refusing or deliberately omitting to permit the disabled person to make use of any benefits or facilities; or
(c) by evicting the disabled person, or subjecting him to any other detriment.

[(3A) Regulations may make provision, for purposes of subsection (3)—

(a) as to who is to be treated as being, or as to who is to be treated as not being, a person who manages premises;
(b) as to who is to be treated as being, or as to who is to be treated as not being, a person occupying premises.]

(4) It is unlawful for any person whose licence or consent is required for the disposal of any premises comprised in, or (in Scotland) the subject of, a tenancy to discriminate against a disabled person by withholding his licence or consent for the disposal of the premises to the disabled person.

(5) Subsection (4) applies to tenancies created before as well as after the passing of this Act.

(6) In this section—

"advertisement" includes every form of advertisement or notice, whether to the public or not;

"dispose", in relation to premises, includes granting a right to occupy the premises, and, in relation to premises comprised in, or (in Scotland) the subject of, a tenancy, includes—

(a) assigning the tenancy, and
(b) sub-letting or parting with possession of the premises or any part of the premises;

and "disposal" shall be construed accordingly;

"estate agent" means a person who, by way of profession or trade, provides services for the purpose of finding premises for persons seeking to acquire them or assisting in the disposal of premises; and

"tenancy" means a tenancy created—

(a) by a lease or sub-lease,
(b) by an agreement for a lease or sub-lease,
(c) by a tenancy agreement, or
(d) in pursuance of any enactment.

(7) In the case of an act which constitutes discrimination by virtue of section 55, this section also applies to discrimination against a person who is not disabled.

(8) This section applies only in relation to premises in the United Kingdom.

[988]

PART I STATUTES

NOTES

Commencement: 2 December 1996.

Sub-s (3A): inserted by the Disability Discrimination Act 2005, s 19(1), Sch 1, Pt 1, paras 1, 16.

Regulations: the Disability Discrimination (Premises) Regulations 2006, SI 2006/887.

[22A Commonholds

(1) It is unlawful for any person whose licence or consent is required for the disposal of an interest in a commonhold unit by the unit-holder to discriminate against a disabled person by withholding his licence or consent for the disposal of the interest in favour of, or to, the disabled person.

(2) Where it is not possible for an interest in a commonhold unit to be disposed of by the unit-holder unless some other person is a party to the disposal of the interest, it is unlawful for that other person to discriminate against a disabled person by deliberately not being a party to the disposal of the interest in favour of, or to, the disabled person.

(3) Regulations may provide for subsection (1) or (2) not to apply, or to apply only, in cases of a prescribed description.

(4) Regulations may make provision, for purposes of this section—

(a) as to what is, or as to what is not, to be included within the meaning of "dispose" (and "disposal");

(b) as to what is, or as to what is not, to be included within the meaning of "interest in a commonhold unit".

(5) In this section "commonhold unit", and "unit-holder" in relation to such a unit, have the same meaning as in Part 1 of the Commonhold and Leasehold Reform Act 2002.

(6) In the case of an act which constitutes discrimination by virtue of section 55, this section also applies to discrimination against a person who is not disabled.

(7) This section applies only in relation to premises in England and Wales.]

[988A]

NOTES

Commencement: 30 June 2005 (for the purpose of exercising any power to make regulations, orders or rules of court); 4 December 2006 (otherwise).

Inserted by the Disability Discrimination Act 2005, s 19(1), Sch 1, Pt 1, paras 1, 17.

Regulations: the Disability Discrimination (Premises) Regulations 2006, SI 2006/887.

23 Exemption for small dwellings

(1) Where the conditions mentioned in subsection (2) are satisfied, subsection (1), (3) or (as the case may be) (4) of section 22 does not apply.

(2) The conditions are that—

(a) the relevant occupier resides, and intends to continue to reside, on the premises;

(b) the relevant occupier shares accommodation on the premises with persons who reside on the premises and are not members of his household;

(c) the shared accommodation is not storage accommodation or a means of access; and

(d) the premises are small premises.

(3) For the purposes of this section, premises are "small premises" if they fall within subsection (4) or (5).

(4) Premises fall within this subsection if—

(a) only the relevant occupier and members of his household reside in the accommodation occupied by him;

(b) the premises comprise, in addition to the accommodation occupied by the relevant occupier, residential accommodation for at least one other household;

(c) the residential accommodation for each other household is let, or available for letting, on a separate tenancy or similar agreement; and

(d) there are not normally more than two such other households.

(5) Premises fall within this subsection if there is not normally residential accommodation on the premises for more than six persons in addition to the relevant occupier and any members of his household.

(6) For the purposes of this section "the relevant occupier" means—

(a) in a case falling within section 22(1), the person with power to dispose of the premises, or a near relative of his;

[(aa) in a case falling within section 22(3), the person managing the premises, or a near relative of his;]

(b) in a case falling within section 22(4), the person whose licence or consent is required for the disposal of the premises, or a near relative of his.

(7) For the purposes of this section—

"near relative" means a person's spouse [or civil partner], partner, parent, child, grandparent, grandchild, or brother or sister (whether of full or half blood or [by marriage or civil partnership)]; and

["partner" means the other member of a couple consisting of—

(a) a man and a woman who are not married to each other but are living together as husband and wife, or

(b) two people of the same sex who are not civil partners of each other but are living together as if they were civil partners.]

[989]

NOTES

Commencement: 2 December 1996.

Sub-s (6): para (aa) inserted by the Disability Discrimination Act 2005, s 19(1), Sch 1, Pt 1, paras 1, 18.

Sub-s (7): in definition "near relative" words in first pair of square brackets inserted and words in second pair of square brackets substituted, and definition "partner" substituted, by the Civil Partnership Act 2004, s 261(1), Sch 27, para 150.

24 Meaning of "discrimination"

(1) For the purposes of [sections 22 and 22A], a person ("A") discriminates against a disabled person if—

(a) for a reason which relates to the disabled person's disability, he treats him less favourably than he treats or would treat others to whom that reason does not or would not apply; and

(b) he cannot show that the treatment in question is justified.

(2) For the purposes of this section, treatment is justified only if—

(a) in A's opinion, one or more of the conditions mentioned in subsection (3) are satisfied; and

(b) it is reasonable, in all the circumstances of the case, for him to hold that opinion.

(3) The conditions are that—

(a) in any case, the treatment is necessary in order not to endanger the health or safety of any person (which may include that of the disabled person);

(b) in any case, the disabled person is incapable of entering into an enforceable agreement, or of giving an informed consent, and for that reason the treatment is reasonable in that case;

(c) in a case falling within section 22(3)(a), the treatment is necessary in order for the disabled person or the occupiers of other premises forming part of the building to make use of the benefit or facility;

(d) in a case falling within section 22(3)(b), the treatment is necessary in order for the occupiers of other premises forming part of the building to make use of the benefit or facility.

[(e) in a case to which subsection (3A) applies, the terms are less favourable in order to recover costs which—

(i) as a result of the disabled person having a disability, are incurred in connection with the disposal of the premises, and

(ii) are not costs incurred in connection with taking steps to avoid liability under section 24G(1);

(f) in a case to which subsection (3B) applies, the disabled person is subjected to the detriment in order to recover costs which—

(i) as a result of the disabled person having a disability, are incurred in connection with the management of the premises, and

(ii) are not costs incurred in connection with taking steps to avoid liability under section 24A(1) or 24G(1).]

[(3A) This subsection applies to a case if—

(a) the case falls within section 22(1)(a);
(b) the premises are to let;
(c) the person with power to dispose of the premises is a controller of them; and
(d) the proposed disposal of the premises would involve the disabled person becoming a person to whom they are let.

(3B) This subsection applies to a case if—
(a) the case falls within section 22(3)(c);
(b) the detriment is not eviction;
(c) the premises are let premises;
(d) the person managing the premises is a controller of them; and
(e) the disabled person is a person to whom the premises are let or, although not a person to whom they are let, is lawfully under the letting an occupier of them.

(3C) Section 24G(3) and (4) apply for the purposes of subsection (3A) as for those of section 24G; and section 24A(3) and (4) apply for the purposes of subsection (3B) as for those of section 24A.]

(4) Regulations may make provision, for purposes of this section, as to circumstances in which—
(a) it is reasonable for a person to hold the opinion mentioned in subsection 2(a);
(b) it is not reasonable for a person to hold that opinion.

[(4A) Regulations may make provision for the condition specified in subsection (3)(b) not to apply in prescribed circumstances.]

(5) Regulations may make provision, for purposes of this section, as to circumstances (other than those mentioned in subsection (3)) in which treatment is to be taken to be justified.
[990]

NOTES

Commencement: 2 December 1996 (sub-ss (1)–(4)); 6 June 1996 (sub-s (5)).
Sub-s (1): words in square brackets substituted by the Disability Discrimination Act 2005, s 19(1), Sch 1, Pt 1, paras 1, 19(1), (2).
Sub-s (3): paras (e), (f) added by the Disability Discrimination Act 2005, s 19(1), Sch 1, Pt 1, paras 1, 19(1), (3).
Sub-ss (3A)–(3C): inserted by the Disability Discrimination Act 2005, s 19(1), Sch 1, Pt 1, paras 1, 19(1), (4).
Sub-s (4A): inserted by the Disability Discrimination Act 2005, s 19(1), Sch 1, Pt 1, paras 1, 19(1), (5).
Regulations: the Disability Discrimination (Premises) Regulations 2006, SI 2006/887.

[24A Let premises: discrimination in failing to comply with duty

(1) It is unlawful for a controller of let premises to discriminate against a disabled person—
(a) who is a person to whom the premises are let; or
(b) who, although not a person to whom the premises are let, is lawfully under the letting an occupier of the premises.

(2) For the purposes of subsection (1), a controller of let premises discriminates against a disabled person if—
(a) he fails to comply with a duty under section 24C or 24D imposed on him by reference to the disabled person; and
(b) he cannot show that failure to comply with the duty is justified (see section 24K).

(3) For the purposes of this section and sections 24B to 24F, a person is a controller of let premises if he is—
(a) a person by whom the premises are let; or
(b) a person who manages the premises.

(4) For the purposes of this section and sections 24B to 24F—
(a) "let" includes sub-let; and
(b) premises shall be treated as let by a person to another where a person has granted another a contractual licence to occupy them.

(5) This section applies only in relation to premises in the United Kingdom.]
[990A]

NOTES

Commencement: 4 December 2006.

Inserted, together with ss 24B–24H, 24J–24L, by the Disability Discrimination Act 2005, s 13.

[24B Exceptions to section 24A(1)

(1) Section 24A(1) does not apply if—

(a) the premises are, or have at any time been, the only or principal home of an individual who is a person by whom they are let; and

(b) since entering into the letting-

(i) the individual has not, and

(ii) where he is not the sole person by whom the premises are let, no other person by whom they are let has,

used for the purpose of managing the premises the services of a person who, by profession or trade, manages let premises.

(2) Section 24A(1) does not apply if the premises are of a prescribed description.

(3) Where the conditions mentioned in section 23(2) are satisfied, section 24A(1) does not apply.

(4) For the purposes of section 23 "the relevant occupier" means, in a case falling within section 24A(1), a controller of the let premises, or a near relative of his; and "near relative" has here the same meaning as in section 23.]

[990B]

NOTES

Commencement: 4 December 2006.

Inserted as noted to s 24A, at **[990A]**.

[24C Duty for purposes of section 24A(2) to provide auxiliary aid or service

(1) Subsection (2) applies where—

(a) a controller of let premises receives a request made by or on behalf of a person to whom the premises are let;

(b) it is reasonable to regard the request as a request that the controller take steps in order to provide an auxiliary aid or service; and

(c) either the first condition, or the second condition, is satisfied.

(2) It is the duty of the controller to take such steps as it is reasonable, in all the circumstances of the case, for him to have to take in order to provide the auxiliary aid or service (but see section 24E(1)).

(3) The first condition is that—

(a) the auxiliary aid or service-

(i) would enable a relevant disabled person to enjoy, or facilitate such a person's enjoyment of, the premises, but

(ii) would be of little or no practical use to the relevant disabled person concerned if he were neither a person to whom the premises are let nor an occupier of them; and

(b) it would, were the auxiliary aid or service not to be provided, be impossible or unreasonably difficult for the relevant disabled person concerned to enjoy the premises.

(4) The second condition is that—

(a) the auxiliary aid or service-

(i) would enable a relevant disabled person to make use, or facilitate such a person's making use, of any benefit, or facility, which by reason of the letting is one of which he is entitled to make use, but

(ii) would be of little or no practical use to the relevant disabled person concerned if he were neither a person to whom the premises are let nor an occupier of them; and

(b) it would, were the auxiliary aid or service not to be provided, be impossible or unreasonably difficult for the relevant disabled person concerned to make use of any benefit, or facility, which by reason of the letting is one of which he is entitled to make use.]

[990C]

NOTES

Commencement: 4 December 2006.
Inserted as noted to s 24A, at **[990A]**.

[24D Duty for purposes of section 24A(2) to change practices, terms etc

(1) Subsection (3) applies where—

(a) a controller of let premises has a practice, policy or procedure which has the effect of making it impossible, or unreasonably difficult, for a relevant disabled person-

(i) to enjoy the premises, or

(ii) to make use of any benefit, or facility, which by reason of the letting is one of which he is entitled to make use, or

(b) a term of the letting has that effect,

and (in either case) the conditions specified in subsection (2) are satisfied.

(2) Those conditions are—

(a) that the practice, policy, procedure or term would not have that effect if the relevant disabled person concerned did not have a disability;

(b) that the controller receives a request made by or on behalf of a person to whom the premises are let; and

(c) that it is reasonable to regard the request as a request that the controller take steps in order to change the practice, policy, procedure or term so as to stop it having that effect.

(3) It is the duty of the controller to take such steps as it is reasonable, in all the circumstances of the case, for him to have to take in order to change the practice, policy, procedure or term so as to stop it having that effect (but see section 24E(1)).]

[990D]

NOTES

Commencement: 4 December 2006.
Inserted as noted to s 24A, at **[990A]**.

[24E Sections 24C and 24D: supplementary and interpretation

(1) For the purposes of sections 24C and 24D, it is never reasonable for a controller of let premises to have to take steps consisting of, or including, the removal or alteration of a physical feature.

(2) Sections 24C and 24D impose duties only for the purpose of determining whether a person has, for the purposes of section 24A, discriminated against another; and accordingly a breach of any such duty is not actionable as such.

(3) In sections 24C and 24D "relevant disabled person", in relation to let premises, means a particular disabled person—

(a) who is a person to whom the premises are let; or

(b) who, although not a person to whom the premises are let, is lawfully under the letting an occupier of the premises.

(4) For the purposes of sections 24C and 24D, the terms of a letting of premises include the terms of any agreement which relates to the letting of the premises.]

[990E]

NOTES

Commencement: 4 December 2006.
Inserted as noted to s 24A, at **[990A]**.

[24F Let premises: victimisation of persons to whom premises are let

(1) Where a duty under section 24C or 24D is imposed on a controller of let premises by reference to a person who, although not a person to whom the premises are let, is lawfully

under the letting an occupier of the premises, it is unlawful for a controller of the let premises to discriminate against a person to whom the premises are let.

(2) For the purposes of subsection (1), a controller of the let premises discriminates against a person to whom the premises are let if—

(a) the controller treats that person ("T") less favourably than he treats or would treat other persons whose circumstances are the same as T's; and

(b) he does so because of costs incurred in connection with taking steps to avoid liability under section 24A(1) for failure to comply with the duty.

(3) In comparing T's circumstances with those of any other person for the purposes of subsection (2)(a), the following (as well as the costs' having been incurred) shall be disregarded—

(a) the making of the request that gave rise to the imposition of the duty; and

(b) the disability of each person who-

(i) is a disabled person or a person who has had a disability, and

(ii) is a person to whom the premises are let or, although not a person to whom the premises are let, is lawfully under the letting an occupier of the premises.]

[990F]

NOTES

Commencement: 4 December 2006.

Inserted as noted to s 24A, at **[990A]**.

[24G Premises that are to let: discrimination in failing to comply with duty

(1) Where—

(a) a person has premises to let, and

(b) a disabled person is considering taking a letting of the premises,

it is unlawful for a controller of the premises to discriminate against the disabled person.

(2) For the purposes of subsection (1), a controller of premises that are to let discriminates against a disabled person if—

(a) he fails to comply with a duty under section 24J imposed on him by reference to the disabled person; and

(b) he cannot show that failure to comply with the duty is justified (see section 24K).

(3) For the purposes of this section and sections 24H and 24J, a person is a controller of premises that are to let if he is—

(a) a person who has the premises to let; or

(b) a person who manages the premises.

(4) For the purposes of this section and sections 24H and 24J—

(a) "let" includes sub-let;

(b) premises shall be treated as to let by a person to another where a person proposes to grant another a contractual licence to occupy them;

and references to a person considering taking a letting of premises shall be construed accordingly.

(5) This section applies only in relation to premises in the United Kingdom.]

[990G]

NOTES

Commencement: 4 December 2006.

Inserted as noted to s 24A, at **[990A]**.

[24H Exceptions to section 24G(1)

(1) Section 24G(1) does not apply in relation to premises that are to let if the premises are, or have at any time been, the only or principal home of an individual who is a person who has them to let and—

(a) the individual does not use, and

(b) where he is not the sole person who has the premises to let, no other person who has the premises to let uses, the services of an estate agent (within the meaning given by section 22(6)) for the purposes of letting the premises.

(2) Section 24G(1) does not apply if the premises are of a prescribed description.

(3) Where the conditions mentioned in section 23(2) are satisfied, section 24G(1) does not apply.

(4) For the purposes of section 23 "the relevant occupier" means, in a case falling within section 24G(1), a controller of the premises that are to let, or a near relative of his; and "near relative" has here the same meaning as in section 23.]

[990H]

NOTES

Commencement: 4 December 2006.
Inserted as noted to s 24A, at **[990A]**.

[24J Duties for purposes of section 24G(2)

(1) Subsection (2) applies where—

(a) a controller of premises that are to let receives a request made by or on behalf of a relevant disabled person;

(b) it is reasonable to regard the request as a request that the controller take steps in order to provide an auxiliary aid or service;

(c) the auxiliary aid or service-

(i) would enable the relevant disabled person to become, or facilitate his becoming, a person to whom the premises are let, but

(ii) would be of little or no practical use to him if he were not considering taking a letting of the premises; and

(d) it would, were the auxiliary aid or service not to be provided, be impossible or unreasonably difficult for the relevant disabled person to become a person to whom the premises are let.

(2) It is the duty of the controller to take such steps as it is reasonable, in all the circumstances of the case, for the controller to have to take in order to provide the auxiliary aid or service (but see subsection (5)).

(3) Subsection (4) applies where—

(a) a controller of premises that are to let has a practice, policy or procedure which has the effect of making it impossible, or unreasonably difficult, for a relevant disabled person to become a person to whom the premises are let;

(b) the practice, policy or procedure would not have that effect if the relevant disabled person did not have a disability;

(c) the controller receives a request made by or on behalf of the relevant disabled person; and

(d) it is reasonable to regard the request as a request that the controller take steps in order to change the practice, policy or procedure so as to stop it having that effect.

(4) It is the duty of the controller to take such steps as it is reasonable, in all the circumstances of the case, for him to have to take in order to change the practice, policy or procedure so as to stop it having that effect (but see subsection (5)).

(5) For the purposes of this section, it is never reasonable for a controller of premises that are to let to have to take steps consisting of, or including, the removal or alteration of a physical feature.

(6) In this section "relevant disabled person", in relation to premises that are to let, means a particular disabled person who is considering taking a letting of the premises.

(7) This section imposes duties only for the purpose of determining whether a person has, for the purposes of section 24G, discriminated against another; and accordingly a breach of any such duty is not actionable as such.]

[990J]

NOTES

Commencement: 4 December 2006.
Inserted as noted to s 24A, at **[990A]**.

[24K Let premises and premises that are to let: justification

(1) For the purposes of sections 24A(2) and 24G(2), a person's failure to comply with a duty is justified only if—

(a) in his opinion, a condition mentioned in subsection (2) is satisfied; and
(b) it is reasonable, in all the circumstances of the case, for him to hold that opinion.

(2) The conditions are—

(a) that it is necessary to refrain from complying with the duty in order not to endanger the health or safety of any person (which may include that of the disabled person concerned);
(b) that the disabled person concerned is incapable of entering into an enforceable agreement, or of giving informed consent, and for that reason the failure is reasonable.

(3) Regulations may—

(a) make provision, for purposes of this section, as to circumstances in which it is, or as to circumstances in which it is not, reasonable for a person to hold the opinion mentioned in subsection (1)(a);
(b) amend or omit a condition specified in subsection (2) or make provision for it not to apply in prescribed circumstances;
(c) make provision, for purposes of this section, as to circumstances (other than any for the time being mentioned in subsection (2)) in which a failure is to be taken to be justified.]

[990K]

NOTES

Commencement: 30 Jun 2005 (for the purpose of exercising any power to make regulations, orders or rules of court); 4 December 2006 (otherwise).
Inserted as noted to s 24A, at **[990A]**.
Regulations: the Disability Discrimination (Premises) Regulations 2006, SI 2006/887.

[24L Sections 24 to 24K: power to make supplementary provision

(1) Regulations may make provision, for purposes of sections 24(3A) and (3B) and 24A to 24K—

(a) as to circumstances in which premises are to be treated as let to a person;
(b) as to circumstances in which premises are to be treated as not let to a person;
(c) as to circumstances in which premises are to be treated as being, or as not being, to let;
(d) as to who is to be treated as being, or as to who is to be treated as not being, a person who, although not a person to whom let premises are let, is lawfully under the letting an occupier of the premises;
(e) as to who is to be treated as being, or as to who is to be treated as not being, a person by whom premises are let;
(f) as to who is to be treated as having, or as to who is to be treated as not having, premises to let;
(g) as to who is to be treated as being, or as to who is to be treated as not being, a person who manages premises;
(h) as to things which are, or as to things which are not, to be treated as auxiliary aids or services;
(i) as to what is, or as to what is not, to be included within the meaning of "practice, policy or procedure";
(j) as to circumstances in which it is, or as to circumstances in which it is not, reasonable for a person to have to take steps of a prescribed description;
(k) as to steps which it is always, or as to steps which it is never, reasonable for a person to have to take;
(l) as to circumstances in which it is, or as to circumstances in which it is not, reasonable to regard a request as being of a particular kind;
(m) as to things which are, or as to things which are not, to be treated as physical features;
(n) as to things which are, or as to things which are not, to be treated as alterations of physical features.

(2) Regulations under subsection (1)(a) may (in particular) provide for premises to be treated as let to a person where they are a commonhold unit of which he is a unit-holder; and

"commonhold unit", and "unit-holder" in relation to such a unit, have here the same meaning as in Part 1 of the Commonhold and Leasehold Reform Act 2002.

(3) The powers under subsections (1)(j) and (k) are subject to sections 24E(1) and 24J(5).]

[990L]

NOTES

Commencement: 30 Jun 2005 (for the purpose of exercising any power to make regulations, orders or rules of court); 4 December 2006 (otherwise).

Inserted as noted to s 24A, at **[990A]**.

Regulations: the Disability Discrimination (Premises) Regulations 2006, SI 2006/887.

[24M Premises provisions do not apply where other provisions operate

(1) Sections 22 to 24L do not apply—

(a) in relation to the provision of premises by a provider of services where he provides the premises in providing services to members of the public;

(b) in relation to the provision, in the course of a Part 2 relationship, of premises by the regulated party to the other party;

(c) in relation to the provision of premises to a student or prospective student—

(i) by a responsible body within the meaning of Chapter 1 or 2 of Part 4, or

(ii) by an authority in discharging any functions mentioned in section 28F(1); or

(d) to anything which is unlawful under section 21F or which would be unlawful under that section but for the operation of any provision in or made under this Act.

(2) Subsection (1)(a) has effect subject to any prescribed exceptions.

(3) In subsection (1)(a) "provider of services", and providing services, have the same meaning as in section 19.

(4) For the purposes of subsection (1)(b)—

(a) "Part 2 relationship" means a relationship during the course of which an act of discrimination against, or harassment of, one party to the relationship by the other party to it is unlawful under sections 4 to 15C; and

(b) in relation to a Part 2 relationship, "regulated party" means the party whose acts of discrimination, or harassment, are made unlawful by sections 4 to 15C.

(5) In subsection (1)(c) "student" includes pupil.]

[990M]

NOTES

Commencement: 4 December 2006.

Inserted by the Disability Discrimination Act 2005, s 19(1), Sch 1, Pt 1, paras 1, 20.

Enforcement, etc

25 Enforcement, remedies and procedure

(1) A claim by any person that another person—

(a) has discriminated against him in a way which is unlawful under this Part; or

(b) is by virtue of section 57 or 58 to be treated as having discriminated against him in such a way,

may be made the subject of civil proceedings in the same way as any other claim in tort or (in Scotland) in reparation for breach of statutory duty.

(2) For the avoidance of doubt it is hereby declared that damages in respect of discrimination in a way which is unlawful under this Part may include compensation for injury to feelings whether or not they include compensation under any other head.

(3) Proceedings in England and Wales shall be brought only in a county court.

(4) (*Applies to Scotland only.*)

(5) The remedies available in such proceedings are those which are available in the High Court or (as the case may be) the Court of Session.

(6) Part II of Schedule 3 makes further provision about the enforcement of this Part and about procedure.

[(6A) Subsection (1) does not apply in relation to a claim by a person that another person—

(a) has discriminated against him in relation to the provision under a group insurance arrangement of facilities by way of insurance; or

(b) is by virtue of section 57 or 58 to be treated as having discriminated against him in relation to the provision under such an arrangement of such facilities.]

[[(7) Subsection (1) does not apply in relation to a claim by a person that another person—

(a) has discriminated against him in relation to the provision of employment services; or

(b) is by virtue of section 57 or 58 to be treated as having discriminated against him in relation to the provision of employment services.

(8) A claim—

(a) of the kind referred to in subsection (6A) or (7), or

(b) by a person that another—

(i) has subjected him to harassment in a way which is unlawful under section 21A(2), or

(ii) is by virtue of section 57 or 58 to be treated as having subjected him to harassment in such a way,

may be presented as a complaint to an employment tribunal.]

(9) Section 17A(1A) to (7) and paragraphs 3 and 4 of Schedule 3 apply in relation to a complaint under subsection (8) as if it were a complaint under section 17A(1) (and paragraphs 6 to 8 of Schedule 3 do not apply in relation to such a complaint).]

[991]

NOTES

Commencement: 2 December 1996.

Sub-s (6A): inserted by the Disability Discrimination Act 2005, s 11(2).

Sub-ss (7), (8): added, together with sub-s (9), by the Disability Discrimination Act 1995 (Amendment) Regulations 2003, SI 2003/1673, regs 3(1), 19(2); substituted by the Disability Discrimination Act 2005, s 19(1), Sch 1, Pt 1, paras 1, 21.

Sub-s (9): added, together with sub-ss (7), (8), by SI 2003/1673, regs 3(1), 19(2).

26 Validity and revision of certain agreements

(1) Any term in a contract for the provision of goods, facilities or services or in any other agreement is void so far as it purports to—

(a) require a person to do anything which would contravene any provision of, or made under, this Part,

(b) exclude or limit the operation of any provision of this Part, or

(c) prevent any person from making a claim under this Part.

[(1A) Subsection (1) does not apply to—

(a) any term in a contract for the provision of employment services;

(b) any term in a contract which is a group insurance arrangement; or

(c) a term which—

(i) is in an agreement which is not a contract of either of those kinds, and

(ii) relates to the provision of employment services or the provision under a group insurance arrangement of facilities by way of insurance.]

(2) Paragraphs (b) and (c) of subsection (1) do not apply to an agreement settling a claim to which section 25 applies.

(3) On the application of any person interested in an agreement to which subsection (1) applies, a county court or a sheriff court may make such order as it thinks just for modifying the agreement to take account of the effect of subsection (1).

(4) No such order shall be made unless all persons affected have been—

(a) given notice of the application; and

(b) afforded an opportunity to make representations to the court.

(5) Subsection (4) applies subject to any rules of court providing for that notice to be dispensed with.

(6) An order under subsection (3) may include provision as respects any period before the making of the order.

[992]

NOTES

Commencement: 2 December 1996.

Sub-s (1A): inserted by the Disability Discrimination Act 1995 (Amendment) Regulations 2003, SI 2003/1673, regs 3(1), 19(3); substituted by the Disability Discrimination Act 2005, s 19(1), Sch 1, Pt 1, paras 1, 22.

27 Alterations to premises occupied under leases

(1) This section applies where—

(a) a provider of services[, a public authority (within the meaning given by section 21B) or an association to which section 21F applies] ("the occupier") occupies premises under a lease;

(b) but for this section, [the occupier] would not be entitled to make a particular alteration to the premises; and

(c) the alteration is one which the occupier proposes to make in order to comply with a section 21 duty [or a duty imposed under section 21E or 21H].

(2) Except to the extent to which it expressly so provides, the lease shall have effect by virtue of this subsection as if it provided—

(a) for the occupier to be entitled to make the alteration with the written consent of the lessor;

(b) for the occupier to have to make a written application to the lessor for consent if he wishes to make the alteration;

(c) if such an application is made, for the lessor not to withhold his consent unreasonably; and

(d) for the lessor to be entitled to make his consent subject to reasonable conditions.

(3) In this section—

"lease" includes a tenancy, sub-lease or sub-tenancy and an agreement for a lease, tenancy, sub-lease or sub-tenancy; and

"sub-lease" and "sub-tenancy" have such meaning as may be prescribed.

(4) If the terms and conditions of a lease—

(a) impose conditions which are to apply if the occupier alters the premises, or

(b) entitle the lessor to impose conditions when consenting to the occupier's altering the premises,

the occupier is to be treated for the purposes of subsection (1) as not being entitled to make the alteration.

(5) Part II of Schedule 4 supplements the provisions of this section.

[993]

NOTES

Commencement: 9 May 2001 (sub-s (3), sub-s (5) certain purposes; 1 October 2004 (sub-ss (1), (2), (4), sub-s (5) remaining purposes).

Sub-s (1): words in square brackets in paras (a), (c) inserted and words in square brackets in para (b) substituted by the Disability Discrimination Act 2005, s 19(1), Sch 1, Pt 1, paras 1, 23.

Modification: modified, in relation to any case where the occupier occupies premises under a sub-lease or sub-tenancy, by the Disability Discrimination (Providers of Services) (Adjustment of Premises) Regulations 2001, SI 2001/3253, reg 9(1)–(3).

Regulations: the Disability Discrimination (Providers of Services) (Adjustment of Premises) Regulations 2001, SI 2001/3253; the Disability Discrimination (Service Providers and Public Authorities Carrying Out Functions) Regulations 2005, SI 2005/2901.

[28 *Conciliation of disputes*

(1) The Commission may make arrangements with any other person for the provision of conciliation services by, or by persons appointed by, that person in relation to disputes arising under this Part.

(2) In deciding what arrangements (if any) to make, the Commission shall have regard to the desirability of securing, so far as reasonably practicable, that conciliation services are available for all disputes arising under this Part which the parties may wish to refer to conciliation.

(3) No member or employee of the Commission may provide conciliation services in relation to disputes arising under this Part.

(4) The Commission shall ensure that any arrangements under this section include appropriate safeguards to prevent the disclosure to members or employees of the Commission of information obtained by a person in connection with the provision of conciliation services in pursuance of the arrangements.

(5) Subsection (4) does not apply to information relating to a dispute which is disclosed with the consent of the parties to that dispute.

(6) Subsection (4) does not apply to information which—

(a) is not identifiable with a particular dispute or a particular person; and

(b) is reasonably required by the Commission for the purpose of monitoring the operation of the arrangements concerned.

(7) Anything communicated to a person while providing conciliation services in pursuance of any arrangements under this section is not admissible in evidence in any proceedings except with the consent of the person who communicated it to that person.

(8) In this section "conciliation services" means advice and assistance provided by a conciliator to the parties to a dispute with a view to promoting its settlement otherwise than through the courts.]

[994]

NOTES

Commencement: 25 April 2000.

Repealed by the Equality Act 2006, ss 40, 91, Sch 3, paras 41, 45, Sch 4, as from a day to be appointed under s 93 of that Act.

Substituted by the Disability Rights Commission Act 1999, s 10.

28A–59A *((Pts IV–VII) outside the scope of this work.)*

PART VIII
MISCELLANEOUS

60–67B *(Outside the scope of this work.)*

68 Interpretation

(1) In this Act—

"accessibility certificate" means a certificate issued under section 41(1)(a); "act" includes a deliberate omission;

"approval certificate" means a certificate issued under section 42(4);

.....

"conciliation officer" means a person designated under section 211 of the Trade Union and Labour Relations (Consolidation) Act 1992;

["criminal investigation" has the meaning given in subsection (1A);]

["criminal proceedings" includes—

(a) proceedings on dealing summarily with a charge under the Army Act 1955 or the Air Force Act 1955 or on summary trial under the Naval Discipline Act 1957;

(b) proceedings before a summary appeal court constituted under any of those Acts;

(c) proceedings before a court-martial constituted under any of those Acts or a disciplinary court constituted under section 52G of the Naval Discipline Act 1957;

(d) proceedings before the Courts-Martial Appeal Court; and

(e) proceedings before a Standing Civilian Court;]

"employment" means, subject to any prescribed provision, employment under a contract of service or of apprenticeship or a contract personally to do any work, and related expressions are to be construed accordingly;

["employment at an establishment in Great Britain" is to be construed in accordance with subsections (2) to (4A);]

["employment services" has the meaning given in section 21A(1);]

"enactment" includes subordinate legislation and any Order in Council[, and … includes an enactment comprised in, or in an instrument made under, an Act of the Scottish Parliament];

["Great Britain" includes such of the territorial waters of the United Kingdom as are adjacent to Great Britain;]

["group insurance arrangement" means an arrangement between an employer and another for the provision by the other of facilities by way of insurance to the employer's employees or to any class of those employees;]

"licensing authority"[, except in section 37A,] means—

(a) in relation to the area to which the Metropolitan Public Carriage Act 1869 applies, the Secretary of State or the holder of any office for the time being designated by the Secretary of State; or

(b) in relation to any other area in England and Wales, the authority responsible for licensing taxis in that area;

"mental impairment" does not have the same meaning as in the Mental Health Act 1983 … but the fact that an impairment would be a mental impairment for the purposes of [that Act] does not prevent it from being a mental impairment for the purposes of this Act;

["Minister of the Crown" includes the Treasury and the Defence Council;]

"occupational pension scheme" has the same meaning as in the Pension Schemes Act 1993;

"premises" includes land of any description;

"prescribed" means prescribed by regulations[, except in section 28D (where it has the meaning given by section 28D(17))];

"profession" includes any vocation or occupation;

"provider of services" has the meaning given in section 19(2)(b);

["public investigator functions" has the meaning given in subsection (1B);]

"public service vehicle" and "regulated public service vehicle" have the meaning given in section 40;

"PSV accessibility regulations" means regulations made under section 40(1);

"rail vehicle" and "regulated rail vehicle" have the meaning given in section 46;

["rail vehicle accessibility compliance certificate" has the meaning given in section 47A(3);]

"rail vehicle accessibility regulations" means regulations made under section 46(1);

"regulations" means regulations made by the Secretary of State[, except in sections 2(3), 28D, 28L(6), 28Q(7), 33, 49D *to 49F* and 67 (provisions where the meaning of "regulations" is apparent)];

.....

"section 21 duty" means any duty imposed by or under section 21;

"subordinate legislation" has the same meaning as in section 21 of the Interpretation Act 1978;

"taxi" and "regulated taxi" have the meaning given in section 32;

"taxi accessibility regulations" means regulations made under section 32(1);

"trade" includes any business;

"trade organisation" has the meaning given in section 13;

"vehicle examiner" means an examiner appointed under section 66A of the Road Traffic Act 1988.

[(1A) In this Act "criminal investigation" means—

(a) any investigation which a person in carrying out functions to which section 21B(1) applies has a duty to conduct with a view to it being ascertained whether a person should be charged with, or in Scotland prosecuted for, an offence, or whether a person charged with or prosecuted for an offence is guilty of it;

(b) any investigation which is conducted by a person in carrying out functions to which section 21B(1) applies and which in the circumstances may lead to a decision by that person to institute criminal proceedings which the person has power to conduct; or

(c) any investigation which is conducted by a person in carrying out functions to which section 21B(1) applies and which in the circumstances may lead to a decision by that person to make a report to the procurator fiscal for the purpose of enabling him to determine whether criminal proceedings should be instituted.

(1B) In this Act "public investigator functions" means functions of conducting criminal investigations or charging offenders.

(1C) In subsections (1A) and (1B)—

"offence" includes *any offence of a kind triable by court-martial under the Army Act 1955, the Air Force Act 1955 or the Naval Discipline Act 1957*, and

"offender" is to be construed accordingly.]

[(2) Employment (including employment on board a ship to which subsection (2B) applies or on an aircraft or hovercraft to which subsection (2C) applies) is to be regarded as being employment at an establishment in Great Britain if the employee—

(a) does his work wholly or partly in Great Britain; or

(b) does his work wholly outside Great Britain and subsection (2A) applies.

(2A) This subsection applies if—

(a) the employer has a place of business at an establishment in Great Britain;

(b) the work is for the purposes of the business carried on at the establishment; and

(c) the employee is ordinarily resident in Great Britain—

(i) at the time when he applies for or is offered the employment, or

(ii) at any time during the course of the employment.

(2B) This subsection applies to a ship if—

(a) it is registered at a port of registry in Great Britain; or

(b) it belongs to or is possessed by Her Majesty in right of the Government of the United Kingdom.

(2C) This subsection applies to an aircraft or hovercraft if—

(a) it is—

(i) registered in the United Kingdom, and

(ii) operated by a person who has his principal place of business, or is ordinarily resident, in Great Britain; or

(b) it belongs to or is possessed by Her Majesty in right of the Government of the United Kingdom.

(2D) The following are not to be regarded as being employment at an establishment in Great Britain—

(a) employment on board a ship to which subsection (2B) does not apply;

(b) employment on an aircraft or hovercraft to which subsection (2C) does not apply.]

(4) Employment of a prescribed kind, or in prescribed circumstances, is to be regarded as not being employment at an establishment in Great Britain.

[(4A) For the purposes of determining if employment concerned with the exploration of the sea bed or sub-soil or the exploitation of their natural resources is outside Great Britain, subsections (2)(a) and (b), (2A) and (2C) of this section each have effect as if "Great Britain" had the same meaning as that given to the last reference to Great Britain in section 10(1) of the Sex Discrimination Act 1975 by section 10(5) of that Act read with the Sex Discrimination and Equal Pay (Offshore Employment) Order 1987.]

(5) …

[995]

NOTES

Commencement: 16 December 1999 (sub-s (2)); 2 December 1996 (sub-ss (3)–(5)); 17 May 1996 (sub-s (1)).

Sub-s (1): definitions "benefits", "section 6 duty" and "section 15 duty" repealed, definitions "employment at an establishment in Great Britain" and "Minister of the Crown" substituted, and definition "Great Britain" inserted by the Disability Discrimination Act 1995 (Amendment) Regulations 2003, SI 2003/1673, regs 3(1), 27(a); definitions "criminal investigation", "criminal proceedings", "employment services", "group insurance arrangement", "public investigator functions" inserted by the Disability Discrimination Act 2005, ss 11(3), 19(1), Sch 1, Pt 1, paras 1, 34(1), (2); in definition "enactment" words in square brackets inserted by the Scotland Act 1998 (Consequential Modifications) Order 2000, SI 2000/2040, art 2(1), Schedule, Pt I, para 18, words omitted repealed by the Disability Discrimination Act 2005, s 19, Sch 1, Pt 1, paras 1, 34(1), (3), Sch 2; in definition "licensing authority" words in square brackets inserted by the Private Hire Vehicles (Carriage of Guide Dogs etc) Act 2002, s 5; in definition "mental impairment" words omitted repealed and words in square brackets substituted by the Disability Discrimination Act 2005, s 19, Sch 1, Pt 1, paras 1, 34(1), (4), Sch 2; in definition "prescribed" words in square brackets inserted by the Disability Discrimination Act 2005, s 19(1), Sch 1, Pt 1, paras 1, 34(1), (5); definition "rail vehicle accessibility compliance certificate" inserted by the Disability Discrimination Act 2005, s 7(3), as from a day to be appointed under s 20(3) of that Act; in definition "regulations" words in square brackets inserted by the Disability Discrimination Act 2005, s 19(1), Sch 1, Pt 1, paras 1, 34(1), (6), words in italics repealed by the Equality Act 2006, ss 40, 91, Sch 3, paras 41, 54, Sch 4, as from a day to be appointed under s 93 of that Act; definition "criminal proceedings" substituted as follows by the Armed Forces Act 2006, s 378(1), Sch 16, para 134(a), as from a day to be appointed—

""criminal proceedings" includes service law proceedings (as defined by section 324(5) of the Armed Forces Act 2006);".

Sub-ss (1A), (1B): inserted, together with sub-s (1C), by the Disability Discrimination Act 2005, s 19(1), Sch 1, Pt 1, paras 1, 34(1), (7).

Sub-s (1C): inserted, together with sub-ss (1A), (1B), by the Disability Discrimination Act 2005, s 19(1), Sch 1, Pt 1, paras 1, 34(1), (7); in definition "offence" for the words in italics there are substituted the words "any service offence within the meaning of the Armed Forces Act 2006" by the Armed Forces Act 2006, s 378(1), Sch 16, para 134(b), as from a day to be appointed.

Sub-ss (2), (2A)–(2D): substituted, for sub-ss (2), (3) as originally enacted, by SI 2003/1673, regs 3(1), 27(b).

Sub-s (4A): inserted by SI 2003/1673, regs 3(1), 27(c).

Sub-s (5): repealed by SI 2003/1673, regs 3(1), 27(d).

69 (*Outside the scope of this work.*)

70 Short title, commencement, extent etc

(1) This Act may be cited as the Disability Discrimination Act 1995.

(2) This section (apart from subsections (4), (5) and (7)) comes into force on the passing of this Act.

(3) The other provisions of this Act come into force on such day as the Secretary of State may by order appoint and different days may be appointed for different purposes.

(4) Schedule 6 makes consequential amendments.

(5) The repeals set out in Schedule 7 shall have effect.

[(5A) Sections 7A[, *7B, 49G, 49H and 53A(1D) and (1E)*] extend to England and Wales only.

(5B) Sections 7C and 7D extend to Scotland only.]

(6) [Subject to subsections (5A) and (5B), this Act extends to England and Wales, Scotland and Northern Ireland;] but in their application to Northern Ireland the provisions of this Act mentioned in Schedule 8 shall have effect subject to the modifications set out in that Schedule.

(7) …

(8) Consultations which are required by any provision of this Act to be held by the Secretary of State may be held by him before the coming into force of that provision.

[996]

NOTES

Commencement: 8 November 1995 (sub-ss (1)–(3), (6), (8)); 17 May 1996 (sub-s (7)); 2 December 1996 (sub-s (4), sub-s (5) certain purposes); to be appointed (sub-s (5), remaining purposes).

Sub-s (5A): inserted, together with sub-s (5B), by the Disability Discrimination Act 1995 (Amendment) Regulations 2003, SI 2003/1673, regs 3(1), 28(a); words in square brackets substituted by the Disability Discrimination Act 2005, s 19(1), Sch 1, Pt 1, paras 1, 35, further substituted by the words "7B and 49G" by the Equality Act 2006, s 40, Sch 3, paras 41, 55, as from a day to be appointed under s 93 of that Act.

Sub-s (5B): inserted, together with sub-s (5A), by SI 2003/1673, regs 3(1), 28(a).

Sub-s (6): words in square brackets substituted by SI 2003/1673, regs 3(1), 28(b).

Sub-s (7): amends the House of Commons Disqualification Act 1975, Sch 1, Pt II and the Northern Ireland Assembly Disqualification Act 1975, Sch 1, Pt II; repealed in part by the Disability Rights Commission Act 1999, s 14(2), Sch 5.

Orders: the Disability Discrimination Act 1995 (Commencement No 1) Order 1995, SI 1995/3330; the Disability Discrimination Act 1995 (Commencement No 2) Order 1996, SI 1996/1336; the Disability Discrimination Act 1995 (Commencement No 3 and Saving and Transitional Provisions) Order 1996, SI 1996/1474; the Disability Discrimination Act 1995 (Commencement No 4) Order 1996, SI 1996/3003; the Disability Discrimination Act 1995 (Commencement No 5) Order 1998, SI 1998/1282; the Disability Discrimination Act 1995 (Commencement Order No 6) Order 1999, SI 1999/1190; the Disability Discrimination Act 1995 (Commencement No 7) Order 2000, SI 2000/1969; the Disability Discrimination Act 1995 (Commencement No 8) Order 2000, SI 2000/2989; the Disability Discrimination Act 1995 (Commencement No 9) Order 2001, SI 2001/2030; the Disability Discrimination Act 1995 (Commencement No 10) (Scotland) Order 2003, SI 2003/215; the Disability Discrimination Act 1995 (Commencement No 11) Order 2005, SI 2005/1122.

SCHEDULES

SCHEDULE 1
PROVISIONS SUPPLEMENTING SECTION 1

Section 1(1)

Impairment

1.—(1) …

(2) Regulations may make provision, for the purposes of this Act—
- (a) for conditions of a prescribed description to be treated as amounting to impairments;
- (b) for conditions of a prescribed description to be treated as not amounting to impairments.

(3) Regulations made under sub-paragraph (2) may make provision as to the meaning of "condition" for the purposes of those regulations.

Long-term effects

2.—(1) The effect of an impairment is a long-term effect if—
- (a) it has lasted at least 12 months;
- (b) the period for which it lasts is likely to be at least 12 months; or
- (c) it is likely to last for the rest of the life of the person affected.

(2) Where an impairment ceases to have a substantial adverse effect on a person's ability to carry out normal day-to-day activities, it is to be treated as continuing to have that effect if that effect is likely to recur.

(3) For the purposes of sub-paragraph (2), the likelihood of an effect recurring shall be disregarded in prescribed circumstances.

(4) Regulations may prescribe circumstances in which, for the purposes of this Act—
- (a) an effect which would not otherwise be a long-term effect is to be treated as such an effect; or
- (b) an effect which would otherwise be a long-term effect is to be treated as not being such an effect.

Severe disfigurement

3.—(1) An impairment which consists of a severe disfigurement is to be treated as having a substantial adverse effect on the ability of the person concerned to carry out normal day-today activities.

(2) Regulations may provide that in prescribed circumstances a severe disfigurement is not to be treated as having that effect.

(3) Regulations under sub-paragraph (2) may, in particular, make provision with respect to deliberately acquired disfigurements.

Normal day-to-day activities

4.—(1) An impairment is to be taken to affect the ability of the person concerned to carry out normal day-to-day activities only if it affects one of the following—
- (a) mobility;
- (b) manual dexterity;
- (c) physical co-ordination;
- (d) continence;
- (e) ability to lift, carry or otherwise move everyday objects;
- (f) speech, hearing or eyesight;
- (g) memory or ability to concentrate, learn or understand; or
- (h) perception of the risk of physical danger.

(2) Regulations may prescribe—

(a) circumstances in which an impairment which does not have an effect falling within sub-paragraph (1) is to be taken to affect the ability of the person concerned to carry out normal day-to-day activities;

(b) circumstances in which an impairment which has an effect falling within subparagraph (1) is to be taken not to affect the ability of the person concerned to carry out normal day-to-day activities.

Substantial adverse effects

5. Regulations may make provision for the purposes of this Act—

(a) for an effect of a prescribed kind on the ability of a person to carry out normal day-to-day activities to be treated as a substantial adverse effect;

(b) for an effect of a prescribed kind on the ability of a person to carry out normal day-to-day activities to be treated as not being a substantial adverse effect.

Effect of medical treatment

6.—(1) An impairment which would be likely to have a substantial adverse effect on the ability of the person concerned to carry out normal day-to-day activities, but for the fact that measures are being taken to treat or correct it, is to be treated as having that effect.

(2) In sub-paragraph (1) "measures" includes, in particular, medical treatment and the use of a prosthesis or other aid.

(3) Sub-paragraph (1) does not apply—

(a) in relation to the impairment of a person's sight, to the extent that the impairment is, in his case, correctable by spectacles or contact lenses or in such other ways as may be prescribed; or

(b) in relation to such other impairments as may be prescribed, in such circumstances as may be prescribed.

[6A.—(1) Subject to sub-paragraph (2), a person who has cancer, HIV infection or multiple sclerosis is to be deemed to have a disability, and hence to be a disabled person.

(2) Regulations may provide for sub-paragraph (1) not to apply in the case of a person who has cancer if he has cancer of a prescribed description.

(3) A description of cancer prescribed under sub-paragraph (2) may (in particular) be framed by reference to consequences for a person of his having it.]

Persons deemed to be disabled

7.—(1) Sub-paragraph (2) applies to any person whose name is, both on 12th January 1995 and on the date when this paragraph comes into force, in the register of disabled persons maintained under section 6 of the Disabled Persons (Employment) Act 1944.

(2) That person is to be deemed—

(a) during the initial period, to have a disability, and hence to be a disabled person; and

(b) afterwards, to have had a disability and hence to have been a disabled person during that period.

(3) A certificate of registration shall be conclusive evidence, in relation to the person with respect to whom it was issued, of the matters certified.

(4) Unless the contrary is shown, any document purporting to be a certificate of registration shall be taken to be such a certificate and to have been validly issued.

(5) Regulations may provide for prescribed descriptions of person to be deemed to have disabilities, and hence to be disabled persons, for the purposes of this Act.

[(5A) The generality of sub-paragraph (5) shall not be taken to be prejudiced by the other provisions of this Schedule.]

(6) Regulations may prescribe circumstances in which a person who has been deemed to be a disabled person by the provisions of sub-paragraph (1) or regulations made under subparagraph (5) is to be treated as no longer being deemed to be such a person.

(7) In this paragraph—

"certificate of registration" means a certificate issued under regulations made under section 6 of the Act of 1944; and

"initial period" means the period of three years beginning with the date on which this paragraph comes into force.

Progressive conditions

8.—(1) Where—

(a) a person has a progressive condition (such as cancer, multiple sclerosis or muscular dystrophy or [HIV infection]),

(b) as a result of that condition, he has an impairment which has (or had) an effect on his ability to carry out normal day-to-day activities, but

(c) that effect is not (or was not) a substantial adverse effect, he shall be taken to have an impairment which has such a substantial adverse effect if the condition is likely to result in his having such an impairment.

(2) Regulations may make provision, for the purposes of this paragraph—

(a) for conditions of a prescribed description to be treated as being progressive;

(b) for conditions of a prescribed description to be treated as not being progressive.

[Interpretation

9. In this Schedule "HIV infection" means infection by a virus capable of causing the Acquired Immune Deficiency Syndrome.]

[997]

NOTES

Commencement: 2 December 1996 (para 7); 17 May 1996 (paras 1–6, 8).

Para 1: sub-para (1) repealed by the Disability Discrimination Act 2005, ss 18(1), (2), 19(2), Sch 2.

Para 6A: inserted by the Disability Discrimination Act 2005, s 18(1), (3).

Para 7: sub-para (5A) inserted by the Disability Discrimination Act 2005, s 18(1), (4).

Para 8: words in square brackets substituted by the Disability Discrimination Act 2005, s 19(1), Sch 1, Pt 1, paras 1, 36.

Para 9: inserted by the Disability Discrimination Act 2005, s 18(1), (5).

Disabled Persons (Employment) Act 1944, s 6: repealed by ss 60(7)(b), 70(5) of, and Sch 7 to, this Act.

Regulations: the Disability Discrimination (Meaning of Disability) Regulations 1996, SI 1996/1455; the Disability Discrimination (Blind and Partially Sighted Persons) Regulations 2003, SI 2003/712.

SCHEDULE 2
PAST DISABILITIES

Section 2(2)

1. The modifications referred to in section 2 are as follows.

2. References in Parts II [to 4] [and 5A] to a disabled person are to be read as references to a person who has had a disability.

[2A. References in Chapter 1 of Part 4 to a disabled pupil are to be read as references to a pupil who has had a disability.

2B. References in Chapter 2 of Part 4 to a disabled student are to be read as references to a student who has had a disability.]

[2C. In *section 3A(5)*, after "not having that particular disability" insert "and who has not had that particular disability".]

[3. In sections 4A(1), 4B(4), 4E(1), [4H(1),] 6B(1), 7B(1), 7D(1), 14(1), 14B(1), 14D(1)[, 15C(1)] and 16A(4), section 21A(4)(a) (in the words to be read as section 19(1)(aa)) and section 21A(6)(a) (in the words to be substituted in section 21(1)), [and section 31AD(1)(d), (2)(c) and (3),] after "not disabled" (in each place it occurs) insert "and who have not had a disability".]

[4. In sections 4A(3)(b), 4E(3)(b), [4H(3)(b),] 6B(3)(b), 7B(4)(b), 7D(3)(b), 14(3)(b), 14B(3)(b), 14D(3)(b)[, 15C(3)(a)] *and 16A(6)*, for "has" (in each place it occurs) substitute "has had".]

[4ZA. In section 24(3)(e)(i) and (f)(i), after "having" insert "had".

4ZB. In sections 24D(2)(a) and 24J(3)(b), for "did not have" substitute "had not had".]

[4A. In section 28B(3)(a) and (4), after "disabled" insert "or that he had had a disability".

4B. In section 28C(1), in paragraphs (a) and (b), after "not disabled" insert "and who have not had a disability"

[4C. In section 28S
 (a) in subsection (3)(a), after "disabled" insert "or that he had had a disability",
 (b) in subsection (6)(a), after "who do not have" insert "and have not had", and
 (c) in subsection (10), for "that particular disability" substitute "and who has not had that particular disability and".]

4D. In [subsections (1), (1A), (1B) (1C) and (1D)] of section 28T, after "not disabled" insert "and who have not had a disability".

4E. In [subsection (1) of that section] as substituted by paragraphs 2 [9, 14 and 21] of Schedule 4C, after "not disabled" insert "and who have not had a disability".]

5. For paragraph 2(1) to (3) of Schedule 1, substitute—

"(1) The effect of an impairment is a long-term effect if it has lasted for at least 12 months.

(2) Where an impairment ceases to have a substantial adverse effect on a person's ability to carry out normal day-to-day activities, it is to be treated as continuing to have that effect if that effect recurs.

(3) For the purposes of sub-paragraph (2), the recurrence of an effect shall be disregarded in prescribed circumstances."

[998]

NOTES

Commencement: 17 May 1996.

Para 2: words in first pair of square brackets substituted by the Special Educational Needs and Disability Act 2001, s 38(1), (11); words in second pair of square brackets inserted by the Disability Discrimination Act 2005, s 19(1), Sch 1, Pt 1, paras 1, 37(1), (2).

Paras 2A, 2B: inserted by the Special Educational Needs and Disability Act 2001, s 38(1), (12).

Para 2C: inserted, in relation to England, Wales and Scotland, by the Disability Discrimination Act 1995 (Amendment) Regulations 2003, SI 2003/1673, regs 3(1), 29(1)(a); words in italics substituted for "sections 3A(5) and 31AB(8)" by the Disability Discrimination Act 2005, s 19(1), Sch 1, Pt 1, paras 1, 37(1), (3), as from a day to be appointed under s 20(3) thereof.

Para 3: substituted, in relation to England, Wales and Scotland, by SI 2003/1673, regs 3(1), 29(1)(b); number in first pair of square brackets inserted by the Disability Discrimination Act 1995 (Pensions) Regulations 2003, SI 2003/2770, regs 2, 4(4)(a); number in second pair of square brackets inserted by the Disability Discrimination Act 2005, s 19(1), Sch 1, Pt 1, paras 1, 37(1), (4)(a); words in third pair of square brackets inserted by the Disability Discrimination Act 2005, s 19(1), Sch 1, Pt 1, paras 1, 37(1), (4)(b), as from a day to be appointed under s 20(3) thereof.

Para 4: substituted, in relation to England, Wales and Scotland, by SI 2003/1673, regs 3(1), 29(1)(c); number in first pair of square brackets inserted by the Disability Discrimination Act 1995 (Pensions) Regulations 2003, SI 2003/2770, regs 2, 4(4)(b);number in second pair of square brackets inserted by the Disability Discrimination Act 2005, s 19(1), Sch 1, Pt 1, paras 1, 37(1), (5)(a); words in italics substituted for words ", 16A(6) and 31AD(4)(b)," by the Disability Discrimination Act 2005, s 19(1), Sch 1, Pt 1, paras 37(1), (5)(b), as from a day to be appointed under s 20(3) thereof.

Paras 4ZA, 4ZB: inserted by the Disability Discrimination Act 2005, s 19(1), Sch 1, Pt 1, paras 1, 37(1), (6).

Paras 4A, 4B: inserted, together with paras 4C–4E, by the Special Educational Needs and Disability Act 2001, s 38(1), (13).

Para 4C: inserted, together with paras 4A, 4B, 4D, 4E, by the Special Educational Needs and Disability Act 2001, s 38(1), (13); substituted by the Disability Discrimination Act 1995 (Amendment) (Further and Higher Education) Regulations 2006, SI 2006/1721, regs 4(1), 18(1), (2).

Paras 4D, 4E: inserted, together with paras 4A–4C, by the Special Educational Needs and Disability Act 2001, s 38(1), (13); words in square brackets substituted by SI 2006/1721, regs 4(1), 18(1), (3), (4).

SCHEDULE 3
ENFORCEMENT AND PROCEDURE

Sections [17A(8)], 25(6)

PART I
EMPLOYMENT

Conciliation

1. …

Restriction on proceedings for breach of Part II

2.—[(1) Except as provided by Part 2, no civil or criminal proceedings may be brought against any person in respect of an act merely because the act is unlawful under that Part.]

(2) Sub-paragraph (1) does not prevent the making of an application for judicial review [or the investigation or determination of any matter in accordance with Part 10 (investigations) of the Pension Schemes Act 1993 by the Pensions Ombudsman].

[(3) Sub-paragraph (1) does not prevent the bringing of proceedings in respect of an offence under section 16B(2B).]

Period within which proceedings must be brought

3.—(1) An [employment tribunal] shall not consider a complaint under [section 17A or 25(8)] unless it is presented before the end of the period of three months beginning when the act complained of was done.

(2) A tribunal may consider any such complaint which is out of time if, in all the circumstances of the case, it considers that it is just and equitable to do so.

(3) For the purposes of sub-paragraph (1)—

(a) where an unlawful act … is attributable to a term in a contract, that act is to be treated as extending throughout the duration of the contract;

(b) any act extending over a period shall be treated as done at the end of that period; and

(c) a deliberate omission shall be treated as done when the person in question decided upon it.

(4) In the absence of evidence establishing the contrary, a person shall be taken for the purposes of this paragraph to decide upon an omission—

(a) when he does an act inconsistent with doing the omitted act; or

(b) if he has done no such inconsistent act, when the period expires within which he might reasonably have been expected to do the omitted act if it was to be done.

Evidence

4.—(1) In any proceedings under [section 17A or 25(8)], a certificate signed by or on behalf of a Minister of the Crown and certifying—

(a) that any conditions or requirements specified in the certificate were imposed by a Minister of the Crown and were in operation at a time or throughout a time so specified, …

(b) …

shall be conclusive evidence of the matters certified.

[(1A) In any proceedings under section 17A or 25(8), a certificate signed by or on behalf of the Scottish Ministers and certifying that any conditions or requirements specified in the certificate—

(a) were imposed by a member of the Scottish Executive, and

(b) were in operation at a time or throughout a time so specified,

shall be conclusive evidence of the matters certified.

(1B) In any proceedings under section 17A or 25(8), a certificate signed by or on behalf of the National Assembly for Wales and certifying that any conditions or requirements specified in the certificate—

(a) were imposed by the Assembly, and

(b) were in operation at a time or throughout a time so specified,

shall be conclusive evidence of the matters certified.]

(2) A document purporting to be such a certificate [as is mentioned in sub-paragraph (1), (1A) or (1B)] shall be received in evidence and, unless the contrary is proved, be deemed to be such a certificate.

[999]

NOTES

Commencement: 2 December 1996.

Enabling section: number in square brackets substituted in relation to England, Wales and Scotland, by the Disability Discrimination Act 1995 (Amendment) Regulations 2003, SI 2003/1673, regs 3(1), 29(2)(a).

Para 1: repealed by the Employment Tribunals Act 1996, s 45, Sch 3, Pt I.

Para 2: sub-para (1) substituted in relation to England, Wales and Scotland, by SI 2003/1673, regs 3(1), 29(2)(b); words in square brackets in sub-para (2) substituted by the Disability Discrimination Act 1995 (Pensions) Regulations 2003, SI 2003/2770, regs 2, 4(5); sub-para (3) inserted by the Disability Discrimination Act 2005, s 19(1), Sch 1, Pt 1, paras 1, 38(1), (2).

Para 3: in sub-para (1) words in first pair of square brackets substituted by the Employment Rights (Dispute Resolution) Act 1998, s 1(2)(a); words in second pair of square brackets in sub-para (1) substituted and words omitted from sub-para (3) omitted in relation to England, Wales and Scotland, by SI 2003/1673, regs 3(1), 29(2)(c), (d).

Para 4: words in square brackets in sub-para (1) substituted, in relation to England, Wales and Scotland, by SI 2003/1673, regs 3(1), 29(2)(e); in sub-para (1) words omitted repealed by the Employment Relations Act 1999, s 44, Sch 9, Table 12; sub-paras (1A), (1B) inserted by the Disability Discrimination Act 2005, s 19(1), Sch 1, Pt 1, paras 1, 38(1), (3); in sub-para (2) words in square brackets inserted by the Disability Discrimination Act 2005, s 19(1), Sch 1, Pt 1, paras 1, 38(1), (4).

By virtue of the Employment Rights (Dispute Resolution) Act 1998, s 1(2), the Industrial Tribunals Act 1996 shall be cited as the Employment Tribunals Act 1996; the reference to the Industrial Tribunals Act 1996 in the note relating to para 1 above has been changed accordingly.

PART II
DISCRIMINATION IN OTHER AREAS

Restriction on proceedings for breach of Part III

5.—(1) Except as provided by section 25 no civil or criminal proceedings may be brought against any person in respect of an act merely because the act is unlawful under Part III.

(2) Sub-paragraph (1) does not prevent the making of an application for judicial review.

Period within which proceedings must be brought

6.—(1) A county court or a sheriff court shall not consider a claim under section 25 unless proceedings in respect of the claim are instituted before the end of the period of six months beginning when the act complained of was done.

(2) *Where, in relation to proceedings or prospective proceedings under section 25, [the dispute concerned is referred for conciliation in pursuance of arrangements under section 28] before the end of the period of six months mentioned in sub-paragraph (1), the period allowed by that sub-paragraph shall be extended by two months.*

(3) A court may consider any claim under section 25 which is out of time if, in all the circumstances of the case, it considers that it is just and equitable to do so.

(4) For the purposes of sub-paragraph (1)—

(a) where an unlawful act of discrimination is attributable to a term in a contract, that act is to be treated as extending throughout the duration of the contract;

(b) any act extending over a period shall be treated as done at the end of that period; and

(c) a deliberate omission shall be treated as done when the person in question decided upon it.

(5) In the absence of evidence establishing the contrary, a person shall be taken for the purposes of this paragraph to decide upon an omission—

(a) when he does an act inconsistent with doing the omitted act; or

(b) if he has done no such inconsistent act, when the period expires within which he might reasonably have been expected to do the omitted act if it was to be done.

[Staying or sisting proceedings on section 21B claim affecting criminal matters

6A.—(1) Sub-paragraph (2) applies where a party to proceedings under section 25 which have arisen by virtue of section 21B(1) has applied for a stay or sist of those proceedings on the grounds of prejudice to—

(a) particular criminal proceedings;

(b) a criminal investigation; or

(c) a decision to institute criminal proceedings.

(2) The court shall grant the stay or sist unless it is satisfied that the continuance of the proceedings under section 25 would not result in the prejudice alleged.

Restriction of remedies for section 21B claim relating to criminal matters

6B.—(1) Sub-paragraph (2) applies to a remedy other than—

(a) damages; or

(b) a declaration or, in Scotland, a declarator.

(2) In proceedings under section 25, the remedy shall be obtainable in respect of a relevant discriminatory act only if the court is satisfied that—

(a) no criminal investigation,

(b) no decision to institute criminal proceedings, and

(c) no criminal proceedings,

would be prejudiced by the remedy.

(3) In sub-paragraph (2) "relevant discriminatory act" means an act—

(a) which is done, or by virtue of section 57 or 58 is treated as done, by a person-

(i) in carrying out public investigator functions, or

(ii) in carrying out functions as a public prosecutor; and

(b) which is unlawful by virtue of section 21B(1).]

Compensation for injury to feelings

7. In any proceedings under section 25, the amount of any damages awarded as compensation for injury to feelings shall not exceed the prescribed amount.

Evidence

8.—(1) In any proceedings under section 25, a certificate signed by or on behalf of a Minister of the Crown and certifying—

(a) that any conditions or requirements specified in the certificate were imposed by a Minister of the Crown and were in operation at a time or throughout a time so specified, or

(b) that an act specified in the certificate was done for the purpose of safeguarding national security,

shall be conclusive evidence of the matters certified.

(2) A document purporting to be such a certificate shall be received in evidence and, unless the contrary is proved, be deemed to be such a certificate.

[(3) In any proceedings under section 25, a certificate signed by or on behalf of the Scottish Ministers and certifying that any conditions or requirements specified in the certificate—

(a) were imposed by a member of the Scottish Executive, and

(b) were in operation at a time or throughout a time so specified,

shall be conclusive evidence of the matters certified.

(4) In any proceedings under section 25, a certificate signed by or on behalf of the National Assembly for Wales and certifying that any conditions or requirements specified in the certificate—

(a) were imposed by the Assembly, and

(b) were in operation at a time or throughout a time so specified,

shall be conclusive evidence of the matters certified.

(5) A document purporting to be such a certificate as is mentioned in sub-paragraph (3) or (4) shall be received in evidence and, unless the contrary is proved, be deemed to be such a certificate.]

[1000]

NOTES

Commencement: 2 December 1996.

Para 6(2): words in square brackets substituted by the Disability Rights Commission Act 1999, s 14(1), Sch 4, para 3(1), (3); substituted as follows by the Equality Act 2006, s 40, Sch 3, paras 41, 56(1), as from a day to be appointed under s 93 thereof:

"(2) Where, in relation to proceedings or prospective proceedings under section 25, the dispute concerned is referred for conciliation in pursuance of arrangements under section 27 of the Equality Act 2006 before the end of the period of six months mentioned in sub-paragraph (1), the period allowed by that sub-paragraph shall be extended by three months."

Paras 6A, 6B: inserted by the Disability Discrimination Act 2005, s 19(1), Sch 1, Pt 1, paras 1, 38(1), (5).

Para 8: sub-paras (3)–(5) added by the Disability Discrimination Act 2005, s 19(1), Sch 1, Pt 1, paras 1, 38(1), (6).

(*Sch 3, Pts 3, 4, as inserted by the Special Educational Needs and Disability Act 2001, ss 19(2), 30(2), Sch 3, paras 1, 2, outside the scope of this work.*)

[SCHEDULE 3A
VALIDITY OF CONTRACTS, COLLECTIVE AGREEMENTS AND RULES OF UNDERTAKINGS

Section 17C

PART 1
VALIDITY AND REVISION OF CONTRACTS

1.—(1) A term of a contract is void where—

(a) the making of the contract is, by reason of the inclusion of the term, unlawful by virtue of this Part of this Act;

(b) it is included in furtherance of an act which is unlawful by virtue of this Part of this Act; or

(c) it provides for the doing of an act which is unlawful by virtue of this Part of this Act.

(2) Sub-paragraph (1) does not apply to a term the inclusion of which constitutes, or is in furtherance of, or provides for, unlawful discrimination against, or harassment of, a party to the contract, but the term shall be unenforceable against that party.

(3) A term in a contract which purports to exclude or limit any provision of this Part of this Act is unenforceable by any person in whose favour the term would operate apart from this paragraph.

(4) Sub-paragraphs (1), (2) and (3) apply whether the contract was entered into before or after the date on which this Schedule comes into force; but in the case of a contract made before that date, those sub-paragraphs do not apply in relation to any period before that date.

2.—(1) Paragraph 1(3) does not apply—

(a) to a contract settling a complaint to which section 17A(1) or 25(8) applies where the contract is made with the assistance of a conciliation officer (within the meaning of the Trade Union and Labour Relations (Consolidation) Act 1992); or

(b) to a contract settling a complaint to which section 17A(1) or 25(8) applies if the conditions regulating compromise contracts under this Schedule are satisfied in relation to the contract.

(2) The conditions regulating compromise contracts under this Schedule are that—

(a) the contract must be in writing;
(b) the contract must relate to the particular complaint;
(c) the complainant must have received advice from a relevant independent adviser as to the terms and effect of the proposed contract and in particular its effect on his ability to pursue a complaint before an employment tribunal;
(d) there must be in force, when the adviser gives the advice, a contract of insurance, or an indemnity provided for members of a profession or professional body, covering the risk of a claim by the complainant in respect of loss arising in consequence of the advice;
(e) the contract must identify the adviser; and
(f) the contract must state that the conditions regulating compromise contracts under this Schedule are satisfied.

(3) A person is a relevant independent adviser for the purposes of sub-paragraph (2)(c)—
(a) if he is a qualified lawyer;
(b) if he is an officer, official, employee or member of an independent trade union who has been certified in writing by the trade union as competent to give advice and as authorised to do so on behalf of the trade union; …
(c) if he works at an advice centre (whether as an employee or a volunteer) and has been certified in writing by the centre as competent to give advice and as authorised to do so on behalf of the centre[; or
(d) if he is a person of a description specified in an order made by the Secretary of State].

(4) But a person is not a relevant independent adviser for the purposes of sub-paragraph (2)(c) in relation to the complainant—
(a) if he is, is employed by or is acting in the matter for the other party or a person who is connected with the other party;
(b) in the case of a person within sub-paragraph (3)(b) or (c), if the trade union or advice centre is the other party or a person who is connected with the other party; or
(c) in the case of a person within sub-paragraph (3)(c), if the complainant makes a payment for the advice received from him.

(5) In sub-paragraph (3)(a) "qualified lawyer" means—
(a) as respects England and Wales, a barrister (whether in practice as such or employed to give legal advice), a solicitor who holds a practising certificate, or a person other than a barrister or solicitor who is an authorised advocate or authorised litigator (within the meaning of the Courts and Legal Services Act 1990); and
(b) as respects Scotland, an advocate (whether in practice as such or employed to give legal advice), or a solicitor who holds a practising certificate.

(6) In sub-paragraph (3)(b) "independent trade union" has the same meaning as in the Trade Union and Labour Relations (Consolidation) Act 1992.

(7) For the purposes of sub-paragraph (4)(a) any two persons are to be treated as connected—
(a) if one is a company of which the other (directly or indirectly) has control; or
(b) if both are companies of which a third person (directly or indirectly) has control.

(8) An agreement under which the parties agree to submit a dispute to arbitration—
(a) shall be regarded for the purposes of sub-paragraph (1)(a) and (b) as being a contract settling a complaint if—
(i) the dispute is covered by a scheme having effect by virtue of an order under section 212A of the Trade Union and Labour Relations (Consolidation) Act 1992, and
(ii) the agreement is to submit it to arbitration in accordance with the scheme; but
(b) shall be regarded as neither being nor including such a contract in any other case.

3.—(1) On the application of a disabled person interested in a contract to which paragraph 1(1) or (2) applies, a county court or a sheriff court may make such order as it thinks fit for—
(a) removing or modifying any term rendered void by paragraph 1(1), or
(b) removing or modifying any term made unenforceable by paragraph 1(2);
but such an order shall not be made unless all persons affected have been given notice in writing of the application (except where under rules of court notice may be dispensed with) and have been afforded an opportunity to make representations to the court.

(2) An order under sub-paragraph (1) may include provision as respects any period before the making of the order (but after the coming into force of this Schedule).]

[1000A]

NOTES

Commencement: 3 July 2003 (so far as enabling anything to be done for the purposes of preparing and bringing into force on or after 1 October 2004 a code of practice under section 53A of this Act); 1 October 2004 (otherwise).

Inserted by the Disability Discrimination Act 1995 (Amendment) Regulations 2003, SI 2003/1673, regs 3(1), 16(2), Schedule.

Para 2: word omitted repealed and words in square brackets inserted by the Disability Discrimination Act 2005, s 19, Sch 1, Pt 1, paras 1, 39(1), (2), Sch 2.

Orders: the Compromise Agreements (Description of Person) Order 2005, SI 2005/2364.

[PART 2
COLLECTIVE AGREEMENTS AND RULES OF UNDERTAKINGS

4.—(1) This Part of this Schedule applies to—

(a) any term of a collective agreement, including an agreement which was not intended, or is presumed not to have been intended, to be a legally enforceable contract;

(b) any rule made by an employer for application to all or any of the persons who are employed by him or who apply to be, or are, considered by him for employment;

(c) any rule made by a trade organisation (within the meaning of section 13) or a qualifications body (within the meaning of section 14A) for application to—

(i) all or any of its members or prospective members; or

(ii) all or any of the persons on whom it has conferred authorisations or qualifications or who are seeking the authorisations or qualifications which it has power to confer.

(2) Any term or rule to which this Part of this Schedule applies is void where—

(a) the making of the collective agreement is, by reason of the inclusion of the term, unlawful by virtue of this Part of this Act;

(b) the term or rule is included in furtherance of an act which is unlawful by virtue of this Part of this Act; or

(c) the term or rule provides for the doing of an act which is unlawful by virtue of this Part of this Act.

(3) Sub-paragraph (2) applies whether the agreement was entered into, or the rule made, before or after the date on which this Schedule comes into force; but in the case of an agreement entered into, or a rule made, before the date on which this Schedule comes into force, that sub-paragraph does not apply in relation to any period before that date.

5. A disabled person to whom this paragraph applies may present a complaint to an employment tribunal that a term or rule is void by virtue of paragraph 4 if he has reason to believe—

(a) that the term or rule may at some future time have effect in relation to him; and

(b) where he alleges that it is void by virtue of paragraph 4(2)(c), that—

(i) an act for the doing of which it provides, may at some such time be done in relation to him, and

(ii) the act would be unlawful by virtue of this Part of this Act if done in relation to him in present circumstances.

6. In the case of a complaint about—

(a) a term of a collective agreement made by or on behalf of—

(i) an employer,

(ii) an organisation of employers of which an employer is a member, or

(iii) an association of such organisations of one of which an employer is a member, or

(b) a rule made by an employer within the meaning of paragraph 4(1)(b),

paragraph 5 applies to any disabled person who is, or is genuinely and actively seeking to become, one of his employees.

7. In the case of a complaint about a rule made by an organisation or body to which paragraph 4(1)(c) applies, paragraph 5 applies to any disabled person—

(a) who is, or is genuinely and actively seeking to become, a member of the organisation or body;

(b) on whom the organisation or body has conferred an authorisation or qualification; or

(c) who is genuinely and actively seeking an authorisation or qualification which the organisation or body has power to confer.

8.—(1) When an employment tribunal finds that a complaint presented to it under paragraph 5 is well-founded the tribunal shall make an order declaring that the term or rule is void.

(2) An order under sub-paragraph (1) may include provision as respects any period before the making of the order (but after the coming into force of this Schedule).

9. The avoidance by virtue of paragraph 4(2) of any term or rule which provides for any person to be discriminated against shall be without prejudice to the following rights (except in so far as they enable any person to require another person to be treated less favourably than himself), namely—

(a) such of the rights of the person to be discriminated against, and

(b) such of the rights of any person who will be treated more favourably in direct or indirect consequence of the discrimination,

as are conferred by or in respect of a contract made or modified wholly or partly in pursuance of, or by reference to, that term or rule.]

[1000B]

NOTES

Commencement: 3 July 2003 (so far as enabling anything to be done for the purposes of preparing and bringing into force on or after 1 October 2004 a code of practice under section 53A of this Act); 1 October 2004 (otherwise).

Inserted by the Disability Discrimination Act 1995 (Amendment) Regulations 2003, SI 2003/1673, regs 3(1), 16(2), Schedule.

[PART 3
INTERPRETATION

10. In this Schedule "collective agreement" means any agreement relating to one or more of the matters mentioned in section 178(2) of the Trade Union and Labour Relations (Consolidation) Act 1992 (meaning of trade dispute), being an agreement made by or on behalf of one or more employers or one or more organisations of employers or associations of such organisations with one or more organisations of workers or associations of such organisations.

[11. Any reference in this Schedule to this Part of this Act shall be taken to include a reference to Part 3 of this Act, to the extent that it relates to—

(a) the provision of employment services; or

(b) the provision under a group insurance arrangement of facilities by way of insurance.

12. Where a term to which section 26(1A)(c) applies is a term in an agreement which is not a contract, Part 1 of this Schedule shall have effect as if the agreement were a contract.]]

[1000C]

NOTES

Commencement: 3 July 2003 (so far as enabling anything to be done for the purposes of preparing and bringing into force on or after 1 October 2004 a code of practice under section 53A of this Act); 1 October 2004 (otherwise).

Inserted by the Disability Discrimination Act 1995 (Amendment) Regulations 2003, SI 2003/1673, regs 3(1), 16(2), Schedule.

Paras 11, 12: substituted, for para 11, by the Disability Discrimination Act 2005, s 19(1), Sch 1, Pt 1, paras 1, 39(1), (3).

SCHEDULE 4
PREMISES OCCUPIED UNDER LEASES

Sections [18A(5)], 27(5)

PART I
OCCUPATION BY [EMPLOYER ETC]

Failure to obtain consent to alteration

1. If any question arises as to whether the occupier has failed to comply with [any duty to make reasonable adjustments], by failing to make a particular alteration to the premises, any constraint attributable to the fact that he occupies the premises under a lease is to be ignored unless he has applied to the lessor in writing for consent to the making of the alteration.

Joining lessors in proceedings under [section 17A …]

2.—(1) In any proceedings [on a complaint under section 17A], in a case to which [section 18A] applies, the complainant or the occupier may ask the tribunal hearing the complaint to direct that the lessor be joined or sisted as a party to the proceedings.

(2) The request shall be granted if it is made before the hearing of the complaint begins.

(3) The tribunal may refuse the request if it is made after the hearing of the complaint begins.

(4) The request may not be granted if it is made after the tribunal has determined the complaint.

(5) Where a lessor has been so joined or sisted as a party to the proceedings, the tribunal may determine—

(a) whether the lessor has—
 (i) refused consent to the alteration, or
 (ii) consented subject to one or more conditions, and
(b) if so, whether the refusal or any of the conditions was unreasonable.

(6) If, under sub-paragraph (5), the tribunal determines that the refusal or any of the conditions was unreasonable it may take one or more of the following steps—

(a) make such declaration as it considers appropriate;
(b) make an order authorising the occupier to make the alteration specified in the order;
(c) order the lessor to pay compensation to the complainant.

(7) An order under sub-paragraph (6)(b) may require the occupier to comply with conditions specified in the order.

(8) Any step taken by the tribunal under sub-paragraph (6) may be in substitution for, or in addition to, any step taken by the tribunal under [section 17A(2)].

(9) If the tribunal orders the lessor to pay compensation it may not make an order under [section 17A(2)] ordering the occupier to do so.

Regulations

3. Regulations may make provision as to circumstances in which—

(a) a lessor is to be taken, for the purposes of [section 18A] and this Part of this Schedule to have—
 (i) withheld his consent;
 (ii) withheld his consent unreasonably;
 (iii) acted reasonably in withholding his consent;
(b) a condition subject to which a lessor has given his consent is to be taken to be reasonable;
(c) a condition subject to which a lessor has given his consent is to be taken to be unreasonable.

Sub-leases etc

4. The Secretary of State may by regulations make provision supplementing, or modifying, the provision made by [section 18A] or any provision made by or under this Part of this Schedule in relation to cases where the occupier occupies premises under a sub-lease or sub-tenancy.

[1001]

NOTES

Commencement: 2 December 1996 (paras 1, 2); 6 June 1996 (para 3); 17 May 1996 (para 4).

Enabling section: number in square brackets substituted in relation to England, Wales and Scotland, by the Disability Discrimination Act 1995 (Amendment) Regulations 2003, SI 2003/1673, regs 3(1), 29(3)(a).

Part heading: words in square brackets substituted, in relation to England, Wales and Scotland, by SI 2003/1673, regs 3(1), 29(3)(b).

Paras 1, 3, 4: words in square brackets substituted, in relation to England, Wales and Scotland, by SI 2003/1673, regs 3(1), 29(3)(c), (e)–(g).

Para 2: words in square brackets in the heading substituted, in relation to England, Wales and Scotland, by SI 2003/1673, regs 3(1), 29(3)(d) and words omitted repealed by the Disability Discrimination Act 2005, s 19(1), Sch 1, Pt 1, paras 1, 40(1), (2); in sub-para (1) words in first pair of square brackets substituted by the Disability Discrimination Act 2005, s 19(1), Sch 1, Pt 1, paras 1, 40(1), (2) and words in second pair of square brackets substituted, in relation to England, Wales and Scotland, by SI 2003/1673, regs 3(1), 29(3)(d); in sub-paras (8), (9) words in second pair of square brackets substituted, in relation to England, Wales and Scotland, by SI 2003/1673, regs 3(1), 29(3)(d).

Regulations: the Disability Discrimination (Employment Field) (Leasehold Premises) Regulations 2004, SI 2004/153.

PART II
OCCUPATION BY [PERSONS SUBJECT TO A DUTY UNDER SECTION 21, 21E OR 21H]

Failure to obtain consent to alteration

5. If any question arises as to whether the occupier has failed to comply with the section 21 duty [or a duty imposed under section 21E or 21H], by failing to make a particular alteration to premises, any constraint attributable to the fact that he occupies the premises under a lease is to be ignored unless he has applied to the lessor in writing for consent to the making of the alteration.

Reference to court

6.—(1) If the occupier has applied in writing to the lessor for consent to the alteration and—

(a) that consent has been refused, or

(b) the lessor has made his consent subject to one or more conditions,

the occupier or a disabled person who has an interest in the proposed alteration to the premises being made, may refer the matter to a county court or, in Scotland, to the sheriff.

(2) In the following provisions of this Schedule "court" includes "sheriff".

(3) On such a reference the court shall determine whether the lessor's refusal was unreasonable or (as the case may be) whether the condition is, or any of the conditions are, unreasonable.

(4) If the court determines—

(a) that the lessor's refusal was unreasonable, or

(b) that the condition is, or any of the conditions are, unreasonable, it may make such declaration as it considers appropriate or an order authorising the occupier to make the alteration specified in the order.

(5) An order under sub-paragraph (4) may require the occupier to comply with conditions specified in the order.

Joining lessors in proceedings under section 25

7.—(1) In any proceedings on a claim [under section 25 in a case to which section 27 applies, other than a claim presented as a complaint under section 25(8),] the plaintiff, the pursuer or the occupier concerned may ask the court to direct that the lessor be joined or sisted as a party to the proceedings.

(2) The request shall be granted if it is made before the hearing of the claim begins.

(3) The court may refuse the request if it is made after the hearing of the claim begins.

(4) The request may not be granted if it is made after the court has determined the claim.

(5) Where a lessor has been so joined or sisted as a party to the proceedings, the court may determine—

(a) whether the lessor has—

(i) refused consent to the alteration, or

(ii) consented subject to one or more conditions, and

(b) if so, whether the refusal or any of the conditions was unreasonable.

(6) If, under sub-paragraph (5), the court determines that the refusal or any of the conditions was unreasonable it may take one or more of the following steps—

(a) make such declaration as it considers appropriate;

(b) make an order authorising the occupier to make the alteration specified in the order;

(c) order the lessor to pay compensation to the complainant.

(7) An order under sub-paragraph (6)(b) may require the occupier to comply with conditions specified in the order.

(8) If the court orders the lessor to pay compensation it may not order the occupier to do so.

[Joining lessors in proceedings relating to group insurance or employment services

7A.—(1) In any proceedings on a complaint under section 25(8) in a case to which section 27 applies, the complainant or the occupier may ask the tribunal hearing the complaint to direct that the lessor be joined or sisted as a party to the proceedings.

(2) The request shall be granted if it is made before the hearing of the complaint begins.

(3) The tribunal may refuse the request if it is made after the hearing of the complaint begins.

(4) The request may not be granted if it is made after the tribunal has determined the complaint.

(5) Where a lessor has been so joined or sisted as a party to the proceedings, the tribunal may determine—

(a) whether the lessor has—

(i) refused consent to the alteration, or

(ii) consented subject to one or more conditions; and

(b) if so, whether the refusal or any of the conditions was unreasonable.

(6) If, under sub-paragraph (5), the tribunal determines that the refusal or any of the conditions was unreasonable it may take one or more of the following steps—

(a) make such declaration as it considers appropriate;

(b) make an order authorising the occupier to make the alteration specified in the order;

(c) order the lessor to pay compensation to the complainant.

(7) An order under sub-paragraph (6)(b) may require the occupier to comply with conditions specified in the order.

(8) Any step taken by the tribunal under sub-paragraph (6) may be in substitution for, or in addition to, any step taken by the tribunal under section 17A(2).

(9) If the tribunal orders the lessor to pay compensation it may not make an order under section 17A(2) ordering the occupier to do so.]

Regulations

8. Regulations may make provision as to circumstances in which—
   (a) a lessor is to be taken, for the purposes of section 27 and this Part of this Schedule to have—
      (i) withheld his consent;
      (ii) withheld his consent unreasonably;
      (iii) acted reasonably in withholding his consent;
   (b) a condition subject to which a lessor has given his consent is to be taken to be reasonable;
   (c) a condition subject to which a lessor has given his consent is to be taken to be unreasonable.

Sub-leases etc

9. The Secretary of State may by regulations make provision supplementing, or modifying, the provision made by section 27 or any provision made by or under this Part of this Schedule in relation to cases where the occupier occupies premises under a sub-lease or sub-tenancy.

[1002]

NOTES

Commencement: 9 May 2001 (paras 8, 9, in relation to England, Wales and Scotland); 31 December 2001 (paras 8, 9, in relation to Northern Ireland); 1 October 2004 (paras 5–7).

Part heading: words in square brackets substituted by the Disability Discrimination Act 2005, s 19(1), Sch 1, Pt 1, paras 1, 40(1), (3).

Para 5: words in square brackets inserted by the Disability Discrimination Act 2005, s 19(1), Sch 1, Pt 1, paras 1, 40(1), (4).

Para 7: words in sub-para (1) substituted by the Disability Discrimination Act 2005, s 19(1), Sch 1, Pt 1, paras 1, 40(1), (5).

Para 7A: inserted by the Disability Discrimination Act 2005, s 19(1), Sch 1, Pt 1, paras 1, 40(1), (6).

Modification: modified, in relation to any case where the occupier occupies premises under a sub-lease or sub-tenancy, by the Disability Discrimination (Providers of Services) (Adjustment of Premises) Regulations 2001, SI 2001/3253, reg 9(1), (4)–(7).

Regulations: the Disability Discrimination (Providers of Services) (Adjustment of Premises) Regulations 2001, SI 2001/3253; the Disability Discrimination (Service Providers and Public Authorities Carrying Out Functions) Regulations 2005, SI 2005/2901.

(*Sch 4, Pt 3, Schs 4A–4C, as inserted by the Special Educational Needs and Disability Act 2001, ss 11(2), 26(2), 29(2), 31(2), Schs 2, 4–6, outside the scope of this work; Sch 5 repealed by the Disability Rights Commission Act 1999, s 14(2), Sch 5; Sch 6 (consequential amendments), Sch 7 (repeals), Sch 8 (modification of this Act in relation to Northern Ireland) outside the scope of this work.*)

FINANCE ACT 1996

(1996 c 8)

An Act to grant certain duties, to alter other duties, and to amend the law relating to the National Debt and the Public Revenue, and to make further provision in connection with Finance.

[29 April 1996]

1–38 ((*Pts I, II*) *outside the scope of this work.*)

PART III
LANDFILL TAX

39–50 (*Outside the scope of this work.*)

Credit

51 Credit: general

(1) Regulations may provide that where—

(a) a person has paid or is liable to pay tax, and

(b) prescribed conditions are fulfilled,

the person shall be entitled to credit of such an amount as is found in accordance with prescribed rules.

(2) Regulations may make provision as to the manner in which a person is to benefit from credit, and in particular may make provision—

(a) that a person shall be entitled to credit by reference to accounting periods;

(b) that a person shall be entitled to deduct an amount equal to his total credit for an accounting period from the total amount of tax due from him for the period;

(c) that if no tax is due from a person for an accounting period but he is entitled to credit for the period, the amount of the credit shall be paid to him by the Commissioners;

(d) that if the amount of credit to which a person is entitled for an accounting period exceeds the amount of tax due from him for the period, an amount equal to the excess shall be paid to him by the Commissioners;

(e) for the whole or part of any credit to be held over to be credited for a subsequent accounting period;

(f) as to the manner in which a person who has ceased to be registrable is to benefit from credit.

(3) Regulations under subsection (2)(c) or (d) above may provide that where at the end of an accounting period an amount is due to a person who has failed to submit returns for an earlier period as required by this Part, the Commissioners may withhold payment of the amount until he has complied with that requirement.

(4) Regulations under subsection (2)(e) above may provide for credit to be held over either on the person's application or in accordance with directions given by the Commissioners from time to time; and the regulations may allow directions to be given generally or with regard to particular cases.

(5) Regulations may provide that—

(a) no benefit shall be conferred in respect of credit except on a claim made in such manner and at such time as may be determined by or under regulations;

(b) payment in respect of credit shall be made subject to such conditions (if any) as the Commissioners think fit to impose, including conditions as to repayment in specified circumstances;

(c) deduction in respect of credit shall be made subject to such conditions (if any) as the Commissioners think fit to impose, including conditions as to the payment to the Commissioners, in specified circumstances, of an amount representing the whole or part of the amount deducted.

(6) Regulations may require a claim by a person to be made in a return required by provision made under section 49 above.

(7) Nothing in section 52 or 53 below shall be taken to derogate from the power to make regulations under this section (whether with regard to bad debts, the environment or any other matter).

[1003]

NOTES

Commencement: 29 April 1996.
Regulations: the Landfill Tax Regulations 1996, SI 1996/1527.

52 Bad debts

(1) Regulations may be made under section 51 above with a view to securing that a person is entitled to credit if—

(a) he carries out a taxable activity as a result of which he becomes entitled to a debt which turns out to be bad (in whole or in part), and

(b) such other conditions as may be prescribed are fulfilled.

(2) The regulations may include provision under section 51(5)(b) or (c) above requiring repayment or payment if it turns out that it was not justified to regard a debt as bad (or to regard it as bad to the extent that it was so regarded).

(3) The regulations may include provision for determining whether, and to what extent, a debt is to be taken to be bad.

[1004]

NOTES

Commencement: 29 April 1996.
Regulations: the Landfill Tax Regulations 1996, SI 1996/1527.

53 Bodies concerned with the environment

(1) Regulations may be made under section 51 above with a view to securing that a person is entitled to credit if—

(a) he pays a sum to a body whose objects are or include the protection of the environment, and
(b) such other conditions as may be prescribed are fulfilled.

(2) The regulations may in particular prescribe conditions—

(a) requiring bodies to which sums are paid (environmental bodies) to be approved by another body (the regulatory body);
(b) requiring the regulatory body to be approved by the Commissioners;
(c) requiring sums to be paid with the intention that they be expended on such matters connected with the protection of the environment as may be prescribed.

(3) The regulations may include provision under section 51(5)(b) or (c) above requiring repayment or payment if—

(a) a sum is not in fact expended on matters prescribed under subsection (2)(c) above, or
(b) a prescribed condition turns out not to have been fulfilled.

(4) The regulations may include—

(a) provision for determining the amount of credit (including provision for limiting it);
(b) provision that matters connected with the protection of the environment include such matters as overheads (including administration) of environmental bodies and the regulatory body;
(c) provision as to the matters by reference to which an environmental body or the regulatory body can be, and remain, approved (including matters relating to the functions and activities of any such body);
(d) provision allowing approval of an environmental body or the regulatory body to be withdrawn (whether prospectively or retrospectively);
(e) provision that, if approval of the regulatory body is withdrawn, another body may be approved in its place or its functions may be performed by the Commissioners;
(f) provision allowing the Commissioners to disclose to the regulatory body information which relates to the tax affairs of persons carrying out taxable activities and which is relevant to the credit scheme established by the regulations.

[1005]

NOTES

Commencement: 29 April 1996.
Regulations: the Landfill Tax Regulations 1996, SI 1996/1527.

54–196 (*Ss 54–71, ss 72–196* (*Pts IV–VI*) *outside the scope of this work.*)

PART VII
MISCELLANEOUS AND SUPPLEMENTAL

197–205 (*Outside the scope of this work.*)

206 Short title

This Act may be cited as the Finance Act 1996.

[1006]

NOTES
Commencement: 29 April 1996.

(Schs 1–41 outside the scope of this work.)

TRUSTS OF LAND AND APPOINTMENT OF TRUSTEES ACT 1996

(1996 c 47)

ARRANGEMENT OF SECTIONS

PART I
TRUSTS OF LAND

Introductory

An Act to make new provision about trusts of land including provision phasing out the Settled Land Act 1925, abolishing the doctrine of conversion and otherwise amending the law about trusts for sale of land; to amend the law about the appointment and retirement of trustees of any trust; and for connected purposes

[24 July 1996]

PART I
TRUSTS OF LANDS

Introductory

1 Meaning of "trust of land"

(1) In this Act—
(a) "trust of land" means (subject to subsection (3)) any trust of property which consists of or includes land, and
(b) "trustees of land" means trustees of a trust of land.

(2) The reference in subsection (1)(a) to a trust—
(a) is to any description of trust (whether express, implied, resulting or constructive), including a trust for sale and a bare trust, and
(b) includes a trust created, or arising, before the commencement of this Act.

(3) The reference to land in subsection (1)(a) does not include land which (despite section 2) is settled land or which is land to which the Universities and College Estates Act 1925 applies.

[1007]

NOTES

Commencement: 1 January 1997.

Settlements and trusts for sale as trusts of land

2 Trusts in place of settlements

(1) No settlement created after the commencement of this Act is a settlement for the purposes of the Settled Land Act 1925; and no settlement shall be deemed to be made under that Act after that commencement.

(2) Subsection (1) does not apply to a settlement created on the occasion of an alteration in any interest in, or of a person becoming entitled under, a settlement which—
(a) is in existence at the commencement of this Act, or
(b) derives from a settlement within paragraph (a) or this paragraph.

(3) But a settlement created as mentioned in subsection (2) is not a settlement for the purposes of the Settled Land Act 1925 if provision to the effect that it is not is made in the instrument, or any of the instruments, by which it is created.

(4) Where at any time after the commencement of this Act there is in the case of any settlement which is a settlement for the purposes of the Settled Land Act 1925 no relevant property which is, or is deemed to be, subject to the settlement, the settlement permanently ceases at that time to be a settlement for the purposes of that Act.

In this subsection "relevant property" means land and personal chattels to which section 67(1) of the Settled Land Act 1925 (heirlooms) applies.

(5) No land held on charitable, ecclesiastical or public trusts shall be or be deemed to be settled land after the commencement of this Act, even if it was or was deemed to be settled land before that commencement.

(6) Schedule 1 has effect to make provision consequential on this section (including provision to impose a trust in circumstances in which, apart from this section, there would be a settlement for the purposes of the Settled Land Act 1925 (and there would not otherwise be a trust)).

[1008]

NOTES

Commencement: 1 January 1997.

3 Abolition of doctrine of conversion

(1) Where land is held by trustees subject to a trust for sale, the land is not to be regarded as personal property; and where personal property is subject to a trust for sale in order that the trustees may acquire land, the personal property is not to be regarded as land.

(2) Subsection (1) does not apply to a trust created by a will if the testator died before the commencement of this Act.

(3) Subject to that, subsection (1) applies to a trust whether it is created, or arises, before or after that commencement.

[1009]

NOTES

Commencement: 1 January 1997.

4 Express trusts for sale as trusts of land

(1) In the case of every trust for sale of land created by a disposition there is to be implied, despite any provision to the contrary made by the disposition, a power for the trustees to postpone sale of the land; and the trustees are not liable in any way for postponing sale of the land, in the exercise of their discretion, for an indefinite period.

(2) Subsection (1) applies to a trust whether it is created, or arises, before or after the commencement of this Act.

(3) Subsection (1) does not affect any liability incurred by trustees before that commencement.

[1010]

NOTES

Commencement: 1 January 1997.

5 Implied trusts for sale as trusts of land

(1) Schedule 2 has effect in relation to statutory provisions which impose a trust for sale of land in certain circumstances so that in those circumstances there is instead a trust of the land (without a duty to sell).

(2) Section 1 of the Settled Land Act 1925 does not apply to land held on any trust arising by virtue of that Schedule (so that any such land is subject to a trust of land).

[1011]

NOTES

Commencement: 1 January 1997.

Functions of trustees of land

6 General powers of trustees

(1) For the purpose of exercising their functions as trustees, the trustees of land have in relation to the land subject to the trust all the powers of an absolute owner.

(2) Where in the case of any land subject to a trust of land each of the beneficiaries interested in the land is a person of full age and capacity who is absolutely entitled to the land,

the powers conferred on the trustees by subsection (1) include the power to convey the land to the beneficiaries even though they have not required the trustees to do so; and where land is conveyed by virtue of this subsection—

(a) the beneficiaries shall do whatever is necessary to secure that it vests in them, and

(b) if they fail to do so, the court may make an order requiring them to do so.

(3) The trustees of land have power to [acquire land under the power conferred by section 8 of the Trustee Act 2000].

(4) …

(5) In exercising the powers conferred by this section trustees shall have regard to the rights of the beneficiaries.

(6) The powers conferred by this section shall not be exercised in contravention of, or of any order made in pursuance of, any other enactment or any rule of law or equity.

(7) The reference in subsection (6) to an order includes an order of any court or of the [Charity Commission].

(8) Where any enactment other than this section confers on trustees authority to act subject to any restriction, limitation or condition, trustees of land may not exercise the powers conferred by this section to do any act which they are prevented from doing under the other enactment by reason of the restriction, limitation or condition.

[(9) The duty of care under section 1 of the Trustee Act 2000 applies to trustees of land when exercising the powers conferred by this section.]

[1012]

NOTES

Commencement: 1 January 1997 (sub-ss (1)–(8)); 1 February 2001 (sub-s (9)).

Sub-s (3): words in square brackets substituted by the Trustee Act 2000, s 40(1), Sch 2, Pt II, para 45(1).

Sub-s (4): repealed by the Trustee Act 2000, s 40(1), (3), Sch 2, Pt II, para 45(2), Sch 4, Pt II.

Sub-s (7): words in square brackets substituted by the Charities Act 2006, s 75(1), Sch 8, para 182.

Sub-s (9): added by the Trustee Act 2000, s 40(1), Sch 2, Pt II, para 45(3).

7 Partition by trustees

(1) The trustees of land may, where beneficiaries of full age are absolutely entitled in undivided shares to land subject to the trust, partition the land, or any part of it, and provide (by way of mortgage or otherwise) for the payment of any equality money.

(2) The trustees shall give effect to any such partition by conveying the partitioned land in severalty (whether or not subject to any legal mortgage created for raising equality money), either absolutely or in trust, in accordance with the rights of those beneficiaries.

(3) Before exercising their powers under subsection (2) the trustees shall obtain the consent of each of those beneficiaries.

(4) Where a share in the land is affected by an incumbrance, the trustees may either give effect to it or provide for its discharge from the property allotted to that share as they think fit.

(5) If a share in the land is absolutely vested in a minor, subsections (1) to (4) apply as if he were of full age, except that the trustees may act on his behalf and retain land or other property representing his share in trust for him.

[(6) Subsection (1) is subject to sections 21 (part-unit: interests) and 22 (part-unit: charging) of the Commonhold and Leasehold Reform Act 2002.]

[1013]

NOTES

Commencement: 1 January 1997.

Sub-s (6): added by the Commonhold and Leasehold Reform Act 2002, s 68, Sch 5, para 8.

8 Exclusion and restriction of powers

(1) Sections 6 and 7 do not apply in the case of a trust of land created by a disposition in so far as provision to the effect that they do not apply is made by the disposition.

(2) If the disposition creating such a trust makes provision requiring any consent to be obtained to the exercise of any power conferred by section 6 or 7, the power may not be exercised without that consent.

(3) Subsection (1) does not apply in the case of charitable, ecclesiastical or public trusts.

(4) Subsections (1) and (2) have effect subject to any enactment which prohibits or restricts the effect of provision of the description mentioned in them.

[1014]

NOTES

Commencement: 1 January 1997.

9 Delegation by trustees

(1) The trustees of land may, by power of attorney, delegate to any beneficiary or beneficiaries of full age and beneficially entitled to an interest in possession in land subject to the trust any of their functions as trustees which relate to the land.

(2) Where trustees purport to delegate to a person by a power of attorney under subsection (1) functions relating to any land and another person in good faith deals with him in relation to the land, he shall be presumed in favour of that other person to have been a person to whom the functions could be delegated unless that other person has knowledge at the time of the transaction that he was not such a person.

And it shall be conclusively presumed in favour of any purchaser whose interest depends on the validity of that transaction that that other person dealt in good faith and did not have such knowledge if that other person makes a statutory declaration to that effect before or within three months after the completion of the purchase.

(3) A power of attorney under subsection (1) shall be given by all the trustees jointly and (unless expressed to be irrevocable and to be given by way of security) may be revoked by any one or more of them; and such a power is revoked by the appointment as a trustee of a person other than those by whom it is given (though not by any of those persons dying or otherwise ceasing to be a trustee).

(4) Where a beneficiary to whom functions are delegated by a power of attorney under subsection (1) ceases to be a person beneficially entitled to an interest in possession in land subject to the trust—

(a) if the functions are delegated to him alone, the power is revoked,

(b) if the functions are delegated to him and to other beneficiaries to be exercised by them jointly (but not separately), the power is revoked if each of the other beneficiaries ceases to be so entitled (but otherwise functions exercisable in accordance with the power are so exercisable by the remaining beneficiary or beneficiaries), and

(c) if the functions are delegated to him and to other beneficiaries to be exercised by them separately (or either separately or jointly), the power is revoked in so far as it relates to him.

(5) A delegation under subsection (1) may be for any period or indefinite.

(6) A power of attorney under subsection (1) cannot be *an enduring power within the meaning of the Enduring Powers of Attorney Act 1985.*

(7) Beneficiaries to whom functions have been delegated under subsection (1) are, in relation to the exercise of the functions, in the same position as trustees (with the same duties and liabilities); but such beneficiaries shall not be regarded as trustees for any other purposes (including, in particular, the purposes of any enactment permitting the delegation of functions by trustees or imposing requirements relating to the payment of capital money).

(8) …

(9) Neither this section nor the repeal by this Act of section 29 of the Law of Property Act 1925 (which is superseded by this section) affects the operation after the commencement of this Act of any delegation effected before that commencement.

[1015]

NOTES

Commencement: 1 January 1997.

PART I STATUTES

Sub-s (6): for the words in italics there are substituted the words "an enduring power of attorney or lasting power of attorney within the meaning of the Mental Capacity Act 2005" by the Mental Capacity Act 2005, s 67(1), Sch 6, para 42(1), (2), as from a day to be appointed under s 68(1) of that Act.

Sub-s (8): repealed by the Trustee Act 2000, s 40(1), (3), Sch 2, Pt II, para 46, Sch 4, Pt II; for effect see s 9A(7) of this Act at **[1016]**.

Law of Property Act 1925, s 29: repealed by s 25(2) of, and Sch 4 to, this Act.

[9A Duties of trustees in connection with delegation etc

(1) The duty of care under section 1 of the Trustee Act 2000 applies to trustees of land in deciding whether to delegate any of their functions under section 9.

(2) Subsection (3) applies if the trustees of land—

(a) delegate any of their functions under section 9, and

(b) the delegation is not irrevocable.

(3) While the delegation continues, the trustees—

(a) must keep the delegation under review,

(b) if circumstances make it appropriate to do so, must consider whether there is a need to exercise any power of intervention that they have, and

(c) if they consider that there is a need to exercise such a power, must do so.

(4) "Power of intervention" includes—

(a) a power to give directions to the beneficiary;

(b) a power to revoke the delegation.

(5) The duty of care under section 1 of the 2000 Act applies to trustees in carrying out any duty under subsection (3).

(6) A trustee of land is not liable for any act or default of the beneficiary, or beneficiaries, unless the trustee fails to comply with the duty of care in deciding to delegate any of the trustees' functions under section 9 or in carrying out any duty under subsection (3).

(7) Neither this section nor the repeal of section 9(8) by the Trustee Act 2000 affects the operation after the commencement of this section of any delegation effected before that commencement.]

[1016]

NOTES

Commencement: 1 February 2001.

Inserted by the Trustee Act 2000, s 40(1), Sch 2, Pt II, para 47.

Consents and consultation.

10 Consents

(1) If a disposition creating a trust of land requires the consent of more than two persons to the exercise by the trustees of any function relating to the land, the consent of any two of them to the exercise of the function is sufficient in favour of a purchaser.

(2) Subsection (1) does not apply to the exercise of a function by trustees of land held on charitable, ecclesiastical or public trusts.

(3) Where at any time a person whose consent is expressed by a disposition creating a trust of land to be required to the exercise by the trustees of any function relating to the land is not of full age—

(a) his consent is not, in favour of a purchaser, required to the exercise of the function, but

(b) the trustees shall obtain the consent of a parent who has parental responsibility for him (within the meaning of the Children Act 1989) or of a guardian of his.

[1017]

NOTES

Commencement: 1 January 1997.

11 Consultation with beneficiaries

(1) The trustees of land shall in the exercise of any function relating to land subject to the trust—

(a) so far as practicable, consult the beneficiaries of full age and beneficially entitled to an interest in possession in the land, and

(b) so far as consistent with the general interest of the trust, give effect to the wishes of those beneficiaries, or (in case of dispute) of the majority (according to the value of their combined interests).

(2) Subsection (1) does not apply—

(a) in relation to a trust created by a disposition in so far as provision that it does not apply is made by the disposition,

(b) in relation to a trust created or arising under a will made before the commencement of this Act, or

(c) in relation to the exercise of the power mentioned in section 6(2).

(3) Subsection (1) does not apply to a trust created before the commencement of this Act by a disposition, or a trust created after that commencement by reference to such a trust, unless provision to the effect that it is to apply is made by a deed executed—

(a) in a case in which the trust was created by one person and he is of full capacity, by that person, or

(b) in a case in which the trust was created by more than one person, by such of the persons who created the trust as are alive and of full capacity.

(4) A deed executed for the purposes of subsection (3) is irrevocable.

[1018]

NOTES

Commencement: 1 January 1997.

Right of beneficiaries to occupy trust land

12 The right to occupy

(1) A beneficiary who is beneficially entitled to an interest in possession in land subject to a trust of land is entitled by reason of his interest to occupy the land at any time if at that time—

(a) the purposes of the trust include making the land available for his occupation (or for the occupation of beneficiaries of a class of which he is a member or of beneficiaries in general), or

(b) the land is held by the trustees so as to be so available.

(2) Subsection (1) does not confer on a beneficiary a right to occupy land if it is either unavailable or unsuitable for occupation by him.

(3) This section is subject to section 13.

[1019]

NOTES

Commencement: 1 January 1997.

13 Exclusion and restriction of right to occupy

(1) Where two or more beneficiaries are (or apart from this subsection would be) entitled under section 12 to occupy land, the trustees of land may exclude or restrict the entitlement of any one or more (but not all) of them.

(2) Trustees may not under subsection (1)—

(a) unreasonably exclude any beneficiary's entitlement to occupy land, or

(b) restrict any such entitlement to an unreasonable extent.

(3) The trustees of land may from time to time impose reasonable conditions on any beneficiary in relation to his occupation of land by reason of his entitlement under section 12.

(4) The matters to which trustees are to have regard in exercising the powers conferred by this section include—

(a) the intentions of the person or persons (if any) who created the trust,
(b) the purposes for which the land is held, and
(c) the circumstances and wishes of each of the beneficiaries who is (or apart from any previous exercise by the trustees of those powers would be) entitled to occupy the land under section 12.

(5) The conditions which may be imposed on a beneficiary under subsection (3) include, in particular, conditions requiring him—
(a) to pay any outgoings or expenses in respect of the land, or
(b) to assume any other obligation in relation to the land or to any activity which is or is proposed to be conducted there.

(6) Where the entitlement of any beneficiary to occupy land under section 12 has been excluded or restricted, the conditions which may be imposed on any other beneficiary under subsection (3) include, in particular, conditions requiring him to—
(a) make payments by way of compensation to the beneficiary whose entitlement has been excluded or restricted, or
(b) forgo any payment or other benefit to which he would otherwise be entitled under the trust so as to benefit that beneficiary.

(7) The powers conferred on trustees by this section may not be exercised—
(a) so as prevent any person who is in occupation of land (whether or not by reason of an entitlement under section 12) from continuing to occupy the land, or
(b) in a manner likely to result in any such person ceasing to occupy the land,

unless he consents or the court has given approval.

(8) The matters to which the court is to have regard in determining whether to give approval under subsection (7) include the matters mentioned in subsection (4)(a) to (c).
[1020]

NOTES
Commencement: 1 January 1997.

Powers of court

14 Applications for order

(1) Any person who is a trustee of land or has an interest in a property subject to a trust of land may make an application to the court for an order under this section.

(2) On an application for an order under this section the court may make any such order—
(a) relating to the exercise by the trustees of any of their functions (including an order relieving them of any obligation to obtain the consent of, or to consult, any person in connection with the exercise of any of their functions), or
(b) declaring the nature or extent of a person's interest in property subject to the trust,

as the court thinks fit.

(3) The court may not under this section make any order as to the appointment or removal of trustees.

(4) The powers conferred on the court by this section are exercisable on an application whether it is made before or after the commencement of this Act.
[1021]

NOTES
Commencement: 1 January 1997.

15 Matters relevant in determining applications

(1) The matters to which the court is to have regard in determining an application for an order under section 14 include—
(a) the intentions of the person or persons (if any) who created the trust,
(b) the purposes for which the property subject to the trust is held,
(c) the welfare of any minor who occupies or might reasonably be expected to occupy any land subject to the trust as his home, and

(d) the interests of any secured creditor of any beneficiary.

(2) In the case of an application relating to the exercise in relation to any land of the powers conferred on the trustees by section 13, the matters to which the court is to have regard also include the circumstances and wishes of each of the beneficiaries who is (or apart from any previous exercise by the trustees of those powers would be) entitled to occupy the land under section 12.

(3) In the case of any other application, other than one relating to the exercise of the power mentioned in section 6(2), the matters to which the court is to have regard also include the circumstances and wishes of any beneficiaries of full age and entitled to an interest in possession in property subject to the trust or (in case of dispute) of the majority (according to the value of their combined interests).

(4) This section does not apply to an application if section 335A of the Insolvency Act 1986 (which is inserted by Schedule 3 and relates to applications by a trustee of a bankrupt) applies to it.

[1022]

NOTES

Commencement: 1 January 1997.

Purchaser protection

16 Protection of purchasers

(1) A purchaser of land which is or has been subject to a trust need not be concerned to see that any requirement imposed on the trustees by section 6(5), 7(3) or 11(1) has been complied with.

(2) Where—

(a) trustees of land who convey land which (immediately before it is conveyed) is subject to the trust contravene section 6(6) or (8), but

(b) the purchaser of the land from the trustees has no actual notice of the contravention,

the contravention does not invalidate the conveyance.

(3) Where the powers of trustees of land are limited by virtue of section 8—

(a) the trustees shall take all reasonable steps to bring the limitation to the notice of any purchaser of the land from them, but

(b) the limitation does not invalidate any conveyance by the trustees to a purchaser who has no actual notice of the limitation.

(4) Where trustees of land convey land which (immediately before it is conveyed) is subject to the trust to persons believed by them to be beneficiaries absolutely entitled to the land under the trust and of full age and capacity—

(a) the trustees shall execute a deed declaring that they are discharged from the trust in relation to that land, and

(b) if they fail to do so, the court may make an order requiring them to do so.

(5) A purchaser of land to which a deed under subsection (4) relates is entitled to assume that, as from the date of the deed, the land is not subject to the trust unless he has actual notice that the trustees were mistaken in their belief that the land was conveyed to beneficiaries absolutely entitled to the land under the trust and of full age and capacity.

(6) Subsections (2) and (3) do not apply to land held on charitable, ecclesiastical or public trusts.

(7) This section does not apply to registered land.

[1023]

NOTES

Commencement: 1 January 1997.

Supplementary

17 Application of provisions to trusts of proceeds of sale

(1) …

(2) Section 14 applies in relation to a trust of proceeds of sale of land and trustees of such a trust as in relation to a trust of land and trustees of land.

(3) In this section "trust of proceeds of sale of land" means (subject to subsection (5)) any trust of property (other than a trust of land) which consists of or includes—
- (a) any proceeds of a disposition of land held in trust (including settled land), or
- (b) any property representing any such proceeds.

(4) The references in subsection (3) to a trust—
- (a) are to any description of trust (whether express, implied, resulting or constructive), including a trust for sale and a bare trust, and
- (b) include a trust created, or arising, before the commencement of this Act.

(5) A trust which (despite section 2) is a settlement for the purposes of the Settled Land Act 1925 cannot be a trust of proceeds of sale of land.

(6) In subsection (3)—
- (a) "disposition" includes any disposition made, or coming into operation, before the commencement of this Act, and
- (b) the reference to settled land includes personal chattels to which section 67(1) of the Settled Land Act 1925 (heirlooms) applies.

[1024]

NOTES

Commencement: 1 January 1997.
Sub-s (1): repealed by the Trustee Act 2000, s 40(1), (3), Sch 2, Pt II, para 48, Sch 4, Pt II.

18 Application of Part to personal representatives

(1) The provisions of this Part relating to trustees, other than sections 10, 11 and 14, apply to personal representatives, but with appropriate modifications and without prejudice to the functions of personal representatives for the purposes of administration.

(2) The appropriate modifications include—
- (a) the substitution of references to persons interested in the due administration of the estate for references to beneficiaries, and
- (b) the substitution of references to the will for references to the disposition creating the trust.

(3) Section 3(1) does not apply to personal representatives if the death occurs before the commencement of this Act.

[1025]

NOTES

Commencement: 1 January 1997.

PART II
APPOINTMENT AND RETIREMENT OF TRUSTEES

19 Appointment and retirement of trustee at instance of beneficiaries

(1) This section applies in the case of a trust where—
- (a) there is no person nominated for the purpose of appointing new trustees by the instrument, if any, creating the trust, and
- (b) the beneficiaries under the trust are of full age and capacity and (taken together) are absolutely entitled to the property subject to the trust.

(2) The beneficiaries may give a direction or directions of either or both of the following descriptions—
- (a) a written direction to a trustee or trustees to retire from the trust, and
- (b) a written direction to the trustees or trustee for the time being (or, if there are

none, to the personal representative of the last person who was a trustee) to appoint by writing to be a trustee or trustees the person or persons specified in the direction.

(3) Where—

(a) a trustee has been given a direction under subsection (2)(a),

(b) reasonable arrangements have been made for the protection of any rights of his in connection with the trust,

(c) after he has retired there will be either a trust corporation or at least two persons to act as trustees to perform the trust, and

(d) either another person is to be appointed to be a new trustee on his retirement (whether in compliance with a direction under subsection (2)(b) or otherwise) or the continuing trustees by deed consent to his retirement,

he shall make a deed declaring his retirement and shall be deemed to have retired and be discharged from the trust.

(4) Where a trustee retires under subsection (3) he and the continuing trustees (together with any new trustee) shall (subject to any arrangements for the protection of his rights) do anything necessary to vest the trust property in the continuing trustees (or the continuing and new trustees).

(5) This section has effect subject to the restrictions imposed by the Trustee Act 1925 on the number of trustees.

[1026]

NOTES

Commencement: 1 January 1997.

20 ***Appointment of substitute for incapable trustee***

(1) This section applies where—

(a) a trustee *is incapable by reason of mental disorder of exercising* his functions as trustee,

(b) there is no person who is both entitled and willing and able to appoint a trustee in place of him under section 36(1) of the Trustee Act 1925, and

(c) the beneficiaries under the trust are of full age and capacity and (taken together) are absolutely entitled to the property subject to the trust.

(2) The beneficiaries may give to—

(a) a receiver of the trustee,

(b) an attorney acting for him under the authority of *a power of attorney created by an instrument which is registered under section 6 of the Enduring Powers of Attorney Act 1985*, or

(c) a person authorised for the purpose by *the authority having jurisdiction under Part VII of the Mental Health Act 1983*,

a written direction to appoint by writing the person or persons specified in the direction to be a trustee or trustees in place of the incapable trustee.

[1027]

NOTES

Commencement: 1 January 1997.

Section heading: substituted by the words "Appointment of substitute for trustee who lacks capacity" by the Mental Capacity Act 2005, s 67(1), Sch 6, para 42(1), (3), as from a day to be appointed under s 68(1) of that Act.

Sub-s (1): for the words in italics there are substituted the words "lacks capacity (within the meaning of the Mental Capacity Act 2005) to exercise" by the Mental Capacity Act 2005, s 67(1), Sch 6, para 42(1), (3)(a), as from a day to be appointed under s 68(1) of that Act.

Sub-s (2): para (a) substituted as follows—

"(a) a deputy appointed for the trustee by the Court of Protection,",

words in italics in para (b) substituted by the words "an enduring power of attorney or lasting power of attorney registered under the Mental Capacity Act 2005" and words in italics in para (c) substituted by the words "the Court of Protection" by the Mental Capacity Act 2005, s 67(1), Sch 6, para 42(1), (3)(b), as from a day to be appointed under s 68(1) of that Act.

21 Supplementary

(1) For the purposes of section 19 or 20 a direction is given by beneficiaries if—

(a) a single direction is jointly given by all of them, or
(b) (subject to subsection (2)) a direction is given by each of them (whether solely or jointly with one or more, but not all, of the others),

and none of them by writing withdraws the direction given by him before it has been complied with.

(2) Where more than one direction is given each must specify for appointment or retirement the same person or persons.

(3) Subsection (7) of section 36 of the Trustee Act 1925 (powers of trustees appointed under that section) applies to a trustee appointed under section 19 or 20 as if he were appointed under that section.

(4) A direction under section 19 or 20 must not specify a person or persons for appointment if the appointment of that person or those persons would be in contravention of section 35(1) of the Trustee Act 1925 or section 24(1) of the Law of Property Act 1925 (requirements as to identity of trustees).

(5) Sections 19 and 20 do not apply in relation to a trust created by a disposition in so far as provision that they do not apply is made by the disposition.

(6) Sections 19 and 20 do not apply in relation to a trust created before the commencement of this Act by a disposition in so far as provision to the effect that they do not apply is made by a deed executed—
(a) in a case in which the trust was created by one person and he is of full capacity, by that person, or
(b) in a case in which the trust was created by more than one person, by such of the persons who created the trust as are alive and of full capacity.

(7) A deed executed for the purposes of subsection (6) is irrevocable.

(8) Where a deed is executed for the purposes of subsection (6)—
(a) it does not affect anything done before its execution to comply with a direction under section 19 or 20, but
(b) a direction under section 19 or 20 which has been given but not complied with before its execution shall cease to have effect.

[1028]

NOTES

Commencement: 1 January 1997.

PART III
SUPPLEMENTARY

22 Meaning of "beneficiary"

(1) In this Act "beneficiary", in relation to a trust, means any person who under the trust has an interest in property subject to the trust (including a person who has such an interest as a trustee or a personal representative).

(2) In this Act references to a beneficiary who is beneficially entitled do not include a beneficiary who has an interest in property subject to the trust only by reason of being a trustee or personal representative.

(3) For the purposes of this Act a person who is a beneficiary only by reason of being an annuitant is not to be regarded as entitled to an interest in possession in land subject to the trust.

[1029]

NOTES

Commencement: 1 January 1997.

23 Other interpretation provisions

(1) In this Act "purchaser" has the same meaning as in Part I of the Law of Property Act 1925.

(2) Subject to that, where an expression used in this Act is given a meaning by the Law of Property Act 1925 it has the same meaning as in that Act unless the context otherwise requires.

(3) In this Act "the court" means—
(a) the High Court, or
(b) a county court.

[1030]

NOTES
Commencement: 1 January 1997.

24 Application to Crown

(1) Subject to subsection (2), this Act binds the Crown.

(2) This Act (except so far as it relates to undivided shares and joint ownership) does not affect or alter the descent, devolution or nature of the estates and interests of or in—
(a) land for the time being vested in Her Majesty in right of the Crown or of the Duchy of Lancaster, or
(b) land for the time being belonging to the Duchy of Cornwall and held in right or respect of the Duchy.

[1031]

NOTES
Commencement: 1 January 1997.

25 Amendments, repeals etc

(1) The enactments mentioned in Schedule 3 have effect subject to the amendments specified in that Schedule (which are minor or consequential on other provisions of this Act).

(2) The enactments mentioned in Schedule 4 are repealed to the extent specified in the third column of that Schedule.

(3) Neither section 2(5) nor the repeal by this Act of section 29 of the Settled Land Act 1925 applies in relation to the deed of settlement set out in the Schedule to the Chequers Estate Act 1917 or the trust instrument set out in the Schedule to the Chevening Estate Act 1959.

(4) The amendments and repeals made by this Act do not affect any entailed interest created before the commencement of this Act.

(5) The amendments and repeals made by this Act in consequence of section 3—
(a) do not affect a trust created by a will if the testator died before the commencement of this Act, and
(b) do not affect personal representatives of a person who died before that commencement;

and the repeal of section 22 of the Partnership Act 1890 does not apply in any circumstances involving the personal representatives of a partner who died before that commencement.

[1032]

NOTES
Commencement: 1 January 1997.

26 Power to make consequential provision

(1) The Lord Chancellor may by order made by statutory instrument make any such supplementary, transitional or incidental provision as appears to him to be appropriate for any of the purposes of this Act or in consequence of any of the provisions of this Act.

(2) An order under subsection (1) may, in particular, include provision modifying any enactment contained in a public general or local Act which is passed before, or in the same Session as, this Act.

(3) A statutory instrument made in the exercise of the power conferred by this section is subject to annulment in pursuance of a resolution of either House of Parliament.

[1033]

NOTES
Commencement: 1 January 1997.

27 Short title, commencement and extent

(1) This Act may be cited as the Trusts of Land and Appointment of Trustees Act 1996.

(2) This Act comes into force on such day as the Lord Chancellor appoints by order made by statutory instrument.

(3) Subject to subsection (4), the provisions of this Act extend only to England and Wales.

(4) The repeal in section 30(2) of the Agriculture Act 1970 extends only to Northern Ireland.

[1034]

NOTES
Commencement: 1 January 1997.
Order: the Trusts of Land and Appointment of Trustees Act 1996 (Commencement) Order 1996, SI 1996/2974.

SCHEDULES

SCHEDULE 1
PROVISIONS CONSEQUENTIAL ON SECTION 2

Section 2

Minors

1.—(1) Where after the commencement of this Act a person purports to convey a legal estate in land to a minor, or two or more minors, alone, the conveyance—
(a) is not effective to pass the legal estate, but
(b) operates as a declaration that the land is held in trust for the minor or minors (or if he purports to convey it to the minor or minors in trust for any persons, for those persons).

(2) Where after the commencement of this Act a person purports to convey a legal estate in land to—
(a) a minor or two or more minors, and
(b) another person who is, or other persons who are, of full age,
the conveyance operates to vest the land in the other person or persons in trust for the minor or minors and the other person or persons (or if he purports to convey it to them in trust for any persons, for those persons).

(3) Where immediately before the commencement of this Act a conveyance is operating (by virtue of section 27 of the Settled Land Act 1925) as an agreement to execute a settlement in favour of a minor or minors—
(a) the agreement ceases to have effect on the commencement of this Act, and
(b) the conveyance subsequently operates instead as a declaration that the land is held in trust for the minor or minors.

2. Where after the commencement of this Act a legal estate in land would, by reason of intestacy or in any other circumstances not dealt with in paragraph 1, vest in a person who is a minor if he were a person of full age, the land is held in trust for the minor.

Family charges

3. Where, by virtue of an instrument coming into operation after the commencement of this Act, land becomes charged voluntarily (or in consideration of marriage [or the formation of a civil partnership]) or by way of family arrangement, whether immediately or after an interval, with the payment of—
(a) a rentcharge for the life of a person or a shorter period, or

(b) capital, annual or periodical sums for the benefit of a person,

the instrument operates as a declaration that the land is held in trust for giving effect to the charge.

Charitable, ecclesiastical and public trusts

4.—(1) This paragraph applies in the case of land held on charitable, ecclesiastical or public trusts (other than land to which the Universities and College Estates Act 1925 applies).

(2) Where there is a conveyance of such land—

(a) if neither section 37(1) nor section 39(1) of the Charities Act 1993 applies to the conveyance, it shall state that the land is held on such trusts, and

(b) if neither section 37(2) nor section 39(2) of that Act has been complied with in relation to the conveyance and a purchaser has notice that the land is held on such trusts, he must see that any consents or orders necessary to authorise the transaction have been obtained.

(3) Where any trustees or the majority of any set of trustees have power to transfer or create any legal estate in the land, the estate shall be transferred or created by them in the names and on behalf of the persons in whom it is vested.

Entailed interests

5.—(1) Where a person purports by an instrument coming into operation after the commencement of this Act to grant to another person an entailed interest in real or personal property, the instrument—

(a) is not effective to grant an entailed interest, but

(b) operates instead as a declaration that the property is held in trust absolutely for the person to whom an entailed interest in the property was purportedly granted.

(2) Where a person purports by an instrument coming into operation after the commencement of this Act to declare himself a tenant in tail of real or personal property, the instrument is not effective to create an entailed interest.

Property held on settlement ceasing to exist

6. Where a settlement ceases to be a settlement for the purposes of the Settled Land Act 1925 because no relevant property (within the meaning of section 2(4)) is, or is deemed to be, subject to the settlement, any property which is or later becomes subject to the settlement is held in trust for the persons interested under the settlement.

[1035]

NOTES

Commencement: 1 January 1997.

Para 3: words in square brackets inserted by the Civil Partnership Act 2004, s 261(1), Sch 27, para 153.

SCHEDULE 2

AMENDMENTS OF STATUTORY PROVISIONS IMPOSING TRUST FOR SALE

Section 5

Mortgaged property held by trustees after redemption barred

1.—(1)–(6) …

(7) The amendments made by this paragraph—

(a) apply whether the right of redemption is discharged before or after the commencement of this Act, but

(b) are without prejudice to any dealings or arrangements made before the commencement of this Act.

Land purchased by trustees of personal property etc

2.—(1) …

(2) The repeal made by this paragraph applies in relation to land purchased after the commencement of this Act whether the trust or will in pursuance of which it is purchased comes into operation before or after the commencement of this Act.

Dispositions to tenants in common

3.—(1)–(5) …

(6) The amendments made by this paragraph apply whether the disposition is made, or comes into operation, before or after the commencement of this Act.

Joint tenancies

4.—(1)–(3) …

(4) The amendments made by this paragraph apply whether the legal estate is limited, or becomes held in trust, before or after the commencement of this Act.

Intestacy

5.—(1)–(4) …

(5) The amendments made by this paragraph apply whether the death occurs before or after the commencement of this Act.

Reverter of sites

6.—(1)–(5) …

(6) The amendments made by this paragraph apply whether the trust arises before or after the commencement of this Act.

Trusts deemed to arise in 1926

7. Where at the commencement of this Act any land is held on trust for sale, or on the statutory trusts, by virtue of Schedule 1 to the Law of Property Act 1925 (transitional provisions), it shall after that commencement be held in trust for the persons interested in the land; and references in that Schedule to trusts for sale or trustees for sale or to the statutory trusts shall be construed accordingly.

[1036]

NOTES

Commencement: 1 January 1997.
Para 1: sub-paras (1)–(6) amend the Law of Property Act 1925, s 31.
Para 2: sub-para (1) repeals the Law of Property Act 1925, s 32.
Para 3: sub-paras (1)–(5) amend the Law of Property Act 1925, s 34.
Para 4: sub-paras (1)–(3) amend the Law of Property Act 1925, s 36(1), (2).
Para 5: sub-paras (1)–(4) amend the Administration of Estates Act 1925, s 33.
Para 6: sub-paras (1)–(5) amend the Reverter of Sites Act 1987, s 1, at **[682]**.

(Sch 3 contains minor and consequential amendments; Sch 4 contains repeals.)

HOUSING ACT 1996

(1996 c 52)

ARRANGEMENT OF SECTIONS

PART I
SOCIAL RENTED SECTOR

CHAPTER I
REGISTERED SOCIAL LANDLORDS

Registration

Regulation of registered social landlords

CHAPTER II
DISPOSAL OF LAND AND RELATED MATTERS

Power of registered social landlord to dispose of land

Control by Relevant Authority of land transactions

Right of tenant to acquire dwelling

CHAPTER III
GRANTS AND OTHER FINANCIAL MATTERS

Grants and other financial assistance

Treatment of disposal proceeds

Recovery, &c of social housing grants

Grants to bodies other than registered social landlords

PART VIII
MISCELLANEOUS AND GENERAL PROVISIONS

Final provisions

An Act to make provision about housing, including provision about the social rented sector, houses in multiple occupation, landlord and tenant matters, the administration of housing benefit, the conduct of tenants, the allocation of housing accommodation by local housing authorities and homelessness; and for connected purposes

[24 July 1996]

NOTES

Transfer of functions in relation to Wales: as to the transfer of functions under this Act from Ministers of the Crown to the National Assembly for Wales, see the National Assembly for Wales (Transfer of Functions) Order 1999, SI 1999/672.

PART I
SOCIAL RENTED SECTOR

CHAPTER I
REGISTERED SOCIAL LANDLORDS

Registration

1 The register of social landlords

(1) The [Relevant Authority] shall maintain a register of social landlords which shall be open to inspection at all reasonable times …

[(1A) In this Part "the Relevant Authority" means the Housing Corporation or the Secretary of State, as provided by section 56.

(1B) The register maintained by the Housing Corporation shall be maintained at its head office.]

(2) …

[1037]

NOTES

Commencement: 1 November 1998 (sub-ss (1A), (1B)); 1 October 1996 (remainder). By virtue of the Housing Act 1996 (Commencement No 3 and Transitional Provisions) Order 1996, SI 1996/2402, art 3, Schedule, para 1, this section applies in relation to matters occurring before 1 October 1996 as it applies in relation to matters arising on or after that date.

Sub-s (1): words in square brackets substituted and words omitted repealed by the Government of Wales Act 1998, ss 140, 152, Sch 16, paras 81, 82(1)(a), (2), Sch 18, Pt VI.

Sub-ss (1A), (1B): inserted by the Government of Wales Act 1998, s 140, Sch 16, paras 81, 83(3).

Sub-s (2): repealed by the Government of Wales Act 1998, ss 140, 152, Sch 16, paras 81, 83(4), Sch 18, Pt VI.

2 Eligibility for registration

(1) A body is eligible for registration as a social landlord if it is—

(a) a registered charity which is a housing association,

(b) a society registered under the Industrial and Provident Societies Act 1965 which satisfies the conditions in subsection (2), or

(c) a company registered under the Companies Act 1985 which satisfies those conditions.

(2) The conditions are that the body is non-profit-making and is established for the purpose of, or has among its objects or powers, the provision, construction, improvement or management of—

(a) houses to be kept available for letting,

(b) houses for occupation by members of the body, where the rules of the body restrict membership to persons entitled or prospectively entitled (as tenants or otherwise) to occupy a house provided or managed by the body, or

(c) hostels,

and that any additional purposes or objects are among those specified in subsection (4).

(3) For the purposes of this section a body is non-profit-making if—

(a) it does not trade for profit, or

(b) its constitution or rules prohibit the issue of capital with interest or dividend exceeding the rate prescribed by the Treasury for the purposes of section 1(1)(b) of the Housing Associations Act 1985.

(4) The permissible additional purposes or objects are—

(a) providing land, amenities or services, or providing, constructing, repairing or improving buildings, for its residents, either exclusively or together with other persons;

(b) acquiring, or repairing and improving, or creating by the conversion of houses or other property, houses to be disposed of on sale, on lease or on shared ownership terms;

(c) constructing houses to be disposed of on shared ownership terms;

(d) managing houses held on leases or other lettings (not being houses within subsection (2)(a) or (b)) or blocks of flats;

(e) providing services of any description for owners or occupiers of houses in arranging or carrying out works of maintenance, repair or improvement, or encouraging or facilitating the carrying out of such works;

(f) encouraging and giving advice on the forming of housing associations or providing services for, and giving advice on the running of, such associations and other voluntary organisations concerned with housing, or matters connected with housing.

(5) A body is not ineligible for registration as a social landlord by reason only that its powers include power—

(a) to acquire commercial premises or businesses as an incidental part of a project or series of projects undertaken for purposes or objects falling within subsection (2) or (4);

(b) to repair, improve or convert commercial premises acquired as mentioned in paragraph (a) or to carry on for a limited period any business so acquired;

(c) to repair or improve houses, or buildings in which houses are situated, after a disposal of the houses by the body by way of sale or lease or on shared ownership terms.

(6) In this section—

"block of flats" means a building containing two or more flats which are held on leases or other lettings and which are occupied or intended to be occupied wholly or mainly for residential purposes; "disposed of on shared ownership terms" means disposed of on a lease—

(a) granted on a payment of a premium calculated by reference to a percentage of the value of the house or of the cost of providing it, or

(b) under which the tenant (or his personal representatives) will or may be entitled to a sum calculated by reference directly or indirectly to the value of the house;

"letting" includes the grant of a licence to occupy;

"residents", in relation to a body, means persons occupying a house or hostel provided or managed by the body; and

"voluntary organisation" means an organisation whose activities are not carried on for profit.

(7) The Secretary of State may by order specify permissible purposes, objects or powers additional to those specified in subsections (4) and (5).

The order may (without prejudice to the inclusion of other incidental or supplementary provisions) contain such provision as the Secretary of State thinks fit with respect to the priority of mortgages entered into in pursuance of any additional purposes, objects or powers.

(8) An order under subsection (7) shall be made by statutory instrument which shall be subject to annulment in pursuance of a resolution of either House of Parliament.

[1038]

NOTES

Commencement: 1 October 1996 (sub-ss (1)–(6)); 1 August 1996 (remainder). By virtue of the Housing Act 1996 (Commencement No 3 and Transitional Provisions) Order 1996, SI 1996/2402, art 3, Schedule, para 1, sub-ss (1)–(6) apply in relation to matters occurring before 1 October 1996 as they apply in relation to matters arising on or after that date.

Orders: the Social Landlords (Permissible Additional Purposes or Objects) Order 1996, SI 1996/2256; the Social Landlords (Additional Purposes or Objects) Order 1999, SI 1999/985; the Social Landlords (Additional Purposes or Objects) (No 2) Order 1999, SI 1999/1206; the Social Landlords (Permissible Additional Purposes) (England) Order 2006, SI 2006/1968; the Caravan Sites Act 1968 and Social Landlords (Permissible Additional Purposes) (England) Order 2006 (Definition of Caravan) (Amendment) (England) Order 2006, SI 2006/2374.

3 Registration

(1) The [Relevant Authority] may register as a social landlord any body which is eligible for such registration.

(2) An application for registration shall be made in such manner, and shall be accompanied by such fee (if any), as the [Relevant Authority] may determine.

(3) As soon as may be after registering a body as a social landlord the [Relevant Authority] shall give notice of the registration—

(a) in the case of a registered charity, to the [Charity Commission],

(b) in the case of an industrial and provident society, to the [Financial Services Authority], and

(c) in the case of a company registered under the Companies Act 1985 (including such a company which is also a registered charity), to the registrar of companies,

who shall record the registration.

(4) A body which at any time is, or was, registered as a social landlord shall, for all purposes other than rectification of the register, be conclusively presumed to be, or to have been, at that time a body eligible for registration as a social landlord.

[1039]

NOTES

Commencement: (sub-ss (1), (3), (4) were brought into force on 1 October 1996; sub-s (2) was brought into force on 1 August 1996 in so far as it confers a power to make determinations, and on 1 October 1996 for remaining purposes. By virtue of the Housing Act 1996 (Commencement No 3 and Transitional Provisions) Order 1996, SI 1996/2402, art 3, Schedule, para 1, sub-ss (1), (3), (4) (and sub-s (2) in so far as it comes into force on 1 October 1996) apply in relation to matters occurring before 1 October 1996 as they apply in relation to matters arising on or after that date.

Sub-ss (1), (2): words in square brackets substituted by the Government of Wales Act 1998, s 140, Sch 16, paras 81, 82(1)(a).

Sub-s (3): words in first pair of square brackets substituted by the Government of Wales Act 1998, s 140, Sch 16, paras 81, 82(1)(a); words in square brackets in para (a) substituted by the Charities Act 2006, s 75(1), Sch 8, paras 183, 184; words in square brackets in para (b) substituted by the Financial Services and Markets Act 2000 (Consequential Amendments and Repeals) Order 2001, SI 2001/3649, art 351.

4 Removal from the register

(1) A body which has been registered as a social landlord shall not be removed from the register except in accordance with this section.

(2) If it appears to the [Relevant Authority] that a body which is on the register of social landlords—

(a) is no longer a body eligible for such registration, or

(b) has ceased to exist or does not operate,

the [Relevant Authority] shall, after giving the body at least 14 days' notice, remove it from the register.

(3) In the case of a body which appears to the [Relevant Authority] to have ceased to exist or not to operate, notice under subsection (2) shall be deemed to be given to the body if it is served at the address last known to the [Relevant Authority] to be the principal place of business of the body.

(4) A body which is registered as a social landlord may request the [Relevant Authority] to remove it from the register and the [Relevant Authority] may do so, subject to the following provisions.

(5) Before removing a body from the register of social landlords under subsection (4) the [Relevant Authority] shall consult the local authorities in whose area the body operates; and the [Relevant Authority] shall also inform those authorities of its decision.

(6) As soon as may be after removing a body from the register of social landlords the [Relevant Authority] shall give notice of the removal—

(a) in the case of a registered charity, to the [Charity Commission],

(b) in the case of an industrial and provident society, to the [Financial Services Authority], and

(c) in the case of a company registered under the Companies Act 1985 (including such a company which is also a registered charity), to the registrar of companies,

who shall record the removal.

[1040]

NOTES

Commencement: 1 October 1996. By virtue of the Housing Act 1996 (Commencement No 3 and Transitional Provisions) Order 1996, SI 1996/2402, art 3, Schedule, para 1, this section applies in relation to matters occurring before 1 October 1996 as it applies in relation to matters arising on or after that date.

Sub-ss (2)–(5): words in square brackets substituted by the Government of Wales Act 1998, s 140, Sch 16, paras 81, 82(1)(a).

Sub-s (6): words in first pair of square brackets substituted by the Government of Wales Act 1998, s 140, Sch 16, paras 81, 82(1)(a); words in square brackets in para (a) substituted by the Charities Act 2006, s 75(1), Sch 8, paras 183, 185; words in square brackets in para (b) substituted by the Financial Services and Markets Act 2000 (Consequential Amendments and Repeals) Order 2001, SI 2001/3649, art 352.

5 Criteria for registration or removal from register

(1) The [Relevant Authority] shall establish (and may from time to time vary) criteria which should be satisfied by a body seeking registration as a social landlord; and in deciding whether to register a body the [Relevant Authority] shall have regard to whether those criteria are met.

(2) The [Relevant Authority] shall establish (and may from time to time vary) criteria which should be satisfied where such a body seeks to be removed from the register of social landlords; and in deciding whether to remove a body from the register the [Relevant Authority] shall have regard to whether those criteria are met.

(3) Before establishing or varying any such criteria the [Relevant Authority] shall consult such bodies representative of registered social landlords, and such bodies representative of local authorities, as it thinks fit.

(4) The [Relevant Authority] shall publish the criteria for registration and the criteria for removal from the register in such manner as the [Relevant Authority] considers appropriate for bringing the criteria to the notice of bodies representative of registered social landlords and bodies representative of local authorities.

[1041]

NOTES

Commencement: 1 August 1996.

Words in square brackets substituted by the Government of Wales Act 1998, s 140, Sch 16, paras 81, 82(1)(a).

6 Appeal against decision on removal

(1) A body which is aggrieved by a decision of the [Relevant Authority]—

(a) not to register it as a social landlord, or

(b) to remove or not to remove it from the register of social landlords,

may appeal against the decision to the High Court.

(2) If an appeal is brought against a decision relating to the removal of a body from the register, the [Relevant Authority] shall not remove the body from the register until the appeal has been finally determined or is withdrawn.

(3) As soon as may be after an appeal is brought against a decision relating to the removal of a body from the register, the [Relevant Authority] shall give notice of the appeal—

(a) in the case of a registered charity, to the [Charity Commission],

(b) in the case of an industrial and provident society, to the [Financial Services Authority], and

(c) in the case of a company registered under the Companies Act 1985 (including such a company which is also a registered charity), to the registrar of companies.

[1042]

NOTES

Commencement: 1 October 1996. By virtue of the Housing Act 1996 (Commencement No 3 and Transitional Provisions) Order 1996, SI 1996/2402, art 3, Schedule, para 3, the right to appeal a decision not to register a landlord or not to remove a landlord from the register does not apply to decisions made before that date.

Sub-ss (1), (2): words in square brackets substituted by the Government of Wales Act 1998, s 140, Sch 16, paras 81, 82(1)(a).

Sub-s (3): words in first pair of square brackets substituted by the Government of Wales Act 1998, s 140, Sch 16, paras 81, 82(1)(a); words in square brackets in para (a) substituted by the Charities Act 2006, s 75(1), Sch 8, paras 183, 186; words in square brackets in para (b) substituted by the Financial Services and Markets Act 2000 (Consequential Amendments and Repeals) Order 2001, SI 2001/3649, art 353.

Regulation of registered social landlords

7 Regulation of registered social landlords

Schedule 1 has effect for the regulation of registered social landlords.

Part I relates to the control of payments to members and similar matters.

Part II relates to the constitution, change of rules, amalgamation or dissolution of a registered social landlord.

Part III relates to accounts and audit.

Part IV relates to inquiries into the affairs of a registered social landlord.

[1043]

NOTES

Commencement: 1 October 1996 (certain purposes); 1 August 1996 (remaining purposes).

CHAPTER II
DISPOSAL OF LAND AND RELATED MATTERS

Power of registered social landlord to dispose of land

8 Power of registered social landlord to dispose of land

(1) A registered social landlord has power by virtue of this section and not otherwise to dispose, in such manner as it thinks fit, of land held by it.

(2) Section 39 of the Settled Land Act 1925 (disposal of land by trustees) does not apply to the disposal of land by a registered social landlord; and accordingly the disposal need not be for the best consideration in money that can reasonably be obtained.

Nothing in this subsection shall be taken to authorise any action on the part of a charity which would conflict with the trusts of the charity.

(3) This section has effect subject to section 9 (control by [Relevant Authority] of land transactions).

[1044]

NOTES

Commencement: 1 October 1996. By virtue of the Housing Act 1996 (Commencement No 3 and Transitional Provisions) Order 1996, SI 1996/2402, art 3, Schedule, para 1, this section applies in relation to matters occurring before 1 October 1996 as it applies in relation to matters arising on or after that date.

Sub-s (3): words in square brackets substituted by the Government of Wales Act 1998, s 140, Sch 16, paras 81, 82(1)(a).

Control by [Relevant Authority] of land transactions

9 Consent required for disposal of land by registered social landlord

(1) The consent of the [Relevant Authority] … is required for any disposal of land by a registered social landlord under section 8.

[(1A) The consent—

(a) if given by the Housing Corporation, shall be given by order under its seal, and

(b) if given by the Secretary of State, shall be given by order in writing.]

(2) The consent of the [Relevant Authority] may be so given—

(a) generally to all registered social landlords or to a particular landlord or description of landlords;

(b) in relation to particular land or in relation to a particular description of land,

and may be given subject to conditions.

(3) Before giving any consent other than a consent in relation to a particular landlord or particular land, the [Relevant Authority] shall consult such bodies representative of registered social landlords as it thinks fit.

(4) A disposal of a house by a registered social landlord made without the consent required by this section is void unless—

(a) the disposal is to an individual (or to two or more individuals),

(b) the disposal does not extend to any other house, and

(c) the landlord reasonably believes that the individual or individuals intend to use the house as their principal dwelling.

(5) Any other disposal by a registered social landlord which requires consent under this section is valid in favour of a person claiming under the landlord notwithstanding that that consent has not been given; and a person dealing with a registered social landlord, or with a person claiming under such a landlord, shall not be concerned to see or inquire whether any such consent has been given.

(6) Where at the time of its removal from the register of social landlords a body owns land, this section continues to apply to that land after the removal as if the body concerned continued to be a registered social landlord.

(7) For the purposes of this section "disposal" means sale, lease, mortgage, charge or any other disposition.

(8) This section has effect subject to section 10 (lettings and other disposals not requiring consent of [Relevant Authority]).

[1045]

NOTES

Words in square brackets in the heading preceding this section substituted by the Government of Wales Act 1998, s 140, Sch 16, paras 81, 82(1)(a).

Commencement: 1 November 1998 (sub-s (1A)); 1 October 1996 (sub-ss (1), (2), (4)–(8)); 1 August 1996 (remainder). By virtue of the Housing Act 1996 (Commencement No 3 and Transitional Provisions) Order 1996, SI 1996/2402, art 3, Schedule, paras 1, 6, sub-ss (1), (2), (4)–(8) apply in relation to matters occurring before 1 October 1996 as they apply in relation to matters arising on or after that date.

Sub-s (1): words in square brackets substituted and words omitted repealed by the Government of Wales Act 1998, ss 140, 152, Sch 16, paras 81, 82(1)(a), 84(1), (2), Sch 18, Pt VI.

Sub-s (1A): inserted by the Government of Wales Act 1998, s 140, Sch 16, paras 81, 84(1), (3).

Sub-ss (2), (3), (8): words in square brackets substituted by the Government of Wales Act 1998, s 140, Sch 16, paras 81, 82(1)(a).

10 Lettings and other disposals not requiring consent of [Relevant Authority]

(1) A letting by a registered social landlord does not require consent under section 9 if it is—

(a) a letting of land under an assured tenancy or an assured agricultural occupancy, or what would be an assured tenancy or an assured agricultural occupancy but for any of paragraphs 4 to 8, or paragraph 12(1)(h), of Schedule 1 to the Housing Act 1988, or

(b) a letting of land under a secure tenancy or what would be a secure tenancy but for any of paragraphs 2 to 12 of Schedule 1 to the Housing Act 1985.

(2) Consent under section 9 is not required in the case of a disposal to which section 81 or 133 of the Housing Act 1988 applies (certain disposals for which the consent of the Secretary of State is required).

(3) Consent under section 9 is not required for a disposal under Part V of the Housing Act 1985 (the right to buy) or under the right conferred by section 16 below (the right to acquire).

[1046]

NOTES

Commencement: 1 October 1996. By virtue of the Housing Act 1996 (Commencement No 3 and Transitional Provisions) Order 1996, SI 1996/2402, art 3, Schedule, para 1, this section applies in relation to matters occurring before 1 October 1996 as it applies in relation to matters arising on or after that date.

Section heading: words in square brackets substituted by the Government of Wales Act 1998, s 140, Sch 16, paras 81, 82(1)(a).

[11 Covenant for repayment of discount on disposal

(1) Where on a disposal of a house by a registered social landlord, in accordance with a consent given by the Relevant Authority under section 9, a discount has been given to the purchaser, and the consent does not provide otherwise, the conveyance, grant or assignment shall contain a covenant binding on the purchaser and his successors in title to the following effect.

(2) The covenant shall be to pay to the landlord such sum (if any) as the landlord may demand in accordance with subsection (3) on the occasion of the first relevant disposal which is not an exempted disposal and which takes place within the period of five years beginning with the conveyance, grant or assignment.

(3) The landlord may demand such sum as he considers appropriate, up to and including the maximum amount specified in this section.

(4) The maximum amount which may be demanded by the landlord is a percentage of the price or premium paid for the first relevant disposal which is equal to the percentage discount given to the purchaser in respect of the disposal of the house by the landlord.

(5) But for each complete year which has elapsed after the conveyance, grant or assignment and before the first relevant disposal the maximum amount which may be demanded by the landlord is reduced by one-fifth.

(6) Subsections (3) to (5) are subject to section 11A.]

[1047]

NOTES

Commencement: 18 January 2005.

Substituted, together with ss 11A, 11B, by the Housing Act 2004, s 199(1), (3), except in any case where the purchaser has accepted an offer for the disposal of the house from the landlord or the landlord has accepted an offer for the disposal of the house from the purchaser, before 18 January 2005.

[11A Increase in value of house attributable to home improvements to be disregarded

(1) In calculating the maximum amount which may be demanded by the landlord under section 11, such amount (if any) of the price or premium paid for the first relevant disposal which is attributable to improvements made to the house—

(a) by the person by whom the disposal is, or is to be, made, and

(b) after the conveyance, grant or assignment and before the disposal,

shall be disregarded.

(2) The amount to be disregarded under this section shall be such amount as may be agreed between the parties or determined by the district valuer.

(3) The district valuer shall not be required by virtue of this section to make a determination for the purposes of this section unless—

(a) it is reasonably practicable for him to do so; and

(b) his reasonable costs in making the determination are paid by the person by whom the disposal is, or is to be, made.

(4) If the district valuer does not make a determination for the purposes of this section (and in default of an agreement), no amount is required to be disregarded under this section.] **[1047A]**

NOTES

Commencement: 18 January 2005.
Substituted as noted to s 11 at **[1047]**.

[11B Liability to repay is a charge on the house

(1) The liability that may arise under the covenant required by section 11 is a charge on the house, taking effect as if it had been created by deed expressed to be by way of legal mortgage.

(2) Where there is a relevant disposal which is an exempted disposal by virtue of section 15(4)(d) or (e) (compulsory disposal or disposal of yard, garden, etc)—

(a) the covenant required by section 11 is not binding on the person to whom the disposal is made or any successor in title of his, and

(b) the covenant and the charge taking effect by virtue of this section cease to apply in relation to the property disposed of.]

[1047B]

NOTES

Commencement: 18 January 2005.
Substituted as noted to s 11 at **[1047]**.

12 Priority of charge for repayment of discount

(1) The charge taking effect by virtue of [section 11B] (charge for repayment of discount) has priority immediately after any legal charge securing an amount—

(a) left outstanding by the purchaser, or

(b) advanced to him by an approved lending institution for the purpose of enabling him to acquire the interest disposed of on the first disposal,

subject to the following provisions.

(2) An advance which is made for a purpose other than that mentioned in subsection (1)(b) and which is secured by a legal charge having priority to the charge taking effect by virtue of [section 11B], and any further advance which is so secured, shall rank in priority to that charge if, and only if, the registered social landlord by notice served on the institution concerned gives consent.

The landlord shall give consent if the purpose of the advance or further advance is an approved purpose.

(3) The registered social landlord may at any time by notice served on an approved lending institution postpone the charge taking effect by virtue of [section 11B] to an advance or further advance which—

(a) is made to the purchaser by that institution, and

(b) is secured by a legal charge not having priority to that charge;

and the landlord shall serve such a notice if the purpose of the advance or further advance is an approved purpose.

(4) The covenant required by [section 11B] does not, by virtue of its binding successors in title of the purchaser, bind a person exercising rights under a charge having priority over the charge taking effect by virtue of that section, or a person deriving title under him.

A provision of the conveyance, grant or assignment, or of a collateral agreement, is void in so far as it purports to authorise a forfeiture, or to impose a penalty or disability, in the event of any such person failing to comply with that covenant.

(5) In this section "approved lending institution" means—

(a) a building society, bank, insurance company or friendly society,

(b) the [Relevant Authority], or

(c) any body specified, or of a class or description specified, in an order made under section 156 of the Housing Act 1985 (which makes corresponding provision in relation to disposals in pursuance of the right to buy).

(6) The following are "approved purposes" for the purposes of this section—

(a) to enable the purchaser to defray, or to defray on his behalf, any of the following—

(i) the cost of any works to the house,

(ii) any service charge payable in respect of the house for works, whether or not to the house, and

(iii) any service charge or other amount payable in respect of the house for insurance, whether or not of the house, and

(b) to enable the purchaser to discharge, or to discharge on his behalf, any of the following—

(i) so much as is still outstanding of any advance or further advance which ranks in priority to the charge taking effect by virtue of [section 11B],

(ii) any arrears of interest on such an advance or further advance, and

(iii) any costs and expenses incurred in enforcing payment of any such interest, or repayment (in whole or in part) of any such advance or further advance.

In this subsection "service charge" has the meaning given by section 621A of the Housing Act 1985.

(7) Where different parts of an advance or further advance are made for different purposes, each of those parts shall be regarded as a separate advance or further advance for the purposes of this section.

[1048]

NOTES

Commencement: 1 October 1996. By virtue of the Housing Act 1996 (Commencement No 3 and Transitional Provisions) Order 1996, SI 1996/2402, art 3, Schedule, para 11, this section applies in relation to covenants and charges arising under the Housing Associations Act 1985, Sch 2, as it applies in relation to those arising under ss 11–15 of this Act.

Sub-ss (1)–(4), (6): words in square brackets substituted by the Housing Act 2004, s 199(2), (3), except in any case where the purchaser has accepted an offer for the disposal of the house from the landlord or the landlord has accepted an offer for the disposal of the house from the purchaser, before 18 January 2005.

Sub-s (5): in para (b) words in square brackets substituted by the Government of Wales Act 1998, s 140, Sch 16, paras 81, 82(1)(a).

[12A Right of first refusal for registered social landlord

(1) Where on a disposal of a house by a registered social landlord, in accordance with a consent given by the Relevant Authority under section 9, a discount has been given to the purchaser, and the consent does not provide otherwise, the conveyance, grant or assignment shall contain the following covenant, which shall be binding on the purchaser and his successors in title.

(2) The covenant shall be to the effect that, until the end of the period of ten years beginning with the conveyance, grant or assignment, there will be no relevant disposal which is not an exempted disposal, unless the prescribed conditions have been satisfied in relation to that or a previous such disposal.

(3) In subsection (2) "the prescribed conditions" means such conditions as are prescribed by regulations under this section at the time when the conveyance, grant or assignment is made.

(4) The Secretary of State may by regulations prescribe such conditions as he considers appropriate for and in connection with conferring on—

(a) a registered social landlord which has made a disposal as mentioned in subsection (1), or

(b) such other person as is determined in accordance with the regulations,

a right of first refusal to have a disposal within subsection (5) made to him for such consideration as is mentioned in section 12B.

(5) The disposals within this subsection are—

(a) a reconveyance or conveyance of the house; and

(b) a surrender or assignment of the lease.

(6) Regulations under this section may, in particular, make provision—

(a) for the purchaser to offer to make such a disposal to such person or persons as may be prescribed;

(b) for a prescribed recipient of such an offer to be able either to accept the offer or to nominate some other person as the person by whom the offer may be accepted;
(c) for the person who may be so nominated to be either a person of a prescribed description or a person whom the prescribed recipient considers, having regard to any prescribed matters, to be a more appropriate person to accept the offer;
(d) for a prescribed recipient making such a nomination to give a notification of the nomination to the person nominated, the purchaser and any other prescribed person;
(e) for authorising a nominated person to accept the offer and for determining which acceptance is to be effective where the offer is accepted by more than one person;
(f) for the period within which the offer may be accepted or within which any other prescribed step is to be, or may be, taken;
(g) for the circumstances in which the right of first refusal lapses (whether following the service of a notice to complete or otherwise) with the result that the purchaser is able to make a disposal on the open market;
(h) for the manner in which any offer, acceptance or notification is to be communicated.

(7) In subsection (6) any reference to the purchaser is a reference to the purchaser or his successor in title.

Nothing in that subsection affects the generality of subsection (4).

(8) Regulations under this section—
(a) may make different provision with respect to different cases or descriptions of case; and
(b) shall be made by statutory instrument which shall be subject to annulment in pursuance of a resolution of either House of Parliament.

(9) The limitation imposed by a covenant within subsection (2) is a local land charge.

(10) The Chief Land Registrar must enter in the register of title a restriction reflecting the limitation imposed by any such covenant.

(11) Where there is a relevant disposal which is an exempted disposal by virtue of section 15(4)(d) or (e) (compulsory disposal or disposal of yard, garden, &c)—
(a) the covenant required by this section is not binding on the person to whom the disposal is made or any successor in title of his, and
(b) the covenant ceases to apply in relation to the property disposed of.]

[1048A]

NOTES

Commencement: 18 January 2005.

Inserted, together with s 12B, by the Housing Act 2004, s 200(1), (3), except in relation to a disposal under s 8 of this Act if the purchaser has accepted an offer for the disposal of the house from the landlord or the landlord has accepted an offer for the disposal of the house from the purchaser, before 18 January 2005.

Regulations: the Housing (Right of First Refusal) (England) Regulations 2005, SI 2005/1917; the Housing (Right of First Refusal) (Wales) Regulations 2005, SI 2005/2680.

[12B Consideration payable for disposal under section 12A

(1) The consideration for a disposal made in respect of a right of first refusal as mentioned in section 12A(4) shall be such amount as may be agreed between the parties, or determined by the district valuer, as being the amount which is to be taken to be the value of the house at the time when the offer is made (as determined in accordance with regulations under that section).

(2) That value shall be taken to be the price which, at that time, the interest to be reconveyed, conveyed, surrendered or assigned would realise if sold on the open market by a willing vendor, on the assumption that any liability under the covenant required by section 11 (repayment of discount on early disposal) would be discharged by the vendor.

(3) If the offer is accepted in accordance with regulations under section 12A, no payment shall be required in pursuance of any such covenant as is mentioned in subsection (2), but the consideration shall be reduced, subject to subsection (4), by such amount (if any) as, on a disposal made at the time the offer was made, being a relevant disposal which is not an exempted disposal, would fall to be paid under that covenant.

(4) Where there is a charge on the house having priority over the charge to secure payment of the sum due under the covenant mentioned in subsection (2), the consideration shall not be reduced under subsection (3) below the amount necessary to discharge the outstanding sum secured by the first-mentioned charge at the date of the offer (as determined in accordance with regulations under section 12A).]

[1048B]

NOTES

Commencement: 18 January 2005.

Inserted as noted to s 12A at **[1048A]**.

13 Restriction on disposal of houses in National Parks, &c

(1) On the disposal by a registered social landlord, in accordance with a consent given by the [Relevant Authority] under section 9, of a house situated in—

(a) a National Park,

(b) an area designated under [section 82 of the Countryside and Rights of Way Act 2000] as an area of outstanding natural beauty, or

(c) an area designated as a rural area by order under section 157 of the Housing Act 1985,

the conveyance, grant or assignment may (unless it contains a condition of a kind mentioned in section 33(2)(b) or (c) of the Housing Act 1985 (right of pre-emption or restriction on assignment) [or a covenant as mentioned in section 12A(2) of this Act (right of first refusal for registered social landlord)]) contain a covenant to the following effect limiting the freedom of the purchaser (including any successor in title of his and any person deriving title under him or such a successor) to dispose of the house.

(2) The limitation is that until such time (if any) as may be notified in writing by the registered social landlord to the purchaser or a successor in title of his, there will be no relevant disposal which is not an exempted disposal without the written consent of the landlord.

(3) That consent shall not be withheld if the person to whom the disposal is made (or, if it is made to more than one person, at least one of them) has, throughout the period of three years immediately preceding the application for consent—

(a) had his place of work in a region designated by order under section 157(3) of the Housing Act 1985 which, or part of which, is comprised in the National Park or area concerned, or

(b) had his only or principal home in such a region,

or if he has had the one in part or parts of that period and the other in the remainder.

The region need not have been the same throughout the period.

(4) A disposal in breach of such a covenant as is mentioned above is void.

(5) The limitation imposed by such a covenant is a local land charge and, [if the first disposal involves registration under the Land Registration Act 2002, the Chief Land Registrar shall enter in the register of title a restriction reflecting the limitation].

(6) In this section "purchaser" means the person acquiring the interest disposed of by the first disposal.

(7) Where there is a relevant disposal which is an exempted disposal by virtue of section 15(4)(d) or (e) (compulsory disposal or disposal of yard, garden, &c), any such covenant as is mentioned in this section ceases to apply in relation to the property disposed of.

[1049]

NOTES

Commencement: 1 October 1996. By virtue of the Housing Act 1996 (Commencement No 3 and Transitional Provisions) Order 1996, SI 1996/2402, art 3, Schedule, para 11, this section applies in relation to covenants and charges arising under the Housing Associations Act 1985, Sch 2, as it applies in relation to those arising under ss 11–15 of this Act.

Sub-s (1): words in first pair of square brackets substituted by the Government of Wales Act 1998, s 140, Sch 16, paras 81, 82(1)(a); words in square brackets in para (b) substituted by the Countryside and Rights of Way Act 2000, s 93, Sch 15, Pt I, para 14; words in third pair of square brackets inserted by the Housing Act 2004, s 200(2), (3), except in relation to a disposal under s 8 of this Act if the purchaser has accepted an offer for the disposal of the house from the landlord or the landlord has accepted an offer for the disposal of the house from the purchaser, before 18 January 2005.

Sub-s (5): words in square brackets substituted by the Land Registration Act 2002, s 133, Sch 11, para 35.

14 Treatment of options

(1) For the purposes of sections 9 to 13 the grant of an option enabling a person to call for a relevant disposal which is not an exempted disposal shall be treated as such a disposal made to him.

(2) For the purposes of section 13(2) (requirement of consent to disposal of house in National Park, &c) consent to such a grant shall be treated as consent to a disposal made in pursuance of the option.

[1050]

NOTES

Commencement: 1 October 1996. By virtue of the Housing Act 1996 (Commencement No 3 and Transitional Provisions) Order 1996, SI 1996/2402, art 3, Schedule, para 11, this section applies in relation to covenants and charges arising under the Housing Associations Act 1985, Sch 2, as it applies in relation to those arising under ss 11–15 of this Act.

15 Relevant and exempted disposals

(1) In sections 11 to 14 the expression "relevant disposal which is not an exempted disposal" shall be construed as follows.

(2) A disposal, whether of the whole or part of the house, is a relevant disposal if it is—

(a) a conveyance of the freehold or an assignment of the lease, or

(b) the grant of a lease or sub-lease (other than a mortgage term) for a term of more than 21 years otherwise than at a rack-rent.

(3) For the purposes of subsection (2)(b) it shall be assumed—

(a) that any option to renew or extend a lease or sub-lease, whether or not forming part of a series of options, is exercised, and

(b) that any option to terminate a lease or sub-lease is not exercised.

(4) A disposal is an exempted disposal if—

(a) it is a disposal of the whole of the house and a conveyance of the freehold or an assignment of the lease and the person or each of the persons to whom it is made is a qualifying person (as defined in subsection (5));

(b) it is a vesting of the whole of the house in a person taking under a will or on an intestacy;

(c) it is a disposal of the whole of the house in pursuance of any such order as is mentioned in subsection (6);

(d) it is a compulsory disposal (as defined in subsection (7));

(e) the property disposed of is a yard, garden, outhouses or appurtenances belonging to a house or usually enjoyed with it.

(5) For the purposes of subsection (4)(a) a person is a qualifying person in relation to a disposal if—

(a) he is the person or one of the persons by whom the disposal is made,

(b) he is the spouse or a former spouse[,or the civil partner or a former civil partner,] of that person or one of those persons, or

(c) he is a member of the family of that person or one of those persons and has resided with him throughout the period of twelve months ending with the disposal.

(6) The orders referred to in subsection (4)(c) are orders under—

(a) section 24 or 24A of the Matrimonial Causes Act 1973 (property adjustment orders or orders for the sale of property in connection with matrimonial proceedings);

(b) section 2 of the Inheritance (Provision for Family and Dependants) Act 1975 (orders as to financial provision to be made from estate);

(c) section 17 of the Matrimonial and Family Proceedings Act 1984 (property adjustment orders or orders for the sale of property after overseas divorce, &c); …

(d) paragraph 1 of Schedule 1 to the Children Act 1989 (orders for financial relief against parents)[; or

(e) Part 2 or 3 of Schedule 5, or paragraph 9 of Schedule 7, to the Civil Partnership

Act 2004 (property adjustment orders, or orders for the sale of property, in connection with civil partnership proceedings or after overseas dissolution of civil partnership, etc).]

(7) For the purposes of subsection (4)(d) a compulsory disposal is a disposal of property which is acquired compulsorily, or is acquired by a person who has made or would have made, or for whom another person has made or would have made, a compulsory purchase order authorising its compulsory purchase for the purposes for which it is acquired.

[1051]

NOTES

Commencement: 1 October 1996. By virtue of the Housing Act 1996 (Commencement No 3 and Transitional Provisions) Order 1996, SI 1996/2402, art 3, Schedule, para 11, this section applies in relation to covenants and charges arising under the Housing Associations Act 1985, Sch 2, as it applies in relation to those arising under ss 11–15 of this Act.

Sub-s (5): words in square brackets in para (b) inserted by the Civil Partnership Act 2004, s 81, Sch 8, para 50(1), (2).

Sub-s (6): word omitted from para (c) repealed and para (e) and word "or" immediately preceding it added by the Civil Partnership Act 2004, ss 81, 261(4), Sch 8, para 50(1), (3), Sch 30.

[15A Treatment of deferred resale agreements for purposes of section 11

(1) If a purchaser or his successor in title enters into an agreement within subsection (3), any liability arising under the covenant required by section 11 shall be determined as if a relevant disposal which is not an exempted disposal had occurred at the appropriate time.

(2) In subsection (1) "the appropriate time" means—

(a) the time when the agreement is entered into, or

(b) if it was made before the beginning of the discount repayment period, immediately after the beginning of that period.

(3) An agreement is within this subsection if it is an agreement between the purchaser or his successor in title and any other person—

(a) which is made (expressly or impliedly) in contemplation of, or in connection with, a disposal to be made, or made, by virtue of section 8,

(b) which is made before the end of the discount repayment period, and

(c) under which a relevant disposal which is not an exempted disposal is or may be required to be made to any person after the end of that period.

(4) Such an agreement is within subsection (3)—

(a) whether or not the date on which the relevant disposal is to take place is specified in the agreement, and

(b) whether or not any requirement to make that disposal is or may be made subject to the fulfilment of any condition.

(5) The Secretary of State may by order provide—

(a) for subsection (1) to apply to agreements of any description specified in the order in addition to those within subsection (3);

(b) for subsection (1) not to apply to agreements of any description so specified to which it would otherwise apply.

(6) An order under subsection (5)—

(a) may make different provision with respect to different cases or descriptions of case; and

(b) shall be made by statutory instrument which shall be subject to annulment in pursuance of a resolution of either House of Parliament.

(7) In this section—

"agreement" includes arrangement;

"the discount repayment period" means the period of three or five years that applies for the purposes of section 11(2) (depending on whether an offer such as is mentioned in section 199(3) of the Housing Act 2004 was made before or on or after the coming into force of that section).]

[1051A]

NOTES

Commencement: 18 January 2005.

Inserted by the Housing Act 2004, s 201, except in relation to any agreement or arrangement made before 18 January 2005.

Right of tenant to acquire dwelling

16 Right of tenant to acquire dwelling

(1) A tenant of a registered social landlord has the right to acquire the dwelling of which he is a tenant if—

(a) he is a tenant under an assured tenancy, other than an assured shorthold tenancy or a long tenancy, or under a secure tenancy,

(b) the dwelling was provided with public money and has remained in the social rented sector, and

(c) he satisfies any further qualifying conditions applicable under Part V of the Housing Act 1985 (the right to buy) as it applies in relation to the right conferred by this section.

(2) For this purpose a dwelling shall be regarded as provided with public money if—

(a) it was provided or acquired wholly or in part by means of a grant under section 18 (social housing grant),

(b) it was provided or acquired wholly or in part by applying or appropriating sums standing in the disposal proceeds fund of a registered social landlord (see section 25), or

(c) it was acquired by a registered social landlord after the commencement of this paragraph on a disposal by a public sector landlord at a time when it was capable of being let as a separate dwelling.

(3) A dwelling shall be regarded for the purposes of this section as having remained within the social rented sector if, since it was so provided or acquired—

(a) the person holding the freehold interest in the dwelling has been either a registered social landlord or a public sector landlord; and

(b) any person holding an interest as lessee (otherwise than as mortgagee) in the dwelling has been—

(i) an individual holding otherwise than under a long tenancy; or

(ii) a registered social landlord or a public sector landlord.

[(3A) In subsection (3)(a) the reference to the freehold interest in the dwelling includes a reference to such an interest in the dwelling as is held by the landlord under a lease granted in pursuance of paragraph 3 of Schedule 9 to the Leasehold Reform, Housing and Urban Development Act 1993 (mandatory leaseback to former freeholder on collective enfranchisement).]

(4) A dwelling shall be regarded for the purposes of this section as provided by means of a grant under section 18 (social housing grant) if, and only if, the [Relevant Authority] when making the grant notified the recipient that the dwelling was to be so regarded.

The [Relevant Authority] shall before making the grant inform the applicant that it proposes to give such a notice and allow him an opportunity to withdraw his application within a specified time.

[(5) But notice must be taken to be given to a registered social landlord under subsection (4) by the Housing Corporation if it is sent using electronic communications to such number or address as the registered social landlord has for the time being notified to the Housing Corporation for that purpose.

(6) The means by which notice is sent by virtue of subsection (5) must be such as to enable the registered social landlord to reproduce the notice by electronic means in a form which is visible and legible.

(7) An electronic communication is a communication transmitted (whether from one person to another, from one device to another, or from a person to a device or vice versa)—

(a) by means of [an electronic communications network]; or

(b) by other means but while in an electronic form.]

[1052]

NOTES

Sub-s (3A): inserted by the Housing Act 2004, s 202(1), (2); for effect see s 202(3) of that Act.

Sub-s (4): words in square brackets substituted by the Government of Wales Act 1998, s 140, Sch 16, paras 81, 82(1)(a).
Sub-ss (5), (6): inserted, together with sub-s (7), in relation to England, by the Housing (Right to Acquire) (Electronic Communications) (England) Order 2001, SI 2001/3257, arts 1(2), 2.
Sub-s (7): inserted, together with sub-ss (5), (6), in relation to England, by SI 2001/3257, arts 1(2), 2; words in square brackets substituted by the Communications Act 2003, s 406(1), Sch 17, para 136.

[16A Extension of section 16 to dwellings funded by grants under section 27A

(1) Section 16 applies in relation to a dwelling ("a funded dwelling") provided or acquired wholly or in part by means of a grant under section 27A (grants to bodies other than registered social landlords) with the following modifications.

(2) In section 16(1) the reference to a registered social landlord includes a reference to any person to whom a grant has been paid under section 27A.

(3) In section 16(2) and (4) any reference to section 18 includes a reference to section 27A.

(4) For the purposes of section 16 a funded dwelling is to be regarded as having remained within the social rented sector in relation to any relevant time if, since it was acquired or provided as mentioned in subsection (1) above, it was used—
- (a) by the recipient of the grant mentioned in that subsection, or
- (b) if section 27B applies in relation to the grant, by each person to whom the grant was, or is treated as having been, paid,

exclusively for the purposes for which the grant was made or any other purposes agreed to by the Relevant Authority.

(5) In subsection (4) "relevant time" means a time when the dwelling would not be treated as being within the social rented sector by virtue of section 16(3).]

[1052A]

NOTES

Commencement: 17 February 2005 (in relation to England); to be appointed (in relation to Wales).
Inserted by the Housing Act 2004, s 221.

17 Right of tenant to acquire dwelling: supplementary provisions

(1) The Secretary of State may by order—
- (a) specify the amount or rate of discount to be given on the exercise of the right conferred by section 16; and
- (b) designate rural areas in relation to dwellings in which the right conferred by that section does not arise.

(2) The provisions of Part V of the Housing Act 1985 apply in relation to the right to acquire under section 16—
- (a) subject to any order under subsection (1) above, and
- (b) subject to such other exceptions, adaptations and other modifications as may be specified by regulations made by the Secretary of State.

(3) The regulations may provide—
- (a) that the powers of the Secretary of State under sections 164 to 170 of that Act (powers to intervene, give directions or assist) do not apply,
- (b) that paragraphs 1 and 3 (exceptions for charities and certain housing associations), and paragraph 11 (right of appeal to Secretary of State), of Schedule 5 to that Act do not apply,
- (c) that the provisions of Part V of that Act relating to the right to acquire on rent to mortgage terms do not apply,
- (d) that the provisions of that Part relating to restrictions on disposals in National Parks, &c do not apply, and
- (e) that the provisions of that Part relating to the preserved right to buy do not apply.

Nothing in this subsection affects the generality of the power conferred by subsection (2).

(4) The specified exceptions, adaptations and other modifications shall take the form of textual amendments of the provisions of Part V of that Act as they apply in relation to the right to buy under that Part; and the first regulations, and any subsequent consolidating regulations, shall set out the provisions of Part V as they so apply.

(5) An order or regulations under this section—

(a) may make different provision for different cases or classes of case including different areas, and

(b) may contain such incidental, supplementary and transitional provisions as the Secretary of State considers appropriate.

(6) Before making an order which would have the effect that an area ceased to be designated under subsection (1)(b), the Secretary of State shall consult—

(a) the local housing authority or authorities in whose district the area or any part of it is situated or, if the order is general in its effect, local housing authorities in general, and

(b) such bodies appearing to him to be representative of registered social landlords as he considers appropriate.

(7) An order or regulations under this section shall be made by statutory instrument which shall be subject to annulment in pursuance of a resolution of either House of Parliament.

[1053]

NOTES

Commencement: 1 August 1996.

Orders and regulations: the Housing (Right to Acquire) (Discount) (Wales) Order 1997, SI 1997/569; the Housing (Right to Acquire) (Discount) Order 1998, SI 1998/2014 (which revokes and replaces the Housing (Right to Acquire) (Discount) Order 1997, SI 1997/626, except in relation to a case where a notice was served claiming to exercise the right to acquire before 9 September 1998); the Housing (Right to Acquire) Regulations 1997, SI 1997/619; the Housing (Right to Acquire or Enfranchise) (Designated Rural Areas) Order 1999, SI 1999/1307; the Housing (Right to Acquire) (Discount) Order 2002, SI 2002/1091; the Housing (Right to Acquire and Right to Buy) (Designated Rural Areas and Designated Regions) (Wales) Order 2003, SI 2003/54; the Housing (Right of First Refusal) (England) Regulations 2005, SI 2005/1917; the Housing (Right of First Refusal) (Wales) Regulations 2005, SI 2005/2680.

CHAPTER III
GRANTS AND OTHER FINANCIAL MATTERS

Grants and other financial assistance

18 Social housing grants

(1) The [Relevant Authority] may make grants to registered social landlords in respect of expenditure incurred or to be incurred by them in connection with their housing activities.

(2) The [Relevant Authority] … shall specify in relation to grants under this section—

(a) the procedure to be followed in relation to applications for grant,

(b) the circumstances in which grant is or is not to be payable,

(c) the method for calculating, and any limitations on, the amount of grant, and

(d) the manner in which, and time or times at which, grant is to be paid.

(3) In making a grant under this section, the [Relevant Authority] may provide that the grant is conditional on compliance by the landlord with such conditions as the [Relevant Authority] may specify.

(4) The [Relevant Authority] may, with the agreement of a local housing authority, appoint the authority to act as its agent in connection with the assessment and payment of grant under this section.

[(5) The appointment—

(a) if made by the Housing Corporation, shall be on such terms as the Housing Corporation may, with the approval of the Secretary of State given with the consent of the Treasury, specify, and

(b) if made by the Secretary of State, shall be on such terms as the Secretary of State may, with the consent of the Treasury, specify;

and, in either case, the authority shall act in accordance with those terms.]

(6) Where—

(a) a grant under this section is payable to a registered social landlord, and

(b) at any time property to which the grant relates becomes vested in, or is leased for a term of years to, or reverts to, another registered social landlord, or trustees for another such landlord,

this section (including this subsection) shall have effect after that time as if the grant, or such proportion of it as is specified or determined under subsection (7), were payable to the other landlord.

(7) The proportion mentioned in subsection (6) is that which, in the circumstances of the particular case—

(a) the [Relevant Authority], acting in accordance with such principles as it may from time to time determine, may specify as being appropriate, or

(b) the [Relevant Authority] may determine to be appropriate.

(8) Where one of the landlords mentioned in subsection (6) is registered by the Housing Corporation and another is registered by [the Secretary of State], the determination mentioned in subsection (7) shall be such as shall be agreed between the [Housing Corporation and the Secretary of State].

[1054]

NOTES

Commencement: sub-ss (1), (3)–(6), (8) were brought into force on 1 April 1997; sub-ss (2), (7) were brought into force on 1 October 1996, in so far as they confer the power to make a determination, and on 1 April 1997 for remaining purposes.

Sub-ss (1), (3), (4), (7), (8): words in square brackets substituted by the Government of Wales Act 1998, s 140, Sch 16, paras 81, 82(1)(a), 85(1), (3).

Sub-s (2): words in square brackets substituted by the Government of Wales Act 1998, s 140, Sch 16, paras 81, 82(1)(a); words omitted repealed by the Housing Act 2004, ss 218, 266, Sch 11, paras 7, 8, Sch 16, as from a day to be appointed under s 270(4) of that Act.

Sub-s (5): substituted by the Government of Wales Act 1998, s 140, Sch 16, paras 81, 85(1), (2).

19 Land subject to housing management agreement

A registered social landlord is not entitled to a grant under section 18 (social housing grant) in respect of land comprised in a management agreement within the meaning of the Housing Act 1985 (see sections 27(2) and 27B(4) of that Act: delegation of housing management functions by certain authorities).

[1055]

NOTES

Commencement: 1 April 1997.

20 Purchase grant where right to acquire exercised

(1) The [Relevant Authority] shall make grants to registered social landlords in respect of discounts given by them to persons exercising the right to acquire conferred by section 16.

(2) The amount of the grant for any year shall be the aggregate value of the discounts given in that year.

(3) The [Relevant Authority] ... shall specify in relation to grants under this section—

(a) the procedure to be followed in relation to applications for grant,

(b) the manner in which, and time or times at which, grant is to be paid.

(4) In making a grant the [Relevant Authority] may provide that the grant is conditional on compliance by the registered social landlord with such conditions as the [Relevant Authority] may specify.

[1056]

NOTES

Commencement: sub-ss (1), (2), (4) were brought into force on 1 April 1997; sub-s (3) was brought into force on 1 October 1996, in so far as it confers the power to make a determination, and on 1 April 1997 for remaining purposes.

Sub-ss (1) (4): words in square brackets substituted by the Government of Wales Act 1998, s 140, Sch 16, paras 81, 82(1)(a).

Sub-s (3): words in square brackets substituted by the Government of Wales Act 1998, s 140, Sch 16, paras 81, 82(1)(a); words omitted repealed by the Housing Act 2004, ss 218, 266, Sch 11, paras 7, 9, Sch 16.

21 Purchase grant in respect of other disposals

(1) The [Relevant Authority] may make grants to registered social landlords in respect of discounts on disposals by them of dwellings to tenants otherwise than in pursuance of the right conferred by section 16.

(2) The [Relevant Authority] shall make such a grant if the tenant was entitled to exercise the right conferred by section 16 in relation to another dwelling of the landlord's.

The amount of the grant in such a case shall not exceed the amount of the discount to which the tenant would have been entitled in respect of the other dwelling.

(3) The [Relevant Authority] ... shall specify in relation to grants under this section—
- (a) the procedure to be followed in relation to applications for grant;
- (b) the circumstances in which grant is or is not to be payable;
- (c) the method for calculating, and any limitations on, the amount of grant; and
- (d) the manner in which, and time or times at which, grant is to be paid.

(4) In making a grant under this section, the [Relevant Authority] may provide that the grant is conditional on compliance by the registered social landlord with such conditions as the [Relevant Authority] may specify.

[1057]

NOTES

Commencement: sub-ss (1), (2), (4) were brought into force on 1 April 1997; sub-s (3) was brought into force on 1 October 1996, in so far as it confers the power to make a determination, and on 1 April 1997 for remaining purposes.

Sub-ss (1), (2), (4): words in square brackets substituted by the Government of Wales Act 1998, s 140, Sch 16, paras 81, 82(1)(a).

Sub-s (3): words in square brackets substituted by the Government of Wales Act 1998, s 140, Sch 16, paras 81, 82(1)(a); words omitted repealed by the Housing Act 2004, ss 218, 266, Sch 11, paras 7, 10, Sch 16.

22 Assistance from local authorities

(1) A local authority may promote—
- (a) the formation of bodies to act as registered social landlords, and
- (b) the extension of the objects or activities of registered social landlords.

(2) A local authority may for the assistance of any registered social landlord subscribe for share or loan capital of the landlord.

(3) A local authority may for the assistance of a registered social landlord—
- (a) make grants or loans to the landlord, or
- (b) guarantee or join in guaranteeing the payment of the principal of, and interest on, money borrowed by the landlord (including money borrowed by the issue of loan capital) or of interest on share capital issued by the landlord.

(4) A local housing authority may sell or supply under a hire-purchase agreement furniture to the occupants of houses provided by a registered social landlord, and may buy furniture for that purpose.

In this subsection "hire-purchase agreement" means a hire-purchase agreement or conditional sale agreement within the meaning of the Consumer Credit Act 1974.

[1058]

NOTES

Commencement: 1 October 1996. By virtue of the Housing Act 1996 (Commencement No 3 and Transitional Provisions) Order 1996, SI 1996/2402, art 3, Schedule, para 1, this section applies in relation to matters occurring before 1 October 1996 as it applies in relation to matters arising on or after that date.

23 Loans by Public Works Loans Commissioners

(1) The Public Works Loans Commissioners may lend money to a registered social landlord—
- (a) for the purpose of constructing or improving, or facilitating or encouraging the construction or improvement, of dwellings,
- (b) for the purchase of dwellings which the landlord desires to purchase with a view to their improvement, and

(c) for the purchase and development of land.

(2) A loan for any of those purposes, and interest on the loan, shall be secured by a mortgage of—

(a) the land in respect of which that purpose is to be carried out, and

(b) such other lands (if any) as may be offered as security for the loan;

and the money lent shall not exceed three-quarters (or, if the payment of the principal of, and interest on, the loan is guaranteed by a local authority, nine-tenths) of the value, to be ascertained to the satisfaction of the Public Works Commissioners, of the estate or interest in the land proposed to be so mortgaged.

(3) Loans may be made by instalments as the building of dwellings or other work on the land mortgaged under subsection (2) progresses (so, however, that the total amount lent does not at any time exceed the amount specified in that subsection); and a mortgage may accordingly be made to secure such loans to be so made.

(4) If the loan exceeds two-thirds of the value referred to in subsection (2), and is not guaranteed as to principal and interest by a local authority, the Public Works Loans Commissioners shall require, in addition to such a mortgage as is mentioned in that subsection, such further security as they think fit.

(5) Subject to subsection (6), the period for repayment of a loan under this section shall not exceed 40 years, and no money shall be lent on mortgage of any land unless the estate proposed to be mortgaged is either an estate in fee simple absolute in possession or an estate for a term of years absolute of which not less than 50 years are unexpired at the date of the loan.

(6) Where a loan under this section is made for the purpose of carrying out a scheme for the provision of houses approved by the Secretary of State, the maximum period for the repayment of the loan is 50 instead of 40 years, and money may be lent on the mortgage of an estate for a term of years absolute of which a period of not less than ten years in excess of the period fixed for the repayment of the sums advanced remains unexpired at the date of the loan.

[1059]

NOTES

Commencement: 1 October 1996. By virtue of the Housing Act 1996 (Commencement No 3 and Transitional Provisions) Order 1996, SI 1996/2402, art 3, Schedule, para 1, this section applies in relation to matters occurring before 1 October 1996 as it applies in relation to matters arising on or after that date.

Treatment of disposal proceeds

24 The disposal proceeds fund

(1) A registered social landlord shall show separately in its accounts for any period ending after the coming into force of this section its net disposal proceeds.

(2) The net disposal proceeds of a registered social landlord are—

(a) the net proceeds of sale received by it in respect of any disposal of land to a tenant—

  (i) in pursuance of the right conferred by section 16 (right of tenant to acquire dwelling), or

  (ii) in respect of which a grant was made under section 21 (purchase grant in respect of other disposals);

(b) payments of grant received by it under section 20 or 21 (purchase grant);

(c) where any such grant has been paid to it, any repayments of discount in respect of which the grant was given; and

(d) such other proceeds of sale or payments of grant (if any) as the [Relevant Authority] may from time to time determine.

(3) The net proceeds of sale means the proceeds of sale less an amount calculated in accordance with a determination by the [Relevant Authority].

(4) The disposal proceeds shall be shown in a fund to be known as a disposal proceeds fund.

(5) The method of constituting the fund and showing it in the landlord's accounts shall be as required by determination of the [Relevant Authority] under paragraph 16 of Schedule 1 (general requirements as to accounts).

(6) Interest shall be added to the fund in accordance with a determination made by the [Relevant Authority].

(7) Where this section applies in relation to the proceeds of sale arising on a disposal, section 27 below (recovery, &c of social housing grants) and section 52 of the Housing Act 1988 (recovery, &c of grants under that Act and earlier enactments) do not apply.

[1060]

NOTES

Commencement: this section was brought into force on 1 August 1996, in so far as conferring a power to consult, to make determinations, to give consents and to delegate functions, and on 1 April 1997 for remaining purposes.

Sub-ss (2), (3), (5), (6): words in square brackets substituted by the Government of Wales Act 1998, Sch 16, paras 81, 82(1)(a).

25 Application or appropriation of disposal proceeds

(1) The sums standing in the disposal proceeds account of a registered social landlord ("disposal proceeds") may only be applied or appropriated by it for such purposes and in such manner as the [Relevant Authority] may determine.

(2) If any disposal proceeds are not applied or appropriated as mentioned in subsection (1) within such time as is specified by determination of the [Relevant Authority], the [Relevant Authority] may direct that the whole or part of them shall be paid to it.

[1061]

NOTES

Commencement: this section was brought into force on 1 October 1996 in so far as conferring a power to make determinations and directions, and on 1 April 1997 for remaining purposes.

Words in square brackets substituted by the Government of Wales Act 1998, s 140, Sch 16, paras 81, 82(1)(a).

26 Disposal proceeds: power to require information

(1) The [Relevant Authority] may give notice—

(a) to all registered social landlords,

(b) to registered social landlords of a particular description, or

(c) to particular registered social landlords,

requiring them to furnish it with such information as it may reasonably require in connection with the exercise of its functions under sections 24 and 25 (treatment of disposal proceeds).

(2) A notice under subsection (1)(a) or (b) may be given by publication in such manner as the [Relevant Authority] considers appropriate for bringing it to the attention of the landlords concerned.

[1062]

NOTES

Commencement: 1 April 1997.

Words in square brackets substituted by the Government of Wales Act 1998, s 140, Sch 16, paras 81, 82(1)(a).

Recovery, &c of social housing grants

27 Recovery, &c of social housing grants

(1) Where a registered social landlord has received a grant under section 18 (social housing grant), the following powers are exercisable in such events as the [Relevant Authority] may from time to time determine.

(2) The [Relevant Authority] may, acting in accordance with such principles as it has determined—

(a) reduce any grant payable by it, or suspend or cancel any instalment of any such grant, or

(b) direct the registered social landlord to apply or appropriate for such purposes as the [Relevant Authority] may specify, or to pay to the [Relevant Authority], such amount as the [Relevant Authority] may specify.

(3) A direction by the [Relevant Authority] under subsection (2)(b) may require the application, appropriation or payment of an amount with interest.

(4) Any such direction shall specify—

(a) the rate or rates of interest (whether fixed or variable) which is or are applicable,

(b) the date from which interest is payable, and

(c) any provision for suspended or reduced interest which is applicable.

The date from which interest is payable must not be earlier than the date of the event giving rise to the exercise of the [Relevant Authority's] powers under this section.

(5) In subsection (4)(c)—

(a) provision for suspended interest means provision to the effect that if the principal amount is applied, appropriated or paid before a date specified in the direction, no interest will be payable for any period after the date of the direction; and

(b) provision for reduced interest means provision to the effect that if the principal amount is so applied, appropriated or paid, any interest payable will be payable at a rate or rates lower than the rate or rates which would otherwise be applicable.

(6) Where—

(a) a registered social landlord has received a payment in respect of a grant under section 18, and

(b) at any time property to which the grant relates becomes vested in, or is leased for a term of years to, or reverts to, some other registered social landlord,

this section (including this subsection) shall have effect in relation to periods after that time as if the grant, or such proportion of it as may be determined by the [Relevant Authority] to be appropriate, had been made to that other registered social landlord.

(7) The matters specified in a direction under subsection (4)(a) to (c), and the proportion mentioned in subsection (6), shall be—

(a) such as the [Relevant Authority], acting in accordance with such principles as it may from time to time determine, may specify as being appropriate, or

(b) such as the [Relevant Authority] may determine to be appropriate in the particular case.

[1063]

NOTES

Commencement: this section was brought into force on 1 October 1996 in so far as conferring a power to make determinations and directions, and on 1 April 1997 for remaining purposes.

Sub-ss (1)–(3), (4), (6), (7): words in square brackets substituted by the Government of Wales Act 1998, s 140, Sch 16, para 82(1).

[Grants to bodies other than registered social landlords

27A Grants to bodies other than registered social landlords

(1) The Relevant Authority may make grants under this section to persons other than registered social landlords.

(2) Grants under this section are grants for any of the following purposes—

(a) acquiring, or repairing and improving, or creating by the conversion of houses or other property, houses to be disposed of—

(i) under equity percentage arrangements, or

(ii) on shared ownership terms;

(b) constructing houses to be disposed of—

(i) under equity percentage arrangements, or

(ii) on shared ownership terms;

(c) providing loans to be secured by mortgages to assist persons to acquire houses for their own occupation;

(d) providing, constructing or improving houses to be kept available for letting;

(e) providing, constructing or improving houses for letting that are to be managed by such registered social landlords, and under arrangements containing such terms, as are approved by the Relevant Authority;

(f) such other purposes as may be specified in an order under subsection (3).

(3) The Secretary of State may by order make such provision in connection with the making of grants under this section as he considers appropriate.

(4) An order under subsection (3) may, in particular, make provision—

(a) defining "equity percentage arrangements" for the purposes of this section;

(b) specifying or describing the bodies from whom loans may be obtained by persons wishing to acquire houses for their own occupation;

(c) dealing with the priority of mortgages entered into by such persons;

(d) specifying purposes additional to those mentioned in subsection (2)(a) to (e).

(5) As regards grants made by the Housing Corporation, an order under subsection (3) may also require the imposition of conditions in connection with such grants, and for this purpose may—

(a) prescribe conditions that are to be so imposed;

(b) prescribe matters about which conditions are to be so imposed and any particular effects that such conditions are to achieve.

(6) The Relevant Authority shall specify in relation to grants under this section—

(a) the procedure to be followed in relation to applications for grant,

(b) the circumstances in which grant is or is not to be payable,

(c) the method for calculating, and any limitations on, the amount of grant, and

(d) the manner in which, and the time or times at which, grant is to be paid.

(7) If, by virtue of subsection (5), an order under subsection (3) requires conditions to be imposed by the Housing Corporation in connection with a grant to a person under this section, the Corporation in making the grant—

(a) must provide that the grant is conditional on compliance by the person with such conditions as are required by the order; and

(b) if it exercises its power to impose conditions under subsection (8), must not impose any that are inconsistent with the requirements of the order.

(8) In making a grant to a person under this section the Relevant Authority may provide that the grant is conditional on compliance by the person with such conditions as the Authority may specify.

(9) The conditions that may be so specified include conditions requiring the payment to the Relevant Authority in specified circumstances of a sum determined by the Authority (with or without interest).

(10) An order under subsection (3) shall be made by statutory instrument which shall be subject to annulment in pursuance of a resolution of either House of Parliament.

(11) In this section—

"disposed of on shared ownership terms" has the meaning given by section 2(6);

"letting" includes the grant of a licence to occupy.]

[1063A]

NOTES

Commencement: 17 February 2005 (in relation to England); to be appointed (in relation to Wales).

Inserted, together with preceding cross-heading and s 27B in relation to England, and inserted as from a day to be appointed under s 270(4), (5) of that Act in relation to Wales, by the Housing Act 2004, s 220.

Orders: Social Housing (Grants to Bodies other than Registered Social Landlords) (Additional Purposes) (England) Order 2006, SI 2006/583.

[27B Transfer of property funded by grants under section 27A

(1) Where—

(a) any grant is paid or payable to any person under section 27A, and

(b) at any time property to which the grant relates becomes vested in, or is leased for a term of years to, or reverts to, another person who is not a registered social landlord,

this Part shall have effect, in relation to times falling after that time, as if the grant, or such proportion of it as is determined or specified under subsection (4), had been paid or (as the case may be) were payable to that other person under section 27A.

(2) Where—

(a) any amount is paid or payable to any person by way of grant under section 27A, and

(b) at any time property to which the grant relates becomes vested in, or is leased for a term of years to, or reverts to, a registered social landlord,

this Part shall have effect, in relation to times falling after that time, as if the grant, or such proportion of it as is determined or specified under subsection (4), had been paid or (as the case may be) were payable to that other person under section 18.

(3) In such a case, the relevant section 18 conditions accordingly apply to that grant or proportion of it, in relation to times falling after that time, in place of those specified under section 27A(8).

"The relevant section 18 conditions" means such conditions specified under section 18(3) as would have applied at the time of the making of the grant if it had been made under section 18 to a registered social landlord.

(4) The proportion mentioned in subsection (1) or (2) is that which, in the circumstances of the particular case—

(a) the Relevant Authority, acting in accordance with such principles as it may from time to time determine, may specify as being appropriate, or

(b) the Relevant Authority may determine to be appropriate.]

[1063B]

NOTES

Commencement: 17 February 2005 (in relation to England); to be appointed (in relation to Wales).
Inserted as noted to s 27A at **[1063A]**.

Grants, &c under earlier enactments

28 Grants under ss 50 to [54] of the Housing Act 1988

(1) No application for a grant under section 50 of the Housing Act 1988 (housing association grant) may be made after the commencement of this subsection.

(2) No application for a grant under section 51 of that Act (revenue deficit grant) may be made after the commencement of this subsection except by an association which had such a deficit as is mentioned in that section for any of the years beginning 1st April 1994, 1st April 1995 or 1st April 1996.

(3)–(5) …

(6) Any reference in sections 50 to [54] of that Act to registration as a housing association shall be construed after the commencement of section 1 of this Act (the register of social landlords) as a reference to registration as a social landlord.

[1064]

NOTES

Commencement: sub-ss (1), (2), (5), (6) were brought into force on 1 April 1997; sub-s (3) was brought into force on 1 October 1996 for the purpose of enabling a determination to be made under the Housing Act 1988, s 52(2), and on 1 April 1997 for remaining purposes; sub-s (4) was brought into force on 1 August 1996.

Section heading: number in square brackets substituted by the Housing Act 2004, s 218, Sch 11, paras 7, 11.

Sub-ss (3)–(5): amend the Housing Act 1988, ss 52, 53, 55.

Sub-s (6): number in square brackets substituted by the Housing Act 2004, s 218, Sch 11, paras 7, 11.

29 Commutation of payments of special residual subsidy

(1) The Secretary of State may, after consultation with a housing association, determine to commute any payments of special residual subsidy payable to the association under paragraph 2 of Part I of Schedule 5 to the Housing Associations Act 1985 for the financial year 1998–99 and subsequent years.

(2) Where the Secretary of State makes such a determination the payments of special residual subsidy payable to a housing association shall be commuted into a single sum calculated in such manner, and payable on such date, as the Secretary of State may consider appropriate.

(3) If after a commuted payment has been made to a housing association it appears to the Secretary of State that the payment was smaller or greater than it should have been, the Secretary of State may make a further payment to the association or require the association to repay to him such sum as he may direct.

(4) The Secretary of State may delegate to the Housing Corporation, to such extent and subject to such conditions as he may specify, any of his functions under this section and, where he does so, references to him in this section shall be construed accordingly.

[1065]

NOTES

Commencement: this section was brought into force on 1 August 1996, in so far as conferring a power to consult, to make determinations, to give consents and to delegate functions, and on 1 April 1997 for remaining purposes.

CHAPTER IV
GENERAL POWERS OF THE [RELEVANT AUTHORITY]

Information

30 General power to obtain information

(1) The [Relevant Authority] may for any purpose connected with the discharge of any of its functions in relation to registered social landlords serve a notice on a person requiring him—

(a) to give to the [Relevant Authority], at a time and place and in the form and manner specified in the notice, such information relating to the affairs of a registered social landlord as may be specified or described in the notice, or

(b) to produce to the [Relevant Authority] or a person authorised by the [Relevant Authority], at a time and place specified in the notice, any documents relating to the affairs of the registered social landlord which are specified or described in the notice and are in his custody or under his control.

(2) A notice under this section may be served on—

(a) a registered social landlord,

(b) any person who is, or has been, an officer, member, employee or agent of a registered social landlord,

(c) a subsidiary or associate of a registered social landlord,

(d) any person who is, or has been, an officer, member, employee or agent of a subsidiary or associate of a registered social landlord, or

(e) any other person whom the [Relevant Authority] has reason to believe is or may be in possession of relevant information.

In this section "agent" includes banker, solicitor and auditor.

(3) No notice shall be served on a person within paragraphs (b) to (e) of subsection (2) unless—

(a) a notice has been served on the registered social landlord and has not been complied with, or

(b) the [Relevant Authority] believes that the information or documents in question are not in the possession of the landlord.

(4) Nothing in this section authorises the [Relevant Authority] to require—

(a) the disclosure of anything which a person would be entitled to refuse to disclose on grounds of legal professional privilege in proceedings in the High Court, or

(b) the disclosure by a banker of anything in breach of any duty of confidentiality owed by him to a person other than a registered social landlord or a subsidiary or associate of a registered social landlord.

[(5) A notice under this section—

(a) if given by the Housing Corporation, shall be given under its seal, and

(b) if given by the Secretary of State, shall be given in writing.]

(6) References in this section to a document are to anything in which information of any description is recorded; and in relation to a document in which information is recorded otherwise than in legible form, references to producing it are to producing it in legible form.

(7) Where by virtue of this section documents are produced to any person, he may take copies of or make extracts from them.

[1066]

NOTES

Words in square brackets in the heading preceding this section substituted by the Government of Wales Act 1998, s 140, Sch 16, paras 81, 82(1).

Commencement: 1 October 1996. By virtue of the Housing Act 1996 (Commencement No 3 and Transitional Provisions) Order 1996, SI 1996/2402, art 3, Schedule, para 1, this section applies in relation to matters occurring before 1 October 1996 as it applies in relation to matters arising on or after that date.

Sub-ss (1)–(4): words in square brackets substituted by the Government of Wales Act 1998, s 140, Sch 16, paras 81, 82(1)(a).

Sub-s (5): substituted by the Government of Wales Act 1998, s 140, Sch 16, paras 81, 86.

31 Enforcement of notice to provide information, &c

(1) A person who without reasonable excuse fails to do anything required of him by a notice under section 30 commits an offence and is liable on summary conviction to a fine not exceeding level 5 on the standard scale.

(2) A person who intentionally alters, suppresses or destroys a document which he has been required by a notice under section 30 to produce commits an offence and is liable—

(a) on summary conviction, to a fine not exceeding the statutory maximum,

[(b) on conviction on indictment, to imprisonment for a term not exceeding two years or to a fine, or both.]

(3) Proceedings for an offence under subsection (1) or (2) may be brought only by or with the consent of the [Relevant Authority] or the Director of Public Prosecutions.

(4) If a person makes default in complying with a notice under section 30, the High Court may, on the application of the [Relevant Authority], make such order as the court thinks fit for requiring the default to be made good.

Any such order may provide that all the costs or expenses of and incidental to the application shall be borne by the person in default or by any officers of a body who are responsible for its default.

[1067]

NOTES

Commencement: 1 October 1996. By virtue of the Housing Act 1996 (Commencement No 3 and Transitional Provisions) Order 1996, SI 1996/2402, art 3, Schedule, para 1, this section applies in relation to matters occurring before 1 October 1996 as it applies in relation to matters arising on or after that date.

Sub-s (2): para (b) substituted by the Housing Act 2004, s 218, Sch 11, paras 7, 12, except in relation to any offence committed before 18 January 2005.

Sub-ss (3), (4): words in square brackets substituted by the Government of Wales Act 1998, s 140, Sch 16, paras 81, 82(1)(a).

32 Disclosure of information to the [Relevant Authority]

(1) A body or person to whom this section applies may, subject to the following provisions, disclose to the [Relevant Authority], for the purpose of enabling the [Relevant Authority] to discharge any of its functions relating to registered social landlords, any information received by that body or person under or for the purposes of any enactment.

(2) This section applies to the following bodies and persons—

(a) any government department (including a Northern Ireland department);

(b) any local authority;

(c) any constable; and

(d) any other body or person discharging functions of a public nature (including a body or person discharging regulatory functions in relation to any description of activities).

(3) This section has effect subject to any express restriction on disclosure imposed by or under any other enactment.

(4) Nothing in this section shall be construed as affecting any power of disclosure exercisable apart from this section.

[1068]

NOTES

Commencement: 1 October 1996. By virtue of the Housing Act 1996 (Commencement No 3 and Transitional Provisions) Order 1996, SI 1996/2402, art 3, Schedule, para 1, this section applies in relation to matters occurring before 1 October 1996 as it applies in relation to matters arising on or after that date.

Section heading: words in square brackets substituted by the Government of Wales Act 1998, s 140, Sch 16, paras 81, 82(1)(a).

Sub-s (1): words in square brackets substituted by the Government of Wales Act 1998, s 140, Sch 16, paras 81, 82(1)(a).

33 Disclosure of information by the [Relevant Authority]

(1) The [Relevant Authority] may disclose to a body or person to whom this section applies any information received by it relating to a registered social landlord—

- (a) for any purpose connected with the discharge of the functions of the [Relevant Authority] in relation to such landlords, or
- (b) for the purpose of enabling or assisting that body or person to discharge any of its or his functions.

(2) This section applies to the following bodies and persons—

- (a) any government department (including a Northern Ireland department);
- (b) any local authority;
- (c) any constable; and
- (d) any other body or person discharging functions of a public nature (including a body or person discharging regulatory functions in relation to any description of activities).

Paragraph (d) extends to any such body or person in a country or territory outside the United Kingdom.

(3) Where any information disclosed to the [Relevant Authority] under section 32 is so disclosed subject to any express restriction on the further disclosure of the information, the [Relevant Authority's] power of disclosure under this section is exercisable subject to that restriction.

A person who discloses information in contravention of any such restriction commits an offence and is liable on summary conviction to a fine not exceeding level 3 on the standard scale.

(4) Any information disclosed by the [Relevant Authority] under this section may be subject by the [Relevant Authority] to any express restriction on the further disclosure of the information.

(5) A person who discloses information in contravention of any such restriction commits an offence and is liable on summary conviction to a fine not exceeding level 3 on the standard scale.

Proceedings for such an offence may be brought only by or with the consent of the [Relevant Authority] or the Director of Public Prosecutions.

(6) Nothing in this section shall be construed as affecting any power of disclosure exercisable apart from this section.

[1069]

NOTES

Commencement: 1 October 1996. By virtue of the Housing Act 1996 (Commencement No 3 and Transitional Provisions) Order 1996, SI 1996/2402, art 3, Schedule, para 1, this section applies in relation to matters occurring before 1 October 1996 as it applies in relation to matters arising on or after that date.

Section heading: words in square brackets substituted by the Government of Wales Act 1998, s 140, Sch 16, paras 81, 82(1)(a).

Sub-ss (1), (3)–(5): words in square brackets substituted by the Government of Wales Act 1998, s 140, Sch 16, paras 81, 82(1).

Standards of performance

34 Standards of performance

The [Relevant Authority] may, after consultation with persons or bodies appearing to it to be representative of registered social landlords, from time to time—

(a) determine such standards of performance in connection with the provision of housing as, in its opinion, ought to be achieved by such landlords, and
(b) arrange for the publication, in such form and in such manner as it considers appropriate, of the standards so determined.

[1070]

NOTES

Commencement: 1 October 1996. By virtue of the Housing Act 1996 (Commencement No 3 and Transitional Provisions) Order 1996, SI 1996/2402, art 3, Schedule, para 1, this section applies in relation to matters occurring before 1 October 1996 as it applies in relation to matters arising on or after that date.

Words in square brackets substituted by the Government of Wales Act 1998, s 140, Sch 16, paras 81, 82(1)(a).

35 Information as to levels of performance

(1) The [Relevant Authority] shall from time to time collect information as to the levels of performance achieved by registered social landlords in connection with the provision of housing.

(2) On or before such date in each year as may be specified in a direction given by the [Relevant Authority], each registered social landlord shall provide the [Relevant Authority], as respects each standard determined under section 34, with such information as to the level of performance achieved by him as may be so specified.

(3) A registered social landlord who without reasonable excuse fails to do anything required of him by a direction under subsection (2) commits an offence and is liable on summary conviction to a fine not exceeding level 5 on the standard scale.

Proceedings for such an offence may be brought only by or with the consent of the [Relevant Authority] or the Director of Public Prosecutions.

(4) The [Relevant Authority] shall at least once in every year arrange for the publication, in such form and in such manner as it considers appropriate, of such of the information collected by or provided to it under this section as appears to it expedient to give to tenants or potential tenants of registered social landlords.

(5) In arranging for the publication of any such information the [Relevant Authority] shall have regard to the need for excluding, so far as that is practicable—
(a) any matter which relates to the affairs of an individual, where publication of that matter would or might, in the opinion of the [Relevant Authority], seriously and prejudicially affect the interests of that individual; and
(b) any matter which relates specifically to the affairs of a particular body of persons, whether corporate or unincorporate, where publication of that matter would or might, in the opinion of the [Relevant Authority], seriously and prejudicially affect the interests of that body.

[1071]

NOTES

Commencement: 1 April 1998 (sub-s (4)); 1 April 1997 (sub-ss (1)–(3), (5)).

Words in square brackets substituted by the Government of Wales Act 1998, s 140, Sch 16, paras 81, 82(1)(a).

Housing management

36 Issue of guidance by the [Relevant Authority]

(1) The [Relevant Authority] may issue guidance with respect to the management of housing accommodation by registered social landlords.

(2) Guidance under [subsection (1)] may, in particular, be issued with respect to—
(a) the housing demands for which provision should be made and the means of meeting those demands;
(b) the allocation of housing accommodation between individuals;
(c) the terms of tenancies and the principles upon which levels of rent should be determined;
(d) standards of maintenance and repair and the means of achieving those standards;

(e) the services to be provided to tenants;
(f) the procedures to be adopted to deal with complaints by tenants against a landlord;
(g) consultation and communication with tenants;
(h) the devolution to tenants of decisions concerning the management of housing accommodation;
[(i) the policy and procedures a landlord is required under section 218A to prepare and from time to time revise in connection with anti-social behaviour.]

[(2A) The Relevant Authority may also issue guidance with respect to—
(a) the governance of bodies that are registered social landlords;
(b) the effective management of such bodies;
(c) establishing and maintaining the financial viability of such bodies.]

[(3) Before issuing any guidance under this section the Relevant Authority shall consult such bodies appearing to the Relevant Authority to be representative of registered social landlords as the Relevant Authority considers appropriate; and where the Relevant Authority issues guidance under this section it shall be issued in such manner as the Relevant Authority considers appropriate for bringing it to the notice of the landlords concerned.

(4) The Housing Corporation shall not issue guidance under this section unless—
(a) it has been submitted in draft to the Secretary of State for his approval, and
(b) the Secretary of State has given his approval to the draft.]

(5) Guidance issued under this section may be revised or withdrawn; and subsections (3) and (4) apply in relation to the revision of guidance as in relation to its issue.

(6) Guidance under this section may make different provision in relation to different cases and, in particular, in relation to different areas, different descriptions of housing accommodation and different descriptions of registered social landlord.

(7) In considering whether action needs to be taken to secure the proper management of the affairs of a registered social landlord or whether there has been [misconduct or] mismanagement, the [Relevant Authority] may have regard (among other matters) to the extent to which any guidance under this section is being or has been followed.

[1072]

NOTES

Commencement: 1 November 1998 (sub-ss (3), (4)); 1 October 1996 (sub-s (7)); 1 August 1996 (sub-ss (1)–(6)). By virtue of the Housing Act 1996 (Commencement No 3 and Transitional Provisions) Order 1996, SI 1996/2402, art 3, Schedule, para 1, sub-s (7) applies in relation to matters occurring before 1 October 1996 as it applies in relation to matters arising on or after that date.

Section heading, sub-s (1): words in square brackets substituted by the Government of Wales Act 1998, s 140, Sch 16, paras 81, 82(1)(a).

Sub-s (2): words in first pair of square brackets substituted by the Housing Act 2004, s 218, Sch 11, paras 7, 13(1), (2); para (i) added by the Anti-social Behaviour Act 2003, s 12(2).

Sub-s (2A): inserted by the Housing Act 2004, s 218, Sch 11, paras 7, 13(1), (3).

Sub-ss (3), (4): substituted by the Government of Wales Act 1998, s 140, Sch 16, paras 81, 87.

Sub-s (7): words in first pair of square brackets inserted by the Housing Act 2004, s 218, Sch 11, paras 7, 13(1), (4); words in second pair of square brackets substituted by the Government of Wales Act 1998, s 140, Sch 16, paras 81, 82(1)(a).

37 Powers of entry

(1) This section applies where it appears to the [Relevant Authority] that a registered social landlord may be failing to maintain or repair any premises in accordance with guidance issued under section 36.

(2) A person authorised by the [Relevant Authority] may at any reasonable time, on giving not less than 28 days' notice of his intention to the landlord concerned, enter any such premises for the purpose of survey and examination.

(3) Where such notice is given to the landlord, the landlord shall give the occupier or occupiers of the premises not less than seven days' notice of the proposed survey and examination.

A landlord who fails to do so commits an offence and is liable on summary conviction to a fine not exceeding level 3 on the standard scale.

(4) Proceedings for an offence under subsection (3) may be brought only by or with the consent of the [Relevant Authority] or the Director of Public Prosecutions.

(5) An authorisation for the purposes of this section shall be in writing stating the particular purpose or purposes for which the entry is authorised and shall, if so required, be produced for inspection by the occupier or anyone acting on his behalf.

(6) The [Relevant Authority] shall give a copy of any survey carried out in exercise of the powers conferred by this section to the landlord concerned.

(7) The [Relevant Authority] may require the landlord concerned to pay to it such amount as the [Relevant Authority] may determine towards the costs of carrying out any survey under this section.

[1073]

NOTES

Commencement: 1 October 1996. By virtue of the Housing Act 1996 (Commencement No 3 and Transitional Provisions) Order 1996, SI 1996/2402, art 3, Schedule, para 1, this section applies in relation to matters occurring before 1 October 1996 as it applies in relation to matters arising on or after that date.

Sub-ss (1), (2), (4), (6), (7): words in square brackets substituted by the Government of Wales Act 1998, s 140, Sch 16, paras 81, 82(1)(a).

38 Penalty for obstruction of person exercising power of entry

(1) It is an offence for a registered social landlord or any of its officers or employees to obstruct a person authorised under section 37 (powers of entry) to enter premises in the performance of anything which he is authorised by that section to do.

(2) A person who commits such an offence is liable on summary conviction to a fine not exceeding level 3 on the standard scale.

(3) Proceedings for such an offence may be brought only by or with the consent of the [Relevant Authority] or the Director of Public Prosecutions.

[1074]

NOTES

Commencement: 1 October 1996. By virtue of the Housing Act 1996 (Commencement No 3 and Transitional Provisions) Order 1996, SI 1996/2402, art 3, Schedule, para 1, this section applies in relation to matters occurring before 1 October 1996 as it applies in relation to matters arising on or after that date.

Sub-s (3): words in square brackets substituted by the Government of Wales Act 1998, s 140, Sch 16, paras 81, 82(1)(a).

39 Insolvency, &c of registered social landlord: scheme of provisions

(1) The following sections make provision—

(a) for notice to be given to the [Relevant Authority] of any proposal to take certain steps in relation to a registered social landlord (section 40), and for further notice to be given when any such step is taken (section 41),

(b) for a moratorium on the disposal of land, and certain other assets, held by the registered social landlord (sections 42 and 43),

(c) for proposals by the [Relevant Authority] as to the future ownership and management of the land held by the landlord (section 44), which are binding if agreed (section 45),

(d) for the appointment of a manager to implement agreed proposals (section 46) and as to the powers of such a manager (sections 47 and 48),

(e) for the giving of assistance by the [Relevant Authority] (section 49), and

(f) for application to the court to secure compliance with the agreed proposals (section 50).

(2) In those sections—

"disposal" means sale, lease, mortgage, charge or any other disposition, and includes the grant of an option;

"secured creditor" means a creditor who holds a mortgage or charge (including a floating charge) over land held by the landlord or any existing or future interest of the landlord in rents or other receipts from land; and

"security" means any mortgage, charge or other security.

(3) The Secretary of State may make provision by order defining for the purposes of those sections what is meant by a step to enforce security over land.

PART I STATUTES

Any such order shall be made by statutory instrument which shall be subject to annulment in pursuance of a resolution of either House of Parliament.

[1075]

NOTES

Commencement: 1 October 1996.

Sub-s (1): words in square brackets substituted by the Government of Wales Act 1998, s 140, Sch 16, paras 81, 82(1)(a).

40 Initial notice to be given to the [Relevant Authority]

(1) Notice must be given to the [Relevant Authority] before any of the steps mentioned below is taken in relation to a registered social landlord.

The person by whom the notice must be given is indicated in the second column.

(2) Where the registered social landlord is an industrial and provident society, the steps and the person by whom notice must be given are—

Any step to enforce any security over land held by the landlord	The person proposing to take the step.
Presenting a petition for the winding up of the landlord.	The petitioner.
Passing a resolution for the winding up of the landlord.	The landlord.

(3) Where the registered social landlord is a company registered under the Companies Act 1985 (including a registered charity), the steps and the person by whom notice must be given are—

Any step to enforce any security over land held by the landlord	The person proposing to take the step.
Applying for an administration order.	The applicant.
Presenting a petition for the winding up of the landlord	The petitioner.
Passing a resolution for the winding up of the landlord.	The landlord.

(4) Where the registered social landlord is a registered charity (other than a company registered under the Companies Act 1985), the steps and the person by whom notice must be given are—

Any step to enforce any security over land held by the landlord.	The person proposing to take the step.

(5) Notice need not be given under this section in relation to a resolution for voluntary winding up where the consent of the [Relevant Authority] is required (see paragraphs 12(4) and 13(6) of Schedule 1).

(6) Any step purportedly taken without the requisite notice being given under this section is ineffective.

[(7) Subsections (8) and (9) apply in relation to the reference in subsection (3) to applying for an administration order.

(8) In a case where an administrator is appointed under paragraph 14 or 22 of Schedule B1 to the Insolvency Act 1986 (appointment by floating charge holder, company or directors)—

(a) the reference includes a reference to appointing an administrator under that paragraph, and

(b) in respect of an appointment under either of those paragraphs the reference to the applicant shall be taken as a reference to the person making the appointment.

(9) In a case where a copy of a notice of intention to appoint an administrator under either of those paragraphs is filed with the court—

(a) the reference shall be taken to include a reference to the filing of the copy of the notice, and

(b) in respect of the filing of a copy of a notice of intention to appoint under either of those paragraphs the reference to the applicant shall be taken as a reference to the person giving the notice.]

[1076]

NOTES

Commencement: 1 October 1996.

Section heading, sub-ss (1), (5): words in square brackets substituted by the Government of Wales Act 1998, s 140, Sch 16, paras 81, 82(1)(a).

Sub-ss (7)–(9): added by the Enterprise Act 2002, s 248(3), Sch 17, paras 50, 51.

41 Further notice to be given to the [Relevant Authority]

(1) Notice must be given to the [Relevant Authority] as soon as may be after any of the steps mentioned below is taken in relation to a registered social landlord.

The person by whom the notice must be given is indicated in the second column.

(2) Where the registered social landlord is an industrial and provident society, the steps and the person by whom notice must be given are—

The taking of a step to enforce any security over land held by the landlord.	The person taking the step.
The making of an order for the winding up of the landlord.	The petitioner.
The passing of a resolution for the winding up of the landlord.	The landlord.

(3) Where the registered social landlord is a company registered under the Companies Act 1985 (including a registered charity), the steps and the person by whom notice must be given are—

The taking of a step to enforce any security over land held by the landlord.	The making of an administration order.
The making of an order for the winding up of the landlord.	The passing of a resolution for the winding up of the landlord.

(4) Where the registered social landlord is a registered charity (other than a company registered under the Companies Act 1985), the steps and the person by whom notice must be given are—

The taking of a step to enforce any security over land held by the landlord.	The person taking the step.
The making of an administration order.	The person who applied for the order.
The making of an order for the winding up of the landlord.	The petitioner.
The passing of a resolution for the winding up of the landlord.	The landlord.

(5) Failure to give notice under this section does not affect the validity of any step taken; but the period of 28 days mentioned in section 43(1) (period after which moratorium on disposal of land, &c ends) does not begin to run until any requisite notice has been given under this section.

[(6) In subsection (3)—

(a) the reference to the making of an administration order includes a reference to appointing an administrator under paragraph 14 or 22 of Schedule B1 to the Insolvency Act 1986 (administration), and

(b) in respect of an appointment under either of those paragraphs the reference to the applicant shall be taken as a reference to the person making the appointment.]

[1077]

NOTES

Commencement: 1 October 1996.

Section heading, sub-s (1): words in square brackets substituted by the Government of Wales Act 1998, s 140, Sch 16, paras 81, 82(1)(a).

Sub-s (6): added by the Enterprise Act 2002, s 248(3), Sch 17, paras 50, 52.

42 Moratorium on disposal of land, &c

(1) Where any of the steps mentioned in section 41 is taken in relation to a registered social landlord, there is a moratorium on the disposal of land held by the landlord.

(2) During the moratorium the consent of the [Relevant Authority] under this section is required (except as mentioned below) for any disposal of land held by the landlord, whether by the landlord itself or any person having a power of disposal in relation to the land.

Consent under this section may be given in advance and may be given subject to conditions.

(3) Consent is not required under this section for any such disposal as is mentioned in section 10(1), (2) or (3) (lettings and other disposals not requiring consent under section 9).

(4) A disposal made without the consent required by this section is void.

(5) Nothing in this section prevents a liquidator from disclaiming any land held by the landlord as onerous property.

(6) The provisions of this section apply in relation to any existing or future interest of the landlord in rent or other receipts arising from land as they apply to an interest in land.

[1078]

NOTES

Commencement: 1 October 1996.

Sub-s (2): words in square brackets substituted by the Government of Wales Act 1998, s 140, Sch 16, paras 81, 82(1)(a).

43 Period of moratorium

(1) The moratorium in consequence of the taking of any step as mentioned in section 41—

(a) begins when the step is taken, and

(b) ends at the end of the period of 28 days beginning with the day on which notice of its having been taken was given to the [Relevant Authority] under that section,

subject to the following provisions.

(2) The taking of any further step as mentioned in section 41 at a time when a moratorium is already in force does not start a further moratorium or affect the duration of the existing one.

(3) A moratorium may be extended from time to time with the consent of all the landlord's secured creditors.

Notice of any such extension shall be given by the [Relevant Authority] to—

(a) the landlord, and

(b) any liquidator, administrative receiver, receiver or administrator appointed in respect of the landlord or any land held by it.

(4) If during a moratorium the [Relevant Authority] considers that the proper management of the landlord's land can be secured without making proposals under section 44 (proposals as to ownership and management of landlord's land), the [Relevant Authority] may direct that the moratorium shall cease to have effect.

Before making any such direction the [Relevant Authority] shall consult the person who took the step which brought about the moratorium.

(5) When a moratorium comes to an end, or ceases to have effect under subsection (4), the [Relevant Authority] shall give notice of that fact to the landlord and the landlord's secured creditors.

(6) When a moratorium comes to an end (but not when it ceases to have effect under subsection (4)), the following provisions of this section apply.

The [Relevant Authority's] notice shall, in such a case, inform the landlord and the landlord's secured creditors of the effect of those provisions.

(7) If any further step as mentioned in section 41 is taken within the period of three years after the end of the original period of the moratorium, the moratorium may be renewed with the consent of all the landlord's secured creditors (which may be given before or after the step is taken).

Notice of any such renewal shall be given by the [Relevant Authority] to the persons to whom notice of an extension is required to be given under subsection (3).

(8) If a moratorium ends without any proposals being agreed, then, for a period of three years the taking of any further step as mentioned in section 41 does not start a further moratorium except with the consent of the landlord's secured creditors as mentioned in subsection (7) above.

[1079]

NOTES

Commencement: 1 October 1996.

Sub-ss (1), (3)–(7): words in square brackets substituted by the Government of Wales Act 1998, s 140, Sch 16, paras 81, 82(1).

44 Proposals as to ownership and management of landlord's land

(1) During the moratorium (see sections 42 and 43) the [Relevant Authority] may make proposals as to the future ownership and management of the land held by the registered social landlord, designed to secure the continued proper management of the landlord's land by a registered social landlord.

(2) In drawing up its proposals the [Relevant Authority]—

(a) shall consult the landlord and, so far as is practicable, its tenants, and

(b) shall have regard to the interests of all the landlord's creditors, both secured and unsecured.

(3) The [Relevant Authority] shall also consult—

(a) where the landlord is an industrial and provident society, the appropriate registrar, and

(b) where the landlord is a registered charity, the [Charity Commission].

(4) No proposals shall be made under which—

(a) a preferential debt of the landlord is to be paid otherwise than in priority to debts which are not preferential debts, or

(b) a preferential creditor is to be paid a smaller proportion of his preferential debt than another preferential creditor, except with the concurrence of the creditor concerned.

In this subsection references to preferential debts and preferential creditors have the same meaning as in the Insolvency Act 1986.

(5) So far as practicable no proposals shall be made which have the effect that unsecured creditors of the landlord are in a worse position than they would otherwise be.

(6) Where the landlord is a charity the proposals shall not require the landlord to act outside the terms of its trusts, and any disposal of housing accommodation occupied under a tenancy or licence from the landlord must be to another charity whose objects appear to the [Relevant Authority] to be, as nearly as practicable, akin to those of the landlord.

(7) The [Relevant Authority] shall serve a copy of its proposals on—

(a) the landlord and its officers,

(b) the secured creditors of the landlord, and

(c) any liquidator, administrator, administrative receiver or receiver appointed in respect of the landlord or its land;

and it shall make such arrangements as it considers appropriate to see that the members, tenants and unsecured creditors of the landlord are informed of the proposals.

[1080]

NOTES

Commencement: 1 October 1996.

Sub-ss (1), (2), (6), (7): words in square brackets substituted by the Government of Wales Act 1998, s 140, Sch 16, paras 81, 82(1)(a).

Sub-s (3): words in first pair of square brackets substituted by the Government of Wales Act 1998, s 140, Sch 16, paras 81, 82(1)(a); words in square brackets in para (b) substituted by the Charities Act 2006, s 75(1), Sch 8, paras 183, 187.

45 Effect of agreed proposals

(1) The following provisions apply if proposals made by the [Relevant Authority] under section 44 are agreed, with or without modifications, by all the secured creditors of the registered social landlord.

(2) Once agreed the proposals are binding on the [Relevant Authority], the landlord, all the landlord's creditors (whether secured or unsecured) and any liquidator, administrator, administrative receiver or receiver appointed in respect of the landlord or its land.

(3) It is the duty of—

(a) the members of the committee where the landlord is an industrial and provident society,

(b) the directors where the landlord is a company registered under the Companies Act 1985 (including a company which is a registered charity), and

(c) the trustees where the landlord is a charitable trust,

to co-operate in the implementation of the proposals.

This does not mean that they have to do anything contrary to any fiduciary or other duty owed by them.

(4) The [Relevant Authority] shall serve a copy of the agreed proposals on—

(a) the landlord and its officers,

(b) the secured creditors of the landlord, and

(c) any liquidator, administrator, administrative receiver or receiver appointed in respect of the landlord or its land, and

(d) where the landlord is an industrial and provident society or registered charity, the [Financial Services Authority] or the [Charity Commission], as the case may be;

and it shall make such arrangements as it considers appropriate to see that the members, tenants and unsecured creditors of the landlord are informed of the proposals.

(5) The proposals may subsequently be amended with the consent of the [Relevant Authority] and all the landlord's secured creditors.

Section 44(2) to (7) and subsections (2) to (4) above apply in relation to the amended proposals as in relation to the original proposals.

[1081]

NOTES

Commencement: 1 October 1996.

Sub-ss (1), (2), (5): words in square brackets substituted by the Government of Wales Act 1998, s 140, Sch 16, paras 81, 82(1)(a).

Sub-s (4): words in first pair of square brackets substituted by the Government of Wales Act 1998, s 140, Sch 16, paras 81, 82(1)(a); words in first pair of square brackets in para (d) substituted by the Financial Services and Markets Act 2000 (Consequential Amendments and Repeals) Order 2001, SI 2001/3649, art 354; words in second pair of square brackets in para (d) substituted by the Charities Act 2006, s 75(1), Sch 8, paras 183, 188.

46 Appointment of manager to implement agreed proposals

(1) Where proposals agreed as mentioned in section 45 so provide, the [Relevant Authority] may by order … appoint a manager to implement the proposals or such of them as are specified in the order.

(2) If the landlord is a registered charity, the [Relevant Authority] shall give notice to the [Charity Commission] of the appointment.

(3) Where proposals make provision for the appointment of a manager, they shall also provide for the payment of his reasonable remuneration and expenses.

(4) The [Relevant Authority] may give the manager directions in relation to the carrying out of his functions.

(5) The manager may apply to the High Court for directions in relation to any particular matter arising in connection with the carrying out of his functions.

A direction of the court supersedes any direction of the [Relevant Authority] in respect of the same matter.

(6) If a vacancy occurs by death, resignation or otherwise in the office of manager, the [Relevant Authority] may by further order … fill the vacancy.

[(7) An order under this section—

(a) if made by the Housing Corporation, shall be made under its seal, and

(b) if made by the Secretary of State, shall be made in writing.]

[1082]

NOTES

Commencement: 1 November 1998 (sub-s (7)); 1 October 1996 (remainder).

Sub-ss (1), (6): words in square brackets substituted and words omitted repealed by the Government of Wales Act 1998, ss 140, 152, Sch 16, paras 81, 82(1)(a), (2), Sch 18, Pt VI.

Sub-s (2): words in first pair of square brackets substituted by the Government of Wales Act 1998, s 140, Sch 16, paras 81, 82(1)(a); words in second pair of square brackets substituted by the Charities Act 2006, s 75(1), Sch 8, paras 183, 189.

Sub-ss (4), (5): words in square brackets substituted by the Government of Wales Act 1998, s 140, Sch 16, paras 81, 82(1)(a).

Sub-s (7): added by the Government of Wales Act 1998, s 140, Sch 16, paras 81, 88(3).

47 Powers of the manager

(1) An order under section 46(1) shall confer on the manager power generally to do all such things as are necessary for carrying out his functions.

(2) The order may include the following specific powers—

1 Power to take possession of the land held by the landlord and for that purpose to take any legal proceedings which seem to him expedient.

2 Power to sell or otherwise dispose of the land by public auction or private contract.

3 Power to raise or borrow money and for that purpose to grant security over the land.

4 Power to appoint a solicitor or accountant or other professionally qualified person to assist him in the performance of his functions.

5 Power to bring or defend legal proceedings relating to the land in the name and on behalf of the landlord.

6 Power to refer to arbitration any question affecting the land.

7 Power to effect and maintain insurance in respect of the land.

8 Power where the landlord is a body corporate to use the seal of the body corporate for purposes relating to the land.

9 Power to do all acts and to execute in the name and on behalf of the landlord any deed, receipt or other document relating to the land.

10 Power to appoint an agent to do anything which he is unable to do for himself or which can more conveniently be done by an agent, and power to employ and dismiss any employees.

11 Power to do all such things (including the carrying out of works) as may be necessary in connection with the management or transfer of the land.

12 Power to make any payment which is necessary or incidental to the performance of his functions.

13 Power to carry on the business of the landlord so far as relating to the management or transfer of the land.

14 Power to grant or accept a surrender of a lease or tenancy of any of the land, and to take a lease or tenancy of any property required or convenient for the landlord's housing activities.

15 Power to make any arrangement or compromise on behalf of the landlord in relation to the management or transfer of the land.

16 Power to do all other things incidental to the exercise of any of the above powers.

(3) In carrying out his functions the manager acts as the landlord's agent and he is not personally liable on a contract which he enters into as manager.

(4) A person dealing with the manager in good faith and for value is not concerned to inquire whether the manager is acting within his powers.

(5) The manager shall, so far as practicable, consult the landlord's tenants about any exercise of his powers which is likely to affect them and inform them about any such exercise of his powers.

[1083]

NOTES

Commencement: 1 October 1996.

48 Powers of the manager: transfer of engagements

(1) An order under section 46(1) may, where the landlord is an industrial and provident society, give the manager power to make and execute on behalf of the society an instrument transferring the engagements of the society.

(2) Any such instrument has the same effect as a transfer of engagements under section 51 or 52 of the Industrial and Provident Societies Act 1965 (transfer of engagements by special resolution to another society or a company).

In particular, its effect is subject to section 54 of that Act (saving for rights of creditors).

(3) A copy of the instrument, signed by the manager, shall be sent to the [Financial Services Authority and registered by it]; and until that copy is so registered the instrument shall not take effect.

(4) It is the duty of the manager to send a copy for registration within 14 days from the day on which the instrument is executed; but this does not invalidate registration after that time.

[1084]

NOTES

Commencement: 1 October 1996.

Sub-s (3): words in square brackets substituted by the Financial Services and Markets Act 2000 (Consequential Amendments and Repeals) Order 2001, SI 2001/3649, art 355.

49 Assistance by the [Relevant Authority]

(1) The [Relevant Authority] may give such assistance as it thinks fit—

(a) to the landlord, for the purpose of preserving the position pending the making of and agreement to proposals;

(b) to the landlord or a manager appointed under section 46, for the purpose of carrying out any agreed proposals.

(2) The [Relevant Authority] may, in particular—

(a) lend staff;

(b) pay or secure payment of the manager's reasonable remuneration and expenses;

(c) give such financial assistance as appears to the [Relevant Authority] to be appropriate.

(3) The [giving by the Housing Corporation of the following forms of assistance requires] the consent of the Secretary of State—

(a) making grants or loans;

(b) agreeing to indemnify the manager in respect of liabilities incurred or loss or damage sustained by him in connection with his functions;

(c) paying or guaranteeing the repayment of the principal of, the payment of interest on and the discharge of any other financial obligation in connection with any sum borrowed (before or after the making of the order) and secured on any land disposed of.

[1085]

NOTES

Commencement: 1 October 1996.

Section heading: words in square brackets substituted by the Government of Wales Act 1998, s 140, Sch 16, paras 81, 82(1)(a).

Words in square brackets substituted by the Government of Wales Act 1998, s 140, Sch 16, paras 81, 82(1)(a), 89.

50 Application to court to secure compliance with agreed proposals

(1) The landlord or any creditor of the landlord may apply to the High Court on the ground that an action of the manager appointed under section 46 is not in accordance with the agreed proposals.

On such an application the court may confirm, reverse or modify any act or decision of the manager, give him directions or make such other order as it thinks fit.

(2) The [Relevant Authority] or any other person bound by agreed proposals may apply to the High Court on the ground that any action, or proposed action, by another person bound by the proposals is not in accordance with those proposals.

On such an application the court may—

(a) declare any such action to be ineffective, and

(b) grant such relief by way of injunction, damages or otherwise as appears to the court appropriate.

[1086]

NOTES

Commencement: 1 October 1996.

Sub-s (2): words in square brackets substituted by the Government of Wales Act 1998, s 140, Sch 16, paras 81, 82(1)(a).

CHAPTER V
MISCELLANEOUS AND GENERAL PROVISIONS

Housing complaints

51 Schemes for investigation of complaints

(1) The provisions of Schedule 2 have effect for the purpose of enabling tenants and other individuals to have complaints against social landlords investigated by a housing ombudsman in accordance with a scheme approved by the Secretary of State.

(2) For the purposes of that Schedule a "social landlord" means—

(a) a registered social landlord [or a body which was at any time a registered social landlord];

(b) a transferee of housing pursuant to a qualifying disposal under section 135 of the Leasehold Reform, Housing and Urban Development Act 1993;

(c) a body which has acquired dwellings under Part IV of the Housing Act 1988 (change of landlord: secure tenants); or

(d) any other body which was at any time registered with the [Housing Corporation, or with Housing for Wales,] and which owns or manages publicly-funded dwellings.

(3) In subsection (2)(d) a "publicly-funded dwelling" means a dwelling which was—

(a) provided by means of a grant under—
section 18 of this Act (social housing grant), or
section 50 of the Housing Act 1988, section 41 of the Housing Associations Act 1985, or section 29 or 29A of the Housing Act 1974 (housing association grant); or

(b) acquired on a disposal by a public sector landlord.

(4) The Secretary of State may by order add to or amend the descriptions of landlords who are to be treated as social landlords for the purposes of Schedule 2.

(5) Before making any such order the Secretary of State shall consult such persons as he considers appropriate.

(6) Any such order shall be made by statutory instrument which shall be subject to annulment in pursuance of a resolution of either House of Parliament.

[(7) This section shall not apply in relation to social landlords in Wales (within the meaning given by [section 41 of the Public Services Ombudsman (Wales) Act 2005]).]

[1087]

NOTES

Commencement: 1 April 1997 (sub-s (1) certain purposes, sub-ss (2)–(6)); 1 August 1996 (sub-s (1) remaining purposes).

Sub-s (2): words in square brackets in para (a) inserted and words in square brackets in para (d) substituted by the Government of Wales Act 1998, s 140, Sch 16, paras 81, 90.

Sub-s (7): added by the Housing Act 2004, s 228(1); words in square brackets substituted by the Public Services Ombudsman (Wales) Act 2005, s 39(1), Sch 6, paras 56, 57.

[51A]–[51C] *(Inserted by the Housing Act 2004, s 228(2), repealed by the Public Services Ombudsman (Wales) Act 2005, s 39, Sch 6, paras 56, 58, Sch 7.)*

Orders and determinations

52 General provisions as to orders

(1) The following provisions apply to any power of the Secretary of State under [section 2, 17, [27A,] 39, 51 or 55 or Schedule 2] to make an order.

(2) An order may make different provision for different cases or descriptions of case.

This includes power to make different provision for different bodies or descriptions of body, different provision for different housing activities and different provision for different areas.

(3) An order may contain such supplementary, incidental, consequential or transitional provisions and savings as the Secretary of State considers appropriate.

[1088]

NOTES

Commencement: 1 August 1996.

Sub-s (1): words in first (outer) square brackets substituted by the Government of Wales Act 1998, s 140, Sch 16, paras 81, 91; number in second (inner) pair of square brackets inserted by the Housing Act 2004, s 265(1), Sch 15, paras 40, 41.

Orders: the Housing Act 1996 (Consequential Provisions) Order 1996, SI 1996/2325; the Housing Act 1996 (Consequential Amendments) (No 2) Order 1997, SI 1997/627.

53 General provisions as to determinations

(1) The following provisions apply to determinations of the [Housing Corporation] or the Secretary of State under this Part.

(2) A determination may make different provision for different cases or descriptions of case.

This includes power to make—

- (a) different provision for different registered social landlords or descriptions of registered social landlord, and
- (b) different provision for different housing activities and different provision for different areas;

and for the purposes of paragraph (b) descriptions may be framed by reference to any matters whatever, including in particular, in the case of housing activities, the manner in which they are financed.

(3) In this Part a general determination means a determination which does not relate solely to a particular case.

(4) Before making a general determination, the [Housing Corporation] or the Secretary of State shall consult such bodies appearing to them to be representative of registered social landlords as they consider appropriate.

(5) After making a general determination, the [Housing Corporation] or the Secretary of State shall publish the determination in such manner as they consider appropriate for bringing the determination to the notice of the landlords concerned.

[1089]

NOTES

Commencement: 1 August 1996.

Sub-ss (1), (4), (5): words in square brackets substituted by the Government of Wales Act 1998, s 140, Sch 16, paras 81, 92.

54 Determinations of the [Housing Corporation] requiring approval

The [Housing Corporation] shall not make—

(a) a general determination under paragraph 16 of Schedule 1 (accounting and audit requirements for registered social landlords) or section 18 (social housing grant), or

(b) any determination under section 27 (recovery, &c of social housing grants), [or

(c) any determination under section 27B (transfer of property funded by grants under s 27A),]

except with the approval of the Secretary of State.

[1090]

NOTES

Commencement: 1 August 1996.

Section heading: words in square brackets substituted by virtue of the Government of Wales Act 1998, s 140, Sch 16, paras 81, 93.

Words in first pair of square brackets substituted by the Government of Wales Act 1998, s 140, Sch 16, paras 81, 93; para (c) and word "or" immediately preceding it added by the Housing Act 2004, s 265(1), Sch 15, paras 40, 42.

Minor and consequential amendments

55 Minor and consequential amendments: Part I

(1) The enactments mentioned in Schedule 3 have effect with the minor amendments specified there.

(2) The Secretary of State may by order make such amendments or repeals of any enactment as appear to him necessary or expedient in consequence of the provisions of this Part.

(3) Any such order shall be made by statutory instrument which shall be subject to annulment in pursuance of a resolution of either House of Parliament.

[1091]

NOTES

Commencement: 1 April 1997 (sub-s (1) certain purposes); 1 October 1996 (sub-s (1) certain purposes); 1 August 1996 (sub-s (1) remaining purposes, sub-s (2), (3)).

Orders: the Housing Act 1996 (Consequential Provisions) Order 1996, SI 1996/2325; the Housing Act 1996 (Consequential Amendments) (No 2) Order 1997, SI 1997/627.

Interpretation

56 Meaning of "the [Relevant Authority]"

(1) In this Part "the [Relevant Authority]" means the Housing Corporation or [the Secretary of State], as follows.

(2) In relation to a registered social landlord, or a body applying for such registration, which is—

(a) a registered charity which has its address for the purposes of registration by the [Charity Commission] in Wales,
(b) an industrial and provident society which has its registered office for the purposes of the Industrial and Provident Societies Act 1965 in Wales, or
(c) a company registered under the Companies Act 1985 which has its registered office for the purposes of that Act in Wales,

"the [Relevant Authority]" means [the Secretary of State].

(3) In relation to any other registered social landlord or body applying for such registration, "the [Relevant Authority]" means the Housing Corporation.

(4) Nothing in this Part shall be construed as requiring the Housing Corporation and [the Secretary of State] to establish the same criteria for registration as a social landlord, or otherwise to act on the same principles in respect of any matter in relation to which they have functions under this Part.

[1092]

NOTES

Commencement: 1 August 1996.

Section heading: words in square brackets substituted by the Government of Wales Act 1998, s 140, Sch 16, paras 81, 82(1)(a).

Sub-ss (1), (3), (4): words in square brackets substituted by the Government of Wales Act 1998, s 140, Sch 16, paras 81, 82(1)(a), 94.

Sub-s (2): words in square brackets in para (a) substituted by the Charities Act 2006, s 75(1), Sch 8, paras 183, 190; words in second and third pairs of square brackets substituted by the Government of Wales Act 1998, s 140, Sch 16, paras 81, 82(1)(a), 94.

57 Definitions relating to industrial and provident societies

(1) In this Part, in relation to an industrial and provident society—

. . . . .

"committee" means the committee of management or other directing body of the society; and

"co-opted member", in relation to the committee, includes any person co-opted to serve on the committee, whether he is a member of the society or not.

(2) Any reference in this Part to a member of the committee of an industrial and provident society includes a co-opted member.

[1093]

NOTES

Commencement: 1 August 1996.

Sub-s (1): definition omitted repealed by the Financial Services and Markets Act 2000 (Consequential Amendments and Repeals) Order 2001, SI 2001/3649, art 356(1).

58 Definitions relating to charities

(1) In this Part—
(a) "charity" and "trusts", in relation to a charity, have the same meaning as in the Charities Act 1993, and "trustee" means a charitable trustee within the meaning of that Act; and
(b) "registered charity" means a charity which is registered *under section 3* of that Act *and is not an exempt charity within the meaning of that Act.*

(2) References in this Part to a company registered under the Companies Act 1985 do not include a company which is a registered charity, except where otherwise provided.

[1094]

NOTES

Commencement: 1 August 1996.

Sub-s (1): for the words in italics in the first place in para (b) there are substituted the words "in accordance with section 3A" and words in italics in the second place repealed by the Charities Act 2006, s 75(1), (2), Sch 8, paras 183, 191, Sch 9, as from a day to be appointed under s 79(2) of that Act.

59 Meaning of "officer" of registered social landlord

(1) References in this Part to an officer of a registered social landlord are—

(a) in the case of a registered charity which is not a company registered under the Companies Act 1985, to any trustee, secretary or treasurer of the charity;
(b) in the case of an industrial and provident society, to any officer of the society as defined in section 74 of the Industrial and Provident Societies Act 1965; and
(c) in the case of a company registered under the Companies Act 1985 (including such a company which is also a registered charity), to any director or other officer of the company within the meaning of that Act.

(2) Any such reference includes, in the case of an industrial and provident society, a co-opted member of the committee of the society.

[1095]

NOTES
Commencement: 1 August 1996.

60 Meaning of "subsidiary"

(1) In this Part "subsidiary", in relation to a registered social landlord, means a company with respect to which one of the following conditions is fulfilled—
(a) the landlord is a member of the company and controls the composition of the board of directors;
(b) the landlord holds more than half in nominal value of the company's equity share capital; or
(c) the company is a subsidiary, within the meaning of the Companies Act 1985 or the Friendly and Industrial and Provident Societies Act 1968, of another company which, by virtue of paragraph (a) or paragraph (b), is itself a subsidiary of the landlord.

(2) For the purposes of subsection (1)(a), the composition of a company's board of directors shall be deemed to be controlled by a registered social landlord if, but only if, the landlord, by the exercise of some power exercisable by him without the consent or concurrence of any other person, can appoint or remove the holders of all or a majority of the directorships.

(3) In relation to a company which is an industrial and provident society—
(a) any reference in this section to the board of directors is a reference to the committee of management of the society; and
(b) the reference in subsection (2) to the holders of all or a majority of the directorships is a reference—
(i) to all or a majority of the members of the committee, or
(ii) if the landlord is himself a member of the committee, such number as together with him would constitute a majority.

(4) In the case of a registered social landlord which is a body of trustees, references in this section to the landlord are to the trustees acting as such.

[1096]

NOTES
Commencement: 1 August 1996.

61 Meaning of "associate"

(1) In this Part "associate", in relation to a registered social landlord, means—
(a) any body of which the landlord is a subsidiary, and
(b) any other subsidiary of such a body.

(2) In this section "subsidiary" has the same meaning as in the Companies Act 1985 or the Friendly and Industrial and Provident Societies Act 1968 or, in the case of a body which is itself a registered social landlord, has the meaning given by section 60.

[1097]

NOTES
Commencement: 1 August 1996.

62 Members of a person's family: Part I

(1) A person is a member of another's family within the meaning of this Part if—

(a) he is the spouse [or civil partner] of that person, or he and that person live together as husband and wife [or as if they were civil partners], or
(b) he is that person's parent, grandparent, child, grandchild, brother, sister, uncle, aunt, nephew or niece.

(2) For the purpose of subsection (1)(b)—
(a) a relationship by marriage [or civil partnership] shall be treated as a relationship by blood,
(b) a relationship of the half-blood shall be treated as a relationship of the whole blood, and
(c) the stepchild of a person shall be treated as his child.

[1098]

NOTES

Commencement: 1 August 1996.

Sub-s (1): words in square brackets in para (a) inserted by the Civil Partnership Act 2004, s 81, Sch 8, para 51(1), (2).

Sub-s (2): words in square brackets in para (a) inserted by the Civil Partnership Act 2004, s 81, Sch 8, para 51(1), (3).

63 Minor definitions: Part I

(1) In this Part—

"dwelling" means a building or part of a building occupied or intended to be occupied as a separate dwelling, together with any yard, garden, outhouses and appurtenances belonging to it or usually enjoyed with it;

"fully mutual", in relation to a housing association, and "co-operative housing association" have the same meaning as in the Housing Associations Act 1985 (see section 1(2) of that Act);

"hostel" means a building in which is provided for persons generally or for a class or classes of persons—
(a) residential accommodation otherwise than in separate and self-contained premises, and
(b) either board or facilities for the preparation of food adequate to the needs of those persons, or both; "house" includes—
(a) any part of a building occupied or intended to be occupied as a separate dwelling, and
(b) any yard, garden, outhouses and appurtenances belonging to it or usually enjoyed with it;

"housing accommodation" includes flats, lodging-houses and hostels;

"housing activities" means, in relation to a registered social landlord, all its activities in pursuance of the purposes, objects and powers mentioned in or specified under section 2;

"information" includes accounts, estimates and returns;

"local authority" has the same meaning as in the Housing Associations Act 1985;

"long tenancy" has the same meaning as in Part V of the Housing Act 1985;

"modifications" includes additions, alterations and omissions and cognate expressions shall be construed accordingly;

"notice" means notice in writing;

"public sector landlord" means any of the authorities or bodies within section 80(1) of the Housing Act 1985 (the landlord condition for secure tenancies);

"registrar of companies" has the same meaning as in the Companies Act 1985;

"statutory tenancy" has the same meaning as in the Housing Act 1985.

(2) References in this Part to the provision of a dwelling or house include the provision of a dwelling or house—
(a) by erecting the dwelling or house, or converting a building into dwellings or a house, or
(b) by altering, enlarging, repairing or improving an existing dwelling or house;

and references to a dwelling or house provided by means of a grant or other financial assistance are to its being so provided directly or indirectly.

[1099]

NOTES

Commencement: 1 August 1996.

64 Index of defined expressions: Part I

The following Table shows provisions defining or otherwise explaining expressions used in this Part (other than provisions defining or explaining an expression used in the same section)—

appointed person (in relation to inquiry into affairs of registered social landlord)	paragraph 20 of Schedule 1
.....	
associate (in relation to a registered social landlord)	section 61(1)
assured tenancy	section 230
assured agricultural occupancy	section 230
assured shorthold tenancy	section 230
Charity	section 58(1)(a)
committee member (in relation to an industrial and provident society)	section 57(2)
company registered under the Companies Act 1985	section 58(2)
co-operative housing association	section 63
co-opted member (of committee of industrial and provident society)	section 57(1)
.....	
disposal proceeds fund	section 24
dwelling	section 63
enactment	section 230
fully mutual housing association	section 63
Hostel	section 63
House	section 63
housing accommodation	section 63
housing activities	section 63
housing association	section 230
industrial and provident society	section 2(1)(b)
information	section 63
lease	section 229
local authority	section 63
long tenancy	section 63
member of family	section 62
modifications	section 63
notice	section 63
officer of registered social landlord	section 59
provision (in relation to dwelling or house)	section 63(2)
public sector landlord	section 63
register, registered and registration (in relation to social landlords)	section 1
registered charity	section 58(1)(b)
registrar of companies	section 63
[the Relevant Authority	section 56]

relevant disposal which is not an exempted disposal (in sections 11 to 14)	section 15
secure tenancy	section 230
social housing grant	section 18(1)
statutory tenancy	section 63
subsidiary (in relation to a registered social landlord)	section 60(1)
trustee and trusts (in relation to a charity)	section 58(1)(a)

[1100]

NOTES

Commencement: 1 August 1996.

Entry relating to "appropriate registrar" omitted repealed by the Financial Services and Markets Act 2000 (Consequential Amendments and Repeals) Order 2001, SI 2001/3649, art 356(2); entry relating to "the Corporation" omitted repealed and entry relating to "the Relevant Authority" inserted by the Government of Wales Act 1998, ss 140, 152, Sch 16, paras 81, 95, Sch 18, Pt VI.

65–218 ((*Pts II–VII*) *outside the scope of this work.*)

PART VIII
MISCELLANEOUS AND GENERAL

218A–230 (*Outside the scope of this work.*)

Final provisions

231 (*Outside the scope of this work.*)

232 Commencement

(1) The following provisions of this Act come into force on Royal Assent—
section 110 (new leases: valuation principles),
section 120 (payment of housing benefit to third parties), and
sections 223 to 226 and 228 to 233 (general provisions).

(2) (*Outside the scope of this work.*)

(3) The other provisions of this Act come into force on a day appointed by order of the Secretary of State, and different days may be appointed for different areas and different purposes.

(4) An order under subsection (3) shall be made by statutory instrument and may contain such transitional provisions and savings as appear to the Secretary of State to be appropriate.
[1101]

NOTES

Orders: the Housing Act 1996 (Commencement No 1) Order 1996, SI 1996/2048; the Housing Act 1996 (Commencement No 2 and Saving) Order 1996, SI 1996/2212; the Housing Act 1996 (Commencement No 3 and Transitional Provisions) Order 1996, SI 1996/2402; the Housing Act 1996 (Commencement No 4) Order 1996, SI 1996/2658; the Housing Act 1996 (Commencement No 5 and Transitional Provisions) Order 1996, SI 1996/2959; the Housing Act 1996 (Commencement No 6 and Savings) Order 1997, SI 1997/66; the Housing Act 1996 (Commencement No 7 and Savings) Order 1997, SI 1997/225; the Housing Act 1996 (Commencement No 8) Order 1997, SI 1997/350; the Housing Act 1996 (Commencement No 9) Order 1997, SI 1997/596; the Housing Act 1996 (Commencement No 10 and Transitional Provisions) Order 1997, SI 1997/618; the Housing Act 1996 (Commencement No 11 and Savings) Order 1997, SI 1997/1851; the Housing Act 1996 (Commencement No 12 and Transitional Provisions) Order 1998, SI 1998/1768; the Housing Act 1996 (Commencement No 13) Order 2001, SI 2001/3164.

233 Short title

This Act may be cited as the Housing Act 1996.

[1102]

SCHEDULES

SCHEDULE 1
REGISTERED SOCIAL LANDLORDS: REGULATION

Section 7

PART I
CONTROL OF PAYMENTS TO MEMBERS, &C

Payments by way of gift, dividend or bonus

1.—(1) A registered social landlord shall not make a gift or pay a sum by way of dividend or bonus to—

(a) a person who is or has been a member of the body,

(b) a person who is a member of the family of a person within paragraph (a), or

(c) a company of which a person within paragraph (a) or (b) is a director,

except as permitted by this paragraph.

(2) The following are permitted—

(a) the payment of a sum which, in accordance with the constitution or rules of the body, is paid as interest on capital lent to the body or subscribed by way of shares in the body;

(b) the payment by a fully mutual housing association to a person who has ceased to be a member of the association of a sum which is due to him either under his tenancy agreement with the association or under the terms of the agreement under which he became a member of the association;

[(c) the payment of a sum, in accordance with the constitution or rules of the body, to a registered social landlord which is a subsidiary or associate of the body.]

(3) Where an industrial and provident society or a company registered under the Companies Act 1985 pays a sum or makes a gift in contravention of this paragraph, the society or company may recover the sum or the value of the gift, and proceedings for its recovery shall be taken if the [Relevant Authority] so directs.

Payments and benefits to officers and employees, &c

2.—(1) A registered social landlord which is an industrial and provident society or a company registered under the Companies Act 1985 shall not make a payment or grant a benefit to—

(a) an officer or employee of the society or company,

(b) a person who at any time within the preceding twelve months has been a person within paragraph (a),

(c) a close relative of a person within paragraph (a) or (b), or

(d) a business trading for profit of which a person falling within paragraph (a), (b) or (c) is a principal proprietor or in the management of which such a person is directly concerned,

except as permitted by this paragraph.

(2) The following are permitted—

(a) payments made or benefits granted to an officer or employee of the society or company under his contract of employment with the society or company;

(b) the payment of remuneration or expenses to an officer of the society or company who does not have a contract of employment with the society or company;

(c) any such payment as may be made in accordance with paragraph 1(2) (interest payable in accordance with the rules and certain sums payable by a fully mutual housing association to a person who has ceased to be a member);

(d) the grant or renewal of a tenancy by a co-operative housing association;

(e) where a tenancy of a house has been granted to, or to a close relative of, a person who later became an officer or employee, the grant to that tenant of a new tenancy whether of the same or another house;

(f) payments made or benefits granted in accordance with any determination made by the [Relevant Authority].

(3) A determination for the purposes of sub-paragraph (2)(f) may specify the class or classes of case in which a payment may be made or benefit granted and specify the maximum amount.

(4) Where a society or company pays a sum or grants a benefit in contravention of this paragraph, the society or company may recover the sum or value of the benefit; and proceedings for its recovery shall be taken if the [Relevant Authority] so directs.

Maximum amounts payable by way of fees, expenses, &c

3.—(1) The [Relevant Authority] may from time to time specify the maximum amounts which may be paid by a registered social landlord which is an industrial and provident society or a company registered under the Companies Act 1985—

(a) by way of fees or other remuneration, or by way of expenses, to a member of the society or company who is not an officer or employee of the society or company, or

(b) by way of remuneration or expenses to an officer of the society or company who does not have a contract of employment with the society or company.

(2) Different amounts may be so specified for different purposes.

(3) Where a society or company makes a payment in excess of the maximum permitted under this paragraph, the society or company may recover the excess, and proceedings for its recovery shall be taken if the [Relevant Authority] so directs.

[1103]

NOTES

Commencement: paras 1, 2(1), (2)(a)–(e), (3), (4), 3(3) were brought into force on 1 October 1996; paras 3(1), (2) were brought into force on 1 August 1996; para 2(2)(f) was brought into force on 1 August 1996 in so far as it confers a power to make determinations, and on 1 October 1996 for remaining purposes.

Para 1: sub-para (2)(c) added by the Housing Act 2004, s 218, Sch 11, paras 7, 14; words in square brackets in sub-para (3) substituted by the Government of Wales Act 1998, s 140, Sch 16, paras 81, 82(1)(a).

Paras 2, 3: words in square brackets substituted by the Government of Wales Act 1998, s 140, Sch 16, paras 81, 82(1)(a).

PART II
CONSTITUTION, CHANGE OF RULES, AMALGAMATION AND DISSOLUTION

General power to remove director, trustee, &c

4.—(1) The [Relevant Authority] may, in accordance with the following provisions, by order remove—

(a) a director or trustee of a registered social landlord which is a registered charity,

(b) a committee member of a registered social landlord which is an industrial and provident society, or

(c) a director of a registered social landlord which is a company registered under the Companies Act 1985.

(2) The [Relevant Authority] may make an order removing any such person if—

(a) he has been adjudged bankrupt or has made an arrangement with his creditors;

(b) he is subject to a disqualification order [or disqualification undertaking] under the Company Directors Disqualification Act 1986 [or to a disqualification order under Part II of the Companies (Northern Ireland) Order 1989] [or disqualification undertaking under the Companies Directors Disqualification (Northern Ireland) Order 2002];

(c) he is subject to an order under section 429(2) of the Insolvency Act 1986 (failure to pay under county court administration order);

(d) he is disqualified under section 72 of the Charities Act 1993 from being a charity trustee;

(e) he is incapable of acting by reason of mental disorder;

(f) he has not acted; or

(g) he cannot be found or does not act and his absence or failure to act is impeding the proper management of the registered social landlord's affairs.

(3) Before making an order the [Relevant Authority] shall give at least 14 days' notice of its intention to do so to the person whom it intends to remove, and to the registered social landlord.

(4) That notice may be given by post, and if so given to the person whom the [Relevant Authority] intend to remove may be addressed to his last known address in the United Kingdom.

(5) A person who is ordered to be removed under this paragraph may appeal against the order to the High Court.

Restriction on power of removal in case of registered charity

5.—(1) The [Relevant Authority] may make an order under paragraph 4 removing a director or trustee of a registered charity only if the charity has, at any time before the power is exercised—

(a) received financial assistance under section 24 of the Local Government Act 1988 (assistance for privately let housing accommodation),

(b) had property transferred to it on a qualifying disposal under section 135 of the Leasehold Reform, Housing and Urban Development Act 1993, or

(c) received a grant or loan under any of the following provisions.

(2) The provisions are—

section 18 of this Act (social housing grants),

section 22 of this Act or section 58 of the Housing Associations Act 1985 (grants or loans by local authorities),

section 50 of the Housing Act 1988, section 41 of the Housing Associations Act 1985 or any enactment replaced by that section (housing association grant),

section 51 of the Housing Act 1988 or section 54 or 55 of the Housing Associations Act 1985 (revenue deficit grant or hostel deficit grant),

section 79 of the Housing Associations Act 1985 (loans by Housing Corporation),

section 31 of the Housing Act 1974 (management grants), or

any enactment mentioned in paragraph 2 or 3 of Schedule 1 to the Housing Associations Act 1985 (pre-1974 grants and certain loans).

Registered charity: power to appoint new director or trustee

6.—(1) The [Relevant Authority] may by order appoint a person to be a director or trustee of a registered social landlord which is a registered charity—

(a) in place of a person removed by the [Relevant Authority],

(b) where there are no directors or no trustees, or

(c) where the [Relevant Authority] is of the opinion that it is necessary for the proper management of the charity's affairs to have an additional director or trustee.

The power conferred by paragraph (c) may be exercised notwithstanding that it will cause the maximum number of directors or trustees permissible under the charity's constitution to be exceeded.

(2) The [Relevant Authority] shall only exercise its power under sub-paragraph (1) if—

(a) the charity has, at any time before the power is exercised, received financial assistance, had property transferred to it, or received a grant or loan as mentioned in paragraph 5, and

(b) the [Relevant Authority] has consulted the [Charity Commission].

(3) A person may be so appointed notwithstanding any restrictions on appointment in the charity's constitution or rules.

(4) A person appointed under this paragraph shall hold office for such period and on such terms as the [Relevant Authority] may specify; and on the expiry of the appointment the [Relevant Authority] may renew the appointment for such period as it may specify.

This does not prevent a person appointed under this paragraph from retiring in accordance with the charity's constitution or rules.

(5) A person appointed under this paragraph as director or trustee of a registered charity is entitled—

(a) to attend, speak and vote at any general meeting of the charity and to receive all notices of and other communications relating to any such meeting which a member is entitled to receive,
(b) to move a resolution at any general meeting of the charity, and
(c) to require a general meeting of the charity to be convened within 21 days of a request to that effect made in writing to the directors or trustees.

Company: power to appoint new director

7.—(1) The [Relevant Authority] may by order appoint a person to be a director of a registered social landlord which is a company registered under the Companies Act 1985—
(a) in place of a director removed by the [Relevant Authority],
(b) where there are no directors, or
(c) where the [Relevant Authority] is of the opinion that it is necessary for the proper management of the company's affairs to have an additional director.

(2) A person may be so appointed whether or not he is a member of the company and notwithstanding anything in the company's articles of association.

(3) Where a person is appointed under this paragraph—
(a) he shall hold office for such period and on such terms as the [Relevant Authority] may specify, and
(b) on the expiry of the appointment the [Relevant Authority] may renew the appointment for such period as it may specify.

This does not prevent a person from retiring in accordance with the company's articles of association.

(4) A person appointed under this paragraph is entitled—
(a) to attend, speak and vote at any general meeting of the company and to receive all notices of and other communications relating to any general meeting which a member of the company is entitled to receive,
(b) to move a resolution at any general meeting of the company, and
(c) to require an extraordinary general meeting of the company to be convened within 21 days of a request to that effect made in writing to the directors of the company.

Industrial and provident society: power to appoint new committee member

8.—(1) The [Relevant Authority] may by order appoint a person to be a committee member of a registered social landlord which is an industrial and provident society—
(a) in place of a person removed by the [Relevant Authority],
(b) where there are no members of the committee, or
(c) where the [Relevant Authority] is of the opinion that it is necessary for the proper management of the society's affairs to have an additional committee member.

The power conferred by paragraph (c) may be exercised notwithstanding that it will cause the maximum number of committee members permissible under the society's constitution to be exceeded.

(2) A person may be so appointed whether or not he is a member of the society and, if he is not, notwithstanding that the rules of the society restrict appointment to members.

(3) A person appointed under this paragraph shall hold office for such period and on such terms as the [Relevant Authority] may specify; and on the expiry of the appointment the [Relevant Authority] may renew the appointment for such period as it may specify.

This does not prevent a person appointed under this paragraph from retiring in accordance with the rules of the society.

(4) A person appointed under this paragraph is entitled—
(a) to attend, speak and vote at any general meeting of the society and to receive all notices of and other communications relating to any general meeting which a member of the society is entitled to receive,
(b) to move a resolution at any general meeting of the society, and
(c) to require a general meeting of the society to be convened within 21 days of a request to that effect made in writing to the committee of the society.

Change of rules, &c by industrial and provident society

9.—(1) This paragraph applies to an industrial and provident society whose registration as a social landlord has been recorded by the [Financial Services Authority].

(2) Notice shall be sent to the [Relevant Authority] of any change of the society's name or of the situation of its registered office.

(3) Any other amendment of the society's rules is not valid without the [Relevant Authority's] consent …

[(3A) Consent under sub-paragraph (3)—

(a) if given by the Housing Corporation, shall be given by order under its seal, and

(b) if given by the Secretary of State, shall be given by order in writing.]

(4) A copy of that consent shall be sent with the copies of the amendment required by section 10(1) of the Industrial and Provident Societies Act 1965 to be sent to the [Financial Services Authority].

(5) The Industrial and Provident Societies Act 1965 applies in relation to the provisions of this paragraph as if they were contained in section 10 of that Act (amendment of registered rules).

Change of objects by certain charities

10.—(1) This paragraph applies to a registered social landlord—

(a) which is a registered charity and is not a company incorporated under the Companies Act 1985, and

(b) whose registration under this Part of this Act has been recorded by the [Charity Commission] in accordance with section 3(3).

(2) No power contained in the provisions establishing the registered social landlord as a charity, or regulating its purposes or administration, to vary or add to its objects may be exercised without the consent of the [Charity Commission].

Before giving [its] consent the [Charity Commission] shall consult the [Relevant Authority].

Change of memorandum or articles of association of company

11.—(1) This paragraph applies to a company registered under the Companies Act 1985 (including such a company which is also a registered charity) whose registration as a social landlord has been recorded by the registrar of companies.

(2) Notice shall be sent to the [Relevant Authority] of any change of the company's name or of the address of its registered office.

(3) Any other alteration of the company's memorandum or articles of which notice is required to be given to the registrar of companies is not valid without the [Relevant Authority's] consent …

[(3A) Consent under sub-paragraph (3)—

(a) if given by the Housing Corporation, shall be given by order under its seal, and

(b) if given by the Secretary of State, shall be given by order in writing.]

(4) A copy of that consent shall be sent with any copy of the alterations required to be sent to the registrar of companies under the Companies Act 1985.

Amalgamation and dissolution &c of industrial and provident society

12.—(1) This paragraph applies to an industrial and provident society whose registration as a social landlord has been recorded by the [Financial Services Authority].

(2) The [Financial Services Authority] shall not register a special resolution which is passed for the purposes of—

(a) section 50 of the Industrial and Provident Societies Act 1965 (amalgamation of societies),

(b) section 51 of that Act (transfer of engagements between societies), or
(c) section 52 of that Act (power of a society to convert itself into, amalgamate with or transfer its engagements to a company registered under the Companies Act 1985),

unless, together with the copy of the resolution, there is sent to [it] a copy of the [Relevant Authority's] consent to the amalgamation, transfer or conversion.

(3) Any new body created by the amalgamation or conversion or, in the case of a transfer of engagements, the transferee, shall be deemed to be registered as a social landlord forthwith upon the amalgamation, conversion or transfer taking effect.

(4) If the society resolves by special resolution that it be wound up voluntarily under the Insolvency Act 1986, the resolution has no effect unless—
(a) before the resolution was passed the [Relevant Authority] gave its consent to its passing, and
(b) a copy of the consent is forwarded to the [Financial Services Authority] together with a copy of the resolution required to be so forwarded in accordance with the Companies Act 1985.

(5) If the society is to be dissolved by instrument of dissolution, the [Financial Services Authority] shall not—
(a) register the instrument in accordance with section 58(5) of the Industrial and Provident Societies Act 1965, or
(b) cause notice of the dissolution to be advertised in accordance with section 58(6) of that Act,

unless together with the instrument there is sent to [it] a copy of the [Relevant Authority's] consent to its making.

(6) The references in this paragraph to the [Relevant Authority's] consent [are—
(a) if it is given by the Housing Corporation, to consent given by order under its seal, and
(b) if it is given by the Secretary of State, to consent given by order in writing].

Arrangement, reconstruction, &c of company

13.—(1) This paragraph applies to a company registered under the Companies Act 1985 whose registration as a social landlord has been recorded by the registrar of companies.

(2) An order of the court given for the purposes of section 425 of the Companies Act 1985 (compromise or arrangement with creditors or members) is not effective unless the [Relevant Authority] has given its consent.

A copy of the consent shall be sent to the registrar of companies along with the office copy of the order delivered to him under that section.

(3) An order of the court given for the purposes of section 427 of the Companies Act 1985 (transfer of undertaking or property for purposes of reconstruction or amalgamation) is not effective unless the [Relevant Authority] has given its consent.

A copy of the consent shall be sent to the registrar of companies along with the office copy of the order delivered to him under that section.

(4) The registrar of companies shall not register any resolution under section 53 of the Industrial and Provident Societies Act 1965 (conversion of company into industrial and provident society), unless, together with the copy of the resolution, there is sent to him a copy of the [Relevant Authority's] consent to the conversion.

(5) Where a director, administrator or liquidator of the company proposes to make a voluntary arrangement with the company's creditors under section 1 of the Insolvency Act 1986, the arrangement shall not take effect under section 5 (effect of approval by members and creditors) of that Act unless the [Relevant Authority] has given its consent to the voluntary arrangement.

(6) If the company resolves by special resolution that it be wound up voluntarily under the Insolvency Act 1986, the resolution has no effect unless—
(a) before the resolution was passed the [Relevant Authority] gave its consent to its passing, and

(b) a copy of the consent is forwarded to the registrar of companies together with a copy of the resolution required to be so forwarded in accordance with section 380 of the Companies Act 1985.

(7) The references in this paragraph to the [Relevant Authority's] consent [are—

(a) if it is given by the Housing Corporation, to consent given by order under its seal, and

(b) if it is given by the Secretary of State, to consent given by order in writing].

(8) Where sub-paragraph (3) or (4) applies, the transferee or, as the case may be, any new body created by the conversion shall be deemed to be registered as a social landlord forthwith upon the transfer or conversion taking effect.

[Relevant Authority's] power to petition for winding up

14.—(1) The [Relevant Authority] may present a petition for the winding up under the Insolvency Act 1986 of a registered social landlord which is—

(a) a company incorporated under the Companies Act 1985 (including such a company which is also a registered charity), or

(b) an industrial and provident society (to which the winding up provisions of the Insolvency Act 1986 apply in accordance with section 55(a) of the Industrial and Provident Societies Act 1965),

on either of the following grounds.

(2) The grounds are—

(a) that the landlord is failing properly to carry out its purposes or objects, or

(b) that the landlord is unable to pay its debts within the meaning of section 123 of the Insolvency Act 1986.

Transfer of net assets on dissolution or winding up

15.—(1) This paragraph applies—

(a) where a registered social landlord which is an industrial and provident society is dissolved as mentioned in section 55(a) or (b) of the Industrial and Provident Societies Act 1965 (winding-up under the Insolvency Act 1986 or by instrument of dissolution), and

(b) where a registered social landlord which is a company registered under the Companies Act 1985 [(including such a company which is also a registered charity)] is wound up under the Insolvency Act 1986.

(2) On such a dissolution or winding-up, so much of the property of the society or company as remains after meeting the claims of its creditors and any other liabilities arising on or before the dissolution or winding-up shall be transferred to the [Relevant Authority] or, if the [Relevant Authority] so directs, to a specified registered social landlord.

The above provision has effect notwithstanding anything in the Industrial and Provident Societies Act 1965, the Companies Act 1985 or the Insolvency Act 1986, or in the rules of the society or, as the case may be, in the memorandum or articles of association of the company.

(3) In order to avoid the necessity for the sale of land belonging to the registered social landlord and thereby secure the transfer of the land under this paragraph, the [Relevant Authority] may, if it appears to it appropriate to do so, make payments to discharge such claims or liabilities as are referred to in sub-paragraph (2).

(4) Where the registered social landlord which is dissolved or wound up is a charity, the [Relevant Authority] may dispose of property transferred to it by virtue of this paragraph only to another registered social landlord—

(a) which is also a charity, and

(b) the objects of which appear to the [Relevant Authority] to be, as nearly as practicable, akin to those of the body which is dissolved or wound up.

[And in such a case any registered social landlord specified in a direction under sub-paragraph (2) must be one to which paragraphs (a) and (b) above apply.]

[(5) In any other case—

(a) the Relevant Authority may dispose of property transferred to it by virtue of this paragraph to a registered social landlord, and

(b) the Housing Corporation may dispose of property transferred to it by virtue of this paragraph to any of its subsidiaries.]

(6) Where property transferred to the [Relevant Authority] by virtue of this paragraph includes land subject to an existing mortgage or charge (whether in favour of the [Relevant Authority] or not), the [Relevant Authority] may, in exercise of its powers under Part III of the Housing Associations Act 1985, dispose of the land either—

(a) subject to that mortgage or charge, or

(b) subject to a new mortgage or charge in favour of the [Relevant Authority] securing such amount as appears to the [Relevant Authority] to be appropriate in the circumstances.

[Transfer of net assets on termination of charity not within paragraph 15(1)

15A.—(1) The Secretary of State may by regulations provide for any provisions of paragraph 15(2) to (6) to apply in relation to a registered social landlord within sub-paragraph (2)—

(a) in such circumstances, and

(b) with such modifications,

as may be specified in the regulations.

(2) A registered social landlord is within this sub-paragraph if—

(a) it is a registered charity, and

(b) it does not fall within sub-paragraph (1) of paragraph 15.

(3) Regulations under this paragraph may in particular provide that any provision of the regulations requiring the transfer of any property of the charity is to have effect notwithstanding—

(a) anything in the terms of its trusts, or

(b) any resolution, order or other thing done for the purposes of, or in connection with, the termination of the charity in any manner specified in the regulations.

(4) Any regulations under this paragraph shall be made by statutory instrument which shall be subject to annulment in pursuance of a resolution of either House of Parliament.]

[1104]

NOTES

Commencement: 1 October 1996.

Para 4: words in square brackets in sub-paras (1), (3), (4) and in first pair of square brackets in sub-para (2) substituted by the Government of Wales Act 1998, s 140, Sch 16, paras 81, 82(1)(a); words in first and second pairs of square brackets in sub-para (2)(b) inserted by the Insolvency Act 2000, s 8, Sch 4, Pt II, para 21; words in third pair of square brackets in sub-para (2)(b) inserted by the Insolvency Act 2000 (Company Directors Disqualification Undertakings) Order 2004, SI 2004/1941, art 3, Schedule, para 8.

Paras 5, 7, 8, 13, 14: words in square brackets substituted by the Government of Wales Act 1998, s 140, Sch 16, paras 81, 82(1)(a).

Para 6: words "Relevant Authority" in square brackets in each place they occur substituted by the Government of Wales Act 1998, s 140, Sch 16, paras 81, 82(1)(a); words in second pair of square brackets in sub-para (2)(b) substituted by the Charities Act 2006, s 75(1), Sch 8, paras 183, 192(1), (2).

Para 9: words in square brackets in sub-paras (1), (4) substituted by the Financial Services and Markets Act 2000 (Consequential Amendments and Repeals) Order 2001, SI 2001/3649, art 357(1), (2); sub-para (3A) inserted, words in square brackets in sub-paras (2), (3) substituted, and words omitted repealed by the Government of Wales Act 1998, ss 140, 152, Sch 16, paras 81, 82(1)(b), 96(1), (2), Sch 18, Pt VI.

Para 10: words in first, second, third and fourth pairs of square brackets substituted by the Charities Act 2006, s 75(1), Sch 8, paras 183, 192(1), (3); words in fifth pair of square brackets substituted by the Government of Wales Act 1998, s 140, Sch 16, paras 81, 82(1)(a).

Para 11: sub-para (3A) inserted, other words in square brackets substituted, and words omitted repealed by the Government of Wales Act 1998, ss 140, 152, Sch 16, paras 81, 82(1)(b), 96(1), (2), Sch 18, Pt VI.

Para 12: references to "Relevant Authority" and "Relevant Authority's" in square brackets and words in second pair of square brackets in sub-para (6) substituted by the Government of Wales Act 1998, s 140, Sch 16, paras 81, 82(1)(a), 96(3); other words in square brackets substituted by SI 2001/3649, art 357(1), (3).

Para 15: words in square brackets in sub-para (1)(b) inserted and words at the end of sub-para (4) added by the Housing Act 2004, s 218, Sch 11, paras 7, 15; other words in square brackets and sub-para (5) substituted by the Government of Wales Act 1998, s 140, Sch 16, paras 81, 82(1)(a), 96(1), (4).

Para 15A: inserted, together with preceding cross-heading, so far as conferring any power to make an order or regulations which is exercisable by the Secretary of State or the National Assembly for Wales, and otherwise as from a day to be appointed, by the Housing Act 2004, s 218, Sch 11, paras 7, 16.

Housing Act 1974, s 31: repealed by the Housing (Consequential Provisions) Act 1985, s 3, Sch 1, Pt I.

PART III
ACCOUNTS AND AUDIT

General requirements as to accounts and audit

16.—(1) The [Relevant Authority] may from time to time determine accounting requirements for registered social landlords with a view to ensuring that the accounts of every registered social landlord—

(a) are prepared in a proper form, and

(b) give a true and fair view of—

(i) the state of affairs of the landlord, so far as its housing activities are concerned, and

(ii) the disposition of funds and assets which are, or at any time have been, in its hands in connection with those activities.

(2) The [Relevant Authority] by a determination under sub-paragraph (1) may lay down a method by which a registered charity is to distinguish in its accounts between its housing activities and other activities.

(3) The accounts of every registered social landlord shall comply with the requirements laid down under this paragraph.

(4) …

[(5) Every registered social landlord shall furnish to the Relevant Authority—

(a) a copy of its accounts, and

(b) (subject to sub-paragraph (7)) a copy of the auditor's report in respect of them,

within six months of the end of the period to which they relate.

(6) The auditor's report shall state, in addition to any other matters which it is required to state, whether in the auditor's opinion the accounts comply with the requirements laid down under this paragraph.

(7) The provisions of sub-paragraphs (5)(b) and (6) do not apply where, by virtue of any enactment—

(a) any accounts of a registered social landlord are not required to be audited, and

(b) instead a report is required to be prepared in respect of them by a person appointed for the purpose ("the reporting accountant"),

and sub-paragraph (8) shall apply in place of those provisions.

(8) In such a case—

(a) the registered social landlord shall furnish to the Relevant Authority a copy of the reporting accountant's report in respect of the accounts within six months of the end of the period to which they relate; and

(b) that report shall state, in addition to any other matters which it is required to state, whether in the reporting accountant's opinion the accounts comply with the requirements laid down under this paragraph.]

[Companies exempt from audit requirements: accountant's report

16A.—(1) This paragraph applies to registered social landlords which are companies registered under the Companies Act 1985 ("RSL companies").

(2) In section 249A of the Companies Act 1985 (exemptions from audit)—

(a) subsection (2) shall apply in relation to an RSL company which meets the total exemption conditions in respect of a financial year (whether it is a charity or not), and

(b) that subsection shall apply in relation to such a company in the same way as it applies in relation to an RSL company which is a charity and meets the report conditions in relation to a financial year; and

(c) subsection (1) accordingly does not have effect in relation to an RSL company.

(3) In section 249C of that Act (report required for the purposes of section 249A(2)), subsection (3) shall apply in relation to an RSL company within sub-paragraph (2)(a) above as if the reference to satisfying the requirements of section 249A(4) were a reference to meeting the total exemption conditions.

(4) The Relevant Authority may, in respect of any relevant financial year of an RSL company, give a direction to the company requiring it—

(a) to appoint a qualified auditor to audit its accounts and balance sheet for that year, and

(b) to furnish to the Relevant Authority a copy of the auditor's report by such date as is specified in the direction.

(5) For the purposes of sub-paragraph (4), a financial year of an RSL company is a "relevant financial year" if—

(a) it precedes that in which the direction is given, and

(b) the company met either the total exemption conditions or the report conditions in respect of that year, and

(c) its accounts and balance sheet for that year were not audited in accordance with Part 7 of the Companies Act 1985.

(6) In this paragraph—

(a) "financial year" has the meaning given by section 223 of the Companies Act 1985;

(b) "qualified auditor" means a person who is eligible for appointment as auditor of the company under Part 2 of the Companies Act 1989;

(c) any reference to a company meeting the report conditions is to be read in accordance with section 249A(4) of the Companies Act 1985; and

(d) any reference to a company meeting the total exemption conditions is to be read in accordance with section 249A(3) or section 249A(3) and (3A) of that Act, depending on whether it is a charity.]

[Industrial and provident societies exempt from audit requirements: accountant's report

17.—(1) This paragraph applies to registered social landlords which are industrial and provident societies.

(2) Section 9A of the Friendly and Industrial and Provident Societies Act 1968 (duty to obtain accountant's reports where section 4 applied) shall have effect, in its application to such a landlord, with the omission of subsection (1)(b) (accountant's report required only where turnover exceeds a specified sum).

(3) The Relevant Authority may, in respect of any relevant year of account of such a landlord, give a direction to the landlord requiring it—

(a) to appoint a qualified auditor to audit its accounts and balance sheet for that year, and

(b) to furnish to the Relevant Authority a copy of the auditor's report by such date as is specified in the direction.

(4) For the purposes of sub-paragraph (3), a year of account of a landlord is a "relevant year of account" if—

(a) it precedes that in which the direction is given, and

(b) at the end of it there is in force in relation to it a disapplication under section 4A(1) of the Friendly and Industrial and Provident Societies Act 1968.

(5) In this paragraph—

"qualified auditor" means a person who is a qualified auditor for the purposes of the Friendly and Industrial and Provident Societies Act 1968;

"year of account" has the meaning given by section 21(1) of that Act.]

Accounting and audit [or reporting] requirements for charities

18.—(1) A registered social landlord which is a registered charity shall, in respect of its housing activities (and separately from its other activities, if any), be subject to the following provisions …

This does not affect any obligation of the charity under sections 41 to 45 of the Charities Act 1993 (charity accounts).

(2) The charity shall in respect of its housing activities—

(a) cause to be kept properly books of account showing its transactions and its assets and liabilities, and

(b) establish and maintain a satisfactory system of control of its books of accounts, its cash holdings and all its receipts and remittances.

The books of account must be such as to enable a true and fair view to be given of the state of affairs of the charity in respect of its housing activities, and to explain its transactions in the course of those activities.

(3) The charity shall for each period of account prepare—

(a) a revenue account giving a true and fair view of the charity's income and expenditure in the period, so far as arising in connection with its housing activities, and

(b) a balance sheet giving a true and fair view as at the end of the period of the state of the charity's affairs.

The revenue account and balance sheet must be signed by at least two directors or trustees of the charity.

[(4) The charity must appoint a qualified auditor ("the auditor") to audit the accounts prepared in accordance with sub-paragraph (3) in respect of each period of account in which—

[(a) the charity's gross income arising in connection with its housing activities exceeds the sum for the time being specified in section 43(1)(a) of the Charities Act 1993, or

(b) the charity's gross income arising in that connection exceeds the accounts threshold and at the end of that period the aggregate value of its assets (before deduction of liabilities) in respect of its housing activities exceeds the sum for the time being specified in section 43(1)(b) of that Act;

and in this sub-paragraph "gross income" and "accounts threshold" have the same meanings as in section 43 of the Charities Act 1993.]

(4A) Where sub-paragraph (4) does not apply in respect of a period of account, the charity must appoint a qualified auditor ("the reporting accountant") to make such a report as is mentioned in paragraph 18A(1) in respect of the period of account.

(4B) In sub-paragraphs (4) and (4A) "qualified auditor" means a person who is eligible for appointment as auditor of the charity under Part 2 of the Companies Act 1989 or who would be so eligible if the charity were a company registered under the Companies Act 1985.]

(5) The auditor shall make a report to the charity on the accounts audited by him, stating whether in his opinion—

(a) the revenue account gives a true and fair view of the state of income and expenditure of the charity in respect of its housing activities and of any other matters to which it relates, and

(b) the balance sheet gives a true and fair view of the state of affairs of the charity as at the end of the period of account.

(6) The auditor in preparing his report shall carry out such investigations as will enable him to form an opinion as to the following matters—

(a) whether the association has kept, in respect of its housing activities, proper books of account in accordance with the requirements of this paragraph,

(b) whether the charity has maintained a satisfactory system of control over its transactions in accordance with those requirements, and

(c) whether the accounts are in agreement with the charity's books;

and if he is of opinion that the charity has failed in any respect to comply with this paragraph, or if the accounts are not in agreement with the books, he shall state that fact in his report.

(7) The auditor—

(a) has a right of access at all times to the books, deeds and accounts of the charity, so far as relating to its housing activities, and to all other documents relating to those activities, and

(b) is entitled to require from officers of the charity such information and explanations as he thinks necessary for the performance of his duties;

and if he fails to obtain all the information and explanations which, to the best of his knowledge and belief, are necessary for the purposes of his audit, he shall state that fact in his report.

(8) A period of account for the purposes of this paragraph is twelve months or such other period not less than six months or more than 18 months as the charity may, with the consent of the [Relevant Authority], determine.

[Charities exempt from audit requirements: accountant's report

18A.—(1) The report referred to in paragraph 18(4A) is a report—

(a) relating to the charity's accounts prepared in accordance with paragraph 18(3) in respect of the period of account in question, and

(b) complying with sub-paragraphs (2) and (3) below.

(2) The report must state whether, in the opinion of the reporting accountant—

(a) the revenue account or accounts and the balance sheet are in agreement with the books of account kept by the charity under paragraph 18(2),

(b) on the basis of the information contained in those books of account, the revenue account or accounts and the balance sheet comply with the requirements of the Charities Act 1993, and

(c) on the basis of the information contained in those books of account, paragraph 18(4A) applied to the charity in respect of the period of account in question.

(3) The report must also state the name of the reporting accountant and be signed by him.

(4) Paragraph 18(7) applies to the reporting accountant and his functions under this paragraph as it applies to an auditor and his functions under paragraph 18.

(5) The Relevant Authority may, in respect of a relevant period of account of a charity, give a direction to the charity requiring it—

(a) to appoint a qualified auditor to audit its accounts for that period, and

(b) to furnish to the Relevant Authority a copy of the auditor's report by such date as is specified in the direction;

and paragraph 18(5) to (7) apply to an auditor so appointed as they apply to an auditor appointed under paragraph 18.

(6) For the purposes of sub-paragraph (5), a period of account of a charity is a relevant period of account if—

(a) it precedes that in which the direction is given; and

(b) paragraph 18(4A) applied in relation to it.

(7) In this paragraph "period of account" and "qualified auditor" have the same meaning as in paragraph 18(4A).]

Responsibility for securing compliance with accounting requirements

19.—(1) Every responsible person, that is to say, every person who—

(a) is directly concerned with the conduct and management of the affairs of a registered social landlord, and

(b) is in that capacity responsible for the preparation and audit of accounts,

shall ensure that paragraph 16 (general requirements as to accounts and audit) and, where applicable, paragraph 18 (accounting and audit requirements for charities) are complied with by the registered social landlord.

(2) If—

(a) paragraph 16(5) (furnishing of accounts and auditor's report) is not complied with,

(b) the accounts furnished to the [Relevant Authority] under that provision do not comply with the accounting requirements laid down under paragraph 16(1),

(c) paragraph 18 (accounting and audit [or reporting] requirements for charities), where applicable, is not complied with,

(d) … or

(e) any notice under section 26 (information relating to disposal proceeds fund) is not complied with,

every responsible person, and the registered social landlord itself, commits a summary offence and is liable on conviction to a fine not exceeding [level 5] on the standard scale.

(3) In proceedings for an offence under this paragraph it is a defence—

(a) for a responsible person to prove that he did everything that could reasonably have been expected of him by way of discharging the relevant duty;

(b) for a registered social landlord to prove that every responsible person did everything that could reasonably have been expected of him by way of discharging the relevant duty in relation to the registered social landlord.

(4) Proceedings for an offence under this paragraph may be brought only by or with the consent of the [Relevant Authority] or the Director of Public Prosecutions.

[(5) Where any of paragraphs (a) to (e) of sub-paragraph (2) applies in respect of any default on the part of a registered social landlord, the High Court may, on the application of the Relevant Authority, make such order as the court thinks fit for requiring the default to be made good.

Any such order may provide that all the costs or expenses of and incidental to the application shall be borne by the registered social landlord or by any of its officers who are responsible for the default.]

[Disclosure of information by auditors etc to the Relevant Authority

19A.—(1) A person who is, or has been, an auditor of a registered social landlord does not contravene any duty to which he is subject merely because he gives to the Relevant Authority—

(a) information on a matter of which he became aware in his capacity as auditor of the registered social landlord, or

(b) his opinion on such a matter,

if he is acting in good faith and he reasonably believes that the information or opinion is relevant to any functions of the Relevant Authority.

(2) Sub-paragraph (1) applies whether or not the person is responding to a request from the Relevant Authority.

(3) This paragraph applies to a person who is, or has been, a reporting accountant as it applies to a person who is, or has been, an auditor.

(4) A "reporting accountant" means a person appointed as mentioned in paragraph 16(7)(b).]

[1105]

NOTES

Commencement: paras 17, 18 were brought into force on 1 October 1996; paras 16(3)–(5), 19 were brought into force on the same date and, by virtue of the Housing Act 1996 (Commencement No 3 and Transitional Provisions) Order 1996, SI 1996/2402, art 3, Schedule, para 5, apply in relation to accounts which relate to periods ending on or before 30 September 1996 and requirements under the Housing Associations Act 1985, s 24 as they apply in relation to periods ending after that date and requirements under para 16; paras 16(1), (2) were brought into force on 1 August 1996.

Para 16: words in square brackets in sub-paras (1), (2) substituted by the Government of Wales Act 1998, s 140, Sch 16, paras 81, 82(1)(a); sub-para (4) repealed and sub-paras (5)–(8) substituted for sub-para (5) as originally enacted, by the Housing Act 2004, ss 218, 266, Sch 11, paras 7, 17, Sch 16.

Para 16A: inserted, together with preceding cross-heading by the Housing Act 2004, s 218, Sch 11, paras 7, 18.

Para 17: substituted, together with preceding cross-heading by the Housing Act 2004, s 218, Sch 11, paras 7, 19.

Para 18: words in square brackets in cross-heading inserted, words omitted from sub-para (1) repealed and sub-paras (4)–(4B) substituted for sub-para (4) as originally enacted by the Housing Act 2004, ss 218, 266, Sch 11, paras 7, 21, Sch 16; sub-para (4)(a), (b) substituted in relation to any financial year of a charity which begins on or after 27 February 2007 by the Charities Act 2006, s 75(1), Sch 8, paras 183, 192(1), (4): see the Charities Act 2006 (Commencement No 1, Transitional Provisions and Savings) Order 2007, SI 2007/309, art 12. Original sub-para (4)(a), (b) read as follows—

"(a) the charity's gross income (within the meaning of the Charities Act 1993) arising in connection with its housing activities, or

(b) its total expenditure arising in connection with those activities,

exceeds the sum for the time being specified in section 43(1) of the Charities Act 1993 (audit required for charities where gross income or total income exceeds the specified sum).";

words in square brackets in sub-para (8) substituted by the Government of Wales Act 1998, s 140, Sch 16, paras 81, 82(1)(a).

Para 18A: inserted, together with preceding cross-heading by the Housing Act 2004, s 218, Sch 11, paras 7, 21.

Para 19: words in square brackets in sub-paras (2)(b), (4) substituted by the Government of Wales Act 1998, s 140, Sch 16, paras 81, 82(1)(a); words in square brackets in sub-para (2)(c) inserted, words omitted from sub-para (2)(d) repealed, words in third pair of square brackets in sub-para (2) substituted except in relation to any offence committed before 18 January 2005, and sub-para (5) added by the Housing Act 2004, ss 218, 266, Sch 11, paras 7, 22, Sch 16.

Para 19A: inserted, together with preceding cross-heading by the Housing Act 2004, s 218, Sch 11, paras 7, 23.

PART IV
INQUIRY INTO AFFAIRS OF REGISTERED SOCIAL LANDLORDS

Inquiry

20.—(1) The [Relevant Authority] may direct an inquiry into the affairs of a registered social landlord if it appears to the [Relevant Authority] that there may have been misconduct or mismanagement.

For this purpose "misconduct" includes any failure to comply with the requirements of this Part of this Act.

(2) Any such inquiry shall be conducted by one or more persons appointed by the [Relevant Authority].

(3) If one person is appointed [by the Housing Corporation to conduct an inquiry] he must be a person who is not a member or an employee of the [Housing Corporation] and has not been such a member or employee within the previous five years; and if more than one person is [so] appointed at least one of them must be such a person.

(4) If the [Relevant Authority] so directs, or if during the course of the inquiry the person or persons conducting the inquiry consider it necessary, the inquiry shall extend to the affairs of any other body which at any material time is or was a subsidiary or associate of the registered social landlord.

[(4A) The person or persons conducting the inquiry may determine the procedure to be followed in connection with the inquiry.]

(5) The person or persons conducting the inquiry may, if they think fit during the course of the inquiry, make one or more interim reports on such matters as appear to them to be appropriate.

(6) On completion of the inquiry the person or persons conducting the inquiry shall make a final report on such matters as the [Relevant Authority] may specify.

(7) An interim or final report shall be in such form as the [Relevant Authority] may specify[, and the Relevant Authority may arrange for the whole or part of an interim or final report to be published in such manner as it considers appropriate.]

[(8) A local authority may, if they think fit, contribute to the expenses of the Relevant Authority in connection with any inquiry under this paragraph.]

[Evidence

20A.—(1) For the purposes of an inquiry the person or persons conducting it may serve a notice on an appropriate person directing him to attend at a specified time and place and do either or both of the following, namely—

(a) give evidence;

(b) produce any specified documents, or documents of a specified description, which are in his custody or under his control and relate to any matter relevant to the inquiry.

(2) The person or persons conducting such an inquiry—

(a) may take evidence on oath and for that purpose administer oaths, or

(b) instead of administering an oath, require the person examined to make and subscribe a declaration of the truth of the matters about which he is examined.

(3) In this paragraph—

"appropriate person" means a person listed in section 30(2);

"document" has the same meaning as in section 30;

"inquiry" means an inquiry under paragraph 20.

(4) A person may not be required under this paragraph to disclose anything that, by virtue of section 30(4), he could not be required to disclose under section 30.

(5) Section 31 (enforcement of notice to provide information, &c) applies in relation to a notice given under this paragraph by the person or persons conducting an inquiry as it applies in relation to a notice given under section 30 by the Relevant Authority, but subject to sub-paragraph (6).

(6) A person guilty of an offence under section 31(1) as it applies in accordance with sub-paragraph (5) is liable—

(a) on summary conviction, to a fine not exceeding the statutory maximum;

(b) on conviction on indictment, to imprisonment for a term not exceeding two years or to a fine, or both.

(7) Any person who, in purported compliance with a notice given under this paragraph by the person or persons conducting an inquiry, knowingly or recklessly provides any information which is false or misleading in a material particular commits an offence and is liable to the penalties mentioned in sub-paragraph (6).

(8) Proceedings for an offence under sub-paragraph (7) may be brought only by or with the consent of the Relevant Authority or the Director of Public Prosecutions.]

Power of appointed person to obtain information

21.—(1) A person appointed by the [Relevant Authority] under paragraph 20 to conduct an inquiry (or, if more than one person is so appointed, each of those persons) has, for the purposes of the inquiry, the same powers as are conferred on the [Relevant Authority] by section 30 (general power to obtain information).

(2) Where by virtue of a notice under that section given by an appointed person any documents are produced to any person, the person to whom they are produced may take copies of or make extracts from them.

(3) Section 31 (enforcement of notice to provide information, &c) applies in relation to a notice given under this paragraph by an appointed person as it applies in relation to a notice given under section 30 by the [Relevant Authority][, but subject to sub-paragraph (4).]

[(4) A person guilty of an offence under section 31(1) as it applies in accordance with sub-paragraph (3) is liable—

(a) on summary conviction, to a fine not exceeding the statutory maximum;

(b) on conviction on indictment, to imprisonment for a term not exceeding two years or to a fine, or both.

(5) Any person who, in purported compliance with a notice given under this paragraph by an appointed person, knowingly or recklessly provides any information which is false or misleading in a material particular commits an offence and is liable to the penalties mentioned in sub-paragraph (4).

(6) Proceedings for an offence under sub-paragraph (5) may be brought only by or with the consent of the Relevant Authority or the Director of Public Prosecutions.]

Extraordinary audit for purposes of inquiry

22.—(1) For the purposes of an inquiry under paragraph 20 the [Relevant Authority] may require the accounts and balance sheet of the registered social landlord concerned, or such of them as the [Relevant Authority] may specify, to be audited by a qualified auditor appointed by the [Relevant Authority].

(2) A person is a qualified auditor for this purpose if he would be eligible for appointment as auditor of the ordinary accounts of the registered social landlord.

(3) On completion of the audit the appointed auditor shall make a report to the [Relevant Authority] on such matters and in such form as the [Relevant Authority] may specify.

(4) The expenses of the audit, including the remuneration of the auditor, shall be paid by the [Relevant Authority].

(5) An audit under this paragraph is additional to, and does not affect, any audit made or to be made under any other enactment.

Powers exercisable on interim basis

23.—(1) The [Relevant Authority] may make an order under this paragraph—
(a) where an inquiry has been directed under paragraph 20 and the [Relevant Authority] has reasonable grounds to believe—
(i) that there has been misconduct or mismanagement in the affairs of the registered social landlord, and
(ii) that immediate action is needed to protect the interests of the tenants of the registered social landlord or to protect the assets of the landlord; or
(b) where an interim report has been made under paragraph 20(5) as a result of which the [Relevant Authority] is satisfied that there has been misconduct or mismanagement in the affairs of a registered social landlord.

(2) The orders that may be made under this paragraph are—
(a) an order suspending any officer, employee or agent of the registered social landlord who appears to the [Relevant Authority] to have been responsible for or privy to the misconduct or mismanagement or by his conduct to have contributed to or facilitated it;
(b) an order directing any bank or other person who holds money or securities on behalf of the registered social landlord not to part with the money or securities without the approval of the [Relevant Authority];
(c) an order restricting the transactions which may be entered into, or the nature or amount of the payments which may be made, by the registered social landlord without the approval of the [Relevant Authority].

(3) An order under this paragraph, if not previously revoked by the [Relevant Authority], shall cease to have effect six months after the making of the final report under paragraph 20(6) unless the [Relevant Authority] renews it, which it may do for a further period of up to six months.

(4) A person suspended by an order under sub-paragraph (2)(a) may appeal against the order to the High Court.

(5) Where a person is suspended by such an order, the [Relevant Authority] may give directions with respect to the performance of his functions and otherwise as to matters arising from his suspension.

The [Relevant Authority] may, in particular, appoint a named person to perform his functions.

(6) A person who contravenes an order under sub-paragraph (2)(b) commits an offence and is liable on summary conviction to a fine not exceeding level 5 on the standard scale *or imprisonment for a term not exceeding three months, or both.*

Proceedings for such an offence may be brought only by or with the consent of the [Relevant Authority] or the Director of Public Prosecutions.

Powers exercisable as a result of final report or audit

24.—(1) Where the [Relevant Authority] is satisfied, as the result of an inquiry under paragraph 20 or an audit under paragraph 22, that there has been misconduct or mismanagement in the affairs of a registered social landlord, it may make an order under this paragraph.

(2) The orders that may be made under this paragraph are—
(a) an order removing any officer, employee or agent of the registered social landlord who appears to the [Relevant Authority] to have been responsible for or privy to the misconduct or mismanagement or by his conduct to have contributed to or facilitated it;
(b) an order suspending any such person for up to six months, pending determination whether he should be removed;
(c) an order directing any bank or other person who holds money or securities on behalf of the registered social landlord not to part with the money or securities without the approval of the [Relevant Authority];

(d) an order restricting the transactions which may be entered into, or the nature or amount of the payments which may be made, by the registered social landlord without the approval of the [Relevant Authority].

(3) Before making an order under sub-paragraph (2)(a) the [Relevant Authority] shall give at least 14 days' notice of its intention to do so—

(a) to the person it intends to remove, and
(b) to the registered social landlord concerned.

Notice under this sub-paragraph may be given by post, and if so given to the person whom the [Relevant Authority] intends to remove may be addressed to his last known address in the United Kingdom.

(4) A person who is ordered to be removed under sub-paragraph (2)(a) or suspended under sub-paragraph (2)(b) may appeal against the order to the High Court.

(5) Where a person is suspended under sub-paragraph (2)(b), the [Relevant Authority] may give directions with respect to the performance of his functions and otherwise as to matters arising from the suspension.

The [Relevant Authority] may, in particular, appoint a named person to perform his functions.

(6) A person who contravenes an order under sub-paragraph (2)(c) commits an offence and is liable on summary conviction to a fine not exceeding level 5 on the standard scale *or imprisonment for a term not exceeding three months, or both.*

Proceedings for such an offence may be brought only by or with the consent of the [Relevant Authority] or the Director of Public Prosecutions.

Disqualification as officer of registered social landlord

25.—(1) A person is disqualified from being an officer of a registered social landlord if the [Relevant Authority] has made an order against him under—

(a) paragraph 24(2)(a) (removal for misconduct or mismanagement), or
(b) section 30(1)(a) of the Housing Associations Act 1985 or section 20(1)(a) of the Housing Act 1974 (corresponding earlier provisions).

(2) The [Relevant Authority] may, on the application of any such person, waive his disqualification either generally or in relation to a particular registered social landlord or particular class of registered social landlord.

(3) Any waiver shall be notified in writing to the person concerned.

(4) For the purposes of this paragraph the [Relevant Authority] shall keep, in such manner as it thinks fit, a register of all persons who have been removed from office by the Corporation under the provisions mentioned in sub-paragraph (1).

(5) The register shall be available for public inspection at all reasonable times.

Persons acting as officer while disqualified

26.—(1) A person who acts as an officer of a registered social landlord while he is disqualified under paragraph 25(1) commits an offence.

A person guilty of such an offence is liable—

(a) on summary conviction, to imprisonment for a term not exceeding six months or to a fine not exceeding the statutory maximum, or both;
(b) on conviction on indictment, to imprisonment for a term not exceeding two years or to a fine, or both.

(2) Proceedings for an offence under sub-paragraph (1) may be brought only by or with the consent of the [Relevant Authority] or the Director of Public Prosecutions.

(3) Acts done as an officer of a registered social landlord by a person who is disqualified under paragraph 25(1) are not invalid by reason only of that disqualification.

(4) Where the [Relevant Authority] is satisfied—

(a) that a person has acted as an officer of a registered social landlord while disqualified under paragraph 25(1), and

(b) that while so acting he has received from the registered social landlord any payments or benefits in connection with his so acting,

it may by order direct him to repay to the registered social landlord the whole or part of any such sums or, as the case may be, to pay to it the whole or part of the monetary value (as determined by it) of any such benefit.

Power to direct transfer of land

27.—(1) Where as a result of an inquiry under paragraph 20 or an audit under paragraph 22 the [Relevant Authority] is satisfied as regards a registered social landlord—

(a) that there has been misconduct or mismanagement in its administration, or
(b) that the management of its land would be improved if its land were transferred in accordance with the provisions of this paragraph,

the [Relevant Authority] may … direct the registered social landlord to make such a transfer.

[The consent of the Secretary of State is required for the giving of directions by the Housing Corporation.]

(2) Where the registered social landlord concerned is a charity, the [Relevant Authority] may only direct a transfer to be made to another registered social landlord—

(a) which is also a charity, and
(b) the objects of which appear to the [Relevant Authority] to be, as nearly as practicable, akin to those of the registered social landlord concerned.

(3) In any other case the [Relevant Authority] may direct a transfer to be made to the [Relevant Authority] or to another registered social landlord.

(4) The transfer shall be on such terms as the [Relevant Authority] may direct on the basis of principles determined by it.

[If the transfer is directed by the Housing Corporation, the consent] of the Secretary of State is required both for the terms of the transfer and for the determination of the principles on which it is based.

(5) The price shall not be less than the amount certified by the district valuer to be the amount the property would command if sold by a willing seller to another registered social landlord.

(6) The terms shall include provision as to the payment of debts and liabilities (including debts and liabilities secured on the land).

Availability of powers in relation to registered charities

28.—(1) The [Relevant Authority] may exercise its powers under paragraphs 20 to 26 in relation to a registered charity only if the charity has, at any time before the powers are exercised—

(a) received financial assistance under section 24 of the Local Government Act 1988 (assistance for privately let housing accommodation),
(b) had property transferred to it on a qualifying disposal under section 135 of the Leasehold Reform, Housing and Urban Development Act 1993, or
(c) received a grant or loan under any of the following provisions.

(2) The provisions are—

section 18 of this Act (social housing grant),
section 22 of this Act or section 58 of the Housing Associations Act 1985 (grants or loans by local authorities),
section 50 of the Housing Act 1988, section 41 of the Housing Associations Act 1985 or any enactment replaced by that section (housing association grant),
section 51 of the Housing Act 1988 or section 54 or 55 of the Housing Associations Act 1985 (revenue deficit grant or hostel deficit grant),
section 79 of the Housing Associations Act 1985 (loans by [Relevant Authority]),
section 31 of the Housing Act 1974 (management grants), or any enactment mentioned in paragraph 2 or 3 of Schedule 1 to the Housing Associations Act 1985 (pre-1974 grants and certain loans).

(3) In relation to a registered charity paragraphs 20 to 26 have effect with the following adaptations—

(a) references to its affairs are confined to its housing activities and such other activities (if any) as are incidental to or connected with its housing activities;
(b) references to its accounts do not include revenue accounts which do not relate to its housing activities, except so far as such accounts are necessary for the auditing of revenue accounts which do so relate or of the balance sheet;
(c) a person is a qualified auditor for the purpose of paragraph 22 (extraordinary audit) only if he is an auditor qualified for the purposes of paragraph 18 (accounting and audit requirements for charities).

(4) The [Relevant Authority] shall notify the [Charity Commission] upon the exercise in relation to a registered charity of its powers under—
(a) paragraph 20(1) (inquiry into affairs of registered social landlord),
(b) paragraph 23(2)(a) (interim suspension of person in connection with misconduct or mismanagement), or
(c) paragraph 24(2)(a) or (b) (removal of person in connection with misconduct or mismanagement or suspension with a view to removal).

29. The [Relevant Authority] may not exercise its powers under paragraph 27 in relation to a registered charity.

[1106]

NOTES

Commencement: paras 20–26, 27(1)–(3), (5), (6), 28, 29 were brought into force on 1 October 1996; para 27(4) was brought into force on 1 August 1996 in so far as it confers the power to make determinations or give consents, and on 1 October 1996 for remaining purposes.

Para 20: words "Relevant Authority" in square brackets in each place they occur and words in second pair of square brackets in sub-para (3) substituted, and words in first and third pairs of square brackets in sub-para (3) inserted, by the Government of Wales Act 1998, s 140, Sch 16, paras 81, 82(1)(a), 96(1), (5); sub-para (4A) inserted, words in second pair of square brackets in sub-para (7) added, and sub-para (8) added, by the Housing Act 2004, s 218, Sch 11, paras 7, 24.

Para 20A: inserted, together with preceding cross-heading by the Housing Act 2004, s 218, Sch 11, paras 7, 25.

Para 21: words in square brackets in sub-para (1) and words in first pair of square brackets in sub-para (3) substituted by the Government of Wales Act 1998, s 140, Sch 16, paras 81, 82(1)(a); words in second pair of square brackets in sub-para (3) added and sub-paras (4)–(6) added by the Housing Act 2004, s 218, Sch 11, paras 7, 26 except in relation to any offence committed or other thing done before 18 January 2005.

Paras 22, 25, 26, 29: words in square brackets substituted by the Government of Wales Act 1998, s 140, Sch 16, paras 81, 82(1)(a), 96(1), (8).

Paras 23, 24: words in square brackets substituted by the Government of Wales Act 1998, s 140, Sch 16, paras 81, 82(1)(a); words in italics repealed by the Criminal Justice Act 2003, s 332, Sch 37, Pt 9, as from a day to be appointed under s 336(3), (4) of that Act.

Para 27: words "Relevant Authority" in square brackets in each place they occur and words in second pair of square brackets in sub-para (4) substituted, words in final pair of square brackets in sub-para (1) inserted, and words omitted from that sub-paragraph repealed, by the Government of Wales Act 1998, ss 140, 152, Sch 16, paras 81, 82(1)(a), 96(1), (6), (7), Sch 18, Pt VI.

Para 28: words "Relevant Authority" in square brackets in each place they occur substituted by the Government of Wales Act 1998, s 140, Sch 16, paras 81, 82(1)(a), 96(1), (8); words in second pair of square brackets in sub-para (4) substituted by the Charities Act 2006, s 75(1), Sch 8, paras 183, 192(1), (5).

Housing Associations Act 1985: s 30 was repealed by s 277 of, and Sch 19, Pt I to, this Act. Ss 41, 54, 55 were repealed by the Housing Act 1988, s 142, Sch 18.

Housing Act 1974, ss 20(1)(a), 31: repealed by the Housing (Consequential Provisions) Act 1985, s 3, Sch 1, Pt I.

SCHEDULE 2
SOCIAL RENTED SECTOR: HOUSING COMPLAINTS

Section 51

Social landlords required to be member of approved scheme

1.—(1) A social landlord must be a member of an approved scheme covering, or more than one approved scheme which together cover, all his housing activities.

(2) If a social landlord fails to comply with the duty imposed by this paragraph, the Secretary of State may apply to the High Court for an order directing him to comply within a specified period and the High Court may, if it thinks fit, make such an order.

(3) Nothing in this Schedule shall be construed as restricting membership of an approved scheme to social landlords.

Matters for which scheme must provide

2.—(1) A scheme shall not be approved for the purposes of this Schedule unless it makes provision for—

1 The establishment or appointment of an independent person to administer the scheme.
2 The criteria for membership for—
(a) social landlords under a duty to be members of an approved scheme, and
(b) other persons.
3 The manner of becoming or ceasing to be a member.
4 The matters about which complaints may be made under the scheme.
5 The grounds on which a matter may be excluded from investigation, including that the matter is the subject of court proceedings or was the subject of court proceedings where judgment on the merits was given.
6 The descriptions of individual who may make a complaint under the scheme.
7 The appointment of an independent individual to be the housing ombudsman under the scheme.
8 The appointment of staff to administer the scheme and to assist the housing ombudsman and the terms upon which they are appointed.
9 A duty of the housing ombudsman to investigate any complaint duly made and not withdrawn, and a power to investigate any complaint duly made but withdrawn, and where he investigates to make a determination.
10 A power of the housing ombudsman to propose alternative methods of resolving a dispute.
11 The powers of the housing ombudsman for the purposes of his investigations, and the procedure to be followed in the conduct of investigations.
12 The powers of the housing ombudsman on making a determination.
13 The making and publication of annual reports by the housing ombudsman on the discharge of his functions.
14 The manner in which determinations are to be—
(a) communicated to the complainant and the person against whom the complaint was made, and
(b) published.
15 The manner in which the expenses of the scheme are to be defrayed by the members.
16 The keeping and auditing of accounts and the submission of accounts to the Secretary of State.
17 The making of annual reports on the administration of the scheme.
18 The manner of amending the scheme.

(2) The Secretary of State may by order amend sub-paragraph (1) by adding to or deleting from it any item or by varying any item for the time being contained in it.

(3) An order under sub-paragraph (2) shall be made by statutory instrument which shall be subject to annulment in pursuance of a resolution of either House of Parliament.

Approval of scheme, or amendment, and withdrawal of approval

3.—(1) An application to the Secretary of State for approval of a scheme shall be made in such manner as the Secretary of State may determine, and shall be accompanied by such information as the Secretary of State may require.

(2) If it appears to the Secretary of State that the scheme—
(a) provides for the matters specified in paragraph 2, and
(b) is a satisfactory scheme for the purposes of this Schedule,

he shall approve the scheme.

(3) An amendment of an approved scheme is not effective unless approved by the Secretary of State.

Sub-paragraph (1) applies in relation to an application for approval of an amendment as it applies to an application for approval of a scheme; and the Secretary of State shall approve the amendment if it appears to him that the scheme as amended meets the conditions in sub-paragraph (2).

(4) The Secretary of State may withdraw his approval of a scheme.

(5) If the Secretary of State proposes to withdraw his approval of a scheme, he shall serve on the person administering the scheme and on the housing ombudsman under the scheme, a notice stating—

(a) that he proposes to withdraw his approval,
(b) the grounds for the proposed withdrawal of his approval, and
(c) that the person receiving the notice may make representations with respect to the proposed withdrawal of approval within such period of not less than 14 days as is specified in the notice;

and he shall, before reaching a decision on whether to withdraw approval, consider any representations duly made to him.

(6) The Secretary of State shall give notice of his decision on a proposal to withdraw approval of a scheme, together with his reasons, to every person on whom he served a notice under sub-paragraph (5).

(7) Withdrawal of approval by the Secretary of State has effect from such date as is specified in the notice of his decision.

(8) Where the person administering a scheme is given notice of a decision to withdraw approval of the scheme, he shall give notice of the decision to every member of the scheme.

Notice to be given of becoming a member of an approved scheme

4.—(1) A social landlord who—

(a) becomes a member of an approved scheme, or
(b) is a member of a scheme which becomes an approved scheme,

shall, within the period of 21 days beginning with the date of becoming a member or, as the case may be, of being informed of the Secretary of State's approval of the scheme, give notice of that fact to the [Relevant Authority].

(2) The [Relevant Authority], on receiving the notice, shall record his membership of an approved scheme.

(3) A person who fails to comply with sub-paragraph (1) commits an offence and is liable on summary conviction to a fine not exceeding level 4 on the standard scale.

Proceedings for such an offence may be brought only by or with the consent of the [Relevant Authority] or the Director of Public Prosecutions.

Withdrawal from approved scheme

5.—(1) A social landlord wishing to withdraw from membership of an approved scheme shall send notice of his proposed withdrawal to the [Relevant Authority].

(2) The notice shall specify—

(a) the housing activities in relation to which he is subject to investigation under the scheme,
(b) the approved scheme or schemes of which he is also a member or will, on his withdrawal, become a member, and
(c) under which scheme or schemes the housing activities mentioned in paragraph (a) will be subject to investigation after his withdrawal.

(3) If the [Relevant Authority] is satisfied that withdrawal by the landlord from the scheme will not result in a failure to comply with his duty under paragraph 1, it shall confirm the landlord's withdrawal from the scheme.

(4) If the [Relevant Authority] is not so satisfied, it shall withhold confirmation of the landlord's withdrawal from the scheme; and the landlord shall continue to be a member of the scheme and bound and entitled under the scheme accordingly.

Register of approved schemes

6.—(1) The [Relevant Authority] shall maintain a register of schemes approved by the Secretary of State for the purposes of this Schedule and of the social landlords who are members of those schemes.

(2) The Secretary of State shall give notice to the [Housing Corporation]—
(a) when he grants or withdraws his approval of a scheme, and
(b) when he approves an amendment of a scheme,

and he shall supply the [Housing Corporation] with copies of any approved scheme or any amendment to a scheme.

(3) A member of the public shall be entitled, upon payment of such fees as the [Relevant Authority] may determine, to receive a copy of an approved scheme and a list of the social landlords who are members of it.

Determinations by housing ombudsman

7.—(1) A housing ombudsman under an approved scheme shall investigate any complaint duly made to him and not withdrawn, and may investigate any complaint duly made but withdrawn, and where he investigates a complaint he shall determine it by reference to what is, in his opinion, fair in all the circumstances of the case.

(2) He may in his determination—
(a) order the member of a scheme against whom the complaint was made to pay compensation to the complainant, and
(b) order that the member or the complainant shall not exercise or require the performance of any of the contractual or other obligations or rights existing between them.

(3) If the member against whom the complaint was made fails to comply with the determination within a reasonable time, the housing ombudsman may order him to publish in such manner as the ombudsman sees fit that he has failed to comply with the determination.

(4) Where the member is not a social landlord, the housing ombudsman may also order that the member—
(a) be expelled from the scheme, and
(b) publish in such manner as the housing ombudsman sees fit that he has been expelled and the reasons for his expulsion.

(5) If a person fails to comply with an order under sub-paragraph (3) or (4)(b), the housing ombudsman may take such steps as he thinks appropriate to publish what the member ought to have published and recover from the member the costs of doing so.

(6) A member who is ordered by the housing ombudsman to pay compensation or take any other steps has power to do so, except that a member which is also a charity shall not do anything contrary to its trusts.

Publication of determinations, &c

8.—(1) A housing ombudsman under an approved scheme may publish—
(a) his determination on any complaint, and
(b) such reports as he thinks fit on the discharge of his functions.

(2) He may include in any such determination or report statements, communications, reports, papers or other documentary evidence obtained in the exercise of his functions.

(3) In publishing any determination or report, a housing ombudsman shall have regard to the need for excluding so far as practicable—
(a) any matter which relates to the private affairs of an individual, where publication would seriously and prejudicially affect the interests of that individual, and
(b) any matter which relates specifically to the affairs of a member of an approved scheme, where publication would seriously and prejudicially affect its interests, unless the inclusion of that matter is necessary for the purposes of the determination or report.

Absolute privilege for communications, &c

9. For the purposes of the law of defamation absolute privilege attaches to—
   (a) any communication between a housing ombudsman under an approved scheme and any person by or against whom a complaint is made to him,
   (b) any determination by such an ombudsman, and
   (c) the publication of such a determination or any report under paragraph 8.

Appointment and status of housing ombudsman

10.—(1) Where an approved scheme provides that it shall be administered by a body corporate, that body shall appoint on such terms as it thinks fit the housing ombudsman for the purposes of the scheme and the appointment and its terms shall be subject to the approval of the Secretary of State.

(2) Where an approved scheme does not so provide—
   (a) the housing ombudsman for the purposes of the scheme shall be appointed by the Secretary of State on such terms as the Secretary of State thinks fit,
   (b) the Secretary of State may by order provide that the housing ombudsman for the purposes of the scheme shall be a corporation sole, and
   (c) the staff to administer the scheme and otherwise assist the ombudsman in the discharge of his functions shall be appointed and employed by him.

(3) The Secretary of State may at any time remove from office a housing ombudsman (whether appointed by him or otherwise).

(4) A housing ombudsman appointed by the Secretary of State or otherwise shall not be regarded as the servant or agent of the Crown or as enjoying any status, privilege or immunity of the Crown or as exempt from any tax, duty, rate, levy or other charge whatsoever, whether general or local, and any property held by him shall not be regarded as property of, or held on behalf of, the Crown.

Subscriptions payable in respect of approved schemes

11.—(1) Members of an approved scheme shall pay a subscription, calculated as set out in the scheme, to the person administering the scheme.

(2) If a social landlord fails to comply with his duty under paragraph 1, the Secretary of State may determine—
   (a) which approved scheme or schemes he should have joined, and
   (b) what sums by way of subscription he should have paid,

and may require him to pay those amounts to the person administering the scheme or schemes.

(3) The person administering an approved scheme may recover sums payable under sub-paragraph (1) or (2) as if they were debts due to him.

(4) The Secretary of State or the [Housing Corporation] may pay grant and provide other financial assistance to—
   (a) a body corporate administering an approved scheme, or
   (b) in a case where paragraph 10(2) applies, to the housing ombudsman under an approved scheme,

for such purposes and upon such terms as the Secretary of State or, as the case may be, the [Housing Corporation] thinks fit.

[1107]

NOTES

Commencement: 1 April 1997 (paras 1, 7–9, 11(2), subject to transitional provisions); 1 August 1996 (paras 2–6, 10, 11(1), (3), (4), subject to transitional provisions): for transitional provisions see the Housing Act 1996 (Commencement No 10 and Transitional Provisions) Order 1997, SI 1997/618, art 2, Schedule, paras 2–6, 10, 11 and the Housing Act 1996 (Commencement No 1 and Transitional Provisions) Order 1996, SI 1996/2048, art 2.

Paras 4–6, 11: words in square brackets substituted by the Government of Wales Act 1998, s 140, Sch 16, paras 81, 82(1)(a), 97.

(*Sch 2A repealed by the Public Services Ombudsman (Wales) Act 2005, s 39, Sch 6, paras 56, 58, Sch 7; Schs 3–19 outside the scope of this work.*)

DATA PROTECTION ACT 1998

(1998 c 29)

ARRANGEMENT OF SECTIONS

PART I
PRELIMINARY

PART II
RIGHTS OF DATA SUBJECTS AND OTHERS

PART III
NOTIFICATION BY DATA CONTROLLERS

PART IV
EXEMPTIONS

PART V
ENFORCEMENT

PART VI
MISCELLANEOUS AND GENERAL

Functions of Commissioner

Unlawful obtaining etc of personal data

Records obtained under data subject's right of access

Information provided to Commissioner or Tribunal

General provisions relating to offences

General

An Act to make new provision for the regulation of the processing of information relating to individuals, including the obtaining, holding, use or disclosure of such information

[16 July 1998]

NOTES

Transfer of functions: as to the transfer of functions under this Act from Ministers of the Crown to the National Assembly for Wales, see the National Assembly for Wales (Transfer of Functions) Order 1999, SI 1999/672.

PART I
PRELIMINARY

1 Basic interpretative provisions

(1) In this Act, unless the context otherwise requires—

"data" means information which—

(a) is being processed by means of equipment operating automatically in response to instructions given for that purpose,

(b) is recorded with the intention that it should be processed by means of such equipment,

(c) is recorded as part of a relevant filing system or with the intention that it should form part of a relevant filing system, …

(d) does not fall within paragraph (a), (b) or (c) but forms part of an accessible record as defined by section 68, [or

(e) is recorded information held by a public authority and does not fall within any of paragraphs (a) to (d);]

"data controller" means, subject to subsection (4), a person who (either alone or jointly or in common with other persons) determines the purposes for which and the manner in which any personal data are, or are to be, processed;

"data processor", in relation to personal data, means any person (other than an employee of the data controller) who processes the data on behalf of the data controller;

"data subject" means an individual who is the subject of personal data;

"personal data" means data which relate to a living individual who can be identified—

(a) from those data, or

(b) from those data and other information which is in the possession of, or is likely to come into the possession of, the data controller,

and includes any expression of opinion about the individual and any indication of the intentions of the data controller or any other person in respect of the individual;

"processing", in relation to information or data, means obtaining, recording or holding the information or data or carrying out any operation or set of operations on the information or data, including—

(a) organisation, adaptation or alteration of the information or data,

(b) retrieval, consultation or use of the information or data,

(c) disclosure of the information or data by transmission, dissemination or otherwise making available, or

(d) alignment, combination, blocking, erasure or destruction of the information or data;

["public authority" means a public authority as defined by the Freedom of Information Act 2000 or a Scottish public authority as defined by the Freedom of Information (Scotland) Act 2002;]

"relevant filing system" means any set of information relating to individuals to the extent that, although the information is not processed by means of equipment operating automatically in response to instructions given for that purpose, the set is structured, either by reference to individuals or by reference to criteria relating to individuals, in such a way that specific information relating to a particular individual is readily accessible.

(2) In this Act, unless the context otherwise requires—

(a) "obtaining" or "recording", in relation to personal data, includes obtaining or recording the information to be contained in the data, and

(b) "using" or "disclosing", in relation to personal data, includes using or disclosing the information contained in the data.

(3) In determining for the purposes of this Act whether any information is recorded with the intention—

(a) that it should be processed by means of equipment operating automatically in response to instructions given for that purpose, or

(b) that it should form part of a relevant filing system,

it is immaterial that it is intended to be so processed or to form part of such a system only after being transferred to a country or territory outside the European Economic Area.

(4) Where personal data are processed only for purposes for which they are required by or under any enactment to be processed, the person on whom the obligation to process the data is imposed by or under that enactment is for the purposes of this Act the data controller.

[(5) In paragraph (e) of the definition of "data" in subsection (1), the reference to information "held" by a public authority shall be construed in accordance with section 3(2) of the Freedom of Information Act 2000 [or section 3(2), (4) and (5) of the Freedom of Information (Scotland) Act 2002].

(6) Where

[(a)] section 7 of the Freedom of Information Act 2000 prevents Parts I to V of that Act [or

(b) section 7(1) of the Freedom of Information (Scotland) Act 2002 prevents that Act,]

from applying to certain information held by a public authority, that information is not to be treated for the purposes of paragraph (e) of the definition of "data" in subsection (1) as held by a public authority.]

[1108]

NOTES

Commencement: 16 July 1998.

Sub-s (1): in definition "data" word omitted from para (c) repealed, and para (e) and word immediately preceding it inserted by the Freedom of Information Act 2000, ss 68(1), (2)(a), 86, Sch 8, Pt III; definition "public authority" (originally inserted by the Freedom of Information Act 2000, s 68(1), (2)(b)) substituted by the Freedom of Information (Scotland) Act 2002 (Consequential Modifications) Order 2004, SI 2004/3089, art 2(1), (2)(a).

Sub-s (5): added by the Freedom of Information Act 2000, s 68(1), (3); words in square brackets inserted by SI 2004/3089, art 2(1), (2)(b).

Sub-s (6): added by the Freedom of Information Act 2000, s 68(1), (3); para (a) numbered as such and para (b) and the word immediately preceding it inserted by SI 2004/3089, art 2(1), (2)(c).

2 Sensitive personal data

In this Act "sensitive personal data" means personal data consisting of information as to—

(a) the racial or ethnic origin of the data subject,

(b) his political opinions,

(c) his religious beliefs or other beliefs of a similar nature,

(d) whether he is a member of a trade union (within the meaning of the Trade Union and Labour Relations (Consolidation) Act 1992,

(e) his physical or mental health or condition,

(f) his sexual life,

(g) the commission or alleged commission by him of any offence, or
(h) any proceedings for any offence committed or alleged to have been committed by him, the disposal of such proceedings or the sentence of any court in such proceedings.

[1109]

NOTES
Commencement: 16 July 1998.

3 The special purposes

In this Act "the special purposes" means any one or more of the following—
(a) the purposes of journalism,
(b) artistic purposes, and
(c) literary purposes.

[1110]

NOTES
Commencement: 16 July 1998.

4 The data protection principles

(1) References in this Act to the data protection principles are to the principles set out in Part I of Schedule 1.

(2) Those principles are to be interpreted in accordance with Part II of Schedule 1.

(3) Schedule 2 (which applies to all personal data) and Schedule 3 (which applies only to sensitive personal data) set out conditions applying for the purposes of the first principle; and Schedule 4 sets out cases in which the eighth principle does not apply.

(4) Subject to section 27(1), it shall be the duty of a data controller to comply with the data protection principles in relation to all personal data with respect to which he is the data controller.

[1111]

NOTES
Commencement: 1 March 2000.

5 Application of Act

(1) Except as otherwise provided by or under section 54, this Act applies to a data controller in respect of any data only if—
(a) the data controller is established in the United Kingdom and the data are processed in the context of that establishment, or
(b) the data controller is established neither in the United Kingdom nor in any other EEA State but uses equipment in the United Kingdom for processing the data otherwise than for the purposes of transit through the United Kingdom.

(2) A data controller falling within subsection (1)(b) must nominate for the purposes of this Act a representative established in the United Kingdom.

(3) For the purposes of subsections (1) and (2), each of the following is to be treated as established in the United Kingdom—
(a) an individual who is ordinarily resident in the United Kingdom,
(b) a body incorporated under the law of, or of any part of, the United Kingdom,
(c) a partnership or other unincorporated association formed under the law of any part of the United Kingdom, and
(d) any person who does not fall within paragraph (a), (b) or (c) but maintains in the United Kingdom—
(i) an office, branch or agency through which he carries on any activity, or
(ii) a regular practice;

and the reference to establishment in any other EEA State has a corresponding meaning.

[1112]

NOTES

Commencement: 1 March 2000.

6 The Commissioner and the Tribunal

[(1) For the purposes of this Act and of the Freedom of Information Act 2000 there shall be an officer known as the Information Commissioner (in this Act referred to as "the Commissioner").]

(2) The Commissioner shall be appointed by Her Majesty by Letters Patent.

[(3) For the purposes of this Act and of the Freedom of Information Act 2000 there shall be a tribunal known as the Information Tribunal (in this Act referred to as "the Tribunal").]

(4) The Tribunal shall consist of—
- (a) a chairman appointed by the Lord Chancellor after consultation with the [Secretary of State],
- (b) such number of deputy chairmen so appointed as the Lord Chancellor may determine, and
- (c) such number of other members appointed by the [Secretary of State] as he may determine.

(5) The members of the Tribunal appointed under subsection (4)(a) and (b) shall be—
- (a) persons who have a 7 year general qualification, within the meaning of section 71 of the Courts and Legal Services Act 1990,
- (b) advocates or solicitors in Scotland of at least 7 years' standing, or
- (c) members of the bar of Northern Ireland or *solicitors of the Supreme Court of Northern Ireland* of at least 7 years' standing.

(6) The members of the Tribunal appointed under subsection (4)(c) shall be—
- (a) persons to represent the interests of data subjects,
- [(aa) persons to represent the interests of those who make requests for information under the Freedom of Information Act 2000,]
- (b) persons to represent the interests of data controllers [and
- (bb) persons to represent the interests of public authorities].

(7) Schedule 5 has effect in relation to the Commissioner and the Tribunal.

[1113]

NOTES

Commencement: 1 March 2000.

Sub-ss (1), (3): substituted by the Freedom of Information Act 2000, s 18(4), Sch 2, Pt 1, para 13.

Sub-s (4): words in square brackets in para (a) substituted by virtue of the Transfer of Functions (Lord Advocate and Secretary of State) Order 1999, SI 1999/678, art 2(1), Schedule; words in square brackets in para (c) substituted by the Secretary of State for Constitutional Affairs Order 2003, SI 2003/1887, art 9, Sch 2, para 9(1)(a).

Sub-s (5): for the words in italics there are substituted the words "solicitors of the Court of Judicature of Northern Ireland" by the Constitutional Reform Act 2005, s 59(5), Sch 11, Pt 3, para 5, as from a day to be appointed under s 148(1) of that Act.

Sub-s (6): para (aa) substituted for original word "and" at the end of para (a), and para (bb) and word immediately preceding it inserted, by the Freedom of Information Act 2000, s 18(4), Sch 2, Pt II, para 16.

PART II
RIGHTS OF DATA SUBJECTS AND OTHERS

7 Right of access to personal data

(1) Subject to the following provisions of this section and to [sections 8, 9 and 9A], an individual is entitled—
- (a) to be informed by any data controller whether personal data of which that individual is the data subject are being processed by or on behalf of that data controller,
- (b) if that is the case, to be given by the data controller a description of—
  - (i) the personal data of which that individual is the data subject,
  - (ii) the purposes for which they are being or are to be processed, and
  - (iii) the recipients or classes of recipients to whom they are or may be disclosed,

(c) to have communicated to him in an intelligible form—
   (i) the information constituting any personal data of which that individual is the data subject, and
   (ii) any information available to the data controller as to the source of those data, and

(d) where the processing by automatic means of personal data of which that individual is the data subject for the purpose of evaluating matters relating to him such as, for example, his performance at work, his creditworthiness, his reliability or his conduct, has constituted or is likely to constitute the sole basis for any decision significantly affecting him, to be informed by the data controller of the logic involved in that decision-taking.

(2) A data controller is not obliged to supply any information under subsection (1) unless he has received—

(a) a request in writing, and
(b) except in prescribed cases, such fee (not exceeding the prescribed maximum) as he may require.

[(3) Where a data controller—

(a) reasonably requires further information in order to satisfy himself as to the identity of the person making a request under this section and to locate the information which that person seeks, and
(b) has informed him of that requirement,

the data controller is not obliged to comply with the request unless he is supplied with that further information.]

(4) Where a data controller cannot comply with the request without disclosing information relating to another individual who can be identified from that information, he is not obliged to comply with the request unless—

(a) the other individual has consented to the disclosure of the information to the person making the request, or
(b) it is reasonable in all the circumstances to comply with the request without the consent of the other individual.

(5) In subsection (4) the reference to information relating to another individual includes a reference to information identifying that individual as the source of the information sought by the request; and that subsection is not to be construed as excusing a data controller from communicating so much of the information sought by the request as can be communicated without disclosing the identity of the other individual concerned, whether by the omission of names or other identifying particulars or otherwise.

(6) In determining for the purposes of subsection (4)(b) whether it is reasonable in all the circumstances to comply with the request without the consent of the other individual concerned, regard shall be had, in particular, to—

(a) any duty of confidentiality owed to the other individual,
(b) any steps taken by the data controller with a view to seeking the consent of the other individual,
(c) whether the other individual is capable of giving consent, and
(d) any express refusal of consent by the other individual.

(7) An individual making a request under this section may, in such cases as may be prescribed, specify that his request is limited to personal data of any prescribed description.

(8) Subject to subsection (4), a data controller shall comply with a request under this section promptly and in any event before the end of the prescribed period beginning with the relevant day.

(9) If a court is satisfied on the application of any person who has made a request under the foregoing provisions of this section that the data controller in question has failed to comply with the request in contravention of those provisions, the court may order him to comply with the request.

(10) In this section—

"prescribed" means prescribed by the [Secretary of State] by regulations;
"the prescribed maximum" means such amount as may be prescribed;
"the prescribed period" means forty days or such other period as may be prescribed;
"the relevant day", in relation to a request under this section, means the day on which the data controller receives the request or, if later, the first day on which the data controller has both the required fee and the information referred to in subsection (3).

(11) Different amounts or periods may be prescribed under this section in relation to different cases.

[1114]

NOTES

Commencement: 1 March 2000 (16 July 1998: sub-s (7) insofar as conferring a power to make subordinate legislation).

Sub-s (1): words in square brackets substituted by the Freedom of Information Act 2000, s 69(1).

Sub-s (3): substituted by the Freedom of Information Act 2000, s 73, Sch 6, para 1.

Sub-s (10): words in square brackets substituted by the Secretary of State for Constitutional Affairs Order 2003, SI 2003/1887, art 9, Sch 2, para 9(1)(a).

Regulations: the Data Protection (Subject Access) (Fees and Miscellaneous Provisions) Regulations 2000, SI 2000/191.

8 Provisions supplementary to section 7

(1) The [Secretary of State] may by regulations provide that, in such cases as may be prescribed, a request for information under any provision of subsection (1) of section 7 is to be treated as extending also to information under other provisions of that subsection.

(2) The obligation imposed by section 7(1)(c)(i) must be complied with by supplying the data subject with a copy of the information in permanent form unless—

(a) the supply of such a copy is not possible or would involve disproportionate effort, or

(b) the data subject agrees otherwise;

and where any of the information referred to in section 7(1)(c)(i) is expressed in terms which are not intelligible without explanation the copy must be accompanied by an explanation of those terms.

(3) Where a data controller has previously complied with a request made under section 7 by an individual, the data controller is not obliged to comply with a subsequent identical or similar request under that section by that individual unless a reasonable interval has elapsed between compliance with the previous request and the making of the current request.

(4) In determining for the purposes of subsection (3) whether requests under section 7 are made at reasonable intervals, regard shall be had to the nature of the data, the purpose for which the data are processed and the frequency with which the data are altered.

(5) Section 7(1)(d) is not to be regarded as requiring the provision of information as to the logic involved in any decision-taking if, and to the extent that, the information constitutes a trade secret.

(6) The information to be supplied pursuant to a request under section 7 must be supplied by reference to the data in question at the time when the request is received, except that it may take account of any amendment or deletion made between that time and the time when the information is supplied, being an amendment or deletion that would have been made regardless of the receipt of the request.

(7) For the purposes of section 7(4) and (5) another individual can be identified from the information being disclosed if he can be identified from that information, or from that and any other information which, in the reasonable belief of the data controller, is likely to be in, or to come into, the possession of the data subject making the request.

[1115]

NOTES

Commencement: 1 March 2000 (16 July 1998: sub-s (1) insofar as conferring a power to make subordinate legislation).

Sub-s (1): words in square brackets substituted by the Secretary of State for Constitutional Affairs Order 2003, SI 2003/1887, art 9, Sch 2, para 9(1)(a).

Regulations: the Data Protection (Subject Access) (Fees and Miscellaneous Provisions) Regulations 2000, SI 2000/191.

9 Application of section 7 where data controller is credit reference agency

(1) Where the data controller is a credit reference agency, section 7 has effect subject to the provisions of this section.

(2) An individual making a request under section 7 may limit his request to personal data relevant to his financial standing, and shall be taken to have so limited his request unless the request shows a contrary intention.

(3) Where the data controller receives a request under section 7 in a case where personal data of which the individual making the request is the data subject are being processed by or on behalf of the data controller, the obligation to supply information under that section includes an obligation to give the individual making the request a statement, in such form as may be prescribed by the [Secretary of State] by regulations, of the individual's rights—

(a) under section 159 of the Consumer Credit Act 1974, and

(b) to the extent required by the prescribed form, under this Act.

[1116]

NOTES

Commencement: 1 March 2000 (16 July 1998: sub-s (3) insofar as conferring a power to make subordinate legislation).

Sub-s (3): words in square brackets substituted by the Secretary of State for Constitutional Affairs Order 2003, SI 2003/1887, art 9, Sch 2, para 9(1)(a).

Regulations: the Consumer Credit (Credit Reference Agency) Regulations 2000, SI 2000/290.

[9A Unstructured personal data held by public authorities

(1) In this section "unstructured personal data" means any personal data falling within paragraph (e) of the definition of "data" in section 1(1), other than information which is recorded as part of, or with the intention that it should form part of, any set of information relating to individuals to the extent that the set is structured by reference to individuals or by reference to criteria relating to individuals.

(2) A public authority is not obliged to comply with subsection (1) of section 7 in relation to any unstructured personal data unless the request under that section contains a description of the data.

(3) Even if the data are described by the data subject in his request, a public authority is not obliged to comply with paragraph (a) of section 7(1) in relation to the unstructured personal data if the authority estimates that the cost of complying with the request so far as relating to those data would exceed the appropriate limit.

(4) Subsection (3) does not exempt the public authority from its obligation to comply with paragraph (a) of section 7(1) in relation to the unstructured personal data unless the estimated cost of complying with that paragraph alone in relation to those data would exceed the appropriate limit.

(5) In subsections (3) and (4) "the appropriate limit" means such amount as may be prescribed by the [Secretary of State] by regulations, and different amounts may be prescribed in relation to different cases.

(6) Any estimate for the purposes of this section must be made in accordance with regulations under s 12(5) of the Freedom of Information Act 2000.]

[1116A]

NOTES

Commencement: 30 November 2000 (for the purpose of making regulations); 1 January 2005 (otherwise).

Inserted by the Freedom of Information Act 2000, s 69(2).

Sub-s (5): words in square brackets substituted by the Secretary of State for Constitutional Affairs Order 2003, SI 2003/1887, art 9, Sch 2, paras 9(1)(a), 12(1)(b).

Regulations: the Freedom of Information and Data Protection (Appropriate Limit and Fees) Regulations 2004, SI 2004/3244.

10 Right to prevent processing likely to cause damage or distress

(1) Subject to subsection (2), an individual is entitled at any time by notice in writing to a data controller to require the data controller at the end of such period as is reasonable in the circumstances to cease, or not to begin, processing, or processing for a specified purpose or in a specified manner, any personal data in respect of which he is the data subject, on the ground that, for specified reasons—

(a) the processing of those data or their processing for that purpose or in that manner is causing or is likely to cause substantial damage or substantial distress to him or to another, and

(b) that damage or distress is or would be unwarranted.

(2) Subsection (1) does not apply—

(a) in a case where any of the conditions in paragraphs 1 to 4 of Schedule 2 is met, or

(b) in such other cases as may be prescribed by the [Secretary of State] by order.

(3) The data controller must within twenty-one days of receiving a notice under subsection (1) ("the data subject notice") give the individual who gave it a written notice—

(a) stating that he has complied or intends to comply with the data subject notice, or

(b) stating his reasons for regarding the data subject notice as to any extent unjustified and the extent (if any) to which he has complied or intends to comply with it.

(4) If a court is satisfied, on the application of any person who has given a notice under subsection (1) which appears to the court to be justified (or to be justified to any extent), that the data controller in question has failed to comply with the notice, the court may order him to take such steps for complying with the notice (or for complying with it to that extent) as the court thinks fit.

(5) The failure by a data subject to exercise the right conferred by subsection (1) or section 11(1) does not affect any other right conferred on him by this Part.

[1117]

NOTES

Commencement: 1 March 2000 (16 July 1998: sub-s (2) insofar as conferring a power to make subordinate legislation).

Sub-s (2): words in square brackets in para (b) substituted by the Secretary of State for Constitutional Affairs Order 2003, SI 2003/1887, art 9, Sch 2, para 9(1)(a).

11 Right to prevent processing for purposes of direct marketing

(1) An individual is entitled at any time by notice in writing to a data controller to require the data controller at the end of such period as is reasonable in the circumstances to cease, or not to begin, processing for the purposes of direct marketing personal data in respect of which he is the data subject.

(2) If the court is satisfied, on the application of any person who has given a notice under subsection (1), that the data controller has failed to comply with the notice, the court may order him to take such steps for complying with the notice as the court thinks fit.

[(2A) This section shall not apply in relation to the processing of such data as are mentioned in paragraph (1) of regulation 8 of the Telecommunications (Data Protection and Privacy) Regulations 1999 (processing of telecommunications billing data for certain marketing purposes) for the purposes mentioned in paragraph (2) of that regulation.]

(3) In this section "direct marketing" means the communication (by whatever means) of any advertising or marketing material which is directed to particular individuals.

[1118]

NOTES

Commencement: 1 March 2000.

Sub-s (2A): inserted by the Telecommunications (Data Protection and Privacy) Regulations 1999, SI 1999/2093, reg 3(3), Sch 1, Pt II, para 3.

12 Rights in relation to automated decision-taking

(1) An individual is entitled at any time, by notice in writing to any data controller, to require the data controller to ensure that no decision taken by or on behalf of the data controller which significantly affects that individual is based solely on the processing by automatic means of personal data in respect of which that individual is the data subject for the purpose of evaluating matters relating to him such as, for example, his performance at work, his creditworthiness, his reliability or his conduct.

(2) Where, in a case where no notice under subsection (1) has effect, a decision which significantly affects an individual is based solely on such processing as is mentioned in subsection (1)—

(a) the data controller must as soon as reasonably practicable notify the individual that the decision was taken on that basis, and

(b) the individual is entitled, within twenty-one days of receiving that notification from the data controller, by notice in writing to require the data controller to reconsider the decision or to take a new decision otherwise than on that basis.

(3) The data controller must, within twenty-one days of receiving a notice under subsection (2)(b) ("the data subject notice") give the individual a written notice specifying the steps that he intends to take to comply with the data subject notice.

(4) A notice under subsection (1) does not have effect in relation to an exempt decision; and nothing in subsection (2) applies to an exempt decision.

(5) In subsection (4) "exempt decision" means any decision—

(a) in respect of which the condition in subsection (6) and the condition in subsection (7) are met, or

(b) which is made in such other circumstances as may be prescribed by the [Secretary of State] by order.

(6) The condition in this subsection is that the decision—

(a) is taken in the course of steps taken—

(i) for the purpose of considering whether to enter into a contract with the data subject,

(ii) with a view to entering into such a contract, or

(iii) in the course of performing such a contract, or

(b) is authorised or required by or under any enactment.

(7) The condition in this subsection is that either—

(a) the effect of the decision is to grant a request of the data subject, or

(b) steps have been taken to safeguard the legitimate interests of the data subject (for example, by allowing him to make representations).

(8) If a court is satisfied on the application of a data subject that a person taking a decision in respect of him ("the responsible person") has failed to comply with subsection (1) or (2)(b), the court may order the responsible person to reconsider the decision, or to take a new decision which is not based solely on such processing as is mentioned in subsection (1).

(9) An order under subsection (8) shall not affect the rights of any person other than the data subject and the responsible person.

[1119]

NOTES

Commencement: 1 March 2000 (16 July 1998: sub-s (5) insofar as conferring a power to make subordinate legislation).

Sub-s (5): words in square brackets in para (b) substituted by the Secretary of State for Constitutional Affairs Order 2003, SI 2003/1887, art 9, Sch 2, para 9(1)(a).

[12A Rights of data subjects in relation to exempt manual data

(1) A data subject is entitled at any time by notice in writing—

(a) to require the data controller to rectify, block, erase or destroy exempt manual data which are inaccurate or incomplete, or

(b) to require the data controller to cease holding exempt manual data in a way incompatible with the legitimate purposes pursued by the data controller.

(2) A notice under subsection (1)(a) or (b) must state the data subject's reasons for believing that the data are inaccurate or incomplete or, as the case may be, his reasons for believing that they are held in a way incompatible with the legitimate purposes pursued by the data controller.

(3) If the court is satisfied, on the application of any person who has given a notice under subsection (1) which appears to the court to be justified (or to be justified to any extent) that the data controller in question has failed to comply with the notice, the court may order him to take such steps for complying with the notice (or for complying with it to that extent) as the court thinks fit.

(4) In this section "exempt manual data" means—

(a) in relation to the first transitional period, as defined by paragraph 1(2) of Schedule 8, data to which paragraph 3 or 4 of that Schedule applies, and

(b) in relation to the second transitional period, as so defined, data to which paragraph 14 [or 14A] of that Schedule applies.

(5) For the purposes of this section personal data are incomplete if, and only if, the data, although not inaccurate, are such that their incompleteness would constitute a contravention of the third or fourth data protection principles, if those principles applied to the data.]

[1120]

NOTES

Commencement: 1 March 2000.

Inserted by s 72, Sch 13, para 1 of this Act, to have effect during the period beginning with the commencement of s 72 and ending on 23 October 2007; see s 72 at **[1179]**.

Sub-s (4): words in square brackets inserted by virtue of the Freedom of Information Act 2000, s 70(4).

13 Compensation for failure to comply with certain requirements

(1) An individual who suffers damage by reason of any contravention by a data controller of any of the requirements of this Act is entitled to compensation from the data controller for that damage.

(2) An individual who suffers distress by reason of any contravention by a data controller of any of the requirements of this Act is entitled to compensation from the data controller for that distress if—

(a) the individual also suffers damage by reason of the contravention, or

(b) the contravention relates to the processing of personal data for the special purposes.

(3) In proceedings brought against a person by virtue of this section it is a defence to prove that he had taken such care as in all the circumstances was reasonably required to comply with the requirement concerned.

[1121]

NOTES

Commencement: 1 March 2000.

14 Rectification, blocking, erasure and destruction

(1) If a court is satisfied on the application of a data subject that personal data of which the applicant is the subject are inaccurate, the court may order the data controller to rectify, block, erase or destroy those data and any other personal data in respect of which he is the data controller and which contain an expression of opinion which appears to the court to be based on the inaccurate data.

(2) Subsection (1) applies whether or not the data accurately record information received or obtained by the data controller from the data subject or a third party but where the data accurately record such information, then—

(a) if the requirements mentioned in paragraph 7 of Part II of Schedule 1 have been complied with, the court may, instead of making an order under subsection (1), make an order requiring the data to be supplemented by such statement of the true facts relating to the matters dealt with by the data as the court may approve, and

(b) if all or any of those requirements have not been complied with, the court may, instead of making an order under that subsection, make such order as it thinks fit for securing compliance with those requirements with or without a further order requiring the data to be supplemented by such a statement as is mentioned in paragraph (a).

(3) Where the court

(a) makes an order under subsection (1), or

(b) is satisfied on the application of a data subject that personal data of which he was the data subject and which have been rectified, blocked, erased or destroyed were inaccurate,

it may, where it considers it reasonably practicable, order the data controller to notify third parties to whom the data have been disclosed of the rectification, blocking, erasure or destruction.

(4) If a court is satisfied on the application of a data subject—

(a) that he has suffered damage by reason of any contravention by a data controller of any of the requirements of this Act in respect of any personal data, in circumstances entitling him to compensation under section 13, and

(b) that there is a substantial risk of further contravention in respect of those data in such circumstances,

the court may order the rectification, blocking, erasure or destruction of any of those data.

(5) Where the court makes an order under subsection (4) it may, where it considers it reasonably practicable, order the data controller to notify third parties to whom the data have been disclosed of the rectification, blocking, erasure or destruction.

(6) In determining whether it is reasonably practicable to require such notification as is mentioned in subsection (3) or (5) the court shall have regard, in particular, to the number of persons who would have to be notified.

[1122]

NOTES

Commencement: 1 March 2000.

15 Jurisdiction and procedure

(1) The jurisdiction conferred by sections 7 to 14 is exercisable by the High Court or a county court or, in Scotland, by the Court of Session or the sheriff.

(2) For the purpose of determining any question whether an applicant under subsection (9) of section 7 is entitled to the information which he seeks (including any question whether any relevant data are exempt from that section by virtue of Part IV) a court may require the information constituting any data processed by or on behalf of the data controller and any information as to the logic involved in any decision-taking as mentioned in section 7(1)(d) to be made available for its own inspection but shall not, pending the determination of that question in the applicant's favour, require the information sought by the applicant to be disclosed to him or his representatives whether by discovery (or, in Scotland, recovery) or otherwise.

[1123]

NOTES

Commencement: 1 March 2000.

PART III
NOTIFICATION BY DATA CONTROLLERS

16 Preliminary

(1) In this Part "the registrable particulars", in relation to a data controller, means—

(a) his name and address,

(b) if he has nominated a representative for the purposes of this Act, the name and address of the representative,

(c) a description of the personal data being or to be processed by or on behalf of the data controller and of the category or categories of data subject to which they relate,

(d) a description of the purpose or purposes for which the data are being or are to be processed,

(e) a description of any recipient or recipients to whom the data controller intends or may wish to disclose the data,

(f) the names, or a description of, any countries or territories outside the European Economic Area to which the data controller directly or indirectly transfers, or intends or may wish directly or indirectly to transfer, the data,

[(ff) where the data controller is a public authority, a statement of that fact,] and

(g) in any case where—

(i) personal data are being, or are intended to be, processed in circumstances in which the prohibition in subsection (1) of section 17 is excluded by subsection (2) or (3) of that section, and

(ii) the notification does not extend to those data,

a statement of that fact.

(2) In this Part—

"fees regulations" means regulations made by the [Secretary of State] under section 18(5) or 19(4) or (7);

"notification regulations" means regulations made by the [Secretary of State] under the other provisions of this Part;

"prescribed", except where used in relation to fees regulations, means prescribed by notification regulations.

(3) For the purposes of this Part, so far as it relates to the addresses of data controllers—

(a) the address of a registered company is that of its registered office, and

(b) the address of a person (other than a registered company) carrying on a business is that of his principal place of business in the United Kingdom.

[1124]

NOTES

Commencement: 1 March 2000.

Sub-s (1): para (ff) inserted by the Freedom of Information Act 2000, s 71.

Sub-s (2): words in square brackets substituted by the Secretary of State for Constitutional Affairs Order 2003, SI 2003/1887, art 9, Sch 2, para 9(1)(a).

17 Prohibition on processing without registration

(1) Subject to the following provisions of this section, personal data must not be processed unless an entry in respect of the data controller is included in the register maintained by the Commissioner under section 19 (or is treated by notification regulations made by virtue of section 19(3) as being so included).

(2) Except where the processing is assessable processing for the purposes of section 22, subsection (1) does not apply in relation to personal data consisting of information which falls neither within paragraph (a) of the definition of "data" in section 1(1) nor within paragraph (b) of that definition.

(3) If it appears to the [Secretary of State] that processing of a particular description is unlikely to prejudice the rights and freedoms of data subjects, notification regulations may provide that, in such cases as may be prescribed, subsection (1) is not to apply in relation to processing of that description.

(4) Subsection (1) does not apply in relation to any processing whose sole purpose is the maintenance of a public register.

[1125]

NOTES

Sub-s (3): words in square brackets substituted by the Secretary of State for Constitutional Affairs Order 2003, SI 2003/1887, art 9, Sch 2, para 9(1)(a).

Regulations: the Data Protection (Notification and Notification Fees) Regulations 2000, SI 2000/188 at **[3290]**.

18 Notification by data controllers

(1) Any data controller who wishes to be included in the register maintained under section 19 shall give a notification to the Commissioner under this section.

(2) A notification under this section must specify in accordance with notification regulations—

(a) the registrable particulars, and

(b) a general description of measures to be taken for the purpose of complying with the seventh data protection principle.

(3) Notification regulations made by virtue of subsection (2) may provide for the determination by the Commissioner, in accordance with any requirements of the regulations, of the form in which the registrable particulars and the description mentioned in subsection (2)(b) are to be specified, including in particular the detail required for the purposes of section 16(1)(c), (d), (e) and (f) and subsection (2)(b).

(4) Notification regulations may make provision as to the giving of notification—

(a) by partnerships, or

(b) in other cases where two or more persons are the data controllers in respect of any personal data.

(5) The notification must be accompanied by such fee as may be prescribed by fees regulations.

(6) Notification regulations may provide for any fee paid under subsection (5) or section 19(4) to be refunded in prescribed circumstances.

[1126]

NOTES

Commencement: 1 March 2000 (16 July 1998: sub-ss (2), (4)–(6) insofar as conferring a power to make subordinate legislation).

Regulations: the Data Protection (Notification and Notification Fees) Regulations 2000, SI 2000/188 at **[3290]**.

19 Register of notifications

(1) The Commissioner shall—

(a) maintain a register of persons who have given notification under section 18, and

(b) make an entry in the register in pursuance of each notification received by him under that section from a person in respect of whom no entry as data controller was for the time being included in the register.

(2) Each entry in the register shall consist of—

(a) the registrable particulars notified under section 18 or, as the case requires, those particulars as amended in pursuance of section 20(4), and

(b) such other information as the Commissioner may be authorised or required by notification regulations to include in the register.

(3) Notification regulations may make provision as to the time as from which any entry in respect of a data controller is to be treated for the purposes of section 17 as having been made in the register.

(4) No entry shall be retained in the register for more than the relevant time except on payment of such fee as may be prescribed by fees regulations.

(5) In subsection (4) "the relevant time" means twelve months or such other period as may be prescribed by notification regulations; and different periods may be prescribed in relation to different cases.

(6) The Commissioner—

(a) shall provide facilities for making the information contained in the entries in the register available for inspection (in visible and legible form) by members of the public at all reasonable hours and free of charge, and

(b) may provide such other facilities for making the information contained in those entries available to the public free of charge as he considers appropriate.

(7) The Commissioner shall, on payment of such fee, if any, as may be prescribed by fees regulations, supply any member of the public with a duly certified copy in writing of the particulars contained in any entry made in the register.

[1127]

NOTES

Commencement: 1 March 2000 (16 July 1998: sub-ss (3), (4), (7) insofar as conferring a power to make subordinate legislation).

Regulations: the Data Protection (Fees under section 19(7)) Regulations 2000, SI 2000/187; the Data Protection (Notification and Notification Fees) Regulations 2000, SI 2000/188 at **[3290]**.

20 Duty to notify changes

(1) For the purpose specified in subsection (2), notification regulations shall include provision imposing on every person in respect of whom an entry as a data controller is for the time being included in the register maintained under section 19 a duty to notify to the Commissioner, in such circumstances and at such time or times and in such form as may be prescribed, such matters relating to the registrable particulars and measures taken as mentioned in section 18(2)(b) as may be prescribed.

(2) The purpose referred to in subsection (1) is that of ensuring, so far as practicable, that at any time—

(a) the entries in the register maintained under section 19 contain current names and addresses and describe the current practice or intentions of the data controller with respect to the processing of personal data, and

(b) the Commissioner is provided with a general description of measures currently being taken as mentioned in section 18(2)(b).

(3) Subsection (3) of section 18 has effect in relation to notification regulations made by virtue of subsection (1) as it has effect in relation to notification regulations made by virtue of subsection (2) of that section.

(4) On receiving any notification under notification regulations made by virtue of subsection (1), the Commissioner shall make such amendments of the relevant entry in the register maintained under section 19 as are necessary to take account of the notification.

[1128]

NOTES

Commencement: 1 March 2000 (16 July 1998: sub-s (1) insofar as conferring a power to make subordinate legislation).

Regulations: the Data Protection (Notification and Notification Fees) Regulations 2000, SI 2000/188 at **[3290]**.

21 Offences

(1) If section 17(1) is contravened, the data controller is guilty of an offence.

(2) Any person who fails to comply with the duty imposed by notification regulations made by virtue of section 20(1) is guilty of an offence.

(3) It shall be a defence for a person charged with an offence under subsection (2) to show that he exercised all due diligence to comply with the duty.

[1129]

NOTES

Commencement: 1 March 2000.

22 Preliminary assessment by Commissioner

(1) In this section "assessable processing" means processing which is of a description specified in an order made by the [Secretary of State] as appearing to him to be particularly likely—

(a) to cause substantial damage or substantial distress to data subjects, or
(b) otherwise significantly to prejudice the rights and freedoms of data subjects.

(2) On receiving notification from any data controller under section 18 or under notification regulations made by virtue of section 20 the Commissioner shall consider—

(a) whether any of the processing to which the notification relates is assessable processing, and
(b) if so, whether the assessable processing is likely to comply with the provisions of this Act.

(3) Subject to subsection (4), the Commissioner shall, within the period of twenty-eight days beginning with the day on which he receives a notification which relates to assessable processing, give a notice to the data controller stating the extent to which the Commissioner is of the opinion that the processing is likely or unlikely to comply with the provisions of this Act.

(4) Before the end of the period referred to in subsection (3) the Commissioner may, by reason of special circumstances, extend that period on one occasion only by notice to the data controller by such further period not exceeding fourteen days as the Commissioner may specify in the notice.

(5) No assessable processing in respect of which a notification has been given the Commissioner as mentioned in subsection (2) shall be carried on unless either—

(a) the period of twenty-eight days beginning with the day on which the notification is received by the Commissioner (or, in a case falling within subsection (4), that period as extended under that subsection) has elapsed, or
(b) before the end of that period (or that period as so extended) the data controller has received a notice from the Commissioner under subsection (3) in respect of the processing.

(6) Where subsection (5) is contravened, the data controller is guilty of an offence.

(7) The [Secretary of State] may by order amend subsections (3), (4) and (5) by substituting for the number of days for the time being specified there a different number specified in the order.

[1130]

NOTES

Commencement: 1 March 2000 (16 July 1998: sub-ss (1), (7) insofar as conferring a power to make subordinate legislation).

Sub-ss (1), (7): words in square brackets substituted by the Secretary of State for Constitutional Affairs Order 2003, SI 2003/1887, art 9, Sch 2, para 9(1)(a).

23 Power to make provision for appointment of data protection supervisors

(1) The [Secretary of State] may by order—

(a) make provision under which a data controller may appoint a person to act as a data protection supervisor responsible in particular for monitoring in an independent manner the data controller's compliance with the provisions of this Act, and

(b) provide that, in relation to any data controller who has appointed a data protection supervisor in accordance with the provisions of the order and who complies with such conditions as may be specified in the order, the provisions of this Part are to have effect subject to such exemptions or other modifications as may be specified in the order.

(2) An order under this section may—

(a) impose duties on data protection supervisors in relation to the Commissioner, and

(b) confer functions on the Commissioner in relation to data protection supervisors.

[1131]

NOTES

Commencement: 1 March 2000 (16 July 1998 (sub-s (1) insofar as conferring a power to make subordinate legislation).

Sub-s (1): words in square brackets substituted by the Secretary of State for Constitutional Affairs Order 2003, SI 2003/1887, art 9, Sch 2, para 9(1)(a).

24 Duty of certain data controllers to make certain information available

(1) Subject to subsection (3), where personal data are processed in a case where—

(a) by virtue of subsection (2) or (3) of section 17, subsection (1) of that section does not apply to the processing, and

(b) the data controller has not notified the relevant particulars in respect of that processing under section 18,

the data controller must, within twenty-one days of receiving a written request from any person, make the relevant particulars available to that person in writing free of charge.

(2) In this section "the relevant particulars" means the particulars referred to in paragraphs (a) to (f) of section 16(1).

(3) This section has effect subject to any exemption conferred for the purposes of this section by notification regulations.

(4) Any data controller who fails to comply with the duty imposed by subsection (1) is guilty of an offence.

(5) It shall be a defence for a person charged with an offence under subsection (4) to show that he exercised all due diligence to comply with the duty.

[1132]

NOTES

Commencement: 1 March 2000 (16 July 1998: sub-s (3) insofar as conferring a power to make subordinate legislation).

25 Functions of Commissioner in relation to making of notification regulations

(1) As soon as practicable after the passing of this Act, the Commissioner shall submit to the Secretary of State proposals as to the provisions to be included in the first notification regulations.

(2) The Commissioner shall keep under review the working of notification regulations and may from time to time submit to the [Secretary of State] proposals as to amendments to be made to the regulations.

(3) The [Secretary of State] may from time to time require the Commissioner to consider any matter relating to notification regulations and to submit to him proposals as to amendments to be made to the regulations in connection with that matter.

(4) Before making any notification regulations, the [Secretary of State] shall—

(a) consider any proposals made to him by the Commissioner under [subsection (2) or (3)], and

(b) consult the Commissioner.

[1133]

NOTES

Commencement: 1 March 2000 (sub-ss (2), (3)); 16 July 1998 (remainder).

Sub-ss (2), (3): words in square brackets substituted by the Secretary of State for Constitutional Affairs Order 2003, SI 2003/1887, art 9, Sch 2, para 9(1)(a).

Sub-s (4): words in first pair of square brackets substituted by SI 2003/1887, art 9, Sch 2, para 9(1)(a); words in second pair of square brackets substituted by the Transfer of Functions (Miscellaneous) Order 2001, SI 2001/3500, art 8, Sch 2, Pt I, para 6(2).

26 Fees regulations

(1) Fees regulations prescribing fees for the purposes of any provision of this Part may provide for different fees to be payable in different cases.

(2) In making any fees regulations, the [Secretary of State] shall have regard to the desirability of securing that the fees payable to the Commissioner are sufficient to offset—

(a) the expenses incurred by the Commissioner and the Tribunal in discharging their functions [under this Act] and any expenses of the [Secretary of State] in respect of the Commissioner or the Tribunal [so far as attributable to their functions under this Act], and

(b) to the extent that the [Secretary of State] considers appropriate—

(i) any deficit previously incurred (whether before or after the passing of this Act) in respect of the expenses mentioned in paragraph (a), and

(ii) expenses incurred or to be incurred by the [Secretary of State] in respect of the inclusion of any officers or staff of the Commissioner in any scheme under section 1 of the Superannuation Act 1972.

[1134]

NOTES

Commencement: 16 July 1998.

Sub-s (2): words in first, third, fifth and sixth pair of square brackets substituted by the Secretary of State for Constitutional Affairs Order 2003, SI 2003/1887, art 9, Sch 2, para 9(1)(a); words in second and fourth pairs of square brackets inserted by the Freedom of Information Act 2000, s 18(4), Sch 2, Pt II, para 17.

Regulations: the Data Protection (Notification and Notification Fees) Regulations 2000, SI 2000/188 at **[3290]**.

PART IV
EXEMPTIONS

27 Preliminary

(1) References in any of the data protection principles or any provision of Parts II and III to personal data or to the processing of personal data do not include references to data or processing which by virtue of this Part are exempt from that principle or other provision.

(2) In this Part "the subject information provisions" means—

(a) the first data protection principle to the extent to which it requires compliance with paragraph 2 of Part II of Schedule 1, and

(b) section 7.

(3) In this Part "the non-disclosure provisions" means the provisions specified in subsection (4) to the extent to which they are inconsistent with the disclosure in question.

(4) The provisions referred to in subsection (3) are—

(a) the first data protection principle, except to the extent to which it requires compliance with the conditions in Schedules 2 and 3,

(b) the second, third, fourth and fifth data protection principles, and

(c) sections 10 and 14(1) to (3).

(5) Except as provided by this Part, the subject information provisions shall have effect notwithstanding any enactment or rule of law prohibiting or restricting the disclosure, or authorising the withholding, of information.

[1135]

NOTES

Commencement: 1 March 2000.

28 National security

(1) Personal data are exempt from any of the provisions of—

(a) the data protection principles,

(b) Parts II, III and V, and

(c) [sections 54A and] 55,

if the exemption from that provision is required for the purpose of safeguarding national security.

(2) Subject to subsection (4), a certificate signed by a Minister of the Crown certifying that exemption from all or any of the provisions mentioned in subsection (1) is or at any time was required for the purpose there mentioned in respect of any personal data shall be conclusive evidence of that fact.

(3) A certificate under subsection (2) may identify the personal data to which it applies by means of a general description and may be expressed to have prospective effect.

(4) Any person directly affected by the issuing of a certificate under subsection (2) may appeal to the Tribunal against the certificate.

(5) If on an appeal under subsection (4), the Tribunal finds that, applying the principles applied by the court on an application for judicial review, the Minister did not have reasonable grounds for issuing the certificate, the Tribunal may allow the appeal and quash the certificate.

(6) Where in any proceedings under or by virtue of this Act it is claimed by a data controller that a certificate under subsection (2) which identifies the personal data to which it applies by means of a general description applies to any personal data, any other party to the proceedings may appeal to the Tribunal on the ground that the certificate does not apply to the personal data in question and, subject to any determination under subsection (7), the certificate shall be conclusively presumed so to apply.

(7) On any appeal under subsection (6), the Tribunal may determine that the certificate does not so apply.

(8) A document purporting to be a certificate under subsection (2) shall be received in evidence and deemed to be such a certificate unless the contrary is proved.

(9) A document which purports to be certified by or on behalf of a Minister of the Crown as a true copy of a certificate issued by that Minister under subsection (2) shall in any legal proceedings be evidence (or, in Scotland, sufficient evidence) of that certificate.

(10) The power conferred by subsection (2) on a Minister of the Crown shall not be exercisable except by a Minister who is a member of the Cabinet or by the Attorney General or the [Advocate General for Scotland].

(11) No power conferred by any provision of Part V may be exercised in relation to personal data which by virtue of this section are exempt from that provision.

(12) Schedule 6 shall have effect in relation to appeals under subsection (4) or (6) and the proceedings of the Tribunal in respect of any such appeal.

[1136]

NOTES

Commencement: 1 March 2000.

Sub-s (1): words in square brackets substituted by the Crime (International Co-operation) Act 2003, s 91(1), Sch 5, paras 68, 69.

Sub-s (10): words in square brackets substituted by the Transfer of Functions (Lord Advocate and Advocate General for Scotland) Order 1999, SI 1999/679, art 2, Schedule.

29 Crime and taxation

(1) Personal data processed for any of the following purposes—

(a) the prevention or detection of crime,

(b) the apprehension or prosecution of offenders, or

(c) the assessment or collection of any tax or duty or of any imposition of a similar nature,

are exempt from the first data protection principle (except to the extent to which it requires compliance with the conditions in Schedules 2 and 3) and section 7 in any case to the extent to which the application of those provisions to the data would be likely to prejudice any of the matters mentioned in this subsection.

(2) Personal data which—

(a) are processed for the purpose of discharging statutory functions, and

(b) consist of information obtained for such a purpose from a person who had it in his possession for any of the purposes mentioned in subsection (1),

are exempt from the subject information provisions to the same extent as personal data processed for any of the purposes mentioned in that subsection.

(3) Personal data are exempt from the non-disclosure provisions in any case in which—

(a) the disclosure is for any of the purposes mentioned in subsection (1), and

(b) the application of those provisions in relation to the disclosure would be likely to prejudice any of the matters mentioned in that subsection.

(4) Personal data in respect of which the data controller is a relevant authority and which—

(a) consist of a classification applied to the data subject as part of a system of risk assessment which is operated by that authority for either of the following purposes—

(i) the assessment or collection of any tax or duty or any imposition of a similar nature, or

(ii) the prevention or detection of crime, or apprehension or prosecution of offenders, where the offence concerned involves any unlawful claim for any payment out of, or any unlawful application of, public funds, and

(b) are processed for either of those purposes,

are exempt from section 7 to the extent to which the exemption is required in the interests of the operation of the system.

(5) In subsection (4)—

"public funds" includes funds provided by any Community institution; "relevant authority" means—

(a) a government department,

(b) a local authority, or

(c) any other authority administering housing benefit or council tax benefit.

[1137]

NOTES

Commencement: 1 March 2000.

30 Health, education and social work

(1) The [Secretary of State] may by order exempt from the subject information provisions, or modify those provisions in relation to, personal data consisting of information as to the physical or mental health or condition of the data subject.

(2) The [Secretary of State] may by order exempt from the subject information provisions, or modify those provisions in relation to—
- (a) personal data in respect of which the data controller is the proprietor of, or a teacher at, a school, and which consist of information relating to persons who are or have been pupils at the school, or
- (b) personal data in respect of which the data controller is an education authority in Scotland, and which consist of information relating to persons who are receiving, or have received, further education provided by the authority.

(3) The [Secretary of State] may by order exempt from the subject information provisions, or modify those provisions in relation to, personal data of such other descriptions as may be specified in the order, being information—
- (a) processed by government departments or local authorities or by voluntary organisations or other bodies designated by or under the order, and
- (b) appearing to him to be processed in the course of, or for the purposes of, carrying out social work in relation to the data subject or other individuals;

but the [Secretary of State] shall not under this subsection confer any exemption or make any modification except so far as he considers that the application to the data of those provisions (or of those provisions without modification) would be likely to prejudice the carrying out of social work.

(4) An order under this section may make different provision in relation to data consisting of information of different descriptions.

(5) In this section—

"education authority" and "further education" have the same meaning as in the Education (Scotland) Act 1980 ("the 1980 Act"), and

"proprietor"—
- (a) in relation to a school in England or Wales, has the same meaning as in the Education Act 1996,
- (b) in relation to a school in Scotland, means—
  - (i) …
  - (ii) in the case of an independent school, the proprietor within the meaning of the 1980 Act,
  - (iii) in the case of a grant-aided school, the managers within the meaning of the 1980 Act, and
  - (iv) in the case of a public school, the education authority within the meaning of the 1980 Act, and
- (c) in relation to a school in Northern Ireland, has the same meaning as in the Education and Libraries (Northern Ireland) Order 1986 and includes, in the case of a controlled school, the Board of Governors of the school.

[1138]

NOTES

Commencement: 1 March 2000 (16 July 1998: sub-ss (1)–(3) insofar as conferring a power to make subordinate legislation).

Sub-ss (1)–(3): words in square brackets substituted by the Secretary of State for Constitutional Affairs Order 2003, SI 2003/1887, art 9, Sch 2, para 9(1)(a).

Sub-s (5): in definition "proprietor" para (b)(i) repealed by the Standards in Scotland's Schools etc Act 2000, s 60(2), Sch 3.

Transfer of functions: the National Assembly for Wales (Transfer of Functions) Order 1999, SI 1999/672, art 2(a), Sch 1 provided that, subject to art 2(b)–(f), all functions of a Minister of the Crown under this section were, in so far as exercisable in relation to Wales, transferred to the National Assembly for Wales. As a consequence of the amendment of Sch 1 to the 1999 Order by the National Assembly for Wales (Transfer of Functions) Order 2000, SI 2000/253, art 4, Sch 3(g), the functions transferred to the Assembly by the 1999 Order ceased to be exercisable by the Assembly and instead (by virtue of art 5 of the 2000 Order) became exercisable by the Minister of the Crown by whom they were exercisable, in relation to Wales, immediately before 1 July 1999.

Orders: the Data Protection (Subject Access Modification) (Health) Order 2000, SI 2000/413; the Data Protection (Subject Access Modification) (Education) Order 2000, SI 2000/414; the Data Protection (Subject Access Modification) (Social Work) Order 2000, SI 2000/415 at **[3340]**.

31 Regulatory activity

(1) Personal data processed for the purposes of discharging functions to which this subsection applies are exempt from the subject information provisions in any case to the extent to which the application of those provisions to the data would be likely to prejudice the proper discharge of those functions.

(2) Subsection (1) applies to any relevant function which is designed—
(a) for protecting members of the public against—
(i) financial loss due to dishonesty, malpractice or other seriously improper conduct by, or the unfitness or incompetence of, persons concerned in the provision of banking, insurance, investment or other financial services or in the management of bodies corporate,
(ii) financial loss due to the conduct of discharged or undischarged bankrupts, or
(iii) dishonesty, malpractice or other seriously improper conduct by, or the unfitness or incompetence of, persons authorised to carry on any profession or other activity,
(b) for protecting charities [or community interest companies] against misconduct or mismanagement (whether by trustees[, directors] or other persons) in their administration,
(c) for protecting the property of charities [or community interest companies] from loss or misapplication,
(d) for the recovery of the property of charities [or community interest companies],
(e) for securing the health, safety and welfare of persons at work, or
(f) for protecting persons other than persons at work against risk to health or safety arising out of or in connection with the actions of persons at work.

(3) In subsection (2) "relevant function" means—
(a) any function conferred on any person by or under any enactment,
(b) any function of the Crown, a Minister of the Crown or a government department, or
(c) any other function which is of a public nature and is exercised in the public interest.

(4) Personal data processed for the purpose of discharging any function which—
(a) is conferred by or under any enactment on—
(i) the Parliamentary Commissioner for Administration,
(ii) the Commission for Local Administration in England […] … ,
(iii) the Health Service Commissioner for England […] … ,
[(iv) the Public Services Ombudsman for Wales,]
(v) the Assembly Ombudsman for Northern Ireland, …
(vi) the Northern Ireland Commissioner for Complaints, [or]
[(vii) the Scottish Public Services Ombudsman, and]
(b) is designed for protecting members of the public against—
(i) maladministration by public bodies,
(ii) failures in services provided by public bodies, or
(iii) a failure of a public body to provide a service which it was a function of the body to provide,

are exempt from the subject information provisions in any case to the extent to which the application of those provisions to the data would be likely to prejudice the proper discharge of that function.

[(4A) Personal data processed for the purpose of discharging any function which is conferred by or under Part XVI of the Financial Services and Markets Act 2000 on the body established by the Financial Services Authority for the purposes of that Part are exempt from the subject information provisions in any case to the extent to which the application of those provisions to the data would be likely to prejudice the proper discharge of the function.]

(5) Personal data processed for the purpose of discharging any function which—
(a) is conferred by or under any enactment on [the Office of Fair Trading], and
(b) is designed—
(i) for protecting members of the public against conduct which may adversely affect their interests by persons carrying on a business,
(ii) for regulating agreements or conduct which have as their object or effect the prevention, restriction or distortion of competition in connection with any commercial activity, or
(iii) for regulating conduct on the part of one or more undertakings which amounts to the abuse of a dominant position in a market,

are exempt from the subject information provisions in any case to the extent to which the application of those provisions to the data would be likely to prejudice the proper discharge of that function.

[(5A) Personal data processed by a CPC enforcer for the purpose of discharging any function conferred on such a body by or under the CPC Regulation are exempt from the subject information provisions in any case to the extent to which the application of those provisions to the data would be likely to prejudice the proper discharge of that function.

(5B) In subsection (5A)—

(a) "CPC enforcer" has the meaning given to it in section 213(5A) of the Enterprise Act 2002 but does not include the Office of Fair Trading;

(b) "CPC Regulation" has the meaning given to it in section 235A of that Act.]

[(6) Personal data processed for the purpose of the function of considering a complaint under [section 14 of the NHS Redress Act 2006,] section 113(1) or (2) or 114(1) or (3) of the Health and Social Care (Community Health and Standards) Act 2003, or section 24D, 26, *26ZA* or 26ZB of the Children Act 1989, are exempt from the subject information provisions in any case to the extent to which the application of those provisions to the data would be likely to prejudice the proper discharge of that function.]

[1139]

NOTES

Commencement: 1 March 2000.

Sub-s (2): words in square brackets inserted by the Companies (Audit, Investigations and Community Enterprise) Act 2004, s 59(3).

Sub-s (4): in para (a)(ii), word omitted from square brackets (as inserted by the Scottish Public Services Ombudsman Act 2002 (Consequential Provisions and Modifications) Order 2004, SI 2004/1823, art 19(a)(i)) repealed by the Public Services Ombudsman (Wales) Act 2005, s 39, Sch 6, para 60(a), Sch 7, and other words omitted repealed by SI 2004/1823, art 19(a)(ii) and the Public Services Ombudsman (Wales) Act 2005, s 39, Sch 6, para 60(a), Sch 7; in para (a)(iii), word omitted from square brackets (as inserted by SI 2004/1823, art 19(b)(i)) repealed by the Public Services Ombudsman (Wales) Act 2005, s 39, Sch 6, para 60(b), Sch 7, and other words omitted repealed by SI 2004/1823, art 19(b)(ii) and the Public Services Ombudsman (Wales) Act 2005, s 39, Sch 6, para 60(b), Sch 7; para (a)(iv) substituted by the Public Services Ombudsman (Wales) Act 2005, s 39(1), Sch 6, para 60(c); word omitted from para (a)(v) repealed, word in square brackets in para (a)(vi) substituted and para (a)(vii) inserted by SI 2004/1823, art 19(c)–(e). For transitional provisions in connection with the amendments made by Public Services Ombudsman (Wales) Act 2005, see the Public Services Ombudsman (Wales) Act 2005 (Commencement No 1 and Transitional Provisions and Savings) Order 2005, SI 2005/2800, arts 6, 7.

Sub-s (4A): inserted by the Financial Services and Markets Act 2000, s 233.

Sub-s (5): words in square brackets substituted by the Enterprise Act 2002, s 278(1), Sch 25, para 37.

Sub-ss (5A), (5B): inserted by the Enterprise Act 2002 (Amendment) Regulations 2006, SI 2006/3363, reg 29.

Sub-s (6): inserted by the Health and Social Care (Community Health and Standards) Act 2003, s 119; words in square brackets inserted by the NHS Redress Act 2006, s 14(10), as from a day to be appointed; figure in italics repealed by the Education and Inspections Act 2006, ss 157, 184, Sch 14, para 32, Sch 18, Pt 5, as from a day to be appointed.

32 Journalism, literature and art

(1) Personal data which are processed only for the special purposes are exempt from any provision to which this subsection relates if—

(a) the processing is undertaken with a view to the publication by any person of any journalistic, literary or artistic material,

(b) the data controller reasonably believes that, having regard in particular to the special importance of the public interest in freedom of expression, publication would be in the public interest, and

(c) the data controller reasonably believes that, in all the circumstances, compliance with that provision is incompatible with the special purposes.

(2) Subsection (1) relates to the provisions of—

(a) the data protection principles except the seventh data protection principle,

(b) section 7,

(c) section 10,

(d) section 12, and

(e) section 14(1) to (3).

(3) In considering for the purposes of subsection (1)(b) whether the belief of a data controller that publication would be in the public interest was or is a reasonable one, regard may be had to his compliance with any code of practice which—

(a) is relevant to the publication in question, and

(b) is designated by the [Secretary of State] by order for the purposes of this subsection.

(4) Where at any time ("the relevant time") in any proceedings against a data controller under section 7(9), 10(4), 12(8) or 14 or by virtue of section 13 the data controller claims, or it appears to the court, that any personal data to which the proceedings relate are being processed—

(a) only for the special purposes, and

(b) with a view to the publication by any person of any journalistic, literary or artistic material which, at the time twenty-four hours immediately before the relevant time, had not previously been published by the data controller,

the court shall stay the proceedings until either of the conditions in subsection (5) is met.

(5) Those conditions are—

(a) that a determination of the Commissioner under section 45 with respect to the data in question takes effect, or

(b) in a case where the proceedings were stayed on the making of a claim, that the claim is withdrawn.

(6) For the purposes of this Act "publish", in relation to journalistic, literary or artistic material, means make available to the public or any section of the public.

[1140]

NOTES

Commencement: 1 March 2000 (16 July 1998: sub-s (3) insofar as conferring a power to make subordinate legislation).

Sub-s (3): words in square brackets in para (b) substituted by the Secretary of State for Constitutional Affairs Order 2003, SI 2003/1887, art 9, Sch 2, para 9(1)(a).

Modifications: by virtue of s 72 of, and Sch 13, para 2 to, this Act at **[1179]**, **[1202]**, for the period beginning with the commencement of s 72 of this Act (1 March 2000) and ending 23 October 2007, sub-s (2) above has effect with the following added after para (d)—

"(dd) section 12A,"

and sub-s (4) above has effect with the figure ", 12A(3)" inserted after "12(8)".

Orders: the Data Protection (Designated Codes of Practice) (No 2) Order 2000, SI 2000/1864.

33 Research, history and statistics

(1) In this section—

"research purposes" includes statistical or historical purposes;

"the relevant conditions", in relation to any processing of personal data, means the conditions—

(a) that the data are not processed to support measures or decisions with respect to particular individuals, and

(b) that the data are not processed in such a way that substantial damage or substantial distress is, or is likely to be, caused to any data subject.

(2) For the purposes of the second data protection principle, the further processing of personal data only for research purposes in compliance with the relevant conditions is not to be regarded as incompatible with the purposes for which they were obtained.

(3) Personal data which are processed only for research purposes in compliance with the relevant conditions may, notwithstanding the fifth data protection principle, be kept indefinitely.

(4) Personal data which are processed only for research purposes are exempt from section 7 if—

(a) they are processed in compliance with the relevant conditions, and

(b) the results of the research or any resulting statistics are not made available in a form which identifies data subjects or any of them.

(5) For the purposes of subsections (2) to (4) personal data are not to be treated as processed otherwise than for research purposes merely because the data are disclosed—

(a) to any person, for research purposes only,

(b) to the data subject or a person acting on his behalf,

(c) at the request, or with the consent, of the data subject or a person acting on his behalf, or

(d) in circumstances in which the person making the disclosure has reasonable grounds for believing that the disclosure falls within paragraph (a), (b) or (c).

[1141]

NOTES

Commencement: 1 March 2000.

[33A Manual data held by authorities

(1) Personal data falling within paragraph (e) of the definition of "data" in section 1(1) are exempt from—

(a) the first, second, third, fifth, seventh and eighth data protection principles,

(b) the sixth data protection principle except so far as it relates to the rights conferred on data subjects by sections 7 and 14,

(c) sections 10 to 12,

(d) section 13, except so far as it relates to damage caused by a contravention of section 7 or of the fourth data protection principle and to any distress which is also suffered by reason of that contravention,

(e) Part III, and

(f) section 55.

(2) Personal data which fall within paragraph (e) of the definition of "data" in section 1(1) and relate to appointments or removals, pay, discipline, superannuation or other personnel matters, in relation to—

(a) service in any of the armed forces of the Crown,

(b) service in any office or employment under the Crown or under any public authority, or

(c) service in any office or employment, or under any contract for services, in respect of which power to take action, or to determine or approve the action taken, in such matters is vested in Her Majesty, any Minister of the Crown, the National Assembly for Wales, any Northern Ireland Minister (within the meaning of the Freedom of Information Act 2000) or any public authority,

are also exempt from the remaining data protection principles and the remaining provisions of Part II.]

[1141A]

NOTES

Commencement: 1 January 2005.

Inserted by the Freedom of Information Act 2000, s 70(1).

34 Information available to the public by or under enactment

Personal data are exempt from—

(a) the subject information provisions,

(b) the fourth data protection principle and section 14(1) to (3), and

(c) the non-disclosure provisions,

if the data consist of information which the data controller is obliged by or under any enactment [other than an enactment contained in the Freedom of Information Act 2000] to make available to the public, whether by publishing it, by making it available for inspection, or otherwise and whether gratuitously or on payment of a fee.

[1142]

NOTES

Commencement: 1 March 2000.

Words in square brackets inserted by the Freedom of Information Act 2000, s 72.

Modification: for the period beginning with the commencement of s 72 of this Act (1 March 2000) and ending 23 October 2007, this section has effect with the words "sections 12A and 14(1) to (3)" substituted for the words "section 14(1) to (3)"; see s 72, Sch 13, para 3 at **[1179]**, **[1202]**.

35 Disclosures required by law or made in connection with legal proceedings etc

(1) Personal data are exempt from the non-disclosure provisions where the disclosure is required by or under any enactment, by any rule of law or by the order of a court.

(2) Personal data are exempt from the non-disclosure provisions where the disclosure is necessary—

(a) for the purpose of, or in connection with, any legal proceedings (including prospective legal proceedings), or

(b) for the purpose of obtaining legal advice,

or is otherwise necessary for the purposes of establishing, exercising or defending legal rights.

[1143]

NOTES

Commencement: 1 March 2000.

[35A Parliamentary Privilege

Personal data are exempt from—

(a) the first data protection principle, except to the extent to which it requires compliance with the conditions in Schedules 2 and 3,

(b) the second, third, fourth and fifth data protection principles,

(c) second 7, and

(d) sections 10 and 14(1) to (3),

if the exemption is required for the purpose of avoiding an infringement of the privileges of either House of Parliament.]

[1143A]

NOTES

Commencement: 1 January 2005.

Inserted by the Freedom of Information Act 2000, s 73, Sch 6, para 2.

36 Domestic purposes

Personal data processed by an individual only for the purposes of that individual's personal, family or household affairs (including recreational purposes) are exempt from the data protection principles and the provisions of Parts II and III.

[1144]

NOTES

Commencement: 1 March 2000.

37 Miscellaneous exemptions

Schedule 7 (which confers further miscellaneous exemptions) has effect.

[1145]

NOTES

Commencement: 1 March 2000.

38 Powers to make further exemptions by order

(1) The [Secretary of State] may by order exempt from the subject information provisions personal data consisting of information the disclosure of which is prohibited or restricted by or under any enactment if and to the extent that he considers it necessary for the safeguarding of the interests of the data subject or the rights and freedoms of any other individual that the prohibition or restriction ought to prevail over those provisions.

(2) The [Secretary of State] may by order exempt from the non-disclosure provisions any disclosures of personal data made in circumstances specified in the order, if he considers the exemption is necessary for the safeguarding of the interests of the data subject or the rights and freedoms of any other individual.

[1146]

NOTES

Commencement: 1 March 2000 (16 July 1998 insofar as conferring a power to make subordinate legislation).

Sub-ss (1), (2): words in square brackets substituted by the Secretary of State for Constitutional Affairs Order 2003, SI 2003/1887, art 9, Sch 2, para 9(1)(a).

Order: the Data Protection (Miscellaneous Subject Access Exemptions) Order 2000, SI 2000/419.

39 Transitional relief

Schedule 8 (which confers transitional exemptions) has effect.

[1147]

NOTES

Commencement: 1 March 2000.

PART V
ENFORCEMENT

40 Enforcement notices

(1) If the Commissioner is satisfied that a data controller has contravened or is contravening any of the data protection principles, the Commissioner may serve him with a notice (in this Act referred to as "an enforcement notice") requiring him, for complying with the principle or principles in question, to do either or both of the following—

(a) to take within such time as may be specified in the notice, or to refrain from taking after such time as may be so specified, such steps as are so specified, or

(b) to refrain from processing any personal data, or any personal data of a description specified in the notice, or to refrain from processing them for a purpose so specified or in a manner so specified, after such time as may be so specified.

(2) In deciding whether to serve an enforcement notice, the Commissioner shall consider whether the contravention has caused or is likely to cause any person damage or distress.

(3) An enforcement notice in respect of a contravention of the fourth data protection principle which requires the data controller to rectify, block, erase or destroy any inaccurate data may also require the data controller to rectify, block, erase or destroy any other data held by him and containing an expression of opinion which appears to the Commissioner to be based on the inaccurate data.

(4) An enforcement notice in respect of a contravention of the fourth data protection principle, in the case of data which accurately record information received or obtained by the data controller from the data subject or a third party, may require the data controller either—

(a) to rectify, block, erase or destroy any inaccurate data and any other data held by him and containing an expression of opinion as mentioned in subsection (3), or

(b) to take such steps as are specified in the notice for securing compliance with the requirements specified in paragraph 7 of Part II of Schedule 1 and, if the Commissioner thinks fit, for supplementing the data with such statement of the true facts relating to the matters dealt with by the data as the Commissioner may approve.

(5) Where—

(a) an enforcement notice requires the data controller to rectify, block, erase or destroy any personal data, or

(b) the Commissioner is satisfied that personal data which have been rectified, blocked, erased or destroyed had been processed in contravention of any of the data protection principles,

an enforcement notice may, if reasonably practicable, require the data controller to notify third parties to whom the data have been disclosed of the rectification, blocking, erasure or destruction; and in determining whether it is reasonably practicable to require such notification regard shall be had, in particular, to the number of persons who would have to be notified.

(6) An enforcement notice must contain—

(a) a statement of the data protection principle or principles which the Commissioner is satisfied have been or are being contravened and his reasons for reaching that conclusion, and

(b) particulars of the rights of appeal conferred by section 48.

(7) Subject to subsection (8), an enforcement notice must not require any of the provisions of the notice to be complied with before the end of the period within which an appeal can be brought against the notice and, if such an appeal is brought, the notice need not be complied with pending the determination or withdrawal of the appeal.

(8) If by reason of special circumstances the Commissioner considers that an enforcement notice should be complied with as a matter of urgency he may include in the notice a statement to that effect and a statement of his reasons for reaching that conclusion; and in that event subsection (7) shall not apply but the notice must not require the provisions of the notice to be complied with before the end of the period of seven days beginning with the day on which the notice is served.

(9) Notification regulations (as defined by section 16(2)) may make provision as to the effect of the service of an enforcement notice on any entry in the register maintained under section 19 which relates to the person on whom the notice is served.

(10) This section has effect subject to section 46(1).

[1148]

NOTES

Commencement: 1 March 2000 (16 July 1998: sub-s (9) insofar as conferring a power to make subordinate legislation).

41 Cancellation of an enforcement notice

(1) If the Commissioner considers that all or any of the provisions of an enforcement notice need not be complied with in order to ensure compliance with the data protection principle or principles to which it relates, he may cancel or vary the notice by written notice to the person on whom it was served.

(2) A person on whom an enforcement notice has been served may, at any time after the expiry of the period during which an appeal can be brought against that notice, apply in writing to the Commissioner for the cancellation or variation of that notice on the ground that, by reason of a change of circumstances, all or any of the provisions of that notice need not be complied with in order to ensure compliance with the data protection principle or principles to which that notice relates.

[1149]

NOTES

Commencement: 1 March 2000.

42 Request for assessment

(1) A request may be made to the Commissioner by or on behalf of any person who is, or believes himself to be, directly affected by any processing of personal data for an assessment as to whether it is likely or unlikely that the processing has been or is being carried out in compliance with the provisions of this Act.

(2) On receiving a request under this section, the Commissioner shall make an assessment in such manner as appears to him to be appropriate, unless he has not been supplied with such information as he may reasonably require in order to—

(a) satisfy himself as to the identity of the person making the request, and
(b) enable him to identify the processing in question.

(3) The matters to which the Commissioner may have regard in determining in what manner it is appropriate to make an assessment include—

(a) the extent to which the request appears to him to raise a matter of substance,
(b) any undue delay in making the request, and
(c) whether or not the person making the request is entitled to make an application under section 7 in respect of the personal data in question.

(4) Where the Commissioner has received a request under this section he shall notify the person who made the request—

(a) whether he has made an assessment as a result of the request, and
(b) to the extent that he considers appropriate, having regard in particular to any exemption from section 7 applying in relation to the personal data concerned, of any view formed or action taken as a result of the request.

[1150]

NOTES

Commencement: 1 March 2000.

43 Information notices

(1) If the Commissioner—

(a) has received a request under section 42 in respect of any processing of personal data, or

(b) reasonably requires any information for the purpose of determining whether the data controller has complied or is complying with the data protection principles,

he may serve the data controller with a notice (in this Act referred to as "an information notice") requiring the data controller, within such time as is specified in the notice, to furnish the Commissioner, in such form as may be so specified, with such information relating to the request or to compliance with the principles as is so specified.

(2) An information notice must contain—

(a) in a case falling within subsection (1)(a), a statement that the Commissioner has received a request under section 42 in relation to the specified processing, or

(b) in a case falling within subsection (1)(b), a statement that the Commissioner regards the specified information as relevant for the purpose of determining whether the data controller has complied, or is complying, with the data protection principles and his reasons for regarding it as relevant for that purpose.

(3) An information notice must also contain particulars of the rights of appeal conferred by section 48.

(4) Subject to subsection (5), the time specified in an information notice shall not expire before the end of the period within which an appeal can be brought against the notice and, if such an appeal is brought, the information need not be furnished pending the determination or withdrawal of the appeal.

(5) If by reason of special circumstances the Commissioner considers that the information is required as a matter of urgency, he may include in the notice a statement to that effect and a statement of his reasons for reaching that conclusion; and in that event subsection (4) shall not apply, but the notice shall not require the information to be furnished before the end of the period of seven days beginning with the day on which the notice is served.

(6) A person shall not be required by virtue of this section to furnish the Commissioner with any information in respect of—

(a) any communication between a professional legal adviser and his client in connection with the giving of legal advice to the client with respect to his obligations, liabilities or rights under this Act, or

(b) any communication between a professional legal adviser and his client, or between such an adviser or his client and any other person, made in connection with or in contemplation of proceedings under or arising out of this Act (including proceedings before the Tribunal) and for the purposes of such proceedings.

(7) In subsection (6) references to the client of a professional legal adviser include references to any person representing such a client.

(8) A person shall not be required by virtue of this section to furnish the Commissioner with any information if the furnishing of that information would, by revealing evidence of the commission of any offence other than an offence under this Act, expose him to proceedings for that offence.

(9) The Commissioner may cancel an information notice by written notice to the person on whom it was served.

(10) This section has effect subject to section 46(3).

[1151]

NOTES

Commencement: 1 March 2000.

44 Special information notices

If the Commissioner—

(a) has received a request under section 42 in respect of any processing of personal data, or

(b) has reasonable grounds for suspecting that, in a case in which proceedings have been stayed under section 32, the personal data to which the proceedings relate—

(i) are not being processed only for the special purposes, or

(ii) are not being processed with a view to the publication by any person of any journalistic, literary or artistic material which has not previously been published by the data controller,

he may serve the data controller with a notice (in this Act referred to as a "special information notice") requiring the data controller, within such time as is specified in the notice, to furnish the Commissioner, in such form as may be so specified, with such information as is so specified for the purpose specified in subsection (2).

(2) That purpose is the purpose of ascertaining—

(a) whether the personal data are being processed only for the special purposes, or

(b) whether they are being processed with a view to the publication by any person of any journalistic, literary or artistic material which has not previously been published by the data controller.

(3) A special information notice must contain—

(a) in a case falling within paragraph (a) of subsection (1), a statement that the Commissioner has received a request under section 42 in relation to the specified processing, or

(b) in a case falling within paragraph (b) of that subsection, a statement of the Commissioner's grounds for suspecting that the personal data are not being processed as mentioned in that paragraph.

(4) A special information notice must also contain particulars of the rights of appeal conferred by section 48.

(5) Subject to subsection (6), the time specified in a special information notice shall not expire before the end of the period within which an appeal can be brought against the notice and, if such an appeal is brought, the information need not be furnished pending the determination or withdrawal of the appeal.

(6) If by reason of special circumstances the Commissioner considers that the information is required as a matter of urgency, he may include in the notice a statement to that effect and a statement of his reasons for reaching that conclusion; and in that event subsection (5) shall not apply, but the notice shall not require the information to be furnished before the end of the period of seven days beginning with the day on which the notice is served.

(7) A person shall not be required by virtue of this section to furnish the Commissioner with any information in respect of—

(a) any communication between a professional legal adviser and his client in connection with the giving of legal advice to the client with respect to his obligations, liabilities or rights under this Act, or

(b) any communication between a professional legal adviser and his client, or between such an adviser or his client and any other person, made in connection with or in contemplation of proceedings under or arising out of this Act (including proceedings before the Tribunal) and for the purposes of such proceedings.

(8) In subsection (7) references to the client of a professional legal adviser include references to any person representing such a client.

(9) A person shall not be required by virtue of this section to furnish the Commissioner with any information if the furnishing of that information would, by revealing evidence of the commission of any offence other than an offence under this Act, expose him to proceedings for that offence.

(10) The Commissioner may cancel a special information notice by written notice to the person on whom it was served.

[1152]

NOTES

Commencement: 1 March 2000.

45 Determination by Commissioner as to the special purposes

(1) Where at any time it appears to the Commissioner (whether as a result of the service of a special information notice or otherwise) that any personal data—

(a) are not being processed only for the special purposes, or

(b) are not being processed with a view to the publication by any person of any journalistic, literary or artistic material which has not previously been published by the data controller, he may make a determination in writing to that effect.

(2) Notice of the determination shall be given to the data controller; and the notice must contain particulars of the right of appeal conferred by section 48.

(3) A determination under subsection (1) shall not take effect until the end of the period within which an appeal can be brought and, where an appeal is brought, shall not take effect pending the determination or withdrawal of the appeal.

[1153]

NOTES

Commencement: 1 March 2000.

46 Restriction on enforcement in case of processing for the special purposes

(1) The Commissioner may not at any time serve an enforcement notice on a data controller with respect to the processing of personal data for the special purposes unless—

(a) a determination under section 45(1) with respect to those data has taken effect, and

(b) the court has granted leave for the notice to be served.

(2) The court shall not grant leave for the purposes of subsection (1)(b) unless it is satisfied—

(a) that the Commissioner has reason to suspect a contravention of the data protection principles which is of substantial public importance, and

(b) except where the case is one of urgency, that the data controller has been given notice, in accordance with rules of court, of the application for leave.

(3) The Commissioner may not serve an information notice on a data controller with respect to the processing of personal data for the special purposes unless a determination under section 45(1) with respect to those data has taken effect.

[1154]

NOTES

Commencement: 1 March 2000.

47 Failure to comply with notice

(1) A person who fails to comply with an enforcement notice, an information notice or a special information notice is guilty of an offence.

(2) A person who, in purported compliance with an information notice or a special information notice—

(a) makes a statement which he knows to be false in a material respect, or

(b) recklessly makes a statement which is false in a material respect,

is guilty of an offence.

(3) It is a defence for a person charged with an offence under subsection (1) to prove that he exercised all due diligence to comply with the notice in question.

[1155]

NOTES

Commencement: 1 March 2000.

48 Rights of appeal

(1) A person on whom an enforcement notice, an information notice or a special information notice has been served may appeal to the Tribunal against the notice.

(2) A person on whom an enforcement notice has been served may appeal to the Tribunal against the refusal of an application under section 41(2) for cancellation or variation of the notice.

(3) Where an enforcement notice, an information notice or a special information notice contains a statement by the Commissioner in accordance with section 40(8), 43(5) or 44(6) then, whether or not the person appeals against the notice, he may appeal against—

(a) the Commissioner's decision to include the statement in the notice, or

(b) the effect of the inclusion of the statement as respects any part of the notice.

(4) A data controller in respect of whom a determination has been made under section 45 may appeal to the Tribunal against the determination.

(5) Schedule 6 has effect in relation to appeals under this section and the proceedings of the Tribunal in respect of any such appeal.

[1156]

NOTES

Commencement: 1 March 2000.

49 Determination of appeals

(1) If on an appeal under section 48(1) the Tribunal considers—

(a) that the notice against which the appeal is brought is not in accordance with the law, or

(b) to the extent that the notice involved an exercise of discretion by the Commissioner, that he ought to have exercised his discretion differently,

the Tribunal shall allow the appeal or substitute such other notice or decision as could have been served or made by the Commissioner; and in any other case the Tribunal shall dismiss the appeal.

(2) On such an appeal, the Tribunal may review any determination of fact on which the notice in question was based.

(3) If on an appeal under section 48(2) the Tribunal considers that the enforcement notice ought to be cancelled or varied by reason of a change in circumstances, the Tribunal shall cancel or vary the notice.

(4) On an appeal under subsection (3) of section 48 the Tribunal may direct—

(a) that the notice in question shall have effect as if it did not contain any such statement as is mentioned in that subsection, or

(b) that the inclusion of the statement shall not have effect in relation to any part of the notice,

and may make such modifications in the notice as may be required for giving effect to the direction.

(5) On an appeal under section 48(4), the Tribunal may cancel the determination of the Commissioner.

(6) Any party to an appeal to the Tribunal under section 48 may appeal from the decision of the Tribunal on a point of law to the appropriate court; and that court shall be—

(a) the High Court of Justice in England if the address of the person who was the appellant before the Tribunal is in England or Wales,

(b) the Court of Session if that address is in Scotland, and

(c) the High Court of Justice in Northern Ireland if that address is in Northern Ireland.

(7) For the purposes of subsection (6)—

(a) the address of a registered company is that of its registered office, and

(b) the address of a person (other than a registered company) carrying on a business is that of his principal place of business in the United Kingdom.

[1157]

NOTES

Commencement: 1 March 2000.

50 Powers of entry and inspection

Schedule 9 (powers of entry and inspection) has effect.

[1158]

NOTES

Commencement: 1 March 2000.

PART VI
MISCELLANEOUS AND GENERAL

Functions of Commissioner

51 General duties of Commissioner

(1) It shall be the duty of the Commissioner to promote the following of good practice by data controllers and, in particular, so to perform his functions under this Act as to promote the observance of the requirements of this Act by data controllers.

(2) The Commissioner shall arrange for the dissemination in such form and manner as he considers appropriate of such information as it may appear to him expedient to give to the public about the operation of this Act, about good practice, and about other matters within the scope of his functions under this Act, and may give advice to any person as to any of those matters.

(3) Where—

(a) the [Secretary of State] so directs by order, or

(b) the Commissioner considers it appropriate to do so,

the Commissioner shall, after such consultation with trade associations, data subjects or persons representing data subjects as appears to him to be appropriate, prepare and disseminate to such persons as he considers appropriate codes of practice for guidance as to good practice.

(4) The Commissioner shall also—

(a) where he considers it appropriate to do so, encourage trade associations to prepare, and to disseminate to their members, such codes of practice, and

(b) where any trade association submits a code of practice to him for his consideration, consider the code and, after such consultation with data subjects or persons representing data subjects as appears to him to be appropriate, notify the trade association whether in his opinion the code promotes the following of good practice.

(5) An order under subsection (3) shall describe the personal data or processing to which the code of practice is to relate, and may also describe the persons or classes of persons to whom it is to relate.

(6) The Commissioner shall arrange for the dissemination in such form and manner as he considers appropriate of—

(a) any Community finding as defined by paragraph 15(2) of Part II of Schedule 1,

(b) any decision of the European Commission, under the procedure provided for in Article 31(2) of the Data Protection Directive, which is made for the purposes of Article 26(3) or (4) of the Directive, and

(c) such other information as it may appear to him to be expedient to give to data controllers in relation to any personal data about the protection of the rights and freedoms of data subjects in relation to the processing of personal data in countries and territories outside the European Economic Area.

(7) The Commissioner may, with the consent of the data controller, assess any processing of personal data for the following of good practice and shall inform the data controller of the results of the assessment.

(8) The Commissioner may charge such sums as he may with the consent of the [Secretary of State] determine for any services provided by the Commissioner by virtue of this Part.

(9) In this section—

"good practice" means such practice in the processing of personal data as appears to the Commissioner to be desirable having regard to the interests of data subjects and others, and includes (but is not limited to) compliance with the requirements of this Act;

"trade association" includes any body representing data controllers.

[1159]

NOTES

Commencement: 1 March 2000 (16 July 1998: sub-s (3) insofar as conferring a power to make subordinate legislation).

Sub-ss (3), (8): words in square brackets substituted by the Secretary of State for Constitutional Affairs Order 2003, SI 2003/1887, art 9, Sch 2, para 9(1)(a).

52 Reports and codes of practice to be laid before Parliament

(1) The Commissioner shall lay annually before each House of Parliament a general report on the exercise of his functions under this Act.

(2) The Commissioner may from time to time lay before each House of Parliament such other reports with respect to those functions as he thinks fit.

(3) The Commissioner shall lay before each House of Parliament any code of practice prepared under section 51(3) for complying with a direction of the [Secretary of State], unless the code is included in any report laid under subsection (1) or (2).

[1160]

NOTES

Commencement: 1 March 2000.

Sub-s (3): words in square brackets substituted by the Secretary of State for Constitutional Affairs Order 2003, SI 2003/1887, art 9, Sch 2, para 9(1)(a).

53 Assistance by Commissioner in cases involving processing for the special purposes

(1) An individual who is an actual or prospective party to any proceedings under section 7(9), 10(4), 12(8) or 14 or by virtue of section 13 which relate to personal data processed for the special purposes may apply to the Commissioner for assistance in relation to those proceedings.

(2) The Commissioner shall, as soon as reasonably practicable after receiving an application under subsection (1), consider it and decide whether and to what extent to grant it, but he shall not grant the application unless, in his opinion, the case involves a matter of substantial public importance.

(3) If the Commissioner decides to provide assistance, he shall, as soon as reasonably practicable after making the decision, notify the applicant, stating the extent of the assistance to be provided.

(4) If the Commissioner decides not to provide assistance, he shall, as soon as reasonably practicable after making the decision, notify the applicant of his decision and, if he thinks fit, the reasons for it.

(5) In this section—
  (a) references to "proceedings" include references to prospective proceedings, and
  (b) "applicant", in relation to assistance under this section, means an individual who applies for assistance.

(6) Schedule 10 has effect for supplementing this section.

[1161]

NOTES

Commencement: 1 March 2000.

Modification: for the period beginning with the commencement of s 72 of this Act (1 March 2000) and ending 23 October 2007, sub-s (1) above has effect with the figure ", 12A(3)" inserted after the figure "12(8)"; see s 72, Sch 13, para 4 at **[1179]**, **[1202]**.

54 International co-operation

(1) The Commissioner—

(a) shall continue to be the designated authority in the United Kingdom for the purposes of Article 13 of the Convention, and
(b) shall be the supervisory authority in the United Kingdom for the purposes of the Data Protection Directive.

(2) The [Secretary of State] may by order make provision as to the functions to be discharged by the Commissioner as the designated authority in the United Kingdom for the purposes of Article 13 of the Convention.

(3) The [Secretary of State] may by order make provision as to co-operation by the Commissioner with the European Commission and with supervisory authorities in other EEA States in connection with the performance of their respective duties and, in particular, as to—
(a) the exchange of information with supervisory authorities in other EEA States or with the European Commission, and
(b) the exercise within the United Kingdom at the request of a supervisory authority in another EEA State, in cases excluded by section 5 from the application of the other provisions of this Act, of functions of the Commissioner specified in the order.

(4) The Commissioner shall also carry out any data protection functions which the [Secretary of State] may by order direct him to carry out for the purpose of enabling Her Majesty's Government in the United Kingdom to give effect to any international obligations of the United Kingdom.

(5) The Commissioner shall, if so directed by the [Secretary of State], provide any authority exercising data protection functions under the law of a colony specified in the direction with such assistance in connection with the discharge of those functions as the [Secretary of State] may direct or approve, on such terms (including terms as to payment) as the [Secretary of State] may direct or approve.

(6) Where the European Commission makes a decision for the purposes of Article 26(3) or (4) of the Data Protection Directive under the procedure provided for in Article 31(2) of the Directive, the Commissioner shall comply with that decision in exercising his functions under paragraph 9 of Schedule 4 or, as the case may be, paragraph 8 of that Schedule.

(7) The Commissioner shall inform the European Commission and the supervisory authorities in other EEA States—
(a) of any approvals granted for the purposes of paragraph 8 of Schedule 4, and
(b) of any authorisations granted for the purposes of paragraph 9 of that Schedule.

(8) In this section—
"the Convention" means the Convention for the Protection of Individuals with regard to Automatic Processing of Personal Data which was opened for signature on 28th January 1981;
"data protection functions" means functions relating to the protection of individuals with respect to the processing of personal information.

[1162]

NOTES

Commencement: 1 March 2000 (16 July 1998: sub-ss (2)–(4)) insofar as conferring a power to make subordinate legislation).

Sub-ss (2)–(5): words in square brackets substituted by the Secretary of State for Constitutional Affairs Order 2003, SI 2003/1887, art 9, Sch 2, para 9(1)(a).

Orders: the Data Protection (Functions of Designated Authority) Order 2000, SI 2000/186; the Data Protection (International Co-operation) Order 2000, SI 2000/190.

[54A Inspection of overseas information systems

(1) The Commissioner may inspect any personal data recorded in—
(a) the Schengen information system,
(b) the Europol information system,
(c) the Customs information system.

(2) The power conferred by subsection (1) is exercisable only for the purpose of assessing whether or not any processing of the data has been or is being carried out in compliance with this Act.

(3) The power includes power to inspect, operate and test equipment which is used for the processing of personal data.

(4) Before exercising the power, the Commissioner must give notice in writing of his intention to do so to the data controller.

(5) But subsection (4) does not apply if the Commissioner considers that the case is one of urgency.

(6) Any person who—
- (a) intentionally obstructs a person exercising the power conferred by subsection (1), or
- (b) fails without reasonable excuse to give any person exercising the power any assistance he may reasonably require,

is guilty of an offence.

(7) In this section—

"the Customs information system" means the information system established under Chapter II of the Convention on the Use of Information Technology for Customs Purposes,

"the Europol information system" means the information system established under Title II of the Convention on the Establishment of a European Police Office,

"the Schengen information system" means the information system established under Title IV of the Convention implementing the Schengen Agreement of 14th June 1985, or any system established in its place in pursuance of any Community obligation.]

[1162A]

NOTES

Commencement: 26 April 2004.
Inserted by the Crime (International Co-operation) Act 2003, s 81.

Unlawful obtaining etc of personal data

55 Unlawful obtaining etc of personal data

(1) A person must not knowingly or recklessly, without the consent of the data controller—
- (a) obtain or disclose personal data or the information contained in personal data, or
- (b) procure the disclosure to another person of the information contained in personal data.

(2) Subsection (1) does not apply to a person who shows—
- (a) that the obtaining, disclosing or procuring—
  - (i) was necessary for the purpose of preventing or detecting crime, or
  - (ii) was required or authorised by or under any enactment, by any rule of law or by the order of a court,
- (b) that he acted in the reasonable belief that he had in law the right to obtain or disclose the data or information or, as the case may be, to procure the disclosure of the information to the other person,
- (c) that he acted in the reasonable belief that he would have had the consent of the data controller if the data controller had known of the obtaining, disclosing or procuring and the circumstances of it, or
- (d) that in the particular circumstances the obtaining, disclosing or procuring was justified as being in the public interest.

(3) A person who contravenes subsection (1) is guilty of an offence.

(4) A person who sells personal data is guilty of an offence if he has obtained the data in contravention of subsection (1).

(5) A person who offers to sell personal data is guilty of an offence if—
- (a) he has obtained the data in contravention of subsection (1), or
- (b) he subsequently obtains the data in contravention of that subsection.

(6) For the purposes of subsection (5), an advertisement indicating that personal data are or may be for sale is an offer to sell the data.

(7) Section 1(2) does not apply for the purposes of this section; and for the purposes of subsections (4) to (6), "personal data" includes information extracted from personal data.

(8) References in this section to personal data do not include references to personal data which by virtue of section 28 [or 33A] are exempt from this section.

[1163]

NOTES

Commencement: 1 March 2000.

Sub-s (8): words in square brackets inserted by the Freedom of Information Act 2000, s 70(2).

Records obtained under data subject's right of access

56 Prohibition of requirement as to production of certain records

(1) A person must not, in connection with—

(a) the recruitment of another person as an employee,

(b) the continued employment of another person, or

(c) any contract for the provision of services to him by another person,

require that other person or a third party to supply him with a relevant record or to produce a relevant record to him.

(2) A person concerned with the provision (for payment or not) of goods, facilities or services to the public or a section of the public must not, as a condition of providing or offering to provide any goods, facilities or services to another person, require that other person or a third party to supply him with a relevant record or to produce a relevant record to him.

(3) Subsections (1) and (2) do not apply to a person who shows—

(a) that the imposition of the requirement was required or authorised by or under any enactment, by any rule of law or by the order of a court, or

(b) that in the particular circumstances the imposition of the requirement was justified as being in the public interest.

(4) Having regard to the provisions of Part V of the Police Act 1997 (certificates of criminal records etc), the imposition of the requirement referred to in subsection (1) or (2) is not to be regarded as being justified as being in the public interest on the ground that it would assist in the prevention or detection of crime.

(5) A person who contravenes subsection (1) or (2) is guilty of an offence.

(6) In this section "a relevant record" means any record which—

(a) has been or is to be obtained by a data subject from any data controller specified in the first column of the Table below in the exercise of the right conferred by section 7, and

(b) contains information relating to any matter specified in relation to that data controller in the second column,

and includes a copy of such a record or a part of such a record.

TABLE

Data controller	*Subject-matter*
1. Any of the following persons— (a) a chief officer of police of a police force in England and Wales. (b) a chief constable of a police force in Scotland. (c) the [Chief Constable of the Police Service of Northern Ireland].	(a) Convictions. (b) Cautions.

Data controller	*Subject-matter*
[(d) the Director General of the Serious Organised Crime Agency.]	
2. The Secretary of State.	(a) Convictions.
	(b) Cautions.
	(c) His functions under [section 92 of the Powers of Criminal Courts (Sentencing) Act 2000], section 205(2) or 208 of the Criminal Procedure (Scotland) Act 1995 or section 73 of the Children and Young Persons Act (Northern Ireland) 1968 in relation to any person sentenced to detention.
	(d) His functions under the Prison Act 1952, the Prisons (Scotland) Act 1989 or the Prison Act (Northern Ireland) 1953 in relation to any person imprisoned or detained.
	(e) His functions under the Social Security Contributions and Benefits Act 1992, the Social Security Administration Act 1992 or the Jobseekers Act 1995.
	(f) His functions under Part V of the Police Act 1997.
	[(g) His functions under the Safeguarding Vulnerable Groups Act 2006.]
3. The Department of Health and Social Services for Northern Ireland.	Its functions under the Social Security Contributions and Benefits (Northern Ireland) Act 1992, the Social Security Administration (Northern Ireland) Act 1992 or the Jobseekers (Northern Ireland) Order 1995.
[4. The Independent Barring Board	Its functions under the Safeguarding Vulnerable Groups Act 2006.]

[(6A) A record is not a relevant record to the extent that it relates, or is to relate, only to personal data falling within paragraph (e) of the definition of "data" in section 1(1).]

(7) In the Table in subsection (6)—

"caution" means a caution given to any person in England and Wales or Northern Ireland in respect of an offence which, at the time when the caution is given, is admitted;

"conviction" has the same meaning as in the Rehabilitation of Offenders Act 1974 or the Rehabilitation of Offenders (Northern Ireland) Order 1978.

(8) The [Secretary of State] may by order amend—

(a) the Table in subsection (6), and

(b) subsection (7).

(9) For the purposes of this section a record which states that a data controller is not processing any personal data relating to a particular matter shall be taken to be a record containing information relating to that matter.

(10) In this section "employee" means an individual who—

(a) works under a contract of employment, as defined by section 230(2) of the Employment Rights Act 1996, or

(b) holds any office,

whether or not he is entitled to remuneration; and "employment" shall be construed accordingly.

[1164]

NOTES

Commencement: 16 July 1998 (sub-s (8) insofar as conferring a power to make subordinate legislation); to be appointed (otherwise).

Sub-s (6): words in square brackets in entry 1(c) of the Table substituted by the Police (Northern Ireland) Act 2000, s 78(2)(a); entry 1(d) of the Table substituted for original entry 1(d), (e) by the Serious Organised Crime and Police Act 2005, s 59, Sch 4, para 112; words in square brackets in entry 2(c) of the Table substituted by the Powers of Criminal Courts (Sentencing) Act 2000, s 165(1), Sch 9, para 191; entries 2(g), 4 of the Table inserted by the Safeguarding Vulnerable Groups Act 2006, s 63(1), Sch 9, Pt 2, para 15(1), (2), as from a day to be appointed.

Sub-s (6A): inserted by the Freedom of Information Act 2000, s 68(4).

Sub-s (8): words in square brackets substituted by the Secretary of State for Constitutional Affairs Order 2003, SI 2003/1887, art 9, Sch 2, para 9(1)(a).

57 Avoidance of certain contractual terms relating to health records

(1) Any term or condition of a contract is void in so far as it purports to require an individual—

(a) to supply any other person with a record to which this section applies, or with a copy of such a record or a part of such a record, or

(b) to produce to any other person such a record, copy or part.

(2) This section applies to any record which—

(a) has been or is to be obtained by a data subject in the exercise of the right conferred by section 7, and

(b) consists of the information contained in any health record as defined by section 68(2).

[1165]

NOTES

Commencement: 1 March 2000.

Information provided to Commissioner or Tribunal

58 Disclosure of information

No enactment or rule of law prohibiting or restricting the disclosure of information shall preclude a person from furnishing the Commissioner or the Tribunal with any information necessary for the discharge of their functions under this Act [or the Freedom of Information Act].

[1166]

NOTES

Commencement: 1 March 2000.

Words in square brackets added by the Freedom of Information Act 2000, s 18(4), Sch 2, Pt II, para 18.

59 Confidentiality of information

(1) No person who is or has been the Commissioner, a member of the Commissioner's staff or an agent of the Commissioner shall disclose any information which—

(a) has been obtained by, or furnished to, the Commissioner under or for the purposes of [the information Acts],

(b) relates to an identified or identifiable individual or business, and

(c) is not at the time of the disclosure, and has not previously been, available to the public from other sources,

unless the disclosure is made with lawful authority.

(2) For the purposes of subsection (1) a disclosure of information is made with lawful authority only if, and to the extent that—

(a) the disclosure is made with the consent of the individual or of the person for the time being carrying on the business,

(b) the information was provided for the purpose of its being made available to the public (in whatever manner) under any provision of [the information Acts],

(c) the disclosure is made for the purposes of, and is necessary for, the discharge of—

(i) any functions under [the information Acts], or

(ii) any Community obligation,

(d) the disclosure is made for the purposes of any proceedings, whether criminal or civil and whether arising under, or by virtue of, [the information Acts] or otherwise, or

(e) having regard to the rights and freedoms or legitimate interests of any person, the disclosure is necessary in the public interest.

(3) Any person who knowingly or recklessly discloses information in contravention of subsection (1) is guilty of an offence.

[(4) In this section "the information Acts" means this Act and the Freedom of Information Act 2000.]

[1167]

NOTES

Commencement: 1 March 2000.

Sub-ss (1), (2): words in square brackets substituted by the Freedom of Information Act 2000, s 18(4), Sch 2, Pt II, para 19(1), (2).

Sub-s (4): added by the Freedom of Information Act 2000, s 18(4), Sch 2, Pt II, para 19(1), (3).

General provisions relating to offences

60 Prosecutions and penalties

(1) No proceedings for an offence under this Act shall be instituted—

(a) in England or Wales, except by the Commissioner or by or with the consent of the Director of Public Prosecutions;

(b) in Northern Ireland, except by the Commissioner or by or with the consent of the Director of Public Prosecutions for Northern Ireland.

(2) A person guilty of an offence under any provision of this Act other than [section 54A and] paragraph 12 of Schedule 9 is liable—

(a) on summary conviction, to a fine not exceeding the statutory maximum, or

(b) on conviction on indictment, to a fine.

(3) A person guilty of an offence under [section 54A and] paragraph 12 of Schedule 9 is liable on summary conviction to a fine not exceeding level 5 on the standard scale.

(4) Subject to subsection (5), the court by or before which a person is convicted of—

(a) an offence under section 21(1), 22(6), 55 or 56,

(b) an offence under section 21(2) relating to processing which is assessable processing for the purposes of section 22, or

(c) an offence under section 47(1) relating to an enforcement notice,

may order any document or other material used in connection with the processing of personal data and appearing to the court to be connected with the commission of the offence to be forfeited, destroyed or erased.

(5) The court shall not make an order under subsection (4) in relation to any material where a person (other than the offender) claiming to be the owner of or otherwise interested in the material applies to be heard by the court, unless an opportunity is given to him to show cause why the order should not be made.

[1168]

NOTES

Commencement: 1 March 2000.

Sub-ss (2), (3): words in square brackets inserted by the Crime (International Co-operation) Act 2003, s 91(1), Sch 5, paras 68, 70.

61 Liability of directors etc

(1) Where an offence under this Act has been committed by a body corporate and is proved to have been committed with the consent or connivance of or to be attributable to any neglect on the part of any director, manager, secretary or similar officer of the body corporate or any person who was purporting to act in any such capacity, he as well as the body corporate shall be guilty of that offence and be liable to be proceeded against and punished accordingly.

(2) Where the affairs of a body corporate are managed by its members subsection (1) shall apply in relation to the acts and defaults of a member in connection with his functions of management as if he were a director of the body corporate.

(3) Where an offence under this Act has been committed by a Scottish partnership and the contravention in question is proved to have occurred with the consent or connivance of, or to be attributable to any neglect on the part of, a partner, he as well as the partnership shall be guilty of that offence and shall be liable to be proceeded against and punished accordingly.
[1169]

NOTES

Commencement: 1 March 2000.

62 (*Amends the Consumer Credit Act 1974, ss 158–160.*)

General

63 Application to Crown

(1) This Act binds the Crown.

(2) For the purposes of this Act each government department shall be treated as a person separate from any other government department.

(3) Where the purposes for which and the manner in which any personal data are, or are to be, processed are determined by any person acting on behalf of the Royal Household, the Duchy of Lancaster or the Duchy of Cornwall, the data controller in respect of those data for the purposes of this Act shall be—

(a) in relation to the Royal Household, the Keeper of the Privy Purse,

(b) in relation to the Duchy of Lancaster, such person as the Chancellor of the Duchy appoints, and

(c) in relation to the Duchy of Cornwall, such person as the Duke of Cornwall, or the possessor for the time being of the Duchy of Cornwall, appoints.

(4) Different persons may be appointed under subsection (3)(b) or (c) for different purposes.

(5) Neither a government department nor a person who is a data controller by virtue of subsection (3) shall be liable to prosecution under this Act, but [sections 54A and] 55 and paragraph 12 of Schedule 9 shall apply to a person in the service of the Crown as they apply to any other person.

[1170]

NOTES

Commencement: 1 March 2000.
Sub-s (5): words in square brackets substituted by the Crime (International Co-operation) Act 2003, s 91(1), Sch 5, paras 68, 71.

[63A Application to Parliament

(1) Subject to the following provisions of this section and to section 35A, this Act applies to the processing of personal data by or on behalf of either House of Parliament as it applies to the processing of personal data by other persons.

(2) Where the purposes for which and the manner in which any personal data are, or are to be, processed are determined by or on behalf of the House of Commons, the data controller in respect of those data for the purposes of this Act shall be the Corporate Officer of that House.

(3) Where the purposes for which and the manner in which any personal data are, or are to be, processed are determined by or on behalf of the House of Lords, the data controller in respect of those data for the purposes of this Act shall be the Corporate Officer of that House.

(4) Nothing in subsection (2) or (3) is to be taken to render the Corporate Officer of the House of Commons or the Corporate Officer of the House of Lords liable to prosecution under this Act, but section 55 and paragraph 12 of Schedule 9 shall apply to a person acting on behalf of either House as they apply to any other person.]

[1170A]

NOTES

Commencement: 1 January 2005.
Inserted by the Freedom of Information Act 2000, s 73, Sch 6, para 3.

64 Transmission of notices etc by electronic or other means

(1) This section applies to—

(a) a notice or request under any provision of Part II,
(b) a notice under subsection (1) of section 24 or particulars made available under that subsection, or
(c) an application under section 41(2), but does not apply to anything which is required to be served in accordance with rules of court.

(2) The requirement that any notice, request, particulars or application to which this section applies should be in writing is satisfied where the text of the notice, request, particulars or application—

(a) is transmitted by electronic means,
(b) is received in legible form, and
(c) is capable of being used for subsequent reference.

(3) The [Secretary of State] may by regulations provide that any requirement that any notice, request, particulars or application to which this section applies should be in writing is not to apply in such circumstances as may be prescribed by the regulations.

[1171]

NOTES

Commencement: 1 March 2000 (16 July 1998: sub-s (3) insofar as conferring a power to make subordinate legislation).
Sub-s (3): words in square brackets substituted by the Secretary of State for Constitutional Affairs Order 2003, SI 2003/1887, art 9, Sch 2, para 9(1)(a).

65 Service of notices by Commissioner

(1) Any notice authorised or required by this Act to be served on or given to any person by the Commissioner may—

(a) if that person is an individual, be served on him—
  (i) by delivering it to him, or
  (ii) by sending it to him by post addressed to him at his usual or last-known place of residence or business, or
  (iii) by leaving it for him at that place;
(b) if that person is a body corporate or unincorporate, be served on that body—
  (i) by sending it by post to the proper officer of the body at its principal office, or
  (ii) by addressing it to the proper officer of the body and leaving it at that office;
(c) if that person is a partnership in Scotland, be served on that partnership—
  (i) by sending it by post to the principal office of the partnership, or
  (ii) by addressing it to that partnership and leaving it at that office.

(2) In subsection (1)(b) "principal office", in relation to a registered company, means its registered office and "proper officer", in relation to any body, means the secretary or other executive officer charged with the conduct of its general affairs.

(3) This section is without prejudice to any other lawful method of serving or giving a notice.

[1172]

NOTES

Commencement: 1 March 2000.

66 Exercise of rights in Scotland by children

(1) Where a question falls to be determined in Scotland as to the legal capacity of a person under the age of sixteen years to exercise any right conferred by any provision of this Act, that person shall be taken to have that capacity where he has a general understanding of what it means to exercise that right.

(2) Without prejudice to the generality of subsection (1), a person of twelve years of age or more shall be presumed to be of sufficient age and maturity to have such understanding as is mentioned in that subsection.

[1173]

NOTES

Commencement: 1 March 2000.

67 Orders, regulations and rules

(1) Any power conferred by this Act on the [Secretary of State] to make an order, regulations or rules shall be exercisable by statutory instrument.

(2) Any order, regulations or rules made by the [Secretary of State] under this Act may—

(a) make different provision for different cases, and

(b) make such supplemental, incidental, consequential or transitional provision or savings as the [Secretary of State] considers appropriate;

and nothing in section 7(11), 19(5), 26(1) or 30(4) limits the generality of paragraph (a).

(3) Before making—

(a) an order under any provision of this Act other than section 75(3),

(b) any regulations under this Act other than notification regulations (as defined by section 16(2)),

the [Secretary of State] shall consult the Commissioner.

(4) A statutory instrument containing (whether alone or with other provisions) an order under—

section 10(2)(b),
section 12(5)(b),
section 22(1),
section 30, section 32(3),
section 38,
section 56(8),
paragraph 10 of Schedule 3, or
paragraph 4 of Schedule 7,

shall not be made unless a draft of the instrument has been laid before and approved by a resolution of each House of Parliament.

(5) A statutory instrument which contains (whether alone or with other provisions)—

(a) an order under—
section 22(7),
section 23,
section 51(3),
section 54(2), (3) or (4),
paragraph 3, 4 or 14 of Part II of Schedule 1,
paragraph 6 of Schedule 2,
paragraph 2, 7 or 9 of Schedule 3,
paragraph 4 of Schedule 4,
paragraph 6 of Schedule 7,

(b) regulations under section 7 which—
(i) prescribe cases for the purposes of subsection (2)(b),
(ii) are made by virtue of subsection (7), or
(iii) relate to the definition of "the prescribed period",

(c) regulations under section 8(1)[, 9(3) or 9A(5)],

(d) regulations under section 64,
(e) notification regulations (as defined by section 16(2)), or
(f) rules under paragraph 7 of Schedule 6,

and which is not subject to the requirement in subsection (4) that a draft of the instrument be laid before and approved by a resolution of each House of Parliament, shall be subject to annulment in pursuance of a resolution of either House of Parliament.

(6) A statutory instrument which contains only—
(a) regulations prescribing fees for the purposes of any provision of this Act, or
(b) regulations under section 7 prescribing fees for the purposes of any other enactment,

shall be laid before Parliament after being made.

[1174]

NOTES

Commencement: 16 July 1998.

Sub-ss (1)–(3): words in square brackets substituted by the Secretary of State for Constitutional Affairs Order 2003, SI 2003/1887, art 9, Sch 2, para 9(1)(a).

Sub-s (5): words in square brackets in para (c) substituted by the Freedom of Information Act 2000, s 69(3).

68 Meaning of "accessible record"

(1) In this Act "accessible record" means—
(a) a health record as defined by subsection (2),
(b) an educational record as defined by Schedule 11, or
(c) an accessible public record as defined by Schedule 12.

(2) In subsection (1)(a) "health record" means any record which—
(a) consists of information relating to the physical or mental health or condition of an individual, and
(b) has been made by or on behalf of a health professional in connection with the care of that individual.

[1175]

NOTES

Commencement: 16 July 1998.

69 Meaning of "health professional"

(1) In this Act "health professional" means any of the following—
(a) a registered medical practitioner,
(b) a registered dentist as defined by section 53(1) of the Dentists Act 1984,
[(c) a registered dispensing optician or a registered optometrist within the meaning of the Opticians Act 1989,]
(d) *a registered pharmaceutical chemist as defined by section 24(1) of the Pharmacy Act 1954* or a registered person as defined by Article 2(2) of the Pharmacy (Northern Ireland) Order 1976,
[(e) a registered nurse or midwife]
(f) a registered osteopath as defined by section 41 of the Osteopaths Act 1993,
(g) a registered chiropractor as defined by section 43 of the Chiropractors Act 1994,
(h) any person who is registered as a member of a profession to which [the Health Professions Order 2001] for the time being extends,
(i) a clinical psychologist [or child psychotherapist],
(j) … and
(k) a scientist employed by such a body as head of a department.

(2) In subsection (1)(a) "registered medical practitioner" includes any person who is provisionally registered under section 15 or 21 of the Medical Act 1983 and is engaged in such employment as is mentioned in subsection (3) of that section.

(3) In subsection (1) "health service body" means—
(a) a [Strategic Health Authority] [established under section 13 of the National Health Service Act 2006],

(b) a Special Health Authority established under [section 28 of that Act, or section 22 of the National Health Service (Wales) Act 2006],

[(bb) a Primary Care Trust established under [section 18 of the National Health Service Act 2006],]

[(bbb) a Local Health Board established under [section 11 of the National Health Service (Wales) Act 2006],]

(c) a Health Board within the meaning of the National Health Service (Scotland) Act 1978,

(d) a Special Health Board within the meaning of that Act,

(e) the managers of a State Hospital provided under section 102 of that Act,

(f) a National Health Service trust first established under section 5 of the National Health Service and Community Care Act 1990[, section 25 of the National Health Service Act 2006, section 18 of the National Health Service (Wales) Act 2006] or section 12A of the National Health Service (Scotland) Act 1978,

[(fa) an NHS foundation trust,]

(g) a Health and Social Services Board established under Article 16 of the Health and Personal Social Services (Northern Ireland) Order 1972,

(h) a special health and social services agency established under the Health and Personal Social Services (Special Agencies) (Northern Ireland) Order 1990, or

(i) a Health and Social Services trust established under Article 10 of the Health and Personal Social Services (Northern Ireland) Order 1991.

[1176]

NOTES

Commencement: 16 July 1998.

Sub-s (1): para (c) substituted by the Opticians Act 1989 (Amendment) Order 2005, SI 2005/848, art 28, Sch 1, Pt 2, para 12; for the words in italics in para (d) there are substituted the words "a registered pharmacist or registered pharmacy technician within the meaning of the Pharmacists and Pharmacy Technicians Order 2007" by the Pharmacists and Pharmacy Technicians Order 2007, SI 2007/289, arts 67, 68(1), Sch 1, Pt 1, para 7, Sch 2, as from a day to be notified in the London, Edinburgh and Belfast Gazettes; para (e) substituted by the Nursery and Midwifery Order 2002, SI 2002/253, art 54(3), Sch 5, para 14; words in square brackets in para (h) substituted by the Health Professions Order 2002, SI 2002/254, art 48(3), Sch 4, para 7; words in square brackets in para (i) substituted, and para (j) repealed, by the Health Professions Order 2003 (Consequential Amendments) Order 2003, SI 2003/1590, art 3, Schedule, Pt 1, para 1.

Sub-s (3): in para (a) words in first pair of square brackets inserted by the National Health Service Reform and Health Care Professions Act 2002 (Supplementary, Consequential etc Provisions) Regulations 2002, SI 2002/2469, reg 4, Sch 1, Pt 1, para 24; words in second pair of square brackets in para (a) and words in square brackets in paras (b), (bb), (bbb) substituted, and words in square brackets in para (f) inserted by the National Health Service (Consequential Provisions) Act 2006, s 2, Sch 1, paras 190, 191; para (bb) inserted by the Health Act 1999 (Supplementary, Consequential etc Provisions) Order 2000, SI 2000/90, art 3(1), Sch 1, para 33; para (bbb) inserted by the National Health Service Reform and Health Care Professions Act 2002, s 6(2), Sch 5, para 41; para (fa) inserted by the Health and Social Care (Community Health and Standards) Act 2003, s 34, Sch 4, paras 106, 107.

70 Supplementary definitions

(1) In this Act, unless the context otherwise requires—

"business" includes any trade or profession;

"the Commissioner" means [the Information Commissioner];

"credit reference agency" has the same meaning as in the Consumer Credit Act 1974;

"the Data Protection Directive" means Directive 95/46/EC on the protection of individuals with regard to the processing of personal data and on the free movement of such data;

"EEA State" means a State which is a contracting party to the Agreement on the European Economic Area signed at Oporto on 2nd May 1992 as adjusted by the Protocol signed at Brussels on 17th March 1993;

"enactment" includes an enactment passed after this Act [and any enactment comprised in, or in any instrument made under, an Act of the Scottish Parliament];

"government department" includes a Northern Ireland department and any body or authority exercising statutory functions on behalf of the Crown;

"Minister of the Crown" has the same meaning as in the Ministers of the Crown Act 1975;

"public register" means any register which pursuant to a requirement imposed—

(a) by or under any enactment, or

(b) in pursuance of any international agreement,

is open to public inspection or open to inspection by any person having a legitimate interest;

"pupil"—

(a) in relation to a school in England and Wales, means a registered pupil within the meaning of the Education Act 1996,

(b) in relation to a school in Scotland, means a pupil within the meaning of the Education (Scotland) Act 1980, and

(c) in relation to a school in Northern Ireland, means a registered pupil within the meaning of the Education and Libraries (Northern Ireland) Order 1986;

"recipient", in relation to any personal data, means any person to whom the data are disclosed, including any person (such as an employee or agent of the data controller, a data processor or an employee or agent of a data processor) to whom they are disclosed in the course of processing the data for the data controller, but does not include any person to whom disclosure is or may be made as a result of, or with a view to, a particular inquiry by or on behalf of that person made in the exercise of any power conferred by law;

"registered company" means a company registered under the enactments relating to companies for the time being in force in the United Kingdom;

"school"—

(a) in relation to England and Wales, has the same meaning as in the Education Act 1996,

(b) in relation to Scotland, has the same meaning as in the Education (Scotland) Act 1980, and

(c) in relation to Northern Ireland, has the same meaning as in the Education and Libraries (Northern Ireland) Order 1986;

"teacher" includes—

(a) in Great Britain, head teacher, and

(b) in Northern Ireland, the principal of a school;

"third party", in relation to personal data, means any person other than—

(a) the data subject,

(b) the data controller, or

(c) any data processor or other person authorised to process data for the data controller or processor;

"the Tribunal" means [the Information Tribunal].

(2) For the purposes of this Act data are inaccurate if they are incorrect or misleading as to any matter of fact.

[1177]

NOTES

Commencement: 16 July 1998.

Sub-s (1): in definitions "the Commissioner" and "the Tribunal" words in square brackets substituted by the Freedom of Information Act 2000, s 18(4), Sch 2, Pt I, para 14; in definition "enactment" words in square brackets added by the Scotland Act 1999 (Consequential Modifications) (No 2) Order 1999, SI 1999/1820, art 4, Sch 2, Pt I, para 133.

Directive 95/46/EC: OJ L281, 23.11.95, p 31.

71 Index of defined expressions

The following Table shows provisions defining or otherwise explaining expressions used in this Act (other than provisions defining or explaining an expression only used in the same section or Schedule)—

accessible record	section 68
address (in Part III)	section 16(3)
business	section 70(1)
the Commissioner	section 70(1)
credit reference agency	section 70(1)
data	section 1(1)
data controller	sections 1(1) and (4) and 63(3)

data processor	section 1(1)
the Data Protection Directive	section 70(1)
data protection principles	section 4 and Schedule 1
data subject	section 1(1)
disclosing (of personal data)	section 1(2)(b)
EEA State	section 70(1)
enactment	section 70(1)
enforcement notice	section 40(1)
fees regulations (in Part III)	section 16(2)
government department	section 70(1)
health professional	section 69
inaccurate (in relation to data)	section 70(2)
information notice	section 43(1)
Minister of the Crown	section 70(1)
the non-disclosure provisions (in Part IV)	section 27(3)
notification regulations (in Part III)	section 16(2)
obtaining (of personal data)	section 1(2)(a)
personal data	section 1(1)
prescribed (in Part III)	section 16(2)
processing (of information or data)	section 1(1) and paragraph 5 of Schedule 8
[public authority	section 1(1)]
public register	section 70(1)
publish (in relation to journalistic, literary or artistic material)	section 32(6)
pupil (in relation to a school)	section 70(1)
recipient (in relation to personal data)	section 70(1)
recording (of personal data)	section 1(2)(a)
registered company	section 70(1)
registrable particulars (in Part III)	section 16(1)
relevant filing system	section 1(1)
school	section 70(1)
sensitive personal data	section 2
special information notice	section 44(1)
the special purposes	section 3
the subject information provisions (in Part IV)	section 27(2)
teacher	section 70(1)
third party (in relation to processing of personal data)	section 70(1)
the Tribunal	section 70(1)
using (of personal data)	section 1(2)(b).

[1178]

NOTES

Commencement: 16 July 1998.

Table: entry "public authority" inserted by the Freedom of Information Act 2000, s 68(5).

72 Modifications of Act

During the period beginning with the commencement of this section and ending with 23rd October 2007, the provisions of this Act shall have effect subject to the modifications set out in Schedule 13.

[1179]

NOTES

Commencement: 1 March 2000.

73 Transitional provisions and savings

Schedule 14 (which contains transitional provisions and savings) has effect.

[1180]

NOTES

Commencement: 1 March 2000.

74 Minor and consequential amendments and repeals and revocations

(1) Schedule 15 (which contains minor and consequential amendments) has effect.

(2) The enactments and instruments specified in Schedule 16 are repealed or revoked to the extent specified.

[1181]

NOTES

Commencement: 1 March 2000.

75 Short title, commencement and extent

(1) This Act may be cited as the Data Protection Act 1998.

(2) The following provisions of this Act—

(a) sections 1 to 3,
(b) section 25(1) and (4),
(c) section 26,
(d) sections 67 to 71,
(e) this section,
(f) paragraph 17 of Schedule 5,
(g) Schedule 11,
(h) Schedule 12, and
(i) so much of any other provision of this Act as confers any power to make subordinate legislation,

shall come into force on the day on which this Act is passed.

(3) The remaining provisions of this Act shall come into force on such day as the [Secretary of State] may by order appoint; and different days may be appointed for different purposes.

(4) The day appointed under subsection (3) for the coming into force of section 56 must not be earlier than the first day on which sections 112, 113 and 115 of the Police Act 1997 (which provide for the issue by the Secretary of State of criminal conviction certificates, criminal record certificates and enhanced criminal record certificates) are all in force.

[(4A) Subsection (4) does not apply to section 56 so far as that section relates to a record containing information relating to—

(a) the Secretary of State's functions under the Safeguarding Vulnerable Groups Act 2006, or
(b) the Independent Barring Board's functions under that Act.]

(5) Subject to subsection (6), this Act extends to Northern Ireland.

(6) Any amendment, repeal or revocation made by Schedule 15 or 16 has the same extent as that of the enactment or instrument to which it relates.

[1182]

NOTES

Commencement: 16 July 1998.

Sub-s (3): words in square brackets substituted by the Secretary of State for Constitutional Affairs Order 2003, SI 2003/1887, art 9, Sch 2, para 9(1)(a).

Sub-s (4A): inserted by the Safeguarding Vulnerable Groups Act 2006, s 63(1), Sch 9, Pt 2, para 15(1), (3), as from a day to be appointed.

Orders: the Data Protection Act 1998 (Commencement) Order 2000, SI 2000/183.

SCHEDULES

SCHEDULE 1
THE DATA PROTECTION PRINCIPLES

Section 4(1) and (2)

PART I
THE PRINCIPLES

1. Personal data shall be processed fairly and lawfully and, in particular, shall not be processed unless—
   (a) at least one of the conditions in Schedule 2 is met, and
   (b) in the case of sensitive personal data, at least one of the conditions in Schedule 3 is also met.

2. Personal data shall be obtained only for one or more specified and lawful purposes, and shall not be further processed in any manner incompatible with that purpose or those purposes.

3. Personal data shall be adequate, relevant and not excessive in relation to the purpose or purposes for which they are processed.

4. Personal data shall be accurate and, where necessary, kept up to date.

5. Personal data processed for any purpose or purposes shall not be kept for longer than is necessary for that purpose or those purposes.

6. Personal data shall be processed in accordance with the rights of data subjects under this Act.

7. Appropriate technical and organisational measures shall be taken against unauthorised or unlawful processing of personal data and against accidental loss or destruction of, or damage to, personal data.

8. Personal data shall not be transferred to a country or territory outside the European Economic Area unless that country or territory ensures an adequate level of protection for the rights and freedoms of data subjects in relation to the processing of personal data.

[1183]

NOTES

Commencement: 1 March 2000.

PART II
INTERPRETATION OF THE PRINCIPLES IN PART I

The first principle

1.—(1) In determining for the purposes of the first principle whether personal data are processed fairly, regard is to be had to the method by which they are obtained, including in particular whether any person from whom they are obtained is deceived or misled as to the purpose or purposes for which they are to be processed.

(2) Subject to paragraph 2, for the purposes of the first principle data are to be treated as obtained fairly if they consist of information obtained from a person who—

(a) is authorised by or under any enactment to supply it, or

(b) is required to supply it by or under any enactment or by any convention or other instrument imposing an international obligation on the United Kingdom.

2.—(1) Subject to paragraph 3, for the purposes of the first principle personal data are not to be treated as processed fairly unless—

(a) in the case of data obtained from the data subject, the data controller ensures so far as practicable that the data subject has, is provided with, or has made readily available to him, the information specified in sub-paragraph (3), and

(b) in any other case, the data controller ensures so far as practicable that, before the relevant time or as soon as practicable after that time, the data subject has, is provided with, or has made readily available to him, the information specified in sub-paragraph (3).

(2) In sub-paragraph (1)(b) "the relevant time" means—

(a) the time when the data controller first processes the data, or

(b) in a case where at that time disclosure to a third party within a reasonable period is envisaged—

(i) if the data are in fact disclosed to such a person within that period, the time when the data are first disclosed,

(ii) if within that period the data controller becomes, or ought to become, aware that the data are unlikely to be disclosed to such a person within that period, the time when the data controller does become, or ought to become, so aware, or

(iii) in any other case, the end of that period.

(3) The information referred to in sub-paragraph (1) is as follows, namely—

(a) the identity of the data controller,

(b) if he has nominated a representative for the purposes of this Act, the identity of that representative,

(c) the purpose or purposes for which the data are intended to be processed, and

(d) any further information which is necessary, having regard to the specific circumstances in which the data are or are to be processed, to enable processing in respect of the data subject to be fair.

3.—(1) Paragraph 2(1)(b) does not apply where either of the primary conditions in subparagraph (2), together with such further conditions as may be prescribed by the [Secretary of State] by order, are met.

(2) The primary conditions referred to in sub-paragraph (1) are—

(a) that the provision of that information would involve a disproportionate effort, or

(b) that the recording of the information to be contained in the data by, or the disclosure of the data by, the data controller is necessary for compliance with any legal obligation to which the data controller is subject, other than an obligation imposed by contract.

4.—(1) Personal data which contain a general identifier falling within a description prescribed by the [Secretary of State] by order are not to be treated as processed fairly and lawfully unless they are processed in compliance with any conditions so prescribed in relation to general identifiers of that description.

(2) In sub-paragraph (1) "a general identifier" means any identifier (such as, for example, a number or code used for identification purposes) which—

(a) relates to an individual, and

(b) forms part of a set of similar identifiers which is of general application.

The second principle

5. The purpose or purposes for which personal data are obtained may in particular be specified—

(a) in a notice given for the purposes of paragraph 2 by the data controller to the data subject, or

(b) in a notification given to the Commissioner under Part III of this Act.

6. In determining whether any disclosure of personal data is compatible with the purpose or purposes for which the data were obtained, regard is to be had to the purpose or purposes for which the personal data are intended to be processed by any person to whom they are disclosed.

The fourth principle

7. The fourth principle is not to be regarded as being contravened by reason of any inaccuracy in personal data which accurately record information obtained by the data controller from the data subject or a third party in a case where—

(a) having regard to the purpose or purposes for which the data were obtained and further processed, the data controller has taken reasonable steps to ensure the accuracy of the data, and

(b) if the data subject has notified the data controller of the data subject's view that the data are inaccurate, the data indicate that fact.

The sixth principle

8. A person is to be regarded as contravening the sixth principle if, but only if—

(a) he contravenes section 7 by failing to supply information in accordance with that section,

(b) he contravenes section 10 by failing to comply with a notice given under subsection (1) of that section to the extent that the notice is justified or by failing to give a notice under subsection (3) of that section,

(c) he contravenes section 11 by failing to comply with a notice given under subsection (1) of that section, or

(d) he contravenes section 12 by failing to comply with a notice given under subsection (1) or (2)(b) of that section or by failing to give a notification under subsection (2)(a) of that section or a notice under subsection (3) of that section.

The seventh principle

9. Having regard to the state of technological development and the cost of implementing any measures, the measures must ensure a level of security appropriate to—

(a) the harm that might result from such unauthorised or unlawful processing or accidental loss, destruction or damage as are mentioned in the seventh principle, and

(b) the nature of the data to be protected.

10. The data controller must take reasonable steps to ensure the reliability of any employees of his who have access to the personal data.

11. Where processing of personal data is carried out by a data processor on behalf of a data controller, the data controller must in order to comply with the seventh principle—

(a) choose a data processor providing sufficient guarantees in respect of the technical and organisational security measures governing the processing to be carried out, and

(b) take reasonable steps to ensure compliance with those measures.

12. Where processing of personal data is carried out by a data processor on behalf of a data controller, the data controller is not to be regarded as complying with the seventh principle unless—

(a) the processing is carried out under a contract—
    (i) which is made or evidenced in writing, and
    (ii) under which the data processor is to act only on instructions from the data controller, and

(b) the contract requires the data processor to comply with obligations equivalent to those imposed on a data controller by the seventh principle.

The eighth principle

13. An adequate level of protection is one which is adequate in all the circumstances of the case, having regard in particular to—
    (a) the nature of the personal data,
    (b) the country or territory of origin of the information contained in the data,
    (c) the country or territory of final destination of that information,
    (d) the purposes for which and period during which the data are intended to be processed,
    (e) the law in force in the country or territory in question,
    (f) the international obligations of that country or territory,
    (g) any relevant codes of conduct or other rules which are enforceable in that country or territory (whether generally or by arrangement in particular cases), and
    (h) any security measures taken in respect of the data in that country or territory.

14. The eighth principle does not apply to a transfer falling within any paragraph of Schedule 4, except in such circumstances and to such extent as the [Secretary of State] may by order provide.

15.—(1) Where—
    (a) in any proceedings under this Act any question arises as to whether the requirement of the eighth principle as to an adequate level of protection is met in relation to the transfer of any personal data to a country or territory outside the European Economic Area, and
    (b) a Community finding has been made in relation to transfers of the kind in question,

that question is to be determined in accordance with that finding.

(2) In sub-paragraph (1) "Community finding" means a finding of the European Commission, under the procedure provided for in Article 31(2) of the Data Protection Directive, that a country or territory outside the European Economic Area does, or does not, ensure an adequate level of protection within the meaning of Article 25(2) of the Directive.
[1184]

NOTES

Commencement: 1 March 2000.

Paras 3, 4, 14: words in square brackets substituted by the Secretary of State for Constitutional Affairs Order 2003, SI 2003/1887, art 9, Sch 2, para 9(1)(b).

Modification: by virtue of s 72 of, and Sch 13, para 5 to, this Act, for the period beginning with the commencement of s 72 (1 March 2000) and ending 23 October 2007, para 8 above has effect with the omission of the word "or" at the end of sub-para (c) and with the following added after sub-para (d)—

"or
    (e) he contravenes section 12A by failing to comply with a notice given under subsection (1) of that section to the extent that the notice is justified.".

Orders: the Data Protection (Conditions under Paragraph 3 of Part II of Schedule 1) Order 2000, SI 2000/185.

SCHEDULE 2
CONDITIONS RELEVANT FOR PURPOSES OF THE FIRST PRINCIPLE: PROCESSING OF ANY PERSONAL DATA

Section 4(3)

1. The data subject has given his consent to the processing.

2. The processing is necessary—
    (a) for the performance of a contract to which the data subject is a party, or
    (b) for the taking of steps at the request of the data subject with a view to entering into a contract.

3. The processing is necessary for compliance with any legal obligation to which the data controller is subject, other than an obligation imposed by contract.

4. The processing is necessary in order to protect the vital interests of the data subject.

5. The processing is necessary—

(a) for the administration of justice,
[(aa) for the exercise of any functions of either House of Parliament,]
(b) for the exercise of any functions conferred on any person by or under any enactment,
(c) for the exercise of any functions of the Crown, a Minister of the Crown or a government department, or
(d) for the exercise of any other functions of a public nature exercised in the public interest by any person.

6.—(1) The processing is necessary for the purposes of legitimate interests pursued by the data controller or by the third party or parties to whom the data are disclosed, except where the processing is unwarranted in any particular case by reason of prejudice to the rights and freedoms or legitimate interests of the data subject.

(2) The [Secretary of State] may by order specify particular circumstances in which this condition is, or is not, to be taken to be satisfied.

[1185]

NOTES

Commencement: 1 March 2000 (16 July 1998: para 6(2) insofar as conferring a power to make subordinate legislation).

Para 5: sub-para (aa) inserted by the Freedom of Information Act, s 73, Sch 6, para 4.

Para 6: words in square brackets in sub-para (2) substituted by the Secretary of State for Constitutional Affairs Order 2003, SI 2003/1887, art 9, Sch 2, para 9(1)(b).

SCHEDULE 3
CONDITIONS RELEVANT FOR PURPOSES OF THE FIRST PRINCIPLE: PROCESSING OF SENSITIVE PERSONAL DATA

Section 4(3)

1. The data subject has given his explicit consent to the processing of the personal data.

2.—(1) The processing is necessary for the purposes of exercising or performing any right or obligation which is conferred or imposed by law on the data controller in connection with employment.

(2) The [Secretary of State] may by order—
(a) exclude the application of sub-paragraph (1) in such cases as may be specified, or
(b) provide that, in such cases as may be specified, the condition in subparagraph (1) is not to be regarded as satisfied unless such further conditions as may be specified in the order are also satisfied.

3. The processing is necessary—
(a) in order to protect the vital interests of the data subject or another person, in a case where—
(i) consent cannot be given by or on behalf of the data subject, or
(ii) the data controller cannot reasonably be expected to obtain the consent of the data subject, or
(b) in order to protect the vital interests of another person, in a case where consent by or on behalf of the data subject has been unreasonably withheld.

4. The processing—
(a) is carried out in the course of its legitimate activities by any body or association which—
(i) is not established or conducted for profit, and
(ii) exists for political, philosophical religious or trade-union purposes,
(b) is carried out with appropriate safeguards for the rights and freedoms of data subjects,
(c) relates only to individuals who either are members of the body or association or have regular contact with it in connection with its purposes, and
(d) does not involve disclosure of the personal data to a third party without the consent of the data subject.

5. The information contained in the personal data has been made public as a result of steps deliberately taken by the data subject.

6. The processing—
   (a) is necessary for the purpose of, or in connection with, any legal proceedings (including prospective legal proceedings),
   (b) is necessary for the purpose of obtaining legal advice, or
   (c) is otherwise necessary for the purposes of establishing, exercising or defending legal rights.

7.—(1) The processing is necessary—
   (a) for the administration of justice,
   [(aa) for the exercise of any functions of either House of Parliament,]
   (b) for the exercise of any functions conferred on any person by or under an enactment, or
   (c) for the exercise of any functions of the Crown, a Minister of the Crown or a government department.

(2) The [Secretary of State] may by order—
   (a) exclude the application of sub-paragraph (1) in such cases as may be specified, or
   (b) provide that, in such cases as may be specified, the condition in subparagraph (1) is not to be regarded as satisfied unless such further conditions as may be specified in the order are also satisfied.

8.—(1) The processing is necessary for medical purposes and is undertaken by—
   (a) a health professional, or
   (b) a person who in the circumstances owes a duty of confidentiality which is equivalent to that which would arise if that person were a health professional.

(2) In this paragraph "medical purposes" includes the purposes of preventative medicine, medical diagnosis, medical research, the provision of care and treatment and the management of healthcare services.

9.—(1) The processing—
   (a) is of sensitive personal data consisting of information as to racial or ethnic origin,
   (b) is necessary for the purpose of identifying or keeping under review the existence or absence of equality of opportunity or treatment between persons of different racial or ethnic origins, with a view to enabling such equality to be promoted or maintained, and
   (c) is carried out with appropriate safeguards for the rights and freedoms of data subjects.

(2) The [Secretary of State] may by order specify circumstances in which processing falling within sub-paragraph (1)(a) and (b) is, or is not, to be taken for the purposes of subparagraph (1)(c) to be carried out with appropriate safeguards for the rights and freedoms of data subjects.

10. The personal data are processed in circumstances specified in an order made by the [Secretary of State] for the purposes of this paragraph.

[1186]

NOTES

Commencement: 1 March 2000 (16 July 1998: paras 2(2), 7(2), 9(2) insofar as conferring a power to make subordinate legislation).

Paras 2, 9, 10: words in square brackets substituted by the Secretary of State for Constitutional Affairs Order 2003, SI 2003/1887, art 9, Sch 2, para 9(1)(b).

Para 7: sub-para (1)(aa) inserted by the Freedom of Information Act 2000, s 73, Sch 6, para 5; words in square brackets in sub-para (2) substituted by SI 2003/1887, art 9, Sch 2, para 9(1)(b).

Orders: the Data Protection (Processing of Sensitive Personal Data) Order 2000, SI 2000/417 at **[3348]**; the Data Protection (Processing of Sensitive Personal Data) (Elected Representatives) Order 2002, SI 2002/2905; the Data Protection (Processing of Sensitive Personal Data) Order 2006, SI 2006/2068.

SCHEDULE 4
CASES WHERE THE EIGHTH PRINCIPLE DOES NOT APPLY

Section 4(3)

1. The data subject has given his consent to the transfer.

2. The transfer is necessary—

(a) for the performance of a contract between the data subject and the data controller, or

(b) for the taking of steps at the request of the data subject with a view to his entering into a contract with the data controller.

3. The transfer is necessary—

(a) for the conclusion of a contract between the data controller and a person other than the data subject which—

(i) is entered into at the request of the data subject, or

(ii) is in the interests of the data subject, or

(b) for the performance of such a contract.

4.—(1) The transfer is necessary for reasons of substantial public interest.

(2) The [Secretary of State] may by order specify—

(a) circumstances in which a transfer is to be taken for the purposes of subparagraph (1) to be necessary for reasons of substantial public interest, and

(b) circumstances in which a transfer which is not required by or under an enactment is not to be taken for the purpose of sub-paragraph (1) to be necessary for reasons of substantial public interest.

5. The transfer—

(a) is necessary for the purpose of, or in connection with, any legal proceedings (including prospective legal proceedings),

(b) is necessary for the purpose of obtaining legal advice, or

(c) is otherwise necessary for the purposes of establishing, exercising or defending legal rights.

6. The transfer is necessary in order to protect the vital interests of the data subject.

7. The transfer is of part of the personal data on a public register and any conditions subject to which the register is open to inspection are complied with by any person to whom the data are or may be disclosed after the transfer.

8. The transfer is made on terms which are of a kind approved by the Commissioner as ensuring adequate safeguards for the rights and freedoms of data subjects.

9. The transfer has been authorised by the Commissioner as being made in such a manner as to ensure adequate safeguards for the rights and freedoms of data subjects.

[1187]

NOTES

Commencement: 1 March 2000 (16 July 1998: para 4(2) insofar as conferring a power to make subordinate legislation).

Para 4: words in square brackets in sub-para (2) substituted by the Secretary of State for Constitutional Affairs Order 2003, SI 2003/1887, art 9, Sch 2, para 9(1)(b).

SCHEDULE 5
THE [INFORMATION COMMISSIONER] AND THE [INFORMATION TRIBUNAL]

Section 6(7)

PART I
THE COMMISSIONER

Status and capacity

1.—(1) The corporation sole by the name of the Data Protection Registrar established by the Data Protection Act 1984 shall continue in existence by the name of the [Information Commissioner].

(2) The Commissioner and his officers and staff are not to be regarded as servants or agents of the Crown.

Tenure of office

2.—(1) Subject to the provisions of this paragraph, the Commissioner shall hold office for such term not exceeding five years as may be determined at the time of his appointment.

(2) The Commissioner may be relieved of his office by Her Majesty at his own request.

(3) The Commissioner may be removed from office by Her Majesty in pursuance of an Address from both Houses of Parliament.

(4) The Commissioner shall in any case vacate his office—
- (a) on completing the year of service in which he attains the age of sixty-five years, or
- (b) if earlier, on completing his fifteenth year of service.

(5) Subject to sub-paragraph (4), a person who ceases to be Commissioner on the expiration of his term of office shall be eligible for re-appointment, but a person may not be re-appointed for a third or subsequent term as Commissioner unless, by reason of special circumstances, the person's re-appointment for such a term is desirable in the public interest.

Salary etc

3.—(1) There shall be paid—
- (a) to the Commissioner such salary, and
- (b) to or in respect of the Commissioner such pension,

as may be specified by a resolution of the House of Commons.

(2) A resolution for the purposes of this paragraph may—
- (a) specify the salary or pension,
- (b) provide that the salary or pension is to be the same as, or calculated on the same basis as, that payable to, or to or in respect of, a person employed in a specified office under, or in a specified capacity in the service of, the Crown, or
- (c) specify the salary or pension and provide for it to be increased by reference to such variables as may be specified in the resolution.

(3) A resolution for the purposes of this paragraph may take effect from the date on which it is passed or from any earlier or later date specified in the resolution.

(4) A resolution for the purposes of this paragraph may make different provision in relation to the pension payable to or in respect of different holders of the office of Commissioner.

(5) Any salary or pension payable under this paragraph shall be charged on and issued out of the Consolidated Fund.

(6) In this paragraph "pension" includes an allowance or gratuity and any reference to the payment of a pension includes a reference to the making of payments towards the provision of a pension.

Officers and staff

4.—(1) The Commissioner—
- (a) shall appoint a deputy commissioner [or two deputy commissioners], and
- (b) may appoint such number of other officers and staff as he may determine.

[(1A) The Commissioner shall, when appointing any second deputy commissioner, specify which of the Commissioner's functions are to be performed, in the circumstances referred to in paragraph 5(1), by each of the deputy commissioners.]

(2) The remuneration and other conditions of service of the persons appointed under this paragraph shall be determined by the Commissioner.

(3) The Commissioner may pay such pensions, allowances or gratuities to or in respect of the persons appointed under this paragraph, or make such payments towards the provision of such pensions, allowances or gratuities, as he may determine.

(4) The references in sub-paragraph (3) to pensions, allowances or gratuities to or in respect of the persons appointed under this paragraph include references to pensions, allowances or gratuities by way of compensation to or in respect of any of those persons who suffer loss of office or employment.

(5) Any determination under sub-paragraph (1)(b), (2) or (3) shall require the approval of the [Secretary of State].

(6) The Employers' Liability (Compulsory Insurance) Act 1969 shall not require insurance to be effected by the Commissioner.

5.—(1) The deputy commissioner [or deputy commissioners] shall perform the functions conferred by this Act [or the Freedom of Information Act 2000] on the Commissioner during any vacancy in that office or at any time when the Commissioner is for any reason unable to act.

(2) Without prejudice to sub-paragraph (1), any functions of the Commissioner under this Act [or the Freedom of Information Act 2000] may, to the extent authorised by him, be performed by any of his officers or staff.

Authentication of seal of the Commissioner

6. The application of the seal of the Commissioner shall be authenticated by his signature or by the signature of some other person authorised for the purpose.

Presumption of authenticity of documents issued by the Commissioner

7. Any document purporting to be an instrument issued by the Commissioner and to be duly executed under the Commissioner's seal or to be signed by or on behalf of the Commissioner shall be received in evidence and shall be deemed to be such an instrument unless the contrary is shown.

Money

8. The [Secretary of State] may make payments to the Commissioner out of money provided by Parliament.

9.—(1) All fees and other sums received by the Commissioner in the exercise of his functions under this Act[, under section 159 of the Consumer Credit Act 1974 or under the Freedom of Information Act 2000] shall be paid by him to the [Secretary of State].

(2) Sub-paragraph (1) shall not apply where the [Secretary of State], with the consent of the Treasury, otherwise directs.

(3) Any sums received by the [Secretary of State] under sub-paragraph (1) shall be paid into the Consolidated Fund.

Accounts

10.—(1) It shall be the duty of the Commissioner—

(a) to keep proper accounts and other records in relation to the accounts,

(b) to prepare in respect of each financial year a statement of account in such form as the [Secretary of State] may direct, and

(c) to send copies of that statement to the Comptroller and Auditor General on or before 31st August next following the end of the year to which the statement relates or on or before such earlier date after the end of that year as the Treasury may direct.

(2) The Comptroller and Auditor General shall examine and certify any statement sent to him under this paragraph and lay copies of it together with his report thereon before each House of Parliament.

(3) In this paragraph "financial year" means a period of twelve months beginning with 1st April.

Application of Part I in Scotland

11. Paragraphs 1(1), 6 and 7 do not extend to Scotland.

[1188]

NOTES

Commencement: 1 March 2000.

Schedule heading: words in square brackets substituted by the Freedom of Information Act 2000, s 18(4), Sch 2, Pt I, para 1.

Para 1: words in square brackets in sub-para (1) substituted by the Freedom of Information Act 2000, s 18(4), Sch 2, Pt I, para 15(1), (2).

Para 4: words in square brackets in sub-para (1)(a), and the whole of sub-para (1A), inserted by the Freedom of Information Act 2000, s 18(4), Sch 2, Pt II, para 20; words in square brackets in sub-para (5) substituted by the Secretary of State for Constitutional Affairs Order 2003, SI 2003/1887, art 9, Sch 2, para 9(1)(c).

Para 5: words in square brackets inserted by the Freedom of Information Act 2000, s 18(4), Sch 2, Pt II, para 21.

Paras 8, 10: words in square brackets substituted by SI 2003/1887, art 9, Sch 2, para 9(1)(c).

Para 9: words in first pair of square brackets substituted by the Freedom of Information Act 2000, s 18(4), Sch 2, Pt II, para 22; words in second, third and fourth pairs of square brackets substituted by SI 2003/1887, art 9, Sch 2, para 9(1)(c).

PART II
THE TRIBUNAL

Tenure of office

12.—(1) Subject to the following provisions of this paragraph, a member of the Tribunal shall hold and vacate his office in accordance with the terms of his appointment and shall, on ceasing to hold office, be eligible for re-appointment.

(2) Any member of the Tribunal may at any time resign his office by notice in writing to the Lord Chancellor … [(in the case of the chairman or a deputy chairman) or to the Secretary of State (in the case of any other member)].

(3) A person who is the chairman or deputy chairman of the Tribunal shall vacate his office on the day on which he attains the age of seventy years; but this sub-paragraph is subject to section 26(4) to (6) of the Judicial Pensions and Retirement Act 1993 (power to authorise continuance in office up to the age of seventy-five years).

Salary etc

13. The [Secretary of State] shall pay to the members of the Tribunal out of money provided by Parliament such remuneration and allowances as he may determine.

Officers and staff

14. The [Secretary of State] may provide the Tribunal with such officers and staff as he thinks necessary for the proper discharge of its functions.

Expenses

15. Such expenses of the Tribunal as the [Secretary of State] may determine shall be defrayed by the [Secretary of State] out of money provided by Parliament.

[1189]–[1190]

NOTES

Commencement: 1 March 2000.

Para 12: in sub-para (2), words omitted repealed by the Transfer of Functions (Miscellaneous) Order 2001, SI 2001/3500, art 8, Sch 2, Pt I, para 6(3); words in square brackets added by the Secretary of State for Constitutional Affairs Order 2003, SI 2003/1887, art 9, Sch 2, para 9(2).

Paras 13–15: words in square brackets substituted by SI 2003/1887, art 9, Sch 2, para 9(1)(c).

(Pt III repealed by the Freedom of Information Act 2000, ss 18(4), 86, Sch 2, Pt I, para 15(1), (3), Sch 8, Pt II.)

SCHEDULE 6
APPEAL PROCEEDINGS

Sections 28(12), 48(5)

Hearing of appeals

1. For the purpose of hearing and determining appeals or any matter preliminary or incidental to an appeal the Tribunal shall sit at such times and in such places as the chairman or a deputy chairman may direct and may sit in two or more divisions.

Constitution of Tribunal in national security cases

2.—(1) The Lord Chancellor shall from time to time designate, from among the chairman and deputy chairmen appointed by him under section 6(4)(a) and (b), those persons who are to be capable of hearing appeals under section 28(4) or (6) [or under section 60(1) or (4) of the Freedom of Information Act 2000].

(2) A designation under sub-paragraph (1) may at any time be revoked by the Lord Chancellor.

[(3) The Lord Chancellor may make, or revoke, a designation under this paragraph only with the concurrence of all of the following—
- (a) the Lord Chief Justice;
- (b) the Lord President of the Court of Session;
- (c) the Lord Chief Justice of Northern Ireland.

(4) The Lord Chief Justice of England and Wales may nominate a judicial office holder (as defined in section 109(4) of the Constitutional Reform Act 2005) to exercise his functions under sub-paragraph (3) so far as they relate to a designation under this paragraph.

(5) The Lord President of the Court of Session may nominate a judge of the Court of Session who is a member of the First or Second Division of the Inner House of that Court to exercise his functions under sub-paragraph (3) so far as they relate to a designation under this paragraph.

(6) The Lord Chief Justice of Northern Ireland may nominate any of the following to exercise his functions under sub-paragraph (3) so far as they relate to a designation under this paragraph—
- (a) the holder of one of the offices listed in Schedule 1 to the Justice (Northern Ireland) Act 2002;
- (b) a Lord Justice of Appeal (as defined in section 88 of that Act).]

[3.—[(1)] The Tribunal shall be duly constituted—
- (a) for an appeal under section 28(4) or (6) in any case where the application of paragraph 6(1) is excluded by rules under paragraph 7, or
- (b) for an appeal under section 60(1) or (4) of the Freedom of Information Act 2000,

if it consists of three of the persons designated under paragraph 2(1), of whom one shall be designated by the Lord Chancellor to preside.

[(2) The Lord Chancellor may designate a person to preside under this paragraph only with the concurrence of all of the following—
- (a) the Lord Chief Justice of England and Wales;
- (b) the Lord President of the Court of Session;
- (c) the Lord Chief Justice of Northern Ireland.

(3) The Lord Chief Justice of England and Wales may nominate a judicial office holder (as defined in section 109(4) of the Constitutional Reform Act 2005) to exercise his functions under this paragraph.

(4) The Lord President of the Court of Session may nominate a judge of the Court of Session who is a member of the First or Second Division of the Inner House of that Court to exercise his functions under this paragraph.

(5) The Lord Chief Justice of Northern Ireland may nominate any of the following to exercise his functions under this paragraph—
- (a) the holder of one of the offices listed in Schedule 1 to the Justice (Northern Ireland) Act 2002;

(b) a Lord Justice of Appeal (as defined in section 88 of that Act).]]

Constitution of Tribunal in other cases

4.—(1) Subject to any rules made under paragraph 7, the Tribunal shall be duly constituted for an appeal under section 48(1), (2) or (4) if it consists of—

(a) the chairman or a deputy chairman (who shall preside), and

(b) an equal number of the members appointed respectively in accordance with paragraphs (a) and (b) of section 6(6).

[(1A) Subject to any rules made under paragraph 7, the Tribunal shall be duly constituted for an appeal under section 57(1) or (2) of the Freedom of Information Act 2000 if it consists of—

(a) the chairman or a deputy chairman (who shall preside), and

(b) an equal number of the members appointed respectively in accordance with paragraphs (aa) and (bb) of section 6(6).]

(2) The members who are to constitute the Tribunal in accordance with subparagraph (1) [or (1A)] shall be nominated by the chairman or, if he is for any reason unable to act, by a deputy chairman.

Determination of questions by full Tribunal

5. The determination of any question before the Tribunal when constituted in accordance with paragraph 3 or 4 shall be according to the opinion of the majority of the members hearing the appeal.

Ex parte proceedings

6.—(1) Subject to any rules made under paragraph 7, the jurisdiction of the Tribunal in respect of an appeal under section 28(4) or (6) shall be exercised ex parte by one or more persons designated under paragraph 2(1).

(2) Subject to any rules made under paragraph 7, the jurisdiction of the Tribunal in respect of an appeal under section 48(3) shall be exercised ex parte by the chairman or a deputy chairman sitting alone.

Rules of procedure

7.—(1) The [Secretary of State] may make rules for [regulating—

(a) the exercise of the rights of appeal conferred—

(i) by sections 28(4) and (6) and 48, and

(ii) by sections 57(1) and (2) and section 60(1) and (4) of the Freedom of Information Act 2000, and

(b) the practice and procedure of the Tribunal.]

(2) Rules under this paragraph may in particular make provision—

(a) with respect to the period within which an appeal can be brought and the burden of proof on an appeal,

[(aa) for the joinder of any person as a party to any proceedings on an appeal under the Freedom of Information Act 2000,

(ab) for the hearing of an appeal under this Act with an appeal under the Freedom of Information Act 2000,]

(b) for the summoning (or, in Scotland, citation) of witnesses and the administration of oaths,

(c) for securing the production of documents and material used for the processing of personal data,

(d) for the inspection, examination, operation and testing of any equipment or material used in connection with the processing of personal data,

(e) for the hearing of an appeal wholly or partly in camera,

(f) for hearing an appeal in the absence of the appellant or for determining an appeal without a hearing,

PART I STATUTES

(g) for enabling an appeal under section 48(1) against an information notice to be determined by the chairman or a deputy chairman,

(h) for enabling any matter preliminary or incidental to an appeal to be dealt with by the chairman or a deputy chairman,

(i) for the awarding of costs or, in Scotland, expenses,

(j) for the publication of reports of the Tribunal's decisions, and

(k) for conferring on the Tribunal such ancillary powers as the [Secretary of State] thinks necessary for the proper discharge of its functions.

(3) In making rules under this paragraph which relate to appeals under section 28(4) or (6) the [Secretary of State] shall have regard, in particular, to the need to secure that information is not disclosed contrary to the public interest.

Obstruction etc

8.—(1) If any person is guilty of any act or omission in relation to proceedings before the Tribunal which, if those proceedings were proceedings before a court having power to commit for contempt, would constitute contempt of court, the Tribunal may certify the offence to the High Court or, in Scotland, the Court of Session.

(2) Where an offence is so certified, the court may inquire into the matter and, after hearing any witness who may be produced against or on behalf of the person charged with the offence, and after hearing any statement that may be offered in defence, deal with him in any manner in which it could deal with him if he had committed the like offence in relation to the court.

[1191]

NOTES

Commencement: 1 March 2000 (16 July 1998: para 7 insofar as conferring a power to make subordinate legislation).

Para 2: words in square brackets in sub-para (1) inserted by the Freedom of Information Act 2000, s 61(1), Sch 4, para 1; sub-paras (3)–(6) added by the Constitutional Reform Act 2005, s 15(1), Sch 4, Pt 1, para 275(1), (2).

Para 3: substituted by the Freedom of Information Act 2000, s 61(1), Sch 4, para 2; sub-para (1) numbered as such and sub-paras (2)–(5) added by the Constitutional Reform Act 2005, s 15(1), Sch 4, Pt 1, para 275(1), (3).

Para 4: sub-para (1A) and words in square brackets in sub-para (2) inserted by the Freedom of Information Act 2000, s 61(1), Sch 4, para 3.

Para 7: words in second pair of square brackets substituted, and sub-para (2)(aa), (ab) inserted, by the Freedom of Information Act 2000, s 61(1), Sch 4, para 4; other words in square brackets substituted by the Secretary of State for Constitutional Affairs Order 2003, SI 2003/1887, art 9, Sch 2, para 9(1)(d).

Rules: the [Information Tribunal] (National Security Appeals) (Telecommunications) Rules 2000, SI 2000/731; the Information Tribunal (National Security Appeals) Rules 2005, SI 2005/13; the Information Tribunal (Enforcement Appeals) Rules 2005, SI 2005/14 at **[3368]**.

SCHEDULE 7
MISCELLANEOUS EXEMPTIONS

Section 37

Confidential references given by the data controller

1. Personal data are exempt from section 7 if they consist of a reference given or to be given in confidence by the data controller for the purposes of—

(a) the education, training or employment, or prospective education, training or employment, of the data subject,

(b) the appointment, or prospective appointment, of the data subject to any office, or

(c) the provision, or prospective provision, by the data subject of any service.

Armed forces

2. Personal data are exempt from the subject information provisions in any case to the extent to which the application of those provisions would be likely to prejudice the combat effectiveness of any of the armed forces of the Crown.

Judicial appointments and honours

3. Personal data processed for the purposes of—
(a) assessing any person's suitability for judicial office or the office of Queen's Counsel, or
(b) the conferring by the Crown of any honour [or dignity],
are exempt from the subject information provisions.

Crown employment and Crown or Ministerial appointments

4.—[(1)] The [Secretary of State] may by order exempt from the subject information provisions personal data processed for the purposes of assessing any person's suitability for—
(a) employment by or under the Crown, or
(b) any office to which appointments are made by Her Majesty, by a Minister of the Crown or by a [Northern Ireland authority].

[(2) In this paragraph "Northern Ireland authority" means the First Minister, the deputy First Minister, a Northern Ireland Minister or a Northern Ireland department.]

Management forecasts etc

5. Personal data processed for the purposes of management forecasting or management planning to assist the data controller in the conduct of any business or other activity are exempt from the subject information provisions in any case to the extent to which the application of those provisions would be likely to prejudice the conduct of that business or other activity.

Corporate finance

6.—(1) Where personal data are processed for the purposes of, or in connection with, a corporate finance service provided by a relevant person—
(a) the data are exempt from the subject information provisions in any case to the extent to which either—
(i) the application of those provisions to the data could affect the price of any instrument which is already in existence or is to be or may be created, or
(ii) the data controller reasonably believes that the application of those provisions to the data could affect the price of any such instrument, and
(b) to the extent that the data are not exempt from the subject information provisions by virtue of paragraph (a), they are exempt from those provisions if the exemption is required for the purpose of safeguarding an important economic or financial interest of the United Kingdom.

(2) For the purposes of sub-paragraph (1)(b) the [Secretary of State] may by order specify—
(a) matters to be taken into account in determining whether exemption from the subject information provisions is required for the purpose of safeguarding an important economic or financial interest of the United Kingdom, or
(b) circumstances in which exemption from those provisions is, or is not, to be taken to be required for that purpose.

(3) In this paragraph—
"corporate finance service" means a service consisting in—
(a) underwriting in respect of issues of, or the placing of issues of, any instrument,
(b) advice to undertakings on capital structure, industrial strategy and related matters and advice and service relating to mergers and the purchase of undertakings, or
(c) services relating to such underwriting as is mentioned in paragraph (a);
"instrument" means any instrument listed in *section B of the Annex to the Council Directive on investment services in the securities field (93/22/EEC)* … ;
"price" includes value;
"relevant person" means—
[(a) any person who, by reason of any permission he has under Part IV of the

Financial Services and Markets Act 2000, is able to carry on a corporate finance service without contravening the general prohibition, within the meaning of section 19 of that Act,

(b) an EEA firm of the kind mentioned in paragraph 5(a) or (b) of Schedule 3 to that Act which has qualified for authorisation under paragraph 12 of that Schedule, and may lawfully carry on a corporate finance service,

(c) any person who is exempt from the general prohibition in respect of any corporate finance service—

(i) as a result of an exemption order made under section 38(1) of that Act, or

(ii) by reason of section 39(1) of that Act (appointed representatives),

(cc) any person, not falling within paragraph (a), (b) or (c) who may lawfully carry on a corporate finance service without contravening the general prohibition,]

(d) any person who, in the course of his employment, provides to his employer a service falling within paragraph (b) or (c) of the definition of "corporate finance service", or

(e) any partner who provides to other partners in the partnership a service falling within either of those paragraphs.

Negotiations

7. Personal data which consist of records of the intentions of the data controller in relation to any negotiations with the data subject are exempt from the subject information provisions in any case to the extent to which the application of those provisions would be likely to prejudice those negotiations.

Examination marks

8.—(1) Section 7 shall have effect subject to the provisions of sub-paragraphs (2) to (4) in the case of personal data consisting of marks or other information processed by a data controller—

(a) for the purpose of determining the results of an academic, professional or other examination or of enabling the results of any such examination to be determined, or

(b) in consequence of the determination of any such results.

(2) Where the relevant day falls before the day on which the results of the examination are announced, the period mentioned in section 7(8) shall be extended until—

(a) the end of five months beginning with the relevant day, or

(b) the end of forty days beginning with the date of the announcement,

whichever is the earlier.

(3) Where by virtue of sub-paragraph (2) a period longer than the prescribed period elapses after the relevant day before the request is complied with, the information to be supplied pursuant to the request shall be supplied both by reference to the data in question at the time when the request is received and (if different) by reference to the data as from time to time held in the period beginning when the request is received and ending when it is complied with.

(4) For the purposes of this paragraph the results of an examination shall be treated as announced when they are first published or (if not published) when they are first made available or communicated to the candidate in question.

(5) In this paragraph—

"examination" includes any process for determining the knowledge, intelligence, skill or ability of a candidate by reference to his performance in any test, work or other activity;

"the prescribed period" means forty days or such other period as is for the time being prescribed under section 7 in relation to the personal data in question;

"relevant day" has the same meaning as in section 7.

Examination scripts etc

9.—(1) Personal data consisting of information recorded by candidates during an academic, professional or other examination are exempt from section 7.

(2) In this paragraph "examination" has the same meaning as in paragraph 8.

Legal professional privilege

10. Personal data are exempt from the subject information provisions if the data consist of information in respect of which a claim to legal professional privilege [or, in Scotland, to confidentiality of communications] could be maintained in legal proceedings.

Self-incrimination

11.—(1) A person need not comply with any request or order under section 7 to the extent that compliance would, by revealing evidence of the commission of any offence other than an offence under this Act, expose him to proceedings for that offence.

(2) Information disclosed by any person in compliance with any request or order under section 7 shall not be admissible against him in proceedings for an offence under this Act.

[1192]

NOTES

Commencement: 1 March 2000 (16 July 1998: paras 4, 6(2) insofar as conferring a power to make subordinate legislation).

Para 3: words in square brackets in sub-para (b) inserted by the Freedom of Information Act 2000, s 73, Sch 6, para 6.

Para 4: sub-para (1) numbered as such, words in square brackets in sub-para (1)(b) substituted, and sub-para (2) added, by the Northern Ireland Act 1998, s 99, Sch 13, para 21; words "Secretary of State" in square brackets substituted by the Secretary of State for Constitutional Affairs Order 2003, SI 2003/1887, art 9, Sch 2, para 9(1)(e).

Para 6: words in square brackets in sub-para (2) substituted by SI 2003/1887, art 9, Sch 2, para 9(1)(e); for the words in italics in definition "instrument" in sub-para (3) there are substituted the words "section C of Annex I to Directive 2004/39/EC of the European Parliament and of the Council of 21 April 2004 on markets in financial instruments" by the Financial Services and Markets Act 2000 (Markets in Financial Instruments) Regulations 2007, SI 2007/126, art 3(6), Sch 6, Pt 1, para 12, as from 1 April 2007 for certain purposes and as from 1 November 2007 otherwise (for purposes see reg 1 of those Regulations); in sub-para (3), words omitted from definition "instrument" repealed, and in definition "relevant person" paras (a)–(c), (cc) substituted, for paras (a)–(c) as originally enacted, by the Financial Services and Markets Act 2000 (Consequential Amendments) Order 2002, SI 2002/1555, art 25.

Para 10: words in square brackets substituted by the Freedom of Information Act 2000, s 73, Sch 6, para 7.

Orders: the Data Protection (Corporate Finance Exemption) Order 2000, SI 2000/184; the Data Protection (Crown Appointments) Order 2000, SI 2000/416.

SCHEDULE 8
TRANSITIONAL RELIEF

Section 39

PART I
INTERPRETATION OF SCHEDULE

1.—(1) For the purposes of this Schedule, personal data are "eligible data" at any time if, and to the extent that, they are at that time subject to processing which was already under way immediately before 24th October 1998.

(2) In this Schedule—

"eligible automated data" means eligible data which fall within paragraph (a) or (b) of the definition of "data" in section 1(1);

"eligible manual data" means eligible data which are not eligible automated data;

"the first transitional period" means the period beginning with the commencement of this Schedule and ending with 23rd October 2001;

"the second transitional period" means the period beginning with 24th October 2001 and ending with 23rd October 2007.

[1193]

NOTES

Commencement: 1 March 2000.

PART II
EXEMPTIONS AVAILABLE BEFORE 24TH OCTOBER 2001

Manual data

2.—(1) Eligible manual data, other than data forming part of an accessible record, are exempt from the data protection principles and Parts II and III of this Act during the first transitional period.

(2) This paragraph does not apply to eligible manual data to which paragraph 4 applies.

3.—(1) This paragraph applies to—
(a) eligible manual data forming part of an accessible record, and
(b) personal data which fall within paragraph (d) of the definition of "data" in section 1(1) but which, because they are not subject to processing which was already under way immediately before 24th October 1998, are not eligible data for the purposes of this Schedule.

(2) During the first transitional period, data to which this paragraph applies are exempt from—
(a) the data protection principles, except the sixth principle so far as relating to sections 7 and 12A,
(b) Part II of this Act, except—
(i) section 7 (as it has effect subject to section 8) and section 12A, and
(ii) section 15 so far as relating to those sections, and
(c) Part III of this Act.

4.—(1) This paragraph applies to eligible manual data which consist of information relevant to the financial standing of the data subject and in respect of which the data controller is a credit reference agency.

(2) During the first transitional period, data to which this paragraph applies are exempt from—
(a) the data protection principles, except the sixth principle so far as relating to sections 7 and 12A,
(b) Part II of this Act, except—
(i) section 7 (as it has effect subject to sections 8 and 9) and section 12A, and
(ii) section 15 so far as relating to those sections, and
(c) Part III of this Act.

Processing otherwise than by reference to the data subject

5. During the first transitional period, for the purposes of this Act (apart from paragraph 1), eligible automated data are not to be regarded as being "processed" unless the processing is by reference to the data subject.

Payrolls and accounts

6.—(1) Subject to sub-paragraph (2), eligible automated data processed by a data controller for one or more of the following purposes—
(a) calculating amounts payable by way of remuneration or pensions in respect of service in any employment or office or making payments of, or of sums deducted from, such remuneration or pensions, or
(b) keeping accounts relating to any business or other activity carried on by the data controller or keeping records of purchases, sales or other transactions for the purpose of ensuring that the requisite payments are made by or to him in respect of those transactions or for the purpose of making financial or management forecasts to assist him in the conduct of any such business or activity,

are exempt from the data protection principles and Parts II and III of this Act during the first transitional period.

(2) It shall be a condition of the exemption of any eligible automated data under this paragraph that the data are not processed for any other purpose, but the exemption is not lost by any processing of the eligible data for any other purpose if the data controller shows that he had taken such care to prevent it as in all the circumstances was reasonably required.

(3) Data processed only for one or more of the purposes mentioned in subparagraph (1)(a) may be disclosed—

(a) to any person, other than the data controller, by whom the remuneration or pensions in question are payable,

(b) for the purpose of obtaining actuarial advice,

(c) for the purpose of giving information as to the persons in any employment or office for use in medical research into the health of, or injuries suffered by, persons engaged in particular occupations or working in particular places or areas,

(d) if the data subject (or a person acting on his behalf) has requested or consented to the disclosure of the data either generally or in the circumstances in which the disclosure in question is made, or

(e) if the person making the disclosure has reasonable grounds for believing that the disclosure falls within paragraph (d).

(4) Data processed for any of the purposes mentioned in sub-paragraph (1) may be disclosed—

(a) for the purpose of audit or where the disclosure is for the purpose only of giving information about the data controller's financial affairs, or

(b) in any case in which disclosure would be permitted by any other provision of this Part of this Act if sub-paragraph (2) were included among the non-disclosure provisions.

(5) In this paragraph "remuneration" includes remuneration in kind and "pensions" includes gratuities or similar benefits.

Unincorporated members' clubs and mailing lists

7. Eligible automated data processed by an unincorporated members' club and relating only to the members of the club are exempt from the data protection principles and Parts II and III of this Act during the first transitional period.

8. Eligible automated data processed by a data controller only for the purposes of distributing, or recording the distribution of, articles or information to the data subjects and consisting only of their names, addresses or other particulars necessary for effecting the distribution, are exempt from the data protection principles and Parts II and III of this Act during the first transitional period.

9. Neither paragraph 7 nor paragraph 8 applies to personal data relating to any data subject unless he has been asked by the club or data controller whether he objects to the data relating to him being processed as mentioned in that paragraph and has not objected.

10. It shall be a condition of the exemption of any data under paragraph 7 that the data are not disclosed except as permitted by paragraph 11 and of the exemption under paragraph 8 that the data are not processed for any purpose other than that mentioned in that paragraph or as permitted by paragraph 11, but—

(a) the exemption under paragraph 7 shall not be lost by any disclosure in breach of that condition, and

(b) the exemption under paragraph 8 shall not be lost by any processing in breach of that condition,

if the data controller shows that he had taken such care to prevent it as in all the circumstances was reasonably required.

11. Data to which paragraph 10 applies may be disclosed—

(a) if the data subject (or a person acting on his behalf) has requested or consented to the disclosure of the data either generally or in the circumstances in which the disclosure in question is made,

(b) if the person making the disclosure has reasonable grounds for believing that the disclosure falls within paragraph (a), or

(c) in any case in which disclosure would be permitted by any other provision of this Part of this Act if paragraph 8 were included among the non-disclosure provisions.

Back-up data

12. Eligible automated data which are processed only for the purpose of replacing other data in the event of the latter being lost, destroyed or impaired are exempt from section 7 during the first transitional period.

Exemption of all eligible automated data from certain requirements

13.—(1) During the first transitional period, eligible automated data are exempt from the following provisions—

(a) the first data protection principle to the extent to which it requires compliance with—
  (i) paragraph 2 of Part II of Schedule 1,
  (ii) the conditions in Schedule 2, and
  (iii) the conditions in Schedule 3,

(b) the seventh data protection principle to the extent to which it requires compliance with paragraph 12 of Part II of Schedule 1;

(c) the eighth data protection principle,

(d) in section 7(1), paragraphs (b), (c)(ii) and (d),

(e) sections 10 and 11,

(f) section 12, and

(g) section 13, except so far as relating to—
  (i) any contravention of the fourth data protection principle,
  (ii) any disclosure without the consent of the data controller,
  (iii) loss or destruction of data without the consent of the data controller, or
  (iv) processing for the special purposes.

(2) The specific exemptions conferred by sub-paragraph (1)(a), (c) and (e) do not limit the data controller's general duty under the first data protection principle to ensure that processing is fair.

[1194]

NOTES

Commencement: 1 March 2000.

PART III
EXEMPTIONS AVAILABLE AFTER 23RD OCTOBER 2001 BUT BEFORE 24TH OCTOBER 2007

14.—(1) This paragraph applies to—

(a) eligible manual data which were held immediately before 24th October 1998, and

(b) personal data which fall within paragraph (d) of the definition of "data" in section 1(1) but do not fall within paragraph (a) of this subparagraph,

but does not apply to eligible manual data to which the exemption in paragraph 16 applies.

(2) During the second transitional period, data to which this paragraph applies are exempt from the following provisions—

(a) the first data protection principle except to the extent to which it requires compliance with paragraph 2 of Part II of Schedule 1,

(b) the second, third, fourth and fifth data protection principles, and

(c) section 14(1) to (3).

[14A.—(1) This paragraph applies to personal data which fall within paragraph (e) of the definition of "data" in section 1(1) and do not fall within paragraph 14(1)(a), but does not apply to eligible manual data to which the exemption in paragraph 16 applies.

(2) During the second transitional period, data to which this paragraph applies are exempt from—

(a) the fourth data protection principle, and

(b) section 14(1) to (3).]

[1195]

NOTES

Commencement: 1 March 2000.
Para 14A: inserted by the Freedom of Information Act 2000, s 70(3).

PART IV
EXEMPTIONS AFTER 23RD OCTOBER 2001 FOR HISTORICAL RESEARCH

15. In this Part of this Schedule "the relevant conditions" has the same meaning as in section 33.

16.—(1) Eligible manual data which are processed only for the purpose of historical research in compliance with the relevant conditions are exempt from the provisions specified in sub-paragraph (2) after 23rd October 2001.

(2) The provisions referred to in sub-paragraph (1) are—

(a) the first data protection principle except in so far as it requires compliance with paragraph 2 of Part II of Schedule 1,
(b) the second, third, fourth and fifth data protection principles, and
(c) section 14(1) to (3).

17.—(1) After 23rd October 2001 eligible automated data which are processed only for the purpose of historical research in compliance with the relevant conditions are exempt from the first data protection principle to the extent to which it requires compliance with the conditions in Schedules 2 and 3.

(2) Eligible automated data which are processed—

(a) only for the purpose of historical research,
(b) in compliance with the relevant conditions, and
(c) otherwise than by reference to the data subject,

are also exempt from the provisions referred to in sub-paragraph (3) after 23rd October 2001.

(3) The provisions referred to in sub-paragraph (2) are—

(a) the first data protection principle except in so far as it requires compliance with paragraph 2 of Part II of Schedule 1,
(b) the second, third, fourth and fifth data protection principles, and
(c) section 14(1) to (3).

18. For the purposes of this Part of this Schedule personal data are not to be treated as processed otherwise than for the purpose of historical research merely because the data are disclosed—

(a) to any person, for the purpose of historical research only,
(b) to the data subject or a person acting on his behalf,
(c) at the request, or with the consent, of the data subject or a person acting on his behalf, or
(d) in circumstances in which the person making the disclosure has reasonable grounds for believing that the disclosure falls within paragraph (a), (b) or (c).

[1196]

NOTES

Commencement: 1 March 2000.

PART V
EXEMPTION FROM SECTION 22

19. Processing which was already under way immediately before 24th October 1998 is not assessable processing for the purposes of section 22.

[1197]

NOTES

Commencement: 1 March 2000.

SCHEDULE 9
POWERS OF ENTRY AND INSPECTION

Section 50

Issue of warrants

1.—(1) If a circuit judge [or a District Judge (Magistrates' Courts)] is satisfied by information on oath supplied by the Commissioner that there are reasonable grounds for suspecting—

(a) that a data controller has contravened or is contravening any of the data protection principles, or

(b) that an offence under this Act has been or is being committed,

and that evidence of the contravention or of the commission of the offence is to be found on any premises specified in the information, he may, subject to subparagraph (2) and paragraph 2, grant a warrant to the Commissioner.

(2) A judge shall not issue a warrant under this Schedule in respect of any personal data processed for the special purposes unless a determination by the Commissioner under section 45 with respect to those data has taken effect.

(3) A warrant issued under sub-paragraph (1) shall authorise the Commissioner or any of his officers or staff at any time within seven days of the date of the warrant to enter the premises, to search them, to inspect, examine, operate and test any equipment found there which is used or intended to be used for the processing of personal data and to inspect and seize any documents or other material found there which may be such evidence as is mentioned in that sub-paragraph.

2.—(1) A judge shall not issue a warrant under this Schedule unless he is satisfied—

(a) that the Commissioner has given seven days' notice in writing to the occupier of the premises in question demanding access to the premises, and

(b) that either—

(i) access was demanded at a reasonable hour and was unreasonably refused, or

(ii) although entry to the premises was granted, the occupier unreasonably refused to comply with a request by the Commissioner or any of the Commissioner's officers or staff to permit the Commissioner or the officer or member of staff to do any of the things referred to in paragraph 1(3), and

(c) that the occupier, has, after the refusal, been notified by the Commissioner of the application for the warrant and has had an opportunity of being heard by the judge on the question whether or not it should be issued.

(2) Sub-paragraph (1) shall not apply if the judge is satisfied that the case is one of urgency or that compliance with those provisions would defeat the object of the entry.

3. A judge who issues a warrant under this Schedule shall also issue two copies of it and certify them clearly as copies.

Execution of warrants

4. A person executing a warrant issued under this Schedule may use such reasonable force as may be necessary.

5. A warrant issued under this Schedule shall be executed at a reasonable hour unless it appears to the person executing it that there are grounds for suspecting that the evidence in question would not be found if it were so executed.

6. If the person who occupies the premises in respect of which a warrant is issued under this Schedule is present when the warrant is executed, he shall be shown the warrant and supplied with a copy of it; and if that person is not present a copy of the warrant shall be left in a prominent place on the premises.

7.—(1) A person seizing anything in pursuance of a warrant under this Schedule shall give a receipt for it if asked to do so.

(2) Anything so seized may be retained for so long as is necessary in all the circumstances but the person in occupation of the premises in question shall be given a copy of anything that is seized if he so requests and the person executing the warrant considers that it can be done without undue delay.

Matters exempt from inspection and seizure

8. The powers of inspection and seizure conferred by a warrant issued under this Schedule shall not be exercisable in respect of personal data which by virtue of section 28 are exempt from any of the provisions of this Act.

9.—(1) Subject to the provisions of this paragraph, the powers of inspection and seizure conferred by a warrant issued under this Schedule shall not be exercisable in respect of—

(a) any communication between a professional legal adviser and his client in connection with the giving of legal advice to the client with respect to his obligations, liabilities or rights under this Act, or

(b) any communication between a professional legal adviser and his client, or between such an adviser or his client and any other person, made in connection with or in contemplation of proceedings under or arising out of this Act (including proceedings before the Tribunal) and for the purposes of such proceedings.

(2) Sub-paragraph (1) applies also to—

(a) any copy or other record of any such communication as is there mentioned, and

(b) any document or article enclosed with or referred to in any such communication if made in connection with the giving of any advice or, as the case may be, in connection with or in contemplation of and for the purposes of such proceedings as are there mentioned.

(3) This paragraph does not apply to anything in the possession of any person other than the professional legal adviser or his client or to anything held with the intention of furthering a criminal purpose.

(4) In this paragraph references to the client of a professional legal adviser include references to any person representing such a client.

10. If the person in occupation of any premises in respect of which a warrant is issued under this Schedule objects to the inspection or seizure under the warrant of any material on the grounds that it consists partly of matters in respect of which those powers are not exercisable, he shall, if the person executing the warrant so requests, furnish that person with a copy of so much of the material as is not exempt from those powers.

Return of warrants

11. A warrant issued under this Schedule shall be returned to the court from which it was issued—

(a) after being executed, or

(b) if not executed within the time authorised for its execution;

and the person by whom any such warrant is executed shall make an endorsement on it stating what powers have been exercised by him under the warrant.

Offences

12. Any person who—

(a) intentionally obstructs a person in the execution of a warrant issued under this Schedule, or

(b) fails without reasonable excuse to give any person executing such a warrant such assistance as he may reasonably require for the execution of the warrant,

is guilty of an offence.

Vessels, vehicles etc

13. In this Schedule "premises" includes any vessel, vehicle, aircraft or hovercraft, and references to the occupier of any premises include references to the person in charge of any vessel, vehicle, aircraft or hovercraft.

Scotland and Northern Ireland

14. In the application of this Schedule to Scotland—

(a) for any reference to a circuit judge there is substituted a reference to the sheriff,

(b) for any reference to information on oath there is substituted a reference to evidence on oath, and

(c) for the reference to the court from which the warrant was issued there is substituted a reference to the sheriff clerk.

15. In the application of this Schedule to Northern Ireland—

(a) for any reference to a circuit judge there is substituted a reference to a county court judge, and

(b) for any reference to information on oath there is substituted a reference to a complaint on oath.

[1198]

NOTES

Commencement: 1 March 2000.

Para 1: words in square brackets inserted by the Courts Act 2003, s 65, Sch 4, para 8, as from a day to be appointed.

As to the power of seizure under para 1 of this Schedule, see the Criminal Justice and Police Act 2001, s 50, Sch 1, Pt 1, para 65 (additional powers of seizure of material from premises).

SCHEDULE 10
FURTHER PROVISIONS RELATING TO ASSISTANCE UNDER SECTION 53

Section 53(6)

1. In this Schedule "applicant" and "proceedings" have the same meaning as in section 53.

2. The assistance provided under section 53 may include the making of arrangements for, or for the Commissioner to bear the costs of—

(a) the giving of advice or assistance by a solicitor or counsel, and

(b) the representation of the applicant, or the provision to him of such assistance as is usually given by a solicitor or counsel—

(i) in steps preliminary or incidental to the proceedings, or

(ii) in arriving at or giving effect to a compromise to avoid or bring an end to the proceedings.

3. Where assistance is provided with respect to the conduct of proceedings—

(a) it shall include an agreement by the Commissioner to indemnify the applicant (subject only to any exceptions specified in the notification) in respect of any liability to pay costs or expenses arising by virtue of any judgment or order of the court in the proceedings,

(b) it may include an agreement by the Commissioner to indemnify the applicant in respect of any liability to pay costs or expenses arising by virtue of any compromise or settlement arrived at in order to avoid the proceedings or bring the proceedings to an end, and

(c) it may include an agreement by the Commissioner to indemnify the applicant in respect of any liability to pay damages pursuant to an undertaking given on the grant of interlocutory relief (in Scotland, an interim order) to the applicant.

4. Where the Commissioner provides assistance in relation to any proceedings, he shall do so on such terms, or make such other arrangements, as will secure that a person against whom the proceedings have been or are commenced is informed that assistance has been or is being provided by the Commissioner in relation to them.

5. In England and Wales or Northern Ireland, the recovery of expenses incurred by the Commissioner in providing an applicant with assistance (as taxed or assessed in such manner as may be prescribed by rules of court) shall constitute a first charge for the benefit of the Commissioner—
   (a) on any costs which, by virtue of any judgment or order of the court, are payable to the applicant by any other person in respect of the matter in connection with which the assistance is provided, and
   (b) on any sum payable to the applicant under a compromise or settlement arrived at in connection with that matter to avoid or bring to an end any proceedings.

6. In Scotland, the recovery of such expenses (as taxed or assessed in such manner as may be prescribed by rules of court) shall be paid to the Commissioner, in priority to other debts—
   (a) out of any expenses which, by virtue of any judgment or order of the court, are payable to the applicant by any other person in respect of the matter in connection with which the assistance is provided, and
   (b) out of any sum payable to the applicant under a compromise or settlement arrived at in connection with that matter to avoid or bring to an end any proceedings.

[1199]

NOTES

Commencement: 1 March 2000.

SCHEDULE 11
EDUCATIONAL RECORDS

Section 68(1), (6)

Meaning of "educational record"

1. For the purposes of section 68 "educational record" means any record to which paragraph 2, 5 or 7 applies.

England and Wales

2. This paragraph applies to any record of information which—
   (a) is processed by or on behalf of the governing body of, or a teacher at, any school in England and Wales specified in paragraph 3,
   (b) relates to any person who is or has been a pupil at the school, and
   (c) originated from or was supplied by or on behalf of any of the persons specified in paragraph 4,

other than information which is processed by a teacher solely for the teacher's own use.

3. The schools referred to in paragraph 2(a) are—
   (a) a school maintained by a local education authority, and
   (b) a special school, as defined by section 6(2) of the Education Act 1996, which is not so maintained.

4. The persons referred to in paragraph 2(c) are—
   (a) an employee of the local education authority which maintains the school,
   (b) in the case of—
      (i) a voluntary aided, foundation or foundation special school (within the meaning of the School Standards and Framework Act 1998), or
      (ii) a special school which is not maintained by a local education authority,

   a teacher or other employee at the school (including an educational psychologist engaged by the governing body under a contract for services), (c) the pupil to whom the record relates, and (d) a parent, as defined by section 576(1) of the Education Act 1996, of that pupil.

5. This paragraph applies to any record of information which is processed—
   (a) by an education authority in Scotland, and
   (b) for the purpose of the relevant function of the authority,

other than information which is processed by a teacher solely for the teacher's own use.

6. For the purposes of paragraph 5—

(a) "education authority" means an education authority within the meaning of the Education (Scotland) Act 1980 ("the 1980 Act") …,

(b) "the relevant function" means, in relation to each of those authorities, their function under section 1 of the 1980 Act and section 7(1) of the 1989 Act, and

(c) information processed by an education authority is processed for the purpose of the relevant function of the authority if the processing relates to the discharge of that function in respect of a person—

(i) who is or has been a pupil in a school provided by the authority, or

(ii) who receives, or has received, further education (within the meaning of the 1980 Act) so provided.

Northern Ireland

7.—(1) This paragraph applies to any record of information which—

(a) is processed by or on behalf of the Board of Governors of, or a teacher at, any grant-aided school in Northern Ireland,

(b) relates to any person who is or has been a pupil at the school, and

(c) originated from or was supplied by or on behalf of any of the persons specified in paragraph 8,

other than information which is processed by a teacher solely for the teacher's own use.

(2) In sub-paragraph (1) "grant-aided school" has the same meaning as in the Education and Libraries (Northern Ireland) Order 1986.

8. The persons referred to in paragraph 7(1) are—

(a) a teacher at the school,

(b) an employee of an education and library board, other than such a teacher,

(c) the pupil to whom the record relates, and

(d) a parent (as defined by Article 2(2) of the Education and Libraries (Northern Ireland) Order 1986) of that pupil.

England and Wales: transitory provisions

9.—(1) Until the appointed day within the meaning of section 20 of the School Standards and Framework Act 1998, this Schedule shall have effect subject to the following modifications.

(2) Paragraph 3 shall have effect as if for paragraph (b) and the "and" immediately preceding it there were substituted—

"(aa) a grant-maintained school, as defined by section 183(1) of the Education Act 1996,

(ab) a grant-maintained special school, as defined by section 337(4) of that Act, and

(b) a special school, as defined by section 6(2) of that Act, which is neither a maintained special school, as defined by section 337(3) of that Act, nor a grant-maintained special school.".

(3) Paragraph 4(b)(i) shall have effect as if for the words from "foundation", in the first place where it occurs, to "1998)" there were substituted "or grant-maintained school".

[1200]

NOTES

Commencement: 16 July 1998.

Para 6: words omitted from sub-para (a) repealed by the Standards in Scotland's Schools etc Act 2000, s 60(2), Sch 3.

SCHEDULE 12
ACCESSIBLE PUBLIC RECORDS

Section 68(1)(c)

Meaning of "accessible public record"

1. For the purposes of section 68 "accessible public record" means any record which is kept by an authority specified—

(a) as respects England and Wales, in the Table in paragraph 2,

(b) as respects Scotland, in the Table in paragraph 4, or

(c) as respects Northern Ireland, in the Table in paragraph 6,

and is a record of information of a description specified in that Table in relation to that authority.

Housing and social services records: England and Wales

2. The following is the Table referred to in paragraph 1(a).

TABLE OF AUTHORITIES AND INFORMATION

The authorities	*The accessible information*
Housing Act local authority.	Information held for the purpose of any of the authority's tenancies.
Local social services authority.	Information held for any purpose of the authority's social services functions.

3.—(1) The following provisions apply for the interpretation of the Table in paragraph 2.

(2) Any authority which, by virtue of section 4(e) of the Housing Act 1985, is a local authority for the purpose of any provision of that Act is a "Housing Act local authority" for the purposes of this Schedule, and so is any housing action trust established under Part III of the Housing Act 1988.

(3) Information contained in records kept by a Housing Act local authority is "held for the purpose of any of the authority's tenancies" if it is held for any purpose of the relationship of landlord and tenant of a dwelling which subsists, has subsisted or may subsist between the authority and any individual who is, has been or, as the case may be, has applied to be, a tenant of the authority.

(4) Any authority which, by virtue of section 1 or 12 of the Local Authority Social Services Act 1970, is or is treated as a local authority for the purposes of that Act is a "local social services authority" for the purposes of this Schedule; and information contained in records kept by such an authority is "held for any purpose of the authority's social services functions" if it is held for the purpose of any past, current or proposed exercise of such a function in any case.

(5) Any expression used in paragraph 2 or this paragraph and in Part II of the Housing Act 1985 or the Local Authority Social Services Act 1970 has the same meaning as in that Act.

Housing and social services records: Scotland

4. The following is the Table referred to in paragraph 1(b).

TABLE OF AUTHORITIES AND INFORMATION

The authorities	*The accessible information*
Local authority.	Information held for any purpose of any of the body's tenancies.
Scottish Homes.	
Social work authority.	Information held for any purpose of the authority's functions under the Social Work (Scotland) Act 1968 and the enactments referred to in section 5(1B) of that Act.

5.—(1) The following provisions apply for the interpretation of the Table in paragraph 4.

(2) "Local authority" means—

(a) a council constituted under section 2 of the Local Government etc (Scotland) Act 1994,

(b) a joint board or joint committee of two or more of those councils, or

(c) any trust under the control of such a council.

(3) Information contained in records kept by a local authority *or Scottish Homes* is held for the purpose of any of their tenancies if it is held for any purpose of the relationship of landlord and tenant of a dwelling-house which subsists, has subsisted or may subsist between the authority *or, as the case may be, Scottish Homes* and any individual who is, has been or, as the case may be, has applied to be a tenant of theirs.

(4) "Social work authority" means a local authority for the purposes of the Social Work (Scotland) Act 1968; and information contained in records kept by such an authority is held for any purpose of their functions if it is held for the purpose of any past, current or proposed exercise of such a function in any case.

Housing and social services records: Northern Ireland

6. The following is the Table referred to in paragraph 1(c).

TABLE OF AUTHORITIES AND INFORMATION

The authorities	*The accessible information*
The Northern Ireland Housing Executive.	Information held for the purpose of any of the Executive's tenancies.
A Health and Social Services Board.	Information held for the purpose of any past, current or proposed exercise by the Board of any function exercisable, by virtue of directions under Article 17(1) of the Health and Personal Social Services (Northern Ireland) Order 1972, by the Board on behalf of the Department of Health and Social Services with respect to the administration of personal social services under— (a) the Children and Young Persons Act (Northern Ireland) 1968; (b) the Health and Personal Social Services (Northern Ireland) Order 1972; (c) Article 47 of the Matrimonial Causes (Northern Ireland) Order 1978; (d) Article 11 of the Domestic Proceedings (Northern Ireland) Order 1980;

The authorities	*The accessible information*
	(e) the Adoption (Northern Ireland) Order 1987; or
	(f) the Children (Northern Ireland) Order 1995.
An HSS trust.	Information held for the purpose of any past, current or proposed exercise by the trust of any function exercisable, by virtue of an authorisation under Article 3(1) of the Health and Personal Social Services (Northern Ireland) Order 1994, by the trust on behalf of a Health and Social Services Board with respect to the administration of personal social services under any statutory provision mentioned in the last preceding entry.

7.—(1) This paragraph applies for the interpretation of the Table in paragraph 6.

(2) Information contained in records kept by the Northern Ireland Housing Executive is "held for the purpose of any of the Executive's tenancies" if it is held for any purpose of the relationship of landlord and tenant of a dwelling which subsists, has subsisted or may subsist between the Executive and any individual who is, has been or, as the case may be, has applied to be, a tenant of the Executive.

[1201]

NOTES

Commencement: 16 July 1998.

Para 4: entry "Scottish Homes" repealed by the Housing (Scotland) Act 2001, s 112, Sch 10, para 26(a), as from a day to be appointed.

Para 5: words in italics repealed by the Housing (Scotland) Act 2001, s 112, Sch 10, para 26(b), as from a day to be appointed.

SCHEDULE 13
MODIFICATIONS OF ACT HAVING EFFECT BEFORE 24TH OCTOBER 2007
Section 72

1. After section 12 there is inserted—

"12A Rights of data subjects in relation to exempt manual data

(1) A data subject is entitled at any time by notice in writing—

(a) to require the data controller to rectify, block, erase or destroy exempt manual data which are inaccurate or incomplete, or

(b) to require the data controller to cease holding exempt manual data in a way incompatible with the legitimate purposes pursued by the data controller.

(2) A notice under subsection (1)(a) or (b) must state the data subject's reasons for believing that the data are inaccurate or incomplete or, as the case may be, his reasons for believing that they are held in a way incompatible with the legitimate purposes pursued by the data controller.

(3) If the court is satisfied, on the application of any person who has given a notice under subsection (1) which appears to the court to be justified (or to be justified to any extent) that the data controller in question has failed to comply with the notice, the court may order him to take such steps for complying with the notice (or for complying with it to that extent) as the court thinks fit.

(4) In this section "exempt manual data" means—

(a) in relation to the first transitional period, as defined by paragraph 1(2) of Schedule 8, data to which paragraph 3 or 4 of that Schedule applies, and

(b) in relation to the second transitional period, as so defined, data to which paragraph 14 [or 14A] of that Schedule applies.

(5) For the purposes of this section personal data are incomplete if, and only if, the data, although not inaccurate, are such that their incompleteness would constitute a contravention of the third or fourth data protection principles, if those principles applied to the data.".

2. In section 32—
(a) in subsection (2) after "section 12" there is inserted—
"(dd) section 12A,", and
(b) in subsection (4) after "12(8)" there is inserted ", 12A(3)".

3. In section 34 for "section 14(1) to (3)" there is substituted "sections 12A and 14(1) to (3)."

4. In section 53(1) after "12(8)" there is inserted ", 12A(3)".

5. In paragraph 8 of Part II of Schedule 1, the word "or" at the end of paragraph (c) is omitted and after paragraph (d) there is inserted
"or
(e) he contravenes section 12A by failing to comply with a notice given under subsection (1) of that section to the extent that the notice is justified.".

[1202]

NOTES

Commencement: 1 March 2000.

Para 1: words in square brackets in s 12A(4)(b) (as set out above) inserted by the Freedom of Information Act 2000, s 70(4).

SCHEDULE 14
TRANSITIONAL PROVISIONS AND SAVINGS

Section 73

Interpretation

1. In this Schedule—
"the 1984 Act" means the Data Protection Act 1984;
"the old principles" means the data protection principles within the meaning of the 1984 Act;
"the new principles" means the data protection principles within the meaning of this Act.

Effect of registration under Part II of 1984 Act

2.—(1) Subject to sub-paragraphs (4) and (5) any person who, immediately before the commencement of Part III of this Act—
(a) is registered as a data user under Part II of the 1984 Act, or
(b) is treated by virtue of section 7(6) of the 1984 Act as so registered,
is exempt from section 17(1) of this Act until the end of the registration period …

(2) In sub-paragraph (1) "the registration period", in relation to a person, means—
(a) where there is a single entry in respect of that person as a data user, the period at the end of which, if section 8 of the 1984 Act had remained in force, that entry would have fallen to be removed unless renewed, and
(b) where there are two or more entries in respect of that person as a data user, the period at the end of which, if that section had remained in force, the last of those entries to expire would have fallen to be removed unless renewed.

(3) Any application for registration as a data user under Part II of the 1984 Act which is received by the Commissioner before the commencement of Part III of this Act (including any appeal against a refusal of registration) shall be determined in accordance with the old principles and the provisions of the 1984 Act.

(4) If a person falling within paragraph (b) of sub-paragraph (1) receives a notification under section 7(1) of the 1984 Act of the refusal of his application, sub-paragraph (1) shall cease to apply to him—

(a) if no appeal is brought, at the end of the period within which an appeal can be brought against the refusal, or

(b) on the withdrawal or dismissal of the appeal.

(5) If a data controller gives a notification under section 18(1) at a time when he is exempt from section 17(1) by virtue of sub-paragraph (1), he shall cease to be so exempt.

(6) The Commissioner shall include in the register maintained under section 19 an entry in respect of each person who is exempt from section 17(1) by virtue of sub-paragraph (1); and each entry shall consist of the particulars which, immediately before the commencement of Part III of this Act, were included (or treated as included) in respect of that person in the register maintained under section 4 of the 1984 Act.

(7) Notification regulations under Part III of this Act may make provision modifying the duty referred to in section 20(1) in its application to any person in respect of whom an entry in the register maintained under section 19 has been made under sub-paragraph (6).

(8) Notification regulations under Part III of this Act may make further transitional provision in connection with the substitution of Part III of this Act for Part II of the 1984 Act (registration), including provision modifying the application of provisions of Part III in transitional cases.

Rights of data subjects

3.—(1) The repeal of section 21 of the 1984 Act (right of access to personal data) does not affect the application of that section in any case in which the request (together with the information referred to in paragraph (a) of subsection (4) of that section and, in a case where it is required, the consent referred to in paragraph (b) of that subsection) was received before the day on which the repeal comes into force.

(2) Sub-paragraph (1) does not apply where the request is made by reference to this Act.

(3) Any fee paid for the purposes of section 21 of the 1984 Act before the commencement of section 7 in a case not falling within sub-paragraph (1) shall be taken to have been paid for the purposes of section 7.

4. The repeal of section 22 of the 1984 Act (compensation for inaccuracy) and the repeal of section 23 of that Act (compensation for loss or unauthorised disclosure) do not affect the application of those sections in relation to damage or distress suffered at any time by reason of anything done or omitted to be done before the commencement of the repeals.

5. The repeal of section 24 of the 1984 Act (rectification and erasure) does not affect any case in which the application to the court was made before the day on which the repeal comes into force.

6. Subsection (3)(b) of section 14 does not apply where the rectification, blocking, erasure or destruction occurred before the commencement of that section.

Enforcement and transfer prohibition notices served under Part V of 1984 Act

7.—(1) If, immediately before the commencement of section 40—

(a) an enforcement notice under section 10 of the 1984 Act has effect, and

(b) either the time for appealing against the notice has expired or any appeal has been determined,

then, after that commencement, to the extent mentioned in sub-paragraph (3), the notice shall have effect for the purposes of sections 41 and 47 as if it were an enforcement notice under section 40.

(2) Where an enforcement notice has been served under section 10 of the 1984 Act before the commencement of section 40 and immediately before that commencement either—

(a) the time for appealing against the notice has not expired, or

(b) an appeal has not been determined,

PART I STATUTES

the appeal shall be determined in accordance with the provisions of the 1984 Act and the old principles and, unless the notice is quashed on appeal, to the extent mentioned in sub-paragraph (3) the notice shall have effect for the purposes of sections 41 and 47 as if it were an enforcement notice under section 40.

(3) An enforcement notice under section 10 of the 1984 Act has the effect described in sub-paragraph (1) or (2) only to the extent that the steps specified in the notice for complying with the old principle or principles in question are steps which the data controller could be required by an enforcement notice under section 40 to take for complying with the new principles or any of them.

8.—(1) If, immediately before the commencement of section 40—

(a) a transfer prohibition notice under section 12 of the 1984 Act has effect, and

(b) either the time for appealing against the notice has expired or any appeal has been determined,

then, on and after that commencement, to the extent specified in sub-paragraph (3), the notice shall have effect for the purposes of sections 41 and 47 as if it were an enforcement notice under section 40.

(2) Where a transfer prohibition notice has been served under section 12 of the 1984 Act and immediately before the commencement of section 40 either—

(a) the time for appealing against the notice has not expired, or

(b) an appeal has not been determined,

the appeal shall be determined in accordance with the provisions of the 1984 Act and the old principles and, unless the notice is quashed on appeal, to the extent mentioned in sub-paragraph (3) the notice shall have effect for the purposes of sections 41 and 47 as if it were an enforcement notice under section 40.

(3) A transfer prohibition notice under section 12 of the 1984 Act has the effect described in sub-paragraph (1) or (2) only to the extent that the prohibition imposed by the notice is one which could be imposed by an enforcement notice under section 40 for complying with the new principles or any of them.

Notices under new law relating to matters in relation to which 1984 Act had effect

9. The Commissioner may serve an enforcement notice under section 40 on or after the day on which that section comes into force if he is satisfied that, before that day, the data controller contravened the old principles by reason of any act or omission which would also have constituted a contravention of the new principles if they had applied before that day.

10. Subsection (5)(b) of section 40 does not apply where the rectification, blocking, erasure or destruction occurred before the commencement of that section.

11. The Commissioner may serve an information notice under section 43 on or after the day on which that section comes into force if he has reasonable grounds for suspecting that, before that day, the data controller contravened the old principles by reason of any act or omission which would also have constituted a contravention of the new principles if they had applied before that day.

12. Where by virtue of paragraph 11 an information notice is served on the basis of anything done or omitted to be done before the day on which section 43 comes into force, subsection (2)(b) of that section shall have effect as if the reference to the data controller having complied, or complying, with the new principles were a reference to the data controller having contravened the old principles by reason of any such act or omission as is mentioned in paragraph 11.

Self-incrimination, etc

13.—(1) In section 43(8), section 44(9) and paragraph 11 of Schedule 7, any reference to an offence under this Act includes a reference to an offence under the 1984 Act.

(2) In section 34(9) of the 1984 Act, any reference to an offence under that Act includes a reference to an offence under this Act.

Warrants issued under 1984 Act

14. The repeal of Schedule 4 to the 1984 Act does not affect the application of that Schedule in any case where a warrant was issued under that Schedule before the commencement of the repeal.

Complaints under section 36(2) of 1984 Act and requests for assessment under section 42

15. The repeal of section 36(2) of the 1984 Act does not affect the application of that provision in any case where the complaint was received by the Commissioner before the commencement of the repeal.

16. In dealing with a complaint under section 36(2) of the 1984 Act or a request for an assessment under section 42 of this Act, the Commissioner shall have regard to the provisions from time to time applicable to the processing, and accordingly—
- (a) in section 36(2) of the 1984 Act, the reference to the old principles and the provisions of that Act includes, in relation to any time when the new principles and the provisions of this Act have effect, those principles and provisions, and
- (b) in section 42 of this Act, the reference to the provisions of this Act includes, in relation to any time when the old principles and the provisions of the 1984 Act had effect, those principles and provisions.

Applications under Access to Health Records Act 1990 or corresponding Northern Ireland legislation

17.—(1) The repeal of any provision of the Access to Health Records Act 1990 does not affect—
- (a) the application of section 3 or 6 of that Act in any case in which the application under that section was received before the day on which the repeal comes into force, or
- (b) the application of section 8 of that Act in any case in which the application to the court was made before the day on which the repeal comes into force.

(2) Sub-paragraph (1)(a) does not apply in relation to an application for access to information which was made by reference to this Act.

18.—(1) The revocation of any provision of the Access to Health Records (Northern Ireland) Order 1993 does not affect—
- (a) the application of Article 5 or 8 of that Order in any case in which the application under that Article was received before the day on which the repeal comes into force, or
- (b) the application of Article 10 of that Order in any case in which the application to the court was made before the day on which the repeal comes into force.

(2) Sub-paragraph (1)(a) does not apply in relation to an application for access to information which was made by reference to this Act.

Applications under regulations under Access to Personal Files Act 1987 or corresponding Northern Ireland legislation

19.—(1) The repeal of the personal files enactments does not affect the application of regulations under those enactments in relation to—
- (a) any request for information,
- (b) any application for rectification or erasure, or
- (c) any application for review of a decision,

which was made before the day on which the repeal comes into force.

(2) Sub-paragraph (1)(a) does not apply in relation to a request for information which was made by reference to this Act.

(3) In sub-paragraph (1) "the personal files enactments" means—
- (a) in relation to Great Britain, the Access to Personal Files Act 1987, and
- (b) in relation to Northern Ireland, Part II of the Access to Personal Files and Medical Reports (Northern Ireland) Order 1991.

Applications under section 158 of Consumer Credit Act 1974

20. Section 62 does not affect the application of section 158 of the Consumer Credit Act 1974 in any case where the request was received before the commencement of section 62, unless the request is made by reference to this Act.

[1203]

NOTES

Commencement: 1 March 2000.

Para 2: words omitted from sub-para (1) repealed by the Freedom of Information Act 2000, ss 73, 86, Sch 6, para 8, Sch 8, Pt I.

Regulations: the Data Protection (Notification and Notification Fees) Regulations 2000, SI 2000/188 at **[3290]**.

(Sch 15 contains minor and consequential amendments.)

SCHEDULE 16
REPEALS AND REVOCATIONS

Section 74(2)

PART I
REPEALS

Chapter	*Short title*	*Extent of repeal*
1984 c 35.	The Data Protection Act 1984.	The whole Act.
1986 c 60.	The Financial Services Act 1986.	Section 190.
1987 c 37.	The Access to Personal Files Act 1987.	The whole Act.
1988 c 40.	The Education Reform Act 1988.	Section 223.
1988 c 50.	The Housing Act 1988.	In Schedule 17, paragraph 80.
1990 c 23.	The Access to Health Records Act 1990.	In section 1(1), the words from "but does not" to the end.
		In section 3, subsection (1)(a) to (e) and, in subsection (6)(a), the words "in the case of an application made otherwise than by the patient".
		Section 4(1) and (2).
		In section 5(1)(a)(i), the words "of the patient or" and the word "other".
		In section 10, in subsection (2) the words "or orders" and in subsection (3) the words "or an order under section 2(3) above".
		In section 11, the definitions of "child" and "parental responsibility".
1990 c 37.	The Human Fertilisation and Embryology Act 1990.	Section 33(8).
1990 c 41.	The Courts and Legal Services Act 1990.	In Schedule 10, paragraph 58.
1992 c 13.	The Further and Higher Education Act 1992.	Section 86.

Chapter	*Short title*	*Extent of repeal*
1992 c 37.	The Further and Higher Education (Scotland) Act 1992.	Section 59.
1993 c 8.	The Judicial Pensions and Retirement Act 1993.	In Schedule 6, paragraph 50.
1993 c 10.	The Charities Act 1993.	Section 12.
1993 c 21.	The Osteopaths Act 1993.	Section 38.
1994 c 17.	The Chiropractors Act 1994.	Section 38.
1994 c 19.	The Local Government (Wales) Act 1994.	In Schedule 13, paragraph 30.
1994 c 33.	The Criminal Justice and Public Order Act 1994.	Section 161.
1994 c 39.	The Local Government etc (Scotland) Act 1994.	In Schedule 13, paragraph 154.

[1204]

NOTES

Commencement: 1 March 2000.

PART II
REVOCATIONS

Number	*Title*	*Extent of revocation*
SI 1991/1142	The Data Protection Registration Fee Order 1991	The Whole Order.
SI 1991/1707 (NI 14)	The Access to Personal Files and Medical Reports (Northern Ireland) Order 1991	Part II. The Schedule.
SI 1992/3218	The Banking Co-ordination (Second Council Directive) Regulations 1992	In Schedule 10, paragraphs 15 and 40.
SI 1993/1250 (NI 4)	The Access to Health Records (Northern Ireland) Order 1993	In Article 2(2), the definitions of "child" and "parental responsibility". In Article 3(1), the words from "but does not include" to the end. In Article 5, paragraph (1)(a) to (d) and, in paragraph (6)(a), the words "in the case of an application made otherwise than by the patient". Article 6(1) and (2). In Article 7(1)(a)(i), the words "of the patient or" and the word "other".
SI 1994/429 (NI 2)	The Health and Personal Social Services (Northern Ireland) Order 1994	In Schedule 1, the entries relating to the Access to Personal Files and Medical Reports (Northern Ireland) Order 1991.

Number	Title	Extent of revocation
SI 1994/1696	The Insurance Companies (Third Insurance Directives) Regulations 1994	In Schedule 8, paragraph 8.
SI 1995/755 (NI 2)	The Children (Northern Ireland) Order 1995	In Schedule 9, paragraphs 177 and 191.
SI 1995/3275	The Investment Services Regulations 1995	In Schedule 10, paragraphs 3 and 15.
SI 1996/2827	The Open-Ended Investment Companies (Investment Companies with Variable Capital) Regulations 1996	In Schedule 8, paragraphs 3 and 26.

[1205]

NOTES
Commencement: 1 March 2000.

FINANCE ACT 1998

(1998 c 36)

An Act to grant certain duties, to alter other duties, and to amend the law relating to the National Debt and the Public Revenue, and to make further provision in connection with Finance

[31 July 1998]

1–24 ((*Pts I, II*) *outside the scope of this work.*)

PART III
INCOME TAX, CORPORATION TAX AND CAPITAL GAINS TAX

CHAPTER I
INCOME TAX AND CORPORATION TAX

25–46 (*Outside the scope of this work.*)

Gifts to charities

47 (*Repealed by the Finance Act 1999, ss 55(2), (3), 139, Sch 20, Pt III(12), with effect in relation to gifts made on or after 27 July 1999.*)

48 Gifts of money for relief in poor countries

(1) This section applies to any gift of a sum of money by an individual to a charity that has given the required notification to the Board if that gift is made—

(a) in the period beginning with [31st July 1998] and ending with 31st December 2000; and

(b) in circumstances giving rise to a reasonable expectation that the sum given will be applied for, or in connection with, [one or more] of the purposes specified in subsection (2) below.

(2) Those purposes are—

(a) the relief of poverty in any one or more [countries or territories designated for the purposes of this paragraph,] …

(b) the advancement of education in any one or more [countries or territories designated for the purposes of this paragraph,] [and

(c) the relief of poverty in the case of persons from any country or territory designated for the purposes of this paragraph who are refugees or who have suffered displacement as a result of organised intimidation or oppression or of war or other armed conflict].

(3) …

(4) Where—

(a) a relevant gift of less than £100 is made [before 6th April 2000] by an individual to a charity that has given the required notification to the Board,

(b) the aggregate of that gift and any one or more subsequent relevant gifts made by that individual to that charity is £100 or more,

[(bb) the subsequent gift, or at least one of the subsequent gifts, is made on or after 6th April 2000;]

(c) that individual gives an [appropriate declaration] in relation to that aggregate to that charity, and

(d) the condition specified in paragraph

(e) of subsection (2) of section 25 of the Finance Act 1990 (limit on benefit for the donor) would be satisfied if the aggregated gifts constituted a single gift by that individual to that charity made at the time of the making of the last of them to be made,

the aggregated gifts shall be treated for the purposes of that section [(but subject to subsection (4A) below)] as if they together constituted a single qualifying donation made by that individual to that charity at that time.

[(4A) Subsection (10) of section 25 of the Finance Act 1990 (receipts of gifts by a charity to be treated as payments of grossed-up amounts after deduction of basic rate income tax) shall have effect where—

(a) any aggregated gifts are treated under this section as a single qualifying donation made to a charity, and

(b) the aggregated gifts include gifts made in different years of assessment,

as if that single qualifying donation had been received by the charity in the year of assessment in which the first of the aggregated gifts was made and as if that were the relevant year of assessment for the purposes of that subsection.]

(5) The gifts aggregated for the purposes of subsection (4) above must not include either—

(a) a relevant gift of £250 or more; or

(b) more than one relevant gift of £100 or more.

(6), (7) …

The reference in paragraph (c) of subsection (4) above to an appropriate certificate is a reference to a certificate which states—

(a) that each of the gifts being aggregated qualifies as a relevant gift for the purposes of this section;

(b) that if those gifts are treated in accordance with this section as a single qualifying donation made at the time specified in subsection (4) above, the single donation will satisfy the taxation condition; and

(c) that the condition in paragraph (d) of that subsection is satisfied in the case of those gifts taken together.

(7) For the purposes of subsection (6) above the taxation condition in the case of any relevant gift is that, either directly or by deduction from profits or gains brought into charge to tax in the relevant year of assessment, the individual making the gift has paid or will pay to the Board income tax of an amount equal to income tax at the basic rate for the relevant year of assessment on the grossed up amount of that gift.

(8) In this section—

.....

["relevant gift" means a gift to which this section applies—

(a) which satisfies the requirements of subsection (2) of section 25 of the Finance Act 1990 (as amended by section 39 of the Finance Act 2000); or

(b) which would satisfy those requirements if paragraph (e) of that subsection were disregarded;] and

"required notification", in relation to a charity, means a notification (including one given before the passing of this Act) which—

(i) is in such form, and contains such information, as may have been required by the Board, and

(ii) contains a statement to the effect that the charity proposes to accept gifts to which this section applies.

(9) A country or territory is a designated country or territory for the purposes of [paragraph (a), (b) or (c) of subsection (2) above] if—

(a) it is designated as such by an order made for those purposes by the Treasury; or

(b) it is of a description specified in an order so made;

and a description specified in such an order may be expressed by reference to the opinion of any person so specified or by reference to the contents from time to time of a document prepared by a person so specified.

(10) Expressions used in this section and in section 25 of the Finance Act 1990 have the same meanings in this section as in that section.

[1206]

NOTES

Commencement: this Act received Royal Assent on 31 July 1998: for provision as to the application of this section see sub-s (1) above.

Sub-s (1): words in square brackets substituted by the Finance Act 1999, s 56(1), (2), (7), in relation to gifts made on or after 6 April 1999.

Sub-s (2): words in square brackets in paras (a), (b) substituted, word omitted repealed and para (c) and the word immediately preceding it added by the Finance Act 1999, ss 56(1), (3), (7), 139, Sch 20, Pt III(13), in relation to gifts made on or after 6 April 1999.

Sub-s (3): repealed by the Finance Act 2000, ss 42(1), 156, Sch 40, Pt II(1).

Sub-s (4): words in square brackets in para (a), and para (bb), inserted, and words in square brackets in para (c) substituted by the Finance Act 2000, s 42(2); final words in square brackets inserted, with retrospective effect, by the Finance Act 1999, s 57(1), (2).

Sub-s (4A): inserted, with retrospective effect, by the Finance Act 1999, s 57(1), (3).

Sub-ss (6), (7): repealed by the Finance Act 2000, ss 42(1), 156, Sch 40, Pt II(1).

Sub-s (8): definition omitted repealed by the Finance Act 1999, s 139, Sch 20, Pt III(13), in relation to gifts made on or after 6 April 1999; definition "relevant gift" substituted by the Finance Act 2000, s 42(3).

Sub-s (9): words in square brackets substituted by the Finance Act 1999, s 56(1), (4), (7), in relation to gifts made on or after 6 April 1999.

See further, in relation to orders made under sub-s (9) above and in relation to notification given, in relation to a charity, before 27 July 1999: the Finance Act 1999, s 56(5), (6), (8).

Orders: the Gifts for Relief in Poor Countries (Designation) Order 1998, SI 1998/1868; the Gifts for Relief in Poor Countries (Designation of Kosovo) Order 1999, SI 1999/2118.

49–154 (*Ss 49–141, ss 142–154* (*Pts IV, V*) *outside the scope of this work.*)

PART VI
MISCELLANEOUS AND SUPPLEMENTAL

155–163 (*Outside the scope of this work.*)

Supplemental

164, 165 (*Outside the scope of this work.*)

166 Short title

This Act may be cited as the Finance Act 1998.

[1207]

NOTES

Commencement: 31 July 1998.

(*Schs 1–27 outside the scope of this work.*)

NATIONAL MINIMUM WAGE ACT 1998

(1998 c 39)

An Act to make provision for and in connection with a national minimum wage; to provide for the amendment of certain enactments relating to the remuneration of persons employed in agriculture; and for connected purposes

[31 July 1998]

Entitlement to the national minimum wage

1 Workers to be paid at least the minimum wage

(1) A person who qualifies for the national minimum wage shall be remunerated by his employer in respect of his work in any pay reference period at a rate which is not less than the national minimum wage.

(2) A person qualifies for the national minimum wage if he is an individual who—

(a) is a worker;
(b) is working, or ordinarily works, in the United Kingdom under his contract; and
(c) has ceased to be of compulsory school age.

(3) The national minimum wage shall be such single hourly rate as the Secretary of State may from time to time prescribe.

(4) For the purposes of this Act a "pay reference period" is such period as the Secretary of State may prescribe for the purpose.

(5) Subsections (1) to (4) above are subject to the following provisions of this Act.

[1208]

NOTES

Commencement: this section came into force on 31 July 1998, in so far as conferring power to make subordinate legislation, and on 1 April 1999 for remaining purposes.

Regulations: the National Minimum Wage Regulations 1999, SI 1999/584.

2–42 (*Outside the scope of this work.*)

Exclusions

43 (*Outside the scope of this work.*)

44 Voluntary workers

(1) A worker employed by a charity, a voluntary organisation, an associated fund-raising body or a statutory body does not qualify for the national minimum wage in respect of that employment if he receives, and under the terms of his employment (apart from this Act) is entitled to,—

(a) no monetary payments of any description, or no monetary payments except in respect of expenses—
  (i) actually incurred in the performance of his duties; or
  (ii) reasonably estimated as likely to be or to have been so incurred; and
(b) no benefits in kind of any description, or no benefits in kind other than the provision of some or all of his subsistence or of such accommodation as is reasonable in the circumstances of the employment.

(2) A person who would satisfy the conditions in subsection (1) above but for receiving monetary payments made solely for the purpose of providing him with means of subsistence shall be taken to satisfy those conditions if—

(a) he is employed to do the work in question as a result of arrangements made between a charity acting in pursuance of its charitable purposes and the body for which the work is done; and
(b) the work is done for a charity, a voluntary organisation, an associated fund-raising body or a statutory body.

(3) For the purposes of subsection (1)(b) above—

(a) any training (other than that which a person necessarily acquires in the course of doing his work) shall be taken to be a benefit in kind; but

(b) there shall be left out of account any training provided for the sole or main purpose of improving the worker's ability to perform the work which he has agreed to do.

(4) In this section—

"associated fund-raising body" means a body of persons the profits of which are applied wholly for the purposes of a charity or voluntary organisation;

"charity" means a body of persons, or the trustees of a trust, established for charitable purposes only;

"receive", in relation to a monetary payment or a benefit in kind, means receive in respect of, or otherwise in connection with, the employment in question (whether or not under the terms of the employment);

"statutory body" means a body established by or under an enactment (including an enactment comprised in Northern Ireland legislation);

"subsistence" means such subsistence as is reasonable in the circumstances of the employment in question, and does not include accommodation;

"voluntary organisation" means a body of persons, or the trustees of a trust, which is established only for charitable purposes (whether or not those purposes are charitable within the meaning of any rule of law), benevolent purposes or philanthropic purposes, but which is not a charity.

[1209]

NOTES

Commencement: 1 November 1998.

[44A Religious and other communities: resident workers

(1) A residential member of a community to which this section applies does not qualify for the national minimum wage in respect of employment by the community.

(2) Subject to subsection (3), this section applies to a community if—

(a) it is a charity or is established by a charity,

(b) a purpose of the community is to practise or advance a belief of a religious or similar nature, and

(c) all or some of its members live together for that purpose.

(3) This section does not apply to a community which—

(a) is an independent school, or

(b) provides a course of further or higher education.

(4) The residential members of a community are those who live together as mentioned in subsection (2)(c).

(5) In this section—

(a) "charity" has the same meaning as in section 44, and

(b) "independent school" has the same meaning as in section 463 of the Education Act 1996 (in England and Wales), section 135 of the Education (Scotland) Act 1980 (in Scotland) and Article 2 of the Education and Libraries (Northern Ireland) Order 1986 (in Northern Ireland).

(6) In this section "course of further or higher education" means—

(a) in England and Wales, a course of a description referred to in Schedule 6 to the Education Reform Act 1988 or Schedule 2 to the Further and Higher Education Act 1992;

(b) in Scotland, a course or programme of a description mentioned in or falling within section 6(1) or 38 of the Further and Higher Education (Scotland) Act 1992;

(c) in Northern Ireland, a course of a description referred to in Schedule 1 to the Further Education (Northern Ireland) Order 1997 or a course providing further education within the meaning of Article 3 of that Order.]

[1209A]

NOTES

Commencement: 25 October 1999.

Inserted by the Employment Relations Act 1999, s 22.

45–50 (*Outside the scope of this work.*)

Supplementary

51–53 (*Outside the scope of this work.*)

54 Meaning of "worker", "employee" etc

(1) In this Act "employee" means an individual who has entered into or works under (or, where the employment has ceased, worked under) a contract of employment.

(2) In this Act "contract of employment" means a contract of service or apprenticeship, whether express or implied, and (if it is express) whether oral or in writing.

(3) In this Act "worker" (except in the phrases "agency worker" and "home worker") means an individual who has entered into or works under (or, where the employment has ceased, worked under)—

(a) a contract of employment; or

(b) any other contract, whether express or implied and (if it is express) whether oral or in writing, whereby the individual undertakes to do or perform personally any work or services for another party to the contract whose status is not by virtue of the contract that of a client or customer of any profession or business undertaking carried on by the individual;

and any reference to a worker's contract shall be construed accordingly.

(4) In this Act "employer", in relation to an employee or a worker, means the person by whom the employee or worker is (or, where the employment has ceased, was) employed.

(5) In this Act "employment"—

(a) in relation to an employee, means employment under a contract of employment; and

(b) in relation to a worker, means employment under his contract;

and "employed" shall be construed accordingly.

[1210]

NOTES

Commencement: 1 November 1998.

55 (*Outside the scope of this work.*)

56 Short title, commencement and extent

(1) This Act may be cited as the National Minimum Wage Act 1998.

(2) Apart from this section and any powers to make an Order in Council or regulations or an order (which accordingly come into force on the day on which this Act is passed) the provisions of this Act shall come into force on such day or days as the Secretary of State may by order appoint; and different days may be appointed for different purposes.

(3) This Act extends to Northern Ireland.

[1211]

NOTES

Commencement: 31 July 1998.

Orders: the National Minimum Wage Act 1998 (Commencement No 1 and Transitional Provisions) Order 1998, SI 1998/2574; the National Minimum Wage Act 1998 (Commencement No 2 and Transitional Provisions) Order 1999, SI 1999/685.

(*Schs 1–3 outside the scope of this work.*)

HUMAN RIGHTS ACT 1998

(1998 c 42)

An Act to give further effect to rights and freedoms guaranteed under the European Convention on Human Rights; to make provision with respect to holders of certain judicial offices who become judges of the European Court of Human Rights; and for connected purposes

[9 November 1998]

ARRANGEMENT OF SECTIONS

Introduction

1 The Convention Rights

(1) In this Act "the Convention rights" means the rights and fundamental freedoms set out in—
- (a) Articles 2 to 12 and 14 of the Convention,
- (b) Articles 1 to 3 of the First Protocol, and
- (c) [Article 1 of the Thirteenth Protocol],

as read with Articles 16 to 18 of the Convention.

(2) Those Articles are to have effect for the purposes of this Act subject to any designated derogation or reservation (as to which see sections 14 and 15).

(3) The Articles are set out in Schedule 1.

(4) The [Secretary of State] may by order make such amendments to this Act as he considers appropriate to reflect the effect, in relation to the United Kingdom, of a protocol.

(5) In subsection (4) "protocol" means a protocol to the Convention—
- (a) which the United Kingdom has ratified; or
- (b) which the United Kingdom has signed with a view to ratification.

(6) No amendment may be made by an order under subsection (4) so as to come into force before the protocol concerned is in force in relation to the United Kingdom.

[1212]

PART I STATUTES

NOTES

Sub-s (1): words in square brackets in para (c) substituted by the Human Rights Act 1998 (Amendment) Order 2004, SI 2004/1574, art 2(1).

Sub-s (4): words in square brackets substituted by the Secretary of State for Constitutional Affairs Order 2003, SI 2003/1887, art 9, Sch 2, para 10(1).

Orders: the Human Rights Act 1998 (Amendment) Order 2004, SI 2004/1574.

2 Interpretation of Convention rights

(1) A court or tribunal determining a question which has arisen in connection with a Convention right must take into account any—
- (a) judgment, decision, declaration or advisory opinion of the European Court of Human Rights,
- (b) opinion of the Commission given in a report adopted under Article 31 of the Convention,
- (c) decision of the Commission in connection with Article 26 or 27(2) of the Convention, or
- (d) decision of the Committee of Ministers taken under Article 46 of the Convention,

whenever made or given, so far as, in the opinion of the court or tribunal, it is relevant to the proceedings in which that question has arisen.

(2) Evidence of any judgment, decision, declaration or opinion of which account may have to be taken under this section is to be given in proceedings before any court or tribunal in such manner as may be provided by rules.

(3) In this section "rules" means rules of court or, in the case of proceedings before a tribunal, rules made for the purposes of this section—
- (a) by ... [the Lord Chancellor or] the Secretary of State, in relation to any proceedings outside Scotland;
- (b) by the Secretary of State, in relation to proceedings in Scotland; or
- (c) by a Northern Ireland department, in relation to proceedings before a tribunal in Northern Ireland—
  - (i) which deals with transferred matters; and
  - (ii) for which no rules made under paragraph (a) are in force.

[1213]

NOTES

Sub-s (3): words omitted from para (a) repealed by the Secretary of State for Constitutional Affairs Order 2003, SI 2003/1887, art 9, Sch 2, para 10(2); words in square brackets in para (a) inserted by the Transfer of Functions (Lord Chancellor and Secretary of State) Order 2005, SI 2005/3429, art 8, Schedule, para 3.

By the Transfer of Functions (Lord Chancellor and Secretary of State) Order 2005, SI 2005/3429, art 3(2), the functions of the Secretary of State under sub-s (3)(a) are to be exercisable concurrently with the Lord Chancellor.

Legislation

3 Interpretation of legislation

(1) So far as it is possible to do so, primary legislation and subordinate legislation must be read and given effect in a way which is compatible with the Convention rights.

(2) This section—

(a) applies to primary legislation and subordinate legislation whenever enacted;

(b) does not affect the validity, continuing operation or enforcement of any incompatible primary legislation; and

(c) does not affect the validity, continuing operation or enforcement of any incompatible subordinate legislation if (disregarding any possibility of revocation) primary legislation prevents removal of the incompatibility.

[1214]

4 Declaration of incompatibility

(1) Subsection (2) applies in any proceedings in which a court determines whether a provision of primary legislation is compatible with a Convention right.

(2) If the court is satisfied that the provision is incompatible with a Convention right, it may make a declaration of that incompatibility.

(3) Subsection (4) applies in any proceedings in which a court determines whether a provision of subordinate legislation, made in the exercise of a power conferred by primary legislation, is compatible with a Convention right.

(4) If the court is satisfied—

(a) that the provision is incompatible with a Convention right, and

(b) that (disregarding any possibility of revocation) the primary legislation concerned prevents removal of the incompatibility,

it may make a declaration of that incompatibility.

(5) In this section "court" means—

(a) *the House of Lords;*

(b) the Judicial Committee of the Privy Council;

(c) the *Courts-Martial Appeal Court*;

(d) in Scotland, the High Court of Justiciary sitting otherwise than as a trial court or the Court of Session;

(e) in England and Wales or Northern Ireland, the High Court or the Court of Appeal;

[(f) the Court of Protection, in any matter being dealt with by the President of the Family Division, the Vice-Chancellor or a puisne judge of the High Court.]

(6) A declaration under this section ("a declaration of incompatibility")—

(a) does not affect the validity, continuing operation or enforcement of the provision in respect of which it is given; and

(b) is not binding on the parties to the proceedings in which it is made.

[1215]

NOTES

Sub-s (5): for the words in italics in para (c) there are substituted the words "Court Martial Appeal Court" by the Armed Forces Act 2006, s 378, Sch 16, para 156, as from a day to be appointed; para (f) added by the Mental Capacity Act 2005, s 67(1), Sch 6, para 43, as from a day to be appointed under s 68(1) of that Act; para (a) substituted by the Constitutional Reform Act 2005, s 40(4), Sch 9, Pt 1, para 66(1), (2), as from a day to be appointed as follows—

"(a) the Supreme Court;".

5 Right of Crown to intervene

(1) Where a court is considering whether to make a declaration of incompatibility, the Crown is entitled to notice in accordance with rules of court.

(2) In any case to which subsection (1) applies—
(a) a Minister of the Crown (or a person nominated by him),
(b) a member of the Scottish Executive,
(c) a Northern Ireland Minister,
(d) a Northern Ireland department,

is entitled, on giving notice in accordance with rules of court, to be joined as a party to the proceedings.

(3) Notice under subsection (2) may be given at any time during the proceedings.

(4) A person who has been made a party to criminal proceedings (other than in Scotland) as the result of a notice under subsection (2) may, with leave, appeal to the *House of Lords* against any declaration of incompatibility made in the proceedings.

(5) In subsection (4)—
"criminal proceedings" includes all proceedings before the *Courts-Martial Appeal Court*; and
"leave" means leave granted by the court making the declaration of incompatibility or by the *House of Lords*.

[1216]

NOTES

Sub-s (4): for the words in italics there are substituted the words "Supreme Court" by the Constitutional Reform Act 2005, s 40(4), Sch 9, Pt 1, para 66(1), (3), as from a day to be appointed under s 148(1) of that Act.

Sub-s (5): for the words in italics in definition "criminal proceedings" there are substituted the words "Court Martial Appeal Court" by the Armed Forces Act 2006, s 378, Sch 16, para 157, as from a day to be appointed; for the words in italics in definition "leave" there are substituted the words "Supreme Court" by the Constitutional Reform Act 2005, s 40(4), Sch 9, Pt 1, para 66(1), (3), as from a day to be appointed under s 148(1) of that Act.

Transfer of functions: the function under sub-s (2) shall be exercisable by the National Assembly for Wales concurrently with any Minister of the Crown by whom it is exercisable, in so far as it relates to any proceedings in which a court is considering whether to make a declaration of incompatibility within the meaning of s 4 of this Act, in respect of subordinate legislation made by the National Assembly, and subordinate legislation made, in relation to Wales, by a Minister of the Crown in the exercise of a function which is exercisable by the National Assembly: see the National Assembly for Wales (Transfer of Functions) (No 2) Order 2000, SI 2000/1830, art 2.

Public authorities

6 Acts of public authorities

(1) It is unlawful for a public authority to act in a way which is incompatible with a Convention right.

(2) Subsection (1) does not apply to an act if—
(a) as the result of one or more provisions of primary legislation, the authority could not have acted differently; or
(b) in the case of one or more provisions of, or made under, primary legislation which cannot be read or given effect in a way which is compatible with the Convention rights, the authority was acting so as to give effect to or enforce those provisions.

(3) In this section "public authority" includes—
(a) a court or tribunal, and
(b) any person certain of whose functions are functions of a public nature,

but does not include either House of Parliament or a person exercising functions in connection with proceedings in Parliament.

(4) In subsection (3) "Parliament" does not include the House of Lords in its judicial capacity.

(5) In relation to a particular act, a person is not a public authority by virtue only of subsection (3)(b) if the nature of the act is private.

(6) "An act" includes a failure to act but does not include a failure to—
(a) introduce in, or lay before, Parliament a proposal for legislation; or
(b) make any primary legislation or remedial order.

[1217]

NOTES

Sub-s (4): repealed by the Constitutional Reform Act 2005, ss 40(4), 146, Sch 9, Pt 1, para 66(1), (4), Sch 18, Pt 5, as from a day to be appointed under s 148(1) of that Act.

7 Proceedings

(1) A person who claims that a public authority has acted (or proposes to act) in a way which is made unlawful by section 6(1) may—

(a) bring proceedings against the authority under this Act in the appropriate court or tribunal, or

(b) rely on the Convention right or rights concerned in any legal proceedings,

but only if he is (or would be) a victim of the unlawful act.

(2) In subsection (1)(a) "appropriate court or tribunal" means such court or tribunal as may be determined in accordance with rules; and proceedings against an authority include a counterclaim or similar proceeding.

(3) If the proceedings are brought on an application for judicial review, the applicant is to be taken to have a sufficient interest in relation to the unlawful act only if he is, or would be, a victim of that act.

(4) If the proceedings are made by way of a petition for judicial review in Scotland, the applicant shall be taken to have title and interest to sue in relation to the unlawful act only if he is, or would be, a victim of that act.

(5) Proceedings under subsection (1)(a) must be brought before the end of—

(a) the period of one year beginning with the date on which the act complained of took place; or

(b) such longer period as the court or tribunal considers equitable having regard to all the circumstances,

but that is subject to any rule imposing a stricter time limit in relation to the procedure in question.

(6) In subsection (1)(b) "legal proceedings" includes—

(a) proceedings brought by or at the instigation of a public authority; and

(b) an appeal against the decision of a court or tribunal.

(7) For the purposes of this section, a person is a victim of an unlawful act only if he would be a victim for the purposes of Article 34 of the Convention if proceedings were brought in the European Court of Human Rights in respect of that act.

(8) Nothing in this Act creates a criminal offence.

(9) In this section "rules" means—

(a) in relation to proceedings before a court or tribunal outside Scotland, rules made by … [the Lord Chancellor or] the Secretary of State for the purposes of this section or rules of court,

(b) in relation to proceedings before a court or tribunal in Scotland, rules made by the Secretary of State for those purposes,

(c) in relation to proceedings before a tribunal in Northern Ireland—

(i) which deals with transferred matters; and

(ii) for which no rules made under paragraph (a) are in force,

rules made by a Northern Ireland department for those purposes,

and includes provision made by order under section 1 of the Courts and Legal Services Act 1990.

(10) In making rules, regard must be had to section 9.

(11) The Minister who has power to make rules in relation to a particular tribunal may, to the extent he considers it necessary to ensure that the tribunal can provide an appropriate remedy in relation to an act (or proposed act) of a public authority which is (or would be) unlawful as a result of section 6(1), by order add to—

(a) the relief or remedies which the tribunal may grant; or

(b) the grounds on which it may grant any of them.

(12) An order made under subsection (11) may contain such incidental, supplemental, consequential or transitional provision as the Minister making it considers appropriate.

(13) "The Minister" includes the Northern Ireland department concerned.

[1218]

NOTES

Sub-s (9): words omitted from para (a) repealed by the Secretary of State for Constitutional Affairs Order 2003, SI 2003/1887, art 9, Sch 2, para 10(2); words in square brackets inserted by the Transfer of Functions (Lord Chancellor and Secretary of State) Order 2005, SI 2005/3429, art 8, Schedule, para 3.

By the Transfer of Functions (Lord Chancellor and Secretary of State) Order 2005, SI 2005/3429, art 3(2), the functions of the Secretary of State under sub-s (9)(a), and under sub-s (11) by virtue thereof, are to be exercisable concurrently with the Lord Chancellor.

Rules: the Human Rights Act 1998 (Jurisdiction) (Scotland) Rules 2000, SSI 2000/301; the Proscribed Organisations Appeal Commission (Human Rights Act 1998 Proceedings) Rules 2006, SI 2006/2290.

8 Judicial remedies

(1) In relation to any act (or proposed act) of a public authority which the court finds is (or would be) unlawful, it may grant such relief or remedy, or make such order, within its powers as it considers just and appropriate.

(2) But damages may be awarded only by a court which has power to award damages, or to order the payment of compensation, in civil proceedings.

(3) No award of damages is to be made unless, taking account of all the circumstances of the case, including—

(a) any other relief or remedy granted, or order made, in relation to the act in question (by that or any other court), and

(b) the consequences of any decision (of that or any other court) in respect of that act,

the court is satisfied that the award is necessary to afford just satisfaction to the person in whose favour it is made.

(4) In determining—

(a) whether to award damages, or

(b) the amount of an award,

the court must take into account the principles applied by the European Court of Human Rights in relation to the award of compensation under Article 41 of the Convention.

(5) A public authority against which damages are awarded is to be treated—

(a) in Scotland, for the purposes of section 3 of the Law Reform (Miscellaneous Provisions) (Scotland) Act 1940 as if the award were made in an action of damages in which the authority has been found liable in respect of loss or damage to the person to whom the award is made;

(b) for the purposes of the Civil Liability (Contribution) Act 1978 as liable in respect of damage suffered by the person to whom the award is made.

(6) In this section—

"court" includes a tribunal;

"damages" means damages for an unlawful act of a public authority; and

"unlawful" means unlawful under section 6(1).

[1219]

9 Judicial acts

(1) Proceedings under section 7(1)(a) in respect of a judicial act may be brought only—

(a) by exercising a right of appeal;

(b) on an application (in Scotland a petition) for judicial review; or

(c) in such other forum as may be prescribed by rules.

(2) That does not affect any rule of law which prevents a court from being the subject of judicial review.

(3) In proceedings under this Act in respect of a judicial act done in good faith, damages may not be awarded otherwise than to compensate a person to the extent required by Article 5(5) of the Convention.

(4) An award of damages permitted by subsection (3) is to be made against the Crown; but no award may be made unless the appropriate person, if not a party to the proceedings, is joined.

(5) In this section—

"appropriate person" means the Minister responsible for the court concerned, or a person or government department nominated by him;

"court" includes a tribunal;

"judge" includes a member of a tribunal, a justice of the peace [(or, in Northern Ireland, a lay magistrate)] and a clerk or other officer entitled to exercise the jurisdiction of a court;

"judicial act" means a judicial act of a court and includes an act done on the instructions, or on behalf, of a judge; and

"rules" has the same meaning as in section 7(9).

[1220]

NOTES

Sub-s (5): in definition "judge" words in square brackets inserted by the Justice (Northern Ireland) Act 2002, s 10(6), Sch 4, para 39.

Rules: the Human Rights Act 1998 (Jurisdiction) (Scotland) Rules 2000, SSI 2000/301.

Remedial action

10 Power to take remedial action

(1) This section applies if—

(a) a provision of legislation has been declared under section 4 to be incompatible with a Convention right and, if an appeal lies—

(i) all persons who may appeal have stated in writing that they do not intend to do so;

(ii) the time for bringing an appeal has expired and no appeal has been brought within that time; or

(iii) an appeal brought within that time has been determined or abandoned; or

(b) it appears to a Minister of the Crown or Her Majesty in Council that, having regard to a finding of the European Court of Human Rights made after the coming into force of this section in proceedings against the United Kingdom, a provision of legislation is incompatible with an obligation of the United Kingdom arising from the Convention.

(2) If a Minister of the Crown considers that there are compelling reasons for proceeding under this section, he may by order make such amendments to the legislation as he considers necessary to remove the incompatibility.

(3) If, in the case of subordinate legislation, a Minister of the Crown considers—

(a) that it is necessary to amend the primary legislation under which the subordinate legislation in question was made, in order to enable the incompatibility to be removed, and

(b) that there are compelling reasons for proceeding under this section,

he may by order make such amendments to the primary legislation as he considers necessary.

(4) This section also applies where the provision in question is in subordinate legislation and has been quashed, or declared invalid, by reason of incompatibility with a Convention right and the Minister proposes to proceed under paragraph 2(b) of Schedule 2.

(5) If the legislation is an Order in Council, the power conferred by subsection (2) or (3) is exercisable by Her Majesty in Council.

(6) In this section "legislation" does not include a Measure of the Church Assembly or of the General Synod of the Church of England.

(7) Schedule 2 makes further provision about remedial orders.

[1221]

NOTES

Orders: the Mental Health Act 1983 (Remedial) Order 2001, SI 2001/3712; the Naval Discipline Act 1957 (Remedial) Order 2004, SI 2004/66; the Marriage Act 1949 (Remedial) Order 2007, SI 2007/438.

Other rights and proceedings

11 Safeguard for existing human rights

A person's reliance on a Convention right does not restrict—

(a) any other right or freedom conferred on him by or under any law having effect in any part of the United Kingdom; or

(b) his right to make any claim or bring any proceedings which he could make or bring apart from sections 7 to 9.

[1222]

12 Freedom of expression

(1) This section applies if a court is considering whether to grant any relief which, if granted, might affect the exercise of the Convention right to freedom of expression.

(2) If the person against whom the application for relief is made ("the respondent") is neither present nor represented, no such relief is to be granted unless the court is satisfied—

(a) that the applicant has taken all practicable steps to notify the respondent; or

(b) that there are compelling reasons why the respondent should not be notified.

(3) No such relief is to be granted so as to restrain publication before trial unless the court is satisfied that the applicant is likely to establish that publication should not be allowed.

(4) The court must have particular regard to the importance of the Convention right to freedom of expression and, where the proceedings relate to material which the respondent claims, or which appears to the court, to be journalistic, literary or artistic material (or to conduct connected with such material), to—

(a) the extent to which—

(i) the material has, or is about to, become available to the public; or

(ii) it is, or would be, in the public interest for the material to be published;

(b) any relevant privacy code.

(5) In this section—

"court" includes a tribunal; and

"relief" includes any remedy or order (other than in criminal proceedings).

[1223]

13 Freedom of thought, conscience and religion

(1) If a court's determination of any question arising under this Act might affect the exercise by a religious organisation (itself or its members collectively) of the Convention right to freedom of thought, conscience and religion, it must have particular regard to the importance of that right.

(2) In this section "court" includes a tribunal.

[1224]

Derogations and reservations

14 Derogations

(1) In this Act "designated derogation" means—

(a) …

(b) any derogation by the United Kingdom from an Article of the Convention, or of any protocol to the Convention, which is designated for the purposes of this Act in an order made by the [Secretary of State].

(2) …

(3) If a designated derogation is amended or replaced it ceases to be a designated derogation.

(4) But subsection (3) does not prevent the [Secretary of State] from exercising his power under subsection (1) … to make a fresh designation order in respect of the Article concerned.

(5) The [Secretary of State] must by order make such amendments to Schedule 3 as he considers appropriate to reflect—

(a) any designation order; or

(b) the effect of subsection (3).

(6) A designation order may be made in anticipation of the making by the United Kingdom of a proposed derogation.

[1225]

NOTES

Sub-s (1): words omitted repealed by the Human Rights (Amendment) Order 2001, SI 2001/1216, art 2(a); words in square brackets substituted by the Secretary of State for Constitutional Affairs Order 2003, SI 2003/1887, art 9, Sch 2, para 10(1).

Sub-s (2): repealed by SI 2001/1216, art 2(b).

Sub-s (4): words in square brackets substituted by SI 2003/1887, art 9, Sch 2, para 10(1); reference omitted repealed by SI 2001/1216, art 2(c).

Sub-s (5): words in square brackets substituted by SI 2003/1887, art 9, Sch 2, para 10(1).

Orders: the Human Rights Act 1998 (Designated Derogation) Order 2001, SI 2001/3644; the Human Rights Act 1998 (Amendment No 2) Order 2001, SI 2001/4032.

15 Reservations

(1) In this Act "designated reservation" means—

(a) the United Kingdom's reservation to Article 2 of the First Protocol to the Convention; and

(b) any other reservation by the United Kingdom to an Article of the Convention, or of any protocol to the Convention, which is designated for the purposes of this Act in an order made by the [Secretary of State].

(2) The text of the reservation referred to in subsection (1)(a) is set out in Part II of Schedule 3.

(3) If a designated reservation is withdrawn wholly or in part it ceases to be a designated reservation.

(4) But subsection (3) does not prevent the [Secretary of State] from exercising his power under subsection (1)(b) to make a fresh designation order in respect of the Article concerned.

(5) The [Secretary of State] must by order make such amendments to this Act as he considers appropriate to reflect—

(a) any designation order; or

(b) the effect of subsection (3).

[1226]

NOTES

Sub-ss (1), (4), (5): words in square brackets substituted by the Secretary of State for Constitutional Affairs Order 2003, SI 2003/1887, art 9, Sch 2, para 10(1).

16 Period for which designated derogations have effect

(1) If it has not already been withdrawn by the United Kingdom, a designated derogation ceases to have effect for the purposes of this Act … at the end of the period of five years beginning with the date on which the order designating it was made.

(2) At any time before the period—

(a) fixed by subsection (1) … , or

(b) extended by an order under this subsection,

comes to an end, the [Secretary of State] may by order extend it by a further period of five years.

(3) An order under section 14(1) … ceases to have effect at the end of the period for consideration, unless a resolution has been passed by each House approving the order.

(4) Subsection (3) does not affect—

(a) anything done in reliance on the order; or

(b) the power to make a fresh order under section 14(1) …

(5) In subsection (3) "period for consideration" means the period of forty days beginning with the day on which the order was made.

(6) In calculating the period for consideration, no account is to be taken of any time during which—

(a) Parliament is dissolved or prorogued; or
(b) both Houses are adjourned for more than four days.

(7) If a designated derogation is withdrawn by the United Kingdom, the [Secretary of State] must by order make such amendments to this Act as he considers are required to reflect that withdrawal.

[1227]

NOTES

Sub-ss (1), (3), (4): words omitted repealed by the Human Rights Act (Amendment) Order 2001, SI 2001/1216, art 3(a), (c), (d).

Sub-s (2): words omitted repealed by SI 2001/1216, art 3(b); words in square brackets substituted by the Secretary of State for Constitutional Affairs Order 2003, SI 2003/1887, art 9, Sch 2, para 10(1).

Sub-s (7): words in square brackets substituted by SI 2003/1887, art 9, Sch 2, para 10(1).

Orders: the Human Rights Act 1998 (Amendment) Order 2005, SI 2005/1071; the Human Rights Act (Amendment) Order 2001, 2001/1216.

17 Periodic review of designated reservations

(1) The appropriate Minister must review the designated reservation referred to in section 15(1)(a)—
(a) before the end of the period of five years beginning with the date on which section 1(2) came into force; and
(b) if that designation is still in force, before the end of the period of five years beginning with the date on which the last report relating to it was laid under subsection (3).

(2) The appropriate Minister must review each of the other designated reservations (if any)—
(a) before the end of the period of five years beginning with the date on which the order designating the reservation first came into force; and
(b) if the designation is still in force, before the end of the period of five years beginning with the date on which the last report relating to it was laid under subsection (3).

(3) The Minister conducting a review under this section must prepare a report on the result of the review and lay a copy of it before each House of Parliament.

[1228]

Judges of the European Court of Human Rights

18 Appointment to European Court of Human Rights

(1) In this section "judicial office" means the office of—
(a) Lord Justice of Appeal, Justice of the High Court or Circuit judge, in England and Wales;
(b) judge of the Court of Session or sheriff, in Scotland;
(c) Lord Justice of Appeal, judge of the High Court or county court judge, in Northern Ireland.

(2) The holder of a judicial office may become a judge of the European Court of Human Rights ("the Court") without being required to relinquish his office.

(3) But he is not required to perform the duties of his judicial office while he is a judge of the Court.

(4) In respect of any period during which he is a judge of the Court—
(a) a Lord Justice of Appeal or Justice of the High Court is not to count as a judge of the relevant court for the purposes of section 2(1) or 4(1) of the *Supreme Court Act 1981* (maximum number of judges) nor as a judge of the *Supreme Court* for the purposes of section 12(1) to (6) of that Act (salaries etc);
(b) a judge of the Court of Session is not to count as a judge of that court for the purposes of section 1(1) of the Court of Session Act 1988 (maximum number of judges) or of section 9(1)(c) of the Administration of Justice Act 1973 ("the 1973 Act") (salaries etc);
(c) a Lord Justice of Appeal or judge of the High Court in Northern Ireland is not to count as a judge of the relevant court for the purposes of section 2(1) or 3(1) of the

Judicature (Northern Ireland) Act 1978 (maximum number of judges) nor as a judge of the *Supreme Court* of Northern Ireland for the purposes of section 9(1)(d) of the 1973 Act (salaries etc);

(d) a Circuit judge is not to count as such for the purposes of section 18 of the Courts Act 1971 (salaries etc);

(e) a sheriff is not to count as such for the purposes of section 14 of the Sheriff Courts (Scotland) Act 1907 (salaries etc);

(f) a county court judge of Northern Ireland is not to count as such for the purposes of section 106 of the County Courts Act (Northern Ireland) 1959 (salaries etc).

(5) If a sheriff principal is appointed a judge of the Court, section 11(1) of the Sheriff Courts (Scotland) Act 1971 (temporary appointment of sheriff principal) applies, while he holds that appointment, as if his office is vacant.

(6) Schedule 4 makes provision about judicial pensions in relation to the holder of a judicial office who serves as a judge of the Court.

(7) The Lord Chancellor or the Secretary of State may by order make such transitional provision (including, in particular, provision for a temporary increase in the maximum number of judges) as he considers appropriate in relation to any holder of a judicial office who has completed his service as a judge of the Court.

[(7A) The following paragraphs apply to the making of an order under subsection (7) in relation to any holder of a judicial office listed in subsection (1)(a)—

(a) before deciding what transitional provision it is appropriate to make, the person making the order must consult the Lord Chief Justice of England and Wales;

(b) before making the order, that person must consult the Lord Chief Justice of England and Wales.

(7B) The following paragraphs apply to the making of an order under subsection (7) in relation to any holder of a judicial office listed in subsection (1)(c)—

(a) before deciding what transitional provision it is appropriate to make, the person making the order must consult the Lord Chief Justice of Northern Ireland;

(b) before making the order, that person must consult the Lord Chief Justice of Northern Ireland.

(7C) The Lord Chief Justice of England and Wales may nominate a judicial office holder (within the meaning of section 109(4) of the Constitutional Reform Act 2005) to exercise his functions under this section.

(7D) The Lord Chief Justice of Northern Ireland may nominate any of the following to exercise his functions under this section—

(a) the holder of one of the offices listed in Schedule 1 to the Justice (Northern Ireland) Act 2002;

(b) a Lord Justice of Appeal (as defined in section 88 of that Act).]

[1229]

NOTES

Sub-s (4): in para (a) words in italics in the first place where they occur substituted by the words "Senior Courts Act 1981", words in italics in the second place where they occur substituted by the words "Senior Courts" and words in italics in para (c) substituted by the words "Court of Judicature" by the Constitutional Reform Act 2005, s 59(5), Sch 11, Pt 1, para 1(2), Pt 2, para 4(1), (3), Pt 3, para 6(1), (3), as from a day to be appointed.

Sub-ss (7A)–(7D): added by the Constitutional Reform Act 2005, s 15(1), Sch 4, Pt 1, para 278.

Orders: the Judicial Pensions (European Court of Human Rights) Order 1998, SI 1998/2768.

Parliamentary procedure

19 Statements of compatibility

(1) A Minister of the Crown in charge of a Bill in either House of Parliament must, before Second Reading of the Bill—

(a) make a statement to the effect that in his view the provisions of the Bill are compatible with the Convention rights ("a statement of compatibility"); or

(b) make a statement to the effect that although he is unable to make a statement of compatibility the government nevertheless wishes the House to proceed with the Bill.

(2) The statement must be in writing and be published in such manner as the Minister making it considers appropriate.

[1230]

Supplemental

20 Orders etc under this Act

(1) Any power of a Minister of the Crown to make an order under this Act is exercisable by statutory instrument.

(2) The power of … [the Lord Chancellor or] the Secretary of State to make rules (other than rules of court) under section 2(3) or 7(9) is exercisable by statutory instrument.

(3) Any statutory instrument made under section 14, 15 or 16(7) must be laid before Parliament.

(4) No order may be made by … [the Lord Chancellor or] the Secretary of State under section 1(4), 7(11) or 16(2) unless a draft of the order has been laid before, and approved by, each House of Parliament.

(5) Any statutory instrument made under section 18(7) or Schedule 4, or to which subsection (2) applies, shall be subject to annulment in pursuance of a resolution of either House of Parliament.

(6) The power of a Northern Ireland department to make—
- (a) rules under section 2(3)(c) or 7(9)(c), or
- (b) an order under section 7(11),

is exercisable by statutory rule for the purposes of the Statutory Rules (Northern Ireland) Order 1979.

(7) Any rules made under section 2(3)(c) or 7(9)(c) shall be subject to negative resolution; and section 41(6) of the Interpretation Act (Northern Ireland) 1954 (meaning of "subject to negative resolution") shall apply as if the power to make the rules were conferred by an Act of the Northern Ireland Assembly.

(8) No order may be made by a Northern Ireland department under section 7(11) unless a draft of the order has been laid before, and approved by, the Northern Ireland Assembly.

[1231]

NOTES

Sub-ss (2), (4): words omitted repealed by the Secretary of State for Constitutional Affairs Order 2003, SI 2003/1887, art 9, Sch 2, para 10(2); words in square brackets inserted by the Transfer of Functions (Lord Chancellor and Secretary of State) Order 2005, SI 2005/3429, art 8, Schedule, para 3.

21 Interpretation, etc

(1) In this Act—

"amend" includes repeal and apply (with or without modifications);

"the appropriate Minister" means the Minister of the Crown having charge of the appropriate authorised government department (within the meaning of the Crown Proceedings Act 1947);

"the Commission" means the European Commission of Human Rights;

"the Convention" means the Convention for the Protection of Human Rights and Fundamental Freedoms, agreed by the Council of Europe at Rome on 4th November 1950 as it has effect for the time being in relation to the United Kingdom;

"declaration of incompatibility" means a declaration under section 4;

"Minister of the Crown" has the same meaning as in the Ministers of the Crown Act 1975;

"Northern Ireland Minister" includes the First Minister and the deputy First Minister in Northern Ireland;

"primary legislation" means any—
- (a) public general Act;
- (b) local and personal Act;
- (c) private Act;
- (d) Measure of the Church Assembly;
- (e) Measure of the General Synod of the Church of England;

(f) Order in Council—

(i) made in exercise of Her Majesty's Royal Prerogative;

(ii) made under section 38(1)(a) of the Northern Ireland Constitution Act 1973 or the corresponding provision of the Northern Ireland Act 1998; or

(iii) amending an Act of a kind mentioned in paragraph (a), (b) or (c);

and includes an order or other instrument made under primary legislation (otherwise than by the *National Assembly for Wales*, a member of the Scottish Executive, a Northern Ireland Minister or a Northern Ireland department) to the extent to which it operates to bring one or more provisions of that legislation into force or amends any primary legislation;

"the First Protocol" means the protocol to the Convention agreed at Paris on 20th March 1952;

.....

"the Eleventh Protocol" means the protocol to the Convention (restructuring the control machinery established by the Convention) agreed at Strasbourg on 11th May 1994;

["the Thirteenth Protocol" means the protocol to the Convention (concerning the abolition of the death penalty in all circumstances) agreed at Vilnius on 3rd May 2002;]

"remedial order" means an order under section 10;

"subordinate legislation" means any—

(a) Order in Council other than one—

(i) made in exercise of Her Majesty's Royal Prerogative;

(ii) made under section 38(1)(a) of the Northern Ireland Constitution Act 1973 or the corresponding provision of the Northern Ireland Act 1998; or

(iii) amending an Act of a kind mentioned in the definition of primary legislation;

[(ba) Measure of the National Assembly for Wales;

(bb) Act of the National Assembly for Wales;]

(b) Act of the Scottish Parliament;

(c) Act of the Parliament of Northern Ireland;

(d) Measure of the Assembly established under section 1 of the Northern Ireland Assembly Act 1973;

(e) Act of the Northern Ireland Assembly;

(f) order, rules, regulations, scheme, warrant, byelaw or other instrument made under primary legislation (except to the extent to which it operates to bring one or more provisions of that legislation into force or amends any primary legislation);

(g) order, rules, regulations, scheme, warrant, byelaw or other instrument made under legislation mentioned in paragraph (b), (c), (d) or (e) or made under an Order in Council applying only to Northern Ireland;

(h) order, rules, regulations, scheme, warrant, byelaw or other instrument made by a member of the Scottish Executive[, Welsh Ministers, the First Minister for Wales, the Counsel General to the Welsh Assembly Government], a Northern Ireland Minister or a Northern Ireland department in exercise of prerogative or other executive functions of Her Majesty which are exercisable by such a person on behalf of Her Majesty;

"transferred matters" has the same meaning as in the Northern Ireland Act 1998; and

"tribunal" means any tribunal in which legal proceedings may be brought.

(2) The references in paragraphs (b) and (c) of section 2(1) to Articles are to Articles of the Convention as they had effect immediately before the coming into force of the Eleventh Protocol.

(3) The reference in paragraph (d) of section 2(1) to Article 46 includes a reference to Articles 32 and 54 of the Convention as they had effect immediately before the coming into force of the Eleventh Protocol.

(4) The references in section 2(1) to a report or decision of the Commission or a decision of the Committee of Ministers include references to a report or decision made as provided by paragraphs 3, 4 and 6 of Article 5 of the Eleventh Protocol (transitional provisions).

(5) *Any liability under the Army Act 1955, the Air Force Act 1955 or the Naval Discipline Act 1957 to suffer death for an offence is replaced by a liability to imprisonment for life or any less punishment authorised by those Acts; and those Acts shall accordingly have effect with the necessary modifications.*

[1232]

NOTES

Sub-s (1): in definition "primary legislation" for the words in italics there are substituted the words "Welsh Ministers, the First Minister for Wales, the Counsel General to the Welsh Assembly Government", in definition "subordinate legislation" paras (ba), (bb) inserted and words in square brackets in para (h) inserted, by the Government of Wales Act 2006, s 160(1), Sch 10, para 56(1), (2), as from immediately after the ordinary election (under the Government of Wales Act 1998, s 3) held in 2007: see the Government of Wales Act 2006, s 161(1), and for further effect in respect of this commencement see sub-ss (4), (5) of that section; definition "the Sixth Protocol" omitted repealed and definition "the Thirteenth Protocol" inserted by the Human Rights Act 1998 (Amendment) Order 2004, SI 2004/1574, art 2(2).

Sub-s (5): repealed by the Armed Forces Act 2006, s 378(2), Sch 17, as from a day to be appointed.

Emergency regulations made under the Civil Contingencies Act 2004, s 20 are to be treated as subordinate legislation and not primary legislation for the purposes of this Act: see s 30(2) of the 2004 Act.

22 Short title, commencement, application and extent

(1) This Act may be cited as the Human Rights Act 1998.

(2) Sections 18, 20 and 21(5) and this section come into force on the passing of this Act.

(3) The other provisions of this Act come into force on such day as the Secretary of State may by order appoint; and different days may be appointed for different purposes.

(4) Paragraph (b) of subsection (1) of section 7 applies to proceedings brought by or at the instigation of a public authority whenever the act in question took place; but otherwise that subsection does not apply to an act taking place before the coming into force of that section.

(5) This Act binds the Crown.

(6) This Act extends to Northern Ireland.

(7) *Section 21(5), so far as it relates to any provision contained in the Army Act 1955, the Air Force Act 1955 or the Naval Discipline Act 1957, extends to any place to which that provision extends.*

[1233]

NOTES

Sub-s (7): repealed by the Armed Forces Act 2006, s 378(2), Sch 17, as from a day to be appointed.

Orders: the Human Rights Act 1998 (Commencement) Order 1998, SI 1998/2882; the Human Rights Act 1998 (Commencement No 2) Order 2000, SI 2000/1851.

SCHEDULE 1
THE ARTICLES

Section 1(3)

PART I
THE CONVENTION RIGHTS AND FREEDOMS

Article 2
Right to life

1. Everyone's right to life shall be protected by law. No one shall be deprived of his life intentionally save in the execution of a sentence of a court following his conviction of a crime for which this penalty is provided by law.

2. Deprivation of life shall not be regarded as inflicted in contravention of this Article when it results from the use of force which is no more than absolutely necessary—
   (a) in defence of any person from unlawful violence;
   (b) in order to effect a lawful arrest or to prevent the escape of a person lawfully detained;

(c) in action lawfully taken for the purpose of quelling a riot or insurrection.

Article 3
Prohibition of torture

No one shall be subjected to torture or to inhuman or degrading treatment or punishment.

Article 4
Prohibition of slavery and forced labour

1. No one shall be held in slavery or servitude.

2. No one shall be required to perform forced or compulsory labour.

3. For the purpose of this Article the term "forced or compulsory labour" shall not include—

(a) any work required to be done in the ordinary course of detention imposed according to the provisions of Article 5 of this Convention or during conditional release from such detention;
(b) any service of a military character or, in case of conscientious objectors in countries where they are recognised, service exacted instead of compulsory military service;
(c) any service exacted in case of an emergency or calamity threatening the life or well-being of the community;
(d) any work or service which forms part of normal civic obligations.

Article 5
Right to liberty and security

1. Everyone has the right to liberty and security of person. No one shall be deprived of his liberty save in the following cases and in accordance with a procedure prescribed by law—

(a) the lawful detention of a person after conviction by a competent court;
(b) the lawful arrest or detention of a person for non-compliance with the lawful order of a court or in order to secure the fulfilment of any obligation prescribed by law;
(c) the lawful arrest or detention of a person effected for the purpose of bringing him before the competent legal authority on reasonable suspicion of having committed an offence or when it is reasonably considered necessary to prevent his committing an offence or fleeing after having done so;
(d) the detention of a minor by lawful order for the purpose of educational supervision or his lawful detention for the purpose of bringing him before the competent legal authority;
(e) the lawful detention of persons for the prevention of the spreading of infectious diseases, of persons of unsound mind, alcoholics or drug addicts or vagrants;
(f) the lawful arrest or detention of a person to prevent his effecting an unauthorised entry into the country or of a person against whom action is being taken with a view to deportation or extradition.

2. Everyone who is arrested shall be informed promptly, in a language which he understands, of the reasons for his arrest and of any charge against him.

3. Everyone arrested or detained in accordance with the provisions of paragraph 1(c) of this Article shall be brought promptly before a judge or other officer authorised by law to exercise judicial power and shall be entitled to trial within a reasonable time or to release pending trial. Release may be conditioned by guarantees to appear for trial.

4. Everyone who is deprived of his liberty by arrest or detention shall be entitled to take proceedings by which the lawfulness of his detention shall be decided speedily by a court and his release ordered if the detention is not lawful.

5. Everyone who has been the victim of arrest or detention in contravention of the provisions of this Article shall have an enforceable right to compensation.

Article 6
Right to a fair trial

1. In the determination of his civil rights and obligations or of any criminal charge against him, everyone is entitled to a fair and public hearing within a reasonable time by an independent and impartial tribunal established by law. Judgment shall be pronounced publicly but the press and public may be excluded from all or part of the trial in the interest of morals, public order or national security in a democratic society, where the interests of juveniles or the protection of the private life of the parties so require, or to the extent strictly necessary in the opinion of the court in special circumstances where publicity would prejudice the interests of justice.

2. Everyone charged with a criminal offence shall be presumed innocent until proved guilty according to law.

3. Everyone charged with a criminal offence has the following minimum rights—
   (a) to be informed promptly, in a language which he understands and in detail, of the nature and cause of the accusation against him;
   (b) to have adequate time and facilities for the preparation of his defence;
   (c) to defend himself in person or through legal assistance of his own choosing or, if he has not sufficient means to pay for legal assistance, to be given it free when the interests of justice so require;
   (d) to examine or have examined witnesses against him and to obtain the attendance and examination of witnesses on his behalf under the same conditions as witnesses against him;
   (e) to have the free assistance of an interpreter if he cannot understand or speak the language used in court.

Article 7
No punishment without law

1. No one shall be held guilty of any criminal offence on account of any act or omission which did not constitute a criminal offence under national or international law at the time when it was committed. Nor shall a heavier penalty be imposed than the one that was applicable at the time the criminal offence was committed.

2. This Article shall not prejudice the trial and punishment of any person for any act or omission which, at the time when it was committed, was criminal according to the general principles of law recognised by civilised nations.

Article 8
Right to respect for private and family life

1. Everyone has the right to respect for his private and family life, his home and his correspondence.

2. There shall be no interference by a public authority with the exercise of this right except such as is in accordance with the law and is necessary in a democratic society in the interests of national security, public safety or the economic well-being of the country, for the prevention of disorder or crime, for the protection of health or morals, or for the protection of the rights and freedoms of others.

Article 9
Freedom of thought, conscience and religion

1. Everyone has the right to freedom of thought, conscience and religion; this right includes freedom to change his religion or belief and freedom, either alone or in community with others and in public or private, to manifest his religion or belief, in worship, teaching, practice and observance.

2. Freedom to manifest one's religion or beliefs shall be subject only to such limitations as are prescribed by law and are necessary in a democratic society in the interests of public safety, for the protection of public order, health or morals, or for the protection of the rights and freedoms of others.

Article 10
Freedom of expression

1. Everyone has the right to freedom of expression. This right shall include freedom to hold opinions and to receive and impart information and ideas without interference by public authority and regardless of frontiers. This Article shall not prevent States from requiring the licensing of broadcasting, television or cinema enterprises.

2. The exercise of these freedoms, since it carries with it duties and responsibilities, may be subject to such formalities, conditions, restrictions or penalties as are prescribed by law and are necessary in a democratic society, in the interests of national security, territorial integrity or public safety, for the prevention of disorder or crime, for the protection of health or morals, for the protection of the reputation or rights of others, for preventing the disclosure of information received in confidence, or for maintaining the authority and impartiality of the judiciary.

Article 11
Freedom of assembly and association

1. Everyone has the right to freedom of peaceful assembly and to freedom of association with others, including the right to form and to join trade unions for the protection of his interests.

2. No restrictions shall be placed on the exercise of these rights other than such as are prescribed by law and are necessary in a democratic society in the interests of national security or public safety, for the prevention of disorder or crime, for the protection of health or morals or for the protection of the rights and freedoms of others. This Article shall not prevent the imposition of lawful restrictions on the exercise of these rights by members of the armed forces, of the police or of the administration of the State.

Article 12
Right to marry

Men and women of marriageable age have the right to marry and to found a family, according to the national laws governing the exercise of this right.

Article 14
Prohibition of discrimination

The enjoyment of the rights and freedoms set forth in this Convention shall be secured without discrimination on any ground such as sex, race, colour, language, religion, political or other opinion, national or social origin, association with a national minority, property, birth or other status.

Article 16
Restrictions on political activity of aliens

Nothing in Articles 10, 11 and 14 shall be regarded as preventing the High Contracting Parties from imposing restrictions on the political activity of aliens.

Article 17
Prohibition of abuse of rights

Nothing in this Convention may be interpreted as implying for any State, group or person any right to engage in any activity or perform any act aimed at the destruction of any of the rights and freedoms set forth herein or at their limitation to a greater extent than is provided for in the Convention.

Article 18
Limitation on use of restrictions on rights

The restrictions permitted under this Convention to the said rights and freedoms shall not be applied for any purpose other than those for which they have been prescribed.

[1234]

NOTES

Commencement: 2 October 2000.

PART II
THE FIRST PROTOCOL

Article 1
Protection of property

Every natural or legal person is entitled to the peaceful enjoyment of his possessions. No one shall be deprived of his possessions except in the public interest and subject to the conditions provided for by law and by the general principles of international law.

The preceding provisions shall not, however, in any way impair the right of a State to enforce such laws as it deems necessary to control the use of property in accordance with the general interest or to secure the payment of taxes or other contributions or penalties.

Article 2
Right to education

No person shall be denied the right to education. In the exercise of any functions which it assumes in relation to education and to teaching, the State shall respect the right of parents to ensure such education and teaching in conformity with their own religious and philosophical convictions.

Article 3
Right to free elections

The High Contracting Parties undertake to hold free elections at reasonable intervals by secret ballot, under conditions which will ensure the free expression of the opinion of the people in the choice of the legislature.

[1235]

[PART 3
ARTICLE 1 OF THE THIRTEENTH PROTOCOL

Abolition of the death penalty

The death penalty shall be abolished. No one shall be condemned to such penalty or executed.]

[1236]

NOTES

Commencement: 22 June 2004.
Substituted by the Human Rights Act 1998 (Amendment) Order 2004, SI 2004/1574, art 2(3).

SCHEDULE 2
REMEDIAL ORDERS

Section 10

Orders

1.—(1) A remedial order may—

(a) contain such incidental, supplemental, consequential or transitional provision as the person making it considers appropriate;
(b) be made so as to have effect from a date earlier than that on which it is made;
(c) make provision for the delegation of specific functions;
(d) make different provision for different cases.

(2) The power conferred by sub-paragraph (1)(a) includes—
(a) power to amend primary legislation (including primary legislation other than that which contains the incompatible provision); and
(b) power to amend or revoke subordinate legislation (including subordinate legislation other than that which contains the incompatible provision).

(3) A remedial order may be made so as to have the same extent as the legislation which it affects.

(4) No person is to be guilty of an offence solely as a result of the retrospective effect of a remedial order.

Procedure

2. No remedial order may be made unless—
(a) a draft of the order has been approved by a resolution of each House of Parliament made after the end of the period of 60 days beginning with the day on which the draft was laid; or
(b) it is declared in the order that it appears to the person making it that, because of the urgency of the matter, it is necessary to make the order without a draft being so approved.

Orders laid in draft

3.—(1) No draft may be laid under paragraph 2(a) unless—
(a) the person proposing to make the order has laid before Parliament a document which contains a draft of the proposed order and the required information; and
(b) the period of 60 days, beginning with the day on which the document required by this sub-paragraph was laid, has ended.

(2) If representations have been made during that period, the draft laid under paragraph 2(a) must be accompanied by a statement containing—
(a) a summary of the representations; and
(b) if, as a result of the representations, the proposed order has been changed, details of the changes.

Urgent cases

4.—(1) If a remedial order ("the original order") is made without being approved in draft, the person making it must lay it before Parliament, accompanied by the required information, after it is made.

(2) If representations have been made during the period of 60 days beginning with the day on which the original order was made, the person making it must (after the end of that period) lay before Parliament a statement containing—
(a) a summary of the representations; and
(b) if, as a result of the representations, he considers it appropriate to make changes to the original order, details of the changes.

(3) If sub-paragraph (2)(b) applies, the person making the statement must—
(a) make a further remedial order replacing the original order; and
(b) lay the replacement order before Parliament.

(4) If, at the end of the period of 120 days beginning with the day on which the original order was made, a resolution has not been passed by each House approving the original or replacement order, the order ceases to have effect (but without that affecting anything previously done under either order or the power to make a fresh remedial order).

Definitions

5. In this Schedule—

"representations" means representations about a remedial order (or proposed remedial order) made to the person making (or proposing to make) it and includes any relevant Parliamentary report or resolution; and

"required information" means—

(a) an explanation of the incompatibility which the order (or proposed order) seeks to remove, including particulars of the relevant declaration, finding or order; and

(b) a statement of the reasons for proceeding under section 10 and for making an order in those terms.

Calculating periods

6. In calculating any period for the purposes of this Schedule, no account is to be taken of any time during which—

(a) Parliament is dissolved or prorogued; or

(b) both Houses are adjourned for more than four days.

[7.—(1) This paragraph applies in relation to—

(a) any remedial order made, and any draft of such under an order proposed to be made,—

(i) by the Scottish Ministers; or

(ii) within devolved competence (within the meaning of the Scotland Act 1998) by Her Majesty in Council; and

(b) any document or statement to be laid in connection with such an order (or proposed order).

(2) This Schedule has effect in relation to any such order (or proposed order), document or statement subject to the following modifications.

(3) Any reference to Parliament, each House of Parliament or both Houses of Parliament shall be construed as a reference to the Scottish Parliament.

(4) Paragraph 6 does not apply and instead, in calculating the period for the purposes of this Schedule, no account is to be taken of any time during which the Scottish Parliament is dissolved or is in recess for more than four days.]

[1237]–[1238]

NOTES

Para 7: added by the Scotland Act 1998 (Consequential Modifications) Order 2000, SI 2000/2040, art 2(1), Schedule, Pt I, para 21.

Orders: the Mental Health Act 1983 (Remedial) Order 2001, SI 2001/3712; the Naval Discipline Act 1957 (Remedial) Order 2004, SI 2004/66; the Marriage Act 1949 (Remedial) Order 2007, SI 2007/438.

SCHEDULE 3
DEROGATION AND RESERVATION

Sections 14 and 15

(Original Sch 3, Pt I repealed by the Human Rights Act (Amendment) Order 2001, SI 2001/1216; new Sch 3, Pt I inserted by the Human Rights Act (Amendment No 2) Order 2001, SI 2001/4032, art 2, Schedule and repealed by the Human Rights Act 1998 (Amendment) Order 2005, SI 2005/1071, art 2.)

PART II
RESERVATION

At the time of signing the present (First) Protocol, I declare that, in view of certain provisions of the Education Acts in the United Kingdom, the principle affirmed in the second sentence of Article 2 is accepted by the United Kingdom only so far as it is compatible with the provision of efficient instruction and training, and the avoidance of unreasonable public expenditure.

Dated 20 March 1952. Made by the United Kingdom Permanent Representative to the Council of Europe.

[1239]

SCHEDULE 4
JUDICIAL PENSIONS

Section 18(6)

Duty to make orders about pensions

1.—(1) The appropriate Minister must by order make provision with respect to pensions payable to or in respect of any holder of a judicial office who serves as an ECHR judge.

(2) A pensions order must include such provision as the Minister making it considers is necessary to secure that—

(a) an ECHR judge who was, immediately before his appointment as an ECHR judge, a member of a judicial pension scheme is entitled to remain as a member of that scheme;

(b) the terms on which he remains a member of the scheme are those which would have been applicable had he not been appointed as an ECHR judge; and

(c) entitlement to benefits payable in accordance with the scheme continues to be determined as if, while serving as an ECHR judge, his salary was that which would (but for section 18(4)) have been payable to him in respect of his continuing service as the holder of his judicial office.

Contributions

2. A pensions order may, in particular, make provision—

(a) for any contributions which are payable by a person who remains a member of a scheme as a result of the order, and which would otherwise be payable by deduction from his salary, to be made otherwise than by deduction from his salary as an ECHR judge; and

(b) for such contributions to be collected in such manner as may be determined by the administrators of the scheme.

Amendments of other enactments

3. A pensions order may amend any provision of, or made under, a pensions Act in such manner and to such extent as the Minister making the order considers necessary or expedient to ensure the proper administration of any scheme to which it relates.

Definitions

4. In this Schedule—

"appropriate Minister" means—

(a) in relation to any judicial office whose jurisdiction is exercisable exclusively in relation to Scotland, the Secretary of State; and

(b) otherwise, the Lord Chancellor;

"ECHR judge" means the holder of a judicial office who is serving as a judge of the Court;

"judicial pension scheme" means a scheme established by and in accordance with a pensions Act;

"pensions Act" means—

(a) the County Courts Act (Northern Ireland) 1959;

(b) the Sheriffs' Pensions (Scotland) Act 1961;

(c) the Judicial Pensions Act 1981; or

(d) the Judicial Pensions and Retirement Act 1993; and

"pensions order" means an order made under paragraph 1.

[1240]

NOTES

Orders: the Judicial Pensions (European Court of Human Rights) Order 1998, SI 1998/2768.

NATIONAL LOTTERY ACT 1998

(1998 c 22)

ARRANGEMENT OF SECTIONS

PART I
PROVISIONS RELATING TO THE NATIONAL LOTTERY

The Director General and the National Lottery Commission

PART II
THE NATIONAL ENDOWMENT FOR SCIENCE, TECHNOLOGY AND THE ARTS

PART III
SUPPLEMENTAL PROVISIONS

An Act to make further provision in relation to the National Lottery; to make provision for and in connection with the establishment of a body corporate to be endowed out of the National Lottery Distribution Fund and to be known as the National Endowment for Science, Technology and the Arts; and for connected purposes

[2 July 1998]

PART I
PROVISIONS RELATING TO THE NATIONAL LOTTERY

The Director General and the National Lottery Commission

1 Replacement of Director General by National Lottery Commission

(1) There shall cease to be an office of Director General of the National Lottery.

(2) In consequence of subsection (1) above, in the National Lottery etc

Act 1993 (in this Act referred to as "the 1993 Act") section 3 and Schedule 2 (which relate to the Director General of the National Lottery) shall cease to have effect.

(3) …

(4) On the day on which this subsection comes into force under section 27(3) below, the functions conferred or imposed on the Director General of the National Lottery by or under the 1993 Act (including any functions so conferred or imposed by virtue of this Act) shall, by virtue of this subsection, be transferred to the National Lottery Commission.

(5) Schedule 1 to this Act (which makes provision supplemental to, or consequential on, this section) shall have effect.

[1241]–[1243]

NOTES

Commencement: 1 April 1999.
Sub-s (3): inserts the National Lottery etc Act 1993, s 3A at **[874]**.

2–15 (*S 2 (as repealed in part by s 26 of, and Sch 5 to, this Act) inserts the National Lottery etc Act 1993, s 10A at* **[882]**, *in relation to any contravention, after 2 September 1998, of a condition in a licence under section 5 or 6 of the 1993 Act, whenever granted, and amends ss 11, 21(2) of the 1993 Act at* **[884]**, **[893]**; *s 3 inserts s 10B of the 1993 Act at* **[883]**; *s 4 amends Sch 3, Pt II to the 1993 Act; s 5 adds s 33(4)–(10) of the 1993 Act at* **[910]**, *in relation to accounts prepared under subsection (1) of that section so far as they relate to periods beginning on or after 1 April 1999; s 6 amends s 22 of the 1993 Act at* **[894]**; *s 6(1) introduces sub-ss (2)–(6); ss 6(2)–(7), (9), (10), 7, 8(1), (3)–(7), 11(5), (6), 14 repealed by the National Lottery Act 2006, s 21, Sch 3; s 6(8)* amends the National Lottery etc Act 1993, s 44(1) at **[926]**; *s 8(2)* adds the National Lottery etc Act 1993, s 44(3) at **[926]**; *s 9 inserts ss 25(1A), 44(4) of the 1993 Act at* **[897]**, **[926]**; *s 10 inserts s 25(2A), (2B) of the 1993 Act at* **[897]**; *s 11(1)–(4) inserts ss 25A, 26(3A), (4A) of the 1993 Act at* **[898]**, **[902]**, *and amends s 26(4) of the 1993 Act; s 12(1) inserts s 25B of the 1993 Act at* **[899]**; *s 12(2) amends s 44(1) of the 1993 Act at* **[926]**; *s 12(3) (together with Sch 3) inserts Sch 3A to the 1993 Act; s 13 inserts s 25C of the 1993 Act at* **[900]**; *s 15 amends s 60(2), (3), and inserts s 60(2A), (3A), (3B), (6).)*

PART II
THE NATIONAL ENDOWMENT FOR SCIENCE, TECHNOLOGY AND THE ARTS

16 The National Endowment for Science, Technology and the Arts

(1) There shall be a body corporate known as the National Endowment for Science, Technology and the Arts (in this Part of this Act referred to as "NESTA").

(2) Schedule 4 to this Act makes provision in relation to NESTA.

[1244]

NOTES

Commencement: 2 July 1998.

17 Objects

(1) The objects of NESTA are to support and promote talent, innovation and creativity in the fields of science, technology and the arts.

(2) The objects of NESTA are to be achieved by the following means, namely—

- (a) helping talented individuals (or groups of such individuals) in the fields of science, technology and the arts to achieve their potential;
- (b) helping persons to turn inventions or ideas in the fields of science, technology and the arts into products or services—
  - (i) which can be effectively exploited; and
  - (ii) the rights to which can be adequately protected; and
- (c) contributing to public knowledge and appreciation of science, technology and the arts.

(3) At the request of NESTA, the Secretary of State may by order amend subsection (2) above so as to add to, remove or vary any of the means by which NESTA are to achieve their objects.

(4) An order under this section shall be made by statutory instrument; but no such instrument shall be made unless a draft of it has been laid before, and approved by a resolution of, each House of Parliament.

[1245]

NOTES

Commencement: 2 July 1998.

18 General duty and powers

(1) NESTA shall be under a general duty to achieve their objects by the means for the time being specified in section 17(2) above.

(2) Subject to any directions under section 20 or 21 below, NESTA may do anything which appears to them to be necessary or expedient for the purpose of or in connection with achieving their objects, including in particular—

(a) giving financial assistance to persons (whether by way of grant, loan or otherwise);
(b) attaching conditions to any financial assistance given, including conditions requiring repayment, payment of interest or payment of other amounts;
(c) acquiring and disposing of, or exploiting, land and other property;
(d) taking charges or other forms of security over land and other property;
(e) entering into contracts of whatever nature;
(f) forming, or acquiring and disposing of interests in, bodies corporate;
(g) acting with other persons, whether by way of partnership, joint venture or otherwise;
(h) accepting gifts of assistance, money, land and other property; and
(i) investing money not immediately required for the purpose of achieving their objects.

(3) NESTA may not, without the approval of the Secretary of State—
(a) borrow money; or
(b) make or enter into arrangements which give rise to, or may give rise to contingent liabilities of an unusual nature.

(4) Directions under section 21 below may include provision for the purpose of determining whether arrangements are such as give rise to, or may give rise to, contingent liabilities of an unusual nature.

[1246]

NOTES

Commencement: 2 July 1998.

19 Initial and subsequent endowment

(1) For the purpose of providing NESTA with an endowment to enable them to achieve their objects, the Secretary of State may, before the end of the period of one year beginning with the day on which this Act is passed, make one or more payments to NESTA out of money held in the National Lottery Distribution Fund and allocated for expenditure on or connected with health, education or the environment.

(2) For the purpose of increasing the amount of NESTA's endowment, the Secretary of State may, at any time after the end of the period of one year beginning with the day on which this Act is passed, make an order permitting him to pay to NESTA, out of money held in the National Lottery Distribution Fund and allocated for such one or more of the descriptions for the time being mentioned in section 22(3) of the 1993 Act as may be specified in the order, such sum or, as the case may be, such sums (whether or not of equal amounts) as may be so specified.

(3) Before making an order under this section, the Secretary of State shall consult each of the bodies for the time being mentioned in section 23 of the 1993 Act.

(4) Where an order is made under this section, the Secretary of State may make the payment or payments permitted by the order.

(5) NESTA may not spend their endowment, or any part of their endowment, without the approval of the Secretary of State.

(6) In subsections (2) and (5) above, "endowment" means the aggregate of any amounts paid to NESTA under subsection (1) or (4) above.

(7) …

(8) An order under this section shall be made by statutory instrument; but no such instrument shall be made unless a draft of it has been laid before, and approved by a resolution of, each House of Parliament.

[1247]

NOTES

Commencement: 2 July 1998.
Sub-s (7): adds the National Lottery etc Act 1993, s 22(4) at **[894]**.
Orders: the National Endowment for Science, Technology and the Arts (Increase of Endowment) Order 2003, SI 2003/235; the National Endowment for Science, Technology and the Arts (Increase of Endowment) Order 2006, SI 2006/396.

20 Solicitation of gifts and investment of money

(1) NESTA shall be under a duty to seek gifts of assistance, money, land and other property, but in seeking or accepting any such gifts NESTA shall comply with any directions given to them by the Secretary of State.

(2) Except to the extent that directions under section 21 below otherwise provide, NESTA shall pay—

(a) their endowment, and

(b) any other money held by them which is not immediately required by them for the purpose of achieving their objects,

to the National Debt Commissioners for investment by them in accordance with any instructions given to them by NESTA.

(3) In giving instructions to the National Debt Commissioners under subsection (2) above, NESTA shall comply with any directions under section 21 below.

(4) The expenses of the National Debt Commissioners in making any investment under subsection (2) above shall be met by NESTA.

(5) In this section "endowment" has the meaning given by section 19(6) above.

[1248]

NOTES

Commencement: 2 July 1998.

21 Financial directions etc

(1) NESTA shall comply with any directions given to them by the Secretary of State—

(a) in connection with the management, control or investment of their endowment or any other money held by them;

(b) in connection with the management, control, use or exploitation of any property in which they have an interest;

(c) in connection with the control of their administrative costs (including staff costs); or

(d) otherwise in connection with their financial affairs.

(2) If NESTA fail to comply with any direction given to them under this section, the Secretary of State may, after taking into account any representations made by NESTA, require NESTA to pay to him such amount as the Secretary of State thinks appropriate having regard to the extent or degree of that failure.

(3) The amount, or the aggregate of any amounts, which NESTA are required to pay under this section shall not exceed the amount of their endowment.

(4) Any amount which NESTA are required to pay under this section shall be recoverable by the Secretary of State as a debt due to him from NESTA.

(5) The Secretary of State shall pay into the National Lottery Distribution Fund any amount received by him under this section; and any amount so paid shall be treated for the purposes of the 1993 Act as so paid under section 21(2) of that Act.

(6) The Secretary of State shall consult NESTA before giving any directions to them under this section.

(7) In this section "endowment" has the meaning given by section 19(6) above.

[1249]

NOTES

Commencement: 2 July 1998.

22 Annual report and forward plans

(1) As soon as possible after the end of each financial year, NESTA shall make a report to the Secretary of State on the activities of NESTA during that year.

(2) The report shall set out any directions given to NESTA under section 20 or 21 above that had effect during the financial year to which the report relates.

(3) NESTA shall from time to time draw up a forward plan.

(4) As soon as possible after drawing up a forward plan, NESTA—
(a) shall send a copy of the plan to the Secretary of State; and
(b) shall publish and publicise the plan.

(5) The Secretary of State shall lay a copy of every report and forward plan received by him under this section before Parliament.

(6) In this section "forward plan" means a plan for a future period which sets out the strategy which NESTA propose to follow during that period for the purpose of achieving their objects.

[1250]

NOTES
Commencement: 2 July 1998.

23 Accounts

(1) NESTA shall—
(a) keep proper accounts and proper records in relation to the accounts, and
(b) prepare a statement of accounts in respect of each financial year.

(2) The statement shall comply with any directions that may be given by the Secretary of State as to the information to be contained in such a statement, the manner in which such information is to be presented or the methods and principles according to which such a statement is to be prepared.

(3) Copies of the statement shall be sent to the Secretary of State and the Comptroller and Auditor General within such period after the end of the financial year to which the statement relates as the Secretary of State may direct.

(4) The Comptroller and Auditor General shall examine, certify and report on the statement and shall lay copies of the statement and of his report before Parliament.

(5) The Secretary of State shall not give a direction under this section without the Treasury's approval.

[1251]

NOTES
Commencement: 2 July 1998.

24 (*Amends the Income and Corporation Taxes Act 1988, s 507(1) at* **[707]**, *the Taxation of Chargeable Gains Act 1992, s 271(7), the Inheritance Tax Act 1984, Sch 3 at* **[308]**, *the Finance Act 1982, s 129(1) at* **[268]**, *and the Finance Act 1986, s 90(7).*)

25 Interpretation of Part II

(1) In this Part of this Act—
"financial year", in relation to NESTA, means—
(a) the period beginning with the date on which NESTA is established and ending with the next 31st March following that date, and
(b) each successive period of twelve months ending with 31st March;
"the National Lottery Distribution Fund" has the same meaning as in the 1993 Act;
"NESTA" means the National Endowment for Science, Technology and the Arts.

(2) Any reference in this Part of this Act to the arts includes a reference to—
(a) architecture, design or crafts;
(b) the film, audio-visual or broadcasting industries; and
(c) the music industry.

(3) Any reference in this Part of this Act to property includes a reference to intellectual property.

(4) Any directions under this Part of this Act shall be given in writing and may be varied or revoked by subsequent directions.

[1252]

NOTES
Commencement: 2 July 1998.

PART III
SUPPLEMENTAL PROVISIONS

26 (*Introduces Sch 5 to this Act* (*Repeals*).)

27 Short title, interpretation, commencement and extent

(1) This Act may be cited as the National Lottery Act 1998.

(2) In this Act "the 1993 Act" means the National Lottery etc Act 1993.

(3) The following provisions of this Act, namely—

(a) section 1,

(b) Schedule 1, and

(c) Part I of Schedule 5 and section 26 so far as relating to that Part of that Schedule,

shall come into force on such day as the Secretary of State may appoint by order made by statutory instrument; and different days may be so appointed for different purposes.

(4) The following provisions of this Act, namely—

(a) this section,

(b) sections 6 to 12 and 15 to 25,

(c) Schedules 2 to 4, and

(d) section 26 and Part II of Schedule 5, so far as relating to the repeals in section 22 of, and paragraphs 2, 3 and 6 of Schedule 5 to, the 1993 Act,

shall come into force on the day on which this Act is passed.

(5) The remaining provisions of this Act shall come into force at the end of the period of two months beginning with the day on which this Act is passed.

(6) The power conferred by subsection (3) above to make an order includes power to make incidental, consequential, supplemental or transitional provision or savings (including power to amend enactments).

(7) This Act extends to Northern Ireland.

[1253]

NOTES

Commencement: 2 July 1998.
Orders: the National Lottery Act 1998 (Commencement) Order 1999, SI 1999/650.

SCHEDULES

SCHEDULE 1
REPLACEMENT OF DIRECTOR GENERAL BY COMMISSION: SUPPLEMENTARY PROVISIONS

Section 1

PART I
TRANSFERS ETC

Interpretation

1. In this Part of this Schedule—

"the appointed day" means the day on which subsection (4) of the principal section comes into force under section 27(3) of this Act;

"the Commission" means the National Lottery Commission;

"the Director General" means the Director General of the National Lottery;

"instrument" includes orders, rules, regulations, schemes, licences, agreements and other documents;

"the principal section" means section 1 of this Act.

Transfer of property, rights and liabilities

2. On the appointed day, there shall by virtue of this paragraph be transferred to the Commission any property, rights or liabilities to which, immediately before that day, the Director General was entitled or subject in connection with any functions transferred to the Commission by the principal section.

Transfer of staff

3.—(1) This paragraph applies to any person who, immediately before the appointed day, is employed by virtue of paragraph 3 of Schedule 2 to the 1993 Act.

(2) Any contract of employment under which a person to whom this paragraph applies is so employed shall have effect as from the appointed day as if it had originally been made between him and the Commission.

(3) Without prejudice to sub-paragraph (2) above—

(a) all the rights, powers, duties and liabilities of the employer under or in connection with a contract to which that sub-paragraph applies shall by virtue of that subparagraph be transferred to the Commission on the appointed day, and

(b) anything done before that day by or in relation to the employer in respect of that contract or the employee shall be deemed from that day to have been done by or in relation to the Commission.

(4) Sub-paragraphs (2) and (3) above are without prejudice to any right of an employee to terminate his contract of employment if his working conditions are changed substantially to his detriment; but such a change shall not be taken to have occurred by reason only of the change in employer effected by sub-paragraph (2) above.

(5) In sub-paragraph (4) above, the reference to an employee's working conditions includes a reference to any rights (whether accrued or contingent) under any pension or superannuation scheme of which he was a member by virtue of his employment immediately before the appointed day.

Construction of references to the Director General

4. Any enactment or instrument passed or made before the appointed day shall have effect, so far as necessary for the purposes of, or in consequence of, the transfers effected by the principal section and paragraphs 2 and 3 above, as if any reference to the Director General were a reference to the Commission.

Continuing validity of past acts

5.—(1) Nothing in any other provision of the principal section or this Schedule shall affect the validity of anything done by or in relation to the Director General before the coming into force of that provision.

(2) Anything (including legal proceedings) which immediately before the appointed day is in the process of being done by or in relation to the Director General may, if it relates to any of the functions, property, rights or liabilities transferred by the principal section or paragraph 2 or 3 above, be continued by or in relation to the Commission.

(3) Any approval, authorisation, consent, delegation, direction, licence or appointment given, granted or made or other thing whatever done by the Director General for the purposes of any of the functions transferred by the principal section shall, if in force immediately before the appointed day, continue in force and have effect as if similarly given, granted, made or done by the Commission.

Final report and accounts of the Director General

6.—(1) As respects any time on or after the appointed day, the duties imposed on the Director General in relation to—

(a) accounts, and

(b) the making of a report under section 14 of the 1993 Act,

in respect of his last financial year, or any preceding financial year for which those duties have not been discharged, shall be discharged by the Commission.

(2) Any reference in this paragraph to the Director General's last financial year is a reference to the financial year beginning with the 1st April last preceding the appointed day.

(3) The duties imposed on the Commission by sub-paragraph (1) above shall be discharged by them as if the Director General's last financial year ended with the day preceding the appointed day (if it would not in fact do so).

(4) The property transferred to the Commission by virtue of paragraph 2 above shall include the records of the Director General.

(5) For the purposes of this paragraph, the amendments of section 14 of the 1993 Act made by paragraph 13 below shall be disregarded.

(6) In this paragraph "financial year" means the twelve months beginning with 1st April in any year and ending with the 31st March next following.

[1254]

NOTES

Commencement: 1 April 1999.

(Sch 1, Pt II inserts the National Lottery etc Act 1993, Sch 2A; Sch 1, Pt III amends ss 14, 20, 31 of the 1993 Act at **[887]**, **[892]**, **[908]**, *and amends the Public Records Act 1958, Sch 1, the Parliamentary Commissioner Act 1967, Sch 2, the House of Commons Disqualification Act 1975, Sch 1, Pts II, III, the Northern Ireland Assembly Disqualification Act 1975, Sch 1, Pts II, III, and the Tribunals and Inquiries Act 1992, s 7, Sch 1; Sch 2 repealed by the National Lottery Act 2006, s 21, Sch 3; Sch inserts Sch 3A to the 1993 Act.)*

SCHEDULE 4
THE NATIONAL ENDOWMENT FOR SCIENCE, TECHNOLOGY AND THE ARTS

Section 16

Membership

1.—(1) NESTA shall consist of not more than 15 members (in this Schedule referred to as "trustees")—

(a) all of whom shall be appointed by the Secretary of State; and

(b) one of whom shall be so appointed as chairman.

(2) Before making any appointment under this paragraph, the Secretary of State shall consult such persons as appear to him to be representative of those engaged in the fields of science, technology and the arts.

(3) The Secretary of State may by order amend sub-paragraph (1) above so as to increase the number for the time being specified in that sub-paragraph.

(4) An order under this paragraph shall be made by statutory instrument which shall be subject to annulment in pursuance of a resolution of either House of Parliament.

Delegation of functions

2.—(1) NESTA may appoint any other body or person to exercise on their behalf any of their functions under this Part of this Act—

(a) in any particular case, or

(b) in cases of any particular description.

(2) The persons who may be appointed by NESTA under sub-paragraph (1) above include a trustee, member of staff or committee of NESTA.

(3) NESTA may establish a committee for the purpose of exercising on behalf of NESTA any such function as is mentioned in sub-paragraph (1) above.

(4) A committee established under sub-paragraph (3) above—

(a) may consist of or include persons who are trustees of NESTA;

(b) may consist of or include persons who are members of staff of NESTA; and
(c) may consist of or include persons who are neither trustees nor members of staff of NESTA.

(5) Any reference in this paragraph to a trustee of NESTA includes a reference to the chairman of NESTA.

Tenure of office

3.—(1) Subject to the following provisions of this paragraph, a person shall hold and vacate office as chairman or trustee of NESTA in accordance with the terms of his appointment.

(2) The Secretary of State shall not appoint a person to hold office as a trustee of NESTA for a term of more than five years.

(3) A chairman or trustee of NESTA may at any time resign his office by notice in writing addressed to the Secretary of State.

(4) A trustee of NESTA may be removed from office by the Secretary of State on the ground that—
(a) he has been absent for a period longer than three consecutive months from meetings of NESTA, or of any committee of NESTA, without NESTA's consent,
(b) a bankruptcy order has been made against him, or his estate has been sequestrated, or he has made a composition or arrangement with, or granted a trust deed for, his creditors, or
(c) he is unable or unfit to discharge the functions of his office.

(5) If a chairman of NESTA ceases to be a trustee of NESTA he shall also cease to be chairman.

(6) A person who ceases, otherwise than by virtue of sub-paragraph (4) above, to be a trustee or chairman of NESTA shall be eligible for re-appointment.

Remuneration and allowances

4.—(1) If the Secretary of State so determines, NESTA may pay such remuneration to their chairman or any other trustee of NESTA as the Secretary of State may determine.

(2) NESTA may, in accordance with any scheme for the time being approved by the Secretary of State, pay travelling and other allowances to their chairman, to any other trustee of NESTA, to any member of a committee of theirs or to any person who, by virtue of paragraph 2 above, exercises on behalf of NESTA any of their functions under this Part of this Act.

(3) Where the Secretary of State so determines in the case of a holder of the office of chairman of NESTA, or in the case of any other trustee of NESTA, NESTA shall—
(a) pay to or in respect of him such pension, allowances or gratuities, or
(b) make such payments towards the provision of a pension, allowances or gratuities to or in respect of him,

as the Secretary of State may determine.

(4) If the Secretary of State determines that there are special circumstances that make it right for a person ceasing to hold office as chairman of NESTA, or ceasing to be a trustee of NESTA, to receive compensation, NESTA may pay to him such compensation as the Secretary of State may determine.

Staff

5. Subject to any directions under section 21 of this Act, NESTA may appoint such staff as they think fit, on such terms (including terms as to remuneration and pensions) as they think fit.

Proceedings

6.—(1) NESTA may regulate their own procedure and that of any of their committees (and in particular may specify a quorum for meetings).

(2) The validity of any proceedings of NESTA shall not be affected by any vacancy among their trustees, or by any defect in the appointment of any person as chairman or a trustee.

Application of seal and evidence

7. The application of the seal of NESTA shall be authenticated by the signature—
   (a) of any trustee of NESTA, or
   (b) of any other person who has been authorised by NESTA (whether generally or specially) for that purpose.

8. A document purporting to be duly executed under the seal of NESTA or to be signed on their behalf shall be received in evidence and, unless the contrary is proved, taken to be so executed or signed.

Status of NESTA

9. NESTA shall not be regarded as the servant or agent of the Crown or as enjoying any status, immunity or privilege of the Crown.

10. …

Reimbursement

11. The payments which may be made under section 31 of the 1993 Act (payments from Distribution Fund into Consolidated Fund in respect of expenses) shall include a payment of such amount as the Secretary of State with the approval of the Treasury determines to be appropriate for defraying expenses incurred by the Secretary of State before the commencement of this Part of this Act for the purpose of facilitating the establishment of NESTA.

Prior consultation

12. Any consultation undertaken before the commencement of this Schedule in connection with any appointments under paragraph 1 above shall be as effective, in relation to those appointments, as if this Schedule had been in force at the time the consultation was undertaken.

Application to Scotland

13. Paragraphs 7 and 8 above do not extend to Scotland.

[1255]

NOTES

Commencement: 2 July 1998.

Para 10: amends the House of Commons Disqualification Act 1975, Sch 1, Pt III and the Northern Ireland Assembly Disqualification Act 1975, Sch 1, Pt III.

(Sch 5 contains repeals only.)

TRUSTEE DELEGATION ACT 1999

(1999 c 15)

ARRANGEMENT OF SECTIONS

Attorney of trustee with beneficial interest in land

An Act to amend the law relating to the delegation of trustee functions by power of attorney and the exercise of such functions by the donee of a power of attorney; and to make provision about the authority of the donee of a power of attorney to act in relation to land

[15 July 1999]

Attorney of trustee with beneficial interest in land

1 Exercise of trustee functions by attorney

(1) The donee of a power of attorney is not prevented from doing an act in relation to—
- (a) land,
- (b) capital proceeds of a conveyance of land, or
- (c) income from land,

by reason only that the act involves the exercise of a trustee function of the donor if, at the time when the act is done, the donor has a beneficial interest in the land, proceeds or income.

(2) In this section—
- (a) "conveyance" has the same meaning as in the Law of Property Act 1925, and
- (b) references to a trustee function of the donor are to a function which the donor has as trustee (either alone or jointly with any other person or persons).

(3) Subsection (1) above—
- (a) applies only if and so far as a contrary intention is not expressed in the instrument creating the power of attorney, and
- (b) has effect subject to the terms of that instrument.

(4) The donor of the power of attorney—
- (a) is liable for the acts or defaults of the donee in exercising any function by virtue of subsection (1) above in the same manner as if they were acts or defaults of the donor, but
- (b) is not liable by reason only that a function is exercised by the donee by virtue of that subsection.

(5) Subsections (1) and (4) above—
- (a) apply only if and so far as a contrary intention is not expressed in the instrument (if any) creating the trust, and
- (b) have effect subject to the terms of such an instrument.

(6) The fact that it appears that, in dealing with any shares or stock, the donee of the power of attorney is exercising a function by virtue of subsection (1) above does not affect with any notice of any trust a person in whose books the shares are, or stock is, registered or inscribed.

(7) In any case where (by way of exception to section 3(1) of the Trusts of Land and Appointment of Trustees Act 1996) the doctrine of conversion continues to operate, any person who, by reason of the continuing operation of that doctrine, has a beneficial interest in the proceeds of sale of land shall be treated for the purposes of this section and section 2 below as having a beneficial interest in the land.

(8) The donee of a power of attorney is not to be regarded as exercising a trustee function by virtue of subsection (1) above if he is acting under a trustee delegation power; and for this purpose a trustee delegation power is a power of attorney given under—

(a) a statutory provision, or

(b) a provision of the instrument (if any) creating a trust,

under which the donor of the power is expressly authorised to delegate the exercise of all or any of his trustee functions by power of attorney.

(9) Subject to section 4(6) below, this section applies only to powers of attorney created after the commencement of this Act.

[1256]

NOTES

Commencement: 1 March 2000.

2 Evidence of beneficial interest

(1) This section applies where the interest of a purchaser depends on the donee of a power of attorney having power to do an act in relation to any property by virtue of section 1(1) above.

In this subsection "purchaser" has the same meaning as in Part I of the Law of Property Act 1925.

(2) Where this section applies an appropriate statement is, in favour of the purchaser, conclusive evidence of the donor of the power having a beneficial interest in the property at the time of the doing of the act.

(3) In this section "an appropriate statement" means a signed statement made by the donee—

(a) when doing the act in question, or

(b) at any other time within the period of three months beginning with the day on which the act is done,

that the donor has a beneficial interest in the property at the time of the donee doing the act.

(4) If an appropriate statement is false, the donee is liable in the same way as he would be if the statement were contained in a statutory declaration.

[1257]

NOTES

Commencement: 1 March 2000.

3 *(Amends the Powers of Attorney Act 1971, s 10(2).)*

4 Enduring powers

(1) Section 3(3) of the Enduring Powers of Attorney Act 1985 (which entitles the donee of an enduring power to exercise any of the donor's functions as trustee and to give receipt for capital money etc) does not apply to enduring powers created after the commencement of this Act.

(2) Section 3(3) of the Enduring Powers of Attorney Act 1985 ceases to apply to enduring powers created before the commencement of this Act—

(a) where subsection (3) below applies, in accordance with that subsection, and

(b) otherwise, at the end of the period of one year from that commencement.

(3) Where an application for the registration of the instrument creating such an enduring power is made before the commencement of this Act, or during the period of one year from that commencement, section 3(3) of the Enduring Powers of Attorney Act 1985 ceases to apply to the power—

(a) if the instrument is registered pursuant to the application (whether before commencement or during or after that period), when the registration of the instrument is cancelled, and

(b) if the application is finally refused during or after that period, when the application is finally refused.

(4) In subsection (3) above—

(*a*) *"registration" and "registered" mean registration and registered under section 6 of the Enduring Powers of Attorney Act 1985, and*
(*b*) *"cancelled" means cancelled under section 8(4) of that Act.*

(5) *For the purposes of subsection (3)(b) above an application is finally refused—*
(*a*) *if the application is withdrawn or any appeal is abandoned, when the application is withdrawn or the appeal is abandoned, and*
(*b*) *otherwise, when proceedings on the application (including any proceedings on, or in consequence of, an appeal) have been determined and any time for appealing or further appealing has expired.*

(6) *Section 1 above applies to an enduring power created before the commencement of this Act from the time when (in accordance with subsections (2) to (5) above) section 3(3) of the Enduring Powers of Attorney Act 1985 ceases to apply to it.*

[1258]

NOTES

Commencement: 1 March 2000.
Repealed by the Mental Capacity Act 2005, s 67(2), Sch 7, as from a day to be appointed under s 68(1) of that Act.

Trustee delegation under section 25 of the Trustee Act 1925

5 (*Substitutes the Trustee Act 1925, s 25 at* **[28]**, *in relation to powers of attorney created after 1 March 2000, and amends the Pensions Act 1995, s 34(2)(b).*)

6 Section 25 powers as enduring powers

Section 2(8) of the Enduring Powers of Attorney Act 1985 (which prevents a power of attorney under section 25 of the Trustee Act 1925 from being an enduring power) does not apply to powers of attorney created after the commencement of this Act.

[1259]

NOTES

Commencement: 1 March 2000.
Repealed by the Mental Capacity Act 2005, s 67(2), Sch 7, as from a day to be appointed under s 68(1) of that Act.

Miscellaneous provisions about attorney acting for trustee

7 Two-trustee rules

(1) A requirement imposed by an enactment—
(a) that capital money be paid to, or dealt with as directed by, at least two trustees or that a valid receipt for capital money be given otherwise than by a sole trustee, or
(b) that, in order for an interest or power to be overreached, a conveyance or deed be executed by at least two trustees,

is not satisfied by money being paid to or dealt with as directed by, or a receipt for money being given by, a relevant attorney or by a conveyance or deed being executed by such an attorney.

(2) In this section "relevant attorney" means a person (other than a trust corporation within the meaning of the Trustee Act 1925) who is acting either—
(a) both as a trustee and as attorney for one or more other trustees, or
(b) as attorney for two or more trustees,

and who is not acting together with any other person or persons.

(3) This section applies whether a relevant attorney is acting under a power created before or after the commencement of this Act (but in the case of such an attorney acting under an enduring power created before that commencement is without prejudice to any continuing application of section 3(3) of the Enduring Powers of Attorney Act 1985 to the enduring power after that commencement *in accordance with section 4 above*).

[1260]

NOTES

Commencement: 1 March 2000.

Sub-s (3): words in italics repealed by the Mental Capacity Act 2005, s 67(2), Sch 7, as from a day to be appointed under s 68(1) of that Act.

8, 9 (*S 8 inserts the Trustee Act 1925, s 36(6A)–(6D) at* **[38]**, *in relation to cases here the power, or (where more than one) each of them, is created after 1 March 2000; s 9 adds the Law of Property Act 1925, s 22(3), and has effect whether the enduring power was created before or after 1 March 2000.*)

Authority of attorney to act in relation to land

10 Extent of attorney's authority to act in relation to land

(1) Where the donee of a power of attorney is authorised by the power to do an act of any description in relation to any land, his authority to do an act of that description at any time includes authority to do it with respect to any estate or interest in the land which is held at that time by the donor (whether alone or jointly with any other person or persons).

(2) Subsection (1) above—

(a) applies only if and so far as a contrary intention is not expressed in the instrument creating the power of attorney, and

(b) has effect subject to the terms of that instrument.

(3) This section applies only to powers of attorney created after the commencement of this Act.

[1261]

NOTES

Commencement: 1 March 2000.

Supplementary

11 Interpretation

(1) In this Act—

"land" has the same meaning as in the Trustee Act 1925, and

"enduring power" has the same meaning as in the Enduring Powers of Attorney Act 1985.

(2) References in this Act to the creation of a power of attorney are to the execution by the donor of the instrument creating it.

[1262]

NOTES

Commencement: 1 March 2000.

12 (*Introduces the Schedule to this Act* (*Repeals*).)

13 Commencement, extent and short title

(1) The preceding provisions of this Act shall come into force on such day as the Lord Chancellor may by order made by statutory instrument appoint.

(2) This Act extends to England and Wales only.

(3) This Act may be cited as the Trustee Delegation Act 1999.

[1263]

NOTES

Commencement: 15 July 1999.

Orders: the Trustee Delegation Act 1999 (Commencement) Order 2000, SI 2000/216.

(*Schedule* (*Repeals*) *outside the scope of this work.*)

FINANCIAL SERVICES AND MARKETS ACT 2000

(2000 c 8)

ARRANGEMENT OF SECTIONS

PART XXI
MUTUAL SOCIETIES

Friendly societies

Building societies

Industrial and provident societies and credit unions

Supplemental

PART XXX
SUPPLEMENTAL

An Act to make provision about the regulation of financial services and markets; to provide for the transfer of certain statutory functions relating to building societies, friendly societies, industrial and provident societies and certain other mutual societies; and for connected purposes

[14 June 2000]

1–333 ((*Pts I–XX*) *outside the scope of this work.*)

PART XXI
MUTUAL SOCIETIES

Friendly societies

334 The Friendly Societies Commission

(1) The Treasury may by order provide—

(a) for any functions of the Friendly Societies Commission to be transferred to the Authority;

(b) for any functions of the Friendly Societies Commission which have not been, or are not being, transferred to the Authority to be transferred to the Treasury.

(2) If the Treasury consider it appropriate to do so, they may by order provide for the Friendly Societies Commission to cease to exist on a day specified in or determined in accordance with the order.

(3) The enactments relating to friendly societies which are mentioned in Part I of Schedule 18 are amended as set out in that Part.

(4) Part II of Schedule 18—

(a) removes certain restrictions on the ability of incorporated friendly societies to form subsidiaries and control corporate bodies; and

(b) makes connected amendments.

[1263A]

NOTES

Commencement: 25 February 2001 (certain purposes); 1 December 2001 (otherwise).

Friendly Societies Commission: the Commission was established by the Friendly Societies Act 1992, s 1, Sch 1, as originally enacted. Section 1 of the 1992 Act (together with ss 2–4) was substituted by a new s 1 (functions of the Financial Services Authority in relation to friendly societies), and Sch 1 was repealed by the Financial Services and Markets Act 2000 (Mutual Societies) Order 2001, SI 2001/2617, art 13(1), (2), Sch 3, Pt I, paras 53, 54, 119, Sch 4, subject to transitional provisions and savings in art 13(3) of, and Sch 5, paras 8, 9, 16 to, that Order. Provision for the Commission to cease to exist is made by art 10 of the 2001 Order.

Orders: the Financial Services and Markets Act 2000 (Mutual Societies) Order 2001, SI 2001/2617.

335 The Registry of Friendly Societies

(1) The Treasury may by order provide—

(a) for any functions of the Chief Registrar of Friendly Societies, or of an assistant registrar of friendly societies for the central registration area, to be transferred to the Authority;

(b) for any of their functions which have not been, or are not being, transferred to the Authority to be transferred to the Treasury.

(2) The Treasury may by order provide—

(a) for any functions of the central office of the registry of friendly societies to be transferred to the Authority;

(b) for any functions of that office which have not been, or are not being, transferred to the Authority to be transferred to the Treasury.

(3) The Treasury may by order provide—

(a) for any functions of the assistant registrar of friendly societies for Scotland to be transferred to the Authority;

(b) for any functions of the assistant registrar which have not been, or are not being, transferred to the Authority to be transferred to the Treasury.

(4) If the Treasury consider it appropriate to do so, they may by order provide for—

(a) the office of Chief Registrar of Friendly Societies,

(b) the office of assistant registrar of friendly societies for the central registration area,

(c) the central office, or

(d) the office of assistant registrar of friendly societies for Scotland,

to cease to exist on a day specified in or determined in accordance with the order.

[1263B]

NOTES

Commencement: 25 February 2001.

The Registry of Friendly Societies: the offices of Chief Registrar of Friendly Societies, Assistant Registrar of Friendly Societies, and Assistant registrar of Friendly Societies for Scotland were continued by the Friendly Societies Act 1974, s 1. That section was repealed by the Financial Services and Markets Act 2000 (Mutual Societies) Order 2001, SI 2001/2617, art 13(1), (2), Sch 3, Pt I, paras 1, 2, Sch 4, subject to transitional provisions and savings in art 13(3), Sch 5, paras 3, 4 thereof. Provision for these offices to cease to exist is made by art 12 of the 2001 Order.

Orders: the Financial Services and Markets Act 2000 (Mutual Societies) Order 2001, SI 2001/2617.

Building societies

336 The Building Societies Commission

(1) The Treasury may by order provide—

(a) for any functions of the Building Societies Commission to be transferred to the Authority;

(b) for any functions of the Building Societies Commission which have not been, or are not being, transferred to the Authority to be transferred to the Treasury.

(2) If the Treasury consider it appropriate to do so, they may by order provide for the Building Societies Commission to cease to exist on a day specified in or determined in accordance with the order.

(3) The enactments relating to building societies which are mentioned in Part III of Schedule 18 are amended as set out in that Part.

[1263C]

NOTES

Commencement: 25 February 2001 (sub-ss (1), (2)); 1 December 2001 (otherwise).

Building Societies Commission: the Commission was established by the Building Societies Act 1986, s 1, Sch 1, as originally enacted. Section 1 of the 1986 Act (together with ss 2–4) was substituted by a new s 1 (functions of the Financial Services Authority in relation to building societies), and Sch 1 was repealed by the Financial Services and Markets Act 2000 (Mutual Societies) Order 2001, SI 2001/2617, art 13(1), (2), Sch 3, Pt II, paras 131, 132, 199, Sch 4, subject to transitional provisions and savings in art 13(3) of, and Sch 5, paras 17, 18, 27 to, that Order. Provision for the Commission to cease to exist is made by art 9 of the 2001 Order.

Orders: the Financial Services and Markets Act 2000 (Mutual Societies) Order 2001, SI 2001/2617.

337 The Building Societies Investor Protection Board

The Treasury may by order provide for the Building Societies Investor Protection Board to cease to exist on a day specified in or determined in accordance with the order.

[1263D]

NOTES

Commencement: 25 February 2001.

Building Societies Investor Protection Board: the Board was established by the Building Societies Act 1986, s 24, Sch 5 (repealed by the Financial Services and Markets Act 2000 (Mutual Societies) Order 2001, SI 2001/2617, art 13(1), (2), Sch 3, Pt II, paras 131, 139, 202, Sch 4, subject to transitional provisions and savings in art 13(3) of, and Sch 5, paras 17, 19, 29 thereof). Provision for the Board to cease to exist is made by art 11 of the 2001 Order.

Orders: the Financial Services and Markets Act 2000 (Mutual Societies) Order 2001, SI 2001/2617.

Industrial and provident societies and credit unions

338 Industrial and provident societies and credit unions

(1) The Treasury may by order provide for the transfer to the Authority of any functions conferred by—

- (a) the Industrial and Provident Societies Act 1965;
- (b) the Industrial and Provident Societies Act 1967;
- (c) the Friendly and Industrial and Provident Societies Act 1968;
- (d) the Industrial and Provident Societies Act 1975;
- (e) the Industrial and Provident Societies Act 1978;
- (f) the Credit Unions Act 1979.

(2) The Treasury may by order provide for the transfer to the Treasury of any functions under those enactments which have not been, or are not being, transferred to the Authority.

(3) The enactments relating to industrial and provident societies which are mentioned in Part IV of Schedule 18 are amended as set out in that Part.

(4) The enactments relating to credit unions which are mentioned in Part V of Schedule 18 are amended as set out in that Part.

[1263E]

NOTES

Commencement: 25 February 2001 (sub-ss (1), (2)); 1 December 2001 (otherwise).

Note: credit unions in Northern Ireland have not been brought within this Act's regime and remain under the jurisdiction of the Registrar of Friendly Societies in Northern Ireland. A transitional exemption in the Financial Services and Markets Act 2000 (Exemption) Order 2001, SI 2001/1201, art 6 was made permanent in respect of credit unions within the meaning of Credit Unions (Northern Ireland) Order 1985 by the Financial Services and Markets Act 2000 (Exemption) (Amendment) Order 2001, SI 2001/3623, arts 3, 4, which adds a new para 24A to this effect to the Schedule of SI 2001/1201.

Orders: the Financial Services and Markets Act 2000 (Mutual Societies) Order 2001, SI 2001/2617.

Supplemental

339 Supplemental provisions

(1) The additional powers conferred by section 428 on a person making an order under this Act include power for the Treasury, when making an order under section 334, 335, 336 or 338 which transfers functions, to include provision—

(a) for the transfer of any functions of a member of the body, or servant or agent of the body or person, whose functions are transferred by the order;

(b) for the transfer of any property, rights or liabilities held, enjoyed or incurred by any person in connection with transferred functions;

(c) for the carrying on and completion by or under the authority of the person to whom functions are transferred of any proceedings, investigations or other matters commenced, before the order takes effect, by or under the authority of the person from whom the functions are transferred;

(d) amending any enactment relating to transferred functions in connection with their exercise by, or under the authority of, the person to whom they are transferred;

(e) for the substitution of the person to whom functions are transferred for the person from whom they are transferred, in any instrument, contract or legal proceedings made or begun before the order takes effect.

(2) The additional powers conferred by section 428 on a person making an order under this Act include power for the Treasury, when making an order under section 334(2), 335(4), 336(2) or 337, to include provision—

(a) for the transfer of any property, rights or liabilities held, enjoyed or incurred by any person in connection with the office or body which ceases to have effect as a result of the order;

(b) for the carrying on and completion by or under the authority of such person as may be specified in the order of any proceedings, investigations or other matters commenced, before the order takes effect, by or under the authority of the person whose office, or the body which, ceases to exist as a result of the order;

(c) amending any enactment which makes provision with respect to that office or body;

(d) for the substitution of the Authority, the Treasury or such other body as may be specified in the order in any instrument, contract or legal proceedings made or begun before the order takes effect.

(3) On or after the making of an order under any of sections 334 to 338 ("the original order"), the Treasury may by order make any incidental, supplemental, consequential or transitional provision which they had power to include in the original order.

(4) A certificate issued by the Treasury that property vested in a person immediately before an order under this Part takes effect has been transferred as a result of the order is conclusive evidence of the transfer.

(5) Subsections (1) and (2) are not to be read as affecting in any way the powers conferred by section 428.

[1263F]

NOTES

Commencement: 25 February 2001.

Orders: the Financial Services and Markets Act 2000 (Mutual Societies) Order 2001, SI 2001/2617; the Financial Services and Markets Act 2000 (Transitional Provisions, Repeals and Savings) (Financial Services Compensation Scheme) Order 2001, SI 2001/2967; the Financial Services and Markets Act 2000 (Consequential Amendments and Savings) (Industrial Assurance) Order 2001, SI 2001/3647.

340–425 ((*Pts XXII–XXIX*) *outside the scope of this work.*)

PART XXX
SUPPLEMENTAL

426–429 (*Outside the scope of this work.*)

430 Extent

(1) This Act, except Chapter IV of Part XVII, extends to Northern Ireland.

(2) Except where Her Majesty by Order in Council provides otherwise, the extent of any amendment or repeal made by or under this Act is the same as the extent of the provision amended or repealed.

(3) Her Majesty may by Order in Council provide for any provision of or made under this Act relating to a matter which is the subject of other legislation which extends to any of the Channel Islands or the Isle of Man to extend there with such modifications (if any) as may be specified in the Order.

[1263G]

NOTES

Commencement: 14 June 2000.

431 Commencement

(1) The following provisions come into force on the passing of this Act—

- (a) this section;
- (b) sections 428, 430 and 433;
- (c) paragraphs 1 and 2 of Schedule 21.

(2) The other provisions of this Act come into force on such day as the Treasury may by order appoint; and different days may be appointed for different purposes.

[1263H]

NOTES

Commencement: 14 June 2000.

Orders: the Financial Services and Markets Act 2000 (Commencement No 1) Order 2001, SI 2001/516; the Financial Services and Markets Act 2000 (Commencement No 2) Order 2001, SI 2001/1282; the Financial Services and Markets Act 2000 (Commencement No 3) Order 2001, SI 2001/1820; the Financial Services and Markets Act 2000 (Commencement No 4 and Transitional Provision) Order 2001, SI 2001/2364; the Financial Services and Markets Act 2000 (Commencement No 5) Order 2001, SI 2001/2632; the Financial Services and Markets Act 2000 (Commencement No 6) Order 2001, SI 2001/3436; the Financial Services and Markets Act 2000 (Commencement No 7) Order 2001, SI 2001/3538.

432 (*Outside the scope of this work.*)

433 Short title

This Act may be cited as the Financial Services and Markets Act 2000.

[1263I]

NOTES

Commencement: 14 June 2000.

(*Schs 1–29 outside the scope of this work.*)

FINANCE ACT 2000

(2000 c 17)

ARRANGEMENT OF SECTIONS

PART III
INCOME TAX, CORPORATION TAX AND CAPITAL GAINS TAX

CHAPTER II
OTHER PROVISIONS

Giving to charity

An Act to grant certain duties, to alter other duties, and to amend the law relating to the National Debt and the Public Revenue, and to make further provision in connection with Finance

[28 July 2000]

1–30 ((*Pts I, II*) *outside the scope of this work.*)

PART III
INCOME TAX, CORPORATION TAX AND CAPITAL GAINS TAX

31–37 ((*Ch I*) *outside the scope of this work.*)

CHAPTER II
OTHER PROVISIONS

Giving to charity

38 Payroll deduction scheme

(1) Where in accordance with a scheme approved [for the purposes of section 714 of the Income Tax (Earnings and Pensions) Act 2003] (donations to charity: payroll deduction scheme) an agent is to pay to a charity any sum which—

(a) is withheld by [a person] from a payment which [individual] is entitled to receive; and

(b) is paid by the [person] to the agent,

the agent shall, within a period prescribed by regulations made by the Treasury, pay a supplement equal to 10% of that sum to the charity.

(2) On a claim made by an agent in such form as the Board may prescribe, the Board shall pay to the agent out of money provided by Parliament—

(a) such amounts as are required—

(i) to fund the payment of supplements falling to be paid by him; or

(ii) to reimburse him for supplements paid by him the payment of which has not been so funded; and

(b) in the case of an agent which is a charity, an amount which is equal to 10% of the aggregate of sums which—

(i) are withheld and paid as mentioned in paragraphs (a) and (b) of subsection (1) above; and

(ii) are sums to which the agent is itself entitled in its capacity as a charity.

(3) The Treasury may by regulations make provision—

(a) requiring agents to notify the Board of any failures of theirs to comply with subsection (1) above, and of the reasons for those failures;

(b) requiring agents to keep records of supplements paid by them under that subsection; and

(c) for the assessment and recovery under the Taxes Acts of amounts paid to agents under subsection (2) above which ought not to have been so paid.

The regulations may contain such supplementary and incidental provision as appears to the Treasury necessary or expedient.

(4) In this section—

["agent" means an agent approved for the purposes of section 714 of the Income Tax (Earnings and Pensions) Act 2003;]

"charity" has the same meaning as in section 506 of that Act and includes each of the bodies mentioned in section 507 of that Act;

"the Taxes Acts" has the same meaning as in the Taxes Management Act 1970.

(5) ...

(6) Subsections (1) to (4) above shall have effect in relation to supplements or other amounts payable in respect of sums withheld on or after 6th April 2000 and before [6th April 2004]; and no claim under subsection (2) above shall be entertained if made on or after [6th April 2005].

(7) ...

[1264]

NOTES

Commencement: this Act received Royal Assent on 28 July 2000: for provision as to the effect of this section see sub-ss (6), (7) above.

Sub-s (1): words in square brackets substituted by the Income Tax (Earnings and Pensions) Act 2003, ss 722, 723, Sch 6, Pt 2, paras 242, 243(1), (2), with effect for the purposes of income tax, for the tax year 2003–04 and subsequent tax years, and for the purposes of corporation tax, for accounting periods ending after 5 April 2003.

Sub-s (4): definition "agent" substituted for definitions "agent", "employee" and "employer" by the Income Tax (Earnings and Pensions) Act 2003, ss 722, 723, Sch 6, Pt 2, paras 242, 243(1), (3), with effect for the purposes of income tax, for the tax year 2003–04 and subsequent tax years, and for the purposes of corporation tax, for accounting periods ending after 5 April 2003.

Sub-ss (5), (7): repealed by the Income Tax (Earnings and Pensions) Act 2003, ss 723, 724(1), Sch 8, Pt 1, with effect for the purposes of income tax, for the tax year 2003–04 and subsequent tax years, and for the purposes of corporation tax, for accounting periods ending after 5 April 2003.

Sub-s (6): words in square brackets substituted by the Finance Act 2003, s 146.

Regulations: the Charitable Deductions (Approved Schemes) (Amendment No 2) Regulations 2000, SI 2000/2083; the Charitable Deductions (Approved Schemes) (Amendment) Regulations 2003, SI 2003/1745.

39 Gift aid payments by individuals

(1)–(9) ...

(10) This section has effect in relation to—

(a) gifts made on or after 6th April 2000 which are not covenanted payments; and

(b) covenanted payments falling to be made on or after that date;

and any regulations made under subsection (3) of section 25 of the Finance Act 1990 (as substituted by subsection (4) above) within three months of the passing of this Act may be so made as to apply to any payments in relation to which this section has effect.

[1265]

NOTES

Commencement: this Act received Royal Assent on 28 July 2000: for provision as to the effect of this section see sub-s (10) above.

Sub-ss (1)–(9): amend the Finance Act 1990, s 25 at **[733]**, and the Income and Corporation Taxes Act 1988, s 257BB, Sch 13B, para 4.

Regulations: the Donations to Charity by Individuals (Appropriate Declarations) Regulations 2000, SI 2000/2074.

40 Gift aid payments by companies

(1)–(10) ...

(11) This section has effect in relation to payments made on or after 1st April 2000; and—

(a) so much of an accounting period as falls before that date; and

(b) so much of it as falls after 31st March 2000,

shall be treated as separate accounting periods for the purposes of the amendment made by subsection (5) above.

[1266]

NOTES

Commencement: this Act received Royal Assent on 28 July 2000: for provision as to the effect of this section see sub-s (11) above.

Sub-ss (1)–(10): amend the Income and Corporation Taxes Act 1988, ss 338, 339 at **[698]**, **[699]**, and s 209 of the 1998 Act.

41 Covenanted payments to charities

(1)–(7) …

(8) Where a deed of covenant executed by an individual before 6th April 2000 provides for the payment of specified amounts, any amount payable under the deed on or after that date shall be determined as if the individual were entitled to deduct tax from that amount at the basic rate.

(9) This section shall have effect in relation to covenanted payments—

(a) falling to be made by individuals on or after 6th April 2000; or

(b) made by companies on or after 1st April 2000.

[1267]

NOTES

Commencement: this Act received Royal Assent on 28 July 2000: for provision as to the effect of this section see sub-s (9) above.

Sub-ss (1)–(5), (7): amend the Income and Corporation Taxes Act 1988, ss 338, 347A, 349, 505 at **[698]**, **[700]**, **[702]**, **[705]**, and s 348 of the 1988 Act, and repeal the Finance Act 1989, s 59.

Sub-s (6): repealed by the Income Tax (Trading and Other Income) Act 2005, s 884, Sch 3, with effect, for the purposes of income tax for the year 2005–06 and subsequent tax years, and for the purposes of corporation tax for accounting periods ending after 5 April 2005.

42 (*Amends the Finance Act 1998, s 48 at* **[1206]**.)

43 Gifts of shares and securities to charities etc

(1), (2) …

(3) This section has effect in relation to—

(a) disposals made by individuals on or after 6th April 2000; and

(b) disposals made by companies on or after 1st April 2000.

[1268]

NOTES

Commencement: this Act received Royal Assent on 28 July 2000: for provision as to the effect of this section see sub-s (3) above.

Sub-ss (1), (2): inserts the Income and Corporation Taxes Act 1988, s 587B and amends s 338 of the 1988 Act at **[698]**.

44 Gifts to charity from certain trusts

(1)–(3) …

(4) Where in any year of assessment qualifying income arising under a [trust the trustees of which are resident in the United Kingdom (a "UK trust")] exceeds the amount of that income falling within [section 628(1) or 630(1) of ITTOIA 2005], any management expenses for that year shall be rateably apportioned between—

(a) so much of that income as is equal to that amount; and

(b) so much of that income as exceeds that amount.

[(5) In this section—

"qualifying income" has the same meaning as in section 628 of ITTOIA 2005; and

"resident", in relation to the trustees of a trust, shall be construed in accordance with section 110 of the Finance Act 1989.]

(6) This section has effect in relation to qualifying income arising to a UK trust on or after 6th April 2000.

[1269]–[1270]

NOTES

Commencement: this Act received Royal Assent on 28 July 2000: for provision as to the effect of this section see sub-s (6) above.

Sub-ss (1)–(3): repealed by the Income Tax (Trading and Other Income) Act 2005, ss 882(1), 884, Sch 1, Pt 2, paras 511, 512(1), (2), Sch 3, with effect, for the purposes of income tax for the year 2005–06 and subsequent tax years, and for the purposes of corporation tax for accounting periods ending after 5 April 2005.

Sub-s (4): words in square brackets substituted by the Income Tax (Trading and Other Income) Act 2005, s 882(1), Sch 1, Pt 2, paras 511, 512(1), (3), with effect, for the purposes of income tax for the year 2005–06 and subsequent tax years, and for the purposes of corporation tax for accounting periods ending after 5 April 2005.

Sub-s (5): substituted by the Income Tax (Trading and Other Income) Act 2005, s 882(1), Sch 1, Pt 2, paras 511, 512(1), (4), with effect, for the purposes of income tax for the year 2005–06 and subsequent tax years, and for the purposes of corporation tax for accounting periods ending after 5 April 2005.

45 *(Repealed by the Income Tax (Trading and Other Income) Act 2005, ss 882(1), 884, Sch 1, Pt 2, paras 511, 513, Sch 3, with effect, for the purposes of income tax for the year 2005–06 and subsequent tax years, and for the purposes of corporation tax for accounting periods ending after 5 April 2005.)*

46 Exemption for small trades etc

[(1) Subject to subsections (2) and (2A) below, exemption—
(a) from income tax—
(i) under Part 2 of ITTOIA 2005 in respect of a trade carried on wholly or partly in the United Kingdom, or
(ii) under or by virtue of any provision to which section 836B of the Taxes Act 1988 applies, or
(b) from corporation tax under Case I or VI of Schedule D,

shall be granted] on a claim made in that behalf to the Board, in respect of any income of a charity if the requirements of subsection (3) below are satisfied with respect to the income.

[(2) Exemption shall not be granted under subsection (1) above in respect of income which is chargeable to—
(a) income tax under or by virtue of any provision to which section 836B of the Taxes Act 1988 applies, or
(b) corporation tax under Case VI of Schedule D,

by virtue of any of the provisions mentioned in subsection (2A).

(2A) The provisions are—
(a) sections 214, 547(1)(b), 703, 776, 788, 790 or 804 of the Taxes Act 1988;
(b) paragraph 52(4) of Schedule 18 to the Finance Act 1998;
(c) Chapter 9 of Part 4, and Chapter 5 of Part 5, of ITTOIA 2005; and
(d) any other enactment specified in an order made by the Treasury.]

(3) The requirements of this subsection are satisfied with respect to any income for a chargeable period if it is applied solely for the purposes of the charity and either—
(a) the charity's gross income for the chargeable period does not exceed the requisite limit; or
(b) the charity had, at the beginning of the period, a reasonable expectation that its gross income for the period would not exceed that limit.

(4) Subject to subsection (5) below, the requisite limit is whichever is the greater of—
(a) £5,000; and
(b) whichever is the lesser of £50,000 and 25% of all of the charity's incoming resources for the chargeable period.

(5) For a chargeable period of less than twelve months, the amounts of £5,000 and £50,000 specified in subsection (4) above shall be proportionally reduced.

(6) In this section—
"charity" means any body of persons or trust established for charitable purposes only;
"gross income", in relation to a charity, means income before deduction of any expenses;
"income", in relation to a charity, means[—
(a) any profits or other income or gains—
(i) which are chargeable to income tax under Part 2 of ITTOIA 2005 in respect of a trade carried on wholly or partly in the United Kingdom, or
(ii) which are chargeable to income tax under or by virtue of any provision to which section 836B of the Taxes Act 1988 applies,

and which (in either case) are not, apart from this section, exempted from income tax chargeable under or by virtue of that Part or provision, or

(b)] any profits or gains or other income which is chargeable to [corporation] tax under Case I or VI of Schedule D and which is not, apart this section, exempted from tax under that Case.

(7) This section applies for the year 2000–01 and subsequent years of assessment or, in the case of charities which are companies, for accounting periods beginning on or after 1st April 2000.

[1271]

NOTES

Commencement: this Act received Royal Assent on 28 July 2000: for provision as to the effect of this section see sub-s (7) above.

Sub-s (1): words in square brackets substituted by the Income Tax (Trading and Other Income) Act 2005, s 882(1) Sch 1, Pt 2, paras 511, 514(1), (2), with effect, for the purposes of income tax for the year 2005–06 and subsequent tax years, and for the purposes of corporation tax for accounting periods ending after 5 April 2005.

Sub-ss (2), (2A): substituted, for sub-s (2) as originally enacted, by the Income Tax (Trading and Other Income) Act 2005, s 882(1), Sch 1, Pt 2, paras 511, 514(1), (3), with effect, for the purposes of income tax for the year 2005–06 and subsequent tax years, and for the purposes of corporation tax for accounting periods ending after 5 April 2005.

Sub-s (6): in definition "income" para (a) inserted and para (b) numbered as such and word in square brackets inserted by the Income Tax (Trading and Other Income) Act 2005, s 882(1), Sch 1, Pt 2, paras 511, 514(1), (4), with effect, for the purposes of income tax for the year 2005–06 and subsequent tax years, and for the purposes of corporation tax for accounting periods ending after 5 April 2005.

47–142 (*Ss 47–113, ss 114–142 (Pts IV, V) outside the scope of this work.*)

PART VI
MISCELLANEOUS AND SUPPLEMENTARY PROVISIONS

143–154 (*Outside the scope of this work.*)

Supplementary provisions

155, 156 (*Outside the scope of this work.*)

157 Short title

This Act may be cited as the Finance Act 2000.

[1272]

NOTES

Commencement: 28 July 2000.

(*Schs 1–40 outside the scope of this work.*)

TRUSTEE ACT 2000

(2000 c 29)

ARRANGEMENT OF SECTIONS

PART I
THE DUTY OF CARE

PART III
ACQUISITION OF LAND

PART IV
AGENTS, NOMINEES AND CUSTODIANS

Agents

Nominees and custodians

Review of and liability for agents, nominees and custodians etc

Supplementary

PART V
REMUNERATION

PART VI
MISCELLANEOUS AND SUPPLEMENTARY

An Act to amend the law relating to trustees and persons having the investment powers of trustees; and for connected purposes

[23 November 2000]

PART I
THE DUTY OF CARE

1 The duty of care

(1) Whenever the duty under this subsection applies to a trustee, he must exercise such care and skill as is reasonable in the circumstances, having regard in particular—

(a) to any special knowledge or experience that he has or holds himself out as having, and

(b) if he acts as trustee in the course of a business or profession, to any special knowledge or experience that it is reasonable to expect of a person acting in the course of that kind of business or profession.

(2) In this Act the duty under subsection (1) is called "the duty of care".

[1273]

NOTES

Commencement: 1 February 2001.

2 Application of duty of care

Schedule 1 makes provision about when the duty of care applies to a trustee.

[1274]

NOTES

Commencement: 1 February 2001.

PART II
INVESTMENT

3 General power of investment

(1) Subject to the provisions of this Part, a trustee may make any kind of investment that he could make if he were absolutely entitled to the assets of the trust.

(2) In this Act the power under subsection (1) is called "the general power of investment".

(3) The general power of investment does not permit a trustee to make investments in land other than in loans secured on land (but see also section 8).

(4) A person invests in a loan secured on land if he has rights under any contract under which—

(a) one person provides another with credit, and

(b) the obligation of the borrower to repay is secured on land.

(5) "Credit" includes any cash loan or other financial accommodation.

(6) "Cash" includes money in any form.

[1275]

NOTES

Commencement: 1 February 2001.

4 Standard investment criteria

(1) In exercising any power of investment, whether arising under this Part or otherwise, a trustee must have regard to the standard investment criteria.

(2) A trustee must from time to time review the investments of the trust and consider whether, having regard to the standard investment criteria, they should be varied.

(3) The standard investment criteria, in relation to a trust, are—

(a) the suitability to the trust of investments of the same kind as any particular investment proposed to be made or retained and of that particular investment as an investment of that kind, and

(b) the need for diversification of investments of the trust, in so far as is appropriate to the circumstances of the trust.

[1276]

NOTES

Commencement: 1 February 2001.

---

5 Advice

(1) Before exercising any power of investment, whether arising under this Part or otherwise, a trustee must (unless the exception applies) obtain and consider proper advice about the way in which, having regard to the standard investment criteria, the power should be exercised.

(2) When reviewing the investments of the trust, a trustee must (unless the exception applies) obtain and consider proper advice about whether, having regard to the standard investment criteria, the investments should be varied.

(3) The exception is that a trustee need not obtain such advice if he reasonably concludes that in all the circumstances it is unnecessary or inappropriate to do so.

(4) Proper advice is the advice of a person who is reasonably believed by the trustee to be qualified to give it by his ability in and practical experience of financial and other matters relating to the proposed investment.

[1277]

NOTES

Commencement: 1 February 2001.

---

6 Restriction or exclusion of this Part etc

(1) The general power of investment is—

(a) in addition to powers conferred on trustees otherwise than by this Act, but

(b) subject to any restriction or exclusion imposed by the trust instrument or by any enactment or any provision of subordinate legislation.

(2) For the purposes of this Act, an enactment or a provision of subordinate legislation is not to be regarded as being, or as being part of, a trust instrument.

(3) In this Act "subordinate legislation" has the same meaning as in the Interpretation Act 1978.

[1278]

NOTES

Commencement: 1 February 2001.

---

7 Existing trusts

(1) This Part applies in relation to trusts whether created before or after its commencement.

(2) No provision relating to the powers of a trustee contained in a trust instrument made before 3rd August 1961 is to be treated (for the purposes of section 6(1)(b)) as restricting or excluding the general power of investment.

(3) A provision contained in a trust instrument made before the commencement of this Part which—

(a) has effect under section 3(2) of the Trustee Investments Act 1961 as a power to invest under that Act, or

(b) confers power to invest under that Act,

is to be treated as conferring the general power of investment on a trustee.

[1279]

NOTES

Commencement: 1 February 2001.

PART III
ACQUISITION OF LAND

8 Power to acquire freehold and leasehold land

(1) A trustee may acquire freehold or leasehold land in the United Kingdom—

(a) as an investment,

(b) for occupation by a beneficiary, or

(c) for any other reason.

(2) "Freehold or leasehold land" means—

(a) in relation to England and Wales, a legal estate in land,

(b) in relation to Scotland—

(i) the estate or interest of the proprietor of the dominium utile or, in the case of land not held on feudal tenure, the estate or interest of the owner, or

(ii) a tenancy, and

(c) in relation to Northern Ireland, a legal estate in land, including land held under a fee farm grant.

(3) For the purpose of exercising his functions as a trustee, a trustee who acquires land under this section has all the powers of an absolute owner in relation to the land.

[1280]

NOTES

Commencement: 1 February 2001.

9 Restriction or exclusion of this Part etc

The powers conferred by this Part are—

(a) in addition to powers conferred on trustees otherwise than by this Part, but

(b) subject to any restriction or exclusion imposed by the trust instrument or by any enactment or any provision of subordinate legislation.

[1281]

NOTES

Commencement: 1 February 2001.

10 Existing trusts

(1) This Part does not apply in relation to—

(a) a trust of property which consists of or includes land which (despite section 2 of the Trusts of Land and Appointment of Trustees Act 1996) is settled land, or

(b) a trust to which the Universities and College Estates Act 1925 applies.

(2) Subject to subsection (1), this Part applies in relation to trusts whether created before or after its commencement.

[1282]

NOTES

Commencement: 1 February 2001.

PART IV
AGENTS, NOMINEES AND CUSTODIANS

Agents

11 Power to employ agents

(1) Subject to the provisions of this Part, the trustees of a trust may authorise any person to exercise any or all of their delegable functions as their agent.

(2) In the case of a trust other than a charitable trust, the trustees' delegable functions consist of any function other than—

(a) any function relating to whether or in what way any assets of the trust should be distributed,

(b) any power to decide whether any fees or other payment due to be made out of the trust funds should be made out of income or capital,

(c) any power to appoint a person to be a trustee of the trust, or

(d) any power conferred by any other enactment or the trust instrument which permits the trustees to delegate any of their functions or to appoint a person to act as a nominee or custodian.

(3) In the case of a charitable trust, the trustees' delegable functions are—

(a) any function consisting of carrying out a decision that the trustees have taken;

(b) any function relating to the investment of assets subject to the trust (including, in the case of land held as an investment, managing the land and creating or disposing of an interest in the land);

(c) any function relating to the raising of funds for the trust otherwise than by means of profits of a trade which is an integral part of carrying out the trust's charitable purpose;

(d) any other function prescribed by an order made by the Secretary of State.

(4) For the purposes of subsection (3)(c) a trade is an integral part of carrying out a trust's charitable purpose if, whether carried on in the United Kingdom or elsewhere, the profits are applied solely to the purposes of the trust and either—

(a) the trade is exercised in the course of the actual carrying out of a primary purpose of the trust, or

(b) the work in connection with the trade is mainly carried out by beneficiaries of the trust.

(5) The power to make an order under subsection (3)(d) is exercisable by statutory instrument which shall be subject to annulment in pursuance of a resolution of either House of Parliament.

[1283]

NOTES

Commencement: 1 February 2001.

12 Persons who may act as agents

(1) Subject to subsection (2), the persons whom the trustees may under section 11 authorise to exercise functions as their agent include one or more of their number.

(2) The trustees may not authorise two (or more) persons to exercise the same function unless they are to exercise the function jointly.

(3) The trustees may not under section 11 authorise a beneficiary to exercise any function as their agent (even if the beneficiary is also a trustee).

(4) The trustees may under section 11 authorise a person to exercise functions as their agent even though he is also appointed to act as their nominee or custodian (whether under section 16, 17 or 18 or any other power).

[1284]

NOTES

Commencement: 1 February 2001.

13 Linked functions etc

(1) Subject to subsections (2) and (5), a person who is authorised under section 11 to exercise a function is (whatever the terms of the agency) subject to any specific duties or restrictions attached to the function.

For example, a person who is authorised under section 11 to exercise the general power of investment is subject to the duties under section 4 in relation to that power.

(2) A person who is authorised under section 11 to exercise a power which is subject to a requirement to obtain advice is not subject to the requirement if he is the kind of person from whom it would have been proper for the trustees, in compliance with the requirement, to obtain advice.

(3) Subsections (4) and (5) apply to a trust to which section 11(1) of the Trusts of Land and Appointment of Trustees Act 1996 (duties to consult beneficiaries and give effect to their wishes) applies.

(4) The trustees may not under section 11 authorise a person to exercise any of their functions on terms that prevent them from complying with section 11(1) of the 1996 Act.

(5) A person who is authorised under section 11 to exercise any function relating to land subject to the trust is not subject to section 11(1) of the 1996 Act.

[1285]

NOTES

Commencement: 1 February 2001.

14 Terms of agency

(1) Subject to subsection (2) and sections 15(2) and 29 to 32, the trustees may authorise a person to exercise functions as their agent on such terms as to remuneration and other matters as they may determine.

(2) The trustees may not authorise a person to exercise functions as their agent on any of the terms mentioned in subsection (3) unless it is reasonably necessary for them to do so.

(3) The terms are—

(a) a term permitting the agent to appoint a substitute;

(b) a term restricting the liability of the agent or his substitute to the trustees or any beneficiary;

(c) a term permitting the agent to act in circumstances capable of giving rise to a conflict of interest.

[1286]

NOTES

Commencement: 1 February 2001.

15 Asset management: special restrictions

(1) The trustees may not authorise a person to exercise any of their asset management functions as their agent except by an agreement which is in or evidenced in writing.

(2) The trustees may not authorise a person to exercise any of their asset management functions as their agent unless—

(a) they have prepared a statement that gives guidance as to how the functions should be exercised ("a policy statement"), and

(b) the agreement under which the agent is to act includes a term to the effect that he will secure compliance with—

(i) the policy statement, or

(ii) if the policy statement is revised or replaced under section 22, the revised or replacement policy statement.

(3) The trustees must formulate any guidance given in the policy statement with a view to ensuring that the functions will be exercised in the best interests of the trust.

(4) The policy statement must be in or evidenced in writing.

(5) The asset management functions of trustees are their functions relating to—

(a) the investment of assets subject to the trust,

(b) the acquisition of property which is to be subject to the trust, and

(c) managing property which is subject to the trust and disposing of, or creating or disposing of an interest in, such property.

[1287]

NOTES

Commencement: 1 February 2001.

Nominees and custodians

16 Power to appoint nominees

(1) Subject to the provisions of this Part, the trustees of a trust may—

(a) appoint a person to act as their nominee in relation to such of the assets of the trust as they determine (other than settled land), and

(b) take such steps as are necessary to secure that those assets are vested in a person so appointed.

(2) An appointment under this section must be in or evidenced in writing.

(3) This section does not apply to any trust having a custodian trustee or in relation to any assets vested in the official custodian for charities.

[1288]

NOTES

Commencement: 1 February 2001.

17 Power to appoint custodians

(1) Subject to the provisions of this Part, the trustees of a trust may appoint a person to act as a custodian in relation to such of the assets of the trust as they may determine.

(2) For the purposes of this Act a person is a custodian in relation to assets if he undertakes the safe custody of the assets or of any documents or records concerning the assets.

(3) An appointment under this section must be in or evidenced in writing.

(4) This section does not apply to any trust having a custodian trustee or in relation to any assets vested in the official custodian for charities.

[1289]

NOTES

Commencement: 1 February 2001.

18 Investment in bearer securities

(1) If trustees retain or invest in securities payable to bearer, they must appoint a person to act as a custodian of the securities.

(2) Subsection (1) does not apply if the trust instrument or any enactment or provision of subordinate legislation contains provision which (however expressed) permits the trustees to retain or invest in securities payable to bearer without appointing a person to act as a custodian.

(3) An appointment under this section must be in or evidenced in writing.

(4) This section does not apply to any trust having a custodian trustee or in relation to any securities vested in the official custodian for charities.

[1290]

NOTES

Commencement: 1 February 2001.

19 Persons who may be appointed as nominees or custodians

(1) A person may not be appointed under section 16, 17 or 18 as a nominee or custodian unless one of the relevant conditions is satisfied.

(2) The relevant conditions are that—

(a) the person carries on a business which consists of or includes acting as a nominee or custodian;

(b) the person is a body corporate which is controlled by the trustees;

(c) the person is a body corporate recognised under section 9 of the Administration of Justice Act 1985.

(3) The question whether a body corporate is controlled by trustees is to be determined in accordance with section 840 of the Income and Corporation Taxes Act 1988.

(4) The trustees of a charitable trust which is not an exempt charity must act in accordance with any guidance given by the [Charity Commission] concerning the selection of a person for appointment as a nominee or custodian under section 16, 17 or 18.

(5) Subject to subsections (1) and (4), the persons whom the trustees may under section 16, 17 or 18 appoint as a nominee or custodian include—

(a) one of their number, if that one is a trust corporation, or

(b) two (or more) of their number, if they are to act as joint nominees or joint custodians.

(6) The trustees may under section 16 appoint a person to act as their nominee even though he is also—

(a) appointed to act as their custodian (whether under section 17 or 18 or any other power), or

(b) authorised to exercise functions as their agent (whether under section 11 or any other power).

(7) Likewise, the trustees may under section 17 or 18 appoint a person to act as their custodian even though he is also—

(a) appointed to act as their nominee (whether under section 16 or any other power), or

(b) authorised to exercise functions as their agent (whether under section 11 or any other power).

[1291]

NOTES

Commencement: 1 February 2001.

Sub-s (4): words in square brackets substituted by the Charities Act 2006, s 75(1), Sch 8, para 197.

20 Terms of appointment of nominees and custodians

(1) Subject to subsection (2) and sections 29 to 32, the trustees may under section 16, 17 or 18 appoint a person to act as a nominee or custodian on such terms as to remuneration and other matters as they may determine.

(2) The trustees may not under section 16, 17 or 18 appoint a person to act as a nominee or custodian on any of the terms mentioned in subsection (3) unless it is reasonably necessary for them to do so.

(3) The terms are—

(a) a term permitting the nominee or custodian to appoint a substitute;

(b) a term restricting the liability of the nominee or custodian or his substitute to the trustees or to any beneficiary;

(c) a term permitting the nominee or custodian to act in circumstances capable of giving rise to a conflict of interest.

[1292]

NOTES

Commencement: 1 February 2001.

Review of and liability for agents, nominees and custodians etc

21 Application of sections 22 and 23

(1) Sections 22 and 23 apply in a case where trustees have, under section 11, 16, 17 or 18—

(a) authorised a person to exercise functions as their agent, or

(b) appointed a person to act as a nominee or custodian.

(2) Subject to subsection (3), sections 22 and 23 also apply in a case where trustees have, under any power conferred on them by the trust instrument or by any enactment or any provision of subordinate legislation—

(a) authorised a person to exercise functions as their agent, or

(b) appointed a person to act as a nominee or custodian.

(3) If the application of section 22 or 23 is inconsistent with the terms of the trust instrument or the enactment or provision of subordinate legislation, the section in question does not apply.

[1293]

NOTES

Commencement: 1 February 2001.

22 Review of agents, nominees and custodians etc

(1) While the agent, nominee or custodian continues to act for the trust, the trustees—

(a) must keep under review the arrangements under which the agent, nominee or custodian acts and how those arrangements are being put into effect,

(b) if circumstances make it appropriate to do so, must consider whether there is a need to exercise any power of intervention that they have, and

(c) if they consider that there is a need to exercise such a power, must do so.

(2) If the agent has been authorised to exercise asset management functions, the duty under subsection (1) includes, in particular—

(a) a duty to consider whether there is any need to revise or replace the policy statement made for the purposes of section 15,

(b) if they consider that there is a need to revise or replace the policy statement, a duty to do so, and

(c) a duty to assess whether the policy statement (as it has effect for the time being) is being complied with.

(3) Subsections (3) and (4) of section 15 apply to the revision or replacement of a policy statement under this section as they apply to the making of a policy statement under that section.

(4) "Power of intervention" includes—

(a) a power to give directions to the agent, nominee or custodian;

(b) a power to revoke the authorisation or appointment.

[1294]

NOTES

Commencement: 1 February 2001.

23 Liability for agents, nominees and custodians etc

(1) A trustee is not liable for any act or default of the agent, nominee or custodian unless he has failed to comply with the duty of care applicable to him, under paragraph 3 of Schedule 1—

(a) when entering into the arrangements under which the person acts as agent, nominee or custodian, or

(b) when carrying out his duties under section 22.

(2) If a trustee has agreed a term under which the agent, nominee or custodian is permitted to appoint a substitute, the trustee is not liable for any act or default of the substitute unless he has failed to comply with the duty of care applicable to him, under paragraph 3 of Schedule 1—

(a) when agreeing that term, or

(b) when carrying out his duties under section 22 in so far as they relate to the use of the substitute.

[1295]

NOTES

Commencement: 1 February 2001.

Supplementary

24 Effect of trustees exceeding their powers

A failure by the trustees to act within the limits of the powers conferred by this Part—

(a) in authorising a person to exercise a function of theirs as an agent, or

(b) in appointing a person to act as a nominee or custodian,

does not invalidate the authorisation or appointment.

[1296]

NOTES

Commencement: 1 February 2001.

25 Sole trustees

(1) Subject to subsection (2), this Part applies in relation to a trust having a sole trustee as it applies in relation to other trusts (and references in this Part to trustees—except in sections 12(1) and (3) and 19(5)—are to be read accordingly).

(2) Section 18 does not impose a duty on a sole trustee if that trustee is a trust corporation.

[1297]

NOTES

Commencement: 1 February 2001.

26 Restriction or exclusion of this Part etc

The powers conferred by this Part are—

(a) in addition to powers conferred on trustees otherwise than by this Act, but

(b) subject to any restriction or exclusion imposed by the trust instrument or by any enactment or any provision of subordinate legislation.

[1298]

NOTES

Commencement: 1 February 2001.

27 Existing trusts

This Part applies in relation to trusts whether created before or after its commencement.

[1299]

NOTES

Commencement: 1 February 2001.

PART V
REMUNERATION

28 Trustee's entitlement to payment under trust instrument

(1) Except to the extent (if any) to which the trust instrument makes inconsistent provision, subsections (2) to (4) apply to a trustee if—

(a) there is a provision in the trust instrument entitling him to receive payment out of trust funds in respect of services provided by him to or on behalf of the trust, and

(b) the trustee is a trust corporation or is acting in a professional capacity.

(2) The trustee is to be treated as entitled under the trust instrument to receive payment in respect of services even if they are services which are capable of being provided by a lay trustee.

(3) Subsection (2) applies to a trustee of a charitable trust who is not a trust corporation only—

(a) if he is not a sole trustee, and

(b) to the extent that a majority of the other trustees have agreed that it should apply to him.

(4) Any payments to which the trustee is entitled in respect of services are to be treated as remuneration for services (and not as a gift) for the purposes of—

(a) section 15 of the Wills Act 1837 (gifts to an attesting witness to be void), and

(b) section 34(3) of the Administration of Estates Act 1925 (order in which estate to be paid out).

(5) For the purposes of this Part, a trustee acts in a professional capacity if he acts in the course of a profession or business which consists of or includes the provision of services in connection with—

(a) the management or administration of trusts generally or a particular kind of trust, or

(b) any particular aspect of the management or administration of trusts generally or a particular kind of trust,

and the services he provides to or on behalf of the trust fall within that description.

(6) For the purposes of this Part, a person acts as a lay trustee if he—

(a) is not a trust corporation, and

(b) does not act in a professional capacity.

[1300]

NOTES

Commencement: 1 February 2001.

29 Remuneration of certain trustees

(1) Subject to subsection (5), a trustee who—

(a) is a trust corporation, but

(b) is not a trustee of a charitable trust,

is entitled to receive reasonable remuneration out of the trust funds for any services that the trust corporation provides to or on behalf of the trust.

(2) Subject to subsection (5), a trustee who—

(a) acts in a professional capacity, but

(b) is not a trust corporation, a trustee of a charitable trust or a sole trustee,

is entitled to receive reasonable remuneration out of the trust funds for any services that he provides to or on behalf of the trust if each other trustee has agreed in writing that he may be remunerated for the services.

(3) "Reasonable remuneration" means, in relation to the provision of services by a trustee, such remuneration as is reasonable in the circumstances for the provision of those services to or on behalf of that trust by that trustee and for the purposes of subsection (1) includes, in relation to the provision of services by a trustee who is an authorised institution under the Banking Act 1987 and provides the services in that capacity, the institution's reasonable charges for the provision of such services.

(4) A trustee is entitled to remuneration under this section even if the services in question are capable of being provided by a lay trustee.

(5) A trustee is not entitled to remuneration under this section if any provision about his entitlement to remuneration has been made—

(a) by the trust instrument, or

(b) by any enactment or any provision of subordinate legislation.

(6) This section applies to a trustee who has been authorised under a power conferred by Part IV or the trust instrument—

(a) to exercise functions as an agent of the trustees, or

(b) to act as a nominee or custodian,

as it applies to any other trustee.

[1301]

NOTES

Commencement: 1 February 2001.

30 Remuneration of trustees of charitable trusts

(1) The Secretary of State may by regulations make provision for the remuneration of trustees of charitable trusts who are trust corporations or act in a professional capacity.

(2) The power under subsection (1) includes power to make provision for the remuneration of a trustee who has been authorised under a power conferred by Part IV or any other enactment or any provision of subordinate legislation, or by the trust instrument—

(a) to exercise functions as an agent of the trustees, or

(b) to act as a nominee or custodian.

(3) Regulations under this section may—

(a) make different provision for different cases;

(b) contain such supplemental, incidental, consequential and transitional provision as the Secretary of State considers appropriate.

(4) The power to make regulations under this section is exercisable by statutory instrument, but no such instrument shall be made unless a draft of it has been laid before Parliament and approved by a resolution of each House of Parliament.

[1302]

NOTES

Commencement: 1 February 2001.

31 Trustees' expenses

(1) A trustee—

(a) is entitled to be reimbursed from the trust funds, or

(b) may pay out of the trust funds,

expenses properly incurred by him when acting on behalf of the trust.

(2) This section applies to a trustee who has been authorised under a power conferred by Part IV or any other enactment or any provision of subordinate legislation, or by the trust instrument—

(a) to exercise functions as an agent of the trustees, or

(b) to act as a nominee or custodian,

as it applies to any other trustee.

[1303]

NOTES

Commencement: 1 February 2001.

32 Remuneration and expenses of agents, nominees and custodians

(1) This section applies if, under a power conferred by Part IV or any other enactment or any provision of subordinate legislation, or by the trust instrument, a person other than a trustee has been—

(a) authorised to exercise functions as an agent of the trustees, or

(b) appointed to act as a nominee or custodian.

(2) The trustees may remunerate the agent, nominee or custodian out of the trust funds for services if—

(a) he is engaged on terms entitling him to be remunerated for those services, and

(b) the amount does not exceed such remuneration as is reasonable in the circumstances for the provision of those services by him to or on behalf of that trust.

(3) The trustees may reimburse the agent, nominee or custodian out of the trust funds for any expenses properly incurred by him in exercising functions as an agent, nominee or custodian.

[1304]

NOTES

Commencement: 1 February 2001.

33 Application

(1) Subject to subsection (2), sections 28, 29, 31 and 32 apply in relation to services provided to or on behalf of, or (as the case may be) expenses incurred on or after their commencement on behalf of, trusts whenever created.

(2) Nothing in section 28 or 29 is to be treated as affecting the operation of—

(a) section 15 of the Wills Act 1837, or

(b) section 34(3) of the Administration of Estates Act 1925,

in relation to any death occurring before the commencement of section 28 or (as the case may be) section 29.

[1305]

NOTES

Commencement: 1 February 2001.

PART VI
MISCELLANEOUS AND SUPPLEMENTARY

34 Power to insure

(1), (2) …

(3) The amendments made by this section apply in relation to trusts whether created before or after its commencement.

[1306]

NOTES

Commencement: 1 February 2001.
Sub-s (1): substitutes the Trustee Act 1925, s 19.
Sub-s (2): amends the Trustee Act 1925, s 20(1).

35 Personal representatives

(1) Subject to the following provisions of this section, this Act applies in relation to a personal representative administering an estate according to the law as it applies to a trustee carrying out a trust for beneficiaries.

(2) For this purpose this Act is to be read with the appropriate modifications and in particular—

(a) references to the trust instrument are to be read as references to the will,

(b) references to a beneficiary or to beneficiaries, apart from the reference to a beneficiary in section 8(1)(b), are to be read as references to a person or the persons interested in the due administration of the estate, and

(c) the reference to a beneficiary in section 8(1)(b) is to be read as a reference to a person who under the will of the deceased or under the law relating to intestacy is beneficially interested in the estate.

(3) Remuneration to which a personal representative is entitled under section 28 or 29 is to be treated as an administration expense for the purposes of—

(a) section 34(3) of the Administration of Estates Act 1925 (order in which estate to be paid out), and

(b) any provision giving reasonable administration expenses priority over the preferential debts listed in Schedule 6 to the Insolvency Act 1986.

(4) Nothing in subsection (3) is to be treated as affecting the operation of the provisions mentioned in paragraphs (a) and (b) of that subsection in relation to any death occurring before the commencement of this section.

[1307]

NOTES

Commencement: 1 February 2001.

36 Pension schemes

(1) In this section "pension scheme" means an occupational pension scheme (within the meaning of the Pension Schemes Act 1993) established under a trust and subject to the law of England and Wales.

(2) Part I does not apply in so far as it imposes a care of duty in relation to—
- (a) the functions described in paragraphs 1 and 2 of Schedule 1, or
- (b) the functions described in paragraph 3 of that Schedule to the extent that they relate to trustees—
  - (i) authorising a person to exercise their functions with respect to investment, or
  - (ii) appointing a person to act as their nominee or custodian.

(3) Nothing in Part II or III applies to the trustees of any pension scheme.

(4) Part IV applies to the trustees of a pension scheme subject to the restrictions in subsections (5) to (8).

(5) The trustees of a pension scheme may not under Part IV authorise any person to exercise any functions relating to investment as their agent.

(6) The trustees of a pension scheme may not under Part IV authorise a person who is—
- (a) an employer in relation to the scheme, or
- (b) connected with or an associate of such an employer,

to exercise any of their functions as their agent.

(7) For the purposes of subsection (6)—
- (a) "employer", in relation to a scheme, has the same meaning as in the Pensions Act 1995;
- (b) sections 249 and 435 of the Insolvency Act 1986 apply for the purpose of determining whether a person is connected with or an associate of an employer.

(8) Sections 16 to 20 (powers to appoint nominees and custodians) do not apply to the trustees of a pension scheme.

[1308]

NOTES

Commencement: 1 February 2001.

37 Authorised unit trusts

(1) Parts II to IV do not apply to trustees of authorised unit trusts.

(2) "Authorised unit trust" means a unit trust scheme in the case of which an order under section 78 of the Financial Services Act 1986 is in force.

[1309]

NOTES

Commencement: 1 February 2001.

38 Common investment schemes for charities etc

Parts II to IV do not apply to—
- (a) trustees managing a fund under a common investment scheme made, or having effect as if made, under section 24 of the Charities Act 1993, other than such a fund the trusts of which provide that property is not to be transferred to the fund except by or on behalf of a charity the trustees of which are the trustees appointed to manage the fund, or

(b) trustees managing a fund under a common deposit scheme made, or having effect as if made, under section 25 of that Act.

[1310]

NOTES

Commencement: 1 February 2001.

39 Interpretation

(1) In this Act—

"asset" includes any right or interest;

"charitable trust" means a trust under which property is held for charitable purposes and "charitable purposes" has the same meaning as in the Charities Act 1993;

"custodian trustee" has the same meaning as in the Public Trustee Act 1906;

"enactment" includes any provision of a Measure of the Church Assembly or of the General Synod of the Church of England;

"exempt charity" has the same meaning as in the Charities Act 1993;

"functions" includes powers and duties;

"legal mortgage" has the same meaning as in the Law of Property Act 1925;

"personal representative" has the same meaning as in the Trustee Act 1925;

"settled land" has the same meaning as in the Settled Land Act 1925;

"trust corporation" has the same meaning as in the Trustee Act 1925;

"trust funds" means income or capital funds of the trust.

(2) In this Act the expressions listed below are defined or otherwise explained by the provisions indicated—

asset management functions	section 15(5)
custodian	section 17(2)
the duty of care	section 1(2)
the general power of investment	section 3(2)
lay trustee	section 28(6)
power of intervention	section 22(4)
the standard investment criteria	section 4(3)
subordinate legislation	section 6(3)
trustee acting in a professional capacity	section 28(5)
trust instrument	sections 6(2) and 35(2)(a)

[1311]

NOTES

Commencement: 1 February 2001.

40 Minor and consequential amendments etc

(1) Schedule 2 (minor and consequential amendments) shall have effect.

(2) Schedule 3 (transitional provisions and savings) shall have effect.

(3) Schedule 4 (repeals) shall have effect.

[1312]

NOTES

Commencement: 1 February 2001.

41 Power to amend other Acts

(1) A Minister of the Crown may by order make such amendments of any Act, including an Act extending to places outside England and Wales, as appear to him appropriate in consequence of or in connection with Part II or III.

(2) Before exercising the power under subsection (1) in relation to a local, personal or private Act, the Minister may consult any person who appears to him to be affected by any proposed amendment.

(3) An order under this section may—
- (a) contain such transitional provisions and savings as the Minister thinks fit;
- (b) make different provision for different purposes.

(4) The power to make an order under this section is exercisable by statutory instrument which shall be subject to annulment in pursuance of a resolution of either House of Parliament.

(5) "Minister of the Crown" has the same meaning as in the Ministers of the Crown Act 1975.

[1313]

NOTES

Commencement: 23 November 2000.

42 Commencement and extent

(1) Section 41, this section and section 43 shall come into force on the day on which this Act is passed.

(2) The remaining provisions of this Act shall come into force on such day as the Lord Chancellor may appoint by order made by statutory instrument; and different days may be so appointed for different purposes.

(3) An order under subsection (2) may contain such transitional provisions and savings as the Lord Chancellor considers appropriate in connection with the order.

(4) Subject to section 41(1) and subsection (5), this Act extends to England and Wales only.

(5) An amendment or repeal in Part II or III of Schedule 2 or Part II of Schedule 4 has the same extent as the provision amended or repealed.

[1314]

NOTES

Commencement: 23 November 2000.
Orders: the Trustee Act 2000 (Commencement) Order 2001, SI 2001/49.

43 Short title

This Act may be cited as the Trustee Act 2000.

[1315]

NOTES

Commencement: 23 November 2000.

SCHEDULES

SCHEDULE 1
APPLICATION OF DUTY OF CARE

Section 2

Investment

1. The duty of care applies to a trustee—
   - (a) when exercising the general power of investment or any other power of investment, however conferred;
   - (b) when carrying out a duty to which he is subject under section 4 or 5 (duties relating to the exercise of a power of investment or to the review of investments).

Acquisition of land

2. The duty of care applies to a trustee—

(a) when exercising the power under section 8 to acquire land;
(b) when exercising any other power to acquire land, however conferred;
(c) when exercising any power in relation to land acquired under a power mentioned in sub-paragraph (a) or (b).

Agents, nominees and custodians

3.—(1) The duty of care applies to a trustee—
(a) when entering into arrangements under which a person is authorised under section 11 to exercise functions as an agent;
(b) when entering into arrangements under which a person is appointed under section 16 to act as a nominee;
(c) when entering into arrangements under which a person is appointed under section 17 or 18 to act as a custodian;
(d) when entering into arrangements under which, under any other power, however conferred, a person is authorised to exercise functions as an agent or is appointed to act as a nominee or custodian;
(e) when carrying out his duties under section 22 (review of agent, nominee or custodian, etc).

(2) For the purposes of sub-paragraph (1), entering into arrangements under which a person is authorised to exercise functions or is appointed to act as a nominee or custodian includes, in particular—
(a) selecting the person who is to act,
(b) determining any terms on which he is to act, and
(c) if the person is being authorised to exercise asset management functions, the preparation of a policy statement under section 15.

Compounding of liabilities

4. The duty of care applies to a trustee—
(a) when exercising the power under section 15 of the Trustee Act 1925 to do any of the things referred to in that section;
(b) when exercising any corresponding power, however conferred.

Insurance

5. The duty of care applies to a trustee—
(a) when exercising the power under section 19 of the Trustee Act 1925 to insure property;
(b) when exercising any corresponding power, however conferred.

Reversionary interests, valuations and audit

6. The duty of care applies to a trustee—
(a) when exercising the power under section 22(1) or (3) of the Trustee Act 1925 to do any of the things referred to there;
(b) when exercising any corresponding power, however conferred.

Exclusion of duty of care

7. The duty of care does not apply if or in so far as it appears from the trust instrument that the duty is not meant to apply.

[1316]

NOTES
Commencement: 1 February 2001.

(Sch 2: Pt I repeals the Trustee Investments Act 1961, ss 1, 2, 3, 5, 6, 8, 9, 12, 13, 15, 16(1) (in part), Schs 2, 3, Sch 4, para 1(1); repeals the Charities Act 1993, ss 70, 71 and amends

s 86(2) thereof at **[850]***; Pt II repealed in part, remainder amends the Places of Worship Sites Act 1873, s 2; amends the Technical and Industrial Institutions Act 1892, s 9; repeals the Duchy of Cornwall Management Act 1893; amends the Duchy of Lancaster Act 1920, s 1; amends the Settled Land Act 1925, ss 21, 39, 73, 75, 98, 102, 104, 107, inserts s 75A to that Act and repeals ss 96, 100 thereof; repeals the Trustee Act 1925, ss 2–11 (Pt I), 21, 23, 30, amends ss 14, 15, 22, 31 to that Act at* **[17]**, **[18]**, **[25]**, **[33]***; amends the Administration of Estates Act 1925, ss 33, 39; amends the Universities and College Estates Act 1925, s 26; amends the Regimental Charitable Funds Act 1935, s 2; amends the Agricultural Marketing Act 1958, s 16; amends the Horticulture Act 1960, s 13; amends the House of Commons Members' Fund Act 1962, ss 1, 2; amends the Betting, Gaming and Lotteries Act 1963, s 25; amends the Cereals Marketing Act 1965, s 18; amends the Agriculture Act 1967, s 18; amends the Solicitors Act 1974, Sch 2; amends the Policyholders Protection Act 1975, Sch 1, para 7; amends the National Heritage Act 1980, s 6; amends the Licensing (Alcohol Education and Research) Act 1981, s 7; substitutes the Fisheries Act 1981, s 10; substitutes the Duchy of Cornwall Management Act 1982, s 1 and amends ss 6, 11, to that Act; amends the Administration of Justice Act 1982, s 42; amends the Trusts of Land and Appointment of Trustees Act 1996, ss 6, 9, 17 at* **[1012]**, **[1015]**, **[1024]***, and Sch 3 to that Act, and inserts s 9A to that Act at* **[1016]***; Pt III amends various Measures outside the scope of this work.)*

SCHEDULE 3
TRANSITIONAL PROVISIONS AND SAVINGS

Section 40(2)

The Trustee Act 1925 (c 19)

1.—(1) Sub-paragraph (2) applies if, immediately before the day on which Part IV of this Act comes into force, a banker or banking company holds any bearer securities deposited with him under section 7(1) of the 1925 Act (investment in bearer securities).

(2) On and after the day on which Part IV comes into force, the banker or banking company shall be treated as if he had been appointed as custodian of the securities under section 18.

2. The repeal of section 8 of the 1925 Act (loans and investments by trustees not chargeable as breaches of trust) does not affect the operation of that section in relation to loans or investments made before the coming into force of that repeal.

3. The repeal of section 9 of the 1925 Act (liability for loss by reason of improper investment) does not affect the operation of that section in relation to any advance of trust money made before the coming into force of that repeal.

4.—(1) Sub-paragraph (2) applies if, immediately before the day on which Part IV of this Act comes into force, a banker or banking company holds any documents deposited with him under section 21 of the 1925 Act (deposit of documents for safe custody).

(2) On and after the day on which Part IV comes into force, the banker or banking company shall be treated as if he had been appointed as custodian of the documents under section 17.

5.—(1) Sub-paragraph (2) applies if, immediately before the day on which Part IV of this Act comes into force, a person has been appointed to act as or be an agent or attorney under section 23(1) or (3) of the 1925 Act (general power to employ agents etc).

(2) On and after the day on which Part IV comes into force, the agent shall be treated as if he had been authorised to exercise functions as an agent under section 11 (and, if appropriate, as if he had also been appointed under that Part to act as a custodian or nominee).

6. The repeal of section 23(2) of the 1925 Act (power to employ agents in respect of property outside the United Kingdom) does not affect the operation after the commencement of the repeal of an appointment made before that commencement.

The Trustee Investments Act 1961 (*c 62*)

7.—(1) A trustee shall not be liable for breach of trust merely because he continues to hold an investment acquired by virtue of paragraph 14 of Part II of Schedule 1 to the 1961 Act (perpetual rent-charges etc).

(2) A person who—
(a) is not a trustee,
(b) before the commencement of Part II of this Act had powers to invest in the investments described in paragraph 14 of Part II of Schedule 1 to the 1961 Act, and
(c) on that commencement acquired the general power of investment,

shall not be treated as exceeding his powers of investment merely because he continues to hold an investment acquired by virtue of that paragraph.

The Cathedrals Measure 1963 (*No 2*)

8. While section 21 of the Cathedrals Measure 1963 (investment powers, etc of capitular bodies) continues to apply in relation to any cathedral, that section shall have effect as if—
(a) in subsection (1), for paragraph (c) and the words from "and the powers" to the end of the subsection there were substituted—
"(c) power to invest in any investments in which trustees may invest under the general power of investment in section 3 of the Trustee Act 2000 (as restricted by sections 4 and 5 of that Act).", and
(b) in subsection (5), for "subsections (2) and (3) of section six of the Trustee Investments Act 1961" there were substituted "section 5 of the Trustee Act 2000".

[1317]

SCHEDULE 4
REPEALS

PART I
THE TRUSTEE INVESTMENTS ACT 1961 AND THE CHARITIES ACT 1993

Chapter	Short title	Extent of repeal
1961 c 62	The Trustee Investments Act 1961	Sections 1 to 3, 5, 6, 8, 9, 12, 13, 15 and 16(1).
		Schedules 2 and 3.
		In Schedule 4, paragraph 1(1).
1993 c 10	The Charities Act 1993	Sections 70 and 71.
		In section 86(2) in paragraph (a), "70" and paragraph (b).

Note: the repeals in this Part of this Schedule have effect in accordance with Part I of Schedule 2.

[1318]

PART II
OTHER REPEALS

Chapter	Short title	Extent of repeal
1893 c 20	The Duchy of Cornwall Management Act 1893	The whole Act.

Chapter	Short title	Extent of repeal
1925 c 18	The Settled Land Act 1925	Section 96.
		Section 98(1) and (2).
		Section 100.
		In section 104(3)(b) the words "authorised by statute for the investment of trust money".
1925 c 19	The Trustee Act 1925	Part I.
		In section 20(1) the words "whether by fire or otherwise".
		Sections 21, 23 and 30.
1961 No 3	The Clergy Pensions Measure 1961	Section 32(3)
1962 c 53	The House of Commons Members' Fund Act 1962	In section 1, in subsection (2) the words "Subject to the following provisions of this section" and subsections (3) to (5).
		Section 2(1).
1965 c 14	The Cereals Marketing Act 1965	Section 18(3)
1967 c 22	The Agriculture Act 1967	Section 18(3)
1988 No 4	The Church of England (Pensions) Measure 1988	Section 14(b)
1996 c 47	The Trusts of Land and Appointment of Trustees Act 1996	Section 6(4)
		Section 9(8)
		Section 17(1)
		In Schedule 3, paragraph 3(4).
1999 No 1	The Cathedrals Measure 1999	In section 16(1), the words from "and the powers" to the end of the subsection.

[1319]

FREEDOM OF INFORMATION ACT 2000

(2000 c 36)

ARRANGEMENT OF SECTIONS

PART I
ACCESS TO INFORMATION HELD BY PUBLIC AUTHORITIES

Right to information

PART I
ACCESS TO INFORMATION HELD BY PUBLIC AUTHORITIES

Right to information

1 General right of access to information held by public authorities

(1) Any person making a request for information to a public authority is entitled—
- (a) to be informed in writing by the public authority whether it holds information of the description specified in the request, and
- (b) if that is the case, to have that information communicated to him.

(2) Subsection (1) has effect subject to the following provisions of this section and to the provisions of sections 2, 9, 12 and 14.

(3) Where a public authority—
- (a) reasonably requires further information in order to identify and locate the information requested, and

(b) has informed the applicant of that requirement,

the authority is not obliged to comply with subsection (1) unless it is supplied with that further information.

(4) The information—

(a) in respect of which the applicant is to be informed under subsection (1)(a), or

(b) which is to be communicated under subsection (1)(b),

is the information in question held at the time when the request is received, except that account may be taken of any amendment or deletion made between that time and the time when the information is to be communicated under subsection (1)(b), being an amendment or deletion that would have been made regardless of the receipt of the request.

(5) A public authority is to be taken to have complied with subsection (1)(a) in relation to any information if it has communicated the information to the applicant in accordance with subsection (1)(b).

(6) In this Act, the duty of a public authority to comply with subsection (1)(a) is referred to as "the duty to confirm or deny".

[1320]

NOTES

Commencement: 1 January 2005.

2 Effect of the exemptions in Part II

(1) Where any provision of Part II states that the duty to confirm or deny does not arise in relation to any information, the effect of the provision is that where either—

(a) the provision confers absolute exemption, or

(b) in all the circumstances of the case, the public interest in maintaining the exclusion of the duty to confirm or deny outweighs the public interest in disclosing whether the public authority holds the information,

section 1(1)(a) does not apply.

(2) In respect of any information which is exempt information by virtue of any provision of Part II, section 1(1)(b) does not apply if or to the extent that—

(a) the information is exempt information by virtue of a provision conferring absolute exemption, or

(b) in all the circumstances of the case, the public interest in maintaining the exemption outweighs the public interest in disclosing the information.

(3) For the purposes of this section, the following provisions of Part II (and no others) are to be regarded as conferring absolute exemption—

(a) section 21,

(b) section 23,

(c) section 32,

(d) section 34,

(e) section 36 so far as relating to information held by the House of Commons or the House of Lords,

(f) in section 40—

(i) subsection (1), and

(ii) subsection (2) so far as relating to cases where the first condition referred to in that subsection is satisfied by virtue of subsection (3)(a)(i) or (b) of that section,

(g) section 41, and

(h) section 44.

[1321]

NOTES

Commencement: 1 January 2005.

3 Public authorities

(1) In this Act "public authority" means—

(a) subject to section 4(4), any body which, any other person who, or the holder of any office which—

(i) is listed in Schedule 1, or
(ii) is designated by order under section 5, or
(b) a publicly-owned company as defined by section 6.

(2) For the purposes of this Act, information is held by a public authority if—
(a) it is held by the authority, otherwise than on behalf of another person, or
(b) it is held by another person on behalf of the authority.

[1322]

4 Amendment of Schedule 1

(1) The [Secretary of State] may by order amend Schedule 1 by adding to that Schedule a reference to any body or the holder of any office which (in either case) is not for the time being listed in that Schedule but as respects which both the first and the second conditions below are satisfied.

(2) The first condition is that the body or office—
(a) is established by virtue of Her Majesty's prerogative or by an enactment or by subordinate legislation, or
(b) is established in any other way by a Minister of the Crown in his capacity as Minister, by a government department or by the National Assembly for Wales.

(3) The second condition is—
(a) in the case of a body, that the body is wholly or partly constituted by appointment made by the Crown, by a Minister of the Crown, by a government department or by the National Assembly for Wales, or
(b) in the case of an office, that appointments to the office are made by the Crown, by a Minister of the Crown, by a government department or by the National Assembly for Wales.

(4) If either the first or the second condition above ceases to be satisfied as respects any body or office which is listed in Part VI or VII of Schedule 1, that body or the holder of that office shall cease to be a public authority by virtue of the entry in question.

(5) The [Secretary of State] may by order amend Schedule 1 by removing from Part VI or VII of that Schedule an entry relating to any body or office—
(a) which has ceased to exist, or
(b) as respects which either the first or the second condition above has ceased to be satisfied.

(6) An order under subsection (1) may relate to a specified person or office or to persons or offices falling within a specified description.

(7) Before making an order under subsection (1), the [Secretary of State] shall—
(a) if the order adds to Part II, III, IV or VI of Schedule 1 a reference to—
(i) a body whose functions are exercisable only or mainly in or as regards Wales, or
(ii) the holder of an office whose functions are exercisable only or mainly in or as regards Wales, consult the National Assembly for Wales, and
(b) if the order relates to a body which, or the holder of any office who, if the order were made, would be a Northern Ireland public authority, consult the First Minister and deputy First Minister in Northern Ireland.

(8) This section has effect subject to section 80.

(9) In this section "Minister of the Crown" includes a Northern Ireland Minister.

[1323]

NOTES

Sub-ss (1), (5), (7): words in square brackets substituted by the Secretary of State for Constitutional Affairs Order 2003, SI 2003/1887, art 9, Sch 2, para 12(1)(a).

Orders: the Freedom of Information (Additional Public Authorities) Order 2002, SI 2002/2623; the Freedom of Information (Additional Public Authorities) Order 2003, SI 2003/1882; the Freedom of Information (Removal of References to Public Authorities) Order 2003, SI 2003/1883; the Freedom of Information (Additional Public Authorities) Order 2004, SI 2004/938; the Freedom of Information (Removal of References to Public Authorities) Order 2004, SI 2004/1641; the Freedom of Information (Additional Public Authorities) Order 2005, SI 2005/3593; the Freedom of Information (Removal of References to Public Authorities) Order 2005, SI 2005/3594.

5 Further power to designate public authorities

(1) The [Secretary of State] may by order designate as a public authority for the purposes of this Act any person who is neither listed in Schedule 1 nor capable of being added to that Schedule by an order under section 4(1), but who—

(a) appears to the [Secretary of State] to exercise functions of a public nature, or

(b) is providing under a contract made with a public authority any service whose provision is a function of that authority.

(2) An order under this section may designate a specified person or office or persons or offices falling within a specified description.

(3) Before making an order under this section, the [Secretary of State] shall consult every person to whom the order relates, or persons appearing to him to represent such persons.

(4) This section has effect subject to section 80.

[1324]

NOTES

Sub-ss (1), (3): words in square brackets substituted by the Secretary of State for Constitutional Affairs Order 2003, SI 2003/1887, art 9, Sch 2, para 12(1)(a).

6 Publicly-owned companies

(1) A company is a "publicly-owned company" for the purposes of section 3(1)(b) if—

(a) it is wholly owned by the Crown, or

(b) it is wholly owned by any public authority listed in Schedule 1 other than—

(i) a government department, or

(ii) any authority which is listed only in relation to particular information.

(2) For the purposes of this section—

(a) a company is wholly owned by the Crown if it has no members except—

(i) Ministers of the Crown, government departments or companies wholly owned by the Crown, or

(ii) persons acting on behalf of Ministers of the Crown, government departments or companies wholly owned by the Crown, and

(b) a company is wholly owned by a public authority other than a government department if it has no members except—

(i) that public authority or companies wholly owned by that public authority, or

(ii) persons acting on behalf of that public authority or of companies wholly owned by that public authority.

(3) In this section—

"company" includes any body corporate;

"Minister of the Crown" includes a Northern Ireland Minister.

[1325]

7 Public authorities to which Act has limited application

(1) Where a public authority is listed in Schedule 1 only in relation to information of a specified description, nothing in Parts I to V of this Act applies to any other information held by the authority.

(2) An order under section 4(1) may, in adding an entry to Schedule 1, list the public authority only in relation to information of a specified description.

(3) The [Secretary of State] may by order amend Schedule 1—

(a) by limiting to information of a specified description the entry relating to any public authority, or

(b) by removing or amending any limitation to information of a specified description which is for the time being contained in any entry.

(4) Before making an order under subsection (3), the [Secretary of State] shall—

(a) if the order relates to the National Assembly for Wales or a Welsh public authority, consult the National Assembly for Wales,

(b) if the order relates to the Northern Ireland Assembly, consult the Presiding Officer of that Assembly, and

(c) if the order relates to a Northern Ireland department or a Northern Ireland public authority, consult the First Minister and deputy First Minister in Northern Ireland.

(5) An order under section 5(1)(a) must specify the functions of the public authority designated by the order with respect to which the designation is to have effect; and nothing in Parts I to V of this Act applies to information which is held by the authority but does not relate to the exercise of those functions.

(6) An order under section 5(1)(b) must specify the services provided under contract with respect to which the designation is to have effect; and nothing in Parts I to V of this Act applies to information which is held by the public authority designated by the order but does not relate to the provision of those services.

(7) Nothing in Parts I to V of this Act applies in relation to any information held by a publicly-owned company which is excluded information in relation to that company.

(8) In subsection (7) "excluded information", in relation to a publicly-owned company, means information which is of a description specified in relation to that company in an order made by the [Secretary of State] for the purposes of this subsection.

(9) In this section "publicly-owned company" has the meaning given by section 6.
[1326]

NOTES

Sub-ss (3), (4), (8): words in square brackets substituted by the Secretary of State for Constitutional Affairs Order 2003, SI 2003/1887, art 9, Sch 2, para 12(1)(a).

Orders: the Freedom of Information (Additional Public Authorities) Order 2002, SI 2002/2623; the Freedom of Information (Additional Public Authorities) Order 2003, SI 2003/1882; the Freedom of Information (Additional Public Authorities) Order 2005, SI 2005/3593.

8 Request for information

(1) In this Act any reference to a "request for information" is a reference to such a request which—

(a) is in writing,
(b) states the name of the applicant and an address for correspondence, and
(c) describes the information requested.

(2) For the purposes of subsection (1)(a), a request is to be treated as made in writing where the text of the request—

(a) is transmitted by electronic means,
(b) is received in legible form, and
(c) is capable of being used for subsequent reference.

[1327]

9 Fees

(1) A public authority to whom a request for information is made may, within the period for complying with section 1(1), give the applicant a notice in writing (in this Act referred to as a "fees notice") stating that a fee of an amount specified in the notice is to be charged by the authority for complying with section 1(1).

(2) Where a fees notice has been given to the applicant, the public authority is not obliged to comply with section 1(1) unless the fee is paid within the period of three months beginning with the day on which the fees notice is given to the applicant.

(3) Subject to subsection (5), any fee under this section must be determined by the public authority in accordance with regulations made by the [Secretary of State].

(4) Regulations under subsection (3) may, in particular, provide—

(a) that no fee is to be payable in prescribed cases,
(b) that any fee is not to exceed such maximum as may be specified in, or determined in accordance with, the regulations, and
(c) that any fee is to be calculated in such manner as may be prescribed by the regulations.

(5) Subsection (3) does not apply where provision is made by or under any enactment as to the fee that may be charged by the public authority for the disclosure of the information.
[1328]

NOTES

Commencement: 30 November 2000 (in so far as confers powers to make any order, regulations or code of practice); 1 January 2005 (otherwise).

Sub-s (3): words in square brackets substituted by the Secretary of State for Constitutional Affairs Order 2003, SI 2003/1887, art 9, Sch 2, para 12(1)(a).

Regulations: the Freedom of Information and Data Protection (Appropriate Limit and Fees) Regulations 2004, SI 2004/3244.

10 Time for compliance with request

(1) Subject to subsections (2) and (3), a public authority must comply with section 1(1) promptly and in any event not later than the twentieth working day following the date of receipt.

(2) Where the authority has given a fees notice to the applicant and the fee is paid in accordance with section 9(2), the working days in the period beginning with the day on which the fees notice is given to the applicant and ending with the day on which the fee is received by the authority are to be disregarded in calculating for the purposes of subsection (1) the twentieth working day following the date of receipt.

(3) If, and to the extent that—

(a) section 1(1)(a) would not apply if the condition in section 2(1)(b) were satisfied, or

(b) section 1(1)(b) would not apply if the condition in section 2(2)(b) were satisfied,

the public authority need not comply with section 1(1)(a) or (b) until such time as is reasonable in the circumstances; but this subsection does not affect the time by which any notice under section 17(1) must be given.

(4) The [Secretary of State] may by regulations provide that subsections (1) and (2) are to have effect as if any reference to the twentieth working day following the date of receipt were a reference to such other day, not later than the sixtieth working day following the date of receipt, as may be specified in, or determined in accordance with, the regulations.

(5) Regulations under subsection (4) may—

(a) prescribe different days in relation to different cases, and

(b) confer a discretion on the Commissioner.

(6) In this section—

"the date of receipt" means—

(a) the day on which the public authority receives the request for information, or

(b) if later, the day on which it receives the information referred to in section 1(3);

"working day" means any day other than a Saturday, a Sunday, Christmas Day, Good Friday or a day which is a bank holiday under the Banking and Financial Dealings Act 1971 in any part of the United Kingdom.

[1329]

NOTES

Commencement: 30 November 2000 (in so far as confers powers to make any order, regulations or code of practice); 1 January 2005 (otherwise).

Sub-s (4): words in square brackets substituted by the Secretary of State for Constitutional Affairs Order 2003, SI 2003/1887, art 9, Sch 2, para 12(1)(a).

Regulations: the Freedom of Information (Time for Compliance with Request) Regulations 2004, SI 2004/3364.

11 Means by which communication to be made

(1) Where, on making his request for information, the applicant expresses a preference for communication by any one or more of the following means, namely—

(a) the provision to the applicant of a copy of the information in permanent form or in another form acceptable to the applicant,

(b) the provision to the applicant of a reasonable opportunity to inspect a record containing the information, and

(c) the provision to the applicant of a digest or summary of the information in permanent form or in another form acceptable to the applicant, the public authority shall so far as reasonably practicable give effect to that preference.

(2) In determining for the purposes of this section whether it is reasonably practicable to communicate information by particular means, the public authority may have regard to all the circumstances, including the cost of doing so.

(3) Where the public authority determines that it is not reasonably practicable to comply with any preference expressed by the applicant in making his request, the authority shall notify the applicant of the reasons for its determination.

(4) Subject to subsection (1), a public authority may comply with a request by communicating information by any means which are reasonable in the circumstances. **[1330]**

NOTES

Commencement: 1 January 2005.

12 Exemption where cost of compliance exceeds appropriate limit

(1) Section 1(1) does not oblige a public authority to comply with a request for information if the authority estimates that the cost of complying with the request would exceed the appropriate limit.

(2) Subsection (1) does not exempt the public authority from its obligation to comply with paragraph (a) of section 1(1) unless the estimated cost of complying with that paragraph alone would exceed the appropriate limit.

(3) In subsections (1) and (2) "the appropriate limit" means such amount as may be prescribed, and different amounts may be prescribed in relation to different cases.

(4) The [Secretary of State] may by regulations provide that, in such circumstances as may be prescribed, where two or more requests for information are made to a public authority—

(a) by one person, or
(b) by different persons who appear to the public authority to be acting in concert or in pursuance of a campaign,

the estimated cost of complying with any of the requests is to be taken to be the estimated total cost of complying with all of them.

(5) The [Secretary of State] may by regulations make provision for the purposes of this section as to the costs to be estimated and as to the manner in which they are to be estimated. **[1331]**

NOTES

Commencement: 30 November 2000 (in so far as confers powers to make any order, regulations or code of practice); 1 January 2005 (otherwise).

Sub-ss (4), (5): words in square brackets substituted by the Secretary of State for Constitutional Affairs Order 2003, SI 2003/1887, art 9, Sch 2, para 12(1)(a).

Regulations: the Freedom of Information and Data Protection (Appropriate Limit and Fees) Regulations 2004, SI 2004/3244.

13 Fees for disclosure where cost of compliance exceeds appropriate limit

(1) A public authority may charge for the communication of any information whose communication—

(a) is not required by section 1(1) because the cost of complying with the request for information exceeds the amount which is the appropriate limit for the purposes of section 12(1) and (2), and
(b) is not otherwise required by law,

such fee as may be determined by the public authority in accordance with regulations made by the [Secretary of State].

(2) Regulations under this section may, in particular, provide—

(a) that any fee is not to exceed such maximum as may be specified in, or determined in accordance with, the regulations, and
(b) that any fee is to be calculated in such manner as may be prescribed by the regulations.

(3) Subsection (1) does not apply where provision is made by or under any enactment as to the fee that may be charged by the public authority for the disclosure of the information.

[1332]

NOTES

Commencement: 30 November 2000 (in so far as confers powers to make any order, regulations or code of practice); 1 January 2005 (otherwise).

Sub-s (1): words in square brackets substituted by the Secretary of State for Constitutional Affairs Order 2003, SI 2003/1887, art 9, Sch 2, para 12(1)(a).

Regulations: the Freedom of Information and Data Protection (Appropriate Limit and Fees) Regulations 2004, SI 2004/3244.

14 Vexatious or repeated requests

(1) Section 1(1) does not oblige a public authority to comply with a request for information if the request is vexatious.

(2) Where a public authority has previously complied with a request for information which was made by any person, it is not obliged to comply with a subsequent identical or substantially similar request from that person unless a reasonable interval has elapsed between compliance with the previous request and the making of the current request.

[1333]

NOTES

Commencement: 1 January 2005.

15 Special provisions relating to public records transferred to Public Record Office, etc

(1) Where—

- (a) the appropriate records authority receives a request for information which relates to information which is, or if it existed would be, contained in a transferred public record, and
- (b) either of the conditions in subsection (2) is satisfied in relation to any of that information,

that authority shall, within the period for complying with section 1(1), send a copy of the request to the responsible authority.

(2) The conditions referred to in subsection (1)(b) are—

- (a) that the duty to confirm or deny is expressed to be excluded only by a provision of Part II not specified in subsection (3) of section 2, and
- (b) that the information is exempt information only by virtue of a provision of Part II not specified in that subsection.

(3) On receiving the copy, the responsible authority shall, within such time as is reasonable in all the circumstances, inform the appropriate records authority of the determination required by virtue of subsection (3) or (4) of section 66.

(4) In this Act "transferred public record" means a public record which has been transferred—

- (a) to the Public Record Office,
- (b) to another place of deposit appointed by the Lord Chancellor under the Public Records Act 1958, or
- (c) to the Public Record Office of Northern Ireland.

(5) In this Act—

"appropriate records authority", in relation to a transferred public record, means—

- (a) in a case falling within subsection (4)(a), the Public Record Office,
- (b) in a case falling within subsection (4)(b), the Lord Chancellor, and
- (c) in a case falling within subsection (4)(c), the Public Record Office of Northern Ireland;

"responsible authority", in relation to a transferred public record, means—

- (a) in the case of a record transferred as mentioned in subsection (4)(a) or (b) from a government department in the charge of a Minister of the Crown, the Minister of the Crown who appears to the Lord Chancellor to be primarily concerned,

(b) in the case of a record transferred as mentioned in subsection (4)(a) or (b) from any other person, the person who appears to the Lord Chancellor to be primarily concerned,

(c) in the case of a record transferred to the Public Record Office of Northern Ireland from a government department in the charge of a Minister of the Crown, the Minister of the Crown who appears to the appropriate Northern Ireland Minister to be primarily concerned,

(d) in the case of a record transferred to the Public Record Office of Northern Ireland from a Northern Ireland department, the Northern Ireland Minister who appears to the appropriate Northern Ireland Minister to be primarily concerned, or

(e) in the case of a record transferred to the Public Record Office of Northern Ireland from any other person, the person who appears to the appropriate Northern Ireland Minister to be primarily concerned.

[1334]

NOTES

Commencement: 1 January 2005.

16 Duty to provide advice and assistance

(1) It shall be the duty of a public authority to provide advice and assistance, so far as it would be reasonable to expect the authority to do so, to persons who propose to make, or have made, requests for information to it.

(2) Any public authority which, in relation to the provision of advice or assistance in any case, conforms with the code of practice under section 45 is to be taken to comply with the duty imposed by subsection (1) in relation to that case.

[1335]

NOTES

Commencement: 1 January 2005.

Refusal of request

17 Refusal of request

(1) A public authority which, in relation to any request for information, is to any extent relying on a claim that any provision of Part II relating to the duty to confirm or deny is relevant to the request or on a claim that information is exempt information must, within the time for complying with section 1(1), give the applicant a notice which—

(a) states that fact,

(b) specifies the exemption in question, and

(c) states (if that would not otherwise be apparent) why the exemption applies.

(2) Where—

(a) in relation to any request for information, a public authority is, as respects any information, relying on a claim—

(i) that any provision of Part II which relates to the duty to confirm or deny and is not specified in section 2(3) is relevant to the request, or

(ii) that the information is exempt information only by virtue of a provision not specified in section 2(3), and

(b) at the time when the notice under subsection (1) is given to the applicant, the public authority (or, in a case falling within section 66(3) or (4), the responsible authority) has not yet reached a decision as to the application of subsection (1)(b) or (2)(b) of section 2,

the notice under subsection (1) must indicate that no decision as to the application of that provision has yet been reached and must contain an estimate of the date by which the authority expects that such a decision will have been reached.

(3) A public authority which, in relation to any request for information, is to any extent relying on a claim that subsection (1)(b) or (2)(b) of section 2 applies must, either in the notice under subsection (1) or in a separate notice given within such time as is reasonable in the circumstances, state the reasons for claiming—

(a) that, in all the circumstances of the case, the public interest in maintaining the exclusion of the duty to confirm or deny outweighs the public interest in disclosing whether the authority holds the information, or

(b) that, in all the circumstances of the case, the public interest in maintaining the exemption outweighs the public interest in disclosing the information.

(4) A public authority is not obliged to make a statement under subsection (1)(c) or (3) if, or to the extent that, the statement would involve the disclosure of information which would itself be exempt information.

(5) A public authority which, in relation to any request for information, is relying on a claim that section 12 or 14 applies must, within the time for complying with section 1(1), give the applicant a notice stating that fact.

(6) Subsection (5) does not apply where—

(a) the public authority is relying on a claim that section 14 applies,

(b) the authority has given the applicant a notice, in relation to a previous request for information, stating that it is relying on such a claim, and

(c) it would in all the circumstances be unreasonable to expect the authority to serve a further notice under subsection (5) in relation to the current request.

(7) A notice under subsection (1), (3) or (5) must—

(a) contain particulars of any procedure provided by the public authority for dealing with complaints about the handling of requests for information or state that the authority does not provide such a procedure, and

(b) contain particulars of the right conferred by section 50.

[1336]

NOTES

Commencement: 1 January 2005.

The Information Commissioner and the Information Tribunal

18 The Information Commissioner and the Information Tribunal

(1) The Data Protection Commissioner shall be known instead as the Information Commissioner.

(2) The Data Protection Tribunal shall be known instead as the Information Tribunal.

(3) In this Act—

(a) the Information Commissioner is referred to as "the Commissioner", and

(b) the Information Tribunal is referred to as "the Tribunal".

(4) Schedule 2 (which makes provision consequential on subsections (1) and (2) and amendments of the Data Protection Act 1998 relating to the extension by this Act of the functions of the Commissioner and the Tribunal) has effect.

(5) If the person who held office as Data Protection Commissioner immediately before the day on which this Act is passed remains in office as Information Commissioner at the end of the period of two years beginning with that day, he shall vacate his office at the end of that period.

(6) Subsection (5) does not prevent the re-appointment of a person whose appointment is terminated by that subsection.

(7) In the application of paragraph 2(4)(b) and (5) of Schedule 5 to the Data Protection Act 1998 (Commissioner not to serve for more than fifteen years and not to be appointed, except in special circumstances, for a third or subsequent term) to anything done after the passing of this Act, there shall be left out of account any term of office served by virtue of an appointment made before the passing of this Act.

[1337]

NOTES

Commencement: 30 November 2000 (sub-s (4) certain purposes); 30 January 2001 (sub-s (1), sub-s (4) certain purposes); 14 May 2001 (sub-ss (2), (3), (5)–(7), sub-s (4) certain purposes); 30 November 2002 (otherwise).

PART I STATUTES

Publication schemes

19 Publication schemes

(1) It shall be the duty of every public authority—

(a) to adopt and maintain a scheme which relates to the publication of information by the authority and is approved by the Commissioner (in this Act referred to as a "publication scheme"),

(b) to publish information in accordance with its publication scheme, and

(c) from time to time to review its publication scheme.

(2) A publication scheme must—

(a) specify classes of information which the public authority publishes or intends to publish,

(b) specify the manner in which information of each class is, or is intended to be, published, and

(c) specify whether the material is, or is intended to be, available to the public free of charge or on payment.

(3) In adopting or reviewing a publication scheme, a public authority shall have regard to the public interest—

(a) in allowing public access to information held by the authority, and

(b) in the publication of reasons for decisions made by the authority.

(4) A public authority shall publish its publication scheme in such manner as it thinks fit.

(5) The Commissioner may, when approving a scheme, provide that his approval is to expire at the end of a specified period.

(6) Where the Commissioner has approved the publication scheme of any public authority, he may at any time give notice to the public authority revoking his approval of the scheme as from the end of the period of six months beginning with the day on which the notice is given.

(7) Where the Commissioner—

(a) refuses to approve a proposed publication scheme, or

(b) revokes his approval of a publication scheme,

he must give the public authority a statement of his reasons for doing so.

[1338]

NOTES

Commencement (sub-ss (1)–(4)): 30 November 2000 (in so far as relating to the approval of publication schemes); 30 November 2002 (in so far as relating to public authorities listed in Sch 1, paras 1 (except the Crown Prosecution Service and the Serious Fraud Office), 2, 3, 5 to the Act and SI 2002/2812, Sch 1); 28 February 2003 (in so far as relating to the Common Council of the City of London, in respect of information held in its capacity as a local authority or port health authority and public authorities listed in Sch 1, paras 7, 8, 10–16, 18–36 to the Act and SI 2002/2812, Sch 2); 30 June 2003 (in so far as relating to the Crown Prosecution Service and the Serious Fraud Office, the Common Council of the City of London, in respect of information held in its capacity as a police authority, and public authorities listed in Sch 1, paras 6, 57–64 to the Act and SI 2002/2812, Sch 3); 31 October 2003 (in so far as relating to the public authorities listed in Sch 1, Pt III to the Act, the Distinction and Meritorious Service Awards Committee, Invest Northern Ireland and The Northern Ireland Council for Postgraduate Medical and Dental Education); 29 February 2004 (in so far as relating to the public authorities listed in Sch 1, Pt IV to the Act (except for those specified in para 52(b)) and SI 2003/2603, Sch 1 and any publicly-owned company as defined in s 6 of the Act); 30 June 2004 (in so far as relating to all public authorities in respect of which these provisions have not been commenced elsewhere, except for the public authority listed in Sch 1, para 17 to the Act and the consultative Civic Forum referred to in the Northern Ireland Act 1998, s 56(4)); 30 November 2005 (otherwise).

Commencement (sub-ss (5)–(7)): 30 November 2000 (in so far as relating to the approval of publication schemes); 30 November 2002 (otherwise).

20 Model publication schemes

(1) The Commissioner may from time to time approve, in relation to public authorities falling within particular classes, model publication schemes prepared by him or by other persons.

(2) Where a public authority falling within the class to which an approved model scheme relates adopts such a scheme without modification, no further approval of the Commissioner

is required so long as the model scheme remains approved; and where such an authority adopts such a scheme with modifications, the approval of the Commissioner is required only in relation to the modifications.

(3) The Commissioner may, when approving a model publication scheme, provide that his approval is to expire at the end of a specified period.

(4) Where the Commissioner has approved a model publication scheme, he may at any time publish, in such manner as he thinks fit, a notice revoking his approval of the scheme as from the end of the period of six months beginning with the day on which the notice is published.

(5) Where the Commissioner refuses to approve a proposed model publication scheme on the application of any person, he must give the person who applied for approval of the scheme a statement of the reasons for his refusal.

(6) Where the Commissioner refuses to approve any modifications under subsection (2), he must give the public authority a statement of the reasons for his refusal.

(7) Where the Commissioner revokes his approval of a model publication scheme, he must include in the notice under subsection (4) a statement of his reasons for doing so.

[1339]

NOTES

Commencement: 30 November 2000 (so far as relating to the approval and preparation by the Commissioner of model publication schemes); 30 November 2002 (otherwise).

PART II
EXEMPT INFORMATION

21 Information accessible to applicant by other means

(1) Information which is reasonably accessible to the applicant otherwise than under section 1 is exempt information.

(2) For the purposes of subsection (1)—

(a) information may be reasonably accessible to the applicant even though it is accessible only on payment, and

(b) information is to be taken to be reasonably accessible to the applicant if it is information which the public authority or any other person is obliged by or under any enactment to communicate (otherwise than by making the information available for inspection) to members of the public on request, whether free of charge or on payment.

(3) For the purposes of subsection (1), information which is held by a public authority and does not fall within subsection (2)(b) is not to be regarded as reasonably accessible to the applicant merely because the information is available from the public authority itself on request, unless the information is made available in accordance with the authority's publication scheme and any payment required is specified in, or determined in accordance with, the scheme.

[1340]

NOTES

Commencement: 1 January 2005.

22 Information intended for future publication

(1) Information is exempt information if—

(a) the information is held by the public authority with a view to its publication, by the authority or any other person, at some future date (whether determined or not),

(b) the information was already held with a view to such publication at the time when the request for information was made, and

(c) it is reasonable in all the circumstances that the information should be withheld from disclosure until the date referred to in paragraph (a).

(2) The duty to confirm or deny does not arise if, or to the extent that, compliance with section 1(1)(a) would involve the disclosure of any information (whether or not already recorded) which falls within subsection (1).

[1341]

NOTES

Commencement: 1 January 2005.

23 Information supplied by, or relating to, bodies dealing with security matters

(1) Information held by a public authority is exempt information if it was directly or indirectly supplied to the public authority by, or relates to, any of the bodies specified in subsection (3).

(2) A certificate signed by a Minister of the Crown certifying that the information to which it applies was directly or indirectly supplied by, or relates to, any of the bodies specified in subsection (3) shall, subject to section 60, be conclusive evidence of that fact.

(3) The bodies referred to in subsections (1) and (2) are—

(a) the Security Service,
(b) the Secret Intelligence Service,
(c) the Government Communications Headquarters,
(d) the special forces,
(e) the Tribunal established under section 65 of the Regulation of Investigatory Powers Act 2000,
(f) the Tribunal established under section 7 of the Interception of Communications Act 1985,
(g) the Tribunal established under section 5 of the Security Service Act 1989,
(h) the Tribunal established under section 9 of the Intelligence Services Act 1994,
(i) the Security Vetting Appeals Panel,
(j) the Security Commission,
(k) the National Criminal Intelligence Service, …
(l) the Service Authority for the National Criminal Intelligence Service,
[(m) the Serious Organised Crime Agency]

(4) In subsection (3)(c) "the Government Communications Headquarters" includes any unit or part of a unit of the armed forces of the Crown which is for the time being required by the Secretary of State to assist the Government Communications Headquarters in carrying out its functions.

(5) The duty to confirm or deny does not arise if, or to the extent that, compliance with section 1(1)(a) would involve the disclosure of any information (whether or not already recorded) which was directly or indirectly supplied to the public authority by, or relates to, any of the bodies specified in subsection (3).

[1342]

NOTES

Commencement: 1 January 2005.
Sub-s (3): word omitted from para (k) repealed and para (m) inserted by the Serious Organised Crime and Police Act 2005, ss 59, 174(2), Sch 4, paras 158, 159, Sch 17, Pt 2.

24 National security

(1) Information which does not fall within section 23(1) is exempt information if exemption from section 1(1)(b) is required for the purpose of safeguarding national security.

(2) The duty to confirm or deny does not arise if, or to the extent that, exemption from section 1(1)(a) is required for the purpose of safeguarding national security.

(3) A certificate signed by a Minister of the Crown certifying that exemption from section 1(1)(b), or from section 1(1)(a) and (b), is, or at any time was, required for the purpose of safeguarding national security shall, subject to section 60, be conclusive evidence of that fact.

(4) A certificate under subsection (3) may identify the information to which it applies by means of a general description and may be expressed to have prospective effect.

[1343]

NOTES

Commencement: 1 January 2005.

25 Certificates under ss 23 and 24: supplementary provisions

(1) A document purporting to be a certificate under section 23(2) or 24(3) shall be received in evidence and deemed to be such a certificate unless the contrary is proved.

(2) A document which purports to be certified by or on behalf of a Minister of the Crown as a true copy of a certificate issued by that Minister under section 23(2) or 24(3) shall in any legal proceedings be evidence (or, in Scotland, sufficient evidence) of that certificate.

(3) The power conferred by section 23(2) or 24(3) on a Minister of the Crown shall not be exercisable except by a Minister who is a member of the Cabinet or by the Attorney General, the Advocate General for Scotland or the Attorney General for Northern Ireland.

[1344]

NOTES

Commencement: 1 January 2005.

26 Defence

(1) Information is exempt information if its disclosure under this Act would, or would be likely to, prejudice—

(a) the defence of the British Islands or of any colony, or

(b) the capability, effectiveness or security of any relevant forces.

(2) In subsection (1)(b) "relevant forces" means—

(a) the armed forces of the Crown, and

(b) any forces co-operating with those forces,

or any part of any of those forces.

(3) The duty to confirm or deny does not arise if, or to the extent that, compliance with section 1(1)(a) would, or would be likely to, prejudice any of the matters mentioned in subsection (1).

[1345]

NOTES

Commencement: 1 January 2005.

27 International relations

(1) Information is exempt information if its disclosure under this Act would, or would be likely to, prejudice—

(a) relations between the United Kingdom and any other State,

(b) relations between the United Kingdom and any international organisation or international court,

(c) the interests of the United Kingdom abroad, or

(d) the promotion or protection by the United Kingdom of its interests abroad.

(2) Information is also exempt information if it is confidential information obtained from a State other than the United Kingdom or from an international organisation or international court.

(3) For the purposes of this section, any information obtained from a State, organisation or court is confidential at any time while the terms on which it was obtained require it to be held in confidence or while the circumstances in which it was obtained make it reasonable for the State, organisation or court to expect that it will be so held.

(4) The duty to confirm or deny does not arise if, or to the extent that, compliance with section 1(1)(a)—

(a) would, or would be likely to, prejudice any of the matters mentioned in subsection (1), or

(b) would involve the disclosure of any information (whether or not already recorded) which is confidential information obtained from a State other than the United Kingdom or from an international organisation or international court.

(5) In this section—

"international court" means any international court which is not an international organisation and which is established—

(a) by a resolution of an international organisation of which the United Kingdom is a member, or

(b) by an international agreement to which the United Kingdom is a party;

"international organisation" means any international organisation whose members include any two or more States, or any organ of such an organisation;

"State" includes the government of any State and any organ of its government, and references to a State other than the United Kingdom include references to any territory outside the United Kingdom.

[1346]

NOTES

Commencement: 1 January 2005.

28 Relations within the United Kingdom

(1) Information is exempt information if its disclosure under this Act would, or would be likely to, prejudice relations between any administration in the United Kingdom and any other such administration.

(2) In subsection (1) "administration in the United Kingdom" means—

(a) the government of the United Kingdom,

(b) the Scottish Administration,

(c) the Executive Committee of the Northern Ireland Assembly, or

(d) the National Assembly for Wales.

(3) The duty to confirm or deny does not arise if, or to the extent that, compliance with section 1(1)(a) would, or would be likely to, prejudice any of the matters mentioned in subsection (1).

[1347]

NOTES

Commencement: 1 January 2005.

29 The economy

(1) Information is exempt information if its disclosure under this Act would, or would be likely to, prejudice—

(a) the economic interests of the United Kingdom or of any part of the United Kingdom, or

(b) the financial interests of any administration in the United Kingdom, as defined by section 28(2).

(2) The duty to confirm or deny does not arise if, or to the extent that, compliance with section 1(1)(a) would, or would be likely to, prejudice any of the matters mentioned in subsection (1).

[1348]

NOTES

Commencement: 1 January 2005.

30 Investigations and proceedings conducted by public authorities

(1) Information held by a public authority is exempt information if it has at any time been held by the authority for the purposes of—

(a) any investigation which the public authority has a duty to conduct with a view to it being ascertained—

(i) whether a person should be charged with an offence, or

(ii) whether a person charged with an offence is guilty of it,

(b) any investigation which is conducted by the authority and in the circumstances may lead to a decision by the authority to institute criminal proceedings which the authority has power to conduct, or

(c) any criminal proceedings which the authority has power to conduct.

(2) Information held by a public authority is exempt information if—

(a) it was obtained or recorded by the authority for the purposes of its functions relating to—

(i) investigations falling within subsection (1)(a) or (b),

(ii) criminal proceedings which the authority has power to conduct,

(iii) investigations (other than investigations falling within subsection (1)(a) or (b)) which are conducted by the authority for any of the purposes specified in section 31(2) and either by virtue of Her Majesty's prerogative or by virtue of powers conferred by or under any enactment, or

(iv) civil proceedings which are brought by or on behalf of the authority and arise out of such investigations, and

(b) it relates to the obtaining of information from confidential sources.

(3) The duty to confirm or deny does not arise in relation to information which is (or if it were held by the public authority would be) exempt information by virtue of subsection (1) or (2).

(4) In relation to the institution or conduct of criminal proceedings or the power to conduct them, references in subsection (1)(b) or (c) and subsection (2)(a) to the public authority include references—

(a) to any officer of the authority,

(b) in the case of a government department other than a Northern Ireland department, to the Minister of the Crown in charge of the department, and

(c) in the case of a Northern Ireland department, to the Northern Ireland Minister in charge of the department.

(5) *In this section—*

"criminal proceedings" includes—

(*a*) *proceedings before a court-martial constituted under the Army Act 1955, the Air Force Act 1955 or the Naval Discipline Act 1957… ,*

(*b*) *proceedings on dealing summarily with a charge under the Army Act 1955 or the Air Force Act 1955 or on summary trial under the Naval Discipline Act 1957,*

(*c*) *proceedings before a court established by section 83ZA of the Army Act 1955, section 83ZA of the Air Force Act 1955 or section 52FF of the Naval Discipline Act 1957 (summary appeal courts),*

(*d*) *proceedings before the Courts-Martial Appeal Court, and*

(*e*) *proceedings before a Standing Civilian Court;*

"offence" includes any offence under the Army Act 1955, the Air Force Act 1955 or the Naval Discipline Act 1957.

(6) In the application of this section to Scotland—

(a) in subsection (1)(b), for the words from "a decision" to the end there is substituted "a decision by the authority to make a report to the procurator fiscal for the purpose of enabling him to determine whether criminal proceedings should be instituted",

(b) in subsections (1)(c) and (2)(a)(ii) for "which the authority has power to conduct" there is substituted "which have been instituted in consequence of a report made by the authority to the procurator fiscal", and

(c) for any reference to a person being charged with an offence there is substituted a reference to the person being prosecuted for the offence.

[1349]

NOTES

Commencement: 1 January 2005.

Sub-s (5): in definition "criminal proceedings" words omitted from para (a) repealed by the Armed Forces Act 2001, s 38, Sch 7, Pt 1 (note that the Queen's Printer's copy of the 2001 Act erroneously purports to make this amendment to s 29(5) of this Act); substituted by the Armed Forces Act 2006, s 378(1), Sch 16, para 176, as from a day to be appointed, as follows:

"(5) In this section—
"criminal proceedings" includes service law proceedings (as defined by section 324(5) of the Armed Forces Act 2006);
"offence" includes a service offence (as defined by section 50 of that Act).".

31 Law enforcement

(1) Information which is not exempt information by virtue of section 30 is exempt information if its disclosure under this Act would, or would be likely to, prejudice—

- (a) the prevention or detection of crime,
- (b) the apprehension or prosecution of offenders,
- (c) the administration of justice,
- (d) the assessment or collection of any tax or duty or of any imposition of a similar nature,
- (e) the operation of the immigration controls,
- (f) the maintenance of security and good order in prisons or in other institutions where persons are lawfully detained,
- (g) the exercise by any public authority of its functions for any of the purposes specified in subsection (2),
- (h) any civil proceedings which are brought by or on behalf of a public authority and arise out of an investigation conducted, for any of the purposes specified in subsection (2), by or on behalf of the authority by virtue of Her Majesty's prerogative or by virtue of powers conferred by or under an enactment, or
- (i) any inquiry held under the Fatal Accidents and Sudden Deaths Inquiries (Scotland) Act 1976 to the extent that the inquiry arises out of an investigation conducted, for any of the purposes specified in subsection (2), by or on behalf of the authority by virtue of Her Majesty's prerogative or by virtue of powers conferred by or under an enactment.

(2) The purposes referred to in subsection (1)(g) to (i) are—

- (a) the purpose of ascertaining whether any person has failed to comply with the law,
- (b) the purpose of ascertaining whether any person is responsible for any conduct which is improper,
- (c) the purpose of ascertaining whether circumstances which would justify regulatory action in pursuance of any enactment exist or may arise,
- (d) the purpose of ascertaining a person's fitness or competence in relation to the management of bodies corporate or in relation to any profession or other activity which he is, or seeks to become, authorised to carry on,
- (e) the purpose of ascertaining the cause of an accident,
- (f) the purpose of protecting charities against misconduct or mismanagement (whether by trustees or other persons) in their administration,
- (g) the purpose of protecting the property of charities from loss or misapplication,
- (h) the purpose of recovering the property of charities,
- (i) the purpose of securing the health, safety and welfare of persons at work, and
- (j) the purpose of protecting persons other than persons at work against risk to health or safety arising out of or in connection with the actions of persons at work.

(3) The duty to confirm or deny does not arise if, or to the extent that, compliance with section 1(1)(a) would, or would be likely to, prejudice any of the matters mentioned in subsection (1).

[1350]

NOTES

Commencement: 1 January 2005.

32 Court records, etc

(1) Information held by a public authority is exempt information if it is held only by virtue of being contained in—

- (a) any document filed with, or otherwise placed in the custody of, a court for the purposes of proceedings in a particular cause or matter,
- (b) any document served upon, or by, a public authority for the purposes of proceedings in a particular cause or matter, or
- (c) any document created by—
  - (i) a court, or

(ii) a member of the administrative staff of a court,

for the purposes of proceedings in a particular cause or matter.

(2) Information held by a public authority is exempt information if it is held only by virtue of being contained in—

(a) any document placed in the custody of a person conducting an inquiry or arbitration, for the purposes of the inquiry or arbitration, or

(b) any document created by a person conducting an inquiry or arbitration, for the purposes of the inquiry or arbitration.

(3) The duty to confirm or deny does not arise in relation to information which is (or if it were held by the public authority would be) exempt information by virtue of this section.

(4) In this section—

(a) "court" includes any tribunal or body exercising the judicial power of the State,

(b) "proceedings in a particular cause or matter" includes any inquest or post-mortem examination,

(c) "inquiry" means any inquiry or hearing held under any provision contained in, or made under, an enactment, and

(d) except in relation to Scotland, "arbitration" means any arbitration to which Part I of the Arbitration Act 1996 applies.

[1351]

NOTES

Commencement: 1 January 2005.

Disapplication: sub-s (2) is disapplied in relation to information contained in documents that, in pursuance of rules under the Inquiries Act 2005, s 41(1)(b), have been passed to and are held by a public authority, by the Inquiries Act 2005, s 18(3).

33 Audit functions

(1) This section applies to any public authority which has functions in relation to—

(a) the audit of the accounts of other public authorities, or

(b) the examination of the economy, efficiency and effectiveness with which other public authorities use their resources in discharging their functions.

(2) Information held by a public authority to which this section applies is exempt information if its disclosure would, or would be likely to, prejudice the exercise of any of the authority's functions in relation to any of the matters referred to in subsection (1).

(3) The duty to confirm or deny does not arise in relation to a public authority to which this section applies if, or to the extent that, compliance with section 1(1)(a) would, or would be likely to, prejudice the exercise of any of the authority's functions in relation to any of the matters referred to in subsection (1).

[1352]

NOTES

Commencement: 1 January 2005.

34 Parliamentary privilege

(1) Information is exempt information if exemption from section 1(1)(b) is required for the purpose of avoiding an infringement of the privileges of either House of Parliament.

(2) The duty to confirm or deny does not apply if, or to the extent that, exemption from section 1(1)(a) is required for the purpose of avoiding an infringement of the privileges of either House of Parliament.

(3) A certificate signed by the appropriate authority certifying that exemption from section 1(1)(b), or from section 1(1)(a) and (b), is, or at any time was, required for the purpose of avoiding an infringement of the privileges of either House of Parliament shall be conclusive evidence of that fact.

(4) In subsection (3) "the appropriate authority" means—

(a) in relation to the House of Commons, the Speaker of that House, and

(b) in relation to the House of Lords, the Clerk of the Parliaments.

[1353]

NOTES

Commencement: 1 January 2005.

35 Formulation of government policy, etc

(1) Information held by a government department or by the National Assembly for Wales is exempt information if it relates to—

(a) the formulation or development of government policy,

(b) Ministerial communications,

(c) the provision of advice by any of the Law Officers or any request for the provision of such advice, or

(d) the operation of any Ministerial private office.

(2) Once a decision as to government policy has been taken, any statistical information used to provide an informed background to the taking of the decision is not to be regarded—

(a) for the purposes of subsection (1)(a), as relating to the formulation or development of government policy, or

(b) for the purposes of subsection (1)(b), as relating to Ministerial communications.

(3) The duty to confirm or deny does not arise in relation to information which is (or if it were held by the public authority would be) exempt information by virtue of subsection (1).

(4) In making any determination required by section 2(1)(b) or (2)(b) in relation to information which is exempt information by virtue of subsection (1)(a), regard shall be had to the particular public interest in the disclosure of factual information which has been used, or is intended to be used, to provide an informed background to decision-taking.

(5) In this section—

"government policy" includes the policy of the Executive Committee of the Northern Ireland Assembly and the policy of the National Assembly for Wales;

"the Law Officers" means the Attorney General, the Solicitor General, the Advocate General for Scotland, the Lord Advocate, the Solicitor General for Scotland and the Attorney General for Northern Ireland;

"Ministerial communications" means any communications—

(a) between Ministers of the Crown,

(b) between Northern Ireland Ministers, including Northern Ireland junior Ministers, or

(c) between Assembly Secretaries, including the Assembly First Secretary,

and includes, in particular, proceedings of the Cabinet or of any committee of the Cabinet, proceedings of the Executive Committee of the Northern Ireland Assembly, and proceedings of the executive committee of the National Assembly for Wales;

"Ministerial private office" means any part of a government department which provides personal administrative support to a Minister of the Crown, to a Northern Ireland Minister or a Northern Ireland junior Minister or any part of the administration of the National Assembly for Wales providing personal administrative support to the Assembly First Secretary or an Assembly Secretary;

"Northern Ireland junior Minister" means a member of the Northern Ireland Assembly appointed as a junior Minister under section 19 of the Northern Ireland Act 1998.

[1354]

NOTES

Commencement: 1 January 2005.

36 Prejudice to effective conduct of public affairs

(1) This section applies to—

(a) information which is held by a government department or by the National Assembly for Wales and is not exempt information by virtue of section 35, and

(b) information which is held by any other public authority.

(2) Information to which this section applies is exempt information if, in the reasonable opinion of a qualified person, disclosure of the information under this Act—

(a) would, or would be likely to, prejudice—

(i) the maintenance of the convention of the collective responsibility of Ministers of the Crown, or

(ii) the work of the Executive Committee of the Northern Ireland Assembly, or
(iii) the work of the executive committee of the National Assembly for Wales,

(b) would, or would be likely to, inhibit—
(i) the free and frank provision of advice, or
(ii) the free and frank exchange of views for the purposes of deliberation, or

(c) would otherwise prejudice, or would be likely otherwise to prejudice, the effective conduct of public affairs.

(3) The duty to confirm or deny does not arise in relation to information to which this section applies (or would apply if held by the public authority) if, or to the extent that, in the reasonable opinion of a qualified person, compliance with section 1(1)(a) would, or would be likely to, have any of the effects mentioned in subsection (2).

(4) In relation to statistical information, subsections (2) and (3) shall have effect with the omission of the words "in the reasonable opinion of a qualified person".

(5) In subsections (2) and (3) "qualified person"—

(a) in relation to information held by a government department in the charge of a Minister of the Crown, means any Minister of the Crown,

(b) in relation to information held by a Northern Ireland department, means the Northern Ireland Minister in charge of the department,

(c) in relation to information held by any other government department, means the commissioners or other person in charge of that department,

(d) in relation to information held by the House of Commons, means the Speaker of that House,

(e) in relation to information held by the House of Lords, means the Clerk of the Parliaments,

(f) in relation to information held by the Northern Ireland Assembly, means the Presiding Officer,

(g) in relation to information held by the National Assembly for Wales, means the Assembly First Secretary,

(h) in relation to information held by any Welsh public authority other than the Auditor General for Wales, means—
(i) the public authority, or
(ii) any officer or employee of the authority authorised by the Assembly First Secretary,

(i) in relation to information held by the National Audit Office, means the Comptroller and Auditor General,

(j) in relation to information held by the Northern Ireland Audit Office, means the Comptroller and Auditor General for Northern Ireland,

(k) in relation to information held by the Auditor General for Wales, means the Auditor General for Wales,

(l) in relation to information held by any Northern Ireland public authority other than the Northern Ireland Audit Office, means—
(i) the public authority, or
(ii) any officer or employee of the authority authorised by the First Minister and deputy First Minister in Northern Ireland acting jointly,

(m) in relation to information held by the Greater London Authority, means the Mayor of London,

(n) in relation to information held by a functional body within the meaning of the Greater London Authority Act 1999, means the chairman of that functional body, and

(o) in relation to information held by any public authority not falling within any of paragraphs (a) to (n), means—
(i) a Minister of the Crown,
(ii) the public authority, if authorised for the purposes of this section by a Minister of the Crown, or
(iii) any officer or employee of the public authority who is authorised for the purposes of this section by a Minister of the Crown.

(6) Any authorisation for the purposes of this section—

(a) may relate to a specified person or to persons falling within a specified class,

(b) may be general or limited to particular classes of case, and

(c) may be granted subject to conditions.

(7) A certificate signed by the qualified person referred to in subsection (5)(d) or (e) above certifying that in his reasonable opinion—

(a) disclosure of information held by either House of Parliament, or
(b) compliance with section 1(1)(a) by either House,

would, or would be likely to, have any of the effects mentioned in subsection (2) shall be conclusive evidence of that fact.

[1355]

NOTES

Commencement: 1 January 2005.

37 Communications with Her Majesty, etc and honours

(1) Information is exempt information if it relates to—
(a) communications with Her Majesty, with other members of the Royal Family or with the Royal Household, or
(b) the conferring by the Crown of any honour or dignity.

(2) The duty to confirm or deny does not arise in relation to information which is (or if it were held by the public authority would be) exempt information by virtue of subsection (1).

[1356]

NOTES

Commencement: 1 January 2005.

38 Health and safety

(1) Information is exempt information if its disclosure under this Act would, or would be likely to—
(a) endanger the physical or mental health of any individual, or
(b) endanger the safety of any individual.

(2) The duty to confirm or deny does not arise if, or to the extent that, compliance with section 1(1)(a) would, or would be likely to, have either of the effects mentioned in subsection (1).

[1357]

NOTES

Commencement: 1 January 2005.

39 Environmental information

(1) Information is exempt information if the public authority holding it—
(a) is obliged by [environmental information regulations] to make the information available to the public in accordance with the regulations, or
(b) would be so obliged but for any exemption contained in the regulations.

[(1A) In subsection (1) "environmental information regulations" means—
(a) regulations made under section 74, or
(b) regulations made under section 2(2) of the European Communities Act 1972 for the purpose of implementing any Community obligation relating to public access to, and the dissemination of, information on the environment.]

(2) The duty to confirm or deny does not arise in relation to information which is (or if it were held by the public authority would be) exempt information by virtue of subsection (1).

(3) Subsection (1)(a) does not limit the generality of section 21(1).

[1358]

NOTES

Commencement: 1 January 2005.

Sub-s (1): words in square brackets substituted by the Environmental Information Regulations 2004, SI 2004/3391, reg 20(1), (2).

Sub-s (1A): inserted by SI 2004/3391, reg 20(1), (3).

40 Personal information

(1) Any information to which a request for information relates is exempt information if it constitutes personal data of which the applicant is the data subject.

(2) Any information to which a request for information relates is also exempt information if—

(a) it constitutes personal data which do not fall within subsection (1), and
(b) either the first or the second condition below is satisfied.

(3) The first condition is—

(a) in a case where the information falls within any of paragraphs (a) to (d) of the definition of "data" in section 1(1) of the Data Protection Act 1998, that the disclosure of the information to a member of the public otherwise than under this Act would contravene—
   (i) any of the data protection principles, or
   (ii) section 10 of that Act (right to prevent processing likely to cause damage or distress), and
(b) in any other case, that the disclosure of the information to a member of the public otherwise than under this Act would contravene any of the data protection principles if the exemptions in section 33A(1) of the Data Protection Act 1998 (which relate to manual data held by public authorities) were disregarded.

(4) The second condition is that by virtue of any provision of Part IV of the Data Protection Act 1998 the information is exempt from section 7(1)(c) of that Act (data subject's right of access to personal data).

(5) The duty to confirm or deny—

(a) does not arise in relation to information which is (or if it were held by the public authority would be) exempt information by virtue of subsection (1), and
(b) does not arise in relation to other information if or to the extent that either—
   (i) the giving to a member of the public of the confirmation or denial that would have to be given to comply with section 1(1)(a) would (apart from this Act) contravene any of the data protection principles or section 10 of the Data Protection Act 1998 or would do so if the exemptions in section 33A(1) of that Act were disregarded, or
   (ii) by virtue of any provision of Part IV of the Data Protection Act 1998 the information is exempt from section 7(1)(a) of that Act (data subject's right to be informed whether personal data being processed).

(6) In determining for the purposes of this section whether anything done before 24th October 2007 would contravene any of the data protection principles, the exemptions in Part III of Schedule 8 to the Data Protection Act 1998 shall be disregarded.

(7) In this section—

"the data protection principles" means the principles set out in Part I of Schedule 1 to the Data Protection Act 1998, as read subject to Part II of that Schedule and section 27(1) of that Act;
"data subject" has the same meaning as in section 1(1) of that Act;
"personal data" has the same meaning as in section 1(1) of that Act.

[1359]

NOTES

Commencement: 1 January 2005.

41 Information provided in confidence

(1) Information is exempt information if—

(a) it was obtained by the public authority from any other person (including another public authority), and
(b) the disclosure of the information to the public (otherwise than under this Act) by the public authority holding it would constitute a breach of confidence actionable by that or any other person.

(2) The duty to confirm or deny does not arise if, or to the extent that, the confirmation or denial that would have to be given to comply with section 1(1)(a) would (apart from this Act) constitute an actionable breach of confidence.

[1360]

NOTES

Commencement: 1 January 2005.

42 Legal professional privilege

(1) Information in respect of which a claim to legal professional privilege or, in Scotland, to confidentiality of communications could be maintained in legal proceedings is exempt information.

(2) The duty to confirm or deny does not arise if, or to the extent that, compliance with section 1(1)(a) would involve the disclosure of any information (whether or not already recorded) in respect of which such a claim could be maintained in legal proceedings.

[1361]

NOTES

Commencement: 1 January 2005.

43 Commercial interests

(1) Information is exempt information if it constitutes a trade secret.

(2) Information is exempt information if its disclosure under this Act would, or would be likely to, prejudice the commercial interests of any person (including the public authority holding it).

(3) The duty to confirm or deny does not arise if, or to the extent that, compliance with section 1(1)(a) would, or would be likely to, prejudice the interests mentioned in subsection (2).

[1362]

NOTES

Commencement: 1 January 2005.

44 Prohibitions on disclosure

(1) Information is exempt information if its disclosure (otherwise than under this Act) by the public authority holding it—

(a) is prohibited by or under any enactment,
(b) is incompatible with any Community obligation, or
(c) would constitute or be punishable as a contempt of court.

(2) The duty to confirm or deny does not arise if the confirmation or denial that would have to be given to comply with section 1(1)(a) would (apart from this Act) fall within any of paragraphs (a) to (c) of subsection (1).

[1363]

NOTES

Commencement: 1 January 2005.

PART III
GENERAL FUNCTIONS OF … LORD CHANCELLOR AND INFORMATION COMMISSIONER

45 Issue of code of practice …

(1) The [Secretary of State] shall issue, and may from time to time revise, a code of practice providing guidance to public authorities as to the practice which it would, in his opinion, be desirable for them to follow in connection with the discharge of the authorities' functions under Part I.

(2) The code of practice must, in particular, include provision relating to—

(a) the provision of advice and assistance by public authorities to persons who propose to make, or have made, requests for information to them,
(b) the transfer of requests by one public authority to another public authority by which the information requested is or may be held,
(c) consultation with persons to whom the information requested relates or persons whose interests are likely to be affected by the disclosure of information,

(d) the inclusion in contracts entered into by public authorities of terms relating to the disclosure of information, and

(e) the provision by public authorities of procedures for dealing with complaints about the handling by them of requests for information.

(3) The code may make different provision for different public authorities.

(4) Before issuing or revising any code under this section, the [Secretary of State] shall consult the Commissioner.

(5) The [Secretary of State] shall lay before each House of Parliament any code or revised code made under this section.

[1364]

NOTES

Commencement: 30 November 2000 (for the purpose of exercising the power to make codes of practice); 30 November 2002 (otherwise).

Part heading, section heading: words omitted repealed by the Transfer of Functions (Miscellaneous) Order 2001, SI 2001/3500, art 8, Sch 2, Pt I, para 8(1)(h).

Sub-ss (1), (4), (5): words in square brackets substituted by the Secretary of State for Constitutional Affairs Order 2003, SI 2003/1887, art 9, Sch 2, para 12(1)(a).

46 Issue of code of practice by Lord Chancellor

(1) The Lord Chancellor shall issue, and may from time to time revise, a code of practice providing guidance to relevant authorities as to the practice which it would, in his opinion, be desirable for them to follow in connection with the keeping, management and destruction of their records.

(2) For the purpose of facilitating the performance by the Public Record Office, the Public Record Office of Northern Ireland and other public authorities of their functions under this Act in relation to records which are public records for the purposes of the Public Records Act 1958 or the Public Records Act (Northern Ireland) 1923, the code may also include guidance as to—

(a) the practice to be adopted in relation to the transfer of records under section 3(4) of the Public Records Act 1958 or section 3 of the Public Records Act (Northern Ireland) 1923, and

(b) the practice of reviewing records before they are transferred under those provisions.

(3) In exercising his functions under this section, the Lord Chancellor shall have regard to the public interest in allowing public access to information held by relevant authorities.

(4) The code may make different provision for different relevant authorities.

(5) Before issuing or revising any code under this section the Lord Chancellor shall consult—

[(a) the Secretary of State,]

(b) the Commissioner, and

(c) in relation to Northern Ireland, the appropriate Northern Ireland Minister.

(6) The Lord Chancellor shall lay before each House of Parliament any code or revised code made under this section.

(7) In this section "relevant authority" means—

(a) any public authority, and

(b) any office or body which is not a public authority but whose administrative and departmental records are public records for the purposes of the Public Records Act 1958 or the Public Records Act (Northern Ireland) 1923.

[1365]

NOTES

Commencement: 30 November 2000 (for the purpose of exercising the power to make codes of practice); 30 November 2002 (otherwise).

Sub-s (5): original para (a) repealed by the Transfer of Functions (Miscellaneous) Order 2001, SI 2001/3500, art 8, Sch 2, Pt I, para 8(2); new para (a) inserted by the Secretary of State for Constitutional Affairs Order 2003, SI 2003/1887, art 9, Sch 2, para 12(2).

47 General functions of Commissioner

(1) It shall be the duty of the Commissioner to promote the following of good practice by public authorities and, in particular, so to perform his functions under this Act as to promote the observance by public authorities of—

(a) the requirements of this Act, and

(b) the provisions of the codes of practice under sections 45 and 46.

(2) The Commissioner shall arrange for the dissemination in such form and manner as he considers appropriate of such information as it may appear to him expedient to give to the public—

(a) about the operation of this Act,

(b) about good practice, and

(c) about other matters within the scope of his functions under this Act,

and may give advice to any person as to any of those matters.

(3) The Commissioner may, with the consent of any public authority, assess whether that authority is following good practice.

(4) The Commissioner may charge such sums as he may with the consent of the [Secretary of State] determine for any services provided by the Commissioner under this section.

(5) The Commissioner shall from time to time as he considers appropriate—

(a) consult the Keeper of Public Records about the promotion by the Commissioner of the observance by public authorities of the provisions of the code of practice under section 46 in relation to records which are public records for the purposes of the Public Records Act 1958, and

(b) consult the Deputy Keeper of the Records of Northern Ireland about the promotion by the Commissioner of the observance by public authorities of those provisions in relation to records which are public records for the purposes of the Public Records Act (Northern Ireland) 1923.

(6) In this section "good practice", in relation to a public authority, means such practice in the discharge of its functions under this Act as appears to the Commissioner to be desirable, and includes (but is not limited to) compliance with the requirements of this Act and the provisions of the codes of practice under sections 45 and 46.

[1366]

NOTES

Commencement: 30 November 2000 (sub-ss (2)–(6)); 30 November 2002 (otherwise).

Sub-s (4): words in square brackets substituted by the Secretary of State for Constitutional Affairs Order 2003, SI 2003/1887, art 9, Sch 2, para 12(1)(a).

48 Recommendations as to good practice

(1) If it appears to the Commissioner that the practice of a public authority in relation to the exercise of its functions under this Act does not conform with that proposed in the codes of practice under sections 45 and 46, he may give to the authority a recommendation (in this section referred to as a "practice recommendation") specifying the steps which ought in his opinion to be taken for promoting such conformity.

(2) A practice recommendation must be given in writing and must refer to the particular provisions of the code of practice with which, in the Commissioner's opinion, the public authority's practice does not conform.

(3) Before giving to a public authority other than the Public Record Office a practice recommendation which relates to conformity with the code of practice under section 46 in respect of records which are public records for the purposes of the Public Records Act 1958, the Commissioner shall consult the Keeper of Public Records.

(4) Before giving to a public authority other than the Public Record Office of Northern Ireland a practice recommendation which relates to conformity with the code of practice under section 46 in respect of records which are public records for the purposes of the Public Records Act (Northern Ireland) 1923, the Commissioner shall consult the Deputy Keeper of the Records of Northern Ireland.

[1367]

NOTES

Commencement: 30 November 2002 (sub-ss (1), (2), in relation to the issue of practice recommendations relating to the conformity with the code of practice under s 45 hereof of the practice of public authorities in relation to the exercise of their functions under the publication scheme provisions); 1 January 2005 (otherwise).

49 Reports to be laid before Parliament

(1) The Commissioner shall lay annually before each House of Parliament a general report on the exercise of his functions under this Act.

(2) The Commissioner may from time to time lay before each House of Parliament such other reports with respect to those functions as he thinks fit.

[1368]

PART IV
ENFORCEMENT

50 Application for decision by Commissioner

(1) Any person (in this section referred to as "the complainant") may apply to the Commissioner for a decision whether, in any specified respect, a request for information made by the complainant to a public authority has been dealt with in accordance with the requirements of Part I.

(2) On receiving an application under this section, the Commissioner shall make a decision unless it appears to him—

(a) that the complainant has not exhausted any complaints procedure which is provided by the public authority in conformity with the code of practice under section 45,

(b) that there has been undue delay in making the application,

(c) that the application is frivolous or vexatious, or

(d) that the application has been withdrawn or abandoned.

(3) Where the Commissioner has received an application under this section, he shall either—

(a) notify the complainant that he has not made any decision under this section as a result of the application and of his grounds for not doing so, or

(b) serve notice of his decision (in this Act referred to as a "decision notice") on the complainant and the public authority.

(4) Where the Commissioner decides that a public authority—

(a) has failed to communicate information, or to provide confirmation or denial, in a case where it is required to do so by section 1(1), or

(b) has failed to comply with any of the requirements of sections 11 and 17,

the decision notice must specify the steps which must be taken by the authority for complying with that requirement and the period within which they must be taken.

(5) A decision notice must contain particulars of the right of appeal conferred by section 57.

(6) Where a decision notice requires steps to be taken by the public authority within a specified period, the time specified in the notice must not expire before the end of the period within which an appeal can be brought against the notice and, if such an appeal is brought, no step which is affected by the appeal need be taken pending the determination or withdrawal of the appeal.

(7) This section has effect subject to section 53.

[1369]

NOTES

Commencement: 1 January 2005.

51 Information notices

(1) If the Commissioner—

(a) has received an application under section 50, or

(b) reasonably requires any information—

(i) for the purpose of determining whether a public authority has complied or is complying with any of the requirements of Part I, or

(ii) for the purpose of determining whether the practice of a public authority in relation to the exercise of its functions under this Act conforms with that proposed in the codes of practice under sections 45 and 46,

he may serve the authority with a notice (in this Act referred to as "an information notice") requiring it, within such time as is specified in the notice, to furnish the Commissioner, in such form as may be so specified, with such information relating to the application, to compliance with Part I or to conformity with the code of practice as is so specified.

(2) An information notice must contain—

(a) in a case falling within subsection (1)(a), a statement that the Commissioner has received an application under section 50, or

(b) in a case falling within subsection (1)(b), a statement—

(i) that the Commissioner regards the specified information as relevant for either of the purposes referred to in subsection (1)(b), and

(ii) of his reasons for regarding that information as relevant for that purpose.

(3) An information notice must also contain particulars of the right of appeal conferred by section 57.

(4) The time specified in an information notice must not expire before the end of the period within which an appeal can be brought against the notice and, if such an appeal is brought, the information need not be furnished pending the determination or withdrawal of the appeal.

(5) An authority shall not be required by virtue of this section to furnish the Commissioner with any information in respect of—

(a) any communication between a professional legal adviser and his client in connection with the giving of legal advice to the client with respect to his obligations, liabilities or rights under this Act, or

(b) any communication between a professional legal adviser and his client, or between such an adviser or his client and any other person, made in connection with or in contemplation of proceedings under or arising out of this Act (including proceedings before the Tribunal) and for the purposes of such proceedings.

(6) In subsection (5) references to the client of a professional legal adviser include references to any person representing such a client.

(7) The Commissioner may cancel an information notice by written notice to the authority on which it was served.

(8) In this section "information" includes unrecorded information.

[1370]

NOTES

Commencement: 30 November 2002 (in relation to the issue and enforcement of information notices relating to the conformity with the code of practice under s 45 hereof of the practice of public authorities in relation to the exercise of their functions under the publication scheme provisions); 1 January 2005 (otherwise).

52 Enforcement notices

(1) If the Commissioner is satisfied that a public authority has failed to comply with any of the requirements of Part I, the Commissioner may serve the authority with a notice (in this Act referred to as "an enforcement notice") requiring the authority to take, within such time as may be specified in the notice, such steps as may be so specified for complying with those requirements.

(2) An enforcement notice must contain—

(a) a statement of the requirement or requirements of Part I with which the Commissioner is satisfied that the public authority has failed to comply and his reasons for reaching that conclusion, and

(b) particulars of the right of appeal conferred by section 57.

(3) An enforcement notice must not require any of the provisions of the notice to be complied with before the end of the period within which an appeal can be brought against the notice and, if such an appeal is brought, the notice need not be complied with pending the determination or withdrawal of the appeal.

(4) The Commissioner may cancel an enforcement notice by written notice to the authority on which it was served.

(5) This section has effect subject to section 53.

[1371]

NOTES

Commencement: 30 November 2002 (in relation to the enforcement of the requirements on public authorities under the publication scheme provisions); 1 January 2005 (otherwise).

53 Exception from duty to comply with decision notice or enforcement notice

(1) This section applies to a decision notice or enforcement notice which—

(a) is served on—

(i) a government department,

(ii) the National Assembly for Wales, or

(iii) any public authority designated for the purposes of this section by an order made by the [Secretary of State], and

(b) relates to a failure, in respect of one or more requests for information—

(i) to comply with section 1(1)(a) in respect of information which falls within any provision of Part II stating that the duty to confirm or deny does not arise, or

(ii) to comply with section 1(1)(b) in respect of exempt information.

(2) A decision notice or enforcement notice to which this section applies shall cease to have effect if, not later than the twentieth working day following the effective date, the accountable person in relation to that authority gives the Commissioner a certificate signed by him stating that he has on reasonable grounds formed the opinion that, in respect of the request or requests concerned, there was no failure falling within subsection (1)(b).

(3) Where the accountable person gives a certificate to the Commissioner under subsection (2) he shall as soon as practicable thereafter lay a copy of the certificate before—

(a) each House of Parliament,

(b) the Northern Ireland Assembly, in any case where the certificate relates to a decision notice or enforcement notice which has been served on a Northern Ireland department or any Northern Ireland public authority, or

(c) the National Assembly for Wales, in any case where the certificate relates to a decision notice or enforcement notice which has been served on the National Assembly for Wales or any Welsh public authority.

(4) In subsection (2) "the effective date", in relation to a decision notice or enforcement notice, means—

(a) the day on which the notice was given to the public authority, or

(b) where an appeal under section 57 is brought, the day on which that appeal (or any further appeal arising out of it) is determined or withdrawn.

(5) Before making an order under subsection (1)(a)(iii), the [Secretary of State] shall—

(a) if the order relates to a Welsh public authority, consult the National Assembly for Wales,

(b) if the order relates to the Northern Ireland Assembly, consult the Presiding Officer of that Assembly, and

(c) if the order relates to a Northern Ireland public authority, consult the First Minister and deputy First Minister in Northern Ireland.

(6) Where the accountable person gives a certificate to the Commissioner under subsection (2) in relation to a decision notice, the accountable person shall, on doing so or as soon as reasonably practicable after doing so, inform the person who is the complainant for the purposes of section 50 of the reasons for his opinion.

(7) The accountable person is not obliged to provide information under subsection (6) if, or to the extent that, compliance with that subsection would involve the disclosure of exempt information.

(8) In this section "the accountable person"—
- (a) in relation to a Northern Ireland department or any Northern Ireland public authority, means the First Minister and deputy First Minister in Northern Ireland acting jointly,
- (b) in relation to the National Assembly for Wales or any Welsh public authority, means the Assembly First Secretary, and
- (c) in relation to any other public authority, means—
  - (i) a Minister of the Crown who is a member of the Cabinet, or
  - (ii) the Attorney General, the Advocate General for Scotland or the Attorney General for Northern Ireland.

(9) In this section "working day" has the same meaning as in section 10.

[1372]

NOTES

Commencement: 30 November 2000 (so far as confers powers to make any order, regulations or code of practice): 1 January 2005 (otherwise).

Sub-ss (1), (5): words in square brackets substituted by the Secretary of State for Constitutional Affairs Order 2003, SI 2003/1887, art 9, Sch 2, para 12(1)(a).

54 Failure to comply with notice

(1) If a public authority has failed to comply with—
- (a) so much of a decision notice as requires steps to be taken,
- (b) an information notice, or
- (c) an enforcement notice,

the Commissioner may certify in writing to the court that the public authority has failed to comply with that notice.

(2) For the purposes of this section, a public authority which, in purported compliance with an information notice—
- (a) makes a statement which it knows to be false in a material respect, or
- (b) recklessly makes a statement which is false in a material respect,

is to be taken to have failed to comply with the notice.

(3) Where a failure to comply is certified under subsection (1), the court may inquire into the matter and, after hearing any witness who may be produced against or on behalf of the public authority, and after hearing any statement that may be offered in defence, deal with the authority as if it had committed a contempt of court.

(4) In this section "the court" means the High Court or, in Scotland, the Court of Session.

[1373]

NOTES

Commencement: 30 November 2002 (in so far as it relates to the enforcement of the requirements on public authorities under the publication scheme provisions and so far as relates to: (i) the issue of practice recommendations, and (ii) the issue and enforcement of information notices, relating to the conformity with the code of practice under s 45 of the practice of public authorities in relation to the exercise of their functions under the publication scheme provisions); 1 January 2005 (otherwise).

55 Powers of entry and inspection

Schedule 3 (powers of entry and inspection) has effect.

[1374]

NOTES

Commencement: 30 November 2002 (certain purposes); 1 January 2005 (otherwise).

56 No action against public authority

(1) This Act does not confer any right of action in civil proceedings in respect of any failure to comply with any duty imposed by or under this Act.

(2) Subsection (1) does not affect the powers of the Commissioner under section 54.

[1375]

NOTES

Commencement: 30 November 2002.

PART V
APPEALS

57 Appeal against notices served under Part IV

(1) Where a decision notice has been served, the complainant or the public authority may appeal to the Tribunal against the notice.

(2) A public authority on which an information notice or an enforcement notice has been served by the Commissioner may appeal to the Tribunal against the notice.

(3) In relation to a decision notice or enforcement notice which relates—

(a) to information to which section 66 applies, and

(b) to a matter which by virtue of subsection (3) or (4) of that section falls to be determined by the responsible authority instead of the appropriate records authority,

subsections (1) and (2) shall have effect as if the reference to the public authority were a reference to the public authority or the responsible authority.

[1376]

NOTES

Commencement: 30 November 2002 (sub-s (2)); 1 January 2005 (otherwise).

58 Determination of appeals

(1) If on an appeal under section 57 the Tribunal considers—

(a) that the notice against which the appeal is brought is not in accordance with the law, or

(b) to the extent that the notice involved an exercise of discretion by the Commissioner, that he ought to have exercised his discretion differently,

the Tribunal shall allow the appeal or substitute such other notice as could have been served by the Commissioner; and in any other case the Tribunal shall dismiss the appeal.

(2) On such an appeal, the Tribunal may review any finding of fact on which the notice in question was based.

[1377]

NOTES

Commencement: 30 November 2002.

59 Appeals from decision of Tribunal

Any party to an appeal to the Tribunal under section 57 may appeal from the decision of the Tribunal on a point of law to the appropriate court; and that court shall be—

(a) the High Court of Justice in England if the address of the public authority is in England or Wales,

(b) the Court of Session if that address is in Scotland, and

(c) the High Court of Justice in Northern Ireland if that address is in Northern Ireland.

[1378]

NOTES

Commencement: 30 November 2002.

60 Appeals against national security certificate

(1) Where a certificate under section 23(2) or 24(3) has been issued—

(a) the Commissioner, or

(b) any applicant whose request for information is affected by the issue of the certificate, may appeal to the Tribunal against the certificate.

(2) If on an appeal under subsection (1) relating to a certificate under section 23(2), the Tribunal finds that the information referred to in the certificate was not exempt information by virtue of section 23(1), the Tribunal may allow the appeal and quash the certificate.

(3) If on an appeal under subsection (1) relating to a certificate under section 24(3), the Tribunal finds that, applying the principles applied by the court on an application for judicial review, the Minister did not have reasonable grounds for issuing the certificate, the Tribunal may allow the appeal and quash the certificate.

(4) Where in any proceedings under this Act it is claimed by a public authority that a certificate under section 24(3) which identifies the information to which it applies by means of a general description applies to particular information, any other party to the proceedings may appeal to the Tribunal on the ground that the certificate does not apply to the information in question and, subject to any determination under subsection (5), the certificate shall be conclusively presumed so to apply.

(5) On any appeal under subsection (4), the Tribunal may determine that the certificate does not so apply.

[1379]

NOTES

Commencement: 1 January 2005.

61 Appeal proceedings

(1) Schedule 4 (which contains amendments of Schedule 6 to the Data Protection Act 1998 relating to appeal proceedings) has effect.

(2) Accordingly, the provisions of Schedule 6 to the Data Protection Act 1998 have effect (so far as applicable) in relation to appeals under this Part.

[1380]

NOTES

Commencement: 14 May 2001 (sub-s (1), certain purposes); 30 November 2002 (sub-s (1) certain purposes, sub-s (2)); 1 January 2005 (otherwise).

PART VI
HISTORICAL RECORDS AND RECORDS IN PUBLIC RECORD OFFICE OR PUBLIC RECORD OFFICE OF NORTHERN IRELAND

62 Interpretation of Part VI

(1) For the purposes of this Part, a record becomes a "historical record" at the end of the period of thirty years beginning with the year following that in which it was created.

(2) Where records created at different dates are for administrative purposes kept together in one file or other assembly, all the records in that file or other assembly are to be treated for the purposes of this Part as having been created when the latest of those records was created.

(3) In this Part "year" means a calendar year.

[1381]

NOTES

Commencement: 1 January 2005.

63 Removal of exemptions: historical records generally

(1) Information contained in a historical record cannot be exempt information by virtue of section 28, 30(1), 32, 33, 35, 36, 37(1)(a), 42 or 43.

(2) Compliance with section 1(1)(a) in relation to a historical record is not to be taken to be capable of having any of the effects referred to in section 28(3), 33(3), 36(3), 42(2) or 43(3).

(3) Information cannot be exempt information by virtue of section 37(1)(b) after the end of the period of sixty years beginning with the year following that in which the record containing the information was created.

(4) Information cannot be exempt information by virtue of section 31 after the end of the period of one hundred years beginning with the year following that in which the record containing the information was created.

(5) Compliance with section 1(1)(a) in relation to any record is not to be taken, at any time after the end of the period of one hundred years beginning with the year following that in which the record was created, to be capable of prejudicing any of the matters referred to in section 31(1).

[1382]

NOTES

Commencement: 1 January 2005.

64 Removal of exemptions: historical records in public record offices

(1) Information contained in a historical record in the Public Record Office or the Public Record Office of Northern Ireland cannot be exempt information by virtue of section 21 or 22.

(2) In relation to any information falling within section 23(1) which is contained in a historical record in the Public Record Office or the Public Record Office of Northern Ireland, section 2(3) shall have effect with the omission of the reference to section 23.

[1383]

NOTES

Commencement: 1 January 2005.

65 Decisions as to refusal of discretionary disclosure of historical records

(1) Before refusing a request for information relating to information which is contained in a historical record and is exempt information only by virtue of a provision not specified in section 2(3), a public authority shall—

(a) if the historical record is a public record within the meaning of the Public Records Act 1958, consult the Lord Chancellor, or

(b) if the historical record is a public record to which the Public Records Act (Northern Ireland) 1923 applies, consult the appropriate Northern Ireland Minister.

(2) This section does not apply to information to which section 66 applies.

[1384]

NOTES

Commencement: 1 January 2005.

66 Decisions relating to certain transferred public records

(1) This section applies to any information which is (or, if it existed, would be) contained in a transferred public record, other than information which the responsible authority has designated as open information for the purposes of this section.

(2) Before determining whether—

(a) information to which this section applies falls within any provision of Part II relating to the duty to confirm or deny, or

(b) information to which this section applies is exempt information,

the appropriate records authority shall consult the responsible authority.

(3) Where information to which this section applies falls within a provision of Part II relating to the duty to confirm or deny but does not fall within any of the provisions of that Part relating to that duty which are specified in subsection (3) of section 2, any question as to the application of subsection (1)(b) of that section is to be determined by the responsible authority instead of the appropriate records authority.

(4) Where any information to which this section applies is exempt information only by virtue of any provision of Part II not specified in subsection (3) of section 2, any question as

to the application of subsection (2)(b) of that section is to be determined by the responsible authority instead of the appropriate records authority.

(5) Before making by virtue of subsection (3) or (4) any determination that subsection (1)(b) or (2)(b) of section 2 applies, the responsible authority shall consult—

(a) where the transferred public record is a public record within the meaning of the Public Records Act 1958, the Lord Chancellor, and

(b) where the transferred public record is a public record to which the Public Records Act (Northern Ireland) 1923 applies, the appropriate Northern Ireland Minister.

(6) Where the responsible authority in relation to information to which this section applies is not (apart from this subsection) a public authority, it shall be treated as being a public authority for the purposes of Parts III, IV and V of this Act so far as relating to—

(a) the duty imposed by section 15(3), and

(b) the imposition of any requirement to furnish information relating to compliance with Part I in connection with the information to which this section applies.

[1385]

NOTES

Commencement: 1 January 2005.

67–73 (*S 67 introduces Sch 5 to this Act (amendments to the Public Records Act 1958 and the Public Records Act (Northern Ireland) 1923) outside the scope of this work; ss 68–72 amend the Data Protection Act 1998, ss 1, 7, 16, 34, 55, 56, 67, 71, Sch 8, Pt III, Sch 13 at* **[1108]**, **[1114]**, **[1124]**, **[1142]**, **[1163]**, **[1164]**, **[1174]**, **[1178]**, **[1195]**, **[1202]**, *and insert ss 9A, 33A of that Act at* **[1116A]**, **[1141A];** *s 73 introduces Sch 6 to this Act (further amendments to the Data Protection Act 1998).*)

PART VIII
MISCELLANEOUS AND SUPPLEMENTAL

74 Power to make provision relating to environmental information

(1) In this section "the Aarhus Convention" means the Convention on Access to Information, Public Participation in Decision-making and Access to Justice in Environmental Matters signed at Aarhus on 25th June 1998.

(2) For the purposes of this section "the information provisions" of the Aarhus Convention are Article 4, together with Articles 3 and 9 so far as relating to that Article.

(3) The Secretary of State may by regulations make such provision as he considers appropriate—

(a) for the purpose of implementing the information provisions of the Aarhus Convention or any amendment of those provisions made in accordance with Article 14 of the Convention, and

(b) for the purpose of dealing with matters arising out of or related to the implementation of those provisions or of any such amendment.

(4) Regulations under subsection (3) may in particular—

(a) enable charges to be made for making information available in accordance with the regulations,

(b) provide that any obligation imposed by the regulations in relation to the disclosure of information is to have effect notwithstanding any enactment or rule of law,

(c) make provision for the issue by the Secretary of State of a code of practice,

(d) provide for sections 47 and 48 to apply in relation to such a code with such modifications as may be specified,

(e) provide for any of the provisions of Parts IV and V to apply, with such modifications as may be specified in the regulations, in relation to compliance with any requirement of the regulations, and

(f) contain such transitional or consequential provision (including provision modifying any enactment) as the Secretary of State considers appropriate.

(5) This section has effect subject to section 80.

[1386]

75 Power to amend or repeal enactments prohibiting disclosure of information

(1) If, with respect to any enactment which prohibits the disclosure of information held by a public authority, it appears to the [Secretary of State] that by virtue of section 44(1)(a) the enactment is capable of preventing the disclosure of information under section 1, he may by order repeal or amend the enactment for the purpose of removing or relaxing the prohibition.

(2) In subsection (1)—

"enactment" means—

(a) any enactment contained in an Act passed before or in the same Session as this Act, or

(b) any enactment contained in Northern Ireland legislation or subordinate legislation passed or made before the passing of this Act;

"information" includes unrecorded information.

(3) An order under this section may do all or any of the following—

(a) make such modifications of enactments as, in the opinion of the [Secretary of State], are consequential upon, or incidental to, the amendment or repeal of the enactment containing the prohibition;

(b) contain such transitional provisions and savings as appear to the [Secretary of State] to be appropriate;

(c) make different provision for different cases.

[1387]

NOTES

Sub-ss (1), (3): words in square brackets substituted by the Secretary of State for Constitutional Affairs Order 2003, SI 2003/1887, art 9, Sch 2, para 12(1)(c).

Orders: the Freedom of Information (Removal and Relaxation of Statutory Prohibitions on Disclosure of Information) Order 2004, SI 2004/3363.

76 Disclosure of information between Commissioner and ombudsmen

(1) The Commissioner may disclose to a person specified in the first column of the Table below any information obtained by, or furnished to, the Commissioner under or for the purposes of this Act or the Data Protection Act 1998 if it appears to the Commissioner that the information relates to a matter which could be the subject of an investigation by that person under the enactment specified in relation to that person in the second column of that Table.

TABLE

Ombudsman	*Enactment*
The Parliamentary Commissioner for Administration	The Parliamentary Commissioner Act 1967 (c 13).
The Health Service Commissioner for England	The Health Service Commissioners Act 1993 (c 46).
…	…
…	…
A Local Commissioner as defined by section 23(3) of the Local Government Act 1974	Part III of the Local Government Act 1974 (c 7).
[The Scottish Public Services Ombudsman	The Scottish Public Services Ombudsman Act 2002 (asp 11)]
…	…
…	…
[The Public Services Ombudsman for Wales	Part 2 of the Public Services Ombudsman (Wales) Act 2005.]
[…	…]

Ombudsman	*Enactment*
The Northern Ireland Commissioner for Complaints	The Commissioner for Complaints (Northern Ireland) Order 1996 (SI 1996/1297 (NI 7)).
The Assembly Ombudsman for Northern Ireland	The Ombudsman (Northern Ireland) Order 1996 (SI 1996/1298 (NI 8)).
[The Commissioner for Older People in Wales	The Commissioner for Older People (Wales) Act 2006.]

(2) Schedule 7 (which contains amendments relating to information disclosed to ombudsmen under subsection (1) and to the disclosure of information by ombudsmen to the Commissioner) has effect.

[1388]

NOTES

Sub-s (1), Table: entry relating to "The Health Service Commissioner for Wales" (omitted) repealed and entry relating to "The Public Services Ombudsman for Wales" substituted for original entry "The Welsh Administration Ombudsman" by the Public Services Ombudsman (Wales) Act 2005, s 39, Sch 6, paras 70, 71, Sch 7, subject to transitional provisions in SI 2005/2800, arts 6, 7; entries relating to "The Health Service Commissioner for Scotland", "The Commissioner for Local Administration in Scotland" and "The Scottish Parliamentary Commissioner for Administration" (omitted) repealed and entry relating to "The Scottish Public Services Ombudsman" inserted by the Scottish Public Services Ombudsman Act 2002, s 25(1), Sch 6, para 23(1), (2); entry relating to "The Social Housing Ombudsman for Wales" (omitted) inserted by the Housing Act 2004, s 265(1), Sch 15, para 46, and repealed by the Public Services Ombudsman (Wales) Act 2005, s 39, Sch 6, paras 70, 71(a), Sch 7, subject to transitional provisions in SI 2005/2800, arts 6, 7; entry relating to "The Commissioner for Older People in Wales" inserted by the Commissioner for Older People (Wales) Act 2006, s 1(2), Sch 1, para 21(a).

[76A Disclosure between Commissioner and Scottish Information Commissioner

The Commissioner may disclose to the Scottish Information Commissioner any information obtained or furnished as mentioned in section 76(1) of this Act if it appears to the Commissioner that the information is of the same type that could be obtained by, or furnished to, the Scottish Information Commissioner under or for the purposes of the Freedom of Information (Scotland) Act 2002.]

[1389]

NOTES

Commencement: 1 January 2005.

Inserted by the Freedom of Information (Scotland) Act 2002 (Consequential Modifications) Order 2004, SI 2004/3089, art 3(1), (2).

77 Offence of altering etc records with intent to prevent disclosure

(1) Where—

(a) a request for information has been made to a public authority, and

(b) under section 1 of this Act or section 7 of the Data Protection Act 1998, the applicant would have been entitled (subject to payment of any fee) to communication of any information in accordance with that section,

any person to whom this subsection applies is guilty of an offence if he alters, defaces, blocks, erases, destroys or conceals any record held by the public authority, with the intention of preventing the disclosure by that authority of all, or any part, of the information to the communication of which the applicant would have been entitled.

(2) Subsection (1) applies to the public authority and to any person who is employed by, is an officer of, or is subject to the direction of, the public authority.

(3) A person guilty of an offence under this section is liable on summary conviction to a fine not exceeding level 5 on the standard scale.

(4) No proceedings for an offence under this section shall be instituted—

(a) in England or Wales, except by the Commissioner or by or with the consent of the Director of Public Prosecutions;

(b) in Northern Ireland, except by the Commissioner or by or with the consent of the Director of Public Prosecutions for Northern Ireland.

[1390]

NOTES

Commencement: 1 January 2005.

78 Saving for existing powers

Nothing in this Act is to be taken to limit the powers of a public authority to disclose information held by it.

[1391]

79 Defamation

Where any information communicated by a public authority to a person ("the applicant") under section 1 was supplied to the public authority by a third person, the publication to the applicant of any defamatory matter contained in the information shall be privileged unless the publication is shown to have been made with malice.

[1392]

80 Scotland

(1) No order may be made under section 4(1) or 5 in relation to any of the bodies specified in subsection (2); and the power conferred by section 74(3) does not include power to make provision in relation to information held by any of those bodies.

(2) The bodies referred to in subsection (1) are—

(a) the Scottish Parliament,

(b) any part of the Scottish Administration,

(c) the Scottish Parliamentary Corporate Body, or

(d) any Scottish public authority with mixed functions or no reserved functions (within the meaning of the Scotland Act 1998).

[(3) Section 50 of the Copyright, Designs and Patents Act 1988 and paragraph 6 of Schedule 1 to the Copyright and Rights in Databases Regulations 1997 apply in relation to the Freedom of Information (Scotland) Act 2002 as they apply in relation to this Act.]

[1393]

NOTES

Sub-s (3): added by the Freedom of Information (Scotland) Act 2002 (Consequential Modifications) Order 2004, SI 2004/3089, art 3(1), (3).

81 Application to government departments, etc

(1) For the purposes of this Act each government department is to be treated as a person separate from any other government department.

(2) Subsection (1) does not enable—

(a) a government department which is not a Northern Ireland department to claim for the purposes of section 41(1)(b) that the disclosure of any information by it would constitute a breach of confidence actionable by any other government department (not being a Northern Ireland department), or

(b) a Northern Ireland department to claim for those purposes that the disclosure of information by it would constitute a breach of confidence actionable by any other Northern Ireland department.

(3) A government department is not liable to prosecution under this Act, but section 77 and paragraph 12 of Schedule 3 apply to a person in the public service of the Crown as they apply to any other person.

(4) The provisions specified in subsection (3) also apply to a person acting on behalf of either House of Parliament or on behalf of the Northern Ireland Assembly as they apply to any other person.

[1394]

82 Orders and regulations

(1) Any power of the […] Secretary of State to make an order or regulations under this Act shall be exercisable by statutory instrument.

(2) A statutory instrument containing (whether alone or with other provisions)—
(a) an order under section 5, 7(3) or (8), 53(1)(a)(iii) or 75, or
(b) regulations under section 10(4) or 74(3),

shall not be made unless a draft of the instrument has been laid before, and approved by a resolution of, each House of Parliament.

(3) A statutory instrument which contains (whether alone or with other provisions)—
(a) an order under section 4(1), or
(b) regulations under any provision of this Act not specified in subsection (2)(b),

and which is not subject to the requirement in subsection (2) that a draft of the instrument be laid before and approved by a resolution of each House of Parliament, shall be subject to annulment in pursuance of a resolution of either House of Parliament.

(4) An order under section 4(5) shall be laid before Parliament after being made.

(5) If a draft of an order under section 5 or 7(8) would, apart from this subsection, be treated for the purposes of the Standing Orders of either House of Parliament as a hybrid instrument, it shall proceed in that House as if it were not such an instrument.

[1395]

NOTES

Sub-s (1): words omitted from square brackets inserted by the Transfer of Functions (Miscellaneous) Order 2001, SI 2001/3500, art 8, Sch 2, Pt I, para 8(3), and repealed by the Secretary of State for Constitutional Affairs Order 2003, SI 2003/1887, art 9, Sch 2, para 12(3).

83 Meaning of "Welsh public authority"

(1) In this Act "Welsh public authority" means—
(a) any public authority which is listed in Part II, III, IV or VI of Schedule 1 and whose functions are exercisable only or mainly in or as regards Wales, other than an excluded authority, or
(b) any public authority which is an Assembly subsidiary as defined by section 99(4) of the Government of Wales Act 1998.

(2) In paragraph (a) of subsection (1) "excluded authority" means a public authority which is designated by the [Secretary of State] by order as an excluded authority for the purposes of that paragraph.

(3) Before making an order under subsection (2), the [Secretary of State] shall consult the National Assembly for Wales.

[1396]

NOTES

Sub-ss (2), (3): words in square brackets substituted by the Secretary of State for Constitutional Affairs Order 2003, SI 2003/1887, art 9, Sch 2, para 12(1)(c).

Orders: the Freedom of Information (Excluded Welsh Authorities) Order 2002, SI 2002/2832.

84 Interpretation

In this Act, unless the context otherwise requires—

"applicant", in relation to a request for information, means the person who made the request;

"appropriate Northern Ireland Minister" means the Northern Ireland Minister in charge of the Department of Culture, Arts and Leisure in Northern Ireland;

"appropriate records authority", in relation to a transferred public record, has the meaning given by section 15(5);

"body" includes an unincorporated association;

"the Commissioner" means the Information Commissioner;

"decision notice" has the meaning given by section 50;

"the duty to confirm or deny" has the meaning given by section 1(6);

"enactment" includes an enactment contained in Northern Ireland legislation;

"enforcement notice" has the meaning given by section 52;

"executive committee", in relation to the National Assembly for Wales, has the same meaning as in the Government of Wales Act 1998;
"exempt information" means information which is exempt information by virtue of any provision of Part II;
"fees notice" has the meaning given by section 9(1);
"government department" includes a Northern Ireland department, the Northern Ireland Court Service and any other body or authority exercising statutory functions on behalf of the Crown, but does not include—
(a) any of the bodies specified in section 80(2),
(b) the Security Service, the Secret Intelligence Service or the Government Communications Headquarters, or
(c) the National Assembly for Wales;
"information" (subject to sections 51(8) and 75(2)) means information recorded in any form;
"information notice" has the meaning given by section 51;
"Minister of the Crown" has the same meaning as in the Ministers of the Crown Act 1975;
"Northern Ireland Minister" includes the First Minister and deputy First Minister in Northern Ireland;
"Northern Ireland public authority" means any public authority, other than the Northern Ireland Assembly or a Northern Ireland department, whose functions are exercisable only or mainly in or as regards Northern Ireland and relate only or mainly to transferred matters;
"prescribed" means prescribed by regulations made by the [Secretary of State];
"public authority" has the meaning given by section 3(1);
"public record" means a public record within the meaning of the Public Records Act 1958 or a public record to which the Public Records Act (Northern Ireland) 1923 applies;
"publication scheme" has the meaning given by section 19;
"request for information" has the meaning given by section 8;
"responsible authority", in relation to a transferred public record, has the meaning given by section 15(5);
"the special forces" means those units of the armed forces of the Crown the maintenance of whose capabilities is the responsibility of the Director of Special Forces or which are for the time being subject to the operational command of that Director;
"subordinate legislation" has the meaning given by subsection (1) of section 21 of the Interpretation Act 1978, except that the definition of that term in that subsection shall have effect as if "Act" included Northern Ireland legislation;
"transferred matter", in relation to Northern Ireland, has the meaning given by section 4(1) of the Northern Ireland Act 1998;
"transferred public record" has the meaning given by section 15(4);
"the Tribunal" means the Information Tribunal;
"Welsh public authority" has the meaning given by section 83.

[1397]

NOTES

Words in square brackets in definition "prescribed" substituted by the Secretary of State for Constitutional Affairs Order 2003, SI 2003/1887, art 9, Sch 2, para 12(1)(c).

85 Expenses

There shall be paid out of money provided by Parliament—
(a) any increase attributable to this Act in the expenses of the [Secretary of State] in respect of the Commissioner, the Tribunal or the members of the Tribunal,
(b) any administrative expenses of the [Secretary of State] attributable to this Act,
(c) any other expenses incurred in consequence of this Act by a Minister of the Crown or government department or by either House of Parliament, and
(d) any increase attributable to this Act in the sums which under any other Act are payable out of money so provided.

[1398]

NOTES

Words in square brackets in paras (a), (b) substituted by the Secretary of State for Constitutional Affairs Order 2003, SI 2003/1887, art 9, Sch 2, para 12(1)(c).

86 Repeals

Schedule 8 (repeals) has effect.

[1399]

NOTES

Commencement: 30 November 2000 (certain purposes); 30 January 2001 (certain purposes); 1 January 2005 (otherwise).

87 Commencement

(1) The following provisions of this Act shall come into force on the day on which this Act is passed—

(a) sections 3 to 8 and Schedule 1,
(b) section 19 so far as relating to the approval of publication schemes,
(c) section 20 so far as relating to the approval and preparation by the Commissioner of model publication schemes,
(d) section 47(2) to (6),
(e) section 49,
(f) section 74,
(g) section 75,
(h) sections 78 to 85 and this section,
(i) paragraphs 2 and 17 to 22 of Schedule 2 (and section 18(4) so far as relating to those paragraphs),
(j) paragraph 4 of Schedule 5 (and section 67 so far as relating to that paragraph),
(k) paragraph 8 of Schedule 6 (and section 73 so far as relating to that paragraph),
(l) Part I of Schedule 8 (and section 86 so far as relating to that Part), and
(m) so much of any other provision of this Act as confers power to make any order, regulations or code of practice.

(2) The following provisions of this Act shall come into force at the end of the period of two months beginning with the day on which this Act is passed—

(a) section 18(1),
(b) section 76 and Schedule 7,
(c) paragraphs 1(1), 3(1), 4, 6, 7, 8(2), 9(2), 10(a), 13(1) and (2), 14(a) and 15(1) and (2) of Schedule 2 (and section 18(4) so far as relating to those provisions), and
(d) Part II of Schedule 8 (and section 86 so far as relating to that Part).

(3) Except as provided by subsections (1) and (2), this Act shall come into force at the end of the period of five years beginning with the day on which this Act is passed or on such day before the end of that period as the [Secretary of State] may by order appoint; and different days may be appointed for different purposes.

(4) An order under subsection (3) may contain such transitional provisions and savings (including provisions capable of having effect after the end of the period referred to in that subsection) as the [Secretary of State] considers appropriate.

(5) During the twelve months beginning with the day on which this Act is passed, and during each subsequent complete period of twelve months in the period beginning with that day and ending with the first day on which all the provisions of this Act are fully in force, the [Secretary of State] shall—

(a) prepare a report on his proposals for bringing fully into force those provisions of this Act which are not yet fully in force, and
(b) lay a copy of the report before each House of Parliament.

[1400]

NOTES

Sub-ss (3)–(5): words in square brackets substituted by the Secretary of State for Constitutional Affairs Order 2003, SI 2003/1887, art 9, Sch 2, para 12(1)(c).

Orders: the Freedom of Information Act 2000 (Commencement No 1) Order 2001, SI 2001/1637; the Freedom of Information Act 2002 (Commencement No 2) Order 2002, SI 2002/2812; the Freedom of Information Act 2000 (Commencement No 3) Order 2003, SI 2003/2603; the Freedom of Information Act 2000 (Commencement No 4) Order 2004, SI 2004/1909; the Freedom of Information Act 2000 (Commencement No 5) Order 2004, SI 2004/3122.

88 Short title and extent

(1) This Act may be cited as the Freedom of Information Act 2000.

(2) Subject to subsection (3), this Act extends to Northern Ireland.

(3) The amendment or repeal of any enactment by this Act has the same extent as that enactment.

[1401]

NOTES

Commencement: 30 November 2002.

SCHEDULES

SCHEDULE 1
PUBLIC AUTHORITIES

Section 3(1)(a)(i)

PART I
GENERAL

1. Any government department [other than the Office for Standards in Education, Children's Services and Skills].

[1A. The Office for Standards in Education, Children's Services and Skills, in respect of information held for purposes other than those of the functions exercisable by Her Majesty's Chief Inspector of Education, Children's Services and Skills by virtue of section 5(1)(a)(iii) of the Care Standards Act 2000.]

2. The House of Commons.

3. The House of Lords.

4. The Northern Ireland Assembly.

5. The National Assembly for Wales.

6. The armed forces of the Crown, except—
   (a) the special forces, and
   (b) any unit or part of a unit which is for the time being required by the Secretary of State to assist the Government Communications Headquarters in the exercise of its functions.

[1402]

NOTES

Para 1: words in square brackets inserted by the Education and Inspections Act 2006, s 157, Sch 14, para 69(1), (2)(a), as from a day to be appointed.

Para 1A: inserted by the Education and Inspections Act 2006, s 157, Sch 14, para 69(1), (2)(b), as from a day to be appointed.

PART II
LOCAL GOVERNMENT

England and Wales

7. A local authority within the meaning of the Local Government Act 1972, namely—
   (a) in England, a county council, a London borough council, a district council or a parish council,
   (b) in Wales, a county council, a county borough council or a community council.

8. The Greater London Authority.

9. The Common Council of the City of London, in respect of information held in its capacity as a local authority, police authority or port health authority.

10. The Sub-Treasurer of the Inner Temple or the Under-Treasurer of the Middle Temple, in respect of information held in his capacity as a local authority.

11. The Council of the Isles of Scilly.

12. A parish meeting constituted under section 13 of the Local Government Act 1972.

13. Any charter trustees constituted under section 246 of the Local Government Act 1972.

[14. A fire and rescue authority constituted by a scheme under section 2 of the Fire and Rescue Services Act 2004 or a scheme to which section 4 of that Act applies.]

15. A waste disposal authority established by virtue of an order under section 10(1) of the Local Government Act 1985.

16. A port health authority constituted by an order under section 2 of the Public Health (Control of Disease) Act 1984.

17. …

18. An internal drainage board which is continued in being by virtue of section 1 of the Land Drainage Act 1991.

19. A joint authority established under Part IV of the Local Government Act 1985 [(fire and rescue services and transport)].

20. The London Fire and Emergency Planning Authority.

21. A joint fire authority established by virtue of an order under section 42(2) of the Local Government Act 1985 (reorganisation of functions).

22. A body corporate established pursuant to an order under section 67 of the Local Government Act 1985 (transfer of functions to successors of residuary bodies, etc).

23. A body corporate established pursuant to an order under section 22 of the Local Government Act 1992 (residuary bodies).

24. The Broads Authority established by section 1 of the Norfolk and Suffolk Broads Act 1988.

25. A joint committee constituted in accordance with section 102(1)(b) of the Local Government Act 1972.

26. A joint board which is continued in being by virtue of section 263(1) of the Local Government Act 1972.

27. A joint authority established under section 21 of the Local Government Act 1992.

28. A Passenger Transport Executive for a passenger transport area within the meaning of Part II of the Transport Act 1968.

29. Transport for London.

30. The London Transport Users Committee.

31. A joint board the constituent members of which consist of any of the public authorities described in paragraphs 8, 9, 10, 12, 15, 16, 20 to 31, 57 and 58.

32. A National Park authority established by an order under section 63 of the Environment Act 1995.

33. A joint planning board constituted for an area in Wales outside a National Park by an order under section 2(1B) of the Town and Country Planning Act 1990.

34. …

35. The London Development Agency.

[35A. A local fisheries committee for a sea fisheries district established under section 1 of the Sea Fisheries Regulation Act 1966.]

Northern Ireland

36. A district council within the meaning of the Local Government Act (Northern Ireland) 1972.

[1403]

NOTES

Para 14: substituted by the Fire and Rescue Services Act 2004, s 53(1), Sch 1, para 95.

Para 17: repealed by the Licensing Act 2003, s 199, Sch 7, subject to savings in SI 2005/3056, art 4.

Para 19: words in square brackets substituted by the Civil Contingencies Act 2004, s 32(1), Sch 2, Pt 1, para 10(3)(d).

Para 34: repealed by the Courts Act 2003, s 109(1), (3), Sch 8, para 392, Sch 10, subject to transitional provisions in SI 2005/911, arts 2–5.

Para 35A: inserted by virtue of the Freedom of Information (Additional Public Authorities) Order 2004, SI 2004/938, art 2, Sch 1 (as amended by the Freedom of Information (Additional Public Authorities) (Amendment) Order 2004, SI 2004/1870, art 2).

PART III
THE NATIONAL HEALTH SERVICE

England and Wales

[36A. A strategic Health Authority established under [section 13 of the National Health Service Act 2006].]

37. …

38. A special health authority established under [section 28 of the National Health Service Act 2006 or section 22 of the National Health Service (Wales) Act 2006].

39. A primary care trust established under [section 18 of the National Health Service Act 2006].

[39A. A Local Health Board established under [section 11 of the National Health Service (Wales) Act 2006].]

40. A National Health Service trust established under [section 25 of the National Health Service Act 2006 or section 18 of the National Health Service (Wales) Act 2006].

[40A. An NHS foundation trust.]

41. A Community Health Council [established under section 182 of the National Health Service (Wales) Act 2006].

[41A. A Patients' Forum established under [section 237 of the National Health Service Act 2006].]

42, 43. …

[43A. Any person providing primary medical services *or primary dental services*—

(a) in accordance with arrangements made under [section 92 or 107 of the National Health Service Act 2006, or section 50 or 64 of the National Health Service (Wales) Act 2006]; or

(b) under a contract under [section 84 *or 100* of the National Health Service Act 2006 or section 42 or 57 of the National Health Service (Wales) Act 2006];

in respect of information relating to the provision of those services.]

44. Any person providing *general medical services, general dental services,* general ophthalmic services or pharmaceutical services under [the National Health Service Act 2006 or the National Health Service (Wales) Act 2006], in respect of information relating to the provision of those services.

45. *Any person providing personal medical services or personal dental services under arrangements made under section 28C of the National Health Service Act 1977, in respect of information relating to the provision of those services.*

[45A. Any person providing local pharmaceutical services under—

(a) a pilot scheme established under [section 134 of the National Health Service Act 2006 or section 92 of the National Health Service (Wales) Act 2006]; or

(b) an LPS scheme established under [Schedule 12 to the National Health Service Act 2006 or Schedule 7 to the National Health Service (Wales) Act 2006],

in respect of information relating to the provision of those services.]

[45B. The Commission for Patient and Public Involvement in Health.]

Northern Ireland

46. A Health and Social Services Board established under Article 16 of the Health and Personal Social Services (Northern Ireland) Order 1972.

47. A Health and Social Services Council established under Article 4 of the Health and Personal Social Services (Northern Ireland) Order 1991.

48. A Health and Social Services Trust established under Article 10 of the Health and Personal Social Services (Northern Ireland) Order 1991.

49. A special agency established under Article 3 of the Health and Personal Social Services (Special Agencies) (Northern Ireland) Order 1990.

50. The Northern Ireland Central Services Agency for the Health and Social Services established under Article 26 of the Health and Personal Social Services (Northern Ireland) Order 1972.

51. Any person providing [primary medical services], general dental services, general ophthalmic services or pharmaceutical services under Part VI of the Health and Personal Social Services (Northern Ireland) Order 1972, in respect of information relating to the provision of those services.

[1404]

NOTES

Para 36A: inserted by the National Health Service Reform and Health Care Professions Act 2002 (Supplementary, Consequential etc Provisions) Regulations 2002, SI 2002/2649, reg 4, Sch 1, para 29; words in square brackets substituted by the National Health Service (Consequential Provisions) Act 2006, s 2, Sch 1, para 210(a).

Para 37: repealed by the National Health Service (Consequential Provisions) Act 2006, ss 2, 6, Sch 1, para 210(b), Sch 4.

Para 38: words in square brackets substituted by the National Health Service (Consequential Provisions) Act 2006, s 2, Sch 1, para 210(c).

Para 39: words in square brackets substituted by the National Health Service (Consequential Provisions) Act 2006, s 2, Sch 1, para 210(d).

Para 39A: inserted by the National Health Service Reform and Health Care Professions Act 2002, ss 6(2), 19(7), Sch 5, para 48; words in square brackets substituted by the National Health Service (Consequential Provisions) Act 2006, s 2, Sch 1, para 210(e).

Para 40: words in square brackets substituted by the National Health Service (Consequential Provisions) Act 2006, s 2, Sch 1, para 210(f).

Para 40A: inserted by the Health and Social Care (Community Health and Standards) Act 2003, s 34, Sch 4, paras 113, 114.

Para 41: words in square brackets substituted by the National Health Service (Consequential Provisions) Act 2006, s 2, Sch 1, para 210(g).

Para 41A: inserted by the National Health Service Reform and Health Care Professions Act 2002, ss 6(2), 19(7), Sch 5, para 48; words in square brackets substituted by the National Health Service (Consequential Provisions) Act 2006, s 2, Sch 1, para 210(h).

Paras 42, 43: repealed by the Health and Social Care (Community Health and Standards) Act 2003, ss 190(2), 196, Sch 13, para 10, Sch 14, Pts 4, 7.

Para 43A: inserted by the Health and Social Care (Community Health and Standards) Act 2003, s 184, Sch 11, para 68; for the first words in italics there are substituted the words ", primary dental services or primary ophthalmic services" by the Health Act 2006, s 80(1), Sch 8, para 45(1), (2), as from a day to be appointed; words in square brackets in paras (a), (b) substituted by the National Health Service (Consequential Provisions) Act 2006, s 2, Sch 1, para 210(i), (j); words in italics in para (b) substituted for ", 100 or 117" by the Health Act 2006, s 80(1), Sch 8, para 45(1), (2)(b) (as amended by the National Health Service (Consequential Provisions) Act 2006, s 2, Sch 1, paras 281, 300), as from a day to be appointed.

Para 44: words in italics repealed by the Health and Social Care (Community Health and Standards) Act 2003, s 196, Sch 14, Pt 4, partly as from a day to be appointed in relation to Wales; words in square brackets substituted by the National Health Service (Consequential Provisions) Act 2006, s 2, Sch 1, para 210(k).

Para 45: repealed by the Health and Social Care (Community Health and Standards) Act 2003, s 196, Sch 14, Pt 4, partly as from a day to be appointed in relation to Wales.

Para 45A: inserted by the Health and Social Care Act 2001, s 67(1), Sch 5, Pt 1, para 14(1); words in square brackets substituted by the National Health Service (Consequential Provisions) Act 2006, s 2, Sch 1, para 210(l), (m).

Para 45B: inserted by the National Health Service Reform and Health Care Professions Act 2002, s 20(11), Sch 6, para 19.

Para 51: words in square brackets substituted by the Primary Medical Services (Northern Ireland) Order 2004, SI 2004/311, art 10, Sch 1, para 18.

PART IV
MAINTAINED SCHOOLS AND OTHER EDUCATIONAL INSTITUTIONS

England and Wales

[52. The governing body of—
- (a) a maintained school, as defined by section 20(7) of the School Standards and Framework Act 1998, or
- (b) a maintained nursery school, as defined by section 22(9) of that Act.]

53.—(1) The governing body of—
- (a) an institution within the further education sector,
- (b) a university receiving financial support under section 65 of the Further and Higher Education Act 1992,
- (c) an institution conducted by a higher education corporation,
- (d) a designated institution for the purposes of Part II of the Further and Higher Education Act 1992 as defined by section 72(3) of that Act, or
- (e) any college, school, hall or other institution of a university which falls within paragraph (b).

(2) In sub-paragraph (1)—
- (a) "governing body" is to be interpreted in accordance with subsection (1) of section 90 of the Further and Higher Education Act 1992 but without regard to subsection (2) of that section,
- (b) in paragraph (a), the reference to an institution within the further education sector is to be construed in accordance with section 91(3) of the Further and Higher Education Act 1992,
- (c) in paragraph (c), "higher education corporation" has the meaning given by section 90(1) of that Act, and
- (d) in paragraph (e) "college" includes any institution in the nature of a college.

Northern Ireland

54.—(1) The managers of—

(a) a controlled school, voluntary school or grant-maintained integrated school within the meaning of Article 2(2) of the Education and Libraries (Northern Ireland) Order 1986, or

(b) a pupil referral unit as defined by Article 87(1) of the Education (Northern Ireland) Order 1998.

(2) In sub-paragraph (1) "managers" has the meaning given by Article 2(2) of the Education and Libraries (Northern Ireland) Order 1986.

55.—(1) The governing body of—

(a) a university receiving financial support under Article 30 of the Education and Libraries (Northern Ireland) Order 1993,

(b) a college of education … in respect of which grants are paid under Article 66(2) or (3) of the Education and Libraries (Northern Ireland) Order 1986, or

(c) an institution of further education within the meaning of the Further Education (Northern Ireland) Order 1997.

(2) In sub-paragraph (1) "governing body" has the meaning given by Article 30(3) of the Education and Libraries (Northern Ireland) Order 1993.

56. Any person providing further education to whom grants, loans or other payments are made under Article 5(1)(b) of the Further Education (Northern Ireland) Order 1997.

[1405]

NOTES

Para 52: substituted by the Education Act 2002, s 215(1), Sch 21, para 127.

Para 55: words omitted from sub-para (1)(b) repealed by the Colleges of Education (Northern Ireland) Order 2005, SI 2005/1963, art 14, Sch 3, para 4, Sch 4.

PART V
POLICE

England and Wales

57. A police authority established under section 3 of the Police Act 1996.

58. The Metropolitan Police Authority established under section 5B of the Police Act 1996.

59. A chief officer of police of a police force in England or Wales.

Northern Ireland

60. The [Northern Ireland Policing Board].

61. The Chief Constable of the [Police Service of Northern Ireland].

Miscellaneous

62. The British Transport Police.

63. The Ministry of Defence Police established by section 1 of the Ministry of Defence Police Act 1987.

[63A. The Civil Nuclear Police Authority.

63B. The chief constable of the Civil Nuclear Constabulary.]

64. Any person who—

(a) by virtue of any enactment has the function of nominating individuals who may be appointed as special constables by justices of the peace, and

(b) is not a public authority by virtue of any other provision of this Act, in respect of information relating to the exercise by any person appointed on his nomination of the functions of a special constable.

[1406]

NOTES

Paras 60, 61: words in square brackets substituted by the Police (Northern Ireland) Act 2000, s 78(1), Sch 6, para 25(1), (2).

Paras 63A, 63B: inserted by the Energy Act 2004, s 51(2), Sch 10, para 18.

PART VI
OTHER PUBLIC BODIES AND OFFICES: GENERAL

[The Adjudication Panel for Wales.]

The Adjudicator for the Inland Revenue and Customs and Excise.

The Administration of Radioactive Substances Advisory Committee.

[*The Adult Learning Inspectorate*.]

...

The Advisory Board on Restricted Patients.

The Advisory Board on the Registration of Homoeopathic Products.

...

The Advisory Committee for Disabled People in Employment and Training.

The Advisory Committee for the Public Lending Right.

...

The Advisory Committee on Advertising.

The Advisory Committee on Animal Feedingstuffs.

The Advisory Committee on Borderline Substances.

The Advisory Committee on Business and the Environment.

The Advisory Committee on Business Appointments.

The Advisory Committee on Conscientious Objectors.

The Advisory Committee on Consumer Products and the Environment.

The Advisory Committee on Dangerous Pathogens.

The Advisory Committee on Distinction Awards.

An Advisory Committee on General Commissioners of Income Tax.

The Advisory Committee on the Government Art Collection.

The Advisory Committee on Hazardous Substances.

The Advisory Committee on Historic Wreck Sites.

An Advisory Committee on Justices of the Peace in England and Wales.

The Advisory Committee on the Microbiological Safety of Food.

...

The Advisory Committee on Novel Foods and Processes.

[The Advisory Committee on Organic Standards.]

The Advisory Committee on Overseas Economic and Social Research.

The Advisory Committee on Packaging.

The Advisory Committee on Pesticides.

The Advisory Committee on Releases to the Environment.

[The Advisory Committee on Statute Law.]

[The Advisory Committee on Telecommunications for the Disabled and Elderly.]

[The Advisory Council on Historical Manuscripts.]

The Advisory Council on Libraries.

The Advisory Council on the Misuse of Drugs.

[The Advisory Council on National Records and Archives.]

The Advisory Council on Public Records.

The Advisory Group on Hepatitis.

[The Advisory Group on Medical Countermeasures.]

[The Advisory Panel on Beacon Councils.]

[The Advisory Panel on Public Sector Information.]

The Advisory Panel on Standards for the Planning Inspectorate.

The Aerospace Committee.

An Agricultural Dwelling House Advisory Committee.

An Agricultural Wages Board for England and Wales.

An Agricultural Wages Committee.

The Agriculture and Environment Biotechnology Commission.

[The Air Quality Expert Group.]

The Airborne Particles Expert Group.

The Alcohol Education and Research Council.

[The All-Wales Medicines Strategy Group.]

…

The Animal Procedures Committee.

The Animal Welfare Advisory Committee.

…

[The Appointments Commission.]

[The Architects Registration Board.]

The Armed Forces Pay Review Body.

[The Arts and Humanities Research Council.]

The Arts Council of England.

The Arts Council of Wales.

The Audit Commission for Local Authorities and the National Health Service in England and Wales.

The Auditor General for Wales.

The Authorised Conveyancing Practitioners Board.

The Bank of England, in respect of information held for purposes other than those of its functions with respect to—

(a) monetary policy,

(b) financial operations intended to support financial institutions for the purposes of maintaining stability, and

(c) the provision of private banking services and related services.

The Better Regulation Task Force.

The Biotechnology and Biological Sciences Research Council.

[The Board of the Pension Protection Fund.]

Any Board of Visitors established under section 6(2) of the Prison Act 1952.

The Britain-Russia Centre and East-West Centre.

The British Association for Central and Eastern Europe.

The British Broadcasting Corporation, in respect of information held for purposes other than those of journalism, art or literature.

The British Coal Corporation.

The British Council.

The British Educational Communications and Technology Agency.

The British Hallmarking Council.

The British Library.

The British Museum.

The British Pharmacopoeia Commission.

The British Potato Council.

The British Railways Board.

British Shipbuilders.

The British Tourist Authority.

[The British Transport Police Authority.]

The British Waterways Board.

The British Wool Marketing Board.

The Broadcasting Standards Commission.

The Building Regulations Advisory Committee.

[…]

[The Care Council for Wales.]

The Central Advisory Committee on War Pensions.

…

[*The Central Police Training and Development Authority.*]

The Central Rail Users' Consultative Committee.

[The Certification Officer.]

The Channel Four Television Corporation, in respect of information held for purposes other than those of journalism, art or literature.

[The Chemical Weapons Convention National Authority Advisory Committee.]

The Children and Family Court Advisory and Support Service.

[The Children's Commissioner.]

[The Children's Commissioner for Wales.]

The Civil Aviation Authority.

The Civil Justice Council.

The Civil Procedure Rule Committee.

The Civil Service Appeal Board.

The Civil Service Commissioners.

The Coal Authority.

The Commission for Architecture and the Built Environment.

…

[The Commission for Equality and Human Rights]

[The Commission for Healthcare Audit and Inspection, in respect of information held for purposes other than those of its functions exercisable by virtue of paragraph 5(a)(i) of the Care Standards Act 2000.]

[The Commission for Integrated Transport.]

The Commission for Local Administration in England.

…

The Commission for Racial Equality.

[Commission for Rural Communities.]

[The Commission for Social Care Inspection, in respect of information held for purposes other than those of its functions exercisable by virtue of paragraph 5(a)(ii) of the Care Standards Act 2000.]

The Commission for the New Towns.

…

[The Commissioner for Older People in Wales.]

The Commissioner for Public Appointments.

[The Commissioners of Northern Lighthouses.]

The Committee for Monitoring Agreements on Tobacco Advertising and Sponsorship.

…

The Committee on Agricultural Valuation.

The Committee on Carcinogenicity of Chemicals in Food, Consumer Products and the Environment.

The Committee on Chemicals and Materials of Construction For Use in Public Water Supply and Swimming Pools.

The Committee on Medical Aspects of Food and Nutrition Policy.

The Committee on Medical Aspects of Radiation in the Environment.

The Committee on Mutagenicity of Chemicals in Food, Consumer Products and the Environment.

[The Committee on Radioactive Waste Management.]

[The Committee on Safety of Devices.]

The Committee on Standards in Public Life.

The Committee on Toxicity of Chemicals in Food, Consumer Products and the Environment.

The Committee on the Medical Effects of Air Pollutants.

The Committee on the Safety of Medicines.

The Commonwealth Scholarship Commission in the United Kingdom.

[Communications for Business.]

The Community Development Foundation.

The Competition Commission, in relation to information held by it otherwise than as a tribunal.

[The Competition Service.]

[A conservation board established under section 86 of the Countryside and Rights of Way Act 2000.]

The Construction Industry Training Board.

Consumer Communications for England.

[The Consumer Council for Postal Services.]

…

[The Consumer Panel established under section 16 of the Communications Act 2003.]

…

…

[The Council for the Regulation of Health Care Professionals.]

The Council for the Central Laboratory of the Research Councils.

The Council for Science and Technology.

The Council on Tribunals.

…

The Countryside Council for Wales.

[A courts board established under section 4 of the Courts Act 2003.]

The Covent Garden Market Authority.

The Criminal Cases Review Commission.

[The Criminal Injuries Compensation Appeals Panel, in relation to information held by it otherwise than as a tribunal.]

[The Criminal Injuries Compensation Authority.]

The Criminal Justice Consultative Council.

[The Criminal Procedure Rule Committee.]

The Crown Court Rule Committee.

The Dartmoor Steering Group and Working Party.

The Darwin Advisory Committee.

The Defence Nuclear Safety Committee.

The Defence Scientific Advisory Council.

The Design Council.

…

The Diplomatic Service Appeal Board.

[The Director of Fair Access to Higher Education.]

[The Disability Employment Advisory Committee.]

The Disability Living Allowance Advisory Board.

The Disability Rights Commission.

The Disabled Persons Transport Advisory Committee.

[The Distributed Generation Co-Ordinating Group.]

[The East of England Industrial Development Board.]

The Economic and Social Research Council.

…

[The Electoral Commission.]

…

The Engineering Construction Industry Training Board.

The Engineering and Physical Sciences Research Council.

…

…

The English Sports Council.

The English Tourist Board.

The Environment Agency.

The Equal Opportunities Commission.

[The Ethnic Minority Business Forum.]

The Expert Advisory Group on AIDS.

The Expert Group on Cryptosporidium in Water Supplies.

An Expert Panel on Air Quality Standards.

The Export Guarantees Advisory Council.

[The Family Justice Council.]

[The Family Procedure Rule Committee.]

The Family Proceedings Rules Committee.

The Farm Animal Welfare Council.

[The Financial Reporting Advisory Board.]

[The Financial Services Authority.]

The Fire Services Examination Board.

The Firearms Consultative Committee.

The Food Advisory Committee.

Food from Britain.

The Football Licensing Authority.

The Fuel Cell Advisory Panel.

[The Fuel Poverty Advisory Group.]

. . .

[The Gaelic Media Service, in respect of information held for purposes other than those of journalism, art or literature.]

[The Gambling Commission.]

[Gangmasters Licensing Authority.]

. . .

[The Gas and Electricity Consumer Council.]

The Gene Therapy Advisory Committee.

The General Chiropractic Council.

The General Dental Council.

The General Medical Council.

[The General Optical Council.]

The General Osteopathic Council.

[The General Social Care Council.]

[The General Teaching Council for England.]

[The General Teaching Council for Wales.]

The Genetic Testing and Insurance Committee.

The Government Hospitality Advisory Committee for the Purchase of Wine.

[The Government-Industry Forum on Non-Food Use of Crops.]

The Government Chemist.

The Great Britain-China Centre.

[The Health Professions Council.]

[The Health Protection Agency.]

The Health and Safety Commission.

The Health and Safety Executive.

The Health Service Commissioner for England.

…

[The Hearing Aid Council.]

[Her Majesty's Chief Inspector of Education and Training in Wales or Prif Arolygydd Ei Mawrhydi dros Addysg a Hyfforddiant yng Nghymru].

[Her Majesty's Commissioners for Judicial Appointments.]

The Higher Education Funding Council for England.

The Higher Education Funding Council for Wales.

…

…

The Historic Buildings and Monuments Commission for England.

The Historic Royal Palaces Trust.

The Home-Grown Cereals Authority.

…

The Horserace Betting Levy Board.

The Horserace Totalisator Board.

The Horticultural Development Council.

Horticulture Research International.

The House of Lords Appointments Commission.

Any housing action trust established under Part III of the Housing Act 1988.

The Housing Corporation.

The Human Fertilisation and Embryology Authority.

[The Human Tissue Authority.]

The Human Genetics Commission.

The Immigration Services Commissioner.

The Imperial War Museum.

[The Independent Advisory Group on Teenage Pregnancy.]

The Independent Board of Visitors for Military Corrective Training Centres.

The Independent Case Examiner for the Child Support Agency.

[The Independent Groundwater Complaints Administrator.]

The Independent Living Funds.

[The Independent Police Complaints Commission.]

[The Independent Regulator of NHS Foundation Trusts.]

[The Independent Review Panel for Advertising.]

[The Independent Review Panel for Borderline Products.]

[The Independent Scientific Group on Cattle Tuberculosis.]

The Independent Television Commission.

…

The Industrial Development Advisory Board.

The Industrial Injuries Advisory Council.

The Information Commissioner.

The *Inland Waterways Amenity Advisory Council.*

The Insolvency Rules Committee.

…

[The Integrated Administration and Controls System Appeals Panel.]

[The Intellectual Property Advisory Committee.]

Investors in People UK.

The Joint Committee on Vaccination and Immunisation.

The Joint Nature Conservation Committee.

The Joint Prison/Probation Accreditation Panel.

[The Judicial Appointments and Conduct Ombudsman.]

[The Judicial Appointments Commission.]

The Judicial Studies Board.

The Know-How Fund Advisory Board.

The Land Registration Rule Committee.

The Law Commission.

[The Learning and Skills Council for England.]

The Legal Services Commission.

[The Legal Services Complaints Commissioner.]

The Legal Services Consultative Panel.

The Legal Services Ombudsman.

…

The Local Government Boundary Commission for Wales.

The Local Government Commission for England.

A local probation board established under section 4 of the Criminal Justice and Court Services Act 2000.

[The London and South East Industrial Development Board.]

The London Pensions Fund Authority.

The Low Pay Commission.

The Magistrates' Courts Rules Committee.

The Marshall Aid Commemoration Commission.

The Measurement Advisory Committee.

The Meat and Livestock Commission.

…

The Medical Research Council.

…

The Medicines Commission.

The Milk Development Council.

…

The Museum of London.

The National Army Museum.

The National Audit Office.

The National Biological Standards Board (UK).

[The National Care Standards Commission.]

The National Consumer Council.

[…]

…

The National Employers' Liaison Committee.

[The National Employment Panel.]

The National Endowment for Science, Technology and the Arts.

…

[The National Forest Company.]

The National Gallery.

The National Heritage Memorial Fund.

[The National Identity Scheme Commissioner.]

The National Library of Wales.

…

The National Lottery Commission.

The National Maritime Museum.

The National Museum of Science and Industry.

The National Museums and Galleries of Wales.

The National Museums and Galleries on Merseyside.

[The National Policing Improvement Agency.]

The National Portrait Gallery.

…

[Natural England.]

The Natural Environment Research Council.

The Natural History Museum.

The New Deal Task Force.

…

[The North East Industrial Development Board.]

[The North West Industrial Development Board.]

[The Northern Ireland Judicial Appointments Ombudsman.]

[The Nuclear Decommissioning Authority.]

[The Nuclear Research Advisory Council.]

[The Nursing and Midwifery Council.]

…

[The Office of Communications.]

[The Office of Government Commerce.]

[The Office of Manpower Economics.]

The Oil and Pipelines Agency.

[The Olympic Delivery Authority.]

[The Ombudsman for the Board of the Pension Protection Fund.]

The OSO Board.

The Overseas Service Pensions Scheme Advisory Board.

The Panel on Standards for the Planning Inspectorate.

The Parliamentary Boundary Commission for England.

The Parliamentary Boundary Commission for Scotland.

The Parliamentary Boundary Commission for Wales.

The Parliamentary Commissioner for Administration.

The Parole Board.

The Particle Physics and Astronomy Research Council.

[The Patient Information Advisory Group.]

…

The Pensions Ombudsman.

[The Pensions Regulator.]

[The Pesticide Residues Committee.]

[The Pesticides Forum.]

…

…

The Poisons Board.

[The Police Advisory Board for England and Wales.]

…

The Police Information Technology Organisation.

The Police Negotiating Board.

The Political Honours Scrutiny Committee.

[The Postgraduate Medical Education and Training Board.]

The Post Office.

…

…

[The Prison Service Pay Review Body.]

…

[The Public Private Partnership Agreement Arbiter.]

[The Public Service Ombudsman for Wales.]

…

The Qualifications Curriculum Authority.

The Race Education and Employment Forum.

The Race Relations Forum.

The Radio Authority.

The Radioactive Waste Management Advisory Committee.

[…]

A Regional Cultural Consortium.

Any regional development agency established under the Regional Development Agencies Act 1998, other than the London Development Agency.

Any regional flood defence committee.

...

[The Registrar General for England and Wales.]

The Registrar of Public Lending Right.

Remploy Ltd.

The Renewable Energy Advisory Committee.

[The Renewables Advisory Board.]

Resource: The Council for Museums, Archives and Libraries.

The Review Board for Government Contracts.

The Review Body for Nursing Staff, Midwives, Health Visitors and Professions Allied to Medicine.

The Review Body on Doctors and Dentists Remuneration.

The Reviewing Committee on the Export of Works of Art.

The Royal Air Force Museum.

The Royal Armouries.

The Royal Botanic Gardens, Kew.

[The Royal College of Veterinary Surgeons, in respect of information held by it otherwise than as a tribunal.]

The Royal Commission on Ancient and Historical Monuments of Wales.

The Royal Commission on Environmental Pollution.

The Royal Commission on Historical Manuscripts.

[The Royal Hospital at Chelsea.]

...

The Royal Mint Advisory Committee on the Design of Coins, Medals, Seals and Decorations.

[The Royal Pharmaceutical Society of Great Britain, in respect of information held by it otherwise than as a tribunal.]

The School Teachers' Review Body.

[The Scientific Advisory Committee on Nutrition.]

The Scientific Committee on Tobacco and Health.

...

The Scottish Committee of the Council on Tribunals.

The Sea Fish Industry Authority.

[The Security Industry Authority].

The Senior Salaries Review Body.

The Sentencing Advisory Panel.

[The Sentencing Guidelines Council.]

...

Sianel Pedwar Cymru, in respect of information held for purposes other than those of journalism, art or literature.

Sir John Soane's Museum.

...

[The Small Business Council.]

[The Small Business Investment Task Force.]

[The Social Care Institute for Excellence.]

The social fund Commissioner appointed under section 65 of the Social Security Administration Act 1992.

The Social Security Advisory Committee.

The Social Services Inspectorate for Wales Advisory Group.

[The South West Industrial Development Board.]

[The Specialist Advisory Committee on Antimicrobial Research.]

The Spongiform Encephalopathy Advisory Committee.

The Sports Council for Wales.

[The Standards Board for England.]

The Standing Advisory Committee on Industrial Property.

The Standing Advisory Committee on Trunk Road Assessment.

The Standing Dental Advisory Committee.

…

…

…

[The Statistics Commission.]

The Steering Committee on Pharmacy Postgraduate Education.

[The Strategic Investment Board.]

[…]

The subsidence adviser appointed under section 46 of the Coal Industry Act 1994.

The Substance Misuse Advisory Panel.

The Sustainable Development Commission.

…

[The Sustainable Energy Policy Advisory Board.]

The Tate Gallery.

The Teacher Training Agency.

[The Technical Advisory Board.]

The Theatres Trust.

The Traffic Commissioners, in respect of information held by them otherwise than as a tribunal.

[The Training and Development Agency for Schools.]

The Treasure Valuation Committee.

The UK Advisory Panel for Health Care Workers Infected with Bloodborne Viruses.

[The UK Chemicals Stakeholder Forum.]

The UK Sports Council.

The United Kingdom Atomic Energy Authority.

…

…

The United Kingdom Xenotransplantation Interim Regulatory Authority.

[The University for Industry.]

The Unlinked Anonymous Serosurveys Steering Group.

The Unrelated Live Transplant Regulatory Authority.

The Urban Regeneration Agency.

[The Valuation Tribunal Service.]

[The verderers of the New Forest, in respect of information held by them otherwise than as a tribunal.]

The Veterinary Products Committee.

[The Veterinary Residues Committee.]

The Victoria and Albert Museum.

[The Wales Centre for Health.]

…

…

The Wallace Collection.

The War Pensions Committees.

The Water Regulations Advisory Committee.

…

…

The Welsh Committee for Professional Development of Pharmacy.

The Welsh Dental Committee.

…

The Welsh Industrial Development Advisory Board.

The Welsh Language Board.

The Welsh Medical Committee.

…

The Welsh Nursing and Midwifery Committee.

The Welsh Optometric Committee.

The Welsh Pharmaceutical Committee.

The Welsh Scientific Advisory Committee.

[The West Midlands Industrial Development Board.]

The Westminster Foundation for Democracy.

The Wilton Park Academic Council.

The Wine Standards Board of the Vintners' Company.

The Women's National Commission.

[The Yorkshire and the Humber and the East Midlands Industrial Development Board.]

The Youth Justice Board for England and Wales.

The Zoos Forum.

[1407]

NOTES

Entries "The Adjudication Panel for Wales", "The All-Wales Medicines Strategy Group", "The Care Council for Wales", "The Certification Officer", "The Children's Commissioner for Wales", "The Commissioners of Northern Lighthouses", "The Consumer Council for Postal Services", "The Criminal Injuries Compensation Appeals Panel", "The Criminal Injuries Compensation Authority", "The Electoral Commission", "The Gas and Electricity Consumer Council", "The General Social Care Council", "The General Teaching Council for Wales", "The National Care Standards Commission", and "The Standards Board for England" inserted by the Freedom of Information (Additional Public Authorities) Order 2002, SI 2002/2623, art 2, Sch 1.

Entries "The Adult Learning Inspectorate", "The Advisory Committee on Telecommunications for the Disabled and Elderly", "The Advisory Council on Historical Manuscripts", "The Advisory Council on National Records and Archives", "The Advisory Group on Medical Countermeasures", "The Advisory Panel on Beacon Councils", "The Air Quality Expert Group", "The Business Incubation Fund Investment Panel", "The Committee on Safety of Devices", "Communications for Business", "The Competition

Service", "The Disability Employment Advisory Committee", "The Ethnic Minority Business Forum", "The Financial Reporting Advisory Board", "The Financial Services Authority", "The General Teaching Council for England", "The Government–Industry Forum on Non-Food Use of Crops", "The Hearing Aid Council", "The Independent Advisory Group on Teenage Pregnancy", "The Independent Scientific Group on Cattle Tuberculosis", "The Integrated Administration and Controls System Appeals Panel", "The Intellectual Property Advisory Committee", "The Learning and Skills Council for England", "The National Employment Panel", "The National Forest Company", "The Nuclear Research Advisory Council", "The Office of Government Commerce", "The Office of Manpower Economics", "The Pesticide Residues Committee", "The Scientific Advisory Committee on Nutrition", "The Small Business Council", "The Small Business Investment Task Force", "The Social Care Institute for Excellence", "The Specialist Advisory Committee on Antimicrobial Research", "The Statistics Commission", "The Strategic Investment Board", "The Technical Advisory Board", "The UK Chemicals Stakeholder Forum" and "The Veterinary Residues Committee" inserted by the Freedom of Information (Additional Public Authorities) Order 2003, SI 2003/1882, art 2, Sch 1.

Entry "The Adult Learning Inspectorate" repealed by the Education and Inspections Act 2006, ss 157, 184, Sch 14, para 69(1), (3), Sch 18, Pt 5, as from a day to be appointed.

Entries "The Advisory Board on Family Law", "The Advisory Committee for Wales, (in relation to the Environment Agency)", "The Advisory Committee on NHS Drugs", "The Apple and Pear Research Council", "The Consumer Panel", "The Development Awareness Working Group", "The Education Transfer Council", "The Energy Advisory Panel", "The Further Education Funding Council for Wales", "The Gas Consumers' Council", "The Honorary Investment Advisory Council", "The Indian Family Pensions Funds Body of Commissioners", "The Medical Practices Committee", "The Medical Workforce Standing Advisory Committee", "The Place Names Advisory Committee", "The Post Office Users' Councils for Scotland, Wales and Northern Ireland", "The Post Office Users' National Council", "The Sustainable Development Education Panel" and "The Wales New Deal Advisory Task Force", (all omitted) repealed by the Freedom of Information (Removal of References to Public Authorities) Order 2003, SI 2003/1883, art 2, Sch 1.

Entries "The Advisory Committee for Cleaner Coal Technology", "The Hill Farming Advisory Committee", "The Hill Farming Advisory Sub-committee for Wales", "The Property Advisory Group", "The Royal Military College of Science Advisory Council", "The Skills Task Force" and "The United Kingdom Register of Organic Food Standards" (all omitted) repealed by the Freedom of Information (Removal of References to Public Authorities) Order 2004, SI 2004/1641, art 2, Sch 1.

Entries "The Advisory Committee on Organic Standards", "The Advisory Committee on Statute Law", "The Architects Registration Board", "The Chemical Weapons Convention National Authority Advisory Committee", "The Committee on Radioactive Waste Management", "The Distributed Generation Co-Ordinating Group", "The East of England Industrial Development Board", "The Fuel Poverty Advisory Group", "Her Majesty's Commissioners for Judicial Appointments", "The Independent Review Panel for Advertising", "The Independent Review Panel for Borderline Products", "The Legal Services Complaints Commissioner", "The London and South East Industrial Development Board", "The North East Industrial Development Board", "The North West Industrial Development Board", "The Pesticides Forum", "The Police Advisory Board for England and Wales", "The Postgraduate Medical Education and Training Board", "The Prison Service Pay Review Body", "The Public Private Partnership Agreement Arbiter", "The Renewables Advisory Board", "The Royal Hospital at Chelsea", "The South West Industrial Development Board", "The Sustainable Energy Policy Advisory Board", "The West Midlands Industrial Development Board", and "The Yorkshire and the Humber and the East Midlands Industrial Development Board" inserted by the Freedom of Information (Additional Public Authorities) Order 2004, SI 2004/938, art 3, Sch 2.

Entries "The Advisory Panel on Public Sector Information", "The British Transport Police Authority", "The Children's Commissioner", "A conservation board", "A courts board", "The Commission for Integrated Transport", "The Criminal Procedure Rule Committee", "The Family Justice Council", "The Family Procedure Rule Committee", "The Gaelic Media Service", "The General Optical Council", "The Independent Groundwater Complaints Administrator", "The Independent Regulator of NHS Foundation Trusts", "The Registrar General for England and Wales", "The Royal College of Veterinary Surgeons", "The Royal Pharmaceutical Society of Great Britain", "The Sentencing Guidelines Council", "The University for Industry", and "The verderers of the New Forest" inserted by the Freedom of Information (Additional Public Authorities) Order 2005, SI 2005/3593, arts 2, 3, Schs 1, 2.

Entry "The Ancient Monuments Board for Wales" (omitted) repealed by the Ancient Monuments Board for Wales (Abolition) Order 2006, SI 2006/64, art 3(1)(b)(iii).

Entry "The Appointments Commission" inserted by the Health Act 2006, s 80(1), Sch 8, para 45(1), (3).

Entries "The Arts and Humanities Research Council" and "The Director of Fair Access to Higher Education" inserted by the Higher Education Act 2004, s 49, Sch 6, para 10.

Entries "The Board of the Pension Protection Fund", "The Ombudsman for the Board of the Pension Protection Fund" and "The Pensions Regulator" inserted, and entries "The Occupational Pensions Regulatory Authority", "The Pensions Compensation Board", "The Registrar of Occupational and Personal Pension Schemes" (all omitted) repealed, by the Pensions Act 2004, ss 319(1), 320, Sch 12, para 79, Sch 13, Pt 1.

Entry "The British Railways Board" repealed by the Transport Act 2000, s 274, Sch 31, Pt IV, as from a day to be appointed.

Entries "The Broadcasting Standards Commission", "The Independent Television Commission" and "The Radio Authority" repealed as from a day to be appointed, entries "The Scottish Advisory Committee on Telecommunications" and "The Welsh Advisory Committee on Telecommunications" (both omitted) repealed, and entry "The Consumer Panel established under section 16 of the Communications Act 2003" inserted, by the Communications Act 2003, s 406(1), (7), Sch 17, para 164, Sch 19(1).

Entries "The Business Incubation Fund Investment Panel" (as inserted by SI 2003/1882), "The Commissioner for Integrated Transport", "The National Expert Group", "The Pharmacists' Review Panel", "The Standing Medical Advisory Committee", "The Standing Nursing and Midwifery Advisory Committee", and "The Standing Pharmaceutical Advisory Committee" (all omitted) repealed by the Freedom of Information (Removal of References to Public Authorities) Order 2005, SI 2005/3594, art 2, Sch 1.

Entry "The Central Council for Education and Training in Social Work (UK)" (omitted) repealed by the Abolition of the Central Council for Education and Training in Social Work Order 2002, SI 2002/797, art 2(c).

Entry "The Central Police Training and Development Authority" inserted by the Criminal Justice and Police Act 2001, s 102, Sch 4, para 8; repealed by the Police and Justice Act 2006, s 52, Sch 15, Pt 1, as from a day to be appointed.

Entry "The Commission for Equality and Human Rights" inserted by the Equality Act 2006, s 2, Sch 1, Pt 4, para 48.

Entry "The Commission for Health Improvement" (omitted) repealed, and entries "The Commission for Healthcare Audit and Inspection" and "The Commission for Social Care Inspection" inserted, by the Health and Social Care (Community Health and Standards) Act 2003, ss 147, 196, Sch 9, para 31, Sch 14, Pt 2.

Entries "The Commission for Local Administration in Wales", "The Health Service Commissioner for Wales" and "The Welsh Administration Ombudsman" (all omitted) repealed and entry "The Public Services Ombudsman for Wales" inserted by the Public Services Ombudsman Act 2005, s 39, Sch 6, paras 70, 72, Sch 7.

Entries "The Commission for Racial Equality", "The Disability Rights Commission", and "The Equal Opportunities Commission" repealed by the Equality Act 2006, ss 40, 91, Sch 3, para 60, Sch 4, as from a day to be appointed.

Entries "Commission for Rural Communities" and "Natural England" inserted, and entries "The Committee of Investigation for Great Britain", "The consumers' committee for Great Britain", "The Countryside Agency", "English Nature" (all omitted) repealed by the Natural Environment and Rural Communities Act 2006, s 105, Sch 11, Pt 1, para 153, Sch 12.

Entry "The Commissioner for Older People in Wales" inserted by the Commissioner for Older People (Wales) Act 2006, s 1(2), Sch 1, para 21(b).

Entry "The Council for Professions Supplementary to Medicine" (omitted) repealed, and entry "The Health Professions Council" inserted, by the Health Professions Order 2001, SI 2002/254, art 48(3), Sch 4, para 9; for transitional provisions see Sch 2 to that Order.

Entry "The Council for the Regulation of Health Care Professionals" inserted by the National Health Service Reform and Health Care Professions Act 2002, s 25(4), Sch 7, para 24.

Entries "The English National Board for Nursing, Midwifery and Health Visiting", "The United Kingdom Central Council for Nursing, Midwifery and Health Visiting" and "The Welsh National Board for Nursing, Midwifery and Health Visiting" (all omitted) repealed, and entry "The Nursing and Midwifery Council" inserted, by the Nursing and Midwifery Order 2001, SI 2002/253, art 54(3), Sch 5, para 17; for transitional provisions see Sch 2 to that Order.

Entry "The Gambling Commission" substituted for original entry "The Gaming Board for Great Britain" by the Gambling Act 2005, s 356(1), Sch 16, Pt 2, para 16.

Entry "Gangmasters Licensing Authority" inserted by the Gangmasters (Licensing) Act 2004, s 1(6), Sch 1, para 6.

Entry "The Health Protection Agency" inserted and entry "The National Radiological Protection Board" (omitted) repealed, by the Health Protection Agency Act 2004, s 11(1), (2), Sch 3, para 15, Sch 4.

Entry "Her Majesty's Chief Inspector of Education and Training in Wales" substituted by the Learning and Skills Act 2000, s 73(1), (3)(a).

Entry "The Historic Buildings Council for Wales" (omitted) repealed by the Historic Buildings Council for Wales (Abolition) Order 2006, SI 2006/63, art 3(1)(c)(iii).

Entries "The Horserace Betting Levy Board" and "The Horserace Totaliser Board" repealed by the Horserace Betting and Olympic Lottery Act 2004, ss 13, 17(2), 38, Sch 2, para 22, Sch 4, para 9, Sch 6, as from a day to be appointed.

Entry "The Human Tissue Authority" inserted by the Human Tissue Act 2004, s 13(2), Sch 2, para 27.

Entry "The Independent Police Complaints Commission" inserted, and entry "The Police Complaints Authority" (omitted) repealed, by the Police Reform Act 2002, s 107, Sch 7, para 23, Sch 8.

In entry "The Inland Waterways Amenity Advisory Council" for the words in italics there are substituted the words "Inland Waterways Advisory Council" by the Natural Environment and Rural Communities Act 2006, s 105(1), Sch 11, Pt 2, para 175(1)(a), (2), as from a day to be appointed.

Entry "The Insurance Brokers Registration Council" (omitted) repealed by the Financial Services and Markets Act 2000 (Dissolution of the Insurance Brokers Registration Council) (Consequential Provisions) Order 2001, SI 2001/1283, art 3(7).

Entries "The Judicial Appointments Commission" and "The Judicial Appointments and Conduct Ombudsman" inserted by the Constitutional Reform Act 2005, ss 61(2), 62(2), Sch 12, Pt 2, para 36(3), Sch 13, para 17(3).

Entry "The Library and Information Services Council (Wales)" (omitted) repealed by the Library Advisory Council for Wales Abolition and Consequential Amendments Order 2004, SI 2004/803, art 3(3).

Entries "The Millennium Commission", "The National Lottery Charities Board", and "The New Opportunities Fund" (omitted) repealed by the National Lottery Act 2006, s 21, Sch 3.

Entry "The National Council for Education and Training for Wales" (omitted) inserted by SI 2002/2623, art 2, Sch 1; repealed by the National Council for Education and Training for Wales (Transfer of Functions to the National Assembly for Wales and Abolition) Order 2005, SI 2005/3238, art 9(1), Sch 1, para 85.

Entries "The National Crime Squad" and "The Service Authority for the National Crime Squad" (omitted) repealed by the Serious Organised Crime and Police Act 2005, ss 59, 174(2), Sch 4, paras 158, 160, Sch 17, Pt 2.

Entry "The National Identity Scheme Commissioner" inserted by the Identity Cards Act 2006, s 22(8), as from a day to be appointed.

Entry "The Northern Ireland Judicial Appointments Ombudsman" inserted by the Justice (Northern Ireland) Act 2002, s 9A(3), Sch 3A, para 17(3) (as inserted by the Constitutional Reform Act 2005, s 124(3), Sch 15).

Entry "The Nuclear Decommissioning Authority" inserted by the Energy Act 2004, s 2(10), Sch 1, para 18.

Entry "The Office of Communications" inserted by the Office of Communications Act 2002, s 1(10), Schedule, para 22.

Entry "The Olympic Delivery Authority" inserted by the London Olympic Games and Paralympic Games Act 2006, s 3(2), Sch 1, Pt 2, para 23.

Entry "The Patient Information Advisory Group" inserted by the Health and Social Care Act 2001, s 67(1), Sch 5, Pt 3, para 18.

Entry "The Police Information Technology Organisation" repealed and entry "The National Policing Improvement Agency" inserted, by the Police and Justice Act 2006, ss 1(3), 52, Sch 1, Pt 7, para 74, Sch 15, Pt 1, as from a day to be appointed.

Entry "The Qualifications, Curriculum and Assessment Authority for Wales" (omitted) repealed by the Qualifications, Curriculum and Assessment Authority for Wales (Transfer of Functions to the National Assembly for Wales and Abolition) Order 2005, SI 2005/3239, art 9(1), Sch 1, para 31, subject to transitional provisions in art 7 thereof.

Entry "Any Rail Passengers' Committee" (omitted) inserted by SI 2002/2623, art 2, Sch 1; repealed by the Railways Act 2005, s 59(6), Sch 13, Pt 1.

Entry "The Security Industry Authority" inserted by the Private Security Industry Act 2001, s 1, Sch 1, para 23.

Entry "Strategic Rail Authority" (omitted) inserted by the Transport Act 2000, s 204, Sch 14, Pt V, para 30; repealed by the Railways Act 2005, s 59(6), Sch 13, Pt 1.

Entry "The Training and Development Agency for Schools" inserted by the Education Act 2005, s 98, Sch 14, para 22.

Entry "The Valuation Tribunal Service" inserted by the Local Government Act 2003, s 105(9), Sch 4, para 24.

Entry "The Wales Centre for Health" inserted by the Health (Wales) Act 2003, s 7(1), Sch 3, para 15.

Entry "The Wales Tourist Board" (omitted) repealed by the Wales Tourist Board (Transfer of Functions to the National Assembly for Wales and Abolition) Order 2005, SI 2005/3225, art 6(2), Sch 2, Pt 1, para 5, subject to transitional provisions in art 3 thereof.

Entry "The Welsh Development Agency" (omitted) repealed by the Welsh Development Agency (Transfer of Functions to the National Assembly for Wales and Abolition) Order 2005, SI 2005/3226, art 7(1)(b), Sch 2, Pt 1, para 13, subject to transitional provisions in art 3 thereof.

PART VII
OTHER PUBLIC BODIES AND OFFICES: NORTHERN IRELAND

[An advisory committee established under paragraph 25 of the Health and Personal Social Services (Northern Ireland) Order 1972.]

An Advisory Committee on General Commissioners of Income Tax (Northern Ireland).

The Advisory Committee on Justices of the Peace in Northern Ireland.

…

The Advisory Committee on Pesticides for Northern Ireland.

[The Agri-food and Biosciences Institute.]

…

The Agricultural Wages Board for Northern Ireland.

The Arts Council of Northern Ireland.

The Assembly Ombudsman for Northern Ireland.

[The Attorney General for Northern Ireland.]

[The Belfast Harbour Commissioners.]

The Board of Trustees of National Museums and Galleries of Northern Ireland.

…

The Boundary Commission for Northern Ireland.

[A central advisory committee established under paragraph 24 of the Health and Personal Social Services (Northern Ireland) Order 1972.]

[The Certification Officer for Northern Ireland.]

The Charities Advisory Committee.

The Chief Electoral Officer for Northern Ireland.

[The Chief Inspector of Criminal Justice in Northern Ireland.]

The Civil Service Commissioners for Northern Ireland.

[Comhairle na Gaelscolaíochta.]

[Commissioner for Children and Young People for Northern Ireland.]

The Commissioner for Public Appointments for Northern Ireland.

[The Commissioner for Victims and Survivors for Northern Ireland.]

The Construction Industry Training Board.

The consultative Civic Forum referred to in section 56(4) of the Northern Ireland Act 1998.

The Council for Catholic Maintained Schools.

The Council for Nature Conservation and the Countryside.

The County Court Rules Committee (Northern Ireland).

[The Criminal Injuries Compensation Appeals Panel for Northern Ireland, in relation to information held by it otherwise than as a tribunal.]

[A development corporation established under Part III of the Strategic Investment and Regeneration of Sites (Northern Ireland) Order 2003.]

The Disability Living Allowance Advisory Board for Northern Ireland.

The Distinction and Meritorious Service Awards Committee.

[A district policing partnership.]

The Drainage Council for Northern Ireland.

An Education and Library Board established under Article 3 of the Education and Libraries (Northern Ireland) Order 1986.

Enterprise Ulster.

The Equality Commission for Northern Ireland.

The Family Proceedings Rules Committee (Northern Ireland).

…

The Fisheries Conservancy Board for Northern Ireland.

The General Consumer Council for Northern Ireland.

[The General Teaching Council for Northern Ireland.]

[The Governors of the Armargh Observatory and Planetarium.]

[The Harbour of Donaghadee Commissioners.]

The Health and Safety Agency for Northern Ireland.

The Historic Buildings Council.

The Historic Monuments Council.

The Independent Assessor of Military Complaints Procedures in Northern Ireland.

[An independent monitoring board appointed under section 10 of the Prison Act (Northern Ireland) 1953.]

The Independent Reviewer of the Northern Ireland (Emergency Provisions) Act.

The Independent Commissioner for Holding Centres.

…

…

[Invest Northern Ireland.]

…

The Labour Relations Agency.

The Laganside Corporation.

The Law Reform Advisory Committee for Northern Ireland.

The Lay Observer for Northern Ireland.

[…]

The Legal Aid Advisory Committee (Northern Ireland).

[The Life Sentence Review Commissioners appointed under Article 3 of the Life Sentences (Northern Ireland) Order 2001.]

The Livestock & Meat Commission for Northern Ireland.

…

The Local Government Staff Commission.

[The Londonderry Port and Harbour Commissioners.]

The Magistrates' Courts Rules Committee (Northern Ireland).

The Mental Health Commission for Northern Ireland.

…

The Northern Ireland Audit Office.

The Northern Ireland Building Regulations Advisory Committee.

The Northern Ireland Civil Service Appeal Board.

The Northern Ireland Commissioner for Complaints.

The Northern Ireland Community Relations Council.

…

The Northern Ireland Council for the Curriculum, Examinations and Assessment.

…

[The Northern Ireland Court of Judicature Rules Committee.]

The Northern Ireland Crown Court Rules Committee.

…

[The Northern Ireland Events Company.]

[The Northern Ireland Fire and Rescue Service Board.]

The Northern Ireland Fishery Harbour Authority.

[The Northern Ireland Health and Personal Social Services Regulation and Improvement Authority.]

The Northern Ireland Higher Education Council.

The Northern Ireland Housing Executive.

The Northern Ireland Human Rights Commission.

The Northern Ireland Insolvency Rules Committee.

[The Northern Ireland Judicial Appointments Commission.]

[The Northern Ireland Law Commission.]

[The Northern Ireland Legal Services Commission.]

The Northern Ireland Local Government Officers' Superannuation Committee.

The Northern Ireland Museums Council.

The Northern Ireland Pig Production Development Committee.

[The Northern Ireland Practice and Education Council for Nursing and Midwifery.]

[The Northern Ireland Social Care Council.]

The Northern Ireland Supreme Court Rules Committee.

The Northern Ireland Tourist Board.

The Northern Ireland Transport Holding Company.

The Northern Ireland Water Council.

[…]

The Parades Commission.

[The Pharmaceutical Society of Northern Ireland, in respect of information held by it otherwise than as a tribunal.]

[The Poisons Board (Northern Ireland).]

The Police Ombudsman for Northern Ireland.

The Probation Board for Northern Ireland.

The Rural Development Council for Northern Ireland.

The Sentence Review Commissioners appointed under section 1 of the Northern Ireland (Sentences) Act 1998.

The social fund Commissioner appointed under Article 37 of the Social Security (Northern Ireland) Order 1998.

The Sports Council for Northern Ireland.

The Staff Commission for Education and Library Boards.

The Statistics Advisory Committee.

The Statute Law Committee for Northern Ireland.

[A sub-group established under section 21 of the Police (Northern Ireland) Act 2000.]

…

Ulster Supported Employment Ltd.

[The Warrenpoint Harbour Authority.]

[The Waste Management Advisory Board.]

The Youth Council for Northern Ireland.

[1408]

NOTES

Entry "Advisory Committee on Juvenile Court Lay Panel (Northern Ireland)" (omitted) repealed by the Justice (Northern Ireland) Act 2002, s 86, Sch 13.

Entry "The Agri-food and Biosciences Institute" inserted, and entry "The Agricultural Research Institute of Northern Ireland" (omitted) repealed by the Agriculture (Northern Ireland) Order 2004, SI 2004/3327, arts 3(5), 13, Sch 1, para 21, Sch 4.

Entries "The Belfast Harbour Commissioners", "The Certification Officer for Northern Ireland", "The Londonderry Port and Harbour Commissioners", and "The Warrenpoint Harbour Authority" inserted by the Freedom of Information (Additional Public Authorities) Order 2002, SI 2002/2623, art 3, Sch 2.

Entry "Boards of Visitors and Visiting Committees" (omitted) repealed and entry "An independent monitoring board appointed under section 10 of the Prison Act (Northern Ireland) 1953" inserted by the Criminal Justice (Northern Ireland) Order 2005, SI 2005/1965, art 10(2), Sch 1, para 10.

Entries "A central advisory committee established under paragraph 24 of the Health and Personal Social Services (Northern Ireland) Order 1972" and "An advisory committee established under paragraph 25 of the Health and Personal Social Services (Northern Ireland) Order 1972" inserted by the Freedom of Information (Additional Public Authorities) Order 2004, SI 2004/938, art 4, Sch 3.

Entry "The Chief Inspector of Criminal Justice in Northern Ireland" inserted by the Justice (Northern Ireland) Act 2002, s 45(3), Sch 8, para 16.

Entries "Comhairle na Gaelscolaíochta", "The Criminal Injuries Compensation Appeals Panel for Northern Ireland", "The General Teaching Council for Northern Ireland", "The Governors of the Armagh Observatory and Planetarium", "The Harbour of Donaghadee Commissioners", "The Northern Ireland Practice and Education Council for Nursing and Midwifery", "The Northern Ireland Social Care

Council" and "The Waste Management Advisory Board" inserted by the Freedom of Information (Additional Public Authorities) Order 2003, SI 2003/1882, art 3, Sch 2.

Entry "Commissioner for Children and Young People for Northern Ireland" inserted by the Commissioner for Children and Young People (Northern Ireland) Order 2003, SI 2003/439, art 5(3), Sch 2, para 15.

Entry "The Commissioner for Victims and Survivors for Northern Ireland" inserted by the Victims and Survivors (Northern Ireland) Order 2006, SI 2006/2953, art 4(3), Schedule, para 15, as from a day to be appointed.

Entry beginning "A development corporation" inserted by the Strategic Investment and Regeneration of Sites (Northern Ireland) Order 2003, SI 2003/410, art 15(3), Sch 1, para 23.

Entry "A district policing partnership" inserted by the Police (Northern Ireland) Act 2000, s 78(1), Sch 6, para 25(1), (3).

Entry "The Fire Authority for Northern Ireland" (omitted) repealed and entry "The Northern Ireland Fire and Rescue Service Board" inserted by the Fire and Rescue Services (Northern Ireland) Order 2006, SI 2006/1254, arts 3(3), 62(2), Sch 1, para 19, Sch 4.

Entries "Industrial Development Board for Northern Ireland", "Industrial Research and Technology Unit" and "Local Enterprise Development Unit" (all omitted) repealed, and entry "Invest Northern Ireland" inserted, by the Industrial Development Act (Northern Ireland) 2002, ss 1(2), 5(4), Sch 1, para 21, Sch 4.

Entries "The Juvenile Justice Board", "The Northern Ireland Consumer Committee for Electricity", "The Northern Ireland Council for Postgraduate Medical and Dental Education" and "The Training and Employment Agency" (all omitted) repealed by the Freedom of Information (Removal of References to Public Authorities) Order 2004, SI 2004/1641, art 3, Sch 2.

Entry "Law Reform Advisory Committee for Northern Ireland" repealed, and entries "The Attorney General for Northern Ireland" and "The Northern Ireland Law Commission" inserted, by the Justice (Northern Ireland) Act 2002, ss 23(9), 50(7), 86, Sch 9, para 15, Sch 13, as from a day to be appointed.

Entry "The Learning and Skills Advisory Board" inserted by SI 2003/1882, art 3, Sch 2; repealed by SI 2004/1641, art 3, Sch 2.

Entry "The Life Sentence Review Commissioners" inserted by the Life Sentences (Northern Ireland Consequential Amendments) Order 2001, SI 2001/2565, art 4.

Entry "The Northern Ireland Advisory Committee on Telecommunications" repealed by the Communications Act 2003, s 406(7), Sch 19(1).

Entry "The Northern Ireland Court of Judicature Rules Committee" inserted and entry "The Northern Ireland Supreme Court Rules Committee" repealed by the Constitutional Reform Act 2005, ss 59(5), 146, Sch 11, Pt 4, para 34, Sch 18, Pt 5, as from a day to be appointed.

Entries "The Northern Ireland Economic Council" and "Obstetrics Committee" (as inserted by SI 2004/938, art 4, Sch 3) (omitted) repealed by the Freedom of Information (Removal of References to Public Authorities) Order 2005, SI 2005/3594, art 2, Sch 1.

Entries "The Northern Ireland Events Company", "The Northern Ireland Health and Personal Social Services Regulation and Improvement Authority", "The Pharmaceutical Society of Northern Ireland", and "The Poisons Board (Northern Ireland)" inserted by the Freedom of Information (Additional Public Authorities) Order 2005, SI 2005/3593, arts 4, 5, Schs 3, 4.

Entry "The Northern Ireland Judicial Appointments Commission" inserted by the Justice (Northern Ireland) Act 2002, s 3(3), Sch 2, para 20.

Entry "The Northern Ireland Legal Services Commission" inserted by the Access to Justice (Northern Ireland) Order 2003, SI 2003/435, art 49(1), Sch 4, para 15.

Entry relating to "section 21 of the Police (Northern Ireland) Act 2000" inserted by the Police (Northern Ireland) Act 2003, s 19(1), Sch 1, paras 1, 15, as from a day to be appointed.

SCHEDULE 2
THE COMMISSIONER AND THE TRIBUNAL

Section 18(4)

PART I
PROVISION CONSEQUENTIAL ON S 18(1) AND (2)

General

1.—(1) Any reference in any enactment, instrument or document to the Data Protection Commissioner or the Data Protection Registrar shall be construed, in relation to any time after the commencement of section 18(1), as a reference to the Information Commissioner.

(2) Any reference in any enactment, instrument or document to the Data Protection Tribunal shall be construed, in relation to any time after the commencement of section 18(2), as a reference to the Information Tribunal.

2.—(1) Any reference in this Act or in any instrument under this Act to the Commissioner shall be construed, in relation to any time before the commencement of section 18(1), as a reference to the Data Protection Commissioner.

(2) Any reference in this Act or in any instrument under this Act to the Tribunal shall be construed, in relation to any time before the commencement of section 18(2), as a reference to the Data Protection Tribunal.

3–15. …

[1409]

NOTES

Paras 3–15: amend the Data Protection Act 1998, ss 6, 70, Sch 5 at **[1113]**, **[1177]**, **[1188]**, and contain other amendments outside the scope of this work.

(*Pt II amends the Data Protection Act 1998, ss 6, 26, 58, 59, Sch 5 at* **[1113]**, **[1134]**, **[1166]**, **[1167]**, **[1188]**.)

SCHEDULE 3
POWERS OF ENTRY AND INSPECTION

Section 55

Issue of warrants

1.—(1) If a circuit judge [or a District Judge (Magistrates' Courts)] is satisfied by information on oath supplied by the Commissioner that there are reasonable grounds for suspecting—

(a) that a public authority has failed or is failing to comply with—
   (i) any of the requirements of Part I of this Act,
   (ii) so much of a decision notice as requires steps to be taken, or
   (iii) an information notice or an enforcement notice, or
(b) that an offence under section 77 has been or is being committed,

and that evidence of such a failure to comply or of the commission of the offence is to be found on any premises specified in the information, he may, subject to paragraph 2, grant a warrant to the Commissioner.

(2) A warrant issued under sub-paragraph (1) shall authorise the Commissioner or any of his officers or staff at any time within seven days of the date of the warrant—

(a) to enter and search the premises,
(b) to inspect and seize any documents or other material found there which may be such evidence as is mentioned in that sub-paragraph, and
(c) to inspect, examine, operate and test any equipment found there in which information held by the public authority may be recorded.

2.—(1) A judge shall not issue a warrant under this Schedule unless he is satisfied—

(a) that the Commissioner has given seven days' notice in writing to the occupier of the premises in question demanding access to the premises, and
(b) that either—
   (i) access was demanded at a reasonable hour and was unreasonably refused, or
   (ii) although entry to the premises was granted, the occupier unreasonably refused to comply with a request by the Commissioner or any of the Commissioner's officers or staff to permit the Commissioner or the officer or member of staff to do any of the things referred to in paragraph 1(2), and
(c) that the occupier, has, after the refusal, been notified by the Commissioner of the application for the warrant and has had an opportunity of being heard by the judge on the question whether or not it should be issued.

(2) Sub-paragraph (1) shall not apply if the judge is satisfied that the case is one of urgency or that compliance with those provisions would defeat the object of the entry.

3. A judge who issues a warrant under this Schedule shall also issue two copies of it and certify them clearly as copies.

Execution of warrants

4. A person executing a warrant issued under this Schedule may use such reasonable force as may be necessary.

5. A warrant issued under this Schedule shall be executed at a reasonable hour unless it appears to the person executing it that there are grounds for suspecting that the evidence in question would not be found if it were so executed.

6.—(1) If the premises in respect of which a warrant is issued under this Schedule are occupied by a public authority and any officer or employee of the authority is present when the warrant is executed, he shall be shown the warrant and supplied with a copy of it; and if no such officer or employee is present a copy of the warrant shall be left in a prominent place on the premises.

(2) If the premises in respect of which a warrant is issued under this Schedule are occupied by a person other than a public authority and he is present when the warrant is executed, he shall be shown the warrant and supplied with a copy of it; and if that person is not present a copy of the warrant shall be left in a prominent place on the premises.

7.—(1) A person seizing anything in pursuance of a warrant under this Schedule shall give a receipt for it if asked to do so.

(2) Anything so seized may be retained for so long as is necessary in all the circumstances but the person in occupation of the premises in question shall be given a copy of anything that is seized if he so requests and the person executing the warrant considers that it can be done without undue delay.

Matters exempt from inspection and seizure

8. The powers of inspection and seizure conferred by a warrant issued under this Schedule shall not be exercisable in respect of information which is exempt information by virtue of section 23(1) or 24(1).

9.—(1) Subject to the provisions of this paragraph, the powers of inspection and seizure conferred by a warrant issued under this Schedule shall not be exercisable in respect of—

(a) any communication between a professional legal adviser and his client in connection with the giving of legal advice to the client with respect to his obligations, liabilities or rights under this Act, or

(b) any communication between a professional legal adviser and his client, or between such an adviser or his client and any other person, made in connection with or in contemplation of proceedings under or arising out of this Act (including proceedings before the Tribunal) and for the purposes of such proceedings.

(2) Sub-paragraph (1) applies also to—

(a) any copy or other record of any such communication as is there mentioned, and

(b) any document or article enclosed with or referred to in any such communication if made in connection with the giving of any advice or, as the case may be, in connection with or in contemplation of and for the purposes of such proceedings as are there mentioned.

(3) This paragraph does not apply to anything in the possession of any person other than the professional legal adviser or his client or to anything held with the intention of furthering a criminal purpose.

(4) In this paragraph references to the client of a professional legal adviser include references to any person representing such a client.

10. If the person in occupation of any premises in respect of which a warrant is issued under this Schedule objects to the inspection or seizure under the warrant of any material on the grounds that it consists partly of matters in respect of which those powers are not exercisable, he shall, if the person executing the warrant so requests, furnish that person with a copy of so much of the material in relation to which the powers are exercisable.

Return of warrants

11. A warrant issued under this Schedule shall be returned to the court from which it was issued—
 (a) after being executed, or
 (b) if not executed within the time authorised for its execution;

and the person by whom any such warrant is executed shall make an endorsement on it stating what powers have been exercised by him under the warrant.

Offences

12. Any person who—
 (a) intentionally obstructs a person in the execution of a warrant issued under this Schedule, or
 (b) fails without reasonable excuse to give any person executing such a warrant such assistance as he may reasonably require for the execution of the warrant,

is guilty of an offence.

Vessels, vehicles etc

13. In this Schedule "premises" includes any vessel, vehicle, aircraft or hovercraft, and references to the occupier of any premises include references to the person in charge of any vessel, vehicle, aircraft or hovercraft.

Scotland and Northern Ireland

14. In the application of this Schedule to Scotland—
 (a) for any reference to a circuit judge there is substituted a reference to the sheriff, and
 (b) for any reference to information on oath there is substituted a reference to evidence on oath.

15. In the application of this Schedule to Northern Ireland—
 (a) for any reference to a circuit judge there is substituted a reference to a county court judge, and
 (b) or any reference to information on oath there is substituted a reference to a complaint on oath.

[1410]

NOTES

Commencement: 30 November 2002 (in so far as it relates to the enforcement of the requirements on public authorities under the publication scheme provisions and in so far as relates to: (i) the issue of practice recommendations, and (ii) the issue and enforcement of information notices, relating to the conformity with the code of practice under s 45 of the practice of public authorities in relation to the exercise of their functions under the publication scheme provisions); 1 January 2005 (otherwise).

Para 1: words in square brackets in sub-para (1) inserted by the Courts Act 2003, s 65, Sch 4, para 13, as from a day to be appointed.

See further, in relation to additional powers of seizure from premises: the Criminal Justice and Police Act 2001, s 50, Sch 1, Pt 1, para 73.

(Sch 4 amends the Data Protection Act 1998, Sch 6 at **[1191]**; *Sch 5 (amendments of public records legislation) outside the scope of this work; Sch 6 amends s 7 of, Schs 2, 3, 7, 14 to, the 1998 Act at* **[1114]**, **[1185]**, **[1186]**, **[1192]**, **[1203]**, *and inserts ss 35A, 63A of that Act at* **[1143A]**, **[1170A]**; *Sch 7 (amendments relating to disclosure of information by Ombudsmen) outside the scope of this work.)*

SCHEDULE 8
REPEALS

Section 86

PART I
REPEAL COMING INTO FORCE ON PASSING OF ACT

Chapter	*Short title*	*Extent of repeal*
1998 c 29	The Data Protection Act 1998	In Schedule 14, in paragraph 2(1), the words "or, if earlier, 24th October 2001".

[1411]

PART II
REPEALS COMING INTO FORCE IN ACCORDANCE WITH SECTION 87(2)

Chapter	*Short title*	*Extent of repeal*
1958 c 51	The Public Records Act 1958	In Schedule 1, in Part II of the Table in paragraph 3, the entry relating to the Data Protection Commissioner.
1967 c 13	The Parliamentary Commissioner Act 1967	In Schedule 2, the entry relating to the Data Protection Commissioner.
1975 c 24	The House of Commons Disqualification Act 1975	In Schedule 1, in Part III, the entry relating to the Data Protection Commissioner.
1975 c 25	The Northern Ireland Assembly Disqualification Act 1975	In Schedule 1, in Part III, the entry relating to the Data Protection Commissioner.
1998 c 29	The Data Protection Act 1998	In Schedule 5, Part III. In Schedule 15, paragraphs 1(1), 2, 4, 5(2) and 6(2).

[1412]

PART III
REPEALS COMING INTO FORCE IN ACCORDANCE WITH SECTION 87(3)

Chapter	*Short title*	*Extent of repeal*
1958 c 51	The Public Records Act 1958	In section 5, subsections (1), (2) and (4) and, in subsection (5), the words from "and subject to" to the end. Schedule 2.
1975 c 24	The House of Commons Disqualification Act 1975	In Schedule 1, in Part II, the entry relating to the Data Protection Tribunal.
1975 c 25	The Northern Ireland Assembly Disqualification Act 1975'	In Schedule 1, in Part II, the entry relating to the Data Protection Tribunal.

Chapter	*Short title*	*Extent of repeal*
1998 c 29	The Data Protection Act 1998	In section 1(1), in the definition of "data", the word "or" at the end of paragraph (c). In Schedule 15, paragraphs 1(2) and (3), 3, 5(1) and 6(1).

[1413]

NOTES

Commencement: 1 January 2005.

GAMBLING ACT 2005

(2005 c 19)

ARRANGEMENT OF SECTIONS

PART 1
INTERPRETATION OF KEY CONCEPTS

Principal concepts

Maintenance

Duration

PART 11
LOTTERIES

Interpretation

Offences

Miscellaneous

General

PART 14
PRIVATE AND NON-COMMERCIAL GAMING AND BETTING

Non-commercial gaming and betting

PART 18
MISCELLANEOUS AND GENERAL

General

An Act to make provision about gambling

[7 April 2005]

PART 1
INTERPRETATION OF KEY CONCEPTS

Principal concepts

1 The licensing objectives

In this Act a reference to the licensing objectives is a reference to the objectives of—

(a) preventing gambling from being a source of crime or disorder, being associated with crime or disorder or being used to support crime,

(b) ensuring that gambling is conducted in a fair and open way, and

(c) protecting children and other vulnerable persons from being harmed or exploited by gambling.

[1413A]

NOTES

Commencement: 1 October 2005.

2 Licensing authorities

(1) For the purposes of this Act the following are licensing authorities—

(a) in relation to England—

(i) a district council,

(ii) a county council for a county in which there are no district councils,

(iii) a London borough council,

(iv) the Common Council of the City of London, and

(v) the Council of the Isles of Scilly,

(b) in relation to Wales—

(i) a county council, and

(ii) a county borough council, and

(c) in relation to Scotland, a licensing board constituted under section 1 of the Licensing (Scotland) Act 1976 (c 66).

(2) For the purposes of Schedule 13, the Sub-Treasurer of the Inner Temple and the Under-Treasurer of the Middle Temple are licensing authorities.

[1413B]

NOTES

Commencement: 1 October 2005.

3 Gambling

In this Act "gambling" means—

(a) gaming (within the meaning of section 6),

(b) betting (within the meaning of section 9), and

(c) participating in a lottery (within the meaning of section 14 and subject to section 15).

[1413C]

NOTES

Commencement: 1 October 2005.

4–13 (*Outside the scope of this work.*)

Lottery

14 Lottery

(1) For the purposes of this Act an arrangement is a lottery, irrespective of how it is described, if it satisfies one of the descriptions of lottery in subsections (2) and (3).

(2) An arrangement is a simple lottery if—
(a) persons are required to pay in order to participate in the arrangement,
(b) in the course of the arrangement one or more prizes are allocated to one or more members of a class, and
(c) the prizes are allocated by a process which relies wholly on chance.

(3) An arrangement is a complex lottery if—
(a) persons are required to pay in order to participate in the arrangement,
(b) in the course of the arrangement one or more prizes are allocated to one or more members of a class,
(c) the prizes are allocated by a series of processes, and
(d) the first of those processes relies wholly on chance.

(4) In this Act "prize" in relation to lotteries includes any money, articles or services—
(a) whether or not described as a prize, and
(b) whether or not consisting wholly or partly of money paid, or articles or services provided, by the members of the class among whom the prize is allocated.

(5) A process which requires persons to exercise skill or judgment or to display knowledge shall be treated for the purposes of this section as relying wholly on chance if—
(a) the requirement cannot reasonably be expected to prevent a significant proportion of persons who participate in the arrangement of which the process forms part from receiving a prize, and
(b) the requirement cannot reasonably be expected to prevent a significant proportion of persons who wish to participate in that arrangement from doing so.

(6) Schedule 2 makes further provision about when an arrangement is to be or not to be treated for the purposes of this section as requiring persons to pay.

(7) The Secretary of State may by regulations provide that an arrangement of a specified kind is to be or not to be treated as a lottery for the purposes of this Act; and—
(a) the power in this subsection is not constrained by subsections (1) to (6) or Schedule 2, and
(b) regulations under this subsection may amend other provisions of this section or Schedule 2.

[1413D]

NOTES

Commencement: 1 October 2005.

15 National Lottery

(1) Participating in a lottery which forms part of the National Lottery is not gambling for the purposes of this Act (despite section 3(c) but subject to subsections (2) and (3) below).

(2) Participating in a lottery which forms part of the National Lottery is gambling for the purposes of—
(a) section 42, and
(b) section 335.

(3) Where participating in a lottery which forms part of the National Lottery would also constitute gaming within the meaning of section 6, it shall be treated as gaming for the purposes of this Act if and only if a person participating in the lottery is required to participate in, or to be successful in, more than three processes before becoming entitled to a prize.

(4) Participating in a lottery which forms part of the National Lottery shall not be treated as betting for the purposes of this Act where it would—
(a) satisfy the definition of pool betting in section 12, or
(b) satisfy the definition of betting in section 9 by virtue of section 11.

(5) Schedule 3 shall have effect.

[1413E]

NOTES

Commencement: 1 October 2005 (sub-ss (1)–(4), sub-s (5) certain purposes); 1 September 2007 (sub-s (5) for remaining purposes).

Cross-category activities

16 (*Outside the scope of this work.*)

17 Lotteries and gaming

(1) This section applies to an arrangement which satisfies—

(a) the definition of a game of chance in section 6, and

(b) the definition of a lottery in section 14.

(2) An arrangement to which this section applies shall be treated for the purposes of this Act as a game of chance (and not as a lottery) if a person who pays in order to join the class amongst whose members prizes are allocated is required to participate in, or to be successful in, more than three processes before becoming entitled to a prize.

(3) An arrangement to which this section applies shall, subject to subsection (2), be treated for the purposes of this Act as a lottery (and not as a game of chance) if—

(a) it satisfies paragraph 1(1)(a) and (b) of Schedule 11,

(b) it satisfies paragraph 10(1)(a) and (b) of Schedule 11,

(c) it satisfies paragraph 11(1)(a) and (b) of Schedule 11,

(d) it satisfies paragraph 12(1)(a) and (b) of Schedule 11,

(e) it satisfies paragraph 20(1)(a) and (b) of Schedule 11,

(f) it satisfies paragraph 30(1)(a) and (b) of Schedule 11, or

(g) it is promoted in reliance on a lottery operating licence.

(4) Any other arrangement to which this section applies shall be treated for the purposes of this Act as a game of chance (and not as a lottery).

(5) This section is subject to regulations under section 6(6) or 14(7).

[1413F]

NOTES

Commencement: 1 October 2005.

18 Lotteries and betting

(1) This section applies to a transaction which satisfies the definition of participating in a lottery in section 14 and also—

(a) satisfies the definition of pool betting in section 12, or

(b) satisfies the definition of betting in section 9 by virtue of section 11.

(2) A transaction to which this section applies shall be treated for the purposes of this Act as participating in a lottery (and not as betting) if—

(a) it satisfies paragraph 1(1)(a) and (b) of Schedule 11,

(b) it satisfies paragraph 10(1)(a) and (b) of Schedule 11,

(c) it satisfies paragraph 11(1)(a) and (b) of Schedule 11,

(d) it satisfies paragraph 12(1)(a) and (b) of Schedule 11,

(e) it satisfies paragraph 20(1)(a) and (b) of Schedule 11,

(f) it satisfies paragraph 30(1)(a) and (b) of Schedule 11, or

(g) it is promoted in reliance on a lottery operating licence.

(3) Any other transaction to which this section applies shall be treated for the purposes of this Act as betting (and not as participating in a lottery).

(4) This section is subject to regulations under section 14(7).

[1413G]

NOTES

Commencement: 1 October 2005.

Miscellaneous

19 Non-commercial society

(1) For the purposes of this Act a society is non-commercial if it is established and conducted—

(a) for charitable purposes,

(b) for the purpose of enabling participation in, or of supporting, sport, athletics or a cultural activity, or

(c) for any other non-commercial purpose other than that of private gain.

(2) In subsection (1) "charitable purposes" means—

(a) in relation to England and Wales, purposes which are exclusively charitable according to the law of England and Wales, and

(b) in relation to Scotland, purposes which are charitable purposes only (that expression having the same meaning as in the Income Tax Acts).

(3) The provision of a benefit to one or more individuals is not a provision for the purpose of private gain for the purposes of this Act if made in the course of the activities of a society that is a non-commercial society by virtue of subsection (1)(a) or (b).

[1413H]

NOTES

Commencement: 1 October 2005.

20–32 (*Outside the scope of this work.*)

PART 3
GENERAL OFFENCES

Provision of facilities for gambling

33 Provision of facilities for gambling

(1) A person commits an offence if he provides facilities for gambling unless—

(a) an exception provided for in subsection (2) or (3) applies, or

(b) an exception provided for by any of the following provisions applies—

(i) sections 34 and 35,

(ii) sections 269 and 271 (clubs and miners' welfare institutes),

(iii) section 279 (premises with alcohol licence),

(iv) sections 289 to 292 (prize gaming),

(v) section 296 (private gaming and betting), and

(vi) section 298 (non-commercial gaming).

(2) (*Outside the scope of this work.*)

[1413I]

NOTES

Commencement: 1 September 2007; for transitional provisions see the Gambling Act 2005 (Commencement No 6 and Transitional Provisions) Order 2006, SI 2006/3272, art 6, Sch 4.

34 Exception: lotteries

Section 33 shall not apply to the provision of facilities for a lottery.

[1413J]

NOTES

Commencement: 1 September 2007; for transitional provisions see the Gambling Act 2005 (Commencement No 6 and Transitional Provisions) Order 2006, SI 2006/3272, art 6, Sch 4.

35–64 (*Outside the scope of this work.*)

PART 5
OPERATING LICENCES

Introductory

65 Nature of licence

(1) The Commission may issue operating licences in accordance with the provisions of this Part.

(2) An operating licence is a licence which states that it authorises the licensee—

(a)–(i) (*outside the scope of this work*)

(j) to promote a lottery (a "lottery operating licence").

(3)–(5) (*Outside the scope of this work.*)

[1413K]

NOTES

Commencement: 1 October 2005 (sub-s (2)); 1 January 2007 (sub-s (1) for the purpose of enabling advance applications for operating licences to be made, considered and determined; and enabling such licences to be issued before 1st September 2007); 1 September 2007 (sub-s (1) for remaining purposes); for transitional provisions see the Gambling Act 2005 (Commencement No 6 and Transitional Provisions) Order 2006, SI 2006/3272, art 6, Sch 4.

66 Form of licence

(1) An operating licence must specify—

(a) the person to whom it is issued,

(b) the period during which it is to have effect, and

(c) any condition attached by the Commission under section 75 or 77.

(2) The Secretary of State may by regulations require the Commission to ensure that an operating licence—

(a) is issued in such form as the regulations may specify, and

(b) contains, in addition to the matters specified in subsection (1), such information as the regulations may specify (which may, in particular, include information about conditions attached to the licence by virtue of section 78).

[1413L]

NOTES

Commencement: 1 January 2007 (for the purpose of enabling advance applications for operating licences to be made, considered and determined; and enabling such licences to be issued before 1st September 2007); 1 September 2007 (for remaining purposes); for transitional provisions see the Gambling Act 2005 (Commencement No 6 and Transitional Provisions) Order 2006, SI 2006/3272, art 6, Sch 4.

67–74 (*Outside the scope of this work.*)

Conditions

75 General conditions imposed by Commission

(1) The Commission may specify conditions to be attached to—

(a) each operating licence, or

(b) each operating licence falling within a specified class.

(2) For the purposes of subsection (1)(b) a class may be defined wholly or partly by reference to—

(a) the nature of the licensed activities;

(b) the circumstances in which the licensed activities are carried on;

(c) the nature or circumstances of the licensee or of another person involved or likely to be involved in the conduct of the licensed activities.

(3) Where the Commission issues an operating licence it shall attach to the licence any condition specified under subsection (1) as a condition to be attached to operating licences of a class within which the licence falls.

[1413M]

NOTES

Commencement: 1 October 2005 (sub-ss (1), (2)); 1 January 2007 (sub-s (3)); for transitional provisions see the Gambling Act 2005 (Commencement No 6 and Transitional Provisions) Order 2006, SI 2006/3272, art 6, Sch 4.

76 (*Outside the scope of this work.*)

77 Individual condition imposed by Commission

Where the Commission issues an operating licence it may attach a condition to the licence. **[1413N]**

NOTES

Commencement: 1 January 2007; for transitional provisions see the Gambling Act 2005 (Commencement No 6 and Transitional Provisions) Order 2006, SI 2006/3272, art 6, Sch 4.

78 Condition imposed by Secretary of State

(1) The Secretary of State may by regulations provide for a specified condition to be attached to operating licences falling within a specified description.

(2) Transitional provision of regulations under this section (made by virtue of section 355(1)(c)) may, in particular, apply a condition (with or without modification) to licences issued before the regulations are made (or come into force). **[1413O]**

NOTES

Commencement: 1 January 2007; for transitional provisions see the Gambling Act 2005 (Commencement No 6 and Transitional Provisions) Order 2006, SI 2006/3272, art 6, Sch 4.

79–88 (*Outside the scope of this work.*)

Rules for particular kinds of licence

89–97 (*Outside the scope of this work.*)

98 Lottery operating licences

(1) A lottery operating licence may be issued only to—
- (a) a non-commercial society,
- (b) a local authority, or
- (c) a person proposing to act as external lottery manager on behalf of a non-commercial society or a local authority.

(2) A lottery operating licence may authorise—
- (a) promotion generally or only specified promoting activities;
- (b) the promotion of lotteries generally or only the promotion of lotteries of a specified kind or in specified circumstances;
- (c) action as an external lottery manager (in which case it is known as a "lottery manager's operating licence").

(3) In issuing a lottery operating licence to a society or authority the Commission—
- (a) may attach a condition under section 75 or 77 requiring that the society or authority ensure that all the arrangements for the lottery are made by the holder of a lottery manager's operating licence, and
- (b) may, if they attach a condition under paragraph (a), issue the lottery licence to the society or authority without consideration of the matters specified in section 70(1)(b).

(4) A lottery operating licence shall, by virtue of this subsection, permit the delivery of lottery tickets by post.

(5) The effect of the term implied by subsection (4) may not be disapplied or restricted by a condition attached under section 75, 77 or 78.

(6) In issuing a lottery operating licence the Commission may attach a condition under section 75 or 77 preventing, restricting or controlling the use of a rollover.

(7) In this section "local authority" means—

(a) in relation to England—

(i) a district council,

(ii) a county council,

(iii) a parish council,

(iv) a London borough council,

(v) the Common Council of the City of London, and

(vi) the Council of the Isles of Scilly,

(b) in relation to Wales—

(i) a county council,

(ii) a county borough council, and

(iii) a community council, and

(c) in relation to Scotland, a council constituted under section 2 of the Local Government etc (Scotland) Act 1994 (c 39).

[1413P]

NOTES

Commencement: 1 January 2007; for transitional provisions see the Gambling Act 2005 (Commencement No 6 and Transitional Provisions) Order 2006, SI 2006/3272, art 6, Sch 4.

99 Mandatory conditions of lottery operating licence

(1) In issuing a lottery operating licence to a non-commercial society or to a local authority the Commission shall attach conditions under section 75 or 77 for the purpose of achieving the requirements specified in this section.

(2) The first requirement is that at least 20% of the proceeds of any lottery promoted in reliance on the licence are applied—

(a) in the case of a licence issued to a non-commercial society, to a purpose for which the promoting society is conducted, and

(b) in the case of a licence issued to a local authority, for a purpose for which the authority has power to incur expenditure.

(3) The second requirement is that—

(a) the proceeds of any lottery promoted in reliance on the licence may not exceed £2,000,000, and

(b) the aggregate of the proceeds of lotteries promoted wholly or partly in a calendar year in reliance on the licence may not exceed £10,000,000.

(4) The third requirement is that it must not be possible for the purchaser of a ticket in a lottery promoted in reliance on the licence to win by virtue of that ticket (whether in money, money's worth, or partly the one and partly the other) more than—

(a) £25,000, or

(b) if more, 10% of the proceeds of the lottery;

and any rollover must comply with this subsection.

(5) The fourth requirement is that where a person purchases a lottery ticket in a lottery promoted by a non-commercial society in reliance on the licence he receives a document which—

(a) identifies the promoting society,

(b) states the name and address of a member of the society who is designated, by persons acting on behalf of the society, as having responsibility within the society for the promotion of the lottery, and

(c) either—

(i) states the date of the draw (or each draw) in the lottery, or

(ii) enables the date of the draw (or each draw) in the lottery to be determined.

(6) The fifth requirement is that the price payable for purchasing each ticket in a lottery promoted in reliance on the licence—

(a) must be the same,

(b) must be shown on the ticket or in a document received by the purchaser, and

(c) must be paid to the promoter of the lottery before any person is given a ticket or any right in respect of membership of the class among whom prizes are to be allocated.

(7) For the purpose of subsections (5) and (6) a reference to a person receiving a document includes, in particular, a reference to a message being sent or displayed to him electronically in a manner which enables him, without incurring significant expense or delay, to—

(a) retain the message electronically, or
(b) print it.

(8) The sixth requirement is that membership of the class among whom prizes in any lottery promoted in reliance on the licence are allocated may not be dependent on making any payment (apart from payment of the price of a ticket).

(9) Where—

(a) conditions are attached to a lottery operating licence in accordance with this section, and
(b) the lottery operating licence is also subject to a condition under section 98(3)(a) requiring arrangements for the lottery to be made by the holder of a lottery manager's operating licence,

the conditions specified in paragraph (a) above shall, by virtue of this subsection, attach to the lottery manager's operating licence in so far as it is relied upon in pursuance of the condition specified in paragraph (b) above.

(10) Nothing in this section prevents the Commission from attaching a condition to a lottery operating licence of a kind similar to but more onerous than a requirement of this section.

(11) The Secretary of State may by order vary a monetary amount or a percentage in this section.

[1413Q]

NOTES

Commencement: 1 January 2007; for transitional provisions see the Gambling Act 2005 (Commencement No 6 and Transitional Provisions) Order 2006, SI 2006/3272, art 6, Sch 4.

Maintenance

100 Annual fee

(1) The holder of an operating licence—

(a) shall pay a first annual fee to the Commission within such period after the issue of the licence as may be prescribed, and
(b) shall pay an annual fee to the Commission before each anniversary of the issue of the licence.

(2) In this section—

"annual fee" means a fee of such amount as may be prescribed, and
"prescribed" means prescribed by the Secretary of State by regulations.

(3) Regulations under this section may, in particular, make different provision for—

(a) different kinds of operating licence, or
(b) different circumstances.

(4) Subsection (1)(b) does not apply in relation to an anniversary of the issue of a licence on or immediately before which the licence ceases to have effect by virtue of section 111.

[1413R]

NOTES

Commencement: 1 January 2007; for transitional provisions see the Gambling Act 2005 (Commencement No 6 and Transitional Provisions) Order 2006, SI 2006/3272, art 6, Sch 4.

101–103 (*Outside the scope of this work.*)

104 Application to vary licence

(1) The holder of an operating licence may apply to the Commission to vary the licence by—

(a) adding, amending or removing a licensed activity,

(b) amending another detail of the licence, or

(c) adding, amending or removing a condition attached to the licence under section 77.

(2) A licence may not be varied under this section so as to authorise anyone other than the person to whom it was issued to provide facilities for gambling.

(3) The provisions of this Part shall apply in relation to an application for variation as they apply in relation to an application for a licence—

(a) subject to the provisions of this section, and

(b) with any other necessary modifications.

(4) Regulations under this Part which relate to an application for an operating licence may make—

(a) provision which applies only in the case of an application for variation;

(b) provision which does not apply in the case of an application for variation;

(c) different provision in relation to an application for variation from that made in relation to an application for an operating licence;

(d) different provision in relation to applications for variations of different kinds.

(5) An application for variation must (in addition to anything required by section 69) be accompanied by—

(a) a statement of the variation sought, and

(b) either—

(i) the licence to be varied, or

(ii) a statement explaining why it is not reasonably practicable to produce the licence.

(6) In granting an application for variation the Commission—

(a) shall specify a time when the variation shall begin to have effect, and

(b) may make transitional provision.

[1413S]

NOTES

Commencement: 1 January 2007; for transitional provisions see the Gambling Act 2005 (Commencement No 6 and Transitional Provisions) Order 2006, SI 2006/3272, art 6, Sch 4.

Regulations: the Gambling (Operating Licence and Single-Machine Permit Fees) Regulations 2006, SI 2006/3284; the Gambling (Personal Licence Fees) Regulations 2006, SI 2006/3285.

105 Amendment

(1) The Commission may require the holder of an operating licence to submit it to the Commission for the purpose of amendment to reflect—

(a) a general variation of conditions under section 75,

(b) a change notified under section 101,

(c) the grant of an application for variation under section 104,

(d) the attachment of an additional condition, or the amendment of a condition, under section 117,

(e) the grant of an application for renewal under section 112, or

(f) anything done in relation to a personal licence under Part 6.

(2) A licensee shall comply with a requirement under subsection (1) within the period of 14 days beginning with the day on which he receives notice of the requirement.

(3) A person commits an offence if he fails without reasonable excuse to comply with a requirement imposed under subsection (1).

(4) A person guilty of an offence under subsection (3) shall be liable on summary conviction to a fine not exceeding level 2 on the standard scale.

(5) Subsection (1)(a) is without prejudice to section 76(4)(c).

[1413T]

NOTES

Commencement: 1 January 2007; for transitional provisions see the Gambling Act 2005 (Commencement No 6 and Transitional Provisions) Order 2006, SI 2006/3272, art 6, Sch 4.

106 Register of operating licences

(1) The Commission shall—

(a) maintain a register of operating licences containing such details of and relating to each licence as the Commission thinks appropriate,

(b) make the register available for inspection by members of the public at all reasonable times, and

(c) make arrangements for the provision of a copy of an entry in the register to a member of the public on request.

(2) The Commission may refuse to provide access to the register or to provide a copy of an entry unless the person seeking access or a copy pays a fee specified by the Commission.

(3) The Commission may not specify a fee under subsection (2) which exceeds the reasonable cost of providing the service sought (but in calculating the cost of providing a service to a person the Commission may include a reasonable share of expenditure which is referable only indirectly to the provision of that service).

[1413U]

NOTES

Commencement: 1 January 2007; for transitional provisions see the Gambling Act 2005 (Commencement No 6 and Transitional Provisions) Order 2006, SI 2006/3272, art 6, Sch 4.

107 Copy of licence

(1) The Commission may make arrangements to issue to a licensee on request a copy of an operating licence which has been lost, stolen or damaged.

(2) The arrangements may, in particular, include a requirement—

(a) for the payment of a fee not exceeding such sum as may be prescribed for the purposes of this subsection by the Secretary of State by regulations;

(b) in the case of a licence being lost or stolen, that the licensee has complied with specified arrangements for reporting the loss or theft to the police.

(3) A copy of a licence issued under this section shall be treated as if it were the licence.

[1413V]

NOTES

Commencement: 1 January 2007; for transitional provisions see the Gambling Act 2005 (Commencement No 6 and Transitional Provisions) Order 2006, SI 2006/3272, art 6, Sch 4.

Regulations: the Gambling (Operating Licence and Single-Machine Permit Fees) Regulations 2006, SI 2006/3284; the Gambling (Personal Licence Fees) Regulations 2006, SI 2006/3285.

108 Production of licence

(1) A constable or enforcement officer may require the holder of an operating licence to produce it to the constable or enforcement officer within a specified period.

(2) A licensee commits an offence if he fails without reasonable excuse to comply with a requirement under subsection (1).

(3) A person guilty of an offence under subsection (2) shall be liable on summary conviction to a fine not exceeding level 2 on the standard scale.

[1413W]

NOTES

Commencement: 1 September 2007; for transitional provisions see the Gambling Act 2005 (Commencement No 6 and Transitional Provisions) Order 2006, SI 2006/3272, art 6, Sch 4.

109 Conviction

(1) If the holder of an operating licence is convicted of an offence by or before a court in Great Britain he shall as soon as is reasonably practicable notify the Commission of—

(a) his conviction, and

(b) any sentence passed in respect of it.

(2) If the holder of an operating licence is convicted of a relevant offence by or before a court in Great Britain he shall immediately inform the court that he is the holder of an operating licence.

(3) If the holder of an operating licence is convicted of a relevant offence by or before a court outside Great Britain he shall as soon as is reasonably practicable notify the Commission of—

(a) his conviction, and
(b) any sentence passed in respect of it.

(4) A person commits an offence if he fails without reasonable excuse to comply with any of subsections (1) to (3).

(5) A person guilty of an offence under subsection (4) shall be liable on summary conviction to a fine not exceeding level 2 on the standard scale.

[1413X]

NOTES

Commencement: 1 January 2007; for transitional provisions see the Gambling Act 2005 (Commencement No 6 and Transitional Provisions) Order 2006, SI 2006/3272, art 6, Sch 4.

Duration

110 Indefinite duration

An operating licence shall continue to have effect unless and until it ceases to have effect in accordance with—

(a) a determination under section 111, or
(b) section 113, 114, 115, 118 or 119.

[1413Y]

NOTES

Commencement: 1 September 2007; for transitional provisions see the Gambling Act 2005 (Commencement No 6 and Transitional Provisions) Order 2006, SI 2006/3272, art 6, Sch 4.

111 Power to limit duration

(1) The Commission may determine that operating licences, or a specified class of operating licence, shall cease to have effect at the end of a specified period (unless terminated earlier in accordance with section 113, 114, 115 or 119).

(2) The period specified under subsection (1)—

(a) in the case of an operating licence issued after the determination, must begin with the date on which the licence is issued, and
(b) in the case of an operating licence issued before the determination, must begin with the date of the determination.

(3) The Commission—

(a) may determine different periods under subsection (1) for operating licences authorising different classes of activity (but may not otherwise determine different periods for different licences),
(b) may alter a determination under subsection (1) (but an alteration shall have effect only in relation to licences issued after the alteration), and
(c) may revoke a determination under subsection (1) (in which case the determination shall cease to have effect in relation to licences already issued).

(4) The Commission shall publish any determination under subsection (1) as part of a statement (or revised statement) under section 23.

[1413Z]

NOTES

Commencement: 1 September 2007; for transitional provisions see the Gambling Act 2005 (Commencement No 6 and Transitional Provisions) Order 2006, SI 2006/3272, art 6, Sch 4.

112 Renewal of licence

(1) Where an operating licence is subject to a determination under section 111, the licensee may apply to the Commission for renewal of the licence.

(2) The provisions of this Part shall apply in relation to an application for renewal as they apply in relation to an application for a licence—
(a) subject to the provisions of this section, and
(b) with any other necessary modifications.

(3) An application for renewal of an operating licence may be made only during the period which—
(a) begins three months before the date on which the licence would otherwise expire by virtue of section 111, and
(b) ends one month before the date on which the licence would otherwise expire by virtue of that section.

(4) Where an application for renewal of an operating licence is awaiting determination on the date when it would expire by virtue of section 111, the licence shall continue to have effect by virtue of this subsection until the application is determined (unless it ceases to have effect by virtue of section 113, 114, 115, 118 or 119).

(5) A direction or regulations under this Part which relate to an application for an operating licence may make—
(a) provision which applies only in the case of an application for renewal;
(b) provision which does not apply in the case of an application for renewal;
(c) different provision in relation to an application for renewal from that made in relation to an application for an operating licence.

(6) An application for renewal must (in addition to anything required by section 69) be accompanied by—
(a) the licence to be renewed, or
(b) a statement explaining why it is not reasonably practicable to submit the licence to be renewed.

(7) The Commission shall determine the period during which a renewed operating licence is to have effect (subject to sections 113, 114, 115, 118 and 119); and the Commission—
(a) may determine different periods for operating licences authorising different classes of activity (but may not otherwise determine different periods for different licences),
(b) may alter a determination (but an alteration shall have effect only in relation to licences issued after the alteration), and
(c) shall publish any determination under this subsection as part of a statement (or revised statement) under section 23.

(8) The Secretary of State may by order amend subsection (3) so as to substitute a different time for a time specified.

[1413ZA]

NOTES

Commencement: 1 September 2007; for transitional provisions see the Gambling Act 2005 (Commencement No 6 and Transitional Provisions) Order 2006, SI 2006/3272, art 6, Sch 4.

113 Surrender

An operating licence shall cease to have effect if the licensee—
(a) notifies the Commission of his intention to surrender the licence, and
(b) gives the Commission either—
(i) the licence, or
(ii) a written statement explaining why it is not reasonably practicable to produce the licence.

[1413ZB]

NOTES

Commencement: 1 January 2007; for transitional provisions see the Gambling Act 2005 (Commencement No 6 and Transitional Provisions) Order 2006, SI 2006/3272, art 6, Sch 4.

114 Lapse

(1) In the case of an operating licence issued to an individual, the licence shall lapse if—
(a) the licensee dies,

(b) the licensee becomes, in the opinion of the Commission as notified to the licensee, incapable of carrying on the licensed activities by reason of mental or physical incapacity,
(c) the licensee becomes bankrupt (within the meaning of section 381 of the Insolvency Act 1986 (c 45)), or
(d) sequestration of the licensee's estate is awarded under section 12(1) of the Bankruptcy (Scotland) Act 1985 (c 66).

(2) In any other case an operating licence shall lapse if the licensee—
(a) ceases to exist, or
(b) goes into liquidation (within the meaning of section 247(2) of the Insolvency Act 1986).

[1413ZC]

NOTES

Commencement: 1 January 2007; for transitional provisions see the Gambling Act 2005 (Commencement No 6 and Transitional Provisions) Order 2006, SI 2006/3272, art 6, Sch 4.

115 Forfeiture

(1) Where the holder of an operating licence is convicted of a relevant offence by or before a court in Great Britain the court may order forfeiture of the licence.

(2) Forfeiture under this section shall be on such terms (which may include terms as to suspension) as may be specified by—
(a) the court which orders forfeiture,
(b) a court to which an appeal against the conviction, or against any order made on the conviction, has been or could be made, or
(c) the High Court, if hearing proceedings relating to the conviction.

(3) Subject to any express provision made under subsection (2), an operating licence shall cease to have effect on the making of a forfeiture order under subsection (1).

(4) The terms on which a forfeiture order is made under this section shall, in particular, include a requirement that the licensee deliver to the Commission, within such time as the order may specify—
(a) the licence, or
(b) a statement explaining why it is not reasonably practicable to produce the licence.

(5) As soon as is reasonably practicable after making an order for forfeiture under this section the court shall notify the Commission.

[1413ZD]

NOTES

Commencement: 1 January 2007; for transitional provisions see the Gambling Act 2005 (Commencement No 6 and Transitional Provisions) Order 2006, SI 2006/3272, art 6, Sch 4.

116–251 (*Outside the scope of this work.*)

PART 11
LOTTERIES

Interpretation

252 Promoting a lottery

(1) For the purposes of this Act a person promotes a lottery if he makes or participates in making the arrangements for a lottery.

(2) In particular, a person promotes a lottery if he—
(a) makes arrangements for the printing of lottery tickets,
(b) makes arrangements for the printing of promotional material,
(c) arranges for the distribution or publication of promotional material,
(d) possesses promotional material with a view to its distribution or publication,
(e) makes other arrangements to advertise a lottery,

(f) invites a person to participate in a lottery,
(g) sells or supplies a lottery ticket,
(h) offers to sell or supply a lottery ticket,
(i) possesses a lottery ticket with a view to its sale or supply,
(j) does or offers to do anything by virtue of which a person becomes a member of a class among whom prizes in a lottery are to be allocated, or
(k) uses premises for the purpose of allocating prizes or for any other purpose connected with the administration of a lottery.

(3) In subsection (2) "promotional material" means a document which—
(a) advertises a specified lottery,
(b) invites participation in a specified lottery,
(c) contains information about how to participate in a specified lottery, or
(d) lists winners in a specified lottery.

(4) Where arrangements for a lottery are made by an external lottery manager on behalf of a society or authority, for the purposes of this Act both the external lottery manager and the society or authority promote the lottery.

[1413ZE]

NOTES

Commencement: 1 January 2007 (for transitional provisions see the Gambling Act 2005 (Commencement No 6 and Transitional Provisions) Order 2006, SI 2006/3272, art 6, Sch 4).

253 Lottery ticket

(1) For the purposes of this Act a document or article is a lottery ticket if it confers, or can be used to prove, membership of a class for the purpose of the allocation of prizes in a lottery.

(2) A reference in this Act to the sale or supply of a lottery ticket by a person includes a reference to a person doing anything as a result of which another person becomes a member of the class among whom prizes in a lottery are to be allocated.

(3) A reference in this Act to purchase of a lottery ticket includes a reference to any action by a person as a result of which he becomes a member of the class among whom prizes in a lottery are to be allocated.

[1413ZF]

NOTES

Commencement: 1 January 2007 (for transitional provisions see the Gambling Act 2005 (Commencement No 6 and Transitional Provisions) Order 2006, SI 2006/3272, art 6, Sch 4).

254 Proceeds and profits

(1) In this Act a reference to the proceeds of a lottery is a reference to the aggregate of amounts paid in respect of the purchase of lottery tickets.

(2) In this Act a reference to the profits of a lottery is a reference to—
(a) the proceeds of the lottery, minus
(b) amounts deducted by the promoters of the lottery in respect of—
(i) the provision of prizes,
(ii) sums to be made available for allocation in another lottery in accordance with a rollover, or
(iii) other costs reasonably incurred in organising the lottery.

[1413ZG]

NOTES

Commencement: 1 January 2007 (for transitional provisions see the Gambling Act 2005 (Commencement No 6 and Transitional Provisions) Order 2006, SI 2006/3272, art 6, Sch 4).

255 Draw

In this Act "draw", in relation to a lottery, includes any process by which a prize in the lottery is allocated.

[1413ZH]

NOTES

Commencement: 1 January 2007 (for transitional provisions see the Gambling Act 2005 (Commencement No 6 and Transitional Provisions) Order 2006, SI 2006/3272, art 6, Sch 4).

256 Rollover

(1) In this Act "rollover" in relation to a lottery means an arrangement whereby the fact that a prize is not allocated or claimed in one lottery increases the value of the prizes available for allocation in another lottery.

(2) For the purposes of this Act where prizes are allocated by means of more than one draw—

(a) the draws together constitute a single lottery if the class of persons among whom prizes are allocated is (and, by virtue of arrangements for the sale or supply of tickets, must be) the same in the case of each draw, and

(b) otherwise, the arrangements for each draw constitute a separate lottery.

[1413ZI]

NOTES

Commencement: 1 January 2007 (for transitional provisions see the Gambling Act 2005 (Commencement No 6 and Transitional Provisions) Order 2006, SI 2006/3272, art 6, Sch 4).

257 External lottery manager

A person acts as an external lottery manager for the purposes of this Act if he makes arrangements for a lottery on behalf of a society or authority of which he is not—

(a) a member,

(b) an officer, or

(c) an employee under a contract of employment.

[1413ZJ]

NOTES

Commencement: 1 January 2007 (for transitional provisions see the Gambling Act 2005 (Commencement No 6 and Transitional Provisions) Order 2006, SI 2006/3272, art 6, Sch 4).

Offences

258 Promotion of lottery

(1) A person commits an offence if he promotes a lottery unless—

(a) the exception in subsection (2) or (3) applies, or

(b) the lottery is an exempt lottery.

(2) This section does not apply to activity by a person if—

(a) he holds an operating licence authorising the activity, and

(b) he acts in accordance with the terms and conditions of the licence.

(3) This section does not apply to activity by a person if—

(a) he acts, otherwise than as an external lottery manager, on behalf of a person who holds an operating licence authorising the activity, and

(b) the activity is carried on in accordance with the terms and conditions of the licence.

(4) It is a defence for a person charged with an offence under this section to show that he reasonably believed that—

(a) he was not committing the offence by reason of subsection (1)(b), (2) or (3),

(b) that the arrangement to which the charge relates was not a lottery, or

(c) that the arrangement to which the charge relates was a lottery forming part of the National Lottery.

(5) In this Act "exempt lottery" means a lottery which is exempt by virtue of a provision of Schedule 11.

[1413ZK]

NOTES

Commencement: 1 October 2005 (sub-s (5) for certain purposes); 1 September 2007 (sub-ss (1)–(4), sub-s (5) for remaining purposes) (for transitional provisions see the Gambling Act 2005 (Commencement No 6 and Transitional Provisions) Order 2006, SI 2006/3272, art 6, Sch 4).

259 Facilitating a lottery

(1) A person commits an offence if he facilitates a lottery unless—

(a) the exception in subsection (3) applies, or

(b) the lottery is an exempt lottery.

(2) For the purposes of this section a person facilitates a lottery if (and only if) he—

(a) prints lottery tickets for a specified lottery,

(b) prints promotional material for a specified lottery, or

(c) advertises a specified lottery.

(3) This section does not apply to activity by a person if he acts in accordance with the terms and conditions of an operating licence.

(4) It is a defence for a person charged with an offence under this section to show that he reasonably believed—

(a) that he was not committing the offence by reason of subsection (1)(b) or (3), or

(b) that the arrangement to which the charge relates was not a lottery, or

(c) that the arrangement to which the charge relates was a lottery forming part of the National Lottery.

(5) In subsection (2)(b) "promotional material" means a document which—

(a) advertises a specified lottery,

(b) invites participation in a specified lottery,

(c) contains information about how to participate in a specified lottery, or

(d) lists winners in a specified lottery.

[1413ZL]

NOTES

Commencement: 1 September 2007 (for transitional provisions see the Gambling Act 2005 (Commencement No 6 and Transitional Provisions) Order 2006, SI 2006/3272, art 6, Sch 4).

260 Misusing profits of lottery

(1) This section applies to a lottery in respect of which the promoter has stated (in whatever terms) a fund-raising purpose for the promotion of the lottery.

(2) A person commits an offence if he uses any part of the profits of a lottery to which this section applies for a purpose other than that stated.

(3) The reference in subsection (2) to using profits includes a reference to permitting profits to be used.

(4) In subsection (1) the reference to a statement of a purpose for the promotion of a lottery is a reference to a statement appearing—

(a) on lottery tickets, or

(b) in an advertisement for the lottery.

(5) In subsection (4)(b) "advertisement" in relation to a lottery includes any written notice announcing that a lottery will take place or inviting people to participate in a lottery (in either case whether or not it also gives other information).

[1413ZM]

NOTES

Commencement: 1 September 2007 (for transitional provisions see the Gambling Act 2005 (Commencement No 6 and Transitional Provisions) Order 2006, SI 2006/3272, art 6, Sch 4).

261 Misusing profits of exempt lottery

(1) This section applies to the following kinds of lottery—

(a) an incidental non-commercial lottery (within the meaning of Part 1 of Schedule 11),
(b) a private society lottery (within the meaning of Part 2 of that Schedule), and
(c) a small society lottery (within the meaning of Part 4 of that Schedule).

(2) A person commits an offence if he uses any part of the profits of a lottery to which this section applies for a purpose other than one for which the lottery is permitted to be promoted in accordance with Schedule 11.

(3) Subsection (3) of section 260 shall have effect for the purpose of this section as it has effect for the purpose of that section.

[1413ZN]

NOTES

Commencement: 1 September 2007 (for transitional provisions see the Gambling Act 2005 (Commencement No 6 and Transitional Provisions) Order 2006, SI 2006/3272, art 6, Sch 4).

262 Small society lottery: breach of condition

A non-commercial society commits an offence if—

(a) a lottery, purporting to be an exempt lottery under Part 4 of Schedule 11, is promoted on the society's behalf wholly or partly at a time when the society is not registered with a local authority in accordance with Part 5 of that Schedule,
(b) the society fails to comply with the requirements of paragraph 39 of that Schedule, or
(c) the society provides false or misleading information for the purposes of paragraph 39 of that Schedule.

[1413ZO]

NOTES

Commencement: 1 September 2007 (for transitional provisions see the Gambling Act 2005 (Commencement No 6 and Transitional Provisions) Order 2006, SI 2006/3272, art 6, Sch 4).

263 Penalty

(1) A person guilty of an offence under this Part shall be liable on summary conviction to—

(a) imprisonment for a term not exceeding 51 weeks,
(b) a fine not exceeding level 5 on the standard scale, or
(c) both.

(2) In the application of subsection (1) to Scotland the reference to 51 weeks shall have effect as a reference to six months.

[1413ZP]

NOTES

Commencement: 1 September 2007 (for transitional provisions see the Gambling Act 2005 (Commencement No 6 and Transitional Provisions) Order 2006, SI 2006/3272, art 6, Sch 4).

Miscellaneous

264 Exclusion of the National Lottery

The preceding provisions of this Part do not apply to the National Lottery.

[1413ZQ]

NOTES

Commencement: 1 September 2007 (for transitional provisions see the Gambling Act 2005 (Commencement No 6 and Transitional Provisions) Order 2006, SI 2006/3272, art 6, Sch 4).

General

265 Territorial application

(1) This Part applies to anything done in relation to a lottery—

(a) in Great Britain, or

(b) by the provision of, or by means of, remote gambling equipment situated in Great Britain.

(2) But this Part does not apply in relation to a lottery if—

(a) no person in Great Britain does anything by virtue of which he becomes a participant in the lottery, and

(b) no person in Great Britain possesses tickets for the lottery with a view to selling or supplying them to a person in Great Britain who thereby becomes a participant in the lottery.

(3) It is a defence for a person charged with an offence under section 258 or 259 to show that he reasonably believed that this Part did not and would not apply to the lottery, by reason of subsection (2) above.

[1413ZR]

NOTES

Commencement: 1 September 2007 (for transitional provisions see the Gambling Act 2005 (Commencement No 6 and Transitional Provisions) Order 2006, SI 2006/3272, art 6, Sch 4).

266–294 (*Outside the scope of this work.*)

PART 14
PRIVATE AND NON-COMMERCIAL GAMING AND BETTING

295, 296 (*Outside the scope of this work.*)

Non-commercial gaming and betting

297 Interpretation

(1) For the purposes of this Act gaming is non-commercial if it takes place at a non-commercial event (whether as an incidental activity or as the principal or only activity).

(2) An event is non-commercial if the arrangements for the event are such that no part of the proceeds is to be appropriated for the purpose of private gain.

(3) For the purposes of subsection (2) the proceeds of an event are—

(a) the sums raised by the organisers (whether by way of fees for entrance or for participation, by way of sponsorship, by way of commission from traders or otherwise), minus

(b) amounts deducted by the organisers in respect of costs reasonably incurred in organising the event.

[1413ZS]

NOTES

Commencement: 1 September 2007 (for transitional provisions see the Gambling Act 2005 (Commencement No 6 and Transitional Provisions) Order 2006, SI 2006/3272, art 6, Sch 4).

298 Exceptions to offences

(1) A person does not commit an offence under section 33 by providing facilities for—

(a) non-commercial prize gaming which complies with the conditions in section 299, or

(b) non-commercial equal chance gaming which complies with the conditions in section 300.

(2) Section 37 shall not apply to or in respect of the use of premises to carry on—

(a) non-commercial prize gaming which complies with the conditions in section 299, or

(b) non-commercial equal chance gaming which complies with the conditions in section 300.

[1413ZT]

PART I STATUTES

NOTES

Commencement: 1 September 2007 (for transitional provisions see the Gambling Act 2005 (Commencement No 6 and Transitional Provisions) Order 2006, SI 2006/3272, art 6, Sch 4).

299 Conditions for non-commercial prize gaming

(1) This section specifies the conditions for non-commercial prize gaming mentioned in section 298.

(2) The first condition is that players are informed that the purpose of the gaming is to raise money for a specified purpose other than that of private gain.

(3) The second condition is that the arrangements for the gaming are such that the profits will be applied for a purpose other than that of private gain.

(4) The third condition is that the non-commercial event of which the gaming is part does not take place—

- (a) on premises, other than a track, in respect of which a premises licence has effect,
- (b) on a track at a time when activities are being carried on in reliance on a premises licence, or
- (c) on premises at a time when activities are being carried on in reliance on a temporary use notice.

(5) The fourth condition is that the gaming is not remote.

(6) In this section "profits" in relation to gaming means—

- (a) the aggregate of amounts—
  - (i) paid by way of stakes, or
  - (ii) otherwise accruing to the person organising the gaming directly in connection with it, minus
- (b) amounts deducted by the person organising the gaming in respect of—
  - (i) the provision of prizes, or
  - (ii) other costs reasonably incurred in organising or providing facilities for the gaming.

[1413ZU]

NOTES

Commencement: 1 September 2007 (for transitional provisions see the Gambling Act 2005 (Commencement No 6 and Transitional Provisions) Order 2006, SI 2006/3272, art 6, Sch 4).

300 Conditions for non-commercial equal-chance gaming

(1) This section specifies the conditions for non-commercial equal-chance gaming mentioned in section 298.

(2) The first condition is that persons participating in the gaming are informed that the purpose of the gaming is to raise money for a specified purpose other than that of private gain.

(3) The second condition is that the arrangements for the gaming are such that the profits will be applied for a purpose other than that of private gain.

(4) The third condition is that the arrangements for the gaming ensure compliance with regulations of the Secretary of State—

- (a) limiting amounts staked;
- (b) limiting participation fees;
- (c) limiting other amounts paid by a person in connection with the gaming;
- (d) limiting a combination of matters specified in paragraphs (a) to (c);
- (e) limiting the amount or value of a prize;
- (f) limiting the aggregate amount or value of prizes.

(5) Regulations under subsection (4) may, in particular—

- (a) make provision by reference to whether or not a game is part of a series;
- (b) make provision by reference to whether or not the non-commercial event of which the gaming is part is associated, as defined by the regulations, with another event;
- (c) limit stakes in relation to a participant in more than one game;
- (d) make different provision for different kinds of game or for games played in different circumstances.

(6) The fourth condition is that the non-commercial event of which the gaming is part does not take place—
- (a) on premises, other than a track, in respect of which a premises licence has effect,
- (b) on a track at a time when activities are being carried on in reliance on a premises licence, or
- (c) on premises at a time when activities are being carried on in reliance on a temporary use notice.

(7) The fifth condition is that the gaming is non-remote.

(8) In this section "profits" in relation to gaming means—
- (a) the aggregate of amounts—
  - (i) paid by way of stakes, or
  - (ii) otherwise accruing to the person organising the gaming directly in connection with it, minus
- (b) amounts deducted by the person organising the gaming in respect of—
  - (i) the provision of prizes, or
  - (ii) other costs reasonably incurred in organising or providing facilities for the gaming.

[1413ZV]

NOTES

Commencement: 1 September 2007 (for transitional provisions see the Gambling Act 2005 (Commencement No 6 and Transitional Provisions) Order 2006, SI 2006/3272, art 6, Sch 4).

301 Misusing profits of non-commercial prize gaming

(1) This section applies to—
- (a) non-commercial prize gaming in respect of which a fund-raising purpose has been specified as mentioned in section 299(2), and
- (b) non-commercial equal-chance gaming in respect of which a fund-raising purpose has been specified as mentioned in section 300(2).

(2) A person commits an offence if he uses any part of the profits of gaming to which this section applies for a purpose other than that specified.

(3) The reference in subsection (2) to the use of profits includes a reference to permitting profits to be used.

(4) A person guilty of an offence under this section shall be liable on summary conviction to—
- (a) imprisonment for a term not exceeding 51 weeks,
- (b) a fine not exceeding level 5 on the standard scale, or
- (c) both.

(5) In the application of subsection (4) to Scotland the reference to 51 weeks shall have effect as a reference to six months.

(6) In this section "profits" has the same meaning as in sections 299 and 300.

[1413ZW]

NOTES

Commencement: 1 September 2007 (for transitional provisions see the Gambling Act 2005 (Commencement No 6 and Transitional Provisions) Order 2006, SI 2006/3272, art 6, Sch 4).

302 Non-commercial betting

For the purposes of this Act a betting transaction is non-commercial betting if no party to the transaction—
- (a) enters it in the course of a business, or
- (b) holds himself out as being in business in relation to the acceptance of bets.

[1413ZX]

NOTES

Commencement: 1 September 2007 (for transitional provisions see the Gambling Act 2005 (Commencement No 6 and Transitional Provisions) Order 2006, SI 2006/3272, art 6, Sch 4).

303–338 (*Outside the scope of this work.*)

PART 18
MISCELLANEOUS AND GENERAL

339–352 (*Outside the scope of this work.*)

General

353 Interpretation

(1) In this Act, except where the context otherwise requires—
"adult" means an individual who is not a child or young person,

.....

"child" has the meaning given by section 45,

.....

"the Commission" means the Gambling Commission,

.....

"draw", in relation to a lottery, has the meaning given by section 255,

.....

"enforcement officer" means a person designated or appointed as an enforcement officer under section 303,
"equal chance gaming" has the meaning given by section 8,
"exempt lottery" has the meaning given by section 258,
"external lottery manager" has the meaning given by section 257,

.....

"gambling" has the meaning given by section 3,

.....

"game of chance" has the meaning given by section 6,
"gaming" has the meaning given by that section,

.....

"lottery" has the meaning given by section 14 (and section 256),
"lottery manager's operating licence" has the meaning given by section 98,
"lottery ticket" has the meaning given by section 253,

.....

"the National Lottery" has the meaning given by section 1 of the National Lottery etc Act 1993 (c 39)),

.....

"non-commercial gaming" has the meaning given by section 297,
"non-commercial society" has the meaning given by section 19,

.....

"operating licence" means a licence issued under Part 5,

.....

"participation fee" has the meaning given by section 344,

.....

"premises" includes any place and, in particular—
(a) a vessel, and
(b) a vehicle,
"premises licence" means a licence issued under Part 8,

.....

"private gain" is to be construed in accordance with section 19(3),

.....

"prize" in relation to a lottery has the meaning given by section 14,
"prize gaming" has the meaning given by section 288,

.....

"proceeds", in relation to a lottery, has the meaning given by section 254,
"profits", in relation to a lottery, has the meaning given by that section,

.....

"relevant offence" has the meaning given by section 126 and Schedule 7,
"remote communication" has the meaning given by section 4,
"remote gambling" has the meaning given by that section,
"remote gambling equipment" has the meaning given by section 36,

.....

"rollover", in relation to a lottery, has the meaning given by section 256,

.....

"society" includes a branch or section of a society,

"stake" means an amount paid or risked in connection with gambling and which either—

(a) is used in calculating the amount of the winnings or the value of the prize that the person making the stake receives if successful, or

(b) is used in calculating the total amount of winnings or value of prizes in respect of the gambling in which the person making the stake participates,

"supply" includes—

(a) sale,

(b) lease, and

(c) placing on premises with permission or in accordance with a contract or other arrangement,

"temporary use notice" has the meaning given by section 215,

"track" means a horse-race course, dog track or other premises on any part of which a race or other sporting event takes place or is intended to take place,

.....

"vehicle" includes—

(a) a train,

(b) an aircraft,

(c) a seaplane, and

(d) an amphibious vehicle (other than a hovercraft within the meaning of the Hovercraft Act 1968 (c 59)),

"vessel" includes—

(a) anything, other than a seaplane or an amphibious vehicle, designed or adapted for navigation or other use in, on or over water,

(b) a hovercraft (within the meaning of the Hovercraft Act 1968), and

(c) anything, or any part of any place, situated in or on water,

.....

"young person" has the meaning given by section 45.

(2) In this Act, except where the context otherwise requires—

(a) a reference to accepting a bet includes a reference to negotiating a bet,

(b) a reference to advertising is to be construed in accordance with section 327,

(c) a reference to participating in a lottery is to be construed in accordance with section 14,

(d)–(f) (*outside the scope of this work*)

(g) a reference to premises includes a reference to part of premises,

(h) a reference to promoting a lottery is to be construed in accordance with section 252,

(i) a reference to providing facilities for gambling is to be construed in accordance with section 5,

(j) a reference to publication includes a reference to display, and

(k) a reference to the sale, supply or purchase of a lottery ticket is to be construed in accordance with section 253.

(3) (*Outside the scope of this work.*)

(4) A requirement under this Act to give a notice (or to notify) is a requirement to give notice in writing; and for that purpose—

(a) a message sent by facsimile transmission or electronic mail shall be treated as a notice given in writing, and

(b) a notice sent to a licensee at the address specified for that purpose in the licence shall, unless the contrary is proved, be treated as reaching him within a period within which it could reasonably be expected to reach him in the ordinary course of events.

(5) A reference in this Act to an act which is authorised by a licence or other document does not include a reference to an act which would be authorised by the licence or document but for failure to comply with a term or condition.

[1413ZY]

NOTES

Commencement: 1 January 2007 (for transitional provisions see the Gambling Act 2005 (Commencement No 6 and Transitional Provisions) Order 2006, SI 2006/3272, art 6, Sch 4.

The definitions omitted from sub-s (1) are outside the scope of this work.

354–357 (*Outside the scope of this work.*)

358 Commencement

(1) The preceding provisions of this Act shall come into force in accordance with provision made by the Secretary of State by order.

(2) An order under subsection (1) may (without prejudice to the generality of section 355(1))—
- (a) bring only specified provisions into force;
- (b) bring different provisions into force at different times;
- (c) bring a provision into force for a specified purpose only;
- (d) bring a provision into force at different times for different purposes;
- (e) in particular, bring Part 2 into force only for specified preliminary purposes relating to the establishment of the Commission (which may include the assumption of functions of the Gaming Board for Great Britain pending the commencement of repeals made by this Act);
- (f) in particular, bring a provision of this Act into force for the purpose of enabling an advance application for a licence or permit to be made, considered and determined;
- (g) in particular, bring an offence or other provision of this Act into force only in relation to gambling of a specified class or in specified circumstances;
- (h) include transitional provision modifying the application of a provision of this Act pending the commencement of, or pending the doing of anything under, a provision of another enactment.

(3) Schedule 18 (transitional) shall have effect.

(4) Without prejudice to the generality of section 355(1)(c) or of Schedule 18, an order under this section may—
- (a) make savings (with or without modification) or transitional provision in connection with Part 1 or 2 of the Horserace Betting and Olympic Lottery Act 2004 (c 25) (sale of the Horserace Totalisator Board ("the Tote") and abolition of the horserace betting levy system);
- (b) modify a provision of this Act in its application in relation to a matter addressed by Part 1 or 2 of that Act or so as to reflect a provision of Part 1 or 2 of that Act;
- (c) modify a provision of Part 1 or 2 of that Act (including a provision which amends another enactment) so as to reflect a provision of this Act.

(5) If the Secretary of State brings into force a repeal effected by this Act at a time when the appointed day for the purposes of Part 1 of that Act has not been appointed or has not arrived, he may by order—
- (a) save, with or without modification, a provision repealed by this Act in so far as it relates to the Tote;
- (b) make provision in connection with the Tote of a kind similar to provision made by a provision repealed by this Act;
- (c) modify a provision of this Act for a purpose connected with the Tote;
- (d) modify a provision of Part 1 of that Act (including a provision which amends another enactment) so as to reflect a provision of this Act.

(6) If the Secretary of State wholly or partly brings into force the repeal by this Act of the Betting, Gaming and Lotteries Act 1963 (c 2) at a time when the provisions listed in section 15(1)(a) to (c) of the Horserace Betting and Olympic Lottery Act 2004 (horserace betting levy system) have not been entirely repealed by order under that section, he may by order—
- (a) save any of those provisions, with or without modification;
- (b) make provision of a kind similar to any of those provisions;
- (c) modify a provision of this Act for a purpose connected with a matter addressed by any of those provisions or by Part 2 of that Act;
- (d) modify a provision of Part 2 of that Act (including a provision which amends another enactment) so as to reflect a provision of this Act.

[1413ZZ]

NOTES

Commencement: 7 April 2005.

Orders: Gambling Act 2005 (Commencement No 1) Order 2005, SI 2005/2425; Gambling Act 2005 (Commencement No 2 and Transitional Provisions) Order 2005, SI 2005/2455; Gambling Act 2005

(Commencement No 3) Order 2006, SI 2006/631; Gambling Act 2005 (Commencement No 4) Order 2006, SI 2006/2964; Gambling Act 2005 (Commencement No 5) Order 2006, SI 2006/3220; the Gambling Act 2005 (Commencement No 6 and Transitional Provisions) Order 2006, SI 2006/3272.

359–361 (*Outside the scope of this work.*)

362 Short title

This Act may be cited as the Gambling Act 2005.

[1413ZZA]

NOTES

Commencement: 7 April 2005.

SCHEDULES

(*Sch 1 outside the scope of this work.*)

SCHEDULE 2
LOTTERIES: DEFINITION OF PAYMENT TO ENTER

Section 14

Introduction

1. This Schedule makes provision about the circumstances in which an arrangement is to be or not to be treated for the purposes of section 14 as requiring persons to pay in order to participate in an arrangement.

Meaning of payment

2. For the purposes of section 14 and this Schedule a reference to paying includes a reference to—

(a) paying money,

(b) transferring money's worth, and

(c) paying for goods or services at a price or rate which reflects the opportunity to participate in an arrangement.

3. It is immaterial for the purposes of section 14 and this Schedule—

(a) to whom a payment is made, and

(b) who receives benefit from a payment.

4. It is also immaterial for the purposes of section 14 and this Schedule whether a person knows when he makes a payment that he thereby participates in an arrangement.

Stamps, telephone calls, &c

5.—(1) For the purposes of section 14 and this Schedule a reference to paying does not include a reference to incurring the expense, at a normal rate, of—

(a) sending a letter by ordinary post,

(b) making a telephone call, or

(c) using any other method of communication.

(2) For the purpose of sub-paragraph (1)—

(a) a "normal rate" is a rate which does not reflect the opportunity to enter a lottery, and

(b) ordinary post means ordinary first-class or second-class post (without special arrangements for delivery).

Payment to discover whether prize won

6. For the purposes of section 14 and this Schedule a requirement to pay in order to discover whether a prize has been won under an arrangement shall be treated as a requirement to pay in order to participate in the arrangement.

Payment to claim prize

7. For the purposes of section 14 and this Schedule a requirement to pay in order to take possession of a prize which has or may have been allocated to a person under an arrangement shall be treated as a requirement to pay in order to participate in the arrangement.

Choice of free entry

8.—(1) For the purposes of section 14 and this Schedule an arrangement shall not be treated as requiring persons to pay in order to participate if under the arrangement—

(a) each individual who is eligible to participate has a choice whether to participate by paying or by sending a communication,

(b) the communication mentioned in paragraph (a) may be—

(i) a letter sent by ordinary post, or

(ii) another method of communication which is neither more expensive nor less convenient than entering the lottery by paying,

(c) the choice is publicised in such a way as to be likely to come to the attention of each individual who proposes to participate, and

(d) the system for allocating prizes does not differentiate between those who participate by paying and those who participate by sending a communication.

(2) In this paragraph "ordinary post" has the meaning given by paragraph 5(2)(b).

Power to make regulations

9. Regulations under section 14(7) may, in particular, provide that an activity of a specified kind or performed in specified circumstances is to be or not to be treated as paying to enter a lottery.

[1413ZZB]

NOTES

Commencement: 1 October 2005.

(Schs 3–10: outside the scope of this work.)

SCHEDULE 11
EXEMPT LOTTERIES

Section 258

PART 1
INCIDENTAL NON-COMMERCIAL LOTTERIES

The exemption

1.—(1) A lottery is exempt if—

(a) it is incidental to a non-commercial event within the meaning of paragraph 2 ("the connected event"), and

(b) the conditions specified in this Part are satisfied.

(2) A lottery to which sub-paragraph (1) applies is referred to in this Part as an incidental non-commercial lottery.

2. An event is non-commercial if no sum raised by the organisers of the event (whether by way of fees for entrance or for participation, by way of sponsorship, by way of commission from traders or otherwise) is appropriated for the purpose of private gain.

Deductions from proceeds

3. The promoters of an incidental non-commercial lottery may not deduct from the proceeds of the lottery more than the prescribed sum in respect of the cost of the prizes (irrespective of their actual cost).

4. The promoters of an incidental non-commercial lottery may not deduct from the proceeds of the lottery more than the prescribed sum in respect of costs incurred in organising the lottery (irrespective of the amount of the costs incurred).

Purpose of lottery

5. An incidental non-commercial lottery must be promoted wholly for a purpose other than that of private gain.

No rollover

6. The arrangements for an incidental non-commercial lottery must not include a rollover.

Connection between lottery and event

7.—(1) No lottery ticket for an incidental non-commercial lottery may be sold or supplied otherwise than—

(a) on the premises on which the connected event takes place, and
(b) while the connected event is taking place.

(2) The results of the lottery must be made public while the connected event is taking place.

Interpretation: "prescribed"

8. In this Part "prescribed" means prescribed by the Secretary of State by regulations.
[1413ZZC]

NOTES

Commencement: 1 October 2005 (for certain purposes); 1 September 2007 (for remaining purposes). For transitional provisions see the Gambling Act 2005 (Commencement No 6 and Transitional Provisions) Order 2006, SI 2006/3272, art 6, Sch 4.

(Parts 2 and 3 outside the scope of this work.)

PART 4
SMALL SOCIETY LOTTERIES

The exemption

30.—(1) A lottery is exempt if—

(a) it is promoted wholly on behalf of a non-commercial society ("the promoting society"),
(b) it is a small lottery (within the meaning of paragraph 31), and
(c) the other conditions of a small society lottery specified in this Part are satisfied.

(2) A lottery promoted wholly on behalf of a non-commercial society is referred to in this Part as a small society lottery.

31.—(1) For the purposes of this Part a society lottery is a small lottery unless it is a large lottery by virtue of any of sub-paragraphs (2) to (5).

(2) A society lottery is a large lottery if the arrangements for it are such that its proceeds may exceed £20,000.

(3) A society lottery is a large lottery if it is promoted wholly or partly at a time in a calendar year at which the aggregate of the promoting society's proceeds from society lotteries promoted wholly or partly during that year exceeds £250,000.

(4) A society lottery is a large lottery if the arrangements for it are such that (disregarding any other society lottery the sale of tickets for which is not concluded) it may during its promotion become a large lottery by virtue of sub-paragraph (3).

(5) If a society promotes a lottery that is a large society lottery by virtue of sub-paragraph (2), (3) or (4) ("the first lottery"), any other society lottery promoted by that society is a large lottery if it is wholly or partly promoted—

(a) after the beginning of the promotion of the first lottery and in a calendar year during which the first lottery is wholly or partly promoted, or

(b) in any of the three calendar years successively following the last calendar year during which the first lottery was wholly or partly promoted.

Purpose of lottery

32. A small society lottery may be promoted for any of the purposes for which the promoting society is conducted.

Minimum distribution for fund-raising purpose

33. The arrangements for a small society lottery must ensure that at least 20% of the proceeds of the lottery are applied to a purpose for which the society is conducted.

Maximum prize

34. It must not be possible for the purchaser of a ticket in a small society lottery to win by virtue of that ticket (whether in money, money's worth, or partly the one and partly the other) more than £25,000.

Rollover

35.—(1) The arrangements for a small society lottery may include a rollover only if each other lottery which may be affected by the rollover is a small society lottery promoted by or on behalf of the same society.

(2) This paragraph is subject to paragraph 34.

Tickets

36.—(1) Where a person purchases a lottery ticket in a small society lottery he must receive a document which—

(a) identifies the promoting society,

(b) states the price of the ticket,

(c) states the name and an address of—

  (i) a member of the society who is designated, by persons acting on behalf of the society, as having responsibility within the society for the promotion of the lottery, or

  (ii) if there is one, the external lottery manager, and

(d) either—

  (i) states the date of the draw (or each draw) in the lottery, or

  (ii) enables the date of the draw (or each draw) in the lottery to be determined.

(2) For the purpose of sub-paragraph (1) a reference to a person receiving a document includes, in particular, a reference to a message being sent or displayed to him electronically in a manner which enables him to—

(a) retain the message electronically, or

(b) print it.

Price

37.—(1) The price payable for each ticket in a small society lottery—
 (a) must be the same, and
 (b) must be paid to the promoter of the lottery before any person is given the ticket or any right in respect of membership of the class among whom prizes are to be allocated.

(2) Membership of the class among whom prizes in a small society lottery are allocated may not be dependent on making any payment (apart from payment of the price of a ticket).

Registration

38. The promoting society of a small society lottery must, throughout the period during which the lottery is promoted, be registered with a local authority in accordance with Part 5 of this Schedule.

Filing of records

39.—(1) The promoting society of a small society lottery must send to the local authority with which the society is registered under Part 5 of this Schedule a statement of the matters specified in sub-paragraph (2).

(2) Those matters are—
 (a) the arrangements for the lottery (including the dates on which tickets were available for sale or supply, the dates of any draw and the arrangements for prizes (including any rollover),
 (b) the proceeds of the lottery,
 (c) the amounts deducted by the promoters of the lottery in respect of the provision of prizes (including the provision of prizes in accordance with any rollover),
 (d) the amounts deducted by the promoters of the lottery in respect of other costs incurred in organising the lottery,
 (e) any amount applied to a purpose for which the promoting society is conducted, and
 (f) whether any expenses in connection with the lottery were defrayed otherwise than by deduction from proceeds, and, if they were—
  (i) the amount of the expenses, and
  (ii) the sources from which they were defrayed.

(3) The statement must be sent to the local authority during the period of three months beginning with the day on which the draw (or the last draw) in the lottery takes place.

(4) The statement must be—
 (a) signed by two members of the society who are appointed for the purpose in writing by the society or, if it has one, its governing body, and
 (b) accompanied by a copy of the appointment under paragraph (a).

(5) A member signing a statement in accordance with sub-paragraph (4) must be an adult.

40.—(1) If after receiving a statement under paragraph 39 a local authority think that the lottery to which the statement relates was a large lottery, they shall notify the Commission in writing.

(2) A notice under sub-paragraph (1) shall be accompanied by a copy of—
 (a) the statement relating to the lottery, and
 (b) the statement relating to any other lottery as a result of which the lottery mentioned in paragraph (a) is a large lottery.

[1413ZZD]

NOTES

Commencement: 1 October 2005 (paras 30, 31 for certain purposes); 1 September 2007 (paras 30, 31 for remaining purposes, paras 32–40). For transitional provisions see the Gambling Act 2005 (Commencement No 6 and Transitional Provisions) Order 2006, SI 2006/3272, art 6, Sch 4.

PART 5
REGISTRATION WITH LOCAL AUTHORITY

Local authority

41. In this Part "local authority" means—
(a) in relation to England—
(i) a district council,
(ii) a county council for a county in which there are no district councils,
(iii) a London borough council,
(iv) the Common Council of the City of London, and
(v) the Council of the Isles of Scilly,
(b) in relation to Wales,
(i) a county council, and
(ii) a county borough council, and
(c) in relation to Scotland, a licensing board constituted under section 1 of the Licensing (Scotland) Act 1976 (c 66).

Application

42.—(1) A society may apply to the relevant local authority for registration under this Part.

(2) An application under this paragraph—
(a) must be in the prescribed form,
(b) must specify the purposes for which the society is conducted,
(c) must contain such other information, and be accompanied by such documents, as may be prescribed, and
(d) must be accompanied by the prescribed fee.

43. In relation to the registration of a society, the relevant local authority is the local authority for the area in which the principal premises of the society are situated.

Registration

44. As soon as is reasonably practicable after receipt of an application under paragraph 42 a local authority shall, subject to paragraphs 47 and 48—
(a) enter the applicant, together with such information as may be prescribed, in a register kept by the authority for the purposes of this Part,
(b) notify the applicant of his registration, and
(c) notify the Commission of the registration.

Gambling Commission

45. As soon as is reasonably practicable after receipt of notice of a registration under paragraph 44(c) the Commission shall record the registration.

46.—(1) A notice under paragraph 44(c) must be accompanied by such part of the application fee as may be prescribed.

(2) In sub-paragraph (1) "application fee" means the fee accompanying an application under paragraph 42.

Refusal of registration

47. A local authority shall refuse an application for registration if in the period of five years ending with the date of the application—
(a) an operating licence held by the applicant for registration has been revoked under section 119(1), or
(b) an application for an operating licence made by the applicant for registration has been refused.

48. A local authority may refuse an application for registration if they think that—

(a) the applicant is not a non-commercial society,
(b) a person who will or may be connected with the promotion of the lottery has been convicted of a relevant offence, or
(c) information provided in or with the application for registration is false or misleading.

49. A local authority may not refuse an application for registration unless they have given the applicant an opportunity to make representations.

Revocation

50.—(1) A local authority may revoke a registration under this Part if they think that they would be obliged or permitted to refuse an application for the registration were it being made anew.

(2) Where a local authority revoke a registration under this Part they shall specify that the revocation takes effect—
(a) immediately, or
(b) at the end of such period, beginning with the day of the revocation and not exceeding two months, as they may specify.

(3) A local authority may not revoke a registration under this Part unless they have given the registered society an opportunity to make representations.

Appeal

51.—(1) If a local authority refuse or revoke registration under this Part—
(a) the authority shall notify the applicant society or the formerly registered society as soon as is reasonably practicable, and
(b) the society may appeal to a magistrates' court.

(2) An appeal under this paragraph must be instituted—
(a) in a magistrates' court for a local justice area which is wholly or partly within the area of the local authority against whose decision the appeal is brought,
(b) by notice of appeal given to the designated officer, and
(c) in the period of 21 days beginning with the day on which the society is notified of the refusal or revocation of registration, and

(3) On an appeal under this paragraph a magistrates' court may—
(a) affirm the local authority's decision;
(b) reverse the local authority's decision;
(c) make any other order (which may include transitional provision).

(4) In relation to registration in Scotland—
(a) sub-paragraph (1)(b) shall have effect as if the reference to a magistrate's court were a reference to a sheriff whose sheriffdom is wholly or partly within the area of the local authority against whose decision the appeal is brought,
(b) sub-paragraph (2)(a) and (b) shall not have effect, and
(c) sub-paragraph (3) shall have effect as if the reference to a magistrate's court were a reference to the sheriff.

Cancellation

52. A registered society may apply in writing to the registering authority for the registration to be cancelled.

53. As soon as is reasonably practicable after receipt of an application under paragraph 52 a local authority shall—
(a) cancel the registration,
(b) notify the formerly registered society of the cancellation, and
(c) notify the Commission of the cancellation.

Annual fee

54.—(1) A registered society shall pay an annual fee to the registering local authority.

(2) An annual fee—

(a) shall be paid within such period before each anniversary of the registration as may be prescribed, and

(b) shall be of the prescribed amount.

(3) If a registered society fails to comply with this paragraph the registering authority may cancel the society's registration.

(4) If a local authority cancel a registration under sub-paragraph (3) the authority shall as soon as is reasonably practicable notify—

(a) the formerly registered society, and

(b) the Commission.

Retention of records

55.—(1) Where a statement is sent to a local authority under paragraph 39 the authority shall—

(a) retain it for at least 18 months,

(b) make it available for inspection by members of the public at all reasonable times, and

(c) make arrangements for the provision of a copy of it or part of it to any member of the public on request.

(2) But a local authority may refuse to provide access or a copy unless the person seeking access or a copy pays a fee specified by the authority.

(3) A local authority may not specify a fee under sub-paragraph (2) which exceeds the reasonable cost of providing the service sought (but in calculating the cost of providing a service to a person the authority may include a reasonable share of expenditure which is referable only indirectly to the provision of that service).

Interpretation: "prescribed"

56. In this Part "prescribed" means prescribed by the Secretary of State by regulations except that, in the following provisions, it means prescribed by the Scottish Ministers by regulations—

(a) in paragraph 42(2)(d), where the application is made to a local authority in Scotland,

(b) in paragraph 46(1), where the local authority giving notice is in Scotland, and

(c) in paragraph 54(2)(b), where the registering local authority is in Scotland.

[1413ZZE]

NOTES

Commencement: 1 September 2007 (for transitional provisions see the Gambling Act 2005 (Commencement No 6 and Transitional Provisions) Order 2006, SI 2006/3272, art 6, Sch 4).

PART 6
POWERS TO IMPOSE ADDITIONAL RESTRICTIONS, &C

Distributing lottery tickets by post

57.—(1) The Secretary of State may by regulations impose a condition in relation to exempt lotteries requiring that tickets purchased be delivered to the purchaser by hand at the time of purchase and not by post.

(2) Regulations under this paragraph may apply generally, only in relation to a specified class of lottery or only in specified circumstances.

Rollover

58.—(1) The Secretary of State may by regulations impose in relation to exempt lotteries conditions or limitations in respect of the use of a rollover (in addition to any conditions or limitations set out in this Schedule).

(2) Regulations under this paragraph may apply generally, only in relation to a specified class of lottery or only in specified circumstances.

Other additional provision

59.—(1) The Secretary of State may by order impose in relation to a class of lottery a condition (in addition to any specified in this Schedule) with which a lottery must comply if it is to be an exempt lottery within the meaning of this Schedule.

(2) A condition imposed under this paragraph may, in particular, relate to—
- (a) the persons who may sell or supply lottery tickets;
- (b) the persons who may buy lottery tickets;
- (c) the circumstances in which lottery tickets are sold or supplied;
- (d) the nature of lottery tickets and information appearing on them;
- (e) arrangements for advertising the lottery;
- (f) the deductions which promoters may make from the proceeds of a lottery.

(3) The Secretary of State may by order restrict the extent to which a person may carry on activities in reliance on an exemption under this Schedule.

(4) An order under sub-paragraph (3) may, in particular, make provision—
- (a) restricting the number of lotteries that may be promoted on behalf of a person wholly or partly within a specified period;
- (b) prescribing a minimum interval between activity in connection with one lottery promoted on behalf of a person and activity in connection with another lottery promoted on behalf of that person.

(5) Before making an order under this paragraph the Secretary of State must consult the Commission.

Variation of monetary limits and percentages

60. The Secretary of State may by order vary a monetary amount or a percentage in this Schedule.

[1413ZZF]

NOTES

Commencement: 1 September 2007 (for transitional provisions see the Gambling Act 2005 (Commencement No 6 and Transitional Provisions) Order 2006, SI 2006/3272, art 6, Sch 4).

PART 7
GENERAL

Interpretation: advertisement

61. For the purposes of this Schedule—
- (a) "advertisement", in relation to a lottery, includes any document, or electronic communication, announcing that a lottery will take place or inviting people to participate in a lottery (in either case whether or not it also gives other information),
- (b) a reference to displaying an advertisement includes a reference to publishing a notice, and
- (c) in the case of an advertisement in the form of an electronic communication, the communication is to be treated as being—
  - (i) distributed to any place at which a person can access it, and
  - (ii) sent to any premises at which a person can access it.

Interpretation: business

62. In this Schedule "business" includes trade and profession.

Vessels

63. Nothing in Part 2 or 3 of this Schedule applies to anything done on a vessel.
[1413ZZG]

NOTES

Commencement: 1 September 2007 (for transitional provisions see the Gambling Act 2005 (Commencement No 6 and Transitional Provisions) Order 2006, SI 2006/3272, art 6, Sch 4).

COMPANIES ACT 2006

(2006 c 46)

NOTES

Commencement: the commencement of this Act is provided for by s 1300 at **[2116]**. See also the Companies Act 2006 (Commencement No 1, Transitional Provisions and Savings) Order 2006, SI 2006/3428. Note that art 3(3) of the 2006 Order provides that, in so far as not already brought into force by s 1300(1) of the 2006 Act, or arts 2, 3(1), (2) of the 2006 Order, this Act shall come into force on 20 January 2007 for the purpose of enabling the exercise of powers to make Orders or Regulations by statutory instrument. The commencement of these Order and Regulation making powers has not been noted on individual provisions of this Act.

Application to unregistered companies: as to the application of certain parts of this Act to unregistered companies, see the Companies Acts (Unregistered Companies) Regulations 2007, SI 2007/318 (made under s 1043 of this Act).

ARRANGEMENT OF SECTIONS

PART 1
GENERAL INTRODUCTORY PROVISIONS

Companies and Companies Acts

Types of company

PART 2
COMPANY FORMATION

General

Requirements for registration

Registration and its effect

PART 3
A COMPANY'S CONSTITUTION

CHAPTER 1
INTRODUCTORY

CHAPTER 2
ARTICLES OF ASSOCIATION

General

Alteration of articles

Supplementary

CHAPTER 3
RESOLUTIONS AND AGREEMENTS AFFECTING A COMPANY'S CONSTITUTION

CHAPTER 4
MISCELLANEOUS AND SUPPLEMENTARY PROVISIONS

Statement of company's objects

Other provisions with respect to a company's constitution

Supplementary provisions

PART 4
A COMPANY'S CAPACITY AND RELATED MATTERS

Capacity of company and power of directors to bind it

Formalities of doing business under the law of England and Wales or Northern Ireland

CHAPTER 6
TRADING DISCLOSURES

PART 6
A COMPANY'S REGISTERED OFFICE

General

Welsh companies

PART 7
RE-REGISTRATION AS A MEANS OF ALTERING A COMPANY'S STATUS

Introductory

Private limited company becoming unlimited

Unlimited private company becoming limited

PART 8
A COMPANY'S MEMBERS

CHAPTER 1
THE MEMBERS OF A COMPANY

CHAPTER 2
REGISTER OF MEMBERS

General

Special cases

Supplementary

CHAPTER 3
OVERSEAS BRANCH REGISTERS

CHAPTER 4
PROHIBITION ON SUBSIDIARY BEING MEMBER OF ITS HOLDING COMPANY

General prohibition

Subsidiary acting as personal representative or trustee

Supplementary

PART 9
EXERCISE OF MEMBERS' RIGHTS

Effect of provisions in company's articles

Information rights

Exercise of rights where shares held on behalf of others

PART 10
A COMPANY'S DIRECTORS

CHAPTER 1
APPOINTMENT AND REMOVAL OF DIRECTORS

Requirement to have directors

Appointment

Register of directors, etc

PART I
STATUTES

Records of meetings of directors

Meaning of "director" and "shadow director"

Other definitions

General

PART 11
DERIVATIVE CLAIMS AND PROCEEDINGS BY MEMBERS

CHAPTER 1
DERIVATIVE CLAIMS IN ENGLAND AND WALES OR NORTHERN IRELAND

PART 12
COMPANY SECRETARIES

Private companies

Provisions applying to private companies with a secretary and to public companies

PART 13
RESOLUTIONS AND MEETINGS

CHAPTER 1
GENERAL PROVISIONS ABOUT RESOLUTIONS

CHAPTER 2
WRITTEN RESOLUTIONS

General provisions about written resolutions

Circulation of written resolutions

Agreeing to written resolutions

Supplementary

CHAPTER 3
RESOLUTIONS AT MEETINGS

General provisions about resolutions at meetings

Calling meetings

Notice of meetings

Members' statements

Procedure at meetings

Proxies

Adjourned meetings

Accounting and reporting standards

Companies qualifying as medium-sized

General power to make further provision about accounts and reports

Other supplementary provisions

PART 16
AUDIT

CHAPTER 1
REQUIREMENT FOR AUDITED ACCOUNTS

Requirement for audited accounts

Exemption from audit: small companies

Exemption from audit: dormant companies

Companies subject to public sector audit

General power of amendment by regulations

CHAPTER 2
APPOINTMENT OF AUDITORS

Private companies

General provisions

CHAPTER 3
FUNCTIONS OF AUDITOR

Auditor's report

Duties and rights of auditors

CHAPTER 7
SUPPLEMENTARY PROVISIONS

PART 17
A COMPANY'S SHARE CAPITAL

CHAPTER 1
SHARES AND SHARE CAPITAL OF A COMPANY

Shares

Share capital

CHAPTER 2
ALLOTMENT OF SHARES: GENERAL PROVISIONS

Power of directors to allot shares

Prohibition of commissions, discounts and allowances

Registration of allotment

Return of allotment

Supplementary provisions

CHAPTER 3
ALLOTMENT OF EQUITY SECURITIES: EXISTING SHAREHOLDERS' RIGHT OF PRE-EMPTION

Introductory

Existing shareholders' right of pre-emption

Exceptions to right of pre-emption

Exclusion of right of pre-emption

CHAPTER 9
CLASSES OF SHARE AND CLASS RIGHTS

Introductory

Variation of class rights

Matters to be notified to the registrar

CHAPTER 10
REDUCTION OF SHARE CAPITAL

Introductory

Private companies: reduction of capital supported by solvency statement

Reduction of capital confirmed by the court

Public company reducing capital below authorised minimum

Effect of reduction of capital

CHAPTER 11
MISCELLANEOUS AND SUPPLEMENTARY PROVISIONS

PART 18
ACQUISITION BY LIMITED COMPANY OF ITS OWN SHARES

CHAPTER 1
GENERAL PROVISIONS

Introductory

Shares held by company's nominee

PART 36
OFFENCES UNDER THE COMPANIES ACTS

Liability of officer in default

Offences under the Companies Act 1985

PART 37
COMPANIES: SUPPLEMENTARY PROVISIONS

Company records

Service addresses

Sending or supplying documents or information

PART 38
COMPANIES: INTERPRETATION

Meaning of "UK-registered company"

Meaning of "subsidiary" and related expressions

Meaning of "undertaking" and related expressions

Other definitions

General

An Act to reform company law and restate the greater part of the enactments relating to companies; to make other provision relating to companies and other forms of business organisation; to make provision about directors' disqualification, business names, auditors and actuaries; to amend Part 9 of the Enterprise Act 2002; and for connected purposes

[8 November 2006]

PART 1
GENERAL INTRODUCTORY PROVISIONS

Companies and Companies Acts

1 Companies

(1) In the Companies Acts, unless the context otherwise requires—
"company" means a company formed and registered under this Act, that is—

(a) a company so formed and registered after the commencement of this Part, or

(b) a company that immediately before the commencement of this Part—

(i) was formed and registered under the Companies Act 1985 (c 6) or the Companies (Northern Ireland) Order 1986 (SI 1986/1032 (NI 6)), or

(ii) was an existing company for the purposes of that Act or that Order,

(which is to be treated on commencement as if formed and registered under this Act).

(2) Certain provisions of the Companies Acts apply to—

(a) companies registered, but not formed, under this Act (see Chapter 1 of Part 33), and

(b) bodies incorporated in the United Kingdom but not registered under this Act (see Chapter 2 of that Part).

(3) For provisions applying to companies incorporated outside the United Kingdom, see Part 34 (overseas companies).

[1414]

NOTES

Commencement: to be appointed (see the introductory note to this Act).

2 The Companies Acts

(1) In this Act "the Companies Acts" means—

(a) the company law provisions of this Act,

(b) Part 2 of the Companies (Audit, Investigations and Community Enterprise) Act 2004 (c 27) (community interest companies), and

(c) the provisions of the Companies Act 1985 (c 6) and the Companies Consolidation (Consequential Provisions) Act 1985 (c 9) that remain in force.

(2) The company law provisions of this Act are—

(a) the provisions of Parts 1 to 39 of this Act, and

(b) the provisions of Parts 45 to 47 of this Act so far as they apply for the purposes of those Parts.

[1415]

NOTES

Commencement: 1 January 2007 (certain purposes); 20 January 2007 (certain purposes); to be appointed (otherwise) (see the notes below and the introductory note to this Act).

Note: the Companies Act 2006 (Commencement No 1, Transitional Provisions and Savings) Order 2006, SI 2006/3428, art 2(2) provides that this section shall come into force on 1 January 2007 in so far as is necessary for the purposes of the provisions mentioned in art 2(1) of that Order. Those provisions are: ss 1068(5), 1077–1080, 1085–1092, 1102–1107, 1111. Article 3(2) of the 2006 Order further provides that this section shall come into force on 20 January 2007 in so far as is necessary for the purposes of the provisions mentioned in art 3(1) of that Order. Those provisions are: ss 308, 309, 333, 463, 791–810, 811(1)–(3), 813, 815–828, 1143–1148 and Schs 4 and 5.

Transitional adaptations: art 5 of the Companies Act 2006 (Commencement No 1, Transitional Provisions and Savings) Order 2006, SI 2006/3428 provides that the provisions brought into force by arts 2–4 of 2006 Order shall have effect subject to any transitional adaptations specified in Sch 1 to that Order. Schedule 1, para 1 to the Order provides as follows—

1.—(1) Section 2 (the Companies Acts) has effect with the following adaptation.

(2) For subsection (1)(c) substitute—

"(c) the provisions of the Companies Acts as defined in section 744 of the Companies Act 1985, and the Companies Orders as defined in Article 2(3) of the Companies (Northern Ireland) Order 1986, that remain in force.".

Types of company

3 Limited and unlimited companies

(1) A company is a "limited company" if the liability of its members is limited by its constitution.

It may be limited by shares or limited by guarantee.

(2) If their liability is limited to the amount, if any, unpaid on the shares held by them, the company is "limited by shares".

(3) If their liability is limited to such amount as the members undertake to contribute to the assets of the company in the event of its being wound up, the company is "limited by guarantee".

(4) If there is no limit on the liability of its members, the company is an "unlimited company".

[1416]

NOTES

Commencement: to be appointed (see the introductory note to this Act).

4 Private and public companies

(1) A "private company" is any company that is not a public company.

(2) A "public company" is a company limited by shares or limited by guarantee and having a share capital—

(a) whose certificate of incorporation states that it is a public company, and
(b) in relation to which the requirements of this Act, or the former Companies Acts, as to registration or re-registration as a public company have been complied with on or after the relevant date.

(3) For the purposes of subsection (2)(b) the relevant date is—

(a) in relation to registration or re-registration in Great Britain, 22nd December 1980;
(b) in relation to registration or re-registration in Northern Ireland, 1st July 1983.

(4) For the two major differences between private and public companies, see Part 20.

[1417]

NOTES

Commencement: to be appointed (see the introductory note to this Act).

5 Companies limited by guarantee and having share capital

(1) A company cannot be formed as, or become, a company limited by guarantee with a share capital.

(2) Provision to this effect has been in force—

(a) in Great Britain since 22nd December 1980, and
(b) in Northern Ireland since 1st July 1983.

(3) Any provision in the constitution of a company limited by guarantee that purports to divide the company's undertaking into shares or interests is a provision for a share capital.

This applies whether or not the nominal value or number of the shares or interests is specified by the provision.

[1418]

NOTES

Commencement: to be appointed (see the introductory note to this Act).

6 Community interest companies

(1) In accordance with Part 2 of the Companies (Audit, Investigations and Community Enterprise) Act 2004 (c 27)—

(a) a company limited by shares or a company limited by guarantee and not having a share capital may be formed as or become a community interest company, and
(b) a company limited by guarantee and having a share capital may become a community interest company.

(2) The other provisions of the Companies Acts have effect subject to that Part.

[1419]

NOTES

Commencement: to be appointed (see the introductory note to this Act).

PART 2
COMPANY FORMATION

General

7 Method of forming company

(1) A company is formed under this Act by one or more persons—

(a) subscribing their names to a memorandum of association (see section 8), and

(b) complying with the requirements of this Act as to registration (see sections 9 to 13).

(2) A company may not be so formed for an unlawful purpose.

[1420]

NOTES

Commencement: to be appointed (see the introductory note to this Act).

8 Memorandum of association

(1) A memorandum of association is a memorandum stating that the subscribers—

(a) wish to form a company under this Act, and

(b) agree to become members of the company and, in the case of a company that is to have a share capital, to take at least one share each.

(2) The memorandum must be in the prescribed form and must be authenticated by each subscriber.

[1421]

NOTES

Commencement: to be appointed (see the introductory note to this Act).

Requirements for registration

9 Registration documents

(1) The memorandum of association must be delivered to the registrar together with an application for registration of the company, the documents required by this section and a statement of compliance.

(2) The application for registration must state—

(a) the company's proposed name,

(b) whether the company's registered office is to be situated in England and Wales (or in Wales), in Scotland or in Northern Ireland,

(c) whether the liability of the members of the company is to be limited, and if so whether it is to be limited by shares or by guarantee, and

(d) whether the company is to be a private or a public company.

(3) If the application is delivered by a person as agent for the subscribers to the memorandum of association, it must state his name and address.

(4) The application must contain—

(a) in the case of a company that is to have a share capital, a statement of capital and initial shareholdings (see section 10);

(b) in the case of a company that is to be limited by guarantee, a statement of guarantee (see section 11);

(c) a statement of the company's proposed officers (see section 12).

(5) The application must also contain—

(a) a statement of the intended address of the company's registered office; and

(b) a copy of any proposed articles of association (to the extent that these are not supplied by the default application of model articles: see section 20).

(6) The application must be delivered—

(a) to the registrar of companies for England and Wales, if the registered office of the company is to be situated in England and Wales (or in Wales);

(b) to the registrar of companies for Scotland, if the registered office of the company is to be situated in Scotland;

(c) to the registrar of companies for Northern Ireland, if the registered office of the company is to be situated in Northern Ireland.

[1422]

NOTES

Commencement: to be appointed (see the introductory note to this Act).

10 Statement of capital and initial shareholdings

(1) The statement of capital and initial shareholdings required to be delivered in the case of a company that is to have a share capital must comply with this section.

(2) It must state—

(a) the total number of shares of the company to be taken on formation by the subscribers to the memorandum of association,

(b) the aggregate nominal value of those shares,

(c) for each class of shares—

(i) prescribed particulars of the rights attached to the shares,

(ii) the total number of shares of that class, and

(iii) the aggregate nominal value of shares of that class, and

(d) the amount to be paid up and the amount (if any) to be unpaid on each share (whether on account of the nominal value of the share or by way of premium).

(3) It must contain such information as may be prescribed for the purpose of identifying the subscribers to the memorandum of association.

(4) It must state, with respect to each subscriber to the memorandum—

(a) the number, nominal value (of each share) and class of shares to be taken by him on formation, and

(b) the amount to be paid up and the amount (if any) to be unpaid on each share (whether on account of the nominal value of the share or by way of premium).

(5) Where a subscriber to the memorandum is to take shares of more than one class, the information required under subsection (4)(a) is required for each class.

[1423]

NOTES

Commencement: to be appointed (see the introductory note to this Act).

11 Statement of guarantee

(1) The statement of guarantee required to be delivered in the case of a company that is to be limited by guarantee must comply with this section.

(2) It must contain such information as may be prescribed for the purpose of identifying the subscribers to the memorandum of association.

(3) It must state that each member undertakes that, if the company is wound up while he is a member, or within one year after he ceases to be a member, he will contribute to the assets of the company such amount as may be required for—

(a) payment of the debts and liabilities of the company contracted before he ceases to be a member,

(b) payment of the costs, charges and expenses of winding up, and

(c) adjustment of the rights of the contributories among themselves,

not exceeding a specified amount.

[1424]

NOTES

Commencement: to be appointed (see the introductory note to this Act).

12 Statement of proposed officers

(1) The statement of the company's proposed officers required to be delivered to the registrar must contain the required particulars of—

(a) the person who is, or persons who are, to be the first director or directors of the company;

(b) in the case of a company that is to be a private company, any person who is (or any persons who are) to be the first secretary (or joint secretaries) of the company;

(c) in the case of a company that is to be a public company, the person who is (or the persons who are) to be the first secretary (or joint secretaries) of the company.

(2) The required particulars are the particulars that will be required to be stated—

(a) in the case of a director, in the company's register of directors and register of directors' residential addresses (see sections 162 to 166);

(b) in the case of a secretary, in the company's register of secretaries (see sections 277 to 279).

(3) The statement must also contain a consent by each of the persons named as a director, as secretary or as one of joint secretaries, to act in the relevant capacity.

If all the partners in a firm are to be joint secretaries, consent may be given by one partner on behalf of all of them.

[1425]

NOTES

Commencement: to be appointed (see the introductory note to this Act).

13 Statement of compliance

(1) The statement of compliance required to be delivered to the registrar is a statement that the requirements of this Act as to registration have been complied with.

(2) The registrar may accept the statement of compliance as sufficient evidence of compliance.

[1426]

NOTES

Commencement: to be appointed (see the introductory note to this Act).

Registration and its effect

14 Registration

If the registrar is satisfied that the requirements of this Act as to registration are complied with, he shall register the documents delivered to him.

[1427]

NOTES

Commencement: to be appointed (see the introductory note to this Act).

15 Issue of certificate of incorporation

(1) On the registration of a company, the registrar of companies shall give a certificate that the company is incorporated.

(2) The certificate must state—

(a) the name and registered number of the company,

(b) the date of its incorporation,

(c) whether it is a limited or unlimited company, and if it is limited whether it is limited by shares or limited by guarantee,

(d) whether it is a private or a public company, and
(e) whether the company's registered office is situated in England and Wales (or in Wales), in Scotland or in Northern Ireland.

(3) The certificate must be signed by the registrar or authenticated by the registrar's official seal.

(4) The certificate is conclusive evidence that the requirements of this Act as to registration have been complied with and that the company is duly registered under this Act.
[1428]

NOTES
Commencement: to be appointed (see the introductory note to this Act).

16 Effect of registration

(1) The registration of a company has the following effects as from the date of incorporation.

(2) The subscribers to the memorandum, together with such other persons as may from time to time become members of the company, are a body corporate by the name stated in the certificate of incorporation.

(3) That body corporate is capable of exercising all the functions of an incorporated company.

(4) The status and registered office of the company are as stated in, or in connection with, the application for registration.

(5) In the case of a company having a share capital, the subscribers to the memorandum become holders of the shares specified in the statement of capital and initial shareholdings.

(6) The persons named in the statement of proposed officers—
(a) as director, or
(b) as secretary or joint secretary of the company,
are deemed to have been appointed to that office.
[1429]

NOTES
Commencement: to be appointed (see the introductory note to this Act).

PART 3
A COMPANY'S CONSTITUTION

CHAPTER 1
INTRODUCTORY

17 A company's constitution

Unless the context otherwise requires, references in the Companies Acts to a company's constitution include—
(a) the company's articles, and
(b) any resolutions and agreements to which Chapter 3 applies (see section 29).
[1430]

NOTES
Commencement: to be appointed (see the introductory note to this Act).

CHAPTER 2
ARTICLES OF ASSOCIATION

General

18 Articles of association

(1) A company must have articles of association prescribing regulations for the company.

(2) Unless it is a company to which model articles apply by virtue of section 20 (default application of model articles in case of limited company), it must register articles of association.

(3) Articles of association registered by a company must—
- (a) be contained in a single document, and
- (b) be divided into paragraphs numbered consecutively.

(4) References in the Companies Acts to a company's "articles" are to its articles of association.

[1431]

NOTES

Commencement: to be appointed (see the introductory note to this Act).

19 Power of Secretary of State to prescribe model articles

(1) The Secretary of State may by regulations prescribe model articles of association for companies.

(2) Different model articles may be prescribed for different descriptions of company.

(3) A company may adopt all or any of the provisions of model articles.

(4) Any amendment of model articles by regulations under this section does not affect a company registered before the amendment takes effect.

"Amendment" here includes addition, alteration or repeal.

(5) Regulations under this section are subject to negative resolution procedure.

[1432]

NOTES

Commencement: to be appointed (see the introductory note to this Act).

20 Default application of model articles

(1) On the formation of a limited company—
- (a) if articles are not registered, or
- (b) if articles are registered, in so far as they do not exclude or modify the relevant model articles,

the relevant model articles (so far as applicable) form part of the company's articles in the same manner and to the same extent as if articles in the form of those articles had been duly registered.

(2) The "relevant model articles" means the model articles prescribed for a company of that description as in force at the date on which the company is registered.

[1433]

NOTES

Commencement: to be appointed (see the introductory note to this Act).

Alteration of articles

21 Amendment of articles

(1) A company may amend its articles by special resolution.

(2) In the case of a company that is a charity, this is subject to—
- (a) in England and Wales, section 64 of the Charities Act 1993 (c 10);
- (b) in Northern Ireland, Article 9 of the Charities (Northern Ireland) Order 1987 (SI 1987/2048 (NI 19)).

(3) In the case of a company that is registered in the Scottish Charity Register, this is subject to—
- (a) section 112 of the Companies Act 1989 (c 40), and

(b) section 16 of the Charities and Trustee Investment (Scotland) Act 2005 (asp 10). **[1434]**

NOTES

Commencement: to be appointed (see the introductory note to this Act).

22 Entrenched provisions of the articles

(1) A company's articles may contain provision ("provision for entrenchment") to the effect that specified provisions of the articles may be amended or repealed only if conditions are met, or procedures are complied with, that are more restrictive than those applicable in the case of a special resolution.

(2) Provision for entrenchment may only be made—

(a) in the company's articles on formation, or

(b) by an amendment of the company's articles agreed to by all the members of the company.

(3) Provision for entrenchment does not prevent amendment of the company's articles—

(a) by agreement of all the members of the company, or

(b) by order of a court or other authority having power to alter the company's articles.

(4) Nothing in this section affects any power of a court or other authority to alter a company's articles.

[1435]

NOTES

Commencement: to be appointed (see the introductory note to this Act).

23 Notice to registrar of existence of restriction on amendment of articles

(1) Where a company's articles—

(a) on formation contain provision for entrenchment,

(b) are amended so as to include such provision, or

(c) are altered by order of a court or other authority so as to restrict or exclude the power of the company to amend its articles,

the company must give notice of that fact to the registrar.

(2) Where a company's articles—

(a) are amended so as to remove provision for entrenchment, or

(b) are altered by order of a court or other authority—

(i) so as to remove such provision, or

(ii) so as to remove any other restriction on, or any exclusion of, the power of the company to amend its articles,

the company must give notice of that fact to the registrar.

[1436]

NOTES

Commencement: to be appointed (see the introductory note to this Act).

24 Statement of compliance where amendment of articles restricted

(1) This section applies where a company's articles are subject—

(a) to provision for entrenchment, or

(b) to an order of a court or other authority restricting or excluding the company's power to amend the articles.

(2) If the company—

(a) amends its articles, and

(b) is required to send to the registrar a document making or evidencing the amendment,

the company must deliver with that document a statement of compliance.

(3) The statement of compliance required is a statement certifying that the amendment has been made in accordance with the company's articles and, where relevant, any applicable order of a court or other authority.

(4) The registrar may rely on the statement of compliance as sufficient evidence of the matters stated in it.

[1437]

PART I STATUTES

NOTES

Commencement: to be appointed (see the introductory note to this Act).

25 Effect of alteration of articles on company's members

(1) A member of a company is not bound by an alteration to its articles after the date on which he became a member, if and so far as the alteration—

(a) requires him to take or subscribe for more shares than the number held by him at the date on which the alteration is made, or

(b) in any way increases his liability as at that date to contribute to the company's share capital or otherwise to pay money to the company.

(2) Subsection (1) does not apply in a case where the member agrees in writing, either before or after the alteration is made, to be bound by the alteration.

[1438]

NOTES

Commencement: to be appointed (see the introductory note to this Act).

26 Registrar to be sent copy of amended articles

(1) Where a company amends its articles it must send to the registrar a copy of the articles as amended not later than 15 days after the amendment takes effect.

(2) This section does not require a company to set out in its articles any provisions of model articles that—

(a) are applied by the articles, or

(b) apply by virtue of section 20 (default application of model articles).

(3) If a company fails to comply with this section an offence is committed by—

(a) the company, and

(b) every officer of the company who is in default.

(4) A person guilty of an offence under this section is liable on summary conviction to a fine not exceeding level 3 on the standard scale and, for continued contravention, a daily default fine not exceeding one-tenth of level 3 on the standard scale.

[1439]

NOTES

Commencement: to be appointed (see the introductory note to this Act).

27 Registrar's notice to comply in case of failure with respect to amended articles

(1) If it appears to the registrar that a company has failed to comply with any enactment requiring it—

(a) to send to the registrar a document making or evidencing an alteration in the company's articles, or

(b) to send to the registrar a copy of the company's articles as amended,

the registrar may give notice to the company requiring it to comply.

(2) The notice must—

(a) state the date on which it is issued, and

(b) require the company to comply within 28 days from that date.

(3) If the company complies with the notice within the specified time, no criminal proceedings may be brought in respect of the failure to comply with the enactment mentioned in subsection (1).

(4) If the company does not comply with the notice within the specified time, it is liable to a civil penalty of £200.

This is in addition to any liability to criminal proceedings in respect of the failure mentioned in subsection (1).

(5) The penalty may be recovered by the registrar and is to be paid into the Consolidated Fund.

[1440]

NOTES

Commencement: to be appointed (see the introductory note to this Act).

Supplementary

28 Existing companies: provisions of memorandum treated as provisions of articles

(1) Provisions that immediately before the commencement of this Part were contained in a company's memorandum but are not provisions of the kind mentioned in section 8 (provisions of new-style memorandum) are to be treated after the commencement of this Part as provisions of the company's articles.

(2) This applies not only to substantive provisions but also to provision for entrenchment (as defined in section 22).

(3) The provisions of this Part about provision for entrenchment apply to such provision as they apply to provision made on the company's formation, except that the duty under section 23(1)(a) to give notice to the registrar does not apply.

[1441]

NOTES

Commencement: to be appointed (see the introductory note to this Act).

CHAPTER 3
RESOLUTIONS AND AGREEMENTS AFFECTING A COMPANY'S CONSTITUTION

29 Resolutions and agreements affecting a company's constitution

(1) This Chapter applies to—

(a) any special resolution;

(b) any resolution or agreement agreed to by all the members of a company that, if not so agreed to, would not have been effective for its purpose unless passed as a special resolution;

(c) any resolution or agreement agreed to by all the members of a class of shareholders that, if not so agreed to, would not have been effective for its purpose unless passed by some particular majority or otherwise in some particular manner;

(d) any resolution or agreement that effectively binds all members of a class of shareholders though not agreed to by all those members;

(e) any other resolution or agreement to which this Chapter applies by virtue of any enactment.

(2) References in subsection (1) to a member of a company, or of a class of members of a company, do not include the company itself where it is such a member by virtue only of its holding shares as treasury shares.

[1442]

NOTES

Commencement: to be appointed (see the introductory note to this Act).

30 Copies of resolutions or agreements to be forwarded to registrar

(1) A copy of every resolution or agreement to which this Chapter applies, or (in the case of a resolution or agreement that is not in writing) a written memorandum setting out its terms, must be forwarded to the registrar within 15 days after it is passed or made.

(2) If a company fails to comply with this section, an offence is committed by—
(a) the company, and
(b) every officer of it who is in default.

(3) A person guilty of an offence under this section is liable on summary conviction to a fine not exceeding level 3 on the standard scale and, for continued contravention, a daily default fine not exceeding one-tenth of level 3 on the standard scale.

(4) For the purposes of this section, a liquidator of the company is treated as an officer of it.

[1443]

NOTES

Commencement: to be appointed (see the introductory note to this Act).

CHAPTER 4
MISCELLANEOUS AND SUPPLEMENTARY PROVISIONS

Statement of company's objects

31 Statement of company's objects

(1) Unless a company's articles specifically restrict the objects of the company, its objects are unrestricted.

(2) Where a company amends its articles so as to add, remove or alter a statement of the company's objects—
(a) it must give notice to the registrar,
(b) on receipt of the notice, the registrar shall register it, and
(c) the amendment is not effective until entry of that notice on the register.

(3) Any such amendment does not affect any rights or obligations of the company or render defective any legal proceedings by or against it.

(4) In the case of a company that is a charity, the provisions of this section have effect subject to—
(a) in England and Wales, section 64 of the Charities Act 1993 (c 10);
(b) in Northern Ireland, Article 9 of the Charities (Northern Ireland) Order 1987 (SI 1987/2048 (NI 19)).

(5) In the case of a company that is entered in the Scottish Charity Register, the provisions of this section have effect subject to the provisions of the Charities and Trustee Investment (Scotland) Act 2005 (asp 10).

[1444]

NOTES

Commencement: to be appointed (see the introductory note to this Act).

Other provisions with respect to a company's constitution

32 Constitutional documents to be provided to members

(1) A company must, on request by any member, send to him the following documents—
(a) an up-to-date copy of the company's articles;
(b) a copy of any resolution or agreement relating to the company to which Chapter 3 applies (resolutions and agreements affecting a company's constitution) and that is for the time being in force;
(c) a copy of any document required to be sent to the registrar under—
(i) section 34(2) (notice where company's constitution altered by enactment), or
(ii) section 35(2)(a) (notice where order of court or other authority alters company's constitution);
(d) a copy of any court order under section 899 (order sanctioning compromise or arrangement) or section 900 (order facilitating reconstruction or amalgamation);

(e) a copy of any court order under section 996 (protection of members against unfair prejudice: powers of the court) that alters the company's constitution;
(f) a copy of the company's current certificate of incorporation, and of any past certificates of incorporation;
(g) in the case of a company with a share capital, a current statement of capital;
(h) in the case of a company limited by guarantee, a copy of the statement of guarantee.

(2) The statement of capital required by subsection (1)(g) is a statement of—
(a) the total number of shares of the company,
(b) the aggregate nominal value of those shares,
(c) for each class of shares—
(i) prescribed particulars of the rights attached to the shares,
(ii) the total number of shares of that class, and
(iii) the aggregate nominal value of shares of that class, and
(d) the amount paid up and the amount (if any) unpaid on each share (whether on account of the nominal value of the share or by way of premium).

(3) If a company makes default in complying with this section, an offence is committed by every officer of the company who is in default.

(4) A person guilty of an offence under this section is liable on summary conviction to a fine not exceeding level 3 on the standard scale.

[1445]

NOTES

Commencement: to be appointed (see the introductory note to this Act).

33 Effect of company's constitution

(1) The provisions of a company's constitution bind the company and its members to the same extent as if there were covenants on the part of the company and of each member to observe those provisions.

(2) Money payable by a member to the company under its constitution is a debt due from him to the company.

In England and Wales and Northern Ireland it is of the nature of an ordinary contract debt.

[1446]

NOTES

Commencement: to be appointed (see the introductory note to this Act).

34 Notice to registrar where company's constitution altered by enactment

(1) This section applies where a company's constitution is altered by an enactment, other than an enactment amending the general law.

(2) The company must give notice of the alteration to the registrar, specifying the enactment, not later than 15 days after the enactment comes into force.

In the case of a special enactment the notice must be accompanied by a copy of the enactment.

(3) If the enactment amends—
(a) the company's articles, or
(b) a resolution or agreement to which Chapter 3 applies (resolutions and agreements affecting a company's constitution),

the notice must be accompanied by a copy of the company's articles, or the resolution or agreement in question, as amended.

(4) A "special enactment" means an enactment that is not a public general enactment, and includes—
(a) an Act for confirming a provisional order,
(b) any provision of a public general Act in relation to the passing of which any of the standing orders of the House of Lords or the House of Commons relating to Private Business applied, or

(c) any enactment to the extent that it is incorporated in or applied for the purposes of a special enactment.

(5) If a company fails to comply with this section an offence is committed by—

(a) the company, and

(b) every officer of the company who is in default.

(6) A person guilty of an offence under this section is liable on summary conviction to a fine not exceeding level 3 on the standard scale and, for continued contravention, a daily default fine not exceeding one-tenth of level 3 on the standard scale.

[1447]

NOTES

Commencement: to be appointed (see the introductory note to this Act).

35 Notice to registrar where company's constitution altered by order

(1) Where a company's constitution is altered by an order of a court or other authority, the company must give notice to the registrar of the alteration not later than 15 days after the alteration takes effect.

(2) The notice must be accompanied by—

(a) a copy of the order, and

(b) if the order amends—

(i) the company's articles, or

(ii) a resolution or agreement to which Chapter 3 applies (resolutions and agreements affecting the company's constitution),

a copy of the company's articles, or the resolution or agreement in question, as amended.

(3) If a company fails to comply with this section an offence is committed by—

(a) the company, and

(b) every officer of the company who is in default.

(4) A person guilty of an offence under this section is liable on summary conviction to a fine not exceeding level 3 on the standard scale and, for continued contravention, a daily default fine not exceeding one-tenth of level 3 on the standard scale.

(5) This section does not apply where provision is made by another enactment for the delivery to the registrar of a copy of the order in question.

[1448]

NOTES

Commencement: to be appointed (see the introductory note to this Act).

36 Documents to be incorporated in or accompany copies of articles issued by company

(1) Every copy of a company's articles issued by the company must be accompanied by—

(a) a copy of any resolution or agreement relating to the company to which Chapter 3 applies (resolutions and agreements affecting a company's constitution),

(b) where the company has been required to give notice to the registrar under section 34(2) (notice where company's constitution altered by enactment), a statement that the enactment in question alters the effect of the company's constitution,

(c) where the company's constitution is altered by a special enactment (see section 34(4)), a copy of the enactment, and

(d) a copy of any order required to be sent to the registrar under section 35(2)(a) (order of court or other authority altering company's constitution).

(2) This does not require the articles to be accompanied by a copy of a document or by a statement if—

(a) the effect of the resolution, agreement, enactment or order (as the case may be) on the company's constitution has been incorporated into the articles by amendment, or

(b) the resolution, agreement, enactment or order (as the case may be) is not for the time being in force.

(3) If the company fails to comply with this section, an offence is committed by every officer of the company who is in default.

(4) A person guilty of an offence under this section is liable on summary conviction to a fine not exceeding level 3 on the standard scale for each occasion on which copies are issued, or, as the case may be, requested.

(5) For the purposes of this section, a liquidator of the company is treated as an officer of it.

[1449]

NOTES

Commencement: to be appointed (see the introductory note to this Act).

Supplementary provisions

37 Right to participate in profits otherwise than as member void

In the case of a company limited by guarantee and not having a share capital any provision in the company's articles, or in any resolution of the company, purporting to give a person a right to participate in the divisible profits of the company otherwise than as a member is void.

[1450]

NOTES

Commencement: to be appointed (see the introductory note to this Act).

38 Application to single member companies of enactments and rules of law

Any enactment or rule of law applicable to companies formed by two or more persons or having two or more members applies with any necessary modification in relation to a company formed by one person or having only one person as a member.

[1451]

NOTES

Commencement: to be appointed (see the introductory note to this Act).

PART 4
A COMPANY'S CAPACITY AND RELATED MATTERS

Capacity of company and power of directors to bind it

39 A company's capacity

(1) The validity of an act done by a company shall not be called into question on the ground of lack of capacity by reason of anything in the company's constitution.

(2) This section has effect subject to section 42 (companies that are charities).

[1452]

NOTES

Commencement: to be appointed (see the introductory note to this Act).

40 Power of directors to bind the company

(1) In favour of a person dealing with a company in good faith, the power of the directors to bind the company, or authorise others to do so, is deemed to be free of any limitation under the company's constitution.

(2) For this purpose—

(a) a person "deals with" a company if he is a party to any transaction or other act to which the company is a party,

(b) a person dealing with a company—
  (i) is not bound to enquire as to any limitation on the powers of the directors to bind the company or authorise others to do so,
  (ii) is presumed to have acted in good faith unless the contrary is proved, and
  (iii) is not to be regarded as acting in bad faith by reason only of his knowing that an act is beyond the powers of the directors under the company's constitution.

(3) The references above to limitations on the directors' powers under the company's constitution include limitations deriving—
(a) from a resolution of the company or of any class of shareholders, or
(b) from any agreement between the members of the company or of any class of shareholders.

(4) This section does not affect any right of a member of the company to bring proceedings to restrain the doing of an action that is beyond the powers of the directors.

But no such proceedings lie in respect of an act to be done in fulfilment of a legal obligation arising from a previous act of the company.

(5) This section does not affect any liability incurred by the directors, or any other person, by reason of the directors' exceeding their powers.

(6) This section has effect subject to—
section 41 (transactions with directors or their associates), and
section 42 (companies that are charities).

[1453]

NOTES

Commencement: to be appointed (see the introductory note to this Act).

41 Constitutional limitations: transactions involving directors or their associates

(1) This section applies to a transaction if or to the extent that its validity depends on section 40 (power of directors deemed to be free of limitations under company's constitution in favour of person dealing with company in good faith).

Nothing in this section shall be read as excluding the operation of any other enactment or rule of law by virtue of which the transaction may be called in question or any liability to the company may arise.

(2) Where—
(a) a company enters into such a transaction, and
(b) the parties to the transaction include—
  (i) a director of the company or of its holding company, or
  (ii) a person connected with any such director,

the transaction is voidable at the instance of the company.

(3) Whether or not it is avoided, any such party to the transaction as is mentioned in subsection (2)(b)(i) or (ii), and any director of the company who authorised the transaction, is liable—
(a) to account to the company for any gain he has made directly or indirectly by the transaction, and
(b) to indemnify the company for any loss or damage resulting from the transaction.

(4) The transaction ceases to be voidable if—
(a) restitution of any money or other asset which was the subject matter of the transaction is no longer possible, or
(b) the company is indemnified for any loss or damage resulting from the transaction, or
(c) rights acquired bona fide for value and without actual notice of the directors' exceeding their powers by a person who is not party to the transaction would be affected by the avoidance, or
(d) the transaction is affirmed by the company.

(5) A person other than a director of the company is not liable under subsection (3) if he shows that at the time the transaction was entered into he did not know that the directors were exceeding their powers.

(6) Nothing in the preceding provisions of this section affects the rights of any party to the transaction not within subsection (2)(b)(i) or (ii).

But the court may, on the application of the company or any such party, make an order affirming, severing or setting aside the transaction on such terms as appear to the court to be just.

(7) In this section—

(a) "transaction" includes any act; and

(b) the reference to a person connected with a director has the same meaning as in Part 10 (company directors).

[1454]

NOTES

Commencement: to be appointed (see the introductory note to this Act).

42 Constitutional limitations: companies that are charities

(1) Sections 39 and 40 (company's capacity and power of directors to bind company) do not apply to the acts of a company that is a charity except in favour of a person who—

(a) does not know at the time the act is done that the company is a charity, or

(b) gives full consideration in money or money's worth in relation to the act in question and does not know (as the case may be)—

(i) that the act is not permitted by the company's constitution, or

(ii) that the act is beyond the powers of the directors.

(2) Where a company that is a charity purports to transfer or grant an interest in property, the fact that (as the case may be)—

(a) the act was not permitted by the company's constitution, or

(b) the directors in connection with the act exceeded any limitation on their powers under the company's constitution,

does not affect the title of a person who subsequently acquires the property or any interest in it for full consideration without actual notice of any such circumstances affecting the validity of the company's act.

(3) In any proceedings arising out of subsection (1) or (2) the burden of proving—

(a) that a person knew that the company was a charity, or

(b) that a person knew that an act was not permitted by the company's constitution or was beyond the powers of the directors,

lies on the person asserting that fact.

(4) In the case of a company that is a charity the affirmation of a transaction to which section 41 applies (transactions with directors or their associates) is ineffective without the prior written consent of—

(a) in England and Wales, the Charity Commission;

(b) in Northern Ireland, the Department for Social Development.

(5) This section does not extend to Scotland (but see section 112 of the Companies Act 1989 (c 40)).

[1455]

NOTES

Commencement: to be appointed (see the introductory note to this Act).

Formalities of doing business under the law of England and Wales or Northern Ireland

43 Company contracts

(1) Under the law of England and Wales or Northern Ireland a contract may be made—

(a) by a company, by writing under its common seal, or

(b) on behalf of a company, by a person acting under its authority, express or implied.

(2) Any formalities required by law in the case of a contract made by an individual also apply, unless a contrary intention appears, to a contract made by or on behalf of a company.

[1456]

NOTES

Commencement: to be appointed (see the introductory note to this Act).

44 Execution of documents

(1) Under the law of England and Wales or Northern Ireland a document is executed by a company—

(a) by the affixing of its common seal, or
(b) by signature in accordance with the following provisions.

(2) A document is validly executed by a company if it is signed on behalf of the company—

(a) by two authorised signatories, or
(b) by a director of the company in the presence of a witness who attests the signature.

(3) The following are "authorised signatories" for the purposes of subsection (2)—

(a) every director of the company, and
(b) in the case of a private company with a secretary or a public company, the secretary (or any joint secretary) of the company.

(4) A document signed in accordance with subsection (2) and expressed, in whatever words, to be executed by the company has the same effect as if executed under the common seal of the company.

(5) In favour of a purchaser a document is deemed to have been duly executed by a company if it purports to be signed in accordance with subsection (2).

A "purchaser" means a purchaser in good faith for valuable consideration and includes a lessee, mortgagee or other person who for valuable consideration acquires an interest in property.

(6) Where a document is to be signed by a person on behalf of more than one company, it is not duly signed by that person for the purposes of this section unless he signs it separately in each capacity.

(7) References in this section to a document being (or purporting to be) signed by a director or secretary are to be read, in a case where that office is held by a firm, as references to its being (or purporting to be) signed by an individual authorised by the firm to sign on its behalf.

(8) This section applies to a document that is (or purports to be) executed by a company in the name of or on behalf of another person whether or not that person is also a company.
[1457]

NOTES

Commencement: to be appointed (see the introductory note to this Act).

45 Common seal

(1) A company may have a common seal, but need not have one.

(2) A company which has a common seal shall have its name engraved in legible characters on the seal.

(3) If a company fails to comply with subsection (2) an offence is committed by—

(a) the company, and
(b) every officer of the company who is in default.

(4) An officer of a company, or a person acting on behalf of a company, commits an offence if he uses, or authorises the use of, a seal purporting to be a seal of the company on which its name is not engraved as required by subsection (2).

(5) A person guilty of an offence under this section is liable on summary conviction to a fine not exceeding level 3 on the standard scale.

(6) This section does not form part of the law of Scotland.
[1458]

NOTES

Commencement: to be appointed (see the introductory note to this Act).

46 Execution of deeds

(1) A document is validly executed by a company as a deed for the purposes of section 1(2)(b) of the Law of Property (Miscellaneous Provisions) Act 1989 (c 34) and for the purposes of the law of Northern Ireland if, and only if—

(a) it is duly executed by the company, and

(b) it is delivered as a deed.

(2) For the purposes of subsection (1)(b) a document is presumed to be delivered upon its being executed, unless a contrary intention is proved.

[1459]

NOTES

Commencement: to be appointed (see the introductory note to this Act).

47 Execution of deeds or other documents by attorney

(1) Under the law of England and Wales or Northern Ireland a company may, by instrument executed as a deed, empower a person, either generally or in respect of specified matters, as its attorney to execute deeds or other documents on its behalf.

(2) A deed or other document so executed, whether in the United Kingdom or elsewhere, has effect as if executed by the company.

[1460]

NOTES

Commencement: to be appointed (see the introductory note to this Act).

Formalities of doing business under the law of Scotland

48 Execution of documents by companies

(1) The following provisions form part of the law of Scotland only.

(2) Notwithstanding the provisions of any enactment, a company need not have a company seal.

(3) For the purposes of any enactment—

(a) providing for a document to be executed by a company by affixing its common seal, or

(b) referring (in whatever terms) to a document so executed,

a document signed or subscribed by or on behalf of the company in accordance with the provisions of the Requirements of Writing (Scotland) Act 1995 (c 7) has effect as if so executed.

[1461]

NOTES

Commencement: to be appointed (see the introductory note to this Act).

Other matters

49 Official seal for use abroad

(1) A company that has a common seal may have an official seal for use outside the United Kingdom.

(2) The official seal must be a facsimile of the company's common seal, with the addition on its face of the place or places where it is to be used.

(3) The official seal when duly affixed to a document has the same effect as the company's common seal.

This subsection does not extend to Scotland.

(4) A company having an official seal for use outside the United Kingdom may—

(a) by writing under its common seal, or

(b) as respects Scotland, by writing subscribed in accordance with the Requirements of Writing (Scotland) Act 1995,

authorise any person appointed for the purpose to affix the official seal to any deed or other document to which the company is party.

(5) As between the company and a person dealing with such an agent, the agent's authority continues—

(a) during the period mentioned in the instrument conferring the authority, or

(b) if no period is mentioned, until notice of the revocation or termination of the agent's authority has been given to the person dealing with him.

(6) The person affixing the official seal must certify in writing on the deed or other document to which the seal is affixed the date on which, and place at which, it is affixed.

[1462]

NOTES

Commencement: to be appointed (see the introductory note to this Act).

50 Official seal for share certificates etc

(1) A company that has a common seal may have an official seal for use—

(a) for sealing securities issued by the company, or

(b) for sealing documents creating or evidencing securities so issued.

(2) The official seal—

(a) must be a facsimile of the company's common seal, with the addition on its face of the word "Securities", and

(b) when duly affixed to the document has the same effect as the company's common seal.

[1463]

NOTES

Commencement: to be appointed (see the introductory note to this Act).

51 Pre-incorporation contracts, deeds and obligations

(1) A contract that purports to be made by or on behalf of a company at a time when the company has not been formed has effect, subject to any agreement to the contrary, as one made with the person purporting to act for the company or as agent for it, and he is personally liable on the contract accordingly.

(2) Subsection (1) applies—

(a) to the making of a deed under the law of England and Wales or Northern Ireland, and

(b) to the undertaking of an obligation under the law of Scotland,

as it applies to the making of a contract.

[1464]

NOTES

Commencement: to be appointed (see the introductory note to this Act).

52 Bills of exchange and promissory notes

A bill of exchange or promissory note is deemed to have been made, accepted or endorsed on behalf of a company if made, accepted or endorsed in the name of, or by or on behalf or on account of, the company by a person acting under its authority.

[1465]

NOTES

Commencement: to be appointed (see the introductory note to this Act).

PART 5
A COMPANY'S NAME

CHAPTER 1
GENERAL REQUIREMENTS

Prohibited names

53 Prohibited names

A company must not be registered under this Act by a name if, in the opinion of the Secretary of State—

(a) its use by the company would constitute an offence, or

(b) it is offensive.

[1466]

NOTES

Commencement: to be appointed (see the introductory note to this Act).

Sensitive words and expressions

54 Names suggesting connection with government or public authority

(1) The approval of the Secretary of State is required for a company to be registered under this Act by a name that would be likely to give the impression that the company is connected with—

(a) Her Majesty's Government, any part of the Scottish administration or Her Majesty's Government in Northern Ireland,

(b) a local authority, or

(c) any public authority specified for the purposes of this section by regulations made by the Secretary of State.

(2) For the purposes of this section—

"local authority" means—

(a) a local authority within the meaning of the Local Government Act 1972 (c 70), the Common Council of the City of London or the Council of the Isles of Scilly,

(b) a council constituted under section 2 of the Local Government etc (Scotland) Act 1994 (c 39), or

(c) a district council in Northern Ireland;

"public authority" includes any person or body having functions of a public nature.

(3) Regulations under this section are subject to affirmative resolution procedure.

[1467]

NOTES

Commencement: to be appointed (see the introductory note to this Act).

55 Other sensitive words or expressions

(1) The approval of the Secretary of State is required for a company to be registered under this Act by a name that includes a word or expression for the time being specified in regulations made by the Secretary of State under this section.

(2) Regulations under this section are subject to approval after being made.

[1468]

NOTES

Commencement: to be appointed (see the introductory note to this Act).

56 Duty to seek comments of government department or other specified body

(1) The Secretary of State may by regulations under—

(a) section 54 (name suggesting connection with government or public authority), or

(b) section 55 (other sensitive words or expressions),

require that, in connection with an application for the approval of the Secretary of State under that section, the applicant must seek the view of a specified Government department or other body.

(2) Where such a requirement applies, the applicant must request the specified department or other body (in writing) to indicate whether (and if so why) it has any objections to the proposed name.

(3) Where a request under this section is made in connection with an application for the registration of a company under this Act, the application must—

(a) include a statement that a request under this section has been made, and

(b) be accompanied by a copy of any response received.

(4) Where a request under this section is made in connection with a change in a company's name, the notice of the change sent to the registrar must be accompanied by—

(a) a statement by a director or secretary of the company that a request under this section has been made, and

(b) a copy of any response received.

(5) In this section "specified" means specified in the regulations.

[1469]

NOTES

Commencement: to be appointed (see the introductory note to this Act).

Permitted characters etc

57 Permitted characters etc

(1) The Secretary of State may make provision by regulations—

(a) as to the letters or other characters, signs or symbols (including accents and other diacritical marks) and punctuation that may be used in the name of a company registered under this Act; and

(b) specifying a standard style or format for the name of a company for the purposes of registration.

(2) The regulations may prohibit the use of specified characters, signs or symbols when appearing in a specified position (in particular, at the beginning of a name).

(3) A company may not be registered under this Act by a name that consists of or includes anything that is not permitted in accordance with regulations under this section.

(4) Regulations under this section are subject to negative resolution procedure.

(5) In this section "specified" means specified in the regulations.

[1470]

NOTES

Commencement: to be appointed (see the introductory note to this Act).

CHAPTER 2
INDICATIONS OF COMPANY TYPE OR LEGAL FORM

Required indications for limited companies

58 Public limited companies

(1) The name of a limited company that is a public company must end with "public limited company" or "p.l.c.".

(2) In the case of a Welsh company, its name may instead end with "cwmni cyfyngedig cyhoeddus" or "c.c.c.".

(3) This section does not apply to community interest companies (but see section 33(3) and (4) of the Companies (Audit, Investigations and Community Enterprise) Act 2004 (c 27)).
[1471]

NOTES
Commencement: to be appointed (see the introductory note to this Act).

59 Private limited companies

(1) The name of a limited company that is a private company must end with "limited" or "ltd.".

(2) In the case of a Welsh company, its name may instead end with "cyfyngedig" or "cyf.".

(3) Certain companies are exempt from this requirement (see section 60).

(4) This section does not apply to community interest companies (but see section 33(1) and (2) of the Companies (Audit, Investigations and Community Enterprise) Act 2004).
[1472]

NOTES
Commencement: to be appointed (see the introductory note to this Act).

60 Exemption from requirement as to use of "limited"

(1) A private company is exempt from section 59 (requirement to have name ending with "limited" or permitted alternative) if—
- (a) it is a charity,
- (b) it is exempted from the requirement of that section by regulations made by the Secretary of State, or
- (c) it meets the conditions specified in—
  section 61 (continuation of existing exemption: companies limited by shares), or
  section 62 (continuation of existing exemption: companies limited by guarantee).

(2) The registrar may refuse to register a private limited company by a name that does not include the word "limited" (or a permitted alternative) unless a statement has been delivered to him that the company meets the conditions for exemption.

(3) The registrar may accept the statement as sufficient evidence of the matters stated in it.

(4) Regulations under this section are subject to negative resolution procedure.
[1473]

NOTES
Commencement: to be appointed (see the introductory note to this Act).

61 Continuation of existing exemption: companies limited by shares

(1) This section applies to a private company limited by shares—
- (a) that on 25th February 1982—
  - (i) was registered in Great Britain, and

(ii) had a name that, by virtue of a licence under section 19 of the Companies Act 1948 (c 38) (or corresponding earlier legislation), did not include the word "limited" or any of the permitted alternatives, or

(b) that on 30th June 1983—

(i) was registered in Northern Ireland, and

(ii) had a name that, by virtue of a licence under section 19 of the Companies Act (Northern Ireland) 1960 (c 22 (NI)) (or corresponding earlier legislation), did not include the word "limited" or any of the permitted alternatives.

(2) A company to which this section applies is exempt from section 59 (requirement to have name ending with "limited" or permitted alternative) so long as—

(a) it continues to meet the following two conditions, and

(b) it does not change its name.

(3) The first condition is that the objects of the company are the promotion of commerce, art, science, education, religion, charity or any profession, and anything incidental or conducive to any of those objects.

(4) The second condition is that the company's articles—

(a) require its income to be applied in promoting its objects,

(b) prohibit the payment of dividends, or any return of capital, to its members, and

(c) require all the assets that would otherwise be available to its members generally to be transferred on its winding up either—

(i) to another body with objects similar to its own, or

(ii) to another body the objects of which are the promotion of charity and anything incidental or conducive thereto,

(whether or not the body is a member of the company).

[1474]

NOTES

Commencement: to be appointed (see the introductory note to this Act).

62 Continuation of existing exemption: companies limited by guarantee

(1) A private company limited by guarantee that immediately before the commencement of this Part—

(a) was exempt by virtue of section 30 of the Companies Act 1985 (c 6) or Article 40 of the Companies (Northern Ireland) Order 1986 (SI 1986/ 1032 (NI 6)) from the requirement to have a name including the word "limited" or a permitted alternative, and

(b) had a name that did not include the word "limited" or any of the permitted alternatives,

is exempt from section 59 (requirement to have name ending with "limited" or permitted alternative) so long as it continues to meet the following two conditions and does not change its name.

(2) The first condition is that the objects of the company are the promotion of commerce, art, science, education, religion, charity or any profession, and anything incidental or conducive to any of those objects.

(3) The second condition is that the company's articles—

(a) require its income to be applied in promoting its objects,

(b) prohibit the payment of dividends to its members, and

(c) require all the assets that would otherwise be available to its members generally to be transferred on its winding up either—

(i) to another body with objects similar to its own, or

(ii) to another body the objects of which are the promotion of charity and anything incidental or conducive thereto,

(whether or not the body is a member of the company).

[1475]

NOTES

Commencement: to be appointed (see the introductory note to this Act).

63 Exempt company: restriction on amendment of articles

(1) A private company—

(a) that is exempt under section 61 or 62 from the requirement to use "limited" (or a permitted alternative) as part of its name, and

(b) whose name does not include "limited" or any of the permitted alternatives,

must not amend its articles so that it ceases to comply with the conditions for exemption under that section.

(2) If subsection (1) above is contravened an offence is committed by—

(a) the company, and

(b) every officer of the company who is in default.

For this purpose a shadow director is treated as an officer of the company.

(3) A person guilty of an offence under this section is liable on summary conviction to a fine not exceeding level 5 on the standard scale and, for continued contravention, a daily default fine not exceeding one-tenth of level 5 on the standard scale.

(4) Where immediately before the commencement of this section—

(a) a company was exempt by virtue of section 30 of the Companies Act 1985 (c 6) or Article 40 of the Companies (Northern Ireland) Order 1986 (SI 1986/1032 (NI 6)) from the requirement to have a name including the word "limited" (or a permitted alternative), and

(b) the company's memorandum or articles contained provision preventing an alteration of them without the approval of—

(i) the Board of Trade or a Northern Ireland department (or any other department or Minister), or

(ii) the Charity Commission,

that provision, and any condition of any such licence as is mentioned in section 61(1)(a)(ii) or (b)(ii) requiring such provision, shall cease to have effect.

This does not apply if, or to the extent that, the provision is required by or under any other enactment.

(5) It is hereby declared that any such provision as is mentioned in subsection (4)(b) formerly contained in a company's memorandum was at all material times capable, with the appropriate approval, of being altered or removed under section 17 of the Companies Act 1985 or Article 28 of the Companies (Northern Ireland) Order 1986 (SI 1986/1032 (NI 6)) (or corresponding earlier enactments).

[1476]

NOTES

Commencement: to be appointed (see the introductory note to this Act).

64 Power to direct change of name in case of company ceasing to be entitled to exemption

(1) If it appears to the Secretary of State that a company whose name does not include "limited" or any of the permitted alternatives—

(a) has ceased to be entitled to exemption under section 60(1)(a) or (b), or

(b) in the case of a company within section 61 or 62 (which impose conditions as to the objects and articles of the company)—

(i) has carried on any business other than the promotion of any of the objects mentioned in subsection (3) of section 61 or, as the case may be, subsection (2) of section 62, or

(ii) has acted inconsistently with the provision required by subsection (4)(a) or (b) of section 61 or, as the case may be, subsection (3)(a) or (b) of section 62,

the Secretary of State may direct the company to change its name so that it ends with "limited" or one of the permitted alternatives.

(2) The direction must be in writing and must specify the period within which the company is to change its name.

(3) A change of name in order to comply with a direction under this section may be made by resolution of the directors.

This is without prejudice to any other method of changing the company's name.

(4) Where a resolution of the directors is passed in accordance with subsection (3), the company must give notice to the registrar of the change.

Sections 80 and 81 apply as regards the registration and effect of the change.

(5) If the company fails to comply with a direction under this section an offence is committed by—

- (a) the company, and
- (b) every officer of the company who is in default.

(6) A person guilty of an offence under this section is liable on summary conviction to a fine not exceeding level 5 on the standard scale and, for continued contravention, a daily default fine not exceeding one-tenth of level 5 on the standard scale.

(7) A company that has been directed to change its name under this section may not, without the approval of the Secretary of State, subsequently change its name so that it does not include "limited" or one of the permitted alternatives. This does not apply to a change of name on re-registration or on conversion to a community interest company.

[1477]

NOTES

Commencement: to be appointed (see the introductory note to this Act).

Inappropriate use of indications of company type or legal form

65 Inappropriate use of indications of company type or legal form

(1) The Secretary of State may make provision by regulations prohibiting the use in a company name of specified words, expressions or other indications —

- (a) that are associated with a particular type of company or form of organisation, or
- (b) that are similar to words, expressions or other indications associated with a particular type of company or form of organisation.

(2) The regulations may prohibit the use of words, expressions or other indications—

- (a) in a specified part, or otherwise than in a specified part, of a company's name;
- (b) in conjunction with, or otherwise than in conjunction with, such other words, expressions or indications as may be specified.

(3) A company must not be registered under this Act by a name that consists of or includes anything prohibited by regulations under this section.

(4) In this section "specified" means specified in the regulations.

(5) Regulations under this section are subject to negative resolution procedure.

[1478]

NOTES

Commencement: to be appointed (see the introductory note to this Act).

CHAPTER 3
SIMILARITY TO OTHER NAMES

Similarity to other name on registrar's index

66 Name not to be the same as another in the index

(1) A company must not be registered under this Act by a name that is the same as another name appearing in the registrar's index of company names.

(2) The Secretary of State may make provision by regulations supplementing this section.

(3) The regulations may make provision—

- (a) as to matters that are to be disregarded, and

(b) as to words, expressions, signs or symbols that are, or are not, to be regarded as the same,

for the purposes of this section.

(4) The regulations may provide—

(a) that registration by a name that would otherwise be prohibited under this section is permitted—

(i) in specified circumstances, or

(ii) with specified consent, and

(b) that if those circumstances obtain or that consent is given at the time a company is registered by a name, a subsequent change of circumstances or withdrawal of consent does not affect the registration.

(5) Regulations under this section are subject to negative resolution procedure.

(6) In this section "specified" means specified in the regulations.

[1479]

NOTES

Commencement: to be appointed (see the introductory note to this Act).

67 Power to direct change of name in case of similarity to existing name

(1) The Secretary of State may direct a company to change its name if it has been registered in a name that is the same as or, in the opinion of the Secretary of State, too like—

(a) a name appearing at the time of the registration in the registrar's index of company names, or

(b) a name that should have appeared in that index at that time.

(2) The Secretary of State may make provision by regulations supplementing this section.

(3) The regulations may make provision—

(a) as to matters that are to be disregarded, and

(b) as to words, expressions, signs or symbols that are, or are not, to be regarded as the same,

for the purposes of this section.

(4) The regulations may provide—

(a) that no direction is to be given under this section in respect of a name—

(i) in specified circumstances, or

(ii) if specified consent is given, and

(b) that a subsequent change of circumstances or withdrawal of consent does not give rise to grounds for a direction under this section.

(5) Regulations under this section are subject to negative resolution procedure.

(6) In this section "specified" means specified in the regulations.

[1480]

NOTES

Commencement: to be appointed (see the introductory note to this Act).

68 Direction to change name: supplementary provisions

(1) The following provisions have effect in relation to a direction under section 67 (power to direct change of name in case of similarity to existing name).

(2) Any such direction—

(a) must be given within twelve months of the company's registration by the name in question, and

(b) must specify the period within which the company is to change its name.

(3) The Secretary of State may by a further direction extend that period.

Any such direction must be given before the end of the period for the time being specified.

(4) A direction under section 67 or this section must be in writing.

(5) If a company fails to comply with the direction, an offence is committed by—
(a) the company, and
(b) every officer of the company who is in default.

For this purpose a shadow director is treated as an officer of the company.

(6) A person guilty of an offence under this section is liable on summary conviction to a fine not exceeding level 3 on the standard scale and, for continued contravention, a daily default fine not exceeding one-tenth of level 3 on the standard scale.

[1481]

NOTES

Commencement: to be appointed (see the introductory note to this Act).

Similarity to other name in which person has goodwill

69 Objection to company's registered name

(1) A person ("the applicant") may object to a company's registered name on the ground—
(a) that it is the same as a name associated with the applicant in which he has goodwill, or
(b) that it is sufficiently similar to such a name that its use in the United Kingdom would be likely to mislead by suggesting a connection between the company and the applicant.

(2) The objection must be made by application to a company names adjudicator (see section 70).

(3) The company concerned shall be the primary respondent to the application. Any of its members or directors may be joined as respondents.

(4) If the ground specified in subsection (1)(a) or (b) is established, it is for the respondents to show—
(a) that the name was registered before the commencement of the activities on which the applicant relies to show goodwill; or
(b) that the company—
(i) is operating under the name, or
(ii) is proposing to do so and has incurred substantial start-up costs in preparation, or
(iii) was formerly operating under the name and is now dormant;
or
(c) that the name was registered in the ordinary course of a company formation business and the company is available for sale to the applicant on the standard terms of that business; or
(d) that the name was adopted in good faith; or
(e) that the interests of the applicant are not adversely affected to any significant extent.

If none of those is shown, the objection shall be upheld.

(5) If the facts mentioned in subsection (4)(a), (b) or (c) are established, the objection shall nevertheless be upheld if the applicant shows that the main purpose of the respondents (or any of them) in registering the name was to obtain money (or other consideration) from the applicant or prevent him from registering the name.

(6) If the objection is not upheld under subsection (4) or (5), it shall be dismissed.

(7) In this section "goodwill" includes reputation of any description.

[1482]

NOTES

Commencement: to be appointed (see the introductory note to this Act).

70 Company names adjudicators

(1) The Secretary of State shall appoint persons to be company names adjudicators.

(2) The persons appointed must have such legal or other experience as, in the Secretary of State's opinion, makes them suitable for appointment.

(3) An adjudicator—
- (a) holds office in accordance with the terms of his appointment,
- (b) is eligible for re-appointment when his term of office ends,
- (c) may resign at any time by notice in writing given to the Secretary of State, and
- (d) may be dismissed by the Secretary of State on the ground of incapacity or misconduct.

(4) One of the adjudicators shall be appointed Chief Adjudicator.

He shall perform such functions as the Secretary of State may assign to him.

(5) The other adjudicators shall undertake such duties as the Chief Adjudicator may determine.

(6) The Secretary of State may—
- (a) appoint staff for the adjudicators;
- (b) pay remuneration and expenses to the adjudicators and their staff;
- (c) defray other costs arising in relation to the performance by the adjudicators of their functions;
- (d) compensate persons for ceasing to be adjudicators.

[1483]

NOTES

Commencement: to be appointed (see the introductory note to this Act).

71 Procedural rules

(1) The Secretary of State may make rules about proceedings before a company names adjudicator.

(2) The rules may, in particular, make provision—
- (a) as to how an application is to be made and the form and content of an application or other documents;
- (b) for fees to be charged;
- (c) about the service of documents and the consequences of failure to serve them;
- (d) as to the form and manner in which evidence is to be given;
- (e) for circumstances in which hearings are required and those in which they are not;
- (f) for cases to be heard by more than one adjudicator;
- (g) setting time limits for anything required to be done in connection with the proceedings (and allowing for such limits to be extended, even if they have expired);
- (h) enabling the adjudicator to strike out an application, or any defence, in whole or in part—
  - (i) on the ground that it is vexatious, has no reasonable prospect of success or is otherwise misconceived, or
  - (ii) for failure to comply with the requirements of the rules;
- (i) conferring power to order security for costs (in Scotland, caution for expenses);
- (j) as to how far proceedings are to be held in public;
- (k) requiring one party to bear the costs (in Scotland, expenses) of another and as to the taxing (or settling) the amount of such costs (or expenses).

(3) The rules may confer on the Chief Adjudicator power to determine any matter that could be the subject of provision in the rules.

(4) Rules under this section shall be made by statutory instrument which shall be subject to annulment in pursuance of a resolution of either House of Parliament.

[1484]

NOTES

Commencement: to be appointed (see the introductory note to this Act).

72 Decision of adjudicator to be made available to public

(1) A company names adjudicator must, within 90 days of determining an application under section 69, make his decision and his reasons for it available to the public.

(2) He may do so by means of a website or by such other means as appear to him to be appropriate.

[1485]

NOTES

Commencement: to be appointed (see the introductory note to this Act).

73 Order requiring name to be changed

(1) If an application under section 69 is upheld, the adjudicator shall make an order—

(a) requiring the respondent company to change its name to one that is not an offending name, and

(b) requiring all the respondents—

(i) to take all such steps as are within their power to make, or facilitate the making, of that change, and

(ii) not to cause or permit any steps to be taken calculated to result in another company being registered with a name that is an offending name.

(2) An "offending name" means a name that, by reason of its similarity to the name associated with the applicant in which he claims goodwill, would be likely—

(a) to be the subject of a direction under section 67 (power of Secretary of State to direct change of name), or

(b) to give rise to a further application under section 69.

(3) The order must specify a date by which the respondent company's name is to be changed and may be enforced—

(a) in England and Wales or Northern Ireland, in the same way as an order of the High Court;

(b) in Scotland, in the same way as a decree of the Court of Session.

(4) If the respondent company's name is not changed in accordance with the order by the specified date, the adjudicator may determine a new name for the company.

(5) If the adjudicator determines a new name for the respondent company he must give notice of his determination—

(a) to the applicant,

(b) to the respondents, and

(c) to the registrar.

(6) For the purposes of this section a company's name is changed when the change takes effect in accordance with section 81(1) (on the issue of the new certification of incorporation).

[1486]

NOTES

Commencement: to be appointed (see the introductory note to this Act).

74 Appeal from adjudicator's decision

(1) An appeal lies to the court from any decision of a company names adjudicator to uphold or dismiss an application under section 69.

(2) Notice of appeal against a decision upholding an application must be given before the date specified in the adjudicator's order by which the respondent company's name is to be changed.

(3) If notice of appeal is given against a decision upholding an application, the effect of the adjudicator's order is suspended.

(4) If on appeal the court—

(a) affirms the decision of the adjudicator to uphold the application, or

(b) reverses the decision of the adjudicator to dismiss the application,

the court may (as the case may require) specify the date by which the adjudicator's order is to be complied with, remit the matter to the adjudicator or make any order or determination that the adjudicator might have made.

(5) If the court determines a new name for the company it must give notice of the determination—

(a) to the parties to the appeal, and
(b) to the registrar.

[1487]

NOTES

Commencement: to be appointed (see the introductory note to this Act).

CHAPTER 4
OTHER POWERS OF THE SECRETARY OF STATE

75 Provision of misleading information etc

(1) If it appears to the Secretary of State—
(a) that misleading information has been given for the purposes of a company's registration by a particular name, or
(b) that an undertaking or assurance has been given for that purpose and has not been fulfilled,

the Secretary of State may direct the company to change its name.

(2) Any such direction—
(a) must be given within five years of the company's registration by that name, and
(b) must specify the period within which the company is to change its name.

(3) The Secretary of State may by a further direction extend the period within which the company is to change its name.

Any such direction must be given before the end of the period for the time being specified.

(4) A direction under this section must be in writing.

(5) If a company fails to comply with a direction under this section, an offence is committed by—
(a) the company, and
(b) every officer of the company who is in default.

For this purpose a shadow director is treated as an officer of the company.

(6) A person guilty of an offence under this section is liable on summary conviction to a fine not exceeding level 3 on the standard scale and, for continued contravention, a daily default fine not exceeding one-tenth of level 3 on the standard scale.

[1488]

NOTES

Commencement: to be appointed (see the introductory note to this Act).

---

76 Misleading indication of activities

(1) If in the opinion of the Secretary of State the name by which a company is registered gives so misleading an indication of the nature of its activities as to be likely to cause harm to the public, the Secretary of State may direct the company to change its name.

(2) The direction must be in writing.

(3) The direction must be complied with within a period of six weeks from the date of the direction or such longer period as the Secretary of State may think fit to allow.

This does not apply if an application is duly made to the court under the following provisions.

(4) The company may apply to the court to set the direction aside.

The application must be made within the period of three weeks from the date of the direction.

(5) The court may set the direction aside or confirm it.

If the direction is confirmed, the court shall specify the period within which the direction is to be complied with.

(6) If a company fails to comply with a direction under this section, an offence is committed by—
- (a) the company, and
- (b) every officer of the company who is in default.

For this purpose a shadow director is treated as an officer of the company.

(7) A person guilty of an offence under this section is liable on summary conviction to a fine not exceeding level 3 on the standard scale and, for continued contravention, a daily default fine not exceeding one-tenth of level 3 on the standard scale.

[1489]

NOTES

Commencement: to be appointed (see the introductory note to this Act).

CHAPTER 5
CHANGE OF NAME

77 Change of name

(1) A company may change its name—
- (a) by special resolution (see section 78), or
- (b) by other means provided for by the company's articles (see section 79).

(2) The name of a company may also be changed—
- (a) by resolution of the directors acting under section 64 (change of name to comply with direction of Secretary of State under that section);
- (b) on the determination of a new name by a company names adjudicator under section 73 (powers of adjudicator on upholding objection to company name);
- (c) on the determination of a new name by the court under section 74 (appeal against decision of company names adjudicator);
- (d) under section 1033 (company's name on restoration to the register).

[1490]

NOTES

Commencement: to be appointed (see the introductory note to this Act).

78 Change of name by special resolution

(1) Where a change of name has been agreed to by a company by special resolution, the company must give notice to the registrar.

This is in addition to the obligation to forward a copy of the resolution to the registrar.

(2) Where a change of name by special resolution is conditional on the occurrence of an event, the notice given to the registrar of the change must—
- (a) specify that the change is conditional, and
- (b) state whether the event has occurred.

(3) If the notice states that the event has not occurred—
- (a) the registrar is not required to act under section 80 (registration and issue of new certificate of incorporation) until further notice,
- (b) when the event occurs, the company must give notice to the registrar stating that it has occurred, and
- (c) the registrar may rely on the statement as sufficient evidence of the matters stated in it.

[1491]

NOTES

Commencement: to be appointed (see the introductory note to this Act).

79 Change of name by means provided for in company's articles

(1) Where a change of a company's name has been made by other means provided for by its articles—
- (a) the company must give notice to the registrar, and

(b) the notice must be accompanied by a statement that the change of name has been made by means provided for by the company's articles.

(2) The registrar may rely on the statement as sufficient evidence of the matters stated in it.

[1492]

NOTES

Commencement: to be appointed (see the introductory note to this Act).

80 Change of name: registration and issue of new certificate of incorporation

(1) This section applies where the registrar receives notice of a change of a company's name.

(2) If the registrar is satisfied—

(a) that the new name complies with the requirements of this Part, and

(b) that the requirements of the Companies Acts, and any relevant requirements of the company's articles, with respect to a change of name are complied with,

the registrar must enter the new name on the register in place of the former name.

(3) On the registration of the new name, the registrar must issue a certificate of incorporation altered to meet the circumstances of the case.

[1493]

NOTES

Commencement: to be appointed (see the introductory note to this Act).

81 Change of name: effect

(1) A change of a company's name has effect from the date on which the new certificate of incorporation is issued.

(2) The change does not affect any rights or obligations of the company or render defective any legal proceedings by or against it.

(3) Any legal proceedings that might have been continued or commenced against it by its former name may be continued or commenced against it by its new name.

[1494]

NOTES

Commencement: to be appointed (see the introductory note to this Act).

CHAPTER 6
TRADING DISCLOSURES

82 Requirement to disclose company name etc

(1) The Secretary of State may by regulations make provision requiring companies—

(a) to display specified information in specified locations,

(b) to state specified information in specified descriptions of document or communication, and

(c) to provide specified information on request to those they deal with in the course of their business.

(2) The regulations—

(a) must in every case require disclosure of the name of the company, and

(b) may make provision as to the manner in which any specified information is to be displayed, stated or provided.

(3) The regulations may provide that, for the purposes of any requirement to disclose a company's name, any variation between a word or words required to be part of the name and a permitted abbreviation of that word or those words (or vice versa) shall be disregarded.

(4) In this section "specified" means specified in the regulations.

(5) Regulations under this section are subject to affirmative resolution procedure.

[1495]

NOTES

Commencement: to be appointed (see the introductory note to this Act).

83 Civil consequences of failure to make required disclosure

(1) This section applies to any legal proceedings brought by a company to which section 82 applies (requirement to disclose company name etc) to enforce a right arising out of a contract made in the course of a business in respect of which the company was, at the time the contract was made, in breach of regulations under that section.

(2) The proceedings shall be dismissed if the defendant (in Scotland, the defender) to the proceedings shows—

- (a) that he has a claim against the claimant (pursuer) arising out of the contract that he has been unable to pursue by reason of the latter's breach of the regulations, or
- (b) that he has suffered some financial loss in connection with the contract by reason of the claimant's (pursuer's) breach of the regulations,

unless the court before which the proceedings are brought is satisfied that it is just and equitable to permit the proceedings to continue.

(3) This section does not affect the right of any person to enforce such rights as he may have against another person in any proceedings brought by that person.

[1496]

NOTES

Commencement: to be appointed (see the introductory note to this Act).

84 Criminal consequences of failure to make required disclosures

(1) Regulations under section 82 may provide—

- (a) that where a company fails, without reasonable excuse, to comply with any specified requirement of regulations under that section an offence is committed by—
  - (i) the company, and
  - (ii) every officer of the company who is in default;
- (b) that a person guilty of such an offence is liable on summary conviction to a fine not exceeding level 3 on the standard scale and, for continued contravention, a daily default fine not exceeding one-tenth of level 3 on the standard scale.

(2) The regulations may provide that, for the purposes of any provision made under subsection (1), a shadow director of the company is to be treated as an officer of the company.

(3) In subsection (1)(a) "specified" means specified in the regulations.

[1497]

NOTES

Commencement: to be appointed (see the introductory note to this Act).

85 Minor variations in form of name to be left out of account

(1) For the purposes of this Chapter, in considering a company's name no account is to be taken of—

- (a) whether upper or lower case characters (or a combination of the two) are used,
- (b) whether diacritical marks or punctuation are present or absent,
- (c) whether the name is in the same format or style as is specified under section 57(1)(b) for the purposes of registration,

provided there is no real likelihood of names differing only in those respects being taken to be different names.

(2) This does not affect the operation of regulations under section 57(1)(a) permitting only specified characters, diacritical marks or punctuation.

[1498]

NOTES

Commencement: to be appointed (see the introductory note to this Act).

PART 6
A COMPANY'S REGISTERED OFFICE

General

86 A company's registered office

A company must at all times have a registered office to which all communications and notices may be addressed.

[1499]

NOTES

Commencement: to be appointed (see the introductory note to this Act).

87 Change of address of registered office

(1) A company may change the address of its registered office by giving notice to the registrar.

(2) The change takes effect upon the notice being registered by the registrar, but until the end of the period of 14 days beginning with the date on which it is registered a person may validly serve any document on the company at the address previously registered.

(3) For the purposes of any duty of a company—

(a) to keep available for inspection at its registered office any register, index or other document, or

(b) to mention the address of its registered office in any document,

a company that has given notice to the registrar of a change in the address of its registered office may act on the change as from such date, not more than 14 days after the notice is given, as it may determine.

(4) Where a company unavoidably ceases to perform at its registered office any such duty as is mentioned in subsection (3)(a) in circumstances in which it was not practicable to give prior notice to the registrar of a change in the address of its registered office, but—

(a) resumes performance of that duty at other premises as soon as practicable, and

(b) gives notice accordingly to the registrar of a change in the situation of its registered office within 14 days of doing so,

it is not to be treated as having failed to comply with that duty.

[1500]

NOTES

Commencement: to be appointed (see the introductory note to this Act).

Welsh companies

88 Welsh companies

(1) In the Companies Acts a "Welsh company" means a company as to which it is stated in the register that its registered office is to be situated in Wales.

(2) A company—

(a) whose registered office is in Wales, and

(b) as to which it is stated in the register that its registered office is to be situated in England and Wales,

may by special resolution require the register to be amended so that it states that the company's registered office is to be situated in Wales.

(3) A company—

(a) whose registered office is in Wales, and
(b) as to which it is stated in the register that its registered office is to be situated in Wales,

may by special resolution require the register to be amended so that it states that the company's registered office is to be situated in England and Wales.

(4) Where a company passes a resolution under this section it must give notice to the registrar, who shall—

(a) amend the register accordingly, and
(b) issue a new certificate of incorporation altered to meet the circumstances of the case.

[1501]

NOTES

Commencement: to be appointed (see the introductory note to this Act).

PART 7
RE-REGISTRATION AS A MEANS OF ALTERING A COMPANY'S STATUS

Introductory

89 Alteration of status by re-registration

A company may by re-registration under this Part alter its status—

(a) from a private company to a public company (see sections 90 to 96);
(b) from a public company to a private company (see sections 97 to 101);
(c) from a private limited company to an unlimited company (see sections 102 to 104);
(d) from an unlimited private company to a limited company (see sections 105 to 108);
(e) from a public company to an unlimited private company (see sections 109 to 111).

[1502]

NOTES

Commencement: to be appointed (see the introductory note to this Act).

90–101 (*Outside the scope of this work.*)

Private limited company becoming unlimited

102 Re-registration of private limited company as unlimited

(1) A private limited company may be re-registered as an unlimited company if—

(a) all the members of the company have assented to its being so re-registered,
(b) the condition specified below is met, and
(c) an application for re-registration is delivered to the registrar in accordance with section 103, together with—
 (i) the other documents required by that section, and
 (ii) a statement of compliance.

(2) The condition is that the company has not previously been re-registered as limited.

(3) The company must make such changes in its name and its articles—

(a) as are necessary in connection with its becoming an unlimited company; and
(b) if it is to have a share capital, as are necessary in connection with its becoming an unlimited company having a share capital.

(4) For the purposes of this section—

(a) a trustee in bankruptcy of a member of the company is entitled, to the exclusion of the member, to assent to the company's becoming unlimited; and
(b) the personal representative of a deceased member of the company may assent on behalf of the deceased.

(5) In subsection (4)(a), "a trustee in bankruptcy of a member of the company" includes—

(a) a permanent trustee or an interim trustee (within the meaning of the Bankruptcy (Scotland) Act 1985 (c 66)) on the sequestrated estate of a member of the company;

(b) a trustee under a protected trustee deed (within the meaning of the Bankruptcy (Scotland) Act 1985) granted by a member of the company.

[1503]

NOTES

Commencement: to be appointed (see the introductory note to this Act).

103 Application and accompanying documents

(1) An application for re-registration as an unlimited company must contain a statement of the company's proposed name on re-registration.

(2) The application must be accompanied by—

(a) the prescribed form of assent to the company's being registered as an unlimited company, authenticated by or on behalf of all the members of the company;

(b) a copy of the company's articles as proposed to be amended.

(3) The statement of compliance required to be delivered together with the application is a statement that the requirements of this Part as to re-registration as an unlimited company have been complied with.

(4) The statement must contain a statement by the directors of the company—

(a) that the persons by whom or on whose behalf the form of assent is authenticated constitute the whole membership of the company, and

(b) if any of the members have not authenticated that form themselves, that the directors have taken all reasonable steps to satisfy themselves that each person who authenticated it on behalf of a member was lawfully empowered to do so.

(5) The registrar may accept the statement of compliance as sufficient evidence that the company is entitled to be re-registered as an unlimited company.

[1504]

NOTES

Commencement: to be appointed (see the introductory note to this Act).

104 Issue of certificate of incorporation on re-registration

(1) If on an application for re-registration of a private limited company as an unlimited company the registrar is satisfied that the company is entitled to be so re-registered, the company shall be re-registered accordingly.

(2) The registrar must issue a certificate of incorporation altered to meet the circumstances of the case.

(3) The certificate must state that it is issued on re-registration and the date on which it is issued.

(4) On the issue of the certificate—

(a) the company by virtue of the issue of the certificate becomes an unlimited company, and

(b) the changes in the company's name and articles take effect.

(5) The certificate is conclusive evidence that the requirements of this Act as to re-registration have been complied with.

[1505]

NOTES

Commencement: to be appointed (see the introductory note to this Act).

Unlimited private company becoming limited

105 Re-registration of unlimited company as limited

(1) An unlimited company may be re-registered as a private limited company if—

(a) a special resolution that it should be so re-registered is passed,

(b) the condition specified below is met, and

(c) an application for re-registration is delivered to the registrar in accordance with section 106, together with—

(i) the other documents required by that section, and

(ii) a statement of compliance.

(2) The condition is that the company has not previously been re-registered as unlimited.

(3) The special resolution must state whether the company is to be limited by shares or by guarantee.

(4) The company must make such changes—

(a) in its name, and

(b) in its articles,

as are necessary in connection with its becoming a company limited by shares or, as the case may be, by guarantee.

[1506]

NOTES

Commencement: to be appointed (see the introductory note to this Act).

106 Application and accompanying documents

(1) An application for re-registration as a limited company must contain a statement of the company's proposed name on re-registration.

(2) The application must be accompanied by—

(a) a copy of the resolution that the company should re-register as a private limited company (unless a copy has already been forwarded to the registrar under Chapter 3 of Part 3);

(b) if the company is to be limited by guarantee, a statement of guarantee;

(c) a copy of the company's articles as proposed to be amended.

(3) The statement of guarantee required to be delivered in the case of a company that is to be limited by guarantee must state that each member undertakes that, if the company is wound up while he is a member, or within one year after he ceases to be a member, he will contribute to the assets of the company such amount as may be required for—

(a) payment of the debts and liabilities of the company contracted before he ceases to be a member,

(b) payment of the costs, charges and expenses of winding up, and

(c) adjustment of the rights of the contributories among themselves,

not exceeding a specified amount.

(4) The statement of compliance required to be delivered together with the application is a statement that the requirements of this Part as to re-registration as a limited company have been complied with.

(5) The registrar may accept the statement of compliance as sufficient evidence that the company is entitled to be re-registered as a limited company.

[1507]

NOTES

Commencement: to be appointed (see the introductory note to this Act).

107 Issue of certificate of incorporation on re-registration

(1) If on an application for re-registration of an unlimited company as a limited company the registrar is satisfied that the company is entitled to be so re-registered, the company shall be re-registered accordingly.

(2) The registrar must issue a certificate of incorporation altered to meet the circumstances of the case.

(3) The certificate must state that it is issued on re-registration and the date on which it is so issued.

(4) On the issue of the certificate—

(a) the company by virtue of the issue of the certificate becomes a limited company, and

(b) the changes in the company's name and articles take effect.

(5) The certificate is conclusive evidence that the requirements of this Act as to re-registration have been complied with.

[1508]

NOTES

Commencement: to be appointed (see the introductory note to this Act).

108 Statement of capital required where company already has share capital

(1) A company which on re-registration under section 107 already has allotted share capital must within 15 days after the re-registration deliver a statement of capital to the registrar.

(2) This does not apply if the information which would be included in the statement has already been sent to the registrar in—

(a) a statement of capital and initial shareholdings (see section 10), or

(b) a statement of capital contained in an annual return (see section 856(2)).

(3) The statement of capital must state with respect to the company's share capital on re-registration—

(a) the total number of shares of the company,

(b) the aggregate nominal value of those shares,

(c) for each class of shares—

(i) prescribed particulars of the rights attached to the shares,

(ii) the total number of shares of that class, and

(iii) the aggregate nominal value of shares of that class, and

(d) the amount paid up and the amount (if any) unpaid on each share (whether on account of the nominal value of the share or by way of premium).

(4) If default is made in complying with this section, an offence is committed by—

(a) the company, and

(b) every officer of the company who is in default.

(5) A person guilty of an offence under this section is liable on summary conviction to a fine not exceeding level 3 on the standard scale and, for continued contravention, a daily default fine not exceeding one-tenth of level 3 on the standard scale.

[1509]

NOTES

Commencement: to be appointed (see the introductory note to this Act).

109–111 (*Outside the scope of this work.*)

PART 8
A COMPANY'S MEMBERS

CHAPTER 1
THE MEMBERS OF A COMPANY

112 The members of a company

(1) The subscribers of a company's memorandum are deemed to have agreed to become members of the company, and on its registration become members and must be entered as such in its register of members.

(2) Every other person who agrees to become a member of a company, and whose name is entered in its register of members, is a member of the company.

[1510]

NOTES

Commencement: to be appointed (see the introductory note to this Act).

CHAPTER 2
REGISTER OF MEMBERS

General

113 Register of members

(1) Every company must keep a register of its members.

(2) There must be entered in the register—
- (a) the names and addresses of the members,
- (b) the date on which each person was registered as a member, and
- (c) the date at which any person ceased to be a member.

(3) In the case of a company having a share capital, there must be entered in the register, with the names and addresses of the members, a statement of—
- (a) the shares held by each member, distinguishing each share—
  - (i) by its number (so long as the share has a number), and
  - (ii) where the company has more than one class of issued shares, by its class, and
- (b) the amount paid or agreed to be considered as paid on the shares of each member.

(4) If the company has converted any of its shares into stock, and given notice of the conversion to the registrar, the register of members must show the amount and class of stock held by each member instead of the amount of shares and the particulars relating to shares specified above.

(5) In the case of joint holders of shares or stock in a company, the company's register of members must state the names of each joint holder.

In other respects joint holders are regarded for the purposes of this Chapter as a single member (so that the register must show a single address).

(6) In the case of a company that does not have a share capital but has more than one class of members, there must be entered in the register, with the names and addresses of the members, a statement of the class to which each member belongs.

(7) If a company makes default in complying with this section an offence is committed by—
- (a) the company, and
- (b) every officer of the company who is in default.

(8) A person guilty of an offence under this section is liable on summary conviction to a fine not exceeding level 3 on the standard scale and, for continued contravention, a daily default fine not exceeding one-tenth of level 3 on the standard scale.

[1511]

NOTES

Commencement: to be appointed (see the introductory note to this Act).

114 Register to be kept available for inspection

(1) A company's register of members must be kept available for inspection—
- (a) at its registered office, or
- (b) at a place specified in regulations under section 1136.

(2) A company must give notice to the registrar of the place where its register of members is kept available for inspection and of any change in that place.

(3) No such notice is required if the register has, at all times since it came into existence (or, in the case of a register in existence on the relevant date, at all times since then) been kept available for inspection at the company's registered office.

(4) The relevant date for the purposes of subsection (3) is—
(a) 1st July 1948 in the case of a company registered in Great Britain, and
(b) 1st April 1961 in the case of a company registered in Northern Ireland.

(5) If a company makes default for 14 days in complying with subsection (2), an offence is committed by—
(a) the company, and
(b) every officer of the company who is in default.

(6) A person guilty of an offence under this section is liable on summary conviction to a fine not exceeding level 3 on the standard scale and, for continued contravention, a daily default fine not exceeding one-tenth of level 3 on the standard scale.

[1512]

NOTES

Commencement: to be appointed (see the introductory note to this Act).

115 Index of members

(1) Every company having more than 50 members must keep an index of the names of the members of the company, unless the register of members is in such a form as to constitute in itself an index.

(2) The company must make any necessary alteration in the index within 14 days after the date on which any alteration is made in the register of members.

(3) The index must contain, in respect of each member, a sufficient indication to enable the account of that member in the register to be readily found.

(4) The index must be at all times kept available for inspection at the same place as the register of members.

(5) If default is made in complying with this section, an offence is committed by—
(a) the company, and
(b) every officer of the company who is in default.

(6) A person guilty of an offence under this section is liable on summary conviction to a fine not exceeding level 3 on the standard scale and, for continued contravention, a daily default fine not exceeding one-tenth of level 3 on the standard scale.

[1513]

NOTES

Commencement: to be appointed (see the introductory note to this Act).

116 Rights to inspect and require copies

(1) The register and the index of members' names must be open to the inspection—
(a) of any member of the company without charge, and
(b) of any other person on payment of such fee as may be prescribed.

(2) Any person may require a copy of a company's register of members, or of any part of it, on payment of such fee as may be prescribed.

(3) A person seeking to exercise either of the rights conferred by this section must make a request to the company to that effect.

(4) The request must contain the following information—
(a) in the case of an individual, his name and address;
(b) in the case of an organisation, the name and address of an individual responsible for making the request on behalf of the organisation;
(c) the purpose for which the information is to be used; and
(d) whether the information will be disclosed to any other person, and if so—
(i) where that person is an individual, his name and address,
(ii) where that person is an organisation, the name and address of an individual responsible for receiving the information on its behalf, and
(iii) the purpose for which the information is to be used by that person.

[1514]

NOTES

Commencement: to be appointed (see the introductory note to this Act).

117 Register of members: response to request for inspection or copy

(1) Where a company receives a request under section 116 (register of members: right to inspect and require copy), it must within five working days either—

(a) comply with the request, or

(b) apply to the court.

(2) If it applies to the court it must notify the person making the request.

(3) If on an application under this section the court is satisfied that the inspection or copy is not sought for a proper purpose—

(a) it shall direct the company not to comply with the request, and

(b) it may further order that the company's costs (in Scotland, expenses) on the application be paid in whole or in part by the person who made the request, even if he is not a party to the application.

(4) If the court makes such a direction and it appears to the court that the company is or may be subject to other requests made for a similar purpose (whether made by the same person or different persons), it may direct that the company is not to comply with any such request.

The order must contain such provision as appears to the court appropriate to identify the requests to which it applies.

(5) If on an application under this section the court does not direct the company not to comply with the request, the company must comply with the request immediately upon the court giving its decision or, as the case may be, the proceedings being discontinued.

[1515]

NOTES

Commencement: to be appointed (see the introductory note to this Act).

118 Register of members: refusal of inspection or default in providing copy

(1) If an inspection required under section 116 (register of members: right to inspect and require copy) is refused or default is made in providing a copy required under that section, otherwise than in accordance with an order of the court, an offence is committed by—

(a) the company, and

(b) every officer of the company who is in default.

(2) A person guilty of an offence under this section is liable on summary conviction to a fine not exceeding level 3 on the standard scale and, for continued contravention, a daily default fine not exceeding one-tenth of level 3 on the standard scale.

(3) In the case of any such refusal or default the court may by order compel an immediate inspection or, as the case may be, direct that the copy required be sent to the person requesting it.

[1516]

NOTES

Commencement: to be appointed (see the introductory note to this Act).

119 Register of members: offences in connection with request for or disclosure of information

(1) It is an offence for a person knowingly or recklessly to make in a request under section 116 (register of members: right to inspect or require copy) a statement that is misleading, false or deceptive in a material particular.

(2) It is an offence for a person in possession of information obtained by exercise of either of the rights conferred by that section—

(a) to do anything that results in the information being disclosed to another person, or

(b) to fail to do anything with the result that the information is disclosed to another person,

knowing, or having reason to suspect, that person may use the information for a purpose that is not a proper purpose.

(3) A person guilty of an offence under this section is liable—

(a) on conviction on indictment, to imprisonment for a term not exceeding two years or a fine (or both);

(b) on summary conviction—

(i) in England and Wales, to imprisonment for a term not exceeding twelve months or to a fine not exceeding the statutory maximum (or both);

(ii) in Scotland or Northern Ireland, to imprisonment for a term not exceeding six months, or to a fine not exceeding the statutory maximum (or both).

[1517]

NOTES

Commencement: to be appointed (see the introductory note to this Act).

120 Information as to state of register and index

(1) When a person inspects the register, or the company provides him with a copy of the register or any part of it, the company must inform him of the most recent date (if any) on which alterations were made to the register and there were no further alterations to be made.

(2) When a person inspects the index of members' names, the company must inform him whether there is any alteration to the register that is not reflected in the index.

(3) If a company fails to provide the information required under subsection (1) or (2), an offence is committed by—

(a) the company, and

(b) every officer of the company who is in default.

(4) A person guilty of an offence under this section is liable on summary conviction to a fine not exceeding level 3 on the standard scale.

[1518]

NOTES

Commencement: to be appointed (see the introductory note to this Act).

121 Removal of entries relating to former members

An entry relating to a former member of the company may be removed from the register after the expiration of ten years from the date on which he ceased to be a member.

[1519]

NOTES

Commencement: to be appointed (see the introductory note to this Act).

122 *(Outside the scope of this work.)*

123 Single member companies

(1) If a limited company is formed under this Act with only one member there shall be entered in the company's register of members, with the name and address of the sole member, a statement that the company has only one member.

(2) If the number of members of a limited company falls to one, or if an unlimited company with only one member becomes a limited company on re-registration, there shall upon the occurrence of that event be entered in the company's register of members, with the name and address of the sole member—

(a) a statement that the company has only one member, and

(b) the date on which the company became a company having only one member.

(3) If the membership of a limited company increases from one to two or more members, there shall upon the occurrence of that event be entered in the company's register of members, with the name and address of the person who was formerly the sole member—

(a) a statement that the company has ceased to have only one member, and
(b) the date on which that event occurred.

(4) If a company makes default in complying with this section, an offence is committed by—

(a) the company, and
(b) every officer of the company who is in default.

(5) A person guilty of an offence under this section is liable on summary conviction to a fine not exceeding level 3 on the standard scale and, for continued contravention, a daily default fine not exceeding one-tenth of level 3 on the standard scale.

[1520]

NOTES

Commencement: to be appointed (see the introductory note to this Act).

124 (*Outside the scope of this work.*)

Supplementary

125 Power of court to rectify register

(1) If—

(a) the name of any person is, without sufficient cause, entered in or omitted from a company's register of members, or
(b) default is made or unnecessary delay takes place in entering on the register the fact of any person having ceased to be a member,

the person aggrieved, or any member of the company, or the company, may apply to the court for rectification of the register.

(2) The court may either refuse the application or may order rectification of the register and payment by the company of any damages sustained by any party aggrieved.

(3) On such an application the court may decide any question relating to the title of a person who is a party to the application to have his name entered in or omitted from the register, whether the question arises between members or alleged members, or between members or alleged members on the one hand and the company on the other hand, and generally may decide any question necessary or expedient to be decided for rectification of the register.

(4) In the case of a company required by this Act to send a list of its members to the registrar of companies, the court, when making an order for rectification of the register, shall by its order direct notice of the rectification to be given to the registrar.

[1521]

NOTES

Commencement: to be appointed (see the introductory note to this Act).

126 Trusts not to be entered on register

No notice of any trust, expressed, implied or constructive, shall be entered on the register of members of a company registered in England and Wales or Northern Ireland, or be receivable by the registrar.

[1522]

NOTES

Commencement: to be appointed (see the introductory note to this Act).

127 Register to be evidence

The register of members is prima facie evidence of any matters which are by this Act directed or authorised to be inserted in it.

[1523]

NOTES

Commencement: to be appointed (see the introductory note to this Act).

128 Time limit for claims arising from entry in register

(1) Liability incurred by a company—

(a) from the making or deletion of an entry in the register of members, or

(b) from a failure to make or delete any such entry,

is not enforceable more than ten years after the date on which the entry was made or deleted or, as the case may be, the failure first occurred.

(2) This is without prejudice to any lesser period of limitation (and, in Scotland, to any rule that the obligation giving rise to the liability prescribes before the expiry of that period). **[1524]**

NOTES

Commencement: to be appointed (see the introductory note to this Act).

CHAPTER 3
OVERSEAS BRANCH REGISTERS

129 Overseas branch registers

(1) A company having a share capital may, if it transacts business in a country or territory to which this Chapter applies, cause to be kept there a branch register of members resident there (an "overseas branch register").

(2) This Chapter applies to—

(a) any part of Her Majesty's dominions outside the United Kingdom, the Channel Islands and the Isle of Man, and

(b) the countries or territories listed below.

Bangladesh
Cyprus
Dominica
The Gambia
Ghana
Guyana
The Hong Kong Special Administrative Region of the People's Republic of China
India
Ireland
Kenya
Kiribati
Lesotho
Malawi
Malaysia
Malta
Nigeria
Pakistan
Seychelles
Sierra Leone
Singapore
South Africa
Sri Lanka
Swaziland
Trinidad and Tobago
Uganda
Zimbabwe

(3) The Secretary of State may make provision by regulations as to the circumstances in which a company is to be regarded as keeping a register in a particular country or territory.

(4) Regulations under this section are subject to negative resolution procedure.

(5) References—

(a) in any Act or instrument (including, in particular, a company's articles) to a dominion register, or

(b) in articles registered before 1st November 1929 to a colonial register, are to be read (unless the context otherwise requires) as a reference to an overseas branch register kept under this section.

[1525]

NOTES

Commencement: to be appointed (see the introductory note to this Act).

130 Notice of opening of overseas branch register

(1) A company that begins to keep an overseas branch register must give notice to the registrar within 14 days of doing so, stating the country or territory in which the register is kept.

(2) If default is made in complying with subsection (1), an offence is committed by—

(a) the company, and

(b) every officer of the company who is in default.

(3) A person guilty of an offence under subsection (2) is liable on summary conviction to a fine not exceeding level 3 on the standard scale and, for continued contravention, a daily default fine not exceeding one-tenth of level 3 on the standard scale.

[1526]

NOTES

Commencement: to be appointed (see the introductory note to this Act).

131 Keeping of overseas branch register

(1) An overseas branch register is regarded as part of the company's register of members ("the main register").

(2) The Secretary of State may make provision by regulations modifying any provision of Chapter 2 (register of members) as it applies in relation to an overseas branch register.

(3) Regulations under this section are subject to negative resolution procedure.

(4) Subject to the provisions of this Act, a company may by its articles make such provision as it thinks fit as to the keeping of overseas branch registers.

[1527]

NOTES

Commencement: to be appointed (see the introductory note to this Act).

132 Register or duplicate to be kept available for inspection in UK

(1) A company that keeps an overseas branch register must keep available for inspection—

(a) the register, or

(b) a duplicate of the register duly entered up from time to time,

at the place in the United Kingdom where the company's main register is kept available for inspection.

(2) Any such duplicate is treated for all purposes of this Act as part of the main register.

(3) If default is made in complying with subsection (1), an offence is committed by—

(a) the company, and

(b) every officer of the company who is in default.

(4) A person guilty of an offence under subsection (3) is liable on summary conviction to a fine not exceeding level 3 on the standard scale and, for continued contravention, a daily default fine not exceeding one-tenth of level 3 on the standard scale.

[1528]

NOTES

Commencement: to be appointed (see the introductory note to this Act).

133 Transactions in shares registered in overseas branch register

(1) Shares registered in an overseas branch register must be distinguished from those registered in the main register.

(2) No transaction with respect to shares registered in an overseas branch register may be registered in any other register.

(3) An instrument of transfer of a share registered in an overseas branch register—

(a) is regarded as a transfer of property situated outside the United Kingdom, and

(b) unless executed in a part of the United Kingdom, is exempt from stamp duty.

[1529]

NOTES

Commencement: to be appointed (see the introductory note to this Act).

134 Jurisdiction of local courts

(1) A competent court in a country or territory where an overseas branch register is kept may exercise the same jurisdiction as is exercisable by a court in the United Kingdom—

(a) to rectify the register (see section 125), or

(b) in relation to a request for inspection or a copy of the register (see section 117).

(2) The offences—

(a) of refusing inspection or failing to provide a copy of the register (see section 118), and

(b) of making a false, misleading or deceptive statement in a request for inspection or a copy (see section 119),

may be prosecuted summarily before any tribunal having summary criminal jurisdiction in the country or territory where the register is kept.

(3) This section extends only to those countries and territories to which paragraph 3 of Schedule 14 to the Companies Act 1985 (c 6) (which made similar provision) extended immediately before the coming into force of this Chapter.

[1530]

NOTES

Commencement: to be appointed (see the introductory note to this Act).

135 Discontinuance of overseas branch register

(1) A company may discontinue an overseas branch register.

(2) If it does so all the entries in that register must be transferred—

(a) to some other overseas branch register kept in the same country or territory, or

(b) to the main register.

(3) The company must give notice to the registrar within 14 days of the discontinuance.

(4) If default is made in complying with subsection (3), an offence is committed by—

(a) the company, and

(b) every officer of the company who is in default.

(5) A person guilty of an offence under subsection (4) is liable on summary conviction to a fine not exceeding level 3 on the standard scale and, for continued contravention, a daily default fine not exceeding one-tenth of level 3 on the standard scale.

[1531]

NOTES

Commencement: to be appointed (see the introductory note to this Act).

CHAPTER 4
PROHIBITION ON SUBSIDIARY BEING MEMBER OF ITS HOLDING COMPANY

General prohibition

136 Prohibition on subsidiary being a member of its holding company

(1) Except as provided by this Chapter—

(a) a body corporate cannot be a member of a company that is its holding company, and

(b) any allotment or transfer of shares in a company to its subsidiary is void.

(2) The exceptions are provided for in—
section 138 (subsidiary acting as personal representative or trustee), and
section 141 (subsidiary acting as authorised dealer in securities).

[1532]

NOTES

Commencement: to be appointed (see the introductory note to this Act).

137 Shares acquired before prohibition became applicable

(1) Where a body corporate became a holder of shares in a company—

(a) before the relevant date, or

(b) on or after that date and before the commencement of this Chapter in circumstances in which the prohibition in section 23(1) of the Companies Act 1985 or Article 33(1) of the Companies (Northern Ireland) Order 1986 (SI 1986/1032 (NI 6)) (or any corresponding earlier enactment), as it then had effect, did not apply, or

(c) on or after the commencement of this Chapter in circumstances in which the prohibition in section 136 did not apply,

it may continue to be a member of the company.

(2) The relevant date for the purposes of subsection (1)(a) is—

(a) 1st July 1948 in the case of a company registered in Great Britain, and

(b) 1st April 1961 in the case of a company registered in Northern Ireland.

(3) So long as it is permitted to continue as a member of a company by virtue of this section, an allotment to it of fully paid shares in the company may be validly made by way of capitalisation of reserves of the company.

(4) But, so long as the prohibition in section 136 would (apart from this section) apply, it has no right to vote in respect of the shares mentioned in subsection (1) above, or any shares allotted as mentioned in subsection (3) above, on a written resolution or at meetings of the company or of any class of its members.

[1533]

NOTES

Commencement: to be appointed (see the introductory note to this Act).

Subsidiary acting as personal representative or trustee

138 Subsidiary acting as personal representative or trustee

(1) The prohibition in section 136 (prohibition on subsidiary being a member of its holding company) does not apply where the subsidiary is concerned only—

(a) as personal representative, or

(b) as trustee,

unless, in the latter case, the holding company or a subsidiary of it is beneficially interested under the trust.

(2) For the purpose of ascertaining whether the holding company or a subsidiary is so interested, there shall be disregarded—

(a) any interest held only by way of security for the purposes of a transaction entered into by the holding company or subsidiary in the ordinary course of a business that includes the lending of money;

(b) any interest within—
section 139 (interests to be disregarded: residual interest under pension scheme or employees' share scheme), or
section 140 (interests to be disregarded: employer's rights of recovery under pension scheme or employees' share scheme);

(c) any rights that the company or subsidiary has in its capacity as trustee, including in particular—
  (i) any right to recover its expenses or be remunerated out of the trust property, and
  (ii) any right to be indemnified out of the trust property for any liability incurred by reason of any act or omission in the performance of its duties as trustee.

[1534]

NOTES

Commencement: to be appointed (see the introductory note to this Act).

139 Interests to be disregarded: residual interest under pension scheme or employees' share scheme

(1) Where shares in a company are held on trust for the purposes of a pension scheme or employees' share scheme, there shall be disregarded for the purposes of section 138 any residual interest that has not vested in possession.

(2) A "residual interest" means a right of the company or subsidiary ("the residual beneficiary") to receive any of the trust property in the event of—

(a) all the liabilities arising under the scheme having been satisfied or provided for, or
(b) the residual beneficiary ceasing to participate in the scheme, or
(c) the trust property at any time exceeding what is necessary for satisfying the liabilities arising or expected to arise under the scheme.

(3) In subsection (2)—

(a) the reference to a right includes a right dependent on the exercise of a discretion vested by the scheme in the trustee or another person, and
(b) the reference to liabilities arising under a scheme includes liabilities that have resulted, or may result, from the exercise of any such discretion.

(4) For the purposes of this section a residual interest vests in possession—

(a) in a case within subsection (2)(a), on the occurrence of the event mentioned there (whether or not the amount of the property receivable pursuant to the right is ascertained);
(b) in a case within subsection (2)(b) or (c), when the residual beneficiary becomes entitled to require the trustee to transfer to him any of the property receivable pursuant to the right.

(5) In this section "pension scheme" means a scheme for the provision of benefits consisting of or including relevant benefits for or in respect of employees or former employees.

(6) In subsection (5)—

(a) "relevant benefits" means any pension, lump sum, gratuity or other like benefit given or to be given on retirement or on death or in anticipation of retirement or, in connection with past service, after retirement or death; and
(b) "employee" shall be read as if a director of a company were employed by it.

[1535]

NOTES

Commencement: to be appointed (see the introductory note to this Act).

140 Interests to be disregarded: employer's rights of recovery under pension scheme or employees' share scheme

(1) Where shares in a company are held on trust for the purposes of a pension scheme or employees' share scheme, there shall be disregarded for the purposes of section 138 any

charge or lien on, or set-off against, any benefit or other right or interest under the scheme for the purpose of enabling the employer or former employer of a member of the scheme to obtain the discharge of a monetary obligation due to him from the member.

(2) In the case of a trust for the purposes of a pension scheme there shall also be disregarded any right to receive from the trustee of the scheme, or as trustee of the scheme to retain, an amount that can be recovered or retained, under section 61 of the Pension Schemes Act 1993 (c 48) or section 57 of the Pension Schemes (Northern Ireland) Act 1993 (c 49) (deduction of contributions equivalent premium from refund of scheme contributions) or otherwise, as reimbursement or partial reimbursement for any contributions equivalent premium paid in connection with the scheme under Part 3 of that Act.

(3) In this section "pension scheme" means a scheme for the provision of benefits consisting of or including relevant benefits for or in respect of employees or former employees.

"Relevant benefits" here means any pension, lump sum, gratuity or other like benefit given or to be given on retirement or on death or in anticipation of retirement or, in connection with past service, after retirement or death.

(4) In this section "employer" and "employee" shall be read as if a director of a company were employed by it.

[1536]

NOTES

Commencement: to be appointed (see the introductory note to this Act).

141–142 (*Outside the scope of this work.*)

Supplementary

143 Application of provisions to companies not limited by shares

In relation to a company other than a company limited by shares, the references in this Chapter to shares shall be read as references to the interest of its members as such, whatever the form of that interest.

[1537]

NOTES

Commencement: to be appointed (see the introductory note to this Act).

144 Application of provisions to nominees

The provisions of this Chapter apply to a nominee acting on behalf of a subsidiary as to the subsidiary itself.

[1538]

NOTES

Commencement: to be appointed (see the introductory note to this Act).

PART 9
EXERCISE OF MEMBERS' RIGHTS

Effect of provisions in company's articles

145 Effect of provisions of articles as to enjoyment or exercise of members' rights

(1) This section applies where provision is made by a company's articles enabling a member to nominate another person or persons as entitled to enjoy or exercise all or any specified rights of the member in relation to the company.

(2) So far as is necessary to give effect to that provision, anything required or authorised by any provision of the Companies Acts to be done by or in relation to the member shall

instead be done, or (as the case may be) may instead be done, by or in relation to the nominated person (or each of them) as if he were a member of the company.

(3) This applies, in particular, to the rights conferred by—
- (a) sections 291 and 293 (right to be sent proposed written resolution);
- (b) section 292 (right to require circulation of written resolution);
- (c) section 303 (right to require directors to call general meeting);
- (d) section 310 (right to notice of general meetings);
- (e) section 314 (right to require circulation of a statement);
- (f) section 324 (right to appoint proxy to act at meeting);
- (g) section 338 (right to require circulation of resolution for AGM of public company); and
- (h) section 423 (right to be sent a copy of annual accounts and reports).

(4) This section and any such provision as is mentioned in subsection (1)—
- (a) do not confer rights enforceable against the company by anyone other than the member, and
- (b) do not affect the requirements for an effective transfer or other disposition of the whole or part of a member's interest in the company.

[1539]

NOTES

Commencement: to be appointed (see the introductory note to this Act).

Information rights

146 Traded companies: nomination of persons to enjoy information rights

(1) This section applies to a company whose shares are admitted to trading on a regulated market.

(2) A member of such a company who holds shares on behalf of another person may nominate that person to enjoy information rights.

(3) "Information rights" means—
- (a) the right to receive a copy of all communications that the company sends to its members generally or to any class of its members that includes the person making the nomination, and
- (b) the rights conferred by—
  - (i) section 431 or 432 (right to require copies of accounts and reports), and
  - (ii) section 1145 (right to require hard copy version of document or information provided in another form).

(4) The reference in subsection (3)(a) to communications that a company sends to its members generally includes the company's annual accounts and reports. For the application of section 426 (option to provide summary financial statement) in relation to a person nominated to enjoy information rights, see subsection (5) of that section.

(5) A company need not act on a nomination purporting to relate to certain information rights only.

[1540]

NOTES

Commencement: to be appointed (see the introductory note to this Act).

147 Information rights: form in which copies to be provided

(1) This section applies as regards the form in which copies are to be provided to a person nominated under section 146 (nomination of person to enjoy information rights).

(2) If the person to be nominated wishes to receive hard copy communications, he must—
- (a) request the person making the nomination to notify the company of that fact, and
- (b) provide an address to which such copies may be sent.

This must be done before the nomination is made.

(3) If having received such a request the person making the nomination—

(a) notifies the company that the nominated person wishes to receive hard copy communications, and

(b) provides the company with that address,

the right of the nominated person is to receive hard copy communications accordingly.

(4) This is subject to the provisions of Parts 3 and 4 of Schedule 5 (communications by company) under which the company may take steps to enable it to communicate in electronic form or by means of a website.

(5) If no such notification is given (or no address is provided), the nominated person is taken to have agreed that documents or information may be sent or supplied to him by the company by means of a website.

(6) That agreement—

(a) may be revoked by the nominated person, and

(b) does not affect his right under section 1145 to require a hard copy version of a document or information provided in any other form.

[1541]

NOTES

Commencement: to be appointed (see the introductory note to this Act).

148 Termination or suspension of nomination

(1) The following provisions have effect in relation to a nomination under section 146 (nomination of person to enjoy information rights).

(2) The nomination may be terminated at the request of the member or of the nominated person.

(3) The nomination ceases to have effect on the occurrence in relation to the member or the nominated person of any of the following—

(a) in the case of an individual, death or bankruptcy;

(b) in the case of a body corporate, dissolution or the making of an order for the winding up of the body otherwise than for the purposes of reconstruction.

(4) In subsection (3)—

(a) the reference to bankruptcy includes—

(i) the sequestration of a person's estate, and

(ii) a person's estate being the subject of a protected trust deed (within the meaning of the Bankruptcy (Scotland) Act 1985 (c 66)); and

(b) the reference to the making of an order for winding up is to—

(i) the making of such an order under the Insolvency Act 1986 (c 45) or the Insolvency (Northern Ireland) Order 1989 (SI 1989/2405 (NI 19)), or

(ii) any corresponding proceeding under the law of a country or territory outside the United Kingdom.

(5) The effect of any nominations made by a member is suspended at any time when there are more nominated persons than the member has shares in the company.

(6) Where—

(a) the member holds different classes of shares with different information rights, and

(b) there are more nominated persons than he has shares conferring a particular right,

the effect of any nominations made by him is suspended to the extent that they confer that right.

(7) Where the company—

(a) enquires of a nominated person whether he wishes to retain information rights, and

(b) does not receive a response within the period of 28 days beginning with the date on which the company's enquiry was sent,

the nomination ceases to have effect at the end of that period.

Such an enquiry is not to be made of a person more than once in any twelve-month period.

(8) The termination or suspension of a nomination means that the company is not required to act on it.

It does not prevent the company from continuing to do so, to such extent or for such period as it thinks fit.

[1542]

NOTES

Commencement: to be appointed (see the introductory note to this Act).

149 Information as to possible rights in relation to voting

(1) This section applies where a company sends a copy of a notice of a meeting to a person nominated under section 146 (nomination of person to enjoy information rights)

(2) The copy of the notice must be accompanied by a statement that—

(a) he may have a right under an agreement between him and the member by whom he was nominated to be appointed, or to have someone else appointed, as a proxy for the meeting, and

(b) if he has no such right or does not wish to exercise it, he may have a right under such an agreement to give instructions to the member as to the exercise of voting rights.

(3) Section 325 (notice of meeting to contain statement of member's rights in relation to appointment of proxy) does not apply to the copy, and the company must either—

(a) omit the notice required by that section, or

(b) include it but state that it does not apply to the nominated person.

[1543]

NOTES

Commencement: to be appointed (see the introductory note to this Act).

150 Information rights: status of rights

(1) This section has effect as regards the rights conferred by a nomination under section 146 (nomination of person to enjoy information rights).

(2) Enjoyment by the nominated person of the rights conferred by the nomination is enforceable against the company by the member as if they were rights conferred by the company's articles.

(3) Any enactment, and any provision of the company's articles, having effect in relation to communications with members has a corresponding effect (subject to any necessary adaptations) in relation to communications with the nominated person.

(4) In particular—

(a) where under any enactment, or any provision of the company's articles, the members of a company entitled to receive a document or information are determined as at a date or time before it is sent or supplied, the company need not send or supply it to a nominated person—

(i) whose nomination was received by the company after that date or time, or

(ii) if that date or time falls in a period of suspension of his nomination; and

(b) where under any enactment, or any provision of the company's articles, the right of a member to receive a document or information depends on the company having a current address for him, the same applies to any person nominated by him.

(5) The rights conferred by the nomination—

(a) are in addition to the rights of the member himself, and

(b) do not affect any rights exercisable by virtue of any such provision as is mentioned in section 145 (provisions of company's articles as to enjoyment or exercise of members' rights).

(6) A failure to give effect to the rights conferred by the nomination does not affect the validity of anything done by or on behalf of the company.

(7) References in this section to the rights conferred by the nomination are to—

(a) the rights referred to in section 146(3) (information rights), and

(b) where applicable, the rights conferred by section 147(3) (right to hard copy communications) and section 149 (information as to possible voting rights).

[1544]

NOTES

Commencement: to be appointed (see the introductory note to this Act).

151 Information rights: power to amend

(1) The Secretary of State may by regulations amend the provisions of sections 146 to 150 (information rights) so as to—

(a) extend or restrict the classes of companies to which section 146 applies,

(b) make other provision as to the circumstances in which a nomination may be made under that section, or

(c) extend or restrict the rights conferred by such a nomination.

(2) The regulations may make such consequential modifications of any other provisions of this Part, or of any other enactment, as appear to the Secretary of State to be necessary.

(3) Regulations under this section are subject to affirmative resolution procedure.

[1545]

NOTES

Commencement: to be appointed (see the introductory note to this Act).

Exercise of rights where shares held on behalf of others

152 Exercise of rights where shares held on behalf of others: exercise in different ways

(1) Where a member holds shares in a company on behalf of more than one person—

(a) rights attached to the shares, and

(b) rights under any enactment exercisable by virtue of holding the shares,

need not all be exercised, and if exercised, need not all be exercised in the same way.

(2) A member who exercises such rights but does not exercise all his rights, must inform the company to what extent he is exercising the rights.

(3) A member who exercises such rights in different ways must inform the company of the ways in which he is exercising them and to what extent they are exercised in each way.

(4) If a member exercises such rights without informing the company—

(a) that he is not exercising all his rights, or

(b) that he is exercising his rights in different ways,

the company is entitled to assume that he is exercising all his rights and is exercising them in the same way.

[1546]

NOTES

Commencement: to be appointed (see the introductory note to this Act).

153 Exercise of rights where shares held on behalf of others: members' requests

(1) This section applies for the purposes of—

(a) section 314 (power to require circulation of statement),

(b) section 338 (public companies: power to require circulation of resolution for AGM),

(c) section 342 (power to require independent report on poll), and

(d) section 527 (power to require website publication of audit concerns).

(2) A company is required to act under any of those sections if it receives a request in relation to which the following conditions are met—

(a) it is made by at least 100 persons;

(b) it is authenticated by all the persons making it;

(c) in the case of any of those persons who is not a member of the company, it is accompanied by a statement—

(i) of the full name and address of a person ("the member") who is a member of the company and holds shares on behalf of that person,

(ii) that the member is holding those shares on behalf of that person in the course of a business,
(iii) of the number of shares in the company that the member holds on behalf of that person,
(iv) of the total amount paid up on those shares,
(v) that those shares are not held on behalf of anyone else or, if they are, that the other person or persons are not among the other persons making the request,
(vi) that some or all of those shares confer voting rights that are relevant for the purposes of making a request under the section in question, and
(vii) that the person has the right to instruct the member how to exercise those rights;

(d) in the case of any of those persons who is a member of the company, it is accompanied by a statement—
(i) that he holds shares otherwise than on behalf of another person, or
(ii) that he holds shares on behalf of one or more other persons but those persons are not among the other persons making the request;

(e) it is accompanied by such evidence as the company may reasonably require of the matters mentioned in paragraph (c) and (d);

(f) the total amount of the sums paid up on—
(i) shares held as mentioned in paragraph (c), and
(ii) shares held as mentioned in paragraph (d),

divided by the number of persons making the request, is not less than £100;

(g) the request complies with any other requirements of the section in question as to contents, timing and otherwise.

[1547]

NOTES

Commencement: to be appointed (see the introductory note to this Act).

PART 10
A COMPANY'S DIRECTORS

CHAPTER 1
APPOINTMENT AND REMOVAL OF DIRECTORS

Requirement to have directors

154 Companies required to have directors

(1) A private company must have at least one director.

(2) A public company must have at least two directors.

[1548]

NOTES

Commencement: to be appointed (see the introductory note to this Act).

155 Companies required to have at least one director who is a natural person

(1) A company must have at least one director who is a natural person.

(2) This requirement is met if the office of director is held by a natural person as a corporation sole or otherwise by virtue of an office.

[1549]

NOTES

Commencement: to be appointed (see the introductory note to this Act).

156 Direction requiring company to make appointment

(1) If it appears to the Secretary of State that a company is in breach of—
section 154 (requirements as to number of directors), or

section 155 (requirement to have at least one director who is a natural person), the Secretary of State may give the company a direction under this section.

(2) The direction must specify—

(a) the statutory requirement the company appears to be in breach of,
(b) what the company must do in order to comply with the direction, and
(c) the period within which it must do so.

That period must be not less than one month or more than three months after the date on which the direction is given.

(3) The direction must also inform the company of the consequences of failing to comply.

(4) Where the company is in breach of section 154 or 155 it must comply with the direction by—

(a) making the necessary appointment or appointments, and
(b) giving notice of them under section 167,

before the end of the period specified in the direction.

(5) If the company has already made the necessary appointment or appointments (or so far as it has done so), it must comply with the direction by giving notice of them under section 167 before the end of the period specified in the direction.

(6) If a company fails to comply with a direction under this section, an offence is committed by—

(a) the company, and
(b) every officer of the company who is in default.

For this purpose a shadow director is treated as an officer of the company.

(7) A person guilty of an offence under this section is liable on summary conviction to a fine not exceeding level 5 on the standard scale and, for continued contravention, a daily default fine not exceeding one-tenth of level 5 on the standard scale.

[1550]

NOTES

Commencement: to be appointed (see the introductory note to this Act).

Appointment

157 Minimum age for appointment as director

(1) A person may not be appointed a director of a company unless he has attained the age of 16 years.

(2) This does not affect the validity of an appointment that is not to take effect until the person appointed attains that age.

(3) Where the office of director of a company is held by a corporation sole, or otherwise by virtue of another office, the appointment to that other office of a person who has not attained the age of 16 years is not effective also to make him a director of the company until he attains the age of 16 years.

(4) An appointment made in contravention of this section is void.

(5) Nothing in this section affects any liability of a person under any provision of the Companies Acts if he—

(a) purports to act as director, or
(b) acts as a shadow director,

although he could not, by virtue of this section, be validly appointed as a director.

(6) This section has effect subject to section 158 (power to provide for exceptions from minimum age requirement).

[1551]

NOTES

Commencement: to be appointed (see the introductory note to this Act).

158 Power to provide for exceptions from minimum age requirement

(1) The Secretary of State may make provision by regulations for cases in which a person who has not attained the age of 16 years may be appointed a director of a company.

(2) The regulations must specify the circumstances in which, and any conditions subject to which, the appointment may be made.

(3) If the specified circumstances cease to obtain, or any specified conditions cease to be met, a person who was appointed by virtue of the regulations and who has not since attained the age of 16 years ceases to hold office.

(4) The regulations may make different provision for different parts of the United Kingdom.

This is without prejudice to the general power to make different provision for different cases.

(5) Regulations under this section are subject to negative resolution procedure.

[1552]

NOTES

Commencement: to be appointed (see the introductory note to this Act).

159 Existing under-age directors

(1) This section applies where—

(a) a person appointed a director of a company before section 157 (minimum age for appointment as director) comes into force has not attained the age of 16 when that section comes into force, or

(b) the office of director of a company is held by a corporation sole, or otherwise by virtue of another office, and the person appointed to that other office has not attained the age of 16 years when that section comes into force,

and the case is not one excepted from that section by regulations under section 158.

(2) That person ceases to be a director on section 157 coming into force.

(3) The company must make the necessary consequential alteration in its register of directors but need not give notice to the registrar of the change.

(4) If it appears to the registrar (from other information) that a person has ceased by virtue of this section to be a director of a company, the registrar shall note that fact on the register.

[1553]

NOTES

Commencement: to be appointed (see the introductory note to this Act).

160 (*Outside the scope of this work.*)

161 Validity of acts of directors

(1) The acts of a person acting as a director are valid notwithstanding that it is afterwards discovered—

(a) that there was a defect in his appointment;

(b) that he was disqualified from holding office;

(c) that he had ceased to hold office;

(d) that he was not entitled to vote on the matter in question.

(2) This applies even if the resolution for his appointment is void under section 160 (appointment of directors of public company to be voted on individually).

[1554]

NOTES

Commencement: to be appointed (see the introductory note to this Act).

Register of directors, etc

162 Register of directors

(1) Every company must keep a register of its directors.

(2) The register must contain the required particulars (see sections 163, 164 and 166) of each person who is a director of the company.

(3) The register must be kept available for inspection—

(a) at the company's registered office, or

(b) at a place specified in regulations under section 1136.

(4) The company must give notice to the registrar—

(a) of the place at which the register is kept available for inspection, and

(b) of any change in that place,

unless it has at all times been kept at the company's registered office.

(5) The register must be open to the inspection—

(a) of any member of the company without charge, and

(b) of any other person on payment of such fee as may be prescribed.

(6) If default is made in complying with subsection (1), (2) or (3) or if default is made for 14 days in complying with subsection (4), or if an inspection required under subsection (5) is refused, an offence is committed by—

(a) the company, and

(b) every officer of the company who is in default.

For this purpose a shadow director is treated as an officer of the company.

(7) A person guilty of an offence under this section is liable on summary conviction to a fine not exceeding level 5 on the standard scale and, for continued contravention, a daily default fine not exceeding one-tenth of level 5 on the standard scale.

(8) In the case of a refusal of inspection of the register, the court may by order compel an immediate inspection of it.

[1555]

NOTES

Commencement: to be appointed (see the introductory note to this Act).

163 Particulars of directors to be registered: individuals

(1) A company's register of directors must contain the following particulars in the case of an individual—

(a) name and any former name;

(b) a service address;

(c) the country or state (or part of the United Kingdom) in which he is usually resident;

(d) nationality;

(e) business occupation (if any);

(f) date of birth.

(2) For the purposes of this section "name" means a person's Christian name (or other forename) and surname, except that in the case of—

(a) a peer, or

(b) an individual usually known by a title,

the title may be stated instead of his Christian name (or other forename) and surname or in addition to either or both of them.

(3) For the purposes of this section a "former name" means a name by which the individual was formerly known for business purposes.

Where a person is or was formerly known by more than one such name, each of them must be stated.

(4) It is not necessary for the register to contain particulars of a former name in the following cases—

(a) in the case of a peer or an individual normally known by a British title, where the name is one by which the person was known previous to the adoption of or succession to the title;

(b) in the case of any person, where the former name—

(i) was changed or disused before the person attained the age of 16 years, or

(ii) has been changed or disused for 20 years or more.

(5) A person's service address may be stated to be "The company's registered office". **[1556]**

NOTES

Commencement: to be appointed (see the introductory note to this Act).

164 Particulars of directors to be registered: corporate directors and firms

A company's register of directors must contain the following particulars in the case of a body corporate, or a firm that is a legal person under the law by which it is governed—

(a) corporate or firm name;

(b) registered or principal office;

(c) in the case of an EEA company to which the First Company Law Directive (68/151/EEC) applies, particulars of—

(i) the register in which the company file mentioned in Article 3 of that Directive is kept (including details of the relevant state), and

(ii) the registration number in that register;

(d) in any other case, particulars of—

(i) the legal form of the company or firm and the law by which it is governed, and

(ii) if applicable, the register in which it is entered (including details of the state) and its registration number in that register.

[1557]

NOTES

Commencement: to be appointed (see the introductory note to this Act).

165 Register of directors' residential addresses

(1) Every company must keep a register of directors' residential addresses.

(2) The register must state the usual residential address of each of the company's directors.

(3) If a director's usual residential address is the same as his service address (as stated in the company's register of directors), the register of directors' residential addresses need only contain an entry to that effect.

This does not apply if his service address is stated to be "The company's registered office".

(4) If default is made in complying with this section, an offence is committed by—

(a) the company, and

(b) every officer of the company who is in default.

For this purpose a shadow director is treated as an officer of the company.

(5) A person guilty of an offence under this section is liable on summary conviction to a fine not exceeding level 5 on the standard scale and, for continued contravention, a daily default fine not exceeding one-tenth of level 5 on the standard scale.

(6) This section applies only to directors who are individuals, not where the director is a body corporate or a firm that is a legal person under the law by which it is governed.

[1558]

NOTES

Commencement: to be appointed (see the introductory note to this Act).

166 Particulars of directors to be registered: power to make regulations

(1) The Secretary of State may make provision by regulations amending—
section 163 (particulars of directors to be registered: individuals),

section 164 (particulars of directors to be registered: corporate directors and firms), or
section 165 (register of directors' residential addresses),

so as to add to or remove items from the particulars required to be contained in a company's register of directors or register of directors' residential addresses.

(2) Regulations under this section are subject to affirmative resolution procedure.

[1559]

NOTES

Commencement: to be appointed (see the introductory note to this Act).

167 Duty to notify registrar of changes

(1) A company must, within the period of 14 days from—
- (a) a person becoming or ceasing to be a director, or
- (b) the occurrence of any change in the particulars contained in its register of directors or its register of directors' residential addresses,

give notice to the registrar of the change and of the date on which it occurred.

(2) Notice of a person having become a director of the company must—
- (a) contain a statement of the particulars of the new director that are required to be included in the company's register of directors and its register of directors' residential addresses, and
- (b) be accompanied by a consent, by that person, to act in that capacity.

(3) Where—
- (a) a company gives notice of a change of a director's service address as stated in the company's register of directors, and
- (b) the notice is not accompanied by notice of any resulting change in the particulars contained in the company's register of directors' residential addresses,

the notice must be accompanied by a statement that no such change is required.

(4) If default is made in complying with this section, an offence is committed by—
- (a) the company, and
- (b) every officer of the company who is in default.

For this purpose a shadow director is treated as an officer of the company.

(5) A person guilty of an offence under this section is liable on summary conviction to a fine not exceeding level 5 on the standard scale and, for continued contravention, a daily default fine not exceeding one-tenth of level 5 on the standard scale.

[1560]

NOTES

Commencement: to be appointed (see the introductory note to this Act).

Removal

168 Resolution to remove director

(1) A company may by ordinary resolution at a meeting remove a director before the expiration of his period of office, notwithstanding anything in any agreement between it and him.

(2) Special notice is required of a resolution to remove a director under this section or to appoint somebody instead of a director so removed at the meeting at which he is removed.

(3) A vacancy created by the removal of a director under this section, if not filled at the meeting at which he is removed, may be filled as a casual vacancy.

(4) A person appointed director in place of a person removed under this section is treated, for the purpose of determining the time at which he or any other director is to retire, as if he had become director on the day on which the person in whose place he is appointed was last appointed a director.

(5) This section is not to be taken—
- (a) as depriving a person removed under it of compensation or damages payable to

him in respect of the termination of his appointment as director or of any appointment terminating with that as director, or

(b) as derogating from any power to remove a director that may exist apart from this section.

[1561]

NOTES

Commencement: to be appointed (see the introductory note to this Act).

169 Director's right to protest against removal

(1) On receipt of notice of an intended resolution to remove a director under section 168, the company must forthwith send a copy of the notice to the director concerned.

(2) The director (whether or not a member of the company) is entitled to be heard on the resolution at the meeting.

(3) Where notice is given of an intended resolution to remove a director under that section, and the director concerned makes with respect to it representations in writing to the company (not exceeding a reasonable length) and requests their notification to members of the company, the company shall, unless the representations are received by it too late for it to do so—

(a) in any notice of the resolution given to members of the company state the fact of the representations having been made; and

(b) send a copy of the representations to every member of the company to whom notice of the meeting is sent (whether before or after receipt of the representations by the company).

(4) If a copy of the representations is not sent as required by subsection (3) because received too late or because of the company's default, the director may (without prejudice to his right to be heard orally) require that the representations shall be read out at the meeting.

(5) Copies of the representations need not be sent out and the representations need not be read out at the meeting if, on the application either of the company or of any other person who claims to be aggrieved, the court is satisfied that the rights conferred by this section are being abused.

(6) The court may order the company's costs (in Scotland, expenses) on an application under subsection (5) to be paid in whole or in part by the director, notwithstanding that he is not a party to the application.

[1562]

NOTES

Commencement: to be appointed (see the introductory note to this Act).

CHAPTER 2
GENERAL DUTIES OF DIRECTORS

Introductory

170 Scope and nature of general duties

(1) The general duties specified in sections 171 to 177 are owed by a director of a company to the company.

(2) A person who ceases to be a director continues to be subject—

(a) to the duty in section 175 (duty to avoid conflicts of interest) as regards the exploitation of any property, information or opportunity of which he became aware at a time when he was a director, and

(b) to the duty in section 176 (duty not to accept benefits from third parties) as regards things done or omitted by him before he ceased to be a director.

To that extent those duties apply to a former director as to a director, subject to any necessary adaptations.

(3) The general duties are based on certain common law rules and equitable principles as they apply in relation to directors and have effect in place of those rules and principles as regards the duties owed to a company by a director.

(4) The general duties shall be interpreted and applied in the same way as common law rules or equitable principles, and regard shall be had to the corresponding common law rules and equitable principles in interpreting and applying the general duties.

(5) The general duties apply to shadow directors where, and to the extent that, the corresponding common law rules or equitable principles so apply.

[1563]

NOTES

Commencement: to be appointed (see the introductory note to this Act).

The general duties

171 Duty to act within powers

A director of a company must—

(a) act in accordance with the company's constitution, and

(b) only exercise powers for the purposes for which they are conferred.

[1564]

NOTES

Commencement: to be appointed (see the introductory note to this Act).

172 Duty to promote the success of the company

(1) A director of a company must act in the way he considers, in good faith, would be most likely to promote the success of the company for the benefit of its members as a whole, and in doing so have regard (amongst other matters) to—

(a) the likely consequences of any decision in the long term,

(b) the interests of the company's employees,

(c) the need to foster the company's business relationships with suppliers, customers and others,

(d) the impact of the company's operations on the community and the environment,

(e) the desirability of the company maintaining a reputation for high standards of business conduct, and

(f) the need to act fairly as between members of the company.

(2) Where or to the extent that the purposes of the company consist of or include purposes other than the benefit of its members, subsection (1) has effect as if the reference to promoting the success of the company for the benefit of its members were to achieving those purposes.

(3) The duty imposed by this section has effect subject to any enactment or rule of law requiring directors, in certain circumstances, to consider or act in the interests of creditors of the company.

[1565]

NOTES

Commencement: to be appointed (see the introductory note to this Act).

173 Duty to exercise independent judgment

(1) A director of a company must exercise independent judgment.

(2) This duty is not infringed by his acting—

(a) in accordance with an agreement duly entered into by the company that restricts the future exercise of discretion by its directors, or

(b) in a way authorised by the company's constitution.

[1566]

NOTES

Commencement: to be appointed (see the introductory note to this Act).

174 Duty to exercise reasonable care, skill and diligence

(1) A director of a company must exercise reasonable care, skill and diligence.

(2) This means the care, skill and diligence that would be exercised by a reasonably diligent person with—

(a) the general knowledge, skill and experience that may reasonably be expected of a person carrying out the functions carried out by the director in relation to the company, and

(b) the general knowledge, skill and experience that the director has.

[1567]

NOTES

Commencement: to be appointed (see the introductory note to this Act).

175 Duty to avoid conflicts of interest

(1) A director of a company must avoid a situation in which he has, or can have, a direct or indirect interest that conflicts, or possibly may conflict, with the interests of the company.

(2) This applies in particular to the exploitation of any property, information or opportunity (and it is immaterial whether the company could take advantage of the property, information or opportunity).

(3) This duty does not apply to a conflict of interest arising in relation to a transaction or arrangement with the company.

(4) This duty is not infringed—

(a) if the situation cannot reasonably be regarded as likely to give rise to a conflict of interest; or

(b) if the matter has been authorised by the directors.

(5) Authorisation may be given by the directors—

(a) where the company is a private company and nothing in the company's constitution invalidates such authorisation, by the matter being proposed to and authorised by the directors; or

(b) where the company is a public company and its constitution includes provision enabling the directors to authorise the matter, by the matter being proposed to and authorised by them in accordance with the constitution.

(6) The authorisation is effective only if—

(a) any requirement as to the quorum at the meeting at which the matter is considered is met without counting the director in question or any other interested director, and

(b) the matter was agreed to without their voting or would have been agreed to if their votes had not been counted.

(7) Any reference in this section to a conflict of interest includes a conflict of interest and duty and a conflict of duties.

[1568]

NOTES

Commencement: to be appointed (see the introductory note to this Act).

176 Duty not to accept benefits from third parties

(1) A director of a company must not accept a benefit from a third party conferred by reason of—

(a) his being a director, or

(b) his doing (or not doing) anything as director.

(2) A "third party" means a person other than the company, an associated body corporate or a person acting on behalf of the company or an associated body corporate.

(3) Benefits received by a director from a person by whom his services (as a director or otherwise) are provided to the company are not regarded as conferred by a third party.

(4) This duty is not infringed if the acceptance of the benefit cannot reasonably be regarded as likely to give rise to a conflict of interest.

(5) Any reference in this section to a conflict of interest includes a conflict of interest and duty and a conflict of duties.

[1569]

NOTES

Commencement: to be appointed (see the introductory note to this Act).

177 Duty to declare interest in proposed transaction or arrangement

(1) If a director of a company is in any way, directly or indirectly, interested in a proposed transaction or arrangement with the company, he must declare the nature and extent of that interest to the other directors.

(2) The declaration may (but need not) be made—
- (a) at a meeting of the directors, or
- (b) by notice to the directors in accordance with—
  - (i) section 184 (notice in writing), or
  - (ii) section 185 (general notice).

(3) If a declaration of interest under this section proves to be, or becomes, inaccurate or incomplete, a further declaration must be made.

(4) Any declaration required by this section must be made before the company enters into the transaction or arrangement.

(5) This section does not require a declaration of an interest of which the director is not aware or where the director is not aware of the transaction or arrangement in question.

For this purpose a director is treated as being aware of matters of which he ought reasonably to be aware.

(6) A director need not declare an interest—
- (a) if it cannot reasonably be regarded as likely to give rise to a conflict of interest;
- (b) if, or to the extent that, the other directors are already aware of it (and for this purpose the other directors are treated as aware of anything of which they ought reasonably to be aware); or
- (c) if, or to the extent that, it concerns terms of his service contract that have been or are to be considered—
  - (i) by a meeting of the directors, or
  - (ii) by a committee of the directors appointed for the purpose under the company's constitution.

[1570]

NOTES

Commencement: to be appointed (see the introductory note to this Act).

Supplementary provisions

178 Civil consequences of breach of general duties

(1) The consequences of breach (or threatened breach) of sections 171 to 177 are the same as would apply if the corresponding common law rule or equitable principle applied.

(2) The duties in those sections (with the exception of section 174 (duty to exercise reasonable care, skill and diligence)) are, accordingly, enforceable in the same way as any other fiduciary duty owed to a company by its directors.

[1571]

NOTES

Commencement: to be appointed (see the introductory note to this Act).

179 Cases within more than one of the general duties

Except as otherwise provided, more than one of the general duties may apply in any given case.

[1572]

NOTES

Commencement: to be appointed (see the introductory note to this Act).

180 Consent, approval or authorisation by members

(1) In a case where—

(a) section 175 (duty to avoid conflicts of interest) is complied with by authorisation by the directors, or

(b) section 177 (duty to declare interest in proposed transaction or arrangement) is complied with,

the transaction or arrangement is not liable to be set aside by virtue of any common law rule or equitable principle requiring the consent or approval of the members of the company.

This is without prejudice to any enactment, or provision of the company's constitution, requiring such consent or approval.

(2) The application of the general duties is not affected by the fact that the case also falls within Chapter 4 (transactions requiring approval of members), except that where that Chapter applies and— (a) approval is given under that Chapter, or (b) the matter is one as to which it is provided that approval is not needed, it is not necessary also to comply with section 175 (duty to avoid conflicts of interest) or section 176 (duty not to accept benefits from third parties).

(3) Compliance with the general duties does not remove the need for approval under any applicable provision of Chapter 4 (transactions requiring approval of members).

(4) The general duties—

(a) have effect subject to any rule of law enabling the company to give authority, specifically or generally, for anything to be done (or omitted) by the directors, or any of them, that would otherwise be a breach of duty, and

(b) where the company's articles contain provisions for dealing with conflicts of interest, are not infringed by anything done (or omitted) by the directors, or any of them, in accordance with those provisions.

(5) Otherwise, the general duties have effect (except as otherwise provided or the context otherwise requires) notwithstanding any enactment or rule of law.

[1573]

NOTES

Commencement: to be appointed (see the introductory note to this Act).

181 Modification of provisions in relation to charitable companies

(1) In their application to a company that is a charity, the provisions of this Chapter have effect subject to this section.

(2) Section 175 (duty to avoid conflicts of interest) has effect as if—

(a) for subsection (3) (which disapplies the duty to avoid conflicts of interest in the case of a transaction or arrangement with the company) there were substituted—

"(3) This duty does not apply to a conflict of interest arising in relation to a transaction or arrangement with the company if or to the extent that the company's articles allow that duty to be so disapplied, which they may do only in relation to descriptions of transaction or arrangement specified in the company's articles.";

(b) for subsection (5) (which specifies how directors of a company may give authority under that section for a transaction or arrangement) there were substituted—

"(5) Authorisation may be given by the directors where the company's constitution includes provision enabling them to authorise the matter, by the matter being proposed to and authorised by them in accordance with the constitution.".

(3) Section 180(2)(b) (which disapplies certain duties under this Chapter in relation to cases excepted from requirement to obtain approval by members under Chapter 4) applies only if or to the extent that the company's articles allow those duties to be so disapplied, which they may do only in relation to descriptions of transaction or arrangement specified in the company's articles.

(4) After section 26(5) of the Charities Act 1993 (c 10) (power of Charity Commission to authorise dealings with charity property etc) insert—

> "(5A) In the case of a charity that is a company, an order under this section may authorise an act notwithstanding that it involves the breach of a duty imposed on a director of the company under Chapter 2 of Part 10 of the Companies Act 2006 (general duties of directors).".

(5) This section does not extend to Scotland.

[1574]

NOTES

Commencement: to be appointed (see the introductory note to this Act).

CHAPTER 3
DECLARATION OF INTEREST IN EXISTING TRANSACTION OR ARRANGEMENT

182 Declaration of interest in existing transaction or arrangement

(1) Where a director of a company is in any way, directly or indirectly, interested in a transaction or arrangement that has been entered into by the company, he must declare the nature and extent of the interest to the other directors in accordance with this section.

This section does not apply if or to the extent that the interest has been declared under section 177 (duty to declare interest in proposed transaction or arrangement).

(2) The declaration must be made—

- (a) at a meeting of the directors, or
- (b) by notice in writing (see section 184), or
- (c) by general notice (see section 185).

(3) If a declaration of interest under this section proves to be, or becomes, inaccurate or incomplete, a further declaration must be made.

(4) Any declaration required by this section must be made as soon as is reasonably practicable.

Failure to comply with this requirement does not affect the underlying duty to make the declaration.

(5) This section does not require a declaration of an interest of which the director is not aware or where the director is not aware of the transaction or arrangement in question.

For this purpose a director is treated as being aware of matters of which he ought reasonably to be aware.

(6) A director need not declare an interest under this section—

- (a) if it cannot reasonably be regarded as likely to give rise to a conflict of interest;
- (b) if, or to the extent that, the other directors are already aware of it (and for this purpose the other directors are treated as aware of anything of which they ought reasonably to be aware); or
- (c) if, or to the extent that, it concerns terms of his service contract that have been or are to be considered—
  - (i) by a meeting of the directors, or
  - (ii) by a committee of the directors appointed for the purpose under the company's constitution.

[1575]

NOTES

Commencement: to be appointed (see the introductory note to this Act).

183 Offence of failure to declare interest

(1) A director who fails to comply with the requirements of section 182 (declaration of interest in existing transaction or arrangement) commits an offence.

(2) A person guilty of an offence under this section is liable—

(a) on conviction on indictment, to a fine;
(b) on summary conviction, to a fine not exceeding the statutory maximum.

[1576]

NOTES

Commencement: to be appointed (see the introductory note to this Act).

184 Declaration made by notice in writing

(1) This section applies to a declaration of interest made by notice in writing.

(2) The director must send the notice to the other directors.

(3) The notice may be sent in hard copy form or, if the recipient has agreed to receive it in electronic form, in an agreed electronic form.

(4) The notice may be sent—
(a) by hand or by post, or
(b) if the recipient has agreed to receive it by electronic means, by agreed electronic means.

(5) Where a director declares an interest by notice in writing in accordance with this section—
(a) the making of the declaration is deemed to form part of the proceedings at the next meeting of the directors after the notice is given, and
(b) the provisions of section 248 (minutes of meetings of directors) apply as if the declaration had been made at that meeting.

[1577]

NOTES

Commencement: to be appointed (see the introductory note to this Act).

185 General notice treated as sufficient declaration

(1) General notice in accordance with this section is a sufficient declaration of interest in relation to the matters to which it relates.

(2) General notice is notice given to the directors of a company to the effect that the director—
(a) has an interest (as member, officer, employee or otherwise) in a specified body corporate or firm and is to be regarded as interested in any transaction or arrangement that may, after the date of the notice, be made with that body corporate or firm, or
(b) is connected with a specified person (other than a body corporate or firm) and is to be regarded as interested in any transaction or arrangement that may, after the date of the notice, be made with that person.

(3) The notice must state the nature and extent of the director's interest in the body corporate or firm or, as the case may be, the nature of his connection with the person.

(4) General notice is not effective unless—
(a) it is given at a meeting of the directors, or
(b) the director takes reasonable steps to secure that it is brought up and read at the next meeting of the directors after it is given.

[1578]

NOTES

Commencement: to be appointed (see the introductory note to this Act).

186 Declaration of interest in case of company with sole director

(1) Where a declaration of interest under section 182 (duty to declare interest in existing transaction or arrangement) is required of a sole director of a company that is required to have more than one director—
(a) the declaration must be recorded in writing,
(b) the making of the declaration is deemed to form part of the proceedings at the next meeting of the directors after the notice is given, and

(c) the provisions of section 248 (minutes of meetings of directors) apply as if the declaration had been made at that meeting.

(2) Nothing in this section affects the operation of section 231 (contract with sole member who is also a director: terms to be set out in writing or recorded in minutes).

[1579]

NOTES

Commencement: to be appointed (see the introductory note to this Act).

187 Declaration of interest in existing transaction by shadow director

(1) The provisions of this Chapter relating to the duty under section 182 (duty to declare interest in existing transaction or arrangement) apply to a shadow director as to a director, but with the following adaptations.

(2) Subsection (2)(a) of that section (declaration at meeting of directors) does not apply.

(3) In section 185 (general notice treated as sufficient declaration), subsection (4) (notice to be given at or brought up and read at meeting of directors) does not apply.

(4) General notice by a shadow director is not effective unless given by notice in writing in accordance with section 184.

[1580]

NOTES

Commencement: to be appointed (see the introductory note to this Act).

CHAPTER 4
TRANSACTIONS WITH DIRECTORS REQUIRING APPROVAL OF MEMBERS

Service contracts

188 Directors' long-term service contracts: requirement of members' approval

(1) This section applies to provision under which the guaranteed term of a director's employment—

(a) with the company of which he is a director, or

(b) where he is the director of a holding company, within the group consisting of that company and its subsidiaries,

is, or may be, longer than two years.

(2) A company may not agree to such provision unless it has been approved—

(a) by resolution of the members of the company, and

(b) in the case of a director of a holding company, by resolution of the members of that company.

(3) The guaranteed term of a director's employment is—

(a) the period (if any) during which the director's employment—

(i) is to continue, or may be continued otherwise than at the instance of the company (whether under the original agreement or under a new agreement entered into in pursuance of it), and

(ii) cannot be terminated by the company by notice, or can be so terminated only in specified circumstances, or

(b) in the case of employment terminable by the company by notice, the period of notice required to be given,

or, in the case of employment having a period within paragraph (a) and a period within paragraph (b), the aggregate of those periods.

(4) If more than six months before the end of the guaranteed term of a director's employment the company enters into a further service contract (otherwise than in pursuance of a right conferred, by or under the original contract, on the other party to it), this section applies as if there were added to the guaranteed term of the new contract the unexpired period of the guaranteed term of the original contract.

(5) A resolution approving provision to which this section applies must not be passed unless a memorandum setting out the proposed contract incorporating the provision is made available to members—

(a) in the case of a written resolution, by being sent or submitted to every eligible member at or before the time at which the proposed resolution is sent or submitted to him;

(b) in the case of a resolution at a meeting, by being made available for inspection by members of the company both—

(i) at the company's registered office for not less than 15 days ending with the date of the meeting, and

(ii) at the meeting itself.

(6) No approval is required under this section on the part of the members of a body corporate that—

(a) is not a UK-registered company, or

(b) is a wholly-owned subsidiary of another body corporate.

(7) In this section "employment" means any employment under a director's service contract.

[1581]

NOTES

Commencement: to be appointed (see the introductory note to this Act).

189 Directors' long-term service contracts: civil consequences of contravention

If a company agrees to provision in contravention of section 188 (directors' long-term service contracts: requirement of members' approval)—

(a) the provision is void, to the extent of the contravention, and

(b) the contract is deemed to contain a term entitling the company to terminate it at any time by the giving of reasonable notice.

[1582]

NOTES

Commencement: to be appointed (see the introductory note to this Act).

Substantial property transactions

190 Substantial property transactions: requirement of members' approval

(1) A company may not enter into an arrangement under which—

(a) a director of the company or of its holding company, or a person connected with such a director, acquires or is to acquire from the company (directly or indirectly) a substantial non-cash asset, or

(b) the company acquires or is to acquire a substantial non-cash asset (directly or indirectly) from such a director or a person so connected,

unless the arrangement has been approved by a resolution of the members of the company or is conditional on such approval being obtained.

For the meaning of "substantial non-cash asset" see section 191.

(2) If the director or connected person is a director of the company's holding company or a person connected with such a director, the arrangement must also have been approved by a resolution of the members of the holding company or be conditional on such approval being obtained.

(3) A company shall not be subject to any liability by reason of a failure to obtain approval required by this section.

(4) No approval is required under this section on the part of the members of a body corporate that—

(a) is not a UK-registered company, or

(b) is a wholly-owned subsidiary of another body corporate.

(5) For the purposes of this section—

(a) an arrangement involving more than one non-cash asset, or

(b) an arrangement that is one of a series involving non-cash assets,

shall be treated as if they involved a non-cash asset of a value equal to the aggregate value of all the non-cash assets involved in the arrangement or, as the case may be, the series.

(6) This section does not apply to a transaction so far as it relates—

(a) to anything to which a director of a company is entitled under his service contract, or

(b) to payment for loss of office as defined in section 215 (payments requiring members' approval).

[1583]

NOTES

Commencement: to be appointed (see the introductory note to this Act).

191 Meaning of "substantial"

(1) This section explains what is meant in section 190 (requirement of approval for substantial property transactions) by a "substantial" non-cash asset.

(2) An asset is a substantial asset in relation to a company if its value—

(a) exceeds 10% of the company's asset value and is more than £5,000, or

(b) exceeds £100,000.

(3) For this purpose a company's "asset value" at any time is—

(a) the value of the company's net assets determined by reference to its most recent statutory accounts, or

(b) if no statutory accounts have been prepared, the amount of the company's called-up share capital.

(4) A company's "statutory accounts" means its annual accounts prepared in accordance with Part 15, and its "most recent" statutory accounts means those in relation to which the time for sending them out to members (see section 424) is most recent.

(5) Whether an asset is a substantial asset shall be determined as at the time the arrangement is entered into.

[1584]

NOTES

Commencement: to be appointed (see the introductory note to this Act).

192 Exception for transactions with members or other group companies

Approval is not required under section 190 (requirement of members' approval for substantial property transactions)—

(a) for a transaction between a company and a person in his character as a member of that company, or

(b) for a transaction between—

(i) a holding company and its wholly-owned subsidiary, or

(ii) two wholly-owned subsidiaries of the same holding company.

[1585]

NOTES

Commencement: to be appointed (see the introductory note to this Act).

193 Exception in case of company in winding up or administration

(1) This section applies to a company—

(a) that is being wound up (unless the winding up is a members' voluntary winding up), or

(b) that is in administration within the meaning of Schedule B1 to the Insolvency Act 1986 (c 45) or the Insolvency (Northern Ireland) Order 1989 (SI 1989/2405 (NI 19)).

(2) Approval is not required under section 190 (requirement of members' approval for substantial property transactions)—

(a) on the part of the members of a company to which this section applies, or
(b) for an arrangement entered into by a company to which this section applies.

[1586]

NOTES

Commencement: to be appointed (see the introductory note to this Act).

194 (*Outside the scope of this work.*)

195 Property transactions: civil consequences of contravention

(1) This section applies where a company enters into an arrangement in contravention of section 190 (requirement of members' approval for substantial property transactions).

(2) The arrangement, and any transaction entered into in pursuance of the arrangement (whether by the company or any other person), is voidable at the instance of the company, unless—

(a) restitution of any money or other asset that was the subject matter of the arrangement or transaction is no longer possible,
(b) the company has been indemnified in pursuance of this section by any other persons for the loss or damage suffered by it, or
(c) rights acquired in good faith, for value and without actual notice of the contravention by a person who is not a party to the arrangement or transaction would be affected by the avoidance.

(3) Whether or not the arrangement or any such transaction has been avoided, each of the persons specified in subsection (4) is liable—

(a) to account to the company for any gain that he has made directly or indirectly by the arrangement or transaction, and
(b) (jointly and severally with any other person so liable under this section) to indemnify the company for any loss or damage resulting from the arrangement or transaction.

(4) The persons so liable are—

(a) any director of the company or of its holding company with whom the company entered into the arrangement in contravention of section 190,
(b) any person with whom the company entered into the arrangement in contravention of that section who is connected with a director of the company or of its holding company,
(c) the director of the company or of its holding company with whom any such person is connected, and
(d) any other director of the company who authorised the arrangement or any transaction entered into in pursuance of such an arrangement.

(5) Subsections (3) and (4) are subject to the following two subsections.

(6) In the case of an arrangement entered into by a company in contravention of section 190 with a person connected with a director of the company or of its holding company, that director is not liable by virtue of subsection (4)(c) if he shows that he took all reasonable steps to secure the company's compliance with that section.

(7) In any case—

(a) a person so connected is not liable by virtue of subsection (4)(b), and
(b) a director is not liable by virtue of subsection (4)(d),

if he shows that, at the time the arrangement was entered into, he did not know the relevant circumstances constituting the contravention.

(8) Nothing in this section shall be read as excluding the operation of any other enactment or rule of law by virtue of which the arrangement or transaction may be called in question or any liability to the company may arise.

[1587]

NOTES

Commencement: to be appointed (see the introductory note to this Act).

196 Property transactions: effect of subsequent affirmation

Where a transaction or arrangement is entered into by a company in contravention of section 190 (requirement of members' approval) but, within a reasonable period, it is affirmed—

(a) in the case of a contravention of subsection (1) of that section, by resolution of the members of the company, and

(b) in the case of a contravention of subsection (2) of that section, by resolution of the members of the holding company,

the transaction or arrangement may no longer be avoided under section 195.

[1588]

NOTES

Commencement: to be appointed (see the introductory note to this Act).

Loans, quasi-loans and credit transactions

197 Loans to directors: requirement of members' approval

(1) A company may not—

(a) make a loan to a director of the company or of its holding company, or

(b) give a guarantee or provide security in connection with a loan made by any person to such a director,

unless the transaction has been approved by a resolution of the members of the company.

(2) If the director is a director of the company's holding company, the transaction must also have been approved by a resolution of the members of the holding company.

(3) A resolution approving a transaction to which this section applies must not be passed unless a memorandum setting out the matters mentioned in subsection (4) is made available to members—

(a) in the case of a written resolution, by being sent or submitted to every eligible member at or before the time at which the proposed resolution is sent or submitted to him;

(b) in the case of a resolution at a meeting, by being made available for inspection by members of the company both—

(i) at the company's registered office for not less than 15 days ending with the date of the meeting, and

(ii) at the meeting itself.

(4) The matters to be disclosed are—

(a) the nature of the transaction,

(b) the amount of the loan and the purpose for which it is required, and

(c) the extent of the company's liability under any transaction connected with the loan.

(5) No approval is required under this section on the part of the members of a body corporate that—

(a) is not a UK-registered company, or

(b) is a wholly-owned subsidiary of another body corporate.

[1589]

NOTES

Commencement: to be appointed (see the introductory note to this Act).

198 Quasi-loans to directors: requirement of members' approval

(1) This section applies to a company if it is—

(a) a public company, or

(b) a company associated with a public company.

(2) A company to which this section applies may not—

(a) make a quasi-loan to a director of the company or of its holding company, or

(b) give a guarantee or provide security in connection with a quasi-loan made by any person to such a director, unless the transaction has been approved by a resolution of the members of the company.

(3) If the director is a director of the company's holding company, the transaction must also have been approved by a resolution of the members of the holding company.

(4) A resolution approving a transaction to which this section applies must not be passed unless a memorandum setting out the matters mentioned in subsection (5) is made available to members—

(a) in the case of a written resolution, by being sent or submitted to every eligible member at or before the time at which the proposed resolution is sent or submitted to him;

(b) in the case of a resolution at a meeting, by being made available for inspection by members of the company both—

(i) at the company's registered office for not less than 15 days ending with the date of the meeting, and

(ii) at the meeting itself.

(5) The matters to be disclosed are—

(a) the nature of the transaction,

(b) the amount of the quasi-loan and the purpose for which it is required, and

(c) the extent of the company's liability under any transaction connected with the quasi-loan.

(6) No approval is required under this section on the part of the members of a body corporate that—

(a) is not a UK-registered company, or

(b) is a wholly-owned subsidiary of another body corporate.

[1590]

NOTES

Commencement: to be appointed (see the introductory note to this Act).

199 Meaning of "quasi-loan" and related expressions

(1) A "quasi-loan" is a transaction under which one party ("the creditor") agrees to pay, or pays otherwise than in pursuance of an agreement, a sum for another ("the borrower") or agrees to reimburse, or reimburses otherwise than in pursuance of an agreement, expenditure incurred by another party for another ("the borrower")—

(a) on terms that the borrower (or a person on his behalf) will reimburse the creditor; or

(b) in circumstances giving rise to a liability on the borrower to reimburse the creditor.

(2) Any reference to the person to whom a quasi-loan is made is a reference to the borrower.

(3) The liabilities of the borrower under a quasi-loan include the liabilities of any person who has agreed to reimburse the creditor on behalf of the borrower.

[1591]

NOTES

Commencement: to be appointed (see the introductory note to this Act).

200 Loans or quasi-loans to persons connected with directors: requirement of members' approval

(1) This section applies to a company if it is—

(a) a public company, or

(b) a company associated with a public company.

(2) A company to which this section applies may not—

(a) make a loan or quasi-loan to a person connected with a director of the company or of its holding company, or

(b) give a guarantee or provide security in connection with a loan or quasi-loan made by any person to a person connected with such a director,

unless the transaction has been approved by a resolution of the members of the company.

(3) If the connected person is a person connected with a director of the company's holding company, the transaction must also have been approved by a resolution of the members of the holding company.

(4) A resolution approving a transaction to which this section applies must not be passed unless a memorandum setting out the matters mentioned in subsection (5) is made available to members—

- (a) in the case of a written resolution, by being sent or submitted to every eligible member at or before the time at which the proposed resolution is sent or submitted to him;
- (b) in the case of a resolution at a meeting, by being made available for inspection by members of the company both—
  - (i) at the company's registered office for not less than 15 days ending with the date of the meeting, and
  - (ii) at the meeting itself.

(5) The matters to be disclosed are—

- (a) the nature of the transaction,
- (b) the amount of the loan or quasi-loan and the purpose for which it is required, and
- (c) the extent of the company's liability under any transaction connected with the loan or quasi-loan.

(6) No approval is required under this section on the part of the members of a body corporate that—

- (a) is not a UK-registered company, or
- (b) is a wholly-owned subsidiary of another body corporate.

[1592]

NOTES

Commencement: to be appointed (see the introductory note to this Act).

201–202 (*Outside the scope of this work.*)

203 Related arrangements: requirement of members' approval

(1) A company may not—

- (a) take part in an arrangement under which—
  - (i) another person enters into a transaction that, if it had been entered into by the company, would have required approval under section 197, 198, 200 or 201, and
  - (ii) that person, in pursuance of the arrangement, obtains a benefit from the company or a body corporate associated with it, or
- (b) arrange for the assignment to it, or assumption by it, of any rights, obligations or liabilities under a transaction that, if it had been entered into by the company, would have required such approval,

unless the arrangement in question has been approved by a resolution of the members of the company.

(2) If the director or connected person for whom the transaction is entered into is a director of its holding company or a person connected with such a director, the arrangement must also have been approved by a resolution of the members of the holding company.

(3) A resolution approving an arrangement to which this section applies must not be passed unless a memorandum setting out the matters mentioned in subsection (4) is made available to members—

- (a) in the case of a written resolution, by being sent or submitted to every eligible member at or before the time at which the proposed resolution is sent or submitted to him;
- (b) in the case of a resolution at a meeting, by being made available for inspection by members of the company both—
  - (i) at the company's registered office for not less than 15 days ending with the date of the meeting, and
  - (ii) at the meeting itself.

(4) The matters to be disclosed are—

- (a) the matters that would have to be disclosed if the company were seeking approval of the transaction to which the arrangement relates,

(b) the nature of the arrangement, and
(c) the extent of the company's liability under the arrangement or any transaction connected with it.

(5) No approval is required under this section on the part of the members of a body corporate that—
(a) is not a UK-registered company, or
(b) is a wholly-owned subsidiary of another body corporate.

(6) In determining for the purposes of this section whether a transaction is one that would have required approval under section 197, 198, 200 or 201 if it had been entered into by the company, the transaction shall be treated as having been entered into on the date of the arrangement.

[1593]

NOTES

Commencement: to be appointed (see the introductory note to this Act).

---

204 Exception for expenditure on company business

(1) Approval is not required under section 197, 198, 200 or 201 (requirement of members' approval for loans etc) for anything done by a company—
(a) to provide a director of the company or of its holding company, or a person connected with any such director, with funds to meet expenditure incurred or to be incurred by him—
(i) for the purposes of the company, or
(ii) for the purpose of enabling him properly to perform his duties as an officer of the company, or
(b) to enable any such person to avoid incurring such expenditure.

(2) This section does not authorise a company to enter into a transaction if the aggregate of—
(a) the value of the transaction in question, and
(b) the value of any other relevant transactions or arrangements,

exceeds £50,000.

[1594]

NOTES

Commencement: to be appointed (see the introductory note to this Act).

---

205 Exception for expenditure on defending proceedings etc

(1) Approval is not required under section 197, 198, 200 or 201 (requirement of members' approval for loans etc) for anything done by a company—
(a) to provide a director of the company or of its holding company with funds to meet expenditure incurred or to be incurred by him—
(i) in defending any criminal or civil proceedings in connection with any alleged negligence, default, breach of duty or breach of trust by him in relation to the company or an associated company, or
(ii) in connection with an application for relief (see subsection (5)), or
(b) to enable any such director to avoid incurring such expenditure,

if it is done on the following terms.

(2) The terms are—
(a) that the loan is to be repaid, or (as the case may be) any liability of the company incurred under any transaction connected with the thing done is to be discharged, in the event of—
(i) the director being convicted in the proceedings,
(ii) judgment being given against him in the proceedings, or
(iii) the court refusing to grant him relief on the application; and
(b) that it is to be so repaid or discharged not later than—
(i) the date when the conviction becomes final,
(ii) the date when the judgment becomes final, or
(iii) the date when the refusal of relief becomes final.

(3) For this purpose a conviction, judgment or refusal of relief becomes final—
(a) if not appealed against, at the end of the period for bringing an appeal;
(b) if appealed against, when the appeal (or any further appeal) is disposed of.

(4) An appeal is disposed of—
(a) if it is determined and the period for bringing any further appeal has ended, or
(b) if it is abandoned or otherwise ceases to have effect.

(5) The reference in subsection (1)(a)(ii) to an application for relief is to an application for relief under—
section 661(3) or (4) (power of court to grant relief in case of acquisition of shares by innocent nominee), or
section 1157 (general power of court to grant relief in case of honest and reasonable conduct).

[1595]

NOTES
Commencement: to be appointed (see the introductory note to this Act).

206 Exception for expenditure in connection with regulatory action or investigation

Approval is not required under section 197, 198, 200 or 201 (requirement of members' approval for loans etc) for anything done by a company—
(a) to provide a director of the company or of its holding company with funds to meet expenditure incurred or to be incurred by him in defending himself—
(i) in an investigation by a regulatory authority, or
(ii) against action proposed to be taken by a regulatory authority,
in connection with any alleged negligence, default, breach of duty or breach of trust by him in relation to the company or an associated company, or
(b) to enable any such director to avoid incurring such expenditure.

[1596]

NOTES
Commencement: to be appointed (see the introductory note to this Act).

207 Exceptions for minor and business transactions

(1) Approval is not required under section 197, 198 or 200 for a company to make a loan or quasi-loan, or to give a guarantee or provide security in connection with a loan or quasi-loan, if the aggregate of—
(a) the value of the transaction, and
(b) the value of any other relevant transactions or arrangements,
does not exceed £10,000.

(2) Approval is not required under section 201 for a company to enter into a credit transaction, or to give a guarantee or provide security in connection with a credit transaction, if the aggregate of—
(a) the value of the transaction (that is, of the credit transaction, guarantee or security), and
(b) the value of any other relevant transactions or arrangements,
does not exceed £15,000.

(3) Approval is not required under section 201 for a company to enter into a credit transaction, or to give a guarantee or provide security in connection with a credit transaction, if—
(a) the transaction is entered into by the company in the ordinary course of the company's business, and
(b) the value of the transaction is not greater, and the terms on which it is entered into are not more favourable, than it is reasonable to expect the company would have offered to, or in respect of, a person of the same financial standing but unconnected with the company.

[1597]

NOTES
Commencement: to be appointed (see the introductory note to this Act).

208 Exceptions for intra-group transactions

(1) Approval is not required under section 197, 198 or 200 for—

(a) the making of a loan or quasi-loan to an associated body corporate, or

(b) the giving of a guarantee or provision of security in connection with a loan or quasi-loan made to an associated body corporate.

(2) Approval is not required under section 201—

(a) to enter into a credit transaction as creditor for the benefit of an associated body corporate, or

(b) to give a guarantee or provide security in connection with a credit transaction entered into by any person for the benefit of an associated body corporate.

[1598]

NOTES

Commencement: to be appointed (see the introductory note to this Act).

209 (*Outside the scope of this work.*)

210 Other relevant transactions or arrangements

(1) This section has effect for determining what are "other relevant transactions or arrangements" for the purposes of any exception to section 197, 198, 200 or 201. In the following provisions "the relevant exception" means the exception for the purposes of which that falls to be determined.

(2) Other relevant transactions or arrangements are those previously entered into, or entered into at the same time as the transaction or arrangement in question in relation to which the following conditions are met.

(3) Where the transaction or arrangement in question is entered into—

(a) for a director of the company entering into it, or

(b) for a person connected with such a director,

the conditions are that the transaction or arrangement was (or is) entered into for that director, or a person connected with him, by virtue of the relevant exception by that company or by any of its subsidiaries.

(4) Where the transaction or arrangement in question is entered into—

(a) for a director of the holding company of the company entering into it, or

(b) for a person connected with such a director,

the conditions are that the transaction or arrangement was (or is) entered into for that director, or a person connected with him, by virtue of the relevant exception by the holding company or by any of its subsidiaries.

(5) A transaction or arrangement entered into by a company that at the time it was entered into—

(a) was a subsidiary of the company entering into the transaction or arrangement in question, or

(b) was a subsidiary of that company's holding company,

is not a relevant transaction or arrangement if, at the time the question arises whether the transaction or arrangement in question falls within a relevant exception, it is no longer such a subsidiary.

[1599]

NOTES

Commencement: to be appointed (see the introductory note to this Act).

211 The value of transactions and arrangements

(1) For the purposes of sections 197 to 214 (loans etc)—

(a) the value of a transaction or arrangement is determined as follows, and

(b) the value of any other relevant transaction or arrangement is taken to be the value so determined reduced by any amount by which the liabilities of the person for whom the transaction or arrangement was made have been reduced.

(2) The value of a loan is the amount of its principal.

(3) The value of a quasi-loan is the amount, or maximum amount, that the person to whom the quasi-loan is made is liable to reimburse the creditor.

(4) The value of a credit transaction is the price that it is reasonable to expect could be obtained for the goods, services or land to which the transaction relates if they had been supplied (at the time the transaction is entered into) in the ordinary course of business and on the same terms (apart from price) as they have been supplied, or are to be supplied, under the transaction in question.

(5) The value of a guarantee or security is the amount guaranteed or secured.

(6) The value of an arrangement to which section 203 (related arrangements) applies is the value of the transaction to which the arrangement relates.

(7) If the value of a transaction or arrangement is not capable of being expressed as a specific sum of money—

(a) whether because the amount of any liability arising under the transaction or arrangement is unascertainable, or for any other reason, and

(b) whether or not any liability under the transaction or arrangement has been reduced,

its value is deemed to exceed £50,000.

[1600]

NOTES

Commencement: to be appointed (see the introductory note to this Act).

212 The person for whom a transaction or arrangement is entered into

For the purposes of sections 197 to 214 (loans etc) the person for whom a transaction or arrangement is entered into is—

(a) in the case of a loan or quasi-loan, the person to whom it is made;

(b) in the case of a credit transaction, the person to whom goods, land or services are supplied, sold, hired, leased or otherwise disposed of under the transaction;

(c) in the case of a guarantee or security, the person for whom the transaction is made in connection with which the guarantee or security is entered into;

(d) in the case of an arrangement within section 203 (related arrangements), the person for whom the transaction is made to which the arrangement relates.

[1601]

NOTES

Commencement: to be appointed (see the introductory note to this Act).

213 Loans etc: civil consequences of contravention

(1) This section applies where a company enters into a transaction or arrangement in contravention of section 197, 198, 200, 201 or 203 (requirement of members' approval for loans etc).

(2) The transaction or arrangement is voidable at the instance of the company, unless—

(a) restitution of any money or other asset that was the subject matter of the transaction or arrangement is no longer possible,

(b) the company has been indemnified for any loss or damage resulting from the transaction or arrangement, or

(c) rights acquired in good faith, for value and without actual notice of the contravention by a person who is not a party to the transaction or arrangement would be affected by the avoidance.

(3) Whether or not the transaction or arrangement has been avoided, each of the persons specified in subsection (4) is liable—

(a) to account to the company for any gain that he has made directly or indirectly by the transaction or arrangement, and

(b) (jointly and severally with any other person so liable under this section) to indemnify the company for any loss or damage resulting from the transaction or arrangement.

(4) The persons so liable are—

(a) any director of the company or of its holding company with whom the company entered into the transaction or arrangement in contravention of section 197, 198, 201 or 203,

(b) any person with whom the company entered into the transaction or arrangement in contravention of any of those sections who is connected with a director of the company or of its holding company,

(c) the director of the company or of its holding company with whom any such person is connected, and

(d) any other director of the company who authorised the transaction or arrangement.

(5) Subsections (3) and (4) are subject to the following two subsections.

(6) In the case of a transaction or arrangement entered into by a company in contravention of section 200, 201 or 203 with a person connected with a director of the company or of its holding company, that director is not liable by virtue of subsection (4)(c) if he shows that he took all reasonable steps to secure the company's compliance with the section concerned.

(7) In any case—

(a) a person so connected is not liable by virtue of subsection (4)(b), and

(b) a director is not liable by virtue of subsection (4)(d),

if he shows that, at the time the transaction or arrangement was entered into, he did not know the relevant circumstances constituting the contravention.

(8) Nothing in this section shall be read as excluding the operation of any other enactment or rule of law by virtue of which the transaction or arrangement may be called in question or any liability to the company may arise.

[1602]

NOTES

Commencement: to be appointed (see the introductory note to this Act).

214 Loans etc: effect of subsequent affirmation

Where a transaction or arrangement is entered into by a company in contravention of section 197, 198, 200, 201 or 203 (requirement of members' approval for loans etc) but, within a reasonable period, it is affirmed—

(a) in the case of a contravention of the requirement for a resolution of the members of the company, by a resolution of the members of the company, and

(b) in the case of a contravention of the requirement for a resolution of the members of the company's holding company, by a resolution of the members of the holding company,

the transaction or arrangement may no longer be avoided under section 213.

[1603]

NOTES

Commencement: to be appointed (see the introductory note to this Act).

Payments for loss of office

215 Payments for loss of office

(1) In this Chapter a "payment for loss of office" means a payment made to a director or past director of a company—

(a) by way of compensation for loss of office as director of the company,

(b) by way of compensation for loss, while director of the company or in connection with his ceasing to be a director of it, of—

  (i) any other office or employment in connection with the management of the affairs of the company, or

  (ii) any office (as director or otherwise) or employment in connection with the management of the affairs of any subsidiary undertaking of the company,

(c) as consideration for or in connection with his retirement from his office as director of the company, or

(d) as consideration for or in connection with his retirement, while director of the company or in connection with his ceasing to be a director of it, from—
  (i) any other office or employment in connection with the management of the affairs of the company, or
  (ii) any office (as director or otherwise) or employment in connection with the management of the affairs of any subsidiary undertaking of the company.

(2) The references to compensation and consideration include benefits otherwise than in cash and references in this Chapter to payment have a corresponding meaning.

(3) For the purposes of sections 217 to 221 (payments requiring members' approval)—
(a) payment to a person connected with a director, or
(b) payment to any person at the direction of, or for the benefit of, a director or a person connected with him,

is treated as payment to the director.

(4) References in those sections to payment by a person include payment by another person at the direction of, or on behalf of, the person referred to.

[1604]

NOTES

Commencement: to be appointed (see the introductory note to this Act).

216 Amounts taken to be payments for loss of office

(1) This section applies where in connection with any such transfer as is mentioned in section 218 or 219 (payment in connection with transfer of undertaking, property or shares) a director of the company—
(a) is to cease to hold office, or
(b) is to cease to be the holder of—
  (i) any other office or employment in connection with the management of the affairs of the company, or
  (ii) any office (as director or otherwise) or employment in connection with the management of the affairs of any subsidiary undertaking of the company.

(2) If in connection with any such transfer—
(a) the price to be paid to the director for any shares in the company held by him is in excess of the price which could at the time have been obtained by other holders of like shares, or
(b) any valuable consideration is given to the director by a person other than the company,

the excess or, as the case may be, the money value of the consideration is taken for the purposes of those sections to have been a payment for loss of office.

[1605]

NOTES

Commencement: to be appointed (see the introductory note to this Act).

217 Payment by company: requirement of members' approval

(1) A company may not make a payment for loss of office to a director of the company unless the payment has been approved by a resolution of the members of the company.

(2) A company may not make a payment for loss of office to a director of its holding company unless the payment has been approved by a resolution of the members of each of those companies.

(3) A resolution approving a payment to which this section applies must not be passed unless a memorandum setting out particulars of the proposed payment (including its amount) is made available to the members of the company whose approval is sought—
(a) in the case of a written resolution, by being sent or submitted to every eligible member at or before the time at which the proposed resolution is sent or submitted to him;
(b) in the case of a resolution at a meeting, by being made available for inspection by the members both—

(i) at the company's registered office for not less than 15 days ending with the date of the meeting, and

(ii) at the meeting itself.

(4) No approval is required under this section on the part of the members of a body corporate that—

(a) is not a UK-registered company, or

(b) is a wholly-owned subsidiary of another body corporate.

[1606]

NOTES

Commencement: to be appointed (see the introductory note to this Act).

218 Payment in connection with transfer of undertaking etc: requirement of members' approval

(1) No payment for loss of office may be made by any person to a director of a company in connection with the transfer of the whole or any part of the undertaking or property of the company unless the payment has been approved by a resolution of the members of the company.

(2) No payment for loss of office may be made by any person to a director of a company in connection with the transfer of the whole or any part of the undertaking or property of a subsidiary of the company unless the payment has been approved by a resolution of the members of each of the companies.

(3) A resolution approving a payment to which this section applies must not be passed unless a memorandum setting out particulars of the proposed payment (including its amount) is made available to the members of the company whose approval is sought—

(a) in the case of a written resolution, by being sent or submitted to every eligible member at or before the time at which the proposed resolution is sent or submitted to him;

(b) in the case of a resolution at a meeting, by being made available for inspection by the members both—

(i) at the company's registered office for not less than 15 days ending with the date of the meeting, and

(ii) at the meeting itself.

(4) No approval is required under this section on the part of the members of a body corporate that—

(a) is not a UK-registered company, or

(b) is a wholly-owned subsidiary of another body corporate.

(5) A payment made in pursuance of an arrangement—

(a) entered into as part of the agreement for the transfer in question, or within one year before or two years after that agreement, and

(b) to which the company whose undertaking or property is transferred, or any person to whom the transfer is made, is privy,

is presumed, except in so far as the contrary is shown, to be a payment to which this section applies.

[1607]

NOTES

Commencement: to be appointed (see the introductory note to this Act).

219 Payment in connection with share transfer: requirement of members' approval

(1) No payment for loss of office may be made by any person to a director of a company in connection with a transfer of shares in the company, or in a subsidiary of the company, resulting from a takeover bid unless the payment has been approved by a resolution of the relevant shareholders.

(2) The relevant shareholders are the holders of the shares to which the bid relates and any holders of shares of the same class as any of those shares.

(3) A resolution approving a payment to which this section applies must not be passed unless a memorandum setting out particulars of the proposed payment (including its amount) is made available to the members of the company whose approval is sought—

(a) in the case of a written resolution, by being sent or submitted to every eligible member at or before the time at which the proposed resolution is sent or submitted to him;

(b) in the case of a resolution at a meeting, by being made available for inspection by the members both—

(i) at the company's registered office for not less than 15 days ending with the date of the meeting, and

(ii) at the meeting itself.

(4) Neither the person making the offer, nor any associate of his (as defined in section 988), is entitled to vote on the resolution, but—

(a) where the resolution is proposed as a written resolution, they are entitled (if they would otherwise be so entitled) to be sent a copy of it, and

(b) at any meeting to consider the resolution they are entitled (if they would otherwise be so entitled) to be given notice of the meeting, to attend and speak and if present (in person or by proxy) to count towards the quorum.

(5) If at a meeting to consider the resolution a quorum is not present, and after the meeting has been adjourned to a later date a quorum is again not present, the payment is (for the purposes of this section) deemed to have been approved.

(6) No approval is required under this section on the part of shareholders in a body corporate that—

(a) is not a UK-registered company, or

(b) is a wholly-owned subsidiary of another body corporate.

(7) A payment made in pursuance of an arrangement—

(a) entered into as part of the agreement for the transfer in question, or within one year before or two years after that agreement, and

(b) to which the company whose shares are the subject of the bid, or any person to whom the transfer is made, is privy,

is presumed, except in so far as the contrary is shown, to be a payment to which this section applies.

[1608]

NOTES

Commencement: to be appointed (see the introductory note to this Act).

220 Exception for payments in discharge of legal obligations etc

(1) Approval is not required under section 217, 218 or 219 (payments requiring members' approval) for a payment made in good faith—

(a) in discharge of an existing legal obligation (as defined below),

(b) by way of damages for breach of such an obligation,

(c) by way of settlement or compromise of any claim arising in connection with the termination of a person's office or employment, or

(d) by way of pension in respect of past services.

(2) In relation to a payment within section 217 (payment by company) an existing legal obligation means an obligation of the company, or any body corporate associated with it, that was not entered into in connection with, or in consequence of, the event giving rise to the payment for loss of office.

(3) In relation to a payment within section 218 or 219 (payment in connection with transfer of undertaking, property or shares) an existing legal obligation means an obligation of the person making the payment that was not entered into for the purposes of, in connection with or in consequence of, the transfer in question.

(4) In the case of a payment within both section 217 and section 218, or within both section 217 and section 219, subsection (2) above applies and not subsection (3).

(5) A payment part of which falls within subsection (1) above and part of which does not is treated as if the parts were separate payments.

[1609]

NOTES

Commencement: to be appointed (see the introductory note to this Act).

221 Exception for small payments

(1) Approval is not required under section 217, 218 or 219 (payments requiring members' approval) if—

(a) the payment in question is made by the company or any of its subsidiaries, and

(b) the amount or value of the payment, together with the amount or value of any other relevant payments, does not exceed £200.

(2) For this purpose "other relevant payments" are payments for loss of office in relation to which the following conditions are met.

(3) Where the payment in question is one to which section 217 (payment by company) applies, the conditions are that the other payment was or is paid—

(a) by the company making the payment in question or any of its subsidiaries,

(b) to the director to whom that payment is made, and

(c) in connection with the same event.

(4) Where the payment in question is one to which section 218 or 219 applies (payment in connection with transfer of undertaking, property or shares), the conditions are that the other payment was (or is) paid in connection with the same transfer—

(a) to the director to whom the payment in question was made, and

(b) by the company making the payment or any of its subsidiaries.

[1610]

NOTES

Commencement: to be appointed (see the introductory note to this Act).

222 Payments made without approval: civil consequences

(1) If a payment is made in contravention of section 217 (payment by company)—

(a) it is held by the recipient on trust for the company making the payment, and

(b) any director who authorised the payment is jointly and severally liable to indemnify the company that made the payment for any loss resulting from it.

(2) If a payment is made in contravention of section 218 (payment in connection with transfer of undertaking etc), it is held by the recipient on trust for the company whose undertaking or property is or is proposed to be transferred.

(3) If a payment is made in contravention of section 219 (payment in connection with share transfer)—

(a) it is held by the recipient on trust for persons who have sold their shares as a result of the offer made, and

(b) the expenses incurred by the recipient in distributing that sum amongst those persons shall be borne by him and not retained out of that sum.

(4) If a payment is in contravention of section 217 and section 218, subsection (2) of this section applies rather than subsection (1).

(5) If a payment is in contravention of section 217 and section 219, subsection (3) of this section applies rather than subsection (1), unless the court directs otherwise.

[1611]

NOTES

Commencement: to be appointed (see the introductory note to this Act).

Supplementary

223 Transactions requiring members' approval: application of provisions to shadow directors

(1) For the purposes of—

(a) sections 188 and 189 (directors' service contracts),

(b) sections 190 to 196 (property transactions),

(c) sections 197 to 214 (loans etc), and

(d) sections 215 to 222 (payments for loss of office),

a shadow director is treated as a director.

(2) Any reference in those provisions to loss of office as a director does not apply in relation to loss of a person's status as a shadow director.

[1612]

NOTES

Commencement: to be appointed (see the introductory note to this Act).

224 Approval by written resolution: accidental failure to send memorandum

(1) Where—

(a) approval under this Chapter is sought by written resolution, and

(b) a memorandum is required under this Chapter to be sent or submitted to every eligible member before the resolution is passed,

any accidental failure to send or submit the memorandum to one or more members shall be disregarded for the purpose of determining whether the requirement has been met.

(2) Subsection (1) has effect subject to any provision of the company's articles.

[1613]

NOTES

Commencement: to be appointed (see the introductory note to this Act).

225 Cases where approval is required under more than one provision

(1) Approval may be required under more than one provision of this Chapter.

(2) If so, the requirements of each applicable provision must be met.

(3) This does not require a separate resolution for the purposes of each provision.

[1614]

NOTES

Commencement: to be appointed (see the introductory note to this Act).

226 (*Substitutes the Charities Act 1993, ss 66, 66A at* **[830]**, **[830A]**.)

CHAPTER 5
DIRECTORS' SERVICE CONTRACTS

227 Directors' service contracts

(1) For the purposes of this Part a director's "service contract", in relation to a company, means a contract under which—

(a) a director of the company undertakes personally to perform services (as director or otherwise) for the company, or for a subsidiary of the company, or

(b) services (as director or otherwise) that a director of the company undertakes personally to perform are made available by a third party to the company, or to a subsidiary of the company.

(2) The provisions of this Part relating to directors' service contracts apply to the terms of a person's appointment as a director of a company.

They are not restricted to contracts for the performance of services outside the scope of the ordinary duties of a director.

[1615]

NOTES

Commencement: to be appointed (see the introductory note to this Act).

228 Copy of contract or memorandum of terms to be available for inspection

(1) A company must keep available for inspection—

(a) a copy of every director's service contract with the company or with a subsidiary of the company, or

(b) if the contract is not in writing, a written memorandum setting out the terms of the contract.

(2) All the copies and memoranda must be kept available for inspection at—

(a) the company's registered office, or

(b) a place specified in regulations under section 1136.

(3) The copies and memoranda must be retained by the company for at least one year from the date of termination or expiry of the contract and must be kept available for inspection during that time.

(4) The company must give notice to the registrar—

(a) of the place at which the copies and memoranda are kept available for inspection, and

(b) of any change in that place,

unless they have at all times been kept at the company's registered office.

(5) If default is made in complying with subsection (1), (2) or (3), or default is made for 14 days in complying with subsection (4), an offence is committed by every officer of the company who is in default.

(6) A person guilty of an offence under this section is liable on summary conviction to a fine not exceeding level 3 on the standard scale and, for continued contravention, a daily default fine not exceeding one-tenth of level 3 on the standard scale.

(7) The provisions of this section apply to a variation of a director's service contract as they apply to the original contract.

[1616]

NOTES

Commencement: to be appointed (see the introductory note to this Act).

229 Right of member to inspect and request copy

(1) Every copy or memorandum required to be kept under section 228 must be open to inspection by any member of the company without charge.

(2) Any member of the company is entitled, on request and on payment of such fee as may be prescribed, to be provided with a copy of any such copy or memorandum.

The copy must be provided within seven days after the request is received by the company.

(3) If an inspection required under subsection (1) is refused, or default is made in complying with subsection (2), an offence is committed by every officer of the company who is in default.

(4) A person guilty of an offence under this section is liable on summary conviction to a fine not exceeding level 3 on the standard scale and, for continued contravention, a daily default fine not exceeding one-tenth of level 3 on the standard scale.

(5) In the case of any such refusal or default the court may by order compel an immediate inspection or, as the case may be, direct that the copy required be sent to the person requiring it.

[1617]

NOTES

Commencement: to be appointed (see the introductory note to this Act).

230 Directors' service contracts: application of provisions to shadow directors

A shadow director is treated as a director for the purposes of the provisions of this Chapter.

[1618]

NOTES

Commencement: to be appointed (see the introductory note to this Act).

CHAPTER 6
CONTRACTS WITH SOLE MEMBERS WHO ARE DIRECTORS

231 Contract with sole member who is also a director

(1) This section applies where—

(a) a limited company having only one member enters into a contract with the sole member,

(b) the sole member is also a director of the company, and

(c) the contract is not entered into in the ordinary course of the company's business.

(2) The company must, unless the contract is in writing, ensure that the terms of the contract are either—

(a) set out in a written memorandum, or

(b) recorded in the minutes of the first meeting of the directors of the company following the making of the contract.

(3) If a company fails to comply with this section an offence is committed by every officer of the company who is in default.

(4) A person guilty of an offence under this section is liable on summary conviction to a fine not exceeding level 5 on the standard scale.

(5) For the purposes of this section a shadow director is treated as a director.

(6) Failure to comply with this section in relation to a contract does not affect the validity of the contract.

(7) Nothing in this section shall be read as excluding the operation of any other enactment or rule of law applying to contracts between a company and a director of the company.

[1619]

NOTES

Commencement: to be appointed (see the introductory note to this Act).

CHAPTER 7
DIRECTORS' LIABILITIES

Provision protecting directors from liability

232 Provisions protecting directors from liability

(1) Any provision that purports to exempt a director of a company (to any extent) from any liability that would otherwise attach to him in connection with any negligence, default, breach of duty or breach of trust in relation to the company is void.

(2) Any provision by which a company directly or indirectly provides an indemnity (to any extent) for a director of the company, or of an associated company, against any liability attaching to him in connection with any negligence, default, breach of duty or breach of trust in relation to the company of which he is a director is void, except as permitted by—

(a) section 233 (provision of insurance),

(b) section 234 (qualifying third party indemnity provision), or

(c) section 235 (qualifying pension scheme indemnity provision).

(3) This section applies to any provision, whether contained in a company's articles or in any contract with the company or otherwise.

(4) Nothing in this section prevents a company's articles from making such provision as has previously been lawful for dealing with conflicts of interest.

[1620]

NOTES

Commencement: to be appointed (see the introductory note to this Act).

233 Provision of insurance

Section 232(2) (voidness of provisions for indemnifying directors) does not prevent a company from purchasing and maintaining for a director of the company, or of an associated company, insurance against any such liability as is mentioned in that subsection.

[1621]

NOTES

Commencement: to be appointed (see the introductory note to this Act).

234 Qualifying third party indemnity provision

(1) Section 232(2) (voidness of provisions for indemnifying directors) does not apply to qualifying third party indemnity provision.

(2) Third party indemnity provision means provision for indemnity against liability incurred by the director to a person other than the company or an associated company.

Such provision is qualifying third party indemnity provision if the following requirements are met.

(3) The provision must not provide any indemnity against—

(a) any liability of the director to pay—

(i) a fine imposed in criminal proceedings, or

(ii) a sum payable to a regulatory authority by way of a penalty in respect of non-compliance with any requirement of a regulatory nature (however arising); or

(b) any liability incurred by the director—

(i) in defending criminal proceedings in which he is convicted, or

(ii) in defending civil proceedings brought by the company, or an associated company, in which judgment is given against him, or

(iii) in connection with an application for relief (see subsection (6)) in which the court refuses to grant him relief.

(4) The references in subsection (3)(b) to a conviction, judgment or refusal of relief are to the final decision in the proceedings.

(5) For this purpose—

(a) a conviction, judgment or refusal of relief becomes final—

(i) if not appealed against, at the end of the period for bringing an appeal, or

(ii) if appealed against, at the time when the appeal (or any further appeal) is disposed of; and

(b) an appeal is disposed of—

(i) if it is determined and the period for bringing any further appeal has ended, or

(ii) if it is abandoned or otherwise ceases to have effect.

(6) The reference in subsection (3)(b)(iii) to an application for relief is to an application for relief under—

section 661(3) or (4) (power of court to grant relief in case of acquisition of shares by innocent nominee), or

section 1157 (general power of court to grant relief in case of honest and reasonable conduct).

[1622]

NOTES

Commencement: to be appointed (see the introductory note to this Act).

235 Qualifying pension scheme indemnity provision

(1) Section 232(2) (voidness of provisions for indemnifying directors) does not apply to qualifying pension scheme indemnity provision.

(2) Pension scheme indemnity provision means provision indemnifying a director of a company that is a trustee of an occupational pension scheme against liability incurred in connection with the company's activities as trustee of the scheme.

Such provision is qualifying pension scheme indemnity provision if the following requirements are met.

(3) The provision must not provide any indemnity against—
 (a) any liability of the director to pay—
  (i) a fine imposed in criminal proceedings, or
  (ii) a sum payable to a regulatory authority by way of a penalty in respect of non-compliance with any requirement of a regulatory nature (however arising); or
 (b) any liability incurred by the director in defending criminal proceedings in which he is convicted.

(4) The reference in subsection (3)(b) to a conviction is to the final decision in the proceedings.

(5) For this purpose—
 (a) a conviction becomes final—
  (i) if not appealed against, at the end of the period for bringing an appeal, or
  (ii) if appealed against, at the time when the appeal (or any further appeal) is disposed of; and
 (b) an appeal is disposed of—
  (i) if it is determined and the period for bringing any further appeal has ended, or
  (ii) if it is abandoned or otherwise ceases to have effect.

(6) In this section "occupational pension scheme" means an occupational pension scheme as defined in section 150(5) of the Finance Act 2004 (c 12) that is established under a trust.

[1623]

NOTES

Commencement: to be appointed (see the introductory note to this Act).

236 Qualifying indemnity provision to be disclosed in directors' report

(1) This section requires disclosure in the directors' report of—
 (a) qualifying third party indemnity provision, and
 (b) qualifying pension scheme indemnity provision.

Such provision is referred to in this section as "qualifying indemnity provision".

(2) If when a directors' report is approved any qualifying indemnity provision (whether made by the company or otherwise) is in force for the benefit of one or more directors of the company, the report must state that such provision is in force.

(3) If at any time during the financial year to which a directors' report relates any such provision was in force for the benefit of one or more persons who were then directors of the company, the report must state that such provision was in force.

(4) If when a directors' report is approved qualifying indemnity provision made by the company is in force for the benefit of one or more directors of an associated company, the report must state that such provision is in force.

(5) If at any time during the financial year to which a directors' report relates any such provision was in force for the benefit of one or more persons who were then directors of an associated company, the report must state that such provision was in force.

[1624]

NOTES

Commencement: to be appointed (see the introductory note to this Act).

237 Copy of qualifying indemnity provision to be available for inspection

(1) This section has effect where qualifying indemnity provision is made for a director of a company, and applies—
 (a) to the company of which he is a director (whether the provision is made by that company or an associated company), and
 (b) where the provision is made by an associated company, to that company.

(2) That company or, as the case may be, each of them must keep available for inspection—
(a) a copy of the qualifying indemnity provision, or
(b) if the provision is not in writing, a written memorandum setting out its terms.

(3) The copy or memorandum must be kept available for inspection at—
(a) the company's registered office, or
(b) a place specified in regulations under section 1136.

(4) The copy or memorandum must be retained by the company for at least one year from the date of termination or expiry of the provision and must be kept available for inspection during that time.

(5) The company must give notice to the registrar—
(a) of the place at which the copy or memorandum is kept available for inspection, and
(b) of any change in that place,
unless it has at all times been kept at the company's registered office.

(6) If default is made in complying with subsection (2), (3) or (4), or default is made for 14 days in complying with subsection (5), an offence is committed by every officer of the company who is in default.

(7) A person guilty of an offence under this section is liable on summary conviction to a fine not exceeding level 3 on the standard scale and, for continued contravention, a daily default fine not exceeding one-tenth of level 3 on the standard scale.

(8) The provisions of this section apply to a variation of a qualifying indemnity provision as they apply to the original provision.

(9) In this section "qualifying indemnity provision" means—
(a) qualifying third party indemnity provision, and
(b) qualifying pension scheme indemnity provision.

[1625]

NOTES

Commencement: to be appointed (see the introductory note to this Act).

238 Right of member to inspect and request copy

(1) Every copy or memorandum required to be kept by a company under section 237 must be open to inspection by any member of the company without charge.

(2) Any member of the company is entitled, on request and on payment of such fee as may be prescribed, to be provided with a copy of any such copy or memorandum.

The copy must be provided within seven days after the request is received by the company.

(3) If an inspection required under subsection (1) is refused, or default is made in complying with subsection (2), an offence is committed by every officer of the company who is in default.

(4) A person guilty of an offence under this section is liable on summary conviction to a fine not exceeding level 3 on the standard scale and, for continued contravention, a daily default fine not exceeding one-tenth of level 3 on the standard scale.

(5) In the case of any such refusal or default the court may by order compel an immediate inspection or, as the case may be, direct that the copy required be sent to the person requiring it.

[1626]

NOTES

Commencement: to be appointed (see the introductory note to this Act).

Ratification of acts giving rise to liability

239 Ratification of acts of directors

(1) This section applies to the ratification by a company of conduct by a director amounting to negligence, default, breach of duty or breach of trust in relation to the company.

(2) The decision of the company to ratify such conduct must be made by resolution of the members of the company.

(3) Where the resolution is proposed as a written resolution neither the director (if a member of the company) nor any member connected with him is an eligible member.

(4) Where the resolution is proposed at a meeting, it is passed only if the necessary majority is obtained disregarding votes in favour of the resolution by the director (if a member of the company) and any member connected with him. This does not prevent the director or any such member from attending, being counted towards the quorum and taking part in the proceedings at any meeting at which the decision is considered.

(5) For the purposes of this section—
- (a) "conduct" includes acts and omissions;
- (b) "director" includes a former director;
- (c) a shadow director is treated as a director; and
- (d) in section 252 (meaning of "connected person"), subsection (3) does not apply (exclusion of person who is himself a director).

(6) Nothing in this section affects—
- (a) the validity of a decision taken by unanimous consent of the members of the company, or
- (b) any power of the directors to agree not to sue, or to settle or release a claim made by them on behalf of the company.

(7) This section does not affect any other enactment or rule of law imposing additional requirements for valid ratification or any rule of law as to acts that are incapable of being ratified by the company.

[1627]

NOTES

Commencement: to be appointed (see the introductory note to this Act).

CHAPTER 8
DIRECTORS' RESIDENTIAL ADDRESSES: PROTECTION FROM DISCLOSURE

240 Protected information

(1) This Chapter makes provision for protecting, in the case of a company director who is an individual—
- (a) information as to his usual residential address;
- (b) the information that his service address is his usual residential address.

(2) That information is referred to in this Chapter as "protected information".

(3) Information does not cease to be protected information on the individual ceasing to be a director of the company.

References in this Chapter to a director include, to that extent, a former director.

[1628]

NOTES

Commencement: to be appointed (see the introductory note to this Act).

241 Protected information: restriction on use or disclosure by company

(1) A company must not use or disclose protected information about any of its directors, except—
- (a) for communicating with the director concerned,
- (b) in order to comply with any requirement of the Companies Acts as to particulars to be sent to the registrar, or

(c) in accordance with section 244 (disclosure under court order).

(2) Subsection (1) does not prohibit any use or disclosure of protected information with the consent of the director concerned.

[1629]

NOTES

Commencement: to be appointed (see the introductory note to this Act).

242 Protected information: restriction on use or disclosure by registrar

(1) The registrar must omit protected information from the material on the register that is available for inspection where—

(a) it is contained in a document delivered to him in which such information is required to be stated, and

(b) in the case of a document having more than one part, it is contained in a part of the document in which such information is required to be stated.

(2) The registrar is not obliged—

(a) to check other documents or (as the case may be) other parts of the document to ensure the absence of protected information, or

(b) to omit from the material that is available for public inspection anything registered before this Chapter comes into force.

(3) The registrar must not use or disclose protected information except—

(a) as permitted by section 243 (permitted use or disclosure by registrar), or

(b) in accordance with section 244 (disclosure under court order).

[1630]

NOTES

Commencement: to be appointed (see the introductory note to this Act).

243 Permitted use or disclosure by the registrar

(1) The registrar may use protected information for communicating with the director in question.

(2) The registrar may disclose protected information—

(a) to a public authority specified for the purposes of this section by regulations made by the Secretary of State, or

(b) to a credit reference agency.

(3) The Secretary of State may make provision by regulations—

(a) specifying conditions for the disclosure of protected information in accordance with this section, and

(b) providing for the charging of fees.

(4) The Secretary of State may make provision by regulations requiring the registrar, on application, to refrain from disclosing protected information relating to a director to a credit reference agency.

(5) Regulations under subsection (4) may make provision as to—

(a) who may make an application,

(b) the grounds on which an application may be made,

(c) the information to be included in and documents to accompany an application, and

(d) how an application is to be determined.

(6) Provision under subsection (5)(d) may in particular—

(a) confer a discretion on the registrar;

(b) provide for a question to be referred to a person other than the registrar for the purposes of determining the application.

(7) In this section—

"credit reference agency" means a person carrying on a business comprising the furnishing of information relevant to the financial standing of individuals, being information collected by the agency for that purpose; and

"public authority" includes any person or body having functions of a public nature.

(8) Regulations under this section are subject to negative resolution procedure.

[1631]

NOTES

Commencement: to be appointed (see the introductory note to this Act).

244 Disclosure under court order

(1) The court may make an order for the disclosure of protected information by the company or by the registrar if—

(a) there is evidence that service of documents at a service address other than the director's usual residential address is not effective to bring them to the notice of the director, or

(b) it is necessary or expedient for the information to be provided in connection with the enforcement of an order or decree of the court,

and the court is otherwise satisfied that it is appropriate to make the order.

(2) An order for disclosure by the registrar is to be made only if the company—

(a) does not have the director's usual residential address, or

(b) has been dissolved.

(3) The order may be made on the application of a liquidator, creditor or member of the company, or any other person appearing to the court to have a sufficient interest.

(4) The order must specify the persons to whom, and purposes for which, disclosure is authorised.

[1632]

NOTES

Commencement: to be appointed (see the introductory note to this Act).

245 Circumstances in which registrar may put address on the public record

(1) The registrar may put a director's usual residential address on the public record if—

(a) communications sent by the registrar to the director and requiring a response within a specified period remain unanswered, or

(b) there is evidence that service of documents at a service address provided in place of the director's usual residential address is not effective to bring them to the notice of the director.

(2) The registrar must give notice of the proposal—

(a) to the director, and

(b) to every company of which the registrar has been notified that the individual is a director.

(3) The notice must—

(a) state the grounds on which it is proposed to put the director's usual residential address on the public record, and

(b) specify a period within which representations may be made before that is done.

(4) It must be sent to the director at his usual residential address, unless it appears to the registrar that service at that address may be ineffective to bring it to the individual's notice, in which case it may be sent to any service address provided in place of that address.

(5) The registrar must take account of any representations received within the specified period.

(6) What is meant by putting the address on the public record is explained in section 246.

[1633]

NOTES

Commencement: to be appointed (see the introductory note to this Act).

246 Putting the address on the public record

(1) The registrar, on deciding in accordance with section 245 that a director's usual residential address is to be put on the public record, shall proceed as if notice of a change of registered particulars had been given—

(a) stating that address as the director's service address, and
(b) stating that the director's usual residential address is the same as his service address.

(2) The registrar must give notice of having done so—
(a) to the director, and
(b) to the company.

(3) On receipt of the notice the company must—
(a) enter the director's usual residential address in its register of directors as his service address, and
(b) state in its register of directors' residential addresses that his usual residential address is the same as his service address.

(4) If the company has been notified by the director in question of a more recent address as his usual residential address, it must—
(a) enter that address in its register of directors as the director's service address, and
(b) give notice to the registrar as on a change of registered particulars.

(5) If a company fails to comply with subsection (3) or (4), an offence is committed by—
(a) the company, and
(b) every officer of the company who is in default.

(6) A person guilty of an offence under subsection (5) is liable on summary conviction to a fine not exceeding level 5 on the standard scale and, for continued contravention, a daily default fine not exceeding one-tenth of level 5 on the standard scale.

(7) A director whose usual residential address has been put on the public record by the registrar under this section may not register a service address other than his usual residential address for a period of five years from the date of the registrar's decision.

[1634]

NOTES

Commencement: to be appointed (see the introductory note to this Act).

CHAPTER 9
SUPPLEMENTARY PROVISIONS

Provision for employees on cessation or transfer of business

247 Power to make provision for employees on cessation or transfer of business

(1) The powers of the directors of a company include (if they would not otherwise do so) power to make provision for the benefit of persons employed or formerly employed by the company, or any of its subsidiaries, in connection with the cessation or the transfer to any person of the whole or part of the undertaking of the company or that subsidiary.

(2) This power is exercisable notwithstanding the general duty imposed by section 172 (duty to promote the success of the company).

(3) In the case of a company that is a charity it is exercisable notwithstanding any restrictions on the directors' powers (or the company's capacity) flowing from the objects of the company.

(4) The power may only be exercised if sanctioned—
(a) by a resolution of the company, or
(b) by a resolution of the directors,
in accordance with the following provisions.

(5) A resolution of the directors—
(a) must be authorised by the company's articles, and
(b) is not sufficient sanction for payments to or for the benefit of directors, former directors or shadow directors.

(6) Any other requirements of the company's articles as to the exercise of the power conferred by this section must be complied with.

(7) Any payment under this section must be made—

(a) before the commencement of any winding up of the company, and
(b) out of profits of the company that are available for dividend.

[1635]

NOTES

Commencement: to be appointed (see the introductory note to this Act).

Records of meetings of directors

248 Minutes of directors' meetings

(1) Every company must cause minutes of all proceedings at meetings of its directors to be recorded.

(2) The records must be kept for at least ten years from the date of the meeting.

(3) If a company fails to comply with this section, an offence is committed by every officer of the company who is in default.

(4) A person guilty of an offence under this section is liable on summary conviction to a fine not exceeding level 3 on the standard scale and, for continued contravention, a daily default fine not exceeding one-tenth of level 3 on the standard scale.

[1636]

NOTES

Commencement: to be appointed (see the introductory note to this Act).

249 Minutes as evidence

(1) Minutes recorded in accordance with section 248, if purporting to be authenticated by the chairman of the meeting or by the chairman of the next directors' meeting, are evidence (in Scotland, sufficient evidence) of the proceedings at the meeting.

(2) Where minutes have been made in accordance with that section of the proceedings of a meeting of directors, then, until the contrary is proved—

(a) the meeting is deemed duly held and convened,
(b) all proceedings at the meeting are deemed to have duly taken place, and
(c) all appointments at the meeting are deemed valid.

[1637]

NOTES

Commencement: to be appointed (see the introductory note to this Act).

Meaning of "director" and "shadow director"

250 "Director"

In the Companies Acts "director" includes any person occupying the position of director, by whatever name called.

[1638]

NOTES

Commencement: to be appointed (see the introductory note to this Act).

251 "Shadow director"

(1) In the Companies Acts "shadow director", in relation to a company, means a person in accordance with whose directions or instructions the directors of the company are accustomed to act.

(2) A person is not to be regarded as a shadow director by reason only that the directors act on advice given by him in a professional capacity.

(3) A body corporate is not to be regarded as a shadow director of any of its subsidiary companies for the purposes of—

Chapter 2 (general duties of directors),
Chapter 4 (transactions requiring members' approval), or
Chapter 6 (contract with sole member who is also a director),

by reason only that the directors of the subsidiary are accustomed to act in accordance with its directions or instructions.

[1639]

NOTES

Commencement: to be appointed (see the introductory note to this Act).

Other definitions

252 Persons connected with a director

(1) This section defines what is meant by references in this Part to a person being "connected" with a director of a company (or a director being "connected" with a person).

(2) The following persons (and only those persons) are connected with a director of a company—

(a) members of the director's family (see section 253);
(b) a body corporate with which the director is connected (as defined in section 254);
(c) a person acting in his capacity as trustee of a trust—
  (i) the beneficiaries of which include the director or a person who by virtue of paragraph (a) or (b) is connected with him, or
  (ii) the terms of which confer a power on the trustees that may be exercised for the benefit of the director or any such person,

other than a trust for the purposes of an employees' share scheme or a pension scheme;

(d) a person acting in his capacity as partner—
  (i) of the director, or
  (ii) of a person who, by virtue of paragraph (a), (b) or (c), is connected with that director;
(e) a firm that is a legal person under the law by which it is governed and in which—
  (i) the director is a partner,
  (ii) a partner is a person who, by virtue of paragraph (a), (b) or (c) is connected with the director, or
  (iii) a partner is a firm in which the director is a partner or in which there is a partner who, by virtue of paragraph (a), (b) or (c), is connected with the director.

(3) References in this Part to a person connected with a director of a company do not include a person who is himself a director of the company.

[1640]

NOTES

Commencement: to be appointed (see the introductory note to this Act).

253 Members of a director's family

(1) This section defines what is meant by references in this Part to members of a director's family.

(2) For the purposes of this Part the members of a director's family are—

(a) the director's spouse or civil partner;
(b) any other person (whether of a different sex or the same sex) with whom the director lives as partner in an enduring family relationship;
(c) the director's children or step-children;
(d) any children or step-children of a person within paragraph (b) (and who are not children or step-children of the director) who live with the director and have not attained the age of 18;
(e) the director's parents.

(3) Subsection (2)(b) does not apply if the other person is the director's grandparent or grandchild, sister, brother, aunt or uncle, or nephew or niece.

[1641]

NOTES

Commencement: to be appointed (see the introductory note to this Act).

254 Director "connected with" a body corporate

(1) This section defines what is meant by references in this Part to a director being "connected with" a body corporate.

(2) A director is connected with a body corporate if, but only if, he and the persons connected with him together—

(a) are interested in shares comprised in the equity share capital of that body corporate of a nominal value equal to at least 20% of that share capital, or

(b) are entitled to exercise or control the exercise of more than 20% of the voting power at any general meeting of that body.

(3) The rules set out in Schedule 1 (references to interest in shares or debentures) apply for the purposes of this section.

(4) References in this section to voting power the exercise of which is controlled by a director include voting power whose exercise is controlled by a body corporate controlled by him.

(5) Shares in a company held as treasury shares, and any voting rights attached to such shares, are disregarded for the purposes of this section.

(6) For the avoidance of circularity in the application of section 252 (meaning of "connected person") —

(a) a body corporate with which a director is connected is not treated for the purposes of this section as connected with him unless it is also connected with him by virtue of subsection (2)(c) or (d) of that section (connection as trustee or partner); and

(b) a trustee of a trust the beneficiaries of which include (or may include) a body corporate with which a director is connected is not treated for the purposes of this section as connected with a director by reason only of that fact.

[1642]

NOTES

Commencement: to be appointed (see the introductory note to this Act).

255 Director "controlling" a body corporate

(1) This section defines what is meant by references in this Part to a director "controlling" a body corporate.

(2) A director of a company is taken to control a body corporate if, but only if—

(a) he or any person connected with him—

  (i) is interested in any part of the equity share capital of that body, or

  (ii) is entitled to exercise or control the exercise of any part of the voting power at any general meeting of that body, and

(b) he, the persons connected with him and the other directors of that company, together—

  (i) are interested in more than 50% of that share capital, or

  (ii) are entitled to exercise or control the exercise of more than 50% of that voting power.

(3) The rules set out in Schedule 1 (references to interest in shares or debentures) apply for the purposes of this section.

(4) References in this section to voting power the exercise of which is controlled by a director include voting power whose exercise is controlled by a body corporate controlled by him.

(5) Shares in a company held as treasury shares, and any voting rights attached to such shares, are disregarded for the purposes of this section.

(6) For the avoidance of circularity in the application of section 252 (meaning of "connected person")—

(a) a body corporate with which a director is connected is not treated for the purposes of this section as connected with him unless it is also connected with him by virtue of subsection (2)(c) or (d) of that section (connection as trustee or partner); and

(b) a trustee of a trust the beneficiaries of which include (or may include) a body corporate with which a director is connected is not treated for the purposes of this section as connected with a director by reason only of that fact.

[1643]

NOTES

Commencement: to be appointed (see the introductory note to this Act).

256 Associated bodies corporate

For the purposes of this Part—

(a) bodies corporate are associated if one is a subsidiary of the other or both are subsidiaries of the same body corporate, and

(b) companies are associated if one is a subsidiary of the other or both are subsidiaries of the same body corporate.

[1644]

NOTES

Commencement: to be appointed (see the introductory note to this Act).

257 References to company's constitution

(1) References in this Part to a company's constitution include—

(a) any resolution or other decision come to in accordance with the constitution, and

(b) any decision by the members of the company, or a class of members, that is treated by virtue of any enactment or rule of law as equivalent to a decision by the company.

(2) This is in addition to the matters mentioned in section 17 (general provision as to matters contained in company's constitution).

[1645]

NOTES

Commencement: to be appointed (see the introductory note to this Act).

General

258 Power to increase financial limits

(1) The Secretary of State may by order substitute for any sum of money specified in this Part a larger sum specified in the order.

(2) An order under this section is subject to negative resolution procedure.

(3) An order does not have effect in relation to anything done or not done before it comes into force.

Accordingly, proceedings in respect of any liability incurred before that time may be continued or instituted as if the order had not been made.

[1646]

NOTES

Commencement: to be appointed (see the introductory note to this Act).

259 Transactions under foreign law

For the purposes of this Part it is immaterial whether the law that (apart from this Act) governs an arrangement or transaction is the law of the United Kingdom, or a part of it, or not.

[1647]

NOTES

Commencement: to be appointed (see the introductory note to this Act).

PART 11
DERIVATIVE CLAIMS AND PROCEEDINGS BY MEMBERS

CHAPTER 1
DERIVATIVE CLAIMS IN ENGLAND AND WALES OR NORTHERN IRELAND

260 Derivative claims

(1) This Chapter applies to proceedings in England and Wales or Northern Ireland by a member of a company—

(a) in respect of a cause of action vested in the company, and
(b) seeking relief on behalf of the company.

This is referred to in this Chapter as a "derivative claim".

(2) A derivative claim may only be brought—

(a) under this Chapter, or
(b) in pursuance of an order of the court in proceedings under section 994 (proceedings for protection of members against unfair prejudice).

(3) A derivative claim under this Chapter may be brought only in respect of a cause of action arising from an actual or proposed act or omission involving negligence, default, breach of duty or breach of trust by a director of the company.

The cause of action may be against the director or another person (or both).

(4) It is immaterial whether the cause of action arose before or after the person seeking to bring or continue the derivative claim became a member of the company.

(5) For the purposes of this Chapter—

(a) "director" includes a former director;
(b) a shadow director is treated as a director; and
(c) references to a member of a company include a person who is not a member but to whom shares in the company have been transferred or transmitted by operation of law.

[1648]

NOTES

Commencement: to be appointed (see the introductory note to this Act).

261 Application for permission to continue derivative claim

(1) A member of a company who brings a derivative claim under this Chapter must apply to the court for permission (in Northern Ireland, leave) to continue it.

(2) If it appears to the court that the application and the evidence filed by the applicant in support of it do not disclose a prima facie case for giving permission (or leave), the court—

(a) must dismiss the application, and
(b) may make any consequential order it considers appropriate.

(3) If the application is not dismissed under subsection (2), the court—

(a) may give directions as to the evidence to be provided by the company, and
(b) may adjourn the proceedings to enable the evidence to be obtained.

(4) On hearing the application, the court may—

(a) give permission (or leave) to continue the claim on such terms as it thinks fit,
(b) refuse permission (or leave) and dismiss the claim, or
(c) adjourn the proceedings on the application and give such directions as it thinks fit.

[1649]

NOTES

Commencement: to be appointed (see the introductory note to this Act).

262 Application for permission to continue claim as a derivative claim

(1) This section applies where—
(a) a company has brought a claim, and
(b) the cause of action on which the claim is based could be pursued as a derivative claim under this Chapter.

(2) A member of the company may apply to the court for permission (in Northern Ireland, leave) to continue the claim as a derivative claim on the ground that—
(a) the manner in which the company commenced or continued the claim amounts to an abuse of the process of the court,
(b) the company has failed to prosecute the claim diligently, and
(c) it is appropriate for the member to continue the claim as a derivative claim.

(3) If it appears to the court that the application and the evidence filed by the applicant in support of it do not disclose a prima facie case for giving permission (or leave), the court—
(a) must dismiss the application, and
(b) may make any consequential order it considers appropriate.

(4) If the application is not dismissed under subsection (3), the court—
(a) may give directions as to the evidence to be provided by the company, and
(b) may adjourn the proceedings to enable the evidence to be obtained.

(5) On hearing the application, the court may—
(a) give permission (or leave) to continue the claim as a derivative claim on such terms as it thinks fit,
(b) refuse permission (or leave) and dismiss the application, or
(c) adjourn the proceedings on the application and give such directions as it thinks fit.
[1650]

NOTES
Commencement: to be appointed (see the introductory note to this Act).

263 Whether permission to be given

(1) The following provisions have effect where a member of a company applies for permission (in Northern Ireland, leave) under section 261 or 262.

(2) Permission (or leave) must be refused if the court is satisfied—
(a) that a person acting in accordance with section 172 (duty to promote the success of the company) would not seek to continue the claim, or
(b) where the cause of action arises from an act or omission that is yet to occur, that the act or omission has been authorised by the company, or
(c) where the cause of action arises from an act or omission that has already occurred, that the act or omission—
  (i) was authorised by the company before it occurred, or
  (ii) has been ratified by the company since it occurred.

(3) In considering whether to give permission (or leave) the court must take into account, in particular—
(a) whether the member is acting in good faith in seeking to continue the claim;
(b) the importance that a person acting in accordance with section 172 (duty to promote the success of the company) would attach to continuing it;
(c) where the cause of action results from an act or omission that is yet to occur, whether the act or omission could be, and in the circumstances would be likely to be—
  (i) authorised by the company before it occurs, or
  (ii) ratified by the company after it occurs;
(d) where the cause of action arises from an act or omission that has already occurred, whether the act or omission could be, and in the circumstances would be likely to be, ratified by the company;
(e) whether the company has decided not to pursue the claim;
(f) whether the act or omission in respect of which the claim is brought gives rise to a cause of action that the member could pursue in his own right rather than on behalf of the company.

(4) In considering whether to give permission (or leave) the court shall have particular regard to any evidence before it as to the views of members of the company who have no personal interest, direct or indirect, in the matter.

(5) The Secretary of State may by regulations—
- (a) amend subsection (2) so as to alter or add to the circumstances in which permission (or leave) is to be refused;
- (b) amend subsection (3) so as to alter or add to the matters that the court is required to take into account in considering whether to give permission (or leave).

(6) Before making any such regulations the Secretary of State shall consult such persons as he considers appropriate.

(7) Regulations under this section are subject to affirmative resolution procedure.

[1651]

NOTES

Commencement: to be appointed (see the introductory note to this Act).

264 Application for permission to continue derivative claim brought by another member

(1) This section applies where a member of a company ("the claimant")—
- (a) has brought a derivative claim,
- (b) has continued as a derivative claim a claim brought by the company, or
- (c) has continued a derivative claim under this section.

(2) Another member of the company ("the applicant") may apply to the court for permission (in Northern Ireland, leave) to continue the claim on the ground that—
- (a) the manner in which the proceedings have been commenced or continued by the claimant amounts to an abuse of the process of the court,
- (b) the claimant has failed to prosecute the claim diligently, and
- (c) it is appropriate for the applicant to continue the claim as a derivative claim.

(3) If it appears to the court that the application and the evidence filed by the applicant in support of it do not disclose a prima facie case for giving permission (or leave), the court—
- (a) must dismiss the application, and
- (b) may make any consequential order it considers appropriate.

(4) If the application is not dismissed under subsection (3), the court—
- (a) may give directions as to the evidence to be provided by the company, and
- (b) may adjourn the proceedings to enable the evidence to be obtained.

(5) On hearing the application, the court may—
- (a) give permission (or leave) to continue the claim on such terms as it thinks fit,
- (b) refuse permission (or leave) and dismiss the application, or
- (c) adjourn the proceedings on the application and give such directions as it thinks fit.

[1652]

NOTES

Commencement: to be appointed (see the introductory note to this Act).

265–269 (*Outside the scope of this work.*)

PART 12
COMPANY SECRETARIES

Private companies

270 Private company not required to have secretary

(1) A private company is not required to have a secretary.

(2) References in the Companies Acts to a private company "without a secretary" are to a private company that for the time being is taking advantage of the exemption in subsection (1); and references to a private company "with a secretary" shall be construed accordingly.

(3) In the case of a private company without a secretary—
  (a) anything authorised or required to be given or sent to, or served on, the company by being sent to its secretary—
    (i) may be given or sent to, or served on, the company itself, and
    (ii) if addressed to the secretary shall be treated as addressed to the company; and
  (b) anything else required or authorised to be done by or to the secretary of the company may be done by or to—
    (i) a director, or
    (ii) a person authorised generally or specifically in that behalf by the directors.

[1653]

NOTES

Commencement: to be appointed (see the introductory note to this Act).

271–273 (*Outside the scope of this work.*)

Provisions applying to private companies with a secretary and to public companies

274 Discharge of functions where office vacant or secretary unable to act

Where in the case of any company the office of secretary is vacant, or there is for any other reason no secretary capable of acting, anything required or authorised to be done by or to the secretary may be done—
  (a) by or to an assistant or deputy secretary (if any), or
  (b) if there is no assistant or deputy secretary or none capable of acting, by or to any person authorised generally or specifically in that behalf by the directors.

[1654]

NOTES

Commencement: to be appointed (see the introductory note to this Act).

275 Duty to keep register of secretaries

(1) A company must keep a register of its secretaries.

(2) The register must contain the required particulars (see sections 277 to 279) of the person who is, or persons who are, the secretary or joint secretaries of the company.

(3) The register must be kept available for inspection—
  (a) at the company's registered office, or
  (b) at a place specified in regulations under section 1136.

(4) The company must give notice to the registrar—
  (a) of the place at which the register is kept available for inspection, and
  (b) of any change in that place,

unless it has at all times been kept at the company's registered office.

(5) The register must be open to the inspection—
  (a) of any member of the company without charge, and
  (b) of any other person on payment of such fee as may be prescribed.

(6) If default is made in complying with subsection (1), (2) or (3), or if default is made for 14 days in complying with subsection (4), or if an inspection required under subsection (5) is refused, an offence is committed by—
  (a) the company, and
  (b) every officer of the company who is in default.

For this purpose a shadow director is treated as an officer of the company.

(7) A person guilty of an offence under this section is liable on summary conviction to a fine not exceeding level 5 on the standard scale and, for continued contravention, a daily default fine not exceeding one-tenth of level 5 on the standard scale.

(8) In the case of a refusal of inspection of the register, the court may by order compel an immediate inspection of it.

[1655]

NOTES

Commencement: to be appointed (see the introductory note to this Act).

276 Duty to notify registrar of changes

(1) A company must, within the period of 14 days from—

(a) a person becoming or ceasing to be its secretary or one of its joint secretaries, or

(b) the occurrence of any change in the particulars contained in its register of secretaries,

give notice to the registrar of the change and of the date on which it occurred.

(2) Notice of a person having become secretary, or one of joint secretaries, of the company must be accompanied by a consent by that person to act in the relevant capacity.

(3) If default is made in complying with this section, an offence is committed by every officer of the company who is in default.

For this purpose a shadow director is treated as an officer of the company.

(4) A person guilty of an offence under this section is liable on summary conviction to a fine not exceeding level 5 on the standard scale and, for continued contravention, a daily default fine not exceeding one-tenth of level 5 on the standard scale.

[1656]

NOTES

Commencement: to be appointed (see the introductory note to this Act).

277 Particulars of secretaries to be registered: individuals

(1) A company's register of secretaries must contain the following particulars in the case of an individual—

(a) name and any former name;

(b) address.

(2) For the purposes of this section "name" means a person's Christian name (or other forename) and surname, except that in the case of—

(a) a peer, or

(b) an individual usually known by a title,

the title may be stated instead of his Christian name (or other forename) and surname or in addition to either or both of them.

(3) For the purposes of this section a "former name" means a name by which the individual was formerly known for business purposes.

Where a person is or was formerly known by more than one such name, each of them must be stated.

(4) It is not necessary for the register to contain particulars of a former name in the following cases—

(a) in the case of a peer or an individual normally known by a British title, where the name is one by which the person was known previous to the adoption of or succession to the title;

(b) in the case of any person, where the former name—

(i) was changed or disused before the person attained the age of 16 years, or

(ii) has been changed or disused for 20 years or more.

(5) The address required to be stated in the register is a service address. This may be stated to be "The company's registered office".

[1657]

NOTES

Commencement: to be appointed (see the introductory note to this Act).

278 Particulars of secretaries to be registered: corporate secretaries and firms

(1) A company's register of secretaries must contain the following particulars in the case of a body corporate, or a firm that is a legal person under the law by which it is governed—

(a) corporate or firm name;
(b) registered or principal office;
(c) in the case of an EEA company to which the First Company Law Directive (68/151/EEC) applies, particulars of—
  (i) the register in which the company file mentioned in Article 3 of that Directive is kept (including details of the relevant state), and
  (ii) the registration number in that register;
(d) in any other case, particulars of—
  (i) the legal form of the company or firm and the law by which it is governed, and
  (ii) if applicable, the register in which it is entered (including details of the state) and its registration number in that register.

(2) If all the partners in a firm are joint secretaries it is sufficient to state the particulars that would be required if the firm were a legal person and the firm had been appointed secretary.

[1658]

NOTES

Commencement: to be appointed (see the introductory note to this Act).

279 Particulars of secretaries to be registered: power to make regulations

(1) The Secretary of State may make provision by regulations amending—
section 277 (particulars of secretaries to be registered: individuals), or
section 278 (particulars of secretaries to be registered: corporate secretaries and firms),
so as to add to or remove items from the particulars required to be contained in a company's register of secretaries.

(2) Regulations under this section are subject to affirmative resolution procedure.

[1659]

NOTES

Commencement: to be appointed (see the introductory note to this Act).

280 Acts done by person in dual capacity

A provision requiring or authorising a thing to be done by or to a director and the secretary of a company is not satisfied by its being done by or to the same person acting both as director and as, or in place of, the secretary.

[1660]

NOTES

Commencement: to be appointed (see the introductory note to this Act).

PART 13
RESOLUTIONS AND MEETINGS

CHAPTER 1
GENERAL PROVISIONS ABOUT RESOLUTIONS

281 Resolutions

(1) A resolution of the members (or of a class of members) of a private company must be passed—
(a) as a written resolution in accordance with Chapter 2, or
(b) at a meeting of the members (to which the provisions of Chapter 3 apply).

(2) A resolution of the members (or of a class of members) of a public company must be passed at a meeting of the members (to which the provisions of Chapter 3 and, where relevant, Chapter 4 apply).

(3) Where a provision of the Companies Acts—

(a) requires a resolution of a company, or of the members (or a class of members) of a company, and

(b) does not specify what kind of resolution is required,

what is required is an ordinary resolution unless the company's articles require a higher majority (or unanimity).

(4) Nothing in this Part affects any enactment or rule of law as to—

(a) things done otherwise than by passing a resolution,

(b) circumstances in which a resolution is or is not treated as having been passed, or

(c) cases in which a person is precluded from alleging that a resolution has not been duly passed.

[1661]

NOTES

Commencement: to be appointed (see the introductory note to this Act).

282 Ordinary resolutions

(1) An ordinary resolution of the members (or of a class of members) of a company means a resolution that is passed by a simple majority.

(2) A written resolution is passed by a simple majority if it is passed by members representing a simple majority of the total voting rights of eligible members (see Chapter 2).

(3) A resolution passed at a meeting on a show of hands is passed by a simple majority if it is passed by a simple majority of—

(a) the members who, being entitled to do so, vote in person on the resolution, and

(b) the persons who vote on the resolution as duly appointed proxies of members entitled to vote on it.

(4) A resolution passed on a poll taken at a meeting is passed by a simple majority if it is passed by members representing a simple majority of the total voting rights of members who (being entitled to do so) vote in person or by proxy on the resolution.

(5) Anything that may be done by ordinary resolution may also be done by special resolution.

[1662]

NOTES

Commencement: to be appointed (see the introductory note to this Act).

283 Special resolutions

(1) A special resolution of the members (or of a class of members) of a company means a resolution passed by a majority of not less than 75%.

(2) A written resolution is passed by a majority of not less than 75% if it is passed by members representing not less than 75% of the total voting rights of eligible members (see Chapter 2).

(3) Where a resolution of a private company is passed as a written resolution—

(a) the resolution is not a special resolution unless it stated that it was proposed as a special resolution, and

(b) if the resolution so stated, it may only be passed as a special resolution.

(4) A resolution passed at a meeting on a show of hands is passed by a majority of not less than 75% if it is passed by not less than 75% of—

(a) the members who, being entitled to do so, vote in person on the resolution, and

(b) the persons who vote on the resolution as duly appointed proxies of members entitled to vote on it.

(5) A resolution passed on a poll taken at a meeting is passed by a majority of not less than 75% if it is passed by members representing not less than 75% of the total voting rights of the members who (being entitled to do so) vote in person or by proxy on the resolution.

(6) Where a resolution is passed at a meeting—

(a) the resolution is not a special resolution unless the notice of the meeting included the text of the resolution and specified the intention to propose the resolution as a special resolution, and

(b) if the notice of the meeting so specified, the resolution may only be passed as a special resolution.

[1663]

NOTES

Commencement: to be appointed (see the introductory note to this Act).

284 Votes: general rules

(1) On a vote on a written resolution—

(a) in the case of a company having a share capital, every member has one vote in respect of each share or each £10 of stock held by him, and

(b) in any other case, every member has one vote.

(2) On a vote on a resolution on a show of hands at a meeting—

(a) every member present in person has one vote, and

(b) every proxy present who has been duly appointed by a member entitled to vote on the resolution has one vote.

(3) On a vote on a resolution on a poll taken at a meeting—

(a) in the case of a company having a share capital, every member has one vote in respect of each share or each £10 of stock held by him, and

(b) in any other case, every member has one vote.

(4) The provisions of this section have effect subject to any provision of the company's articles.

[1664]

NOTES

Commencement: to be appointed (see the introductory note to this Act).

285 Votes: specific requirements

(1) Where a member entitled to vote on a resolution has appointed one proxy only, and the company's articles provide that the proxy has fewer votes in a vote on a resolution on a show of hands taken at a meeting than the member would have if he were present in person—

(a) the provision about how many votes the proxy has on a show of hands is void, and

(b) the proxy has the same number of votes on a show of hands as the member who appointed him would have if he were present at the meeting.

(2) Where a member entitled to vote on a resolution has appointed more than one proxy, subsection (1) applies as if the references to the proxy were references to the proxies taken together.

(3) In relation to a resolution required or authorised by an enactment, if a private company's articles provide that a member has a different number of votes in relation to a resolution when it is passed as a written resolution and when it is passed on a poll taken at a meeting—

(a) the provision about how many votes a member has in relation to the resolution passed on a poll is void, and

(b) a member has the same number of votes in relation to the resolution when it is passed on a poll as he has when it is passed as a written resolution.

[1665]

NOTES

Commencement: to be appointed (see the introductory note to this Act).

286 Votes of joint holders of shares

(1) In the case of joint holders of shares of a company, only the vote of the senior holder who votes (and any proxies duly authorised by him) may be counted by the company.

(2) For the purposes of this section, the senior holder of a share is determined by the order in which the names of the joint holders appear in the register of members.

(3) Subsections (1) and (2) have effect subject to any provision of the company's articles.

[1666]

NOTES

Commencement: to be appointed (see the introductory note to this Act).

287 Saving for provisions of articles as to determination of entitlement to vote

Nothing in this Chapter affects—

(a) any provision of a company's articles—

(i) requiring an objection to a person's entitlement to vote on a resolution to be made in accordance with the articles, and

(ii) for the determination of any such objection to be final and conclusive, or

(b) the grounds on which such a determination may be questioned in legal proceedings.

[1667]

NOTES

Commencement: to be appointed (see the introductory note to this Act).

CHAPTER 2
WRITTEN RESOLUTIONS

General provisions about written resolutions

288 Written resolutions of private companies

(1) In the Companies Acts a "written resolution" means a resolution of a private company proposed and passed in accordance with this Chapter.

(2) The following may not be passed as a written resolution—

(a) a resolution under section 168 removing a director before the expiration of his period of office;

(b) a resolution under section 510 removing an auditor before the expiration of his term of office.

(3) A resolution may be proposed as a written resolution—

(a) by the directors of a private company (see section 291), or

(b) by the members of a private company (see sections 292 to 295).

(4) References in enactments passed or made before this Chapter comes into force to—

(a) a resolution of a company in general meeting, or

(b) a resolution of a meeting of a class of members of the company,

have effect as if they included references to a written resolution of the members, or of a class of members, of a private company (as appropriate).

(5) A written resolution of a private company has effect as if passed (as the case may be)—

(a) by the company in general meeting, or

(b) by a meeting of a class of members of the company,

and references in enactments passed or made before this section comes into force to a meeting at which a resolution is passed or to members voting in favour of a resolution shall be construed accordingly.

[1668]

NOTES

Commencement: to be appointed (see the introductory note to this Act).

289 Eligible members

(1) In relation to a resolution proposed as a written resolution of a private company, the eligible members are the members who would have been entitled to vote on the resolution on the circulation date of the resolution (see section 290).

(2) If the persons entitled to vote on a written resolution change during the course of the day that is the circulation date of the resolution, the eligible members are the persons entitled to vote on the resolution at the time that the first copy of the resolution is sent or submitted to a member for his agreement.

[1669]

NOTES

Commencement: to be appointed (see the introductory note to this Act).

Circulation of written resolutions

290 Circulation date

References in this Part to the circulation date of a written resolution are to the date on which copies of it are sent or submitted to members in accordance with this Chapter (or if copies are sent or submitted to members on different days, to the first of those days).

[1670]

NOTES

Commencement: to be appointed (see the introductory note to this Act).

291 Circulation of written resolutions proposed by directors

(1) This section applies to a resolution proposed as a written resolution by the directors of the company.

(2) The company must send or submit a copy of the resolution to every eligible member.

(3) The company must do so—

(a) by sending copies at the same time (so far as reasonably practicable) to all eligible members in hard copy form, in electronic form or by means of a website, or

(b) if it is possible to do so without undue delay, by submitting the same copy to each eligible member in turn (or different copies to each of a number of eligible members in turn),

or by sending copies to some members in accordance with paragraph (a) and submitting a copy or copies to other members in accordance with paragraph (b).

(4) The copy of the resolution must be accompanied by a statement informing the member—

(a) how to signify agreement to the resolution (see section 296), and

(b) as to the date by which the resolution must be passed if it is not to lapse (see section 297).

(5) In the event of default in complying with this section, an offence is committed by every officer of the company who is in default.

(6) A person guilty of an offence under this section is liable—

(a) on conviction on indictment, to a fine;

(b) on summary conviction, to a fine not exceeding the statutory maximum.

(7) The validity of the resolution, if passed, is not affected by a failure to comply with this section.

[1671]

NOTES

Commencement: to be appointed (see the introductory note to this Act).

292 Members' power to require circulation of written resolution

(1) The members of a private company may require the company to circulate a resolution that may properly be moved and is proposed to be moved as a written resolution.

(2) Any resolution may properly be moved as a written resolution unless—

(a) it would, if passed, be ineffective (whether by reason of inconsistency with any enactment or the company's constitution or otherwise),

(b) it is defamatory of any person, or
(c) it is frivolous or vexatious.

(3) Where the members require a company to circulate a resolution they may require the company to circulate with it a statement of not more than 1,000 words on the subject matter of the resolution.

(4) A company is required to circulate the resolution and any accompanying statement once it has received requests that it do so from members representing not less than the requisite percentage of the total voting rights of all members entitled to vote on the resolution.

(5) The "requisite percentage" is 5% or such lower percentage as is specified for this purpose in the company's articles.

(6) A request—
(a) may be in hard copy form or in electronic form,
(b) must identify the resolution and any accompanying statement, and
(c) must be authenticated by the person or persons making it.

[1672]

NOTES

Commencement: to be appointed (see the introductory note to this Act).

293 Circulation of written resolution proposed by members

(1) A company that is required under section 292 to circulate a resolution must send or submit to every eligible member—
(a) a copy of the resolution, and
(b) a copy of any accompanying statement.

This is subject to section 294(2) (deposit or tender of sum in respect of expenses of circulation) and section 295 (application not to circulate members' statement).

(2) The company must do so—
(a) by sending copies at the same time (so far as reasonably practicable) to all eligible members in hard copy form, in electronic form or by means of a website, or
(b) if it is possible to do so without undue delay, by submitting the same copy to each eligible member in turn (or different copies to each of a number of eligible members in turn),

or by sending copies to some members in accordance with paragraph (a) and submitting a copy or copies to other members in accordance with paragraph (b).

(3) The company must send or submit the copies (or, if copies are sent or submitted to members on different days, the first of those copies) not more than 21 days after it becomes subject to the requirement under section 292 to circulate the resolution.

(4) The copy of the resolution must be accompanied by guidance as to—
(a) how to signify agreement to the resolution (see section 296), and
(b) the date by which the resolution must be passed if it is not to lapse (see section 297).

(5) In the event of default in complying with this section, an offence is committed by every officer of the company who is in default.

(6) A person guilty of an offence under this section is liable—
(a) on conviction on indictment, to a fine;
(b) on summary conviction, to a fine not exceeding the statutory maximum.

(7) The validity of the resolution, if passed, is not affected by a failure to comply with this section.

[1673]

NOTES

Commencement: to be appointed (see the introductory note to this Act).

294 Expenses of circulation

(1) The expenses of the company in complying with section 293 must be paid by the members who requested the circulation of the resolution unless the company resolves otherwise.

(2) Unless the company has previously so resolved, it is not bound to comply with that section unless there is deposited with or tendered to it a sum reasonably sufficient to meet its expenses in doing so.

[1674]

NOTES

Commencement: to be appointed (see the introductory note to this Act).

295 Application not to circulate members' statement

(1) A company is not required to circulate a members' statement under section 293 if, on an application by the company or another person who claims to be aggrieved, the court is satisfied that the rights conferred by section 292 and that section are being abused.

(2) The court may order the members who requested the circulation of the statement to pay the whole or part of the company's costs (in Scotland, expenses) on such an application, even if they are not parties to the application.

[1675]

NOTES

Commencement: to be appointed (see the introductory note to this Act).

Agreeing to written resolutions

296 Procedure for signifying agreement to written resolution

(1) A member signifies his agreement to a proposed written resolution when the company receives from him (or from someone acting on his behalf) an authenticated document—

(a) identifying the resolution to which it relates, and
(b) indicating his agreement to the resolution.

(2) The document must be sent to the company in hard copy form or in electronic form.

(3) A member's agreement to a written resolution, once signified, may not be revoked.

(4) A written resolution is passed when the required majority of eligible members have signified their agreement to it.

[1676]

NOTES

Commencement: to be appointed (see the introductory note to this Act).

297 Period for agreeing to written resolution

(1) A proposed written resolution lapses if it is not passed before the end of—

(a) the period specified for this purpose in the company's articles, or
(b) if none is specified, the period of 28 days beginning with the circulation date.

(2) The agreement of a member to a written resolution is ineffective if signified after the expiry of that period.

[1677]

NOTES

Commencement: to be appointed (see the introductory note to this Act).

Supplementary

298 Sending documents relating to written resolutions by electronic means

(1) Where a company has given an electronic address in any document containing or accompanying a proposed written resolution, it is deemed to have agreed that any document

or information relating to that resolution may be sent by electronic means to that address (subject to any conditions or limitations specified in the document).

(2) In this section "electronic address" means any address or number used for the purposes of sending or receiving documents or information by electronic means.

[1678]

NOTES

Commencement: to be appointed (see the introductory note to this Act).

299 Publication of written resolution on website

(1) This section applies where a company sends—

(a) a written resolution, or

(b) a statement relating to a written resolution,

to a person by means of a website.

(2) The resolution or statement is not validly sent for the purposes of this Chapter unless the resolution is available on the website throughout the period beginning with the circulation date and ending on the date on which the resolution lapses under section 297.

[1679]

NOTES

Commencement: to be appointed (see the introductory note to this Act).

300 Relationship between this Chapter and provisions of company's articles

A provision of the articles of a private company is void in so far as it would have the effect that a resolution that is required by or otherwise provided for in an enactment could not be proposed and passed as a written resolution.

[1680]

NOTES

Commencement: to be appointed (see the introductory note to this Act).

CHAPTER 3
RESOLUTIONS AT MEETINGS

General provisions about resolutions at meetings

301 Resolutions at general meetings

A resolution of the members of a company is validly passed at a general meeting if—

(a) notice of the meeting and of the resolution is given, and

(b) the meeting is held and conducted,

in accordance with the provisions of this Chapter (and, where relevant, Chapter 4) and the company's articles.

[1681]

NOTES

Commencement: to be appointed (see the introductory note to this Act).

Calling meetings

302 Directors' power to call general meetings

The directors of a company may call a general meeting of the company.

[1682]

NOTES

Commencement: to be appointed (see the introductory note to this Act).

303 Members' power to require directors to call general meeting

(1) The members of a company may require the directors to call a general meeting of the company.

(2) The directors are required to call a general meeting once the company has received requests to do so from—

(a) members representing at least the required percentage of such of the paid-up capital of the company as carries the right of voting at general meetings of the company (excluding any paid-up capital held as treasury shares); or

(b) in the case of a company not having a share capital, members who represent at least the required percentage of the total voting rights of all the members having a right to vote at general meetings.

(3) The required percentage is 10% unless, in the case of a private company, more than twelve months has elapsed since the end of the last general meeting—

(a) called in pursuance of a requirement under this section, or

(b) in relation to which any members of the company had (by virtue of an enactment, the company's articles or otherwise) rights with respect to the circulation of a resolution no less extensive than they would have had if the meeting had been so called at their request,

in which case the required percentage is 5%.

(4) A request—

(a) must state the general nature of the business to be dealt with at the meeting, and

(b) may include the text of a resolution that may properly be moved and is intended to be moved at the meeting.

(5) A resolution may properly be moved at a meeting unless—

(a) it would, if passed, be ineffective (whether by reason of inconsistency with any enactment or the company's constitution or otherwise),

(b) it is defamatory of any person, or

(c) it is frivolous or vexatious.

(6) A request—

(a) may be in hard copy form or in electronic form, and

(b) must be authenticated by the person or persons making it.

[1683]

NOTES

Commencement: to be appointed (see the introductory note to this Act).

304 Directors' duty to call meetings required by members

(1) Directors required under section 303 to call a general meeting of the company must call a meeting—

(a) within 21 days from the date on which they become subject to the requirement, and

(b) to be held on a date not more than 28 days after the date of the notice convening the meeting.

(2) If the requests received by the company identify a resolution intended to be moved at the meeting, the notice of the meeting must include notice of the resolution.

(3) The business that may be dealt with at the meeting includes a resolution of which notice is given in accordance with this section.

(4) If the resolution is to be proposed as a special resolution, the directors are treated as not having duly called the meeting if they do not give the required notice of the resolution in accordance with section 283.

[1684]

NOTES

Commencement: to be appointed (see the introductory note to this Act).

305 Power of members to call meeting at company's expense

(1) If the directors—

(a) are required under section 303 to call a meeting, and
(b) do not do so in accordance with section 304,

the members who requested the meeting, or any of them representing more than one half of the total voting rights of all of them, may themselves call a general meeting.

(2) Where the requests received by the company included the text of a resolution intended to be moved at the meeting, the notice of the meeting must include notice of the resolution.

(3) The meeting must be called for a date not more than three months after the date on which the directors become subject to the requirement to call a meeting.

(4) The meeting must be called in the same manner, as nearly as possible, as that in which meetings are required to be called by directors of the company.

(5) The business which may be dealt with at the meeting includes a resolution of which notice is given in accordance with this section.

(6) Any reasonable expenses incurred by the members requesting the meeting by reason of the failure of the directors duly to call a meeting must be reimbursed by the company.

(7) Any sum so reimbursed shall be retained by the company out of any sums due or to become due from the company by way of fees or other remuneration in respect of the services of such of the directors as were in default.

[1685]

NOTES

Commencement: to be appointed (see the introductory note to this Act).

306 Power of court to order meeting

(1) This section applies if for any reason it is impracticable—
(a) to call a meeting of a company in any manner in which meetings of that company may be called, or
(b) to conduct the meeting in the manner prescribed by the company's articles or this Act.

(2) The court may, either of its own motion or on the application—
(a) of a director of the company, or
(b) of a member of the company who would be entitled to vote at the meeting,

order a meeting to be called, held and conducted in any manner the court thinks fit.

(3) Where such an order is made, the court may give such ancillary or consequential directions as it thinks expedient.

(4) Such directions may include a direction that one member of the company present at the meeting be deemed to constitute a quorum.

(5) A meeting called, held and conducted in accordance with an order under this section is deemed for all purposes to be a meeting of the company duly called, held and conducted.

[1686]

NOTES

Commencement: to be appointed (see the introductory note to this Act).

Notice of meetings

307 Notice required of general meeting

(1) A general meeting of a private company (other than an adjourned meeting) must be called by notice of at least 14 days.

(2) A general meeting of a public company (other than an adjourned meeting) must be called by notice of—
(a) in the case of an annual general meeting, at least 21 days, and
(b) in any other case, at least 14 days.

(3) The company's articles may require a longer period of notice than that specified in subsection (1) or (2).

(4) A general meeting may be called by shorter notice than that otherwise required if shorter notice is agreed by the members.

(5) The shorter notice must be agreed to by a majority in number of the members having a right to attend and vote at the meeting, being a majority who—
- (a) together hold not less than the requisite percentage in nominal value of the shares giving a right to attend and vote at the meeting (excluding any shares in the company held as treasury shares), or
- (b) in the case of a company not having a share capital, together represent not less than the requisite percentage of the total voting rights at that meeting of all the members.

(6) The requisite percentage is—
- (a) in the case of a private company, 90% or such higher percentage (not exceeding 95%) as may be specified in the company's articles;
- (b) in the case of a public company, 95%.

(7) Subsections (5) and (6) do not apply to an annual general meeting of a public company (see instead section 337(2)).

[1687]

NOTES

Commencement: to be appointed (see the introductory note to this Act).

308 Manner in which notice to be given

Notice of a general meeting of a company must be given—
- (a) in hard copy form,
- (b) in electronic form, or
- (c) by means of a website (see section 309),

or partly by one such means and partly by another.

[1688]

NOTES

Commencement: 20 January 2007.

309 Publication of notice of meeting on website

(1) Notice of a meeting is not validly given by a company by means of a website unless it is given in accordance with this section.

(2) When the company notifies a member of the presence of the notice on the website the notification must—
- (a) state that it concerns a notice of a company meeting,
- (b) specify the place, date and time of the meeting, and
- (c) in the case of a public company, state whether the meeting will be an annual general meeting.

(3) The notice must be available on the website throughout the period beginning with the date of that notification and ending with the conclusion of the meeting.

[1689]

NOTES

Commencement: 20 January 2007.

310 Persons entitled to receive notice of meetings

(1) Notice of a general meeting of a company must be sent to—
- (a) every member of the company, and
- (b) every director.

(2) In subsection (1), the reference to members includes any person who is entitled to a share in consequence of the death or bankruptcy of a member, if the company has been notified of their entitlement.

(3) In subsection (2), the reference to the bankruptcy of a member includes—
(a) the sequestration of the estate of a member;
(b) a member's estate being the subject of a protected trust deed (within the meaning of the Bankruptcy (Scotland) Act 1985 (c 66)).

(4) This section has effect subject to—
(a) any enactment, and
(b) any provision of the company's articles.

[1690]

NOTES

Commencement: to be appointed (see the introductory note to this Act).

311 Contents of notices of meetings

(1) Notice of a general meeting of a company must state—
(a) the time and date of the meeting, and
(b) the place of the meeting.

(2) Notice of a general meeting of a company must state the general nature of the business to be dealt with at the meeting.

This subsection has effect subject to any provision of the company's articles.

[1691]

NOTES

Commencement: to be appointed (see the introductory note to this Act).

312 Resolution requiring special notice

(1) Where by any provision of the Companies Acts special notice is required of a resolution, the resolution is not effective unless notice of the intention to move it has been given to the company at least 28 days before the meeting at which it is moved.

(2) The company must, where practicable, give its members notice of any such resolution in the same manner and at the same time as it gives notice of the meeting.

(3) Where that is not practicable, the company must give its members notice at least 14 days before the meeting—
(a) by advertisement in a newspaper having an appropriate circulation, or
(b) in any other manner allowed by the company's articles.

(4) If, after notice of the intention to move such a resolution has been given to the company, a meeting is called for a date 28 days or less after the notice has been given, the notice is deemed to have been properly given, though not given within the time required.

[1692]

NOTES

Commencement: to be appointed (see the introductory note to this Act).

313 Accidental failure to give notice of resolution or meeting

(1) Where a company gives notice of—
(a) a general meeting, or
(b) a resolution intended to be moved at a general meeting,

any accidental failure to give notice to one or more persons shall be disregarded for the purpose of determining whether notice of the meeting or resolution (as the case may be) is duly given.

(2) Except in relation to notice given under—
(a) section 304 (notice of meetings required by members),
(b) section 305 (notice of meetings called by members), or
(c) section 339 (notice of resolutions at AGMs proposed by members),

subsection (1) has effect subject to any provision of the company's articles.

[1693]

NOTES

Commencement: to be appointed (see the introductory note to this Act).

Members' statements

314 Members' power to require circulation of statements

(1) The members of a company may require the company to circulate, to members of the company entitled to receive notice of a general meeting, a statement of not more than 1,000 words with respect to—

(a) a matter referred to in a proposed resolution to be dealt with at that meeting, or
(b) other business to be dealt with at that meeting.

(2) A company is required to circulate a statement once it has received requests to do so from—

(a) members representing at least 5% of the total voting rights of all the members who have a relevant right to vote (excluding any voting rights attached to any shares in the company held as treasury shares), or
(b) at least 100 members who have a relevant right to vote and hold shares in the company on which there has been paid up an average sum, per member, of at least £100.

See also section 153 (exercise of rights where shares held on behalf of others).

(3) In subsection (2), a "relevant right to vote" means—

(a) in relation to a statement with respect to a matter referred to in a proposed resolution, a right to vote on that resolution at the meeting to which the requests relate, and
(b) in relation to any other statement, a right to vote at the meeting to which the requests relate.

(4) A request—

(a) may be in hard copy form or in electronic form,
(b) must identify the statement to be circulated,
(c) must be authenticated by the person or persons making it, and
(d) must be received by the company at least one week before the meeting to which it relates.

[1694]

NOTES

Commencement: to be appointed (see the introductory note to this Act).

315 Company's duty to circulate members' statement

(1) A company that is required under section 314, to circulate a statement must send a copy of it to each member of the company entitled to receive notice of the meeting—

(a) in the same manner as the notice of the meeting, and
(b) at the same time as, or as soon as reasonably practicable after, it gives notice of the meeting.

(2) Subsection (1) has effect subject to section 316(2) (deposit or tender of sum in respect of expenses of circulation) and section 317 (application not to circulate members' statement).

(3) In the event of default in complying with this section, an offence is committed by every officer of the company who is in default.

(4) A person guilty of an offence under this section is liable—

(a) on conviction on indictment, to a fine;
(b) on summary conviction, to a fine not exceeding the statutory maximum.

[1695]

NOTES

Commencement: to be appointed (see the introductory note to this Act).

316 Expenses of circulating members' statement

(1) The expenses of the company in complying with section 315 need not be paid by the members who requested the circulation of the statement if—

(a) the meeting to which the requests relate is an annual general meeting of a public company, and

(b) requests sufficient to require the company to circulate the statement are received before the end of the financial year preceding the meeting.

(2) Otherwise—

(a) the expenses of the company in complying with that section must be paid by the members who requested the circulation of the statement unless the company resolves otherwise, and

(b) unless the company has previously so resolved, it is not bound to comply with that section unless there is deposited with or tendered to it, not later than one week before the meeting, a sum reasonably sufficient to meet its expenses in doing so.

[1696]

NOTES

Commencement: to be appointed (see the introductory note to this Act).

317 Application not to circulate members' statement

(1) A company is not required to circulate a members' statement under section 315 if, on an application by the company or another person who claims to be aggrieved, the court is satisfied that the rights conferred by section 314 and that section are being abused.

(2) The court may order the members who requested the circulation of the statement to pay the whole or part of the company's costs (in Scotland, expenses) on such an application, even if they are not parties to the application.

[1697]

NOTES

Commencement: to be appointed (see the introductory note to this Act).

Procedure at meetings

318 Quorum at meetings

(1) In the case of a company limited by shares or guarantee and having only one member, one qualifying person present at a meeting is a quorum.

(2) In any other case, subject to the provisions of the company's articles, two qualifying persons present at a meeting are a quorum, unless—

(a) each is a qualifying person only because he is authorised under section 323 to act as the representative of a corporation in relation to the meeting, and they are representatives of the same corporation; or

(b) each is a qualifying person only because he is appointed as proxy of a member in relation to the meeting, and they are proxies of the same member.

(3) For the purposes of this section a "qualifying person" means—

(a) an individual who is a member of the company,

(b) a person authorised under section 323 (representation of corporations at meetings) to act as the representative of a corporation in relation to the meeting, or

(c) a person appointed as proxy of a member in relation to the meeting.

[1698]

NOTES

Commencement: to be appointed (see the introductory note to this Act).

319 Chairman of meeting

(1) A member may be elected to be the chairman of a general meeting by a resolution of the company passed at the meeting.

(2) Subsection (1) is subject to any provision of the company's articles that states who may or may not be chairman.

[1699]

NOTES

Commencement: to be appointed (see the introductory note to this Act).

320 Declaration by chairman on a show of hands

(1) On a vote on a resolution at a meeting on a show of hands, a declaration by the chairman that the resolution—

(a) has or has not been passed, or
(b) passed with a particular majority,

is conclusive evidence of that fact without proof of the number or proportion of the votes recorded in favour of or against the resolution.

(2) An entry in respect of such a declaration in minutes of the meeting recorded in accordance with section 355 is also conclusive evidence of that fact without such proof.

(3) This section does not have effect if a poll is demanded in respect of the resolution (and the demand is not subsequently withdrawn).

[1700]

NOTES

Commencement: to be appointed (see the introductory note to this Act).

321 Right to demand a poll

(1) A provision of a company's articles is void in so far as it would have the effect of excluding the right to demand a poll at a general meeting on any question other than—

(a) the election of the chairman of the meeting, or
(b) the adjournment of the meeting.

(2) A provision of a company's articles is void in so far as it would have the effect of making ineffective a demand for a poll on any such question which is made—

(a) by not less than 5 members having the right to vote on the resolution; or
(b) by a member or members representing not less than 10% of the total voting rights of all the members having the right to vote on the resolution (excluding any voting rights attached to any shares in the company held as treasury shares); or
(c) by a member or members holding shares in the company conferring a right to vote on the resolution, being shares on which an aggregate sum has been paid up equal to not less than 10% of the total sum paid up on all the shares conferring that right (excluding shares in the company conferring a right to vote on the resolution which are held as treasury shares).

[1701]

NOTES

Commencement: to be appointed (see the introductory note to this Act).

322 Voting on a poll

On a poll taken at a general meeting of a company, a member entitled to more than one vote need not, if he votes, use all his votes or cast all the votes he uses in the same way.

[1702]

NOTES

Commencement: to be appointed (see the introductory note to this Act).

323 Representation of corporations at meetings

(1) If a corporation (whether or not a company within the meaning of this Act) is a member of a company, it may by resolution of its directors or other governing body authorise a person or persons to act as its representative or representatives at any meeting of the company.

(2) Where the corporation authorises only one person, he is entitled to exercise the same powers on behalf of the corporation as the corporation could exercise if it were an individual member of the company.

(3) Where the corporation authorises more than one person, any one of them is entitled to exercise the same powers on behalf of the corporation as the corporation could exercise if it were an individual member of the company.

(4) Where the corporation authorises more than one person and more than one of them purport to exercise a power under subsection (3)—

(a) if they purport to exercise the power in the same way, the power is treated as exercised in that way,

(b) if they do not purport to exercise the power in the same way, the power is treated as not exercised.

[1703]

NOTES

Commencement: to be appointed (see the introductory note to this Act).

Proxies

324 Rights to appoint proxies

(1) A member of a company is entitled to appoint another person as his proxy to exercise all or any of his rights to attend and to speak and vote at a meeting of the company.

(2) In the case of a company having a share capital, a member may appoint more than one proxy in relation to a meeting, provided that each proxy is appointed to exercise the rights attached to a different share or shares held by him, or (as the case may be) to a different £10, or multiple of £10, of stock held by him.

[1704]

NOTES

Commencement: to be appointed (see the introductory note to this Act).

325 Notice of meeting to contain statement of rights

(1) In every notice calling a meeting of a company there must appear, with reasonable prominence, a statement informing the member of—

(a) his rights under section 324, and

(b) any more extensive rights conferred by the company's articles to appoint more than one proxy.

(2) Failure to comply with this section does not affect the validity of the meeting or of anything done at the meeting.

(3) If this section is not complied with as respects any meeting, an offence is committed by every officer of the company who is in default.

(4) A person guilty of an offence under this section is liable on summary conviction to a fine not exceeding level 3 on the standard scale.

[1705]

NOTES

Commencement: to be appointed (see the introductory note to this Act).

326 Company-sponsored invitations to appoint proxies

(1) If for the purposes of a meeting there are issued at the company's expense invitations to members to appoint as proxy a specified person or a number of specified persons, the invitations must be issued to all members entitled to vote at the meeting.

(2) Subsection (1) is not contravened if—

(a) there is issued to a member at his request a form of appointment naming the proxy or a list of persons willing to act as proxy, and

(b) the form or list is available on request to all members entitled to vote at the meeting.

(3) If subsection (1) is contravened as respects a meeting, an offence is committed by every officer of the company who is in default.

(4) A person guilty of an offence under this section is liable on summary conviction to a fine not exceeding level 3 on the standard scale.

[1706]

NOTES

Commencement: to be appointed (see the introductory note to this Act).

327 Notice required of appointment of proxy etc

(1) This section applies to—

(a) the appointment of a proxy, and

(b) any document necessary to show the validity of, or otherwise relating to, the appointment of a proxy.

(2) Any provision of the company's articles is void in so far as it would have the effect of requiring any such appointment or document to be received by the company or another person earlier than the following time—

(a) in the case of a meeting or adjourned meeting, 48 hours before the time for holding the meeting or adjourned meeting;

(b) in the case of a poll taken more than 48 hours after it was demanded, 24 hours before the time appointed for the taking of the poll;

(c) in the case of a poll taken not more than 48 hours after it was demanded, the time at which it was demanded.

(3) In calculating the periods mentioned in subsection (2) no account shall be taken of any part of a day that is not a working day.

[1707]

NOTES

Commencement: to be appointed (see the introductory note to this Act).

328 Chairing meetings

(1) A proxy may be elected to be the chairman of a general meeting by a resolution of the company passed at the meeting.

(2) Subsection (1) is subject to any provision of the company's articles that states who may or who may not be chairman.

[1708]

NOTES

Commencement: to be appointed (see the introductory note to this Act).

329 Right of proxy to demand a poll

(1) The appointment of a proxy to vote on a matter at a meeting of a company authorises the proxy to demand, or join in demanding, a poll on that matter.

(2) In applying the provisions of section 321(2) (requirements for effective demand), a demand by a proxy counts—

(a) for the purposes of paragraph (a), as a demand by the member;

(b) for the purposes of paragraph (b), as a demand by a member representing the voting rights that the proxy is authorised to exercise;

(c) for the purposes of paragraph (c), as a demand by a member holding the shares to which those rights are attached.

[1709]

NOTES

Commencement: to be appointed (see the introductory note to this Act).

330 Notice required of termination of proxy's authority

(1) This section applies to notice that the authority of a person to act as proxy is terminated ("notice of termination").

(2) The termination of the authority of a person to act as proxy does not affect—
- (a) whether he counts in deciding whether there is a quorum at a meeting,
- (b) the validity of anything he does as chairman of a meeting, or
- (c) the validity of a poll demanded by him at a meeting,

unless the company receives notice of the termination before the commencement of the meeting.

(3) The termination of the authority of a person to act as proxy does not affect the validity of a vote given by that person unless the company receives notice of the termination—
- (a) before the commencement of the meeting or adjourned meeting at which the vote is given, or
- (b) in the case of a poll taken more than 48 hours after it is demanded, before the time appointed for taking the poll.

(4) If the company's articles require or permit members to give notice of termination to a person other than the company, the references above to the company receiving notice have effect as if they were or (as the case may be) included a reference to that person.

(5) Subsections (2) and (3) have effect subject to any provision of the company's articles which has the effect of requiring notice of termination to be received by the company or another person at a time earlier than that specified in those subsections.

This is subject to subsection (6).

(6) Any provision of the company's articles is void in so far as it would have the effect of requiring notice of termination to be received by the company or another person earlier than the following time—
- (a) in the case of a meeting or adjourned meeting, 48 hours before the time for holding the meeting or adjourned meeting;
- (b) in the case of a poll taken more than 48 hours after it was demanded, 24 hours before the time appointed for the taking of the poll;
- (c) in the case of a poll taken not more than 48 hours after it was demanded, the time at which it was demanded.

(7) In calculating the periods mentioned in subsections (3)(b) and (6) no account shall be taken of any part of a day that is not a working day.

[1710]

NOTES

Commencement: to be appointed (see the introductory note to this Act).

331 Saving for more extensive rights conferred by articles

Nothing in sections 324 to 330 (proxies) prevents a company's articles from conferring more extensive rights on members or proxies than are conferred by those sections.

[1711]

NOTES

Commencement: to be appointed (see the introductory note to this Act).

Adjourned meetings

332 Resolution passed at adjourned meeting

Where a resolution is passed at an adjourned meeting of a company, the resolution is for all purposes to be treated as having been passed on the date on which it was in fact passed, and is not to be deemed passed on any earlier date.

[1712]

NOTES

Commencement: to be appointed (see the introductory note to this Act).

Electronic communications

333 Sending documents relating to meetings etc in electronic form

(1) Where a company has given an electronic address in a notice calling a meeting, it is deemed to have agreed that any document or information relating to proceedings at the meeting may be sent by electronic means to that address (subject to any conditions or limitations specified in the notice).

(2) Where a company has given an electronic address—

(a) in an instrument of proxy sent out by the company in relation to the meeting, or

(b) in an invitation to appoint a proxy issued by the company in relation to the meeting,

it is deemed to have agreed that any document or information relating to proxies for that meeting may be sent by electronic means to that address (subject to any conditions or limitations specified in the notice).

(3) In subsection (2), documents relating to proxies include—

(a) the appointment of a proxy in relation to a meeting,

(b) any document necessary to show the validity of, or otherwise relating to, the appointment of a proxy, and

(c) notice of the termination of the authority of a proxy.

(4) In this section "electronic address" means any address or number used for the purposes of sending or receiving documents or information by electronic means.

[1713]

NOTES

Commencement: 20 January 2007.

Application to class meetings

334 Application to class meetings

(1) The provisions of this Chapter apply (with necessary modifications) in relation to a meeting of holders of a class of shares as they apply in relation to a general meeting.

This is subject to subsections (2) and (3).

(2) The following provisions of this Chapter do not apply in relation to a meeting of holders of a class of shares—

(a) sections 303 to 305 (members' power to require directors to call general meeting), and

(b) section 306 (power of court to order meeting).

(3) The following provisions (in addition to those mentioned in subsection (2)) do not apply in relation to a meeting in connection with the variation of rights attached to a class of shares (a "variation of class rights meeting")—

(a) section 318 (quorum), and

(b) section 321 (right to demand a poll).

(4) The quorum for a variation of class rights meeting is—

(a) for a meeting other than an adjourned meeting, two persons present holding at least one-third in nominal value of the issued shares of the class in question (excluding any shares of that class held as treasury shares);

(b) for an adjourned meeting, one person present holding shares of the class in question.

(5) For the purposes of subsection (4), where a person is present by proxy or proxies, he is treated as holding only the shares in respect of which those proxies are authorised to exercise voting rights.

(6) At a variation of class rights meeting, any holder of shares of the class in question present may demand a poll.

(7) For the purposes of this section—

(a) any amendment of a provision contained in a company's articles for the variation of the rights attached to a class of shares, or the insertion of any such provision into the articles, is itself to be treated as a variation of those rights, and

(b) references to the variation of rights attached to a class of shares include references to their abrogation.

[1714]

NOTES

Commencement: to be appointed (see the introductory note to this Act).

335 Application to class meetings: companies without a share capital

(1) The provisions of this Chapter apply (with necessary modifications) in relation to a meeting of a class of members of a company without a share capital as they apply in relation to a general meeting.

This is subject to subsections (2) and (3).

(2) The following provisions of this Chapter do not apply in relation to a meeting of a class of members—

(a) sections 303 to 305 (members' power to require directors to call general meeting), and

(b) section 306 (power of court to order meeting).

(3) The following provisions (in addition to those mentioned in subsection (2)) do not apply in relation to a meeting in connection with the variation of the rights of a class of members (a "variation of class rights meeting")—

(a) section 318 (quorum), and

(b) section 321 (right to demand a poll).

(4) The quorum for a variation of class rights meeting is—

(a) for a meeting other than an adjourned meeting, two members of the class present (in person or by proxy) who together represent at least one-third of the voting rights of the class;

(b) for an adjourned meeting, one member of the class present (in person or by proxy).

(5) At a variation of class rights meeting, any member present (in person or by proxy) may demand a poll.

(6) For the purposes of this section—

(a) any amendment of a provision contained in a company's articles for the variation of the rights of a class of members, or the insertion of any such provision into the articles, is itself to be treated as a variation of those rights, and

(b) references to the variation of rights of a class of members include references to their abrogation.

[1715]

NOTES

Commencement: to be appointed (see the introductory note to this Act).

336–354 ((*Chapters 4, 5) outside the scope of this work.*)

CHAPTER 6
RECORDS OF RESOLUTIONS AND MEETINGS

355 Records of resolutions and meetings etc

(1) Every company must keep records comprising—

(a) copies of all resolutions of members passed otherwise than at general meetings,

(b) minutes of all proceedings of general meetings, and

(c) details provided to the company in accordance with section 357 (decisions of sole member).

(2) The records must be kept for at least ten years from the date of the resolution, meeting or decision (as appropriate).

(3) If a company fails to comply with this section, an offence is committed by every officer of the company who is in default.

(4) A person guilty of an offence under this section is liable on summary conviction to a fine not exceeding level 3 on the standard scale and, for continued contravention, a daily default fine not exceeding one-tenth of level 3 on the standard scale.

[1716]

NOTES

Commencement: to be appointed (see the introductory note to this Act).

356 Records as evidence of resolutions etc

(1) This section applies to the records kept in accordance with section 355.

(2) The record of a resolution passed otherwise than at a general meeting, if purporting to be signed by a director of the company or by the company secretary, is evidence (in Scotland, sufficient evidence) of the passing of the resolution.

(3) Where there is a record of a written resolution of a private company, the requirements of this Act with respect to the passing of the resolution are deemed to be complied with unless the contrary is proved.

(4) The minutes of proceedings of a general meeting, if purporting to be signed by the chairman of that meeting or by the chairman of the next general meeting, are evidence (in Scotland, sufficient evidence) of the proceedings at the meeting.

(5) Where there is a record of proceedings of a general meeting of a company, then, until the contrary is proved—
- (a) the meeting is deemed duly held and convened,
- (b) all proceedings at the meeting are deemed to have duly taken place, and
- (c) all appointments at the meeting are deemed valid.

[1717]

NOTES

Commencement: to be appointed (see the introductory note to this Act).

357 Records of decisions by sole member

(1) This section applies to a company limited by shares or by guarantee that has only one member.

(2) Where the member takes any decision that—
- (a) may be taken by the company in general meeting, and
- (b) has effect as if agreed by the company in general meeting,

he must (unless that decision is taken by way of a written resolution) provide the company with details of that decision.

(3) If a person fails to comply with this section he commits an offence.

(4) A person guilty of an offence under this section is liable on summary conviction to a fine not exceeding level 2 on the standard scale.

(5) Failure to comply with this section does not affect the validity of any decision referred to in subsection (2).

[1718]

NOTES

Commencement: to be appointed (see the introductory note to this Act).

358 Inspection of records of resolutions and meetings

(1) The records referred to in section 355 (records of resolutions etc) relating to the previous ten years must be kept available for inspection—
- (a) at the company's registered office, or
- (b) at a place specified in regulations under section 1136.

(2) The company must give notice to the registrar—

(a) of the place at which the records are kept available for inspection, and
(b) of any change in that place,

unless they have at all times been kept at the company's registered office.

(3) The records must be open to the inspection of any member of the company without charge.

(4) Any member may require a copy of any of the records on payment of such fee as may be prescribed.

(5) If default is made for 14 days in complying with subsection (2) or an inspection required under subsection (3) is refused, or a copy requested under subsection (4) is not sent, an offence is committed by every officer of the company who is in default.

(6) A person guilty of an offence under this section is liable on summary conviction to a fine not exceeding level 3 on the standard scale and, for continued contravention, a daily default fine not exceeding one-tenth of level 3 on the standard scale.

(7) In a case in which an inspection required under subsection (3) is refused or a copy requested under subsection (4) is not sent, the court may by order compel an immediate inspection of the records or direct that the copies required be sent to the persons who requested them.

[1719]

NOTES

Commencement: to be appointed (see the introductory note to this Act).

359 Records of resolutions and meetings of class of members

The provisions of this Chapter apply (with necessary modifications) in relation to resolutions and meetings of—

(a) holders of a class of shares, and
(b) in the case of a company without a share capital, a class of members,

as they apply in relation to resolutions of members generally and to general meetings.

[1720]

NOTES

Commencement: to be appointed (see the introductory note to this Act).

CHAPTER 7
SUPPLEMENTARY PROVISIONS

360 Computation of periods of notice etc: clear day rule

(1) This section applies for the purposes of the following provisions of this Part—

section 307(1) and (2) (notice required of general meeting),
section 312(1) and (3) (resolution requiring special notice),
section 314(4)(d) (request to circulate members' statement),
section 316(2)(b) (expenses of circulating statement to be deposited or tendered before meeting),
section 338(4)(d)(i) (request to circulate member's resolution at AGM of public company), and
section 340(2)(b)(i) (expenses of circulating statement to be deposited or tendered before meeting).

(2) Any reference in those provisions to a period of notice, or to a period before a meeting by which a request must be received or sum deposited or tendered, is to a period of the specified length excluding—

(a) the day of the meeting, and
(b) the day on which the notice is given, the request received or the sum deposited or tendered.

[1721]

NOTES

Commencement: to be appointed (see the introductory note to this Act).

361 Meaning of "quoted company"

In this Part "quoted company" has the same meaning as in Part 15 of this Act.

[1722]

NOTES

Commencement: to be appointed (see the introductory note to this Act).

PART 14
CONTROL OF POLITICAL DONATIONS AND EXPENDITURE

Introductory

362 Introductory

This Part has effect for controlling—

(a) political donations made by companies to political parties, to other political organisations and to independent election candidates, and

(b) political expenditure incurred by companies.

[1723]

NOTES

Commencement: to be appointed (see the introductory note to this Act).

Donations and expenditure to which this Part applies

363 Political parties, organisations etc to which this Part applies

(1) This Part applies to a political party if—

(a) it is registered under Part 2 of the Political Parties, Elections and Referendums Act 2000 (c 41), or

(b) it carries on, or proposes to carry on, activities for the purposes of or in connection with the participation of the party in any election or elections to public office held in a member State other than the United Kingdom.

(2) This Part applies to an organisation (a "political organisation") if it carries on, or proposes to carry on, activities that are capable of being reasonably regarded as intended—

(a) to affect public support for a political party to which, or an independent election candidate to whom, this Part applies, or

(b) to influence voters in relation to any national or regional referendum held under the law of the United Kingdom or another member State.

(3) This Part applies to an independent election candidate at any election to public office held in the United Kingdom or another member State.

(4) Any reference in the following provisions of this Part to a political party, political organisation or independent election candidate, or to political expenditure, is to a party, organisation, independent candidate or expenditure to which this Part applies.

[1724]

NOTES

Commencement: to be appointed (see the introductory note to this Act).

364 Meaning of "political donation"

(1) The following provisions have effect for the purposes of this Part as regards the meaning of "political donation".

(2) In relation to a political party or other political organisation—

(a) "political donation" means anything that in accordance with sections 50 to 52 of the Political Parties, Elections and Referendums Act 2000—

(i) constitutes a donation for the purposes of Chapter 1 of Part 4 of that Act (control of donations to registered parties), or

(ii) would constitute such a donation reading references in those sections to a registered party as references to any political party or other political organisation,

and

(b) section 53 of that Act applies, in the same way, for the purpose of determining the value of a donation.

(3) In relation to an independent election candidate—

(a) "political donation" means anything that, in accordance with sections 50 to 52 of that Act, would constitute a donation for the purposes of Chapter 1 of Part 4 of that Act (control of donations to registered parties) reading references in those sections to a registered party as references to the independent election candidate, and

(b) section 53 of that Act applies, in the same way, for the purpose of determining the value of a donation.

(4) For the purposes of this section, sections 50 and 53 of the Political Parties, Elections and Referendums Act 2000 (c 41) (definition of "donation" and value of donations) shall be treated as if the amendments to those sections made by the Electoral Administration Act 2006 (which remove from the definition of "donation" loans made otherwise than on commercial terms) had not been made.

[1725]

NOTES

Commencement: to be appointed (see the introductory note to this Act).

365 Meaning of "political expenditure"

(1) In this Part "political expenditure", in relation to a company, means expenditure incurred by the company on—

(a) the preparation, publication or dissemination of advertising or other promotional or publicity material—

(i) of whatever nature, and

(ii) however published or otherwise disseminated,

that, at the time of publication or dissemination, is capable of being reasonably regarded as intended to affect public support for a political party or other political organisation, or an independent election candidate, or

(b) activities on the part of the company that are capable of being reasonably regarded as intended—

(i) to affect public support for a political party or other political organisation, or an independent election candidate, or

(ii) to influence voters in relation to any national or regional referendum held under the law of a member State.

(2) For the purposes of this Part a political donation does not count as political expenditure.

[1726]

NOTES

Commencement: to be appointed (see the introductory note to this Act).

Authorisation required for donations or expenditure

366 Authorisation required for donations or expenditure

(1) A company must not—

(a) make a political donation to a political party or other political organisation, or to an independent election candidate, or

(b) incur any political expenditure,

unless the donation or expenditure is authorised in accordance with the following provisions.

(2) The donation or expenditure must be authorised—

(a) in the case of a company that is not a subsidiary of another company, by a resolution of the members of the company;

(b) in the case of a company that is a subsidiary of another company by—
(i) a resolution of the members of the company, and
(ii) a resolution of the members of any relevant holding company.

(3) No resolution is required on the part of a company that is a wholly-owned subsidiary of a UK-registered company.

(4) For the purposes of subsection (2)(b)(ii) a "relevant holding company" means a company that, at the time the donation was made or the expenditure was incurred—
(a) was a holding company of the company by which the donation was made or the expenditure was incurred,
(b) was a UK-registered company, and
(c) was not a subsidiary of another UK-registered company.

(5) The resolution or resolutions required by this section—
(a) must comply with section 367 (form of authorising resolution), and
(b) must be passed before the donation is made or the expenditure incurred.

(6) Nothing in this section enables a company to be authorised to do anything that it could not lawfully do apart from this section.

[1727]

NOTES

Commencement: to be appointed (see the introductory note to this Act).

367 Form of authorising resolution

(1) A resolution conferring authorisation for the purposes of this Part may relate to—
(a) the company passing the resolution,
(b) one or more subsidiaries of that company, or
(c) the company passing the resolution and one or more subsidiaries of that company.

(2) A resolution may be expressed to relate to all companies that are subsidiaries of the company passing the resolution—
(a) at the time the resolution is passed, or
(b) at any time during the period for which the resolution has effect,
without identifying them individually.

(3) The resolution may authorise donations or expenditure under one or more of the following heads—
(a) donations to political parties or independent election candidates;
(b) donations to political organisations other than political parties;
(c) political expenditure.

(4) The resolution must specify a head or heads—
(a) in the case of a resolution under subsection (2), for all of the companies to which it relates taken together;
(b) in the case of any other resolution, for each company to which it relates.

(5) The resolution must be expressed in general terms conforming with subsection (2) and must not purport to authorise particular donations or expenditure.

(6) For each of the specified heads the resolution must authorise donations or, as the case may be, expenditure up to a specified amount in the period for which the resolution has effect (see section 368).

(7) The resolution must specify such amounts—
(a) in the case of a resolution under subsection (2), for all of the companies to which it relates taken together;
(b) in the case of any other resolution, for each company to which it relates.

[1728]

NOTES

Commencement: to be appointed (see the introductory note to this Act).

368 Period for which resolution has effect

(1) A resolution conferring authorisation for the purposes of this Part has effect for a period of four years beginning with the date on which it is passed unless the directors determine, or the articles require, that it is to have effect for a shorter period beginning with that date.

(2) The power of the directors to make a determination under this section is subject to any provision of the articles that operates to prevent them from doing so.

[1729]

NOTES

Commencement: to be appointed (see the introductory note to this Act).

Remedies in case of unauthorised donations or expenditure

369 Liability of directors in case of unauthorised donation or expenditure

(1) This section applies where a company has made a political donation or incurred political expenditure without the authorisation required by this Part.

(2) The directors in default are jointly and severally liable—

(a) to make good to the company the amount of the unauthorised donation or expenditure, with interest, and

(b) to compensate the company for any loss or damage sustained by it as a result of the unauthorised donation or expenditure having been made.

(3) The directors in default are—

(a) those who, at the time the unauthorised donation was made or the unauthorised expenditure was incurred, were directors of the company by which the donation was made or the expenditure was incurred, and

(b) where—

(i) that company was a subsidiary of a relevant holding company, and

(ii) the directors of the relevant holding company failed to take all reasonable steps to prevent the donation being made or the expenditure being incurred,

the directors of the relevant holding company.

(4) For the purposes of subsection (3)(b) a "relevant holding company" means a company that, at the time the donation was made or the expenditure was incurred—

(a) was a holding company of the company by which the donation was made or the expenditure was incurred,

(b) was a UK-registered company, and

(c) was not a subsidiary of another UK-registered company.

(5) The interest referred to in subsection (2)(a) is interest on the amount of the unauthorised donation or expenditure, so far as not made good to the company—

(a) in respect of the period beginning with the date when the donation was made or the expenditure was incurred, and

(b) at such rate as the Secretary of State may prescribe by regulations.

Section 379(2) (construction of references to date when donation made or expenditure incurred) does not apply for the purposes of this subsection.

(6) Where only part of a donation or expenditure was unauthorised, this section applies only to so much of it as was unauthorised.

[1730]

NOTES

Commencement: to be appointed (see the introductory note to this Act).

370 Enforcement of directors' liabilities by shareholder action

(1) Any liability of a director under section 369 is enforceable—

(a) in the case of a liability of a director of a company to that company, by proceedings brought under this section in the name of the company by an authorised group of its members;

(b) in the case of a liability of a director of a holding company to a subsidiary, by proceedings brought under this section in the name of the subsidiary by—
(i) an authorised group of members of the subsidiary, or
(ii) an authorised group of members of the holding company.

(2) This is in addition to the right of the company to which the liability is owed to bring proceedings itself to enforce the liability.

(3) An "authorised group" of members of a company means—
(a) the holders of not less than 5% in nominal value of the company's issued share capital,
(b) if the company is not limited by shares, not less than 5% of its members, or
(c) not less than 50 of the company's members.

(4) The right to bring proceedings under this section is subject to the provisions of section 371.

(5) Nothing in this section affects any right of a member of a company to bring or continue proceedings under Part 11 (derivative claims or proceedings).

[1731]

NOTES

Commencement: to be appointed (see the introductory note to this Act).

371 Enforcement of directors' liabilities by shareholder action: supplementary

(1) A group of members may not bring proceedings under section 370 in the name of a company unless—
(a) the group has given written notice to the company stating—
(i) the cause of action and a summary of the facts on which the proceedings are to be based,
(ii) the names and addresses of the members comprising the group, and
(iii) the grounds on which it is alleged that those members constitute an authorised group; and
(b) not less than 28 days have elapsed between the date of the giving of the notice to the company and the bringing of the proceedings.

(2) Where such a notice is given to a company, any director of the company may apply to the court within the period of 28 days beginning with the date of the giving of the notice for an order directing that the proposed proceedings shall not be brought, on one or more of the following grounds—
(a) that the unauthorised amount has been made good to the company;
(b) that proceedings to enforce the liability have been brought, and are being pursued with due diligence, by the company;
(c) that the members proposing to bring proceedings under this section do not constitute an authorised group.

(3) Where an application is made on the ground mentioned in subsection (2)(b), the court may as an alternative to directing that the proposed proceedings under section 370 are not to be brought, direct—
(a) that such proceedings may be brought on such terms and conditions as the court thinks fit, and
(b) that the proceedings brought by the company—
(i) shall be discontinued, or
(ii) may be continued on such terms and conditions as the court thinks fit.

(4) The members by whom proceedings are brought under section 370 owe to the company in whose name they are brought the same duties in relation to the proceedings as would be owed by the company's directors if the proceedings were being brought by the company.

But proceedings to enforce any such duty may be brought by the company only with the permission of the court.

(5) Proceedings brought under section 370 may not be discontinued or settled by the group except with the permission of the court, which may be given on such terms as the court thinks fit.

[1732]

NOTES

Commencement: to be appointed (see the introductory note to this Act).

372 Costs of shareholder action

(1) This section applies in relation to proceedings brought under section 370 in the name of a company ("the company") by an authorised group ("the group").

(2) The group may apply to the court for an order directing the company to indemnify the group in respect of costs incurred or to be incurred by the group in connection with the proceedings.

The court may make such an order on such terms as it thinks fit.

(3) The group is not entitled to be paid any such costs out of the assets of the company except by virtue of such an order.

(4) If no such order has been made with respect to the proceedings, then—
- (a) if the company is awarded costs in connection with the proceedings, or it is agreed that costs incurred by the company in connection with the proceedings should be paid by any defendant, the costs shall be paid to the group; and
- (b) if any defendant is awarded costs in connection with the proceedings, or it is agreed that any defendant should be paid costs incurred by him in connection with the proceedings, the costs shall be paid by the group.

(5) (*Outside the scope of this work.*)

[1733]

NOTES

Commencement: to be appointed (see the introductory note to this Act).

373 Information for purposes of shareholder action

(1) Where proceedings have been brought under section 370 in the name of a company by an authorised group, the group is entitled to require the company to provide it with all information relating to the subject matter of the proceedings that is in the company's possession or under its control or which is reasonably obtainable by it.

(2) If the company, having been required by the group to do so, refuses to provide the group with all or any of that information, the court may, on an application made by the group, make an order directing—
- (a) the company, and
- (b) any of its officers or employees specified in the application,

to provide the group with the information in question in such form and by such means as the court may direct.

[1734]

NOTES

Commencement: to be appointed (see the introductory note to this Act).

Exemptions

374 Trade unions

(1) A donation to a trade union, other than a contribution to the union's political fund, is not a political donation for the purposes of this Part.

(2) A trade union is not a political organisation for the purposes of section 365 (meaning of "political expenditure").

(3) In this section—

"trade union" has the meaning given by section 1 of Trade Union and Labour Relations (Consolidation) Act 1992 (c 52) or Article 3 of the Industrial Relations (Northern Ireland) Order 1992 (SI 1992/807 (NI 5));

"political fund" means the fund from which payments by a trade union in the furtherance of political objects are required to be made by virtue of section 82(1)(a) of that Act or Article 57(2)(a) of that Order.

[1735]

NOTES

Commencement: to be appointed (see the introductory note to this Act).

375 Subscription for membership of trade association

(1) A subscription paid to a trade association for membership of the association is not a political donation for the purposes of this Part.

(2) For this purpose—

"trade association" means an organisation formed for the purpose of furthering the trade interests of its members, or of persons represented by its members, and

"subscription" does not include a payment to the association to the extent that it is made for the purpose of financing any particular activity of the association.

[1736]

NOTES

Commencement: to be appointed (see the introductory note to this Act).

376 All-party parliamentary groups

(1) An all-party parliamentary group is not a political organisation for the purposes of this Part.

(2) An "all-party parliamentary group" means an all-party group composed of members of one or both of the Houses of Parliament (or of such members and other persons).

[1737]

NOTES

Commencement: to be appointed (see the introductory note to this Act).

377 Political expenditure exempted by order

(1) Authorisation under this Part is not needed for political expenditure that is exempt by virtue of an order of the Secretary of State under this section.

(2) An order may confer an exemption in relation to—

(a) companies of any description or category specified in the order, or

(b) expenditure of any description or category so specified (whether framed by reference to goods, services or other matters in respect of which such expenditure is incurred or otherwise),

or both.

(3) If or to the extent that expenditure is exempt from the requirement of authorisation under this Part by virtue of an order under this section, it shall be disregarded in determining what donations are authorised by any resolution of the company passed for the purposes of this Part.

(4) An order under this section is subject to affirmative resolution procedure.

[1738]

NOTES

Commencement: to be appointed (see the introductory note to this Act).

378 Donations not amounting to more than £5,000 in any twelve month period

(1) Authorisation under this Part is not needed for a donation except to the extent that the total amount of—

(a) that donation, and

(b) other relevant donations made in the period of 12 months ending with the date on which that donation is made, exceeds £5,000.

(2) In this section—

"donation" means a donation to a political party or other political organisation or to an independent election candidate; and

"other relevant donations" means—

(a) in relation to a donation made by a company that is not a subsidiary, any other donations made by that company or by any of its subsidiaries;

(b) in relation to a donation made by a company that is a subsidiary, any other donations made by that company, by any holding company of that company or by any other subsidiary of any such holding company.

(3) If or to the extent that a donation is exempt by virtue of this section from the requirement of authorisation under this Part, it shall be disregarded in determining what donations are authorised by any resolution passed for the purposes of this Part.

[1739]

NOTES

Commencement: to be appointed (see the introductory note to this Act).

Supplementary provisions

379 Minor definitions

(1) In this Part—

"director" includes shadow director; and

"organisation" includes any body corporate or unincorporated association and any combination of persons.

(2) Except as otherwise provided, any reference in this Part to the time at which a donation is made or expenditure is incurred is, in a case where the donation is made or expenditure incurred in pursuance of a contract, any earlier time at which that contract is entered into by the company.

[1740]

NOTES

Commencement: to be appointed (see the introductory note to this Act).

PART 15
ACCOUNTS AND REPORTS

CHAPTER 1
INTRODUCTION

General

380 Scheme of this Part

(1) The requirements of this Part as to accounts and reports apply in relation to each financial year of a company.

(2) In certain respects different provisions apply to different kinds of company.

(3) The main distinctions for this purpose are—

(a) between companies subject to the small companies regime (see section 381) and companies that are not subject to that regime; and

(b) between quoted companies (see section 385) and companies that are not quoted.

(4) In this Part, where provisions do not apply to all kinds of company—

(a) provisions applying to companies subject to the small companies regime appear before the provisions applying to other companies,

(b) provisions applying to private companies appear before the provisions applying to public companies, and

(c) provisions applying to quoted companies appear after the provisions applying to other companies.

[1741]

NOTES

Commencement: to be appointed (see the introductory note to this Act).

Companies subject to the small companies regime

381 Companies subject to the small companies regime

The small companies regime for accounts and reports applies to a company for a financial year in relation to which the company—

(a) qualifies as small (see sections 382 and 383), and

(b) is not excluded from the regime (see section 384).

[1742]

NOTES

Commencement: to be appointed (see the introductory note to this Act).

382 Companies qualifying as small: general

(1) A company qualifies as small in relation to its first financial year if the qualifying conditions are met in that year.

(2) A company qualifies as small in relation to a subsequent financial year—

(a) if the qualifying conditions are met in that year and the preceding financial year;

(b) if the qualifying conditions are met in that year and the company qualified as small in relation to the preceding financial year;

(c) if the qualifying conditions were met in the preceding financial year and the company qualified as small in relation to that year.

(3) The qualifying conditions are met by a company in a year in which it satisfies two or more of the following requirements—

1 Turnover	Not more than £5.6 million
2 Balance sheet total	Not more than £2.8 million
3 Number of employees	Not more than 50

(4) For a period that is a company's financial year but not in fact a year the maximum figures for turnover must be proportionately adjusted.

(5) The balance sheet total means the aggregate of the amounts shown as assets in the company's balance sheet.

(6) The number of employees means the average number of persons employed by the company in the year, determined as follows—

(a) find for each month in the financial year the number of persons employed under contracts of service by the company in that month (whether throughout the month or not),

(b) add together the monthly totals, and

(c) divide by the number of months in the financial year.

(7) This section is subject to section 383 (companies qualifying as small: parent companies).

[1743]

NOTES

Commencement: to be appointed (see the introductory note to this Act).

383 Companies qualifying as small: parent companies

(1) A parent company qualifies as a small company in relation to a financial year only if the group headed by it qualifies as a small group.

(2) A group qualifies as small in relation to the parent company's first financial year if the qualifying conditions are met in that year.

(3) A group qualifies as small in relation to a subsequent financial year of the parent company—

(a) if the qualifying conditions are met in that year and the preceding financial year;
(b) if the qualifying conditions are met in that year and the group qualified as small in relation to the preceding financial year;
(c) if the qualifying conditions were met in the preceding financial year and the group qualified as small in relation to that year.

(4) The qualifying conditions are met by a group in a year in which it satisfies two or more of the following requirements—

1. Aggregate turnover	Not more than £5.6 million net (or £6.72 million gross)
2. Aggregate balance sheet total	Not more than £2.8 million net (or £3.36 million gross)
3. Aggregate number of employees	Not more than 50

(5) The aggregate figures are ascertained by aggregating the relevant figures determined in accordance with section 382 for each member of the group.

(6) In relation to the aggregate figures for turnover and balance sheet total—

"net" means after any set-offs and other adjustments made to eliminate group transactions—

(a) in the case of Companies Act accounts, in accordance with regulations under section 404,
(b) in the case of IAS accounts, in accordance with international accounting standards; and

"gross" means without those set-offs and other adjustments.

A company may satisfy any relevant requirement on the basis of either the net or the gross figure.

(7) The figures for each subsidiary undertaking shall be those included in its individual accounts for the relevant financial year, that is—

(a) if its financial year ends with that of the parent company, that financial year, and
(b) if not, its financial year ending last before the end of the financial year of the parent company.

If those figures cannot be obtained without disproportionate expense or undue delay, the latest available figures shall be taken.

[1744]

NOTES

Commencement: to be appointed (see the introductory note to this Act).

384–385 (*Outside the scope of this work.*)

CHAPTER 2
ACCOUNTING RECORDS

386 Duty to keep accounting records

(1) Every company must keep adequate accounting records.

(2) Adequate accounting records means records that are sufficient—

(a) to show and explain the company's transactions,

(b) to disclose with reasonable accuracy, at any time, the financial position of the company at that time, and

(c) to enable the directors to ensure that any accounts required to be prepared comply with the requirements of this Act (and, where applicable, of Article 4 of the IAS Regulation).

(3) Accounting records must, in particular, contain—

(a) entries from day to day of all sums of money received and expended by the company and the matters in respect of which the receipt and expenditure takes place, and

(b) a record of the assets and liabilities of the company.

(4) If the company's business involves dealing in goods, the accounting records must contain—

(a) statements of stock held by the company at the end of each financial year of the company,

(b) all statements of stocktakings from which any statement of stock as is mentioned in paragraph (a) has been or is to be prepared, and

(c) except in the case of goods sold by way of ordinary retail trade, statements of all goods sold and purchased, showing the goods and the buyers and sellers in sufficient detail to enable all these to be identified.

(5) A parent company that has a subsidiary undertaking in relation to which the above requirements do not apply must take reasonable steps to secure that the undertaking keeps such accounting records as to enable the directors of the parent company to ensure that any accounts required to be prepared under this Part comply with the requirements of this Act (and, where applicable, of Article 4 of the IAS Regulation).

[1745]

NOTES

Commencement: to be appointed (see the introductory note to this Act).

387 Duty to keep accounting records: offence

(1) If a company fails to comply with any provision of section 386 (duty to keep accounting records), an offence is committed by every officer of the company who is in default.

(2) It is a defence for a person charged with such an offence to show that he acted honestly and that in the circumstances in which the company's business was carried on the default was excusable.

(3) A person guilty of an offence under this section is liable—

(a) on conviction on indictment, to imprisonment for a term not exceeding two years or a fine (or both);

(b) on summary conviction—

(i) in England and Wales, to imprisonment for a term not exceeding twelve months or to a fine not exceeding the statutory maximum (or both);

(ii) in Scotland or Northern Ireland, to imprisonment for a term not exceeding six months, or to a fine not exceeding the statutory maximum (or both).

[1746]

NOTES

Commencement: to be appointed (see the introductory note to this Act).

388 Where and for how long records to be kept

(1) A company's accounting records—

(a) must be kept at its registered office or such other place as the directors think fit, and

(b) must at all times be open to inspection by the company's officers.

(2) If accounting records are kept at a place outside the United Kingdom, accounts and returns with respect to the business dealt with in the accounting records so kept must be sent to, and kept at, a place in the United Kingdom, and must at all times be open to such inspection.

(3) The accounts and returns to be sent to the United Kingdom must be such as to—
- (a) disclose with reasonable accuracy the financial position of the business in question at intervals of not more than six months, and
- (b) enable the directors to ensure that the accounts required to be prepared under this Part comply with the requirements of this Act (and, where applicable, of Article 4 of the IAS Regulation).

(4) Accounting records that a company is required by section 386 to keep must be preserved by it—
- (a) in the case of a private company, for three years from the date on which they are made;
- (b) in the case of a public company, for six years from the date on which they are made.

(5) Subsection (4) is subject to any provision contained in rules made under section 411 of the Insolvency Act 1986 (c 45) (company insolvency rules) or Article 359 of the Insolvency (Northern Ireland) Order 1989 (SI 1989/2405 (NI 19)).

[1747]

NOTES

Commencement: to be appointed (see the introductory note to this Act).

389 Where and for how long records to be kept: offences

(1) If a company fails to comply with any provision of subsections (1) to (3) of section 388 (requirements as to keeping of accounting records), an offence is committed by every officer of the company who is in default.

(2) It is a defence for a person charged with such an offence to show that he acted honestly and that in the circumstances in which the company's business was carried on the default was excusable.

(3) An officer of a company commits an offence if he—
- (a) fails to take all reasonable steps for securing compliance by the company with subsection (4) of that section (period for which records to be preserved), or
- (b) intentionally causes any default by the company under that subsection.

(4) A person guilty of an offence under this section is liable—
- (a) on conviction on indictment, to imprisonment for a term not exceeding two years or a fine (or both);
- (b) on summary conviction—
  - (i) in England and Wales, to imprisonment for a term not exceeding twelve months or to a fine not exceeding the statutory maximum (or both);
  - (ii) in Scotland or Northern Ireland, to imprisonment for a term not exceeding six months, or to a fine not exceeding the statutory maximum (or both).

[1748]

NOTES

Commencement: to be appointed (see the introductory note to this Act).

CHAPTER 3
A COMPANY'S FINANCIAL YEAR

390 A company's financial year

(1) A company's financial year is determined as follows.

(2) Its first financial year—
- (a) begins with the first day of its first accounting reference period, and
- (b) ends with the last day of that period or such other date, not more than seven days before or after the end of that period, as the directors may determine.

(3) Subsequent financial years—
- (a) begin with the day immediately following the end of the company's previous financial year, and

(b) end with the last day of its next accounting reference period or such other date, not more than seven days before or after the end of that period, as the directors may determine.

(4) In relation to an undertaking that is not a company, references in this Act to its financial year are to any period in respect of which a profit and loss account of the undertaking is required to be made up (by its constitution or by the law under which it is established), whether that period is a year or not.

(5) The directors of a parent company must secure that, except where in their opinion there are good reasons against it, the financial year of each of its subsidiary undertakings coincides with the company's own financial year.

[1749]

NOTES

Commencement: to be appointed (see the introductory note to this Act).

391 Accounting reference periods and accounting reference date

(1) A company's accounting reference periods are determined according to its accounting reference date in each calendar year.

(2) The accounting reference date of a company incorporated in Great Britain before 1st April 1996 is—

(a) the date specified by notice to the registrar in accordance with section 224(2) of the Companies Act 1985 (c 6) (notice specifying accounting reference date given within nine months of incorporation), or

(b) failing such notice—

(i) in the case of a company incorporated before 1st April 1990, 31st March, and

(ii) in the case of a company incorporated on or after 1st April 1990, the last day of the month in which the anniversary of its incorporation falls.

(3) The accounting reference date of a company incorporated in Northern Ireland before 22nd August 1997 is—

(a) the date specified by notice to the registrar in accordance with article 232(2) of the Companies (Northern Ireland) Order 1986 (SI 1986/1032 (NI 6)) (notice specifying accounting reference date given within nine months of incorporation), or

(b) failing such notice—

(i) in the case of a company incorporated before the coming into operation of Article 5 of the Companies (Northern Ireland) Order 1990 (SI 1990/593 (NI 5)), 31st March, and

(ii) in the case of a company incorporated after the coming into operation of that Article, the last day of the month in which the anniversary of its incorporation falls.

(4) The accounting reference date of a company incorporated—

(a) in Great Britain on or after 1st April 1996 and before the commencement of this Act,

(b) in Northern Ireland on or after 22nd August 1997 and before the commencement of this Act, or

(c) after the commencement of this Act,

is the last day of the month in which the anniversary of its incorporation falls.

(5) A company's first accounting reference period is the period of more than six months, but not more than 18 months, beginning with the date of its incorporation and ending with its accounting reference date.

(6) Its subsequent accounting reference periods are successive periods of twelve months beginning immediately after the end of the previous accounting reference period and ending with its accounting reference date.

(7) This section has effect subject to the provisions of section 392 (alteration of accounting reference date).

[1750]

NOTES

Commencement: to be appointed (see the introductory note to this Act).

392 Alteration of accounting reference date

(1) A company may by notice given to the registrar specify a new accounting reference date having effect in relation to—

(a) the company's current accounting reference period and subsequent periods, or

(b) the company's previous accounting reference period and subsequent periods.

A company's "previous accounting reference period" means the one immediately preceding its current accounting reference period.

(2) The notice must state whether the current or previous accounting reference period—

(a) is to be shortened, so as to come to an end on the first occasion on which the new accounting reference date falls or fell after the beginning of the period, or

(b) is to be extended, so as to come to an end on the second occasion on which that date falls or fell after the beginning of the period.

(3) A notice extending a company's current or previous accounting reference period is not effective if given less than five years after the end of an earlier accounting reference period of the company that was extended under this section.

This does not apply—

(a) to a notice given by a company that is a subsidiary undertaking or parent undertaking of another EEA undertaking if the new accounting reference date coincides with that of the other EEA undertaking or, where that undertaking is not a company, with the last day of its financial year, or

(b) where the company is in administration under Part 2 of the Insolvency Act 1986 (c 45) or Part 3 of the Insolvency (Northern Ireland) Order 1989 (SI 1989/2405 (NI 19)), or

(c) where the Secretary of State directs that it should not apply, which he may do with respect to a notice that has been given or that may be given.

(4) A notice under this section may not be given in respect of a previous accounting reference period if the period for filing accounts and reports for the financial year determined by reference to that accounting reference period has already expired.

(5) An accounting reference period may not be extended so as to exceed 18 months and a notice under this section is ineffective if the current or previous accounting reference period as extended in accordance with the notice would exceed that limit.

This does not apply where the company is in administration under Part 2 of the Insolvency Act 1986 (c 45) or Part 3 of the Insolvency (Northern Ireland) Order 1989 (SI 1989/2405 (NI 19)).

(6) In this section "EEA undertaking" means an undertaking established under the law of any part of the United Kingdom or the law of any other EEA State.

[1751]

NOTES

Commencement: to be appointed (see the introductory note to this Act).

CHAPTER 4
ANNUAL ACCOUNTS

General

393 Accounts to give true and fair view

(1) The directors of a company must not approve accounts for the purposes of this Chapter unless they are satisfied that they give a true and fair view of the assets, liabilities, financial position and profit or loss—

(a) in the case of the company's individual accounts, of the company;

(b) in the case of the company's group accounts, of the undertakings included in the consolidation as a whole, so far as concerns members of the company.

(2) The auditor of a company in carrying out his functions under this Act in relation to the company's annual accounts must have regard to the directors' duty under subsection (1).
[1752]

NOTES

Commencement: to be appointed (see the introductory note to this Act).

Individual accounts

394 Duty to prepare individual accounts

The directors of every company must prepare accounts for the company for each of its financial years.

Those accounts are referred to as the company's "individual accounts".
[1753]

NOTES

Commencement: to be appointed (see the introductory note to this Act).

395 Individual accounts: applicable accounting framework

(1) A company's individual accounts may be prepared—

(a) in accordance with section 396 ("Companies Act individual accounts"), or

(b) in accordance with international accounting standards ("IAS individual accounts").

This is subject to the following provisions of this section and to section 407 (consistency of financial reporting within group).

(2) The individual accounts of a company that is a charity must be Companies Act individual accounts.

(3) After the first financial year in which the directors of a company prepare IAS individual accounts ("the first IAS year"), all subsequent individual accounts of the company must be prepared in accordance with international accounting standards unless there is a relevant change of circumstance.

(4) There is a relevant change of circumstance if, at any time during or after the first IAS year—

(a) the company becomes a subsidiary undertaking of another undertaking that does not prepare IAS individual accounts,

(b) the company ceases to be a company with securities admitted to trading on a regulated market in an EEA State, or

(c) a parent undertaking of the company ceases to be an undertaking with securities admitted to trading on a regulated market in an EEA State.

(5) If, having changed to preparing Companies Act individual accounts following a relevant change of circumstance, the directors again prepare IAS individual accounts for the company, subsections (3) and (4) apply again as if the first financial year for which such accounts are again prepared were the first IAS year.
[1754]

NOTES

Commencement: to be appointed (see the introductory note to this Act).

396 Companies Act individual accounts

(1) Companies Act individual accounts must comprise—

(a) a balance sheet as at the last day of the financial year, and

(b) a profit and loss account.

(2) The accounts must—

(a) in the case of the balance sheet, give a true and fair view of the state of affairs of the company as at the end of the financial year, and

(b) in the case of the profit and loss account, give a true and fair view of the profit or loss of the company for the financial year.

(3) The accounts must comply with provision made by the Secretary of State by regulations as to—

(a) the form and content of the balance sheet and profit and loss account, and

(b) additional information to be provided by way of notes to the accounts.

(4) If compliance with the regulations, and any other provision made by or under this Act as to the matters to be included in a company's individual accounts or in notes to those accounts, would not be sufficient to give a true and fair view, the necessary additional information must be given in the accounts or in a note to them.

(5) If in special circumstances compliance with any of those provisions is inconsistent with the requirement to give a true and fair view, the directors must depart from that provision to the extent necessary to give a true and fair view.

Particulars of any such departure, the reasons for it and its effect must be given in a note to the accounts.

[1755]

NOTES

Commencement: to be appointed (see the introductory note to this Act).

397 IAS individual accounts

Where the directors of a company prepare IAS individual accounts, they must state in the notes to the accounts that the accounts have been prepared in accordance with international accounting standards.

[1756]

NOTES

Commencement: to be appointed (see the introductory note to this Act).

Group accounts: small companies

398 Option to prepare group accounts

If at the end of a financial year a company subject to the small companies regime is a parent company the directors, as well as preparing individual accounts for the year, may prepare group accounts for the year.

[1757]

NOTES

Commencement: to be appointed (see the introductory note to this Act).

399–402 (*Outside the scope of this work.*)

Group accounts: general

403 Group accounts: applicable accounting framework

(1) The group accounts of certain parent companies are required by Article 4 of the IAS Regulation to be prepared in accordance with international accounting standards ("IAS group accounts").

(2) The group accounts of other companies may be prepared—

(a) in accordance with section 404 ("Companies Act group accounts"), or

(b) in accordance with international accounting standards ("IAS group accounts").

This is subject to the following provisions of this section.

(3) The group accounts of a parent company that is a charity must be Companies Act group accounts.

(4) After the first financial year in which the directors of a parent company prepare IAS group accounts ("the first IAS year"), all subsequent group accounts of the company must be prepared in accordance with international accounting standards unless there is a relevant change of circumstance.

(5) There is a relevant change of circumstance if, at any time during or after the first IAS year—

(a) the company becomes a subsidiary undertaking of another undertaking that does not prepare IAS group accounts,

(b) the company ceases to be a company with securities admitted to trading on a regulated market in an EEA State, or

(c) a parent undertaking of the company ceases to be an undertaking with securities admitted to trading on a regulated market in an EEA State.

(6) If, having changed to preparing Companies Act group accounts following a relevant change of circumstance, the directors again prepare IAS group accounts for the company, subsections (4) and (5) apply again as if the first financial year for which such accounts are again prepared were the first IAS year.

[1757A]

NOTES

Commencement: to be appointed (see the introductory note to this Act).

404 Companies Act group accounts

(1) Companies Act group accounts must comprise—

(a) a consolidated balance sheet dealing with the state of affairs of the parent company and its subsidiary undertakings, and

(b) a consolidated profit and loss account dealing with the profit or loss of the parent company and its subsidiary undertakings.

(2) The accounts must give a true and fair view of the state of affairs as at the end of the financial year, and the profit or loss for the financial year, of the undertakings included in the consolidation as a whole, so far as concerns members of the company.

(3) The accounts must comply with provision made by the Secretary of State by regulations as to—

(a) the form and content of the consolidated balance sheet and consolidated profit and loss account, and

(b) additional information to be provided by way of notes to the accounts.

(4) If compliance with the regulations, and any other provision made by or under this Act as to the matters to be included in a company's group accounts or in notes to those accounts, would not be sufficient to give a true and fair view, the necessary additional information must be given in the accounts or in a note to them.

(5) If in special circumstances compliance with any of those provisions is inconsistent with the requirement to give a true and fair view, the directors must depart from that provision to the extent necessary to give a true and fair view.

Particulars of any such departure, the reasons for it and its effect must be given in a note to the accounts.

[1758]

NOTES

Commencement: to be appointed (see the introductory note to this Act).

405 Companies Act group accounts: subsidiary undertakings included in the consolidation

(1) Where a parent company prepares Companies Act group accounts, all the subsidiary undertakings of the company must be included in the consolidation, subject to the following exceptions.

(2) A subsidiary undertaking may be excluded from consolidation if its inclusion is not material for the purpose of giving a true and fair view (but two or more undertakings may be excluded only if they are not material taken together).

(3) A subsidiary undertaking may be excluded from consolidation where—
- (a) severe long-term restrictions substantially hinder the exercise of the rights of the parent company over the assets or management of that undertaking, or
- (b) the information necessary for the preparation of group accounts cannot be obtained without disproportionate expense or undue delay, or
- (c) the interest of the parent company is held exclusively with a view to subsequent resale.

(4) The reference in subsection (3)(a) to the rights of the parent company and the reference in subsection (3)(c) to the interest of the parent company are, respectively, to rights and interests held by or attributed to the company for the purposes of the definition of "parent undertaking" (see section 1162) in the absence of which it would not be the parent company. **[1759]**

NOTES

Commencement: to be appointed (see the introductory note to this Act).

406 IAS group accounts

Where the directors of a company prepare IAS group accounts, they must state in the notes to those accounts that the accounts have been prepared in accordance with international accounting standards.

[1760]

NOTES

Commencement: to be appointed (see the introductory note to this Act).

407 Consistency of financial reporting within group

(1) The directors of a parent company must secure that the individual accounts of—
- (a) the parent company, and
- (b) each of its subsidiary undertakings,

are all prepared using the same financial reporting framework, except to the extent that in their opinion there are good reasons for not doing so.

(2) Subsection (1) does not apply if the directors do not prepare group accounts for the parent company.

(3) Subsection (1) only applies to accounts of subsidiary undertakings that are required to be prepared under this Part.

(4) Subsection (1) does not require accounts of undertakings that are charities to be prepared using the same financial reporting framework as accounts of undertakings which are not charities.

(5) Subsection (1)(a) does not apply where the directors of a parent company prepare IAS group accounts and IAS individual accounts.

[1761]

NOTES

Commencement: to be appointed (see the introductory note to this Act).

408 Individual profit and loss account where group accounts prepared

(1) This section applies where—
- (a) a company prepares group accounts in accordance with this Act, and
- (b) the notes to the company's individual balance sheet show the company's profit or loss for the financial year determined in accordance with this Act.

(2) The profit and loss account need not contain the information specified in section 411 (information about employee numbers and costs).

(3) The company's individual profit and loss account must be approved in accordance with section 414(1) (approval by directors) but may be omitted from the company's annual accounts for the purposes of the other provisions of the Companies Acts.

(4) The exemption conferred by this section is conditional upon its being disclosed in the company's annual accounts that the exemption applies.

[1762]

NOTES

Commencement: to be appointed (see the introductory note to this Act).

Information to be given in notes to the accounts

409 Information about related undertakings

(1) The Secretary of State may make provision by regulations requiring information about related undertakings to be given in notes to a company's annual accounts.

(2) The regulations—

(a) may make different provision according to whether or not the company prepares group accounts, and

(b) may specify the descriptions of undertaking in relation to which they apply, and make different provision in relation to different descriptions of related undertaking.

(3) The regulations may provide that information need not be disclosed with respect to an undertaking that—

(a) is established under the law of a country outside the United Kingdom, or

(b) carries on business outside the United Kingdom,

if the following conditions are met.

(4) The conditions are—

(a) that in the opinion of the directors of the company the disclosure would be seriously prejudicial to the business of—

(i) that undertaking,

(ii) the company,

(iii) any of the company's subsidiary undertakings, or

(iv) any other undertaking which is included in the consolidation;

(b) that the Secretary of State agrees that the information need not be disclosed.

(5) Where advantage is taken of any such exemption, that fact must be stated in a note to the company's annual accounts.

[1763]

NOTES

Commencement: to be appointed (see the introductory note to this Act).

410 Information about related undertakings: alternative compliance

(1) This section applies where the directors of a company are of the opinion that the number of undertakings in respect of which the company is required to disclose information under any provision of regulations under section 409 (related undertakings) is such that compliance with that provision would result in information of excessive length being given in notes to the company's annual accounts.

(2) The information need only be given in respect of—

(a) the undertakings whose results or financial position, in the opinion of the directors, principally affected the figures shown in the company's annual accounts, and

(b) where the company prepares group accounts, undertakings excluded from consolidation under section 405(3) (undertakings excluded on grounds other than materiality).

(3) If advantage is taken of subsection (2)—

(a) there must be included in the notes to the company's annual accounts a statement that the information is given only with respect to such undertakings as are mentioned in that subsection, and

(b) the full information (both that which is disclosed in the notes to the accounts and that which is not) must be annexed to the company's next annual return.

For this purpose the "next annual return" means that next delivered to the registrar after the accounts in question have been approved under section 414.

(4) If a company fails to comply with subsection (3)(b), an offence is committed by—

(a) the company, and

(b) every officer of the company who is in default.

(5) A person guilty of an offence under subsection (4) is liable on summary conviction to a fine not exceeding level 3 on the standard scale and, for continued contravention, a daily default fine not exceeding one-tenth of level 3 on the standard scale.

[1764]

NOTES

Commencement: to be appointed (see the introductory note to this Act).

411 Information about employee numbers and costs

(1) In the case of a company not subject to the small companies regime, the following information with respect to the employees of the company must be given in notes to the company's annual accounts—

(a) the average number of persons employed by the company in the financial year, and

(b) the average number of persons so employed within each category of persons employed by the company.

(2) The categories by reference to which the number required to be disclosed by subsection (1)(b) is to be determined must be such as the directors may select having regard to the manner in which the company's activities are organised.

(3) The average number required by subsection (1)(a) or (b) is determined by dividing the relevant annual number by the number of months in the financial year.

(4) The relevant annual number is determined by ascertaining for each month in the financial year—

(a) for the purposes of subsection (1)(a), the number of persons employed under contracts of service by the company in that month (whether throughout the month or not);

(b) for the purposes of subsection (1)(b), the number of persons in the category in question of persons so employed;

and adding together all the monthly numbers.

(5) In respect of all persons employed by the company during the financial year who are taken into account in determining the relevant annual number for the purposes of subsection (1)(a) there must also be stated the aggregate amounts respectively of—

(a) wages and salaries paid or payable in respect of that year to those persons;

(b) social security costs incurred by the company on their behalf; and

(c) other pension costs so incurred.

This does not apply in so far as those amounts, or any of them, are stated elsewhere in the company's accounts.

(6) In subsection (5)—

"pension costs" includes any costs incurred by the company in respect of—

(a) any pension scheme established for the purpose of providing pensions for persons currently or formerly employed by the company,

(b) any sums set aside for the future payment of pensions directly by the company to current or former employees, and

(c) any pensions paid directly to such persons without having first been set aside;

"social security costs" means any contributions by the company to any state social security or pension scheme, fund or arrangement.

(7) Where the company prepares group accounts, this section applies as if the undertakings included in the consolidation were a single company.

[1765]

NOTES

Commencement: to be appointed (see the introductory note to this Act).

412 Information about directors' benefits: remuneration

(1) The Secretary of State may make provision by regulations requiring information to be given in notes to a company's annual accounts about directors' remuneration.

(2) The matters about which information may be required include—

(a) gains made by directors on the exercise of share options;

(b) benefits received or receivable by directors under long-term incentive schemes;

(c) payments for loss of office (as defined in section 215);

(d) benefits receivable, and contributions for the purpose of providing benefits, in respect of past services of a person as director or in any other capacity while director;

(e) consideration paid to or receivable by third parties for making available the services of a person as director or in any other capacity while director.

(3) Without prejudice to the generality of subsection (1), regulations under this section may make any such provision as was made immediately before the commencement of this Part by Part 1 of Schedule 6 to the Companies Act 1985 (c 6).

(4) For the purposes of this section, and regulations made under it, amounts paid to or receivable by—

(a) a person connected with a director, or

(b) a body corporate controlled by a director,

are treated as paid to or receivable by the director.

The expressions "connected with" and "controlled by" in this subsection have the same meaning as in Part 10 (company directors).

(5) It is the duty of—

(a) any director of a company, and

(b) any person who is or has at any time in the preceding five years been a director of the company,

to give notice to the company of such matters relating to himself as may be necessary for the purposes of regulations under this section.

(6) A person who makes default in complying with subsection (5) commits an offence and is liable on summary conviction to a fine not exceeding level 3 on the standard scale.

[1766]

NOTES

Commencement: to be appointed (see the introductory note to this Act).

413 Information about directors' benefits: advances, credit and guarantees

(1) In the case of a company that does not prepare group accounts, details of—

(a) advances and credits granted by the company to its directors, and

(b) guarantees of any kind entered into by the company on behalf of its directors,

must be shown in the notes to its individual accounts.

(2) In the case of a parent company that prepares group accounts, details of—

(a) advances and credits granted to the directors of the parent company, by that company or by any of its subsidiary undertakings, and

(b) guarantees of any kind entered into on behalf of the directors of the parent company, by that company or by any of its subsidiary undertakings,

must be shown in the notes to the group accounts.

(3) The details required of an advance or credit are—

(a) its amount,

(b) an indication of the interest rate,

(c) its main conditions, and
(d) any amounts repaid.

(4) The details required of a guarantee are—
(a) its main terms,
(b) the amount of the maximum liability that may be incurred by the company (or its subsidiary), and
(c) any amount paid and any liability incurred by the company (or its subsidiary) for the purpose of fulfilling the guarantee (including any loss incurred by reason of enforcement of the guarantee).

(5) There must also be stated in the notes to the accounts the totals—
(a) of amounts stated under subsection (3)(a),
(b) of amounts stated under subsection (3)(d),
(c) of amounts stated under subsection (4)(b), and
(d) of amounts stated under subsection (4)(c).

(6) References in this section to the directors of a company are to the persons who were a director at any time in the financial year to which the accounts relate.

(7) The requirements of this section apply in relation to every advance, credit or guarantee subsisting at any time in the financial year to which the accounts relate—
(a) whenever it was entered into,
(b) whether or not the person concerned was a director of the company in question at the time it was entered into, and
(c) in the case of an advance, credit or guarantee involving a subsidiary undertaking of that company, whether or not that undertaking was such a subsidiary undertaking at the time it was entered into.

(8) Banking companies and the holding companies of credit institutions need only state the details required by subsections (3)(a) and (4)(b).

[1767]

NOTES

Commencement: to be appointed (see the introductory note to this Act).

Approval and signing of accounts

414 Approval and signing of accounts

(1) A company's annual accounts must be approved by the board of directors and signed on behalf of the board by a director of the company.

(2) The signature must be on the company's balance sheet.

(3) If the accounts are prepared in accordance with the provisions applicable to companies subject to the small companies regime, the balance sheet must contain a statement to that effect in a prominent position above the signature.

(4) If annual accounts are approved that do not comply with the requirements of this Act (and, where applicable, of Article 4 of the IAS Regulation), every director of the company who—
(a) knew that they did not comply, or was reckless as to whether they complied, and
(b) failed to take reasonable steps to secure compliance with those requirements or, as the case may be, to prevent the accounts from being approved,

commits an offence.

(5) A person guilty of an offence under this section is liable—
(a) on conviction on indictment, to a fine;
(b) on summary conviction, to a fine not exceeding the statutory maximum.

[1768]

NOTES

Commencement: to be appointed (see the introductory note to this Act).

CHAPTER 5
DIRECTORS' REPORT

Directors' report

415 Duty to prepare directors' report

(1) The directors of a company must prepare a directors' report for each financial year of the company.

(2) For a financial year in which—
(a) the company is a parent company, and
(b) the directors of the company prepare group accounts,
the directors' report must be a consolidated report (a "group directors' report") relating to the undertakings included in the consolidation.

(3) A group directors' report may, where appropriate, give greater emphasis to the matters that are significant to the undertakings included in the consolidation, taken as a whole.

(4) In the case of failure to comply with the requirement to prepare a directors' report, an offence is committed by every person who—
(a) was a director of the company immediately before the end of the period for filing accounts and reports for the financial year in question, and
(b) failed to take all reasonable steps for securing compliance with that requirement.

(5) A person guilty of an offence under this section is liable—
(a) on conviction on indictment, to a fine;
(b) on summary conviction, to a fine not exceeding the statutory maximum.

[1769]

NOTES

Commencement: to be appointed (see the introductory note to this Act).

416 Contents of directors' report: general

(1) The directors' report for a financial year must state—
(a) the names of the persons who, at any time during the financial year, were directors of the company, and
(b) the principal activities of the company in the course of the year.

(2) In relation to a group directors' report subsection (1)(b) has effect as if the reference to the company was to the undertakings included in the consolidation.

(3) Except in the case of a company subject to the small companies regime, the report must state the amount (if any) that the directors recommend should be paid by way of dividend.

(4) The Secretary of State may make provision by regulations as to other matters that must be disclosed in a directors' report.

Without prejudice to the generality of this power, the regulations may make any such provision as was formerly made by Schedule 7 to the Companies Act 1985.

[1770]

NOTES

Commencement: to be appointed (see the introductory note to this Act).

417 Contents of directors' report: business review

(1) Unless the company is subject to the small companies' regime, the directors' report must contain a business review.

(2) The purpose of the business review is to inform members of the company and help them assess how the directors have performed their duty under section 172 (duty to promote the success of the company).

(3) The business review must contain—

(a) a fair review of the company's business, and

(b) a description of the principal risks and uncertainties facing the company.

(4) The review required is a balanced and comprehensive analysis of—

(a) the development and performance of the company's business during the financial year, and

(b) the position of the company's business at the end of that year,

consistent with the size and complexity of the business.

(5) In the case of a quoted company the business review must, to the extent necessary for an understanding of the development, performance or position of the company's business, include—

(a) the main trends and factors likely to affect the future development, performance and position of the company's business; and

(b) information about—

(i) environmental matters (including the impact of the company's business on the environment),

(ii) the company's employees, and

(iii) social and community issues,

including information about any policies of the company in relation to those matters and the effectiveness of those policies; and

(c) subject to subsection (11), information about persons with whom the company has contractual or other arrangements which are essential to the business of the company.

If the review does not contain information of each kind mentioned in paragraphs (b)(i), (ii) and (iii) and (c), it must state which of those kinds of information it does not contain.

(6) The review must, to the extent necessary for an understanding of the development, performance or position of the company's business, include—

(a) analysis using financial key performance indicators, and

(b) where appropriate, analysis using other key performance indicators, including information relating to environmental matters and employee matters.

"Key performance indicators" means factors by reference to which the development, performance or position of the company's business can be measured effectively.

(7) Where a company qualifies as medium-sized in relation to a financial year (see sections 465 to 467), the directors' report for the year need not comply with the requirements of subsection (6) so far as they relate to non-financial information.

(8) The review must, where appropriate, include references to, and additional explanations of, amounts included in the company's annual accounts.

(9) In relation to a group directors' report this section has effect as if the references to the company were references to the undertakings included in the consolidation.

(10) Nothing in this section requires the disclosure of information about impending developments or matters in the course of negotiation if the disclosure would, in the opinion of the directors, be seriously prejudicial to the interests of the company.

(11) Nothing in subsection (5)(c) requires the disclosure of information about a person if the disclosure would, in the opinion of the directors, be seriously prejudicial to that person and contrary to the public interest.

[1771]

NOTES

Commencement: to be appointed (see the introductory note to this Act).

418 Contents of directors' report: statement as to disclosure to auditors

(1) This section applies to a company unless—

(a) it is exempt for the financial year in question from the requirements of Part 16 as to audit of accounts, and

(b) the directors take advantage of that exemption.

(2) The directors' report must contain a statement to the effect that, in the case of each of the persons who are directors at the time the report is approved—

(a) so far as the director is aware, there is no relevant audit information of which the company's auditor is unaware, and

(b) he has taken all the steps that he ought to have taken as a director in order to make himself aware of any relevant audit information and to establish that the company's auditor is aware of that information.

(3) "Relevant audit information" means information needed by the company's auditor in connection with preparing his report.

(4) A director is regarded as having taken all the steps that he ought to have taken as a director in order to do the things mentioned in subsection (2)(b) if he has—

(a) made such enquiries of his fellow directors and of the company's auditors for that purpose, and

(b) taken such other steps (if any) for that purpose,

as are required by his duty as a director of the company to exercise reasonable care, skill and diligence.

(5) Where a directors' report containing the statement required by this section is approved but the statement is false, every director of the company who—

(a) knew that the statement was false, or was reckless as to whether it was false, and

(b) failed to take reasonable steps to prevent the report from being approved,

commits an offence.

(6) A person guilty of an offence under subsection (5) is liable—

(a) on conviction on indictment, to imprisonment for a term not exceeding two years or a fine (or both);

(b) on summary conviction—

(i) in England and Wales, to imprisonment for a term not exceeding twelve months or to a fine not exceeding the statutory maximum (or both);

(ii) in Scotland or Northern Ireland, to imprisonment for a term not exceeding six months, or to a fine not exceeding the statutory maximum (or both).

[1772]

NOTES

Commencement: to be appointed (see the introductory note to this Act).

419 Approval and signing of directors' report

(1) The directors' report must be approved by the board of directors and signed on behalf of the board by a director or the secretary of the company.

(2) If the report is prepared in accordance with the small companies regime, it must contain a statement to that effect in a prominent position above the signature.

(3) If a directors' report is approved that does not comply with the requirements of this Act, every director of the company who—

(a) knew that it did not comply, or was reckless as to whether it complied, and

(b) failed to take reasonable steps to secure compliance with those requirements or, as the case may be, to prevent the report from being approved,

commits an offence.

(4) A person guilty of an offence under this section is liable—

(a) on conviction on indictment, to a fine;

(b) on summary conviction, to a fine not exceeding the statutory maximum.

[1773]

NOTES

Commencement: to be appointed (see the introductory note to this Act).

420–422 ((*Chapter 6*) *outside the scope of this work.*)

CHAPTER 7
PUBLICATION OF ACCOUNTS AND REPORTS

Duty to circulate copies of accounts and reports

423 Duty to circulate copies of annual accounts and reports

(1) Every company must send a copy of its annual accounts and reports for each financial year to—

(a) every member of the company,
(b) every holder of the company's debentures, and
(c) every person who is entitled to receive notice of general meetings.

(2) Copies need not be sent to a person for whom the company does not have a current address.

(3) A company has a "current address" for a person if—

(a) an address has been notified to the company by the person as one at which documents may be sent to him, and
(b) the company has no reason to believe that documents sent to him at that address will not reach him.

(4) In the case of a company not having a share capital, copies need not be sent to anyone who is not entitled to receive notices of general meetings of the company.

(5) Where copies are sent out over a period of days, references in the Companies Acts to the day on which copies are sent out shall be read as references to the last day of that period.

(6) This section has effect subject to section 426 (option to provide summary financial statement).

[1774]

NOTES

Commencement: to be appointed (see the introductory note to this Act).

424 Time allowed for sending out copies of accounts and reports

(1) The time allowed for sending out copies of the company's annual accounts and reports is as follows.

(2) A private company must comply with section 423 not later than—

(a) the end of the period for filing accounts and reports, or
(b) if earlier, the date on which it actually delivers its accounts and reports to the registrar.

(3) A public company must comply with section 423 at least 21 days before the date of the relevant accounts meeting.

(4) If in the case of a public company copies are sent out later than is required by subsection (3), they shall, despite that, be deemed to have been duly sent if it is so agreed by all the members entitled to attend and vote at the relevant accounts meeting.

(5) Whether the time allowed is that for a private company or a public company is determined by reference to the company's status immediately before the end of the accounting reference period by reference to which the financial year for the accounts in question was determined.

(6) In this section the "relevant accounts meeting" means the accounts meeting of the company at which the accounts and reports in question are to be laid.

[1775]

NOTES

Commencement: to be appointed (see the introductory note to this Act).

425 Default in sending out copies of accounts and reports: offences

(1) If default is made in complying with section 423 or 424, an offence is committed by—

(a) the company, and
(b) every officer of the company who is in default.

(2) A person guilty of an offence under this section is liable—
(a) on conviction on indictment, to a fine;
(b) on summary conviction, to a fine not exceeding the statutory maximum.

[1776]

NOTES

Commencement: to be appointed (see the introductory note to this Act).

Option to provide summary financial statement

426 Option to provide summary financial statement

(1) A company may—
(a) in such cases as may be specified by regulations made by the Secretary of State, and
(b) provided any conditions so specified are complied with,

provide a summary financial statement instead of copies of the accounts and reports required to be sent out in accordance with section 423.

(2) Copies of those accounts and reports must, however, be sent to any person entitled to be sent them in accordance with that section and who wishes to receive them.

(3) The Secretary of State may make provision by regulations as to the manner in which it is to be ascertained, whether before or after a person becomes entitled to be sent a copy of those accounts and reports, whether he wishes to receive them.

(4) A summary financial statement must comply with the requirements of—
section 427 (form and contents of summary financial statement: unquoted companies), or
section 428 (form and contents of summary financial statement: quoted companies).

(5) This section applies to copies of accounts and reports required to be sent out by virtue of section 146 to a person nominated to enjoy information rights as it applies to copies of accounts and reports required to be sent out in accordance with section 423 to a member of the company.

(6) Regulations under this section are subject to negative resolution procedure.

[1777]

NOTES

Commencement: to be appointed (see the introductory note to this Act).

427 Form and contents of summary financial statement: unquoted companies

(1) A summary financial statement by a company that is not a quoted company must—
(a) be derived from the company's annual accounts, and
(b) be prepared in accordance with this section and regulations made under it.

(2) The summary financial statement must be in such form, and contain such information, as the Secretary of State may specify by regulations.

The regulations may require the statement to include information derived from the directors' report.

(3) Nothing in this section or regulations made under it prevents a company from including in a summary financial statement additional information derived from the company's annual accounts or the directors' report.

(4) The summary financial statement must—
(a) state that it is only a summary of information derived from the company's annual accounts;
(b) state whether it contains additional information derived from the directors' report and, if so, that it does not contain the full text of that report;

(c) state how a person entitled to them can obtain a full copy of the company's annual accounts and the directors' report;

(d) contain a statement by the company's auditor of his opinion as to whether the summary financial statement—

(i) is consistent with the company's annual accounts and, where information derived from the directors' report is included in the statement, with that report, and

(ii) complies with the requirements of this section and regulations made under it;

(e) state whether the auditor's report on the annual accounts was unqualified or qualified and, if it was qualified, set out the report in full together with any further material needed to understand the qualification;

(f) state whether, in that report, the auditor's statement under section 496 (whether directors' report consistent with accounts) was qualified or unqualified and, if it was qualified, set out the qualified statement in full together with any further material needed to understand the qualification;

(g) state whether that auditor's report contained a statement under—

(i) section 498(2)(a) or (b) (accounting records or returns inadequate or accounts not agreeing with records and returns), or

(ii) section 498(3) (failure to obtain necessary information and explanations),

and if so, set out the statement in full.

(5) Regulations under this section may provide that any specified material may, instead of being included in the summary financial statement, be sent separately at the same time as the statement.

(6) Regulations under this section are subject to negative resolution procedure.

[1778]

NOTES

Commencement: to be appointed (see the introductory note to this Act).

428 (*Outside the scope of this work.*)

429 Summary financial statements: offences

(1) If default is made in complying with any provision of section 426, 427 or 428, or of regulations under any of those sections, an offence is committed by—

(a) the company, and

(b) every officer of the company who is in default.

(2) A person guilty of an offence under this section is liable on summary conviction to a fine not exceeding level 3 on the standard scale.

[1779]

NOTES

Commencement: to be appointed (see the introductory note to this Act).

430 (*Outside the scope of this work.*)

Right of member or debenture holder to demand copies of accounts and reports

431 Right of member or debenture holder to copies of accounts and reports: unquoted companies

(1) A member of, or holder of debentures of, an unquoted company is entitled to be provided, on demand and without charge, with a copy of—

(a) the company's last annual accounts,

(b) the last directors' report, and

(c) the auditor's report on those accounts (including the statement on that report).

(2) The entitlement under this section is to a single copy of those documents, but that is in addition to any copy to which a person may be entitled under section 423.

(3) If a demand made under this section is not complied with within seven days of receipt by the company, an offence is committed by—

(a) the company, and

(b) every officer of the company who is in default.

(4) A person guilty of an offence under this section is liable on summary conviction to a fine not exceeding level 3 on the standard scale and, for continued contravention, a daily default fine not exceeding one-tenth of level 3 on the standard scale.

[1780]

NOTES

Commencement: to be appointed (see the introductory note to this Act).

432 (*Outside the scope of this work.*)

Requirements in connection with publication of accounts and reports

433 Name of signatory to be stated in published copies of accounts and reports

(1) Every copy of a document to which this section applies that is published by or on behalf of the company must state the name of the person who signed it on behalf of the board.

(2) In the case of an unquoted company, this section applies to copies of—

(a) the company's balance sheet, and

(b) the directors' report.

(3) In the case of a quoted company, this section applies to copies of—

(a) the company's balance sheet,

(b) the directors' remuneration report, and

(c) the directors' report.

(4) If a copy is published without the required statement of the signatory's name, an offence is committed by—

(a) the company, and

(b) every officer of the company who is in default.

(5) A person guilty of an offence under this section is liable on summary conviction to a fine not exceeding level 3 on the standard scale.

[1781]

NOTES

Commencement: to be appointed (see the introductory note to this Act).

434 Requirements in connection with publication of statutory accounts

(1) If a company publishes any of its statutory accounts, they must be accompanied by the auditor's report on those accounts (unless the company is exempt from audit and the directors have taken advantage of that exemption).

(2) A company that prepares statutory group accounts for a financial year must not publish its statutory individual accounts for that year without also publishing with them its statutory group accounts.

(3) A company's "statutory accounts" are its accounts for a financial year as required to be delivered to the registrar under section 441.

(4) If a company contravenes any provision of this section, an offence is committed by—

(a) the company, and

(b) every officer of the company who is in default.

(5) A person guilty of an offence under this section is liable on summary conviction to a fine not exceeding level 3 on the standard scale.

(6) This section does not apply in relation to the provision by a company of a summary financial statement (see section 426).

[1782]

NOTES

Commencement: to be appointed (see the introductory note to this Act).

435 Requirements in connection with publication of non-statutory accounts

(1) If a company publishes non-statutory accounts, it must publish with them a statement indicating—

(a) that they are not the company's statutory accounts,

(b) whether statutory accounts dealing with any financial year with which the non-statutory accounts purport to deal have been delivered to the registrar, and

(c) whether an auditor's report has been made on the company's statutory accounts for any such financial year, and if so whether the report—

(i) was qualified or unqualified, or included a reference to any matters to which the auditor drew attention by way of emphasis without qualifying the report, or

(ii) contained a statement under section 498(2) (accounting records or returns inadequate or accounts or directors' remuneration report not agreeing with records and returns), or section 498(3) (failure to obtain necessary information and explanations).

(2) The company must not publish with non-statutory accounts the auditor's report on the company's statutory accounts.

(3) References in this section to the publication by a company of "non-statutory accounts" are to the publication of—

(a) any balance sheet or profit and loss account relating to, or purporting to deal with, a financial year of the company, or

(b) an account in any form purporting to be a balance sheet or profit and loss account for a group headed by the company relating to, or purporting to deal with, a financial year of the company,

otherwise than as part of the company's statutory accounts.

(4) In subsection (3)(b) "a group headed by the company" means a group consisting of the company and any other undertaking (regardless of whether it is a subsidiary undertaking of the company) other than a parent undertaking of the company.

(5) If a company contravenes any provision of this section, an offence is committed by—

(a) the company, and

(b) every officer of the company who is in default.

(6) A person guilty of an offence under this section is liable on summary conviction to a fine not exceeding level 3 on the standard scale.

(7) This section does not apply in relation to the provision by a company of a summary financial statement (see section 426).

[1783]

NOTES

Commencement: to be appointed (see the introductory note to this Act).

436 Meaning of "publication" in relation to accounts and reports

(1) This section has effect for the purposes of—

section 433 (name of signatory to be stated in published copies of accounts and reports),
section 434 (requirements in connection with publication of statutory accounts), and
section 435 (requirements in connection with publication of non-statutory accounts).

(2) For the purposes of those sections a company is regarded as publishing a document if it publishes, issues or circulates it or otherwise makes it available for public inspection in a manner calculated to invite members of the public generally, or any class of members of the public, to read it.

[1784]

NOTES

Commencement: to be appointed (see the introductory note to this Act).

437–440 ((*Chapters 8, 9*) *outside the scope of this work.*)

CHAPTER 10
FILING OF ACCOUNTS AND REPORTS

Duty to file accounts and reports

441 Duty to file accounts and reports with the registrar

(1) The directors of a company must deliver to the registrar for each financial year the accounts and reports required by—

section 444 (filing obligations of companies subject to small companies regime),
section 445 (filing obligations of medium-sized companies),
section 446 (filing obligations of unquoted companies), or
section 447 (filing obligations of quoted companies).

(2) This is subject to section 448 (unlimited companies exempt from filing obligations).
[1785]

NOTES

Commencement: to be appointed (see the introductory note to this Act).

442 Period allowed for filing accounts

(1) This section specifies the period allowed for the directors of a company to comply with their obligation under section 441 to deliver accounts and reports for a financial year to the registrar.

This is referred to in the Companies Acts as the "period for filing" those accounts and reports.

(2) The period is—

(a) for a private company, nine months after the end of the relevant accounting reference period, and
(b) for a public company, six months after the end of that period.

This is subject to the following provisions of this section.

(3) If the relevant accounting reference period is the company's first and is a period of more than twelve months, the period is—

(a) nine months or six months, as the case may be, from the first anniversary of the incorporation of the company, or
(b) three months after the end of the accounting reference period,

whichever last expires.

(4) If the relevant accounting reference period is treated as shortened by virtue of a notice given by the company under section 392 (alteration of accounting reference date), the period is—

(a) that applicable in accordance with the above provisions, or
(b) three months from the date of the notice under that section,

whichever last expires.

(5) If for any special reason the Secretary of State thinks fit he may, on an application made before the expiry of the period otherwise allowed, by notice in writing to a company extend that period by such further period as may be specified in the notice.

(6) Whether the period allowed is that for a private company or a public company is determined by reference to the company's status immediately before the end of the relevant accounting reference period.

(7) In this section "the relevant accounting reference period" means the accounting reference period by reference to which the financial year for the accounts in question was determined.

[1786]

NOTES

Commencement: to be appointed (see the introductory note to this Act).

443 Calculation of period allowed

(1) This section applies for the purposes of calculating the period for filing a company's accounts and reports which is expressed as a specified number of months from a specified date or after the end of a specified previous period.

(2) Subject to the following provisions, the period ends with the date in the appropriate month corresponding to the specified date or the last day of the specified previous period.

(3) If the specified date, or the last day of the specified previous period, is the last day of a month, the period ends with the last day of the appropriate month (whether or not that is the corresponding date).

(4) If—

(a) the specified date, or the last day of the specified previous period, is not the last day of a month but is the 29th or 30th, and

(b) the appropriate month is February,

the period ends with the last day of February.

(5) "The appropriate month" means the month that is the specified number of months after the month in which the specified date, or the end of the specified previous period, falls.
[1787]

NOTES

Commencement: to be appointed (see the introductory note to this Act).

Filing obligations of different descriptions of company

444 Filing obligations of companies subject to small companies regime

(1) The directors of a company subject to the small companies regime—

(a) must deliver to the registrar for each financial year a copy of a balance sheet drawn up as at the last day of that year, and

(b) may also deliver to the registrar—

(i) a copy of the company's profit and loss account for that year, and

(ii) a copy of the directors' report for that year.

(2) The directors must also deliver to the registrar a copy of the auditor's report on those accounts (and on the directors' report).

This does not apply if the company is exempt from audit and the directors have taken advantage of that exemption.

(3) The copies of accounts and reports delivered to the registrar must be copies of the company's annual accounts and reports, except that where the company prepares Companies Act accounts—

(a) the directors may deliver to the registrar a copy of a balance sheet drawn up in accordance with regulations made by the Secretary of State, and

(b) there may be omitted from the copy profit and loss account delivered to the registrar such items as may be specified by the regulations.

These are referred to in this Part as "abbreviated accounts".

(4) If abbreviated accounts are delivered to the registrar the obligation to deliver a copy of the auditor's report on the accounts is to deliver a copy of the special auditor's report required by section 449.

(5) Where the directors of a company subject to the small companies regime deliver to the registrar IAS accounts, or Companies Act accounts that are not abbreviated accounts, and in accordance with this section—

(a) do not deliver to the registrar a copy of the company's profit and loss account, or

(b) do not deliver to the registrar a copy of the directors' report,

the copy of the balance sheet delivered to the registrar must contain in a prominent position a statement that the company's annual accounts and reports have been delivered in accordance with the provisions applicable to companies subject to the small companies regime.

(6) The copies of the balance sheet and any directors' report delivered to the registrar under this section must state the name of the person who signed it on behalf of the board.

(7) The copy of the auditor's report delivered to the registrar under this section must—

(a) state the name of the auditor and (where the auditor is a firm) the name of the person who signed it as senior statutory auditor, or

(b) if the conditions in section 506 (circumstances in which names may be omitted) are met, state that a resolution has been passed and notified to the Secretary of State in accordance with that section.

[1788]

NOTES

Commencement: to be appointed (see the introductory note to this Act).

445 Filing obligations of medium-sized companies

(1) The directors of a company that qualifies as a medium-sized company in relation to a financial year (see sections 465 to 467) must deliver to the registrar a copy of—

(a) the company's annual accounts, and

(b) the directors' report.

(2) They must also deliver to the registrar a copy of the auditor's report on those accounts (and on the directors' report).

This does not apply if the company is exempt from audit and the directors have taken advantage of that exemption.

(3) Where the company prepares Companies Act accounts, the directors may deliver to the registrar a copy of the company's annual accounts for the financial year—

(a) that includes a profit and loss account in which items are combined in accordance with regulations made by the Secretary of State, and

(b) that does not contain items whose omission is authorised by the regulations.

These are referred to in this Part as "abbreviated accounts".

(4) If abbreviated accounts are delivered to the registrar the obligation to deliver a copy of the auditor's report on the accounts is to deliver a copy of the special auditor's report required by section 449.

(5) The copies of the balance sheet and directors' report delivered to the registrar under this section must state the name of the person who signed it on behalf of the board.

(6) The copy of the auditor's report delivered to the registrar under this section must—

(a) state the name of the auditor and (where the auditor is a firm) the name of the person who signed it as senior statutory auditor, or

(b) if the conditions in section 506 (circumstances in which names may be omitted) are met, state that a resolution has been passed and notified to the Secretary of State in accordance with that section.

(7) This section does not apply to companies within section 444 (filing obligations of companies subject to the small companies regime).

[1789]

NOTES

Commencement: to be appointed (see the introductory note to this Act).

446 Filing obligations of unquoted companies

(1) The directors of an unquoted company must deliver to the registrar for each financial year of the company a copy of—

(a) the company's annual accounts, and

(b) the directors' report.

(2) The directors must also deliver to the registrar a copy of the auditor's report on those accounts (and the directors' report).

This does not apply if the company is exempt from audit and the directors have taken advantage of that exemption.

(3) The copies of the balance sheet and directors' report delivered to the registrar under this section must state the name of the person who signed it on behalf of the board.

(4) The copy of the auditor's report delivered to the registrar under this section must—
(a) state the name of the auditor and (where the auditor is a firm) the name of the person who signed it as senior statutory auditor, or
(b) if the conditions in section 506 (circumstances in which names may be omitted) are met, state that a resolution has been passed and notified to the Secretary of State in accordance with that section.

(5) This section does not apply to companies within—
(a) section 444 (filing obligations of companies subject to the small companies regime), or
(b) section 445 (filing obligations of medium-sized companies).

[1790]

NOTES

Commencement: to be appointed (see the introductory note to this Act).

447 (*Outside the scope of this work.*)

448 Unlimited companies exempt from obligation to file accounts

(1) The directors of an unlimited company are not required to deliver accounts and reports to the registrar in respect of a financial year if the following conditions are met.

(2) The conditions are that at no time during the relevant accounting reference period—
(a) has the company been, to its knowledge, a subsidiary undertaking of an undertaking which was then limited, or
(b) have there been, to its knowledge, exercisable by or on behalf of two or more undertakings which were then limited, rights which if exercisable by one of them would have made the company a subsidiary undertaking of it, or
(c) has the company been a parent company of an undertaking which was then limited.

The references above to an undertaking being limited at a particular time are to an undertaking (under whatever law established) the liability of whose members is at that time limited.

(3) The exemption conferred by this section does not apply if—
(a) the company is a banking or insurance company or the parent company of a banking or insurance group, or
(b) the company is a qualifying company within the meaning of the Partnerships and Unlimited Companies (Accounts) Regulations 1993 (SI 1993/1820).

(4) Where a company is exempt by virtue of this section from the obligation to deliver accounts—
(a) section 434(3) (requirements in connection with publication of statutory accounts: meaning of "statutory accounts") has effect with the substitution for the words "as required to be delivered to the registrar under section 441" of the words "as prepared in accordance with this Part and approved by the board of directors"; and
(b) section 435(1)(b) (requirements in connection with publication of non-statutory accounts: statement whether statutory accounts delivered) has effect with the substitution for the words from "whether statutory accounts" to "have been delivered to the registrar" of the words "that the company is exempt from the requirement to deliver statutory accounts".

(5) In this section the "relevant accounting reference period", in relation to a financial year, means the accounting reference period by reference to which that financial year was determined.

[1791]

NOTES

Commencement: to be appointed (see the introductory note to this Act).

Requirements where abbreviated accounts delivered

449 Special auditor's report where abbreviated accounts delivered

(1) This section applies where—

(a) the directors of a company deliver abbreviated accounts to the registrar, and
(b) the company is not exempt from audit (or the directors have not taken advantage of any such exemption).

(2) The directors must also deliver to the registrar a copy of a special report of the company's auditor stating that in his opinion—
(a) the company is entitled to deliver abbreviated accounts in accordance with the section in question, and
(b) the abbreviated accounts to be delivered are properly prepared in accordance with regulations under that section.

(3) The auditor's report on the company's annual accounts need not be delivered, but—
(a) if that report was qualified, the special report must set out that report in full together with any further material necessary to understand the qualification, and
(b) if that report contained a statement under—
(i) section 498(2)(a) or (b) (accounts, records or returns inadequate or accounts not agreeing with records and returns), or
(ii) section 498(3) (failure to obtain necessary information and explanations),
the special report must set out that statement in full.

(4) The provisions of—
sections 503 to 506 (signature of auditor's report), and
sections 507 to 509 (offences in connection with auditor's report),
apply to a special report under this section as they apply to an auditor's report on the company's annual accounts prepared under Part 16.

(5) If abbreviated accounts are delivered to the registrar, the references in section 434 or 435 (requirements in connection with publication of accounts) to the auditor's report on the company's annual accounts shall be read as references to the special auditor's report required by this section.

[1792]

NOTES
Commencement: to be appointed (see the introductory note to this Act).

450 Approval and signing of abbreviated accounts

(1) Abbreviated accounts must be approved by the board of directors and signed on behalf of the board by a director of the company.

(2) The signature must be on the balance sheet.

(3) The balance sheet must contain in a prominent position above the signature a statement to the effect that it is prepared in accordance with the special provisions of this Act relating (as the case may be) to companies subject to the small companies regime or to medium-sized companies.

(4) If abbreviated accounts are approved that do not comply with the requirements of regulations under the relevant section, every director of the company who—
(a) knew that they did not comply, or was reckless as to whether they complied, and
(b) failed to take reasonable steps to prevent them from being approved,
commits an offence.

(5) A person guilty of an offence under subsection (4) is liable—
(a) on conviction on indictment, to a fine;
(b) on summary conviction, to a fine not exceeding the statutory maximum.

[1793]

NOTES
Commencement: to be appointed (see the introductory note to this Act).

Failure to file accounts and reports

451 Default in filing accounts and reports: offences

(1) If the requirements of section 441 (duty to file accounts and reports) are not complied with in relation to a company's accounts and reports for a financial year before the end of the

period for filing those accounts and reports, every person who immediately before the end of that period was a director of the company commits an offence.

(2) It is a defence for a person charged with such an offence to prove that he took all reasonable steps for securing that those requirements would be complied with before the end of that period.

(3) It is not a defence to prove that the documents in question were not in fact prepared as required by this Part.

(4) A person guilty of an offence under this section is liable on summary conviction to a fine not exceeding level 5 on the standard scale and, for continued contravention, a daily default fine not exceeding one-tenth of level 5 on the standard scale.

[1794]

PART I STATUTES

NOTES

Commencement: to be appointed (see the introductory note to this Act).

452 Default in filing accounts and reports: court order

(1) If—

(a) the requirements of section 441 (duty to file accounts and reports) are not complied with in relation to a company's accounts and reports for a financial year before the end of the period for filing those accounts and reports, and

(b) the directors of the company fail to make good the default within 14 days after the service of a notice on them requiring compliance,

the court may, on the application of any member or creditor of the company or of the registrar, make an order directing the directors (or any of them) to make good the default within such time as may be specified in the order.

(2) The court's order may provide that all costs (in Scotland, expenses) of and incidental to the application are to be borne by the directors.

[1795]

NOTES

Commencement: to be appointed (see the introductory note to this Act).

453 Civil penalty for failure to file accounts and reports

(1) Where the requirements of section 441 are not complied with in relation to a company's accounts and reports for a financial year before the end of the period for filing those accounts and reports, the company is liable to a civil penalty.

This is in addition to any liability of the directors under section 451.

(2) The amount of the penalty shall be determined in accordance with regulations made by the Secretary of State by reference to—

(a) the length of the period between the end of the period for filing the accounts and reports in question and the day on which the requirements are complied with, and

(b) whether the company is a private or public company.

(3) The penalty may be recovered by the registrar and is to be paid into the Consolidated Fund.

(4) It is not a defence in proceedings under this section to prove that the documents in question were not in fact prepared as required by this Part.

(5) Regulations under this section having the effect of increasing the penalty payable in any case are subject to affirmative resolution procedure. Otherwise, the regulations are subject to negative resolution procedure.

[1796]

NOTES

Commencement: to be appointed (see the introductory note to this Act).

CHAPTER 11
REVISION OF DEFECTIVE ACCOUNTS AND REPORTS

Voluntary revision

454 Voluntary revision of accounts etc

(1) If it appears to the directors of a company that—

(a) the company's annual accounts,

(b) the directors' remuneration report or the directors' report, or

(c) a summary financial statement of the company,

did not comply with the requirements of this Act (or, where applicable, of Article 4 of the IAS Regulation), they may prepare revised accounts or a revised report or statement.

(2) Where copies of the previous accounts or report have been sent out to members, delivered to the registrar or (in the case of a public company) laid before the company in general meeting, the revisions must be confined to—

(a) the correction of those respects in which the previous accounts or report did not comply with the requirements of this Act (or, where applicable, of Article 4 of the IAS Regulation), and

(b) the making of any necessary consequential alterations.

(3) The Secretary of State may make provision by regulations as to the application of the provisions of this Act in relation to—

(a) revised annual accounts,

(b) a revised directors' remuneration report or directors' report, or

(c) a revised summary financial statement.

(4) The regulations may, in particular—

(a) make different provision according to whether the previous accounts, report or statement are replaced or are supplemented by a document indicating the corrections to be made;

(b) make provision with respect to the functions of the company's auditor in relation to the revised accounts, report or statement;

(c) require the directors to take such steps as may be specified in the regulations where the previous accounts or report have been—

(i) sent out to members and others under section 423,

(ii) laid before the company in general meeting, or

(iii) delivered to the registrar,

or where a summary financial statement containing information derived from the previous accounts or report has been sent to members under section 426;

(d) apply the provisions of this Act (including those creating criminal offences) subject to such additions, exceptions and modifications as are specified in the regulations.

(5) Regulations under this section are subject to negative resolution procedure.

[1797]

NOTES

Commencement: to be appointed (see the introductory note to this Act).

Secretary of State's notice

455 Secretary of State's notice in respect of accounts or reports

(1) This section applies where—

(a) copies of a company's annual accounts or directors' report have been sent out under section 423, or

(b) a copy of a company's annual accounts or directors' report has been delivered to the registrar or (in the case of a public company) laid before the company in general meeting,

and it appears to the Secretary of State that there is, or may be, a question whether the accounts or report comply with the requirements of this Act (or, where applicable, of Article 4 of the IAS Regulation).

(2) The Secretary of State may give notice to the directors of the company indicating the respects in which it appears that such a question arises or may arise.

(3) The notice must specify a period of not less than one month for the directors to give an explanation of the accounts or report or prepare revised accounts or a revised report.

(4) If at the end of the specified period, or such longer period as the Secretary of State may allow, it appears to the Secretary of State that the directors have not—

(a) given a satisfactory explanation of the accounts or report, or

(b) revised the accounts or report so as to comply with the requirements of this Act (or, where applicable, of Article 4 of the IAS Regulation),

the Secretary of State may apply to the court.

(5) The provisions of this section apply equally to revised annual accounts and revised directors' reports, in which case they have effect as if the references to revised accounts or reports were references to further revised accounts or reports.

[1798]

NOTES

Commencement: to be appointed (see the introductory note to this Act).

Application to court

456 Application to court in respect of defective accounts or reports

(1) An application may be made to the court—

(a) by the Secretary of State, after having complied with section 455, or

(b) by a person authorised by the Secretary of State for the purposes of this section,

for a declaration (in Scotland, a declarator) that the annual accounts of a company do not comply, or a directors' report does not comply, with the requirements of this Act (or, where applicable, of Article 4 of the IAS Regulation) and for an order requiring the directors of the company to prepare revised accounts or a revised report.

(2) Notice of the application, together with a general statement of the matters at issue in the proceedings, shall be given by the applicant to the registrar for registration.

(3) If the court orders the preparation of revised accounts, it may give directions as to—

(a) the auditing of the accounts,

(b) the revision of any directors' remuneration report, directors' report or summary financial statement, and

(c) the taking of steps by the directors to bring the making of the order to the notice of persons likely to rely on the previous accounts,

and such other matters as the court thinks fit.

(4) If the court orders the preparation of a revised directors' report it may give directions as to—

(a) the review of the report by the auditors,

(b) the revision of any summary financial statement,

(c) the taking of steps by the directors to bring the making of the order to the notice of persons likely to rely on the previous report, and

(d) such other matters as the court thinks fit.

(5) If the court finds that the accounts or report did not comply with the requirements of this Act (or, where applicable, of Article 4 of the IAS Regulation) it may order that all or part of—

(a) the costs (in Scotland, expenses) of and incidental to the application, and

(b) any reasonable expenses incurred by the company in connection with or in consequence of the preparation of revised accounts or a revised report,

are to be borne by such of the directors as were party to the approval of the defective accounts or report.

For this purpose every director of the company at the time of the approval of the accounts or report shall be taken to have been a party to the approval unless he shows that he took all reasonable steps to prevent that approval.

(6) Where the court makes an order under subsection (5) it shall have regard to whether the directors party to the approval of the defective accounts or report knew or ought to have

known that the accounts or report did not comply with the requirements of this Act (or, where applicable, of Article 4 of the IAS Regulation), and it may exclude one or more directors from the order or order the payment of different amounts by different directors.

(7) On the conclusion of proceedings on an application under this section, the applicant must send to the registrar for registration a copy of the court order or, as the case may be, give notice to the registrar that the application has failed or been withdrawn.

(8) The provisions of this section apply equally to revised annual accounts and revised directors' reports, in which case they have effect as if the references to revised accounts or reports were references to further revised accounts or reports.

[1799]

NOTES

Commencement: to be appointed (see the introductory note to this Act).

457 Other persons authorised to apply to the court

(1) The Secretary of State may by order (an "authorisation order") authorise for the purposes of section 456 any person appearing to him—

(a) to have an interest in, and to have satisfactory procedures directed to securing, compliance by companies with the requirements of this Act (or, where applicable, of Article 4 of the IAS Regulation) relating to accounts and directors' reports,

(b) to have satisfactory procedures for receiving and investigating complaints about companies' annual accounts and directors' reports, and

(c) otherwise to be a fit and proper person to be authorised.

(2) A person may be authorised generally or in respect of particular classes of case, and different persons may be authorised in respect of different classes of case.

(3) The Secretary of State may refuse to authorise a person if he considers that his authorisation is unnecessary having regard to the fact that there are one or more other persons who have been or are likely to be authorised.

(4) If the authorised person is an unincorporated association, proceedings brought in, or in connection with, the exercise of any function by the association as an authorised person may be brought by or against the association in the name of a body corporate whose constitution provides for the establishment of the association.

(5) An authorisation order may contain such requirements or other provisions relating to the exercise of functions by the authorised person as appear to the Secretary of State to be appropriate.

No such order is to be made unless it appears to the Secretary of State that the person would, if authorised, exercise his functions as an authorised person in accordance with the provisions proposed.

(6) Where authorisation is revoked, the revoking order may make such provision as the Secretary of State thinks fit with respect to pending proceedings.

(7) An order under this section is subject to negative resolution procedure.

[1800]

NOTES

Commencement: to be appointed (see the introductory note to this Act).

458 Disclosure of information by tax authorities

(1) The Commissioners for Her Majesty's Revenue and Customs may disclose information to a person authorised under section 457 for the purpose of facilitating—

(a) the taking of steps by that person to discover whether there are grounds for an application to the court under section 456 (application in respect of defective accounts etc), or

(b) a decision by the authorised person whether to make such an application.

(2) This section applies despite any statutory or other restriction on the disclosure of information.

Provided that, in the case of personal data within the meaning of the Data Protection Act 1998 (c 29), information is not to be disclosed in contravention of that Act.

(3) Information disclosed to an authorised person under this section—
(a) may not be used except in or in connection with—
(i) taking steps to discover whether there are grounds for an application to the court under section 456, or
(ii) deciding whether or not to make such an application,
or in, or in connection with, proceedings on such an application; and
(b) must not be further disclosed except—
(i) to the person to whom the information relates, or
(ii) in, or in connection with, proceedings on any such application to the court.

(4) A person who contravenes subsection (3) commits an offence unless—
(a) he did not know, and had no reason to suspect, that the information had been disclosed under this section, or
(b) he took all reasonable steps and exercised all due diligence to avoid the commission of the offence.

(5) A person guilty of an offence under subsection (4) is liable—
(a) on conviction on indictment, to imprisonment for a term not exceeding two years or a fine (or both);
(b) on summary conviction—
(i) in England and Wales, to imprisonment for a term not exceeding twelve months or to a fine not exceeding the statutory maximum (or both);
(ii) in Scotland or Northern Ireland, to imprisonment for a term not exceeding six months, or to a fine not exceeding the statutory maximum (or both).

[1801]

NOTES

Commencement: to be appointed (see the introductory note to this Act).

Power of authorised person to require documents etc

459 Power of authorised person to require documents, information and explanations

(1) This section applies where it appears to a person who is authorised under section 457 that there is, or may be, a question whether a company's annual accounts or directors' report comply with the requirements of this Act (or, where applicable, of Article 4 of the IAS Regulation).

(2) The authorised person may require any of the persons mentioned in subsection (3) to produce any document, or to provide him with any information or explanations, that he may reasonably require for the purpose of—
(a) discovering whether there are grounds for an application to the court under section 456, or
(b) deciding whether to make such an application.

(3) Those persons are—
(a) the company;
(b) any officer, employee, or auditor of the company;
(c) any persons who fell within paragraph (b) at a time to which the document or information required by the authorised person relates.

(4) If a person fails to comply with such a requirement, the authorised person may apply to the court.

(5) If it appears to the court that the person has failed to comply with a requirement under subsection (2), it may order the person to take such steps as it directs for securing that the documents are produced or the information or explanations are provided.

(6) A statement made by a person in response to a requirement under subsection (2) or an order under subsection (5) may not be used in evidence against him in any criminal proceedings.

(7) Nothing in this section compels any person to disclose documents or information in respect of which a claim to legal professional privilege (in Scotland, to confidentiality of communications) could be maintained in legal proceedings.

(8) In this section "document" includes information recorded in any form.

[1802]

NOTES

Commencement: to be appointed (see the introductory note to this Act).

460 Restrictions on disclosure of information obtained under compulsory powers

(1) This section applies to information (in whatever form) obtained in pursuance of a requirement or order under section 459 (power of authorised person to require documents etc) that relates to the private affairs of an individual or to any particular business.

(2) No such information may, during the lifetime of that individual or so long as that business continues to be carried on, be disclosed without the consent of that individual or the person for the time being carrying on that business.

(3) This does not apply—

(a) to disclosure permitted by section 461 (permitted disclosure of information obtained under compulsory powers), or

(b) to the disclosure of information that is or has been available to the public from another source.

(4) A person who discloses information in contravention of this section commits an offence, unless—

(a) he did not know, and had no reason to suspect, that the information had been disclosed under section 459, or

(b) he took all reasonable steps and exercised all due diligence to avoid the commission of the offence.

(5) A person guilty of an offence under this section is liable—

(a) on conviction on indictment, to imprisonment for a term not exceeding two years or a fine (or both);

(b) on summary conviction—

(i) in England and Wales, to imprisonment for a term not exceeding twelve months or to a fine not exceeding the statutory maximum (or both);

(ii) in Scotland or Northern Ireland, to imprisonment for a term not exceeding six months, or to a fine not exceeding the statutory maximum (or both).

[1803]

NOTES

Commencement: to be appointed (see the introductory note to this Act).

461 Permitted disclosure of information obtained under compulsory powers

(1) The prohibition in section 460 of the disclosure of information obtained in pursuance of a requirement or order under section 459 (power of authorised person to require documents etc) that relates to the private affairs of an individual or to any particular business has effect subject to the following exceptions.

(2) It does not apply to the disclosure of information for the purpose of facilitating the carrying out by the authorised person of his functions under section 456.

(3) It does not apply to disclosure to—

(a) the Secretary of State,

(b) the Department of Enterprise, Trade and Investment for Northern Ireland,

(c) the Treasury,

(d) the Bank of England,

(e) the Financial Services Authority, or

(f) the Commissioners for Her Majesty's Revenue and Customs.

(4) It does not apply to disclosure—

(a) for the purpose of assisting a body designated by an order under section 46 of the Companies Act 1989 (c 40) (delegation of functions of the Secretary of State) to exercise its functions under Part 2 of that Act;

(b) with a view to the institution of, or otherwise for the purposes of, disciplinary proceedings relating to the performance by an accountant or auditor of his professional duties;

(c) for the purpose of enabling or assisting the Secretary of State or the Treasury to exercise any of their functions under any of the following—

(i) the Companies Acts,
(ii) Part 5 of the Criminal Justice Act 1993 (c 36) (insider dealing),
(iii) the Insolvency Act 1986 (c 45) or the Insolvency (Northern Ireland) Order 1989 (SI 1989/2405 (NI 19)),
(iv) the Company Directors Disqualification Act 1986 (c 46) or the Company Directors Disqualification (Northern Ireland) Order 2002 (SI 2002/3150 (NI 4)),
(v) the Financial Services and Markets Act 2000 (c 8);

(d) for the purpose of enabling or assisting the Department of Enterprise, Trade and Investment for Northern Ireland to exercise any powers conferred on it by the enactments relating to companies, directors' disqualification or insolvency;
(e) for the purpose of enabling or assisting the Bank of England to exercise its functions;
(f) for the purpose of enabling or assisting the Commissioners for Her Majesty's Revenue and Customs to exercise their functions;
(g) for the purpose of enabling or assisting the Financial Services Authority to exercise its functions under any of the following—
(i) the legislation relating to friendly societies or to industrial and provident societies,
(ii) the Building Societies Act 1986 (c 53),
(iii) Part 7 of the Companies Act 1989 (c 40),
(iv) the Financial Services and Markets Act 2000; or
(h) in pursuance of any Community obligation.

(5) It does not apply to disclosure to a body exercising functions of a public nature under legislation in any country or territory outside the United Kingdom that appear to the authorised person to be similar to his functions under section 456 for the purpose of enabling or assisting that body to exercise those functions.

(6) In determining whether to disclose information to a body in accordance with subsection (5), the authorised person must have regard to the following considerations—
(a) whether the use which the body is likely to make of the information is sufficiently important to justify making the disclosure;
(b) whether the body has adequate arrangements to prevent the information from being used or further disclosed other than—
(i) for the purposes of carrying out the functions mentioned in that subsection, or
(ii) for other purposes substantially similar to those for which information disclosed to the authorised person could be used or further disclosed.

(7) Nothing in this section authorises the making of a disclosure in contravention of the Data Protection Act 1998 (c 29).

[1804]

NOTES

Commencement: to be appointed (see the introductory note to this Act).

462 Power to amend categories of permitted disclosure

(1) The Secretary of State may by order amend section 461(3), (4) and (5).

(2) An order under this section must not—
(a) amend subsection (3) of that section (UK public authorities) by specifying a person unless the person exercises functions of a public nature (whether or not he exercises any other function);
(b) amend subsection (4) of that section (purposes for which disclosure permitted) by adding or modifying a description of disclosure unless the purpose for which the disclosure is permitted is likely to facilitate the exercise of a function of a public nature;
(c) amend subsection (5) of that section (overseas regulatory authorities) so as to have the effect of permitting disclosures to be made to a body other than one that exercises functions of a public nature in a country or territory outside the United Kingdom.

(3) An order under this section is subject to negative resolution procedure.

[1805]

NOTES

Commencement: to be appointed (see the introductory note to this Act).

CHAPTER 12
SUPPLEMENTARY PROVISIONS

Liability for false or misleading statements in reports

463 Liability for false or misleading statements in reports

(1) The reports to which this section applies are—
- (a) the directors' report,
- (b) the directors' remuneration report, and
- (c) a summary financial statement so far as it is derived from either of those reports.

(2) A director of a company is liable to compensate the company for any loss suffered by it as a result of—
- (a) any untrue or misleading statement in a report to which this section applies, or
- (b) the omission from a report to which this section applies of anything required to be included in it.

(3) He is so liable only if—
- (a) he knew the statement to be untrue or misleading or was reckless as to whether it was untrue or misleading, or
- (b) he knew the omission to be dishonest concealment of a material fact.

(4) No person shall be subject to any liability to a person other than the company resulting from reliance, by that person or another, on information in a report to which this section applies.

(5) The reference in subsection (4) to a person being subject to a liability includes a reference to another person being entitled as against him to be granted any civil remedy or to rescind or repudiate an agreement.

(6) This section does not affect—
- (a) liability for a civil penalty, or
- (b) liability for a criminal offence.

[1806]

NOTES

Commencement: 20 January 2007 (for transitional provisions see the note below).

Transitional provisions: the Companies Act 2006 (Commencement No 1, Transitional Provisions and Savings) Order 2006, SI 2006/3428, Sch 5, para 3 provides as follows—

3 False or misleading statements in reports

Section 463 of the Companies Act 2006 (liability for false or misleading statements in reports) does not apply to a directors' report, directors' remuneration report or summary financial statement first sent to members and others under section 238 or 251 of the 1985 Act, or Article 246 or 259 of the 1986 Order, before 20th January 2007.

Accounting and reporting standards

464 Accounting standards

(1) In this Part "accounting standards" means statements of standard accounting practice issued by such body or bodies as may be prescribed by regulations.

(2) References in this Part to accounting standards applicable to a company's annual accounts are to such standards as are, in accordance with their terms, relevant to the company's circumstances and to the accounts.

(3) Regulations under this section may contain such transitional and other supplementary and incidental provisions as appear to the Secretary of State to be appropriate.

[1807]

NOTES

Commencement: to be appointed (see the introductory note to this Act).

Companies qualifying as medium-sized

465 Companies qualifying as medium-sized: general

(1) A company qualifies as medium-sized in relation to its first financial year if the qualifying conditions are met in that year.

(2) A company qualifies as medium-sized in relation to a subsequent financial year—

(a) if the qualifying conditions are met in that year and the preceding financial year;

(b) if the qualifying conditions are met in that year and the company qualified as medium-sized in relation to the preceding financial year;

(c) if the qualifying conditions were met in the preceding financial year and the company qualified as medium-sized in relation to that year.

(3) The qualifying conditions are met by a company in a year in which it satisfies two or more of the following requirements—

1 Turnover	Not more than £22.8 million
2 Balance sheet total	Not more than £11.4 million
3 Number of employees	Not more than 250

(4) For a period that is a company's financial year but not in fact a year the maximum figures for turnover must be proportionately adjusted.

(5) The balance sheet total means the aggregate of the amounts shown as assets in the company's balance sheet.

(6) The number of employees means the average number of persons employed by the company in the year, determined as follows—

(a) find for each month in the financial year the number of persons employed under contracts of service by the company in that month (whether throughout the month or not),

(b) add together the monthly totals, and

(c) divide by the number of months in the financial year.

(7) This section is subject to section 466 (companies qualifying as medium-sized: parent companies).

[1808]

NOTES

Commencement: to be appointed (see the introductory note to this Act).

466 Companies qualifying as medium-sized: parent companies

(1) A parent company qualifies as a medium-sized company in relation to a financial year only if the group headed by it qualifies as a medium-sized group.

(2) A group qualifies as medium-sized in relation to the parent company's first financial year if the qualifying conditions are met in that year.

(3) A group qualifies as medium-sized in relation to a subsequent financial year of the parent company—

(a) if the qualifying conditions are met in that year and the preceding financial year;

(b) if the qualifying conditions are met in that year and the group qualified as medium-sized in relation to the preceding financial year;

(c) if the qualifying conditions were met in the preceding financial year and the group qualified as medium-sized in relation to that year.

(4) The qualifying conditions are met by a group in a year in which it satisfies two or more of the following requirements—

1 Aggregate turnover	Not more than £22.8 million net (or £27.36 million gross)
2 Aggregate balance sheet total	Not more than £11.4 million net (or £13.68 million gross)
3 Aggregate number of employees	Not more than 250

(5) The aggregate figures are ascertained by aggregating the relevant figures determined in accordance with section 465 for each member of the group.

(6) In relation to the aggregate figures for turnover and balance sheet total—

"net" means after any set-offs and other adjustments made to eliminate group transactions—

(a) in the case of Companies Act accounts, in accordance with regulations under section 404,

(b) in the case of IAS accounts, in accordance with international accounting standards; and

"gross" means without those set-offs and other adjustments.

A company may satisfy any relevant requirement on the basis of either the net or the gross figure.

(7) The figures for each subsidiary undertaking shall be those included in its individual accounts for the relevant financial year, that is—

(a) if its financial year ends with that of the parent company, that financial year, and

(b) if not, its financial year ending last before the end of the financial year of the parent company.

If those figures cannot be obtained without disproportionate expense or undue delay, the latest available figures shall be taken.

[1809]

NOTES

Commencement: to be appointed (see the introductory note to this Act).

467 Companies excluded from being treated as medium-sized

(1) A company is not entitled to take advantage of any of the provisions of this Part relating to companies qualifying as medium-sized if it was at any time within the financial year in question—

(a) a public company,

(b) a company that—

(i) has permission under Part 4 of the Financial Services and Markets Act 2000 (c 8) to carry on a regulated activity, or

(ii) carries on insurance market activity, or

(c) a member of an ineligible group.

(2) A group is ineligible if any of its members is—

(a) a public company,

(b) a body corporate (other than a company) whose shares are admitted to trading on a regulated market,

(c) a person (other than a small company) who has permission under Part 4 of the Financial Services and Markets Act 2000 to carry on a regulated activity,

(d) a small company that is an authorised insurance company, a banking company, an e-money issuer, an ISD investment firm or a UCITS management company, or

(e) a person who carries on insurance market activity.

(3) A company is a small company for the purposes of subsection (2) if it qualified as small in relation to its last financial year ending on or before the end of the financial year in question.

[1810]

NOTES

Commencement: to be appointed (see the introductory note to this Act).

General power to make further provision about accounts and reports

468 General power to make further provision about accounts and reports

(1) The Secretary of State may make provision by regulations about—

(a) the accounts and reports that companies are required to prepare;

(b) the categories of companies required to prepare accounts and reports of any description;

(c) the form and content of the accounts and reports that companies are required to prepare;

(d) the obligations of companies and others as regards—

(i) the approval of accounts and reports,

(ii) the sending of accounts and reports to members and others,

(iii) the laying of accounts and reports before the company in general meeting,

(iv) the delivery of copies of accounts and reports to the registrar, and

(v) the publication of accounts and reports.

(2) The regulations may amend this Part by adding, altering or repealing provisions.

(3) But they must not amend (other than consequentially)—

(a) section 393 (accounts to give true and fair view), or

(b) the provisions of Chapter 11 (revision of defective accounts and reports).

(4) The regulations may create criminal offences in cases corresponding to those in which an offence is created by an existing provision of this Part.

The maximum penalty for any such offence may not be greater than is provided in relation to an offence under the existing provision.

(5) The regulations may provide for civil penalties in circumstances corresponding to those within section 453(1) (civil penalty for failure to file accounts and reports).

The provisions of section 453(2) to (5) apply in relation to any such penalty.

[1811]

NOTES

Commencement: to be appointed (see the introductory note to this Act).

Other supplementary provisions

469 Preparation and filing of accounts in euros

(1) The amounts set out in the annual accounts of a company may also be shown in the same accounts translated into euros.

(2) When complying with section 441 (duty to file accounts and reports), the directors of a company may deliver to the registrar an additional copy of the company's annual accounts in which the amounts have been translated into euros.

(3) In both cases—

(a) the amounts must have been translated at the exchange rate prevailing on the date to which the balance sheet is made up, and

(b) that rate must be disclosed in the notes to the accounts.

(4) For the purposes of sections 434 and 435 (requirements in connection with published accounts) any additional copy of the company's annual accounts delivered to the registrar under subsection (2) above shall be treated as statutory accounts of the company.

In the case of such a copy, references in those sections to the auditor's report on the company's annual accounts shall be read as references to the auditor's report on the annual accounts of which it is a copy.

[1812]

NOTES

Commencement: to be appointed (see the introductory note to this Act).

470 (*Outside the scope of this work.*)

471 Meaning of "annual accounts" and related expressions

(1) In this Part a company's "annual accounts", in relation to a financial year, means—

(a) the company's individual accounts for that year (see section 394), and

(b) any group accounts prepared by the company for that year (see sections 398 and 399).

This is subject to section 408 (option to omit individual profit and loss account from annual accounts where information given in group accounts).

(2) In the case of an unquoted company, its "annual accounts and reports" for a financial year are—

(a) its annual accounts,

(b) the directors' report, and

(c) the auditor's report on those accounts and the directors' report (unless the company is exempt from audit).

(3) In the case of a quoted company, its "annual accounts and reports" for a financial year are—

(a) its annual accounts,

(b) the directors' remuneration report,

(c) the directors' report, and

(d) the auditor's report on those accounts, on the auditable part of the directors' remuneration report and on the directors' report.

[1813]

NOTES

Commencement: to be appointed (see the introductory note to this Act).

472 Notes to the accounts

(1) Information required by this Part to be given in notes to a company's annual accounts may be contained in the accounts or in a separate document annexed to the accounts.

(2) References in this Part to a company's annual accounts, or to a balance sheet or profit and loss account, include notes to the accounts giving information which is required by any provision of this Act or international accounting standards, and required or allowed by any such provision to be given in a note to company accounts.

[1814]

NOTES

Commencement: to be appointed (see the introductory note to this Act).

473 Parliamentary procedure for certain regulations under this Part

(1) This section applies to regulations under the following provisions of this Part—

section 396 (Companies Act individual accounts),
section 404 (Companies Act group accounts),
section 409 (information about related undertakings),
section 412 (information about directors' benefits: remuneration, pensions and compensation for loss of office),
section 416 (contents of directors' report: general),
section 421 (contents of directors' remuneration report),
section 444 (filing obligations of companies subject to small companies regime),
section 445 (filing obligations of medium-sized companies),
section 468 (general power to make further provision about accounts and reports).

(2) Any such regulations may make consequential amendments or repeals in other provisions of this Act, or in other enactments.

(3) Regulations that—

(a) restrict the classes of company which have the benefit of any exemption, exception or special provision,

(b) require additional matter to be included in a document of any class, or

(c) otherwise render the requirements of this Part more onerous,

are subject to affirmative resolution procedure.

(4) Otherwise, the regulations are subject to negative resolution procedure.

[1815]

NOTES

Commencement: to be appointed (see the introductory note to this Act).

474 Minor definitions

(1) In this Part—

"e-money issuer" means a person who has permission under Part 4 of the Financial Services and Markets Act 2000 (c 8) to carry on the activity of issuing electronic money within the meaning of article 9B of the Financial Services and Markets Act 2000 (Regulated Activities) Order 2001 (SI 2001/544);

"group" means a parent undertaking and its subsidiary undertakings;

"IAS Regulation" means EC Regulation No 1606/2002 of the European Parliament and of the Council of 19 July 2002 on the application of international accounting standards;

"included in the consolidation", in relation to group accounts, or "included in consolidated group accounts", means that the undertaking is included in the accounts by the method of full (and not proportional) consolidation, and references to an undertaking excluded from consolidation shall be construed accordingly;

"international accounting standards" means the international accounting standards, within the meaning of the IAS Regulation, adopted from time to time by the European Commission in accordance with that Regulation;

"ISD investment firm" has the meaning given by the Glossary forming part of the Handbook made by the Financial Services Authority under the Financial Services and Markets Act 2000;

"profit and loss account", in relation to a company that prepares IAS accounts, includes an income statement or other equivalent financial statement required to be prepared by international accounting standards;

"regulated activity" has the meaning given in section 22 of the Financial Services and Markets Act 2000, except that it does not include activities of the kind specified in any of the following provisions of the Financial Services and Markets Act 2000 (Regulated Activities) Order 2001 (SI 2001/544)—

(a) article 25A (arranging regulated mortgage contracts),

(b) article 25B (arranging regulated home reversion plans),

(c) article 25C (arranging regulated home purchase plans),

(d) article 39A (assisting administration and performance of a contract of insurance),

(e) article 53A (advising on regulated mortgage contracts),

(f) article 53B (advising on regulated home reversion plans),

(g) article 53C (advising on regulated home purchase plans),

(h) article 21 (dealing as agent), article 25 (arranging deals in investments) or article 53 (advising on investments) where the activity concerns relevant investments that are not contractually based investments (within the meaning of article 3 of that Order), or

(i) article 64 (agreeing to carry on a regulated activity of the kind mentioned in paragraphs (a) to (h));

"turnover", in relation to a company, means the amounts derived from the provision of goods and services falling within the company's ordinary activities, after deduction of—

(a) trade discounts,

(b) value added tax, and

(c) any other taxes based on the amounts so derived;

"UCITS management company" has the meaning given by the Glossary forming part of the Handbook made by the Financial Services Authority under the Financial Services and Markets Act 2000 (c 8).

(2) In the case of an undertaking not trading for profit, any reference in this Part to a profit and loss account is to an income and expenditure account. References to profit and loss and, in relation to group accounts, to a consolidated profit and loss account shall be construed accordingly.

[1816]

NOTES

Commencement: to be appointed (see the introductory note to this Act).

PART 16
AUDIT

CHAPTER 1
REQUIREMENT FOR AUDITED ACCOUNTS

Requirement for audited accounts

475 Requirement for audited accounts

(1) A company's annual accounts for a financial year must be audited in accordance with this Part unless the company—

(a) is exempt from audit under—
section 477 (small companies), or
section 480 (dormant companies);

or

(b) is exempt from the requirements of this Part under section 482 (non-profit-making companies subject to public sector audit).

(2) A company is not entitled to any such exemption unless its balance sheet contains a statement by the directors to that effect.

(3) A company is not entitled to exemption under any of the provisions mentioned in subsection (1)(a) unless its balance sheet contains a statement by the directors to the effect that—

(a) the members have not required the company to obtain an audit of its accounts for the year in question in accordance with section 476, and

(b) the directors acknowledge their responsibilities for complying with the requirements of this Act with respect to accounting records and the preparation of accounts.

(4) The statement required by subsection (2) or (3) must appear on the balance sheet above the signature required by section 414.

[1817]

NOTES

Commencement: to be appointed (see the introductory note to this Act).

476 Right of members to require audit

(1) The members of a company that would otherwise be entitled to exemption from audit under any of the provisions mentioned in section 475(1)(a) may by notice under this section require it to obtain an audit of its accounts for a financial year.

(2) The notice must be given by—

(a) members representing not less in total than 10% in nominal value of the company's issued share capital, or any class of it, or

(b) if the company does not have a share capital, not less than 10% in number of the members of the company.

(3) The notice may not be given before the financial year to which it relates and must be given not later than one month before the end of that year.

[1818]

NOTES

Commencement: to be appointed (see the introductory note to this Act).

Exemption from audit: small companies

477 Small companies: conditions for exemption from audit

(1) A company that meets the following conditions in respect of a financial year is exempt from the requirements of this Act relating to the audit of accounts for that year.

(2) The conditions are—

(a) that the company qualifies as a small company in relation to that year,

(b) that its turnover in that year is not more than £5.6 million, and

(c) that its balance sheet total for that year is not more than £2.8 million.

(3) For a period which is a company's financial year but not in fact a year the maximum figure for turnover shall be proportionately adjusted.

(4) For the purposes of this section—

(a) whether a company qualifies as a small company shall be determined in accordance with section 382(1) to (6), and

(b) "balance sheet total" has the same meaning as in that section.

(5) This section has effect subject to—

section 475(2) and (3) (requirements as to statements to be contained in balance sheet),
section 476 (right of members to require audit),
section 478 (companies excluded from small companies exemption), and
section 479 (availability of small companies exemption in case of group company).

[1819]

NOTES

Commencement: to be appointed (see the introductory note to this Act).

478 Companies excluded from small companies exemption

A company is not entitled to the exemption conferred by section 477 (small companies) if it was at any time within the financial year in question—

(a) a public company,

(b) a company that—

(i) is an authorised insurance company, a banking company, an e-money issuer, an ISD investment firm or a UCITS management company, or

(ii) carries on insurance market activity, or

(c) a special register body as defined in section 117(1) of the Trade Union and Labour Relations (Consolidation) Act 1992 (c 52) or an employers' association as defined in section 122 of that Act or Article 4 of the Industrial Relations (Northern Ireland) Order 1992 (SI 1992/807 (NI 5)).

[1820]

NOTES

Commencement: to be appointed (see the introductory note to this Act).

479 Availability of small companies exemption in case of group company

(1) A company is not entitled to the exemption conferred by section 477 (small companies) in respect of a financial year during any part of which it was a group company unless—

(a) the conditions specified in subsection (2) below are met, or

(b) subsection (3) applies.

(2) The conditions are—

(a) that the group—

(i) qualifies as a small group in relation to that financial year, and

(ii) was not at any time in that year an ineligible group;

(b) that the group's aggregate turnover in that year is not more than £5.6 million net (or £6.72 million gross);

(c) that the group's aggregate balance sheet total for that year is not more than £2.8 million net (or £3.36 million gross).

(3) A company is not excluded by subsection (1) if, throughout the whole of the period or periods during the financial year when it was a group company, it was both a subsidiary undertaking and dormant.

(4) In this section—
(a) "group company" means a company that is a parent company or a subsidiary undertaking, and
(b) "the group", in relation to a group company, means that company together with all its associated undertakings.

For this purpose undertakings are associated if one is a subsidiary undertaking of the other or both are subsidiary undertakings of a third undertaking.

(5) For the purposes of this section—
(a) whether a group qualifies as small shall be determined in accordance with section 383 (companies qualifying as small: parent companies);
(b) "ineligible group" has the meaning given by section 384(2) and (3);
(c) a group's aggregate turnover and aggregate balance sheet total shall be determined as for the purposes of section 383;
(d) "net" and "gross" have the same meaning as in that section;
(e) a company may meet any relevant requirement on the basis of either the gross or the net figure.

(6) The provisions mentioned in subsection (5) apply for the purposes of this section as if all the bodies corporate in the group were companies.

[1821]

NOTES

Commencement: to be appointed (see the introductory note to this Act).

Exemption from audit: dormant companies

480 Dormant companies: conditions for exemption from audit

(1) A company is exempt from the requirements of this Act relating to the audit of accounts in respect of a financial year if—
(a) it has been dormant since its formation, or
(b) it has been dormant since the end of the previous financial year and the following conditions are met.

(2) The conditions are that the company—
(a) as regards its individual accounts for the financial year in question—
(i) is entitled to prepare accounts in accordance with the small companies regime (see sections 381 to 384), or
(ii) would be so entitled but for having been a public company or a member of an ineligible group, and
(b) is not required to prepare group accounts for that year.

(3) This section has effect subject to—
section 475(2) and (3) (requirements as to statements to be contained in balance sheet),
section 476 (right of members to require audit), and
section 481 (companies excluded from dormant companies exemption).

[1822]

NOTES

Commencement: to be appointed (see the introductory note to this Act).

481 Companies excluded from dormant companies exemption

A company is not entitled to the exemption conferred by section 480 (dormant companies) if it was at any time within the financial year in question a company that—
(a) is an authorised insurance company, a banking company, an e-money issuer, an ISD investment firm or a UCITS management company, or
(b) carries on insurance market activity.

[1823]

NOTES

Commencement: to be appointed (see the introductory note to this Act).

Companies subject to public sector audit

482 Non-profit-making companies subject to public sector audit

(1) The requirements of this Part as to audit of accounts do not apply to a company for a financial year if it is non-profit-making and its accounts—

(a) are subject to audit—

(i) by the Comptroller and Auditor General by virtue of an order under section 25(6) of the Government Resources and Accounts Act 2000 (c 20), or

(ii) by the Auditor General for Wales by virtue of section 96, or an order under section 144, of the Government of Wales Act 1998 (c 38);

(b) are accounts—

(i) in relation to which section 21 of the Public Finance and Accountability (Scotland) Act 2000 (asp 1) (audit of accounts: Auditor General for Scotland) applies, or

(ii) that are subject to audit by the Auditor General for Scotland by virtue of an order under section 483 (Scottish public sector companies: audit by Auditor General for Scotland); or

(c) are subject to audit by the Comptroller and Auditor General for Northern Ireland by virtue of an order under Article 5(3) of the Audit and Accountability (Northern Ireland) Order 2003 (SI 2003/418 (NI 5)).

(2) In the case of a company that is a parent company or a subsidiary undertaking, subsection (1) applies only if every group undertaking is non-profit-making.

(3) In this section "non-profit-making" has the same meaning as in Article 48 of the Treaty establishing the European Community.

(4) This section has effect subject to section 475(2) (balance sheet to contain statement that company entitled to exemption under this section).

[1824]

NOTES

Commencement: to be appointed (see the introductory note to this Act).

483 (*Outside the scope of this work.*)

General power of amendment by regulations

484 General power of amendment by regulations

(1) The Secretary of State may by regulations amend this Chapter or section 539 (minor definitions) so far as applying to this Chapter by adding, altering or repealing provisions.

(2) The regulations may make consequential amendments or repeals in other provisions of this Act, or in other enactments.

(3) Regulations under this section imposing new requirements, or rendering existing requirements more onerous, are subject to affirmative resolution procedure.

(4) Other regulations under this section are subject to negative resolution procedure.

[1825]

NOTES

Commencement: to be appointed (see the introductory note to this Act).

CHAPTER 2
APPOINTMENT OF AUDITORS

Private companies

485 Appointment of auditors of private company: general

(1) An auditor or auditors of a private company must be appointed for each financial year of the company, unless the directors reasonably resolve otherwise on the ground that audited accounts are unlikely to be required.

(2) For each financial year for which an auditor or auditors is or are to be appointed (other than the company's first financial year), the appointment must be made before the end of the period of 28 days beginning with—

(a) the end of the time allowed for sending out copies of the company's annual accounts and reports for the previous financial year (see section 424), or

(b) if earlier, the day on which copies of the company's annual accounts and reports for the previous financial year are sent out under section 423.

This is the "period for appointing auditors".

(3) The directors may appoint an auditor or auditors of the company—

(a) at any time before the company's first period for appointing auditors,

(b) following a period during which the company (being exempt from audit) did not have any auditor, at any time before the company's next period for appointing auditors, or

(c) to fill a casual vacancy in the office of auditor.

(4) The members may appoint an auditor or auditors by ordinary resolution—

(a) during a period for appointing auditors,

(b) if the company should have appointed an auditor or auditors during a period for appointing auditors but failed to do so, or

(c) where the directors had power to appoint under subsection (3) but have failed to make an appointment.

(5) An auditor or auditors of a private company may only be appointed—

(a) in accordance with this section, or

(b) in accordance with section 486 (default power of Secretary of State).

This is without prejudice to any deemed re-appointment under section 487.

[1826]

NOTES

Commencement: to be appointed (see the introductory note to this Act).

486 Appointment of auditors of private company: default power of Secretary of State

(1) If a private company fails to appoint an auditor or auditors in accordance with section 485, the Secretary of State may appoint one or more persons to fill the vacancy.

(2) Where subsection (2) of that section applies and the company fails to make the necessary appointment before the end of the period for appointing auditors, the company must within one week of the end of that period give notice to the Secretary of State of his power having become exercisable.

(3) If a company fails to give the notice required by this section, an offence is committed by—

(a) the company, and

(b) every officer of the company who is in default.

(4) A person guilty of an offence under this section is liable on summary conviction to a fine not exceeding level 3 on the standard scale and, for continued contravention, a daily default fine not exceeding one-tenth of level 3 on the standard scale.

[1827]

NOTES

Commencement: to be appointed (see the introductory note to this Act).

487 Term of office of auditors of private company

(1) An auditor or auditors of a private company hold office in accordance with the terms of their appointment, subject to the requirements that—

- (a) they do not take office until any previous auditor or auditors cease to hold office, and
- (b) they cease to hold office at the end of the next period for appointing auditors unless re-appointed.

(2) Where no auditor has been appointed by the end of the next period for appointing auditors, any auditor in office immediately before that time is deemed to be re-appointed at that time, unless—

- (a) he was appointed by the directors, or
- (b) the company's articles require actual re-appointment, or
- (c) the deemed re-appointment is prevented by the members under section 488, or
- (d) the members have resolved that he should not be re-appointed, or
- (e) the directors have resolved that no auditor or auditors should be appointed for the financial year in question.

(3) This is without prejudice to the provisions of this Part as to removal and resignation of auditors.

(4) No account shall be taken of any loss of the opportunity of deemed re-appointment under this section in ascertaining the amount of any compensation or damages payable to an auditor on his ceasing to hold office for any reason.

[1828]

NOTES

Commencement: to be appointed (see the introductory note to this Act).

488 Prevention by members of deemed re-appointment of auditor

(1) An auditor of a private company is not deemed to be re-appointed under section 487(2) if the company has received notices under this section from members representing at least the requisite percentage of the total voting rights of all members who would be entitled to vote on a resolution that the auditor should not be re-appointed.

(2) The "requisite percentage" is 5%, or such lower percentage as is specified for this purpose in the company's articles.

(3) A notice under this section—

- (a) may be in hard copy or electronic form,
- (b) must be authenticated by the person or persons giving it, and
- (c) must be received by the company before the end of the accounting reference period immediately preceding the time when the deemed re-appointment would have effect.

[1829]

NOTES

Commencement: to be appointed (see the introductory note to this Act).

489–491 (*Outside the scope of this work.*)

General provisions

492 Fixing of auditor's remuneration

(1) The remuneration of an auditor appointed by the members of a company must be fixed by the members by ordinary resolution or in such manner as the members may by ordinary resolution determine.

(2) The remuneration of an auditor appointed by the directors of a company must be fixed by the directors.

(3) The remuneration of an auditor appointed by the Secretary of State must be fixed by the Secretary of State.

(4) For the purposes of this section "remuneration" includes sums paid in respect of expenses.

(5) This section applies in relation to benefits in kind as to payments of money.

[1830]

NOTES

Commencement: to be appointed (see the introductory note to this Act).

493 Disclosure of terms of audit appointment

(1) The Secretary of State may make provision by regulations for securing the disclosure of the terms on which a company's auditor is appointed, remunerated or performs his duties.

Nothing in the following provisions of this section affects the generality of this power.

(2) The regulations may—

- (a) require disclosure of—
  - (i) a copy of any terms that are in writing, and
  - (ii) a written memorandum setting out any terms that are not in writing;
- (b) require disclosure to be at such times, in such places and by such means as are specified in the regulations;
- (c) require the place and means of disclosure to be stated—
  - (i) in a note to the company's annual accounts (in the case of its individual accounts) or in such manner as is specified in the regulations (in the case of group accounts),
  - (ii) in the directors' report, or
  - (iii) in the auditor's report on the company's annual accounts.

(3) The provisions of this section apply to a variation of the terms mentioned in subsection (1) as they apply to the original terms.

(4) Regulations under this section are subject to affirmative resolution procedure.

[1831]

NOTES

Commencement: to be appointed (see the introductory note to this Act).

494 Disclosure of services provided by auditor or associates and related remuneration

(1) The Secretary of State may make provision by regulations for securing the disclosure of—

- (a) the nature of any services provided for a company by the company's auditor (whether in his capacity as auditor or otherwise) or by his associates;
- (b) the amount of any remuneration received or receivable by a company's auditor, or his associates, in respect of any such services.

Nothing in the following provisions of this section affects the generality of this power.

(2) The regulations may provide—

- (a) for disclosure of the nature of any services provided to be made by reference to any class or description of services specified in the regulations (or any combination of services, however described);
- (b) for the disclosure of amounts of remuneration received or receivable in respect of services of any class or description specified in the regulations (or any combination of services, however described);
- (c) for the disclosure of separate amounts so received or receivable by the company's auditor or any of his associates, or of aggregate amounts so received or receivable by all or any of those persons.

(3) The regulations may—

- (a) provide that "remuneration" includes sums paid in respect of expenses;
- (b) apply to benefits in kind as well as to payments of money, and require the disclosure of the nature of any such benefits and their estimated money value;
- (c) apply to services provided for associates of a company as well as to those provided for a company;
- (d) define "associate" in relation to an auditor and a company respectively.

(4) The regulations may provide that any disclosure required by the regulations is to be made—

(a) in a note to the company's annual accounts (in the case of its individual accounts) or in such manner as is specified in the regulations (in the case of group accounts),

(b) in the directors' report, or

(c) in the auditor's report on the company's annual accounts.

(5) If the regulations provide that any such disclosure is to be made as mentioned in subsection (4)(a) or (b), the regulations may require the auditor to supply the directors of the company with any information necessary to enable the disclosure to be made.

(6) Regulations under this section are subject to negative resolution procedure.

[1832]

NOTES

Commencement: to be appointed (see the introductory note to this Act).

CHAPTER 3
FUNCTIONS OF AUDITOR

Auditor's report

495 Auditor's report on company's annual accounts

(1) A company's auditor must make a report to the company's members on all annual accounts of the company of which copies are, during his tenure of office—

(a) in the case of a private company, to be sent out to members under section 423;

(b) in the case of a public company, to be laid before the company in general meeting under section 437.

(2) The auditor's report must include—

(a) an introduction identifying the annual accounts that are the subject of the audit and the financial reporting framework that has been applied in their preparation, and

(b) a description of the scope of the audit identifying the auditing standards in accordance with which the audit was conducted.

(3) The report must state clearly whether, in the auditor's opinion, the annual accounts—

(a) give a true and fair view—

(i) in the case of an individual balance sheet, of the state of affairs of the company as at the end of the financial year,

(ii) in the case of an individual profit and loss account, of the profit or loss of the company for the financial year,

(iii) in the case of group accounts, of the state of affairs as at the end of the financial year and of the profit or loss for the financial year of the undertakings included in the consolidation as a whole, so far as concerns members of the company;

(b) have been properly prepared in accordance with the relevant financial reporting framework; and

(c) have been prepared in accordance with the requirements of this Act (and, where applicable, Article 4 of the IAS Regulation).

Expressions used in this subsection that are defined for the purposes of Part 15 (see section 474) have the same meaning as in that Part.

(4) The auditor's report—

(a) must be either unqualified or qualified, and

(b) must include a reference to any matters to which the auditor wishes to draw attention by way of emphasis without qualifying the report.

[1833]

NOTES

Commencement: to be appointed (see the introductory note to this Act).

496 Auditor's report on directors' report

The auditor must state in his report on the company's annual accounts whether in his opinion the information given in the directors' report for the financial year for which the accounts are prepared is consistent with those accounts.

[1834]

NOTES

Commencement: to be appointed (see the introductory note to this Act).

497 Auditor's report on auditable part of directors' remuneration report

(1) If the company is a quoted company, the auditor, in his report on the company's annual accounts for the financial year, must—

(a) report to the company's members on the auditable part of the directors' remuneration report, and

(b) state whether in his opinion that part of the directors' remuneration report has been properly prepared in accordance with this Act.

(2) For the purposes of this Part, "the auditable part" of a directors' remuneration report is the part identified as such by regulations under section 421.

[1835]

NOTES

Commencement: to be appointed (see the introductory note to this Act).

Duties and rights of auditors

498 Duties of auditor

(1) A company's auditor, in preparing his report, must carry out such investigations as will enable him to form an opinion as to—

(a) whether adequate accounting records have been kept by the company and returns adequate for their audit have been received from branches not visited by him, and

(b) whether the company's individual accounts are in agreement with the accounting records and returns, and

(c) in the case of a quoted company, whether the auditable part of the company's directors' remuneration report is in agreement with the accounting records and returns.

(2) If the auditor is of the opinion—

(a) that adequate accounting records have not been kept, or that returns adequate for their audit have not been received from branches not visited by him, or

(b) that the company's individual accounts are not in agreement with the accounting records and returns, or

(c) in the case of a quoted company, that the auditable part of its directors' remuneration report is not in agreement with the accounting records and returns,

the auditor shall state that fact in his report.

(3) If the auditor fails to obtain all the information and explanations which, to the best of his knowledge and belief, are necessary for the purposes of his audit, he shall state that fact in his report.

(4) If—

(a) the requirements of regulations under section 412 (disclosure of directors' benefits: remuneration, pensions and compensation for loss of office) are not complied with in the annual accounts, or

(b) in the case of a quoted company, the requirements of regulations under section 421 as to information forming the auditable part of the directors' remuneration report are not complied with in that report,

the auditor must include in his report, so far as he is reasonably able to do so, a statement giving the required particulars.

(5) If the directors of the company have prepared accounts and reports in accordance with the small companies regime and in the auditor's opinion they were not entitled so to do, the auditor shall state that fact in his report.

[1836]

NOTES

Commencement: to be appointed (see the introductory note to this Act).

499 Auditor's general right to information

(1) An auditor of a company—

(a) has a right of access at all times to the company's books, accounts and vouchers (in whatever form they are held), and

(b) may require any of the following persons to provide him with such information or explanations as he thinks necessary for the performance of his duties as auditor.

(2) Those persons are—

(a) any officer or employee of the company;

(b) any person holding or accountable for any of the company's books, accounts or vouchers;

(c) any subsidiary undertaking of the company which is a body corporate incorporated in the United Kingdom;

(d) any officer, employee or auditor of any such subsidiary undertaking or any person holding or accountable for any books, accounts or vouchers of any such subsidiary undertaking;

(e) any person who fell within any of paragraphs (a) to (d) at a time to which the information or explanations required by the auditor relates or relate.

(3) A statement made by a person in response to a requirement under this section may not be used in evidence against him in criminal proceedings except proceedings for an offence under section 501.

(4) Nothing in this section compels a person to disclose information in respect of which a claim to legal professional privilege (in Scotland, to confidentiality of communications) could be maintained in legal proceedings.

[1837]

NOTES

Commencement: to be appointed (see the introductory note to this Act).

500 Auditor's right to information from overseas subsidiaries

(1) Where a parent company has a subsidiary undertaking that is not a body corporate incorporated in the United Kingdom, the auditor of the parent company may require it to obtain from any of the following persons such information or explanations as he may reasonably require for the purposes of his duties as auditor.

(2) Those persons are—

(a) the undertaking;

(b) any officer, employee or auditor of the undertaking;

(c) any person holding or accountable for any of the undertaking's books, accounts or vouchers;

(d) any person who fell within paragraph (b) or (c) at a time to which the information or explanations relates or relate.

(3) If so required, the parent company must take all such steps as are reasonably open to it to obtain the information or explanations from the person concerned.

(4) A statement made by a person in response to a requirement under this section may not be used in evidence against him in criminal proceedings except proceedings for an offence under section 501.

(5) Nothing in this section compels a person to disclose information in respect of which a claim to legal professional privilege (in Scotland, to confidentiality of communications) could be maintained in legal proceedings.

[1838]

NOTES

Commencement: to be appointed (see the introductory note to this Act).

501 Auditor's rights to information: offences

(1) A person commits an offence who knowingly or recklessly makes to an auditor of a company a statement (oral or written) that—

(a) conveys or purports to convey any information or explanations which the auditor requires, or is entitled to require, under section 499, and

(b) is misleading, false or deceptive in a material particular.

(2) A person guilty of an offence under subsection (1) is liable—

(a) on conviction on indictment, to imprisonment for a term not exceeding two years or a fine (or both);

(b) on summary conviction—

(i) in England and Wales, to imprisonment for a term not exceeding twelve months or to a fine not exceeding the statutory maximum (or both);

(ii) in Scotland or Northern Ireland, to imprisonment for a term not exceeding six months or to a fine not exceeding the statutory maximum (or both).

(3) A person who fails to comply with a requirement under section 499 without delay commits an offence unless it was not reasonably practicable for him to provide the required information or explanations.

(4) If a parent company fails to comply with section 500, an offence is committed by—

(a) the company, and

(b) every officer of the company who is in default.

(5) A person guilty of an offence under subsection (3) or (4) is liable on summary conviction to a fine not exceeding level 3 on the standard scale.

(6) Nothing in this section affects any right of an auditor to apply for an injunction (in Scotland, an interdict or an order for specific performance) to enforce any of his rights under section 499 or 500.

[1839]

NOTES

Commencement: to be appointed (see the introductory note to this Act).

502 Auditor's rights in relation to resolutions and meetings

(1) In relation to a written resolution proposed to be agreed to by a private company, the company's auditor is entitled to receive all such communications relating to the resolution as, by virtue of any provision of Chapter 2 of Part 13 of this Act, are required to be supplied to a member of the company.

(2) A company's auditor is entitled—

(a) to receive all notices of, and other communications relating to, any general meeting which a member of the company is entitled to receive,

(b) to attend any general meeting of the company, and

(c) to be heard at any general meeting which he attends on any part of the business of the meeting which concerns him as auditor.

(3) Where the auditor is a firm, the right to attend or be heard at a meeting is exercisable by an individual authorised by the firm in writing to act as its representative at the meeting.

[1840]

NOTES

Commencement: to be appointed (see the introductory note to this Act).

Signature of auditor's report

503 Signature of auditor's report

(1) The auditor's report must state the name of the auditor and be signed and dated.

(2) Where the auditor is an individual, the report must be signed by him.

(3) Where the auditor is a firm, the report must be signed by the senior statutory auditor in his own name, for and on behalf of the auditor.

[1841]

NOTES

Commencement: to be appointed (see the introductory note to this Act).

504 Senior statutory auditor

(1) The senior statutory auditor means the individual identified by the firm as senior statutory auditor in relation to the audit in accordance with—

(a) standards issued by the European Commission, or

(b) if there is no applicable standard so issued, any relevant guidance issued by—

(i) the Secretary of State, or

(ii) a body appointed by order of the Secretary of State.

(2) The person identified as senior statutory auditor must be eligible for appointment as auditor of the company in question (see Chapter 2 of Part 42 of this Act).

(3) The senior statutory auditor is not, by reason of being named or identified as senior statutory auditor or by reason of his having signed the auditor's report, subject to any civil liability to which he would not otherwise be subject.

(4) An order appointing a body for the purpose of subsection (1)(b)(ii) is subject to negative resolution procedure.

[1842]

NOTES

Commencement: to be appointed (see the introductory note to this Act).

505 Names to be stated in published copies of auditor's report

(1) Every copy of the auditor's report that is published by or on behalf of the company must—

(a) state the name of the auditor and (where the auditor is a firm) the name of the person who signed it as senior statutory auditor, or

(b) if the conditions in section 506 (circumstances in which names may be omitted) are met, state that a resolution has been passed and notified to the Secretary of State in accordance with that section.

(2) For the purposes of this section a company is regarded as publishing the report if it publishes, issues or circulates it or otherwise makes it available for public inspection in a manner calculated to invite members of the public generally, or any class of members of the public, to read it.

(3) If a copy of the auditor's report is published without the statement required by this section, an offence is committed by—

(a) the company, and

(b) every officer of the company who is in default.

(4) A person guilty of an offence under this section is liable on summary conviction to a fine not exceeding level 3 on the standard scale.

[1843]

NOTES

Commencement: to be appointed (see the introductory note to this Act).

506 Circumstances in which names may be omitted

(1) The auditor's name and, where the auditor is a firm, the name of the person who signed the report as senior statutory auditor, may be omitted from—

(a) published copies of the report, and
(b) the copy of the report delivered to the registrar under Chapter 10 of Part 15 (filing of accounts and reports),

if the following conditions are met.

(2) The conditions are that the company—
(a) considering on reasonable grounds that statement of the name would create or be likely to create a serious risk that the auditor or senior statutory auditor, or any other person, would be subject to violence or intimidation, has resolved that the name should not be stated, and
(b) has given notice of the resolution to the Secretary of State, stating—
(i) the name and registered number of the company,
(ii) the financial year of the company to which the report relates, and
(iii) the name of the auditor and (where the auditor is a firm) the name of the person who signed the report as senior statutory auditor.

[1844]

NOTES

Commencement: to be appointed (see the introductory note to this Act).

Offences in connection with auditor's report

507 Offences in connection with auditor's report

(1) A person to whom this section applies commits an offence if he knowingly or recklessly causes a report under section 495 (auditor's report on company's annual accounts) to include any matter that is misleading, false or deceptive in a material particular.

(2) A person to whom this section applies commits an offence if he knowingly or recklessly causes such a report to omit a statement required by—
(a) section 498(2)(b) (statement that company's accounts do not agree with accounting records and returns),
(b) section 498(3) (statement that necessary information and explanations not obtained), or
(c) section 498(5) (statement that directors wrongly took advantage of exemption from obligation to prepare group accounts).

(3) This section applies to—
(a) where the auditor is an individual, that individual and any employee or agent of his who is eligible for appointment as auditor of the company;
(b) where the auditor is a firm, any director, member, employee or agent of the firm who is eligible for appointment as auditor of the company.

(4) A person guilty of an offence under this section is liable—
(a) on conviction on indictment, to a fine;
(b) on summary conviction, to a fine not exceeding the statutory maximum.

[1845]

NOTES

Commencement: to be appointed (see the introductory note to this Act).

508 Guidance for regulatory and prosecuting authorities: England, Wales and Northern Ireland

(1) The Secretary of State may issue guidance for the purpose of helping relevant regulatory and prosecuting authorities to determine how they should carry out their functions in cases where behaviour occurs that—
(a) appears to involve the commission of an offence under section 507 (offences in connection with auditor's report), and
(b) has been, is being or may be investigated pursuant to arrangements—
(i) under paragraph 15 of Schedule 10 (investigation of complaints against auditors and supervisory bodies), or
(ii) of a kind mentioned in paragraph 24 of that Schedule (independent investigation for disciplinary purposes of public interest cases).

(2) The Secretary of State must obtain the consent of the Attorney General before issuing any such guidance.

(3) In this section "relevant regulatory and prosecuting authorities" means—
- (a) supervisory bodies within the meaning of Part 42 of this Act,
- (b) bodies to which the Secretary of State may make grants under section 16(1) of the Companies (Audit, Investigations and Community Enterprise) Act 2004 (c 27) (bodies concerned with accounting standards etc),
- (c) the Director of the Serious Fraud Office,
- (d) the Director of Public Prosecutions or the Director of Public Prosecutions for Northern Ireland, and
- (e) the Secretary of State.

(4) This section does not apply to Scotland.

[1846]

NOTES

Commencement: to be appointed (see the introductory note to this Act).

509 (*Outside the scope of this work.*)

CHAPTER 4
REMOVAL, RESIGNATION, ETC OF AUDITORS

Removal of auditor

510 Resolution removing auditor from office

(1) The members of a company may remove an auditor from office at any time.

(2) This power is exercisable only—
- (a) by ordinary resolution at a meeting, and
- (b) in accordance with section 511 (special notice of resolution to remove auditor).

(3) Nothing in this section is to be taken as depriving the person removed of compensation or damages payable to him in respect of the termination—
- (a) of his appointment as auditor, or
- (b) of any appointment terminating with that as auditor.

(4) An auditor may not be removed from office before the expiration of his term of office except by resolution under this section.

[1847]

NOTES

Commencement: to be appointed (see the introductory note to this Act).

511 Special notice required for resolution removing auditor from office

(1) Special notice is required for a resolution at a general meeting of a company removing an auditor from office.

(2) On receipt of notice of such an intended resolution the company must immediately send a copy of it to the auditor proposed to be removed.

(3) The auditor proposed to be removed may make with respect to the intended resolution representations in writing to the company (not exceeding a reasonable length) and request their notification to members of the company.

(4) The company must (unless the representations are received by it too late for it to do so)—
- (a) in any notice of the resolution given to members of the company, state the fact of the representations having been made, and
- (b) send a copy of the representations to every member of the company to whom notice of the meeting is or has been sent.

(5) If a copy of any such representations is not sent out as required because received too late or because of the company's default, the auditor may (without prejudice to his right to be heard orally) require that the representations be read out at the meeting.

(6) Copies of the representations need not be sent out and the representations need not be read at the meeting if, on the application either of the company or of any other person claiming to be aggrieved, the court is satisfied that the auditor is using the provisions of this section to secure needless publicity for defamatory matter.

The court may order the company's costs (in Scotland, expenses) on the application to be paid in whole or in part by the auditor, notwithstanding that he is not a party to the application.

[1848]

NOTES

Commencement: to be appointed (see the introductory note to this Act).

512 Notice to registrar of resolution removing auditor from office

(1) Where a resolution is passed under section 510 (resolution removing auditor from office), the company must give notice of that fact to the registrar within 14 days.

(2) If a company fails to give the notice required by this section, an offence is committed by—

- (a) the company, and
- (b) every officer of it who is in default.

(3) A person guilty of an offence under this section is liable on summary conviction to a fine not exceeding level 3 on the standard scale and, for continued contravention, a daily default fine not exceeding one-tenth of level 3 on the standard scale.

[1849]

NOTES

Commencement: to be appointed (see the introductory note to this Act).

513 Rights of auditor who has been removed from office

(1) An auditor who has been removed by resolution under section 510 has, notwithstanding his removal, the rights conferred by section 502(2) in relation to any general meeting of the company—

- (a) at which his term of office would otherwise have expired, or
- (b) at which it is proposed to fill the vacancy caused by his removal.

(2) In such a case the references in that section to matters concerning the auditor as auditor shall be construed as references to matters concerning him as a former auditor.

[1850]

NOTES

Commencement: to be appointed (see the introductory note to this Act).

Failure to re-appoint auditor

514 Failure to re-appoint auditor: special procedure required for written resolution

(1) This section applies where a resolution is proposed as a written resolution of a private company whose effect would be to appoint a person as auditor in place of a person (the "outgoing auditor") whose term of office has expired, or is to expire, at the end of the period for appointing auditors.

(2) The following provisions apply if—

- (a) no period for appointing auditors has ended since the outgoing auditor ceased to hold office, or
- (b) such a period has ended and an auditor or auditors should have been appointed but were not.

(3) The company must send a copy of the proposed resolution to the person proposed to be appointed and to the outgoing auditor.

(4) The outgoing auditor may, within 14 days after receiving the notice, make with respect to the proposed resolution representations in writing to the company (not exceeding a reasonable length) and request their circulation to members of the company.

(5) The company must circulate the representations together with the copy or copies of the resolution circulated in accordance with section 291 (resolution proposed by directors) or section 293 (resolution proposed by members).

(6) Where subsection (5) applies—

(a) the period allowed under section 293(3) for service of copies of the proposed resolution is 28 days instead of 21 days, and

(b) the provisions of section 293(5) and (6) (offences) apply in relation to a failure to comply with that subsection as in relation to a default in complying with that section.

(7) Copies of the representations need not be circulated if, on the application either of the company or of any other person claiming to be aggrieved, the court is satisfied that the auditor is using the provisions of this section to secure needless publicity for defamatory matter.

The court may order the company's costs (in Scotland, expenses) on the application to be paid in whole or in part by the auditor, notwithstanding that he is not a party to the application.

(8) If any requirement of this section is not complied with, the resolution is ineffective. **[1851]**

NOTES

Commencement: to be appointed (see the introductory note to this Act).

515 Failure to re-appoint auditor: special notice required for resolution at general meeting

(1) This section applies to a resolution at a general meeting of a company whose effect would be to appoint a person as auditor in place of a person (the "outgoing auditor") whose term of office has ended, or is to end—

(a) in the case of a private company, at the end of the period for appointing auditors;

(b) in the case of a public company, at the end of the next accounts meeting.

(2) Special notice is required of such a resolution if—

(a) in the case of a private company—

(i) no period for appointing auditors has ended since the outgoing auditor ceased to hold office, or

(ii) such a period has ended and an auditor or auditors should have been appointed but were not;

(b) in the case of a public company—

(i) there has been no accounts meeting of the company since the outgoing auditor ceased to hold office, or

(ii) there has been an accounts meeting at which an auditor or auditors should have been appointed but were not.

(3) On receipt of notice of such an intended resolution the company shall forthwith send a copy of it to the person proposed to be appointed and to the outgoing auditor.

(4) The outgoing auditor may make with respect to the intended resolution representations in writing to the company (not exceeding a reasonable length) and request their notification to members of the company.

(5) The company must (unless the representations are received by it too late for it to do so)—

(a) in any notice of the resolution given to members of the company, state the fact of the representations having been made, and

(b) send a copy of the representations to every member of the company to whom notice of the meeting is or has been sent.

(6) If a copy of any such representations is not sent out as required because received too late or because of the company's default, the outgoing auditor may (without prejudice to his right to be heard orally) require that the representations be read out at the meeting.

(7) Copies of the representations need not be sent out and the representations need not be read at the meeting if, on the application either of the company or of any other person claiming to be aggrieved, the court is satisfied that the auditor is using the provisions of this section to secure needless publicity for defamatory matter.

The court may order the company's costs (in Scotland, expenses) on the application to be paid in whole or in part by the outgoing auditor, notwithstanding that he is not a party to the application.

[1852]

NOTES

Commencement: to be appointed (see the introductory note to this Act).

Resignation of auditor

516 Resignation of auditor

(1) An auditor of a company may resign his office by depositing a notice in writing to that effect at the company's registered office.

(2) The notice is not effective unless it is accompanied by the statement required by section 519.

(3) An effective notice of resignation operates to bring the auditor's term of office to an end as of the date on which the notice is deposited or on such later date as may be specified in it.

[1853]

NOTES

Commencement: to be appointed (see the introductory note to this Act).

517 Notice to registrar of resignation of auditor

(1) Where an auditor resigns the company must within 14 days of the deposit of a notice of resignation send a copy of the notice to the registrar of companies.

(2) If default is made in complying with this section, an offence is committed by—

(a) the company, and

(b) every officer of the company who is in default.

(3) A person guilty of an offence under this section is liable—

(a) on conviction on indictment, to a fine;

(b) on summary conviction, to a fine not exceeding the statutory maximum and, for continued contravention, a daily default fine not exceeding one-tenth of the statutory maximum.

[1854]

NOTES

Commencement: to be appointed (see the introductory note to this Act).

518 Rights of resigning auditor

(1) This section applies where an auditor's notice of resignation is accompanied by a statement of the circumstances connected with his resignation (see section 519).

(2) He may deposit with the notice a signed requisition calling on the directors of the company forthwith duly to convene a general meeting of the company for the purpose of receiving and considering such explanation of the circumstances connected with his resignation as he may wish to place before the meeting.

(3) He may request the company to circulate to its members—

(a) before the meeting convened on his requisition, or

(b) before any general meeting at which his term of office would otherwise have expired or at which it is proposed to fill the vacancy caused by his resignation, a statement in writing (not exceeding a reasonable length) of the circumstances connected with his resignation.

(4) The company must (unless the statement is received too late for it to comply)—

(a) in any notice of the meeting given to members of the company, state the fact of the statement having been made, and

(b) send a copy of the statement to every member of the company to whom notice of the meeting is or has been sent.

(5) The directors must within 21 days from the date of the deposit of a requisition under this section proceed duly to convene a meeting for a day not more than 28 days after the date on which the notice convening the meeting is given.

(6) If default is made in complying with subsection (5), every director who failed to take all reasonable steps to secure that a meeting was convened commits an offence.

(7) A person guilty of an offence under this section is liable—

(a) on conviction on indictment, to a fine;

(b) on summary conviction to a fine not exceeding the statutory maximum.

(8) If a copy of the statement mentioned above is not sent out as required because received too late or because of the company's default, the auditor may (without prejudice to his right to be heard orally) require that the statement be read out at the meeting.

(9) Copies of a statement need not be sent out and the statement need not be read out at the meeting if, on the application either of the company or of any other person who claims to be aggrieved, the court is satisfied that the auditor is using the provisions of this section to secure needless publicity for defamatory matter.

The court may order the company's costs (in Scotland, expenses) on such an application to be paid in whole or in part by the auditor, notwithstanding that he is not a party to the application.

(10) An auditor who has resigned has, notwithstanding his resignation, the rights conferred by section 502(2) in relation to any such general meeting of the company as is mentioned in subsection (3)(a) or (b) above.

In such a case the references in that section to matters concerning the auditor as auditor shall be construed as references to matters concerning him as a former auditor.

[1855]

NOTES

Commencement: to be appointed (see the introductory note to this Act).

Statement by auditor on ceasing to hold office

519 Statement by auditor to be deposited with company

(1) Where an auditor of an unquoted company ceases for any reason to hold office, he must deposit at the company's registered office a statement of the circumstances connected with his ceasing to hold office, unless he considers that there are no circumstances in connection with his ceasing to hold office that need to be brought to the attention of members or creditors of the company.

(2) If he considers that there are no circumstances in connection with his ceasing to hold office that need to be brought to the attention of members or creditors of the company, he must deposit at the company's registered office a statement to that effect.

(3) Where an auditor of a quoted company ceases for any reason to hold office, he must deposit at the company's registered office a statement of the circumstances connected with his ceasing to hold office.

(4) The statement required by this section must be deposited—

(a) in the case of resignation, along with the notice of resignation;

(b) in the case of failure to seek re-appointment, not less than 14 days before the end of the time allowed for next appointing an auditor;

(c) in any other case, not later than the end of the period of 14 days beginning with the date on which he ceases to hold office.

(5) A person ceasing to hold office as auditor who fails to comply with this section commits an offence.

(6) In proceedings for such an offence it is a defence for the person charged to show that he took all reasonable steps and exercised all due diligence to avoid the commission of the offence.

(7) A person guilty of an offence under this section is liable—
(a) on conviction on indictment, to a fine;
(b) on summary conviction, to a fine not exceeding the statutory maximum.

[1856]

NOTES

Commencement: to be appointed (see the introductory note to this Act).

520 Company's duties in relation to statement

(1) This section applies where the statement deposited under section 519 states the circumstances connected with the auditor's ceasing to hold office.

(2) The company must within 14 days of the deposit of the statement either—
(a) send a copy of it to every person who under section 423 is entitled to be sent copies of the accounts, or
(b) apply to the court.

(3) If it applies to the court, the company must notify the auditor of the application.

(4) If the court is satisfied that the auditor is using the provisions of section 519 to secure needless publicity for defamatory matter—
(a) it shall direct that copies of the statement need not be sent out, and
(b) it may further order the company's costs (in Scotland, expenses) on the application to be paid in whole or in part by the auditor, even if he is not a party to the application.

The company must within 14 days of the court's decision send to the persons mentioned in subsection (2)(a) a statement setting out the effect of the order.

(5) If no such direction is made the company must send copies of the statement to the persons mentioned in subsection (2)(a) within 14 days of the court's decision or, as the case may be, of the discontinuance of the proceedings.

(6) In the event of default in complying with this section an offence is committed by every officer of the company who is in default.

(7) In proceedings for such an offence it is a defence for the person charged to show that he took all reasonable steps and exercised all due diligence to avoid the commission of the offence.

(8) A person guilty of an offence under this section is liable—
(a) on conviction on indictment, to a fine;
(b) on summary conviction, to a fine not exceeding the statutory maximum.

[1857]

NOTES

Commencement: to be appointed (see the introductory note to this Act).

521 Copy of statement to be sent to registrar

(1) Unless within 21 days beginning with the day on which he deposited the statement under section 519 the auditor receives notice of an application to the court under section 520, he must within a further seven days send a copy of the statement to the registrar.

(2) If an application to the court is made under section 520 and the auditor subsequently receives notice under subsection (5) of that section, he must within seven days of receiving the notice send a copy of the statement to the registrar.

(3) An auditor who fails to comply with subsection (1) or (2) commits an offence.

(4) In proceedings for such an offence it is a defence for the person charged to show that he took all reasonable steps and exercised all due diligence to avoid the commission of the offence.

(5) A person guilty of an offence under this section is liable—
  (a) on conviction on indictment, to a fine;
  (b) on summary conviction, to a fine not exceeding the statutory maximum.

[1858]

NOTES

Commencement: to be appointed (see the introductory note to this Act).

522 Duty of auditor to notify appropriate audit authority

(1) Where—
  (a) in the case of a major audit, an auditor ceases for any reason to hold office, or
  (b) in the case of an audit that is not a major audit, an auditor ceases to hold office before the end of his term of office,

the auditor ceasing to hold office must notify the appropriate audit authority.

(2) The notice must—
  (a) inform the appropriate audit authority that he has ceased to hold office, and
  (b) be accompanied by a copy of the statement deposited by him at the company's registered office in accordance with section 519.

(3) If the statement so deposited is to the effect that he considers that there are no circumstances in connection with his ceasing to hold office that need to be brought to the attention of members or creditors of the company, the notice must also be accompanied by a statement of the reasons for his ceasing to hold office.

(4) The auditor must comply with this section—
  (a) in the case of a major audit, at the same time as he deposits a statement at the company's registered office in accordance with section 519;
  (b) in the case of an audit that is not a major audit, at such time (not being earlier than the time mentioned in paragraph (a)) as the appropriate audit authority may require.

(5) A person ceasing to hold office as auditor who fails to comply with this section commits an offence.

(6) If that person is a firm an offence is committed by—
  (a) the firm, and
  (b) every officer of the firm who is in default.

(7) In proceedings for an offence under this section it is a defence for the person charged to show that he took all reasonable steps and exercised all due diligence to avoid the commission of the offence.

(8) A person guilty of an offence under this section is liable—
  (a) on conviction on indictment, to a fine;
  (b) on summary conviction, to a fine not exceeding the statutory maximum.

[1859]

NOTES

Commencement: to be appointed (see the introductory note to this Act).

523 Duty of company to notify appropriate audit authority

(1) Where an auditor ceases to hold office before the end of his term of office, the company must notify the appropriate audit authority.

(2) The notice must—
  (a) inform the appropriate audit authority that the auditor has ceased to hold office, and
  (b) be accompanied by—
    (i) a statement by the company of the reasons for his ceasing to hold office, or
    (ii) if the copy of the statement deposited by the auditor at the company's registered office in accordance with section 519 contains a statement of circumstances in connection with his ceasing to hold office that need to be brought to the attention of members or creditors of the company, a copy of that statement.

(3) The company must give notice under this section not later than 14 days after the date on which the auditor's statement is deposited at the company's registered office in accordance with section 519.

(4) If a company fails to comply with this section, an offence is committed by—
(a) the company, and
(b) every officer of the company who is in default.

(5) In proceedings for such an offence it is a defence for the person charged to show that he took all reasonable steps and exercised all due diligence to avoid the commission of the offence.

(6) A person guilty of an offence under this section is liable—
(a) on conviction on indictment, to a fine;
(b) on summary conviction, to a fine not exceeding the statutory maximum.

[1860]

NOTES

Commencement: to be appointed (see the introductory note to this Act).

524 Information to be given to accounting authorities

(1) The appropriate audit authority on receiving notice under section 522 or 523 of an auditor's ceasing to hold office—
(a) must inform the accounting authorities, and
(b) may if it thinks fit forward to those authorities a copy of the statement or statements accompanying the notice.

(2) The accounting authorities are—
(a) the Secretary of State, and
(b) any person authorised by the Secretary of State for the purposes of section 456 (revision of defective accounts: persons authorised to apply to court).

(3) If either of the accounting authorities is also the appropriate audit authority it is only necessary to comply with this section as regards any other accounting authority.

(4) If the court has made an order under section 520(4) directing that copies of the statement need not be sent out by the company, sections 460 and 461 (restriction on further disclosure) apply in relation to the copies sent to the accounting authorities as they apply to information obtained under section 459 (power to require documents etc).

[1861]

NOTES

Commencement: to be appointed (see the introductory note to this Act).

525 Meaning of "appropriate audit authority" and "major audit"

(1) In sections 522, 523 and 524 "appropriate audit authority" means—
(a) in the case of a major audit—
(i) the Secretary of State, or
(ii) if the Secretary of State has delegated functions under section 1252 to a body whose functions include receiving the notice in question, that body;
(b) in the case of an audit that is not a major audit, the relevant supervisory body.

"Supervisory body" has the same meaning as in Part 42 (statutory auditors) (see section 1217).

(2) In sections 522 and this section "major audit" means a statutory audit conducted in respect of—
(a) a company any of whose securities have been admitted to the official list (within the meaning of Part 6 of the Financial Services and Markets Act 2000 (c 8)), or
(b) any other person in whose financial condition there is a major public interest.

(3) In determining whether an audit is a major audit within subsection (2)(b), regard shall be had to any guidance issued by any of the authorities mentioned in subsection (1).

[1862]

NOTES

Commencement: to be appointed (see the introductory note to this Act).

Supplementary

526 Effect of casual vacancies

If an auditor ceases to hold office for any reason, any surviving or continuing auditor or auditors may continue to act.

[1863]

NOTES

Commencement: to be appointed (see the introductory note to this Act).

527–531 ((*Chapter 5*) *outside the scope of this work.*)

CHAPTER 6
AUDITORS' LIABILITY

Voidness of provisions protecting auditors from liability

532 Voidness of provisions protecting auditors from liability

(1) This section applies to any provision—

(a) for exempting an auditor of a company (to any extent) from any liability that would otherwise attach to him in connection with any negligence, default, breach of duty or breach of trust in relation to the company occurring in the course of the audit of accounts, or

(b) by which a company directly or indirectly provides an indemnity (to any extent) for an auditor of the company, or of an associated company, against any liability attaching to him in connection with any negligence, default, breach of duty or breach of trust in relation to the company of which he is auditor occurring in the course of the audit of accounts.

(2) Any such provision is void, except as permitted by—

(a) section 533 (indemnity for costs of successfully defending proceedings), or

(b) sections 534 to 536 (liability limitation agreements).

(3) This section applies to any provision, whether contained in a company's articles or in any contract with the company or otherwise.

(4) For the purposes of this section companies are associated if one is a subsidiary of the other or both are subsidiaries of the same body corporate.

[1864]

NOTES

Commencement: to be appointed (see the introductory note to this Act).

Indemnity for costs of defending proceedings

533 Indemnity for costs of successfully defending proceedings

Section 532 (general voidness of provisions protecting auditors from liability) does not prevent a company from indemnifying an auditor against any liability incurred by him—

(a) in defending proceedings (whether civil or criminal) in which judgment is given in his favour or he is acquitted, or

(b) in connection with an application under section 1157 (power of court to grant relief in case of honest and reasonable conduct) in which relief is granted to him by the court.

[1865]

NOTES

Commencement: to be appointed (see the introductory note to this Act).

Liability limitation agreements

534 Liability limitation agreements

(1) A "liability limitation agreement" is an agreement that purports to limit the amount of a liability owed to a company by its auditor in respect of any negligence, default, breach of duty or breach of trust, occurring in the course of the audit of accounts, of which the auditor may be guilty in relation to the company.

(2) Section 532 (general voidness of provisions protecting auditors from liability) does not affect the validity of a liability limitation agreement that—

(a) complies with section 535 (terms of liability limitation agreement) and of any regulations under that section, and

(b) is authorised by the members of the company (see section 536).

(3) Such an agreement—

(a) is effective to the extent provided by section 537, and

(b) is not subject—

(i) in England and Wales or Northern Ireland, to section 2(2) or 3(2)(a) of the Unfair Contract Terms Act 1977 (c 50);

(ii) in Scotland, to section 16(1)(b) or 17(1)(a) of that Act.

[1866]

NOTES

Commencement: to be appointed (see the introductory note to this Act).

535 Terms of liability limitation agreement

(1) A liability limitation agreement—

(a) must not apply in respect of acts or omissions occurring in the course of the audit of accounts for more than one financial year, and

(b) must specify the financial year in relation to which it applies.

(2) The Secretary of State may by regulations—

(a) require liability limitation agreements to contain specified provisions or provisions of a specified description;

(b) prohibit liability limitation agreements from containing specified provisions or provisions of a specified description.

"Specified" here means specified in the regulations.

(3) Without prejudice to the generality of the power conferred by subsection (2), that power may be exercised with a view to preventing adverse effects on competition.

(4) Subject to the preceding provisions of this section, it is immaterial how a liability limitation agreement is framed.

In particular, the limit on the amount of the auditor's liability need not be a sum of money, or a formula, specified in the agreement.

(5) Regulations under this section are subject to negative resolution procedure.

[1867]

NOTES

Commencement: to be appointed (see the introductory note to this Act).

536 Authorisation of agreement by members of the company

(1) A liability limitation agreement is authorised by the members of the company if it has been authorised under this section and that authorisation has not been withdrawn.

(2) A liability limitation agreement between a private company and its auditor may be authorised—

(a) by the company passing a resolution, before it enters into the agreement, waiving the need for approval,
(b) by the company passing a resolution, before it enters into the agreement, approving the agreement's principal terms, or
(c) by the company passing a resolution, after it enters into the agreement, approving the agreement.

(3) A liability limitation agreement between a public company and its auditor may be authorised—
(a) by the company passing a resolution in general meeting, before it enters into the agreement, approving the agreement's principal terms, or
(b) by the company passing a resolution in general meeting, after it enters into the agreement, approving the agreement.

(4) The "principal terms" of an agreement are terms specifying, or relevant to the determination of—
(a) the kind (or kinds) of acts or omissions covered,
(b) the financial year to which the agreement relates, or
(c) the limit to which the auditor's liability is subject.

(5) Authorisation under this section may be withdrawn by the company passing an ordinary resolution to that effect—
(a) at any time before the company enters into the agreement, or
(b) if the company has already entered into the agreement, before the beginning of the financial year to which the agreement relates.

Paragraph (b) has effect notwithstanding anything in the agreement.

[1868]

NOTES

Commencement: to be appointed (see the introductory note to this Act).

537 Effect of liability limitation agreement

(1) A liability limitation agreement is not effective to limit the auditor's liability to less than such amount as is fair and reasonable in all the circumstances of the case having regard (in particular) to—
(a) the auditor's responsibilities under this Part,
(b) the nature and purpose of the auditor's contractual obligations to the company, and
(c) the professional standards expected of him.

(2) A liability limitation agreement that purports to limit the auditor's liability to less than the amount mentioned in subsection (1) shall have effect as if it limited his liability to that amount.

(3) In determining what is fair and reasonable in all the circumstances of the case no account is to be taken of—
(a) matters arising after the loss or damage in question has been incurred, or
(b) matters (whenever arising) affecting the possibility of recovering compensation from other persons liable in respect of the same loss or damage.

[1869]

NOTES

Commencement: to be appointed (see the introductory note to this Act).

538 Disclosure of agreement by company

(1) A company which has entered into a liability limitation agreement must make such disclosure in connection with the agreement as the Secretary of State may require by regulations.

(2) The regulations may provide, in particular, that any disclosure required by the regulations shall be made—
(a) in a note to the company's annual accounts (in the case of its individual accounts) or in such manner as is specified in the regulations (in the case of group accounts), or
(b) in the directors' report.

(3) Regulations under this section are subject to negative resolution procedure.

[1870]

NOTES

Commencement: to be appointed (see the introductory note to this Act).

CHAPTER 7
SUPPLEMENTARY PROVISIONS

539 Minor definitions

In this Part—

"e-money issuer" means a person who has permission under Part 4 of the Financial Services and Markets Act 2000 (c 8) to carry on the activity of issuing electronic money within the meaning of article 9B of the Financial Services and Markets Act 2000 (Regulated Activities) Order 2001 (SI 2001/544);

"ISD investment firm" has the meaning given by the Glossary forming part of the Handbook made by the Financial Services Authority under the Financial Services and Markets Act 2000;

"qualified", in relation to an auditor's report (or a statement contained in an auditor's report), means that the report or statement does not state the auditor's unqualified opinion that the accounts have been properly prepared in accordance with this Act or, in the case of an undertaking not required to prepare accounts in accordance with this Act, under any corresponding legislation under which it is required to prepare accounts;

"turnover", in relation to a company, means the amounts derived from the provision of goods and services falling within the company's ordinary activities, after deduction of—

(a) trade discounts,
(b) value added tax, and
(c) any other taxes based on the amounts so derived;

"UCITS management company" has the meaning given by the Glossary forming part of the Handbook made by the Financial Services Authority under the Financial Services and Markets Act 2000.

[1871]

NOTES

Commencement: to be appointed (see the introductory note to this Act).

PART 17
A COMPANY'S SHARE CAPITAL

CHAPTER 1
SHARES AND SHARE CAPITAL OF A COMPANY

Shares

540 Shares

(1) In the Companies Acts "share", in relation to a company, means share in the company's share capital.

(2) A company's shares may no longer be converted into stock.

(3) Stock created before the commencement of this Part may be reconverted into shares in accordance with section 620.

(4) In the Companies Acts—

(a) references to shares include stock except where a distinction between share and stock is express or implied, and
(b) references to a number of shares include an amount of stock where the context admits of the reference to shares being read as including stock.

[1872]

NOTES

Commencement: to be appointed (see the introductory note to this Act).

541 Nature of shares

The shares or other interest of a member in a company are personal property (or, in Scotland, moveable property) and are not in the nature of real estate (or heritage).

[1873]

NOTES

Commencement: to be appointed (see the introductory note to this Act).

542 Nominal value of shares

(1) Shares in a limited company having a share capital must each have a fixed nominal value.

(2) An allotment of a share that does not have a fixed nominal value is void.

(3) Shares in a limited company having a share capital may be denominated in any currency, and different classes of shares may be denominated in different currencies.

But see section 765 (initial authorised minimum share capital requirement for public company to be met by reference to share capital denominated in sterling or euros).

(4) If a company purports to allot shares in contravention of this section, an offence is committed by every officer of the company who is in default.

(5) A person guilty of an offence under this section is liable—
- (a) on conviction on indictment, to a fine;
- (b) on summary conviction, to a fine not exceeding the statutory maximum.

[1874]

NOTES

Commencement: to be appointed (see the introductory note to this Act).

543 Numbering of shares

(1) Each share in a company having a share capital must be distinguished by its appropriate number, except in the following circumstances.

(2) If at any time—
- (a) all the issued shares in a company are fully paid up and rank *pari passu* for all purposes, or
- (b) all the issued shares of a particular class in a company are fully paid up and rank *pari passu* for all purposes,

none of those shares need thereafter have a distinguishing number so long as it remains fully paid up and ranks *pari passu* for all purposes with all shares of the same class for the time being issued and fully paid up.

[1875]

NOTES

Commencement: to be appointed (see the introductory note to this Act).

544 Transferability of shares

(1) The shares or other interest of any member in a company are transferable in accordance with the company's articles.

(2) This is subject to—
- (a) the Stock Transfer Act 1963 (c 18) or the Stock Transfer Act (Northern Ireland) 1963 (c 24 (NI)) (which enables securities of certain descriptions to be transferred by a simplified process), and
- (b) regulations under Chapter 2 of Part 21 of this Act (which enable title to securities to be evidenced and transferred without a written instrument).

PART I STATUTES

(3) See Part 21 of this Act generally as regards share transfers.

[1876]

NOTES

Commencement: to be appointed (see the introductory note to this Act).

545 Companies having a share capital

References in the Companies Acts to a company having a share capital are to a company that has power under its constitution to issue shares.

[1877]

NOTES

Commencement: to be appointed (see the introductory note to this Act).

546 Issued and allotted share capital

(1) References in the Companies Acts—

(a) to "issued share capital" are to shares of a company that have been issued;

(b) to "allotted share capital" are to shares of a company that have been allotted.

(2) References in the Companies Acts to issued or allotted shares, or to issued or allotted share capital, include shares taken on the formation of the company by the subscribers to the company's memorandum.

[1878]

NOTES

Commencement: to be appointed (see the introductory note to this Act).

Share capital

547 Called-up share capital

In the Companies Acts—

"called-up share capital", in relation to a company, means so much of its share capital as equals the aggregate amount of the calls made on its shares (whether or not those calls have been paid), together with—

(a) any share capital paid up without being called, and

(b) any share capital to be paid on a specified future date under the articles, the terms of allotment of the relevant shares or any other arrangements for payment of those shares; and

"uncalled share capital" is to be construed accordingly.

[1879]

NOTES

Commencement: to be appointed (see the introductory note to this Act).

548 Equity share capital

In the Companies Acts "equity share capital", in relation to a company, means its issued share capital excluding any part of that capital that, neither as respects dividends nor as respects capital, carries any right to participate beyond a specified amount in a distribution.

[1880]

NOTES

Commencement: to be appointed (see the introductory note to this Act).

CHAPTER 2
ALLOTMENT OF SHARES: GENERAL PROVISIONS

Power of directors to allot shares

549 Exercise by directors of power to allot shares etc

(1) The directors of a company must not exercise any power of the company—
- (a) to allot shares in the company, or
- (b) to grant rights to subscribe for, or to convert any security into, shares in the company,

except in accordance with section 550 (private company with single class of shares) or section 551 (authorisation by company).

(2) Subsection (1) does not apply—
- (a) to the allotment of shares in pursuance of an employees' share scheme, or
- (b) to the grant of a right to subscribe for, or to convert any security into, shares so allotted.

(3) If this section applies in relation to the grant of a right to subscribe for, or to convert any security into, shares, it does not apply in relation to the allotment of shares pursuant to that right.

(4) A director who knowingly contravenes, or permits or authorises a contravention of, this section commits an offence.

(5) A person guilty of an offence under this section is liable—
- (a) on conviction on indictment, to a fine;
- (b) on summary conviction, to a fine not exceeding the statutory maximum.

(6) Nothing in this section affects the validity of an allotment or other transaction.

[1881]

NOTES

Commencement: to be appointed (see the introductory note to this Act).

550 Power of directors to allot shares etc: private company with only one class of shares

Where a private company has only one class of shares, the directors may exercise any power of the company—
- (a) to allot shares of that class, or
- (b) to grant rights to subscribe for or to convert any security into such shares,

except to the extent that they are prohibited from doing so by the company's articles.

[1882]

NOTES

Commencement: to be appointed (see the introductory note to this Act).

551 Power of directors to allot shares etc: authorisation by company

(1) The directors of a company may exercise a power of the company—
- (a) to allot shares in the company, or
- (b) to grant rights to subscribe for or to convert any security into shares in the company,

if they are authorised to do so by the company's articles or by resolution of the company.

(2) Authorisation may be given for a particular exercise of the power or for its exercise generally, and may be unconditional or subject to conditions.

(3) Authorisation must—
- (a) state the maximum amount of shares that may be allotted under it, and
- (b) specify the date on which it will expire, which must be not more than five years from—

(i) in the case of authorisation contained in the company's articles at the time of its original incorporation, the date of that incorporation;
(ii) in any other case, the date on which the resolution is passed by virtue of which the authorisation is given.

(4) Authorisation may—
(a) be renewed or further renewed by resolution of the company for a further period not exceeding five years, and
(b) be revoked or varied at any time by resolution of the company.

(5) A resolution renewing authorisation must—
(a) state (or restate) the maximum amount of shares that may be allotted under the authorisation or, as the case may be, the amount remaining to be allotted under it, and
(b) specify the date on which the renewed authorisation will expire.

(6) In relation to rights to subscribe for or to convert any security into shares in the company, references in this section to the maximum amount of shares that may be allotted under the authorisation are to the maximum amount of shares that may be allotted pursuant to the rights.

(7) The directors may allot shares, or grant rights to subscribe for or to convert any security into shares, after authorisation has expired if—
(a) the shares are allotted, or the rights are granted, in pursuance of an offer or agreement made by the company before the authorisation expired, and
(b) the authorisation allowed the company to make an offer or agreement which would or might require shares to be allotted, or rights to be granted, after the authorisation had expired.

(8) A resolution of a company to give, vary, revoke or renew authorisation under this section may be an ordinary resolution, even though it amends the company's articles.

(9) Chapter 3 of Part 3 (resolutions affecting a company's constitution) applies to a resolution under this section.

[1883]

NOTES

Commencement: to be appointed (see the introductory note to this Act).

Prohibition of commissions, discounts and allowances

552 General prohibition of commissions, discounts and allowances

(1) Except as permitted by section 553 (permitted commission), a company must not apply any of its shares or capital money, either directly or indirectly, in payment of any commission, discount or allowance to any person in consideration of his—
(a) subscribing or agreeing to subscribe (whether absolutely or conditionally) for shares in the company, or
(b) procuring or agreeing to procure subscriptions (whether absolute or conditional) for shares in the company.

(2) It is immaterial how the shares or money are so applied, whether by being added to the purchase money of property acquired by the company or to the contract price of work to be executed for the company, or being paid out of the nominal purchase money or contract price, or otherwise.

(3) Nothing in this section affects the payment of such brokerage as has previously been lawful.

[1884]

NOTES

Commencement: to be appointed (see the introductory note to this Act).

553 Permitted commission

(1) A company may, if the following conditions are satisfied, pay a commission to a person in consideration of his subscribing or agreeing to subscribe (whether absolutely or

conditionally) for shares in the company, or procuring or agreeing to procure subscriptions (whether absolute or conditional) for shares in the company.

(2) The conditions are that—
(a) the payment of the commission is authorised by the company's articles; and
(b) the commission paid or agreed to be paid does not exceed—
(i) 10% of the price at which the shares are issued, or
(ii) the amount or rate authorised by the articles,
whichever is the less.

(3) A vendor to, or promoter of, or other person who receives payment in money or shares from, a company may apply any part of the money or shares so received in payment of any commission the payment of which directly by the company would be permitted by this section.

[1885]

NOTES

Commencement: to be appointed (see the introductory note to this Act).

Registration of allotment

554 Registration of allotment

(1) A company must register an allotment of shares as soon as practicable and in any event within two months after the date of the allotment.

(2) This does not apply if the company has issued a share warrant in respect of the shares (see section 779).

(3) If a company fails to comply with this section, an offence is committed by—
(a) the company, and
(b) every officer of the company who is in default.

(4) A person guilty of an offence under this section is liable on summary conviction to a fine not exceeding level 3 on the standard scale and, for continued contravention, a daily default fine not exceeding one-tenth of level 3 on the standard scale.

(5) For the company's duties as to the issue of share certificates etc, see Part 21 (certification and transfer of securities).

[1886]

NOTES

Commencement: to be appointed (see the introductory note to this Act).

Return of allotment

555 Return of allotment by limited company

(1) This section applies to a company limited by shares and to a company limited by guarantee and having a share capital.

(2) The company must, within one month of making an allotment of shares, deliver to the registrar for registration a return of the allotment.

(3) The return must—
(a) contain the prescribed information, and
(b) be accompanied by a statement of capital.

(4) The statement of capital must state with respect to the company's share capital at the date to which the return is made up—
(a) the total number of shares of the company,
(b) the aggregate nominal value of those shares,
(c) for each class of shares—
(i) prescribed particulars of the rights attached to the shares,
(ii) the total number of shares of that class, and
(iii) the aggregate nominal value of shares of that class, and

(d) the amount paid up and the amount (if any) unpaid on each share (whether on account of the nominal value of the share or by way of premium).

[1887]

NOTES

Commencement: to be appointed (see the introductory note to this Act).

556 Return of allotment by unlimited company allotting new class of shares

(1) This section applies to an unlimited company that allots shares of a class with rights that are not in all respects uniform with shares previously allotted.

(2) The company must, within one month of making such an allotment, deliver to the registrar for registration a return of the allotment.

(3) The return must contain the prescribed particulars of the rights attached to the shares.

(4) For the purposes of this section shares are not to be treated as different from shares previously allotted by reason only that the former do not carry the same rights to dividends as the latter during the twelve months immediately following the former's allotment.

[1888]

NOTES

Commencement: to be appointed (see the introductory note to this Act).

557 Offence of failure to make return

(1) If a company makes default in complying with—

section 555 (return of allotment of shares by limited company), or

section 556 (return of allotment of new class of shares by unlimited company),

an offence is committed by every officer of the company who is in default.

(2) A person guilty of an offence under this section is liable—

(a) on conviction on indictment, to a fine;

(b) on summary conviction, to a fine not exceeding the statutory maximum and, for continued contravention, a daily default fine not exceeding one-tenth of the statutory maximum.

(3) In the case of default in delivering to the registrar within one month after the allotment the return required by section 555 or 556—

(a) any person liable for the default may apply to the court for relief, and

(b) the court, if satisfied—

(i) that the omission to deliver the document was accidental or due to inadvertence, or

(ii) that it is just and equitable to grant relief,

may make an order extending the time for delivery of the document for such period as the court thinks proper.

[1889]

NOTES

Commencement: to be appointed (see the introductory note to this Act).

Supplementary provisions

558 When shares are allotted

For the purposes of the Companies Acts shares in a company are taken to be allotted when a person acquires the unconditional right to be included in the company's register of members in respect of the shares.

[1890]

NOTES

Commencement: to be appointed (see the introductory note to this Act).

559 Provisions about allotment not applicable to shares taken on formation

The provisions of this Chapter have no application in relation to the taking of shares by the subscribers to the memorandum on the formation of the company.

[1891]

NOTES

Commencement: to be appointed (see the introductory note to this Act).

CHAPTER 3
ALLOTMENT OF EQUITY SECURITIES: EXISTING SHAREHOLDERS' RIGHT OF PRE-EMPTION

Introductory

560 Meaning of "equity securities" and related expressions

(1) In this Chapter—

"equity securities" means—

(a) ordinary shares in the company, or

(b) rights to subscribe for, or to convert securities into, ordinary shares in the company;

"ordinary shares" means shares other than shares that as respects dividends and capital carry a right to participate only up to a specified amount in a distribution.

(2) References in this Chapter to the allotment of equity securities include—

(a) the grant of a right to subscribe for, or to convert any securities into, ordinary shares in the company, and

(b) the sale of ordinary shares in the company that immediately before the sale are held by the company as treasury shares.

[1892]

NOTES

Commencement: to be appointed (see the introductory note to this Act).

Existing shareholders' right of pre-emption

561 Existing shareholders' right of pre-emption

(1) A company must not allot equity securities to a person on any terms unless—

(a) it has made an offer to each person who holds ordinary shares in the company to allot to him on the same or more favourable terms a proportion of those securities that is as nearly as practicable equal to the proportion in nominal value held by him of the ordinary share capital of the company, and

(b) the period during which any such offer may be accepted has expired or the company has received notice of the acceptance or refusal of every offer so made.

(2) Securities that a company has offered to allot to a holder of ordinary shares may be allotted to him, or anyone in whose favour he has renounced his right to their allotment, without contravening subsection (1)(b).

(3) If subsection (1) applies in relation to the grant of such a right, it does not apply in relation to the allotment of shares in pursuance of that right.

(4) Shares held by the company as treasury shares are disregarded for the purposes of this section, so that—

(a) the company is not treated as a person who holds ordinary shares, and

(b) the shares are not treated as forming part of the ordinary share capital of the company.

(5) This section is subject to—

(a) sections 564 to 566 (exceptions to pre-emption right),

(b) sections 567 and 568 (exclusion of rights of pre-emption),

(c) sections 569 to 573 (disapplication of pre-emption rights), and

(d) section 576 (saving for certain older pre-emption procedures).

[1893]

NOTES

Commencement: to be appointed (see the introductory note to this Act).

562 Communication of pre-emption offers to shareholders

(1) This section has effect as to the manner in which offers required by section 561 are to be made to holders of a company's shares.

(2) The offer may be made in hard copy or electronic form.

(3) If the holder—

(a) has no registered address in an EEA State and has not given to the company an address in an EEA State for the service of notices on him, or

(b) is the holder of a share warrant,

the offer may be made by causing it, or a notice specifying where a copy of it can be obtained or inspected, to be published in the Gazette.

(4) The offer must state a period during which it may be accepted and the offer shall not be withdrawn before the end of that period.

(5) The period must be a period of at least 21 days beginning—

(a) in the case of an offer made in hard copy form, with the date on which the offer is sent or supplied;

(b) in the case of an offer made in electronic form, with the date on which the offer is sent;

(c) in the case of an offer made by publication in the Gazette, with the date of publication.

(6) The Secretary of State may by regulations made by statutory instrument—

(a) reduce the period specified in subsection (5) (but not to less than 14 days), or

(b) increase that period.

(7) A statutory instrument containing regulations made under subsection (6) is subject to affirmative resolution procedure.

[1894]

NOTES

Commencement: to be appointed (see the introductory note to this Act).

563 Liability of company and officers in case of contravention

(1) This section applies where there is a contravention of—

section 561 (existing shareholders' right of pre-emption), or

section 562 (communication of pre-emption offers to shareholders).

(2) The company and every officer of it who knowingly authorised or permitted the contravention are jointly and severally liable to compensate any person to whom an offer should have been made in accordance with those provisions for any loss, damage, costs or expenses which the person has sustained or incurred by reason of the contravention.

(3) No proceedings to recover any such loss, damage, costs or expenses shall be commenced after the expiration of two years—

(a) from the delivery to the registrar of companies of the return of allotment, or

(b) where equity securities other than shares are granted, from the date of the grant.

[1895]

NOTES

Commencement: to be appointed (see the introductory note to this Act).

Exceptions to right of pre-emption

564 Exception to pre-emption right: bonus shares

Section 561(1) (existing shareholders' right of pre-emption) does not apply in relation to the allotment of bonus shares.

[1896]

NOTES

Commencement: to be appointed (see the introductory note to this Act).

565 Exception to pre-emption right: issue for non-cash consideration

Section 561(1) (existing shareholders' right of pre-emption) does not apply to a particular allotment of equity securities if these are, or are to be, wholly or partly paid up otherwise than in cash.

[1897]

NOTES

Commencement: to be appointed (see the introductory note to this Act).

566 Exception to pre-emption right: securities held under employees' share scheme

Section 561 (existing shareholders' right of pre-emption) does not apply to the allotment of securities that would, apart from any renunciation or assignment of the right to their allotment, be held under an employees' share scheme.

[1898]

NOTES

Commencement: to be appointed (see the introductory note to this Act).

Exclusion of right of pre-emption

567 Exclusion of requirements by private companies

(1) All or any of the requirements of—

(a) section 561 (existing shareholders' right of pre-emption), or

(b) section 562 (communication of pre-emption offers to shareholders)

may be excluded by provision contained in the articles of a private company.

(2) They may be excluded—

(a) generally in relation to the allotment by the company of equity securities, or

(b) in relation to allotments of a particular description.

(3) Any requirement or authorisation contained in the articles of a private company that is inconsistent with either of those sections is treated for the purposes of this section as a provision excluding that section.

(4) A provision to which section 568 applies (exclusion of pre-emption right: corresponding right conferred by articles) is not to be treated as inconsistent with section 561.

[1899]

NOTES

Commencement: to be appointed (see the introductory note to this Act).

568 Exclusion of pre-emption right: articles conferring corresponding right

(1) The provisions of this section apply where, in a case in which section 561 (existing shareholders' right of pre-emption) would otherwise apply—

(a) a company's articles contain provision ("pre-emption provision") prohibiting the company from allotting ordinary shares of a particular class unless it has complied with the condition that it makes such an offer as is described in section 561(1) to each person who holds ordinary shares of that class, and

(b) in accordance with that provision—
   (i) the company makes an offer to allot shares to such a holder, and
   (ii) he or anyone in whose favour he has renounced his right to their allotment accepts the offer.

(2) In that case, section 561 does not apply to the allotment of those shares and the company may allot them accordingly.

(3) The provisions of section 562 (communication of pre-emption offers to shareholders) apply in relation to offers made in pursuance of the pre-emption provision of the company's articles.

This is subject to section 567 (exclusion of requirements by private companies).

(4) If there is a contravention of the pre-emption provision of the company's articles, the company, and every officer of it who knowingly authorised or permitted the contravention, are jointly and severally liable to compensate any person to whom an offer should have been made under the provision for any loss, damage, costs or expenses which the person has sustained or incurred by reason of the contravention.

(5) No proceedings to recover any such loss, damage, costs or expenses may be commenced after the expiration of two years—
(a) from the delivery to the registrar of companies of the return of allotment, or
(b) where equity securities other than shares are granted, from the date of the grant.

[1900]

NOTES

Commencement: to be appointed (see the introductory note to this Act).

Disapplication of pre-emption rights

569 Disapplication of pre-emption rights: private company with only one class of shares

(1) The directors of a private company that has only one class of shares may be given power by the articles, or by a special resolution of the company, to allot equity securities of that class as if section 561 (existing shareholders' right of pre-emption)—
(a) did not apply to the allotment, or
(b) applied to the allotment with such modifications as the directors may determine.

(2) Where the directors make an allotment under this section, the provisions of this Chapter have effect accordingly.

[1901]

NOTES

Commencement: to be appointed (see the introductory note to this Act).

570 Disapplication of pre-emption rights: directors acting under general authorisation

(1) Where the directors of a company are generally authorised for the purposes of section 551 (power of directors to allot shares etc: authorisation by company), they may be given power by the articles, or by a special resolution of the company, to allot equity securities pursuant to that authorisation as if section 561 (existing shareholders' right of pre-emption)—
(a) did not apply to the allotment, or
(b) applied to the allotment with such modifications as the directors may determine.

(2) Where the directors make an allotment under this section, the provisions of this Chapter have effect accordingly.

(3) The power conferred by this section ceases to have effect when the authorisation to which it relates—
(a) is revoked, or
(b) would (if not renewed) expire.

But if the authorisation is renewed the power may also be renewed, for a period not longer than that for which the authorisation is renewed, by a special resolution of the company.

(4) Notwithstanding that the power conferred by this section has expired, the directors may allot equity securities in pursuance of an offer or agreement previously made by the company if the power enabled the company to make an offer or agreement that would or might require equity securities to be allotted after it expired.

[1902]

NOTES

Commencement: to be appointed (see the introductory note to this Act).

571 Disapplication of pre-emption rights by special resolution

(1) Where the directors of a company are authorised for the purposes of section 551 (power of directors to allot shares etc: authorisation by company), whether generally or otherwise, the company may by special resolution resolve that section 561 (existing shareholders' right of pre-emption)—

(a) does not apply to a specified allotment of equity securities to be made pursuant to that authorisation, or

(b) applies to such an allotment with such modifications as may be specified in the resolution.

(2) Where such a resolution is passed the provisions of this Chapter have effect accordingly.

(3) A special resolution under this section ceases to have effect when the authorisation to which it relates—

(a) is revoked, or

(b) would (if not renewed) expire.

But if the authorisation is renewed the resolution may also be renewed, for a period not longer than that for which the authorisation is renewed, by a special resolution of the company.

(4) Notwithstanding that any such resolution has expired, the directors may allot equity securities in pursuance of an offer or agreement previously made by the company if the resolution enabled the company to make an offer or agreement that would or might require equity securities to be allotted after it expired.

(5) A special resolution under this section, or a special resolution to renew such a resolution, must not be proposed unless—

(a) it is recommended by the directors, and

(b) the directors have complied with the following provisions.

(6) Before such a resolution is proposed, the directors must make a written statement setting out—

(a) their reasons for making the recommendation,

(b) the amount to be paid to the company in respect of the equity securities to be allotted, and

(c) the directors' justification of that amount.

(7) The directors' statement must—

(a) if the resolution is proposed as a written resolution, be sent or submitted to every eligible member at or before the time at which the proposed resolution is sent or submitted to him;

(b) if the resolution is proposed at a general meeting, be circulated to the members entitled to notice of the meeting with that notice.

[1903]

NOTES

Commencement: to be appointed (see the introductory note to this Act).

572 Liability for false statement in directors' statement

(1) This section applies in relation to a directors' statement under section 571 (special resolution disapplying pre-emption rights) that is sent, submitted or circulated under subsection (7) of that section.

(2) A person who knowingly or recklessly authorises or permits the inclusion of any matter that is misleading, false or deceptive in a material particular in such a statement commits an offence.

(3) A person guilty of an offence under this section is liable—
(a) on conviction on indictment, to imprisonment for a term not exceeding two years or a fine (or both);
(b) on summary conviction—
(i) in England and Wales, to imprisonment for a term not exceeding twelve months or to a fine not exceeding the statutory maximum (or both);
(ii) in Scotland or Northern Ireland, to imprisonment for a term not exceeding six months, or to a fine not exceeding the statutory maximum (or both).

[1904]

NOTES

Commencement: to be appointed (see the introductory note to this Act).

573 (*Outside the scope of this work.*)

Supplementary

574 References to holder of shares in relation to offer

(1) In this Chapter, in relation to an offer to allot securities required by—
(a) section 561 (existing shareholders' right of pre-emption), or
(b) any provision to which section 568 applies (articles conferring corresponding right),

a reference (however expressed) to the holder of shares of any description is to whoever was the holder of shares of that description at the close of business on a date to be specified in the offer.

(2) The specified date must fall within the period of 28 days immediately before the date of the offer.

[1905]

NOTES

Commencement: to be appointed (see the introductory note to this Act).

575 Saving for other restrictions on offer or allotment

(1) The provisions of this Chapter are without prejudice to any other enactment by virtue of which a company is prohibited (whether generally or in specified circumstances) from offering or allotting equity securities to any person.

(2) Where a company cannot by virtue of such an enactment offer or allot equity securities to a holder of ordinary shares of the company, those shares are disregarded for the purposes of section 561 (existing shareholders' right of pre-emption), so that—
(a) the person is not treated as a person who holds ordinary shares, and
(b) the shares are not treated as forming part of the ordinary share capital of the company.

[1906]

NOTES

Commencement: to be appointed (see the introductory note to this Act).

576 Saving for certain older pre-emption requirements

(1) In the case of a public company the provisions of this Chapter do not apply to an allotment of equity securities that are subject to a pre-emption requirement in relation to which section 96(1) of the Companies Act 1985 (c 6) or Article 106(1) of the Companies (Northern Ireland) Order 1986 (SI 1986/1032 (NI 6)) applied immediately before the commencement of this Chapter.

(2) In the case of a private company a pre-emption requirement to which section 96(3) of the Companies Act 1985 or Article 106(3) of the Companies (Northern Ireland) Order 1986

applied immediately before the commencement of this Chapter shall have effect, so long as the company remains a private company, as if it were contained in the company's articles.

(3) A pre-emption requirement to which section 96(4) of the Companies Act 1985 or Article 106(4) of the Companies (Northern Ireland) Order 1986 applied immediately before the commencement of this section shall be treated for the purposes of this Chapter as if it were contained in the company's articles.

[1907]

NOTES

Commencement: to be appointed (see the introductory note to this Act).

577 Provisions about pre-emption not applicable to shares taken on formation

The provisions of this Chapter have no application in relation to the taking of shares by the subscribers to the memorandum on the formation of the company.

[1908]

NOTES

Commencement: to be appointed (see the introductory note to this Act).

578–579 (*(Chapter 4) outside the scope of this work.*)

CHAPTER 5
PAYMENT FOR SHARES

General rules

580 Shares not to be allotted at a discount

(1) A company's shares must not be allotted at a discount.

(2) If shares are allotted in contravention of this section, the allottee is liable to pay the company an amount equal to the amount of the discount, with interest at the appropriate rate.

[1909]

NOTES

Commencement: to be appointed (see the introductory note to this Act).

581 Provision for different amounts to be paid on shares

A company, if so authorised by its articles, may—

(a) make arrangements on the issue of shares for a difference between the shareholders in the amounts and times of payment of calls on their shares;

(b) accept from any member the whole or part of the amount remaining unpaid on any shares held by him, although no part of that amount has been called up;

(c) pay a dividend in proportion to the amount paid up on each share where a larger amount is paid up on some shares than on others.

[1910]

NOTES

Commencement: to be appointed (see the introductory note to this Act).

582 General rule as to means of payment

(1) Shares allotted by a company, and any premium on them, may be paid up in money or money's worth (including goodwill and know-how).

(2) This section does not prevent a company—

(a) from allotting bonus shares to its members, or

(b) from paying up, with sums available for the purpose, any amounts for the time being unpaid on any of its shares (whether on account of the nominal value of the shares or by way of premium).

(3) This section has effect subject to the following provisions of this Chapter (additional rules for public companies).

[1911]

NOTES

Commencement: to be appointed (see the introductory note to this Act).

583 Meaning of payment in cash

(1) The following provisions have effect for the purposes of the Companies Acts.

(2) A share in a company is deemed paid up (as to its nominal value or any premium on it) in cash, or allotted for cash, if the consideration received for the allotment or payment up is a cash consideration.

(3) A "cash consideration" means—

(a) cash received by the company,

(b) a cheque received by the company in good faith that the directors have no reason for suspecting will not be paid,

(c) a release of a liability of the company for a liquidated sum,

(d) an undertaking to pay cash to the company at a future date, or

(e) payment by any other means giving rise to a present or future entitlement (of the company or a person acting on the company's behalf) to a payment, or credit equivalent to payment, in cash.

(4) The Secretary of State may by order provide that particular means of payment specified in the order are to be regarded as falling within subsection (3)(e).

(5) In relation to the allotment or payment up of shares in a company—

(a) the payment of cash to a person other than the company, or

(b) an undertaking to pay cash to a person other than the company,

counts as consideration other than cash.

This does not apply for the purposes of Chapter 3 (allotment of equity securities: existing shareholders' right of pre-emption).

(6) For the purpose of determining whether a share is or is to be allotted for cash, or paid up in cash, "cash" includes foreign currency.

(7) An order under this section is subject to negative resolution procedure.

[1912]

NOTES

Commencement: to be appointed (see the introductory note to this Act).

584–587 (*Outside the scope of this work.*)

Supplementary provisions

588 Liability of subsequent holders of shares

(1) If a person becomes a holder of shares in respect of which—

(a) there has been a contravention of any provision of this Chapter, and

(b) by virtue of that contravention another is liable to pay any amount under the provision contravened,

that person is also liable to pay that amount (jointly and severally with any other person so liable), subject as follows.

(2) A person otherwise liable under subsection (1) is exempted from that liability if either—

(a) he is a purchaser for value and, at the time of the purchase, he did not have actual notice of the contravention concerned, or

(b) he derived title to the shares (directly or indirectly) from a person who became a holder of them after the contravention and was not liable under subsection (1).

(3) References in this section to a holder, in relation to shares in a company, include any person who has an unconditional right—
(a) to be included in the company's register of members in respect of those shares, or
(b) to have an instrument of transfer of the shares executed in his favour.

(4) This section applies in relation to a failure to carry out a term of a contract as mentioned in section 587(4) (public companies: payment by long-term undertaking) as it applies in relation to a contravention of a provision of this Chapter.

[1913]

NOTES

Commencement: to be appointed (see the introductory note to this Act).

589 Power of court to grant relief

(1) This section applies in relation to liability under—
section 585(2) (liability of allottee in case of breach by public company of prohibition on accepting undertaking to do work or perform services),
section 587(2) or (4) (liability of allottee in case of breach by public company of prohibition on payment by long-term undertaking), or
section 588 (liability of subsequent holders of shares),
as it applies in relation to a contravention of those sections.

(2) A person who—
(a) is subject to any such liability to a company in relation to payment in respect of shares in the company, or
(b) is subject to any such liability to a company by virtue of an undertaking given to it in, or in connection with, payment for shares in the company,
may apply to the court to be exempted in whole or in part from the liability.

(3) In the case of a liability within subsection (2)(a), the court may exempt the applicant from the liability only if and to the extent that it appears to the court just and equitable to do so having regard to—
(a) whether the applicant has paid, or is liable to pay, any amount in respect of—
(i) any other liability arising in relation to those shares under any provision of this Chapter or Chapter 6, or
(ii) any liability arising by virtue of any undertaking given in or in connection with payment for those shares;
(b) whether any person other than the applicant has paid or is likely to pay, whether in pursuance of any order of the court or otherwise, any such amount;
(c) whether the applicant or any other person—
(i) has performed in whole or in part, or is likely so to perform any such undertaking, or
(ii) has done or is likely to do any other thing in payment or part payment for the shares.

(4) In the case of a liability within subsection (2)(b), the court may exempt the applicant from the liability only if and to the extent that it appears to the court just and equitable to do so having regard to—
(a) whether the applicant has paid or is liable to pay any amount in respect of liability arising in relation to the shares under any provision of this Chapter or Chapter 6;
(b) whether any person other than the applicant has paid or is likely to pay, whether in pursuance of any order of the court or otherwise, any such amount.

(5) In determining whether it should exempt the applicant in whole or in part from any liability, the court must have regard to the following overriding principles—
(a) a company that has allotted shares should receive money or money's worth at least equal in value to the aggregate of the nominal value of those shares and the whole of any premium or, if the case so requires, so much of that aggregate as is treated as paid up;
(b) subject to that, where a company would, if the court did not grant the exemption, have more than one remedy against a particular person, it should be for the company to decide which remedy it should remain entitled to pursue.

(6) If a person brings proceedings against another ("the contributor") for a contribution in respect of liability to a company arising under any provision of this Chapter or Chapter 6

and it appears to the court that the contributor is liable to make such a contribution, the court may, if and to the extent that it appears to it just and equitable to do so having regard to the respective culpability (in respect of the liability to the company) of the contributor and the person bringing the proceedings—

(a) exempt the contributor in whole or in part from his liability to make such a contribution, or

(b) order the contributor to make a larger contribution than, but for this subsection, he would be liable to make.

[1914]

NOTES

Commencement: to be appointed (see the introductory note to this Act).

590 Penalty for contravention of this Chapter

(1) If a company contravenes any of the provisions of this Chapter, an offence is committed by—

(a) the company, and

(b) every officer of the company who is in default.

(2) A person guilty of an offence under this section is liable—

(a) on conviction on indictment, to a fine;

(b) on summary conviction, to a fine not exceeding the statutory maximum.

[1915]

NOTES

Commencement: to be appointed (see the introductory note to this Act).

591 Enforceability of undertakings to do work etc

(1) An undertaking given by any person, in or in connection with payment for shares in a company, to do work or perform services or to do any other thing, if it is enforceable by the company apart from this Chapter, is so enforceable notwithstanding that there has been a contravention in relation to it of a provision of this Chapter or Chapter 6.

(2) This is without prejudice to section 589 (power of court to grant relief etc in respect of liabilities).

[1916]

NOTES

Commencement: to be appointed (see the introductory note to this Act).

592 The appropriate rate of interest

(1) For the purposes of this Chapter the "appropriate rate" of interest is 5% per annum or such other rate as may be specified by order made by the Secretary of State.

(2) An order under this section is subject to negative resolution procedure.

[1917]

NOTES

Commencement: to be appointed (see the introductory note to this Act).

593–609 ((*Chapter 6*) *outside the scope of this work.*)

CHAPTER 7
SHARE PREMIUMS

The share premium account

610 Application of share premiums

(1) If a company issues shares at a premium, whether for cash or otherwise, a sum equal to the aggregate amount or value of the premiums on those shares must be transferred to an account called "the share premium account".

(2) Where, on issuing shares, a company has transferred a sum to the share premium account, it may use that sum to write off—

(a) the expenses of the issue of those shares;

(b) any commission paid on the issue of those shares.

(3) The company may use the share premium account to pay up new shares to be allotted to members as fully paid bonus shares.

(4) Subject to subsections (2) and (3), the provisions of the Companies Acts relating to the reduction of a company's share capital apply as if the share premium account were part of its paid up share capital.

(5) This section has effect subject to—

section 611 (group reconstruction relief);

section 612 (merger relief);

section 614 (power to make further provisions by regulations).

(6) In this Chapter "the issuing company" means the company issuing shares as mentioned in subsection (1) above.

[1918]

NOTES

Commencement: to be appointed (see the introductory note to this Act).

Relief from requirements as to share premiums

611 Group reconstruction relief

(1) This section applies where the issuing company—

(a) is a wholly-owned subsidiary of another company ("the holding company"), and

(b) allots shares—

(i) to the holding company, or

(ii) to another wholly-owned subsidiary of the holding company,

in consideration for the transfer to the issuing company of non-cash assets of a company ("the transferor company") that is a member of the group of companies that comprises the holding company and all its wholly-owned subsidiaries.

(2) Where the shares in the issuing company allotted in consideration for the transfer are issued at a premium, the issuing company is not required by section 610 to transfer any amount in excess of the minimum premium value to the share premium account.

(3) The minimum premium value means the amount (if any) by which the base value of the consideration for the shares allotted exceeds the aggregate nominal value of the shares.

(4) The base value of the consideration for the shares allotted is the amount by which the base value of the assets transferred exceeds the base value of any liabilities of the transferor company assumed by the issuing company as part of the consideration for the assets transferred.

(5) For the purposes of this section—

(a) the base value of assets transferred is taken as—

(i) the cost of those assets to the transferor company, or

(ii) if less, the amount at which those assets are stated in the transferor company's accounting records immediately before the transfer;

(b) the base value of the liabilities assumed is taken as the amount at which they are stated in the transferor company's accounting records immediately before the transfer.

[1919]

NOTES

Commencement: to be appointed (see the introductory note to this Act).

612 Merger relief

(1) This section applies where the issuing company has secured at least a 90% equity holding in another company in pursuance of an arrangement providing for the allotment of equity shares in the issuing company on terms that the consideration for the shares allotted is to be provided—

(a) by the issue or transfer to the issuing company of equity shares in the other company, or

(b) by the cancellation of any such shares not held by the issuing company.

(2) If the equity shares in the issuing company allotted in pursuance of the arrangement in consideration for the acquisition or cancellation of equity shares in the other company are issued at a premium, section 610 does not apply to the premiums on those shares.

(3) Where the arrangement also provides for the allotment of any shares in the issuing company on terms that the consideration for those shares is to be provided—

(a) by the issue or transfer to the issuing company of non-equity shares in the other company, or

(b) by the cancellation of any such shares in that company not held by the issuing company,

relief under subsection (2) extends to any shares in the issuing company allotted on those terms in pursuance of the arrangement.

(4) This section does not apply in a case falling within section 611 (group reconstruction relief).

[1920]

NOTES

Commencement: to be appointed (see the introductory note to this Act).

613 Merger relief: meaning of 90% equity holding

(1) The following provisions have effect to determine for the purposes of section 612 (merger relief) whether a company ("company A") has secured at least a 90% equity holding in another company ("company B") in pursuance of such an arrangement as is mentioned in subsection (1) of that section.

(2) Company A has secured at least a 90% equity holding in company B if in consequence of an acquisition or cancellation of equity shares in company B (in pursuance of that arrangement) it holds equity shares in company B of an aggregate amount equal to 90% or more of the nominal value of that company's equity share capital.

(3) For this purpose—

(a) it is immaterial whether any of those shares were acquired in pursuance of the arrangement; and

(b) shares in company B held by the company as treasury shares are excluded in determining the nominal value of company B's share capital.

(4) Where the equity share capital of company B is divided into different classes of shares, company A is not regarded as having secured at least a 90% equity holding in company B unless the requirements of subsection (2) are met in relation to each of those classes of shares taken separately.

(5) For the purposes of this section shares held by—

(a) a company that is company A's holding company or subsidiary, or

(b) a subsidiary of company A's holding company, or

(c) its or their nominees,

are treated as held by company A.

[1921]

NOTES

Commencement: to be appointed (see the introductory note to this Act).

614 Power to make further provision by regulations

(1) The Secretary of State may by regulations make such provision as he thinks appropriate—

(a) for relieving companies from the requirements of section 610 (application of share premiums) in relation to premiums other than cash premiums;
(b) for restricting or otherwise modifying any relief from those requirements provided by this Chapter.

(2) Regulations under this section are subject to affirmative resolution procedure.

[1922]

NOTES

Commencement: to be appointed (see the introductory note to this Act).

615 Relief may be reflected in company's balance sheet

An amount corresponding to the amount representing the premiums, or part of the premiums, on shares issued by a company that by virtue of any relief under this Chapter is not included in the company's share premium account may also be disregarded in determining the amount at which any shares or other consideration provided for the shares issued is to be included in the company's balance sheet.

[1923]

NOTES

Commencement: to be appointed (see the introductory note to this Act).

Supplementary provisions

616 Interpretation of this Chapter

(1) In this Chapter—

"arrangement" means any agreement, scheme or arrangement (including an arrangement sanctioned in accordance with—
(a) Part 26 (arrangements and reconstructions), or
(b) section 110 of the Insolvency Act 1986 (c 45) or Article 96 of the Insolvency (Northern Ireland) Order 1989 (SI 1989/2405 (NI 19)) (liquidator in winding up accepting shares as consideration for sale of company property));

"company", except in reference to the issuing company, includes any body corporate;

"equity shares" means shares comprised in a company's equity share capital, and "non-equity shares" means shares (of any class) that are not so comprised;

"the issuing company" has the meaning given by section 610(6).

(2) References in this Chapter (however expressed) to—
(a) the acquisition by a company of shares in another company, and
(b) the issue or allotment of shares to, or the transfer of shares to or by, a company,

include (respectively) the acquisition of shares by, and the issue or allotment or transfer of shares to or by, a nominee of that company.

The reference in section 611 to the transferor company shall be read accordingly.

(3) References in this Chapter to the transfer of shares in a company include the transfer of a right to be included in the company's register of members in respect of those shares.

[1924]

NOTES

Commencement: to be appointed (see the introductory note to this Act).

CHAPTER 8
ALTERATION OF SHARE CAPITAL

How share capital may be altered

617 Alteration of share capital of limited company

(1) A limited company having a share capital may not alter its share capital except in the following ways.

(2) The company may—
(a) increase its share capital by allotting new shares in accordance with this Part, or
(b) reduce its share capital in accordance with Chapter 10.

(3) The company may—
(a) sub-divide or consolidate all or any of its share capital in accordance with section 618, or
(b) reconvert stock into shares in accordance with section 620.

(4) The company may redenominate all or any of its shares in accordance with section 622, and may reduce its share capital in accordance with section 626 in connection with such a redenomination.

(5) Nothing in this section affects—
(a) the power of a company to purchase its own shares, or to redeem shares, in accordance with Part 18;
(b) the power of a company to purchase its own shares in pursuance of an order of the court under—
(i) section 98 (application to court to cancel resolution for re-registration as a private company),
(ii) section 721(6) (powers of court on objection to redemption or purchase of shares out of capital),
(iii) section 759 (remedial order in case of breach of prohibition of public offers by private company), or
(iv) Part 30 (protection of members against unfair prejudice);
(c) the forfeiture of shares, or the acceptance of shares surrendered in lieu, in pursuance of the company's articles, for failure to pay any sum payable in respect of the shares;
(d) the cancellation of shares under section 662 (duty to cancel shares held by or for a public company);
(e) the power of a company—
(i) to enter into a compromise or arrangement in accordance with Part 26 (arrangements and reconstructions), or
(ii) to do anything required to comply with an order of the court on an application under that Part.

[1925]

NOTES

Commencement: to be appointed (see the introductory note to this Act).

Subdivision or consolidation of shares

618 Sub-division or consolidation of shares

(1) A limited company having a share capital may—
(a) sub-divide its shares, or any of them, into shares of a smaller nominal amount than its existing shares, or
(b) consolidate and divide all or any of its share capital into shares of a larger nominal amount than its existing shares.

(2) In any sub-division, consolidation or division of shares under this section, the proportion between the amount paid and the amount (if any) unpaid on each resulting share must be the same as it was in the case of the share from which that share is derived.

(3) A company may exercise a power conferred by this section only if its members have passed a resolution authorising it to do so.

(4) A resolution under subsection (3) may authorise a company—
(a) to exercise more than one of the powers conferred by this section;
(b) to exercise a power on more than one occasion;
(c) to exercise a power at a specified time or in specified circumstances.

(5) The company's articles may exclude or restrict the exercise of any power conferred by this section.

[1926]

NOTES

Commencement: to be appointed (see the introductory note to this Act).

619 Notice to registrar of sub-division or consolidation

(1) If a company exercises the power conferred by section 618 (sub-division or consolidation of shares) it must within one month after doing so give notice to the registrar, specifying the shares affected.

(2) The notice must be accompanied by a statement of capital.

(3) The statement of capital must state with respect to the company's share capital immediately following the exercise of the power—

(a) the total number of shares of the company,
(b) the aggregate nominal value of those shares,
(c) for each class of shares—
  (i) prescribed particulars of the rights attached to the shares,
  (ii) the total number of shares of that class, and
  (iii) the aggregate nominal value of shares of that class, and
(d) the amount paid up and the amount (if any) unpaid on each share (whether on account of the nominal value of the share or by way of premium).

(4) If default is made in complying with this section, an offence is committed by—

(a) the company, and
(b) every officer of the company who is in default.

(5) A person guilty of an offence under this section is liable on summary conviction to a fine not exceeding level 3 on the standard scale and, for continued contravention, a daily default fine not exceeding one-tenth of level 3 on the standard scale.

[1927]

NOTES

Commencement: to be appointed (see the introductory note to this Act).

620–621 (*Outside the scope of this work.*)

Redenomination of share capital

622 Redenomination of share capital

(1) A limited company having a share capital may by resolution redenominate its share capital or any class of its share capital.

"Redenominate" means convert shares from having a fixed nominal value in one currency to having a fixed nominal value in another currency.

(2) The conversion must be made at an appropriate spot rate of exchange specified in the resolution.

(3) The rate must be either—

(a) a rate prevailing on a day specified in the resolution, or
(b) a rate determined by taking the average of rates prevailing on each consecutive day of a period specified in the resolution.

The day or period specified for the purposes of paragraph (a) or (b) must be within the period of 28 days ending on the day before the resolution is passed.

(4) A resolution under this section may specify conditions which must be met before the redenomination takes effect.

(5) Redenomination in accordance with a resolution under this section takes effect—

(a) on the day on which the resolution is passed, or
(b) on such later day as may be determined in accordance with the resolution.

(6) A resolution under this section lapses if the redenomination for which it provides has not taken effect at the end of the period of 28 days beginning on the date on which it is passed.

(7) A company's articles may prohibit or restrict the exercise of the power conferred by this section.

(8) Chapter 3 of Part 3 (resolutions affecting a company's constitution) applies to a resolution under this section.

[1928]

NOTES

Commencement: to be appointed (see the introductory note to this Act).

623 Calculation of new nominal values

For each class of share the new nominal value of each share is calculated as follows:

Step One

Take the aggregate of the old nominal values of all the shares of that class.

Step Two

Translate that amount into the new currency at the rate of exchange specified in the resolution.

Step Three

Divide that amount by the number of shares in the class.

[1929]

NOTES

Commencement: to be appointed (see the introductory note to this Act).

624 Effect of redenomination

(1) The redenomination of shares does not affect any rights or obligations of members under the company's constitution, or any restrictions affecting members under the company's constitution.

In particular, it does not affect entitlement to dividends (including entitlement to dividends in a particular currency), voting rights or any liability in respect of amounts unpaid on shares.

(2) For this purpose the company's constitution includes the terms on which any shares of the company are allotted or held.

(3) Subject to subsection (1), references to the old nominal value of the shares in any agreement or statement, or in any deed, instrument or document, shall (unless the context otherwise requires) be read after the resolution takes effect as references to the new nominal value of the shares.

[1930]

NOTES

Commencement: to be appointed (see the introductory note to this Act).

625 Notice to registrar of redenomination

(1) If a limited company having a share capital redenominates any of its share capital, it must within one month after doing so give notice to the registrar, specifying the shares redenominated.

(2) The notice must—
- (a) state the date on which the resolution was passed, and
- (b) be accompanied by a statement of capital.

(3) The statement of capital must state with respect to the company's share capital as redenominated by the resolution—
- (a) the total number of shares of the company,
- (b) the aggregate nominal value of those shares,
- (c) for each class of shares—
  - (i) prescribed particulars of the rights attached to the shares,
  - (ii) the total number of shares of that class, and
  - (iii) the aggregate nominal value of shares of that class, and

(d) the amount paid up and the amount (if any) unpaid on each share (whether on account of the nominal value of the share or by way of premium).

(4) If default is made in complying with this section, an offence is committed by—

(a) the company, and

(b) every officer of the company who is in default.

(5) A person guilty of an offence under this section is liable on summary conviction to a fine not exceeding level 3 on the standard scale and, for continued contravention, a daily default fine not exceeding one-tenth of level 3 on the standard scale.

[1931]

NOTES

Commencement: to be appointed (see the introductory note to this Act).

626 Reduction of capital in connection with redenomination

(1) A limited company that passes a resolution redenominating some or all of its shares may, for the purpose of adjusting the nominal values of the redenominated shares to obtain values that are, in the opinion of the company, more suitable, reduce its share capital under this section.

(2) A reduction of capital under this section requires a special resolution of the company.

(3) Any such resolution must be passed within three months of the resolution effecting the redenomination.

(4) The amount by which a company's share capital is reduced under this section must not exceed 10% of the nominal value of the company's allotted share capital immediately after the reduction.

(5) A reduction of capital under this section does not extinguish or reduce any liability in respect of share capital not paid up.

(6) Nothing in Chapter 10 applies to a reduction of capital under this section.

[1932]

NOTES

Commencement: to be appointed (see the introductory note to this Act).

627 Notice to registrar of reduction of capital in connection with redenomination

(1) A company that passes a resolution under section 626 (reduction of capital in connection with redenomination) must within 15 days after the resolution is passed give notice to the registrar stating—

(a) the date of the resolution, and

(b) the date of the resolution under section 622 in connection with which it was passed.

This is in addition to the copies of the resolutions themselves that are required to be delivered to the registrar under Chapter 3 of Part 3.

(2) The notice must be accompanied by a statement of capital.

(3) The statement of capital must state with respect to the company's share capital as reduced by the resolution—

(a) the total number of shares of the company,

(b) the aggregate nominal value of those shares,

(c) for each class of shares—

(i) prescribed particulars of the rights attached to the shares,

(ii) the total number of shares of that class, and

(iii) the aggregate nominal value of shares of that class, and

(d) the amount paid up and the amount (if any) unpaid on each share (whether on account of the nominal value of the share or by way of premium).

(4) The registrar must register the notice and the statement on receipt.

(5) The reduction of capital is not effective until those documents are registered.

(6) The company must also deliver to the registrar, within 15 days after the resolution is passed, a statement by the directors confirming that the reduction in share capital is in accordance with section 626(4) (reduction of capital not to exceed 10% of nominal value of allotted shares immediately after reduction).

(7) If default is made in complying with this section, an offence is committed by—
(a) the company, and
(b) every officer of the company who is in default.

(8) A person guilty of an offence under this section is liable—
(a) on conviction on indictment to a fine, and
(b) on summary conviction to a fine not exceeding the statutory maximum.

[1933]

NOTES

Commencement: to be appointed (see the introductory note to this Act).

628 Redenomination reserve

(1) The amount by which a company's share capital is reduced under section 626 (reduction of capital in connection with redenomination) must be transferred to a reserve, called "the redenomination reserve".

(2) The redenomination reserve may be applied by the company in paying up shares to be allotted to members as fully paid bonus shares.

(3) Subject to that, the provisions of the Companies Acts relating to the reduction of a company's share capital apply as if the redenomination reserve were paid-up share capital of the company.

[1934]

NOTES

Commencement: to be appointed (see the introductory note to this Act).

CHAPTER 9
CLASSES OF SHARE AND CLASS RIGHTS

Introductory

629 Classes of shares

(1) For the purposes of the Companies Acts shares are of one class if the rights attached to them are in all respects uniform.

(2) For this purpose the rights attached to shares are not regarded as different from those attached to other shares by reason only that they do not carry the same rights to dividends in the twelve months immediately following their allotment.

[1935]

NOTES

Commencement: to be appointed (see the introductory note to this Act).

Variation of class rights

630 Variation of class rights: companies having a share capital

(1) This section is concerned with the variation of the rights attached to a class of shares in a company having a share capital.

(2) Rights attached to a class of a company's shares may only be varied—
(a) in accordance with provision in the company's articles for the variation of those rights, or
(b) where the company's articles contain no such provision, if the holders of shares of that class consent to the variation in accordance with this section.

(3) This is without prejudice to any other restrictions on the variation of the rights.

(4) The consent required for the purposes of this section on the part of the holders of a class of a company's shares is—

(a) consent in writing from the holders of at least three-quarters in nominal value of the issued shares of that class (excluding any shares held as treasury shares), or

(b) a special resolution passed at a separate general meeting of the holders of that class sanctioning the variation.

(5) Any amendment of a provision contained in a company's articles for the variation of the rights attached to a class of shares, or the insertion of any such provision into the articles, is itself to be treated as a variation of those rights.

(6) In this section, and (except where the context otherwise requires) in any provision in a company's articles for the variation of the rights attached to a class of shares, references to the variation of those rights include references to their abrogation.

[1936]

NOTES

Commencement: to be appointed (see the introductory note to this Act).

631 Variation of class rights: companies without a share capital

(1) This section is concerned with the variation of the rights of a class of members of a company where the company does not have a share capital.

(2) Rights of a class of members may only be varied—

(a) in accordance with provision in the company's articles for the variation of those rights, or

(b) where the company's articles contain no such provision, if the members of that class consent to the variation in accordance with this section.

(3) This is without prejudice to any other restrictions on the variation of the rights.

(4) The consent required for the purposes of this section on the part of the members of a class is—

(a) consent in writing from at least three-quarters of the members of the class, or

(b) a special resolution passed at a separate general meeting of the members of that class sanctioning the variation.

(5) Any amendment of a provision contained in a company's articles for the variation of the rights of a class of members, or the insertion of any such provision into the articles, is itself to be treated as a variation of those rights.

(6) In this section, and (except where the context otherwise requires) in any provision in a company's articles for the variation of the rights of a class of members, references to the variation of those rights include references to their abrogation.

[1937]

NOTES

Commencement: to be appointed (see the introductory note to this Act).

632 Variation of class rights: saving for court's powers under other provisions

Nothing in section 630 or 631 (variation of class rights) affects the power of the court under—

section 98 (application to cancel resolution for public company to be re-registered as private),

Part 26 (arrangements and reconstructions), or

Part 30 (protection of members against unfair prejudice).

[1938]

NOTES

Commencement: to be appointed (see the introductory note to this Act).

633 Right to object to variation: companies having a share capital

(1) This section applies where the rights attached to any class of shares in a company are varied under section 630 (variation of class rights: companies having a share capital).

(2) The holders of not less in the aggregate than 15% of the issued shares of the class in question (being persons who did not consent to or vote in favour of the resolution for the variation) may apply to the court to have the variation cancelled.

For this purpose any of the company's share capital held as treasury shares is disregarded.

(3) If such an application is made, the variation has no effect unless and until it is confirmed by the court.

(4) Application to the court—
(a) must be made within 21 days after the date on which the consent was given or the resolution was passed (as the case may be), and
(b) may be made on behalf of the shareholders entitled to make the application by such one or more of their number as they may appoint in writing for the purpose.

(5) The court, after hearing the applicant and any other persons who apply to the court to be heard and appear to the court to be interested in the application, may, if satisfied having regard to all the circumstances of the case that the variation would unfairly prejudice the shareholders of the class represented by the applicant, disallow the variation, and shall if not so satisfied confirm it. The decision of the court on any such application is final.

(6) References in this section to the variation of the rights of holders of a class of shares include references to their abrogation.

[1939]

NOTES

Commencement: to be appointed (see the introductory note to this Act).

634 Right to object to variation: companies without a share capital

(1) This section applies where the rights of any class of members of a company are varied under section 631 (variation of class rights: companies without a share capital).

(2) Members amounting to not less than 15% of the members of the class in question (being persons who did not consent to or vote in favour of the resolution for the variation) may apply to the court to have the variation cancelled.

(3) If such an application is made, the variation has no effect unless and until it is confirmed by the court.

(4) Application to the court must be made within 21 days after the date on which the consent was given or the resolution was passed (as the case may be) and may be made on behalf of the members entitled to make the application by such one or more of their number as they may appoint in writing for the purpose.

(5) The court, after hearing the applicant and any other persons who apply to the court to be heard and appear to the court to be interested in the application, may, if satisfied having regard to all the circumstances of the case that the variation would unfairly prejudice the members of the class represented by the applicant, disallow the variation, and shall if not so satisfied confirm it.

The decision of the court on any such application is final.

(6) References in this section to the variation of the rights of a class of members include references to their abrogation.

[1940]

NOTES

Commencement: to be appointed (see the introductory note to this Act).

635 Copy of court order to be forwarded to the registrar

(1) The company must within 15 days after the making of an order by the court on an application under section 633 or 634 (objection to variation of class rights) forward a copy of the order to the registrar.

(2) If default is made in complying with this section an offence is committed by—
(a) the company, and
(b) every officer of the company who is in default.

(3) A person guilty of an offence under this section is liable on summary conviction to a fine not exceeding level 3 on the standard scale and, for continued contravention, a daily default fine not exceeding one-tenth of level 3 on the standard scale.

[1941]

NOTES

Commencement: to be appointed (see the introductory note to this Act).

Matters to be notified to the registrar

636 Notice of name or other designation of class of shares

(1) Where a company assigns a name or other designation, or a new name or other designation, to any class or description of its shares, it must within one month from doing so deliver to the registrar a notice giving particulars of the name or designation so assigned.

(2) If default is made in complying with this section, an offence is committed by—

(a) the company, and

(b) every officer of the company who is in default.

(3) A person guilty of an offence under this section is liable on summary conviction to a fine not exceeding level 3 on the standard scale and, for continued contravention, a daily default fine not exceeding one-tenth of level 3 on the standard scale.

[1942]

NOTES

Commencement: to be appointed (see the introductory note to this Act).

637 Notice of particulars of variation of rights attached to shares

(1) Where the rights attached to any shares of a company are varied, the company must within one month from the date on which the variation is made deliver to the registrar a notice giving particulars of the variation.

(2) If default is made in complying with this section, an offence is committed by—

(a) the company, and

(b) every officer of the company who is in default.

(3) A person guilty of an offence under this section is liable on summary conviction to a fine not exceeding level 3 on the standard scale and, for continued contravention, a daily default fine not exceeding one-tenth of level 3 on the standard scale.

[1943]

NOTES

Commencement: to be appointed (see the introductory note to this Act).

638 Notice of new class of members

(1) If a company not having a share capital creates a new class of members, the company must within one month from the date on which the new class is created deliver to the registrar a notice containing particulars of the rights attached to that class.

(2) If default is made in complying with this section, an offence is committed by—

(a) the company, and

(b) every officer of the company who is in default.

(3) A person guilty of an offence under this section is liable on summary conviction to a fine not exceeding level 3 on the standard scale and, for continued contravention, a daily default fine not exceeding one-tenth of level 3 on the standard scale.

[1944]

NOTES

Commencement: to be appointed (see the introductory note to this Act).

639 Notice of name or other designation of class of members

(1) Where a company not having a share capital assigns a name or other designation, or a new name or other designation, to any class of its members, it must within one month from doing so deliver to the registrar a notice giving particulars of the name or designation so assigned.

(2) If default is made in complying with this section, an offence is committed by—
- (a) the company, and
- (b) every officer of the company who is in default.

(3) A person guilty of an offence under this section is liable on summary conviction to a fine not exceeding level 3 on the standard scale and, for continued contravention, a daily default fine not exceeding one-tenth of level 3 on the standard scale.

[1945]

NOTES

Commencement: to be appointed (see the introductory note to this Act).

640 Notice of particulars of variation of class rights

(1) If the rights of any class of members of a company not having a share capital are varied, the company must within one month from the date on which the variation is made deliver to the registrar a notice containing particulars of the variation.

(2) If default is made in complying with this section, an offence is committed by—
- (a) the company, and
- (b) every officer of the company who is in default.

(3) A person guilty of an offence under this section is liable on summary conviction to a fine not exceeding level 3 on the standard scale and, for continued contravention, a daily default fine not exceeding one-tenth of level 3 on the standard scale.

[1946]

NOTES

Commencement: to be appointed (see the introductory note to this Act).

CHAPTER 10
REDUCTION OF SHARE CAPITAL

Introductory

641 Circumstances in which a company may reduce its share capital

(1) A limited company having a share capital may reduce its share capital—
- (a) in the case of a private company limited by shares, by special resolution supported by a solvency statement (see sections 642 to 644);
- (b) in any case, by special resolution confirmed by the court (see sections 645 to 651).

(2) A company may not reduce its capital under subsection (1)(a) if as a result of the reduction there would no longer be any member of the company holding shares other than redeemable shares.

(3) Subject to that, a company may reduce its share capital under this section in any way.

(4) In particular, a company may—
- (a) extinguish or reduce the liability on any of its shares in respect of share capital not paid up, or
- (b) either with or without extinguishing or reducing liability on any of its shares—
  - (i) cancel any paid-up share capital that is lost or unrepresented by available assets, or
  - (ii) repay any paid-up share capital in excess of the company's wants.

(5) A special resolution under this section may not provide for a reduction of share capital to take effect later than the date on which the resolution has effect in accordance with this Chapter.

(6) This Chapter (apart from subsection (5) above) has effect subject to any provision of the company's articles restricting or prohibiting the reduction of the company's share capital. **[1947]**

NOTES

Commencement: to be appointed (see the introductory note to this Act).

Private companies: reduction of capital supported by solvency statement

642 Reduction of capital supported by solvency statement

(1) A resolution for reducing share capital of a private company limited by shares is supported by a solvency statement if—

(a) the directors of the company make a statement of the solvency of the company in accordance with section 643 (a "solvency statement") not more than 15 days before the date on which the resolution is passed, and

(b) the resolution and solvency statement are registered in accordance with section 644.

(2) Where the resolution is proposed as a written resolution, a copy of the solvency statement must be sent or submitted to every eligible member at or before the time at which the proposed resolution is sent or submitted to him.

(3) Where the resolution is proposed at a general meeting, a copy of the solvency statement must be made available for inspection by members of the company throughout that meeting.

(4) The validity of a resolution is not affected by a failure to comply with subsection (2) or (3).

[1948]

NOTES

Commencement: to be appointed (see the introductory note to this Act).

643 Solvency statement

(1) A solvency statement is a statement that each of the directors—

(a) has formed the opinion, as regards the company's situation at the date of the statement, that there is no ground on which the company could then be found to be unable to pay (or otherwise discharge) its debts; and

(b) has also formed the opinion—

(i) if it is intended to commence the winding up of the company within twelve months of that date, that the company will be able to pay (or otherwise discharge) its debts in full within twelve months of the commencement of the winding up; or

(ii) in any other case, that the company will be able to pay (or otherwise discharge) its debts as they fall due during the year immediately following that date.

(2) In forming those opinions, the directors must take into account all of the company's liabilities (including any contingent or prospective liabilities).

(3) The solvency statement must be in the prescribed form and must state—

(a) the date on which it is made, and

(b) the name of each director of the company.

(4) If the directors make a solvency statement without having reasonable grounds for the opinions expressed in it, and the statement is delivered to the registrar, an offence is committed by every director who is in default.

(5) A person guilty of an offence under subsection (4) is liable—

(a) on conviction on indictment, to imprisonment for a term not exceeding two years or a fine (or both);

(b) on summary conviction—

(i) in England and Wales, to imprisonment for a term not exceeding twelve months or to a fine not exceeding the statutory maximum (or both);

(ii) in Scotland or Northern Ireland, to imprisonment for a term not exceeding six months, or to a fine not exceeding the statutory maximum (or both).

[1949]

NOTES

Commencement: to be appointed (see the introductory note to this Act).

644 Registration of resolution and supporting documents

(1) Within 15 days after the resolution for reducing share capital is passed the company must deliver to the registrar—

(a) a copy of the solvency statement, and

(b) a statement of capital.

This is in addition to the copy of the resolution itself that is required to be delivered to the registrar under Chapter 3 of Part 3.

(2) The statement of capital must state with respect to the company's share capital as reduced by the resolution—

(a) the total number of shares of the company,

(b) the aggregate nominal value of those shares,

(c) for each class of shares—

(i) prescribed particulars of the rights attached to the shares,

(ii) the total number of shares of that class, and

(iii) the aggregate nominal value of shares of that class, and

(d) the amount paid up and the amount (if any) unpaid on each share (whether on account of the nominal value of the share or by way of premium).

(3) The registrar must register the documents delivered to him under subsection (1) on receipt.

(4) The resolution does not take effect until those documents are registered.

(5) The company must also deliver to the registrar, within 15 days after the resolution is passed, a statement by the directors confirming that the solvency statement was—

(a) made not more than 15 days before the date on which the resolution was passed, and

(b) provided to members in accordance with section 642(2) or (3).

(6) The validity of a resolution is not affected by—

(a) a failure to deliver the documents required to be delivered to the registrar under subsection (1) within the time specified in that subsection, or

(b) a failure to comply with subsection (5).

(7) If the company delivers to the registrar a solvency statement that was not provided to members in accordance with section 642(2) or (3), an offence is committed by every officer of the company who is in default.

(8) If default is made in complying with this section, an offence is committed by—

(a) the company, and

(b) every officer of the company who is in default.

(9) A person guilty of an offence under subsection (7) or (8) is liable—

(a) on conviction on indictment, to a fine;

(b) on summary conviction, to a fine not exceeding the statutory maximum.

[1950]

NOTES

Commencement: to be appointed (see the introductory note to this Act).

Reduction of capital confirmed by the court

645 Application to court for order of confirmation

(1) Where a company has passed a resolution for reducing share capital, it may apply to the court for an order confirming the reduction.

(2) If the proposed reduction of capital involves either—
(a) diminution of liability in respect of unpaid share capital, or
(b) the payment to a shareholder of any paid-up share capital,

section 646 (creditors entitled to object to reduction) applies unless the court directs otherwise.

(3) The court may, if having regard to any special circumstances of the case it thinks proper to do so, direct that section 646 is not to apply as regards any class or classes of creditors.

(4) The court may direct that section 646 is to apply in any other case.

[1951]

NOTES

Commencement: to be appointed (see the introductory note to this Act).

646 Creditors entitled to object to reduction

(1) Where this section applies (see section 645(2) and (4)), every creditor of the company who at the date fixed by the court is entitled to any debt or claim that, if that date were the commencement of the winding up of the company would be admissible in proof against the company, is entitled to object to the reduction of capital.

(2) The court shall settle a list of creditors entitled to object.

(3) For that purpose the court—
(a) shall ascertain, as far as possible without requiring an application from any creditor, the names of those creditors and the nature and amount of their debts or claims, and
(b) may publish notices fixing a day or days within which creditors not entered on the list are to claim to be so entered or are to be excluded from the right of objecting to the reduction of capital.

(4) If a creditor entered on the list whose debt or claim is not discharged or has not determined does not consent to the reduction, the court may, if it thinks fit, dispense with the consent of that creditor on the company securing payment of his debt or claim.

(5) For this purpose the debt or claim must be secured by appropriating (as the court may direct) the following amount—
(a) if the company admits the full amount of the debt or claim or, though not admitting it, is willing to provide for it, the full amount of the debt or claim;
(b) if the company does not admit, and is not willing to provide for, the full amount of the debt or claim, or if the amount is contingent or not ascertained, an amount fixed by the court after the like enquiry and adjudication as if the company were being wound up by the court.

[1952]

NOTES

Commencement: to be appointed (see the introductory note to this Act).

647 Offences in connection with list of creditors

(1) If an officer of the company—
(a) intentionally or recklessly—
(i) conceals the name of a creditor entitled to object to the reduction of capital, or
(ii) misrepresents the nature or amount of the debt or claim of a creditor, or
(b) is knowingly concerned in any such concealment or misrepresentation,

he commits an offence.

(2) A person guilty of an offence under this section is liable—
(a) on conviction on indictment, to a fine;
(b) on summary conviction, to a fine not exceeding the statutory maximum.

[1953]

NOTES

Commencement: to be appointed (see the introductory note to this Act).

648 Court order confirming reduction

(1) The court may make an order confirming the reduction of capital on such terms and conditions as it thinks fit.

(2) The court must not confirm the reduction unless it is satisfied, with respect to every creditor of the company who is entitled to object to the reduction of capital that either—
(a) his consent to the reduction has been obtained, or
(b) his debt or claim has been discharged, or has determined or has been secured.

(3) Where the court confirms the reduction, it may order the company to publish (as the court directs) the reasons for reduction of capital, or such other information in regard to it as the court thinks expedient with a view to giving proper information to the public, and (if the court thinks fit) the causes that led to the reduction.

(4) The court may, if for any special reason it thinks proper to do so, make an order directing that the company must, during such period (commencing on or at any time after the date of the order) as is specified in the order, add to its name as its last words the words "and reduced".

If such an order is made, those words are, until the end of the period specified in the order, deemed to be part of the company's name.

[1954]

NOTES

Commencement: to be appointed (see the introductory note to this Act).

649 Registration of order and statement of capital

(1) The registrar, on production of an order of the court confirming the reduction of a company's share capital and the delivery of a copy of the order and of a statement of capital (approved by the court), shall register the order and statement.

This is subject to section 650 (public company reducing capital below authorised minimum).

(2) The statement of capital must state with respect to the company's share capital as altered by the order—
(a) the total number of shares of the company,
(b) the aggregate nominal value of those shares,
(c) for each class of shares—
(i) prescribed particulars of the rights attached to the shares,
(ii) the total number of shares of that class, and
(iii) the aggregate nominal value of shares of that class, and
(d) the amount paid up and the amount (if any) unpaid on each share (whether on account of the nominal value of the share or by way of premium).

(3) The resolution for reducing share capital, as confirmed by the court's order, takes effect—
(a) in the case of a reduction of share capital that forms part of a compromise or arrangement sanctioned by the court under Part 26 (arrangements and reconstructions)—
(i) on delivery of the order and statement of capital to the registrar, or
(ii) if the court so orders, on the registration of the order and statement of capital;
(b) in any other case, on the registration of the order and statement of capital.

(4) Notice of the registration of the order and statement of capital must be published in such manner as the court may direct.

(5) The registrar must certify the registration of the order and statement of capital.

(6) The certificate—
(a) must be signed by the registrar or authenticated by the registrar's official seal, and
(b) is conclusive evidence—
(i) that the requirements of this Act with respect to the reduction of share capital have been complied with, and
(ii) that the company's share capital is as stated in the statement of capital.

[1955]

NOTES

Commencement: to be appointed (see the introductory note to this Act).

Public company reducing capital below authorised minimum

650 (*Outside the scope of this work.*)

651 Expedited procedure for re-registration as a private company

(1) The court may authorise the company to be re-registered as a private company without its having passed the special resolution required by section 97.

(2) If it does so, the court must specify in the order the changes to the company's name and articles to be made in connection with the re-registration.

(3) The company may then be re-registered as a private company if an application to that effect is delivered to the registrar together with—

(a) a copy of the court's order, and

(b) notice of the company's name, and a copy of the company's articles, as altered by the court's order.

(4) On receipt of such an application the registrar must issue a certificate of incorporation altered to meet the circumstances of the case.

(5) The certificate must state that it is issued on re-registration and the date on which it is issued.

(6) On the issue of the certificate—

(a) the company by virtue of the issue of the certificate becomes a private company, and

(b) the changes in the company's name and articles take effect.

(7) The certificate is conclusive evidence that the requirements of this Act as to re-registration have been complied with.

[1956]

NOTES

Commencement: to be appointed (see the introductory note to this Act).

Effect of reduction of capital

652 Liability of members following reduction of capital

(1) Where a company's share capital is reduced a member of the company (past or present) is not liable in respect of any share to any call or contribution exceeding in amount the difference (if any) between—

(a) the nominal amount of the share as notified to the registrar in the statement of capital delivered under section 644 or 649, and

(b) the amount paid on the share or the reduced amount (if any) which is deemed to have been paid on it, as the case may be.

(2) This is subject to section 653 (liability to creditor in case of omission from list).

(3) Nothing in this section affects the rights of the contributories among themselves.

[1957]

NOTES

Commencement: to be appointed (see the introductory note to this Act).

653 Liability to creditor in case of omission from list of creditors

(1) This section applies where, in the case of a reduction of capital confirmed by the court—

(a) a creditor entitled to object to the reduction of share capital is by reason of his ignorance—
(i) of the proceedings for reduction of share capital, or
(ii) of their nature and effect with respect to his debt or claim,

not entered on the list of creditors, and

(b) after the reduction of capital the company is unable to pay the amount of his debt or claim.

(2) Every person who was a member of the company at the date on which the resolution for reducing capital took effect under section 649(3) is liable to contribute for the payment of the debt or claim an amount not exceeding that which he would have been liable to contribute if the company had commenced to be wound up on the day before that date.

(3) If the company is wound up, the court on the application of the creditor in question, and proof of ignorance as mentioned in subsection (1)(a), may if it thinks fit—

(a) settle accordingly a list of persons liable to contribute under this section, and
(b) make and enforce calls and orders on them as if they were ordinary contributories in a winding up.

(4) The reference in subsection (1)(b) to a company being unable to pay the amount of a debt or claim has the same meaning as in section 123 of the Insolvency Act 1986 (c 45) or Article 103 of the Insolvency (Northern Ireland) Order 1989 (SI 1989/2405 (NI 19)).

[1958]

NOTES

Commencement: to be appointed (see the introductory note to this Act).

CHAPTER 11
MISCELLANEOUS AND SUPPLEMENTARY PROVISIONS

654 Treatment of reserve arising from reduction of capital

(1) A reserve arising from the reduction of a company's share capital is not distributable, subject to any provision made by order under this section.

(2) The Secretary of State may by order specify cases in which—

(a) the prohibition in subsection (1) does not apply, and
(b) the reserve is to be treated for the purposes of Part 23 (distributions) as a realised profit.

(3) An order under this section is subject to affirmative resolution procedure.

[1959]

NOTES

Commencement: to be appointed (see the introductory note to this Act).

655 Shares no bar to damages against company

A person is not debarred from obtaining damages or other compensation from a company by reason only of his holding or having held shares in the company or any right to apply or subscribe for shares or to be included in the company's register of members in respect of shares.

[1960]

NOTES

Commencement: to be appointed (see the introductory note to this Act).

656 (*Outside the scope of this work.*)

657 General power to make further provision by regulations

(1) The Secretary of State may by regulations modify the following provisions of this Part—

sections 552 and 553 (prohibited commissions, discounts and allowances),
Chapter 5 (payment for shares),

Chapter 6 (public companies: independent valuation of non-cash consideration),
Chapter 7 (share premiums),
sections 622 to 628 (redenomination of share capital),
Chapter 10 (reduction of capital), and
section 656 (public companies: duty of directors to call meeting on serious loss of capital).

(2) The regulations may—
(a) amend or repeal any of those provisions, or
(b) make such other provision as appears to the Secretary of State appropriate in place of any of those provisions.

(3) Regulations under this section may make consequential amendments or repeals in other provisions of this Act, or in other enactments.

(4) Regulations under this section are subject to affirmative resolution procedure.

[1961]

NOTES

Commencement: to be appointed (see the introductory note to this Act).

PART 18
ACQUISITION BY LIMITED COMPANY OF ITS OWN SHARES

CHAPTER 1
GENERAL PROVISIONS

Introductory

658 General rule against limited company acquiring its own shares

(1) A limited company must not acquire its own shares, whether by purchase, subscription or otherwise, except in accordance with the provisions of this Part.

(2) If a company purports to act in contravention of this section—
(a) an offence is committed by—
(i) the company, and
(ii) every officer of the company who is in default, and
(b) the purported acquisition is void.

(3) A person guilty of an offence under this section is liable—
(a) on conviction on indictment, to imprisonment for a term not exceeding two years or a fine (or both);
(b) on summary conviction—
(i) in England and Wales, to imprisonment for a term not exceeding twelve months or a fine not exceeding the statutory maximum (or both);
(ii) in Scotland or Northern Ireland, to imprisonment for a term not exceeding six months or a fine not exceeding the statutory maximum (or both).

[1962]

NOTES

Commencement: to be appointed (see the introductory note to this Act).

659 Exceptions to general rule

(1) A limited company may acquire any of its own fully paid shares otherwise than for valuable consideration.

(2) Section 658 does not prohibit—
(a) the acquisition of shares in a reduction of capital duly made;
(b) the purchase of shares in pursuance of an order of the court under—
(i) section 98 (application to court to cancel resolution for re-registration as a private company),
(ii) section 721(6) (powers of court on objection to redemption or purchase of shares out of capital),

(iii) section 759 (remedial order in case of breach of prohibition of public offers by private company), or
(iv) Part 30 (protection of members against unfair prejudice);

(c) the forfeiture of shares, or the acceptance of shares surrendered in lieu, in pursuance of the company's articles, for failure to pay any sum payable in respect of the shares.

[1963]

NOTES

Commencement: to be appointed (see the introductory note to this Act).

Shares held by company's nominee

660 Treatment of shares held by nominee

(1) This section applies where shares in a limited company—
(a) are taken by a subscriber to the memorandum as nominee of the company,
(b) are issued to a nominee of the company, or
(c) are acquired by a nominee of the company, partly paid up, from a third person.

(2) For all purposes—
(a) the shares are to be treated as held by the nominee on his own account, and
(b) the company is to be regarded as having no beneficial interest in them.

(3) This section does not apply—
(a) to shares acquired otherwise than by subscription by a nominee of a public company, where—
(i) a person acquires shares in the company with financial assistance given to him, directly or indirectly, by the company for the purpose of or in connection with the acquisition, and
(ii) the company has a beneficial interest in the shares;
(b) to shares acquired by a nominee of the company when the company has no beneficial interest in the shares.

[1964]

NOTES

Commencement: to be appointed (see the introductory note to this Act).

661 Liability of others where nominee fails to make payment in respect of shares

(1) This section applies where shares in a limited company—
(a) are taken by a subscriber to the memorandum as nominee of the company,
(b) are issued to a nominee of the company, or
(c) are acquired by a nominee of the company, partly paid up, from a third person.

(2) If the nominee, having been called on to pay any amount for the purposes of paying up, or paying any premium on, the shares, fails to pay that amount within 21 days from being called on to do so, then—
(a) in the case of shares that he agreed to take as subscriber to the memorandum, the other subscribers to the memorandum, and
(b) in any other case, the directors of the company when the shares were issued to or acquired by him,

are jointly and severally liable with him to pay that amount.

(3) If in proceedings for the recovery of an amount under subsection (2) it appears to the court that the subscriber or director—
(a) has acted honestly and reasonably, and
(b) having regard to all the circumstances of the case, ought fairly to be relieved from liability,

the court may relieve him, either wholly or in part, from his liability on such terms as the court thinks fit.

(4) If a subscriber to a company's memorandum or a director of a company has reason to apprehend that a claim will or might be made for the recovery of any such amount from him—

(a) he may apply to the court for relief, and
(b) the court has the same power to relieve him as it would have had in proceedings for recovery of that amount.

(5) This section does not apply to shares acquired by a nominee of the company when the company has no beneficial interest in the shares.

[1965]

NOTES

Commencement: to be appointed (see the introductory note to this Act).

662–670 (*Outside the scope of this work.*)

Supplementary provisions

671 Interests to be disregarded in determining whether company has beneficial interest

In determining for the purposes of this Chapter whether a company has a beneficial interest in shares, there shall be disregarded any such interest as is mentioned in—

section 672 (residual interest under pension scheme or employees' share scheme),
section 673 (employer's charges and other rights of recovery), or
section 674 (rights as personal representative or trustee).

[1966]

NOTES

Commencement: to be appointed (see the introductory note to this Act).

672 Residual interest under pension scheme or employees' share scheme

(1) Where the shares are held on trust for the purposes of a pension scheme or employees' share scheme, there shall be disregarded any residual interest of the company that has not vested in possession.

(2) A "residual interest" means a right of the company to receive any of the trust property in the event of—

(a) all the liabilities arising under the scheme having been satisfied or provided for, or
(b) the company ceasing to participate in the scheme, or
(c) the trust property at any time exceeding what is necessary for satisfying the liabilities arising or expected to arise under the scheme.

(3) In subsection (2)—

(a) the reference to a right includes a right dependent on the exercise of a discretion vested by the scheme in the trustee or another person, and
(b) the reference to liabilities arising under a scheme includes liabilities that have resulted, or may result, from the exercise of any such discretion.

(4) For the purposes of this section a residual interest vests in possession—

(a) in a case within subsection (2)(a), on the occurrence of the event mentioned there (whether or not the amount of the property receivable pursuant to the right is ascertained);
(b) in a case within subsection (2)(b) or (c), when the company becomes entitled to require the trustee to transfer to it any of the property receivable pursuant to that right.

(5) Where by virtue of this section shares are exempt from section 660 or 661 (shares held by company's nominee) at the time they are taken, issued or acquired but the residual interest in question vests in possession before they are disposed of or fully paid up, those sections apply to the shares as if they had been taken, issued or acquired on the date on which that interest vests in possession.

(6) Where by virtue of this section shares are exempt from sections 662 to 668 (shares held by or for public company) at the time they are acquired but the residual interest in question vests in possession before they are disposed of, those sections apply to the shares as if they had been acquired on the date on which the interest vests in possession.

[1967]

NOTES

Commencement: to be appointed (see the introductory note to this Act).

673 Employer's charges and other rights of recovery

(1) Where the shares are held on trust for the purposes of a pension scheme there shall be disregarded—

(a) any charge or lien on, or set-off against, any benefit or other right or interest under the scheme for the purpose of enabling the employer or former employer of a member of the scheme to obtain the discharge of a monetary obligation due to him from the member;

(b) any right to receive from the trustee of the scheme, or as trustee of the scheme to retain, an amount that can be recovered or retained—

(i) under section 61 of the Pension Schemes Act 1993 (c 48), or otherwise, as reimbursement or partial reimbursement for any contributions equivalent premium paid in connection with the scheme under Part 3 of that Act, or

(ii) under section 57 of the Pension Schemes (Northern Ireland) Act 1993 (c 49), or otherwise, as reimbursement or partial reimbursement for any contributions equivalent premium paid in connection with the scheme under Part 3 of that Act.

(2) Where the shares are held on trust for the purposes of an employees' share scheme, there shall be disregarded any charge or lien on, or set-off against, any benefit or other right or interest under the scheme for the purpose of enabling the employer or former employer of a member of the scheme to obtain the discharge of a monetary obligation due to him from the member.

[1968]

NOTES

Commencement: to be appointed (see the introductory note to this Act).

674 Rights as personal representative or trustee

Where the company is a personal representative or trustee, there shall be disregarded any rights that the company has in that capacity including, in particular—

(a) any right to recover its expenses or be remunerated out of the estate or trust property, and

(b) any right to be indemnified out of that property for any liability incurred by reason of any act or omission of the company in the performance of its duties as personal representative or trustee.

[1969]

NOTES

Commencement: to be appointed (see the introductory note to this Act).

675 Meaning of "pension scheme"

(1) In this Chapter "pension scheme" means a scheme for the provision of benefits consisting of or including relevant benefits for or in respect of employees or former employees.

(2) In subsection (1) "relevant benefits" means any pension, lump sum, gratuity or other like benefit given or to be given on retirement or on death or in anticipation of retirement or, in connection with past service, after retirement or death.

[1970]

NOTES

Commencement: to be appointed (see the introductory note to this Act).

676 Application of provisions to directors

For the purposes of this Chapter references to "employer" and "employee", in the context of a pension scheme or employees' share scheme, shall be read as if a director of a company were employed by it.

[1971]–[1972]

NOTES

Commencement: to be appointed (see the introductory note to this Act).

677–754 *((Pt 18, Chapters 2–7, Pt 19) outside the scope of this work.)*

PART 20
PRIVATE AND PUBLIC COMPANIES

CHAPTER 1
PROHIBITION OF PUBLIC OFFERS BY PRIVATE COMPANIES

755 Prohibition of public offers by private company

(1) A private company limited by shares or limited by guarantee and having a share capital must not—

(a) offer to the public any securities of the company, or

(b) allot or agree to allot any securities of the company with a view to their being offered to the public.

(2) Unless the contrary is proved, an allotment or agreement to allot securities is presumed to be made with a view to their being offered to the public if an offer of the securities (or any of them) to the public is made—

(a) within six months after the allotment or agreement to allot, or

(b) before the receipt by the company of the whole of the consideration to be received by it in respect of the securities.

(3) A company does not contravene this section if—

(a) it acts in good faith in pursuance of arrangements under which it is to re-register as a public company before the securities are allotted, or

(b) as part of the terms of the offer it undertakes to re-register as a public company within a specified period, and that undertaking is complied with.

(4) The specified period for the purposes of subsection (3)(b) must be a period ending not later than six months after the day on which the offer is made (or, in the case of an offer made on different days, first made).

(5) In this Chapter "securities" means shares or debentures.

[1973]

NOTES

Commencement: to be appointed (see the introductory note to this Act).

756 Meaning of "offer to the public"

(1) This section explains what is meant in this Chapter by an offer of securities to the public.

(2) An offer to the public includes an offer to any section of the public, however selected.

(3) An offer is not regarded as an offer to the public if it can properly be regarded, in all the circumstances, as—

(a) not being calculated to result, directly or indirectly, in securities of the company becoming available to persons other than those receiving the offer, or

(b) otherwise being a private concern of the person receiving it and the person making it.

(4) An offer is to be regarded (unless the contrary is proved) as being a private concern of the person receiving it and the person making it if—

(a) it is made to a person already connected with the company and, where it is made on terms allowing that person to renounce his rights, the rights may only be renounced in favour of another person already connected with the company; or

(b) it is an offer to subscribe for securities to be held under an employees' share scheme and, where it is made on terms allowing that person to renounce his rights, the rights may only be renounced in favour of—

(i) another person entitled to hold securities under the scheme, or
(ii) a person already connected with the company.

(5) For the purposes of this section "person already connected with the company" means—
(a) an existing member or employee of the company,
(b) a member of the family of a person who is or was a member or employee of the company,
(c) the widow or widower, or surviving civil partner, of a person who was a member or employee of the company,
(d) an existing debenture holder of the company, or
(e) a trustee (acting in his capacity as such) of a trust of which the principal beneficiary is a person within any of paragraphs (a) to (d).

(6) For the purposes of subsection (5)(b) the members of a person's family are the person's spouse or civil partner and children (including step-children) and their descendants.

[1974]

NOTES

Commencement: to be appointed (see the introductory note to this Act).

757 Enforcement of prohibition: order restraining proposed contravention

(1) If it appears to the court—
(a) on an application under this section, or
(b) in proceedings under Part 30 (protection of members against unfair prejudice),

that a company is proposing to act in contravention of section 755 (prohibition of public offers by private companies), the court shall make an order under this section.

(2) An order under this section is an order restraining the company from contravening that section.

(3) An application for an order under this section may be made by—
(a) a member or creditor of the company, or
(b) the Secretary of State.

[1975]

NOTES

Commencement: to be appointed (see the introductory note to this Act).

758 Enforcement of prohibition: orders available to the court after contravention

(1) This section applies if it appears to the court—
(a) on an application under this section, or
(b) in proceedings under Part 30 (protection of members against unfair prejudice),

that a company has acted in contravention of section 755 (prohibition of public offers by private companies).

(2) The court must make an order requiring the company to re-register as a public company unless it appears to the court—
(a) that the company does not meet the requirements for re-registration as a public company, and
(b) that it is impractical or undesirable to require it to take steps to do so.

(3) If it does not make an order for re-registration, the court may make either or both of the following—
(a) a remedial order (see section 759), or
(b) an order for the compulsory winding up of the company.

(4) An application under this section may be made by—
(a) a member of the company who—
(i) was a member at the time the offer was made (or, if the offer was made over a period, at any time during that period), or
(ii) became a member as a result of the offer,
(b) a creditor of the company who was a creditor at the time the offer was made (or, if the offer was made over a period, at any time during that period), or

(c) the Secretary of State.

[1976]

NOTES

Commencement: to be appointed (see the introductory note to this Act).

759 Enforcement of prohibition: remedial order

(1) A "remedial order" is an order for the purpose of putting a person affected by anything done in contravention of section 755 (prohibition of public offers by private company) in the position he would have been in if it had not been done.

(2) The following provisions are without prejudice to the generality of the power to make such an order.

(3) Where a private company has—

(a) allotted securities pursuant to an offer to the public, or

(b) allotted or agreed to allot securities with a view to their being offered to the public,

a remedial order may require any person knowingly concerned in the contravention of section 755 to offer to purchase any of those securities at such price and on such other terms as the court thinks fit.

(4) A remedial order may be made—

(a) against any person knowingly concerned in the contravention, whether or not an officer of the company;

(b) notwithstanding anything in the company's constitution (which includes, for this purpose, the terms on which any securities of the company are allotted or held);

(c) whether or not the holder of the securities subject to the order is the person to whom the company allotted or agreed to allot them.

(5) Where a remedial order is made against the company itself, the court may provide for the reduction of the company's capital accordingly.

[1977]

NOTES

Commencement: to be appointed (see the introductory note to this Act).

760 Validity of allotment etc not affected

Nothing in this Chapter affects the validity of any allotment or sale of securities or of any agreement to allot or sell securities.

[1978]

NOTES

Commencement: to be appointed (see the introductory note to this Act).

761–767 (*(Chapter 2) outside the scope of this work.*)

PART 21
CERTIFICATION AND TRANSFER OF SECURITIES

CHAPTER 1
CERTIFICATION AND TRANSFER OF SECURITIES: GENERAL

Share certificates

768 Share certificate to be evidence of title

(1) In the case of a company registered in England and Wales or Northern Ireland, a certificate under the common seal of the company specifying any shares held by a member is prima facie evidence of his title to the shares.

(2) (*Outside the scope of this work.*)

[1979]

NOTES

Commencement: to be appointed (see the introductory note to this Act).

Issue of certificates etc on allotment

769 Duty of company as to issue of certificates etc on allotment

(1) A company must, within two months after the allotment of any of its shares, debentures or debenture stock, complete and have ready for delivery—

(a) the certificates of the shares allotted,
(b) the debentures allotted, or
(c) the certificates of the debenture stock allotted.

(2) Subsection (1) does not apply—

(a) if the conditions of issue of the shares, debentures or debenture stock provide otherwise,
(b) in the case of allotment to a financial institution (see section 778), or
(c) in the case of an allotment of shares if, following the allotment, the company has issued a share warrant in respect of the shares (see section 779).

(3) If default is made in complying with subsection (1) an offence is committed by every officer of the company who is in default.

(4) A person guilty of an offence under subsection (3) is liable on summary conviction to a fine not exceeding level 3 on the standard scale and, for continued contravention, a daily default fine not exceeding one-tenth of level 3 on the standard scale.

[1980]

NOTES

Commencement: to be appointed (see the introductory note to this Act).

Transfer of securities

770 Registration of transfer

(1) A company may not register a transfer of shares in or debentures of the company unless—

(a) a proper instrument of transfer has been delivered to it, or
(b) the transfer—
  (i) is an exempt transfer within the Stock Transfer Act 1982 (c 41), or
  (ii) is in accordance with regulations under Chapter 2 of this Part.

(2) Subsection (1) does not affect any power of the company to register as shareholder or debenture holder a person to whom the right to any shares in or debentures of the company has been transmitted by operation of law.

[1981]

NOTES

Commencement: to be appointed (see the introductory note to this Act).

771 Procedure on transfer being lodged

(1) When a transfer of shares in or debentures of a company has been lodged with the company, the company must either—

(a) register the transfer, or
(b) give the transferee notice of refusal to register the transfer, together with its reasons for the refusal,

as soon as practicable and in any event within two months after the date on which the transfer is lodged with it.

(2) If the company refuses to register the transfer, it must provide the transferee with such further information about the reasons for the refusal as the transferee may reasonably request.

This does not include copies of minutes of meetings of directors.

(3) If a company fails to comply with this section, an offence is committed by—
- (a) the company, and
- (b) every officer of the company who is in default.

(4) A person guilty of an offence under this section is liable on summary conviction to a fine not exceeding level 3 on the standard scale and, for continued contravention, a daily default fine not exceeding one-tenth of level 3 on the standard scale.

(5) This section does not apply—
- (a) in relation to a transfer of shares if the company has issued a share warrant in respect of the shares (see section 779);
- (b) in relation to the transmission of shares or debentures by operation of law.

[1982]

NOTES

Commencement: to be appointed (see the introductory note to this Act).

772 Transfer of shares on application of transferor

On the application of the transferor of any share or interest in a company, the company shall enter in its register of members the name of the transferee in the same manner and subject to the same conditions as if the application for the entry were made by the transferee.

[1983]

NOTES

Commencement: to be appointed (see the introductory note to this Act).

773 Execution of share transfer by personal representative

An instrument of transfer of the share or other interest of a deceased member of a company—
- (a) may be made by his personal representative although the personal representative is not himself a member of the company, and
- (b) is as effective as if the personal representative had been such a member at the time of the execution of the instrument.

[1984]

NOTES

Commencement: to be appointed (see the introductory note to this Act).

774 Evidence of grant of probate etc

The production to a company of any document that is by law sufficient evidence of the grant of—
- (a) probate of the will of a deceased person,
- (b) letters of administration of the estate of a deceased person, or
- (c) confirmation as executor of a deceased person,

shall be accepted by the company as sufficient evidence of the grant.

[1985]

NOTES

Commencement: to be appointed (see the introductory note to this Act).

775 Certification of instrument of transfer

(1) The certification by a company of an instrument of transfer of any shares in, or debentures of, the company is to be taken as a representation by the company to any person acting on the faith of the certification that there have been produced to the company such documents as on their face show a prima facie title to the shares or debentures in the transferor named in the instrument.

(2) The certification is not to be taken as a representation that the transferor has any title to the shares or debentures.

(3) Where a person acts on the faith of a false certification by a company made negligently, the company is under the same liability to him as if the certification had been made fraudulently.

(4) For the purposes of this section—

(a) an instrument of transfer is certificated if it bears the words "certificate lodged" (or words to the like effect);

(b) the certification of an instrument of transfer is made by a company if—

(i) the person issuing the instrument is a person authorised to issue certificated instruments of transfer on the company's behalf, and

(ii) the certification is signed by a person authorised to certificate transfers on the company's behalf or by an officer or employee either of the company or of a body corporate so authorised;

(c) a certification is treated as signed by a person if—

(i) it purports to be authenticated by his signature or initials (whether handwritten or not), and

(ii) it is not shown that the signature or initials was or were placed there neither by himself nor by a person authorised to use the signature or initials for the purpose of certificating transfers on the company's behalf.

[1986]

NOTES

Commencement: to be appointed (see the introductory note to this Act).

Issue of certificates etc on transfer

776 Duty of company as to issue of certificates etc on transfer

(1) A company must, within two months after the date on which a transfer of any of its shares, debentures or debenture stock is lodged with the company, complete and have ready for delivery—

(a) the certificates of the shares transferred,

(b) the debentures transferred, or

(c) the certificates of the debenture stock transferred.

(2) For this purpose a "transfer" means—

(a) a transfer duly stamped and otherwise valid, or

(b) an exempt transfer within the Stock Transfer Act 1982 (c 41),

but does not include a transfer that the company is for any reason entitled to refuse to register and does not register.

(3) Subsection (1) does not apply—

(a) if the conditions of issue of the shares, debentures or debenture stock provide otherwise,

(b) in the case of a transfer to a financial institution (see section 778), or

(c) in the case of a transfer of shares if, following the transfer, the company has issued a share warrant in respect of the shares (see section 779).

(4) Subsection (1) has effect subject to section 777 (cases where the Stock Transfer Act 1982 applies).

(5) If default is made in complying with subsection (1) an offence is committed by every officer of the company who is in default.

(6) A person guilty of an offence under this section is liable on summary conviction to a fine not exceeding level 3 on the standard scale and, for continued contravention, a daily default fine not exceeding one-tenth of level 3 on the standard scale.

[1987]

NOTES

Commencement: to be appointed (see the introductory note to this Act).

777 Issue of certificates etc: cases within the Stock Transfer Act 1982

(1) Section 776(1) (duty of company as to issue of certificates etc on transfer) does not apply in the case of a transfer to a person where, by virtue of regulations under section 3 of the Stock Transfer Act 1982, he is not entitled to a certificate or other document of or evidencing title in respect of the securities transferred.

(2) But if in such a case the transferee—

(a) subsequently becomes entitled to such a certificate or other document by virtue of any provision of those regulations, and

(b) gives notice in writing of that fact to the company,

section 776 (duty to company as to issue of certificates etc) has effect as if the reference in subsection (1) of that section to the date of the lodging of the transfer were a reference to the date of the notice.

[1988]

NOTES

Commencement: to be appointed (see the introductory note to this Act).

778–853 *(Outside the scope of this work.)*

PART 24
A COMPANY'S ANNUAL RETURN

854 Duty to deliver annual returns

(1) Every company must deliver to the registrar successive annual returns each of which is made up to a date not later than the date that is from time to time the company's return date.

(2) The company's return date is—

(a) the anniversary of the company's incorporation, or

(b) if the company's last return delivered in accordance with this Part was made up to a different date, the anniversary of that date.

(3) Each return must—

(a) contain the information required by or under the following provisions of this Part, and

(b) be delivered to the registrar within 28 days after the date to which it is made up.

[1989]

NOTES

Commencement: to be appointed (see the introductory note to this Act).

855 Contents of annual return: general

(1) Every annual return must state the date to which it is made up and contain the following information—

(a) the address of the company's registered office;

(b) the type of company it is and its principal business activities;

(c) the prescribed particulars of—

(i) the directors of the company, and

(ii) in the case of a private company with a secretary or a public company, the secretary or joint secretaries;

(d) if the register of members is not kept available for inspection at the company's registered office, the address of the place where it is kept available for inspection;

(e) if any register of debenture holders (or a duplicate of any such register or a part of it) is not kept available for inspection at the company's registered office, the address of the place where it is kept available for inspection.

(2) The information as to the company's type must be given by reference to the classification scheme prescribed for the purposes of this section.

(3) The information as to the company's principal business activities may be given by reference to one or more categories of any prescribed system of classifying business activities.

[1990]

NOTES

Commencement: to be appointed (see the introductory note to this Act).

856 Contents of annual return: information about share capital and shareholders

(1) The annual return of a company having a share capital must also contain—

(a) a statement of capital, and

(b) the particulars required by subsections (3) to (6) about the members of the company.

(2) The statement of capital must state with respect to the company's share capital at the date to which the return is made up—

(a) the total number of shares of the company,

(b) the aggregate nominal value of those shares,

(c) for each class of shares—

(i) prescribed particulars of the rights attached to the shares,

(ii) the total number of shares of that class, and

(iii) the aggregate nominal value of shares of that class, and

(d) the amount paid up and the amount (if any) unpaid on each share (whether on account of the nominal value of the share or by way of premium).

(3) The return must contain the prescribed particulars of every person who—

(a) is a member of the company on the date to which the return is made up, or

(b) has ceased to be a member of the company since the date to which the last return was made up (or, in the case of the first return, since the incorporation of the company).

The return must conform to such requirements as may be prescribed for the purpose of enabling the entries relating to any given person to be easily found.

(4) The return must also state—

(a) the number of shares of each class held by each member of the company at the date to which the return is made up,

(b) the number of shares of each class transferred—

(i) since the date to which the last return was made up, or

(ii) in the case of the first return, since the incorporation of the company,

by each member or person who has ceased to be a member, and

(c) the dates of registration of the transfers.

(5) If either of the two immediately preceding returns has given the full particulars required by subsections (3) and (4), the return need only give such particulars as relate—

(a) to persons ceasing to be or becoming members since the date of the last return, and

(b) to shares transferred since that date.

(6) Where the company has converted any of its shares into stock, the return must give the corresponding information in relation to that stock, stating the amount of stock instead of the number or nominal value of shares.

[1991]

NOTES

Commencement: to be appointed (see the introductory note to this Act).

857 Contents of annual return: power to make further provision by regulations

(1) The Secretary of State may by regulations make further provision as to the information to be given in a company's annual return.

(2) The regulations may—

(a) amend or repeal the provisions of sections 855 and 856, and

(b) provide for exceptions from the requirements of those sections as they have effect from time to time.

(3) Regulations under this section are subject to negative resolution procedure.

[1992]

NOTES

Commencement: to be appointed (see the introductory note to this Act).

858 Failure to deliver annual return

(1) If a company fails to deliver an annual return before the end of the period of 28 days after a return date, an offence is committed by—

- (a) the company,
- (b) subject to subsection (4)—
  - (i) every director of the company, and
  - (ii) in the case of a private company with a secretary or a public company, every secretary of the company, and
- (c) every other officer of the company who is in default.

(2) A person guilty of an offence under subsection (1) is liable on summary conviction to a fine not exceeding level 5 on the standard scale and, for continued contravention, a daily default fine not exceeding one-tenth of level 5 on the standard scale.

(3) The contravention continues until such time as an annual return made up to that return date is delivered by the company to the registrar.

(4) It is a defence for a director or secretary charged with an offence under subsection (1)(b) to prove that he took all reasonable steps to avoid the commission or continuation of the offence.

(5) In the case of continued contravention, an offence is also committed by every officer of the company who did not commit an offence under subsection (1) in relation to the initial contravention but is in default in relation to the continued contravention.

A person guilty of an offence under this subsection is liable on summary conviction to a fine not exceeding one-tenth of level 5 on the standard scale for each day on which the contravention continues and he is in default.

[1993]

NOTES

Commencement: to be appointed (see the introductory note to this Act).

859 Application of provisions to shadow directors

For the purposes of this Part a shadow director is treated as a director.

[1994]

NOTES

Commencement: to be appointed (see the introductory note to this Act).

PART 25
COMPANY CHARGES

CHAPTER 1
COMPANIES REGISTERED IN ENGLAND AND WALES OR IN NORTHERN IRELAND

Requirement to register company charges

860 Charges created by a company

(1) A company that creates a charge to which this section applies must deliver the prescribed particulars of the charge, together with the instrument (if any) by which the charge is created or evidenced, to the registrar for registration before the end of the period allowed for registration.

(2) Registration of a charge to which this section applies may instead be effected on the application of a person interested in it.

(3) Where registration is effected on the application of some person other than the company, that person is entitled to recover from the company the amount of any fees properly paid by him to the registrar on registration.

(4) If a company fails to comply with subsection (1), an offence is committed by—
(a) the company, and
(b) every officer of it who is in default.

(5) A person guilty of an offence under this section is liable—
(a) on conviction on indictment, to a fine;
(b) on summary conviction, to a fine not exceeding the statutory maximum.

(6) Subsection (4) does not apply if registration of the charge has been effected on the application of some other person.

(7) This section applies to the following charges—
(a) a charge on land or any interest in land, other than a charge for any rent or other periodical sum issuing out of land,
(b) a charge created or evidenced by an instrument which, if executed by an individual, would require registration as a bill of sale,
(c) a charge for the purposes of securing any issue of debentures,
(d) a charge on uncalled share capital of the company,
(e) a charge on calls made but not paid,
(f) a charge on book debts of the company,
(g) a floating charge on the company's property or undertaking,
(h) a charge on a ship or aircraft, or any share in a ship,
(i) a charge on goodwill or on any intellectual property.

[1995]

NOTES

Commencement: to be appointed (see the introductory note to this Act).

861 Charges which have to be registered: supplementary

(1) The holding of debentures entitling the holder to a charge on land is not, for the purposes of section 860(7)(a), an interest in the land.

(2) It is immaterial for the purposes of this Chapter where land subject to a charge is situated.

(3) The deposit by way of security of a negotiable instrument given to secure the payment of book debts is not, for the purposes of section 860(7)(f), a charge on those book debts.

(4) For the purposes of section 860(7)(i), "intellectual property" means—
(a) any patent, trade mark, registered design, copyright or design right;
(b) any licence under or in respect of any such right.

(5) In this Chapter—
"charge" includes mortgage, and
"company" means a company registered in England and Wales or in Northern Ireland.

[1996]

NOTES

Commencement: to be appointed (see the introductory note to this Act).

862 Charges existing on property acquired

(1) This section applies where a company acquires property which is subject to a charge of a kind which would, if it had been created by the company after the acquisition of the property, have been required to be registered under this Chapter.

(2) The company must deliver the prescribed particulars of the charge, together with a certified copy of the instrument (if any) by which the charge is created or evidenced, to the registrar for registration.

(3) Subsection (2) must be complied with before the end of the period allowed for registration.

(4) If default is made in complying with this section, an offence is committed by—
(a) the company, and
(b) every officer of it who is in default.

(5) A person guilty of an offence under this section is liable—
(a) on conviction on indictment, to a fine;
(b) on summary conviction, to a fine not exceeding the statutory maximum.

[1997]

NOTES

Commencement: to be appointed (see the introductory note to this Act).

Special rules about debentures

863 Charge in series of debentures

(1) Where a series of debentures containing, or giving by reference to another instrument, any charge to the benefit of which debenture holders of that series are entitled *pari passu* is created by a company, it is for the purposes of section 860(1) sufficient if the required particulars, together with the deed containing the charge (or, if there is no such deed, one of the debentures of the series), are delivered to the registrar before the end of the period allowed for registration.

(2) The following are the required particulars—
(a) the total amount secured by the whole series, and
(b) the dates of the resolutions authorising the issue of the series and the date of the covering deed (if any) by which the series is created or defined, and
(c) a general description of the property charged, and
(d) the names of the trustees (if any) for the debenture holders.

(3) Particulars of the date and amount of each issue of debentures of a series of the kind mentioned in subsection (1) must be sent to the registrar for entry in the register of charges.

(4) Failure to comply with subsection (3) does not affect the validity of the debentures issued.

(5) Subsections (2) to (6) of section 860 apply for the purposes of this section as they apply for the purposes of that section, but as if references to the registration of a charge were references to the registration of a series of debentures.

[1998]

NOTES

Commencement: to be appointed (see the introductory note to this Act).

864 Additional registration requirement for commission etc in relation to debentures

(1) Where any commission, allowance or discount has been paid or made either directly or indirectly by a company to a person in consideration of his—
(a) subscribing or agreeing to subscribe, whether absolutely or conditionally, for debentures in a company, or
(b) procuring or agreeing to procure subscriptions, whether absolute or conditional, for such debentures,

the particulars required to be sent for registration under section 860 shall include particulars as to the amount or rate per cent. of the commission, discount or allowance so paid or made.

(2) The deposit of debentures as security for a debt of the company is not, for the purposes of this section, treated as the issue of debentures at a discount.

(3) Failure to comply with this section does not affect the validity of the debentures issued.

[1999]

NOTES

Commencement: to be appointed (see the introductory note to this Act).

865 Endorsement of certificate on debentures

(1) The company shall cause a copy of every certificate of registration given under section 869 to be endorsed on every debenture or certificate of debenture stock which is issued by the company, and the payment of which is secured by the charge so registered.

(2) But this does not require a company to cause a certificate of registration of any charge so given to be endorsed on any debenture or certificate of debenture stock issued by the company before the charge was created.

(3) If a person knowingly and wilfully authorises or permits the delivery of a debenture or certificate of debenture stock which under this section is required to have endorsed on it a copy of a certificate of registration, without the copy being so endorsed upon it, he commits an offence.

(4) A person guilty of an offence under this section is liable on summary conviction to a fine not exceeding level 3 on the standard scale.

[2000]

NOTES

Commencement: to be appointed (see the introductory note to this Act).

Charges in other jurisdictions

866 Charges created in, or over property in, jurisdictions outside the United Kingdom

(1) Where a charge is created outside the United Kingdom comprising property situated outside the United Kingdom, the delivery to the registrar of a verified copy of the instrument by which the charge is created or evidenced has the same effect for the purposes of this Chapter as the delivery of the instrument itself.

(2) Where a charge is created in the United Kingdom but comprises property outside the United Kingdom, the instrument creating or purporting to create the charge may be sent for registration under section 860 even if further proceedings may be necessary to make the charge valid or effectual according to the law of the country in which the property is situated.

[2001]

NOTES

Commencement: to be appointed (see the introductory note to this Act).

867 Charges created in, or over property in, another United Kingdom jurisdiction

(1) Subsection (2) applies where—

(a) a charge comprises property situated in a part of the United Kingdom other than the part in which the company is registered, and

(b) registration in that other part is necessary to make the charge valid or effectual under the law of that part of the United Kingdom.

(2) The delivery to the registrar of a verified copy of the instrument by which the charge is created or evidenced, together with a certificate stating that the charge was presented for registration in that other part of the United Kingdom on the date on which it was so presented has, for the purposes of this Chapter, the same effect as the delivery of the instrument itself.

[2002]

NOTES

Commencement: to be appointed (see the introductory note to this Act).

Orders charging land: Northern Ireland

868 Northern Ireland: registration of certain charges etc affecting land

(1) Where a charge imposed by an order under Article 46 of the 1981 Order or notice of such a charge is registered in the Land Registry against registered land or any estate in

registered land of a company, the Registrar of Titles shall as soon as may be cause two copies of the order made under Article 46 of that Order or of any notice under Article 48 of that Order to be delivered to the registrar.

(2) Where a charge imposed by an order under Article 46 of the 1981 Order is registered in the Registry of Deeds against any unregistered land or estate in land of a company, the Registrar of Deeds shall as soon as may be cause two copies of the order to be delivered to the registrar.

(3) On delivery of copies under this section, the registrar shall—

(a) register one of them in accordance with section 869, and

(b) not later than 7 days from that date of delivery, cause the other copy together with a certificate of registration under section 869(5) to be sent to the company against which judgment was given.

(4) Where a charge to which subsection (1) or (2) applies is vacated, the Registrar of Titles or, as the case may be, the Registrar of Deeds shall cause a certified copy of the certificate of satisfaction lodged under Article 132(1) of the 1981 Order to be delivered to the registrar for entry of a memorandum of satisfaction in accordance with section 872.

(5) In this section—

"the 1981 Order" means the Judgments Enforcement (Northern Ireland) Order 1981 (SI 1981/226 (NI 6));

"the Registrar of Deeds" means the registrar appointed under the Registration of Deeds Act (Northern Ireland) 1970 (c 25);

"Registry of Deeds" has the same meaning as in the Registration of Deeds Acts;

"Registration of Deeds Acts" means the Registration of Deeds Act (Northern Ireland) 1970 and every statutory provision for the time being in force amending that Act or otherwise relating to the registry of deeds, or the registration of deeds, orders or other instruments or documents in such registry;

"the Land Registry" and "the Registrar of Titles" are to be construed in accordance with section 1 of the Land Registration Act (Northern Ireland) 1970 (c 18);

"registered land" and "unregistered land" have the same meaning as in Part 3 of the Land Registration Act (Northern Ireland) 1970.

[2003]

NOTES

Commencement: to be appointed (see the introductory note to this Act).

The register of charges

869 Register of charges to be kept by registrar

(1) The registrar shall keep, with respect to each company, a register of all the charges requiring registration under this Chapter.

(2) In the case of a charge to the benefit of which holders of a series of debentures are entitled, the registrar shall enter in the register the required particulars specified in section 863(2).

(3) In the case of a charge imposed by the Enforcement of Judgments Office under Article 46 of the Judgments Enforcement (Northern Ireland) Order 1981, the registrar shall enter in the register the date on which the charge became effective.

(4) In the case of any other charge, the registrar shall enter in the register the following particulars—

(a) if it is a charge created by a company, the date of its creation and, if it is a charge which was existing on property acquired by the company, the date of the acquisition,

(b) the amount secured by the charge,

(c) short particulars of the property charged, and

(d) the persons entitled to the charge.

(5) The registrar shall give a certificate of the registration of any charge registered in pursuance of this Chapter, stating the amount secured by the charge.

(6) The certificate—

(a) shall be signed by the registrar or authenticated by the registrar's official seal, and
(b) is conclusive evidence that the requirements of this Chapter as to registration have been satisfied.

(7) The register kept in pursuance of this section shall be open to inspection by any person.

[2004]

NOTES

Commencement: to be appointed (see the introductory note to this Act).

870 The period allowed for registration

(1) The period allowed for registration of a charge created by a company is—

(a) 21 days beginning with the day after the day on which the charge is created, or
(b) if the charge is created outside the United Kingdom, 21 days beginning with the day after the day on which the instrument by which the charge is created or evidenced (or a copy of it) could, in due course of post (and if despatched with due diligence) have been received in the United Kingdom.

(2) The period allowed for registration of a charge to which property acquired by a company is subject is—

(a) 21 days beginning with the day after the day on which the acquisition is completed, or
(b) if the property is situated and the charge was created outside the United Kingdom, 21 days beginning with the day after the day on which the instrument by which the charge is created or evidenced (or a copy of it) could, in due course of post (and if despatched with due diligence) have been received in the United Kingdom.

(3) The period allowed for registration of particulars of a series of debentures as a result of section 863 is—

(a) if there is a deed containing the charge mentioned in section 863(1), 21 days beginning with the day after the day on which that deed is executed, or
(b) if there is no such deed, 21 days beginning with the day after the day on which the first debenture of the series is executed.

[2005]

NOTES

Commencement: to be appointed (see the introductory note to this Act).

871 Registration of enforcement of security

(1) If a person obtains an order for the appointment of a receiver or manager of a company's property, or appoints such a receiver or manager under powers contained in an instrument, he shall within 7 days of the order or of the appointment under those powers, give notice of the fact to the registrar.

(2) Where a person appointed receiver or manager of a company's property under powers contained in an instrument ceases to act as such receiver or manager, he shall, on so ceasing, give the registrar notice to that effect.

(3) The registrar must enter a fact of which he is given notice under this section in the register of charges.

(4) A person who makes default in complying with the requirements of this section commits an offence.

(5) A person guilty of an offence under this section is liable on summary conviction to a fine not exceeding level 3 on the standard scale and, for continued contravention, a daily default fine not exceeding one-tenth of level 3 on the standard scale.

[2006]

NOTES

Commencement: to be appointed (see the introductory note to this Act).

872 Entries of satisfaction and release

(1) Subsection (2) applies if a statement is delivered to the registrar verifying with respect to a registered charge—

(a) that the debt for which the charge was given has been paid or satisfied in whole or in part, or

(b) that part of the property or undertaking charged has been released from the charge or has ceased to form part of the company's property or undertaking.

(2) The registrar may enter on the register a memorandum of satisfaction in whole or in part, or of the fact part of the property or undertaking has been released from the charge or has ceased to form part of the company's property or undertaking (as the case may be).

(3) Where the registrar enters a memorandum of satisfaction in whole, the registrar shall if required send the company a copy of it.

[2007]

NOTES

Commencement: to be appointed (see the introductory note to this Act).

873 Rectification of register of charges

(1) Subsection (2) applies if the court is satisfied—

(a) that the failure to register a charge before the end of the period allowed for registration, or the omission or mis-statement of any particular with respect to any such charge or in a memorandum of satisfaction—

(i) was accidental or due to inadvertence or to some other sufficient cause, or

(ii) is not of a nature to prejudice the position of creditors or shareholders of the company, or

(b) that on other grounds it is just and equitable to grant relief.

(2) The court may, on the application of the company or a person interested, and on such terms and conditions as seem to the court just and expedient, order that the period allowed for registration shall be extended or, as the case may be, that the omission or mis-statement shall be rectified.

[2008]

NOTES

Commencement: to be appointed (see the introductory note to this Act).

Avoidance of certain charges

874 Consequence of failure to register charges created by a company

(1) If a company creates a charge to which section 860 applies, the charge is void (so far as any security on the company's property or undertaking is conferred by it) against—

(a) a liquidator of the company,

(b) an administrator of the company, and

(c) a creditor of the company,

unless that section is complied with.

(2) Subsection (1) is subject to the provisions of this Chapter.

(3) Subsection (1) is without prejudice to any contract or obligation for repayment of the money secured by the charge; and when a charge becomes void under this section, the money secured by it immediately becomes payable.

[2009]

NOTES

Commencement: to be appointed (see the introductory note to this Act).

Companies' records and registers

875 Companies to keep copies of instruments creating charges

(1) A company must keep available for inspection a copy of every instrument creating a charge requiring registration under this Chapter, including any document delivered to the company under section 868(3)(b) (Northern Ireland: orders imposing charges affecting land).

(2) In the case of a series of uniform debentures, a copy of one of the debentures of the series is sufficient.

[2010]

NOTES

Commencement: to be appointed (see the introductory note to this Act).

876 Company's register of charges

(1) Every limited company shall keep available for inspection a register of charges and enter in it—

(a) all charges specifically affecting property of the company, and

(b) all floating charges on the whole or part of the company's property or undertaking.

(2) The entry shall in each case give a short description of the property charged, the amount of the charge and, except in the cases of securities to bearer, the names of the persons entitled to it.

(3) If an officer of the company knowingly and wilfully authorises or permits the omission of an entry required to be made in pursuance of this section, he commits an offence.

(4) A person guilty of an offence under this section is liable—

(a) on conviction on indictment, to a fine;

(b) on summary conviction, to a fine not exceeding the statutory maximum.

[2011]

NOTES

Commencement: to be appointed (see the introductory note to this Act).

877 Instruments creating charges and register of charges to be available for inspection

(1) This section applies to—

(a) documents required to be kept available for inspection under section 875 (copies of instruments creating charges), and

(b) a company's register of charges kept in pursuance of section 876.

(2) The documents and register must be kept available for inspection—

(a) at the company's registered office, or

(b) at a place specified in regulations under section 1136.

(3) The company must give notice to the registrar—

(a) of the place at which the documents and register are kept available for inspection, and

(b) of any change in that place,

unless they have at all times been kept at the company's registered office.

(4) The documents and register shall be open to the inspection—

(a) of any creditor or member of the company without charge, and

(b) of any other person on payment of such fee as may be prescribed.

(5) If default is made for 14 days in complying with subsection (3) or an inspection required under subsection (4) is refused, an offence is committed by—

(a) the company, and

(b) every officer of the company who is in default.

(6) A person guilty of an offence under this section is liable on summary conviction to a fine not exceeding level 3 on the standard scale and, for continued contravention, a daily default fine not exceeding one-tenth of level 3 on the standard scale.

(7) If an inspection required under subsection (4) is refused the court may by order compel an immediate inspection.

[2012]

NOTES

Commencement: to be appointed (see the introductory note to this Act).

878–992 (*Outside the scope of this work.*)

PART 29
FRAUDULENT TRADING

993 Offence of fraudulent trading

(1) If any business of a company is carried on with intent to defraud creditors of the company or creditors of any other person, or for any fraudulent purpose, every person who is knowingly a party to the carrying on of the business in that manner commits an offence.

(2) This applies whether or not the company has been, or is in the course of being, wound up.

(3) A person guilty of an offence under this section is liable—

(a) on conviction on indictment, to imprisonment for a term not exceeding ten years or a fine (or both);

(b) on summary conviction—

(i) in England and Wales, to imprisonment for a term not exceeding twelve months or a fine not exceeding the statutory maximum (or both);

(ii) in Scotland or Northern Ireland, to imprisonment for a term not exceeding six months or a fine not exceeding the statutory maximum (or both).

[2013]

NOTES

Commencement: to be appointed (see the introductory note to this Act).

994–999 (*Outside the scope of this work.*)

PART 31
DISSOLUTION AND RESTORATION TO THE REGISTER

1000–1011 (*Outside the scope of this work.*)

CHAPTER 2
PROPERTY OF DISSOLVED COMPANY

1012–1022 (*Outside the scope of this work.*)

Supplementary provisions

1023 Liability for rentcharge on company's land after dissolution

(1) This section applies where on the dissolution of a company land in England and Wales or Northern Ireland that is subject to a rentcharge vests by operation of law in the Crown or any other person ("the proprietor").

(2) Neither the proprietor nor his successors in title are subject to any personal liability in respect of sums becoming due under the rentcharge, except sums becoming due after the proprietor, or some person claiming under or through him, has taken possession or control of the land or has entered into occupation of it.

(3) In this section "company" includes any body corporate.

[2014]

NOTES

Commencement: to be appointed (see the introductory note to this Act).

1024–1039 (*Outside the scope of this work.*)

PART 33
UK COMPANIES NOT FORMED UNDER COMPANIES LEGISLATION

CHAPTER 1
COMPANIES NOT FORMED UNDER COMPANIES LEGISLATION BUT AUTHORISED TO REGISTER

1040 Companies authorised to register under this Act

(1) This section applies to—

(a) any company that was in existence on 2nd November 1862 (including any company registered under the Joint Stock Companies Acts), and

(b) any company formed after that date (whether before or after the commencement of this Act)—

(i) in pursuance of an Act of Parliament other than this Act or any of the former Companies Acts,

(ii) in pursuance of letters patent, or

(iii) that is otherwise duly constituted according to law.

(2) Any such company may on making application register under this Act.

(3) Subject to the following provisions, it may register as an unlimited company, as a company limited by shares or as a company limited by guarantee.

(4) A company having the liability of its members limited by Act of Parliament or letters patent—

(a) may not register under this section unless it is a joint stock company, and

(b) may not register under this section as an unlimited company or a company limited by guarantee.

(5) A company that is not a joint stock company may not register under this section as a company limited by shares.

(6) The registration of a company under this section is not invalid by reason that it has taken place with a view to the company's being wound up.

[2015]

NOTES

Commencement: to be appointed (see the introductory note to this Act).

1041 Definition of "joint stock company"

(1) For the purposes of section 1040 (companies authorised to register under this Act) "joint stock company" means a company—

(a) having a permanent paid-up or nominal share capital of fixed amount divided into shares, also of fixed amount, or held and transferable as stock, or divided and held partly in one way and partly in the other, and

(b) formed on the principle of having for its members the holders of those shares or that stock, and no other persons.

(2) Such a company when registered with limited liability under this Act is deemed a company limited by shares.

[2016]

NOTES

Commencement: to be appointed (see the introductory note to this Act).

1042 Power to make provision by regulations

(1) The Secretary of State may make provision by regulations—

(a) for and in connection with registration under section 1040 (companies authorised to register under this Act), and
(b) as to the application to companies so registered of the provisions of the Companies Acts.

(2) Without prejudice to the generality of that power, regulations under this section may make provision corresponding to any provision formerly made by Chapter 2 of Part 22 of the Companies Act 1985 (c 6).

(3) Regulations under this section are subject to negative resolution procedure.

[2017]

NOTES

Commencement: to be appointed (see the introductory note to this Act).

1043–1059 (*Outside the scope of this work.*)

PART 35
THE REGISTRAR OF COMPANIES

The registrar

1060 The registrar

(1) There shall continue to be—
(a) a registrar of companies for England and Wales,
(b) a registrar of companies for Scotland, and
(c) a registrar of companies for Northern Ireland.

(2) The registrars shall be appointed by the Secretary of State.

(3) In the Companies Acts "the registrar of companies" and "the registrar" mean the registrar of companies for England and Wales, Scotland or Northern Ireland, as the case may require.

(4) References in the Companies Acts to registration in a particular part of the United Kingdom are to registration by the registrar for that part of the United Kingdom.

[2018]

NOTES

Commencement: 6 April 2007 (certain purposes); to be appointed (otherwise) (see the note below and the introductory note to this Act).

Note: the Companies Act 2006 (Commencement No 1, Transitional Provisions and Savings) Order 2006, SI 2006/3428, art 4(3) provides that this section shall come into force on 6 April 2007 in so far as is necessary for the purposes of the provisions mentioned in art 4(1), (2) of that Order. Those provisions are: ss 1063, 1176–1179, 1281, 1295, Sch 16.

1061 The registrar's functions

(1) The registrar shall continue—
(a) to perform the functions conferred on the registrar—
(i) under the Companies Acts, and
(ii) under the enactments listed in subsection (2), and
(b) to perform such functions on behalf of the Secretary of State, in relation to the registration of companies or other matters, as the Secretary of State may from time to time direct.

(2) The enactments are—
the Joint Stock Companies Acts;
the Newspaper Libel and Registration Act 1881 (c 60);
the Limited Partnerships Act 1907 (c 24);
section 53 of the Industrial and Provident Societies Act 1965 (c 12) or, for Northern Ireland, section 62 of the Industrial and Provident Societies Act (Northern Ireland) 1969 (c 24 (NI));
the Insolvency Act 1986 (c 45) or, for Northern Ireland, the Insolvency (Northern Ireland) Order 1989 (SI 1989/2405 (NI 19));

section 12 of the Statutory Water Companies Act 1991 (c 58);
sections 3, 4, 6, 63 and 64 of, and Schedule 1 to, the Housing Act 1996 (c 52) or, for Northern Ireland, Articles 3 and 16 to 32 of the Housing (Northern Ireland) Order 1992 (SI 1992/1725 (NI 15));
sections 2, 4 and 26 of the Commonwealth Development Corporation Act 1999 (c 20);
Part 6 and section 366 of the Financial Services and Markets Act 2000 (c 8);
the Limited Liability Partnerships Act 2000 (c 12);
section 14 of the Insolvency Act 2000 (c 39) or, for Northern Ireland, Article 11 of the Insolvency (Northern Ireland) Order 2002 (SI 2002/ 3152 (NI 6));
section 121 of the Land Registration Act 2002 (c 9);
section 1248 of this Act.

(3) References in this Act to the functions of the registrar are to functions within subsection (1)(a) or (b).

[2019]

NOTES

Commencement: 6 April 2007 (certain purposes); to be appointed (otherwise) (see the note below and the introductory note to this Act).

Note: the Companies Act 2006 (Commencement No 1, Transitional Provisions and Savings) Order 2006, SI 2006/3428, art 4(3) provides that this section shall come into force on 6 April 2007 in so far as is necessary for the purposes of the provisions mentioned in art 4(1), (2) of that Order. Those provisions are: ss 1063, 1176–1179, 1281, 1295, Sch 16.

1062 The registrar's official seal

The registrar shall have an official seal for the authentication of documents in connection with the performance of the registrar's functions.

[2020]

NOTES

Commencement: to be appointed (see the introductory note to this Act).

1063 Fees payable to registrar

(1) The Secretary of State may make provision by regulations requiring the payment to the registrar of fees in respect of—

(a) the performance of any of the registrar's functions, or

(b) the provision by the registrar of services or facilities for purposes incidental to, or otherwise connected with, the performance of any of the registrar's functions.

(2) The matters for which fees may be charged include—

(a) the performance of a duty imposed on the registrar or the Secretary of State,

(b) the receipt of documents delivered to the registrar, and

(c) the inspection, or provision of copies, of documents kept by the registrar.

(3) The regulations may—

(a) provide for the amount of the fees to be fixed by or determined under the regulations;

(b) provide for different fees to be payable in respect of the same matter in different circumstances;

(c) specify the person by whom any fee payable under the regulations is to be paid;

(d) specify when and how fees are to be paid.

(4) Regulations under this section are subject to negative resolution procedure.

(5) In respect of the performance of functions or the provision of services or facilities—

(a) for which fees are not provided for by regulations, or

(b) in circumstances other than those for which fees are provided for by regulations,

the registrar may determine from time to time what fees (if any) are chargeable.

(6) Fees received by the registrar are to be paid into the Consolidated Fund.

(7) The Limited Partnerships Act 1907 (c 24) is amended as follows—

(a) in section 16(1) (inspection of statements registered)—

(i) omit the words ", and there shall be paid for such inspection such fees as may be appointed by the Board of Trade, not exceeding 5p for each inspection", and
(ii) omit the words from "and there shall be paid for such certificate" to the end;

(b) in section 17 (power to make rules)—
(i) omit the words "(but as to fees with the concurrence of the Treasury)", and
(ii) omit paragraph (a).

[2021]

NOTES

Commencement: 20 January 2007 (certain purposes); 6 April 2007 (otherwise) (see the introductory note to this Act).

Transitional provisions: the Companies Act 2006 (Commencement No 1, Transitional Provisions and Savings) Order 2006, SI 2006/3428, Sch 5, para 6(1), (2) provides as follows—

6 Saving for existing provisions relating to fees

(1) The coming into force of section 1063 of the Companies Act 2006 (fees payable to the registrar) does not affect the continued operation of any other provision under which the payment of fees to the registrar of companies may be required until—

(a) the coming into force of the repeal of the other provision; or

(b) the exercise of the power in section 1063 in a manner inconsistent with its continued operation.

(2) Notwithstanding the coming into force of the repeals in section 16 of the Limited Partnerships Act 1907 and the repeal of section 17(a) of that Act, the fees appointed under the said section 16 and having effect immediately before 6th April 2007 shall continue to be payable, and the rules in force under the said section 17(a) immediately before 6th April 2007 shall continue to have effect.

Note: the commencement of this section on 6 April 2007 by SI 2006/3428 does not extend to Northern Ireland (see art 4(4) of that Order).

Certificates of incorporation

1064 Public notice of issue of certificate of incorporation

(1) The registrar must cause to be published—

(a) in the Gazette, or

(b) in accordance with section 1116 (alternative means of giving public notice),

notice of the issue by the registrar of any certificate of incorporation of a company.

(2) The notice must state the name and registered number of the company and the date of issue of the certificate.

(3) This section applies to a certificate of incorporation issued under—

(a) section 80 (change of name),

(b) section 88 (Welsh companies), or

(c) any provision of Part 7 (re-registration),

as well as to the certificate issued on a company's formation.

[2022]

NOTES

Commencement: to be appointed (see the introductory note to this Act).

1065 Right to certificate of incorporation

Any person may require the registrar to provide him with a copy of any certificate of incorporation of a company, signed by the registrar or authenticated by the registrar's seal.

[2023]

NOTES

Commencement: to be appointed (see the introductory note to this Act).

Registered numbers

1066 Company's registered numbers

(1) The registrar shall allocate to every company a number, which shall be known as the company's registered number.

(2) Companies' registered numbers shall be in such form, consisting of one or more sequences of figures or letters, as the registrar may determine.

(3) The registrar may on adopting a new form of registered number make such changes of existing registered numbers as appear necessary.

(4) A change of a company's registered number has effect from the date on which the company is notified by the registrar of the change.

(5) For a period of three years beginning with that date any requirement to disclose the company's registered number imposed by regulations under section 82 or section 1051 (trading disclosures) is satisfied by the use of either the old number or the new.

(6) In this section "company" includes an overseas company whose particulars have been registered under section 1046, other than a company that appears to the registrar not to be required to register particulars under that section.

[2024]

NOTES

Commencement: to be appointed (see the introductory note to this Act).

1067 Registered numbers of branches of overseas company

(1) The registrar shall allocate to every branch of an overseas company whose particulars are registered under section 1046 a number, which shall be known as the branch's registered number.

(2) Branches' registered numbers shall be in such form, consisting of one or more sequences of figures or letters, as the registrar may determine.

(3) The registrar may on adopting a new form of registered number make such changes of existing registered numbers as appear necessary.

(4) A change of a branch's registered number has effect from the date on which the company is notified by the registrar of the change.

(5) For a period of three years beginning with that date any requirement to disclose the branch's registered number imposed by regulations under section 1051 (trading disclosures) is satisfied by the use of either the old number or the new.

[2025]

NOTES

Commencement: to be appointed (see the introductory note to this Act).

Delivery of documents to the registrar

1068 Registrar's requirements as to form, authentication and manner of delivery

(1) The registrar may impose requirements as to the form, authentication and manner of delivery of documents required or authorised to be delivered to the registrar under any enactment.

(2) As regards the form of the document, the registrar may—
- (a) require the contents of the document to be in a standard form;
- (b) impose requirements for the purpose of enabling the document to be scanned or copied.

(3) As regards authentication, the registrar may—
- (a) require the document to be authenticated by a particular person or a person of a particular description;
- (b) specify the means of authentication;

(c) require the document to contain or be accompanied by the name or registered number of the company to which it relates (or both).

(4) As regards the manner of delivery, the registrar may specify requirements as to—

(a) the physical form of the document (for example, hard copy or electronic form);

(b) the means to be used for delivering the document (for example, by post or electronic means);

(c) the address to which the document is to be sent;

(d) in the case of a document to be delivered by electronic means, the hardware and software to be used, and technical specifications (for example, matters relating to protocol, security, anti-virus protection or encryption).

(5) The registrar must secure that as from 1st January 2007 all documents subject to the Directive disclosure requirements (see section 1078) may be delivered to the registrar by electronic means.

(6) The power conferred by this section does not authorise the registrar to require documents to be delivered by electronic means (see section 1069).

(7) Requirements imposed under this section must not be inconsistent with requirements imposed by any enactment with respect to the form, authentication or manner of delivery of the document concerned.

[2026]

NOTES

Commencement: 1 January 2007 (sub-s (5), and sub-ss (1)–(4), (6), (7) for certain purposes only); to be appointed (otherwise) (see the note below and the introductory note to this Act).

Note: the Companies Act 2006 (Commencement No 1, Transitional Provisions and Savings) Order 2006, SI 2006/3428, art 2(2) provides that sub-ss (1)–(4), (6), (7) above shall come into force on 1 January 2007 in so far as is necessary for the purposes of the provisions mentioned in art 2(1) of that Order. Those provisions are: ss 1068(5), 1077–1080, 1085–1092, 1102–1107, 1111.

1069 Power to require delivery by electronic means

(1) The Secretary of State may make regulations requiring documents that are authorised or required to be delivered to the registrar to be delivered by electronic means.

(2) Any such requirement to deliver documents by electronic means is effective only if registrar's rules have been published with respect to the detailed requirements for such delivery.

(3) Regulations under this section are subject to affirmative resolution procedure.

[2027]

NOTES

Commencement: to be appointed (see the introductory note to this Act).

1070 Agreement for delivery by electronic means

(1) The registrar may agree with a company that documents relating to the company that are required or authorised to be delivered to the registrar—

(a) will be delivered by electronic means, except as provided for in the agreement, and

(b) will conform to such requirements as may be specified in the agreement or specified by the registrar in accordance with the agreement.

(2) An agreement under this section may relate to all or any description of documents to be delivered to the registrar.

(3) Documents in relation to which an agreement is in force under this section must be delivered in accordance with the agreement.

[2028]

NOTES

Commencement: to be appointed (see the introductory note to this Act).

1071 Document not delivered until received

(1) A document is not delivered to the registrar until it is received by the registrar.

(2) Provision may be made by registrar's rules as to when a document is to be regarded as received.

[2029]

NOTES

Commencement: to be appointed (see the introductory note to this Act).

Requirements for proper delivery

1072 Requirements for proper delivery

(1) A document delivered to the registrar is not properly delivered unless all the following requirements are met—

(a) the requirements of the provision under which the document is to be delivered to the registrar as regards—
  (i) the contents of the document, and
  (ii) form, authentication and manner of delivery;

(b) any applicable requirements under—
section 1068 (registrar's requirements as to form, authentication and manner of delivery),
section 1069 (power to require delivery by electronic means), or
section 1070 (agreement for delivery by electronic means);

(c) any requirements of this Part as to the language in which the document is drawn up and delivered or as to its being accompanied on delivery by a certified translation into English;

(d) in so far as it consists of or includes names and addresses, any requirements of this Part as to permitted characters, letters or symbols or as to its being accompanied on delivery by a certificate as to the transliteration of any element;

(e) any applicable requirements under section 1111 (registrar's requirements as to certification or verification);

(f) any requirement of regulations under section 1082 (use of unique identifiers);

(g) any requirements as regards payment of a fee in respect of its receipt by the registrar.

(2) A document that is not properly delivered is treated for the purposes of the provision requiring or authorising it to be delivered as not having been delivered, subject to the provisions of section 1073 (power to accept documents not meeting requirements for proper delivery).

[2030]

NOTES

Commencement: to be appointed (see the introductory note to this Act).

1073 Power to accept documents not meeting requirements for proper delivery

(1) The registrar may accept (and register) a document that does not comply with the requirements for proper delivery.

(2) A document accepted by the registrar under this section is treated as received by the registrar for the purposes of section 1077 (public notice of receipt of certain documents).

(3) No objection may be taken to the legal consequences of a document's being accepted (or registered) by the registrar under this section on the ground that the requirements for proper delivery were not met.

(4) The acceptance of a document by the registrar under this section does not affect—

(a) the continuing obligation to comply with the requirements for proper delivery, or

(b) subject as follows, any liability for failure to comply with those requirements.

(5) For the purposes of—

(a) section 453 (civil penalty for failure to file accounts and reports), and

(b) any enactment imposing a daily default fine for failure to deliver the document,

the period after the document is accepted does not count as a period during which there is default in complying with the requirements for proper delivery.

(6) But if, subsequently—
(a) the registrar issues a notice under section 1094(4) in respect of the document (notice of administrative removal from the register), and
(b) the requirements for proper delivery are not complied with before the end of the period of 14 days after the issue of that notice,

any subsequent period of default does count for the purposes of those provisions.

[2031]

NOTES

Commencement: to be appointed (see the introductory note to this Act).

1074 Documents containing unnecessary material

(1) This section applies where a document delivered to the registrar contains unnecessary material.

(2) "Unnecessary material" means material that—
(a) is not necessary in order to comply with an obligation under any enactment, and
(b) is not specifically authorised to be delivered to the registrar.

(3) For this purpose an obligation to deliver a document of a particular description, or conforming to certain requirements, is regarded as not extending to anything that is not needed for a document of that description or, as the case may be, conforming to those requirements.

(4) If the unnecessary material cannot readily be separated from the rest of the document, the document is treated as not meeting the requirements for proper delivery.

(5) If the unnecessary material can readily be separated from the rest of the document, the registrar may register the document either—
(a) with the omission of the unnecessary material, or
(b) as delivered.

[2032]

NOTES

Commencement: to be appointed (see the introductory note to this Act).

1075 Informal correction of document

(1) A document delivered to the registrar may be corrected by the registrar if it appears to the registrar to be incomplete or internally inconsistent.

(2) This power is exercisable only—
(a) on instructions, and
(b) if the company has given (and has not withdrawn) its consent to instructions being given under this section.

(3) The following requirements must be met as regards the instructions—
(a) the instructions must be given in response to an enquiry by the registrar;
(b) the registrar must be satisfied that the person giving the instructions is authorised to do so—
  (i) by the person by whom the document was delivered, or
  (ii) by the company to which the document relates;
(c) the instructions must meet any requirements of registrar's rules as to—
  (i) the form and manner in which they are given, and
  (ii) authentication.

(4) The company's consent to instructions being given under this section (and any withdrawal of such consent)—
(a) may be in hard copy or electronic form, and
(b) must be notified to the registrar.

(5) This section applies in relation to documents delivered under Part 25 (company charges) by a person other than the company as if the references to the company were to the company or the person by whom the document was delivered.

(6) A document that is corrected under this section is treated, for the purposes of any enactment relating to its delivery, as having been delivered when the correction is made.

(7) The power conferred by this section is not exercisable if the document has been registered under section 1073 (power to accept documents not meeting requirements for proper delivery).

[2033]

NOTES

Commencement: to be appointed (see the introductory note to this Act).

1076 Replacement of document not meeting requirements for proper delivery

(1) The registrar may accept a replacement for a document previously delivered that—

(a) did not comply with the requirements for proper delivery, or

(b) contained unnecessary material (within the meaning of section 1074).

(2) A replacement document must not be accepted unless the registrar is satisfied that it is delivered by—

(a) the person by whom the original document was delivered, or

(b) the company to which the original document relates, and that it complies with the requirements for proper delivery.

(3) The power of the registrar to impose requirements as to the form and manner of delivery includes power to impose requirements as to the identification of the original document and the delivery of the replacement in a form and manner enabling it to be associated with the original.

(4) This section does not apply where the original document was delivered under Part 25 (company charges) (but see sections 873 and 888 (rectification of register of charges)).

[2034]

NOTES

Commencement: to be appointed (see the introductory note to this Act).

Public notice of receipt of certain documents

1077 Public notice of receipt of certain documents

(1) The registrar must cause to be published—

(a) in the Gazette, or

(b) in accordance with section 1116 (alternative means of giving public notice),

notice of the receipt by the registrar of any document that, on receipt, is subject to the Directive disclosure requirements (see section 1078).

(2) The notice must state the name and registered number of the company, the description of document and the date of receipt.

(3) The registrar is not required to cause notice of the receipt of a document to be published before the date of incorporation of the company to which the document relates.

[2035]

NOTES

Commencement: 1 January 2007.

Transitional adaptations: art 5 of the Companies Act 2006 (Commencement No 1, Transitional Provisions and Savings) Order 2006, SI 2006/3428 provides that the provisions brought into force by arts 2–4 of 2006 Order shall have effect subject to any transitional adaptations specified in Sch 1 to that Order. Schedule 1, para 4 to the Order provides as follows—

4.—(1) Section 1077 (public notice of receipt of certain documents) has effect with the following adaptation.

(2) Omit subsection (1)(b).

1078–1079 (*Outside the scope of this work.*)

The register

1080 The register

(1) The registrar shall continue to keep records of—
- (a) the information contained in documents delivered to the registrar under any enactment,
- (b) certificates of incorporation issued by the registrar, and
- (c) certificates issued by the registrar under section 869(5) or 885(4) (certificates of registration of charge).

(2) The records relating to companies are referred to collectively in the Companies Acts as "the register".

(3) Information deriving from documents subject to the Directive disclosure requirements (see section 1078) that are delivered to the registrar on or after 1st January 2007 must be kept by the registrar in electronic form.

(4) Subject to that, information contained in documents delivered to the registrar may be recorded and kept in any form the registrar thinks fit, provided it is possible to inspect it and produce a copy of it.

This is sufficient compliance with any duty of the registrar to keep, file or register the document or to record the information contained in it.

(5) The records kept by the registrar must be such that information relating to a company is associated with that company, in such manner as the registrar may determine, so as to enable all the information relating to the company to be retrieved.

[2036]

NOTES

Commencement: 1 January 2007.

Transitional adaptations: art 5 of the Companies Act 2006 (Commencement No 1, Transitional Provisions and Savings) Order 2006, SI 2006/3428 provides that the provisions brought into force by arts 2–4 of 2006 Order shall have effect subject to any transitional adaptations specified in Sch 1 to that Order. Schedule 1, para 7 to the Order provides as follows—

7.—(1) Section 1080 (the register) has effect with the following adaptation.

(2) In subsection (1)(c), for "section 869(5) or 885(4)" substitute "section 401(2) or 418 of the Companies Act 1985 or Article 409(3) of the Companies (Northern Ireland) Order 1986".

1081 Annotation of the register

(1) The registrar must place a note in the register recording—
- (a) the date on which a document is delivered to the registrar;
- (b) if a document is corrected under section 1075, the nature and date of the correction;
- (c) if a document is replaced (whether or not material derived from it is removed), the fact that it has been replaced and the date of delivery of the replacement;
- (d) if material is removed—
  - (i) what was removed (giving a general description of its contents),
  - (ii) under what power, and
  - (iii) the date on which that was done.

(2) The Secretary of State may make provision by regulations—
- (a) authorising or requiring the registrar to annotate the register in such other circumstances as may be specified in the regulations, and
- (b) as to the contents of any such annotation.

(3) No annotation is required in the case of a document that by virtue of section 1072(2) (documents not meeting requirements for proper delivery) is treated as not having been delivered.

(4) A note may be removed if it no longer serves any useful purpose.

(5) Any duty or power of the registrar with respect to annotation of the register is subject to the court's power under section 1097 (powers of court on ordering removal of material from the register) to direct—
- (a) that a note be removed from the register, or

(b) that no note shall be made of the removal of material that is the subject of the court's order.

(6) Notes placed in the register in accordance with subsection (1), or in pursuance of regulations under subsection (2), are part of the register for all purposes of the Companies Acts.

(7) Regulations under this section are subject to negative resolution procedure.

[2037]

NOTES

Commencement: to be appointed (see the introductory note to this Act).

1082 Allocation of unique identifiers

(1) The Secretary of State may make provision for the use, in connection with the register, of reference numbers ("unique identifiers") to identify each person who—

(a) is a director of a company,
(b) is secretary (or a joint secretary) of a company, or
(c) in the case of an overseas company whose particulars are registered under section 1046, holds any such position as may be specified for the purposes of this section by regulations under that section.

(2) The regulations may—

(a) provide that a unique identifier may be in such form, consisting of one or more sequences of letters or numbers, as the registrar may from time to time determine;
(b) make provision for the allocation of unique identifiers by the registrar;
(c) require there to be included, in any specified description of documents delivered to the registrar, as well as a statement of the person's name—
  (i) a statement of the person's unique identifier, or
  (ii) a statement that the person has not been allocated a unique identifier;
(d) enable the registrar to take steps where a person appears to have more than one unique identifier to discontinue the use of all but one of them.

(3) The regulations may contain provision for the application of the scheme in relation to persons appointed, and documents registered, before the commencement of this Act.

(4) The regulations may make different provision for different descriptions of person and different descriptions of document.

(5) Regulations under this section are subject to affirmative resolution procedure.

[2038]

NOTES

Commencement: to be appointed (see the introductory note to this Act).

1083 Preservation of original documents

(1) The originals of documents delivered to the registrar in hard copy form must be kept for three years after they are received by the registrar, after which they may be destroyed provided the information contained in them has been recorded in the register.

This is subject to section 1087(3) (extent of obligation to retain material not available for public inspection).

(2) The registrar is under no obligation to keep the originals of documents delivered in electronic form, provided the information contained in them has been recorded in the register.

(3) This section applies to documents held by the registrar when this section comes into force as well as to documents subsequently received.

[2039]

NOTES

Commencement: to be appointed (see the introductory note to this Act).

1084 Records relating to companies that have been dissolved etc

(1) This section applies where—

(a) a company is dissolved,

(b) an overseas company ceases to have any connection with the United Kingdom by virtue of which it is required to register particulars under section 1046, or

(c) a credit or financial institution ceases to be within section 1050 (overseas institutions required to file accounts with the registrar).

(2) At any time after two years from the date on which it appears to the registrar that—

(a) the company has been dissolved,

(b) the overseas company has ceased to have any connection with the United Kingdom by virtue of which it is required to register particulars under section 1046, or

(c) the credit or financial institution has ceased to be within section 1050 (overseas institutions required to file accounts with the registrar),

the registrar may direct that records relating to the company or institution may be removed to the Public Record Office or, as the case may be, the Public Record Office of Northern Ireland.

(3) Records in respect of which such a direction is given shall be disposed of under the enactments relating to that Office and the rules made under them.

(4) In subsection (1)(a) "company" includes a company provisionally or completely registered under the Joint Stock Companies Act 1844 (c 110).

(5) This section does not extend to Scotland.

[2040]

NOTES

Commencement: to be appointed (see the introductory note to this Act).

Inspection etc of the register

1085 Inspection of the register

(1) Any person may inspect the register.

(2) The right of inspection extends to the originals of documents delivered to the registrar in hard copy form if, and only if, the record kept by the registrar of the contents of the document is illegible or unavailable.

The period for which such originals are to be kept is limited by section 1083(1).

(3) This section has effect subject to section 1087 (material not available for public inspection).

[2041]

NOTES

Commencement: 1 January 2007.

Transitional adaptations: art 5 of the Companies Act 2006 (Commencement No 1, Transitional Provisions and Savings) Order 2006, SI 2006/3428 provides that the provisions brought into force by arts 2–4 of 2006 Order shall have effect subject to any transitional adaptations specified in Sch 1 to that Order. Schedule 1, para 8 to the Order provides as follows—

8.—(1) Section 1085 (inspection of the register) has effect with the following adaptation.

(2) In subsection (2) for "section 1083(1)" substitute "section 707A(2) of the Companies Act 1985 or Article 656A(2) of the Companies (Northern Ireland) Order 1986".

1086 Right to copy of material on the register

(1) Any person may require a copy of any material on the register.

(2) The fee for any such copy of material derived from a document subject to the Directive disclosure requirements (see section 1078), whether in hard copy or electronic form, must not exceed the administrative cost of providing it.

(3) This section has effect subject to section 1087 (material not available for public inspection).

[2042]

NOTES

Commencement: 1 January 2007.

1087 Material not available for public inspection

(1) The following material must not be made available by the registrar for public inspection—

(a) the contents of any document sent to the registrar containing views expressed pursuant to section 56 (comments on proposal by company to use certain words or expressions in company name);

(b) protected information within section 242(1) (directors' residential addresses: restriction on disclosure by registrar) or any corresponding provision of regulations under section 1046 (overseas companies);

(c) any application to the registrar under section 1024 (application for administrative restoration to the register) that has not yet been determined or was not successful;

(d) any document received by the registrar in connection with the giving or withdrawal of consent under section 1075 (informal correction of documents);

(e) any application or other document delivered to the registrar under section 1088 (application to make address unavailable for public inspection) and any address in respect of which such an application is successful;

(f) any application or other document delivered to the registrar under section 1095 (application for rectification of register);

(g) any court order under section 1096 (rectification of the register under court order) that the court has directed under section 1097 (powers of court on ordering removal of material from the register) is not to be made available for public inspection;

(h) the contents of—

(i) any instrument creating or evidencing a charge and delivered to the registrar under section 860 (registration of company charges: England and Wales or Northern Ireland), or

(ii) any certified copy of an instrument creating or evidencing a charge and delivered to the registrar under section 878 (registration of company charges: Scotland);

(i) any e-mail address, identification code or password deriving from a document delivered for the purpose of authorising or facilitating electronic filing procedures or providing information by telephone;

(j) the contents of any documents held by the registrar pending a decision of the Regulator of Community Interest Companies under section 36 or 38 of the Companies (Audit, Investigations and Community Enterprise) Act 2004 (c 27) (decision on eligibility for registration as community interest company) and that the registrar is not later required to record;

(k) any other material excluded from public inspection by or under any other enactment.

(2) A restriction applying by reference to material deriving from a particular description of document does not affect the availability for public inspection of the same information contained in material derived from another description of document in relation to which no such restriction applies.

(3) Material to which this section applies need not be retained by the registrar for longer than appears to the registrar reasonably necessary for the purposes for which the material was delivered to the registrar.

[2043]

NOTES

Commencement: 1 January 2007.

Transitional adaptations: art 5 of the Companies Act 2006 (Commencement No 1, Transitional Provisions and Savings) Order 2006, SI 2006/3428 provides that the provisions brought into force by arts 2–4 of 2006 Order shall have effect subject to any transitional adaptations specified in Sch 1 to that Order. Schedule 1, para 9 to the Order provides as follows—

9.—(1) Section 1087 (material not available for public inspection) has effect with the following adaptations.

(2) In subsection (1)(a) for "views expressed pursuant to section 56" substitute "a statement that a request has been made pursuant to section 29(2) of the Companies Act 1985 or Article 39(2) of the Companies (Northern Ireland) Order 1986 or any response to such a request".

(3) For subsection (1)(b) substitute—

"(b) at any time when an order made under section 723B of the Companies Act 1985 is in force in relation to an individual, so much of any record kept by the registrar as contains information which is recorded as particulars of the individual's residential address that were contained in a document delivered to the registrar after the order came into force;".

(4) Omit subsection (1)(c) to (g).

(5) In subsection (1)(h)(i), for "section 860" substitute "section 395 of the Companies Act 1985 or Article 402 of the Companies (Northern Ireland) Order 1986".

(6) In subsection (1)(h)(ii), for "section 878" substitute "section 410 of the Companies Act 1985".

1088 Application to registrar to make address unavailable for public inspection

(1) The Secretary of State may make provision by regulations requiring the registrar, on application, to make an address on the register unavailable for public inspection.

(2) The regulations may make provision as to—

(a) who may make an application,
(b) the grounds on which an application may be made,
(c) the information to be included in and documents to accompany an application,
(d) the notice to be given of an application and of its outcome, and
(e) how an application is to be determined.

(3) Provision under subsection (2)(e) may in particular—

(a) confer a discretion on the registrar;
(b) provide for a question to be referred to a person other than the registrar for the purposes of determining the application.

(4) An application must specify the address to be removed from the register and indicate where on the register it is.

(5) The regulations may provide—

(a) that an address is not to be made unavailable for public inspection under this section unless replaced by a service address, and
(b) that in such a case the application must specify a service address.

(6) Regulations under this section are subject to affirmative resolution procedure.

[2044]

NOTES

Commencement: 1 January 2007.

1089 Form of application for inspection or copy

(1) The registrar may specify the form and manner in which application is to be made for—

(a) inspection under section 1085, or
(b) a copy under section 1086.

(2) As from 1st January 2007, applications in respect of documents subject to the Directive disclosure requirements may be submitted to the registrar in hard copy or electronic form, as the applicant chooses.

This does not affect the registrar's power under subsection (1) above to impose requirements in respect of other matters.

[2045]

NOTES

Commencement: 1 January 2007.

1090 Form and manner in which copies to be provided

(1) The following provisions apply as regards the form and manner in which copies are to be provided under section 1086.

(2) As from 1st January 2007, copies of documents subject to the Directive disclosure requirements must be provided in hard copy or electronic form, as the applicant chooses.

This is subject to the following proviso.

(3) The registrar is not obliged by subsection (2) to provide copies in electronic form of a document that was delivered to the registrar in hard copy form if—

(a) the document was delivered to the registrar on or before 31st December 1996, or

(b) the document was delivered to the registrar on or before 31st December 2006 and ten years or more elapsed between the date of delivery and the date of receipt of the first application for a copy on or after 1st January 2007.

(4) Subject to the preceding provisions of this section, the registrar may determine the form and manner in which copies are to be provided.

[2046]

NOTES

Commencement: 1 January 2007.

1091 Certification of copies as accurate

(1) Copies provided under section 1086 in hard copy form must be certified as true copies unless the applicant dispenses with such certification.

(2) Copies so provided in electronic form must not be certified as true copies unless the applicant expressly requests such certification.

(3) A copy provided under section 1086, certified by the registrar (whose official position it is unnecessary to prove) to be an accurate record of the contents of the original document, is in all legal proceedings admissible in evidence—

(a) as of equal validity with the original document, and

(b) as evidence (in Scotland, sufficient evidence) of any fact stated in the original document of which direct oral evidence would be admissible.

(4) The Secretary of State may make provision by regulations as to the manner in which such a certificate is to be provided in a case where the copy is provided in electronic form.

(5) Except in the case of documents that are subject to the Directive disclosure requirements (see section 1078), copies provided by the registrar may, instead of being certified in writing to be an accurate record, be sealed with the registrar's official seal.

[2047]

NOTES

Commencement: 1 January 2007.

Regulations: the Companies (Registrar, Languages and Trading Disclosures) Regulations 2006, SI 2006/3429.

1092 Issue of process for production of records kept by the registrar

(1) No process for compelling the production of a record kept by the registrar shall issue from any court except with the permission of the court.

(2) Any such process shall bear on it a statement that it is issued with the permission of the court.

[2048]

NOTES

Commencement: 1 January 2007.

Correction or removal of material on the register

1093 Registrar's notice to resolve inconsistency on the register

(1) Where it appears to the registrar that the information contained in a document delivered to the registrar is inconsistent with other information on the register, the registrar may give notice to the company to which the document relates—

(a) stating in what respects the information contained in it appears to be inconsistent with other information on the register, and
(b) requiring the company to take steps to resolve the inconsistency.

(2) The notice must—
(a) state the date on which it is issued, and
(b) require the delivery to the registrar, within 14 days after that date, of such replacement or additional documents as may be required to resolve the inconsistency.

(3) If the necessary documents are not delivered within the period specified, an offence is committed by—
(a) the company, and
(b) every officer of the company who is in default.

(4) A person guilty of an offence under subsection (3) is liable on summary conviction to a fine not exceeding level 5 on the standard scale and, for continued contravention, a daily default fine not exceeding one-tenth of level 5 on the standard scale.

[2049]

NOTES

Commencement: to be appointed (see the introductory note to this Act).

1094–1098 (*Outside the scope of this work.*)

The registrar's index of company names

1099 The registrar's index of company names

(1) The registrar of companies must keep an index of the names of the companies and other bodies to which this section applies.

This is "the registrar's index of company names".

(2) This section applies to—
(a) UK-registered companies;
(b) any body to which any provision of the Companies Acts applies by virtue of regulations under section 1043 (unregistered companies); and
(c) overseas companies that have registered particulars with the registrar under section 1046, other than companies that appear to the registrar not to be required to do so.

(3) This section also applies to—
(a) limited partnerships registered in the United Kingdom;
(b) limited liability partnerships incorporated in the United Kingdom;
(c) European Economic Interest Groupings registered in the United Kingdom;
(d) open-ended investment companies authorised in the United Kingdom;
(e) societies registered under the Industrial and Provident Societies Act 1965 (c 12) or the Industrial and Provident Societies Act (Northern Ireland) 1969 (c 24 (NI)).

(4) The Secretary of State may by order amend subsection (3)—
(a) by the addition of any description of body;
(b) by the deletion of any description of body.

(5) Any such order is subject to negative resolution procedure.

[2050]

NOTES

Commencement: to be appointed (see the introductory note to this Act).

1100 Right to inspect index

Any person may inspect the registrar's index of company names.

[2051]

NOTES

Commencement: to be appointed (see the introductory note to this Act).

1101 Power to amend enactments relating to bodies other than companies

(1) The Secretary of State may by regulations amend the enactments relating to any description of body for the time being within section 1099(3) (bodies other than companies whose names are to be entered in the registrar's index), so as to—

(a) require the registrar to be provided with information as to the names of bodies registered, incorporated, authorised or otherwise regulated under those enactments, and

(b) make provision in relation to such bodies corresponding to that made by—
section 66 (company name not to be the same as another in the index), and
sections 67 and 68 (power to direct change of company name in case of similarity to existing name).

(2) Regulations under this section are subject to affirmative resolution procedure.

[2052]

NOTES

Commencement: to be appointed (see the introductory note to this Act).

Language requirements: translation

1102 Application of language requirements

(1) The provisions listed below apply to all documents required to be delivered to the registrar under any provision of—

(a) the Companies Acts, or

(b) the Insolvency Act 1986 (c 45) or the Insolvency (Northern Ireland) Order 1989 (SI 1989/2405 (NI 19)).

(2) The Secretary of State may make provision by regulations applying all or any of the listed provisions, with or without modifications, in relation to documents delivered to the registrar under any other enactment.

(3) The provisions are—
section 1103 (documents to be drawn up and delivered in English),
section 1104 (documents relating to Welsh companies),
section 1105 (documents that may be drawn up and delivered in other languages),
section 1107 (certified translations).

(4) Regulations under this section are subject to negative resolution procedure.

[2053]

NOTES

Commencement: 1 January 2007.

1103 Documents to be drawn up and delivered in English

(1) The general rule is that all documents required to be delivered to the registrar must be drawn up and delivered in English.

(2) This is subject to—
section 1104 (documents relating to Welsh companies) and
section 1105 (documents that may be drawn up and delivered in other languages).

[2054]

NOTES

Commencement: 1 January 2007.

Transitional adaptations: art 5 of the Companies Act 2006 (Commencement No 1, Transitional Provisions and Savings) Order 2006, SI 2006/3428 provides that the provisions brought into force by arts 2–4 of 2006 Order shall have effect subject to any transitional adaptations specified in Sch 1 to that Order. Schedule 1, para 10 to the Order provides as follows—

10.—(1) Section 1103 (documents to be drawn up and delivered in English) has effect with the following adaptation.

(2) After subsection (2) insert—

"(3) This section does not affect the operation of the following provisions (under which documents may be delivered in a language other than English if a certified translation is delivered)—

(a) section 228(2)(f) or 228A(2)(g) of the Companies Act 1985 or Article 236(2)(f) of the Companies (Northern Ireland) Order 1986 (conditions for exemption from duty to prepare group accounts: delivery of certain accounts and reports);

(b) section 242(1) of that Act or Article 250(1) of that Order (main requirements as to accounts and reports);

(c) section 272(5) of that Act or Article 280(5) of that Order (interim accounts prepared for a proposed distribution by a public company);

(d) section 273(7) of that Act or Article 281(7) of that Order (initial accounts prepared for a proposed distribution by a public company);

(e) paragraph 7(3) of Part 2 of Schedule 9 to that Act or paragraph 7(3) of Part 2 of Schedule 9 to that Order (information as to undertaking in which shares held as a result of financial assistance operation).".

1104 Documents relating to Welsh companies

(1) Documents relating to a Welsh company may be drawn up and delivered to the registrar in Welsh.

(2) On delivery to the registrar any such document must be accompanied by a certified translation into English, unless it is—

(a) of a description excepted from that requirement by regulations made by the Secretary of State, or

(b) in a form prescribed in Welsh (or partly in Welsh and partly in English) by virtue of section 26 of the Welsh Language Act 1993 (c 38).

(3) Where a document is properly delivered to the registrar in Welsh without a certified translation into English, the registrar must obtain such a translation if the document is to be available for public inspection.

The translation is treated as if delivered to the registrar in accordance with the same provision as the original.

(4) A Welsh company may deliver to the registrar a certified translation into Welsh of any document in English that relates to the company and is or has been delivered to the registrar.

(5) Section 1105 (which requires certified translations into English of documents delivered to the registrar in another language) does not apply to a document relating to a Welsh company that is drawn up and delivered in Welsh.

[2055]

NOTES

Commencement: 1 January 2007.

Transitional adaptations: art 5 of the Companies Act 2006 (Commencement No 1, Transitional Provisions and Savings) Order 2006, SI 2006/3428 provides that the provisions brought into force by arts 2–4 of 2006 Order shall have effect subject to any transitional adaptations specified in Sch 1 to that Order. Schedule 1, para 11 to the Order provides as follows—

11.—(1) Section 1104 (documents relating to Welsh companies) has effect with the following adaptations.

(2) For subsection (5) substitute—

"(5) None of the following provisions (which require certified translations into English of documents delivered to the registrar in another language) applies to a document relating to a Welsh company that is drawn up and delivered in Welsh—

(a) section 228(2)(f) and section 228A(2)(g) of the Companies Act 1985;

(b) section 242(1) of that Act;

(c) section 272(5) of that Act;

(d) section 273(7) of that Act;

(e) paragraph 7(3) of Part 2 of Schedule 9 to that Act;

(f) section 1105 of this Act.".

(3) After that subsection insert—

"(6) In this section, "a Welsh company" means a company whose memorandum states that its registered office is to be situated in Wales.".

1105 Documents that may be drawn up and delivered in other languages

(1) Documents to which this section applies may be drawn up and delivered to the registrar in a language other than English, but when delivered to the registrar they must be accompanied by a certified translation into English.

(2) This section applies to—

(a) agreements required to be forwarded to the registrar under Chapter 3 of Part 3 (agreements affecting the company's constitution);

(b) documents required to be delivered under section 400(2)(e) or section 401(2)(f) (company included in accounts of larger group: required to deliver copy of group accounts);

(c) instruments or copy instruments required to be delivered under Part 25 (company charges);

(d) documents of any other description specified in regulations made by the Secretary of State.

(3) Regulations under this section are subject to negative resolution procedure.

[2056]

NOTES

Commencement: 1 January 2007.

Transitional adaptations: art 5 of the Companies Act 2006 (Commencement No 1, Transitional Provisions and Savings) Order 2006, SI 2006/3428 provides that the provisions brought into force by arts 2–4 of 2006 Order shall have effect subject to any transitional adaptations specified in Sch 1 to that Order. Schedule 1, para 121 to the Order provides as follows—

12.—(1) Section 1105 (documents that may be drawn up and delivered in other languages) has effect with the following adaptations.

(2) In subsection (2)(a) for "Chapter 3 of Part 3" substitute "section 380 of the Companies Act 1985 or Article 388 of the Companies (Northern Ireland) Order 1986".

(3) In subsection (2)(b) for "section 400(2)(e) or section 401(2)(f)" substitute "section 228(2)(e) or section 228A(2)(f) of the Companies Act 1985 or Article 236(2)(e) of the Companies (Northern Ireland) Order 1986".

(4) In subsection (2)(c) for "Part 25" substitute "Part 12 of the Companies Act 1985 or Part 13 of the Companies (Northern Ireland) Order 1986".

Regulations: the Companies (Registrar, Languages and Trading Disclosures) Regulations 2006, SI 2006/3429.

1106 Voluntary filing of translations

(1) A company may deliver to the registrar one or more certified translations of any document relating to the company that is or has been delivered to the registrar.

(2) The Secretary of State may by regulations specify—

(a) the languages, and

(b) the descriptions of document,

in relation to which this facility is available.

(3) The regulations must provide that it is available as from 1st January 2007—

(a) in relation to all the official languages of the European Union, and

(b) in relation to all documents subject to the Directive disclosure requirements (see section 1078).

(4) The power of the registrar to impose requirements as to the form and manner of delivery includes power to impose requirements as to the identification of the original document and the delivery of the translation in a form and manner enabling it to be associated with the original.

(5) Regulations under this section are subject to negative resolution procedure.

(6) This section does not apply where the original document was delivered to the registrar before this section came into force.

[2057]

NOTES

Commencement: 1 January 2007.

Regulations: the Companies (Registrar, Languages and Trading Disclosures) Regulations 2006, SI 2006/3429.

1107 Certified translations

(1) In this Part a "certified translation" means a translation certified to be a correct translation.

(2) In the case of any discrepancy between the original language version of a document and a certified translation—

(a) the company may not rely on the translation as against a third party, but

(b) a third party may rely on the translation unless the company shows that the third party had knowledge of the original.

(3) A "third party" means a person other than the company or the registrar.

[2058]

NOTES

Commencement: 1 January 2007.

Language requirements: transliteration

1108 Transliteration of names and addresses: permitted characters

(1) Names and addresses in a document delivered to the registrar must contain only letters, characters and symbols (including accents and other diacritical marks) that are permitted.

(2) The Secretary of State may make provision by regulations—

(a) as to the letters, characters and symbols (including accents and other diacritical marks) that are permitted, and

(b) permitting or requiring the delivery of documents in which names and addresses have not been transliterated into a permitted form.

(3) Regulations under this section are subject to negative resolution procedure.

[2059]

NOTES

Commencement: to be appointed (see the introductory note to this Act).

1109 Transliteration of names and addresses: voluntary transliteration into Roman characters

(1) Where a name or address is or has been delivered to the registrar in a permitted form using other than Roman characters, the company may deliver to the registrar a transliteration into Roman characters.

(2) The power of the registrar to impose requirements as to the form and manner of delivery includes power to impose requirements as to the identification of the original document and the delivery of the transliteration in a form and manner enabling it to be associated with the original.

[2060]

NOTES

Commencement: to be appointed (see the introductory note to this Act).

1110 Transliteration of names and addresses: certification

(1) The Secretary of State may make provision by regulations requiring the certification of transliterations and prescribing the form of certification.

(2) Different provision may be made for compulsory and voluntary transliterations.

(3) Regulations under this section are subject to negative resolution procedure.

[2061]

NOTES

Commencement: to be appointed (see the introductory note to this Act).

Supplementary provisions

1111 Registrar's requirements as to certification or verification

(1) Where a document required or authorised to be delivered to the registrar under any enactment is required—

(a) to be certified as an accurate translation or transliteration, or

(b) to be certified as a correct copy or verified,

the registrar may impose requirements as to the person, or description of person, by whom the certificate or verification is to be given.

(2) The power conferred by section 1068 (registrar's requirements as to form, authentication and manner of delivery) is exercisable in relation to the certificate or verification as if it were a separate document.

(3) Requirements imposed under this section must not be inconsistent with requirements imposed by any enactment with respect to the certification or verification of the document concerned.

[2062]

NOTES

Commencement: 1 January 2007.

1112 General false statement offence

(1) It is an offence for a person knowingly or recklessly—

(a) to deliver or cause to be delivered to the registrar, for any purpose of the Companies Acts, a document, or

(b) to make to the registrar, for any such purpose, a statement,

that is misleading, false or deceptive in a material particular.

(2) A person guilty of an offence under this section is liable—

(a) on conviction on indictment, to imprisonment for a term not exceeding two years or a fine (or both);

(b) on summary conviction—

(i) in England and Wales, to imprisonment for a term not exceeding twelve months or to a fine not exceeding the statutory maximum (or both);

(ii) in Scotland or Northern Ireland, to imprisonment for a term not exceeding six months, or to a fine not exceeding the statutory maximum (or both).

[2063]

NOTES

Commencement: to be appointed (see the introductory note to this Act).

1113 Enforcement of company's filing obligations

(1) This section applies where a company has made default in complying with any obligation under the Companies Acts—

(a) to deliver a document to the registrar, or

(b) to give notice to the registrar of any matter.

(2) The registrar, or any member or creditor of the company, may give notice to the company requiring it to comply with the obligation.

(3) If the company fails to make good the default within 14 days after service of the notice, the registrar, or any member or creditor of the company, may apply to the court for an order directing the company, and any specified officer of it, to make good the default within a specified time.

(4) The court's order may provide that all costs (in Scotland, expenses) of or incidental to the application are to be borne by the company or by any officers of it responsible for the default.

(5) This section does not affect the operation of any enactment making it an offence, or imposing a civil penalty, for the default.

[2064]

NOTES

Commencement: to be appointed (see the introductory note to this Act).

1114 Application of provisions about documents and delivery

(1) In this Part—

(a) "document" means information recorded in any form, and

(b) references to delivering a document include forwarding, lodging, registering, sending, producing or submitting it or (in the case of a notice) giving it.

(2) Except as otherwise provided, this Part applies in relation to the supply to the registrar of information otherwise than in documentary form as it applies in relation to the delivery of a document.

[2065]

NOTES

Commencement: 1 January 2007 (certain purposes); to be appointed (otherwise) (see the note below and the introductory note to this Act).

Note: the Companies Act 2006 (Commencement No 1, Transitional Provisions and Savings) Order 2006, SI 2006/3428, art 2(2) provides that this section shall come into force on 1 January 2007 in so far as is necessary for the purposes of the provisions mentioned in art 2(1) of that Order. Those provisions are: ss 1068(5), 1077–1080, 1085–1092, 1102–1107, 1111.

1115 Supplementary provisions relating to electronic communications

(1) Registrar's rules may require a company to give any necessary consents to the use of electronic means for communications by the registrar to the company as a condition of making use of any facility to deliver material to the registrar by electronic means.

(2) A document that is required to be signed by the registrar or authenticated by the registrar's seal shall, if sent by electronic means, be authenticated in such manner as may be specified by registrar's rules.

[2066]

NOTES

Commencement: to be appointed (see the introductory note to this Act).

1116 Alternative to publication in the Gazette

(1) Notices that would otherwise need to be published by the registrar in the Gazette may instead be published by such means as may from time to time be approved by the registrar in accordance with regulations made by the Secretary of State.

(2) The Secretary of State may make provision by regulations as to what alternative means may be approved.

(3) The regulations may, in particular—

(a) require the use of electronic means;

(b) require the same means to be used—

(i) for all notices or for all notices of specified descriptions, and

(ii) whether the company is registered in England and Wales, Scotland or Northern Ireland;

(c) impose conditions as to the manner in which access to the notices is to be made available.

(4) Regulations under this section are subject to negative resolution procedure.

(5) Before starting to publish notices by means approved under this section the registrar must publish at least one notice to that effect in the Gazette.

(6) Nothing in this section prevents the registrar from giving public notice both in the Gazette and by means approved under this section.

In that case, the requirement of public notice is met when notice is first given by either means.

[2067]

NOTES

Commencement: to be appointed (see the introductory note to this Act).

1117 Registrar's rules

(1) Where any provision of this Part enables the registrar to make provision, or impose requirements, as to any matter, the registrar may make such provision or impose such requirements by means of rules under this section.

This is without prejudice to the making of such provision or the imposing of such requirements by other means.

(2) Registrar's rules—
- (a) may make different provision for different cases, and
- (b) may allow the registrar to disapply or modify any of the rules.

(3) The registrar must—
- (a) publicise the rules in a manner appropriate to bring them to the notice of persons affected by them, and
- (b) make copies of the rules available to the public (in hard copy or electronic form).

[2068]

NOTES

Commencement: 1 January 2007 (certain purposes); to be appointed (otherwise) (see the note below and the introductory note to this Act).

Note: the Companies Act 2006 (Commencement No 1, Transitional Provisions and Savings) Order 2006, SI 2006/3428, art 2(2) provides that this section shall come into force on 1 January 2007 in so far as is necessary for the purposes of the provisions mentioned in art 2(1) of that Order. Those provisions are: ss 1068(5), 1077–1080, 1085–1092, 1102–1107, 1111.

1118 Payments into the Consolidated Fund

Nothing in the Companies Acts or any other enactment as to the payment of receipts into the Consolidated Fund shall be read as affecting the operation in relation to the registrar of section 3(1) of the Government Trading Funds Act 1973 (c 63).

[2069]

NOTES

Commencement: to be appointed (see the introductory note to this Act).

1119 Contracting out of registrar's functions

(1) Where by virtue of an order made under section 69 of the Deregulation and Contracting Out Act 1994 (c 40) a person is authorised by the registrar to accept delivery of any class of documents that are under any enactment to be delivered to the registrar, the registrar may direct that documents of that class shall be delivered to a specified address of the authorised person.

Any such direction must be printed and made available to the public (with or without payment).

(2) A document of that class that is delivered to an address other than the specified address is treated as not having been delivered.

(3) Registrar's rules are not subordinate legislation for the purposes of section 71 of the Deregulation and Contracting Out Act 1994 (functions excluded from contracting out).

[2070]

NOTES

Commencement: to be appointed (see the introductory note to this Act).

1120 Application of this Part to overseas companies

Unless the context otherwise requires, the provisions of this Part apply to an overseas company as they apply to a company as defined in section 1.

[2071]

NOTES

Commencement: 1 January 2007 (certain purposes); to be appointed (otherwise) (see the note below and the introductory note to this Act).

Note: the Companies Act 2006 (Commencement No 1, Transitional Provisions and Savings) Order 2006, SI 2006/3428, art 2(2) provides that this section shall come into force on 1 January 2007 in so far as is necessary for the purposes of the provisions mentioned in art 2(1) of that Order. Those provisions are: ss 1068(5), 1077–1080, 1085–1092, 1102–1107, 1111.

Transitional adaptations: art 5 of the Companies Act 2006 (Commencement No 1, Transitional Provisions and Savings) Order 2006, SI 2006/3428 provides that the provisions brought into force by arts 2–4 of 2006 Order shall have effect subject to any transitional adaptations specified in Sch 1 to that Order. Schedule 1, para 13 to the Order provides as follows—

13.—(1) Section 1120 (application of Part 35 to overseas companies) has effect with the following adaptations.

(2) For "an overseas company" substitute "an oversea company (as defined in section 744 of the Companies Act 1985) or a Part 23 company (as defined in Article 640 of the Companies (Northern Ireland) Order 1986)".

(3) For "a company as defined in section 1" substitute "a company as defined in section 735(1) of that Act or Article 3(1) of that Order".

PART 36
OFFENCES UNDER THE COMPANIES ACTS

Liability of officer in default

1121 Liability of officer in default

(1) This section has effect for the purposes of any provision of the Companies Acts to the effect that, in the event of contravention of an enactment in relation to a company, an offence is committed by every officer of the company who is in default.

(2) For this purpose "officer" includes—
- (a) any director, manager or secretary, and
- (b) any person who is to be treated as an officer of the company for the purposes of the provision in question.

(3) An officer is "in default" for the purposes of the provision if he authorises or permits, participates in, or fails to take all reasonable steps to prevent, the contravention.

[2072]

NOTES

Commencement: 20 January 2007 (certain purposes); to be appointed (otherwise) (see the note below and the introductory note to this Act).

Note: the Companies Act 2006 (Commencement No 1, Transitional Provisions and Savings) Order 2006, SI 2006/3428, art 3(2) provides that this section shall come into force on 20 January 2007 in so far as is necessary for the purposes of the provisions mentioned in art 3(1) of that Order. Those provisions are: ss 308, 309, 333, 463, 791–810, 811(1)–(3), 813, 815–828, 1143–1148 and Schs 4 and 5.

1122 Liability of company as officer in default

(1) Where a company is an officer of another company, it does not commit an offence as an officer in default unless one of its officers is in default.

(2) Where any such offence is committed by a company the officer in question also commits the offence and is liable to be proceeded against and punished accordingly.

(3) In this section "officer" and "in default" have the meanings given by section 1121.

[2073]

NOTES

Commencement: 20 January 2007 (certain purposes); to be appointed (otherwise) (see the note below and the introductory note to this Act).

Note: the Companies Act 2006 (Commencement No 1, Transitional Provisions and Savings) Order 2006, SI 2006/3428, art 3(2) provides that this section shall come into force on 20 January 2007 in so far as is necessary for the purposes of the provisions mentioned in art 3(1) of that Order. Those provisions are: ss 308, 309, 333, 463, 791–810, 811(1)–(3), 813, 815–828, 1143–1148 and Schs 4 and 5.

1123 Application to bodies other than companies

(1) Section 1121 (liability of officers in default) applies to a body other than a company as it applies to a company.

(2) As it applies in relation to a body corporate other than a company—
- (a) the reference to a director of the company shall be read as referring—
  - (i) where the body's affairs are managed by its members, to a member of the body,
  - (ii) in any other case, to any corresponding officer of the body, and
- (b) the reference to a manager or secretary of the company shall be read as referring to any manager, secretary or similar officer of the body.

(3) As it applies in relation to a partnership—
- (a) the reference to a director of the company shall be read as referring to a member of the partnership, and
- (b) the reference to a manager or secretary of the company shall be read as referring to any manager, secretary or similar officer of the partnership.

(4) As it applies in relation to an unincorporated body other than a partnership—
- (a) the reference to a director of the company shall be read as referring—
  - (i) where the body's affairs are managed by its members, to a member of the body,
  - (ii) in any other case, to a member of the governing body, and
- (b) the reference to a manager or secretary of the company shall be read as referring to any manager, secretary or similar officer of the body.

[2074]

NOTES

Commencement: to be appointed (see the introductory note to this Act).

Offences under the Companies Act 1985

1124 Amendments of the Companies Act 1985

Schedule 3 contains amendments of the Companies Act 1985 (c 6) relating to offences.

[2075]

NOTES

Commencement: to be appointed (see the introductory note to this Act).

1125–1133 (*Outside the scope of this work.*)

PART 37
COMPANIES: SUPPLEMENTARY PROVISIONS

Company records

1134 Meaning of "company records"

In this Part "company records" means—
- (a) any register, index, accounting records, agreement, memorandum, minutes or other document required by the Companies Acts to be kept by a company, and
- (b) any register kept by a company of its debenture holders.

[2076]

NOTES

Commencement: to be appointed (see the introductory note to this Act).

1135 Form of company records

(1) Company records—

(a) may be kept in hard copy or electronic form, and

(b) may be arranged in such manner as the directors of the company think fit,

provided the information in question is adequately recorded for future reference.

(2) Where the records are kept in electronic form, they must be capable of being reproduced in hard copy form.

(3) If a company fails to comply with this section, an offence is committed by every officer of the company who is in default.

(4) A person guilty of an offence under this section is liable on summary conviction to a fine not exceeding level 3 on the standard scale and, for continued contravention, a daily default fine not exceeding one-tenth of level 3 on the standard scale.

(5) Any provision of an instrument made by a company before 12th February 1979 that requires a register of holders of the company's debentures to be kept in hard copy form is to be read as requiring it to be kept in hard copy or electronic form.

[2077]

NOTES

Commencement: to be appointed (see the introductory note to this Act).

1136 Regulations about where certain company records to be kept available for inspection

(1) The Secretary of State may make provision by regulations specifying places other than a company's registered office at which company records required to be kept available for inspection under a relevant provision may be so kept in compliance with that provision.

(2) The "relevant provisions" are—

section 114 (register of members);
section 162 (register of directors);
section 228 (directors' service contracts);
section 237 (directors' indemnities);
section 275 (register of secretaries);
section 358 (records of resolutions etc);
section 702 (contracts relating to purchase of own shares);
section 720 (documents relating to redemption or purchase of own shares out of capital by private company);
section 743 (register of debenture holders);
section 805 (report to members of outcome of investigation by public company into interests in its shares);
section 809 (register of interests in shares disclosed to public company);
section 877 (instruments creating charges and register of charges: England and Wales);
section 892 (instruments creating charges and register of charges: Scotland).

(3) The regulations may specify a place by reference to the company's principal place of business, the part of the United Kingdom in which the company is registered, the place at which the company keeps any other records available for inspection or in any other way.

(4) The regulations may provide that a company does not comply with a relevant provision by keeping company records available for inspection at a place specified in the regulations unless conditions specified in the regulations are met.

(5) The regulations—

(a) need not specify a place in relation to each relevant provision;

(b) may specify more than one place in relation to a relevant provision.

(6) A requirement under a relevant provision to keep company records available for inspection is not complied with by keeping them available for inspection at a place specified in the regulations unless all the company's records subject to the requirement are kept there.

(7) Regulations under this section are subject to negative resolution procedure.

[2078]

NOTES

Commencement: to be appointed (see the introductory note to this Act).

1137 Regulations about inspection of records and provision of copies

(1) The Secretary of State may make provision by regulations as to the obligations of a company that is required by any provision of the Companies Acts—

(a) to keep available for inspection any company records, or

(b) to provide copies of any company records.

(2) A company that fails to comply with the regulations is treated as having refused inspection or, as the case may be, having failed to provide a copy.

(3) The regulations may—

(a) make provision as to the time, duration and manner of inspection, including the circumstances in which and extent to which the copying of information is permitted in the course of inspection, and

(b) define what may be required of the company as regards the nature, extent and manner of extracting or presenting any information for the purposes of inspection or the provision of copies.

(4) Where there is power to charge a fee, the regulations may make provision as to the amount of the fee and the basis of its calculation.

(5) Nothing in any provision of this Act or in the regulations shall be read as preventing a company—

(a) from affording more extensive facilities than are required by the regulations, or

(b) where a fee may be charged, from charging a lesser fee than that prescribed or none at all.

(6) Regulations under this section are subject to negative resolution procedure.

[2079]

NOTES

Commencement: to be appointed (see the introductory note to this Act).

1138 Duty to take precautions against falsification

(1) Where company records are kept otherwise than in bound books, adequate precautions must be taken—

(a) to guard against falsification, and

(b) to facilitate the discovery of falsification.

(2) If a company fails to comply with this section, an offence is committed by every officer of the company who is in default.

(3) A person guilty of an offence under this section is liable on summary conviction to a fine not exceeding level 3 on the standard scale and, for continued contravention, a daily default fine not exceeding one-tenth of level 3 on the standard scale.

(4) This section does not apply to the documents required to be kept under—

(a) section 228 (copy of director's service contract or memorandum of its terms); or

(b) section 237 (qualifying indemnity provision).

[2080]

NOTES

Commencement: to be appointed (see the introductory note to this Act).

Service addresses

1139 Service of documents on company

(1) A document may be served on a company registered under this Act by leaving it at, or sending it by post to, the company's registered office.

(2) A document may be served on an overseas company whose particulars are registered under section 1046—

(a) by leaving it at, or sending it by post to, the registered address of any person resident in the United Kingdom who is authorised to accept service of documents on the company's behalf, or

(b) if there is no such person, or if any such person refuses service or service cannot for any other reason be effected, by leaving it at or sending by post to any place of business of the company in the United Kingdom.

(3) For the purposes of this section a person's "registered address" means any address for the time being shown as a current address in relation to that person in the part of the register available for public inspection.

(4) Where a company registered in Scotland or Northern Ireland carries on business in England and Wales, the process of any court in England and Wales may be served on the company by leaving it at, or sending it by post to, the company's principal place of business in England and Wales, addressed to the manager or other head officer in England and Wales of the company.

Where process is served on a company under this subsection, the person issuing out the process must send a copy of it by post to the company's registered office.

(5) Further provision as to service and other matters is made in the company communications provisions (see section 1143).

[2081]

NOTES

Commencement: to be appointed (see the introductory note to this Act).

1140 Service of documents on directors, secretaries and others

(1) A document may be served on a person to whom this section applies by leaving it at, or sending it by post to, the person's registered address.

(2) This section applies to—

(a) a director or secretary of a company;

(b) in the case of an overseas company whose particulars are registered under section 1046, a person holding any such position as may be specified for the purposes of this section by regulations under that section;

(c) a person appointed in relation to a company as—

(i) a judicial factor (in Scotland),

(ii) a receiver and manager appointed under section 18 of the Charities Act 1993 (c 10), or

(iii) a manager appointed under section 47 of the Companies (Audit, Investigations and Community Enterprise) Act 2004 (c 27).

(3) This section applies whatever the purpose of the document in question.

It is not restricted to service for purposes arising out of or in connection with the appointment or position mentioned in subsection (2) or in connection with the company concerned.

(4) For the purposes of this section a person's "registered address" means any address for the time being shown as a current address in relation to that person in the part of the register available for public inspection.

(5) If notice of a change of that address is given to the registrar, a person may validly serve a document at the address previously registered until the end of the period of 14 days beginning with the date on which notice of the change is registered.

(6) Service may not be effected by virtue of this section at an address—

(a) if notice has been registered of the termination of the appointment in relation to which the address was registered and the address is not a registered address of the person concerned in relation to any other appointment;

(b) in the case of a person holding any such position as is mentioned in subsection (2)(b), if the overseas company has ceased to have any connection with the United Kingdom by virtue of which it is required to register particulars under section 1046.

(7) Further provision as to service and other matters is made in the company communications provisions (see section 1143).

(8) Nothing in this section shall be read as affecting any enactment or rule of law under which permission is required for service out of the jurisdiction.

[2082]

NOTES

Commencement: to be appointed (see the introductory note to this Act).

1141 Service addresses

(1) In the Companies Acts a "service address", in relation to a person, means an address at which documents may be effectively served on that person.

(2) The Secretary of State may by regulations specify conditions with which a service address must comply.

(3) Regulations under this section are subject to negative resolution procedure.

[2083]

NOTES

Commencement: to be appointed (see the introductory note to this Act).

1142 Requirement to give service address

Any obligation under the Companies Acts to give a person's address is, unless otherwise expressly provided, to give a service address for that person.

[2084]

NOTES

Commencement: to be appointed (see the introductory note to this Act).

Sending or supplying documents or information

1143 The company communications provisions

(1) The provisions of sections 1144 to 1148 and Schedules 4 and 5 ("the company communications provisions") have effect for the purposes of any provision of the Companies Acts that authorises or requires documents or information to be sent or supplied by or to a company.

(2) The company communications provisions have effect subject to any requirements imposed, or contrary provision made, by or under any enactment.

(3) In particular, in their application in relation to documents or information to be sent or supplied to the registrar, they have effect subject to the provisions of Part 35.

(4) For the purposes of subsection (2), provision is not to be regarded as contrary to the company communications provisions by reason only of the fact that it expressly authorises a document or information to be sent or supplied in hard copy form, in electronic form or by means of a website.

[2085]

NOTES

Commencement: 20 January 2007.

Transitional adaptations: art 5 of the Companies Act 2006 (Commencement No 1, Transitional Provisions and Savings) Order 2006, SI 2006/3428 provides that the provisions brought into force by arts 2–4 of 2006 Order shall have effect subject to any transitional adaptations specified in Sch 1 to that Order. Schedule 1, para 14 to the Order provides as follows—

14 The company communications provisions

(1) Section 1143 (the company communications provisions) has effect with the following adaptation.

(2) In subsection (3), after "Part 35" insert "and, to the extent that they remain in force, Part 24 of the Companies Act 1985 and Part 24 of the Companies (Northern Ireland) Order 1986".

1144 Sending or supplying documents or information

(1) Documents or information to be sent or supplied to a company must be sent or supplied in accordance with the provisions of Schedule 4.

(2) Documents or information to be sent or supplied by a company must be sent or supplied in accordance with the provisions of Schedule 5.

(3) The provisions referred to in subsection (2) apply (and those referred to in subsection (1) do not apply) in relation to documents or information that are to be sent or supplied by one company to another.

[2086]

NOTES

Commencement: 20 January 2007.

1145 Right to hard copy version

(1) Where a member of a company or a holder of a company's debentures has received a document or information from the company otherwise than in hard copy form, he is entitled to require the company to send him a version of the document or information in hard copy form.

(2) The company must send the document or information in hard copy form within 21 days of receipt of the request from the member or debenture holder.

(3) The company may not make a charge for providing the document or information in that form.

(4) If a company fails to comply with this section, an offence is committed by the company and every officer of it who is in default.

(5) A person guilty of an offence under this section is liable on summary conviction to a fine not exceeding level 3 on the standard scale and, for continued contravention, a daily default fine not exceeding one-tenth of level 3 on the standard scale.

[2087]

NOTES

Commencement: 20 January 2007.

1146 Requirement of authentication

(1) This section applies in relation to the authentication of a document or information sent or supplied by a person to a company.

(2) A document or information sent or supplied in hard copy form is sufficiently authenticated if it is signed by the person sending or supplying it.

(3) A document or information sent or supplied in electronic form is sufficiently authenticated—

(a) if the identity of the sender is confirmed in a manner specified by the company, or

(b) where no such manner has been specified by the company, if the communication contains or is accompanied by a statement of the

identity of the sender and the company has no reason to doubt the truth of that statement.

(4) Where a document or information is sent or supplied by one person on behalf of another, nothing in this section affects any provision of the company's articles under which the company may require reasonable evidence of the authority of the former to act on behalf of the latter.

[2088]

NOTES

Commencement: 20 January 2007.

1147 Deemed delivery of documents and information

(1) This section applies in relation to documents and information sent or supplied by a company.

(2) Where—
(a) the document or information is sent by post (whether in hard copy or electronic form) to an address in the United Kingdom, and
(b) the company is able to show that it was properly addressed, prepaid and posted,

it is deemed to have been received by the intended recipient 48 hours after it was posted.

(3) Where—
(a) the document or information is sent or supplied by electronic means, and
(b) the company is able to show that it was properly addressed,

it is deemed to have been received by the intended recipient 48 hours after it was sent.

(4) Where the document or information is sent or supplied by means of a website, it is deemed to have been received by the intended recipient—
(a) when the material was first made available on the website, or
(b) if later, when the recipient received (or is deemed to have received) notice of the fact that the material was available on the website.

(5) In calculating a period of hours for the purposes of this section, no account shall be taken of any part of a day that is not a working day.

(6) This section has effect subject to—
(a) in its application to documents or information sent or supplied by a company to its members, any contrary provision of the company's articles;
(b) in its application to documents or information sent or supplied by a company to its debentures holders, any contrary provision in the instrument constituting the debentures;
(c) in its application to documents or information sent or supplied by a company to a person otherwise than in his capacity as a member or debenture holder, any contrary provision in an agreement between the company and that person.

[2089]

NOTES

Commencement: 20 January 2007.

1148 Interpretation of company communications provisions

(1) In the company communications provisions—

"address" includes a number or address used for the purposes of sending or receiving documents or information by electronic means;

"company" includes any body corporate;

"document" includes summons, notice, order or other legal process and registers.

(2) References in the company communications provisions to provisions of the Companies Acts authorising or requiring a document or information to be sent or supplied include all such provisions, whatever expression is used, and references to documents or information being sent or supplied shall be construed accordingly.

(3) References in the company communications provisions to documents or information being sent or supplied by or to a company include references to documents or information being sent or supplied by or to the directors of a company acting on behalf of the company.

[2090]

NOTES

Commencement: 20 January 2007.

1149–1157 (*Outside the scope of this work.*)

PART 38
COMPANIES: INTERPRETATION

Meaning of "UK-registered company"

1158 Meaning of "UK-registered company"

In the Companies Acts "UK-registered company" means a company registered under this Act.

The expression does not include an overseas company that has registered particulars under section 1046.

[2091]

NOTES

Commencement: to be appointed (see the introductory note to this Act).

Meaning of "subsidiary" and related expressions

1159 Meaning of "subsidiary" etc

(1) A company is a "subsidiary" of another company, its "holding company", if that other company—

(a) holds a majority of the voting rights in it, or

(b) is a member of it and has the right to appoint or remove a majority of its board of directors, or

(c) is a member of it and controls alone, pursuant to an agreement with other members, a majority of the voting rights in it,

or if it is a subsidiary of a company that is itself a subsidiary of that other company.

(2) A company is a "wholly-owned subsidiary" of another company if it has no members except that other and that other's wholly-owned subsidiaries or persons acting on behalf of that other or its wholly-owned subsidiaries.

(3) Schedule 6 contains provisions explaining expressions used in this section and otherwise supplementing this section.

(4) In this section and that Schedule "company" includes any body corporate.

[2092]

NOTES

Commencement: to be appointed (see the introductory note to this Act).

1160 Meaning of "subsidiary" etc: power to amend

(1) The Secretary of State may by regulations amend the provisions of section 1159 (meaning of "subsidiary" etc) and Schedule 6 (meaning of "subsidiary" etc: supplementary provisions) so as to alter the meaning of the expressions "subsidiary", "holding company" or "wholly-owned subsidiary".

(2) Regulations under this section are subject to negative resolution procedure.

(3) Any amendment made by regulations under this section does not apply for the purposes of enactments outside the Companies Acts unless the regulations so provide.

(4) So much of section 23(3) of the Interpretation Act 1978 (c 30) as applies section 17(2)(a) of that Act (effect of repeal and re-enactment) to deeds, instruments and documents other than enactments does not apply in relation to any repeal and re-enactment effected by regulations under this section.

[2093]

NOTES

Commencement: to be appointed (see the introductory note to this Act).

Meaning of "undertaking" and related expressions

1161 Meaning of "undertaking" and related expressions

(1) In the Companies Acts "undertaking" means—

(a) a body corporate or partnership, or

(b) an unincorporated association carrying on a trade or business, with or without a view to profit.

(2) In the Companies Acts references to shares—

(a) in relation to an undertaking with capital but no share capital, are to rights to share in the capital of the undertaking; and
(b) in relation to an undertaking without capital, are to interests—
  (i) conferring any right to share in the profits or liability to contribute to the losses of the undertaking, or
  (ii) giving rise to an obligation to contribute to the debts or expenses of the undertaking in the event of a winding up.

(3) Other expressions appropriate to companies shall be construed, in relation to an undertaking which is not a company, as references to the corresponding persons, officers, documents or organs, as the case may be, appropriate to undertakings of that description.

This is subject to provision in any specific context providing for the translation of such expressions.

(4) References in the Companies Acts to "fellow subsidiary undertakings" are to undertakings which are subsidiary undertakings of the same parent undertaking but are not parent undertakings or subsidiary undertakings of each other.

(5) In the Companies Acts "group undertaking", in relation to an undertaking, means an undertaking which is—
(a) a parent undertaking or subsidiary undertaking of that undertaking, or
(b) a subsidiary undertaking of any parent undertaking of that undertaking.

[2094]

NOTES

Commencement: to be appointed (see the introductory note to this Act).

1162 Parent and subsidiary undertakings

(1) This section (together with Schedule 7) defines "parent undertaking" and "subsidiary undertaking" for the purposes of the Companies Acts.

(2) An undertaking is a parent undertaking in relation to another undertaking, a subsidiary undertaking, if—
(a) it holds a majority of the voting rights in the undertaking, or
(b) it is a member of the undertaking and has the right to appoint or remove a majority of its board of directors, or
(c) it has the right to exercise a dominant influence over the undertaking—
  (i) by virtue of provisions contained in the undertaking's articles, or
  (ii) by virtue of a control contract, or
(d) it is a member of the undertaking and controls alone, pursuant to an agreement with other shareholders or members, a majority of the voting rights in the undertaking.

(3) For the purposes of subsection (2) an undertaking shall be treated as a member of another undertaking—
(a) if any of its subsidiary undertakings is a member of that undertaking, or
(b) if any shares in that other undertaking are held by a person acting on behalf of the undertaking or any of its subsidiary undertakings.

(4) An undertaking is also a parent undertaking in relation to another undertaking, a subsidiary undertaking, if—
(a) it has the power to exercise, or actually exercises, dominant influence or control over it, or
(b) it and the subsidiary undertaking are managed on a unified basis.

(5) A parent undertaking shall be treated as the parent undertaking of undertakings in relation to which any of its subsidiary undertakings are, or are to be treated as, parent undertakings; and references to its subsidiary undertakings shall be construed accordingly.

(6) Schedule 7 contains provisions explaining expressions used in this section and otherwise supplementing this section.

(7) In this section and that Schedule references to shares, in relation to an undertaking, are to allotted shares.

[2095]

NOTES

Commencement: to be appointed (see the introductory note to this Act).

Other definitions

1163 "Non-cash asset"

(1) In the Companies Acts "non-cash asset" means any property or interest in property, other than cash.

For this purpose "cash" includes foreign currency.

(2) A reference to the transfer or acquisition of a non-cash asset includes—

(a) the creation or extinction of an estate or interest in, or a right over, any property, and

(b) the discharge of a liability of any person, other than a liability for a liquidated sum.

[2096]

NOTES

Commencement: to be appointed (see the introductory note to this Act).

1164–1166 (*Outside the scope of this work.*)

1167 Meaning of "prescribed"

In the Companies Acts "prescribed" means prescribed (by order or by regulations) by the Secretary of State.

[2097]

NOTES

Commencement: to be appointed (see the introductory note to this Act).

1168 Hard copy and electronic form and related expressions

(1) The following provisions apply for the purposes of the Companies Acts.

(2) A document or information is sent or supplied in hard copy form if it is sent or supplied in a paper copy or similar form capable of being read.

References to hard copy have a corresponding meaning.

(3) A document or information is sent or supplied in electronic form if it is sent or supplied—

(a) by electronic means (for example, by e-mail or fax), or

(b) by any other means while in an electronic form (for example, sending a disk by post).

References to electronic copy have a corresponding meaning.

(4) A document or information is sent or supplied by electronic means if it is—

(a) sent initially and received at its destination by means of electronic equipment for the processing (which expression includes digital compression) or storage of data, and

(b) entirely transmitted, conveyed and received by wire, by radio, by optical means or by other electromagnetic means.

References to electronic means have a corresponding meaning.

(5) A document or information authorised or required to be sent or supplied in electronic form must be sent or supplied in a form, and by a means, that the sender or supplier reasonably considers will enable the recipient—

(a) to read it, and

(b) to retain a copy of it.

(6) For the purposes of this section, a document or information can be read only if—

(a) it can be read with the naked eye, or
(b) to the extent that it consists of images (for example photographs, pictures, maps, plans or drawings), it can be seen with the naked eye.

(7) The provisions of this section apply whether the provision of the Companies Acts in question uses the words "sent" or "supplied" or uses other words (such as "deliver", "provide", "produce" or, in the case of a notice, "give") to refer to the sending or supplying of a document or information.

[2098]

NOTES

Commencement: 1 January 2007 (certain purposes); 20 January 2007 (certain purposes); to be appointed (otherwise) (see the notes below and the introductory note to this Act).

Note: the Companies Act 2006 (Commencement No 1, Transitional Provisions and Savings) Order 2006, SI 2006/3428, art 2(2) provides that this section shall come into force on 1 January 2007 in so far as is necessary for the purposes of the provisions mentioned in art 2(1) of that Order. Those provisions are: ss 1068(5), 1077–1080, 1085–1092, 1102–1107, 1111. Article 3(2) of the 2006 Order further provides that this section shall come into force on 20 January 2007 in so far as is necessary for the purposes of the provisions mentioned in art 3(1) of that Order. Those provisions are: ss 308, 309, 333, 463, 791–810, 811(1)–(3), 813, 815–828, 1143–1148 and Schs 4 and 5.

1169 Dormant companies

(1) For the purposes of the Companies Acts a company is "dormant" during any period in which it has no significant accounting transaction.

(2) A "significant accounting transaction" means a transaction that is required by section 386 to be entered in the company's accounting records.

(3) In determining whether or when a company is dormant, there shall be disregarded—
(a) any transaction arising from the taking of shares in the company by a subscriber to the memorandum as a result of an undertaking of his in connection with the formation of the company;
(b) any transaction consisting of the payment of—
(i) a fee to the registrar on a change of the company's name,
(ii) a fee to the registrar on the re-registration of the company,
(iii) a penalty under section 453 (penalty for failure to file accounts), or
(iv) a fee to the registrar for the registration of an annual return.

(4) Any reference in the Companies Acts to a body corporate other than a company being dormant has a corresponding meaning.

[2099]

NOTES

Commencement: to be appointed (see the introductory note to this Act).

1170 Meaning of "EEA State" and related expressions

In the Companies Acts—

"EEA State" means a state which is a Contracting Party to the Agreement on the European Economic Area signed at Oporto on 2nd May 1992 (as it has effect from time to time);

"EEA company" and "EEA undertaking" mean a company or undertaking governed by the law of an EEA State.

[2100]

NOTES

Commencement: to be appointed (see the introductory note to this Act).

1171 The former Companies Acts

In the Companies Acts—

"the former Companies Acts" means—
(a) the Joint Stock Companies Acts, the Companies Act 1862 (c 89), the Companies (Consolidation) Act 1908 (c 69), the Companies Act 1929 (c 23), the Companies Act (Northern Ireland) 1932 (c 7 (NI)), the

Companies Acts 1948 to 1983, the Companies Act (Northern Ireland) 1960 (c 22 (NI)), the Companies (Northern Ireland) Order 1986 (SI 1986/1032 (NI 6)) and the Companies Consolidation (Consequential Provisions) (Northern Ireland) Order 1986 (SI 1986/1035 (NI 9)), and

(b) the provisions of the Companies Act 1985 (c 6) and the Companies Consolidation (Consequential Provisions) Act 1985 (c 9) that are no longer in force;

"the Joint Stock Companies Acts" means the Joint Stock Companies Act 1856 (c 47), the Joint Stock Companies Acts 1856, 1857 (20 & 21 Vict c 14), the Joint Stock Banking Companies Act 1857 (c 49), and the Act to enable Joint Stock Banking Companies to be formed on the principle of limited liability (1858 c 91), but does not include the Joint Stock Companies Act 1844 (c 110).

[2101]

NOTES

Commencement: to be appointed (see the introductory note to this Act).

General

1172 References to requirements of this Act

References in the company law provisions of this Act to the requirements of this Act include the requirements of regulations and orders made under it.

[2102]

NOTES

Commencement: to be appointed (see the introductory note to this Act).

1173 Minor definitions: general

(1) In the Companies Acts—

"body corporate" and "corporation" include a body incorporated outside the United Kingdom, but do not include—

(a) a corporation sole, or

(b) a partnership that, whether or not a legal person, is not regarded as a body corporate under the law by which it is governed;

"credit institution" means a credit institution as defined in Article 4.1(a) of Directive 2006/48/EC of the European Parliament and of the Council relating to the taking up and pursuit of the business of credit institutions;

"financial institution" means a financial institution within the meaning of Article 1.1 of the Council Directive on the obligations of branches established in a Member State of credit and financial institutions having their head offices outside that Member State regarding the publication of annual accounting documents (the Bank Branches Directive, 89/ 117/EEC);

"firm" means any entity, whether or not a legal person, that is not an individual and includes a body corporate, a corporation sole and a partnership or other unincorporated association;

"the Gazette" means—

(a) as respects companies registered in England and Wales, the London Gazette,

(b) as respects companies registered in Scotland, the Edinburgh Gazette, and

(c) as respects companies registered in Northern Ireland, the Belfast Gazette;

"hire-purchase agreement" has the same meaning as in the Consumer Credit Act 1974 (c 39);

"officer", in relation to a body corporate, includes a director, manager or secretary;

"parent company" means a company that is a parent undertaking (see section 1162 and Schedule 7);

"regulated activity" has the meaning given in section 22 of the Financial Services and Markets Act 2000 (c 8);

"regulated market" has the same meaning as in Directive 2004/39/EC of the European Parliament and of the Council on markets in financial instruments (see Article 4.1(14));

"working day", in relation to a company, means a day that is not a Saturday or Sunday, Christmas Day, Good Friday or any day that is a bank holiday under the Banking and Financial Dealings Act 1971 (c 80) in the part of the United Kingdom where the company is registered.

(2) In relation to an EEA State that has not implemented Directive 2004/39/EC of the European Parliament and of the Council on markets in financial instruments, the following definition of "regulated market" has effect in place of that in subsection (1)—

"regulated market" has the same meaning as it has in Council Directive 93/22/EEC on investment services in the securities field.

[2103]

NOTES

Commencement: 1 January 2007 (certain purposes); 20 January 2007 (certain purposes); to be appointed (otherwise) (see the notes below and the introductory note to this Act).

Note: the Companies Act 2006 (Commencement No 1, Transitional Provisions and Savings) Order 2006, SI 2006/3428, art 2(2) provides that the definitions "Gazette" and "working day" shall come into force on 1 January 2007 in so far as is necessary for the purposes of the provisions mentioned in art 2(1) of that Order. Those provisions are: ss 1068(5), 1077–1080, 1085–1092, 1102–1107, 1111. Article 3(2) of the 2006 Order further provides that the definition "working day" shall come into force on 20 January 2007 in so far as is necessary for the purposes of the provisions mentioned in art 3(1) of that Order. Those provisions are: ss 308, 309, 333, 463, 791–810, 811(1)–(3), 813, 815–828, 1143–1148 and Schs 4 and 5.

1174 Index of defined expressions

Schedule 8 contains an index of provisions defining or otherwise explaining expressions used in the Companies Acts.

[2104]

NOTES

Commencement: to be appointed (see the introductory note to this Act).

PART 39
COMPANIES: MINOR AMENDMENTS

1175 Removal of special provisions about accounts and audit of charitable companies

(1) Part 7 of the Companies Act 1985 (c 6) and Part 8 of the Companies (Northern Ireland) Order 1986 (accounts and audit) are amended in accordance with Schedule 9 to this Act so as to remove the special provisions about companies that are charities.

(2) In that Schedule—

Part 1 contains repeals and consequential amendments of provisions of the Companies Act 1985;

Part 2 contains repeals and consequential amendments of provisions of the Companies (Northern Ireland) Order 1986.

[2105]

NOTES

Commencement: to be appointed (see the introductory note to this Act).

1176–1191 (*Outside the scope of this work.*)

PART 41
BUSINESS NAMES

CHAPTER 1
RESTRICTED OR PROHIBITED NAMES

Introductory

1192 Application of this Chapter

(1) This Chapter applies to any person carrying on business in the United Kingdom.

(2) The provisions of this Chapter do not prevent—

(a) an individual carrying on business under a name consisting of his surname without any addition other than a permitted addition, or

(b) individuals carrying on business in partnership under a name consisting of the surnames of all the partners without any addition other than a permitted addition.

(3) The following are the permitted additions—

(a) in the case of an individual, his forename or initial;

(b) in the case of a partnership—

(i) the forenames of individual partners or the initials of those forenames, or

(ii) where two or more individual partners have the same surname, the addition of "s" at the end of that surname;

(c) in either case, an addition merely indicating that the business is carried on in succession to a former owner of the business.

[2106]

NOTES

Commencement: to be appointed (see the introductory note to this Act).

Sensitive words or expressions

1193 Name suggesting connection with government or public authority

(1) A person must not, without the approval of the Secretary of State, carry on business in the United Kingdom under a name that would be likely to give the impression that the business is connected with—

(a) Her Majesty's Government, any part of the Scottish administration or Her Majesty's Government in Northern Ireland,

(b) any local authority, or

(c) any public authority specified for the purposes of this section by regulations made by the Secretary of State.

(2) For the purposes of this section—

"local authority" means—

(a) a local authority within the meaning of the Local Government Act 1972 (c 70), the Common Council of the City of London or the Council of the Isles of Scilly,

(b) a council constituted under section 2 of the Local Government etc (Scotland) Act 1994 (c 39), or

(c) a district council in Northern Ireland;

"public authority" includes any person or body having functions of a public nature.

(3) Regulations under this section are subject to affirmative resolution procedure.

(4) A person who contravenes this section commits an offence.

(5) Where an offence under this section is committed by a body corporate, an offence is also committed by every officer of the body who is in default.

(6) A person guilty of an offence under this section is liable on summary conviction to a fine not exceeding level 3 on the standard scale and, for continued contravention, a daily default fine not exceeding one-tenth of level 3 on the standard scale.

[2107]

NOTES

Commencement: to be appointed (see the introductory note to this Act).

1194 Other sensitive words or expressions

(1) A person must not, without the approval of the Secretary of State, carry on business in the United Kingdom under a name that includes a word or expression for the time being specified in regulations made by the Secretary of State under this section.

(2) Regulations under this section are subject to approval after being made.

(3) A person who contravenes this section commits an offence.

(4) Where an offence under this section is committed by a body corporate, an offence is also committed by every officer of the body who is in default.

(5) A person guilty of an offence under this section is liable on summary conviction to a fine not exceeding level 3 on the standard scale and, for continued contravention, a daily default fine not exceeding one-tenth of level 3 on the standard scale.

[2108]

NOTES

Commencement: to be appointed (see the introductory note to this Act).

1195 Requirement to seek comments of government department or other relevant body

(1) The Secretary of State may by regulations under—

(a) section 1193 (name suggesting connection with government or public authority), or

(b) section 1194 (other sensitive words or expressions),

require that, in connection with an application for the approval of the Secretary of State under that section, the applicant must seek the view of a specified Government department or other body.

(2) Where such a requirement applies, the applicant must request the specified department or other body (in writing) to indicate whether (and if so why) it has any objections to the proposed name.

(3) He must submit to the Secretary of State a statement that such a request has been made and a copy of any response received from the specified body.

(4) If these requirements are not complied with, the Secretary of State may refuse to consider the application for approval.

(5) In this section "specified" means specified in the regulations.

[2109]

NOTES

Commencement: to be appointed (see the introductory note to this Act).

1196 Withdrawal of Secretary of State's approval

(1) This section applies to approval given for the purposes of—

section 1193 (name suggesting connection with government or public authority), or
section 1194 (other sensitive words or expressions).

(2) If it appears to the Secretary of State that there are overriding considerations of public policy that require such approval to be withdrawn, the approval may be withdrawn by notice in writing given to the person concerned.

(3) The notice must state the date as from which approval is withdrawn.

[2110]

NOTES

Commencement: to be appointed (see the introductory note to this Act).

Misleading names

1197 Name containing inappropriate indication of company type or legal form

(1) The Secretary of State may make provision by regulations prohibiting a person from carrying on business in the United Kingdom under a name consisting of or containing specified words, expressions or other indications—

(a) that are associated with a particular type of company or form of organisation, or

(b) that are similar to words, expressions or other indications associated with a particular type of company or form of organisation.

(2) The regulations may prohibit the use of words, expressions or other indications—

(a) in a specified part, or otherwise than in a specified part, of a name;

(b) in conjunction with, or otherwise than in conjunction with, such other words, expressions or indications as may be specified.

(3) In this section "specified" means specified in the regulations.

(4) Regulations under this section are subject to negative resolution procedure.

(5) A person who uses a name in contravention of regulations under this section commits an offence.

(6) Where an offence under this section is committed by a body corporate, an offence is also committed by every officer of the body who is in default.

(7) A person guilty of an offence under this section is liable on summary conviction to a fine not exceeding level 3 on the standard scale and, for continued contravention, a daily default fine not exceeding one-tenth of level 3 on the standard scale.

[2111]

NOTES

Commencement: to be appointed (see the introductory note to this Act).

1198 Name giving misleading indication of activities

(1) A person must not carry on business in the United Kingdom under a name that gives so misleading an indication of the nature of the activities of the business as to be likely to cause harm to the public.

(2) A person who uses a name in contravention of this section commits an offence.

(3) Where an offence under this section is committed by a body corporate, an offence is also committed by every officer of the body who is in default.

(4) A person guilty of an offence under this section is liable on summary conviction to a fine not exceeding level 3 on the standard scale and, for continued contravention, a daily default fine not exceeding one-tenth of level 3 on the standard scale.

[2112]

NOTES

Commencement: to be appointed (see the introductory note to this Act).

Supplementary

1199 Savings for existing lawful business names

(1) This section has effect in relation to—

sections 1192 to 1196 (sensitive words or expressions), and

section 1197 (inappropriate indication of company type or legal form).

(2) Those sections do not apply to the carrying on of a business by a person who—

(a) carried on the business immediately before the date on which this Chapter came into force, and

(b) continues to carry it on under the name that immediately before that date was its lawful business name.

(3) Where—

(a) a business is transferred to a person on or after the date on which this Chapter came into force, and

(b) that person carries on the business under the name that was its lawful business name immediately before the transfer,

those sections do not apply in relation to the carrying on of the business under that name during the period of twelve months beginning with the date of the transfer.

(4) In this section "lawful business name", in relation to a business, means a name under which the business was carried on without contravening—

(a) section 2(1) of the Business Names Act 1985 (c 7) or Article 4(1) of the Business Names (Northern Ireland) Order 1986 (SI 1986/1033 NI 7)), or

(b) after this Chapter has come into force, the provisions of this Chapter.

[2113]

NOTES

Commencement: to be appointed (see the introductory note to this Act).

1200–1297 (*Outside the scope of this work.*)

PART 47
FINAL PROVISIONS

1298 Short title

The short title of this Act is the Companies Act 2006.

[2114]

NOTES

Commencement: 8 November 2006.

1299 Extent

Except as otherwise provided (or the context otherwise requires), the provisions of this Act extend to the whole of the United Kingdom.

[2115]

NOTES

Commencement: 8 November 2006.

1300 Commencement

(1) The following provisions come into force on the day this Act is passed—

(a) Part 43 (transparency obligations and related matters), except the amendment in paragraph 11(2) of Schedule 15 of the definition of "regulated market" in Part 6 of the Financial Services and Markets Act 2000 (c 8),

(b) in Part 44 (miscellaneous provisions)—
section 1274 (grants to bodies concerned with actuarial standards etc), and
section 1276 (application of provisions to Scotland and Northern Ireland),

(c) Part 46 (general supplementary provisions), except section 1295 and Schedule 16 (repeals), and

(d) this Part.

(2) The other provisions of this Act come into force on such day as may be appointed by order of the Secretary of State or the Treasury.

[2116]

NOTES

Commencement: 8 November 2006.

Orders: the Companies Act 2006 (Commencement No 1, Transitional Provisions and Savings) Order 2006, SI 2006/3428.

SCHEDULES

SCHEDULE 1
CONNECTED PERSONS: REFERENCES TO AN INTEREST IN SHARES OR DEBENTURES

Sections 254 and 255

Introduction

1.—(1) The provisions of this Schedule have effect for the interpretation of references in sections 254 and 255 (directors connected with or controlling a body corporate) to an interest in shares or debentures.

(2) The provisions are expressed in relation to shares but apply to debentures as they apply to shares.

General provisions

2.—(1) A reference to an interest in shares includes any interest of any kind whatsoever in shares.

(2) Any restraints or restrictions to which the exercise of any right attached to the interest is or may be subject shall be disregarded.

(3) It is immaterial that the shares in which a person has an interest are not identifiable.

(4) Persons having a joint interest in shares are deemed each of them to have that interest.

Rights to acquire shares

3.—(1) A person is taken to have an interest in shares if he enters into a contract to acquire them.

(2) A person is taken to have an interest in shares if—
- (a) he has a right to call for delivery of the shares to himself or to his order, or
- (b) he has a right to acquire an interest in shares or is under an obligation to take an interest in shares,

whether the right or obligation is conditional or absolute.

(3) Rights or obligations to subscribe for shares are not to be taken for the purposes of sub-paragraph (2) to be rights to acquire or obligations to take an interest in shares.

(4) A person ceases to have an interest in shares by virtue of this paragraph—
- (a) on the shares being delivered to another person at his order—
  - (i) in fulfilment of a contract for their acquisition by him, or
  - (ii) in satisfaction of a right of his to call for their delivery;
- (b) on a failure to deliver the shares in accordance with the terms of such a contract or on which such a right falls to be satisfied;
- (c) on the lapse of his right to call for the delivery of shares.

Right to exercise or control exercise of rights

4.—(1) A person is taken to have an interest in shares if, not being the registered holder, he is entitled—
- (a) to exercise any right conferred by the holding of the shares, or
- (b) to control the exercise of any such right.

(2) For this purpose a person is taken to be entitled to exercise or control the exercise of a right conferred by the holding of shares if he—
- (a) has a right (whether subject to conditions or not) the exercise of which would make him so entitled, or
- (b) is under an obligation (whether or not so subject) the fulfilment of which would make him so entitled.

(3) A person is not by virtue of this paragraph taken to be interested in shares by reason only that—

(a) he has been appointed a proxy to exercise any of the rights attached to the shares, or

(b) he has been appointed by a body corporate to act as its representative at any meeting of a company or of any class of its members.

Bodies corporate

5.—(1) A person is taken to be interested in shares if a body corporate is interested in them and—

(a) the body corporate or its directors are accustomed to act in accordance with his directions or instructions, or

(b) he is entitled to exercise or control the exercise of more than one-half of the voting power at general meetings of the body corporate.

(2) For the purposes of sub-paragraph (1)(b) where—

(a) a person is entitled to exercise or control the exercise of more than one-half of the voting power at general meetings of a body corporate, and

(b) that body corporate is entitled to exercise or control the exercise of any of the voting power at general meetings of another body corporate,

the voting power mentioned in paragraph (b) above is taken to be exercisable by that person.

Trusts

6.—(1) Where an interest in shares is comprised in property held on trust, every beneficiary of the trust is taken to have an interest in shares, subject as follows.

(2) So long as a person is entitled to receive, during the lifetime of himself or another, income from trust property comprising shares, an interest in the shares in reversion or remainder or (as regards Scotland) in fee shall be disregarded.

(3) A person is treated as not interested in shares if and so long as he holds them—

(a) under the law in force in any part of the United Kingdom, as a bare trustee or as a custodian trustee, or

(b) under the law in force in Scotland, as a simple trustee.

(4) There shall be disregarded any interest of a person subsisting by virtue of—

(a) an authorised unit trust scheme (within the meaning of section 237 of the Financial Services and Markets Act 2000 (c 8));

(b) a scheme made under section 22 or 22A of the Charities Act 1960 (c 58), section 25 of the Charities Act (Northern Ireland) 1964 (c 33 (NI)) or section 24 or 25 of the Charities Act 1993 (c 10), section 11 of the Trustee Investments Act 1961 (c 62) or section 42 of the Administration of Justice Act 1982 (c 53); or

(c) the scheme set out in the Schedule to the Church Funds Investment Measure 1958 (1958 No 1).

(5) There shall be disregarded any interest—

(a) of the Church of Scotland General Trustees or of the Church of Scotland Trust in shares held by them;

(b) of any other person in shares held by those Trustees or that Trust otherwise than as simple trustees.

"The Church of Scotland General Trustees" are the body incorporated by the order confirmed by the Church of Scotland (General Trustees) Order Confirmation Act 1921 (1921 c xxv), and "the Church of Scotland Trust" is the body incorporated by the order confirmed by the Church of Scotland Trust Order Confirmation Act 1932 (1932 c xxi).

[2117]

NOTES

Commencement: to be appointed (see the introductory note to this Act).

(*Schs 2, 3 outside the scope of this work.*)

SCHEDULE 4
DOCUMENTS AND INFORMATION SENT OR SUPPLIED TO A COMPANY
Section 1144(1)

PART 1
INTRODUCTION

Application of Schedule

1.—(1) This Schedule applies to documents or information sent or supplied to a company.

(2) It does not apply to documents or information sent or supplied by another company (see section 1144(3) and Schedule 5).

[2118]

NOTES

Commencement: 20 January 2007.

PART 2
COMMUNICATIONS IN HARD COPY FORM

Introduction

2. A document or information is validly sent or supplied to a company if it is sent or supplied in hard copy form in accordance with this Part of this Schedule.

Method of communication in hard copy form

3.—(1) A document or information in hard copy form may be sent or supplied by hand or by post to an address (in accordance with paragraph 4).

(2) For the purposes of this Schedule, a person sends a document or information by post if he posts a prepaid envelope containing the document or information.

Address for communications in hard copy form

4. A document or information in hard copy form may be sent or supplied—
- (a) to an address specified by the company for the purpose;
- (b) to the company's registered office;
- (c) to an address to which any provision of the Companies Acts authorises the document or information to be sent or supplied.

[2119]

NOTES

Commencement: 20 January 2007.

PART 3
COMMUNICATIONS IN ELECTRONIC FORM

Introduction

5. A document or information is validly sent or supplied to a company if it is sent or supplied in electronic form in accordance with this Part of this Schedule.

Conditions for use of communications in electronic form

6. A document or information may only be sent or supplied to a company in electronic form if—

(a) the company has agreed (generally or specifically) that the document or information may be sent or supplied in that form (and has not revoked that agreement), or
(b) the company is deemed to have so agreed by a provision in the Companies Acts.

Address for communications in electronic form

7.—(1) Where the document or information is sent or supplied by electronic means, it may only be sent or supplied to an address—
(a) specified for the purpose by the company (generally or specifically), or
(b) deemed by a provision in the Companies Acts to have been so specified.

(2) Where the document or information is sent or supplied in electronic form by hand or by post, it must be sent or supplied to an address to which it could be validly sent if it were in hard copy form.

[2120]

NOTES

Commencement: 20 January 2007.

PART 4
OTHER AGREED FORMS OF COMMUNICATION

8. A document or information that is sent or supplied to a company otherwise than in hard copy form or electronic form is validly sent or supplied if it is sent or supplied in a form or manner that has been agreed by the company.

[2121]

NOTES

Commencement: 20 January 2007.

SCHEDULE 5
COMMUNICATIONS BY A COMPANY

Section 1144(2)

PART 1
INTRODUCTION

Application of this Schedule

1. This Schedule applies to documents or information sent or supplied by a company.

[2122]

NOTES

Commencement: 20 January 2007.

PART 2
COMMUNICATIONS IN HARD COPY FORM

Introduction

2. A document or information is validly sent or supplied by a company if it is sent or supplied in hard copy form in accordance with this Part of this Schedule.

Method of communication in hard copy form

3.—(1) A document or information in hard copy form must be—

(a) handed to the intended recipient, or
(b) sent or supplied by hand or by post to an address (in accordance with paragraph 4).

(2) For the purposes of this Schedule, a person sends a document or information by post if he posts a prepaid envelope containing the document or information.

Address for communications in hard copy form

4.—(1) A document or information in hard copy form may be sent or supplied by the company—
(a) to an address specified for the purpose by the intended recipient;
(b) to a company at its registered office;
(c) to a person in his capacity as a member of the company at his address as shown in the company's register of members;
(d) to a person in his capacity as a director of the company at his address as shown in the company's register of directors;
(e) to an address to which any provision of the Companies Acts authorises the document or information to be sent or supplied.

(2) Where the company is unable to obtain an address falling within sub-paragraph (1), the document or information may be sent or supplied to the intended recipient's last address known to the company.

[2123]

NOTES
Commencement: 20 January 2007.

PART 3
COMMUNICATIONS IN ELECTRONIC FORM

Introduction

5. A document or information is validly sent or supplied by a company if it is sent in electronic form in accordance with this Part of this Schedule.

Agreement to communications in electronic form

6. A document or information may only be sent or supplied by a company in electronic form—
(a) to a person who has agreed (generally or specifically) that the document or information may be sent or supplied in that form (and has not revoked that agreement), or
(b) to a company that is deemed to have so agreed by a provision in the Companies Acts.

Address for communications in electronic form

7.—(1) Where the document or information is sent or supplied by electronic means, it may only be sent or supplied to an address—
(a) specified for the purpose by the intended recipient (generally or specifically), or
(b) where the intended recipient is a company, deemed by a provision of the Companies Acts to have been so specified.

(2) Where the document or information is sent or supplied in electronic form by hand or by post, it must be—
(a) handed to the intended recipient, or
(b) sent or supplied to an address to which it could be validly sent if it were in hard copy form.

[2124]

NOTES

Commencement: 20 January 2007.

PART 4
COMMUNICATIONS BY MEANS OF A WEBSITE

Use of website

8. A document or information is validly sent or supplied by a company if it is made available on a website in accordance with this Part of this Schedule.

Agreement to use of website

9. A document or information may only be sent or supplied by the company to a person by being made available on a website if the person—

(a) has agreed (generally or specifically) that the document or information may be sent or supplied to him in that manner, or

(b) is taken to have so agreed under—

(i) paragraph 10 (members of the company etc), or

(ii) paragraph 11 (debenture holders),

and has not revoked that agreement.

Deemed agreement of members of company etc to use of website

10.—(1) This paragraph applies to a document or information to be sent or supplied to a person—

(a) as a member of the company, or

(b) as a person nominated by a member in accordance with the company's articles to enjoy or exercise all or any specified rights of the member in relation to the company, or

(c) as a person nominated by a member under section 146 to enjoy information rights.

(2) To the extent that—

(a) the members of the company have resolved that the company may send or supply documents or information to members by making them available on a website, or

(b) the company's articles contain provision to that effect,

a person in relation to whom the following conditions are met is taken to have agreed that the company may send or supply documents or information to him in that manner.

(3) The conditions are that—

(a) the person has been asked individually by the company to agree that the company may send or supply documents or information generally, or the documents or information in question, to him by means of a website, and

(b) the company has not received a response within the period of 28 days beginning with the date on which the company's request was sent.

(4) A person is not taken to have so agreed if the company's request—

(a) did not state clearly what the effect of a failure to respond would be, or

(b) was sent less than twelve months after a previous request made to him for the purposes of this paragraph in respect of the same or a similar class of documents or information.

(5) Chapter 3 of Part 3 (resolutions affecting a company's constitution) applies to a resolution under this paragraph.

Deemed agreement of debenture holders to use of website

11.—(1) This paragraph applies to a document or information to be sent or supplied to a person as holder of a company's debentures.

(2) To the extent that—

(a) the relevant debenture holders have duly resolved that the company may send or supply documents or information to them by making them available on a website, or

(b) the instrument creating the debenture in question contains provision to that effect,

a debenture holder in relation to whom the following conditions are met is taken to have agreed that the company may send or supply documents or information to him in that manner.

(3) The conditions are that—

(a) the debenture holder has been asked individually by the company to agree that the company may send or supply documents or information generally, or the documents or information in question, to him by means of a website, and

(b) the company has not received a response within the period of 28 days beginning with the date on which the company's request was sent.

(4) A person is not taken to have so agreed if the company's request—

(a) did not state clearly what the effect of a failure to respond would be, or

(b) was sent less than twelve months after a previous request made to him for the purposes of this paragraph in respect of the same or a similar class of documents or information.

(5) For the purposes of this paragraph—

(a) the relevant debenture holders are the holders of debentures of the company ranking *pari passu* for all purposes with the intended recipient, and

(b) a resolution of the relevant debenture holders is duly passed if they agree in accordance with the provisions of the instruments creating the debentures.

Availability of document or information

12.—(1) A document or information authorised or required to be sent or supplied by means of a website must be made available in a form, and by a means, that the company reasonably considers will enable the recipient—

(a) to read it, and

(b) to retain a copy of it.

(2) For this purpose a document or information can be read only if—

(a) it can be read with the naked eye, or

(b) to the extent that it consists of images (for example photographs, pictures, maps, plans or drawings), it can be seen with the naked eye.

Notification of availability

13.—(1) The company must notify the intended recipient of—

(a) the presence of the document or information on the website,

(b) the address of the website,

(c) the place on the website where it may be accessed, and

(d) how to access the document or information.

(2) The document or information is taken to be sent—

(a) on the date on which the notification required by this paragraph is sent, or

(b) if later, the date on which the document or information first appears on the website after that notification is sent.

Period of availability on website

14.—(1) The company must make the document or information available on the website throughout—

(a) the period specified by any applicable provision of the Companies Acts, or

(b) if no such period is specified, the period of 28 days beginning with the date on which the notification required under paragraph 13 is sent to the person in question.

(2) For the purposes of this paragraph, a failure to make a document or information available on a website throughout the period mentioned in sub-paragraph (1) shall be disregarded if—

(a) it is made available on the website for part of that period, and

(b) the failure to make it available throughout that period is wholly attributable to circumstances that it would not be reasonable to have expected the company to prevent or avoid.

[2125]

NOTES

Commencement: 20 January 2007.

Transitional adaptations: art 5 of the Companies Act 2006 (Commencement No 1, Transitional Provisions and Savings) Order 2006, SI 2006/3428 provides that the provisions brought into force by arts 2–4 of 2006 Order shall have effect subject to any transitional adaptations specified in Sch 1 to that Order. Schedule 1, para 16 to the Order provides as follows—

16 Communications by a company

(1) Schedule 5 (communications by a company) has effect with the following adaptation.

(2) In paragraph 10(5), for "Chapter 3 of Part 3" substitute "section 380 of the Companies Act 1985 or Article 388 of the Companies (Northern Ireland) Order 1986".

PART 5
OTHER AGREED FORMS OF COMMUNICATION

15. A document or information that is sent or supplied otherwise than in hard copy or electronic form or by means of a website is validly sent or supplied if it is sent or supplied in a form or manner that has been agreed by the intended recipient.

[2126]

NOTES

Commencement: 20 January 2007.

PART 6
SUPPLEMENTARY PROVISIONS

Joint holders of shares or debentures

16.—(1) This paragraph applies in relation to documents or information to be sent or supplied to joint holders of shares or debentures of a company.

(2) Anything to be agreed or specified by the holder must be agreed or specified by all the joint holders.

(3) Anything authorised or required to be sent or supplied to the holder may be sent or supplied either—

(a) to each of the joint holders, or
(b) to the holder whose name appears first in the register of members or the relevant register of debenture holders.

(4) This paragraph has effect subject to anything in the company's articles.

Death or bankruptcy of holder of shares

17.—(1) This paragraph has effect in the case of the death or bankruptcy of a holder of a company's shares.

(2) Documents or information required or authorised to be sent or supplied to the member may be sent or supplied to the persons claiming to be entitled to the shares in consequence of the death or bankruptcy—

(a) by name, or
(b) by the title of representatives of the deceased, or trustee of the bankrupt, or by any like description,

at the address in the United Kingdom supplied for the purpose by those so claiming.

(3) Until such an address has been so supplied, a document or information may be sent or supplied in any manner in which it might have been sent or supplied if the death or bankruptcy had not occurred.

(4) This paragraph has effect subject to anything in the company's articles.

(5) References in this paragraph to the bankruptcy of a person include—
(a) the sequestration of the estate of a person;
(b) a person's estate being the subject of a protected trust deed (within the meaning of the Bankruptcy (Scotland) Act 1985 (c 66)).

In such a case the reference in sub-paragraph (2)(b) to the trustee of the bankrupt is to be read as the permanent or interim trustee (within the meaning of that Act) on the sequestrated estate or, as the case may be, the trustee under the protected deed.

[2127]

NOTES

Commencement: 20 January 2007.

SCHEDULE 6
MEANING OF "SUBSIDIARY" ETC: SUPPLEMENTARY PROVISIONS

Section 1159

Introduction

1. The provisions of this Part of this Schedule explain expressions used in section 1159 (meaning of "subsidiary" etc) and otherwise supplement that section.

Voting rights in a company

2. In section 1159(1)(a) and (c) the references to the voting rights in a company are to the rights conferred on shareholders in respect of their shares or, in the case of a company not having a share capital, on members, to vote at general meetings of the company on all, or substantially all, matters.

Right to appoint or remove a majority of the directors

3.—(1) In section 1159(1)(b) the reference to the right to appoint or remove a majority of the board of directors is to the right to appoint or remove directors holding a majority of the voting rights at meetings of the board on all, or substantially all, matters.

(2) A company shall be treated as having the right to appoint to a directorship if—
(a) a person's appointment to it follows necessarily from his appointment as director of the company, or
(b) the directorship is held by the company itself.

(3) A right to appoint or remove which is exercisable only with the consent or concurrence of another person shall be left out of account unless no other person has a right to appoint or, as the case may be, remove in relation to that directorship.

Rights exercisable only in certain circumstances or temporarily incapable of exercise

4.—(1) Rights which are exercisable only in certain circumstances shall be taken into account only—
(a) when the circumstances have arisen, and for so long as they continue to obtain, or
(b) when the circumstances are within the control of the person having the rights.

(2) Rights which are normally exercisable but are temporarily incapable of exercise shall continue to be taken into account.

Rights held by one person on behalf of another

5. Rights held by a person in a fiduciary capacity shall be treated as not held by him.

6.—(1) Rights held by a person as nominee for another shall be treated as held by the other.

(2) Rights shall be regarded as held as nominee for another if they are exercisable only on his instructions or with his consent or concurrence.

Rights attached to shares held by way of security

7. Rights attached to shares held by way of security shall be treated as held by the person providing the security—

(a) where apart from the right to exercise them for the purpose of preserving the value of the security, or of realising it, the rights are exercisable only in accordance with his instructions, and

(b) where the shares are held in connection with the granting of loans as part of normal business activities and apart from the right to exercise them for the purpose of preserving the value of the security, or of realising it, the rights are exercisable only in his interests.

Rights attributed to holding company

8.—(1) Rights shall be treated as held by a holding company if they are held by any of its subsidiary companies.

(2) Nothing in paragraph 6 or 7 shall be construed as requiring rights held by a holding company to be treated as held by any of its subsidiaries.

(3) For the purposes of paragraph 7 rights shall be treated as being exercisable in accordance with the instructions or in the interests of a company if they are exercisable in accordance with the instructions of or, as the case may be, in the interests of—

(a) any subsidiary or holding company of that company, or

(b) any subsidiary of a holding company of that company.

Disregard of certain rights

9. The voting rights in a company shall be reduced by any rights held by the company itself.

Supplementary

10. References in any provision of paragraphs 5 to 9 to rights held by a person include rights falling to be treated as held by him by virtue of any other provision of those paragraphs but not rights which by virtue of any such provision are to be treated as not held by him.

[2128]

NOTES

Commencement: to be appointed (see the introductory note to this Act).

SCHEDULE 7

PARENT AND SUBSIDIARY UNDERTAKINGS: SUPPLEMENTARY PROVISIONS

Section 1162

Introduction

1. The provisions of this Schedule explain expressions used in section 1162 (parent and subsidiary undertakings) and otherwise supplement that section.

Voting rights in an undertaking

2.—(1) In section 1162(2)(a) and (d) the references to the voting rights in an undertaking are to the rights conferred on shareholders in respect of their shares or, in the case of an undertaking not having a share capital, on members, to vote at general meetings of the undertaking on all, or substantially all, matters.

(2) In relation to an undertaking which does not have general meetings at which matters are decided by the exercise of voting rights the references to holding a majority of the voting rights in the undertaking shall be construed as references to having the right under the constitution of the undertaking to direct the overall policy of the undertaking or to alter the terms of its constitution.

Right to appoint or remove a majority of the directors

3.—(1) In section 1162(2)(b) the reference to the right to appoint or remove a majority of the board of directors is to the right to appoint or remove directors holding a majority of the voting rights at meetings of the board on all, or substantially all, matters.

(2) An undertaking shall be treated as having the right to appoint to a directorship if—
- (a) a person's appointment to it follows necessarily from his appointment as director of the undertaking, or
- (b) the directorship is held by the undertaking itself.

(3) A right to appoint or remove which is exercisable only with the consent or concurrence of another person shall be left out of account unless no other person has a right to appoint or, as the case may be, remove in relation to that directorship.

Right to exercise dominant influence

4.—(1) For the purposes of section 1162(2)(c) an undertaking shall not be regarded as having the right to exercise a dominant influence over another undertaking unless it has a right to give directions with respect to the operating and financial policies of that other undertaking which its directors are obliged to comply with whether or not they are for the benefit of that other undertaking.

(2) A "control contract" means a contract in writing conferring such a right which—
- (a) is of a kind authorised by the articles of the undertaking in relation to which the right is exercisable, and
- (b) is permitted by the law under which that undertaking is established.

(3) This paragraph shall not be read as affecting the construction of section 1162(4)(a).

Rights exercisable only in certain circumstances or temporarily incapable of exercise

5.—(1) Rights which are exercisable only in certain circumstances shall be taken into account only—
- (a) when the circumstances have arisen, and for so long as they continue to obtain, or
- (b) when the circumstances are within the control of the person having the rights.

(2) Rights which are normally exercisable but are temporarily incapable of exercise shall continue to be taken into account.

Rights held by one person on behalf of another

6. Rights held by a person in a fiduciary capacity shall be treated as not held by him.

7.—(1) Rights held by a person as nominee for another shall be treated as held by the other.

(2) Rights shall be regarded as held as nominee for another if they are exercisable only on his instructions or with his consent or concurrence.

Rights attached to shares held by way of security

8. Rights attached to shares held by way of security shall be treated as held by the person providing the security—
- (a) where apart from the right to exercise them for the purpose of preserving the value of the security, or of realising it, the rights are exercisable only in accordance with his instructions, and
- (b) where the shares are held in connection with the granting of loans as part of

normal business activities and apart from the right to exercise them for the purpose of preserving the value of the security, or of realising it, the rights are exercisable only in his interests.

Rights attributed to parent undertaking

9.—(1) Rights shall be treated as held by a parent undertaking if they are held by any of its subsidiary undertakings.

(2) Nothing in paragraph 7 or 8 shall be construed as requiring rights held by a parent undertaking to be treated as held by any of its subsidiary undertakings.

(3) For the purposes of paragraph 8 rights shall be treated as being exercisable in accordance with the instructions or in the interests of an undertaking if they are exercisable in accordance with the instructions of or, as the case may be, in the interests of any group undertaking.

Disregard of certain rights

10. The voting rights in an undertaking shall be reduced by any rights held by the undertaking itself.

Supplementary

11. References in any provision of paragraphs 6 to 10 to rights held by a person include rights falling to be treated as held by him by virtue of any other provision of those paragraphs but not rights which by virtue of any such provision are to be treated as not held by him.
[2129]

NOTES

Commencement: to be appointed (see the introductory note to this Act).

SCHEDULE 8
INDEX OF DEFINED EXPRESSIONS

Section 1174

abbreviated accounts (in Part 15)	sections 444(4) and 445(3)
accounting reference date and accounting reference period	section 391
accounting standards (in Part 15)	section 464
accounts meeting	section 437(3)
acquisition, in relation to a non-cash asset	section 1163(2)
address	
— generally in the Companies Acts	section 1142
— in the company communications provisions	section 1148(1)
affirmative resolution procedure, in relation to regulations and orders	section 1290
allotment (time of)	section 558
allotment of equity securities (in Chapter 3 of Part 17)	section 560(2)
allotted share capital and allotted shares	section 546(1)(b) and (2)
annual accounts (in Part 15)	section 471
annual accounts and reports (in Part 15)	section 471

annual general meeting	section 336
annual return	section 854
appropriate audit authority (in sections 522, 523 and 524)	section 525(1)
appropriate rate of interest	
— in Chapter 5 of Part 17	section 592
— in Chapter 6 of Part 17	section 609
approval after being made, in relation to regulations and orders	section 1291
arrangement	
— in Chapter 7 of Part 17	section 616(1)
— in Part 26	section 895(2)
articles	section 18
associate (in Chapter 3 of Part 28)	section 988
associated bodies corporate and associated company (in Part 10)	section 256
authenticated, in relation to a document or information sent or supplied to a company	section 1146
authorised group, of members of a company (in Part 14)	section 370(3)
authorised insurance company	section 1165(2)
authorised minimum (in relation to share capital of public company)	section 763
available profits (in Chapter 5 of Part 18)	sections 711 and 712
banking company and banking group	section 1164
body corporate	section 1173(1)
called-up share capital	section 547
capital redemption reserve	section 733
capitalisation in relation to a company's profits (in Part 23)	section 853(3)
cash (in relation to paying up or allotting shares)	section 583
cause of action, in relation to derivative proceedings (in Chapter 2 of Part 11)	section 265(7)
certified translation (in Part 35)	section 1107
charge (in Chapter 1 of Part 25)	section 861(5)
circulation date, in relation to a written resolution (in Part 13)	section 290
class of shares	section 629
the Companies Acts	section 2
Companies Act accounts	sections 395(1)(a) and 403(2)(a)
Companies Act group accounts	section 403(2)(a)
Companies Act individual accounts	section 395(1)(a)
companies involved in the division (in Part 27)	section 919(2)
company	
— generally in the Companies Acts	section 1
— in Chapter 7 of Part 17	section 616(1)
— in Chapter 1 of Part 25	section 861(5)

PART I
STATUTES

— in Chapter 2 of Part 25	section 879(6)
— in Part 26	section 895(2)
— in Chapter 3 of Part 28	section 991(1)
— in the company communications provisions	section 1148(1)
the company communications provisions	section 1143
the company law provisions of this Act	section 2(2)
company records (in Part 37)	section 1134
connected with, in relation to a director (in Part 10)	sections 252 to 254
constitution, of a company	
— generally in the Companies Acts	section 17
— in Part 10	section 257
controlling, of a body corporate by a director (in Part 10)	section 255
corporation	section 1173(1)
the court	section 1156
credit institution	section 1173(1)
credit transaction (in Chapter 4 of Part 10)	section 202
creditor (in Chapter 1 of Part 31)	section 1011
daily default fine	section 1125
date of the offer (in Chapter 3 of Part 28)	section 991(1)
debenture	section 738
derivative claim (in Chapter 1 of Part 11)	section 260
derivative proceedings (in Chapter 2 of Part 11)	section 265
Directive disclosure requirements	section 1078
director	
— generally in the Companies Acts	section 250
— in Chapter 8 of Part 10	section 240(3)
— in Chapter 1 of Part 11	section 260(5)
— in Chapter 2 of Part 11	section 265(7)
— in Part 14	section 379(1)
directors' remuneration report	section 420
directors' report	section 415
distributable profits	
— in Chapter 2 of Part 18	section 683(1)
— elsewhere in Part 18	section 736
distribution	
— in Chapter 2 of Part 18	section 683(1)
— in Part 23	section 829
division (in Part 27)	section 919
document	
— in Part 35	section 1114(1)
— in the company communications provisions	section 1148(1)

dormant, in relation to a company or other body corporate	section 1169
EEA State and related expressions	section 1170
electronic form, electronic copy, electronic means	
— generally in the Companies Acts	section 1168(3) and (4)
— in relation to communications to a company	Part 3 of Schedule 4
— in relation to communications by a company	Part 3 of Schedule 5
eligible members, in relation to a written resolution	section 289
e-money issuer	
— in Part 15	section 474(1)
— in Part 16	section 539
employees' share scheme	section 1166
employer and employee (in Chapter 1 of Part 18)	section 676
enactment	section 1293
equity securities (in Chapter 3 of Part 17)	section 560(1)
equity share capital	section 548
equity shares (in Chapter 7 of Part 17)	section 616(1)
existing company (in Part 27)	section 902(2)
fellow subsidiary undertakings	section 1161(4)
financial assistance (in Chapter 2 of Part 18)	section 677
financial institution	section 1173(1)
financial year, of a company	section 390
firm	section 1173(1)
fixed assets (in Part 23)	section 853
the former Companies Acts	section 1171
the Gazette	section 1173(1)
group (in Part 15)	section 474(1)
group undertaking	section 1161(5)
hard copy form and hard copy	
— generally in the Companies Acts	section 1168(2)
— in relation to communications to a company	Part 2 of Schedule 4
— in relation to communications by a company	Part 2 of Schedule 5
hire-purchase agreement	section 1173(1)
holder of shares (in Chapter 3 of Part 17)	section 574
holding company	section 1159 (and see section 1160 and Schedule 6)
IAS accounts	sections 395(1)(b) and 403(1) and (2)(b)
IAS group accounts	section 403(1) and (2)(b)
IAS individual accounts	section 395(1)(b)
IAS Regulation (in Part 15)	section 474(1)

included in the consolidation, in relation to group accounts (in Part 15)	section 474(1)
individual accounts	section 394
information rights (in Part 9)	section 146(3)
insurance company	section 1165(3)
insurance group	section 1165(5)
insurance market activity	section 1165(7)
interest in shares (for the purposes of Part 22)	sections 820 to 825
international accounting standards (in Part 15)	section 474(1)
investment company (in Part 23)	section 833
ISD investment firm	
— in Part 15	section 474(1)
— in Part 16	section 539
issued share capital and issued shares	section 546(1)(a) and (2)
the issuing company (in Chapter 7 of Part 17)	section 610(6)
the Joint Stock Companies Acts	section 1171
liabilities (in Part 27)	section 941
liability, references to incurring, reducing or discharging (in Chapter 2 of Part 18)	section 683(2)
limited by guarantee	section 3(3)
limited by shares	section 3(2)
limited company	section 3
the main register (of members) (in Chapter 3 of Part 8)	section 131(1)
major audit (in sections 522 and 525)	section 525(2)
market purchase, by a company of its own shares (in Chapter 4 of Part 18)	section 693(4)
member, of a company	
— generally in the Companies Acts	section 112
— in Chapter 1 of Part 11	section 260(5)
— in Chapter 2 of Part 11	section 265(7)
memorandum of association	section 8
merger (in Part 27)	section 904
merging companies (in Part 27)	section 904(2)
merger by absorption (in Part 27)	section 904(1)(a)
merger by formation of a new company (in Part 27)	section 904(1)(b)
negative resolution procedure, in relation to regulations and orders	section 1289
net assets (in Part 7)	section 92
new company (in Part 27)	section 902(2)
non-cash asset	section 1163
non-voting shares (in Chapter 3 of Part 28)	section 991(1)
number, in relation to shares	section 540(4)(b)
off-market purchase, by a company of its own shares (in Chapter 4 of Part 18)	section 693(2)

offer period (in Chapter 2 of Part 28)	section 971(1)
offer to the public (in Chapter 1 of Part 20)	section 756
offeror	
— in Chapter 2 of Part 28	section 971(1)
— in Chapter 3 of Part 28	section 991(1)
officer, in relation to a body corporate	section 1173(1)
officer in default	section 1121
official seal, of registrar	section 1062
opted-in company (in Chapter 2 of Part 28)	section 971(1)
opting-in resolution (in Chapter 2 of Part 28)	section 966(1)
opting-out resolution (in Chapter 2 of Part 28)	section 966(5)
ordinary resolution	section 282
ordinary shares (in Chapter 3 of Part 17)	section 560(1)
organisation (in Part 14)	section 379(1)
other relevant transactions or arrangements (in Chapter 4 of Part 10)	section 210
overseas company	section 1044
overseas branch register	section 129(1)
paid up	section 583
the Panel (in Part 28)	section 942
parent company	section 1173(1)
parent undertaking	section 1162 (and see Schedule 7)
payment for loss of office (in Chapter 4 of Part 10)	section 215
pension scheme (in Chapter 1 of Part 18)	section 675
period for appointing auditors, in relation to a private company	section 485(2)
period for filing, in relation to accounts and reports for a financial year	section 442
permissible capital payment (in Chapter 5 of Part 18)	section 710
political donation (in Part 14)	section 364
political expenditure (in Part 14)	section 365
political organisation (in Part 14)	section 363(2)
prescribed	section 1167
private company	section 4
profit and loss account (in Part 15)	section 474(1) and (2)
profits and losses (in Part 23)	section 853(2)
profits available for distribution (for the purposes of Part 23)	section 830(2)
property (in Part 27)	section 941
protected information (in Chapter 8 of Part 10)	section 240
provision for entrenchment, in relation to a company's articles	section 22
public company	section 4
publication, in relation to accounts and reports (in sections 433 to 435)	section 436

qualified, in relation to an auditor's report etc (in Part 16)	section 539
qualifying shares (in Chapter 6 of Part 18)	section 724(2)
qualifying third party indemnity provision (in Chapter 7 of Part 10)	section 234
qualifying pension scheme indemnity provision (in Chapter 7 of Part 10)	section 235
quasi-loan (in Chapter 4 of Part 10)	section 199
quoted company	
— in Part 13	section 361
— in Part 15	section 385
— in Chapter 5 of Part 16	section 531 (and section 385)
realised profits and losses (in Part 23)	section 853(4)
redeemable shares	section 684(1)
redenominate	section 622(1)
redenomination reserve	section 628
the register	section 1080
register of charges, kept by registrar	
— in England and Wales and Northern Ireland	section 869
— in Scotland	section 885
register of directors	section 162
register of directors' residential addresses	section 165
register of members	section 113
register of secretaries	section 275
registered number, of a branch of an overseas company	section 1067
registered number, of a company	section 1066
registered office, of a company	section 86
registrar and registrar of companies	section 1060
registrar's index of company names	section 1099
registrar's rules	section 1117
registration in a particular part of the United Kingdom	section 1060(4)
regulated activity	
— generally in the Companies Acts	section 1173(1)
— in Part 15	section 474(1)
regulated market	section 1173(1)
relevant accounts (in Part 23)	section 836(2)
requirements for proper delivery (in Part 35)	section 1072 (and see section 1073)
requirements of this Act	section 1172
securities (and related expressions)	
— in Chapter 1 of Part 20	section 755(5)
— in Chapter 2 of Part 21	section 783
senior statutory auditor	section 504

sent or supplied, in relation to documents or information (in the company communications provisions)	section 1148(2) and (3)
service address	section 1141
service contract, of a director (in Part 10)	section 227
shadow director	section 251
share	
— generally in the Companies Acts	section 540 (and see section 1161(2))
— in Part 22	section 792
— in section 1162 and Schedule 7	section 1162(7)
share capital, company having a	section 545
share exchange ratio	
— in Chapter 2 of Part 27	section 905(2)
— in Chapter 3 of Part 27	section 920(2)
share premium account	section 610(1)
share warrant	section 779(1)
small companies regime, for accounts and reports	section 381
solvency statement (in sections 641 to 644)	section 643
special notice, in relation to a resolution	section 312
special resolution	section 283
statutory accounts	section 434(3)
subsidiary	section 1159 (and see section 1160 and Schedule 6)
subsidiary undertaking	section 1162 (and see Schedule 7)
summary financial statement	section 426
takeover bid (in Chapter 2 of Part 28)	section 971(1)
takeover offer (in Chapter 3 of Part 28)	section 974
the Takeovers Directive	
— in Chapter 1 of Part 28	section 943(8)
— in Chapter 2 of Part 28	section 971(1)
trading certificate	section 761(1)
transfer, in relation to a non-cash asset	section 1163(2)
treasury shares	section 724(5)
turnover	
— in Part 15	section 474(1)
— in Part 16	section 539
UCITS management company	
— in Part 15	section 474(1)
— in Part 16	section 539
UK-registered company	section 1158
uncalled share capital	section 547
unconditional, in relation to a contract to acquire shares (in Chapter 3 of Part 28)	section 991(2)
undistributable reserves	section 831(4)
undertaking	section 1161(1)

unique identifier	section 1082
unlimited company	section 3
unquoted company (in Part 15)	section 385
voting rights	
— in Chapter 2 of Part 28	section 971(1)
— in Chapter 3 of Part 28	section 991(1)
— in section 1159 and Schedule 6	paragraph 2 of Schedule 6
— in section 1162 and Schedule 7	paragraph 2 of Schedule 7
voting shares	
— in Chapter 2 of Part 28	section 971(1)
— in Chapter 3 of Part 28	section 991(1)
website, communication by a company by means of	Part 4 of Schedule 5
Welsh company	section 88
wholly-owned subsidiary	section 1159(2) (and see section 1160 and Schedule 6)
working day, in relation to a company	section 1173(1)
written resolution	section 288

[2130]

NOTES

Commencement: to be appointed (see the introductory note to this Act).

(*Schs 9–16 outside the scope of this work.*)

CHARITIES ACT 2006

(2006 c 50)

NOTES

The following table shows the commencement of this Act as at 1 March 2007, and includes the commencements made by s 79 and the Charities Act 2006 (Commencement No 1, Transitional Provisions and Savings) Order 2007, SI 2007/309.

Commencement Table for the Charities Act 2006

Provision			
s 1			Not in force
s 2	(1)	(a)	Not in force
		(b)	27 Feb 2007 (for the purposes of the definition of the Charity Commission's public benefit objective (as defined by the Charities Act 1993, s 1B(3), (4)) and to enable the Charity Commission to issue guidance in pursuance of that objective) (SI 2007/309)
			Not in force (otherwise)
	(2)–(8)		Not in force

Commencement Table for the Charities Act 2006

Provision		
s 3	(1)	27 Feb 2007 (for the purpose of enabling the Charity Commission to issue guidance under s 4 in pursuance of its public benefit objective) (SI 2007/309)
		Not in force (otherwise)
	(2)–(4)	Not in force
s 4	(1)–(5)	27 Feb 2007 (SI 2007/309)
	(6)	Not in force
s 5		Not in force
s 6		27 Feb 2007 (SI 2007/309)
s 7		27 Feb 2007 (except so far as it inserts Charities Act 1993, ss 1C(2), para 4, 1C(5), 1E(3) (SI 2007/309)
		Not in force (exceptions noted above)
s 8	(1)	27 Feb 2007 (so far as inserts Charities Act 1993, ss 2B(1)–(4), (8), (9), 2C(5)(b) for the purpose of enabling the Lord Chancellor to exercise the power to make subordinate legislation) (SI 2007/309)
		Not in force (otherwise)
	(2)	See Sch 3 below
	(3)	See Sch 4 below
s 9		27 Feb 2007 (so far as inserts Charities Act 1993, ss 3A(2)(c), (4)(b), (5), 3B(2)(b) for the purpose of enabling the Minister to exercise the power to make subordinate legislation) (SI 2007/309)
		Not in force (otherwise)
s 10		27 Feb 2007 (SI 2007/309)
s 11	(1)–(10)	Not in force
	(11)–(14)	27 Feb 2007 (SI 2007/309)
s 12		See Sch 5 below
s 13	(1)–(3)	Not in force
	(4), (5)	8 Nov 2006 (s 79(1)(a))
ss 14–16		Not in force
s 17		27 Feb 2007 (so far as inserts Charities Act 1993, s 14A(9)) (SI 2007/309)
		Not in force (otherwise)
ss 18–21		Not in force
ss 22–28		27 Feb 2007 (SI 2007/309)
s 29		Not in force
s 30	(1)	Not in force
	(2)	See Sch 6 below
s 31		Not in force
s 32		27 Feb 2007 (SI 2007/309)
s 33		Not in force
s 34		See Sch 7 below
s 35		27 Feb 2007 (SI 2007/309)
ss 36, 37		Not in force

Commencement Table for the Charities Act 2006

Provision

s 38		27 Feb 2007 (except so far as inserts Charities Act 1993, s 73E(2)(b) and refers to group accounts as required to be prepared under Sch 5A to that Act) (SI 2007/309)
		Not in force (exception noted above)
s 39		27 Feb 2007 (SI 2007/309)
ss 40, 41		Not in force
s 42		27 Feb 2007 (SI 2007/309)
ss 43–67		Not in force
s 68		27 Feb 2007 (so far as inserts Charities Act 1992, s 60B(6) for the purpose of enabling the Minister to exercise the power to make subordinate legislation) (SI 2007/309)
		Not in force (otherwise)
s 69		27 Feb 2007 (SI 2007/309)
s 70		1 Apr 2007 (SI 2007/309)
ss 71, 72		27 Feb 2007 (SI 2007/309)
s 73		Not in force
s 74		8 Nov 2006 (s 79(1)(b))
s 75	(1)	See Sch 8 below
	(2)	See Sch 9 below
	(3)	See Sch 10 below
	(4), (5)	8 Nov 2006 (s 79(1)(c))
	(6)	27 Feb 2007 (SI 2007/309)
s 76		27 Feb 2007 (SI 2007/309)
s 77		8 Nov 2006 (s 79(1)(e))
s 78		8 Nov 2006 (s 79(1)(d))
ss 79, 80		8 Nov 2006 (s 79(1)(f))
Schs 1, 2		27 Feb 2007 (SI 2007/309)
Sch 3		Not in force
Sch 4		27 Feb 2007 (so far as inserts Charities Act 1993, Sch 1C, para 6 for the purpose of enabling the Minister to exercise the power to make subordinate legislation) (SI 2007/309)
		Not in force (otherwise)
Sch 5		Not in force
Sch 6		27 Feb 2007 (so far as inserts Charities Act 1993, Sch 5A, paras 3(3)(b), (4), (5), 4(2), (3), 6(2), 8, 10(2), (3), 15 for the purpose of enabling the Minister to exercise the power to make subordinate legislation) (SI 2007/309)
		Not in force (otherwise)
Sch 7, para	1	27 Feb 2007 (so far as inserts Charities Act 1993, Pt 8A, ss 69B(3), (5), 69E(2)(b), 69G(5)(d), 69H(4), 69J, 69N, 69Q for the purpose of enabling the Minister (and the Charity Commission in relation to s 69B(5)) to exercise the power to make subordinate legislation) (SI 2007/309)
		Not in force (otherwise)

Commencement Table for the Charities Act 2006

Provision			
	2		27 Feb 2007 (so far as inserts Charities Act 1993, Sch 5B, paras 10(2), (3), 13 for the purpose of enabling the Minister to exercise the power to make subordinate legislation) (SI 2007/309)
			Not in force (otherwise)
	3–5		Not in force
	6		27 Feb 2007 (SI 2007/309)
	7		Not in force
Sch 8, para	1		27 Feb 2007 (SI 2007/309)
	2	(a)	Not in force
		(b)	27 Feb 2007 (SI 2007/309)
	3–14		27 Feb 2007 (SI 2007/309)
	15		Not in force
	16–38		27 Feb 2007 (SI 2007/309)
	39, 40		Not in force
	41–50		27 Feb 2007 (SI 2007/309)
	51	(1)–(4)	27 Feb 2007 (SI 2007/309)
		(5)	Not in force
	52–65		27 Feb 2007 (SI 2007/309)
	66		Not in force
	67–72		27 Feb 2007 (SI 2007/309)
	73		Not in force
	74		27 Feb 2007 (SI 2007/309)
	75		Not in force
	76		27 Feb 2007 (SI 2007/309)
	77	(1), (2)	27 Feb 2007 (SI 2007/309)
		(3)	Not in force
	78, 79		27 Feb 2007 (SI 2007/309)
	80	(1)–(5)	27 Feb 2007 (SI 2007/309)
		(6)(a)	Not in force
		(6)(b)–(d)	27 Feb 2007 (SI 2007/309)
		(6)(e)	Not in force
		(7)	27 Feb 2007 (SI 2007/309)
		(8)	Not in force
		(9), (10)	27 Feb 2007 (SI 2007/309)
	81		27 Feb 2007 (SI 2007/309)
	82	(1), (2)	27 Feb 2007 (SI 2007/309)
		(3)	Not in force
		(4)–(7)	27 Feb 2007 (SI 2007/309)
	83	(1), (2)	27 Feb 2007 (SI 2007/309)
		(3), (4)	Not in force
	84		27 Feb 2007 (SI 2007/309)
	85		Not in force
	86		27 Feb 2007 (SI 2007/309)
	87, 88		Not in force
	89		27 Feb 2007 (SI 2007/309)

Commencement Table for the Charities Act 2006

Provision		
90 (1)		Not in force
	(2)	8 Nov 2006 (s 79(1)(g))
	(3), (4)	Not in force
91–93		27 Feb 2007 (SI 2007/309)
94, 95		Not in force
96–98		27 Feb 2007 (SI 2007/309)[1]
99	(1), (2)	27 Feb 2007 (SI 2007/309)
	(3)	Not in force
	(4)(a)	Not in force
	(4)(b), (c)	27 Feb 2007 (SI 2007/309)
	(5)(a)	Not in force
	(5)(b)	27 Feb 2007 (SI 2007/309)
	(5)(c)	Not in force
100	(1), (2)	27 Feb 2007 (SI 2007/309)
	(3)	Not in force
101–103		27 Feb 2007 (SI 2007/309)
104		8 Nov 2006 (so far as it confers power to make regulations) (s 79(1)(g))
		27 Feb 2007 (except so far as inserts Charities Act 1993, s 10B or refers thereto) (SI 2007/309)[1]
		Not in force (exception noted above)
105–108		27 Feb 2007 (SI 2007/309)
109	(1)–(11)	27 Feb 2007 (SI 2007/309)
	(12)	Not in force
	(13)	27 Feb 2007 (SI 2007/309)
110		27 Feb 2007 (SI 2007/309)
111	(1)–(6)	27 Feb 2007 (SI 2007/309)
	(7)	Not in force
	(8)–(10)	27 Feb 2007 (SI 2007/309)
112		27 Feb 2007 (SI 2007/309)
113		27 Feb 2007 (except so far as refers to Charities Act 1993, ss 18A, 19A, 19B) (SI 2007/309)
		Not in force (exception noted above)
114–132		27 Feb 2007 (SI 2007/309)[1]
133		Not in force
134–138		27 Feb 2007 (SI 2007/309)[1]
139	(1), (2)	27 Feb 2007 (SI 2007/309)
	(3), (4)	Not in force
	(5)	27 Feb 2007 (SI 2007/309)
	(6), (7)	Not in force
140–142		27 Feb 2007 (SI 2007/309)[1]
143	(1), (2)	27 Feb 2007 (SI 2007/309)
	(3)(a), (b)	27 Feb 2007 (SI 2007/309)
	(3)(c)	Not in force
144–161		27 Feb 2007 (SI 2007/309)

Commencement Table for the Charities Act 2006

Provision		
162		27 Feb 2007 (except so far as sub-para (2) inserts Charities Act 1993, s 80(1)(c)) (SI 2007/309)
		Not in force (exception noted above)
163	(1)–(3)	27 Feb 2007 (SI 2007/309)
	(4)	Not in force
	(5)	27 Feb 2007 (SI 2007/309)
164		27 Feb 2007 (SI 2007/309)
165	(1)	27 Feb 2007 (SI 2007/309)
	(2)	27 Feb 2007 (SI 2007/309)
		Not in force
	(3), (4)	27 Feb 2007 (SI 2007/309)
166		27 Feb 2007 (SI 2007/309)
167	(1)	27 Feb 2007 (SI 2007/309)
	(2)	Not in force
	(3)–(5)	27 Feb 2007 (SI 2007/309)
168–170		27 Feb 2007 (SI 2007/309)
171		Not in force
172		27 Feb 2007 (SI 2007/309)
173	(1)	27 Feb 2007 (SI 2007/309)
	(2), (3)	Not in force
	(4)	27 Feb 2007 (SI 2007/309)
174	(a)	Not in force
	(b), (c)	27 Feb 2007 (SI 2007/309)
	(d)	8 Nov 2006 (s 79(1)(g))
175		27 Feb 2007 (except so far as refers to Charities Act 1993, Pt 8A) (SI 2007/309)
		Not in force (exception noted above)
176		27 Feb 2007 (except so far as refers to Charities Act 1993, s 10B) (SI 2007/309)
		Not in force (exception noted above)
177–190		27 Feb 2007 (SI 2007/309)[1]
191		Not in force
192		27 Feb 2007 (SI 2007/309)[1]
193–195		Not in force
196–198		27 Feb 2007 (SI 2007/309)
199		Not in force
200–207		27 Feb 2007 (SI 2007/309)
208		Not in force
209		27 Feb 2007 (SI 2007/309)
210	(a)	27 Feb 2007 (SI 2007/309)
	(b), (c)	Not in force
211		27 Feb 2007 (SI 2007/309)
212	(1), (2)	27 Feb 2007 (SI 2007/309)
	(3)	Not in force
Sch 9		27 Feb 2007 (SI 2007/309) repeals of or in–
		Charities Act 1992, Pt 3, ss 76, 77, Sch 6;

Commencement Table for the Charities Act 2006

Provision		
		Charities Act 1993, ss 1, 2, 23, 44, 61, Sch 1;
		Local Government (Wales) Act 1994
		Not in force, repeals of or in—
		Police, Factories, &c (Miscellaneous Provisions) Act 1916;
		Recreational Charities Act 1958;
		Church Funds Investment Measure 1958;
		Charities Act 1960;
		Housing Act 1985;
		Reverter of Sites Act 1987;
		Charities Act 1992, Pt 1, s 79, Schs 5, 7;
		Charities Act 1993, ss 4, 6, 9, 16, 17, 18, 24, 28, 33, 46, 73, 92, 96, Schs 2, 6;
		National Lottery etc Act 1993;
		Deregulation and Contracting Out Act 1994;
		Housing Act 1996;
		Teaching and Higher Education Act 1998;
		School Standards and Framework Act 1998;
		Intervention Board for Agricultural Produce (Abolition) Regulations 2001, SI 2001/3686;
		Regulatory Reform (National Health Service Charitable and Non-Charitable Trust Accounts and Audit) Order 2005, SI 2005/1074
Sch 10, para	1	27 Feb 2007 (SI 2007/309)
	2–5	Not in force
	6, 7	27 Feb 2007 (SI 2007/309)
	8	Not in force
	9	27 Feb 2007 (SI 2007/309)
	10	Not in force
	11	27 Feb 2007 (SI 2007/309)
	12	Not in force
	13	27 Feb 2007 (SI 2007/309)
	14, 15	Not in force
	16	27 Feb 2007 (SI 2007/309)
	17, 18	Not in force
	19, 20	27 Feb 2007 (SI 2007/309)
	21–29	Not in force

[1] For transitional provisions and savings, see SI 2007/309, arts 4–13

ARRANGEMENT OF SECTIONS

PART 1
MEANING OF "CHARITY" AND "CHARITABLE PURPOSE"

PART 2
REGULATION OF CHARITIES

CHAPTER 1
THE CHARITY COMMISSION

Establishment of Charity Commission

CHAPTER 2
THE CHARITY TRIBUNAL

CHAPTER 3
REGISTRATION OF CHARITIES

General

Exempt charities: registration and regulation

PART 3
FUNDING FOR CHARITABLE, BENEVOLENT OR PHILANTHROPIC INSTITUTIONS

CHAPTER 1
PUBLIC CHARITABLE COLLECTIONS

Preliminary

Restrictions on conducting collections

Public collections certificates

Permits

Supplementary

CHAPTER 3
FINANCIAL ASSISTANCE

PART 4
MISCELLANEOUS AND GENERAL

Miscellaneous

General

An Act to provide for the establishment and functions of the Charity Commission for England and Wales and the Charity Tribunal; to make other amendments of the law about charities, including provision about charitable incorporated organisations; to make further provision about public charitable collections and other fund-raising carried on in connection with charities and other institutions; to make other provision about the funding of such institutions; and for connected purposes

[8 November 2006]

PART 1
MEANING OF "CHARITY" AND "CHARITABLE PURPOSE"

1 Meaning of "charity"

(1) For the purposes of the law of England and Wales, "charity" means an institution which—

(a) is established for charitable purposes only, and

(b) falls to be subject to the control of the High Court in the exercise of its jurisdiction with respect to charities.

(2) The definition of "charity" in subsection (1) does not apply for the purposes of an enactment if a different definition of that term applies for those purposes by virtue of that or any other enactment.

(3) A reference in any enactment or document to a charity within the meaning of the Charitable Uses Act 1601 (c 4) or the preamble to it is to be construed as a reference to a charity as defined by subsection (1).

[2131]

NOTES

Commencement: to be appointed.

Charitable Uses Act 1601: repealed by the Mortmain and Charitable Uses Act 1888, which expressly preserved the preamble at **[1]** (s 13(2)). The 1888 Act was repealed by the Charities Act 1960, ss 38(1), 48(2), Sch 7, Pt II.

2 Meaning of "charitable purpose"

(1) For the purposes of the law of England and Wales, a charitable purpose is a purpose which—

(a) falls within subsection (2), and

(b) is for the public benefit (see section 3).

(2) A purpose falls within this subsection if it falls within any of the following descriptions of purposes—

(a) the prevention or relief of poverty;

(b) the advancement of education;

(c) the advancement of religion;

(d) the advancement of health or the saving of lives;

(e) the advancement of citizenship or community development;
(f) the advancement of the arts, culture, heritage or science;
(g) the advancement of amateur sport;
(h) the advancement of human rights, conflict resolution or reconciliation or the promotion of religious or racial harmony or equality and diversity;
(i) the advancement of environmental protection or improvement;
(j) the relief of those in need by reason of youth, age, ill-health, disability, financial hardship or other disadvantage;
(k) the advancement of animal welfare;
(l) the promotion of the efficiency of the armed forces of the Crown, or of the efficiency of the police, fire and rescue services or ambulance services;
(m) any other purposes within subsection (4).

(3) In subsection (2)—
(a) in paragraph (c) "religion" includes—
(i) a religion which involves belief in more than one god, and
(ii) a religion which does not involve belief in a god;
(b) in paragraph (d) "the advancement of health" includes the prevention or relief of sickness, disease or human suffering;
(c) paragraph (e) includes—
(i) rural or urban regeneration, and
(ii) the promotion of civic responsibility, volunteering, the voluntary sector or the effectiveness or efficiency of charities;
(d) in paragraph (g) "sport" means sports or games which promote health by involving physical or mental skill or exertion;
(e) paragraph (j) includes relief given by the provision of accommodation or care to the persons mentioned in that paragraph; and
(f) in paragraph (l) "fire and rescue services" means services provided by fire and rescue authorities under Part 2 of the Fire and Rescue Services Act 2004 (c 21).

(4) The purposes within this subsection (see subsection (2)(m)) are—
(a) any purposes not within paragraphs (a) to (l) of subsection (2) but recognised as charitable purposes under existing charity law or by virtue of section 1 of the Recreational Charities Act 1958 (c 17);
(b) any purposes that may reasonably be regarded as analogous to, or within the spirit of, any purposes falling within any of those paragraphs or paragraph (a) above; and
(c) any purposes that may reasonably be regarded as analogous to, or within the spirit of, any purposes which have been recognised under charity law as falling within paragraph (b) above or this paragraph.

(5) Where any of the terms used in any of paragraphs (a) to (l) of subsection (2), or in subsection (3), has a particular meaning under charity law, the term is to be taken as having the same meaning where it appears in that provision.

(6) Any reference in any enactment or document (in whatever terms)—
(a) to charitable purposes, or
(b) to institutions having purposes that are charitable under charity law,

is to be construed in accordance with subsection (1).

(7) Subsection (6)—
(a) applies whether the enactment or document was passed or made before or after the passing of this Act, but
(b) does not apply where the context otherwise requires.

(8) In this section—
"charity law" means the law relating to charities in England and Wales; and
"existing charity law" means charity law as in force immediately before the day on which this section comes into force.

[2132]

NOTES

Commencement: 27 February 2007 (sub-s (1)(b) for the purpose of the definition of the Charity Commission's public benefit objective (as defined by the Charities Act 1993, s 1B(3), (4)) and for the purpose of enabling the Charity Commission to issue guidance in pursuance of that objective); to be appointed (remainder).

3 The "public benefit" test

(1) This section applies in connection with the requirement in section 2(1)(b) that a purpose falling within section 2(2) must be for the public benefit if it is to be a charitable purpose.

(2) In determining whether that requirement is satisfied in relation to any such purpose, it is not to be presumed that a purpose of a particular description is for the public benefit.

(3) In this Part any reference to the public benefit is a reference to the public benefit as that term is understood for the purposes of the law relating to charities in England and Wales.

(4) Subsection (3) applies subject to subsection (2).

[2133]

NOTES

Commencement: 27 February 2007 (sub-s (1) for the purpose of enabling the Charity Commission to issue guidance under s 4 in pursuance of its public benefit objective); to be appointed (remainder).

4 Guidance as to operation of public benefit requirement

(1) The Charity Commission for England and Wales (see section 6 of this Act) must issue guidance in pursuance of its public benefit objective.

(2) That objective is to promote awareness and understanding of the operation of the requirement mentioned in section 3(1) (see section 1B(3) and (4) of the Charities Act 1993 (c 10), as inserted by section 7 of this Act).

(3) The Commission may from time to time revise any guidance issued under this section.

(4) The Commission must carry out such public and other consultation as it considers appropriate—

(a) before issuing any guidance under this section, or

(b) (unless it considers that it is unnecessary to do so) before revising any such guidance.

(5) The Commission must publish any guidance issued or revised under this section in such manner as it considers appropriate.

(6) The charity trustees of a charity must have regard to any such guidance when exercising any powers or duties to which the guidance is relevant.

[2134]

NOTES

Commencement: 27 February 2007 (sub-ss (1)–(5)); to be appointed (sub-s (6)).

5 Special provisions about recreational charities, sports clubs etc

(1)–(3) …

(4) A registered sports club established for charitable purposes is to be treated as not being so established, and accordingly cannot be a charity.

(5) In subsection (4) a "registered sports club" means a club for the time being registered under Schedule 18 to the Finance Act 2002 (c 23) (relief for community amateur sports club).

[2135]

NOTES

Commencement: to be appointed.

Sub-ss (1)–(3): substitute the Recreational Charities Act 1958, s 1(2), (2A) at **[92]** and repeal s 2 thereof at **[93]**.

PART 2
REGULATION OF CHARITIES

CHAPTER 1
THE CHARITY COMMISSION

Establishment of Charity Commission

6 The Charity Commission

(1) …

(2) Schedule 1 (which inserts the new Schedule 1A into the 1993 Act) has effect.

(3) The office of Charity Commissioner for England and Wales is abolished.

(4) The functions of the Charity Commissioners for England and Wales and their property, rights and liabilities are by virtue of this subsection transferred to the Charity Commission for England and Wales.

(5) Any enactment or document has effect, so far as necessary for the purposes of or in consequence of the transfer effected by subsection (4), as if any reference to the Charity Commissioners for England and Wales or to any Charity Commissioner for England and Wales were a reference to the Charity Commission for England and Wales.

(6) …

(7) Schedule 2 (which contains supplementary provision relating to the establishment of the Charity Commission for England and Wales) has effect.

[2136]

NOTES

Commencement: 27 February 2007.

Sub-s (1): inserts the Charities Act 1993, s 1A at **[766A]**.

Sub-s (6): repeals the Charities Act 1993, s 1, Sch 1.

Commission's objectives, general functions etc

7 (*Inserts the Charities Act 1993, ss 1B–1D at* **[766B]**–**[766D]**.)

CHAPTER 2
THE CHARITY TRIBUNAL

8 The Charity Tribunal

(1) …

(2) Schedule 3 (which inserts the new Schedule 1B into the 1993 Act) has effect.

(3) Schedule 4 (which inserts the new Schedules 1C and 1D into the 1993 Act) has effect.

[2137]

NOTES

Commencement: 27 February 2007 (sub-s (1) so far as inserts Charities Act 1993, ss 2B(1)–(4), (8), (9), 2C(5)(b) for the purpose of enabling the Lord Chancellor to exercise the power to make subordinate legislation; sub-s (3) certain purposes); to be appointed (remainder).

Sub-s (1): inserts the Charities Act 1993, ss 2A–2D at **[767A]**–**[767D]**.

CHAPTER 3
REGISTRATION OF CHARITIES

General

9 (*Substitutes the Charities Act 1993, ss 3–3B at* **[768]**–**[768B]**.)

10 Interim changes in threshold for registration of small charities

(1) At any time before the appointed day, the Minister may by order amend section 3 of the 1993 Act (the register of charities) so as to—

(a) replace section 3(5)(c) (threshold for registration of small charities) with a provision referring to a charity whose gross income does not exceed such sum as is prescribed in the order, and

(b) define "gross income" for the purposes of that provision.

(2) Subsection (1) does not affect the existing power under section 3(12) of that Act to increase the financial limit specified in section 3(5)(c).

(3) This section ceases to have effect on the appointed day.

(4) In this section "the appointed day" means the day on which section 3A(1) to (5) of the 1993 Act (as substituted by section 9 of this Act) come into force by virtue of an order under section 79 of this Act.

[2138]

NOTES

Commencement: 27 February 2007.

Exempt charities: registration and regulation

11 Changes in exempt charities

(1)–(10) …

(11) The Minister may by order make such further amendments of Schedule 2 to the 1993 Act as he considers appropriate for securing—

(a) that (so far as they are charities) institutions of a particular description become or (as the case may be) cease to be exempt charities, or

(b) that (so far as it is a charity) a particular institution becomes or (as the case may be) ceases to be an exempt charity,

or for removing from that Schedule an institution that has ceased to exist.

(12) An order under subsection (11) may only be made for the purpose mentioned in paragraph (a) or (b) of that subsection if the Minister is satisfied that the order is desirable in the interests of ensuring appropriate or effective regulation of the charities or charity concerned in connection with compliance by the charity trustees of the charities or charity with their legal obligations in exercising control and management of the administration of the charities or charity.

(13) The Minister may by order make such amendments or other modifications of any enactment as he considers appropriate in connection with—

(a) charities of a particular description becoming, or ceasing to be, exempt charities, or

(b) a particular charity becoming, or ceasing to be, an exempt charity,

by virtue of any provision made by or under this section.

(14) In this section "exempt charity" has the same meaning as in the 1993 Act.

[2139]

NOTES

Commencement: 27 February 2007 (sub-ss (11)–(14)); to be appointed (sub-ss (1)–(10)).
Sub-ss (1)–(9): amend the Charities Act 1993, Sch 2 at **[866]**.
Sub-s (10): amends the Charities Act 1993, s 24(8) at **[792]**.

12 Increased regulation of exempt charities under 1993 Act

The 1993 Act is amended in accordance with Schedule 5 (which has effect for increasing the extent to which exempt charities are subject to regulation under that Act).

[2140]

NOTES

Commencement: to be appointed.

13 General duty of principal regulator in relation to exempt charity

(1) This section applies to any body or Minister of the Crown who is the principal regulator in relation to an exempt charity.

(2) The body or Minister must do all that it or he reasonably can to meet the compliance objective in relation to the charity.

(3) The compliance objective is to promote compliance by the charity trustees with their legal obligations in exercising control and management of the administration of the charity.

(4) In this section—
(a) "exempt charity" has the same meaning as in the 1993 Act; and
(b) "principal regulator", in relation to an exempt charity, means such body or Minister of the Crown as is prescribed as its principal regulator by regulations made by the Minister.

(5) Regulations under subsection (4)(b) may make such amendments or other modifications of any enactment as the Minister considers appropriate for the purpose of facilitating, or otherwise in connection with, the discharge by a principal regulator of the duty under subsection (2).

[2141]

NOTES

Commencement: 8 November 2006 (sub-ss (4), (5)); remainder to be appointed.

14–44 (S 14 inserts the Charities Act 1993, s 86A at **[850A]**. Chapter 4: s 15 amends the Charities Act 1993, s 13 at **[777]**; s 16 amends the Charities Act 1993, s 14 at **[778]**; s 17 inserts the Charities Act 1993, s 14A at **[778A]**; s 18 inserts the Charities Act 1993, s 14B at **[778B]**. Chapter 5: s 19 inserts the Charities Act 1993, s 18A at **[782A]**; s 20 inserts the Charities Act 1993, s 19A at **[783A]**; s 21 inserts the Charities Act 1993, s 19B at **[783B]**; s 22 substitutes the Charities Act 1993, ss 20, 20A at **[784]**, **[784A]**; s 23(1) inserts the Charities Act 1993, s 23(3A), (3B) at **[787]**; s 23(2) amends the Charities Act 1993, s 25(2) at **[789]**; s 23(3) inserts the Charities Act 1993, s 25(4)–(6) at **[789]**; s 23(4) inserts the Charities Act 1993, s 25A at **[789A]**; s 23(5) amends the Charities Act 1993, s 100(4) at **[864]**; s 24 substitutes the Charities Act 1993, s 29 at **[793]**; s 25 inserts the Charities Act 1993, s 29A at **[793A]**; s 26(1) inserts the Charities Act 1993, s 31A at **[795A]**; s 26(2) inserts the Criminal Justice and Police Act 2001, Sch 1, Pt 1, para 56A; s 27 amends the Charities Act 1993, s 38 at **[802]**. Chapter 6: s 28 amends the Charities Act 1993, s 43 at **[807]**; s 29(1) inserts the Charities Act 1993, s 44A at **[808A]**; s 29(2) amends the Charities Act 1993, s 46 at **[810]**; s 30(1) inserts the Charities Act 1993, s 49A at **[813A]**; s 30(2) introduces Sch 6 to this Act. Chapter 7: s 31 amends the Charities Act 1993, s 64 at **[828]**; s 32 amends the Companies Act 1985, s 249A(4) at **[395]** and 249B(1C)at **[397]**; s 33 inserts the Charities Act 1993, s 68A at **[832A]**. Chapter 8: s 34 introduces Sch 7 to this Act. Chapter 9: s 35 inserts the Charities Act 1993, s 72(4A) at **[836]**; s 36 inserts the Charities Act 1993, ss 73A, 73B at **[837A]**, **[837B]**; s 37 inserts the Charities Act 1993, s 73C at **[837C]**; s 38 inserts the Charities Act 1993, ss 73D, 73E at **[837C]**, **[837D]**; s 39 inserts the Charities Act 1993, s 73F at **[837F]**. Chapter 10: s 40 substitutes the Charities Act 1993, ss 74–74B at **[838]**–**[838B]**; s 41 inserts the Charities Act 1993, s 74C at **[838C]**; s 42 inserts the Charities Act 1993, s 74D at **[838D]**. Chapter 11: s 43 substitutes the Charities Act 1993, ss 75–75B at **[839]**–**[839B]**; s 44 inserts the Charities Act 1993, ss 75C–75F at **[839C]**–**[839F]**.)

PART 3
FUNDING FOR CHARITABLE, BENEVOLENT OR PHILANTHROPIC INSTITUTIONS

CHAPTER 1
PUBLIC CHARITABLE COLLECTIONS

Preliminary

45 Regulation of public charitable collections

(1) This Chapter regulates public charitable collections, which are of the following two types—
(a) collections in a public place; and

(b) door to door collections.

(2) For the purposes of this Chapter—

(a) "public charitable collection" means (subject to section 46) a charitable appeal which is made—

(i) in any public place, or

(ii) by means of visits to houses or business premises (or both);

(b) "charitable appeal" means an appeal to members of the public which is—

(i) an appeal to them to give money or other property, or

(ii) an appeal falling within subsection (4),

(or both) and which is made in association with a representation that the whole or any part of its proceeds is to be applied for charitable, benevolent or philanthropic purposes;

(c) a "collection in a public place" is a public charitable collection that is made in a public place, as mentioned in paragraph (a)(i);

(d) a "door to door collection" is a public charitable collection that is made by means of visits to houses or business premises (or both), as mentioned in paragraph (a)(ii).

(3) For the purposes of subsection (2)(b)—

(a) the reference to the giving of money is to doing so by whatever means; and

(b) it does not matter whether the giving of money or other property is for consideration or otherwise.

(4) An appeal falls within this subsection if it consists in or includes—

(a) the making of an offer to sell goods or to supply services, or

(b) the exposing of goods for sale,

to members of the public.

(5) In this section—

"business premises" means any premises used for business or other commercial purposes;

"house" includes any part of a building constituting a separate dwelling;

"public place" means—

(a) any highway, and

(b) (subject to subsection (6)) any other place to which, at any time when the appeal is made, members of the public have or are permitted to have access and which either—

(i) is not within a building, or

(ii) if within a building, is a public area within any station, airport or shopping precinct or any other similar public area.

(6) In subsection (5), paragraph (b) of the definition of "public place" does not include—

(a) any place to which members of the public are permitted to have access only if any payment or ticket required as a condition of access has been made or purchased; or

(b) any place to which members of the public are permitted to have access only by virtue of permission given for the purposes of the appeal in question.

[2142]

NOTES

Commencement: to be appointed.

46 Charitable appeals that are not public charitable collections

(1) A charitable appeal is not a public charitable collection if the appeal—

(a) is made in the course of a public meeting; or

(b) is made—

(i) on land within a churchyard or burial ground contiguous or adjacent to a place of public worship, or

(ii) on other land occupied for the purposes of a place of public worship and contiguous or adjacent to it,

where the land is enclosed or substantially enclosed (whether by any wall or building or otherwise); or

(c) is made on land to which members of the public have access only—

(i) by virtue of the express or implied permission of the occupier of the land, or

(ii) by virtue of any enactment,

and the occupier is the promoter of the collection; or

(d) is an appeal to members of the public to give money or other property by placing it in an unattended receptacle.

(2) For the purposes of subsection (1)(c) "the occupier", in relation to unoccupied land, means the person entitled to occupy it.

(3) For the purposes of subsection (1)(d) a receptacle is unattended if it is not in the possession or custody of a person acting as a collector.

[2143]

NOTES

Commencement: to be appointed.

47 Other definitions for purposes of this Chapter

(1) In this Chapter—

"charitable, benevolent or philanthropic institution" means—

(a) a charity, or

(b) an institution (other than a charity) which is established for charitable, benevolent, or philanthropic purposes;

"collector", in relation to a public charitable collection, means any person by whom the appeal in question is made (whether made by him alone or with others and whether made by him for remuneration or otherwise);

"local authority" means a unitary authority, the council of a district so far as it is not a unitary authority, the council of a London borough or of a Welsh county or county borough, the Common Council of the City of London or the Council of the Isles of Scilly;

"prescribed" means prescribed by regulations under section 63;

"proceeds", in relation to a public charitable collection, means all money or other property given (whether for consideration or otherwise) in response to the charitable appeal in question;

"promoter", in relation to a public charitable collection, means—

(a) a person who (whether alone or with others and whether for remuneration or otherwise) organises or controls the conduct of the charitable appeal in question, or

(b) where there is no person acting as mentioned in paragraph (a), any person who acts as a collector in respect of the collection,

and associated expressions are to be construed accordingly;

"public collections certificate" means a certificate issued by the Commission under section 52.

(2) In subsection (1) "unitary authority" means—

(a) the council of a county so far as it is the council for an area for which there are no district councils;

(b) the council of any district comprised in an area for which there is no county council.

(3) The functions exercisable under this Chapter by a local authority are to be exercisable—

(a) as respects the Inner Temple, by its Sub-Treasurer, and

(b) as respects the Middle Temple, by its Under Treasurer;

and references in this Chapter to a local authority or to the area of a local authority are to be construed accordingly.

[2144]

NOTES

Commencement: to be appointed.

Restrictions on conducting collections

48 Restrictions on conducting collections in a public place

(1) A collection in a public place must not be conducted unless—

(a) the promoters of the collection hold a public collections certificate in force under section 52 in respect of the collection, and
(b) the collection is conducted in accordance with a permit issued under section 59 by the local authority in whose area it is conducted.

(2) Subsection (1) does not apply to a public charitable collection which is an exempt collection by virtue of section 50 (local, short-term collections).

(3) Where—
(a) a collection in a public place is conducted in contravention of subsection (1), and
(b) the circumstances of the case do not fall within section 50(6),

every promoter of the collection is guilty of an offence and liable on summary conviction to a fine not exceeding level 5 on the standard scale.

[2145]

NOTES

Commencement: to be appointed.

49 Restrictions on conducting door to door collections

(1) A door to door collection must not be conducted unless the promoters of the collection—
(a) hold a public collections certificate in force under section 52 in respect of the collection, and
(b) have within the prescribed period falling before the day (or the first of the days) on which the collection takes place—
(i) notified the local authority in whose area the collection is to be conducted of the matters mentioned in subsection (3), and
(ii) provided that authority with a copy of the certificate mentioned in paragraph (a).

(2) Subsection (1) does not apply to a door to door collection which is an exempt collection by virtue of section 50 (local, short-term collections).

(3) The matters referred to in subsection (1)(b)(i) are—
(a) the purpose for which the proceeds of the appeal are to be applied;
(b) the prescribed particulars of when the collection is to be conducted;
(c) the locality within which the collection is to be conducted; and
(d) such other matters as may be prescribed.

(4) Where—
(a) a door to door collection is conducted in contravention of subsection (1), and
(b) the circumstances of the case do not fall within section 50(6),

every promoter of the collection is guilty of an offence and liable on summary conviction to a fine not exceeding level 5 on the standard scale.

This is subject to subsection (5).

(5) Where—
(a) a door to door collection is conducted in contravention of subsection (1),
(b) the appeal is for goods only, and
(c) the circumstances of the case do not fall within section 50(6),

every promoter of the collection is guilty of an offence and liable on summary conviction to a fine not exceeding level 3 on the standard scale.

(6) In subsection (5) "goods" includes all personal chattels other than things in action and money.

[2146]

NOTES

Commencement: to be appointed.

50 Exemption for local, short-term collections

(1) A public charitable collection is an exempt collection if—
(a) it is a local, short-term collection (see subsection (2)), and
(b) the promoters notify the local authority in whose area it is to be conducted of the

matters mentioned in subsection (3) within the prescribed period falling before the day (or the first of the days) on which the collection takes place,

unless, within the prescribed period beginning with the date when they are so notified, the local authority serve a notice under subsection (4) on the promoters.

(2) A public charitable collection is a local, short term collection if—

(a) the appeal is local in character; and

(b) the duration of the appeal does not exceed the prescribed period of time.

(3) The matters referred to in subsection (1)(b) are—

(a) the purpose for which the proceeds of the appeal are to be applied;

(b) the date or dates on which the collection is to be conducted;

(c) the place at which, or the locality within which, the collection is to be conducted; and

(d) such other matters as may be prescribed.

(4) Where it appears to the local authority—

(a) that the collection is not a local, short-term collection, or

(b) that the promoters or any of them have or has on any occasion—

(i) breached any provision of regulations made under section 63, or

(ii) been convicted of an offence within section 53(2)(a)(i) to (v),

they must serve on the promoters written notice of their decision to that effect and the reasons for their decision.

(5) That notice must also state the right of appeal conferred by section 62(1) and the time within which such an appeal must be brought.

(6) Where—

(a) a collection in a public place is conducted otherwise than in accordance with section 48(1) or a door to door collection is conducted otherwise than in accordance with section 49(1), and

(b) the collection is a local, short term collection but the promoters do not notify the local authority as mentioned in subsection (1)(b),

every promoter of the collection is guilty of an offence and liable on summary conviction to a fine not exceeding level 3 on the standard scale.

[2147]

NOTES

Commencement: to be appointed.

Public collections certificates

51 Applications for certificates

(1) A person or persons proposing to promote public charitable collections (other than exempt collections) may apply to the Charity Commission for a public collections certificate in respect of those collections.

(2) The application must be made—

(a) within the specified period falling before the first of the collections is to commence, or

(b) before such later date as the Commission may allow in the case of that application.

(3) The application must—

(a) be made in such form as may be specified,

(b) specify the period for which the certificate is sought (which must be no more than 5 years), and

(c) contain such other information as may be specified.

(4) An application under this section may be made for a public collections certificate in respect of a single collection; and the references in this Chapter, in the context of such certificates, to public charitable collections are to be read accordingly.

(5) In subsections (2) and (3) "specified" means specified in regulations made by the Commission after consulting such persons or bodies of persons as it considers appropriate.

(6) Regulations under subsection (5)—
(a) must be published in such manner as the Commission considers appropriate,
(b) may make different provision for different cases or descriptions of case, and
(c) may make such incidental, supplementary, consequential or transitional provision as the Commission considers appropriate.

(7) In this section "exempt collection" means a public charitable collection which is an exempt collection by virtue of section 50.

[2148]

NOTES

Commencement: to be appointed.

52 Determination of applications and issue of certificates

(1) On receiving an application for a public collections certificate made in accordance with section 51, the Commission may make such inquiries (whether under section 54 or otherwise) as it thinks fit.

(2) The Commission must, after making any such inquiries, determine the application by either—
(a) issuing a public collections certificate in respect of the collections, or
(b) refusing the application on one or more of the grounds specified in section 53(1).

(3) A public collections certificate—
(a) must specify such matters as may be prescribed, and
(b) shall (subject to section 56) be in force for—
(i) the period specified in the application in accordance with section 51(3)(b), or
(ii) such shorter period as the Commission thinks fit.

(4) The Commission may, at the time of issuing a public collections certificate, attach to it such conditions as it thinks fit.

(5) Conditions attached under subsection (4) may include conditions prescribed for the purposes of that subsection.

(6) The Commission must secure that the terms of any conditions attached under subsection (4) are consistent with the provisions of any regulations under section 63 (whether or not prescribing conditions for the purposes of that subsection).

(7) Where the Commission—
(a) refuses to issue a certificate, or
(b) attaches any condition to it,

it must serve on the applicant written notice of its decision and the reasons for its decision.

(8) That notice must also state the right of appeal conferred by section 57(1) and the time within which such an appeal must be brought.

[2149]

NOTES

Commencement: to be appointed.

53 Grounds for refusing to issue a certificate

(1) The grounds on which the Commission may refuse an application for a public collections certificate are—
(a) that the applicant has been convicted of a relevant offence;
(b) where the applicant is a person other than a charitable, benevolent or philanthropic institution for whose benefit the collections are proposed to be conducted, that the Commission is not satisfied that the applicant is authorised (whether by any such institution or by any person acting on behalf of any such institution) to promote the collections;
(c) that it appears to the Commission that the applicant, in promoting any other collection authorised under this Chapter or under section 119 of the 1982 Act, failed to exercise the required due diligence;

(d) that the Commission is not satisfied that the applicant will exercise the required due diligence in promoting the proposed collections;

(e) that it appears to the Commission that the amount likely to be applied for charitable, benevolent or philanthropic purposes in consequence of the proposed collections would be inadequate, having regard to the likely amount of the proceeds of the collections;

(f) that it appears to the Commission that the applicant or any other person would be likely to receive an amount by way of remuneration in connection with the collections that would be excessive, having regard to all the circumstances;

(g) that the applicant has failed to provide information—
 (i) required for the purposes of the application for the certificate or a previous application, or
 (ii) in response to a request under section 54(1);

(h) that it appears to the Commission that information so provided to it by the applicant is false or misleading in a material particular;

(i) that it appears to the Commission that the applicant or any person authorised by him—
 (i) has breached any conditions attached to a previous public collections certificate, or
 (ii) has persistently breached any conditions attached to a permit issued under section 59;

(j) that it appears to the Commission that the applicant or any person authorised by him has on any occasion breached any provision of regulations made under section 63(1)(b).

(2) For the purposes of subsection (1)—

(a) a "relevant offence" is—
 (i) an offence under section 5 of the 1916 Act;
 (ii) an offence under the 1939 Act;
 (iii) an offence under section 119 of the 1982 Act or regulations made under it;
 (iv) an offence under this Chapter;
 (v) an offence involving dishonesty; or
 (vi) an offence of a kind the commission of which would, in the opinion of the Commission, be likely to be facilitated by the issuing to the applicant of a public collections certificate; and

(b) the "required due diligence" is due diligence—
 (i) to secure that persons authorised by the applicant to act as collectors for the purposes of the collection were (or will be) fit and proper persons;
 (ii) to secure that such persons complied (or will comply) with the provisions of regulations under section 63(1)(b) of this Act or (as the case may be) section 119 of the 1982 Act; or
 (iii) to prevent badges or certificates of authority being obtained by persons other than those the applicant had so authorised.

(3) Where an application for a certificate is made by more than one person, any reference to the applicant in subsection (1) or (2) is to be construed as a reference to any of the applicants.

(4) Subject to subsections (5) and (6), the reference in subsection (2)(b)(iii) to badges or certificates of authority is a reference to badges or certificates of authority in a form prescribed by regulations under section 63(1)(b) of this Act or (as the case may be) under section 119 of the 1982 Act.

(5) Subsection (2)(b) applies to the conduct of the applicant (or any of the applicants) in relation to any public charitable collection authorised—

(a) under regulations made under section 5 of the 1916 Act (collection of money or sale of articles in a street or other public place), or

(b) under the 1939 Act (collection of money or other property by means of visits from house to house),

as it applies to his conduct in relation to a collection authorised under this Chapter, but subject to the modifications set out in subsection (6).

(6) The modifications are—

(a) in the case of a collection authorised under regulations made under the 1916 Act—
 (i) the reference in subsection (2)(b)(ii) to regulations under section 63(1)(b)

of this Act is to be construed as a reference to the regulations under which the collection in question was authorised, and

(ii) the reference in subsection (2)(b)(iii) to badges or certificates of authority is to be construed as a reference to any written authority provided to a collector pursuant to those regulations; and

(b) in the case of a collection authorised under the 1939 Act—

(i) the reference in subsection (2)(b)(ii) to regulations under section 63(1)(b) of this Act is to be construed as a reference to regulations under section 4 of that Act, and

(ii) the reference in subsection (2)(b)(iii) to badges or certificates of authority is to be construed as a reference to badges or certificates of authority in a form prescribed by such regulations.

(7) In subsections (1)(c) and (5) a reference to a collection authorised under this Chapter is a reference to a public charitable collection that—

(a) is conducted in accordance with section 48 or section 49 (as the case may be), or

(b) is an exempt collection by virtue of section 50.

(8) In this section—

"the 1916 Act" means the Police, Factories, &c. (Miscellaneous Provisions) Act 1916 (c 31);

"the 1939 Act" means the House to House Collections Act 1939 (c 44); and

"the 1982 Act" means the Civic Government (Scotland) Act 1982 (c 45).

[2150]

NOTES

Commencement: to be appointed.

54 Power to call for information and documents

(1) The Commission may request—

(a) any applicant for a public collections certificate, or

(b) any person to whom such a certificate has been issued,

to provide it with any information in his possession, or document in his custody or under this control, which is relevant to the exercise of any of its functions under this Chapter.

(2) Nothing in this section affects the power conferred on the Commission by section 9 of the 1993 Act.

[2151]

NOTES

Commencement: to be appointed.

55 Transfer of certificate between trustees of unincorporated charity

(1) One or more individuals to whom a public collections certificate has been issued ("the holders") may apply to the Commission for a direction that the certificate be transferred to one or more other individuals ("the recipients").

(2) An application under subsection (1) must—

(a) be in such form as may be specified, and

(b) contain such information as may be specified.

(3) The Commission may direct that the certificate be transferred if it is satisfied that—

(a) each of the holders is or was a trustee of a charity which is not a body corporate;

(b) each of the recipients is a trustee of that charity and consents to the transfer; and

(c) the charity trustees consent to the transfer.

(4) Where the Commission refuses to direct that a certificate be transferred, it must serve on the holders written notice of—

(a) its decision, and

(b) the reasons for its decision.

(5) That notice must also state the right of appeal conferred by section 57(2) and the time within which such an appeal must be brought.

(6) Subsections (5) and (6) of section 51 apply for the purposes of subsection (2) of this section as they apply for the purposes of subsection (3) of that section.

(7) Except as provided by this section, a public collections certificate is not transferable.
[2152]

NOTES

Commencement: to be appointed.

56 Withdrawal or variation etc of certificates

(1) Where subsection (2), (3) or (4) applies, the Commission may—

(a) withdraw a public collections certificate,

(b) suspend such a certificate,

(c) attach any condition (or further condition) to such a certificate, or

(d) vary any existing condition of such a certificate.

(2) This subsection applies where the Commission—

(a) has reason to believe there has been a change in the circumstances which prevailed at the time when it issued the certificate, and

(b) is of the opinion that, if the application for the certificate had been made in the new circumstances, it would not have issued the certificate or would have issued it subject to different or additional conditions.

(3) This subsection applies where—

(a) the holder of a certificate has unreasonably refused to provide any information or document in response to a request under section 54(1), or

(b) the Commission has reason to believe that information provided to it by the holder of a certificate (or, where there is more than one holder, by any of them) for the purposes of the application for the certificate, or in response to such a request, was false or misleading in a material particular.

(4) This subsection applies where the Commission has reason to believe that there has been or is likely to be a breach of any condition of a certificate, or that a breach of such a condition is continuing.

(5) Any condition imposed at any time by the Commission under subsection (1) (whether by attaching a new condition to the certificate or by varying an existing condition) must be one that it would be appropriate for the Commission to attach to the certificate under section 52(4) if the holder was applying for it in the circumstances prevailing at that time.

(6) The exercise by the Commission of the power conferred by paragraph (b), (c) or (d) of subsection (1) on one occasion does not prevent it from exercising any of the powers conferred by that subsection on a subsequent occasion; and on any subsequent occasion the reference in subsection (2)(a) to the time when the Commission issued the certificate is a reference to the time when it last exercised any of those powers.

(7) Where the Commission—

(a) withdraws or suspends a certificate,

(b) attaches a condition to a certificate, or

(c) varies an existing condition of a certificate,

it must serve on the holder written notice of its decision and the reasons for its decision.

(8) That notice must also state the right of appeal conferred by section 57(3) and the time within which such an appeal must be brought.

(9) If the Commission—

(a) considers that the interests of the public require a decision by it under this section to have immediate effect, and

(b) includes a statement to that effect and the reasons for it in the notice served under subsection (7),

the decision takes effect when that notice is served on the holder.

(10) In any other case the certificate shall continue to have effect as if it had not been withdrawn or suspended or (as the case may be) as if the condition had not been attached or varied—

(a) until the time for bringing an appeal under section 57(3) has expired, or

(b) if such an appeal is duly brought, until the determination or abandonment of the appeal.

(11) A certificate suspended under this section shall (subject to any appeal and any withdrawal of the certificate) remain suspended until—

(a) such time as the Commission may by notice direct that the certificate is again in force, or

(b) the end of the period of six months beginning with the date on which the suspension takes effect,

whichever is the sooner.

[2153]

NOTES

Commencement: to be appointed.

57 Appeals against decisions of the Commission

(1) A person who has duly applied to the Commission for a public collections certificate may appeal to the Charity Tribunal ("the Tribunal") against a decision of the Commission under section 52—

(a) to refuse to issue the certificate, or

(b) to attach any condition to it.

(2) A person to whom a public collections certificate has been issued may appeal to the Tribunal against a decision of the Commission not to direct that the certificate be transferred under section 55.

(3) A person to whom a public collections certificate has been issued may appeal to the Tribunal against a decision of the Commission under section 56—

(a) to withdraw or suspend the certificate,

(b) to attach a condition to the certificate, or

(c) to vary an existing condition of the certificate.

(4) The Attorney General may appeal to the Tribunal against a decision of the Commission—

(a) to issue, or to refuse to issue, a certificate,

(b) to attach, or not to attach, any condition to a certificate (whether under section 52 or section 56),

(c) to direct, or not to direct, that a certificate be transferred under section 55,

(d) to withdraw or suspend, or not to withdraw or suspend, a certificate, or

(e) to vary, or not to vary, an existing condition of a certificate.

(5) In determining an appeal under this section, the Tribunal—

(a) must consider afresh the decision appealed against, and

(b) may take into account evidence which was not available to the Commission.

(6) On an appeal under this section, the Tribunal may—

(a) dismiss the appeal,

(b) quash the decision, or

(c) substitute for the decision another decision of a kind that the Commission could have made;

and in any case the Tribunal may give such directions as it thinks fit, having regard to the provisions of this Chapter and of regulations under section 63.

(7) If the Tribunal quashes the decision, it may remit the matter to the Commission (either generally or for determination in accordance with a finding made or direction given by the Tribunal).

[2154]

NOTES

Commencement: to be appointed.

Permits

58 Applications for permits to conduct collections in public places

(1) A person or persons proposing to promote a collection in a public place (other than an exempt collection) in the area of a local authority may apply to the authority for a permit to conduct that collection.

(2) The application must be made within the prescribed period falling before the day (or the first of the days) on which the collection is to take place, except as provided in subsection (4).

(3) The application must—
- (a) specify the date or dates in respect of which it is desired that the permit, if issued, should have effect (which, in the case of two or more dates, must not span a period of more than 12 months);
- (b) be accompanied by a copy of the public collections certificate in force under section 52 in respect of the proposed collection; and
- (c) contain such information as may be prescribed.

(4) Where an application ("the certificate application") has been made in accordance with section 51 for a public collections certificate in respect of the collection and either—
- (a) the certificate application has not been determined by the end of the period mentioned in subsection (2) above, or
- (b) the certificate application has been determined by the issue of such a certificate but at a time when there is insufficient time remaining for the application mentioned in subsection (2) ("the permit application") to be made by the end of that period,

the permit application must be made as early as practicable before the day (or the first of the days) on which the collection is to take place.

(5) In this section "exempt collection" means a collection in a public place which is an exempt collection by virtue of section 50.

[2155]

NOTES

Commencement: to be appointed.

59 Determination of applications and issue of permits

(1) On receiving an application made in accordance with section 58 for a permit in respect of a collection in a public place, a local authority must determine the application within the prescribed period by either—
- (a) issuing a permit in respect of the collection, or
- (b) refusing the application on the ground specified in section 60(1).

(2) Where a local authority issue such a permit, it shall (subject to section 61) have effect in respect of the date or dates specified in the application in accordance with section 58(3)(a).

(3) At the time of issuing a permit under this section, a local authority may attach to it such conditions within paragraphs (a) to (d) below as they think fit, having regard to the local circumstances of the collection—
- (a) conditions specifying the day of the week, date, time or frequency of the collection;
- (b) conditions specifying the locality or localities within their area in which the collection may be conducted;
- (c) conditions regulating the manner in which the collection is to be conducted;
- (d) such other conditions as may be prescribed for the purposes of this subsection.

(4) A local authority must secure that the terms of any conditions attached under subsection (3) are consistent with the provisions of any regulations under section 63 (whether or not prescribing conditions for the purposes of that subsection).

(5) Where a local authority—
- (a) refuse to issue a permit, or
- (b) attach any condition to it,

they must serve on the applicant written notice of their decision and the reasons for their decision.

(6) That notice must also state the right of appeal conferred by section 62(2) and the time within which such an appeal must be brought.

[2156]

NOTES

Commencement: to be appointed.

60 Refusal of permits

(1) The only ground on which a local authority may refuse an application for a permit to conduct a collection in a public place is that it appears to them that the collection would cause undue inconvenience to members of the public by reason of—

(a) the day or the week or date on or in which,
(b) the time at which,
(c) the frequency with which, or
(d) the locality or localities in which,

it is proposed to be conducted.

(2) In making a decision under subsection (1), a local authority may have regard to the fact (where it is the case) that the collection is proposed to be conducted—

(a) wholly or partly in a locality in which another collection in a public place is already authorised to be conducted under this Chapter, and
(b) on a day on which that other collection is already so authorised, or on the day falling immediately before, or immediately after, any such day.

(3) A local authority must not, however, have regard to the matters mentioned in subsection (2) if it appears to them—

(a) that the proposed collection would be conducted only in one location, which is on land to which members of the public would have access only—
  (i) by virtue of the express or implied permission of the occupier of the land, or
  (ii) by virtue of any enactment, and
(b) that the occupier of the land consents to that collection being conducted there;

and for this purpose "the occupier", in relation to unoccupied land, means the person entitled to occupy it.

(4) In this section a reference to a collection in a public place authorised under this Chapter is a reference to a collection in a public place that—

(a) is conducted in accordance with section 48, or
(b) is an exempt collection by virtue of section 50.

[2157]

NOTES

Commencement: to be appointed.

61 Withdrawal or variation etc of permits

(1) Where subsection (2), (3) or (4) applies, a local authority who have issued a permit under section 59 may—

(a) withdraw the permit,
(b) attach any condition (or further condition) to the permit, or
(c) vary any existing condition of the permit.

(2) This subsection applies where the local authority—

(a) have reason to believe that there has been a change in the circumstances which prevailed at the time when they issued the permit, and
(b) are of the opinion that, if the application for the permit had been made in the new circumstances, they would not have issued the permit or would have issued it subject to different or additional conditions.

(3) This subsection applies where the local authority have reason to believe that any information provided to them by the holder of a permit (or, where there is more than one holder, by any of them) for the purposes of the application for the permit was false or misleading in a material particular.

(4) This subsection applies where the local authority have reason to believe that there has been or is likely to be a breach of any condition of a permit issued by them, or that a breach of such a condition is continuing.

(5) Any condition imposed at any time by a local authority under subsection (1) (whether by attaching a new condition to the permit or by varying an existing condition) must be one that it would be appropriate for the authority to attach to the permit under section 59(3) if the holder was applying for it in the circumstances prevailing at that time.

(6) The exercise by a local authority of the power conferred by paragraph (b) or (c) of subsection (1) on one occasion does not prevent them from exercising any of the powers conferred by that subsection on a subsequent occasion; and on any subsequent occasion the reference in subsection (2)(a) to the time when the local authority issued the permit is a reference to the time when they last exercised any of those powers.

(7) Where under this section a local authority—
(a) withdraw a permit,
(b) attach a condition to a permit, or
(c) vary an existing condition of a permit,

they must serve on the holder written notice of their decision and the reasons for their decision.

(8) That notice must also state the right of appeal conferred by section 62(3) and the time within which such an appeal must be brought.

(9) Where a local authority withdraw a permit under this section, they must send a copy of their decision and the reasons for it to the Commission.

(10) Where a local authority under this section withdraw a permit, attach any condition to a permit, or vary an existing condition of a permit, the permit shall continue to have effect as if it had not been withdrawn or (as the case may be) as if the condition had not been attached or varied—
(a) until the time for bringing an appeal under section 62(3) has expired, or
(b) if such an appeal is duly brought, until the determination or abandonment of the appeal.

[2158]

NOTES

Commencement: to be appointed.

62 Appeals against decisions of local authority

(1) A person who, in relation to a public charitable collection, has duly notified a local authority of the matters mentioned in section 50(3) may appeal to a magistrates' court against a decision of the local authority under section 50(4)—
(a) that the collection is not a local, short-term collection, or
(b) that the promoters or any of them has breached any such provision, or been convicted of any such offence, as is mentioned in paragraph (b) of that subsection.

(2) A person who has duly applied to a local authority for a permit to conduct a collection in a public place in the authority's area may appeal to a magistrates' court against a decision of the authority under section 59—
(a) to refuse to issue a permit, or
(b) to attach any condition to it.

(3) A person to whom a permit has been issued may appeal to a magistrates' court against a decision of the local authority under section 61—
(a) to withdraw the permit,
(b) to attach a condition to the permit, or
(c) to vary an existing condition of the permit.

(4) An appeal under subsection (1), (2) or (3) shall be by way of complaint for an order, and the Magistrates' Courts Act 1980 (c 43) shall apply to the proceedings.

(5) Any such appeal shall be brought within 14 days of the date of service on the person in question of the relevant notice under section 50(4), section 59(5) or (as the case may be) section 61(7); and for the purposes of this section an appeal shall be taken to be brought when the complaint is made.

(6) An appeal against the decision of a magistrates' court on an appeal under subsection (1), (2) or (3) may be brought to the Crown Court.

(7) On an appeal to a magistrates' court or the Crown Court under this section, the court may confirm, vary or reverse the local authority's decision and generally give such directions as it thinks fit, having regard to the provisions of this Chapter and of any regulations under section 63.

(8) On an appeal against a decision of a local authority under section 50(4), directions under subsection (7) may include a direction that the collection may be conducted—

(a) on the date or dates notified in accordance with section 50(3)(b), or

(b) on such other date or dates as may be specified in the direction;

and if so conducted the collection is to be regarded as one that is an exempt collection by virtue of section 50.

(9) It shall be the duty of the local authority to comply with any directions given by the court under subsection (7); but the authority need not comply with any directions given by a magistrates' court—

(a) until the time for bringing an appeal under subsection (6) has expired, or

(b) if such an appeal is duly brought, until the determination or abandonment of the appeal.

[2159]

NOTES

Commencement: to be appointed.

Supplementary

63 Regulations

(1) The Minister may make regulations—

(a) prescribing the matters which a local authority are to take into account in determining whether a collection is local in character for the purposes of section 50(2)(a);

(b) for the purpose of regulating the conduct of public charitable collections;

(c) prescribing anything falling to be prescribed by virtue of any provision of this Chapter.

(2) The matters which may be prescribed by regulations under subsection (1)(a) include—

(a) the extent of the area within which the appeal is to be conducted;

(b) whether the appeal forms part of a series of appeals;

(c) the number of collectors making the appeal and whether they are acting for remuneration or otherwise;

(d) the financial resources (of any description) of any charitable, benevolent or philanthropic institution for whose benefit the appeal is to be conducted;

(e) where the promoters live or have any place of business.

(3) Regulations under subsection (1)(b) may make provision—

(a) about the keeping and publication of accounts;

(b) for the prevention of annoyance to members of the public;

(c) with respect to the use by collectors of badges and certificates of authority, or badges incorporating such certificates, including, in particular, provision—

(i) prescribing the form of such badges and certificates;

(ii) requiring a collector, on request, to permit his badge, or any certificate of authority held by him of the purposes of the collection, to be inspected by a constable or a duly authorised officer of a local authority, or by an occupier of any premises visited by him in the course of the collection;

(d) for prohibiting persons under a prescribed age from acting as collectors, and prohibiting others from causing them so to act.

(4) Nothing in subsection (2) or (3) prejudices the generality of subsection (1)(a) or (b).

(5) Regulations under this section may provide that any failure to comply with a specified provision of the regulations is to be an offence punishable on summary conviction by a fine not exceeding level 2 on the standard scale.

(6) Before making regulations under this section the Minister must consult such persons or bodies of persons as he considers appropriate.

[2160]

NOTES

Commencement: to be appointed.

64 Offences

(1) A person commits an offence if, in connection with any charitable appeal, he displays or uses—

(a) a prescribed badge or prescribed certificate of authority which is not for the time being held by him for the purposes of the appeal pursuant to regulations under section 63, or

(b) any badge or article, or any certificate or other document, so nearly resembling a prescribed badge or (as the case may be) a prescribed certificate of authority as to be likely to deceive a member of the public.

(2) A person commits an offence if—

(a) for the purposes of an application made under section 51 or section 58, or

(b) for the purposes of section 49 or section 50,

he knowingly or recklessly furnishes any information which is false or misleading in a material particular.

(3) A person guilty of an offence under this section is liable on summary conviction to a fine not exceeding level 5 on the standard scale.

(4) In subsection (1) "prescribed badge" and "prescribed certificate of authority" mean respectively a badge and a certificate of authority in such form as may be prescribed.

[2161]

NOTES

Commencement: to be appointed.

65 Offences by bodies corporate

(1) Where any offence under this Chapter or any regulations made under it—

(a) is committed by a body corporate, and

(b) is proved to have been committed with the consent or connivance of, or to be attributable to any neglect on the part of, any director, manager, secretary or other similar officer of the body corporate, or any person who was purporting to act in any such capacity,

he as well as the body corporate shall be guilty of that offence and shall be liable to be proceeded against and punished accordingly.

(2) In subsection (1) "director", in relation to a body corporate whose affairs are managed by its members, means a member of the body corporate.

[2162]

NOTES

Commencement: to be appointed.

66 Service of documents

(1) This section applies to any notice required to be served under this Chapter.

(2) A notice to which this section applies may be served on a person (other than a body corporate)—

(a) by delivering it to that person;

(b) by leaving it at his last known address in the United Kingdom; or

(c) by sending it by post to him at that address.

(3) A notice to which this section applies may be served on a body corporate by delivering it or sending it by post—

(a) to the registered or principal office of the body in the United Kingdom, or

(b) if it has no such office in the United Kingdom, to any place in the United Kingdom where it carries on business or conducts its activities (as the case may be).

(4) A notice to which this section applies may also be served on a person (including a body corporate) by sending it by post to that person at an address notified by that person for the purposes of this subsection to the person or persons by whom it is required to be served. **[2163]**

NOTES

Commencement: to be appointed.

67–69 (*Chapter 2: s 67 amends the Charities Act 1992, s 60 at* **[746]**; *s 68 inserts the Charities Act 1992, ss 60A, 60B at* **[746A]**, **[746B]**; *s 69 inserts the Charities Act 1992, s 64A at* **[750A]**.)

CHAPTER 3
FINANCIAL ASSISTANCE

70 Power of relevant Minister to give financial assistance to charitable, benevolent or philanthropic institutions

(1) A relevant Minister may give financial assistance to any charitable, benevolent or philanthropic institution in respect of any of the institution's activities which directly or indirectly benefit the whole or any part of England (whether or not they also benefit any other area).

(2) Financial assistance under subsection (1) may be given in any form and, in particular, may be given by way of—
- (a) grants,
- (b) loans,
- (c) guarantees, or
- (d) incurring expenditure for the benefit of the person assisted.

(3) Financial assistance under subsection (1) may be given on such terms and conditions as the relevant Minister considers appropriate.

(4) Those terms and conditions may, in particular, include provision as to—
- (a) the purposes for which the assistance may be used;
- (b) circumstances in which the assistance is to be repaid, or otherwise made good, to the relevant Minister, and the manner in which that is to be done;
- (c) the making of reports to the relevant Minister regarding the uses to which the assistance has been put;
- (d) the keeping, and making available for inspection, of accounts and other records;
- (e) the carrying out of examinations by the Comptroller and Auditor General into the economy, efficiency and effectiveness with which the assistance has been used;
- (f) the giving by the institution of financial assistance in any form to other persons on such terms and conditions as the institution or the relevant Minister considers appropriate.

(5) A person receiving assistance under this section must comply with the terms and conditions on which it is given, and compliance may be enforced by the relevant Minister.

(6) A relevant Minister may make arrangements for—
- (a) assistance under subsection (1) to be given, or
- (b) any other of his functions under this section to be exercised,

by some other person.

(7) Arrangements under subsection (6) may make provision for the functions concerned to be so exercised—
- (a) either wholly or to such extent as may be specified in the arrangements, and
- (b) either generally or in such cases or circumstances as may be so specified,

but do not prevent the functions concerned from being exercised by a relevant Minister.

(8) As soon as possible after 31st March in each year, a relevant Minister must make a report on any exercise by him of any powers under this section during the period of 12 months ending on that day.

(9) The relevant Minister must lay a copy of the report before each House of Parliament.

(10) In this section "charitable, benevolent or philanthropic institution" means—
(a) a charity, or
(b) an institution (other than a charity) which is established for charitable, benevolent or philanthropic purposes.

(11) In this section "relevant Minister" means the Secretary of State or the Minister for the Cabinet Office.

[2164]

NOTES
Commencement: to be appointed.

71 Power of National Assembly for Wales to give financial assistance to charitable, benevolent or philanthropic institutions

(1) The National Assembly for Wales may give financial assistance to any charitable, benevolent or philanthropic institution in respect of any of the institution's activities which directly or indirectly benefit the whole or any part of Wales (whether or not they also benefit any other area).

(2) Financial assistance under subsection (1) may be given in any form and, in particular, may be given by way of—
(a) grants,
(b) loans,
(c) guarantees, or
(d) incurring expenditure for the benefit of the person assisted.

(3) Financial assistance under subsection (1) may be given on such terms and conditions as the Assembly considers appropriate.

(4) Those terms and conditions may, in particular, include provision as to—
(a) the purposes for which the assistance may be used;
(b) circumstances in which the assistance is to be repaid, or otherwise made good, to the Assembly, and the manner in which that is to be done;
(c) the making of reports to the Assembly regarding the uses to which the assistance has been put;
(d) the keeping, and making available for inspection, of accounts and other records;
(e) the carrying out of examinations by the Auditor General for Wales into the economy, efficiency and effectiveness with which the assistance has been used;
(f) the giving by the institution of financial assistance in any form to other persons on such terms and conditions as the institution or the Assembly considers appropriate.

(5) A person receiving assistance under this section must comply with the terms and conditions on which it is given, and compliance may be enforced by the Assembly.

(6) The Assembly may make arrangements for—
(a) assistance under subsection (1) to be given, or
(b) any other of its functions under this section to be exercised,

by some other person.

(7) Arrangements under subsection (6) may make provision for the functions concerned to be so exercised—
(a) either wholly or to such extent as may be specified in the arrangements, and
(b) either generally or in such cases or circumstances as may be so specified,

but do not prevent the functions concerned from being exercised by the Assembly.

(8) After 31st March in each year, the Assembly must publish a report on the exercise of powers under this section during the period of 12 months ending on that day.

(9) In this section "charitable, benevolent or philanthropic institution" means—
(a) a charity, or
(b) an institution (other than a charity) which is established for charitable, benevolent or philanthropic purposes.

[2165]

NOTES

Commencement: 27 February 2007.

PART 4
MISCELLANEOUS AND GENERAL

Miscellaneous

72 Disclosure of information to and by Northern Ireland regulator

(1) This section applies if a body (referred to in this section as "the Northern Ireland regulator") is established to exercise functions in Northern Ireland which are similar in nature to the functions exercised in England and Wales by the Charity Commission.

(2) The Minister may by regulations authorise relevant public authorities to disclose information to the Northern Ireland regulator for the purpose of enabling or assisting the Northern Ireland regulator to discharge any of its functions.

(3) If the regulations authorise the disclosure of Revenue and Customs information, they must contain provision in relation to that disclosure which corresponds to the provision made in relation to the disclosure of such information by section 10(2) to (4) of the 1993 Act (as substituted by paragraph 104 of Schedule 8 to this Act).

(4) In the case of information disclosed to the Northern Ireland regulator pursuant to regulations made under this section, any power of the Northern Ireland regulator to disclose the information is exercisable subject to any express restriction subject to which the information was disclosed to the Northern Ireland regulator.

(5) Subsection (4) does not apply in relation to Revenue and Customs information disclosed to the Northern Ireland regulator pursuant to regulations made under this section; but any such information may not be further disclosed except with the consent of the Commissioners for Her Majesty's Revenue and Customs.

(6) Any person specified, or of a description specified, in regulations made under this section who discloses information in contravention of subsection (5) is guilty of an offence and liable—

(a) on summary conviction, to imprisonment for a term not exceeding 12 months or to a fine not exceeding the statutory maximum, or both;

(b) on conviction on indictment, to imprisonment for a term not exceeding two years or to a fine, or both.

(7) It is a defence for a person charged with an offence under subsection (5) of disclosing information to prove that he reasonably believed—

(a) that the disclosure was lawful, or

(b) that the information had already and lawfully been made available to the public.

(8) In the application of this section to Scotland or Northern Ireland, the reference to 12 months in subsection (6) is to be read as a reference to 6 months.

(9) In this section—

"relevant public authority" means—

(a) any government department (other than a Northern Ireland department),

(b) any local authority in England, Wales or Scotland,

(c) any person who is a constable in England and Wales or Scotland,

(d) any other body or person discharging functions of a public nature (including a body or person discharging regulatory functions in relation to any description of activities), except a body or person whose functions are exercisable only or mainly in or as regards Northern Ireland and relate only or mainly to transferred matters;

"Revenue and Customs information" means information held as mentioned in section 18(1) of the Commissioners for Revenue and Customs Act 2005 (c 11);

"transferred matter" has the same meaning as in the Northern Ireland Act 1998 (c 47).

[2166]

NOTES

Commencement: 27 February 2007.

73 Report on operation of this Act

(1) The Minister must, before the end of the period of five years beginning with the day on which this Act is passed, appoint a person to review generally the operation of this Act.

(2) The review must address, in particular, the following matters—

(a) the effect of the Act on—

(i) excepted charities,

(ii) public confidence in charities,

(iii) the level of charitable donations, and

(iv) the willingness of individuals to volunteer,

(b) the status of the Charity Commission as a government department, and

(c) any other matters the Minister considers appropriate.

(3) After the person appointed under subsection (1) has completed his review, he must compile a report of his conclusions.

(4) The Minister must lay before Parliament a copy of the report mentioned in subsection (3).

(5) For the purposes of this section a charity is an excepted charity if—

(a) it falls within paragraph (b) or (c) of section 3A(2) of the 1993 Act (as amended by section 9 of this Act), or

(b) it does not fall within either of those paragraphs but, immediately before the appointed day (within the meaning of section 10 of this Act), it fell within section 3(5)(b) or (5B)(b) of the 1993 Act.

[2167]

NOTES

Commencement: to be appointed.

General

74 Orders and regulations

(1) Any power of a relevant Minister to make an order or regulations under this Act is exercisable by statutory instrument.

(2) Any such power—

(a) may be exercised so as to make different provision for different cases or descriptions of case or different purposes or areas, and

(b) includes power to make such incidental, supplementary, consequential, transitory, transitional or saving provision as the relevant Minister considers appropriate.

(3) Subject to subsection (4), orders or regulations made by a relevant Minister under this Act are to be subject to annulment in pursuance of a resolution of either House of Parliament.

(4) Subsection (3) does not apply to—

(a) any order under section 11,

(b) any regulations under section 13(4)(b) which amend any provision of an Act,

(c) any regulations under section 72,

(d) any order under section 75(4) which amends or repeals any provision of an Act or an Act of the Scottish Parliament,

(e) any order under section 76 or 77, or

(f) any order under section 79(2).

(5) No order or regulations within subsection (4)(a), (b), (c), (d) or (e) may be made by a relevant Minister (whether alone or with other provisions) unless a draft of the order or regulations has been laid before, and approved by resolution of, each House of Parliament.

(6) If a draft of an instrument containing an order under section 11 would, apart from this subsection, be treated for the purposes of the Standing Orders of either House of Parliament as a hybrid instrument, it is to proceed in that House as if it were not such an instrument.

(7) In this section "relevant Minister" means the Secretary of State or the Minister for the Cabinet Office.

[2168]

NOTES

Commencement: 8 November 2006.

75 Amendments, repeals, revocations and transitional provisions

(1) Schedule 8 contains minor and consequential amendments.

(2) Schedule 9 makes provision for the repeal and revocation of enactments (including enactments which are spent).

(3) Schedule 10 contains transitional provisions and savings.

(4) A relevant Minister may by order make—

(a) such supplementary, incidental or consequential provision, or

(b) such transitory, transitional or saving provision,

as he considers appropriate for the general purposes, or any particular purposes, of this Act or in consequence of, or for giving full effect to, any provision made by this Act.

(5) An order under subsection (4) may amend, repeal, revoke or otherwise modify any enactment (including an enactment restating, with or without modifications, an enactment amended by this Act).

(6) In this section "relevant Minister" means the Secretary of State or the Minister for the Cabinet Office.

[2169]

NOTES

Commencement: 8 November 2006 (sub-s (1) certain purposes, sub-ss (4), (5)); 27 February 2007 (sub-ss (1)–(3) certain purposes, sub-s (6)); remaining purposes to be appointed.

76 Pre-consolidation amendments

(1) The Minister may by order make such amendments of the enactments relating to charities as in his opinion facilitate, or are otherwise desirable in connection with, the consolidation of the whole or part of those enactments.

(2) An order under this section shall not come into force unless—

(a) a single Act, or

(b) a group of two or more Acts,

is passed consolidating the whole or part of the enactments relating to charities (with or without any other enactments).

(3) If such an Act or group of Acts is passed, the order shall (by virtue of this subsection) come into force immediately before the Act or group of Acts comes into force.

(4) Once an order under this section has come into force, no further order may be made under this section.

(5) In this section—

"amendments" includes repeals, revocations and modifications, and

"the enactments relating to charities" means—

(a) the Charities Act 1992 (c 41), the Charities Act 1993 (c 10) and this Act,

(b) any other enactment relating to institutions which fall within section 1(1) of this Act, and

(c) any other enactment, so far as forming part of the law of England and Wales, which makes provision relating to bodies or other institutions which are charities under the law of Scotland or Northern Ireland,

and section 78(2)(a) (definition of "charity") does not apply for the purposes of this section.

[2170]

NOTES

Commencement: 27 February 2007.

77 Amendments reflecting changes in company law audit provisions

(1) The Minister may by order make such amendments of the 1993 Act or this Act as he considers appropriate—

(a) in consequence of, or in connection with, any changes made or to be made by any enactment to the provisions of company law relating to the accounts of charitable companies or to the auditing of, or preparation of reports in respect of, such accounts;

(b) for the purposes of, or in connection with, applying provisions of Schedule 5A to the 1993 Act (group accounts) to charitable companies that are not required to produce group accounts under company law.

(2) In this section—

"accounts" includes group accounts;

"amendments" includes repeals and modifications;

"charitable companies" means companies which are charities;

"company law" means the enactments relating to companies.

[2171]

NOTES

Commencement: 8 November 2006.

78 Interpretation

(1) In this Act—

"the 1992 Act" means the Charities Act 1992 (c 41);

"the 1993 Act" means the Charities Act 1993 (c 10).

(2) In this Act—

(a) "charity" has the meaning given by section 1(1);

(b) "charitable purposes" has (in accordance with section 2(6)) the meaning given by section 2(1); and

(c) "charity trustees" has the same meaning as in the 1993 Act;

but (subject to subsection (3) below) the exclusions contained in section 96(2) of the 1993 Act (ecclesiastical corporations etc) have effect in relation to references to a charity in this Act as they have effect in relation to such references in that Act.

(3) Those exclusions do not have effect in relation to references in section 1 or any reference to the law relating to charities in England and Wales.

(4) In this Act "enactment" includes—

(a) any provision of subordinate legislation (within the meaning of the Interpretation Act 1978 (c 30)),

(b) a provision of a Measure of the Church Assembly or of the General Synod of the Church of England, and

(c) (in the context of section 6(5) or 75(5)) any provision made by or under an Act of the Scottish Parliament or Northern Ireland legislation,

and references to enactments include enactments passed or made after the passing of this Act.

(5) In this Act "institution" means an institution whether incorporated or not, and includes a trust or undertaking.

(6) In this Act "the Minister" means the Minister for the Cabinet Office.

(7) Subsections (2) to (5) apply except where the context otherwise requires.

[2172]

NOTES

Commencement: 8 November 2006.

79 Commencement

(1) The following provisions come into force on the day on which this Act is passed—

(a) section 13(4) and (5),

(b) section 74,

(c) section 75(4) and (5),

(d) section 78,

(e) section 77,
(f) this section and section 80, and
(g) the following provisions of Schedule 8—
paragraph 90(2),
paragraph 104 so far as it confers power to make regulations, and
paragraph 174(d),
and section 75(1) so far as relating to those provisions.

(2) Otherwise, this Act comes into force on such day as the Minister may by order appoint.

(3) An order under subsection (2)—
(a) may appoint different days for different purposes or different areas;
(b) make such provision as the Minister considers necessary or expedient for transitory, transitional or saving purposes in connection with the coming into force of any provision of this Act.

[2173]

NOTES

Commencement: 8 November 2006.

Orders: the Charities Act 2006 (Commencement No 1, Transitional Provisions and Savings) Order 2007, SI 2007/309 (see the table at the beginning of this Act for further details of the provisions brought into force by this order).

80 Short title and extent

(1) This Act may be cited as the Charities Act 2006.

(2) Subject to subsections (3) to (7), this Act extends to England and Wales only.

(3) The following provisions extend also to Scotland—
(a) sections 1 to 3 and 5,
(b) section 6(5),
(c) sections 72 and 74,
(d) section 75(2) and (3) and Schedules 9 and 10 so far as relating to the Recreational Charities Act 1958 (c 17), and
(e) section 75(4) and (5), sections 76 to 79 and this section.

(4) But the provisions referred to in subsection (3)(a) and (d) affect the law of Scotland only so far as they affect the construction of references to charities or charitable purposes in enactments which relate to matters falling within Section A1 of Part 2 of Schedule 5 to the Scotland Act 1998 (c 46) (reserved matters: fiscal policy etc); and so far as they so affect the law of Scotland—
(a) references in sections 1(1) and 2(1) to the law of England and Wales are to be read as references to the law of Scotland, and
(b) the reference in section 1(1) to the High Court is to be read as a reference to the Court of Session.

(5) The following provisions extend also to Northern Ireland—
(a) sections 1 to 3 and 5,
(b) section 6(5),
(c) section 23,
(d) sections 72 and 74,
(e) section 75(2) and (3) and Schedules 9 and 10 so far as relating to the Recreational Charities Act 1958 (c 17), and
(f) section 75(4) and (5), sections 76 to 79 and this section.

(6) But the provisions referred to in subsection (5)(a) and (e) affect the law of Northern Ireland only so far as they affect the construction of references to charities or charitable purposes in enactments which relate to matters falling within paragraph 9 of Schedule 2 to the Northern Ireland Act 1998 (c 47) (excepted matters: taxes and duties); and so far as they so affect the law of Northern Ireland—
(a) references in sections 1(1) and 2(1) to the law of England and Wales are to be read as references to the law of Northern Ireland, and
(b) the reference in section 1(1) to the High Court is to be read as a reference to the High Court in Northern Ireland.

(7) Any amendment, repeal or revocation made by this Act has the same extent as the enactment to which it relates.

(8) But subsection (7) does not apply to any amendment or repeal made in the Recreational Charities Act 1958 by a provision referred to in subsection (3) or (5).

(9) Subsection (7) also does not apply to—

(a) the amendments made by section 32 in the Companies Act 1985 (c 6), or

(b) those made by Schedule 8 in the Police, Factories, &c. (Miscellaneous Provisions) Act 1916 (c 31), or

(c) the repeal made in that Act by Schedule 9,

which extend to England and Wales only.

[2174]

NOTES

Commencement: 8 November 2006.

SCHEDULES

(*Sch 1 (The Charity Commission): para 1 inserts the Charities Act 1993, Sch 1A at* **[865A]***; paras 2, 3 are outside the scope of this work.*)

SCHEDULE 2

ESTABLISHMENT OF THE CHARITY COMMISSION: SUPPLEMENTARY

Section 6

1. In this Schedule—

"commencement" means the coming into force of section 6, and

"the Commission" means the Charity Commission.

Appointments to Commission

2.—(1) The person who immediately before commencement was the Chief Charity Commissioner for England and Wales is on commencement to become the chairman of the Commission as if duly appointed under paragraph 1 of Schedule 1A to the 1993 Act.

(2) Any other person who immediately before commencement was a Charity Commissioner for England and Wales is on commencement to become a member of the Commission as if duly appointed under that paragraph.

(3) While a person holds office as a member of the Commission by virtue of this paragraph he shall—

(a) continue to be deemed to be employed in the civil service of the Crown, and

(b) hold that office on the terms on which he held office as a Charity Commissioner for England and Wales immediately before commencement.

(4) Sub-paragraph (3)(b) is subject to—

(a) sub-paragraph (5),

(b) paragraph 3(4) and (5) of Schedule 1A to the 1993 Act, and

(c) any necessary modifications to the terms in question.

(5) No person may hold office as a member of the Commission by virtue of this paragraph for a term exceeding three years from commencement.

(6) Paragraphs 2 and 3(1) to (3) of Schedule 1A to the 1993 Act, and paragraphs 2 and 3 of Schedule 1 to this Act, shall not apply in relation to a person while he holds office as a member of the Commission by virtue of this paragraph.

Effect of transfers under section 6

3.—(1) Anything which—

(a) has been done (or has effect as if done) by or in relation to the Commissioners, and

(b) is in effect immediately before commencement,

is to be treated as if done by or in relation to the Commission.

(2) Anything (including legal proceedings) which—
- (a) relates to anything transferred by section 6(4), and
- (b) is in the process of being done by or in relation to the Commissioners,

may be continued by or in relation to the Commission.

(3) But nothing in section 6 or this paragraph affects the validity of anything done by or in relation to the Commissioners.

(4) In this paragraph "the Commissioners" means the Charity Commissioners for England and Wales (and includes any person acting for them by virtue of paragraph 3(3) of Schedule 1 to the 1993 Act).

First annual report of Commission

4.—(1) This paragraph applies if there is a period of one or more days which—
- (a) began on the day after the end of the last year for which the Charity Commissioners for England and Wales made a report under section 1(5) of the 1993 Act, and
- (b) ended on the day before commencement.

(2) The first report published by the Commission under paragraph 11 of Schedule 1A to the 1993 Act shall also be a report on the operations of the Charity Commissioners for England and Wales during the period mentioned in sub-paragraph (1).

Resource accounts of Commission

5.—(1) The new Commission and the old Commission shall be treated as being the same government department for the purposes of section 5 of the Government Resources and Accounts Act 2000 (c 20).

(2) Resource accounts sent to the Comptroller and Auditor General by the new Commission in respect of any period before commencement shall be resource accounts in the name of the new Commission.

(3) In this paragraph—

"the new Commission" means the Charity Commission established by section 6, and
"the old Commission" means the government department known as the Charity Commission and existing immediately before commencement.

[2175]

NOTES

Commencement: 27 February 2007.

(*Sch 3 (The Charity Tribunal): para 1 inserts the Charities Act 1993, Sch 1B at* **[865B]***; paras 2–5 are outside the scope of this work. Sch 4 (Appeals and applications to the Charity Tribunal) inserts the Charities Act 1993, Schs 1C, 1D at* **[865C]**, **[865D]**. *Sch 5 (Exempt charities: increased regulation under 1993 Act) amends the Charities Act 1993, ss 6, 8, 9, 16, 17, 18, 28, 33, 73 at* **[771]**, **[773]**, **[774]**, **[780]**, **[781]**, **[782]**, **[792]**, **[797]**, **[837]**. *Sch 6 (Group accounts) inserts the Charities Act 1993, Sch 5A at* **[869A]**. *Sch 7 (Charitable incorporated organisations): Pt 1, para 1 inserts the Charities Act 1993, ss 69A–69Q (Pt 8A) at* **[833A]**–**[833Q]***; Pt 1, para 2 inserts the Charities Act 1993, Sch 5B at* **[869B]***; Pt 2 amends the Charities Act 1993, ss 45, 48, 86, 97 at* **[809]**, **[812]**, **[850]**, **[861]**. *Sch 8 (Minor and consequential amendments) amends the Charities Act 1992 at* **[739]** *et seq and the Charities Act 1993 at* **[766]** *et seq, and contains various amendments to other legislation which, in so far as relevant to this work, are incorporated at the appropriate place. Sch 9 (Repeals and revocations) contains repeals and revocations only which, in so far as relevant to this work, are incorporated at the appropriate place.*)

SCHEDULE 10
TRANSITIONAL PROVISIONS AND SAVINGS

Section 75

Section 4: guidance as to operation of public benefit requirement

1. Any consultation initiated by the Charity Commissioners for England and Wales before the day on which section 4 of this Act comes into force is to be as effective for the purposes of section 4(4)(a) as if it had been initiated by the Commission on or after that day.

Section 5: recreational charities etc

2. Where section 2 of the Recreational Charities Act 1958 (c 17) applies to any trusts immediately before the day on which subsection (3) of section 5 of this Act comes into force, that subsection does not prevent the trusts from continuing to be charitable if they constitute a charity in accordance with section 1(1) of this Act.

Section 18: cy-près schemes

3. The amendment made by section 18 applies to property given for charitable purposes whether before or on or after the day on which that section comes into force.

Section 19: suspension or removal of trustee etc from membership of charity

4. The amendment made by section 19 applies where the misconduct or other relevant conduct on the part of the person suspended or removed from his office or employment took place on or after the day on which section 19 comes into force.

Section 20: specific directions for protection of charity

5. The amendment made by section 20 applies whether the inquiry under section 8 of the 1993 Act was instituted before or on or after the day on which section 20 comes into force.

Section 26: offence of obstructing power of entry

6. In relation to an offence committed before the commencement of section 281(5) of the Criminal Justice Act 2003 (c 44) (alteration of penalties for summary offences), the reference to 51 weeks in section 31A(11) of the 1993 Act (as inserted by section 26 of this Act) is to be read as a reference to 3 months.

Section 28: audit or examination of accounts of charity which is not a company

7. The amendments made by section 28 apply in relation to any financial year of a charity which begins on or after the day on which that section comes into force.

Section 29: auditor etc of charity which is not a company to report matters to Commission

8.—(1) The amendments made by section 29 apply in relation to matters ("pre-commencement matters") of which a person became aware at any time falling—
   (a) before the day on which that section comes into force, and
   (b) during a financial year ending on or after that day,

as well as in relation to matters of which he becomes aware on or after that day.

(2) Any duty imposed by or by virtue of the new section 44A(2) or 46(2A) of the 1993 Act inserted by section 29 must be complied with in relation to any such pre-commencement matters as soon as practicable after section 29 comes into force.

Section 32: audit or examination of accounts of charitable companies

9. The amendments made by section 32 apply in relation to any financial year of a charity which begins on or after the day on which that section comes into force.

Section 33: auditor etc of charitable company to report matters to Commission

10.—(1) The amendment made by section 33 applies in relation to matters ("pre-commencement matters") of which a person became aware at any time falling—

(a) before the day on which that section comes into force, and

(b) during a financial year ending on or after that day,

as well as in relation to matters of which he becomes aware on or after that day.

(2) Any duty imposed by virtue of the new section 68A(1) of the 1993 Act inserted by section 33 must be complied with in relation to any such pre-commencement matters as soon as practicable after section 33 comes into force.

Section 35: waiver of trustee's disqualification

11. The amendment made by section 35 applies whether the disqualification took effect before, on or after the day on which that section comes into force.

Section 36: remuneration of trustees etc providing services to charity

12. The amendment made by section 36 does not affect the payment of remuneration or provision of services in accordance with an agreement made before the day on which that section comes into force.

Section 38: relief from liability for breach of trust or duty

13. Sections 73D and 73E of the 1993 Act (as inserted by section 38 of this Act) have effect in relation to acts or omissions occurring before the day on which section 38 comes into force as well as in relation to those occurring on or after that day.

Section 44: registration of charity mergers

14. Section 75C of the 1993 Act (as inserted by section 44 of this Act) applies to relevant charity mergers taking place before the day on which section 44 comes into force as well as to ones taking place on or after that day.

Section 67: statements relating to fund-raising

15. The amendments made by section 67 apply in relation to any solicitation or representation to which section 60(1), (2) or (3) of the 1992 Act applies and which is made on or after the day on which section 67 comes into force.

Section 72: Disclosure of information to and by Northern Ireland regulator

16. In relation to an offence committed in England and Wales before the commencement of section 154(1) of the Criminal Justice Act 2003 (c 44) (general limit on magistrates' court's power to impose imprisonment), the reference to 12 months in section 72(6) is to be read as a reference to 6 months.

Schedule 6: group accounts

17. Paragraph 3(2) of the new Schedule 5A inserted in the 1993 Act by Schedule 6 to this Act does not apply in relation to any financial year of a parent charity beginning before the day on which paragraph 3(2) comes into force.

Schedule 8: minor and consequential amendments

18. The following provisions, namely—
   (a) paragraphs 80(6) and (8), 83(3) and (4), 99(3), (4)(a) and (5)(a) and (c), 109(12), 111(7) and 171 of Schedule 8, and
   (b) the corresponding entries in Schedule 9,

do not affect the operation of the Coal Industry Act 1987 (c 3), the Reverter of Sites Act 1987 (c 15) or the 1993 Act in relation to any appeal brought in the High Court before the day on which those provisions come into force.

19. Paragraph 98(2) of Schedule 8 does not affect the validity of any designation made by the Charity Commissioners for England and Wales under section 2(2) of the 1993 Act which is in effect immediately before that paragraph comes into force.

20. In relation to an offence committed in England and Wales before the commencement of section 154(1) of the Criminal Justice Act 2003 (c 44) (general limit on magistrates' court's power to impose imprisonment), the reference to 12 months in section 10A(4) of the 1993 Act (as inserted by paragraph 104 of Schedule 8 to this Act) is to be read as a reference to 6 months.

Schedule 9: savings on repeal of provisions of Charities Act 1960

21.—(1) This paragraph applies where, immediately before the coming into force of the repeal by this Act of section 35(6) of the Charities Act 1960 (c 58) (transfer and evidence of title to property vested in trustees), any relevant provision had effect, in accordance with that provision, as if contained in a conveyance or other document declaring the trusts on which land was held at the commencement of that Act.

(2) In such a case the relevant provision continues to have effect as if so contained despite the repeal of section 35(6) of that Act.

(3) A "relevant provision" means a provision of any of the following Acts providing for the appointment of trustees—
   (a) the Trustee Appointment Act 1850 (c 28),
   (b) the Trustee Appointment Act 1869 (c 26),
   (c) the Trustees Appointment Act 1890 (c 19), or
   (d) the School Sites Act 1852 (c 49) so far as applying any of the above Acts,

as in force at the commencement of the Charities Act 1960.

22. The repeal by this Act of section 39(2) of the Charities Act 1960 (repeal of obsolete enactments) does not affect the continued operation of any trusts which, at the commencement of that Act, were wholly or partly comprised in an enactment specified in Schedule 5 to that Act (enactments repealed as obsolete).

23. The repeal by this Act of section 48(1) of, and Schedule 6 to, the Charities Act 1960 (consequential amendments etc) does not affect the amendments made by Schedule 6 in—
   (a) section 9 of the Places of Worship Registration Act 1855 (c 81),
   (b) section 4(1) of the Open Spaces Act 1906 (c 25),
   (c) section 24(4) of the Landlord and Tenant Act 1927 (c 36), or
   (d) section 14(1) or 31 of the New Parishes Measure 1943.

24. Despite the repeal by this Act of section 48(3) of the Charities Act 1960, section 30(3) to (5) of the 1993 Act continue to apply to documents enrolled by or deposited with the Charity Commissioners under the Charitable Trusts Acts 1853 to 1939.

25. Despite the repeal by this Act of section 48(4) of the Charities Act 1960—
   (a) any scheme, order, certificate or other document issued under or for the purposes

PART I STATUTES

of the Charitable Trusts Acts 1853 to 1939 and having effect in accordance with section 48(4) immediately before the commencement of that repeal continues to have the same effect (and to be enforceable or liable to be discharged in the same way) as would have been the case if that repeal had not come into force, and

(b) any such document, and any document under the seal of the official trustees of charitable funds, may be proved as if the 1960 Act had not been passed.

26.—(1) Despite the repeal by this Act of section 48(6) of the Charities Act 1960 (c 58), the official custodian for charities is to continue to be treated as the successor for all purposes both of the official trustee of charity lands and of the official trustees of charitable funds as if—

(a) the functions of the official trustee or trustees had been functions of the official custodian, and

(b) as if the official trustee or trustees had been, and had discharged his or their functions as, holder of the office of the official custodian.

(2) Despite the repeal of section 48(6) (and without affecting the generality of sub-paragraph (1))—

(a) any property which immediately before the commencement of that repeal was, by virtue of section 48(6), held by the official custodian as if vested in him under section 21 of the 1993 Act continues to be so held, and

(b) any enactment or document referring to the official trustee or trustees mentioned above continues to have effect, so far as the context permits, as if the official custodian had been mentioned instead.

27. The repeal by this Act of the Charities Act 1960 does not affect any transitional provision or saving contained in that Act which is capable of having continuing effect but whose effect is not preserved by any other provision of this Schedule.

Schedule 9: savings on repeal of provisions of Charities Act 1992

28. The repeal by this Act of section 49 of, and Schedule 5 to, the 1992 Act (amendments relating to redundant churches etc) does not affect the amendments made by that Schedule in the Redundant Churches and Other Religious Buildings Act 1969.

Schedule 9: repeal of certain repeals made by Charities Acts 1960 and 1992

29.—(1) It is hereby declared that (in accordance with sections 15 and 16 of the Interpretation Act 1978 (c 30)) the repeal by this Act of any of the provisions mentioned in sub-paragraph (2) does not revive so much of any enactment or document as ceased to have effect by virtue of that provision.

(2) The provisions are—

(a) section 28(9) of the Charities Act 1960 (repeal of provisions regulating taking of charity proceedings),

(b) section 36 of the 1992 Act (repeal of provisions requiring Charity Commissioners' consent to dealings with charity land), and

(c) section 50 of that Act (repeal of provisions requiring amount of contributions towards maintenance etc of almshouses to be sanctioned by Charity Commissioners).

[2176]–[3000]

NOTES

Commencement: 27 February 2007 (paras 1, 6, 7, 9, 11, 13, 16, 19, 20); to be appointed (remainder).

Recreational Charities Act 1958, s 2: repealed by ss 5(1), (3), 75(2) of, and Sch 9 to, this Act as from a day to be appointed.

Charities Act 1960: repealed by s 75(3) of, and Sch 9 to, this Act as from a day to be appointed.

Trustee Appointment Act 1850; Trustee Appointment Act 1869; Trustees Appointment Act 1890: repealed by the Charities Act 1960, ss 35(6), 48(2), Sch 7, Pt I.

School Sites Act 1852: repealed, so far as applying the Trustee Appointment Act 1850, the Trustee Appointment Act 1869, and the Trustees Appointment Act 1890, by the Charities Act 1960, s 35(6).

Charitable Trusts Acts 1853 to 1939: repealed by the Charities Act 1960, s 48(2), Sch 7.

PART II
STATUTORY INSTRUMENTS

PART II
STATUTORY INSTRUMENTS

HOUSE TO HOUSE COLLECTIONS REGULATIONS 1947

(SI 1947/2662)

NOTES

Made: 12 December 1947.

Authority: House to House Collections Act 1939, s 4. The 1939 Act is repealed by the Charities Act 1992, s 78(2), Sch 7, as from a day to be appointed; these regulations will accordingly lapse on that date (unless previously revoked).

Commencement: 29 December 1947.

ARRANGEMENT OF REGULATIONS

NOTES

Modification: by virtue of the Local Authorities etc (Miscellaneous Provision) (No 2) Order 1974, SI 1974/595, reg 4(2) these regulations have effect as if for any reference to a police authority there were substituted a reference to a licensing authority within the meaning of the House to House Collections Act 1939, s 2(1A) (prospectively repealed), and any reference in the regulations to a police area is to be construed accordingly.

1 Title and extent

(1) These regulations may be cited as the House to House Collections Regulations, 1947, and shall come into operation on the twenty-ninth day of December, 1947.

(2) These regulations shall not extend to Scotland.

[3013]

NOTES

These regulations will lapse on the repeal of their enabling power by the Charities Act 1992, s 78(2), Sch 7, as from a day to be appointed under s 79(2) thereof.

2 Interpretation

(1) In these regulations, unless the context otherwise requires,—

"the Act" means the House to House Collections Act, 1939;

"chief promoter", in relation to a collection, means a person to whom a licence has been granted authorising him to promote that collection or in respect of whom an order has been made directing that he shall be exempt from the provisions of subsection (2) of section 1 of the Act as respects that collection;

"collecting box" means a box or other receptacle for monetary contributions, securely closed and sealed in such a way that it cannot be opened without breaking the seal;

"licence" means a licence granted by a police authority under section 2 of the Act;

"order" means an order made by the Secretary of State under section 3 of the Act;

"prescribed badge" means a badge in the form set out in the Fourth Schedule to these regulations;

"prescribed certificate of authority" means a certificate in the form set out in the Third Schedule to these regulations;

"receipt book" means a book of detachable forms of receipt consecutively numbered with counterfoils or duplicates correspondingly numbered;

"street collection" means a collection or sale to which regulations made under section 5 of the Police, Factories, etc (Miscellaneous Provisions) Act, 1916, apply.

(2) A mark shall for the purposes of these regulations be deemed to have been made on a collecting box if it is made on a wrapper securely gummed to the collecting box.

(3) The Interpretation Act 1889, applies to the interpretation of these regulations as it applies to the interpretation of an Act of Parliament.

[3014]

NOTES

These regulations will lapse as noted to reg 1 at **[3013]**.
The Interpretation Act 1889: see now the Interpretation Act 1978.

3 Local collections of a transitory nature

(1) Every certificate granted under subsection (4) of section 1 of the Act shall be in the form set out in the First Schedule to these regulations, and sections 5 and 6 and subsections (4) and (5) of section 8 of the Act shall be set forth on the back of every such certificate.

(2) Where such a certificate is granted as aforesaid, the provisions of these regulations shall not apply, in relation to a collection made for the purpose specified on the certificate, within the locality and within the period so specified, to the person to whom the certificate is granted or to any person authorised by him to act as a collector for the purposes of that collection.

[3015]

NOTES

These regulations will lapse as noted to reg 1 at **[3013]**.

4 Applications for licences and orders

(1) An application for a licence shall be in the form set out in the Second Schedule to these regulations, and shall give the particulars there specified.

(2) An application for a licence or for an order shall be made not later than the first day of the month preceding that in which it is proposed to commence the collection:

Provided that the police authority or, as the case may be, the Secretary of State may grant the application notwithstanding that it was not made within the time required by this paragraph if satisfied that there are special reasons for so doing.

[3016]

NOTES

These regulations will lapse as noted to reg 1 at **[3013]**.

5 Responsibility of promoters as respects collectors

Every promoter of a collection shall exercise all due diligence—

(a) to secure that persons authorised to act as collectors for the purposes of the collection are fit and proper persons; and

(*b*) *to secure compliance on the part of persons so authorised with the provisions of these regulations.*

[3017]

NOTES

These regulations will lapse as noted to reg 1 at **[3013]**.

6 Certificates of authority, badges, collecting boxes and receipt books

(1) No promoter of a collection shall permit any person to act as a collector, unless he has issued or caused to be issued to that person—

(*a*) *a prescribed certificate of authority duly completed (except as regards the signature of the collector) and signed by or on behalf of the chief promoter of the collection;*

(*b*) *a prescribed badge, having inserted therein or annexed thereto a general indication of the purpose of the collection; and*

(*c*) *if money is to be collected, a collecting box or receipt book marked with a clear indication of the purpose of the collection and a distinguishing number, which indication and number shall, in the case of a receipt book, also be marked on every receipt contained therein in addition to the consecutive number of the receipt.*

(2) *Every promoter of a collection shall exercise all due diligence to secure—*

(*a*) *that no prescribed certificate of authority, prescribed badge, collecting box or receipt book is issued, unless the name and address of the collector to whom it is issued have been entered on a list showing in respect of any collecting box or receipt book the distinguishing number thereof; and*

(*b*) *that every prescribed certificate of authority, prescribed badge, collecting box or receipt book issued by him or on his behalf is returned when the collection is completed or when for any other reason a collector ceases to act as such.*

(*3*) *In the case of a collection in respect of which a licence has been granted—*

(*a*) *every prescribed certificate of authority shall be given on a form obtained from His Majesty's Stationery Office, and every prescribed badge shall be so obtained; and*

(*b*) *every prescribed certificate of authority shall be authenticated, and the general indication on every prescribed badge of the purpose of the collection shall be inserted therein or annexed thereto, in a manner approved by the chief officer of police for the area in respect of which the licence was granted.*

[3018]

NOTES

These regulations will lapse as noted to reg 1 at **[3013]**.

7 Duties of collectors in relation to certificates and badges

Every collector shall—

(*a*) *sign his name on the prescribed certificate of authority issued to him and produce it on the demand of any police constable or of any occupant of a house visited by him for the purpose of collection;*

(*b*) *sign his name on the prescribed badge issued to him and wear the badge prominently whenever he is engaged in collecting; and*

(*c*) *keep such certificate and badge in his possession and return them to a promoter of the collection on replacement thereof or when the collection is completed or at any other time on the demand of a promoter of the collection.*

[3019]

NOTES

These regulations will lapse as noted to reg 1 at **[3013]**.

[8 Age limit

No person under the age of 16 years shall act or be authorised to act as a collector of money.]

[3020]

PART II STATUTORY INSTRUMENTS

NOTES

Substituted by the House to House Collections Regulations 1963, SI 1963/684, reg 1.
These regulations will lapse as noted to reg 1 at **[3013]**.

9 Importuning

No collector shall importune any person to the annoyance of such person, or remain in, or at the door of, any house if requested to leave by any occupant thereof.

[3021]

NOTES

These regulations will lapse as noted to reg 1 at **[3013]**.

10 Collection of money

(1) Where a collector is collecting money by means of a collecting box, he shall not receive any contribution save by permitting the person from whom it is received to place it in a collecting box issued to him by a promoter of the collection.

(2) Where a collector is collecting money by other means than a collecting box, he shall, upon receiving a contribution from any person, forthwith and in the presence of such person enter on a form of receipt in a receipt book issued to him by a promoter of the collection and on the corresponding counterfoil or duplicate the date, the name of the contributor and the amount contributed, and shall sign the form of receipt, the entries and signature being in ink or indelible pencil, and shall hand the form of receipt to the person from whom he received the contribution.

[3022]

NOTES

These regulations will lapse as noted to reg 1 at **[3013]**.

11 Duty of collectors to return boxes and books

Every collector, to whom a collecting box or receipt book has been issued, shall—

- *(a) when the collecting box is full or the receipt book is exhausted, or*
- *(b) upon the demand of a promoter of the collection, or*
- *(c) when he does not desire to act as a collector, or*
- *(d) upon the completion of the collection,*

return to a promoter of the collection that collecting box with the seal unbroken or that receipt book with a sum equal to the total amount of the contributions (if any) entered therein.

[3023]

NOTES

These regulations will lapse as noted to reg 1 at **[3013]**.

12 Examination of boxes and books

(1) Subject as provided in paragraph (2) of this regulation, a collecting box when returned shall be examined by, and, if it contains money, be opened in the presence of, a promoter of the collection and another responsible person.

(2) Where a collecting box is delivered unopened to a bank, it may be examined and opened by an official of the bank in the absence of a promoter of the collection.

(3) As soon as a collecting box has been opened, the contents shall be counted and the amount shall be entered with the distinguishing number of the collecting box on a list, which shall be certified by the persons making the examination.

(4) Every receipt book when returned and all sums received therewith shall be examined by a promoter of the collection and another responsible person, and the amount of the contributions entered in the receipt book shall be checked with the money and entered with the distinguishing number of the receipt book on a list, which shall be certified by the persons making the examination.

[3024]

NOTES

These regulations will lapse as noted to reg 1 at **[3013]**.

13 Provision for envelope collections

(1) Where the promoter of a collection to whom an order has been granted informs the Secretary of State that he desires to promote an envelope collection, and the Secretary of State is of opinion that the collection is for a charitable purpose of major importance and is suitably administered, the Secretary of State may, if he thinks fit, give permission for the promotion of an envelope collection.

(2) Where an envelope collection is made in accordance with this regulation—

- *(a) every envelope used shall have a gummed flap by means of which it can be securely closed;*
- *(b) no collector shall receive a contribution except in an envelope which has been so closed; and*
- *(c) these regulations shall have effect subject to the following modifications:—*
  - *(i) sub-paragraph (c) of paragraph (1) of regulation 6 shall not apply;*
  - *(ii) regulation 10 shall not apply;*
  - *(iii) regulations 11 and 12 shall have effect as if each envelope in which a contribution is received were a collecting box;*
  - *(iv) in regulation 11 for the words "with the seal unbroken" there shall be substituted the word "unopened";*
  - *(v) in paragraph (3) of regulation 12 for the words "As soon as a collecting box has been opened" there shall be substituted the words "As soon as the envelope has been opened" and the words "with the distinguishing number of the collecting box" shall be omitted.*

(3) In this regulation "envelope collection" means a collection made by persons going from house to house leaving envelopes in which money may be placed and which are subsequently called for.

[3025]

NOTES

These regulations will lapse as noted to reg 1 at **[3013]**.

14 Promoters to furnish accounts

(1) The chief promoter of a collection in respect of which a licence has been granted shall furnish an account of the collection to the police authority by which the licence was granted within one month of the expiry of the licence:

Provided that if licences are granted to the same person for collections to be made for the same purpose in more than one police area, a combined account of the collections made in all or any of those police areas may, by agreement between the chief promoter and the respective police authorities, be made only to such of the respective police authorities as may be so agreed.

(2) The chief promoter of a collection in respect of which an order has been made shall furnish an account annually to the Secretary of State so long as the order remains in force, and if the order is revoked a final account shall be furnished within three months of the date of the revocation of the order.

(3) The police authority or the Secretary of State may extend the period within which an account is required to be furnished to the authority or to him, as the case may be, if satisfied that there are special reasons for so doing.

(4) The chief promoter of a collection which is made in connection in whole or in part with a street collection of which an account is required to be furnished to a police authority by regulations made under section 5 of the Police, Factories, etc. (Miscellaneous Provisions) Act, 1916, may, if the said police authority agrees, combine the accounts of the house to house collection, in so far as it is made in connection with the street collection, with the accounts of the street collection, and the amount so included in the combined account shall not be required to form part of the account required to be furnished under paragraph (1) or, as the case may be, paragraph (2) of this regulation, so, however, that in the case of an account furnished under the said paragraph (2) the account shall show, in addition to an account in

respect of moneys received from house to house collections not made in connection with a street collection, a statement showing the total proceeds of all combined collections, the total expenses and the balance applied to charitable purposes.

[3026]

NOTES

These regulations will lapse as noted to reg 1 at **[3013]**.

15 Form and certification of accounts

The account required by the preceding regulation—

(*a*) *where money has been collected, shall be furnished in the form set out in the Fifth Schedule to these regulations and, where property has been collected and sold, shall be furnished in the form set out in the Sixth Schedule to these regulations, and in either case shall be certified by the chief promoter of the collection and by an independent responsible person as auditor; and*

(*b*) *where property (other than money) has been collected and given away or used, shall be furnished in the form set out in the Seventh Schedule to these regulations and shall be certified by the chief promoter and by every person responsible for the disposal of the property collected.*

[3027]

NOTES

These regulations will lapse as noted to reg 1 at **[3013]**.

16 Vouching of accounts

(*1*) *Every account furnished under paragraph* (*a*) *of regulation 15 of these regulations shall be accompanied by vouchers for each item of the expenses and application of the proceeds and, in the case of a collection of money, by every receipt book used for the purposes of the collection and by the list referred to in paragraph* (2) *of regulation 6 of these regulations and the list referred to in regulation 12 of these regulations.*

(2) *Paragraph* (*1*) *of this regulation shall not apply to an account certified by an auditor who is a member of an association or society of accountants incorporated at the date of these regulations or is on other grounds accepted as competent by the authority to which the account is submitted, but where in such a case the vouchers, receipt books and lists mentioned in the said paragraph* (*1*) *are not submitted with an account, the chief promoter shall ensure that they are available for three months after the account is submitted and shall, if the authority to which the account was submitted so requires at any time within that period, submit them to that authority.*

[3028]

NOTES

These regulations will lapse as noted to reg 1 at **[3013]**.

17 Disposal of disused certificates of authority, etc

The chief promoter of a collection shall exercise all due diligence to secure that all forms of prescribed certificates of authority and prescribed badges obtained by him for the purposes of the collection are destroyed when no longer required in connection with that collection or in connection with a further collection which he has been authorised to promote for the same purpose.

[3029]

NOTES

These regulations will lapse as noted to reg 1 at **[3013]**.

SCHEDULES

FIRST SCHEDULE

Regulation 3

Form of Certificate of Exemption of a Local Collection of a Transitory Nature

In pursuance of section 1(4) of the House to House Collections Act 1939, I hereby certify that I am satisfied that the collection, of which particulars are given below, is for a charitable purpose which is local in character, and is likely to be completed within a short period of time.

Accordingly the provisions of that Act (other than those set forth over-leaf) will not apply, in relation to a collection made for the purpose and within the locality and period indicated below, to the promoter(s) named below or to any person authorised by him/them to act as a collector for the purposes of the collection.*

(Signed)..

Particulars of Collection

Name(s) of promoter(s).

Purpose of collection.

Locality to which collection is to be confined.

Date of commencement of collection.

Date beyond which collection must not continue.

**Sections 5, 6, 8(4) and 8(5) of the Act are to be set forth on the back of the certificate.*

[3030]

NOTES

These regulations will lapse as noted to reg 1 at **[3013]**.

SECOND SCHEDULE

Regulation 4

Form of Application for Licence

To the Police Authority for (here insert name of police area).

In pursuance of section 2 of the House to House Collections Act 1939, I hereby apply for a licence authorising me to promote the collection, of which particulars are given below.

Date...................................... *(Signed)*..

Particulars of Collection

1. Surname of applicant (in block letters).

Other names.

2. Address of applicant.

3. Particulars of charitable purposes to which proceeds of collection are to be applied. (Full particulars should be given and, where possible, the most recent account of any charity which is to benefit should be enclosed.)

4. Over what parts of the police area is it proposed that the collection should extend?

5. During what period of the year is it proposed that the collection should be made?

6. Is it proposed to collect money?

7. Is it proposed to collect other property? If so, of what nature? and is it proposed to sell such property or to give it away or to use it?

8. Approximately how many persons is it proposed to authorise to act as collectors in the area of the police authority to which the application is addressed?

9. Is it proposed that remuneration should be paid out of the proceeds of the collection—

(a) to collectors?

(b) to other persons?

If so, at what rates and to what classes of persons?

10. Is application being made for licences for collections for the same purpose in other police areas?

If so, to what police authorities?

And, approximately, how many persons in all is it proposed to authorise to act as collectors?

11. Has the applicant, or to the knowledge of the applicant, anyone associated with the promotion of the collection, been refused a licence or order under the Act, or had a licence or order revoked?

If so, give particulars.

12. Is it proposed to promote this collection in conjunction with a street collection? If so, is it desired that the accounts of this collection should be combined wholly or in part with the account of the street collection?
13. If the collection is for a War Charity, state if such charity has been registered or exempted from registration under the War Charities Act 1940, and give name of registration authority and date of registration or exemption.

[3031]

NOTES
These regulations will lapse as noted to reg 1 at **[3013]**.

THIRD SCHEDULE

Regulations 2 and 6

FORM OF PRESCRIBED CERTIFICATE OF AUTHORITY

House to House Collections Act
Collector's Certificate of Authority
(Here insert name of collector in block letters)
of (here insert address of collector)
is hereby authorised to collect for
(here insert the purpose of the collection)
in (here insert the area within which the collector is authorised to collect, being an area within which the collection has been authorised)
*during the period (here insert the period during which the collector is authorised to collect, being a period during which the collection has been authorised)
Signature of collector— Signed—

** This entry may be omitted in the case of a collection in respect of which an order has been made. Regulation 7 is to be set forth on the back of the certificate.*

[3032]

NOTES
These regulations will lapse as noted to reg 1 at **[3013]**.

FOURTH SCHEDULE

Regulations 2 and 6

Form of Prescribed Badge

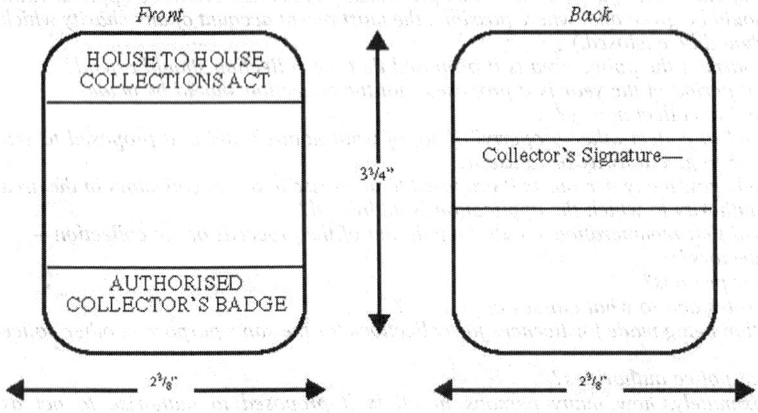

[3033]

NOTES
These regulations will lapse as noted to reg 1 at **[3013]**.

FIFTH SCHEDULE

Regulation 15

Form of Account of Expenses, Proceeds and Application of Proceeds of Collection of Money

(a) Surname of chief promoter (in block letters).
(b) Other names (in block letters).
Address of chief promoter.
Purpose of collection.
Area to which account relates.
Period to which account relates.

All amounts to be entered gross

PROCEEDS OF COLLECTION		*EXPENSES AND APPLICATION OF PROCEEDS*	
	£ s d		*£ s d*
From collectors, as in lists of collectors and amounts attached hereto.		*Printing and stationery*	
		Postage	
		Advertising	
Bank Interest		*Collecting boxes*	
Other items (if any):—		*Other items (if any):—*	
....		....	
....		....	
		Disposal of Balance (insert particulars):—	
		....	
		....	
		....	
Total		*Total*	

Certificate of Chief Promoter

I certify that to the best of my knowledge and belief the above is a true account of the expenses, proceeds and application of the proceeds of the collection to which it relates.

Date..................................... *(Signed)*...

Certificate of Auditor

I certify that I have obtained all the information and explanations required by me as auditor and that the above is in my opinion a true account of the expenses, proceeds and application of the proceeds of the collection to which it relates.

Date .... *(Signed)* ....

Qualifications ....

[3034]

NOTES

These regulations will lapse as noted to reg 1 at **[3013]**.

SIXTH SCHEDULE

Regulation 15

Form of Account of Expenses, Proceeds and Application of Proceeds of Collection of Property Sold or Collected for Sale

(a) Surname of chief promoter (in block letters).
(b) Other names (in block letters).
Address of chief promoter.
Purpose of collection.
Area to which account relates.
Period to which account relates.

Cash Account

All amounts to be entered gross

MONETARY RECEIPTS		*EXPENSES AND APPLICATION OF MONETARY RECEIPTS*		
	£ s d		*£ s d*	*£ s d*
Amount obtained during period of account by sales of property collected		*Items of expense incurred during period of account, other than expenses incurred for the purpose of converting property collected into cash, viz:—*		
Bank Interest		....		
Other items (if any):—		....		
....		....		
....				£
		Items of expense incurred during period of account for the purpose of converting property collected into cash, viz—		
		....		
		....		£
		Disposal of Balance (insert particulars):—		
		....		
		....		
				£
Total		*Total*		

Valuation of Property Collected

Estimated value of property collected during period of account ....
If the estimated value is not equal to the difference between the "amount obtained by sales of property collected" and the total of the "items of expense incurred during period of account for the purpose of converting property collected into cash", as stated in the cash account, an explanation should be given.

Certificate of Chief Promoter

I certify that to the best of my knowledge and belief the above is a true account of the expenses and the value and application of the proceeds of the collection to which it relates, and that none of the property to which it relates has been disposed of otherwise than by sale, unless found useless and destroyed or otherwise disposed of as rubbish.

Date....................................... *(Signed)*..

Certificate of Auditor

I certify that I have obtained all the information and explanations required by me as auditor and that the above is in my opinion a true account of the monetary receipts and expenses and application of the monetary receipts of the collection to which it relates.

Date..................................... (*Signed*).......................................

[3035]

NOTES

These regulations will lapse as noted to reg 1 at **[3013]**.

SEVENTH SCHEDULE

Regulation 15

Form of Account of Collection of Property (Other than Money) Given away used or Collected for Giving Away

(*a*) *Surname of chief promoter* (*in block letters*).
(*b*) *Other names* (*in block letters*).
Address of chief promoter.
Purpose of collection.
Area to which account relates.
Period to which account relates.
I certify that to the best of my knowledge and belief all property collected in the collection of which particulars are given above (*unless found useless and destroyed or otherwise disposed of as rubbish*) *has been given away or used for charitable purposes as follows:—*
(*Here insert particulars of disposal of property collected.*)

(*Signed*) .... *Chief promoter.*

....

....

Date..........................

I further certify that the above certificate has been signed by every person responsible for the disposal of the property collected.

Date................................ (*Signed*).......................................

Chief promoter.

[3036]

NOTES

These regulations will lapse as noted to reg 1 at **[3013]**.

CHARITIES (EXCEPTION OF VOLUNTARY SCHOOLS FROM REGISTRATION) REGULATIONS 1960

(SI 1960/2366)

NOTES

Made: 15 December 1960.

Authority: Charities Act 1960, ss 4(4), 43 (repealed).

These Regulations now have effect as if made under the Charities Act 1993, ss 3(5), 86, by virtue of the Interpretation Act 1978, s 17(2)(b). S 3 of the 1993 Act is substituted by the Charities Act 2006, s 9, as from a day to be appointed, and by virtue of s 3A(4)(a) of the 1993 Act (as substituted) these regulations will take effect under s 3A(2)(c) thereof on that date.

Commencement: 1 January 1961.

1 These regulations may be cited as the Charities (Exception of Voluntary Schools from Registration) Regulations, 1960, and shall come into operation on the first day of January, 1961.

[3037]

2 All voluntary schools, within the meaning of the Education Acts, 1944 to 1959, being charities and having no permanent endowment other than the premises of, or connected with, the school, are hereby excepted from the duty to be registered under subsection (2) of section 4 of the Charities Act, 1960.

[3038]

NOTES

Charities Act 1960, s 4: repealed; see now the Charities Act 1993, s 3 at **[768]**.

Education Acts 1944 to 1959: repealed; see now the School Standards and Framework Act 1998, ss 20, 21, Sch 2.

CHARITIES (EXCEPTION OF CERTAIN CHARITIES FOR BOY SCOUTS AND GIRL GUIDES FROM REGISTRATION) REGULATIONS 1961

(SI 1961/1044)

NOTES

Made: 1 June 1961.

Authority: the Charities Act 1960, ss 4(4), 43 (repealed).

These Regulations now have effect as if made under the Charities Act 1993, ss 3(5), 86, by virtue of the Interpretation Act 1978, s 17(2)(b). S 3 of the 1993 Act is substituted by the Charities Act 2006, s 9, as from a day to be appointed, and by virtue of s 3A(4)(a) of the 1993 Act (as substituted) these regulations will take effect under s 3A(2)(c) thereof on that date.

Commencement: 22 June 1961.

1 These regulations may be cited as the Charities (Exception of Certain Charities for Boy Scouts and Girl Guides from Registration) Regulations, 1961, and shall come into operation on the 22nd day of June, 1961.

[3039]

2 Charities comprising funds, not being permanent endowments, belonging to units, or to trustees for units, of the Boy Scouts Association or the Girl Guides Association, which are being accumulated for the purposes of the unit and which produce an income of more than £15 a year, are hereby excepted from the duty to be registered under subsection (2) of section 4 of the Charities Act 1960.

[3040]

NOTES

Charities Act 1960, s 4: repealed; see now the Charities Act 1993, s 3 at **[768]**.

EXEMPT CHARITIES ORDER 1962

(SI 1962/1343)

NOTES

Made: 27 June 1962.

Authority: the Charities Act 1960, Sch 2, para (c) (repealed).

This Order now has effect as if made under the Charities Act 1993, Sch 2, para (c), by virtue of the Interpretation Act 1978, s 17(2)(b).

Commencement: 9 July 1962.

1 The universities, university colleges and other institutions specified in the Schedule to this Order are hereby declared to be exempt charities for the purposes of the Charities Act 1960.

[3041]

2 This Order may be cited as the Exempt Charities Order 1962 and shall come into operation on 9th July 1962.

[3042]

SCHEDULE

Article 1

UNIVERSITIES AND UNIVERSITY COLLEGES

University of Keele.

University of Sussex.

University of Wales.

University College of Wales, Aberystwyth.

University College of North Wales.

University College of South Wales and Monmouthshire.

University College of Swansea.

INSTITUTIONS CONNECTED WITH THE UNIVERSITY OF LONDON

General

The Chairman Council and Governors of Bedford College for Women.

Birkbeck College.

Imperial College of Science and Technology.

The London School of Economics and Political Science.

The Principal and Governors of Queen Elizabeth College.

Queen Mary College.

The Royal Holloway College.

The Royal Veterinary College.

The School of Oriental and African Studies.

The School of Pharmacy, University of London.

The Principal and Governors of Westfield College London.

The College of St. Gregory and St Martin at Wye.

Medical

Charing Cross Hospital Medical School.

The Council of Governors of Guy's Hospital Medical School.

King's College Hospital Medical School (University of London).

The London Hospital Medical College.

The Middlesex Hospital Medical School.

The Royal Dental Hospital of London School of Dental Surgery.

Royal Free Hospital School of Medicine.

The Medical College of St Bartholomew's Hospital in the City of London.

St George's Hospital Medical School.

St Mary's Hospital Medical School.

St Thomas's Hospital Medical School.

University College Hospital Medical School.

Westminster Medical School.

Postgraduate Medical

The British Postgraduate Medical Federation:—

Postgraduate Medical School of London.

The Institute of Cancer Research: Royal Cancer Hospital.

The Institute of Cardiology.

The Institute of Child Health.

The Institute of Dental Surgery.

The Institute of Dermatology.

The Institute of Diseases of the Chest.

The Institute of Laryngology and Otology.

Institute of Neurology (Queen Square).

The Institute of Obstetrics and Gynaecology.

The Institute of Ophthalmology.

The Institute of Orthopaedics.

The Institute of Psychiatry.

The Institute of Urology.

The London School of Hygiene and Tropical Medicine.

INSTITUTIONS CONNECTED WITH THE UNIVERSITY OF WALES

Welsh National School of Medicine.

[3043]

NOTES

Further orders: the Orders in Council listed below, which were made, or now have effect, under the Charities Act 1993, Sch 2, para (c), declare the following universities, university colleges and other institutions to be exempt charities:

Order	Universities, etc
SI 1965/1715	*Universities*
	University of East Anglia.
	University of Essex.
	University of Kent.
	University of Lancaster.
	University of Warwick.
	University of York.
	University College
	St David's College, Lampeter.
SI 1966/1460	*Universities*
	University of Surrey.
	University of Aston in Birmingham.
	University of Bradford.
	Loughborough University of Technology.
	Institution connected with the University of Manchester
	University of Manchester Institute of Science and Technology.
SI 1967/821	*Universities*
	Bath University of Technology.

	Brunel University.
	City University.
	University of Salford.
	Institution connected with the University of London
	Chelsea College of Science and Technology.
SI 1969/1496	Open University.
SI 1978/453	University College London.
SI 1982/1661	United Medical Schools of Guy's and St Thomas's Hospitals.
SI 1983/1516	United Medical and Dental Schools of Guy's and St Thomas's Hospitals.
SI 1984/1976	University of Wales College of Medicine.
SI 1987/1823	Institute of Education, University of London.
SI 1989/2394	Goldsmiths' College, University of London.
SI 1993/2359	Cranfield University.
SI 1994/1905	London Guildhall University.
SI 1994/2956	University of Greenwich.
SI 1995/2998	University of Derby.
SI 1996/1637	London Business School.
SI 1996/1932	University of Westminster.
SI 1996/1933	University of North London.
SI 1999/3139	South Bank University.
SI 2000/1826	Royal College of Art.
SI 2002/1626	Courtauld Institute of Art
SI 2003/1881	University College Chichester
SI 2004/1995	Roehampton University
SI 2006/1452	University of Winchester

CHARITIES (EXCEPTION FROM REGISTRATION AND ACCOUNTS) REGULATIONS 1965

(SI 1965/1056)

NOTES

Made: 29 April 1965.

Authority: Charities Act 1960, ss 4(4), 8(1), 43, 45(6) (repealed).

In so far as made under ss 4(4), 43, 45(6), these Regulations now have effect as if made under the Charities Act 1993, ss 3(5), (13), 86, by virtue of the Interpretation Act 1978, s 17(2)(b). S 3 of the 1993 Act is substituted by the Charities Act 2006, s 9, as from a day to be appointed, and by virtue of s 3A(4)(a) of the 1993 Act (as substituted) these regulations will take effect under s 3A(2)(c) thereof on that date.

Commencement: 15 May 1965.

1 A charity to which these Regulations apply is hereby excepted from the duty to be registered under section 4(2) of the Charities Act 1960, and it shall be an excepted charity for the purposes of section 8(1) of that Act.

[3044]

NOTES

Charities Act 1960, ss 4, 8: repealed; in relation to s 4, see now the Charities Act 1993, s 3 at **[768]**.

2 These Regulations shall apply to a charity wholly or mainly concerned with the promotion of the efficiency of any of the armed forces of the Crown, not being—

PART II STATUTORY INSTRUMENTS

(a) a charity having any land in England and Wales for any estate or interest greater than a tenancy from year to year;
(b) a charity whose objects extend to the relief or assistance of any person not being a serving member of those forces; or
(c) a charity for the exhibition or preservation of articles of historical interest.

[3045]

3 The Interpretation Act 1889 shall apply for the interpretation of these Regulations as it applies for the interpretation of an Act of Parliament.

[3046]

NOTES

The Interpretation Act 1889: see now the Interpretation Act 1978.

4 These Regulations may be cited as the Charities (Exception from Registration and Accounts) Regulations 1965 and shall come into operation on 15th May 1965.

[3047]

CHARITIES (EXCEPTION OF UNIVERSITIES FROM REGISTRATION) REGULATIONS 1966

(SI 1966/965)

NOTES

Made: 2 August 1966.
Charities Act 1960, ss 4(4), 43 (repealed).
These Regulations now have effect as if made under the Charities Act 1993, ss 3(5), 86, by virtue of the Interpretation Act 1978, s 17(2)(b). S 3 of the 1993 Act is substituted by the Charities Act 2006, s 9, as from a day to be appointed, and by virtue of s 3A(4)(a) of the 1993 Act (as substituted) these regulations will take effect under s 3A(2)(c) thereof on that date.
Commencement: 11 August 1966.

1 Citation and commencement

These regulations may be cited as the Charities (Exception of Universities from Registration) Regulations 1966 and shall come into operation on 11th August 1966.

[3048]

2 Exception of Universities from Registration

Every university which is not an exempt charity within the meaning of the Charities Act 1960 shall be excepted from registration under the Act.

[3049]

NOTES

Charities Act 1960, s 4: repealed; see now the Charities Act 1993, s 3 at **[768]**.

CHARITABLE COLLECTIONS (TRANSITIONAL PROVISIONS) ORDER 1974

(SI 1974/140)

NOTES

Made: 30 January 1974.
Authority: Local Government Act 1972, s 254.
Commencement: 15 February 1974.

1—(1) This Order may be cited as the Charitable Collections (Transitional Provisions) Order 1974 and shall come into operation on 15th February 1974.

(2) This Order shall not apply to the Metropolitan Police District or the City of London.
[3050]

2–8 (*Lapsed.*)

SCHEDULE
MODEL STREET COLLECTION REGULATIONS

1. In these Regulations, unless the context otherwise requires—

"collection" means a collection of money or a sale of articles for the benefit of charitable or other purposes and the word "collector" shall be construed accordingly;

"promoter" means a person who causes others to act as collectors;

"the licensing authority" means (Insert the name of the licensing authority granting the permit);

"permit" means a permit for a collection;

"contributor" means a person who contributes to a collection and includes a purchaser of articles for sale for the benefit of charitable or other purposes;

"collecting box" means a box or other receptacle for the reception of money from contributors.

2. No collection, other than a collection taken at a meeting in the open air, shall be made in any street or public place within (Insert the name of the new licensing area) unless a promoter shall have obtained from the licensing authority a permit.

3. Application for a permit shall be made in writing not later than one month before the date on which it is proposed to make the collection:

Provided that the licensing authority may reduce the period of one month if satisfied that there are special reasons for so doing.

4. No collection shall be made except upon the day and between the hours stated in the permit.

5. The licensing authority may, in granting a permit, limit the collection to such streets or public places or such parts thereof as it thinks fit.

6.—(1) No person may assist or take part in any collection without the written authority of a promoter.

(2) Any person authorised under paragraph (1) above shall produce such written authority forthwith for inspection on being requested to do so by a duly authorised officer of the licensing authority or any constable.

7. No collection shall be made in any part of the carriage way of any street which has a footway:

Provided that the licensing authority may, if it thinks fit, allow a collection to take place on the said carriage way where such collection has been authorised to be held in connection with a procession.

8. No collection shall be made in a manner likely to inconvenience or annoy any person.

9. No collector shall importune any person to the annoyance of such person.

10. While collecting—
- (a) a collector shall remain stationary; and
- (b) a collector or two collectors together shall not be nearer to another collector than 25 metres:

Provided that the licensing authority may, if it thinks fit, waive the requirements of this Regulation in respect of a collection which has been authorised to be held in connection with a procession.

PART II
STATUTORY INSTRUMENTS

11. No promoter, collector or person who is otherwise connected with a collection shall permit a person under the age of sixteen years to act as a collector.

12.—(1) Every collector shall carry a collecting box.

(2) All collecting boxes shall be numbered consecutively and shall be securely closed and sealed in such a way as to prevent them being opened without the seal being broken.

(3) All money received by a collector from contributors shall immediately be placed in a collecting box.

(4) Every collector shall deliver, unopened, all collecting boxes in his possession to a promoter.

13. A collector shall not carry or use any collecting box, receptacle or tray which does not bear displayed prominently thereon the name of the charity or fund which is to benefit nor any collecting box which is not duly numbered.

14.—(1) Subject to paragraph (2) below a collecting box shall be opened in the presence of a promoter and another responsible person.

(2) Where a collecting box is delivered, unopened, to a bank, it may be opened by an official of the bank.

(3) As soon as a collecting box has been opened, the person opening it shall count the contents and shall enter the amount with the number of the collecting box on a list which shall be certified by that person.

15.—(1) No payment shall be made to any collector.

(2) No payment shall be made out of the proceeds of a collection, either directly or indirectly, to any other person connected with the promotion or conduct of such collection for, or in respect of, services connected therewith, except such payments as may have been approved by the licensing authority.

16.—(1) Within one month after the date of any collection the person to whom a permit has been granted shall forward to the licensing authority—

(a) a statement in the form set out in the Schedule to these Regulations, or in a form to the like effect, showing the amount received and the expenses and payments incurred in connection with such collection, and certified by that person and a qualified accountant;

(b) a list of the collectors;

(c) a list of the amounts contained in each collecting box;

and shall, if required by the licensing authority, satisfy it as to the proper application of the proceeds of the collection.

(2) The said person shall also, within the same period, at the expense of that person and after a qualified accountant has given his certificate under paragraph (1)(a) above, publish in such newspaper or newspapers as the licensing authority may direct a statement showing the name of the person to whom the permit has been granted, the area to which the permit relates, the name of the charity or fund to benefit, the date of the collection, the amount collected, and the amount of the expenses and payments incurred in connection with such collection.

(3) The licensing authority may, if satisfied there are special reasons for so doing extend the period of one month referred to in paragraph (1) above.

(4) For the purposes of this Regulation "a qualified accountant" means a member of one or more of the following bodies:—

the Institute of Chartered Accountants in England and Wales;
the Institute of Chartered Accountants of Scotland;
the Association of Certified Accountants;
the Institute of Chartered Accountants in Ireland.

17. These regulations shall not apply—

(a) in respect of a collection taken at a meeting in the open air; or

(b) to the selling of articles in any street or public place when the articles are sold in the ordinary course of trade.

18. Any person who acts in contravention of any of the foregoing regulations shall be liable on summary conviction to a fine not exceeding two pounds or in the case of a second or subsequent offence not exceeding five pounds.

[3051]

SCHEDULE

Form of Statement

Name of the person to whom the permit was granted ....

Address of the person to whom the permit was granted ....

Name of the charity or fund which is to benefit ....

Date of Collection ....

Show nil entries					
Proceeds of Collection	Amount	Total	Expenses and Application of Proceeds	Amount	Total
From collecting boxes Interest on proceeds Other items:—			Printing & Stationery Postage Advertising Collecting Boxes Badges Emblems Other items:— .... Payments approved under Regulation 15(2) Disposal of Balance (insert particulars)		
TOTAL £			TOTAL £		

Certificate of the person to whom the permit was granted

I certify that to the best of my knowledge and belief the above is a true account of the proceeds, expenses and application of the proceeds of the collection.

Date .... (Signed) ....

Certificate of Accountant

I certify that I have obtained all the information and explanations required by me and that the above is in my opinion a true account of the proceeds, expenses and application of the proceeds of the collection.

Date .... (Signed) ....

Qualifications ....

[3052]–[3055]

COMPANY AND BUSINESS NAMES REGULATIONS 1981

(SI 1981/1685)

NOTES

Made: 24 November 1981.

Authority: the Companies Act 1981, ss 31, 32.

These regulations now have effect as if made under the Companies Act 1985, s 29, and the Business Names Act 1985, ss 3, 6. The Business Names Act 1985 and the Companies Act 1985, s 29 are repealed by the Companies Act 2006, s 1295, Sch 9, as from a day to be appointed; by virtue s 1297 thereof, these regulations will take effect under s 55 of the 2006 from that date.

Commencement: 26 February 1982.

1 These Regulations may be cited as the Company and Business Names Regulations 1981 and shall come into operation on 26th February 1982.

[3056]

2 In these Regulations, unless the context otherwise requires, "the Act" means the Companies Act 1981.

[3057]

NOTES

Companies Act 1981: repealed and replaced by CA 1985.

3 The words and expressions stated in column (1) of the Schedule hereto [together with the plural and the possessive forms of those words and expressions] are hereby specified as words and expressions for the registration of which as or as part of a company's corporate name the approval of the Secretary of State is required by section 22(2)(b) of the Act or for the use of which as or as part of a business name his approval is required by section 28(2)(b) of the Act.

[3058]

NOTES

Words in square brackets inserted by the Company and Business Names (Amendment) Regulations 1992, SI 1992/1196, reg 2(1), (2).

Sections 22(2)(b), 28(2)(b) of the Act: see now the Companies Act 1985, s 26(2)(b at **[335]**), the Business Names Act 1985, s 2(1)(b) at **[583]**, respectively.

4 Subject to Regulation 5, each Government department or other body stated in column (2) of the Schedule hereto is hereby specified as the relevant body for the purposes of section 31(2) and (3) of the Act in relation to the word or expression [and the plural and the possessive forms of that word or expression] opposite to it in column (1).

[3059]

NOTES

Words in square brackets inserted by the Company and Business Names (Amendment) Regulations 1992, SI 1992/1196, reg 2(1), (3).

Section 31(2), (3) of the Act: see now the Companies Act 1985, s 29(2), (3) at **[338]** and the Business Names Act 1985, s 3(2) at **[584]**.

5 Where two Government departments or other bodies are specified in the alternative in Column (2) of the Schedule hereto the second alternative is to be treated as specified,

(a) in the case of the corporate name of a company,

(i) if the company has not yet been registered and its principal or only place of business in Great Britain is to be in Scotland or, if it will have no place of business in Great Britain, its proposed registered office is in Scotland, and

(ii) if the company is already registered and its principal or only place of business in Great Britain is in Scotland or, if it has no place of business in Great Britain, its registered office is in Scotland, and

(b) in the case of a business name, if the principal or only place of the business carried on or to be carried on in Great Britain is or is to be in Scotland,

and the first alternative is to be treated as specified in any other case.

[3060]

SCHEDULE

SPECIFICATION OF WORDS, EXPRESSIONS AND RELEVANT BODIES

Regulations 3–5

Column (1) *Word or expression*	*Column (2)* *Relevant body*
Abortion	Department of Health (formerly of Health and Social Security)
Apothecary	[Worshipful Society of Apothecaries of London] or Pharmaceutical Society of Great Britain
Association	
Assurance	
Assurer	
Authority	
Benevolent	
Board	
…	
British	
…	
[Chamber (or Chambers) of Business (or their Welsh equivalents, Siambr Fusnes; Siambrau Busnes)	
Chamber (or Chambers) of Commerce (or their Welsh equivalents, Siambr Fasnach; Siambrau Masnach)	
Chamber (or Chambers) of Commerce and Industry (or their Welsh equivalents, Siambr Masnach a Diwydiant; Siambrau Masnach a Diwydiant)	
Chamber (or Chambers) of Commerce, Training and Enterprise (or their Welsh equivalents, Siambr Masnach, Hyfforddiant a Menter; Siambrau Masnach, Hyfforddiant a Menter)	
Chamber (or Chambers) of Enterprise (or their Welsh equivalents, Siambr Fenter; Siambrau Menter)	
Chamber (or Chambers) of Industry (or their Welsh equivalents, Siambr Ddiwydiant; Siambrau Diwydiant)	
Chamber (or Chambers) of Trade (or their Welsh equivalents, Siambr Fasnach; Siambrau Masnach)	
Chamber (or Chambers) of Trade and Industry (or their Welsh equivalents, Siambr Masnach a Diwydiant; Siambrau Masnach a Diwydiant)	

Column (1) *Word or expression*	*Column (2)* *Relevant body*
Chamber (or Chambers) of Training (or their Welsh equivalents, Siambr Hyfforddiant; Siambrau Hyfforddiant)	
Chamber (or Chambers) of Training and Enterprise (or their Welsh equivalents, Siambr Hyfforddiant a Menter; Siambrau Hyfforddiant a Menter)]	
Chamber of Industry	
Chamber of Trade	
Charitable	Charity Commission or [the Scottish Ministers]
Charity	Charity Commission or [the Scottish Ministers]
Charter	
Chartered	
[Chemist	
Chemistry]	
Contact Lens	General Optical Council
Co-operative	
Council	
Dental	General Dental Council
Dentistry	General Dental Council
District Nurse	[Nursing and Midwifery Council]
Duke	Home Office or [the Scottish Ministers]
England	
English	
European	
Federation	
Friendly Society	
Foundation	
Fund	
Giro	
Great Britain	
Group	
Health Centre	Department of Health (formerly of Health and Social Security)
Health Service	Department of Health (formerly of Health and Social Security)
Health Visitor	[Nursing and Midwifery Council]
Her Majesty	Home Office or [the Scottish Ministers]
His Majesty	Home Office or [the Scottish Ministers]
Holding	
Industrial and Provident Society	
Institute	
Institution	

Column (1) *Word or expression*	*Column (2)* *Relevant body*
Insurance	
Insurer	
International	
Ireland	
Irish	
King	Home Office or [the Scottish Ministers]
Midwife	[Nursing and Midwifery Council]
Midwifery	[Nursing and Midwifery Council]
National	
Nurse	[Nursing and Midwifery Council]
Nursing	[Nursing and Midwifery Council]
…	
Patent	
Patentee	
Police	Home Office or [the Scottish Ministers]
[Polytechnic]	[Department for Education and Skills]
Post Office	
Pregnancy Termination	Department of Health (formerly of Health and Social Security)
Prince	Home Office or [the Scottish Ministers]
Princess	Home Office or [the Scottish Ministers]
Queen	Home Office or [the Scottish Ministers]
Reassurance	
Reassurer	
Register	
Registered	
Reinsurance	
Reinsurer	
Royal	Home Office or [the Scottish Ministers]
Royale	Home Office or [the Scottish Ministers]
Royalty	Home Office or [the Scottish Ministers]
Scotland	
Scottish	
Sheffield	
Society	
Special School	[Department for Education and Skills]
Stock Exchange	
Trade Union	
Trust	
United Kingdom	
[University]	[The Privy Council]
Wales	

PART II STATUTORY INSTRUMENTS

Column (1) *Word or expression*	*Column (2)* *Relevant body*
Welsh	
Windsor	Home Office or [the Scottish Ministers]

[**Note:** The reference in Column (2) to the Home Office shall be treated as a reference to the Lord Chancellor's Department in relation to the following entries in Column (1)—

(a) Duke,
(b) Her Majesty,
(c) His Majesty,
(d) King,
(e) Prince,
(f) Princess,
(g) Queen,
(h) Royal,
(i) Royale,
(j) Royalty, and
(k) Windsor.]

[3061]

NOTES

In entry "Apothecary" words in square brackets substituted by the Company and Business Names (Amendment) Regulations 1982, SI 1982/1653, reg 2(a), as from 1 January 1983.

Entries "Breed", "Breeder", "Breeding" and "Nursing Home" revoked by the Company and Business Names (Amendment) Regulations 1995, SI 1995/3022, reg 3(b), as from 1 January 1996.

Entry "Building Society" revoked by the Company and Business Names (Amendment) Regulations 1992, SI 1992/1196, reg 2(1), (4), as from 12 June 1992.

Entries from "Chamber (or Chambers) of Business" to "Chamber (or Chambers) of Training and Enterprise" substituted, for entries "Chamber of Commerce", "Chamber of Industry", "Chamber of Commerce, Training and Enterprise" (originally inserted by SI 1995/3022, reg 3(a)) and "Chamber of Trade" by the Companies and Business Names (Amendment) Regulations 2001, SI 2001/259, reg 3, as from 10 May 2001.

In column (2), the words "the Scottish Ministers" in square brackets in each place they appear substituted by the Scotland Act 1998 (Consequential Modifications) (No 2) Order 1999, SI 1999/1820, art 4, Sch 2, Pt II, para 139, as from 1 July 1999.

Entries "Chemist", "Chemistry", "Polytechnic" and "University" inserted by SI 1982/1653, reg 2(b), (c), as from 1 January 1983.

Words "Nursing and Midwifery Council" in square brackets in Column 2 opposite entries for "District Nurse", "Health Visitor", "Midwife", "Midwifery", "Nurse", and "Nursing" substituted by the Health Act 1999 (Consequential Amendments) (Nursing and Midwifery) Order 2004, SI 2004/1771, art 3, Schedule, Pt 2, para 52, as from 1 August 2004.

In column (2) words "Department for Education and Skills" in square brackets in each place they appear substituted by the Secretaries of State for Education and Skills and for Work and Pensions Order 2002, SI 2002/1397, art 12, Schedule, Pt II, para 17, as from 27 June 2002.

In entry "University" words in square brackets substituted by SI 1992/1196, reg 2(1), (5).

Note in final pair of square brackets added by the Transfer of Functions (Miscellaneous) Order 2001, SI 2001/3500, art 8, Sch 2, Pt II, para 14, as from 26 November 2001.

COMPANIES (TABLES A TO F) REGULATIONS 1985

(SI 1985/805)

NOTES

Made: 22 May 1985.
Authority: the Companies Act 1985, ss 3, 8.
Commencement: 1 July 1985.

1 These Regulations may be cited as the Companies (Tables A to F) Regulations 1985 and shall come into operation on 1st July 1985.

[3062]

2 The regulations in Table A and the forms in Tables B, C, D, E and F in the Schedule to these Regulations shall be the regulations and forms of memorandum and articles of association for the purposes of sections 3 and 8 of the Companies Act 1985.

[3063]

3 (*Revokes the Companies (Alteration of Table A etc) Regulations 1984, SI 1984/717.*)

SCHEDULE

TABLE A
REGULATIONS FOR MANAGEMENT OF A COMPANY LIMITED BY SHARES

INTERPRETATION

1. In these regulations—

"the Act" means the Companies Act 1985 including any statutory modification or re-enactment thereof for the time being in force.

"the articles" means the articles of the company.

"clear days" in relation to the period of a notice means that period excluding the day when the notice is given or deemed to be given and the day for which it is given or on which it is to take effect.

["communication" means the same as in the Electronic Communications Act 2000.]

["electronic communication" means the same as in the Electronic Communications Act 2000.]

"executed" includes any mode of execution.

"office" means the registered office of the company.

"the holder" in relation to shares means the member whose name is entered in the register of members as the holder of the shares.

"the seal" means the common seal of the company.

"secretary" means the secretary of the company or any other person appointed to perform the duties of the secretary of the company, including a joint, assistant or deputy secretary.

"the United Kingdom" means Great Britain and Northern Ireland.

Unless the context otherwise requires, words or expressions contained in these regulations bear the same meaning as in the Act but excluding any statutory modification thereof not in force when these regulations become binding on the company.

NOTES

Definitions in square brackets inserted by the Companies Act 1985 (Electronic Communications) Order 2000, SI 2000/3373, art 32(1), Sch 1, para 1, as from 22 December 2000.

SHARE CAPITAL

2. Subject to the provisions of the Act and without prejudice to any rights attached to any existing shares, any share may be issued with such rights or restrictions as the company may by ordinary resolution determine.

3. Subject to the provisions of the Act, shares may be issued which are to be redeemed or are to be liable to be redeemed at the option of the company or the holder on such terms and in such manner as may be provided by the articles.

4. The company may exercise the powers of paying commissions conferred by the Act. Subject to the [provisions] of the Act, any such commission may be satisfied by the payment of cash or by the allotment of fully or partly paid shares or partly in one way and partly in the other.

NOTES

Word in square brackets substituted for original word "provision" by the Companies (Tables A to F) (Amendment) Regulations 1985, SI 1985/1052, reg 2, as from 1 August 1985.

5. Except as required by law, no person shall be recognised by the company as holding any share upon any trust and (except as otherwise provided by the articles or by law) the company shall not be bound by or recognise any interest in any share except an absolute right to the entirety thereof in the holder.

SHARE CERTIFICATES

6. Every member, upon becoming the holder of any shares, shall be entitled without payment to one certificate for all the shares of each class held by him (and, upon transferring a part of his holding of shares of any class, to a certificate for the balance of such holding) or several certificates each for one or more of his shares upon payment for every certificate after the first of such reasonable sum as the directors may determine. Every certificate shall be sealed with the seal and shall specify the number, class and distinguishing numbers (if any) of the shares to which it relates and the amount or respective amounts paid up thereon. The company shall not be bound to issue more than one certificate for shares held jointly by several persons and delivery of a certificate to one joint holder shall be a sufficient delivery to all of them.

7. If a share certificate is defaced, worn-out, lost or destroyed, it may be renewed on such terms (if any) as to evidence and indemnity and payment of the expenses reasonably incurred by the company in investigating evidence as the directors may determine but otherwise free of charge, and (in the case of defacement or wearing-out) on delivery up of the old certificate.

LIEN

8. The company shall have a first and paramount lien on every share (not being a fully paid share) for all moneys (whether presently payable or not) payable at a fixed time or called in respect of that share. The directors may at any time declare any share to be wholly or in part exempt from the provisions of this regulation. The company's lien on a share shall extend to any amount payable in respect of it.

9. The company may sell in such manner as the directors determine any shares on which the company has a lien if a sum in respect of which the lien exists is presently payable and is not paid within fourteen clear days after notice has been given to the holder of the share or to the person entitled to it in consequence of the death or bankruptcy of the holder, demanding payment and stating that if the notice is not complied with the shares may be sold.

10. To give effect to a sale the directors may authorise some person to execute an instrument of transfer of the shares sold to, or in accordance with the directions of, the purchaser. The title of the transferee to the shares shall not be affected by any irregularity in or invalidity of the proceedings in reference to the sale.

11. The net proceeds of the sale, after payment of the costs, shall be applied in payment of so much of the sum for which the lien exists as is presently payable, and any residue shall (upon surrender to the company for cancellation of the certificate for the shares sold and subject to a like lien for any moneys not presently payable as existed upon the shares before the sale) be paid to the person entitled to the shares at the date of the sale.

CALLS ON SHARES AND FORFEITURE

12. Subject to the terms of allotment, the directors may make calls upon the members in respect of any moneys unpaid on their shares (whether in respect of nominal value or premium) and each member shall (subject to receiving at least fourteen clear days' notice specifying when and where payment is to be made) pay to the company as required by the notice the amount called on his shares. A call may be required to be paid by instalments. A call may, before receipt by the company of any sum due thereunder, be revoked in whole or part and payment of a call may be postponed in whole or part. A person upon whom a call is made shall remain liable for calls made upon him notwithstanding the subsequent transfer of the shares in respect whereof the call was made.

13. A call shall be deemed to have been made at the time when the resolution of the directors authorising the call was passed.

14. The joint holders of a share shall be jointly and severally liable to pay all calls in respect thereof.

15. If a call remains unpaid after it has become due and payable the person from whom it is due and payable shall pay interest on the amount unpaid from the day it became due and payable until it is paid at the rate fixed by the terms of allotment of the share or in the notice

of the call or, if no rate is fixed, at the appropriate rate (as defined by the Act) but the directors may waive payment of the interest wholly or in part.

16. An amount payable in respect of a share on allotment or at any fixed date, whether in respect of nominal value or premium or as an instalment of a call, shall be deemed to be a call and if it is not paid the provisions of the articles shall apply as if that amount had become due and payable by virtue of a call.

17. Subject to the terms of allotment, the directors may make arrangements on the issue of shares for a difference between the holders in the amounts and times of payment of calls on their shares.

18. If a call remains unpaid after it has become due and payable the directors may give to the person from whom it is due not less than fourteen clear days' notice requiring payment of the amount unpaid together with any interest which may have accrued. The notice shall name the place where payment is to be made and shall state that if the notice is not complied with the shares in respect of which the call was made will be liable to be forfeited.

19. If the notice is not complied with any share in respect of which it was given may, before the payment required by the notice has been made, be forfeited by a resolution of the directors and the forfeiture shall include all dividends or other moneys payable in respect of the forfeited shares and not paid before the forfeiture.

20. Subject to the provisions of the Act, a forfeited share may be sold, re-allotted or otherwise disposed of on such terms and in such manner as the directors determine either to the person who was before the forfeiture the holder or to any other person and at any time before sale, re-allotment or other disposition, the forfeiture may be cancelled on such terms as the directors think fit. Where for the purposes of its disposal a forfeited share is to be transferred to any person the directors may authorise some person to execute an instrument of transfer of the share to that person.

21. A person any of whose shares have been forfeited shall cease to be a member in respect of them and shall surrender to the company for cancellation the certificate for the shares forfeited but shall remain liable to the company for all moneys which at the date of forfeiture were presently payable by him to the company in respect of those shares with interest at the rate at which interest was payable on those moneys before the forfeiture or, if no interest was so payable, at the appropriate rate (as defined in the Act) from the date of forfeiture until payment but the directors may waive payment wholly or in part or enforce payment without any allowance for the value of the shares at the time of forfeiture or for any consideration received on their disposal.

22. A statutory declaration by a director or the secretary that a share has been forfeited on a specified date shall be conclusive evidence of the facts stated in it as against all persons claiming to be entitled to the share and the declaration shall (subject to the execution of an instrument of transfer if necessary) constitute a good title to the share and the person to whom the share is disposed of shall not be bound to see to the application of the consideration, if any, nor shall his title to the share be affected by any irregularity in or invalidity of the proceedings in reference to the forfeiture or disposal of the share.

TRANSFER OF SHARES

23. The instrument of transfer of a share may be in any usual form or in any other form which the directors may approve and shall be executed by or on behalf of the transferor and, unless the share is fully paid, by or on behalf of the transferee.

24. The directors may refuse to register the transfer of a share which is not fully paid to a person of whom they do not approve and they may refuse to register the transfer of a share on which the company has a lien. They may also refuse to register a transfer unless—

(a) it is lodged at the office or at such other place as the directors may appoint and is accompanied by the certificate for the shares to which it relates and such other evidence as the directors may reasonably require to show the right of the transferor to make the transfer;

(b) it is in respect of only one class of shares; and

(c) it is in favour of not more than four transferees.

25. If the directors refuse to register a transfer of a share, they shall within two months after the date on which the transfer was lodged with the company send to the transferee notice of the refusal.

26. The registration of transfers of shares or of transfers of any class of shares may be suspended at such times and for such periods (not exceeding thirty days in any year) as the directors may determine.

27. No fee shall be charged for the registration of any instrument of transfer or other document relating to or affecting the title to any share.

28. The company shall be entitled to retain any instrument of transfer which is registered, but any instrument of transfer which the directors refuse to register shall be returned to the person lodging it when notice of the refusal is given.

TRANSMISSION OF SHARES

29. If a member dies the survivor or survivors where he was a joint holder, and his personal representatives where he was a sole holder or the only survivor of joint holders, shall be the only persons recognised by the company as having any title to his interest; but nothing herein contained shall release the estate of a deceased member from any liability in respect of any share which had been jointly held by him.

30. A person becoming entitled to a share in consequence of the death or bankruptcy of a member may, upon such evidence being produced as the directors may properly require, elect either to become the holder of the share or to have some person nominated by him registered as the transferee. If he elects to become the holder he shall give notice to the company to that effect. If he elects to have another person registered he shall execute an instrument of transfer of the share to that person. All the articles relating to the transfer of shares shall apply to the notice or instrument of transfer as if it were an instrument of transfer executed by the member and the death or bankruptcy of the member had not occurred.

31. A person becoming entitled to a share in consequence of the death or bankruptcy of a member shall have the rights to which he would be entitled if he were the holder of the share, except that he shall not, before being registered as the holder of the share, be entitled in respect of it to attend or vote at any meeting of the company or at any separate meeting of the holders of any class of shares in the company.

ALTERATION OF SHARE CAPITAL

32. The company may by ordinary resolution—
- (a) increase its share capital by new shares of such amount as the resolution prescribes;
- (b) consolidate and divide all or any of its share capital into shares of larger amount than its existing shares;
- (c) subject to the provisions of the Act, sub-divide its shares, or any of them, into shares of smaller amount and the resolution may determine that, as between the shares resulting from the sub-division, any of them may have any preference or advantage as compared with the others; and
- (d) cancel shares which, at the date of the passing of the resolution, have not been taken or agreed to be taken by any person and diminish the amount of its share capital by the amount of the shares so cancelled.

33. Whenever as a result of a consolidation of shares any members would become entitled to fractions of a share, the directors may, on behalf of those members, sell the shares representing the fractions for the best price reasonably obtainable to any person (including, subject to the provisions of the Act, the company) and distribute the net proceeds of sale in due proportion among those members, and the directors may authorise some person to execute an instrument of transfer of the shares to, or in accordance with the directions of, the purchaser. The transferee shall not be bound to see to the application of the purchase money nor shall his title to the shares be affected by any irregularity in or invalidity of the proceedings in reference to the sale.

34. Subject to the provisions of the Act, the company may by special resolution reduce its share capital, any capital redemption reserve and any share premium account in any way.

PURCHASE OF OWN SHARES

35. Subject to the provisions of the Act, the company may purchase its own shares (including any redeemable shares) and, if it is a private company, make a payment in respect of the redemption or purchase of its own shares otherwise than out of distributable profits of the company or the proceeds of a fresh issue of shares.

GENERAL MEETINGS

36. All general meetings other than annual general meetings shall be called extraordinary general meetings.

37. The directors may call general meetings and, on the requisition of members pursuant to the provisions of the Act, shall forthwith proceed to convene an extraordinary general meeting for a date not later than eight weeks after receipt of the requisition. If there are not within the United Kingdom sufficient directors to call a general meeting, any director or any member of the company may call a general meeting.

NOTICE OF GENERAL MEETINGS

38. An annual general meeting and an extraordinary general meeting called for the passing of a special resolution or a resolution appointing a person as a director shall be called by at least twenty-one clear days' notice. All other extraordinary general meetings shall be called by at least fourteen clear days' notice but a general meeting may be called by shorter notice if it is so agreed—

(a) in the case of an annual general meeting, by all the members entitled to attend and vote thereat; and

(b) in the case of any other meeting by a majority in number of the members having a right to attend and vote being a majority together holding not less than ninety-five per cent in nominal value of the shares giving that right.

The notice shall specify the time and place of the meeting and the general nature of the business to be transacted and, in the case of an annual general meeting, shall specify the meeting as such.

Subject to the provisions of the articles and to any restrictions imposed on any shares, the notice shall be given to all the members, to all persons entitled to a share in consequence of the death or bankruptcy of a member and to the directors and auditors.

39. The accidental omission to give notice of a meeting to, or the non-receipt of notice of a meeting by, any person entitled to receive notice shall not invalidate the proceedings at that meeting.

PROCEEDINGS AT GENERAL MEETINGS

40. No business shall be transacted at any meeting unless a quorum is present. Two persons entitled to vote upon the business to be transacted, each being a member or a proxy for a member or a duly authorised representative of a corporation, shall be a quorum.

41. If such a quorum is not present within half an hour from the time appointed for the meeting, or if during a meeting such a quorum ceases to be present, the meeting shall stand adjourned to the same day in the next week at the same time and place or [to] such time and place as the directors may determine.

NOTES

Word in square brackets inserted by the Companies (Tables A to F) (Amendment) Regulations 1985, SI 1985/1052, reg 2, as from 1 August 1985.

42. The chairman, if any, of the board of directors or in his absence some other director nominated by the directors shall preside as chairman of the meeting, but if neither the chairman nor such other director (if any) be present within fifteen minutes after the time appointed for holding the meeting and willing to act, the directors present shall elect one of their number to be chairman and, if there is only one director present and willing to act, he shall be chairman.

PART II
STATUTORY INSTRUMENTS

43. If no director is willing to act as chairman, or if no director is present within fifteen minutes after the time appointed for holding the meeting, the members present and entitled to vote shall choose one of their number to be chairman.

44. A director shall, notwithstanding that he is not a member, be entitled to attend and speak at any general meeting and at any separate meeting of the holders of any class of shares in the company.

45. The chairman may, with the consent of a meeting at which a quorum is present (and shall if so directed by the meeting), adjourn the meeting from time to time and from place to place, but no business shall be transacted at an adjourned meeting other than business which might properly have been transacted at the meeting had the adjournment not taken place. When a meeting is adjourned for fourteen days or more, at least seven clear days' notice shall be given specifying the time and place of the adjourned meeting and the general nature of the business to be transacted. Otherwise it shall not be necessary to give any such notice.

46. A resolution put to the vote of a meeting shall be decided on a show of hands unless before, or on the declaration of the result of, the show of hands a poll is duly demanded. Subject to the provisions of the Act, a poll may be demanded—

(a) by the chairman; or
(b) by at least two members having the right to vote at the meeting; or
(c) by a member or members representing not less than one-tenth of the total voting rights of all the members having the right to vote at the meeting; or
(d) by a member or members holding shares conferring a right to vote at the meeting being shares on which an aggregate sum has been paid up equal to not less than one-tenth of the total sum paid up on all the shares conferring that right;

and a demand by a person as proxy for a member shall be the same as a demand by the member.

47. Unless a poll is duly demanded a declaration by the chairman that a resolution has been carried or carried unanimously, or by a particular majority, or lost, or not carried by a particular majority and an entry to that effect in the minutes of the meeting shall be conclusive evidence of the fact without proof of the number or proportion of the votes recorded in favour of or against the resolution.

48. The demand for a poll may, before the poll is taken, be withdrawn but only with the consent of the chairman and a demand so withdrawn shall not be taken to have invalidated the result of a show of hands declared before the demand was made.

49. A poll shall be taken as the chairman directs and he may appoint scrutineers (who need not be members) and fix a time and place for declaring the result of the poll. The result of the poll shall be deemed to be the resolution of the meeting at which the poll was demanded.

50. In the case of an equality of votes, whether on a show of hands or on a poll, the chairman shall be entitled to a casting vote in addition to any other vote he may have.

51. A poll demanded on the election of a chairman or on a question of adjournment shall be taken forthwith. A poll demanded on any other question shall be taken either forthwith or at such time and place as the chairman directs not being more than thirty days after the poll is demanded. The demand for a poll shall not prevent the continuance of a meeting for the transaction of any business other than the question on which the poll was demanded. If a poll is demanded before the declaration of the result of a show of hands and the demand is duly withdrawn, the meeting shall continue as if the demand had not been made.

52. No notice need be given of a poll not taken forthwith if the time and place at which it is to be taken are announced at the meeting at which it is demanded. In any other case at least seven clear days' notice shall be given specifying the time and place at which the poll is to be taken.

53. A resolution in writing executed by or on behalf of each member who would have been entitled to vote upon it if it had been proposed at a general meeting at which he was present shall be as effectual as if it had been passed at a general meeting duly convened and held and may consist of several instruments in the like form each executed by or on behalf of one or more members.

VOTES OF MEMBERS

54. Subject to any rights or restrictions attached to any shares, on a show of hands every member who (being an individual) is present in person or (being a corporation) is present by a duly authorised representative, not being himself a member entitled to vote, shall have one vote and on a poll every member shall have one vote for every share of which he is the holder.

55. In the case of joint holders the vote of the senior who tenders a vote, whether in person or by proxy, shall be accepted to the exclusion of the votes of the other joint holders; and seniority shall be determined by the order in which the names of the holders stand in the register of members.

56. A member in respect of whom an order has been made by any court having jurisdiction (whether in the United Kingdom or elsewhere) in matters concerning mental disorder may vote, whether on a show of hands or on a poll, by his receiver, curator bonis or other person authorised in that behalf appointed by that court, and any such receiver, curator bonis or other person may, on a poll, vote by proxy. Evidence to the satisfaction of the directors of the authority of the person claiming to exercise the right to vote shall be deposited at the office, or at such other place as is specified in accordance with the articles for the deposit of instruments of proxy, not less than 48 hours before the time appointed for holding the meeting or adjourned meeting at which the right to vote is to be exercised and in default the right to vote shall not be exercisable.

57. No member shall vote at any general meeting or at any separate meeting of the holders of any class of shares in the company, either in person or by proxy, in respect of any share held by him unless all moneys presently payable by him in respect of that share have been paid.

58. No objection shall be raised to the qualification of any voter except at the meeting or adjourned meeting at which the vote objected to is tendered, and every vote not disallowed at the meeting shall be valid. Any objection made in due time shall be referred to the chairman whose decision shall be final and conclusive.

59. On a poll votes may be given either personally or by proxy. A member may appoint more than one proxy to attend on the same occasion.

60. [The appointment of] a proxy shall be *in writing* executed by or on behalf of the appointor and shall be in the following form (or in a form as near thereto as circumstances allow or in any other form which is usual or which the directors may approve)—

"... PLC/Limited
I/We, ... of ....
being a member/members of the above-named company,
hereby appoint .... of ....,
or failing him, ... of ....,
as my/our proxy to vote in my/our name[s] and on my/our behalf at the annual/extraordinary general meeting of the company, to be held on
.... 19...... , and at any adjournment thereof.
Signed on .... 19...... "

NOTES

Words in square brackets substituted for original words "An instrument appointing" and words in italics revoked by the Companies Act 1985 (Electronic Communications) Order 2000, SI 2000/3373, art 32(1), Sch 1, para 2, as from 22 December 2000.

61. Where it is desired to afford members an opportunity of instructing the proxy how he shall act the [appointment of] a proxy shall be in the following form (or in a form as near thereto as circumstances allow or in any other form which is usual or which the directors may approve)—

"... PLC/Limited
I/We, ... of ....
being a member/members of the above-named company,
hereby appoint .... of ....,
or failing him, ... of ....,

as my/our proxy to vote in my/our name[s] and on my/our behalf at the annual/extraordinary general meeting of the company, to be held on
.... 19......, and at any adjournment thereof.
This form is to be used in respect of the resolutions mentioned below as follows:
Resolution No 1 *for *against
Resolution No 2 *for *against.
* Strike out whichever is not desired.
Unless otherwise instructed, the proxy may vote as he thinks fit or abstain from voting.
Signed this .... day of .... 19..... "

NOTES

Words in square brackets substituted for original words "instrument appointing" by the Companies Act 1985 (Electronic Communications) Order 2000, SI 2000/3373, art 32(1), Sch 1, para 3, as from 22 December 2000.

62. [The appointment of] a proxy and any authority under which it is executed or a copy of such authority certified notarially or in some other way approved by the directors may—

(a) [in the case of an instrument in writing] be deposited at the office or at such other place within the United Kingdom as is specified in the notice convening the meeting or in any instrument of proxy sent out by the company in relation to the meeting not less than 48 hours before the time for holding the meeting or adjourned meeting at which the person named in the instrument proposes to vote; or

[(aa) in the case of an appointment contained in an electronic communication, where an address has been specified for the purpose of receiving electronic communications—

(i) in the notice convening the meeting, or

(ii) in any instrument of proxy sent out by the company in relation to the meeting, or

(iii) in any invitation contained in an electronic communication to appoint a proxy issued by the company in relation to the meeting,

be received at such address not less than 48 hours before the time for holding the meeting or adjourned meeting at which the person named in the appointment proposes to vote;]

(b) in the case of a poll taken more than 48 hours after it is demanded, be deposited [or received] as aforesaid after the poll has been demanded and not less than 24 hours before the time appointed for the taking of the poll; or

(c) where the poll is not taken forthwith but is taken not more than 48 hours after it was demanded, be delivered at the meeting at which the poll was demanded to the chairman or to the secretary or to any director;

[and an appointment of proxy which is not deposited, delivered or received] in a manner so permitted shall be invalid.

[In this regulation and the next, "address", in relation to electronic communications, includes any number or address used for the purposes of such communications.]

NOTES

Words in first pair of square brackets substituted for original words "The instrument appointing", words in fifth pair of square brackets substituted for original words "and an instrument of proxy which is not deposited or delivered", and other words in square brackets inserted, by the Companies Act 1985 (Electronic Communications) Order 2000, SI 2000/3373, art 32(1), Sch 1, para 4, as from 22 December 2000.

63. A vote given or poll demanded by proxy or by the duly authorised representative of a corporation shall be valid notwithstanding the previous determination of the authority of the person voting or demanding a poll unless notice of the determination was received by the company at the office or at such other place at which the instrument of proxy was duly deposited [or, where the appointment of the proxy was contained in an electronic communication, at the address at which such appointment was duly received] before the commencement of the meeting or adjourned meeting at which the vote is given or the poll demanded or (in the case of a poll taken otherwise than on the same day as the meeting or adjourned meeting) the time appointed for taking the poll.

NOTES

Words in square brackets inserted by the Companies Act 1985 (Electronic Communications) Order 2000, SI 2000/3373, art 32(1), Sch 1, para 5, as from 22 December 2000.

NUMBER OF DIRECTORS

64. Unless otherwise determined by ordinary resolution, the number of directors (other than alternate directors) shall not be subject to any maximum but shall be not less than two.

ALTERNATE DIRECTORS

65. Any director (other than an alternate director) may appoint any other director, or any other person approved by resolution of the directors and willing to act, to be an alternate director and may remove from office an alternate director so appointed by him.

66. An alternate director shall be entitled to receive notice of all meetings of directors and of all meetings of committees of directors of which his appointor is a member, to attend and vote at any such meeting at which the director appointing him is not personally present, and generally to perform all the functions of his appointor as a director in his absence but shall not be entitled to receive any remuneration from the company for his services as an alternate director. But it shall not be necessary to give notice of such a meeting to an alternate director who is absent from the United Kingdom.

67. An alternate director shall cease to be an alternate director if his appointor ceases to be a director; but, if a director retires by rotation or otherwise but is reappointed or deemed to have been reappointed at the meeting at which he retires, any appointment of an alternate director made by him which was in force immediately prior to his retirement shall continue after his reappointment.

68. Any appointment or removal of an alternate director shall be by notice to the company signed by the director making or revoking the appointment or in any other manner approved by the directors.

69. Save as otherwise provided in the articles, an alternate director shall be deemed for all purposes to be a director and shall alone be responsible for his own acts and defaults and he shall not be deemed to be the agent of the director appointing him.

POWERS OF DIRECTORS

70. Subject to the provisions of the Act, the memorandum and the articles and to any directions given by special resolution, the business of the company shall be managed by the directors who may exercise all the powers of the company. No alteration of the memorandum or articles and no such direction shall invalidate any prior act of the directors which would have been valid if that alteration had not been made or that direction had not been given. The powers given by this regulation shall not be limited by any special power given to the directors by the articles and a meeting of directors at which a quorum is present may exercise all powers exercisable by the directors.

71. The directors may, by power of attorney or otherwise, appoint any person to be the agent of the company for such purposes and on such conditions as they determine, including authority for the agent to delegate all or any of his powers.

DELEGATION OF DIRECTORS' POWERS

72. The directors may delegate any of their powers to any committee consisting of one or more directors. They may also delegate to any managing director or any director holding any other executive office such of their powers as they consider desirable to be exercised by him. Any such delegation may be made subject to any conditions the directors may impose, and either collaterally with or to the exclusion of their own powers and may be revoked or altered. Subject to any such conditions, the proceedings of a committee with two or more members shall be governed by the articles regulating the proceedings of directors so far as they are capable of applying.

APPOINTMENT AND RETIREMENT OF DIRECTORS

73. At the first annual general meeting all the directors shall retire from office, and at every subsequent annual general meeting one-third of the directors who are subject to retirement by rotation or, if their number is not three or a multiple of three, the number nearest to one-third shall retire from office; but, if there is only one director who is subject to retirement by rotation, he shall retire.

74. Subject to the provisions of the Act, the directors to retire by rotation shall be those who have been longest in office since their last appointment or reappointment, but as between persons who became or were last reappointed directors on the same day those to retire shall (unless they otherwise agree among themselves) be determined by lot.

75. If the company, at the meeting at which a director retires by rotation, does not fill the vacancy the retiring director shall, if willing to act, be deemed to have been reappointed unless at the meeting it is resolved not to fill the vacancy or unless a resolution for the reappointment of the director is put to the meeting and lost.

76. No person other than a director retiring by rotation shall be appointed or reappointed a director at any general meeting unless—
(a) he is recommended by the directors; or
(b) not less than fourteen nor more than thirty-five clear days before the date appointed for the meeting, notice executed by a member qualified to vote at the meeting has been given to the company of the intention to propose that person for appointment or reappointment stating the particulars which would, if he were so appointed or reappointed, be required to be included in the company's register of directors together with notice executed by that person of his willingness to be appointed or reappointed.

77. Not less than seven nor more than twenty-eight clear days before the date appointed for holding a general meeting notice shall be given to all who are entitled to receive notice of the meeting of any person (other than a director retiring by rotation at the meeting) who is recommended by the directors for appointment or reappointment as a director at the meeting or in respect of whom notice has been duly given to the company of the intention to propose him at the meeting for appointment or reappointment as a director. The notice shall give the particulars of that person which would, if he were so appointed or reappointed, be required to be included in the company's register of directors.

78. Subject as aforesaid, the company may by ordinary resolution appoint a person who is willing to act to be a director either to fill a vacancy or as an additional director and may also determine the rotation in which any additional directors are to retire.

79. The directors may appoint a person who is willing to act to be a director, either to fill a vacancy or as an additional director, provided that the appointment does not cause the number of directors to exceed any number fixed by or in accordance with the articles as the maximum number of directors. A director so appointed shall hold office only until the next following annual general meeting and shall not be taken into account in determining the directors who are to retire by rotation at the meeting. If not reappointed at such annual general meeting, he shall vacate office at the conclusion thereof.

80. Subject as aforesaid, a director who retires at an annual general meeting may, if willing to act, be reappointed. If he is not reappointed, he shall retain office until the meeting appoints someone in his place, or if it does not do so, until the end of the meeting.

DISQUALIFICATION AND REMOVAL OF DIRECTORS

81. The office of a director shall be vacated if—
(a) he ceases to be a director by virtue of any provision of the Act or he becomes prohibited by law from being a director; or
(b) he becomes bankrupt or makes any arrangement or composition with his creditors generally; or
(c) he is, or may be, suffering from mental disorder and either—
(i) he is admitted to hospital in pursuance of an application for admission for treatment under the Mental Health Act 1983 or, in Scotland, an application for admission under the Mental Health (Scotland) Act 1960, or

(ii) an order is made by a court having jurisdiction (whether in the United Kingdom or elsewhere) in matters concerning mental disorder for his detention or for the appointment of a receiver, curator bonis or other person to exercise powers with respect to his property or affairs; or

(d) he resigns his office by notice to the company; or

(e) he shall for more than six consecutive months have been absent without permission of the directors from meetings of directors held during that period and the directors resolve that his office be vacated.

REMUNERATION OF DIRECTORS

82. The directors shall be entitled to such remuneration as the company may by ordinary resolution determine and, unless the resolution provides otherwise, the remuneration shall be deemed to accrue from day to day.

DIRECTORS' EXPENSES

83. The directors may be paid all travelling, hotel, and other expenses properly incurred by them in connection with their attendance at meetings of directors or committees of directors or general meetings or separate meetings of the holders of any class of shares or of debentures of the company or otherwise in connection with the discharge of their duties.

DIRECTORS' APPOINTMENTS AND INTERESTS

84. Subject to the provisions of the Act, the directors may appoint one or more of their number to the office of managing director or to any other executive office under the company and may enter into an agreement or arrangement with any director for his employment by the company or for the provision by him of any services outside the scope of the ordinary duties of a director. Any such appointment, agreement or arrangement may be made upon such terms as the directors determine and they may remunerate any such director for his services as they think fit. Any appointment of a director to an executive office shall terminate if he ceases to be a director but without prejudice to any claim to damages for breach of the contract of service between the director and the company. A managing director and a director holding any other executive office shall not be subject to retirement by rotation.

85. Subject to the provisions of the Act, and provided that he has disclosed to the directors the nature and extent of any material interest of his, a director notwithstanding his office—

(a) may be a party to, or otherwise interested in, any transaction or arrangement with the company or in which the company is otherwise interested;

(b) may be a director or other officer of, or employed by, or a party to any transaction or arrangement with, or otherwise interested in, any body corporate promoted by the company or in which the company is otherwise interested; and

(c) shall not, by reason of his office, be accountable to the company for any benefit which he derives from any such office or employment or from any such transaction or arrangement or from any interest in any such body corporate and no such transaction or arrangement shall be liable to be avoided on the ground of any such interest or benefit.

86. For the purposes of regulation 85—

(a) a general notice given to the directors that a director is to be regarded as having an interest of the nature and extent specified in the notice in any transaction or arrangement in which a specified person or class of persons is interested shall be deemed to be a disclosure that the director has an interest in any such transaction of the nature and extent so specified; and

(b) an interest of which a director has no knowledge and of which it is unreasonable to expect him to have knowledge shall not be treated as an interest of his.

DIRECTORS' GRATUITIES AND PENSIONS

87. The directors may provide benefits, whether by the payment of gratuities or pensions or by insurance or otherwise, for any director who has held but no longer holds any executive office or employment with the company or with any body corporate which is or has been a subsidiary of the company or a predecessor in business of the company or of any such subsidiary, and for any member of his family (including a spouse and a former spouse) or any

person who is or was dependent on him, and may (as well before as after he ceases to hold such office or employment) contribute to any fund and pay premiums for the purchase or provision of any such benefit.

PROCEEDINGS OF DIRECTORS

88. Subject to the provisions of the articles, the directors may regulate their proceedings as they think fit. A director may, and the secretary at the request of a director shall, call a meeting of the directors. It shall not be necessary to give notice of a meeting to a director who is absent from the United Kingdom. Questions arising at a meeting shall be decided by a majority of votes. In the case of an equality of votes, the chairman shall have a second or casting vote. A director who is also an alternate director shall be entitled in the absence of his appointor to a separate vote on behalf of his appointor in addition to his own vote.

89. The quorum for the transaction of the business of the directors may be fixed by the directors and unless so fixed at any other number shall be two. A person who holds office only as an alternate director shall, if his appointor is not present, be counted in the quorum.

90. The continuing directors or a sole continuing director may act notwithstanding any vacancies in their number, but, if the number of directors is less than the number fixed as the quorum, the continuing directors or director may act only for the purpose of filling vacancies or of calling a general meeting.

91. The directors may appoint one of their number to be the chairman of the board of directors and may at any time remove him from that office. Unless he is unwilling to do so, the director so appointed shall preside at every meeting of directors at which he is present. But if there is no director holding that office, or if the director holding it is unwilling to preside or is not present within five minutes after the time appointed for the meeting, the directors present may appoint one of their number to be chairman of the meeting.

92. All acts done by a meeting of directors, or of a committee of directors, or by a person acting as a director shall, notwithstanding that it be afterwards discovered that there was a defect in the appointment of any director or that any of them were disqualified from holding office, or had vacated office, or were not entitled to vote, be as valid as if every such person had been duly appointed and was qualified and had continued to be a director and had been entitled to vote.

93. A resolution in writing signed by all the directors entitled to receive notice of a meeting of directors or of a committee of directors shall be as valid and effectual as if it had been passed at a meeting of directors or (as the case may be) a committee of directors duly convened and held and may consist of several documents in the like form each signed by one or more directors; but a resolution signed by an alternate director need not also be signed by his appointor and, if it is signed by a director who has appointed an alternate director, it need not be signed by the alternate director in that capacity.

94. Save as otherwise provided by the articles, a director shall not vote at a meeting of directors or of a committee of directors on any resolution concerning a matter in which he has, directly or indirectly, an interest or duty which is material and which conflicts or may conflict with the interests of the company unless his interest or duty arises only because the case falls within one or more of the following paragraphs—

(a) the resolution relates to the giving to him of a guarantee, security, or indemnity in respect of money lent to, or an obligation incurred by him for the benefit of, the company or any of its subsidiaries;

(b) the resolution relates to the giving to a third party of a guarantee, security, or indemnity in respect of an obligation of the company or any of its subsidiaries for which the director has assumed responsibility in whole or part and whether alone or jointly with others under a guarantee or indemnity or by the giving of security;

(c) his interest arises by virtue of his subscribing or agreeing to subscribe for any shares, debentures or other securities of the company or any of its subsidiaries, or by virtue of his being, or intending to become, a participant in the underwriting or sub-underwriting of an offer of any such shares, debentures, or other securities by the company or any of its subsidiaries for subscription, purchase or exchange;

(d) the resolution relates in any way to a retirement benefits scheme which has been approved, or is conditional upon approval, by the Board of Inland Revenue for taxation purposes.

For the purposes of this regulation, an interest of a person who is, for any purpose of the Act (excluding any statutory modification thereof not in force when this regulation becomes binding on the company), connected with a director shall be treated as an interest of the director and, in relation to an alternate director, an interest of his appointor shall be treated as an interest of the alternate director without prejudice to any interest which the alternate director has otherwise.

95. A director shall not be counted in the quorum present at a meeting in relation to a resolution on which he is not entitled to vote.

96. The company may by ordinary resolution suspend or relax to any extent, either generally or in respect of any particular matter, any provision of the articles prohibiting a director from voting at a meeting of directors or of a committee of directors.

97. Where proposals are under consideration concerning the appointment of two or more directors to offices or employments with the company or any body corporate in which the company is interested the proposals may be divided and considered in relation to each director separately and (provided he is not for another reason precluded from voting) each of the directors concerned shall be entitled to vote and be counted in the quorum in respect of each resolution except that concerning his own appointment.

98. If a question arises at a meeting of directors or of a committee of directors as to the right of a director to vote, the question may, before the conclusion of the meeting, be referred to the chairman of the meeting and his ruling in relation to any director other than himself shall be final and conclusive.

SECRETARY

99. Subject to the provisions of the Act, the secretary shall be appointed by the directors for such term, at such remuneration and upon such conditions as they may think fit; and any secretary so appointed may be removed by them.

MINUTES

100. The directors shall cause minutes to be made in books kept for the purpose—
- (a) of all appointments of officers made by the directors; and
- (b) of all proceedings at meetings of the company, of the holders of any class of shares in the company, and of the directors, and of committees of directors, including the names of the directors present at each such meeting.

THE SEAL

101. The seal shall only be used by the authority of the directors or of a committee of directors authorised by the directors. The directors may determine who shall sign any instrument to which the seal is affixed and unless otherwise so determined it shall be signed by a director and by the secretary or by a second director.

DIVIDENDS

102. Subject to the provisions of the Act, the company may by ordinary resolution declare dividends in accordance with the respective rights of the members, but no dividend shall exceed the amount recommended by the directors.

103. Subject to the provisions of the Act, the directors may pay interim dividends if it appears to them that they are justified by the profits of the company available for distribution. If the share capital is divided into different classes, the directors may pay interim dividends on shares which confer deferred or non-preferred rights with regard to dividend as well as on shares which confer preferential rights with regard to dividend, but no interim dividend shall be paid on shares carrying deferred or non-preferred rights if, at the time of payment, any preferential dividend is in arrear. The directors may also pay at intervals settled by them any dividend payable at a fixed rate if it appears to them that the profits available for distribution justify the payment. Provided the directors act in good faith they shall not incur any liability to the holders of shares conferring preferred rights for any loss they may suffer by the lawful payment of an interim dividend on any shares having deferred or non-preferred rights.

104. Except as otherwise provided by the rights attached to shares, all dividends shall be declared and paid according to the amounts paid up on the shares on which the dividend is paid. All dividends shall be apportioned and paid proportionately to the amounts paid up on the shares during any portion or portions of the period in respect of which the dividend is paid; but, if any share is issued on terms providing that it shall rank for dividend as from a particular date, that share shall rank for dividend accordingly.

105. A general meeting declaring a dividend may, upon the recommendation of the directors, direct that it shall be satisfied wholly or partly by the distribution of assets and, where any difficulty arises in regard to the distribution, the directors may settle the same and in particular may issue fractional certificates and fix the value for distribution of any assets and may determine that cash shall be paid to any member upon the footing of the value so fixed in order to adjust the rights of members and may vest any assets in trustees.

106. Any dividend or other moneys payable in respect of a share may be paid by cheque sent by post to the registered address of the person entitled or, if two or more persons are the holders of the share or are jointly entitled to it by reason of the death or bankruptcy of the holder, to the registered address of that one of those persons who is first named in the register of members or to such person and to such address as the person or persons entitled may in writing direct. Every cheque shall be made payable to the order of the person or persons entitled or to such other person as the person or persons entitled may in writing direct and payment of the cheque shall be a good discharge to the company. Any joint holder or other person jointly entitled to a share as aforesaid may give receipts for any dividend or other moneys payable in respect of the share.

107. No dividend or other moneys payable in respect of a share shall bear interest against the company unless otherwise provided by the rights attached to the share.

108. Any dividend which has remained unclaimed for twelve years from the date when it became due for payment shall, if the directors so resolve, be forfeited and cease to remain owing by the company.

ACCOUNTS

109. No member shall (as such) have any right of inspecting any accounting records or other book or document of the company except as conferred by statute or authorised by the directors or by ordinary resolution of the company.

CAPITALISATION OF PROFITS

110. The directors may with the authority of an ordinary resolution of the company—

(a) subject as hereinafter provided, resolve to capitalise any undivided profits of the company not required for paying any preferential dividend (whether or not they are available for distribution) or any sum standing to the credit of the company's share premium account or capital redemption reserve;

(b) appropriate the sum resolved to be capitalised to the members who would have been entitled to it if it were distributed by way of dividend and in the same proportions and apply such sum on their behalf either in or towards paying up the amounts, if any, for the time being unpaid on any shares held by them respectively, or in paying up in full unissued shares or debentures of the company of a nominal amount equal to that sum, and allot the shares or debentures credited as fully paid to those members, or as they may direct, in those proportions, or partly in one way and partly in the other: but the share premium account, the capital redemption reserve, and any profits which are not available for distribution may, for the purposes of this regulation, only be applied in paying up unissued shares to be allotted to members credited as fully paid;

(c) make such provision by the issue of fractional certificates or by payment in cash or otherwise as they determine in the case of shares or debentures becoming distributable under this regulation in fractions; and

(d) authorise any person to enter on behalf of all the members concerned into an agreement with the company providing for the allotment to them respectively, credited as fully paid, of any shares or debentures to which they are entitled upon such capitalisation, any agreement made under such authority being binding on all such members.

NOTICES

[111. Any notice to be given to or by any person pursuant to the articles (other than a notice calling a meeting of the directors) shall be in writing or shall be given using electronic communications to an address for the time being notified for that purpose to the person giving the notice.

In this regulation, "address", in relation to electronic communications, includes any number or address used for the purposes of such communications.]

NOTES

Substituted by the Companies Act 1985 (Electronic Communications) Order 2000, SI 2000/3373, art 32(1), Sch 1, para 6, as from 22 December 2000. The original reg 111 read as follows—

"111. Any notice to be given to or by any person pursuant to the articles shall be in writing except that a notice calling a meeting of the directors need not be in writing.".

112. The company may give any notice to a member either personally or by sending it by post in a prepaid envelope addressed to the member at his registered address or by leaving it at that address [or by giving it using electronic communications to an address for the time being notified to the company by the member]. In the case of joint holders of a share, all notices shall be given to the joint holder whose name stands first in the register of members in respect of the joint holding and notice so given shall be sufficient notice to all the joint holders. A member whose registered address is not within the United Kingdom and who gives to the company an address within the United Kingdom at which notices may be given to him[, or an address to which notices may be sent using electronic communications,] shall be entitled to have notices given to him at that address, but otherwise no such member shall be entitled to receive any notice from the company.

[In this regulation and the next, "address", in relation to electronic communications, includes any number or address used for the purposes of such communications.]

NOTES

Words in square brackets inserted by the Companies Act 1985 (Electronic Communications) Order 2000, SI 2000/3373, art 32(1), Sch 1, para 7, as from 22 December 2000.

113. A member present, either in person or by proxy, at any meeting of the company or of the holders of any class of shares in the company shall be deemed to have received notice of the meeting and, where requisite, of the purposes for which it was called.

114. Every person who becomes entitled to a share shall be bound by any notice in respect of that share which, before his name is entered in the register of members, has been duly given to a person from whom he derives his title.

115. Proof that an envelope containing a notice was properly addressed, prepaid and posted shall be conclusive evidence that the notice was given. [Proof that a notice contained in an electronic communication was sent in accordance with guidance issued by the Institute of Chartered Secretaries and Administrators shall be conclusive evidence that the notice was given.] A notice shall, *unless the contrary is proved,* be deemed to be given at the expiration of 48 hours after the envelope containing it was posted [or, in the case of a notice contained in an electronic communication, at the expiration of 48 hours after the time it was sent].

NOTES

Words in square brackets inserted by the Companies Act 1985 (Electronic Communications) Order 2000, SI 2000/3373, art 32(1), Sch 1, para 8, as from 22 December 2000; words in italics revoked by the Companies (Tables A to F) (Amendment) Regulations 1985, SI 1985/1052, reg 2, as from 1 August 1985.

116. A notice may be given by the company to the persons entitled to a share in consequence of the death or bankruptcy of a member by sending or delivering it, in any manner authorised by the articles for the giving of notice to a member, addressed to them by name, or by the title of representatives of the deceased, or trustee of the bankrupt or by any like description at the address, if any, within the United Kingdom supplied for that purpose by

the persons claiming to be so entitled. Until such an address has been supplied, a notice may be given in any manner in which it might have been given if the death or bankruptcy had not occurred.

WINDING UP

117. If the company is wound up, the liquidator may, with the sanction of an extraordinary resolution of the company and any other sanction required by the Act, divide among the members in specie the whole or any part of the assets of the company and may, for that purpose, value any assets and determine how the division shall be carried out as between the members or different classes of members. The liquidator may, with the like sanction, vest the whole or any part of the assets in trustees upon such trusts for the benefit of the members as he with the like sanction determines, but no member shall be compelled to accept any assets upon which there is a liability.

INDEMNITY

118. Subject to the provisions of the Act but without prejudice to any indemnity to which a director may otherwise be entitled, every director or other officer or auditor of the company shall be indemnified out of the assets of the company against any liability incurred by him in defending any proceedings, whether civil or criminal, in which judgment is given in his favour or in which he is acquitted or in connection with any application in which relief is granted to him by the court from liability for negligence, default, breach of duty or breach of trust in relation to the affairs of the company.

[3064]

(*Table B outside the scope of this work.*)

TABLE C
A COMPANY LIMITED BY GUARANTEE AND NOT HAVING A SHARE CAPITAL
MEMORANDUM OF ASSOCIATION

1. The company's name is "The Dundee School Association Limited".
2. The company's registered office is to be situated in Scotland.
3. The company's objects are the carrying on of a school for boys and girls in Dundee and the doing of all such other things as are incidental or conducive to the attainment of that object.
4. The liability of the members is limited.
5. Every member of the company undertakes to contribute such amount as may be required (not exceeding £100) to the company's assets if it should be wound up while he is a member or within one year after he ceases to be a member, for payment of the company's debts and liabilities contracted before he ceases to be a member, and of the costs, charges and expenses of winding up, and for the adjustment of the rights of the contributories among themselves.
We, the subscribers to this memorandum of association, wish to be formed into a company pursuant to this memorandum.
Names and Addresses of Subscribers.
1. Kenneth Brodie, 14 Bute Street, Dundee.
2. Ian Davis, 2 Burns Avenue, Dundee.
Dated 19 .
Witness to the above signatures.
Anne Brown, 149 Princes Street, Edinburgh.

ARTICLES OF ASSOCIATION

PRELIMINARY

1. Regulations 2 to 35 inclusive, 54, 55, 57, 59, 102 to 108 inclusive, 110, 114, 116 and 117 of Table A, shall not apply to the company but the articles hereinafter contained and, subject to the modifications hereinafter expressed, the remaining regulations of Table A shall constitute the articles of association of the company.

INTERPRETATION

2. In regulation 1 of Table A, the definition of "the holder" shall be omitted.

MEMBERS

3. The subscribers to the memorandum of association of the company and such other persons as are admitted to membership in accordance with the articles shall be members of

the company. No person shall be admitted a member of the company unless he is approved by the directors. Every person who wishes to become a member shall deliver to the company an application for membership in such form as the directors require executed by him.

4. A member may at any time withdraw from the company by giving at least seven clear days' notice to the company. Membership shall not be transferable and shall cease on death.

NOTICE OF GENERAL MEETINGS

5. In regulation 38 of Table A—
   (a) in paragraph (b) the words "of the total voting rights at the meeting of all the members" shall be substituted for "in nominal value of the shares giving that right" and
   (b) the words "The notice shall be given to all the members and to the directors and auditors" shall be substituted for the last sentence.

PROCEEDINGS AT GENERAL MEETINGS

6. The words "and at any separate meeting of the holders of any class of shares in the company" shall be omitted from regulation 44 of Table A.

7. Paragraph (d) of regulation 46 of Table A shall be omitted.

VOTES OF MEMBERS

8. On a show of hands every member present in person shall have one vote. On a poll every member present in person or by proxy shall have one vote.

DIRECTORS' EXPENSES

9. The words "of any class of shares or" shall be omitted from regulation 83 of Table A.

PROCEEDINGS OF DIRECTORS

10. In paragraph (c) of regulation 94 of Table A the word "debentures" shall be substituted for the words "shares, debentures or other securities" in both places where they occur.

MINUTES

11. The words "of the holders of any class of shares in the company" shall be omitted from regulation 100 of Table A.

NOTICES

12. The second sentence of regulation 112 of Table A shall be omitted.

13. The words "or of the holders of any class of shares in the company" shall be omitted from regulation 113 of Table A.

[3065]

(*Table D outside the scope of this work.*)

TABLE E
AN UNLIMITED COMPANY HAVING A SHARE CAPITAL
MEMORANDUM OF ASSOCIATION

1. The company's name is "The Woodford Engineering Company".
2. The company's registered office is to be situated in England and Wales.
3. The company's objects are the working of certain patented inventions relating to the application of microchip technology to the improvement of food processing, and the doing of all such other things as are incidental or conducive to the attainment of that object.
We, the subscribers to this memorandum of association, wish to be formed into a company pursuant to this memorandum; and we agree to take the number of shares shown opposite our respective names.

PART II
STATUTORY INSTRUMENTS

Names and Addresses of Subscribers	Number of shares taken by each Subscriber
1. Brian Smith, 24 Nibley Road, Wotton-under-Edge, Gloucestershire.	3
2. William Green, 278 High Street, Chipping Sodbury, Avon.	5
Total shares taken	8

Dated 19
Witness to the above signatures,
Anne Brown, 108 Park Way, Bristol 8.

ARTICLES OF ASSOCIATION

1. Regulations 3, 32, 34 and 35 of Table A shall not apply to the company, but the articles hereinafter contained and, subject to the modification hereinafter expressed, the remaining regulations of Table A shall constitute the articles of association of the company.

2. The words "at least seven clear days' notice" shall be substituted for the words "at least fourteen clear days' notice" in regulation 38 of Table A.

3. The share capital of the company is £20,000 divided into 20,000 shares of £1 each.

4. The company may by special resolution—
   - (a) increase the share capital by such sum to be divided into shares of such amount as the resolution may prescribe;
   - (b) consolidate and divide all or any of its share capital into shares of a larger amount than its existing shares;
   - (c) subdivide its shares, or any of them, into shares of a smaller amount than its existing shares;
   - (d) cancel any shares which at the date of the passing of the resolution have not been taken or agreed to be taken by any person;
   - (e) reduce its share capital and any share premium account in any way.

[3066]

(*Table F outside the scope of this work.*)

CHARITABLE DEDUCTIONS (APPROVED SCHEMES) REGULATIONS 1986

(SI 1986/2211)

NOTES

Made: 15 December 1986.
Authority: Finance Act 1986, s 28.
These Regulations now have effect as if made under the Income Tax (Earnings and Pensions) Act 2003, s 715.
Commencement: 8 January 1987.

ARRANGEMENT OF REGULATIONS

1 Citation and commencement

These Regulations may be cited as the Charitable Deductions (Approved Schemes) Regulations 1986, and shall come into operation on 8th January 1987.

[3067]

2 Interpretation

In these Regulations unless the context otherwise requires:—

"approved agency" means a body approved as agent in accordance with Regulation 5;
"approved scheme" means a scheme approved in accordance with Regulation 3;
"employer" means a person paying emoluments;
"employee" means any person entitled to receive payments of emoluments;
"emoluments" means income to be taken into account in assessing liability to income tax under Schedule E, from payments of which income tax falls to be deducted by virtue of section 204 of the Taxes Act and regulations under that section;
"income tax month" means the period beginning on the 6th day of any calendar month and ending on the 5th day of the following calendar month;
"scheme" includes a kind of scheme;
["supplement" means the supplement payable under section 38 of the Finance Act 2000;]
"year" means the period beginning on any 6th day of April and ending on the following 5th day of April.

[3068]

NOTES

Definition "supplement" inserted by the Charitable Deductions (Approved Schemes) (Amendment No 2) Regulations 2000, SI 2000/2083, reg 3 with effect in relation to supplements payable in respect of sums withheld on or after 6 April 2000 and before 6 April 2003; substituted by the Charitable Deductions (Approved Schemes) (Amendment) Regulations 2003, SI 2003/1745, reg 3 with effect in relation to supplements payable in respect of sums withheld on or after 6 April 2003 and before 6 April 2004.

Taxes Act, s 204: repealed; see now the Income Tax (Earnings and Pensions) Act 2003, s 684.

3 Approval of schemes

The Board may grant approval of a scheme for the purposes of section 27 of the Finance Act 1986 if it is satisfied on an application by an approved agency that the scheme provides:—

(a) for a contract between the approved agency and an employer to give effect to the scheme;

(b) that any employee to whom thc employer pays emoluments on or after 6th April 1987 may … request the employer, in such form as the Board may approve or prescribe, to withhold from such emoluments such sum as the employee may specify pursuant to the scheme to be paid (subject to the provisions of the scheme) either by way of gift to such charity or charities as the employee may specify or in exchange for vouchers which the employee may surrender by way of gift to the charity or charities of his choice;

(c) that under the scheme the employer is constituted the agent of the approved agency in holding moneys withheld from employees pursuant to the scheme;

(d) for any minimum sum which may be withheld pursuant to the scheme and for any limit which may be imposed on the number of charities which one employee may specify pursuant to the scheme;

(e) …

(f) that no sum so withheld shall be due to the specified charity pursuant to a deed of covenant or, where the sum withheld is paid in exchange for vouchers, that the value of those vouchers shall not be due to the charity or charities to which they are surrendered pursuant to a deed of covenant;

(g) that the employer is to be bound to pay over to the approved agency sums withheld from employees pursuant to the scheme in any income tax month within 14 days of the end of that income tax month;

(h) that the approved agency will if so requested give written receipts to the employer in respect of sums paid over to it;

PART II STATUTORY INSTRUMENTS

(i) that in no circumstances will sums duly withheld and paid over to the approved agency be returnable to the employer or to any employee;

(j) that the approved agency will, subject to any deduction in respect of its charges, pay sums paid to it by the employer pursuant to the scheme to the charities respectively specified by the employees or provide the employees with vouchers to be surrendered to the charities of their choice;

[(ja) that the approved agency will pay to the charities specified by the employees the sums paid to it by the employer pursuant to the scheme within a period which does not exceed the period set out in regulation 4A;]

(k) that the approved agency will if so requested by an employee at the end of any year give him a certificate of the amounts which the approved agency has paid to charities specified by him in respect of sums withheld from his emoluments in that year and of the maximum time elapsing in any period specified by the employee between the receipt of such sums from the employer and the payment to the charities of amounts in respect of such sums;

(l) that if for any reason it becomes impossible for the approved agency to pay any amount to a charity specified by an employee the approved agency shall pay that amount to such other charity as it may consider has objects similar to those of the charity specified by the employee, but so that it shall not in any circumstances appropriate that amount to its own funds; and that on so paying that amount to that other charity the approved agency will give notice to the employee that it has done so;

(m) that where an employee has been provided with a voucher by which payment may be made to a charity and that voucher has not been presented to the approved agency by way of payment within a time prescribed by the approved agency the approved agency will pay the amount represented by that voucher to such other charity as it sees fit, but so that it shall not in any circumstances appropriate that amount to its own funds; and that on so paying that amount to that other charity the approved agency will give notice to the employee that it has done so;

(n) for the method by which the approved agency's charges in relation to the operation of the scheme will be met and for the determining of the amount of such charges.

[3069]

NOTES

Words omitted from para (b) and whole of para (e) revoked by the Charitable Deductions (Approved Schemes) (Amendment No 2) Regulations 2000, SI 2000/2083, reg 4; para (ja) inserted by the Charitable Deductions (Approved Schemes) (Amendment) Regulations 2000, SI 2000/759, reg 3.

Finance Act 1986, s 27: repealed; see now the Income Tax (Earnings and Pensions) Act 2003, s 684.

4 Applications by an approved agency in accordance with Regulation 3 shall be in such form as the Board may approve or prescribe.

[3070]

[4A Period for payment by agencies to charities

(1) An approved agency shall, notwithstanding anything in the provisions of an approved scheme or in a contract entered into with the employer to give effect to an approved scheme, pay to the charities specified by the employees the sums paid to it by the employer pursuant to the scheme not later than 60 days following either—

(a) the date on which it receives the sums paid to it from the employer or, if later,

(b) the date on which it receives notification of the charity or charities specified by an employee.

(2) Where an employee has been provided with a voucher by which payment may be made to a charity, the date on which a charity presents that voucher to the approved agency for payment shall be treated for the purposes of paragraph (1)(b) as the date on which the approved agency receives notification of the specification of that charity by the employee.

[(3) The prescribed period for the purposes of section 38(1) of the Finance Act 2000 shall be—

(a) the period of 7 days following the coming into force of the Charitable Deductions (Approved Schemes) (Amendment) Regulations 2003, or

(b) if it ends later, the period within which payment of the sums paid to the approved agency by the employer pursuant to the scheme is to be made under this regulation.]]

[3071]

NOTES

Inserted by the Charitable Deductions (Approved Schemes) (Amendment) Regulations 2000, SI 2000/759, reg 4, in relation to sums withheld on or after 6 April 2000.

Para (3): added by the Charitable Deductions (Approved Schemes) (Amendment No 2) Regulations 2000, SI 2000/2083, reg 5, with effect in relation to supplements payable in respect of sums withheld on or after 6 April 2000 and before 6 April 2003; substituted by the Charitable Deductions (Approved Schemes) (Amendment) Regulations 2003, SI 2003/1745, reg 4 with effect in relation to supplements payable in respect of sums withheld on or after 6 April 2003 and before 6 April 2004.

5 Approval of agencies

The Board may grant approval as an agent for the purposes of section 27 of the Finance Act 1986 to any charity which the Board is satisfied is prepared and able to act as an approved agency in relation to approved schemes and to comply with the provisions of these Regulations.

[3072]

NOTES

Finance Act 1986, s 27: repealed; see now the Income Tax (Earnings and Pensions) Act 2003, s 684.

6 Applications by a charity for approval as an agent in accordance with Regulation 5 shall be in such form as the Board may approve or prescribe.

[3073]

7 Withdrawal of approval of agencies

If at any time the Board is of opinion that an approved agency has ceased to be a charity or has failed to act properly in relation to an approved scheme or has failed to comply with these Regulations, it may give notice of withdrawal of approval to the approved agency and thereupon, from such date as the Board may specify in its notice, the agency shall cease to be approved and all schemes which have been approved on its application shall cease to be approved and all contracts to give effect to such schemes shall determine. When the Board gives such notice it shall inform every employer who has a contract with the approved agency to give effect to an approved scheme that it has so given notice.

[3074]

8 Appeals

(1) Any person aggrieved by the Board's refusal to grant him approval as an agent in accordance with Regulation 5 or by the Board's withdrawal of such approval in accordance with Regulation 7 may, by notice in writing given to the Board within 30 days from the date on which he is notified of the Board's refusal or withdrawal of approval, require the matter to be determined by the Special Commissioners, and the Special Commissioners shall hear and determine the matter in like manner as an appeal.

(2) Any approved agency aggrieved by the Board's refusal to grant approval of a scheme in accordance with Regulation 3, may, by notice in writing given to the Board within 30 days from the date on which it is notified of the Board's refusal, require the matter to be determined by the Special Commissioners, and the Special Commissioners shall hear and determine the matter in like manner as an appeal.

[3075]

9 Information, returns and records

(1) Every approved agency shall, within 30 days of entering into a contract with an employer giving effect to an approved scheme, inform the Board, in such form as the Board may approve or prescribe, of the date of the contract and of the name and address of the employer.

(2) Where a contract giving effect to an approved scheme is terminated the approved agency shall, within 30 days, inform the Board of such termination.

[(3) Where an approved agency has not paid to the charities specified by the employees—

(a) the sums paid to it by the employer pursuant to the scheme within the period set out in regulation 4A(1) and (2), or

(b) any supplements relating to those sums within the period prescribed by regulation 4A(3),

the approved agency shall, not later than 7 days following the last day on which it should have paid those sums or supplements to the charities, inform the Board by furnishing a statement of those sums or supplements and the reasons why it has not been able to comply with regulation 4A.]

[3076]

NOTES

Para (3): substituted by the Charitable Deductions (Approved Schemes) (Amendment No 2) Regulations 2000, SI 2000/2083, reg 6, with effect in relation to supplements payable in respect of sums withheld on or after 6 April 2000 and before 6 April 2003; further substituted by the Charitable Deductions (Approved Schemes) (Amendment) Regulations 2003, SI 2003/1745, reg 5 with effect in relation to supplements payable in respect of sums withheld on or after 6 April 2003 and before 6 April 2004.

10 On the ending of each year every approved agency shall, within 30 days of the end of such year or within such further time as the Board may allow, furnish a return to the Board, in such form as the Board may approve or prescribe, of the sums received from each employer with whom it has at any time within the year had a subsisting contract to give effect to an approved scheme, of the numbers of employees from whose emoluments such sums have been withheld, of the number of vouchers issued pursuant to any contract and the total values of such vouchers, of the amounts paid by it to each charity in relation to such approved schemes, and of its charges in relation to the operation of schemes.

[3077]

11—(1) Every approved agency shall retain:—

(a) records of approved schemes,

(b) records of contracts with employers until 3 years from the termination of each contract, . . .

(c) for not less than 3 years, records of sums received from employers, records of amounts paid to all charities specified by employers, and records of vouchers for charities issued by it to employees pursuant to approved schemes, [and

(d) for not less than 3 years, records of all supplements paid to charities specified by employees and records of all amounts received from the Board under section 38 of the Finance Act 2000.]

(2) Every approved agency, when so required by notice served on it by the Board, shall within 30 days of such service produce for inspection by an officer of the Board all records required to be retained by it by paragraph (1) of this Regulation.

[3078]

NOTES

Para (1): word omitted from sub-para (b) revoked by the Charitable Deductions (Approved Schemes) (Amendment No 2) Regulations 2000, SI 2000/2083, reg 7(a), with effect in relation to supplements payable in respect of sums withheld on or after 6 April 2000 and before 6 April 2003.

Para (1)(d) (and word immediately preceding it): inserted by the Charitable Deductions (Approved Schemes) (Amendment No 2) Regulations 2000, SI 2000/2083, reg 7(b), with effect in relation to supplements payable in respect of sums withheld on or after 6 April 2000 and before 6 April 2003; substituted by the Charitable Deductions (Approved Schemes) (Amendment) Regulations 2003, SI 2003/1745, reg 6 with effect in relation to supplements payable in respect of sums withheld on or after 6 April 2003 and before 6 April 2004.

12—(1) Every employer who has entered into a contract with an approved agency pursuant to an approved scheme shall retain:—

(a) a copy of such contract until 3 years from the termination of the contract,

(b) all forms of request to deduct given by employees pursuant to the approved scheme until 3 years from the revocation or lapse of such request and,

(c) for not less than 3 years, records of all sums withheld from such employees pursuant to the approved scheme and evidence of all payments made to the approved agency pursuant to the approved scheme.

(2) Every employer who has entered into a contract with an approved agency pursuant to an approved scheme, when so required by notice served on him by the Board, shall within 30 days of such service produce for inspection by an officer of the Board all documents and records required to be retained by him pursuant to paragraph (1) of this Regulation.

[3079]

13 Termination of contracts

If at any time an employer who has contracted to give effect to a scheme has without reasonable excuse failed in a significant respect to give effect to the scheme in accordance with his contract the approved agency shall forthwith give notice to the employer of termination of the contract.

[3080]

14 Employee leaving employment

Where an employee who has requested his employer to withhold any sum pursuant to an approved scheme leaves his employment, the employer shall provide the employee with a statement, in such form as the Board may approve or prescribe, of the total amount so withheld from the employee's emoluments from that employment in the year in which the employee so leaves his employment.

[3081]

15 Service by post

Any notice which is authorised or required to be given or served under these Regulations may be sent by post.

[3082]

[16 Overpayment of supplement to be treated as unpaid tax

Where the Board has made an overpayment under section 38 of the Finance Act 2000 to an approved agent, the amount of that overpayment may be assessed and recovered as if it were an amount of unpaid tax for the purposes of the Taxes Acts.]

[3083]

NOTES

Added by the Charitable Deductions (Approved Schemes) (Amendment No 2) Regulations 2000, SI 2000/2083, reg 8, with effect in relation to supplements payable in respect of sums withheld on or after 6 April 2000 and before 6 April 2003; substituted by the Charitable Deductions (Approved Schemes) (Amendment) Regulations 2003, SI 2003/1745, reg 7 with effect in relation to supplements payable in respect of sums withheld on or after 6 April 2003 and before 6 April 2004.

CONSUMER CREDIT (EXEMPT AGREEMENTS) ORDER 1989

(SI 1989/869)

NOTES

Made: 19 May 1989.
Authority: Consumer Credit Act 1974, ss 16(1), (4)–(6), 182(2), (4).
Commencement: 19 June 1989.

ARRANGEMENT OF ARTICLES

PART II STATUTORY INSTRUMENTS

1 Citation, commencement, interpretation and revocation

(1) This Order may be cited as the Consumer Credit (Exempt Agreements) Order 1989 and shall come into force on 19th June 1989.

(2) In this Order—

"the Act" means the Consumer Credit Act 1974;

"business premises" means premises for occupation for the purposes of a business (including any activity carried on by a body of persons, whether corporate or unincorporate) or for those and other purposes;

and references to the total charge for credit and the rate thereof are respectively references to the total charge for credit and the rate thereof calculated in accordance with the Consumer Credit (Total Charge for Credit) Regulations 1980.

(3) The Orders specified in Schedule 2 to this Order are hereby revoked.

[3084]

2 Exemption of certain consumer credit agreements secured on land

(1) The Act shall not regulate a consumer credit agreement which falls within section 16(2) of the Act, being an agreement to which this paragraph applies.

(2) Where the creditor is a body specified in Part I of Schedule 1 to this Order, [or a deposit taker (within the meaning given by section 16(10) of the Act),] paragraph (1) above applies only to—

(a) a debtor-creditor-supplier agreement falling within section 16(2)(a) or (c) of the Act;

(b) a debtor-creditor agreement secured by any land mortgage to finance—

(i) the purchase of land; or

(ii) the provision of dwellings or business premises on any land; or

(iii) subject to paragraph (3) below, the alteration, enlarging, repair or improvement of a dwelling or business premises on any land;

(c) a debtor-creditor agreement secured by any land mortgage to refinance any existing indebtedness of the debtor, whether to the creditor or another person, under any agreement by which the debtor was provided with credit for any of the purposes specified in heads (i) to (iii) of sub-paragraph (b) above.

(3) Head (iii) of sub-paragraph (b) of paragraph (2) above applies only—

(i) where the creditor is the creditor under—

(a) an agreement (whenever made) by which the debtor is provided with credit for any of the purposes specified in head (i) and head (ii) of that sub-paragraph; or

(b) an agreement (whenever made) refinancing an agreement under which the debtor is provided with credit for any of the said purposes,

being, in either case, an agreement relating to the land referred to in the said head (iii) and secured by a land mortgage on that land; or

(ii) where a debtor-creditor agreement to finance the alteration, enlarging, repair or improvement of a dwelling, secured by a land mortgage on that dwelling, is made as a result of any such services as are described in [section 4(3)(e) of the Housing Associations Act 1985] which are certified as having been provided by—

(a) a local authority;

(b) a housing association within the meaning of section 1 of the Housing Associations Act 1985 or [Article 3 of the Housing (Northern Ireland) Order 1992];

(c) a body established by such a housing association for the purpose of providing such services as are described in the said [section 4(3)(e) of the Housing Associations Act 1985];

(d) a charity;

(e) the National Home Improvement Council; ...

(f) the Northern Ireland Housing Executive[; or

(g) a body, or a body of any description, that has been approved by the Secretary of State under section 169(4)(c) of the Local Government and Housing Act 1989 [or the Department of the Environment for Northern Ireland under article 103(4)(c) of the Housing (Northern Ireland) Order 1992.]]

(4) Where the creditor is a body specified in Part II of Schedule 1 to this Order, paragraph (1) above applies only to an agreement of a description specified in that Part in relation to that body and made pursuant to an enactment or for a purpose so specified.

(5) Where the creditor is a body specified in Part III of Schedule 1 to this Order, paragraph (1) above applies only to an agreement of a description falling within Article 2(2)(a) to (c) above, being an agreement advancing money on the security of a dwelling-house.

[3085]

NOTES

Para (2): words in square brackets substituted by the Financial Services and Markets Act 2000 (Consequential Amendments and Repeals) Order 2001 SI 2001/3649, art 396.

Para (3): words in first, second and third pairs of square brackets substituted and words in final (inner) pair of square brackets added by the Consumer Credit (Exempt Agreements) (Amendment) (No 2) Order 1993, SI 1993/2922, art 2(a); word omitted revoked and para (g) and word immediately preceding it added, by the Consumer Credit (Exempt Agreements) (Amendment) (No 3) Order 1991, SI 1991/2844, art 2(a).

3 Exemption of certain consumer credit agreements by reference to the number of payments to be made by the debtor

(1) The Act shall not regulate a consumer credit agreement which is an agreement of one of the following descriptions, that is to say—

(a) a debtor-creditor-supplier agreement being either—

(i) an agreement for fixed-sum credit under which the total number of payments to be made by the debtor does not exceed four, and those payments are required to be made within a period not exceeding 12 months beginning with the date of the agreement; or

(ii) an agreement for running-account credit which provides for the making of payments by the debtor in relation to specified periods and requires that the number of payments to be made by the debtor in repayment of the whole amount of the credit provided in each such period shall not exceed one;

not being, in either case, an agreement of a description specified in paragraph (2) below; and in this sub-paragraph, "payment" means a payment comprising an amount in respect of credit with or without any other amount;

(b) a debtor-creditor-supplier agreement financing the purchase of land being an agreement under which the number of payments to be made by the debtor does not exceed four; and in this sub-paragraph, "payment" means a payment comprising or including an amount in respect of credit or the total charge for credit (if any);

(c) a debtor-creditor-supplier agreement for fixed-sum credit to finance a premium under a contract of insurance relating to any land or to anything thereon where—

(i) the creditor is the creditor under an agreement secured by a land mortgage on that land which either is an exempt agreement by virtue of section 16(1) of the Act or of article 2 above, or is a personal credit agreement which would be an exempt agreement by virtue of either of those provisions if the credit provided were not to exceed £15,000;

(ii) the amount of the credit is to be repaid within the period to which the premium relates, not being a period exceeding 12 months; and

(iii) there is no charge forming part of the total charge for credit under the agreement other than interest at a rate not exceeding the rate of interest from time to time payable under the agreement mentioned in head (i) above,

and the number of payments to be made by the debtor does not exceed twelve; and in this sub-paragraph "payment" has the same meaning as it has in paragraph (1)(b) above; and

(d) a debtor-creditor-supplier agreement for fixed-sum credit where—

(i) the creditor is the creditor under an agreement secured by a land mortgage on any land which either is an exempt agreement by virtue of section 16(1) of the Act or of article 2 above, or is a personal credit agreement which would be an exempt agreement by virtue of either of those provisions if the credit provided were not to exceed £15,000;

(ii) the agreement is to finance a premium under a contract of life insurance which provides, in the event of the death before the credit under the agreement referred to in head (i) above has been repaid of the person on whose life the contract is effected, for payment of a sum not exceeding the amount sufficient to defray the sums which, immediately after that credit has been advanced, would be payable to the creditor in respect of that credit and of the total charge for that credit; and

(iii) there is no charge forming part of the total charge for credit under the agreement other than interest at a rate not exceeding the rate of interest from time to time payable under the agreement referred to in head (i) above,

and the number of payments to be made by the debtor does not exceed twelve; and in this sub-paragraph, "payment" has the same meaning as it has in sub-paragraph (1)(b) above.

(2) The descriptions of agreement referred to in sub-paragraph (a) of paragraph (1) above and to which accordingly that sub-paragraph does not apply are—

(a) agreements financing the purchase of land;

(b) agreements which are conditional sale agreements or hire-purchase agreements; and

(c) agreements secured by a pledge (other than a pledge of documents of title or of bearer bonds).

[3086]

[4 Exemption of certain consumer credit agreements by reference to the rate of the total charge for credit

(1) The Act shall not regulate—

(a) a debtor-creditor agreement where the creditor is a credit union and the rate of the total charge for credit does not exceed [26.9 per cent];

(b) (subject to paragraph (2) below) a debtor-creditor agreement—

(i) which is an agreement of a type offered to a particular class, or particular classes, of individuals and not offered to the public generally; and

(ii) under the terms of which the only charge included in the total charge for credit is interest which cannot at any time exceed the sum of one per cent and the highest of the base rates published by the banks named in paragraph (3) below, being the latest rates in operation on the date 28 days before any such time; or

(c) (subject to paragraph (2) below) a debtor-creditor agreement—

(i) which is an agreement of a type offered to a particular class, or particular classes, of individuals and not offered to the public generally;

(ii) under which there can be no increase after the relevant date in the rate or amount of any item which is included in the total charge for credit or which would be included but for regulation 14 of the Total Charge for Credit Regulations; and

(iii) in respect of which the rate of the total charge for credit does not exceed the sum of one per cent and the highest of the base rates published by the banks named in paragraph (3) below, being the latest rates in operation on the date 28 days before the date on which the agreement is made.

(2) Paragraph (1)(b) and (c) above does not apply to an agreement under which the total amount to be repaid by the debtor to discharge his indebtedness in respect of the amount of credit provided may vary according to a formula which is specified in the agreement and which has effect by reference to movements in the level of any index or to any other factor.

(3) The banks referred to in paragraph (1)(b) and (c) above are—

Bank of England
Bank of Scotland
Barclays Bank PLC
Clydesdale Bank PLC
Co-operative Bank Public Limited Company
Coutts & Co
Lloyds TSB Bank plc
Midland Bank Public Limited Company
National Westminster Bank Public Limited Company
The Royal Bank of Scotland plc

(4) In this article—

"credit union" means—

(a) a society registered under the Industrial and Provident Societies Act 1965 by virtue of section 1 of the Credit Unions Act 1979; or

(b) a society registered under the Credit Unions (Northern Ireland) Order 1985 or a society registered under the Industrial and Provident Societies Act (Northern Ireland) 1969 as a credit union;

"interest" means interest at a rate determined in accordance with the formula set out in regulation 7(1) of the Total Charge for Credit Regulations, and in that formula as applied by paragraph (1)(b) above;

"period rate of charge" has the meaning given in regulation 7(2) of those Regulations;

"the relevant date" has the meaning given in regulation 1(2) of the Total Charge for Credit Regulations; and

"the Total Charge for Credit Regulations" means the Consumer Credit (Total Charge for Credit) Regulations 1980.]

[3087]

NOTES

Commencement: 1 August 1999.

Substituted by the Consumer Credit (Exempt Agreements) (Amendment) Order 1999, SI 1999/1956, art 3.

Para (1)(a): words in square brackets substituted by the Consumer Credit (Exempt Agreements) (Amendment) Order 2006, SI 2006/1273, arts 2, 3.

5 Exemption of certain consumer credit agreements having a connection with a country outside the United Kingdom

The Act shall not regulate a consumer credit agreement made—

(a) in connection with trade in goods or services between the United Kingdom and a country outside the United Kingdom or within a country or between countries outside the United Kingdom, being an agreement under which credit is provided to the debtor in the course of a business carried on by him; or

(b) between a creditor listed in Part IV of Schedule 1 to this Order and a debtor who is—

(i) a member of any of the armed forces of the United States of America;

(ii) an employee not habitually resident in the United Kingdom of any of those forces; or

(iii) any such member's or employee's wife or husband or any other person (whether or not a child of his) whom he wholly or partly maintains and treats as a child of the family.

[3088]

6 Exemption of certain consumer hire agreements

The Act shall not regulate a consumer hire agreement where the owner is a body corporate authorised by or under any enactment to supply [gas,] electricity or water and the subject of the agreement is a meter or metering equipment used or to be used in connection with the supply of [gas,] electricity or water, as the case may be.

[3089]

NOTES

Words in square brackets inserted by the Consumer Credit (Exempt Agreements) (Amendment) Order 1991, SI 1991/1393, art 2(b).

SCHEDULES

SCHEDULE 1
BODIES WHOSE AGREEMENTS OF THE SPECIFIED DESCRIPTION ARE EXEMPT AGREEMENTS

Articles 2 and 5

PART I

...

FRIENDLY SOCIETIES

The Ancient Order of Foresters Friendly Society

Anglo-Saxons Friendly Society

Blackburn Philanthropic Mutual Assurance Society

British Benefit Society

British Order of Ancient Free Gardeners' Friendly Society

…

Brunel Assurance Society

Cirencester Benefit Society

…

Civil Servants' Annuities Assurance Society

Colmore Friendly Society

Coventry Assurance Society

Dentists' Provident Society

…

Devon and Exeter Women's Equitable Benefit Society

[The Exeter Equitable Friendly Society]

Grand United Order of Oddfellows Friendly Society

The Hampshire and General Friendly Society

Harvest Friendly Society

…

Hearts of Oak Benefit Society

…

The Ideal Benefit Society

Independent Order of Oddfellows Kingston Unity Friendly Society

The Independent Order of Odd Fellows Manchester Unity Friendly Society

The Independent Order of Rechabites, Salford Unity, Friendly Society

Leeds District of the Ancient Order of Foresters Investment Association

Leek Assurance Collecting Society

The Leicester District Foresters' Investment Society

Liverpool Victoria Friendly Society

…

…

The Manchester and Districts of the Ancient Order of Foresters Investment Association

National Deposit Friendly Society

National Equalized Druids Friendly Society

National United Order of Free Gardeners Friendly Society

New Tab Friendly Society

Northumberland and Durham Miners' Permanent Relief Fund Friendly Society

[Nottingham Oddfellows Assurance Friendly Society]

…

The Order of Druids Friendly Society

The Order of the Sons of Temperance Friendly Society

Original Holloway Society

Pioneer Benefit Society

Preston Catholic Collecting Society

Preston Shelley Assurance Collecting Society

Provident Reliance Friendly Society

Rational and County Assurance Society

Royal Liver Friendly Society

Scottish Friendly Assurance Society

The Scottish Legal Life Assurance Society

[The Shepherds Friendly Society]

Sons of Scotland Temperance Friendly Society

Stepney District Distressed Members' Pension Benevolent Fund

. . .

The Sussex Widow and Orphans Society

Teachers Provident Society

Time Assurance Society

Tunbridge Wells Equitable Friendly Society

Tunstall and District Assurance Collecting Society

United Ancient Order of Druids Friendly Society

United Kingdom Civil Service Benefit Society

United Patriots' National Benefit Society

West Surrey General Benefit Society

Widow and Orphan Fund of the Woolwich District of the Independent Order of Odd Fellows Manchester Unity Friendly Society

Widow and Orphans' Fund, Stepney District of the Independent Order of Odd Fellows, Manchester Unity Friendly Society

. . .

Widow, Widowers and Orphans' Fund of the Godalming District of the Independent Order of Oddfellows, Manchester Unity, Friendly Society

Wiltshire Holloway Benefit Society

CHARITIES

The Central Board of Finance of the Church of England

Church Commissioners

The Church of England Pensions Board

The Church of Scotland

The Church of Scotland General Trustees

Church of Scotland Trust

[The Representative Body of the Church in Wales]

Timber Trades Benevolent Society

The Winchester Diocesan Board of Finance

York Diocesan Board of Finance Limited

. . .

[3090]–[3093]

NOTES

Entries omitted in the first and final places outside the scope of this work; entries omitted in the second, eighth and tenth places revoked by the Consumer Credit (Exempt Agreements) (Amendment) (No 3)

PART II STATUTORY INSTRUMENTS

Order 1991, SI 1991/2844, art 2(b); entries omitted in the third, fourth, fifth, sixth and ninth places revoked, entry "The Exeter Equitable Friendly Society" substituted for original entry "Devon and Exeter Men's Equitable Benefit Society", and entry "City of Glasgow Friendly Society" substituted by entry "Scottish Friendly Assurance Society" (which was already contained in the list), by the Consumer Credit (Exempt Agreements) (Amendment) Order 1993, SI 1993/346, art 2(a); entry omitted in the seventh place revoked, entry "Nottingham Oddfellows Assurance Friendly Society" substituted and entries "The Shepherds Friendly Society" and "The Representative Body of the Church in Wales" inserted by the Consumer Credit (Exempt Agreements) (Amendment) Order 1991, SI 1991/1393, art 2(c); entry omitted in the eleventh place revoked by the Consumer Credit (Exempt Agreements) (Amendment) (No 2) Order 1993, SI 1993/2922, art 2(b)(i).

(Pts II–IV outside the scope of this work; Sch 2 contains revocations.)

CHARITIES (MISLEADING NAMES) REGULATIONS 1992

(SI 1992/1901)

NOTES

Made: 28 July 1992.

Authority: Charities Act 1992, s 4(2)(c) (repealed).

These Regulations now have effect as if made under the Charities Act 1993, s 6(2)(c), by virtue of the Interpretation Act 1978, s 17(2)(b).

Commencement: 1 September 1992.

1 These Regulations may be cited as the Charities (Misleading Names) Regulations 1992 and shall come into force on 1st September 1992.

[3094]

2 The words and expressions set out in the Schedule to these Regulations, together (where appropriate) with the plural and possessive forms of those words and expressions and any abbreviation of them, are hereby specified for the purposes of section 4(2)(c) of the Charities Act 1992.

[3095]

NOTES

Charities Act 1992, s 4(2)(c): repealed; see now Charities Act 1993, s 6(2)(c).

SCHEDULE
SPECIFICATION OF WORDS AND EXPRESSIONS FOR THE PURPOSES OF SECTION 4(2)(C) OF THE CHARITIES ACT 1992

Regulation 2

Assurance

Authority

Bank

Benevolent

British

Building Society

Church

Co-operative

England

English

Europe

European

Friendly Society

Grant-Maintained

Great Britain

Great British

Her Majesty

His Majesty

Industrial & Provident Society

International

Ireland

Irish

King

National

Nationwide

Northern Ireland

Northern Irish

Official

Polytechnic

Prince

Princess

Queen

Registered

Royal

Royale

Royalty

School

Scotland

Scottish

Trade Union

United Kingdom

University

Wales

Welsh

Windsor

[3096]

CHARITIES (RECEIVER AND MANAGER) REGULATIONS 1992

(SI 1992/2355)

NOTES

Made: 1 October 1992.

Authority: Charities Act 1960, ss 20A(6), (7), 43 (repealed).

These Regulations now have effect as if made under the Charities Act 1993, ss 19(6), (7), 86, by virtue of the Interpretation Act 1978, s 17(2)(b).

Commencement: 1 November 1992.

1 Citation, commencement and interpretation

(1) These Regulations may be cited as the Charities (Receiver and Manager) Regulations 1992 and shall come into force on 1st November 1992.

(2) In these Regulations—

"the 1960 Act" means the Charities Act 1960;

"the appointed person" means a person appointed by order under section 20(1)(vii) of the 1960 Act to be receiver and manager in respect of the property and affairs of a charity;

"the relevant charity" means the charity in respect of which that person was appointed; and

"the relevant order" means the order by which that person was appointed.

[3097]

NOTES

Charities Act 1960, s 20(1)(vii): repealed; see now Charities Act 1993, s 19.

2 Security by appointed person

The Commissioners are hereby authorised to require the appointed person to give security to them for the due discharge of his functions within such time and in such form as they may specify.

[3098]

3 Remuneration of appointed person

(1) The Commissioners are hereby authorised to determine the amount of an appointed person's remuneration.

(2) The remuneration of an appointed person shall be payable out of the income of the relevant charity.

(3) The Commissioners are hereby authorised to disallow any amount of remuneration of an appointed person where, on the expiry of the time specified in the notice referred to in regulation 4(2) below and after consideration of such representations, if any, as are duly made in response to such a notice, they are satisfied that he has failed in such manner as is set out in paragraph (a) or (b) of regulation 4(1) below and specified in such a notice.

[3099]

4 Notice of failure to, and removal of, appointed person

(1) Where it appears to the Commissioners that an appointed person has failed—

(a) to give security within such time or in such form as they have specified, or

(b) satisfactorily to discharge any function imposed on him by or by virtue of the relevant order or by regulation 5 below,

and they wish to consider exercising their powers under regulation 3(3) above or paragraph (3) below, they shall give him, whether in person or by post, a written notice complying with paragraph (2) below.

(2) A notice given to an appointed person under paragraph (1) above shall inform him of—

(a) any failure under paragraph (1)(a) or (b) above in respect of which the notice is issued;

(b) of the Commissioners' power under regulation 3(3) above to authorise the disallowance of any amount of remuneration if satisfied as to any such failure;

(c) of their power under paragraph (3) below to remove him if satisfied as to any such failure; and

(d) of his right to make representations to them in respect of any such alleged failure within such reasonable time as is specified in the notice.

(3) On the expiry of the time specified in the notice referred to in paragraph (2) above and after consideration of such representations, if any, as are duly made in response to such a notice, the Commissioners may remove an appointed person where they are satisfied that he has failed in such manner as is set out in paragraph (1)(a) or (b) above and specified in such notice (whether or not they also exercise the power conferred by regulation 3(3) above).

[3100]

5 Reports by appointed person

(1) This regulation makes provision in respect of the reports which are to be made by an appointed person to the Commissioners (and which, in addition to the matters which are required to be included by virtue of paragraphs (2) to (4) below, may also include particulars of any matter which, in his opinion, should be brought to their attention).

(2) An appointed person shall make a report to the Commissioners not later than three months after the date of his appointment setting out—

(a) an estimate by him of the total value of the property of the relevant charity on, or shortly after, the date of his appointment;

(b) such information about the property and affairs of the relevant charity immediately prior to his appointment as he believes should be included in the report, notwithstanding that it may also be eventually included in a report under section 6 of the 1960 Act; and

(c) his strategy for discharging the functions conferred on him by or by virtue of the relevant order.

(3) For as long as an appointed person holds office as such, he shall make a report to the Commissioners not later than one month after each anniversary of his appointment setting out—

(a) an estimate by him of the total value of the property of the relevant charity on that anniversary of his appointment in respect of which the report is required to be made;

(b) a summary of the discharge by him of the functions conferred on him by or by virtue of the relevant order during the twelve months ending with that anniversary; and

(c) where there are changes to his strategy as last set out in a report in accordance with paragraph (2)(c) above or, as the case may be, this sub-paragraph, those changes.

(4) Subject to paragraph (5) below, an appointed person shall make a report to the Commissioners not later than three months after the date when he ceased to hold office as such setting out—

(a) an estimate by him of the total value of the property of the relevant charity on that date; and

(b) a summary of the discharge by him of the functions conferred on him by or by virtue of the relevant order during the period ending with that date and beginning with either—

(i) the date of his appointment; or

(ii) if that date is more than twelve months before the date when he ceased to hold office as an appointed person, the day immediately after the last anniversary of his appointment.

(5) Paragraph (4) above does not apply where an appointed person ceased to hold office one month or less after an anniversary of his appointment and a report had been made to the Commissioners in accordance with paragraph (3) above in respect of that anniversary.

[3101]

PART II STATUTORY INSTRUMENTS

CHARITIES (QUALIFIED SURVEYORS' REPORTS) REGULATIONS 1992

(SI 1992/2980)

NOTES

Made: 29 November 1992.

Authority: Charities Act 1992, ss 32(4) (repealed), 77(3).

These Regulations now have effect as if made under the Charities Act 1993, ss 36(4), 86, by virtue of the Interpretation Act 1978, s 17(2)(b).

Commencement: 1 January 1993.

1—(1) These Regulations may be cited as the Charities (Qualified Surveyors' Reports) Regulations 1992 and shall come into force on 1st January 1993.

(2) In these Regulations—

"relevant land" means the land in respect of which a report is being obtained for the purposes of section 32(3) of the Charities Act 1992; and

"the surveyor" means the qualified surveyor from whom such a report is being obtained.

[3102]

NOTES

Charities Act 1992, s 32(3): repealed; see now Charities Act 1993, s 36(3).

2 A report prepared for the purposes of section 32(3) of the Charities Act 1992 (requirements to be complied with in respect of the disposition of land held by or in trust for a charity otherwise than with an order of the court or of the Charity Commissioners or where section 32(5) of that Act applies) shall contain such information and deal with such matters as are prescribed by the Schedule to these Regulations (together with such other information and such other matters as the surveyor believes should be drawn to the attention of the charity trustees).

[3103]

NOTES

Charities Act 1992, s 32(3): repealed; see now Charities Act 1993, s 36(3).

SCHEDULE
INFORMATION TO BE CONTAINED IN, AND MATTERS TO BE DEALT WITH BY, QUALIFIED SURVEYORS' REPORTS

Regulation 2

1.—(1) A description of the relevant land and its location, to include—

(a) the measurements of the relevant land;

(b) its current use;

(c) the number of buildings (if any) included in the relevant land;

(d) the measurements of any such buildings; and

(e) the number of rooms in any such buildings and the measurements of those rooms.

(2) Where any information required by sub-paragraph (1) above may be clearly given by means of a plan, it may be so given and any such plan need not be drawn to scale.

2. Whether the relevant land, or any part of it, is leased by or from the charity trustees and, if it is, details of—

(a) the length of the lease and the period of it which is outstanding;

(b) the rent payable under the lease;

(c) any service charge which is so payable;

(d) the provisions in the lease for any review of the rent payable under it or any service charge so payable;

(e) the liability under the lease for repairs and dilapidations; and

(f) any other provision in the lease which, in the opinion of the surveyor, affects the value of the relevant land.

3. Whether the relevant land is subject to the burden of, or enjoys the benefit of, any easement or restrictive covenant or is subject to any annual or other periodic sum charged on or issuing out of the land except rent reserved by a lease or tenancy.

4. Whether any buildings included in the relevant land are in good repair and, if not, the surveyor's advice—

(a) as to whether or not it would be in the best interests of the charity for repairs to be carried out prior to the proposed disposition;

(b) as to what those repairs, if any, should be; and

(c) as to the estimated cost of any repairs he advises.

5. Where, in the opinion of the surveyor, it would be in the best interests of the charity to alter any buildings included in the relevant land prior to disposition (because, for example, adaptations to the buildings for their current use are not such as to command the best market price on the proposed disposition), that opinion and an estimate of the outlay required for any alterations which he suggests.

6. Advice as to the manner of disposing of the relevant land so that the terms on which it is disposed of are the best that can reasonably be obtained for the charity, including—

(a) where appropriate, a recommendation that the land should be divided for the purposes of the disposition;

(b) unless the surveyor's advice is that it would not be in the best interests of the charity to advertise the proposed disposition, the period for which and the manner in which the proposed disposition should be advertised;

(c) where the surveyor's advice is that it would not be in the best interests of the charity to advertise the proposed disposition, his reasons for that advice (for example, that the proposed disposition is the renewal of a lease to someone who enjoys statutory protection or that he believes someone with a special interest in acquiring the relevant land will pay considerably more than the market price for it); and

(d) any view the surveyor may have on the desirability or otherwise of delaying the proposed disposition and, if he believes such delay is desirable, what the period of that delay should be.

7.—(1) Where the surveyor feels able to give such advice and where such advice is relevant, advice as to the chargeability or otherwise of value added tax on the proposed disposition and the effect of such advice on the valuations given under paragraph 8 below.

(2) Where either the surveyor does not feel able to give such advice or such advice is not in his opinion relevant, a statement to that effect.

8. The surveyor's opinion as to—

(a) the current value of the relevant land having regard to its current state of repair and current circumstances (such as the presence of a tenant who enjoys statutory protection) or, where the proposed disposition is a lease, the rent which could be obtained under it having regard to such matters;

(b) what the value of the relevant land or what the rent under the proposed disposition would be—

(i) where he has given advice under paragraph 4 above, if that advice is followed; or

(ii) where he has expressed an opinion under paragraph 5 above, if that opinion is acted upon; or

(iii) if both that advice is followed and that opinion is acted upon;

(c) where he has made a recommendation under paragraph 6(a) above, the increase in the value of the relevant land or rent in respect of it if the recommendation were followed;

(d) where his advice is that it would not be in the best interests of the charity to advertise the proposed disposition because he believes a higher price can be obtained by not doing so, the amount by which that price exceeds the price that could be obtained if the proposed disposition were advertised; and

(e) where he has advised a delay in the proposed disposition under paragraph 6(d) above, the amount by which he believes the price which could be obtained consequent on such a delay exceeds the price that could be obtained without it.

9. Where the surveyor is of the opinion that the proposed disposition is not in the best interests of the charity because it is not a disposition that makes the best use of the relevant land, that opinion and the reasons for it, together with his advice as to the type of disposition which would constitute the best use of the land (including such advice as may be relevant as to the prospects of buying out any sitting tenant or of succeeding in an application for change of use of the land under the laws relating to town and country planning etc).

[3104]

CHARITY COMMISSIONERS' FEES (COPIES AND EXTRACTS) REGULATIONS 1992

(SI 1992/2986)

NOTES

Made: 29 November 1992.
Authority: Charities Act 1992, ss 51(1), (2) (repealed), 77(3).

PART II STATUTORY INSTRUMENTS

These Regulations now have effect as if made under the Charities Act 1993, ss 85(1), (2), 86, by virtue of the Interpretation Act 1978, s 17(2)(b).
Commencement: 1 January 1993.

1—(1) These Regulations may be cited as the Charity Commissioners' Fees (Copies and Extracts) Regulations 1992 and shall come into force on 1st January 1993.

(2) In these Regulations "relevant document" means any document which is kept by the Commissioners under the enactments relating to charities and of or from which section 9 of the Charities Act 1960 or section 7 of the Charitable Trustees Incorporation Act 1872 requires the Commissioners to furnish copies or extracts at the request of any person.

[3105]

NOTES

Charities Act 1960, s 9; Charitable Trustees Incorporation Act 1872, s 7: repealed; see now Charities Act 1993, ss 57, 84.

2 Where a photocopier is used in response to a request to furnish a copy of, or extract from, a relevant document, there shall, subject to regulation 6 below, be payable to the Commissioners for such a copy or extract—

(a) where there are not more than six sheets of photocopied material, a fee of £1.80; and

(b) where there are more than six sheets of photocopied material, a fee of £1.80 and an additional 30p for each such sheet in excess of the first six.

[3106]

3—(1) Where a request is made for a copy of, or extract from, a relevant document and the information contained in that document is recorded otherwise than in legible form, there shall, subject to paragraph (2) and regulation 6 below, be payable to the Commissioners for such a copy or extract (which, by virtue of section 46(2) of the Charities Act 1960, must be furnished in legible form) a fee of 60p for each sheet of paper on which such a copy or extract is printed.

(2) Paragraph (1) above shall not apply for the purposes of the calculation of the fee payable on the furnishing of extracts from a relevant document where—

(a) the extracts requested are such that the request is capable of being dealt with as a request under regulation 4 below, and

(b) the fee payable under that regulation for such extracts is lower than the fee which would otherwise be payable under paragraph (1) above.

[3107]

NOTES

Charities Act 1960, s 46(2): repealed; see now Charities Act 1993, s 97(2).

4—(1) This regulation applies to a request for an extract (or extracts) from the register of charities (which is a relevant document because section 9 of the Charities Act 1960 applies to it by virtue of the requirement in section 4(7) of that Act that the register be kept open to public inspection) where—

(a) the information contained in that register is recorded otherwise than in legible form, and

(b) the request is in respect of any registered charity (or charities) identified by either its name (or their names) or the number under which it is registered (or the numbers under which they are registered).

(2) Subject to regulation 6 below, where a request of the kind described in paragraph (1) above is for a short extract (or extracts) from the register of charities, there shall be payable to the Commissioners in respect of furnishing it (or them) a fee of £2 with an additional 15p for each charity in respect of which a short extract is so furnished.

(3) Subject to regulation 6 below, where a request of the kind described in paragraph (1) above is for a standard extract (or extracts) from the register of charities, there shall be payable to the Commissioners in respect of furnishing it (or them) a fee of £2 with an additional 20p for each charity in respect of which a standard extract is so furnished.

(4) Subject to regulation 6 below, where a request of the kind described in paragraph (1) above is for a detailed extract (or extracts) from the register of charities, there shall be payable to the Commissioners in respect of furnishing it (or them) a fee of £2 with an additional 25p for each charity in respect of which a detailed extract is so furnished or, where it is not possible to furnish such an extract (because the criterion which distinguishes a detailed extract from a standard extract and is referred to in paragraph (5) below is not satisfied) 20p for each charity in respect of which a standard extract is so furnished.

(5) In this regulation and regulation 5 below—

"a short extract" means an extract (not being a standard or detailed extract) which includes the name and registration number of the charity in question;

"a standard extract" means an extract (not being a detailed extract) which, in addition to the information about the charity in question included in a short extract, also includes the purposes of that charity and an address for correspondence with the charity trustees; and

"a detailed extract" means an extract which, in addition to the information about the charity in question included in a standard extract, also includes the names of any other (subsidiary) charity registered in the register of charities under the same number as that charity.

[3108]

NOTES

Charities Act 1960, s 9: repealed; see now Charities Act 1993, s 84.

5—(1) This regulation applies to a request for an extract (or extracts) from the register of charities where—

(a) the information contained in that register is recorded otherwise than in legible form, and

(b) the request is framed by reference to criteria other than the name of any registered charity (or charities) or the number under which it is registered (or the numbers under which they are registered).

(2) Subject to regulation 6 below, there shall be payable to the Commissioners in respect of the furnishing of an extract (or extracts) from the register of charities in response to a request of the kind described in paragraph (1) above a fee of £2 with an additional £40 for each criterion by reference to which the extracts are to be identified, and an additional—

(a) 15p for each extract which is a short extract;

(b) 20p for each extract which is a standard extract; or

(c) 25p for each extract which is a detailed extract.

[3109]

6 Where it appears to the Commissioners appropriate to do so, they may confer such exemption as they see fit from the liability to pay a fee prescribed by regulations 2 to 5 above.

[3110]

CHARITIES (CY-PRÈS ADVERTISEMENTS, INQUIRIES AND DISCLAIMER) REGULATIONS 1993

NOTES

These regulations were not made by Statutory Instrument but pursuant to the power conferred on the Charity Commission under the Charities Act 1960, s 14(1), (5A), and now contained in the Charities Act 1993, s 14(8) and (9).

1—(1) These regulations may be cited as the Charity (Cy-près Advertisements, Inquiries and Disclaimer) Regulations 1993 and shall come into force on the date on which they are made.

(2) In these Regulations—

"the Act" means the Charities Act 1960;

"advertisement" means an advertisement published in pursuance of section 14(1)(a)(i) of the Act;

"appeal" means an invitation to the public or a section of the public whether in writing, or by means of television or radio or otherwise;

"property" means property given for specific charitable purposes which have failed.

[3111]

NOTES

Charities Act 1960: largely repealed by the Charities Act 1993, s 98(2), Sch 7. The provisions of s 14 of the 1960 Act are now contained in s 14 of the 1993 Act.

2—(1) Advertisements shall be in the form specified in Schedule 1 to these Regulations or in a form equivalent to that form in any other language required or permitted by paragraph (2) of this Regulation.

(2) Advertisements shall be published—

- (a) in English in every case; and
- (b) where the appeal was published in another language, in that language; and may, in addition, be published in Welsh in any case where the appeal was not made in Welsh.

[3112]

3 Any advertisement published in pursuance of section 14(1)(a)(i) of the Act shall be published in the manner specified in Schedule 2 to these Regulations.

[3113]

4 Any inquiry made in pursuance of section 14(1)(a)(i) of the Act shall—

- (a) be made in writing;
- (b) be sent by post to the address of each donor recorded in the records of the trustees of the property; and
- (c) contain at least the information specified in Schedule 3 to these Regulations.

[3113A]

5 The period prescribed for the purposes of section 14(1)(a)(ii) of the Act shall be three months.

[3114]

6 Any disclaimer executed in pursuance of section 14(1)(b) of the Act shall either—

- (a) be executed in English in the form specified in Schedule 4 to these Regulations; or
- (b) be executed in Welsh in the form equivalent in that language to the form specified in Schedule 4 to these Regulations.

[3115]

SCHEDULES

SCHEDULE 1

Regulation 2

FORM OF ADVERTISEMENT PRESCRIBED FOR THE PURPOSES OF SECTION 14(1)(A)(I) OF THE CHARITIES ACT 1960

"**Advertisement**

Name of charity (if applicable):
Registered charity number (if applicable):
Purpose for which money or other property was given:
NOTICE is given that money and other property given for this purpose cannot be used for that purpose because [state reasons].
2. If you gave money or other property for that purpose you are entitled to claim it back. If you wish to do so you must tell [insert name] of [insert address] within 3 months of [specify date: see note below]. If you wish the money or other property to go to a similar charitable purpose and to disclaim your right to the return of the money or other property, you must ask the person named above for a form of disclaimer.
3. If you do not either make a claim within the 3 months or sign a disclaimer, the Charity Commissioners may make a Scheme applying the property to other charitable purposes. You will still be able to claim the return of your money or other property (less expenses), but **only if you do so within 6 months from the date of any Scheme made by the Commissioners**.

4. Date of this notice: [specify date: see note below]"

[Note: [This Note does not form part of the prescribed advertisement] If this advertisement is to be published in a newspaper or other periodical, the words "the date of this publication" should be inserted in paragraphs 2 and 4 above.

If this advertisement is to be published on a public notice board, the date inserted here should be the date on which the advertisement was fixed to the public notice board.]

[3116]

SCHEDULE 2

Regulation 3

MANNER OF PUBLISHING ADVERTISEMENTS IN PURSUANCE OF SECTION 14(1)(A)(I) OF THE ACT

1. Every advertisement shall be published in a newspaper or other periodical which is:
   (a) written in the same language as the advertisement; and
   (b) is sold or distributed throughout the area in which the appeal was made.

2. Where the purposes of the appeal were directed towards the benefit of an area contained wholly or mainly within a local authority district or a London Borough or the City of London, a copy of every advertisement published under paragraph 1 shall also be published by fixing copies of it to two public notice boards in the relevant area.

[3117]

SCHEDULE 3

Regulation 4

INFORMATION TO BE CONTAINED IN INQUIRIES TO BE MADE IN PURSUANCE OF SECTION 14(1)(A)(I) OF THE ACT

1. The name and address of the charity to which the property was given by the donor;

2. A description of the specific charitable purpose for which the property was given by the donor;

3. The reasons why that purpose has failed;

4. A description of the property (including the amount of any money) given for that purpose by the donor;

5. A statement of the donor's right to have the property returned;

6. A statement that the donor may disclaim the right to have the property described in paragraph 4 above returned by executing a disclaimer in the prescribed form;

7. A statement that, where the donor disclaims his right in respect of such property, the property may be applied for other charitable purposes similar to those for which it was given by a Scheme established by the Commissioners or by the court; and

8. A statement that, where the donor has not replied in writing to the inquiry within three months from the date of service of the inquiry, he will be treated for the purposes of section 14(1)(a) as a donor who cannot be identified or found, but that he will be able to claim the property, less expenses, within six months from the date of any Scheme made by the Commissioners or the court.

[3118]

SCHEDULE 4

Regulation 6

FORM OF DISCLAIMER PRESCRIBED FOR THE PURPOSES OF SECTION 14(1)(A)(II) OF THE CHARITIES ACT 1960

"Disclaimer

I HEREBY DISCLAIM my right to the return of *the sum of £....... / the property consisting of* (*insert description of property*)* given by me for (insert name of charity to which, or description of purposes for which, the money or property was given).

Signed ....
Name in capitals ....
Address ....
Date ....

Signed# ....
Name in capitals ....
Address ....
Date ....

* Delete as appropriate.
# This paragraph may be repeated if further signatures are required."

The Seal of the Charity Commissioners for England and Wales was affixed hereto by order of the Commissioners.

[3119]

LOTTERIES REGULATIONS 1993

(SI 1993/3223)

NOTES

Made: 18 December 1993.

Lotteries and Amusements Act 1976, s 12. The 1976 Act is repealed by the Gambling Act 2005, s 356(3)(i), (4), Sch 17, as from 1 September 2007; it is thought that these regulations will accordingly lapse on that date (unless previously revoked).

Commencement: 3 May 1994.

1—(1) These Regulations may be cited as the Lotteries Regulations 1993.

(2) These Regulations shall come into force on 3rd May 1994 except that they shall not have effect in relation to any lottery in respect of which any tickets or chances have been sold before that day.

(3) The Regulations specified in Schedule 1 to these Regulations are hereby revoked.

[3120]

NOTES

It is thought that these regulations will lapse on the repeal of their enabling power by the Gambling Act 2005, s 356(3)(i), (4), Sch 17, as from 1 September 2007.

2—(1) A scheme approved by a society or local authority for the promotion of a lottery or any modification of such a scheme shall comply with the provisions of Schedule 2 to these Regulations.

(2) This regulation does not prevent the inclusion in a scheme of provisions not required by that Schedule.

[3121]

NOTES

These regulations will lapse as noted to reg 1 at **[3120]**.

3 No ticket or chance in a society's lottery or local lottery shall be sold by or to a person who has not attained the age of sixteen years.

[3122]

NOTES

These regulations will lapse as noted to reg 1 at **[3120]**.

4—(1) Subject to paragraph (2) below, no ticket or chance in a society's lottery or local lottery shall be sold to a person in any street.

(2) Paragraph (1) above shall not have effect in relation to the sale of a ticket or chance by a person present in a kiosk or shop premises having no space for the accommodation of customers.

(3) In this regulation, "street" includes any bridge, road, lane, footway, subway, court, alley or passage, whether a thoroughfare or not, which is for the time being open to the public without payment.

[3123]

NOTES

These regulations will lapse as noted to reg 1 at **[3120]**.

5 No ticket or chance in a society's lottery or local lottery shall be sold by means of a machine.

[3124]–[3125]

NOTES

These regulations will lapse as noted to reg 1 at **[3120]**.

6 (Repealed by the Lotteries (Amendment) Regulations 1996, SI 1996/3106, except in relation to any lottery in respect of which any tickets or chances were sold before 6 June 1996.)

7 Every ticket distributed or sold in a society's lottery shall either specify the name of the registration authority with which the society is registered under Schedule 1 to the Lotteries and Amusements Act 1976 or, as the case may be, specify that the society is registered under Schedule 1A to that Act with the Gaming Board for Great Britain.

[3126]

NOTES

These regulations will lapse as noted to reg 1 at **[3120]**.

Gaming Board for Great Britain: the functions of the Gaming Board for Great Britain were transferred to the Gambling Commission under the Gambling Act 2005, s 21, Sch 5.

8 Every ticket distributed or sold in a local lottery shall specify the name of the local authority promoting the lottery, the date of the lottery and that the authority have registered a scheme with the Gaming Board for Great Britain under Schedule 2 to the Lotteries and Amusements Act 1976.

[3127]

NOTES

These regulations will lapse as noted to reg 1 at **[3120]**.

Gaming Board for Great Britain: the functions of the Gaming Board for Great Britain were transferred to the Gambling Commission under the Gambling Act 2005, s 21, Sch 5.

9 Where two or more lotteries are promoted by a society or local authority on the same date, the tickets to be sold in each such lottery shall indicate in which lottery they are sold by means of a serial number.

[3128]

NOTES

These regulations will lapse as noted to reg 1 at **[3120]**.

10 Where the information appearing on a ticket in a society's lottery or local lottery includes any reference in writing to a person who, for reward, is acting or assisting, or has acted or assisted, in the promotion of the lottery—

(*a*) *the size of the lettering used in such reference shall not exceed the size of the smallest lettering used in the same ticket to specify the name of the society on whose behalf the lottery is promoted or, as the case may be, the name of the local authority promoting the lottery, and*

(*b*) *that reference shall be afforded no greater prominence than is afforded to that name in the same ticket.*

[3129]

NOTES

These regulations will lapse as noted to reg 1 at **[3120]**.

11—(1) No request or requirement shall be made to any person supplying lottery tickets to which this regulation applies for use in a society's lottery or local lottery to the effect that those tickets shall be supplied in such a manner, or so marked, as to enable a ticket to be identified, before it is sold in the lottery, as a winning ticket.

(2) This regulation applies to lottery tickets manufactured or designed so as to conceal such information appearing in or on each ticket by way of words, figures, signs, symbols or other features as would, if revealed, indicate that the ticket is a winning ticket or is not.

(3) In this regulation, "winning ticket" means a ticket which, when sold in a lottery, entitles the holder of the ticket to claim a prize in the lottery.

[3130]

NOTES

These regulations will lapse as noted to reg 1 at **[3120]**.

12—(1) Subject to paragraph (2) below, no prize in a society's lottery or local lottery shall be offered on such terms that the winning of the prize depends upon the purchase of more than one ticket or chance in the lottery.

(2) The winning of a prize in a society's lottery or local lottery may depend upon the purchase of more than one chance provided that the price of the number of chances required to win a prize does not exceed the amount for the time being specified for the purposes of section 11(2) of the Lotteries and Amusements Act 1976.

[3131]

NOTES

These regulations will lapse as noted to reg 1 at **[3120]**.

13—(1) No person shall be invited to purchase any group of tickets or chances in a set of lotteries in which the determination of the winners in the lotteries is designed to secure that a person holding a group of winning tickets or chances is a winner of a prize in each lottery in the set of lotteries to which that group of tickets or chances relates.

(2) In paragraph (1) above, a reference to a set of lotteries is a reference to two or more lotteries in a set consisting of society's lotteries or local lotteries or both.

[3132]

NOTES

These regulations will lapse as noted to reg 1 at **[3120]**.

SCHEDULES

(Sch 1 contains revocations.)

SCHEDULE 2
LOTTERY SCHEMES

Regulation 2

1. The scheme shall specify the name and address of the society or local authority by which the scheme was approved.

2.—(1) Sub-paragraph (2) below applies where—
- *(a) a scheme is approved by a society; and*
- *(b) the society is registered under Schedule 1 to the Lotteries and Amusements Act 1976.*

(2) The scheme shall specify the following matters relating to the registration of the society for the purposes of section 5(3) of that Act (power of certain societies to promote lotteries), that is to say:—
- *(a) the name and address of the registration authority;*
- *(b) the date of registration; and*
- *(c) the reference number (if any) of the registration.*

3. Where a scheme is modified by a society or local authority, the scheme shall specify the date on which the modifications shall come into effect.

4. A scheme approved by a society or local authority shall specify the maximum number of lotteries which are intended to be promoted under it in any period of 12 months and the scheme shall require that the number so specified shall not be exceeded.

5.—(1) The scheme shall specify a proportion (not exceeding one half) as being the proportion of the whole proceeds of any lottery under the scheme which may be appropriated for the provision of prizes in that lottery; and shall require that the proportion so specified shall not be exceeded except in the special circumstances mentioned in sub-paragraph (2) below.

(2) The special circumstances referred to above are that—
- *(a) the proceeds of the lottery fall short of the sum reasonably estimated; and*
- *(b) the appropriation is made in order to fulfil an unconditional undertaking as to prizes given in connection with the sale of the relevant tickets or chances; and*
- *(c) the total amount appropriated in respect of prizes does not exceed the amount which could have been appropriated out of the proceeds of the lottery if the proceeds had amounted to the sum reasonably estimated.*

6. In the case of a scheme approved by a local authority, the scheme shall make provision as to whether all or any class of—
- *(a) members of the authority; and*
- *(b) officers of the authority,*

are to be precluded from buying tickets or chances in any lottery under the scheme, or not.
[3133]

NOTES

These regulations will lapse as noted to reg 1 at **[3120]**.

CHARITABLE INSTITUTIONS (FUND-RAISING) REGULATIONS 1994

(SI 1994/3024)

NOTES

Made: 28 November 1994.
Authority: Charities Act 1992, ss 64, 77(3).

PART II
STATUTORY INSTRUMENTS

Commencement: 1 March 1995.

ARRANGEMENT OF REGULATIONS

1 Citation, commencement and interpretation

(1) These Regulations may be cited as the Charitable Institutions (Fund-Raising) Regulations 1994 and shall come into force on 1st March 1995.

[(2) In these Regulations, "authorised deposit taker" means—

(a) the Bank of England;

(b) a person who has permission under Part 4 of the Financial Services and Markets Act 2000 to accept deposits; or

(c) an EEA firm of the kind mentioned in paragraph 5(b) of Schedule 3 to that Act, which has permission under paragraph 15 of that Schedule (as a result of qualifying for authorisation under paragraph 12(1) of that Schedule) to accept deposits.]

[(2A) Paragraph (2) must be read with—

(a) section 22 of the Financial Services and Markets Act 2000;

(b) any relevant order under that section; and

(c) Schedule 3 to that Act.]

(3) In these Regulations, any reference, in relation to an agreement made for the purposes of section 59 of the Charities Act 1992, to a charitable institution, commercial participator or professional fund-raiser, shall, unless the contrary intention appears, be construed as a reference to any charitable institution, commercial participator or professional fund-raiser, respectively, which is or who is a party to the agreement.

[3134]

NOTES

Para (2) substituted, and para (2A) inserted, by the Financial Services and Markets Act 2000 (Consequential Amendments and Repeals) Order 2001, SI 2001/3649, art 480.

2 Agreements between charitable institutions and professional fund-raisers

(1) The requirements as to form and content of an agreement made for the purposes of section 59(1) of the Charities Act 1992 are those set out in the following provisions of this regulation.

(2) Such an agreement (hereafter in this regulation referred to as "the agreement") shall be in writing and shall be signed by or on behalf of the charitable institution and the professional fund-raiser.

(3) The agreement shall specify—

(a) the name and address of each of the parties to the agreement;

(b) the date on which the agreement was signed by or on behalf of each of those parties;

(c) the period for which the agreement is to subsist;

(d) any terms relating to the termination of the agreement prior to the date on which that period expires; and

(e) any terms relating to the variation of the agreement during that period.

(4) The agreement shall also contain—

(a) a statement of its principal objectives and the methods to be used in pursuit of those objectives;

(b) if there is more than one charitable institution party to the agreement, provision as to the manner in which the proportion in which the institutions which are so party are respectively to benefit under the agreement is to be determined; and

(c) provision as to the amount by way of remuneration or expenses which the professional fund-raiser is to be entitled to receive in respect of things done by him in pursuance of the agreement and the manner in which that amount is to be determined.

[3135]

3 Agreements between charitable institutions and commercial participators

(1) The requirements as to form and content of an agreement made for the purposes of section 59(2) of the Charities Act 1992 are those set out in the following provisions of this regulation.

(2) Such an agreement (hereafter in this regulation referred to as "the agreement") shall be in writing and shall be signed by or on behalf of the charitable institution and the commercial participator.

(3) The agreement shall specify—

(a) the name and address of each of the parties to the agreement;

(b) the date on which the agreement was signed by or on behalf of each of those parties;

(c) the period for which the agreement is to subsist;

(d) any terms relating to the termination of the agreement prior to the date on which that period expires; and

(e) any terms relating to the variation of the agreement during that period.

(4) The agreement shall also contain—

(a) a statement of its principal objectives and the methods to be used in pursuit of those objectives;

(b) provision as to the manner in which are to be determined—

(i) if there is more than one charitable institution party to the agreement, the proportion in which the institutions which are so party are respectively to benefit under the agreement; and

(ii) the proportion of the consideration given for goods or services sold or supplied by the commercial participator, or of any other proceeds of a promotional venture undertaken by him, which is to be given to or applied for the benefit of the charitable institution, or

(iii) the sums by way of donations by the commercial participator in connection with the sale or supply of any goods or services sold or supplied by him which are to be so given or applied,

as the case may require; and

(c) provision as to any amount by way of remuneration or expenses which the commercial participator is to be entitled to receive in respect of things done by him in pursuance of the agreement and the manner in which any such amount is to be determined.

(5) The statement of methods referred to in paragraph (4)(a) above shall include, in relation to each method specified, a description of the type of charitable contributions which are to be given to or applied for the benefit of the charitable institution and of the circumstances in which they are to be so given or applied.

[3136]

4 Notice prior to injunction to prevent unauthorised fund-raising

A notice served under subsection (3) of section 62 of the Charities Act 1992 shall, in addition to satisfying the requirements of that subsection, specify the circumstances which gave rise to the serving of the notice and the grounds on which an application under that section is to be made.

[3137]

5 Availability of books, documents or other records

(1) A professional fund-raiser or commercial participator who is a party to an agreement made for the purposes of section 59 of the Charities Act 1992 shall, on request and at all reasonable times, make available to any charitable institution which is a party to that agreement any books, documents or other records (however kept) which relate to that institution and are kept for the purposes of the agreement.

(2) In the case of any record which is kept otherwise than in legible form, the reference in paragraph (1) above to making that record available shall be construed as a reference to making it available in legible form.

[3138]

6 Transmission of money and other property to charitable institutions

(1) Any money or other property acquired by a professional fund-raiser or commercial participator for the benefit of, or otherwise falling to be given to or applied by such a person for the benefit of, a charitable institution (including such money or other property as is referred to in section 64(3) of the Charities Act 1992) shall, notwithstanding any inconsistent term in an agreement made for the purposes of section 59 of that Act, be transmitted to that institution in accordance with the following provisions of this regulation.

(2) A professional fund-raiser or commercial participator holding any such money or property as is referred to in paragraph (1) above shall, unless he has a reasonable excuse—

(a) in the case of any money, and any negotiable instrument which is payable to or to the account of the charitable institution, as soon as is reasonably practicable after its receipt and in any event not later than the expiration of 28 days after that receipt or such other period as may be agreed with the institution—

(i) pay it to the person or persons having the general control and management of the administration of the institution; or

(ii) pay it into an account held by [an authorised deposit taker] in the name of or on behalf of the institution which is under the control of the person, or any of the persons, specified in sub-paragraph (i) above; and

(b) in the case of any other property, deal with it in accordance with any instructions given for that purpose, either generally or in a particular case, by the charitable institution:

Provided that—

(i) any property in the possession of the professional fund-raiser or commercial participator either pending the obtaining of such instructions as are referred to above or in accordance with such instructions shall be securely held by him;

(ii) the proceeds of the sale or other disposal of any property shall, from the time of their receipt by the professional fund-raiser or commercial participator, be subject to the requirements of sub-paragraph (a) above.

[3139]

NOTES

Para (2)(a)(ii): words in square brackets substituted by the Financial Services and Markets Act 2000 (Consequential Amendments and Repeals) Order 2001, SI 2001/3649, art 480(1), (4).

7 Fund-raising for charitable etc purposes otherwise than by professional fund-raisers or commercial participators

(1) This regulation applies to any person who carries on for gain a business other than a fund-raising business but, in the course of that business, engages in any promotional venture in the course of which it is represented that charitable contributions are to be applied for charitable, benevolent or philanthropic purposes of any description (rather than for the benefit of one or more particular charitable institutions).

(2) Where any person to whom this regulation applies makes a representation to the effect that charitable contributions are to be applied for such charitable, benevolent or philanthropic purposes as are mentioned in paragraph (1) above he shall, unless he has a reasonable excuse, ensure that the representation is accompanied by a statement clearly indicating—

(a) the fact that the charitable contributions referred to in the representation are to be applied for those purposes and not for the benefit of any particular charitable institution or institutions;

(b) (in general terms) the method by which it is to be determined—

(i) what proportion of the consideration given for goods or services sold or supplied by him, or of any other proceeds of a promotional venture undertaken by him, is to be applied for those purposes, or

(ii) what sums by way of donations by him in connection with the sale or supply of any such goods or services are to be so applied,

as the case may require; and

(c) the method by which it is to be determined how the charitable contributions referred to in the representation are to be distributed between different charitable institutions.

[3140]

8 Offences and penalties

(1) Failure to comply with any of the provisions of these Regulations specified in paragraph (2) below shall be an offence punishable on summary conviction by a fine not exceeding the second level on the standard scale.

(2) The provisions referred to in paragraph (1) above are—

(a) regulation 5(1);
(b) regulation 6(2); and
(c) regulation 7(2).

[3141]

LOCAL GOVERNMENT CHANGES FOR ENGLAND (PROPERTY TRANSFER AND TRANSITIONAL PAYMENTS) REGULATIONS 1995

(SI 1995/402)

NOTES

Made: 20 February 1995.
Authority: Local Government Act 1992, ss 19, 26.
Commencement: 14 March 1995.

ARRANGEMENT OF REGULATIONS

PART I
GENERAL

1 Citation and commencement

These Regulations may be cited as the Local Government Changes for England (Property Transfer and Transitional Payments) Regulations 1995 and shall come into force on 14th March 1995.

[3142]

2 Interpretation

(1) In these Regulations—

"the Act" means the Local Government Act 1992;

["the 1947 Act" means the Fire Services Act 1947;]

"the 1989 Act" means the Local Government and Housing Act 1989;

"the 1992 Act" means the Local Government Finance Act 1992;

"abolished authority" means a principal council which is or is to be wound up and dissolved by a section 17 order;

"council tax base", in relation to any authority, means the amount calculated by the authority as its council tax base for a financial year in accordance with the relevant rules;

["HRA dwelling" means a dwelling comprised in HRA property;

"HRA property" means property in respect of which a local housing authority is required under section 74 of the 1989 Act to keep an account, called the "Housing Revenue Account", of sums falling to be credited or debited in respect of that property;]

"investment" does not include any land held as an investment;

"relevant instrument" means a statutory instrument made under the Act or, in connection with the Act or such an instrument, under any other Act;

"relevant rules", in relation to the council tax base for a financial year, means the rules for the time being effective as regards the financial year under regulations made by the Secretary of State under section 33(5) or, as the case may require, section 44(5) of the 1992 Act;

"the reorganisation date", in relation to an authority, means the date (being 1st April in any year) which is specified as such in a section 17 order;

"the Residuary Body" means the Local Government Residuary Body (England);

"section 17 order" means an order under section 17 of the Act; and

"successor authority", in relation to an abolished authority, means—

(a) where a section 17 order gives effect to a structural change, [a principal council] to which any functions of the abolished authority are or are to be transferred on the reorganisation date; and

(b) where such an order gives effect to a boundary change, [a principal council] whose area, on and after that date, includes, or is to include, an area which, before that date, is the whole or any part of the area of the abolished authority.

(2) In these Regulations—

(a) any reference to a transferred area is a reference to an area in relation to which, immediately before the reorganisation date, a principal council (other than an abolished authority) ("the relinquishing authority") exercises functions which, by virtue of a structural or boundary change effected by a section 17 order, it ceases to exercise on that date; and

(b) any reference to the acquiring authority in relation to such an area is a reference to [the principal council] which, by virtue of such a change, exercises or is to exercise those functions in relation to the area on and after that date.

(3) Any reference in these Regulations to any rights or liabilities of an authority includes a reference to rights or liabilities acquired or incurred by any predecessor in title of the authority.

[3143]

NOTES

Para (1): definition "1947 Act" inserted, and in definition "successor authority" words in square brackets substituted, by the Local Government Changes for England (Property Transfer and Transitional Payments) (Amendment) Regulations 1995, SI 1995/2796, reg 2(2)(a); definitions "HRA dwelling" and "HRA property" inserted by the Local Government Changes for England (Property Transfer and Transitional Payments) (Amendment) Regulations 1996, SI 1996/312, reg 2(2).

Para (2): words in square brackets in sub-para (b) substituted by SI 1995/2796, reg 2(2)(b).

PART II
TRANSFER OF PROPERTY RIGHTS AND LIABILITIES

3 Application and interpretation of Part

(1) This Part does not apply with respect to the transfer of—

(a) any property, rights or liabilities for the transfer of which provision is made in the Local Government Changes for England (Finance) Regulations 1994;

[(aa) any property which is held by a fire authority solely in connection with the provision of fire services and any rights or liabilities held or incurred by such an authority in respect of—

(i) any contract of employment with a person who is a member of, or employed wholly or mainly for the purposes of, the fire brigade maintained by such an authority in pursuance of the 1947 Act;

(ii) the [Firefighters' Pension Scheme] as set out in Schedule 2 to the Firemen's Pension Scheme Order 1992; or

(iii) any contract for the provision of services or the delivery of goods solely in connection with the provision of fire services;]

(b) any superannuation fund maintained by a principal council by virtue of regulations made under section 7 of the Superannuation Act 1972; or

(c) any rights or liabilities of such a council in respect of such a fund.

(2) In this Part—

"associated property", in relation to any land of an abolished authority or, as the case may be, the relinquishing authority in relation to a transferred area, means—

(a) property in or on the land which is used or intended to be used by the authority exclusively for the discharge of functions on the land;

(b) property which is so used or intended to be so used and which is kept elsewhere when not in use;

(c) investments or cash which relate exclusively to the land; or

(d) records which relate exclusively to the land;

"charitable purposes" has the same meaning as in the Charities Act 1993;

["combination scheme" means a combination scheme made under the 1947 Act;

"combined fire authority" means an authority which for the time being is constituted a fire authority by a combination scheme;]

"contract" includes any enforceable undertaking;

["fire authority" has the same meaning as in the 1947 Act;]

"the preliminary period", in relation to an authority, means the period specified as such in a section 17 order;

"record" includes material in whatever form or medium which conveys or is capable of conveying information; and

"relevant shares" means shares held in a company which is under the control of a local authority within the meaning of section 68 of the 1989 Act (but with the omission of the words "unless the Secretary of State otherwise directs" in subsection (1) of that section); and "share" has the same meaning as in the Companies Act 1985.

[3144]

NOTES

Para (1): sub-para (aa) inserted by Local Government Changes for England (Property Transfer and Transitional Payments) (Amendment) Regulations 1995, SI 1995/2796, reg 2(3)(a); words in square brackets substituted by virtue of the Firefighters' Pension Scheme (England and Scotland) Order 2004, SI 2004/2306, art 4.

Para (2): definitions "combination scheme", "combined fire authority" and "fire authority" inserted by SI 1995/2796, reg 2(3)(b).

4 Information for facilitating implementation

(1) This regulation has effect for the purpose of facilitating the implementation of these Regulations.

(2) An abolished authority shall, within the relevant period, supply to any successor authority—

(a) details of any relevant contract; and

(b) all such information relating to the abolished authority's property, rights or liabilities as the successor authority may reasonably request.

(3) The relinquishing authority in relation to a transferred area shall, within the relevant period, supply to the acquiring authority in relation to that area—

(a) details of any relevant contract in relation to which such rights or liabilities as are mentioned in paragraph (5)(a) of regulation 5 arise; and

(b) all such information relating to any rights or liabilities so mentioned, or to property to which paragraph (6) of that regulation applies, as the acquiring authority may reasonably request.

(4) Any person authorized in that behalf by a successor authority in relation to an abolished authority or, as the case may be, the acquiring authority in relation to a transferred area shall be entitled, at all reasonable times, on producing, if so required, evidence of his authority—

(a) to inspect any record belonging to or under the control of the abolished authority or, as the case may be, the relinquishing authority which relates to any relevant contract, or any property, rights or liabilities, mentioned in paragraph (2) or (3) above; and

(b) to take, or be supplied with, a copy of any such record or part of it.

(5) The rights conferred by paragraph (4) above include the right to require any record which is not in legible form to be made available in legible form for the purposes of inspection or copying or being supplied with copies.

(6) In this regulation—

"the final period" means the period of six weeks ending on the date immediately before the reorganisation date;

"relevant contract" means a contract entered into by an abolished authority or the relinquishing authority the period of which extends or may, under the terms of the contract, be extended beyond that date; and

"relevant period" means—

(a) for the purposes of paragraph (2)(a) and (3)(a) above—

(i) in a case where the relevant contract was entered into before the date on which the preliminary period begins, the period of 3 months beginning with that date;

(ii) in a case where the relevant contract is entered into on or after that date and before the beginning of the final period, the period of six weeks beginning with the date on which the contract is entered into; and

(iii) in a case where the relevant contract is entered into after the beginning of the final period, that period; and

(b) for the purposes of paragraph (2)(b) or (3)(b) above—

(i) in a case where the request for information is made before the beginning of the final period, the period of six weeks beginning with the date of the making of the request; and

(ii) in a case where the request is made after the beginning of the final period, that period; and

a reference to a successor authority [in paragraph (2)(b) and (4) above,] includes, where there are two or more successor authorities in relation to an abolished authority, a reference to the Residuary Body.

[(7) Paragraphs (2)(b), (3)(b) and (4) above shall have effect in relation to a combined fire authority constituted before the reorganisation date, with respect to an area which is, at the date the authority is constituted, the whole or part of the area of a fire authority which is an abolished authority or the relinquishing authority in relation to a transferred area as if—

(a) the references to a successor authority or, as the case may be, the acquiring authority in relation to that area included a reference to the combined fire authority;

(b) the references to property were references to property held or used by the abolished authority or the relinquishing authority concerned partly for the purposes of the provision of fire services and partly for other purposes; and

(c) the references to rights or liabilities were omitted.]

[3145]

NOTES

Para (6): words in square brackets inserted by the Local Government Changes for England (Miscellaneous Provision) Regulations 1995, SI 1995/1748, reg 3.

Para (7): inserted by Local Government Changes for England (Property Transfer and Transitional Payments) (Amendment) Regulations 1995, SI 1995/2796, reg 2(4).

5 Agreements for the transfer of property etc

(1) Nothing in this regulation [or regulation 5A] applies to—

(a) any [property of an authority consisting of cash or investments] which are not associated property or relevant shares;

(b) any property held by an authority, as sole trustee, exclusively for charitable purposes;

(c) any rights or liabilities of an authority in respect of … such property; or

(d) any rights or liabilities of an authority in respect of money borrowed by the authority.

[(1A) Where a section 17 order includes provision modifying the 1947 Act for the purposes of the making, before the reorganisation date, of a combination scheme with respect to an area which is, at the date the order is made, the whole or part of the area of a fire authority which is an abolished authority or the relinquishing authority in relation to a transferred area, nothing in this regulation shall apply to any property held or used by such an authority partly for the purposes of the provision of fire services and partly for other purposes.]

(2) Where there are two or more successor authorities in relation to an abolished authority, the successor authorities shall, during the preliminary period, use their best endeavours to make agreements which, subject to [paragraphs (2A) and (3)] below—

(a) identify all the property, rights or liabilities of the abolished authority;

(b) in relation to any property so identified, specify one of the successor authorities for the purposes of regulation 6(4);

(c) in relation to any rights or liabilities so identified, specify one, or two or more, of the successor authorities for those purposes; and

(d) in the case of any property mentioned in sub-paragraph (b) above which is land—

(i) identify such, if any, of it as will not be required by any of them for the purposes of, or in connection with, the exercise of functions on and after the reorganisation date; and

(ii) provide for the distribution among all the successor authorities of receipts from its disposal in accordance with regulation 10.

[(2A) An agreement pursuant to paragraph (2) above shall not identify any HRA dwellings pursuant to paragraph (2)(d)(i).]

(3) An agreement pursuant to paragraph (2) above shall not specify different successor authorities in relation to—

(a) any property identified in the agreement which forms part of a relevant collection; or

(b) any rights or liabilities exclusively in respect of any such property;

and, for these purposes, "relevant collection" means—

(i) any collection of archives or other records of general or local interest held as such by an abolished authority; or

(ii) any collection of a museum or gallery provided or maintained by such an authority.

(4) Where the successor authorities in relation to an abolished authority are unable to make an agreement under paragraph (2) above in respect of any relevant shares held by that authority, any of the successor authorities may, before the reorganisation date, serve on the other successor authorities a notice stating that a difference has arisen in respect of such of those shares as are specified in the notice.

PART II STATUTORY INSTRUMENTS

(5) The relinquishing authority and the acquiring authority in relation to a transferred area shall, during the preliminary period, use their best endeavours to make agreements which—

(a) identify property of the relinquishing authority to which paragraph (6) below applies and any rights or liabilities acquired or incurred by that authority in respect of any such property or the exercise of any functions in or in relation to the transferred area;

(b) in relation to any property so identified (other than property ("surplus land") mentioned in sub-paragraph (b)(ii) of that paragraph), specify the acquiring authority for the purposes of paragraph (1) of regulation 8; and

(c) in relation to any rights or liabilities so identified (other than rights or liabilities in respect of surplus land), specify that authority for those purposes or that authority and the relinquishing authority for the purposes of paragraph (3) of that regulation.

(6) This paragraph applies to property—

(a) which is situated in the transferred area or is held for the purposes of, or in connection with, the exercise of functions in or in relation to that area; and

(b) which either—

(i) is required by the acquiring authority for the purposes of, or in connection with, the exercise of functions in or in relation to that area on and after the reorganisation date; or

(ii) in the case of property [other than a HRA dwelling] which is land, is neither so required nor required by the relinquishing authority for the purposes of, or in connection with, the exercise of functions, on and after that date, in or in relation to its area.

(7) Where the relinquishing authority and the acquiring authority in relation to a transferred area are unable to make an agreement under paragraph (5) above in respect of any property, rights or liabilities mentioned in sub-paragraph (a) of that paragraph [(other than HRA dwellings)], either of those authorities may, before the reorganisation date, serve on the other a notice specifying that property, or those rights or liabilities, for the purposes of paragraph (4) of regulation 8.

(8) Except where the context otherwise requires, any reference in any of the following provisions of these Regulations to an agreement is a reference to an agreement made under the preceding paragraphs of this regulation; and any such agreement shall be in writing and be sealed, before the end of the preliminary period, by—

(a) in the case of an agreement under paragraph (2) above, all the successor authorities; and

(b) in the case of an agreement under paragraph (5) above, the relinquishing authority and the acquiring authority.

[3146]

NOTES

Para (1): words in first pair of square brackets inserted, words in second pair of square brackets substituted, and words omitted revoked, by the Local Government Changes for England (Property Transfer and Transitional Payments) (Amendment) Regulations 1995, SI 1995/2796, reg 2(5)(a).

Para (1A): inserted by SI 1995/2796, reg 2(5)(b).

Para (2): words in square brackets substituted by the Local Government Changes for England (Property Transfer and Transitional Payments) (Amendment) Regulations 1996, SI 1996/312, reg 2(3)(a).

Para (2A): inserted by SI 1996/312, reg 2(3)(b).

Paras (6), (7): words in square brackets inserted by SI 1996/312, reg 2(3)(c), (d).

[5A Agreements for the transfer of property etc of fire authorities

(1) Where a section 17 order includes such provision as is mentioned in regulation 5(1A) and a combined fire authority is constituted, before the reorganisation date, with respect to an area which is, at the date the order is made, the whole or part of the area of a fire authority which is an abolished authority or the relinquishing authority in relation to a transferred area, the relevant authorities in relation to such a fire authority shall, during the relevant period, use their best endeavours to make agreements which identify—

(a) any property of the fire authority concerned to which paragraph (2) below applies; and

(b) in the case of any such property which is land, such, if any, of it as will not be required by any of them for the purposes of, or in connection with, the exercise of functions on and after the reorganisation date ("surplus land").

(2) This paragraph applies to any property held or used partly for the purposes of the provision of fire services and partly for other purposes.

(3) Where an agreement under paragraph (1) above identifies any property of a fire authority which is an abolished authority—

(a) in the case of surplus land, the relevant authorities in relation to that authority shall, during the relevant period, use their best endeavours to make agreements which—

(i) specify one of the successor authorities for the purposes of regulation 5B(1); and

(ii) provide for the distribution among all of the successor authorities of receipts from its disposal in accordance with regulation 10; and

(b) in any other case, the relevant authorities shall, during the relevant period, use their best endeavours to make agreements which specify one of the relevant authorities for the purposes of regulation 5B(1).

(4) Where an agreement under paragraph (1) above identifies any property (other than surplus land) of a fire authority which is the relinquishing authority in relation to a transferred area, the relevant authorities shall, during the relevant period, use their best endeavours to make agreements which—

(a) specify one of the relevant authorities (other than the relinquishing authority) for the purposes of regulation 5B(1); or

(b) provide for its retention by the relinquishing authority.

(5) Where the relevant authorities in relation to a fire authority which is the relinquishing authority in relation to a transferred area are unable to make an agreement under paragraph (4) above in respect of any property to which paragraph (2) above applies, any of those authorities may, before the reorganisation date, serve on the other such authorities a notice specifying that property for the purposes of paragraph (5) of regulation 5B.

(6) Any agreement under this regulation shall be in writing and be sealed, before the end of the relevant period, by all the relevant authorities concerned.

(7) In this regulation and regulation 5B—

"the relevant authorities", in relation to a fire authority, means—

(a) where that authority is an abolished authority, any successor authority in relation to that authority and the combined fire authority concerned; or

(b) where the fire authority is the relinquishing authority in relation to a transferred area, that authority, any authority which is the acquiring authority in relation to a transferred area which is part of the area with respect to which the combination scheme in question is made and the combined fire authority concerned; and

"the relevant period" means the period beginning with the date on which the combined fire authority concerned is constituted and ending with the date immediately before the reorganisation date.]

[3147]

NOTES

Inserted by the Local Government Changes for England (Property Transfer and Transitional Payments) (Amendment) Regulations 1995, SI 1995/2796, reg 2(6).

[5B Vesting of property of fire authorities

(1) Where an agreement under paragraph (3) or (4) of regulation 5A provides for the transfer of any property of a fire authority to a relevant authority, the property shall, on the reorganisation date, vest in that authority.

(2) Paragraph (1) above shall not apply to vest any surplus land, or any associated property in relation to that land, where an agreement under paragraph (3) of regulation 5A does not include the provision mentioned in sub-paragraph (a)(ii) of that paragraph.

(3) Where any land of a fire authority which is an abolished authority vests in a relevant authority by virtue of paragraph (1) above and any associated property in relation to the land does not vest in that authority or another relevant authority by virtue of that paragraph, the associated property shall, on the reorganisation date, vest in the relevant authority in which the land is vested.

(4) Any of the relevant authorities in relation to a fire authority which is the relinquishing authority in relation to a transferred area may, during the period of six months beginning with the reorganisation date, serve on the other such authorities a notice specifying, for the purposes of paragraph (5) below, any property to which regulation 5A(2) applies which was not identified before that date.

(5) During the period of six months beginning with the reorganisation date, the relevant authorities in relation to a fire authority which is the relinquishing authority in relation to a transferred area shall make agreements under this paragraph providing for the transfer to a relevant authority (other than the relinquishing authority), or the retention by that authority, of any property which has been specified for the purposes of this paragraph in a notice under regulation 5A(5) or paragraph (4) above.

(6) Where an agreement under paragraph (5) above provides for the transfer to a relevant authority of any property mentioned in that paragraph, the property shall, on such date as shall be specified in the agreement for the purposes of this paragraph, vest in that relevant authority.]

[3148]

NOTES

Inserted by the Local Government Changes for England (Property Transfer and Transitional Payments) (Amendment) Regulations 1995, SI 1995/2796, reg 2(6).

6 Vesting of property etc of abolished authorities

(1) Nothing in this regulation shall apply to any property held, as sole trustee, exclusively for charitable purposes by an abolished authority or to any rights or liabilities in respect of such property.

(2) All the property, rights and liabilities of an abolished authority in relation to which there is only one successor authority shall, on the reorganisation date, vest in that successor authority.

(3) The following paragraphs of this regulation, and regulation 7, shall have effect where there are two or more successor authorities in relation to an abolished authority.

(4) Subject to paragraph (5) below—

(a) any property of the abolished authority which is identified in an agreement and in relation to which a successor authority is specified for the purposes of this paragraph shall, on the reorganisation date, vest in that authority; and

(b) any rights or liabilities of an abolished authority which are so identified and in relation to which a successor authority, or two or more successor authorities, are specified for the purposes of this paragraph shall, on that date, vest in that authority or, as the case may be, in those authorities jointly and severally.

(5) Paragraph (4) above shall not apply to vest—

(a) any land identified in an agreement as mentioned in sub-paragraph (d)(i) of paragraph (2) of regulation 5, or any associated property in relation to that land, where the agreement does not include the provision mentioned in sub-paragraph (d)(ii) of that paragraph; or

(b) any rights and liabilities exclusively in respect of such property [or in respect of any such property as is mentioned in regulation 5B(2)], including, in the case of property which is land, rights and liabilities in respect of a contract for the provision of services on, or the delivery of goods to, the land.

[(5A)

(a) This paragraph applies to HRA dwellings of an abolished authority and to other HRA property specified in sub-paragraph (c) all of which HRA dwellings and HRA property are not vested by virtue of paragraph (4) above.

(b) Any HRA dwelling shall, on the reorganisation date, vest in the successor authority for the area in which it is situated.

(c) Any HRA property which is exclusively enjoyed or used in connection with any dwelling vested by virtue of sub-paragraph (b) above shall, on the reorganisation date, vest in the authority in which the dwelling vests on that date.]

(6) Where any land of the abolished authority vests in a successor authority by virtue of [paragraph (4) or (5A)] above and any associated property in relation to the land does not vest

in that authority or another successor authority by virtue of [either paragraph], the associated property shall, on the reorganisation date, vest in the successor authority in which the land is vested.

(7) This paragraph applies to—

(a) any relevant shares of the abolished authority which have been specified in a notice under regulation 5(4);

(b) any property of the abolished authority consisting of cash or investments which is not vested by virtue of paragraph (4) or (6) above;

(c) any rights or liabilities in respect of such shares or such property; and

(d) any rights or liabilities in respect of money borrowed by the abolished authority.

(8) Any property, rights and liabilities to which paragraph (7) above applies shall, on the reorganisation date, vest in the successor authority specified in a section 17 order as the designated authority in relation to this paragraph.

(9) This paragraph applies to—

(a) any property of the abolished authority which is not vested by virtue of [one of the foregoing provisions of this Part]; and

(b) any rights or liabilities exclusively in respect of such property [(other than rights or liabilities in respect of a claim by any person for personal injury or damage to property)], including, in the case of property which is land, rights or liabilities in respect of a contract for the provision of services on, or the delivery of goods to, the land.

(10) Any property, rights or liabilities to which paragraph (9) above applies shall, on the reorganisation date, vest in the Residuary Body.

[3149]

NOTES

Para (5): words in square brackets in sub-para (b) inserted by the Local Government Changes for England (Property Transfer and Transitional Payments) (Amendment) Regulations 1995, SI 1995/2796, reg 2(7)(a).

Para (5A): inserted by the Local Government Changes for England (Property Transfer and Transitional Payments) (Amendment) Regulations 1996, SI 1996/312, reg 2(4)(a).

Para (6): words in square brackets substituted by SI 1996/312, reg 2(4)(b).

Para (9): words in square brackets in sub-para (a) substituted by SI 1995/2796, reg 2(7)(b); words in square brackets in sub-para (b) inserted by SI 1996/312, reg 2(4)(c).

7 Vesting of residual rights and liabilities of abolished authorities

(1) This paragraph applies to any rights or liabilities arising in relation to any contract for the provision of services, or the delivery of goods, by or to the abolished authority which are not vested by virtue of paragraph (4) or (10) of regulation 6.

(2) Any rights or liabilities to which paragraph (1) above applies shall, on the reorganisation date, vest—

(a) where the contract relates exclusively to land which is vested in a successor authority by virtue of [one of the foregoing provisions of this Part], in that authority;

(b) where the contract relates to land which is [so vested] in a successor authority and to land which is so vested in another successor authority, in those authorities jointly and severally;

(c) where the contract relates to land which is [so vested] and to land which is vested in the Residuary Body by virtue of paragraph (10) of that regulation, in that authority and the Residuary Body jointly and severally;

(d) where the contract relates exclusively to the area of one successor authority, in that authority; and

(e) where the contract relates to the area of two or more successor authorities, in those authorities jointly and severally.

(3) This paragraph applies to any rights or liabilities arising in relation to any transaction whereby an abolished authority undertook (whether voluntarily or by virtue of a statutory provision) any liability for—

(a) the management, maintenance, repair or improvement of any property situated within its area which is vested in any other person ("the relevant property"); or

(b) a guarantee, indemnity or financial assistance by way of grant or otherwise in respect of any such property.

(4) Any rights or liabilities to which paragraph (3) above applies shall, on the reorganisation date, vest in the successor authority in whose area the relevant property is situated or, where it is situated in the area of more than one successor authority, in those authorities jointly and severally.

[(4A) Where any property of the abolished authority vests in a successor authority by virtue of any of the foregoing provisions of this Part and any rights or liabilities exclusively in respect of such property are not vested by virtue of any such provision, the rights or liabilities shall, on the reorganisation date, vest in the successor authority in which the property is vested.

(4B) Any rights or liabilities of the abolished authority—

(a) which arise in relation to anything which, by virtue of regulation 4 of the Local Government Changes for England Regulations 1994, has effect as if done, by or in relation to a successor authority or two or more successor authorities; and

(b) which are not vested by any of the foregoing provisions of this Part,

shall, on the reorganisation date, vest in that successor authority or, as the case may be, those successor authorities jointly and severally.]

(5) Any rights or liabilities of the abolished authority which are not vested by virtue of [one of the foregoing provisions of this Part] shall, on the reorganisation date, vest in all the successor authorities jointly and severally.

[3150]

NOTES

Paras (2), (5): words in square brackets substituted by Local Government Changes for England (Property Transfer and Transitional Payments) (Amendment) Regulations 1995, SI 1995/2796, reg 2(8)(a), (c).

Paras (4A), (4B): inserted by SI 1995/2796, reg 2(8)(b).

8 Vesting of property etc of relinquishing authorities

(1) The following property shall, on the reorganisation date, vest in the acquiring authority in relation to a transferred area—

(a) any property of the relinquishing authority in relation to that area which is identified in an agreement and in relation to which the acquiring authority is specified for the purposes of this paragraph; and

(b) any associated property in relation to such property (other than associated property specified in a notice under regulation 5(7)).

(2) Any rights or liabilities of the relinquishing authority in relation to a transferred area in respect of any associated property which, by virtue of paragraph (1) above, vests in the acquiring authority in relation to that area shall, on the reorganisation date, vest in that authority.

(3) Any rights or liabilities of the relinquishing authority in relation to a transferred area which are identified in an agreement and in relation to which the acquiring authority or, as the case may be, that authority and the relinquishing authority, are specified for the purposes of this paragraph shall, on the reorganisation date, vest in the acquiring authority or, as the case may be, in that authority and the relinquishing authority jointly and severally.

[(3A) [Subject to paragraph (6) below] the relinquishing authority in relation to a transferred area or the acquiring authority in relation to that area may, during the period of six months beginning with the reorganisation date, serve on the other a notice specifying, for the purposes of paragraph (4) below, any property, rights or liabilities mentioned in regulation 5(5)(a) which were not identified before that date.]

(4) During the period of six months beginning with the reorganisation date, the relinquishing authority and the acquiring authority in relation to a transferred area shall make agreements under this paragraph providing for—

(a) the transfer to the acquiring authority, or the retention by the relinquishing authority, of any property specified for the purposes of this paragraph in a notice under regulation 5(7) [or paragraph (3A) above]; and

(b) either—

(i) the transfer to the acquiring authority, or to that authority and the relinquishing authority jointly and severally, of any rights or liabilities so specified; or

(ii) the retention by the relinquishing authority of any such rights or liabilities.

(5) Where an agreement under paragraph (4) above provides for the transfer of any property, rights or liabilities as mentioned in that paragraph, on such date as shall be specified in the agreement for the purposes of this paragraph—

(a) the property shall vest in the acquiring authority; and

(b) the rights and liabilities shall, according as the agreement provides, vest in that authority or that authority and the relinquishing authority jointly and severally.

[(6)

(a) This paragraph applies where the relinquishing authority and the acquiring authority in relation to a transferred area are unable to make an agreement under regulation 5(5) in respect of—

(i) any HRA dwelling situated in the transferred area,

(ii) any HRA property exclusively enjoyed or used in connection with such an HRA dwelling, or

(iii) any rights or liabilities exclusively in respect of any such dwelling or other property including in the case of property which is land, rights or liabilities in respect of a contract for the provision of services on, or delivery of goods to, the land.

(b) Sub-paragraph (a)(iii) above shall not apply to any liability of a former tenant or licensee of the relinquishing authority to pay rent or other sums in respect of any HRA dwelling or other HRA property.

(c) Any dwelling, other property and rights or liabilities specified in sub-paragraph (a) and not excluded by sub-paragraph (b) shall, on the reorganisation date, vest in the acquiring authority and shall not be specified for the purposes of paragraph (4) in a notice under paragraph (3A) above.]

[3151]

NOTES

Para (3A): inserted by the Local Government Changes for England (Property Transfer and Transitional Payments) (Amendment) Regulations 1995, SI 1995/2796, reg 2(9)(a); words in square brackets inserted by the Local Government Changes for England (Property Transfer and Transitional Payments) (Amendment) Regulations 1996, SI 1996/312, reg 2(5)(a).

Para (4): words in square brackets inserted by SI 1995/2796, reg 2(9)(b).

Para (6): added by SI 1996/312, reg 2(5)(b).

9 Charities

(1) This paragraph applies to any property which, immediately before the reorganisation date, is held, as sole trustee, exclusively for charitable purposes by an abolished authority.

(2) Where any property to which paragraph (1) above applies is held for the benefit of, or of the inhabitants of, or of any particular class or body of persons in, a specified area, the property shall, on the reorganisation date, vest (on the same trusts) in the successor authority the area of which, on and after that date, comprises the whole or the greater part of that specified area.

(3) Where any property to which paragraph (1) above applies is not held for such a benefit as is mentioned in paragraph (2) above, the property shall, on the reorganisation date, vest (on the same trusts) in the successor authority the area of which, on and after that date, comprises an area which, immediately before that date, is the whole or the greater part of the area of the abolished authority.

(4) Any property to which paragraph (1) above applies which is not vested in a successor authority by virtue of paragraph (2) or (3) above shall, on the reorganisation date, vest (on the same trusts) in such one of the successor authorities as may be agreed between them not later than three months before the reorganisation date or, in default of such agreement, in such successor authority as the Charity Commissioners shall determine.

(5) Where, immediately before the reorganisation date, any property is held, as sole trustee, exclusively for charitable purposes by the relinquishing authority in relation to a transferred area and is so held for the benefit of, or of the inhabitants of, or of any particular class or body of persons in, a specified area the whole or the greater part of which is comprised in the transferred area, the property shall, on that date, vest (on the same trusts) in the acquiring authority in relation to that area.

(6) Any rights and liabilities—

(a) of an abolished authority in respect of any property to which paragraph (1) above applies; or

(b) of the relinquishing authority in relation to a transferred area in respect of any property which is held as mentioned in paragraph (5) above,

shall, on the reorganisation date, vest in the authority in which the property is vested.

(7) Where, immediately before the reorganisation date, any power with respect to a relevant charity is under the trusts of the charity or by virtue of any enactment vested in, or in the holder of an office connected with, an abolished authority or, as the case may be, the relinquishing authority in relation to a transferred area, that power shall, on that date, vest in, or in the holder of the corresponding office connected with, or (if there is no such office) the proper officer of, the authority in which the property of the charity would have been vested under paragraphs (2) to (5) above if that property had been property to which paragraph (1) above applied or, as the case may be, held as mentioned in paragraph (5) above.

(8) References in paragraph (7) above to a power with respect to a relevant charity do not include references to a power of any person by virtue of being a charity trustee of the charity; but where, under the trusts of such a charity, the charity trustees immediately before the reorganisation date include an abolished authority or the relinquishing authority in relation to a transferred area, or the holder of an office connected with such an authority, those trustees shall instead include the authority in which the property of the charity would have been vested as mentioned in paragraph (7) above or, as the case may be, the holder of the corresponding office connected with, or (if there is no such office) the proper officer of, that authority.

(9) Nothing in this regulation shall affect any power of Her Majesty, the court or any other person to alter the trusts of any charity.

(10) In this regulation—

"charity", "charity trustees", "company", "the court" and "trusts" have the same meanings as in the Charities Act 1993;

"proper officer" has the same meaning as in the Local Government Act 1972; and

"relevant charity" means a charity other than a charity which is incorporated by charter or a company.

[3152]

10 Disposal of surplus land

(1) An authority in whom any surplus land is vested on the reorganisation date ("the custodian authority")—

(a) shall use its best endeavours to secure that the land is disposed of as soon as is reasonably practicable; and

(b) shall not, except with the consent of the Secretary of State, dispose of it for a consideration which is less than the best that can reasonably be obtained.

(2) Where the custodian authority is a successor authority, the authority shall, as soon as is reasonably practicable after a disposal under paragraph (1) above—

(a) deduct the amount of any relevant expenditure from the amount received in respect of the disposal ("the disposal receipt"); and

(b) if the amount found after that deduction is a positive amount, distribute that amount in accordance with provisions included in an agreement as mentioned in regulation 5(2)(d)(ii).

(3) Where the custodian authority is the relinquishing authority in relation to a transferred area, the authority shall, as soon as is reasonably practicable after a disposal under paragraph (1) above—

(a) deduct the relevant proportion of any relevant expenditure from the appropriate proportion of the disposal receipt; and

(b) if the amount found after that deduction is a positive amount, pay that amount to the acquiring authority in relation to the area.

(4) For the purposes of paragraph (3) above—

(a) the appropriate proportion is the proportion equal to the proportion which the population of the transferred area bears to the population of the area which, immediately before the reorganisation date, was the area of the relinquishing authority; and

(b) the population of an area shall be taken to be the number estimated by the Registrar General by reference to the date which, at the reorganisation date, is the latest date in respect of which such an estimate is available.

(5) Where the whole of a custodian authority's relevant expenditure is not met by a deduction of such expenditure from the amount of a disposal receipt as mentioned in

paragraph (2) or (3) above, that authority may recover an amount equal to the relevant proportion of any relevant expenditure which is not so met from—

(a) where the custodian authority is a successor authority in relation to an abolished authority, any other successor authority in relation to that authority; or

(b) where the custodian authority is the relinquishing authority in relation to a transferred area, the acquiring authority in relation to that area.

(6) For the purposes of paragraphs (3) and (5) above, the relevant proportion means such proportion as the authorities concerned may agree, or failing such agreement—

(a) where those authorities are successor authorities in relation to an abolished authority, the proportion equal to the proportion which the council tax base of the authority from whom an amount is to be recovered for the financial year in which the disposal takes place bears to the aggregate of the council tax bases for that financial year of all the successor authorities; and

(b) where the authorities concerned are the relinquishing authority and the acquiring authority in relation to a transferred area, the proportion equal to the proportion which the relinquishing authority's estimate of the council tax base of the transferred area for that financial year bears to that authority's estimate of the council tax base for that year of the area which, immediately before the reorganisation date, was the area of that authority.

(7) In this regulation—

"relevant expenditure" means a sum equal to the amount by which the total of expenditure properly incurred by the custodian authority in connection with the management or disposal of surplus land exceeds the total of payments (other than the disposal receipt) received by that authority in respect of the land; and

"surplus land" means any land identified in an agreement as mentioned in paragraph (2)(d)(i) or, as the case may be, (6)(b)(ii) of regulation 5 [or paragraph (1)(b) of regulation 5A].

[3153]

NOTES

Para (7): words in square brackets in definition "surplus land" added by the Local Government Changes for England (Property Transfer and Transitional Payments) (Amendment) Regulations 1995, SI 1995/2796, reg 2(10).

11 Rights of access to records

(1) Where—

(a) any records of a relevant authority are vested by virtue of these Regulations or any other relevant instrument in any body; and

(b) the records relate to—

(i) any property, rights or liabilities which are so vested in another body; or

(ii) any function which is exercisable, on and after the reorganisation date, by such other body,

that other body shall be entitled during ordinary office hours, through any person authorised in that behalf, to inspect those records and to take, or be supplied with, copies of those records or of any part of them.

(2) The rights conferred by paragraph (1) above include the right to require any record which is not in legible form to be made available in legible form for the purposes of inspection or copying or being supplied with copies.

(3) In this regulation and regulation 12, "relevant authority" means—

(i) an abolished authority; or

(ii) the relinquishing authority in relation to a transferred area.

[3154]

12 Continuity of matters

(1) All contracts, deeds, bonds, agreements, licences and other instruments subsisting in favour of, or against, and all notices in force which were given, or have effect as if given, by or to, a relevant authority in respect of any transferred matters shall be of full force and effect in favour of, or against, the body to whom such matters are transferred.

(2) Any action or proceeding, or any cause of action or proceeding, pending or existing at the reorganisation date by or against a relevant authority in respect of any transferred matters may be continued, prosecuted and enforced by or against the body to which such matters are transferred.

(3) In this regulation, "transferred matters" means any property, rights or liabilities transferred by virtue of these Regulations or any other relevant instrument.

[3155]

PART III
TRANSITIONAL PAYMENTS

13 Interpretation of Part and general provision

(1) In this Part—

"the final accounts" means the accounts of the relevant authority for the final year;

"the accounts date" means the date on which the responsible financial officer signs the statement of accounts prepared in relation to the final accounts;

"designated authority" means—

(a) in a case where there are two or more successor authorities in relation to an abolished authority … , the successor authority which is specified in a section 17 order as the designated authority in relation to this Part; and

(b) in the case of the relinquishing authority and the acquiring authority in relation to a transferred area, the relinquishing authority;

"the final year" means the financial year ending immediately before the reorganisation date;

"participant authority", in relation to a designated authority, means—

(i) in a case where the designated authority is one of two or more successor authorities in relation to an abolished authority … , any other such successor authority; and

(ii) in a case where the designated authority is the relinquishing authority in relation to a transferred area, the acquiring authority in relation to that area;

"the relevant authority", in relation to a designated authority and any participant authority, means—

(a) where those authorities are successor authorities in relation to an abolished authority, the abolished authority; and

(b) where the designated authority is the relinquishing authority in relation to a transferred area and the participant authority is the acquiring authority in relation to that area, the relinquishing authority.

(2) Any notice under this Part which sets out calculations made in accordance with [the Schedule to these Regulations ("the Schedule")] shall include an explanation of the basis on which the amount or value ascribed to each of the items of the formulae in that Schedule was determined.

(3) Any notification by a participant authority under this Part that it disagrees with any calculations made by the designated authority in accordance with [the Schedule] shall state the reasons for the disagreement.

(4) A participant authority may, within one month of service by a designated authority of a notice under this Part, request that authority to supply such information relating to the contents of the notice as may be specified in the request; and the designated authority shall, as soon as is reasonably practicable, supply the information.

[3156]

NOTES

Para (1): words omitted revoked by the Local Government Changes for England (Property Transfer and Transitional Payments) (Amendment) Regulations 1995, SI 1995/2796, reg 2(11)(a).

Paras (2), (3): words in square brackets substituted by SI 1995/2796, reg 2(11)(b), (c).

14 Initial calculations

(1) A designated authority—

(a) within such period as that authority and each participant authority may agree or, failing such agreement, the period of one month beginning with the accounts date, shall make calculations in relation to each participant authority in accordance with [the Schedule]; and

(b) as soon as is reasonably practicable, shall serve on each participant authority a notice setting out the calculations it has made in relation to that authority and any other participant authority.

(2) At any time within the period of two months beginning with the date of service of the notice mentioned in paragraph (1) above, a designated authority may serve on each participant authority one further notice setting out calculations made in accordance with [the Schedule] in substitution for the calculations set out in the first-mentioned notice.

(3) A notice under paragraph (2) above shall include a statement of the designated authority's reasons for serving it.

(4) Not later than the expiry of the period of two months beginning with the date of service of a notice under paragraph (1) or, where a notice has been served under paragraph (2) above, the date of service of that notice ("the relevant period"), each participant authority shall notify the designated authority and any other participant authority in writing whether or not it agrees with the calculations set out in the notice.

(5) Where a participant authority, pursuant to paragraph (4) above, notifies the designated authority that it does not agree with the calculations set out in a notice under paragraph (1) or, as the case may be, paragraph (2) above, the designated authority shall, not later than the expiry of the period of one month beginning with the end of the relevant period, serve on each participant authority a notice which either—

(a) sets out calculations made in accordance with [the Schedule] in substitution for the calculations set out in the notice under paragraph (1) or, as the case may be, paragraph (2) above; or

(b) states that the designated authority does not intend to make any such calculations and the reasons for not doing so.

(6) A participant authority may, within the period of two months beginning with the date of service of a notice under paragraph (5) above, notify the designated authority and any other participant authority in writing that it disagrees with any substitute calculations set out in the notice or, where the notice does not set out such calculations, in respect of the calculations set out in the notice under paragraph (1) or, as the case may be, paragraph (2) above.

[3157]

NOTES

Paras (1), (2), (5): words in square brackets substituted by the Local Government Changes for England (Property Transfer and Transitional Payments) (Amendment) Regulations 1995, SI 1995/2796, reg 2(12).

15 Further calculations

(1) As soon as is reasonably practicable after the conclusion of the audit of the final accounts, a designated authority shall make calculations in relation to each participant authority in accordance with [the Schedule] and shall serve on each such authority a notice setting out the calculations it has made in relation to that authority and any other participant authority.

(2) A participant authority may, not later than the expiry of the period of two months beginning with the date of service of the notice under paragraph (1) above, notify the designated authority and any other participant authority in writing that it disagrees with the calculations set out in the notice.

[3158]

NOTES

Para (1): words in square brackets substituted by the Local Government Changes for England (Property Transfer and Transitional Payments) (Amendment) Regulations 1995, SI 1995/2796, reg 2(12).

16 Calculations following determination of differences

(1) As soon as is reasonably practicable after the determination under regulation 19 of a difference notified under regulation 14(6) or 15(2), a designated authority shall, subject to paragraph (2) below, make calculations in relation to each participant authority in accordance with [the Schedule] and shall serve on each such authority a notice setting out the calculations it has made in relation to that authority and any other participant authority.

(2) Where amounts or values are ascribed in the determination to any items of the formulae in [the Schedule], the designated authority shall ascribe those amounts or values to those items when making the calculations required by paragraph (1) above.

[3159]

NOTES

Paras (1), (2): words in square brackets substituted by the Local Government Changes for England (Property Transfer and Transitional Payments) (Amendment) Regulations 1995, SI 1995/2796, reg 2(12).

17 Payments by or to the designated authority

(1) Subject to paragraph (2) below—

(a) where the amount calculated in relation to a participant authority in accordance with the formula in paragraph 8 of [the Schedule] is a positive amount, the designated authority shall pay to the participant authority a sum equal to that amount; and

(b) where the amount so calculated is a negative amount, the participant authority shall pay to the designated authority a sum equal to that amount expressed as a positive amount.

(2) Where notification has been given by a participant authority under regulation 14(6) or 15(2) that it disagrees with any calculations made by the designated authority, any sum required, by virtue of paragraph (1) above, to be paid by that authority, any other participant authority or the designated authority in respect of those calculations shall be reduced by 20%.

(3) Any sum payable by virtue of paragraph (1) above shall be paid on or before—

(a) such date as the authority by whom ("the paying authority") and the authority to whom ("the payee authority") the payment is to be made may have agreed during the period of two months beginning with the date of service of the notice setting out the calculations which give rise to the liability to pay; or

(b) failing such agreement, the day (other than a Saturday, a Sunday or a Bank Holiday) which falls two weeks after the end of that period.

(4) Where the authorities concerned so agree, any liability to pay a sum by virtue of this Part may be discharged, in whole or in part, by the transfer to the payee authority of investments held by the paying authority.

(5) At any time after the reorganisation date, the designated authority or a participant authority may each make a payment on account to the other in respect of any sum which the authority estimates it will be liable to pay to the other in consequence of calculations to be made in accordance with paragraph 6 of [the Schedule].

[3160]

NOTES

Paras (1), (5): words in square brackets substituted by the Local Government Changes for England (Property Transfer and Transitional Payments) (Amendment) Regulations 1995, SI 1995/2796, reg 2(12).

18 Interest

(1) The paying authority shall pay interest to the payee authority in respect of any sum which has become payable by virtue of this Part and has not been paid by the due date.

(2) Interest payable under paragraph (1) above—

(a) shall be calculated in accordance with such method as may be agreed between the paying authority and the payee authority or, failing such agreement, shall be simple interest calculated on the unpaid amount in respect of the period beginning with the due date and ending with the day before the day on which the sum is paid at a rate equivalent to two per cent above the highest base rate quoted by any of the reference banks at any time during that period; and

(b) shall be paid at the same time as the sum is paid.

[(3) For the purposes of paragraph (2) above, the reference banks are the seven largest persons for the time being who—

(a) have permission under Part 4 of the Financial Services and Markets Act 2000 to accept deposits,

(b) are incorporated in the United Kingdom and carrying on there a regulated activity of accepting deposits, and

(c) quote a base rate in sterling.]

(4) For the purposes of paragraph (3) above, the size of [a person] is to be determined by reference to [his] consolidated gross assets denominated in sterling, as shown in [his] audited end-year accounts last published before the period for which interest is payable begins.

(5) In this regulation—

"consolidated gross assets" of [a person] is a reference to the gross assets of [that person] together with any subsidiary (within the meaning of section 736 of the Companies Act 1985);

…

"the due date" for payment of a sum is a reference to the date on or before which the sum is required to be paid; and

"sum" includes a reference to a part of a sum.

[(6) Paragraph (3)(a) and (b) must be read with—

(a) section 22 of the Financial Services and Markets Act 2000;

(b) any relevant order under that section; and

(c) Schedule 22 to that Act.]

[3161]

NOTES

Para (3) substituted, words in square brackets in paras (4), (5) substituted, definition "deposit-taking business" (omitted from para (5)) revoked and para (6) added by the Financial Services and Markets Act 2000 (Consequential Amendments and Repeals) Order 2001, SI 2001/3649, art 486.

PART IV
MISCELLANEOUS

19 Disputes

(1) Any question as to the interpretation or application of any provision of these Regulations [or any provision of [any other relevant instrument] which relates to the vesting of any property, rights or liabilities] may be determined—

(a) in the case of a question as to the interpretation or application of regulation 9, by the Charity Commissioners; and

(b) in any other case, by a person agreed on by the parties concerned or, in default of their agreement, appointed by the Secretary of State;

and—

(i) any matter which falls to be agreed under regulation [5B(5) or] 8(4) and is not so agreed; or

(ii) any difference notified under regulation 5(4), 14(6) or 15(2),

shall be determined by such a person.

(2) Where any question as to the interpretation or application of any provision of these Regulations [or [any other relevant instrument]] which relates to the vesting of any property, rights or liabilities is referred for determination under paragraph (1) above before the expiry of the period of 12 months beginning with the reorganisation date—

(a) the provision … which is in question (other than [regulation 6(5A) or (8)]) shall not have, or shall cease to have, effect for the purposes of the vesting of the property, rights or liabilities concerned; and

(b) pending the determination of the question—

(i) in a case which concerns any property of an abolished authority or any rights or liabilities of such an authority exclusively in respect of such property, the property, rights or liabilities shall vest in the Residuary Body; and

(ii) in a case which concerns any other rights or liabilities of such an authority, the rights or liabilities shall vest in the successor authority specified in a section 17 order as the designated authority in relation to regulation 6(8).

(3) The determination of—

(a) any question such as is mentioned in paragraph (2) above;

(b) any such matter as is mentioned in paragraph (1)(i) above; or

(c) any difference notified under regulation 5(4)

PART II STATUTORY INSTRUMENTS

may make any provision that might be contained in an agreement under section 20 of the Act in respect of property, rights or liabilities [and may, in respect of any property which is land, identify the land as surplus land for the purposes of regulation 10].

(4) Where a determination provides for the transfer of any property, rights or liabilities to an authority specified in the determination or, in the case of rights or liabilities, jointly and severally to two or more authorities so specified—

(a) the property, rights or liabilities concerned shall, by virtue of the determination, vest in the authority so specified or, as the case may be, jointly and severally in the authorities so specified; and

(b) the provisions of these Regulations which would have applied to the property, rights or liabilities if the vesting had been effected by virtue of [the provision in question] shall apply to the property, rights or liabilities.

(5) In paragraph (4) above, "authority" includes the Residuary Body.

(6) Section 31 of the Arbitration Act 1950 shall have effect for the purposes of a determination under this regulation by any person mentioned in paragraph (1)(b) above as if such a determination were an arbitration under any other Act within the meaning of that section.

[3162]

NOTES

Para (1): words in first (outer) and final pairs of square brackets inserted by the Local Government Changes for England (Property Transfer and Transitional Payments) (Amendment) Regulations 1995, SI 1995/2796, reg 2(13)(a), (c), words in second (inner) pair of square brackets substituted by the Local Government Changes for England (Property Transfer and Transitional Payments) (Amendment) (No 2) Regulations 1996, SI 1996/2825, reg 2(2).

Para (2): words in first (outer) pair of square brackets inserted and words omitted revoked by SI 1995/2796, reg 2(13)(b), words in second (inner) pair of square brackets substituted by SI 1996/2825, reg 2(2); words in final pair of square brackets substituted by the Local Government Changes for England (Property Transfer and Transitional Payments) (Amendment) Regulations 1996, SI 1996/312, reg 2(6).

Para (3): words in square brackets added by SI 1995/2796, reg 2(13)(a), (c).

Para (4): words in square brackets substituted by SI 1995/2796, reg 2(13)(d).

20 Disputes in respect of transitional payments: further provision

(1) Where the audit of the final accounts of the relevant authority is concluded after notification of a difference has been given under regulation 14(6), the designated authority concerned shall notify that fact to the person who is to determine the difference.

(2) A notification under paragraph (1) above shall be given by the designated authority within three working days of the reference of the difference to the person who is to determine it or, if later, the conclusion of the audit.

(3) Where a notification under paragraph (1) above is given before the determination of the difference, the person who is to determine it shall do so by reference to the final accounts as they stand at the conclusion of the audit.

(4) In this regulation—

"the final accounts" and "the relevant authority" have the same meanings as in Part III of these Regulations; and

"working day" means a day other than a Saturday, a Sunday or a bank holiday.

[3163]

21 Designated authorities: recovery of expenditure and distribution of surpluses

(1) Subject to paragraph (2) below, [where, pursuant to a provision of a relevant instrument, an authority is the designated authority in relation to any such provision, that authority] may recover from each participant authority such proportion of any eligible expenditure as may be agreed between them or, failing such agreement, the appropriate proportion.

(2) Where the designated authority is a successor authority in relation to an abolished authority, the amount of any eligible expenditure shall, for the purposes of paragraph (1) above, be reduced by an amount equal to [the designated authority's estimate of] the total of any interest or other sums received [or to be received by that authority] in respect of investments vested in that authority by virtue of regulation 6(8).

(3) Where the designated authority is a successor authority in relation to an abolished authority and the total of any sums received by the designated authority in any financial year

in carrying out its functions as a designated authority exceeds the amount of any eligible expenditure in respect of that year, the designated authority shall, as soon as is reasonably practicable after the end of that year, pay to each participant authority the appropriate proportion of the excess.

(4) In this regulation—

"the appropriate proportion", in relation to any participant authority, means—

(a) where the participant authority is a successor authority in relation to an abolished authority, the proportion equal to the proportion which the council tax base of the participant authority for the financial year in which an amount is recovered under paragraph (1) above, or paid under paragraph (3) above, bears to the aggregate of the council tax bases for that financial year of the designated authority and all participant authorities; and

(b) where the participant authority is the acquiring authority in relation to a transferred area, the proportion equal to the proportion which the relinquishing authority's estimate of the council tax base of the transferred area for that financial year bears to that authority's estimate of the council tax base for that year of the area which, immediately before the reorganisation date, was the area of that authority;

"eligible expenditure", in relation to a designated authority, means expenditure properly incurred by the authority in carrying out any of its functions as a designated authority for the meeting of which provision is not otherwise made in a relevant instrument; and

"participant authority" has the same meaning as in Part III of these Regulations.

[3164]

NOTES

Para (1): words in square brackets substituted by the Local Government Changes for England (Property Transfer and Transitional Payments) (Amendment) (No 2) Regulations 1996, SI 1996/2825, reg 2(3).

Para (2): words in first pair of square brackets inserted, and words in second pair of square brackets substituted, by the Local Government Changes for England (Property Transfer and Transitional Payments) (Amendment) Regulations 1995, SI 1995/2796, reg 2(14).

SCHEDULE
TRANSITIONAL PAYMENTS

Article 14, 15, 16

CALCULATIONS BY DESIGNATED AUTHORITIES

1.—(1) In this Schedule—

["final Housing Revenue Account" means the Housing Revenue Account of the relevant authority for the final year;]

"the participant authority" means the participant authority in relation to which calculations are being made in accordance with this Schedule;

"relevant area", in relation to the participant authority, means any area which, immediately before the reorganisation date, was the whole or part of the area of the relevant authority and which, on and after that date, is the whole or part of the area of the participant authority (whether or not it was also the whole or part of that authority's area immediately before that date);

"relevant capital receipts" means the usable part of capital receipts (within the meaning of Part IV of the 1989 Act) which has not been applied as mentioned in section 60(2) of that Act;

["relevant PCL" means any amount set aside by the relevant authority (whether voluntarily or pursuant to a requirement under Part IV of the 1989 Act) as provision to meet credit liabilities and not applied as mentioned in section 64 of that Act (use of amounts set aside to meet credit liabilities);]

"relevant provision" means any amount set aside by the relevant authority as mentioned in section 41(3)(b) of the 1989 Act (other than an amount set aside in respect of debts owed to the authority or stocks) and not used before the reorganisation date; and

"transferred", in relation to any property, rights or liabilities, means transferred by virtue of a provision of Part II of these Regulations, a determination under regulation 19 or a provision of any other relevant instrument.

(2) In this Schedule—

(a) any reference to property does not include property held by an authority, as sole

PART II STATUTORY INSTRUMENTS

trustee, exclusively for charitable purposes and any reference to rights or liabilities does not include rights or liabilities in respect of such property;

(b) any reference to an item in the final accounts, or its book value or net book value, is a reference to the item, or its book value or net book value, on the day immediately before the reorganisation date as shown in the final accounts;

(c) in the case of a relevant authority which is a relinquishing authority in relation to a transferred area and a billing authority (within the meaning of the 1992 Act), any reference to an item in the final accounts does not include any item which relates to the collection fund maintained by the authority pursuant to section 89 of the Local Government Finance Act 1988;

(d) any reference to the item of account which relates to debts owed by the relevant authority does not include so much (if any) of that item as relates to credit arrangements entered into by that authority;

(e) any reference to the appropriate amount or appropriate value of any item in the final accounts is a reference to such amount or value as may be agreed between the designated authority and the participant authority or, failing such [agreement—

(i) except for an item which relates to rent and service charge arrears, as is determined by the designated authority, and

(ii) in the case of an item which relates to rent and service charge arrears, as is determined by deducting from the arrears an amount calculated in accordance with the Table below; ...]

(f) references to subsection (3) of section 50 of the 1989 Act include references to that subsection as applied by section 51(4) of that Act (variations of credit arrangements) [and

(g) any reference to the credit ceiling of a local authority on any day is a reference to that authority's credit ceiling on that day as determined under Part III of Schedule 3 to the 1989 Act (credit ceiling)].

(3) Where—

(a) a calculation in accordance with a formula in this Schedule requires an amount to be found by reference to an item of account which relates to any rights or liabilities of the relevant authority which have been transferred to the designated authority or the participant authority; and

(b) the rights or liabilities have been transferred jointly and severally to both of those authorities or to either of those authorities and another participant authority or the Residuary Body,

the amount or value of the item of account to be ascribed to the participant authority or the designated authority for the purposes of the calculation shall be such proportion of the amount or value of the item as may be agreed by all the authorities to whom the rights or liabilities have jointly and severally been transferred or, in default of such agreement, as the designated authority shall determine.

(4) An amount ascribed to an item of a formula in accordance with the following paragraphs of this Schedule may be nil or, as the case may be, a negative amount.

[(5) Any reference to an amount in paragraphs 2 to 5 shall exclude any amounts for which separate provision is made by their inclusion in the calculation of Z in paragraph 6A.

TABLE
RENT AND SERVICE CHARGE ARREARS

Arrears of tenants or licensees of the authority at the date of transfer: weeks overdue		Deduction from the amount of the arrears as a percentage
Exceeding	*Not Exceeding*	
—	4	0
4	13	10
13	26	25
26	39	50
39	52	75
52	—	95]

2. The first calculation is—

$$A+B+\frac{(C\times d)}{D}$$

where—

A is the amount which is the aggregate of—

(a) the appropriate amount of so much of any financial reserves in the final accounts as is attributable to amounts set aside—

(i) in connection with any property which has been transferred to the participant authority; or

(ii) for the purpose of meeting any liabilities which have been so transferred; and

(b) so much of any relevant provisions in those accounts as is attributable to amounts which were set aside or applied in that connection or for that purpose;

B is the amount found by subtracting the aggregate of—

(a) the appropriate value of so much of the item in the final accounts which relates to debts owed to the relevant authority as is attributable to debts the right to which has been transferred to the participant authority; and

(b) the appropriate value of so much of the item in those accounts which relates to stocks as is attributable to property which has been so transferred;

from the aggregate of—

(a) the net book value of debts the right to which has been transferred to the participant authority; and

(b) the net book value of stocks which are attributable to property which has been so transferred;

C is an amount determined in accordance with paragraph 3 below;

D is the amount calculated by the relevant authority as its council tax base for the final year in accordance with the relevant rules; and

d is the designated authority's estimate of so much of that amount as relates to any relevant area.

3. The amount of C shall be determined in accordance with the formula—

$E-(F+(GA-GB)+H)$

where—

E is the amount which is the difference between—

(a) the aggregate of financial reserves and relevant provisions in the final accounts; and

(b) the aggregate of any revenue account deficits in those accounts or the accounts in respect of any preceding financial year for which provision has not already been made;

F is the amount which is—

(a) where the designated authority is a successor authority in relation to an abolished authority, the aggregate of—

(i) the appropriate amount of so much of any financial reserves in the final accounts as is attributable to amounts set aside—

(a) in connection with any property which has been transferred to the designated authority; or

(b) for the purpose of meeting any liabilities which have been so transferred; and

(ii) so much of any relevant provisions in those accounts as is attributable to amounts which were set aside or applied in that connection or for that purpose; and

(b) where the designated authority is the relinquishing authority in relation to a transferred area, the aggregate of—

(i) the appropriate amount of so much of any financial reserves in the final accounts as is attributable to amounts set aside—

(a) in connection with property other than property which has been transferred to [any other authority]; or

(b) for the purpose of meeting any liabilities other than liabilities which have been so transferred; and

PART II STATUTORY INSTRUMENTS

(ii) so much of any relevant provisions in those accounts as is attributable to amounts which were set aside or applied in that connection or for that purpose;

GA is—

(a) in a case where the designated authority is a successor authority in relation to an abolished authority, the amount which is the aggregate of—

(i) the net book value of debts owed to the abolished authority the right to which has been transferred to the designated authority; and

(ii) the net book value of stocks which are attributable to property which has been so transferred; and

(b) in a case where the designated authority is the relinquishing authority in relation to a transferred area, the amount which is the aggregate of—

(i) the net book value of debts owed to that authority other than debts the right to which has been transferred to [any other authority]; and

(ii) the net book value of stocks which are attributable to property other than property which has been so transferred;

GB is—

(a) in a case where the designated authority is a successor authority in relation to an abolished authority, the amount which is the aggregate of—

(i) the appropriate value of so much of the item in the final accounts which relates to debts owed to the abolished authority as is attributable to debts the right to which has been transferred to the designated authority; and

(ii) the appropriate value of so much of the item in those accounts which relates to stocks as is attributable to property which has been so transferred; and

(b) in a case where the designated authority is the relinquishing authority in relation to a transferred area, the amount which is the aggregate of—

(i) the appropriate value of so much of the item in the final accounts which relates to debts owed to that authority as is not attributable to debts the right to which has been transferred to [any other authority]; and

(ii) the appropriate value of so much of the item in those accounts which relates to stocks as is not attributable to any property which has been so transferred; and

H is the aggregate of the amounts found ... in respect of items A and B in paragraph 2 above [in relation to—

(a) in a case where the designated authority is a successor authority in relation to an abolished authority, all participant authorities; and

(b) in a case where the designated authority is the relinquishing authority in relation to a transferred area, the participant authority and any other principal council which is the acquiring authority in relation to a transferred area which, immediately before the reorganisation date, was comprised in the area of the relinquishing authority.]

4. [Subject to paragraph 4A below, the second] calculation is—

$$(I + J + K) - (L + M)$$

where—

I is the amount found by the first calculation in paragraph 2 above;

J is the aggregate of—

(i) the book value of so much of the item in the final accounts which relates to debts owed by the relevant authority as is attributable to debts the liability for which has been transferred to the participant authority; and

(ii) so much of the item in those accounts relating to receipts in advance as, in the designated authority's opinion, is attributable to the participant authority;

K is an amount in respect of relevant capital receipts determined in accordance with paragraph 5 below;

L is the amount which is the aggregate of—

(a) the net book value of so much of the item in the final accounts which relates to stocks as is attributable to property which has been transferred to the participant authority; and

(b) so much of the item in those accounts relating to payments in advance as, in the designated authority's opinion, is attributable to the participant authority;

M is the net book value of so much of the item in the final accounts which relates to debts owed to the relevant authority as is attributable to debts the right to which has been transferred to the participant authority.

[4A. Where the condition in paragraph 4B below is fulfilled, the second calculation shall be—

$$(I + J + K + KK) - (L + M)$$

where, I, J, K, L and M have the same meaning as in paragraph 4 above and KK is an amount in respect of relevant PCL determined in accordance with paragraph 5A below.

4B. The condition mentioned in paragraph 4A above is that the relevant authority, on the day immediately before the reorganisation date, had a credit ceiling which is a negative amount and no money outstanding by way of borrowing other than—

(a) short-term borrowing (within the meaning of section 45(6) of the 1989 Act); or

(b) borrowing undertaken before 24th August 1995 (other than by the issue of stock on or after 15th December 1993) from a person who is not one of the following—

(i) the Public Works Loan Board;

(ii) the Bank of England;

(iii) the European Investment Bank;

(iv) a body mentioned in any of paragraphs 1 to 17, 28 or 29 of Part II of the Schedule to the Local Authorities (Capital Finance) (Approved Investments) Regulations 1990;

(v) an authorised institution within the meaning of the Banking Act 1987; or

(vi) a building society within the meaning of the Building Societies Act 1986.]

5. The amount of K shall be determined in such manner as the designated authority and the participant authority may agree or, in default of such agreement, in accordance with the formula—

$$\frac{KA \times d}{D}$$

where—

KA is an amount equal to the total of the item in the final accounts which relates to relevant capital receipts; and

D and d have the same meaning as in paragraph 2 above.

[5A.—(1) Subject to paragraph (2) below, the amount of KK shall be determined in such manner as the designated authority and the participant authority may agree or, in default of such agreement, in accordance with the formula—

$$\frac{(KB - KC) \times d}{D}$$

where—

KB is an amount equal to the lesser of—

(a) the total of the item in the final accounts which relates to relevant PCL; or

(b) the amount by which the relevant authority's credit ceiling on the day immediately before the reorganisation date is less than nil;

KC is the aggregate of amounts determined in accordance with paragraph 5B below in respect of any credit arrangements entered into by the relevant authority at any time before the reorganisation date and in respect of which rights and liabilities exist on that date ("existing credit arrangements"); and

D and d have the same meaning as in paragraph 2 above.

(2) The amount of KK determined in a manner agreed between the designated authority and the participant authority shall not exceed such amount as is determined in accordance with the formula—

$$KB - KC$$

where KB and KG have the same meanings as in paragraph (1) above.

5B. For the purposes of item KC, the amount in respect of each existing credit arrangement shall be determined in accordance with the formula—

$$(kd + ke + kf + kg) - kh$$

where—

kd is the amount which is the aggregate of—

(i) any amount of the usable part of capital receipts which the relevant authority applied in relation to the existing credit arrangement as mentioned in paragraph (b) of subsection (3) of section 50 of the 1989 Act (credit cover for credit arrangements); and

(ii) any amount set aside from a revenue account by that authority in relation to that credit arrangement as mentioned in paragraph (c) of that subsection;

ke is the aggregate of amounts determined in respect of notional interest on the existing credit arrangement for the purposes of paragraph 15(1)(b) of Schedule 3 to the 1989 Act for each financial year ("relevant year") beginning with the financial year immediately following the financial year in which the existing credit arrangement concerned was entered into and ending with the final year;

kf is the total of principal amounts for each relevant year, and, for these purposes, a principal amount for a relevant year is so much of the amount in respect of principal referred to in paragraph 15(1)(a) of Schedule 3 to the 1989 Act for that year as the designated authority and the participant authority agree is attributable to the existing credit arrangement or, in default of such agreement, as the designated authority determines to be so attributable;

kg is the amount which is the aggregate of—

(i) the amount by which the total amounts shown in the accounts of the relevant authority for each relevant year as amounts set aside from a revenue account as provision to meet credit liabilities in relation to the existing credit arrangement (otherwise than in accordance with a determination under paragraph (c) of subsection (3) of section 50 of the 1989 Act) exceeds the amount which is the principal amount for that year for the purposes of item kf above; and

(ii) the total of amounts shown in such accounts as the usable part of capital receipts applied as provision to meet credit liabilities in relation to the existing credit arrangement (otherwise than as mentioned in paragraph (b) of that subsection); and

kh is the aggregate of amounts shown in the accounts of the relevant authority for each relevant year as amounts applied under section 64(1)(b) of the 1989 Act in respect of the existing credit arrangement.]

6. The third calculation is—

$$(N + P + Z) - Q]$$

where—

N is the amount found by the calculation made in accordance with paragraph 4 above;

P is the aggregate of amounts determined in accordance with paragraph 7 below in respect of any credit arrangements entered into by the relevant authority in respect of which the rights and liabilities have been transferred to the participant authority ("relevant credit arrangements"); …

Q is the total of any investments or cash which have been transferred to the participant authority [and

Z is the amount calculated in accordance with paragraph 6A.]

[6A. The amount of Z shall be calculated in accordance with the formula—

$$(HA + HJ - HL - HM) + \frac{(HC \times Hd)}{(HD)}$$

where—

HA is the appropriate amount of so much of the closing balance of the final Housing Revenue Account as is attributable to amounts set aside—

(i) in connection with any HRA property which has been transferred to the participant authority; or

(ii) for the purpose of meeting any liabilities which have been so transferred;

HJ is the aggregate of—

(i) the book value of so much of the item in the final accounts which relates to debts owed by the relevant authority in connection with HRA property as is attributable to such debts the liability for which has been transferred to the participant authority; and

(ii) so much of the item in those accounts relating to receipts in advance in connection with HRA property as, in the designated authority's opinion, is attributable to the participant authority;

HL is the amount which is the aggregate of—

(i) the appropriate value of so much of the item in the final accounts which relates to stocks held in connection with HRA property which has been transferred to the participant authority; and

(ii) so much of the item in those accounts relating to payments in advance in connection with HRA property as, in the designated authority's opinion, is attributable to the participant authority;

HM is the aggregate of the appropriate value of so much of the items in the final accounts which relate to rent and service charge arrears in connection with HRA property and other debts in connection with that property owed to the relevant authority as is attributable to such arrears and debts the right to which has been transferred to the participant authority;

HC is the difference between the closing balance of the final Housing Revenue Account and the aggregate either—

(i) where the designated authority is a successor authority to an abolished authority, of—

(a) the aggregate of the amounts found in relation to all participant authorities [for HA]; and

(b) the amount found in relation to the designated authority if [an amount for HA] had been calculated in respect of the property, rights and liabilities transferred to the designated authority; or

(ii) where the designated authority is the relinquishing authority in relation to a transferred area, of—

(a) the aggregate of the amounts found [for HA] above in relation to the participant authority and any other principal council which is the acquiring authority in relation to a transferred area which, immediately before the reorganisation date, was comprised in the area of the relinquishing authority, and

(b) the amount found in relation to the designated authority if [an amount for HA] had been calculated in respect of property, rights and liabilities of that authority which have not been transferred to any other authority;

Hd is the number of HRA dwellings transferred to the participant authority; and

HD is the total number of HRA dwellings of the relevant authority on the final day of the final year.]

7. For the purposes of item P, the amount of each relevant credit arrangement shall be determined in accordance with the formula—

$$(R + S + T + U) - V$$

where—

R is the amount which is the aggregate of—

(a) any amount of the usable part of capital receipts which the relevant authority applied in relation to the relevant credit arrangement as mentioned in paragraph (b) of subsection (3) of section 50 of the 1989 Act (credit cover for credit arrangements); and

(b) any amount set aside from a revenue account by that authority in relation to that credit arrangement as mentioned in paragraph (c) of that subsection;

S is the aggregate of amounts determined in respect of notional interest on the relevant credit arrangement for the purposes of paragraph 15(1)(b) of Schedule 3 to the 1989 Act for each financial year ("relevant year") beginning with the financial year immediately following the financial year in which the relevant credit arrangement was entered into ("the first year") and ending with the final year;

T is the aggregate of principal amounts for each relevant year; and, for these purposes, a principal amount for a relevant year is so much of the amount in respect of principal referred to in paragraph 15(1)(a) of Schedule 3 to the 1989 Act for that year as the designated authority and the participant authority agree is attributable to the relevant credit arrangement or, in default of such agreement, as the designated authority determines to be so attributable;

U is the amount which is the aggregate of—

(a) the amount by which the total of amounts shown in the accounts of the relevant authority for each relevant year as amounts set aside from a revenue account as provision to meet credit liabilities in relation to the relevant credit arrangement (otherwise than in accordance with a determination under paragraph (c) of subsection (3) of section 50 of the 1989 Act) exceeds the amount which is the principal amount for that year for the purposes of item T above; and

(b) the total of amounts shown in such accounts as the usable part of capital receipts applied as provision to meet credit liabilities in relation to the relevant credit arrangement (otherwise than as mentioned in paragraph (b) of that subsection); and

V is the aggregate of amounts shown in the accounts of the relevant authority for each relevant year as amounts applied under section 64(1)(b) of the 1989 Act in respect of the relevant credit arrangement.

8. The fourth calculation is—

W – (X – Y)

where—

W is the amount found by the calculation made in accordance with paragraph 6 above;

X is the aggregate of—

(a) amounts paid by the designated authority to the participant authority by virtue of paragraph (1) of regulation 17 in consequence of calculations previously made in accordance with paragraph 6 above; and

(b) amounts so paid by virtue of paragraph (5) of that regulation; and

Y is the aggregate of—

(a) amounts paid by the participant authority to the designated authority by virtue of paragraph (1) of regulation 17 in consequence of such calculations; and

(b) amounts so paid by virtue of paragraph (5) of that regulation.

[3165]

NOTES

Para 1: in sub-para (1) definition "final Housing Revenue Account" inserted by the Local Government Changes for England (Property Transfer and Transitional Payments) (Amendment) Regulations 1996, SI 1996/312, reg 2(7)(a), definition "relevant PCL" inserted by the Local Government Changes for England (Property Transfer and Transitional Payments) (Amendment) (No 2) Regulations 1996, SI 1996/2825, reg 2(4)(a); in sub-para (2)(e) words in square brackets substituted by SI 1996/312, reg 2(7)(a), word omitted revoked by SI 1996/2825, reg 2(4)(b); sub-para (2)(g) inserted by SI 1996/2825, reg 2(4)(b); sub-para (5) inserted by SI 1996/312, reg 2(7)(a).

Para 3: words in square brackets in items F, GA, GB substituted, and in item H words omitted revoked and words in square brackets inserted by Local Government Changes for England (Property Transfer and Transitional Payments) (Amendment) Regulations 1995, SI 1995/2796, reg 2(15).

Para 4: words in square brackets substituted by SI 1996/2825, reg 2(5).

Paras 4A, 4B, 5A, 5B: inserted by SI 1996/2825, reg 2(6), (7).

Para 6: formula in square brackets substituted, word omitted revoked, and words in final pair of square brackets inserted, by SI 1996/312, reg 2(7)(b).

Para 6A: inserted by SI 1996/312, reg 2(7)(c); words in square brackets substituted by SI 1996/2825, reg 2(8).

LOCAL AUTHORITIES (COMPANIES) ORDER 1995

(SI 1995/849)

NOTES

Made: 21 March 1995.

Authority: Local Government and Housing Act 1989, ss 39(5)–(7), 67(4), 70(1), (5), 71(1)(b). S 39 is repealed by the Local Government Act 2003, s 127(1), (2), Sch 7, paras 28, 29, Sch 8, Pt 1, subject to transitional provisions and savings in SI 2003/2938, art 8, Schedule, paras 1–11 (England), and SI 2003/3034, art 3, Sch 2, paras 2, 3 (Wales), and in SI 2004/533, art 3, and this order has accordingly lapsed to the extent that it was made under the said s 39, subject to those transitional provisions and savings. In addition, Pt V of the order is revoked, subject to savings, by SI 2004/533, art 9, to the extent that it has not already lapsed by virtue of the repeal of s 39(5)–(7).

Commencement: 1 July 1995 (art 4, arts 5–10, certain purposes); 1 April 1995 (arts 5–10 remaining purposes, arts 1–3, 11–18, Schedule).

ARRANGEMENT OF ARTICLES

PART I
GENERAL

PART II
REGULATION OF CONTROLLED AND
INFLUENCED COMPANIES

PART III
CONTROLLED COMPANIES WHICH ARE NOT
ARM'S LENGTH COMPANIES

PART IV
MINORITY INTERESTS

PART I
GENERAL

1 Citation, commencement and interpretation

(1) This Order may be cited as the Local Authorities (Companies) Order 1995 and shall come into force as provided in paragraph (2) below.

(2) This Order shall come into force—
(a) for the purposes of article 4, on 1st July 1995;
(b) for the purposes of articles 5 to 10 in so far as they relate to companies formed on or before 31st March 1995, on 1st July 1995; and
(c) for all other purposes on 1st April 1995.

(3) Except where the context otherwise requires, any reference in this Order to a section or Part is to a section or Part of the 1989 Act.

(4) In this Order—
"the 1985 Act" means the Companies Act 1985;
"the 1989 Act" means the Local Government and Housing Act 1989;
"the Audit Commission" means the Audit Commission for Local Authorities and the National Health Service in England and Wales;
"controlled company" means a company (other than a company within a description set out in the Schedule to this Order) which for the purposes of Part V is under the control of a local authority or is treated as being under the control of each of two or more local authorities;
"director", except in so far as the context otherwise requires, includes, in relation to a company which is an industrial and provident society, a member of the committee of management of the society and its chief officer;
"relevant authority", in relation to a regulated company, means any local authority having control of that company or to whose influence the company is subject, or which is, by virtue of section 73 (authorities acting jointly, etc) treated as having such control or influence;

and any reference to a regulated company is a reference to a company which is for the time being either—
(a) a controlled company, or
(b) a company which for the purposes of Part V is, or is treated as, subject to the influence of a local authority (the "relevant authority") and which—
(i) is an unlimited company or a society registered or deemed to be registered

under the Industrial and Provident Societies Act 1965 or under the Industrial and Provident Societies Act (Northern Ireland) 1969; or

(ii) satisfies either or both of the first and second conditions set out in paragraphs (5) and (7) below,

but is not within any description set out in the Schedule to this Order.

(5) The first condition mentioned in paragraph (4)(b)(ii) above is that the relevant authority would, if it were a company registered under the 1985 Act, be treated by virtue of section 258 of that Act as having the right to exercise, or as having, during the relevant period, actually exercised, a dominant influence over the company in question.

(6) For the purposes of paragraph (5) above "the relevant period", in relation to any duty or any action referred to in Part II of this Order, means the financial year of the relevant authority which ended immediately before the financial year in which, if the company in question were a regulated company, that duty would fall to be fulfilled, or in which that action is performed.

(7) The second condition mentioned in paragraph (4)(b)(ii) above is that if the authority were a company registered under the 1985 Act it would be required, by virtue of section 227 of that Act, or of accounting standards such as would, by virtue of that Act, be applicable in the circumstances, to prepare group accounts in respect of the company in question.

(8) For the purposes of paragraph (7) above, in determining whether a local authority would be required to prepare group accounts it shall be assumed that no exclusion of or exemption from such requirement, other than those referred to in section 229(3)(a) and (c) of the 1985 Act, would be applicable by virtue of that Act.

[3166]

2 Companies subject to the influence of local authorities

In determining for the purposes of this Order whether a company is subject to the influence of a local authority no account shall be taken of any condition specified in any paragraph of subsection (1) or (3) of section 69, in so far as that condition is fulfilled by reference only to another company which is of a description mentioned in the Schedule to this Order, or to a person who is both an employee and either a director, manager, secretary or similar officer of such a company.

[3167]

3 Application of the Order

No provision in this Order shall be construed as requiring a company to act (or refrain from acting) in breach of any provision made by or under any enactment, or any obligation subsisting on the day on which such provision comes into force.

[3168]

PART II

REGULATION OF CONTROLLED AND INFLUENCED COMPANIES

4 Identification of companies

(1) A regulated company shall have mentioned on all relevant documents the fact that it is a company controlled, or, as the case may be, influenced, by a local authority, within the meaning of Part V; and naming the relevant authority or authorities.

(2) In this article "relevant documents" means business letters, notices and other documents of the company, being of any kind mentioned in paragraphs (a) to (d) of section 349(1) of the 1985 Act.

[3169]

5 Requirements applicable to regulated companies

(1) A regulated company shall not—

(a) in respect of the carrying out of any relevant duty, pay to a regulated director remuneration in excess of the maximum amount;

(b) in respect of expenditure on travelling or subsistence in connection with the carrying out of a relevant duty, pay to a regulated director an allowance, or reimburse expenses, in excess of the maximum amount;

(c) publish any material which the relevant authority would be prohibited from publishing by section 2 of the Local Government Act 1986.

(2) Where a director becomes disqualified for membership of a local authority otherwise than by being employed by a local authority or a controlled company, the company shall make such arrangements as may be necessary for a resolution to be moved for his removal in accordance with section 303 of the 1985 Act.

(3) In this article—

(a) for the purposes of paragraph (1)(a), the maximum amount is the greatest amount which would for the time being be payable by the relevant authority in respect of a comparable duty performed on behalf of that authority, less any amount paid by that authority in respect of the relevant duty to the regulated director in question;

(b) for the purposes of paragraph (1)(b), the maximum amount in relation to a director is the maximum amount of travelling or subsistence allowance which would for the time being be payable to that director by the local authority of which he is a member if the relevant duty were an approved duty for the purposes of section 174 of the Local Government Act 1972;

(c) "regulated director" means a director of the company who is also a member of a relevant authority; and

(d) "relevant duty" means a duty carried out on behalf of the company.

[3170]

6 Provision of information to authority's auditor

A regulated company shall provide, and authorise or instruct its auditors to provide—

(a) to the person who is for the time being the auditor in relation to the accounts of the relevant authority, such information and explanation about the affairs of the company as that person may require for the purposes of the audit of the local authority's accounts; and

(b) to any person authorised by the Audit Commission, such information as that person or the Commission may require for the discharge of any function under Part III of the Local Government Finance Act 1982.

[3171]

7 Provision of information to members of local authority

(1) Subject to paragraph (2), a regulated company shall provide to a member of a relevant authority such information about the affairs of the company as the member reasonably requires for the proper discharge of his duties.

(2) Nothing in this article shall require a company to provide information in breach of any enactment, or of an obligation owed to any person.

[3172]–[3173]

8 *(Revoked by the Local Authorities (Capital Finance) (Consequential, Transitional and Saving Provisions) Order 2004, SI 2004/533, art 9(1), subject to savings in relation to financial years beginning before 1 April 2004.)*

9 Appointment of auditor

A controlled company shall, before it first appoints any person as auditor of the company, obtain the [the consent of—

(a) where the company is under the control of one or more local authorities, all of which are local government bodies in Wales within the meaning of section 12 of the Public Audit (Wales) Act 2004, the Auditor General for Wales;

(b) in any other case, the Audit Commission,

to the appointment of that person.]

[3174]

NOTES

Words in square bracket substituted by the Public Audit (Wales) Act 2004 (Consequential Amendments) (Wales) Order 2005, SI 2005/757, art 2.

PART III
CONTROLLED COMPANIES WHICH ARE NOT ARM'S LENGTH COMPANIES

10 Public inspection of minutes

(1) A controlled company which is not an arm's length company shall, until the expiry of the period of four years beginning with the date of the meeting, make available for inspection by any member of the public a copy of the minutes of any general meeting of the company.

(2) Nothing in paragraph (1) requires any copy to be made available which includes any matter the disclosure of which would be in breach of any enactment, or of an obligation owed to any person.

(3) Nothing in this article shall require a company to make available for inspection the minutes of any meeting held before the date on which this Order comes into force.

[3175]

PART IV
MINORITY INTERESTS

11 Authorised companies

There are hereby specified for the purposes of section 71 (control of minority interests) companies, other than regulated companies and companies within any description set out in the Schedule to this Order, in which any person associated with a local authority (within the meaning of section 69(5)) has a right to vote at a general meeting or of which any such person is a director.

[3176]–[3183]

(*Part V revoked by the Local Authorities* (*Capital Finance*) (*Consequential, Transitional and Saving Provisions*) *Order 2004, SI 2004/533, art 9*(*1*)*, subject to savings in relation to financial years beginning before 1 April 2004.*)

SCHEDULE
COMPANIES NOT SUBJECT TO THE ORDER

Articles 1(2), 11

1. A public transport company within the meaning of section 72 of the Transport Act 1985.

2. A public airport company within the meaning of Part II of the Airports Act 1986.

3. A company which is under the control or subject to the influence of a Passenger Transport Executive.

4. A company which by virtue of section 73 of the 1989 Act is treated as under the control or subject to the influence of two or more authorities, where each of those authorities is a Passenger Transport Executive.

5. A company which, in relation to a company ("the holding company") within any description in paragraphs 1 to 4, would, if the holding company were a local authority within the meaning of Part V, be under the control of that authority.

[3184]–[3205]

CHARITIES (EXCEPTION FROM REGISTRATION) REGULATIONS 1996

(SI 1996/180)

NOTES

Made: 1 February 1996.

Authority: Charities Act 1993, ss 3(5), (13), 86(3). S 3 is substituted for ss 3, 3A, 3B by the Charities Act 2006, s 9 as from a date to be appointed.

Commencement: 1 March 1996.

1 Citation and commencement

These Regulations may be cited as the Charities (Exception from Registration) Regulations 1996 and shall come into force on 1st March 1996.

[3206]

NOTES

Commencement: 1 March 1996.

2 Interpretation

In these Regulations—

"advancement of religion" includes the relief of ministers and former ministers of religion and their families;

"the Act" means the Charities Act 1993.

[3207]

NOTES

Commencement: 1 March 1996.

3 (*Revokes the Charities (Exception from Registration and Accounts) Regulations 1963, SI 1963/2074 and the Charities (Exception from Registration and Accounts) Regulations 1964, SI 1964/1825.*)

4 Temporary exception of certain religious charities connected with certain bodies

(1) A charity to which this regulation applies is hereby excepted until 1st March 2001 from the duty to be registered under section 3(2) of the Act.

(2) This regulation shall apply to a charity wholly or mainly concerned with the advancement of religion, being a charity connected with a body named in paragraph (3) below and either—

(a) having as a trustee a trust corporation connected with that body; or

(b) established wholly or mainly to make provision for public religious worship; or

(c) in respect of which accounts are sent annually to the Methodist Conference, a Methodist Synod or any connexional or other committee or department appointed or established by the Methodist Conference.

(3) The bodies referred to in paragraph (2) above are—

a church within the meaning of section 2 of the Baptist and Congregational Trusts Act 1951;

a church which is affiliated to the Fellowship of Independent Evangelical Churches;

a church which is a member of the General Assembly of Unitarian and Free Christian Churches;

the Calvinistic Methodist or Presbyterian Church of Wales;

the Church of England;

the Church in Wales;

the Methodist Church;

the Religious Society of Friends;

the United Reformed Church.

[3208]

NOTES

Commencement: 1 March 1996.

Para (1): words in square brackets substituted by the Charities (Exception From Registration) (Amendment) Regulations 2002, SI 2002/1598, reg 2.

5 Permanent exception of trusts conditional upon the upkeep of graves

(1) A charity to which this regulation applies is hereby excepted from the duty to be registered under section 3(2) of the Act.

PART II
STATUTORY INSTRUMENTS

(2) This regulation shall apply to a charity for the advancement of religion where—

(a) the application of its income in a particular manner is conditional upon a grave, tomb or personal monument being kept in good order; and

(b) the income of the charity does not amount to more than £1,000 a year.

[3209]

NOTES

Commencement: 1 March 1996.

LOCAL GOVERNMENT REORGANISATION (WALES) (CHARITIES) ORDER 1996

(SI 1996/183)

NOTES

Made: 29 January 1996.
Local Government (Wales) Act 1994, ss 49(6), 63(5)(a).
Commencement: 1 April 1996.

1 Citation and commencement

This Order may be cited as the Local Government Reorganisation (Wales) (Charities) Order 1996 and shall come into force on 1st April 1996.

[3210]

NOTES

Commencement: 1 April 1996.

2 Supplemental provision to section 49 of the Local Government (Wales) Act 1994

(1) The following provisions shall have effect in relation to the application of section 49 of the Local Government (Wales) Act 1994 (Charities).

(2) Where, immediately before the commencement of section 49, any power with respect to a charity was vested in an old authority, that power shall vest in the appropriate council as determined in accordance with the provisions of section 49(4) or, where section 49(4) does not apply, in accordance with section 49(5).

(3) References in paragraph (2) and section 49(2) to a power with respect to a charity do not include any power vested in an old authority, proper officer or other office holder by virtue of being a trustee thereof.

(4) Where—

(a) section 49(2) applies, but section 49(1) does not apply, or

(b) section 49(3) applies,

the provisions of subsection (4) shall nevertheless apply if the property of the charity in question is held for the benefit of any area or persons as referred to in that subsection.

(5) Where there are more than two principal councils in whose areas fall—

(a) the specified area under section 49(4), or

(b) the area of the old authority in question under section 49(5),

the reference in each of those provisions to "the greater part" shall, in any such case, be construed as a reference to "the greatest part".

(6) Any rights and liabilities of an old authority arising from that authority holding as trustee property to which section 49 applies shall transfer to the new principal council in which the property is vested.

[3211]

NOTES

Commencement: 1 April 1996.

TRUSTEE INVESTMENTS (DIVISION OF TRUST FUND) ORDER 1996

(SI 1996/845)

NOTES

Made: 18 March 1996.
Authority: Trustee Investments Act 1961, s 13(1).
Commencement: 11 May 1996.

1 This Order may be cited as the Trustee Investments (Division of Trust Fund) Order 1996 and shall come into force on the tenth day after the day on which it is approved by resolution of each House of Parliament.

[3212]

NOTES

Commencement: 11 May 1996.

2 It is hereby directed that, subject to section 4(3) of the Trustee Investments Act 1961, any division of a trust fund made in pursuance of section 2(1) of that Act shall be made so that the value of the wider-range part at the time of the division bears to the then value of the narrower-range part the proportion of three to one.

[3213]

NOTES

Commencement: 11 May 1996.

LANDFILL TAX REGULATIONS 1996

(SI 1996/1527)

NOTES

Made: 12 June 1996.
Authority: Finance Act 1996, ss 47(9), 48(1), (2), 49, 51(1)–(6), 52(1)–(3), 53(1)–(4), 58(1), (4)–(6), 61(2), 62(1)–(3), (5), (6), 68(1)–(6), Sch 5, paras 2(1)–(3), 13(1), (6), 14(5), 20(3), 23(1), 42(1)–(5), 43(1)–(5).
Commencement: 1 August 1996.

ARRANGEMENT OF REGULATIONS

PART I
PRELIMINARY

PART II
REGISTRATION AND PROVISION FOR SPECIAL CASES

PART III
ACCOUNTING, PAYMENT AND RECORDS

PART I
PRELIMINARY

1 Citation and commencement

These Regulations may be cited as the Landfill Tax Regulations 1996 and shall come into force on 1st August 1996.

[3214]

NOTES

Commencement: 1 August 1996.

2 Interpretation

(1) In these Regulations—

"accounting period" means—

(a) in the case of a registered person, each period of three months ending on the dates notified to him by the Commissioners, whether by means of a registration certificate issued by them or otherwise;

(b) in the case of a registrable person who is not registered, each quarter; or

(c) in the case of any registrable person, such other period in relation to which he is required by or under regulation 11 to make a return;

and, in every case, the first accounting period of a registrable person shall begin on the effective date of registration;

"the Act" means the Finance Act 1996;

"Collector" means a Collector, Deputy Collector or Assistant Collector of Customs and Excise;

"credit", except where the context otherwise requires, means credit which a person is entitled to claim under Part IV of these Regulations;

"disposal" means a landfill disposal (which expression has the meaning given in section 70(2) of the Act) made on or after 1st October 1996 and "disposed of" shall be construed accordingly;

"effective date of registration" means the date determined in accordance with section 47 of the Act upon which the person was or should have been registered;

"landfill invoice" means an invoice of the description in regulation 37;

"landfill site" has the meaning given in section 66 of the Act;

"landfill tax account" has the meaning given in regulation 12;

"landfill tax bad debt account" has the meaning given in regulation 26;

"quarter" means a period of three months ending at the end of March, June, September or December;

"registered person" means a person who is registered under section 47 of the Act and "register" and "registration" shall be construed accordingly;

"registrable person" has the meaning given in section 47(10) of the Act;

"registration number" means the identifying number allocated to a registered person and notified to him by the Commissioners;

"return" means a return which is required to be made in accordance with regulation 11;

"taxable business" means a business or part of a business in the course of which taxable activities are carried out;

["transfer note" is a transfer note within the meaning of—

(a) the Environmental Protection (Duty of Care) Regulations 1991; or

(b) the Controlled Waste (Duty of Care) Regulations (Northern Ireland) 2002;]

"working day" means any day of the week except Saturday and Sunday and a bank holiday or public holiday, in either case, for England.

(2) In these Regulations any question whether a person is connected with another shall be determined in accordance with section 839 of the Taxes Act 1988.

(3) Any reference in these Regulations to "this Part" is a reference to the Part of these Regulations in which that reference is made.

(4) Any reference in these Regulations to a form prescribed in the Schedule to these Regulations shall include a reference to a form which the Commissioners are satisfied is a form to the like effect.

[3215]

NOTES

Commencement: 1 August 1996.

Para (1): definition "transfer note" substituted by the Landfill Tax (Amendment) Regulations 2004, SI 2004/769, reg 2.

3 Designation, direction or approval

Any designation, direction or approval by the Commissioners under or for the purposes of these Regulations shall be made or given by a notice in writing.

[3216]

NOTES

Commencement: 1 August 1996.

PART II
REGISTRATION AND PROVISION FOR SPECIAL CASES

4 Notification of liability to be registered

(1) A person who is required by section 47(3) of the Act to notify the Commissioners of his intention to carry out taxable activities shall do so on the form numbered 1 in the Schedule to these Regulations.

(2) Where the notification referred to in this regulation is made by a person who operates or intends to operate more than one landfill site, it shall include the particulars set out on the form numbered 2 in the Schedule to these Regulations.

(3) Where the notification referred to in this regulation is made by a partnership, it shall include the particulars set out on the form numbered 3 in the Schedule to these Regulations.

(4) The notification referred to in this regulation shall be made within 30 days of the earliest date after 1st August 1996 on which the person either forms or continues to have the intention to carry out taxable activities.

[3217]

NOTES

Commencement: 1 August 1996.

5 Changes in particulars

(1) A person who has made a notification under regulation 4, whether or not it was made in accordance with paragraph (4) of that regulation, shall, within 30 days of—

(a) discovering any inaccuracy in; or

(b) any change occurring which causes to become inaccurate,

any of the information which was contained in or provided with the notification, notify the Commissioners in writing and furnish them with full particulars.

(2) Without prejudice to paragraph (1) above, a registrable person shall, within 30 days of any change occurring in any of the circumstances referred to in paragraph (4) below, notify the Commissioners in writing and furnish them with particulars of—

(a) the change; and

(b) the date on which the change occurred.

(3) A registrable person who discovers that any information contained in or provided with a notification under paragraph (1) or (2) above was inaccurate shall, within 30 days of his discovering the inaccuracy, notify the Commissioners in writing and furnish them with particulars of—

(a) the inaccuracy;
(b) the date on which the inaccuracy was discovered;
(c) how the information was inaccurate; and
(d) the correct information.

(4) The circumstances mentioned in paragraph (2) above are the following circumstances relating to the registrable person or any taxable business carried on by him—
(a) his name, his trading name (if different), his address and the landfill sites he operates;
(b) his status, namely whether he carries on business as a sole proprietor, body corporate, partnership or other unincorporated body;
(c) in the case of a partnership, the name and address of any partner.

(5) Any person failing to comply with a requirement imposed in any of paragraphs (1) to (3) above shall be liable to a penalty of £250.

(6) Where in relation to a registered person the Commissioners are satisfied that any of the information recorded in the register is or has become inaccurate they may correct the register accordingly.

(7) For the purposes of paragraph (6) above, it is immaterial whether or not the registered person has notified the Commissioners of any change which has occurred in accordance with paragraphs (1) to (3) above.

[3218]

NOTES
Commencement: 1 August 1996.

6 Notification of cessation of taxable activities

A person who is required by section 47(4) of the Act to notify the Commissioners of his having ceased to have the intention to carry out taxable activities shall, within 30 days of his so having ceased, notify the Commissioners in writing and shall therein inform them of—
(a) the date on which he ceased to have the intention of carrying out taxable activities; and
(b) if different, the date on which he ceased to carry out taxable activities.

[3219]

NOTES
Commencement: 1 August 1996.

7 Transfer of a going concern

(1) Where—
(a) a taxable business is transferred as a going concern;
(b) the registration of the transferor has not already been cancelled;
(c) as a result of the transfer of the business the registration of the transferor is to be cancelled and the transferee has become liable to be registered; and
(d) an application is made on the form numbered 4 in the Schedule to these Regulations by both the transferor and the transferee,

the Commissioners may with effect from the date of the transfer cancel the registration of the transferor and register the transferee with the registration number previously allocated to the transferor.

(2) An application under paragraph (1) above shall be treated as the notification referred to in regulation 6.

(3) Where the transferee of a business has been registered under paragraph (1) above with the registration number previously allocated to the transferor—
(a) any liability of the transferor existing at the date of the transfer to make a return or account for or pay any tax under Part III of these Regulations shall become the liability of the transferee;
(b) any entitlement of the transferor, whether or not existing at the date of the transfer, to credit or payment under Part IV of these Regulations shall become the entitlement of the transferee.

PART II STATUTORY INSTRUMENTS

(4) In addition to the provisions set out in paragraph (3) above, where the transferee of a business has been registered under paragraph (1) above with the registration number previously allocated to the transferor during an accounting period subsequent to that in which the transfer took place (but with effect from the date of the transfer) and any—

(a) return has been made;
(b) tax has been accounted for; or
(c) entitlement to credit has been claimed,

by either the transferor or the transferee, it shall be treated as having been done by the transferee.

(5) Where—

(a) a taxable business is transferred as a going concern;
(b) the transferee removes material as described in regulation 21(2) or (4); and
(c) the transferor has paid tax on the disposal concerned,

then, whether or not the transferee has been registered under paragraph (1) above with the registration number previously allocated to the transferor, any entitlement to credit arising under Part V of these Regulations shall become the entitlement of the transferee.

[3220]

NOTES

Commencement: 1 August 1996.

8 Representation of unincorporated body

(1) Where anything is required to be done by or under the Act (whether by these Regulations or otherwise) by or on behalf of an unincorporated body other than a partnership, it shall be the joint and several responsibility of—

(a) every member holding office as president, chairman, treasurer, secretary or any similar office; or
(b) if there is no such office, every member holding office as a member of a committee by which the affairs of the body are managed; or
(c) if there is no such office or committee, every member;

but, subject to paragraph (2) below, if it is done by any of the persons referred to above that shall be sufficient compliance with any such requirement.

(2) Where an unincorporated body other than a partnership is required to make any notification such as is referred to in regulations 4 to 6, it shall not be sufficient compliance unless the notification is made by a person upon whom a responsibility for making it is imposed by paragraph (1) above.

(3) Where anything is required to be done by or under the Act (whether by these Regulations or otherwise) by or on behalf of a partnership, it shall be the joint and several responsibility of every partner; but if it is done by one partner or, in the case of a partnership whose principal place of business is in Scotland, by any other person authorised by the partnership with respect thereto that shall be sufficient compliance with any such requirement.

[3221]

NOTES

Commencement: 1 August 1996.

9 Bankruptcy or incapacity of registrable persons

(1) If a registrable person becomes bankrupt or incapacitated, the Commissioners may, from the date on which he became bankrupt or incapacitated, as the case may be, treat as a registrable person any person carrying on any taxable business of his; and any legislation relating to landfill tax shall apply to any person so treated as though he were a registered person.

(2) Any person carrying on such business as aforesaid shall, within 30 days of commencing to do so, inform the Commissioners in writing of that fact and the date of the bankruptcy order or of the nature of the incapacity and the date on which it began.

(3) Where the Commissioners have treated a person carrying on a business as a registrable person under paragraph (1) above, they shall cease so to treat him if—

(a) the registration of the registrable person is cancelled, whether or not any other person is registered with the registration number previously allocated to him;

(b) the bankruptcy is discharged or the incapacity ceases; or
(c) he ceases carrying on the business of the registrable person.

(4) In relation to a registrable person which is a company, the references in this regulation to the registrable person becoming incapacitated shall be construed as references to its going into liquidation or receivership or [entering administration]; and references to the incapacity ceasing shall be construed accordingly.

[3222]

NOTES

Commencement: 1 August 1996.
Para (4): words in square brackets substituted by the Enterprise Act 2002 (Insolvency) Order 2003, SI 2003/2096, art 5, Schedule, Pt 2, paras 65, 66.

PART III
ACCOUNTING, PAYMENT AND RECORDS

10 Interpretation

In this Part, "accounting period" has the meaning given in regulation 2(1).

[3223]

NOTES

Commencement: 1 August 1996.

11 Making of returns

(1) Subject to paragraph (3) below and save as the Commissioners may otherwise allow, a registrable person shall, in respect of each accounting period, make a return to the Controller, Central Collection Unit (LT), on the form numbered 5 in the Schedule to these Regulations.

(2) Subject to paragraph (3) below, a registrable person shall make each return not later than the last working day of the month next following the end of the period to which it relates.

(3) Where the Commissioners consider it necessary in the circumstances of any particular case, they may—
(a) vary the length of any accounting period or the date on which it begins or ends or by which any return must be made;
(b) allow or direct the registrable person to make a return in accordance with sub-paragraph (a) above;
(c) allow or direct a registrable person to make returns to a specified address,

and any person to whom the Commissioners give any direction such as is referred to in this regulation shall comply therewith.

[3224]

NOTES

Commencement: 1 August 1996.

12 Landfill tax account

(1) Every registrable person shall make and maintain an account to be known as "the landfill tax account".

(2) The landfill tax account shall be in such form and contain such particulars as may be stipulated in a notice published by the Commissioners and not withdrawn by a further notice.

[3225]

NOTES

Commencement: 1 August 1996.

13 Correction of errors

(1) In this regulation—

PART II STATUTORY INSTRUMENTS

"overdeclaration" means, in relation to any return, the amount (if any) which was wrongly treated as tax due for the accounting period concerned and which caused the amount of tax which was payable to be overstated, or the entitlement to a payment under regulation 20 to be understated (or both) or would have caused such an overstatement or understatement were it not for the existence of an underdeclaration in relation to that return;

"underdeclaration" means, in relation to any return, the aggregate of—

(a) the amount (if any) of tax due for the accounting period concerned which was not taken into account; and

(b) the amount (if any) which was wrongly deducted as credit,

and which caused the amount of tax which was payable to be understated, or the entitlement to a payment under regulation 20 to be overstated (or both) or would have caused such an understatement or overstatement were it not for the existence of an overdeclaration in relation to that return.

(2) This regulation applies where a registrable person has made a return which was inaccurate as the result of an overdeclaration or underdeclaration.

(3) Where in any accounting period a registrable person has discovered one or more overdeclarations, he may enter the overdeclarations in the return for the accounting period in which they were discovered by including their amount in the box opposite the legend "Overdeclarations from previous periods (no limit)".

(4) Where in any accounting period—

(a) a registrable person discovers one or more underdeclarations; and

(b) having treated the amount of those underdeclarations as reduced by the amount of any overdeclarations for the same accounting periods, the total of those underdeclarations does not exceed £2,000,

he may enter the underdeclarations in his return for the accounting period in which they were discovered by including their amount in the box opposite the legend "Underdeclarations from previous periods (must not exceed £2,000, see general notes)".

(5) Where a registrable person enters an amount in a return in accordance with paragraph (3) or (4) above he shall calculate the tax payable by him or the payment to which he is entitled accordingly.

(6) Where an amount has been entered in accordance with this regulation in a return which has been made—

(a) the return shall be regarded as correcting any earlier return to which that amount relates; and

(b) the registrable person shall be taken to have furnished information with respect to the inaccuracy in the prescribed form and manner for the purposes of paragraph 20 of Schedule 5 to the Act.

(7) No amount shall be entered in a return in respect of any overdeclaration or underdeclaration except in accordance with this regulation; and as regards any underdeclaration that cannot be corrected under paragraph (4) above a person shall not be taken to have furnished information with respect to an inaccuracy in the prescribed form and manner for the purposes of paragraph 20 of Schedule 5 to the Act unless he provides such information to the Commissioners in writing.

[3226]

NOTES

Commencement: 1 August 1996.

14 Claims for overpaid tax

Except where the amount to which the claim relates has been entered in a return in accordance with regulation 13 or is included in an amount so entered, any claim under paragraph 14 of Schedule 5 to the Act shall be made in writing to the Commissioners and shall, by reference to such documentary evidence as is in the possession of the claimant, state the amount of the claim and the method by which that amount was calculated.

[3227]

NOTES

Commencement: 1 August 1996.

[14A Interpretation of regulations 14A to 14H

In this regulation and in regulations 14B to 14H below—

"claim" means a claim made (irrespective of when it was made) under paragraph 14 of Schedule 5 to the Act for repayment of an amount paid to the Commissioners by way of tax which was not tax due to them; and "claimed" and "claimant" shall be construed accordingly;

"reimbursement arrangements" means any arrangements (whether made before, on or after 30th January 1998) for the purposes of a claim which—

(a) are made by a claimant for the purpose of securing that he is not unjustly enriched by the repayment of any amount in pursuance of the claim; and

(b) provide for the reimbursement of persons (consumers) who have, for practical purposes, borne the whole or any part of the cost of the original payment of that amount to the Commissioners;

"relevant amount" means that part (which may be the whole) of the amount of a claim which the claimant has reimbursed or intends to reimburse to consumers.]

[3228]

NOTES

Commencement: 11 February 1998.

Inserted, together with regs 14B–14H, by the Landfill Tax (Amendment) Regulations 1998, SI 1998/61, reg 2.

[14B Reimbursement arrangements—general

Without prejudice to regulation 14H below, for the purposes of paragraph 14(3) of Schedule 5 to the Act (defence by the Commissioners that repayment by them of an amount claimed would unjustly enrich the claimant) reimbursement arrangements made by a claimant shall be disregarded except where they—

(a) include the provisions described in regulation 14C below; and

(b) are supported by the undertakings described in regulation 14G below.]

[3229]

NOTES

Commencement: 11 February 1998.

Inserted as noted to reg 14A at **[3228]**.

[14C Reimbursement arrangements—provisions to be included

The provisions referred to in regulation 14B(a) above are that—

(a) reimbursement for which the arrangements provide will be completed by no later than 90 days after the repayment to which it relates;

(b) no deduction will be made from the relevant amount by way of fee or charge (howsoever expressed or effected);

(c) reimbursement will be made only in cash or by cheque;

(d) any part of the relevant amount that is not reimbursed by the time mentioned in paragraph (a) above will be repaid by the claimant to the Commissioners;

(e) any interest paid by the Commissioners on any relevant amount repaid by them will also be treated by the claimant in the same way as the relevant amount falls to be treated under paragraphs (a) and (b) above; and

(f) the records described in regulation 14E below will be kept by the claimant and produced by him to the Commissioners, or to an officer of theirs in accordance with regulation 14F below.]

[3230]

NOTES

Commencement: 11 February 1998.

Inserted as noted to reg 14A at **[3228]**.

[14D Repayments to the Commissioners

The claimant shall, without prior demand, make any repayment to the Commissioners that he is required to make by virtue of regulation 14C(d) and (e) above within 14 days of the expiration of the period of 90 days referred to in regulation 14C(a) above.]

[3231]

NOTES

Commencement: 11 February 1998.
Inserted as noted to reg 14A at **[3228]**.

[14E Records

The claimant shall keep records of the following matters—

(a) the names and addresses of those consumers whom he has reimbursed or whom he intends to reimburse;

(b) the total amount reimbursed to each such consumer;

(c) the amount of interest included in each total amount reimbursed to each consumer;

(d) the date that each reimbursement is made.]

[3232]

NOTES

Commencement: 11 February 1998.
Inserted as noted to reg 14A at **[3228]**.

[14F Production of records

(1) Where a claimant is given notice in accordance with paragraph (2) below, he shall, in accordance with such notice produce to the Commissioners, or to an officer of theirs, the records that he is required to keep pursuant to regulation 14E above.

(2) A notice given for the purposes of paragraph (1) above shall—

(a) be in writing;

(b) state the place and time at which, and the date on which the records are to be produced; and

(c) be signed and dated by the Commissioners, or by an officer of theirs,

and may be given before or after, or both before and after the Commissioners have paid the relevant amount to the claimant.]

[3233]

NOTES

Commencement: 11 February 1998.
Inserted as noted to reg 14A at **[3228]**.

[14G Undertakings

(1) Without prejudice to regulation 14H(b) below, the undertakings referred to in regulation 14B(b) above shall be given to the Commissioners by the claimant no later than the time at which he makes the claim for which the reimbursement arrangements have been made.

(2) The undertakings shall be in writing, shall be signed and dated by the claimant, and shall be to the effect that—

(a) at the date of the undertakings he is able to identify the names and addresses of those consumers whom he has reimbursed or whom he intends to reimburse;

(b) he will apply the whole of the relevant amount repaid to him, without any deduction by way of fee or charge or otherwise, to the reimbursement in cash or by cheque, of such consumers by no later than 90 days after his receipt of that amount (except insofar as he has already so reimbursed them);

(c) he will apply any interest paid to him on the relevant amount repaid to him wholly to the reimbursement of such consumers by no later than 90 days after his receipt of that interest;

(d) he will repay to the Commissioners without demand the whole or such part of the relevant amount repaid to him or of any interest paid to him as he fails to apply in accordance with the undertakings mentioned in sub-paragraphs (b) and (c) above;

(e) he will keep the records described in regulation 14E above; and

(f) he will comply with any notice given to him in accordance with regulation 14F above concerning the production of such records.]

[3234]

NOTES

Commencement: 11 February 1998.
Inserted as noted to reg 14A at **[3228]**.

[14H Reimbursement arrangements made before 11th February 1998

Reimbursement arrangements made by a claimant before 11th February 1998 shall not be disregarded for the purposes of paragraph 14(3) of Schedule 5 to the Act if, not later than 11th March 1998—

(a) he includes in those arrangements (if they are not already included) the provisions described in regulation 14C above; and
(b) gives the undertakings described in regulation 14G above.]

[3235]

NOTES

Commencement: 11 February 1998.
Inserted as noted to reg 14A at **[3228]**.

15 Payment of tax

Save as the Commissioners may otherwise allow or direct, any person required to make a return shall pay to the Controller, Central Collection Unit (LT), such amount of tax as is payable by him in respect of the accounting period to which the return relates no later than the last day on which he was required to make the return.

[3236]

NOTES

Commencement: 1 August 1996.

16 Records

(1) Every registrable person shall, for the purpose of accounting for tax, preserve the following—

(a) his business and accounting records;
(b) his landfill tax account;
(c) transfer notes and any other original or copy records in relation to material brought onto or removed from the landfill site (including any record made for the purpose of Part IX of these Regulations);
(d) all invoices (including landfill invoices) and similar documents issued to him and copies of such invoices and similar documents issued by him;
(e) all credit or debit notes or other documents received by him which evidence an increase or decrease in the amount of any consideration for a relevant transaction, and copies of such documents that are issued by him;
(f) such other records as the Commissioners may specify in a notice published by them and not withdrawn by a further notice.

(2) Subject to paragraphs (3) and (4) below, every registrable person shall preserve the records specified in paragraph (1) above for a period of six years.

(3) Subject to paragraph (4) below, a registrable person who has made a landfill tax bad debt account shall preserve that account for a period of five years from the date of the claim made under Part VI of these Regulations.

(4) The Commissioners may direct that registrable persons shall preserve the records specified in paragraph (1) above for a shorter period than that specified in this regulation; and such direction may be made so as to apply generally or in such cases as the Commissioners may stipulate.

(5) In paragraph (1) above—

(a) the reference to material being brought onto a landfill site is a reference to material that is brought onto the site for the purpose of a relevant transaction;
(b) the reference to material being removed from a landfill site is a reference to material being removed that has at some previous time fallen wholly or partly within paragraph (a) above.

(6) In this regulation "relevant transaction" means a disposal or anything that would be a disposal but for the fact that the material is not disposed of as waste.

[3237]

NOTES

Commencement: 1 August 1996.

PART IV
CREDIT: GENERAL

17 Interpretation

In this Part—

"relevant accounting period" means—

(a) in the case of an entitlement to credit arising under Part V of these Regulations, the accounting period in which the reuse condition or, as the case may be, the enforced removal condition was satisfied;

(b) in the case of an entitlement to credit arising under Part VI of these Regulations, the accounting period in which the period of one year from the date of the issue of the landfill invoice expired;

(c) in the case of an entitlement arising under Part VII of these Regulations, the accounting period in which the qualifying contribution was made;

"relevant amount" means the amount of the credit as determined in accordance with Part V, VI or VII of these Regulations, as the case may be;

"relevant tax" means the tax, if any, that was required to have been paid as a condition of the entitlement to credit.

[3238]

NOTES

Commencement: 1 August 1996.

18 Scope

(1) This Part applies to entitlements to credit arising under Part V, VI or VII of these Regulations.

(2) No credit arising under any provision of these Regulations may be claimed except in accordance with this Part.

[3239]

NOTES

Commencement: 1 August 1996.

19 Claims in returns

(1) Subject to paragraphs (2) and (3) below, a person entitled to credit may claim it by deducting its amount from any tax due from him for the relevant accounting period or any subsequent accounting period and, where he does so, he shall make his return for that accounting period accordingly.

(2) Where the entitlement to credit arises under Part VII of these Regulations paragraph (1) above shall apply as if there were substituted for "or any subsequent accounting period" the words "or any subsequent accounting period in the same contribution year as determined in relation to that person under regulation 31".

(3) The Commissioners may make directions generally or with regard to particular cases prescribing rules in accordance with which credit may or shall be held over to be credited in an accounting period subsequent to the relevant accounting period; and where such a direction has been made that credit, subject to any subsequent such direction varying or withdrawing the rules, may only be claimed in accordance with those rules.

[3240]

NOTES

Commencement: 1 August 1996.

20 Payments in respect of credit

(1) Subject to paragraph (5) below, where the total credit claimed by a registrable person in accordance with this Part exceeds the total of the tax due from him for the accounting period, the Commissioners shall pay to him an amount equal to the excess.

(2) Where the Commissioners have cancelled the registration of a person in accordance with section 47(6) of the Act, and he is not a registrable person, he shall make any claim in respect of credit to which this Part applies by making an application in writing.

(3) A person making an application under paragraph (2) above shall furnish to the Commissioners full particulars in relation to the credit claimed, including (but not restricted to)—

(a) except in the case of an entitlement to credit arising under Part VII of these Regulations, the return in which the relevant tax was accounted for;

(b) except in the case of an entitlement to credit arising under Part VII of these Regulations, the amount of the tax and the date and manner of its payment;

(c) the events by virtue of which the entitlement to credit arose.

(4) Subject to paragraph (5) below, where the Commissioners are satisfied that a person who has made a claim in accordance with paragraphs (2) and (3) above is entitled to credit, and that he has not previously had the benefit of that credit, they shall pay to him an amount equal to the credit.

(5) The Commissioners shall not be liable to make any payment under this regulation unless and until the person has made all the returns which he was required to make.

[3241]

NOTES

Commencement: 1 August 1996.

PART V

CREDIT: PERMANENT REMOVALS ETC

21 Entitlement to credit

(1) An entitlement to credit arises under this Part where—

(a) a registered person has accounted for an amount of tax and, except where the removal by virtue of which sub-paragraph (b) below is satisfied takes place in the accounting period in which credit arising under this Part is claimed in accordance with Part IV of these Regulations, he has paid that tax; and

(b) in relation to the disposal on which that tax was charged, either—

(i) the reuse condition has been satisfied; or

(ii) the enforced removal condition has been satisfied.

(2) The reuse condition is satisfied where—

(a) the disposal has been made with the intention that the material comprised in it—

(i) would be recycled or incinerated, or

(ii) removed for use (other than by way of a further disposal) at a place other than a relevant site;

(b) that material, or some of it, has been recycled, incinerated or permanently removed from the landfill site, as the case may be, in accordance with that intention;

(c) that recycling, incineration or removal—

(i) has taken place no later than one year after the date of the disposal; or

(ii) where water had been added to the material in order to facilitate its disposal, has taken place no later than five years after the date of the disposal; and

(d) the registered person has, before the disposal, notified the Commissioners in writing that he intends to make one or more removals of material in relation to which sub-paragraphs (a) to (c) above will be satisfied.

(3) For the purpose of paragraph (2)(a)(ii) above a relevant site is the landfill site at which the disposal was made or any other landfill site.

(4) The enforced removal condition is satisfied where—

(a) the disposal is in breach of the terms of the licence[, resolution or permit], as the case may be, by virtue of which the land constitutes a landfill site;
(b) the registered person has been directed to remove the material comprised in the disposal, or some of it, by a relevant authority and he has removed it, or some of it; and
(c) a further taxable disposal of the material has been made and, except where the registered person is the person liable for the tax chargeable on that further disposal, he has paid to the site operator an amount representing that tax.

(5) For the purpose of paragraph (4)(b) above the following are relevant authorities—
(a) the Environment Agency;
(b) the Scottish Environment Protection Agency;
(c) the Department of the Environment for Northern Ireland;
(d) a district council in Northern Ireland.

(6) The amount of the credit arising under this Part shall be equal to the tax that was charged on the disposal; except that where only some of the material comprised in that disposal is removed, the amount of the credit shall be such proportion of that tax as the material removed forms of the total of the material.

[3242]

NOTES

Commencement: 1 August 1996.
Para (4): in para (a) words in square brackets substituted by the Landfill Tax (Amendment) Regulations 2005, SI 2005/759, regs 2, 3.

PART VI
CREDIT: BAD DEBTS

22 Interpretation

In this Part—

"claim" means a claim in accordance with Part IV of these Regulations for an amount of credit arising under this Part and "claimant" shall be construed accordingly;
"customer" means a person for whom a taxable activity is carried out by the claimant;
"outstanding amount" means, in relation to any claim—
(a) if at the time of the claim the claimant has received no payment in respect of the amount written off in his accounts, the amount so written off; or
(b) if at that time he has received a payment, the amount by which the amount written off exceeds the payment (or the aggregate of the payments);
"relevant disposal" means any taxable disposal upon which a claim is based;
"security" means—
(a) in relation to England, Wales and Northern Ireland, any mortgage, charge, lien or other security; and
(b) in relation to Scotland, any security (whether heritable or moveable), any floating charge and any right of lien or preference and right of retention (other than a right of compensation or set-off).

[3243]

NOTES

Commencement: 1 August 1996.

23 Scope

An entitlement to credit arises under this Part where—
(a) a registered person has carried out a taxable activity for a consideration in money for a customer with whom he is not connected;
(b) he has accounted for and paid tax on the disposal concerned;
(c) the whole or any part of the consideration for the disposal has been written off in his accounts as a bad debt;
(d) he has issued a landfill invoice in respect of the disposal which shows the amount of tax chargeable;
(e) that invoice was issued—
(i) within 14 days of the date of the disposal, or

(ii) within such other period as may have been specified in a direction of the Commissioners made under section 61(3) of the Act;

(f) a period of one year (beginning with the date of the issue of that invoice) has elapsed; and

(g) the following provisions of this Part have been complied with.

[3244]

NOTES

Commencement: 1 August 1996.

24 Amount of credit

The credit arising under this Part shall be of an amount equal to such proportion of the tax charged on the relevant disposal as the outstanding amount forms of the total consideration.

[3245]

NOTES

Commencement: 1 August 1996.

25 Evidence required in support of claim

The claimant, before he makes a claim, shall hold in respect of each relevant disposal—

(a) a copy of the landfill invoice issued by him;

(b) records or any other documents showing that he has accounted for and paid tax on the disposal; and

(c) records or any other documents showing that the consideration has been written off in his accounts as a bad debt.

[3246]

NOTES

Commencement: 1 August 1996.

26 Records required to be kept

(1) Any person who makes a claim shall make a record of that claim.

(2) The record referred to in paragraph (1) above shall contain the following information in respect of each claim made:

(a) in respect of each relevant disposal—

(i) the amount of tax charged;

(ii) the return in which that tax was accounted for and when it was paid;

(iii) the date and identifying number of the landfill invoice that was issued;

(iv) any consideration that has been received (whether before the claim was made or subsequently);

(v) the details of any transfer note;

(b) the outstanding amount;

(c) the amount of the claim;

(d) the return in which the claim was made.

(3) Any records made in pursuance of this regulation shall be kept in a single account known as "the landfill tax bad debt account".

[3247]

NOTES

Commencement: 1 August 1996.

27 Attribution of payments

(1) Where—

(a) the claimant has carried out a taxable activity for a customer;

(b) there exist one or more other matters in respect of which the claimant is entitled to a debt owed by the customer (whether they involve a taxable disposal or not and whether they are connected with waste or not); and

(c) a payment has been received by the claimant from the customer,

the payment shall be attributed to the taxable activity and the other matters in accordance with the rule set out in paragraphs (2) and (3) below (and the debts arising in respect of the taxable activity and the other matters are collectively referred to in those paragraphs as debts).

(2) The payment shall be attributed to the debt which arose earliest and, if not wholly attributed to that debt, thereafter to debts in the order of the dates on which they arose, except that attribution under this paragraph shall not be made if the payment was allocated to a debt by the customer at the time of payment and the debt was paid in full.

(3) Where—

(a) the earliest debt and the other debts to which the whole of the payment could be attributed arose on the same day; or

(b) the debts to which the balance of the payment could be attributed in accordance with paragraph (2) above arose on the same day,

the payment shall be attributed to those debts by multiplying, for each such debt, the payment made by a fraction of which the numerator is the amount remaining unpaid in respect of that debt and the denominator is the amount remaining unpaid in respect of all those debts.

[3248]

NOTES

Commencement: 1 August 1996.

28 Repayment of credit

(1) Where a claimant—

(a) has benefited from an amount of credit to which he was entitled under this Part; and

(b) either—

(i) a payment for the relevant disposal is subsequently received; or

(ii) a payment is, by virtue of regulation 27, treated as attributed to the relevant disposal,

he shall repay to the Commissioners such amount as equals the amount of the credit, or the balance thereof, multiplied by a fraction of which the numerator is the amount so received or attributed, and the denominator is the amount of the outstanding consideration,

(2) Where the claimant—

(a) fails to comply with the requirements of regulation 26; or

(b) in relation to the documents mentioned in that regulation, fails to comply with either—

(i) regulation 16; or

(ii) any obligation arising under paragraph 3 of Schedule 5 to the Act,

he shall repay to the Commissioners the amount of the claim to which the failure to comply relates.

[3249]

NOTES

Commencement: 1 August 1996.

29 Writing off debts

(1) This regulation shall apply for the purpose of determining whether, and to what extent, the consideration is to be taken to have been written off as a bad debt.

(2) The whole or any part of the consideration for a taxable activity shall be taken to have been written off as a bad debt where—

(a) the claimant has written it off in his accounts as a bad debt; and

(b) he has made an entry in relation to that activity in the landfill tax bad debt account in accordance with regulation 26 (and this shall apply regardless of whether a claim can be made in relation to that activity at that time).

(3) Where the claimant owes an amount of money to the customer which can be set off, the consideration written off in the landfill tax bad debt account shall be reduced by the amount so owed.

(4) Where the claimant holds in relation to the customer an enforceable security, the consideration written off in the landfill tax bad debt account shall be reduced by the value of the security.

[3250]

NOTES

Commencement: 1 August 1996.

PART VII

CREDIT: BODIES CONCERNED WITH THE ENVIRONMENT

30 Interpretation and general provisions

(1) In this Part—

"approved body" means a body approved for the time being under regulation 34;

"approved object" has the meaning given in regulation 33;

["contributing third party" means a person who has made or agreed to make (whether or not under a legally binding agreement) a payment to a registered person to secure the making by him of a qualifying contribution or to reimburse him, in whole or in part, for any such contribution he has made;]

"income" includes interest;

"qualifying contribution" has the meaning given in regulation 32;

"the regulatory body" means such body, if any, as in relation to which an approval of the Commissioners under regulation 35 has effect for the time being;

"running costs" includes any cost incurred in connection with the management and administration of a body or its assets.

(2) A body shall only be taken to spend a qualifying contribution in the course or furtherance of its approved objects—

(a) in a case where the contribution is made subject to a condition that it may only be invested for the purpose of generating income, where the body so spends all of that income;

(b) in a case not falling within sub-paragraph (a) above, where the body becomes entitled to income, where it so spends both the whole of the qualifying contribution and all of that income;

(c) in a case not falling within either of sub-paragraphs (a) and (b) above, where the body so spends the whole of the qualifying contribution; or

(d) where—

(i) it transfers any qualifying contribution or income derived therefrom to another approved body, and

(ii) that transfer is subject to a condition that the sum transferred shall be spent only in the course or furtherance of that other body's approved objects.

(3) Any approval, or revocation of such approval, by the Commissioners or the regulatory body shall be given by notice in writing to the body affected and shall take effect from the date the notice is given or such later date as the Commissioners or, as the case may be, the regulatory body may specify in it.

[3251]

NOTES

Commencement: 1 August 1996.

Para (1): definition "contributing third party" inserted by the Landfill Tax (Amendment) Regulations 1999, SI 1999/3270, regs 2, 3.

31 Entitlement to credit

(1) Subject to the following provisions of this regulation, an entitlement to credit arises under this Part in respect of qualifying contributions made by registered persons.

(2) Subject to paragraph (3) below, a person shall be entitled to credit in respect of 90 per cent of the amount of each qualifying contribution made by him in any accounting period; and for this purpose a qualifying contribution made—

[(a) in one accounting period;]

(b) before the return for the previous accounting period has been made; and

(c) before the period within which that return is required to be made has expired, shall be treated as having been made in the accounting period mentioned in sub-paragraph (b) above (and not in the accounting period in which it was in fact made).

(3) In respect of the qualifying contributions made in each contribution year, a person shall not be entitled to credit of an amount greater than [6.7] per cent of his relevant tax liability.

[(4) For the purpose of paragraphs (2) and (3) the contribution year of a person is his first contribution year and then each period of 12 months beginning on 1st April.

(5) The reference in paragraph (4) to the first contribution year of a person is a reference to the period beginning with his effective date of registration and ending on the day immediately preceding the first day of the next contribution year.

(6) Where one contribution year ends and another contribution year begins in an accounting period, the amount of any qualifying contribution which, by virtue of paragraph (2), is treated as made in that period shall be apportioned, in accordance with paragraph (6A), between those contribution years.]

[[(6A) The apportionment shall be on the basis of either—

(a) the number of days of the accounting period that fall before 1st April and the number of days that fall on and after that day; or

(b) the amount of tax charged on taxable disposals made in the accounting period before 1st April and the amount of tax charged on taxable disposals made in that period on and after that day,

whichever the registered person may choose.]

(6B) …

(6C) …

(6D) …

(6E) …]

(7) Subject to [paragraph (10)] below, the reference in paragraph (3) above to the relevant tax liability of a person is a reference to the aggregate of—

(a) the tax payable by him, if any, in respect of the accounting period in relation to which that liability falls to be determined; and

(b) the tax payable by him, if any, in respect of any earlier accounting period or periods which fall within the same contribution year as that accounting period;

and where in respect of any accounting period he is entitled to a payment under regulation 20 the aggregate of the tax payable by him in respect of the accounting periods mentioned in sub-paragraphs (a) and (b) above shall be reduced by the amount of that payment.

(8) …

(9) …

(10) For the purposes of [paragraph (7)] above any entitlement to credit arising under this Part shall be disregarded in determining the tax payable by a person in respect of any period.

[3252]

NOTES

Commencement: 1 January 2000 (paras 6A)–(6E)); 1 August 1996 (remainder).

Paras (2): sub-para (a) substituted by the Landfill Tax (Amendment) Regulations 1999, SI 1999/3270, regs 2, 4(a).

Para (3): reference in square brackets substituted by the Landfill Tax (Amendment) Regulations 2006, SI 2006/865, reg 2.

Paras (4)–(6): substituted by the Landfill Tax (Amendment) Regulations 2003, SI 2003/605, regs 2, 3(b)–(d).

Paras (6A)–(6E): inserted by SI 1999/3270, regs 2, 4(d).

Para (6A): substituted by SI 2003/605, regs 2, 3(d).

Paras (6B)–(6E): revoked by SI 2003/605, regs 2, 3(e).

Para (7): words in square brackets substituted by SI 1999/3270, regs 2, 4(e).

Paras (8), (9): revoked by SI 1999/3270, regs 2, 4(f).

Para (10): words in square brackets substituted by SI 1999/3270, regs 2, 4(g).

32 Qualifying contributions

(1) A payment is a qualifying contribution if—

(a) it is made by a registered person to an approved body;

(b) it is made subject to a condition that the body shall spend the sum paid or any income derived from it or both only in the course or furtherance of its approved objects;

(c) the requirements of [paragraphs (2) to (2B)] below have been complied with in relation to that payment; and

(d) it is not repaid to him[, or a contributing third party,] in the same accounting period as that in which it was made.

(2) A person claiming credit arising under this Part shall make a record containing the following information—

(a) the amount and date of each payment he has made to an approved body;

(b) the name and enrolment number of that body;

[(c) the name and address of any contributing third party; and

(d) the amount of the payment made or to be made by the contributing third party and the date, or as the case may require, dates on which payment of the whole or any part of that amount—

(i) was received, or

(ii) is expected to be received.]

[(2A) A person claiming credit under this Part for a contribution in relation to which there is a contributing third party shall have provided to the regulatory body or, if they are performing the functions specified in regulation 34(1) below, to the Commissioners the following information—

(a) the name and address of the contributing third party;

(b) the amount of the payment made or to be made by the contributing third party and the date, or as the case may require, dates on which payment of the whole or any part of that amount—

(i) was received, or

(ii) is expected to be received;

(c) the enrolment number of the approved body to whom the contribution was made.

(2B) A person claiming credit under this Part for a contribution in relation to which there is a contributing third party shall have informed the approved body to which the contribution is made of the name and address of the contributing third party.]

[(3) For the purposes of this Part where any qualifying contribution or income derived therefrom is transferred to a body as described in regulation 30(2)(d)—

(a) the body to whom the sum is transferred shall be treated as having received qualifying contributions of the amount concerned; and

(b) that body shall be treated as having received those qualifying contributions from the registered person or persons who originally paid them (but this shall not give rise to any further entitlement to credit in respect of those contributions).]

[3253]

NOTES

Commencement: 1 January 2000 (paras (2A), (2B), (3)); 1 August 1996 (remainder).

Para (1): in sub-para (c) words in square brackets substituted, and in sub-para (d) words in square brackets inserted, by the Landfill Tax (Amendment) Regulations 1999, SI 1999/3270, regs 2, 5(a), (b).

Para (2): sub-paras (c), (d) inserted by SI 1999/3270, regs 2, 5(c).

Paras (2A), (2B): inserted by SI 1999/3270, regs 2, 5(d).

Para (3): substituted by SI 1999/3270, regs 2, 5(e).

33 Bodies eligible for approval

(1) [A body is eligible to be approved if—]

(a) it is—

(i) a body corporate, or

(ii) a trust, partnership or other unincorporated body;

(b) its objects are or include any of the objects within paragraph (2) below (approved objects);

(c) it is precluded from distributing and does not distribute any profit it makes or other income it receives;

(d) it applies any profit or other income to the furtherance of its objects (whether or not approved objects);

[(e) it is precluded from applying any of its funds for the benefit of any of the persons—

(i) who have made qualifying contributions to it, or

(ii) who were a contributing third party in relation to such contributions,

except that such persons may benefit where they belong to a class of persons that benefits generally;] …

[(f) it is not controlled by one or more of the persons and bodies listed in paragraphs (1A) and (1B) below;

(g) none of the persons or bodies listed in paragraph (1B) below is concerned in its management; and

(h) it pays to the regulatory body an application fee of £100 or such lesser sum as the regulatory body may require.]

[(1A) The persons and bodies mentioned in paragraph (1)(f) above are:

(a) a local authority;

(b) a body corporate controlled by one or more local authorities;

(c) a registered person;

(d) a person connected with any of the persons or bodies mentioned in sub-paragraphs (a) to (c) above.

(1B) The persons and bodies mentioned in paragraph 1(f) and (g) above are:

(a) a person who controlled or was concerned in the management of a body the approval of which was revoked otherwise than under regulation 34(1)(ee);

(b) a person who has been convicted of an indictable offence;

(c) a person who is disqualified for being a charity trustee or a trustee for a charity by virtue of section 72 of the Charities Act 1993;

(d) a person connected with any of the persons or bodies mentioned in sub-paragraphs (a) to (c) above;

(e) a person who is incapable by reason of mental disorder.

(1C) For the purpose of paragraph (1B)(e) above, a person shall be treated as incapable by reason of mental disorder where—

(a) in England and Wales, the judge has exercised any of his functions under Part VII of the Mental Health Act 1983;

(b) in Scotland, the court has appointed a curator bonis, tutor or judicial factor; or

(c) in Northern Ireland, the court has exercised any of its powers under Part VIII of the Mental Health (Northern Ireland) Order 1986 (whether or not by virtue of Article 97(2) of that Order),

but shall cease to be so treated where the judge or court concerned has made a finding that he is not or is no longer incapable of managing and administering his property and affairs.]

(2) The objects of a body are approved objects insofar as they are any of the following objects—

(a) in relation to any land the use of which for any economic, social or environmental purpose has been prevented or restricted because of the carrying on of an activity on the land which has ceased—

(i) reclamation, remediation or restoration; or

(ii) any other operation intended to facilitate economic, social or environmental use;

but this is subject to paragraph (3) below;

(b) in relation to any land the condition of which, by reason of the carrying on of an activity on the land which has ceased, is such that pollution (whether of that land or not) is being or may be caused—

(i) any operation intended to prevent or reduce any potential for pollution; or

(ii) any operation intended to remedy or mitigate the effects of any pollution that has been caused,

but this is subject to paragraph (3) below;

(c) …

[(cc) …]

(d) where it is for the protection of the environment, the provision, maintenance or improvement of—

(i) a public park; or

(ii) another public amenity,

in the vicinity of a landfill site, provided the conditions in paragraph (6) below are satisfied;

[(da) where it is for the protection of the environment, and subject to paragraph (3A) below, the conservation or promotion of biological diversity through—

(i) the provision, conservation, restoration or enhancement of a natural habitat; or

(ii) the maintenance or recovery of a species in its natural habitat,

on land or in water situated in the vicinity of a landfill site;]

(e) where it is for the protection of the environment, the maintenance, repair or restoration of a building or other structure which—

(i) is a place of religious worship or of historic or architectural interest,

(ii) is open to the public, and

(iii)is situated in the vicinity of a landfill site,

provided the conditions in paragraph (6) below are satisfied;

(f) the provision of financial, administration and other similar services to bodies which are within this regulation and only such bodies.

[(2A) In paragraph (2)(da) above "biological diversity" has the same meaning as in the United Nations Environmental Programme Convention on Biological Diversity of 1992.]

(3) An object shall not be, or shall no longer be, regarded as falling within paragraph (2)(a) or (b) above if the reclamation, remediation, restoration or other operation—

(a) is such that any benefit from it will accrue to any person who has carried out or knowingly permitted the activity which has ceased;

(b) involves works which are required to be carried out by a notice or order within paragraph (4) below; or

(c) is wholly or partly required to be carried out by a relevant condition.

[(3A) An object shall not be, or shall no longer be, regarded as falling within paragraph (2)(da) above if it involves works which—

(a) are required to be carried out by a notice or order within paragraph (4) below;

(b) are required to be carried out in accordance with an agreement made under section 16 of the National Parks and Access to the Countryside Act 1949;

(c) are required to be carried out in accordance with an agreement made under section 15 of the Countryside Act 1968;

(d) give effect to any provision of a management scheme under section 28J of the Wildlife and Countryside Act 1981 or are required to be carried out by a notice served under section 28K of that Act;

(e) are wholly or partly required to be carried out by a relevant condition; or

(f) are carried out with a view to profit.]

(4) The notices and order mentioned in paragraph (3) above are—

(a) a works notice served under section 46A of the Control of Pollution Act 1974;

(b) an enforcement notice served under section 13 of the Environmental Protection Act 1990;

(c) a prohibition notice served under section 14 of the Environmental Protection Act 1990;

(d) an order under section 26 of the Environmental Protection Act 1990;

(e) a remediation notice served under section 78E of the Environmental Protection Act 1990;

(f) an enforcement notice served under section 90B of the Water Resources Act 1991;

(g) a works notice served under section 161A of the Water Resources Act 1991;

[(h) an enforcement notice served under regulation 24 of the Pollution Prevention and Control (England and Wales) Regulations 2000;

(i) a suspension notice served under regulation 25 of those Regulations;

(j) an order under regulation 35 of those Regulations];

[(k) a notice served under regulation 28(2) of the Water Environment (Controlled Activities) (Scotland) Regulations 2005;]

[(k) an enforcement notice under regulation 24 of the Pollution Prevention and Control Regulations (Northern Ireland) 2003;

(l) a suspension notice served under regulation 25 of those Regulations;

(m) an order under regulation 36 of those Regulations].

(5) …

(6) The conditions mentioned in sub-paragraphs (d) and (e) of paragraph (2) above are—

PART II STATUTORY INSTRUMENTS

(a) in a case falling within sub-paragraph (d), that the provision of the park or amenity is not required by a relevant condition; and
(b) in a case falling within either of those sub-paragraphs, that the park, amenity, building or structure (as the case may be) is not to be operated with a view to profit.

(7) Where the objects of a body are or include any of the objects set out in paragraph (2) above, the following shall also be regarded as objects within that paragraph—
(a) the use of qualifying contributions in paying the running costs of the body, but this is subject to paragraph (8) below;
(b) ... the use of qualifying contributions in paying a contribution to the running costs of the regulatory body.

(8) The use of qualifying contributions in paying the running costs of the body shall only be regarded as an approved object if the body determines so to use no more than such proportion of the total of qualifying contributions, together with any income derived from them, (or, in the case of a contribution within regulation 30(2)(a), only that income) as the proportion of that total forms of the total funds at its disposal and does not in fact use a greater amount.

(9) For the purposes of paragraph (1) above [a body or person (in either case, for the purposes of this paragraph, "the person")] shall be taken to control a body where—
(a) in the case of a body which is a body corporate, the person is empowered by statute to control that body's activities or if he is that body's holding company within the meaning of section 736 of the Companies Act 1985, and an individual shall be taken to control a body corporate if he, were he a company, would be that body's holding company within the meaning of that Act;
(b) in the case of a body which is a trust or a partnership, where—
(i) the person, taken together with any nominee of his, or
(ii) any nominee of the person, taken together with any nominee of that nominee or any other nominee of the person,
forms a majority of the total number of trustees or partners, as the case may be;
(c) in the case of any other body, where the person, whether directly or through any nominee, has the power—
(i) to appoint or remove any officer of the body;
(ii) to determine the objects of the body;
(iii) to determine how any of the body's funds may be applied.

(10) For the purposes of paragraphs (3)[, (3A)] and (6) above a condition is relevant if it is—
(a) a condition of any planning permission or other statutory consent or approval granted on the application of any person making a qualifying contribution to the body, or
[(b) a term of an agreement made under—
(i) section 106 of the Town and Country Planning Act 1990,
(ii) section 75 of the Town and Country Planning (Scotland) Act 1997, or
(iii) article 40 of the Planning (Northern Ireland) Order 1991,
to which such a person is a party.]

[3254]

NOTES

Commencement: 1 January 2000 (paras (1A)–(1C)); 1 August 1996 (remainder).

Para (1): words in square brackets substituted, and word omitted revoked, by the Landfill Tax (Amendment) Regulations 1999, SI 1999/3270, regs 2, 6(a)–(d).

Paras (1A)–(1C): inserted by SI 1999/3270, regs 2, 6(e).

Para (2): sub-para (c) revoked by the Landfill Tax (Amendment) Regulations 2003, SI 2003/605, regs 2, 4.

Para (2): sub-para (cc) inserted by SI 1999/3270, regs 2, 6(f), revoked by SI 2003/605, regs 2, 4.

Para (2): sub-para (da) inserted by the Landfill Tax (Amendment) (No 2) Regulations 2003, SI 2003/2313, regs 2, 3(a).

Para (2A): inserted by SI 2003/2313, regs 2, 3(b).

Para (3A): inserted by SI 2003/2313, regs 2, 3(c).

Para (4): sub-paras (h)–(j) inserted by the Pollution Prevention and Control (England and Wales) Regulations 2000, SI 2000/1973, reg 39, Sch 10, Pt 2, para 41.

Para (4): first sub-para (k) inserted, in relation to Scotland, by the Water Environment and Water Services (Scotland) Act 2003 (Consequential Provisions and Modifications) Order 2006, SI 2006/1054, art 2, Sch 1, Pt 2, para 3.

Para (4): second sub-para (k) and sub-paras (l), (m) inserted by the Pollution Prevention and Control Regulations (Northern Ireland) 2003, SR 2003/46, reg 41, Sch 11, para 6.

Para (5): revoked by SI 2003/605, regs 2, 4.
Para (7): in sub-para (b) words omitted revoked by SI 1999/3270, regs 2, 6(h).
Para (9): words in square brackets substituted by SI 1999/3270, regs 2, 6(i), (j).
Para (10): words in square brackets inserted by SI 2003/2313, regs 2, 3(d).
Para (10): sub-para (b) substituted by SI 1999/3270, regs 2, 6(j).
Modification: by virtue of the Adults with Incapacity (Scotland) Act 2000, s 88(2), Sch 5, para 1, the references in para (1C)(b) to a curator bonis and to a tutor shall be construed as references to a guardian with similar powers appointed under that Act.

[33A Obligations of approved bodies

(1) An approved body shall—

(a) continue to meet all the requirements of regulation 33 above;

(b) apply qualifying contributions and any income derived therefrom only to approved objects;

(c) not apply any of its funds for the benefit of any of the persons who have made qualifying contributions to it or who were contributing third parties in relation to such contributions (except to the extent that they benefit by virtue of belonging to a class of persons that benefits generally);

(d) make and retain records of the following—

(i) the name, address and registration number of each registered person making a qualifying contribution to the body;

(ii) the name and address of any contributing third party in relation to a qualifying contribution received by the body;

(iii) the amount and date of receipt of each qualifying contribution and the amount and date of receipt of any income derived therefrom;

(iv) in the case of a transfer of the whole or part of any qualifying contribution or income derived therefrom to or from the body, the date of the transfer, the amount transferred, the name and enrolment number of the body from or, as the case may require, to which it was transferred, the name, address and registration number of the person who made the qualifying contribution and the name and address of any contributing third party in relation to the qualifying contribution;

(v) in respect of each qualifying contribution and any income derived therefrom, including any such amount transferred to the body by another approved body, the date of and all other details relating to its expenditure;

(e) provide the following information to the regulatory body or, if they are performing the functions specified in regulation 34(1) below, to the Commissioners within 7 days of the receipt by it of any qualifying contribution—

(i) the amount of the contribution;

(ii) the date it was received;

(iii) the name and registration number of the person making the contribution;

(iv) the name and address of any contributing third party in relation to the contribution notified to it by virtue of regulation 32(2B) above;

(f) notify the regulatory body within seven days of any transfer to or by it of qualifying contributions or of income derived therefrom of—

(i) the date of the transfer;

(ii) the enrolment number of the approved body by or, as the case may require, to which the transfer was made;

(iii) the amount transferred;

(iv) the name and registration number of the person who made the qualifying contribution;

(v) the name and address of any contributing third party in relation to the contribution; and

(vi) the approved objects to which the transferred funds are to be applied;

(g) provide the regulatory body or, if they are performing the functions specified in regulation 34(1) below, the Commissioners with information from or access to the records referred to in [sub-paragraph (d)] above within 14 days (or such longer period as the regulatory body or, as the case may require, the Commissioners may allow) of a request being made for such information or access;

(h) submit to the regulatory body or, if they are performing the functions specified in regulation 34(1) below, to the Commissioners within 14 days of the end of the relevant period determined in accordance with paragraph (2) below details of—

(i) qualifying contributions and any other income or profit whatsoever received by it,

PART II STATUTORY INSTRUMENTS

(ii) any expenditure made by it during the period, and
(iii) any balances held by it at the end of the period;

(i) submit to the regulatory body within 9 months of the end of its financial year independently audited financial accounts for that year; and

(j) pay to the regulatory body an amount equal to 5 per cent of each qualifying contribution it receives, or such lesser amount as the regulatory body may require, towards its running costs within 14 days of receipt of a demand for payment.

(2) For the purposes of paragraph (1)(h) above, the relevant period in respect of an approved body is—

(a) in the case of the first such period—
(i) the period of 6 months, or
(ii) where the aggregate of the qualifying contributions and income therefrom received by the body in the period referred to in sub-paragraph (i) above is no greater than £100,000, the period of 12 months,

commencing with the date on which the body was approved; and

(b) in the case of subsequent periods—
(i) the period of 6 months, or
(ii) where the aggregate of the qualifying contributions and income therefrom received by the body during the period referred to in sub-paragraph (i) above and the period of 6 months preceding that does not exceed £100,000, the period of 12 months,

commencing with the day after the end of the first or, as the case may require, a subsequent period.]

[3255]

NOTES

Commencement: 1 January 2000.
Inserted by the Landfill Tax (Amendment) Regulations 1999, SI 1999/3270, regs 2, 7.
Para (1): in sub-para (g) words in square brackets substituted by the Landfill Tax (Amendment) Regulations 2002, SI 2002/1, regs 2, 3.

34 Functions of the regulatory body

(1) The regulatory body—

[(a) shall, on application being made to it by a body which is eligible to be approved under regulation 33 above, approve that body;]

(b)–(d) …

[(e) may revoke the approval of any body which fails to comply with any requirement of regulation 33A(1);

(ee) shall revoke the approval of any body which applies for its approval to be revoked;]

(f) shall maintain a roll of bodies which it has approved;

(g) shall allocate an identifying number (the enrolment number) to each such body;

(h) shall remove from the roll any body whose approval it has revoked;

(i) shall satisfy itself, by reference to such records or other documents or information it thinks fit, that the qualifying contributions received by the body have been spent by it only in the course or furtherance of its approved objects; …

(j) shall publish information regarding which bodies it has approved and which approvals it has revoked[; and

(k) shall, when notified by an approved body of the transfer to or by it of the whole or part of a qualifying contribution or of income derived therefrom, notify the registered person who made the qualifying contribution, and any contributing third party in relation to it, of—
(i) the date of the transfer,
(ii) the name and enrolment number of the body by or, as the case may require, to whom the transfer was made;
(iii) the amount transferred; and
(iv) the approved objects to which the transferred funds are to be applied].

(2) Where—

(a) the Commissioners revoke their approval of the regulatory body without approving another body with effect from the day after the revocation takes effect; and

(b) they have not given notice in writing to each body which has been enrolled (and which has not been removed from the roll), no later than the date such revocation takes effect, that they [will be] performing any of the functions specified in paragraph (1) above,

the approval of all such bodies shall be deemed to have been revoked on the day the Commissioners revoked their approval.

[3256]

NOTES

Commencement: 1 August 1996.

Para (1): words in square brackets substituted, words omitted revoked, and sub-para (k) and word immediately preceding it inserted, by the Landfill Tax (Amendment) Regulations 1999, SI 1999/3270, regs 2, 8(a)–(e).

Para (2): in sub-para (b) words in square brackets substituted by SI 1999/3270, regs 2, 8(f).

35 Functions of the Commissioners

(1) The Commissioners—

[(a) may approve a body to carry out the functions prescribed by regulation 34(1) above;]

(b) ...

(c) may revoke the approval;

(d) shall not approve a body without first revoking the approval for any other body with effect from a time earlier than that for which the new approval is to take effect;

(e) for any time as regards which no approval has effect, may perform any of the functions specified in regulation 34(1);

(f) may disclose to the [regulatory] body information which relates to the tax affairs of registered persons and which is relevant to the credit scheme established by this Part; and

(g) having regard to any information received from the [regulatory] body, may serve notices under regulation 36.

[(2) Without prejudice to the generality of paragraph (1)(c) above, the Commissioners may revoke their approval of the regulatory body where it appears to them necessary to do so for the proper operation of the credit scheme established by this Part.]

[3257]

NOTES

Commencement: 1 January 2000 (para (2)); 1 August 1996 (remainder).

Para (1): sub-para (a) substituted, sub-para (b) revoked and in sub-paras (f), (g) words in square brackets inserted by the Landfill Tax (Amendment) Regulations 1999, SI 1999/3270, regs 2, 9(a)–(c).

Para (2): substituted by SI 1999/3270, regs 2, 9(d).

36 Repayment of credit

(1) Where a person has benefited from an amount of credit to which he was entitled under this Part and the Commissioners serve upon him a notice in relation to a qualifying contribution paid to an approved body—

(a) specifying that—

(i) they are not satisfied that the contribution has been spent by the body only in the course or furtherance of its approved objects; or

(ii) they are not satisfied that any income derived from the contribution has been so spent by the body;

(b) specifying a breach of a condition to which the approval of the body was made subject and which occurred before the contribution was spent by the body; or

(c) specifying that—

(i) the approval of the body has been revoked; and

(ii) the contribution had not been spent by the body before that revocation took effect,

he shall repay to the Commissioners the credit claimed in respect of the qualifying contribution.

(2) For the purpose of paragraph (1) above where—

(a) repayment is required in relation to credit that has been claimed in respect of more than one qualifying contribution in an accounting period; and

PART II STATUTORY INSTRUMENTS

(b) regulation 31(3) applied so that the amount of credit was restricted,

the person shall be deemed to have claimed credit in respect of such proportion of each contribution made in that accounting period as the total credit claimed in accordance with that regulation forms of the total of the contributions made.

[(3) Where—

(a) a person has benefited from an amount of credit to which he was entitled under this Part; and

(b) the whole or a part of the qualifying contribution in respect of which the entitlement to credit arose has been repaid to him or a person who was a contributing third party in relation to the qualifying contribution,

he shall pay to the Commissioners an amount equal to 90 per cent of the amount repaid to him or, as the case may require, to the contributing third party.]

(4) Paragraph (5) below applies where—

(a) a person has benefited from an amount of credit to which he was entitled under this Part; and

(b) he is entitled to a payment under regulation 20 in respect of a later accounting period in the same contribution year as the accounting period in respect of which that credit was claimed.

(5) Where this paragraph applies the person shall pay to the Commissioners an amount equal to the difference between—

(a) the aggregate of—

(i) the amount of the credit from which he has benefited, and

(ii) any other amounts of credit arising under this Part which he is or was entitled to claim,

in respect of that contribution year; and

(b) the amount of credit which he would have been entitled to claim if he had in fact claimed the aggregate amount mentioned in sub-paragraph (a) above in the return for the accounting period in respect of which he was entitled to the payment under regulation 20.

(6) Where—

(a) a person has benefited from an amount of credit to which he was entitled under this Part;

(b) he acquires an asset from a body to which he has made a qualifying contribution for—

(i) no consideration, or

(ii) a consideration which is less than the open market value of the asset,

he shall pay to the Commissioners an amount equal to 90 per cent of the amount by which the open market value exceeds the consideration; but this is subject to paragraph (7) below.

(7) A person required to pay an amount to the Commissioners by paragraph (6) above—

(a) shall not be required to pay more than the total amount of relevant credit;

(b) shall not be entitled to claim any further amounts of credit in respect of qualifying contributions made by him to the body in question on or after the date on which he acquired the asset.

(8) For the purposes of paragraphs (6) and (7) above

(a) "asset" includes land, goods or services and any interest in any of these;

(b) the open market value of an asset is the amount of the consideration in money that would be payable for the asset by a person standing in no such relationship with any person as would affect that consideration;

(c) "relevant credit" means credit arising under this Part—

(i) from which a person has benefited, and

(ii) which has arisen in respect of qualifying contributions made by him to the body in question or treated by virtue of regulation 32(3) as having been received by that body from him.

[3258]

NOTES

Commencement: 1 January 2000 (para (3)); 1 August 1996 (remainder).

Para (3): substituted by the Landfill Tax (Amendment) Regulations 1999, SI 1999/3270, regs 2, 10.

PART VIII
LANDFILL INVOICES

37 Contents of a landfill invoice

(1) An invoice is a landfill invoice if it contains the following information—
- (a) an identifying number;
- (b) the date of its issue;
- (c) the date of the disposal or disposals in respect of which it is issued or, where a series of disposals is made for the same person, the dates between which the disposals were made;
- (d) the name, address and registration number of the person issuing it;
- (e) the name and address of the person to whom it is issued;
- (f) the weight of the material disposed of;
- (g) a description of the material disposed of;
- (h) the rate of tax chargeable in relation to the disposal or, if the invoice relates to more than one disposal and the rate of tax for each of them is not the same, the rate of tax chargeable for each disposal;
- (i) the total amount payable for which the invoice is issued; and
- (j) where the amount of tax is shown separately, a statement confirming that that tax may not be treated as the input tax of any person.

(2) In paragraph (1)(j) above "input tax" has the same meaning as in section 24(1) of the Value Added Tax Act 1994.

[3259]

NOTES

Commencement: 1 August 1996.

PART IX
TEMPORARY DISPOSALS

38 Scope and effect

(1) A disposal to which this Part applies—
- (a) shall not be treated as made at the time when apart from this Part it would be regarded as made; and
- (b) shall be treated as having been made—
  - (i) when it is treated as being an exempt disposal by virtue of regulation 39, or
  - (ii) to the extent that it is not so treated, at the time when it is treated as having been made by virtue of regulation 40.

(2) This Part applies to a disposal where—
- (a) an authorised person has designated an area (the designated area) for the purpose of this Part;
- (b) material is disposed of in the designated area at a time when the designation has effect;
- (c) [the material comprised in the disposal is held temporarily] pending all of the material being put to a qualifying use within the relevant period; and
- (d) such other conditions as the Commissioners or an authorised person may specify for the purpose of this Part, whether generally or with regard to particular cases, are satisfied.

(3) A designation ceases to have effect if—
- (a) notice to that effect is given in writing by the Commissioners or by an authorised person;
- (b) any period for which the designation was to have effect by virtue of a condition specified in relation thereto expires;
- (c) any disposal to which this Part does not apply (whether because [the material comprised in it is not held in accordance with paragraph (2)(c) above] or for some other reason) is made in the designated area; or
- (d) a disposal is treated by virtue of regulation 40 as having been made at a certain time and all of the material comprised in that disposal is not removed from the designated area within seven days of that time.

[(4) A use is a qualifying use if, within the relevant period, the material is—
(a) re-cycled or incinerated; or
(b) used (other than by way of a further disposal)—
(i) at a place other than a relevant site; or
(ii) for site restoration purposes at the landfill site at which the disposal was made.

(4A) Sorting of material pending—
(i) its use by way of any qualifying use within paragraph (4) above, or
(ii) its disposal within the relevant period,
is also a qualifying use.]

(5) For the purposes of [paragraphs (4) and (4A)] above—
(a) a use is not a qualifying use if it would constitute a breach of any condition relating to the use of the material to be disposed of which has been specified in relation to that designated area or generally;
[(aa) material is used for site restoration purposes if—
(i) the material is treated for the purposes of section 42 of the Act as qualifying material;
(ii) before the material is used the operator of the landfill site notifies the Commissioners in writing that he is commencing the restoration of all or a part of the site and provides such other written information as the Commissioners may require generally or in the particular case; and
(iii) the material is used in the restoration of the site or part specified in the notification under paragraph (ii) above;
(ab) "restoration" means work, other than capping waste, which is required by a relevant instrument to be carried out to restore a landfill site to use on completion of waste disposal operations;
(ac) the following are relevant instruments—
(i) a planning consent;
(ii) a waste management licence;
(iii) a resolution authorising the disposal of waste on or in land;]
[(iv) a permit authorising the disposal of waste on or in land;]
(b) a relevant site is the landfill site at which the disposal was made or any other landfill site;
(c) …

[(6) Subject to paragraph (7) below, the relevant period is the period of one year commencing with the date of the disposal or such other period as the Commissioners or an authorised person may approve or direct.

(7) In relation to site restoration which is a qualifying use falling within paragraph (4)(b)(ii) above, the relevant period is the period of three years commencing with the date of the disposal or such other period as the Commissioners or an authorised person may approve or direct.]

[3260]

NOTES

Commencement: 1 August 1996.
Para (2): in sub-para (c) words in square brackets substituted by the Landfill Tax (Amendment) Regulations 2002, SI 2002/1, regs 2, 4(a).
Para (3): in sub-para (c) words in square brackets substituted by SI 2002/1, regs 2, 4(b).
Paras (4), (4A): substituted, for para (4) as originally enacted, by SI 2002/1, regs 2, 4(c).
Para (5): words in square brackets substituted by SI 2002/1, regs 2, 4(d)(i).
Para (5): sub-paras (aa)–(ac) inserted by SI 2002/1, regs 2, 4(d)(ii).
Para (5): sub-para (ac)(iv) inserted by the Landfill Tax (Amendment) Regulations 2005, SI 2005/759, regs 2, 5.
Para (5): sub-para (c) revoked by SI 2002/1, regs 2, 4(d)(iii).
Paras (6), (7): inserted by SI 2002/1, regs 2, 4(e).

39 Disposals to be treated as exempt

(1) Where there is a disposal to which this Part applies and—
(a) the material comprised in the disposal has been put to a qualifying use within the relevant period, if it would otherwise be a taxable disposal that disposal shall be treated as not being a taxable disposal (shall be treated as being an exempt disposal); but this is subject to paragraph (2) below;
(b) some of the material comprised in a disposal has been put to a qualifying use

within the relevant period (and some has not), the disposal shall be treated as being an exempt disposal to the extent of the part so dealt with and the remaining part shall be treated in accordance with regulation 40.

(2) A disposal shall not be treated as being an exempt disposal unless the landfill site operator concerned has made and, in relation to that disposal, maintained the record specified in paragraph (3) below (the temporary disposal record).

(3) The temporary disposal record mentioned in paragraph (2) above is a record, in relation to the designated area, of—

(a) the weight and description of all material disposed of;

[(b) the intended destination or use of all such material and, where any material has been removed or used, the actual destination or use of that material;]

(c) the weight and description of any material [sorted or] removed.

[3261]

NOTES

Commencement: 1 August 1996.

Para (3): sub-para (b) substituted by the Landfill Tax (Amendment) Regulations 2002, SI 2002/1, regs 2, 5(a).

Para (3): in sub-para (c) words in square brackets inserted by SI 2002/1, regs 2, 5(b).

40 Disposals to be treated as made at certain times

(1) Where in the case of a disposal to which this Part applies the disposal is not wholly treated as being an exempt disposal it shall, to the extent that it is not so treated, be treated as having been made at the earliest of the following times—

(a) when the relevant period has expired;

(b) when the designation ceases to have effect;

(c) when there has been a breach of any condition specified by the Commissioners or an authorised person;

(d) when there has been a failure to make the temporary disposal record;

(e) when there has been a failure to maintain the temporary disposal record;

(f) when any of the material concerned is used (other than by way of a further disposal) at the same or another landfill site (but not in the same designated area).

(2) The reference in paragraph (1)(e) above to a failure to maintain the temporary disposal record is a reference to an omission to enter in a record that has been made the information specified in regulation 39(3) in relation to any disposal made after the record was made.

[3262]

NOTES

Commencement: 1 August 1996.

PART X
DETERMINATION OF WEIGHT OF MATERIAL DISPOSED OF

41 Scope

This Part applies for the purpose of determining the weight of material comprised in a disposal; and references in this Part to weight shall be construed as references to the weight of such material.

[3263]

NOTES

Commencement: 1 August 1996.

42 Basic method

(1) Except where regulation 43 or 44 applies and subject to paragraph (2) below, a registrable person shall determine weight by weighing the material concerned.

PART II STATUTORY INSTRUMENTS

(2) The weighing of the material shall be carried out at the time of the disposal; and for this purpose any time at which section 61 of the Act or Part IX of these Regulations require the disposal to be treated as made shall be disregarded.

[3264]

NOTES

Commencement: 1 August 1996.

43 Specified methods

(1) Except where regulation 44 applies, this regulation applies where the Commissioners have specified rules for determining weight in a notice published by them and not withdrawn by a further notice.

(2) A specification made by the Commissioners as described in paragraph (1) above may make provision for—

(a) the method by which weight is to be determined;

(b) the time by reference to which weight is to be determined.

(3) A specification made by the Commissioners as described in paragraph (1) above may provide—

(a) that it is to have effect only in relation to disposals of such descriptions as may be set out in the specification;

(b) that it is not to have effect in relation to particular disposals unless the Commissioners are satisfied that such conditions as may be set out in the specification are met in relation to the disposals.

(4) Where this regulation applies the registrable person shall determine weight in accordance with the rules in the specification (and not in accordance with the rule in regulation 42).

[3265]

NOTES

Commencement: 1 August 1996.

44 Agreed methods

(1) This regulation applies where—

(a) the registrable person and an authorised person have agreed in writing that weight shall be determined in accordance with rules other than those described in regulation 42 or specified under regulation 43; and

(b) a direction under paragraph (3) below has not been made.

(2) Rules may be agreed under this regulation as regards—

(a) the method by which weight is to be determined;

(b) the time by reference to which weight is to be determined;

(c) the discounting of water forming a constituent of material disposed of, but this is subject to paragraph (5) below.

(3) Where rules have been agreed under this regulation and the Commissioners believe that they should no longer be applied because they do not give an accurate indication of the weight or they are not being fully observed or for some other reason they may direct that the agreed rules shall no longer have effect.

(4) Where this regulation applies the registrable person shall determine weight in accordance with the rules agreed (and not in accordance with the rule in regulation 42 or 43).

(5) Subject to paragraphs (6) to (8) below, rules may be agreed regarding the discounting of water if, and only if—

(a) no water is present in the material naturally and the water is present because—

(i) it has been added for the purpose of enabling the material to be transported for disposal;

(ii) it has been used for the purpose of extracting any mineral; or

(iii) it has arisen, or has been added, in the course of an industrial process; or

(b) the material is the residue from the treatment of effluent or sewage by a water treatment works.

(6) Rules may not be agreed under paragraph (5) above where any of the material is capable of escaping from the landfill site concerned by leaching unless—
- (a) it is likely to do so in the form of water only; or
- (b) the leachate is to be collected on the site concerned and treated in order to eliminate any potential it has to cause harm.

(7) Where the material falls within paragraph (5)(a) above rules may not be agreed under paragraph (5) above unless the total water which has been added, or (in a case falling within paragraph (5)(a)(iii) above) has arisen or has been added or both, constitutes 25 per cent or more of the weight at the time of the disposal.

(8) Where the material falls within paragraph (5)(b) above rules may not be agreed under paragraph (5) above except for the discounting of water which has been added prior to disposal (and not of water which is present in the material naturally).

(9) For the purposes of paragraph (8) above any water which has been extracted prior to disposal shall be deemed to be water that has been added, except that where the water extracted exceeds the quantity of water added that excess shall be deemed to have been present naturally.

[3266]

NOTES

Commencement: 1 August 1996.

PART II STATUTORY INSTRUMENTS

PART XI
SET-OFF OF AMOUNTS

45 Landfill tax amount owed to Commissioners

(1) Subject to regulation 47, this regulation applies where—
- (a) a person is under a duty to pay to the Commissioners at any time an amount or amounts in respect of landfill tax; and
- (b) the Commissioners are under a duty to pay to that person at the same time an amount or amounts in respect of any tax or taxes under their care and management.

(2) Where the total of the amount or amounts mentioned in paragraph (1)(a) above exceeds the total of the amount or amounts mentioned in paragraph (1)(b) above, the latter shall be set off against the former.

(3) Where the total of the amount or amounts mentioned in paragraph (1)(b) above exceeds the total of the amount or amounts mentioned in paragraph (1)(a) above, the Commissioners may set off the latter in paying the former.

(4) Where the total of the amount or amounts mentioned in paragraph (1)(a) above is the same as the total of the amount or amounts mentioned in paragraph (1)(b) above, no payment need be made in respect of either.

(5) Where this regulation applies and an amount has been set off in accordance with any of paragraphs (2) to (4) above, the duty of both the person and the Commissioners to pay the amount or amounts concerned shall be treated as having been discharged accordingly.

(6) References in paragraph (1) above to an amount in respect of a particular tax include references not only to an amount of tax itself but also to amounts of penalty, surcharge or interest.

(7) In this regulation "tax" includes "duty".

[3267]

NOTES

Commencement: 1 August 1996.

46 Landfill tax amount owed by Commissioners

(1) Subject to regulation 47, this regulation applies where—
- (a) a person is under a duty to pay to the Commissioners at any time an amount or amounts in respect of any tax or taxes under their care and management; and

(b) the Commissioners are under a duty to pay to that person at the same time an amount or amounts in respect of landfill tax.

(2) Where the total of the amount or amounts mentioned in paragraph (1)(a) above exceeds the total of the amount or amounts mentioned in paragraph (1)(b) above, the latter shall be set off against the former.

(3) Where the total of the amount or amounts mentioned in paragraph (1)(b) above exceeds the total of the amount or amounts mentioned in paragraph (1)(a) above, the Commissioners may set off the latter in paying the former.

(4) Where the total of the amount or amounts mentioned in paragraph (1)(a) above is the same as the total of the amount or amounts mentioned in paragraph (1)(b) above, no payment need be made in respect of either.

(5) Where this regulation applies and an amount has been set off in accordance with any of paragraphs (2) to (4) above, the duty of both the person and the Commissioners to pay the amount or amounts concerned shall be treated as having been discharged accordingly.

(6) Paragraphs (6) and (7) of regulation 45 shall apply in relation to this regulation as they apply in relation to that regulation.

[3268]

NOTES

Commencement: 1 August 1996.

47 No set-off where insolvency procedure applied

(1) Neither regulation 45 nor 46 shall require any such amount as is mentioned in paragraph (1)(b) of those regulations (in either case, "the credit") to be set against any such sum as is mentioned in paragraph (1)(a) of those regulations (in either case, "the debit") in any case where—

(a) an insolvency procedure has been applied to the person entitled to the credit;
(b) the credit became due after that procedure was so applied;
(c) the liability to pay the debit either arose before that procedure was so applied or (having risen afterwards) relates to, or to matters occurring in the course of—
  (i) the carrying on of any business; or
  (ii) in the case of any sum such as is mentioned in regulation 46(1)(b), the carrying out of taxable activities,

at times before the procedure was so applied.

(2) Subject to paragraph (3) below, the following are the times when an insolvency procedure is to be taken, for the purposes of this regulation, to have been applied to any person, that is to say—

(a) when a bankruptcy order, winding-up order, … or award of sequestration is made in relation to that person [or that person enters administration];
(b) when that person is put into administrative receivership;
(c) when that person, being a corporation, passes a resolution for voluntary winding-up;
(d) when any voluntary arrangement approved in accordance with Part I or Part VIII of the Insolvency Act 1986, or Part II or Chapter II of Part VIII of the Insolvency (Northern Ireland) Order 1989, comes into force in relation to that person;
(e) when a deed of arrangement registered in accordance with the Deeds of Arrangement Act 1914 or Chapter I of Part VIII of that Order of 1989 takes effect in relation to that person;
(f) when that person's estate becomes vested in any other person as that person's trustee under a trust deed.

(3) References in this regulation, in relation to any person, to the application of an insolvency procedure to that person shall not include—

(a) the making of a bankruptcy order, winding-up order, … or award of sequestration [or that person entering administration] at a time when any such arrangements or deed as is mentioned in paragraph (2)(d) to (f) above is in force in relation to that person;
(b) the making of a winding-up order at any of the following times—
  (i) immediately upon [the appointment of the administrator ceasing to have effect];

(ii) when that person is being wound-up voluntarily;
(iii) when that person is in administrative receivership; or

(c) the making of an administration order in relation to that person at any time when that person is in administrative receivership.

(4) For the purposes of this regulation a person shall be regarded as being in administrative receivership throughout any continuous period for which (disregarding any temporary vacancy in the office of receiver) there is an administrative receiver of that person, and the reference in paragraph (2) above to a person being put into administrative receivership shall be construed accordingly.

[3269]

NOTES

Commencement: 1 August 1996.

Para (2): in sub-para (a) words omitted revoked by the Enterprise Act 2002 (Insolvency) Order 2003, SI 2003/2096, art 5, Schedule, Pt 2, paras 65, 67(a).

Para (2): in sub-para (a) words in square brackets inserted by SI 2003/2096, art 5, Schedule, Pt 2, paras 65, 67(a).

Para (3): in sub-para (a) words omitted revoked, and words in square brackets inserted, by SI 2003/2096, art 5, Schedule, Pt 2, paras 65, 67(b)(i).

Para (3): in sub-para (b)(i) words in square brackets substituted by SI 2003/2096, art 5, Schedule, Pt 2, paras 65, 67(b)(ii).

PART XII
DISTRESS AND DILIGENCE

[A48 In this Part—

"Job Band" followed by a number between "1" and "12" means the band for the purposes of pay and grading in which the job an officer performs is ranked in the system applicable to Customs and Excise.]

[3270]

NOTES

Commencement: 2 September 1996.

Inserted by the Landfill Tax (Amendment) Regulations 1996, SI 1996/2100, reg 3.

48 *(Revoked by the Distress for Customs and Excise Duties and Other Indirect Taxes Regulations 1997, SI 1997/1431, reg 3(1), Sch 3.)*

49 Diligence

In Scotland the following provisions shall have effect—

(a) where the Commissioners are empowered to apply to the sheriff for a warrant to authorise a sheriff officer to recover any amount of tax or sum recoverable as if it were tax remaining due and unpaid, any application, and any certificate required to accompany that application, may be made on their behalf by a Collector or an officer of rank not below that of [Job Band 7];

(b) where during the course of [an attachment] the Commissioners are entitled as a creditor to do any act, then any such act, with the exception of the exercise of the power contained in [section 30(4) of the Debt Arrangement and Attachment (Scotland) Act 2002 (asp 17)], may be done on their behalf by a Collector or an officer of rank not below that of [Job Band 7].

[3271]

NOTES

Commencement: 1 August 1996.

Paras (a), (b): words in square brackets substituted by the Landfill Tax (Amendment) Regulations 1996, SI 1996/2100, reg 4(1).

In para (b) words in square brackets substituted by the Debt Arrangement and Attachment (Scotland) Act 2002, s 61, Sch 3, Pt 2, para 36.

(Schedule contains Forms 1–5 which are not reproduced in this work.)

GIFTS FOR RELIEF IN POOR COUNTRIES (DESIGNATION) ORDER 1998

(SI 1998/1868)

NOTES
Made: 31 July 1998.
Authority: Finance Act 1998, ss 47(8), 48(9).
Commencement: 21 August 1998.

1 This Order may be cited as the Gifts for Relief in Poor Countries (Designation) Order 1998 and shall come into force on 21st August 1998.

[3272]

NOTES
Commencement: 21 August 1998.

2 The descriptions of countries specified for the purposes of sections 47 and 48 of the Finance Act 1998 are—

(a) the countries included in the lists of countries which are eligible for lending by the International Development Association ("the Association"), and by the Association and the International Bank for Reconstruction and Development ("the Bank"), published by the Association and the Bank (under the name of The World Bank) in Appendix 5 to The World Bank Annual Report 1997, under the headings "Countries eligible for IDA funds only" and "Countries eligible for a blend of IBRD and IDA funds", and

(b) any further countries included in those lists as published in The World Bank Annual Reports issued between the date on which this Order is made and 31st December 2000.

[3273]

NOTES
Commencement: 21 August 1998.

CIVIL PROCEDURE RULES 1998

(SI 1998/3132)

NOTES
Made: 10 December 1998.
Authority: Civil Procedure Act 1997, s 2.
Commencement: 26 April 1999.

Rules 1–63 (*Outside the scope of this work.*)

[PART 64
ESTATES, TRUST AND CHARITIES

[64.1 General

(1) This Part contains rules—

(a) in Section I, about claims relating to—

(i) the administration of estates of deceased persons, and

(ii) trusts; and

(b) in Section II, about charity proceedings.

(2) In this Part and its practice directions, where appropriate, references to trustees include executors and administrators.

(3) All proceedings in the High Court to which this Part applies must be brought in the Chancery Division.]

[3274]

NOTES

Commencement: 2 December 2002.
Inserted by the Civil Procedure (Amendment) Rules 2002, SI 2002/2058, r 26(a), Sch 5.

Rules 64.2–64.4 (*Outside the scope of this work.*)

[SECTION II: CHARITY PROCEEDINGS

64.5 Scope of this Section and interpretation

(1) This Section applies to charity proceedings.

(2) In this Section—
(a) "the Act" means the Charities Act 1993;
(b) "charity proceedings" has the same meaning as in section 33(8) of the Act; and
(c) "the Commissioners" means the Charity Commissioners for England and Wales.]

[3275]

NOTES

Commencement: 2 December 2002.
Inserted by the Civil Procedure (Amendment) Rules 2002, SI 2002/2058, r 26(a), Sch 5.

[64.6 Application for permission to take charity proceedings

(1) An application to the High Court under section 33(5) of the Act for permission to start charity proceedings must be made within 21 days after the refusal by the Commissioners of an order authorising proceedings.

(2) The application must be made by issuing a Part 8 claim form, which must contain the information specified in the practice direction.

(3) The Commissioners must be made defendants to the claim, but the claim form need not be served on them or on any other person.

(4) The judge considering the application may direct the Commissioners to file a written statement of their reasons for their decision.

(5) The court will serve on the applicant a copy of any statement filed under paragraph (4).

(6) The judge may either—
(a) give permission without a hearing; or
(b) fix a hearing.]

[3276]–[3279]

NOTES

Commencement: 2 December 2002.
Inserted by the Civil Procedure (Amendment) Rules 2002, SI 2002/2058, r 26(a), Sch 5.

Rules 65–76, Glossary, Schs 1, 2 (*Outside the scope of this work.*)

GIFTS FOR RELIEF IN POOR COUNTRIES (DESIGNATION OF KOSOVO) ORDER 1999

(SI 1999/2118)

NOTES

Made: 27 July 1999.
Authority: Finance Act 1998, s 48(9); Finance Act 1999, s 56(8).

Commencement: 21 August 1999.

1 This Order may be cited as the Gifts for Relief in Poor Countries (Designation of Kosovo) Order 1999 and shall come into force on 21st August 1999, but shall have effect in relation to gifts made on or after 6th April 1999.

[3280]

NOTES

Commencement: 21 August 1999.

2 This Order designates Kosovo (in the Federation of Yugoslavia) as a territory for the purposes of paragraph (c) of section 48(2) of the Finance Act 1998.

[3281]–[3284]

NOTES

Commencement: 21 August 1998.

DATA PROTECTION (CONDITIONS UNDER PARAGRAPH 3 OF PART II OF SCHEDULE 1) ORDER 2000

(SI 2000/185)

NOTES

Made: 31 January 2000.
Authority: Data Protection Act 1998, s 67(2), Sch 1, Pt II, para 3(1).
Commencement: 1 March 2000.

1 Citation and commencement

This Order may be cited as the Data Protection (Conditions under Paragraph 3 of Part II of Schedule 1) Order 2000 and shall come into force on 1st March 2000.

[3285]

NOTES

Commencement: 1 March 2000.

2 Interpretation

In this Order, "Part II" means Part II of Schedule 1 to the Data Protection Act 1998.

[3286]

NOTES

Commencement: 1 March 2000.

3 General provisions

(1) In cases where the primary condition referred to in paragraph 3(2)(a) of Part II is met, the provisions of articles 4 and 5 apply.

(2) In cases where the primary condition referred to in paragraph 3(2)(b) of that Part is met by virtue of the fact that the recording of the information to be contained in the data by, or the disclosure of the data by, the data controller is not a function conferred on him by or under any enactment or an obligation imposed on him by order of a court, but is necessary for compliance with any legal obligation to which the data controller is subject, other than an obligation imposed by contract, the provisions of article 4 apply.

[3287]

NOTES

Commencement: 1 March 2000.

4 Notices in writing

(1) One of the further conditions prescribed in paragraph (2) must be met if paragraph 2(1)(b) of Part II is to be disapplied in respect of any particular data subject.

(2) The conditions referred to in paragraph (1) are that—
(a) no notice in writing has been received at any time by the data controller from an individual, requiring that data controller to provide the information set out in paragraph 2(3) of that Part before the relevant time (as defined in paragraph 2(2) of that Part) or as soon as practicable after that time; or
(b) where such notice in writing has been received but the data controller does not have sufficient information about the individual in order readily to determine whether he is processing personal data about that individual, the data controller shall send to the individual a written notice stating that he cannot provide the information set out in paragraph 2(3) of that Part because of his inability to make that determination, and explaining the reasons for that inability.

(3) The requirement in paragraph (2) that notice should be in writing is satisfied where the text of the notice—
(a) is transmitted by electronic means,
(b) is received in legible form, and
(c) is capable of being used for subsequent reference.

[3288]

NOTES
Commencement: 1 March 2000.

5 Further condition in cases of disproportionate effort

(1) The further condition prescribed in paragraph (2) must be met for paragraph 2(1)(b) of Part II to be disapplied in respect of any data.

(2) The condition referred to in paragraph (1) is that the data controller shall record the reasons for his view that the primary condition referred to in article 3(1) is met in respect of the data.

[3289]

NOTES
Commencement: 1 March 2000.

PART II STATUTORY INSTRUMENTS

DATA PROTECTION (NOTIFICATION AND NOTIFICATION FEES) REGULATIONS 2000

(SI 2000/188)

NOTES
Made: 31 January 2000.
Authority: Data Protection Act 1998, ss 17(3), 18(2), (4), (5), 19(2), (3), (4), (5), 20(1), 26(1), 67(2), Sch 14, para 2(7), (8).
Commencement: 1 March 2000.

ARRANGEMENT OF REGULATIONS

1 Citation and commencement

These Regulations may be cited as the Data Protection (Notification and Notification Fees) Regulations 2000 and shall come into force on 1st March 2000.

[3290]

NOTES

Commencement: 1 March 2000.

2 Interpretation

In these Regulations—

"the Act" means the Data Protection Act 1998;

"the register" means the register maintained by the Commissioner under section 19 of the Act.

[3291]

NOTES

Commencement: 1 March 2000.

3 Exemptions from notification

Except where the processing is assessable processing for the purposes of section 22 of the Act, section 17(1) of the Act shall not apply in relation to processing—

(a) falling within one or more of the descriptions of processing set out in paragraphs 2 to 5 of the Schedule to these Regulations (being processing appearing to the Secretary of State to be unlikely to prejudice the rights and freedoms of data subjects); or

(b) which does not fall within one or more of those descriptions solely by virtue of the fact that disclosure of the personal data to a person other than those specified in the descriptions—

(i) is required by or under any enactment, by any rule of law or by the order of a court, or

(ii) may be made by virtue of an exemption from the non-disclosure provisions (as defined in section 27(3) of the Act).

[3292]

NOTES

Commencement: 1 March 2000.

4 Form of giving notification

(1) Subject to regulations 5 and 6 below, the Commissioner shall determine the form in which the registrable particulars (within the meaning of section 16(1) of the Act) and the description mentioned in section 18(2)(b) of the Act are to be specified, including in particular the detail required for the purposes of that description and section 16(1)(c), (d), (e) and (f) of the Act.

(2) Subject to regulations 5 and 6 below, the Commissioner shall determine the form in which a notification under regulation 12 (including that regulation as modified by regulation 13) is to be specified.

[3293]

NOTES

Commencement: 1 March 2000.

5 Notification in respect of partnerships

(1) In any case in which two or more persons carrying on a business in partnership are the data controllers in respect of any personal data for the purposes of that business, a notification under section 18 of the Act or under regulation 12 below may be given in respect of those persons in the name of the firm.

(2) Where a notification is given in the name of a firm under paragraph (1) above—

(a) the name to be specified for the purposes of section 16(1)(a) of the Act is the name of the firm, and

(b) the address to be specified for the purposes of section 16(1)(a) of the Act is the address of the firm's principal place of business.

[3294]

NOTES

Commencement: 1 March 2000.

6 Notification in respect of the governing body of, and head teacher at, any school

(1) In any case in which a governing body of, and a head teacher at, any school are, in those capacities, the data controllers in respect of any personal data, a notification under section 18 of the Act or under regulation 12 below may be given in respect of that governing body and head teacher in the name of the school.

(2) Where a notification is given in the name of a school under paragraph (1) above, the name and address to be specified for the purposes of section 16(1)(a) of the Act are those of the school.

(3) In this regulation, "head teacher" includes in Northern Ireland the principal of a school.

[3295]

NOTES

Commencement: 1 March 2000.

7 Fees to accompany notification under section 18 of the Act

(1) This regulation applies to any notification under section 18 of the Act, including a notification which, by virtue of regulation 5 or 6 above, is given in respect of more than one data controller.

(2) A notification to which this regulation applies must be accompanied by a fee of £35.

[3296]

NOTES

Commencement: 1 March 2000.

8 Date of entry in the register

(1) The time from which an entry in respect of a data controller who has given a notification under section 18 of the Act in accordance with these Regulations is to be treated for the purposes of section 17 of the Act as having been made in the register shall be determined as follows.

(2) In the case of a data controller who has given the notification by sending it by registered post or the recorded delivery service, that time is the day after the day on which it is received for dispatch by the [postal operator (within the meaning of the Postal Services Act 2000) concerned].

(3) In the case of a data controller who has given a notification by some other means, that time is the day on which it is received by the Commissioner.

[3297]

NOTES

Commencement: 1 March 2000.

Para (2): words in square brackets substituted by the Postal Services Act 2000 (Consequential Modifications No 1) Order 2001, SI 2001/1149, art 3(1), Sch 1, para 137.

PART II
STATUTORY INSTRUMENTS

9 Acknowledgment of receipt of notification in the case of assessable processing

(1) In any case in which the Commissioner considers under section 22(2)(a) of the Act that any of the processing to which a notification relates is assessable processing within the meaning of that section he shall, within 10 days of receipt of the notification, give a written notice to the data controller who has given the notification, acknowledging its receipt.

(2) A notice under paragraph (1) above shall indicate—
(a) the date on which the Commissioner received the notification, and
(b) the processing which the Commissioner considers to be assessable processing.

[3298]

NOTES
Commencement: 1 March 2000.

10 Confirmation of register entries

(1) The Commissioner shall, as soon as practicable and in any event within a period of 28 days after making an entry in the register under section 19(1)(b) of the Act or amending an entry in the register under section 20(4) of the Act, give the data controller to whom the register entry relates notice confirming the register entry.

(2) A notice under paragraph (1) above shall include a statement of—
(a) the date on which—
(i) in the case of an entry made under section 19(1)(b) of the Act, the entry is treated as having been included by virtue of regulation 8 above, or
(ii) in the case of an entry made under section 20(4) of the Act, the notification was received by the Commissioner;
(b) the particulars entered in the register, or the amendment made, in pursuance of the notification; and
(c) in the case of a notification under section 18 of the Act, the date by which the fee payable under regulation 14 below must be paid in order for the entry to be retained in the register as provided by section 19(4) of the Act.

[3299]

NOTES
Commencement: 1 March 2000.

11 Additional information in register entries

In addition to the matters mentioned in section 19(2)(a) of the Act, the Commissioner may include in a register entry—
(a) a registration number issued by the Commissioner in respect of that entry;
(b) the date on which the entry is treated, by virtue of regulation 8 above, as having been included in pursuance of a notification under section 18 of theAct;
(c) the date on which the entry falls or may fall to be removed by virtue of regulation 14 or 15 below; and
(d) information additional to the registrable particulars for the purpose of assisting persons consulting the register to communicate with any data controller to whom the entry relates concerning matters relating to the processing of personal data.

[3300]

NOTES
Commencement: 1 March 2000.

12 Duty to notify changes to matters previously notified

(1) Subject to regulation 13 below, every person in respect of whom an entry is for the time being included in the register is under a duty to give the Commissioner a notification specifying any respect in which—
(a) that entry becomes inaccurate or incomplete as a statement of his current registrable particulars, or
(b) the general description of measures notified under section 18(2)(b) of the Act or, as the case may be, that description as amended in pursuance of a notification under this regulation, becomes inaccurate or incomplete,

and setting out the changes which need to be made to that entry or general description in order to make it accurate and complete.

(2) Such a notification must be given as soon as practicable and in any event within a period of 28 days from the date on which the entry or, as the case may be, the general description, becomes inaccurate or incomplete.

(3) References in this regulation to an entry being included in the register include any entry being treated under regulation 8 above as being so included.

[3301]

NOTES

Commencement: 1 March 2000.

13 Duty to notify changes—transitional modifications

(1) This regulation applies to persons in respect of whom an entry in the register has been made under paragraph 2(6) of Schedule 14 to the Act.

(2) In the case of a person to whom this regulation applies, the duty imposed by regulation 12 above shall be modified so as to have effect as follows.

(3) Every person in respect of whom an entry is for the time being included in the register is under a duty to give the Commissioner a notification specifying—

(a) his name and address, in any case in which a change to his name or address results in the entry in respect of him no longer including his current name and address;

(b) to the extent to which the entry relates to eligible data—

(i) a description of any eligible data being or to be processed by him or on his behalf, in any case in which such processing is of personal data of a description not included in that entry;

(ii) a description of the category or categories of data subject to which eligible data relate, in any case in which such category or categories are of a description not included in that entry;

(iii) a description of the purpose or purposes for which eligible data are being or are to be processed in any case in which such processing is for a purpose or purposes of a description not included in that entry;

(iv) a description of the source or sources from which he intends or may wish to obtain eligible data, in any case in which such obtaining is from a source of a description not included in that entry;

(v) a description of any recipient or recipients to whom he intends or may wish to disclose eligible data, in any case in which such disclosure is to a recipient or recipients of a description not included in that entry; and

(vi) the names, or a description of, any countries or territories outside the United Kingdom to which he directly or indirectly transfers, or intends or may wish directly or indirectly to transfer, eligible data, in any case in which such transfer would be to a country or territory not named or described in that entry; and

(c) to the extent to which sub-paragraph (b) above does not apply, any respect in which the entry is or becomes inaccurate or incomplete as—

(i) a statement of his current registrable particulars to the extent mentioned in section 16(1)(c), (d) and (e) of the Act;

(ii) a description of the source or sources from which he currently intends or may wish to obtain personal data; and

(iii) the names or a description of any countries or territories outside the United Kingdom to which he currently intends or may wish directly or indirectly to transfer personal data;

and setting out the changes which need to be made to that entry in order to make it accurate and complete in those respects.

(4) Such a notification must be given as soon as practicable and in any event within a period of 28 days from the date on which—

(a) in the case of a notification under paragraph (3)(a) above, the entry no longer includes the current name and address;

(b) in the case of a notification under paragraph (3)(b) above, the specified practice or intentions are in the particulars there mentioned of a description not included in the entry; and

PART II STATUTORY INSTRUMENTS

(c) in the case of a notification under paragraph (3)(c) above, the entry becomes inaccurate or incomplete in the particulars there mentioned.

(5) For the purposes of this regulation, personal data are "eligible data" at any time if, and to the extent that, they are at that time subject to processing which was already under way immediately before 24th October 1998.

[3302]

NOTES

Commencement: 1 March 2000.

14 Retention of register entries

(1) This regulation applies to any entry in respect of a person which is for the time being included, or by virtue of regulation 8 is treated as being included, in the register, other than an entry to which regulation 15 below applies.

(2) In relation to an entry to which this regulation applies, the fee referred to in section 19(4) of the Act is £35.

[3303]

NOTES

Commencement: 1 March 2000.

15 Retention of register entries—transitional provisions

(1) This regulation applies to any entry in respect of a person which is for the time being included in the register under paragraph 2(6) of Schedule 14 to the Act or, as the case may be, such an entry as amended in pursuance of regulation 12 (including that regulation as modified by regulation 13).

(2) Section 19(4) and (5) of the Act applies to entries to which this regulation applies subject to the modifications in paragraph (3) below.

(3) Section 19(4) and (5) of the Act shall be modified so as to have effect as follows—

"(4) No entry shall be retained in the register after—

(a) the end of the registration period, or

(b) …

[(b)] the date on which the data controller gives a notification under section 18 of the Act,

whichever occurs first.

(5) In subsection (4) "the registration period" has the same meaning as in paragraph 2(2) of Schedule 14.".

[3304]

NOTES

Commencement: 1 March 2000.

Para (3): sub-para (b) revoked, and original sub-para (c) lettered as sub-para (b), by the Data Protection (Notification and Notification Fees) (Amendment) Regulations 2001, SI 2001/3214, reg 2.

SCHEDULE
PROCESSING TO WHICH SECTION 17(1) DOES NOT APPLY

Regulation 3

1 Interpretation

In this Schedule—

"exempt purposes" in paragraphs 2 to 4 shall mean the purposes specified in sub-paragraph (a) of those paragraphs and in paragraph 5 shall mean the purposes specified in sub-paragraph (b) of that paragraph;

"staff" includes employees or office holders, workers within the meaning given in section 296 of the Trade Union and Labour Relations (Consolidation) Act 1992, persons working under any contract for services, and volunteers.

2 Staff administration exemption

The processing—

(a) is for the purposes of appointments or removals, pay, discipline, superannuation, work management or other personnel matters in relation to the staff of the data controller;

(b) is of personal data in respect of which the data subject is—

(i) a past, existing or prospective member of staff of the data controller; or

(ii) any person the processing of whose personal data is necessary for the exempt purposes;

(c) is of personal data consisting of the name, address and other identifiers of the data subject or information as to—

(i) qualifications, work experience or pay; or

(ii) other matters the processing of which is necessary for the exempt purposes;

(d) does not involve disclosure of the personal data to any third party other than—

(i) with the consent of the data subject; or

(ii) where it is necessary to make such disclosure for the exempt purposes; and

(e) does not involve keeping the personal data after the relationship between the data controller and staff member ends, unless and for so long as it is necessary to do so for the exempt purposes.

3 Advertising, marketing and public relations exemption

The processing—

(a) is for the purposes of advertising or marketing the data controller's business, activity, goods or services and promoting public relations in connection with that business or activity, or those goods or services;

(b) is of personal data in respect of which the data subject is—

(i) a past, existing or prospective customer or supplier; or

(ii) any person the processing of whose personal data is necessary for the exempt purposes;

(c) is of personal data consisting of the name, address and other identifiers of the data subject or information as to other matters the processing of which is necessary for the exempt purposes;

(d) does not involve disclosure of the personal data to any third party other than—

(i) with the consent of the data subject; or

(ii) where it is necessary to make such disclosure for the exempt purposes; and

(e) does not involve keeping the personal data after the relationship between the data controller and customer or supplier ends, unless and for so long as it is necessary to do so for the exempt purposes.

4 Accounts and records exemption

(1) The processing—

(a) is for the purposes of keeping accounts relating to any business or other activity carried on by the data controller, or deciding whether to accept any person as a customer or supplier, or keeping records of purchases, sales or other transactions for the purpose of ensuring that the requisite payments and deliveries are made or services provided by or to the data controller in respect of those transactions, or for the purpose of making financial or management forecasts to assist him in the conduct of any such business or activity;

(b) is of personal data in respect of which the data subject is—

(i) a past, existing or prospective customer or supplier; or

(ii) any person the processing of whose personal data is necessary for the exempt purposes;

(c) is of personal data consisting of the name, address and other identifiers of the data subject or information as to—

(i) financial standing; or

(ii) other matters the processing of which is necessary for the exempt purposes;

(d) does not involve disclosure of the personal data to any third party other than—

(i) with the consent of the data subject; or

(ii) where it is necessary to make such disclosure for the exempt purposes; and

(e) does not involve keeping the personal data after the relationship between the data controller and customer or supplier ends, unless and for so long as it is necessary to do so for the exempt purposes.

(2) Sub-paragraph (1)(c) shall not be taken as including personal data processed by or obtained from a credit reference agency.

5 Non profit-making organisations exemptions

The processing—

(a) is carried out by a data controller which is a body or association which is not established or conducted for profit;

(b) is for the purposes of establishing or maintaining membership of or support for the body or association, or providing or administering activities for individuals who are either members of the body or association or have regular contact with it;

(c) is of personal data in respect of which the data subject is—

 (i) a past, existing or prospective member of the body or organisation;

 (ii) any person who has regular contact with the body or organisation in connection with the exempt purposes; or

 (iii) any person the processing of whose personal data is necessary for the exempt purposes;

(d) is of personal data consisting of the name, address and other identifiers of the data subject or information as to—

 (i) eligibility for membership of the body or association; or

 (ii) other matters the processing of which is necessary for the exempt purposes;

(e) does not involve disclosure of the personal data to any third party other than—

 (i) with the consent of the data subject; or

 (ii) where it is necessary to make such disclosure for the exempt purposes; and

(f) does not involve keeping the personal data after the relationship between the data controller and data subject ends, unless and for so long as it is necessary to do so for the exempt purposes.

[3305]–[3332]

NOTES

Commencement: 1 March 2000.

DATA PROTECTION (SUBJECT ACCESS) (FEES AND MISCELLANEOUS PROVISIONS) REGULATIONS 2000

(SI 2000/191)

NOTES

Made: 31 January 2000.
Authority: Data Protection Act 1998, ss 7(2), (7), (8), (11).
Commencement: 1 March 2000.

ARRANGEMENT OF REGULATIONS

1 Citation, commencement and interpretation

(1) These Regulations may be cited as the Data Protection (Subject Access) (Fees and Miscellaneous Provisions) Regulations 2000 and shall come into force on 1st March 2000.

(2) In these Regulations "the Act" means the Data Protection Act 1998.

[3333]

NOTES

Commencement: 1 March 2000.

2 Extent of subject access requests

(1) A request for information under any provision of section 7(1)(a), (b) or (c) of the Act is to be treated as extending also to information under all other provisions of section 7(1)(a), (b) and (c).

(2) A request for information under any provision of section 7(1) of the Act is to be treated as extending to information under the provisions of section 7(1)(d) only where the request shows an express intention to that effect.

(3) A request for information under the provisions of section 7(1)(d) of the Act is to be treated as extending also to information under any other provision of section 7(1) only where the request shows an express intention to that effect.

[3334]

NOTES

Commencement: 1 March 2000.

3 Maximum subject access fee

Except as otherwise provided by regulations 4, 5 and 6 below, the maximum fee which may be required by a data controller under section 7(2)(b) of the Act is £10.

[3335]

NOTES

Commencement: 1 March 2000.

4 Limited requests for subject access where data controller is credit reference agency

(1) In any case in which a request under section 7 of the Act has been made to a data controller who is a credit reference agency, and has been limited, or by virtue of section 9(2) of the Act is taken to have been limited, to personal data relevant to an individual's financial standing—

(a) the maximum fee which may be required by a data controller under section 7(2)(b) of the Act is £2, and

(b) the prescribed period for the purposes of section 7(8) of the Act is seven working days.

(2) In this regulation "working day" means any day other than—

(a) Saturday or Sunday,

(b) Christmas Day or Good Friday,

(c) a bank holiday, within the meaning of section 1 of the Banking and Financial Dealings Act 1971, in the part of the United Kingdom in which the data controller's address is situated.

(3) For the purposes of paragraph (2)(c) above—

(a) the address of a registered company is that of its registered office, and

(b) the address of a person (other than a registered company) carrying on a business is that of his principal place of business in the United Kingdom.

[3336]

NOTES

Commencement: 1 March 2000.

5 Subject access requests in respect of educational records

(1) This regulation applies to any case in which a request made under section 7 of the Act relates wholly or partly to personal data forming part of an accessible record which is an educational record within the meaning of Schedule 11 to the Act.

(2) Except as provided by paragraph (3) below, a data controller may not require a fee under section 7(2)(b) of the Act in any case to which this regulation applies.

(3) Where, in a case to which this regulation applies, the obligation imposed by section 7(1)(c)(i) of the Act is to be complied with by supplying the data subject with a copy

PART II STATUTORY INSTRUMENTS

of information in permanent form, the maximum fee which may be required by a data controller under section 7(2)(b) of the Act is that applicable to the case under the Schedule to these Regulations.

(4) In any case to which this regulation applies, and in which the address of the data controller to whom the request is made is situated in England and Wales, the prescribed period for the purposes of section 7(8) of the Act is fifteen school days within the meaning of section 579(1) of the Education Act 1996.

[3337]

NOTES

Commencement: 1 March 2000.

6 Certain subject access requests in respect of health records ...

(1) This regulation applies only to cases in which a request made under section 7 of the Act—

(a) relates wholly or partly to personal data forming part of an accessible record which is a health record within the meaning of section 68(2) of the Act [and],

(b) does not relate exclusively to data within paragraphs (a) and (b) of the definition of "data" in section 1(1) of the Act ...

(c) ...

(2) Where in a case to which this regulation applies, the obligation imposed by section 7(1)(c)(i) of the Act is to be complied with by supplying the data subject with a copy of information in permanent form, the maximum fee which may be required by a data controller under section 7(2)(b) of the Act is £50.

(3) Except in a case to which paragraph (2) above applies, a data controller may not require a fee under section 7(2)(b) of the Act where, in a case to which this regulation applies, the request relates solely to personal data which—

(a) form part of an accessible record—

(i) which is a health record within the meaning of section 68(2) of the Act, and

(ii) at least some of which was made after the beginning of the period of 40 days immediately preceding the date of the request; and

(b) do not fall within paragraph (a) or (b) of the definition of "data" in section 1(1) of the Act.

(4) For the purposes of paragraph (3) above, an individual making a request in any case to which this regulation applies may specify that his request is limited to personal data of the description set out in that paragraph.

[3338]

NOTES

Commencement: 1 March 2000.

Provision heading: words omitted revoked by the Data Protection (Subject Access (Fees and Miscellaneous Provisions) (Amendment) Regulations 2001, SI 2001/3223, reg 2(1), (2).

Para (1): word in square brackets in sub-para (a) added, and sub-para (c) and the word immediately preceding it revoked, by SI 2001/3223, reg 2(1), (3).

SCHEDULE
MAXIMUM SUBJECT ACCESS FEES WHERE A COPY OF INFORMATION CONTAINED IN AN EDUCATIONAL RECORD IS SUPPLIED IN PERMANENT FORM

Regulation 5(3)

1. In any case in which the copy referred to in regulation 5(3) includes material in any form other than a record in writing on paper, the maximum fee applicable for the purposes of regulation 5(3) is £50.

2. In any case in which the copy referred to in regulation 5(3) consists solely of a record in writing on paper, the maximum fee applicable for the purposes of regulation 5(3) is set out in the table below.

TABLE

number of pages of information comprising the copy	*maximum fee*
fewer than 20	£1
20–29	£2
30–39	£3
40–49	£4
50–59	£5
60–69	£6
70–79	£7
80–89	£8
90–99	£9
100–149	£10
150–199	£15
200–249	£20
250–299	£25
300–349	£30
350–399	£35
400–449	£40
450–499	£45
500 or more	£50

[3339]

NOTES
Commencement: 1 March 2000.

DATA PROTECTION (SUBJECT ACCESS MODIFICATION) (SOCIAL WORK) ORDER 2000

(SI 2000/415)

NOTES
Made: 17 February 2000.
Authority: Data Protection Act 1998, s 30(3), (4), 67(2).
Commencement: 1 March 2000.

ARRANGEMENT OF ARTICLES

1 Citation and commencement

This Order may be cited as the Data Protection (Subject Access Modification) (Social Work) Order 2000 and shall come into force on 1st March 2000.

[3340]

NOTES

Commencement: 1 March 2000.

2 Interpretation

(1) In this Order—

"the Act" means the Data Protection Act 1998;

"compulsory school age" in paragraph 1(f) of the Schedule has the same meaning as in section 8 of the Education Act 1996, and in paragraph 1(g) of the Schedule has the same meaning as in Article 46 of the Education and Libraries (Northern Ireland) Order 1986;

"Health and Social Services Board" means a Health and Social Services Board established under Article 16 of the Health and Personal Social Services (Northern Ireland) Order 1972;

"Health and Social Services Trust" means a Health and Social Services Trust established under the Health and Personal Social Services (Northern Ireland) Order 1991;

"Principal Reporter" means the Principal Reporter appointed under section 127 of the Local Government etc (Scotland) Act 1994 or any officer of the Scottish Children's Reporter Administration to whom there is delegated under section 131(1) of that Act any function of the Principal Reporter;

"request" means a request made under section 7;

"school age" in paragraph 1(h) of the Schedule has the same meaning as in section 31 of the Education (Scotland) Act 1980;

"section 7" means section 7 of the Act; and

"social work authority" in article 6 means a local authority for the purposes of the Social Work (Scotland) Act 1968.

(2) Any reference in this Order to a local authority in relation to data processed or formerly processed by it includes a reference to the Council of the Isles of Scilly in relation to data processed or formerly processed by the Council in connection with any functions mentioned in paragraph 1(a)(ii) of the Schedule which are or have been conferred upon the Council by or under any enactment.

[3341]

NOTES

Commencement: 1 March 2000.

3 Personal data to which Order applies

(1) Subject to paragraph (2), this Order applies to personal data falling within any of the descriptions set out in paragraphs 1 and 2 of the Schedule.

(2) This Order does not apply—

(a) to any data consisting of information as to the physical or mental health or condition of the data subject to which the Data Protection (Subject Access Modification) (Health) Order 2000 or the Data Protection (Subject Access Modification) (Education) Order 2000 applies; or

(b) to any data which are exempted from section 7 by an order made under section 38(1) of the Act.

[3342]

NOTES

Commencement: 1 March 2000.

4 Exemption from subject information provisions

Personal data to which this Order applies by virtue of paragraph 2 of the Schedule are exempt from the subject information provisions.

[3343]

NOTES

Commencement: 1 March 2000.

5 Exemption from section 7

(1) Personal data to which this Order applies by virtue of paragraph 1 of the Schedule are exempt from the obligations in section 7(1)(b) to (d) of the Act in any case to the extent to which the application of those provisions would be likely to prejudice the carrying out of social work by reason of the fact that serious harm to the physical or mental health or condition of the data subject or any other person would be likely to be caused.

(2) In paragraph (1) the "carrying out of social work" shall be construed as including—

(a) the exercise of any functions mentioned in paragraph 1(a)(i), (d), (f) to (j), (m)[, (o), (r), (s) or (t)] of the Schedule;

(b) the provision of any service mentioned in paragraph 1(b), (c) or (k) of the Schedule; and

(c) the exercise of the functions of any body mentioned in paragraph 1(e) of the Schedule or any person mentioned in paragraph 1(p) or (q) of the Schedule.

(3) Where any person falling within paragraph (4) is enabled by or under any enactment or rule of law to make a request on behalf of a data subject and has made such a request, personal data to which this Order applies are exempt from section 7 in any case to the extent to which the application of that section would disclose information—

(a) provided by the data subject in the expectation that it would not be disclosed to the person making the request;

(b) obtained as a result of any examination or investigation to which the data subject consented in the expectation that the information would not be so disclosed; or

(c) which the data subject has expressly indicated should not be so disclosed,

provided that sub-paragraphs (a) and (b) shall not prevent disclosure where the data subject has expressly indicated that he no longer has the expectation referred to therein.

(4) A person falls within this paragraph if—

(a) except in relation to Scotland, the data subject is a child, and that person has parental responsibility for that data subject;

(b) in relation to Scotland, the data subject is a person under the age of sixteen, and that person has parental responsibilities for that data subject; or

(c) the data subject is incapable of managing his own affairs and that person has been appointed by a court to manage those affairs.

[3344]

NOTES

Commencement: 1 March 2000.

Sub-s (2): words in square brackets substituted by the Data Protection (Subject Access Modification) (Social Work) (Amendment) Order 2005, SI 2005/467, art 3.

6 Modification of section 7 relating to Principal Reporter

Where in Scotland a data controller who is a social work authority receives a request relating to information constituting data to which this Order applies and which originated from or was supplied by the Principal Reporter acting in pursuance of his statutory duties, other than information which the data subject is entitled to receive from the Principal Reporter, section 7 shall be modified so that—

(a) the data controller shall, within fourteen days of the relevant day (within the meaning of section 7(10) of the Act), inform the Principal Reporter that a request has been made; and

(b) the data controller shall not communicate information to the data subject pursuant to that section unless the Principal Reporter has informed that data controller that, in his opinion, the exemption specified in article 5(1) does not apply with respect to the information.

[3345]

NOTES

Commencement: 1 March 2000.

7 Further modifications of section 7

(1) In relation to data to which this Order applies by virtue of paragraph 1 of the Schedule—

PART II STATUTORY INSTRUMENTS

(a) section 7(4) shall have effect as if there were inserted after paragraph (b) of that subsection "or, (c) the other individual is a relevant person";

(b) section 7(9) shall have effect as if—

(i) there was substituted—

"(9) If a court is satisfied on the application of—

(a) any person who has made a request under the foregoing provisions of this section, or

(b) any person to whom serious harm to his physical or mental health or condition would be likely to be caused by compliance with any such request in contravention of those provisions,

that the data controller in question is about to comply with or has failed to comply with the request in contravention of those provisions, the court may order him not to comply or, as the case may be, to comply with the request."; and

(ii) the reference to a contravention of the foregoing provisions of that section included a reference to a contravention of the provisions contained in this Order.

(2) [In relation to data to which this Order applies by virtue of paragraph 1 of the Schedule, section 7 shall have effect as if after subsection (11) there were inserted—]

"(12) A person is a relevant person for the purposes of subsection (4)(c) if he—

(a) is a person referred to in paragraph 1(p) or (q) of the Schedule to the Data Protection (Subject Access Modification) (Social Work) Order 2000; or

(b) is or has been employed by any person or body referred to in paragraph 1 of that Schedule in connection with functions which are or have been exercised in relation to the data consisting of the information; or

(c) has provided for reward a service similar to a service provided in the exercise of any functions specified in paragraph 1(a)(i), (b), (c) or (d) of that Schedule,

and the information relates to him or he supplied the information in his official capacity or, as the case may be, in connection with the provision of that service.".

[3346]

NOTES

Commencement: 1 March 2000.

Sub-s (2): words in square brackets substituted by the Data Protection (Subject Access Modification) (Social Work) (Amendment) Order 2005, SI 2005/467, art 4.

SCHEDULE
PERSONAL DATA TO WHICH THIS ORDER APPLIES

Article 3

1. This paragraph applies to personal data falling within any of the following descriptions—

(a) data processed by a local authority—

(i) in connection with its social services functions within the meaning of the Local Authority Social Services Act 1970 or any functions exercised by local authorities under the Social Work (Scotland) Act 1968 or referred to in section 5(1B) of that Act, or

(ii) in the exercise of other functions but obtained or consisting of information obtained in connection with any of those functions;

(b) data processed by a Health and Social Services Board in connection with the provision of personal social services within the meaning of the Health and Personal Social Services (Northern Ireland) Order 1972 or processed by the Health and Social Services Board in the exercise of other functions but obtained or consisting of information obtained in connection with the provision of those services;

(c) data processed by a Health and Social Services Trust in connection with the provision of personal social services within the meaning of the Health and Personal Social Services (Northern Ireland) Order 1972 on behalf of a Health and Social Services Board by virtue of an authorisation made under Article 3(1) of the Health and Personal Social Services (Northern Ireland) Order 1994 or processed by the Health and Social Services Trust in the exercise of other functions but obtained or consisting of information obtained in connection with the provision of those services;

(d) data processed by a council in the exercise of its functions under Part II of Schedule 9 to the Health and Social Services and Social Security Adjudications Act 1983;

(e) data processed by a probation committee established by section 3 of the Probation Service Act 1993 or the Probation Board for Northern Ireland established by the Probation Board (Northern Ireland) Order 1982;

(f) data processed by a local education authority in the exercise of its functions under section 36 of the Children Act 1989 or Chapter II of Part VI of the Education Act 1996 so far as those functions relate to ensuring that children of compulsory school age receive suitable education whether by attendance at school or otherwise;

(g) data processed by an education and library board in the exercise of its functions under article 55 of the Children (Northern Ireland) Order 1995 or article 45 of, and Schedule 13 to, the Education and Libraries (Northern Ireland) Order 1986 so far as those functions relate to ensuring that children of compulsory school age receive efficient full-time education suitable to their age, ability and aptitude and to any special educational needs they may have, either by regular attendance at school or otherwise;

(h) data processed by an education authority in the exercise of its functions under sections 35 to 42 of the Education (Scotland) Act 1980 so far as those functions relate to ensuring that children of school age receive efficient education suitable to their age, ability and aptitude, whether by attendance at school or otherwise;

(i) data relating to persons detained in a special hospital provided under section 4 of the National Health Service Act 1977 and processed by a special health authority established under section 11 of that Act in the exercise of any functions similar to any social services functions of a local authority;

(j) data relating to persons detained in special accommodation provided under article 110 of the Mental Health (Northern Ireland) Order 1986 and processed by a Health and Social Services Trust in the exercise of any functions similar to any social services functions of a local authority;

(k) data processed by the National Society for the Prevention of Cruelty to Children or by any other voluntary organisation or other body designated under this sub-paragraph by the Secretary of State or the Department of Health, Social Services and Public Safety and appearing to the Secretary of State or the Department, as the case may be, to be processed for the purposes of the provision of any service similar to a service provided in the exercise of any functions specified in sub-paragraphs (a)(i), (b), (c) or (d) above;

(l) data processed by—

[(zi) a Strategic Health Authority established under section 8 of the National Health Service Act 1977;]

(i) a Health Authority established under section 8 of the National Health Service Act 1977;

(ii) an NHS Trust established under section 5 of the National Health Service and Community Care Act 1990; . . .

[(iiza) an NHS foundation trust within the meaning of section 1(1) of the Health and Social Care (Community Health and Standards) Act 2003;]

[(iia) a Primary Care Trust established under section 16A of the National Health Service Act 1977; or]

(iii) a Health Board established under section 2 of the National Health Service (Scotland) Act 1978,

which were obtained or consisted of information which was obtained from any authority or body mentioned above or government department and which, whilst processed by that authority or body or government department, fell within any sub-paragraph of this paragraph;

(m) data processed by an NHS Trust as referred to in sub-paragraph (l)(ii) above in the exercise of any functions similar to any social services functions of a local authority;

[(mm) data processed by an NHS foundation trust as referred to in sub-paragraph (l)(iiza) above in the exercise of any functions similar to any social services functions of a local authority;]

(n) data processed by a government department and obtained or consisting of information obtained from any authority or body mentioned above and which, whilst processed by that authority or body, fell within any of the preceding sub-paragraphs of this paragraph;

(o) data processed for the purposes of the functions of the Secretary of State pursuant to section 82(5) of the Children Act 1989;

PART II STATUTORY INSTRUMENTS

[(p) data processed by any children's guardian appointed under [rule 4.10 of the Family Proceedings Rules 1991 or rule 10 of the Family Proceedings Courts (Children Act 1989) Rules 1991], by any guardian ad litem appointed under Article 60 of the Children (Northern Ireland) Order 1995 or Article 66 of the Adoption (Northern Ireland) Order 1987 or by a safeguarder appointed under section 41 of the Children (Scotland) Act 1995;]

(q) data processed by the Principal Reporter;

[(r) data processed by any officer of the Children and Family Court Advisory and Support Service for the purpose of his functions under section 7 of the Children Act 1989, rules 4.11 and 4.11B of the Family Proceedings Rules 1991, and rules 11 and 11B of the Family Proceedings Courts (Children Act 1989) Rules 1991;

(s) data processed by any officer of the service appointed as guardian ad litem under rule 9.5(1) of the Family Proceedings Rules 1991;

(t) data processed by the Children and Family Court Advisory and Support Service for the purpose of its functions under section 12(1) and (2) and section 13(1), (2) and (4) of the Criminal Justice and Court Services Act 2000];

[(u) data processed for the purposes of the functions of the appropriate Minister pursuant to section 12 of the Adoption and Children Act 2002 (independent review of determinations)].

2. This paragraph applies to personal data processed by a court and consisting of information supplied in a report or other evidence given to the court by a local authority, Health and Social Services Board, Health and Social Services Trust, probation officer[, officer of the Children and Family Court Advisory and Support Service] or other person in the course of any proceedings to which the Family Proceedings Courts (Children Act 1989) Rules 1991, the Magistrates' Courts (Children and Young Persons) Rules 1992, the Magistrates' Courts (Criminal Justice (Children)) Rules (Northern Ireland) 1999, the Act of Sederunt (Child Care and Maintenance Rules) 1997[, the Children's Hearings (Scotland) Rules 1996 or the Family Proceedings Rules 1991] apply where, in accordance with a provision of any of those Rules, the information may be withheld by the court in whole or in part from the data subject.

[3347]

NOTES

Commencement: 1 March 2000.

Para 1: sub-para (l)(zi), (iia) inserted, and the word omitted from sub-para (l)(ii) revoked, by the National Health Service Reform and Health Care Professions Act 2002 (Supplementary, Consequential etc Provisions) Regulations 2002, SI 2002/2469, reg 4, Sch 1, Pt 2, para 88; sub-paras (l)(iiza), (mm) inserted by the Health and Social Care (Community Health and Standards) Act 2003 (Supplementary and Consequential Provision) (NHS Foundation Trusts) Order 2004, SI 2004/696, art 3(1), Sch 1, para 34; sub-para (p) substituted by the Children and Family Court Advisory Support Service (Miscellaneous Amendments) Order 2002, SI 2002/3220, art 3; words in square brackets in sub-para (p) substituted and sub-paras (r), (s), (t) inserted by the Data Protection (Subject Access Modification) (Social Work) (Amendment) Order 2005, SI 2005/467, art 5(1)–(3); sub-para (u) inserted by the Adoption and Children Act 2002 (Consequential Amendments) Order 2005, SI 2005/3504, art 2(2).

Para 2: words in first pair of square brackets inserted and words in second pair of square brackets substituted by SI 2005/467, art 5(1), (4).

DATA PROTECTION (PROCESSING OF SENSITIVE PERSONAL DATA) ORDER 2000

(SI 2000/417)

NOTES

Made: 17 February 2000.

Authority: Data Protection Act 1998, s 67(2), Sch 3, para 10.

Commencement: 1 March 2000.

1—(1) This Order may be cited as the Data Protection (Processing of Sensitive Personal Data) Order 2000 and shall come into force on 1st March 2000.

(2) In this Order, "the Act" means the Data Protection Act 1998.

[3348]

NOTES

Commencement: 1 March 2000.

2 For the purposes of paragraph 10 of Schedule 3 to the Act, the circumstances specified in any of the paragraphs in the Schedule to this Order are circumstances in which sensitive personal data may be processed.

[3349]

NOTES

Commencement: 1 March 2000.

SCHEDULE

CIRCUMSTANCES IN WHICH SENSITIVE PERSONAL DATA MAY BE PROCESSED

Article 2

1.—(1) The processing—

(a) is in the substantial public interest;

(b) is necessary for the purposes of the prevention or detection of any unlawful act; and

(c) must necessarily be carried out without the explicit consent of the data subject being sought so as not to prejudice those purposes.

(2) In this paragraph, "act" includes a failure to act.

2. The processing—

(a) is in the substantial public interest;

(b) is necessary for the discharge of any function which is designed for protecting members of the public against—

(i) dishonesty, malpractice, or other seriously improper conduct by, or the unfitness or incompetence of, any person, or

(ii) mismanagement in the administration of, or failures in services provided by, any body or association; and

(c) must necessarily be carried out without the explicit consent of the data subject being sought so as not to prejudice the discharge of that function.

3.—(1) The disclosure of personal data—

(a) is in the substantial public interest;

(b) is in connection with—

(i) the commission by any person of any unlawful act (whether alleged or established),

(ii) dishonesty, malpractice, or other seriously improper conduct by, or the unfitness or incompetence of, any person (whether alleged or established), or

(iii) mismanagement in the administration of, or failures in services provided by, any body or association (whether alleged or established);

(c) is for the special purposes as defined in section 3 of the Act; and

(d) is made with a view to the publication of those data by any person and the data controller reasonably believes that such publication would be in the public interest.

(2) In this paragraph, "act" includes a failure to act.

4. The processing—

(a) is in the substantial public interest;

(b) is necessary for the discharge of any function which is designed for the provision of confidential counselling, advice, support or any other service; and

(c) is carried out without the explicit consent of the data subject because the processing—

(i) is necessary in a case where consent cannot be given by the data subject,

(ii) is necessary in a case where the data controller cannot reasonably be expected to obtain the explicit consent of the data subject, or

(iii) must necessarily be carried out without the explicit consent of the data subject being sought so as not to prejudice the provision of that counselling, advice, support or other service.

5.—(1) The processing—

(a) is necessary for the purpose of—

(i) carrying on insurance business, or

(ii) making determinations in connection with eligibility for, and benefits payable under, an occupational pension scheme as defined in section 1 of the Pension Schemes Act 1993;

(b) is of sensitive personal data consisting of information falling within section 2(e) of the Act relating to a data subject who is the parent, grandparent, great grandparent or sibling of—

(i) in the case of paragraph (a)(i), the insured person, or

(ii) in the case of paragraph (a)(ii), the member of the scheme;

(c) is necessary in a case where the data controller cannot reasonably be expected to obtain the explicit consent of that data subject and the data controller is not aware of the data subject withholding his consent; and

(d) does not support measures or decisions with respect to that data subject.

(2) In this paragraph—

[(a) "insurance business" means business which consists of effecting or carrying out contracts of insurance of the following kind—

(i) life and annuity,

(ii) linked long term,

(iii) permanent health,

(iv) accident, or

(v) sickness; and]

(b) "insured" and "member" includes an individual who is seeking to become an insured person or member of the scheme respectively.

[(2A) The definition of "insurance business" in sub-paragraph (2) above must be read with—

(a) section 22 of the Financial Services and Markets Act 2000;

(b) any relevant order under that section; and

(c) Schedule 2 to that Act.]

6. The processing—

(a) is of sensitive personal data in relation to any particular data subject that are subject to processing which was already under way immediately before the coming into force of this Order;

(b) is necessary for the purpose of—

[(i) effecting or carrying out contracts of long-term insurance of the kind mentioned in sub-paragraph (2)(a)(i), (ii) or (iii) of paragraph 5 above;]

(ii) establishing or administering an occupational pension scheme as defined in section 1 of the Pension Schemes Act 1993; and

(c) either—

(i) is necessary in a case where the data controller cannot reasonably be expected to obtain the explicit consent of the data subject and that data subject has not informed the data controller that he does not so consent, or

(ii) must necessarily be carried out even without the explicit consent of the data subject so as not to prejudice those purposes.

7.—(1) Subject to the provisions of sub-paragraph (2), the processing—

(a) is of sensitive personal data consisting of information falling within section 2(c) or (e) of the Act;

(b) is necessary for the purpose of identifying or keeping under review the existence or absence of equality of opportunity or treatment between persons—

(i) holding different beliefs as described in section 2(c) of the Act, or

(ii) of different states of physical or mental health or different physical or mental conditions as described in section 2(e) of the Act,

with a view to enabling such equality to be promoted or maintained;

(c) does not support measures or decisions with respect to any particular data subject otherwise than with the explicit consent of that data subject; and

(d) does not cause, nor is likely to cause, substantial damage or substantial distress to the data subject or any other person.

(2) Where any individual has given notice in writing to any data controller who is processing personal data under the provisions of sub-paragraph (1) requiring that data controller to cease processing personal data in respect of which that individual is the data subject at the end of such period as is reasonable in the circumstances, that data controller must have ceased processing those personal data at the end of that period.

8.—(1) Subject to the provisions of sub-paragraph (2), the processing—

(a) is of sensitive personal data consisting of information falling within section 2(b) of the Act;

(b) is carried out by any person or organisation included in the register maintained pursuant to section 1 of the Registration of Political Parties Act 1998 in the course of his or its legitimate political activities; and

(c) does not cause, nor is likely to cause, substantial damage or substantial distress to the data subject or any other person.

(2) Where any individual has given notice in writing to any data controller who is processing personal data under the provisions of sub-paragraph (1) requiring that data controller to cease processing personal data in respect of which that individual is the data subject at the end of such period as is reasonable in the circumstances, that data controller must have ceased processing those personal data at the end of that period.

9. The processing—

(a) is in the substantial public interest;

(b) is necessary for research purposes (which expression shall have the same meaning as in section 33 of the Act);

(c) does not support measures or decisions with respect to any particular data subject otherwise than with the explicit consent of that data subject; and

(d) does not cause, nor is likely to cause, substantial damage or substantial distress to the data subject or any other person.

10. The processing is necessary for the exercise of any functions conferred on a constable by any rule of law.

[3350]

NOTES

Commencement: 1 March 2000.

Para 5: sub-para (2)(a) substituted, and sub-para (2A) inserted, by the Financial Services and Markets Act 2000 (Consequential Amendments and Repeals) Order 2001, SI 2001/3649, art 587(1)–(3).

Para 6: sub-para (b)(i) substituted by SI 2001/3649, art 587(1), (4).

PART II STATUTORY INSTRUMENTS

DONATIONS TO CHARITY BY INDIVIDUALS (APPROPRIATE DECLARATIONS) REGULATIONS 2000

(SI 2000/2074)

NOTES

Made: 28 July 2000.

Authority: Finance Act 1990, s 25(3); Finance Act 1999, ss 132(1)(a), (2)(a), (8), (9), (10), 133(1), (2); Finance Act 2000, s 39(10).

Commencement: 21 August 2000.

ARRANGEMENT OF REGULATIONS

1 Citation, commencement and effect

(1) These Regulations may be cited as the Donations to Charity by Individuals (Appropriate Declarations) Regulations 2000 and shall come into force on 21st August 2000.

(2) These Regulations shall have effect in relation to—

(a) gifts made on or after 6th April 2000 which are not covenanted payments; and

(b) covenanted payments falling to be made on or after that date.

[3351]

NOTES

Commencement: 21 August 2000.

2 Interpretation

In these Regulations—

"appropriate declaration" has the same meaning as in section 25(1)(c) of the Finance Act 1990;

["the Commissioners" means the Commissioners for Her Majesty's Revenue and Customs;]

"donor" has the same meaning as in section 25(1) of the Finance Act 1990;

["electronic communications" includes any communications conveyed by means of an electronic communications network].

[3352]

NOTES

Commencement: 21 August 2000.

Definition "the Commissioners" substituted, for definition "the Board" as originally enacted, by the Donations to Charity by Individuals (Appropriate Declarations) (Amendment) Regulations 2005, SI 2005/2790, regs 2, 3.

Definition "electronic communications" substituted by the Communications Act 2003 (Consequential Amendments) Order 2003, SI 2003/2155, art 3(1), Sch 1, Pt 5, para 23(1)(c), (2).

3 Manner in which an appropriate declaration may be given

An appropriate declaration may be given by a donor to a charity—

(a) in writing; [or

(b) orally;

including the use of written or oral methods of electronic communications, as the case may be].

[3353]

NOTES

Commencement: 21 August 2000.

Words in square brackets substituted by the Donations to Charity by Individuals (Appropriate Declarations) (Amendment) Regulations 2005, SI 2005/2790, regs 2, 4.

[4 Giving appropriate declarations]

[(1) An appropriate declaration must—

(a) contain the name and home address of the donor,

(b) name the charity (or be made in circumstances where the charity is identified),

(c) identify the gift or gifts to which the declaration relates, and

(d) confirm that the identified gift or gifts are to be qualifying donations for the purposes of section 25 of the Finance Act 1990 (Donations to charity by individuals).

(2) The explanation of section 25(8) of the Finance Act 1990 referred to in regulation 5(2)(b) or (4)(b), as the case may be, must be given to the donor in order for an appropriate declaration to have effect (subject to regulation 6).]

[3354]

NOTES

Commencement: 21 August 2000.

Substituted by the Donations to Charity by Individuals (Appropriate Declarations) (Amendment) Regulations 2005, SI 2005/2790, regs 2, 5.

[5 Recording and audit of appropriate declarations]

[(1) A charity must either—

(a) maintain an auditable record of appropriate declarations given to it, or

(b) comply with paragraphs (4) to (6) in relation to each declaration.

This is subject to paragraph (3).

(2) An auditable record is a record of evidence—

(a) of appropriate declarations and the making of them, and

(b) that (whether or not separate from the declaration) statements explaining the effect of section 25(8) of the Finance Act 1990 were given to donors at the time the declarations were made,

in a form, and to a standard, which can be inspected and audited by the Commissioners.

(3) If the Commissioners notify the charity that the record, or the records relating to particular declarations or classes of declarations, do not meet with their satisfaction, the charity must comply with paragraphs (4) to (6) in relation to the declarations in question.

(4) Where paragraph (1)(b) or (3) applies, the charity shall in each case send the donor a statement in writing ("written statement") containing—

(a) the information required by regulation 4(1)(a) to (d),

(b) an explanation of the effect of section 25(8) of the Finance Act 1990,

(c) the date on which the charity sends the statement to the donor, and

(d) a statement that the donor is entitled to cancel his declaration by giving notice in writing to the charity not later than 30 days following the date in sub-paragraph (c).

(5) Where paragraph (4) applies, the donor is entitled to cancel the declaration by giving notice of cancellation to the charity in accordance with paragraph (4)(d).

(6) The charity shall maintain an auditable record of—

(a) written statements, and

(b) any cancellation notices,

in a form, and to a standard, which can be inspected and audited by the Commissioners.

(7) Where a donor who has given an appropriate declaration to a charity notifies the charity of any change to his name or home address, the charity must keep a record of those changes with the declaration.]

[3355]

NOTES

Commencement: 21 August 2000.

Substituted by the Donations to Charity by Individuals (Appropriate Declarations) (Amendment) Regulations 2005, SI 2005/2790, regs 2, 5.

[6 Prescribed circumstances in which appropriate declarations are deemed never to have had effect]

[An appropriate declaration shall be treated for the purposes of the Taxes Acts as never having had effect where—

(a) the charity has not sent the written statement to the donor in a case where it is required to do so by regulation 5(4);

(b) the donor cancels the declaration by giving notice in accordance with regulation 5(5); or

(c) the Commissioners notify the charity that the records relating to that declaration under regulation 5(6) do not meet with their satisfaction.]

[3356]

NOTES

Commencement: 21 August 2000.

Substituted by SI 2005/2790, regs 2, 5.

[7 Prescribed circumstances in which appropriate declarations cease to have effect]

[An appropriate declaration shall cease to have effect for the purposes of the Taxes Acts where—

(a) the donor notifies the charity of the cancellation of his declaration (other than in accordance with regulation 5(5)), and

(b) the cancellation takes effect from (or after) the date of its receipt by the charity.]

[3357]

NOTES

Commencement: 21 August 2000.

Substituted by the Donations to Charity by Individuals (Appropriate Declarations) (Amendment) Regulations 2005, SI 2005/2790, regs 2, 5.

LAND REGISTRATION RULES 2003

SI 2003/1417

NOTES

Made: 19 May 2003.

Authority: Land Registration Act 2002, ss 1(2), 6(6), 13(a), (b), 14(a), (b), 16(2), 18(1)(b), (2), (4), 19(2), 20(3)(a), (b), (c), 21(2)(a), (b), (c), (d), 22, 25(1), 27(6), 34(2), 35(3), 36(3), (4), 37(2), 39, 43(2)(a), (b), (c), (d), 44(2), 45(2), 46(4), 47(a), (b), 48(2)(a), (b), 49(2), (3)(b), (4)(b), 50, 57, 60(3), (4), 61(2), 64(2), 66(2), 67(3), 68(1)(d), (2)(a), (b), 69(2), 70, 71(a), (b), 72(6)(a), (b), 73(2), (3), (4), 75(2), 76(2), 81(2), 82, 86(3), 87(4), 89, 95(a), 98(7), Sch 2, paras 2(2), 7(3), Sch 4, paras 4(a), (b), (c), 7(a), (b), (c), (d), Sch 6, paras 2(1)(d), 3(2), 14, 15, Sch 8, para 9, Sch 10, paras 1(1)(a), (b), 3(a), (b), (c), 5, 6(a), (b), (c), (d), (e), 7, 8, Sch 12, paras 2(4), 18(5), the Charities Act 1993, ss 37(7), 39(1), (1A), the Leasehold Reform, Housing and Urban Development Act 1993, ss 34(10), 57(11) and the Family Law Act 1996, Sch 4, para 4(4).

Commencement: 13 October 2003.

ARRANGEMENT OF RULES

PRELIMINARY

PART 14
MISCELLANEOUS AND SPECIAL CASES

Charities

Companies and other corporations

PART 15
GENERAL PROVISIONS

PRELIMINARY

1 Citation and commencement

These rules may be cited as the Land Registration Rules 2003 and shall come into force on the day that section 1 of the Act comes into force.

[3358]

NOTES

Commencement: 13 October 2003.

2–160 ((*Pts 1–13*) *outside the scope of this work.*)

PART 14
MISCELLANEOUS AND SPECIAL CASES

161–175 (*Outside the scope of this work.*)

Charities

176 Non-exempt charities—restrictions

(1) The restriction which the registrar is required by section 37(8) or section 39(1B) of the Charities Act 1993 to enter in the register where one of those subsections applies must be the appropriate restriction.

(2) Any of the following applications must, if they relate to a registered or unregistered estate held by or in trust for a non-exempt charity, be accompanied by an application for entry of the appropriate restriction unless, in the case of a registered estate, that restriction is already in the register—

(a) an application for first registration of an unregistered estate unless the disposition which triggers the requirement of registration is effected by an instrument containing the statement set out in rule 179(b) or rule 180(2)(b) or (c),

(b) an application to register a transfer of a registered estate unless the disposition is effected by an instrument containing the statement set out in rule 179(b),

(c) an application under rule 161 to register the vesting of a registered estate in a person other than the proprietor of that estate.

(3) Where a registered estate is held by or in trust for a corporation and the corporation becomes a non-exempt charity, the charity trustees must apply for entry of the appropriate restriction.

(4) In this rule "the appropriate restriction" means a restriction in Form E.

[3359]

NOTES

Commencement: 13 October 2003.

177 Registration of trustees incorporated under Part VII of the Charities Act 1993

In any registrable disposition in favour of charity trustees incorporated under Part VII of the Charities Act 1993 they must be described as "a body corporate under Part VII of the Charities Act 1993" and the application to register the disposition must be accompanied by the certificate granted by the Charity Commissioners under section 50 of that Act.

[3360]

NOTES

Commencement: 13 October 2003.

178 Registration of official custodian

(1) An application to register the official custodian as proprietor of a registered estate or a registered charge must be accompanied by—

(a) an order of the court made under section 21(1) of the Charities Act 1993, or

(b) an order of the Charity Commissioners made under sections 16 or 18 of the Charities Act 1993.

(2) Where the estate or charge is vested in the official custodian by virtue of an order under section 18 of the Charities Act 1993, an application to register him as proprietor (whether under Chapter 1 of Part 2 of the Act or following a registrable disposition) must be accompanied by an application for the entry of a restriction in Form F.

(3) Where the official custodian is registered as proprietor of a registered estate or a registered charge, except where the estate or charge is vested in him by virtue of an order under section 18 of the Charities Act 1993, the address of the charity trustees or, where the registered estate or registered charge is held on behalf of a charity which is a corporation, the address of the charity, must be entered in the register as his address for service under rule 198.
[3361]

NOTES

Commencement: 13 October 2003.

179 Statements to be contained in dispositions in favour of a charity

The statement required by section 37(5) of the Charities Act 1993 must, in an instrument to which section 37(7) of that Act applies, be in one of the following forms—

(a) "The land transferred (*or as the case may be*) will, as a result of this transfer (*or as the case may be*) be held by (or in trust for) (*charity*), an exempt charity."

(b) "The land transferred (*or as the case may be*) will, as a result of this transfer (*or as the case may be*) be held by (*or* in trust for) (*charity*), a non-exempt charity, and the restrictions on disposition imposed by section 36 of the Charities Act 1993 will apply to the land (subject to section 36(9) of that Act).".
[3362]

NOTES

Commencement: 13 October 2003.

180 Statements to be contained in dispositions by a charity

(1) The statement required by section 37(1) of the Charities Act 1993 must, in an instrument to which section 37(7) of that Act applies, be in one of the following forms—

(a) "The land transferred (*or as the case may be*) is held by [(*proprietors*) in trust for] (*charity*), an exempt charity."

(b) "The land transferred (*or as the case may be*) is held by [(*proprietors*) in trust for] (*charity*), a non-exempt charity, but this transfer (*or as the case may be*) is one falling within paragraph ((a), (b) or (c) *as the case may be*) of section 36(9) of the Charities Act 1993."

(c) "The land transferred (*or as the case may be*) is held by [(*proprietors*) in trust for] (*charity*), a non-exempt charity, and this transfer (*or as the case may be*) is not one falling within paragraph (a), (b) or (c) of section 36(9) of the Charities Act 1993, so that the restrictions on disposition imposed by section 36 of that Act apply to the land.".

(2) The statement required by section 39(1) of the Charities Act 1993 must, in a mortgage which is a registrable disposition or to which section 4(1)(g) of the Act applies, be in one of the following forms—

(a) "The land charged is held by (*or* in trust for) (*charity*), an exempt charity."

(b) "The land charged is held by (*or* in trust for) (*charity*), a non-exempt charity, but this charge (*or* mortgage) is one falling within section 38(5) of the Charities Act 1993."

(c) "The land charged is held by (*or* in trust for) (*charity*), a non-exempt charity, and this charge (*or* mortgage) is not one falling within section 38(5) of the Charities Act 1993, so that the restrictions imposed by section 38 of that Act apply.".

(3) The statement required by section 39(1A)(b) of the Charities Act 1993 must be in the following form—

"The restrictions on disposition imposed by section 36 of the Charities Act 1993 also apply to the land (subject to section 36(9) of that Act).".

[3363]

NOTES

Commencement: 13 October 2003.

Companies and other corporations

181 Registration of companies and limited liability partnerships

(1) Where a company registered in England and Wales or Scotland under the Companies Acts applies to be registered as proprietor of a registered estate or of a registered charge, the application must state the company's registered number.

(2) If the company is a registered social landlord within the meaning of the Housing Act 1996, the application must also contain or be accompanied by a certificate to that effect.

(3) If the company is an unregistered housing association within the meaning of the Housing Associations Act 1985 and the application relates to grant-aided land as defined in Schedule 1 to that Act, the application must also contain or be accompanied by a certificate to that effect.

(4) Where a limited liability partnership incorporated under the Limited Liability Partnerships Act 2000 applies to be registered as proprietor of a registered estate or of a registered charge, the application must state the limited liability partnership's registered number.

[3364]

NOTES

Commencement: 13 October 2003.

182 Registration of trustees of charitable, ecclesiastical or public trust

(1) Subject to paragraph (4), where a corporation or body of trustees holding on charitable, ecclesiastical or public trusts applies to be registered as proprietor of a registered estate or registered charge, the application must be accompanied by the document creating the trust.

(2) If the registered estate or registered charge to which the application relates is held on trust for a registered social landlord within the meaning of the Housing Act 1996, the application must also contain or be accompanied by a certificate to that effect.

(3) If the registered estate or registered charge to which the application relates is held on trust for an unregistered housing association within the meaning of the Housing Associations Act 1985 and is grant-aided land as defined in Schedule 1 to that Act, the application must also contain or be accompanied by a certificate to that effect.

(4) Paragraph (1) of this rule does not apply in the case of a registered estate or a registered charge held by or in trust for a non-exempt charity.

[3365]

NOTES

Commencement: 13 October 2003.

183 Registration of other corporations

(1) Where a corporation aggregate, to which rules 181 and 182 do not apply, makes an application to be registered as proprietor of a registered estate or registered charge the application must also be accompanied by evidence of the extent of its powers to hold and sell, mortgage, lease and otherwise deal with land and, in the case of a charge, to lend money on mortgage.

(2) The evidence must include the charter, statute, rules, memorandum and articles of association or other documents constituting the corporation, together with such further evidence as the registrar may require.

(3) If the corporation is a registered social landlord within the meaning of the Housing Act 1996, the application must contain or be accompanied by a certificate to that effect.

(4) If the corporation is an unregistered housing association within the meaning of the Housing Associations Act 1985 and the application relates to grant-aided land as defined in Schedule 1 to that Act, the application must contain or be accompanied by a certificate to that effect.

[3366]

NOTES

Commencement: 13 October 2003.

184–196 (*Outside the scope of this work.*)

PART 15
GENERAL PROVISIONS

197–216 (*Outside the scope of this work.*)

217 General Interpretation

(1) In these rules—

"the Act" means the Land Registration Act 2002,

"affecting franchise" means a franchise which relates to a defined area of land and is an adverse right affecting, or capable of affecting, the title to an estate or charge,

"business day" means a day when the land registry is open to the public under rule 216,

"caution plan" has the meaning given by rule 41(4),

"caution title number" has the meaning given by rule 41(1),

"certified copy" means a copy of a document which a conveyancer, or such other person as the registrar may permit, has certified on its face to be a true copy of the original and endorsed with his name and address, and the reference to a conveyancer includes where the document is one referred to in—

(a) rule 168(2)(a) or 168(3), the bankrupt's trustee in bankruptcy or the official receiver,

(b) rule 184(2), the company's administrator,

(c) rule 184(5), the company's liquidator,

"charges register" is the register so named in rule 4 the contents of which are described in rule 9,

"charity" and "charity trustees" have the same meaning as in sections 96 and 97(1) of the Charities Act 1993 respectively,

"Companies Acts" means the Companies Act 1985, any Act amending or replacing that Act and any former enactment relating to companies,

"control" in relation to a document of which a person has control means physical possession, or the right to possession, or right to take copies of the document,

"conveyancer" means—

(a) a solicitor, or

(b) a licensed conveyancer within the meaning of section 11(2) of the Administration of Justice Act 1985, or

(c) a fellow of the Institute of Legal Executives, [or

(d) a duly certificated notary public,]

and a reference to a person's conveyancer is a reference to a solicitor, licensed conveyancer[, fellow of the Institute of Legal Executives or duly certificated notary public] who is acting on that person's behalf,

"day list" has the same meaning given by rule 12,

"exempt charity" has the same meaning as in section 96 of the Charities Act 1993 and "non-exempt charity" means a charity which is not an exempt charity,

["home rights notice" means a notice registered under section 31(10)(a) or section 32 of, and paragraph 4(3)(a) or 4(3)(b) of Schedule 4 to, the Family Law Act 1996, or section 2(8) or section 5(3)(b) of the Matrimonial Homes Act 1983, or section 2(7) or section 5(3)(b) of the Matrimonial Homes Act 1967,]

"index map" has the meaning given by rule 10(1)(a),

"index of proprietors' names" has the meaning given by rule 11(1),

"index of relating franchises and manors" is the index described in rule 10(1)(b),

"individual caution register" is the register so named in rule 41(1) the arrangement of which is described in rule 41(2),

"individual register" is the register so named in rule 2 the contents and arrangement of which are described in rules 3 and 4,

"inheritance tax notice" means a notice in respect of an Inland Revenue charge arising under Part III of the Finance Act 1975 or section 237 of the Inheritance Tax Act 1984,

"matrimonial home rights caution" means a caution registered under the Matrimonial Homes Act 1967 before 14 February 1983,

.. ...

"official custodian" means the official custodian for charities,

"old tenancy" means a tenancy as defined in section 28 of the Landlord and Tenant (Covenants) Act 1995 which is not a new tenancy as defined in section 1 of that Act,

"overseas company" means a company incorporated outside Great Britain,

"property register" is the register so named in rule 4 the contents of which are described in rules 5, 6 and 7,

"proprietorship register" is the register so named in rule 4 the contents of which are described in rule 8,

"registered title" means an individual register and any title plan referred to in that register,

"relating franchise" means a franchise which is not an affecting franchise,

"Schedule 1 form" means a form in Schedule 1,

"Schedule 3 form" means a form in Schedule 3,

"scheduled form" means a Schedule 1 form or a Schedule 3 form,

"section 33(5) order" means an order made under section 33(5) of the Family Law Act 1996,

"statutory declaration" includes affidavit,

"title number" has the meaning given by rule 4,

"title plan" has the meaning given by rule 5,

"trust corporation" has the same meaning as in the Settled Land Act 1925,

"trusts" in relation to a charity has the same meaning as in section 97(1) of the Charities Act 1993,

"unregistered company" means a body corporate to which section 718(1) of the Companies Act 1985 applies.

(2) Subject to paragraph (3), a reference in these rules to a form by letter, or by number, or by a combination of both is to a scheduled form.

(3) A reference in these rules to Forms A to Y and [Forms AA to LL] (in each case inclusive) is to the standard form of restriction bearing that letter in Schedule 4.

[3367]

NOTES

Commencement: 13 October 2003.

Para (1): definition "conveyancer": para (d) inserted (with preceding word "or") and words in square brackets in final para of that definition substituted by the Land Registration (Amendment) Rules 2005, SI 2005/1766.

Para (1): definition "home rights notice": inserted by the Land Registration (Amendment) (No 2) Rules 2005, SI 2005/1982, r 16.

Para (1): definition "matrimonial home rights notice" (omitted): revoked by SI 2005/1982, r 16.

Para (3): words in square brackets substituted by SI 2005/1766, r 9(2).

218–224 ((*Pt 16*) *outside the scope of this work.*)

(*Schs 1–9 outside the scope of this work.*)

INFORMATION TRIBUNAL (ENFORCEMENT APPEALS) RULES 2005

(SI 2005/14)

NOTES

Made: 7 January 2005.

Authority: Data Protection Act 1998, s 67(2), Sch 6, para 7.

Commencement: 1 February 2005.

ARRANGEMENT OF RULES

1 Citation and commencement

These Rules may be cited as the Information Tribunal (Enforcement Appeals) Rules 2005 and shall come into force on 1st February 2005.

[3368]

NOTES

Commencement: 1 February 2005.

2 (*Revokes the Data Protection Tribunal (Enforcement Appeals) Rules 2000, SI 2000/189 and the Information Tribunal (Enforcement Appeals) (Amendment) Rules 2002, SI 2002/2722.*)

3 Application and interpretation

(1) These Rules apply to appeals under section 48 of the 1998 Act, section 57 of the 2000 Act, and section 57 of the 2000 Act as applied, as modified, by regulation 18 of the 2004 Regulations and the provisions of these Rules are to be construed accordingly.

(2) In these Rules—

"the 1998 Act" means the Data Protection Act 1998;

"the 2000 Act" means the Freedom of Information Act 2000;

"the 2004 Regulations" means the Environmental Information Regulations 2004;

"appeal" means an appeal under—

- (a) section 48 of the 1998 Act,
- (b) section 57 of the 2000 Act, or
- (c) section 57 of the 2000 Act as applied, as modified, by regulation 18 of the 2004 Regulations,

as the case may be;

"appellant" means—

- (a) a person who brings or intends to bring an appeal under section 48 of the 1998 Act, or
- (b) a complainant who, or a public authority which brings, or intends to bring, an appeal under section 57(1) of the 2000 Act or section 57(1) of the 2000 Act as applied, as modified, by regulation 18 of the 2004 Regulations, or
- (c) a public authority which brings or intends to bring an appeal under section 57(2) of the 2000 Act or section 57(2) of the 2000 Act as applied, as modified, by regulation 18 of the 2004 Regulations,

as the case may be;

"chairman" means the chairman of the Tribunal, and includes a deputy chairman of the Tribunal presiding or sitting alone;

"costs"—

(a) except in Scotland, includes fees, charges, disbursements, expenses and remuneration;

(b) in Scotland means expenses, and includes fees, charges, disbursements and remuneration;

"disputed decision" means—

(a) in relation to an appeal under section 48 of the 1998 Act other than an appeal under section 48(3)(b) of that Act, the decision of the Commissioner,

(b) in relation to an appeal under section 48(3)(b) of the 1998 Act, the effect of a decision of the Commissioner, and

(c) in relation to an appeal under section 57 of the 2000 Act or section 57 as applied, as modified, by regulation 18 of the 2004 Regulations, the decision of the Commissioner,

against which the appellant appeals or intends to appeal to the Tribunal, as the case may be;

"hearing" means a sitting of the Tribunal for the purposes of enabling the Tribunal to take a decision on an appeal, or on any matter raised in relation to an appeal, at which the parties are entitled to attend and be heard;

"party" has the meaning given in paragraph (3) below; and

"proper officer" in relation to a rule means an officer or member of staff provided to the Tribunal under paragraph 14 of Schedule 5 to the 1998 Act and appointed by the chairman to perform the duties of a proper officer under that rule.

(3) In these Rules, "party" means the appellant, or the Commissioner, or a person joined to an appeal in accordance with rule 7 below and, except where the context otherwise requires, references in these Rules to a party (including a reference in rule 15 below) include a person appointed under rule 19(1) to represent his interests.

(4) In relation to proceedings before the Tribunal in Scotland, for the words "on the trial of an action" in rules 14(5), 15(8) and 27(2) below there is substituted "in a proof".

(5) Appeals brought before 1st January 2005 shall be determined in accordance with the Data Protection Tribunal (Enforcement Appeals) Rules 2000 and the Information Tribunal (Enforcement Appeals) (Amendment) Rules 2002.

[3369]

NOTES

Commencement: 1 February 2005.

PART II STATUTORY INSTRUMENTS

4 Method of appealing—notice of appeal

(1) An appeal must be brought by a written notice of appeal served on the Tribunal.

(2) The notice of appeal shall—

(a) identify the disputed decision and the date on which the notice relating to the disputed decision was served on or given to the appellant; and

(b) state—

(i) the name and address of the appellant;

(ii) the grounds of the appeal;

(iii) whether or not the appellant considers that he is likely to wish a hearing to be held;

[(iv) where the appeal is brought under a provision of the 2000 Act, or the 2000 Act as applied, as modified, by regulation 18 of the 2004 Regulations, the name and address of the public authority to which the disputed decision relates;]

(v) where applicable, the special circumstances which the appellant considers justify the Tribunal's accepting jurisdiction under rule 5(2) below; and

(vi) an address for service of notices and other documents on the appellant.

(c) be signed by or on behalf of the appellant.

(3) Where an appeal is brought under section 48(1) of the 1998 Act, section 57(2) of the 2000 Act or section 57(2) as applied, as modified, by regulation 18 of the 2004 Regulations in relation to an information notice, the notice of appeal shall also contain a statement of any

representations the appellant wishes to make as to why it might be necessary in the interests of justice for the appeal to be heard and determined otherwise than by the chairman sitting alone as provided by rule 21(2) below.

(4) A notice of appeal may include a request for an early determination of the appeal and the reasons for that request.

[3370]

NOTES

Commencement: 1 February 2005.

Para (2): sub-para (b)(iv) substituted by the Information Tribunal (Enforcement Appeals) (Amendment) Rules 2005, SI 2005/450, rr 2, 3.

5 Time limit for appealing

(1) Subject to paragraph (2) below, a notice of appeal must be served on the Tribunal within 28 days of the date on which the notice relating to the disputed decision was served on or given to the appellant.

(2) The Tribunal may accept a notice of appeal served after the expiry of the period permitted by paragraph (1) above if it is of the opinion that, by reason of special circumstances, it is just and right to do so.

(3) A notice of appeal shall, if sent by post in accordance with rule 31(2) below, be treated as having been served on the date on which it is received for dispatch by the Post Office.

[3371]

NOTES

Commencement: 1 February 2005.

6 Acknowledgement of notice of appeal and notification to the Commissioner

(1) Upon receipt of a notice of appeal, the proper officer shall send—

(a) an acknowledgement of the service of a notice of appeal to the appellant, or to his representative if one has been appointed; and

(b) subject to paragraph (3) below, a copy of the notice of appeal to the Commissioner and to any other party to the proceedings.

(2) An acknowledgement of service under paragraph (1)(a) above shall be accompanied by a statement of the Tribunal's powers to award costs against an appellant under rule 29 below.

(3) Paragraph (1)(b) above does not apply to a notice of appeal under section 48(3) of the 1998 Act, but in such a case—

(a) the proper officer shall send a copy of the notice of appeal to the Commissioner if the Tribunal is of the opinion that the interests of justice require the Commissioner to assist it by giving evidence or being heard on any matter relating to the appeal, and

(b) where a copy is sent to the Commissioner under subparagraph (a) above, the jurisdiction referred to in paragraph 6(2) of Schedule 6 to the 1998 Act shall not be exercised ex parte.

[3372]

NOTES

Commencement: 1 February 2005.

7 Joinder of other persons to appeals

(1) This rule applies to an appeal under section 57 of the 2000 Act and section 57 of the 2000 Act as applied, as modified, by regulation 18(1) of the 2004 Regulations.

(2) If the Tribunal considers, whether on the application of a party or otherwise, that it is desirable that any person be made a party to an appeal, the Tribunal may order that person to be joined as a party.

(3) Any person who receives a copy of a notice of appeal or reply naming him as a person having an interest in the proceedings, or who otherwise claims an interest in the proceedings, may give notice ("a joinder notice") to the Tribunal that he wishes to be joined to the appeal.

(4) Where the Tribunal decides to make a person a party to an appeal, it shall—
(a) issue that person with an order to that effect ("an order of joinder"), and
(b) send a copy of that order, together with a copy of the joinder notice given in accordance with paragraphs (3) and (6) of this rule, to all other parties to the appeal.

(5) The Tribunal may give directions with regard to the joining of persons to appeals.

(6) A joinder notice must be in writing and must include—
(a) the full name and address of the person seeking to be joined to the appeal;
(b) a statement of the person's interest and whether or not he opposes the appeal, together with any reasons on which he relies in support of his interest; and
(c) the name and address of any representative the person appoints, and whether the Tribunal should send correspondence and notices concerning the appeal to the representative instead.

(7) A person who wishes to be joined as a party to an appeal must also deliver to the Tribunal at least 3 copies of the joinder notice and any accompanying documents to enable the Tribunal to send a copy to each of the other parties.

(8) A joinder notice given under this rule shall, if the person giving it is made a party to the appeal, be treated as that person's reply to the notice of appeal.

[3373]

NOTES

Commencement: 1 February 2005.

PART II STATUTORY INSTRUMENTS

8 Reply by Commissioner

(1) The Commissioner shall take the steps specified in paragraph (2) below—

(a) where he receives a copy of a notice of appeal under rule 6(1)(b) above, within 21 days of the date of that receipt, and

(b) where he receives a copy of a notice of appeal under rule 6(3)(a) above, within such time, not exceeding 21 days from the date of that receipt, as the Tribunal may allow.

(2) The steps are that the Commissioner must—

(a) send to the Tribunal a copy of the notice relating to the disputed decision, and

(b) send to the Tribunal and the appellant a written reply acknowledging service upon him of the notice of appeal, and stating—
(i) whether or not he intends to oppose the appeal and, if so,
(ii) the grounds upon which he relies in opposing the appeal.

(3) Before the expiry of the period referred to in paragraph (1) above which applies to the case, the Commissioner may apply to the Tribunal for an extension of that period, showing cause why, by reason of special circumstances, it would be just and right to do so, and the Tribunal may grant such extension as it considers appropriate.

(4) Where the appellant's notice of appeal has stated that he is not likely to wish a hearing to be held, the Commissioner shall in his reply inform the Tribunal and the appellant whether he considers that a hearing is likely to be desirable.

(5) Where an appeal is brought under section 48(1) of the 1998 Act, section 57(2) of the 2000 Act or section 57(2) of the 2000 Act as applied, as modified, by regulation 18 of the 2004 Regulations in relation to an information notice, the Commissioner may include in his reply a statement of representations as to why it might be necessary in the interests of justice for the appeal to be heard and determined otherwise than by the chairman sitting alone as provided by rule 21(2) below.

(6) A reply under this rule may include a request for an early determination of the appeal and the reasons for that request.

[3374]

NOTES

Commencement: 1 February 2005.

9 Application for striking out

(1) Subject to paragraph (3) below, where the Commissioner is of the opinion that an appeal does not lie to, or cannot be entertained by, the Tribunal, or that the notice of appeal discloses no reasonable grounds of appeal, he may include in his reply under rule 8(2) above a notice to that effect stating the grounds for such contention and applying for the appeal to be struck out.

(2) An application under this rule may be heard as a preliminary issue or at the beginning of the substantive appeal.

(3) This rule does not apply in the case of an appeal under section 48(3) of the 1998 Act. **[3375]**

NOTES

Commencement: 1 February 2005.

10 Summary disposal of appeals

(1) Where, having considered—

(a) the notice of appeal, and

(b) any reply to the notice of appeal,

the Tribunal is of the opinion that the appeal is of such a nature that it can properly be determined by dismissing it forthwith it may, subject to the provisions of this rule, so determine the appeal.

(2) Where the Tribunal proposes to determine an appeal under paragraph (1) above, it must first notify the appellant of the proposal.

(3) A notification to the appellant under paragraph (2) above must contain particulars of the appellant's entitlements set out in paragraph (4) below.

(4) An appellant notified in accordance with paragraph (2) above is entitled, within such time as the Tribunal may reasonably allow—

(a) to make written representations, and

(b) to request the Tribunal to hear oral representations

against the proposal to determine the appeal under paragraph (1) above.

(5) Where an appellant requests a hearing under paragraph (4)(b) above the Tribunal shall, as soon as practicable and with due regard to the convenience of the appellant, appoint a time and place for a hearing.

(6) The proper officer shall send to the appellant a notice informing him of—

(a) the time and place of any hearing under paragraph (5) above which, unless the appellant otherwise agrees, shall not be earlier than 14 days after the date on which the notice is sent, and

(b) the effect of rule 20 below.

(7) The Tribunal must, as soon as practicable, notify the appellant and any other party if, having given a notice under paragraph (2) above, it ceases to propose to determine the appeal under paragraph (1) above.

[3376]

NOTES

Commencement: 1 February 2005.

11 Amendment and supplementary grounds

(1) With the leave of the Tribunal, the appellant may amend his notice of appeal or deliver supplementary grounds of appeal.

(2) Paragraphs (1) and (3) of rule 6 above apply to an amended notice of appeal and supplementary grounds of appeal provided under paragraph (1) above as they do to a notice of appeal.

(3) Upon receipt of a copy of an amended notice of appeal or of supplementary grounds of appeal under rule 6(1)(b) or (3)(a) above, the Commissioner may amend his reply to the notice of appeal, and must send the amended reply to the Tribunal, the appellant and any other person that has been joined as a party to the appeal—

(a) Where he receives a copy of an amended notice of appeal under rule 6(1)(b) above, within 21 days of the date of that receipt, and

(b) Where he receives a copy of an amended notice of appeal under rule 6(3)(a) above, within such time, not exceeding 21 days from the date of that receipt, as the Tribunal may allow.

(4) Rule 8(3) above applies to the periods referred to in paragraph (3) above.

(5) Upon receipt of a copy of an amended notice of appeal or of supplementary grounds of appeal under rule 6(1)(b) above, a person who has been joined as a party to the appeal in accordance with rule 7 above may amend his reply to the notice of appeal, and must send the amended reply to the Tribunal, the appellant and any other party to the appeal within 21 days of the date of that receipt.

(6) Without prejudice to paragraph (3) above, the Commissioner may, with the leave of the Tribunal, amend his reply to the notice of appeal and must send the amended reply to the Tribunal, the appellant and any other party to the appeal.

[3377]

NOTES

Commencement: 1 February 2005.

12 Withdrawal of appeal

(1) The appellant may at any time before the determination of the appeal withdraw his appeal by sending to the Tribunal a notice of withdrawal, and the proper officer shall send a copy of that notice to the Commissioner.

(2) A notice of withdrawal given under this rule shall be in writing and shall be signed by the appellant or on his behalf.

(3) A notice of withdrawal shall, if sent by post in accordance with rule 31(2) below, have effect on the date on which it is received for dispatch by the Post Office.

(4) Where an appeal is withdrawn under this rule, a fresh appeal may not be brought by the appellant in relation to the same disputed decision except with the leave of the Tribunal.

[3378]

NOTES

Commencement: 1 February 2005.

13 Consolidation of appeals

(1) Subject to paragraph (2) below, where in the case of two or more appeals to which these Rules apply it appears to the Tribunal—

(a) that some common question of law or fact arises in both or all of them, or

(b) that for some other reason it is desirable to proceed with the appeals under this rule,

the Tribunal may order that the appeals be consolidated or heard together.

(2) The Tribunal shall not make an order under this rule without giving the parties an opportunity to show cause why such an order should not be made.

[3379]

NOTES

Commencement: 1 February 2005.

14 Directions

(1) Subject to paragraphs (5) and (6) below, the Tribunal may at any time of its own motion or on the application of any party give such directions as it thinks proper to enable the parties to prepare for the hearing or to assist the Tribunal to determine the issues.

PART II
STATUTORY INSTRUMENTS

(2) Such directions may in particular—

(a) provide for a particular matter to be dealt with as a preliminary issue and for a pre-hearing review to be held;

(b) provide for—

(i) the exchange between the parties of lists of documents held by them which are relevant to the appeal;

(ii) the inspection by the parties of the documents so listed;

(iii) the exchange between the parties of statements of evidence; and

(iv) the provision by the parties to the Tribunal of statements or lists of agreed matters;

(c) make provision as to applications for the joinder of other persons to appeals, including giving directions as to the delivery of notices and other documents in such cases;

(d) require any party to send to the Tribunal and to any other party—

(i) statements of facts and statements of the evidence which will be adduced, including such statements provided in modified or edited form;

(ii) a skeleton argument which summarises the submissions which will be made and cites the authorities which will be relied upon, identifying any particular passages to be relied upon;

(iii) a chronology of events;

(iv) any other particulars or supplementary statements which may reasonably be required for the determination of the appeal;

(v) any document or other material which the Tribunal may require and which it is in the power of that party to deliver;

(vi) an estimate of the time which will be needed for any hearing; and

(vii) a list of the witnesses the party intends to call to give evidence at any hearing;

(e) limit the length of oral submissions and the time allowed for examination and cross-examination of witnesses; and

(f) limit the number of expert witnesses to be heard on either side.

(3) If, following the determination of any matter at a pre-hearing review, the Tribunal is of the opinion that its decision as to that matter substantially disposes of the whole appeal, the Tribunal may treat the pre-hearing review as the hearing of the appeal and may give such direction as it thinks fit to dispose of the appeal.

(4) The Tribunal may, subject to any specific provision in these Rules, specify time limits for steps to be taken in the proceedings and may extend any time limit.

(5) Nothing in this rule may require the production of any document or other material which the party could not be compelled to produce on the trial of an action in a court of law in that part of the United Kingdom where the appeal is to be determined.

(6) It shall be a condition of the supply of any information or material provided under this rule that any recipient of that information or material may use it only for the purposes of the appeal.

(7) The power to give directions may be exercised in the absence of the parties.

(8) Notice of any directions given under this rule shall be served on the parties, and the Tribunal may, on the application of any party, set aside or vary such directions.

[(9) If a party does not comply with any direction given under these Rules, the Tribunal may—

(a) dismiss the whole or part of the appeal or application; or

(b) strike out the whole or part of a public authority's, the Commissioner's or another party's notice in reply and where it does so, it may direct that any of them shall not contest the appeal.]

(10) But the Tribunal must not dismiss an appeal, strike out a reply or notice in reply or give a direction unless it has sent a notice to the party who has not complied giving that party the opportunity to comply within such period as the Tribunal may specify in the notice or to show cause why the Tribunal should not dismiss, strike out or so direct.

[3380]

NOTES

Commencement: 1 February 2005.

Para (9): substituted by the Information Tribunal (Enforcement Appeals) (Amendment) Rules 2005, SI 2005/450, rr 2, 4.

15 Power to require entry of premises for testing of equipment or material

(1) Subject to paragraph (8) below, the Tribunal may, for the purpose of determining an appeal, make an order requiring the occupier of any premises ("the occupier") to permit the Tribunal to enter those premises at a specified time and inspect, examine, operate or test any equipment on those premises used or intended to be used in connection with the processing of personal data or the storage or recording of other information, and to inspect, examine or test any documents or other material on those premises connected with the processing of personal data or the storage or recording of other information.

(2) An order under paragraph (1) above shall also require the occupier to permit the Tribunal to be accompanied by—

- (a) the parties, and
- (b) such number of the officers or members of staff provided to the Tribunal under paragraph 14 of Schedule 5 to the 1998 Act as it considers necessary.

(3) The Tribunal shall serve a copy of the order on the occupier and the parties.

(4) The time specified in the order shall not be earlier than 7 days after the date of service of the copy.

(5) The Tribunal may upon the application of the occupier set the order aside.

(6) Subject to paragraph (4) above, the Tribunal may upon the application of any person mentioned in paragraph (3) above alter the time specified in the order without being obliged to serve further copies under that paragraph, but shall notify the other persons so mentioned of the revised time.

(7) This rule also applies where the occupier is a party to the appeal.

(8) Documents or other material which the appellant could not be compelled to produce on the trial of an action in that part of the United Kingdom where the appeal is to be determined shall be immune from inspection, examination or testing under this rule.

[3381]

NOTES

Commencement: 1 February 2005.

16 Determination of appeal without a hearing

(1) Subject to these Rules, the Tribunal may determine an appeal without a hearing.

(2) Where a party makes a request for a hearing, the Tribunal shall grant the request unless it is satisfied that the appeal can properly be determined without a hearing.

(3) Where the Tribunal decides to refuse a request for a hearing, it shall send written notice to the party making the request either before or at the same time as it makes its decision.

(4) A notice sent under paragraph (3) above shall specify the Tribunal's reasons for refusing the request.

(5) The Tribunal may of its own motion and at any stage of an appeal, direct a hearing.

[3382]

NOTES

Commencement: 1 February 2005.

17 Time and place of hearings

(1) Subject to rules 14(3) and 16 above, where the Tribunal has directed that a hearing shall take place, the Tribunal shall appoint a time and place for the hearing as soon as practicable and with due regard to the convenience of the parties and any request made under rule 4(4) or 8(6) above.

(2) The proper officer shall send to each party a notice informing him of the time and place of any hearing.

(3) The reference to a "party" in paragraph (2) above does not include the Commissioner in the case of an appeal under section 48(3) of the 1998 Act other than a case to which rule 6(3)(a) above applies.

(4) The time notified under paragraph (1) above shall not be earlier than 14 days after the date on which the notice is sent unless—

(a) the parties agree otherwise, or

(b) the appellant agrees otherwise, and the hearing relates to an appeal under section 48(3) of the 1998 Act.

(5) A notice to a party under this rule shall inform him of the effect of rule 20 below.

(6) The Tribunal may—

(a) postpone the time appointed for any hearing;

(b) adjourn a hearing to such time as the Tribunal may determine; or

(c) alter the time and place appointed for any hearing;

and, if it exercises any of the above powers, it shall notify each party previously notified of that hearing under this rule, and any person summoned under rule 18 below to attend as a witness at that hearing, of the revised arrangements.

[3383]

NOTES

Commencement: 1 February 2005.

18 Summoning of witnesses

(1) Subject to paragraph (2) below, the Tribunal may by summons require any person in the United Kingdom to attend as a witness at a hearing of an appeal at such time and place as may be specified in the summons and, subject to rule 27(2) and (3) below, at the hearing to answer any questions or produce any documents in his custody or under his control which relate to any matter in question in the appeal.

(2) No person shall be required to attend in obedience to a summons under paragraph (1) above unless he has been given at least 7 days' notice of the hearing or, if less than 7 days, he has informed the Tribunal that he accepts such notice as he has been given.

(3) The Tribunal may, upon the application of a person summoned under this rule, set the summons aside.

(4) A person who has attended a hearing as a witness in obedience to a summons shall be entitled to such sum as the Tribunal considers reasonable in respect of his attendance at, and his travelling to and from, the hearing; and where the summons was issued at the request of a party such sum shall be paid or tendered to him by that party.

(5) In relation to proceedings before the Tribunal in Scotland, in this rule "summons" means citation and the provisions of this rule are to be construed accordingly.

[3384]

NOTES

Commencement: 1 February 2005.

19 Representation at a hearing

(1) At any hearing by the Tribunal a party may conduct his case himself or may appear and be represented by any person whom he may appoint for the purpose.

(2) In this rule, references to a "party" do not include the Commissioner in the case of an appeal under section 48(3) of the 1998 Act other than a case to which rule 6(3)(a) above applies.

(3) If the appellant does not intend to attend or be represented at a hearing, he must inform the Tribunal of his intention, and in such a case may send to the Tribunal additional written representations in support of his appeal.

[3385]

NOTES

Commencement: 1 February 2005.

20 Default of appearance at hearing

If, without furnishing the Tribunal with sufficient reason for his absence, a party fails to appear at a hearing, having been duly notified of the hearing, the Tribunal may, if that party is the appellant, dismiss the appeal or, in any case, hear and determine the appeal, or any particular issue, in the party's absence and may make such order as to costs as it thinks fit.

[3386]

NOTES

Commencement: 1 February 2005.

21 Hearings and determinations in the case of appeals against an information notice

(1) This rule applies to any appeal under section 48(1) of the 1998 Act, section 57(2) of the 2000 Act or section 57(2) as applied, as modified, by regulation 18 of the 2004 Regulations in respect of an information notice.

(2) Subject to paragraph (3) below, any hearing of or relating to an appeal to which this rule applies shall be by the chairman sitting alone, and any appeal or issue relating to an appeal to which this rule applies shall be determined by the chairman sitting alone.

(3) Paragraph (2) above does not apply where it appears to the chairman that a hearing or determination by the Tribunal constituted in accordance with paragraph 4 of Schedule 6 to the 1998 Act is necessary in the interests of justice, taking into account any representations made under rule 4(3) or 8(5) above.

[3387]

NOTES

Commencement: 1 February 2005.

22 Hearings in public or in private

(1) All hearings by the Tribunal (including preliminary hearings) shall be in public unless, having heard representations on the matter from the parties and having regard to the desirability of safeguarding—

- (a) the privacy of data subjects; or
- (b) commercially sensitive information; or
- (c) any matter in respect of which an exemption contained in Part II of the 2000 Act is claimed,

the Tribunal directs that the hearing or any part of the hearing shall take place in private.

(2) Without prejudice to paragraph (3) and rule 23 below, the following persons, in addition to the parties, may attend a hearing notwithstanding that it is in private—

- (a) the chairman or any deputy chairman or member of the Tribunal in his capacity as such, notwithstanding that they do not constitute the Tribunal for the purpose of the hearing; and
- (b) any other person with the leave of the Tribunal and the consent of the parties present.

(3) Whether or not a hearing is held in public, a member of the Council on Tribunals or the Scottish Committee of the Council on Tribunals in his capacity as such may attend the hearing, and may remain present during the deliberations of the Tribunal but must not take part in the deliberations.

[3388]

NOTES

Commencement: 1 February 2005.

23 Power to exclude parties from hearings

(1) Where an application is made to the Tribunal by a Minister of the Crown for a party or parties to the appeal to be excluded from the proceedings or any part of them, the Tribunal shall grant such application and exclude that party or parties, if and only if it is satisfied that it is necessary for reasons of substantial public interest to do so.

(2) An application under paragraph (1) above shall be made to the Tribunal ex parte.

(3) Where the Tribunal considers it necessary, for reasons of substantial public interest, for any party to be excluded from the proceedings, it must—

(a) direct accordingly,

(b) inform the party or parties excluded of it reasons, to the extent that it is possible to do so without disclosing information contrary to the public interest, and

(c) inform the relevant Minister.

[3389]

NOTES

Commencement: 1 February 2005.

24 Conduct of proceedings at hearing

(1) Subject to rules 20 and 23 above, the Tribunal shall at the hearing of an appeal give to each party an opportunity—

(a) to address the Tribunal and to amplify orally written statements previously furnished under these Rules, to give evidence and to call witnesses, and to put questions to any person giving evidence before the Tribunal, and

(b) to make representations on the evidence (if any) and on the subject matter of the appeal generally but, where evidence is taken, such opportunity shall not be given before the completion of the taking of evidence.

(2) Subject to paragraph (3) below, in this rule, references to a "party" do not include the Commissioner in the case of an appeal under section 48(3) of the 1998 Act.

(3) In a case to which rule 6(3)(a) above applies, the Tribunal shall give the Commissioner the opportunity referred to in paragraph (1) above to the extent that it is of the opinion that the interests of justice require the Commissioner to assist it by giving evidence or being heard on any matter relating to the appeal.

(4) Except as provided by these Rules, the Tribunal shall conduct the proceedings in such manner as it considers appropriate in the circumstances for discharging its functions and shall so far as appears to it appropriate seek to avoid formality in its proceedings.

[3390]

NOTES

Commencement: 1 February 2005.

25 Preliminary and incidental matters

As regards matters preliminary or incidental to an appeal the chairman may act for the Tribunal under rules 5(2), 8(1) and (3), [10 to 16], 17(1) and (6)(a) and (c), 18 and 24(1) and (3).

[3391]

NOTES

Commencement: 1 February 2005.

Words in square brackets substituted by the Information Tribunal (Enforcement Appeals) (Amendment) Rules 2005, SI 2005/450, rr 2, 5.

26 Burden of proof

In any proceedings before the Tribunal relating to an appeal to which these Rules apply, other than an appeal under section 48(3) of the 1998 Act [or section 57(1) of the 2000 Act], it shall be for the Commissioner to satisfy the Tribunal that the disputed decision should be upheld.

[3392]

NOTES

Commencement: 1 February 2005.

Words in square brackets inserted by the Information Tribunal (Enforcement Appeals) (Amendment) Rules 2005, SI 2005/450, rr 2, 6.

27 Evidence

(1) The Tribunal may receive in evidence any document or information notwithstanding that such document or information would be inadmissible in a court of law.

(2) No person shall be compelled to given any evidence or produce any document which he could not be compelled to produce on the trial of an action in a court of law in that part of the United Kingdom where the appeal is to be determined.

(3) The Tribunal may require oral evidence of a witness (including a party) to be given on oath or affirmation and for that purpose the chairman or the proper officer shall have power to administer oaths or take affirmations.

[3393]

NOTES

Commencement: 1 February 2005.

28 Determination of appeal

(1) As soon as practicable after the Tribunal has determined an appeal, the chairman shall certify in writing that determination and sign and date the certificate.

(2) If and to the extent that it is possible to do so without disclosing information which is or would be exempt by virtue of any provision in Part II of the 2000 Act, the certificate shall include—

(a) any material finding of fact, and
(b) the reasons for the decision.

(3) The proper officer shall send a copy of the certificate to the parties.

(4) The Tribunal shall make arrangements for the publication of its determination but in doing so shall have regard to the desirability of safeguarding —

(a) the privacy of data subjects,
(b) commercially sensitive information, and
(c) any information which is or would be exempt by virtue of any provision in Part II of the 2000 Act,

and for that purpose may make any necessary amendments to the text of the certificate.

[3394]

NOTES

Commencement: 1 February 2005.

29 Costs

(1) In any appeal before the Tribunal, including one withdrawn under rule 12 above, the Tribunal may make an order awarding costs—

(a) against the appellant and in favour of the Commissioner where it considers that the appeal was manifestly unreasonable;
(b) against the Commissioner and in favour of the appellant where it considers that the disputed decision was manifestly unreasonable;
(c) where it considers that a party has been responsible for frivolous, vexatious, improper or unreasonable action, or for any failure to comply with a direction or any delay which with diligence could have been avoided, against that party and in favour of any other.

(2) The Tribunal shall not make an order under paragraph (1) above awarding costs against a party without first giving that party an opportunity of making representations against the making of the order.

(3) An order under paragraph (1) above may be to the party or parties in question to pay to the other party or parties either a specified sum in respect of the costs incurred by that other party or parties in connection with the proceedings or the whole or part of such costs as taxed (if not otherwise agreed).

(4) Any costs required by an order under this rule to be taxed may be taxed in the county court according to such of the scales prescribed by the county court rules for proceedings in the county court as shall be directed by the order.

(5) In relation to proceedings before the Tribunal in Scotland, for the purposes of the application of paragraph (4) above, for the reference to the county court and the county court rules there shall be substituted reference to the sheriff court and the sheriff court rules and for the reference to proceedings there shall be substituted a reference to civil proceedings.

[3395]

PART II STATUTORY INSTRUMENTS

NOTES

Commencement: 1 February 2005.

30 Irregularities

(1) Any irregularity resulting from failure to comply with any provision of these Rules or of any direction of the Tribunal before the Tribunal has reached a decision shall not of itself render the proceedings void, but the Tribunal may, and shall if it considers that any person may have been prejudiced by that irregularity, give such directions or take such steps as it thinks fit before reaching its decision to cure or waive the irregularity, whether by amendment of any document, the giving of notice or otherwise.

(2) Clerical mistakes in any document recording or certifying a direction, decision or determination of the Tribunal or chairman, or errors arising in such a document from an accidental slip or omission may, at any time, be corrected by the chairman, by certificate signed by him.

[3396]

NOTES

Commencement: 1 February 2005.

31 Notices, etc

(1) Any document or other notice required or authorised by these Rules to be served on or sent to any person or authority may be—

(a) sent by post in a registered letter or by the recorded delivery service, or delivered by hand in accordance with paragraph (2) below, or

(b) by means of electronic communication in accordance with paragraph (3) below.

(2) A document or other notice required or authorised by these Rules to be served on or sent to any person or authority that is sent by post in a registered letter or by the recorded delivery service, or is delivered by hand, must be sent or delivered—

(a) in the case of the Tribunal, to the proper officer of the Tribunal;

(b) in the case of the Commissioner, to him at his office;

(c) in the case of an appellant or any other party, to him or his representative at the address for service under these Rules; and

(d) in the case of an occupier within the provisions of rule 14 above, to him at the premises in question.

(3) A document or other notice required or authorised by these Rules to be served on or sent to any person or authority that is sent by means of an electronic communication, must be sent—

(a) in the case of the Tribunal, by such means and to such address as the proper officer of the Tribunal may specify;

(b) in the case of the Commissioner, by such means and to such address as may be specified by the Commissioner for such purposes;

(c) in the case of an appellant, a respondent data controller or any other party, by such means and to such address as he may specify for such purposes.

(4) Without prejudice to paragraph (3) above, no person shall be required to accept service of documents sent by electronic means unless they have indicated that they are prepared to accept such service.

(5) A party may at any time by notice to the Tribunal change his address for service under these Rules.

[3397]

NOTES

Commencement: 1 February 2005.

CHARITIES (ACCOUNTS AND REPORTS) REGULATIONS 2005

(SI 2005/572)

NOTES

Made: 7 March 2005.
Authority: Charities Act 1993, ss 42, 44, 45 and 86(3).
Commencement: 31 March 2005.

ARRANGEMENT OF REGULATIONS

1 Citation and commencement

(1) These Regulations may be cited as the Charities (Accounts and Reports) Regulations 2005 and, subject to paragraph (2), shall come into force on 31st March 2005.

(2) Paragraph 2(iii) of Part VI of Schedule 2 shall come into force on the date when section 1 of the Civil Partnership Act 2004 comes into force in relation to England and Wales.
[3398]

NOTES

Commencement: 31 March 2005.

2 Interpretation

In these Regulations—

"auditable charity" means a charity the accounts of which for the financial year in question are required to be audited in pursuance of any statutory requirement;

"authorised person" has the same meaning as in the Financial Services and Markets Act 2000;

"charity trustee" includes, in relation to an investment fund, any person who discharges any of the functions of a charity trustee in relation to the investment fund;

"charity trustees" means, in relation to an investment fund, the person or persons appointed to manage the investment fund, except where the scheme or schemes regulating the investment fund allocate responsibility for discharging a particular function to a particular person or persons, when, in relation to that function, "the charity trustees" means that person or those persons;

"common deposit fund" means a common deposit fund established by a scheme under section 22A of the Charities Act 1960 or section 25 of the 1993 Act (which is deemed to be a charity by virtue of section 24(8), as applied by section 25(2), of the 1993 Act);

"common investment fund" means a common investment fund established by a scheme under section 22 of the 1960 Act or section 24 of the 1993 Act (which is deemed to be a charity by virtue of section 24(8) of the 1993 Act), other than a common investment fund the trusts of which provide for property to be transferred to the investment fund only by or on behalf of a participating charity of which the charity trustees are the trustees appointed to manage the investment fund;

"director" includes any person occupying the position of a director, by whatever name called, and in relation to a body corporate whose affairs are managed by its members means a member of the body corporate;

"ex gratia payment" means any such application of the property of a charity, or any such waiver by a charity of any entitlement to receive any property, as is capable of being authorised under section 27(1) of the 1993 Act;

"financial year" shall be construed in accordance with regulation 6 below;

"fixed assets" means the assets of a charity which are intended for use or investment on a continuing basis;

"fund" means particular assets of a charity held on trusts which, as respects the purposes for which those assets are held, or as respects the powers of the charity trustees to use or apply those assets, are not identical to those on which other assets of the charity are held;

"institution or body corporate connected with the charity", in relation to a charity, means an institution or body corporate which—

(a) in the case of an institution, is controlled by,

(b) in the case of a body corporate, in which a substantial interest is held by,

the charity or any one or more of the charity trustees acting in his or their capacity as such, and "substantial interest" shall be construed in accordance with paragraph 4 of Schedule 5 to the 1993 Act;

"investment fund" means a common deposit fund or a common investment fund;

"reserves" means those assets in the unrestricted fund of a charity which the charity trustees have, or can make, available to apply for all or any of its purposes, once they have provided for the liabilities of the unrestricted fund, together with any commitments of the charity and other planned expenditure intended to be met from the assets of the unrestricted fund;

"special case charity" means a charity which is either—

(a) a registered social landlord within the meaning of the Housing Act 1996 and whose registration has been the subject of a notice under section 3(3)(a) of that Act; or

(b) has during the financial year in question—

(i) conducted an institution in relation to which a designation made, or having effect as if made, under section 129 of the Education Reform Act 1988 has effect;

(ii) received financial support from funds administered by a higher education funding council within the meaning of the Further and Higher Education Act 1992 in respect of expenditure incurred or to be incurred by the charity in connection with that institution; and

(iii) incurred no expenditure for charitable purposes other than the purposes of that institution or any other such institution;

"the 1960 Act" means the Charities Act 1960;

"the 1993 Act" means the Charities Act 1993;

"the 1995 Regulations" means the Charities (Accounts and Reports) Regulations 1995;

"the 2000 Regulations" means the Charities (Accounts and Reports) Regulations 2000;

"the SORP" means the Statement of Recommended Practice for Accounting and Reporting by Charities, issued by the Commissioners on 4th March 2005;

"trustee for a charity" means any person (other than the charity itself, or a charity trustee of the charity) who holds the title to property belonging to the charity, and so includes a custodian trustee and a nominee; and

"unrestricted fund" means a fund which is to be used or applied in any way determined by the charity trustees for the furtherance of the objects of a charity, and "restricted fund" means any other fund of a charity.

[3399]

NOTES

Commencement: 31 March 2005.

3 Form and contents of statements of accounts

(1) This regulation applies to a statement of accounts prepared by the charity trustees of a charity, other than an investment fund, or a special case charity, in accordance with section 42(1) of the 1993 Act in respect of a financial year—

(a) which begins on or after 1st April 2005; or

(b) which begins before that date if—

(i) the charity trustees determine that this regulation, rather than regulation 3 of the 2000 Regulations, shall apply to the statement of accounts; and

(ii) the charity trustees have not, before the date when these Regulations come into force, either approved the accounts of the charity in respect of that financial year, or authorised the signature of an annual report in respect of that financial year in accordance with regulation 7(3)(c) of the 2000 Regulations.

(2) If the charity trustees make a determination under sub-paragraph (b) above, they shall also make a determination under regulation 11(1)(b) below, if they are required to prepare an annual report in respect of the financial year in question.

(3) The requirements as to form and contents of a statement of accounts to which this regulation applies are those set out in the following provisions of this regulation.

(4) The statement shall consist of—

(a) a statement of financial activities which shall show the total incoming resources and application of the resources, together with any other movements in the total resources, of the charity during the financial year in respect of which the statement is prepared; and

(b) a balance sheet which shall show the state of affairs of the charity as at the end of the financial year in respect of which the statement is prepared.

(5) The statement shall be prepared in accordance with the following principles, namely that—

(a) the statement of financial activities shall give a true and fair view of the incoming resources and application of the resources of the charity in the financial year in respect of which the statement is prepared;

(b) the balance sheet shall give a true and fair view of the state of affairs of the charity at the end of that year;

(c) where compliance with the following requirements of this regulation would not be sufficient to give a true and fair view, the necessary additional information shall be given in the statement of accounts or in notes to the accounts;

(d) if in special circumstances compliance with any of those requirements would be inconsistent with giving a true and fair view, the charity trustees shall depart from the requirement to the extent necessary to give a true and fair view.

(6) The statement—

(a) shall be prepared in accordance with the methods and principles set out in the SORP; and

(b) subject to the following three paragraphs of this regulation, shall, with respect to any amount required to be shown in the statement of financial activities or in the balance sheet, also show the corresponding amount for the financial year immediately preceding that to which the statement or balance sheet relates.

(7) Where that corresponding amount is not comparable with the amount to be shown for the item in question in respect of the financial year to which the statement of financial activities or balance sheet relates, the former amount shall be adjusted.

(8) Where in the financial year to which the statement of accounts relates the effect of paragraph (5) and paragraph (6)(a) above is that there is nothing required to be shown in respect of a particular item, but an amount was required to be shown in respect of that item in the statement of accounts for the immediately preceding financial year, those provisions shall have effect as if such an amount were required to be shown in the statement of accounts in the financial year to which the statement relates, and that amount were nil.

(9) Where a charity has more than one fund, only amounts corresponding to the entries in the statement of financial activities relating to the totals of both or all of the funds of the charity need be shown.

(10) There shall be provided by way of notes to the accounts the information specified in Schedule 1 to these Regulations.

(11) The balance sheet shall be signed by one or more of the charity trustees of the charity, each of whom has been authorised to do so, and shall specify the date on which the statement of accounts of which the balance sheet forms part was approved by the charity trustees.

[3400]

NOTES

Commencement: 31 March 2005.

4 Form and contents of statements of accounts: investment funds

(1) This regulation applies to a statement of accounts prepared in the case of an investment fund in accordance with section 42(1) of the 1993 Act in respect of a financial year—

(a) which begins on or after 1st April 2005; or

(b) which begins before that date if—

(i) the charity trustees determine that this regulation, rather than regulation 4 of the 1995 Regulations, shall apply to the statement of accounts; and

(ii) the charity trustees have not, before the date when these Regulations come into force, either approved the accounts of the investment fund in respect of that financial year, or authorised the signature of an annual report in respect of that financial year in accordance with regulation 10(1)(c) of the 1995 Regulations.

(2) If the charity trustees make a determination under sub-paragraph (b) above, they shall also make a determination under regulation 12(1)(b) below, if they are required to prepare an annual report in respect of the financial year in question.

(3) Subject to paragraph (8) below, the statement shall consist of the following, that is to say—

(a) a statement of total return which satisfies the requirements set out in Part I of Schedule 2 to these Regulations;

(b) a statement of movement in funds which satisfies the requirements set out in Part II of Schedule 2 to these Regulations; and

(c) a balance sheet which satisfies the requirements set out in Part III of Schedule 2 to these Regulations.

(4) The statement shall be prepared in accordance with the methods and principles specified and referred to in Part IV of Schedule 2 to these Regulations.

(5) There shall be provided by way of notes to the accounts the information specified in Part V of Schedule 2 to these Regulations.

(6) Part VI of Schedule 2 to these Regulations shall have effect for the purposes of defining expressions used in that Schedule.

(7) The balance sheet shall be signed—

(a) if the scheme or schemes regulating the investment fund allocates responsibility for preparing the accounts to a particular person, by that person; and otherwise,

(b) by one or more of the charity trustees of the investment fund, each of whom has been authorised to do so, in which case the balance sheet shall specify the date on which the statement of accounts of which the balance sheet forms part was approved by the charity trustees.

(8) In the case of any financial year of a common deposit fund in which there are no gains or losses on disposal or revaluation of assets, paragraph (3) above shall have effect as if sub-paragraph (b) were omitted.

[3401]

NOTES

Commencement: 31 March 2005.

5 Form and contents of statements of accounts: special case charities

(1) This regulation applies to a statement of accounts prepared by the charity trustees of a special case charity in accordance with section 42(1) of the 1993 Act in respect of a financial year which begins on or after 1st April 2005.

(2) The requirements as to form and contents of a statement of accounts to which this regulation applies are those set out in the following provisions of this regulation.

(3) The statement shall consist of an income and expenditure account and a balance sheet as at the end of the financial year in respect of which the statement of accounts is prepared.

(4) The statement shall be prepared in accordance with the following principles, namely that—

(a) the income and expenditure account shall give a true and fair view of the income and expenditure of the charity for the financial year in respect of which the statement of accounts is prepared; and

(b) the balance sheet shall give a true and fair view of the state of affairs of the charity at the end of that year.

(5) The balance sheet shall be signed by one or more of the charity trustees of the charity, each of whom has been authorised to do so, and shall specify the date on which the statement of accounts of which the balance sheet forms part was approved by the charity trustees.

[3402]

NOTES

Commencement: 31 March 2005.

6 Financial year

(1) The financial year of a charity shall, for the purposes of the 1993 Act and regulations made thereunder, be determined in accordance with the following provisions of this regulation.

(2) The first financial year of a charity shall be the period beginning with the day on which the charity is established and ending with the accounting reference date of the charity or such other date, not more than seven days before or after the accounting reference date, as the charity trustees may determine.

(3) Subsequent financial years of a charity begin with the day immediately following the end of the charity's previous financial year and end with its accounting reference date or such other date, not more than seven days before or after the accounting reference date, as the charity trustees may determine.

(4) The accounting reference date of a charity shall, for the purposes of this regulation, be—

(a) in the first financial year of a charity such date, not less than 6 months nor more than 18 months after the date on which the charity was established, as the charity trustees may determine; and

(b) in any subsequent financial year of a charity, the date 12 months after the previous accounting reference date of the charity or such other date, not less than 6 months nor more than 18 months after the previous accounting reference date of the charity as the trustees may determine:

Provided that—

(i) the charity trustees shall not, without the prior consent of the Commissioners, exercise their powers under sub-paragraph (b) of this paragraph so as to determine an accounting reference date in respect of any financial year which is consecutive, or follows immediately after a financial year which is consecutive, to a previous financial year in respect of which that power was exercised; and

(ii) the charity trustees shall exercise their powers under sub-paragraph (b) of this paragraph so as to determine a date earlier or later than 12 months from the beginning of the financial year only where satisfied that there are exceptional reasons to do so (which reasons shall, in the case of a charity subject to the requirements of regulation 3(10) or 4(5) above, be disclosed in a note to the accounts).

[3403]

NOTES

Commencement: 31 March 2005.

PART II STATUTORY INSTRUMENTS

7 Annual audit of charity accounts

(1) The duties of an auditor carrying out an audit of the accounts of a charity under section 43 of the 1993 Act shall be those specified in the following provisions of this regulation.

(2) Where a statement of accounts has been prepared under section 42(1) of the 1993 Act for the financial year in question the auditor shall make a report on that statement to the charity trustees which—

(a) states the name and address of the auditor and the name of the charity concerned;

(b) is signed by him or, where the office of auditor is held by a body corporate or partnership, in its name by a person authorised to sign on its behalf and states that the auditor is a person falling within paragraph (a) or, as the case may be, (b) of section 43(2) of the 1993 Act;

(c) is dated and specifies the financial year in respect of which the accounts to which it relates have been prepared;

(d) specifies that it is a report in respect of an audit carried out under section 43 of the 1993 Act and in accordance with regulations made under section 44 of that Act;

(e) states whether in the auditor's opinion—

(i) the statement of accounts complies with the requirements of regulation 3 or, as the case may be, 4, or 5 above;

(ii) the balance sheet gives a true and fair view of the state of affairs of the charity at the end of the financial year in question; and

(iii)

(aa) where regulation 3 applies, the statement of financial activities gives a true and fair view of the incoming resources and application of the resources of the charity in the financial year in question;

(bb) where regulation 4 applies, the statement of total return gives a true and fair view of the incoming resources and application of the resources of the investment fund in the financial year in question;

(cc) where regulation 4 applies, the statement of movement in funds gives a true and fair view of the movements in the net assets of the investment fund between their position at the beginning of that year and their position at the end of that year; and

(dd) where regulation 5 applies, the income and expenditure account gives a true and fair view of the income and expenditure of the charity in the financial year in question.

(f) Where the auditor has formed the opinion—

(i) that accounting records have not been kept in respect of the charity in accordance with section 41 of the 1993 Act; or

(ii) that the statement of accounts does not accord with those records; or

(iii) that any information contained in the statement of accounts is inconsistent in any material respect with any report of the charity trustees prepared under section 45 of the 1993 Act in respect of the financial year in question; or

(iv) that any information or explanation to which he is entitled under regulation 9 below has not been afforded to him,

contains a statement of that opinion and of his grounds for forming it.

(3) Where a receipts and payments account and statement of assets and liabilities have been prepared under section 42(3) of the 1993 Act for the financial year in question the auditor shall make a report on that account and statement to the charity trustees which—

(a) states the name and address of the auditor and the name of the charity concerned;

(b) is signed by him or, where the office of auditor is held by a body corporate or partnership, in its name by a person authorised to sign on its behalf and states that the auditor is a person falling within paragraph (a) or, as the case may be, (b) of section 43(2) of the 1993 Act;

(c) is dated and specifies the financial year in respect of which the accounts to which it relates have been prepared;

(d) specifies that it is a report in respect of an audit carried out under section 43 of the 1993 Act and in accordance with regulations made under section 44 of that Act;

(e) states whether in the auditor's opinion—

(i) the account and statement properly present the receipts and payments of the charity for the financial year in question and its assets and liabilities as at the end of that year; and

(ii) the account and statement adequately distinguish any material special trust or other restricted fund of the charity;

(f) where the auditor has formed the opinion—

(i) that accounting records have not been kept in respect of the charity in accordance with section 41 of the 1993 Act; or

(ii) that the account and statement do not accord with those records; or

(iii) that any information or explanation to which he is entitled under regulation 9 below has not been afforded to him,

contains a statement of that opinion and of his grounds for forming it.

(4) The auditor shall, in preparing his report for the purposes of paragraph (2) or, as the case may be, (3) above, carry out such investigations as will enable him to form an opinion as to the matters specified in sub-paragraph (e) and (f) of that paragraph.

(5) The auditor shall immediately make a written report to the Commissioners on any matter of which the auditor becomes aware in his capacity as such which relates to the activities or affairs of the charity or of any institution or body corporate connected with the charity and which the auditor has reasonable cause to believe is, or is likely to be, of material significance for the exercise, in relation to the charity of the Commissioners' functions under section 8 (general power to institute inquiries) or 18 (power to act for protection of charities) of the 1993 Act.

(6) Where an auditor appointed by charity trustees ceases for any reason to hold office he shall send to the charity trustees a statement of any circumstances connected with his ceasing to hold office which he considers should be brought to their attention or, if he considers that there are no such circumstances, a statement that there are none; and the auditor shall send a copy of any statement sent to the charity trustees under this paragraph (except a statement that there are no such circumstances) to the Commissioners.

(7) In the case of an auditor appointed by the Commissioners, the report required by paragraph (2) or, as the case may be, (3) above shall be made to the Commissioners instead of to the charity trustees.

[3404]

NOTES

Commencement: 31 March 2005.

8 Independent examination of charity accounts

An independent examiner who has carried out an examination of the accounts of a charity under section 43 of the 1993 Act shall make a report to the charity trustees which—

(a) states his name and address and the name of the charity concerned;

(b) is signed by him and specifies any relevant professional qualifications or professional body of which he is a member;

(c) is dated and specifies the financial year in respect of which the accounts to which it relates have been prepared;

(d) specifies that it is a report in respect of an examination carried out under section 43 of the 1993 Act and in accordance with any directions given by the Commissioners under subsection (7)(b) of that section which are applicable;

(e) states whether or not any matter has come to the examiner's attention in connection with the examination which gives him reasonable cause to believe that in any material respect—

(i) accounting records have not been kept in respect of the charity in accordance with section 41 of the 1993 Act; or

(ii) the accounts do not accord with those records; or

(iii) in the case of an examination of a statement of accounts which has been prepared under section 42(1) of the 1993 Act, the statement of accounts does not comply with any of the requirements of regulation 3 or, as the case may be, 4 or 5 above, other than any requirement to give a true and fair view;

(f) states whether or not any matter has come to the examiner's attention in connection with the examination to which, in his opinion, attention should be drawn in the report in order to enable a proper understanding of the accounts to be reached;

(g) contains a statement as to any of the following matters that has become apparent to the examiner during the course of the examination, namely, that—

(i) there has been any material expenditure or action which appears not to be in accordance with the trusts of the charity; or

(ii) any information or explanation to which he is entitled under regulation 9 below has not been afforded to him; or

(iii) in the case of an examination of accounts a statement of which has been prepared under section 42(1) of the 1993 Act, any information contained in the statement of accounts is inconsistent in any material respect with any report of the charity trustees prepared under section 45 of the 1993 Act in respect of the financial year in question.

[3405]

NOTES

Commencement: 31 March 2005.

9 Audit and independent examination: supplementary provisions

(1) An auditor or independent examiner carrying out an audit or examination of the accounts of a charity under section 43 of the 1993 Act shall have a right of access to any books, documents and other records (however kept) which relate to the charity concerned and which the auditor or examiner in question considers it necessary to inspect for the purpose of carrying out the audit or, as the case may be, examination.

(2) Such an auditor or independent examiner shall be entitled to require, in the case of the charity concerned, such information and explanations from past or present charity trustees or trustees for the charity, or from past or present officers or employees of the charity, as he considers it necessary to obtain for the purposes of carrying out the audit or, as the case may be, examination.

[3406]

NOTES

Commencement: 31 March 2005.

10 Dispensations from audit or examination requirements

(1) The Commissioners may, in the circumstances specified in paragraph (2) below, dispense with the requirements of section 43(2) or (3) of the 1993 Act in the case of a particular charity or of a particular financial year of a charity.

(2) The circumstances referred to in paragraph (1) above are where the Commissioners—

(a) are satisfied that the accounts of the charity concerned are required to be audited in accordance with any statutory provision contained in or having effect under an Act of Parliament which, in the opinion of the Commissioners, imposes requirements which are sufficiently similar to the requirements of section 43(2) for those requirements to be dispensed with;

(b) are satisfied that the accounts of the charity concerned have been audited by the Comptroller and Auditor General or by the Auditor General for Wales;

(c) are satisfied that the accounts of the charity concerned for the financial year in question have been, or will be, audited or, as the case may be, examined in accordance with requirements or arrangements which, in the opinion of the Commissioners, are sufficiently similar to the relevant requirements of section 43 of the 1993 Act applicable to that financial year of that charity for those requirements to be dispensed with;

(d) are satisfied that there has in the financial year in question been no transaction on the part of the charity concerned which would be required to be shown and explained in the accounting records kept in pursuance of section 41 of the 1993 Act;

(e) consider that, although the financial year in question of the charity concerned is one to which subsection (2) of section 43 of the 1993 Act applies, there are exceptional circumstances which justify the examination of the accounts by an independent examiner instead of their audit in accordance with that subsection.

(3) A dispensation under any of paragraphs 2(a) to (c) of this regulation is conditional on the charity trustees supplying to the Commissioners any report made to them with respect to the accounts of that charity for the financial year in question which the Commissioners have requested, and paragraph (2)(e) of this regulation is conditional on compliance by the charity

trustees with all the requirements which would have applied if they had been able to make, and had in fact made, an election under section 43(3)(a) of the 1993 Act with respect to the accounts of the charity for the financial year in question.

[3407]

NOTES

Commencement: 31 March 2005.

11 Annual reports

(1) This regulation applies to an annual report prepared by the charity trustees of a charity (other than an investment fund) in accordance with section 45(1) of the 1993 Act in respect of a financial year—

(a) which begins on or after 1st April 2005; or

(b) which begins before that date if—

(i) the charity trustees determine that this regulation, rather than regulation 7 of the 2000 Regulations, shall apply to the annual report; and

(ii) the charity trustees have not, before the date when these Regulations come into force, either authorised the signature of an annual report in respect of that financial year in accordance with regulation 7 of the 2000 Regulations or approved a statement of accounts which has been prepared for the charity in respect of that financial year under regulation 3 of those Regulations.

(2) If the charity trustees make a determination under sub-paragraph (b) above, they shall also make a determination under regulation 3(1)(b) above, if they prepare a statement of accounts under section 42(1) of the 1993 Act in respect of the financial year in question and the charity is one to which regulation 3 above may apply.

(3) The report on the activities of a charity during the year which is required to be contained in the annual report in respect of each financial year of the charity prepared under section 45 of the 1993 Act shall specify the financial year to which it relates and shall—

(a) in the case of a charity which is not an auditable charity be a brief summary of the main activities and achievements of the charity during the year in relation to its objects;

(b) in the case of a charity which is an auditable charity—

(i) be a review of significant activities, including—

(aa) details of the aims and objectives which the charity trustees have set for the charity in the year, and details of the strategies adopted, and of significant activities undertaken, in order to achieve those aims and objectives;

(bb) details of the achievements of the charity during the year, measured by reference to the aims and objectives which have been set; and

(cc) details of any significant contribution of volunteers to these activities; and

(dd) details of the principal funding sources of the charity; and

(ii) contain a statement as to whether the charity trustees have—

(aa) given consideration to the major risks to which the charity is exposed; and

(bb) established systems or procedures in order to manage those risks; and

(c) in either case—

(i) where any fund of the charity was materially in deficit at the beginning of the financial year in question, and the charity is one in respect of which a statement of accounts has been prepared under section 42(1) of the 1993 Act for the financial year, contain particulars of the steps taken by the charity trustees to eliminate that deficit; and

(ii) be dated and be signed by one or more of the charity trustees, each of whom has been authorised to do so.

(4) Subject to paragraphs (5) to (8) below, the information relating to a charity and to its trustees and officers which is required to be contained in the annual report shall be—

(a) the name of the charity as it appears in the register of charities and any other name by which it makes itself known;

(b) the number assigned to it in the register and, in the case of a charitable company, the number with which it is registered as a company;

(c) the principal address of the charity and, in the case of a charitable company, the address of its registered office;
(d) the name of any person who is a charity trustee of the charity on the date when the authority referred to in paragraph (3)(c)(ii) above is given, and, where any charity trustee on that date is a body corporate, the name of any person who is a director of the body corporate on that date;
(e) the name of any other person who has, at any time during the financial year in question, been a charity trustee of the charity;
(f) the name of any person who is a trustee for the charity on the date referred to in sub-paragraph (d) above;
(g) the name of any other person who has, at any time during the financial year in question, been a trustee for the charity;
(h) particulars, including the date if known, of any deed or other document containing provisions which regulate the purposes and administration of the charity;
(i) the name of any person or body of persons entitled by the trusts of the charity to appoint one or more new charity trustees, and a description of the method provided by those trusts for such appointment;
(j) a description of the policies and procedures (if any) which have been adopted by the charity trustees for the induction and training of charity trustees, and where no such policies have been adopted a statement to this effect;
(k) a description of the organisational structure of the charity;
(l) a summary of the objects of the charity;
(m) a description of the policies (if any) which have been adopted by the charity trustees for the selection of individuals and institutions who are to receive grants, or other forms of financial support, out of the assets of the charity;
(n) a statement regarding the performance during the financial year of the investments belonging to the charity (if any);
(o) where material investments are held by a charity, a description of the policies (if any) which have been adopted by the charity trustees for the selection, retention and realisation of investments for the charity, including the extent (if any) to which social, environmental or ethical considerations are taken into account;
(p) a description of the policies (if any) which have been adopted by the charity trustees for the purpose of determining the level of reserves which it is appropriate for the charity to maintain in order to meet effectively the needs designated by its trusts, together with details of the amount and purpose of any material commitments and planned expenditure not provided for in the balance sheet which have been deducted from the assets in the unrestricted fund of the charity in calculating the amount of reserves, and where no such policies have been adopted, a statement to this effect;
(q) a description of the aims and objectives which the charity trustees have set for the charity in the future, and of the activities contemplated in furtherance of those aims and objectives; and
(r) a description of any assets held by the charity or by any charity trustee of, or trustee for, the charity, on behalf of another charity, and particulars of any special arrangements made with respect to the safe custody of such assets and their segregation from assets of the charity not so held and a description of the objects of the charity on whose behalf the assets are held.

(5) The Commissioners may, where they are satisfied that, in the case of a particular charity or class of charities, or in the case of a particular financial year of a charity or class of charities—

(a) the disclosure of the name of any person whose name is required by any of sub-paragraphs (d), (e), (f), (g) and (i) of paragraph (4) above to be contained in the annual report of a charity could lead to that person being placed in any personal danger; or
(b) the disclosure of the principal address of the charity in accordance with paragraph (4)(c) above could lead to any such person being placed in any personal danger,

dispense with the requirement—

(i) in any of sub-paragraphs (d), (e), (f), (g) or (i) of that paragraph, so far as it applies to the name of any such person; or
(ii) in sub-paragraph (c) of that paragraph, so far as it applies to the principal address of the charity,

as the case may require.

(6) In the case of a charity having more than 50 charity trustees on the date referred to in paragraph (4)(d) above—

(a) that sub-paragraph shall have effect as if for the words "name of any person who is a charity trustee of the charity" there were substituted the words "names of not less than 50 of the charity trustees of the charity, including any charity trustee who is also an officer of the charity"; and

(b) paragraph (4)(e) shall have effect as if, at the end of the sub-paragraph, there were inserted the words "other than the name of any charity trustee whose name has been excluded from the report in pursuance of sub-paragraph (d) above".

(7) In the case of a report prepared under section 46(5) of the 1993 Act (excepted charities which are not registered), paragraph (4) above shall have effect as if—

(a) in sub-paragraph (a) the words from "as it appears in the register of charities" to the end, and

(b) in sub-paragraph (b) the words "the number assigned to it in the register and,",

were omitted.

(8) In the case of a report in respect of a financial year of a charity which is not an auditable charity, paragraph (4) above shall have effect as if sub-paragraphs (j), (k), (m), (n), (o) and (q) were omitted.

[3408]

NOTES

Commencement: 31 March 2005.

12 Annual Reports: Investment Funds

(1) This regulation applies to an annual report prepared in respect of an investment fund in accordance with section 45(1) of the 1993 Act in respect of a financial year—

(a) which begins on or after 1st April 2005; or

(b) which begins before that date if—

(i) the charity trustees determine that this regulation, rather than regulation 10 of the 1995 Regulations, shall apply to the annual report; and

(ii) the charity trustees have not, before the date when these Regulations come into force, either authorised the signature of an annual report in respect of that financial year in accordance with regulation 10 of the 1995 Regulations or approved a statement of accounts which has been prepared for the charity in respect of that financial year under regulation 4 of those Regulations.

(2) If the charity trustees make a determination under sub-paragraph (b) above, they shall also make a determination under regulation 4(1)(b) above, if they prepare a statement of accounts under section 42(1) of the 1993 Act in respect of the financial year in question.

(3) The report on the activities of an investment fund during the year which is required to be contained in the annual report in respect of each financial year of the charity prepared under section 45 of the 1993 Act shall specify the financial year to which it relates and shall—

(a) be a review of the investment activities of the investment fund during that year, including details of the objectives of the investment fund during the year, and of the policies adopted for achieving those objectives;

(b) provide any other significant information which the charity trustees consider would assist charities participating in the investment fund to make an informed judgement on the suitability to the charity of the investment fund as an investment for the charity;

(c) specify any material events affecting the investment fund which have occurred since the end of the year;

(d) contain a statement as to the steps (if any) taken to consider whether any person to whom functions in respect of the management of the investment fund has been delegated has complied with the terms of the delegation; and

(e) be signed—

(i) if the scheme or schemes regulating the investment fund allocates responsibility for preparing the report to a particular person, by that person; and otherwise,

(ii) by one or more of the charity trustees of the investment fund, each of whom has been authorised to do so.

PART II STATUTORY INSTRUMENTS

(4) The information relating to an investment fund and to its trustees and officers which is required to be contained in the annual report shall be—

(a) the name of the investment fund as it appears in the register of charities and any other name by which it makes itself known;

(b) the number assigned to the investment fund in the register;

(c) the principal address of the investment fund;

(d) particulars, including the date, of any scheme or schemes containing provisions which regulate the purposes and administration of the investment fund;

(e) the name of any person or body of persons entitled under any such scheme or schemes to appoint any charity trustee of the investment fund, and a description of the method provided by any such scheme or schemes for such appointment;

(f) a description of the objects of the investment fund;

(g) a description of the organisational structure of the investment fund;

(h) the name of any charity trustee of the investment fund, on the date of the signature of the report, where paragraph 3(e)(i) above applies, and otherwise on the date when the authority referred to in paragraph (3)(e)(ii) above is given, and, where any such person is a body corporate, the name of any person who is a director of the body corporate on that date;

(i) the professional qualifications of any individual person referred to in sub-paragraphs (e) or (h);

(j) the name of any other person who has, at any time during the financial year in question, been a charity trustee of the investment fund;

(k) the name of any person who is, in relation to the investment fund, a trustee for the charity on the date referred to in sub-paragraph (h) above;

(l) the name of any other person who has, at any time during the financial year in question, been, in relation to the investment fund, a trustee for the charity;

(m) a description of any functions relating to the management of the investment fund which have been delegated (including the maintenance of the register of charities participating in the investment fund), and of the procedures adopted to ensure that those functions are discharged consistently with the scheme or schemes by which the investment fund is regulated, and with the investment policies adopted for the investment fund;

(n) the name and address of any person to whom any such functions in respect of the management of the investment fund have been delegated or who have been instructed to provide advice on investment matters; and

(o) a statement as to which, if any, of the persons whose names are given in accordance with the provisions of sub-paragraphs (h), (j), (k), (l) or (n) above, are authorised persons.

[3409]

NOTES

Commencement: 31 March 2005.

13 Revocation

The 1995 and 2000 Regulations will, except where these Regulations otherwise provide, continue to have effect in relation to the accounts and annual reports of charities for financial years beginning on or before 31st March 2005, but subject to that are hereby revoked.

[3410]

NOTES

Commencement: 31 March 2005.

SCHEDULES

SCHEDULE 1
NOTES TO THE ACCOUNTS

Regulation 3(10)

1 Subject to paragraph 2 below, the information to be provided by way of notes to the accounts shall, insofar as not provided in the statement of financial activities or in the balance sheet, be as follows:

(a) particulars of any material adjustment made pursuant to regulation 3(7) above;

(b) a description of each of the accounting policies which have been adopted by the charity trustees, and which are material in the context of the accounts of the charity, together with a description of those estimation techniques adopted which are material to the presentation of the accounts;

(c) a description of any material change to these policies and techniques, the reason for such change and its effect (if material) on the accounts, in accordance with the methods and principles set out in the SORP;

(d) a description of the nature and purpose of all material funds of the charity in accordance with the methods and principles set out in the SORP;

(e) such particulars of the related party transactions of the charity, or of any institution or body corporate connected with the charity, as may be required by the SORP to be disclosed;

(f) such particulars of the cost to the charity of employing and providing pensions for staff as may be required by the SORP to be disclosed;

(g) such particulars of the emoluments of staff employed by the charity as may be required by the SORP to be disclosed;

(h) a description of any incoming resources which represent capital, according to whether or not that capital is permanent endowment;

(i) an itemised analysis of any material movement between any of the restricted funds of the charity, or between a restricted and an unrestricted fund of the charity, together with an explanation of the nature and purpose of each of those funds;

(j) the name of any institution or body corporate connected with the charity, together with a description of the nature of the charity's relationship with that institution or body corporate and of its activities, including, where material, its turnover and net profit or loss for the corresponding financial year of the institution or body corporate and any qualification expressed in an auditor's report on its accounts;

(k) particulars of any guarantee given by the charity, where any potential liability under the guarantee is outstanding at the date of the balance sheet;

(l) particulars of any loan outstanding at the date of the balance sheet—
   (i) which was made to the charity, and which is secured by an express charge on any of the assets of the charity; or
   (ii) which was made by the charity to any institution or body corporate connected with the charity;

(m) particulars of any fund of the charity which is materially in deficit at the date of the balance sheet;

(n) particulars of any remuneration paid to an auditor or independent examiner in respect of auditing or examining the accounts of the charity and particulars of any remuneration paid to the auditor or independent examiner in respect of any other services rendered to the charity;

(o) such particulars of any grant made by the charity as may be required by the SORP to be disclosed;

(p) particulars of any ex gratia payment made by the charity;

(q) an analysis of any entry in the statement of financial activities relating to resources expended on charitable activities as may be required by the SORP to be disclosed;

(r) such particulars of any support costs incurred by the charity as may be required by the SORP to be disclosed;

(s) an analysis of any entry in the balance sheet relating to fixed assets, debtors and creditors, according to the categories set out in the SORP;

(t) an analysis of all material changes during the financial year in question in the values of fixed assets, in accordance with the methods and principles set out in the SORP;

(u) in the case of any amount required by any of the preceding sub-paragraphs (other than sub-paragraph (i), (o) or (t) to be disclosed), the corresponding amount for the financial year immediately preceding that to which the accounts relate;

(v) a statement as to whether or not the accounts have been prepared in accordance with any applicable accounting standards and statements of recommended practice and particulars of any material departure from those standards and statements of practice and the reasons for such departure;

(w) where the charity trustees have exercised their powers under sub-paragraph (b) of regulation 6(4) above so as to determine an accounting reference date earlier or later than 12 months from the beginning of the financial year, a statement of their reasons for doing so;

(x) if, in accordance with regulation 3(5)(d) above, the charity trustees have departed from any requirement of that regulation, particulars of any such departure, the reasons for it, and its effect; and

(y) any additional information—
(i) which is required to ensure that the statement of accounts complies with the requirements of regulation 3 above; or
(ii) which may reasonably assist the user to understand the statement of accounts.

2 Sub-paragraph (v) of paragraph 1 above shall not apply in the case of any financial year of a charity which is not an auditable charity.

[3411]

NOTES

Commencement: 31 March 2005.

SCHEDULE 2
FORM AND CONTENTS OF STATEMENTS OF ACCOUNTS: INVESTMENT FUNDS
Regulation 4

PART I
STATEMENT OF TOTAL RETURN

1 The statement of total return shall show the net gain or loss on investments, gross income, total expenditure and total return of the investment fund, and the total amount distributed or due, including interest paid or payable, to participating charities out of the investment fund, during the financial year in respect of which the statement of accounts is prepared.

2 The information required by paragraph 1 above shall be analysed by reference to—
(a) net gains or losses on investments, indicated by—
(i) gains or losses on investments sold during the financial year in question, based on the historical cost of the investment sold;
(ii) any net appreciation or depreciation of such investments recognised in earlier accounting periods;
(iii) the gains or losses on such investments based on their value as shown in the accounts (that is to say, the difference between or, as the case may be, the sum of the amounts entered in pursuance of paragraphs (i) and (ii) above); and
(iv) net unrealised appreciation or depreciation of investments during the financial year in question;
(b) gains or losses on other assets;
(c) gross income, divided into—
(i) dividends in respect of shares;
(ii) scrip dividends;
(iii) interest on securities;
(iv) interest on deposits at banks and building societies;
(v) underwriting commission; and
(vi) other income;
(d) expenditure incurred in the administration of the investment fund, divided into—
(i) any fees payable in respect of investment management services provided to the investment fund;
(ii) any fees payable in respect of the maintenance of the register of charities participating in the investment fund;
(iii) any fees payable in respect of any audit of the accounts of the investment fund;
(iv) any fees payable to the person carrying out such an audit in respect of other services for the investment fund provided by him;
(v) any fees payable in respect of the safe custody of the assets of the investment fund;
(vi) any fees payable in respect of other administrative services provided to the investment fund; and
(vii) other expenditure divided into such categories as reasonably enable the user to gain an appreciation of the expenditure incurred;
(e) net income before taxation (that is to say, the total amounts entered in pursuance of sub-paragraph (c) above less the total amounts entered in pursuance of sub-paragraph (d) above);

(f) tax borne by the investment fund in respect of income, profits or gains during the financial year in question, divided into—
  (i) income tax or capital gains tax to which the investment fund is liable in the United Kingdom; and
  (ii) overseas tax;

(g) net income after taxation (that is to say, the total amount entered in pursuance of sub-paragraph (e) above, less the total amount entered in pursuance of sub-paragraph (f) above);

(h) total return (that is to say, the total of the amounts entered in pursuance of sub-paragraphs (a), (b) and (g) above);

(i) the amount distributed or due in respect of income and accumulation shares, and interest paid or payable to charities who have deposited sums, during the financial year in question; and

(j) net increase or decrease in the value of the investment fund resulting from its activities (that is to say, the difference between the amounts entered in pursuance of sub-paragraphs (h) and (i) above).

3 In the case of a common investment fund established by a scheme which, in pursuance of section 22(5) of the 1960 Act or section 24(5) of the 1993 Act, includes provision for enabling sums to be deposited by or on behalf of a charity on the basis that (subject to the provisions of the scheme) the charity shall be entitled to repayment of the sums deposited and to interest thereon at a rate determined by or under the scheme, the analysis required by paragraph 2 above shall distinguish between the amount of capital and income to be shared between charities participating otherwise than by way of deposit and the amounts excluded from such amount under provision made in pursuance of section 22(5) of the 1960 Act or 24(5) of the 1993 Act (that is, such amounts as are from time to time reasonably required in respect of the liabilities of the investment fund for the repayment of deposits and for the interest on deposits, including amounts required by way of reserve).

4 In respect of any information required by a sub-paragraph of paragraph 2 above to be divided into separate categories denoted by paragraphs of that sub-paragraph, the division of that information into such separate categories may, if the charity trustees so elect, be effected by means of a note to the accounts made in pursuance of Part V of this Schedule rather than by division in pursuance of that sub-paragraph.

[3412]

NOTES

Commencement: 31 March 2005.

PART II
STATEMENT OF MOVEMENT IN FUNDS

1 The statement of movement in funds shall provide a reconciliation between the net assets of the investment fund at the beginning of the financial year in respect of which the statement of accounts is prepared and the net assets of the investment fund at the end of that year.

2 The reconciliation referred to in paragraph 1 above shall show—

(a) the value of the net assets at the beginning of the financial year in question;

(b) in the case of a common investment fund, the amount or value of any property transferred to or withdrawn from the investment fund during that year by participating charities;

(c) the net increase or decrease in the value of the investment fund resulting from its activities during that year (that is to say, the amount entered in pursuance of sub-paragraph (j) of paragraph 2 of Part I of this Schedule);

(d) in the case of a common investment fund, the amount of any distribution of income due in respect of accumulation shares;

(e) particulars of any other items necessary to provide the reconciliation required by paragraph 1 above; and

(f) the value of the net assets at the end of the financial year in question.

3 In the case of a common investment fund such as is described in paragraph 3 of Part I of this Schedule, the analysis required by paragraph 2 above shall distinguish between the amount of capital and income to be shared between charities participating otherwise than by

way of deposit and the amounts excluded from such amount under provision made in pursuance of section 22(5) of the 1960 Act or section 24(5) of the 1993 Act.

[3413]

NOTES

Commencement: 31 March 2005.

PART III
BALANCE SHEET

1 The balance sheet shall show, by reference to the information specified in paragraph 2 or, as the case may be, 3 below, the state of affairs of the investment fund as at the end of the financial year.

2 Subject to paragraph 4 below, in the case of a common investment fund, the information referred to in paragraph 1 above is as follows:

- (a) tangible fixed assets for use by the investment fund;
- (b) investments;
- (c) current assets, divided into—
  - (i) debtors;
  - (ii) deposits and loans;
  - (iii) cash at bank and in hand; and
  - (iv) others;
- (d) liabilities, divided into—
  - (i) creditors;
  - (ii) bank overdrafts;
  - (iii) other loans; and
  - (iv) distributions payable to participating charities;
- (e) net current assets less liabilities (that is to say, the difference between the total amount entered in pursuance of sub-paragraph (c) above and the total amount entered in pursuance of sub-paragraph (d) above); and
- (f) net assets (that is to say, the total of the amounts entered in pursuance of sub-paragraphs (a), (b) and (e) above); and
- (g) total funds of the common investment fund.

3 In the case of a common deposit fund, the information referred to in paragraph 1 above is as follows:

- (a) cash at bank and in hand;
- (b) debtors;
- (c) deposits and investments, divided into—
  - (i) deposits at the Bank of England;
  - (ii) deposits with a person who has permission under Part 4 of the Financial Services and Markets Act 2000 to accept deposits;
  - (iii) other bank deposits;
  - (iv) other deposits; and
  - (v) other investments;
- (d) current assets not included in any of paragraphs (a) to (c) above;
- (e) tangible fixed assets for use by the investment fund;
- (f) gross assets (that is to say, the total of the amounts entered in pursuance of sub-paragraphs (a) to (e) above);
- (g) sums deposited by participating charities;
- (h) other liabilities, divided into—
  - (i) creditors;
  - (ii) bank overdrafts;
  - (iii) other loans; and
  - (iv) interest accrued or payable to participating charities;
- (i) sums held as an income reserve on trust for existing depositors; and
- (j) total liabilities (that is to say, the total of the amounts entered in pursuance of sub-paragraphs (g), (h) and (i) above);

4 In the case of a common investment fund such as is described in paragraph 3 of Part I of this Schedule, the information referred to in paragraph 1 above is—

(a) in relation to the amount of capital and income to be shared between charities participating otherwise than by way of deposit, the information specified in paragraph 2 above; and

(b) in relation to the amounts excluded from such amount under provision made in pursuance of section 22(5) of the 1960 Act or section 24(5) of the 1993 Act, the information specified in paragraph 3 above.

5 In respect of any information required by sub-paragraph (c) of paragraph 3 above to be divided into separate categories denoted by paragraphs of that sub-paragraph, the division of that information into such separate categories may, if the charity trustees so elect, be effected by means of a note to the accounts made in pursuance of Part V of this Schedule rather than by division in pursuance of that sub-paragraph.

[3414]

NOTES

Commencement: 31 March 2005.

PART IV
METHODS AND PRINCIPLES

1—(1) The statement of total return shall give a true and fair view of the incoming resources and application of the resources of the investment fund in, and the balance sheet shall give a true and fair view of the state of affairs of the investment fund at the end of, the financial year in respect of which the statement of accounts is prepared.

(2) The statement of movement in funds shall give a true and fair view of the movements in the net assets of the investment fund between their position at the beginning of that year and their position at the end of that year.

(3) Where compliance with Part I, II, III or V of Schedule 2 to these Regulations would not be sufficient to give a true and fair view, the necessary additional information shall be given in the accounts or a note to them.

(4) If in special circumstances compliance with any of those provisions is inconsistent with the requirement to give a true and fair view, the charity trustees shall depart from that provision to the extent necessary to give a true and fair view; particulars of any such departure, the reasons for it and its effect shall be given in a note to the accounts.

2—(1) In respect of every amount required by paragraph 2 of Part I of Schedule 2 to these Regulations to be shown in the statement of total return, or by paragraph 2 of Part II of that Schedule to be shown in the statement of movement in funds, or by paragraph 2 or, as the case may be, 3 of Part III of that Schedule to be shown in the balance sheet, the corresponding amount for the financial year immediately preceding that to which the statement or balance sheet relates shall also be shown.

(2) Where that corresponding amount is not comparable with the amount to be shown for the item in question in respect of the financial year to which the statement of total return, statement of movement in funds or balance sheet relates, the former amount shall be adjusted; particulars of any material adjustment under this sub-paragraph shall be disclosed in a note to the accounts.

(3) Where in the financial year to which the statement of accounts relates there is nothing required to be shown by one or more of the provisions specified in sub-paragraph (1) above but an amount was required to be shown by that provision in the immediately preceding financial year, this paragraph shall have effect as if such an amount were required to be shown in the financial year to which the statement of accounts relates and that amount were nil.

3 The values at which assets and liabilities of an investment fund are recorded in the balance sheet, and the recognition bases for gains and losses, shall be determined in accordance with the methods and principles set out in the IMA SORP.

[3415]

NOTES

Commencement: 31 March 2005.

PART V
NOTES TO THE ACCOUNTS

The information to be provided by way of notes to the accounts shall, insofar as not provided in the statement of accounts, be as follows:

(a) a description of the accounting policies adopted for the investment fund, particularly regarding the basis of valuation of investments, the recognition of dividend income or interest and the conversion of any amounts expressed in currency other than pounds sterling, and of the accounting assumptions made by them, including any material change in these, the reason for such change and its effect (if material) on the accounts;

(b) where the charity trustees have during the financial year in question entered into any transaction, agreement or arrangement, made for the purpose of minimising the risk of loss to the investment fund in consequence of fluctuations in interest rates or in the market value of securities or in the rates of foreign exchange, or entered into any other transaction in financial futures or options relating to shares, securities, foreign currency or into any other financial instrument the value of which is dependent on or derived from the price movements in one or more underlying assets, the nature of, and reason for, entering into that transaction, agreement or arrangement and the total value of, and the maximum extent of financial exposure as at the date of the balance sheet resulting from, that transaction, agreement or arrangement;

(c) a statement as to whether any remuneration or other benefits (together with the amount of such remuneration or, as the case may be, the monetary value of such benefits) has been paid or is payable to any person who is a charity trustee of the investment fund, or to any person to whom functions in relation to management of the investment fund has been delegated, or to any person connected with such a charity trustee or manager, directly or indirectly from the property of the investment fund or from the property of any institution or body corporate connected with the investment fund, and the name of that person;

(d) particulars of any transaction undertaken in the name of or on behalf of the investment fund in which any person referred to in sub-paragraph (c) above has a material interest;

(e) an analysis of the amount and date of any distribution in respect of income and accumulation shares or payment of interest to participating charities;

(f) a note of any adjustments made in the statement of total return to reflect the amount of income included in the creation or cancellation price of a unit or share in the investment fund;

(g) the name of any institution or body corporate connected with the investment fund, together with a description of the nature of the investment fund's relationship with that institution or body corporate and of its activities, including, where material, its turnover and net profit or loss for the corresponding financial year of the institution or body corporate and any qualification expressed in an auditor's report on its accounts;

(h) particulars of any loan or guarantee secured against any of the assets of the investment fund;

(i) an explanation of any amount entered in pursuance of paragraph 2(f)(i) of Part I of this Schedule (United Kingdom tax);

(j) an analysis of any entry in the balance sheet relating to:

 (i) tangible fixed assets for use by the investment fund, according to the following categories—

  (aa) freehold interests in land and buildings;

  (bb) any other interest in land and buildings;

  (cc) payments on account and assets in course of construction; and

  (dd) plant, machinery, fixtures, fittings and equipment;

 (ii) debtors, according to the following categories—

  (aa) in the case of a common investment fund, amounts receivable in respect of property transferred to the investment fund;

  (bb) amounts receivable in respect of securities sold;

  (cc) accrued income; and

  (dd) other debtors; and

 (iii) creditors, according to the following categories—

  (aa) in the case of a common investment fund, amounts payable in respect of property withdrawn from the investment fund;

  (bb) amounts payable in respect of securities purchased;

  (cc) accrued expenses; and

  (dd) other creditors;

(k) in the case of a common investment fund, the following statements, made up to the date of the balance sheet, that is to say—
   (i) a portfolio statement, specifying—
      (aa) details of each investment held by or on behalf of the investment fund, including its market value at that date;
      (bb) whether or not the investment in question is listed on a recognised stock exchange;
      (cc) the category of each such investment, according to its geographical area or industrial sector;
      (dd) where the investment fund invests in more than one class of assets, the market value at that date of each class of investment funds;
      (ee) the percentage of net assets represented by each investment so held and by each category of investment specified under sub-paragraph (cc) above;
      (ff) the percentage of investment assets represented by each class of investments specified under sub-paragraph (dd) above; and
      (gg) an analysis of the credit rating of any interest-bearing securities held at that date, as may be required by the IMA SORP to be given;
   (ii) a statement of major changes in the portfolio, specifying—
      (aa) where the aggregate value of purchases or sales of a particular investment during the financial year in question exceeds 2 per cent of net assets at the beginning of that year, or, in the case of the first financial year of an investment fund, exceeds 2 per cent of the net assets at the end of that year, that value;
      (bb) unless disclosed in pursuance of paragraph (aa) above, the value of the 20 largest purchases and sales of a particular investment during the financial year in question; and
      (cc) the total cost of purchase and net proceeds from sales of investments during the financial year in question;
   (iii) a statement of the number of shares issued as at the beginning of the year and as at the date of the balance sheet and the value of each income or accumulation share as at each of those dates, calculated by reference to the net asset value of the investment fund; and
   (iv) a statement of the amount, if any, in the dividend equalisation reserve;

(l) in the case of a common deposit fund, details of sums deposited by participating charities as at the date of the balance sheet, divided into—
   (i) sums repayable on demand; and
   (ii) deposits with agreed maturity dates or periods of notice, divided into—
      (aa) those repayable in not more than three months;
      (bb) those repayable in more than three months but not more than one year;
      (cc) those repayable in more than one year but not more than five years; and
      (dd) those repayable in more than five years;

(m) in the case of a common deposit fund, details as at the date of the balance sheet of—
   (i) sums placed on deposit, divided into—
      (aa) sums repayable on demand; and
      (bb) other deposits, indicating whether they are repayable in not more than 3 months, more than 3 months but not more than 1 year, more than 1 year but not more than 5 years or more than 5 years; and
   (ii) investments other than deposits, analysed in accordance with sub-paragraph (k)(i) above;

(n) the following particulars of any contingent liability, that is to say, its amount or estimated amount, its legal nature and whether any valuable security has been provided by the investment fund in connection with that liability and, if so, what;

(o) particulars of any other financial commitments which have not been provided for and are relevant to assessment of the state of affairs of the investment fund;

(p) in the case of any amount required by any of the preceding sub-paragraphs (other than sub-paragraph (k)(i) and (ii)) to be disclosed, or the percentage of net assets represented by each category of investment required by sub-paragraph (k)(i)(ee) above to be disclosed, or the percentage of investment assets represented by each class of investment required by sub-paragraph (k)(i)(ff) above, to be disclosed, the corresponding amount or percentage for the financial year immediately preceding that to which the accounts relate;

(q) a statement as to whether or not the accounts have been prepared in accordance

PART II
STATUTORY INSTRUMENTS

with any applicable accounting standards and statements of recommended practice and particulars of any material departure from those standards and practices and the reasons for such departure;

(r) where the charity trustees have exercised their powers under regulation 6(4)(b) above, a statement of their reasons for doing so; and

(s) any other information which is required by these Regulations to be disclosed in a note to the accounts or which may reasonably assist the user to understand the statement of accounts.

[3416]

NOTES

Commencement: 31 March 2005.

PART VI
INTERPRETATION

1 In this Schedule—

"dividend equalisation reserve" means income withheld from distribution with a view to avoiding fluctuations in the amounts distributed;

"the IMA SORP" means the Statement of Recommended Practice for Financial Statements of Authorised Funds issued by the Investment Management Association in November 2003; and

"recognised stock exchange" has the same meaning as in the Income and Corporation Taxes Act 1988;

2 For the purposes of this Schedule, a person is connected with a trustee or a person to whom functions in relation to the management of the investment fund have been delegated if—

(i) he is the child, parent, grandchild, grandparent, brother or sister of any such trustee or manager;

(ii) he is the spouse of any such trustee or manager or of any person connected with a trustee or manager by virtue of sub-paragraph (i) above;

(iii) he is the civil partner of any such trustee or manager or of any person connected with a trustee or manager by virtue of sub-paragraph (i) above;

(iv) he is the trustee of any trust, not being a charity, the beneficiaries or potential beneficiaries of which include a trustee or manager or any person connected with the trustee or manager by virtue of sub-paragraph (i), (ii) or (iii) above and is acting in his capacity as such;

(v) he is a partner of a trustee or manager or of any person connected with a trustee or manager by virtue of sub-paragraph (i), (ii), (iii) or (iv) above and is acting in his capacity as such; or

(vi) the person is a body corporate, not being a company which is connected with a charitable institution within the meaning of section 58(5) of the Charities Act 1992, in which the trustee or manager has, or the trustee or manager and any other trustee or manager or charity trustees or managers or person or persons connected with him or them by virtue of sub-paragraph (i), (ii), (iii), (iv) or (v) above, taken together, have, a substantial interest.

3 Any expression in paragraph 2 above which also appears in Schedule 5 to the 1993 Act shall be construed in accordance with paragraphs 2 to 4 of that Schedule.

[3417]

NOTES

Commencement: 5 Dec 2005 (para 2(iii)); 31 March 2005 (otherwise).

BIG LOTTERY FUND (PRESCRIBED EXPENDITURE) ORDER 2006

(SI 2006/3202)

NOTES

Made: 30 November 2006.
Authority: National Lottery etc Act 1993, ss 22(3A), (3B), 36B(3), (4).
Commencement: 1 December 2006.

1 Citation, commencement and interpretation

(1) This Order may be cited as the Big Lottery Fund (Prescribed Expenditure) Order 2006 and shall come into force on 1st December 2006 or on the day after the day on which it is made, whichever is the later.

(2) In this Order—
"the Act" means the National Lottery etc Act 1993; and
"the Fund" means the Big Lottery Fund.

[3418]

NOTES

Commencement: 1 December 2006.

2 Devolved expenditure

(1) Expenditure that is charitable or connected with health, education or the environment of the descriptions specified in paragraph (2) is prescribed in relation to each of England, Wales, Scotland, Northern Ireland and the Isle of Man for the purposes of section 22(3)(d) of the Act.

(2) The descriptions of expenditure are—
(a) expenditure on or connected with the promotion of community learning;
(b) expenditure on or connected with the promotion of community safety and cohesion;
(c) expenditure on or connected with the promotion of physical and mental well being.

(3) The reference in paragraph (2)(b) to promoting community safety is to making communities places in which it is, or is perceived to be, safer to live or work, in particular by the reduction of actual or perceived levels of crime and other anti-social behaviour.

[3419]

NOTES

Commencement: 1 December 2006.

3 Devolved expenditure: small grants

(1) Expenditure that is charitable or connected with health, education or the environment of the description specified in paragraph (2) is prescribed in relation to each of England, Wales, Scotland and Northern Ireland for the purposes of section 22(3)(d) of the Act.

(2) The description of expenditure is expenditure on or connected with small scale projects in local communities which involve people within those communities.

[3420]

NOTES

Commencement: 1 December 2006.

4 Non-devolved expenditure: transformational grants

(1) Expenditure that is charitable or connected with health, education or the environment of the description specified in paragraph (2) is prescribed for the purposes of section 22(3)(d) of the Act.

(2) The description of expenditure is expenditure on or connected with projects which are intended to transform communities, regions or the nation as a whole.

(3) The maximum amount that may be distributed by the Fund before 1st April 2008 under section 36B(1) of the Act for such expenditure shall be £140 million.

[3421]–[5000]

NOTES

Commencement: 1 December 2006.

PART III

ACCOUNTING AND REPORTING BY CHARITIES: STATEMENT OF RECOMMENDED PRACTICE

ACCOUNTING AND REPORTING BY CHARITIES: STATEMENT OF RECOMMENDED PRACTICE

(Revised 2005)

STATEMENT BY THE ACCOUNTING STANDARDS BOARD ON THE SORP 'ACCOUNTING AND REPORTING BY CHARITIES: STATEMENT OF RECOMMENDED PRACTICE'

The aims of the Accounting Standards Board (the ASB) are to establish and improve standards of financial accounting and reporting, for the benefit of users, preparers, and auditors of financial information. To this end, the ASB issues accounting standards that are primarily applicable to general purpose company financial statements. In particular industries or sectors, further guidance may be required in order to implement accounting standards effectively. This guidance is issued, in the form of Statements of Recommended Practice (SORPs), by bodies recognised for the purpose by the ASB.

The Charity Commission has confirmed that it shares the ASB's aim of advancing and maintaining standards of financial reporting in the public interest and has been recognised by the ASB for the purpose of issuing SORPs. As a condition of recognition, the Commission has agreed to follow the ASB's code of practice for bodies recognised for issuing SORPs.

The code of practice sets out procedures to be followed in the development of SORPs. These procedures do not include a comprehensive review of the proposed SORP by the ASB, but a review of limited scope is performed.

On the basis of its review, the ASB has concluded that the SORP has been developed in accordance with the ASB's code of practice and does not appear to contain any fundamental points of principle that are unacceptable in the context of accounting practice or to conflict with an accounting standard or the ASB's plans for future standards.

Dated 28 February 2005

STATEMENT BY THE CHARITY COMMISSION FOR ENGLAND AND WALES

The Charity Commission is pleased to publish this revised edition of the Charities SORP.

The accounting recommendations of this SORP are based on Financial Reporting Standards currently in issue and have been developed in conjunction with the Charities SORP committee, an advisory committee made up of charity finance directors, charity auditors, academics, charity advisers and charity regulators. The committee is also structured to reflect the different charity jurisdictions of the UK.

Sector involvement has been a central part of producing this SORP. The research, input and feedback provided by the sector and the SORP Committee has informed each stage of its development. The resulting document provides a platform for transparent and consistent reporting by charities. The Commission would like to thank the SORP Committee, and all those who responded to the consultation on the exposure draft as well as all those who prepared research papers and publications that have informed this SORP's development.

This revision creates a new focus for charity reporting, building on existing SORP principles and recommendations. It provides a framework that enables charities to explain what they aim to do, how they go about it and what they achieve. It does so in a way that pulls together narrative and financial reporting into a coherent package focused on activities undertaken.

We, in the UK, are fortunate in benefiting from a dynamic and energetic charity sector that encompasses a huge diversity in terms of size of charity and the activities they undertake. Retaining and enhancing the high reputation of the sector is a responsibility that we share with the sector. This SORP has a key role to play in this respect by assisting charities in providing financial information about their activities and resources that is of interest to many people and to meet legal requirements that such accounts give a "true and fair" view.

Dated 4 March 2005

TABLE OF CONTENTS

ACCOUNTING AND REPORTING BY CHARITIES STATEMENT OF RECOMMENDED PRACTICE (REVISED 2005)

INTRODUCTION

Effective Date of Commencement

1 This Charities Statement of Recommended Practice (SORP) is applicable to all accounting periods beginning on or after 1 April 2005. Early adoption is encouraged.

[5001]

The Objectives

2 The objectives of publishing these recommendations include:

(a) improving the quality of financial reporting by charities
(b) enhancing the relevance, comparability and understandability of information presented in accounts;
(c) providing clarification, explanation and interpretation of accounting standards and of their application in the charities sector and to sector specific transactions; and thereby
(d) assisting those who are responsible for the preparation of the Trustees' Annual Report and Accounts.

[5002]

Scope

3 The accounting recommendations of this SORP apply to all charities in the United Kingdom that prepare accounts on the accruals basis to give a true and fair view of a charity's financial activities and financial position regardless of their size, constitution or complexity.

4 Each accounting recommendation should be considered in the context of what is material (Glossary GL 42) to the particular charity.

5 Where a separate SORP exists for a particular class of charities (e g SORPs applicable to Registered Social Landlords and to Further and Higher Education institutions), the charity trustees of charities in that class should adhere to that SORP and any reporting requirements placed on such charities by charity law.

6 The accounting recommendations of this SORP do not apply to charities preparing cash-based receipts and payments accounts, though such charities are encouraged to adopt the activity approach provided in this SORP (see paragraph 93) to the analysis of their receipts and payments (see appendix 5).

7 The SORP recognises that particular accounting disclosures and the activity basis for the analysis of income and cost within the SoFA may not be relevant information for the users of accruals accounts prepared by smaller charities. The concessions for smaller charities are summarised in Appendix 5.

8 Whilst charities in the Republic of Ireland do not fall within the scope of this SORP they may choose to comply with its recommendations. If a charity based in the Republic of Ireland chooses to adopt this SORP's recommendations they are encouraged to disclose that fact.

9 Charity accounts are accompanied and complemented by information that does not form part of the financial statements. Within the United Kingdom such accompanying information is primarily provided by charities through a Trustees' Annual Report. As is explained in paragraph 24, the legal requirements for an annual report and its contents differ according to the charity reporting frameworks that apply within the separate legal jurisdictions of the UK. The SORP recognises that such accompanying information is of high importance for users of charity accounts in understanding the activities and achievements of a charity as a whole and therefore provides best practice recommendations for the content of such reports. In England and Wales these best practice recommendations are underpinned by law, in Scotland and Northern Ireland whilst the recommendations are considered to be consistent with the law they should be regarded as voluntary best practice recommendations supplementing legal requirements.

[5003]

Purpose of Trustees' Annual Report and Accounts

10 The purpose of preparing a Trustees' Annual Report and Accounts is to discharge the charity trustees' duty of public accountability and stewardship. This SORP sets out recommended accounting practice for this purpose but charity trustees should consider providing such additional information as is needed to give donors, beneficiaries and the general public a greater insight into the charity's activities and achievements. Accounts prepared on the basis of this SORP are not a substitute for management accounts required to run the charity on a daily basis, though both will draw on the same primary financial records.

11 Charities are highly disparate in character, so any comparison of the financial information they produce should be undertaken with care, even if the charities involved seem to be similar. Essentially the accounts should include all the money and other assets entrusted to the charity for whatever purpose, and show how they have been expended during the year and how the balance of each fund is deployed at the end of the accounting period.

12 The balance sheet is not necessarily a measure of the wealth of the charity but does show the resources available, what form those resources take and how they are held in the different funds, and provides information about the liquidity of assets and general solvency.

13 The Statement of Financial Activities provides information as to how a charity receives and applies its resources to meet its objectives. It is not intended to demonstrate a charity's efficiency.

14 Accounts focus on financial performance and in isolation do not give the reader a perspective of what has been achieved from the activities undertaken and the resources expended in their delivery. The SORP recognises these limitations and places significant weight on the Trustees' Annual Report to provide a necessary link between objectives, strategies, activities and the achievements that flow from them. Without this information the value of the accounts to the reader may be significantly diminished.

15 The Trustees' Annual Report and Accounts should therefore:

a) provide timely and regular information on the charity and its funds;
b) enable the reader to understand the charity's objectives, structure, activities and achievements; and

PART III SORP 2005

c) enable the reader to gain a full and proper appreciation of the charity's financial transactions during the year and of the position of its funds at the end of the year.

[5004]

How to Use the SORP

16 This SORP recommends particular accounting treatments and provides guidance on the application of accounting standards (compliance with which is considered necessary, in all save exceptional circumstances, to meet the legal requirement to give a true and fair view) in a manner which takes account of the particular circumstances of charities. In all but exceptional circumstances, charities preparing accruals accounts should follow this SORP's accounting recommendations to assist in ensuring that their accounts give a true and fair view.

17 There will be few, if any, charities preparing accruals accounts to which all parts of this SORP apply since it caters for a wide variety of charity activities and transactions. Charities do not have to follow those sections which do not apply to them. For example, advice on how to account for gifts in kind and the proceeds of trading activities will not apply to all charities. Readers whose charity does not have receipts from those sources may safely pass over the sections dealing with them and any other sections which do not apply to their charity's own activities. However, there are several sections which will apply to all or nearly all charities.

18 The main text of the SORP deals with the normal accounting practice for those charities producing accruals accounts. Small charities that are not subject to a statutory audit requirement may choose to apply a number of concessions available under the SORP in relation to both reporting disclosures and presentation. These concessions are summarised in Appendix 5.

19 Certain charities will have to meet additional requirements due to the transactions undertaken or the legal or operating structures adopted. The following sections set out additional recommendations applicable for:

(a) Consolidation of Subsidiary Undertakings – paragraphs 381–406.
(b) Accounting for Associates, Joint Ventures and Joint Arrangements – paragraphs 407–418.
(c) Charitable Companies – paragraphs 419–429.
(d) Accounting for Retirement Benefits – paragraphs 430–448.
(e) Common Investment Funds and Investment Pooling Schemes – paragraphs 449–451.

20 The accounting disclosure requirements have been separately identified throughout the SORP. Generally charities are only excused from a particular disclosure requirement where the item in question is not relevant to a charity or where disclosure would be immaterial for the user of the accounts. For example, investment disclosures are not required if a charity has no investments. Certain other disclosures, for example, remuneration of trustees, provide information of significance to the reader and require a "nil" disclosure in the event of no remuneration being paid. Where such a "nil" disclosure is required, this is specifically stated in the relevant disclosure recommendation.

21 The main obligation of charity trustees in preparing accruals accounts is to give a true and fair view of the charity's incoming resources and application of resources during the year and of its state of affairs at the end of the year. To achieve this, the charity trustees' judgement may dictate the disclosure of more information than specifically recommended in this SORP. Similarly charity trustees may occasionally find that following a recommendation is incompatible with the obligation to give a true and fair view. They should then use the alternative accounting treatment which gives a true and fair view and provide particulars within the accounting policy notes (in accordance with paragraph 359) of any material departure from the recommendations in this SORP. A departure from the SORP is not justified simply because it gives the reader a more appealing picture of the financial position or results of the charity.

[5005]

The SORP and the Law

22 The SORP is compatible with the requirements of the law. The SORP clarifies how charity accounting is affected by legal requirements, including aspects of trust law. It provides the charity sector with an interpretation of accounting standards and principles and clarifies the accounting treatment for sector specific transactions. In so doing, applying the SORP enables the preparers of charity accounts to meet their legal or other reporting duties for their accounts to give a true and fair view.

23 Charity trustees should include any additional information which they are required by law to report and in order for the accounts to comply with current statutory requirements or the requirements of the charity's governing document to the extent that these exceed statutory requirements.

24 The legal requirements for a Trustees' Annual Report and its contents differ according to the charity reporting frameworks that apply within the separate legal jurisdictions of the UK. The SORP provides best practice recommendations that in England and Wales are underpinned by law. In Scotland and Northern Ireland, whilst the recommendations are considered to be consistent with the law they should be regarded a voluntary best practice recommendations supplementing legal requirements.

25 The charity trustees (see glossary GL 7) are jointly responsible for the preparation of the Annual Report and Accounts which should be approved by the charity trustees as a body in accordance with their usual procedures and both documents should be signed on behalf of the charity trustees by one of their number authorised so to do or as otherwise required by law. The date of approval should be stated.

26 Any audit, independent examination or other statutory report on the accounts should be attached to the accounts when they are distributed or made available to users of financial information.

27 The primary legislative sources that contain requirements relating to the form and content of charity accounts and reports prepared under this SORP include:

(a) The Charities Act 1993 and Regulations made thereunder,
(b) The Companies Act 1985 and 1989,
(c) The Industrial and Provident Societies Acts 1965 to 2002,
(d) The Law Reform (Miscellaneous Provisions) (Scotland) Act 1990 and Regulations made thereunder, currently the Charities Accounts (Scotland) Regulations 1992, unless and until these are repealed;

28 Charitable companies governed by the requirements of the Companies Act 1985 should refer to paragraphs 419 to 429 that provide recommendations as to how the particular requirements of company law should be addressed within charity accounts.

29 Table 1 below summarises the legislative framework applying to the accounts of charities within the UK not reporting under company law.

TABLE 1. LEGISLATIVE FRAMEWORK FOR CHARITY ACCOUNTS IN THE UNITED KINGDOM

Country	Charity authority	Act(s) Governing Charities	Registration and Filing of Accounts	Preparation of Accounts
England and Wales	Charity Commission for England and Wales	Part VI Charities Act 1993, and applicable Regulations	The Charity Commission is responsible for the supervision and regulation of charities that are not exempt and maintains a public register of charities that are not exempt or excepted. Trustees' Annual Report and accounts must be filed by all registered charities with gross income or total expenditure of over £10,000.	All charities required to prepare accounts. Registered and excepted charities follow Regulations. Exempt charities follow relevant legislation or governing documents or prepare income and expenditure account and balance sheet.

PART III
SORP 2005

Country	Charity authority	Act(s) Governing Charities	Registration and Filing of Accounts	Preparation of Accounts
Scotland	Office of the Scottish Charity Regulator	Law Reform (Miscellaneous Provisions) (Scotland) Act 1990 and Regulations made thereunder (currently the Charities Accounts (Scotland) Regulations 1992) unless and until these are repealed	Recognition of Scottish Charities is a function of the Inland Revenue. Whilst there is no statutory requirement to file accounts, the Office of the Scottish Charity Regulator is developing a monitoring programme which is likely to include a requirement to submit an annual return and accounts.	Accounts prepared by non-company Scottish charities are subject to the 1990 Act, which requires an Income and Expenditure Account, and the 1992 Regulations, which require specific disclosures additional to those in this SORP including lower thresholds for accruals accounts and inclusion of a Cash Flow Statement (see Appendix 4).
Northern Ireland	Department for Social Development	Charities Act (Northern Ireland) 1964 and the Charities (Northern Ireland) Order 1987	There is no register of charities for Northern Ireland, and no requirement for accounts to be filed with the Department except where this is specifically directed by the High Court of Justice in Northern Ireland or the Department acting under specific statutory powers.	Section 27 of the Charities Act (Northern Ireland) 1964 requires the trustees of a charity to keep proper accounts and to preserve them for at least 7 years.

[5006]

Accounts Structure

30 Charity accruals accounts should comprise:

(a) a **Statement of Financial Activities** for the year that shows all incoming resources and all resources expended by it and reconciles all changes in its funds. The statement should consist of a single set of accounting statements and be presented in columnar form if the charity operates more than one class of fund;

(b) an **income and expenditure account** where this is a legal requirement. This applies to unincorporated charities in Scotland, and to certain charitable companies. In certain circumstances the Statement of Financial Activities will also meet the legal requirements for an Income and Expenditure Account. Where the two statements are combined this should be identified in the heading of the statement. Paragraphs 423 to 426 fully describe the circumstances in which a summary income and expenditure account is necessary for companies in addition to the Statement of Financial Activities;

(c) a **balance sheet** that shows the recognised assets, the liabilities and the different categories of fund of the charity;

(d) a **cash flow statement**, where required, in accordance with accounting standards; and

(e) **notes** explaining the accounting policies adopted (as set out in paragraphs 356 to 370) and other notes which explain or expand upon the information contained in the accounting statements referred to above or which provide further useful information. This will include notes analysing the figures in the accounts and explaining the relationships between them.

31 The corresponding figures for the previous accounting period should be provided in the accounts in accordance with generally accepted accounting practice. The duration of the current and previous accounting periods should also be shown.

32 The Statement of Financial Activities, the income and expenditure account (or summary), the balance sheet and the cash flow statement (where required), are all considered to be "primary statements", and should therefore be given equal prominence in the accounts and should not be relegated to the notes to the accounts.

33 Where any charity is, or its trustees are, acting as custodian trustees, they should not include the funds they hold as custodian in their own balance sheet but should disclose them by way of a note to their accounts and provide the details, set out in paragraph 59 below, in their Trustees' Annual Report.

[5007]

Summary Financial Information

34 Where summary financial information of any kind is prepared (including financial information contained in publicity or fundraising material and annual reviews), charity trustees are reminded that these accounts should always be fair and accurate. This is dealt with in paragraphs 371 to 379.

[5008]

Trustees' Annual Report

35 Charity accounts alone do not meet all the information needs of users who will usually have to supplement the information they obtain from the accounts with information from other sources. Accounts also have inherent limitations in terms of their ability to reflect the full impact of transactions or activities undertaken and do not provide information on matters such as structures, governance and management arrangements adopted by a charity. The accounts of a charity cannot alone easily portray what the charity has done (its outputs) or achieved (its outcomes) or what difference it has made (its impact). This is mainly because many of these areas cannot be measured in monetary terms: indeed some areas are difficult to measure with any numbers at all. The Trustees' Annual Report provides the opportunity for charity trustees to explain the areas that the accounts do not explain.

36 Charity accounts should therefore be accompanied and complemented by information contained within the Trustees' Annual Report. The Trustees' Annual Report should be a coherent document that meets the requirements of law and regulation and provides a fair review of the charity's structure, aims, objectives, activities and performance. Good reporting will explain what the charity is trying to do and how it is going about it. It will assist the user of accounts in addressing the progress made by the charity against its objectives for the year and in understanding its plans for the future. Good reporting will also explain the charity's governance and management structure and enable the reader to understand how the numerical part of the accounts relates to the organisational structure and activities of the charity (see paragraphs 44 to 59). As part of the report, or attached to it, a statement containing the reference and administrative details of the charity as described in paragraphs 41 to 43 will inform the reader who are the charity's trustees and its advisers and will provide other relevant legal or administrative information.

37 Responsibility for preparing the Trustees' Annual Report rests with the charity trustees. It provides important accompanying information to the accounts and should therefore be attached to the accounts whenever a full set of accounts is distributed or otherwise made available.

38 Legal requirements and this SORP do not limit the inclusion of other information within the Trustees' Annual Report or as additional information accompanying the accounts. Charity trustees may incorporate other material into their annual reporting, for example a chairman's report, environment report, impact assessment or an operating and financial review (see Glossary GL 43).

39 Charities may additionally use other means of providing information, outside of the accounting and reporting framework, about who they are and what they do. Such information is often tailored for the needs of particular audiences and presented through annual reviews, newsletters and websites. Whilst charity trustees might usefully refer to these other sources of information within their Trustees' Annual Report, such additional information should not be seen as a substitute for good statutory annual reporting.

40 Charitable companies must also prepare a Directors' Report (see paragraph 420) in order to meet the requirement of Section 234 of the Companies Act 1985 and applicable parts of Schedule 7. A separate Trustees' Annual Report is not required provided that any statutory Directors' Report prepared also contains all the information required to be provided in the Trustees' Annual Report.

[5009]

CONTENT OF THE TRUSTEES' ANNUAL REPORT

Reference and Administrative Details of the Charity, its Trustees and Advisers

41 The report should provide the following reference and administrative information about the charity, its trustees and advisers:

(a) The name of the charity, which in the case of a registered charity means the name by which it is registered. Any other name by which a charity makes itself known should also be provided.

(b) The charity registration number (in Scotland the Scottish Charity Number) and, if applicable, the company registration number.

(c) The address of the principal office of the charity and in the case of a charitable company the address of its registered office.

(d) The names of all of those who were the charity's trustees (Glossary GL 7) or a trustee for the charity (Glossary GL 59) on the date the report was approved. Where there are more than 50 charity trustees, the names of at least 50 of those trustees (including all the officers of the charity, eg chair, treasurer etc) should be provided. Where any charity trustee disclosed is a body corporate, the names of the directors of the body corporate on that date.

(e) The name of any other person who served as a charity trustee (Glossary GL 7) or as a trustee for the charity (Glossary GL 59) in the financial year in question.

(f) The name of any Chief Executive Officer or other senior staff member(s) to whom day to day management of the charity is delegated by the charity trustees.

(g) The names and addresses of any other relevant organisations or persons. This should include the names and addresses of those acting as bankers, solicitors, auditor (or independent examiner or reporting accountant) and investment or other principal advisers.

42 Where the disclosure of the names of any charity trustees, trustee for the charity, senior staff member, or persons with the power of appointment, or of the charity's principal address could lead to that person being placed in personal danger (eg in the case of a women's refuge), the charity trustees may dispense with the disclosure provided that (for charities in England and Wales) the Charity Commission has given the trustees the authority to do so. It is recommended that the reasons for such non-disclosure should be given in the report. The directors of charitable companies should note that there is no corresponding dispensation in relation to the disclosure requirements for the statutory directors' report.

43 Charities that are not subject to a statutory audit requirement may omit the disclosures in 41(f) and 41(g) above. However the disclosure of these items is encouraged as a matter of good practice.

[5010]

Structure, Governance and Management

44 The report should provide the reader with an understanding of how the charity is constituted, its organisational structure and how its trustees are appointed and trained and assist the reader to understand better how the charity's decision-making processes operate. The level of detail provided in the report is likely to be dependent on the size and complexity of the charity and be proportionate to the needs of the users of the report. In particular, the report should explain:

(a) The nature of the governing document (eg trust deed; memorandum and articles of association; Charity Commission Scheme; Royal Charter; etc) and how the charity is (or its trustees are) constituted (eg limited company; unincorporated association; trustees incorporated as a body; etc).

(b) The methods adopted for the recruitment and appointment of new trustees, including details of any constitutional provisions relating to appointments, for example, election to post. Where any other person or body external to the charity is entitled to appoint one or more of the charity trustees this should be explained together with the name of that person or body (subject to paragraph 42 above – where disclosure of a person's name could lead to personal danger).

(c) The policies and procedures adopted for the induction and training of trustees.

(d) The organisational structure of the charity and how decisions are made. For example, which types of decisions are taken by the charity trustees and which are delegated to staff.
(e) Where the charity is part of a wider network (for example charities affiliated within an umbrella group) then the relationship involved should also be explained where this impacts on the operating policies adopted by the charity.
(f) The relationships between the charity and related parties, including its subsidiaries (see paragraphs 221 to 229 and Glossary GL 50) and with any other charities and organisations with which it co-operates in the pursuit of its charitable objectives.

45 A statement should be provided confirming that the major risks to which the charity is exposed, as identified by the trustees, have been reviewed and systems or procedures have been established to manage those risks.

46 Charities that are not subject to a statutory audit requirement may limit their disclosures within this section to those set out in paragraph 44 (a) and (b) above. The additional disclosures of this section are encouraged as a matter of good practice.

[5011]

Objectives and Activities

47 The report should help the reader understand the aims and objectives set by the charity, and the strategies and activities undertaken to achieve them. The report may also, where relevant, explain how the objectives set for the year relate to longer term strategies and objectives set by the charity. Where significant activities are undertaken through subsidiary undertakings, these should be explained in the report. In particular the report should provide:
(a) A summary of the objects of the charity as set out in its governing document.
(b) An explanation of the charity's aims including the changes or differences it seeks to make through its activities.
(c) An explanation of the charity's main objectives for the year.
(d) An explanation of the charity's strategies for achieving its stated objectives.
(e) Details of significant activities (including its main programmes, projects, or services provided) that contribute to the achievement of the stated objectives.

48 The details of significant activities provided should focus on those activities that the charity trustees consider to be significant in the circumstances of the charity as a whole. The details of activities should, as a minimum, explain the objectives, activities, projects or services identified within the analysis note accompanying charitable activities in the Statement of Financial Activities (see paragraphs 191 to 194).

49 Where the charity conducts a material part of its activities through grantmaking, a statement should be provided setting out its grantmaking policies.

50 Where social or programme related investment (Glossary GL 47) activities are material in the context of charitable activities undertaken, the policies adopted in making such investments should be explained.

51 Where a charity makes significant use of volunteers in the course of undertaking its charitable or income generating activities this should be explained. Whilst measurement issues, including attributing an economic value to such unpaid voluntary contributions, prevents the inclusion of such contributions within the Statement of Financial Activities (see paragraph 133), it is nevertheless important for readers to be provided with sufficient information to understand the role and contribution of volunteers. Such information may, for example, explain the activities that volunteers help provide, quantify the contribution in terms of hours or staff equivalents, and may present an indicative value of this contribution.

52 Charities that are not subject to a statutory audit requirement may limit their disclosures within this section to that set out in paragraph 47(a) above, together with providing a summary of the main activities undertaken in relation to those objects. The additional disclosures of this section are encouraged as a matter of good practice.

[5012]

Achievements and Performance

53 The report should contain information that enables the reader to understand and assess the achievements of the charity and its subsidiary undertakings in the year. It should provide a review of its performance against objectives that have been set. The report is likely to provide both qualitative and quantitative information that helps explain achievement and performance. It will often be helpful to identify any indicators, milestones and benchmarks against which the achievement of objectives is assessed by the charity. In particular, the report should contain:

(a) A review of charitable activities undertaken that explains the performance achieved against objectives set. Where qualitative or quantitative information is used to assess the outcome of activities, a summary of the measures or indicators used to assess achievement should be included.

(b) Where material fundraising activities are undertaken, details of the performance achieved against fundraising objectives set, commenting on any material expenditure for future income generation and explaining the effect on the current period's fundraising return and anticipated income generation in future periods.

(c) Where material investments are held, details of the investment performance achieved against the investment objectives set.

(d) Comment on those factors within and outside the charity's control which are relevant to the achievement of its objectives; these might include relationship with employees, users, beneficiaries, funders and the charity's position in the wider community.

54 Charities that are not subject to a statutory audit requirement may limit their disclosures within this section to providing a summary of the main achievements of the charity during the year. The additional disclosures of this section are encouraged as a matter of good practice.

[5013]

Financial Review

55 The report should contain a review of the financial position of the charity and its subsidiaries and a statement of the principal financial management policies adopted in the year. In particular, the report should explain the charity's:

(a) Policy on reserves (Glossary GL 51) stating the level of reserves held and why they are held. Where material funds have been designated, the reserves policy statement should quantify and explain the purpose of the designations and, where set aside for future expenditure, the likely timing of that expenditure.

(b) Where any fund is materially in deficit, the circumstances giving rise to the deficit and details of the steps being taken to eliminate the deficit.

(c) Principal funding sources and how expenditure in the year under review has supported the key objectives of the charity.

(d) Where material investments are held, the investment policy and objectives, including the extent (if any) to which social, environmental or ethical considerations are taken into account.

56 Charities that are not subject to a statutory audit requirement may limit their disclosures within this section to those set out in paragraph 55(a) and 55(b) above.

[5014]

Plans for Future Periods

57 The report should explain the charity's plans for the future including the aims and key objectives it has set for future periods together with details of any activities planned to achieve them.

58 Charities that are not subject to a statutory audit requirement may omit this disclosure although disclosure of this matter is encouraged as a matter of good practice.

[5015]

Funds Held as Custodian Trustee on Behalf of Others

59 Where a charity is, or its trustees are, acting as custodian trustees, the following matters should be disclosed in the report:

(a) A description of the assets which they hold in this capacity.

(b) The name and objects of the charity (or charities) on whose behalf the assets are held and how this activity falls within their own objects.

(c) Details of the arrangements for safe custody and segregation of such assets from the charity's own assets.

[5016]

GENERAL ACCOUNTING PRINCIPLES

Fundamental Accounting Concepts

60 Accounts intending to show a true and fair view must be prepared on the going concern assumption and the accruals concept and provide information that is relevant, reliable, comparable and understandable (see Appendix 2: FRS 18).

[5017]

Accounting Standards

61 In meeting the obligation to prepare accounts showing a true and fair view (see paragraph 21) accruals accounts should follow the standards and principles issued or adopted by the Accounting Standards Board, or its predecessors or successors and set out in:

(a) Statements of Standard Accounting Practice (SSAPs);
(b) Financial Reporting Standards (FRSs);
(c) Urgent Issues Task Force abstracts (UITFs);

and in addition take note of:

(d) The Interpretation for Public Benefit Entities of the Statement of Principles for Financial Reporting (a discussion paper issued by the Accounting Standards Board in May 2003).

This SORP provides guidance and recommendations that supplement accounting standards in the light of the special factors prevailing or transactions undertaken with the charity sector, and, as with the law, does not seek to repeat all of their requirements. Appendix 2 provides a summary of these accounting standards and of their general applicability to charities.

62 Appendix 5 explains how the Financial Reporting Standard for Smaller Entities (FRSSE) can be applied by charities (whether or not they are companies) which are under the thresholds for small companies as described in the Companies Acts (see Appendix 4).

63 UK accounting standards provide the financial reporting framework under which this SORP has been developed. In the UK, compliance with companies' legislation presently requires compliance with UK accounting standards as does charity legislation in England and Wales through its adoption of the methods and principles of this SORP. Regulations made under the Companies Act 1985 allowing companies to adopt International Financial Reporting Standards (IFRS) in either their individual or consolidated accounts does not apply to charitable companies.

64 Currently the Accounting Standards Board is undertaking a phased approach to convergence of UK accounting standards with IFRS. This includes new standards effective in 2005 and 2006 and thereafter a series of 'step changes' replacing one or more existing UK accounting standards with standards based on IFRS as their development is completed. This SORP will continue to be reviewed in line with the Accounting Standards Board's Policy and Code of Practice to reflect changes in UK standards, including those arising from the convergence process.

[5018]

Accounting for Separate Funds

65 The main purpose of the accounts is to give an overall view of the total incoming resources during the year and how they have been expended, with a balance sheet to show the overall financial position at the year end. There are additional requirements for charities that have to account for more than one fund (Glossary GL 27) under their control. The accounts should provide a summary of the main funds, differentiating in particular between the unrestricted income funds, restricted income funds and endowment funds (see figure 1). The columnar format of the Statement of Financial Activities (and of the balance sheet, where the option is taken to use a columnar presentation of funds) is designed to achieve this. Depending on the materiality (Glossary GL 42) of each, the notes to the accounts should group the restricted funds under one or more heads.

66 Charities need to account for the proper administration of the individual funds in accordance with their respective terms of trust and accounting records must be kept in a way which will adequately separate transactions between different funds. Some charities may hold one or more restricted funds, some of which may be permanent or expendable endowment funds. Appendix 3 explains in detail the legal position as regards transactions involving these various funds. The position is summarised in the following paragraphs 67 to 76.

Figure 1 – The types of funds of charities

[5019]

Unrestricted Income Funds (Including Designated Funds) (see also Appendix 3)

67 Nearly all charities have a fund which is available to the trustees to apply for the general purposes of the charity as set out in its governing document. This is the charity's "unrestricted" fund (sometimes called a "general" fund) because the trustees are free to use it for any of the charity's purposes. Income generated from assets held in an unrestricted fund will be unrestricted income.

PART III SORP 2005

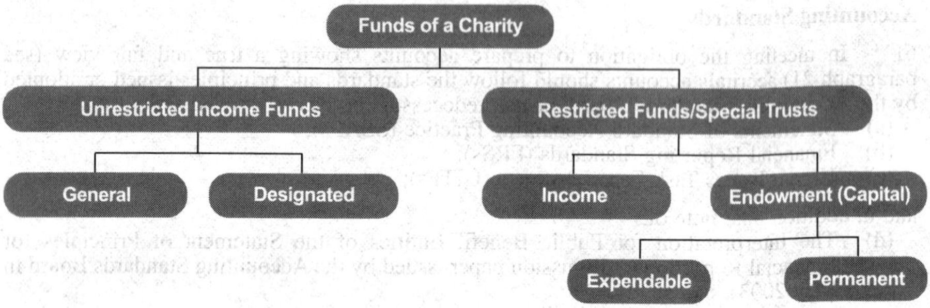

68 The trustees may earmark part of the charity's unrestricted funds to be used for particular purposes in the future. Such sums are described as "designated funds" and should be accounted for as part of the charity's unrestricted funds. The trustees have the power to re-designate such funds within unrestricted funds. When a designation has been made at the balance sheet date, the amount of the designation may be adjusted subsequent to the year end if more accurate information becomes available (see appendix 2 FRS 21).

[5020]

Restricted Funds (see also Appendix 3)

69 Many charities hold funds that can only be applied for particular purposes within their objects. These are restricted funds and have to be separately accounted for. The restriction may apply to the use of income or capital or both. Income generated from assets held in a restricted fund (e g interest) will be legally subject to the same restriction as the original fund unless either:

(a) the terms of the original restriction specifically say otherwise (for example, the expressed wishes of a donor or the terms of an appeal), or

(b) the restricted fund is an endowment fund, the income of which is expendable at the discretion of the trustees.

[5021]

Endowment Funds (see also Appendix 3)

70 One form of restricted fund is an "endowment", which is held on trust to be retained for the benefit of the charity as a capital fund. Where the trustees must permanently maintain the whole of the fund it is known as permanent endowment. Such a fund may consist of investment assets and/or assets that are used for the purposes of the charity. Such a fund cannot normally be spent as if it were income.

71 In some instances the trustees may have a power of discretion to convert endowed capital into income in which case the fund is known as expendable endowment.

72 The initial gift and subsequent increases and decreases in the amount of any endowment funds should be shown in the Statement of Financial Activities as part of those funds.

[5022]

Gains and Losses

73 Realised and unrealised gains and losses on assets held in a particular fund form part of that fund. Similarly, provisions for depreciation, or for a permanent fall in value of assets form part of the fund in which the asset is held.

[5023]

Reconciliation of Funds

74 The Statement of Financial Activities should reflect the principal movements between the opening and closing balances on all the funds of the charity. It should be analysed between unrestricted income funds, restricted income funds and endowment funds (permanent and expendable combined).

[5024]

Particulars of Individual Funds and Notes to the Accounts

75 The notes to the accounts should provide information on the structure of the charity's funds so as to disclose the fund balances and the reasons for them, differentiating between

unrestricted income funds (both general and designated), restricted income funds, permanent endowment and expendable endowment as well as identifying any material individual funds among them. In particular:

(a) The assets and liabilities representing each type of fund of the charity should be clearly summarised and analysed (e g investments, fixed assets, net current assets) between those funds unless this information is presented in a columnar balance sheet (see paragraph 248).

(b) Disclosure of how each of the funds has arisen (including designated funds), the restrictions imposed and the purpose of each fund should be provided. An indication should also be given as to whether or not sufficient resources are held in an appropriate form to enable each fund to be applied in accordance with any restrictions. For example, if a charity has a fund which is to be spent in the near future, it should be made clear in the notes whether or not the assets held (or expected to be received) in the fund are liquid assets.

(c) Any funds in deficit should always be separately disclosed. An explanation should be given in the Trustees' Annual Report (see paragraph 55(b)). Designated funds should never be in deficit.

(d) Material transfers between different funds and allocations to designated funds should be separately disclosed, without netting off, and should be accompanied by an explanation of the nature of the transfers or allocations and the reasons for them.

(e) Where, in relation to permanent endowment, a total return approach to investments has been adopted, the notes to the accounts should give particulars of the movements in the value of the unapplied total return for the financial year. The note should reconcile the balance held as unapplied total return at the beginning with that at the end of the financial year. (See Appendix 3 paragraphs 3(g) to 3(k))

76 Separate sets of statements may be produced for each major fund and linked to a total summary. The trustees should decide on the most suitable form of presentation, bearing in mind:

(a) the complexity of the fund structure,

(b) the need for the total provided in the summary to agree to the primary statements (Statement of Financial Activities and Balance Sheet), and

(c) the need to avoid confusion between the movements on the various funds.

An example of a suitable summary is given in Table 2:

TABLE 2. OUTLINE SUMMARY OF FUND MOVEMENTS

Fund Name	Fund Balances brought forward	Incoming Resources	Outgoing Resources	Transfers	Gains and Losses	Fund Balances carried forward
Major Fund 1						
Major Fund 2						
Major Fund 3						
Other Funds						
Total Funds						

[5025]

Branches

77 Before preparing accounts, trustees must be quite clear as to the legal structure of the charity. A charity may operate through "branches" to raise funds and/or carry out its charitable purposes. Branches as defined in the Glossary (GL 4) will be accounted for as part of the whole charity. But if both reporting charity and the "branch(es)" are companies, company law requires each entity to prepare its own accounts. In such a case, one Trustees' Annual Report should normally be prepared to cover both the reporting charity and its branch(es) and consolidated accounts should be prepared in accordance with paragraphs 381 to 406.

PART III SORP 2005

78 Separate legal entities which may be known as branches but do not fall within the definition of a branch in the Glossary should prepare their own Annual Report and Accounts and, if they are connected charities, the relationship should be explained in the Trustees' Annual Report (see paragraph 44(f)).

79 All branch transactions should be accounted for gross in the reporting charity's own accounts excluding those transactions which net off e g branch to branch transactions or those between the branches and the head office. Similarly all assets and liabilities of the branch including, for example, funds raised but not remitted to the reporting charity at the year end, should be incorporated into the reporting charity's own balance sheet. This provision need not apply where the transactions and balances of the branches in aggregate are not material to the charity's accounts.

80 Funds raised by a branch for the general charitable purposes of the reporting charity will be accounted for as unrestricted funds in the accounts of the reporting charity. Funds raised by a branch for specific purposes of the reporting charity will need to be accounted for as restricted funds in the accounts of the reporting charity. Funds held for the general purposes of a branch which is a separate charity should usually be accounted for as restricted funds in the accounts of the reporting charity.

81 Where a branch is not a separate legal entity, its accounts must form part of the accounts of the reporting charity, but it may be in the interests of local supporters and beneficiaries for additional accounts to be prepared covering only the branch.

[5026]

STATEMENT OF FINANCIAL ACTIVITIES

Introduction

82 The Statement of Financial Activities is a single accounting statement with the objective of showing *all* incoming resources and resources expended by the charity in the year on *all* its funds.

It is designed to show how the charity has used its resources in furtherance of its objects for the provision of benefit to its beneficiaries. It shows whether there has been a net inflow or outflow of resources, including capital gains and losses on assets, and provides a reconciliation of all movements in the charity's funds.

[5027]

Presentation of Information

Structure of the Statement

83 In the Statement of Financial Activities the charity's incoming resources and resources expended should be analysed so that the reader can see where its resources came from and what it spent its resources on during the year. As a minimum it must also distinguish between unrestricted income funds, restricted income funds and the endowment funds of the charity. All of the charity's incoming resources and resources expended can be categorised between these funds (see Figure 1), but a charity will not necessarily have funds of all three types.

84 If it has more than one type of fund, the statement should show, in columns, the movements in the different types of funds as well as the total movements of all the funds. Comparative figures for the previous financial year, given on the face of the statement will normally only be given for the row totals (e g voluntary income, investment income etc) rather than for the analysis of each row across the various categories of funds.

[5028]

Adaptation of Formats

85 The structure, format and activity categories of the Statement of Financial Activities are shown in Table 3 below.

86 The Statement of Financial Activities may be adapted to give a true and fair view, but disclosure requirements should always be met and the underlying structure should not be changed. Trustees should balance the provision of information with clarity.

87 The three columns in the Statement of Financial Activities providing an aggregate total for unrestricted, restricted and endowment funds of a charity will often contain several individual funds which will be explained in greater detail in the notes to the accounts (see paragraph 76). If any one of these funds (or a group of these funds) is of particular materiality and the charity trustees wish to draw the attention of readers to it, they may add additional

columns to the Statement of Financial Activities to display such funds on the face of the SOFA rather than in notes. For example a school may have two unrestricted fund columns, one containing the resource movement connected with teaching, another welfare and other costs. Similarly a charity engaged in collecting funds to acquire fixed assets may have two restricted fund columns, one including all funds related to fixed assets acquisition and another for other restricted funds. Any additional analysis of this type provided on the face of the Statement of Financial Activities should make clear the type of fund (unrestricted, restricted or endowment) in the title and not mix up different types of fund.

88 Some charities may also find it informative to their readers to insert additional subtotals. For example, after row B1c (investment management costs), an additional subtotal "net incoming resources available for charitable application" may be added.

89 Charities should expand the structure, where necessary using notes, in order to present a true and fair view and convey a proper understanding of the nature of all their activities. Charities should, where possible, have a clear link between the incoming and outgoing resources and in particular activity analysis. Two examples of this are:

(a) a charity running a care home could use the sub-heading "Residential Care Fees" within row A2 (incoming resources from charitable activities) and "Residential Care Costs" in row B2 (resources expended on charitable activities);

(b) a charity fundraising through a shop could use the sub-heading "shops" within row A1b (activities for generating funds) and row B1b (fundraising trading costs).

Thus incoming resources and resources expended can be linked together by using similar or identical headings in different parts of the Statement of Financial Activities.

90 In order to comply with FRS 3, where a charity has discontinued any of its operations or acquired new ones, the accounts should distinguish between continuing, discontinued and acquired operations. This will normally apply to the whole of a distinctive type of activity of a charity but not to the development or cessation of new projects within that activity.

91 Category headings should be omitted where there is nothing to report in both the current and proceeding periods. A charity may also vary the order in which it presents activity categories within the incoming resources and resources expended sections of the Statement of Financial Activities to meet its own presentational needs.

92 Where, as a result of adopting the activity approach, the categories shown in the Statement of Financial Activities change from those used in the prior year, comparatives will also need to be restated in accordance with FRS 18 (Appendix 2).

93 The classification of incoming resources and resources expended by activity is encouraged for all charities preparing accruals accounts. Smaller charities may be excused from adopting this approach by legislation recognising that such information is likely to be less relevant to the users of small charity accounts. Where a small charity adopts an alternative approach to analysis within the Statement of Financial Activities certain note disclosures may no longer be necessary, for example, where these disclosures relate to the constituent costs of an activity category or where relevant information is provided on the face of the Statement of Financial Activity. These concessions for smaller charities are summarised in Appendix 5.

TABLE 3. STATEMENT OF FINANCIAL ACTIVITIES

Reference		Unrestricted Funds	Restricted Funds	Endowment Funds	Total Funds	Prior Year Total Funds	Further Details
A	Incoming resources						
A1	Incoming resources from generated funds						
A1a	Voluntary income						121–136
A1b	Activities for generating funds						137–139
A1c	Investment income						140–142
A2	Incoming resources from charitable activities						143–146
A3	Other incoming resources						147
	Total incoming resources						
B	Resources expended						
B1	Costs of generating funds						178–179
B1a	Costs of generating voluntary income						180–184
B1b	Fundraising trading: cost of goods sold and other costs						185–186
B1c	Investment management costs						187
B2	Charitable activities						188–209
B3	Governance costs						210–212

Reference		Unrestricted Funds	Restricted Funds	Endowment Funds	Total Funds	Prior Year Total Funds	Further Details
B4	Other resources expended						213
	Total resources expended						
	Net incoming/ outgoing resources before transfers						
	Transfers						
C	Gross transfers between funds						214–216
	Net incoming resources before other recognised gains and losses						
D	Other recognised gains/losses						
D1	Gains on revaluation of fixed assets for charity's own use						217–218
D2	Gains/losses on investment assets						219
D3	Actuarial gains/losses on defined benefit pension schemes						220
	Net movement in funds						

PART III
SORP 2005

Reference		Unrestricted Funds	Restricted Funds	Endowment Funds	Total Funds	Prior Year Total Funds	Further Details
E	Reconciliation of Funds						
	Total funds brought forward						
	Total funds carried forward						

[5029]

INCOMING RESOURCES

General Rules on the Recognition of Incoming Resources

94 Incoming resources – both for income and endowment funds – should be recognised in the Statement of Financial Activities when the effect of a transaction or other event results in an increase in the charity's assets. This will be dependent on the following three factors being met:

- (a) entitlement – normally arises when there is control over the rights or other access to the resource, enabling the charity to determine its future application;
- (b) certainty – when it is virtually certain that the incoming resource will be received;
- (c) measurement – when the monetary value of the incoming resource can be measured with sufficient reliability.

95 All incoming resources should be reported gross when raised by the charity (or by volunteers working at the charity's direction) or its agents. However where funds are raised or collected for the charity by individuals not employed or contracted by the charity, the gross incoming resources of the charity are the proceeds remitted to the charity by the organisers of the event, after deducting their expenses.

96 Within the charity sector entitlement to incoming resources may arise from a wide variety of transactions varying from contractual (ie in exchange for goods or services of approximately equal value between a seller and a purchaser) to the receipt of unrestricted grants or donations (resources given to use on any of the charity's purposes).

97 This SORP seeks to provide guidance on how such differing transactions can be distinguished. However, judgement will still be required in deciding how any individual transaction fits into this framework and in identifying those factors that are likely to lead to different accounting treatments for their recognition. The recommendations provided below set out how accounting standards and principles should be applied in the context of transactions that are commonly undertaken within the charity sector. In order to understand how accounting standards apply to different funding arrangements, charity trustees need to determine for each source of funds:

- What legal arrangements (eg contract or trust law) govern the terms of the arrangement and how any disputes arising are to be settled.
- Whether entitlement to the funding requires a specific performance to be achieved (a contract or performance related grant).
- Whether funds can be used for any of the purposes of the charity, or whether they can only be used for a specific purpose.

[5030]

Contractual Arrangements

98 Some charities earn income by providing goods and/or services in return for a fee as part of their charitable activities. Such contractual income is recognised as incoming resources in the Statement of Financial Activities to the extent that the charity has provided the goods and/or services. Where such incoming resources are received in advance then a charity may not have entitlement to these resources until the goods or services have been provided. In this situation incoming resources received in advance should be deferred (Glossary: GL 15) until the charity becomes entitled to the resources.

99 Certain grant funding arrangements may contain conditions that closely specify the service to be performed by the charity. The terms of such funding may be set out in a service level agreement where the conditions for payment are linked to the performance of a particular level of service or units of output delivered, for example, number of meals provided or the opening hours of a facility used by beneficiaries. Entitlement to the incoming resources derived from such performance-related grants (Glossary GL 45) may be conditional upon the delivery of the specified level of service and in such circumstances should be recognised as incoming resources to the extent that the charity has provided the services or goods.

100 Simply because a grant is restricted to a particular purpose of the recipient charity does not mean it should necessarily be recognised as a performance related grant. For a performance related grant entitlement to the incoming resource only arises with the performance of a specific output identified as a condition for the grant. Entitlement to the grant in such cases only arises as the performance conditions are met. This can be contrasted with a restriction that whilst limiting how a charity may expend funds to particular purposes does not require a specific and measurable output to be delivered by the recipient charity as a condition of a charity's entitlement to the funds. Such restricted grants are recognised on the basis set out in paragraphs 104 to 111.

101 Where charities receive membership subscriptions, these may be in the nature of a gift, or they may effectively buy services or access to certain privileges. Where the substance of the subscription is that of a gift, the incoming resource should be recognised on the same basis as a donation. If the subscription purchases the right to services or benefits, the incoming resource should be recognised as the service or benefit is provided. If the subscriber receives rights to such benefits evenly over the period of membership then recognising such membership income on a pro-rata basis for the period of time covered by the subscription may be an appropriate estimation technique for income recognition.

102 Charities may also, on occasions, undertake activities under a long-term contract. Owing to the length of time taken to complete such contracts, it is appropriate to take credit for ascertainable incoming resources and the cost of any resources expended while contracts are in progress in accordance with the guidance given in SSAP 9.

103 Application Note G to FRS 5 provides specific guidance on revenue recognition under long-term contractual arrangements. A charity should recognise incoming resources in respect of its performance under a long-term contract when, and to the extent that, it obtains entitlement to consideration. This should be derived from an assessment of the fair value of the goods or services provided to its reporting date as a proportion of the total fair value of the contract. There will be contracts where costs incurred to date reflect the work performed and in such circumstances it would be appropriate to calculate incoming resources recognised at the balance sheet date based on the proportion of costs incurred to date in comparison with total expenditure. In the case of services, it may be appropriate to use the time spent as a proportion of the total time to be spent to fulfil the contract where this provides a reasonable estimate of a charity's performance and therefore entitlement. The incurrence of costs by the charity, does not, in itself, justify the recognition of revenue.

[5031]

Grants and Donations Receivable

104 A pre-requisite of recognition of a promised grant or donation is evidence of entitlement. Evidence will normally exist when the grant is formally expressed in writing. Where entitlement is demonstrable, and no conditions are attached, such promises should be recognised as incoming resources once the criteria of certainty and measurability are met.

105 Charities often receive grants or donations with conditions attached that must be fulfilled before the entity has unconditional entitlement (control) of the resources. Meeting such conditions may be either within the recipient charity's control or reliant on external factors outside its control. Where meeting such conditions is within the charity's control and there is sufficient evidence that the conditions will be met, then the incoming resource should be recognised. Where uncertainty exists as to whether the recipient charity can meet conditions within its control, the incoming resource should not be recognised but deferred as a liability until certainty exists that the conditions imposed can be met.

106 For example, a grant may be conditional on a charity obtaining matched funding, or subject to a successful planning consent. Meeting the conditions attaching to such grants would not be either certain or wholly within the control of the recipient charity. The charity would not therefore have unconditional entitlement (control) of the incoming resource until these conditions were met. The incoming resource and corresponding asset should not be recognised until the conditions set have been met.

107 Conditions such as the submission of accounts or certification of expenditure can be seen as simply an administrative requirement as opposed to a condition that might prevent the recognition of incoming resources.

108 Incoming resources may also be subject to donor imposed conditions that specify the time period in which the expenditure of resources can take place. Such a pre-condition for use limits the charity's ability to expend the resource until the time condition is met. For example, the receipt in advance of a grant for expenditure that must take place in a future accounting period should be accounted for as deferred income and recognised as a liability until the accounting period in which the recipient charity is allowed by the condition to expend the resource.

109 Where the existence of a condition prevents the recognition of an incoming resource, a contingent asset should be disclosed where it is probable (but not virtually certain) that the condition will be met in the future (see paragraphs 340 to 348).

110 Charities are normally entitled to incoming resources when they are receivable. Recognition of a grant or donation without pre-conditions should not be deferred (Glossary GL 15) even if the resources are received in advance of the expenditure on the activity funded by the grant or donation. In such cases the charity has entitlement to the resource with the timing of the expenditure being within the discretion of the charity. Such incoming resources cannot be deferred simply because the related expenditure has not been incurred. Similarly, a condition that allows for the recovery by the donor of any unexpended part of a grant does not prevent recognition. A liability for any repayment is recognised when repayment becomes probable.

111 Where either incoming resources are given specifically to provide a fixed asset or a fixed asset is donated (a gift in kind), the charity will normally have entitlement to the incoming resources when they are receivable. At this point, all of the incoming resources should be recognised in the Statement of Financial Activities and not deferred over the life of the asset. As explained in paragraph 110 the possibility of having to repay the incoming resources does not affect their recognition in the first instance. Once acquired, the use of the asset will either be restricted or unrestricted (see paragraph 117). If its use is unrestricted the trustees may consider creating a designated fund reflecting the book value of the asset. The relevant fund will then be reduced over the useful economic life of the asset in line with its depreciation. This treatment accords with the requirements under accounting standards for the recognition of assets and liabilities and provides the most appropriate interpretation of SSAP 4 for charities (see Appendix 2: SSAP 4).
[5032]

Funds Received as Agent

112 Some incoming resources do not belong to the charity, for instance where it receives the resources in circumstances where the trustees, acting as agents (and not as custodian trustees), are legally bound to pay them over to a third party and have no responsibility for their ultimate application. In these circumstances the transaction is legally a transfer of resources from the original payer (who remains the principal) to the specified third party. If the original payer retains the legal responsibility for ensuring the charitable application of the funds, the intermediary charity should not recognise the resources in the Statement of Financial Activities or the balance sheet (see paragraph 319).

113 However, in some cases an intermediary charity may control the use of resources prior to their transfer to a third party and its trustees will act as principal and have responsibility for their charitable application. For instance, where the trustees of the intermediary charity may have applied for the grant of the resources or are able to direct how the grant should be used by the third party or both. Other forms of funding arrangements involving intermediary charities may need their trustees to accept the legal responsibility for the transfer of the grant to the third party (and for its charitable application, where the third party is not a charity). In all of these circumstances the resources should then be included in the intermediary charity's Statement of Financial Activities and balance sheet (see paragraph 320).

Disclosure

114 Where any incoming resources have been deferred, the notes to the accounts should explain the reasons for the deferrals and analyse the movement on the deferred account between incoming resources deferred in the current year and amounts released from previous years. Incoming resources of a similar nature can be grouped together in the notes as appropriate.

115 Where a charity has held resources for a third party which have not been included in the Statement of Financial Activities, the notes to the accounts should analyse the movement of these resources during the year relating to each party or type of party where material. Where resources have been held for related parties the required disclosure of paragraphs 227 to 228 should be given.

[5033]

Incoming Resources Subject to Restrictions

116 The fact that a grant or donation is for a restricted purpose does not affect the basis of its recognition within the Statement of Financial Activities. There is an important difference for accounting purposes between restrictions placed on the purposes for which a particular resource may be used and conditions which must be fulfilled prior to entitlement or use by the charity. The existence of a restriction does not prevent the recognition of the incoming resource as the charity has entitlement to (control of) the resource and is simply limited by the restriction as to the purposes to which the resource can be applied.

117 Funds received for the restricted purpose of providing fixed assets should be accounted for immediately as restricted funds. The treatment of the fixed assets provided with those funds will depend on the basis on which they are held. The terms on which the funds were received may either require the fixed asset acquired to be held in a restricted fund or the fixed assets' acquisition may discharge the restriction and the asset will be held in the unrestricted funds (see also paragraph 111). There is no general rule and the treatment will depend upon the circumstance of each individual case (see Appendix 3). Where assets are re-allocated from one fund to another, this should be reflected as a transfer between the relevant funds.

[5034]

A: Incoming Resources

118 Incoming resources should be analysed according to the activity that produced the resources. The analysis adopted should follow that given in table 3, in particular grouping separately those resources generated by charitable activity from those activities aimed primarily at generating funds.

119 In most cases it will be clear which activity generated a particular resource. When the resources are generated from several activities then it is permissible to apportion the resources between the activities on a reasonable, justifiable and consistent basis.

Disclosure

120 Where any apportionment has taken place the method of apportionment should be disclosed in the accounting policy notes to the accounts.

[5035]

A1: Incoming Resources from Generated Funds

A1a: Voluntary Income

121 Voluntary income (Glossary GL 61) includes incoming resources generated from the following sources:

(a) gifts, donations and any related gift aid claimed, including legacies (see paragraph 123), given by the founders, patrons, supporters, the general public and businesses;

(b) grants which provide core funding or are of a general nature provided by government and charitable foundations but will not include those grants which are specifically for the performance of a service or production of charitable goods, for instance a service agreement with a local authority;

(c) membership subscriptions and sponsorships where these are, in substance, donations rather than payment for goods or services;

(d) gifts in kind (see paragraph 129) and donated services and facilities (see paragraph 133).

Disclosure

122 Where material, details of the types of activities undertaken to generate voluntary income should be provided either on the face of the Statement of Financial Activities or in the notes to the accounts. As far as possible the analysis categories provided here should match the detailed analysis provided for the costs of generating voluntary income.

[5036]

Legacies

123 It is good practice to monitor a legacy from the time when notification is received to its final receipt. A charity should not, however, regard a legacy as receivable simply because it has been told about it. It should only do so when the legacy has been received or if, before receipt, there is sufficient evidence to provide the necessary certainty that the legacy will be received and the value of the incoming resources can be measured with sufficient reliability (see paragraph 94).

124 There will normally be sufficient certainty of receipt, for example, as soon as a charity receives a letter from the personal representatives of the estate advising that payment of the legacy will be made or that the property bequeathed will be transferred. It is likely that the value of the resource will also be measurable from this time. However, legacies which are not immediately payable should not be treated as receivable until the conditions associated with payment have been fulfilled (e g the death of a life tenant).

125 It is unlikely in practice that the entitlement, certainty of receipt and measurability conditions will be satisfied before the receipt of a letter from the personal representatives advising of an intended payment or transfer. The amount which is available in the estate for distribution to the beneficiaries may not have been finalised and, even if it has, there may still be outstanding matters relating to the precise division of the amount. In these circumstances entitlement may be in doubt or it may not be possible to provide a reasonable estimate of the legacy receivable, in which case it should not be included in the Statement of Financial Activities.

126 Where a charity receives a payment on account of its interest in an estate or a letter advising that such a payment will be made, the payment, or intended payment, on account should be treated as receivable.

127 Similarly, where a payment is received or notified as receivable (by the personal representatives) after the accounting year end, but it is clear that it had been agreed by the personal representatives prior to the year end (hence providing evidence of a condition that existed at the balance sheet date), then it should be accrued in the Statement of Financial Activities and the balance sheet.

Disclosure

128 Where the charity has been notified of material legacies which have not been included in the Statement of Financial Activities (because the conditions for recognition have not been met), this fact and an estimate of the amounts receivable should be disclosed in the notes to the accounts. Similarly, an indication should be provided of the nature of any material assets bequeathed to the charity but subject to a life tenancy interest held by a third party. Where material, the accounting policy notes should distinguish between the accounting treatments adopted for pecuniary and residuary legacies and legacies subject to a life interest held by another party.

[5037]

Gifts in Kind

129 Incoming resources in the form of gifts in kind should be included in the Statement of Financial Activities in the following ways:

(a) Assets given and held as stock for distribution by the charity should be recognised as incoming resources for the year within "voluntary income" only when distributed with an equivalent amount being included as resources expended under the appropriate category of the Statement of Financial Activities to reflect its distribution.

(b) Assets given for use by the charity (e g property for its own occupation) should be recognised as incoming resources and within the relevant fixed asset category of the balance sheet when receivable (see paragraph 111).

(c) Where a gift has been made in kind but on trust for conversion into cash and subsequent application by the charity, the incoming resource should normally be recognised in the accounting period when receivable and where material, an adjustment should be made to the original valuation upon subsequent realisation of the gift. However in certain cases this will not be practicable and the incoming resources should be included in the accounting period in which the gift is sold. The most common example is that of second-hand goods donated for resale, which, whilst regarded as a donation in legal terms, is in economic terms similar to trading and should be included within "activities for generating funds".

130 In all cases the amount at which gifts in kind are included in the Statement of Financial Activities should be either a reasonable estimate of their gross value to the charity or

the amount actually realised as in the case of second-hand goods donated for resale. Where gifts in kind are included in the Statement of Financial Activities at their estimated gross value, the current value will usually be the price that it estimates it would have to pay in the open market for an equivalent item.

Disclosure

131 The basis of any valuation should be disclosed in the accounting policies.

132 Referring to 129(a) above, where there are undistributed assets at the year end, a general description of the items involved and an estimate of their value should be given by way of a note to the accounts provided such value is material.

[5038]

Donated Services and Facilities

133 A charity may receive assistance in the form of donated facilities, beneficial loan arrangements or donated services. Such incoming resources should be included in the Statement of Financial Activities where the benefit to the charity is reasonably quantifiable and measurable. The value placed on these resources should be the estimated value to the charity of the service or facility received: this will be the price the charity estimates it would pay in the open market for a service or facility of equivalent utility to the charity.

134 Donated services and facilities recognised in financial statements would include those usually provided by an individual or entity as part of their trade or profession for a fee. In contrast, the contribution of volunteers should be excluded from the Statement of Financial Activities as the value of their contribution to the charity cannot be reasonably quantified in financial terms. Commercial discounts should not be recognised as incoming resource except where they clearly represent a donation.

135 Where donated services or facilities are recognised, an equivalent amount should be included as expenditure under the appropriate heading in the Statement of Financial Activities.

Disclosure

136 The notes to the accounts should give an analysis of donated services or facilities included in the Statement of Financial Activities distinguishing appropriately between the different major items e g seconded staff, loaned assets etc. The accounting policy notes should also indicate the basis of valuation used. Where donated services are received but not included in the Statement of Financial Activities (e g volunteers) this should be disclosed in the Trustees' Annual Report if this information is necessary for the reader to gain a better understanding of the charity's activities.

[5039]

A1b: Activities for Generating Funds

137 Activities for generating funds are the trading and other fundraising activities carried out by a charity primarily to generate incoming resources which will be used to undertake its charitable activities. The activities included within this category involve an element of exchange, with the charity receiving income in return for providing goods, services or an entry to an event. This category will include:

(a) fundraising events such as jumble sales, firework displays and concerts (which are legally considered to be trading activities);
(b) those sponsorships and social lotteries which cannot be considered as pure donations;
(c) shop income from selling donated goods and bought in goods;
(d) providing goods and services other than for the benefit of the charity's beneficiaries,
(e) letting and licensing arrangements of property held primarily for functional use by the charity but temporarily surplus to operational requirements.

138 Whilst selling donated goods is legally considered to be the realisation of a donation in kind (see paragraph 129(c)), in economic terms it is similar to a trading activity and should be included in this section.

139 It may be possible to identify the incoming resources and resources expended for each different component of an activity (this may have to be done for tax purposes) but often these will be viewed as contributing to a single economic activity. Charity trustees should consider the balance of the activities being undertaken to determine the most appropriate place to include the incoming resources from such enterprises but having done this the components of incoming resources need not be analysed further. For example, a shop may mainly sell donated and bought in goods but it may also sell a small amount of goods made by

its beneficiaries and incidentally provide information about the charity. It would be acceptable to classify all the incoming resources from the shop as "shop income" under activities for generating funds.

[5040]

A1c: Investment Income

140 Investment income includes incoming resources from investment assets, including dividends, interest and rents but excluding realised and unrealised investment gains and losses.

141 Where a charity has subsidiary undertakings:

(a) all payments to the charity by its subsidiary undertakings and all dividend entitlements from them, other than amounts receivable by the charity for the provision of goods and services to subsidiaries, should be separately recognised as incoming resources and appropriately described under investment income in the parent charity's accounts.

(b) The exact amount of a gift aid payment from a subsidiary undertaking relating to a financial year can often only be precisely determined subsequent to the year end, for example with the calculation of taxable profits. Provided that a liability for the gift aid payment existed at the year end, the amount of the liability should be adjusted where calculations subsequent to the year end provide greater accuracy (see Appendix 2: FRS 21).

(c) Gift aid payments from subsidiary undertakings should be separately disclosed in the charity's Statement of Financial Activities within investment income, or, if not material, in the notes to the accounts. The subsidiary undertakings themselves will only be accounted for by the charity in its consolidated Statement of Financial Activities of the group (see paragraphs 381 to 406).

Disclosure

142 The notes to the accounts should show the gross investment income arising from each class of investment shown in paragraph 303.

[5041]

A2: Incoming Resources from Charitable Activities

143 This category includes any incoming resources received which are a payment for goods and services provided for the benefit of the charity's beneficiaries. It will include trading activities undertaken in furtherance of the charity's objects and those grants (although legally donations) which have conditions which make them similar in economic terms to trading income, such as service level agreements with local authorities.

144 This category will not include grants which are for core funding or do not have particular service requirements or are in response to an appeal. Such grants should be included in the section for voluntary income (see paragraph 121(b)).

145 Incoming resources from charitable activities should include:

(a) the sale of goods or services as part of the direct charitable activities of the charity (known as primary purpose trading);

(b) the sale of goods or services made or provided by the beneficiaries of the charity;

(c) the letting of non-investment property in furtherance of the charity's objects;

(d) contractual payments from government or public authorities where these are received in the normal course of trading under (a) to (c), e g fees for respite care;

(e) grants specifically for the provision of goods and services to be provided as part of charitable activities or services to beneficiaries;

(f) ancillary trades connected to a primary purpose in (a) to (e).

Disclosure

146 An analysis of incoming resources from charitable activities should be given in the notes to the accounts to supplement the analysis on the face of the Statement of Financial Activities. It should be sufficiently detailed so that the reader of the accounts understands the main activities carried out by the charity and the main components of the gross incoming resources receivable from each material charitable activity. As far as possible, incoming resources should be analysed using the same analysis categories as used for resources expended on charitable activities.

[5042]

A3: Other Incoming Resources

147 Other incoming resources will include the receipt of any resources which the charity has not been able to analyse within the main incoming resource categories. This will be a

minority of incoming resources and most charities will not need to use this category. Examples of items that fall within this category include a gain on the disposal of a tangible fixed asset held for the charity's own use (paragraph 218) and a gain on the disposal of a programme related investment (paragraph 310).

[5043]

EXPENDITURE AND COSTS

General Rules on the Recognition of Resources Expended

148 Expenditure should be recognised when and to the extent that a liability is incurred or increased without a commensurate increase in recognised assets or a reduction in liabilities. In accounts prepared on the accruals basis, liabilities are recognised as resources expended as soon as there is a legal or constructive obligation committing the charity to the expenditure as described in Financial Reporting Standards 5 and 12. A liability will arise when a charity is under an obligation to make a transfer of value to a third party as a result of past transactions or events.

149 Just as charities may receive funds under a variety of arrangements (see paragraphs 96–97) so may charities expend their funds in a variety of ways ranging from meeting contractual liabilities to the payments of grants or donations. This SORP seeks to provide guidance on how such differing transactions can be distinguished. However, judgement will still be required in deciding how any individual transaction fits into this framework. The recommendations below set out how accounting standards and principles should be applied in the context of transactions that are commonly undertaken within the charity sector.

[5044]

Contractual Arrangements

150 Where a charity enters into a contract for the supply of goods or services, expenditure is recognised once the supplier of the goods or services has performed their part of the contract, for example, the delivery of goods or the provision of a service.

151 Certain grants made may contain specific conditions that closely specify a particular service to be performed by the recipient of the grant. The terms of such grants may be set out in a service level agreement where the conditions for payment are linked to the performance of a particular level of service or units of output delivered, for example, number of meals provided or the opening hours of a facility used by beneficiaries. Often, in such cases, the grant maker will have negotiated the services to be provided to it or its beneficiaries. Expenditure on such performance-related grants (Glossary GL 45) should be recognised as resources expended to the extent that the recipient of the grant has provided the specified service or goods.

152 A grant that is merely restricted to a particular purpose of the recipient does not create a performance-related grant unless the grant also includes specific performance terms that meet the criteria set out above. Similarly, certain restricted grants may fund a programme of work to be undertaken over a number of years by the recipient. Again, this does not mean it should necessarily be recognised as a performance-related grant simply because of the period of the funding commitment or because the grantor is involved in monitoring or influencing the focus of the work as part of its grantmaking procedures.

153 For example, a grantmaking charity may fund a three year research programme enabling the recipient to undertake a programme of work identified by the recipient as necessary to meet its own objectives or that adds to the stock of knowledge on a topic. In order to provide funding, the work undertaken will need to be consistent with the legal objects of the grantmaker which may also, as part of its own grant approval processes, be involved in monitoring or influencing the focus of the work. Such an arrangement would not create a performance-related grant (see Glossary GL 45) if the funding is not directed at providing a specified service to the grantmaker or its beneficiaries as a condition of payment. Grants without such performance conditions that are directed at enabling the recipient to follow its own programme of work or increasing the pool of knowledge in an area of work should be recognised as a liability where a constructive obligation arises to make the grant payment (see Paragraph 155).

[5045]

Grants Payable and Constructive Obligations

154 In the case of grants (other than performance-related grants) and certain other expenditure relating directly to charitable activities, an exchange for consideration does not

arise. Such expenditure is incurred to further the charity's objects but without creating a contractual or quasi-contractual relationship with the recipient of the grant or the charity's beneficiaries. Nevertheless, the charity may still have a liability (Glossary GL 40) which needs to be recognised.

155 Liabilities may arise from a constructive or a legal obligation (Glossary GL 10). A constructive obligation arises under FRS 12 where events have created a valid expectation in other parties that the charity will discharge its obligations. Evidence that a valid expectation has been created might be provided by the charity's current and past practice in discharging such obligations and the specific communication of a commitment to the recipient. A constructive obligation always involves a commitment to another party that has been communicated to those affected in a sufficiently specific manner to raise a valid expectation on the part of the recipient that the charity will discharge its obligations. Because an obligation always involves a commitment to another party, it follows that a funding decision by a charity's trustees does not give rise to a constructive obligation at the balance sheet date unless the decision has been communicated before the balance sheet date to those affected in a sufficiently specific manner to raise a valid expectation in them that the charity will discharge its responsibilities.

156 Charities may on occasions make general or policy statements of their future intentions, for example, of an intention or aim of relieving famine in a particular location or to improve the quality of care provided to a particular group of people. Such statements can be communicated in a variety of ways including mission statements, setting out future plans in a Trustees' Annual Report or simply by making a general policy statement. Statements such as these do not create a constructive obligation as discretion is retained by the charity as to their implementation. A term in a grant agreement or offer that relieved a donor charity from a future obligation in the event of lack of funds at a future settlement date would not normally prevent the recognition of a liability by the donor charity. The liability would however be derecognised when an event requires the funding offer to be rescinded.

157 A constructive obligation is likely to arise where:

(a) a specific commitment, or promise to provide goods, services or grant funding is given, and

(b) this is communicated directly to a beneficiary or grant recipient.

In such circumstances, the charity is unlikely to have a realistic alternative but to meet the obligation. However, the recognition of any resulting liability will be dependent on any conditions attaching to such commitments.

158 A charity may enter into commitments which are dependent upon explicit conditions being met either by itself or by the recipient before payment is made or upon future reviews. A liability, and hence expenditure, should be recognised once such conditions fall outside the control of the giving charity. If the conditions set remain within the control of giving charity, then the charity retains the discretion to avoid the expenditure and therefore a liability should not be recognised.

159 By way of illustration, where a charity makes a specific commitment to grant fund a project over a three year period, the following situations may arise:

(a) If the multi-year grant obligation:

(i) is conditional on an annual review of progress that determines whether future funding is provided; and

(ii) discretion is retained by the giving charity to terminate the grant;

then provided evidence exists (eg from past review practice) that the discretion retained by the charity has substance, this amounts to a condition and an immediate liability arises only for the first year of the funding commitment.

If the annual review process, although set out in the conditions of the grant, is not in practice used to determine whether funding is provided in the subsequent years of the commitment, then the review stipulation should not be interpreted as a condition and a liability for the full three years of the grant should be recognised.

(b) If there is no condition attaching to the grant that enables the charity to realistically avoid the commitment, the liability for the full three years of the funding should be recognised.

160 Commitments may contain conditions that are outside the control of the giving charity. For example, a charity may promise a grant payment on the condition that the recipient finds matching funding. As the condition falls outside the control of the giving charity, a liability arises and expenditure should be recognised.

[5046]

General Issues

161 Where a liability is not accrued, because conditions have not been met, such a commitment should normally be treated as a contingent liability. The balance sheet treatment for both outstanding commitments and contingent liabilities is given in paragraphs 340 to 348.

162 The trustees may wish to designate some of the charity's income funds to represent contingent liabilities and other planned expenditure which may not have created a liability.

163 Where later events make the recognition of a liability no longer appropriate, the liability should be cancelled by credit against the relevant expenditure heading in the Statement of Financial Activities. The credit should mirror the treatment originally used to recognise the expenditure for the liability and should be disclosed separately.

[5047]

Support Costs

164 In undertaking any activity there may be support costs (Glossary GL 54) incurred that, whilst necessary to deliver an activity, do not themselves produce or constitute the output of the charitable activity. Similarly, costs will be incurred in supporting income generation activities such as fundraising, and in supporting the governance of the charity. Support costs include the central or regional office functions such as general management, payroll administration, budgeting and accounting, information technology, human resources, and financing.

165 Support costs do not, in themselves, constitute an activity, instead they enable output-creating activities to be undertaken. Support costs are therefore allocated to the relevant activity cost category they support on the bases set out in paragraphs 168 to 174. This enables the total cost of an activity category to be disclosed in the Statement of Financial Activities and for the cost of the constituent sub-activities to be presented at a service, programme or project level within the notes to the accounts. There is nevertheless legitimate user interest in both the level of support costs incurred and the policies adopted for their allocation to the relevant activity cost categories that should be addressed through relevant note disclosures.

Disclosure

166 The notes to the accounts should provide details of the total support costs incurred and of material items or categories of expenditure included within support costs.

167 Where support costs are material, an explanation should be provided in the notes of how these costs have been allocated to each of the activity cost categories disclosed in the Statement of Financial Activities or the supporting notes to the accounts. The explanation may include percentages or amounts allocated, details of the methods of apportionment used or a table showing the detailed allocations such as that shown below in Table 4:

PART III SORP 2005

TABLE 4. EXAMPLE OF SUPPORT COST BREAKDOWN BY ACTIVITY

Support Cost (Examples)	Fund-raising	Activity 1	Activity 2	Activity 3	Activity 4	Activity 5	Basis of allocation
Management	£x	£x	£x	£x	£x	£x	Text describing method
Finance	£x	£x	£x	£x	£x	£x	Text describing method
Information Technology	£x	£x	£x	£x	£x	£x	Text describing method
Human Resources	£x	£x	£x	£x	£x	£x	Text describing method
Total	£x	£x	£x	£x	£x	£x	

[5048]

Allocation of Costs

168 A reliable approach to cost allocation should be adopted but a charity should also consider the materiality of the amounts involved and the cost benefit advantages of the approach in that greater accuracy may on occasions only be achievable at a high incremental cost.

169 In attributing costs between activity categories, the following principles should be applied:

(a) Where appropriate, expenditure should be allocated directly to an activity cost category.

(b) Items of expenditure which contribute directly to the output of more than one activity cost category, for example, the cost of a staff member whose time is divided between a fundraising activity and working on a charitable project, should be apportioned on a reasonable, justifiable and consistent basis.

(c) Depreciation, amortisation, impairment or losses on disposal of fixed assets should be attributed in accordance with the same principles.

(d) Support costs may not be attributable to single activity but rather provide the organisational infrastructure that enables output producing activities to take place. Such costs should therefore also be apportioned on a reasonable, justifiable and consistent basis to the activity cost categories being supported.

170 There are a number of bases for apportionment that may be applied. Examples include:

(a) usage – eg on the same basis as expenditure incurred directly in undertaking an activity;

(b) per capita – ie on the number of people employed within an activity;

(c) on the basis of floor area occupied by an activity;

(d) on the basis of time (eg where staff duties are multi-activity).

171 The bases for apportionment adopted by a charity should be appropriate to the cost concerned and to the charity's particular circumstances and selected to enable its accounts to give a true and fair view. The bases adopted for apportionment will normally be consistent between accounting periods.

172 Particular issues arise where a charity provides information about its activities in the context of a fundraising activity. Information about the aims, objectives and projects of a charity is frequently provided in the context of mail shots, websites, collections and telephone fundraising. In determining whether a multi-purpose activity arises, and therefore a need to apportion costs, a distinction should be drawn between:

(a) publicity or information costs involved in raising the profile of a charity which is associated with fundraising (costs of generating funds) and

(b) publicity or information that is provided in an educational manner in furtherance of the charity's objectives (charitable expenditure).

173 In the context of a fundraising activity, for publicity or information to be regarded as charitable expenditure, it must be supplied in an educational manner. To achieve an educational purpose, information supplied would be:

(a) targeted at beneficiaries or others who can use the information to further the charity's objectives; and

(b) information or advice on which the recipient can act upon in an informed manner to further the charity's objectives; and

(c) related to other educational activities or objectives undertaken by the charity.

Where information provided in conjunction with a fundraising activity does not meet these criteria, it should be regarded as targeted at potential donors and therefore relating wholly to the fundraising activity.

174 For example, a health education charity that targeted high-risk beneficiary groups or the medical profession supplying information as to health risks or symptom recognition and advising on steps that should be taken. Such information would fall within charitable expenditure in that it is targeted at beneficiaries, advises on steps that can be taken and is likely to link to the charity's activities or objectives in health education. Therefore when such information is provided in the context of a fundraising activity, a joint cost would arise with costs apportioned between the fundraising and charitable activities.

Disclosure

175 The accounting policy notes should explain the policy adopted for the apportionment of costs between activities and any estimation technique(s) used to calculate their apportionment.

176 Where any fundraising activity is identified as meeting the criteria of a multi-purpose activity (see paragraphs 172 to 174) and part of the costs of the multi-purpose activity are allocated to charitable activities then the policy for the identification of such multi-purpose costs should be explained in the accounting policy notes together with the basis on which any allocation to charitable activities is made.

[5049]

B: Resources Expended

177 The Statement of Financial Activities provides an analysis of the resources expended by a charity based on the nature of the activities undertaken. Resources expended are split into three main activity categories, being:
- (a) the costs of generating funds (paragraph 178–187)
- (b) the costs of charitable activities (paragraph 188–209) and
- (c) the governance costs (paragraph 210 to 212).

The Statement of Financial Activities or the notes to the accounts should include an analysis of the sub-activities, services, programmes, projects or other initiatives that contribute to a particular activity category.

[5050]

B1: Costs of Generating Funds

178 These are the costs which are associated with generating incoming resources from all sources other than from undertaking charitable activities. The main components of costs within this category are:
- (a) costs of generating voluntary income (Glossary GL 13 and see paragraphs 180 to 184);
- (b) costs of fundraising trading, including cost of goods sold and other associated costs (see paragraphs 185 to 186); and
- (c) costs of managing investments for both income generation and capital maintenance (see paragraph 187).

179 Costs of generating funds should **not** include:
- (a) costs associated with delivering or supporting the provision of goods and services in the furtherance of the charity's objects; nor
- (b) the costs of any subsequent negotiation, monitoring or reporting relating to the provision of goods or services under the terms of a grant, contract or performance-related grant.

[5051]

B1a: Costs of Generating Voluntary Income

180 Costs of generating voluntary income are defined in the Glossary (GL 13). All such fundraising costs, including agents' costs where fundraising agents are used, should be included within this category. In the case of consolidated accounts any such costs incurred by any subsidiary companies or other entities should be consolidated on a line-by-line basis.

181 Some fundraising costs may be incurred in starting up a new source of future income such as legacies, or in developing a supporter database.
- (a) Start-up costs of a new fundraising activity should be treated in the same manner as similar cost incurred as part of a charity's ongoing activities. In most cases, it will be inappropriate to carry forward start-up costs as prepayments or deferred expenditure as the future economic benefits that may be derived are usually not sufficiently certain (see Appendix 2: UITF Abstract 24 – Accounting for Start-up Costs).
- (b) Data capture costs of internally developed databases may only be capitalised where future benefit can be demonstrated and the resulting database has a readily ascertainable value.

182 The start-up costs of a new fundraising activity may be material in the context of the overall fundraising activity and may, because of their exceptional size or incidence, require separate disclosure to explain performance.

Disclosure

183 Where the costs of generating voluntary income are material, details of the types of activity on which the costs were expended should be shown in the notes to the accounts. Types of activity could include collections (eg street and house-to-house collections), sponsorship, legacy development and direct mail. As far as possible the analysis provided here should match the detailed analysis of voluntary incoming resources (see paragraphs 121 to 122).

PART III SORP 2005

184 Exceptional costs that arise in the context of generating voluntary income should not be presented as a separate category of costs on the face of the Statement of Financial Activities but, rather, should be included as an exceptional item within the relevant activity cost category. The amount of each exceptional item, either individually or as an aggregate of items of a similar type, should be disclosed in the notes to the accounts or on the face of the Statement of Financial Activities (within the activity category to which the cost relates) if that degree of prominence is necessary to give a true and fair view. An adequate description should be given to enable its nature to be understood.

[5052]

B1b: Fundraising Trading: Cost of goods sold and other costs

185 This category should include all those costs that are incurred by trading for a fundraising purpose in either donated or bought-in goods or in providing non-charitable services to generate income. This includes:

(a) the cost of goods sold or services provided;
(b) other costs related to the trade, including staff costs, premises costs and other costs incurred in the activity including allocated support costs; and
(c) costs related to the licensing of a charity logo.

In consolidated accounts this category will include the costs incurred by both the charity and any subsidiaries or other entities consolidated on a line-by-line basis.

Disclosure

186 Where the costs associated with fundraising trading are material, details should be given in the notes to the accounts to distinguish the cost of separate trading activities in a way that matches the analysis of income.

[5053]

B1c: Investment Management Costs

187 Investment management costs are defined in the Glossary (GL 38). Where investment management fees are deducted from investment income by investment managers, the charity should show as investment income the gross investment income before fees and report the fees within this cost category (see paragraph 140). As explained in Appendix 3, paragraph 3(c), investment management costs associated with endowment fund investments should generally be charged to the endowment fund in the Statement of Financial Activities.

[5054]

B2: Charitable Activities

188 Resources expended on charitable activities comprise all the resources applied by the charity in undertaking its work to meet its charitable objectives as opposed to the cost of raising the funds to finance these activities and governance costs. Charitable activities are all the resources expended by the charity in the delivery of goods and services, including its programme and project work that is directed at the achievement of its charitable aims and objectives. Such costs include the direct costs of the charitable activities together with those support costs incurred that enable these activities to be undertaken.

189 Charities may carry out their activities through a combination of direct service provision and grant funding of third parties to undertake work that contributes to the charity's objectives or programme of work. In such cases, the total cost of the activity involves both costs incurred directly by the charity and funding provided to third parties through grantmaking activities.

190 Where incoming resources are received either under contract or by a restricted grant to provide a specified service, further analysis of charitable activities expenditure may be provided in the notes to the accounts to demonstrate the link between the incoming resource and the charitable activity that it funds.

Disclosure

191 Resources expended on charitable activities should be analysed on the face of the Statement of Financial Activities or in a prominent note to the accounts. This analysis should provide an understanding of the nature of the activities undertaken and the resources expended on their provision. This analysis may, for example, set out the activity cost of the main services provided by the charity, or set out the resources expended on material programmes or projects undertaken by the charity.

192 The note to the accounts should identify the amount of support costs allocated to charitable activities.

193 Where activities are carried out through a combination of direct service or programme activity and grant funding of third parties, the notes to the accounts should identify the amount of grantmaking expenditure using the note to explain the activity funded.

194 The disclosures required may, for example, be presented in a table such as Table 5 (with totals reconciling with the Statement of Financial Activities and other notes as appropriate):

TABLE 5. BREAKDOWN OF COSTS OF CHARITABLE ACTIVITY

Activity or Programme	Activities undertaken directly	Grant funding of activities	Support costs	Total
	£	£	£	£
Activity 1				
Activity 2				
Activity 3				
Total				

[5055]

Grantmaking

195 Costs associated with grantmaking activity include the grants actually made and the support costs associated with the activity. The term grant is defined in the Glossary (GL 29) and associated support costs are explained further at paragraph 164 above.

196 Support costs related to grantmaking will include:

(a) costs incurred before grants are made (pre-grant costs) as part of the decision making process;

(b) post-grant costs e g monitoring of grants; and

(c) costs of any central or regional office functions such as general management, payroll administration, budgeting and accounting, information technology, human resources, and financing.

197 Grantmaking charities may undertake their entire programme of work through grantmaking activities, whilst other charities may undertake their activities through a combination of direct service provision and grant funding of third parties. In either case, further analysis of grantmaking, where material, should be provided.

198 The further information provided in relation to grantmaking should provide the reader with a reasonable understanding of the nature of the activities or projects that are being funded and whether the financial support is provided directly to individuals or to assist an institution undertake its activities or projects. In the case of institutional grants, information as to the recipient(s) of the funding should be provided so that the reader can appreciate the type and range of institutions supported.

199 An individual grant is one that is made for the direct benefit of the individual who receives it, for example, to relieve financial hardship or for an educational bursary. All other grants should be regarded as institutional. For example, a grant which is made to an individual to carry out a research project should be regarded as a grant to the institution with which the individual is connected rather than as a grant to the individual.

200 Information provided in relation to grantmaking may be limited or excluded when:

(a) grants are made to individuals – in which case details of the recipient are not required;

(b) grantmaking activities in total are not material in the context of a charity's overall charitable activities – in which case no disclosures are required ;

(c) total grants to a particular institution are not material in the context of institutional grants – in which case the name of the recipient institution need not be disclosed;

(d) disclosure of a particular institutional grant would seriously prejudice either the grant maker or the recipient.

Disclosure

201 The analysis and explanation should help the reader of the accounts understand how the grants made relate to the objects of the charity and the policy adopted by the trustees in pursuing these objects.

PART III SORP 2005

202 The notes to the accounts should identify the amount of support costs associated with grantmaking activities.

203 The analysis and explanation in the notes should provide details, with amounts that reconcile with the total of grants payable of:

(a) the total amount of grants analysed between grants to individuals and grants to institutions,

(b) an analysis of the total amount of grants paid by nature or type of activity or project being supported.

This statement may, for example, be structured as shown in Table 6:

TABLE 6. ANALYSIS OF GRANTS

Analysis	Grants to Institutions Total amount £	Grants to Individuals Total amount £
Activity or Project 1		
Activity or Project 2		
Activity or Project 3		
Total		

204 The analysis of grants should provide the reader with an understanding of the nature of the activities or projects being funded by the grantmaker. This analysis of grants should relate to the charity's objectives, for example, categories may be social welfare, medical research, the performing arts, welfare of people in financial need, help to people seeking to further their education, depending on the nature of the charity. Some charities may decide that it is appropriate to provide further or alternative levels of analysis perhaps for example, showing a geographical analysis of the value of grants made.

205 The trustees may give further analysis and explanation of the purposes for which grants were made as part of the Trustees' Annual Report or by means of a separate publication. Such further analysis does not excuse the trustees from providing sufficient detail in the notes to the accounts as is needed to provide a true and fair view.

206 If a charity has made grants to particular institutions that are material in the context of grantmaking, the charity should disclose details, as specified in paragraph 207, of a sufficient number of institutional grants to provide a reasonable understanding of the range of institutions it has supported. This information may be provided either in the notes to the accounts, or as part of the Trustees' Annual Report or by means of a separate publication. Where the analysis is contained in a separate publication, it should be made available by the charity to the public on request. The notes to the accounts should identify the publication and state how copies of it can be obtained.

207 The disclosure of institutional grants should give the name of the institution and total value of grants made to that institution in the accounting year. Where grants have been made to a particular institution to undertake different activities or projects, the total value of the grants made for each activity or purpose should be disclosed. For example, a charity may have made grants to different officers or departments of a particular university for different projects. Such grants should be treated as having been made to the same institution.

208 Very exceptionally, even though the grants to a particular institution are material, it is possible that the disclosure of the details of one or more of those grants could **seriously prejudice** the furtherance of the purposes either of the *recipient institution* or of the *charity itself*. Situations where serious prejudice is clearly indicated include those where disclosure could result in serious personal injury.

209 Where the circumstances amount to serious prejudice, a charity may withhold details of the recipient of any institutional grant concerned but should in such circumstances:

(a) disclose in the notes to the accounts the total number, value and general purpose of those grants the details of which have not been disclosed;

(b) give in writing to the charity's regulatory body:

(i) the full details of any grants not disclosed, and

(ii) a full explanation of the reasons why those details have not been disclosed in the accounts;

(c) state in the notes to the accounts whether or not those details have been given to the charity's regulatory body.

It is unlikely in practice that all the material institutional grants of a charity would fall within this exception.

[5056]

B3: Governance Costs

210 Governance costs (defined in Glossary GL 28) include the costs of governance arrangements which relate to the general running of the charity as opposed to the direct management functions inherent in generating funds, service delivery and programme or project work. These activities provide the governance infrastructure which allows the charity to operate and to generate the information required for public accountability. They include the strategic planning processes that contribute to future development of the charity.

211 Expenditure on the governance of the charity will normally include both direct and related support costs. Direct costs will include such items as internal and external audit, legal advice for trustees and costs associated with constitutional and statutory requirements eg the cost of trustee meetings and preparing statutory accounts. Where material, there should also be an apportionment of shared and indirect costs involved in supporting the governance activities (as distinct from supporting its charitable or income generation activities).

Disclosure

212 The accounting policy notes should explain the nature of costs allocated to the governance category, and an analysis may be provided within the notes to the accounts of the main items of expenditure included within this category where it is considered to provide useful information to the users of the accounts.

[5057]

B4: Other Resources Expended

213 Other resources expended will include the payment of any resources which the charity has not been able to analyse within the main resources expended categories. This category should not be used for support costs which can be allocated to other activity costs.

[5058]

C: Transfers

214 All transfers between the different categories of funds should be shown on the transfer row of the Statement of Financial Activities. The transfer row will be used for several purposes including:

(a) when capital funds are released to an income fund from expendable endowment;
(b) where a charity has authority to adopt a total return approach to investment (see Appendix 3 paragraph 3(g)) to record the release of funds to income from the unapplied total return fund held within the permanent endowment fund;
(c) where restricted assets have been released and reallocated to unrestricted income funds;
(d) to transfer assets from unrestricted income funds to finance a deficit on a restricted fund; and
(e) to transfer of the value of fixed assets from restricted to unrestricted funds when the asset has been purchased from a restricted fund donation but the asset is held for a general and not a restricted purpose.

215 Material transfers should not be netted off but should be shown gross on the face of the Statement of Financial Activities.

Disclosure

216 The notes to the accounts should provide an explanation of the nature of each material transfer between funds.

[5059]

D Other Recognised Gains and Losses

D1: Gains and Losses on Fixed Assets

217 Gains and losses arising on disposal, revaluation or impairment of fixed assets – whether held for the charity's own use or for investment purposes – will form part of the particular fund in which the investment or other asset concerned is or was held at the time of disposal, revaluation or impairment.

PART III
SORP 2005

218 Such gains and losses should be recognised as follows:

(a) impairment losses of assets held for the charity's own use (ie not investments) should be regarded as additional depreciation of the impaired asset and included appropriately in the resources expended section of the Statement of Financial Activities;

(b) gains on the disposal of fixed assets for the charity's own use should be included under the heading "other incoming resources". Losses on disposal should be treated as additional depreciation and included appropriately in the resources expended section of the Statement of Financial Activities; and

(c) revaluation gains or losses (which are not considered to be impairment losses (see paragraphs 267–272)) on assets held for the charity's own use should be included in the section on gains and losses on revaluations of fixed assets for the charity's own use.

[5060]

D2: Gains and Losses on Investment Assets

219 Any gains and losses on investment assets (including property investments) should be included under the gains and losses on the revaluation and disposal of investment assets. Realised and unrealised gains and losses may be included in a single row on the Statement of Financial Activities. In particular this approach will be necessary where a charity adopts a "marking to market" or continuous revaluation approach in relation to its investment portfolio.

[5061]

D3: Actuarial Gains or Losses on Defined Benefit Pension Schemes

220 Actuarial gains or losses on defined benefit pension schemes should be separately disclosed in the gains and losses section of the Statement of Financial Activities (See paragraphs 430 to 448 – Accounting for Retirement Benefits).

[5062]

OTHER MATTERS TO BE COVERED IN NOTES TO THE ACCOUNTS

Related Party Transactions

221 Subject to paragraph 229 below, disclosure in a note to the accounts is required of any transactions which the reporting charity or any institution connected with it (Glossary GL 9) has entered into with a related party. Such transactions might inhibit the charity from pursuing its own separate interests.

222 Related parties are defined in the Glossary (GL 50).

223 Any decision by a charity to enter into a transaction ought to be influenced only by the consideration of the charity's own interests. This requirement is reinforced by legal rules which, in certain circumstances, can invalidate transactions where the charity trustees have a conflict of interest. This does not necessarily mean that all transactions with related persons are influenced by the consideration of interests other than the charity's nor that they are liable to invalidation.

224 Transparency is particularly important where the relationship between the charity and the other party or parties to a transaction suggests that the transaction could possibly have been influenced by interests other than the charity's. It is possible that the reported financial position and results may have been affected by such transactions and information about these transactions is therefore necessary for the users of the charity's accounts.

225 Related party transactions potentially include (exceptions in paragraph 229):

(a) purchases, sales, leases and donations (including donations which are made in furtherance of the charity's objects) of goods, property, money and other assets such as intellectual property rights to or from the related party;

(b) the supply of services by the related party to the charity, and the supply of services by the charity to the related party. Supplying services includes providing the use of goods, property and other assets and finance arrangements such as making loans and giving guarantees and indemnities; and

(c) any other payments and other benefits which are made to trustees under express provisions of the governing document of a charity or in fulfilment of its charitable objectives.

[5063]

Required Disclosure

226 Trustee remuneration or other benefits should always be regarded as material (subject to paragraph 229(f)). Material transactions with related parties should be disclosed irrespective of whether or not they are undertaken on an arm's length basis.

227 The required disclosure is as follows (also see paragraph 303(c) re investments):
(a) the name(s) of the transacting related party or parties;
(b) a description of the relationship between the parties (including the interest of the related party or parties in the transaction);
(c) a description of the transaction;
(d) the amounts involved;
(e) outstanding balances with related parties at the balance sheet date and any provisions for doubtful debts from such persons;
(f) any amounts written off from such balances during the accounting year; and
(g) any other elements of the transactions which are necessary for the understanding of the accounts.

228 The disclosure can be given in aggregate for similar transactions and type of related party, unless disclosure of an individual transaction or connected transactions:
(a) is necessary for an understanding of the impact of the transactions on the accounts of the charity; or
(b) is a legal requirement, for example, in relation to trustee remuneration (see paragraph 230(b)).

[5064]

Disclosures not Required

229 Some related party transactions are such that they are unlikely to influence the pursuance of the separate independent interests of the charity. These need not be disclosed unless there is evidence to the contrary. Examples are:
(a) donations received by the reporting charity from a related party, so long as the donor has not attached conditions which would, or might, require the charity to alter significantly the nature of its existing activities if it were to accept the donation (but any material grant by the reporting charity to a charity which is a related party should be disclosed);
(b) minor or routine unremunerated services provided to a charity by people related to it;
(c) contracts of employment between a charity and its employees (except where the employees are the charity trustees or people connected with them);
(d) contributions by a charity to a pension fund for the benefit of employees; (also see paragraph 235);
(e) the purchase from a charity by a related party of minor articles which are offered for sale to the general public on the same terms as are offered to the general public;
(f) the provision of services to a related party (including a charity trustee or person connected with a charity trustee), where the related party receives the services as part of a wider beneficiary class, and on the same terms as other members of the class (for example, the use of a village hall by members of its committee of management, as inhabitants of the area of benefit); and
(g) the payment or reimbursement of out-of-pocket expenses to a related party (including a charity trustee or person connected with a charity trustee – but see paragraphs 231 to 233).

[5065]

Trustee Remuneration and Benefits

230 Unlike in the case of the directors of commercial companies, it is not the normal practice for charity trustees, or people connected with them, to receive remuneration, or other benefits, from the charities for which they are responsible, or from institutions connected with those charities. Detailed disclosures of remuneration and benefits are therefore required where the related party is a charity trustee, or a person connected with a charity trustee. The following points should be borne in mind when reporting on transactions, where the related party is a charity trustee or a person connected with a trustee.
(a) Unless one of the exceptions in paragraph 229 applies, the transaction should always be regarded as material, and should therefore be disclosed regardless of its size.
(b) Each type of related party transaction must be separately disclosed. This means, for example, that particulars of remuneration paid to each charity trustee or person connected with a charity trustee, should be given individually in the notes. Where the charity has made any pension arrangements for charity trustees or persons connected

PART III SORP 2005

with them, the amount of contributions paid and the benefits accruing must be disclosed in the notes for each related party.

(c) Where remuneration has been paid to a charity trustee or a person connected with a charity trustee, the legal authority under which the payment was made (e g provision in the governing document of the charity, order of the Court or Charity Commission) should also be given, as should the reason for such remuneration.

(d) Where neither the trustees nor any persons connected with them have received any such remuneration, this fact should be stated.

[5066]

Trustees' Expenses

231 Where a charity has met individual expenses incurred by trustees for services provided to the charity, either by reimbursement of the trustee or by providing the trustee with an allowance or by direct payment to a third party, the aggregate amount of those expenses should be disclosed in a note to the accounts. The note should also indicate the nature of the expenses (e g travel, subsistence, entertainment etc) and the number of trustees involved.

232 Sometimes trustees act as agents for the charity and make purchases on its behalf and are reimbursed for this expenditure, e g payment for stationery or office equipment. Such expenditure is not related to the services provided by a trustee and there is no need to disclose it. Likewise there is no need to disclose routine expenditure which is attributable collectively to the services provided to the trustees, such as the hire of a room for meetings or providing reasonable refreshment at the meeting.

233 Where the trustees have received no such expenses, this fact should be stated.

[5067]

Staff Costs and Emoluments

234 It is important that the accounts disclose the costs of employing staff who work for the charity whether or not the charity itself has incurred those costs. This includes seconded and agency staff and staff employed by connected or independent companies. For instance, staff working for a charity may have contracts with and be paid by a connected company. Payments may also be made to independent third parties for the provision of staff. Where such arrangements are in place and the costs involved are material (in relation to the charity's own expenditure) there should be disclosure by way of note which outlines the arrangement in place, the reasons for them and the amounts involved.

235 The total staff costs should be shown in the notes to the accounts giving the split between gross wages and salaries, employer's national insurance costs and pension costs (those pension costs included within resources expended excluding pension finance costs) for the year. The average number of staff during the year should be provided and where material to the disclosure, e g due to the number of part-time staff, an estimate of the average number of full time equivalent employees for the year may be provided in the notes to the accounts providing sub-categories according to the manner in which the charity's activities are organised.

236 Where a charity is subject to a statutory audit then the notes should also show the number of employees whose emoluments for the year (including taxable benefits in kind but not employer pension costs) fell within each band of £10,000 from £60,000 upwards. Bands in which no employee's emoluments fell should not be listed.

237 In addition the following pension details should be disclosed in total for higher paid staff as defined in paragraph 236:

(a) contributions in the year for the provision of defined contribution scheme (normally money purchase schemes); and

(b) the number of staff to whom retirement benefits are accruing under defined contribution schemes and defined benefit schemes respectively. (Further information on accounting for Retirement Benefit Schemes is given in paragraphs 430 to 448).

238 If there are no employees with emoluments above £60,000 this fact should be stated.

[5068]

Cost of Audit, Independent Examination or Reporting Accountant Services and other Financial Services

239 The notes to the accounts should disclose separately the amounts payable to the auditor, independent examiner or reporting accountant in respect of:

(a) the costs of their respective external scrutiny; and

(b) other financial services such as taxation advice, consultancy, financial advice and accountancy.

[5069]

Ex-Gratia Payments

240 The total amount or value of any:

(a) payment; or
(b) non-monetary benefit; or
(c) other expenditure of any kind; or
(d) waiver of rights to property to which a charity is entitled,

which is made not as an application of funds or property for charitable purposes but in fulfilment of a compelling moral obligation should be disclosed in the notes to the accounts. Where trustees require and obtain the authority of the Court, the Attorney General or the Charity Commission, the nature and date of the authority for each such payment should also be disclosed. (The Charity Commission has provided further guidance on such payments, that is applicable to charities in England and Wales, in its publication (CC7) – Ex Gratia Payments by Charities).

241 Payments which the trustees reasonably consider to be in the interests of the charity (more than a moral obligation) should not be treated as ex-gratia, even though there is no legal obligation to make them. For example, the trustees may think that it will motivate retained staff and hence benefit the charity if they make redundancy payments over and above the minimum legally required.

[5070]

Analysis of the Net Movement in Funds

242 The net movement of funds represents the increase or decrease in resources available to a charity to deploy in undertaking future activities. Unlike profit or loss in a commercial entity, it should not necessarily be regarded as an indicator of a charity's performance. Charities also further their objectives by investing in tangible fixed assets to provide services or by making investments of a programme or social related nature. Such applications are charitable but do not decrease the funds of a charity. Charities may also receive gifts of an endowed nature, which are identified separately in the primary accounting statements. Whilst endowments provide a source of income or service generation in future periods they are not available to finance expenditure.

243 Information on such charitable applications and sources can be ascertained from a charity's cash flow statement (when prepared). A note summarising these effects, when material, can provide valuable information to readers of accounts in interpreting net movements in funds and help the reader understand the impact of such transactions on the liquid funds of the charity. Where relevant a charity may choose to provide in the notes to the accounts the following information:

(a) total net movement in funds for the year;
(b) net endowment receipts for the year (value of endowment receipts less any release of expendable endowment to income funds);
(c) net expenditure on additions to functional fixed assets (cost of additions less proceeds of any disposals) for the year; and
(d) net investment in programme related investments (cost of additions less proceeds of any disposals) for the year.

[5071]

BALANCE SHEET

Introduction

244 The balance sheet provides a snapshot of the charity's assets and liabilities at the end of its accounting year and how assets are split between the different types of funds. The balance sheet will not always include all of the assets and liabilities of a charity, nor attach an up-to-date valuation for all assets. Some heritage assets (see paragraphs 279 to 294), or contingent liabilities (see paragraphs 340 to 348) may be omitted. Where such assets or contingent liabilities exist and are not included in the balance sheet, details should be provided in the notes to the accounts.

245 The objective of the balance sheet is to show the resources available to the charity and whether these are freely available or have to be used for specific purposes because of legal restrictions on their use. It may also show which of the resources the trustees have

designated for specific future use. It will normally be necessary to read the reserves policy and plans for the future in the Trustees' Annual Report (see paragraphs 55(a) and 57) to gain a fuller understanding of the availability and planned use of the charity's funds.

[5072]

Presentation

Structure of the Balance Sheet

246 Table 7 sets out the format and the asset, liability and fund categories of the balance sheet.

247 The assets and liabilities are analysed within the balance sheet according to the category of the asset or liability as set out in Table 7. The balance sheet should also distinguish, as a minimum, between, the total funds held as unrestricted income funds, restricted income funds and as endowment funds. Distinctions between funds held as permanent and expendable endowment and held as designated funds may also be shown on the face of the balance sheet. The order in which the categories of funds are presented within the balance sheet (Section E of Table 7) may be varied to accommodate an individual charity's presentational preference.

248 Charities may choose to adopt a columnar presentation of its assets, liabilities and funds in the balance sheet. Such a presentation shows the asset and liability categories analysed in columns between each fund group in a similar way to the Statement of Financial Activities showing incoming resources and resources expended by type of fund. This presentation is not mandatory, but using it ensures charities present the required analysis of assets and liabilities by category of fund. Where a charity does not have funds of a particular category, the column related to that category of fund is omitted. If this columnar presentation is not adopted then the assets and liabilities (e g investments, fixed assets, net current assets) representing each category of fund should be summarised and analysed between those funds in the notes to the accounts (see paragraph 75(a)).

249 Further details of the assets and liabilities should be given in the balance sheet or the notes to the accounts. This analysis should enable the reader to gain a proper appreciation of their spread and character. For example, long-term debtors should, where the total is material, be separately stated in the balance sheet – otherwise the total amount of the category (see paragraph 314) should be analysed in the notes to the accounts.

250 If for any category of assets (row in Table 7 – the balance sheet) there are no amounts for the current and prior year then no entries need to be made on the balance sheet and the headings can be omitted.

251 As explained in paragraph 4(b) of Appendix 3, expenditure may be incurred in anticipation of the receipt of restricted income, possibly leading to a negative balance on a specific fund. Where such balances are material they should be shown separately as negative balances and not simply be netted off against positive balances on the fund category in the balance sheet. Therefore the balance sheet may show both positive and negative balances on restricted funds.

TABLE 7. BALANCE SHEET

Reference			Total Funds	Prior Year Funds	Reference
A	Fixed assets:				
A1	Intangible assets				252
A2	Tangible assets				253 to 278
A3	Heritage assets				279 to 294
A4	Investments:				
A4a		Investments			295 to 307
A4b		Programme related investments			308 to 312
		Total fixed assets			
B	Current assets:				313 to 316

Reference		Total Funds	Prior Year Funds	Reference
B1	Stocks and work-in-progress			
B2	Debtors			314
B3	Investments			316
B4	Cash at bank and in hand			
	Total current assets			
C	Liabilities:			
C1	Creditors: Amounts falling due within one year			317 to 320
	Net current assets or liabilities			
	Total assets less current liabilities			
C2	Creditors: Amounts falling due after more than one year			317 to 320
C3	Provisions for liabilities and charges			321 to 329
	Net asset or liabilities excluding pension asset or liability			
D	Defined benefit pension scheme asset or liability			330–332
	Net assets or liabilities including pension asset or liability			
E	The funds of the charity:			
E1	Endowment funds			
E2	Restricted income funds			
E3	Unrestricted income funds			
E3a	Share capital			333
E3b	Unrestricted income funds			
E3c	Revaluation reserve			334
	Unrestricted income funds excluding pension asset/liability			
E3d	Pension reserve			335
	Total unrestricted funds			
	Total charity funds			

PART III SORP 2005

[5073]

CONTENT OF THE BALANCE SHEET

A1: Intangible Fixed Assets

252 Intangible fixed assets should be included in the balance sheet in accordance with FRS 10 "Goodwill and Intangible Assets" (see appendix 2 FRS 10).

[5074]

A2: Tangible Fixed Assets (other than Investments)

253 FRS 15 "Tangible Fixed Assets" requires that:

(a) all tangible fixed assets should be capitalised on initial acquisition and included in the balance sheet at cost or valuation;

(b) tangible fixed assets may be periodically revalued;

(c) subsequent expenditure which enhances (rather than maintains) the performance of tangible fixed assets should be capitalised.

254 Within charities, tangible fixed assets (other than investments) fall into two categories, those held for charity use (including those used for the running and administration of the charity) and those classed as heritage assets (Glossary GL 32). Paragraphs 255 to 278 describe the general rules for inclusion of tangible fixed assets in the balance sheet. In principle heritage assets meet the definition of an asset and should be recognised and included within a charity's balance sheet. However, particular considerations arise where the cost or valuation of heritage assets can only be obtained at significant cost or where such information lacks sufficient reliability. Specific recommendations for the accounting treatment of heritage assets are set out in paragraphs 279 to 294.

[5075]

General Rules for Tangible Fixed Assets

255 Tangible fixed assets should initially be included in the balance sheet using the following bases.

(a) The cost of acquisition including costs that are directly attributable to bringing the assets into working condition for their intended use. This can include costs of interest on loans to finance the construction of such assets but only where the charity has adopted this as a policy for all tangible fixed assets and capitalisation of interest should cease when the asset is ready for use. This applies whether assets are bought outright or through hire purchase or finance leasing.

(b) If a functional fixed asset is acquired in full or in part from the proceeds of a grant it should be included at its full acquisition cost (or in the case of a joint arrangement at the gross value of the charity's share in the asset (see paragraph 416)) without netting off the grant proceeds.

(c) Where functional fixed assets have been donated, they should be included in the balance sheet at their current value at the date of the gift and also included in the Statement of Financial Activities (see paragraph 111) as an incoming resource.

(d) Where functional fixed assets are capitalised some time after being acquired, for example, as a result of a change in accounting policy, they should be included at original cost or at the value at which the gift was included in the Statement of Financial Activities less an amount for depreciation. However, if neither of these amounts is ascertainable, a reasonable estimate of the asset's cost or current value to the charity should be used. Such a valuation will be regarded as the asset's initial carrying amount and will not be regarded as a revaluation (see paragraphs 262 to 266).

256 Where the net book value of a fixed asset is higher than its recoverable amount, it will be impaired and should be written down to its recoverable amount. This is covered in more detail in paragraphs 267 to 272.

[5076]

Rules for Mixed use of Fixed Assets (Functional and Investment)

257 Where land and buildings are held for mixed purposes, i e partly as functional property and partly as investment, the balance sheet category in which they should be included depends upon the primary purpose for holding the asset and the extent to which they are separable. The following criteria for balance sheet analysis should be adopted:

(a) Land and buildings held primarily for charity use of which a part is leased at a commercial rent should be regarded as functional fixed assets and included within tangible fixed assets provided the asset is wholly or mainly used for charitable purposes.

(b) Land and buildings held primarily for investment purposes (Glossary GL 39) where the asset is wholly or mainly used for investment purposes should be included within the fixed asset investment category of the balance sheet.

(c) Land and buildings which contain clearly distinguishable parts which are held for different purposes i e partly functional and partly investment and do not fall under (a) or (b) above, should be apportioned and analysed in the balance sheet between functional and investment assets.

[5077]

Depreciation of Tangible Fixed Assets (other than Investments)

258 Most tangible fixed assets depreciate; that is they wear out, are consumed or otherwise suffer a reduction in their useful life through use, the passing of time or obsolescence. Their value is thus gradually expended over their useful economic life. This expenditure should be recognised by means of an annual depreciation charge in the Statement of Financial Activities and shown in the balance sheet as accumulated depreciation deducted from the value of the relevant fixed assets.

259 Tangible fixed assets held for use by the charity which are included in the balance sheet should be depreciated at rates appropriate to their useful economic life. The only exceptions to charging depreciation arise where any of the following conditions apply:

(a) the asset is freehold land which is considered to have an indefinitely long useful life; ***or***

(b) both the depreciation charge and the accumulated depreciation are not material because:

  (i) the asset has a very long useful life; or

  (ii) the estimated residual value (based on prices at the time of acquisition or subsequent revaluation) of the asset is not materially different from the carrying amount of the asset;

  If depreciation is not charged because of immateriality, FRS 15 requires that the asset is subject to an annual impairment review (except for charities under the threshold for following the FRSSE); ***or***

(c) the assets are heritage assets and have not been included in the balance sheet (see paragraphs 279 to 294).

260 The useful economic lives and residual values of fixed assets should be reviewed at the end of the accounting period and, where there is a material change, the value of the asset should be depreciated over its remaining useful life.

261 Where a fixed asset for charity use comprises two or more major components with substantially different useful lives, each component should be accounted for as a separate asset and depreciated over its individual useful life.

[5078]

Revaluation of Tangible Fixed Assets (other than Investments)

262 In accordance with FRS 15, tangible fixed assets (other than investment assets) do not need to be revalued unless the charity adopts a policy of revaluation. Where such a policy is adopted, whilst it need not be applied to all fixed assets it must be applied to entire classes of fixed assets. Therefore if an individual fixed asset is revalued, all other assets in that class must also be revalued. Classes of assets can be narrowly defined, within reason, according to the operations of the charity (see paragraph 273).

263 When an asset is donated or when it is capitalised as a result of the change in an accounting policy, its initial valuation will not be regarded as a revaluation and hence will not require the entire class of such assets to be revalued.

264 Similarly, where a charity was holding assets at a revalued amount at the date FRS 15 requirements first applied, (for accounting periods ending on or after 23rd March 2000) this will not be regarded as a revaluation and no requirement exists for such assets to be revalued periodically unless the trustees so choose.

265 Where there is a policy to revalue fixed assets, their value must be updated on a regular basis. The trustees may use any reasonable approach to valuation at least every five years, subject only to obtaining advice as to the possibility of any material movements between individual valuations. Where a charity has a number of such assets, it will be acceptable for valuations to be carried out on a rolling basis over a five-year period. Independent formal professional valuations are not mandatory in the case of a charity, which instead may obtain a valuation from a suitably qualified person who could be a trustee or employee (see Appendix 2 FRS 15).

266 In the case of assets other than properties, such as motor vehicles, there may be an active second-hand market for the asset, or appropriate indices may exist allowing a valuation to be made with reasonable certainty by an appropriate person (but not necessarily a qualified valuer) either internal or external to the charity. Where this method of valuation is used the assets' values must be updated annually. As an alternative to market value such assets can be recorded at depreciated replacement cost (see Glossary GL 18).

[5079]

Impairment of Fixed Assets for Use by the Charity

267 On rare occasions a functional fixed asset may become impaired. This occurs if its carrying value (net book value, at cost or valuation) is higher than its recoverable amount. In such a case FRS 11 would require it to be written down to its recoverable amount. The recoverable amount is the higher of the net realisable value and the value in use.

268 Value in use is normally the present value of the future cash flows obtainable as a result of an asset's continued use. However many charities have fixed assets that are not held

for the main purpose of generating cash flows either by themselves or in conjunction with other assets. In these cases it is not appropriate to measure the value in use of the asset at an amount based on expected future cash flows. Instead an alternative measure of its service potential will be more relevant, such as the intrinsic worth of the service delivery or the replacement cost of the asset. Each charity can determine its own measure of service delivery but this must be reasonable, justifiable and consistently operated.

269 Impairment reviews should only be carried out where there is some indication that the recoverable amount of a functional fixed asset is below its net book value. Such a review should, as far as possible, be carried out on individual assets or where this is not possible then categories of assets can be grouped (see FRS 11 paragraphs 24 to 28). Events or changes which may indicate an impairment include:

(a) physical deterioration, change or obsolescence of the fixed asset;
(b) social, demographic or environmental changes resulting in a reduction of beneficiaries for a charity;
(c) changes in the law, other regulations or standards which adversely affect the activities of a charity;
(d) management commitments to undertake a significant reorganisation;
(e) a major loss of key employees associated with particular activities of a charity;
(f) operating losses on activities using fixed assets primarily to generate incoming resources.

270 Where an impairment review is required, the charity should first determine the net realisable value of the asset. If this is lower than the net book value, the value in use will need to be considered. If the value in use is considered to be above the net book value, the asset should be valued at the net book value. If a decision is made to sell the asset, it should be valued at its expected net realisable value.

271 Value in use calculations should not be used to manipulate the write down of fixed assets. For instance when a new specialised asset is purchased, although it may have a low net realisable value, it is unlikely that it will suffer an impairment in service delivery within the first years after acquisition.

272 Where there is an impairment loss that needs to be recognised, charities should determine this in accordance with the requirements of FRS 11 (whilst being able to use alternative valuation methods for some assets). The loss should be treated as additional depreciation and included in the Statement of Financial Activities in accordance with paragraph 218. The revised carrying amount of the asset should be depreciated over its remaining useful economic life.

Disclosure

273 Tangible fixed assets for use by the charity should be analysed in the notes to the accounts within the following categories:

(a) freehold interest in land and buildings;
(b) leasehold and other interests in land and buildings;
(c) plant and machinery including motor vehicles;
(d) fixtures, fittings and equipment; and
(e) payments on account and assets in the course of construction.

These are broad categories and any charity may, within reason, split the headings or adopt other narrower classes that meet the definition of a class of tangible fixed assets and are appropriate to its operations.

274 The notes should summarise all material changes in the values of each class of tangible fixed assets and reconcile the opening and closing balances. This may be achieved by using a table such as Table 8 below omitting any rows and columns that are not needed for a charity's particular circumstances:

TABLE 8. ANALYSIS OF MOVEMENT OF FIXED ASSETS

	Freehold land & Buildings	Leasehold land & Buildings	Plant and Machinery	Fixtures, Fittings and Equipment	Payments on account & assets under construction	Total
	£	£	£	£	£	£
Asset cost, valuation or revalued amount						
Balance brought forward						
Additions						
Disposals						
Revaluations						
Transfers						
Balance carried forward						
Accumulated depreciation and impairment provisions						
Balance brought forward						
Disposals						
Revaluations						
Impairment charges						
Transfers						
Charge for year						
Balance carried forward						
Net Book Value						
Brought forward						
Carried forward						

275 The methods of depreciation used and useful economic lives or depreciation rates should be disclosed in the accounting policy notes (see paragraph 364).

276 There is often a considerable difference between the carrying value and market value of interests in land and buildings not held as investments. Where the trustees consider this to be so material that it needs to be drawn to the attention of the users of the accounts then the difference should be included, with such precision as is practicable, in the notes to the accounts. If it is not practicable to quantify the difference, a written explanation will suffice.

277 Where any class of tangible fixed assets of a charity has been revalued, the notes to the accounts should give:

(a) the name and qualification (if any) of the valuer and whether they are a member of staff or a trustee or external to the charity;

(b) the basis or bases of valuation;

(c) where records are available, the historical cost less depreciation;

(d) date of the previous full valuation;

(e) if the value has not been updated in the reporting period, a statement by the trustees that they are not aware of any material changes since the last valuation.

278 The methods used in the impairment review to determine net realisable value and value in use should be disclosed in the notes to the accounts. This should include details required in paragraph 277.

[5080]

A3: Heritage Assets

279 FRS 15 requires that all tangible fixed assets should be capitalised in the balance sheet (see paragraph 253). In principle this includes tangible fixed assets which are of historical, artistic or scientific importance that are held to advance preservation and conservation objectives of a charity.

280 However, charities will not necessarily need to capitalise such heritage assets (Glossary GL 32) that were acquired in past accounting periods and omitted from previous balance sheets when the circumstances in paragraph 283 below apply.

281 To fall within the definition of heritage assets, the charity must hold the relevant assets in pursuit of preservation or conservation objectives. The objective of the charity may be specifically of a preservation or conservation nature, or the heritage assets may be integral to a broader objective such as educating the public in history, the arts or science as in the case of museums and galleries.

282 Newly purchased heritage assets should be initially measured and recognised at their cost.

283 When heritage assets were acquired in past accounting periods and not capitalised, it may be difficult or costly to attribute a cost or value to them. In such cases these assets may only be excluded from the balance sheet if:

(a) reliable cost information is not available and conventional valuation approaches lack sufficient reliability; or
(b) significant costs are involved in the reconstruction or analysis of past accounting records or in valuation which are onerous compared with the additional benefit derived by users of the accounts in assessing the trustees' stewardship of the assets.

284 The assessment of the costs involved in establishing a cost or valuation for heritage assets and the benefits derived by users of accounts from this information will involve the separate consideration of any material sub-classes of assets held within the heritage asset category. Whilst the cost/benefit test may not be practical to apply on an individual asset by asset basis, it should considered in the context of particular parts or sub-classes of an overall collection. For example, in the context of a general museum valuing a fossil collection may be onerous but valuing its collection of vintage cars may not.

285 FRS 15 provides details of appropriate valuation bases. However, certain heritage buildings, structures or sites may present particular valuation issues. Whilst most specialised buildings can be valued using depreciated replacement cost (see Glossary GL 18), particular issues can arise in attempting to estimate the replacement cost of achieving the same service potential of certain historic buildings. The uniqueness of certain structures that are associated with particular locations, events, individuals or periods in history may be irreplaceable in terms of recreating the same service potential. The same service potential in terms of its heritage value or educational benefit to the public may only be achieved through the original structure or site.

286 Examples of heritage assets for which a cost or valuation may be difficult to attribute include:

(a) museum and gallery collections and other collections including the national archives;
(b) medieval castles, archaeological sites, burial mounds, ruins, monuments and statues.

287 It may also be difficult or costly to attribute a cost or valuation to heritage assets which are donated where such assets are rarely sold on the open market. Where assets are purchased by a party who then shortly afterwards donates the asset to the charity, the purchase price should be considered as reliable cost information and could be used as a reference point for the fair value of donations of similar assets. Where an asset is partly purchased by the charity and partly donated, a reasonable estimate of the cost or value to the charity should be able to be made. Gifts on death or lifetime transfers of significant value may also carry valuations for inheritance tax purposes that may provide sufficient reliability.

288 Heritage assets should be included in a separate row in the balance sheet and can be further analysed, in the notes to the accounts, into classes appropriate to each charity e g collections, artefacts, and historic houses. An appropriate depreciation policy should be applied in accordance with paragraphs 258 to 261. As explained in paragraph 259 certain heritage assets may have an indefinite useful life and a high residual value resulting in any depreciation charge being immaterial.

289 Where assets of historical, scientific or artistic importance are held by a charity but not for preservation or conservation purposes, they cannot be regarded as heritage assets. Examples of assets that do not fall within the heritage assets category include situations where a charity:

(a) holds and occupies an historic building as its administrative offices or as part of a property investment portfolio unrelated to any preservation or educational purpose;
(b) has in its possession works of art, or a collection of historic importance, or antique furnishings within its boardroom, as a store of wealth, the retention of which is unrelated to any objectives of preservation or education;
(c) occupies a functional property that is used to house or display a collection of heritage assets (unless the property itself is held for preservation or conservation purposes).

290 Charities may be required by trust law to retain an asset indefinitely for its own use/benefit and are effectively prohibited from its disposal without external consent. Such assets are termed inalienable. Inalienability, of itself, does not preclude capitalisation of an asset.

291 Inalienable assets that do not fall within the definition of heritage assets, should be capitalised and disclosed in the relevant categories of balance sheet and in related notes. For example:

(a) An investment property will be included as an investment within fixed assets, valued at open market value and disclosed as part of investment properties within the investment notes.
(b) Functional properties used by a charity in undertaking its activities are included within tangible fixed assets and are included at cost or valued on an existing use basis unless of a specialised nature when a depreciated replacement cost (see Glossary GL 18) valuation is adopted.
(c) Tangible fixed assets other than properties are included at cost or valued at open market value.

292 Inalienable assets, by their nature, will belong to a charity's restricted funds, often being permanent endowment.

293 Abbeys, Monasteries, Cathedrals, historic Churches and ancient centres of learning may not meet the heritage asset definition as the preservation of the buildings they occupy is unlikely to be the primary objective of the charity. Such assets might nevertheless be considered integral to the activities of the charity and this may give rise to difficulties in ascertaining an estimate of the current cost of construction of an asset that has the same service potential as the existing one. For example, a new structure could recreate the floor area and seating capacity of a medieval Cathedral but such a structure would not recreate the uniqueness of the original in terms of the religious and historical significance. In such cases a valuation of previously non-capitalised assets may be impractical and the notes should contain a statement to that effect explaining why conventional valuation techniques cannot be applied. Similar issues may arise in the context of artefacts contained within and associated with such structures e g religious artefacts contained within a cathedral or historic church.

Disclosure

294 Information on heritage assets (whether or not they have been capitalised) should be given in the notes to the accounts. The notes should contain:

(a) an analysis or narrative that enables the user to appreciate the age, scale and nature of the heritage assets held and the use made of them;
(b) either:
  (i) details of the cost (or value) of additions and disposals of heritage assets during the year; or
  (ii) where details of cost or value are not available (non-capitalisation in previous periods), a brief description of the nature of the assets acquired or disposed of, together with the sales proceeds of any disposals;
(c) accounting policy notes explaining the charity's capitalisation policy in relation to heritage assets and the measurement bases adopted for their inclusion in the accounts.

[5081]

A4: Investment Assets

295 Investment assets (including investments and investment properties (Glossary GL 39) and cash held for investment purposes) should be classified as a separate category within

fixed assets except where the intention is to realise the asset without reinvestment of the sale proceeds. In such a case, it should be reclassified as a current asset. The reason for this is that investment assets are generally held with the overall intention of retaining them long-term (ie as fixed assets) for the continuing benefit of the charity in the form of income and capital appreciation.

[5082]

Valuation of Investment Assets

296 All investment assets other than programme related investments (see paragraph 308), should be shown in the balance sheet at market value or at the trustees' best estimate of market value as described below. Market value best represents a true and fair view of the value of these assets to the charity, given the duty of the trustees to administer the portfolio of investment assets so as to obtain the best investment performance without undue risk. Investment assets should not be depreciated. All changes in value in the year, whether or not realised, should be reported in the "gains and losses on investment assets" section of the Statement of Financial Activities (see paragraph 219).

297 Most freely tradable investments will have a readily available market price eg shares on a recognised stock exchange. For investment assets for which there is no readily identifiable market price the trustees should adopt a reasonable approach. For example:

(a) Shares in unlisted companies may be valued by reference to their underlying net assets or earnings or the dividend record, as appropriate.

(b) Where the cost of obtaining a valuation by one of the methods in (a) above outweighs the benefit to the users of the accounts, or lacks reliability, the investment may be included at cost.

298 For investment assets other than shares or securities (eg property), the trustees may use any reasonable approach to market valuations which must be done at least every five years, subject only to obtaining advice as to the possibility of any material movements between individual valuations. If there is a material movement the assets must be revalued. Where a charity has a number of such assets it will be acceptable for valuations to be carried out on a rolling basis over a five-year period.

Disclosure

299 The investment asset note to the accounts should disclose separately:

(a) investments held primarily to provide an investment return for the charity; and

(b) programme related investments (Glossary GL 47) that the charity makes primarily as part of its charitable activities.

300 Where values are determined other than by reference to readily available market prices (Glossary GL 41), the notes to the accounts should disclose who has made the valuation, giving:

(a) the name and qualification (if any) of the valuer and whether they are a member of staff or a trustee or external to the charity; and

(b) the basis or bases of valuation.

301 In the rare case where the size or nature of a holding of securities is such that the market is thought by the trustees not to be capable of absorbing the sale of the shareholding without a material effect on the quoted price, the trustees should summarise the position in the notes to the accounts. If they are able to do so, the trustees should give an opinion in the notes to the accounts on how much the market price should be adjusted to take this fact into consideration.

302 The notes to the accounts should show all changes in values of investment assets and reconcile the opening and closing book values. This information may be provided in a table format as set out in Table 9:

TABLE 9. ANALYSIS OF MOVEMENT OF INVESTMENTS

	£
Carrying value (market value) at beginning of year	
Add: Additions to investments at cost	
Less: Disposals at carrying value	
Add/deduct Net gain/(loss) on revaluation	
Carrying value (market value) at end of year	

303 The notes should also show the total value of investment assets at the end of the financial year divided between distinct classes of investment. This would normally include:
- (a) investment properties;
- (b) investments listed on a recognised stock exchange or ones valued by reference to such investments, such as common investment funds, open ended investment companies, and unit trusts;
- (c) investments in subsidiary or associated undertakings or in companies which are connected persons (Glossary GL 50);
- (d) other unlisted securities;
- (e) cash and settlements pending, held as part of the investment portfolio;
- (f) any other investments.

304 Items in categories (a) to (f) of paragraph 303 above should be further analysed between:
- (i) investment assets in the UK (see paragraph 305 below);
- (ii) investment assets outside the UK.

305 The total value of shares or investment schemes (including common investment funds, open ended investment companies and unit trusts) relating to companies listed on a UK stock exchange or incorporated in the UK are treated as investment assets in the UK and no further analysis is required of whether such entities invest their funds in the UK or outside the UK.

306 Further details should be given in the notes to the accounts of any particular investment that is considered material in the context of the investment portfolio.

307 The notes to the accounts should indicate the value of investments held in each category of fund. This may be included in the overall analysis of assets held in the different category of funds (see paragraph 75(a)).

[5083]

A4b: Programme Related Investments

308 Programme related investments are defined in the Glossary (GL 47) and should be disclosed separately within the investment asset category from those investments intended primarily to generate a financial return for the charity.

309 Programme related investments should generally be included in the balance sheet at the amount invested less any impairments (in the case of equity or loans) and any amounts repaid (in the case of loans). Impairments should be charged to resources expended on charitable activities. Similarly a loan subsequently converted to a grant would be charged to charitable activities.

310 Where a gain is made on the disposal of a programme related investment, then the gain should either be set off against any prior impairment loss or included as a gain on disposal of fixed assets for the charity's own use and recorded under "other incoming resources" (see paragraph 147).

Disclosure

311 Where the use of programme related investments forms a material part of the work of the charity, or the amounts form a material part of the investment assets of the charity, the notes to the accounts should show all changes in carrying values of programme related investments, including any impairment losses, and reconcile the opening and closing carrying values of such investments.

312 The notes should also analyse programme related investments held between equity, loan and other investments and indicate the charitable objectives, programmes or projects the investment supports.

[5084]

B: Current Assets

313 Current assets other than current asset investments (see paragraph 296) should normally be recognised at the lower of their cost and net realisable value.

Disclosure

314 Where there are debtors which do not fit into any of the following categories, the headings may be added to or adapted as appropriate to the type of debtor or creditor and nature of the charity. Debtors should be analysed in the notes to the accounts between short term and long term (after more than one year) giving amounts for the following:
- (a) trade debtors;
- (b) amounts due from subsidiary and associated undertakings;
- (c) other debtors;
- (d) prepayments and accrued income.

315 Where long term debtors are material in the context of the total net current assets, they should be separately shown in the balance sheet (see paragraph 249).

316 Where investments are held as current assets the same disclosure is required as for fixed asset investments (see paragraphs 299 to 307).

[5085]

C: Current Liabilities and Long-term Creditors

317 Liabilities should normally be recognised at their settlement value. In the case of provisions, this will be the amount that an entity would rationally pay to settle the obligation at the balance sheet date or to transfer it to a third party at that time and may therefore involve discounting (see paragraph 323).

Disclosure

318 Where there are creditors which do not fit into any of the following categories, the headings may be added to or adapted as appropriate to the type of creditor and nature of the charity. The totals for both short-term and long-term creditors should each be separately analysed in the notes giving amounts for the following:
- (a) loans and overdrafts;
- (b) trade creditors;
- (c) amounts due to subsidiary and associated undertakings;
- (d) other creditors;
- (e) accruals and deferred income.

319 Where a charity is acting as an intermediary agent (as opposed to a custodian trustee) for another organisation, as described in paragraph 112, then any assets held and the associated liabilities should be separately identified in the notes to the accounts but not included in the balance sheet. The notes to the accounts should provide sufficient detail so that the reader of the accounts understands the relationship and nature of the transactions between the charity, the funding organisation and the recipient of the funds.

320 The details in paragraph 319 should also be provided when the charity is acting as an intermediary but is the principal as described in paragraph 113. However, in this case the assets and liabilities will be included in the balance sheet.

[5086]

C3: Provisions for Liabilities and Charges

321 Expenditure resulting from provisions that arise due to a legal or constructive obligation (as per FRS 12) should be accounted for in the Statement of Financial Activities in accordance with paragraphs 148 to 163. Such provisions should be appropriately analysed in the balance sheet between liabilities due within one year and those falling due after one year.

322 The amount recognised as a liability should be the best estimate of the expenditure required to settle the present obligation at the balance sheet date or to transfer it to a third party at that time. When calculating this amount consideration should be given to:
- (a) the timing of the cash flows;
- (b) future events and uncertainties which may affect the amount required to settle the obligation.

323 Where provisions are accrued in the current financial year but are to be paid over several years then future payments may have a reduced value in today's terms (current value). Where the effect is material, the outflow of resources required to settle the obligation at the balance sheet date should be discounted to their present value. The discount rate used should

reflect the current assessments of the time value of money and the risks specific to the provision. The interest rate either for the cost of borrowing or investment could be an appropriate discount rate.

324 The best estimate of the liability should be reviewed at the balance sheet date and adjusted appropriately. If a transfer of resources is no longer needed to settle the obligation then the amount of the liability no longer representing an obligation should be deducted from the resources expended category to which it was originally charged in the Statement of Financial Activities.

325 Where a charity has earmarked part of its unrestricted funds for a particular future purpose, this intention to expend funds in the future is not recognised as a provision for a liability in the accounts. Such earmarked amounts may be recorded by setting up a designated fund (see paragraph 68).

Disclosure

326 Particulars of all material provisions for liabilities and charges accrued in the balance sheet as liabilities should be disclosed in the notes. Similarly, particulars of all material commitments in respect of specific charitable projects should be disclosed if they have not been charged in the accounts.

327 These particulars should include the amounts involved, when the commitments are likely to be met and the movements on commitments previously reported. Particulars of all other material binding commitments should also be disclosed (e g operating leases).

328 The notes should distinguish between those commitments included in the balance sheet as liabilities and those that are intentions to spend and are not included, but in both cases should detail:

(a) the reason for the commitments, giving separate disclosure for material projects;
(b) the total amount of the commitments, including amounts already charged in the accounts;
(c) the amount of commitments outstanding at the start of the year;
(d) any amounts charged in the Statement of Financial Activities for the year;
(e) any amounts released during the year due to a change in the value in the commitments;
(f) the amount of commitments outstanding at the end of the year and an indication as to how much is payable within one year and over one year.

329 Any designated funds relating to intentions to spend not included as liabilities should be separately disclosed as part of the unrestricted funds of the charity and appropriately described in the notes. The purpose of the disclosure is to identify that portion of the unrestricted funds that has been set aside to meet the commitments. Activities that are to be wholly financed from future income would not form part of such designation.

[5087]

D: Defined Benefit Pension Scheme Asset/Liability

330 Any asset or liability derived from a surplus or deficit in a defined benefit pension scheme (calculated in accordance with FRS 17: Retirement Benefits) should be included within this category and disclosed on the face of the balance sheet.

331 A surplus or deficit in a defined benefit scheme will normally give rise to an asset or liability within the unrestricted funds of the reporting charity. The circumstances in which the pension asset or liability may accrue to a restricted fund are set out in paragraphs 433 to 442.

332 Recommendations on the application of FRS 17 to charities and the required accounting methods and disclosures are set out in a separate section on accounting for retirement benefits in paragraphs 430 to 448.

[5088]

E3a: Share Capital

333 A number of charities, e g Industrial and Provident Societies, are constituted with a share capital. A small number of charities incorporated as companies under the Companies Act may also have share capital. Usually this is a nominal amount (such as £10) and although this is legally "owners equity", the prohibition on owners benefiting from this share ownership effectively means that money contributed for share capital forms part of the unrestricted funds of the charity. Nevertheless, company law requires share capital to be shown separately in the balance sheet.

[5089]

E3c: Revaluation Reserve

334 Charities that are companies are required to report, in respect of their unrestricted funds, the difference between the historic cost of fixed assets (including investment assets) and their revalued amount as a revaluation reserve.

[5090]

E3d: Pension Reserve

335 When there is a surplus or a deficit on a defined benefit pension scheme that results in an asset or a liability being recognised by the charity, the recognition of the pension asset or liability will result in the creation of a pension reserve. This reserve will be negative in the case of a liability. If the pension asset or liability relates only to unrestricted funds then this reserve will be part of unrestricted funds. If, however, the criteria set out in paragraphs 438 to 442, are met and the pension asset/liability is allocated to a restricted fund, then the pension reserve will be part of that restricted fund.

[5091]

OTHER BALANCE SHEET MATTERS TO BE COVERED IN THE NOTES TO THE ACCOUNTS

Guarantees

336 All material guarantees given by the charity, and the conditions under which liabilities might arise as a result of such guarantees, should be disclosed in a note to the accounts.

[5092]

Financial Derivative Disclosure

337 There are occasions where charities make use of financial derivative products to ameliorate the risk associated with normal operations (eg currency forward contracts), holding investments or borrowing (eg interest rate hedging). Such derivatives as are used will be in response to a charity's risk management and an explanation of the reasons for their use should be provided as part of the discussion of risk in the Trustees' Annual Report.

338 It is not normally appropriate for charities to hold derivatives for any other reason than to ameliorate risk as this would involve establishing a non-charitable trade. As a result, it would not normally be necessary to value the derivative products separately from the underlying investment or debt.

Disclosure

339 The notes to the accounts should indicate what derivative products are in use by the charity and indicate their impact on the risks of the underlying asset or liability to which they relate. The description of the products held should be in sufficient detail so that the reader of the accounts can understand what the charity's position would have been with, and without the derivatives, and should give an indication of the costs and benefits of the derivative products.

[5093]

Contingent Assets and Liabilities

340 A charity may have contingent assets and liabilities as defined in FRS 12 (Glossary GL 11 and GL 12 and Appendix 2: FRS 12).

341 A charity should not recognise incoming or outgoing resources or gains and losses arising respectively from contingent assets or contingent liabilities in the Statement of Financial Activities or the balance sheet.

342 Contingent assets are not recognised because it could result in the recognition of incoming resources that may never be realised. However, when the realisation of the incoming resources is virtually certain, then the asset is not a contingent asset and the resource/gain arising should be included in the Statement of Financial Activities as an incoming resource and in the balance sheet as a debtor.

343 Where it becomes probable that there will be a future outflow of resources to settle an item previously regarded as a contingent liability, it should cease to be contingent and should be accrued in the accounts. The amount of the liability should (except in extremely rare circumstances where no reliable estimate can be made) be capable of being estimated with reasonable accuracy at the date on which the accounts are approved.

344 The probability of a contingent asset or liability resulting in a future transfer of resources (to or from the charity) should be continually assessed and the recognition of the asset or liability should be reviewed as appropriate.

Disclosure

345 Material contingent assets and liabilities should be disclosed in the notes to the accounts unless the probability of a future transfer of resources (to or from the charity) is extremely remote – in which case no disclosure is necessary.

346 The accounts should disclose the nature of each contingency, the uncertainties that are expected to affect the outcome, and a prudent estimate of the financial effect where an amount has not been accrued. If such an estimate cannot be made, the accounts should explain why it is not practicable to make such an estimate.

347 Where there is more than one contingent asset or liability, they may be sufficiently similar in nature for them to be grouped together as one class and be disclosed in a single statement.

348 Where a liability has been accrued but there is still a contingent liability arising from the same set of circumstances then the notes to the accounts should link the provision and the contingent liability.

[5094]

Loan Liabilities

349 If any specific assets (whether land or other property) of the charity are subject to a mortgage or charge given as security for a loan or other liability, a note to the accounts should disclose:

(a) particulars of the assets which are subject to the mortgage or charge;
(b) the amount of the loan or liability and its proportion to the value of the assets mortgaged or charged.

350 The amounts and interest and repayment terms of all inter-fund loans (including any loans from permanent endowment and summarised, if necessary) should be disclosed in the notes to the accounts. Loans made to trading subsidiaries, the security provided, the interest payable and the repayment terms should be disclosed as a separate item in the notes to the accounts.

[5095]

CASH FLOW STATEMENT

Application

351 The preparation of a cash flow statement is a requirement of FRS 1 for all charities above the small companies thresholds (see Appendix 2: FRS 1). An additional threshold applies to Scottish charities regarding the production of cash flow statements and is set down in regulations made under the Law Reform (Miscellaneous Provisions) (Scotland) Act 1990. The object of the cash flow statement is to show the cash received and used by the charity in the accounting period.

352 Wherever a cash flow statement is prepared it should comply with the requirements of FRS 1 subject to the following paragraphs.

353 The analysis of the cash movements should accord with the charity's operations as reported in its Statement of Financial Activities, and be given in appropriate detail. The starting point will normally be "net incoming/outgoing resources before other recognised gains and losses" in Table 3.

354 Movements in endowments should not be included in cash flows from "operating activities" but should be treated as increases or decreases in the financing section. This is achieved as follows:

(a) cash donations to endowment should be treated as additions to endowment in the "financing" section;
(b) the receipts and payments from the acquisition and disposal of investments should be shown gross in the "capital expenditure and financial investment" section of the cash flow statement. A single row should then be included in this section showing the net movement in cash flows attributable to endowment investments. A corresponding row should be included in the "financing" section for the same amount. The row in the

"financing" section should reflect the cash into/(cash out of) the endowment fund whereas it will be the opposite direction in the "capital expenditure and financial investment" section;

(c) on the rare occasion when payments are made out of permanent endowment this should be shown as a decrease in the "financing" section;

(d) transactions which do not result in cash flows should not be reported in the cash flow statement (e g depreciation, revaluations, accruals,) but may need to be disclosed (see paragraph 355).

Disclosure

355 The disclosure requirements of FRS 1 will depend upon the exact basis of preparation and content of the cash flow statement for each charity but the following are some of the more common disclosures:

(a) major transactions not resulting in cash movements should be disclosed in the notes if necessary for an understanding of the underlying transactions. For instance the release of expendable endowment;

(b) cash (and any financing) movements should be reconciled to the appropriate opening and closing balance sheet amounts; and

(c) a reconciliation of cash flows from "operating activities" within the cash flow statement to the net incoming resources/expenditure row of the Statement of Financial Activities.

[5096]

DISCLOSURE OF ACCOUNTING POLICIES

The Basis of the Preparation of Accounts

356 Charity accounts should include notes on the accounting policies chosen. These should be the most appropriate in the particular circumstances of each charity for the purpose of giving a true and fair view. The policies should be consistent with this SORP, Accounting Standards and relevant legislation. FRS 18: Accounting Policies explains how accounting policies should be determined.

357 Accounting policies are the principles, bases, conventions and rules by which transactions are recognised, measured and presented in the accounts. They are supplemented by estimation techniques where judgement is required in recording the value of incoming and outgoing resources and of assets and liabilities. It is essential that the accounts are accompanied by an explanation of the basis and estimation techniques on which they have been prepared. Accounts are normally prepared on the basis that the charity is a going concern and must include relevant, reliable, comparable and understandable information.

358 The notes regarding the basis of preparation of the accounts should state that the accounts have been prepared in accordance with:

(a) this SORP and accounting standards or with this SORP and the FRSSE (see Appendix 5 paragraphs 5.2.1 to 5.2.2);

(b) the Charities Act or the Companies Act or other legislative requirement; and

(c) the historic cost basis of accounting except for investments (and if applicable, fixed assets) which have been included at revalued amounts.

359 If the accounts depart from accounting standards in any material respect, this should be stated in the accounting policies giving the reason and justification for the departure and the financial impact. Similarly the following details should be given for any material departure from this SORP:

(a) a brief description of how the treatment adopted departs from this SORP;

(b) the reasons why the trustees judge that the treatment adopted is more appropriate to the charity's particular circumstances; and

(c) an estimate of the financial effect on the accounts where this is needed for the accounts to give a true and fair view.

360 If any branches (Glossary GL 4) have been omitted from the accounts, the reason for omission should be given although the individual branches do not need to be named. Reference should also be made to any related organisations (such as supporters associations or subsidiaries not consolidated) explaining the accounting treatment adopted.

[5097]

Specific Policies

361 Trustees should explain in the notes to the accounts the accounting policies they have adopted to deal with material items. Explanations need only be brief but they should be clear,

fair and accurate. Changes to any of the policies that result in a material adjustment to prior periods should be disclosed in detail. The following are some examples of matters for which the accounting policies should be explained where the amounts involved are material. Trustees should only include those notes which are relevant to their charity.

[5098]

Incoming Resources Policy Notes

362 The policy for including each type of material incoming resource should be given. This will normally be on a receivable basis but may need further details in some cases, for instance:

(a) a description of when a legacy is regarded as receivable;
(b) the basis of recognition of gifts in kind and donated services and facilities, specifically covering when such items are not included in the Statement of Financial Activities and the methods of valuation;
(c) the basis of recognition of all grants receivable, including those for fixed assets, and how the grants are analysed between the different types of incoming resources;
(d) whether any incoming resources are deferred and the basis for any deferrals;
(e) the basis for including subscriptions for life membership;
(f) whether the incoming resources from endowment funds are unrestricted or restricted;
(g) whether any incoming resources have been included in the Statement of Financial Activities net of expenditure and the reason for this.

[5099]

Resources Expended Policy Notes

363 These policy notes may include:

(a) The policy for the recognition of liabilities including constructive obligations should be given. Where the liabilities are included as provisions, the point at which the provision is considered to become binding and the basis of any discount factors used in current value calculations for long term commitments should be given. This is particularly applicable to grants, the policy for which should be separately identified.
(b) The policy for including items within the relevant activity categories of resources expended should be given. In particular the policy for including items within:
    (i) costs of generating funds;
    (ii) charitable activities;
    (iii) governance costs.
(c) The methods and principles for the allocation and apportionment of all costs between the different activity categories of resources expended in (b). This disclosure should include the underlying principle i e whether based on staff time, staff salaries, space occupied or other. Where the costs apportioned are material, then further clarification on the method of apportionment used is necessary, including the proportions used to undertake the calculations.

[5100]

Assets Policy Notes

364 The policy for capitalisation of fixed assets for charity use should be stated including:

(a) whether each class of asset is included at cost, valuation or revaluation and the method of valuation where applicable;
(b) the value below which fixed assets are not capitalised;
(c) whether or not heritage assets are capitalised and if not, the reason why (e g lack of reliable information, cost/benefit reason etc: see paragraph 283 to 287), specifying the acquisition and disposal policies for such assets;
(d) the rates of depreciation applying to each class of fixed asset; and
(e) the policy with respect to impairment reviews of fixed assets.

365 The policy for including investments in the accounts should be given. This should be at market value but may need to be modified for the valuation of:

(a) investments not listed on a recognised stock exchange;
(b) investment properties; and
(c) investments in subsidiary undertakings.

366 The basis of inclusion in the Statement of Financial Activities of unrealised and realised gains and losses on investments should be stated.

367 The basis for inclusion of stocks and work in progress (where relevant the amount of unsold or unused goods and materials should be given).

[5101]

Funds Structure Policy Notes

368 A brief description should be given of the different types of fund held by the charity, including the policy for any transfers between funds and allocations to or from designated funds. Transfers may arise, for example, where there is a release of restricted or endowed funds to unrestricted funds or charges are made from the unrestricted to other funds.

369 The policy for determining each designated fund should be stated.

[5102]

Other Policy Notes

370 These could include policies for the recognition of the following:
- (a) pension costs and any pension asset or liability;
- (b) foreign exchange gains and losses;
- (c) treatment of exceptional items;
- (d) treatment of finance and operating leases;
- (e) treatment of irrecoverable VAT.

[5103]

SUMMARY FINANCIAL INFORMATION AND STATEMENTS

General Principles

371 Some charities publish financial information or summaries in a format different from the statutory accounts. Such information or summaries are often included in a non-statutory annual review or in fundraising literature. There are two basic types of such summaries:
- (a) Summarised financial statements which should be based on the full financial statements and communicate key financial information without providing the greater detail required in the full accounts (for example, as contained in the notes to the accounts).
- (b) Summary financial information which presents information on a particular aspect of a charity's finances for example, an analysis of incoming resources or expenditure on particular activities of a charity. Such information does not purport to summarise the full statutory accounts.

372 The distinction between summarised financial statements and summary information is set out in Table 10 below:

TABLE 10. CONTRASTING CHARACTERISTICS OF SUMMARISED FINANCIAL STATEMENTS AND INFORMATION

Characteristics of:	
Summarised financial statements	**Summary financial information**
Includes a summary of the Statement of Financial Activities and/or Balance Sheet.	Draws information from only parts of the accounts.
The summary is derived from statutory accounts.	May be based interim accounts or other financial information as well as statutory accounts.
A financial statement that purports to be a Statement of Activities or Balance Sheet or summary thereof.	Makes no reference to either of these primary statements.
Represents the entire finances of a charity or a charity group.	Represents analysis e g of a particular activity or region.

373 As charitable companies are not listed companies, the provisions of section 252 of the Companies Act 1985 concerning statutory summarised financial statements do not apply. However the provisions of section 240 of the Companies Act 1985 relating to the publication of non-statutory financial statements do apply. The recommendations set out below in relation to summarised financial statements are consistent with these statutory provisions applying to companies. There are no legal provisions for other charities.

374 As the form in which such information or summaries will be produced will vary considerably, depending on the purpose for which they have been prepared, it is not

practicable to give detailed recommendations on the content of summary financial information or summarised financial statements. The general principles which should be followed are set out below.

375 Regardless of the intended circulation of any summary financial information or summarised financial statements, the full Annual Report and accounts must always be produced. Any summarised financial statements:

(a) should contain information on both the Statement of Financial Activities and the balance sheet,
(b) should be consistent with the statutory accounts and
(c) should not be misleading by either omission or inappropriate amalgamation of information.

376 Summary financial information will not necessarily contain information on both the Statement of Financial Activities and balance sheet but should nevertheless present information consistent with the statutory accounts and not be misleading by either omission or inappropriate amalgamation of information.

[5104]

Summarised Financial Statements

377 Summarised financial statements should be accompanied by a statement, signed on behalf of the trustees, indicating:

(a) that they are not the statutory accounts but a summary of information relating to both the Statement of Financial Activities and the balance sheet;
(b) whether or not the full accounts from which the summarised financial statements are derived have as yet been externally scrutinised (whether audit, independent examination, or reporting accountant's report); and
(c) where they have been externally scrutinised, whether the report contained any concerns such as a qualified opinion, limitation of scope, etc;
(d) where the report contains any concerns, e g is qualified, contains an explanatory paragraph or emphasis of matter, sufficient details should be provided in the summarised financial statements to enable the reader to appreciate the significance of the report;
(e) where accounts are produced only for a branch of the charity (see paragraph 77), it must be clearly stated that the summarised financial statements are for the branch only and have been extracted from the full accounts of the reporting charity (giving its name);
(f) details of how the full annual accounts, the external scrutiny report (as applicable) and the Trustees' Annual Report can be obtained;
(g) the date on which the annual accounts were approved; and
(h) for charities registered in England and Wales, say whether or not the Trustees' Annual Report and accounts have been submitted to the Charity Commission.

378 If the full accounts have been externally scrutinised, a statement from the external scrutineer, giving an opinion as to whether or not the summarised financial statements are consistent with the full annual accounts, should be attached.

[5105]

PART III SORP 2005

Summary Financial Information

379 Any other summary financial information, in whatever form, should be accompanied by a statement on behalf of the trustees as to:

(a) the purpose of the information;
(b) whether or not it is from the full annual accounts;
(c) whether or not these accounts have been audited, independently examined or subject to a reporting accountant's report;
(d) details of how the full annual accounts, trustees' report and external scrutiny report (as appropriate) can be obtained.

[5106]

SPECIAL SECTIONS

380 The main text of the SORP deals with the recommended accounting practice for those charities producing full accruals accounts. Some charities will have to meet additional requirements and the following sections have therefore been provided to explain the additional recommendations applicable to particular arrangements or structures that charities may adopt.

(a) Consolidation of Subsidiary Undertakings – paragraphs 381 to 406.

(b) Accounting for Associates, Joint Ventures and Joint Arrangements – paragraphs 407 to 418.
(c) Charitable Companies – paragraphs 419 to 429.
(d) Accounting for Retirement Benefits – paragraphs 430 to 448.
(e) Accounting for Common Investment Funds and Investment Pooling Schemes – paragraphs 449 to 451.

[5107]

CONSOLIDATION OF SUBSIDIARY UNDERTAKINGS

Purpose and Scope

381 The purpose of consolidated accounts is to present a true and fair view of the state of financial affairs of all the group interests of the reporting charity including its subsidiary undertakings. The principles and methods of consolidation are covered by FRS 2. These principles should be applied irrespective of whether the parent charity and its subsidiaries are companies or otherwise constituted.

382 Consolidated accounts are a set of accounts prepared in addition to those prepared for the parent itself and to those prepared for each of the subsidiary undertakings in its own right.

383 A parent charity (Glossary GL 44) should prepare consolidated accounts including all its subsidiary undertakings (Glossary GL 44) except where:

(a) FRS 2 provides for the exclusion of certain subsidiary undertakings from consolidation (see paragraph 384); or
(b) The gross income, after consolidation adjustments, (Glossary GL 31) of the group in the accounting period is no more than the threshold for a statutory charity audit (see Appendix 4); or
(c) The results of the subsidiary undertaking(s) are not material to the group; or
(d) The subsidiary is not a company and, by virtue of being a special trust or a charity subject to a uniting direction under s 96 (5) or (6) of the Charities Act 1993, has had its accounts aggregated with that of the parent charity.

384 FRS 2 allows subsidiaries to be excluded from consolidation in certain limited circumstances (severe long-term restrictions which substantially hinder the exercise of the parent undertaking's rights over the subsidiary undertaking's assets or management or subsidiary held only for sale). It is unlikely that these exclusions will generally apply to a charitable group.

385 Charities utilise subsidiary undertakings for a variety of purposes including undertaking non-charitable trading, for investment purposes and carrying out charitable activities. The difference between profit and not-for-profit undertakings is not sufficient of itself to justify non-consolidation. However, where a subsidiary undertaking is a registered company which is insolvent and is being wound up then the subsidiary undertaking can be excluded from consolidation.

[5108]

Charitable Subsidiaries

386 Most non-company charitable subsidiaries will be included in the aggregated accounts of the controlling charity, as they will either be restricted funds or endowment funds of the charity (see Paragraph 383(d)). However, on occasions, a charity may control another charitable entity that does not meet the definition of a special trust, for example, because the objects of the subsidiary are wider than those of the parent charity. Where the tests for control (the parent's ability to direct and benefit) are met, the charitable subsidiary should be consolidated. Benefit to a parent charity may arise where the services and benefits provided by the charitable subsidiary to its own beneficiaries also contribute to the objectives of the parent charity or in terms of cash flow to the parent charity. Where (unusually) a subsidiary charity's objects are substantially different from the parent charity, the benefit test of control will not be met and so no consolidation should take place.

387 A subsidiary that is a charity with objects narrower than its parent will need to be accounted for by the use of one or more restricted fund columns in the consolidated accounts.

[5108A]

Determining whether a Subsidiary undertaking meets the Control test

388 Subsidiary undertakings can be identified by the measure of control (Glossary GL 44) exercised by the parent charity. FRS 2 outlines how such control can be determined in the context of:

(a) voting rights (mainly stemming from share ownership) and/or
(b) dominant influence over the board or activities of the subsidiary.

This embodies the requirements of the Companies Act 1985 which should be followed by those undertakings registered under this Act.

389 A similar relationship to that of a parent and subsidiary undertaking may arise where the parent charity transacts with another undertaking in such a way that all the risks and rewards of the transactions remain with the parent undertaking. An example is when the ownership of the assets is transferred to another entity whilst retaining exclusive use of those assets and meeting the costs of maintaining them. Such undertakings are regarded as quasi-subsidiaries and should be accounted for in accordance with FRS 5.

390 A charity, however constituted, should be regarded as a subsidiary undertaking where the parent charity has the power to exercise, or actually exercises, dominant influence or control over the subsidiary or the parent and subsidiary are managed on a unified basis. Control can arise in any of the following situations:

(a) the charity trustees and/or members and or employees of the parent charity are, or have the right to appoint or remove, a majority of the charity trustees of the subsidiary charity; or
(b) the governing document of the subsidiary charity reserves to the parent charity's trustees and/or members the right to direct, or to give consent to, the exercise of significant discretion by the trustees of the subsidiary charity.

391 The basis for treating a non-company charity as a subsidiary is that the connection between it and some other charity is such that the operating and financial policies of the former are likely to be set in accordance with the wishes of the latter. This is likely to be the case where one of the relationships described in the previous paragraph exists, but trustees may, in a particular case, be able to produce evidence to the contrary.

392 Where the objects of a charity are substantially or exclusively confined to the benefit of another charity, the issue of control requires particular consideration. For example, friends' groups, on occasions, form separate charities to give support to an established charity whilst retaining legal discretion as to the nature and timing of its support. In such cases the formal powers identified in paragraph 390 may not exist but dominant influence may arise less formally. For example, the benefiting charity may set out in outline the nature or timing of the support it wants to achieve. Alternatively the parent charity may intervene on a critical matter. Where evidence exists of such dominant influence being exercised the criteria for consolidation should be regarded as being met.

[5109]

Method of Consolidation

393 The normal rules will apply regarding the method of consolidation, which should be carried out on a line-by-line basis as set out in FRS 2.

394 All items of incoming resources and resources expended should be shown gross after the removal of intra-group transactions. Clearly it is desirable that similar items are treated in the same way. For instance, incoming resources from activities to generate funds in the charity should be combined with similar activities in the subsidiary, and charitable activities within the charity should be combined with similar activities in the subsidiary. Similarly, costs of generating funds and/or governance costs in the subsidiary should be aggregated with those of the charity.

395 Each charity should choose appropriate category headings within the permissible format of the Statement of Financial Activities and suitable amalgamations of activities. The headings used should reflect the underlying activities of the group. If it is not possible to exactly match items between the subsidiary undertaking and the parent charity, segmental information should be provided so that the results of the parent charity and each subsidiary undertaking are transparent (see paragraph 405).

[5110]

Filing of Accounts with Charity Commission (England and Wales)

396 Although consolidated accounts must be prepared under accounting standards, in England and Wales the Charities Act 1993 requires the individual charity's accounts to be filed with the Charity Commission. To meet these requirements, where the group and parent charity's accounts are included in the same set of consolidated accounts, as well as two balance sheets there should be two Statements of Financial Activities (one for the group and one for the parent).

397 However, consolidated accounts are often filed with the Commission omitting the Statement of Financial Activities for the parent charity. The Commission is prepared to accept these accounts as long as gross income/turnover and results of the parent charity are clearly disclosed in the notes. The group accounts must still contain the entity balance sheet of the parent charity. The Commission retains the power to require the production and filing of any individual charity Statement of Financial Activities and similarly members of the public have a legal right to request this statement.

Disclosure

398 There should be a separate comment in the Trustees' Annual Report concerning the activities and performance of each of the charity's material subsidiary undertakings (see paragraph 53).

399 Where consolidated accounts are prepared, the policy notes should state the method of consolidation and which subsidiaries or associated entities are included and excluded from the consolidation.

400 The notes to the consolidated accounts should give the position of the group as well as the parent undertaking.

401 The notes to the accounts should state the aggregate amount of the total investment of the charity in its subsidiary undertakings and, unless the subsidiary is not material, in relation to each one:

(a) its name;
(b) particulars of the parent charity's shareholding or other means of control;
(c) how its activities relate to those of the charity;
(d) the aggregate amount of its assets, liabilities and funds;
(e) a summary of its turnover and expenditure and its profit or loss for the year (or equivalent categories for charitable subsidiary undertakings).

402 If there are any minority interests external to the group, similar details to those in the above paragraph should be provided relating to the minority interest held in the subsidiary undertakings including any restrictions that may be placed on the group's activities.

403 If a charity has a large number of subsidiary undertakings such that the disclosure in paragraph 401 would result in information of excessive length being given, the information need only be given in respect of those undertakings whose results or financial position materially affected the figures shown in the charity's annual accounts. The full disclosure should be made available (in the same way as the accounts) to any member of the public upon request.

404 In addition, if, following paragraphs 383 to 384, subsidiary undertakings are excluded or consolidated accounts are not prepared then the trustees should explain the reasons in a note to the charity's accounts with reference to each excluded subsidiary undertaking.

405 As stated in paragraph 395 segmental information may need to be provided where the aggregation and adjustments required to consolidate financial information may obscure information about the different undertakings and the activities included in the consolidated accounts. It is important that the presentation adopted and disclosure in the notes is sufficiently detailed to distinguish the key results of the charity from those of its subsidiary undertakings. Examples of those items that should be separately disclosed include the costs of generating funds, the costs of charitable activities and governance costs.

406 In consolidated accounts, funds or reserves retained by subsidiary undertakings other than funds available to be used in carrying out the charity's objects should be included under an appropriate separate fund heading in the balance sheet (eg funds retained within a non-charitable subsidiary).

[5111]

ASSOCIATES, JOINT VENTURES AND JOINT ARRANGEMENTS

Introduction

407 This section explains the additional accounting requirements in consolidated accounts where a charity has associates, joint ventures or joint arrangements.

[5112]

Identification

408 FRS 9 covers the accounting for associates, joint ventures and joint arrangements and provides detailed guidance on how to determine the relationship between the entities involved. Where these exist, consolidated accounts should be prepared subject to the exemptions in paragraph 383.

409 Where a charity has a long term participating interest in another undertaking and exercises significant influence over its operating and financial policy then this is likely to be an associate undertaking. Where a charity beneficially holds 20% or more of the voting rights in any undertaking, it will be presumed to have a participating interest and significant influence over its operating and financial policy, unless the contrary is shown.

410 Charities providing grants or making programme related investments may on occasions combine funding with the provision of advice or expertise and on occasions may be invited by the recipient charity to provide or nominate a charity trustee with particular skills or expertise. Where the recipient charity operates with a small trustee body, this might be construed as creating an associate. An associate will be created if the nomination or appointment is used in conjunction with a formal or informal agreement to exercise significant influence through direct involvement in setting the recipient charity's operating and financial polices. Where the charity trustee appointment is simply used to provide advice or expertise to the recipient charity whilst allowing the charity to adopt its own policies and strategies then an associate relationship is unlikely to be created.

411 In a joint venture situation, a separate entity is jointly controlled by two or more undertakings, all of which have a say in the operations of the joint venture, so that no single investing undertaking controls the joint venture but all together can do so. It is possible for a charity to beneficially hold 20% or more of the voting rights in an undertaking but for the management arrangements to be such that control is clearly shared with the other partners and hence the undertaking is a joint venture as opposed to an associate.

412 Often charities also undertake joint arrangements where they may carry out activities in partnership with other bodies but without establishing a separate legal entity.

[5113]

Methods of Accounting for Associates, Joint Ventures and Joint Arrangements

413 **Associates** should be included in the accounts based on the net equity method. The consolidated Statement of Financial Activities should show the net interest in the results for the year in the associates as a separate row after the "net incoming resources/(resources expended) before transfers" row . In the balance sheet, the net interest in associates should be shown as a separate row within fixed asset investments. Where the charity's rights to the associate's assets are severely limited (eg because the majority prohibit any dividend distribution) then this should be reflected in the valuation.

414 **Joint ventures** should be accounted for on a gross equity method. This method requires the reporting entity to present its share of the gross incoming resources of joint ventures on the face of the consolidated profit and loss account (Statement of Financial Activities in charities). However, this does not form part of the group incoming resources and must be clearly distinguished. For charities this can be achieved by including gross incoming resources from joint ventures in the Statement of Financial Activities on a line-by-line basis with an additional row showing the total share of gross incoming resources from joint ventures as a reduction in total incoming resources. In addition a row showing the net interest in the results for the year in the joint ventures as a separate row after the "net incoming resources/(resources expended)" row must be included (this may be combined with that of the associates). In the balance sheet the share of the gross assets and the gross liabilities should be shown in a linked presentation within fixed assets investments.

415 Where there are gains and losses on investments and unrealised gains on other fixed assets, the net share relating to associates should be shown on a separate row, with the gross share relating to joint ventures being shown either on a separate row or combined with the appropriate lines on the Statement of Financial Activities.

416 Where there is a **joint arrangement**, the charity's gross share of the incoming resources and resources expended and the assets and liabilities should be included in the accounts in the same way as for a branch per paragraphs 77 to 81. If under the arrangement the charity is jointly and severally liable for an obligation, it should accrue the part of the obligation for which it is responsible and treat the part of the obligation which is expected to be met by the other parties as a contingent liability.

Disclosure

417 The following disclosure should be given in respect of each associate and joint venture and this will normally be compliant with FRS 9:

(a) its name;
(b) the charity's shareholding and other interests in it;
(c) the nature of the activities of the associate or joint venture;

(d) the charity's interest in the results showing separately its share in:
  (i) gross incoming resources by type;
  (ii) costs of generating funds;
  (iii) expenditure on charitable activities;
  (iv) expenditure on governance;
  (these first four items may need to be adapted in the case of associates or joint ventures that are not charities)
  (v) the net results (where tax is payable, the share of the results pre and post tax and the share in the tax should be shown);
  (vi) gains or losses on investments and the share in unrealised gains on other fixed assets;
  (vii) fixed assets;
  (viii) current assets;
  (ix) liabilities under one year;
  (x) liabilities over one year;
  (xi) the different funds of the charity;
  (xii) contingent liabilities and other commitments;

(e) particulars of any qualifications contained in any audit or other statutory report on its accounts, and any note or reservation in those accounts to call attention to a matter which, apart from the note or reservation, would properly have been referred to in such a qualification.

418 For joint arrangements, the notes to the accounts should provide appropriate details of the charity's commitments in the arrangement.

[5114]

THE SORP IN RELATION TO CHARITABLE COMPANIES IN THE UK

Introduction

419 This section explains the position of this SORP with respect to charitable companies. In following this SORP, charitable companies will normally meet most of the reporting requirements under the Companies Act. However, the SORP does not reproduce these requirements in full and a charity should have regard to its own circumstances when considering the application of the Companies Act. In addition to following the main section of this SORP and the other special sections as applicable, there are certain further requirements which must be met by charitable companies. Ways of meeting the most common of these requirements are suggested below, but these too should be considered in the light of the company's individual circumstances.

[5115]

Accounts and Reports

420 Charitable companies must comply with the Companies Act 1985 with respect to the form and content of their accounts. This Act also stipulates the contents of the annual (directors') report. In England and Wales, strictly, the directors of charitable companies have to prepare both that report, and the Trustees' Annual Report under Part VI of the Charities Act 1993, but the Charity Commission is prepared to accept the directors' report for filing under Part VI if it also contains the information required under Part VI. Charitable companies (unlike non company charities) do not have an exemption to leave out the names of the directors from the Annual Report.

421 The Companies Act 1985 requires a company to prepare annual financial statements which give a true and fair view of its state of affairs at the end of the year and of its profit and loss for that year. In addition, Paragraph 3.(3) of Part 1, section A of Schedule 4 to this Act requires the directors to adapt the headings and subheadings of the balance sheet and profit and loss account in any case where the special nature of the company's business requires such adaptation.

422 The requirement to show a true and fair view and to adapt the accounts for the special nature of charity means that there is a strong presumption that charitable companies will, in all but exceptional circumstances, have to comply with this SORP in order to meet the requirements of company law. Particulars of any material departures from this SORP are required to be disclosed in accordance with paragraph 359.

[5116]

The Statement of Financial Activities and the Summary Income and Expenditure Account

423 All charitable companies registered under the Companies Act 1985 must include an income and expenditure account in their financial statements. The Statement of Financial

Activities is designed to include all the gains and losses of a charity which would be found in both the income and expenditure account *and* the statement of total recognised gains and losses as required by FRS 3. A separate income and expenditure account is therefore not necessarily required. Circumstances where it will probably be required may arise where the income and expenditure account cannot be separately identified within the Statement of Financial Activities and there are items which may be open to challenge if they are included in an income and expenditure account, such as:

(a) movement on endowment (capital) funds during the year; and
(b) unrealised gains and losses arising during the year.

Whilst unrealised gains and losses are not allowed in the income and expenditure account, most of these are included in the Statement of Financial Activities below the point at which a conventional income and expenditure account would end as explained in paragraph 424. Furthermore – where charities adopt a policy of continuous revaluation of investments (as explained in paragraph 219) there may be no realised gains to report and all the revaluation movements will be classified as unrealised gains.

424 Where the Statement of Financial Activities of a charitable company does not include any of the items in paragraph 423, it may not need to produce a separate summary income and expenditure account but the headings in the Statement of Financial Activities should be changed so that:

(a) the title clearly indicates that it includes an income and expenditure account and statement of total recognised gains and losses (if required); and
(b) there is a prominent sub total entitled "net income/(expenditure) for the year" which replaces or is in addition to the heading of "net incoming/(outgoing) resources for the year".

Care should also be taken to ensure that all realised gains and losses are included in the Statement of Financial Activities in such a way that they fall within the bounds of the headings for (a) and (b) within the income and expenditure account. Particular attention may need to be given to impairment losses and reversals which, in accordance with the guidance in FRS 11, are realised in some circumstances and unrealised in others.

425 Where a summary income and expenditure account is required, it should be derived from and cross-referenced to the corresponding figures in the Statement of Financial Activities. It need not distinguish between unrestricted and restricted income funds but the accounting basis on which items are included must be the same as in the Statement of Financial Activities. It should show separately in respect of continuing operations, acquisitions and discontinued operations:

(a) gross income from all sources;
(b) net gains/losses from disposals of all fixed assets belonging to the charity's income funds;
(c) transfers from endowment funds of amounts previously received as capital resources and now converted into income funds for expending;
(d) total income (this will be the total of all incoming resources – other than revaluation gains – of all the income funds but not for any endowment funds);
(e) total expenditure out of the charity's income funds;
(f) net income or expenditure for the year. In practice, the format may need to be modified to comply with specific statutory requirements or those of the charity's own governing document.

426 Charitable companies which require a summary income and expenditure account and which prepare consolidated accounts should prepare a summary income and expenditure account for the group.

[5117]

Revaluation Reserve

427 Where fixed assets are revalued upwards, a revaluation reserve will arise being the difference between the original depreciated cost or valuation of the asset and the revalued amount. Separate reporting of the reserve is not significant for charities as they do not distribute profits, but a revaluation reserve will, nevertheless, arise. This will form part of the funds in which the revalued assets are held. In certain circumstances (as described in FRSs 11 and 15), impairment losses or other downward revaluations can be offset against the revaluation reserve.

428 To comply with the Companies Act 1985, charitable companies must separately disclose the revaluation reserve in respect of their unrestricted funds within the relevant funds section on the face of the balance sheet but may change the heading as appropriate. This may be best effected by use of a prominent inset.

[5118]

Summary Financial Information

429 Charitable companies should follow the recommendations in paragraphs 371 to 379 but their summary financial information should also include a statement indicating whether or not the statutory accounts for the relevant year(s) have been delivered to the Registrar of Companies.

[5119]

ACCOUNTING FOR RETIREMENT BENEFITS

Introduction

430 There are two main types of retirement benefit schemes: defined contribution schemes and defined benefit schemes. Definitions for both appear in the glossary (GL 16 & GL 17). Details of how to account for each are included in this section.

431 A charity participating in a multi-employer defined benefit scheme, where the contributions are set in relation to the current service period only, or where the charity is unable to identify its share of the underlying assets and liabilities on a consistent or reasonable basis, should account for its contributions to the scheme as if it were a defined contribution scheme. Where a charity is unable to identify its share of the underlying assets and liabilities of the scheme, the disclosures set out in paragraph 446 should be provided.

[5120]

Defined Contribution Schemes

432 The cost of a defined contribution scheme recognised in the accounts is equal to the contributions payable to the scheme in the accounting period. These pension costs should be allocated across the relevant resources expended categories of the Statement of Financial Activities set out in paragraph 177. The note disclosures in relation to such schemes are set out in paragraph 445.

[5121]

Defined Benefit Schemes

433 FRS 17: Retirement Benefits substantially affects charities that operate defined benefit schemes (see Appendix 2: FRS 17). The surplus/deficit in a defined benefit scheme is the excess/shortfall of the value of the assets in the scheme over/below the present value of the scheme liabilities. In accordance with FRS 17 principles:

(a) An asset should be recognised to the extent that the employer charity is able to recover a surplus either through reduced contributions in the future or through refunds from the scheme.

(b) A liability should be recognised to the extent that it reflects its legal or constructive obligation of the employer charity.

Similar principles should also be adopted in relation to the provision of death-in-service and incapacity benefits, that are not wholly insured, and provided through a defined benefit pension scheme.

434 Full actuarial valuations of a defined benefit scheme should be undertaken by an independent, qualified actuary at intervals not exceeding three years and updated annually at the charity's balance sheet date to reflect current conditions.

435 A surplus or deficit in a defined benefit scheme normally gives rise to an asset or liability within unrestricted funds of the reporting charity. The reporting charity will normally be the employer and have control as to the future use of a surplus recovered either in the form of reduced contributions or a refund from the scheme. Similarly, where a liability arises through a legal or constructive obligation to make good a deficit, this liability will normally rest with the main charity's unrestricted funds.

[5122]

Allocation of Retirement Benefit Costs and Gains

436 The change in the defined benefit asset or liability (other than that arising from contributions payable to the scheme which affect the surplus or deficit in the scheme) should be analysed into the components identified in FRS 17. However these will only be recognised through the Statement of Financial Activities on full implementation of FRS 17. (See Appendix 2 for FRS 17 implementation date and transitional arrangements).

437 Pension costs may be allocated between the resources expended categories of the Statement of Financial Activities on the basis of the charity's own computations. The basis of

the allocation should be reasonable and consistent. Allocations of pension costs based on the staff costs of employees within the scheme is one approach, although other approaches (eg allocation based on pension contributions payable) may also produce an equitable allocation. Allocation of the components should be based on the following:

(a) The changes relating to current or past service costs and gains, and losses on settlements and curtailments should be allocated to the appropriate resources expended categories set out in paragraph 432.
(b) Pension finance costs arising from changes in the net of the interest costs and expected return on assets should be allocated to the appropriate resources expended categories set out in paragraph 432. Income arising from these changes should be recognised as an incoming resource and separately disclosed where material.
(c) Where past service costs, or gains or losses on settlements or curtailment, are material in the context of the particular expenditure (or income) category in which they are recognised, the amounts should be disclosed as exceptional in accordance with FRS 3 – Reporting Financial Performance (see Appendix 2).
(d) Actuarial gains and losses arising should be recognised within the "gains and losses" categories of the Statement of Financial Activities under the heading "actuarial gains and losses on defined benefit pension scheme".

[5123]

Restricted Funds

438 A pension asset should be recognised as accruing to a restricted fund only where it can be demonstrated that the economic benefit of the asset will accrue to a particular fund through reduced contributions or refunds. Similarly, a pension liability should be allocated to a particular fund only where it is demonstrable that a constructive liability arises to fund the deficit and could properly be met from the particular fund. Such a situation may arise where staff are specifically engaged on a long-term project funded from restricted income. This allocation may be undertaken on the basis of the charity's own computations. Liaison with the provider of a particular restricted fund may be necessary in order to establish the basis on which any pension asset or liability is allocated to that fund and therefore the pension costs that may be properly charged through it.

439 Any allocation of a pension asset or liability to a restricted fund should be reviewed on an annual basis. Where staff changes or cessation of a particular project indicate that the economic benefits or obligations will no longer accrue to that particular fund then the asset or liability should be allocated to the unrestricted funds by means of a transfer of funds through the Statement of Financial Activities.

440 Where the criteria for the recognition of a pension asset or liability within restricted funds are met, the related pension costs should be recognised within the restricted funds column of the Statement of Financial Activities. The components of the pension cost should be recognised within the same Statement of Financial Activities categories and on the same basis as set out in the preceding paragraphs.

441 A restricted fund may, however, incur staff costs without the criteria for the recognition of a pension asset or liability within the restricted fund's balance sheet being met. For example, a restricted fund may be of a short-term nature or staff may be frequently transferred between activities creating uncertainty as to the fund which will ultimately recover any surplus or meet future contributions resulting from any deficit. In such circumstances, the restricted funds column of the Statement of Financial Activities may still be recharged with an appropriate portion of the current service cost component of the pension cost relating to the staff engaged in activities within restricted funds. Such a recharge within the Statement of Financial Activities would, as with any recharge, also necessitate a balance sheet adjustment between fund balances. The balance sheet of the unrestricted funds should, however, continue to recognise the overall pension asset or liability.

442 When past service costs and gains and losses on curtailments and settlements arise, such costs may be recharged to restricted funds only when a charity can demonstrate the costs relate to present staff engaged in the activities of the restricted funds.

Disclosures

443 The disclosure requirements for pension scheme contributions are given in FRS 17. This section summarises the key points.

444 Where a defined contribution scheme is operated by a charity, the notes to the accounts should disclose:

(a) the nature of the scheme,
(b) the costs for the accounting period and

PART III SORP 2005

(c) the amount of any outstanding or prepaid contributions at the year end.

445 FRS 17 disclosure requirements for defined benefit pension schemes are detailed and charities should refer to the text of the standard in completing their disclosure notes. The notes to the accounts should include the following information:

(a) the nature of the scheme;
(b) the date of the most recent full actuarial valuation;
(c) the contributions made in the accounting period and any agreed contribution rates for future years;
(d) the main financial assumptions used at the beginning of the period and at the balance sheet date;
(e) the fair value of scheme assets analysed between equities, bonds and other assets and their expected rates of returns;
(f) the present value of the scheme liabilities and the resulting surplus or deficit compared with the fair value of the scheme assets;
(g) an analysis of the amounts for each of the component parts of the defined benefit costs charged or credited through the Statement of Financial Activities.

446 Where a charity operating a defined benefit scheme has established that the employer's share of underlying assets and liabilities cannot be identified on a consistent and reasonable basis (e g by confirmation from the scheme administrators or actuaries) this fact should be disclosed. Any available information about the existence of the surplus or deficit in the scheme and the implications of that surplus or deficit for the employing charity should be disclosed together with a brief explanation of the general circumstances giving rise to this position.

447 When a charity operating a defined benefit scheme discloses a material pension liability, the notes to the accounts (or Trustees' Annual Report in the explanation of the policy on reserves) should explain the impact, if any, on resources available for general application. If a pension liability exceeds the balance on unrestricted funds, the note should also explain any limitations placed on any restricted fund of the charity to contribute to any resource requirements arising from the disclosed liability.

448 If a material pension asset is disclosed, the notes to the accounts (or Trustees' Annual Report) should explain the nature of the economic benefit derived from the asset and give an indication of the period over which any benefit in terms of reduced contributions will accrue to the charity.

[5124]

COMMON INVESTMENT FUNDS AND INVESTMENT POOLING SCHEMES

449 The trustees of Common Investment Funds (CIFs) in England and Wales, other than pooling scheme funds (see paragraph 450), should prepare their accounts and Trustees' Annual Report in accordance with the relevant accounts and reports regulations for CIFs made under part VI of the Charities Act 1993 (regulations planned for 2005 will ensure these requirements are consistent with the SORP for Authorised Funds issued by the Investment Management Association in November 2003) and any subsequent regulations which may be made. The trustees of Common Deposit Funds (CDFs) should also meet the relevant requirements that regulations place on such funds.

450 Some charities may operate a pooling scheme (Glossary GL 46) for the investments under the control of a single body of trustees common to the investing charities. Sometimes such arrangements are governed by a formal Charity Commission scheme but the pooling of investments may also be an informal arrangement under the Trustee Act 2000. This SORP does not provide details on how to operate or manage pooling schemes where underlying investments funds are apportioned between the investing charities or their funds on a similar basis to that adopted by unit trusts.

451 Where a pooling scheme holds investments for the separate funds of a single reporting charity, the scheme will form a restricted fund of the reporting charity. The assets of the pooled fund are the investments held and its liabilities are the share of these investments due to the funds of the reporting charity which have invested through the pooling arrangements. Its income and costs will accrue to the funds investing in the pool. Therefore, when accounts are prepared for the reporting charity, the assets, investment income and related costs of the pooling scheme fund will appear in the funds investing in the pool. The notes to the accounts simply disclose the pooling of investments with the underlying investments, income and costs being disclosed as part of the investment disclosures of the reporting charity. Thus to the reader of the accounts the pool will not be visible as a separate fund.

[5125]

APPENDICES

APPENDIX 1
GLOSSARY

GL 1 Activity Classification of costs

1.1 An "activity classification of costs" is the aggregation of costs incurred in pursuit of a defined activity (e g provision of services to elderly people or counselling), and is achieved by adding together all the costs (salaries, rents, depreciation etc) relating to that specific activity.

1.2 The three main 'high level' activities that charities preparing accruals accounts will report on are generating funds, charitable activity and governance costs of the charity.

GL 2 Actuarial Gains and Losses

2.1 Changes in the actuarial deficits or surpluses that arise because the actuarial assumptions, in relation to pension or other retirement benefit schemes, have changed or events have not coincided with the actuarial assumptions made for the last valuation.

GL 3 Audit Threshold

3.1 This is the threshold (which may include income, expenditure and asset limits) above which a charity will be required to have a statutory audit.

GL 4 Branches

4.1 "Branches" (which may also be known as supporters' groups, friends' groups, members' groups, communities or parishes which are part of a common trust etc.) are entities or administrative bodies set up, for example, to conduct a particular aspect of the activities of the reporting charity, or to conduct the activities of the reporting charity in a particular geographical area. They may or may not be legal entities which are separate from the reporting charity.

4.2 For the purpose of this SORP a "branch" is either:
- (a) simply part of the administrative machinery of the reporting charity; or
- (b) a fund shown in the accounts as a restricted or endowment fund. Two types of entity are covered by this category, each of which should be treated as linked to the reporting charity for accounting purposes:
  - (i) a separate *legal entity* which is administered by, or *on behalf of*, the reporting charity and whose funds are held for specific purposes which are within the general purposes of the reporting charity. "*Legal entity*" means a trust or unincorporated association or other body formed for a charitable purpose. The words "*on behalf of*" should be taken to mean that, under the constitution of the separate entity, a substantial degree of influence can be exerted by the reporting charity over the administration of its affairs; or,
  - (ii) in England and Wales, a separate legal entity not falling within (i) which the Charity Commission has united by a direction under section 96(5) or 96(6) of the Charities Act 1993 should be treated as linked to the reporting charity for accounting purposes.

4.3 This definition has been adopted to reflect the provisions of the Charities Act 1993 allocating responsibility for accounting in the case of multicellular charities. FRS 2 expressly disapplies its requirements where they are not consistent with a particular statutory accounting framework. Consequently, charitable bodies which are controlled by other charitable bodies will not normally be subject to the requirements of that standard where they are treated as "special trusts" under the Charities Act 1993 or are the subject of a direction as mentioned above in paragraph 4.2(b)(ii). Also see the definition of "parent undertaking and subsidiary undertaking" (see GL 44 below).

4.4 Some of the characteristics of a branch are:
- (a) it uses the name of the reporting charity within its title;
- (b) it exclusively raises funds for the reporting charity and/or for its own local activities;
- (c) it uses the reporting charity's registration number to receive tax relief on its activities;
- (d) it is perceived by the public to be the reporting charity's local representative or its representative for a particular purpose;
- (e) it receives support from the reporting charity through advice, publicity materials, etc.

4.5 If the branch exists to carry out the primary objects of the charity, typically it will receive funds from the reporting charity for its work and may be staffed by employees of the reporting charity.

PART III
SORP 2005

4.6 If the branch is not a separate legal entity, all funds held by a branch will be the legal property of the reporting charity, whether or not the branch has a separate bank account.

Organisations which are not Branches

4.7 Some charities may be known as "branches" within a particular organisational or network structure, but if their level of administrative autonomy from the reporting charity – as determined by their constitutions – is such that legislation requires them to be treated as separate accounting entities, then they should not be regarded as "branches" for accounting purposes but should prepare separate accounts for submission to the appropriate regulatory authority. Such "branches" may also be subsidiaries.

4.8 Other examples of organisations which are not "branches" for the purpose of these recommendations include:

(a) groups of people who occasionally gather together to raise funds for one or a number of different charities and

(b) special interest groups who are affiliated to a particular charity, but do not themselves undertake charitable activities (including fundraising for the charity).

GL 5 Capital

5.1 In the context of charity law "capital" means resources which become available to a charity and which the trustees are legally required to invest or retain and use for its purposes. "Capital" may be permanent endowment, where the trustees have no power to convert it into income and apply it as such, or expendable endowment, where they do have this power (see Appendix 3).

5.2 Capital is also used in its various accounting meanings, such as the capital elements of fixed assets, working capital or share capital.

GL 6 Charity

6.1 A "charity" is any institution established for purposes which are exclusively charitable. Where the institution is involved in more than one activity, operates more than one fund, or is not centralised into one unit of operation, the term is used in this statement to include all those activities, units and funds which fall within the scope of either a single governing instrument (or instruments supplemental to the main instrument) or for which the trustees are otherwise legally liable to account (eg branches, as defined in paragraph GL 4 above).

GL 7 Charity Trustees

7.1 "Charity trustees" has the same meaning as in s 97(1) of the Charities Act 1993, that is the persons having the general control and management of the administration of a charity regardless of what they are called. Custodian trustees and nominees are not within this definition (see GL 59).

7.2 For instance, in the case of an unincorporated association the executive or management committee are its charity trustees, and in the case of a charitable company it is the directors who are the charity trustees.

7.3 Those concerned in any way with the administration of charities should note that the status of a charity trustee is defined in terms of the function to be performed, and not by reference to the title given to any office, or membership of any committee or committees.

GL 8 Common Investment Funds

8.1 Common Investment Funds (CIFs) are collective investment schemes that are similar to authorised unit trusts and are for charity investors only. They are investment vehicles providing diversification of investment to reduce risk, and are tax efficient, administratively simple and cost efficient. They are deemed by law to be charities themselves and enjoy the same tax status as other charities.

8.2 CIFs set up by schemes made by the Charity Commission under section 22 of the Charities Act 1960 or section 24 of the Charities Act are open only to charities in England and Wales.

GL 9 Connected Charities

9.1 "Connected charities" are those which have common, parallel or related objects and activities; and either:

(a) common control; or

(b) unity of administration (eg shared management).

9.2 Within this category may be charities which come together under one umbrella organisation or are part of a federal structure. Also see related parties (GL 50).

GL 10 Constructive Obligation

10.1 An obligation that derives from an entity's actions where:

(a) by an established pattern of past practice, published policies or a sufficiently specific current statement, the entity has indicated to other parties that it will accept certain responsibilities; and

(b) as a result, the entity has created a valid expectation on the part of those other parties that it will discharge those responsibilities.

GL 11 Contingent Asset

11.1 A possible asset that arises from past events and whose existence will be confirmed only by the occurrence of one or more uncertain future events not wholly within the entity's control.

GL 12 Contingent Liability

12.1 This is ***either***:

(a) A possible obligation that arises from past events and whose existence will be confirmed only by the occurrence of one or more uncertain future events not wholly within the entity's control; ***or***

(b) a present obligation that arises from past events but is not recognised in the primary statements because:

- (i) it is not probable that a transfer of economic benefits will be required to settle the obligation; or
- (ii) the amount of the obligation cannot be measured with sufficient reliability.

GL 13 Costs of Generating Voluntary Income

13.1 Costs of generating voluntary income comprise the costs actually incurred by a charity, or by an agent, in inducing others to make gifts to it that are voluntary income (see GL 61).

(a) Such costs will include the costs of producing fundraising advertising, marketing and direct mail materials, as well as any remuneration payable to an agent. It will normally include publicity costs but not those used in an educational manner in furtherance of the charity's objects.

(b) Such costs will exclude fundraising trading costs (see GL 26).

GL 14 Custodian Trustee

14.1 "Custodian Trustee" includes for present purposes any other non-executive trustee in whose name property belonging to the charity is held. (See also "trustee for a charity" GL 59).

GL 15 Deferred Income

15.1 Deferred income consists of resources (normally cash) received by a charity that do not meet the criteria for recognition as incoming resources in the Statement of Financial Activities as entitlement to the incoming resource does not exist at the balance sheet date. This will arise for example, in the case of resources received but not yet earned (in the case of a contract) which is deferred to match with performance under the contract or where the conditions attaching to a grant prevents its immediate recognition.

15.2 Deferred income is not recognised in the Statement of Financial Activities until the charity is entitled to the incoming resource and instead is disclosed as a liability in the balance sheet (see paragraph 318).

GL 16 Defined Benefit Pension Scheme

16.1 A pension or other retirement benefit scheme other than a defined contribution scheme (see GL 17). Usually, the scheme rules define the benefits independently of the contributions payable, and the benefits are not directly related to the investments of the scheme.

GL 17 Defined Contribution Pension Scheme

17.1 A pension or other retirement benefit scheme into which an employer pays regular contributions fixed as an amount or as a percentage of pay and will have no legal or constructive obligations to pay further contributions if the scheme does not have sufficient assets to pay all employee benefits relating to employee service in the current and prior

PART III
SORP 2005

periods. An individual member's benefits are determined by reference to contributions paid into the scheme in respect of that member, usually increased by an amount based on the investment return on those contributions.

GL 18 Depreciated Replacement Cost

18.1 Depreciated Replacement Cost is defined in FRS 15.

18.2 The objective of depreciated replacement cost is to make a realistic estimate of the current cost of constructing an asset that has the same service potential as the existing asset.

GL 19 Designated Fund

19.1 See Appendix 3 (App 3.1).

GL 20 Donated Services and Facilities

20.1 Donated services and facilities could include gifts of facilities, beneficial loan arrangements, or services from volunteers. Used to be known as intangible income (see GL 37).

GL 21 Endowment Fund

21.1 See Appendix 3 (App 3.3).

GL 22 Ex gratia Payment

22.1 Ex gratia payments are payments made at the discretion of trustees and not as a result of a contract or other legal obligation.

22.2 Ex gratia payments are of two distinct types:

(a) Those made by a charity in relation to its charitable activities (eg extra payments to retiring employees). These will not normally need to be disclosed.

(b) Those where a charity believes it is expedient to make in relation to an obligation which is not within its charitable objects and powers. This may be, for example, to settle a claim in respect of a legacy that would otherwise consume charitable resources in legal expenses. (see paragraph 240)

GL 23 Fair Value

23.1 Fair value is the amount for which an asset could be exchanged or a liability settled between knowledgeable, willing parties in an arm's length transaction.

23.2 The object of fair value measurement is to estimate an exchange price for the asset or liability being measured in the absence of an actual transaction for that asset or liability.

GL 24 Financial Derivative

24.1 A financial derivative is a security, such as an option or futures contract, whose value depends on the performance of an underlying security. In their simplest form derivatives can be used to reduce the cost and/or risk associated with holding or acquiring assets.

GL 25 Functional Fixed Assets

25.1 "Functional fixed assets" are those assets which are used for charitable purposes (ie to undertake the activities that are within the charity's objectives).

GL 26 Fundraising Costs

26.1 Fundraising costs consist of two categories:

(a) Costs of generating voluntary income – see GL 13 above and

(b) Fundraising trading costs which comprise the costs of trading to raise funds including the cost of goods sold and any other costs associated with a trading operation.

GL 27 Funds

27.1 A "fund" is a pool of resources, held and maintained separately from other pools because of the circumstances in which the resources were originally received or the way in which they have subsequently been treated. At the broadest level a fund will be one of two kinds: a restricted fund or an unrestricted fund (see Appendix 3 for the legal position as regards the various funds of a charity.)

GL 28 Governance Costs

28.1 These are the costs associated with the governance arrangements of the charity which relate to the general running of the charity as opposed to those costs associated with fundraising or charitable activity. The costs will normally include internal and external audit, legal advice for trustees and costs associated with constitutional and statutory requirements e g the cost of trustee meetings and preparing statutory accounts. Included within this category are any costs associated with the strategic as opposed to day to day management of the charity's activities.

GL 29 Grant

29.1 A grant is any voluntary payment (or other transfer of property) in favour of a person or institution. Grant payments, when made by a charity, are any such voluntary payments made in furtherance of its objects. The payment or transfer may be for the general purposes of the recipient, or for some specific purpose such as the supply of a particular service. It may be unconditional, or be subject to conditions which, if not satisfied by the recipient, may lead to the grant, or property acquired with the aid of the grant, or part of it, being reclaimed.

GL 30 Grants and/or Contract Income

30.1 A payment made to a charity for the purpose of providing goods or services may be by way of grant or contract. The main distinction is that grant payments are voluntary whereas contracts are normally legally binding between the payer and the charity: the payment is not then voluntary and is not a grant. The distinction is important because:

(a) a contractual payment will normally be unrestricted income of the charity, but a grant for the supply of specific services will normally be restricted income;

(b) the nature of the payment may be relevant to its VAT treatment.

30.2 It is not always easy in practice to decide whether a particular arrangement is or is not intended by the parties to be a legally binding contract for the supply of services. If, under the arrangement, the payer, rather than the recipient charity, has taken the lead in identifying the services to be provided, or if the arrangement provides for damages to be paid in the case of a breach of its terms, rather than, say, for total or partial refund of the payment, it is more probable that there is a contract for the supply of services. If there is no such contract, the rights and obligations of the parties will depend primarily on the law of trusts and conditional gifts, rather than on the law of contract.

30.3 Certain grant arrangements may not be contractual in law but nevertheless have the characteristics of a contract, in that the conditions attaching to the grant only give entitlement to the recipient of the funding (and a liability to the grant provider) as the goods or services specified in the grant terms are provided. Such arrangements are termed performance related grants (see GL 45 Performance-related Grants).

GL 31 Gross Income

31.1 Gross income is a term used within the Charities Act 1993 to determine the thresholds made by Regulations under that Act (and the Companies Act in relation to Charitable Companies). The thresholds govern the requirements (in England and Wales) for accounts' scrutiny, the preparation of accruals accounts by non-company charities, submission of reports, accounts and an annual return to the Charity Commission. Gross income does not include the gains from disposals of fixed assets and investments, nor asset revaluation gains nor any resources being received into the endowment funds. It will however include funds released from endowments.

31.2 Gross income is separately defined for the statutory thresholds that apply in Scotland. The detailed definition is contained in The Charities Accounts (Scotland) Regulations 1992 (SI 1992: No 2165).

31.3 In relation to consolidated accounts, gross income will relate to the gross income of the group after any adjustments arising from consolidation (e g inter-group sales).

GL 32 Heritage Assets

32.1 Heritage assets are assets of historical, artistic or scientific importance that are held to advance preservation, conservation and educational objectives of charities and through public access contribute to the nation's culture and education either at a national or local level. Such assets are central to the achievement of the purposes of such charities and include the land, buildings, structures, collections, exhibits or artefacts that are preserved or conserved and are central to the educational objectives of such charities.

32.2 Examples of these assets are:

(a) Charities with preservation objectives may hold specified or historic buildings or a complex of historic or architectural importance or a site where a building has been or where its remains can be seen.

(b) Conservation charities may hold land relating to the habitat needs of species, or the environment generally, including areas of natural beauty or scientific interest.

(c) Museums and art galleries hold collections and artefacts to educate the public and to promote the arts and sciences.

GL 33 Historic Asset

33.1 See GL 32 above: Heritage Assets.

GL 34 Inalienable Asset

34.1 An asset which a charity is required by law to retain indefinitely for its own use/benefit and therefore cannot dispose of without external consent, whether prohibited by its governing document, the donor's wishes or in some other way. Normally the asset will belong to the charity's "permanent endowment", where it is held on trusts which contemplate its retention and continuing use but not its disposal. However, in the case of a gift-in-kind of a "wasting asset", such as a building, a long lease or a non-durable artefact, the terms of trust may not have provided for its maintenance in perpetuity or its replacement. In that case the endowment will be expended to the extent of the aggregate amount of its depreciation or amortisation properly provided for in the annual accounts (ie based on its currently anticipated useful life).

GL 35 Income

35.1 In the context of charity law, income refers to resources received that must be expended within a reasonable time of their being received. This contrasts with capital funds (see definition GL 5 above).

35.2 The term income is also used in its more general accounting sense.

GL 36 Incoming Resources

36.1 Incoming resources means all resources which become available to a charity including contributions to endowment (capital) funds but excluding gains and losses on investment assets. Gross incoming resources includes all trading and investment income, legacies, donations, grants and gains from disposals of fixed assets for use by the charity. Incoming resources should be recognised in the Statement of Financial Activities when the effect of a transaction or other event results in an increase in the charity's assets.

36.2 This term is to be distinguished from the statutory terms gross income (see GL 31) and gross receipts (relating to Scottish Charities) that are used for threshold purposes.

GL 37 Intangible Income

37.1 Intangible income is the term used by previous Charity SORPs to refer to what is now known as Donated Services and Facilities (see GL 20).

GL 38 Investment Management Costs

38.1 Investment management costs include the costs of:

(a) portfolio management;
(b) obtaining investment advice;
(c) administration of the investments;
(d) rent collection, property repairs and maintenance charges.

38.2 Valuation fees incurred for accounting purposes would normally be charged to the governance cost category of the relevant funds that hold the properties being valued.

38.3 Costs associated with acquiring and disposing of investments would normally form part of the acquisition cost of the investment or reduce the return on disposals. These costs are therefore not part of investment management costs.

GL 39 Investment Property

39.1 Subject to the exceptions in paragraph 39.2 below, an investment property is an interest in land and/or buildings:

(a) in respect of which construction work and development have been completed; and
(b) which is held for its investment potential, any rental income being negotiated at arm's length.

39.2 The following are exceptions from the definition:

(a) A property which is owned and occupied by a company for its own purposes is not an investment property.
(b) A property let to and occupied by another group company is not an investment property for the purposes of its own accounts or the group accounts.

GL 40 Liability

40.1 A liability is an obligation of an entity to transfer economic benefits which:

(a) is expected to be settled by the entity parting with assets or in some way losing an economic benefit; and

(b) results from past transactions or events; and

(c) embodies a present duty or responsibility to one or more other entities that entails settlement at a specified or determinable future date, on the occurrence of a specified event, or on demand; and

(d) results from a duty or responsibility which obligates the entity either legally, or practically (a constructive obligation), because it would be financially or otherwise operationally damaging to the entity not to discharge the duty or responsibility.

A moral obligation – such as results from the making of a non-contractual promise – does not create a liability unless it meets the definition above.

GL 41 Market Value

41.1 "Market Value" is the price at which an asset could be, or could be expected to be, sold or acquired in a public market between a willing buyer and willing seller. For traded securities in which there is an established market, the market value basis that is to be used in the valuation for the balance sheet is defined as the midpoint of the quotation in the Stock Exchange Daily Official List or at a similar recognised market value. For other assets it is the trustees' or valuers' best estimate of such a value.

GL 42 Material

42.1 Materiality is the final test of what information should be given in a particular set of accounts. An item of information is material to the accounts if its misstatement or omission might reasonably be expected to influence the economic decisions of users of those accounts, including their assessments of stewardship. Immaterial information will need to be excluded to avoid clutter which impairs the understandability of other information provided.

42.2 Whether information is material will depend on the size and nature of the item in question judged in the particular circumstances of the case. Materiality is not capable of general mathematical definition as it has both qualitative and quantitative aspects. The principal factors to be taken into account are set out below. It will usually be a combination of these factors, rather than any one in particular, that will determine materiality.

(a) The item's size is judged in the context both of the accounts as a whole and of the other information available to users that would affect their evaluation of the accounts. This includes, for example, considering how the item affects the evaluation of trends and similar considerations.

(b) Consideration is given to the item's nature in relation to:

  (i) the transactions or other events giving rise to it;

  (ii) the legality, sensitivity, normality and potential consequences of the event or transaction;

  (iii) the identity of the parties involved; and

  (iv) the particular headings and disclosures that are affected.

42.3 If there are two or more similar items, the materiality of the items in aggregate as well as of the items individually needs to be considered.

42.4 Trustees are responsible for deciding whether an item is or is not material. In cases of doubt an item should be treated as material.

42.5 This process may result in different materiality considerations being applied depending on the aspect of the accounts being considered. For example, the expected degree of accuracy expected in the case of certain statutory disclosures e g trustees' remuneration, may make normal materiality considerations irrelevant.

GL 43 Operating and Financial Review

43.1 An operating and financial review (OFR) is a form of reporting currently adopted by many quoted companies and is designed to provide a balanced and comprehensive analysis of:

(a) the development and performance of the business of the entity during the financial year;

(b) the position of the entity at the end of the year;

(c) the main trends and factors underlying the development, performance and position of the business of the entity during the financial year; and

(d) the main trends and factors which are likely to affect their future development, performance and position, prepared so as to assist investors to assess the strategies adopted by the entity and the potential for those strategies to succeed.

43.2 The Government proposes that quoted companies will be required to prepare an OFR for financial years beginning on or after 1 April 2005. There is currently no requirement for charities to prepare an operating and financial review although a number of this SORP's reporting recommendations for the content of the Trustees' Annual Report are consistent with OFR reporting. The Accounting Standards Board issued an Exposure Draft of Reporting Standard 1: Operating and Financial Review on 30 November 2004.

GL 44 Parent Undertaking and Subsidiary Undertaking

44.1 In relation to a charity, an undertaking is the parent undertaking of another undertaking, called a subsidiary undertaking, where the charity controls the subsidiary. Control requires that the parent can both direct and derive benefit from the subsidiary.

(a) Direction is achieved if the charity or its trustees:
  (i) hold or control the majority of the voting rights, or
  (ii) have the right to appoint or remove a majority of the board of directors or trustees of the subsidiary undertaking, or
  (iii) have the power to exercise, or actually exercise, a dominant influence over the subsidiary undertaking or
  (iv) manage the charity and the subsidiary on a unified basis.

  For a fuller definition, reference should be made to sections 258 and 259 Companies Act 1985.

(b) Benefit derived can either be economic benefit that results in a net cash inflow to the charity or can arise through the provision of goods or services to the benefit of the charity or its beneficiaries.

44.2 Paragraphs 381 to 406 explain how to account for subsidiary undertakings within the consolidated accounts of a parent undertaking. This includes the exemptions from consolidation and the particular circumstances in which a charity can be considered to be a subsidiary undertaking of another charity.

GL 45 Performance Related Grant

45.1 The term performance-related grant is used to describe a grant that has the characteristics of a contract in that:

(a) the terms of the grant require the performance of a specified service that furthers the objectives of the grant maker and
(b) where payment of the grant receivable is conditional on a specified output being provided by the grant recipient.

GL 46 Pooling Scheme (see also GL 8)

46.1 A Pooling Scheme is a class of Common Investment Fund that provides for the pooling of investments belonging to two or more charities (which may be special trusts) which are administered by the same trustee body as the body managing the Pooling Scheme. Such schemes are referred to as Pool Charities and may be established with or without a formal scheme of the Charity Commission or the Courts.

GL 47 Programme Related Investments

47.1 Programme related investments (also known as social investments) are made directly in pursuit of the organisation's charitable purposes. Although they can generate some financial return (funding may or may not be provided on commercial terms), the primary motivation for making them is not financial but to further the objects of the funding charity. Such investments could include loans to individual beneficiaries (eg for housing deposits) or to other charities (for example, in relation to regeneration projects).

GL 48 Provision

48.1 A provision (as defined in FRS 12) is a liability of uncertain timing or amount. It is recognised when a charity has a present obligation (a legal or constructive obligation exists at the balance sheet date) as a result of a past event, it is probable that a transfer of economic benefits will be required to settle the obligation and the amount can be reliably estimated.

GL 49 Public Benefit Entity

49.1 The Accounting Standards Board's Proposed Interpretation of the Statement of Principles for Public Benefit Entities defines such entities as follows:

49.2 "Public benefit entities are reporting entities whose primary objective is to provide goods or services for the general public or social benefit and where any risk capital has been provided with a view to supporting that primary objective rather than for a financial return to equity shareholders."

GL 50 Related Parties

50.1 Related parties include all of the following:

(a) any charity trustee and custodian trustee of the charity;

(b) any person or body with:

(i) *either* the power to appoint or remove a significant proportion of the charity trustees of the charity. All or a majority of the trustees should always be treated as a "significant proportion". Fewer than 50% of the trustees may be a "significant proportion" if they collectively have a dominant influence on the operation of the charity, as, for example, is likely to be the case if one body has the power to appoint/remove 7 of a body of 15 trustees, and 8 other different bodies had the right to appoint/remove 1 each.

(ii) *or* whose consent is required to the exercise of any of the discretions of those trustees,

(iii) *or* who is entitled to give directions to those trustees as to the exercise of any of those discretions;

(c) any institution connected with the charity, and any director of such an institution. An institution is connected with a charity if *either*:

(i) it is controlled by (in Scotland managed or controlled by) the charity. "Controlled" means that the charity is able to secure that the affairs of the institution are conducted in accordance with its wishes. A charity will control another if it is trustee of that charity or has power to appoint or remove a significant proportion of its trustees. Or

(ii) a participating interest in it is beneficially owned by the charity. "Participating interest" means that the charity:

(a) is interested in shares comprised in the equity share capital of the body of a nominal value of more than one fifth of that share capital; or

(b) is entitled to exercise or control the exercise of more than one-fifth of the voting power at any general meeting of that body;

(d) any other charity with which it is commonly controlled. Common control exists if:

(i) the same person, or persons have the right to appoint a majority of the charity trustees of both or all the charities; or

(ii) the same person, or persons, hold a majority of the voting rights in the administration of both or all of the charities.

Persons who are related with each other through family or business relationships should be treated as the same person for the present purposes.

A charity is not necessarily related to another charity simply because a particular person happens to be a trustee of both. It will only be related if one charity subordinates its interests to the other charity in any transaction because of this relationship;

(e) any pension fund for the benefit of:

(i) the employees of the charity, and/or

(ii) of any other person who is a related party of the charity;

(f) any officer, agent or employee of the charity having authority or responsibility for directing or controlling the major activities or resources of the charity; and

(g) any person connected to a person who is related to the charity including:

(i) members of the same family or household of the charity trustee or related person who may be expected to influence, or be influenced by, that person in their dealings with the charity;

(ii) the trustees of any trust, not being a charity, the beneficiaries or potential beneficiaries of which include a charity trustee or related person or a person referred to in (i) as being connected with a charity trustee or to a related person, as the case may be

(iii) any business partner of a charity trustee or related person, or of any person referred to in (i) or (ii) as being connected with a charity trustee or to a related person, as the case may be

(iv) any body corporate, not being a company which is controlled entirely by one or more charitable institutions, in which:

(a) the charity trustee has, or the charity trustee and any other charity trustee or trustees or person or persons referred to in (i), (ii) or (iii) above as being connected with a charity trustee, taken together, have a participating interest; or

(b) the related person has, or the related person and any other related parties of the charity, taken together, have a participating interest;

(v) any person or body who makes available to the charity the services of any person or body as a charity trustee is connected with a charity trustee.

PART III
SORP 2005

GL 51 Reserves

51.1 The term "reserves" has a variety of technical and ordinary meanings, depending on the context in which it is used. In this SORP the term "reserves" (unless otherwise indicated) describes that part of a charity's income funds that is freely available.

51.2 This definition of reserves therefore normally excludes:
(a) permanent endowment funds;
(b) expendable endowment funds;
(c) restricted funds;

and any part of unrestricted funds not readily available for spending, specifically:
(d) income funds which could only be realised by disposing of fixed assets held for charity use and performance related investments.

51.3 Individual charities may have more or less reserves available to them than this simple calculation suggests for example:
(a) Expendable endowments may be readily available for spending or
(b) Unrestricted funds may be earmarked or designated for essential future spending and reduce the amount readily available.

51.4 For further information, see the Charity Commission's publication CC19 on Charities' Reserves.

GL 52 Resources Expended

52.1 Resources expended means all costs incurred in the course of expending or utilising the charity's funds. This includes all claims against the charity upon being recognised as liabilities by the trustees, as well as all accruals and payments made by the trustees of a charity, and all losses on the disposal of fixed assets (other than investments), together with all provisions for impairment of tangible fixed assets or programme related investments.

52.2 This is to be distinguished from total expenditure (see GL 55 below).

GL 53 Restricted Fund

53.1 See Appendix 3 (App 3.2).

GL 54 Support Costs

54.1 Support costs are those costs that, whilst necessary to deliver an activity, do not themselves produce or constitute the output of the charitable activity. Similarly, costs will be incurred in supporting income generation activities such as fundraising, and in supporting the governance of the charity. Support costs include the central or regional office functions such as general management, payroll administration, budgeting and accounting, information technology, human resources, and financing.

GL 55 Total Expenditure

55.1 Total expenditure is a term used within the Charities Act 1993 to determine the thresholds that govern the requirements (in England and Wales) for accounts scrutiny, submission of reports, accounts and an annual return to the Charity Commission. The Charities Accounts (Scotland) Regulations 1992 define a similar term 'Gross Expenditure'. Total Expenditure does not include losses on the disposal of fixed assets nor amounts paid for the acquisition of fixed assets nor any amounts paid out of endowment funds.

GL 56 Total Return Approach to Investment

56.1 The total return approach to investment management allows trustees to manage investments without the need to take account of whether the return is income (dividends, interest, etc.) or capital gains and losses. Normally a total return approach cannot be adopted in relation to permanent endowment funds, though the Charity Commission can enable this for charities in England and Wales. Further details are given in Appendix 3 (paragraph 3(g)).

GL 57 Trading

57.1 In a strict legal sense, trading activities are those carried out under contract, whether at the point of sale or otherwise, where goods and services are provided in return for consideration for those goods or services. Normally, trading activities are carried out on a regular basis with a view to making profits, though it is possible that some one-off activities could be regarded as trading.

57.2 However, in an economic sense, trading can be regarded as the provision of goods and services in return for a payment whether or not this payment is in fact under contract. Therefore, certain incoming grants which are, in a legal sense, donations, but which have specific terms attached to them such that a charity becomes entitled to the payment on the provision of specified goods or services, are in the context of this SORP recognised on the same basis as trading income (see Performance Related Grant: GL 45). This is because the charity has an obligation to provide the specific services or goods in the same way that it would have to provide them under contract. If it fails to provide the goods or services then, if the funds are by way of grant, this will be a breach of trust, but if they are by way of contract, this will be by way of breach of contract. The legal remedies of the funding body are different depending upon the circumstances.

57.3 Similarly, the sale of donated goods is in a legal sense regarded as the realisation of a donation. However, in the context of this SORP it is regarded as trading, and recognised as an activity for generating funds (See paragraph 137), because it is so similar to the sale of bought in goods as to be indistinguishable in the actual processes involved except for the legal distinction.

57.4 For income, corporation and value added tax purposes trading must be interpreted within the meaning of the legislation governing those taxes.

GL 58 Trustees

58.1 Has the same meaning as charity trustees.

GL 59 Trustee for a Charity

59.1 "Trustee for a charity" means any person (other than the charity itself, or a charity trustee of the charity) who holds the title to property belonging to the charity, and so includes a custodian trustee and a nominee.

GL 60 Unrestricted Fund

60.1 See Appendix 3 (App 3.1).

GL 61 Voluntary Income

61.1 Voluntary income comprises gifts that will not normally provide any return to the donor other than the knowledge that someone will benefit from the donation. They will thus exclude any gifts that are quasi-contractual (in that a certain service to a certain level must be provided) but they would include gifts that must be spent on some particular area of work (ie restricted funds) or given to be held as endowment. Voluntary income will normally include gifts in kind and donated services, for example gifts in kind as part of an international aid programme.

Glossary of terms relating to Pension Scheme Accounting under FRS 17

The following definitions are specifically needed to understand pension scheme accounting. Where definitions are more generally applicable they are included in the main glossary above.

GL 62 (Pensions) Actuarial gains and losses

62.1 See definition GL 2 in the main glossary

GL 63 (Pensions) Current service costs

63.1 The increase in the present value of scheme liabilities expected to arise from employee service in the current period.

GL 64 (Pensions) Curtailment

64.1 An event reducing the expected years of future service of present employees or reducing for a number of employees the accrual of defined benefits for future years service, eg early termination of employees' services or termination or amendment of scheme terms affecting benefits accrued by future service.

GL 65 (Pensions) Defined benefit pension scheme

65.1 See definition GL 16 in the main glossary.

GL 66 (Pensions) Defined contribution pension scheme

66.1 See definition GL 17 in the main glossary.

GL 67 (Pensions) Expected rate of return on assets

67.1 Average rate of return, including income and changes in fair value but net of expenses, expected over the remaining life of the related obligation on the assets held by the scheme.

GL 68 (Pensions) Interest cost

68.1 The expected increase during the period in the present value of the scheme liabilities because the benefits are one period closer to settlement.

GL 69 (Pensions) Multi-employer pension scheme

69.1 This is a defined contribution pension scheme or a defined benefit pension scheme where more than one employer participates.

GL 70 (Pensions) Past service cost:

70.1 The increase in the present value of scheme liabilities relating to employee service in prior periods arising in the current period as a result of the introduction of, or improvements to, retirement benefits.

GL 71 (Pensions) Projected unit method:

71.1 An accrued benefits valuation method in which the scheme liabilities make allowance for projected earnings. An accrued benefits valuation method is a valuation method in which the scheme liabilities at the valuation date relate to:

(a) the benefits for pensioners and deferred pensioners (ie individuals who have ceased to be active members but are entitled to benefits payable at a later date) and their dependants, allowing where appropriate for future increases, and

(b) the accrued benefits for members in service on the valuation date.

The accrued benefits are the benefits for service up to a given point in time, whether vested rights or not.

GL 72 (Pensions) Retirement benefit:

72.1 All forms of consideration given by an employer in exchange for services rendered by employees that are payable after the completion of employment.

GL 73 (Pensions) Scheme liabilities:

73.1 The liabilities of a defined benefit scheme for outgoings due after the valuation date.

GL 74 (Pensions) Settlement:

74.1 An irrevocable action that relieves the employer (or the defined benefit scheme) of the primary responsibility for a pension obligation and eliminates significant risks relating to the obligation and the assets used to effect the settlement. For example, the payment of a lump sum in exchange for surrender of rights, the purchase of an annuity to cover benefits, or the transfer of scheme assets and liabilities relating to employees leaving the scheme.

[5126]

APPENDIX 2
APPLICATION OF ACCOUNTING STANDARDS

App 2.1 Accounting standards are developed in the UK by the Accounting Standards Board and are referred to as Financial Reporting Standards (FRSs). Accounting standards developed by its predecessor body the Accounting Standards Committee and adopted by the ASB continue to be known as Statements of Standard Accounting Practice or SSAPs. Accounting standards are authoritative statements of how particular types of transaction and other events should be reflected in accounts and accordingly compliance with accounting standards will normally be necessary for accounts to give a true and fair view. Accounting standards need not be applied to immaterial items. In applying accounting standards it is important to be guided by the spirit and reasoning behind them.

App 2.2 The main role of the Urgent Issues Task Force (UITF) is to assist the ASB with important or significant accounting issues where unsatisfactory or conflicting interpretations of standards have developed. UITF Abstracts apply where accounts are intended to give a true and fair view. They should be regarded as part of the body of practices forming the basis for determining what constitutes a true and fair view and should be read in conjunction with accounting standards. UITF Abstracts need not be applied to immaterial items. As with accounting standards it is important when applying UITF Abstracts to be guided by the spirit and reasoning behind them.

App 2.3 Subsequent to the consultation on this SORP, in December 2004 the Accounting Standards Board issued five new accounting standards (FRS 22 to FRS 26) as part of its strategy for convergence with International Financial Reporting Standards. In addition FRS 2:

Accounting for Subsidiary Undertakings has been amended to reflect recent changes to the Companies Act 1985 and a new standard, FRS 27: Life Assurance, applying to life insurance businesses, was issued.

App 2.4 The following table includes a brief summary of these new standards. Four of these standards will become fully mandatory for charities who adopt fair value measurement rules (unless the FRSSE is applied) for accounting periods beginning on or after 1 January 2006. Where allowed by the relevant standard, charities may adopt them early, and where charities so do, reference should be made directly to the relevant standard. The presentational requirements of FRS 25 Financial Instruments: Disclosure and Presentation apply to charities for accounting periods beginning on or after 1 January 2005. Although charities are unlikely to issue equity, this standard will also be relevant in determining the classification of liabilities based on the substance of the arrangement.

App 2.5 The following table provides a summary of the accounting standards and Urgent Issues Task Force abstracts extant at the date of issue of this SORP and their applicability to charities. The standards should only be applied in so far as they are relevant to activities being carried out by an individual charity. Where this is the case the summaries below should not be relied upon as a substitute for reading the full text of the standard.

Statements of Standard Accounting Practice (SSAPs)

SSAP 4 Accounting Treatment of Government Grants	SSAP 4 deals with the accounting treatment and disclosure of government grants and other forms of government assistance, including grants, equity finance, subsidised loans and advisory assistance. It is also indicative of best practice for accounting for grants and assistance from other sources.	*A gift of a tangible fixed asset (or grant to purchase) is recognised in full with the recipient charity's entitlement to the asset. Any restriction on the asset's future use is recognised by allocating the asset to a restricted fund rather than deferring the recognition of the asset. Any residual liability to the donor arising from, for example, the asset's future sale, is disclosed as a contingent liability unless the event that would trigger repayment of the grant becomes probable in which case a liability for repayment is recognised.* *This SORP provides the most appropriate interpretation of SSAP 4 for charities. In particular, grants for fixed assets should not be deferred though normally they will have to be accounted for in a separate fund (see paragraph 111).*

PART III SORP 2005

SSAP 5 Accounting For Value Added Tax (VAT)	SSAP 5 follows the general principle that the treatment of VAT in the accounts should reflect an entity's role as a collector of the tax and VAT should not be included in income or in expenditure whether of a capital or revenue nature. However, where the VAT is irrecoverable, it should be included in the cost of the items reported in the financial statements.	*Many if not all charities will suffer irrecoverable VAT either because they are not registered or have a mixture of activities which are zero and standard rated, exempt and outside the scope of VAT. The irrecoverable tax should be included in the relevant cost headings on the face of the Statement of Financial Activities and not shown as a separate item though separate disclosure of the amount may be made in the notes to the accounts.*
SSAP 9 Stocks and Long-term Contracts	SSAP 9 gives guidance on the values to be included in the balance sheet of stocks and long-term contracts and the criteria for recognition of income and expenditure on such items within the profit and loss account (Statement of Financial Activities for charities).	*Equally applicable to charities as to other entities.*
SSAP 13 Accounting for Research and Development	SSAP 13 provides guidance on three broad categories of activity, namely pure research, applied research and development. The standard defines these categories and specifies the accounting policies that may be followed for each.	*Equally applicable to charities as to other entities.*
SSAP 17 Accounting for Post Balance Sheet Events	SSAP 17 defines the period for post balance sheet events and describes the accounting treatment for adjusting and non-adjusting events. Adjusting events are those which provide additional evidence of conditions existing at the balance sheet date. Non-adjusting events are those which concern conditions that did not exist at the balance sheet date. SSAP 17 has been replaced by FRS 21 for accounting periods beginning on or after 1 January 2005.	*Equally applicable to charities as to other entities.*
SSAP 19 Accounting for Investment Properties	SSAP 19 requires investment properties to be included in the balance sheet at their open market value, but without charging depreciation.	*Equally applicable to charities as to other entities.*

SSAP 20 Foreign Currency Translation	SSAP 20 generally requires, in individual financial statements, that each transaction should be translated into the entity's local currency using the exchange rate in operation at the date of the transaction. In consolidated accounts the standard allows two alternative methods of translation of a foreign entity's financial statements, depending on whether the enterprise is a separate quasi-independent entity, or a direct extension of the trade of the investing entity. See also FRS 23 and FRS 24.	*Generally applicable to charities entering directly into transactions overseas or with branches or subsidiaries overseas. Gains should be recorded as other income in the Statement of Financial Activities and losses as a support cost of the relevant activity category. Where the standard permits gains and losses to be taken to reserves, these should be shown as a separate row in the Statement of Financial Activities after "net incoming/outgoing resources."*
SSAP 21 Accounting for Leases and Hire Purchase Contracts	SSAP 21 describes how to identify and account for finance leases, operating leases and hire purchase contracts both for the lessee and the lessor.	*Equally applicable to charities as to other entities.*
SSAP 25 Segmental Reporting	SSAP 25 requires the disclosure by class of business and by geographical segment of turnover, segment result and segment net assets. The turnover disclosure is required by all companies otherwise the disclosure is mandatory only for PLCs, banking and insurance companies and those over ten times the threshold for medium sized companies.	*This will only be applicable to the largest charities. The disclosure requirements in the SORP for details of activities by function meets the spirit of SSAP 25 for turnover by class of activity. The disclosure by geographical region and segment net assets would be additional.*

Financial Reporting Standards (FRSs)

FRS 1 Cash Flow Statements (Revised 1996)	FRS 1 (Revised 1996) requires reporting entities within its scope (two of £5.8m gross turnover; £2.8m gross assets; 50 employees) to prepare a cash flow statement in the manner set out in the FRS. (Non company charities in Scotland are bound by the limits in the Scottish Regulations 1992 being £2m gross income and £975,000 gross assets.)	*Paragraphs 351 to 355 explain the applicability of FRS 1 to charities.*
FRS 2 Accounting for Subsidiary Undertakings	FRS 2 sets out the conditions under which an entity qualifies as a parent undertaking which should prepare consolidated financial statements for its group, the parent and its subsidiaries. It also sets out the manner in which consolidated financial statements are to be prepared.	*Paragraphs 381 to 397 explain consolidation and the applicability of FRS 2 to charities.*

FRS 3 Reporting Financial Performance	FRS 3 requires a layered format for the profit and loss (income and expenditure) account split between continuing, newly acquired and discontinued operations. It has effectively outlawed extraordinary items. The standard also requires a statement of total recognised gains and losses to be shown as a primary statement. A note of historical profits, which is a memorandum item, is also required as is the disclosure of earnings per share.	*The Statement of Financial Activities combines both the income and expenditure account and the statement of total recognised gains and losses and meets charity law. Exceptional items should be disclosed on a separate row within the activity to which they relate. The additional requirements for charitable companies are explained in paragraphs 423 to 426. Earnings per share is not relevant to charities.*
FRS 4 Capital Instruments	FRS 4 requires capital instruments to be presented in financial statements in a way that reflects the obligations of the issuer and the impact on shareholders equity. Most parts of this standard are superseded by FRS 25.	*Not generally applicable to charities following this SORP.*
FRS 5 Reporting the Substance of Transactions	FRS 5 requires that the substance of an entity's transactions is reported in its financial statements. This requires that the commercial effect of a transaction and any resulting assets, liabilities, gains and losses are shown and that the accounts do not merely report the legal form of a transaction.	*Equally applicable to charities as to other entities.*
FRS 6 Accounting For Acquisitions and Mergers	FRS 6 sets out the circumstances in which the two methods of accounting for a business combination (acquisition accounting and merger accounting) are to be used. The FRS sets out five criteria that must be met for merger accounting to be used. If they are not met then acquisition accounting should be used.	*The principles of merger accounting are applicable to charities where two or more charities merge. However where funds are merely transferred from one charity to another this may constitute a gift or in the case of a restricted fund simply the administrative transfer of the restricted fund from one set of trustees to another. Two of the five criteria apply to shareholders funds and so will not be applicable to charities. Charities cannot merge with non-charitable companies and so acquisition accounting will have to be used where such companies are acquired.*

FRS 7 Fair Values in Acquisition Accounting	FRS 7 sets out the principles of accounting for a business combination under the acquisition method of accounting. It explains what "identifiable assets and liabilities" means and how to determine their fair values. The difference between the sum of these fair values and the cost of acquisition is recognised as goodwill or negative goodwill.	*Equally applicable to charities as to other entities where acquisition accounting is used.*
FRS 8 Related Party Disclosures	FRS 8 determines who and what are "related parties" and the disclosures necessary to draw attention to the possibility that the reported financial position and results may have been affected by the existence of related parties and by material transactions with them.	*Paragraphs 221 to 233 explain the application of FRS 8 with respect to charities.*
FRS 9 Associates and Joint Ventures	FRS 9 sets out the definitions and accounting treatments for associates and joint ventures, two types of interests that a reporting entity may have in other entities. The FRS also deals with joint arrangements that are not entities.	*Paragraphs 407 to 418 explain the applicability of FRS 9 to charities.*
FRS 10 Goodwill and Intangible Assets	FRS 10 requires purchased goodwill and intangible fixed assets (where marketable) to be capitalised on the balance sheet and amortised over their life, normally regarded as 20 years, subject to impairment reviews.	*FRS 10 covers common occurrences of goodwill and intangible assets. Where a charity has an intangible asset which does not meet the criteria under the standard it should not be included in the primary statements but details of the asset and its financial effect should be disclosed in the notes to the accounts.*
FRS 11 Impairment of Fixed Assets and Goodwill	FRS 11 sets out the principles and methodology for accounting for impairments of fixed assets and goodwill. The carrying amount of an asset is compared with its recoverable amount and, if the carrying amount is higher, the asset is written down. Recoverable amount is defined as the higher of the amount that could be obtained by selling the asset (net realisable value) and the amount that could be obtained through using the asset (value in use). Impairment tests are only required when there has been some indication that an impairment has occurred.	*Paragraphs 267 to 272 explain the applicability of FRS 11 to charities.*

FRS 12 Provisions, Contingent Liabilities and Contingent Assets	FRS 12 describes the circumstances in which a provision (a liability that is of uncertain timing or amount) may arise and how it should be measured and recognised in the financial statements. It also describes how to account for contingent assets and liabilities.	*FRS 12 is generally applicable to charities. Paragraphs 148 to 163 and 321 to 329 describe some particular application points to charities.*
FRS 13 Derivatives and other Financial Instruments	The Financial Reporting Standard on derivatives (FRS 13) must be followed by a reporting entity that has any of its capital instruments listed or publicly traded on a stock exchange or market. A capital instrument is an instrument issued by a reporting entity as a means of raising finance and includes shares, debentures, loans and debt instruments. The FRS is therefore neither applicable to nor designed for charities.	*Although FRS 13 is not applicable to charities, much of what would need to be disclosed is required in the SORP. In particular:* • *Amongst the requirements of the FRS are those to disclose details of financial assets and liabilities, which can include most current assets and current liabilities, investments and derivatives. Disclosure of all these items is required by the SORP.* • *FRS 13 requires disclosure of the financial risk profile of the entity. Disclosure of risks, including financial risk, is required in the Trustees' Annual Report as part of the general disclosure on risk.* • *The FRS also requires an explanation of derivatives in particular and this is also required in the SORP.* • *The SORP also indicates that the notes to the accounts should disclose what derivative products are in use by the charity and the role that financial instruments play in creating or changing the risks that the entity faces in its activities.(see paragraphs 337 to 339).*
FRS 14 Earnings Per Share	This is superseded by FRS 21 for accounting periods beginning on or after 1/1/2005.	*Not applicable to charities.*

FRS 15 Tangible Fixed Assets	FRS 15 sets out the principles of accounting for tangible fixed assets, with the exception of investment properties. In principle all fixed assets should be capitalised at cost or at revalued amount. However, where an enterprise chooses to adopt a policy of revaluing some assets, all assets of the same class must be revalued and the valuations kept up to date.	*The principles of FRS 15 are generally applicable to charities and are embodied in the balance sheet section of this SORP. However, there are relaxed criteria for the valuations of charity assets and certain heritage assets need not be capitalised in certain circumstances as explained in paragraphs 279 to 294.* *As noted in paragraph 265 and 266 where a charity adopts a policy of revaluation of tangible fixed assets, the SORP allows in the case of land and buildings such valuations to be undertaken by a suitably qualified trustee or employee.*
FRS 16 Current Tax		*FRS 16 is generally not applicable to charities. However, the government have paid compensation payments to charities for 5 years from April 1999 for the removal of ACT credits on the payment of UK dividends. These payments should be included as part of a charity's investment income.*
FRS 17 Retirement Benefits	FRS 17 sets out the accounting treatment for retirement benefits such as pensions and medical care during retirement. On the full implementation of the standard the main requirements are: (a) pension assets are measured using fair values, (b) pension scheme liabilities are measured using the projected unit method and discounted using the current rate of return on a high quality corporate bond of equivalent term and currency to the liabilities, (c) the pension scheme surplus (to the extent it can be recovered) or deficit is recognised on the balance sheet, (d) the movement in the scheme surplus/deficit is analysed into: • the current service cost and any past service cost, recognised in operating profit, • the interest cost and expected return on assets, recognised as other finance costs, and	*Equally applicable to charities. Specific guidance on the application of the standard is given in the special section beginning at paragraph 430.*

- actuarial gains and losses recognised in the statement of total recognised gains and losses.

FRS 17 (As amended in November 2002) includes the following transitional arrangements:

(a) For accounting periods ending on or after 22 June 2001, closing balance sheet information (no comparatives required) is to be given in the notes only.

(b) For accounting periods ending on or after 22 June 2002, opening and closing balance sheet information and performance statement information for the period (no comparatives required) is to be given in the notes only.

(c) For accounting periods beginning on or after 1 January 2005, the standard is fully effective.

FRS 18 Accounting Policies

FRS 18 sets out the principles to be followed in selecting accounting policies and the disclosures needed to help users to understand the accounting policies adopted and how they have been applied. Its objective is to ensure that:

- an entity adopts the accounting policies most appropriate to its particular circumstances for the purposes of giving a true and fair view;
- the accounting policies adopted are reviewed regularly to ensure that they remain appropriate, and are changed when a new policy becomes more appropriate to the entity's particular circumstances; and
- sufficient information is disclosed in the financial statements to enable users to understand the accounting policies adopted and how they have been implemented.

Equally applicable to charities as other entities. The disclosure of compliance with any relevant SORP has particular relevance in the context of the charity sector where adherence to this SORP is expected.

The implementation of this SORP may involve the analysis and presentation of incoming resources and resources expended across different SoFA categories and the allocation of support costs to activity categories within the SoFA. The SoFA for the preceding period should be restated to ensure consistent presentation.

	It requires disclosure of the extent to which financial statements comply with any relevant SORP. Where an entity's financial statements fall within the scope of a SORP, the entity should state the title of the SORP and whether its financial statements have been prepared in accordance with the SORP's provisions currently in effect. In the event of a departure, the entity should give a brief description of the departure from recommended practice, the reasons why the treatment adopted is judged more appropriate, details of any disclosures recommended by the SORP that have not been provided and the reasons why they have not been provided. The appropriateness of accounting policies adopted are judged against the objectives of: (a) relevance, (b) reliability, (c) comparability, and (d) understandability.	*Although this SORP does not change the basis of asset and liability recognition, it does provide more detailed guidance on the recognition of performance related grants which may result in some charities amending their accounting policies and where the effect of such a policy change is material, a restatement of comparative amounts will be necessary.*
FRS 19 Deferred Tax	FRS 19 requires full provision to be made for deferred tax assets and liabilities arising from timing differences between the recognition of gains and losses in the financial statements and their recognition in a tax computation. The general principle underlying the requirements is that deferred tax should be recognised as a liability or asset if the transactions or events that give the entity an obligation to pay more tax in the future or the right to pay less tax in the future have occurred at the balance sheet date.	*Not generally applicable to charities due to tax exemptions available. However the standard will be of relevance in consolidated accounts that include non-charitable subsidiaries particularly those that adopt a policy of full or partial profits retention rather than full distribution of taxable profits through gift aid provisions.* *Where it is a subsidiary's practice to make a gift aid payment of all of its taxable profits to its parent charity, subsequent to its reporting year end, which qualifies for tax relief in that earlier period a provision for deferred tax is unlikely to be necessary.*
FRS 20 Share-based Payments		*Not applicable to charities*

FRS 21 (IAS 10) Post Balance sheet events	FRS 21 sets out the recognition and measurement requirements for two types of event after the balance sheet date:	*Equally applicable to charities as other entities.*
	• Those that provide evidence of conditions that existed at the balance sheet date for which the entity shall adjust the amounts recognised in its financial statements or recognise items that were not previously recognised (adjusting events). For example, the settlement of a court case that confirms the entity had a present obligation at the balance sheet date. • Those that are indicative of conditions that arose after the balance sheet date for which the entity does not adjust the amounts recognised in its financial statements (non-adjusting events). For example, a decline in market value of investments between the balance sheet date and the date when the financial statements are authorised for issue.	*The determination after the balance sheet date of the amount of a gift aid payment to a parent charity by a subsidiary undertaking is an adjusting event, if the subsidiary had a present legal (e g a deed) or a constructive obligation at the balance sheet date. Where a present obligation is demonstrable at the year end, an adjustment is made where post balance sheet calculations provide greater accuracy in the measurement of the existing liability e g to equate the gift aid liability more closely to taxable profits.*
	FRS 21 applies for accounting periods beginning on or after 1 January 2005.	*Designations reflect intentions as to the future application of funds held at a particular balance sheet date and do not reflect an external transaction or present obligation to a third party. As such they fall outside the scope of FRS 21. However, the spirit and reasoning behind the standard would suggest that charities would designate for future projects or plans envisaged at the balance sheet date and adjust such estimates to accord with any more accurate information that became available after the year end.*
FRS 22 (IAS 33) Earnings per share	This standard only applies to entities whose ordinary shares are traded or in the process of issuing such shares. This standard supersedes FRS 14 for accounting periods beginning on or after 1 January 2005.	*Not Applicable to Charities.*

FRS 23 (IAS 21) The Effects of Changes of Foreign Exchange Rates	An entity may carry on foreign activities in two ways. It may have transactions in foreign currencies or it may have foreign operations. In addition, an entity may present its financial statements in a foreign currency. This standard prescribes how entities should include foreign currency transactions and foreign operations in their financial statements and how they should translate financial statements into a presentation currency. The standard applies to entities applying FRS 26, In effect this means listed entities are required to apply the standard for accounting periods beginning on or after 1 January 2005 and unlisted entities preparing their accounts in accordance with the fair value accounting rules set out in the Companies Act 1985 will be required to adopt it for accounting periods beginning on or after 1 January 2006. This standard replaces the requirements set out in SSAP 20 from when the new standard is applied.	*Applicable to charities that are applying FRS 26.*
FRS 24 (IAS 29) Financial Reporting in Hyperinflationary economies	FRS 24 prescribes how an entity whose functional currency is the currency of a hyperinflationary economy should report its operating results and financial position. It also provides guidance on determining whether an economy is a hyperinflationary economy. The standard applies to entities applying FRS 26. In effect, this means listed entities are required to apply the standard for accounting periods beginning on or after 1 January 2005 and unlisted entities preparing their accounts in accordance with the fair value accounting rules set out in the Companies Act 1985 will be required to adopt it for accounting periods beginning on or after 1 January 2006. Where this standard is applied it replaces UITF 9.	*Will not apply to charities unless the functional currency in which they report is subject to hyperinflation and FRS 26 has been adopted.*

FRS 25 (IAS 32) Financial Instruments: Disclosure and Presentation	The objective of FRS 25 is to enhance the understanding of users of accounts of the significance of financial instruments to an entity's financial position, performance and cash flow. The presentation requirements of this standard deal with the classification of capital instruments issued between debt and equity and the implications of that classification for dividends and interest expense. The presentational disclosures required by the standard apply to accounting periods beginning on or after 1 January 2005 with earlier adoption not being permitted. The disclosure requirements apply to entities applying FRS 26 only. In effect this means listed entities are required to apply the standard for accounting periods beginning on or after 1 January 2005 and unlisted entities preparing their accounts in accordance with the fair value accounting rules set out in the Companies Act 1985 will be required to adopt it for accounting periods beginning on or after 1 January 2006.	*Presentational requirements apply to charities for accounting periods beginning on or after 1 January 2005. Disclosure requirements apply to charities that are applying FRS 26.*
FRS 26 (IAS 39) Financial Instruments: Measurement	This standard introduces for the first time requirements for the measurement of financial instruments. It implements in full the measurement and hedge accounting provisions of IAS 39 as published by the International Accounting Standards Board. This standard applies to listed entities for accounting periods beginning on or after 1 January 2005. Unlisted entities preparing accounts in accordance with fair value accounting rules set out in the Companies Act 1985 are required to apply the standard for accounting periods beginning on or after 1 January 2006 and may voluntarily apply it for accounting periods beginning on or after 1 January 2005.	*Applicable to charities that are companies and adopt an accounting policy that measures financial instruments at fair value for accounting periods beginning on or after 1 January 2006.*

FRS 27 Life Assurance	FRS 27 applies to all entities with a life assurance business (including a life reinsurance business), and is effective for accounting periods ending on or after 23 December 2005, except that some smaller friendly societies are exempt until 2006 or 2007.	*Will only apply to charities in the even of them undertaking life insurance business.*
FRSSE Financial Reporting Standard for Smaller Entities	The FRSSE brings together the relevant accounting requirements and disclosures from the other accounting standards and UITF abstracts, simplified and modified as appropriate for smaller entities. The FRSSE is an optional standard but entities adopting it are exempt from applying all the other accounting standards and UITF abstracts. Financial reporting is continually evolving and therefore the FRSSE needs to be updated, roughly on an annual basis, to reflect new or revised accounting standards and UITF abstracts.	*Paragraphs 5.2.1 to 5.2.2 in Appendix 5 explain the applicability of the FRSSE to smaller charities. Whilst it can be followed there are certain principles and notes within this SORP which apply to all charities and should be included in the accounts.*
Urgent Issues Task Force (UITF) Abstracts		
UITF Abstract 4 Presentation of long-term debtors in current assets	Such items should be separately disclosed on the face of the balance sheet or in the notes to the accounts.	*Equally applicable to charities as to other entities.*
UITF Abstract 5 Transfers from current assets to fixed assets		*Applicable in principle to charities but unlikely to arise in practice.*
UITF Abstract 9 Accounting for operations in hyper-inflationary economies	See also FRS 24.	*Only applicable to charities which operate in countries where such conditions exist.*
UITF Abstract 11 Capital instruments: issue call options	See also FRS 25 and FRS 26.	*Not generally applicable to charities.*
UITF Abstract 15 Disclosure of substantial acquisitions		*Not applicable to charities.*
UITF Abstract 17 Employee share schemes		*Not applicable to charities.*

PART III SORP 2005

UITF Abstract 18 Pensions costs following the 1997 tax changes in respect of dividend income (to be replaced by FRED 20)	The probable reduction in actuarial value as a result of pension schemes no longer being able to claim tax credits on dividends should be spread over the remaining service lives of current employees in line with SSAP 24.	*Equally applicable to charities as to other entities.*
UITF Abstract 19 Tax on gains and losses on foreign currency borrowings that hedge an investment in a foreign enterprise		*Not generally applicable to charities.*
UITF Abstract 21 Accounting issues arising from the proposed introduction of the Euro		*Generally applicable to charities though it will have limited impact unless the UK adopts the Euro.*
UITF Abstract 22 The acquisition of a Lloyd's business		*Not applicable to charities.*
UITF Abstract 23 Application of the transitional rules in FRS 15	Provides transitional rules on the use of prior period adjustments where tangible fixed assets which were previously treated as a single asset are identified as having two or more major components with substantially different useful economic lives.	*Equally applicable to charities as to other entities.*
UITF Abstract 24 Accounting for Start-up Costs	Addresses whether start-up costs that cannot be included within the cost of a fixed asset may nevertheless be carried forward. Start-up costs that do not meet the recognition criteria under relevant accounting standards should not be carried forward, but recognised as an expense when incurred.	*Equally applicable to charities as to other entities.*
UITF Abstract 25 National Insurance contributions on share option gains		*Not applicable to charities.*

UITF Abstract 26 Barter transaction for advertising	An entity involved in publishing or broadcasting may agree to provide advertising in exchange for advertising services provided by its customers, rather than for cash consideration. Income from advertising undertaken on such a barter basis is only recognised where persuasive evidence exists that the advertising opportunity could have been sold for an equivalent sum of cash.	*Equally applicable to charities as to other entities.*
UITF Abstract 27 Revisions to estimates of useful economic lives of goodwill and intangible assets	This abstract states that a change from non-amortisation of goodwill or intangible assets, on the grounds that the life of the asset is indefinite, to amortisation over a period of 20 years or less, should not be reported as a change in accounting policy. In such a circumstance, the carrying amount of the goodwill or intangible asset should be amortised over the revised remaining useful life.	*Goodwill rarely arises in the context of charity accounts; the treatment of intangible assets applies equally to charities as to other entities.*
UITF Abstract 28 Operating lease incentives	A lessor may provide an incentive for the lessee to enter into a new or renewed operating lease. It requires that the relevant income or expense be recognised over the life of the asset, or until a market rent will be payable, on a straight-line basis unless another systematic basis is more representative of benefit flows.	*Equally applicable to charities as other entities.*
UITF Abstract 29 Website development costs	Websites are used for a variety of activities, including promotion of services and goods, taking orders and provision of information. Many entities incur significant costs in developing such websites. Certain website development costs may be capitalised only where they lead to the creation of an enduring asset delivering benefits at least as great as the amount capitalised.	*Generally applicable to charities. Charities' websites may however also provide economic benefit without being related to cash flow, for example, the provision of educational information to beneficiaries of the charity. To the extent that the relationship to such benefits is sufficiently certain such costs may be capitalised.*
UITF Abstract 30 Date of award to employees of shares or rights to shares		*Not applicable to charities.*

UITF Abstract 31 Exchanges of businesses or other non-monetary assets for an interest in a subsidiary, joint venture or associate	Entities may transfer businesses or other non-monetary assets in exchange for equity in a subsidiary, joint venture or associate. This abstract deals with accounting for such transactions in consolidated accounts, in particular issues surrounding reporting the transaction at fair values or book values.	*Equally applicable to charities as other entities.*
UITF Abstract 32 Employee benefit trusts and other intermediate payment arrangements	This abstract applies when an entity sets up and transfers funds to an employee benefit trust (or other intermediary) and the trust's accumulated assets are used to remunerate the entity's employees (or other service providers). The abstract clarifies how the principles for FRS 5 – Reporting the Substance of Transactions should be applied.	*Not generally applicable to charities.*
UITF Abstract 33 Obligations in capital instruments	This abstract deals with the classification of capital instruments. A capital instrument, other than a share, which involves an obligation to transfer economic benefits will be treated as a liability in the single entity financial statements of the issuer unless that obligation would not be considered in accordance with the going concern concept. See also FRS 25 and FRS 26.	*Equally applicable to charities as other entities.*
UITF Abstract 34 Pre-contract costs	This abstract is intended to bring consistency to the treatment of costs incurred in bidding for and securing contracts to supply products or services. It requires costs incurred before it is virtually certain that a contract will be obtained to be charged immediately as expenses. Directly attributable costs incurred after that point should be recognised as an asset and charged as expenses during the period of the contract.	*Equally applicable to charities as other entities.*

UITF Abstract 35 Death-in-service and incapacity benefits	This Abstract clarifies the accounting required by FRS 17 'Retirement Benefits' for the cost of death-in-service and incapacity benefits, where such benefits are provided through a defined benefit pension scheme. The Abstract requires that, where the benefits are not wholly insured, the uninsured scheme liability and the cost for the accounting period should be measured, in line with other retirement benefits, using the projected unit method. The effect is that the valuation of uninsured benefits reflects the current period's portion of the full benefits ultimately payable in respect of current members of the scheme; the cost of insured benefits is determined by the relevant insurance premiums.	*Equally applicable to charities as other entities.*
UITF Abstract 36 Contracts for sales of capacity	Entities in some industries (such as telecommunications and electricity) sell rights to use capacity on their networks, sometimes entering into exchange or reciprocal transactions ('capacity swaps'). This Abstract sets out the limited circumstances under which transactions in capacity should be reported as sales, and the proceeds reported as turnover.	*Not generally applicable to charities.*
UITF Abstract 37 Purchase and sale of own shares	See also FRS 25 and FRS 26.	*Not applicable to charities.*
UITF Abstract 38 Accounting for ESOP Trusts		*Not applicable to charities.*

[5127]

APPENDIX 3
THE FUNDS OF A CHARITY

The purpose of this appendix is to explain the legal position as regards the various funds of a charity and the implications this has for the way in which the funds are accounted for.

App 3.1 Unrestricted Funds (including designated funds)

1(a) Unrestricted funds are expendable at the discretion of the trustees in furtherance of the charity's objects. If part of an unrestricted fund is earmarked for a particular project it may be designated as a separate fund, but the designation has an administrative purpose only, and does not legally restrict the trustees' discretion to apply the fund. Some trustees have power to declare specific trusts over unrestricted funds. If such a power is available and is exercised, the assets affected will form a restricted fund, and the trustees' discretion to apply the fund will be legally restricted.

1(b) Whether or not trustees have the power to create restricted funds by declaring a trust, unrestricted funds can be spent on the same purposes as restricted funds, for example by spending more on a project for which a restricted grant has provided funding. In practice therefore unrestricted funds may be transferred to meet any overspending on a restricted fund.

1(c) A power of accumulation will allow trustees to create or augment endowment funds (restricted capital funds) from income funds (restricted or unrestricted). Without this power trustees may not create endowment from income funds. Trustees need to be aware that if they use income funds to erect, extend or improve a building on land which is an endowment asset, then those income funds will normally become permanent endowment.

App 3.2 Restricted Funds

2(a) Restricted funds are funds subject to specific trusts, which may be declared by the donor(s) or with their authority (eg in a public appeal) or created through legal process, but still within the wider objects of the charity. Restricted funds may be restricted income funds, which are expendable at the discretion of the trustees in furtherance of some particular aspect(s) of the objects of the charity. Or they may be capital (ie endowment) funds, where the assets are required to be invested, or retained for actual use, rather than expended.

2(b) Where incoming resources are for goods or services and, upon full performance of the service, any surplus funds can be retained and used for general purposes, the incoming resources and related expenditure will most likely be unrestricted. However, if upon full performance any surplus is retrievable by the donor then the resources are most likely to be restricted.

2(c) Where funds are provided for fixed assets, the treatment of the fixed assets acquired with those funds will depend on the basis on which they are held. The terms on which the funds were received may require that the fixed asset which is provided should be held by the charity on trust for a specific purpose. Alternatively, if the charity's governing instrument allows them to do so, the trustees may choose to settle the fixed asset on trust for a specific purpose implied by the appeal (this will be legally binding as opposed to an administrative decision taken by the trustees to include assets in a designated fund). In either case the asset will form part of restricted funds, as will a fixed asset which has itself been given to the charity on trust for a specific purpose. There is, however, no general rule and the treatment will depend upon the circumstances of each individual case.

App 3.3 Endowment funds

Introduction

3(a) An endowment fund where there is no power to convert the capital into income is known as a permanent endowment fund, which must generally be held indefinitely. This concept of "permanence" does not however necessarily mean that the assets held in the endowment fund cannot be exchanged (though in some cases the trusts will require the retention of a specific asset for actual use eg a historic building), nor does it mean that they are incapable of depreciation or loss. What it does mean is that the permanent endowment fund cannot be used as if it were income (ie to make payments or grants to others), however certain payments must be made out of the endowment, such as the payment of investment management fees where these relate to investments held within the endowment. Where assets held in a permanent endowment fund are exchanged, their place in the fund must be taken by the assets received in exchange. "Exchange" here may simply mean a change of investment, but it may also mean, for example, the application of the proceeds of sale of freehold land and buildings in the purchase or improvement of freehold property.

3(b) Trustees may have the power to convert endowment funds into expendable income; such funds are known as expendable endowments. Expendable endowment is distinguishable from "income" in that there is no actual requirement to spend the capital unless, or until, the charity trustees decide to. The fund must be invested to produce income which should be spent for the purposes of the charity within a reasonable time of receipt. If such a power to expend the capital of the expendable endowment is exercised, the relevant funds become restricted or unrestricted income, depending upon whether the trusts permit expenditure for any of the purposes of the charity, or only for specific purposes.

Expenses Related to Endowment Investments

3(c) Any expenses incurred in the administration, or protection of endowment investments should be charged to capital. For example, the fees of someone who manages endowment investments, or the cost of improvements to land held as an endowment investment. Only where the trusts of the charity provide to the contrary, or there are insufficient funds in the endowment to meet such costs, can they be charged against the other funds held by the charity.

3(d) However where charities have land held as endowment investments, then rent collection, property repairs and maintenance charges would normally be charged against the relevant income fund as would the cost of rent reviews. Valuation fees and other expenses incurred in connection with the sale of such land would normally be charged to capital, ie against the gain (or added to the loss) realised on the disposal.

3(e) Valuation fees incurred for accounting purposes would normally, in the case of endowment investments, be charged to capital and recorded in governance category of resources expended.

3(f) All incoming resources derived from assets held as endowment investments should be included in the Statement of Financial Activities. Normally the income forms part of the unrestricted funds but if the application of the income is restricted to a particular purpose the income and corresponding expenditure should be appropriately identified in the restricted funds. Any income not spent at the year end should be carried forward in the appropriate unrestricted or restricted fund.

Total Return on Investment for Permanent Endowment

3(g) In England and Wales, the Charity Commission may give the power to adopt a total return approach to investment (for definition see Glossary: GL 56) to charities with permanent endowment. This power may be taken by new charities and will normally be given to existing charities by Order under section 26 of the Charities Act 1993 which specifies required accounting and reporting disclosures. New charities with such a power are expected by the Charity Commission to mirror these disclosures. The key elements of this approach are:

(i) The charity concerned must hold a permanently endowed fund, the assets of which are required to be invested to produce an investment return.

(ii) Because the return received from investment will not be "labelled" as either income or capital (as it would be under the standard rules), trustees can allocate the return between the present and future beneficiaries in the way *they* consider best gives effect to their duty to be fair to all beneficiaries.

(iii) In any one year, total return is the whole of the investment return received by a charity, regardless of how it has arisen.

(iv) The accumulated total return, less any part of the return which the trustees have previously applied for the purposes of the charity, or have previously allocated to income funds, is referred to as the unapplied total return.

(v) The accounting treatment, where the total return approach to investment is adopted, is specified in the order granting the power and is summarised below.

Accounting Treatment for Total Return

3(h) Where a charity with the necessary authority adopts a total return approach to investment (See Glossary GL 56), the entire investment return initially accrues to an *unapplied total return fund.* Any income earned on the endowment investments and any capital gains or losses will be shown in the relevant row of the Statement of Financial Activities in the endowment column.

3(i) The total return, less any part of the return which has previously been applied for the purposes of the charity, or has previously been allocated to income funds remains in the *unapplied total return fund.* This fund remains part of the permanent endowment until such time as a transfer is made to income funds.

3(j) Any transfer from the unapplied total return fund to either unrestricted or restricted income funds will be shown on the transfer row of the Statement of Financial Activities as appropriate.

3(k) Paragraph 75(e) of the SORP sets out necessary note disclosures in relation to transfers between funds and movements in the *unapplied total return.*

App 3.4 General Points

Asset Gains and Losses

4(a) If a gain is made on the disposal of an asset, the gain will form part of the fund in which the asset was held. An unrealised gain on an asset will also form part of the fund in which the asset is held. Similarly, unrealised losses and provisions for depreciation and impairment of an asset will reduce the fund in which the asset is (or, in the case of a realised loss, was) held. In order to ensure that gains, losses and provisions are added to or deducted from the correct fund, it is therefore essential to know which assets and liabilities are held in which fund.

Restricted Income and Expenditure

4(b) The trustees of a charity will be in breach of trust if they expend restricted income otherwise than in furtherance of that aspect or those aspects of the objects of the charity to which expenditure is restricted. It is therefore essential that due care is taken to spend out of a particular restricted income fund only where the trusts so permit. Expenditure may be charged to a restricted fund which is not at the time in credit, or not in sufficient credit, where there is a genuine anticipation of receipts which can properly be credited to the fund in order to meet the expenditure (eg where a decision has been taken to invite donations for that fund). The fund which is actually drawn upon to finance the expenditure should be held upon trusts which are wide enough to permit the expenditure (in case the expected receipts do not materialise). But if expenditure has been charged to an unrestricted fund, it should not subsequently be recharged to restricted fund receipts simply in order to increase the fund of unrestricted income.

App 3.5 Fund Assets and Liabilities

5(a) It is also important for the trustees to ensure that the assets and liabilities held in a fund are consistent with the fund type; if a fund which, because of donor restrictions, must be applied in the short term is represented by assets which cannot reasonably be expected to be realised in the short term, there is a real possibility that the charity will not be able to apply the funds as directed.

App 3.6 Income Application

6(a) Where restricted income has been invested prior to application for a suitable charitable purpose, any income/gains derived from the investment will be added to, and form part of, the restricted income fund in question. Income derived from the investment of capital (endowment) funds may be applied for the general purposes of the charity (unrestricted income), unless a specific purpose has been declared by the donor for the application of the income from the capital fund in question. Such income will be applicable for that purpose and will be restricted income. Gains from the realisation of investments in a capital (endowment) fund form part of the fund itself.

[5128]

APPENDIX 4
THRESHOLDS

App 4.1 Companies Act 1985 Thresholds for small companies

1.1 The current thresholds in the Companies Act 1985 s 247(3) for qualification as a small company are as follows:

Any 2 of the following 3 conditions:

(i) Annual turnover (gross income for charities) not exceeding – £5,600,000;
(ii) Balance sheet total not exceeding – £2,800,000;
(iii) Average number of employees not exceeding – 50.

For accounting periods which are shorter or longer than 12 months the thresholds should be adjusted in proportion to the accounting period.

The size parameters are subject to periodic amendment. The latest change was in January 2004 under SI 2004/16 and applies to accounting periods ending on or after 30 January 2004.

App 4.2 Thresholds for FRSSE

2.1 Any charity which comes under the above thresholds, ***whether or not it is a company***, may be able to apply the Financial Reporting Standard For Smaller Entities (FRSSE) as described in Appendix 5 paragraphs 5.2.1 to 5.2.2.

App 4.3 Charities Act 1993 (England and Wales) Threshold for the preparation of accruals accounts

3.1 As at 30 April 2004: Gross income above £100,000 (set by SI 1995: No 2696. The Charities Act 1993 (Substitution of Sums) Order 1995).

App 4.4 Charities Act 1993 (England and Wales) Threshold for audit

4.1 As at 30 April 2004: Gross income or total expenditure above £250,000 (set by SI 1995: No 2696. The Charities Act 1993 (Substitution of Sums) Order 1995) (unless and until this is revised).

App 4.5 Law Reform (Miscellaneous Provisions) (Scotland) Act 1990 Threshold for the preparation of accruals accounts (unless and until this is repealed)

5.1 Charities where gross receipts do not exceed £25,000 can prepare receipts and payments accounts unless the founding deed says that the accounts should be audited (set by SI 1992: No 2165 (s 216) The Charities Accounts (Scotland) Regulations 1992).

App 4.6 Law Reform (Miscellaneous Provisions) (Scotland) Act 1990 Threshold for Audit (unless and until this is repealed)

6.1 An audit is required if the charity's gross income or total expenditure exceeds £100,000 in the financial year or in any of the preceding two financial years or if an audit is required under the terms of the charity's founding document (set by SI 1992: No 2165 (s 216) The Charities Accounts (Scotland) Regulations 1992).

[5129]

APPENDIX 5
ACCOUNTING FOR SMALLER CHARITIES

Particular accounting disclosures and the activity basis for the analysis of income and costs within the Statement of Financial Activities may not be relevant information for the users of accounts prepared by smaller charities. Similarly, the level of detail provided in the Trustees' Annual Report is likely to be dependent on the structure, size and complexity of the charity and be proportionate to the needs of the users of the report. This appendix lists the concessions at the date of publication of this SORP.

App 5.1 Cash-Based Receipts and Payments Accounts

5.1.1 There are many relatively small charities with very simple structures and no control of other organisations. The vast majority of them will have cash and deposit accounts but few other assets. Apart from charitable companies (see 5.1.4) these charities will often find that cash-based receipts and payments accounts meet both their needs and those of others who read their accounts. This form of accounts contains a summary of money received and money spent during the year and a list of assets at the end of the year.

5.1.2 In England and Wales, charities whose accounts 'form and content' are governed by the Charities Act 1993, may choose between preparing accruals accounts and receipts and payments accounts provided their gross income is not over £100,000.

5.1.3 Scottish Charities whose accounts are prepared under regulations made under the Law Reform (Miscellaneous Provisions) (Scotland) Act 1990, may prepare receipts and payments accounts provided their gross receipts are not over £25,000.

5.1.4 Small charitable companies must always prepare accruals accounts and are not covered by these concessions.

5.1.5 As this SORP is applicable to accruals accounts, no specific recommendations on cash-based receipts and payment accounts are provided within this SORP although as explained in paragraph 6 such charities are encouraged to analyse their receipts and payments based on the activities undertaken. The Charity Commission for England and Wales produces detailed guidance on the preparation of cash-based accounts.

App 5.2 The Financial Reporting Standard for Smaller Entities (FRSSE)

5.2.1 Any **charity** (whether or not it is a company) which is under the thresholds for small companies, as described in the Companies Acts (see Appendix 4), can follow the Financial Reporting Standard for Smaller Entities (FRSSE) in preparing its financial accounts except where it conflicts with this Charities SORP, in which case this SORP should be followed. Charities which follow another SORP or have to prepare additional accounts in a format required by other bodies, such as HM Treasury, may find that they cannot follow the FRSSE for these purposes. The FRSSE is not relevant to charities preparing cash-based (receipts and payments) accounts.

5.2.2 In following the FRSSE, the accounts will meet most of the requirements of the SORP for smaller entities. However:

(a) The accounts should include a Statement of Financial Activities in place of a profit and loss account and statement of total recognised gains and losses.
(b) The principles of fund accounting should be adopted throughout the accounts. This will include appropriate descriptions of the funds and notes showing the composition of the funds and the differentiation of funds on the balance sheet.
(c) All investments, including investment properties, must be shown at market value.

(d) Those foreign exchange gains and losses which may be allowed to be taken to reserves (as prescribed in the FRSSE) must be shown in the gains and losses section of the Statement of Financial Activities.
(e) Those exceptional items which are required to be shown after operating profit must be shown in an appropriate place on the Statement of Financial Activities.
(f) If a charity applying the FRSSE prepares consolidated accounts, it should apply the relevant accounting practices and disclosures required by accounting standards and the SORP in relation to consolidated accounts.

App 5.3 Accounting statements of Smaller Charities

5.3.1 The SORP provides a number of concessions for smaller charities that are not subject to a statutory audit (see Appendix 4 Audit thresholds). The concessions cover the Statement of Financial Activities and notes to the accounts:
(a) In relation to the Statement of Financial Activities, smaller charities do not need to analyse either resources expended or incoming resources by activity categories within the Statement of Financial Activities. They may instead choose resource classifications to suit their circumstances.
(b) Where a small charity adopts an alternative approach to analysis within the Statement of Financial Activities certain note disclosures may no longer be necessary, for example, where these disclosures relate to the constituent costs of an activity category or where relevant information is provided on the face of the Statement of Financial Activities . The disclosure paragraphs affected by this are:

Details	Paragraph References
Analysis of activities that have generated funds	122
Analysis of incoming resources from charitable activities	146
Support Costs analysis	166–167
Apportionment of Costs	175–176
Breakdown of costs of generating voluntary income	183–184
Analysis of fundraising trading costs	186
Analysis of charitable activity costs	191–194
Analysis of grantmaking or associated support costs by activity	202, 203(b)
Analysis of governance costs	212

(c) Smaller charities are not required to give details of staff emoluments in bands (paragraph 236).

5.3.2 These concessions are intended to reduce the detail of reporting requirements placed on smaller charities, though any such charity wishing to follow the full recommendations of the SORP is encouraged to do so.

App 5.4 Trustees' Annual Reports of Smaller Charities in England and Wales

5.4.1 In England and Wales, all registered charities are required to produce a Trustees' Annual Report. Regulations made under the Charities Act 1993 provide for charities that are not subject to a statutory audit (see Appendix 4 Audit thresholds) to produce an abbreviated Trustees' Annual Report. This concession applies to all charities required to produce the report, and includes charitable companies.

5.4.2 The minimum content of the abbreviated Trustees' Annual Report is summarised in table 11 below.

TABLE 11. CONTENTS OF THE TRUSTEES' ANNUAL REPORT FOR A SMALLER CHARITY (ENGLAND AND WALES – NOT SUBJECT TO A STATUTORY AUDIT)

		SORP Paragraph
Reference and administrative information	The name of the charity	41(a)
	Any other name by which a charity makes itself known	41(a)
	The charity registration number (or Scottish Charity Number) (if any)	41(b)
	The company registration number (if applicable)	41(b)
	The address of the principal office of the charity	41(c)
	The names of the charity's trustees or trustee(s) for the charity on the date the report was approved (where any charity trustee is a body corporate, the names of the directors of that body corporate should also be provided)	41(d)
	The names of any other person who served as a charity trustee in the financial year	41(e)
Structure Governance and Management	The nature of the governing document and how the charity is (or its trustees are) constituted	44(a)
	The methods adopted for the recruitment and appointment of new trustees	44(b)
Objectives and Activities	A summary of the objects of the charity as set out in its governing document	47(a)
	Summary of the main activities undertaken in relation to those objects	47(e)
Achievements and Performance	A summary of the main achievements of the charity during the year	(54)
Financial Review	Policy on reserves	55(a)
	Details of any fund materially in deficit and the circumstances giving rise to the deficit and steps being taken to eliminate the deficit	55(b)
Funds held as Custodian Trustee	A description of the assets which they hold in this capacity	
	The name and objects of the charity (or charities) on whose behalf the assets are held and how this activity falls within their own objects	59
	Details of the arrangements for safe custody and segregation of such assets from the charity's own assets	

APPENDIX 6
THE CHARITY ACCOUNTING REVIEW COMMITTEE (2003/5)

Membership

Chairman

David Taylor

Members

Denis Cathcart

Andrew Dobson

James Dutton

Pesh Framjee

Keith Hickey

Richard Hellewell

Gareth Jones

Raymond Jones

Roger Morris

Paul Palmer

Adrian Randall

Kate Sayer

Ian Smith

Committee Secretary

John Kerry

Technical Secretary

Ken Ashford

[5131]

PART IV
MISCELLANEOUS MATERIALS

HMRC NOTICE: 701/1 CHARITIES

May 2004

NOTES

This HM Revenue & Customs Notice can be found at http://customs.hmrc.gov.uk/channelsPortalWebApp/channelsPortalWebApp.portal?_nfpb=true&_pageLabel=pageVAT_ShowContent&id=HMCE_CL_000097&propertyType=document.

This leaflet is reproduced as amended by Update 1 (June 2004).

CONTENTS

9. Glossary of terms
Do you have any comments?

Foreword

This notice cancels and replaces Notice 701/1 (January 1995). Details of any changes to the previous version can be found in paragraph 1.2 of this notice.

Further help and advice

If you need general advice or more copies of Customs and Excise notices, please ring the **National Advice Service** on **0845 010 9000. You can call between 8.00 am and 8.00 pm, Monday to Friday.**

If you have **hearing difficulties**, please ring the **Textphone** service on **0845 000 0200**.

If you would like to speak to someone in **Welsh**, please ring **0845 010 0300, between 8.00 am and 6.00 pm, Monday to Friday.**

All calls are charged at the local rate within the UK. Charges may differ for mobile phones.

Other notices on this or related subjects

700 The Vat guide I 700/1 Should I be registered for VAT? I 700/2 Group or divisional registration I 701/2 Welfare I 701/5 Clubs and associations I 701/6 Charity funded equipment for medical, veterinary etc uses I 701/7 Reliefs for disabled people I 701/10 Zero-rating of books etc I 701/19 Fuel and power I 701/30 Education and vocational training I 700/34 Staff I 701/41 Sponsorship I 701/45 Sport; I 701/47 Culture I 701/58 Charity advertising and goods connected with collecting donations I 703 Exports and removals of goods from the United Kingdom I 706 Partial exemption I 708 Buildings and construction I 708/6 Energy-saving materials I 709/1 Catering and take-away food I 709/5 Tour Operator's Margin Scheme I 742 Land and property I 742A Opting to tax land and buildings I 48 Extra-statutory concessions I 317 Imports by charities free of duty and VAT I 998 VAT refund scheme for National museums and galleries I CCL2 An introduction to climate change levy I CWL 4 Fund-raising events: exemption for charities and other qualifying bodies

1. INTRODUCTION

1.1 What is this notice about?

This notice explains:

- what a charity is;
- how VAT affects charities;
- how a charity's income is treated for VAT purposes; and
- what VAT reliefs a charity can obtain on its purchases whether or not it is registered for VAT.

You will find a glossary of terms used in this notice at section 9.

Because of the diversity of activities undertaken by charities it is not possible to cover every situation within this notice. If you find that the area you are interested in is not covered by this notice please contact our National Advice Service on 0845 010 9000 for assistance.

1.2 What has changed?

The contents of this notice have been totally updated. It has also been restructured and rewritten to improve readability.

You can access details of any changes to this notice since May 2004 either on our Internet website at www.hmce.gov.uk or by telephoning the National Advice Service on 0845 010 9000.

This notice and others mentioned are available both on paper and on our website.

1.3 Who should read this notice?

You should read this notice if you are:

- involved in a charity;
- involved in a business who makes supplies to or has other dealings with charities;
- a fund-raiser for charities; or
- a user of charity services.

1.4 What law covers this notice?

Because of the diversity of activities undertaken by charities it is not possible to list every relevant section of legislation. The areas of legislation offering specific reliefs to charities are as follows:

The Value Added Tax Act 1994 Section 29A reduced-rates goods and services listed in Schedule 7A to the Act:

- the supply to charities of fuel and power in buildings used by charities for non-business purposes is reduced-rated under Group 1 of Schedule 7A; and
- the supply to charities of energy saving materials, and installation of those materials, in a building intended to be used solely for a relevant charitable purpose is reduced-rated under Group 2 of Schedule 7A.

The Value Added Tax Act 1994 Section 30 zero-rates goods and services listed in Schedule 8 to the Act:

- the supply to charities of talking books for the blind and disabled and wireless sets for the blind is zero-rated under Group 4 of Schedule 8;
- the first grant of a major interest in, and the construction of buildings to be used solely for a relevant charitable purpose is zero-rated under Group 5 of Schedule 8;
- the first grant of a major interest in a substantially reconstructed listed building and approved alterations to a listed building used or intended to be used solely for a relevant charitable purpose are zero-rated under Group 6 of Schedule 8;
- the supply to charities of sea rescue equipment and of repair and maintenance to that equipment is zero-rated under Group 8 of Schedule 8;
- the supply to charities of aids for use by the disabled is zero-rated under Group 12 of Schedule 8; and
- the supply of certain goods and services by and to charities or with funds provided by charities is zero-rated under Group 15 of Schedule 8.

The Value Added Tax Act 1994 Section 31 exempts from VAT goods and services listed in Schedule 9 to the Act:

- the supply by a charity of welfare services and the supply of goods and services in connection with spiritual welfare services is exempted from VAT under Group 7 of Schedule 9; and
- fund-raising events held by charities and other qualifying bodies are exempted from VAT under Group 12 of Schedule 9.

[6001]

2. WHAT IS A CHARITY?

2.1 What is a charity?

A body is considered to be a 'charity' if it has charitable status. A non-profit making body does not necessarily have charitable status.

2.2 Proof of charitable status

There is no distinction for VAT purposes between those charities that are registered with the one of the charity regulators and those that are not. However, charities not registered with a regulator who want to claim VAT relief may need to demonstrate to Customs that they have 'charitable status' through recognition of that charitable status by the Inland Revenue.

Most charities in England and Wales are registered with the Charity Commission which confirms their charitable status. However some charities are not required to be registered: some are exempted by statute, such as universities; others are excepted because they are too small. In the case of a charity not registered with the Charity Commission, recognition of charitable status by the Inland Revenue is sufficient proof.

The Office of the Scottish Charities Regulator opened in December 2003. It is anticipated that bodies in Scotland will be required to register with that regulator, and we will accept that such a body has charitable status. In the meantime, recognition of a body's charitable status by the Inland Revenue is sufficient proof.

There is currently no regulatory body for Northern Ireland charities. The Inland Revenue decides whether bodies in Northern Ireland have charitable status.

2.3 Trading subsidiaries

Charity law allows charities to carry out trading activities in the course of carrying out their primary purpose. For example, the provision of residential accommodation by a care charity in return for a payment, or the holding of an art exhibition by a charitable art gallery or museum in return for admission charges. This is called 'primary purpose trading'.

Charities may also wish to use trading activities as a way of raising money. For example, a charity whose primary purpose is providing education may sell Christmas cards and gifts through a catalogue. This is called 'non-primary purpose trading'.

Charity law does not permit charities to carry out non-primary purpose trading in their own right, on a substantial basis. This is because of the general expectation that contributions made to a charity will be used for its primary purpose or invested prudently, rather than being risked in trading activities simply to raise money.

In order to carry out non-primary purpose trading on a significant scale, charities have to establish 'subsidiary trading companies'. These are trading companies controlled by one or more charities but are not themselves charities.

Most of the VAT reliefs available to charities are **not** available to subsidiary trading companies.

If a charity and its trading subsidiaries are VAT registered it may be possible, under certain conditions, for them to register as a VAT group. Please see Notice 700/2 Group and divisional registration for more information.

2.4 Are you still uncertain?

If you are still uncertain of your position, you can contact the:

- Charity Commission on **0870 333 0123** or on their Internet website;
- Office of the Scottish Charities Regulator on their Internet website; or
- Inland Revenue on **0845 302 0203** or on their Internet website.

[6002]

3. IMPLICATIONS OF VAT FOR CHARITIES

3.1 What is VAT?

VAT is a tax on consumer expenditure. It is collected on business transactions, imports and acquisitions.

3.2 Who needs to register for VAT?

Any business (and this may include a charity or its trading subsidiary) that makes taxable sales in excess of a set figure (known as the VAT registration threshold) must register for VAT. Taxable sales are business transactions that are liable to VAT at the standard, reduced or zero rate. Guidance on whether something is a business transaction can be found in section 4. Many charities make taxable sales and if their level of income from those sales exceeds the VAT registration threshold they will need to register for VAT. This is not optional and there are penalties if you fail to register on time. You can find details of the current VAT registration threshold on our website at www.hmce.gov.uk or by contacting our National Advice Service on 0845 010 9000.

Charities whose business activities take place wholly outside the UK, can register for VAT if those activities would be taxable were they to take place in the UK.

If a charity's income from taxable sales is below the VAT registration threshold they can register for VAT voluntarily. But if a charity's income from taxable sales is below the threshold, and they do not want to register for VAT, the charity does not need to charge VAT on any of its income. The charity should check regularly that it is not exceeding the VAT registration threshold.

However a charity that makes no taxable sales (either because the charity has no business activities or because their sales or income are exempt from VAT) cannot register for VAT.

For more information on VAT registration please see Notice 700/1 Should I be registered for VAT?

3.3 How does VAT affect charities?

VAT affects charities in a number of ways:

- charities receive income from a variety of sources, some of which may be liable to VAT if the charity is VAT registered;
- charities will be able to claim relief from VAT on some of the goods and services they buy, regardless of whether the charity is registered for VAT;

- many of the goods and services that charities buy will be subject to VAT, regardless of whether the charity is registered for VAT; and
- charities that are VAT registered may be able to reclaim some of the VAT they are charged from Customs.

3.4 When will VAT be charged?

Goods and services are divided into different categories, which determine whether VAT will be charged:

3.4.1 Outside the scope

Certain activities carried out by charities are not covered by the VAT system and are not subject to VAT. A typical example of outside the scope income is a freely given donation where the donor receives nothing in return for their money. A typical example of an outside the scope expense is payment of employees' wages.

3.4.2 Taxable

These are goods and services that are standard-rated, reduced-rated or zero-rated when sold by a business (which could include a charity) that is registered for VAT:

- the standard rate (currently 17.5%) is charged on most goods and services;
- the reduced rate (currently 5%) is charged on goods and services listed in Schedule 7A to the VAT Act. Examples include children's car seats and domestic fuel and power; and
- the zero rate (nil) applies to goods and services listed in Schedule 8 to the VAT Act. Examples include food, books and passenger transport.

3.4.3 Exempt

Some goods and services are exempt from VAT when sold by a business (which could include a charity). This means that no VAT is payable – but, equally, the organisation making the supply cannot normally reclaim any of the VAT on the related expenses (please see paragraph 3.7.3 for more information).

Goods and services that are exempt from VAT are listed in Schedule 9 to the VAT Act. Examples include insurance and health care.

3.5 What VAT do charities have to charge?

A VAT registered charity must charge VAT on all the standard-rated and reduced-rated goods and services they sell. The charity does not charge VAT on any income from non-business, zero-rated or exempt sales. The treatment for VAT purposes of a number of activities commonly carried out by charities can be found in section 5.

3.6 What VAT does a charity have to pay?

A charity will pay VAT on all standard-rated or reduced-rated goods and services they buy from VAT registered businesses.

VAT registered businesses can sell certain goods and services to charities at the reduced-rate or zero-rate. Please see section 6 for more information.

3.7 What VAT can a charity reclaim?

A charity needs to consider the VAT on its expenses in three stages.

3.7.1 Stage one – non-business (outside the scope)

A charity **cannot** reclaim **any** VAT it is charged on purchases that directly relate to non-business (outside the scope) activities. Section 4 gives further advice on how to decide if a charity's activities are non-business.

Once a VAT registered charity has decided which of its activities are non-business it will also have to consider how much of the VAT on its general expenses (such as phone and electricity) relate to those activities. The charity will **not** be able to reclaim the proportion of VAT that relates to non-business activities. There are a number of methods a charity can use to calculate this proportion. Some methods are detailed in Notice 700 The VAT guide. VAT that the charity establishes as relating to its business activities is input tax.

3.7.2 Stage two – taxable sales

A VAT registered charity can reclaim all the input tax it is charged on purchases which directly relate to taxable goods or services it sells.

PART IV
MISCELLANEOUS MATERIALS

A charity that is not VAT registered will not be able to recover the VAT it is charged on standard-rated or reduced-rated goods it buys from VAT registered businesses.

3.7.3 Stage three – exempt

A VAT registered charity is not able to reclaim the input tax it has been charged on purchases that relate to exempt activities **unless** these are below a set level (known as the de minimis limit).

In order to determine whether a charity is below the de minimis limit in any VAT accounting period or tax year it needs to:

1 Calculate the input tax that directly relates to exempt activities
2 Calculate the proportion of input tax on general expenses (after adjustment for non-business activities), such as phone and electricity, that relates to exempt activities
3 Add up the input tax at step 1 and 2

If the total input tax at step 3 is below the de minimis limit, then the charity can reclaim all the VAT. For details of the current de minimis limit and further information on how to calculate the proportion of VAT reclaimable please see Notice 706 Partial exemption.

3.8 Accounting for VAT

At set intervals, normally every 3 months, a VAT registered charity will complete a VAT return. This details the VAT the charity has charged on sales of standard-rated and reduced-rated goods and services, and the VAT it has paid on goods and services it has purchased that relate to taxable sales. If the VAT on the charity's sales is more than the VAT on its purchases the charity must pay the excess to Customs. However, if the VAT on the purchases is more than the VAT due on the sales the charity can reclaim the difference from Customs.

There are a number of different accounting schemes available for VAT registered businesses including monthly accounting, cash accounting and annual accounting. For more information on the options available please contact our National Advice Service on 0845 010 9000.

If a charity and its trading subsidiaries are VAT registered it may be possible, under certain conditions, for them to register as a VAT group. Please see Notice 700/2 Group and divisional registration for more information.

[6003]

4. DECIDING WHETHER YOUR ACTIVITIES ARE BUSINESS OR NON-BUSINESS

Although charities may not be deemed to have any business activities under other laws, the definition of business for VAT purposes is governed by specific rules and regulations. These rules and regulations are based on European Community VAT law, as well as UK VAT law, and the findings of many VAT Tribunal and High Court decisions. This means that even though an activity may be performed for the benefit of the community or in the furtherance of charitable aims and objectives, it may still be deemed a business activity for the purposes of VAT.

4.1 Business test

An organisation that is run on a not-for-profit basis may still be regarded as carrying on a business activity for VAT purposes.

The normal questions which need to be considered when determining whether an activity is business for VAT purposes or not are:

- is the activity a serious undertaking earnestly pursued? (This considers whether the activity is carried on for business or daily work rather than pleasure or daily enjoyment.)
- is the activity an occupation or function which is actively pursued with reasonable or recognisable continuity? (When considering this test you should consider how frequently the supplies will be made.)
- does the activity have a certain measure of substance in terms of the quarterly or annual value of taxable supplies made?
- is the activity conducted in a regular manner and on sound and recognised business principles?

- is the activity predominately concerned with the making of taxable supplies for a consideration?
- are the taxable supplies that are being made of a kind which, subject to differences of detail, are commonly made by those who seek to profit from them?

When considering these questions please remember that exempt supplies as well as taxable supplies are business.

These questions do not form a checklist: a business activity may have some but not all of the features indicated. Instead they should be seen as a set of tools designed to help you compare an activity you are uncertain about with features of activities that are clearly business. They are derived from tribunal cases where business status has been disputed and have general application in deciding when an activity is in the course of business. An area of particular difficulty for charities when considering whether their activities are in the course of business is receipt of grant funding. Further information on grant funding can be found in paragraph 5.10.

The activity may still be business if the amount charged does no more than cover the cost to the charity of making the supply or where the charge is less than cost. (However, please see paragraph 5.18.2 if the charity makes supplies of welfare.) If the charity makes no charge at all the activity is unlikely to be considered business.

If you need help in deciding whether an activity is business you should contact our National Advice Service on 0845 010 9000.

[6004]

5. VAT TREATMENT OF INCOME RECEIVED BY CHARITIES

This section explains the VAT treatment of the most common income producing activities undertaken by charities. This list is not exhaustive. If the activity that you are contemplating does not appear below, you will first need to determine whether or not it is a business activity – see paragraph 4.1.

Business activities in the UK can be assumed to be taxable at the standard rate unless specifically reduced-rated, zero-rated or exempted from VAT in law. For more information see Notice 700 The VAT Guide.

If you have concerns as to the correct liability of the activity, you should contact our National Advice Service on 0845 010 9000.

5.1 Admission to premises

Some charities admit visitors to places of interest such as historical monuments, gardens, exhibitions, concerts etc. Where this is done for a charge it is a business activity.

5.1.1 How should charities treat income received from fixed admission charges?

If the charity is registered for VAT then they must account for VAT on this income at the standard rate. However, there are two exceptions:

(a) if the income received is for admittance to a fund-raising event, then the income is exempt from VAT (see paragraph 5.9 and leaflet CWL4 Fund-raising events: exemption for charities and other qualifying bodies).

(b) if the income received is covered by the exemption for admission to cultural events. Charities may be able to treat admission to museums, galleries, art exhibitions, zoos and theatrical, musical or choreographic performances as exempt from VAT. Further information on the conditions for the cultural exemption can be found in Notice 701/47 Culture.

5.1.2 How should charities treat requested donations in return for admission?

In order for a donation to be outside the scope of VAT it should be freely given, with nothing received in return. If admission to the premises is conditional upon payment, the monies received are not donations and VAT must be accounted for at the standard rate. But if admission to the premises is not dependant on a payment then the monies received are donations and are outside the scope of VAT. A charity which "suggests" an amount that visitors may wish to contribute, but does not insist on payment of that amount before allowing admission can treat the amounts received as donations. (But see paragraph 5.9 and leaflet CWL4 Fund-raising events: exemption for charities and other qualifying bodies if admission is to a fund-raising event).

5.1.3 What if the charity makes no charge for admission?

If a charge is not made then there is no business activity and any monies received can be treated as a donation and outside the scope of VAT (but see paragraph 5.12 if the charity is a museum or gallery).

5.2 Advertising services

Charities sometimes sell advertising space in their own brochures, programmes, annual reports or similar. The sale of such advertising space is a business activity and is normally standard-rated (the sale of such space can be zero-rated if supplied to another charity – see paragraph 6.1.1).

However, if **50 per cent or more** of the total adverts in a publication are clearly placed by private individuals the charity can treat **all** the sums received as donations and outside the scope of VAT.

5.2.1 What is a private advertisement?

A private advertisement makes no reference to a business. An example of a private advertisement is one that says 'Good wishes from (or 'space donated by') John and Susan Smith'; but not those with otherwise similar wording taken out by say, 'John and Susan Smith, Grocers, 49 High Street, Anytown'.

5.2.2 Fund-raising events

The sale of advertising space in brochures or programmes for a fund-raising event is exempt from VAT. However, the sale of such space to another charity can be zero-rated. See leaflet CWL 4 Fund-raising events: exemption for charities and other qualifying bodies.

5.3 Affinity credit cards

A charity may receive payments from a bank, building society or other financial institution in return for the charity endorsing that institution's credit card and recommending its use to the charity's members or supporters. This is a business activity and the payments would normally be treated as standard-rated as being in return for marketing services provided to the financial institution.

However, we recognise that a large element of these payments could be a contribution towards charitable funds and not payment for services rendered so we allow charities to treat part of these payments as standard-rated and the remainder as outside the scope of VAT. For more information see section 8.

5.3.1 What if the charity provides more than marketing services and actually acts as an intermediary?

A charity will be acting as an intermediary in arranging a contract between its members and a credit card provider where it:

- stands between the parties to a contract in the performance of a distinct act of negotiation, without having any interest of its own in the terms of the contract;
- brings the two parties to the contract together; and
- undertakes preparatory work, such as completing or assisting with completion of application forms, forwarding forms to the credit card company, and making representations on behalf of either party.

We do not see clerical tasks, such as providing a list of names or access to a database as intermediary services. If a charity is providing intermediary services the payment they receive from the credit card provider is exempt from VAT.

5.4 Ambulance services

5.4.1 What is the liability of ambulance services?

The supply of transport services for sick or injured persons is exempt from VAT, subject to the following conditions:

- the passengers being transported must be sick or injured;
- the transport must form part of a journey to or from a place of medical treatment; and
- the vehicle in which the person is transported must be 'specially designed' for the purpose of providing such transport.

5.4.2 What is 'specially designed'?

To qualify as 'specially designed', a vehicle must have the facility to secure a recumbent person on a stretcher or be fitted with a ramp or a lift, and clamps sufficient to enable a person in a wheelchair to be safely wheeled on, transported in, and wheeled off the vehicle. The term 'specially designed' is not restricted to road vehicles, and can apply in principle to helicopter air ambulances and other forms of rescue transport. Neither is the term restricted to emergency vehicles.

Charities providing ambulance services are also entitled to relief from VAT on the purchase of a 'specially designed' vehicle, the adaptation of a vehicle to a 'specially designed' vehicle and the repair and maintenance of such a vehicle. For more information, see Notice 701/6 Charity funded equipment for medical, veterinary etc uses.

5.4.3 What if the charity provides transport other than in an ambulance?

Passenger transport in vehicles not 'specially designed' such as cars, minibuses etc is normally standard-rated. However, passenger transport in vehicles designed to carry **not less than 10 people** may qualify for zero-rating (see Notice 744A Passenger transport for more information).

5.5 Charity shops and sales of goods

The sale of donated and bought-in goods by charities and their trading subsidiaries is a business activity. The VAT treatment of the income from these sales depends upon the circumstances and the nature of the goods.

5.5.1 How do charities treat income received from the sale or hire of donated goods?

The sale, hire or export of donated goods by a charity or its trading subsidiary (where that subsidiary distributes its profits to the parent charity) is zero-rated. Zero-rating is subject to the following conditions:

- the goods must have been donated to the charity or trading subsidiary; and
- the goods must be made available to the general public, or to two or more persons who are disabled and/or receiving certain means tested benefits.

Please note that certain goods, such as second-hand toys and electrical equipment, which are prevented under safety legislation from being sold to the general public, will still qualify for zero-rating when sold to scrap merchants, as would the sale of scrap clothing to rag merchants.

Zero-rating will **not** apply if:

- the sale, hire or export of the goods is made as a result of any arrangement between the donor, the charity, the trading subsidiary or the purchaser prior to the goods being made available to the public; or
- the goods are used for any other purpose after donation other than being available for sale, hire or export to the general public. So, for example, items of office furniture donated for sale but which are first used by the charity in its offices will not qualify for zero-rating.

5.5.2 What if the charity sells donated goods at a fund-raising event?

If a charity sells donated goods at a qualifying fund-raising event, for example by auction, then the income is zero-rated. Please see paragraph 5.9 and leaflet CWL4 Fund-raising events: exemption for charities and other qualifying bodies.

5.5.3 What if the charity buys in goods to sell?

If a charity buys in goods to sell on it will have to account for VAT at the standard rate on the sale of them, unless they are goods that are zero-rated by statute such as children's clothes, books etc. For more information on zero-rated goods please contact our National Advice Service on 0845 010 9000 or refer to Notice 700 The VAT Guide.

Bought-in goods sold at qualifying fund-raising events are exempt from VAT, please see paragraph 5.9 and leaflet CWL4 Fund-raising events: exemption for charities and other qualifying bodies.

Remember, the charity's entitlement to reclaim the VAT it has been charged on the purchase of the goods will be affected if it sells them exempt from VAT.

5.5.4 How do VAT registered businesses treat goods donated to a charity for sale?

A VAT registered business can zero-rate the donation of goods to a charity or its trading subsidiary provided that the goods are to be offered for sale.

5.6 Catering

Catering is a business activity, normally liable to VAT at the standard rate. Please see Notice 709/1 Catering and take-away food for more information. However some catering can be exempt from VAT when carried on by a charity. For example, catering supplied as part of welfare services (see paragraph 5.18), such as meals for residents of care homes, and supplies of food and drink (but not alcohol) from trolleys, canteens and shops to patients in hospitals or inmates in prisons.

5.6.1 Catering provided as part of a fund-raising event.

Where catering is provided as part of a fund-raising event (see paragraph 5.9 and leaflet CWL 4 Fund-raising events: exemption for charities and other qualifying bodies, the proceeds are exempt from VAT.

5.7 Education, research and training

Charities that supply education, research or training should read Notice 701/30 Education and vocational training for more information.

5.8 Free export of goods

The supply of goods from the UK to a place outside the EC free of charge (usually in the form of relief-aid) is a business activity and is taxable at the zero rate. This enables charities that export aid to register for VAT and reclaim any input tax that they are charged on obtaining and exporting the goods.

5.9 Fund-raising

Fund-raising can take a number of forms; from the soliciting of donations and sponsorship to a wide range of business activities, some of which already appear in this section. Set out below are some of the most common ways of raising funds. If you are uncertain as to the VAT implications of any fund-raising scheme that you are planning, please contact our National Advice Service on 0845 010 9000.

5.9.1 Donations

A donation is outside the scope of VAT provided that it is freely given, with nothing supplied in return. VAT will not have to be accounted for on any monies received.

5.9.2 Fund-raising events that qualify for exemption

Events clearly organised and promoted primarily to raise money for the benefit of the charity are exempt from VAT, subject to certain conditions. The exemption covers admission fees for the event and any other income generated at the event e g sale of commemorative items, food etc.

Only certain types of event are eligible and these events are restricted to 15 events of the same kind in a financial year at any one location by the charity.

The exemption does not extend to the normal trading activities of the charity nor to income generated after the event e g the sale of surplus commemorative items or the sale of video and audio recordings of the event after the event has taken place.

The exemption does not extend to certain 'charity challenge events' (see paragraph 5.9.4).

More information on the fund-raising exemption can be found in leaflet CWL4 Fund-raising events: exemption for charities and other qualifying bodies.

5.9.3 Sponsored events in the UK

Many charities organise walks, runs, swims and other similar sponsored events or arrange for teams of representatives to participate in these events in order to raise funds.

If a charity is organising and promoting the event it may be able to take advantage of the fund-raising exemption. More information on the fund-raising exemption can be found in leaflet CWL4 Fund-raising events: exemption for charities and other qualifying bodies.

Sometimes a charity may be able to organise an exempt fund-raising event in association with a different event (which may or may not be an exempt fund-raising event in its own right). An example might be a national sporting event where the charity plans to have a marquee and hold an auction of sporting memorabilia. The charity can use the fund-raising exemption as long as the event it is organising meets the conditions set out in Notice CWL4 Fund-raising events:exemption for charities and other eligible bodies.

However, many events that individuals take part in to raise funds for charity will not fall within the fund-raising exemption, for example a commercially organised sports event such as a marathon or triathalon. Charities need to carefully consider the VAT implications of the income they receive from such events.

In many cases the charity will pay for places within a commercially organised event, and then offer those places to individuals. Where a charity allows individuals to take part in the event regardless of the amount they raise, and the individuals do not receive any benefits in return, the monies they raise can be treated as a donation and outside the scope of VAT.

We do **not** consider the following to be benefits:

- provision of free training and health advice;
- a free t-shirt, running vest or similar that clearly portrays the charity the individual is taking part on behalf of;
- free massages and support for physical well-being during the event;
- free pre-event meeting, which may include free professional advice or support, a simple meal, energy drinks and encouragement from the charity and other participants; and
- free post-event meeting, which may include medical treatment or advice, changing facilities, light refreshments and gives the charity the opportunity to thank participants.

Provision of free travel or accommodation and other benefits or 'gifts', such as bikes or watches are benefits. If a charity provides such benefits the amount raised by the participant will be taxable at the standard rate.

Some charities require individuals to pay a registration fee or insist that they raise a minimum amount of sponsorship before they can take part in the event. This is effectively an entry fee and is taxable at the standard rate. Any payment in excess of the minimum amount can be treated as a donation and outside the scope of VAT. Where this situation occurs the charity will be entitled to reclaim some of the VAT it incurs on its expenses.

If a charity asks individuals to 'pledge' or 'commit' to raise a certain amount of sponsorship, but do not insist on any payment before allowing the individual to take part in the event, the total amounts raised can be treated as donations and outside the scope of VAT. A charity can encourage individuals to pass on sponsorship money as they receive it, but cannot insist on receiving a certain amount before allowing the individual to take part.

Some charities offer prizes to top fund-raisers. These are not benefits for VAT purposes and does not affect the VAT treatment of income from participants.

5.9.4 Charity challenge events

Many charities organise treks, bike rides and other sponsored events in order to raise funds. These are usually arranged to include travel and accommodation and are often known as 'charity challenge events'.

Fund-raising events that include both travel and accommodation and events that include more than two nights accommodation do not qualify for fund-raising exemption. The provision of travel and accommodation is likely to bring the event within the Tour Operator's Margin Scheme (TOMS). Detailed advice on the TOMS can be found in Notice 709/5 Tour Operator's Margin Scheme.

5.9.5 Sponsorship of a charity

Many charities receive money, goods or services from sponsors. Where the charity is obliged to provide the sponsor with a significant benefit in return the sponsorship is a business activity and is taxable at the standard rate. However, if no significant benefits are provided the charity may be able to treat the income as non-business. We accept that giving a flag or sticker to a donor, or naming a donor in a list of supporters is insignificant. For more information please see Notice 701/41 Sponsorship. Small charities should remember that income from taxable sponsorship could put them over the VAT registration limit.

5.10 Grant funding

Charities often receive funding to support their charitable activities. If funding is freely given, with nothing supplied in return, then no VAT is due as the funding is not consideration for any supply and therefore is outside the scope of VAT.

However, some funding may be given in return for goods or services supplied by the charity. Such funding is consideration for a supply and VAT may be due on the income if the goods and/or services supplied by the charity in return are taxable at either the standard or reduced rate.

Often funding is given subject to the provisions of a contract or agreement, the terms of which may be indicative of the nature of the funding.

However, it is important to note that many such contracts or agreements are drawn up purely to ensure that the funds are used for the intended purpose. It is important not to confuse 'good housekeeping' with supplies of goods or services. Attaching conditions or safeguards to the payment of grants to ensure that the money is spent correctly does not turn it into consideration for a supply. Please remember that a contract or agreement can be oral as well as written.

Additionally, certain 'benefits' to the funder, for example copies of reports, may arise as a result of necessary safeguards to ensure the money is spent correctly and that the end product is put to proper use. Usually where these are incidental to the primary purpose of the project and are minimal in relation to the amount of funding, the funding is not seen as consideration for a supply.

5.10.1 How does a charity decide whether funding is consideration for a supply?

To decide whether funding is consideration for a supply a charity must ask itself the following questions:

- does the donor receive anything in return for the funding?
- if the donor does not benefit, does a third party benefit instead? And if so, is there a direct link between the money paid by the funder and the supply received by the third party? (See example below.)
- are any conditions attached to the funding, which go beyond the requirement to account for the funds (commonly referred to as 'good housekeeping')?

If the answer to one of the questions is 'yes' it indicates that the funding may not be freely given and may be consideration for a supply.

The following example may help to illustrate the difference between 'grant funding' which falls outside the scope of VAT and 'third party funding' which is payment by one party on behalf of someone else and is subject to VAT.

A Citizens Advice Bureau (CAB) provided free legal, and other, advice. It received grant funding from, amongst others, the local authority. The local authority, as a condition of grant funding, required a service level agreement to be entered into by the CAB, detailing opening times, levels of service etc. On this basis the CAB viewed the funding, and linked agreement, to be consideration for a taxable supply of services to the local authority.

On appeal to the VAT tribunal it was found that there was nothing in the service level agreement to support the CAB's view. In the Tribunal's view, although strings were attached to the grant given by the local authority, that in itself did not create a supply. This was because the local authority did not derive any direct benefit from the advice given. Its only benefit was the indirect knowledge that it had helped fund a service that might be of benefit to its citizens. The strings attached to the grant funding were simply good housekeeping measures by the local authority. The only supplies made were to the local citizens and, as these were mainly free of charge, there was no supply for VAT purposes.

The only exception is where legal advice is given by a CAB to a citizen who qualifies for legal aid. In such cases the legal advice given is subject to VAT. This is because the CAB has received specific payment, from a third party, for specific advice given to a citizen.

If you need help deciding whether a charity is making a supply, or on the VAT liability of a supply, please contact our National Advice Service on 0845 010 9000.

5.10.2 Does the use of the funding have any VAT implications?

Where a charity is supported by outside the scope funding, this does not determine the nature of any supplies it makes. In other words, it does not follow that outside the scope income means that the charity will only have non-business activities.

A charity needs to ask itself what activities it will be spending the funding on and whether those activities are business for the purposes of VAT. Please see section 4 for more guidance on business. If you need help deciding whether you are in business please contact our National Advice Service on 0845 010 9000.

5.11 Hiring out buildings, including village halls

The hiring out of a building for a fee is normally a business activity and the fees received are normally exempt from VAT. However, if a charity (as landlord) has opted to tax the building it must treat the fees received as standard-rated. But, if the person hiring the building (or part of a building) from the charity is:

- intending to use it as a dwelling (such as a residential flat above a charity shop);

- another charity who intends to use it for a relevant charitable purpose (for use as a village hall or similarly, or for a non-business purpose); or
- intending to use it for a relevant residential purpose (such as a residential home for children or disabled people, or a hospice),

the option to tax will generally not apply.

Where the hire of the building (or part of a building) is incidental to the provision of facilities, such as the hiring of facilities for playing sport, the supply will normally be standard-rated. (However, where rooms are hired as facilities for playing sport for a period exceeding 24 hours or for a series of 10 or more sessions the supply may be exempt, subject to certain conditions.)

Please see Notices 742 Land and Property and 742A Opting to tax land and buildings for more information. If you are hiring out a building we suggest you contact our National Advice Service on 0845010 9000 for advice on the liability of your supply.

5.12 Museums and galleries

Admission to a museum or gallery for no charge is a non-business activity. Normally this means that no input tax can be reclaimed. This paragraph explains special rules for some museums and galleries. If the charity makes an admission charge please read paragraph 5.1.

5.12.1 When can a museum or gallery offering free admission reclaim VAT?

Free access to a museum or gallery is a non-business activity, and any VAT on goods and services purchased in respect of this activity is normally irrecoverable. However, in certain circumstances the government will reimburse this otherwise irrecoverable VAT. For this to be the case, the provisions of section 33A of the VAT Act 1994 must apply, and the museum or gallery must be named in an order made by HM Treasury.

The museum or gallery may have other business activities, for example catering and the sale of books and postcards, for which normal VAT recovery rules will apply.

For full details of this scheme please refer to Notice 998 VAT refund scheme for National museums and galleries.

5.13 Membership

The provision of membership benefits to members of a club or association is a business activity. The VAT liability of a membership subscription will depend on the benefits being supplied.

In most cases a package of benefits is supplied and the provider has to decide, on the basis of guidance contained in VAT Information Sheet 2/01 (July 2001) Single or Multiple supplies-How to Decide whether he is making a single or multiple supply. If there is one principal benefit, to which all of the other benefits are incidental, the whole subscription is treated as a single supply and the VAT liability will follow that of the principal benefit. For example, if the principle benefit offered by a theatre club to its members is free theatre tickets, and other benefits, such as the right to receive copies of advertising literature, are incidental, then the theatre club would treat the subscription as a single supply of the right of admission. This would either be taxable at the standard rate or exempt if the provider was entitled to exempt its admission charges under the cultural exemption (see paragraph 5.1).

However, as a concession, charities and non-profit making organisations can treat their single supplies of membership benefits as multiple supplies. This means that the VAT treatment of each benefit can be considered individually and the subscription charge apportioned. This means that the supply of magazines or handbooks to members can normally be zero-rated. For more information see Notice 701/5 Clubs and Associations and Notice 701/10 Zero-rating of books etc.

5.14 Patron and supporter schemes

Many cultural organisations operate patron or supporter schemes, which offer benefits in return for a minimum payment. Benefits may include free admission to special exhibitions, the right to receive regular publications, discounts on shop purchases etc. The minimum payment is business income and is standard-rated. However, if one of the benefits to patrons or supporters is the right to receive publications you may be able to treat part of the payment as zero-rated. Please see VAT Information Sheet 2/01 (July 2001) Single or Multiple Supplies – How to Decide.

If a patron or supporter pays more than the minimum amount you can treat the excess as a donation and outside the scope of VAT as long as the patron or supporter is aware that scheme benefits are available for a given amount, and that anything in excess of that amount is a voluntary donation. This should be explicit in the patron or supporter scheme literature.

5.15 Sea rescue

The supply of sea rescue services for no charge is a non-business activity.

5.16 Sports membership and sporting events

The provision of certain kinds of membership to sports clubs and associations, and admission to some sporting events, by certain non-profit making organisations is a business activity, but is exempt from VAT.

Please see Notice 701/45 Sport and leaflet CWL4 Fund-raising events: exemption for charities and other qualifying bodies.

5.17 Supplies of staff between charities

Income received for the supply of staff is a business activity and is normally taxable at the standard-rate. However, if staff are jointly employed there is no supply of staff for VAT purposes. Staff are regarded as jointly employed if their contracts of employment or letters of appointment make it clear that they have more then one employer and who the employers are. Please see Notice 700/34 Staff for more information.

In some circumstances the income from the hire or loan of staff from one charity or voluntary organisation to another can be treated as non-business and outside the scope of VAT. This is subject to the following conditions:

- the employee has been engaged only in the non-business activities of the lending charity/organisation and is being seconded to assist in the non-business activities of the borrowing charity/organisation; and
- the payment for the supply of the employee's services does not exceed the employee's normal remuneration.

A 'voluntary organisation' is a body who operates otherwise than for profit, but does not include any public or local authority. 'Normal remuneration' means the total costs incurred by the lending charity/organisation in employing the member of staff including National Insurance and pension scheme contributions etc.

5.18 Welfare

Welfare services provided by charities, public bodies and state-regulated private welfare institutions or agencies are normally seen as business and are exempt from VAT (but please see paragraph 5.18.2). You can find more information in Notice 701/2 Welfare.

5.18.1 What are welfare services?

In brief, welfare services cover the following supplies:

- care, treatment or instruction designed to promote physical or mental welfare of elderly, sick, distressed or disabled people;
- care and protection of children or young people; and
- spiritual welfare provided by a religious institution as part of a course of instruction or a retreat, not being designed primarily to provide recreation or a holiday.

Please see Notice 701/2 Welfare for more information.

5.18.2 What welfare services can be treated as non-business?

Charities that provide welfare services at significantly below cost, to distressed persons for the relief of their distress, may treat these supplies as non-business and outside the scope of VAT.

'Significantly below cost' means subsidised by at least 15%, and the subsidy must be available to everyone. The charity must be providing the service to the distressed individual, and not a local authority.

By 'distressed' we mean someone who is suffering pain, grief, anguish, severe poverty etc.

An example of a non-business welfare service would be a night shelter for the homeless where a nominal charge of £1 per bed per night is made by the charity. However, the cost to the charity of providing the shelter might be £10 per bed per night.

[6005]

6. VAT RELIEFS CHARITIES CAN OBTAIN ON THEIR PURCHASES

Certain goods and services are zero-rated or reduced-rated when purchased by charities, regardless of whether the charities are registered for VAT or not.

For each of these reliefs specific conditions have to be met. Charities wishing to take advantage of these reliefs **must** provide their suppliers with eligibility declarations certifying that the conditions have been met for that relief. Please see paragraph 6.2 for more information on eligibility declarations.

6.1 VAT reliefs available

6.1.1 Advertising and goods connected with collecting donations

The supply of advertising to a charity is zero-rated. The zero-rating covers advertisements on any subject, including staff recruitment. A charity can also purchase pre-printed collecting boxes, envelopes and appeal letters at the zero rate. Low cost lapel stickers, emblems and badges that a charity gives in acknowledgement of a donation can also be zero-rated. More information can be found in Notice 701/58 Charity advertising and goods connected with collecting donations.

If a printer produces a package of printed material for a charity, some of which is zero-rated and some of which is standard-rated, the printer may be able to zero rate the entire package. This is known as the package test. More information on the package test can be found in Notice 701/10 Zero-rating of books etc.

6.1.2 Aids for the disabled

Supplies to charities of certain goods and services which the charities make available to disabled people for their personal or domestic use are zero-rated.

More information can be found in Notice 701/7 Reliefs for disabled people and Notice 701/59 Motor vehicles for disabled people.

6.1.3 Construction

The construction of buildings, and certain works to protected buildings, intended to be used for solely non-business purposes or as a village hall or similar can be zero-rated subject to certain criteria being met. More information can be found in Notice 708 Buildings and construction.

In certain circumstances a charity can also benefit from zero-rating for the construction of a ramp, widening a doorway or passage, or providing, extending or adapting a washroom or lavatory. For more information see Notice 701/7 Reliefs for disabled people.

The construction reliefs are complex and we recommend that charities contact our National Advice Service on 0845 010 9000 to check entitlement to zero-rating before commencing a project.

6.1.4 Drugs and chemicals

A charity engaged in medical or veterinary research can purchase substances directly used for testing, or for mixing with other substances in the course of that research, at the zero rate.

A 'substance' can be natural or artificial, and can be in solid or liquid form or in the form of a gas or vapour. If the substance is purchased in the form of gas the zero-rating will also apply to the cylinder rental.

6.1.5 Energy-saving materials

The installation of energy-saving materials, such as central heating and insulation, in residential accommodation or in a building used solely for relevant charitable purposes (which means used for non-business purposes or as a village hall or similarly) is liable to VAT at the reduced-rate. See Notice 708/6 Energy-saving materials for details.

6.1.6 Equipment for producing 'talking' books and newspapers

Charities and voluntary bodies caring for the blind and the severely visually impaired can obtain zero-rating for purchases of sound recording and reproduction equipment (or parts and accessories for such equipment) that has been designed or specially adapted for recording or reproducing speech for the benefit of such persons. In the case of reproduction equipment, zero-rating will not apply where the equipment is available for use by anyone other than the blind or severely visually impaired. The zero-rating also covers radios and cassette recorders purchased by charities for free loan to the blind, and the repair or maintenance of any equipment mentioned in this paragraph.

However, the supply of cassette tapes is standard-rated.

6.1.7 Lifeboats, slipways and launching and recovery equipment

A charity providing rescue or assistance at sea can purchase the following goods and services at the zero rate:

- any vessel for use as a lifeboat, and its repair and maintenance;
- lifeboat launching and recovery equipment, and its repair and maintenance;
- the construction and modification of lifeboat slipways, and their repair and maintenance;
- spare parts and accessories for use with the above vessels, equipment and slipways; and
- equipment of a kind ordinarily installed, incorporated or used in a lifeboat.

6.1.8 Medical and scientific equipment etc

The supply to a charity of certain goods that the charity will donate to an eligible body, such as a UK health authority, a hospital, a research institution or certain other charitable institutions, can be zero-rated.

Where a charity is also an eligible body it may purchase certain goods at the zero rate for its own use. Zero-rating will also apply to certain goods purchased by a charity whose sole purpose is to provide a range of care services to meet the personal needs of disabled people, or who provides transport services for disabled people.

More information on the goods that qualify for zero-rating can be found in Notice 701/6 Charity funded equipment for medical, veterinary etc uses.

6.1.9 Medicinal products

A charity engaged in the treatment or care of people or animals, or in medical or veterinary research, can purchase medicinal products at the zero rate.

A 'medicinal product' is a substance presented as a medicine, or an ingredient for a medicine, capable of being administered to people or animals for a medicinal purpose. The zero rate covers medicinal products purchased by a charity for the purpose of testing the efficiency of those products.

'Medicinal purpose' means:

- treating or preventing disease;
- diagnosing disease, or ascertaining the existence or degree of a physiological condition;
- contraception;
- inducing anaesthesia;
- otherwise preventing or interfering with the normal operation of a physiological function, whether permanently or temporarily, and whether by terminating, reducing or postponing, or increasing or accelerating the operation of that function, or in any other way.

6.1.10 Rescue equipment

Charities providing first aid or rescue can purchase specialist communication, light enhancing and heat detecting equipment at the zero-rate.

For more information, see Notice 701/6 Charity funded equipment for medical, veterinary etc uses.

6.1.11 Resuscitation training models

The supply to a charity of a resuscitation training model that is to be used in first-aid training in cardiopulmonary resuscitation or defibrillation techniques is zero-rated. 'Cardiopulmonary resuscitation' means a combination of expired air ventilation and chest compression.

6.2 Eligibility declarations

An eligibility declaration must be completed by the charity for each of the reliefs detailed in this section. Examples of these declarations can be found in Notice 701/6 (Supplement).

It is the supplier's responsibility to ensure that the correct VAT rate is applied. He must take reasonable steps to check with the charity any condition that he cannot verify for himself. Any additional verifications carried out should be recorded and kept with the declaration of eligibility.

If a supplier has taken reasonable steps to check the validity of a declaration but fails to identify an inaccuracy and in good faith makes the supplies concerned at the zero rate,

Customs will not seek to recover the tax due from the supplier. It is important that suppliers carefully check declarations received. (See the concession on incorrect customer declarations in Notice 48 Extra-statutory concessions.)

A charity must give its supplier evidence that it is a charity. If asked for further evidence the charity must be able and willing to give it before VAT relief can be given.

6.3 What if a charity purchases goods from another EC Member State?

VAT registered charities that buy goods in other Member States of the EC as part of their business activities are not normally required to pay VAT when they bring the goods back to the UK. These goods are referred to as acquisitions. Instead of paying VAT on entry the charity must account for any VAT due on the acquisitions at the appropriate UK VAT rate on their next VAT return. No tax will therefore be due on the acquisition of goods which would be zero-rated if purchased by a charity in the UK. You can find more information on purchasing goods within the EC and the accounting requirements in Notice 725 The Single Market.

6.4 What if a charity purchases goods from outside the EC?

When a business (which may include a charity or its trading subsidiary) imports goods into the UK from a place outside the EC VAT is normally due at place of entry to the UK. However charities may be able to claim relief from VAT on some imports. Please see Notice 317 Imports by charities free of duty and VAT for more information.

[6006]

NOTES

Para 6.1.3: first paragraph replaced by Update 1 (June 2004), to correct a typographical error.

7. FUEL AND POWER

7.1 Reduced rate of VAT

Charities have to pay VAT on supplies of fuel and power. However charities can claim the reduced rate where fuel and power is supplied for a qualifying use. Qualifying use means:

- supplied for use in a dwelling or certain other types of residential accommodation, such as a children's home, hospice or care home for the elderly or disabled; or
- supplied for use in charitable non-business activities, such as free day care for the disabled.

Additionally, deliveries of certain small quantities of fuel and power are automatically treated as being for a qualifying use. For example, electricity supplied at a rate not exceeding 1000 kilowatt hours a month or a delivery of not more than 2300 litres of gas oil, will qualify for the reduced rate whatever the use of the building.

If the fuel and power is supplied partly for a qualifying use the supplier may have to apportion the supply. Charities should provide the supplier with a certificate declaring the percentage of the fuel and power that will be used for a qualifying purpose. For more information please see Notice 701/19 Fuel and power.

7.2 Climate Change Levy

If a charity qualifies for the reduced rate for fuel and power, it will be excluded from the climate change levy.

See Notice CCL2 An introduction to climate change levy for further information.

[6007]

8. TREATMENT OF INCOME FROM AFFINITY CREDIT CARDS

8.1 How to treat income from affinity credit cards

Charities may treat income from affinity credit cards as follows, as long as they are not acting as an intermediary between the card provider and the applicant. Please see paragraph 5.3.1 for more information on intermediaries. Please note that this treatment only applies to income from affinity credit cards and does not extend to any other financial products.

A typical qualifying agreement between the charity and the card provider will provide for the supply by the former (or its trading subsidiary) to the latter of the following services:

- access to the charity's membership or mailing lists and/or mailing of the card provider's promotional literature to members.
- endorsement of the card and marketing of the card by the charity to its members/supporters.
- the right to use the charity's name and logo on the card and on the card provider's promotional literature.

Subject to the agreements between the charity and card provider being structured in a qualifying manner, the bulk of the monies received by a charity from the card provider can be treated as outside the scope of VAT.

Typically a card provider will pay an agreed amount to the charity (or its trading subsidiary) on the issue of each new card. Thereafter the card provider pays the charity a percentage of the turnover (value of purchases) on the card.

8.2 How the relief works

The basis of the relief is that payments by card providers to a charity, made solely in respect of the use of the charity's name and logo, can be treated as contributions for which the charity is not obliged to do anything in return.

To benefit from this treatment there must be two separate agreements:

- One agreement, between the charity (or its trading subsidiary) and the card provider should provide for the supply by the charity (or its trading subsidiary) of the necessary marketing and publicity services, access to membership lists and other promotional activity for the card (marketing services). These supplies are taxable at the standard rate.
- A second and separate agreement between the charity and the card provider should provide for contributions to be made by the card provider in respect of the use only of the charity's name and/or logo. Contributions made under this agreement can be treated as outside the scope.

This being the case, part (at least 20%) of the initial payment can be treated as the consideration for the standard-rated business supplies by the charity. The remaining 80% or less of the initial payment, and **all** subsequent payments based on turnover will be outside the scope of VAT.

[6008]

9. GLOSSARY OF TERMS

Acquisition: Goods coming into the UK from another EC Member State.

Business: An economic activity, not necessarily for profit – see section 4. Only charities carrying out business activities and making taxable supplies can register for VAT.

Consideration: Consideration means any form of payment either wholly in money, partly in money and partly in something else (such as in part-exchange transactions) or not in money at all (such as in barter transactions).

Exempt: Some business activities are exempt from VAT, for example, the provision of welfare services by a charity. If a charity is carrying out an exempt business activity it does not have to charge VAT, but it cannot normally reclaim any VAT on the goods and services purchased in respect of that activity (see paragraph 3.7.3). For more information on what goods and services are exempt from VAT see Notice 700 The VAT Guide. Charities (and any other business), whose business activities are wholly exempt, are not able to register for VAT.

Input tax: Most goods and services that charities purchase from a VAT-registered business will bear VAT (but please see Section 6 for details of reliefs available to charities). The VAT paid on goods and services purchased by a charity in respect of any business activity it carries out is input tax. VAT paid on goods and services a charity purchases for any non-business activity it carries out is not input tax (see paragraph 3.7.1). Charities can only reclaim input tax in respect of taxable business activities, with some exceptions (see Notices 700/64 Motoring expenses and 700/65 Business entertainment. Charities cannot normally reclaim any input tax in respect of exempt business activities (see paragraph 3.7.3 and Notice 706 Partial exemption).

Non-business: Any activity which is not a business activity.

Output tax: The VAT that a charity must charge and account for on supplies of taxable goods and services.

Outside the scope: Activities that are not covered by VAT law, for example activities that are non-business, or business activities that take place outside the UK. Charities whose activities are wholly non-business are not allowed to register for VAT. Charities whose business activities take place wholly outside the UK, can register for VAT if those activities would be taxable were they to take place in the UK.

Reduced rate: This is the rate of VAT (currently 5%) liable on supplies of certain goods and services, for example, domestic fuel and power, children's car seats, residential renovations and conversions. For more information about what goods or services are reduced-rated see Notice 700 The VAT Guide.

Standard rate: This is the rate of VAT (currently 17.5%) liable on all business supplies of goods and services that are not specifically exempted, zero-rated or reduced-rated.

Taxable person: An individual, firm, company, charity etc who is, or is required to be, registered for VAT. A person who makes taxable supplies above certain value limits is required to be registered.

Taxable supply: Goods and services that are standard-rated, reduced-rated or zero-rated when sold by a business (or charity) that is registered for VAT.

Trading subsidiary: A non-charitable trading company controlled by one or more charities. Most of the VAT reliefs available to charities are **not** available to trading subsidiaries.

Zero rate: This is the rate of VAT (0%), liable on supplies of certain goods and services, for example, food and children's clothes. For more information on what goods and services are zero-rated see Notice 700 The VAT Guide. Although no VAT is charged on these supplies, any input tax incurred by a charity in the making of zero-rated supplies is recoverable. Unlike exempt activities, charities (and any other business), whose business activities are wholly zero-rated, are able to register for VAT.

Do you have any comments?

We would be pleased to receive any comments or suggestions you may have about this notice. Please write to:

HM Customs and Excise
Construction, Charities and Health Team
4th Floor West
New Kings Beam House
22 Upper Ground
London
SE1 9PJ

Please note this address is **not for general enquiries**. You should ring our National Advice Service about those.

If you have a complaint or suggestion

If you have a complaint please try to resolve it on the spot with our officer. If you are unable to do so, or have a suggestion about how we can improve our service, you should contact one of our Regional Complaints Units. You will find the telephone number under 'Customs and Excise – complaints and suggestions' in your local telephone book. Ask for a copy of our code of practice 'Complaints and putting things right' (Notice 1000). You will find further information on our website at http://www.hmce.gov.uk.

If we are unable to resolve your complaint to your satisfaction you can ask the Adjudicator to look into it. The Adjudicator, whose services are free, is a fair and unbiased referee whose recommendations are independent of Customs and Excise.

You can contact the Adjudicator at:

The Adjudicator's Office
Haymarket House
28 Haymarket
LONDON
SW1Y 4SP

Phone: (020) 7930 2292
Fax: (020) 7930 2298
E-mail: **adjudicators@gtnet.gov.uk**
Internet: **http://www.adjudicatorsoffice.gov.uk/**

[6009]

FUND-RAISING EVENTS: EXEMPTION FOR CHARITIES AND OTHER QUALIFYING BODIES

NOTES

This HM Revenue & Customs Help Sheet can be found at www.hmrc.gov.uk/charities/fund-raising-events.htm.

CONTENTS

INTRODUCTION

Who Is This Help Sheet For?

This Help Sheet is aimed at charities and qualifying bodies that raise money through fund-raising events. This Help Sheet sets out the conditions for direct tax and the VAT exemption that apply to fund-raising events held on or after 1 April 2000. Customs VAT Notice 701/1 'Charities' (including Update 1 dated February 1997) sets out the law and guidance on the VAT exemption for fund-raising events held before 1 April 2000.

This Help Sheet applies to all fund-raising events including small scale events directly conducted by charities, and other qualifying bodies, and larger fund-raising events conducted by the trading subsidiaries of charities.

Direct Taxes

If the event held by a charity meets the criteria for VAT exemption then it will automatically qualify for the purposes of the HMRC Extra-Statutory Concession ESC C4 for exemption from income tax and corporation tax as long as the profits are applied charitably. This concession only applies to events organised by charities and voluntary organisations.

ESC C4

"Certain events arranged by voluntary organisations or charities for the purpose of raising funds for charity may fall within the definition of "trade" in Section 832 ICTA 1988, with the result that any profits will be liable to income tax or corporation tax. Tax will not be charged on such profits provided.

a) the event is of a kind which falls within the exemption from VAT under Group 12 of Schedule 9 to the VAT Act 1994 and

b) the profits are transferred to charities or otherwise applied for charitable purposes."

The fact that an activity is exempt from VAT, and that any profit will not be taxed, does not necessarily mean that charities can undertake the activity directly rather than through a trading company.

Further information about the direct tax treatment of trades carried on by charities can be found in Trading by Charities at **[6016]**.

When Should A Charity Register For VAT?

For VAT purposes, a charity's activities could be entirely non-business, exempt business or taxable business (standard rate, reduced rate and zero rate), or any combination of these.

However, for VAT registration purposes charities only need to take account of the income from their taxable business activities. When that exceeds certain limits charities must notify their local VAT Business Advice Centre. These limits and the procedure for registering for VAT can be found in VAT Notice 700/1 'Should I be registered for VAT?'. The registration limit is reviewed annually. Charities can also apply to register voluntarily if they make taxable supplies below those limits.

Exempt supplies (business supplies which have no VAT charged on them at either the standard or zero rate, such as qualifying fund-raising events) do not form part of your taxable turnover. If you are registered for VAT and make some exempt supplies, it may restrict the amount of VAT recoverable on overhead expenses. You can find further information in VAT Notice 706 'Partial exemption'.

VAT Law

The exemption for charitable fund-raising is based upon Article 13A(1)(o) of the EC Sixth Directive on VAT which was first adopted by the UK in 1989. It is designed to allow charities, and other qualifying bodies, to exempt supplies of goods and services which they make as part of an event held to raise funds for their activities.

Not all fund-raising events will qualify for exemption as this could give charities and other qualifying bodies an unfair advantage over commercial providers. European Community member states may introduce any necessary restrictions they consider necessary in order to prevent distortion of competition.

Charities also need to take account of charity law which limits the fund-raising events they can hold. For more information about this you should read the Charity Commission's publication CC20 'Charities and Fund-raising' which is available on the Internet site charity-commission or telephone the Charity Commission on 0870 3330125.

The current UK law on the VAT exemption for fund-raising events is set out in Group 12, Schedule 9 of the Value Added Tax Act 1994. The law changed significantly from 1 April 2000. The Value Added Tax Act 1994 in guidance book V1–2 'VAT law' and in Notice 701/39 'VAT liability law'.

[6010]

WHO QUALIFIES FOR FUND RAISING EVENTS EXEMPTION?

Charities

Bodies have charitable status when they are registered, excepted or exempted from registration with the Charity Commission in England and Wales. Or are registered by the Office of the Scottish Charity Regulator (OSCR) in Scotland. Or are bodies in Northern Ireland, which are treated by the HM Revenue & Customs as charitable. Not all non-profit making organisations are charities. The term 'charity' has no precise definition in any law. Its scope has been determined by case law. You therefore need to establish whether your organisation is a charity using the following guidelines.

- Charities are non-profit distributing bodies established to advance education, advance religion, relieve poverty, sickness or infirmity or carry out certain other activities beneficial to the community.
- In England and Wales charities must normally register with Charity Commission (not to be confused with VAT registration explained in paragraph 1.3). Some very small charities do not need to register with Charity Commission. There are also some other special cases where particular bodies do not need to register. If you are uncertain of your position contact the Charity Commission on 0870 330 123.
- In Scotland all charities must be registered with the Office of the Scottish Charity Regulator (OSCR). HM Revenue and Customs decides whether bodies in Northern Ireland are eligible to claim the direct tax exemptions. For further information contact HMRC Charities on 08453 02 02 03.

There is no distinction for VAT purposes between those charities registered with the Charity Commission or OSCR and those that are not. However, unregistered charities claiming VAT relief may need to demonstrate that they have 'charitable status'. This may be evident from their written constitution or by the recognition of their charitable status by HM Revenue and Customs.

Bodies Corporate Connected With Charities

Only a body corporate which is wholly owned by a charity and whose profits (from whatever source) are payable to a charity, will be eligible under this relief and may therefore qualify for VAT exemption on fund-raising events. This means that a charity's own trading company can hold fund-raising events on behalf of the charity.

Please note the HMRC Extra-Statutory Concession does not extend to the trading companies of charities as they can shed their profits using the Gift Aid scheme.

Qualifying Bodies

For the purposes of this relief, 'qualifying body' means

- any non-profit making organisation mentioned in item 1 of Group 9, Schedule 9 to the VAT Act 1994
- any body that is an eligible body for the purposes of Group 10, Schedule 9 to the VAT Act 1994, and whose principal purpose is the provision of facilities for persons to take part in sport or physical education, or
- any body that is an eligible body for the purposes of item 2 of Group 13, Schedule 9 to the VAT Act 1994.

This is explained further in the Appendix. For further information see VAT Notices 701/33 'Trade unions, professional bodies and learned societies', 701/45 'Sport and physical education' and 701/47 'Culture'.

Voluntary Organisations

The term 'voluntary organisation' can cover a wide range of groups and associations. Generally, they are not-for-profit organisations with a public benefit purpose and are not for the private benefit of their members. A body within the definition of a qualifying body for VAT purposes will not necessarily be a voluntary organisation.

[6011]

FUND-RAISING EVENTS

Do All Events Held By A Charity Or Qualifying Body Qualify For Exemption?

There are a few restrictions, which are covered in the following paragraphs, to prevent distortion of competition with other organisations holding similar events which do not have the benefit of VAT exemption.

What Is A Fund-Raising Event?

For tax purposes, it is an event clearly organised and promoted primarily to raise money for the benefit of the charity or qualifying body. Social events which incidentally make a profit do not fall within the exemption. People attending or participating in the event must be aware of its primary fund-raising purpose.

An 'event' is an incident with an outcome or a result. This means that activities of a semiregular or continuous nature, such as the frequent operation of a shop or bar, cannot therefore be an event. The relief is not intended to exempt normal trading activities from VAT.

What Kinds Of Events Are Covered By The Exemption?

The following are examples of different kinds of events which may be held for fund-raising purposes.

- A ball, dinner dance, disco or barn dance.
- A performance – such as concert, stage production, and any other event which has a paying audience.
- The showing of a film.
- A fete, fair or festival.
- A horticultural show.
- An exhibition – such as art, history or science.
- A bazaar, jumble sale, car boot sale, or a good-as-new sale.
- Sporting participation (including spectators), such as a sponsored walk or swim.
- A sporting performance.
- A game of skill, a contest, or a quiz.
- Participation in an endurance event.
- A fireworks display.
- A dinner, lunch or barbecue.
- An auction of bought in goods (an auction of donated goods is zero-rated).

This is not an exhaustive list.

Is There A Limit To The Number Of Events Held?

Yes. Eligible events are restricted to 15 events of the same kind in your financial year at any one location by a charity (including its trading subsidiary) or qualifying body. The restriction prevents distortion of competition with other suppliers of similar events which do not benefit from tax exemption. If you hold 16 or more events of the same kind at the same location during your financial year none of the events will qualify for exemption.

What Does 'Location' Mean?

Location means in the same place. Similar kinds of events held in different locations would qualify for exemption provided all other conditions were met. For example, 20 balls held by a national charity each in different towns in the same financial year would all qualify for relief.

Clearly, events which need to be held on special premises, such as a sports ground, swimming pool or theatre are easy to define. Each of these will be accepted as a different location.

If the event is held in a complex of cinemas, theatres or concert halls, the location is the specific cinema, theatre or concert hall in which the fund-raising event takes place.

We regard a charity's entire website as a location for events held over the Internet.

The rule is designed to be generous to charities which may hold a number of events of the same type in different locations, but in the same town. We will not accept arrangements such as weekly boot sales each held in different, but adjacent fields, as constituting a separate location without considering whether such an arrangement is potentially distorting competition.

Does An Event Run Over Several Days At The Same Location Comprise A Single Event Or A Number Of Separate Events?

Where an event, such as a concert, is repeated on successive evenings each performance is a separate event and counts towards the maximum number of 15 allowed within the exemption. A single event which takes place at the same location for more than one day, such as a golf tournament, is accepted as one event.

Where a concert or similar event is offered as part of a travel package this may not be exempt.

Which Events Do Not Qualify For Exemption?

- Each event which counts towards 16 or more of the same kind held at the same location during your financial year.
- Events which are not organised and promoted for fund-raising purposes, such as events which form part of a social calendar for members.
- Events which are organised and promoted primarily for another purpose, such as an annual general meeting.
- Asking the public for donations through street collections, flag days etc. The receipt of donations is not a business activity and so they are not subject to VAT.
- The activity of selling goods is not an event and so is not eligible for relief under these provisions, even where all the proceeds are received by, or donated to, a charity. Where the sale of goods takes place in the context of a qualifying fund-raising event it is covered by the relief and zero-rating may be available in certain circumstances, see paragraph below.
- Travel packages which fall within the Tour Operator's Margin Scheme, see paragraph below.

See paragraph below for the VAT treatment of income for a non-qualifying event.

Is There An Option To Charge VAT On Fund-Raising Events?

No. VAT exemption is mandatory for any event that fulfils all the conditions. An event which does not meet one or more of the conditions will not qualify for exemption as a fund-raising event.

If A Charity Runs More Than 15 Events Of The Same Kind At A Location Are The First 15 Events VAT Exempt And VAT Charged Only From The 16th Event Onwards?

No. Every event in a programme of 16 or more events will be taxable at the standard rate. The exemption applies up to 15 events of the same kind at a location. To exempt the first 15 events in a longer sequence risks distortion of competition. If you hold 16 or more events of the same kind at the same location during your financial year none of the events will qualify for exemption.

What About Frequent Small Scale Events?

The 15 event limit does not apply to fund-raising events where the gross takings from all similar events, such as coffee mornings, are no more than £1000 per week. Such activities carried out more than once or twice a week are likely to be trading activities and not eligible for exemption, see paragraph above.

What Happens If Small Scale Events Take Over £1000 In A Week?

All the events in that week will not qualify as small scale events and each will count towards the 15 event allowance.

Can The Hire Of A Room Or Other Costs Be Offset Against The £1000?

No. The £1000 limit relates to the income of the events prior to any costs being deducted.

Can Zero-Rated Supplies Be Made At An Exempt Event?

Yes. The sale of printed matter, such as programmes and commemorative brochures or any other goods which are eligible for the zero rate relief from VAT, may still be zero-rated when supplied at a fund-raising event.

This means that a VAT registered charity or other qualifying body will be able to recover any input tax which is directly attributable to the taxable supply of those goods.

Examples of zero-rated items are

- the sale of donated goods by a charity
- eligible food
- eligible printed matter
- young children's clothing
- the supply of advertising time or space to a charity
- any other goods which qualify for zero-rating.

Why Is There An Anti-Competition Clause?

The restriction prevents distortion of competition with other suppliers of similar events which do not benefit from tax exemption. We will only use this measure where

- this relief is likely to distort the market, or
- there is significant and systematic evidence of commercial distortion.

If a commercial organisation alleged competitive disadvantage, we would look carefully into the matter and any subsequent action would depend upon the particular circumstances. A charity would have the right of appeal against the decision.

Are Fund-Raising Holidays Or Day Trips VAT Exempt?

No. Any fund-raising activity which falls within the Tour Operator's Margin Scheme, such as a package of travel and accommodation, or which includes more than two nights' accommodation does not qualify for the fund-raising exemption. Further information about the Scheme may be found in Notice 709/5 'Tour Operator's Margin Scheme'.

What Evidence Must I Hold To Show That The Event Was Organised And Promoted Primarily To Raise Funds?

There is no single document that you must hold to demonstrate that the event was organised primarily to raise funds. Minutes of meetings, costing and similar documents should show that the main purpose for holding the event is to raise funds for charitable purposes or a qualifying body's own benefit.

The event must be promoted in such a way that those attending the event are aware that its main purpose is to raise funds. Publicity material, tickets etc should therefore clearly refer to fund-raising. For example

- 'fund-raising for'
- 'in aid of'
- 'help us to build'
- 'help us to raise money for'.

Examples of publicity material, tickets etc, should be retained to support evidence of exemption.

Do Charities Still Need Wholly-Owned Trading Companies For Fund-Raising Activities?

Charity law governs which activities charities may carry out directly and which must be conducted through a trading company. For more information you should read the Charity Commission's publication CC20 'Charities and Fund-raising' which is available on their Internet site charity-commission or telephone 0870 3330125 for a copy.

What Fund-Raising Activities Can Be Carried Out Within A Charity?

You need to bear in mind the following guidance from the Charity Commission on fund-raising activities.

Your charity's governing document may mean that the charity lacks the necessary powers to undertake a fund-raising activity which is exempt from VAT and the profit of which will not be taxed. The new tax relief rules do not change that situation. Charities in England and Wales seeking power to undertake a fund-raising activity should approach the Charity Commission to see if their governing document can be amended.

If your charity has powers which appear to cover the proposed fund-raising activity the charity trustees need to consider carefully whether they in fact do so. Any body which does have the power to engage in substantial trading activities, which involve significant risk to its property is unlikely to be a charity. A charity's assets have been given for charitable purposes and should not be exposed to any serious or substantial risk of loss from fund-raising activities. Risks which might be acceptable commercially will not necessarily be acceptable for your charity to undertake directly. Large scale events such as celebrity concerts or sporting events can be a valuable way of raising funds. However, experience shows that they also carry a high degree of risk and your charity trustees should not normally undertake such activities within your charity.

The Charity Commission strongly advises trustees to take professional advice before doing anything to expand a charity's direct fund-raising activities in any way that falls outside the direct tax exemptions in place before 1 April 2000 and the revised Extra-Statutory Concession

ESC C4. The best way for your charity to raise funds and take full advantage of the new tax regime is to have a wholly owned trading subsidiary which pays all its profits to your charity under the Gift Aid scheme.

[6012]

SCOPE OF THE RELIEF

Are All The Purchases For Qualifying Fund-Raising Events Also VAT Exempt?

No. Normal VAT treatment will apply to the goods and services you purchase.

Does The Exemption Apply To An Individual Or Independent Groups Which Organise Events As Part Of A National Fund-Raising Campaign?

Where an individual or an independent group holds events as part of a national fund-raising campaign such as Comic Relief, Children in Need and Blue Peter Appeals, it is unlikely that they will have charitable status or be a qualifying body. If the group does not have charitable status or is not a qualifying body the exemption would not apply to such events and the group should see VAT Notice 700/1 'Should I be registered for VAT?'. Input tax incurred on expenditure cannot be reclaimed if the individual or independent group is not registered for VAT.

A branch of a charity may or may not be a separate charity to which the exemption applies. This will depend on how the branch and its parent are set up.

Will An Event Organised By Two Or More Charities Or Two Or More Qualifying Bodies Qualify For Exemption?

Yes, but only if all the charities (including their trading subsidiaries) and qualifying bodies have organised, either individually or with others, less than 15 exempt events, of that kind, in that location, in their financial year.

Can A Joint Event Organised By A Charity And A Qualifying Body Be Exempt?

Yes, but only if the charity (including its trading subsidiaries) and the qualifying body, have organised, either individually or with others, less than 15 events in their financial year.

Can A Joint Event Organised By A Charity Or Qualifying Body And Someone Else Be An Exempt Fund-Raising Event?

No. Only events organised exclusively by charities, their trading subsidiaries and qualifying bodies may be exempt fund-raising events.

What About Events Organised By Professional Fund-Raisers Or Agents?

Events held by a charity, trading subsidiary or qualifying body which are organised by professional fund-raisers or other agents may qualify for exemption.

Generally, the VAT incurred by the charity or qualifying body in connection with an exempt event will not be recoverable. You may recover the VAT incurred in making taxable supplies within the event. This applies if the charity or qualifying body makes all the arrangements for the event.

If the agent charges or retains any part of the gross receipts, this is consideration for agency services and will be subject to VAT. This applies even if the amount is less than or equal to the cost of arranging the event.

What Income Is Included In The Exemption?

All the income for supplies of goods and services in connection with an event is exempt, for example

- all admission charges
- the sale of commemorative brochures (may be zero-rated, see paragraph above)
- the sale of advertising space in those brochures (may be zero-rated, see paragraph above)
- other items sold by the charity such as T-shirts, non-donated auctioned goods etc. Where items are normally supplied zero-rated such as children's T-shirts, then zero-rating rather than exemption can be applied (see paragraph above), and
- sponsorship payments directly connected with a qualifying event.

What Income Is Not Included In The Exemption?

Commemorative goods and souvenirs sold for a period after the qualifying fund-raising event. For example

- video and audio recordings of the fund-raising event sold after the event has taken place will be standard-rated
- surplus commemorative items such as adult T-shirts, mugs etc will be standard-rated
- commemorative programmes will remain zero-rated
- children's T-shirts will remain zero-rated
- donated goods for sale may still be sold VAT free provided the normal conditions are met.

Will All The Income For A Non-Qualifying Event Be Subject To VAT?

When a fund-raising event does not qualify for exemption, it is open to a charity or any other body to set a basic minimum charge which will be standard-rated, and to invite those attending the event to supplement this with a voluntary donation.

The extra contributions will be outside the scope of VAT if all the following conditions are met.

- It is clearly stated on all publicity material, including tickets, that anyone paying only the minimum charge will be admitted without further payment.
- The extra payment does not give any particular benefit (for example, admission to a better position in the stadium or auditorium).
- The extent of further contributions is ultimately left to ticket holders to decide, even if the organiser indicates a desired level of donations.
- For film or theatre performances, concerts, sporting fixtures, etc, the minimum charge is not less than the usual price of the particular seats at a normal commercial event of the same type.
- For dances, and similar functions, the minimum total sum upon which the organisers are liable to account for VAT is not less than their total costs incurred in arranging the event.

If the publicity material for a fund-raising event suggests that those paying a recommended extra amount are more likely to be admitted than those paying merely the basic ticket price, then the extra amount becomes part of the consideration for a supply of services, rather than a donation, and as such is subject to VAT at the standard rate.

Further information about admission charges may be found in Notice 700/22 'Admissions'.

What Is The VAT Treatment Of Fund-Raising Events Which Took Place Before 1 April 2000?

Please see Notice 701/1 'Charities' for guidance.

[6013]

FURTHER HELP AND ADVICE

If you need further help and advice on any points covered by this leaflet, please contact HMRC Charities on 08453 02 02 03.

To help us give the best service, always give us the full facts and if you have a detailed query please put it in writing.

You can also obtain help and advice about how to keep your VAT affairs in order from members of the tax accountancy profession. However, you do not have to employ an accountant, but if you choose to do so, responsibility for the accuracy of your VAT affairs remains with you, the registered person.

What Can I Do If I Am Not Happy With The Service I Receive From You?

Naturally we hope this question will not arise, but, with many thousands of enquiries every day, misunderstandings and errors can happen.

If you have a complaint about the way in which we have handled your affairs, first write to the officer in charge of the office concerned. He or she will then do everything possible to resolve the problem quickly.

If the HMRC does not settle your complaint to your satisfaction, you can ask the Adjudicator for HM Revenue & Customs to look into it and recommend appropriate action.

The Adjudicator, whose services are free, acts as an impartial referee where people feel their affairs have been badly handled. The Adjudicator's recommendations are independent. The address is

The Adjudicator's Office
Haymarket House
28 Haymarket
London SW1Y 4SP

Telephone: 020 7930 2292
Fax: 020 7930 2298
e-mail: adjudicator

Finally you can ask a Member of Parliament to refer your complaint to the Independent Parliamentary Commissioner for Administration, commonly known as the 'Ombudsman'. Further information is available from

The Parliamentary Commissioner for Administration
Millbank Tower
Millbank
London SW1P 4QP
Telephone: 020 7217 4163
Fax: 020 7217 4160
e-mail: opca-enqu
Internet: ombudsman.

[6014]

APPENDIX – (SEE PARAGRAPH 2.3)

Check List To Decide If An Event Qualifies For VAT Exemption

1. Are you
- an organisation whose purposes are exclusively charitable
- a wholly owned subsidiary of a charity
- formally appointed agent of a charity
- a non-profit making body mentioned in item 1 of Group 9:
  - a trade union (or other staff association)
  - professional association
  - an association for the advancement of knowledge etc
  - an association for making representations to Government on business and professional interests of members, or
  - a body which has objects which are in the public domain and are of a political, religious, patriotic, philosophical, philanthropic or civic nature
- a non-profit-making body mentioned in Group 10 of Schedule 9 of the Value Added Tax 1994 established for the principal purpose of providing facilities for participating in sport or physical education, or
- a non-profit making cultural body mentioned in item 2 of Group 13 of Schedule 9 of the Value Added Tax Act 1994 which is managed and administered on a voluntary basis by persons who have no financial interest in its activities?

2. Is the event being held primarily for the purpose of raising funds and is this being made clear in the publicity for the event or on the tickets?

3. Are all the funds raised by the event
- for your organisation's own benefit and used in carrying out its objectives
- for the benefit of your parent charity, if you are a wholly owned subsidiary, or
- for the benefit of the charity which has appointed you as its agent?

4. Is the event one of 15 or less of that kind being held at the location during your financial year?

5. Does the event fall within the Tour Operator's Margin Scheme?

If the answer to any of the questions 1–4 is 'no', or the answer to question 5 is 'yes', the event does not qualify for exemption.

These notes are for guidance only and reflect the position at the time of writing.

They do not affect your right of appeal about your tax, National Insurance or VAT.

[6015]

TRADING BY CHARITIES

Clubs and Charities Series

NOTES

This HM Revenue & Customs Help Sheet can be found at www.hmrc.gov.uk/charities/trading-by-charities.htm.

CONTENTS

Many charities carry on trades, either as part of their charitable activities or to raise funds. This explains how the HM Revenue & Customs treats the trading profits of charities for tax purposes. It describes the tax exemptions which are available and explains how these apply to different types of trading activity.

INTRODUCTION

When charities carry on trades, provided certain conditions are met, the profits of these trades are exempted from tax. Charities need to be aware of the tax rules that apply to trading profits when they are deciding the best way to arrange their trading activities.

This help sheet gives some guidance on calculating the profits of a trade carried on by a charity and describes ways in which non-exempt trading profits can be passed to charity so that no tax is payable. Finally, the booklet looks at factors to take into account when a charity invests in a trading company.

If you need any further help or information, you can contact HMRC (Charities).

PART IV MISCELLANEOUS MATERIALS

HMRC (Charities)
St John's House
Merton Road
BOOTLE
Merseyside
L69 9BB

You can also call the Charities Help line on **08453 02 02 03** 8.00 am to 6.00 pm.

If possible, you should always quote your charity tax reference number in any correspondence with HMRC (Charities).

What about VAT?

This help sheet does not cover Value Added Tax (VAT). Customs & Excise Notice 701/1 explains the VAT rules which affect charities and their business activities.

If income or corporation tax relief is available for particular trading activities, this does not automatically mean that relief from VAT is also available. VAT applies to a wide range of goods and services supplied in the course of business. (For VAT purposes 'business' has a wider meaning than trading.) It can also apply to any charitable activities which involve the supply of goods or services.

Many areas in which charities operate, such as the supply of certain health and welfare services, are, however, exempt from VAT. There are also some special reliefs for charities which are explained in the Notice. This help sheet refers you to the Notice whenever activities are mentioned which qualify for relief.

If you require further guidance on VAT, for charities you should contact the HMRC Charities helpline on 08453 02 02 03 8.00 am to 6.00 pm.

[6016]

WHAT IS A TRADE?

Normally, a trade involves the sale of goods or services to customers as part of a commercial enterprise. A one-off or occasional venture may be treated as a trade for tax purposes if it involves the sale of goods or services for profit.

In most cases, it will be clear whether an activity is, or is not, a trade. However, in some cases, such as a one-off transaction, this is not always obvious and in these cases it will be necessary for HMRC (Charities) to look at all the circumstances surrounding the activity in order to make a decision. The fact that the profits are intended to be used for charitable purposes is irrelevant in deciding whether an activity is a trade.

Trading by charities

Trading by charities can take a number of different forms, but most fall into one of two broad categories

- trades which form a Primary Purpose of the charity (for example, a religious charity selling bibles) or trades which are carried on mainly by its beneficiaries (for example, the manufacture and sale of goods by disabled people), or
- trades which are not part of the Primary Purpose of the charity, but which are intended to raise funds for charitable purposes (for example, sales of promotional items).

The distinction between primary purpose trades and other trades is important because it may determine how the trade is treated for tax purposes.

The definition of primary purpose trades are explained in more detail under 'What is a primary purpose trade?'.

The following sections describe the tax rules which apply to trades carried on by charities and explain how those rules apply to different sorts of trades.

[6017]

WHEN ARE CHARITIES' TRADING PROFITS EXEMPT FROM TAX?

There is a limited exemption from tax for the profits of trades carried on by charities. To qualify for exemption, the profits must be used only for the purposes of the charity and the trade must meet one of the following three conditions.

The trade must be part of a primary purpose of the charity (a 'primary purpose trade') or ancillary to this primary purpose trade (see 'What is a primary purpose trade?').

The work in connection with the trade must be mainly carried out by beneficiaries of the charity (see 'What rules apply to trades where the work is carried out by beneficiaries?').

The turnover of a non-primary purpose trade must fall below certain limits (see 'Is small trading exempt from tax?').

Some fund-raising events may qualify for concessional relief under an Extra-Statutory Concession (ESC). See 'What is the Extra-Statutory Concession?' or more details. In addition, there are special rules relating to agricultural shows and lotteries.

Agricultural shows

There is a separate statutory exemption from tax for the profits of exhibitions or shows held by agricultural societies which are not charities. These profits will not be taxable if
- the exhibition or show is held for the purposes of the society, and
- the profits are used only for the purposes of the society.

Lotteries

Charities may run lotteries in order to raise funds for their charitable purposes as defined in Section 3 and 5 of the Lotteries and Amusements Act 1976.

The profits of such lotteries, that are promoted by charities or by subsidiary companies on their behalf, are exempt from tax, as long as the lottery meets the conditions of this Act and the profits are used only for the purposes of the charity.

In cases where the subsidiary company, rather than the charity, is registered as the society under Section 5 of the Lotteries and Amusements Act 1976, the lottery profits will belong to the company and not to the charity, for tax purposes. The exemption will therefore not apply and the company will need to pass the profits to the charity under Gift Aid to get relief from tax (see 'The Gift Aid scheme').

[6018]

WHAT IS A PRIMARY PURPOSE TRADE?

A 'primary purpose trade' is one that forms part of the primary purposes or charitable objectives of the charity. These are set out in the charity's trust deed, constitution or other governing document. Profits from primary purpose trades and from trades which are ancillary to primary purpose trades are exempt from tax.

Primary purpose trades

Examples of trades which may be seen as primary purpose trades are
- the provision of educational services by a school or college in return for course fees
- the holding of an exhibition by an art gallery or museum in return for admission fees
- the sale of tickets for a theatrical production staged by a theatre
- the provision of healthcare services by a hospital in return for payment
- the provision of residential accommodation by a residential care charity in return for payment
- the sale of certain educational goods by an art gallery or museum.

In each of these examples, the organisation carrying on the activity must be a charity and the activity must form part of the charity's objectives.

Trades which are ancillary to primary purpose trades

The exemption from tax also extends to other trades which are not primary purpose activities, but which are ancillary to a primary purpose. Examples of trades which qualify as primary purpose trades in this way include
- the sale of relevant goods or services (for example, text books) for the benefit of students, by a school or college
- the provision of a creche for students' children, by a college in return for payment
- the sale of food and drink in a cafeteria to art gallery or museum visitors
- the sale of food and drink in a restaurant or bar to theatre audiences
- the sale of confectionery, toiletries and flowers to patients and visitors by a hospital.

Trades which are not wholly primary purpose trades

In some cases, a trade may amount, in part, but not wholly, to a primary purpose trade. For example, the trade might offer a range of goods or services, only some of which are within a primary purpose, or the trade might serve some customers who are not beneficiaries or patrons of the charity, as well as those who are. Examples of such trades are

- a shop in a museum, selling a range of goods, some of which are related to a primary purpose of the charity (ie education and the preservation of property for the public benefit). In this case, the sale of direct reproductions of exhibits and catalogues would be related to the primary purpose, but the sale of promotional pens, mugs, tea towels, stamps etc, would not
- a school or college letting accommodation to students (the beneficiaries of the charity) in term-time, and to tourists out of term-time
- a theatre restaurant selling food and drink to the theatre audience (the beneficiaries of the charity), but also to the general public.

In these circumstances, the trade might not qualify as a primary purpose trade because part of the trade is not related to a primary purpose. In practice, the HMRC will accept that all of the profits of the trade will be exempt from tax if

- the turnover of the part of the trade which is not within a primary purpose is not 'large' (ie not more than £50,000), and
- the turnover of that part of the trade is less than 10% of the turnover of the wholetrade.

The following examples illustrate this

Example 1

Charity A carries on a trade with an annual turnover of £60,000, of which £55,000 is primary purpose and £5,000 is not. Because the non-primary purpose turnover is less than 10% of the total and less than £50,000, the whole trade is treated as primary purpose and the profits are therefore exempt from tax.

Example 2

Charity B carries on a trade with an annual turnover of £100,000, of which £85,000 is primary purpose and £15,000 is not. Because the non-primary purpose turnover is more than 10% of the total, the whole trade is treated as non-primary purpose.

If the trade does not fall within the definition of the charity's primary purpose trade, the profits may still be exempt from tax, either because the trade is mainly carried out by the beneficiaries of the charity or because they fall within the exemption for small trading if the statutory requirements are met (see 'Is small trading exempt from tax?').

[6019]

WHAT RULES APPLY TO TRADES WHERE THE WORK IS CARRIED OUT BY BENEFICIARIES?

Where a trade is carried out by beneficiaries of a charity, whether or not the work has a therapeutic, remedial or educational value, the profit from the trade will often qualify for exemption from tax as a primary purpose trade.

Examples of trades commonly carried on by charities where the work is mainly carried out by beneficiaries are

- a farm operated by students of an agricultural college
- a restaurant run by students as part of a catering course at a college
- the sale of goods manufactured by disabled people who are beneficiaries of a disability charity.

In some cases, part of the work of the trade may be carried out by people who are not beneficiaries of the charity. As long as the charity can prove that most of the work is done by beneficiaries, the profits will be exempt from tax.

A charity may pay salaries to beneficiaries who work in a trade carried on by the charity, meaning that the beneficiaries become employees of the charity. Provided that they can still properly be regarded as beneficiaries of the charity, this does not affect the exemption of the trading profits from tax.

PAYE must be operated on the earnings of beneficiaries who are employed by a charity in the same way as for other employees.

[6020]

IS SMALL TRADING EXEMPT FROM TAX?

There is a statutory tax exemption for the profits of small trading carried on by charities, for profits that are not already otherwise exempt. Before a charity considers whether this particular statutory exemption applies to its own trading activities, it should first determine whether the Extra-Statutory Concession for fund raising activities is relevant. (See 'What is the Extra Statutory Concession for fund raising activities?').

How does the exemption apply?

The exemption applies to the profits of all trading activities that are not already exempt from tax, provided

- the total turnover from all of the activities does not exceed the annual turnover limit, or
- if the total turnover exceeds the annual turnover limit, the charity had a reasonable expectation that it would not do so, and
- the profits are used solely for the purposes of the charity.

What is the annual turnover limit?

The annual turnover limit is

- £5,000, or
- if the turnover is greater than £5,000, 25% of the charity's gross income, but
- no more than £50,000.

The following table illustrates the application of these rules

Total gross income of the charity	Maximum sales turnover
Under £20,000	£5,000
£20,000 to £200,000	25% of charity's total gross income
Over £200,000	£50,000

For the purpose of this limit, 'gross income' means the total receipts of the charity for the year from all sources (grants, donations, investment income, trading receipts, etc), calculated in accordance with the normal charity accounting rules.

Example 3

Charity C sells Christmas cards to raise funds to enable it to carry out its primary purpose. Selling Christmas cards is not itself a primary purpose and neither can it be considered under the Extra-Statutory Concession because it does not form part of the income from a fund-raising event (see 'What is the Extra Statutory Concession for fund raising events?').

The sales turnover from the Christmas cards amounts to £4,500 in the year. Assuming this is the charity's only taxable trading activity, any profits will be exempt from tax, because this is less than £5,000.

Example 4

Charity D has a sales turnover, from a non-exempt trade, of £40,000 for the year. Its gross income for the year (including this £40,000) is £150,000.

The £40,000 sales turnover exceeds the annual turnover limit (25% of £150,000 = £37,500).

Therefore, the profits on sales would not be exempt from tax for this year unless the charity had a reasonable expectation at the start of the year that its sales turnover would not exceed the limit (see 'The reasonable expectation test' below).

The reasonable expectation test

If a charity's total turnover of taxable fund-raising activities exceeds the annual turnover limits, its profits will still be exempt if the charity can show that, at the start of the tax year, it was reasonable for it to expect that the turnover would not exceed the limit. This might be the case if either

- the charity expected its non-exempt turnover to be lower than it turned out to be, or
- the charity expected its gross income would be higher than it turned out to be.

The first might happen if, for example, the income from an activity the charity had been carrying on for a number of years increased unexpectedly, or if it the income from a new activity brought in more income than the charity expected it to.

The second could happen if, for example, the charity did not receive a grant for which it had budgeted.

PART IV
MISCELLANEOUS MATERIALS

The H M Revenue & Customs will consider any evidence the charity may have to satisfy the reasonable expectation test, such as

- minutes of meetings at which financial matters were discussed
- copies of cash flow forecasts
- business plans
- the previous year's accounts.

If the charity expects to be regularly trading at or around the annual turnover limits, it might be better to use a trading subsidiary in order to minimise its tax liability. (See 'When should a charity use a trading company?').

[6021]

WHAT IS THE EXTRA-STATUTORY CONCESSION FOR FUND-RAISING ACTIVITIES?

Any profits from trading activities carried on by a charity, which are not covered by one of the three statutory exemptions described above, will be taxable. However, it may be possible for the charity to take advantage of an Extra-Statutory Concession that applies specifically to fund-raising events. If an event falls within the concession, the profits from it will not be taxable.

The full text of this concession is as follows

The concession

"Certain events arranged by voluntary organisations or charities for the purpose of raising funds for charity may fall within the definition of 'trade' in Section 832 ICTA 1988, with the result that any profits will be liable to income tax or corporation tax. Tax will not be charged on such profits provided:

a. the event is of a kind which falls within the exemption from VAT under Group 12 of Schedule 9 to the VAT Act 1994 and

b. the profits are transferred to charities or otherwise applied for charitable purposes."

How does the concession apply?

HMRC will decide whether the Extra-Statutory Concession applies in individual cases. If fund-raising activities meet the criteria for the VAT exemption, they will automatically qualify for the exemption from income tax and corporation tax. Charities should therefore read our help sheet CWL4, 'Fund-raising events: Exemption for charities and other qualifying bodies', which explains when tax exemption is available. You can get copies of this leaflet help sheet from HMRC Charities.

If a charity carries on a substantial, regular trade it may be required by charity law to set up a subsidiary company to carry on the trade, even if the profits are exempt from tax under the concession. Setting up a subsidiary would protect charitable property from being used for non-charitable trading purposes. (See the Charity Commission booklet CC35 'Charities and Trading'.)

What is a fund-raising event?

HMRC considers that the following events may be held for fund-raising purposes, within the concession.

- Balls, dinner dances, discos or barn dances
- Performances; such as concerts, stage productions, and any other events which have a paying audience
- Film showings
- Fetes, fairs or festivals
- Horticultural shows
- Exhibitions – such as art, history or science
- Bazaars, jumble sales, car boot sales, good as new sales
- Sporting participations (including spectating), such as sponsored walks or swims
- Sporting performances
- Games of skill, contests, quizzes
- Endurance participations
- Firework displays
- Dinners, lunches, barbecues
- Auctions of bought-in goods

HMRC will consider factors such as how often and where the events are held, their turnover and any special circumstances, in order to determine whether activities in the above list will be exempt from tax.

What will happen if an event is not covered by the concession?

If an event falls outside the terms of the concession, and it is not covered by the statutory exemptions, the profits may be taxable. If HMRC advises the charity that a particular event will not fall within the exemption from VAT, it should contact HMRC (Charities) at the address shown at the beginning of this booklet.

If the charity believes that a particular event or series of events will not fall within the concession, it may be possible to organise the event to minimise the amount of tax payable.

For example, the charity might set a basic minimum charge (which will be taxable) and invite those attending the event to supplement this with a voluntary donation. The additional contributions will not be taxable if all the following conditions are met.

- All publicity materials, including tickets, clearly state that anyone paying only the minimum charge will be admitted without further payment.
- The additional payment does not secure any particular benefit (for example, admission to a better seat in the auditorium).
- The value of the further contributions is left to ticket-holders to decide (even if the organiser indicates a desired level of donation). These further contributions may be made under Gift Aid, subject to them meeting the requirements of the scheme.
- For film or theatre performances, concerts, sporting fixtures, and similar events, the minimum charge is not less than the usual price for the particular seats at a normal commercial event of the same type.
- For dances, dinners and similar functions, the sum of the basic minimum charges is not less than the total costs incurred in arranging the event.

The concession described above is of general application, but it must be borne in mind that in a particular case there may be special circumstances which have to be taken into account in considering the application of the concession.

The concession will not be given in any case where an attempt is made to use it for tax avoidance.

[6022]

WHAT ABOUT OTHER INCOME?

Sale of donated goods

Many charities raise funds by selling donated goods, either regularly in a shop or on a market stall, or occasionally at a jumble sale or auction. Although such activity is similar to retailing by commercial businesses, the fact that the goods are donated means that such sales are treated differently for tax purposes. This is because, when a charity sells donated goods, it is realising the value of a gift, rather than reselling goods which it has manufactured or purchased for resale.

The same applies even if the donated items are sorted, cleaned and given minor repairs. However, if the goods are significantly altered or processed so that they are sold in a different state from that in which they were donated, the sale proceeds may be regarded as trading income. For example, if a charity makes donated fabric into clothes for sale, this will amount to a trade.

Profits from lettings

Any income a charity receives from renting land or buildings is exempt from tax, as long as the income is used for charitable purposes. Ways in which charities might raise funds from their land or buildings when they are not being used for the charity's own activities include

- a college letting its buildings for conferences outside term time
- a charity letting excess space in its office premises
- a school letting its gymnasium for use by clubs after school hours
- a church charging the public to park in its car park when it is not needed by the congregation.

The profits from such lettings are not treated as trading profits, but as rental income and are therefore not subject to tax. However, if the charity provides services connected with the use of the land or buildings (for example, caretaker, food or laundry services) the letting activities might amount to trading. Therefore, each case must be considered individually.

Business sponsorship

Businesses often provide sponsorship to charities, to support either the charity's work in general, or a particular project. Such links with charity offer publicity or public relations benefits to the business providing the sponsorship.

The tax treatment of payments received by charities under sponsorship arrangements will depend on the nature of the arrangement. The payments may be regarded as

- the income of a stand-alone trade, such as a charity providing mailing lists to a business
- part of the income of a wider trade, such as a theatre offering a stage performance in exchange for payment, or
- some other kind of income.

If, before a sponsor makes a payment to a charity, a commercial participator agreement (required by the Charity Commission under Section 59 of the Charities Act 1992) is in place, the tax treatment of the payment may be determined by the wording of the agreement. Otherwise, the tax treatment of the payment will be determined by the particular facts of the case.

For tax purposes, a donation from a business which results in marketing opportunities for that business is not generally regarded as part of the charity's trading income, but as a donation. This is because the charity is not actually providing goods or services in return for the donation and it is the business, not the charity, which exploits the marketing opportunities offered by the link.

However, if the charity itself also publicises the link with the sponsor, or provides any other goods or services in exchange for the donation, this may be regarded as a trade. This will depend on the extent of the publicity.

- If this publicity amounts to no more than acknowledgement of the sponsorship in the charity's publications, posters, etc, then the publicity activity will not be regarded as a trade.
- If the references to a sponsor in the publicity materials amount to advertisements for the business, then the payments will be treated as trading income. HMRC will regard a reference to a sponsor as an advertisement if it incorporates any of the following
  - large and prominent displays of the sponsor's logo,
  - large and prominent displays of the sponsor's corporate colours, or – a description of the sponsor's products or services.

For example, if a project organised by a charity is sponsored by a business, and the business's name and logo are inserted in the corner of a project report, this would not amount to advertising. However, if the name and logo were widely displayed throughout the report, this might be considered to be advertising in return for the sponsorship payment.

There are other services that a charity might provide in return for sponsorship payments that will be factors in determining whether the payments are trading income. Examples of such services are

- use of the charity's mailing list
- use of the charity's logo
- endorsement of the sponsor's products or services
- exclusive rights to sell goods or services on the charity's premises.

Once it has been determined that sponsorship payments form part of a charity's trading income, the next step is to consider whether the sponsorship arrangement is a trade in its own right or part of the income of a wider trade.

If the sponsorship is intended to fund an activity of the charity which is itself a trade, the payments will be treated in the same way as the other profits of that trade. For example, if a business sponsors a stage production by a theatre, the sponsorship payments will be regarded as part of the income of the trade of putting on the stage production, which is the theatre's primary purpose, and the profits will be exempted from tax. However, if the sponsorship income forms part of the sales turnover from a non-primary purpose trade, the profits may be taxable.

Payments for use of a charity's logo

If a charity accepts payment in return for allowing its logo to be used by a business to endorse the business's products or services, and the charity promotes the endorsement in its own literature, the payments are likely to be treated as trading income of the charity.

Sometimes businesses make annual payments solely for the use of a charity's logo. Whether these payments are considered to be annual payments will depend on the terms of the agreement for the use of the logo. The charity can reclaim the tax that the sponsor deducts when making annual payments, provided the payments

- are applied solely for charitable purposes
- are made under a legal obligation

- recur each year
- are treated as a pure donation in the hands of the charity.

[6023]

HOW DO CHARITIES CALCULATE THE PROFITS OF THEIR TRADES?

The profits of trades carried on by charities which are not covered by the statutory and concessional exemptions described above are taxable. Even if part of the activities of a trade might be covered by one of the exemptions, the whole of the profits will be taxable. In this case, the profits, including capital allowances if applicable, should be calculated in the same way as for any other organisation. However, there are a number of factors that may be particularly relevant when calculating the profits of a trade carried on by a charity.

Allocation of indirect overheads

As well as deducting expenditure relating solely to the trade when calculating the trade's profits, the charity should also deduct a proportion of its overheads which are attributable to the trade. For example, if the trade is carried on in the charity's premises, it will normally be able to deduct part of the running costs, such as

- heating and lighting
- rent
- building repairs and maintenance.

As well as the use of premises, other indirect overheads that may be partly attributable to the trade are

- employee salaries
- computer costs
- telephone charges
- postage costs
- accountancy and legal fees
- general administration.

The share of overhead costs attributable to the trade will depend on the nature of the trade. For example,

- the share of costs for the use of premises might be based on the amount of floor space allocated to the trade
- the share of the running costs of student accommodation let to tourists out of term might be based on the number of days in the year when the premises are allocated to the trade
- the share of employee salaries might be based on the amount of employee time devoted to the trade compared to total employee time.

Goods or services provided at undervalue

Charities often receive goods or services at no cost, or at less than their full market price. For example

- a supplier might sell trading stock or equipment to a charity at cost price
- a professional adviser might provide services free of charge
- helpers and beneficiaries might do work on a voluntary basis.

If a trade is not covered by the concessional exemptions, the charity can deduct a notional amount when calculating the profits of that trade, based on the commercial value of the donated goods or services, as though they had paid this amount for them.

However, the notional amount must be calculated on a 'reasonable basis'. So, for example, if a celebrity acts as a volunteer waiter at a gala dinner, the notional cost would be no more than the going rate for the employment of a waiter, not that of the celebrity.

[6024]

WHAT HAPPENS IF A CHARITY MAKES TRADING LOSSES?

Charities may make trading losses. If the trading activities which make the loss are within the charity's primary purposes, the losses will be regarded as charitable expenditure. However, if the trading activities are not within the charitable objectives, the losses may be regarded as non-charitable expenditure. The exemptions from tax for charities' profits only apply if the profits are used for charitable purposes. Therefore, the exemptions may not apply if the charity makes the loss through non-charitable expenditure. The exemption will depend on the individual circumstances of each case.

Where a trading loss arises as a result of the deduction of a notional market price for goods or services provided free or less than market price (see 'Goods or services provided at undervalue'), the loss will not be regarded as non-charitable expenditure.

Similarly, a trading loss might arise as a result of the allocation of a proportion of the charity's fixed costs. (See 'Allocation of indirect overheads'.) Again, the loss will not be regarded as non-charitable expenditure, provided that

- the charity has a surplus of profit, discounting the allocation of a proportion of indirect costs, after deduction of direct costs, and
- the fixed costs would have been incurred by the charity in any event.

[6025]

WHEN SHOULD A CHARITY USE A TRADING COMPANY?

When charities carry on trades which are not covered by the statutory and concessional exemptions, they will usually set up a wholly-owned trading company to carry on the work. Companies owned by charities are liable to pay tax on trading profits in the same way as other companies. However, they will often donate their whole profits to the charity, which means that they get tax relief. In the hands of the charity, the donation will not be regarded as trading income but as a donation, so that it will be exempted from tax (provided, of course, it is used for charitable purposes).

From 1 April 2000, companies make payments to charities under the Gift Aid scheme, which means that tax is not deducted and therefore does not need to be reclaimed.

The Gift Aid scheme

From 1 April 2000, a trading company can donate its trading profits to the parent charity without deduction of tax, under the Gift Aid scheme.

When deciding how much of their profits to give to charity, companies may need to take into account

- the limits on the amount they can pay out, which are set out in the Insolvency Act 1986
- that they must keep sufficient profits to avoid a cash drain (see 'Investing in a company which sheds its profits to the charity')
- any restrictions imposed by the company's Memorandum and Articles of Association

and any other requirements that may be imposed upon them.

Tax relief for payments under the Gift Aid scheme

When the company has decided how much of its profits to pass to the charity, in most cases, it can make payments for a particular accounting period up to nine months after the end of the accounting period and still qualify for tax relief for the accounting period to which the payments relate.

The company gets tax relief for the Gift Aid payments it makes as a deduction in its corporation tax calculation.

Making the Gift Aid payments

From 1 April 2000, the company does not have to deduct any income tax when making a donation to charity. It gets relief for the actual payment it makes to the charity. This applies to any payment companies make after 1 April 2000, even if they relate to accounting periods before that date. (See 'Investing in a company which sheds its profits to the charity'.)

The company will need to keep normal accounting records and copies of any correspondence to support its claim for relief. It does not need to have any certificate or form of declaration to the charity.

A company can make a Gift Aid payment by making a payment of money to the charity. The company and charity should hold separate bank accounts so that this transfer can take place.

If a company is not wholly-owned by a charity, it can deduct a Gift Aid payment in its corporation tax calculation only for the accounting period in which it actually makes the payment. It cannot carry back the deduction into an earlier period, or carry it forward into a later period.

Calculating profits to be passed to the charity

If the trading company shares the charity's premises, staff or services, it should include an appropriate allocation of the costs in its accounts. The amount the charity charges for the shared resources should generally not exceed the cost, as any profit it makes in this way would be regarded as non-exempt trading income.

See 'How do charities calculate the profits of their trade?' for more information on how to calculate the profits of a trade.

[6026]

HOW DOES A CHARITY FINANCE A TRADING COMPANY?

Charities which set up wholly-owned companies to carry on non-exempt trading activities will usually need to invest funds in the company when it is set up. The company may also need further financial support to fund expansion or development later on.

Charity investments and tax

There are special rules in the Taxes Acts for charities investing funds in trading companies. The charity must follow these rules or may risk losing some or all of its tax exemptions. To qualify for relief, the charity must make an investment

- for charitable purposes only
- for the benefit of the charity, and
- not for the avoidance of tax.

Investments will be regarded as being made for charitable purposes and for the benefit of the charity if they are commercially sound. Usually, this means that charities must ensure that the investments

- are secure
- carry a fair rate of return, and
- in the case of loans, provide for recovery of the amount lent.

Under charity law, when charities make investments, they must

- be objective in their selection of investments
- avoid undue risk or speculation, and
- make a proper spread of investments.

Charities also need to consider the requirements of the Trustee Investment Act 1961 as well as their own investment powers as set out in the charity's governing document. The charity should keep proper records of all investment decisions, including the factors on which the decisions were based. Depending on the size of a proposed investment, the charity may make its decision based on the following.

- Business plans
- Cash flow forecasts
- Projections of future profits.

It should also review its investments regularly.

Investing in a company which sheds its profits to the charity

Most commercial companies use their profits to maintain and develop their business. If a company intends to distribute all of its profits every year, this may leave it without these necessary funds. To avoid this problem, when a charity sets up a trading company, it should ensure that it provides the company with enough capital to enable it to shed its profits every year and stay in business.

If the company is left with insufficient cash to continue its business after passing its profits to the charity, the charity may find it needs to provide it with further funding.

However, if the charity does this very frequently, this can affect both the charity's tax exemptions and the company's deductions for its Gift Aid payments. Therefore, in some cases, it may be necessary for the company to change its practice so that it keeps part of its profits. This part of the profits, because it is not being passed to the charity, will be taxable.

Charities considering making investments in a trading company should seek professional accountancy and legal advice.

[6027]

GIVING TO CHARITY BY BUSINESS

NOTES

This HM Revenue & Customs Help Sheet can be found at www.hmrc.gov.uk/charities/giving-to-charities-bus.htm.

INTRODUCTION

This Help Sheet sets out the tax reliefs available to encourage businesses to give to charity.

The sheet explains the different rules that might apply depending on whether your business is a company, a sole trader or a partnership.

It sets out the position from April 2003 and covers the following topics.

- Gifts of money
- Gifts of land, buildings, shares and securities
- Gifts of equipment or trading stock to charity
- Secondment of employees to charity
- Sponsorship payments

[6028]

GIFTS OF MONEY

Businesses can get tax relief when they give money, whether as a one-off or a regular payment, under the Gift Aid scheme. There is no longer a separate tax relief for payments to charity under a deed of covenant. There is no limit to the amount that the business can give, but the way you get tax relief will depend upon whether the business is a company, a sole trader or a partnership.

How does a company get relief?

If your company decides to give money to charity, it simply makes the payment through Gift Aid and deducts the amount as a 'charge' when working out its profits for corporation tax purposes. You make the full payment to the charity. You do not need to deduct any tax from the payment and the charity does not claim back any tax on the gift. You no longer have to provide a Gift Aid certificate to the charity or provide a new form of declaration. If your company has no corporation tax liability in an accounting period, there are special rules regarding how any loss created by the donation can be used. You should contact the HMRC office that deals with your company's corporation tax affairs if you need further information on this point.

If you are a close company, generally one under the control of five people or less, there is a limit on the benefit which the company, or a person connected with the company, can receive from the charity in return for the payment. (There is an explanation of connected persons in our leaflet CGT1 'Capital gains tax. An Introduction'.)

How do sole traders get relief?

From April 2003, you can treat Gift Aid payments made between the end of the tax year and the date you send us your Self Assessment return as if they were made in the tax year the return is for. To do this, you must send us your Self Assessment return in time to reach us by the filing date.

How do partnerships get relief?

We treat any gift by a partnership as made by the individual partners. We will treat you and your partners as each giving an equal share of the gift, unless you tell us that the partnership has decided to split the gift in a different way. We will treat your gift as paid out of your taxed income and the charity will reclaim the basic rate tax on it from us. If you are a higher rate taxpayer, you can get relief on the difference between the basic rate and the higher rate of tax on the gross amount of your share of the gift.

Unless one partner has power, under the partnership agreement or some other document, to make a Gift Aid declaration on behalf of the partnership, each partner will need to make a Gift Aid declaration in favour of the charity. This can be done on one declaration, providing the name and address of each partner is shown. In Scotland, where partnerships have a legal personality, a partner may make a Gift Aid declaration on behalf of the partnership simply showing the partnership's name and address.

What evidence do I need of payment to the charity?

If required, you will need to provide us with reasonable evidence of all the payments you have made to charities in the year in the same way as for other items in your Self Assessment tax return. For instance, a cancelled cheque, an entry in a bank or credit card statement, or an acknowledgement from the charity.

What are the limits on benefits I can receive in respect of my gift?

The following table sets out the maximum benefits an individual, partner or close company donor is allowed to receive in any tax year in respect of gifts to any one charity. Your business can make gifts to as many charities as you choose, but the total benefits received must not exceed £250 from each charity.

[6029]

GIFTS OF LAND, BUILDINGS, SHARES AND SECURITIES

Businesses can get tax relief for gifts to charity of any qualifying investments. These include certain shares, securities and land and buildings. This is in addition to the relief you can claim for them when calculating capital gains.

How does the tax relief apply?

You can claim the relief if you give, or sell at less than market value, a 'qualifying investment' to a UK charity. However, a company cannot get relief for a gift of its own shares.

What land, buildings, shares and securities qualify?

The following categories qualify.

- Shares and securities listed or dealt in on the UK Stock Exchange, including the Alternative Investment Market.
- Shares and securities listed or dealt in on recognised foreign stock exchanges.
- Units in an authorised unit trust.
- Shares in a UK open-ended investment company.
- Holdings in certain foreign collective investment schemes.
- A qualifying interest in land. A qualifying interest in land is the whole of a person's beneficial interest in freehold or leasehold land in the UK.

If in doubt, we can tell you whether the gift or sale will qualify for relief.

How do I calculate the amount of relief?

The amount of relief you can claim is

- the market value of the net benefit to the charity * at the time you give or sell them the qualifying investment, **plus**
- any incidental costs (for example, brokers' fees or legal fees), less
- any disposal proceeds or other money, or the value of other benefits you or a person connected with you (such as, a relative or connected company), receive in consequence of you giving or selling the qualifying investment to charity.

* The value of the net benefit to the charity is normally the market value of the qualifying investment. However, if the charity is, or becomes, subject to an obligation to any person such that:—

- it is reasonable to suppose that the disposal of the qualifying investment would not have been made in the absence of the obligation; or
- the obligation is connected to the charity receiving the qualifying investment or a related investment,

the market value of the qualifying investment is reduced by the aggregate of the related liabilities of the charity resulting from the exercising of the obligation.

Are there any forms that need to be completed?

No. Evidence of the gift of shares or securities having been made to the charity may be in the form of a copy of the stock transfer form or a letter from the charity acknowledging receipt of the gift.

For gifts of real property, you will need a certificate from the charity that must contain all of the following information.

- A description of the qualifying interest in land, which is the subject of the disposal.
- The date of the disposal.
- A statement that the charity has acquired the qualifying interest in land.

How do I claim the relief?

Companies should deduct the relief as a charge on income for the accounting period in which they make the gift. The amount should be entered on your Corporation Tax Self Assessment return as a charge.

If you are a partner or sole trader, you should deduct the relief when you calculate your income for the tax year in which you make the gift of shares, securities or real property. You should enter the amount on your Self Assessment return. A tax year runs from 6 April one year to 5 April the next.

What date should I take as the date of disposal for the purpose of establishing the market value of the shares, securities or interest in land?

The date on which the qualifying investments are transferred to the charity. In the case of shares and securities, this is likely to be the date that you sign and hand over the stock transfer document. For gifts of land you should take the date on which you disposed of your beneficial interest in the land.

Normally this will be the date on which you transferred the property to the charity. However, if the disposal was made under a contract, perhaps a sale at below market value, you should take the date on which the contract was made.

If the contract was conditional then the date of disposal will be the date on which all the conditions were satisfied. If the gift was made by a declaration of trust you should take that date. If you have granted a lease to a charity you should take the date you granted the lease. There is further information to help you identify the market value at that date in our Help Sheet 'Giving land, buildings, shares and securities to charity'.

[6030]

GIFTS OF EQUIPMENT OR TRADING STOCK TO CHARITY

If your business gives to a charity

- an item manufactured or sold in the course of your trade, or
- machinery or plant used in the course of your trade

then the business can get relief. To qualify, the business must be a trading company, a sole trader, or a trading partnership.

How do I get the relief?

When you give away an article manufactured or sold in the course of your trade, the normal treatment is to include the market value of the gift as a trading receipt when calculating your profits for tax purposes. Where such articles are given to a charity, nothing is included as a trading receipt. In that way, you get relief for the cost of the article in calculating the taxable profits of the trade.

In the case of machinery or plant used in the course of your trade, treat it as having been disposed of at nil value for capital allowances purposes (rather than at market value, as would otherwise be the case). The total capital allowances given to you in respect of the article will be equal to its cost.

[6031]

SECONDMENT OF EMPLOYEES TO CHARITY

Trading or investment companies, sole traders, or trading partnerships that provide assistance to charities by seconding employees to them on a temporary basis can claim relief for the employment costs that they continue to incur.

How do I get relief?

Any costs incurred by your business in connection with the employment of a person on secondment to a charity (including salary payments) should be treated as a business expense when calculating your chargeable profits for tax purposes.

[6032]

SPONSORSHIP PAYMENTS

Trading companies, sole traders or trading partnerships sponsoring a charitable activity can claim relief for sponsorship payments, provided the payments are made wholly and exclusively for the purposes of your trade and are not of a capital nature. (Capital expenditure is expenditure incurred for the purpose of acquiring, improving or extending an asset held for use in the business.)

What sort of payments might qualify?

A payment made to get publicity for your name or product, which represents a reasonable return for the amount paid. Whether a payment qualifies for relief will depend on the facts. If you are in doubt, contact your HMRC Office.

How do I get relief?

You deduct the sponsorship payments in calculating your trading profits for tax purposes.

What happens if sponsorship payments do not meet the conditions for relief?

No relief is available unless all the conditions are met. For example, if you make a sponsorship payment to a charitable activity, which results in your business acquiring an asset from the charity (for instance, office equipment or vehicles), you cannot deduct the payment when calculating the trading profits of the business for tax purposes.

Similarly, if you make a payment that is partly for commercial reasons and partly for charitable reasons, you cannot deduct it in calculating the trading profits of the business for tax purposes. However, you might be able to get relief for such payments as Gift Aid donations. If you are in doubt about how we will treat a particular payment for tax purposes, ask your HMRC Office before making it.

[6033]

FURTHER INFORMATION

This Help Sheet does not cover every point.

If you have any questions, you can contact our Charity Helpline on **0845 3 02 02 03**, which is open from 8.30am to 6.00pm, Monday to Friday.

[6034]

GIVING TO CHARITIES BY INDIVIDUALS

NOTES

Issued by the External Communications Unit of the Inland Revenue (February 2004).

This HM Revenue & Customs Help Sheet can be found at www.hmrc.gov.uk/charities/giving-to-charities-indiv.htm.

CONTENTS

Introduction

If you are thinking of making a gift to charity you should consider the benefits of tax-efficient giving.

This can make it cheaper to donate to charity or it can benefit your chosen charity by making your donation go further.

There are a number of schemes operated by the Inland Revenue, which make it easy to give to charity in a tax-efficient way. This Help Sheet explains the following ways in which you can give.

- Gift Aid.
- Gifts of land, buildings, shares and securities.
- Payroll Giving.

It sets out the position from April 2003, but is only a brief guide.

Gift Aid

If you pay tax in the UK, then Gift Aid is a simple way to increase the value of your gift to a charity. Making your donation using Gift Aid will enable the charity to reclaim the basic rate tax on your gift to them. This means that if you give £10 to charity using Gift Aid in the tax year 2003–04, that gift is worth £12.82 to the charity.

You can make payments by cash, cheque, postal order, direct debit, standing order, debit or credit card or even in a foreign currency (including the euro).

Subject to a few rules, you can give any amount, large or small, regular or one-off and the charity can reclaim the tax.

If you are a higher rate taxpayer, you can claim relief on the difference between the basic rate and higher rate of tax.

If you do not pay tax, you should **not** use Gift Aid.

How does my gift qualify for Gift Aid?

Your chosen charity will normally ask you to consider making your donation using Gift Aid. They will give you a simple form to complete declaring that you wish to make donations under Gift Aid.

The charity can only reclaim the basic rate of tax if you have paid enough tax in the tax year to cover the amount reclaimed on your gifts. The tax year runs from 6 April one year to 5 April the next.

How do I know I have paid enough tax?

For most people it will normally be easy to determine if you have paid enough tax to cover the amount the charities will reclaim. That tax paid can be income tax or capital gains tax at any rate and can include tax paid on savings and income.

You can calculate the amount of tax the charity will reclaim using the following formula.

Amount of gift X basic rate of income tax

100 minus the basic rate

So, with the basic rate 22%, the charity reclaims 22/78ths of your gift.

Example 1

During the tax year you give a total of £400 to various charities.

With the basic rate at 22%, the amount of tax the charities can reclaim is £112.82 (£400 x 22/78).

If you have paid tax totalling £112.82 or more then you can make the donations using Gift Aid, making your donation worth £512.82 (£400 + £112.82) to the charities.

If you have paid less tax than £112.82, you should not make the donations under Gift Aid. You can still give the money to charity and not complete a Gift Aid declaration.

I am a higher rate taxpayer. Can my chosen charity reclaim the higher rate tax paid?

No. The charity can only reclaim tax on your gift at the basic rate. If you are a higher rate taxpayer, you can claim the difference between the higher rate at tax at 40% and the basic rate of tax of 22% in your Self Assessment return.

So, in the example above, you may reclaim higher rate relief of £92.30 (£512.82 at 18%) on your gross donation of £512.82.

From April 2004 you will be able to gift repayments to a charity of your choice. This means that your original gift could be worth even more to the charity.

Do I have to make a declaration with every gift?

No. One declaration will cover all the gifts you make to a charity for whatever period you wish. For example, it can cover gifts you might already have made to a particular charity since 6 April 2000 or it can cover the gifts you make in the future.

Can I receive benefits from the charity in respect of my gift?

There are limits to what benefits can be received in any tax year. These limits are set out in the following table.

Amount of donation	Value of benefits
£0–100	25% of the value of the gift
£101–1,000	£25
£1,001–10,000	2.5% of the value of the gift

The total benefits must not exceed £250.

Can I pay my membership subscriptions through Gift Aid?

You can pay membership subscriptions to a charity through Gift Aid, provided any membership benefits do not exceed the limits on the previous page. Where a charity offers you free or reduced entry to view heritage property or wildlife, the preservation of which is the charity's main aim, the value of that benefit is disregarded.

What is the carry back of Gift Aid relief about?

From 6 April 2003, if you make a gift to charity using Gift Aid, you can elect to have any higher rate tax relief due carried back to the previous year of assessment. The election can be made for any or all Gift Aid payments made between the end of the tax year and the following 31 January (as long as the return has not already been sent in).

Example 2

Mr Jones, a higher rate taxpayer, makes a Gift Aid donation of £1,000 on 1 June 2004.

He has two choices in how he obtains tax relief. He can either claim relief for the payment made for the year 2004–2005 or carry back the relief to the year 2003–2004.

If he elects to carry the relief back he must do so before 31 January 2005. However, if he sent in his return on 30 June 2004 and did not elect to carry back the donation, he can only claim it for the year 2004–2005. It is not possible to amend the return in order to elect to carry back the donation.

How is the relief claimed?

By simply entering the donations in the appropriate Gift Aid box on your Self Assessment return.

Can I use Gift Aid to pay the proceeds of fund-raising events to charity?

If you have been sponsored for an event, and each sponsor has given a Gift Aid declaration, then the charity can recover the tax on the amounts covered by declarations. Charities may produce sponsorship forms for this.

Does a gift I make jointly with someone else qualify for Gift Aid?

Yes, but you must tell the charity how much is from each of you and you will both need to give declarations if the whole amount is to qualify.

Can I use charity vouchers to make Gift Aid donations?

Some organisations, which are charities themselves, offer charity accounts and provide you with a charity card or charity 'cheque book' of vouchers so that you can give directly to the charities of your choice. In this case, you give your money to the organisation issuing the charity card or vouchers. They will ask you for a declaration and will reclaim basic rate tax on your gift. The value of your charity account or the vouchers issued to you will include the tax reclaimed.

Can I get relief for a gift to a foreign charity?

No. Gift Aid applies only to charities established in the UK, but many foreign charities are established in the UK through branches.

Can I make a Gift Aid payment to a UK charity if I do not live in the UK?

In certain circumstances. You may do so if you are a Crown employee serving overseas. You can also use Gift Aid if you are not a UK resident, but you make your gift out of income or gains charged to UK tax.

Will Gift Aid affect my age-related personal allowance or married couples allowance?

The gross amount of any Gift Aid donations you make reduces the level of your income when calculating any entitlement you may have to the age- related personal allowance or married couple's allowance. If you are aged over 65, or (for the married couples allowance) you or your spouse were born before 6 April 1935, it is important that you enter details of your Gift Aid payments on your tax return. Without this information you may not receive all the allowances you are entitled to.

If you are entitled to these allowances and do not receive a tax return, you should notify your Tax Office of the gross amount of any Gift Aid payments you have made in order to ensure that you receive your full entitlement to the allowances.

Gifts of land, buildings, shares and securities

You can now also claim relief on gifts of certain assets to charity. This includes selling the asset to a charity at less than market value. A company cannot, however, get relief for a gift of its own shares.

What land, buildings, shares and securities qualify?

The following categories qualify.

- Shares and securities listed or dealt in on the UK Stock Exchange, including the Alternative Investment Market.
- Shares and securities listed or dealt in on recognised foreign stock exchanges.
- Units in an authorised unit trust.
- Shares in a UK open-ended investment company.
- Holdings in certain foreign collective investment schemes.
- A qualifying interest in land. A qualifying interest in land is the whole of a person's beneficial interest in freehold or leasehold land in the UK.

If in doubt, we can tell you whether the gift or sale will qualify for relief.

How do I calculate the amount of relief?

The amount of relief you can claim is

- the market value of the qualifying investment at the time you give them or sell them to charity, **plus**
- any incidental costs (for example, brokers fees or legal fees), **less**
- any disposal proceeds or other money, or the value of other benefits you or a person connected with you (such as, a relative or connected company), receive in consequence of you giving or selling the qualifying investment to charity.

Are there any forms that need to be completed?

No, evidence of the gift of shares or securities having been made to the charity may be in the form of a copy of the stock transfer form or letter from the charity acknowledging receipt of the gift.

For gifts of real property, you will need a certificate from the charity that must contain all the following information.

- A description of the qualifying interest in land, which is the subject of the disposal.
- The date of the disposal.
- A statement that the charity has acquired the qualifying interest in land.

How do I claim the relief?

Calculate the amount of relief as described on the previous page. The amount should be entered on your Self Assessment return.

If you are a partner or a sole trader, you should deduct the relief when you calculate your income for the tax year in which you make the gift of shares, securities or real property. You should enter the amount on your Self Assessment return.

Payroll Giving

If your employer operates a Payroll Giving scheme, you can make donations to charity direct from your pay packet. It's a simple way for you to give regularly to charity from your pay and get tax relief on your gifts.

If your employer does not operate a Payroll Giving scheme, you might want to ask if they would be willing to start one. Your employer can find out how easy it is to run a scheme by calling **0845 3020203**.

Can all employees join in Payroll Giving?

Yes, provided you are an employee or pensioner and your employer deducts tax from your pay or pension.

How much or how little can I give?

There are no limits on how much or how little you can give. It is entirely up to you.

How does Payroll Giving work?

Once you have authorised your employer to deduct a gift from your pay, they will deduct this amount from your pay and hand it over to a Payroll Giving agency approved by the Inland Revenue. The agency will then distribute the money to the charity or charities of your choice. Some agencies can provide you with a charity card or cheque book so that you can give directly to any charity whenever you want to.

How do I get tax relief?

Your gift is deducted from your pay or pension before your tax is worked out. So you pay tax only on the balance. This means that you get your tax relief immediately at your highest rate of tax. (Your National Insurance contributions are not affected.)

Example 3

Basic rate taxpayer
You authorise a monthly deduction of £10.00
You save income tax at 22% £2.20
Net cost to you £7.80

Higher rate taxpayer
You authorise a monthly deduction of £10.00
You save income tax at 40% £4.00

Net cost to you £6.00

Charity
Charity receives £10.00
Plus 10 per cent Government supplement (until April 2004) £1.00

Total £11.00

Can I give to any charity?

Yes, you can give to any UK charity and you may give to more than one charity if you wish. You can nominate a large, national charity or a smaller, local one. You can nominate your church, village hall, Parent Teacher Association or scout group, etc, providing they are charities.

Will my employer have to know which charity I want to support?

No, you can keep your choice confidential if you wish. The Payroll Giving agency will provide you with a charity nomination form, which you can complete and return direct to the agency. (Alternatively, the agency may be able to offer the charity card or cheque book.)

Can I change the charities I wish to support?

Yes, by simply telling the Payroll Giving agency.

Can I stop giving?

Yes, at any time. Simply tell your employer's payroll department.

Can I ask for a refund of my donations?

No, once a gift has been deducted from your pay, it must go to charity.

Will the Payroll Giving agency deduct a handling charge?

All the agencies are charities in their own right. A small fee – usually no more than 4 per cent or 35p per donation, whichever is the greater – may be deducted from your gift to meet the agency's administration costs. However, some employers will pay the agency's charges so that the full amount of your gift can go to your chosen charity.

Will this affect the other gifts I make to charity?

No, you can make any other gifts you want to, for example, under Gift Aid.

Is more information available?

Yes, there are Payroll Giving guides for employers and for employees available from the Inland Revenue. These give more information about the scheme and can be obtained by calling **0845 3020203**. The guide for employers contains a list of all the approved Payroll Giving agencies. It also contains a list of all the promotional fundraising organisations, which will help employers set up and run a Payroll Giving scheme.

Further Information

Inheritance tax

Outright gifts and bequests to UK charities are completely free of inheritance tax.

Capital gains tax

You are not liable to capital gains tax when you make a gift of assets, such as land or stocks and shares, to charity, even if the asset is worth more when you donate it than when you acquired it.

Contact with the Tax Office

This Help Sheet does not cover every point. If you have any questions, the staff at your local Inland Revenue Enquiry Centre or Tax Office will be happy to answer them. Addresses are in your local telephone book under 'Inland Revenue'. Most offices are open to the public from 8.30am to 5.00pm, Monday to Friday.

Alternatively you can contact our Charity helpline on **0845 3020203** (option 3), which is open from 8.30am to 6.00pm, Monday to Friday.

These notes are for guidance only and reflect the position at the time of writing. They do not affect any right of appeal.

[6035]

LIST OF USEFUL ADDRESSES

Charity Commission

Tel: 0870 3000 218

London Office
Harmsworth House
13–15 Bouverie Street
London EC4Y 8DP
Fax: 020 7674 2300

Liverpool Office
12 Princes Dock
Princes Parade
Liverpool L3 1DE
Fax: 0151 703 1555

Taunton Office
Woodfield House
Tangier
Taunton
Somerset TA1 4BL
Fax: 01823 345003

Newport Office
8th Floor
Clarence House
Clarence Place
Newport NP19 7AA
Fax: 01633 225549

Association of Charitable Foundations

Central House
14 Upper Woburn Place
London WC1H 0AE
Tel: 020 7255 4499
Fax: 020 7255 4496
www.acf.org.uk

Association of Chief Executives of Voluntary Organisations

1 New Oxford Street
London WC1A 1NU
Tel: 0845 345 8481
Fax: 0845 345 8482
www.acevo.org.uk

CCLA Investment Management Ltd

80 Cheapside
London EC2V 6DZ
Tel: 0808 220 2252
Fax: 0808 220 3291
www.ccla.co.uk

Centre for Effective Dispute Resolution

International Dispute Resolution Centre
70 Fleet Street
London EC4Y 1EU
Tel: 020 7536 6000
Fax: 020 7536 6001
www.cedr.co.uk

Charities Aid Foundation

25 Kings Hill Avenue	Tel: 01732 520000
Kings Hill	Fax: 01732 520001
West Malling	www.cafonline.org
Kent ME19 4TA	

Charity Finance Directors' Group

3rd Floor, Downstream Building	Tel: 0845 345 3192
1 London Bridge	Fax: 0845 345 3193
London SE1 9BG	www.cfdg.org.uk

Charity Law Association

c/o Blake Lapthorn Tarlo Lyons	Tel: 02392 221122 ext 625
Harbour Court, Compass Road	Fax: 02392 221123
North Harbour	www.charitylawassociation.org.uk
Portsmouth PO6 4ST	

Inland Revenue Financial Intermediaries and Claims Office (FICO)

St John's House	Tel: 0151 472 6036
Merton Road	Fax:0151 472 6268
Bootle	www.hmrc.gov.uk
Merseyside L69 9BB	

Institute of Fundraising

Park Place	Tel: 020 7840 1000
12 Lawn Lane	Fax: 020 7840 1001
London	www.institute-of-fundraising.org.uk
SW8 1UD	

National Council for Voluntary Organisations

Regent's Wharf	Tel: 020 7713 6161
8 All Saints Street	Fax: 020 7713 6300
London	www.ncvo-vol.org.uk
N1 9RL	

[6036]

USEFUL WEBSITE ADDRESSES

Charity Commission	www.charity-commission.gov.uk
Advisory Conciliation and Arbitration Service	www.acas.org.uk
Big Lottery Fund	www.biglotteryfund.org.uk
Charities Aid Foundation	www.cafonline.org
Companies House	www.companies-house.gov.uk
Department for Communities and Local Government	www.communities.gov.uk
Department for Constitutional Affairs	www.dca.gov.uk
Department for Culture, Media and Sport	www.culture.gov.uk
Department for Education and Skills	www.dfes.gov.uk
Department for the Environment, Food and Rural Affairs	www.defra.gov.uk
Department of Health	www.dh.gov.uk
Department for International Development	www.dfid.gov.uk
Department of Trade and Industry	www.dti.gov.uk
Department for Transport	www.dft.gov.uk
Department for Work and Pensions	www.dwp.gov.uk
Disability Rights Commission	www.drc-gb.org
Financial Services Authority	www.fsa.gov.uk
Home Office	www.homeoffice.gov.uk
Information Commissioner's Office	www.ico.gov.uk
Insolvency Service	www.insolvency.gov.uk
HM Land Registry	www.landreg.gov.uk
HM Revenue & Customs	www.hmrc.gov.uk
HM Treasury	www.hm-treasury.gov.uk

[6037]

Index

A

D

E

I